P9-CLD-532

THE TWELFTH MENTAL MEASUREMENTS YEARBOOK

EARLIER PUBLICATIONS IN THIS SERIES

EDUCATIONAL, PSYCHOLOGICAL, AND PERSONALITY TESTS OF 1933 AND 1934

EDUCATIONAL, PSYCHOLOGICAL, AND PERSONALITY TESTS OF 1933, 1934, AND 1935

EDUCATIONAL, PSYCHOLOGICAL, AND PERSONALITY TESTS OF 1936

THE NINETEEN THIRTY-EIGHT MENTAL MEASUREMENTS YEARBOOK

THE NINETEEN FORTY MENTAL MEASUREMENTS YEARBOOK

THE THIRD MENTAL MEASUREMENTS YEARBOOK

THE FOURTH MENTAL MEASUREMENTS YEARBOOK

THE FIFTH MENTAL MEASUREMENTS YEARBOOK

TESTS IN PRINT

THE SIXTH MENTAL MEASUREMENTS YEARBOOK

READING TESTS AND REVIEWS

PERSONALITY TESTS AND REVIEWS

THE SEVENTH MENTAL MEASUREMENTS YEARBOOK

TESTS IN PRINT II

ENGLISH TESTS AND REVIEWS

FOREIGN LANGUAGE TESTS AND REVIEWS

INTELLIGENCE TESTS AND REVIEWS

MATHEMATICS TESTS AND REVIEWS

PERSONALITY TESTS AND REVIEWS II

READING TESTS AND REVIEWS II

SCIENCE TESTS AND REVIEWS

SOCIAL STUDIES TESTS AND REVIEWS

VOCATIONAL TESTS AND REVIEWS

THE EIGHTH MENTAL MEASUREMENTS YEARBOOK

TESTS IN PRINT III

THE NINTH MENTAL MEASUREMENTS YEARBOOK

THE SUPPLEMENT TO THE NINTH MENTAL MEASUREMENTS YEARBOOK

THE TENTH MENTAL MEASUREMENTS YEARBOOK

THE SUPPLEMENT TO THE TENTH MENTAL MEASUREMENTS YEARBOOK

THE ELEVENTH MENTAL MEASUREMENTS YEARBOOK

TESTS IN PRINT IV

THE SUPPLEMENT TO THE ELEVENTH MENTAL MEASUREMENTS YEARBOOK

BUROS DESK REFERENCE: PSYCHOLOGICAL ASSESSMENT IN THE SCHOOLS

THE TWELFTH MENTAL MEASUREMENTS YEARBOOK

Jane Close Conoley and James C. Impara

Editors

Linda L. Murphy
Managing Editor

The Buros Institute of Mental Measurements
The University of Nebraska-Lincoln
Lincoln, Nebraska

1995
Distributed by The University of Nebraska Press

LC 39-3422
ISBN 910674-40-X

Manufactured in the United States of America.

The paper used in this publication meets the minimum requirements of American National Standard for Information Sciences–Permanence of Paper for Printed Library Materials, ANSI Z39.48-1984.

Note to Users

The staff of the Buros Institute of Mental Measurements has made every effort to ensure the accuracy of the test information included in this work. However, the Buros Institute of Mental Measurements and the Editors of *The Twelfth Mental Measurements Yearbook* do not assume, and hereby expressly and absolutely disclaim, any liability to any party for any loss or damage caused by errors or omissions or statements of any kind in *The Twelfth Mental Measurements Yearbook*. This disclaimer also includes judgments or statements of any kind made by test reviewers, who were extended the professional freedom appropriate to their task. The reviews are the sole opinion of the individual reviewers and do not necessarily represent any general consensus of the professional community or any professional organizations. The judgments and opinions of the reviewers are their own, uninfluenced in any way by the Buros Institute or the Editors.

All material included in *The Twelfth Mental Measurements Yearbook* is intended solely for the use of our readers. None of this material, including reviewer statements, may be used in advertising or for any other commercial purpose.

TABLE OF CONTENTS

DEDICATION

Dedicated to Luella Gubrud Buros
1901–1995

In June, 1995, the testing profession lost an important friend and contributor, Luella Gubrud Buros.

Luella Buros was a very talented woman. She began her career as an artist. Her talent was widely recognized and her paintings were displayed in many well respected shows and galleries. After her marriage to Oscar, and after he began the publication of the *Mental Measurements Yearbooks*, she realized he needed her help to continue that publication. As a devoted wife and helpmate to Oscar, she put aside her career ambitions to help him fulfill his life mission: providing candidly critical evaluations of commercially available tests. Luella and Oscar worked together in his crusade to protect the public and the public interest.

Luella's role as Oscar's companion and colleague in the preparation of test reviews provided her an opportunity to bring her creative eye and artistic talent to the field of publishing. Many of the formatting features of the *Yearbooks* were due to Luella's creative talent. She contributed in many ways including designing the layout of the content of the book and in selecting the colors of the covers. Even though Luella was not furthering her personal career as an artist, she transferred the application of those skills to enhance the products of her work with Oscar. We often consulted Luella regarding artistic aspects of our publishing efforts and were delighted by the enthusiasm she brought to these tasks up to just months before her death.

Luella and Oscar worked side by side on the work of the Institute. When Oscar died in 1978, Luella made sure that the *Eighth Mental Measurements Yearbook*, which was in the final stages of completion at that time, was completed. Then she sought a new home for the Buros Institute so their work would be continued.

Her support of the field of assessment did not end when the Institute was transferred from Highland Park, New Jersey to the University of Nebraska-Lincoln. Luella continued to provide support, this time in terms of money. Early on she contributed funds to help the new Institute get started and she contributed Oscar's extensive collection of measurement and statistics books to start a reference library.

Over the years, she continued her devotion to the Buros Institute and to testing. She made generous financial gifts to the Buros Institute to support the Oscar K. Buros Library of Mental Measurements, a library that has probably the most extensive test collection in the world. Shortly before her death she provided a major financial contribution to expand the scope of the Buros Institute by creating the Oscar and Luella Buros Center for Testing. The Center contains three Institutes: (1) The Buros Institute of Mental Measurements; (2) The Buros Institute for Assessment Consultation and Outreach; and (3) The Buros Institute for Research on Innovative Testing Strategies. Her vision and financial support will translate into a major contribution to assessment education, research, and service. Her estate will continue to provide a base of support for the *Mental Measurements Yearbooks* for many years in the future.

In addition to her financial support, Mrs. Buros's moral support for the continuation of the Buros tradition is noteworthy. She was absolutely committed to improved testing practices and she served as a true inspiration to the entire Buros staff. We will continue to be inspired by her through her paintings, which were willed to the Institute after her death and which are hung on the walls of the Institute and in the Oscar K. Buros Library of Mental Measurements.

The testing field has been doubly blessed by having the talents and dedication of both Oscar and Luella Buros. We had the special privilege of knowing Luella Buros for 17 years. Her love for Oscar continued through her amazing loyalty to the Institute's mission. She will be missed by many and especially by us.

The Staff of the Buros Institute of Mental Measurements

INTRODUCTION

The publication of *The Twelfth Mental Measurements Yearbook* (*12th MMY*) continues the historic mission of the Buros Institute of Mental Measurements to provide test users with descriptive information, references, and critical reviews of tests. Criteria for inclusion of a test in the *12th MMY* are that the test be (a) new or revised since last reviewed in the *MMY* series, (b) commercially available, and (c) published in the English language. Descriptive information about the contents and use of the newest Buros Institute of Mental Measurements publication is provided below.

THE TWELFTH MENTAL MEASUREMENTS YEARBOOK

The *12th MMY* contains reviews of tests that are new or significantly revised since the publication of the *11th MMY* in 1992. Reviews, descriptions, and references associated with many older tests can be located in other Buros publications: *MMY*s and *Tests in Print IV*.

Content. The contents of the *12th MMY* include: (a) a bibliography of 418 commercially available tests, new or revised, published as separates for use with English-speaking subjects; (b) 803 critical test reviews by well-qualified professional people who were selected by the editors on the basis of their expertise in measurement and, often, the content of the test being reviewed; (c) bibliographies of references for specific tests related to the construction, validity, or use of the tests in various settings; (d) a test title index with appropriate cross-references; (e) a classified subject index; (f) a publishers directory and index, including addresses and test listings by publisher; (g) a name index including the names of authors of all tests, reviews, or references included in this *MMY*; (h) an index of acronyms for easy reference when a test acronym, not the full title, is known; and (i) a score index to refer readers to tests featuring particular scores of interest to them.

Organization. The volume is organized like an encyclopedia, with tests being ordered alphabetically by title. If the title of a test is known, the reader can locate the test immediately without having to consult the Index of Titles.

The page headings reflect the encyclopedic organization. The page heading of the left-hand page cites the number and title of the first test listed on that page, and the page heading of the right-hand page cites the number and title of the last test listed on that page. All numbers presented in the various indexes are test numbers, not page numbers. Page numbers are important only for the Table of Contents and are indicated at the bottom of each page.

TESTS AND REVIEWS

The *12th MMY* contains descriptive information on 418 tests as well as 803 test reviews by 494 different authors. The reviewed tests have generated 2,055 references in the professional literature (gathered since the 1994 publication of *Tests in Print IV*) and reviewers have supplied 1,231 additional references in their reviews.

Statistics on the number and percentage of tests in each of 18 major classifications are contained in Table 1. One area, Science, had no tests included in the *12th MMY*.

TABLE 1
TESTS BY MAJOR CLASSIFICATIONS

Classification	Number	Percentage
Personality	85	20.3
Vocations	73	17.5
Intelligence	36	8.6
Miscellaneous	35	8.4
Developmental	29	6.9
Speech and Hearing	25	6.0
English	23	5.5
Behavior Assessment	23	5.5
Education	16	3.8
Reading	16	3.8
Achievement	15	3.6
Neuropsychological	13	3.1
Sensory-Motor	9	2.2
Mathematics	6	1.4
Fine Arts	4	1.0
Multi-Aptitude Batteries	4	1.0
Foreign Languages	3	.7
Social Studies	2	.5
Total	418	100.0

The percentages of new and revised or supplemented tests according to major classifications are contained in Table 2. Overall, almost three-fourths of the tests included in the *12th MMY* are new and have not been listed in a previous *MMY* although all descriptions were included in *Tests in Print IV* (1994). The Index of Titles can be consulted to determine if a test is new or revised.

TABLE 2
NEW AND REVISED OR SUPPLEMENTED TESTS BY MAJOR CLASSIFICATIONS

Classification	Number of Tests	Percentage New	Percentage Revised
Achievement	15	73.3	26.7
Behavior Assessment	23	78.3	21.7
Developmental	29	69.0	31.0
Education	16	87.5	12.5
English	23	78.3	21.8
Fine Arts	4	50.0	50.0
Foreign Languages	3	100.0	.0
Intelligence and Scholastic Aptitude	36	58.3	41.7
Mathematics	6	66.7	33.3
Miscellaneous	35	85.7	14.3
Multi-Aptitude Batteries	4	50.0	50.0
Neuropsychological	13	84.6	15.4
Personality	85	68.2	31.8
Reading	16	50.0	50.0
Sensory-Motor	9	66.7	33.3
Social Studies	2	50.0	50.0
Speech and Hearing	25	88.0	12.0
Vocations	74	63.5	36.5
Total	418	70.8	28.2

Test Selection. Our goal is to include reviews of virtually all English language, commercially published tests that are new or revised. No minimal standards exist and inclusion of a test in the *MMY* does not mean that a test has met any standard of "goodness." We attempt to gather all tests, good and bad alike. We select our reviewers carefully and let them and well-informed readers decide for themselves about the quality of the tests. Some new or revised tests are not included because they were received too late to undergo the review process and still permit timely publication, or because some reviewers did not meet their commitment to review the test.

There are some new or revised tests for which there will be no reviews although all these tests are described in *Tests in Print IV*. In the *10th* and *11th MMY*s, a number of tests were included without reviews but with descriptive information. The absence of reviews occurred for a variety of reasons including: We could not identify qualified reviewers, the test materials were incomplete so reviews were not possible, the tests were sufficiently obscure that reviews were deemed unnecessary, or the tests were published in South Africa during the time we felt morally obligated to boycott their products. Descriptions of all these tests still in print have been published in *TIP IV*. There continue to be some tests that meet the above conditions that are not reviewed in this volume. The names of those tests are listed in Table 3. Descriptions of the tests may be found in *TIP IV*.

TABLE 3
NEW OR REVISED TESTS NOT REVIEWED
(Descriptions in Tests in Print IV)

ACER Advanced Test BL-BQ, New Zealand Revision
ACER Higher Test PL-PQ, New Zealand Revision
Appraise Your World
Aptitude for and Sensitivity to Music
Aptitude Test Battery for Adults
Arithmetic Reasoning Test
Assessment of Developmental Levels by Observation
California Brief Life History Inventory
The Callier-Azusa Scale: G Edition
Canadian Dental Aptitude Test
Cardall Test of Practical Judgement
The Chessington O. T. Neurological Assessment Battery
Chronic Pain Battery
Combined Cognitive Preference Inventory
Continuous Symbol Checking Test
Current and Past Psychopathology Scales
Developmental History Checklist for Children
Diagnostic Tests in Mathematics
Explore the World of Work
Family Satisfaction Scale
50 Grammar Quizzes for Practice and Review
A Form Series Test (Industrial Version)
High Level Estimation Test
High Level Figure Classification Test
Industrial Test Battery
Jung Personality Questionnaire
Junior Rating Scale
Junior Scholastic Proficiency Battery
Junior South African Individual Scales
Kolbe Conative Index, Forms B and C
La Prueba de Realización, Segunda Edición
Leadership Effectiveness Analysis
Levine-Pilowsky [Depression] Questionnaire

TABLE 3 CONT'D
NEW OR REVISED TESTS NOT REVIEWED
(DESCRIPTIONS IN TESTS IN PRINT IV)

Library Skills
Listening Comprehension Test in English
Looking at MySELF
Management Effectiveness Analysis
MATE [Marital ATtitude Evaluation]
Mental Status Checklist for Adults, 1988 Revision
The Meta Contrast Technique, 4th Edition
Musical Aptitude Test
Non-Language Multi-Mental Test
Personal Achievement Formula
Picture Vocational Interest Questionnaire for Adults
Problem Behavior Inventory [Adult & Adolescent Screening Forms]
Proficiency Battery in English and Mathematics for Indian South Africans
Programmer Aptitude Battery
Quick Quizzes for U.S. History Classes
Readiness for Kindergarten
The Revised Sheridan Gardiner Test of Visual Acuity
Rothwell-Miller Interest Blank
The Rutgers Drawing Test
Sales Effectiveness Analysis
A Schedule of Adaptive Mechanisms in CAT Responses
Scholastic Aptitude Test Battery for Pupils in Standards 2 and 3
School-Readiness Evaluation by Trained Teachers
Sentence Completion Tests
Service Excellence
Sexual Adaptation and Functioning Test
The South African Individual Scale for the Blind
South African Wechsler Adult Individual Intelligence Scale
South African Written Language Test
Standard Progressive Matrices [Australian Edition]
Standard Progressive Matrices, New Zealand Standardization
Student Educational Assessment Screening
Test for Auditory Figure-Ground Discrimination
Test for Oral Language Production
Tests of Basic Literacy in the Sotho Languages
Thanatometer
Timed Typings for Holidays
Trade Aptitude Test Battery
Vocational Information Profile
Wide Range Intelligence-Personality Test [1978 Edition]
Wolf Expressive/Receptive Language & Speech Checklist
Wolf Student Behavior Screening

Reviewer Selection. The selection of reviewers was done with great care. The objective was to secure measurement and subject specialists who represent a variety of different viewpoints. It was also important to find individuals who would write critical reviews competently, judiciously, and fairly. Reviewers were identified by means of extensive searches of the professional literature, attendance at professional meetings, and recommendations from leaders in various professional fields. Perusal of reviews in this volume will also reveal that reviewers work in and represent a cross-section of the places in which tests are taught and used: universities, public schools, businesses, and community agencies. These reviewers represent an outstanding array of professional talent, and their contributions are obviously of primary importance in making this *Yearbook* a valuable resource. A list of the individuals reviewing in this volume is included at the beginning of the Index section.

Readers of test reviews in the *12th MMY* are encouraged to exercise an active, analytical, and evaluative perspective in reading the reviews. Just as one would evaluate a test, the reader should evaluate critically the reviewer's comments about the test. The reviewers selected are competent professionals in their respective fields, but it is inevitable that their reviews also reflect their individual perspectives. The *Mental Measurements Yearbooks* are intended to stimulate critical thinking about the selection of the best available test for a given purpose, not the passive acceptance of reviewer judgment. Active, evaluative reading is the key to the most effective use of the professional expertise offered in each of the reviews.

REFERENCES

This yearbook lists a total of 3,286 references related to the development, psychometric quality, and use of specific tests. The "Reviewer's References" section groups the reviewer's references in one convenient listing for easy identification and use by the reader. Of the total of 3,286 references, 2,055 are included under "Test References" and 1,231 are included under "Reviewer's References."

All references listed under "Test References" have been selected by Buros Institute staff who searched through hundreds of professional journals. Because of the great proliferation of tests in recent years, it was decided to increase test and review coverage but to limit the increase in references by not including theses, dissertations, or presentations at professional meetings.

Buros Institute publications traditionally list all references chronologically and then alphabetically by author within year. Our format for references in journals is author, year, title, journal, volume, and page numbers; for books it is author, year, title, place of publication, and publisher. A large number of additional references are listed in *Tests in Print IV*, published in 1994.

All tests in this yearbook that generated 10 or more references are listed in Table 4. Within the table the tests are also rank-ordered according to number of references. The references are valuable as additions to our cumulative knowledge about specific tests, and they are also a useful resource for further research into test quality.

INDEXES

As mentioned above, the *12th MMY* includes six indexes invaluable as aids to effective use: (*a*) Index of Titles, (*b*) Index of Acronyms, (*c*) Classified Subject Index, (*d*) Publishers Directory and Index, (*e*) Index of Names, and (*f*) Score Index. Additional comment on these indexes is presented below.

TABLE 4
NUMBER OF REFERENCES FOR MOST FREQUENTLY CITED TESTS

NAME OF TEST	NUMBER OF REFERENCES
Schedule for Affective Disorders and Schizophrenia, Third Edition	414
Wechsler Intelligence Scale for Children—Third Edition	409
Wide Range Achievement Test 3	111
General Health Questionnaire	88
National Adult Reading Test, Second Edition	77
Family Environment Scale, Second Edition	76
Scale for the Assessment of Negative Symptoms	75
Woodcock-Johnson Psycho-Educational Battery—Revised	56
Revised NEO Personality Inventory	50
Scale for the Assessment of Positive Symptoms	44
Strong Interest Inventory [Fourth Edition]	43
Eating Disorder Inventory-2	38
Sixteen Personality Factor Questionnaire, Fifth Edition	38
Metropolitan Achievement Tests, Seventh Edition	37
Enhanced ACT Assessment	35
Job Descriptive Index and Retirement Descriptive Index	33
Developmental Test of Visual-Motor Integration [Third Revision]	25
Sensory Integration and Praxis Tests	18
Differential Aptitude Tests, Fifth Edition	16
Dissociative Experiences Scale	16
Slosson Intelligence Test [1991 Edition]	16
Positive and Negative Syndrome Scale	15
Grooved Pegboard Test	14
Rokeach Value Survey	14
Comprehensive Assessment of Symptoms and History	12
Menstrual Distress Questionnaire	12
Social Skills Rating System	10

Index of Titles. Because the organization of the *11th MMY* is encyclopedic in nature, with the tests ordered alphabetically by title throughout the volume, the test title index does not have to be consulted to find a test if the title is known. However, the title index has some features that make it useful beyond its function as a complete title listing. First, it includes cross-reference information useful for tests with superseded or alternative titles or tests commonly (and sometimes inaccurately) known by multiple titles. Second, it identifies tests that are new or revised. Third, it may cue the user to other tests with similar titles that may be useful. It is important to keep in mind that the numbers in this index, like those for all *MMY* indexes, are test numbers and not page numbers.

Index of Acronyms. Some tests seem to be better known by their acronyms than by their full titles. The Index of Acronyms can help in these instances; it refers the reader to the full title of the test and to the relevant descriptive information and reviews.

Classified Subject Index. The Classified Subject Index classifies all tests listed in the *12th MMY* into 18 major categories: Achievement, Behavior Assessment, Developmental, Education, English, Fine Arts, Foreign Language, Intelligence and Scholastic Aptitude, Mathematics, Miscellaneous, Multi-Aptitude Batteries, Neuropsychological, Personality, Reading, Sensory-Motor, Social Studies, Speech and Hearing, and Vocations. Each test entry in this index includes test title, population for which the test is intended, and test number. The Classified Subject Index is of great help to readers who seek a listing of tests in given subject areas. The Classified Subject Index represents a starting point for readers who know their area of interest but do not know how to further focus that interest in order to identify the best test(s) for their particular purposes.

Publishers Directory and Index. The Publishers Directory and Index includes the names and addresses of the publishers of all tests included in the *12th MMY* plus a listing of test numbers for each individual publisher. This index can be particularly useful in obtaining addresses for specimen sets or catalogs after the test reviews have been read and evaluated. It can also be useful when a reader knows the publisher of a certain test but is uncertain about the test title, or when a reader is interested in the range of tests published by a given publisher.

Index of Names. The Index of Names provides a comprehensive list of names, indicating authorship of a test, test review, or reference.

Score Index. The Score Index is an index to all scores generated by the tests in the *12th MMY*. Test titles are sometimes misleading or ambiguous, and test content may be difficult to define with precision. But test scores represent operational definitions of the variables the test author is trying to measure, and as such they often define test purpose and content more adequately than other descriptive information. A search for a particular test is most often a search for a test that measures some specific variable(s). Test scores and their associated labels can often be the best definitions of the variable(s) of interest. The Score Index is a detailed subject index based on the most critical operational features of any test—the scores and their associated labels.

HOW TO USE THIS YEARBOOK

A reference work like *The Twelfth Mental Measurements Yearbook* can be of far greater benefit to a reader if some time is taken to become familiar with what it has to offer and how it might be used most effectively to obtain the information wanted.

Step one: Read the Introduction to the *12th MMY* in its entirety.

Step two: Become familiar with the six indexes and particularly with the instructions preceding each index listing.

Step three: Use the book by looking up needed information. This step is simple if one keeps in mind the following possibilities:

1. Go directly to the test entry using the alphabetical page headings if you know the title of the test.

2. Consult the Index of Titles for possible variants of the title or consult the appropriate subject area of the Classified Subject Index for other possible leads or for similar or related tests in the same area, if you do not know, cannot find, or are unsure of the title of a test. (Other uses for both of these indexes were described earlier.)

3. Consult the Index of Names if you know the author of a test but not the title or publisher. Look up the author's titles until you find the test you want.

4. Consult the Publishers Directory and Index if you know the test publisher but not the title or author. Look up the publisher's titles until you find the test you want.

5. Consult the Score Index and locate the test or tests that include the score variable of interest if you are looking for a test that yields a particular kind of score, but have no knowledge of which test that might be.

6. Once you have found the test or tests you are looking for, read the descriptive entries for these tests carefully so that you can take advantage of the information provided. A description of the information provided in these test entries is presented later in this section.

7. Read the test reviews carefully and analytically, as suggested above. The information and evaluation contained in these reviews are meant to assist test consumers in making well-informed decisions about the choice and applications of tests.

8. Once you have read the descriptive information and test reviews, you may want to order a specimen set for a particular test so that you can examine it firsthand. The Publishers Directory and Index has the address information needed to obtain specimen sets or catalogs.

Making Effective Use of the Test Entries. The test entries include extensive information. For each test, descriptive information is presented in the following order:

a) TITLES. Test titles are printed in boldface type. Secondary or series titles are set off from main titles by a colon.

b) PURPOSE. For each test there is a brief, clear statement describing the purpose of the test. Often these statements are quotations from the test manual.

c) POPULATION. This describes the groups for which the test is intended. The grade, chronological age, semester range, or employment category is usually given. For example, "grades 1.5–2.5, 2–3, 4–12, 13–17" means that there are four test booklets: a booklet for the middle of first grade through the middle of the second grade, a booklet for the beginning of the second grade through the end of third grade, a booklet for grades 4 through 12 inclusive, and a booklet for undergraduate and graduate students in colleges and universities.

d) PUBLICATION DATE. The inclusive range of publication dates for the various forms, accessories, and editions of a test is reported.

e) ACRONYM. When a test is often referred to by an acronym, the acronym is given in the test entry immediately following the publication date.

f) SCORES. The number of part scores is presented along with their titles or descriptions of what they are intended to represent or measure.

g) ADMINISTRATION. Individual or group administration is indicated. A test is considered a group test unless it may be administered *only* individually.

h) FORMS, PARTS, AND LEVELS. All available forms, parts, and levels are listed.

i) MANUAL. Notation is made if no manual is available. All other manual information is included under Price Data.

j) RESTRICTED DISTRIBUTION. This is noted only for tests that are put on a special market by the publisher. Educational and psychological restrictions are not noted (unless a special training course is required for use).

k) PRICE DATA. Price information is reported for test packages (usually 20 to 35 tests), answer sheets, all other accessories, and specimen sets. The statement "$17.50 per 35 tests" means that all accessories are included unless otherwise indicated by the reporting of separate prices for accessories. The statement also means 35 tests of one level, one edition, or one part unless stated otherwise. Because test prices can change very quickly, the year that the listed test prices were obtained is also given. Foreign currency is assigned the appropriate symbol. When prices are given in foreign dollars, a qualifying symbol is added (e.g., A$16.50 refers to 16 dollars and 50 cents in Australian currency). Along with cost, the publication date and number of pages on which print occurs is reported for manuals and technical reports (e.g., '93, 102 pages). All types of machine-scorable answer sheets available for use with a specific test are also reported in the descriptive entry. Scoring and reporting services provided by publishers are reported along with information on costs. In a few cases, special computerized scoring and interpretation services are noted at the end of the price information.

l) FOREIGN LANGUAGE AND OTHER SPECIAL EDITIONS. This section concerns foreign language editions published by the same publisher who sells the English edition. It also indicates special editions (e.g., Braille, large type) available from the same or a different publisher.

m) TIME. The number of minutes of actual working time allowed examinees and the approximate length of time needed for administering a test are reported whenever obtainable. The latter figure is always enclosed in parentheses. Thus, "50(60) minutes" indicates that the examinees are allowed 50 minutes of working time and that a total of 60 minutes is needed to administer the test. A time of "40–50 minutes" indicates an untimed test that takes approximately 45 minutes to administer, or—in a few instances—a test so timed that working time and administration time are very difficult to disentangle. When the time necessary to administer a test is not reported or suggested in the test materials but has been obtained through correspondence with the test publisher or author, the time is enclosed in brackets.

n) COMMENTS. Some entries contain special notations, such as: "for research use only"; "revision of the ABC Test"; "tests administered monthly at centers throughout the United States"; "subtests available as separates"; and "verbal creativity." A statement such as "verbal creativity" is intended to further describe what the test claims to measure. Some of the test entries include factual statements that imply criticism of the test, such as "1990 test identical with test copyrighted 1980."

o) AUTHOR. For most tests, all authors are reported. In the case of tests that appear in a new form each year, only authors of the most recent forms are listed. Names are reported exactly as printed on test booklets. Names of editors generally are not reported.

p) PUBLISHER. The name of the publisher or distributor is reported for each test. Foreign publishers are identified by listing the country in brackets immediately following the name of the publisher. The Publishers Directory and Index must be consulted for a publisher's address.

q) FOREIGN ADAPTATIONS. Revisions and adaptations of tests for foreign use are listed in a separate paragraph following the original edition.

r) SUBLISTINGS. Levels, editions, subtests, or parts of a test available in separate booklets are sometimes presented as sublistings with titles set in small capitals. Sub-sublistings are indented and titles are set in italic type.

s) CROSS REFERENCES. For tests that have been listed previously in a Buros Institute publication, a test entry includes—if relevant—a final item containing a cross reference to the reviews, excerpts, and references for that test in those volumes. In the cross references, "T4:467" refers to test 467 in *Tests in Print IV*, "8:1023" refers to test 1023 in *The Eighth Mental Measurements Yearbook*, "T3:144" refers to test 144 in *Tests in Print III*, "7:637" refers to test 637 in *The Seventh Mental Measurements Yearbook*, "P:262" refers to test 262 in *Personality Tests and Reviews I*, "2:1427" refers to test 1427 in *The 1940 Yearbook*, and "1:1110" refers to test 1110 in *The 1938 Yearbook*. In the case of batteries and programs, the paragraph also includes cross references—from the battery to the separately listed subtests and vice versa—to entries in this volume and to entries and reviews in earlier *Yearbooks*. Test numbers not preceded by a colon refer to tests in this *Yearbook*; for example, "see 45" refers to test 45 in this *Yearbook*.

If a reader finds something in a test description that is not understood, the descriptive material presented above can be referred to again and can often help to clarify the matter.

ACKNOWLEDGEMENTS

The publication of the *12th Mental Measurements Yearbook* could not have been accomplished without the contributions of many individuals. The editors acknowledge gratefully the talent, expertise, and dedication of all those who have assisted in the publication process.

Linda Murphy, Managing Editor, is steadfast in her constant effort, knowledge, editorial skill, and cheerful attitude. She makes our job as editors easier than we could have imagined. Nor would the publication of this volume be possible without the efforts of Gary Anderson, Editorial Assistant, and Rosemary Sieck, Word Processing Specialist. As always, their efforts go far beyond that required as part of normal job responsibilities. We appreciate Jack Kramer's early editorial contribution to this volume prior to his leaving the Institute. We are also pleased to acknowledge the continuous assistance available from the Director of the Buros Institute, Dr. Barbara Plake. Her enthusiasm for our work, visionary leadership, and skill in building a cohesive team effort are important to us all. The sense of accomplishment and pride we feel with the publication of the *12th MMY* is shared by our entire staff and our heartfelt thank you is extended to the individuals mentioned above.

Our gratitude is also extended to the many reviewers who have prepared test reviews for the Buros Institute. Their willingness to take time from busy professional schedules to share their expertise in the form of thoughtful test reviews is appreciated. *The Mental Measurements Yearbook* would not exist were it not for their efforts.

Many graduate students have contributed to the publication of this volume. Their efforts have included writing test descriptions, fact checking reviews, looking for test references, and innumerable other tasks. We thank Janet Allison, Dennison Bhola, Robert Bergman, Molly Geil, Jessica Jonson, Kwong Liem Kwan, Annie Mitchell, Heidi Paa, Maria Potenza, Michelle Schicke, Mark Shriver, Robert Spies, Tracy Thorndike-Christ, Paul Turner, Lori Wennstedt, and Kris Yates for their assistance.

Appreciation is also extended to our National and Departmental Advisory Committees for their willingness to assist in the operation of the Buros Institute.

During the period in which this volume was prepared the National Advisory Committee has included Luella Buros, Richard M. Jaeger, Timothy Keith, Barbara Kerr, Frank Schmidt, and Linda Wightman.

The Buros Institute is part of the Department of Educational Psychology of the University of Nebraska-Lincoln and we have benefitted from the many departmental colleagues who have contributed to our Departmental Advisory Committee. The current members are Deborah Bandalos, Terry Gutkin, Ellen McWhirter, and Gregg Schraw. We are also grateful for the contribution of the University of Nebraska Press, which provides expert consultation and serves as distributor of the MMY series.

This volume would have taken much longer to produce were it not for the efforts of Tim Myers at the UNL Computing Resource Center. We thank him for his assistance in organizing our information for printing.

Our thanks also go to Ken Tornvall and his staff at Port City Press, Inc. for their care and pride in the composition, printing, and binding of this and previous volumes.

Finally, none of what we accomplish as editors would be as meaningful without the support of our families. Thanks Collie, Brian, Colleen, Collin, and Barbara.

SUMMARY

The *MMY* series is a valuable resource for people interested in studying or using tests. Once the process of using the series is understood, a reader can gain rapid access to a wealth of information. Our hope is that with the publication of the *12th MMY*, test authors and publishers will consider carefully the comments made by the reviewers and continue to refine and perfect their assessment products.

Jane Close Conoley
James C. Impara
September 1995

Tests and Reviews

[1]

Aberrant Behavior Checklist.

Purpose: Constructed to rate "inappropriate and maladaptive behavior of mentally retarded individuals in residential settings."

Population: Mentally retarded adolescents and adults.

Publication Date: 1986.

Acronym: ABC.

Scores, 5: Irritability, Lethargy, Stereotypy, Hyperactivity, Inappropriate Speech.

Administration: Individual.

Price Data, 1992: $35 per complete kit including manual (32 pages); $18 per 50 checklists/score sheets.

Time: (5) minutes.

Comments: Ratings by direct care or professional staff member acquainted with individual.

Authors: Michael G. Aman and Nirbhay N. Singh.

Publisher: Slosson Educational Publications, Inc.

Cross References: See T4:4 (2 references).

TEST REFERENCES

1. Bihm, E. M., Poindexter, A. R., Kienlen, T. L., & Smith, B. L. (1992). Staff perceptions of reinforcer responsiveness and aberrant behaviors in people with mental retardation. *Journal of Autism and Developmental Disorders, 22*(1), 83-93.

2. Marshburn, E. C., & Aman, M. G. (1992). Factor validity and norms for the Aberrant Behavior Checklist in a community sample of children with mental retardation. *Journal of Autism and Developmental Disorders, 22*(3), 357-373.

3. Kobe, F. H., Mulick, J. A., Rash, T. A., & Martin, J. (1994). Nonambulatory persons with profound mental retardation: Physical, developmental, and behavioral characteristics. *Research in Developmental Disabilities, 15*, 413-423.

4. Pearson, D. A., & Aman, M. G. (1994). Rating hyperactivity and developmental indices: Should clinicians correct for developmental level. *Journal of Autism and Developmental Disorders, 24*, 395-411.

5. Rimland, B., & Edelson, S. M. (1995). Brief report: A pilot study of auditory integration training in autism. *Journal of Autism and Developmental Disorders, 25*, 61-70.

Review of the Aberrant Behavior Checklist by LENA R. GADDIS, Assistant Professor of Educational Psychology, Northern Arizona University, Flagstaff, AZ:

The Aberrant Behavior Checklist (ABC) is a rating scale "for rating inappropriate and maladaptive behavior of mentally retarded individuals in residential settings" (manual, p. ii). Specifically, it is designed to evaluate treatment effects for those individuals. The scale consists of 58 items for which an informant rates the behavior described in the item on a Likert scale of zero to 3, with "0" indicating *not at all a problem* and "3" indicating *the problem is severe in degree*. The manual does not specify the length of time the rater should be familiar with the subject prior to completion of the instrument, but rather it is suggested that he or she have a "knowledge" of a subject's behavior in a variety of settings. The authors provide excellent operational definitions for each item, with which the informant should be thoroughly familiar. With familiarity, the rater should be able to complete the ABC within 5 minutes. Scoring is also easily accomplished.

The authors indicate that the scale was empirically derived via factor analyses, which yielded the following five subscales: Irritability, Lethargy, Stereotypy, Hyperactivity, and Inappropriate Speech. Scores are derived by summing the items that comprise each scale. The subscale raw scores may then be compared to the average scores of subjects stratified by gender, age, and national origin (New Zealand vs. United States).

The sample is not described fully in the manual, rather the user is referred to an outside source (i.e., Aman, Singh, Stewart, & Field, 1985). A general description may be gleaned from two tables presented in the manual. It appears as if the ABC was standardized on a total of 754 New Zealanders aged 5 to 51+ years and 508 (age 7 to 51+ years) individuals from the United States. Subjects were in residential facilities, with levels of retardation ranging from moderate to profound. Nonambulatory and blind residents were excluded from the sample. The sample comprises approximately 60% male and 40% female individuals. Each category of retardation and gender is adequately represented within the sample. It is questionable as to whether there is sufficient number of subjects at each age level to be considered representative with regard to this variable; this is particularly obvious for children and adolescents. However, further norms have been developed since publication of the test manual. Marshburn and Aman (1992) report normative information for 666 students (6 to 21 years of age) enrolled in special classes.

RELIABILITY. Internal consistency, as measured by Cronbach's coefficient alphas, for each of the subscales are very good, ranging from .86 to .95. Thirteen nurses rated 184 hospital residents on two occasions, with a 4-week interval being noted between ratings in order to evaluate test-retest reliability. Coefficients ranged from .96 to .99 for the subscales, suggesting excellent temporal stability. The ABC did not fare quite as well regarding interrater reliability. Correlations between pairs of raters of residents revealed overall subscale means of the coefficients across the studies ranged from .55 to .69. The authors contend that such coefficients are "quite acceptable for research purposes" (p. 11), but are less than adequate for clinical use if the methodology employed involves use of multiple raters.

VALIDITY. Content validity seems reasonably well established. Items were developed via inspection of case records of 400 residents of a hospital for the mentally retarded and of other scales associated with mental retardation and childhood psychopathology. Concurrent validity was investigated by examination of the correlational relationships between the ABC and other instruments associated with mental retardation (e.g., intelligence, adaptive behavior). Results revealed many moderate correlational relationships (in the expected directions) between the ABC subscales and measures of adaptive behavior. Additionally, behavioral observation categories similar to those tapped by the ABC were found to discriminate between "high" and "low" scorers on four of the five subscales of the ABC. In support of construct validity, the authors identified two characteristics "thought to reflect differing levels of maladaptive behavior in a residential-type facility" (p. 13). These were attendance (versus nonattendance) at an available training program and whether or not the resident had Down's syndrome, with the rationale being that those with higher degrees of maladaptive behavior would include residents who had been excluded from training facilities and those without Down's syndrome. Results of these studies supported the authors' premise. Other similar studies are alluded to in the manual, but there are insufficient details presented to judge adequately the relevance of the studies to the validity of the ABC. Factorial validity is noted to be quite strong. The factor structure of the ABC has proven to be quite robust across various populations as is evidenced by numerous studies since the test's publication date (Aman, Singh, & Turbott, 1987; Bihm & Poindexter, 1991; Mashburn & Aman, 1992; Rojahn & Helsel, 1991).

The authors note that "there are relatively few data pertaining to the sensitivity of the ABC to drug effects" (p. 18), which is unfortunate given the stated purpose of the scale. The two studies that used the final version of the ABC yielded some evidence the subscales of the ABC are sensitive to the effects of drug treatment. Specifically, statistically significant improvements were noted in many of the subscales following the introduction of psychotropic medications (pimozide, imipramine). This could indicate, as the authors suggest, that the ABC is more sensitive to subtle behavioral changes than are systematic observations.

CONCLUSIONS. The ABC is a rating scale designed to be used with individuals with moderate to profound retardation in residential placements, with the stated purpose being to identify treatment effects (i.e., psychotropic drugs) in these individuals. Although the original work focused on ratings by health care personnel in residential facilities, the use of the scale has been extended in the literature to children and adolescents in school-based programs and to ratings by parents and teachers. Completion and scoring of the scale are easily accomplished but the interrater reliability is only moderate overall. The instrument has many notable strengths, including item development, suggesting strong content and factorial validity. With the exception of the problems noted for interrater reliability, estimates of reliability are excellent. The manual is lacking, however, in many respects. It frequently refers the consumer to outside sources to gain crucial information that would have been better included in the text of the manual. Also, details to many of the studies presented as evidence of validation lacked enough details for proper evaluation. The major weakness of the instrument is the limited evidence of its sensitivity to treatment effects. This is of considerable concern in that this is the clearly stated purpose of the test. This reviewer concurs with the authors that the instrument possesses adequate psychometric qualities for research purposes. However, results of research devoted to investigation of the effects of drug treatments should be viewed with caution until further validation data are obtained. A review of the literature revealed a study (Bihm, Poindexter, Kienlen, &

Smith, 1992) that focused on the use of the ABC to evaluate responsiveness to reinforcers; this is intriguing and suggests that the ABC may also prove useful in the detection of treatment effects such as those associated with behavioral interventions.

REVIEWER'S REFERENCES

Aman, M. G., Singh, N. N., Stewart, A. W., & Field, C. J. (1985). The Aberrant Behavior Checklist: A behavior rating scale for the assessment of treatment effects. *American Journal of Mental Deficiency, 89*, 485-491.

Aman, M. G., Singh, N. N., & Turbott, S. H. (1987). Reliability of the Aberrant Behavior Checklist and the effects of variations in instructions. *American Journal of Mental Deficiency, 92*, 237-240.

Bihm, E. M., & Poindexter, A. R. (1991). Cross-validation of the factor structure of the Aberrant Behavior Checklist for persons with mental retardation. *American Journal of Mental Retardation, 96*, 209-211.

Rojahn, J., & Helsel, W. J. (1991). The Aberrant Behavior Checklist with children and adolescents with dual diagnosis. *Journal of Autism and Developmental Disorders, 21*, 17-28.

Bihm, E. M., Poindexter, A. R., Kienlen, T. L., & Smith, B. L. (1992). Staff perceptions of reinforcer responsiveness and aberrant behaviors in people with mental retardation. *Journal of Autism and Developmental Disorders, 22*, 83-93.

Mashburn, E. C., & Aman, M. G. (1992). Factor validity and norms for the Aberrant Behavior Checklist in a community sample of children with mental retardation. *Journal of Autism and Developmental Disorders, 22*, 357-373.

Review of the Aberrant Behavior Checklist by J. JEFFREY GRILL, Special Education Coordinator, Ingram State Community College, Deatsville, AL:

The Aberrant Behavior Checklist (ABC) is intended for use as a scale for "rating inappropriate and maladaptive behavior of mentally retarded individuals in residential settings" (manual, p. ii). The 58 items of the ABC are presented as descriptive phrases (e.g., Item 5, "Seeks isolation from others," Item 44, "Easily distractible") to be rated on a scale of 0 (*not at all a problem*) to 3 (*the problem is severe in degree*). The scale, originally developed in New Zealand and cross validated in the United States, may be completed in as little as 5 minutes by "anyone who has a good knowledge of the subject's behavior" (p. 4), including psychologists, teachers, aides, volunteers, or nurses.

Ratings are completed on the inner faces of the protocol, a folded, 11 x 17-inch sheet. These faces include brief directions and the items. One outer face includes space for demographic, pertinent training, medical, and current medication information about the subject; the other is blank. A separate sheet is used to transfer ratings to five columns representing a reordering of items into the five ABC subscales: I, Irritability (15 items); II, Lethargy (16 items); III, Stereotypy (7 items); IV, Hyperactivity (16 items); V, Inappropriate Speech (4 items). For each subscale, the ratings are summed to yield a raw score. No scaled or standard scores are provided because the authors believe that "it makes no sense to speak in terms of 'norms' for institutional residents" (p. 8), and they provide several legitimate reasons for eschewing norms. They suggest that ABC users develop local norms that are relevant to the institutions and populations where the scale is used. However, the manual includes tabular presentation of mean subscale raw scores, by age and sex groups for 454 male and 300 female residents at institutions in New Zealand, and for 306 male and 202 female residents of a large institution in the United States.

The ABC is clearly identified as a research tool that may be useful in monitoring the effects of pharmacological, behavioral, dietary supplement, and other treatments. The authors recommend it be used to supplement, but not to replace, other means of assessing treatment effects. The ABC is narrowly focused, with a well-defined and limited use.

Development of the ABC was careful and thorough, beginning with the selection of a pool of 125 problem behaviors to be written as scale items, and derived from case records of institutionalized individuals at a 400-bed hospital for the mentally retarded, and from review of extant rating scales. This initial scale was used to rate 465 residents, of whom 418 met criteria as ambulatory, and moderately to profoundly retarded. A total of 76 items remained after a factor analysis of those items that applied to at least 10% of this sample. A second independent group of 509 subjects was rated with the 76-item scale. Results of these ratings were also subjected to a factor analysis, and yielded similar results. That is, both analyses yielded five factor solutions, and these factors resulted in the subscales listed above. Comparisons of factor analyses led to further reduction of the items to 58.

Within the Subscales I, II, III, and IV, some items seem redundant. But, pages 5–7 of the manual include specific examples of behaviors identified for each item, thus resolving these apparent redundancies. ABC users should note that these resolutions involve subtle, but clear distinctions between items.

Three types of reliability data are reported: internal consistency, interrater, and test-retest. To estimate internal consistency, coefficients alpha were calculated for each subscale separately for the New Zealand and United States samples. Ranges of .86 to .95 and .88 to .94 for the two samples respectively suggest adequate to high internal consistency. Interrater reliability coefficients, however, ranged only from .55 to .69 for the subscales, in two studies in which pairs of nurses rated groups of 25 residents. Test-retest reliability (reported as Spearman rank order correlation coefficients) ranged from .96 to .99, but these coefficients, based on ratings of 184 hospital residents by 13 nurses, seem unexpectedly high, even to the test authors. And, one must ask why Spearman rather than Pearson coefficients were used to estimate test-retest reliability.

Validity data include results of criterion group studies, correlations with other instruments, and comparisons of ABC ratings with behavioral observations. Criterion group studies (i.e., training facility attenders versus nonattenders, and Down's syndrome versus non-Down's syndrome individuals) resulted in significant differences between groups on mean raw scores for four and five subscales, respectively. Correlations with other instruments suggest that the ABC is (*a*) minimally related to IQ (i.e., Slosson Intelligence Test); (*b*) moderately, negatively related to scales of adaptive behavior (i.e., Fairview Self Help Scale, Vineland Social Maturity Scale, and Part I of the AAMD Adaptive Behavior Scale [ABS]); and (*c*) significantly, positively correlated with analogous domains of the AAMD ABS Part II (e.g., Withdrawal, Stereotyped, and Self Abusive Behavior). Behavior observations of 36 individuals discriminated between subgroups of "high" and "low" scorers at statistically significant levels for Subscales II through V.

Relationship of the ABC to drug treatment was investigated in three studies reported in the manual. Two indicated some sensitivity of the Irritability and Hyperactivity subscales to methylphenidate and to pimozide. The third, a double-blind, placebo controlled study of imipramine in 10 profoundly retarded individuals, revealed a sensitivity of the Irritability, Lethargy, and Hyperactivity subscales to behavior changes effected by the drug. Comparison of mean subscale raw scores of individuals from the New Zealand and United States groups who were receiving no drugs, with those receiving various medications (including antipsychotic, hypnotic, anticonvulsant, antihistamine, or antidepressant medication), revealed that Subscales I through IV, for the New Zealand group, and I, III, and IV for the United States group, discriminated, at statistically significant levels, between those receiving and not receiving drugs.

SUMMARY. The ABC is a carefully developed instrument with some weaknesses. Interrater reliability, important for any rating scale, is weak; internal consistency and test-retest reliabilities are adequate to high. Validity seems adequate, but more evidence on the scale's usefulness with pharmacological treatments is needed. And the manual would benefit from inclusion of much research and descriptive data that is cited but not fully presented. Yet, the ABC appears to be a valuable tool for its primary purpose, research with a clearly, narrowly defined population.

[2]

Access Management Survey.

Purpose: Designed to measure the extent to which a manager provides opportunities and support for employee involvement, and the necessary resources for people to influence work-life issues.
Population: Adults.
Publication Date: 1989.
Acronym: AMS.
Scores, 5: Access to the Problem, Access to People, Access to Information and Resources, Access to Support, Access to the Solution.
Administration: Group.
Price Data, 1993: $6.95 per survey.
Time: Untimed.
Comments: Self-assessment survey.
Author: Jay Hall.
Publisher: Teleometrics International.

Review of the Access Management Survey by THOMAS M. HALADYNA, Professor of Educational Psychology, and ROBERT M. HESS, Assistant Professor of Education, Arizona State University West, Phoenix, AZ:

The Access Management Survey (AMS) was developed for managers involved and interested in managing social aspects of the work force under each manager's responsibility. It is "designed to measure the extent to which managers provide their employees with the opportunities and support for genuine employee involvement" (p. 17). The instrument is based on Jay Hall's Star Model of Access Management for Employment Involvement. This instrument is clearly in the experimental, development stage at this time.

This self-scorable instrument contains 25 items. Instead of using a conventional rating scale, respondents are asked to read a statement and allocate 5 points representing the strength of affinity to bipolar statement. The 25 responses are added up in five columns to arrive at five subscales: access to (*a*) the problem itself, (*b*) people involved, (*c*) needed information and resources, (*d*) emotional and procedural supports, and (*e*) the solution. Scores range from zero to 25 for each scale, relating to the allocation procedure of 5 points for each item. The instrument is available in a number of languages (e.g., Spanish, Swedish, French, German). Norms are provided in a graphical manner so the user can chart the raw scores on the norm figure and instantly read the result: excellent, good, fair, or poor.

The test booklet contains a nine-page section on interpreting results. This section explains the background for the use of the instrument, its history, the underlying rationale for its use, and a related research project is reviewed. Then another section deals with the concept of access management, as measured by this instrument. Although the author is employing a *norming* strategy for users to interpret their individual scores, it is difficult to accept this technique as representative of some type of standardization. The author offers a "normative profile based on the scores of a number of individuals [is] provided via a percentile scaling technique" (p. 17). The limited technical information available in the user scorable manual provides inadequate evidence of the standards by which the test is *normed*.

Alpha reliability is described in the user manual at .86 for the instrument, which is puzzling because the instrument yields five distinct subscores. The assumption is that this value was obtained with the total score rather than the subscores. No supportive information is provided on the sample for estimating reliability.

The author provides a single paragraph explaining that the AMS's validity is *concurrent*; stating that concurrent validity is fair in discriminating among high, average, and low achieving managers. No published study or data are provided. It appears this type of instrument, based as it is upon a theoretical model of management, should be attempting to establish its construct validity first before attempting to establish a rationale for another type of validity. The lack of supportive studies or evidence related to the validity of the instrument is a serious flaw that must be corrected. Personal communication with the publisher indicated that a technical manual is under development but was not available at the time of this review.

The AMS author maintains that the AMS is suitable only for concept training and as a stimulus for team discussion and critique. Even this limited application should be undertaken with prudence. The results of any test lacking empirical supportive evidence and employed for individual evaluation should be interpreted with extreme caution.

Given the lack of validation evidence, it would be difficult to support the use of the instrument for any purpose other than what the author claims. Perhaps this is an instrument that may be used for experimental or research applications but, considering the lack of reliability and validity evidence and the absence of established norms, the instrument would not be used at this time beyond the author's recommendation of its use to stimulate discussion among group members.

Review of the Access Management Survey by MARY A. LEWIS, Manager, Human Resources, PPG Architectural Finishes, Pittsburgh, PA:

The Access Management Survey (AMS) is a self-report inventory designed to measure the extent to which a manager provides opportunities and support for employee involvement. It has 25 situational items with what amounts to a five-option behaviorally anchored rating scale that is described on page 17 of the booklet as "forced-choice, paired-comparison scaling technique." The AMS has five scale scores with five items per scale measuring access to: the problem, the people, information and resources, supports for sustained involvement, and the solution. The items are presented in a 17-page booklet that serves both as a self-administered questionnaire and as a scoring and interpretive guide.

Although the administrative manual contains a great deal of narrative data about the theory supporting the concept of involvement, the normative charts for the Personal Reaction Index on page 8 of the booklet are confusing. The technical development information for the AMS is on page 17. If this instrument is to be evaluated against professional standards (American Educational Research Association, American Psychological Association, & National Council on Measurement in Education, 1985), then it fails miserably.

No technical data are presented to support the design of the items or the scales. No technical data are presented to support the metric used for item response. The author states on page 17 of the manual that "Internal consistency of the AMS is excellent as evidenced by the Alpha of .86," but does not describe the sample used to calculate the alpha, does not indicate how a single alpha was calculated on five separate scales, and does not give any indication of the interscale correlation, or the correlation of the scales with external measures.

The description of the norms is also free of information. In fact, the author merely describes the norms as a method of comparing scores to other working people, and then says on page 17 that the normative data was "based on the score of a number of individuals." From this, I can assume only that more than one person was involved in the sample.

In summary, there is no evidence the scales on the AMS are consistently measuring anything. There is no evidence the scales of the AMS relate in any way to effectiveness of teams, managers, or organizations.

There is a pattern to Hall's lack of technical support for marketed measurement tools that is reflected in reviews of some of his other instruments. I found 17 reviews of various instruments authored by Hall and published by Telemetrics in the last four editions of the *Mental Measurements Yearbooks*: Managerial Competence Index (Geisinger, 1992); Team Process Diagnostic (Aleamoni, 1992); Teamness Index (Lachar, 1992; Leong, 1992); Management Appraisal Survey (Thornton, 1989; Bernardin, 1989); Personal Reaction Index (Alexander, 1985; Spencer, 1985); Power Management Inventory (Benson, 1985; Owens, 1985); Power Management Profile (Gutenberg, 1985); Process Diagnostic (Thayer, 1978); Team Effectiveness Survey (Mollenkopf, 1978); Sales Transaction Audit (Cohen, 1978); Conflict Management Survey (Landy, 1978); Styles of Leadership and Management (Korman, 1978); Personal Relations Survey (Guion, 1978). Those reviews consistently cite a lack of psychometric evidence of reliability and validity. The same reviews also document a lack of content validity, that is, the author does not even provide logical evidence for scale construction and the relationship of the scale to some outcome.

The AMS is designed as a developmental tool intended to change the way managers interact with the people in their organizations. Based on its lack of sound theoretical and empirical evidence, I would not recommend the use of the AMS for any purpose. There are other tools that can be used developmentally for building teams and involvement, that have a much more solid theoretical and empirical base. These instruments may be located by perusing the content section of this and earlier versions of the *Mental Measurements Yearbook*. I would further suggest that any reader who encounters a Hall instrument published by Telemetrics should strongly consider looking elsewhere for a better tool.

REVIEWER'S REFERENCES

Cohen, S. L. (1978). [Review of the Sales Transaction Audit.] In O. K. Buros (Ed.), *The eighth mental measurements yearbook* (pp. 1711-1712). Highland Park, NJ: The Gryphon Press.

Guion, R. M. (1978). [Review of the Personal Relations Survey.] In O. K. Buros (Ed.), *The eighth mental measurements yearbook* (pp. 1760-1761). Highland Park, NJ: The Gryphon Press.

Korman, A. K. (1978). [Review of the Styles of Leadership and Management.] In O. K. Buros (Ed.), *The eighth mental measurements yearbook* (p. 1763). Highland Park, NJ: The Gryphon Press.

Landy, F. J. (1978). [Review of the Conflict Management Survey.] In O. K. Buros (Ed.), *The eighth mental measurements yearbook* (pp. 1741-1742). Highland Park, NJ: The Gryphon Press.

Mollenkopf, W. G. (1978). [Review of the Team Effectiveness Survey.] In O. K. Buros (Ed.), *The eighth mental measurements yearbook* (p. 1682). Highland Park, NJ: The Gryphon Press.

Thayer, P. W. (1978). [Review of the Process Diagnostic.] In O. K. Buros (Ed.), *The eighth mental measurements yearbook* (pp. 1680-1681). Highland Park, NJ: The Gryphon Press.

Alexander, R. A. (1985). [Review of the Personal Reaction Index.] In J. V. Mitchell, Jr., (Ed.), *The ninth mental measurements yearbook* (pp. 1148-1149). Lincoln, NE: The Buros Institute of Mental Measurements.

American Educational Research Association, American Psychological Association, & National Council on Measurement in Education. (1985). *Standards for educational and psychological testing*. Washington, DC: American Psychological Association, Inc.

Benson, P. G. (1985). [Review of the Power Management Inventory.] In J. V. Mitchell, Jr., (Ed.), *The ninth mental measurements yearbook* (p. 1178). Lincoln, NE: The Buros Institute of Mental Measurements.

Gutenberg, R. L. (1985). [Review of the Power Management Profile.] In J. V. Mitchell, Jr., (Ed.), *The ninth mental measurements yearbook* (pp. 1179-1180). Lincoln, NE: The Buros Institute of Mental Measurements.

Spencer, D. G. (1985). [Review of the Personal Reaction Index.] In J. V. Mitchell, Jr., (Ed.), *The ninth mental measurements yearbook* (p. 1149). Lincoln, NE: The Buros Institute of Mental Measurements.

Owens, W. A. (1985). [Review of the Power Management Inventory.] In J. V. Mitchell, Jr., (Ed.), *The ninth mental measurements yearbook* (pp. 1178-1179). Lincoln, NE: The Buros Institute of Mental Measurements.

Bernardin, H. J. (1989). [Review of the Management Appraisal Survey.] In J. C. Conoley & J. J. Kramer (Eds.), *The tenth mental measurements yearbook* (pp. 458-459). Lincoln, NE: The Buros Institute of Mental Measurements.

Thornton, G. C., III. (1989). [Review of the Management Appraisal Survey.] In J. C. Conoley & J. J. Kramer (Eds.), *The tenth mental measurements yearbook* (pp. 459-460). Lincoln, NE: The Buros Institute of Mental Measurements.

Aleamoni, L. M. (1992). [Review of the Team Process Diagnostic.] In J. J. Kramer & J. C. Conoley (Eds.), *The eleventh mental measurements yearbook* (pp. 919-920). Lincoln, NE: The Buros Institute of Mental Measurements.

Geisinger, K. F. (1992). [Review of the Managerial Competence Index.] In J. J. Kramer & J. C. Conoley (Eds.), *The eleventh mental measurements yearbook* (pp. 502-503). Lincoln, NE: The Buros Institute of Mental Measurements.

Lachar, B. (1992). [Review of the Teamness Index.] In J. J. Kramer & J. C. Conoley (Eds.), *The eleventh mental measurements yearbook* (pp. 920-921). Lincoln, NE: The Buros Institute of Mental Measurements.

Leong, F. T. L. (1992). [Review of the Teamness Index.] In J. J. Kramer & J. C. Conoley (Eds.), *The eleventh mental measurements yearbook* (pp. 921-923). Lincoln, NE: The Buros Institute of Mental Measurements.

[3]

Accounting Program Admission Test.

Purpose: Designed as "an objective measure of student achievement in elementary accounting."

Population: College level elementary accounting students.

Publication Date: 1988.

Acronym: APAT.

Scores, 3: Financial Accounting, Managerial Accounting, Total.

Administration: Group.

Price Data: Available from publisher.

Time: 100(110) minutes.

Comments: Formerly called the AICPA Accounting Program Admission Test; no longer affiliated with the AICPA.

Author: American Institute of Certified Public Accountants.

Publisher: The Psychological Corporation.

Review of the Accounting Program Admission Test by JoELLEN CARLSON, Director of Testing Standards, New York Stock Exchange, Inc., New York, NY:

The Accounting Program Admission Test (APAT) is designed to provide colleges and universities with a standardized measure of achievement in elementary accounting. It purports to measure knowledge of financial and managerial accounting principles typically covered in first-year elementary accounting courses. The test consists of 75 items—45 covering Financial Accounting and 30, Managerial Accounting. It is intended to be used in conjunction with other measures, such as overall grade-point average and principles of accounting course grades, for evaluating students' preparation for admission to intermediate accounting courses. Equated scaled scores and percentile ranks are reported for each of the two content areas and for the total test. The APAT score scale ranges from 50 to 350, with a median of 200.

The test was prepared originally under the direction of the American Institute of Certified Public Accountants (AICPA). Some of the publisher's materials mention that accounting educators with expertise in the areas covered by the test have written and reviewed the items, and that such experts review the test content annually, although there is no further description of the procedures and criteria for selecting these educators or the conditions under which the items are written and reviewed. Marketing materials indicate that all items are subjected to a national item tryout and psychometric evaluation, but no further information on item tryout or the psychometric characteristics of the items was provided for this review.

The documentation of test development procedures and psychometric characteristics of this test is inadequate. In the absence of a technical manual, the publisher made available upon request several items providing background information, but without explanation of their relationships. Among the items were a paper that appears to be a proposal for development of the test, a raw-score-scaled-score conversion table, a scaled-score-to-percentile conversion table for two forms of the test, and a printout of traditional test statistics. Although a reasonable approach to item tryouts, norming and equating is described, it is unclear whether the study was carried out as planned, given inconsistencies among the paper and the other materials.

Plans for norming with a geographically representative sample of institutions, stratified by type of institution, is also described. Although the numbers are inconsistent, the marketing materials describe a composition that roughly parallels the plan in proportionate representation of the types of institutions, including 84 institutions and approximately 10,000 students who had completed one year of accounting study. Forty-four percent of the students were from universities with schools of business, 36% from liberal arts colleges, and 20% from two-year community or technical colleges. It is not clear when the norming and equating study was completed.

The authors of the paper and marketing materials cite correlations between .43 and .53 between first-year accounting achievement test scores and elementary accounting grades, and between .32 and .60, with a median of .48, between test scores and intermediate accounting grades. Although it appears that some of the studies may have used this test, it is not completely clear, and additional information should be provided.

It is not clear how many forms of the test exist, as the plan calls for at least four by 1989, but the administration manual and raw-score-to-scaled-score conversion table are for two forms, the scaled-score-to-percentile conversion table is for one form, and the test statistics printout is for only one form. The reported mean score is 43.777, with a standard deviation of 11.359 and standard error of measurement of 3.803. A single reliability estimate is given, a KR20 of .888.

Marketing materials advertise measurement assistance with local data collection, validity studies, and norms development, but there was no information available to this reviewer describing what instructions are given to the institutions using the results. The 1993 Candidate Information Bulletin contains the following quote: "The Psychological Corporation does not set a standard for what is an acceptable score. Each school decides how scores will be used" (p. 10). Authors of the Bulletin instruct students to contact the appropriate accounting department with questions regarding performance standards and their use of examination scores. Understandably, schools would set their own performance standards, but the publisher must be responsible for giving guidance about appropriate interpretations of the scores.

Each institution using the test results is responsible for its own test administration, beginning with informing students of the test requirement and distributing copies of the Candidate Information Booklet. The test fee is determined and collected by the institution administering the APAT, and the fee is allowed to vary with the institution. After administration, the institution returns completed answer sheets to the publisher for electronic scanning and scoring. Marketing materials contain citations about quality control procedures, both computerized and manual, during and after the scoring process, to ensure the accuracy of scores. Test booklets are not made available for review, and candidates are not able to obtain a list of the items they answered incorrectly or correctly, but they are informed of this in advance. Scores are sent to the examinees and up to two schools if requested within 6 weeks following the date of testing.

The Manual of Directions for Examiners is quite thorough and well organized. It provides specific directions for all aspects of test center preparation, test administration, security, and follow-up, and stresses the importance of following the directions exactly as given in the manual. The directions to be read to the examinees are precise and clear. In addition to cautioning the test administrator against answering questions about specific test content or the meanings of words and against commenting on an examinee's performance, the manual includes some frequently asked questions and provides samples of acceptable responses, important precautions with such a test administered by the user.

The Candidate Information Bulletin, recently revised for administrations of the examination after September 1, 1993, is well organized and informative for the potential examinee. It contains relevant information about the purpose of the test, fees and logistics of registering for the test, the general content of the test, and what to expect and do after the test. Notable is the detailed information given for contacting the publisher with requests, along with a toll-free number. Ten sample items, roughly representative of the topic areas in the test, are provided with the correct response options, but no rationales are provided for the correct options. The Candidate Information Bulletin contains detailed instructions for candidates with disabilities who require extra time or assistance, and there is no additional fee for nonstandard administrations for candidates with disabilities. There are no special norms for scores obtained under nonstandard conditions.

Candidates are not allowed to use calculators in taking this test. Although the computations are simple and straightforward, disallowing the use of calculators does not seem to present a realistic situation. On the other hand, this provides standardization of an important aspect of the test administration, as it would be quite difficult to standardize the calculators across the various institutions administering the test.

In the one form of the test provided for review, the items are generally quite well edited, but a few contain minor flaws. There are several "classic" elementary-level accounting items, with financial and managerial accounting items mixed.

The presentation and content of the test, the Candidate Information Bulletin, and the Manual of Directions for Examiners are all of high quality. The publisher needs now to devote attention to planning and carrying out a systematic program of research on the psychometric characteristics of the test, and to documenting the developmental and technical aspects of the testing program.

Review of the Accounting Program Admission Test by WILLIAM R. KOCH, Professor of Educational Psychology, The University of Texas, Austin, TX:

DESCRIPTION. The Accounting Program Admission Test (APAT) is a timed, group-administered, multiple-choice achievement test consisting of 75 items having four answer options each, only one of which is correct. Examinees are allowed 100 minutes to complete the test. The stated purpose of the APAT is to provide colleges and universities with a standardized measure of academic achievement in elementary (first-year) accounting. Institutions may use APAT scores as part of an admissions process for upper division accounting programs or to evaluate the performance of students who have completed their first-year accounting programs relative to national norms. Forty-five of the items measure the content area of elementary Financial Accounting and 30 items cover elementary Managerial Accounting, so two subscores are provided in addition to the total composite score. Two alternate forms of the test are available.

The APAT was first published in 1988 by The Psychological Corporation and was known as the AICPA Accounting Program because it was authored by accounting educators and professionals who were members of the American Institute of Certified Public Accountants. However, the AICPA is no longer affiliated formally with the publication of the APAT. Materials available from the publisher include a Manual of Directions for Examiners and a Candidate Information Booklet, both of which are of high quality and provide useful, up-to-date information. The former has very explicit and clear instructions for examiners that no doubt would enhance the standardization of test administrations, whereas the latter contains suggested test-taking strategies along with 10 sample test questions and their answers. Unfortunately, no technical manual has yet been published for the APAT. However, the publisher was able to supply the reviewer with a few brief internal documents and working papers that describe some of the test development procedures and provide very limited information about norms and the psychometric characteristics of the APAT.

NORMS. Apparently two forms of the APAT were developed and administered to a norming group composed of more than 80 post-secondary institutions from 33 states around the U.S., most of which were community colleges or small regional universities with few exceptions. No information was provided about the numbers of students from each institution who were included in the norms. A frequency distribution was available of the raw scores obtained from the administration of one form of the APAT; the distribution was approximately normal based on a sample of 3,427 students with 99% of the raw scores falling in the range from 18 to 70.

TECHNICAL ELEMENTS. Conversion tables were provided that indicated the raw score to scaled score relationships and scaled score to percentile rank relationships for the two subtests and the total test composite score. Scaled scores range from 50 to 350 with a median equal to 200 (corresponding to a percentile rank of 50%). No information was available about the type of procedure used to equate the test forms nor about the degree of accuracy of the equating results.

The only information provided about the reliability of the APAT was one KR-20 internal consistency reliability estimate (KR-20 = .89) based on total scores from the sample of 3,427 students. No data were available as to test-retest or alternate forms reliability estimates.

The face validity of the APAT is readily apparent in that the items quite obviously measure academic achievement in accounting. Presumably some content validity was built into the test by having accounting educators involved in writing the items, classifying them as either financial or managerial accounting in the content measured, and in deciding on the 60% versus 40% breakdown of financial to managerial items to reflect the curriculum of first-year accounting courses. Unfortunately, no information is available about the criterion-related or construct validity of the APAT.

SUMMARY. The APAT cannot be recommended for use for its intended purposes in the absence of the usual types of information routinely provided in a technical manual. It is difficult even to justify the claim made by the publisher that the APAT is a standardized test in light of the dearth of information about the standardization procedures, the norming group, equating methods, and reliability and validity data. It would be irresponsible to use the APAT for evaluating the quality of first-year accounting programs, for admissions decisions (unless perhaps if local norms and other psychometric information were available), or for interpreting a student's scores relative to norms having an unknown origin.

[4]

ACER Advanced Test B90: New Zealand Edition.

Purpose: "Designed to measure general intellectual ability."
Population: College students and adults.
Publication Date: 1991.
Scores: Total score only.
Administration: Group.

Price Data: Price information available from publisher for test materials including administrator's manual (5 pages).
Time: 50(55) minutes.
Comments: "Selected items from the ACER Advanced Test B40 and the ACER Test of Cognitive Ability."
Authors: Australian Council for Educational Research and manual by Neil Reid and Cedric Croft.
Publisher: New Zealand Council for Educational Research [New Zealand].
Cross References: For a review of ACER Advanced Test B40 by Harriet C. Cobb, see 9:4; see also T2:323 (6 references) and 7:328 (4 references); for a review of ACER Advanced Test B40 by C. Sanders, see 5:296 (3 references).

Review of the ACER Advanced Test B90: New Zealand Edition by JOHN RUST, Senior Lecturer in Psychometrics, Goldsmith's College, University of London, London, England:

The 70-item ACER Advanced Test B90: New Zealand Edition is a new instrument that has been specifically developed for New Zealand but borrows items from the Australian ACER Advanced Test B40 (1983; 9:4) and the ACER Test of Cognitive Ability (1983; 9:23). Items were modified or rewritten, as appropriate, for the New Zealand market. The revisions involved item substitutions and repositioning, as well as changes in both question stems and options to provide a local flavour. The test consists of verbal and quantitative items, but does not include tasks involving nonverbal or perceptual material which, the authors say, would have been included if the test had been intended to give a balanced measure of general cognitive ability. The test is reported as "utilizing a number of types of item which are judged to contribute to an assessment of the general ability factor (*g*), as described by Spearman" (manual, p. 1). It is aimed at the higher ranges of ability. Its intended use is with "students already taking or planning to undertake tertiary courses, and with adults in a selection/training context where emphasis is likely to be placed on relatively superior intellectual abilities" (p. 1).

Item analysis was carried out within the New Zealand Ministry of Defense with recruits and trainees of suitable age and experience in training establishments throughout the country. Further minor revisions were made as a result. Standardization, however, is based on 251 male and 625 female students who were taking courses on testing, measurement, and evaluation within five university psychology departments and two university education departments. There is no explanation of why this atypical sample was used in preference to the military recruits used in the pilot study. Standardization is to a stanine score, which is appropriate for the circumstances. No information on ethnic or linguistic origin was reported. In the light of this they make the apt comment that the test is "inappropriate for use with individuals whose cultural or linguistic backgrounds are such that they could be regarded as disadvantaged in taking tests of this nature" (p. 1). The implications of this in the light of the publisher's suggestion that the test can be used with adults in a selection context does, however, warrant more attention. Sex differences were found which replicated the gender bias that exists in the parent Test of Cognitive Ability, with men obtaining higher scores than women.

No new evidence is given of reliability and validity. The user is referred to the manuals of the two ACER tests from which the items were derived. This obviously fails to meet any reasonable standard for the production of a test manual. Although it might make sense to report an adaptation and restandardization of one of the source tests alone on this basis, no indication is given of the relative contribution of each source test to the new edition. It is clear that, in the absence of any direct data, some estimate of reliability and validity might be obtained from the source tests. However, this should have been reported together with some rationale for the estimation procedure.

In some ways, the authors of this test fail to do themselves justice. The items contain a certain face validity; some strategy must have led to the original test specification which clearly could have been reported. The similarity of the content to tests in use in other countries suggests the test is potentially reliable and valid, at least for assessing the level of reasoning among college students. As it is, the manual provided fails to meet the minimum standards of reporting expected by today's psychology professionals. In the absence of proper reliability and validity data as well as of appropriate norms, it is of some concern that the test should be recommended for use with adults within a selection/training context.

[5]

ACER Applied Reading Test.

Purpose: Designed to measure ability to read and understand technical material.
Population: Apprentices, trainees, technical and trade personnel.
Publication Dates: 1989–90.
Scores: Total score only.
Administration: Group.
Forms, 2: A, B.
Price Data, 1994: A$4.75 per test booklet; $4.50 per 10 answer sheets; $4.20 per score key; $23.50 per manual ('90, 24 pages); $42 per specimen set.
Time: 40–45 minutes.
Authors: J. M. van den Berg and I. R. Woff.
Publisher: Australian Council for Educational Research Ltd. [Australia].

Review of the ACER Applied Reading Test by MARK H. DANIEL, Senior Scientist, American Guidance Service, Circle Pines, MN:

The ACER Applied Reading Test (ART) addresses a need for an Australian test of the ability to read and understand technical material. It is intended for selecting applicants into training or apprenticeship programs or for identifying trainees or employees who need remedial reading instruction.

Each of the two forms has six passages which are each followed by four to seven multiple-choice questions. The passages, in the form of memoranda, instructions, and tables, are adapted from or modeled on actual documents and have an authentic flavor.

A challenge to tests of this type is to present reading materials that are technical enough to be realistic, yet not so technical as to measure knowledge of the subject area. The ART items appear to require only a basic knowledge of technical terms and concepts (such as names of tools and parts), making the test appropriate in this respect for its intended examinees. Most items cannot be answered without reading the passage, but some on each form are passage-independent and can be answered solely from prior knowledge. Fortunately, each form's passages cover diverse topics (e.g., food preparation, plumbing, and safety procedures).

The passages seem to be written at a fairly high general reading level. Each form's initial passage has a Flesch-Kincaid readability index (computed by this reviewer) of grade 9 or 10. It would have been better to start with easier material, so that the test could measure at lower reading levels. There is almost no hint of Australian origin; this reviewer found only two variant spellings ("organisation" and "minimise") and one uncommon term ("n.b.").

The items are literal rather than inferential, few requiring even the ability to understand a paraphrase of the original text. About 10% to 20% of the items on each form are of the complex multiple-choice type in which the examinee must decide which of four sets of one, two, or more "answers" is correct. Because this item format adds difficulty and introduces a reasoning factor, it seems out of place in a test designed to measure reading comprehension.

The test manual, labeled "interim," covers a broad range of important topics but with little depth. The data indicate that the instrument is sound, but additional information is needed, particularly in the areas of validation and equivalence of forms.

NORMS. Norms are presented as percentile ranks, stanines, *T* scores, and *z* scores. The separate norm samples for Forms A ($N = 284$) and B ($N = 372$) consist of Australian applicants to skilled-trades apprenticeships or technical training programs, aged 15 to 38. The samples differ in the types of trades being applied for, and the norm tables for the two forms differ substantially, with median raw scores of 20.4 and 22.7 for Forms A and B. A raw score that yields a percentile of 29 on Form B yields a 49 on Form A; one that yields the 69th percentile on Form B gives the 81st on Form A.

Whether the norm tables differ because the samples vary in ability or because the forms are not equivalent is difficult to say. The manual reports an equivalence study of 88 technical-school students who took both forms in counterbalanced order; Form B's mean score was only slightly (about .1 *SD*) higher, indicating close agreement. The fact that the study revealed a negative practice effect, which the authors attribute to low motivation, weakens its credibility.

Unfortunately, the manual's presentation of divergent norms for the two forms invites misinterpretation. If the forms are approximately equivalent, it is inappropriate to provide different norms based on different samples for each. This has the effect of yielding higher normative scores for examinees who happen to take Form A. It would have been more reasonable, under the assumption of equivalence, to derive a single set of norms from the combined samples for both forms. Form-specific norms would only be appropriate if they served to correct a lack of equivalence between the forms, and then care would have to be taken to make the norm groups comparable.

Without persuasive evidence on form equivalence, anyone using this test for selection or placement should use only one form to avoid normative comparisons among people who took different forms. If both forms must be used, it probably would be best to base comparisons on raw scores or on a single set of norms (such as those for Form A).

RELIABILITY. An impressive alternate-forms reliability of .85 is reported for 88 technical-school students aged 15–17. Surprisingly, internal-consistency reliability is somewhat lower. Coefficient alpha is .83 and .82 for the Forms A and B norm samples, respectively. The norm tables indicate that both forms have adequate floor and ceiling for those populations, the median raw score being about 22 in a possible range of 0 to 32. The 30-minute time limit is assumed to be adequate to avoid introducing a speed factor, based on the authors' observation of the performance of tryout samples on 36-item versions of the forms and on the 32-item final version. However, no data are given on the percentage of norm-sample examinees completing the test within the time limit.

VALIDITY. Information on the validity of the ART consists solely of correlations with other tests. The most relevant is a correlation of .82 with the Industrial Reading Test (IRT) for a sample of 61 technical students aged 15–17. Because the IRT and ART have similar objectives and target populations, this result supports the ART's construct validity. Most of the norm-sample cases also took an ACER mathematics test, which correlates about .6 with the ART, and several USES General Aptitude Test Battery (GATB) subtests (Three-dimensional Space, *r* about .3; Shape Matching, about .25; and Figure Matching and Mark Making, about .15). The pattern of correlations is what one would expect for a highly *g*-loaded test, as reading tests generally are. There is no information on the scores of different occupational groups or on the relationship of ART scores to success in training or on the job.

SUMMARY. The ACER Applied Reading Test is an up-to-date, attractive measure of the ability to understand technical reading material. Its strengths include realistic content, good reliability, and a high correlation with another test of the same construct. Its general reading level may be high for some applicant or trainee groups, and its inclusion of compound items unnecessarily introduces a reasoning component. Because the two forms are not clearly equivalent and are normed on noncomparable samples, users should restrict their use to one form and should be particularly careful to avoid between-form comparison of normative scores. Given these cautions, the ART is a useful new measure of technical reading skill.

Review of the ACER Applied Reading Test by MICHAEL S. TREVISAN, Assistant Professor of Educational Leadership and Counseling Psychology, Washington State University, Pullman, WA:

In an attempt to provide validity and rigor to the selection of "apprentices, trainees, technical, and trade personnel" (manual, p. 1) in Australia, the Australian Council for Educational Research (ACER) developed the Applied Reading Test. This is a group-administered test designed to assess reading comprehension of technical material, essential for successful performance in trade or technical occupations. In addition to assisting the selection of trainees and technical personnel, the authors offer this test "in the counseling of individuals who work within or aspire to these occupations, and in the identification of those apprentices and other technical students who would benefit from remedial assistance with reading" (p. 1). The test was published in 1990.

DEVELOPMENT. There are two forms of the test, referred to as Form A and Form B, respectively. Each test is constructed of 32 four-option multiple-choice items keyed to six passages. The passages were adapted from actual text found in technical reading, in order to represent "real-world technical written material" (p. 1), a positive feature of the ACER Reading Test. Sound procedures for test development were followed, which include rigorous item writing, trial administration of the items, and elimination of items with poor technical quality.

ADMINISTRATION AND SCORING. The Interim Manual for the Applied Reading Test contains what the authors refer to as "preliminary" and "detailed" (p. 4) instructions for administration. The preliminary instructions include suggestions for room arrangements during testing and required materials. The detailed instructions contain the actual print to be read to test takers by the test proctor. Both the preliminary and detailed instructions were used during the norming of the test and should be followed explicitly for proper score comparison. Testing time requires 30 minutes. The authors suggest 45 minutes for administration.

Two options for scoring are available. The first is handscoring. A transparent overlay key, included with the test material, provides a convenient and accurate means of handscoring. An individual's score is simply the number of correct answers. A second means of scoring is to use the ACER scoring service. Directions are provided in the manual for this option.

INTERPRETATION AND NORMS. Derived scores in the form of *T*-scores, *z*-scores, percentiles, and stanines are available to add norm-referenced meaning to the number correct. These scores are obtained either through the scoring service, or if handscoring, by comparing the number correct to tabled derived scores in the manual. Additionally, descriptive ratings based on stanines are offered by the authors as a more comprehensible means of apprising candidates about their test performance.

Two hundred eighty-four subjects for Form A and 372 subjects for Form B constitute the norm group. Subjects were obtained from a technical training school and two colleges in Melbourne, Australia. An attempt was made to represent various trade occupations in the sample. The norm group "was predominantly male."

RELIABILITY. Two types of reliability data are provided. The first, equivalent forms reliability, was computed by correlating the two forms of the test. The correlation is .85. The second type, internal consistency, is.83 for Form A and .82 for Form B. Although these reliability data are acceptable for many applications of standardized norm-referenced tests, they are inadequate, given the "high-stakes" purposes of the test intended by the authors. More work concerning the comparability of the forms and the consistency within forms is needed.

VALIDITY. The authors' approach to developing a validity argument adds rigor to the technical aspects of the test. By correlating this test with several other tests the authors built a case for "the influence of a school achievement factor" (p. 16). Also, the authors found no relationship between age and performance on the ACER Applied Reading Test nor between gender and performance. A weakness, however, is that these analyses were conducted with small sample sizes. The authors acknowledge this in several places in the Interim Manual, and imply that additional analyses will be conducted as more data are collected.

FURTHER CONSIDERATIONS. Schools or companies in the United States that may want to use this test should be forewarned about comparing candidates in the United States with an Australian norm group.

There is some evidence that British psychologists successfully compare British subjects to U.S. norms on the Stanford-Binet (Wright & Stone, 1985). No study could be found which has investigated whether or not U.S. subjects can be successfully compared to Australian norms.

This reviewer found only one competing test, the Industrial Reading Test, published in 1978. A recent test review was critical of the passages in this test because they were constructed of general knowledge information (Sabers, 1985). Consequently, assuming general knowledge, one could perform well on that test without reading the passages. The ACER Applied Reading Test is clearly a developmental step above the Industrial Reading Test in this regard. Passages constructed from actual technical material reflect more content than general knowledge and, therefore, require reading to correctly answer the items. This difference gives the ACER Reading Test the potential to provide meaningful performance information to decision makers and inform candidates of their strengths and weaknesses.

SUMMARY. The ACER Applied Reading Test is an attempt to provide a means of selecting students into trade school or selecting personnel for trade occupations. Although proper test development procedures were followed, the technical characteristics of the test are insufficient for the selection of candidates and, therefore, this reviewer cannot recommend using the test for its intended purpose at this time. The ACER Applied Reading Test does have the potential to become a beneficial aid for selecting candidates into Australian trade and technical schools or occupations, after more data are collected and the technical inadequacies corrected. An empirical investigation concerning the viability of comparing U.S. candidates to Australian norms should be done before this test is used in the U.S.

REVIEWER'S REFERENCES

Sabers, D. L. (1985). [Review of the Industrial Reading Test.] In J. V. Mitchell, Jr. (Ed.), *The ninth mental measurements yearbook* (pp. 684-685). Lincoln, NE: Buros Institute of Mental Measurements.

Wright, B. D., & Stone, M. H. (1985). [Review of the British Ability Scales.] In J. V. Mitchell, Jr. (Ed.), *The ninth mental measurements yearbook* (pp. 232-235). Lincoln, NE: Buros Institute of Mental Measurements.

[6]

ACER Test of Reasoning Ability.

Purpose: "Designed to measure general intellectual ability."
Population: Educational years 9–11 in Australian school system.
Publication Dates: 1986–90.
Scores: Total score only.
Administration: Group.
Price Data: Not available.
Time: 45(60) minutes.
Author: Marion M. de Lemos.
Publisher: Australian Council for Educational Research Ltd. [Australia].

[The publisher advised in January 1994 that this test is now out of print—Ed.]

Review of the ACER Test of Reasoning Ability by PHILIP NAGY, Associate Professor of Measurement, Evaluation, and Computer Applications, The Ontario Institute for Studies in Education, Toronto, Ontario, Canada:

The ACER Test of Reasoning Ability is a 70-item test of "general intellectual ability" for students in years 9, 10, and 11 of Australian schools. Adult norms are provided as well. The test was developed as a multiple-choice version of the ACER Test of Cognitive Ability, an open-ended test normed in 1978 using students in years 10, 11, and 12. The change in age range is not explained. Although the test is described as suitable for use in large-scale testing programs, the author emphasizes interpretation of individual rather than group scores, for purposes related to educational guidance and vocational counselling. The manual advises appropriate cautions concerning the qualifications of test administrators and score interpreters. Respondents are advised to answer even if not absolutely sure, but not to guess wildly.

In the norming sample, there are inevitable anomalies between the actual and expected proportions of students by several variables: geography, type of school, sex, language background, and socioeconomic background. Thoughtful explanations and discussions on the potential impact of most of these are provided, including a calculation that the overrepresentation of independent schools distorts the tables by only .5 to 1.0 points.

A more serious, though far from fatal distortion is not handled satisfactorily: The norming sample has almost twice the expected proportions of students from managerial and professional homes, and only half the expected from semiskilled and unskilled homes. These discrepancies make the conversions from raw to derived scores about 2.3 points too low, but these values are not calculated for the test user as are those for the school-type discrepancies. This problem could be easily remedied in a future edition.

The adult norming sample is inadequate. It consists of 741 people who were applying for positions as police: 69% male, 82% under 25, and only 6% with more than high school education. Scores vary as expected depending on education, and remain relatively constant as a function of age (except for a drastic drop at age 35, based on only 12 people). Although these data are reported with many caveats on their use, it would have been better to omit them entirely from the manual, treat them as developmental work in progress, and market the test for use with school students only.

The administration directions are clear, but there are some problems with the practice questions that exemplify the difficulties of multiple-choice items.

Practice Item 2 (there are 10 like it in the test) presents six mammals and asks which two are different. My first choice, not offered, was the pair of herbivores, sheep and giraffe; the keyed response was the pair of domesticated animals, sheep and dog. Such dubious questions should not be included, particularly as a practice exercise.

Practice Item 5 presents a 3-by-3 matrix, and asks the respondent to provide one of three missing numbers. My initial magic square strategy, in which all rows and columns have the same total, did not work. The route to the keyed response is that a simple operation (e.g., add 3, add 2) is required to go from one row or column to the next. I presented this problem to two colleagues; one used the nonproductive magic square route, whereas the other got the right answer using a holistic strategy that he described as "balance." It seems that a respondent is expected to learn the method for the three similar questions of this type from the practice exercise. However, the scripted explanation of some 230+ words is followed, as in all the examples, with "Answer any questions. Explain further if necessary." In this particular case, such open-ended directions, although common, might lead to some serious lack of standardization in administration.

The test was normed on about 400 students in each of the three years, along with two other tests, in a balanced order to examine practice effects; these were negligible. KR-21 reliability values are high, between .84 and .89, but a confidence interval for a derived score of 100 would still be 90–109. This calculation is not done for readers of the manual, who might not be aware of the wide confidence range of individual scores on such tests. In fairness, this is a problem with most such test manuals.

As validity evidence, the author cites correlations with the Standard Progressive Matrices of .63 for the timed version and .56 for the untimed. This difference might reflect a speed factor, as the test requires 70 items in 45 minutes. Correlations with teacher ratings of English, mathematics, and scholastic ability are in the same range, but if teacher ratings are a validating yardstick, then development of standardized tests seems like a lot of trouble. Correlations with the ACER Word Knowledge Test are around .75, indicating this test might be more verbal than quantitative in what it is measuring. However, the items may be roughly categorized as 31 verbal, 28 numerical, 7 logic, and 4 spatial, which seems a reasonable balance for a general measure.

No individual item or subscore information is provided in the manual. This is an unfortunate but understandable precaution against misinterpretation, for much can be learned from item difficulties, discrimination indices, and percentage omissions.

In summary, educators and psychologists in smaller countries such as Australia and Canada should not have to rely on generic tests marketed by multinational corporations. The ACER is an adequate test for use with Australian students in years 9, 10, and 11. It should not be given to adults with the present norming data. It has adequate reliability and validity evidence, and some excellent advice on interpreting scores in their context. It could be improved by some emphasis on the confidence intervals for individual scores, and by the provision, for those qualified and interested, of some item data.

Review of the ACER Test of Reasoning Ability by JOHN RUST, Senior Lecturer in Psychometrics, Goldsmith's College, University of London, London, England:

The 70-item ACER Test of Reasoning Ability is a multiple-choice version of the earlier ACER Test of Cognitive Ability (1983; 9:23) and is designed principally for the Australian market. The ACER Test of Cognitive Ability had been developed in 1976–77 as a replacement for the Otis Higher Test on the basis of an item analysis of responses to approximately 200 pilot items by students in Australian school years 10, 11, and 12, and by first year college students. The main modifications for the new test are the elimination of five items considered unsuitable for a multiple-choice version, the provision of machine-readable scoring sheets, and a restandardization on over 1,200 subjects.

The authors argue the test is a measure of Spearman's "*g*." No particular consideration is given in the manual to the switch from "intelligence" through "cognitive ability" and now to "reasoning" as the underlying trait of interest. However, the authors are not alone in this and they do state their assumption that the test is measuring "a 'general factor' underlying performance on a wide range of cognitive tasks which involve the ability to see relationships and to solve problems" (manual, p. 1). Inspection of the items does suggest a slant towards verbal intelligence, and it would be helpful to have more details of the test specification on which the original construction of items was based. The renaming exercise is somewhat undermined by the use of the classical IQ format of mean = 100, *s.d.* = 15 for standardization that invites the user to interpret scores in terms of classical IQ. As it stands, the test is open to the traditional abuses of IQ tests and the caveats the manual provides underplay the issue and offer little alleviation.

The new standardization was carried out on a stratified random sample of Australian school children in years 9, 10, and 11. The manual gives helpful details of the various subgroups involved, and describes in some detail the analysis of data from the approximately 10% of subjects for whom English was not the first language. Ethnic minority data are also described, although for a non-Australian the failure to mention the indigenous ethnic minority is striking. One problem encountered seems to be the existence of gender bias in the test, with men scoring higher than women. Although this does receive some consideration it warrants more, particularly as the test is specifically recommended for selection purposes in occupational settings.

Kuder-Richardson internal consistency is given as reliability and is .85 for year 9 (N = 450), .89 for year 10 (N = 394), and .89 for year 11 (N = 369). Validity is based on concurrent validation with the Standard Progressive Matrices (T4:2544). The matrices were administered in either timed or untimed format, and correlations, calculated separately for each year group, ranged between .53 and .67 (samples sizes were between 167 and 221). These are high given the differing nature of the instruments involved. Correlations between test scores and teachers' ratings of school ability were also examined and ranged between .58 (N = 360) and .61 (N = 310). These results demonstrate that the test is a reasonably reliable and valid instrument for assessment related to educational and vocational guidance in educational settings, as is suggested in the manual.

Validity within an occupational environment has not been demonstrated, and this issue does need to be addressed, particularly in the light of the aforementioned gender bias. The school student norms are recommended for use with adults so long as the appropriate Australian school year is used for the "minimum level of education required" for the educational level of the employment category in question. Some data are supplied from a sample of 741 applicants for entry to the Victoria Police Force, some of which is described helpfully. However, the provision of an IQ transformation based on this sample is again a reversion to previous bad practice so far as the use of IQ scores are concerned. *T* score and stanine are more appropriate and are also provided, although these unfortunately appear alongside the "IQs."

In summary, the ACER Test of Reasoning Ability is a group test of intelligence which has been shown to be reliable for use in years 9 to 11 of the Australian school system. Validity within an educational environment is also evident to some degree. However, the authors fail to take account of recent conceptions of "*g*" as a culturally dependent measure of the ability to thrive within the formal education system of a modern industrialized society. The use of the IQ format for the norms is certain to encourage the continuation of bad practice in the field. Of greater concern is the encouragement to use the IQ format within adult occupational settings, particularly when it is so evidently not based on a representative sample of the Australian population. The sampling and detailed analyses of the standardization study with school students appears to have been well thought out and could have formed the basis of recommendations for good practice in the development of valid and fair selection and assessment policies. The authors seem to have lacked the courage of their good intentions and have all too readily retreated along the well-trodden but blighted path of the classical IQ test.

[7]

ACER Tests of Basic Skills—Blue Series.

Purpose: Developed to assess skills in literacy and numeracy learning.
Publication Dates: 1989–91.
Administration: Group.
Price Data: Not available.
Comments: See 8 for Green Series.
Authors: Jan Lokan, Suzanne Jones (Year 3 manual), Susan Zammit (tests), Lynn Robinson (tests), John Lindsey (tests), Brian Doig (tests).
Publisher: Australian Council for Educational Research Ltd. [Australia].

a) YEAR 3.
Population: Year 3 in Australian school system.
Scores, 3: Reading, Number, Total.
Time: 65 minutes.

b) YEAR 6.
Population: Year 6 in Australian school system.
Scores, 6: Reading, Language, Number, Measurement, Space, Total.
Time: 100 minutes.

[The publisher advised in January 1994 that this test is now out of print—Ed.]

Review of the ACER Tests of Basic Skills—Blue Series by DARREL N. CAULLEY, Senior Lecturer, Graduate School of Education, La Trobe University, Bundoora, Australia, ELAINE FURNISS, UNICEF, Hanoi, Vietnam, and MICHAEL McNAMARA, Graduate School of Education, La Trobe University, Bundoora, Australia:

The tests are presented attractively being printed in blue with many illustrations. Each test covers a wide range of skills. The Year 3 Numeracy test contains questions on numeration and the four basic operations of addition, subtraction, multiplication, and division. The Year 6 Numeracy test also assesses these skills of number but in addition tests fractions and percentages. In addition, the section on measurement contains questions on topics such as length, area, volume, mass, time, and temperature, and space includes both two-dimensional and three-dimensional representations.

There are two parts to the Year 3 Literacy test. The first part is composed of three stories, each involving several sentences. Each sentence contains a blank and the student is required to choose a word from four alternative words to fill in the blank. For the second part a context is provided for the questions by the provision of a four-page magazine called *Young Aussie* printed in two colors and thus providing appealing and visually stimulating material. The emphasis is on practical, everyday, real-life reading skills and so a range of types of texts is included. This range of texts or genres is a very positive feature of the test.

The real-life textual approach is also featured in the Year 3 Numeracy test through its use of a school playground and a store sale as themes. The themes were chosen by the authors in the belief that everyday "contexts" would be helpful to students because test questions become meaningful and correct answers are more verifiable. However, paper-and-pencil tests are by their nature limited because they cannot create a sense of purpose and motivation for students, which they would have in literacy and numeracy tasks in students' everyday life and contexts. The use of the word "contexts" by the authors is misleading because paper-and-pencil tests are inevitably context stripping. It would be better to say that the test tasks closely resemble those encountered by the students in their everyday life, which, of course, is a strength of the tests.

Similar kinds of comments made in relation to the Year 3 tests can be made about the Year 6 tests. The Year 6 Literacy test consists of two parts. The first part is a reading test of a simulated newspaper with questions relating to advertisements, an index, captions, and a TV timetable as well as the more traditional passages of narrative, scientific, and other types of text. The impression given is that everyday skills are being tested, but hardly any of the articles in the newspaper are authentic pieces that would be found in a newspaper except for the TV guide section. The second part of the Year 6 Literacy test asks students to edit a hand-written text by underlining errors, and this requires a knowledge of spelling, punctuation, capitalization, and English usage. A simulated sale catalog is the accompanying material for the Year 6 Numeracy test.

The items in the Numeracy tests are given in words and thus require a certain degree of reading ability from students. Consequently, the test user should be concerned with the extent students' measured mathematics abilities are being lowered by their ability to read the word problems. However, the authors have attempted, and succeeded we feel, to keep the language simple and everyday rather than formal and mathematical.

With the exception of the Year 6 test of editing text, the questions are in a multiple-choice format, nearly all questions having four alternative answers from which to choose. Australian Year 3 students are not accustomed to answering tests in multiple-choice format and experienced elementary school teachers indicate that students find this format difficult. American students are more familiar with this format. The tests were originally developed for statewide testing in New South Wales, the Australian state with the highest population, and this necessitated that item responses be machine readable for scoring. It is unfortunate that provision for machine scoring has led to the exclusion of direct, supply type answers. This severely restricts the range of real-life skills represented, because many situations encountered by students in their everyday life require personal construction of a response.

A handful of questions are common to the Literacy and Numeracy tests at both Years 3 and 6. Thus, it is possible to gauge the amount of learning that takes place between Year 3 and Year 6.

For each of the Year 3 tests a set of three skill levels, or "bands," is defined. The highest skill levels involve integrating several pieces of information from written text and working out which operations to use in solving problems with more than one step. At the lowest level are selection of simple words related to everyday experiences and coping with straightforward counting, addition, and subtraction of small numbers. For each of the five strands in the Year 6 tests a set of four skill levels is defined. The highest skill levels involve multistep problem-solving processes and quite complex interpretations of written material. At the lowest level are simple one-step problems and the location of straightforward information in short pieces of text.

What can the tests tell the classroom teacher? The simplest information that can be inferred is relative scores of students in a class. It is possible from knowing a student's score to place the student in one of the skill bands discussed above. With the aid of a special chart in the manual it is possible to diagnose each student's strengths and weaknesses. With the aid of another special chart it is possible to identify a class's strengths and weaknesses showing in what topics the class excels and in what topics they may need help as a group.

Although the tests claim to reflect universally important learning objectives, they are set in the context of New South Wales curricula. To compare the choice of competencies selected for assessment with local curriculum requirements, teachers in the wider educational community would require access to tables of specification.

The tests were constructed with the use of Item Response Theory (IRT). In a personal communication with the first-named author of the tests, she explained that the IRT analyses done on the test data and the way in which items for the final versions of the tests are selected guarantee the reliability of the tests in the traditional sense. However, to support this statement she recently carried out traditional item analysis on a sample of the data from the 1992 Year 6 tests. The resulting KR-20 indices were .94 for Literacy and .88 for Numeracy, based on the responses of about 8,000 students.

To sum up, a significant strength of the tests is the provision of suggestions for the analysis of test responses to obtain a range of detailed information about the performance of individual students, as well as strengths and weaknesses of the class as a whole. Although it is impossible to make tests that test skills exactly as they are used in real life, the authors of the tests have made a very good attempt. It would be useful if tables of specification had been given so any potential user could assess how well the tests fit the user's local curriculum.

Review of the ACER Tests of Basic Skills—Blue Series by DEAN NAFZIGER, Executive Director, and JO-ANNE L. JENSEN, Research Associate, Far West Laboratory for Educational Research and Development, San Francisco, CA:

The Australian Council for Educational Research (ACER) Tests of Basic Skills are designed to assess students' skills in two key areas—Literacy and Numeracy. Although the tests were developed as part of the Basic Skills Testing Program in New South Wales, the authors note that the tests are designed to reflect universally important learning objectives. Recognizing the importance of contextualized materials, the Tests of Basic Skills include specially developed materials for both the Literacy and Numeracy subtests. The tests, originally published in 1991, are currently out of print.

Aspects of Literacy (Year 6) includes two primary skills: Reading and Language. This subtest requires one consumable test book per pupil and one reusable *News Today* per pupil. The *News Today* is a two-page newspaper specifically designed for this assessment. It includes an index, advertisements, captions, and a TV timetable. The passages include a variety of text types. The authors emphasize the assessment of "practical, everyday, real-life reading skills."

All of the items in the reading section involve the traditional multiple-choice format. The test booklet provides clues to students to help them locate the appropriate information from the newspaper to use in answering the questions, but some of the clues appear misleading. Further, the index references articles and features that are not included in the two pages from which the students are working, so the index cannot assist students in locating information from the actual text they have before them. The test questions involve the traditional cloze items and reading comprehension questions. Although the presentation of the text is unique and eye-appealing, the test does not represent a substantial departure from traditional reading assessments. The language section asks students to demonstrate knowledge of conventions of English by underlining errors presented in four stories. With this format it is not possible to determine if the student truly understands the nature of the error. A student might correctly identify a word of phrase as being incorrect, but the selection may have been based on the wrong reason. This format might lead to an overestimate of a student's knowledge of language conventions.

Aspects of Numeracy (Year 6) assesses students' knowledge of Number, Measurement, and Space. Within each of these broad areas, the mathematical concepts have been broken down further. The concept of Number includes the four basic mathematical operations as well as fractions and percentages. Measurement involves length, area, volume, mass, time, and temperature. Space addresses both two-and three-dimensional representations. The Numeracy test requires one consumable test booklet per student and a reusable simulated two-color, four-page sale catalog. As with the newspaper, the sale catalog has been used in the belief that the questions would be more meaningful and answers more verifiable if presented in context.

The Numeracy test does a better job of orienting the students to the correct location of the necessary information when compared to the Reading subtest. Some questions are included in the test that are based on items appearing in the sale catalog but do not require information from the catalog to answer the questions correctly. A third type of item does not refer to the catalog at all. The order of test questions involves a mixture of all three item types that could be potentially confusing to students. Because students answer items using a variety of formats (e.g., trace pathway, color figures), students may need more than the few practice questions provided to feel comfortable with the format. True to the curriculum on which it is based, the test includes questions on the metric system and a monetary system based on notes and pounds.

ADMINISTRATION. Complete instructions for administration are included in the teacher's manual. Students are encouraged to attempt all questions because there is no penalty for guessing. Individual test questions are not to be read or explained to the students, but instructions about a method of answering may be repeated or clarified. The test can be administered under timed or untimed conditions.

ANALYSIS AND INTERPRETATION. Once the tests are handscored, a variety of report options are available. Record sheets have been provided by the publisher to permit the tracking of a given individual or class' strengths and weaknesses. In order to track individual strengths and weaknesses, a DIAMAP is completed on each student. The student's item-level correct, incorrect, and blank responses are tabulated in relation to the overall difficulty of the items and the student's overall number correct score. The DIAMAP helps in identifying those items that are within the range of difficulty that the student answered incorrectly as well as those answered correctly that are above the level of difficulty expected for the student.

Group analysis charts are included to help identify those skill areas on which groups of students are and are not performing well. The Correct Answer Tallies (CAT) are used to tabulate the number and percentage of students who answered each question correctly. The publisher also has included an Incorrect Answers Record (IAR) in which the students' actual incorrect response options to items are indicated in addition to those items that the students answered correctly. In addition to the percentage of students answering each question correctly, it can help to identify common misunderstandings held by students. As noted, if the spread of responses if fairly evenly distributed, the information provided by the IAR is of little value. Although these tallies can be informative and guide remedial instruction, they are very labor intensive. The amount of time required to complete such analyses may be viewed as too prohibitive by most classroom teachers.

The publishers also have provided Skill Bands designed to assess a student's progress towards achieving complex skills. A student's raw correct score is translated into a band that represents the skill levels typical of students at the same band. They have been developed for the subskills for both Literacy and Numeracy tests. The Skill Bands are based on a developmental view of learning that is keyed to the New South Wales curriculum. The publishers provide the appropriate cautions when interpreting the bands (e.g., individual variability, similarity of curriculum content and sequence, adherence to standard testing procedures.)

SUMMARY. The ACER Tests of Basic Skills provides a test of basic literacy and numeracy skills with formats that extend beyond the traditional multiple-choice format. The use of supplemental materials is likely to make the testing situation more interesting to students, but as formatted there are opportunities for confusion. Although a variety of summary report measures are provided, they are labor intensive and require tabulation of individual student responses. The amount of effort involved is likely to limit their use. Further, the interpretation of DIAMAPs and Skill Bands is based on adherence to the developmental curriculum of New South Wales. A full evaluation of this assessment requires a review of the measurement and statistical properties of the test. Such information is not provided in the teacher's manual.

[8]

ACER Tests of Basic Skills—Green Series.

Purpose: Developed to assess skills in literacy and numeracy learning.
Publication Dates: 1990–92.
Administration: Group.
Price Data, 1994: A$16 per 10 literacy test booklets (specify level); $16 per 10 numeracy test booklets (specify level); $39 per specimen set (specify level).
Comments: See 7 for Blue Series.
Authors: Jan Lokan, Margaret Forster (Year 3 tests), Suzanne Jones (Year 3 tests), John Lindsey (tests), Brian Doig (tests), Susan Zammit (Year 6 tests), and Lyn Robinson (Year 6 tests).
Publisher: Australian Council for Educational Research Ltd. [Australia].

a) YEAR 3.
Population: Year 3 in Australian school system.
Scores, 2: Literacy, Numeracy.
Price Data: $10.50 per 10 "Young Aussie" magazines; $33 per teacher's manual ('92, 31 pages).
Time: 87 minutes.

b) YEAR 6.
Population: Year 6 in Australian school system.
Scores, 5: Reading, Language, Number, Measurement, Space.
Price Data: $19 per 10 "Planet" magazines; $33 per teacher's manual ('92, 32 pages).
Time: 113 minutes.

Review of the ACER Tests of Basic Skills—Green Series by LEWIS R. AIKEN, Professor of Psychology, Pepperdine University, Malibu, CA:

These tests were developed for the Basic Skills Testing Program in New South Wales and standardized on large samples of children in Year 3 and Year 6 government schools in Australia during the summer of 1990. The main objectives of this program are "to provide teachers and parents with confidential information about their students' or their child's strengths and weaknesses in important literacy and numeracy skills" (manual, p. 5).

The tests in the Green Series, which are reviewed here, consist of an *Aspects of Literacy* test booklet containing two parts (Part A with 23 items and Part B with 29 items), an *Aspects of Numeracy* test booklet containing 30 items, a teacher's manual, and a simulated magazine. The Year 3 magazine is called the *YOUNG AUSSIE: Green Series*; the Year 6 magazine is *THE PLANET*. The test items for the Green Series 3 test booklets, which were the only ones viewed by this reviewer, are interesting and entertaining.

The Numeracy tests emphasize the four basic number operations, and the Literacy tests assess reading comprehension and language skills (English usage, spelling, punctuation, and capitalization). All items on the Literacy tests are in multiple-choice format, whereas some questions in the Numeracy tests require more extensive responses (e.g., completing a bar graph, coloring in appropriate coins or number cards). Some of the tasks, words, and spelling are different from those found in basic skills tests in the United States (e.g., mum, torch, colour), but these are minimal. The test booklets and magazines are attractively illustrated and printed clearly in color.

The time limits for administering the tests seem rather flexible according to American standards. For *Aspects of Literacy*, the time limits are 10 minutes for Part A (Language Skills), 2 minutes for silent reading of *Young Aussie*, and 30 minutes for Part B (Reading

Skills). Time limits on the Numeracy tests are 40–45 minutes. A break of 20 minutes is permitted between the Literacy and Numeracy tests. In any case, only the test booklets, the accompanying magazine, and pencils are permitted. Specific procedures for administering the test are given in the manual.

Four skill levels, or "bands," are assessed by the Green Series 3 tests; these skill bands are defined in Appendix 1 of the teacher's manual. Table 1 gives the score ranges on the Literacy and Numeracy tests corresponding to each skill band. Precisely how these skill bands were arrived at is not made clear in the manual; perhaps they are quartiles. Special record sheets called DIAMAPs ("diagnostic maps") and Group Analysis Charts are provided for analyzing the strengths and weakness of a school class or to give more information about the performance of individual students. Student performance on the test items may be plotted on a scale showing the position of the "number right" scores in relation to the difficulty levels of the test questions.

The Green Series of these tests is said to be more comprehensive and better standardized than their predecessor, the Blue Series. However, other than the sample sizes of 57,000 for the Year 3 tests and 55,000 for the Year 6 tests of the Green Series, the nature of the samples and how they were selected are not described. Presumably, the resulting norms, the computation of which is not described in the teacher's manual, are representative of the Year 3 and Year 6 population of students in New South Wales. It is also unclear how the DIAMAPs were constructed, although one can guess that they were plotted from the average total scores of those answering each item correctly (or incorrectly as the case may be). As such, plotting the Literacy and Numeracy DIAMAPs for each student may provide useful diagnostic information. The Group Answer Tallies Chart on page 18 of the manual can be completed to determine the number or percentage of students answering each item correctly. Similarly, the Incorrect Answers Record on pages 16–17 can be completed to determine the number or percentage of students answering each item incorrectly.

As might be expected, little statistical information concerning these tests is given in the teacher's manual. Presumably one could write to the Australian Council for Educational Research for quantitative information concerning construction of the skill bands and the DIAMAP scales. A bit of reliability information is given on page 25 of the teacher's manual: KR-20 reliability coefficients, based on over 5,800 students, are .93 for *Aspects of Literacy* and .87 for *Aspects of Numeracy*. These coefficients are in line with those of comparable basic skills achievement tests in primary school. With respect to validity, it is argued that, as a result of care in item construction and consultation during the construction process, the items resemble tasks that students might undertake in their regular classroom activities. This content validity argument could be bolstered by a table of specifications, which is unfortunately lacking.

Reviewing this test was interesting, as much as anything for the insight that it afforded on the differences between the standardized test construction procedures employed in Australia and in the United States. In the United States, we appear to place emphasis on statistical analysis and specifications of procedures for constructing, scoring, standardizing, and psychometric evaluation (reliability, validity, etc.) of test instruments. This does not mean that our procedures are necessarily better, just more precise. For what it is worth, I understand that it is much cheaper to develop a standardized test in Australia than in the United States. Perhaps the explanation is to be found in the difference between the two countries in their concern with psychometric quality. The question is, does that concern invariably produce a better instrument?

Review of the ACER Tests of Basic Skills—Green Series by DELWYN L. HARNISCH, Associate Professor of Educational Psychology, University of Illinois at Urbana-Champaign, Champaign, IL:

NATURE OF THE TEST. The Australian Council for Educational Research (ACER) Tests of Basic Skills—Green Series 6 is primarily an achievement test designed to assess middle to upper primary school students' literacy and numeracy skills. Although originally developed for the Basic Skills Testing Program in New South Wales, Australia, the test can be used by a wider educational community. The purpose of the test is to provide teachers and parents confidential information regarding their students' or their child's strengths and weaknesses in important literacy and numeracy skills. In line with this purpose, the test provides means for the user to construct an analytical report of the test taker's strengths and weaknesses.

Basic skills that are assessed in the test are not minimal surviving skills. They are, in fact, skills essential to successfully pursuing school learning. Therefore, the focus of the ACER Tests of Basic Skills—Green Series 6 is determining degree to which Year 6 (or U.S. grade 6) students satisfy most important learning objectives in literacy and numeracy.

GENERAL DESCRIPTION OF THE TEST. As of June 1990 the tests in the Green Series were administered statewide by classroom teachers to about 55,000 Year 6 students in New South Wales government schools. A complete set of the tests includes the *Aspects of Literacy* test book; the *Aspects of Numeracy* test book; and *THE PLANET* simulated magazine, which is reusable and is necessary for both the Literacy test and the Numeracy test. *Aspects of Numeracy* consists of items drawn from three curriculum strands that are classified as Number, Measurement, and Space. To simulate the real life situation, a range of different types of texts is included in the form of a full-color magazine that is a specially constructed stimulus to be used for answering questions in the test.

TEST CONTENT AND ITEM TYPE. One subtest, *Aspects of Numeracy*, contains 44 items, all of which are multiple-choice questions. These test items cover Number, Measurement, and Space. The other subtest, *Aspects of Literacy*, includes two parts: The first part contains 45 multiple-choice questions assessing test takers' reading skills; the second part consists of 17 multiple-choice questions on conventional English usage and two passages with circled words for error recognition. The second part was designed to test students' mastery of conventional written English, or the language skills as the authors of the test put it. Different from most achievement tests, the ACER tests do not require the students to record their responses on a separate sheet. All responses are made in the test book. The responses are machine scorable.

A unique feature of the test is that, instead of the usual narrative passages reprinted on the test booklet, the ACER test includes as a part of the test package a simulated magazine, printed in full color, from which students may find clues or answers to the test questions. Reflecting the idea that it is more important to assess students' skills in real-life situations, test items cover advertisement, an index, cartoon captions, and procedures such as making lemonade, as well as narrative, scientific, and other types of tests. The questions in the Numeracy test also reflect the authors' efforts to relate mathematical concepts to everyday themes and experiences in students' lives.

TEST ADMINISTRATION AND SCORING. The ACER test can be administered using standard procedures where 58 minutes are required for the Literacy test and 55 minutes for the Numeracy test. If the standard mode is selected, time restrictions and administration guidelines should be strictly followed. The test can also be administered as a power test where students can take as much time as they need to finish the test. Obviously, test scores resulting from power tests should not be compared with test results where standard admission procedures are used. It is not clear, however, whether the score table in the teacher's manual is for the test with standard procedures or for the power test. It is our assumption that the score table is for tests with standard admission procedures.

The user's manual does not specifically mention if the test should be scored by the test publisher or the test user, but it appears that the user will be responsible for the scoring. By comparing the students' responses with the keys provided in the teacher's manual, the user will be able to get the "number right scores." What is more informative, however, is the corresponding skill band associated with the number right score. The teacher's manual contains a detailed description defining skills that students have mastered at each skill band. A word of caution is in order here. The skill bands were established on the basis of a single book *Profiles of Learning: The Basic Skills Testing Program in New South Wales 1989* (Masters et al., 1990). Therefore, it is difficult to determine the degree to which these skill bands accurately and validly depict the skills that students possess. Besides, no information is available concerning the dimensionality of the test items. If the test items are multidimensional as is often the case, it is inappropriate simply to associate the number right scores with a particular skill band. The reason is obvious. There are numerous ways to arrive at a particular number right score, and to get the first 10 items correct, for instance, does not equate to getting the last 10 items correct. And the students' underlying abilities and skills may be vastly different.

The user may also construct student DIAMAP charts using the ready-made DIAMAP chart supplied with the test package. DIAMAP refers to the diagnostic assessment of the individual student's performance with regard to his or her relative strengths and weaknesses in the skills covered by the test. The ready-made DIAMAP is constructed based on the difficulty level of test items. Procedures for using the DIAMAP were provided in the teacher's manual. Basically each item is predetermined to measure a certain skill (e.g., usage). Apart from being arranged on the basis of the difficulty level, each item in the ready-made DIAMAP also carries a symbol with it indicating the particular skill that the item is intended to measure. The user may first determine the number of the items that the student answered correctly, and draw a line across the map. The line will serve as an indicator of the student's potential. It is then easy to locate those items that the student should have answered correctly according to the ability indicator, but that the student has missed, and those items that are beyond the student's potential, but that he or she has answered correctly. Further, the user may analyze these items to see if the student exhibits a certain pattern of relative strengths and weaknesses of the skills being measured.

A third product of the test package is the Group Analysis Charts. Two kinds of Group Analysis Charts are provided which were designed to assist the user in diagnosing areas in the skills assessed by the tests with which students are coping well or poorly. The Correct Answer Tallies Chart (CAT) simply tells the user the number or percentage of the students who answered each question correctly. The Incorrect Answers Record (IAR) Chart produces more diagnostic information indicating to the user what common misunderstandings students have. Basically, the user should fill the ready-made IAR chart with students' incorrect answers by giving the answer that the student has chosen. This enables the user to identify whether it is a student-specific problem or if it is a problem for the whole group. For example, if most students in the group answered "B" when the correct answer should be "A," the user should look at the item closely and find out the sources for the common misunderstanding.

TECHNICAL ASPECTS OF THE TEST. The technical data supplied by the publisher are insufficient. The only available information concerns the reliability of the test. The KR-20 reliability coefficient of *Aspects of Literacy*, based on over 7,000 students, was reported to be .92, whereas that for *Aspects of Numeracy* was .88.

Although claims for validity are made in the teacher's manual, no substantiating information is supplied. Another deficiency is that no information is available on norm groups. Such a deficiency is not excusable as the ACER test is a norm-referenced achievement test.

In sum, the ACER test, if used appropriately, is able to provide important information regarding students' strengths and weaknesses in literacy and numeracy skills. The test not only provides scores as most tests do, but also attempts to associate test scores with skills that students have mastered. Cautions should be taken, however, in associating number right scores with the skill bands. It is arguable that the same number right score may indicate different skills that students possess.

As discussed earlier, the biggest deficiency of the test is the lack of information on the technical aspects of tests as set forth in the approved test standards (APA, AERA, & NCME, 1985). This deficiency is particularly discouraging as the test was originally developed for statewide use in New South Wales, Australia. Without sufficient test data, the user will find it hard to evaluate the appropriateness of the test, and thus, it will be difficult to interpret test results in an appropriate manner. If the test is to be used by a wider educational community as was mentioned in the teacher's manual, the authors and publisher of the test should provide more technical information. A table of contents and information on content validity are especially important as this will enable the user to evaluate the appropriateness of the test for the intended test takers.

REVIEWER'S REFERENCES

American Educational Research Association, American Psychological Association, & National Council on Measurement in Education. (1985). *Standards for educational and psychological testing*. Washington, DC: American Psychological Association, Inc.

Masters, G., Lokan, J., Doig, B., Toon, K. S., Lindsey, J., Robinson, L., & Zammit, S. (1990). *Profiles of learning: The basic skills testing program in New South Wales 1989*. Hawthorn, Australia: Australian Council for Educational Research.

[9]

Ackerman-Schoendorf Scales for Parent Evaluation of Custody.

Purpose: "A clinical tool designed to aid mental health professionals in making child custody recommendations."

Population: Parents engaged in a dispute over custody of their children.

Publication Date: 1992.

Acronym: ASPECT.

Scores: 3 scales (Observational, Social, Cognitive-Emotional) yielding 1 score: Parental Custody Index (PCI).

Administration: Individual.

Price Data, 1995: $110 per kit including 20 parent questionnaires, 10 hand scored answer sheets, manual (77 pages), 2 prepaid mail-in WPS test report answer sheets for computer scoring and interpretation; $29.50 per 20 answer forms; $19.50 per 20 parent questionnaires; $48.50 per manual; $19.50 or less per mail-in answer sheet; $12.50 each for test report fax service.

Time: Administration time not reported.

Comments: For complete set of information to score, need results of each parent's MMPI or MMPI-2, Rorschach, WAIS-R, and WRAT-R or NEAT tests.

Authors: Marc J. Ackerman and Kathleen Schoendorf.

Publisher: Western Psychological Services.

Review of the Ackerman-Schoendorf Scales for Parent Evaluation of Custody by JOYCE A. ARDITTI, Assistant Professor of Family and Child Development, Virginia Polytechnic Institute and State University, Blacksburg, VA:

The Ackerman-Schoendorf Scales for Parent Evaluation of Custody (ASPECT) is "a clinical tool designed to aid mental health professionals in making child custody recommendations" (manual, p. 1). Consisting of a group of standardized scales developed to evaluate parent fitness for custody, the ASPECT also incorporates several commonly used instruments, as well as clinical observations, to quantify characteristics related to effective custodial parenting. Administration of the ASPECT entails several assessment steps, which may be carried out in any order. Each parent is asked to complete a Parent Questionnaire (included in the packet) along with several psychological tests (not included in the packet). The parent questionnaire consists of 57 open-ended questions assessing various characteristics of each parent including demographic information, key elements of parent's psychological and family history, motivations for seeking custody, strengths and weaknesses as a parent, perceptions of the other parent's strengths and weaknesses, each parent's "ideal" custody and visitation arrangements, child rearing philosophy, disciplinary techniques currently used by parent, current and future child care arrangements, basic caregiving practices, and sources of social contact regularly available for the child.

In addition, each parent must be interviewed individually. Interviews are unstructured, however, basic questions should be asked concerning the motivations of each parent to obtain custody, concerns parents have about the other parent, future plans, etc. Observations of parents' general hygiene and appearance, as well as parents' expressions of emotion and negativity, should be noted during the interview process. Child interviews should also be unstructured assessing the child's feeling about each parent, the evaluation process, and possible outcomes of the custody hearing.

Guidelines are given for completing the ASPECT Parental Custody Index (PCI). The manual includes scoring criteria for the PCI—a 56-item index yielding a total score as well as three subscores. The PCI was constructed to assess the general appropriateness of the parent's self-presentation (Observational Scale), the suitability of the social environment provided by the parent (Social Scale), and the extent of the parent's cognitive and emotional capacity to provide effective parenting (Cognitive-Emotional Scale). Sources for completing each item include the parent questionnaire, interviews, observation, psychological test results, and corroborating sources of information (such as court records) when deemed necessary. Criteria for determining whether an item receives a "yes" or "no" response, based on the previous named sources, is offered in the manual. When more than one child is involved in the custody evaluation the word child should be interpreted as representing the majority of the children. *T*-scores are derived by converting raw scores into standard scores. Computerized scoring and interpretation is available for the ASPECT through WPS TEST REPORT mail-in service yielding: (*a*) a report consisting of demographic information for each parent; (*b*) PCI and subscale scores, graphic profile of both parent's ASPECT scores; (*c*) interpretive report comparing PCI scores of one parent with the other; (*d*) a list of critical items for each parent; and (*e*) the WPS Chromograph. Handscoring will yield items *a* through *d* only.

The ASPECT also has 12 critical items shown in Table 3 of the manual. The term "critical" is used to refer to items that may indicate more serious deficits in parenting than are summarized in the PCI or individual subscale scores. Critical items tend to center around parents' understanding of the effects of divorce on children, any prior arrests or involvement in sexual/physical abuse, history of alcohol or substance abuse, cooperation with previous court orders pertaining to custody and visitation, and indicators of psychopathology.

RELIABILITY AND VALIDITY. Reliability estimates and Standard Error of Measurement of the ASPECT Scales (PCI and subscales) are given. Alpha coefficients for internal reliability range from .50 to .76—which is adequate but lower than what is typically desirable. The fact that the Observational and Cognitive/Emotional subscales have alphas of only .50 is noteworthy. The authors rightly acknowledge the low internal consistencies of both of these scales and recommend exercising caution when interpreting subscale scores. Low alphas suggest that the subscales, which may have some practical value, are probably not theoretically valid. Factor analyses, which were not conducted, would be helpful to consider the organization and grouping properties of the 56 items. Also, factor analyses would reveal how important each item is in relation to a given subscale—perhaps lending a different type of rationale and statistical support to the notion of "critical items." Item-to-total correlations of ASPECT subscales are given ranging from .03 to .39 and are generally much lower than desirable. It is likely, given the low alphas and low item-to-total correlations, that factor analyses would not support the grouping of the 56 items into the three factors as they currently appear. Given this possibility, the PCI is probably best used as a total score. Interrater reliability ranges from .92 to .96 and is adequate.

The content validity is thoroughly discussed in chapter 5 of the manual. The manual provides information pertaining to the development and derivation of the ASPECT items, which were rooted in the theoretical and empirical literature pertaining to the divorce experience and children. In reality, predictive validity has yet to be established by the ASPECT. An analysis of the predictive validity of the ASPECT is provided, based only on judges' awards of custody. The overall "hit rate" (ASPECT recommendation consistent with judges decision) was 75%. Obviously, judges' awards of custody may not be the best criterion to use in determining the predictive validity of the instrument. Future research needs to specifically evaluate child adjustment in cases where ASPECT based recommendations determined placement, for comparison with cases in which custody was decided contrary to such recommendation. Concurrent validity also has not been established on the ASPECT. It would be extremely helpful to determine the interrelationships between the ASPECT and other means for assessing parental fitness.

NORMS AND STANDARDIZATION. Information pertaining to norms and the standardization process is provided in chapter 5 of the manual. It should be noted that the demographics of the standardization sample (n = 200) is predominantly white and relatively homogenous. Thus, the ASPECT may not be appropriate for use with racially or ethnically diverse families, as standardized scores and norms represent the experience of white parents (96.9% of sample) and may not be sensitive to cultural variations in parenting practices.

The ASPECT represents an important effort to quantify elements associated with parental effectiveness, as well as provide a sophisticated interpretation of test results. Its major shortcomings are its lack of internal validity and cumbersome administration, given the battery of tests deemed necessary. It may be a useful component of a custody investigation, however, as the authors clearly state, it is not intended to be the sole criterion from which custody is decided. Clearly, corroborating sources of information are needed, as well as home visits and observational data sensitive to cultural and regional influences. Furthermore, the ASPECT lacks important information pertaining to each parent's involvement in various caregiving activities during infancy and early childhood that would have bearing on the development of parent-child attachment and qualitative aspects of the parent-child relationship. The authors stress the inappropriateness of "parental devastation" should custody be awarded to the other parent, as well as parents being too emotionally dependent on their children. However, it seems reasonable that a parent's investment in basic caregiving throughout a child's development has much bearing on how one would respond to these issues.

Review of the Ackerman-Schoendorf Scales for Parent Evaluation of Custody by GARY B. MELTON, Director, Institute for Families in Society, University of South Carolina, Columbia, SC:

About a decade ago, my colleagues and I (Melton, Weithorn, & Slobogin, 1985), surveyed a sample of trial court judges about the frequency with which they received mental health reports or testimony on various issues and the quality of the mental health evidence that they did obtain. Perhaps contrary to conventional wisdom, the judges indicated that they rarely received expert opinions in child custody cases. Nearly half indicated that such testimony is no more than occasionally useful. Similar views have been provided by family lawyers (Felner, Rowlison, Farber, Primavera, & Bishop, 1987).

Many scholarly commentators on forensic assessment (e.g., Melton, Petrila, Poythress, & Slobogin, 1987; Weithorn & Grisso, 1987) have echoed the view that mental health professionals have not distinguished themselves in evaluations for child custody in divorce. Critics have been particularly vociferous on two points. First, mental health professionals often have provided opinions on matters that are questions of morality and law (e.g., the best interests of the child) and thus have overreached their legitimate role. Second, even on matters that are potentially within their expertise (e.g., the effects of particular custody or visitation arrangements on children with particular characteristics), mental health professionals often have ignored, misapplied, or reached beyond research findings.

Amid such debate and criticism, it is unsurprising that clinicians would be in search of guidance in conducting evaluations on child custody. Accordingly, the Ackerman-Schoendorf Scales for Parent Evaluation of Custody (ASPECT) is "a clinical tool designed to aid mental health professionals in making child custody recommendations" by providing scores on "a group of standardized scales devised to evaluate parent fitness for custody" (manual, p. 1). In that regard, the ASPECT is really a test battery combining clinical observations (reduced to yes/no replies to questions such as, "Does father appreciate the effects of the divorce on the child?"), parent questionnaires, and scores from several commonly used tests (i.e., the MMPI or MMPI-2, the Rorschach, the WAIS-R, and the WRAT-R or the NEAT administered to parents; the Draw-a-Family Test, the TAT or the CAT, and "an age-appropriate IQ test" administered to the child[ren]).

Unfortunately, clinicians who use the ASPECT are not likely to improve the quality and ethical propriety of their work. Instead, the ASPECT incorporates and exacerbates most of the problems that have attracted commentators' criticisms. Most fundamentally, Ackerman and Schoendorf urge overreaching by clinicians by suggesting that clinicians recommend particular custody dispositions, even though the determination of best interests is a legal conclusion outside mental health professionals' expertise and certainly not reducible to a Parental Custody Index (PCI) score.

The ASPECT also induces evaluation on matters that are within the province of psychologists (e.g., parental reading level) but that have no clear relation to the outcomes of custody dispositions. Ackerman and Schoendorf claim that by "using measures from . . . established and widely used instruments, and by weighting them equally, the ASPECT facilitates an evenhanded assessment and reduces examiner bias" and "simplifies comparisons between the two parents" (manual, p. 2). Such an assessment may be simple, but there is no reason to believe that it is valid.

As this point illustrates, it would be unwise to rely on PCI scores for custody recommendations even if provision of opinions on ultimate legal issues were a proper exercise for mental health professionals (cf. Guidelines, 1994, noting a lack of consensus on the issue). Covering just four pages of a 56-page manual, the evidence for validity and reliability of the ASPECT is scant. The item choice rests on unvalidated assumptions about the relation of particular variables (e.g., whether the parent's IQ is more than 5 points below that of the child; which parent the child is placed beside in the family drawing) to parental competence and, more important, child outcomes. Indeed, the manual includes an acknowledgment of an absence of empirical foundation for conclusions about the relationship between ASPECT scores and child outcomes.

Ackerman and Schoendorf's claim of content validity for the ASPECT is based exclusively on a logical analysis. No other experts evaluated the validity of the item selection.

What Ackerman and Schoendorf call (incorrectly) construct validity is demonstrated in the manual by a study of ultimate dispositional decisions in 118 cases in the normative sample of 200 in which a recommendation was made and information about disposition was available. The sample was highly unrepresentative in that nearly half of the cases resulted in father custody, a proportion substantially larger than in most populations. Even with such an inflated base rate, the hit rate in predicting custody dispositions (75%) was surprisingly low, given that the ASPECT results likely were used in making the custody recommendations. [Editor's note: The 75% hit rate was reported erroneously in the manual—the correct figure is 91%.]

The normative sample, which also served as the sample for validity and reliability studies, was unrepresentative in many ways. It was nearly all-white and skewed toward high socioeconomic status. A particularly serious problem is that the sample consisted entirely of clients of private practitioners. No information is given about the number of offices or localities from which the sample was drawn.

Information about the reliability of the ASPECT is also limited. Ackerman and Schoendorf indicate that the internal consistency of two of the three ASPECT scales was "fairly low" in two instances in which the reported *r* was .00. Two studies of interrater reliability were reported, but both focused on small subsamples of the normative sample and relied on only two raters.

The item selection and scoring standards were conceptually flawed. The item-by-item description in the manual provides minimal attention to research on custody outcomes. In fairness, however, the most extensive study of custody dispositions (Maccoby & Mnookin, 1992) probably appeared in print after the ASPECT manual went to press.

The scoring procedures obscure clinical realities by requiring clinicians to average scores on particular items across the children in a family. Incidentally, how does one "average" two responses (if there are two children) in a yes-no format? The format itself requires transformation of continua to dichotomous, subjectively perceived variables. Moreover, the instrument reduces complex constructs to narrow behavior slices that seem unlikely to provide valid pictures of family life (e.g., bedtime rituals as indicators of parental warmth).

The ASPECT also does not include thorough assessment of factors (e.g., support by third parties, such as stepparents and teachers) that are not susceptible to measurement by traditional psychological instruments but that may have considerable relevance to the likely effects of particular dispositions. In that instance, Ackerman and Schoendorf explain that direct assessment of third-party involvement is "needlessly time-consuming and intrusive" (p. 42) when the parent can be asked about his or her perceptions of the third party.

In short, the ASPECT was ill-conceived; an instrument that results in a score showing the parent who should be preferred in a custody decision necessarily results in overreaching by experts who use it. Even if the idea had merit, though, the psychometric properties of the ASPECT remain essentially unknown, and the item selection and scoring procedures appear to pull for often irrelevant conclusions.

REVIEWER'S REFERENCES

Melton, G. B., Weithorn, L. A., & Slobogin, C. (1985). *Community mental health centers and the courts: An evaluation of community-based forensic services*. Lincoln, NE: University of Nebraska Press.

Felner, R. D., Rowlison, R. T., Farber, S. S., Primavera, J., & Bishop, T. A. (1987). Child custody resolution: A study of social science involvement and impact. *Professional Psychology: Research and Practice, 18*, 468-474.

Melton, G. B., Petrila, J., Poythress, N. G., & Slobogin, C. (1987). *Psychological evaluations for the courts: A handbook for mental health professionals and lawyers*. New York: Guilford.

Weithorn, L. A., & Grisso, T. (1987). Psychological evaluations in divorce custody: Problems, principles, and procedures. In L. A. Weithorn (Ed.), *Psychology and child custody determinations: Knowledge, roles, and expertise* (pp. 157-181). Lincoln, NE: University of Nebraska Press.

Maccoby, E. E., & Mnookin, R. H. (1992). *Dividing the child: Social and legal dimensions of child custody*. Cambridge, MA: Harvard University Press.

Guidelines for child custody evaluations in divorce proceedings. (1994). *American Psychologist, 49*, 677-680.

[10]

The ACT Evaluation/Survey Service.

Purpose: A service "to assist educational institutions and agencies in the collection, interpretation, and use of student survey data" and to investigate the opinions, plans, goals, and impressions of students and/or prospective students.
Population: High school and college students and prospective adult learners/students.
Publication Dates: 1979–93.
Acronym: ESS.
Administration: Group or individual.
Comments: For measurement of groups, not individuals.
Author: American College Testing.
Publisher: American College Testing.

a) SECONDARY SCHOOL LEVEL.
Population: High school.
Publication Dates: 1979–92.
Price Data, 1993: $7.50 per specimen set including one copy of each secondary-level instrument, sample report pages, user's guide ('92, 29 pages), sample subgroup form and ESS order form; $10 per 25 survey instruments; $5 per User's Guide; $25 per normative data reports; $6 per item catalog; $80–$100 per institutional reporting/handling fee; $45 per tape or diskette containing scoring data.
Time: (15–25) minutes.

1) *High School Student Opinion Survey.*
Publication Dates: 1980–90.
Scores: Student's perceptions in 6 areas: High School Environment, Occupational Preparation, Educational Preparation, High School Characteristics, Additional Questions, Comments and Suggestions.

2) *Student Needs Assessment Questionnaire.*
Publication Dates: 1979–89.
Scores: Student's personal and educational needs in 4 areas: Life Goals, Individual Growth/Development/Planning, Additional Questions, Comments and Suggestions.

3) *High School Follow-Up Survey.*
Publication Date: 1990.
Scores: Student's satisfaction with high school in 5 areas: Continuing Education, Employment History,

High School Experiences, Additional Questions, Comments and Suggestions.

b) POSTSECONDARY SCHOOL LEVEL.

Population: College.

Publication Dates: 1981–93.

Price Data: $8.50 per specimen set including one copy of each post-secondary instrument, sample report pages, user's guide ('92, 44 pages), sample subgrouping form, and ESS order form; $10 per 25 four-page survey instruments; $7.50 per 25 two-page survey instruments; $5 per user's guide; $6 per item catalog; $25 per normative data reports; $80–$100 per institutional reporting/handling fee; $45 per tape or diskette containing student data.

Time: (15–25) minutes.

1) *Adult Learner Needs Assessment Survey.*

Publication Date: 1981.

Scores: Adult student's educational and personal needs in 4 areas: Personal and Educational Needs, Educational Plans and Preferences, Additional Questions, Comments and Suggestions.

2) *Alumni Survey.*

Publication Dates: 1981–89.

Scores: Impact of college on graduates in 5 areas: Continuing Education, College Experiences, Employment History, Additional Questions, Comments and Suggestions.

3) *Alumni Survey (2-Year College Form).*

Publication Dates: 1981–89.

Scores: Same as 2 above.

4) *Alumni Outcomes Survey.*

Publication Date: 1993.

Scores: Alumni outcomes in 6 areas: Employment History and Experiences, Educational Outcomes, Educational Experiences, Activities and Organizations, Additional Questions, Comments and Suggestions.

5) *College Outcomes Survey.*

Publication Date: 1992.

Scores: Student's perception of their college experience in 4 areas: College Outcomes, Satisfaction with Given Aspects of This College, Additional Questions, Comments and Suggestions.

6) *College Student Needs Assessment Survey.*

Scores: Student's educational and personal needs in 4 areas: Career and Life Goals, Educational and Personal Needs, Additional Questions, Comments and Suggestions.

7) *Entering Student Survey.*

Publication Dates: 1982–90.

Scores: Student's expectations for college in 4 areas: Educational Plans and Preferences, College Impressions, Additional Questions, Comments and Suggestions.

8) *Student Opinion Survey.*

Publication Dates: 1981–90.

Scores: Student's perceptions of the institution in 4 areas: College Services, College Environment, Additional Questions, Comments and Suggestions.

9) *Student Opinion Survey (2-Year College Form).*

Publication Dates: 1981–90.

Scores: Student's perceptions of the 2-year college in 5 areas: College Impressions, College Services, College Environment, Additional Items, Comments and Suggestions.

10) *Survey of Academic Advising.*

Publication Date: 1990.

Scores: Student's perception of academic advising services in 6 areas: Advising Information, Academic Advising Needs, Impressions of Your Advisor, Additional Advising Information, Additional Questions, Comments and Suggestions.

11) *Survey of Current Activities and Plans.*

Publication Date: 1988.

Scores: Student's current educational status in 5 areas: Impressions of This College, Educational Plans and Activities, Employment Plans, Additional Questions, Comments and Suggestions.

12) *Survey of Postsecondary Plans.*

Publication Dates: 1982–89.

Scores: Student's educational plans in 5 areas: Occupational Plans After High School, Educational Plans After High School, Impressions of This College, Additional Questions, Comments and Suggestions.

13) *Withdrawing/Nonreturning Student Survey.*

Publication Dates: 1979–90.

Scores: Student's reasons for leaving an institution in 4 areas: Reasons for Leaving This College, College Services and Characteristics, Optional Questions, Comments and Suggestions.

14) *Withdrawing/Nonreturning Student Survey (short form).*

Publication Dates: 1981–90.

Scores: Student's reasons for leaving an institution in 2 areas: Reasons for Leaving This College, Additional Questions.

Cross References: See T4:61 (5 references); for a review of an earlier edition by Rodney T. Hartnett, see 9:44.

Review of The ACT Evaluation/Survey Service by MARCIA J. BELCHER, Associate Dean, Office of Institutional Research, Miami-Dade Community College, Miami, FL:

The ACT Evaluation/Survey Service (ESS) is designed to meet the increased data demands required in today's shifting educational environment. The ESS offers a variety of instruments crafted to elicit information at either the secondary (3 instruments) or postsecondary (14 instruments) level. Targeted respondents include entering and currently enrolled students, alumni, leavers, potential enrollees, and students who were accepted at college but who chose not to enroll. The results can be used in a number of ways including to meet the increased demands for accountability, to satisfy accreditation requirements, or for institutional or program improvement.

The surveys have been well planned and well focused. Although some questions may not be appropriate for some institutions or situations, the surveys cover most if not all important areas. To further individualize the survey, users may add up to 30 questions of their own at the end of the survey. An item catalog is provided, though users are not limited to only these items.

Users also may select up to 15 student subgroups, and receive separate summary information for each subgroup. The groups can be identified from either one item (e.g., select if grade point average over 3.0) or a combination of two items (e.g., select if gender is male and racial/ethnic group is African-American).

ACT reports the validity of the items included in the various instruments depends on the care taken in the design and construction of the surveys. The user's guide authors outline the steps taken in instrument development including review of literature and other instruments, evaluation by professionals in the field, pilot-testing, and post-survey interviews with students completing the instruments. The care taken in completing these steps is evident in the final surveys. With few exceptions, the items are important, straightforward, and ask for information that students could best supply.

With surveys of this type, the traditional reliability techniques cannot be used. ACT responded to this difficulty in several ways. Using the Student Opinion Survey, they reported that between 90%–98% of responses were identical on two administrations of the categorical items. On the five-choice (Likert) items, about 65% chose the same response, whereas 93%–95% were within one point on two administrations, depending on the section. In addition, correlations between the average ratings of satisfaction-related items were .92 for the section on college programs and services and .95 for the college environment. Using a form of interrater reliability, reliability estimates above .90 (and many at .99) were found for the Student Opinion Survey, the Entering Student Survey, and the Adult Learner Needs Assessment Survey. Reliability information was not available in the user's guide, however, on the 11 remaining post-secondary instruments or any of the 3 secondary instruments. This should be remedied in future publications.

A call to ACT resulted in obtaining further information on the use of the Student Opinion Survey in predicting changes in college. Colleges that were reusing the survey were asked what had changed at their institutions and which items should reflect those changes. Results showed that about 70% of the time the items showed the changes. In a second approach, colleges that showed large changes in some items could explain these changes when asked, another indicator of validity for this instrument.

ACT will provide normative reports to users interested in comparing their results with other institutions. However, ACT is clear that the norms are "user norms" and should not be construed as providing "nationally representative" comparisons. With this caution in mind, however, users may compare their results to a total group of users as well as selected subgroups. Normative data on the Student Opinion Survey listed all the institutions included so users could further decide on the value of the comparative information. Although normative data for other instruments were not studied, it is assumed that this same helpful feature would be included with norm reports on other surveys. In addition, users can request norms information for a smaller group of institutions with characteristics similar to their own.

In general, ACT has produced a comprehensive and useful set of instruments. The process for gathering, reporting, and interpreting the information also appears to be thorough and user oriented. Users are walked through the steps needed to design, administer, score, and interpret the survey and its results by information in the user's guide. More individualized support is also available. Users looking for a fairly painless way to gather data on student needs, student outcomes, program evaluation, accountability, or accreditation should consider the ESS.

Review of The ACT Evaluation/Survey Service by CLAUDIA J. MORNER, Associate University Librarian for Access Services, Boston College, Chestnut Hill, MA:

The American College Testing Program, a recognized leader in the field of educational measurement, offers from its Evaluation/Survey Service (ACTE/SS) a series of easy-to-administer and well-thought-out instruments for college and university administrators who want to learn more about the institutional perceptions of their students, potential students, and alumni. (Because the secondary school materials were not supplied to this reviewer, this evaluation is based only on the post-secondary instruments.) These surveys are designed to measure group responses, not individual ones; to obtain an overall idea of trends and impressions from the group of persons who are surveyed. Both questions and the machine-readable answer sheet are incorporated into the two- or four-page survey, which makes the instruments compact and easy to administer.

The items are clear, concise, and appear to cover the topic of the given survey. Additionally, the survey instruments each have space for 30 college-generated items, allowing the institution to tailor the survey to local issues/concerns. ACTE/SS makes available a $6 item catalog of sample items that can be used to identify additional items. This catalog is a good idea because clear, unambiguous items are difficult and time-consuming to develop. Use of these items appears to be free with the purchase of the item catalog and survey instrument(s).

The reviewed survey packet includes one copy of each survey and a number of helpful brochures. A 54-

page pamphlet, "ESS in Action," gives information on how a number of specific (named) institutions used the ACT surveys. These "good use models" are designed to help institutions learn "how to maximize the benefits from using the survey(s)." Names and phone numbers are given for contact persons at each institution, for obtaining further information. A four-page booklet, "Steps to a Successful Survey," covers the whole process from designing the study to interpreting the results, including sampling, administration, and scoring. Detailed information on handling a mailing and followup of unreturned instruments is given, with even a sample follow-up postcard. This information is generally useful in survey research whether used with ACT instruments or self-developed surveys. Although brief, it is clearly written, with references for further reading on research methods.

The packet also includes a series of sheets on the most frequently asked questions. All of the above materials avoid using terms such as "dependent variables," making them more accessible to a broad audience, especially those who may have limited or no experience in survey research.

Norms are given for colleges and universities that have used the instruments from 1984 to 1991. These norms were not generated from a random sample, however, nor were the test administrations controlled, so using them for comparison purposes should be done with caution. A list of institutions on which the norms are based is available by state. ACTE/SS will provide norms based on any subset of institutions that are seen as comparable, for an additional fee.

Because ACTE/SS scores and maintains a database of survey results, surveys can be administered each year and reports obtained that show trends or changes in perception or attitudes. Scoring is done on an NCS-OPSCAN 9101. This is not found on many campuses. ACTE/SS provides the scoring and reports available at the fees listed above. Any number of specialized services and reports are also available from the ACTE/SS. Potential users of these services are invited to inquire to ACTE/SS staff.

Content validity of the instruments is based on literature review, content experts' evaluation, and pilot testing of instruments on 15,000 current and former students. The items in the post-secondary surveys appear to this reviewer to be valid. Reliability data are given for three instruments, Student Opinion Survey, Entering Student Survey, and Adult Learner Needs Assessment Survey. Here stability was established at one institution based on test-retest. Three classes of graduate and undergraduate students were given the instruments with a 2-week interval between survey administrations. Standard internal consistency measures such as KR-20 and coefficient alpha are inappropriate for this kind of survey, as ACTE/SS correctly reports, because these surveys have no scales on which to base a total score. Each item is distinct and group data on the item gives information independent from other items. Stability results, therefore, unlike most instruments that measure individual performance, are reported by giving the average percent of identical item responses on the two administrations of the instrument. These averages range from 90% to 98% for categorical items such as sex, race, age, hours worked per week, educational goals, etc. and range from 57% to 67% on the five-choice satisfaction items. These last percentages are raised from 93% to 97% when the percent of responses are within one scale point of the identical response. For example, if at the first administration an item was answered "satisfied" and the second time answered "very satisfied," this would be within one scale point. Expansion of this reliability data to include all the surveys and with a larger sample of students should be a goal of ACTE/SS. However, because norm data were based on 119,228 students from 232 institutions who took the surveys between 1988 and 1991, it shows the success and broad acceptance of these survey instruments.

ACTE/SS has done a thorough and professional job of producing attractive and easy-to-use survey instruments and helpful instructions and other literature to ensure that administrators gather useful data about their institutions from their students and alumni. These surveys are recommended for any institution of higher learning, but should be a boon for those with limited research staff and resources.

[11]

ACT Study Power Assessment and Inventory.

Purpose: To assess students' study skills.
Population: Grades 10–12.
Publication Dates: 1987–89.
Scores, 7: Managing Time and Environment, Reading Textbooks, Taking Class Notes, Using Resources, Preparing for Tests, Taking Tests, Total.
Administration: Group or individual.
Price Data: Available from publisher for test materials including technical manual ('89, 35 pages).
Time: Administration time not reported.
Comments: Based in part on Effective Study Materials series originated and formerly published by Dr. William F. Brown.
Author: American College Testing.
Publisher: American College Testing.

a) THE STUDY POWER ASSESSMENT.
Acronym: SPA.
Comments: 100-item, self-scoring, true-false cognitive test.

b) THE STUDY POWER INVENTORY.
Acronym: SPI.
Comments: 85-item, self-scoring, multiple-choice behavioral survey.

Review of the ACT Study Power Assessment and Inventory by KENNETH A. KIEWRA, Associate Professor of

Educational Psychology, University of Nebraska-Lincoln, Lincoln, NE:

Study skills training is being implemented in increasing numbers of secondary schools. A problem is that few secondary personnel are trained in evaluating students' current skills and providing skills training. Fortunately, there are several evaluation and instruction programs marketed for this purpose. This review describes the evaluation instruments from one such secondary school program, developed by the American College Testing Program (ACT), called Study Power.

Study Power is composed of six student workbooks, a leader's guide, and two evaluative instruments—the Study Power Assessment and the Study Power Inventory. The workbooks help students acquire knowledge and skills for studying. The instruments, which may be used in conjunction with the workbooks or independently, assess study skills knowledge (The Study Power Assessment) or behaviors (The Study Power Inventory) pertaining to the same six topics covered in the workbooks. This review pertains solely to the evaluation instruments. I describe them jointly in terms of (*a*) purpose; (*b*) composition; (*c*) administration, scoring and interpretation; (*d*) test characteristics; and (*e*) conclusions.

PURPOSE. The Study Power Assessment measures knowledge of study skills; the Study Power Inventory measures study skill behaviors. Both inventories are used to (*a*) screen students requiring academic assistance, (*b*) pinpoint the general needs of a group or class, and (*c*) motivate academically able students to improve study techniques.

COMPOSITION. The Study Power Assessment is a true-false test comprising 100 items divided into six scales: Managing Time and Environment (10 items), Reading Textbooks (20 items), Taking Class Notes (20 items), Using Resources (20 items), Preparing for Tests (20 items), and Taking Tests (10 items).

The Study Power Inventory is a behavioral survey comprising 85 items across the same six scales. The number of items per scale ranges from 9 (Taking Tests) to 17 (Preparing for Tests).

The items in both inventories seemed clear, uniformly constructed, and age appropriate. A range of important topics is addressed within each scale. The Reading Textbooks scale, for example, addressed (among other things) marking text, obeying text signals, using charts and graphs, and drawing relationships.

A major drawback of the instruments, however, is the absence of an assessment of behaviors crucial to studying. These include: (*a*) generating complete lecture notes; (*b*) developing charts, graphs, and illustrations to represent facts and relationships; (*c*) recording and studying a range of examples; (*d*) studying differently for different types of tests (e.g., declarative and procedural); and (*e*) employing motivational and metacognitive strategies in support of academic strategies.

ADMINISTRATION, SCORING, AND INTERPRETATION. The Study Power Assessment and Study Power Inventory are both designed for self-administration and scoring by students, each within a typical classroom period.

Both instruments appear in booklet form. The front covers provide straightforward instructions for completing the inventory. Inside the booklets students circle T or F (true or false) for each statement in the Study Power Assessment and circle the letter that corresponds to their actual study activities (ranging from (*a*) *not often true* to (*b*) *almost always true*) in the Study Power Inventory.

As students mark their booklet, their responses show through onto a scoring key contained within the booklet. Keys are revealed only when a tab is removed alongside the booklet. The appropriate responses for the Study Power Assessment appear as a "1," and inappropriate responses as a "0." The "1s" are quickly tallied for each scale and summed on the back to derive a total score. Responses for the Study Power Inventory appear as 1, 2, 3, or 4. "Four" is the most desirable response and "1" is the least desirable response. Scores are derived by summing item scores within each scale. Total score is derived by summing scale scores. Although a scoring worksheet accompanies the Study Power Inventory, scoring is a bit cumbersome and prone to error. Providing the number of items for each scale on the scoring worksheet would help students to check scoring accuracy.

The Study Power Assessment is easily interpreted by students who circle their raw scores on a printed table that provides scaled scores and a shaded area showing how typical high school students perform. Quickly a student determines how his/her scores compare with other high school students and identifies areas of individual strength and weakness.

Interpretation of the Study Power Inventory is left to the teacher. Interpretation guidelines, however, are not offered. A major drawback of the Inventory, and the Study Power Assessment instrument as well, is that scores are not interpretable relative to what actually constitutes adequate knowledge and behavior regarding studying. Interpretative guidelines established by a panel of experts would be useful in interpreting both Study Power instruments.

TEST CHARACTERISTICS. Test characteristics are described with respect to development, reliability, test intercorrelations, and validity.

Test development was sound. Items were developed by experts in test construction in consultation with high school and college study skills instructors. Ideally, test developers should have also consulted with educational researchers who investigate study skills. Perhaps the content omissions previously cited would not have occurred. Test development also included large-scale item pretesting and item revisions. Norms were established using a representative sample encompassing over 9,000 high school students from 30 schools. Norms tables are provided in a Technical Manual.

Reliability estimates for the Study Power Assessment and Inventory were appropriately high (Kuder-Richardson-20 = .94 and .92, respectively). These internal consistency measures indicate that each instrument measures common knowledge or behaviors.

Intercorrelations among scale scores were appropriately moderate indicating that the scales within each instrument measure relatively unique behaviors or knowledge. The moderate correlation of .47 between the Study Power Assessment and Inventory confirmed that the two instruments shared a common ground but measured unique things.

The criterion validity of the instruments was assessed by comparing scores to three different external variables or criteria. These included grade-point average, future educational and career plans, and previous study skills instruction. Data tables suggested that high scorers on the instruments have higher grade-point averages, choose 4-year college rather than employment as their next career step, and have more study skills experience than do low scorers on the instruments. Although the raw data are impressive, interpret their magnitude cautiously in the absence of significance tests and unexplored influences such as intelligence or time on task.

More damaging to the issue of criterion validity is the absence of behavioral indicants of study skills. There is no evidence that students who score higher on these instruments actually engage in greater or more effective study behaviors. Whether students who perform well on the Taking Class Notes scale actually take effective notes, for example, is untested.

The instruments' content validity rests largely on the view of experts in determining whether items reflect current theory and research about studying. My own view is that the presented items reflect much of current theory and research. Omissions pertaining to (*a*) generating complete lecture notes, (*b*) developing representations, (*c*) recording and studying examples, (*d*) studying differently for different types of tests, and (*e*) employing motivational and metacognitive support strategies are problematic.

CONCLUSIONS. The Study Power Assessment and Inventory are good instruments for measuring study skills knowledge and behaviors. They are reliable, well constructed, and generally simple to administer and score. Their limitation revolves around validity. Important content is omitted from the inventories and self-reported behaviors are not validated by assessing actual study behaviors. In the end, the inventories reveal how well a student's knowledge and behaviors correspond with peers. How extensive the knowledge and effective the strategies is uncertain.

[Acknowledgment: I thank Dr. Steve Wise, University of Nebraska-Lincoln, for his assistance in preparing this review.]

Review of the ACT Study Power Assessment and Inventory by KUSUM SINGH, Assistant Professor of Educational Research and Evaluation, Virginia Polytechnic and State University, Blacksburg, VA:

The ACT Study Power Assessment and Inventory is a set of two instruments designed to assess the high school student's study skills. Although the Study Power Assessment (SPA) and Study Power Inventory (SPI) are both evaluative instruments and may be used independently or in combination, the SPA is a cognitive test to assess the knowledge of effective study strategies and the SPI is a behavioral survey to assess the study behaviors. Because the two instruments are different in structure as well as in purpose, their unique features are reviewed separately and then, comments on the common features of the two instruments are made.

The Study Power Assessment (SPA) is a true-false test designed to assess the knowledge of 10th to 12th grade students regarding effective study skills. It consists of 100 items divided into six scales: Managing Time and Environment (10 items), Reading Textbooks (20 items), Taking Class Notes (20 items), Using Resources (20 items), Preparing for Tests (20 items), and Taking Tests (10 items). It is a self-scoring test to be administered in a classroom setting. It is easily scored, yielding six subscores and a total score. A scaled score profile is provided so individual raw scores can be compared to a standard scaled score distribution from the norming sample with a mean of 50 and a standard deviation of 10. Relatively high and low scores in the six content areas indicate personal strengths and deficiencies in the knowledge of related content areas. Norms were developed on a national probability sample of 9,232 students (3,301 10th graders; 3,089 11th graders; and 2,842 12th graders). The Study Power technical manual provides information about the norming study and the racial background of the norming sample. No other descriptive data or the demographic characteristics of the standardization sample are provided. This information would have been useful to potential users of the instruments. The technical manual includes normative data for use in interpreting scores in percentile ranks for 10th, 11th, and 12th graders. The authors rightly caution against the application of these norms to other grade levels and recommend the development of local norms.

Psychometric characteristics of the instrument are in the acceptable range. Reliabilities for the SPA and its subscales are reported as Kuder-Richardson-20 (KR-20) estimates of internal consistency. These range from .50 to .85 for the scales and .94 for the total score. The lowest reliability is that of the Managing Time and Environment Scale, indicating the scale is not tapping a single concept. The authors point out that the attempts to maximize content validity by choosing items representative of the wide domain of the scale resulted in the low estimate of internal consistency.

Validity evidence of the SPA is presented in a variety of ways. Because the SPA is curriculum based and specifies a domain of content, content validity is of primary concern. Steps taken to maximize the content validity are described in the Study Power technical manual. The content specifications were developed from a review of related curriculum materials and from experts in the area of study skills and study skills instruction. Items were pretested and selected on the basis of content specifications and statistical specifications. Data on criterion-related validity are provided by relationships of mean SPA scores with self-reported grade point average (GPA), future educational plans, and previous study skills instruction. The correlations of self-reported GPA with SPA subscales range from .28 to .31 and the correlation of the SPA total score with GPA is .36. In addition, the intercorrelations for the six scales are reported. These coefficients range from .43 to .68, suggesting that scales are sufficiently independent.

The ACT Study Power Inventory (SPI) is a behavioral survey of study habits consisting of 85 items across six scales: Managing Time and Environment (11 items), Reading Textbooks (16 items), Taking Class Notes (16 items), Using Resources (16 items), Preparing for Tests (17 items), and Taking Tests (9 items). Items have four response options based on the frequency with which the behavior occurs: *Not Often* (0–15% of the time), *Sometimes* (16–50% of the time), *Frequently or Usually* (51–85% of the time), and *Almost Always* (86–100% of the time). The SPI is a self-scoring multiple-choice test to be administered in an untimed setting. Each scale score is indicative of the relative frequency of a particular behavior related to a skill area.

Reported estimates of reliability and validity of the instrument seem adequate. Reliabilities for the SPI and its subscales are reported as Kuder-Richardson-20 (KR-20) estimates of internal consistency. These range from .43 to .79 for the subscales and .92 for the total scale. The lowest reliability estimate (.43) for Test Taking suggests that it does not tap a single concept. Although the authors explain this as a function of high content validity of the subscale, I suggest the items of the scale be examined for their content. The criterion-related evidence for validity is provided by the relationship of the mean SPI scores to self-reported GPA, future education/career plans, and previous study skills instruction. The correlations of the six scale scores and the total score with self-reported GPA range from .25 to .35 and .41 respectively, suggesting that approximately 17% variance in GPA is related to the total SPI score.

Because test-retest reliability was not estimated for either instrument, nothing can be stated about the stability of scores over repeated administration. Secondly, although the instruments have face validity and are based on earlier work in study skills assessment and instruction, no theoretical or empirical reasons are provided for the content areas. Such information and references would be useful to the researchers. A number of uses for the instruments (SPA and SPI) are clearly stated including identification of students whose lack of knowledge about the effective study skills and poor study habits contribute to their low academic performance, and assessment of general study-skills-related deficiencies in a group or in a school. Thus, the uses of the instruments are primarily diagnostic.

In summary, the SPA and SPI are instruments with some promising psychometric information that may prove useful in assessment of study-skills-related knowledge and behaviors. Both instruments rank high for ease of administration, scoring, and interpretation. One strength of the kit is its focus on a link to instruction and intervention. The American College Testing Program (ACT) has developed Study Power workbooks that form the basis of an instructional program to improve the students' study skills. The SPA and SPI may be good diagnostic tools to be used with or without the study skills instruction program. However, the authors have rightly pointed out that when instructional strategies are planned, it is important to use other information about the students' academic performance in conjunctions with the data from the SPA and SPI.

[12]

ACT Study Skills Assessment and Inventory (College Edition).

Purpose: To assess students' study skills.
Population: College students.
Publication Dates: 1988-89.
Scores, 6: Managing Time and Environment, Reading Textbooks, Taking Class Notes, Using Information Resources, Preparing For and Taking Examinations, Total.
Administration: Group or individual.
Price Data: Available from publisher.
Time: (30–40) minutes per test.
Comments: Based in part on materials originated and formerly published by Dr. William F. Brown.
Authors: American College Testing.
Publisher: American College Testing.

a) ACT STUDY SKILLS ASSESSMENT.
Acronym: SSA.

b) ACT STUDY SKILLS INVENTORY.
Acronym: SSI.

Review of the ACT Study Skills Assessment and Inventory (College Edition) by GERALD S. HANNA, Professor of Educational Psychology and Measurement, Kansas State University, Manhattan, KS:

The ACT Study Skills Assessment (SSA) and Study Skills Inventory (SSI) each consists of five subscales: Managing Time and Environment, Reading Textbooks, Taking Class Notes, Using Information Resources, and Preparing For and Taking Examinations. Although the content of each is based on the ACT textbook, *Building Better Study Skills*, it is also designed to be used independently.

The SSA is a 100-item true-false *test* of knowledge concerning useful study skills. Each of its subtests consists of 20 items. The SSI is an 85-item, self-report, verbal-frequency *survey* of study skills having subparts of 17 items each. The SSA and the SSI are respectively designed to provide measures of maximum behavior and typical behavior in the five content domains.

Recommended uses of the instruments in their respective guides for administration and interpretation include screening, assessment of group study-skill needs, motivation, and diagnosis of weakness for individuals.

RELIABILITY. Internal consistency reliability coefficients are reported for both instruments. The coefficient for the total SSA and SSI, respectively, are .85 and .93, whereas the median coefficient alpha for the respective subtests are .73 and .77. These coefficients for subtests seem high enough to support cautious interpretation of one subtest at a time, but rather low for the recommended profile examination for the purpose of revealing relative strengths and weaknesses.

No data are supplied on the important attribute of score stability.

Unfortunately, standard errors of measurement are reported only for the entire distributions rather than for each of several score levels for each instrument.

SSA items appear to be too easy for maximum discrimination in the total population. The midpoint between the chance-level score and a perfect score corresponds to a percentile rank of only 8. Thus, the SSA would be more reliable when used to identify students who especially need instruction than it is with students in general. Therefore, the reported internal consistency coefficient of .85 significantly underestimates the accuracy of the device for the major purpose of screening.

VALIDITY. The instruments' content seems appropriate, reasonable, and balanced. I find only two items in the Using Information Resources section of the SSA with which to quibble. They relate to library card catalogs. My own college-age children have been using computer catalogs since elementary school.

Although the scales were developed to parallel one particular textbook and are referred to as curriculum-based instruments, I judge the content to be sufficiently general for use in courses and other interventions based on other instructional materials. Empirical validity data in which scores of each instrument are related to high school grades, educational aspirations, and prior study skills instruction are also offered in support of each instrument's validity.

Intercorrelations of scales within the SSA and SSI are relatively high, having medians of .66 and .78, respectively, after correction for attenuation. Thus, the discriminant validity within each scale among the five subconstructs is only modest. This limits the instruments' utility for individual diagnosis of relative strengths and weaknesses.

A parallel issue is the discriminant validity between corresponding scales of the SSA and SSI. This could be investigated by examining the disattenuated correlations. Unfortunately, they are not reported. Thus, the validity of the conceptually appealing distinction between the constructs assessed by the SSA, which is a test of knowledge, and the SSI, which is a self-report inventory of typical behavior, is not addressed. Consistent with this absence of data, the Guides authors do not discuss the distinction. This seems very odd, given the close parallelism between the companion instruments.

INTERPRETABILITY. The authors of the Guides very appropriately encourage development of local, institutional norms, and provide helpful instructions on how to do so. Pending this, external norms would, of course, be useful.

Normative data for the SSA are based on 819 first-year students in seven post-secondary institutions. SSI norms are based on 940 first-year students in eight institutions. The Guides contain laudable cautions that the relevance of these data for a given user will depend on the degree of similarity between the norming institutions and the user's institution. Unfortunately, the characteristics of the norming institutions are not described in sufficient detail for users to be able to reach a very informed judgment concerning this degree of similarity.

Although the Guides do not include mention of the possibility, it seems to me that an important potential use of the instruments might be based on comparison of the total scores of the SSA and SSI. Suppose, for example, that a student scored very low on both measures and another scored high on the SSA but low on the SSI. The first student might benefit from instruction in sound study skills, whereas the second might gain more from an intervention designed to motivate day-to-day implementation of what is already known. This simultaneous use of the companion instruments would require (in addition to evidence of discriminant validity) comparable derived scores. Unfortunately, they are not available. Not only were the two instruments normed on (at least somewhat) different groups of college students, but neither group is described in sufficient detail to enable one to judge their degree of comparability.

The Guides encourage students to compare their *raw* scores on the five subscales of each instrument in order to get a general idea of their relative strengths and weaknesses. A visual aid for the SSA further encourages criterion-referenced profile comparisons among raw scores. This seems highly questionable for comparisons among five separate domains of content (e.g., would one want to compare raw scores on a spelling test with raw scores on a language usage test when one test might, by chance, happen to consist of harder items than the other?). Particularly on the SSI, in which the raw scores of the means of the five subparts vary over a range of nearly one standard deviation, the direct, criterion-referenced comparison of raw scores seems extremely ill-advised.

SUMMARY. The recommendations in the Guides concerning diagnostic use of the instruments based on raw scores merit rejection. Not only are the five raw scores within each instrument limited in comparability, but the more-than-minor correlations among the scales, coupled with the limited reliability of the individual scales, even renders normative comparisons hazardous. Local norms could remedy the first, but not the other, of these problems.

Although the SSA and SSI have significant shortcomings, each might prove very helpful in institutions prepared to develop local norms, as recommended by the Guides. Each device might be valuable for formative purposes with individual students in study skills courses. Similarly, each could be used to assess the needs of group. The SSA could be used as a pre or post test, particularly in courses using the ACT textbook. Finally, the difficulty level and unfakable nature of the SSA render it potentially very useful for screening first-year students for study skills knowledge deficits.

Review of the ACT Study Skills Assessment and Inventory (College Edition) by CAROL KEHR TITTLE, Professor of Educational Psychology, Graduate School, City University of New York, New York, NY:

The ACT Study Skills Assessment (SSA) and Inventory (SSI) are presented on self-scoring answer folders, and are intended to tap knowledge and understanding of study skills (SSA) and self-reported study behaviors (SSI). Both provide five scores, as well as a total score: Managing Time and Environment, Reading Textbooks, Taking Class Notes, Using Information Resources, and Preparing For and Taking Examinations. The SSA has 20 items per subscale, and a true-false response format. The SSI has 17 items per subscale, and a 4-point response scale (*Not Often, Sometimes, Frequently, Almost Always*), with responses weighted from 1 to 4.

Time limits are adequate and scoring of the SSA is straightforward. Scoring of the SSI requires care because points for preferred answers can be at either end of the response scale. The directions should remind students to mark firmly, otherwise marks are faint on the scoring pages. The SSA form provides a profile form on the back; the SSI does not.

A Guide to Administering and Interpreting for each inventory consists of 4–5 pages. Reliability estimates (alphas) are in the .70s for the SSI subscales and are similar for the SSA. The intercorrelations of subscales for both the SSI (.44 to .68) and SSA (.41 to .57) are fairly substantial, and the subscale-total correlations average .76 for the SSA and .82 for the SSI. Local norms are encouraged and reference norms are provided for both the SSA and SSI, although on different samples (N = 819 for SSA and 940 for SSI). Little information is given about the norming institutions. The reference norm distributions for subscales are highly skewed for the SSA, with only about 10% of the sample getting 15 or fewer of the 20 items wrong. The distributions are better for the SSI, where there is a possible score of 68 for each subscale.

Validity is not well documented. For content validity, a description of development is given that is too general; detailed test specifications are not available. In the SSI, for example, Using Information Resources includes very disparate items, from locating sources, to discriminating between scholarly and general periodicals, to separating fact from fiction when reading, to initiating contact with an instructor about the appropriateness of a topic, to proofreading a research paper before submitting it. Similarly, Preparing For and Taking an Examination (SSI) includes a confidence item (75) very different from the other behavioral items.

Just as problematic are the suggested non-normative interpretations that require validity-related evidence: as a screening device; to identify areas for instructional or counseling intervention for a large group; as a motivational tool (SSI); and (for individual students) to compare strengths and weaknesses across the five scores. In the last instance, students are encouraged to identify "large differences" between subscales, with no definition of such differences. Criterion-related data cited to justify these different uses are mean SSA and SSI scores for students' self-reported (*a*) high school GPA (D to A); (*b*) level of educational aspiration; and (*c*) previous study skills instruction.

The highly skewed distributions for the SSA indicate a problem suggested by earlier reviews of study skills instruments such as the Survey of Study Habits and Attitudes (SSHA; T4:2663) and the Learning and Study Strategies Inventory (LASSI; T4:1417) (e.g., Shay, 1972, and Hayes, 1992). Although both the SSI and SSA items have face validity, they are self-reports. The discrepancy between knowledge and behaviors, and the extent of socially desirable responses, is unknown.

For the SSI and SSA, the validity-related evidence that would be meaningful to users must be developed in the context to use. The psychometric properties are not as important as research data providing: (*a*) evidence on whether individual (self-selected or otherwise) students can make sense out of the information and change their behaviors, or (*b*) evidence on whether large scale screening identifies and places students in "treatments" that are successful, that is, have differential validity. From this perspective, the SSI and SSA need evidence on their validity *in context*, the context of use that includes the textbook, the study skills course, counselor, or other instructional settings. Validity arguments should be developed for these contexts, rather than arguing from correlational data with high school self-report data.

Technical information is minimal, and unsatisfactory in the case of validity. The theoretical or content-related validity arguments become critical and need far greater documentation than they have received. For example, the LASSI provided a broader, more theoretically based set of 10 subscales that draw on research on motivation, attitudes, and study strategies. The SSI and SSA, along with other study skills inventories, also focus primarily on study skills and knowledge where teaching is based on a lecture model, omitting laboratory-based subjects and an increasing use of student study groups and project-based activities in a variety of subjects. Prospective users will require analyses of the content of the SSI and SSA in relation to student learning and instructional environments on their own campuses, and to describe the instructional contexts in which they plan to use such instruments. Existing information on the SSA and SSI provide little guidance for users in this task.

REVIEWER'S REFERENCES

Shay, C. B. (1972). [Review of the Survey of Study Habits and Attitudes]. In O. K. Buros (Ed.), *The seventh mental measurements yearbook* (pp. 1210-1211). Highland Park, NJ: Gryphon Press.

Hayes, S. C. (1992). [Review of the Learning and Study Strategies Inventory]. In J. J. Kramer & J. C. Conoley (Eds.), *The eleventh mental measurements yearbook* (p. 450). Lincoln, NE: Buros Institute of Mental Measurements.

[13]

Adapted Sequenced Inventory of Communication Development.

Purpose: "To assist in the identification of current communicative abilities of clients."
Population: Normal and retarded children functioning between 4 months and 4 years.
Publication Date: 1989.
Acronym: A-SICD.
Scores, 3: Receptive Scale, Expressive Scale, Skills Checklist.
Administration: Individual.
Price Data, 1989: $250 per complete kit; $40 per Interpretation Manual (88 pages) and Administration Manual (39 pages); $45 per 50 Assessment Booklets; $25 per 50 Receptive Skills Profiles and Checklists; $25 per 50 Expressive Skills Profiles and Checklists.
Time: (30–60) minutes.
Author: Sandra E. McClennen.
Publisher: University of Washington Press.

Review of the Adapted Sequenced Inventory of Communication Development by KAREN T. CAREY, Associate Professor of Psychology, California State University, Fresno, Fresno, CA:

The Adapted Sequenced Inventory of Communication Development for Adolescents and Adults with Severe Handicaps (A-SICD) was developed for adolescents and adults who do not possess any speech skills or have only minimal skills. The inventory assesses both receptive and expressive skills at age-appropriate levels and allows the examinee to respond through gestures, signing, picture board communication, or voice communication. The kit includes an administration manual, an interpretation manual, "real objects" (e.g., bell, spoons, combs) as well as pictures of common objects (e.g., book, shoe, cars). The author states that the utilization of a continuum from real objects to pictures allows the examiner to assess the symbolic abstraction skills of the client.

The A-SICD is an adapted version of the Sequenced Inventory of Communication Development—Revised Edition (T4:2438). The inventory was developed to provide an overview of communication skills and to identify a client's current communication abilities, discrepancies between receptive and expressive skills, and areas for further assessment.

Receptive and expressive skills are measured by two separate scales, each containing at least 26 items. Basal and ceiling levels are established separately for each scale with three correct answers resulting in the basal level, and four consecutive errors resulting in the ceiling, for each scale. The examiner is encouraged to make adaptations to the directions and wording of items if such adaptations will assist the examinee's understanding of the task. The author does state that major changes in wording should be noted on the protocol. In addition, the examiner must be sensitive to responses made by the examinee and accept the mode of communication used by the examinee. It would seem essential that the examiner would have had a number of opportunities to observe and work with the examinee to make certain that the examinee's communication style is clearly understood.

The inventory is scored based on the total number of errors for each scale. Some items contain subitems, and criteria for obtaining a correct answer for the entire item is reported for each such item (e.g., three or four of four subitems, the item is considered correct). Each scale is divided into two profiles for scoring and interpretation, and scoring booklets for each are provided. The Receptive Scale is composed of the receptive processing profile and the receptive concepts profile, and the Expressive Scale is composed of the expressive processing profile and the expressive behavioral profile.

Validation studies were conducted with 40 subjects in three different geographical locations who ranged in age from 16 to 55 years. The SICD-R and the A-SICD were administered to the subjects in counterbalanced order. Interrater reliability on 10 subjects ranged from 88% to 100% on the Receptive Scale and from 90% to 100% on the Expressive Scale. Internal consistency was .78 for the Receptive Scale and .91 for the Expressive Scale of the A-SICD. Although the author admits that the sample size for these studies was small, a caveat is provided stating that the number of severely handicapped individuals is also small. Unfortunately, an inventory with a sample population of 40 subjects seems to have limiting generalization effects.

The inventory is not a norm-referenced tool or a curriculum tool. It appears that the examiner must use clinical judgment in interpreting the inventory. The examiner is told to note errors made by the examinee and to test the limits on items on which the examinee does not make the correct response. The interpretation manual concludes with several case studies describing examinees' performances on the inventory.

In summary, it would appear that much of the same information could be obtained through structured observations of the examinee in the educational, vocational, or home situation. Interpretation is based on the examiner's clinical skills and as the inventory is designed to assist in identifying the examinee's communication abilities, it would seem most beneficial to gather such information in natural settings in which the examinee is familiar and comfortable.

Review of the Adapted Sequenced Inventory of Communication Development by HARLAN J. STIENTJES, School Psychologist, Grant Wood Area Education Agency, Cedar Rapids, IA:

The Adapted Sequenced Inventory of Communication Development for Adolescents and Adults with Severe Handicaps (A-SICD) was developed to assist with the assessment of adolescents and adults with severe handicaps whose communication skills, as measured by other available instruments, is in the range of birth to 4 years. An attempt has been made with this instrument to use more age-appropriate materials and interactions for adolescents and adults who have little or no speech, or who are understood only by those closest to them.

Like the Sequenced Inventory of Communication Development—Revised Edition (SICD-R; T4:2438), on which it is based, the A-SICD was developed to provide an overview of communication skills. Its purpose is to assist in the identification of current communication abilities of clients in order to assist in enhancing communication with and about this special population. Specifically, the A-SICD can be used to provide an overview of both receptive and expressive communication, to identify performance discrepancies between receptive and expressive communication, and to suggest areas for further in-depth assessment for some clients. Because of its focus on individuals with severe disabilities, the A-SICD would not provide useful information about clients who already have a functional expressive language system.

Although many inventories of early communication use normative age referents, the A-SICD uses "order of difficulty," which is based upon the sequence of skill development within the validation group. This sequence describes the expected order of acquisition of skills based on norms, but without age referents. Adolescents and adults with severe disabilities have had extensive learning experiences with some very atypical results and, therefore, the typical normative sequence is not to be assumed. On an individual basis, the assessment items passed will not always correspond exactly to their order of difficulty as determined by the norm group. Variations from one client to another reflect the particular experience, skills, and abilities of each individual.

Overall, the A-SICD appears to be a very significant improvement over using instruments devised for assessing young children to assess the communication skills of adolescents and adults with severe disabilities. Directions for administration and scoring are clear and understandable. The materials and administration procedures are more age appropriate, and tend to enhance the dignity of both the assessor and the clients.

The order of difficulty as presented is based upon administration to a relatively small validation sample of 40 individuals. Age, type of current residence, type of communication used, additional handicapping condition, degree of retardation, and previous history of institutionalization were all represented. A case can be made that, because the population of adolescents and adults with severe disabilities is small, the sample can also be small. However, the variability of these individuals is great and it is difficult to assure that a typical sequence (as defined by order of difficulty) of atypical development can be devised.

Nevertheless, interrater reliability of the A-SICD at 86% to 100% is acceptable, although this did not include the interview portion, for which interrater reliability was not determined (about 30% of the test). The internal consistency of the Expressive Scale (r = .91) is within the recommended range for tests used for individual decision making (above .90), but internal consistency of the Receptive Scale (r = .78) is below this figure. The difference is believed to be in the relative similarity of difficulty level in the Receptive Scale. The high interrater reliability and the internal consistency for the combined test at .86 is probably acceptable for the proposed uses of the A-SICD.

The A-SICD is worthy of use as an instrument for assessment of receptive and expressive communication of severely disabled adolescents and adults. It is a significant improvement over the alternatives previously available. The small validation sample size is unfortunate but acceptable with this population. The individual items and the profiles derived seem to suggest teachable expressive and receptive skills. The alternative forms of communication allowed are most necessary and appropriate for this challenging but highly variable population. Further research to extend the validity of this valuable addition to communication assessment is encouraged.

[14]

Adaptive Behavior Evaluation Scale.

Purpose: "Used as a measure of adaptive behavior in the identification of mentally retarded, behaviorally disordered, learning disabled, vision or hearing impaired, and physically handicapped students."
Population: Ages 4.5–21.
Publication Dates: 1983–88.
Acronym: ABES.
Administration: Individual.
Price Data, 1992: $81 per complete kit including technical manual ('88, 48 pages), 50 school rating forms, Parent Rating of Student Behavior technical manual ('87, 29 pages), 25 parent rating forms, and Adaptive Behavior Intervention Manual ('87, 168 pages); $20 per Adaptive Behavior Intervention Manual; $12 per computerized ABES quick score (Apple II).
Author: Stephen B. McCarney.
Publisher: Hawthorne Educational Services, Inc.

a) ADAPTIVE BEHAVIOR EVALUATION SCALE, SCHOOL VERSION.
Scores, 4: Environmental/Interpersonal, Self-Related, Task-Related, Total.
Price Data: $12 per technical manual; $30 per 50 school rating forms
Time: (15–20) minutes.

b) PARENT RATING OF STUDENT BEHAVIOR.
Acronym: PRSB.
Price Data: $19 per complete kit including technical manual ('87, 29 pages) and 25 rating forms; $6 per Parent Rating of Student Behavior technical manual; $13 per 25 rating forms.
Time: (12–15) minutes.

Review of the Adaptive Behavior Evaluation Scale by MARY ROSS MORAN, Professor of Special Education, University of Kansas, Lawrence, KS:

The Adaptive Behavior Scale (ABES) was designed, in the words of the accompanying manual, to include "those educationally relevant behaviors which may be identified as contributing to more appropriate diagnosis, placement, and programming for students with behavioral, learning, and intellectual handicaps" (p. 4). Although the Parent Rating of Student Behavior (PRSB) does offer one figure to show results for both students with mental retardation and behavior disorders, the ABES interpretation section addresses only students with mental retardation and offers no profiles to show how they might differ from those with behavioral or learning handicaps. Therefore, the usefulness of the ABES for diagnosis or placement purposes appears limited.

The authors of the ABES manual state the instrument serves to screen, develop goals and objectives for the IEP, identify instructional activities for identified problem areas, and document entry points, progress that occurs as a result of interventions, and identify exit points from special service delivery, if appropriate. This is asking a lot of a single 60-item instrument! In the case of the ABES, there are separate manual subheads suggesting multiple ways of using the instrument. The information provided fails to make clear to users how screening data might differ from diagnostic data. Activities useful for program planning are provided in an optional book sold separately, not in the section covering interpretation in the ABES manual.

MATERIALS. A purchaser of the complete kit receives two scales with manuals—a 60-item school form called The Adaptive Behavior Evaluation Scales (ABES), to be completed by observers in the natural educational environment, and another 52-item Parent Rating of Student Behavior (PRSB).

ITEM SELECTION. In addition to "a careful literature review" (p. 19) the ABES item pool was solicited from 73 "educational diagnosticians and special education personnel" who were asked to provide lists of behaviors not "measured by academic skills testing" (p. 11). Indeed, no items on the ABES appear to overlap with academic achievement test items, although at least 7 of the 10 Task-Related items overlap with analysis of direct work products.

From the initial lists, a pool of 78 items was constructed by collapsing and combining related statements. The pool was submitted to a focus group of 62 diagnosticians and special educators who selected 63 items, which were then subjected to field testing by 154 elementary and secondary teachers in 12 Missouri districts. It is unclear how 63 items were reduced to the 60 on the final form.

The ABES items are organized in three subscales—Environmental/Interpersonal Behaviors (Items 1 through 37), Self-Related Behaviors (Items 38 through 49), and Task-Related Behaviors (Items 50 through 60). Within the 37 Environmental/Interpersonal items and 12 Self-Related statements are 29 that require an observer to judge whether or not the action is "appropriate," 3 that require a judgment of whether some action or object is "necessary" or "needed," two that ask for judgments of "positive" interactions, and one each requiring a judgment of "typical" or "friendly" exchanges with peers or whether an action occurs "without difficulty." Only 15 of a possible 49 items in the Environment/Interpersonal and Self-Related Behavior sections are free of inferential qualifiers.

Among the remaining 10 Task-Related items that are to be answered from observation without records are at least 7 that could be better documented from examination of work products over a period of time so that judgments about task completion and accuracy could be data-based rather than impressionistic. I can find no justification for using this less accurate procedure.

The format for response by observers to all 60 ABES items is consistent across the three parts of the scale. Respondents rate each item on the extent to which the student: (*a*) Cannot perform the behavior, (*b*) requires physical assistance in performing the behavior, (*c*) requires verbal assistance in performing the behavior, (*d*) performs the behavior successfully but on an inconsistent basis, or (*e*) performs the behavior successfully and independently. Each of these alternatives is explained with examples on pages 23 and 24 of the manual.

Use of the first alternative may underestimate a subject's skill because an inference that a student cannot perform should not be drawn from an observation that the student does not perform. This constitutes a leap from the observed to the unknown. Indeed, the manual description of this alternative explicitly states that "if the student does not engage in or demonstrate the behavior, he/she is to be rated with quantifier Number One: Cannot perform the behavior" (p. 23).

Alternatives 4 and 5 do not appear to constitute parallel statements on a continuum. To perform "inconsistently" is not related to performing "independently." It would appear that Alternative 5 would be better served by the word "consistently" instead of "independently." The question of whether or not the action is observed as "independent" or not would appear to be answered instead by whether alternatives 2 or 3 were applied instead of 5.

Items for the Parent Rating of Student Behavior (PRSB) came from 284 parents and guardians. Instead of using a focus group to select final items as was done for the ABES, PRSB final items were selected by face validity, item analysis, and factor analysis. Another section of the manual (p. 11) contains the suggestion the same focus group that reviewed the school-form ABES was asked to review the home-based scale as well.

The 52 items on the PRSB are organized into subscales called Social Responsibility, Self-Care, and Personal Independence. Unlike the ABES, the subscales do not consist of consecutive items but are spread across the instrument. In comparison to the school form, the home items rely slightly less on qualifiers. Only 16 of 52 items ask parents to judge the appropriateness of an action; one each asks parents to judge what is "typical," "common," "friendly," "needed," "positive," "without difficulty," or "possibly harmful." Approximately one-third of the items on the PRSB are the same as those on the ABES. Quantifiers identical to those for the ABES are used for the PRSB.

NORMATIVE DATA. The ABES norming sample appears adequate in terms of geographical representation, race, sex, rural or urban residence, and parents' occupational status—all of which closely parallel figures in the 1980 Statistical Abstract of the United States. Norming took place in 1984 over 2,059 students in 18 states with a sample of 159 teachers using the ABES across age levels 4.5 through 21 years. Normative data are similar to those for the Vineland Social Maturity Scale (Doll, 1965), and better than many scales that limit norming samples to residents of a single state.

Norms for the PRSB were derived from 1,378 students in 1986. Demographic data approximated figures in the 1980 Statistical Abstract of the United States. Although norms for the ABES extend to 18 years plus, those for the PRSB stop at grade 12.

RELIABILITY. The ABES manual author reports internal consistency as .98 for the total score. Test-retest reliability is reported as .95. Interrater reliability ranged from .97 to .99, high for an instrument that contains qualifiers such as "appropriate" across the majority of items. Internal consistency correlations ranging from .53 to .83, test-retest reliability of .91, and interrater agreement ranging from .93 to .95 are reported in the manual.

VALIDITY. ABES content validity is inferred as "assured with the meticulous review by the educational diagnosticians and special education personnel" who comprised the focus group (p. 19). Criterion-related validity was measured by comparing 58 previously identified mentally retarded students on the ABES and the Vineland Social Maturity Scale (Doll, 1965). (No mention is made of why the 1985 version of the Vineland Social Maturity Scale was not used instead of the 1965 version.) Correlation for the total scales was .64 or .65. The correlation is reported differently between the text and Table 10 in the manual.

PRSB content validity is also claimed on the basis of the focus group review. Criterion-related validity is reported as a correlation of .71 with the Behavior Rating Profile Parent Rating Scale (Brown & Hammill, 1978). An atypical report of "diagnostic validity" features a comparison of data for identified students with mental retardation and emotional disturbance/behavior disorders. It may be that an analysis of different groups could add to the construct validity of the measure if it purports to be of diagnostic value.

SUMMARY. The ABES and PRSB combine to provide over 90 discrete items and about 15 that overlap across the two scales, rating desirable but not unacceptable behaviors. Norming, reliability, and validity data reported are within acceptable standards. The ABES dependence on qualifiers calls into question the extent to which informants could agree, but reliability data are persuasive. Inconsistent statements in manuals (focus group versus face validity mentioned above for the PRSB) and numerous copyediting errors ("principle components analysis" on p. 20; "lead itself" on p. 5) are distracting but not substantive. The scoring process is based on alternatives that are not parallel and thus have limited usefulness as the end of a continuum.

Users seeking a school scale will find the ABES less comprehensive than the AAMD—School Edition (Lambert & Windmiller, 1981), which adds money handling, shopping, numbers, and time as well as unacceptable behaviors. Unlike the Adaptive Behavior Inventory for Children (Mercer & Lewis, 1978), the ABES correlation with measured intelligence quotient (p. 4) renders it less useful as a discreet and supplementary measure but identifies it rather as a duplication. Like the Vineland Adaptive Behavior Scales (Sparrow, Balla, & Cicchetti, 1985) the ABES/PRSB offers scaled scores with a mean of 100 and a standard deviation of 15 for direct comparison to widely used measures of intellectual functioning.

Upon comparison with other available adaptive behavior scales, the combined ABES/PRSB resembles the 1985 Vineland classroom edition but offers fewer items (112 versus 244). The ABES/PRSB offers some advantageous features. Nevertheless, some of the claims in the manual for this instrument's usefulness are not demonstrated in directions for interpretation. Both ABES/PRSB manuals could profit from, for example, sample profiles and interpretations illustrating how to use data for the multiple purposes claimed by thc authors.

REVIEWER'S REFERENCES

Doll, E. A. (1965). Vineland Social Maturity Scale. Circle Pines, MN: American Guidance Service.

Brown, L. L., & Hammill, D. J. (1978). Behavior Rating Profile. Austin, TX: PRO-ED, Inc.

Mercer, J. R., & Lewis, J. (1978). Adaptive Behavior Inventory for Children in The System of Multicultural Pluralistic Assessment. New York: The Psychological Corporation.

Lambert, N., & Windmiller, M. (1981). AAMD Adaptive Behavior Scale—School Edition. Monterey, CA: McGraw-Hill.

Sparrow, S. S., Balla, D. A., & Cicchetti, D. V. (1985). Vineland Adaptive Behavior Scales. Circle Pines, MN: American Guidance Service.

Review of the Adaptive Behavior Evaluation Scale by HARVEY N. SWITZKY, Professor of Educational Psychology, Counseling, and Special Education, Northern Illinois University, DeKalb, IL:

The Adaptive Behavior Evaluation Scale (ABES) is a clinical tool that claims to allow educators to evaluate the adaptive behavior of all students who experience behavior and learning problems in the learning environment regardless of the severity or suspected handicapping condition. This assertion seems quite a challenging undertaking to this reviewer.

The ABES is a general measure of adaptive behavior based on the theoretical model of adaptive behavior derived from Grossman (1973). In order to answer the question regarding the level of adaptive behavior (i.e., the degree to which an individual demonstrates age and culturally appropriate independent functioning, assumes personal responsibility, and accepts social responsibilities in the environment) of a student, McCarney, the author of the ABES manual, suggests that "an adaptive behavior scale should provide a clear indication or profile of a student's adaptive behavior, based on the most commonly recognized theoretical construct/definition of adaptive behavior, and [that] this should be done in comparison to other students, functioning in the same cultural environment as that student" (manual, p. 4). McCarney suggest the ABES provides this profile.

The ABES was designed to "(a) screen for adaptive behavior problems, (b) provide an adaptive behavior measure for any referred student, (c) provide information which may contribute to the diagnosis of mental retardation, (d) develop goals and objectives for the IEP [the Individual Education Plan], (e) identify instructional activities for identified problem areas, and (f) document entry points, progress which occurs as a result of interventions, and identify exit points from special service delivery, if appropriate" (manual, p. 4). The ABES has extremely ambitious and lofty goals.

The ABES consists of 60 items assessing adaptive behaviors, which are not measured by academic skills testing but are necessary for success in an educational setting. The ABES is organized into three subscales determined by factor analytic techniques. The first scale is Environmental/Interpersonal Behaviors.

> *Environmental* is defined as: acceptable patterns which demonstrate the ability to adapt to school and general community expectations. (manual, p. 7)
>
> *Interpersonal* is defined as: acceptance of authority, response to conflict and criticism, behaviors utilized in seeking attention and assistance, ability to listen and respond appropriately, conduct in play/academic activities, attitudes toward others, interaction with peers, and attitude toward one's own and others' property. (manual, pp. 7–8)

The second scale is Self-Related Behaviors.

> *Self-Related* is defined as: ability to accept consequences and responsibilities as well as the ability to maintain oneself in the environment relative to self-help and independent functioning. (p. 8)

The third scale is Task-Related Behaviors.

> *Task-Related* is defined as: work-study skills including task focus, task completion, following directions, and classroom participation. (p. 8)

The rater or raters, usually the classroom teacher or other professionals with extensive experience in observing the student (e.g., aid, counselor, other teachers), on each item on the ABES identify the extent to which the student: (*a*) cannot perform the behavior, (*b*) requires physical assistance in performing the behavior, (*c*) requires verbal assistance in performing the behavior, (*d*) performs the behavior successfully but on an inconsistent basis, and (*e*) performs the behavior successfully and independently. The manual author does a good job in defining the quantifiers for the raters.

Raw scores on each subscale are converted to subscale standard scores by age (4.5–6.0 years, 6.0–8.0 years, 8.0–12.0 years, 12.0–17.0 years, and 17.0–21.0 years) and sex. The sum of subscale standard scores can be converted to an Adaptive Behavior Quotient or percentile rank also by age and sex. In the manual the author provides useful guidelines for rating the students and for using and deriving the subscale standard scores and the Adaptive Behavior Quotients.

The normative American sample of 2,059 special education students was drawn from the four major geographic regions of the United States. An additional sample of regular education students (number unknown) was also obtained.

Scale development used 73 special education personnel and educational diagnosticians who supplied a list of behavioral items assessing those adaptive behaviors necessary for success in an educational setting that are not measured by academic skills testing. Items were selected on the basis of their apparent match to one of the four characteristics of adaptive behavior as suggested by the theoretical model of adaptive behavior adopted by the ABES (i.e., Environmental, Interpersonal, Self-Related, and Task-Related).

The reviewer has no problem with this strategy of test construction as far as initial test item generation goes. One of the major problems for the ABES is that currently researchers and practitioners cannot agree on a model of adaptive behavior or exactly how to measure its various components (American Association on Mental Retardation, 1992; Author, 1993; Evans, 1991; Greenspan & Granfield, 1992; Greenspan & Switzky, in press; Jacobson & Mulick, 1992, in press; Michelson, 1993; Switzky, 1992; Switzky & Greenspan, in press; Switzky & Utley, 1991), which may severely impair the usefulness of the ABES in terms of its theoretical model and its extremely ambitious goals.

The characteristics of the standardization sample are biased toward urban white populations. This, of course, limits the test's usefulness with African-American, Hispanic-American, and Asian-American students. These are fast growing populations in our schools. The ABES does not, therefore, assist educators in measuring adaptive behaviors of these nonwhite students in terms of culturally appropriate functioning.

The ABES sampled very little from the 4.5–6.0-year (approximately 132 cases) and 17.0–21.0-year (approximately 112 cases) subpopulations. Sampling was dominated by the 8.0–12.0-year (approximately 752 cases) and 12.0–17.0-year (approximately 778 cases) subpopulations. The 6.0–8.0-year (approximately 294 cases) subpopulation was intermediate.

Because of biased sampling procedures, there is very little evidence supporting the claims of the ABES as useful in evaluating the adaptive behavior of *any student* who experiences behavior and learning problems in the learning environment regardless of the severity or suspected handicapping condition.

In terms of the factor-analyses done on the ABES, principal components analysis really supports the presence of only one factor that accounted for half of the variance. Varimax rotation was interpreted in terms of three factors (Environmental/Interpersonal Behaviors, Task-Related Behaviors, and Self-Related Behaviors). However, the subscales are highly intercorrelated suggesting the presence of only one factor if higher order factor-analytic techniques were attempted.

Coefficient alpha showed very high internal consistency reliabilities for the three subscales. Test-retest and interrater reliabilities appeared to be robust. The evidence is unclear exactly what construct the ABES is measuring.

The validity evidence for the ABES is moderate. Content validity, the weakest form of validity, (Switzky & Heal, 1990) was good. Criterion-related validity was assessed using the older version of the Vineland Social Maturity Scale (Doll, 1965), on 58 mentally retarded students (ages 4.5–21 years). This is really too small a sample to be convincing but the comparison showed moderate correlations on the Environmental/Interpersonal and Self-Related Subscales and a low correlation on the Task-Related Subscale, although the correlation with total score was moderate.

Diagnostic validity was determined by comparing 103 randomly selected retarded and 103 nonretarded students (4.5–21 years) on the ABES drawn from the standardization sample. Good discriminative validity was shown on the mean subscale standard scores and on the mean total Adaptive Behavior Quotient. Item-validities were acceptable.

In summary, the strength of the ABES is in its bold attempt to invent a sound measure of the vague construct of adaptive behavior based on the theoretical model of Grossman (1973). The ABES provides a strategy on how this may be accomplished, and how the information obtained can be used by educators.

The major weaknesses of the ABES concern its: (*a*) unrealistic goal of assessing the adaptive behavior of any student (ages 4.5–21.0 years) with a learning problem regardless of the severity or suspected handicapping condition; (*b*) extremely inadequate standardization sample, which almost completely ignores minority populations; (*c*) weak claim to three separate subscales of adaptive behavior; and (*d*) dated theoretical concept of adaptive behavior.

The ABES was derived almost 10 years ago and a paradigm shift has recently occurred regarding exactly what adaptive behaviors are and how to measure them. These theoretical developments may impair the usefulness of the ABES to measure adaptive behavior because the experts have not yet reached consensus on the construct.

Alternative measures of adaptive behavior that may prove as useful or better than the ABES include: (*a*) AAMD Adaptive Behavior Scale—School Edition (Lambert, Windmeyer, Tharinger, & Cole, 1981); (*b*) the Revised Vineland Adaptive Behavior Scales (Sparrow, Balla, & Cicchetti, 1984); (*c*) The Scales of Independent Behavior (Bruininks, Woodcock, Weatherman, & Hill, 1984); and (*d*) Comprehensive Test of Adaptive Behavior (Adams, 1984). In addition, models of assessment based on ecological inventories and environmental assessments, which are designed to identify a pool of skills and activities considered important for a student across domains of life skill, may be useful to educators as well (Ford, Schnorr, Meyer, Davern, Black, & Dempsey, 1989).

REVIEWER'S REFERENCES

Doll, E. A. (1965). Vineland Social Maturity Scale. Circle Pines, MN: American Guidance Service.

Grossman, H. J. (1973). *Manual on terminology and classification in mental retardation* (rev. ed.). Baltimore: Garamond/Pridemark.

Lambert, N. M., Windmeyer, M. B., Tharinger, D., & Cole, L. J. (1981). *AAMD Adaptive Behavior Scale—School Edition*. Monterey, CA: CTB/McGraw-Hill.

Adams, J. M. (1984). Comprehensive Test of Adaptive Behavior. San Antonio, TX: The Psychological Corporation.

Bruininks, R. H., Woodcock, R. W., Weatherman, R. F., & Hill, B. K. (1984). Scales of Independent Behavior. Chicago: Riverside Publishing Co.

Sparrow, S. S., Balla, D. A., & Cicchetti, D. V. (1984). Vineland Adaptive Behavior Scales. Circle Pines, MN: American Guidance Service.

Ford, A., Schnorr, R., Meyer, L., Davern, L., Black, J., & Dempsey, P. (1989). *The Syracuse community-referenced curriculum guide*. Baltimore: Paul H. Brookes Publishing Co.

Switzky, H. N., & Heal, L. W. (1990). Research methods in special education. In R. Gaylor-Ross (Ed.), *Issues and research in special education* (pp. 1-81). New York: Teachers College Press.

Evans, I. M. (1991). Testing and diagnosis: A review and evaluation. In L. H. Meyer, C. A. Peck, & L. Brown (Eds.), *Critical issues in the lives of people with severe disabilities* (pp. 25-44). Baltimore: Paul H. Brookes Publishing Co.

Switzky, H. N., & Utley, C. (1991). Sociocultural perspectives on the classification of persons with mental retardation. *AAMR Psychology Division Newsletter, 1*(2), 1-4.

American Association on Mental Retardation. (1992). *Mental retardation: Definition, classification, and systems of supports* (9th ed.). Washington, DC: Author.

Greenspan, S., & Granfield, J. M. (1992). Reconsidering the construct of mental retardation: Implications of a model of social competence. *American Journal of Mental Retardation, 96*, 442-455.

Jacoboson, J. W., & Mulick, J. A. (1992). A new definition of MR or a new definition of practice? *APA Psychology in Mental Retardation and Developmental Disabilities Newsletter, 18*(1), 9-14.

Switzky, H. N. (1992, November). *Mental retardation: The new definition, useful or useless?* Illinois Council for Exceptional Children Fall Conference, Arlington Heights, IL.

Author. (1993). The AAMR manual revisions: CEC-MR responds assessment of the changes and their implications for special educators. *MR Express, 3*, 3.

Michaelson, R. (1993). Tug-of-war is developing over defining mental retardation. *The APA Monitor, 24*(5), 34-35.

Greenspan, S., & Switzky, H. N. (in press). Assessment of adaptive functioning. In J. W. Jacobson & J. A. Mulick (Eds.), *Manual of diagnosis and professional practice in mental retardation*. Washington, DC: APA Books.

Jacobson, J. W., & Mulick, J. A. (Eds.). (in press). *Manual of diagnosis and professional practice in mental retardation*. Washington, DC: APA Books.

Switzky, H. N., & Greenspan, S. (in press). Adaptive behavior, everyday intelligence, and the constitutive definition of mental retardation. In A. Rutatori (Ed.), *Advances in special education* (vol. 2). Greenwich, CT: JAI Press.

[15]

ADD-H: Comprehensive Teacher's Rating Scale, Second Edition.

Purpose: "Designed to help identify attention disorder, with or without hyperactivity."
Population: Grades K–8.
Publication Dates: 1986–91.
Acronym: ACTeRS.
Scores, 4: Attention, Hyperactivity, Social Skills, Oppositional Behavior.
Administration: Individual.
Editions, 2: Paper-and-pencil; microcomputer.
Price Data, 1994: $58 per examiner's kit including manual ('91, 26 pages) and 100 rating/profile forms; $46 per 100 rating/profile forms; $145 per microcomputer version (includes manual, IBM-PC only); $12 per introductory kit; $12 per manual.
Time: [5–10] minutes.
Comments: IBM-PC necessary for administration of microcomputer edition.
Authors: RNA K. Alumna, Esther K. Sleator, and Robert L. Sprague.
Publisher: MetriTech, Inc.
Cross References: See T4:89 (1 reference); for reviews by Ellen H. Bacon and Ayres G. D'Costa of an earlier edition, see 11:7 (2 references).

TEST REFERENCES

1. Kelly, D., Forney, J., Parker-Fisher, S., & Jones, M. (1993). The challenge of attention deficit disorder in children who are deaf or hard of hearing. *American Annals of the Deaf, 138*, 343-348.

2. McKinney, J. D., Montague, M., & Hocutt, A. M. (1993). Educational assessment of students with attention deficit disorder. *Exceptional Children, 60*, 125-131.

Review of the ADD-H: Comprehensive Teacher's Rating Scale, Second Edition by ROBERT J. MILLER, Associate Professor of Special Education, Mankato State University, Mankato, MN:

The ADD-H: Comprehensive Teacher's Rating Scale (ACTeRS) is a short, concise teacher rating scale designed to be a practical tool for the diagnosis and treatment monitoring of attention deficit disorder. ACTeRS was designed with three goals including: "(1) to put the appropriate emphasis on attention; (2) to be useful to clinicians for diagnosis of ADD and monitoring of treatment effects; and (3) to reveal individual differences in the behavior of children who manifest a deficit in attention, both before and during treatment" (manual, p. 1). The instrument consists of 24 items related to classroom behavior and is available in two formats including a paper-and-pencil form and a microcomputer form. Each of the 24 items included in the behavior scale is gender neutral and consists of a simple statement or phrase of from 1 to 11 words. The teacher completing the ACTeRS rating scale is to read each short phrase and rate the child's behavior on a 5-point Likert-type scale ranging from a rating of 1 = *almost never* to 5 = *almost always*. The teacher completing the rating scale is directed to compare the child's behavior with that of his or her classmates.

The 24 test items are arranged in four factors including: Attention (six items), Hyperactivity (five items), Social Skills (seven items), and Oppositional Behavior (six items). Interpretation of raw scores is based on percentiles with separate profiles included in the test for boys and girls. The teacher completing the scale transfers the raw score for each of the four scales to the gender-specific profile and reads the resulting percentile rank for the student. The authors suggest that one can confidently feel that a diagnosis of ADD is legitimate if the subject scores at or below the 10th percentile on the Attention subscale regardless of other scale scores. A child who scores above the 10th but below the 25th percentile on the Attention subscale is considered handicapped and a score at or below the 25th percentile on any subscale should be considered an indicator of a major deficit. Scores ranging from the 25th to 40th percentile are labeled as moderate problems and from the 40th to 50th percentile as mild problems. Included in this edition of ACTeRS is a table to convert raw scores to normalized *T* scores with separate tables included for boys and girls. As with the earlier edition of this instrument, the discussion in the manual of the rationale for specific percentile scores to represent major, moderate, or mild problems is inadequate. No adequate empirical justification is provided for these percentile cutoffs.

ACTeRS was first developed in the mid-1980s and initial norms were based on 1,339 students from kindergarten through fifth grade. This current edition of ACTeRS has expanded norms through eighth grade. The instrument has been restandardized based on a sample of 2,362 students from 23 schools who had been rated by a total of 84 teachers. This new standardization was based on sampling at grades 6 (N = 518), 7 (N = 448), and 8 (N = 493), as well as approximately 150 students for each of the grades K–5 to provide a check on the stability of the existing norms. No additional information is included in the manual regarding the norming sample. No information is included regarding the geographical location of the 23 schools used for norming the instrument. No information is included as to the socioeconomic status of the norming sample. No information is included regarding minority group representation, or whether the sample was gathered from rural, urban, or suburban locations. It is, therefore, difficult to gauge whether the population to which the instrument is normed is reflective of any larger population. Given the lack of information provided in the manual there exists a strong possibility of bias. This lack of pertinent information regarding the norm sample limits the usefulness of the instrument as a diagnostic tool.

The reliability coefficients for the ACTeRS subscales are presented in table format using three methods including internal consistency method, test-retest method, and interjudge method. The internal consistency of the instrument is presented for the initial sample of 1,339 children grades K–5 with a range of .93–.97 for the four subscales. The internal consistency of the instrument is also included for the 1990 restandardization and norm expansion of 2,362 children grades K–8 with a range of .92–.97 for the four subscales. These data suggest that the instrument is extremely consistent when used by the same person observing the same student.

Reliability coefficients for test-retest method are included with a range of .78–.82 for the four subscales. Although these coefficients for the subscales are very adequate, no information is included as to the length of time between test and retest. Further, the test-retest data were based on a sample of only 80 boys and girls, which represents a total of less than nine subjects per grade level if equally distributed over all the grade levels for which this test is currently normed.

Interrater reliability is of much importance if the instrument is to be used as a tool for diagnosis of attention deficit disorder. Reliability coefficients for the Interjudge Method include: .61 on the Attention subscale; .73 for the Hyperactivity subscale; .51 for the Social subscale; and .59 for the Oppositional subscale. These coefficients are based on data from 124 children with each child rated by two teachers. The reliability coefficients are quite low to support the use of the instrument as a diagnostic tool and the number of subjects on which these interrater reliability data are based are small. The manual lacks any significant discussion of any of the reliability information.

The discussion of validity provided by the authors is inadequate. Numerous research studies are presented to provide "validity evidence." However, the major focus of this section appears to be on the usefulness of the ACTeRS in screening students with learning disabilities from children with ADD and ADD-H. A systematic discussion of validity is needed regarding the instrument.

This reviewer found the microcomputer version of the ACTeRS to be user friendly. Test information was easy to enter into the program and the resulting individual profile was adequate. Up to 12 separate observations of an individual can be entered to simplify longitudinal comparisons and the effects of treatment interventions. One limitation of the current software is that it cannot be run with the newer Windows operating environment active.

This new edition of ACTeRS expands the test from an instrument normed to a K–5 population to an instrument for a K–8 population. However, too little information has been provided by the manual discussing the reliability and validity of the instrument. Information regarding the norm sample is inadequate. With these limitations cited, the high levels of internal consistency supports the use of the instrument for monitoring treatment effects. The lower levels of reliability as measured by the interrater method suggest a more limited value to the instrument for use in diagnosis of ADD.

Review of the ADD-H: Comprehensive Teacher's Rating Scale by JUDY OEHLER-STINNETT, Associate Professor of Applied Behavioral Studies, Oklahoma State University, Stillwater, OK:

The ADD-H: Comprehensive Teacher's Rating Scale (ACTeRS) was developed as a clinical tool for diagnosis and monitoring of treatment effects in children with attention deficits, based on the knowledge that teacher ratings are highly reliable and valid measures of children's behavior. Although DSM III nomenclature (ADHD) did not differentiate between attention-deficit and hyperactivity, the ACTeRS was developed from the theoretical and clinical standpoint that the primary condition is attention deficit, with hyperactivity, conduct disorder, and social skill deficits being secondary contributing factors to maladjustment. Thus, the scale yields scores for four factors chosen for their salience in diagnosis and treatment of attention-deficit children: Attention, Hyperactivity, Social Skills, and Oppositional. Development of the scale focused on developing independent, psychometrically sound factors which could be easily interpreted. Therefore, the scale has only 24 items, and no item loads on more than one factor. Items were drawn from previous research-based items which were shown to be relevant to the subconstructs of interest; additional items were added based on the recommendation of experienced school psychologists. The final 24 items were retained after the original 43 items were subjected to a principal components factor analysis with an Oblimin rotation; a cross-validation factor analysis was also conducted. Norms for grades K–8 were collected from 1987 to 1989 and are based on 3,636 students from Illinois. Males and females are equally represented and separate norms are available by gender based on gender differences found on the subscales. Because "age corrections would have had little practical effect" (manual, p. 3), norms are collapsed across age ranges. Although not stated in the manual, the test publishers indicated in a phone interview with this reviewer that approximately 14% of the sample was black and that norms for Hispanic students are currently being collected. A clearer description of the norm sample in the manual would be helpful, and until a national normative sample is developed, users should consider whether the regional norms on which scores are based are likely to be representative of the children they are rating.

Reliability is reported as internal consistency (alpha), test-retest, and interrater. Test-retest reliability (n = 80) ranges from .78 to .82; retest interval is not reported. Alpha coefficients, based on the standardization sample, ranged from .92 to .97, indicating excellent internal consistency. Interrater reliability (n = 124) ranged from .51 to .73; these lower coefficients are typical of interrater reliability, which underscores the importance of judging students across situations and teachers. Standard error of measurement is not reported in the reliability or interpretation sections of the manual. Calculation based on the test-retest reliability coefficient for the Attention factor (.78) yields a *T*-score *SEM* of 4.42. Users should consider *SEM* and calculate confidence intervals when interpreting *T*-scores.

In addition to the factor analytic and internal consistency data, validity has been addressed through group difference and response to medication studies. The ACTeRS Attention, Hyperactivity, and Social Skills (but not Conduct Disorder) factors have been shown to discriminate significantly between learning disabled and ADD-H children; the Attention and Hyperactivity factors discriminated among reading disabled, ADD, and normal children (Peoples, 1989; Ullmann, 1985). McClaren (1990) utilized the ACTeRS in forming experimental normal, ADD, and ADD children with conduct disorders groups and found the ADD groups to have more difficulty than the normal group on a task of sustained attention. Harding-Roundy (1989) used the ACTeRS to describe the relationship between attention deficits and language disorders. Although the structure of the scale would indicate usefulness in differentiating ADD from ADD-H, this group comparison was not reported. Examination of the factor intercorrelations does lend further support to the discriminant validity of the factors. In general, the subscales that describe prosocial behavior (Attention, Social Skills) are more highly correlated and the scales describing maladaptive behavior (Hyperactivity and Oppositional) are more highly correlated with each other than with the other scales. Attention is more highly correlated with Social Skills than with Hyperactivity, suggesting some discriminant validity. However, the .46 correlation between Attention and Hyperactivity suggests that although the factors are discrete, the behaviors measured on them do co-occur. Unfortunately, no multitrait/multimethod correlational studies utilizing other behavioral measures are reported, making it difficult to compare the ACTeRS to other similar measures. Further validity studies are needed. The authors use appropriate caution in describing use of the Attention and Hyperactivity factors by suggesting using them in conjunction rather than as separate tools for differential diagnosis of ADD and ADD-H.

Some of the strongest support for the ACTeRS comes from medication trial studies. Ullmann and Sleator (1985) demonstrated that ACTeRS ratings can accurately determine optimal medication dosage. The Attention and Hyperactivity subscales showed the most response to medication, whereas the Oppositional and Social Skills subscales showed little effect. Ullmann and Sleator state that clinicians should be aware that these behaviors are relatively unresponsive to stimulant medication and require alternative treatment methods. Use of the four-factor ACTeRS over the Conners' 10-item scale is recommended in order to design more effective interventions for children. Ullmann and Sleator (1986) also found that ACTeRS could correctly identify children who respond to medication, those who respond to placebos, and those who respond to neither. Clinicians are cautioned to use double-blind procedures "to avoid medicating children who respond to nonspecific effects of drugs" (manual, p. 14). These medication studies frequently employed two pretests before medication was initiated. Due to regression to the mean reported with other rating scales, and the test-retest reliability coefficients, this procedure is recommended for treatment effect studies.

Interpretation of the ACTeRS is typically accomplished through percentile scores rather than standard scores. Although a *T*-score conversion chart appears in the manual, the protocol provides space only for raw to percentile conversions. Additionally, scoring is in a positive direction. Although conceptually this is a good idea, it may be confusing to practitioners who are used to rating scales that score in a negative direction and makes it more difficult to compare results to other scales. Cutoff score interpretation guidelines for the Attention factor indicate that any score below average (the 50th percentile) may indicate a problem, below the 40th percentile is moderate, below the 25th percentile is "considerably handicapped," and below the 10th percentile is a definite ADD diagnosis. These cutoffs do not correspond to traditional standard deviation cutoffs but are based on the clinical research of the authors in medication response studies. Although the cutoffs have demonstrated utility based on the research literature, a clear rationale for them, or of *T*-score interpretation and interpretation of the other factors, is not provided in the manual. Because of the lack of correspondence between recommended cutoffs and *T*-score standard deviation cutoffs, use of the percentiles is recommended.

Interpretation emphasis is placed on diagnosis of attention deficit with the Attention factor; the authors do indicate that the Attention and Hyperactivity subscales be used in conjunction with each other to determine the severity of the problem, that the cutoffs above not be used rigidly, and that decisions be made based on all available data. The Oppositional and Social Skills scales are not recommended for isolated use for diagnostic purposes, but for determination of whether a child with attention problems also has behavior and social problems which need to be addressed. Validity studies indicate these subscales could also be used as screening measures and more comprehensive scales could be administered if indicated. Although current interpretation guides appear to be effective, a more detailed interpretative guide for all four factors, including standard score interpretation, would be useful.

The protocol and percentile scoring are user friendly. A new, color version of the protocol is now available. The administration and scoring are self-contained on the protocol, making the ACTeRS a convenient, brief instrument to use for teachers and clinicians. A microcomputer administration and scoring version of the ACTeRS is also available, which allows clinicians to store profile data on a case-by-case basis. Although additional validity work should be completed, the ACTeRS is a practical, brief instrument that can be used for diagnosis and treatment of children with attention problems. The ACTeRS is recommended for use over the Conners' Rating Scales (T4:636) (particularly the 10-item scales) based on the ACTeRS' factor purity and relevance of items, and separation of attention from hyperactivity. Although the Conners' scales are based on a national sample, it was obtained in Canada. There are also limitations to interpretation due to item overlap in the factors, and little validity work has been conducted on the factor structure now in use. Another new attention scale, the Children's Attention and Adjustment Survey (75), is noteworthy because it separates impulsivity from attention and hyperactivity, has a clean factor structure, and has home and school versions. However, it also is based on regional norms and does not provide response to medication validity studies.

REVIEWER'S REFERENCES

Ullmann, R. K. (1985). ACTeRS useful in screening learning disabled from attention deficit disordered (ADD-H) children. *Psychopharmacology Bulletin, 21*, 339-344.

Ullmann, R. K, & Sleator, E. K. (1985). Attention Deficit Disorder children with or without hyperactivity: Which behaviors are helped by stimulants? *Clinical Pediatrics, 24*, 547-551.

Ullmann, R. K., & Sleator, E. K. (1986). Responders, nonresponders, and placebo responders among children with attention deficit disorder. *Clinical Pediatrics, 25*, 594-599.

Harding-Roundy, J. A. (1989). *Attention-deficit hyperactivity disorder in relation to visuospatial processing, affect recognition, and receptive language*. Unpublished doctoral dissertation, Brigham Young University, Provo, UT.

Peoples, J. B. (1989). *Attention-Deficit Hyperactivity Disorder as a reflection of frontal lobe dysfunction: An empirical study*. Unpublished doctoral dissertation, University of Kentucky, Lexington.

McLaren, J. (1990). *The development of selective and sustained attention in normal and attentionally disordered children.* Unpublished doctoral dissertation, Dalhousie University, Halifax, Nova Scotia.

[16]

Adolescent Diagnostic Interview.

Purpose: "Assesses psychoactive substance use disorders."
Population: Ages 12–18.
Publication Date: 1993.
Acronym: ADI.
Scores: 8 sections to indicate presence or absence of a DSM-III-R diagnosis of psychoactive substance use disorder: Sociodemographic Factors, Psychosocial Stressors, Substance Use/Consumption History, Alcohol Use Symptoms, Cannabis Use Symptoms, Additional Drug Use Symptoms, Level of Functioning Domains, Orientation and Memory Screen; plus 8 psychiatric status screens: Depression, Mania, Eating Disorder, Delusional Thinking, Hallucinations, Attention Deficit Disorder, Anxiety Disorder, Conduct Disorder.
Administration: Individual.
Price Data, 1995: $75 per complete kit including 5 administration booklets and manual (46 pages); $32.50 per 5 administration booklets; $45 per manual.
Time: (45–55) minutes.
Comments: Structured interview for use with adolescents.
Authors: Ken C. Winters and George A. Henly.
Publisher: Western Psychological Services.

Review of the Adolescent Diagnostic Interview by TONY TONEATTO, Scientist, Addiction Research Foundation, Toronto, Ontario, Canada:

The Adolescent Diagnostic Interview (ADI) is a structured interview designed to diagnose psychoactive substance use disorders. In addition to providing diagnoses of abuse/dependence the ADI also assesses Psychosocial Stressors, Substance Use/Consumption History, Level of Functioning Domains (i.e., peer and opposite-sex relations, school social functioning, academic functioning, leisure activities, home behavior, home environment, psychiatric status, legal status), and screens for orientation and memory problems.

Developing valid instruments to assess adolescent substance use is certainly a useful endeavor. However, the ADI does not appear to meet the criteria for such an instrument. One limitation is the congruence of the ADI with the *DSM* criteria. The materials provided this reviewer were consistent with the *DSM III-R* criteria, but not with the *DSM IV.* Although the publisher mentioned no plans to revise the ADI to reflect anticipated changes in diagnostic criteria (Grant, 1993), revisions of the ADI are now in place.

The authors also fail to establish how the ADI improves upon competing diagnostic instructions such as the Structured Clinical Interview for DSM-III-R (SCID; Williams, Gibbon, First et al., 1992) and the Diagnostic Interview Schedule (DIS; Robins, Helzer, Croughan, & Ratcliff, 1991), both of which can also be used with adolescents.

The authors also do not clarify the utility of formal diagnoses. As the authors themselves state, meeting criteria for dependence rarely impacts upon the nature or course of treatment, which is frequently a function of treatment philosophy, theoretical orientation, waiting list, etc. Although the primary interpretive value of an ADI diagnosis is the determination of the general level of the need for drug treatment no more than one paragraph is allotted to interpreting ADI diagnoses. It can be argued that treatment need is determined by the individual, not diagnoses of dependence. Thus, the ADI is an instrument that will shortly be outdated, has yet to be demonstrated to have value over existing instruments, and which yields diagnoses for which there are limited treatment implications.

There are many problems with the ADI itself. For example, the authors stress that the ADI is a highly structured instrument that excludes clinical intuition (similar to the DIS). Yet, this kind of inference is critical in making a valid diagnosis. In contrast, the SCID, also structured, permits the clinician to score an item as positive if the individual's pattern of responses and nonverbal behavior contradict their response to a specific item (e.g., denial of sadness despite evidence of clinical depression).

Identifying all of the stressful life events that have occurred within the past 12 months seems to be of dubious value. If an adolescent endorses even a few items (not an unlikely occurrence given the turbulence of adolescence in general) the interview will quickly extend beyond the 45–55-minutes administration time. Would not the issues identified in such an exercise, especially important ones surrounding family relations and abuse, be better, and more sensitively, assessed within the framework of a clinical interview? Furthermore, although the ADI searches for evidence of disorder and stress, social supports, coping skills, and positive values are not assessed. These domains of functioning are at least as crucial for treatment planning and referrals as problem identification.

The screening for other psychiatric disorders is very poorly developed, highly selective and inconsistent in the choice of screening questions, and frequently outright inaccurate. To screen for depression an item on crying is included although this is not part of the DSM diagnosis for depression but resembles grief or an adjustment disorder. The question on sleep problems asks only about insomnia and neglects hypersomnia. Two of the three questions under the category of delusional thinking clearly apply to schizophrenia yet no mention of this disorder is made. The questions for auditory hallucinations confuses imagination and hallucinations. Among the anxiety disorders, social phobia and post-traumatic stress disorder, certainly potentially common among adolescents, are not inquired about whereas questions for which a "yes" might be normal (i.e., concern about peer relations and the future) are taken to be indicants of a possible anxiety disorder. Given that serious errors of inference are possible on the basis of this selective solicitation of psychiatric symptomatology it would have been preferable had existing psychiatric screens been used or to have omitted this section altogether.

The assessment of alcohol and drug information is inconsistent and confusing. For example, quantity is assessed only for alcohol. Questions specific to alcohol or cannabis are frequently redundant with each other (asking separate questions for frequency of intoxication in the lifetime and in the past year). With the burgeoning interest in nicotine addiction, especially in treatment of other substance abuse, tobacco use should have been included.

Interrater reliability is favorable for the ADI based on a sample of 72 adolescents who were administered the test. Kappas for diagnosis of dependence/abuse for all substances was quite high (ranging from .53–1.00 with the majority >.75). High kappas were also reported for individual symptoms of alcohol/cannabis dependence (ranging from .66–.97 with most >.80) as well as for the screens for other psychiatric disorders, ranging from .58–.98 but with most kappa values >.85. A one-week test-retest assessment of reliability for assessment of alcohol/cannabis abuse and dependence, and individual symptoms of dependence for these two substances, although lower, was marginally acceptable with values ranging from .52–.83; 6 out of 20 comparisons fell between .65 and .75. Reliability data for the other components of the ADI were not reported.

Assessment of the validity of the ADI is very limited. Data are presented only for criterion validity which uses another test developed by the authors (the Personal Experience Inventory). No assessment of the ADI's predictive or construct validity is presented although such work is reported to be underway.

Finally, very limited data on norms for the various domains of functioning are provided. With such incomplete data it is impossible to know whether or not the adolescent falls within the range of normal development. The authors assign evaluative scores (i.e., good-average-poor) to the individuals' responses but do not provide a compelling empirical base to support the descriptions.

The limited evidence for the validity of the ADI, the limited norms, and the limitations in the rationale, conceptualization, and actual content of the ADI enumerated above cast serious doubt on the value of this instrument as a whole. The authors attempt to do too much by screening for psychiatric disorders, assessing stress, levels of functioning, etc., and consequently the entire instrument suffers. Should a diagnosis of dependence be required a well-validated instrument such as the SCID will certainly suffice.

REVIEWER'S REFERENCES

Robins, L. N., Helzer, J. E., Croughan, J., & Ratcliff, K. S. (1981). *NIMH Dianostic Interview Schedule: Version III.* Rockville, MD: National Institute of Mental Health.

Williams, J. B., Gibbon, M., First, M. B., Spitzer, R. L., Davies, M., Borus, J., Howes, M. J., Kane, J., Pope, H. G., Rounsaville, B., & Wittchen, H. U. (1992). The Structured Clinical Interview for DSM-III-R (SCID): II. Multisite test-retest reliability. *Archives of General Psychiatry, 49,* 630-636.

Grant, B. F. (1993). ICD-10 and proposed DSM-IV harmful use of alcohol/alcohol abuse and dependence, United States 1988: A nosological comparison. *Alcoholism: Clinical and Experimental Research, 17,* 1093-1101.

Review of the Adolescent Diagnostic Interview by LOGAN WRIGHT, Associate Professor of Psychology, and DONNA FORD and KARYLL KISER, Research Assistants, University of Central Oklahoma, Edmond, OK:

The Adolescent Diagnostic Interview (ADI) is designed to assess psychoactive substance abuse disorder in adolescents aged 12 to 18 years. The ADI is a criterion-referenced diagnostic instrument, in which the individual is "evaluated against a specific set of standards or criteria" (manual, p. 23). These diagnostic criteria are taken from the *Diagnostic and Statistical Manual of Mental Disorders, Third Edition, Revised* (*DSM-III-R*; American Psychiatric Association, 1987). The ADI is one of three instruments comprising the Minnesota Chemical Dependence Adolescent Assessment Package (MCDAAP). This package also contains the Personal Experience Screening Questionnaire (PESQ; 286) and the Personal Experience Inventory (PEI; T4:1971). It is recommended that the ADI be used in conjunction with other MCDAAP instruments; however, it can be used independently.

The ADI is individually administered, follows a structured interview protocol, and consists of 306 possible items. The eight sections of the ADI require approximately 45 minutes to complete when the client's psychoactive substance use is restricted to alcohol and/or cannabis. Administration time increases with the number of additional drugs involved. The following nine classes of substance abuse and dependency can also be evaluated: amphetamines, barbiturates, cocaine, opioids, hallucinogens, PCP, inhalants, unspecified or combination drug use, and polysubstance. The ADI is hand scored rather than machine scored.

The ADI is based entirely on the self-reports of the adolescents, and the instrument has been field tested on only white English-speaking individuals. In addition to the diagnostic evaluation of psychoactive substance use disorder of the ADI, its Psychiatric Status Screens section is designed as a screening tool for: affective, anxiety, psychotic, eating, attention deficit, and conduct disorders. Clients are assigned a Global Severity Rating for psychosocial stressors. The ADI also assesses additional variables that may be related to substance abuse (e.g., peer relations, opposite sex relations, home behaviors, academics, etc.).

Items for each interview section of the ADI were generated from: (*a*) a review of existing structured interviews for children and adolescents, (*b*) existing substance abuse interviews, and (*c*) items suggested by an unspecified number of "chemical dependence counselors, clinicians, and experts" (manual, p. 23). Items were also generated from the description of substance abuse in the *DSM-III-R* of the American Psychiatric Association and from the diagnostic categories in the International Classification of Diseases of the World Health Organization. Finally, items were generated based on the authors' impressions of "the essential features of psychoactive substance abuse and dependence disorders" (manual, p. 2) prevailing in the mental health field.

The ADI manual authors refer to an initial item pool; however, it appears that all items in the original pool were retained. If, in fact, some items were discarded, nothing on the nature of the items retained versus discarded, or the basis for such decisions, is provided.

Details of the test construction, reliability, and validity are described in the test manual and in a related study by Winters, Stinchfield, Fulkerson, and Henly (1993). Reliability of the ADI was assessed for both interrater agreement and test-retest stability. No internal consistency information is available for the 15 ADI categories or its Psychiatric Status Screens or the Psychosocial Stressors Global Severity Rating.

To assess interrater reliability, initial interviews were recorded and subsequently rated by four judges. Interrater reliability for the 15 dependence and abuse categories was estimated for 72 subjects. The resulting kappas for the 15 categories, using Cohen's (1960) percentage of agreement technique to correct for the degree of agreement which might be expected by chance alone, fell between .53 to 1.00.

Estimates of interrater reliability for the Psychiatric Status Screen and the Psychosocial Stressors Global Severity Rating segments of the ADI are described only as having "exceeded chance expectations" (manual, p. 26). Interrater reliability for these segments of the ADI was also estimated using *T* indices, to indicate the actual magnitude of agreement when greater than chance-expected agreement is found. The degrees of agreement on these latter two segments ranged from .58 to .98. Agreement or disagreement on the Psychiatric Status Screens was based on a 3-point scale for *no indication*, *some indication*, or *strong indication* of psychiatric disorder. Interrater agreement for the Psychosocial Stressors Global Severity Rating was based on a 5-point scale of stressor severity.

Test-retest reliability for the ADI is estimated for only two (alcohol and cannabis) of the substance categories. No test-retest reliability data are available for the abuse components of the 10 substance categories. Likewise, no test-retest reliability data are available for the Psychiatric Status Screens or Psychosocial Stressors Global Severity Ratings components.

Test-retest reliability for alcohol dependence and cannabis dependence was estimated using a different sample of 49 adolescent drug users. The subjects were retested by the same interviewer one week following an initial administration using a simple binomial (yes/no) scale. Observed agreement between first and second interviews, again employing Cohen's kappa, was .83 for alcohol and .80 for cannabis. Percent of agreement for the alcohol and cannabis dependence and abuse symptoms ranged from 78 to 92%, whereas the resulting kappas ranged from .52 to .79. The short interval between test-retest may have inflated these test-retest results. The authors suggest that future test-retest studies include longer intervals between the initial and second administrations.

Validity of the ADI was evaluated by correlating ratings for the ADI substance use disorder groups with staff ratings for Heilman's (1973) warning signs of addiction, using 278 subjects recruited from an outpatient adolescent substance abuse evaluation center, residential evaluation centers, and aftercare programs. The resulting correlations of .72 and .78 were significant at $p<.001$.

In summary, the interrater and test-retest reliability of the ADI appear to have been established, at least to a minimal degree. However, the ADI's validity remains essentially undetermined, as does its advantage over other available instruments in the area of substance abuse diagnosis. Additional validity studies are certainly in order. In the meantime, the ADI may serve as a useful clinical tool, but should not be regarded as a validated research or clinical instrument.

REVIEWER'S REFERENCES

Cohen, J. (1960). A coefficient of agreement for nominal scales. *Educational and Psychological Measurement, 20*, 37-46.

Heilman, R. O. (1973). *Early recognition of alcoholism and other drug dependence*. Center City, MN: Hazelden Educational Materials.

American Psychiatric Association. (1987). *Diagnostic and statistical manual of mental disorders* (DSM-III-R; rev. 3rd ed.). Washington, DC: Author.

Winters, K. C., Stinchfield, R. D., Fulkerson, J., & Henly, G. A. (1993). Measuring alcohol and cannabis use disorders in an adolescent clinical sample. *Psychology of Addictive Behaviors, 7*(3), 185-196.

[17]

Adolescent Drinking Index.

Purpose: Constructed to screen for alcohol abuse.
Population: Ages 12–17.
Publication Dates: 1985–89.
Acronym: ADI.
Scores, 3: Self-Medicated Drinking (MED), Aggressive/Rebellious Behavior (REB), Total.
Administration: Group or individual.
Price Data, 1994: $47 per complete kit including manual ('89, 34 pages) and 25 test booklets.
Time: (5) minutes.
Comments: Test booklet title is Drinking & You.
Authors: Adele V. Harrell and Philip W. Wirtz.
Publisher: Psychological Assessment Resources, Inc.

Review of the Adolescent Drinking Index by THOMAS F. DONLON, Director, Office of Test Development and Research, Thomas Edison State College, Trenton, NJ:

The Adolescent Drinking Index (ADI) is a 24-item scale that attempts to measure the severity of any drinking problem that an adolescent may have. The Index is based upon a conceptual framework that delineates four domains or facets of developmentally dysfunctional drinking: (*a*) loss of control over drinking, so that there is drinking at inappropriate times, places, or in inappropriate amounts; (*b*) interference with significant interpersonal relationships through drinking; (*c*) drinking to alter mood or state of relaxation; and (*d*) physical changes through drinking: memory losses or increased tolerance for alcohol.

Two of these four domains are important enough in their own right to be assessed by a subscale: The Self-Medicated Drinking (MED) scale is a four-item indicator of drinking to alter mood, and the Rebelliousness (REB) scale is a seven-item index of aggressive, rebellious behavior, interfering with interpersonal relationships.

The purposes of the ADI are assisting in identifying issues to be addressed in treatment, in clarifying differences in male and female adolescent base rates for alcohol use, and in reducing the tendency to overlook problem drinking in self-medicating adolescents whose drinking problem is unobtrusive. The instrument is described as "*not* designed to serve as a school-wide screening instrument for the detection of alcohol abuse among adolescents in general" (manual, p. 3). However, one part of its validation is based on data collected from a sample selected "to represent a general population of adolescents," and the normative data for these 583 subjects is presented first in the appendices. It was not clear to this reviewer what specific limitations were seen by the authors to rule out its use among adolescents in general.

The content of the 24 questions calls for very direct self-reports, through simple Likert scales indicating the extent to which the statement provided is valid for the subject: *like me a lot* to *not like me at all*, and, for frequency data: *4 or more times* to *never*. The four-item MED scale asks about motivation for drinking in order to counter anger, loneliness, sadness, and tension. The seven-item REB scale asks about "fighting" and "getting into trouble"; however, there is some logical overlap between its questions: One question asks "how often in the past year did you get into a fight over drinking," and another asks "how often in the past year did you fight with your parents about your drinking." The two frequencies reported could obviously be the same events for some students and different events for others, depending on the interpretation of the language. "Get into a fight" may not mean a physical fight to every student.

The manual authors present substantial data on the psychometric characteristics of the instrument, including a confirmatory factor analysis of the scale structure, an analysis of variance testing the age by gender interaction, and the use of a sequence of discriminant analyses in the service of deriving cutoff scores. These analyses are conducted on three samples: the 583-person "school sample" from the general population; the 233-person "treatment sample" consisting of adolescents actively under treatment for alcohol abuse; and the 261-person "validation sample" consisting of adolescents referred to clinicians for some psychological, emotional, or behavioral problem.

Some of these psychometric analyses, however, are based upon complex logical edifices that make them unconvincing. Thus, the confirmatory factor analysis tested the probability that the three hypothesized scales were not perfectly identical. Such statistical significance, even though demonstrated, may not support any practical significance. Given the small numbers of items in the two scales, and the inclusion of these items in the total score (referred to as the primary scale, severity of drinking), it is doubtful that the subscales have useful meaning. Of the seven REB scale items, for example, only one shows a higher correlation with its scale total than with the ADI total in the validation sample; only two of these items show such a higher correlation in the treatment sample. The subscales are called "research scales," and their suggested use is in "generating hypotheses about potential forms of treatment and further methods of evaluation." However, they appear to this reviewer to be somewhat oversold in the manual.

The authors note that "in general, male adolescents . . . have higher rates of alcohol abuse" (p. 13). However, females aged 16–17 show higher ADI total scores than males in the validation sample (20.39 vs. 16.98), and in the treatment sample (32.19 vs. 31.76), and a similar pattern is observed for females and males ages 12–15. Only the school sample showed data conforming to the expectation (females 16–17 averaging 8.11 vs. comparable males 11.84, and females 12–15 averaging 5.63 vs. males 5.92). An analysis of variance testing age-gender interactions, performed *only* on the school sample, is interpreted as "consistent with the general finding of increased alcohol use by males" (p. 13). There was a need for a fuller and more detailed analysis to clarify these results.

A cutoff score of 15 was derived by drawing a series of 25 random samples of 130 subjects (50% of the group sampled) from the validation sample. A discriminant analysis was used to establish in each sample the cutoff score that would best differentiate the severe drinkers from the others in this group. The modal value of the distribution of such cutoffs was 15, and this was chosen as the operational cutoff value. These procedures seem rational, but the cutoff so determined will identify a large proportion of persons whose drinking problem is "moderate." The average score for the 65 "moderate" drinkers in the validation sample was 15.42. There are obviously some choices to be made in devising the cutoff. The use of the cutoff in the other samples showed that 17% of the school sample would demonstrate scores above the cutoff, whereas 78% of the treatment sample would demonstrate such scores. The index seems likely to err in the direction of overidentifying problem drinkers.

The ADI appears to be a commonsense way of screening adolescents in order to identify those with a severe drinking problem. It requires a cooperating subject, and it could be easily manipulated by anyone who wished to conceal a problem. It seems well designed for its intended function as an aid to clinicians making a judgment as to needed additional referral. Although it obviously offers information as to a complex framework with respect to aggressivity and the use of alcohol to control mood, the data do not support the use of the two research scales for anything more than just that: research.

Review of the Adolescent Drinking Index by KEVIN J. McCARTHY, Ph.D Candidate, Associate in Psychology Department, E. Hunt Correctional Center, St. Gabriel, LA, and PENELOPE W. DRALLE, Associate Professor of Psychiatry, Louisiana State University School of Medicine, New Orleans, LA:

The Adolescent Drinking Index (ADI) is a four-page booklet consisting of 24 questions about alcohol usage among teenagers. The assessment instrument is simple and direct. The Index can be self-administered in a few minutes and uses a format that divides the instrument into two component scales. Questions 1–10 address the issue of alcohol use and emotions. Data are collected on a modified 3-point Likert-type scale with answers ranging from *like me a lot* to *not like me at all*. Questions 11–24 focus on the issue of behaviors while under the influence of alcohol. It uses a modified 4-point Likert-type scale with answers ranging from *never* to *4 or more times*. This straightforward approach to drinking practices permits the client to focus on the issue of severity of use and subsequent behavioral problems and minimizes resistance commonly associated with longer instruments.

The Index's two subscales focus on Self-Medicated Drinking (MED) and Aggressive/Rebellious Behavior (REB) related to the use of alcohol. The authors caution that "the MED and REB subscales are research scales, their use should be restricted to generating hypotheses about potential forms of treatment and further methods of evaluation" (manual, p. 6).

The ADI manual authors state the instrument is not designed "to serve as a school-wide screening instrument for the detection of alcohol abuse among adolescents in general" (manual, p. 3). Also the authors state in the manual that "In no case will ADI data be sufficient in making a formal diagnosis of an alcohol abuse disorder" (p. 3). Thus, it has a rather limited primary function, to assess the severity of an adolescent's drinking problems. However, because the treatment study sample consisted of several groups of adolescents hospitalized for alcohol abuse and included several programs offering treatment for substance abuse without treatment differentiation between alcohol and other drugs usage, there is some confusion regarding whether the ADI assesses alcohol use or polysubstance use. The authors report that "Some of the subjects in this sample, therefore, may not have had drinking problems" (p. 9).

The majority of adolescents hospitalized for substance abuse are usually involuntarily admitted by a parent or guardian secondary to some precipitating event involving the use of alcohol or other drugs. Frequently, newly admitted patients minimize their using behaviors or deny the existence of an alcohol abuse problem. Because the ADI contains no measure of test-taking attitude, its usefulness seems to be restricted to those patients who have overcome denial about their drinking behaviors. The manual authors do not report which phase of treatment patients in the normative population were in at the time of assessment.

Substantive data regarding reliability and validity are provided in the manual. The ADI, developed from an item pool of 40 questions, went through pilot testing including qualitative and quantitative item analysis. This yielded an internal consistency reliability alpha coefficient of .92 for the final version, whereas analysis of the three samples comprising the normative population yielded an alpha coefficient exceeding .90. The authors report test-retest reliability at .78.

Convergent validity was assessed using the Michigan Alcoholism Screening Test (MAST) as an indicator yielding a correlation of r = .60–.63 for scores 2 and 1. Discriminant validity data suggest this index is a measure of alcohol abuse among adolescents, but some question remains regarding polysubstance abuse. The manual authors note that analysis of variance was used to conduct criterion group comparisons focusing on severity of adolescent drinking problems. The analysis revealed significant difference among three groups, ranging from minor to no problems to substantial problems.

The fact the ADI's REB subscale is designed to assess drinking behaviors over the last 12 months limits analysis of the data to recent past and current levels of using behaviors while avoiding the complexities of a more longitudinal perspective. This time frame permits the clinician to focus upon those behaviors that are currently problematic. The generalizability of the instrument is enhanced by including in the validation study data from six different sites in five different states tapping many of the regional differences found within the country. However, the regional utility of the instrument would be increased by including sites with larger representations of African-American youth and by specifying the composition of the "other" category.

The questions have not been counterbalanced, which may enhance response set bias. Alternating the social desirability of the items might increase the likelihood the client would read each item before responding. In the manual, the authors note that "The administrator should be available during testing to answer questions concerning test administration or the meaning of items" (p. 5), but they have not provided guidelines for standardized responses to such inequities.

In addition, the authors choose to break their sample into two age groups: 12–15-year-olds and 16–17-year-olds. There are significant developmental differences between 12-year-olds and 15-year-olds. Data presented in this format might be more effectively reorganized into three developmentally equitable groups (i.e., 12–13-year-olds, 14–15-year-olds, and 16–17-year-olds). This grouping would also correspond to the peer groups commonly found in local school districts (i.e., middle school, early and late high school).

The manual layout was rather difficult to follow. Matching data presented in graphs and charts to contextual components was difficult and frequently cumbersome.

In summary, the Adolescent Drinking Index's primary focus is limited to assessing the severity of drinking behaviors among a population of adolescents "referred for emotional or behavioral disorders" (p. 3). Its principal advantage is its brevity and succinctness as well as its ease of administration. When used in conjunction with historical and familial data, the ADI may aid the clinician in assessing drinking problems among receptive patients.

[18]

Adult Career Concerns Inventory.

Purpose: "Designed to measure career planning and one's concerns with the career development tasks at various life stages."
Population: Ages 24 and over.
Publication Date: 1988.
Acronym: ACCI.
Scores, 13: 12 subscales in 4 career stages: Exploration Stage (Crystallization, Specification, Implementation), Establishment Stage (Stabilizing, Consolidating, Advancing), Maintenance Stage (Holding, Updating, Innovating), Disengagement Stage (Deceleration, Retirement Planning, Retirement Living), plus Career Change Status.
Administration: Group.
Price Data, 1992: $9 per 25 test booklets and profiles; $32 per 50 not prepaid answer sheets; $30 per manual (63 pages); $31 per specimen set.
Time: (15–30) minutes.
Comments: Self-administered and self-scored; research edition; a measure of Donald Super's hierarchy of life stages for adults; manual title is Manual for Research and Exploratory Use in Counseling.
Authors: Donald E. Super, Albert S. Thompson, and Richard H. Lindeman.
Publisher: Consulting Psychologists Press, Inc.
Cross References: See T4:103 (5 references).

TEST REFERENCES

1. Savickas, M. L., Passen, A. J., & Jarjoura, D. G. (1988). Career concern and coping as indicators of adult vocational development. *Journal of Vocational Behavior*, *33*, 82-98.

2. Niles, S. G., & Anderson, W. P., Jr. (1993). Career development and adjustment: The relation between concerns and stress. *Journal of Employment Counseling*, *30*, 79-87.

3. Smart, R. M., & Peterson, C. C. (1994). Super's stages and the four-factor structure of the Adult Career Concerns Inventory in an Australian sample. *Measurement and Evaluation in Counseling and Development*, *26*, 243-257.

4. Anderson, W. P., Jr., & Niles, S. G. (1995). Career and personal concerns expressed by career counseling clients. *Career Development Quarterly*, *43*, 240-245.

Review of the Adult Career Concerns Inventory by RICHARD W. JOHNSON, Adjunct Professor of Counseling Psychology, and Associate Director of Counseling & Consultation Center, University of Wisconsin-Madison, Madison, WI:

The Adult Career Concerns Inventory (ACCI) was originally published for research purposes as the Career Development Inventory, Adult Form. In contrast with adolescents and young adults tested by means of the Career Development Inventory, High School or College and University Forms, the authors found that mature adults frequently recycle through earlier stages in their career development as they adjust to changes in their careers. They also found that adults need more specialized occupational information depending upon their particular situation than do youths. For these reasons, they decided to limit their assessment to the different types of concerns that adults might express in attempting to adapt to their careers in the course of a lifetime. They refocused and retitled the inventory as a measure of career concerns instead of career development. In addition to its use in research on the theory of career development, the ACCI can be used for career counseling and planning, for assessing the needs of different groups of people, and for evaluating the effectiveness of different career interventions.

In its present form, the ACCI includes 15 items for each of four career stages (Exploration, Establishment, Maintenance, and Disengagement) included in Donald Super's theory of career development. Each stage is further divided into three substages with five items for each substage. Each item is answered in terms of a five-step scale ranging from *No Concern* to *Great Concern*. All of the items for each stage and substage are listed together, thus facilitating scoring and interpreting the results. The ACCI includes one additional item (Item 61) that reflects career status (i.e., the extent to which the client is considering a career change). The answer to Item 61 is helpful in interpreting the scores on the other parts of the inventory.

The manual provides "preliminary norms" that are limited both in terms of size and representativeness. The sample sizes for the sex-by-age norms (four age groups for each sex) range from 25 to 78. The individuals who volunteered to be included in the norm groups possessed above average education and occupational status. Ultimately, the authors intend to provide more representative norms for different age groups as well as separate norms for different occupational and career-status groups. In the meantime, they recommend the use of local norms for interindividual comparisons. They also stress the value of intraindividual (ipsative) comparisons as a means of identifying quickly the predominant concerns of individuals.

Both the stage and substage scale scores showed high interitem consistency according to two studies reported in the manual. The four stage scales produced alpha coefficients ranging from .92 to .96. The alpha coefficients for the 12 subscales all exceeded .80 with one exception. No test-retest reliabilities are reported in the manual. Although long-term test-retest consistency would not be expected for a measure of career concerns hypothesized to change over time, test-retest scores over short time periods (2 to 4 weeks) should be relatively consistent. Information on this topic should be provided.

Studies of the validity of the CDI show that most people obtain their highest scores on stages that are appropriate for their age according to Super's theory of career development. A number of validity studies reported in the manual show that the relationship between stage scores and age is moderated by such factors as career field, educational level, sex differences, and job performance. The most crucial moderator variable appears to be a person's career status. For example, individuals in the process of changing careers are likely to express exploratory needs regardless of their age. The ACCI appears to provide a valid measure for adults of career concerns that vary according to one's age, career status, and related factors in a predictable fashion.

The scores on the ACCI should be helpful in planning career interventions. For example, clients who score high on the Updating subscale in the Maintenance stage should profit from training opportunities such as workshops, seminars, professional conferences, field trips, and work demonstrations. Presumably, scores on the ACCI could be used to predict the effectiveness of different types of career interventions. Predictive validity studies of this type would provide valuable information for counselors.

Factor analytic research indicates that the ACCI taps four independent factors associated with the four stage scales, which support the construct validity of the instrument. These four factors account for approximately one-half of the variance in the ACCI scores. Because a considerable amount of the variance is not explained by the four factors, counselors should also inspect the subscale scores as well as the individual items to identify possible concerns not adequately represented by the factors.

The ACCI is limited in scope. It principally assesses the adult's needs for career planning and adaptation. It does not measure career planning competencies such as decision-making skills, job-hunting skills, and work-effectiveness skills, which should also be considered in the course of counseling the adult. In the counseling process itself, the ACCI must be supplemented with measures of a client's interests, values, and abilities in regard to different educational and occupational opportunities.

The ACCI should be used when one wishes to assess career concerns that might occur throughout one's work life. Despite the need for additional normative, reliability, and validity studies, the ACCI appears to be better suited for this purpose than any other instrument.

Review of the Adult Career Concerns Inventory by CAROLINE MANUELE-ADKINS, Professor of Educational Foundations and Counseling Programs, Hunter College, City University of New York, New York, NY:

The Adult Career Concerns Inventory (ACCI) was designed to assess career development in adults by identifying the career concerns they have that relate to the various stages, substages, and tasks of career development. The ACCI is a 61-item self-report measure in which respondents are asked to rate the extent of their concern, on a scale of 1 (*no concern*) to 5 (*great concern*), about such statements as "avoiding occupational pressures I formerly handled more easily"; or "advancing to a more responsible position." The ACCI is based on Super's theory of career development. His theory reflects years of research and study on the career development and adjustment of people from early adolescence through middle and late adulthood.

Super's theory postulates that there are four stages of career development. Each stage includes specific substages and developmental tasks that people need to confront and cope with at different ages and times of their lives. The ACCI's scales and scores are the same as Super's stages and substages of career development. Thus, individuals who express varying degrees of concerns about specified career development tasks yield scores that may place them in one of these stages.

As described in the ACCI manual these stages include: (*a*) the Exploration Stage (average age 15–25) where individuals explore and develop ideas about the type of work they want to do, move from general to specific preferences, and begin to implement plans for "getting started in their chosen field"; (*b*) the Establishment Stage (average age 25–45), which involves getting established in a career, becoming committed to an occupation or career after serious trial, and obtaining security and advancing in an occupation and/or organization; (*c*) the Maintenance Stage (average age 45–60 or 65) denotes career behavior and concerns that relate to holding onto a position, updating and keeping abreast of new developments, innovating and advancing in a chosen area of work; (*d*) the Disengagement Stage (average age 65 and beyond), formerly known as the Decline stage, is accompanied by the need for reducing the pace, load, and involvement of work as individuals grow older. Planning for retirement, becoming retired, and learning to function in different work and leisure roles are common for individuals in the final stage of career development.

According to the manual, the ACCI is designed to be self-administered and can be either self-scored or machine scored. It may be used with individuals or groups and on the average takes 15 to 30 minutes to complete. The inventory includes 61 statements of career concerns items, a machine-scorable answer sheet, and a hand-scoring sheet that includes directions for scoring. Once the responses are tallied, weighted, summed, and averaged a profile of concerns emerges that identifies the stage(s) and substages that are of most importance at the current time.

The manual suggests that hand scoring is the preferred alternative when it is being used for immediate feedback "in workshops, courses and counseling intake settings." Test-outs of the hand-scoring method indicate that the authors may be overly optimistic in their estimates of the time required for hand scoring. Although the calculations are not difficult, some individuals have trouble grasping the scoring principles.

The authors even recommend that a calculator is helpful. In a group of 15 individuals the user should allow as much as an hour for hand scoring of the profiles. Many counselors, however, will find that the advantages of immediate feedback far outweigh any disadvantage in the time required for hand scoring.

Machine scoring is available from the publisher and is recommended when groups of any size are tested and when the user may be concerned with "surveying and evaluating the career development needs of large groups who may be employed in specific organizations or occupations." An advantage of machine scoring is that statistical analyses of the group data are provided that include demographic analyses, and means and standard deviations for extent of satisfaction with current employment, career stage status, and career stage concerns.

Most respondents will find the ACCI easy to read and understand unless they have some literacy problems. The items are clearly stated and appear to have good "face validity" in that they express in simple terms typical career issues that people experience at different points of their careers. Professionals who use the ACCI will find the manual well written and easy to understand if they have a background in career development theory and career counseling. This is as it should be because the authors recommend that the ACCI only be used by people "who are familiar with career development theory" and its primary use is for career counseling and planning.

The manual for the ACCI presents evidence for the validity and reliability of the measure. In interpreting these data it is important to distinguish between analyses that were done with prior versions of the ACCI and those that were done with the current form. The majority of studies relate to prior versions of the ACCI but are an important part of its development. A summary of data on content, construct, and concurrent validity of earlier versions and the current one suggests that the results are mixed. According to the authors, item analysis and factor analysis verified that the items in the measure were homogenous for each scale. Although extensive descriptive data are provided about the derivation of the ACCI from many prior versions, related to Super's Career Pattern Study and beyond, no direct evidence for item scale correlations is presented. Factor analytic studies of previous versions and the current one reveal significant clusters that relate conceptually to the stages (scales) in the ACCI but more analyses of this type, for this version, would be important.

Content validity, according to the manual, is established by the fact that the items were derived over time by much of the research, models, and concepts of Super's Career Pattern Study. Concurrent and predictive validity studies are described that explore the relationship between ACCI scores (including scores obtained on previous versions) and stages of adult development, job attitudes, job performance, psychological characteristics, sex differences, exposure to career training and counseling, choice of curriculum, and career adaptability.

An evaluation of all of these studies suggests that about one-half of them are able to demonstrate a significant relationship between stages of career development (as defined by the ACCI) and these variables. Descriptions of many of these validity studies are not accompanied by actual data or tables except for the one done on this published version. Clearly, more validity studies of the current form are needed. At the same time the user should understand that the ACCI is the result of many years of investigation about the career behavior of adults and its development is a product of serious attempts to define and assess it. The authors describe the ACCI as an "instrument for research" and at this point in its development there is sufficient evidence for practitioners to proceed with their use of the measure. At the same time there is a need for further research to produce a fully developed and validated version of the ACCI.

Reliability data for the ACCI are reported on its current form consisting principally of internal consistency reliability (alpha) coefficients ranging from .76 (for the Deceleration Stage) to .95. The majority of the coefficients are in the .90s, suggesting that the reliability of the ACCI is robust. No test-retest reliability data are reported. These analyses have yet to be completed. Additional reliability analyses with a variety of samples are also needed.

Normative data for the ACCI are very limited. The authors describe their normative group as "a small, preliminary sample of an ill-defined universe of adults." This sample includes 373 people (136 males, 225 females) in different age groups who are principally college and professionally educated. Means, standard deviations, and rank importance of career concerns are described for this group. This sample will provide the counselor with some interesting information about how an individual client compares to this sample, but interpretations must be made with caution. Larger samples that include sufficient numbers in all the age groups are needed. More information on the career concerns of different groups is also needed. The manual identifies the need for such samples and suggests that future samples include blue-collar workers, homemakers, people who are unemployed, white-collar workers, the handicapped, and others. One hopes that the authors will continue with these studies. In addition to contributing to the power of the ACCI, the normative data would provide us with substantial information about the career development and behavior of different groups. Given the limited norms, the most appropriate interpretation for ACCI results is an "ipsative" one in which an individual is "compared with him or herself" and is "the norm rather than some external group." This method of interpretation is the one most favored by the authors of the ACCI at the current time.

In summary, the ACCI appears to be an interesting exploratory measure of adult career development. It is unique in its attempt to assess developmental career concerns beyond the high school years. In its current form the ACCI is principally a counseling tool that can be used to encourage adults, and older adolescents, to explore their own career choices and development. The manual provides the counselor with useful suggestions for understanding an individual's career behavior in the context of career adaptability, recycling, re-exploration, gender issues, age, and values. Researchers will also find the measure valuable for exploring the occupational needs and behaviors of different groups in society.

The ACCI is, however, still in an initial stage of development. More validity, reliability, and normative data are needed. Future studies of the ACCI will also be valuable in the sense that many of Super's theoretical constructs are operationalized in this measure. The results of these studies should provide more normative information about adult career behavior and development. Apart from these concerns the ACCI appears to be a measure that will be well received by counselors who are guided by theories of career development to assist them with understanding their client's needs.

[19]

Adult Neuropsychological Questionnaire.

Purpose: To screen for brain dysfunction.
Population: Adults.
Publication Date: 1978.
Acronym: ANQ.
Scores: 8 content areas: General Health, Substance Abuse, Psychiatric Problems, General Neurological, Right Hemisphere, Left Hemisphere, Subcortical/Cerebellar/Spinal, Sensory/Perceptual.
Administration: Individual.
Price Data, 1995: $30 per complete kit including manual (11 pages) and 50 questionnaires.
Time: (5–10) minutes.
Comments: Can be used as adjunct to general intake interview; may be self-administered.
Author: Fernando Melendez.
Publisher: Psychological Assessment Resources, Inc.

Review of the Adult Neuropsychological Questionnaire by ROBERT A. BORNSTEIN, Professor and Associate Chairman, Department of Psychiatry, The Ohio State University, Columbus, OH:

The Adult Neuropsychological Questionnaire consists of 54 items designed to be administered as a semistructured interview. It can also be self-administered. The purpose of the questionnaire is to "inquire about complaints, symptoms, and signs that may suggest underlying brain dysfunction or other organic conditions" (manual, p. 1). It was developed initially as an aid for students who were not well versed in signs and symptoms associated with neurologic conditions. A well-organized neuropsychologically oriented inquiry of history and symptoms would be of considerable value primarily to students or general clinicians. The test manual is essentially an interpretive guide that contains a rationale for the items that have been included. The authors suggest that formal assessment will often confirm or clarify the symptoms endorsed, although no data are presented to support this assertion. Similarly, no reliability or validity data of any kind are presented. The purported relationship between formal assessment and symptom endorsement as relevant for forensic work is fully unsubstantiated. Similarly, there is no support that this questionnaire has any value as a "reliable monitor in following the course of recovery (or decline) over a period of time" (manual, p. 1). The final paragraph of the manual introduction regards this questionnaire as "an assessment procedure," however, there are not even the most rudimentary evaluative data to support this assertion.

Apart from the lack of any supportive psychometric data, the inherent organization and content of the questionnaire leaves much to be desired. The items consist of a melange of questions directed at specific symptoms, personal medical history, and family medical history. Several of the questions are not directed at neurological or neuropsychological questions or conditions. These items, such as Number 5 related to tobacco consumption, are acknowledged to have no neuropsychological correlates, but are included to be used in subsequent medical referrals. It is unclear why questions about the identity and address of the patient's physician, or the date of the last physical examination (Items 38 and 39) should be part of the body of the questionnaire.

The ordering of questions is poorly organized with a random array of questions. This is particularly problematic because the presumed goal of this questionnaire is to help non-neuropsychologists conduct an organized neuropsychological inquiry. It would be of greater value if items were organized in coherent units related to current symptoms, personal history, and family history.

In addition to the poor organization, the content and wording of the questions are inconsistent, and in some cases ambiguous. For example, Item 9 inquires directly about changes in vision, and Item 32 inquires about changes in sense of smell. However, changes in hearing are addressed only indirectly by Item 17, "sometimes when people talk to you, do they seem to mumble?" Although several questions are devoted to possible symptoms of dizziness or loss of balance, there is no direct inquiry about changes in temperament, or problems with attention and concentration, both of which are common symptoms in neurologic populations. There is direct inquiry about relatively rare conditions such as syphilis (Item 46), but there is no direct inquiry regarding whether the patient has ever had a seizure. This is only indirectly, and poorly, addressed by Item 21 which inquires about family history of epilepsy.

The questionnaire also includes items which are very common in the general population, and almost certain to have no discriminative validity. The rationale offered for inclusion of these items (e.g., 19) is that failure to endorse the item represents a form of denial, lack of understanding, or lack of insight. There is no justification offered for this assertion. Many of the item interpretations and explanations offered in the manual are poorly justified, fail to recognize more common neurologic or psychiatric explanations, and dangerously oversimplify the questions under review, particularly in view of the intended audience for this questionnaire.

The dangerous and flawed interpretation of some items is exemplified by the major question categories that are included on the last page of the manual. Without any proper caution in the manual, these question groups could be viewed by the unsophisticated user as quasi-assessment indexes, indicative of specific disorders. The assignment of items to the "right hemisphere" and "left hemisphere" question groups amply demonstrate the problem. There are four "right hemisphere" questions; the first of which (change in sense of direction) may have some validity in relation to right hemisphere function. The other three items (change in memory, experience of déjà-vu, and change in handwriting) have no clear association with right hemisphere function. Although memory function clearly can be affected with right hemisphere function, patients are unlikely to complain spontaneously of the kind of memory deficit typically associated with right hemisphere disorders. Similarly, because memory complaints are so ubiquitous, this item could easily be included in the question categories related to psychiatric problems, general neurologic problems, and subcortical dysfunction.

The "left hemisphere" question group, which consists of five items, suffers from similar flaws. Although some of the items (e.g., 11) may bear some relation to left hemisphere symptoms, other items are not clearly related. For example, Item 18 (slurring your words) suggests dysarthria, which has no necessary association with left hemisphere function. The memory item is equally inappropriate for the left hemisphere question group for the same reasons as indicated above.

Finally, Item 24, related to temporary blindness in one or both eyes, although correctly attributed to cerebrovascular phenomena, has no association with the left hemisphere. Virtually, all of the eight symptom groupings suffer from similar flawed associations and attributions.

In summary, this questionnaire is designed to help students and non-neuropsychologists inquire about symptoms, history, or other complaints that may be associated with neuropsychological disorders. The questionnaire is poorly organized, ambiguous and inconsistent in its inquiry, and severely overinterpretive about the significance and possible attribution of specific symptoms. On the other hand, some important areas of inquiry are entirely omitted. This is a particular problem for a questionnaire intended for unsophisticated users. Furthermore, the implication that this questionnaire represents some form of quasi assessment, as suggested by the question groupings, is likely to lead to grossly incorrect interpretations. Although a well-organized inquiry of history and symptoms would be of significant value for the audience intended, this questionnaire falls seriously short of the mark. It is not recommended for use.

Review of the Adult Neuropsychological Questionnaire by JULIAN FABRY, Counseling Psychologist, Omaha Psychiatric Institute, Omaha, NE:

The Adult Neuropsychological Questionnaire is a self-report approach to evaluating an adult's neuropsychological "complaints, symptoms, or signs" (manual, p. 1) which "suggest organic brain dysfunction." The author developed this appraisal because of the apparent gap between social and psychological information and as a means to make appropriate medical referrals.

The Adult Neuropsychological Questionnaire can be used as an adjunct to a general intake interview, to make medical referrals, and to monitor recovery or deterioration of individuals as well as organize information about them. The questionnaire can be self-administered or a practitioner can ask questions focusing on the frequency, intensity, and duration of the occurrence of a particular symptom. It has been advocated that the person who uses this questionnaire be a practitioner with some fund of basic neuropsychological information.

In addition to a revised manual, the questionnaire itself consists of a booklet that can be used by the practitioner or examinee during the course of the interview or evaluation. The questionnaire consists of 54 items and they are arranged so that an appropriate response can be made (either yes/no or descriptive). The items cover a broad spectrum of information ranging from eating habits to sleep patterns, from alcohol consumption to types of headaches, losses, and changes in physical or mental functioning. It appears the author has rationally grouped the questions according to the following categories: General Health; Substance Abuse; Psychiatric Problems; General Neurological; Right Hemisphere; Left Hemisphere; Subcortical, Cerebellar, Spinal; and Sensory, Perceptual.

The manual contains no technical information regarding reliability and validity. A review of the literature did not provide any information regarding current use of the instrument.

The questionnaire would, therefore, have obvious limited use with no empirical support for differentiating subjects into pathological groups. It seems to be an instrument that is helpful in organizing clinically obtained information for the purpose of making medical referrals.

The most immediate needs are norms based on whether the instrument is used as one that is self-administered or rated by a practitioner. The hit rates for various pathological groups utilizing the preceding rationally derived categories would also extend the usefulness and predictive validity of this instrument.

This questionnaire could also benefit from being computerized to assist in organizing the information obtained for either the researcher or the practitioner. At present it remains a clinical aid that needs empirical validation.

[20]

Adult Personality Inventory.

Purpose: Designed as "a tool for analyzing and reporting individual differences in personality, interpersonal style, and career/life-style preferences."
Population: Ages 16–Adult.
Publication Dates: 1982–88.
Acronym: API.
Scores, 25: Personality Scores (Extroverted, Adjusted, Tough-Minded, Independent, Disciplined, Creative, Enterprising); Interpersonal Style Scores (Caring, Adapting, Withdrawn, Submissive, Uncaring, Non-Conforming, Sociable, Assertive); Career/Life-Style Scores (Practical, Scientific, Aesthetic, Social, Competitive, Structured); Validity Scores (Good Impression, Bad Impression, Infrequency, Uncertainty).
Administration: Group or individual.
Time: (45–60) minutes.
Comments: Self-report; computer scored and interpreted.
Author: Samuel E. Krug.
Publisher: MetriTech, Inc.

a) API NARRATIVE REPORTS.
Purpose: "Oriented to the test taker and features an interpretive narrative that provides extensive feedback."
Price Data, 1994: $49 per Narrative Report Kit including manual ('88, 15 pages), processing of 5 reports, 2 reusable test booklets, and 5 answer sheets; $6.75–$9.75 per narrative report including processing and answer sheets; $16.50 per manual; $16 per 10 reusable test booklets.

b) API/TEST PLUS.
Purpose: Oriented to the test administrator and includes a decision model feature.
Price Data: $795 per API/Test Plus microcomputer version; $48 per occupational decision model disk; $38 per TPEXTERN program; $16 per 10 reusable test booklets; $12 per 50 answer sheets; $18.50 per 50 scannable answer sheets; $36 per 50 decision model worksheets.
Comments: Supports both on-line or off-line testing; IBM version only; optional 189-item short version requires 25–35 minutes for administration.

c) API/CAREER PROFILE.
Purpose: Oriented to the test administrator and compares individual test taker with Occupational Decision Models and user created models..
Price Data: $8.50–$11.50 per report.
Comments: Support both on-line or off-line testing; IBM version only; optional 189-item short version requires 25–35 minutes for administration.

Cross References: See T4:106 (4 references); for a review by Brian Bolton of an earlier edition, see 9:54.

Review of the Adult Personality Inventory by RIK CARL D'AMATO, Professor and Director, Programs in School Psychology, Division of Professional Psychology, University of Northern Colorado, Greeley, CO:

The Adult Personality Inventory (API) by Samuel E. Krug is a 324-question self-report instrument designed to measure personality differences in normal individuals. A computer-generated report provides practical information from a quantitative base. The test is seen as having relevance for vocational counseling, marriage and family therapy, personality assessment, and human development programs. With a 4th grade reading level, the test is offered as appropriate for adults age 16 and older. The API may be considered an updated version of the 16PF (Bolton, 1985, 1991).

The API evolved from the research of Raymond B. Cattell and his associates in the 1950s. Samuel Krug worked with Cattell first as a graduate student and later at the Institute for Personality and Ability Testing. The Institute developed and published the Sixteen Personality Factor Questionnaire (16PF) as well as many other related instruments. The API is an extension of this work, with 564 items from the 16PF serving as a pool of beginning items. Careful consideration was given to revamping the venerable 16PF, and statistical analyses were conducted to simplify, shorten, and finely hone this long standing scale. Items were rewritten to represent updating and a more standardized response format. The API was created when 324 items were selected and judged to represent 21 trait scales. The step-by-step process that was followed is clearly spelled out in the API manual. The API was then evaluated in light of Cattell's personality paradigm and was viewed as covering all areas deemed to be important to this model.

The API provides information from 21 trait scales. The scales are derived from multivariate statistics; thus handscoring is not feasible. Unfortunately, the development of some of the scales is not discussed thoroughly in the manual, and this leads to some confusion regarding the instrument's theoretical foundation.

The first seven scales are designated as Personal/Motivational factors.. Of those, the first five correspond to the second-order factors among the 16PF trait scales. These scales have been documented in the available literature (e.g., Krug, 1991). These scales include Extroverted, Adjusted, Tough-Minded, Independent, and Disciplined. Two new additions included the Creative scale and the Enterprising scale. The Creative scale was developed by studying highly innovative and productive individuals and the Enterprising scale was developed by studying achievement needs in other standardized tests.

The next eight scales reflect Interpersonal Style and evaluate how the individual relates to others. The scales cover the areas of Caring, Adapting, Withdrawn, Submissive, Hostile, Rebellious, Sociable, and Assertive. Many of these scales are closely related to 16PF scales. In fact, some have been seen as psychometrically questionable due to substantial overlap (Bolton, 1985). Of all the API scales, the development of these eight is most obscure.

The final cluster of six scales is seen as Career/Life-Style factors. This area is argued to be related to career choices, job satisfaction, and life-style preferences. The scales are labeled as Practical, Scientific, Aesthetic, Social, Competitive, and Structured. Obviously, these scales are similar to Holland's occupational themes. Thus, many of these constructs are familiar and will find easy application to vocational settings. Research is beginning to support the congruence between the API career factors and Holland occupational types (Ahadi, 1991). The career factors were identified beginning with an analysis of occupational group scores from the 16PF.

The final four scales are Validity scales that indicate the response style of the respondent completing the test. The Good Impression scale suggests that the individual attempted to "fake" good, whereas the Bad Impression scale suggests that the individual tried to "fake" bad. The Infrequency scale identifies items that are not endorsed regularly, and an Uncertainty scale suggests middle or uncertain responses.

The test can be individually or group administered. Special training is not required to administer the test. Directions for testing are clear and can be found on the testing forms, in the manual, or on the computer. Testing can be completed in a variety of fashions. Individuals can complete the API on consumable answer sheets using reusable question booklets. However, completed answer sheets cannot be hand scored and must be computer entered later or sent directly to the publisher for scoring and report generation. Testing can occur on a personal computer with scoring and report generation taking place on-line. Individuals usually complete the test in about one hour or less, although no time limits are suggested in the manual.

The normative sample of the test consists of over 1,000 adults, ranging in age from 16 to 70, from a number of locations across the country. Although the author argues that the norms are appropriate, no breakdown by gender, age, race, or geographic region is offered. Such a lack of information is alarming, especially given the large age range of the instrument. Although preliminary at best, research suggests that race has not been a significant source of bias on the test (Krug, 1986).

Although construct validity information is reported in the manual (including a comparison of the API with other measures) it is limited and sketchy. Moreover, intercorrelations among the 21 scales could not be found in the manual and criterion-referenced validity was lacking as well. Three reliability studies are reported with sample sizes ranging from 31 to 612 subjects. Although initial data appear acceptable, additional studies are certainly needed. Information concerning the standard error of measurement was not included. Due to the great lack of normative information and psychometric characteristics of the test, reviewers have asked repeatedly for a technical supplement (Bolton, 1985; Drummond, 1987).

Several computer programs are available to assist with the API. The computer program called Test Plus suggests routinely using a short form (189-item version) of the API, although the regular form is available if specified when ordering the system. Test Plus requires an IBM-compatible personal computer (PC-DOS, version 2.10 or later) and is accompanied by what seems to be a complete manual. When testing on the computer, the program continuously monitors the testing session, verifying each answer to produce what is offered as error-free testing. Unlimited test usage is also available with a one-time purchase price. Individual records can be stored up to a maximum of 100 reports. Information concerning the Career Profile program (available only for IBM or compatible computers) is not as well developed.

The API represents a unique melding of information representing an individual's personality, interpersonal style, and career factors. Interestingly, although all these areas are surely important in vocational evaluations, counseling, human development, and research, few tests have secured the areas together so suitably. In addition, the manual and generated reports offer a wealth of information, including graphic illustrations that are relevant and helpful. The test also has a low reading level and offers computerized reports on site. The API holds great promise as the instrument of choice for normal adults, pending some normative and technical additions to the manual. Given these changes, the API may become the standard for evaluating normal individuals in many settings.

REVIEWER'S REFERENCES

Bolton, B. (1985). [Review of the Adult Personality Inventory.] In J. V. Mitchell, Jr. (Ed.), *The ninth mental measurements yearbook* (pp. 55-56). Lincoln, NE: Buros Institute of Mental Measurements.

Krug, S. E. (1986). Preliminary evidence regarding Black-White differences in scores on the Adult Personality Inventory. *Psychological Reports, 58*, 203-206.

Drummond, R. J. (1987). [Review of The Adult Personality Inventory.] In D. J. Keyser & R. C. Sweetland (Eds.), *Test critiques: Volume VI* (pp. 21-25). Kansas City, MO: Test Corporation of America.

Ahadi, S. A. (1991). The use of API career factors as Holland occupational types. *Educational and Psychological Measurement, 51*, 167-173.

Bolton, B. (1991). Comments on "The Adult Personality Inventory." *Journal of Counseling & Development, 69*, 272-273.

Krug, S. E. (1991). The Adult Personality Inventory. *Journal of Counseling & Development, 69*, 266-271.

[21]

Adult Suicidal Ideation Questionnaire.

Purpose: "Designed to evaluate the presence and frequency of suicidal thoughts."
Population: Ages 18 and over.
Publication Dates: 1987–91.
Acronym: ASIQ.
Scores: Total score only.
Administration: Individual or group.
Price Data, 1994: $42 per complete kit including manual ('91, 62 pages) and 25 respondent forms; $20 per manual; $26 per 25 respondent forms.
Time: (5–10) minutes.
Author: William M. Reynolds.
Publisher: Psychological Assessment Resources, Inc.

Review of the Adult Suicidal Ideation Questionnaire by DEBRA E. COLE, Director of Partial Hospitalization, Virginia Treatment Center for Children, Medical College of Virginia, Richmond, VA:

The Adult Suicidal Ideation Questionnaire (ASIQ) is a 25-question self-report instrument developed to assess suicidal ideation in adults. It was derived from the Suicidal Ideation Questionnaire (SIQ; Reynolds, 1987; T4:2627), a 30-item measure of suicidal ideation in adolescents. In field testing the SIQ on 55 adults from a psychiatric outpatient setting, five items of relevance in assessing adolescent suicidal ideation were determined to be normative in adults and eliminated from the ASIQ.

The ASIQ was normed on two samples—over 1,100 college students from three midwestern universities and over 500 community-dwelling adults. In addition, 361 adults with *DSM-III-R* psychiatric diagnoses were tested to ascertain descriptive statistics for a psychiatric outpatient sample. From this descriptive information, the author reports that suicidal ideation is relatively rare in the nonclinical adult samples, whereas the clinical group, particularly those individuals with major depression, shows more clinically significant levels of suicidal ideation as measured by the ASIQ.

The ASIQ measures suicidal ideation by asking the respondents to rate the frequency of thoughts in the past month on a 7-point scale ranging from *almost every day* to *I never had this thought*. In the test manual, the author discusses suicidal behavior as classified on a continuum ranging from suicidal ideation to completed suicide. He discusses the suicidal ideation end of the continuum as ranging from relatively passive thoughts about wishing not to be alive to having a specific plan for taking one's life. The ASIQ assesses these poles of suicidal ideation as well as thoughts related to self-worth, death, and serious self-injurious behaviors. The scale examines perceptions about the responses of others to suicidal behaviors or the death of the respondent.

A cutoff score and suggestions for further evaluation for those scoring at or above the cutoff are provided in the manual. In addition, six statements that relate to actual thoughts or plans for suicide are designated as "critical items." Respondents who earn scores of 5 or 6 on two or more of these items are viewed as in need of further evaluation, independent of ASIQ raw scores.

The ASIQ manual contains a particularly helpful description of suicidal behavior, and the author is careful to say what this scale does and does not do. Although suicidal ideation is a *potential* precursor to more serious forms of suicidal behavior, the ASIQ does not predict suicide nor does a score above the cutoff give a probability estimate of risk of suicide. The ASIQ does provide a quick and easy screen of those who in the past month have been thinking suicidal thoughts. Of course, no instrument or clinical interview will be able to uncover suicidal thoughts or behaviors if an individual is determined to conceal them. The ASIQ cutoff and critical items do give the evaluating clinician an idea of who is in need of immediate clinical followup.

Multiple forms of validity and reliability evidence are presented in the ASIQ manual. The author presents internal consistency studies for the two normative samples and the psychiatric sample, which yield Cronbach's alpha ranging from .960 to .967. Similarly high coefficients were found for males and females across all three samples. Test-retest reliability studies conducted with a sample of college students and a mixed sample of psychiatric and community adults yielded reliability coefficients ranging from .86 to .95 for 2- and 1-week time periods respectively.

A wide range of validation procedures are employed to show that the ASIQ is a valid measure of suicidal ideation to adults. To establish content validity, the author presents the theoretical continuum of suicidal thoughts that create the construct of suicidal ideation and shows how ASIQ item content reflects this continuum. The author points out that this approach is descriptive rather than empirical. Convergent validity was investigated by comparing the ASIQ with the Hamilton Depression Rating Scale (HDRS; Hamilton, 1960, 1967), a semistructured clinical interview widely used in research investigations. A correlation coefficient of $r = .77$ was found. Construct validity is supported in the form of convergent and discriminant validity. Significant correlations were found between the ASIQ and the following other measures of psychological distress and well-being: depression, anxiety, low self-esteem, and history of prior suicide attempts. A multiple regression analysis indicated significant correlation coefficients associated with measures of depression, hopelessness, suicide attempts, self-esteem, and anxiety. Discriminant validity was shown by low correlations between ASIQ scores and measures of academic achievement and social desirability. A factor analysis identified four clusters of suicidal ideation, which were consistent with the test's conceptual bases.

When addressing any potentially lethal behavior, the use of a cutoff score may be questioned. The author addresses the clinical efficacy of the cutoff score of 31 by providing statistical comparisons of individuals who have attempted suicide with those that have not. This analysis suggests that the cutoff of 31 yields significant distinctions between normals and mixed psychiatric groups separated by diagnosis. However, it should be noted that normal controls with a history of attempted suicide failed to surpass the cutoff of 31, almost 42% of major depressives exceeded the cutoff but had never attempted suicide. Overall, this suggests a balance between specificity and sensitivity which favors sensitivity (true positives). This, in addition to the "safety net" of critical items, provides sufficient safeguards to warrant the use of the cutoff score. Users are encouraged to always consider the clinical population with whom they are working when evaluating scores.

The ASIQ is a quick, easy, well-researched, and well-designed instrument that assesses suicidal thoughts in adults. As the author cautions, it is not intended to be predictive of suicide, but may provide a way for seriously at-risk individuals to "cry for help" rather than act on dangerous thoughts. As such this measure should be administered in settings that allow for appropriate follow-up contact. The ASIQ should be commended for striving to quantify and standardize the elusive clinical construct of suicidal ideation. Continued use of this measure should contribute significantly to the current understanding of the steps leading to suicide.

REVIEWER'S REFERENCES

Hamilton, M. (1960). A rating scale for depression. *Journal of Neurology, Neurosurgery, and Psychiatry*, *23*, 56-62.

Reynolds, W. M. (1987). Suicidal Ideation Questionnaire. Odessa, FL: Psychological Assessment Resources.

Review of the Adult Suicidal Ideation Questionnaire by ISADORE NEWMAN, Professor and Associate Director for the Institute of Life-Span Development and Gerontology, The University of Akron, and Adjunct Professor of Psychiatry, N.E. Ohio Universities College of Medicine, Akron, OH:

PURPOSE OF THE INSTRUMENT. The Adult Suicidal Ideation Questionnaire (ASIQ) is specifically designed to assess suicidal thoughts of adult clients. The test consists of 25 items, each of which is rated by the subject on a 7-point scale, assessing the frequency of occurrence within the past month. The maximum possible score is 150 and cut scores are provided for clinical relevance.

The ASIQ has been used in a number of clinical studies with adults having various *DSM-III-R* psychopathologies, as well as with outpatient and nonpsychiatric normal adults who have reported histories of suicide attempts.

DESCRIPTION OF SCORING. Chapter 3 of the manual contains information related to the administration, scoring, and interpretation of the inventory. The ASIQ questionnaire is a two-part carbonless response form. The back side of the form contains a summary table for recording the raw score and the related normative score. It also has space to record the number of critical items endorsed. The scoring of the instrument has built-in validity checks that allow one to scan for repeated patterns as well as inconsistencies in responses. A formula for prorating scores if not more than three items are omitted is also included.

The authors stress that the interpretation of the ASIQ is for the clinical assessment of the suicide ideation in a person. It is *not* a predictive or diagnostic measure, although the authors strongly indicate that the ASIQ "provides valuable clinical information" (manual, p. 9).

The scores range from 0 to 150, with a mean score between 7 and 8 for a community adult normative sample and a mean score of 11 for a college sample. The cut score of 31 is used for identifying a need for further evaluation for psychopathology and suicide behavior. It is approximately 2 standard deviations above the normative means. The authors suggest that this cut score will tend to result in an overidentification of cases, therefore, further emphasizing that the ASIQ should be used more as a screening device to identify need for further evaluation.

Of the 25 items, 6 are considered critical and indicative of the potency for serious self-destructive behavior. Chapter 3 of the manual concludes with clear and useful examples to aid the user in interpretation.

TECHNICAL DATA. In the community adult and college student samples, there are virtually no sex differences on the ASIQ, with the college student sample, on the average, scoring higher. The manual includes good descriptive statistics with a total normative sample size of approximately 2,000. The mean, standard deviations, medians, and skewness is presented for each of the normative groups.

The authors clearly state that suicide ideation is not normally distributed in the population and, therefore, the interpretation of standardized scores could be misleading. However, on page 27 of the manual, they indicate that they used a derived linear *T* score, which is a standardized score, without any evidence that they normalized their distribution first. One should be aware of this inconsistency.

Tables with normative information on gender and age differences, ethnicity, and history of suicide attempts are provided. The tables also contain item characteristic information that includes the correlations between items and sex, and items and the total score, as well as reliability estimates based on Cronbach's alpha and the mean interitem correlation, the median item-to-sample correlation, test-retest reliabilities, and standard error of estimate measures. These reliabilities tend to be quite high, with the interitem reliabilities within the mid range, between .50 and .54. The standard error of measurement tends to range around 3 points. Given the possible range of ASIQ scores from 0 to 150, this error variance is quite small. Internal consistency reliabilities were very high and the test-retest reliabilities indicate a stable measurement over a brief period of time.

The validity estimates were based upon a number of validity studies including content validity, criterion-related validity, construct validity, factorial validity, clinical validity (contrasting groups), and the effectiveness of cut scores. It appears that the ASIQ has more validity support than most instruments in the literature in measuring suicide ideation. It is interesting to note that the correlation between the ASIQ and prior suicide attempts for college student samples, as reported in Tables 21 and 22, ranges between .3 and .38, indicating that approximately 9% to 14% of the variability in suicide attempts is being accounted for by the ASIQ scores. A phi^2 coefficient between ASIQ cut scores and suicide behaviors with the Hamilton Depression Rating Scale Suicide Behavior Questionnaire Interview Technique was .6. Also, a Kappa coefficient of 59 and Y (Yule) of .64 were all significant at $p<.0001$.

The authors present multiple regression analyses in which they used depression, hopelessness, suicide attempts, self-esteem, and anxiety to predict ASIQ scores. Some of the data indicate there may be an interaction between gender and suicide attempts. This apparently was not pursued. In addition, no shrinkage estimates were presented to estimate the stability of the regression weights. Most importantly, it seems that a more meaningful analysis would have been using suicide attempts as the criterion variable and the ASIQ as the predictor variable, covarying depression, hopelessness, self-esteem, anxiety, and gender. This would have given us an estimate of the unique variance accounted for by the ASIQ.

The manual contains a number of factor analyses run on different samples. These factor analyses tended to show a 3- or 4-factor solution with a predominant 1 factor. The authors indicate that this supports their construct validity in that there is a strong 1-factor solution. However, these same data can be interpreted as supporting the ASIQ as a multidimensional instrument. It would be interesting to see if the multidimensional subscales suggested by the factor analysis improves some of the validity estimates. It would also be valuable to look at the stability of the factor structures across the subgroups, using something similar to the Kaiser Factor Matching technique.

Overall, it appears that the ASIQ is a valuable tool for clinicians and researchers in the mental health profession. Authors reported strong reliability, good validity estimates, and clinical utility. The ASIQ's sample size of over 2,000 was sufficient and the validation procedures seemed to be logically derived from the nomological net of suicide ideation. It is strongly suggested that this instrument *not* be used as the sole predictor of suicide or high risk behavior, but rather that it be used as part of a battery and/or screening device for further assessment.

[22]

Advanced Measures of Music Audiation.

Purpose: Developed to measure music aptitude.

Population: Junior high school through college.

Publication Date: 1989.
Scores, 3: Tonal, Rhythm, Total.
Administration: Group.
Price Data, 1992: $37 per complete kit including audiocassette, 100 answer sheets, and manual (54 pages); $15 per 100 answer sheets; $20 per set of scoring stencils; scoring service available from publisher at $1 per student.
Time: 16(20) minutes.
Comments: Audiocassette recorder necessary for administration; upward extension of the Intermediate Measures of Music Audiation (T4:1249).
Author: Edwin E. Gordon.
Publisher: G.I.A. Publications, Inc.

Review of the Advanced Measures of Music Audiation by RUDOLF E. RADOCY, Professor of Music Education and Music Therapy, University of Kansas, Lawrence, KS:

PURPOSE. The Advanced Measures of Music Audiation (AMMA) represent the latest segment of the testing portion of Edwin Gordon's music education materials. As are the older Primary (PMMA; T4:2099) and Intermediate Measures of Music Audiation (IMMA; T4:1249), the AMMA are based on Gordon's concept of "audiation," where a person mentally hears and comprehends musical patterns without immediate aural stimulation. Audiation includes the recall of familiar and unfamiliar material, with or without musical notation, writing familiar music patterns, and the silent creation and performance of music. The comprehension aspect means that audiation is more than imitation or memorization. Gordon believes that audiation is the basis of musical aptitude, and that judgments of aptitude based on musical achievement may be misleading; therefore, an audiation-based measure for use in counseling college and university students and adjusting music instruction is useful. The AMMA are that measure. The test also is appropriate for high school students, and the specimen set which this reviewer examined included a table of seventh and eighth grade norms.

TEST CONTENT. The AMMA contain 30 items, plus three practice items. Each item includes a "musical question," followed after 4 seconds of silence by a "musical answer." The subject's task is to specify whether the "answer" is the same as the "question," differs tonally, or differs rhythmically. Paired question-answer combinations always contain an identical number of tones. Tonal differences, which occur for 10 items, may be due to change in individual pitch, mode, tonal center, or combinations thereof. Ten items involve changes in rhythm due to altered durations, meters, tempi, or combinations thereof. No change occurs for 10 items; no item includes both tonal and rhythmic differences. All items are performed by a professional musician on a Yamaha DX-7 synthesizer.

SCORES AND NORMS. Although the test yields a separate Tonal (40 points possible) and Rhythm (40 points possible) as well as a Total (80 points possible) score, the AMMA really is one test, not a "battery." The items with particular discrepancies are interspersed throughout. Gordon believes strongly that the student's indication that a discrepancy in tone or rhythm occurs when in fact neither or the opposite type occurs is just as relevant as the student's indication that no discrepancy occurs when in fact one of either type occurs, so the scores are adjusted to take misjudgments into account. The basic tonal score (T_1) and rhythm score (R_1) are determined by counting the number of correct indications of the particular discrepancy plus, in each case, correct indications of sameness. Twenty is added to T_1 and R_1. Then, the number of erroneous tonal responses T_2 is subtracted from $T_1 + 20$, and the number of erroneous rhythm responses (R_2) is subtracted from $R_1 + 20$. The Total score is $[(T_1 + 20) - T_2] + [(R_1 + 20) - R_2]$. Omitted items neither count for nor against any score. Adjustment for type of error is not simply a correction for guessing.

The AMMA were normed during the 1988–89 school year over a representative sample of 5,336 college and university students (3,206 music majors, 2,130 non-music majors) in 27 states, and 872 high school students. The manual includes percentile ranks for adjusted raw scores for high school, college music major, and college non-music major students.

RELIABILITY AND VALIDITY. Split-halves reliabilities were estimated via a "unique" procedure (p. 41 of the manual) whereby the 20 items constituting the T_1 and R_1 tests each were divided into half on the basis of similar item discrimination and difficulty indexes. For each student, one half of the T_1 test was combined with one half of the T_2 test; one half of the R_1 test was combined with one half of the R_2 test; the remaining halves for each section were combined. The halves for the Tonal Test were formed by combining appropriate Tonal and Rhythm scores. The customary correlations, corrected by the Spearman-Brown prophecy formula, showed split-halves reliability estimates ranging from .80 (for the Tonal and Rhythm Tests for non-music majors) to .88 (for the Tonal Test for music majors). Test-retest reliability estimates, based on a group of 70 students' scores, ranged from .80 (Tonal Test, non-music majors) to .89 (Total Test, music majors).

Validity basically depends on the test in fact being a measure of audiation. If one agrees that audiation exists, and that the test indeed depends on that construct, then one may say, albeit without empirical evidence, that the AMMA has construct validity. Through his arguments, Gordon establishes what he calls "subjective" validity. "Objective" validity is not established due to an alleged lack of appropriate criteria: Gordon states in the manual (p. 41) that "Until valid criterion measures can be established, it is not possible to investigate the criterion-related (objective) validity of the AMMA." Empirically, Gordon presents correlations with his Musical Aptitude Profile (MAP) as a measure of "congruent" validity: These purportedly are "higher than expected" (p. 50), because the MAP is not intended for college students, and range from .43 (for MAP Musical Sensitivity Total and AMMA Rhythm scores) to .85 (for MAP Rhythm Imagery-Meter and AMMA Total scores).

OVERALL EVALUATION. From a technical and administrative standpoint, Gordon's AMMA is excellent. The manual includes the rationale, norms, scoring procedures, and statistical information in great detail. Virtually any adult who is literate in English could administer and score the test, without any musical background. The manual includes 39 references for readers who wish to learn more about musical aptitude and its measurement, although the only citations appearing in the text of the manual are to Gordon's own works.

The AMMA is part of a marketing package. Gordon has worked for over a quarter of a century in the development of his concept of music learning and the measurement and prediction of musical ability. The other audiation tests, the Musical Aptitude Profile (251), a set of sequential musical patterns, vocal and instrumental music curricula, a set of audiation practice tapes, and other materials are marketed to the AMMA purchaser. This is quite appropriate, given that "true believers" in Gordon's approach are likely to want all related materials.

To use the AMMA (and the earlier PMMA and IMMA) with confidence that one is measuring an important human musical skill and can employ the scores in a meaningful way, the test user must buy the concept of audiation completely. In using a test of audiation with older students, one must believe that musical achievement in the sense of performance success and academic grades in music does not indicate true musical ability. Gordon makes a very compelling argument for this, and the AMMA certainly requires skill in holding a musical pattern in memory, making a comparison, and judging the presence and type of discrepancy. Further studies of validity, conducted by individuals other than Gordon or his students, in which musicians' and nonmusicians' AMMA scores are evaluated in accordance with diverse criteria for musical success, imperfect though any single criterion may be, may help determine the true significance of the information provided by the AMMA.

Review of the Advanced Measures of Music Audiation by JAMES W. SHERBON, Professor of Music, Director of Graduate Studies in Music, School of Music, University of North Carolina at Greensboro, Greensboro, NC:

The Advanced Measures of Music Audiation (AMMA) is the most recent of Edwin Gordon's many contributions to the measurement of music aptitude. To meet the needs of music educators and administrators at the college level, the test was designed to be short and easily scorable. The author states the AMMA is a music aptitude test designed specifically for undergraduate and graduate students in colleges and universities as well as high school students. Music literacy or performance skills are not prerequisites for administration.

Gordon lists seven primary purposes for which the test is intended: (*a*) "To serve as a part of the criteria for entrance to a college or university department or school of music"; (*b*) "To identify college and university students, non-music as well as music majors, who possess the music aptitude to achieve high standards in music"; (*c*) "To establish objective and realistic expectations for the music achievement of college and university music and non-music majors"; (*d*) "To efficiently and diagnostically adapt music teaching in private instruction and within a classroom or an ensemble to the individual musical differences found among college and university students"; (*e*) "To assign college and university students to specific music classes, ensembles, and types of private instruction that are designed to meet their individual musical needs"; (*f*) "To assist college and university music students in making career decisions"; and (*g*) "To efficiently and diagnostically adapt music teaching within a classroom or an ensemble and in private instruction to the individual musical differences found among high school students" (manual, pp. 7–8). As the title implies, the AMMA is founded on audiation as the basis of music aptitude. Introduced by Gordon in 1976, the term "audiation" has become relatively common in the fields of psychology, education, and music education and is defined by Gordon as the ability "to hear and comprehend music for which the sound is not physically present" (manual, p. 12).

The AMMA test package consists of a manual, a cassette audio tape, answer sheets, and a set of four scoring masks. The manual is complete, clearly written, and packs a considerable amount of information about aptitude, testing, and the AMMA into 54 pages. Typical of Gordon's thorough manner, the manual includes discussions on aptitude and audiation as well as specific information on the AMMA regarding purposes, rationale, content, design, administration, scoring, interpretation, and application. A bibliography is also included. Of particular strength is an 18-page section including technical aspects of the AMMA such as procedures used for standardization, the establishment of norms, reliability, validity, intercorrelation of scores, and item difficulty and discrimination, plus related material on standard error of measurement, standard error of a difference, central tendency, and variability. Gordon has used discretion when including tables to augment the narrative as there is a balance of text and tabled information—each appropriately supporting the other. Discounting the inability to include completed studies on validity and other test applications, the manual is an excellent reference for users, from the experienced researcher to the novice test administrator. The cassette recording is of high quality, the 11-inch x 4.25-inch answer sheet is functional and easy to handle, and the four scoring masks are traditional. The hand-scoring process requires use of the four masks on each answer sheet plus a simple mathematical adjustment to obtain three raw scores. Machine-scoring service is available from GIA Publications.

The AMMA is a 30-item test recorded on a 16-minute cassette tape with total test administration time suggested as 20 minutes. The test items are like those in the Musical Aptitude Profile (251) although of greater difficulty. The stimuli consist of original music written specifically for the test with some contemporary atonal or arrhythmic items. The stimuli were programmed on an Apple Macintosh computer and performed on a Yamaha DX-7 synthesizer by a professional musician. Each item consists of a musical statement followed by a musical answer with the same number of notes as the statement; the student determines if the answer is the "same" or "different." If different, the answer sheet is marked according to the difference being attributed to a tonal or a rhythmical change. Gordon considers the AMMA to be a single test as opposed to a more common test structure containing several subtests. The 30 items, however, produce three scores, Tonal, Rhythm, and Total—the latter being a sum of Tonal and Rhythm scores obtained through a "unique procedure" used for scoring.

For the collegiate standardization sample, Gordon used data from the Higher Education Arts Data Service (HEADS) report for the National Association of Schools of Music member institutions. Based on these data, a proportional number of institutions and subjects were selected from six geographic regions of the country using categories of institutional size and status (public or private) to gain representativeness. The sample comprised 54 institutions of higher education in 27 states yielding a total of 5,336 students—3,206 undergraduate and graduate music majors and 2,130 undergraduate and graduate non-music majors. The high school standardization was derived from 872 students in grades 9, 10, 11, and 12. Tabled percentile rank norms for the Tonal, Rhythm, and Total scores are provided for three groups—college music majors, college non-music majors, and high school. Analyses indicated that geographic location, institutional size and status, classification (undergraduate or graduate), and gender were factors not requiring separate norms. It is important to note that Gordon's obvious focus when developing and standardizing the AMMA was on applications in higher education, not secondary schools. He states the program of standardization and sample proportionality and representativeness was less extensive for high school students (manual, p. 38). It will, however, be interesting to see the results of additional research with high school and, perhaps, middle school students.

Split-halves and test-retest reliability coefficients are reported for the three groups. The entire standardization sample was used for the split-halves procedure; however, because the scoring process produced adjusted scores, Gordon used an adapted procedure for determining split-halves reliability coefficients. Retest reliability was determined with standard procedures but with only 33 undergraduate music majors and 37 undergraduate non-music majors. The reliabilities obtained from the two procedures, however, are very similar and all coefficients are surprisingly high considering the concision of the test. For undergraduate and graduate music majors the split-halves reliabilities are Tonal, .84; Rhythm, .85; and Total, .88; retest reliabilities are Tonal, .86; Rhythm, .87; and Total, .89. Undergraduate and graduate non-music major split-halves reliabilities are Tonal, .80; Rhythm, .80; and Total, .81; retest reliabilities are Tonal, .80; Rhythm, .81; and Total, .83. High school split-halves reliabilities are Tonal, .81; Rhythm, .82; and Total, .84; retest reliabilities are not provided.

Gordon initiates a discussion in the manual on kinds of test validity, cites several related studies, and reports favorable correlations of AMMA scores with Musical Aptitude Profile scores. The reader is directed to the GIA Monograph Series (Gordon, 1990; Gordon, 1991) for reports of completed research on the AMMA. Gordon (1990) conducted a one-year longitudinal predictive validity study of the AMMA with 114 university students enrolled in orchestra, choir, and band. The students were administered the test in September 1989 and their performances were independently evaluated the following May. Gordon reports a longitudinal predictive validity coefficient of .82 for Total AMMA scores with the combined performance evaluation ratings. In a factor analytic study of the AMMA Gordon (1991) investigated whether factors of "sameness" and "difference," used as response items in the AMMA, are attended to by subjects in the stabilized music aptitude stage. He concluded that adults are primarily concerned with these factors. Gordon (1991) also studied the scoring procedure used in the AMMA with the principal focus being on the feasibility of an adjusted score versus an unadjusted score. This study was conducted with 129 students attending the Hochschule in Bremen, Germany. Gordon concluded that the scoring procedure should remain unchanged.

I administered the test to 10 university graduate students. The trial produced generally favorable responses; however, one comment is worthy of mention. All students commented the items were too long, which is not a justifiable concern; however, the taped instruction stating "You will hear short musical statements" may create a false expectation among students regarding item length.

The AMMA is a welcome addition to Gordon's extensive work with the evaluation of music aptitude and it should fill a space that has been empty much too long. Of particular merit is the test's brevity in view of the substantial reliabilities. The discussion and information presented in the manual on high school applications at times appear to be an afterthought. The material, however, on applications in higher education is clear, complete, and thorough. The AMMA is solid in a theoretical and practical sense and, if recognized and accepted by college and university faculty, should fill many needs for assessment of music aptitude in an area where published standardized music aptitude tests have not existed. With Gordon's continued study on the validity of the AMMA and subsequent publications dealing with research on applications, the test should become well known as an expedient means of evaluating music aptitude in higher levels of education.

REVIEWER'S REFERENCES

Gordon, E. E. (1990). *Predictive validity study of AMMA: A one-year longitudinal predictive validity study of the Advanced Measures of Music Audiation* (GIA Monograph Series No. G-3528). Chicago: GIA.

Gordon, E. E. (1991). *A factor analytic study of the Advanced Measures of Music Audiation and taking another look at scoring the Advanced Measures of Music Audiation: The German study* (GIA Monograph Series No. G-3706). Chicago, GIA.

[23]

Age Projection Test.

Purpose: Designed as "an imagery test aimed at revealing self-images at various age [and self] levels and their associated structures of imagèry functioning useful toward the understanding of a presented problem or a symptom."
Population: Adults.
Publication Date: 1988.
Acronym: APT.
Scores: No scores.
Administration: Individual.
Price Data, 1992: $20 per manual (76 pages) including test.
Time: [60–120] minutes.
Author: Akhter Ahsen.
Publisher: Brandon House, Inc.

Review of the Age Projection Test by EDWARD ARONOW, Associate Professor of Psychology, Montclair State College, Upper Montclair, NJ:

The Age Projection Test is designed as "an imagery test aimed at revealing self images at various age levels" (manual, p. 1). First, it should be noted that calling this instrument a "test" is a misnomer. Although the author attempts to ground the term "test" in classic studies of orientation and perception, this clearly is not a test as dealt with in common usage. There are no data presented as to such psychometric characteristics as reliability and validity, there are no norms, no evidence on freedom from response set, etc. In fact, the Age Projection Test is not really a test at all, but, rather, a suggested clinical procedure for the treatment of various psychological symptoms.

The theoretical grounding of the procedure is somewhat vague. The author attempts to link perceptual research with projective techniques, and the theoretical grounding runs the gamut from the behavioral to the psychoanalytic. The theoretical grounding thus is not in any one theoretical camp, which at times can be an advantage, but is not in this case.

The procedure itself makes for very difficult reading, with turgid and often impenetrable prose. The last section of the test on *symptom oscillation* is remarkably difficult to understand.

The administration itself of the procedure is also unclear. The author appears to impose upsetting images on patients in the hope that this will produce ameliorative effects. However, it would seem more logical to have the subject himself or herself suggest the upsetting images for clinical usage, as is commonly done in cognitive and behavioral approaches to psychotherapy.

I would also remark that age projection as such is not really central to the technique. One might think from the title that a subject is asked to picture the self at different ages. This is not the case.

In short, this test is not recommended for use. It is in fact not a test at all, but a clinical procedure for the treatment of psychological symptoms. Even as such a clinical procedure, it suffers from vagueness, lack of clarity, and lack of a firm grounding in psychological theory.

Review of the Age Projection Test by MICHAEL D. BOTWIN, Assistant Professor of Psychology, California State University, Fresno, Fresno, CA:

The subtitle of the Age Projection Test (APT) states that the intent of the test is to provide "short term imagery treatment of hysterias, phobias, and other themes." This places the APT in the domain of psychotherapeutic techniques rather than the domain of psychological assessment. This technique is based on the assumption that an individual can be regressed to a point in time prior to the event that caused the onset of traumatizing symptoms in an individual. Once the person is regressed to that point in time the subject (patient) will be relieved of their symptoms.

There are five preliminary steps in the administration of the APT. In the first two steps, the subject reports his or her symptoms and concerns about the symptoms. Third, the moderator (test administrator) reviews a list of body organs in an attempt to determine if the individual has "bad feelings" about any part of his or her body. Fourth, the moderator asks for the subject's name and any nicknames they may have in an attempt to assess the individual's various identities. Fifth, this preliminary information is organized into a "symptom table."

Following the gathering of the preliminary information the APT is administered in several stages. The first stage involves a mood induction technique in which the symptom is "warmed up." The moderator repeats the details of the symptom to the subject "over and over again" to activate the symptom within the subject. The symptoms are "gradually activated and brought to an unbearable pitch in which the subject shows signs of pain and anxiety" (manual, p. 17). While the symptoms are being constantly restated the moderator repeatedly addresses the subject by the various permutations of the subject's name.

Once the subject "has been carefully brought to a high pitch of suffering" (manual, p. 17), the moderator pauses the proceedings and begins talking about a time, prior to the onset of the symptoms, when the subject was happy. The subject is then instructed to form an image of themself at this point in time. The author of the test believes this enlightens the subject as to the nature of their distress. The subject is then instructed to imagine they are in the home they were raised in, with their parents standing before them. The subject then is instructed to imagine having a tantrum and is instructed to throw down an article of clothing on the floor in front of the parent images. One of the parent images retrieves the article of clothing and the subject's image is instructed to follow the parental image about the house and watch where the article of clothing is deposited. Both the article of clothing and the location that is placed supposedly provide the subject with insight about the symptom and aids in the resolution of the malady.

The manual states this test should be administered by an individual trained in this procedure, although the author does state that the test can be self-administered if necessary. Several case studies are presented to illustrate the administration of the APT. Use and applications of the instrument are also discussed. There is no information on the norms, validity, and reliability of this test. Furthermore, the author does not seem to believe this information is required for a test of this type.

While reviewing this test I became concerned when the author stated that "the APT is an exact psychological test" (manual, p. 14). After completing this review I felt compelled to regress myself back to a time when test manuals had normative data and presented information on reliability and validity of the instrument. My imaginary parents were not amused.

[24]

AGS Early Screening Profiles.

Purpose: Constructed to screen children for possible developmental problems or giftedness.
Population: Ages 2-0 to 6-11.
Publication Date: 1990.
Scores: 3 Profile Scores: Cognitive/Language, Motor, Self-Help/Social (Parent or Teacher), and 4 Survey Scores: Articulation, Home, Behavior (Cognitive/Language, Motor).
Administration: Individual.
Price Data, 1993: $249.95 per complete kit including test plates in easel, 25 test records, 25 Self-Help/Social Profile questionnaires, Sample Home/Health History survey, 25 score summaries, tape measure, beads and string, Motor Profile administration manual (19 pages), and manual (311 pages, including reproducible Report to Parents and blackline masters "Guide for Training Examiners"); $24.95 per 25 test records; $14.95 per 25 Self-Help/Social Profile questionnaires; $14.95 per 25 Home/Health History surveys; $8.95 per 25 score summaries; $34.95 per manual.
Time: [15–40] minutes.
Comments: Two levels of scoring: Level I scores are 6 "screening indexes" and 3 descriptive categories; Level II scores are standard scores, percentile ranks, and age equivalents; ecological assessment with ratings by parents and teachers as well as direct assessment of the child.
Authors: Patti L. Harrison (coordinating author and manual author), Alan S. Kaufman (Cognitive/Language Profile), Nadeen L. Kaufman (Cognitive/Language Profile), Robert H. Bruininks (Motor Profile), John Rynders (Motor Profile), Steven Ilmer (Motor Profile), Sara S. Sparrow (Self-Help/Social Profile), and Domenic V. Cicchetti (Self-Help/Social Profile)
Publisher: American Guidance Service.

TEST REFERENCES

1. Boivin, M. J., Green, S. D. R., Davies, A. G., Giordani, B., Mokili, J. K. L., & Cutting, W. A. M. (1995). A preliminary evaluation of the cognitive and motor effects of pediatric HIV infection in Zairian children. *Health Psychology, 14*, 13-21.

Review of the AGS Early Screening Profiles by DAVID W. BARNETT, Professor of School Psychology, University of Cincinnati, Cincinnati, OH:

The AGS Early Screening Profiles (ESP) represents an effort by distinguished researchers to create an instrument to help meet the needs of at-risk children. Readers of this review are probably most interested in two questions. Given the many criticisms of early screening efforts, "Does this screening instrument overcome shortcomings of other screening devices?" or if not, "How should young children be screened?"

The criteria applied by the test authors, that the instrument "meets *accepted* psychometric standards" (p. v, emphasis added), is not the only framework applied in this review. The critique that follows draws on existing standards, but also *emerging* and needed standards for technical adequacy based on an analysis of research with prototypic screening instruments, research on decision making, and principles of intervention design. These deal primarily with reliability and validity of *decision outcomes* and expected intervention utility.

DESCRIPTION OF THE EARLY SCREENING PROFILES. The Early Screening Profiles are designed to evaluate the "major areas of functioning of children and their families" (p. v). The ESP consists of seven different "profiles" generated through child testing or caregiver questionnaires that may be used separately or in various combinations. The Developmental Profiles include: Cognitive/Language, Motor, and Self-Help/Social. In addition, other profiles include Articulation, Home, Health History, and Behavior "surveys." The ESP may be administered by paraprofessionals.

Like other screening instruments, children are asked to point to or name objects, select matching objects, and demonstrate knowledge of numbers and concepts. Similarly, Motor skills include imitating movements, walking on a line, and stringing beads. The Self-Help and Socialization domains and the Articulation survey also are predictable from other scales (i.e., adaptive behavior measures, naming objects) purporting to measure these constructs. The Home survey asks questions about types of play material, content and frequency of parent-child interactions (i.e., reading), and responsibilities given to the child. The Health History also is straightforward. However, the Behavior survey is far less than what most professionals would expect. Ratings include activity level, attention span, cooperativeness, and independence based on observations over the course of testing.

The ESP generates a sea of numbers. Two scoring levels are available for the analysis of individual performances. For Level I, scores are available for the Cognitive/Language, Motor, and Self-Help/Social profiles and for total screening. Other possibilities include combining various subtests, or separating subtests such as cognitive and language subscales for ethnic minorities or children with hearing and language problems. The Level I scoring system yields "screening indexes" (six broad categories of performance based on normal curve deviations) to help identify at-risk (or gifted) children. Level II scoring provides an array of interpretive options for broad subscales and total scale (i.e., NCEs, stanines, age equivalents, etc.), and for more detailed analysis of patterns (e.g., expressive and receptive language). Age equivalents are score options from the ESP. These appear in examples, despite the wide criticism they have received. Similarly, the ESP authors state that professional judgment is required, but this quality of an instrument should be no great source of confidence for users or consumers.

PURPOSES. The "major use of the AGS Early Screening Profiles is to provide an ecologically valid, early, developmental screening of young children" (p. 6). The description of the ESP as ecologically valid is questionable. Although there are several definitions of ecological validity, perhaps the most widely accepted is an extension of classical validity: "The extent to which the environment experienced by the subjects in a scientific investigation has the properties it is supposed or assumed to have by the investigator" (Bronfenbrenner, 1977, p. 516). Neisser (1976) described ecological validity in the following ways: "if the theory has something to say about what people do in real, culturally significant situations" (p. 2), and "[H]ow people act in or interact with the ordinary world" (p. 7). Martens and Witt (1988) characterized ecological validity by the extent that interventions lead to desired outcomes without disrupting significant and desirable patterns of behaviors present in the environment. Thus, based on existing definitions of ecological validity, the ESP falls short or, at best, ecological validity remains unexamined.

Other purported uses of the ESP include screening for readiness programs (a widely criticized practice), and use of the Home survey "for a home intervention program" (p. 6) (unlikely, based on principles of intervention design). The scale is also described as useful for program evaluation efforts.

The scale authors suggest follow-up assessments for screening outcomes are necessary but recommend various assessment devices that have been criticized for their inability to yield meaningful developmental profiles and for their lack of treatment utility (Barnett, Macmann, & Carey, 1992). Furthermore, based on other analyses, the results of following screening with other similar assessment techniques will not improve overall outcomes for children. In fact, there is likely to be indefinite triangulation regarding which children need services, and the qualities of effective services will not be addressed (Barnett, Macmann, & Carey, 1992).

TECHNICAL ADEQUACY. Norms were built on a representative sample of 1,149 children from ages 2 years to 6 years and 11 months. Like other test instruments, however, the age levels samples actually used for interpretive purposes are much smaller and vary by age and scale (i.e., for Self-Help/Social: Teacher at age 5-0 to 5-5 (n = 65). The well-established tradition of setting the mean at 100 with a standard deviation of 15 is maintained.

Although many of the coefficient alpha reliabilities are in the .90s, others do not meet accepted standards of technical adequacy (Motor, Behavior), and others are quite low (Home). Test-retest (5 to 21 days) reliabilities range from .66 to .91. The stability of test-retest screening indexes ranged from .56 to .82, which connotes potentially significant variability in *decisions* (that would be noted by children who change screening categories based on different test occasions).

Validity evidence is mustered in many standard ways: through demonstrating a developmental progression in scores, by correlations between subparts and total scores, and by patterns of intercorrelations between scales. Correlations with other measures (such as Kaufman Assessment Battery for Children [K-ABC], Stanford-Binet Intelligence Scale [S-B], etc.) are similar to many other studies (e.g., coefficients range from .40s to .80s). However, the evidence presented also shows inconsistent patterns of divergence and convergence that may translate to remarkably variable interpretations and child outcomes (see Table 8.14, manual, p. 104).

Agreement with other screening instruments (i.e., DIAL-R, BATTELLE) is quite problematic (Table 8.18 and 8.19, pp. 107–108). The specific agreement in Table 8.24 (p. 116) with regard to categories and services also is quite low (i.e., calculations show that specific agreement is .16 for LD). Taken together, these data demonstrate insufficient evidence of concurrent and predictive validity.

On the positive side, information in the manual demonstrates a serious effort at scale development. Beyond the usual content, the authors include discussions related to such important factors as the analysis of errors around cut scores and the effects of base rates. Also, although not developed fully as a sequential decision strategy, the authors mention that a logical step between initial screening and referral for a comprehensive assessment is to simply rescreen. In sum, however, the ESP does not overcome the significant shortcomings of prototypic screening instruments. New directions are necessary.

Conclusions: Toward Robust Screening Efforts.

ECOLOGICAL VALIDITY. The *absence* of evidence that the ESP has ecological validity is a central criticism. In describing the instrument as ecologically valid, the authors are confusing the use of parent and teacher reports (multimethod assessment) about the child's functioning with significant ecological principles. The first steps in screening that stem from an ecologically valid approach are systems analysis and organizational development (e.g., Adelman, 1982). Ecobehavioral (e.g., Rogers-Warren, 1984) screening seeks to identify problem situations and factors related to problem maintenance and change (Barnett, Macmann, & Carey, 1992). Another potential benefit of ecologically valid screening efforts is that of supporting children with special needs in natural environments.

REGARDING SCREENING EXPERTISE AND INTERVENTION DESIGN. The authors of the manual state that "screening coordinators should have a good understanding of theory and research in areas such as child development, education, psychology, tests and measurement, assessment, and childhood exceptionality" (p. 9). In contrast, screening coordinators should be well founded in *intervention design*, which has to do with altering developmental trajectories, and the basics of parent and teacher consultation. In being guided in this way, professional actions and child, parent, and teacher outcomes are likely to be very different from the comprehensive assessment outcomes suggested by the ESP manual (Barnett & Carey, 1992).

TECHNICAL ADEQUACY. Criteria for at-risk status are based on the normal curve. No other criteria are applied, and agencies set their own (i.e., 1 standard deviation below the mean versus 2). However, young children move in and out of risk situations. Interpretations based on score deviations are frail with respect to changes in items, test occasions, and other factors. An appropriate estimate of error would address the robustness and usefulness of decisions and other inferences over time.

The ESP authors note the interdependence of developmental skills. However, the nature of intercorrelated skills results in a practical impasse regarding individual profile interpretations. For example, the reliability of differences between Cognitive/Language and Motor for a child at age 4 (for illustration purposes) would not meet interpretative standards. Given a Cognitive/Language x Motor correlation of .63, a reliability estimate for Cognitive/Language of .93, a reliability estimate for Motor of .78, the reliability of the *difference* would be about .61. Overall interpretations of developmental patterns would be extremely unstable. Furthermore, the extensive number of comparisons that could be made is likely to lead to a high rate of chance-related conclusions.

In response to the questions raised at the beginning of the review, differences between relatively similar screening measures simply may not matter that much. The ESP may be state of the art but it may not necessarily lead to reliable and beneficial outcomes for children. New approaches are necessary based on ecobehavioral theory, principles of intervention design, the analysis of innovative decision strategies such as multiple gating, and the analysis of decision outcomes (Barnett, Macmann, & Carey, 1992).

REVIEWER'S REFERENCES

Neisser, U. (1976). *Cognition and reality: Principles and implications of cognitive psychology*. San Francisco: Freeman.

Bronfenbrenner, U. (1977). Toward an experimental ecology of human development. *American Psychologist*, *32*, 513-531.

Adelman, H. S. (1982). Identifying learning problems at an early age: A critical appraisal. *Journal of Clinical Child Psychology*, *11*, 255-261.

Rogers-Warren, A. K. (1984). Ecobehavioral analysis. *Education and Treatment of Children*, 7, 283-303.

Martens, B. K., & Witt, J. C. (1988). On the ecological validity of behavior modification. In J. C. Witt, S. N. Elliott, & F. M. Gresham (Eds.), *Handbook of behavior therapy in education* (pp. 325-341). New York: Plenum.

Barnett, D. W., & Carey, K. T. (1992). *Designing interventions for preschool learning and behavior problems*. San Francisco: Jossey-Bass.

Barnett, D. W., Macmann, G. M., & Carey, K. T. (1992). Early intervention and the assessment of developmental skills: Challenges and directions. *Topics in Early Childhood Special Education*, *12*, 21-43.

Review of the AGS Early Screening Profiles by CATHY TELZROW, Psychologist and Director, Educational Assessment Project, Cuyahoga Special Education Service Center, Cleveland, OH:

The AGS Early Screening Profiles offer a multisource, multimethod scale for identifying children who may require further assessment to determine the presence of either deficits or excellence in performance. The measure provides maximum flexibility in selection among its seven components. Examiners may administer one or all of three direct testing scales (Cognitive/Language profile, Motor profile, and Articulation survey), two parent questionnaires (Home survey and Health survey), a parent or teacher questionnaire (Self-Help/Social profile), and a Behavior survey (Examiner Questionnaire). Selection of the Early Screening Profiles components may be guided by an agency's screening purposes, such as speech/language screening, health screening, or screening for school readiness or accelerated programs.

Development of the Early Screening Profiles was guided by professional theory and practice in early childhood identification. In addition to general principles of screening related to cost, efficiency, and ease of administration, the author was committed to an ecological approach, identified as one which incorporates "multiple settings, multiple individuals within settings, and multiple behavioral domains" (p. 63). The foundations for three of these behavioral domains were provided by other AGS-published instruments and Authors: the Kaufman Assessment Battery for Children (K-ABC; Kaufman & Kaufman, 1983; 9:562), and the Vineland Adaptive Behavior Scale (VABS; Sparrow, Balla, & Cicchetti, 1984; 10:381). In some instances, item types and administrative formats were borrowed from these earlier measures; for example, the Cognitive/Language profile shares many common features with the K-ABC. In the case of the Self-Help/Social profile, the link with the VABS is even more direct, in that the VABS interview edition items were modified to an abbreviated, self-report format for the Early Screening Profiles. Incorporation of the most salient elements of these technically superior instruments into an early childhood screening measure is one of the most noteworthy strengths of the Early Screening Profiles.

Although not derived so directly from other published measures, development of the remaining four components of the Early Screening Profiles also was guided by previous research. The Articulation survey, for example, masterfully reduces the sound production of 2–6-year-olds to a 20-word sample using developmentally appropriate vocabulary. The original pool of items for the Home survey was derived from the research (including the Home Observation for Measurement of the Environment [HOME; Caldwell & Bradley, 1984; 9:481]) and the author's clinical experiences. Final item selection occurred through a stepwise multiple regression procedure, with priority given to those items producing a significant increase in multiple correlations with the three Profile or Total Screening scores. Health History and Behavior surveys were constructed through a review of other similar scales and professional critiques.

Organization of the Early Screening Profiles is generally clear and concise. The easel format facilitates administration of the Cognitive/Language profile and the Articulation survey. Directions for administering and scoring the Motor profile are in a separate, self-contained book; although these are precise, they are somewhat long and complex, and will require considerable familiarity and practice on the part of examiners. Scores for these three direct test measures (Cognitive/Language profile, Articulation survey, Motor profile), as well as examiner ratings on the Behavior survey, are all recorded on a single test record. The Home survey and Health survey are incorporated into a single questionnaire, as is the Self-Help/Social profile. Results of the Early Screening Profiles are summarized on a one-page Score Summary. Expanded scoring and parent report forms, which can be duplicated for use, are included in the manual.

The Early Screening Profiles provides for two types of scoring. Level I scoring produces screening index scores for each of the profiles individually, subscales of the Cognitive/Language profile, and a total screening score, which is composed of the three profiles (parent version of Self-Help/Social profile must be used). Screening index scores, which range from 1 to 6, describe the range of performance from -3 to +3 standard deviations. Level II scores include such normative data as standard scores with bands of error, percentile ranks, normal curve equivalents, and age equivalents. Raw score performance on the Articulation survey, the Home survey, and the Behavior survey is reported in descriptive categories only (e.g., below average, average, above average). The Health survey is not scored, but is to be reviewed for recommendations regarding followup.

The technical properties of the Early Screening Profiles are thoroughly reported in the manual. Normative data are based on a representative, national sample of 1,149 children stratified according to 1990 census estimates by sex, ethnic group, geographic region, and parents' education level. Median internal consistency reliability coefficients for the profiles ranged from .68 to .95, and for the surveys from .41 to .89. The lowest internal consistency score occurred for the Home survey; the author hypothesizes that because of the "heterogeneous and diverse items" on this survey "perhaps high internal consistency should not be expected" (p. 87). Test-retest reliability coefficients for the Screening indexes ranged from .56 to .82 (immediate) and from .31 to .87 (delayed intervals of 22 to 75 days). Interrater reliability coefficients for the Motor profile ranged from .80 to .99.

The Early Screening Profiles manual includes a table summarizing samples and measures employed in 10 concurrent and predictive validity studies. Correlations between the Cognitive/Language Profile and other measures of cognitive ability (K-ABC; Stanford-Binet Intelligence Scale, Fourth Edition [Thorndike, Hagen, & Sattler, 1985; 10:342]) were moderate to high (.48–.84). As would be expected given the origin of the Motor profile and the Self-Help/Social profile, correlations with their foundation scales (Bruininks-Oseretsky, VABS) were generally in the range of .50 and .60. Correlations with other screening tests (Battelle Developmental Inventory [BDI; Newborg, Stock, Wnek, Guidubaldi, & Svinicki, 1984], Bracken Basic Concepts Test [Bracken, 1985], Denver Developmental Screening Test [Frankenburg, Dodds, & Fandal, 1970], Developmental Indicators for the Assessment of Learning—Revised [DIAL-R; Mardel-Czudnowski, & Goldberg, 1983]) varied widely from study to study, from some negligible and even negative correlations (with the BDI in one study) to moderate *r*s with the DIAL-R. Predictive validity studies reported moderate to high correlations with group aptitude and achievement measures.

The comprehensive manual for the Early Screening Profiles incorporates several excellent features. In addition to thorough information regarding the development, standardization, and technical merits of the scale, there are additional features which help distinguish this from other early childhood screening measures. The manual includes a detailed description of both Level I and Level II scores, including an excellent discussion of the limitations of age equivalent scores. In addition, the manual incorporates a discussion of decision theory as related to selecting "cutoff" scores for reaching screening decisions. Finally, excellent training materials, which can be used for introducing professionals and nonprofessionals to screening young children in general and in the use of the Early Screening Profiles in particular, are provided. These features, together with its high technical quality, make the Early Screening Profiles a scholarly, comprehensive addition to a total program in early childhood identification and service delivery.

REVIEWER'S REFERENCES

Frankenburg, W. K., Dodds, J. B., & Fandal, A. W. (1970). Denver Developmental Screening Test. Denver: LADOCA.

Bruininks, R. H. (1978). Bruininks-Oseretsky Test of Motor Proficiency. Circle Pines, MN: American Guidance Service.

Kaufman, A. S., & Kaufman, N. L. (1983). Kaufman Assessment Battery for Children. Circle Pines, MN: American Guidance Service.

Mardell-Czudnowski, C. D., & Goldenberg, D. S. (1983). Developmental Indicators for the Assessment of Learning—Revised. Edison, NJ: Childcraft.

Caldwell, B. M., & Bradley, R. H. (1984). Home Observation for Measurement of the Environment. Little Rock: University of Arkansas at Little Rock.

Newborg, J., Stock, J. R., Wnek, L., Guidubaldi, J., & Svinicki, J. (1984). Battelle Developmental Inventory. Allen, TX: DLM Teaching Resources.

Sparrow, S. S., Balla, D. A., & Cicchetti, D. V. (1984). Vineland Adaptive Behavior Scales. Circle Pines, MN: American Guidance Service.

Bracken, B. A. (1985). Bracken Basic Concepts Scale. San Antonio, TX: The Psychological Corporation.

Thorndike, R. L., Hagen, E. P., & Sattler, J. M. (1985). Stanford-Binet Intelligence Scale (4th ed.). Chicago: The Riverside Publishing Co.

[25]

Alcohol Use Inventory.

Purpose: "To assess the nature of an individual's alcohol use pattern, and problems associated with that pattern."
Population: Adults suspected of problem drinking.
Publication Date: 1987.
Acronym: AUI.
Scores, 24: Social Improvement, Mental Improvement, Manage Moods, Marital Coping, Gregarious, Compulsive, Sustained, Loss of Control, Role Maladaptation, Delirium, Hangover, Marital Problems, Quantity, Guilt and Worry, Help Before, Receptivity, Awareness, Enhanced, Obsessed, Disruption 1, Disruption 2, Anxious Concern, Receptive Awareness, Alcohol Involvement.
Administration: Group.
Price Data, 1991: $18.85 per 10 reusable test booklets; $21.95 per hand-scoring key; $5.65 per 25 hand-scored answer sheets; $6.95 per Profile Report; $13.50 per Interpretive Report; $5.45 per 25 profile sheets; $11.95 per manual ('87, 95 pages); $8.50 per Interpretive Report User's Guide.
Time: (35–60) minutes.
Comments: Reports are available via immediate on-site microcomputer scoring as well as through a mail-in scoring service.
Authors: John L. Horn, Kenneth W. Wanberg, and F. Mark Foster.
Publisher: National Computer Systems, Inc.

TEST REFERENCES

1. Noordsy, D. L., Drake, R. E., Teague, G. B., Osher, F. C., Hurlbut, S. C., Beaudett, M. S., & Paskus, T. S. (1991). Subjective experiences related to alcohol use among schizophrenics. *The Journal of Nervous and Mental Disease, 179,* 410-414.

2. McMillen, D. L., Adams, M. S., Wells-Parker, E., Pang, M. G., & Anderson, B. J. (1992). Personality traits and behaviors of alcohol-impaired drivers: A comparison of first and multiple offenders. *Addictive Behaviors, 17,* 407-414.

3. Moore, R. H. (1994). Underage female DUI offenders: Personality characteristics, psychological stressors, alcohol and other drug use, and driving-risk. *Psychological Reports, 74,* 435-445.

Review of the Alcohol Use Inventory by ROBERT J. DRUMMOND, Professor of Counselor Education, University of North Florida, Jacksonville, FL:

The Alcohol Use Inventory (AUI) is a self-report inventory designed to assess patterns of behavior, attitudes, and symptoms pertaining to the use of alcohol of individuals 16 years of age or older who drink to some extent. It was developed for use with individuals admitted to an alcoholism treatment program. The AUI is not appropriate for use with individuals who do not drink. The AUI reflects the multiple condition theory about drinking problems and has evolved from numerous research studies originally begun in the 1960s and from previous instruments such as the Alcohol Use Questionnaire (Horn, Skinner, Wanberg, & Foster, 1984) and the Alcohol Use Inventory (Horn, 1974) known as the Drinking History Questionnaire.

The current (1987) edition of the AUI has several new features. There are three new scales: RECEP-

TIV, AWARENESS, and RECPAWAR. The scale concerning the use of nonalcohol drugs was deleted. The arrangements of the scales have been altered and some of the scales renamed. Some experimental items that have been added for research purposes are not utilized in the scoring of any of the scales. Different norms are also mentioned as a new feature. Overall, there are 24 scales that assess dimensions of behavior at three different levels: primary, second-level, and third-level.

The scales appear to be reasonably associated with problem drinking. The Primary Scales focus on the "benefits," "styles," "consequences," and "concerns and acknowledgments" of drinking; for example, SOCIALIM (drink to improve sociability), MENTALIM (drink to improve mental functioning), MANGMOOD (drink to manage mood), MARICOPE (drink to deal with marital problems), GREGARUS (drink in bars, parties, with friends) and the like. There are six second-level scales derived from factor analysis of the relationships among the primary scales; for example, OBSESSED (obsessive, compulsive, sustained drinking).

Factor analysis was used to construct the scales of the AUI. The authors, however, do not present the results of the factor analysis in the manual or provide a matrix of the intercorrelations among the items or primary scales.

The AUI presents internal consistency reliabilities and test-retest information on the scales from a number of different years and groups. The third-level scale and second-level scales have higher coefficients than the primary scales as expected. Of the Primary Scales, QUANTITY has the lowest coefficient. Most of the reliability coefficients range from .65 to .80 for the scales.

Point-biserial correlations are presented to report gender and age differences rather than the more traditional T or F comparisons. A review of the data suggests there should be separate sex norms and norms by age levels. Comparisons are presented among Native Americans, White, African Americans, and Hispanic groups with F ratios given but no multiple comparison results presented to show between which groups the differences were found. There is not a good demographic description of the makeup of the norming group. No standard errors of measurement are given for the scales. The manual authors provide the user with salient information on interpreting the scale and on the BSCS approach (Benefits, Styles, Consequences, and Concerns) associated with the use and abuse of alcohol. A sample computerized report is also presented. The manual is not especially user friendly. There are a number of gaps in the information presented in the manual as previously indicated. The information in the manual is a justification of the approaches used rather than a translation of the information in a way counselors and psychologists could use to better understand the concepts.

Overall, the AUI has as its aim "to obtain measurements that are useful with different kinds of people (are hardy), have satisfactory breadth (bandwidth), adequate internal consistency (fidelity), genuine independence and appropriate stability over time" (manual, p. 22). The AUI appears to have made good progress in meeting these goals and is based on sound research and development. Counselors will find this a useful assessment tool when working with individuals with alcohol problems.

REVIEWERS REFERENCES

Horn, J. L. (1974). Alcohol Use Inventory. Washington, DC: U.S. Patent Office.

Horn, J. L., Skinner, H. A., Wanberg, K. W., & Foster, F. M. (1984). Alcohol Use Questionnaire (AUQ). Toronto, Canada: Addiction Research Foundation.

Review of the Alcohol Use Inventory by SHARON McNEELY, Associate Professor of Educational Foundations, Northeastern Illinois University, Chicago, IL:

The Alcohol Use Inventory (AUI) evolved out of research that sought to provide a multiple-condition assessment of alcohol-related problems. The AUI is designed to provide operational indicators to describe patterns of alcohol use, allowing mental health workers to identify and understand different kinds of alcoholics.

The AUI has 24 scales, three new to this edition. Sixteen of the 17 primary scales rely on responses to less than 10 items (range 3–9) for analysis. The six second-level scales have 11 to 21 items each. The third (broad) scale relies on responses to 40 items. In all, there are 228 self-report items which are answered "Yes" or "No" or with selected frequencies of behaviors.

The primary scales provide four separate domains related to drinking behaviors. The benefits domain provides explanations as to why the respondent drinks. The styles domain shows where and when drinking occurs. The consequences domain presents results the drinker faces. The concerns and acknowledgements domain allows the respondent to admit to feelings associated with the drinking and ways help has been sought and is currently desired.

The second-level scales are not merely combinations of the primary scales, but are derived from factor analysis of the primary scales' relationships. The ENHANCED scale represents benefits of using alcohol. The OBSESSED scale presents the general drinking style of the respondent. The DISRUPT1 scale presents the consequences of drinking in terms of disruptions. Most of the items in this scale are frequently measured indicators of signs of alcoholism. The respondent may recognize and lie about these items so to not seem alcoholic. The DISRUPT2 scale also indicates uncontrolled life disruption. It provides less typical indicators of alcoholism and thus may provide more honest responses. The ANXCONCN scale measures fears and other feelings about drinking. The RECPAWAR scale shows self-awareness of drinking problems.

The third-level factor measures broad involvement with alcohol on the ALCINVOL scale. This may be used as a general indicator of alcohol-related problems.

The manual authors state that most people 16 years of age or older can read and understand the language of the test. Ideally the respondent should be alcohol-free for 8 hours or more before test administration. The respondent should be able to complete the items in 35–60 minutes. With careful reading, the instruction page may take a couple of minutes to read. Although most of the items may be readable for those 16 years and older, they require absolute honesty and a good memory for completion. If the respondent ponders items or has difficulty in reading, completion may take longer than one hour.

Because so many of the items clearly define alcohol as a problem in the item stem, the respondent may be hesitant to answer honestly for fear of being portrayed as a chronic alcoholic. Some of the items also have problems in that the possible responses do not agree with the stems, (e.g., some items should begin with "How often" instead of "Have you").

The AUI is clearly labeled as a test in bold on the cover and title pages, which may lead some respondents to believe there is a best or correct answer. The title page descriptor does not clarify this, for those who may, having taken other tests, skip the instructions page.

The internal consistency reliabilities and test-retest reliabilities are both good across all but two scales (QUANTITY—amount consumed, and MARIPROB—marital problems resulting from drinking). In addition to the scales being fairly stable as long as the respondent's circumstances remain relatively the same, the scales also have good operational independence.

The authors suggest the AUI has strong content validity because only content relevant for decision making in treatment programs was included. The lack of further clarification as to types of treatment programs and types of decisions that relate to the content raise questions about the appropriateness of this validity for decision making. The criterion validity (criterion of alcohol dependence) is also supported. Correlates with the Michigan Alcoholism Screening Test (Selzer, 1971) vary considerably by scale, as would be expected. The manual author provides information for hand scoring and guidelines for interpretation and clinical use. The interpretations are provided in general only for high scale scores, thereby limiting other interpretations and clinical uses. Most of the norming and supportive studies have involved primarily Caucasians, possibly limiting applicability to other groups.

In summary, the AUI is one way for a clinician to obtain information about the multiple dimensions of alcoholism in clients who are fairly capable, honest, and cooperative. The AUI seems to have good reliability and validity, and to be appropriate for use with Caucasian populations. Lack of information about use with other populations should encourage cautious use and interpretation until further studies are undertaken.

REVIEWER'S REFERENCE

Selzer, M. L. (1971). The Michigan Alcoholism Screening Test: The quest for a new diagnostic instrument. *American Journal of Psychiatry*, *127*, 1653-1658.

[26]

Allied Health Professions Admission Test.

Purpose: Developed to measure general academic ability and scientific knowledge.
Population: Applicants to 4-year allied health programs.
Publication Dates: 1979–93.
Acronym: AHPAT.
Scores, 5: Verbal Ability, Quantitative Ability, Biology, Chemistry, Reading Comprehension.
Administration: Group.
Restricted Distribution: Distribution restricted and test administered at licensed testing centers; details may be obtained from publisher.
Price Data: Available from publisher.
Time: 160–175 minutes.
Author: The Psychological Corporation.
Publisher: The Psychological Corporation.

Review of the Allied Health Professions Admission Test by ALAN C. BUGBEE, JR., Director of Educational Systems/Associate Professor of Psychology, The American College, Bryn Mawr, PA:

The Allied Health Professions Admission Test (AHPAT) is a national examination to assess applicants for over 40 programs in allied health professions, ranging from Blood Banking Technology to Surgical Technology, Art Therapy to Speech Pathology and Audiology. It is intended to appraise the general academic and scientific knowledge of persons applying for bachelor's and post-bachelor's degrees in allied health programs. The AHPAT particularly seeks to measure "those skills prerequisite to successful completion of upper-division undergraduate allied health programs" (Information Booklet, The Psychological Corporation, 1991, p. 24). It "should alleviate admissions committees' difficulties in evaluating applicants on the basis of commonly used criteria such as GPAs which come from a wide variety of sources which may be several years old and are not designed for allied health programs" (Summary of Validity Studies, The Psychological Corporation, 1986, p. 1).

To accomplish its objective, the AHPAT covers five areas: Verbal Ability, Quantitative Ability, Biology, Chemistry, and Reading Comprehension. The

Verbal Ability section covers the test taker's general vocabulary and verbal reasoning. This section has about 75 questions and is 20 minutes long. Interestingly enough, the Verbal Ability section is given all at once, even though it has two distinct parts, synonyms and antonyms. Each has a single separate sentence of direction, but are treated as one section.

The Quantitative Ability section is designed to test nonverbal ability in mathematics, including algebra, geometry, and basic trigonometry. This section has 50 test items and is 40 minutes long.

The Biology section covers the principles and concepts of basic biology. Emphasis in these questions is on human biology. The topics covered are in cell biology, genetics, bacteria, viruses, plants, human structure and function, and evolution. About 50 questions are given in 25 minutes.

The Chemistry section addresses principles and concepts of basic chemistry. The questions here may be on atoms and molecules, element and periodic relationships, acids and bases, kinetics, nuclear chemistry, formulas, equations, bonding, electrochemistry, states of matter, and organic chemistry. This section is 25 minutes long and contains 50 questions.

The Reading Comprehension section is also 25 minutes long. It contains approximately 45 items which deal with the test taker's ability to read fairly short (several paragraphs) passages and be able to analyze and interpret them. This section contains a total of approximately 45 questions. In the test form provided for review (1E), this section had three passages, with three, three, and two paragraphs, respectively. The first passage had 10 questions, the second had 15 questions, and the third had 20 questions.

No information was provided on the reliability, or norms and scoring. A summary of validity studies (The Psychological Còrporation, 1986) provides useful information about the AHPAT as a predictor of success in various health professions. These studies demonstrate that the AHPAT is a useful component for prediction in conjunction with grade-point average (GPA) and other variables, including, interestingly enough, age of the applicant (Wiesseman, 1981). The reported coefficients of determination (The Psychological Corporation, 1986, p. 2) range from a low of .16 (predicting success of candidates in Medical Technology using GPA, type of school, and total AHPAT score) to a high of .86 (predicting success of candidates in Medical Records Administration using GPA, age, and AHPAT scores). Most of these studies also show a growth in explained variance in predicting success in various allied health professions when the AHPAT is included as a predictor variable.

It is unclear to me what the primary purpose of the AHPAT is. Although the stated purpose of the test is for selection in Allied Health professions, it seems that it is more for the selection of students for admission to majors in undergraduate programs rather than for admissions to schools. It is not clear why schools and their individual programs need a test to be used to admit students to a major at that school, although, as mentioned above, reasons are given in the validity studies summary. Is it not more proper for schools to set required courses for students to complete, and, when the students successfully pass these courses, to admit them into a major? If the AHPAT is really intended more for admission to post-bachelor's study, then it should be testing for skills acquired in upper division undergraduate studies, not those skills preceding it.

The Allied Health Professions Admission Test is an achievement-type assessment instrument designed to measure whether the test taker has acquired the basic knowledge and skills necessary for either admission to an allied health sciences major in undergraduate school or to post-bachelor's allied health sciences study. Studies show that it contributes significantly to predicting success in at least some allied health professions. Although no information was provided on the test's reliability or norms or scoring method, it is reasonable to assume that the test's manufacturer, The Psychological Corporation, has probably made strides to assure that it fulfills the standards for tests of this kind. Broadly speaking, it appears that the Allied Health Professions Admission Test is useful in determining whether students are adequately prepared for the successful completion of upper-level undergraduate allied health programs, its objective. Whether or not this is necessary is another question.

REVIEWER'S REFERENCES

Wiesseman, J. (1981). *Does the AHPAT add enough predictive ability to the college GPA to justify its use?* Unpublished manuscript, Loma Linda University, Loma Linda, CA.

The Psychological Corporation. (1986). *Allied Health Professions Admission Test: Summary of validity studies.* San Antonio, TX: Author.

The Psychological Corporation. (1991). *Allied Health Professions Admission Test: 1991-1992 candidate information booklet with application.* San Antonio, TX: Author.

Review of the Allied Health Professions Admission Test by RICHARD C. PUGH, Professor of Education, Indiana University, Bloomington, IN:

The Allied Health Professions Admission Test (AHPAT) is a test battery that provides measures of academic ability and knowledge related to the health professions. It is described in the Candidate Information Booklet as helping to identify qualified applicants to academic programs in allied health. It is described as a segment of the admission process by schools of allied health offering baccalaureate and post-baccalaureate programs in allied health. The Candidate Information Booklet states that the AHPAT is designed to measure those skills prerequisite to successful completion of upper-division undergraduate allied health programs.

This is a test battery that takes approximately 4 hours of testing time plus additional time to administer. The content areas assessed by the AHPAT were selected through surveying university allied health programs. Items were contributed by allied health professionals and edited by professional staff. This procedure addresses the content validity of the items. The test consists of five content areas—Verbal Ability, Quantitative Ability, Biology, Chemistry, and Reading Comprehension. The items are in a multiple-choice format with four alternatives. The test is organized into six parts with a 10-minute rest break after the completion of the first three parts.

The Verbal Ability section consists of general vocabulary and verbal reasoning using synonyms and antonyms. In the test booklet, both Parts I and VI are entitled Verbal Ability with 75 items to be completed in 20 minutes in Part I plus another 75 items to be completed in 30 minutes in Part VI. Presumably these two parts are combined to generate a Verbal Ability score.

The Quantitative Ability section (Part II) consists of items that are mixed between ability to reason and understand quantitative concepts and relationships in arithmetic fundamentals and applications in algebra, geometry, and basic trigonometry. There are 50 items in this section with a time limit of 40 minutes. It is suggested that the margin of the test booklet be used for any calculation work. The directions explicitly state that all calculators including watch calculators or any other aids are prohibited.

The Biology section (Part III) has items in which the contents address knowledge of the principles and concepts of basic biology with an emphasis on human biology. Topics stated in the Information Booklet include cell biology, heredity, human structure and function, bacteria and viruses, evolution, and plants. The time limit for this section is 25 minutes. There are 50 items in this section with some items clustered around a common central diagram, common figure, or common graphic.

The Chemistry section (Part IV) consists of items that relate to knowledge of the principles and concepts of basic chemistry. Chemistry topics include atoms and molecules, formulas, equations, bonding, element and periodic relationships, states of matter, solutions, chemical equilibrium, acids, bases, electrochemistry, kinetics, and nuclear and organic chemistry. Similar to the format of the Biology section, the Chemistry section has a time limit of 25 minutes during which examinees have 50 items to complete. Some items are grouped together around a central problem that might include a graph.

The Reading Comprehension section (Part V) is designed using reading passages dealing with science-oriented topics. Items in this section relate to one's ability to comprehend, analyze, understand, and interpret these passages. For Form 1E, there were three reading passages with a total of 45 items to be completed in 25 minutes.

An annotated sample personal score report is found in the Appendix of the Candidate Information Booklet. Based on this sample report, it is evident that five raw scores are generated based on the number of questions answered correctly in each section. There is no composite score reported. Additionally, examinee's percentiles for each section of the test are reported. These percentiles were determined by administering the test to applicants from throughout the United States seeking admission to 4-year allied health programs. The actual procedure for generating the normative data for the AHPAT is not discussed in the Candidate Information Booklet, the Manual of Directions for Examiners, nor the Summary of Validity Studies provided to this reviewer. There is no indication of any lack of cooperation associated with requests by the publisher for participation nor an indication of when the standardization data were collected. The lack of a description of the sampling procedures makes it difficult to determine the representativeness of the norms for this test. However, a typical test manual which would describe the norming procedure was not provided with the materials for this review.

The absence of a typical test manual presented another difficulty. There was no evidence reported on the reliability of the five scores for the AHPAT. However, given the number of items, the length of testing time, the test development procedures, and the homogeneity of content coverage for the five sections it is estimated that the typical internal consistency of the scores would be quite high. However, some caution about the interpretation of scores based on the standard error of measurement should have been reported in the explanation of the annotated sample personal score report and none was found.

In assessing validity of the AHPAT, several studies have been conducted. Criteria such as admittance to the program (when AHPAT was not used as a screening variable), completion of the program, and first-year or cumulative GPA in allied health programs have been used. Predictive validity coefficients based on Pearson product-moment correlations across 15 colleges between AHPAT scores and program GPA ranged from .31 to .84 (all significant at the .01 level) for programs within individual universities. Multiple correlations using AHPAT scores in combination with entering GPAs ranged from .43 to .67 using first-year GPAs within allied health specialties as the criterion. These validity coefficients are substantial but caution must be exercised with the interpretation because there was a general absence of information about the descriptive statistics associated with these studies. No indication is given whether these values are based on samples that were representative or whether the performance was typical.

In summary, this test appears to make a useful contribution to admissions decisions in the allied health professions. Its development undoubtedly followed well-regarded procedures and promises to substantiate its content validity. Although the norm group and reliability information are not reported in detail with the materials provided to this reviewer, the test appears to be appropriate for use as an indicator in selecting applicants to allied health education programs. This conclusion is based on its content and predictive validities.

[27]

The American Drug and Alcohol Survey.

Purpose: Designed to estimate levels of drug use in schools.
Population: Schools and school districts.
Publication Dates: 1989–90.
Scores: Item scores only.
Administration: Group.
Levels, 2: Grades 4–6, Grades 6–12 and college.
Price Data: Available from publisher.
Time: (20–30) minutes.
Comments: Results tabulated by publisher.
Authors: Eugene R. Oetting, Frederick Beauvais, and Ruth Edwards.
Publisher: Rocky Mountain Behavioral Science Institute, Inc.
Cross References: See T4:155 (1 reference).

Review of the American Drug and Alcohol Survey by JEFFREY JENKINS, Attorney, Narvaez & Jenkins, P.A., Albuquerque, NM:

The American Drug and Alcohol Survey (ADAS) was developed to identify the nature and extent of substance abuse among children and adolescents, and is intended for use by communities and local school districts. Different forms are available for children (grades 4–6) and adolescents (grades 6–12). In addition to the questionnaire itself, the publisher of the ADAS provides analysis and reporting of the results, as well as considerable support for public presentation and dissemination of the results. As a survey, the ADAS is not intended to provide a measure of an individual's drug or alcohol use, but an overall picture of the patterns of substance abuse within a local community.

The adolescent form of the ADAS consists of 57 multipart items in a Likert scale or yes/no format. The items are presented on an easy-to-read four-page computer-scannable form. The form collects some demographic information on each respondent (grade, age, sex, ethnicity) for use in reporting categorical results. The first 15 items request information about alcohol use, including how often alcohol was used and where such use occurred. Questions on the extent of alcohol use are also included, as well as whether drinking ever caused the respondent any of a series of problems, including legal, financial, school, or family problems. The remainder of the items address drug use. The items progress from questions about marijuana and inhalants to stimulants, narcotics, and steroids. Several questions also ask about the use of specific drugs such as amphetamines, crack, LSD, and heroin. Three items address tobacco usage.

The children's form of the ADAS consists of 39 items on both sides of a single computer-scannable form. The items are stated clearly in language appropriate for children, and address the use of alcohol, marijuana, inhalants, tobacco, and crack. Several items on the children's form, as well as on the adolescent form, deal with peer issues, such as "How much would your friends try to stop you from getting drunk?"; "How many of your friends use marijuana?"; and "How often have your friends asked you to sniff something to get high?"

The ADAS provides users with extensive analysis and reporting services. The results for the adolescent survey are delivered in a three-ring binder with tabbed sections labeled Executive Summary, Detailed Reports, Media Kit, Resource Guide, and Survey. The results of the survey are reported in descriptive text, tables of percentage breakdowns, and pie charts, and are presented in three parts. The first part is a brief overview of drug and alcohol use among respondents, addressing how many students have tried drugs, what drugs they have used, and the extent or amount of such use. Students at each grade level are also classified at "High Risk," "Moderate Risk," or "Low Risk" from their drug or alcohol use. The second part summarizes students' "experiences and attitudes regarding drugs and alcohol" (manual, p. 15) and analyzes the availability and opportunity for drug use, and the attitudes of students about the harmfulness and problems involved in drug use. Part 3 discusses the use of individual drugs, and provides a brief description of the various drugs surveyed. The report for the children's form follows a different, somewhat simplified format, but provides similar information.

The Media Kit is also a useful part of the report. It includes a presentation script that can be adapted for presentation of the results in a local community, and provides transparencies of pie charts and bar graphs summarizing the results.

The report binder for the ADAS briefly described the reliability and validity of the survey. The publishers generally report performing approximately 40 "consistency checks" among pairs of items in the survey to detect random or otherwise inaccurate responses. They also report an internal consistency coefficient to be approximately .80 "for the 12 major drug categories" (p. 2, Survey section of manual). Although the publishers correctly note that .80 is satisfactory for this type of measure, it is not clear how the coefficient is arrived at or what the reliability of the discrete areas of the survey are. Given the generally responsible and professional manner in which the survey appears to have been developed, this shortcoming in accurately reporting separate reliability estimates as well as a reliability coefficient for the full survey should be remedied. The publisher also addresses the validity of the ADAS by discussing protections taken against false responses, an area of clear concern in a survey of this type. These protections include listing a "fake drug" on the survey, as well as flagging unusual patterns of reported drug use. The publisher also states that "extensive research" has been done "on the relationships of the drug use questions to the questions on student characteristics and attitudes" (p. 3, Survey section of the manual). The publisher should summarize some of this research and make available any technical reports or papers resulting from this work. In addition, the publisher notes that results obtained from the ADAS are similar to those obtained from other drug and alcohol surveys, including the University of Michigan National Senior Survey. No specific comparative data are reported, however. Without more information about these studies, it is not possible to make a conclusive determination about the validity of the ADAS.

Despite these shortcomings in ascertaining the technical characteristics for the ADAS, the survey appears to be a well-constructed and useful tool for assessing the drug and alcohol use of students. A particular strength of the survey is its clear and understandable analysis and summary of the results. School districts should find the ADAS beneficial in assessing the extent of substance abuse among young people in their local communities.

Review of the American Drug and Alcohol Survey by STEVEN SCHINKE, Professor, Columbia University School of Social Work, New York, NY:

The American Drug and Alcohol Survey is a self-report, paper-and-pencil questionnaire intended for anonymous administration to students in the 4th through 12th grades. Survey items ask students about their drug and alcohol use and the frequency and intensity of their current drug and alcohol use. With the responses to the survey's questions, it is possible to describe the adolescents' drug-use type (multi-drug user, occasional drug user, etc.) and to determine their risk level for future drug use. Other questions help determine when students are first experimenting with substances and where students are using substances most frequently (school, parties, home). This information is critical for intervention. Data gleaned by the survey also help drug and alcohol programs determine the nature and extent of substance use in the schools and community. Such knowledge is necessary for successful community campaigns against adolescent substance abuse.

The American Drug and Alcohol Survey has for years effectively measured substance abuse among children and adolescents. Chief among the strengths of the survey are its ease of delivery, conciseness, and documented reliability and validity. The authors validate consistency in survey responses by asking about each drug several different times. Consistency checks are made 40 times during data analyses; students who report two or more inconsistencies are deleted from the report data.

Other safeguards in the survey detect erroneous or exaggerated responses. For example, the survey includes "fake" drugs to detect exaggeration. The authors found that on average only 1.2% of 12th graders and 3.6% of 8th graders indicated that they used these "fake" drugs. Surveys are also checked for implausible responses, such as the student who reports heroin use but not marijuana use. Reliability coefficients for the drug use scales average around .90. The internal consistency reliability index for the 12 major drug categories is about .80. Further testifying to the reliability of the survey is its production of data that bear a strong similarity to data found in other national surveys.

Besides the actual surveys, the American Drug and Alcohol Survey kit provides tabulation analyses and interpretation of results, multicolored overhead transparencies, press releases, and other user-friendly materials. Such a turn-key operation has obvious advantages. Professional, factual reporting of reliable survey results helps ensure attention to the community-wide problem of adolescent substance abuse. This survey is an excellent measure for assessing substance abuse among adolescents.

[28]

The American Occupational Therapy Association, Inc. Fieldwork Evaluation for the Occupational Therapist.

Purpose: Constructed to evaluate "student competence at the completion of each Level II fieldwork experience."
Population: Occupational therapy students.
Publication Dates: 1973–87.
Scores, 3: Performance, Judgment, Attitude.
Administration: Individual.
Price Data: Available from publisher.
Time: Administration time not reported.
Comments: Ratings by supervisor; revision of the Field Work Performance Report (T3:885).
Authors: The American Occupational Therapy Association, Inc.
Publisher: The American Occupational Therapy Association, Inc.
Cross References: For information on the Field Work Performance Report, see T3:885 (2 references) and 8:1107 (1 reference).

Review of The American Occupational Therapy Association, Inc. Fieldwork Evaluation for the Occupational Therapist by JAMES T. AUSTIN, Assistant Professor of Psychology, The Ohio State University, Columbus, OH:

Occupational therapy (OT) is among the fastest growing healthcare specialties in this country. Accountability to the public has led to revisions of the educational and credentialing requirements of the field (cf. American Occupational Therapy Association & American Medical Association, 1991). One method for assessing achievement is to observe and evaluate behaviors on the job or during training (Morgan & Irby, 1978). Such field experiences for OTs are divided into Level I (in-school) and Level II (post-school). The instrument under review, named the Fieldwork Evaluation for the Occupational Therapist (FWEOT), is the third in a series of behavioral rating forms developed for the evaluation of OTs during and after Level II fieldwork (which usually comprises two placements, one psychosocial and one physical disabilities). The first of eight pages contains information about the ratee, fieldwork site and administrative details, a rating summary, and space for comments and signatures. The second page contains instructions to raters, directions for scoring, and performance subcategory definitions. Pages 3–7 present the scale proper, consisting of 51 task statements. Each statement is rated on three dimensions: Performance, Judgment, and Attitude, using 5-point scales (from *Poor* = 1 to *Excellent* = 5). The three dimensions are defined at the top of each page. The Performance dimension is divided into five subcategories (numbers of items in parentheses): Assessment (12), Planning (10), Treatment (12), Problem Solving (8), and Administration/Professionalism (9); whereas Judgment and Attitude dimensions are scored on an overall basis using the sum over all 51 tasks. The form can be completed by self-rating or by one or more supervisors. The final page gives instructions on using the scale for midterm evaluation, suggesting a 3-point rating scale and self-and-supervisor evaluation recommended for this purpose.

Although the goals of the rating form, which are to provide feedback during and at completion of fieldwork experiences and to evaluate readiness for entry to a certification exam, are laudable, the lack of accompanying description about development, interpretation, and usage cannot be praised. When I received the instrument for review, there were no supporting materials. Past editions of the *Mental Measurements Yearbook* revealed several publications dealing with earlier versions of the rating form in the *American Journal of Occupational Therapy* (e.g., Crocker, Muthard, Slaymaker, & Samson, 1975; Slaymaker, Crocker, & Muthard, 1974), but nothing is mentioned on the current form itself. Given that important decisions about OT trainees are made on the basis of the ratings, this deficit is troublesome. The provision of cutoff scores with no apparent evidence is also problematic. In a nutshell, developers and providers have an obligation to present manuals along with the assessment instruments so that users have some guidance concerning limitations of the instrument. Laudable goals cannot compensate for this lack! This is troubling because it mirrors a similar lack of manual for one assessment of Level I fieldwork, the Wisconsin Fieldwork Evaluation Form (cf. Swinehart & Meyers, 1993). In my view the provision of a manual with a measuring instrument implies a commitment on the part of developers to put forth their assumptions, logic, and relevant data bearing on score interpretations (cf. American Educational Research Association, American Psychological Association, & National Council on Measurement in Education, 1985).

In the remainder of this review I will evaluate the validation evidence contained in the references cited above and suggest additional topics for research. First, an operational test and validation study of the current version of the FWEOT was conducted by Cooper and Hickerson-Crist (1988). Preliminary steps included a literature review, survey of educators, and writing of a pool of 499 task statements. This pool was reduced to 99 items and given to two samples for Q-sorting in order to check clarity and content priority. The version tested contained 53 task statements. A national sample of 597 educators and 517 students in Level II trainee positions constituted the sample, which was the result of an attempt to provide a census of the entire population of those undergoing fieldwork experience that fall (N = 646 centers). Response rates were, therefore, 92% and 80%, respectively. Most ratees (72%) were on their first Level II fieldwork assignment (23% were on their second and 5% were on their third). Student reactions were used to assess the "fit" of the items relative to actual fieldwork experiences, an approach that seems close to the idea of content validity. Results indicated very good fit for the Performance dimension and good fit for the Judgment and Attitude items. My interpretation of this is that the former dimension is probably emphasized more during early stages of the OT career, whereas the latter two dimensions become important later. Alpha estimates of .929, .941, and .961 were obtained for the Performance, Judgment, and Attitude ratings (each for 53 items). The estimates for the subcategories of the Performance dimension were also high, ranging from .91 to .94. Finally, educator-raters were asked to categorize student-ratees into five groupings in terms of competence. The resulting data were used to set cutoff scores for the three dimensions.

In providing suggestions for additional research I am guided by an ongoing project that combines qualitative and action research strategies (Mattingly & Gillette, 1991). A core principle guiding this project, entitled the *Clinical Reasoning Study*, is provided by the work of Schon (1983), who contends that knowledge in professions defined on the basis of practice is transactional in nature (the client-practitioner interface) and involves both declarative and procedural components. Put another way, not only must student-practitioners acquire propositions about anatomical, physiological, and psychosocial knowledge, but they must also be able to integrate this knowledge into specific techniques for assessment, treatment planning, and problem solving within an ethical framework (DeMars, Fleming, & Benham, 1991). One implication of this perspective for quantitative evaluation of the Fieldwork Evaluation form is that the client serves as a source of variance in performance or that therapist and client comprise a system. Generalizability theory (Shavelson & Webb, 1991) could be used to elucidate the strength of this source of variance in observational ratings of OT performance. Testing such views requires evaluating multiple clients and one OT trainee, or multiple OT trainees working with a single client. Additionally, given the psychosocial and structural focus of the discipline, perhaps severity of client disabling condition determines performance differences. Using a range of disabling conditions along a severity dimension would enable assessment of this hypothesis. Finally, although I prefer a quantitative rather than qualitative approach to assessment, I see no reason why there could not be a rapprochement between paradigms (cf. Moss, 1992). Consider the collaborative project studying clinical reasoning headed by Mattingly and Gillette (1991). Those researchers videotaped therapists interacting with clients and then presented the videotaped sequences back to the therapists in order to elicit their thoughts about certain decisions. This method provides promise for evaluation, feedback, and training purposes and is commendable. It could be modified for future research on the FWEOT. As one suggestion, perhaps one or more patient-therapist interactions could be videotaped and presented as a standardization for raters.

SUMMARY. This instrument has shown improvement over its revisions and is based on a sound premise: *clinical competence is crucial to the practice of the OT profession and should be evaluated in a standardized manner during fieldwork*. This modification was specifically designed to reduce the ceiling effect found with previous versions in which ratees clustered at the high ends of a 4-point scale. Its standardization across the profession is a strong reason for its continued usage; however, there are still several issues for research. One issue concerns additional evidence for the reliability of the measure—retest and multiple rater estimates would be desirable, perhaps within a generalizability theory framework (as noted above). In such a framework, occasions and raters would be facets in a psychometric design. Another issue concerns the role of rater training, which arises in discussions of the usage of the FWEOT (cf. Hickerson-Crist & Cooper, 1988). A question for research is whether training would improve psychometric or usability measures for this rating. Industrial-organizational psychologists have addressed this topic extensively (Smith, 1986). Another issue concerns validity evidence for the scale, which is still lacking. Further investigations of content validity are desirable, perhaps using the method developed by Bownas, Bosshardt, and Donnelly (1985) for matching training program content to job content. Factor analysis to assess the structure of the rating form is another possibility. Next, even though the FWEOT is used as a criterion measure it could still be validated (cf. Austin & Villanova, 1992). One suggestion would be to correlate FWEOT scores with certification exam scores, making appropriate corrections for range restriction. Additionally, measures of subsequent role performance should be obtained and correlated with FWEOT scores, in the sense that this measure represents an immediate criterion which should predict intermediate criterion measures. Finally, cutoff scores were set somewhat arbitrarily at two standard deviations below the averages obtained from the national sample during the test and evaluation of the FWEOT. Further study is needed to validate these fairly low levels, which would permit nearly 95% of all ratees to qualify for the certification exam (and suggests range restriction). This is important both for scientific reasons and accountability to the public. Both developers and the national leadership are encouraged to build on their good start and continue to collaborate in studying and improving this instrument. An indication that this will occur is that the instrument is to be reviewed on a 5-year cycle, which suggests that efforts are (or should be) underway.

REVIEWER'S REFERENCES

Slaymaker, J. E., Crocker, L. M., & Muthard, J. E. (1974). *Fieldwork performance report manual: Use, history, and development.* Rockville, MD: American Occupational Therapy Association.

Crocker, L. M., Muthard, J. E., Slaymaker, J. E., & Samson, L. (1975). A performance rating scale for evaluating clinical competence of occupational therapy students. *American Journal of Occupational Therapy, 29*, 81-86.

Morgan, M. K., & Irby, D. M. (Eds.). (1978). *Evaluating clinical competence in the health professions.* St. Louis, MO: Mosby.

Schon, D. A. (1983). *The reflective practitioner: How professionals think in action.* New York: Basic Books.

American Educational Research Association, American Psychological Association, & National Council on Measurement in Education. (1985). *Standards for educational and psychological testing.* Washington, DC: American Psychological Association, Inc.

Bownas, D. A., Bosshardt, M. J., & Donnelly, L. F. (1985). A quantitative approach to evaluating training curriculum content sampling adequacy. *Personnel Psychology, 38*, 117-131.

Smith, D. E. (1986). Training programs for performance appraisal: A review. *Academy of Management Review, 11*, 22-40.

Cooper, R. G., & Hickerson-Crist, P. A. (1988). Field test analysis and reliability of the fieldwork evaluation for the occupational therapist. *The Occupational Therapy Journal of Research, 8*, 369-379.

Hickerson-Crist, P. A., & Cooper, R. G. (1988). Evaluating clinical competence with the new fieldwork evaluation. *American Journal of Occupational Therapy, 42*, 771-773.

American Occupational Therapy Association, Inc., & the American Medical Association. (1991). Essentials and guidelines for an accredited educational program for the occupational therapist. *American Journal of Occupational Therapy, 45*, 1077-1084.

DeMars, P. A., Fleming, J. D., & Benham, P. A. (1991). Ethics across the occupational therapy continuum. *American Journal of Occupational Therapy, 45*, 782-787.

Mattingly, C., & Gillette, N. (1991). Anthropology, occupational therapy, and action research. *American Journal of Occupational Therapy*, *45*, 972-978.

Shavelson, R. J., & Webb, N. M. (1991). *Generalizability theory: A primer*. Newbury Park, CA: Sage.

Austin, J. T., & Villanova, P. (1992). The criterion problem: 1917-1992. *Journal of Applied Psychology*, 77, 836-874.

Moss, P. A. (1992). Shifting conceptions of validity in educational measurement: Implications for performance assessment. *Review of Educational Research*, *62*, 229-258.

Swinehart, S., & Meyers, S. K. (1993). Level I fieldwork: Creating a positive experience. *American Journal of Occupational Therapy*, *47*, 68-73.

Review of The American Occupational Therapy Association, Inc. Fieldwork Evaluation for the Occupational Therapist by BRIAN BOLTON, University Professor, Arkansas Research and Training Center in Vocational Rehabilitation, University of Arkansas, Fayetteville, AR:

The Fieldwork Evaluation for the Occupational Therapist is a revision of the Fieldwork Performance Report (FWPR). The FWPR was developed in 1973 for the purpose of assessing the competence of occupational therapy students during their fieldwork experiences. Subsequent critical reviews and suggestions from professionals persuaded the American Occupational Therapy Association's (AOTA) Representative Assembly in 1982 to authorize a revision of the FWPR that would reflect current entry-level requirements.

A task force consisting of six members, including both clinicians and educators, assisted by consultants from two organizations specializing in personnel assessment, worked for 4 years to complete the revision. The revised instrument was retitled the Fieldwork Evaluation for the Occupational Therapist (FWE). The FWE was approved by the AOTA's Commission on Education and Representative Assembly in 1986 and implemented in January 1987.

Working from three AOTA policy documents that specify entry-level roles, uniform terminology, and essentials for accredited educational programs, the task force developed a preliminary pool of 500 items for the FWE. The task force then edited the initial pool down to 100 items, which were distributed to a nationwide sample of clinicians and fieldwork educators for the purpose of increasing the clarity of the items and assuring thorough coverage of essential tasks.

The professional review resulted in a final set of 53 items that were included on the field test form of the FWE. For the field test, more than 500 occupational therapy students were rated by their fieldwork supervisors on the 53 items. Each student was judged on each item using a 5-point scale (poor, fair, good, very good, excellent) in three areas of competence: Performance, Judgment, and Attitude. The fieldwork supervisors also placed each student into one of five categories from the top 20% to the bottom 20% of students that they had supervised and then either recommended or did not recommend each student for entry-level employment.

Two of the 53 FWE items were deleted from further consideration because they were judged to be of questionable relevance by the fieldwork supervisors. Factor analyses of the remaining 51 items for each of the three areas of competence, separately, resulted in five subscales for Performance (assessment, planning, treatment, problem solving, and administration), but only supported total scores for Judgment and Attitude. A total score is also calculated for Performance.

Internal consistency reliability estimates for the five performance subscales and the three total scores ranged from .92 to .96. Correlations between the three total scores were .88, .91, and .94. Mean FWE scores for students located by their supervisors in five categories from the top 20% to bottom 20% were markedly different and in the hypothesized order from high to low. The corresponding correlations for the rankings were .70, .68, and .64 for the three total competency scores. The mean scores for recommended and not recommended students were also consistent with expectations, with corresponding correlations of .41, .40, and .40, respectively.

Minimum passing scores on Performance, Judgment, and Attitude were established at two standard deviations below the mean scores of those students who were recommended for entry-level employment by their supervisors. The AOTA suggests that students should have passing scores in all three areas of competence. Yet, the AOTA also recommends that individual schools implement their own standards and grading systems for the fieldwork experience.

Several problems with the FWE merit attention. Despite the criticism that rater error plagued the earlier instrument, no interrater reliability data are presented for the FWE. Although factor analysis supported the scoring of five subscales for the Performance area, minimum passing scores are not given for these distinguishable components of student performance. In contrast, separate scores are calculated for each of the three areas of competence, even though their high intercorrelations do not justify the practice. Furthermore, field work supervisors found the Judgment and Attitude scales much more difficult to use. The Judgment and Attitude ratings could be deleted (or subsumed into the Performance ratings) without any loss of information.

No rationale is given for the procedure used for setting minimum passing scores. Norm tables providing percentile equivalents for the recommended and not recommended groups of students would be more helpful to educational institutions in developing their own standards and grading systems. The absence of a manual to accompany the FWE is an inexcusable omission, when almost all of the relevant information, including statistical data and clinical objectives for raters, is available in a few unpublished reports and documents. The AOTA should arrange for the preparation and publication of a manual as quickly as possible.

SUMMARY. The Fieldwork Evaluation for the Occupational Therapist is the product of several years of careful work by a dedicated committee of professionals. The FWE's outstanding attribute is its strong foundation in occupational therapy principles and practices that established excellent content validity for the instrument. The scoring procedures should be modified to better reflect the statistical results and to provide more useful information for educators and students. It can be concluded that the FWE is a potentially valuable tool for assessing student achievement in occupational therapy fieldwork sites.

[29]

The Anomalous Sentences Repetition Test.

Purpose: Constructed to differentiate between dementia and depression.
Population: Ages 55 and over.
Publication Date: 1988.
Acronym: ASRT.
Scores: Total error score only.
Administration: Individual.
Price Data, 1992: £40.25 per complete kit including 25 record forms and manual (24 pages); £23 per 25 record forms.
Time: (5) minutes.
Author: David J. Weeks.
Publisher: NFER-Nelson Publishing Co., Ltd. [England].

Review of the Anomalous Sentences Repetition Test by MICHAEL G. KAVAN, Director of Behavioral Sciences and Associate Professor of Family Practice, Creighton University School of Medicine, Omaha, NE:

The Anomalous Sentences Repetition Test (ASRT) is composed of four parallel six-item tests. Its major purpose is to assist in the discrimination between early dementing illnesses and major depressive disorders in persons over the age of 55 years. However, the author claims that it may also be used to discriminate typical alcoholic Korsakoff psychosis patients from patients with Alzheimer-type dementia, assess cognitive and language abilities in younger patients where it is necessary to distinguish between a functional disorder and neuropsychological impairment, and determine the level of impairment in patients with known deficits in the above areas. Test development is based on the supposition that repetition of some sentences that are syntactically complex, meaningless, or very long discriminate between patients with cerebral damage and normals (Newcombe & Marshall, 1967).

ADMINISTRATION AND SCORING. The ASRT may be administered to individual patients by a variety of educational and health care specialists including general practitioners, educational and clinical psychologists, speech therapists, occupational specialists, teachers, and nurses. No mention is made within the manual of any specialized training required in order to administer the ASRT. The author recommends that for diagnostic purposes the ASRT be used in conjunction with a concurrent assessment of the patient's mental status. In addition, it is recommended that the tester postpone testing if noticeable signs of oversedation or untoward medication side effects are present and/or if a moderate to severe hearing impairment is present and not alleviated by hearing aids. After accounting for these factors, the tester completes a Record Form that includes current personal information regarding the patient and testing conditions. The patient is then read each of six anomalous (i.e., meaningless) sentences, one at a time, and asked to repeat these word-for-word. Apparently, the tester copies these verbatim into a space provided after each sentence. Test administration conveniently takes less than 5 minutes. An error score is obtained for each sentence and then summed for a Total Error Score. These are then converted to an age-transformed score due to findings suggesting significant increases in errors with age in the dementia group, but not with the major depression group. Errors may be classified according to errors of omission, transposition, phonetic confusion, addition, substitution, and tense error. Cutoff scores for determining probable dementia or organic impairment were determined by finding the midpoint between the mean scores of elderly patients with dementia and those with depression within each of four age groups (i.e., 55–70, 71–75, 76–80, over 81 [*sic*]). According to the author, use of recommended cutoff scores within the standardization study resulted in sensitivity of 81% (i.e., 19% of patients with dementia will be missed) and specificity of 85% (i.e., 15% of patients will be mistakenly classified as such). The predictive value is 84%.

RELIABILITY. The manual provides information on two reliability studies. Ten-week test-retest reliability for 98 community-dwelling elderly (mean age = 72.9 years) was .84, whereas 23-week test-retest data on 51 "control subjects" (mean age = 51.2 years) was .86. However, no other information is provided within the manual about this sample. Weeks (1986) describes this latter group as a "pool of community volunteers" (6 males; 45 females). Alternate-form reliability for these two groups was found to range from .79 to .91 and .81 to .90, respectively. Although no other reliability information is supplied within the manual, Weeks gives a Spearman-Brown reliability coefficient for the 51 control subjects as .859.

VALIDITY. The manual provides data from the standardization study supporting the ability of the ASRT to discriminate between normal subjects, patients with depression, and patients with dementia. The difference in the number of total errors on the ASRT between the groups with depression and dementia was significant. However, Rai, Stewart, and Scott (1990) used the ASRT in a sample of 16 patients with a diagnosis of dementia of the Alzheimer's type, 18 patients with depression, and 16 normal elderly persons and found no difference in the age-adjusted ASRT scores between the three groups. From these results, Rai et al. concluded that the ASRT is not a useful measure for providing evidence for the existence of cognitive impairment nor for differentiating between dementing and nondementing illness. The manual also provides concurrent validity data regarding the relationship between the ASRT and a battery of psychometric tests administered to varying groups of clinical patients and to a group of elderly community controls. Although most correlations are in the expected direction, some results show inconsistencies. The manual also cites a study conducted by Weeks (1986) in which 45 patients with diagnoses including Alzheimer-type dementia, Korsakoff's psychosis, psychotic depression, cerebro-vascular accident, schizophrenia, anoxic brain damage, closed head injury, cerebral tumor, syphilis, hypomania, and cerebral encephalitis received neuropsychological testing and computerized axial tomography (CAT) to determine the degree of cortical atrophy and cerebral ventricular enlargement. Pearson product-moment correlations were significant between the number of errors on the ASRT and the degree of cortical atrophy (.433) and degree of ventricular enlargement (.47). However, the manual gives no breakdown of correlations between these various diagnoses and CAT findings. Kopelman (1986) is cited within the manual as supporting the ability of anomalous sentences to discriminate between patients with depression, Korsakoff amnesia, and Alzheimer-type dementia; however, these sentences were selected from a list employed by Newcombe and Marshall (1967) as opposed to the ASRT. No other validity data are cited within the manual.

NORMS. Normative data consisting of means and standard deviations are provided for normal elderly living in the community (n = 98), elderly patients with depression (n = 100), and elderly patients with dementia (n = 100). A table presenting means, standard deviations, and standard errors from "all studies to date" (p. 8) is also supplied within the manual. Data are given on younger normal community controls and depressed patients, neurotic depressed patients, psychotic depressed patients, recovered younger depressives, younger neurologically impaired patients, and chronic alcoholic patients (range of n = 35–164). The manual includes limited information on several of these groups.

SUMMARY. The ASRT is a brief, easy-to-use, clinician-administered instrument designed to discriminate between early dementing illnesses and major depressive disorders in persons 55 and older. The author reports that it may also be used to differentiate alcoholic Korsakoff psychosis patients from patients with Alzheimer-type dementia, test cognitive and language abilities in younger patients where one must distinguish between a functional disorder and a neuropsychological impairment, and determine the level of such impairment. At present, conflicting research exists regarding the ability of the ASRT to discriminate between depressed, demented, and normal groups. In addition, limited evidence is presented to support other claims. Because of this, the ASRT should be used cautiously in clinical settings until further research can be completed on these issues. Because of the risk for false positives and missed cases with many brief screening measures, instruments such as the ASRT should not be used by themselves to determine a diagnosis of dementia. Instead, clinicians should remember that a thorough clinical evaluation including history from the patient and significant others, laboratory testing, physical examination, and functional assessment is the most important component of any initial evaluation for dementia (National Institutes of Health, 1987).

REVIEWER'S REFERENCES

Newcombe, F., & Marshall, J. C. (1967). Immediate recall of "sentences" by subjects with unilateral cerebral lesions. *Neuropsychologia, 5*, 329-334.

Kopelman, M. D. (1986). Recall of anomalous sentences in dementia and amnesia. *Brain and Language, 29*, 154-170.

Weeks, D. J. (1986). The Anomalous Sentences Repetition Test: Replication and validation study. *Journal of Clinical Psychology, 42*, 635-638.

National Institutes of Health Consensus Conference. (1987). Differential diagnosis of dementing diseases. *Journal of the American Medical Association, 258*, 3411-3416.

Rai, G. S., Stewart, K., & Scott, L. C. (1990). Assessment of Anomalous Sentences Repetition Test. *Journal of Neurology, Neurosurgery and Psychiatry, 53*, 611-612.

Review of the Anomalous Sentences Repetition Test by CHARLES A. PETERSON, Director of Training in Psychology, VA Minneapolis Medical Center, and Associate Clinical Professor of Psychology at the University of Minnesota, Minneapolis, MN:

INTRODUCTION. Imagine reading an entry in the *Mental Measurements Yearbook* that began like this: "This test, which the guitar baked on lampshade, excitedly luncheon meat a tubular sparrow." What would be the differential diagnosis? *(a)* Printer's error; *(b)* demented reviewer; *(c)* lapse in editorial judgment; *(d)* clever way to introduce a test that uses anomalous sentences to assist in the "discrimination between early dementing illness and major depressive disorders in patients over the age of 55" (manual, p. 1). The answer, most certainly, is *(d)*. Despite the clinically familiar difficulty in diagnostically differentiating early dementia from depression, the Anomalous Sentences Repetition Test (hereafter ASRT) is touted as a "simple, brief," "clinical tool" or "psychometric aid" that may efficiently address Lezak's (1983) "knottiest problem." This test presumably draws on two unquestionable glittering generalities, that neuropsychiatric illness alters and impairs cognition, and that meaningless, confusing, complex, or bizarre stimuli present a greater challenge to efficient and adaptive cognition.

TEST DESCRIPTION. The anomalous (which most dictionaries equate with irregular and abnormal) sentences (6 to 10 words each) were constructed according to carefully balanced norms (e.g., concreteness, pleasantness, familiarity, etc.) on word usage. The six sentences in each of four parallel forms were subjected to varying degrees of semantic (meaning) and syntactic (structure) degradation, and are likely to be experienced by the test subject as peculiar.

ADMINISTRATION. The test manual offers reasonable guidance and caution: When used to discriminate dementia from depression, the ASRT should not be used with subjects younger than age 55. The ASRT should always be used in conjunction with a concurrent assessment of the patient's mental status, including a quantitative evaluation of depression. Testing should be postponed if there is obvious sedation or side-effects from high doses of psychotropic medications. Hearing must be adequate; alleviation of impairment by hearing aid is acceptable. The patient is instructed to repeat carefully enunciated sentences immediately after the examiner, who then records the patient's responses. Two practice sentences are first completed and followed by examiner clarification of "gross misunderstandings" of the task's demands (the author underappreciates such questions for their contribution to the diagnostic process).

SCORING. The patient's verbatim repetitions of six sentences are recorded and subsequently marked and summed for a total error score. The scoring categories are familiar to anyone who has done a language examination: errors of omission, transposition, phonetic confusion, addition, substitution, and tense change. Errors of addition and substitution are further classified as intralist intrusions, extralist intrusions, or semantic confusion. No differential diagnostic implications are noted for different errors. The total error score can then be converted into an age-transformed score, with a familiar mean of 100 and a standard deviation of 15.

STANDARDIZATION. Three roughly equivalent (by sex, age, social class, education, and IQ) groups (approximately 100 in each) of subjects were compared: (*a*) The "normal subjects" were drawn from a cross section of community-dwelling elderly. There is no indication of whether these subjects were screened and excluded for psychopathology or other medical conditions (e.g., hypertension, diabetes, coronary heart disease) that might affect mentation; therefore, these subjects might more safely be considered "not obviously patients" than normals. (*b*) "Depressed patients" were diagnosed per DSM-III, RDC, and scores on quantitative measures of depression, including the Hamilton (questionable with the elderly) and the Geriatric Depression Scale(s). (*c*) "Demented patients" were diagnosed per DSM-III and at least three occurrences within 6 months of at least 5 out of 10 checklist symptoms (e.g., disorientation, memory loss, nocturnal wandering, etc.). There is no information on the stage of the dementia. Depressed and demented patients had been followed for at least 18 months to establish the diagnosis with reasonable certainty. These subjects were also compared on a variety of concurrent measures (e.g., naming, verbal fluency, reading, etc.).

ASRT scores were able to statistically differentiate demented from depressed patients and normal subjects with good sensitivity (81%) and specificity (85%). Cutoffs were established for different ages: For example, more than 17 errors in a 55–70-year-old patient would suggest dementia, whereas more than 27 errors would be required to suggest dementia in a patient over age 81. Additional studies/data suggest that the ASRT may be sensitive to the progressive deterioration associated with dementia, and may be reasonably free of confounding influences such as amount of psychotropic medication, number and recency of previous ECT treatments, and association with some minor neurotic symptoms. The four parallel forms show psychometrically adequate equivalence and test-retest coefficients (median correlation .85).

SUGGESTIONS. (*a*) The manual should specify—and limit!—who should use this test: Visiting nurses and doctoral level clinical neuropsychologists will not use this test in an equivalent manner. There simply is no substitute for a consultation with a good neuropsychologist. (*b*) The manual should not hint that scoring this test is an easy task. No scoring examples were provided; the ASRT novice would benefit from being able to compare their fledgling efforts with clear criteria. No report of interrater reliability was offered. As scoring reliability goes, so goes validity. (*c*) The test-retest and parallel form equivalence studies should be broadened to include clinical subjects, not just "normal control subjects," who might be expected to inflate the test-retest coefficients, as opposed to more erratically performing demented subjects. (*d*) The manual should stress that the ASRT be used as part of a battery of neuropsychological tests. No matter how promising the ASRT might be, one caution looms large: Just as one swallow does not make a summer, an impairment in language repetition does not make a dementia. (*e*) Given the impact of local/ward base rates on cutting scores (Meehl & Rosen, 1955), it is psychometrically irresponsible for the manual to propose one score to differentiate dementia from pseudodementia. (*f*) Finally, further research will answer the crucial question of degree of association between the ASRT and measures of depression and attention concentration (e.g., the author states that the ASRT is "relatively unaffected by poor concentration" [p. 1] but later reports a correlation of .52 between the ASRT and a measure of short-term concentration [p. 16]).

SUMMARY. The ASRT is a plausible and carefully constructed psychometric incarnation of a reasonable idea. Although unlikely to replace the more routinely used instruments in clinical neuropsychology, the few, imperfect studies in this corner of "soft psychology" (where plausibility rivals falsifiability [Meehl, 1978]), suggest that the ASRT may prove useful to neuropsychologists in both clinical and research settings. However, the promising beginnings must now be subjected to tighter research design and anonymous repetition by labs other than that of the test's author.

REVIEWER'S REFERENCES

Meehl, P. E., & Rosen, A. (1955). Antecedent probability and the efficiency of psychometric signs, patterns, or cutting scores. *Psychological Bulletin, 52*, 194-216.

Meehl, P. E. (1978). Theoretical risks and tabular asterisks: Sir Karl, Sir Ronald, and the slow progress of soft psychology. *Journal of Consulting and Clinical Psychology, 46*, 806-834.

Lezak, M. D. (1983). *Neuropsychological assessment* (2nd ed.). New York: Oxford University Press.

[30]

Anxiety Scales for Children and Adults.

Purpose: "To determine the presence and intensity of anxiety in adults and school-age children."
Population: Grade 2–adult.
Publication Date: 1993.
Acronym: ASCA.
Scores: Total score only.
Administration: Group.
Editions, 2: Youth, Adult.
Price Data, 1994: $84 per complete kit including examiner's manual (26 pages), 50 Forms Q, 50 Forms M, scoring acetate, and administration audiocassette; $31 per examiner's manual; $19 per 50 Form Q; $19 per 50 Form M; $6 per scoring acetate; $14 per administration audiocassette.
Time: (10–15) minutes.
Comments: Self-report; Form Q for children and Form M for adults.
Author: James Battle.
Publisher: PRO-ED, Inc.

Review of the Anxiety Scales for Children and Adults by PETER F. MERENDA, Professor Emeritus of Psychology and Statistics, University of Rhode Island, Kingston, RI:

Test authors are expected to be thoroughly familiar with the principles of psychometrics and the standards for evaluating sound construction and effective test use. So it appears to be, at first glance, with the author of these scales. Reference is made early in the examiner's manual to the first in the series of these published *Standards* (American Psychological Association, 1954). The APA published these first principles of good test development and use nearly 40 years ago. Subsequent editions of these standards have been prepared by a joint committee comprising members from the three major national associations with great interest in testing (AERA, APA, & NCME, 1985). It is puzzling to this reviewer why the author makes reference to the first outdated *Standards* and not to the current ones with which test authors are expected to comply.

The initial paragraph on the first page of the examiner's manual not only begins with unsubstantiated claims, but in stating these the author asserts that both the children and adult scales have been *proved* to be reliable and valid. Even if the missing studies had been referenced, the claims would be open to critical review. Research findings based on statistical analysis of empirical data lead only to conclusions dependent upon probability and power levels. They do not ever lead legitimately to the definite conclusion at the level of *proof*.

There are two levels of these anxiety scales: Form Q is the children's form, and Form M is the adult form. It is not stated at which age Form Q should give way to Form M although one can surmise by reading the tables in the Appendix the break comes at the level of junior high school. Form Q is composed of 25 dichotomously scored (yes/no) items selected by the author to measure levels of anxiety in children. Form M is composed of 40 items selected by the author to measure levels of anxiety in adults. The response category for each item is a 5-point Likert scale ranging from *always* (5) to *never* (1). The specific sources of the item pools from which the author selected the items are unknown. It is merely stated the items represent symptoms typically reported by individuals experiencing anxiety. The final items that appear on the scales apparently have never been subjected to item analysis, internal consistency analysis, and factor analysis, all of which are standard scale construction procedures.

The first psychometric property discussed in the manual is *reliability*. This is a property that is evaluated after the scale itself has been developed. The reported test-retest coefficients are in a respectable range (.82–.96, with median = .86). However, the time intervals between testing were only 1 week for Form Q and 2 weeks for Form M. Hence, no evidence of long-range stability over time is presented so the reliability of the scales must be judged only in terms of state anxiety, not trait anxiety. However, there may also be a problem in accepting the accuracy of statistical relationships inferred by the Pearson correlations reported between the first and second testings of Form Q. Given that the maximum attainable score is 25, the distributions for all administrations are markedly positively skewed. They are even multimodal. Beyond these severe departures from normality, the distributions appear to belong to a different class of curves (other than the ordinary frequency distributions that yield the reasonable joint bivariate distributions required for calculating good approximation of the population parameter of the Pearson-Product Correlation Coefficient.) This class is the *Poisson* Distribution. (Note the closeness of the Mean and Standard Deviation in each of the tables for Form Q.)

A serious error occurs in the manual relating to percentile ranks and *T* scores. This error is in the form of a misstatement, "T score conversions permit normalization of a distribution of scores" (p. 9). This is not true. A nonlinear transformation must be made to normalize the distributions with the positive skewness presented in Tables 25–31 of the Appendix. The simple linear transmutation of raw scores to standard scores via the formula, SS = 50 + 10z, merely changes the unit values on the abscissa (x-axis) and does nothing whatsoever to the values on the ordinate (y-axis). Hence, the skewed shape of the raw score distribution is retained by the standard scores. *T* scores that have been normalized range from 20–80. (Note the extent of the varying *T* scores in Tables 25–31.) On this issue, the author and the readers of this review are referred to McNemar (1969) for a discussion of the difference between "ordinary" standard scores and normal or normalized *T* scores (pp. 37–39).

Very little is reported in the manual on *validity* and what is reported is highly questionable. The little that is reported relates to *concurrent* validity (i.e., the relationship between scores on these scales and some other similar ones). For measurement in the affective domain where *anxiety* is located, *construct* validity is both of primary and paramount importance. However, the author did not engage himself in developmental research during the construction phases (or at least does not report in the manual that he has done so). Hence, the nature and dimensionality of the generic construct, anxiety, are at this point, quite elusive. Also, there are no data to indicate or suggest what aspects of anxiety, if that be the case, the items measure and how well they do it. This is a necessary although not sufficient step in attempting to establish the *construct* validity of scales. The single paragraph in the manual in which the author vaguely describes his efforts at demonstrating the *construct* validity of the scales is of no value whatsoever. It is merely a subjective statement that is supported neither by empirical data nor by the description of well-designed and controlled research studies.

The validity of tests and scales is the most important consideration in evaluating their merits. Validity is defined in the current *Standards* (AERA, APA, & NCME, 1985) as a "unitary concept" for which evidence over time supports the inferences that are made from the scores that are forthcoming from the scales. Such evidences for these anxiety scales are, at the moment, lacking, especially those related to *construct* and *predictive* validity. Potential users are cautioned to demand such evidences of validity prior to adopting scales for operational use.

In summary, the Anxiety Scales for Children and Adults are claimed by the author and inferred by the publisher to be of a quality with respect to psychometric properties that is unattainable by any psychological assessment instruments, techniques, or devices. None can be *proved* to be reliable or valid. With respect to validity this is especially true when one considers that, as stated in the APA *Standards* (AERA, APA, & NCME, 1985), it is "the inferences regarding specific uses of a test that are validated, not the test itself" (p. 9). Hence, scales themselves cannot be evaluated as valid, proven or otherwise. Regarding reliability, the evaluation of this psychometric property is always associated with its ubiquitous non-zero errors of measurement. These errors are not even mentioned in the manual. Rather, the misleading statement is made, "These high correlations indicate that the instrument has acceptable test-retest stability" (p. 2) inferring the anxiety scores persist for a long time period. There is no evidence presented to support this claim. Potential users of the scales are therefore advised to be guided by the unfortunate motto in the field of psychological testing: CAVEAT EMPTOR.

REVIEWER'S REFERFENCES

American Psychological Association. (1954). Technical recommendations for psychological tests and diagnostic techniques. *Psychological Bulletin, 51* (Supplement), 13-28.

McNemar, Q. (1969). *Psychological statistics* (4th ed.). New York: Wiley & Sons.

American Educational Research Association, American Psychological Association, & National Council on Measurement in Education. (1985). *Standards for educational and psychological testing.* Washington, DC: American Psychological Association, Inc.

Review of the Anxiety Scales for Children and Adults by JUDY OEHLER-STINNETT, Associate Professor of Applied Behavioral Studies, Oklahoma State University, Stillwater, OK:

The Anxiety Scales for Children and Adults is intended to measure objectively the construct of anxiety in the general population as well as clinical settings. According to the manual the scales can be used for diagnoses, treatment outcome, and research. Use of critical items for an adjunct to interviewing procedures and treatment direction is also recommended.

Although in chapter 1 the author indicates interpretation should be conducted with the aid of a psychologist or other appropriately trained personnel, the Preface lacks such a cautionary statement and indicates the scales may be used by "a wide range of professionals . . . in the helping professions" (p. vii).

There are two levels, a 25-item scale for children in second through ninth grades (Form Q), and a 40-item scale for adults in tenth grade through adulthood (Form M). The scales represent a well-intentioned but elementary approach to test construction and do not offer any advantages over more well-known anxiety measures or personality measures that include an anxiety subscale.

The scales do not appear to be based on any particular model of anxiety, such as empirical-criterion keying, DSM classification schemes, theories of fear and anxiety, or subgroupings of fear contexts. The manual contains three definitions of anxiety including subjective report (e.g., apprehension, uneasiness) and physiological symptoms (e.g., accelerated heart and blood pressure rates). Motor reactions such as crying or avoidant behavior are not included in the definition; however, panic is mentioned. No differentiation is made between real and imagined stimulus threats or state versus trait anxiety, and the relationship among the terms anxiety, clinical fear, phobia, and panic is not described. Developmental appropriateness, stimulus specificity, setting, intensity, severity, and chronicity are also not explicated. There is no attempt to discriminate anxiety from related constructs such as depression; in fact, depression and low self-esteem are described as "manifestations of excessive levels of anxiety" (p. vii).

Items for the scales were developed through work with students and clients, review of other instruments, and interviews with anxious people. Items for Form Q were reduced from 95 to 25 and for Form M from 200 to 40 through field work which purportedly demonstrated retained items "represent symptoms typically reported by individuals experiencing anxiety" (p. 1). However, item analyses and tryout data to support this contention are not reported in the manual. No factor analyses, internal consistency coefficients, or empirical-criterion keying (item scores for anxious versus nonanxious persons or treatment effects studies) are reported. No controls for faking are indicated. Although developmental differences between elementary (second through sixth grades) and junior high (seventh through ninth grades) students were reported, no other age changes are indicated. Particularly important would be an examination of high school students versus adults and age changes through each elementary grade. A face/content examination indicates the majority of items relate to generalized anxiety and physiological symptoms, with some attention to setting and stimulus triggers. Some items compound the concept of being tense with being scared or nervous. Items do appear to relate to the original description of anxiety as subjective with physiological symptoms; however, items do not appear to adequately represent the construct of anxiety.

There is no overt description of the normative sample in the manual. An examination of the sample description for the reliability and validity studies, and of the *n* reported for the standard score conversion tables, suggests the norm samples overlap with reliability/validity study groups. Published results of these studies suggest data were collected in 1987 or 1988. Norms for Form Q are based on 365 elementary and 433 junior high students from the Midwest, with approximate equal representation of males and females. Norms for Form M are based on 247 adults aged 15 to 63 from the Midwest; there are more than twice as many females as males. There is no description of representativeness in terms of minority representation, SES levels, clinical populations, or number of subjects at each age/grade. Separate norms are available for males and females.

Reliability is reported as test-retest only. These 2-week retest coefficients are acceptable for elementary and junior high subjects on Form Q (r = .84; .86, respectively) and excellent for Form M (r = .96). Reporting of test-retest coefficients implies the scales should measure trait rather than state anxiety; however, the brief retest interval and lack of state/trait studies disallow strong confirmation of this hypothesis. Additionally, for the scale to be acceptable as a measure of treatment effects, all coefficients should be in the .90s. As noted, no internal consistency coefficients (alpha) were reported; therefore consistency of the scales in measuring the construct of anxiety cannot be examined. Standard error of measurement was also not reported in the reliability, scoring, or interpretation sections. My calculation of the *T*-score *SEM*s from the reliability coefficients indicates an *SEM* of 4 for Form Q and 2 for Form M. Use of these for interpretation are recommended.

For test validity, concurrent studies are reported. Form Q is correlated with the State-Trait Anxiety Inventory for Children (r = .64; separate coefficients for state versus trait are not reported) and the Nervous Symptoms subtest of the California Test of Personality (r = .66). These coefficients would be acceptable in terms of convergent validity; however, the scale is also correlated with the North American Depression Inventory for Children (r = .82) and the Culture-Free Self-Esteem Inventory (r = -.68). Form M was correlated with the Taylor Anxiety Scale for Adults (r = .75) and the Nervous Symptoms subscale of the California Test of Personality (r = .63). Correlations with related constructs were as high or higher (r with the North American Depression Inventory for Adults = .89; r with the Culture Free Self-Esteem Inventory = -.77). The fact the scales are correlated as high or higher with measures of related constructs as with those of similar constructs is not discussed in terms of convergent/discriminant validity. Validity coefficients by gender indicated similar patterns for males and females, but no breakdown by age or race was reported.

T-tests indicated no significant gender differences on Form Q for the combined elementary and junior high sample. On Form M, females scored significantly higher than males (p = .04). However, the actual mean difference was slight. Data did not clearly support separate norms by gender.

As noted, there is no reporting of factor analyses, item-validity, alpha coefficients, or age changes. There are no group differences studies indicating the scales can distinguish between anxious and nonanxious persons. There are no treatment validity studies supporting pre-test/posttest changes in scores. There are no data to support use of individual items in diagnostic and treatment decisions or any predictive validity studies demonstrating the scales can predict actual behavior.

Administration is relatively straightforward. For Form Q, children respond in a Yes/No fashion; Form M has a 5-point Likert format, which allows for an examination of symptom intensity. Although the scales have a paper-and-pencil format, oral administration and modification of items are acceptable to increase comprehension for younger and lower-functioning persons. Group administration is also permissible, and there is a taped version available. Effects of alternate formats and administration techniques are not reported.

Raw scores are summed and classification tables based on these sums are recommended to label level of anxiety from very low to very high. There are also conversion tables for percentile ranks and *T*-scores. There is a small place on the protocol for recording the raw score, classification, percentile rank, and *T*-score. There is an adequate description of what percentile ranks and *T*-scores are, but discussion of their use for interpretation purposes is minimal. There are no classification tables based on standard scores and the justification for raw score classifications is not apparent. A comparison of the raw score classification tables to the raw to *T*-score conversion tables revealed that, for example, a *T*-score within +1 standard deviation from the mean would be indicative of "High" anxiety, and a *T*-score +1 or more standard deviations from the mean would be considered "Very High" anxiety. There is no discrimination between +1 and +2 standard deviations from the mean, and there is nothing relating scoring cutoffs to the traditionally accepted +2 standard deviations as being significantly different from average. Given the limited nature of the norm groups, standard scores should also be interpreted with caution and *SEM* should be utilized to take into consideration measurement error.

Although it is recommended that items be used for diagnostic and treatment purposes, there is no clear rationale or empirical support for this procedure. Given the lack of item representativeness and lack of subscales, it is not clear the scales have clinical utility even without using the scoring system. Perhaps using the scales as quick screeners or a way to elicit further information in an interview may be appropriate.

In summary, there are major theoretical and empirical limitations to the Anxiety Scales for Children and Adults. Most notably, sufficient test development was not reported, norms are inadequate, and validity for the purpose for which the scales are intended has not been demonstrated. Perhaps sufficient descriptions of the field work would suggest more support for the scales. Until such support is established, use of these scales cannot be recommended.

There is no caution, either in the manual or in the PRO-ED catalog description, of the limitations of these scales. In fact, according to the catalog: norms are based on 1,200 children and 600 adults (in contrast to the sample sizes of 798 and 247 reported in the manual); there is sufficient item validity to warrant use of each item as a "discrete anxiety trigger"; and a relationship with research conducted by Yamamoto (Yamamoto, Soliman, Parsons, & Davies, 1987) exists when no statistical comparisons to that data were made.

Readers are referred to the State-Trait Anxiety Inventory (T4:2563) and the Revised Children's Manifest Anxiety Scale (T4:2257) for measures specific to anxiety. The Fear Survey Schedule for Children—Revised can be used to determine relevant stimulus conditions (Ollendick, 1983). However, norms for all these instruments are outdated. For differential diagnosis, the Minnesota Multiphasic Personality Inventory (MMPI-2 [T4:1645] and MMPI-A [138]), the Multiple Affect Adjective Checklist, Revised Trait Form (T4:1690) and the Revised NEO Personality Inventory (330) should be considered for adults and adolescents. For children, the Child Behavior Checklist (T4:433) and the Behavior Assessment System for Children (T4:275) are recommended. See also Barrios and Hartmann (1988) for an extensive listing of children's measures of fear and anxiety.

REVIEWER'S REFERENCES

Ollendick, T. H. (1983). Reliability and validity of the Revised Fear Survey Schedule for Children (FSSC-R). *Behaviour Research and Therapy, 21*, 685-692.

Yamamoto, E., Soliman, A., Parsons, J., & Davies, O. L. (1987). Voices in unison: Stressful events in the lives of children in six countries. *Journal of Child Psychology and Psychiatry, 28*, 855-864.

Barrios, B. A., & Hartmann, D. P. (1988). Fears and anxieties. In E. J. Mash & L. G. Terdal (Eds.), *Behavioral assessment of childhood disorders* (pp. 196-262). New York: The Guilford Press.

[31]

The Arizona Battery For Communication Disorders of Dementia.

Purpose: To measure "the effects and severity of Alzheimer's Disease."

Population: Alzheimer's patients.

Publication Dates: 1991–93.

Acronym: ABCD.

Scores, 6: Mental Status, Episodic Memory, Linguistic Expression, Linguistic Comprehension, Visuospatial Construction, Total.

Administration: Individual.

Price Data, 1995: $200 per complete kit including manual (77 pages), scoring and interpretation card, 25 response record forms, stimulus book A, stimulus book B, and nail and envelope.

Time: (45–90) minutes.

Authors: Kathryn A. Bayles and Cheryl K. Tomoeda.

Publisher: Canyonlands Publishing, Inc.

Review of The Arizona Battery for Communicative Disorders of Dementia by CHARLES J. LONG, Profes-

sor of Psychology, and WENDY VAN WYHE, Research Assistant, Department of Psychology, The University of Memphis, Memphis, TN:

The Arizona Battery for Communicative Disorders of Dementia (ABCD) is designed to evaluate impairment in linguistic communication in patients suffering Alzheimer's Disease (AD) or other patients with cognitive-linguistic impairment. Administration is both written and oral and appears to be best suited for the evaluation of linguistic/cognitive functioning in patients with mild to moderate dementia without severe perceptual or linguistic deficits. The authors carefully address various problems that may render the test unreliable or invalid (e.g., speech discrimination deficit, visual perceptual problems, visual agnosia, illiteracy, depression, and apraxia), and the battery initially screens each patient to insure that he or she has sufficient auditory, visual, and linguistic functions for meaningful test performance.

The ABCD appears to have evolved from a considerable body of research which, during recent years, has demonstrated that AD patients have problems with speech initiative, preservation, and impoverished vocabulary, as well as exhibiting deficits in word naming, speech comprehension, word finding, verbal explanations, and visual recognition. A number of these studies have been conducted by the first author of the test battery.

The battery consists of four screening tasks and 15 subtests, and it requires 45 to 90 minutes to administer. Basic cognitive processes such as mental status, visual and auditory comprehension, and verbal episodic and semantic memory are assessed.

The testing stimulus books A and B are very functional. Large, labeled tabs separate the subtests, thus providing easy access to each test. The pages are thick, and print is high quality with high resolution. The pictures, too, are of excellent quality and clearly depict what they are intended to show. The binding is large and loose, and all pages can be turned easily and effortlessly. The examiner's booklet contains easy-to-understand information regarding the administration of each test and provides test rationale, standardization information, and references. The testing score sheets are clear, readable, and quite functional. All test blanks are clearly marked, and there is plenty of room for comments.

Scoring is adequately described, and the scoring reference guide indicates how the raw scores for each subtest are converted into summary scores (1 to 5) roughly based on percentiles. Selected summary scores are averaged to provide five construct scores representing Mental Status, Episodic Memory, Linguistic Expression, Linguistic Comprehension, and Visuospatial Construction. The average of the five constructs are summed to obtain a total overall score.

The standardization sample consisted of 86 patients with probable Alzheimer's Disease, whose performance was compared with 8 demented Parkinson's Disease subjects, 62 nondemented Parkinson's subjects, and 86 age-matched normal elderly individuals who served as controls. The cutoff value was selected to approximate the 5th percentile of normal performance. It is estimated that an undiagnosed individual performing below this cutoff value would be considered at risk for AD. The AD test scores fall significantly below the 5th percentile cutoff in nearly all the tests. It should be noted, however, that depressed individuals may perform within the demented range. The test administrator should carefully consider the contribution of a subject's emotional state when interpreting results.

There is a helpful interpretation score sheet that allows for comparisons of raw scores and summary scores to those of both young and old normal controls, mild AD, moderate AD, demented Parkinson's Disease, and nondemented Parkinson's Disease. However, the manual authors provide little information regarding the interpretation of the various scores. Missing is a discussion regarding which subtest(s), construct, or total scores should be used and which values provide the best discrimination. In fact, the authors indicate that scores in the demented range do not necessarily mean that the subject has dementia. The authors instead suggest that interpretation should be made by individuals who are knowledgeable of dementia syndrome and that two provided references should be consulted. The authors do, however, provide normative data that serve as reference points.

The authors discuss the use of four particular subtests for screening purposes. The Story Retelling (Delayed) and the three components of the Word Learning subtests are presented with suggested cutoff scores indicating significant differences in performance between normal elderly adults and AD patients. Although the performances of the two groups appears to differ greatly, there was little discussion as to the discriminative ability of the other subtests. If the Story Retelling and Word Learning subtests, for example, provide excellent discrimination between AD and controls, one wonders the purpose of the other subtests, although they may be important to answer more specific questions. The authors claim the test battery results provide information regarding the patient's ability to read, name, describe, define, repeat, make comparative judgments, follow commands, retell a story, recall and recognize words, copy figures, and draw; although, as the authors indicate, it may take an authority on dementias to draw conclusions on these abilities.

Interjudge reliability for four of the subtests (Concept Definition, Object Description, Figure Copying, and Generative Drawing) was reported to be around 93%. Both test-retest reliability and internal consistency of the subtests appear to be good. The four screening subtests also appear to correlate well with three accepted measures of dementia severity: the Global Deterioration Scale, Mini-Mental State Examination, and Wechsler Adult Intelligence Scale—Revised (WAIS-R) Block Design Subtest.

Overall the test battery appears to be well designed but has a number of limitations. For example, the examiner's manual lacks a discussion regarding pass-fail decisions on the visual field screening task. Furthermore, discussion of the five constructs is limited in the manual and there is a disappointing omission of a clear presentation or discussion of strategies for interpretation. The interpretation must be performed by someone knowledgeable of dementia. Unfortunately, the authors provide very little assistance with regard to how the specific scores on the various tests relate to the existing literature. Although most data presented relate to the ability of each subtest to discriminate between AD and controls, little mention is made of the five concepts or the overall score.

The battery appears to be a collection of modified versions of a dozen frequently used neuropsychological tests and was designed for ease of administration by technicians. If someone desires to have nice testing materials and a clear guide for standard scores on AD patient performance, then this test battery is worth the expense. However, for those persons who have infrequent contact with AD patients or who have access to numerous neuropsychological testing materials, the battery is unnecessary.

Review of The Arizona Battery for Communication Disorders of Dementia by KENNETH SAKAUYE, Associate Professor of Clinical Psychiatry, LSU Medical School in New Orleans, New Orleans, LA:

DESCRIPTION OF INSTRUMENT. The Arizona Battery for Communicative Disorders of Dementia (ABCD) contains screening tasks of speech discrimination, visual perception, literacy, visual field, and visual agnosia. Subtests are constructed in the following areas: (*a*) Mental Status; (*b*) Episodic Memory (Story Retelling, Immediate and Delayed); (*c*) Word Learning in three conditions: free recall, cued recall, and recognition; (*d*) Linguistic Expression (Object Description, Generative Naming, Confrontation Naming, Concept Definition); (*e*) Linguistics Comprehension (Following Commands, Comparative Questions, Repetition, Reading Comprehension); and (*f*) Visuospatial Construction (Generative Drawing, Figure Copying). One can assume from the content the subtests were constructed to provide more items relevant to the impaired population the test is designed to assess (i.e., a low floor).

METHOD OF ADMINISTRATION. Testing can be divided into sections to allow administration in several short sessions if needed. The Hamilton Depression Scale (HAM-D) and the Apraxia subtest of the Western Aphasia Battery are recommended to screen for depression and apraxia. In addition, screening for premorbid intelligence using an equation with demographic information by Wilson, Rosenbaum, and Brown is suggested. The estimated time needed to complete the full battery is 45–90 minutes.

CONTEXT OF DEVELOPMENT AND SUBSEQUENT USE. The current test is the research edition. The ABCD is still being given to patients with Alzheimer's Disease (AD) and other types of dementia to create a final normed edition based on these standardization studies. Although the context for the development of this test was not mentioned, the authors have stated that pragmatic language skills and communication deficits are among the most profound problems in AD. Deficits include difficulty maintaining conversation, empty discourse, imprecise answers to questions, reduced vocabulary, and dysnmoia in mildly demented patients, and progress to paraphasia, perseveration, and egocentric, irrelevant discourse. The test has not been used extensively beyond use by its developers.

SAMPLE. The ABCD was standardized using 50 AD subjects and 50 normal elderly control subjects matched for age, education, handedness, and estimated intelligence. AD subjects met NINCDS-ADRDA diagnostic criteria for AD. All were in good health. Mean, median, standard deviation, and interquartile ranges were computed for the samples. Recruitment of the standardization sample took 3 years.

SCORING. Raw scores are calculated following directions on response records. Raw scores are converted to summary scale scores ranging from 1–5. Construct scores of the five constructs (Mental Status, Episodic Memory, Linguistic Expression, Linguistic Comprehension, and Visuospatial Construction) are derived from the total summary scores of the subtests associated with each construct category. The overall performance score is obtained by summing the five construct scores. The authors note that depression can have profound negative effects on cognitive scores.

FORMAL TESTS OF RELIABILITY. Of the 50 AD patients, 20 were retested approximately 1 week after initial testing. Retest analyses show high test-retest correlations for most subtests. A lack of variability in Story Retelling-Delayed (0 for AD) prevented analyses on that item. Cronbach's alpha was calculated for subtests with discrete variables and predetermined ceiling scores to test item variance. Interitem reliability proved to be high. High interscorer reliability was found for the other ABCD measures for which the calculation of interitem reliability was inappropriate. For nine subtests, alpha exceeded .8.

FORMAL TESTS OF VALIDITY. Cutoff values for each subtest approximated the 5th percentile of normal performances based on the sample of 50 normal elderly. The null hypothesis that equal proportions of normal and AD subjects would fall below the specified cutoff was rejected with a two-sided $p<.0005$ using chi squared. Concurrent validity was established by correlating scores of 50 AD patients with the Global Deterioration Scale (GDS), Mini-Mental State Examination (MMSE), and Block Design subtests of the Wechsler Adult Intelligence Scale—Revised (WAIS-R). Most of the ABCD subtests are highly correlated with GDS, MMSE, and Block Design, at a P (of concordance) >.7. Story Retelling-Delayed was minimally correlated, perhaps due to the lack of variability of responses on this subtest.

USABILITY ON OLDER POPULATIONS. The test has been validated only for AD. Analyses of the specificity of error patterns in differential diagnosis are being conducted with Parkinson disease patients, stroke, and brain-injured patients with and without dementia.

GENERAL COMMENTS AND RECOMMENDATIONS. The manual lacks background on the development of the instrument and reasons for its development. It is not clear what benefit this battery has over the clinical approach of selecting one's own battery of "stand-alone" subtests from other scales such as the Wechsler Memory Scale—Revised (WMS-R), Boston Naming Test, and others that have established reliability and validity for both normal and clinical populations.

The benefits of the ABCD are its relative brevity and its clinical scoring approach, using cutoff scores to alert users to clinically important levels of dysfunction (set at the lower 5th percentile of normal performances). However, the absence of data on its ability to discriminate among various causes of cognitive impairment limits it to use as a research instrument for several more years.

[32]

ASPIRE (A Sales Potential Inventory for Real Estate).

Purpose: "A selection system developed . . . to aid in the selection of residential real estate sales associates."
Population: Real estate sales candidates.
Publication Dates: 1989–90.
Acronym: ASPIRE.
Scores: 1 overall rating plus 5 life history dimensions: Social Skills, Self-Assurance, Sales Disposition, Sales Environment Familiarity, Real Estate Career Commitment (Experienced Form only).
Administration: Group.
Forms, 2: Inexperienced, Experienced.
Price Data: Not available.
Time: (45) minutes.
Comments: Additional services available including Environmental Adequacy Report, Site Recruiting Report, ASPIRE Interview Guide, and New Sales Associate Tracking System; computer administered; all communication with the ASPIRE host system through electronic mail; IBM compatible PC required.
Author: Life Insurance Marketing and Research Association, Inc.
Publisher: Life Insurance Marketing and Research Association, Inc.
[The publisher advised in January 1994 that this test is now out of print.—Ed.]

Review of the ASPIRE (A Sales Potential Inventory for Real Estate) by CRAIG N. MILLS, Executive Director, Testing and Services, Graduate Record Examinations Program, Educational Testing Service, Princeton, NJ:

The purpose of ASPIRE (A Sales Potential Inventory for Real Estate) is to provide a valid biodata assessment for the selection of real estate sales persons. Two versions are available: an "Inexperienced" version, which consists of 67 items and an "Experienced" version, which contains the same 67 items plus 9 additional items related to previous sales performance. Little documentation was provided for this review, so much of it is based on assumptions derived from the information that was provided (a 10-page report entitled "A Sales Potential Inventory for Real Estate [ASPIRE]: Scoring Key Development and Validation").

TEST DEVELOPMENT AND SCORING. No information was provided to allow determination of the types of questions asked in the assessment. Similarly, the test development process was not described although the inventory apparently originally had more than 67 items. In the study described, items were retained if the item score correlated significantly with a criterion measure (a standardized measure of commissions earned in a 6-month period) for the study sample (the top and bottom two-thirds of a sample of "inexperienced" real estate sales persons). Items are scored on a scale ranging from +2 to -2, summed, and then converted to a 5-point total score. The manner in which scores are converted was not described. Four subscales are reported for the Inexperienced version. These scales were selected based on a factor analysis and a minimum internal consistency reliability of .60. Subscales are reported on a 3-point scale developed similarly to the total test 5-point scale. A fifth subscale is reported for the Experienced version based on the additional items in that test. The manner in which items were assigned to subscales is not described. Intercorrelations among subscales are not provided.

TEST USE. Although the test is designed to be used as a selection device, no information was provided concerning the manner in which the test results should be used. Correlations between test scores and success (where success is defined as being in the top 50% of the sample in commissions earned) are the only guidance provided. No cut score is mentioned nor is there any evidence that a cut score study was conducted.

TECHNICAL INFORMATION. Little technical information is provided. Overall test reliability is not reported. Score distributions are not included in the report. However, a small validation study is reported. The results of that study suggest that there may be value to this instrument, although there is certainly insufficient information provided upon which to base an adoption decision.

The validity study had three main components. In the first, data from 980 individuals were available. Two-thirds were selected as a "developmental" sample with the remaining third used for cross-validation. The developmental sample was again reduced to include only the "top" and "bottom" performers. This sample of 435 persons (from an initial survey mailing of 4,939) was used to establish item weights and score keys. For the entire development group, scores correlated .43 with commissions earned. The correlation was .30 for the cross-validation sample.

In the second component of the validation study, survey results collected for newly hired sales personnel were correlated with two measures of earned commissions (collected 6 and 12 months following administration of the survey). Samples were small (less than 200 in all analyses). The converted score correlations with the commissions variables ranged from .18 to .26 across the four analyses.

The third component of the study was administration of the experienced version of the instrument. However, it is unclear whether this was administered to the same sample used in the previous portions of the study or whether a second, truly experienced sample was drawn. If it was the former, the results should be discounted.

Tables are provided showing the percent of the sample that was successful for each converted score level. Although the tables provide comfort (the highest percent successful was for those with the highest converted score and the lowest success rate was for the lowest scoring group), no information about the distribution of scores is provided. As a result, the tables are only minimally useful.

No analyses are provided by gender or ethnic group. There should have been data for gender analyses (about two-thirds of the group was female), but additional data collection is needed before analyses by racial group can be conducted (only 47 minority individuals responded).

SUMMARY. ASPIRE (A Sales Potential Inventory for Real Estate) is an assessment designed to provide prospective employers with biographical information that will assist them in selecting real estate sales personnel. The results of a preliminary, small validation study suggest that the assessment may have some utility. However, there are clearly insufficient data to state that this is necessarily so. Furthermore, the lack of information concerning other important aspects of the test (how items were developed, relationship of the test to important job skills, technical information about the test, usefulness with subpopulations, score distributions, etc.) should make individuals wary of using it. At best, the information available suggests that there is sufficient promise to the measure that additional data should be collected and analyzed to determine whether or not the test can be used in real selection contexts.

[33]

Assessing Specific Competencies.

Purpose: Designed to assess examinees on skills related to employability and work maturity/job retention.
Population: Individuals seeking employment.
Publication Dates: 1984–93.
Administration: Group or individual.
Manual: No manual.
Time: (45–55) minutes.
Comments: Available on computer software; earlier version entitled Assessing Specific Employability Skill Competencies.
Author: Education Associates, Inc.
Publisher: Education Associates, Inc.

a) PRE-ASSESSING SPECIFIC COMPETENCIES.
Scores: 11 skill areas: Making Career Decisions, Using Labor Market Information, Developing a Resume, Completing an Application, Interviewing for a Job, Being Consistently Punctual, Maintaining Regular Attendance, Demonstrating Positive Attitudes/Behavior, Presenting Appropriate Appearance, Exhibiting Good Interpersonal Relations, Completing Tasks Effectively.
Price Data, 1993: $2.09 per pre-test; $129 per Apple or IBM pre-test diskette; $159 per Windows version.

b) POST-ASSESSING SPECIFIC COMPETENCIES.
Scores: Same as *a* above.
Price Data: $2.09 per post-test; $129 per Apple or IBM post-test diskette; $159 per Windows version.

Review of Assessing Specific Competencies by ROBERT FITZPATRICK, Consulting Industrial Psychologist, Cranberry Township, PA:

According to the publisher's catalog, the Assessing Specific Competencies (ASC) tests "establish the baseline of students' knowledge and document gains in the areas of employability skills and work maturity." The 11 skill areas are those specified by the U.S. Department of Labor for job training programs. It appears that students are normally at the high school level and age.

Almost 60% of the test items are true-false; the rest are multiple choice. Numbers of items vary from 13 for Maintaining Regular Attendance to 44 for Interviewing for a Job.

Many items appear to be carelessly or naively written and edited. A number of true-false items include more than one assertion. Some items contain or imply the answers to other items. A few items are duplicated, or nearly so, in the same test form. In some cases, wording is awkward or ungrammatical. Needed information is omitted and unnecessary detail included in some of the item stems. A few items seem to be placed in the wrong subtests.

It seems likely that scores on the tests are highly correlated with intelligence, scholastic achievement, and test-wiseness. This is probably unavoidable, but it would be helpful if the publisher gathered evidence to assess the extent to which it is true and tried to minimize that extent.

The tests are designed to be used with the publisher's training materials, but it is said that "they can be used successfully with any skills training program." A potential user is advised to review the content carefully. Much of the knowledge tested appears to be based on specific course content and style. One can infer from test items that the training materials teach students that, for example, tardiness is a form of dishonesty, that it is best to tackle difficult tasks before easy ones, and that a supervisor who takes all the credit and none of the blame is an "ego-maniac." Each of these assertions is perhaps defensible in the context of an elementary employability training course, but none of them would necessarily be a part of such a course.

The catalog implies that the pre- and post-tests are equivalent, though there seems to be no evidence of this beyond the general similarity of the items. The publisher seems to be suggesting that if a student scores higher on the post-test after training than on the pre-test before training the training has been successful. However, it is likely that only quite large score gains would be meaningful, in view of the general unreliability of gain scores and of the role played by chance in scores on multiple-choice and, especially, on true-false tests.

Some of the pre-test questions seem inappropriate because they deal with specific training content. For example, the publisher's training apparently suggests the use of "job lead cards" to help a job seeker keep track of various possible openings. Items on the pre-test ask about the use of job lead cards. These items would be difficult for an examinee who knows the technique but not the term.

For the printed versions of the tests, no specific directions are provided for either the test administrator or the examinee. No time limits are specified, nor is the examinee advised whether to guess when he or she does not know the correct answer to an item. Answers are to be marked directly on the test booklets, and scoring is by hand. Scores are number correct for each subtest, with no correction for guessing.

Limited directions are given with the computer versions. At the completion of each subtest, the computer displays number and percent correct for the examinee.

The publisher offers training—or retraining—recommendations for examinees with scores judged to be less than satisfactory. For each skill area (or subtest) of the post-test, the cutoff is set at approximately 70% correct. This percentage is said to be mandated by a Labor Department regulation, and hence to be a necessity for government-supported programs. Nevertheless, it is a dubious practice. The problem of setting a meaningful passing score for this type of test is a severe one, but one which the publisher must be asked to undertake. An alternative, even more challenging, would be to adjust the average difficulty level of the items, so that 70% is a rational cutoff point.

The deficiency is compounded for the pre-test, for each subtest of which the publisher suggests 5 separate cutoffs. The lowest cutoff in each case has been set to be a little higher than 70% of the items, the next one in the high 70 percents, then the mid-80s, the next one in the low 90s, and the final at or near 100%. Each cutoff comes with a recommendation that the student complete one or more of the publisher's training modules. It is completely implausible that the subtests measure with sufficient precision to support so many cutoffs. Also disturbing is the fact that the low cutoff is more severe for the pre-test than for the post-test. Thus, for example, a student who has sat through the training and misses seven items on the post-test for Completing Tasks Effectively gets exactly the same recommendation as the untutored examinee who takes the pre-test for the same skill area and misses six items.

No information about reliability, validity, or norms has been published at this writing. However, studies are said to be under way to provide some information of this sort. Preliminary data that were made available for this review suggest that reliability may be satisfactory for each test as a whole, and marginally so for the subtests. Potential users are advised to contact the publisher. It is to be hoped that the publisher will provide a manual, along with revised versions of the tests, when the studies in progress are completed.

In a general way, the content of the items appears to be appropriate for evaluation of an elementary orientation to job hunting and good work habits. Thus, some users are likely to find the tests in their current form to have an adequate degree of content-related validity. One might question whether a purely cognitive understanding of the work world will translate into appropriate behaviors in seeking and retaining a job. But the knowledge is obviously necessary, however insufficient.

It is unfortunately rare for trainers to seriously evaluate the learning of their students and the effectiveness of their training efforts. The ASC tests represent a laudable effort in this direction, although an extensive pruning and editing of the items is needed. Some evidence concerning norms, reliability, and validity of the tests is expected to become available. For those who are engaged in this type of training and need an objective paper-and-pencil test of trainee knowledge for either pre- or post-training use, a review of content relevance and up-to-date evidence of functioning for the ASC tests is recommended.

Review of Assessing Specific Competencies by ROBERT C. REINEHR, Professor of Psychology, Southwestern University, Georgetown, TX:

Assessing Specific Competencies is a 318-item self-administered scale divided into 11 content areas related to employability (the original name of the scale is Assessing Specific Employability Skill Competencies). The scale is provided in both a written version and on a computer diskette. The only instructions provided pertain to how to make the diskette version run on a personal computer. There is no manual, and no information is provided about the intended user population, the characteristics of the scores obtained, or the publications and software referred to in the recommendations section of the test.

The written version of the scale comes with a scoring key and a face sheet labeled "pre-test," that contains a brief section for recording the participant's name, address, social security number, telephone number, and the name of the school or training program. Although the scale is self-administered, the space below the demographic information is reserved for the use of an instructor, implying that the scale is not to be self-interpreted.

For each summary score, there are three different possible recommendations, each of which refers the respondent to further study with specified written material or with a specified software package. Neither the written material nor the software is furnished with the test materials and no information is furnished regarding the sources from which these materials may be obtained. The diskette-based version applies the same scoring criteria as the written version and offers the same range of possible recommendations.

The scale consists of 11–12 true-false questions and 4–6 multiple-choice questions for each of the 11 competencies. The written version is printed in a low-contrast color that makes it difficult to read in any but the best lighting conditions. The software version is reasonably easy to use, but is extremely plain and almost entirely without visual appeal. Unlike the written version, the software version of the scale provides the respondent with the correct answer immediately after every question is answered. it also offers encouraging comments ("great job," "way to go") when the correct answer is given to a multiple-choice item.

This instrument has very little to recommend it. No information is provided regarding reliability or validity and no normative information of any sort is included in the test package. There is no information provided concerning the target population or to the manner in which the instrument is intended to be utilized. There is no way for a user to make use of, or even to understand, the recommendations. The written version is poorly organized and poorly printed, and the software version has the unprofessional appearance of a Shareware product or of a product in development. The lack of accompanying documentation renders both the written and software versions essentially useless to users unfamiliar with the instrument.

[34]

Assessment of Conceptual Organization (ACO): Improving Writing, Thinking, and Reading Skills.

Purpose: Developed to assess "understanding of conceptual organization in written language."
Population: Grades 4–6, 7–12, 10–adult.
Publication Date: 1991.
Acronym: ACO.
Scores: 3 criteria: Correct Superordinate Word Chosen, Appropriateness of Topic Sentence, Relatedness of Topic Sentence and Three Other Sentences.
Administration: Group.
Price Data, 1991: $24.95 per set of 20 assessment and 20 scoring forms (select level); $29.95 per manual (57 pages).
Time: (15–20) minutes.
Comments: Optional administration and scoring procedures available for "reluctant" writers.
Author: Christian Gerhard.
Publisher: Research for Better Schools.

Review of the Assessment of Conceptual Organization (ACO): Improving Writing, Thinking, and Reading Skills by DEBORAH L. BANDALOS, Assistant Professor of Educational Psychology, University of Nebraska-Lincoln, Lincoln, NE:

The Assessment of Conceptual Organization (ACO) was developed to provide "classroom teachers, resource personnel, and tutors with a practical way of determining whether students have a usable understanding of how ideas are organized" (p. 1). Three lists of related words are provided from which the examinee is required to choose one to use in composing a paragraph. In each list of words, one word is designated as the organizing or "superordinate" word. Examinees are instructed to determine which of the words fits this role, and to use it in forming the first sentence of a paragraph. The other words are to be used in separate sentences which make up the remainder of the paragraph. An example of a typical set of words is "table, chair, bed, furniture," where "furniture" would be the superordinate word. There are three form levels: basic, for grades 4 through 6; intermediate, for middle or high school range; and advanced, for more advanced high school students or adults. The forms differ only in the number and difficulty of the words given.

Development of the ACO was based on the theory that categorization skills are fundamental to the ability to organize one's perceptions as well as to process and convey information. Extensive work with teachers and students in formulating ways of teaching and measuring these skills led to the development of the instrument.

The ACO is intended for use as a classroom assessment device and all scoring is done by the classroom teacher. Students are assessed on three criteria: correct selection of the superordinate word, writing an appropriate topic sentence, and writing three (or more) related sentences. Each criterion is rated as either met or not met. Instructions including examples of unsatisfactory sentences are provided for this assessment, followed by a very useful section on using the results in class. However, because assessment depends entirely on the judgement of the teacher, the consistency of these ratings is questionable. The possibility of halo and leniency effects in particular is a concern, particularly as no information on reliability or any other psychometric information is provided in the manual. Although interrater reliability is of primary importance in an instrument of this type, test-retest reliability estimates would also be of interest.

The lack of psychometric information mentioned previously also extends to area of validity. This subject is not addressed specifically in the manual, although two studies are alluded to in describing the development of the instrument. In one study done by the test author, chi-square tests were used to show that ACO scores were not related to age, race, gender, reading comprehension, or vocabulary scores on a standardized test, or with the similarities, block design, or performance scales of the Wechsler Intelligence Scale for Children. Aside from the fact that the chi-square test would not appear to be appropriate for some of these analyses, it is not clear how these relationships, or the lack of them, bears on the usefulness of the ACO.

The ACO appears to be a well thought out instrument based on a great deal of practical experience. However, it cannot be recommended for general use at this time because of the lack of norms or of any form of reliability or validity evidence.

Review of the Assessment of Conceptual Organization (ACO): Improving Writing, Thinking, and Reading Skills by DALE P. SCANNELL, Professor of Education, Indiana University and Purdue University at Indianapolis, Indianapolis, IN:

The Assessment of Conceptual Organization (ACO): Improving Writing, Thinking, and Reading Skills is a very good example of the current emphasis on trying to relate assessments more closely to the activities of classroom teachers and others who work directly with students. The scores produced by this assessment are a set of judgments made by the person who administers the instrument. In some cases, the accuracy of the judgment is quite apparent (e.g., the correct word was identified). In other cases, the judgments are more subjective (e.g., the sentence written by the examinee was appropriate).

Each test is a single page; examinees enter identifying information at the top. The directions tell examinees they will be writing a paragraph using words in one of three groups presented below. Examinees choose the group, identify the word in the list that is the organizing concept for the other words, and then write a paragraph of a specified number of sentences using all of the words in the list. Space is provided for examinees to write the title word and to write the paragraph.

Scoring includes a yes/no decision about the superordinate word, the topic sentence, and whether the sentences are appropriately related to each other. Examiners are to record how many hints they had to give and are to assess behaviors of the examinees during the test.

The quality of instruments such as this can be judged in terms of the research and theory that provide the foundation for the assessment and the appropriateness of the suggestions made for the use of the information produced by the test. These topics are covered in a well-written, comprehensive, and persuasive manual for the ACO.

The manual includes a section on categorization. The importance of this skill in learning and using knowledge and how the skill can be assessed are covered. The research background is described briefly and includes attention to the theoretical background and research conducted by the author and others.

The manual also includes a section in which the instrument is described and instructions for administration are provided. These are quite adequate and well written. The section of the manual describing how the results of the assessment can be used in class is also well done.

Some might classify this instrument as an instructional device rather than as a test. Regardless, this instrument is presented as a means of collecting information to assist teachers in targeting instruction more appropriately for students who most likely will be at different levels of skill in categorizing and presenting ideas in writing. It fulfills its purported purpose admirably.

[35]

Assessment of Core Goals.

Purpose: Constructed to define core goals and to identify activities that will lead to satisfaction of these goals.
Population: High school and over.
Publication Date: 1991.
Acronym: ACG.
Scores: No scores.
Administration: Group or individual.
Price Data, 1994: $40 per sampler set; $90 per one-year permission to reproduce workbook and manual (38 pages).

Time: (60–600) minutes.
Comments: Method and length of administration depends on desired depth of information.
Author: C. W. Nichols.
Publisher: Mind Garden.

Review of the Assessment of Core Goals by GARY J. DEAN, Associate Professor and Department Chairperson, Department of Counseling, Adult Education, and Student Affairs, Indiana University of Pennsylvania, Indiana, PA:

GENERAL COMMENTS. The Assessment of Core Goals (ACG) is a nonstandardized interactive process that consists of a 37-page workbook ($15 each) and a 33-page manual ($20 each). The ACG can be administered in a variety of settings and for several different purposes. According to the author the "primary purpose of the ACG is to help a person define his or her core goals accurately enough so that they can be used to identify activities that will lead to satisfaction or diagnose the sources of current dissatisfaction" (manual, p. 3). All uses of the ACG revolve around this stated purpose.

THEORETICAL BASIS. The ACG is based on the concept that each individual has certain unique core goals. The author provides a lengthy definition of core goals consisting of the following elements: Core goals are cognitive representations of desired consequences; they represent internal emotional states; they are individual constructions not universal constructs; they must be desired as ends in themselves, not as means to achieving other more important or basic goals; they are highly stable over time; each person has a limited set of core goals (usually one to five); they have both positive and negative aspects; strong positive or negative feeling may be triggered by the attainment of a core goal; and core goals function outside of conscious awareness.

Several points should be considered when evaluating the theoretical base of the ACG. The author builds a strong argument for the concept of core goals in the manual but does state that core goals is a relatively new theoretical construct. One premise of core goals is that they are unique to each person. The author places them in juxtaposition to the concept of universal human goals (or needs) as described by theoreticians like Maslow. He also states the ACG was developed from clinical practice based on a previous instrument given to over 2,000 people. Several questions can be raised regarding the core goals identified for those 2,000 cases: Was there evidence of repetition of core goals among the respondents? What is the relationship of those core goals to the universal hierarchy of needs identified by Maslow (in other words, can the core goals be restated in Maslow's terms)? What relationships exist between core goals and basic human emotions? These are not trivial points because the validity of the ACG rests on the assumption that core goals are unique for each person. Another relevant question is: Are there a finite set of core goals which every person experiences somewhat differently due to differences in genetic makeup and life experiences?

Another concern is in defining what is and what is not a core goal. The author states that core goals are ends in themselves and not means to achieving other goals. Nevertheless, examples of core goals provided in the workbook and manual can be interpreted in light of Maslow's hierarchy or other universal needs and goals systems. For example, the core goal "to feel that others care" can be seen as instrumental to achieving a sense of belongingness (or perhaps it is a restatement of that need). It would appear that more research is needed to fully establish the viability of the core goal concept.

ADMINISTRATION AND TARGET AUDIENCE. Administration can be accomplished in a variety of formats. The author outlines five formats: 1-hour group administration, 3-hour group administration, 6–8-hour group administration, 3–6-hour individual administration (in 1-hour counseling sessions), and 6–10 hours of individual counseling sessions. The shorter formats serve to introduce the core goal concept to participants or allow them to explore their core goals in a cursory manner. The more in-depth formats promote a more thorough understanding of one's core goals.

The target population is "a broad range of people from high school students to retired individuals" (manual, p. 3). The author does note some caveats, however, in the use of the ACG with some individuals. People who may have more difficulty than others in completing the ACG include those with: limited life experiences, reading levels below the ninth grade, less ability to focus, a tendency to repress or deny aspects of self, lower overall intelligence (including memory), and less motivation to identify their goals. (It should be noted that this list was compiled from two different sections of the manual, pages 3 and 27.) The author recommends individual counseling over group administration and an extended number of sessions over a brief review of the process. From the reviewer's experience it would appear that these caveats regarding the target population and administration formats are appropriate.

No special training is required to administer the ACG. The author recommends only that the helper be familiar with the ACG, be able to identify patterns of experiences and affective responses, and be able to define core goals. Nevertheless, it would appear that counselors may need considerable guided experience in order to do these activities with insight, caring, and reliability.

PROCEDURE AND APPLICATIONS. The workbook contains a four-step procedure for identifying core goals: listing satisfying activities and experiences, examining each experience closely, identifying core goals, and defining the positive and negative side of the core goals. Each step in the workbook consists of a carefully prepared series of steps. The directions in the workbook are encouraging and quite clear and easy to follow. The examples in the back of the workbook are helpful, especially for individuals attempting to complete the process on their own. The grids, charts, and diagrams in the workbook provide a visual display that aids in the self-exploration activities. In Step 1, the individual is asked to identify up to 25 life experiences that have provided a great deal of satisfaction. In Step 2, 15 of the experiences are selected and analyzed in-depth. This analysis involves making the experience as specific as possible and then identifying the feelings associated with the experience. In Step 3 the experiences are grouped based on like feelings and then core goals are identified from the feelings. In Step 4, the positive and negative aspects of each core goal are identified.

Five applications of the ACG are identified in the manual: to increase satisfaction in current activities, to identify new satisfying activities, to decide among options, to increase self-knowledge, and to define and understand one's experience. Each of these applications depends on different uses of the knowledge gained from identifying one's core goals. The author claims that people who have completed the ACG gain a better understanding of themselves and their behavior. No research, however, is cited to support this contention.

CONCLUSION. The four-step process outlined in the workbook is clear and can be used in a variety of formats as suggested by the author. Because the ACG is not a standardized test in the traditional sense, the validity of the instrument rests on its theoretical foundation. Despite the lack of theoretical clarity and evidence of the instrument's benefits, the ACG may have some positive applications. It may be useful for the purposes identified and with the target audience as specified (with the caveats). The amount of supervision required to use the ACG and its cost may indicate a somewhat selective use of the instrument. If the ACG can increase self-understanding and possibly lead to more effective behavior, its use could be justified.

Review of the Assessment of Core Goals by CAROL KEHR TITTLE, Professor of Educational Psychology, Graduate School, City University of New York, New York, NY:

The Assessment of Core Goals (ACG) is "a structured process of self-inquiry designed to guide a person to a definition of his or her unique and most important sources of satisfaction" (manual, p. 4). Core goals are defined as representing desired internal emotional states (e.g., wanting to feel a sense of belonging or to feel an increased sense of self-direction). The ACG is described as most appropriate for individuals who have more life experience (than high school students), have self-knowledge, and have at least a ninth grade reading level.

The workbook consists of a sequence of instructions and worksheets. The worksheets are intended to: list satisfying experiences, identify best moments and associated feelings, group the experiences, identify core goals, describe positive and negative sides of core goals, and apply knowledge of core goals. The workbook also has supplementary text to aid in getting started and to provide examples of the process of arriving at core goals. The manual author presents several alternatives for administration, ranging from a 1-hour general introduction, a 3-hour working session identifying several core goals, a 1-day group workshop or individual administrations, to long-term individual counseling.

The manual author identifies theoretical constructs related to the ACG. However, there are few empirical or clinical data presented to argue for the validity—meaning and use—of the ACG. Results of using an early version of part of the ACG are mentioned but not documented. A single-subject design study (nine persons) used experts to evaluate whether work-related distressing episodes were due to frustration of core goals. As pointed out in the manual, the ACG is a *process*. Although potential users may not expect to see reliability data, they may justifiably expect to find construct-related validity evidence, clinical case studies, and validity-related data on individual learning (change or development) processes as a function of the different administration procedures recommended. Other validity-related evidence would be based on use of the ACG by counselors in practice, and their treatment or outcome findings.

Overall, use of the ACG requires a skilled counselor who finds the ACG has a theoretical framework and structured set of procedures that are meaningful to her or him, and who works with college-educated individuals or groups who are highly motivated. Individuals are unlikely to complete the ACG on their own because of its length and complexity. Counselors who focus on career, vocational or work-related goals, interests, and values have a variety of instruments to use that provide extensive validity-related evidence (e.g., Katz, 1993), in contrast to the virtual absence of validity data for the ACG.

REVIEWER'S REFERENCE

Katz, M. R. (1993). *Computer-assisted decision making: The guide in the machine.* Hillsdale, NJ: Lawrence Erlbaum Associates.

[36]

The Assessment of Phonological Processes—Revised.

Purpose: Designed to identify and evaluate the severity of phonological disorders.

Population: Preschool children, ages 9–10.

Publication Date: 1986.
Acronym: APP-R.
Scores, 13: Phonological Omissions (Syllable Reduction, Consonant Sequence Reduction, Consonant Singleton Omissions [Prevocalic, Postvocalic]), Class Deficiencies (Stridents, Velar Obstruents, Liquid-l, Liquid-r, Nasals, Glides), Total, Phonological Deviancy Score, Severity Interval Rating for Phonology; Miscellaneous Error Patterns also available.
Administration: Individual.
Levels, 2: Preschool, Multisyllabic.
Price Data, 1994: $69 per complete kit including 50 Phonological Screening Forms—Preschool, 50 Phonological Screening Forms—Multisyllabic, 50 recording forms, 50 Analysis of Phonological Processes Forms, 50 Phonological Analysis Summary Forms, and examiner's manual (92 pages); $9 per 50 screening forms; $9 per 50 recording forms; $9 per 50 analysis forms; $9 per 50 analysis summary forms; $21 per manual.
Time: (15–20) minutes.
Comments: Several additional items needed for administration must be supplied by examiner.
Author: Barbara Williams Hodson.
Publisher: PRO-ED, Inc.
Cross References: See T4:220 (4 references); for a review by Sheldon L. Stick of an earlier version, see 9:91 (1 reference).

Review of the Assessment of Phonological Processes—Revised by ALLAN O. DIEFENDORF, Associate Professor, MICHAEL K. WYNNE, Associate Professor, and KATHY KESSLER, Clinical Lecturer, Department of Otolaryngology, Indiana University School of Medicine, Indianapolis, IN:

The original Assessment of Phonological Processes (APP) was created to assess phonological processes in children's speech. The test was specifically designed to provide clinicians a measurement tool to evaluate the phonological processes produced by highly unintelligible children and a direction for planning remediation. The revised version of this protocol, the Assessment of Phonological Processes—Revised (APP-R), has major changes that evolved as the result of ongoing clinical research in schools, clinics, and universities. It was designed to meet speech-language pathologists' needs to have a phonological assessment instrument that (*a*) is quick and easy to administer; (*b*) indicates the presence, nature, and severity of any phonological disorder; (*c*) provides a direction for planning intervention; and (*d*) addresses efficacy issues of the remediation program. Revisions to the 50 stimulus words have yielded targets that are more appropriate to the vocabulary level of preschool children while maintaining similar phonetic structures and scoring opportunities for occurrences of phonological processes. All English consonants are included in the stimulus words, and each word allows the assessment of more than one phonological process, providing at least 10 opportunities to measure the occurrences for each omission or class deficiency phonological process. The assessment protocol contains both monosyllabic and multisyllabic stimulus words, with several words containing common consonant clusters. The APP-R presents a simplified analysis form compared to the analysis form found in the original APP, requiring less time to complete. A multisyllabic screening protocol has been added for older elementary school children who have difficulties producing complex multisyllabic words. Finally, the revised version offers a formula for calculating severity ratings based on the degree of intelligibility of the child's speech, the estimated total remediation time required for the child to achieve intelligible speech, and the child's chronological age. Although a complete set of picture stimuli and objects is not provided by the test kit, the stimulus words can be readily found in pictures in many magazines and most of the objects can be obtained at a very reasonable cost at most discount department stores.

After the stimulus items have been elicited through picture and/or object identification, a brief continuous speech sample has been obtained, and the speech samples have been transcribed and verified, the transcriptions are transferred to an analysis form using the guidelines described in the manual. Deviations from the appropriate speech pattern for each word are scored in columns that correspond to the phonological processes specific to that pattern. Ten omission and class deficiency categories are provided and described in adequate detail for scoring. Miscellaneous error patterns can be recorded in any one of 16 phonemic substitution categories, 5 assimilation categories, 3 voicing alterations, 2 place shifts, and/or in another error patterns/preferences category. Percent-of-Occurrence Scores are determined from the 10 omission and class deficiency categories that form the basic phonological processes. Taking an "average" of these scores and adjusting them for age and other speech factors, a Phonological Deviancy Score is computed and a Severity Interval ranging from mild to profound is determined. Although the miscellaneous phonological error process scores do not contribute to the Phonological Deviancy Score and Severity Interval, they are useful in determining stimulus items in therapy and provide an additional measure of speech intelligibility and efficacy of the remediation program.

The manual does not contain any descriptions or references regarding the reliability of the APP-R. Reliability data are presented in research studies and suggest excellent intra- and interrater reliability; however, these studies used individuals who received extensive training in the protocol from the author. Information is not available describing the reliability of raters who did not receive this training. These issues are not isolated to the application of the APP-R as most measures of phonological systems are influenced by these problems.

An accurate, reliable, and valid assessment of phonological processes in the speech of children is based on several critical assumptions. The violation of any of these assumptions may likely lead to erroneous results and inappropriate interpretations. First, the clinician should be familiar with phonetics and phonetic transcription, which in turn is dependent on the clinician's ability to hear and recognize phonetic differences. Additionally, the clinician should be familiar with the speech sound systems present in the language of phonologically normal children, considering the language and cultural diversity across populations of children. Finally, phonological assessment should be part of a comprehensive evaluation of the child's communication system. This evaluation should assess aspects such as general functioning, hearing, structure and integrity of the speech mechanism, voice, fluency, language, and pragmatics.

The strength of the APP-R lies in the direction it provides the clinician in planning and carrying out a remediation program for a child's phonological disorder. As an integral component to the cycles phonological remediation approach (Hodson, 1985, 1989; Hodson & Paden, 1991), the APP-R manual contains a brief introduction to the author's approach to phonological remediation. However, we found that reading the Hodson and Paden (1991) text greatly eased the transition between assessment and remediation. Moreover, for many inexperienced clinicians, the Hodson text would be highly recommended prior to APP-R administration.

The APP and the APP-R have also successfully been used to describe the phonological analysis of the speech produced by children from culturally diverse populations (Cabello, Contreras, & Hodson, 1987; Hodson, Diamond, Meza, Cornejo, & Becker, 1987; Nye, 1987) and of the speech produced by children with other concomitant communication disorders (Churchill, Hodson, Jones, & Novak, 1988; Gordon-Brannan, Hodson, & Wynne, 1992; Hodson, Chin, Redmond, & Simpson, 1983; McMahon, Hodson, & Allen, 1983). A third strength of the APP-R is its accompanying screening protocols. With the preschool and multisyllabic screening protocols, the clinician is provided with a broad base of identification and assessment protocols designed to evaluate a child's speech skills.

The major weakness of the APP-R is the lack of empirical data describing its validity and reliability. The author acknowledges the manual's lack of data describing normal phonological systems in children, but she identifies several resources that contain this information. Unfortunately, examiners who are unfamiliar with this research or who are unable to review these resources may invalidate test interpretation based on their own inexperience.

In summary, the APP-R is a useful clinical assessment instrument for identifying, evaluating, and planning the remediation of phonological disorders in children. It was designed by a clinician for clinicians. After several assessments with this protocol, we were impressed by the quantity and quality of the information provided by this test. The APP-R is highly recommended for clinicians who provide evaluations and remediation programs for children within phonological disorders.

REVIEWERS' REFERENCES

Hodson, B. W., Chin, L., Redmond, B., & Simpson, R. (1983). Phonological evaluation and remediation of speech deviations of a child with a repaired cleft palate: A case study. *Journal of Speech and Hearing Disorders, 48*, 93-98.

McMahon, K., Hodson, B., & Allen, E. (1983). Phonological analysis of cerebral palsied children's utterances. *Journal of Childhood Communication Disorders, 7*, 25-31.

Hodson, B. (Author). (1985). Basis of Phonological remediation [Videotape]. Bellingham, WA: VTI Videotapes.

Cabello, A., Contreras, S., & Hodson, B. (1987). Salvadorean and Mexican-American children's phonological systems: Intelligible and unintelligible. In L. Cole, V. R. Deal, M. Fain, A. Massey, & M. McIntosh (Eds.), *Minority focus: Selected abstracts for ASHA conventions 1980-1990* (p. 79). Rockville, MD: American Speech-Language-Hearing Association.

Hodson, B., Diamond, F., Meza, P., Cornejo, R., & Becker, M. (1987). Phonological analysis of Spanish utterances of Mexican-American children. In L. Cole, V. R. Deal, M. Fain, A. Massey, & M. McIntosh (Eds.), *Minority focus: Selected abstracts from ASHA conventions 1980-1990* (p. 27). Rockville, MD: American Speech-Language-Hearing Association.

Nye, C. (1987). Assessing language development in Native American Navajo children. In L. Cole, V. R. Deal, M. Fain, A. Massey, & M. McIntosh (Eds.), *Minority focus: Selected abstracts from ASHA conventions 1980-1990* (p. 113). Rockville, MD: American Speech-Language-Hearing Association.

Churchill, J. D., Hodson, B. W., Jones, B. W., & Novak, R. E. (1988). Phonological systems of speech-disordered clients with positive/negative histories of otitis media. *Language, Speech, and Hearing Services in Schools, 19*, 100-107.

Hodson, B. (1989). Phonological remediation: A cycles approach. In N. A. Creaghead, P. W. Newman, & W. A. Secord (Eds.), *Assessment and remediation of articulatory and phonological disorders* (2nd ed.) (pp. 323-333). Columbus, OH: Merrill.

Hodson, B. W., & Paden, E. P. (1991). *Targeting intelligible speech: A phonological approach to remediation* (2nd ed.). Austin, TX: PRO-ED.

Gordon-Brannan, M., Hodson, B., & Wynne, M. K. (1992). Remediation unintelligible utterances of a child with a mild hearing loss. *American Journal of Speech-Language Pathology, 1*, 28-38.

Review of the Assessment of Phonological Processes—Revised by KATHRYN W. KENNEY, Director, Kenney Associates, Certified Speech-Language Pathologists, Gilbert, AZ:

The Assessment of Phonological Processes (APP) was first published in 1980 and has been reviewed (Stick, 1985). The reader may find it helpful to refer to the review of the earlier version of the APP because many aspects of the test remain unchanged. The comments in the original review are appropriate for the 1986 revisions with exceptions for changes in test construction which will be examined in detail in this review. Other features of the APP including validity and reliability remain essentially unchanged.

The Assessment of Phonological Processess—Revised (APP-R) published in 1986 consists of a manual, two sets of pictures, and five packets of phonological forms. Differences between the original and revised versions include changes in the test stimuli and recording forms. Five of the original test items have been eliminated (doll, rouge, spring, that, and tub). Another seven words (bed, gun, quarter, rug, sled, smooth, and squirrel) have been replaced with new test stimuli that have phonetic structures similar to the original (boats, gum, queen, rock, slide, smoke, and square). The new stimuli are purported to provide comparable opportunities for the occurrence of phonological processes. The result is a revised APP-R consisting of 50 stimulus words. Picture cards are provided for 12 of the 50 APP-R stimulus words for which it may be difficult to find objects (basket, cowboy hat, ice cubes, jump rope, music box, queen, Santa Claus, slide, smoke, square, television, and vase). As in the earlier version the author still recommends the use of objects to elicit responses and indicates that objects are not provided with the test due to cost constraints.

The analysis form which allows the clinician to identify specific phonological processes has been simplified. The new form includes slightly different categorizations and has been reorganized to facilitate scoring. The new categories include two types of basic processes: Omissions and Class Deficiencies. There are four types of omissions: Syllable, Consonant Sequence, Prevocalic Singleton, and Postvocalic Singleton. The six class deficiencies include: Stridents, Velar Obstruents, Liquid (l), Liquid (r), Nasals, and Glides. Miscellaneous processes are organized into 14 phonemic substitutions, 5 assimilations, 3 voice alterations, 2 place shifts, and a category including all "other pattern error pattern preferences." Eliminating 5 test stimuli and 12 processes has provided room for the print to be enlarged making this form much easier to use. It has also been reorganized so that similar processes are clustered together on the left hand side of the analysis form. This should facilitate the transfer of data from the recording form to the analysis form. A scoring key has been provided along with two examples of completed analysis forms to aid examiners in learning the complex scoring procedure. As with the original APP, additional examples on how to score the test would still be helpful. Computer software is available to complete the phonological analysis; however, it is not included with the test. The software was tried and it is a nice improvement over the original manual scoring system.

A significant change in scoring has been the establishment of a formula for calculating severity ratings. The author states the formula evolved from the study of degree of unintelligibility, total remediation time to achieve intelligibility, and chronological age for several hundred clients. The formula is based upon percentage-of-occurrence scores for the basic processes plus compensatory points based on age, average phonological process use, and frequency of occurrence of backing. Severity intervals have been designated as mild, moderate, severe, and profound. Details on how the Severity Interval was formulated or data to support its validity or reliability are lacking.

A further change has been simplification of the preschool screening protocol. The preschool screening tool consists of 12 items (boats, fork, glasses, gum, leaf, nose, rock, soap, spoon, star, watch, and zipper), 8 less than the original version. The author reports the words in the revised edition are familiar to most children prior to age 3. Transcription is provided for the target stimuli and analyses include consonant omissions and class deficiencies for stridents, velars, and liquids. Room is provided on the form to record other error patterns.

A Multisyllabic Screening Protocol has been added to the APP-R. The protocol consists of a recording sheet and an 8.5-inch X 11-inch posterboard containing pictures of the 12 stimuli (aluminum foil, fire extinguisher, hippopotamus, jewelry box, measuring spoons, movie projector, refrigerator, Sleeping Beauty, spaghetti, stethoscope, telephone message, and thermometer). The protocol is designed for "older elementary-school children who evidence difficulty producing complex multisyllabic words when reading" (p. x). A recording sheet is provided with room for phonetic transcription of the stimuli. Productions are analyzed for consonant omissions in singletons and sequences, metathesis migration, assimilation, and/or other patterns.

The author's stated purpose of the APP-R remains the same: to develop a phonological assessment instrument for children with highly unintelligible speech. Although the author has made several improvements in test construction, information on reliability, validity, and normative data lacking in the original APP are still not provided. This is unfortunate because the test has been nicely improved in other areas and it has the potential to become a highly useful tool for clinical treatment and research.

SUMMARY. The APP-R has face validity and much effort was spent on test construction. However, little or no information is provided on any type of validity, reliability, or normative evidence making it difficult to recommend use of the APP-R. Although it also has limitations, the Khan-Lewis Phonological Analysis (Kahn & Lewis, 1986; T4:1356) is a better standardized instrument. It was normed on 852 children from age 2-0 through 5-11 and includes information on both validity and reliability.

REVIEWER'S REFERENCES

Stick, S. L. (1985). [Review of the Assessment of Phonological Processes]. In James V. Mitchell, Jr. (Ed.), *The ninth mental measurements yearbook* (pp. 98-100). Lincoln, NE: Buros Institute of Mental Measurements.

Khan, L. M. L., & Lewis, N. P. (1986). Khan-Lewis Phonological Analysis. Circle Pines, MN: American Guidance Service.

[37]

Athletic Motivation Inventory.

Purpose: Constructed to measure the personality and motivation of athletes participating in competitive sports.

Population: Male and female athletes ages 13 and older and coaches.
Publication Dates: 1969–87.
Acronym: AMI.
Scores, 14: Drive, Aggressiveness, Determination, Responsibility, Leadership, Self-Confidence, Emotional Control, Mental Toughness, Coachability, Conscientiousness, Trust, Validity Scales (Accuracy, Desirability, Completion Rate).
Administration: Group or individual.
Price Data, 1991: $40 per athlete for non-profit teams (scoring and reports by publisher included in price); $85 per questionnaire for professional and recreational athletes (scoring and reports by publisher included in price).
Foreign Language Editions: French and Spanish editions available.
Time: (40–50) minutes.
Authors: Thomas A. Tutko, Leland P. Lyon, and Bruce C. Oglive.
Publisher: Institute of Athletic Motivation.
Comments: May be used for individual self-assessment.
Cross References: For a review by Andrew L. Comrey, see 8:409 (19 references).

Review of the Athletic Motivation Inventory by JOHN W. SHEPARD, Associate Professor of Counselor Education, The University of Toledo, Toledo, OH:

The authors of the Athletic Motivation Inventory (AMI) appear to have designed an instrument that meets its stated purpose of measuring the attitudes of athletes. The format of the AMI addresses 11 key attitudinal components necessary to develop and perform successfully as an athlete. Responses are based on participant self-appraisals. Questionnaire items appear relevant to athletics and understandable for readers functioning at or above a fifth to sixth grade level. Interpretive reports are generated to coaches and/or their potential players. These reports, though written in somewhat definitive terms, are readable, comprehensive, and personally constructive in nature. The AMI's technical manual is well organized, descriptive, and generally complete. All materials associated with the Inventory's use are visually attractive and easy to access. This group-administered measure is time effective but it is relatively expensive to use. All major sports are represented in the AMI's norming and interpretive information.

The AMI's Preliminary Technical manual is generally user friendly. The index is well laid out with helpful descriptions of the Inventory's format, purpose, history, and design. With few exception, technical information is complete and portrayed via numerous tables strategically placed throughout the manual. Cautionary statements regarding the instrument's use, applicability, and interpretation are stated in a realistic and useful manner.

Statistical analysis of the AMI reveals positive results in most areas. Test items were generated through a polling of coaches in a variety of sports. A pool of questions were field tested on approximately 500 athletes and an item analysis was conducted. A final inventory item count of 190 was utilized. Internal reliability is good and test-retest reliability fair to poor. Test-retest coefficients ranged from .46–.80 with most scores falling in the .60s. The number of subjects used in the above studies were limited to 100 and 56, respectively. Data were collected in 1972. The test-retest interval was 9 weeks.

As previously indicated, the AMI's content validity appears good in terms of items selected for inclusion. The construction of the test, however, probably occurred more than 20 years ago. It is not known whether test items are still appropriately current. No descriptions of item revisions/changes were given. Concurrent validity information was based on numerous, but again dated, studies comparing the scale with other proven measures of personality traits relevant to athletics. Cited study findings were supportive but by no means conclusive in validating the AMI's usefulness. No efforts to establish predictive validity were cited.

The manual's shortcoming involves its description of normative data. One table provides a breakdown of reference group participants by type and level of sport. No information regarding the dates or locality of the data collection was identified. Group size by sport and level of competition ranged from 100 to 5,364 with most group sizes falling below an N of 500. The authors state that group sizes will eventually be upgraded until a minimum of 1,000 for each sport/level is achieved. Progress toward this goal is not mentioned in the manual (copyright 1977). Parts of the interpretative reports appear to have been updated in 1989, but no explanation is given.

In summary, the AMI looks to be soundly constructed and useful in carrying out its stated purposes of recruiting, understanding, and preparing athletes to compete in sports. AMI materials are expensive but well laid out and practical to employ. The Inventory's normative data, however, are speciously dated. A revision/update of the manual's statistical contents appears to be in order.

[38]

Attention Deficit Disorders Evaluation Scale.

Purpose: Designed to "evaluate and diagnose Attention Deficit Disorders in children and youth from input provided by teachers and parents."
Population: Ages 4.5–18.
Publication Dates: 1989–90.
Acronym: ADDES.
Scores, 4: Inattentive, Impulsive, Hyperactive, Total.
Administration: Individual.
Price Data, 1993: $159 per complete kit including 50 pre-referral checklist forms, 50 pre-referral intervention strategy documentation forms, School Version technical manual ('89, 37 pages), 50 School Version rating forms, Home Version technical manual ('89, 40 pages), 25 Home Version rating forms, intervention manual ('89, 167 pages),

and intervention manual for parents ('90, 157 pages); $25 per 50 pre-referral checklist forms; $25 per 50 pre-referral intervention strategies documentation forms; $22 per intervention manual; $149 per computerized intervention manual (IBM, Apple II, or Macintosh).

Comments: Manual titles are: The Attention Deficit Disorders Intervention Manual and The Parent's Guide to Attention Deficit Disorders.

Authors: Stephen B. McCarney and Angela Marie Bauer.

Publisher: Hawthorne Educational Services, Inc.

a) SCHOOL VERSION.

Price Data: $12 per School Version technical manual; $30 per 50 School Version rating forms; $12 per computerized School Version quick score (IBM or Apple II).

Time: (15–20) minutes.

b) HOME VERSION.

Price Data: $12 per Home Version technical manual; $20 per 25 Home version rating forms; $13 per The Parent's Guide to Attention Deficit Disorders; $12 per computerized Home Version quick score (IBM or Apple II).

Time: (12–17) minutes.

TEST REFERENCES

1. McKinney, J. D., Montague, M., & Hocutt, A. M. (1993). Educational assessment of students with attention deficit disorder. *Exceptional Children, 60,* 125-131.

Review of the Attention Deficit Disorders Evaluation Scale by DEBORAH COLLINS, Deputy Director, Center for Survey Research, Virginia Polytechnic Institute and State University, Blacksburg, VA:

ATTENTION DEFICIT DISORDERS EVALUATION SCALE: HOME AND SCHOOL VERSION RATING FORMS. The Attention Deficit Disorders Evaluation Scale (ADDES) is designed to provide measures on three behavioral constructs of attention deficit disorders as defined in the American Psychiatric Association's *Diagnostic and Statistical Manual of Mental Disorders, 3rd Edition* (*DSM-III*): inattention, impulsiveness, and hyperactivity. Two versions of the ADDES scale have been prepared—one for administration in an educational or school setting (ADDES-School) and one for the home (ADDES-Home). The School Version includes 60 items arrayed across the three construct areas (inattention, impulsiveness, and hyperactivity). Quantifiers are recorded for each item by one or more appropriate observer(s) to indicate the frequency of various behaviors within each of the three subscales. Raw scores are summed for each subscale and converted to standard scores via conversion tables normed to eight age-sex standardization groups. The standard subscale scores may then be summed for conversion to a percentile score, which allows comparison of the assessed student to students in the standardization sample. The ADDES-Home version is likewise designed except that a total of 46 items are included in that scale and nine age-sex standardization groups were identified for normative comparisons.

Normative data for the School Version involved 4,876 (attention deficit as well as nonattention deficit) students aged 4.5 to 21 years and 1,567 teachers in 72 school systems spread across 19 states. The Home Version was normed on 1,754 children aged 4 to 20 years evaluated by 3,172 parents/guardians across 12 states.

Reliability measures for both versions include test-retest reliability, interrater reliability, and internal consistency reliability measures. Standard errors of measurement are provided for each subscale by age-sex group for both the School and Home Versions. All measures suggest a high degree of reliability from administration to administration, across different raters, and within and among construct subscale areas. Content validity of both scales was investigated through repetitive reviews of ADD descriptors by diagnosticians, parents, and educators. Item pools were further refined through item analysis of response distributions and item/total score correlations. Factor analysis empirically confirmed the construct validity of the three subscales developed for both instruments. Construct validity was further supported by ratings of non-ADD versus identified ADD children and youth from the home and school standardization groups. The results strongly supported the scale's ability to identify ADD behaviors. Convergent validity studies revealed positive and significant correlations between the ADDES scale measures and similar measures obtained using the revised versions of the Conners' Teacher Rating Scale and the Conners' Parent Rating Scale.

A separate technical manual for each version of the ADDES provides detailed information on reliability and validity, normative data, administration and scoring procedures, and interpretation of results. Appendices provide the necessary conversion tables for converting raw subscale scores to standard subscale scores and standard scores to a percentile score. A companion manual to the School Version is The Attention Deficit Disorders Intervention Manual designed to assist educators in identifying behavioral goals and interventions directly linked to the problem behaviors identified through administration of the ADDES. The companion manual to the Home Version of the ADDES is similarly designed to provide strategies for addressing problem behaviors identified through the ADDES-Home.

Precise definition of ADD has a long history of revision, the most recent of which has been outlined in *DSM-IV*. Nevertheless, subcategories of symptoms (i.e., inattention, impulsiveness, and hyperactivity) as used in *DSM-III* are widely supported along with recognition of the need to address application across age ranges and comorbidities. In McKinney, Montague, and Hocutt's (1993) review of educational assessment practices, the authors suggest that a comprehensive assessment protocol for the identification of ADD should employ multiple methods and multiple sources of information across multiple situations or settings. Moreover, the use of DSM-keyed, multifactor instruments that can also be used to assess co-occurring problems would further assist adequate assessment and referral.

The ADDES assessment materials meet several of the criteria suggested by McKinney (1993) for providing a comprehensive assessment procedure. Both the Home and School Versions of the ADDES instrument include an expansive item pool that has been shown to measure the three primary constructs of inattention, impulsivity, and hyperactivity as specified in *DSM-III*. This scale does not, however, distinguish itself in efforts toward further diagnosis or assessment in the area of non-hyperactive ADD students. Nevertheless, the use of observation techniques coupled with rating scales provides a valuable source of assessment data which can be compared to normative data for purposes of treatment and/or referral. Moreover, differentiation of scale scores by age-sex groups increases the sensitivity of this assessment tool in identifying ADD behaviors manifested more or less intensely at different ages by boys and girls. Finally, the ADDES instruments lend themselves to data collection from a number of perspectives—parents and educators—across various settings—school and home.

The content of some items in the ADDES scales does not allow for measurement across various situations within the home or school. However, the instrument is amenable to repeated use over the course of an observation or treatment period to assess not only the presence of ADD behaviors but also the persistence of these behaviors. A more serious concern resides in the ADDES's apparent inability to address co-occurring conditions. Learning disabilities, for example, often occur with ADD and present particular problems in distinguishing ADD specific behaviors. Moreover, treatment of one disorder without acknowledgment of other accompanying problems may thwart treatment efforts. The authors do not address this issue in any way. Perhaps further studies will be conducted to investigate the extent to which this scale may be used to point to or indicate other, co-occurring disabilities.

Finally, the ADDES instruments should prove very useful in identifying ADD behaviors. Standardization across age-sex levels is a particularly important asset of this scale as is the range of items provided within each of the subscale construct areas. The companion manuals provided to identify interventions or strategies for addressing identified ADD behaviors is very comprehensive but may, in fact, prove overwhelming. Future editions of these materials may seek to summarize interventions at the subscale level prior to delineation of interventions for each of the 46 to 60 behaviors.

REVIEWER'S REFERENCE

McKinney, J. D., Montague, M., & Hocutt, A. M. (1993). Educational assessment of students with attention deficit disorder. *Exceptional Children, 60*, 125-131.

Review of the Attention Deficit Disorders Evaluation Scale by STEPHEN OLEJNIK, Professor of Educational Psychology, University of Georgia, Athens, GA:

The Attention Deficit Disorders Evaluation Scales (School Version and Home Version) were developed to document the occurrence of behaviors in school and home environments that have been associated with the attention-deficit disorder in children. Sixty behavioral statements comprise the School Version. The Home Version contains 46 behaviors, many of which paraphrase the School Version but reflect activities that occur in a home setting. Items on these scales were chosen to operationalize the definition of attention-deficit disorder accepted by The American Psychiatric Association as "inappropriate degrees of inattention, impulsiveness, and hyperactivity."

Each scale can be completed in less than 20 minutes. An evaluator can be any individual having extended contact with the child, having observed or worked with the child for more than one month. For each statement the evaluator quantifies each behavior as *does not engage in the behavior* (0) to occurs *one to several times a month* (1), *week* (2), *day* (3), or *an hour* (4).

Scales can be scored quickly and easily by hand. Four scores are provided: Inattentive, Impulsive, Hyperactive, and Total. Raw scores obtained by summing the quantifiers for items identified as measuring each subscale are transformed to standard scores having a mean of 10 and standard deviation of 3. The subscale standard scores can be summed and converted to a percentile rank. The author suggests that a standard score less than 7 for any subscale indicates a potential behavioral problem and standard scores below 4 should be considered a severe problem. It is worth noting the standard score transformation for this test is nonlinear. Score points are set at 5% increments on the percentile scale.

National normative data are available for each scale. A great deal of care and effort was extended to obtain a representative sample of students ranging from 4 to 20 years of age. An adequate sample from each age group participated in the development of the norms. The School Version was normed on a sample of 4,876 students and 1,567 teachers from 72 school districts and 19 states. The Home Version was normed on a sample of 1,754 students and 3,172 parents from 12 states. Students participating in the data collection included both attention deficit and noninvolved students. Several demographics on the participating sample appear to reflect national demographics.

Eight separate conversion tables are available for each subscale on the School Version and nine tables for each subscale on the Home Version. Separate tables for male and female students in several age groupings are provided.

Both the School and the Home Versions have good psychometric properties. Both scales have estimates of subscale reliability in the form of test-retest, internal consistency, and interrater. Test-retest correlations over a 30-day period range between .89 and .97 for the School Version and between .90 and .92 for the Home Version. Internal consistency based on the Kuder-Richardson 20 (KR-20) formula exceeded .90 for all three subscales on both the School and the Home Versions. To compute the KR-20 item responses must have been dichotomized. The authors do not discuss this nor do they provide a rationale for treating the data in this manner. Using the current 5-point item scale, internal consistency could have been computed using coefficient alpha (Popham, 1981, p. 145).

Interrater correlations for 13 age groups ranged between .81 and .90 for the School Version and between .80 and .84 for four age groups on the Home Version. The standard error of measurement is also reported for each subscale for six gender/age groups on the School Version and for nine gender/age groups on the Home Version. For all of the gender/age groupings measurement errors are relatively small providing support for the precision of the subscales. Unfortunately, however, there are some errors in the manuals in the demonstration of the standard error of measurement. Future editions of the Home and School Versions should correct these inaccuracies.

Evidence supporting the content, concurrent, diagnostic, and construct validity of both the School and Home Versions is provided. Support for the content validity of each scale was obtained through a review of the scale items (initially written based on a review of the attention-deficit disorder literature) by a sample of diagnosticians, educators, and parents who had experience with students having attention-deficit disorder. The number of individuals involved in this process is not reported and no degree of consensus is reported.

Factor analysis using principal components analysis with varimax rotation was used to support the construct validity of the scales. Although some evidence for the adequacy of a 3-factor solution is provided for both scales, the results of the analyses are far from convincing. Many of the items have significant secondary loadings. The subscales appear to be highly related, so a principal axes factor analysis with oblique rotation would likely provide a more adequate factor solution.

The diagnostic value of both the School and Home Versions was demonstrated with a comparative analysis of standard scores from a sample of ADD students and a random sample from the normative group. Differences greater than two standard deviations on the standard scores were obtained for both the males and females. These results clearly support the discriminating power of the subscales.

Subscale scores from the School Version were also correlated with ratings of a sample of students based on the Conners' Teacher Rating Scale—Revised. All correlations were statistically significant at the .05 level and ranged between .389 and .828. Subscale scores from the Home Version were correlated with the Conners' Parent Rating Scale-48. All correlations were statistically significant at the .05 level and ranged between .305 and .830. These results support the concurrent validity of the subscales for both versions of the instrument.

Overall, both the School Version and the Home Version of the Attention Deficit Disorders Evaluation Scale appear to be excellent assessment tools. They are both theoretically sound and very easy to complete and score. The amount of time and effort that went into the development of norms is very impressive. Finally, the author has provided considerable psychometric evidence supporting the subscale reliability and validity. Additional factor analytic work should be carried out, however, to strengthen the construct validity of the instruments. Nevertheless, these are very good instruments. They should provide extremely useful data to identify students with attention-deficit disorder and to provide some guidance in the development of intervention strategies for these students.

REVIEWER'S REFERENCE

Popham, J. W. (1981). *Modern educational measurement.* Englewood Cliffs, NJ: Prentice-Hall, Inc.

[39]

Attitudes Toward Mainstreaming Scale.

Purpose: "Developed to measure attitudes toward the integration of handicapped students into the regular classroom."
Population: Teachers.
Publication Dates: 1980–89.
Acronym: ATMS.
Scores, 4: Learning Capability, General Mainstreaming, Traditional Limiting Disabilities, Total.
Administration: Group.
Price Data: Available from publisher.
Time: Administration time not reported.
Authors: Joan D. Berryman, W. R. Neal, Jr., and Charles Berryman.
Publisher: University of Georgia.
Cross References: See T4:228 (4 references); for reviews by Mary Elizabeth Hannah and Michael D. Orlansky, see 9:98 (1 reference); see also T3:224 (3 references).

TEST REFERENCES

1. Leysler, Y., Wang, W., & Kapperman, G. (1993). Teacher attitudes toward the educational mainstreaming of exceptional students: A comparison

between Chinese and American educators. *College Student Journal*, 27, 372-379.

2. Roberts, C., & Zubrick, S. (1993). Factors influencing the social status of children with mild academic disabilities in regular classrooms. *Exceptional Children*, 59, 192-202.

Review of the Attitudes Toward Mainstreaming Scale by ERNEST A. BAUER, Research, Evaluation and Testing Consultant, Oakland Schools, Waterford, MI:

The Attitudes Toward Mainstreaming Scale (ATMS) was designed to measure "attitudes toward the integration of handicapped students into the regular classroom" because "widespread use of mainstreaming resulted in a need to evaluate the attitudes of individuals concerned with the process" (manual, p. 1). The ATMS consists of 18 six-point Likert-type items. The authors state the ATMS was designed to meet five criteria. Two of them are clearly met: The survey is short and it is easy to administer. Unfortunately, evidence supporting the other three criteria (usefulness, validity, and reliability) is sorely lacking.

In the five-page, half-sheet-sized (5.5-inch x 8.5-inch) manual the authors report the items were "derived from a pool of attitudinal statements concerning the efficacy of mainstreaming" (p. 1). The scale asks simply if students with any of the following handicapping conditions should be in regular classrooms: educable mentally retarded, visually handicapped, blind, hearing impaired, deaf, physically handicapped and confined to wheelchair, physically handicapped but not confined to wheelchair, cerebral palsy, stutter, speech difficult to understand, epilepsy, diabetes, behavior disorders, and persistent disciplinary problems. There is no evidence in the manual about how the "pool" was made or how these 14 items came to be selected for the scale. Some of the language (e.g., "confined") is not consistent with current usage.

Those 14 items are accompanied by two items asking for respondents' reaction to statements that mainstreaming is a desirable practice. One item asks if mainstreaming is feasible. Another statement is "Students should have the right to be in regular classrooms." Perhaps if some item analysis strategies and results were included in the manual the rationale for item selection would become more clear. Unfortunately, there are absolutely no item analysis data in the manual.

The authors used two factor analyses (159 preservice teachers and 164 inservice teachers) in which "each of the analyses yielded the same three potentially measurable constructs" (p. 2). They conclude, therefore, they had "supported the construct validity of the scale." Although the authors cite their previous studies, none of the results from the analyses supporting their conclusion are included in the manual. Even if the data were provided, two factor analyses that produce similar results are not necessarily evidence of construct validity. The manual reports that "moderate factor intercorrelations indicated that the three factors are reasonably independent." The correlations are, however, not reported in the manual.

Additional validity data should be made available before the scale is used for any substantial purpose. Validity data could be gathered by interviewing the respondents, their colleagues, their supervisors, the children they serve, or parents of the children they serve.

The authors also report they did a third factor analysis using data from 404 adults described only as "a general adult population." The relevancy of these data is questionable, however, because the survey is intended "to evaluate the attitudes of individuals concerned with the process (mainstreaming)" (p. 1).

The relationship between the handicapping conditions contained in the items and the factor labels is not obvious. "Students with diabetes should be in regular classrooms" is part of a factor called Learning Capability. Attitudes toward students who are blind, hearing impaired, and deaf become a factor labeled Traditional Limiting Disabilities. The data that are presented suggest that a "general adult population" has attitudes toward mainstreaming that differentiate between handicapping conditions with more specificity (four factors) than those of teachers (three factors).

A split-half reliability coefficient is reported for the total score. Alpha coefficients for the three scales are also reported. Although the authors suggest that the scale can be used to measure attitudinal change, there are no data in the manual regarding the stability of the scores over time.

Scale means and standard deviations are reported but it is not clear how these should be used, especially in light of the inadequate descriptions of the two groups of respondents. Both teachers and other adults had scale means of 54, half of the total possible score of 108. Should this be interpreted to mean that each group had ambivalent attitudes toward mainstreaming?

The survey form asks for respondents' year of birth and sex. Nothing in the manual suggests why these two pieces of data ought to be available to users of the survey. The directions to respondents include "Do not omit a response to any item." There are no directions to scorers about what to do if a respondent fails to heed these directions.

The authors do give potential users permission to reproduce the survey, but, given the concerns about the items that are included and analyses presented in the manual, this reviewer cannot recommend its use. This review, by the way, is about the same length as the text of the manual.

Review of the Attitudes Toward Mainstreaming Scale by PATRICIA B. KEITH, Assistant Professor of Psychology, Alfred University, Alfred, NY:

The Attitudes Toward Mainstreaming Scale (ATMS) was developed in response to PL 94-142.

It purports to measure adults' attitudes toward the efficacy of mainstreaming or integrating students with disabilities into regular education classes. Mainstreaming is defined as one method of meeting the current legal requirements (PL 101-476) for placing students in the least restrictive environment (LRE) for educational purposes. Originally developed in 1980, the ATMS-R is an 18-item 6-point (*strong agree* to *strongly disagree*) Likert scale containing statements about LRE and teaching regular and special education students in the same classroom. Previous test reviewers Hannah (1985) and Orlansky (1985), although welcoming the instrument into the field, cited many serious psychometric (e.g., lack of norms) and practical limitations (e.g., lack of items for students with learning disabilities).

This brief instrument is supported by a manual that is also brief. Perhaps because of this brevity, the reader is left with many questions about the instrument and its potential use. The manual is not well written. The authors appear to have taken many short cuts (e.g., citing their work instead of succinctly summarizing it) and provide limited reliability, validity, and standardization group information. Furthermore, it would be helpful for the manual to contain complete information about test administration, estimated or average time needed to complete the test, and how to score and interpret the test.

The test has 18 statements. Four statements deal with homogenous grouping of "normal" and "handicapped students" for classroom instruction and the other 14 statements deal with the "feasibility of the least restrictive educational placement." The manual authors report these statements constitute a three-factor structure for preservice and inservice teachers (Learning Capability, General Mainstreaming, Traditional Limiting Disabilities) and a four-factor structure (Classroom Functioning, Learning Capability I, Learning Capability II, and General Mainstreaming) for lay adults. Although a series of basic factor analysis procedures were done at various times by the authors, items did not consistently load on the same factor, and the number of factors varied, as did the labeling of some of the factors. Indeed, Wilczenski (1992) questioned the basic factor structure of the instrument and recommended caution in interpreting results.

The norm group is not described adequately. A sample of unselected adults and a group representing preservice and inservice students is said to have been used, but more complete information is needed in the manual. Means and standard deviations for factor scores are presented based on these groups. The reliability information in the manual is limited and presented in an unclear manner. Reliability coefficients range between .76 and .92 for several poorly described samples (including the norm group); additional supportive documentation would be helpful.

Cross validation procedures were used to support the construct validity of the instrument. But meager information is presented to determine the validity of the test. The authors state that moderate factor intercorrelations demonstrate that the three factors are reasonably independent. Further explanation is warranted to support that statement.

Review of the author's cited work suggests that perhaps typical test construction procedures (Thorndike, Cunningham, Thorndike, & Hagen, 1991) may not have been used when developing the ATMS or in revising the ATMS-R. This instrument, although possessing a noble goal and mission, falls short of the mark. Its development and refinement may have been data driven rather than research based or theory driven.

Although there may be a need to measure educators' and others' attitudes about the placement of students with disabilities in the LRE or regular education classes with supportive services provided by special education teachers or support personnel, this instrument may not meet many basic psychometric standards for tests and is not recommended for use. Previous reviewers were hopeful this instrument would be further refined and offered many excellent recommendations for needed modifications. Unfortunately, it appears the test authors may not have considered the test reviewers' suggestions when the ATMS was revised. Another instrument which could be reviewed for possible use is the Attitudes Toward Mainstreaming scale developed by Peter Chow and Margaret M. Winzer (1992). This test provides a sound three-factor model (positive effect of mainstreaming on students and setting, negative effects of mainstreaming on children, and teaching load incurred by mainstreaming); was analyzed using item-response theory (IRT) and LISREL; and uses terminology and theoretical constructions that are relevant to educators of students with disabilities in the 1990s.

REVIEWER'S REFERENCES

Hannah, M. E. (1985). [Review of the Attitudes Toward Mainstreaming Scale.] In J. V. Mitchell, Jr. (Ed.), *The ninth mental measurements yearbook* (pp. 110-111). Lincoln, NE: Buros Institute of Mental Measurements.

Orlansky, M. D. (1985). [Review of the Attitudes Toward Mainstreaming Scale.] In J. V. Mitchell, Jr. (Ed.), *The ninth mental measurements yearbook* (p. 111). Lincoln, NE: Buros Institute of Mental Measurements.

Thorndike, R. M., Cunningham, G. K., Thorndike, R. L., & Hagen, E. P. (1991). *Measurement and evaluation in psychology and education* (5th ed.). New York: Macmillan Publishing Co.

Chow, P., & Winzer, M. M. (1992). Reliability and validity of a scale measuring attitudes toward mainstreaming. *Educational and Psychological Measurement*, *52*, 223-228.

Wilczenski, F. L. (1992). Reevaluating the factor structure of the Attitudes Toward Mainstreaming Scale. *Educational and Psychological Measurement*, *52*, 499-504.

[40]

The Auditory Discrimination and Attention Test.

Purpose: Designed to assess "auditory discrimination and attention for speech."

Population: Children ages 3.5–12 years referred for speech therapy.
Publication Date: 1988.
Scores: Total error score only.
Administration: Individual.
Price Data, 1992: £69 per complete set; £10.10 per 25 score sheets.
Time: (20) minutes.
Author: Rosemarie MorganBarry.
Publisher: NFER-Nelson Publishing Co., Ltd. [England].

Review of The Auditory Discrimination and Attention Test by KAREN T. CAREY, Associate Professor of Psychology, California State University, Fresno, Fresno, CA:

The Auditory Discrimination and Attention Test assesses a child's ability to discriminate and attend to differences between 17 pairs of words. Presented in a picture-book format the pairs have one "broad" feature, consisting of a voicing group (i.e., pear/bear), place group (i.e., key/tea), manner group (i.e., mat/bat), and a cluster group (i.e., crown/clown). Twelve colored counters are provided and the child responds to the stimulus word by placing one of the counters in slots provided on the book frame beneath the appropriate picture.

The first item presented is a demonstration item and scoring of this item is not included as a part of the 17-item test. The test is not recommended for children who fail to understand the test instructions or the demonstration procedures, nor for children who have poor concentration.

Each pair of pictures is presented to the child and the child is asked to name each word. The child is then told to place a counter in the slot underneath the picture of the word said by the examiner. The examiner gives three repetitions of each word in the pair to children $3^1/_2$ to 5 years old and six repetitions of each word in the pair to children 5 to 12 years of age. As each item is presented to the child, the examiner is to make certain the child cannot see his/her face (although how this is to be accomplished is not described). Repetitions of words at the request of the child are scored as errors, fluctuations in the child's ability to attend should result in test termination, and for children who are unable to place counters in the appropriate slots, eye-point responses may be made and the examiner inserts the counter into the slot indicated by the child.

Raw scores are obtained based on the total error score and standard scores, expressed as standard deviations from the mean, are obtained based on the child's age. In order to interpret the test, a score of -2 standard deviations from the mean indicates the child is functioning in the "danger" zone. Unfortunately, according to the author, it is difficult to ascertain whether such deviations occur because of a child's auditory discrimination difficulties or due to attentional problems. The author states that a score in the danger range would indicate the child to be in need of "auditory attention-to-discrimination tasks."

The test was standardized on children in England ranging in age from 3 years 6 months to 12 years. The actual number of subjects included in the sample cannot be deciphered from the information presented in the manual. A serious limitation of the tool is the minimal technical information provided. Sample sizes of groups on whom validity and reliability studies were conducted are not included in the manual. For example, no correlation was found between hearing loss (between 20 and 50 decibels) and error rates on the test. The number of children included in this study is not reported. Another study investigating the correlation between attention and auditory discrimination was conducted (r = .8). According to the test author, the 23 children included in this study were identified as having attention problems based on descriptions by Cooper, Moodley, and Reynell (1978). These descriptions are not included, however, in the manual. Internal consistency studies cannot be analyzed because descriptions of the samples and sample sizes are not included in the manual. Furthermore the same information is lacking in the section describing two reliability studies.

A correlation study of The Auditory Discrimination and Attention Test and the Auditory Discrimination Test (ADT, Wepman, 1973) with 13 subjects (mean age = 5.8 years) revealed a correlation of .328. The author describes the low correlation as a result of differences between the content of the two tests and that each test requires additional skills beyond auditory discrimination. The reason for selecting the ADT for this study rather than Wepman's more recent Auditory Discrimination Test, Second Edition (Wepman & Reynolds, 1987; 11:467) is not described.

The use of The Auditory Discrimination and Attention Test must be questioned at this time. There is not enough technical information included in the manual, the number of test items is small (i.e., 17), and the actual sample sizes upon which psychometric data are based are not described. No information is given related to socioeconomic status of the students, parents' level of education, number of years the children had been attending school, and whether or not the children included in the standardization sample had other difficulties beyond speech impairments. Finally, it seems the information that can be obtained from this instrument could be gathered in natural environments through the use of structured observations.

REVIEWER'S REFERENCES

Wepman, J. (1973). The Auditory Discrimination Test. Chicago: Language Research Association, Inc.

Cooper, J., Moodley, M., & Reynell, J. (1978). *Helping language development.* London: Edward Arnold.

Wepman, J., & Reynolds, M. (1987). Wepman's Auditory Discrimination Test, Second Edition. Los Angeles: Western Psychological Services.

Review of The Auditory Discrimination and Attention Test by GERALD TINDAL, Associate Professor of Special Education, University of Oregon, Eugene, OR:

This test by MorganBarry (1988) is designed to ascertain whether children (ages 3.5 to 12 years old) can/do discriminate between the initial and final sounds of word pairs that are very similar (entitled a "minimal pairs paradigm" by the author). A series of pictures are presented on cards (two pictures per card and 17 pairs of words in total) and the student is asked to imitate and produce the word each picture represents. For each pair, the student is given 3–6 trials. The test "was designed for use with all children who have been referred for speech therapy, and whose perceptual abilities are thought to need investigation" (manual, p. 2). As the author notes, the name of the test implies that failure to make auditory discriminations may be due to perception problems (can complete the behavior) or attention problems (do complete the behavior).

The manual author provides a very complete description of the domain from which the words were sampled, emphasizing those features that are consistent with the purpose of the test. The pictures are all well displayed on the cards and represent words of high frequency in the everyday speech of children. Administration directions are clear and unambiguous; the total testing time is brief (less than 20 minutes). The administration protocol emphasizes first the child's production of the word with presentation of each picture, and then if incorrect (appropriately matched word but articulated incorrectly or use of the wrong word to depict the picture), the tester's teaching of the word with subsequent student imitations. Finally, the student's "auditory discrimination" is tested by having the child post a chip under the picture representing the word stated by the tester; each word is presented more than once (three times for children ages 3.6–4.11 and six times for children ages 5–11.11). The directions emphasize the need for uniformity of verbalization on the part of the tester.

The child's score comprises a count of the number of errors and is then converted to a standard score. Normative charts are presented for calculating the student's score with a *z*-score of -2.2 highlighted as the "danger point" (manual, p. 7). These normative tables provide deviation scores in three age groups: preschool (3.6–4.11 years old), primary (5–6.11 years old), and junior (7–11.11 years old). The data from these normative tables were generated by testing 300 children between the ages of 3–12 throughout England. Within this group, subsets of children thought to have speech, language, and attention problems were identified and analyzed separately. Although the geographic regions are presented where children were sampled, no specific sampling plan is further explicated (e.g., the number per area or use of any other blocking factor such as race or SES).

Reliability data are presented comparing "experimental" (speech-impaired) and normal students; the data are based on an unknown number of students. Differences between these groups are found only in the school-age students. No further information is presented about the methods of this pilot study which was conducted in 1984. Interrater reliability (.80) and test-retest (.90) data are reported (based on separate samples). However, no information is provided about this study (either describing the subjects or the methods of research).

There are significant differences in item difficulty across the word pairs. The most difficult pairs for all groups are "sum–sun," "fan–van," and "mouth–mouse." Further validity data are reported that reflect low correlation between hearing loss and performance on this test (for a "small group of children with hearing losses of between 20 and 50 decibels"); however, for a group of children found to have attention difficulties, a reasonably high correlation was found between their scores on this test and their attention levels. No information is provided about either of these studies (i.e., who was tested, how many, what measures were used, or what assessment procedures were followed).

Finally, concurrent validity information is provided by correlating performance on this test and the Auditory Discrimination Test (Wepman, 1973). A small sample study ($N = 13$) suggested a rather low correlation between the two measures (.33). The rationale for choosing the Auditory Discrimination Test is not well stated.

In summary, The Auditory Discrimination and Attention Test is a clear and easy to use test that may provide some information on a child's perception of sound discriminations. The behavior sampled is of questionable educational value, but it may provide low level (medically relevant) perception information. The normative values must be interpreted with great caution, particularly given the exclusively British composition of the group, a problem which may occur because of differences in accents that inherently recalibrate the error rates in U.S. English speaking populations. The reliability data reported are marginal and are not used in establishing standard errors of measurement. Validity data are likewise weak and fail to provide any convincing data that the decisions made from this instrument can help students educationally. The instrument should be used solely to obtain clinical samples of behavior.

REVIEWER'S REFERENCE

Wepman, J. (1973). The Auditory Discrimination Test. Chicago: Language Research Association, Inc.

[41]

Bankson-Bernthal Test of Phonology.

Purpose: "Designed for use by speech-language clinicians to assess the phonology of preschool and school-age children."

Population: Ages 3–9.
Publication Dates: 1989–90.
Acronym: BBTOP.
Scores, 3: Word Inventory, Consonants Composite, Phonological Processes Composite.
Administration: Individual.
Price Data, 1991: $88.98 per complete kit; $34.98 per picture book; $18 per 24 record forms; $19.98 per easel and carrying case; $24.99 per manual ('90, 111 pages).
Time: (10–15) minutes.
Authors: Nicholas W. Bankson and John E. Bernthal.
Publisher: The Riverside Publishing Co.

Review of the Bankson-Bernthal Test of Phonology by LYNN S. BLISS, Professor of Communication Disorders and Sciences, Wayne State University, Detroit, MI:

The Bankson-Bernthal Test of Phonology (BBTOP) was designed to describe consonant production and phonological error patterns and to compare a child's phonological ability with other children of comparable age.

The BBTOP includes a picture book consisting of 80 illustrations depicting objects within the vocabulary of young children. A portable easel is also available. The record form includes sections for transcription and scoring, interpretation, standardization, and design information.

The BBTOP is designed for speech-language clinicians. It is quickly and easily administered. The clinician asks the child to name the picture and scores each response. Descriptions of scoring procedures and practice protocols are presented in the manual. Three scores are obtained. The Word Inventory score is derived by totaling the words in which all consonants were produced accurately. This measure represents an overall index of a child's phonological performance. The score is converted into a percentile rank and standard score. Consonant errors are recorded in initial and final positions. A scale score is derived for each position. The Consonants Composite score represents the sum of the two scale scores and is transformed into a percentile rank and a standard score. A phonological process analysis is included that yields a Phonological Process Composite score, percentile rank, and standard score. The following processes are evaluated: assimilation, fronting, final consonant deletion, weak syllable deletion, stopping, gliding, cluster simplification, depalatization, deaffrication, and vocalization. Interpretation of the scores is described in the manual.

The BBTOP was standardized at 61 sites within the United States on a sample of 1,070 nonimpaired children between the ages of 3 and 9. There was an approximately even ratio of males to females. The percentage of Caucasian children tested is similar to the percentage in the U.S. population. African-American and Hispanic children are somewhat underrepresented in the standardization pool. Scores for the age groups of 3 to 6 were used to derive the normative data. Percentile ranks were converted into standard scores and a stanine (M = 5, SD = 2) was selected for the standard metric.

Internal consistency coefficients are presented to estimate test reliability. The split-half reliability coefficients are all above .92. The stability of test performance was investigated with a subgroup of 34 4-year-old children. They were retested approximately 8 weeks after the initial test. Significant correlations were obtained between the test scores and significant differences were found for many of the scores. High interrater agreement was obtained on 4- and 8-year-old children.

Content validity was addressed by demonstrating the theoretical and research basis for target selection and scoring procedures. Construct validity was evident in age-related sequencing of test data and in relationships among the subcomponents of the test. The data show the BBTOP evaluates a variety of dimensions of phonological performance.

The strengths of the BBTOP are in its ease of administration, clear illustrations, numerous examples presented in the manual, adequate age range of a normative population, and appropriate reliability and validity information. This test will be very useful to practicing speech-language clinicians. Two disadvantages are evident. The first is the description of the derivation of the scale scores is difficult to follow both in the manual and on the response forms. The examples in the manual are useful and help to offset this limitation. However, a clinician must spend time learning how to obtain these scores. The second disadvantage is the reduced number of African-American and Hispanic children included in the normative scores. Clinicians working with children from diverse ethnic backgrounds may wish to collect additional normative data. In summary, the BBTOP is a well-constructed phonological assessment measure that will be useful for speech-language clinicians.

Review of the Bankson-Bernthal Test of Phonology by LAWRENCE J. TURTON, Professor of Speech-Language Pathology, Indiana University of Pennsylvania, Indiana, PA:

As they accepted the mantle of the leading experts in phonological (nee articulation) disorders, Nicholas Bankson and John Bernthal brought new standards of scholarship and clinical leadership to the forefront of the topic. Their text (1988) is now a standard for the student interested in the field of speech sound problems. With the publication of this test, the Bankson-Bernthal Test of Phonology (BBTOP), they have made two additional significant contributions to the profession. First and foremost, they have provided convincing evidence that articulation tests can be subjected to the rigors of psychometric analysis. A perusal of the previous editions of the Buros *Mental Measure-*

ments Yearbook series provides numerous examples of "articulation" tests for which the authors have disregarded the standards of tests and measurement or have paid only lip service to them. If nothing else, this test will become the standard against which all future articulation tests can be compared for psychometric quality. No longer will a test developer be able to claim face validity or self-judgements of reliability as being sufficient.

Their second contribution rests in the availability of an instrument for developing data sets on phonological processes that can be used by the practicing clinician. The procedures are an efficient compromise between the hybrid attempt of the Khan-Lewis system (1986; 10:164) and the rigorous detail demanded by the research methodology of Shriberg and Kwiatkowski (1980) or Ingram (1981). Bankson and Bernthal chose seven processes that their analysis of the literature suggested were used beyond 3 years of age and three that are common to other analytical systems. Unfortunately, they did not provide references or data to suggest that these 10 processes are most common in the speech of children enrolled in articulation therapy, a significant factor for decision making.

The manual is explicitly clear both for an experienced clinician who is versed in phonological theory and for the young graduate student who is acquiring basic skills in phonological assessment. It allows the user to move easily through each step from testing through interpretation of the results. The picture stimuli are age-appropriate in terms of vocabulary difficulty and quality of the color drawings. On page 6, the authors do make the time-honored error in the profession of requiring "phonetic transcription" when their examples are only phonemically transcribed. Ironically, allophonic variation, the heart of phonology of spoken language, is ignored in this test of phonology.

Three values are derived from the data set: a word inventory score, a consonant score, and a phonological process inventory. The word inventory is a clever procedure to insure that the child actually knows the word and that phonological variations in a child's speech are independent of lexical difficulties. The authors are to be commended for this scoring procedure and future test developers would be wise to adopt this strategy.

Consonants are scored only in the initial and final word positions and in clusters. Thus, unless the tester pays close attention to the productions in the relatively few multisyllabic words, intervocalic allophones are eliminated from consideration in determining the status of a child's system. Bankson and Bernthal do not provide a viable explanation for this decision; a serious omission in light of the fact that Final Consonant Deletion, Weak Syllable Deletion, and Cluster Simplification have their roots in the early stages of phonological acquisition when the syllable structures and word relationships are tenuous. The nature of the pattern of the word structure in a child's speech may be predictive of the persistence of a process.

All of the scores are easily converted to standard psychometric and/or linguistic values by an experienced clinician. The tables are easily followed and evidence of a statistical linkage among the values is readily available in the manual. The tables of special interest are those found on pages 15, 76, and 78 because they provide data on age-related scores for the words and sounds tested, a data set of some comfort for those who are still attuned to making decisions on the basis of age of acquisition. Bankson and Bernthal graciously created a new set of developmental norms for their test, a unique event in the history of articulation testing. Unlike some of their predecessors (Fisher & Logemann, 1971; Goldman & Fristoe, 1969), they did not resort to using the traditional Templin (1957) norms, which may not be applicable to a different set of lexical items. Once again, they are to be commended for this change in professional practice. More importantly, the test can be used as a consonant articulation test separate from the phonological processing concepts.

Consistent with the pattern established by Bankson in his other test (Bankson Language Test-2 [1990; 11:26]), the BBTOP has a plethora of data on reliability and validity. Using a sample of 1,070 children drawn from across the nation through a network of quality colleagues, the authors present psychometric analyses that more than vindicate their decision to publish this test. The correlations for temporal reliability ranged from .74 for Consonants Composite to .89 for the Word Inventory. The values are based on only 34 children with an 8-week spread of time and could use data from a larger sample to substantiate the claims for stability. However, we do have a base from which future research can be built.

Split-half reliability coefficients for all three measures are extremely high across all age groups (3-0 years to 9-0 years) covered by this test. The coefficients ranged from, for example, .92 for phonological processes at age 8-0 years to .98 for all three measures at 9-0 years. Standard Errors of Measurement are well within acceptable limits for all age groups. The amount of variability of an obtained score is small, suggesting the scores do reflect some consistent pattern of behavior by the child. Unfortunately, the authors report only correlational type data for interobserver reliability, albeit, very high coefficients (.85 to .99). A data set on percentages of agreement is necessary for this kind of test because the analysis is not based on total number of errors but the specific error per item. Data on the consistency of phonemic transcription per item per tester would greatly strengthen the claims for reliable scoring and valid analyses. Furthermore, the data base for all reliability measures must be extended to children who are in therapy so that the profession will be able to judge the adequacy of the test for the children who are the real target population for these inventories.

As with reliability, Bankson and Bernthal made the effort to present the user with a logical, coherent body of evidence for content and construct validity, eliminating the need to justify the test on the basis of face validity. On the other hand, they omitted an analysis of concurrent validity, which should have been easy to obtain, assuming they determined the normality of their standardization population with the same tests. Furthermore, the lack of data sets to allow for comparisons relative to the standard systems developed by Weiner (1979), Shriberg and Kwiatkowski (1980), and Ingram (1981) leaves another gap that needs to be filled by subsequent research. These analyses would have told the reader how well the scores from the BBTOP correlate with natural speech productions, the essence of phonological development.

Construct validity values were obtained from correlational studies of score patterns and were followed up by detailed factor analyses. The data indicated that the ability to name the items was independent from the ability to produce the sounds. A tester can be confident that phonology and not the lexicon is the major focus of the test. The factor analyses also suggest a predictable pattern of independence for the phonemic units and the phonological processes. The data suggest that children do utilize the processes as separate sets and not as a single, unitary skill.

There is, however, a critical component of phonological theory that is not addressed in the manual by the authors. If phonological processes are supposed to be strategies employed by children to learn adult forms (Stampe, 1979), and if they tend to disappear at about age 4-0 years, what is actually being tested by the BBTOP? Are we attempting to identify developmental strategies for the language learner or phonological rules that control the child's developed, adult system? In Tables 4.2 and 9.5 of the manual strong evidence is presented that the developmental process for the standardization group ended at age 6-0 years. All consonants and clusters items were produced above the 90% level or higher (except for final clusters); all processes appear to have disappeared except in a few children as can be noted by the size of the standard deviation at age 6-0 years as compared to the mean score. The children in the standardization group followed the predicted pattern of phasing out processes early in life.

An understanding of phonological processes within the system of a child or a group of children requires knowledge of their level of language development because we cannot determine if a phonological variation is a process or a phonological rule unless we know what the relationship of these patterns is to lexical, morphological, and syntactic development. As a profession, we would be suspect were we to engage children in a treatment program for *normal* developmental strategies as opposed to aberrant phonological rules.

Utilization of this test and any other process measure demands the use of supportive data on language acquisition; samples of conversational speech; and detailed, in-depth, follow-up testing of the processes (rules) identified by the test results. The authors report the BBTOP can be administered in 10 to 15 minutes. Any good clinician dealing with young children will do language testing; they need only spend 20 to 30 additional minutes to obtain evidence in the way of a sample to determine whether the child is using rules or processes. Phonological processes could turn out to be the coarticulation phenomenon of the '90s. McDonald (1964) presented the profession with a partial concept and created a test and therapy model before adequate research was done to substantiate the model. We are at risk now with phonological concepts unless we clearly distinguish between developmental phenomena and adult rules.

A final problem with the concept of phonological processes as used in the profession is that we have failed to generate new therapy principles and techniques to match the developmental model (other than minimal pairs [Weiner, 1981]). We can make decisions differently; but, we have not freed ourselves from the restrictions of traditional or sensory-motor therapies. (See Hodson & Paden [1990] for an example of phonological decision making but traditional therapy techniques.) Phonological information will be of its greatest significance when it can generate treatment programs that simulate normal developmental sequences that can be justified by modern concepts of phonology and biology.

These issues are not unique to the BBTOP, but they do permeate this test as well as other writings in this developmental domain. However, Bankson and Bernthal have made a valiant effort to upgrade the quality of testing in the area of articulation. They are to be complimented for advancing the state of the art for all of us who work with children. Whether one uses this test as a general test for articulation or as a "phonological" test, it is simply the best on the market today. The other commercial instruments that failed to follow psychometric procedures for test development can be retired and replaced by the BBTOP because with this procedure one will know what is being tested and what the scores actually mean. The other concerns about reliability and validity raised in this review are easily dealt with in traditional psychometric research and will, no doubt, be available in the professional journals in the future.

REVIEWER'S REFERENCES

Templin, M. C. (1957). *Certain language skills in children.* Minneapolis, MN: The University of Minnesota Press.

McDonald, E. T. (1964). *Articulation testing and treatment: A sensory-motor approach.* Pittsburgh, PA: Stanwix House, Inc.

Goldman, R., & Fristoe, M. (1969). Goldman-Fristoe Test of Articulation. Circle Pines, MN: American Guidance Service.

Fisher, H. B., & Logemann, J. A. (1971). The Fisher-Logemann Test of Articulation Competence. Chicago: The Riverside Publishing Co.

Stampe, D. (1979). *A dissertation on natural phonology.* New York: Garland Publishing, Inc.

Weiner, F. F. (1979). *Phonological process analysis.* Baltimore, MD: University Park Press.

Shriberg, L. D., & Kwiatkowski, J. (1980). *Natural process analysis (NPA): A procedure for phonological analysis of continuous speech samples.* New York: John Wiley & Sons.

Ingram, D. (1981). *Procedures for the phonological analysis of children's language.* Baltimore, MD: University Park Press.

Weiner, F. F. (1981). Treatment of phonological disability using the method of meaningful minimal contrast: Two case studies. *Journal of Speech and Hearing Disorders, 46,* 97-103.

Khan, L. M., & Lewis, N. P. (1986). Khan-Lewis Phonological Analysis. Circle Pines, MN: American Guidance Service.

Bernthal, J. E., & Bankson, N. W. (1988). *Articulation and phonological disorders* (2nd ed.). Englewood Cliffs, NJ: Prentice-Hall, Inc.

Bankson, N. W. (1990). Bankson Language Test-2. Austin, TX: PRO-ED, Inc.

Hodson, B. W., & Paden, E. P. (1991). Targeting Intelligible Speech: A Phonological Approach to Remediation. Austin, TX: PRO-ED, Inc.

[42]

Basic Personality Inventory.

Purpose: Constructed to be a "measure of personality and psychopathology."
Population: Ages 12 and over.
Publication Dates: 1984–89.
Acronym: BPI.
Scores, 12: Hypochondriasis, Depression, Denial, Interpersonal Problems, Alienation, Persecutory Ideas, Anxiety, Thinking Disorder, Impulse Expression, Social Introversion, Self Depreciation, Deviation.
Administration: Individual or group.
Price Data, 1991: $44 per examination kit including 10 reusable test booklets, 25 answer sheets, scoring template, 25 profile sheets, answer sheet and coupon for BPI report, and manual ('89, 87 pages); $22.75 per 25 test booklets; $5.50–$9 (depending on volume) per 25 answer sheets; $8 per scoring template; $5.50–$9 (depending on volume) per 25 profile sheets (select adult or adolescent norms); $22 per manual; scoring service offered by publisher.
Time: [35] minutes.
Author: Douglas N. Jackson.
Publisher: Sigma Assessment Systems, Inc., Research Psychologists Press Division.

TEST REFERENCES

1. Kroner, D. G., & Reddon, J. R. (1994). Relationships among clinical and validity scales of the Basic Personality Inventory. *Journal of Clinical Psychology, 50,* 522-528.

Review of the Basic Personality Inventory by SUSANA URBINA, Associate Professor of Psychology, University of North Florida, Jacksonville, FL:

The Basic Personality Inventory (BPI) is a test designed to meet two clear goals: (*a*) to identify and measure a set of constructs broadly spanning the domain of psychopathology, and (*b*) to do so in a manner that incorporates modern methods and stringent standards of test construction. Jackson, the test author, chose to accomplish the first goal by trying to isolate the constructs that underlie the empirically derived diagnostic efficiency of the Minnesota Multiphasic Personality Inventory (MMPI). Then, he attempted to reconstitute them in the context of a set of "purer" (i.e., more homogeneous), more meaningful (i.e., bipolar rather than unipolar), more widely useful (i.e., with both normal and dysfunctional individuals), and nonoverlapping dimensional scales.

The BPI was also designed to correct or minimize undesirable features, such as objectionable item content and the use of pejorative terms in scale names, that have plagued the MMPI and other older inventories such as the Millon Clinical Multiaxial Inventory (MCMI). With a total of 240 items, the BPI is a fairly short test that can be completed in about a half hour by persons with reading comprehension as low as the 5th grade level. The paper-and-pencil version can be easily scored by hand with a single template. The test is also available in formats suitable for computer administration, scoring, and interpretation; unfortunately, some scales for assessing response style are available only through computer scoring.

DEVELOPMENT. Although the BPI was published in the late 1980s, Jackson and his collaborators have been working on it since the mid 1970s and have accumulated a fair amount of research on the test. The construction of the BPI started with factor analyses of the MMPI and the Differential Personality Inventory (DPI), which is a comprehensive but still unpublished measure of 28 major and distinct dimensions of psychopathology that Douglas Jackson and Samuel Messick are developing. Eleven of the factors that emerged from these analyses were common to both tests and showed a good deal of convergence; these dimensions provided the conceptual basis for the 11 content scales of the BPI. A 12th scale, composed of critical items dealing with deviant tendencies and behaviors, was added later to assess distortion of responses in the negative direction; this Deviation scale is the only one in the BPI that does not measure a homogeneous psychological trait.

Once the traits to be assessed by the BPI scales had been defined and conceptualized, original items were prepared. Item preparation took into account the need for homogeneity of the scales and for suppression of evaluative response biases. The selection of the 20 items for each scale (half keyed in the "True" direction and half in the "False" direction) was based on all the previously specified editorial criteria. In addition, a number of statistical indices, such as an item's variance and its correlations with its own scale, with irrelevant scales, and with a desirability scale, were used to select items.

NORMS. The BPI provides separate norms for adults and for adolescents and, because of consistent sex differences, for males and females as well. The adult norms are based on the responses of 709 men and 710 women selected randomly from telephone directories in the United States and voters records in Canada. In order to obtain high response rates to the mailed inventories, each adult in the sample was sent only a subset of one third of the BPI or 4 out of the 12 scales. The United States adults, who made up the vast majority of the sample, were almost all white (95.6%) and had more education and higher occupational levels than the general population. The adolescent norms were gathered on 880 males and 1,380 females from two Canadian provinces who did take the entire BPI and did so in person rather than by mail (D. N. Jackson, personal communication, February 25, 1993).

The profile sheets for adolescents and adults, separated by sex, show clear differences in the ranges of the scale scores for the two age groups. The distributions of the adults' scores show far less variability than those of the adolescents, possibly as a result of the restricted demographic composition of the adult sample. On the Self Depreciation scale, for example, the lowest tabled raw score (0) yields a *T* score equivalent of 43 and the highest raw score (15) yields a *T* score of 110 for adult males, whereas for adolescent males the lowest and highest raw scores (0 and 20) yield *T* scores of 38 and 104 respectively. At any rate, it appears the normative samples of the BPI, at the adult level, may not be representative of the general population. The author himself suggests that accumulation of separate norms for nonwhite subgroups is indispensable in order to use the test with ethnic minorities and promises this is being planned for the future.

PSYCHOMETRIC PROPERTIES. The extraordinary care devoted to the conceptual aspects of the BPI is evident in the quality and variety of investigations of its psychometric properties. On the issue of reliability, for instance, the manual presents data on internal consistency (KR 20) reliabilities for 9 samples and test-retest reliabilities for two groups; these coefficients range from .49 to .90, with central values in the .70s. Moreover, the reliability of the BPI is also described from the standpoints of factor structure at the item level and of congruence among desirability ratings and frequencies of endorsement across items. Although the reliability indices presented are not uniformly high, the patterns in their fluctuations are largely consonant with what would be expected given the premises that underlie the scales.

Jackson's commitment to a construct-based approach to personality testing is also evident in the data he and his collaborators have gathered to examine the validity of the BPI scales. Evidence of convergent and discriminant validity has been collected using the multitrait-multimethod framework and includes several factor analytic studies and studies of criterion-related validity, including a multiple discriminant analysis of delinquent and nondelinquent groups. Attention to proper procedure in the gathering of these data extends to highly desirable yet seldom seen practices such as establishing the reliability of *criterion* data by more than one method.

Because the BPI was designed to tap the constructs underlying the MMPI clinical scales, data comparing results on the two inventories are particularly relevant. A factor analytic study using 235 male alcoholics suggests the two inventories share a substantial amount of common variance that can be accounted for almost completely by five factors whose loadings are conceptually consistent across both measures. Comparisons of the BPI scales with the Wiggins MMPI content scales fare rather well for the most part. Correlations between the BPI and the Millon Clinical Multiaxial Inventory, the State-Trait Anxiety Inventory, and the Adjective Check List are also presented but, not surprisingly, they are not as good as those between the BPI and the MMPI.

SUMMARY. At this point in its development, the BPI is still far from establishing diagnostic utility on a par with that of the MMPI (11:244). However, it has already achieved its primary goal of providing a shorter and psychometrically purer alternative for the study of personality and psychopathology. The BPI also shows promise as a tool for individual assessment of delinquent and nondelinquent adolescents. In order to enhance its potential usefulness in the assessment of adult psychopathology, the BPI must have a more representative set of adult norms as well as norms for ethnic subgroups and more studies of clinical populations.

Review of the Basic Personality Inventory by TAMELA YELLAND, Psychologist, Veterans Administration, Anaheim Vet Center, Anaheim, CA:

The Basic Personality Inventory (BPI) was designed to tap similar personality dimensions as the Minnesota Multiphasic Personality Inventory (MMPI), but with fewer items, more construct-oriented scale development, and less item overlap between scales. The BPI has 240 true-false questions rated to the 5th grade reading level. It has 12 scales, including one measure of overall psychopathology, one measure of the test taker's approach to the test, and 10 constructs of psychopathology.

The test has been targeted for psychiatric adult and deviant adolescent populations. It is self-administered, using paper-and-pencil or computer administration and scoring. The raw scores are easily plotted on a profile setup like the MMPI with standard *T* scores and a mean of 50. Unlike the MMPI, however, there is no cutoff score for clinical significance, because the scales were designed to distinguish between polar opposites. The author suggests that the lower (below 50) scores may be used to infer areas of personality strength and normal personality functioning. It is important to caution against utilizing these scores for anything more than inferences. Interpretation of the lower scores for normal populations has not been established as a valid use of this test.

Norms for male and female adults (age 19 and over), and adolescents (ages 12–18) have been established. Adult norms were based on U.S. and Canadian samples, which were well stratified except for race. Because 95.6% of the sample was white, the generalizability of the test is severely limited. It is not recommended for use with nonwhite populations until further norming data are added. The adolescent norms were derived from both normal and delinquent populations.

Scale definitions and expanded interpretations are provided, and are based on professional opinions. The manual author states the expanded interpretations are for use with delinquent adolescent populations. Unfortunately, no expanded interpretations are provided for any other population. The scale definitions are generally descriptive of behavior but are difficult to translate into diagnoses. This is one of the weaknesses of the test. Information necessary for the interpretation of the profiles and the translation of results into diagnoses, treatment plans, and insight into functioning is sorely lacking for adults and nondelinquent adolescents.

Profile validity is also difficult to differentiate. The "Denial" scale was created to tap the test taker's approach to the test and tendencies to suppress or exaggerate symptomatology. This particular scale was not developed through careful factoring as were the other scales, and does not appear to differentiate the motives of the test taker adequately.

The strengths of the BPI center on its design and psychometric quality. The author based the BPI on an earlier measure that had 28 scales, and through a series of factor analyses and modifications of the constructs, identified 10 scales. Items were edited to limit social desirability, reduce intercorrelations between scales, and to maximize content validity and internal consistency reliability for each scale. Internal consistency was established with adult and adolescent populations, and test-retest stability was demonstrated with young adults. Attempts were made to establish convergent and discriminant validity for the test, which the author admits is a difficult undertaking for a general personality measure. The results of these attempts and the solid construct and content analyses provide confidence in the validity of the measure for its intended use as a measure of psychopathology.

In conclusion then, the BPI is well designed, short, and easy to administer and score, and provides promising insights into the psychopathological functioning of adults and adolescents. It is not recommended for use with nonwhite populations, for interpretation of normal functioning solely, or for interpretation of psychopathological functioning without corollary measures. When further norms and interpretive data have been gathered, this instrument will no doubt be a valuable asset.

[43]

Basic Reading Inventory, Fifth Edition.

Purpose: Designed to assess the student's performance level in reading by a series of graded word lists and graded passages.
Population: Grades Pre-primer–8.
Publication Dates: 1978–91.
Acronym: BRI.
Scores, 3: 3 reading level scores (Independent, Instructional, Frustration) for each of 3 subtests (Word Recognition in Isolation, Word Recognition in Context, Comprehension).
Administration: Individual.
Forms, 5: A, B, C, LN, LE (suggested that A be used for an oral reading measure, B for a silent reading measure, C for a listening measure or posttest, LN for a narrative passages measure, and LE for an expository passages measure; Forms A, B, and C contain word lists and passages ranging from the beginning reader level (pre-primer) through the 8th grade; Forms LN and LE for third to eighth grade in difficulty).
Price Data: Price data for test materials including manual ('91, 284 pages) available from publisher.
Time: Administration time not reported.
Author: Jerry L. Johns.
Publisher: Kendall/Hunt Publishing Company.
Cross References: For a review by Gus P. Plessas of the second edition, see 9:119.

TEST REFERENCES

1. Brozo, W. G. (1989). Learning how at-risk readers learn best: A case for interactive assessment. *Journal of Reading*, *33*, 522-527.
2. Shapiro, J., & White, W. (1991). Reading attitudes and perceptions in traditional and nontraditional reading programs. *Reading Research and Instruction*, *30*(4), 52-66.
3. Rasinski, T. J., Padack, N., Linek, W., & Sturtevant, E. (1994). Effects of fluency development on urban second-grade readers. *Journal of Educational Research*, *87*, 158-165.

Review of the Basic Reading Inventory, Fifth Edition by JERRILYN V. ANDREWS, Assistant for Assessment and Data Collection, Office of School Administration, Montgomery County Public Schools, Rockville, MD:

The Basic Reading Inventory (BRI), an individually administered, informal reading inventory (IRI), is intended for use by classroom teachers, reading specialists, special educators, and students taking courses in reading and diagnosis. The BRI is designed to help a teacher ascertain a student's Independent, Instructional, and Frustration reading levels as well as identify strategies the student uses for word identification, the student's strengths and weaknesses in answering various types of comprehension questions, and listening level.

The 284-page manual includes all five forms of the BRI, instructions for administering and scoring, sample strategies to help students overcome some reading difficulties, a good brief review of the literature on IRIs, and a description of the procedures used in revising the BRI. Although this seems relatively complete, the organization of the manual renders it less useful and user friendly than it could have been. There are two distinct sets of instructions for administering and scoring the BRI; the manual presents the timesaving procedures, intended for people who already understand administering and scoring reading inventories and who want to shorten testing time, in Section 2 and the regular procedures in Section 3. There are some substantial differences between the two sets of instructions and no data are presented to indicate how well the results of different testing procedures correlate. For new users, who are likely to read a manual from front to back, confusion is likely as they go from a general introduction to timesaving administration, which assumes they know quite a bit, followed by regular administration.

To illustrate this problem, the timesaving instructions for scoring Word Recognition in Isolation direct the user to total the correct responses in the "timed" and "untimed" columns. The column headings in the example and the terms used elsewhere in the manual are "sight" and "analysis." An experienced IRI user might quickly understand this change, but a novice probably will not. In addition, in Section 2 the user is told to decide whether to count total miscues or significant miscues before these terms have been introduced or defined. Both sets of instructions for administering and scoring the tests allow a great deal of flexibility and various alternatives are suggested. This flexibility may seriously reduce the likelihood that two testers would come to the same conclusions about a student.

In the review of the IRI literature (Section 7), the manual notes that questions of reliability and validity of IRIs continue to be raised. The BRI certainly illustrates this problem. This fifth edition of the BRI still contains no reliability, validity, or normative data. The manual authors say that for this edition components were refined that "warranted revision, clarification, expansion, and updating" (p. ix) but give no idea of what was changed or why. It explains how the graded word lists were created and field tested on 309 students in grades 1–8 in the U.S. and Canada, but no data are presented to show that there are appropriate differences in difficulty between each level. The authors explain the forms of the BRI were equated in difficulty and generally how that was done; however, the only data presented to support this claim of equivalence are the number of 1-, 2-, and 3-syllable words on each form. In describing the process of revising the reading passages and the comprehension questions, several clearly appropriate steps are listed but again no data are provided regarding the outcome of the procedures. The field testing of this edition is also described, but the only data are the number of students who read each passage on Forms LN and LE. If technical data are available, they should be reported so potential users can make informed judgments about the quality of the test. If basic technical data have not been gathered on a test that is in its fifth edition, then clearly users are being expected to take far too much on faith.

For diagnostic use the authors suggest dividing the comprehension questions into five types: fact, topic, evaluation, inference, and vocabulary. A caution is offered that "these categories of comprehension questions, while widely used in basic reading programs and reading comprehension tests, have little or no empirical support" (p. 59). It is particularly notable that for a given form and grade level the BRI contains five fact, one topic, one evaluation, one vocabulary, and two inference questions. A student might be given four levels of the BRI but four items may not make a very reliable scale. Further, the user is told it is permissible to omit some questions.

A second suggested strategy involves dividing the comprehension questions into lower level (fact) and higher level (the other four) ones. Using this strategy students' relative strengths in lower and higher order skills can be calculated (see p. 63 for an example). A difference of proportions test done by this reviewer, however, found no significant difference between the proportion of correct answers on lower and higher level questions. No clear idea of how to decide if a difference is educationally significant is provided.

In summary, although this is clearly labeled an IRI, the lack of any basic technical information makes it impossible for this reviewer to recommend the use of the BRI for placing and diagnosing students. Graded passages and word lists from a reading program would serve the purpose just as well. Further, the organization of the manual does not make the BRI a good choice for teaching preservice and inservice teachers how to use an IRI.

Review of the Basic Reading Inventory, Fifth Edition by ROBERT T. WILLIAMS, Professor of Occupational and Educational Studies, Colorado State University, Fort Collins, CO:

This inventory is intended for the individual informal assessment of oral reading, silent reading, and listening comprehension in the classroom or clinic. A series of graded word lists and 100 word passages make up the assessment material. There are also longer graded passages (approximately 250 words) of both narrative and expository text. The manual includes guidelines for the quantitative and qualitative evaluation of reading performance and the evaluation of comprehension through comprehension questions, reader retelling, or a combination of the two.

The Basic Reading Inventory seems confused about whether it wants to be a quantitative tool to categorize a reader's performance in traditional terms or a qualitative tool to describe a reader's interaction with written language. The Basic Reading Inventory lacks a consistent philosophy of the reading process, therefore, the use and interpretation of the results seems inconsistent. Although instructions allow one to "count miscues in two different ways so different philosophies or perspectives in scoring can be accommodated" (p. 31), the Inventory would have been more clear and more useful if the assumptions of the various philosophies or perspectives had been summarized and the procedures for each philosophy or perspective had been identified. The various philosophies or perspectives are suggested by statements sprinkled throughout the manual. They are not formally presented so that a user may select a philosophy or perspective and consistently employ it.

The Basic Reading Inventory has no statistically established validity or reliability. This lack might be acceptable in an informal inventory where the purpose was to evaluate or estimate an individual reader's ability to read and comprehend material to be used for instructional and/or recreational reading. If this were the purpose, the evaluator would want to use the material from which the reader would read or learn. The Basic Reading Inventory does not serve well for placement in instructional or recreational reading material because it does not use appropriate material. The use of informal assessment to guide instructional decisions in the classroom or clinic is laudable. The use of material other than that which will be used for instruction is questionable.

The Basic Reading Inventory and its accompanying materials do not help teachers or others involved in the evaluation process develop a background in psycholinguistics, learning theory, or the nature of the reading process. Use of the Basic Reading Inventory may lead preservice or beginning teachers, diagnosticians, or clinicians to assume there is no consistent foundation of reading and that one is left to interpret reading performance as one chooses. Educators, reading diagnosticians, and therapists with strong academic, experiential, professional, and personal foundations in the interactive, psycholinguistic nature of the reading/thinking process would probably not use the Basic Reading Inventory. They would most likely "build" their own reading experiences based upon the expectations they have of the language users with whom they are interacting.

In summary, the use of graded passages for evaluating reading performance in the clinic and for practice by preservice and inservice professionals is valuable. Procedures and practices that recognize and evaluate the dynamic, interactive nature of the reading process are preferred by this reviewer. For the classroom teacher who understands and appreciates this dynamic, interactive aspect of reading, material used for classroom instruction or recreational reading is more effective than the Basic Reading Inventory to evaluate a reader's competencies.

[44]

Bay Area Functional Performance Evaluation, Second Edition.

Purpose: Developed to assess "general components of functioning that are needed to perform activities of daily living."

Population: Psychiatric patients.

Publication Dates: 1978–87.

Acronym: BaFPE.

Administration: Individual.

Price Data, 1988: $135 per complete kit including 25 sorting shells rating sheets, 25 money and marketing rating sheets, 25 home drawing rating sheets, 25 block design rating sheets, 25 kinetic person drawing rating sheets, 25 marketing worksheets, 25 blank checks, seashell set, block design set, 25 SIS assessment forms, 25 TOA assessment forms, 25 SIS rating and summary score sheets, 25 TOA summary score sheets, and manual('87, 97 pages); $63 per 25 refill sets of all 11 expendable forms; $6.50 per 25 sorting shells rating sheets, money and marketing rating sheets, home drawing rating sheets, or kinetic person drawing rating sheets; $5.75 per 25 SIS assessment forms, SIS rating and summary score sheets, or TOA assessment forms; $3.75 per 25 TOA summary score sheets, marketing worksheets, or blank checks; $20 per seashell set; $19 per block design set; $2.25 per set of reusable instruction/demonstration cards; $39.50 per manual.

Comments: Task-Oriented Assessment and Social Interaction Scale may be used separately.

Authors: Susan Lang Williams and Judith Bloomer.

Publisher: Consulting Psychologists Press, Inc.

a) TASK-ORIENTED ASSESSMENT.

Acronym: TOA.

Scores, 138: 16 Component scores: Cognitive (Memory for Written/Verbal Instruction, Organization of Time and Materials, Attention Span, Evidence of Thought Disorder, Ability to Abstract, Total), Performance (Task Completion, Errors, Efficiency, Total), Affective (Motivation/Compliance, Frustration Tolerance, Self-Confidence, General Affective Impression, Total), Total for the following 11 Parameters: Sorting Shells, Money/Marketing, Home Drawing, Block Design, Kinetic Person Drawing, Total; also 11 Qualitative Signs and Referral Indicators ratings: Language, Comprehension, Hemispatial Neglect, Memory, Abstraction, Task-Specific Observations, Total for the above parameters.

Time: (30–45) minutes.

b) SOCIAL INTERACTION SCALE.

Acronym: SIS.

Scores, 13: Parameter scores (Verbal Communication, Psychomotor Behavior, Socially Appropriate Behavior, Response to Authority Figures, Degree of Independence/Dependence, Ability to Work with Others,

Participation in Group Activities), Social Situations (One-to-One, Mealtime, Unstructured Group, Structured Task or Activity Group, Structured Verbal Group), Total Interaction.

Time: [50–60] minutes.

Cross References: See T4:265 (1 reference).

Review of the Bay Area Functional Performance Evaluation, Second Edition by DEBORAH D. ROMAN, Director, Neuropsychology Laboratory, PM & R and Neurosurgery Departments, University of Minnesota, Minneapolis, MN:

The Bay Area Functional Performance Evaluation (BaFPE), Second Edition consists of two components, the Task-Oriented Assessment (TOA) and the Social Interaction Scale (SIS), which can be used separately or together. The original BaFPE was developed in 1978. Subsequent field tests indicated a need to reduce ambiguity in some test parameters, clarify administration instructions, and improve interpretation guidelines, prompting this revision.

The TOA is designed to assess cognitive, affective, and performance functioning. Five tasks are administered: Sorting Shells, Money and Marketing, Home Drawing Task, Block Design, and Kinetic Person Drawing. Performance is rated on a 4-point scale using 12 functional parameters. In addition to these parameters the examiner also completes the Qualitative Signs and Referral Indicators section, in which the subject is rated on five possible indicators of organicity: expressive language, comprehension of written and auditory language, hemispatial neglect, memory, and abstraction. These ratings are based on qualitative observations and are intended as a means of determining the need for further organic workup.

The SIS rates seven aspects of social behavior using observations in five different social settings. These assessment categories are: Verbal Communication, Psychomotor Behavior, Socially Appropriate Behavior, Response to Authority Figures, Independence/Dependence, Ability to Work with Others, and Participation in Group or Program Activities. An optional self-assessment report may be completed by the patient, but the results are not included in the scoring. Behavior is rated on a 5-point continuum ranging from markedly dysfunctional to almost always functional. The five rating settings include a one-to-one interview, mealtime, an unstructured group situation, a structured activity group, and a structured verbal group. This assessment yields scores for each social situation as well as a total score.

The authors assert, "The Bay Area Functional Performance Evaluation (BaFPE) was developed as a reliable and valid means to assess some general components of functioning that are needed to perform activities of daily living" (manual, p. 1). However, the test developers provide no evidence of the BaFPE's validity and little evidence of its reliability.

Concerning validity, no attempt has been made to determine the relationship between the BaFPE performance and other indicators of functional status. The extent to which BaFPE scores can be used to predict functioning in the community, need for support services, length of hospitalization, and so forth, is unknown. In fact, the authors acknowledge, "It is important for clinicians to understand that at this point TOA scores can not be used to predict patient functioning in the community" (p. 55). But this would seem to be the primary use for an instrument of this kind. Further, the patient studies described in the manual have been limited to psychiatric inpatients. Though the authors suggest this test can be used with other patient populations, its utility with other groups has not been explored.

There are several other validity concerns. First, the TOA may in fact be measuring constructs other than the ones intended by the authors. For example, the authors assume that failure to reproduce a block design from memory denotes a memory impairment. Instead, this may be due to inattention or visuospatial processing deficits. Second, for other TOA subtests, the intended construct of interest is not adequately formulated or clearly described. For instance, what function is the Kinetic Person Drawing Task measuring and how is this relevant to functional level or activities of daily living? Third, each of the five TOA tasks consists of a single item. It is doubtful whether this covers a representative sample of the cognitive functions of interest.

Data on the reliability of the BaFPE are incomplete. Reliability studies for the TOA were based on the assessment of 91 hospitalized psychiatric patients. Reliability studies on the SIS were based on a subset of this sample (45 patients). Subjects ranged in age from 17 to 71; all were diagnosed with acute psychosis. "Interrater correlations" for the various TOA and SIS measures are presented as evidence of "interrater reliability." However, the authors do not appear to be using the term "interrater reliability" in the conventional manner (Anastasi, 1982). The manual is not clear on how the interrater correlations were produced. The interrater correlations seem to represent correlations between scores attained by multiple raters, each assessing different patients. They do not appear to be based on scores gleaned from multiple raters independently assessing the same patients. The TOA was administered only once to each subject and the scores calculated by a single rater, yet "interrater correlations" are provided. Two examiners simultaneously observed subjects during administration of the SIS, but it is unclear whether the statistics provided are based on the two examiners' ratings of the same patients, or of different patients. As such, the statistics provided are difficult to interpret. Correlations ranged from .49 to .98 for the TOA and from .56 to .96 for the SIS.

Test-retest reliability studies were not conducted. Given the small number of items in each of the test domains, it would seem that the likelihood of attaining spurious, nonreplicable outcomes would be great. This would be of particular concern in psychiatric populations, wherein many sources of error variance can occur (such as momentary lapses in interest, motivation, attention, or effort level).

Normative data are also limited. Preliminary norms are provided for psychiatric inpatients. TOA means and standard deviations are provide for four small psychiatric groups (sample sizes ranged from 18 to 25). SIS means and standard deviations are provided for two groups of psychiatric patients (sample sizes were 20 and 25). The authors note that the sample sizes are small and may not be representative of psychiatric populations (all of the patients included in the study were acutely psychotic). They encourage users to develop local norms for their populations. But if the BaFPE is to be employed as a measure of functional status and daily living skills, it would seem more worthwhile to provide normative data for a functionally intact population. The norms provided are of limited value in making inferences about the status of the test subject relative to the normal population.

In summary, the BaFPE provides a structured format for making observations about functional domains. However, evidence of the reliability and validity of the instrument as a quantitative measure of adaptive living skills or cognitive abilities is lacking. As such, its use for these purposes is not recommended. A better measure of adaptive living skills would be the Vineland Adaptive Behavior Scales (Sparrow, Balla, & Cicchetti, 1984; T4:2882), which samples a wide range of adaptive living skills (including communication, daily living skills, socialization, and motor skills) and offers good normative data for children and adults. The AAMD Adaptive Behavior Scale (Nihira, Foster, Shellhaas, & Leland, 1975), which featured an indepth survey of living skills and inappropriate behaviors, was a useful instrument specifically designed for use with the mentally retarded. [Editor's Note: This instrument has been replaced by the AAMR Adaptive Behavior Scale—Residential and Community, Second Edition; Nihira, Leland, & Lambert, 1993; T4:1.] A variety of psychometrically sound cognitive measures, such as the Wechsler Adult Intelligence Scales—Revised (Wechsler, 1981; T4:2937), offer a more comprehensive, valid appraisal of cognitive skills, and provide alternatives to the TOA.

REVIEWER'S REFERENCES

Nihira, K., Foster, R., Shellhaas, M., & Leland, H. (1975). *AAMD Adaptive Behavior Scale manual*. Washington, DC: AAMD.

Wechsler, D. (1981). *Wechsler Adult Intelligence Scale—Revised manual*. San Antonio, TX: The Psychological Corporation.

Anastasi, A. (1982). *Psychological testing* (5th ed.). NY: Macmillan Publishing Co., Inc.

Sparrow, S. S., Balla, D. A., & Cicchetti, D. V. (1984). *Vineland Adaptive Behavior Scales interview edition survey form manual*. Circle Pines, MN: American Guidance Service.

Review of the Bay Area Functional Performance Evaluation by OREST E. WASYLIW, Senior Clinical Psychologist, Isaac Ray Center, Chicago, IL:

The Bay Area Functional Performance Evaluation (BaFPE) is an assessment battery designed primarily for psychiatric and neurological patients. Its intent is to assess basic independent living skills through sampling various domains of problem solving and social interactions. The BaFPE is composed of two major sections: The Task-Oriented Assessment (TOA) is designed to measure specific ways in which a person acts in goal-directed ways on the environment. The TOA is composed of five individual tests: Sorting Shells requires categorization and visual discrimination. Money and Marketing uses play and actual money in a variety of shopping-list-development and change-making tasks. Block Design is similar to the Wechsler Adult Intelligence Scale—Revised (WAIS-R) subtest of the same name, but has different stimulus designs. Home Drawing requires a drawing of floor plans. Finally, Kinetic Family Drawings is similar in form to projective drawing tests. The second section of the BaFPE is the Social Interaction Scale (SIS), designed to assess how appropriately a person interacts with others in practical situations. The SIS requires scoring in seven parameters of social behavior, observed in five different social settings. A patient self-assessment form is also included. However, because correlations between the self-assessment form and other BaFPE scores were found to be low (few above .40), this last form is included as an optional information-gathering device.

The Second Edition of the BaFPE has several structural and name changes from the original. The "Bank Deposit" and "House Floor Plan" sections in the original were renamed to "Money and Marketing" and "Home Drawing" respectively, to better communicate their domains. The TOA and SIS scores are no longer combined, to eliminate biases found in the original procedure, and the timing of TOA tasks was formalized. An organic screening instrument was added, derived from observations on the other tasks. This form was not separately validated, but relies on a qualitative "sign" approach (Lezak, 1983). Finally, the SIS was revised to specify five social settings rather than a single overall rating. A reliability study was then conducted. This involved four pairs of OTRs (occupational therapists), who administered the BaFPE to different groups of 25 randomly selected inpatients, all of whom were over 16 years old and had been diagnosed with an acute DSM-III psychiatric disorder. This study was conducted within one week of patients' admission at a single acute-care psychiatric hospital, representing one geographic area. The reported interrater reliabilities are within psychometrically acceptable standards. Differential reliability data are reported for the various subtests of the BaFPE as well as for various component scores. The authors report that 80% of the correlations were at .80 or above. They note differences in reliabilities among and within scorer groups, and suggest that some of these differences may relate to demographic or diagnostic factors. Significant differences between the four patient groups are reported on age, sex, and diagnosis. However, separate reliabilities for different demographic or diagnostic groups are not reported. Also, reliability studies for normal adults are planned, but not yet performed. (Such data were available for the original edition of the BaFPE.) Internal consistency data are also reported for functional parameters and component data. Test-retest studies were apparently planned, but not reported.

The most serious limitation of the BaFPE is that no validity studies have been performed. Basically, the means and standard deviations for the reliability study (N = 91) are the only normative data available to the evaluator. No differential normative data are provided for such variables as age, sex, educational level, or diagnosis. The authors acknowledge this limitation, and suggest that users develop their own local norms. They recommend that evaluators compare patients to the most similar reliability-study groups, but these groups differ significantly on multiple parameters. The sole rationale for the structure of the BaFPE provided by the authors is a brief summary of various theories of functional behavior that have been influential in the field of occupational therapy. These theories are described as "compatible with the approach utilized in developing the BaFPE" (manual, p. 2). No specific rationale is provided for the initial selection of tasks, such as block design, shell sorting, or kinetic drawings. Also, no concurrent validity studies are reported. For example, there have been no attempts to correlate performance on the BaFPE and WAIS-R forms of the Block Design Test, and no attempts to correlate derivative measures, such as memory scores, with other, well-researched memory tests.

It is unfortunate that validity studies are lacking, because the BaFPE does show potential merits. The derivative score categories appear well conceptualized and comprehensive. Scoring categories for the TOA, for example, include memory for written/verbal instructions, organization of time and materials, attention span, evidence of though disorder, ability to abstract, task completion, errors, efficiency, motivation, frustration tolerance, self-confidence, and general affective impression. Although they vary according to the amount of rater subjectivity involved, these assessment categories are potentially useful to occupational therapists, psychologists, or neuropsychologists. Additionally, the use of both familiar and unfamiliar materials offers a potential advantage of this instrument over many standard psychological tests, particularly in the evaluation of the elderly, as elderly patients often perform more poorly in novel situations than in familiar ones (La Rue, 1992). The authors may have missed an opportunity in this regard to develop comparison scores on novel tasks, such as Block Design, and more familiar tasks such as Money and Marketing. The BaFPE does allow for measurement of possible differences in such capacities as memory or attention span in different types of tasks. The authors encourage evaluators to consider such differences, but provide only subjective guidelines for doing so. Some form of difference scores, comparing similar abilities on different tasks, could provide a useful addition to this instrument.

The BaFPE may constitute a useful exploratory technique for occupational therapists to assess areas that may be in need of intervention, or to assess changes in functioning over time. It is very comprehensive in its intended scope. However, it lacks sufficient normative data. Local base rates are desirable, but are not a substitute for comprehensive, demographically specific norms. Without expanded norms or any validity studies, the BaFPE cannot purport to qualify as a psychometric instrument. Without validation studies, it cannot even be asserted that BaFPE measures are more accurate than the self-assessment measures with which they have low correlations. At best, this instrument should be viewed as an exploratory or screening procedure, to point out possible areas for examination by means of better-validated procedures.

REVIEWER'S REFERENCES

Lezak, M. D. (1983). *Neuropsychological assessment* (2nd ed.). New York: Oxford University Press.

La Rue, A. (1992). *Aging and neuropsychological assessment*. New York: Plenum Press.

[45]

Beery Picture Vocabulary Test and Beery Picture Vocabulary Screening Series.

Purpose: Designed to assess recall vocabulary.
Publication Dates: 1990–92.
Price Data, 1994: $99 per complete kit including manual ('92, 91 pages), stimulus card set, 25 Beery PVT record forms, and one each of 11 Beery PVS test booklets; $20 per manual.
Authors: Keith E. Beery and Colleen M. Taheri.
Publisher: Psychological Assessment Resources, Inc.

a) BEERY PICTURE VOCABULARY TEST.
Purpose: Designed to "measure expressive nominal vocabulary."
Population: Ages 2-6 to 39-11.
Acronym: PVT.
Administration: Individual.
Scores: Total score only.
Price Data: $18 per 25 Beery PVT record forms; $60 per Beery PVT stimulus card set.
Time: (10–15) minutes.

b) BEERY PICTURE VOCABULARY SCREENING SERIES.
Purpose: "Classroom screening and/or pretesting."
Population: Grades 2–12.

Acronym: PVS.
Administration: Individual or group.
Scores: Total score only.
Price Data: $22 per 35 Beery PVS test booklets grades 2–12.
Time: (10) minutes.

Review of the Beery Picture Vocabulary Test and the Beery Picture Vocabulary Screening Series by BRUCE G. ROGERS, Professor of Educational Psychology and Foundations, University of Northern Iowa, Cedar Falls, IA:

The Beery Picture Vocabulary Screening Series (PVS) was designed for use by teachers in a classroom setting to evaluate vocabulary development by having students write the name of objects. For those students who are identified (screened) as having difficulty with this task, the Beery Picture Vocabulary Test (PVT) can be used as a follow-up, in-depth instrument for individual administration. The authors believe that because vocabulary is a fundamental component of reading achievement, a sound educational program will include an evaluation of vocabulary development in the annual evaluation program.

Both instruments use "expressive formats" (a term that the authors use when referring to supply-type items) in contrast with most other similar tests, such as the Peabody Picture Vocabulary Test—Revised (PPVT-R), which use a multiple-choice format (p. 1; page numbers in this review refer to the Professional Manual). Although the authors are complimentary of the PPVT-R, they felt that, because of its multiple-choice format, there was a need for an instrument with an expressive format and with nationally representative normative data. From this perspective, they attempted to construct an improved measuring instrument.

DESCRIPTION OF THE PVS AND PVT. In the PVS series, there are 11 tests covering grades 2 through 12, and each is based on 16 nouns representing common objects and some famous people. A black-and-white line drawing, in a 2-inch by 3-inch box, is used to represent the noun, and the student writes a word underneath the drawing. The pictures are neat and professionally drawn. For each grade level, items were selected that showed about 75% correct responses and reasonable discrimination among students in that grade level. The items were also chosen based on "age-appropriate distribution among experience categories" (p. 29), and nine experience categories are listed. How these categories were selected needs to be explained and the age-appropriate distributions need to be described for users who want a better understanding of the test.

The PVT is a set of pictures of nouns on cards, ordered from ages 3 to 40. Mounted on an easel, the cards create a professional appearance. All of the pictures have the same type of line drawing used in the PVS. A careful examination of these two tests suggests that both were constructed in conformity with high standards.

Administering the PVT begins as the teacher estimates the mental age of the child to decide where to start in the age-ordered sequence of pictures. Clear instructions and examples are given to establish a basal score and a ceiling score to generate a standard score and a percentile. Judging from these examples, the teacher can expect to administer about 15 to 20 items to the typical student, which would span 3 or 4 years in the sequence, because there are five items per year for the school-age range.

For the evaluation of the written and spoken responses, guidelines are discussed and the answer key shows some examples of acceptable alternate words and misspellings. What is missing is a discussion of the difficulties teachers have had in deciphering poor penmanship and evaluating alternate words and misspelled words. The teacher is told that, if a student gives a word that is not listed, the "word must . . . —in your judgment—be more sophisticated than those listed" (p. 9). This points out the importance of careful judgment, but the section on Professional Requirements states that "scoring can be performed by anyone who is familiar with the procedures given in this manual" (p. 8). Is it reasonable to assume that the reading of the manual alone will create the ability to make the necessary judgments about the sophistication of the words? Here the manual appears to downplay the need for professional training to administer and score the tests, yet the proper use of these tests depends upon making these "sophisticated judgments."

SCORES AND NORMS. The PVS was normed in a national sample of over 1,000 pupils in grades 2 through 12. A similar size norming sample, ranging in age from 2 to 40, was used for the PVT. The authors state that both standardization samples "were representative of the 1990 U.S. Census" (p. 30) but there are no census data shown in the manual. This oversight should be corrected in an addendum so that potential users can evaluate the representativeness of the sample. From the norming data, raw scores were converted into scaled scores, NCEs, *T* scores, and percentiles, which are laid out in readable tables. Because the norms for the PVS were based on only about 100 students per grade, users must employ appropriate caution in their interpretations, and this concern should also extend to the PVT score interpretations. Data from the PVT were used to create a developmental normative curve, the purpose of which is to show that the average total score increases with both age and grade level. A description of the procedure used for drawing the curve would be helpful, along with information on how close the data fit the curve.

RELIABILITY. To estimate interscorer reliability, the two coauthors each independently scored 25 PVS and 25 PVT fifth-grade record forms and found the resulting correlations to be above .90. Although these data are encouraging, the results will be much more generalizable if data from samples of teachers across all grade levels can be obtained. To estimate internal consistency reliability, the odd-even procedure was applied to each 1-year age group. For the PVS and the PVT, the median values were .73 and .95, respectively. Test-retest values were similar. Values for KR20, which are commonly reported for most standardized tests, were not reported for these tests. Those values would likely have been smaller than the odd-even values, but they would have been more generalizable. The authors feel that a reliability of .8 is a desirable goal for standardized tests. Although the reported value of .79 for the PVS is slightly less than that, it seems acceptable for a screening instrument. After computing the standard error of measurement for each grade and age level, the authors emphasize the value of constructing two-thirds confidence bands, a commendable procedure.

VALIDITY. The content validity of these tests is primarily "judged by the task selection procedures" (p. 35). An examination of those procedures shows that they are stated in quite general terms that follow accepted test construction guidelines, but more details need to be given. To provide evidence of concurrent validity, the PVS and PVT test scores were correlated with each other and with scores from a widely used measure of reading achievement, namely, the Comprehensive Test of Basic Skills (CTBS) Reading Total, in each grade level. These correlation values were quite consistent, with median values between .5 and .7, suggesting that the PVS scores are moderately good estimators of PVT scores and that both PVS and PVT scores are measuring an important component of reading ability. Evidence for construct validity was provided mainly from the developmental normal curve relationship. Those data are appropriate, but evidence from further studies needs to be gathered to substantiate the claim for construct validity.

SUMMARY. In summary, the PVS is a norm-referenced screening test of vocabulary development requiring written responses to line drawings, whereas the PVT is a follow-up test requiring oral responses to similar stimuli. It appears that standard procedures were used to develop the item sequences and to generate national norms, although the norming sample was small for each grade level. The test-retest reliability values were slightly lower than anticipated, but they are adequate to warrant further study and continued use of the tests. The validity evidence is relevant, but further studies are needed. These two series, when properly used together, will be of value to both researchers and classroom teachers.

Review of the Beery Picture Vocabulary Test and Beery Picture Vocabulary Screening Series by NORA M. THOMPSON, Clinical Assistant Professor, Department of Psychiatry, University of Texas Health Science Center, San Antonio, TX:

PURPOSE. The Beery Picture Vocabulary Screening Series (PVS) was designed for group screening of written expressive vocabulary. Like the Beery Picture Vocabulary Test, the PVS exclusively assesses the knowledge of nouns, described as the foundation of vocabulary. The intended population is students enrolled in grades 2 through 12 with adequate visual and visual-motor capabilities. Because vocabulary is proposed to underlie much of academic development, the authors propose that the PVS is a useful screening tool or pre- and posttest measure for use in the classroom.

CONTENT. The PVS consists of a Professional User's Guide and Class Record, as well as a series of 11 test booklets, one for each grade level 2 through 12. The instructions for administering, scoring, and interpreting the PVS are clearly described in the manual. Each test booklet consists of four pages. Page 1 has space for identifying information and test results as well as printed instructions for the student. Page 2 contains two sample items for training as well as test items 1 through 4. The remaining test items are found on pages 3 and 4. Each test item consists of a black line drawing on a white background. Below each drawing is a blank line with a single letter at the beginning of the line. The student is instructed to write the word that starts with the printed letter and best describes the picture on the blank line. Students are allowed 10 minutes to complete the 16 test items. The number correct (i.e., the raw score) is then converted to a standard score and percentile using the table provided in the manual. The authors recommend that students obtaining a score below the 10th percentile be referred for further evaluation, although the rationale for this cutoff is not stated.

NORMATIVE DATA. The development of the test and the characteristics of the normative sample are well described in the professional manual. The normative sample of 1,174 students was chosen from all five major geographic regions to be representative of the 1990 U.S. Census on the basis of age, ethnicity, gender, and area of residence.

RELIABILITY AND VALIDITY. Reliability findings for the PVS are acceptable. Interscorer, internal consistency, and test-retest reliability average .79. Two forms of validity data are presented in the manual. The PVS correlated with the Beery Picture Vocabulary Test at a median of $r = .61$, supporting the construct validity of the PVS. The correlation of the PVS with a summary reading score was .58, suggesting strong concurrent validity of the PVS with global reading ability. Further studies that systematically identify cutoff levels for referral for further testing would be a useful addition to the PVS.

CONCLUSIONS. The PVS appears to be a reliable and valid screening test for expressive vocabulary which can prove helpful in identifying students who need further evaluation. Carefully developed and well normed, the PVS can be used by teachers as well as education professionals.

PURPOSE. The Beery Picture Vocabulary Test (PVT) was designed for individual, in-depth evaluation of expressive vocabulary for Standard American English. Developed to overcome the limitations of a multiple-choice, recognition format for testing vocabulary, the PVT focuses exclusively on the assessment of nouns, which the authors describe as the foundation of vocabulary. Individuals aged 2 years, 6 months through 40 years with adequate visual and speech capacities represent the intended population. Because vocabulary is proposed to underlie intellectual and academic development, the PVT is also depicted as providing a "quick estimate of verbal aptitude." However, it is not intended as a comprehensive evaluation of intelligence.

CONTENT. The PVT consists of an examiner's manual, a booklet of 165 stimulus cards, and record forms. The record form contains adequate space for identifying information, abbreviated instructions for administration and scoring, and tables for generating and comparing derived scores. The instructions for administering, scoring, and interpreting the PVT are clearly described in the manual. Each stimulus card contains a line drawing on a white background with a single letter approximately one inch below. The examinee is shown a stimulus card and asked to generate a word which begins with the printed letter and describes the picture. Four training items are administered to children under age 10, and at least one and as many as four training items can be administered to older students and adults. Directions for probing general answers and prompting correct responses on training items are provided. Suggested starting points, based on chronological age, are given and testing is discontinued after eight consecutive errors. The number of errors is subtracted from the ceiling item to derive the raw score, which is then converted to a standard score and percentile using tables provided in the manual. A rough method for developing age and grade equivalents is offered, but the value of this procedure is unclear, as the examiner is discouraged from using these scores.

NORMATIVE DATA. The development of the test and the characteristics of the normative sample are well described in the professional manual. The normative sample of 1,189 individuals was chosen from all five major geographic regions to be representative of the 1990 U.S. Census on the basis of age, ethnicity, gender, and area of residence.

RELIABILITY AND VALIDITY. Interscorer, internal consistency, and test-retest reliability all exceed .90, which indicate very strong reliability for the PVT. Two forms of validity data are presented in the manual. The authors present correlation results of the PVT with two other major vocabulary tests, the Peabody Picture Vocabulary Test—Revised (PPVT-R) and the Expressive One-Word Picture Vocabulary Test—Revised (EOWPVT-R). The correlations obtained were moderate to high, supporting the construct validity of the PVT. Concurrent validity of the PVT against global reading scores resulted in high correlations (generally .70 to .80), much higher than correlations of either the PPVT-R or EOWPVT-R with reading measures. The higher predictive power of the PVT for reading may be due in part to the inclusion of a letter cue on the stimulus card.

CONCLUSIONS. The PVT appears to be a reliable and valid measure of expressive vocabulary which can provide useful information across a wide range of age and ability levels. Carefully developed and well normed, the PVT can be used with confidence by professionals in psychology, education, speech/language, or learning disabilities.

[46]

Behavior Disorders Identification Scale.

Purpose: "Developed to contribute to the early identification and service delivery for students with behavior disorders/emotional disturbance" through direct observations by educators and parents.
Population: Ages 4.5–21.
Publication Date: 1988.
Acronym: BDIS.
Scores, 5: Learning, Interpersonal Relations, Inappropriate Behavior Under Normal Circumstances, Unhappiness/Depression, Physical Symptoms/Fears.
Administration: Individual.
Price Data, 1993: $147 per complete kit including 50 pre-referral behavior checklist forms, 50 pre-referral intervention strategies documentations, School Version technical manual (34 pages), 50 School Version rating forms, Home Version technical manual (34 pages), 25 Home Version rating forms, and Teacher's Guide to Behavioral Interventions (291 pages); $25 per 50 pre-referral behavior checklist forms; $25 per 50 pre-referral intervention strategies documentations; $12 per School Version technical manual; $32 per 50 School Version rating forms; $12 per Home Version technical manual; $15 per 25 Home Version rating forms; $26 per Teacher's Guide to Behavioral Interventions; $12 per computerized School Version quick score (IBM or Apple II); $190 per computerized Teacher's Guide to Behavioral Interventions (IBM, Macintosh, or Apple II).
Time: [20] minutes for School Version; [15] minutes for Home Version.
Comments: "Includes both a school and home version to provide an ecological perception of student behavior problems"; "used to measure the student's improvement

as a result of the intervention program developed with the intervention manual."
Authors: Fred Wright and Kathy Cummins Wunderlich (Teacher's Guide to Behavioral Interventions).
Publisher: Hawthorne Educational Services, Inc.

Review of the Behavior Disorders Identification Scale by DOREEN WARD FAIRBANK, Adjunct Assistant Professor of Psychology, Meredith College, Raleigh, NC:

The Behavior Disorders Identification Scale (BDIS) is an individually administered instrument designed to measure emotional disturbance/behavior disorders in the school and home environment for the purposes of early identification and educational service delivery. The authors base the BDIS on the definition of emotional disturbance/behavior disorders contained in PL 94-142. Specifically, the five subareas of the BDIS were designed to correspond to the five dimensions of emotional disturbance/behavior disorders included in the PL 94-142 definition: Learning, Interpersonal Relations, Inappropriate Behavior, Unhappiness/Depression, and Physical Symptoms/Fears. The second part of the PL 94-142 criteria involves the frequency, intensity, and context of the behavior. The BDIS addresses this aspect of the federal mandate in the response categories to items: "Not in my Presence" (score of 1), "One time in several months" (2), "Several Times, up to one time a month" (3), "More than one time a month, up to one time a week" (4), "More than one time a week, up to once a day" (5), "More than once a day, up to once an hour" (6), and "More than once an hour" (7).

The BDIS goes a step further than most tests in helping teachers to comply with the legal requirements of PL 94-142 by providing a manual for developing the student's Individual Educational Plan (IEP) goals and objectives. This manual (titled *Teacher's Guide to Behavioral Intervention*) is a very thorough reference manual that should be especially helpful to the new special education teacher or the regular education teacher who may have a student with emotional disturbance/behavior disorders in her/his classroom. This manual may also prove beneficial for establishing goals for regular classroom students who exhibit minor behavior problems.

The complete BDIS kit consists of a prereferral behavior checklist and a form for documenting prereferral intervention strategies, a School Version technical manual and rating forms, a Home Version technical manual and rating forms, and a Teacher's Guide to Behavioral Intervention. Therefore, a clear strength of the complete BDIS kit is that it provides the examiner with all the materials necessary to comply with the PL 94-142 requirements (the prereferral documentation, the assessment, and the IEP goals and objectives) of serving a student with emotional disturbance/behavioral disorders.

The BDIS, considered ecological in nature, relies both on the school and home environment for the behavioral observations and documentation. The BDIS Home Version rating form is completed by a parent/guardian who has knowledge of the student at home, whereas the School Version rating form is more likely to be completed by a teacher. Administration of each version of the BDIS can be completed in about 20 minutes without the student being present. Scoring the BDIS is completed by converting raw scores to subscale standard scores and the overall percentile score using the technical manual for either the school or home version.

In the norming of this instrument, careful attention was paid to sample size and geographic distribution to acquire a sample that is likely to be representative of the U.S. population of children and youth. The developers of the BDIS appear to have done an excellent job in this regard, especially with respect to stratifying the normative sample by sex and by age. The generalizability of the BDIS could have been enhanced further, however, by enrolling in the normative sample adequate numbers of racial/ethnic minority youth to permit assessment of the psychometric characteristics of the instrument by ethnicity. The authors of the School Version manual indicate that 95% of the 3,188 students in the normative sample were white, and as a result it is unlikely there are sufficient numbers of minority youth in the sample to assess the reliability, validity, and utility of the BDIS for African-American, Latino, and other minority youth by age groupings and sex. Further work examining the sensitivity and specificity of this instrument for detecting behavior disorders in minority children and youth is warranted.

Another clear strength of the BDIS is the care paid to examining the psychometric properties of this instrument. The five factors of the BDIS appear robust. Test-retest and interrater reliabilities are within acceptable ranges. The authors describe the work done to examine statistically the underlying dimensions of the BDIS and its factors using principal components analysis. Concurrent validity was investigated by correlating this instrument with another measure of emotional disturbance and behavior disorder in youth, the Behavior Evaluation Scale (BES; McCarney, Leigh, & Cornbleet, 1983, 9:128). Overall, the findings from these analyses appear supportive of the construct and criterion-related validity of the BDIS. A potential limitation, however, is that the principal components analyses were conducted without breaking down the total sample by important characteristics related to the prevalence of emotional disturbance/behavior disorders (e.g., sex, SES, ethnicity). Future efforts might examine whether underlying dimensions of the BDIS vary by sex by employing confirmatory factor analytic techniques to examine specifically the factor structure of the BDIS separately for males and females.

In summary, the BDIS was developed to assess the existence of behaviors that meet the PL 94-142 criteria for identifying students with emotional disturbance/behavioral disorders, target areas of need for behavioral intervention/improvements, identify IEP goals and objectives, measure behavior change over time due to program implementation, and help identify areas of need for home intervention. Overall, the BDIS is a comprehensive, reliable, and valid instrument that is a welcome addition to the assessment of students with emotional disturbance/behavior disorders.

REVIEWER'S REFERENCE

McCarney, S. B., Leigh, J. E., & Cornbleet, J. E. (1983). Behavior Evaluation Scale. Columbia, MO: Educational Services.

Review of the Behavior Disorders Identification Scale by HARLAN J. STIENTJES, School Psychologist, Grant Wood Area Education Agency, Cedar Rapids, IA:

The Behavior Disorders Identification Scale (BDIS) was developed to assist in the early identification of students (age 4½ to 21 years) with behavior disorders and emotional disturbance. The BDIS includes both a School Version and a Home Version, in an attempt to gather information from knowledgeable individuals in several environments. Both scales are divided into five subscales: Learning Problems, Interpersonal Problems, Inappropriate Behavior or Feeling, Unhappiness/Depression, and Physical Symptoms or Fears. A Teachers' Guide to Behavior Intervention includes a listing of generic behavioral objectives and intervention strategies for 110 behavior problems.

The BDIS manual author outlines many of the faults of other behavior checklists. Claims are made that these faults are remedied in the BDIS. For the most part this is not true. The BDIS is based upon a theoretical construct utilized in the definition of behavior disorders/emotional disturbance that appears in PL 94-142. Throughout the manual unsubstantiated claims are presented without reference to research (e.g., the claim that fears are a more important component to troublesome behavior now than when the definition of behavior disorders was written and therefore, now need to be included). This assumption is not supported by reported data from principal component analysis; nevertheless, a separate subscale combining physical symptoms and fears is included.

In addition, several questionable practices are advocated. The BDIS author encourages interpretation of subscales as individual measures, but does not suggest limits of statistically meaningful variation. The implication is that the subscale profile can lead to appropriate selection of behaviors for programming and intervention. This claim would not appear to be educationally sound or practical. Variation of one standard deviation below the mean on any of the five subscales is said to represent extreme behavior significant enough to qualify the student for special program services. This would seem to be advocating that fully 15% of the student population is behaviorally disordered.

Furthermore, the scaling system, in an attempt to be precise, leaves the rater with an onerous task. For example, some of the 83 items on the school version are 35 to 40 words long. These items must be given a rating between "7 (more than once an hour)" and "1 (not in my presence)." As a result, teacher and parent judgment of acceptability may be quite poor.

The Teachers' Guide to Behavioral Intervention is also of questionable value. Generic goals and objectives are listed for 110 behaviors. Strategies are then listed for each of the behaviors. For the most part, the strategies are vague without enough specifics to make them useable.

Although the idea behind the BDIS has some value, the instrument and intervention guide appear to be of little practical value and cannot be recommended for use in this format.

[47]

Behavior Evaluation Scale—2.

Purpose: To provide information about student behavior.
Population: Grades K–12.
Publication Dates: 1983–90.
Acronym: BES-2.
Scores, 6: Learning Problems, Interpersonal Difficulties, Inappropriate Behaviors, Unhappiness/Depression, Physical Symptoms/Fears, Total.
Administration: Individual.
Price Data, 1993: $111 per complete kit including 50 pre-referral behavior checklist forms, 25 data collection forms, technical manual ('90, 34 pages), 50 student record forms, and BES-2 intervention manual ('93, 244 pages); $20 per 50 pre-referral behavior checklist forms; $25 per 25 data collection forms; $12 per technical manual; $30 per student record form; $24 per intervention manual; $12 per computerized quick score (IBM or Apple II).
Time: (15–20) minutes.
Comments: "Criterion referenced"; ratings by teachers or other school personnel.
Authors: Stephen B. McCarney, Michele T. Jackson, and James E. Leigh.
Publisher: Hawthorne Educational Services, Inc.
Cross References: For reviews by J. Jeffrey Grill, Lester Mann, and Leonard Kenowitz of the earlier edition, see 9:128.

Review of the Behavior Evaluation Scale—2 by BERT A. GOLDMAN, Professor of Education, University of North Carolina at Greensboro, Greensboro, NC:

The Behavior Evaluation Scale—2 (BES-2) by Stephen McCarney and James Leigh has six primary purposes: (*a*) screen for behavior problems; (*b*) assess the behavior of referred students; (*c*) assist in the diagnosis of behavior disorders/emotional disturbance; (*d*) contribute to the development of individual education programs for students in need of special education services; (*e*) document progress resulting from behavioral interventions; and (*f*) collect data for research purposes. The scale can be used with most students from kindergarten through 12th grade who exhibit behavioral or emotional problems. In approximately 15 to 20 minutes classroom teachers and other school personnel who have the opportunity to observe students' behavior over time in a variety of contexts can screen students to identify those who may have problems that warrant further diagnostic evaluation and possible special services.

Each of the 76 items representing a specific behavior is associated with one of five subscales which include: Learning Problems, Interpersonal Difficulties, Inappropriate Behaviors, Unhappiness/Depression, and Physical Symptoms/Fears. Users of the scale rate each behavior item for frequency of occurrence on a 7-point scale as follows: 1–*never or not observed*; 2–*less than once a month*; 3–*approximately once a month*; 4–*approximately once a week*; 5–*more than once a week*; 6–*daily at various times*; and 7–*continuously throughout the day*.

After the items are rated by the user they are multiplied by a designated weight of either 1, 3, or 5 based upon the seriousness of each behavior item. Seriousness was determined by 276 regular and special education teachers. These item scores are then added to determine the five subscale raw scores. Next, by use of a table, the raw scores are converted into standard scores and percentile ranks. Further, the sum of the five subscale standard scores, by using a table, is converted to a behavior quotient and a percentile rank. Also, a standard error of measurement for each subscale standard score and for the behavior quotient is provided in a table. Finally, the behavior quotient and the five subscale standard scores can be plotted on a profile indicating at a glance whether a student's behavior is average or atypical relative to normative data for each characteristic.

A supplemental form, the Data Collection Form, may be used optionally by school personnel to procure daily documentation of the occurrence of any or all of the behaviors on the scale.

Development of the BES-2, as described in the manual, appears to have been accomplished through a series of carefully planned and executed procedures dating back to the preparation of the original 1983 BES. The test authors collaborated with many Missouri teachers of behaviorally disordered students to compile the 47 items of the 1983 BES. The list of 47 items was given to 80 Missouri special education teachers and related professionals for revision resulting in a 50-item scale. Each item was assigned by the authors to one of the five characteristics in the federal definition of behavior disorders/emotional disturbance included in PL 94-142. Next, 104 elementary and secondary level teachers from eight Missouri school districts representing metropolitan, suburban, and rural areas ranging in size from 400 to 10,000 students each conducted two evaluations with the BES, one on a student who exhibited serious classroom behavior problems and one on a student considered to be typical or average in the teacher's class. Suggestions from these 104 teachers and from statistical item analyses formed the basis for the final version of the 1983 scale containing 52 items.

In 1988 a revised 83-item pool was prepared by adding 31 new items to the existing 52 items of the 1983 scale. The new items were suggested by a large number of diagnosticians, teachers, and other school personnel, and two nationally recognized experts in behavior disorders/emotional disturbance. A new set of weightings for each item was established by 276 regular and special education teachers of grades K–12 from 16 states. Following a preliminary item analysis of the 83 items developed from a small sample of Missouri students, another item analysis was conducted from input by 675 teachers from 31 states using over 2,700 students. This work resulted in the elimination of seven items with discriminating power outside a range of .30 to .80, leaving 76 items in the final scale which were judged to be appropriate by at least 95% of the teachers and by a final item analysis.

BES-2 norms are based upon 2,272 students from 31 states representative of the four major United States geographical regions and other demographic characteristics of gender, residence, race, ethnicity, physical/emotional condition, grade level, and parents' educational status. Grade level, gender, race, ethnicity, geographic region, residence, and parents' education all seem to reflect representative proportions of the United States population. Although the authors of the manual indicate the normative sample included 31 states, the acknowledgment section of the manual identifies only 28 states plus the District of Columbia. Whereas the scale is intended for working with behavior problem students, only 2.4% (about 54) of the normative sample consisted of such youngsters.

Item weightings on the original BES items were 1, 2, or 3. Weightings for the BES-2 were determined first by having 276 regular and special education teachers evaluate each item on a 1–9 scale according to its perceived severity. Those items ranking within one standard deviation of the mean weighting for all items received a weighting of 3; those ranking more than one standard deviation below the mean received a 1; and those ranking more than one standard deviation above the mean received a weighting of 5. No further explanation is given for the weighting system except to say it enables measurement of a broad range of severity of behaviors in a more sensitive manner.

The scale appears to be relatively easy for classroom teachers to administer, score, and interpret results.

Clear, step-by-step directions are presented in the manual so that classroom teachers should have little or no difficulty in using the scale. There are, however, two minor errors in the manual. The first error probably goes undetected by most classroom teachers who may not be aware of the subtle difference between percentile and percentile rank. Thus, where the directions instruct the user to record numbers on the Student Record Form in the spaces designated percentile rank, those spaces are actually labeled %ile which stands for percentile not percentile rank. The manual authors' second error is in the example presented to demonstrate how to determine each item's weighted score. In the example, Item 8 was assigned a rating of 4 (approximately once a week) and Item 8 has a weighting of 5. However, in the last sentence of the example, these two numbers, 4 and 5, have been reversed so that the example indicates that the rating of 5 (which should be 4) is to be multiplied by its weighting of 4 (which should be 5). Because the correct result is 20 in either case, this error should cause little if any confusion. However, what may be confusing is that for raw scores, *higher* raw scores indicate greater concern; but when the raw scores are converted to standard scores, *lower* standard scores indicate greater concern.

The sum of the five subscale standard scores is converted to a total scale quotient with a mean of 100 and a standard deviation of 15. Why introduce the concept "quotient" when there is no quotient involved? Further, the manual authors point out the similarity between this procedure and the one introduced by Wechsler for use with his intelligence scale. The use of a scale quotient and its similarity to an intelligence quotient may very well lead some users of the BES-2 to think the BES-2 quotient is an IQ.

Data regarding reliability generally appear satisfactory. In the case of internal consistency, all alpha coefficients for BES-2 scales 1, 2, and 3 were .90 or higher and for Scale 4, the alpha coefficients ranged from .87 to .89. Alpha coefficients for grades K–3 and 4–6, although acceptable, were .78 and .75 respectively for Scale 5. The remaining Scale 5 alpha coefficients for grades 7–9 and 10–12 were better (i.e., .81 and .82 respectively). Total scale alpha coefficients were all .97 except for one .98.

Test-retest reliability (10 to 14 days) coefficients for the five subscales were in the .90s with one .89. The total scale test-retest reliability coefficients were .97 (normal group) and .94 (behaviorally disordered group).

Even though, as the manual authors point out, a student may appear to be withdrawn in one class while exhibiting the opposite behavior in another class, it would be helpful to have some indication of interrater reliability, given that the BES-2 scores are based upon the rater's judgment of the student's behavior.

Three types of validity are presented and although some of the findings are questionable, overall there is convincing evidence of the scale's validity. Evidence of content validity was determined from the combination of statistical item analyses and the professional judgment of 675 professional educators.

Criterion-related validity was based upon two studies. One of the studies involved correlations of the five subscales of BES-2 with the Teacher Rating Scale of the Behavior Rating Profile (BRP). BES-2 Subscales 2, 3, and 5 produced correlations of .73, .81, and .62 respectively with the BRP Teacher Rating Scale that were significant at the .01 level of confidence. BES-2 Subscale 4 produced a .44 correlation significant at the .05 level. BES-2 Subscale 1 (Learning Problems) produced virtually zero correlation (.01) with the BRP scale. The only explanation given for this lack of correlation was that BES-2 Subscale 1 contains items primarily related to academically related problems rather than the social or emotional problems contained in the other BES-2 subscales. However, no description of the content of the BRP scale is given. Also, the reader is not told anything about the validity of the BRP scale.

The second criterion-related validity study was based on 190 regular and special education teachers' overall rating of student's classroom behavior on a 9-point scale and their BES-2 ratings of the student. Each teacher rated one student. Although 9 of the 10 correlations were significant at least at the .01 level, they are based upon the ratings of the same teachers using both the 9-point scale of classroom behavior and the BES-2. It would be more convincing to see the correlation between the ratings on each student from independent evaluators (i.e., one group of teachers using the 9-point scale of classroom behavior and the other group of teachers using the BES-2).

Construct validity was investigated by three studies. The first study compared the BES-2 scores of 108 students (K–12) who had been diagnosed as behaviorally disordered with 102 regular class students randomly selected from the standardization sample. Mean differences between the two groups were statistically significant (.001 level) for each of the five subscales indicating significantly more behavior/emotional problems for the behaviorally disordered students on the five subscales. In a second study the BES-2 subscale and total scale scores of a sample of students were compared with the mean subscale and mean total scale scores of the standardization sample. All mean differences between the two groups were statistically significant beyond the .001 level which supports the diagnostic validity of the scale. Further, all but one subscale intercorrelation ranged between .57 and .75 and all subscale correlations with the total score ranged between .77 and .95 providing evidence that the subscales measure different aspects of the behavioral construct. The one intercorrelation of .90 between Subscales 2 and 3 suggests that these subscales are measuring very similar domains. Finally, 69 of the 76 items (91%) correlated highly enough with their subscales to indicate the items within subscales are measuring the same constructs.

In summary, authors McCarney and Leigh appear to have done a thorough job in developing the Behavior Evaluation Scale—2. The manual is written clearly with only a few minor errors. Classroom teachers should find the directions for administering, scoring, and interpreting the results well explained and easy to follow.

Information concerning the instrument's reliability and validity are given in considerable detail and present strong evidence, with only a few questionable aspects, supporting acceptable reliability and validity. Also, in general, the standardization process appears to be based upon representative samples of students, teachers, and other professional personnel.

The BES-2 appears to be a good instrument to assist teachers and other school personnel to identify students who have serious behavioral and emotional problems.

Review of the Behavior Evaluation Scale—2 by D. JOE OLMI, Assistant Professor of School Psychology, Department of Psychology, University of Southern Mississippi, Hattiesburg, MS:

The Behavior Evaluation Scale—2 (BES-2) is a norm-referenced child behavior rating scale designed to aid in the identification of children in grades K–12 who may be at risk for behavioral disorders/emotional disturbance. It comprises 76 items that encompass five subscales (Learning Problems, Interpersonal Difficulties, Inappropriate Behavior, Unhappiness/Depression, Physical Symptoms/Fears) specific to the five characteristics of behavior disorders/emotional disturbance included in P.L. 94-142. The BES-2 is a revision of its 1983 predecessor, the Behavior Evaluation Scale (BES). As stated by the authors, it has six primary purposes: (*a*) screen for behavior problems; (*b*) assess the behavior of referred students; (*c*) assist in the diagnosis of behavior disorders/emotional disturbance; (*d*) contribute to the development of individual education programs for students in need of special education services; (*e*) document progress resulting from behavioral interventions; and (*f*) collect data for research purposes (p. 2).

The instrument includes a manual, the Student Record Form, and the Data Collection Form. The manual is brief, concise, well organized, and easily understood. It includes an overview of the instrument, information about its development, its statistical properties, the administration guidelines, and interpretation information. The tables and appendices facilitate easy scoring. The Student Record Form is the actual behavior rating protocol, with the Data Collection Form serving as an ongoing assessment device for documenting the observed frequency of the behaviors contained in the scale.

The Student Record Form includes sections detailing demographic data, a behavior profile with shaded regions denoting clinical significance, the 76 items for rating, the Data Summary Section, guidelines for administration, and space for comments. Each item of the BES-2 is to be rated by the teacher(s) of the referred child, after several opportunities for contact or observation, on a Likert scale ranging from 1 (*never or Not Observed*) to 7 (*Continuously Throughout the Day*). Items particular to the five subscales are placed randomly to prevent response bias. The amount of time needed to respond to the items is approximately 15–20 minutes as indicated in the manual. Transferring the ratings to the Data Summary Section and scoring took this reviewer approximately 25 additional minutes.

The rating of behaviors on the BES-2 yields total scale and subscale standard scores with a mean of 10 and standard deviation of 3, percentiles and standard errors of measurement associated with the total scale and subscale scores, and a total scale quotient with a mean of 100 and standard deviation of 15. Subscale standard scores below 8 (25th percentile) are considered behaviorally deviant, as are total scale quotients below 90. The authors point out that scores for the scale tend to "truncate" at the upper end. Because scores at the lower end suggest behavioral deviance this is not a significant problem.

Items selected for inclusion on the BES-2 were derived from the original items of the BES with 31 additional items that were selected based on suggestions by "diagnosticians, teachers, and other school personnel who had used the original BES" (p. 8). Item suggestions were also provided by experts in the field of behavior disorders/emotional disturbance. Item weightings were established by 276 general and special education teachers (K–12) from 16 states who ranked the "perceived severity of the behavior represented by each item" (p. 8) on a scale from 1 to 9 with 9 being the most severe. Three final weighting categories (1, 3, 5) were established by the authors. How that decision was made was not fully discussed by the authors.

Correlations of each item with the total scale and subscale were computed with a .30 to .80 coefficient range generally accepted as the standard for inclusion. In the final analysis, some items with correlations below and above the range were accepted for inclusion due to being considered important behaviors by a significant number of teachers who rated the items. Of the 76 items selected for inclusion, 89% of them satisfied the inclusion criteria. Five items fell below .30 and four items fell above .80, but were retained.

These standards for inclusion are acceptable for an instrument of this nature.

The standardization sample of the BES-2 was composed of 2,272 students across K–12 grade levels from 31 states representing the four geographical regions of the United States. Five hundred sixty-eight teachers administered the instrument to randomly selected students in their classes with the numbers ranging from a low of 137 eleventh graders to a high of 207 fifth graders. The demographic breakdown of students in the sample closely compared to U.S. statistical information compiled in 1980 for gender, race, geographic region, residence, and parents' education level for the general population and school-age population. Children with emotional disturbance/behavior disorders composed 2.4% of the standardization sample.

Normative conversion tables are included in the manual for four grade groupings (K–3, 4–6, 7–9, 10–12) representing lower elementary, upper elementary, middle school, and upper secondary. The authors acknowledge "a statistical justification for developing different normative tables based upon differences in certain subscale mean scores at different grade intervals" (p. 11), but favored the less precise method of grade grouping. One might consider this decision to be a psychometric defect.

Another flaw related to these broad grade-based norms is the assumption that the student referred for evaluation has not been retained due to academic deficits. For example, the referred student might currently be placed in the 5th grade, when in fact he/she would be in the 7th grade had there been no retentions. In this case the student would be compared to a normative sample comprising much younger children.

Coefficients of internal consistency (coefficients alpha) for the subscales and total scale across the four grade groupings ranged from .75 to .98. With a time interval between first and second ratings of behaviors by teachers of 10 to 14 days, test-retest coefficients for subscales and the total scale exceeded or were rounded to .90. These coefficients are acceptable. Criterion-related validity was suggested in comparisons of the BES-2 with the Behavior Rating profile (BRP) Teacher Rating Scale. The correlation between the total scale BES-2 and the BRP was .76, which was significant at the .01 level. Correlations of the subscales were significant at the .05 level (Unhappiness/Depression) and .01 level (Interpersonal Difficulties, Inappropriate Behaviors, Physical Symptoms/Fears). The Learning Problems subscale did not correlate significantly with the BRP. Construct validity coefficients were acceptable.

In summary, the BES-2 is an improvement over its predecessor. When used in conjunction with other assessment procedures, it can be a useful instrument. The manual is brief and easily followed. Forms are well organized, but the user may be less inclined to use the Data Collection Form for follow-up. As part of a more comprehensive battery, the psychologist, school psychologist, school social worker, special education teacher, or diagnostician can be adequately served by the Behavior Evaluation Scale—2.

[48]

Behavior Rating Profile, Second Edition.

Purpose: "To evaluate students' behaviors at home, in school, and in interpersonal relationships."
Population: Ages 6-6 to 18-6.
Publication Dates: 1978–90.
Acronym: BRP-2.
Scores: 5 checklists: Student Rating Scales (Home, School, Peers), Teacher Rating Scale, Parent Rating Scale, plus Sociogram score.
Administration: Group.
Price Data, 1994: $139 per complete kit; $25 per 50 rating scale booklets (specify student, parent, or teacher form); $21 per 50 profile forms; $28 per manual ('90, 75 pages).
Foreign Language Edition: Spanish edition available.
Time: (15–30) minutes per scale.
Authors: Linda Brown and Donald D. Hammill.
Publisher: PRO-ED, Inc.
Cross References: For reviews by Thomas R. Kratochwill and Joseph C. Witt of an earlier edition, see 9:130 (1 reference); see also T3:273 (1 reference).

TEST REFERENCES

1. Maag, J. W., Vasa, S. F., Reid, R., & Torrey, G. K. (1995). Social and behavioral predictors of popular, rejected, and average children. *Educational and Psychological Measurement*, 55, 196-205.

Review of the Behavior Rating Profile, Second Edition by SARAH J. ALLEN, Assistant Professor of School Psychology, University of Cincinnati, Cincinnati, OH:

The Behavior Rating Profile, Second Edition (BRP-2) is a norm-referenced ecological battery of indirect assessment measures designed to evaluate the perceived behavior of children 6-6 through 18-6 years of age in a variety of settings and from several different perspectives. There are six instruments in the BRP-2 battery including: the three Student Rating Scales, the Parent Rating Scale, the Teacher Rating Scale, and the Sociogram. Each scale or sociogram is an independent measure that may be administered individually or in combination with any of the other instruments. The instruments may be administered in any order.

The Student Rating Scales include three self-rating scales that describe behavior in the areas of Home, School, and Peers. Each scale contains 20 items that combine into a single 60-item instrument. Administered in either an individual or group format, students identified for assessment are asked to describe their own behavior by responding "True" or "False" to each item.

The Parent Rating Scale is completed by the child's primary caregivers, usually one or both parents. Composed of 30 items, each item is a sentence stem describing behaviors that may be observed at home. Respondents are asked to classify each behavior using the following rating scale: "Very Much Like My Child," "Like My Child," "Not Much Like My Child," or "Not At All Like My Child."

There also are 30 items on the Teacher Rating Scale. Each item is a sentence stem describing behaviors that may be observed at school. Intended to be completed by one or more of the student's teachers, respondents are asked to rate problem behaviors using four categories similar to those found on the Parent scale (e.g., "Very Much Like the Student" to "Not At All Like the Student").

The final instrument contained in the BRP-2 battery is the Sociogram which is intended to provide peers' perceptions of the target student. Unlike the other instruments in this battery, the Sociogram is not a rating scale but rather a peer nomination procedure. Specifically, pairs of stimulus questions (e.g., "Which of the students in your class would you most like to work with on a project in school?" and "Which of the students in your classroom would you least like to work with on a project in school?") are proposed to the target student's entire class. Each student is then asked to list three classmates whose names would answer the questions.

The BRP-2 (1990) is the most recent edition of an indirect assessment instrument that may be familiar to some readers; earlier editions of the Behavior Rating Profile were published in 1978 and 1983. Although the size of the normative sample has been increased and its demographic characteristics strengthened, the BRP-2 is remarkably similar to its predecessors. In fact, there have been no changes in the items, nor in the way that BRP instruments are administered and scored throughout the life of the battery. As a result, the authors contend the research results pertaining to earlier versions of the instrument can be applied with confidence to the current BRP-2. Unfortunately, however, some of the limitations associated with previous versions of the BRP battery are applicable to this edition as well.

For example, one of the limitations of the BRP-2 is that all of the items on the Student, Parent, and Teacher Rating Scales are worded negatively. An instrument that examines only weaknesses or deficits without any consideration of relative strengths provides an incomplete assessment of a child and increases the respondent's vulnerability to a negative response set and search for pathology.

A second criticism related to item content is that a number of items on the BRP-2 do not operationally define terms or describe specific behaviors. For example, the meaning of descriptions such as "is lazy" (Item 5, Teacher Rating Scale; Item 11, Parent Rating Scale) and "has too rich a fantasy life" (Item 17, Parent Rating Scale) may vary depending upon the interpretation of respondents. The lack of behavioral specificity in item content will impede the use of results derived from these rating scales in identifying target goals, as well as planning and evaluating intervention programs.

With regard to item format, it is important to note that undesirable behavior is indicated by "True" and "Very Much Like" the child on every item. As a result, the Rating Scales are vulnerable to the effects of response bias.

A final concern with the format is that the BRP-2 Rating Scales do not provide specific information about the recency, frequency, duration, or intensity of particular behaviors. Follow-up questioning will be necessary in order to clarify responses such as "True" on the Student Rating Scales and "Very Much Like" the child on both the Teacher and Parent Rating Scales.

A number of positive features identified in the BRP-2 also deserve mention. For example, the BRP-2 was designed to take an ecological approach to behavioral assessment. That is, the battery was constructed so that patterns of behavior across settings could be examined by eliciting the perceptions of at least two different individuals within several settings. The authors caution, however, that these instruments are not intended to be used as a complete appraisal system. Rather the information derived from the BRP-2 should be supplemented by information derived from measures of other domains (e.g., aptitude, achievement) and other assessment methods (e.g., direct observation, testing).

Secondly, the instruments comprising this battery are easy and inexpensive to use, in terms of both time and cost. The rating scales, in particular, are not difficult to learn, nor to implement, and scoring procedures are easy to follow. The Sociogram probably is the most time-consuming portion of the battery to administer and score. In the interest of both efficiency and efficacy, it is noted that each of the instruments comprising the BRP-2 may be used individually or in combination with any of the other instruments depending upon the nature of the problem and/or scope of the assessment without jeopardizing its integrity.

The manual for the BRP-2 is well written and comprehensive. Instructions for administration, scoring, and interpretation of the instruments are clear and can be easily understood. Unlike those accompanying most rating scales, the BRP-2 manual includes a comprehensive description of its construction and statistical characteristics. The psychometric characteristics of these instruments are reported in the manual, thereby allowing the reader an opportunity to evaluate their merits (information that should be, but is not always, readily available to consumers).

Lastly, the psychometric qualities of the BRP-2 exceed those of many other behavior rating scales. Specifically, each of the instruments in the BRP-2 battery is norm-referenced. Expanded with each edition, the normative sample presently includes 2,682 students, 1,948 parents, and 1,452 classroom teachers from 26 states. The demographic characteristics of the sample closely parallel those of the most recent census. Apparently, a Spanish-language version of the BRP-2 (*Perfil de Evaluacion del Comportamiento*, Brown & Hammill, 1982) is available, standardized on a normative sample of students, parents, and teachers in various states of Mexico. Caution should be exercised when attempting to apply those norms to a Spanish-speaking student from the United States.

With regard to reliability, internal consistency and test-retest data were presented, but interrater reliability was not addressed. Coefficient alphas were reported for each BRP-2 rating scale across five grade level ranges. There are discrepancies between text and table (manual, pp. 44 and 45) regarding these coefficients. Internal reliability appears adequate but the manual should be corrected.

Studies of the instrument's test-retest and alternate forms reliability are limited. However, the results of one published study (Ellers, Ellers, & Bradley-Johnson, 1989) examining the test-retest stability of the BRP found the Teacher Rating Scale was sufficiently reliable across grade Levels 1–12 (coefficients all in .90s). The results of the Parent Rating Scale were sufficiently reliable for grades 3–12 (all coefficients in .80s and .90s). The Student Rating Scales were least reliable; only 10 of the 18 correlation coefficients were .80 or above. With the exception of the Teacher Rating Scale, none of the scales held up well at the first and second grade level.

In terms of validity, a number of studies representing both the authors' own and independent research were reported in the manual. Substantial preliminary evidence is provided to demonstrate construct validity.

In summary, the BRP-2 is the most recent edition of a battery of indirect assessment measures designed to evaluate the perceived behavior of children 6-6 through 18-6 years of age. The BRP-2 battery includes three Student Rating Scales (Home, School, and Peer), a Parent Rating Scale, a Teacher Rating Scale, and a Sociogram.

The BRP-2 is distinguished from other behavior rating scales by its reliance on an ecological approach to behavioral assessment. Specifically, the battery was constructed so that patterns of behavior across settings could be examined by eliciting the perceptions of at least two different individuals within several settings. However, the BRP-2 should not be regarded as a comprehensive appraisal system; at best, it is one ecologically founded assessment tool that may be used in conjunction with other assessment procedures.

Unlike many other behavior rating scales, the BRP-2 is norm-referenced. A comprehensive description of instrument development and psychometric characteristics of the BRP-2 accompany the instructions for administration in a well-written manual. The potential utility of the BRP-2 Rating Scales is limited by both item content and an item format that increase respondents' vulnerability to response set bias, emphasize undesirable or inappropriate behaviors, and lack behavioral specificity.

REVIEWER'S REFERENCE

Ellers, R. A., Ellers, S. L., & Bradley-Johnson, S. (1989). Stability reliability of the Behavior Rating Profile. *Journal of School Psychology, 27,* 257-263.

Review of the Behavior Rating Profile, Second Edition by LISA A. BLOOM, Assistant Professor of Special Education, Western Carolina University, Cullowhee, NC:

The Behavior Rating Profile-2 (BRP-2) was designed to assess children's behavior from the perspectives of the teacher, parents, target student, and his/her peers. This instrument includes five behavior rating scales and a sociometric technique. The Student Rating Scale represents three scales to be completed by the child and includes 60 true-false items covering behavior at home, school, and with peers. A Parent Rating Scale to be completed by primary care givers includes 30 items. The Teacher Rating Scale includes 30 items related to school problem behavior. The final component of the BRP-2 is a sociogram based on a peer-nominating technique. The sociogram requires at least 20 of the student's classmates to respond to 1–2 pairs of questions such as "Which of the students in your class would you most like to have as your friend" and "Which of the students in your class would you least like to have as your friend?"

ADMINISTRATION AND SCORING. The BRP-2 is easy to use and score. The examiner is encouraged to obtain completed rating scales from several sources including both parents, several teachers, and several classmates. These ratings are converted to percentile ranks and standard scores and charted on a student profile. The Sociogram is scored by computing a rank of the target student in the class out of the total number of students in the class. This score is also converted to a standard score and percentile rank.

The items, procedures, and scoring of the BRP-2 have remained unchanged since the first edition. Several reviews of the BRP-2 are available elsewhere (see Posey, 1989; Bacon, 1989; Broughton, 1985). This review will focus on the new technical information included with the BRP-2 manual.

ITEM SELECTION. Item selection involved the following. First, similar assessment instruments were reviewed. Second, parents and teachers of students with learning disabilities and emotional disturbances were asked to describe behaviors characteristic of their children. Finally, these pools were used to generate experimental versions of the Rating Scales which consisted of 299 items. The BRP-2 manual authors describe the item selection criteria in much greater detail than in the first edition. To select the best items, two internal criteria were imposed. Item discrimination coefficients had to be statistically significant at .05 or beyond and the magnitude of the coefficients had to be between .30 and .80. Second, items which were indicated in more than half of the subjects in the item analysis group were eliminated. The authors considerably increased the number of protocols for item analysis in the revised edition although only the previously selected 120 items were subjected to the analysis. The authors report a final confirmatory analysis of protocols using the Guilford method from 700 student rating scales, 270 parent rating scales, and 530 teacher rating scales. Median item discrimination coefficients ranged from .43 to .83, which is well within acceptable limits.

In the first edition, raw score conversions to scaled scores were based upon normative data from 1,966 students ages 6-6 to 18-6, 955 teachers, and 1,232 parents in 15 states. In the second edition, 718 students from 11 additional states, 716 parents from 4 additional states, and 497 teachers from 11 additional states were added to the normative sample and resulted in slight changes in the normative tables for converting raw scores to standard scores and percentile ranks. The authors of the new manual present demographic characteristics of the normative samples in tabular form. Sample characteristics are comparable to the U.S. population.

Adequate reliability and internal consistency data are reported. Internal consistency was studied using coefficient alpha. Coefficients ranged from .74 to .98 and were highest for the Teacher Rating Scale.

Test-retest reliability is based on two studies. The first was reported in the original edition. Although the results were favorable, they were based on a small sample of 36 normal high school students. The second study conducted by Ellers, Ellers, and Bradley-Johnson (1989) involved 198 students from grades 1–2, 212 parents, and 176 teachers in central Michigan. These authors report the results for the Teacher Rating Scale were sufficiently reliable for all grade levels. The coefficients were all in the .90s. The Parent Rating Scale was sufficiently reliable for screening purposes for grades 3–12 and for eligibility for grades 3–6 and 11–12. For grades 3–12, coefficients ranged from .80 to .96. However, results suggested the scale was less reliable for grades 1–2 with a coefficient of .69. For the student scales, only 4 of the 18 coefficients were in the .90s and 5 in the .80s with a range of .43 to .92. Like the Parent Rating Scale, the results for grades 1 and 2 were the least reliable. Thus, the parent and student scales must be used with caution for these ages.

Concurrent and construct validity are reported in terms of the intercorrelation of the BRP-2 instruments and the BRP-2's relation to other measures of child behavior. In one study adequate correlations between the BRP and the Walker Problem Behavior Identification Checklist, the Quay-Peterson Behavior Problem Checklist, and the Vineland Social Maturity Scale are reported. However, these correlations are based on only four groups of 27 children each. In the new edition, studies of correlation between the BRP and the Test of Early Socioemotional Development, the Index of Children's Personality Characteristics, the Behavior Evaluation Scale, the Devereux Elementary School Behavior Rating Scale II, and the Children's Manifest Anxiety Scale are reported. The results of these studies suggest that the BRP demonstrates sufficient relationship to other similar instruments to consider it to have concurrent validity. However, the best evidence of concurrent validity would be obtained by relating the BRP to direct observation of behavior. This type of endeavor is not described. Technical information in terms of reliability and validity are not provided for the sociogram component of the BRP.

STRENGTHS AND WEAKNESSES. The BRP-2 represents an attempt to provide new and more detailed information about the technical adequacy of the test. The user should be more confident with the BRP-2 based on this information. The strength of the BRP-2 is that it can provide the user with data from several sources and is flexible enough so that information on school or home behavior alone could be obtained. A weakness of the BRP-2 is that the items describe negative behaviors exclusively. They do not afford the opportunity to identify student strengths. Additionally, the items do not describe observable behaviors, making it difficult to use the BRP for identifying appropriate goals and objectives. Other weaknesses include the lack of technical information on the sociogram and the limited reliability of the student scales. As long as these limitations are considered, the BRP-2 could provide the user with useful ecological information.

REVIEWER'S REFERENCES

Broughton, S. F. (1985). [Critique of the Behavior Rating Profile]. In D. J. Keyser & R. C. Sweetland (Eds.), *Test critiques: Vol. IV* (pp. 92-102). Kansas City, MO: Test Corporation of America.

Bacon, E. H. (1989). [Review of the Behavior Rating Profile]. In J. C. Conoley & J. J. Kramer (Eds.), *The tenth mental measurements yearbook* (pp. 84-86). Lincoln, NE: Buros Institute of Mental Measurements.

Ellers, R. A., Ellers, S. L., & Bradley-Johnson, S. (1989). Stability reliability of the Behavior Rating Profile. *Journal of School Psychology*, *27*, 257-263.

Posey, C. D. (1989). [Review of the Behavior Rating Profile]. In J. C. Conoley & J. J. Kramer (Eds.), *The tenth mental measurements yearbook* (pp. 86-87). Lincoln, NE: Buros Institute of Mental Measurements.

[49]

Behavioral Assessment of Pain Questionnaire.
Purpose: "Used for gaining a better understanding of factors which may be maintaining the subacute and chronic noncancerous pain experience."
Population: Subacute and chronic pain patients.
Publication Dates: 1990–92.
Administration: Individual.
Price Data, 1992: $30 per sample kit including manual ('92, 44 pages); answer sheet and Mercury scoring with interpretive clinical profile, general information, scale descriptions, sample BAP clinical profile, and reprint of journal article; $10 per manual.
Foreign Language Edition: Spanish edition available.
Time: (60) minutes.
Authors: Michael J. Lewandowski and Blake H. Tearnan.
Publisher: Pendrake, Inc.

a) BEHAVIORAL ASSESSMENT OF PAIN.
Acronym: BAP.
Scores, 34: Demographic Information, Activity Interference Scale (Domestic/Household Activities, Heavy Activities, Social Activities, Personal Care Activities, Personal Hygiene Activities), Avoidance Scale, Spouse/Partner Influence Scale (Reinforcement of Pain, Discouragement/Criticism of Pain, Reinforcement of Wellness, Discouragement/Criticism of Wellness), Physician Influence Scale (Discouragement/Criticism of Pain, Reinforcement of Wellness, Discouragement/Criticism of Wellness, Reinforcement of Pain), Physician Qualities Scale, Pain Beliefs Scale (Catastrophizing, Fear of Reinjury, Expectation for Cure, Blaming Self, Entitlement, Future Despair, Social Disbelief, Lack of Medical Comprehensiveness), Perceived Consequences Scale (Social Interference, Physical Harm, Psychological Harm, Pain Exacerbation, Productivity Interference), Coping Scale, Negative Mood Scale (Depression, Anxiety, Muscular Discomfort, Change in Weight).
Price Data: $21.50 per on-site scored interpretive report; $23.50 per Mercury scored interpretive report; $5 per BAP booklet.

b) POST BEHAVIORAL ASSESSMENT OF PAIN.
Acronym: P-BAP.
Scores, 23: Avoidance, Spouse/Partner Influence Scale (Reinforcement of Pain, Discouragement/Criticism of Pain, Reinforcement of Wellness, Discouragement/Criticism of Wellness), Pain Beliefs Scale (Catastrophizing, Fear of Reinjury, Expectation for Cure, Blaming Self, Entitlement, Future Despair, Social Disbelief, Lack of Medical Comprehensiveness), Perceived Consequences Scale (Social Interference, Physical Harm, Psychological Harm, Pain Exacerbation, Productivity Interference), Coping Scale, Negative Mood Scale (Depression, Anxiety, Muscular Discomfort, Change in Weight).
Price Data: $21.50 per on-site scored P-BAP report; $23.50 per Mercury scored P-BAP report; $5 per P-BAP booklet.

Review of the Behavioral Assessment of Pain Questionnaire by GERALD E. DeMAURO, Director, Bureau of Statewide Assessment, New Jersey State Department of Education, Trenton, NJ:

The Behavioral Assessment of Pain Questionnaire (BAP) is designed to gain a better understanding of factors that maintain subacute and chronic noncancerous pain. The BAP takes about an hour to complete. A shorter second questionnaire, the Post-Behavioral Assessment of Pain Questionnaire (P-BAP) enables pre- to post-test comparisons.

The BAP yields nine scales and 34 scores. The P-BAP yields six of these scales and 23 scores, excluding Demographic Information, Activity Interference Scale, Physician Influence Scale, and Physician Qualities Scale. The results should be interpreted only by professionals who are appropriately trained and experienced with chronic and subacute pain patients.

The BAP contains 355 bipolar, Likert-type, self-report items as well as multiple-choice demographic items. The number of items per subscale varies considerably, ranging from 2 to 16. The BAP offers two computerized scoring alternatives.

DEVELOPMENT. The BAP development is based on a large literature on pain maintenance and on patient interviews. The original form of the instrument contained eight scales of 411 eight-point items. The instrument was administered to 307 chronic pain patients who volunteered. Eighteen items were eliminated because 90% or more of the responses were either 0 or 1, or 6 or 7. This rule applied to all subscales but the Activity Now subscale, which was expected to yield a skewed distribution of responses. It is not clear why this criterion was used, as it seems to limit the instrument's capacity to provide information about extreme response patterns.

The questionnaire development rests heavily on factor analyses conducted in two phases. In the first, the responses of 307 patients were subjected to principal-axes analyses followed by either oblique or orthogonal rotations depending upon whether the majority of interfactor correlations were above .50 (oblique) or .50 or less (orthogonal). It appears that separate analyses were made for each scale except the Coping Scale which was nominal in structure.

Items were included in factors if they loaded greater than .30 on a factor and discriminated by .15 or more between factors. As a consequence of the first phase, two belief subscales merged, and a measure emerged from the Negative Mood subscales of Anxiety and Depression. Flesch Test readability and subject interviews indicated that the questionnaire was of appropriate difficulty, interest, and length.

Before the second phase, poorly written items and items that failed to meet the above criteria for factor loading were eliminated, and the Coping Scale was changed from nominal to interval. The demographic and background information was expanded, and the Perceived Consequences Scale was added.

Three-hundred twenty-six volunteer chronic pain patients completed the revised questionnaire. Of these, 181 patients completed the BAP and other instruments that purport to measure related constructs. Five items were eliminated using the skewed distribution criterion described earlier.

An exploratory factor analysis was applied to the new Coping Scale, and eight items were retained composing three subscales. Confirmatory factor analyses, using LISREL VI, were made of seven BAP scales: Physician, Spousal, Current Physical Activity, Avoidance, Beliefs, Negative Mood, and Perceived Consequences. The Before Activity subscale was not analyzed. An interactive modification procedures was used until adequate goodness-of-fit indices were achieved. The Beliefs scale was modified and nine items were eliminated from the Spousal scale.

RELIABILITY. Most subscales achieved Cronbach's alpha indices above .80, but three subscales had values below .50. Higher reliability indices than correlations among subscales suggested unique variance for each scale. Thirty-five subjects also completed the questionnaire again from 10 days to 2 weeks after the first administration. Most scales had test-retest coefficients above .80, but two were below .60.

CONCURRENT VALIDITY. The Depression and Anxiety subscales, the Spouse/Partner Influence subscales, and the Current Activity Level subscales had significant correlations with measures of related constructs. BAP subscales also were related to descriptive and demographic variables relevant to the theories of pain maintenance. A combination of the Belief subscales, Activity Avoidance subscales, Anxiety, Depression, and Perceived Consequences subscales had a 97% correct classification rate of patients who had high or low levels of functional impairment, demonstrating the taxonomic properties of the scales. The strongest support for the discriminant properties of the subscales comes from the factor patterns.

NORMATIVE DATA. A Clinical Profile provided for professionals involved in the care of pain patients contains means and standard deviations based on 315 chronic pain patients. Reports are provided for each scale separately.

DISCUSSION. The BAP has an impressive base in the literature and theory of pain, and seems to address all of the biopsychosocial factors that mediate the pain experience. The reports have a prescriptive value, in their comparison of each patient's scale values to other patients. The BAP developers should consider gathering information about people who are *not* chronic or subacute pain patients, to enable an evaluation of how changes in the patient's scale values or in the biopsychosocial environment are related to changes in perceived pain status.

The second recommendation concerns the nature of the profiles and the research sample sizes. In actuality, the profile reports are scale-by-scale descriptions. The observed unique scale variance should support identification of theoretically meaningful patterns of scale scores and the sensitivity to intervention of patients who exhibit these profiles could be explored. The research sample sizes would need to be expanded considerably to support this type of research.

CONCLUSION. The BAP provides empirical analyses of a series of scales that measure factors related to perceived pain of chronic and subacute pain patients. Support is offered for convergence with measures of theoretically related constructs and also for discriminant and taxonomic properties of the scales. Some attention to uses of the information for intervention would improve the clinical utility of the instrument.

REVIEWER'S REFERENCE

Tearnan, B. H., & Lewandowski, M. J. (1992). The Behavioral Assessment of Pain Questionnaire: The development and validation of a comprehensive self-report instrument. *American Journal of Pain Management, 2,* 181-191.

Review of the Behavioral Assessment of Pain Questionnaire by RONALD J. GANELLEN, Director, Neuropsychology Service, Michael Reese Hospital and Medical Center, and Assistant Professor of Psychiatry and Neurology, University of Illinois at Chicago, Chicago, IL:

The Behavioral Assessment of Pain Questionnaire (BAP) is described as a comprehensive instrument for assessing the environmental, psychological, and biological factors that contribute to the experience of chronic and subacute pain. Tearnan and Lewandowski (1992) introduce the BAP as being an improvement over existing measures used to assess patients with chronic pain which are "empirically untested, psychometrically flawed, or are not comprehensive in nature" (p. 181). The authors assert that the BAP is a highly reliable and valid instrument which can provide clinically useful information for assessing the biopsychosocial aspects of pain and identifying significant areas of impairment. The BAP is described as being appropriate for use by any health care provider working with chronic pain patients, including psychologists, physicians, chiropractors, nurses, and social workers.

The BAP is a 390-item self-report inventory that covers a wide range of dimensions relevant to assessing the psychosocial aspects of chronic pain and how an individual copes with this condition. The BAP provides information about patients' demographic background, health care utilization, medication usage, activity level before and after the onset of pain, the response of their spouse/partner to pain, the influence of their physician on pain and wellness behavior, maladaptive beliefs about pain and the consequences of disability, perception of the consequences if their pain increases, positive and negative strategies used by patients to cope with the experience of pain during physical activity, and the patients' current mood.

Most of these dimensions appear in existing tests developed to assess various aspects of the psychosocial functioning of patients with chronic pain. For instance, the West Haven-Yale Multidimensional Pain Inventory (WHYMPI; Kerns, Turk, & Rudy, 1985) assessed activity level, reinforcing and punishing spouse responses to communications about pain, and coping with pain by distraction, whereas the Coping Strategy Questionnaires (Rosenstiel & Keefe, 1983) measures pain patients' use of cognitive and physical techniques to cope with pain. The only new factor included in the BAP is the scale concerning patients' perceptions of their physicians. Thus, the conceptualization of these important dimensions of psychosocial adaptation to chronic pain upon which the BAP is based is not original, but the BAP does incorporate these dimensions into one instrument.

The development of the BAP is described by Tearnan and Lewandowski (1992). A Medline search found no other published articles using the BAP to date. The BAP was developed based upon an initial sample of 370 chronic pain patients and then refined using an independent sample of 326 chronic pain patients. Confirmatory factor analysis was used to refine the scales that have acceptable internal consistency. Test-retest reliability was reported for only 35 patients, which is barely adequate.

A major concern about the BAP is the very limited empirical data that exist concerning the validity and extra-test correlates of its scales. Tearnan and Lewandowski (1992) report the BAP mood scales are significantly correlated with commonly used measures of anxiety and depression; the Spouse/Partner Influence subscales are significantly correlated with measures of perception of and satisfaction with patients' spouses; and that subscales related to activity level are significantly correlated with similar scales. No data are reported concerning the construct validity of the Pain Beliefs, Perceived Consequences, Coping, and Physician Influence scales. Thus, it has not been demonstrated that these subscales actually measure what they purport to measure.

The reported correlations with similar measures begin to address the construct and concurrent validity of the BAP. More important for the clinician, however, are issues of predictive and discriminant validity. For the BAP to be useful in a clinical setting, it should be demonstrated that scores on BAP scales relate to meaningful variables, such as compliance with treatment, functional impairment, prognosis, or reports of pain intensity. These are issues of predictive validity. It has also not been shown that BAP scores provide useful information in terms of classification of pain patients into groups that might respond differentially to different treatment strategies. For instance, no research has been reported showing what the implications for treatment are if a patient obtains high scores on the Perceived Consequences and low scores on the Coping scales (or vice-versa). Similarly, no data are reported concerning how patients' perceptions of spouse reactions to their pain influence the maintenance of pain behavior, compliance with treatment, or risk of relapse. At this point, recommendations for treatment based on the BAP are speculative because the data addressing these critical questions have not been reported.

The manual authors describe the BAP as being based on the results of a 5-year national study involving "well over 600 subacute and chronic pain patients" (manual, p. 29). However, the manual is basically a reproduction of the Tearnan and Lewandowski (1992) article. The 600 subjects alluded to represent the two samples described above and no additional information is reported in the manual that was not contained in the 1992 article. The manual authors offer little guidance concerning the use of the BAP in clinical practice. The authors apparently assume the computer-generated report provides all the interpretive information needed for clinical usage.

Another potentially important limitation of the BAP is the absence of any validity scales with which to examine whether a patient distorted his or her self-report. This is a serious issue to consider as many patients with chronic pain are involved in litigation related to lost wages, medical benefits, compensation for pain and suffering, etc. The absence of validity scales indicates that clinicians should use the BAP only as an adjunct to other measures that have validity indices. If the BAP is used alone, conclusions based on responses to the BAP should be made with considerable caution.

The BAP can be scored only by computer. One can purchase a program to score the BAP on site for $21 per administration if one has an optical scanner, or the response sheet can be mailed in to be scored for $23 per administration. (The prices per administration decrease slightly if there is high volume.) No templates are available for hand scoring if one should desire to do so.

In summary, the BAP represents an initial, preliminary attempt to synthesize existing approaches to assessing psychosocial aspects of chronic pain into one assessment instrument. Data concerning the BAP are quite limited and primarily address issues related to scale development. Although the BAP items are face valid, data concerning the BAP's construct, predictive, and discriminant validity are lacking or minimal. Given these limitations I believe it is premature to use the BAP in clinical practice as there are no data upon which to base treatment decisions. I would strongly recommend against replacing existing assessment instruments with the BAP until additional research is published that addresses these limitations and demonstrates that BAP scores contribute meaningful information to a comprehensive assessment of the biopsychosocial factors relevant to chronic pain and identification of areas of impairment that should be the focus of treatment interventions.

REVIEWER'S REFERENCES

Rosenstiel, A. K., & Keefe, F. J. (1983). The use of coping strategies in chronic low back pain patients: Relationships to patient characteristics and current adjustment. *Pain, 17*, 33-44.

Kerns, R. D., Turk, D. C., & Rudy, T. E. (1985). The West Haven-Yale Multidimensional Pain Inventory (WHYMPI). *Pain, 23*, 345-356.

Tearnan, B. H., & Lewandowski, M. J. (1992). The Behavioral Assessment of Pain Questionnaire: The development and validation of a comprehensive self-report instrument. *American Journal of Pain Management, 2*, 181-191.

[50]

BENCHMARKS.

Purpose: "To assess individual experiences and link learnings to developmental strategies."

Population: Managers and executives.

Publication Dates: 1990–92.

Scores, 24: Feedback in 16 Skill Areas (Resourcefulness, Doing Whatever It Takes, Being a Quick Study, Decisiveness, Leading Employees, Setting a Developmental Climate, Confronting Problem Employees, Team Orientation, Hiring Talented Staff, Building and Mending Relationships, Compassion/Sensitivity, Straightforwardness/Composure, Balance, Self-Awareness, Putting People at Ease, Flexibility); Feedback in 6 Problem Areas (Interpersonal Relationships, Difficulty in Molding Staff, Difficulty in Making Strategic Transitions, Lack of Follow-through, Overdependence, Strategic Differences with Management), Handling of Critical Jobs, Comparison Score.

Administration: Group.

Restricted Distribution: The publisher requires a 2-day certification program for those who wish to give feedback from BENCHMARKS in their own organization or as a consultant.

Price Data, 1993: $225 per set including 12 questionnaires, computer scoring, summary of results, and the Developmental Learning Guide ('90, 62 pages); $1,000 program fee for certification workshop.

Time: (30) minutes per survey.

Authors: Michael M. Lombardo, Cynthia D. McCauley, Russ Moxley (manual), Maxine Dalton (manual), Claire Usher (feedback report), Esther Hutchinson (Developmental Learning Guide), T. Dan Pryor (Developmental Learning Guide).

Publisher: Center for Creative Leadership.

a) BENCHMARKS GROUP PROFILE.

Purpose: "To assess the strengths and developmental needs of target groups."

Population: Upper and middle managers and executives.

Publication Date: 1990.

Price Data, 1992: $500 per report including management skills and perspectives overview, scales, importance for success, group characteristics, and overheads for class presentation; $375 per report if ordered with initial purchase.

Author: Center for Creative Leadership.

Review of BENCHMARKS by SHELDON ZEDECK, Chair and Professor of Psychology, University of California, Berkeley, CA:

BENCHMARKS is an instrument and process that deals with management development, commonly referred to as 360-degree feedback. Specifically, it provides a manager with a benchmark of how he or she is doing from the perspective of self, superiors, peers, and direct reports. The focus of the 164-item BENCHMARKS questionnaire is to capture what an executive has learned from experiences and the skills they developed; what values and perspectives are learned; and what the blocks are to further development. This orientation is in contrast to other such instruments that might focus on characteristics that are more stable and less susceptible to being modified.

The underlying premise is that a respondent can gain insight into his or her management behavior and with feedback and consultation will improve. This can occur because valuable learning occurs on the job and this learning influences how one manages. Further, only managers who continue to learn will continue to be effective.

The 164-item BENCHMARKS questionnaire covers the skills and perspectives needed to be successful, flaws that can stall or derail careers, and demands of jobs. Section 1 contains 106 statements that pertain to 16 skill areas covering how the management job is handled, how employees are dealt with, and the way others and the self are viewed; the respondent indicates the degree to which the person being rated displays the behavior stated in the item. Section 2 focuses on 26 characteristics or problems that can stall a career; again, the respondent indicates the degree to which the person being rated displays each of the characteristics. Section 3 presents 16 job activities and requests that the rater indicate how effectively the person being rated would handle each of the jobs. Finally, Section 4 presents the 16 skill areas and requests that the respondent pick the 8 that are most important for success in the respondent's organization. The process requires the manager to complete the instrument and that, where possible, evaluations on the same instrument be obtained from superiors, peers, and direct reports.

Key to the success of the endeavor is the feedback that is provided to the respondent. This feedback is presented via training programs and through one-on-one feedback from certified trainers. The publisher, the Center for Creative Leadership, scores the instrument and provides a 38-page report of the results and a 52-page development guide for each manager. My a 52-page development guide for each manager. My one concern is how the value of the instrument and process may become diluted as the Center for Creative Leadership reduces its involvement and "certified" trainers become more evident. Finally, the instrument and process is to be used for self-development only and *not* for selection or promotion purposes.

The package that accompanies BENCHMARKS is quite comprehensive. It includes a manual and trainer's guide, sample feedback reports, and a developmental guide. The manual and trainer's guide describes the philosophy underlying the process; the development of BENCHMARKS; how to give feedback and conduct developmental planning; and examples of instruments and plans as appropriate. The manual contains adequate instruction on how to interpret reports and how to prepare developmental plans. Emphasis is placed on how different groups (e.g., peers) see the respondent relative to the respondent's own assessment. Of particular value is the "Analyzing Your Results" handout that is made available to the respondent to facilitate interpretation of the data. This document contains exercises that allow the respondent to capture a "picture" of one's strengths and weaknesses, how others view him or her, and to identify where there are differences among the varied perspectives.

The research base for the development of BENCHMARKS and the process is generally impressive. Over 400 managers from major corporations participated in various phases, which led to the development of the instrument. The only concern, noted by the authors, is that the sample is predominantly white and male. Obviously, females and racial and ethnic minorities must be included in the data base. Also, it would have been interesting to have available demographic data on the participants such as their age, education, experience, etc. The reliability data are impressive, especially given the fact that three types of reliabilities are reported: (*a*) internal consistency, (*b*) test-retest, and (*c*) interrater agreement. The validity model is generally one of content-oriented validity, with some limited evidence presented for criterion-related validity. What is not known (at least not presented in the manual), however, is how well the developmental process works. That is, after completing the instrument, obtaining feedback, and constructing and implementing a developmental plan, is there a long-term effect such that the respondents improve, become more effective managers, and/or achieve higher level jobs? This question is directed toward the influence of the feedback and the developmental plan.

Norm data are available and continuously being updated. Not only can individuals be compared to a cohort group, but group profiles are available to allow for comparison of one's group to other managers of a similar level. The limitation to the norm base is that it is composed of those managers who were "convenient" for assessment and thus it is not necessarily representative of a broader group of managers across many different types of organizations. On the positive side, the manual contains a March 1992 norm base of over 2,200 respondents, with approximately 27% being female; still, racial and ethnic minorities represent only approximately 11%.

Overall, BENCHMARKS is a useful instrument to gather information about one's management approach; the process has the necessary ingredients for success. It is complete and self-contained. The question to be answered concerns its long-term usefulness—does participation in the process make a difference?

[51]

The Block Survey and S.L.I.D.E.

Purpose: Designed to assess readiness for writing.
Population: Preschool and kindergarten.
Publication Date: 1990.
Scores, 5: Sequence, Language, Identicality, Directionality, Equivalence.
Administration: Individual.
Price Data, 1993: $19 per survey/manual.
Time: (15) minutes.
Comments: Manual contains both The Block Survey and S.L.I.D.E.
Authors: Donna Reid Connell and Theodore A. Callisto.
Publisher: United/DOK Publishers.

Review of The Block Survey and S.L.I.D.E. by CHRISTINE NOVAK, Pediatric Psychologist, Division of Developmental Disabilities, University of Iowa, Iowa City, IA:

The Block Survey consists of five tasks designed to elicit specific "clues" as to a young child's readiness for writing. The tasks include: (*a*) drawing a person, (*b*) completing the picture with colored crayons, (*c*) building a block tower in imitation, (*d*) building a block train in imitation, and (*e*) building the same block train from memory. As the child completes these tasks, the observer notes the detail and accuracy of the child's work, the fine-motor skill and eye-hand coordination used in executing the task, and the child's verbal language skill and articulation relative to naming colors and numbers.

The tasks are organized systematically so that transitions between tasks can occur easily. Necessary materials are listed at the beginning of the survey and are clearly referred to in the task instructions. A scoring form is provided to record the child's performance on each task in reference to the thinking skills (i.e., Sequence [S], Language [L], Identicality [I], Directionality [D], and Equivalence [E]) purportedly measured. The accompanying S.L.I.D.E. manual contains game activities to develop these five thinking skills.

The author states the instrument can help determine whether the child is ready to begin learning written letters and numbers, and if not ready, can help identify which of the component thinking skills need remediation. Unfortunately, guidelines for scoring the child's performance are not clearly presented, which could lead to wide variations in scores. There also are no directions on how to use scores; raw scores computed for each thinking skill cannot be directly compared because there is an unequal number of points possible for each of the thinking skills. Of greatest concern, however, is that these thinking skills are not defined, nor is the relevance of these skills to writing explained or supported. The meager rationale provided in the manual suggests that children develop the use of written symbols through common stages of spontaneous drawing. Although the additional focus on language, sequencing, directionality, and sound-symbol relations hold intuitive appeal, further documentation of the relative importance of these thinking skills to the development of writing is needed to establish the validity of this instrument.

In summary, the Block Survey is unique in its purpose but does not provide sufficient data to support its use in formal decision-making situations. In its current state it is best suited for research purposes, particularly investigations of prerequisite skills for writing.

Review of The Block Survey and S.L.I.D.E. by CLAUDE A. SANDY, Vice President, Research Dimensions, Inc., Richmond, VA:

The Block Survey is designed to help parents or teachers assess children's thinking skills related to mental readiness and eye-hand coordination needed for beginning writing. The manual also includes the S.L.I.D.E. (i.e., Sequence, Language, Identicality, Directionality, and Equivalence), a game approach to the development of the five thinking skills assessed in The Block Survey.

Children must be assessed one-on-one, requiring an estimated 15 minutes each. The author states that a volunteer or teacher aide could be trained to administer the survey. Materials required for the survey are commonly found in a kindergarten classroom. The administrator presents the child with five tasks, each of which addresses two or three of the five thinking skills, following instructions in the manual. Instructions in the manual guide the administrator's observations for each task and a sample scoring form indicates the number of points which can be earned for each behavior observed. In general, instructions in the manual are inadequate to assure reliable scoring among different administrators and there are no directions for scoring a partially correct response. For example, a child duplicating a three-block "train" from memory on Task 5 would receive the top score of 10 points for the skill Identicality. There are no instructions, however, regarding the awarding of points for partial accomplishment (e.g., two of the three blocks correct). Presumably, the child would receive no points and, as this is the only observation of identicality in the survey, directions for assigning points for partial accomplishment of this task seem essential.

The author considers The Block Survey to be an "informal survey" and presents no data regarding the technical qualities of the instrument. Norms are not available. The tasks on the survey are similar to those found on tests of general readiness development, and results from the two would likely be highly correlated. Due to the absence of demonstrated validity, use of The Block Survey should be limited to identifying children's weaknesses in order to focus S.L.I.D.E. instructional activities on those weaknesses. The Block Survey would likely do no harm and the game-like activities in S.L.I.D.E. would likely provide some developmental benefit.

[52]

Boston Assessment of Severe Aphasia.

Purpose: Developed to identify "preserved abilities that might form the beginning steps of rehabilitation programs for severely aphasic patients."
Population: Aphasic adults.
Publication Date: 1989.
Acronym: BASA.
Scores, 5: Auditory Comprehension, Praxis, Oral-Gestural Expression, Reading Comprehension, Other.
Administration: Individual.
Price Data, 1991: $178.98 per complete kit; $39.99 per package of manipulatives; $30 per set of stimulus cards; $30 per custom aluminum clipboard; $24 per 24 record forms; $30 per manual (96 pages); $30 per briefcase; $48.99 per demonstration video (not included in complete kit).
Time: (30–40) minutes.
Authors: Nancy Helm-Estabrooks, Gail Ramsberger, Alisa R. Morgan, and Marjorie Nicholas.
Publisher: The Riverside Publishing Co.

TEST REFERENCES

1. Fuh, J., Liao, K., Wang, S., & Lin, K. (1994). Swallowing difficulty in primary progressive aphasia: A case report. *Cortex, 30,* 701-705.
2. Schacter, D. L., Osowiecki, D., Kaszniak, A. W., Kihlstrom, J. F., & Valdiserri, M. (1994). Source memory: Extending the boundaries of age-related deficits. *Psychology and Aging, 9,* 81-89.
3. Fischer, R. S., Alexander, M. P., D'esposito, M., & Otto, R. (1995). Neuropsychological and neuroanatomical correlates of confabulation. *Journal of Clinical and Experimental Neuropsychology, 17,* 20-28.

Review of the Boston Assessment of Severe Aphasia by STEVEN B. LEDER, Associate Professor of Surgery, Yale University School of Medicine, New Haven, CT:

Patients with newly diagnosed strokes in the acute care setting are a special challenge for clinicians to test and treat. These patients are often too impaired for lengthy testing and the test materials commonly used are too difficult for meaningful information to be obtained. There is a need, therefore, in aphasia diagnostics and rehabilitation for rehabilitation-oriented tests that can be used for initial evaluations, to help plan the beginning rehabilitation strategies, and for longitudinal tracking of progress of severely impaired newly aphasic individuals. The Boston Assessment of Severe Aphasia (BASA) is just such an instrument.

The rationale for the BASA is compelling and completely supported by the review of the literature, and the authors provide additional referenced background information to substantiate the use of each subtest. This provides the clinician not only with an intuitive reason for performing a particular subtest but a scientific one as well. The test manual is comprehensive and lucid. It contains instructions that are clear, concise, and supported by helpful examples directly from the test. Scoring principles are documented and administration and test scoring are fully described with examples. Just as important as proper test administration is appropriate summarization and interpretation of test results. The test manual allows the clinician to perform these two tasks, and then transfer the results to the test booklet in a clear manner that is both helpful for determining level of aphasic involvement and for planning of rehabilitation strategies. Finally, the BASA appears to be fully documented regarding norms development, reliability, and both content and construct validity.

The rationale for selection of the test stimuli used is also based on referenced information. The authors are most concerned with assessing communicative intent, either gestural or verbal, and chose stimuli that had the best capability of eliciting meaningful responses from the aphasic patients. In addition, the stimuli were also selected to assess linguistic or paralinguistic information not normally tested on other aphasic tests. The testing situation is set up for optimum pragmatic language use, from the opening "Good morning/afternoon" to the closing "Good-bye," to assess the patient's gestural (wave) or verbal (bye) response. The authors structured the BASA in this manner because they not only wanted to test the patient's ability to respond in a communicatively appropriate manner but also to base rehabilitation on the communicative responses the patient was capable of using in everyday circumstances.

A very interesting and worthwhile idea expressed by the authors is their invitation to clinicians who use the BASA to participate in ongoing research with the test. It is felt that as the BASA is used more widely by clinicians with severely impaired newly aphasic individuals, with individuals presenting with other neurological diagnoses, and for longitudinal assessment of improvement the BASA data base will grow and be enhanced.

In summary, the BASA fulfills its stated purpose of identifying and quantifying preserved abilities that form the beginning steps of rehabilitation programs for severely aphasic patients. The test has been well thought out, fully documented, can be readily learned, and is straightforward to analyze. It should be of benefit to all clinicians involved in the diagnostic process, initial rehabilitative strategies selections, and longitudinal tracking of severely impaired aphasic individuals.

Review of the Boston Assessment of Severe Aphasia by ROGER L. TOWNE, Assistant Professor of Speech Pathology and Audiology, Illinois State University, Normal, IL:

PURPOSE. The Boston Assessment of Severe Aphasia (BASA) was designed for "identifying and quantifying preserved abilities that might form the beginning steps of rehabilitation programs for severely aphasic patients" (p. 1). It is intended to be administered by a certified speech-language pathologist to individuals with aphasia at their bedside or other standard testing setting. The BASA is relatively short and should take approximately 30 to 40 minutes to administer.

ADMINISTRATION, SCORING, AND INTERPRETATION. Administration of the BASA requires a set of items including objects, drawings, and photographs which are supplied in the test kit. Additional items not supplied include a felt-tipped pen, and a quarter, dime, nickel, and penny. The test consists of 61 items which represent seven clusters of communication abilities: Auditory Comprehension, Praxis, Oral-Gestural Expression, Reading Comprehension, Gesture Recognition, Writing, and Visuo-Spatial Tasks. Items were selected which would elicit either a gestural or verbal response from the patient. Test items, instructions, scoring, and scoring summaries are included in a well-organized record form.

Each test item is scored for the following: no response, response modality (gestural or verbal), quality of response (refusal, noncommunicative, partially communicative, or fully communicative), affective quality, and perseveration. Specific guidelines with examples for scoring are provided. Raw scores consist of the number of responses made in each of these categories. These data are then converted to a percentage of responses in each modality that had communicative value. In addition, standard scores, confidence intervals, and percentile ranks can be obtained from the raw item cluster scores for Auditory Comprehensive, Praxis, Oral-Gestural Expression, Reading Comprehension, Other items, and BASA total score.

Interpretation of BASA results involves interpreting the BASA total score and item cluster scores. The BASA total score "should be considered a general measure of communicative ability" (p. 45), which includes both verbal and gestural comprehension and expression. Further, "looking at the patient's BASA performance in terms of the various modalities and task formats on the test may help the clinician better understand the patient's strengths and weaknesses and identifying a core of spared abilities from which to begin a course of therapy" (p. 46). To facilitate this process the pattern of item cluster scores should be analyzed. To assist in test interpretation, five case studies are presented in the manual, which demonstrate how different patterns of performance can be viewed.

EVALUATION OF TEST ADEQUACY. The BASA was normed on 111 patients with severe aphasia. The authors consider these norms to be preliminary and are presumably in the process of gathering data on additional patients. Reliability was measured and reported for internal consistency (coefficient alpha), standard error of measurement, stability, and interrater reliability. Internal consistency ranged between .71 and .89 and was statistically significant at $p<.001$ for all coefficients. Internal consistency coefficients were used to calculate standard errors of measurement for 68% and 95% confidence levels. Test-retest scores (stability) resulted in reliability coefficients ranging between .27 and .71 for 5 clusters with all but one being statistically significant at $p<.05$ or greater, indicating a gain in patient performance over time. Interrater reliability (agreement) between scoring by one of the authors and a group of 14 clinicians ranged between 67% and 100% for all responses and between 68% and 100% for only fully communicative responses.

Concurrent validity was established by comparing BASA performances for 43 patients who were also administered the Boston Diagnostic Aphasia Examination (BDAE; Goodglass & Kaplan, 1984), a well-accepted diagnostic aphasia test battery. Correlations between BASA and BDAE subtests ranged between .01 and .76 with most being above .40 considered by the authors to be the minimally acceptable level. The levels of reliability and validity established by the authors suggest that the BASA can be administered with confidence by trained clinicians.

The BASA appears to be well designed and suited for the targeted population of individuals with severe aphasia. The design of materials and the selection of test questions have a basis in the aphasia literature. Test items cover a complete range of communicative processes and have been made to be simple and uncomplicated. Perhaps the most unique aspect of the BASA is that both verbal and nonverbal (gestural) communication is assessed and quantified. This necessitates, however, that the examiner "attend to all aspects of the patient's behavior, including facial expressions, vocal inflections, and body gestures" (p. 3). Test performance can be used by itself to establish an individual's pattern of communicative strengths and weaknesses, or can be compared to the performances of other severe aphasic individuals. Although the BASA is relatively uncomplicated to administer, familiarization with the scoring criteria is necessary in order to facilitate accuracy and reliability.

SUMMARY. Few aphasia test batteries are designed to be used with patients demonstrating a severe aphasia. This is necessitated by the need to have test items of sufficient difficulty so that more moderately involved patients can avoid a ceiling effect. The BASA, therefore, fills an important niche in the evaluation choices for speech-language pathologists. The test is relatively short and simple yet supplies considerable information that will be useful in making therapeutic decisions regarding the patient. For the patient with severe aphasia "it may be impossible, impractical, or uninformative to administer a lengthy, comprehensive aphasia test. There is a need instead for a short, portable exam that probes all modalities of output and input and that identifies what may be small islands of preserved ability in the severely aphasic patient" (p. 3). The BASA appears to legitimately fill that need.

REVIEWER'S REFERENCE

Goodglass, H., & Kaplan, E. (1984). The Assessment of Aphasia and Related Disorders. Philadelphia: Lea & Febiger.

[53]

BRIGANCE® K & 1 Screen for Kindergarten and First Grade Children [Revised].

Purpose: Designed to screen for readiness for kindergarten or first grade.
Population: Grades K, 1.
Publication Dates: 1982–92.
Administration: Individual.
Price Data, 1991: $49.50 per manual ('92, 88 pages).
Time: [15–20] minutes per child.
Comments: "Criterion-referenced"; 1987 edition still available.
Author: Albert H. Brigance.
Publisher: Curriculum Associates, Inc.

a) KINDERGARTEN.
Scores, 13: Personal Data Response, Color Recognition, Picture Vocabulary, Visual Discrimination-Forms and Uppercase Letters, Visual-Motor Skills, Gross-Motor Skills, Rote Counting, Identifies Body Parts, Follows Verbal Directions, Numeral Comprehension, Prints Personal Data, Syntax and Fluency, Total.
Price Data: $15.85 per 30 data sheets; $16.85 per 10 class summary folders.

b) FIRST GRADE.
Scores, 14: Personal Data Response, Color Recognition, Picture Vocabulary, Visual Discrimination-Lowercase Letters and Words, Visual-Motor Skills, Rote Counting, Recites Alphabet, Numeral Comprehension, Recognition of Lowercase Letters, Auditory Discrimination, Draw A Person, Prints Personal Data, Numerals in Sequence, Total.
Price Data: $16.15 per 30 data sheets; $17.15 per 10 class summary folders.

Cross References: For reviews of an earlier edition by Ann E. Boehm and Dan Wright, see 9:166.

TEST REFERENCES

1. May, D. C., & Kundert, D. K. (1993). Pre-first placements: How common and how informed? *Psychology in the Schools*, *30*, 161-167.

Review of the BRIGANCE® K & 1 Screen for Kindergarten and First Grade Children [Revised] by RONALD A. BERK, Professor, School of Nursing, The Johns Hopkins University, Baltimore, MD:

The BRIGANCE K & 1 Screen is the third edition of this popular screening instrument (earlier editions were published in 1982 and 1987). It was designed originally as a criterion-referenced test to assess the basic skills of kindergarten and first grade children. Twelve skill areas are covered on the kindergarten screen and 13 on the first grade screen.

The entire assessment consists of four components: (*a*) basic skills tests, (*b*) a screening observation form, (*c*) teacher's rating form, and (*d*) parent's rating form. With the exception of the observation form to be completed by the test user, the other components are prepared in both kindergarten and first grade versions. Inasmuch as the assessment is labeled as "criterion-referenced" and "curriculum-referenced," the user would expect to find the items keyed to a set of objectives or content specifications. No content domain specifications are presented from which the items on any of the component measures were generated. This certainly precludes the interpretation of student performance in terms of specific skills or instructional objectives. The author notes only that the "assessments provide data that can be translated into instructional objectives" (p. iii).

Because this is a revised edition, the changes made must be identified. The author notes four changes: (*a*) The basic assessments for kindergarten and first grade were separated for the convenience of test users (previously, both levels were integrated into one section); (*b*) "do and do not" recommendations were added to specify the limitations of the test and purposes for which the results should be used (this was prompted by reports that the earlier editions were being misused for diagnosing learning difficulties, placement in special education programs, and developing individualized education plans); (*c*) the reference list was updated; and (*d*) the sequence of some items was changed, such as the consonant sounds in the Auditory Discrimination (first grade) area (this was done based on a review of developmental age data and the updated normative data for the BRIGANCE Inventory of Early Development—Revised).

The justification for these four changes appears to be based on some type of data collection from the earlier editions. However, no empirical evidence or specific research is cited to furnish a sound foundation for the changes. Although convenience, score misuse, out-of-date references, and updated norms may be appropriate reasons for the changes, substantial documentation is required to justify the need for a test revision. Clearly the reasons given do not support this 1991 "revision." Other than reordering "some items," no structural or content changes in the items for the 27 skill areas were undertaken. The 1991 edition is essentially the same as the 1982 edition.

The previous edition of the BRIGANCE Screen was reviewed in the *MMY* (9:166). Unfortunately, none of the criticisms noted in those reviews were addressed in the latest edition. In particular, there is no evidence of the technical adequacy of the tests, observation form, and rating forms.

The appropriateness of reliability and validity evidence for any instrument hinges on the specific use of the scores and the inferences drawn from those scores. The purpose of the BRIGANCE K & 1 Screen is "to obtain a broad sampling of a students's skills and behaviors . . . (1) to identify any student who should be referred for a more comprehensive evaluation . . . (2) to help determine the most appropriate initial placement or grouping of students . . . (3) to assist the teacher in planning a more appropriate program for the student" (p. v). These score uses should be viewed in the context of the author's recommendations: "Don't make any decisions based solely on the score obtained from the screening . . . [and] Don't use screening data for making decisions such as exclusion from a program or placement in a special program" (p. xiii).

These statements by the author suggest the scores on the Screen be used primarily to classify students into the appropriate grade level (K or 1) and instructional groups, particularly those students who may have disabilities requiring special placement. This classification decision should be made by a screening team who should use the scores on this Screen in conjunction with other data before formulating a recommendation.

The fact that the author recommends the Screen as a "quick means of sampling the skills of a student" and "the score should be evaluated in light of . . . other data" (p. xiii) does not relieve the author of the responsibility for furnishing evidence on the psychometric soundness of the instrument. If the scores are used to classify students, evidence on the accuracy of those classifications is essential to evaluate the effectiveness of the tool. Discriminant validity evidence in the form of correct classification probabilities and false positives/false negatives would be very helpful. This could be computed based on recommended "cutoff scores" for referral decisions (p. xvi). Evidence of decision reliability should also be reported along with classification accuracy.

Beyond these types of technical information to justify the use of the scores, additional evidence is needed related to (*a*) the match of the items to any domain specifications; (*b*) the representativeness of the items in relation to their respective domains; (*c*) the qualifications of the subject-matter experts who judged content-related validity; (*d*) the appropriateness of the instruments for students who do not speak English and how the assessment should be conducted with such students; (*e*) studies of test design, content, or format that might bias test scores for particular ethnic, cultural, and gender groups; (*f*) the method and rationale for selecting the cutoff scores, including technical analyses; and (*g*) item analysis results and criteria for item selection based on the numerous field tests.

In summary, similar to the 1982 edition, this edition of the Screen remains unproven. It does not satisfy the criteria for a "revised edition." The scores cannot be criterion referenced or norm referenced without the proper content specifications and psychometric analyses to support the intended uses and inferences. The BRIGANCE K & 1 Screen is a screening device of unknown characteristics according to the purposes for which it was developed. Potential users should consider alternative measures that satisfy the requisite standards for instrument construction and supportive technical information.

Review of the BRIGANCE® K & 1 Screen for Kindergarten and First Grade Children [Revised] by T. STEUART WATSON, Assistant Professor of Educational Psychology, Mississippi State University, Starkville, MS:

This test is a revision of the popular 1987 edition. Despite criticisms regarding potential misuses of the test and lack of technical information, the author correctly notes that the previous version of this instrument has enjoyed widespread use.

PURPOSE. Generally, the BRIGANCE K & 1 Screen is a criterion-referenced instrument that was designed to tap several broad key skill areas: language, motor ability, number skills, body awareness, and auditory and visual discrimination. The author contends that assessment of skill development in these areas allows for a better prediction of who will or will not be academically successful, although no predictive or discriminant validity data are presented to support this contention. In addition, the Screen is intended to identify students who may require comprehensive evaluations, place and group students in terms of ability, assist the teacher in designing curriculum objectives, and to comply with federal and state screening mandates.

TEST CONTENT. The basic assessment includes 12 skill tests for kindergartners and 13 for first graders. Although the test seems to have content validity for both groups, there is no specific explanation for the criteria used to select new items or the criteria used to retain items for this version of the test. Only cursory explanations are given as to how the 1991 edition was developed.

A major difficulty with this test is that each stimulus page contains numerous stimulus items. For example, the Visual Discrimination skill test for first graders contains 10 rectangular boxes of four words or letters per box. It would have been preferable to have fewer stimulus items per page, particularly when attempting to assess young children whose attention and/or visual acuity are suspect.

The supplemental assessment battery contains some useful tests designed to sample vocabulary and sight word recognition at the preprimer/primer level, basic number skills, articulation, and verbal expression. The first two tests in the supplemental battery (Responses to Pictures), however, present a cluttered stimulus picture that is confusing and unwieldy. Having to sort through the pictures to access the appropriate information is an unnecessary and interfering task for the examinee.

Screening information forms are provided that allow the examiner to make checklist observations of problematic behaviors during screening. Separate forms for kindergartners and first graders are also included for teachers and parents to note whether certain behaviors are within the child's repertoire of skills. Items on the parent and teacher forms closely resemble those on most measures of adaptive behavior. It is highly unlikely, given the expedient nature of the screening process, that these forms will be used in any meaningful way.

ADMINISTRATION AND SCORING. The manual begins with helpful information regarding screening procedures and directions, assessing functional vision and hearing, general recommendations for screening, and possible explanations for low scores. The information contained in these pages is probably more beneficial to the novice, rather than experienced, examiner. The author also provides sample layouts to expedite the screening process, an orientation to the materials, specific recommendations on the effective use of the screen, and directions for completing the data sheets (with completed models provided). Again, these portions of the test manual are more applicable to someone without a great deal of testing experience.

Although it is stated that teachers and other professionals may administer the screen without specialized training in test administration, there are no data to validate this assertion. Interrater reliability studies should be performed to show that those with and without specialized training administer the test and score items similarly. When assessing children of this age, it is often difficult to elicit responses, especially when the responses are one-word, right or wrong answers. Examiners with test administration training may have an edge in prompting responding in children who are hesitant to complete the tasks, thus obtaining a more valid sample of behavior. Despite its deceptively simple-to-administer format, care must be taken to ensure that tests such as this are administered and scored properly, especially when educational and programming decisions are made that are highly dependent on the results of this test.

Scoring is straightforward and easy. Answers to the stimulus items are generally unambiguous and require little interpretation or queuing. The data sheets, or record forms, are in triplicate and seem too small for the amount of information contained on them. There is not enough room for the examiner to quickly record responses and note behavioral observations within a skill area during testing.

An area of particular concern is the section for placement recommendations on the bottom of the data sheet. This seems to imply that educational placement decisions can be made based on the results of this single instrument, regardless of the author's cautionary statements about such a practice. This information is better left off a data sheet.

TECHNICAL INFORMATION. No reliability or validity data are available for this test. This is surprising given the wide use of the test and the applications for which it is intended. More troubling is the fact the author does not mention technical data, either to explain why none are available for this test or why any are excluded. Does the author assume that because this test is criterion referenced, technical data are superfluous? Or that because the test has gained widespread use and acceptance there is obviously no need for reliability and validity data? The omission of such data is the test's most serious flaw.

RECOMMENDATIONS. Without validity data, it is inappropriate and unethical to recommend this test for something other than as an informal screening measure that may be of minor assistance to teachers in planning some curriculum objectives. There are no data to support its use in making placement or class grouping decisions. Unfortunately, most who use this test will do so for the purpose for which it is least suited.

[54]

Bristol Language Development Scales.

Purpose: To provide "a comprehensive approach to the assessment of language production by children and also to the planning of appropriate therapy."
Population: Ages 1.3 to 5.0.
Publication Date: 1989.
Acronym: BLADES.
Scores, 9: Pragmatics (Function), Semantics (Sentence Meaning, Time and Aspect, Modality), Noun Phrase Elements, Syntactics (Conjunctions, Noun Phrase Structure, Sentence/Clause Structure), Total.
Administration: Individual.
Price Data, 1992: £63.25 per complete kit including 10 record forms, 10 therapy planners, and manual (126 pages); £11.25 per 10 record forms; £14.95 per 10 therapy planners; £28.75 per Language, Learning and Education manual.
Time: Administration time varies (30 minute average recording time).
Comments: The Syntax-free Scale "is intended for use with those children whose symbolic communication is not in English (or contains some non-English elements)"; samples of the child's speech must be tape recorded and transcribed; Therapy Planning Form aids in evaluating gaps in the child's performance and in planning therapy.
Authors: Mary Gutfreund, Maureen Harrison, and Gordon Wells.
Publisher: NFER-Nelson Publishing Co., Ltd. [England].

Review of the Bristol Language Development Scales by WILLIAM M. BART, Professor of Educational Psychology, University of Minnesota, Minneapolis, MN:

According to the authors, use of the Bristol Language Development Scales depends on eliciting at least 180 utterances from the child. These utterances can often be obtained in a conversation of about 30 minutes. The conversation must be recorded with a high-quality cassette recorder and microphone. The recorded conversation is transcribed in accordance with a certain commonsensical transcription form described in the manual. For example, the utterances of the child are placed in one column, the utterances of an adult or another child are placed in another column, and notes to provide the context for the utterances are placed in a third column. The utterances of the child are numbered.

After the conversation is completely transcribed, additional conventions are used to supplement the transcription. For example, if there is a pause in an utterance, then one enters the expression "(pause)" in the transcribed utterance where the pause occurred, as in the following transcribed utterance: I went (pause) to the store.

After the conversation is transcribed with appropriate conventions being incorporated into the transcription, one may code the transcribed utterances of the child using one of the two principal scales: (*a*) the Main Scale, and (*b*) the Therapy Planning Form. With the Main Scale, one classifies the developmental levels of various utterances with respect to Pragmatic, Semantic, and Syntactic features of the utterances on a Main Scale Record Form. There are 10 developmental levels but not all levels are available for each of the three categories of linguistic features (i.e., Pragmatics, Semantics, and Syntactics).

An optional Syntax-Free Record Form is also available to classify the developmental levels of the various utterances with respect to function, sentence meaning, and additional features. The Syntax-Free Record Form can be used with deaf children using a language other than English such as French or American Sign Language.

With either Record Form, not all utterances are coded. For example, utterances that are mere repetitions of other utterances are not coded. Examples of how to code various utterances are provided in the manual.

Specific features for most of the developmental levels with respect to each of the three linguistic categories of Pragmatics, Semantics, and Syntactics are identified on the Main Scale Record Form. A sample of utterances is coded according to those features. Each feature is viewed as an item for a given developmental level and a given linguistic category. After the Main Scale Record Form is completed, one completes a Main Scale Score Sheet. Use of this sheet allows users to record items for the various developmental level x linguistic categories and subcategories. If the score of a child at a given developmental level equals or exceeds the criterion score, then one indicates the criterion for that level was met. The highest attained level is a major factor in determining the developmental level of a child. The correct assignment of a developmental level depends on at least 100 coded utterances.

The completion of the Therapy Planning Form and the Syntax-Free Record Form are similarly detailed and complex. Fortunately, the manual is quite comprehensive.

The manual contains no reliability or validity information. However, the scales are not devoid of interesting psychometric features. The scales were based on the order among the items derived from longitudinal records of 125 children. The psychometric method used to determine the order among the items was an adaptation of the ordering-theoretic method of Bart and Krus (1973) to determine hierarchies among items. The adaptation explained in the manual seems to have a reasonable and interesting rationale. The scales are thus the result of painstaking longitudinal inquiry and rather innovative psychometric analysis. It is somewhat disappointing that with such a well-founded instrument there were no efforts to examine the validity of the instrument in terms of important validity considerations. However, even with such failings, the scales may be of potential use and interest to practitioners who examine the developmental levels of the language of children.

These scales may be quite informative to practitioners interested in child speech. But their use does require patience, diligence, and effort to master. Much study and practice with the scales and the manual will clearly be needed in order to reach proficiency. A great deal of inquiry went into the construction and design of these scales and the manual and a generous amount of effort will have to be expended before mastery of the scales is attained by most prospective users.

REVIEWER'S REFERENCE

Bart, W. M., & Krus, D. J. (1973). An ordering-theoretic method to determine hierarchies among items. *Educational and Psychological Measurement, 33*, 291-300.

Review of the Bristol Language Development Scales by NATALIE L. HEDBERG, Professor of Communication Disorders and Speech Science, University of Colorado, Boulder, CO:

The Bristol Language Development Scales (BLADES) is an outgrowth of Gordon Wells' well-known Bristol Language Project in which conversational data were collected at 3-month intervals from 125 children over the ages of 15 to 60 months. Following the procedure for the study, a lengthy and time-consuming method for obtaining a language sample for assessment purposes is recommended in which the family tape-records 30 minutes of the child's conversations with a variety of persons in different contexts at different times during the day or over a few days to obtain a minimum of 100 codeable utterances. The person making the tape recording is also required to make notes on the contexts of the conversations as well as the activities in which the child engages. A format for transcribing the complete conversation is provided.

Clear, detailed instructions are given for coding instances of three language systems—Pragmatics, Semantics, and Syntax—which are subdivided into a total of eight subsystems. Each subsystem contains examples of language items to be coded. The total number of items coded is then easily transferred to a well-laid-out score sheet called the Main Scale Record Form from which composite scores representing 10 possible developmental levels are obtained. The child's scores are compared to criterion scores based on the number of possible items scored for each level to determine the child's BLADES level. The language levels are then compared to the median ages and ranges for each level in the large Bristol sample to determine the adequacy of the child's language at the time sampled. The manual authors state that a child reaches a level when he or she "exhibits half the items given for that level (and has mastered earlier levels)" (manual, p. 21). Unfortunately, no data are provided to support the selection of "half the items" as the appropriate criterion for reaching a level.

An adaptation of the Main Scale called the Syntax-Free Scale, for use with children who communicate in sign or in a language other than English, appears on the back of the Main Scale. This scale is recommended for determining whether there is a general delay in language development or difficulty only in learning English. Minimal instructions for using the Syntax-Free Scale, which codes only the pragmatic and semantic features of language expressed verbally, in sign, or through gesture, are included in the manual. Although the examiner is cautioned to use a video recording in assessing "non-vocal elements" of communication, neither instructions nor examples for coding such elements are given. Means for differentiating general language delay from delay in learning English are not provided.

The Therapy Planning Form can be used to obtain a more detailed language analysis using additional samples of the child's language. With this form any gaps in information related to the eight language subsystems shown on the Main Scale can be filled in through reference to "keys." The keys for each language subsystem direct the user through the process of correctly identifying each additional language item being coded. Specific words from the samples are recorded on the Therapy Planning Form. The information on this form, used in conjunction with "diagrams" showing the sequence of emergence of linguistic items, provides a comprehensive base for planning a therapy program.

The procedures for analyzing language samples, although lengthy and complex, are quite easy to learn, provide a comprehensive measure of a child's expressive language, and provide clear direction for planning therapy. Unfortunately, however, the manual includes little descriptive information on the normative sample (although information is available in other publications) and no information relative to the reliability or validity of the procedures. A further serious limitation is the method for obtaining the language sample. It would be an unusual situation where the parents of children with language delay or disorder could carry out the lengthy procedures recommended. Although suggestions for obtaining a conversational sample in a clinic or classroom are given, the data on use of language in the home would be significantly less valid for comparison. A further concern for the clinician is the time involved in transcribing 30 minutes of conversation and coding a sample of 100 utterances, especially when the recording was made by someone else. Even if reliability and validity data were forthcoming, the other weaknesses discussed would limit the usefulness of this tool for clinical purposes.

In summary, the BLADES is not recommended as a clinical tool because of the requirement of parental involvement in recording the language sample in the home, the time required to complete the analysis, and the lack of information in the manual on reliability, validity, and the normative group. Developmental Sentence Scoring (Lee, 1974), although limited to the assessment of syntax and morphology, is a preferred measure for analyzing language samples of young children.

REVIEWER'S REFERENCE

Lee, L. L. (1974). Developmental Sentence Analysis: A Grammatical Assessment Procedure for Speech and Language Clinicians. Evanston, IL: Northwestern University Press.

[55]

British Ability Scales: Spelling Scale.

Purpose: To provide diagnostic information about children's spelling errors.
Population: Ages 5-0 to 14-5.
Publication Date: 1992.
Acronym: BAS.
Scores: Total score only.
Subtests, 4: Four spelling lists A–D.
Administration: Individual or group.
Price Data, 1992: £46 per complete set including manual (34 pages), 50 record forms, and 50 worksheets; £13 per 50 record forms and worksheets.
Time: Administration time not reported.
Comments: Developed to supplement The British Ability Scales (9:172); included in Americanized version of BAS published as Differential Ability Scales (11:111).
Author: Colin D. Elliott.
Publisher: NFER-Nelson Publishing Co. Ltd. [England].
Cross References: For reviews by Susan Embretson (Whitely) and by Benjamin D. Wright and Mark H. Stone of The British Ability Scales, see 9:172 (5 references); for reviews by Glen P. Aylward and Robert C. Reinehr of the Differential Ability Scales, see 11:111 (1 reference).

Review of the British Ability Scales: Spelling Scale by STEVE GRAHAM, Professor of Special Education, University of Maryland, College Park, MD:

The British Ability Scales (BAS) Spelling Scale is used to assess the spelling achievement of children in elementary through junior high school. The Spelling Scale was constructed so that it could be used in conjunction with the earlier standardized British Ability Scales, an individually administered intelligence test. When administered as part of the BAS battery, discrepancies between spelling and IQ can be calculated.

Spelling achievement is assessed by examining the child's ability to spell individual words. The Spelling Scale contains 69 words divided into four tests. One test contains all 69 items, whereas the remaining tests contain 20 items each. These short-form tests were designed to assess spelling achievement from 5 to 10 years of age, 8 to 14.5 years of age, and across the full age range, respectively. Although the author provided no guidelines for selecting the test to be administered, it is important to note that the standard error of measurement was larger for the short-form tests than for the test containing all 69 items.

Each of the four spelling tests is easy to administer. The examiner says the target word, uses it in a sentence furnished in the manual, and says the word again. Students write their responses on a worksheet; the number for items on the short-form tests are either circled or printed in red. Despite the inclusion of these markings, some children may have difficulty placing their responses in the correct space when taking the short-form tests. Children also may become frustrated when taking the full test as it is not discontinued until 10 consecutive words are misspelled. The short-form tests, in contrast, require fewer successive misspellings to establish a ceiling. The number of successive failures, however, is not the same for the three short-form tests. The rationale for these differences was not addressed by the author.

The number of words that a student spells correctly can be converted to either a percentile, *T*-score, or a spelling-age score. The author is to be commended for encouraging users of the Scale to compute confidence intervals for percentiles and *T*-scores. It should be noted, however, the standard error of measurement was quite high on all four of the tests at the upper and lower ends of ability.

In addition to scoring a child's responses as either correct or incorrect, the examiner can analyze misspellings according to the type of error committed: pre-spelling (*orh* for *the*), major nonphonetic (*nE* for *on*), nonphonetic order (*adn* for *and*), semiphonetic (*wrk* for *work*), basic phonetic (*bloo* for *blue*), and plausible phonetic (*leppard* for *leopard*). To verify hypotheses about student's spelling strategies based on the results of the error analyses, additional tips and assessment techniques were presented in the manual. Unfortunately, the author provided no reliability or validity data on the procedures for analyzing errors, nor were the teaching implications of these analyses adequately addressed. Moreover, some misspellings can be classified as more than one type of error (e.g., *cieling* for *ceiling* as either a nonphonetic order error or a plausible error).

Although the BAS Spelling Scales were designed to assess spelling achievement from 5 to 14.5 years of age, initial trialing of the test items was based on only 316 children who were in second, third, and fifth grade. The 176 third and fifth grade children were tested on 49 of the spelling items along with the Word Reading Scale from the BAS battery. The 140 second graders were also administered the Word Reading Scale and tested on the remaining 20 items plus 10 of the other 49 items. The Rasch item response model was then used to link and calibrate the spelling items to the existing norms for the BAS Word Reading Scale.

No information was provided on the construction of the short forms of the test, nor was any information on their reliability or validity provided. The author did report reliability coefficients for internal consistency for the full test for the second, third, and fifth grade students participating in the initial trialing of items. All reliability coefficients were .90 or above. To establish the validity of the Spelling Scales, the author referenced studies conducted on the Differential Ability Scales: Spelling Scale. The Differential Ability Scales (DAS) represents the standardization of the BAS, along with the BAS Spelling Scale, in the United States. The DAS Spelling Scale was highly correlated with other spelling tests (.74 and above) and with the Word Reading Scale of the DAS (.81). The author interpreted this later finding as support for using the norms from the BAS Word Reading Scale to calibrate the BAS spelling items. Caution must be used in extrapolating the findings from the DAS studies, however, because the BAS and DAS Spelling Scales are not identical. They use the same format, but not all of the test items are the same.

In summary, two noteworthy aspects of the BAS Spelling Scale include the system for classifying errors and the possibility for calculating the discrepancy between spelling and IQ when the Spelling Scale is administered as part of the full BAS battery. Nonetheless, caution must be exercised when using the instrument, as the reliability and validity of the four spelling tests or the system for classifying errors have yet to be adequately established.

Review of the British Ability Scales: Spelling Scale by WILLIAM D. SCHAFER, Associate Professor of Educational Measurement, Statistics, and Evaluation, University of Maryland, College Park, MD:

The British Ability Scales (BAS) Spelling Scale was developed to augment the original BAS school achievement tests. It is an individually administered test that may be used to assess and interpret spelling ability. The manual author also describes ways to analyze an examinee's spelling errors. The test can be administered using a single-sheet form for the examiner and a single-sheet worksheet and a pencil for the examinee.

The Scale consists of 69 items, progressing from easy to difficult. For each item presented to the examinee, the examiner states the word to be spelled, then uses the word in a predetermined sentence, then repeats the single word. The examinee writes the word on a blank line of the worksheet. This process continues until a specified number of successive failures is observed. Different subsets of the items comprise four possible tests: (*a*) all items, making up a long form; (*b*) the first 20 odd-numbered items, making up an easy form; (*c*) the last 20 odd-numbered items, making up a difficult form; and (*d*) 20 items interspersed throughout the range, making up a short form. Codes are used to identify the items to be presented in the word list. However, there are no directions about which forms to use in which circumstances or about whether to alter pronunciations of the words depending on the dialect of the examinee.

Raw, number-right scores are converted to ability scores that can range from 41 to 222, although the ranges of the shorter forms are less. Standard errors are associated with ability scores and test forms and can be as small as 4 and as large as 13. Within 3- to 6-month age groups, ability scores are converted using a table to percentiles and normalized *T* scores. A possible ambiguity arises from repeated ability scores for different percentile and *T*-score combinations; printing the ability score only opposite the combination to be recorded could have avoided this. Use of another table yields spelling ages. Confidence intervals using the standard errors are possible and recommended, but the record form does not include a space to record them. The worksheet includes a section for examiner comments. This is desirable because irregularities that might invalidate the test can be noted. Unfortunately, there is no space on the record form to transcribe them.

Paralleling the original British Ability Scales and their derivative Differential Ability Scales, the BAS Spelling Scale was developed using the one-parameter logistic (Rasch) model for item analysis and scaling. In a Rasch scaling event, one parameter is estimated for each item and interpreted as that item's difficulty.

Several reasonable sources were used to identify 50 potential words, which were selected also to illustrate types of spelling errors. Subsets of these were administered along with the BAS Word Reading Scale, short form Test B, to two samples of different ages (usable n = 89 on 25 spelling items for a year 3 sample, about 8 years in age, and 87 on 35 spelling items, 10 items overlapping, for a year 5 sample, about 10 years in age). Fit to the Rasch model was achieved for the spelling items and for the combined items in each sample, the latter justifying use of the Word Reading Scale's difficulty scale to calibrate the spelling items. This resulted in 49 scaled items. In order to obtain a downward extension, an additional 20 words were administered along with 10 of the calibrated items and the same Word Reading Scale to a year 2 sample, about 7 years in age (usable n = 140). Following adequate fit statistics, the new words were calibrated to the Word Reading Scale and to the 10 calibrated items. Discrepancies between these two calibrations were reported as minor and for each item the results of the two were averaged for the final calibration.

Data were thus available for 70 words and all but one appear on the BAS Spelling Scale. An appendix gives the spelling rule for each of the remaining 69 words. The one word dropped was deleted because everyone who attempted it spelled it right and it therefore could not be calibrated. Although the authors are to be congratulated for their use of modern, latent trait methods in developing the Scale, perhaps oversampling of items and the use of a discrimination index for each item (e.g., estimation using a two-parameter model or calculating a traditional index) might have allowed culling of words and resulted in an improved test.

Reliability and validity data for the BAS Spelling Scale are sparse. Only internal consistency reliabilities for the data obtained in the calibration are reported. Coefficient alpha was .90 for the 25 year 3 items, .92 for the 35 year 5 items, and .91 for the 20 year 2 items. Although these are indicative of acceptable reliability, score consistency across other factors, such as occasions, remains unevaluated, as does reliability of the full set of items and of those making up the easy, difficult, and short forms.

The Differential Ability Scales (DAS) include a Spelling Scale that is identical to the BAS Spelling Scale in format and many items overlap (the same is true of the BAS and DAS Word Reading Scales). The correlation between the DAS Spelling and Word Reading Scales is .81, which supports the use of a word reading scale to calibrate the BAS Spelling Scale. The correlations of DAS Spelling with DAS Basic Number Skills is .56, with DAS General Conceptual Ability is .52, with DAS Verbal Ability is .49, and with DAS Spatial Ability is .34. Correlations of the DAS Spelling Scale with other spelling tests are .85 and higher. These data are suggestive of convergent and divergent validity but are based on few studies and depend on generalization from a similar test to the BAS Spelling Scale. Further research should be conducted to provide a firmer basis with which to judge the psychometric properties of this recently published test.

The manual author suggests a developmental stage approach to error analysis to yield instructionally useful hypotheses about spelling. Errors are divided into three nonphonetic types (prespelling, major nonphonetic, and nonphonetic order) and three phonetic types (semiphonetic, basic phonetic, and plausible phonetic). Space on the record form is available to check the error type for each word spelled incorrectly. Several examples of error types are given but many examiners will remain unsure about how to classify errors after reading the manual. An example of each of the six types of error, where possible, for each word would have been helpful. Although diagnosis of developmental stage in spelling through error analysis may have value, there is no guidance in the manual about how these error patterns might be translated into instructional prescriptions.

Primarily because the Rasch model was used in item calibration, the BAS Spelling Scale has capitalized on several advantages of modern psychometric theory. For example, even though small numbers of examinees were used, there is evidence that its outcomes are interpretable using the more extensive norms of the BAS Word Reading Scale. The few studies that exist suggest it can be a valuable adjunct to the BAS. However, the more extensive data about reliability and validity that would be needed to support its recommendation for routine use are not yet available.

[56]

Burns/Roe Informal Reading Inventory: Preprimer to Twelfth Grade, Third Edition.

Purpose: Provides information about the reading skills, abilities, and needs of individual students in order to plan an appropriate program of reading instruction.

Population: Beginning readers–grade 12.

Publication Dates: 1985–89.

Acronym: IRI.

Scores, 2: Word Recognition, Comprehension.

Administration: Individual.

Levels, 14: Preprimer, Primer, First Reader, Second Grade, Third Grade, Fourth Grade, Fifth Grade, Sixth Grade, Seventh Grade, Eighth Grade, Ninth Grade, Tenth Grade, Eleventh Grade, Twelfth Grade.

Price Data: Available from publisher.
Time: (40–50) minutes.
Comments: No time limit.
Authors: Betty D. Roe and Paul C. Burns.
Publisher: Houghton Mifflin Co.
Cross References: For reviews by Carolyn Colvin Murphy and Roger H. Bruning and by Edward S. Shapiro of an earlier edition, see 10:37.

TEST REFERENCES

1. Arno, K. S. (1989). Burns/Roe Informal Reading Inventory. *Journal of Reading, 33,* 470-471.
2. Fehrenbach, C. R. (1991). Gifted/average readers: Do they use the same reading strategies? *Gifted Child Quarterly, 35,* 125-127.

Review of the Burns/Roe Informal Reading Inventory: Preprimer to Twelfth Grade, Third Edition by STEVEN V. OWEN, Professor of Educational Psychology, University of Connecticut, Storrs, CT:

The Burns/Roe Informal Reading Inventory (hereafter, Burns/Roe) has enjoyed 15 years of popularity among classroom teachers, reading specialists, learning disabilities personnel, and teacher trainers. It is promoted as an efficient and important tool for gathering information about students' strengths and weaknesses in oral and silent reading, and for making decisions about appropriate reading materials. The Burns/Roe certainly makes the assessment easy. It is loaded with vocabulary lists (two equivalent forms) and graded passages (four equivalent forms) ranging in difficulty from preprimer through 12th grade. Burns and Roe provide detailed—but simple—instructions for using the material, and give a lengthy case study to illustrate the process. Although an attractive and promising package, there is no evidence that the Burns/Roe can fulfill its promises.

Informal reading inventories, including the Burns/Roe, seem to have set the stage for the increasingly popular performance assessments. Both forms of measurement emphasize authentic materials and diagnostic utility. Superficially, performance assessments appear to be used for higher stakes decisions including grades, promotion, graduation, and school funding. Reading specialists might argue that high stakes decisions also issue from informal reading inventories (IRI). When reading placements suggested by an IRI are assigned correctly, students are given appropriately challenging material. If an IRI gives an incorrect placement, then progress in reading may be harmed by frustration or by boredom.

Perhaps the clearest distinction between IRIs and performance assessments is that, as a group, IRIs are published and performed with very little psychometric scrutiny. The Burns/Roe authors and publishers, across three editions, have yet to acknowledge the importance of standard measurement evidence. The Burns/Roe gives no reliability estimates. Following the lead of performance assessments, there should be information about internal consistency, interrater reliability, and equivalent forms reliability (considered simultaneously, perhaps, in a generalizability analysis). Standard errors of measurement should also be published. The Burns/Roe gives no details of content, criterion-related, or construct validity. It is as though the authors and publisher have considered themselves exempt from even the barest psychometric exploration. Ironically, in the near future, developers of diagnostic and performance tests will have even more psychometric detail to consider (Linn, 1994; Nichols, 1994).

I am not the first to take Burns and Roe, and Houghton-Mifflin, to task. *Mental Measurements Yearbook* reviewers have similar complaints about the second edition of the Burns/Roe (Murphy & Bruning, 1989; Shapiro, 1989). Other researchers, concerned about Burns and Roe's psychometric silence, have performed their own investigations and have revealed substandard reliability and validity evidence for the Burns/Roe (as well as for other informal reading inventories). For example, there is compelling evidence that slicing comprehension passages or vocabulary words out of their larger context makes them less dependable as a diagnostic tool. One must use many passages, and put vocabulary words in some context, to compensate for this (Caldwell, 1985; Duffelmeyer, Robinson, & Squier, 1989). Others have found that reading inventory comprehension passages are not very representative of basal readers (Fuchs, Fuchs, & Deno, 1982), and that the actual intervals among reading passage grade levels are at odds with the claimed intervals (Klesius & Homan, 1985).

Should one use the Burns/Roe? There is not much indication one way or the other. Traditionally, test developers gather and present psychometric data so prospective users can make informed judgments. For many years, the *Standards for Educational and Psychological Testing* (AERA, APA, & NCME, 1985) has given clear guidance about how to marshall such evidence. Burns and Roe have taken the opposite tack: Here is a test; you figure out its measurement properties. Their approach borders on measurement misconduct.

REVIEWER'S REFERENCES

Fuchs, L. S., Fuchs, D., & Deno, S. L. (1982). Reliability and validity of curriculum-based Informal Reading Inventories. *Reading Research Quarterly, 18,* 6-25.

American Educational Research Association, American Psychological Association, & National Council on Measurement in Education. (1985). *Standards for educational and psychological testing.* Washington, DC: American Psychological Association, Inc.

Caldwell, J. (1985). A new look at the old Informal Reading Inventory. *The Reading Teacher, 39,* 168-173.

Klesius, J. P., & Homan, S. P. (1985). A validity and reliability update on the informal reading inventory with suggestions for improvement. *Journal of Learning Disabilities, 18,* 71-76.

Duffelmeyer, F. A., Robinson, S. S., & Squier, S. E. (1989). Vocabulary questions on informal reading inventories. *The Reading Teacher, 43,* 142-148.

Murphy, C. C., & Bruning, R. H. (1989). [Review of the Burns/Roe Informal Reading Inventory: Preprimer to Twelfth Grade, Second Edition.] In J. C. Conoley & J. J. Kramer (Eds.), *The tenth mental measurements yearbook* (p. 116). Lincoln, NE: Buros Institute of Mental Measurements.

Shapiro, E. S. (1989). [Review of the Burns/Roe Informal Reading Inventory: Preprimer to Twelfth Grade, Second Edition.] In J. C. Conoley & J. J. Kramer (Eds.), *The tenth mental measurements yearbook* (p. 117-118). Lincoln, NE: Buros Institute of Mental Measurements.

Linn, R. L. (1994). Performance assessment: Policy promises and technical measurement standards. *Educational Researcher, 23*(9), 4-14.

Nichols, P. D. (1994). A framework for developing cognitively diagnostic assessments. *Review of Educational Research, 64*, 575-603.

Review of the Burns/Roe Informal Reading Inventory: Preprimer to Twelfth Grade, Third Edition by STEPHANIE STEIN, Associate Professor of Psychology, Central Washington University, Ellensburg, WA:

The Burns/Roe Informal Reading Inventory is designed to assess students' reading levels and diagnose errors in word identification and comprehension. Specifically, the authors provide guidelines for determining students' independent, instructional, and frustration reading levels and listening comprehension levels. Graded word lists are used to suggest the appropriate level of passage to begin assessment of reading level.

The entire test and manual is combined in a single wire-bound booklet with perforated pages that can be torn out if necessary. Most of the booklet is made up of actual test material. Two sets of words lists and four sets of graded passages are provided for 14 levels of reading: preprimer, primer, and 1st through 12th grade. Each word list and passage has a student copy (large print for the lower levels) and a teacher copy.

The Burns/Roe has some definite strengths. First of all, the authors provide a clear introduction to the use of an informal reading inventory and an overview of the different reading levels. The guidelines on scoring, recording, and interpreting the reading measures are quite extensive and the case study example for scoring and interpreting is helpful in learning about the instrument.

The four sets of equivalent forms enable teachers to reassess students several times during the year without having to worry about practice effects on specific passages. In addition, the teacher forms of the test material are convenient to use, with scoring guidelines included on each page. The authors emphasize the importance of diagnosing miscues (reading errors) and give detailed suggestions on how to record and categorize these errors. Finally, the inclusion of a wide range of reading levels (beginner through 12th grade) will make this instrument especially attractive to teachers at the secondary level.

The limitations of this most recent edition of the Burns/Roe are basically the same as those noted in reviews of earlier editions (Murphy & Bruning, 1989; Shapiro, 1989). There is virtually no technical information provided on the instrument. One of the changes to this edition is supposedly "more complete . . . information on development and testing of new material" (p. viii), yet the entire section on construction of the inventory takes up less than two pages in the appendix. The authors refer to "field testing" of the passages on students in grades 1 through 12, with the number of students ranging from 27 on Form D to 32 on Form B. However, there are no data about the breakdown of number of students at each grade level tested or the demographics of the students. Additionally, they note that "the passages did increase in difficulty as the grade level increased" (p. 208) but they do not explain how this was determined. The authors also fail to provide empirical support for the criteria used to determine reading levels and the validity of comprehension categories.

The complete absence of data about the psychometric properties of the inventory in terms of reliability and validity is particularly disturbing. There are not even alternate forms reliability data to suggest that the "equivalent" forms of the passages really are equivalent. The authors claim that the test can be used for making individual decisions about student placement. However, this claim is inconsistent with accepted guidelines that require sufficient data to indicate that the test yields consistent results and is valid for the specific purpose.

In summary, the Burns/Roe Informal Reading Inventory is a convenient and well-organized set of word lists and reading passages that may or may not be valid for the purposes of placement in a basal reader. Teachers who are looking for a quick and easy reading inventory may not be concerned about the lack of technical data in the Burns/Roe—but they *should* be. The term "informal reading inventory" implies that teachers can use it to ascertain quickly student reading level. However, it should not imply that the instrument can stand alone on its face value without any supporting evidence to back it up. The authors are encouraged to provide more detailed information about the construction of their inventory, the demographics of their student sample, and data about the reliability and validity of the instrument. If additional psychometric data are provided, this could be one of the best informal reading inventories available. However, without this information, there is no way to tell how useful it really is.

REVIEWER'S REFERENCES

Murphy, C. C., & Bruning, R. H. (1989). [Review of the Burns/Roe Informal Reading Inventory: Preprimer to Twelfth Grade, Second Edition.] In J. C. Conoley & J. J. Kramer (Eds.), *The tenth mental measurements yearbook* (p. 116). Lincoln, NE: Buros Institute of Mental Measurements.

Shapiro, E. S. (1989). [Review of the Burns/Roe Informal Reading Inventory: Preprimer to Twelfth Grade, Second Edition.] In J. C. Conoley & J. J. Kramer (Eds.), *The tenth mental measurements yearbook* (p. 117-118). Lincoln, NE: Buros Institute of Mental Measurements.

[57]

The California Critical Thinking Dispositions Inventory.

Purpose: "Measures one's disposition or inclination toward critical thinking."

Population: High school, college, and adult.

Publication Date: 1992.

Acronym: CCTDI.

Scores, 8: Truth-Seeking, Inquisitiveness, Open-Mindedness, Confidence, Analyticity, Systematicity, Cognitive Maturity, Total.

Administration: Group or individual.
Price Data, 1993: $75 per specimen kit including inventory, scoring templates, and manual (27 pages); $30 per 20 copies of inventory ($60 per 50 copies, $110 per 100 copies, and $205 per 225 copies).
Time: (15–20) minutes.
Authors: Peter A. Facione and Noreen C. Facione.
Publisher: The California Academic Press.

Review The California Critical Thinking Dispositions Inventory by CAROLYN M. CALLAHAN, Professor, Curry School of Education, University of Virginia, Charlottesville, VA:

The California Critical Thinking Dispositions Inventory (CCTDI) is designed to assess the affective, attitudinal dimension of critical thinking. The recommended use of the inventory is for student assessment and program evaluation. The authors specifically state the CCTDI is *not* a measure of critical thinking ability or skills.

The manual is clearly written and the instructions for administration and scoring of the test are easily followed. Further, the process of translating the point totals into standard scores is easily executed. However, the interpretation of the resulting standard scores is questionable. These scores are labeled *T*-scores in footnotes which describe their derivation, yet they are not derived from *z*-scores or normative groups. If the scores are presented as *T*-scores, there is a danger of misinterpretation of the scores as representative of standing in some normative group. Further, the authors have presented "cut off scores" based on a theoretical rationale for a positive or negative disposition for critical thinking, but present no empirical evidence that individuals scoring above or below those cutoff scores will be better or worse critical thinkers. No normative data are provided in the manual and data comparing the percentage of undergraduate and graduate students scoring above and below the cut scores are highly questionable given the small number of post-baccalaureate cases (34).

The alpha reliabilities for the total score on the CCTDI are reported as between .90 and .91 across high school and college students (baccalaureate and post-baccalaureate). Although the range of reliabilities on subscores is reported (.60–.78 in the replication sample), the specific reliabilities for individual subtests are not. No stability data are reported and the absence of mean and standard deviation data makes the calculation of the standard error of measurement impossible. (None is provided in the manual.) The test authors indicate the test may be used with any individuals who can read the items, but no reliability data are provided for any adult populations other than college populations. Only vague descriptions are provided of the college populations on which the instrument was developed.

The content validity of the test is based on claims the items are derived from the consensus of 46 theoreticians regarding the dispositional dimension of critical thinking. An original set of 150 statements was reduced to 75 based on the psychometric performance of the items on a pilot version of the instrument. Although the subscales are described in depth, little information is provided on how the characteristics list was translated into the statements on the instrument itself or how these were reviewed for accurate reflection of the characteristic.

The authors' claims of predictive validity and construct validity are not supported by the evidence in the test manual. The correlation of the CCTDI with the California Critical Thinking Skills Test (which appears to be concurrent rather than predictive as described) is questionable given the authors' claims of the independence of the two constructs. Factor analysis is alluded to as the support for the subscales' empirical validity, but neither the methodology nor the resulting factor loadings are presented as evidence of the factor structure and the integrity of the subscales. The authors' claims that further confirmation of the stability and validity of the instrument is supported by assertions the "sub-set of 75 also discriminated among the individuals tested at three separate university settings" (p. 13) is unwarranted.

The authors wisely caution against using the instrument for high-stakes assessment of individuals and their caution should be heeded. A researcher or evaluator who is willing to pursue a careful match between the items and program outcomes or research question and who is willing to establish the stability of the instrument prior to the assessment of program change may find this a useful tool.

Review of The California Critical Thinking Dispositions Inventory by SALVADOR HECTOR OCHOA, Assistant Professor of Educational Psychology, Texas A&M University, College Station, TX:

The California Critical Thinking Dispositions Inventory (CCTDI) is designed to assess an individual's disposition for critical thinking. This instrument is based on the Delphi Report, a consensus by a panel of "experts" on the subject area. Although the test authors provide information describing how their instrument differs from other related measures on the basis of a differential theoretical definition of critical thinking, the CCTDI has several psychometric weaknesses.

The sample used to develop the CCTDI is not well defined. The authors report the use of two samples. The pilot version sample consisted of 164 undergraduate students from only two universities in the United States and one university from Canada. The second sample, prepublication, consisted of 156 subjects who were high school, undergraduate, and post-baccalaureate students. Little data are provided on the prepublication sample. No data are provided with respect to gender, ethnicity, geographical location (i.e., pilot version sample only), and socioeconomic status of participants for both samples. It appears from the manual that these two samples were not used to obtain norms for the CCTDI. Instead, the authors provide recommendations on how to interpret the overall and seven subscale scores. They state a score above 50 indicates that a person evidences a strength in a particular disposition area; whereas a score below 40 means that a weakness is apparent. Moreover, total scores of less than 280 and above 350 are interpreted to be a weakness and strength, respectively, in attitudinal factors associated with critical thinking. Given that the eight scores obtained from the CCTDI are not normed, the authors recommend they not be used for "high stake" purposes.

With respect to the reliability, insufficient information is provided in the manual. Although the overall Cronbach's alpha of .90 and .91 for the pilot and prepublication version, respectively, is acceptable, the test authors do not provide each subscale's reliability. There is no information on test-retest reliability.

The validity of the CCTDI is questionable. The authors provide some evidence of content validity as the selection of items for the CCTDI were based on the Delphi Report. No information, however, is provided on what categorization procedures were used to place items under each subscale. Moreover, no data are provided as to whether multiple judges were used and their interrater agreement. The authors suggest the subscales of the CCTDI should be correlated with other well-established instruments measuring similar constructs in the future. This recommendation should have actually been done by the test authors in order to provide support for the validity of the seven subscales. Although the predictive validity of the CCTDI was established by a .67 correlation with the California Critical Thinking Skills Test, the sample size used in this study was only 20. This correlation is surprising given that the test authors state that "the CCTDI is not intended to be a measure of the person's CT [critical thinking] ability" (manual, p. 3). The test authors report predictive validity research is "being replicated with larger samples" (manual, p. 12). The manual does not contain sufficient information to evaluate the construct validity of the CCTDI. The test authors report that a factor analytic analysis was conducted and supported the seven factors. No data, however, are provided on the number of factors and their respective loading resulting from such analysis. No information is provided as to the suitability of items under each subscale.

The CCTDI authors provided a test manual with both strengths and limitations. With respect to its strengths, a good description of the seven subscales of the test is provided. The manual did contain adequate information on test administration and scoring. The technical sections of the manual, however, were poorly organized, confusing, and lacked important information. One had to search for important information in the endnotes. Given the questionable psychometric properties and insufficient data provided in the manual, the CCTDI should be used with caution.

[58]

California Critical Thinking Skills Test.

Purpose: Designed to be "a standardized assessment instrument targeting core critical thinking skills at the post-secondary level."
Population: College and adult.
Publication Dates: 1990–92.
Acronym: CCTST.
Scores, 6: Analysis, Evaluation, Inference, Inductive Reasoning, Deductive Reasoning, Total.
Administration: Group.
Forms, 2: A, B (alternate).
Price Data, 1992: $60 per specimen kit including Form A, Form B, and manual ('92, 20 pages); $35 per 20 copies of test (volume discounts available); $10 per Delphi Report (22 pages).
Time: 45 minutes.
Author: Peter A. Facione.
Publisher: The California Academic Press.

Review of the California Critical Thinking Skills Test by ROBERT F. McMORRIS, Professor of Educational Psychology and Statistics, State University of New York at Albany, Albany, NY:

In the new Roget's Thesaurus (Chapman, 1992, p. 842), a synonym given for "critical" is "crucial." Certainly critical thinking skills are crucial for individuals and society, and developing an appropriate test to assess critical thinking is no trivial task. The California Critical Thinking Skills Test (CCTST) contains 34 multiple-choice items with a 45-minute time limit. The items cover a variety of topics: Some items are realistic, providing high face validity, but they potentially confound reasoning with content; and some are "nonsense," content-free items for those who prefer a more abstract approach. The items seem reasonably interesting, but occasionally it seems the four or five options do not contain the best answer possible. Was the key independently verified by experts? What criteria were used for item retention? What criteria were used to place an item on a subscale? How speeded is the test?

A Delphi panel developed a consensus definition of critical thinking (CT), core CT skills with examples, and dispositions crucial to becoming a critical thinker. The test contains three subscores based on the panel's work: Analysis, Evaluation, and Inference. The developer, Facione, also apologetically offers two other subscores, Deductive Reasoning and Inductive Reasoning, based on 30 of the 34 items, to meet a

California State University objective. (Given the double use of most items, we will refer to subscores rather than subtests.)

The developer conducted several studies using the CCTST at California State in Fullerton involving 1,196 undergraduates, 20 instructors, five different courses, and three academic departments. These data are bases for validity, reliability, and norm information.

VALIDITY. Test users are urged to study the items to judge validity, especially to estimate whether the test meets their conceptualizations of critical thinking.

According to the CCTST Fact Sheet, "The CCTST measures the growth in CT skills which is an intended outcome of completing a college level general education CT course." Facione has collected considerable pre and post data, some quite cleverly by measuring post at the end of the first semester and pre with similar students at the beginning of the second semester. Gain runs between .04 and 1.45 in mean scores on a 34-item test, statistically significant with large samples but hardly fantastic as a descriptive index of learning. Perhaps the test is not instructionally sensitive, perhaps the instruction was insufficiently potent, or perhaps other noise (e.g., more student motivation pre, or instructor present post) did not balance/cancel. This issue and the data are discussed by Facione (Technical Report #1; 1991).

Pretest scores correlate with college GPA (.20), SAT-V (.55), SAT-M (.44), most Nelson-Denny Reading scores (.40s), and posttest scores (.70). In general, these correlations with tests and with grades seem reasonable and supportive. Given, however, this correlation of .70 between pre- and posttest scores, Technical Report #2 contains a questionable section on Effectiveness of Particular Courses, with posttest means compared to four decimal places with no notion of whether the input for different courses was comparable.

Facione may emphasize statistics instead of meaningfulness in examining gender differences. He notes the male/female difference in posttest means is significant although the pre difference is nonsignificant, and he tries to justify differential gain by an elaborate rationale using SATs and grades. Yet the mean differences pre and post are almost equal and hardly impressive (about $^3/_4$ point). The difference in sample size—479 for pre and 710 post—helps in estimating why the posttest means differ statistically by gender.

Students responded to four questions after the 34 items were presented. Eighty percent of the students answered the item "Critical thinking and being logical are quite easy for me" positively on pretest and 84% answered positively on posttest, yet, as noted by the developer, mean item difficulty on the test was only 49.5. Perhaps on another study, a question could be added such as "How well did this test measure your critical thinking ability?"

Another question, "My GPA is an accurate reflection of how logical my thinking is," drew the author's comment: "It is not clear to this investigator why students perceive their GPA and their CT abilities not to be strongly correlated when in fact they are" (Technical Report #3, p. 13). Although the correlation between GPA and CCTST was statistically significant, the term "strongly correlated" may imply a higher relationship than $r = .20$ supports.

We applaud Facione's considering the question of differential functioning according to ethnicity/race for native English speakers. He was hampered by three tiny sample sizes out of the six groups. We recommend that with additional data he consult a methodologist experienced in conducting bias studies.

Another way to consider validity is through multitrait-multimethod matrices (Campbell & Fiske, 1959). The author sets the stage: "Three [subscores] . . . 'Analysis,' 'Evaluation,' and 'Inference,' correlate strongly with each other and with the overall CCTST . . . same is true of the two CCTST [subscores], 'Deductive Reasoning' and 'Inductive Reasoning,' which divide CCTST items along that more traditional matrix" (Technical Manual #4, p. 2). Treating pre and post as methods and the five subscores as traits, the validity diagonal contained one correlation coefficient in the .30s, two in the .40s, and two in the .50s. The heterotrait-monomethod triangles contained two correlations in the .20s, three in the .30s, and three in the .40s. Three estimates of reliability were provided for the total score: KR20s for pretest (.69) and posttest (.68), and a pre-post correlation (.70). Subscore reliability might be estimated using Spearman-Brown; starting from .70 for the total score, reliability for a half-length test would be approximately .54. Given this estimate of reliability, the validity coefficients among subscores appear to this reviewer as reasonably supportive. I hope the developer will use the multitrait-multimethod matrix approach, for example, to estimate whether results of this measure converge with other measures of critical thinking and yet retain some uniqueness when related to measures of general intellectual ability.

RELIABILITY. To summarize the information given above, total-score internal consistency appears to be close to.70. Subscore reliability, although not provided, might be in the .50s. No standard errors of measurement are provided; for the total score, the standard error is about 2.5 based on either the typical formula or Lord's approximation.

The reliability information does not support interpretation of differences for individuals, either for a profile or for gain. Subscore reliability is too low and intercorrelations too high to allow a profile to be dependable. Assessment of gain appears impossible: With total-score KR20s of .68 and .69, and pre-post correlation of .70, the reliability of the difference is estimated to be 0.

NORMS. As noted above, the norm group is composed of undergraduates from one of the California State colleges. To what extent does this group represent the national college student population? The groups contain both native and nonnative English speakers; subgroup norms could easily have been provided. Percentiles are provided for both pretest and posttest groups and for both total score and the five subscores. Subscores are particularly tricky to interpret: A one-point difference in number of correct items can change the percentile rank by up to 27%.

How might such percentile ranks be used? The developer specifies in the directions for test administrators, "If you plan to furnish students their individual percentile scores, indicate when and how that will be accomplished." What an invitation for mischief! There is little mention of limitations for interpretation, no provision of standard errors of measurement, no information on difference scores, no urging to have counselors or other interpreters available, and so on.

SUMMARY. The Delphi panel's characterization of the ideal critical thinker (Technical Report #1, p. 5; Facione, 1991, p. 2) could also be considered descriptive of those selecting, interpreting, and even reviewing tests. (Indeed, considering either the test or this review, you may join me in feeling like you have encountered an extensive reading passage with a multitude of critical-thinking questions at the end.) Some of the critical thinker's characteristics may even help summarize the developer's traits, for example, "habitually inquisitive, . . . flexible, . . . diligent in seeking relevant information, . . . persistent in seeking results which are as precise as the subject and the circumstances of inquiry permit" (Technical Report #1, p. 5). For such a new test, there is considerable information available with replies for many questions of interpretation. Further, responses to some of the questions raised in the Technical Reports are extended in Facione's 1991 paper, a combination thought provoker, information summarizer, and soft seller.

This test does not have the history, the reliability, or the variety of norm groups of a test like the Watson-Glaser Critical Thinking Appraisal (9:1347). The CCTST is a bit shorter, however, and already has a creative, developing, and somewhat supportive program for validation. Perhaps a systematic study of structural relationships among subsets of items for this test and other measures of critical thinking would help the developer deal with his desire to seek causation and components of interpretation in spite of the interrelatedness of the variables. Such a suggestion is offered hesitatingly, however, given that he may already have overinterpreted tests of hypotheses and underattended to descriptive information. To revisit Thesaurus synonyms for "critical," the developer has sought to be "explanatory," and the user needs to be "judicial."

Test users are urged to remain cautious in interpreting results of this measure, especially for individuals, to avoid interpreting profiles or gain scores, especially for individuals, and to supplement the information on validity, reliability, and norms provided by the developer and summarized here.

REVIEWER'S REFERENCES

Campbell, D. T., & Fiske, D. W. (1959). Convergent and discriminant validation by the multitrait-multimethod matrix. *Psychological Bulletin, 56,* 81-105.

Facione, P. A. (1991). *Using the California Critical Thinking Skills Test in research, evaluation, and assessment.* Millbrae, CA: California Academic Press. (ERIC Document Reproduction Service No. ED 337498)

Chapman, R. L. (Ed.). (1992). *Roget's international thesaurus* (5th ed.). New York: Harper Collins.

Review of the California Critical Thinking Skills Test by WILLIAM B. MICHAEL, Professor of Education and Psychology, University of Southern California, Los Angeles, CA:

Based on more than a decade of research and extensive validation efforts involving 1,196 college students, 20 instructors, and five courses in critical thinking given by three departments at a comprehensive urban state university in California, The California Critical Thinking Skills Test (CCTST) consists of 34 multiple-choice items. The test, which is administered within a period of 45 minutes, affords scores on three subtests intended to represent critical thinking (CT) constructs of Analysis (9 items), Evaluation (14 items), and Inference (11 items). In addition, scores are furnished on two conventional or traditional categories of Deductive Reasoning (16 items—4 from Analysis, 4 from Evaluation,and 8 from Inference) and Inductive Reasoning (14 items—1 from Analysis,10 from Evaluation, and 3 from Inference).

A Delphi panel comprising 46 nationally visible scholars in CT from several different academic disciplines labored 2 years to achieve a consensus concerning the definition of CT for general education at the lower division college level. Besides making several recommendations concerning CT instruction and assessment, the panel members created a list of core CT skills and subskills along with illustrations as well as a compilation of those personal dispositions thought to be crucial to one's becoming a competent and effective critical thinker. Their work culminated in a monograph entitled *Critical Thinking: A Statement of Expert Consensus for Purposes of Educational Assessment and Instruction* (ERIC TM 014423). The monograph may be obtained from ERIC, the American Philosophical Association, and the Institute for Critical Thinking at Montclair (New Jersey).

At the present time, there is no manual to accompany the CCTST. However, four technical reports are available that furnish statistical data, research findings, and percentile norms for the previously mentioned sample of college students. One can gain a reasonably accurate notion of the coverage in these documents from their titles: Technical Report No. 1, *CCTST Experimental Validation and Content Validity*, (ERIC TM 015818); Technical Report No. 2, *Factors Predictive of CT Skills*, (ERIC TM 015819); Technical Report No. 3, *Gender, Ethnicity, Major, CT Self-Esteem, and the CCTST*; and Technical Report No. 4, *Interpreting the CCTST, Group Norms and Sub-Scores*.

During the academic year starting in 1989 and terminating in 1990, pretests were administered prior to students taking one of five possible general education courses in critical thinking (a requirement in the university at which the research was conducted) followed by the administration of posttests to ascertain whether improvement in these skills had occurred. Typically, pretest differences in average performance were not associated with gender, ethnicity, college major, or self-confidence in CT skills. On posttests, males seemed to gain slightly more than females, and significant differences appeared relative to college major and membership in an ethnic group. Substantial correlations were noted between scores on the CCTST and those in verbal and mathematics portions of a scholastic aptitude test as well as those in an English placement measure and an entry level mathematics test. When aptitude test scores and native language were controlled, self-confidence in CT was not a significant factor in accounting for pretest or posttest results. A careful study of the technical reports will provide the potential user of the CCTST a substantial body of information regarding not only the definitions of the constructs of CT but also the complexity of the interrelationships of pretest and posttest scores with demographic, intellectual, and affective variables.

The CCTST would appear to possess substantial content validity—perhaps more than any other competing instrument in light of the collective wisdom of the eminent scholars who contributed to its development. The resulting score distributions, which are normal in form, provide a basis for differentiating quite adequately among the examinees. The 34 items are not easy. On the pretest the highest score for the sample of students studied was 29, and on the posttest 31 with respective means of 15.89 and 17.27. This reviewer has serious reservations concerning the scoring of three of the items and moderate reservations regarding the scoring of four others. There may be some concern relative to the 45-minute time limit. Perhaps one hour would be somewhat less threatening and conducive to a higher level of performance, especially for those students for whom English is not the first language. With a longer period of test administration, systematic empirical investigations relating performance on the CCTST to the host of variables that already have been studied might lead to somewhat different outcomes from those obtained with a shorter time limit.

Data pertaining to the reliability of the total scale as well as to the three subtests are meager. In Technical Report No. 1 internal-consistency estimates (KR-20) of only .69 and .68 occurred for total scores on a pretest and posttest administration. Normative information in the form of percentiles on both the pretest and posttest for the college sample studied is quite helpful, although corresponding data for subtests did not appear in the technical reports.

Although one can have considerable confidence that the content of the test represents a strong consensus among experts, additional research regarding the construct validity of the test would be very much in order. It would appear from the preliminary correlational data that both verbal and quantitative intelligence constitute a significant component of CT. It would be interesting to carry out both exploratory and confirmatory factor analyses of the CCTST with other well-known measures of CT and with tests of verbal and mathematical abilities to ascertain whether the hypothesized constructs can be empirically verified. It would also be rewarding to determine what the relationship of the hypothesized dimensions of the CCTST would be to a number of problem-solving abilities such as those identified by Guilford and his coworkers within the context of the structure-of-intellect model. One can anticipate that CT might conceivably be represented by a hierarchy of factor dimensions comprising both higher-order and first-order constructs.

In summary, preliminary evidence indicates the CCTST possesses considerable content validity. A manual is very much needed to synthesize existing information from the four technical reports. Additional efforts should be directed to obtain evidence regarding the empirical validity of the constructs, to provide reliability estimates of scores on the total scale and subscales, and to present more comprehensive normative data. The potential of the CCTST is great. One can hope that the author will be able to obtain the very much deserved necessary support to expend the additional effort needed to generate the required psychometric information that will permit the widespread use of this instrument in both undergraduate and graduate programs in colleges and universities.

[59]

Campbell Leadership Index.

Purpose: "An adjective checklist designed to be used in the assessment of leadership characteristics."
Population: Leaders.
Publication Date: 1991.
Acronym: CLI.
Scores, 22: Ambitious, Daring, Dynamic, Enterprising, Experienced, Farsighted, Original, Persuasive, Energy, Affectionate, Considerate, Empowering, Entertaining, Friendly, Credible, Organized, Productive, Thrifty, Calm, Flexible, Optimistic, Trusting.
Administration: Group or individual.
Price Data: Available from publisher.

Time: (45–60) minutes.
Comments: Self-ratings plus 3–5 observer ratings.
Author: David Campbell.
Publisher: National Computer Systems, Inc.

Review of the Campbell Leadership Index by GEORGE DOMINO, Professor of Psychology, University of Arizona, Tucson, AZ:

The Campbell Leadership Index (CLI) is a 100-item adjective check list designed to assess leadership characteristics. Respondents rate each adjective and the accompanying definition on a 6-point scale ranging from *always* to *never*. Three to five observers are then also required to rate the respondent using the same items and scale responses.

These ratings yield a total of 22 scores encompassing five "orientations" or areas: *L*eadership (8 scales), *E*nergy (1 scale), *A*ffability (5), *De*pendability (4), and *R*esilience (4). (Note the italicized initials spell LEADeR.) In addition to the 22 scores, the resulting profile also yields two summary scores, one for self and one for observers.

The CLI is a component of the Campbell Work Orientations (CWO), which is a collection of surveys focusing on the psychological aspects of the working environment. Campbell proposes that leadership can be defined as "actions which focus resources to create desirable opportunities" (p. 3), and that leadership can occur in the carrying out of seven tasks: vision, management, empowerment, politics, feedback, entrepreneurship, and personal style. One of the unique aspects of the CLI is that it is both a self-report measure and a method of gathering descriptive information from others. The CLI is intended to be used primarily with people in leadership positions. Typical participants are people attending leadership training programs.

The initial item pool for the CLI consisted of 300 adjectives. This pool underwent a number of revisions primarily in response to respondents' complaints about the length, to the current version of 100 items, of which only 96 are scored. Other considerations in the item reduction such as "eliminating items that proved to be unrelated to leadership effectiveness" (p. 123) are mentioned but no evidence is presented regarding the process.

The 22 scales were developed by using an iterative approach whereby clusters of adjectives were grouped into preliminary scoring scales, then samples of convenience were assessed, and modifications made on the basis of both correlational and logical analyses. For each of the 22 scales a table of item intercorrelations based on $N = 235$ are presented. Some of the coefficients are quite high (e.g., adventurous and daring, $r = .61$), most are in the middle ranges (e.g., hardy and sedentary, $r = .35$), and some are quite low (e.g., naive and well-connected, $r = -.11$). It should be noted that all of the scales are quite brief ranging from three to a maximum of seven items.

Once the 22 scales were developed, their intercorrelations were examined, and the five orientations (LEADeR) were constructed by gathering together the scoring scales with the highest intercorrelations. A subsequent factor analysis supports this five-dimension solution. Scores on the CLI are expressed as *T* scores and are based on some 30 normative groups ranging from college student leaders and nonleaders, to various types of business executives, industrial psychologists, municipal fire chiefs, and military officers. Most of these groups appear to be primarily male, but some female groups were also assessed.

The manual author states that "formulating a simple, general statement about the validity of the CLI has proved to be a difficult task" (p. 129). That indeed seems to be the case, although there is an extensive discussion of various types of validity. Content validity is said to be one of the CLI's strongest points, yet a perusal of the adjectives indicates that "competent" is not included, and that a number of adjectives included in Gough's ACL "military leadership" scale, for example, are missing from the CLI. Several concurrent validity studies are presented indicating that self-ratings on the CLI may not accurately reflect current status, but composite observer ratings do. Both construct and discriminant validities are discussed, with findings supportive of the CLI. Extensive reliability data, including alpha coefficients, interrater reliability coefficients, and test-retest coefficients are presented, generally suggesting adequate to excellent reliability.

Appendix A of the manual gives personological descriptions of high and low scorers on each of the 22 scales, although it is not indicated how these psychodynamic portraits were derived.

The respondent apparently receives a rather detailed computerized feedback in the form of a profile, made up primarily of tables, running some 21 pages in length. There is also a CLI Developmental Planning Guide, apparently written for the individual respondent (however, in this Guide the CLI is described as being composed of 21 scales, yet Table 1 lists 22). The Guide also defines a "consistency check" as showing how often responses were inconsistent, such as checking ALWAYS to both "sensitive" and "insensitive"; yet the manual gives no information on the makeup of this consistency check.

The manual has three goals: (*a*) to describe the background that led to the CLI, (*b*) to serve as an administrative manual, and (*c*) to serve as a technical resource manual. The first two goals are well met. The manual is clearly written, quite detailed, and considers the use of the CLI for self-development, team building, and selection and placement procedures. No extravagant promises are made and potential applications of the CLI to individual cases are well tempered with cautionary comments. The manual is professionally printed and gives an outer appearance of professionalism with just the right touch of erudition. The CLI is a "slick" package, not in a pejorative sense, and shows thoughtful preparation for a specific target audience—business executives who utilize the talents of psychological firms. But the price is steep—$160 is the unit price. This is clearly a measure to be used in an applied setting, and not for research purposes.

Several criticisms of the CLI can be made. First, no published studies are cited. Given that the CLI "has been under development for the better part of a decade" (Preface) and that its author is a most prolific and competent psychologist, the lack of references to peer-reviewed papers is particularly disturbing. Secondly, self-reports are susceptible to faking, social desirability, and other response styles. Any self-respecting manual should address these issues—the CLI does not. A third criticism is that although considerable validity data are presented, there is no evidence to show the relationship of the CLI to any other test measuring dimensions of leadership, nor to any of the standard personality inventories such as the CPI (California Psychological Inventory), that might be relevant to further establish the construct validity of the CLI. Furthermore, no evidence is presented against real life criteria of leadership either in a concurrent or predictive fashion.

In summary, there are many psychological testing programs on the marketplace that have been designed for use in the business environment. It is my impression that most lack the kind of reliability and validity evidence that can be found with the CLI. Thus, the CLI seems to be a real contribution, though more evidence needs to be presented to satisfy academic and professional users.

Review of the Campbell Leadership Index by CHARLES HOUSTON, Director of Planning and Research, Virginia Western Community College, Roanoke, VA:

Dr. David Campbell, co-author of the well-known Strong-Campbell Interest Inventory, has provided the leadership for the development of the Campbell Leadership Index (CLI). The CLI provides a 100-adjective checklist designed to identify leadership characteristics. Comparisons are made between an individual's self-reported leadership characteristics and three to five observers. A quantifiable profile that compares self and observers' perceptions on 22 scales within five orientations is developed in order to help an individual understand specific leadership characteristics. A sample description of CLI Orientations, Scales, Typical Adjectives, and Psychological Interpretation would be as follows: An orientation toward farsighted leadership would be described with adjectives such as insightful or forward-looking and suggests a psychological interpretation such as looks ahead, plans, is a visionary. The implications of these orientations and scales are that effective leaders are rated higher on most, if not all, of these dimensions than are ineffective leaders.

SELF VERSUS OBSERVER DIFFERENCES. Although there are usually some differences between self and observers' ratings, a 10-point difference is suggested as a red flag for discerning discrepancies between self versus observers' ratings. Higher observers' ratings than individual's ratings imply that an individual is too modest, whereas lower observers' ratings imply that observers do not give you as much credit as you give yourself on CLI dimensions. Broad agreements between self and observers' ratings are a "healthy finding" and usually indicate that individuals are seen favorably by most of the people with whom they interact.

Selecting areas needing improvements and capitalizing on areas of strength can improve effectiveness as a leader. Action-planning worksheets are provided because good intentions for improving leadership characteristics are best translated into meaningful deeds when action plans are written down and formulated into goals. In summary, the CLI is proposed as an aid in understanding the characteristics and behaviors which influence potential for leadership. The processes and results of the CLI give a set of self versus observers' views from which individuals can develop action plans for improving leadership potential.

CLI'S STRENGTHS AND WEAKNESSES. The CLI is an outstanding attempt to develop and understand the construct of leadership. The CLI's manual is very comprehensive including overviews, applications, uses, norms, planning guides, validity/reliability considerations, etc. The CLI is also a component of the Campbell Work Orientations (CWO), a collection of surveys focusing on the psychological aspects of the working environment. Both the CLI and the CWO can be used in any setting where well-established, quantifiable psychological measures are useful. Excellent individual and group profiles, which compare self and observers' ratings, are available. The CLI also includes a Development Planning Guide that effectively and efficiently presents the concepts and constructs related to this leadership index. The Development Planning Guide can provide executives and other organizational members with a concise summary of the CLI's objectives, organization, and implications in discerning leadership characteristics.

There are several major limitations in using the CLI. First, the CLI is very complex and certainly requires professionals to explain its uses and interpret its results. Major efforts in workshops, training sessions, educational seminars, and briefing sessions will be needed in order to insure that employees understand the goals and objectives of the CLI inventory. Without these training sessions, it is highly unlikely that desirable organizational outcomes will be achieved. Second, the measures of personal characteristics, the privacy and dignity of the individual respondent, and confidentiality at both the data-collecting and results-reporting stages are critical areas that must be addressed in using the CLI. The potential for negative consequences of observers taking advantage to berate and unfairly criticize an individual can happen even in a healthy organization. Because of these limitations, many small businesses, companies, educational institutions, etc. should consider potential problems in using the CLI with serious caution.

In summary, the CLI is a major development in identifying the underlying factors of leadership. It can certainly assist an organization in identifying leadership characteristics and the complex processes necessary to define this construct; however, the specific uses of the CLI must be considered carefully in terms of "cost-benefits" (not financial cost of the CLI, which is very reasonable) within the organization. Finally, the CLI certainly requires significantly more planning than other standard psychological inventories and may be more appropriate for leadership training or development programs rather than assessing current leadership practices within the organization.

[60]

Campbell Organizational Survey.

Purpose: Designed to measure attitudes of employees regarding the organization.
Population: Working adults.
Publication Dates: 1988–90.
Acronym: COS.
Scores, 14: The Work Itself, Working Conditions, Freedom from Stress, Co-Workers, Supervision, Top Leadership, Pay, Benefits, Job Security, Promotional Opportunities, Feedback/Communications, Organizational Planning, Support for Innovation, Overall Satisfaction Index.
Administration: Group.
Price Data, 1990: $50 per administration kit including manual ('90, 175 pages), booklet, roster sheet, and group/subgroup coding worksheet; $17 per individual for scoring and reporting; $35 per group and subgroup report; $75 per demographic subgroup report.
Time: (15–25) minutes.
Comments: A component of Campbell Development Surveys (CDS); scoring and reporting discounts for 50, 250, 1,000 or 2,500+ examinees.
Author: David Campbell.
Publisher: NCS Assessments.
Cross References: See T4:370 (1 reference).

Review of the Campbell Organizational Survey by RALPH O. MUELLER, Associate Professor of Educational Research, Department of Educational Leadership, Graduate School of Education and Human Development, The George Washington University, Washington, DC:

The Campbell Organizational Survey (COS), an independent component of the Campbell Work Orientations (CWO) battery, is a nationally norm-referenced, self-report attitude survey designed to measure individuals' and groups' feelings regarding their work environment. The COS consists of 44 6-point Likert-type items that form 13 subscales and one overall scale. Intended applications of the instrument include (*a*) the determination of the status quo of an individual's or group's feelings about the work setting; (*b*) the discovery of specific work-related sources of well-being and/or frustration, both for individuals and groups; and (*c*) the observation of trends in individuals' and groups' attitudes about the work setting over a period of time.

THE TEST MANUAL. The manual is an attractive, well-packaged, and well-organized collection of information relevant to both potential users and those individuals already familiar with the instrument who want materials that can readily be used in workshops and seminars. The writing style is nontechnical, offering the nonexpert an easily accessible overview of the purposes and potential areas of application of the instrument. Although of some advantage, this style of presentation unfortunately leads to the omission of some basic technical information usually expected in a test manual. For example, no specific references to the applied and/or theoretical literature on job satisfaction in general—and the COS specifically—are given anywhere in the manual. Perhaps most importantly, socio-demographic and other basic descriptive statistics on the norming and validation samples are missing from the presentation. Such omissions are especially disappointing in light of the public's increasing criticism of standardized tests, particularly with regard to: (*a*) the specific rationale for adding yet another test to the already saturated market; and (*b*) once an instrument is in use, the generalizability of test results across groups of different sexes, races, ages, socioeconomic backgrounds, and geographic locations, among other factors.

The first chapter of the test manual contains a short overview of the instrument, including: (*a*) a list of minimum qualifications anybody administering the COS should meet (e.g., some training in tests and measurement, counseling, and knowledge of the specific environment the instrument will be used); (*b*) expressed permission to reproduce certain tables and figures from the manual to facilitate communication in workshops and seminars; (*c*) a list and discussion of assumptions underlying the use of the COS (topics mentioned are indeed related to job satisfaction and productivity, COS profiles can highlight trade-offs in job satisfaction, individual profiles can aid employees with career planning, and group profiles reflect—and help understand—organizational climate fostered by top leadership); and (*d*) a brief description of each of the 13 subscales and the Overall Satisfaction Index.

Possible applications (individual and group assessments) and specific guidelines and instructions for the administration and scoring (possible only through the publishing company) are given in the second and third chapters of the manual. Chapter 3 concludes with a helpful presentation and interpretation of many sample COS profiles based on actual data taken from both individual and group assessments in a variety of professional settings. Unfortunately, specific information necessary for the interpretation of profile charts is not presented until chapter 4 (e.g., why is a score of 36 on the Job Security scale interpreted as "very low" and indicative of job dissatisfaction?) [p. 22]. Thus, until reading chapter 4, the reader must trust the author's interpretations of data presented in the case studies.

Chapters 5 and 6 contain available data on the validity and reliability of the instrument (reviewed below). Chapter 7 contains an explanation of three procedural checks for the identification of invalid or otherwise peculiar response patterns. The Response Percentage Check, Consistency Check, and Omitted Items Check provide useful information regarding individuals' response patterns although the criteria used for identifying a "peculiar" pattern seem somewhat arbitrary and are presented without justification.

Finally, in chapter 8, the author offered some general observations and resulting implications regarding the use of the survey that were based on "the data presented earlier in this manual, from experience gained in using the COS, and from anecdotes from both professional users and respondents" (manual, p. 111). Given the lack of specific descriptive information on the various samples used throughout the manual and the author's reliance on anecdotal evidence, these observations and implications might help the user in obtaining some informal insights into possible meanings of COS results but should not necessarily be accepted as truths. For example, the justification for not developing industry specific norms (i.e., "Few consistent [mean] differences have appeared, and even those seem to reflect true differences, not normative aberration" [p. 112]) are difficult to evaluate because sample standard deviations, standard errors of the means, and results from statistical tests were omitted from the manual.

SCALE DEVELOPMENT. Aspects regarding the development of the COS are described in chapter 4. Although the chapter contains some helpful information regarding theoretical/technical topics such as an overall rationale for item and scale selection and norming (see below), not enough detail is provided for the reader to gain insight into and understanding of the theoretical/technical background that led to the instrument's development. For example, although the author claimed that the rationale for selection of the 13 topics covered by the COS was based on a "large body of research on topics . . . [and] . . . a variety of research studies" (p. 43), no representative references are given as dictated by the *Standards for Educational and Psychological Testing*, Standards 5.2 and 5.3 (American Educational Research Association, American Psychological Association, & National Council on Measurement in Education, 1985, p. 36).

The 13 subscales of the COS are composites of the 44 individual items. The author justified the particular clustering of items into the subscales by explaining that "first, each item had to have high intercorrelations with the other items, and second, the items in each scale had to meet a commonsense test of similarity" (p. 47). Most of the reported bivariate correlations seem to adequately justify scale composition. The reader should be aware, however, that within the majority of scales (7/13) more than one-third of the item correlations were below .30 and for three-quarters of the scales (10/13) more than one-half of the correlations were below .40.

Some inconsistencies were found after comparing the narrative explanations of scale compositions with the tables of correlation coefficients. For instance, "high" intercorrelations among three items were used to justify the composition of the Pay scale, but inspection of the appropriate table revealed correlation coefficients of .31, .11, and .11, which—if correct—do not seem to support the intended conclusion. To circumvent some of the problems associated with interpreting the application of the above mentioned criteria, a more objective and persuasive alternative to scale justification could be an examination of results from an exploratory factor analysis of the items and a subsequent presentation and interpretation of a confirmatory factor analysis of item scores obtained from a second data set.

NORMING. On first glance, the author is to be applauded for discussing in some detail the difficulties associated with norming an instrument intended for use with individuals and groups from "any setting where well-established, quantifiable psychological measures are useful, such as educational institutions, human resource departments, training and development programs, and individual counseling and therapy" (p. 1). The test author noted that "with an organizational survey intended for broad generic use, the standardization issues are . . . complicated because although the desired conceptual goal is for the 'average score' to represent 'typical employees in typical organizations,' no one really knows who these 'typical employees' are" (p. 50). Given these and other statements by the test author, the current reviewer was perplexed to find *neither* a detailed description of the sampling design, *nor* information on the year(s) of data collection and the sex, race, age, socioeconomic status, and geographic location of participants from the various norming samples. No attempts were made to justify using just one set of norms across any and all of the commonly cited socio-demographic factors (norming tables are not provided in the manual; test profiles furnished by the publishing company seem to report only standard scores, not raw scores).

Descriptions of the 39 samples used in the norming of the COS were limited to (*a*) sample size (ranging from $n = 11$ to $n = 190$) and (*b*) general descriptors such as "Top Executives—Publishing Company" or "Technical Writers (Full-time)." Explanations of the conversion from raw scores to standard scores did not go much beyond a presentation of a *T*-score formula and statements such as "because these [norming] samples collectively were not necessarily representative of the entire working population . . . some arbitrary, but sensible, adjustments were made to assure that the norms represent an average work force" (p. 50). *For a nationally norm-referenced test such as the COS, the omission of detailed socio-demographic data on the norming samples and detailed information on sampling design and other norming procedures constitutes a serious violation of Standards 4.3, 4.4, and 4.5* (AERA, APA, & NCME, 1985, pp. 33-34) *and could seriously impede a valid interpretation of survey results.*

VALIDITY AND RELIABILITY. In chapter 5, evidence of the content and construct validity of the instrument is provided (the author acknowledged that data relevant to the criterion-related validity of the COS are not yet available but, instead, offered hypotheses regarding the predictive validity of the instrument). Data in support of the construct validity were presented in the form of descriptive group and scale comparisons; no results from statistical tests for the purpose of these comparisons were reported. The available data were presented in two ways: (*a*) graphical one-on-one comparisons of various samples on mean results on the 14 COS scales; and (*b*) tables for each of the COS scales containing the means from the norming samples (standard deviations for the individual samples and standard errors of the means were not reported).

Chapter 6 contains data related to the internal consistency and test-retest reliability of the instrument. The conclusion that "the COS scales are internally consistent" (p. 95) was based on scanning the observed correlations among items within each of the 13 subscales; no internal consistency coefficient (such as Cronbach's alpha) was reported. A median correlation of .83 between 6-week test-retest scores on the 13 subscales and the Overall Satisfaction Index based on a sample ($n = 73$) of mainly human resources personnel provides initial evidence of the test-retest reliability of the COS.

Finally, providing descriptive results from two case studies, the author attempted to demonstrate reliability by answering in the affirmative the question "Are the scores similar for repeated samples drawn from the same population?" (p. 95). In the opinion of this reviewer, this question does not address the reliability of an instrument: If two or more *representative* samples are drawn from a given population, average scores on *any* measuring device should *not* differ significantly across the samples, no matter how reliable or unreliable the measure is.

SUMMARY. The Campbell Organizational Survey might be a valid and reliable addition to the existing measures of job satisfaction. Detailed background information was omitted, however, from the manual, which made a technical evaluation of the COS difficult. Perhaps the most serious shortcoming is the lack of a thorough description of the norming/validation samples. Thus, data regarding the validity and reliability of the instrument presented in this version of the manual should be interpreted with some caution. In the opinion of this reviewer, more thorough descriptions and statistical analyses of the existing data, and, if necessary, analysis of new data on well-defined samples and populations, are needed before the potential user should select this instrument with confidence as the measure of choice of individuals' and/or groups' job satisfaction.

REVIEWER'S REFERENCE

American Educational Research Association, American Psychological Association, & National Council on Measurement in Education. (1985). *Standards for educational and psychological testing.* Washington, DC: American Psychological Association, Inc.

Review of the Campbell Organizational Survey by KEVIN R. MURPHY, Professor of Psychology, Colorado State University, Fort Collins, CO:

The Campbell Organizational Survey (COS) is a 44-item computer-scored survey designed to provide measures of job satisfaction and the work attitudes of individuals or groups. This information is thought to be useful in individual counseling, the diagnosis of problems in work teams, organizational development, and for identifying broad sources of satisfaction and dissatisfaction in an organization. An overall satisfaction score and scores on 13 specific, content-oriented scales (e.g., The Work Itself, Pay) are provided.

The topics included in the COS were chosen on the basis of research on job satisfaction, leadership, and organizational behavior. Five of the COS subscales (satisfaction with The Work Itself, Supervision, Co-Workers, Pay, and Promotional Opportunities) are highly similar to those on the widely used Job Descriptive Index (199), whereas others (e.g., satisfaction with Freedom from Stress, Support for Innovation) are not frequently encountered on other satisfaction/work attitude measures. The subscales are all quite short, ranging from a single item (the Benefits subscale) to seven items (the Supervision subscale). Although this contributes to the ease with which the survey can be applied (the survey can be completed in 15–20 minutes), the shortness of the subscales may limit the reliability of some subscales, as is noted below.

The COS manual is extremely user friendly, in the sense that it includes a wealth of information designed to aid users in administering and interpreting the survey. For example, the manual includes several case studies, along with sample profiles, as well as transparency masters (which are helpful in presenting results, especially to large groups). Suggestions for feeding back survey results, and for using these results in individual counseling, organizational diagnosis, etc. are included.

The description of the development of this survey is somewhat informal, in the sense that several technical details are glossed over. For example, the process by which initial subscales were chosen or identified is only superficially described, and little information is provided about how, precisely, scales were developed. Several potentially critical details of item development and scoring are simply omitted. For example, the COS uses a 6-point Likert-type scale (items are rated from *Strongly Agree* to *Strongly Disagree*), and the manual author notes that rather than assigning scores of 1–6 to the possible responses, responses in the top and bottom two response categories (i.e., those that would receive scores of 1 and 2 or 5 and 6 in a linearly scored scale) are adjusted slightly to account for the fact that people vary in their tendency to use the top and bottom two categories. The reader is not told what the precise adjustment is, how it was determined, or what effect it has on the eventual distribution of scores. Similarly, in describing the norming process, the manual author notes the distribution of scores in some normative samples were occasionally modified, but it does not say how such adjustments were made or justified. Finally, the manual contains a number of reasonable-sounding procedural checks, including evaluations of the respondent's distribution of responses and a count of obviously inconsistent responses (e.g., agreeing that you enjoy your work *and* that the work is dull and boring), but little detail is given regarding the derivation or validity of the algorithm that is used to label response profiles as "valid," "marginal," or "doubtful."

The development of norms for the COS was based on an iterative procedure in which new samples were added to the normative data base until substantial convergence on subscale and total scale was reached. The final normative sample includes data on over 2,700 individuals, obtained from 39 separate groups. The overall score and scores on the 13 subscales are reported in terms of *T* scores (Mean = 50, *SD* = 10), based on the mean and *SD* in this normative sample. Detailed information regarding the distribution of scores in this normative group is provided for one of the subscales (i.e., Supervision), and adequate summaries of the normative distributions for the other subscales are given.

The manual contains some evidence for the reliability of COS scores. A small-sample (*N* = 73) test-retest reliability study suggests some level of stability, with test-retest stability coefficients in the .80s for most subscales. Internal consistency reliability estimates are not provided, but the item intercorrelations are shown, making it possible to estimate coefficient alpha. The standardized alpha values are low for many of the shorter subscales (e.g., alpha for the three-item Freedom from Stress subscale is .46), but most subscales exhibit alphas of .70 or higher. Based on the fairly high correlations among the subscales, the alpha value for the total scale is likely to exceed .90.

Detailed evidence that scores on this inventory follow sensible and interpretable patterns is taken as evidence of construct validity by the author. For example, executives show high levels of satisfaction with pay and with the top leadership of their organizations. Workers in organizations that are undergoing restructuring efforts show less satisfaction with job security. Plateaued managers show low levels of satisfaction with promotional opportunities. Although the comparisons of the sort presented in the manual do not provide quantitatively sophisticated assessments of construct validity, their sheer number and consistency are reasonably compelling evidence the scale can be sensibly interpreted. Unfortunately, no evidence of criterion-related validity or of correlations with other attitude measures is presented, making it difficult to evaluate this instrument in comparison to its competitors.

The lack of empirical comparisons with other measures of job satisfaction and related attitudes is disappointing. This survey appears to have many advantages over venerable measures such as the Job Descriptive Index (199) or the Minnesota Importance Questionnaire (T4:1641) including its brevity and the accessibility of the user's manual. However, the complete lack of any comparative research makes it impossible to determine whether the COS measures the same constructs as measured by other surveys, or whether the COS scores are in fact valid measures of the aspects of satisfaction described in the subscale titles.

The COS is a simple measure that has the potential to provide useful feedback to both individuals and groups. There is some evidence that it provides psychometrically acceptable measures, but to date there has been insufficient research establishing the construct validity of subscale or total scale scores. The COS is probably most appropriate in settings where a great deal of psychometric sophistication is not needed (e.g., it might be used to facilitate the process of team building), but where precise measures of well-understood constructs are required, there is at present too little research evidence to justify its use.

[61]

Canadian Cognitive Abilities Test, Form 7.

Purpose: "Designed to assess the development of cognitive abilities related to verbal, quantitative, and nonverbal reasoning and problem solving."
Population: Grades K–2, 3–12.
Publication Dates: 1970–90.
Acronym: CCAT.
Scores, 3: Verbal, Quantitative, Non-Verbal.
Administration: Group.
Price Data, 1994: $7.95 per 10 class record sheets; $21.95 per technical notes ('90, 34 pages).
Comments: Canadian version of Cognitive Abilities Test, Form 4 (T4:537).
Authors: Original edition by Robert L. Thorndike and Elizabeth P. Hagen; Canadian revision by Edgar N. Wright.
Publisher: Nelson Canada [Canada].

a) PRIMARY BATTERIES.
Population: Grades K–1, 2–3.
Levels, 2: Primary 1, 2.
Price Data: $43.95 per 35 test booklets; $5.45 per scoring key; $16.45 per examiner's manual ('89, 85 pages); $27.45 per examination kit.
Time: (90) minutes (untimed).

b) MULTILEVEL EDITION.
Population: Grades 3–12.
Price Data: $9.45 per test booklet (Levels A–H); $3.95 per Level A test booklet; $20.45 per 35 hand/machine scorable answer sheets; $17.45 per examiner's manual ('89, 101 pages); $6.95 per supplemental manual Level A with key; $13.45 per scoring mask; $29 per examination kit.
Time: (90) minutes.

Cross References: For reviews by Giuseppe Costantino and Jack A. Cummings, see 10:42 (3 references); see also T3:361 (5 references) and 8:180 (2 references).

TEST REFERENCES

1. Absi-Simaan, N., Crombie, G., & Freeman, C. (1993). Masculinity and femininity in middle childhood: Developmental and factor analyses. *Sex Roles*, *28*, 187-206.
2. Allon, M., Gutkin, T. B., & Bruning, R. (1994). The relationship between metacognition and intelligence in normal adolescents: Some tentative but surprising findings. *Psychology in the Schools*, *31*, 93-97.
3. Pyryt, M. C., & Mendaglio, S. (1994). The multidimensional self-concept: A comparison of gifted and average-ability adolescents. *Journal for the Education of the Gifted*, *17*, 299-305.

Review of the Canadian Cognitive Abilities Test, Form 7 by JOHN O. ANDERSON, Associate Professor, Faculty of Education, University of Victoria, Victoria, British Columbia, Canada:

The Canadian Cognitive Abilities Test (CCAT) provides measures of three cognitive skills labelled Verbal, Quantitative, and Non-Verbal for students from kindergarten through grade 12. The tests are composed of multiple-choice items that require the respondent to complete tasks of interpretation and use of symbols: words, numbers, and abstract graphics. The primary levels (1 and 2) are contained in separate test booklets in which the students enter their responses, the grades 3 to 12 levels (A to H) are contained in a single multilevel booklet that is to be used with a separate answer sheet. The CCAT is a Canadian adaptation of the Cognitive Abilities Test (T4:537); the adaptation consisted primarily of the development of Canadian norms for the test. The test is supported by two resource documents, the Examiner's Manual and the Technical Manual, and a computerized scoring service.

The Verbal battery consists of two subtests at the primary levels: oral vocabulary and verbal classification. Students are read questions (47 for Level 1 and 56 for Level 2) by the teacher from a script in the Examiner's Manual. They then select and mark the appropriate diagram in their test booklets. In the multilevel booklet, the Verbal battery consists of three subtests: verbal classification, sentence completion, and verbal analogies. Students are required to locate the appropriate level of test they are writing, read the test item, and respond correctly on a separate answer sheet. Each student is to complete 75 items.

The Quantitative battery consists of two subtests at the Primary levels: relational concepts and quantitative concepts. Items (47 for Level 1 and 56 for Level 2) are read by the teacher and students are to select the most appropriate diagram in response. The students completing Levels A to H in the multilevel booklet complete 60 items in three subtests: quantitative concepts, number series, and equation building.

The Non-Verbal battery consists of two subtests at the Primary levels: figure classification and matrices. Level 1 has a total of 46 test items and Level 2 has 53 Non-Verbal items. Students are to complete 65 items in three subtests in the multilevel Non-Verbal battery: figure classification, figure analogies, and figure analysis.

The CCAT yields scores for each of the three batteries: Verbal, Quantitative, and Non-Verbal. The types of scores produced are: Universal Scaled Scores (USS), Standard Age Scores (SAS), percentile scores at different ages and grades, and stanines for different ages and grades. The USS are standard scores derived from an equating study (linking all levels of the CCAT) and reported on a scale that is common for all levels of the CCAT. The USS scale is centered at Level D (approximately grade 6) with a mean of 125 and standard deviation of 20. The SAS is a standard score derived for each age group completing the test; it is analogous to IQ-type scores in that it has a mean of 100 and standard deviation of 16. The percentile scores and stanines are developed both for grade and age. The resource documents describe how these scores were derived and contain tables for converting one score format to another but the manuals fail to discuss the meaning and use of these different kinds of scores. All these types of scores are similar in that they inform the user about an individual's test performance in relation to that of a norm group. So a question that has to be answered is: Why have a USS, SAS, grade and age percentiles, and stanines? A clear discussion of how to use each type of score is clearly in order.

Overall test performance appears to be typical for a test of this nature. The average subtest scores are in the 55% range for grades 3 to 12 (Level A to H) and in the 65–70% range for grades 1 and 2. Kindergarten students average around 55% of the Level 1 tests. Item difficulties range from .40 to .75, and discrimination indices (point biserial correlations) average about .40.

The reliability of the CCAT is described both in terms of internal consistency through KR20 coefficients for the three subtests at all levels, and in terms of stability of scores over time. The internal consistency estimates are in the .81 to .94 range indicating respectable performance. The stability of scores was estimated by considering the average performance within a school district over time and across different grades. The results, although not compelling, do suggest the test does generate consistent results across time at least at the aggregate level. Some indication of stability across time at the individual student level would add further credibility to the quality of the test.

The validity of the CCAT is addressed briefly in the technical manual. The issue of content validity is discussed in terms of what kinds of tasks the test items demand of students: "The tasks require the interpretation and use of symbols" (p 20). Test users are encouraged to examine the test in terms of what it is demanding of students and to compare these demands to the user's conception of cognitive abilities. Although this encouragement is solid advice, it does not, of itself, offer evidence of test validity. The issue of criterion-related validity is addressed by presenting the correlations of CCAT scores with those of the Canadian Tests of Basic Skills (CTBS). Over 300 correlation coefficients are tabulated. They are all moderately positive (.40 to .80) but are not convincing evidence of criterion-related validity. A sound rationale as to why the CTBS is a criterion for CCAT validity should be provided. Construct validity is dealt with by correlating the scores from the Verbal battery of the CCAT with results from another general abilities test, the Henmon-Nelson Ability Test. The positive correlations (.78 to .84 at the different grades) do support concurrent and construct validity for the CCAT.

The resource documents accompanying the CCAT are the examiner's manual and the technical manual. These provide information on the administration of the test, the derivation of the various scores, description of the development of the test, and discussion of interpretation and use of CCAT results. These manuals are well structured and written, offering generally sound comment and caution about test use. The advice to evaluate test items in terms of the test user's conceptualization of cognitive skills is good practice. The caution to regard the skills being measured as developed skills, not innate characteristics, is also sound advice. The discussion and illustration of test interpretation by means of simulated case studies is also informative. The authors also point out the language competence required to successfully respond to many items has to be considered in interpreting results. These and other points are well taken. I hope they will be attended to by test users.

However, there are some areas in the manuals that could be expanded or modified to improve these documents. One such area is the description of the test itself—the nature of cognitive skills the test is designed to measure. The concept of cognitive skills is complex with no single universally accepted definition. The conceptualization used by the authors of the CCAT should be fully articulated for the test user; it is not. A related issue is the provision of reference lists to allow the user to locate research and theoretical literature relevant to CCAT use. Unfortunately, there is a complete absence of references in any of the CCAT documents.

Another area of concern in regard to the manuals relates to the use of composite scores. The authors correctly point out that three distinct cognitive skills are tested with the CCAT: Verbal, Quantitative, and Non-Verbal. They make a cogent argument for interpreting the three separately. Then, in a turnabout, they provide 10 pages of tables for obtaining composite results—one overall cognitive score for each student. The only rationale offered for the use of composite scores is that *regulations* may require them. Shifting from a 3-factor conceptualization of cognitive skills to a single factor (a unidimensional *g* model of intelligence, one might assume) on the basis of administrative regulations certainly undermines any pretensions of construct validity the CCAT has attempted to establish.

In summary, the Canadian Cognitive Abilities Test appears to be a useful instrument to provide information on students' general functioning in the three areas of verbal, quantitative, and pattern-recognition skills. As noted in the examiner's manual (p. 53) the test can serve to identify those students performing well above or below age and grade expectations, and in doing so provide educators with information useful in the development of sound educational intervention.

Review of the Canadian Cognitive Abilities Test, Form 7 by JOHN HATTIE, Professor of Education, The University of North Carolina, Greensboro, NC:

The Canadian Cognitive Abilities Test (CCAT) assesses the development of three major cognitive abilities: verbal, quantitative, and nonverbal reasoning and problem solving. There is a battery of six tests for grades K–3 and another battery of nine tests for grades 3–12.

The test has been developed from Thorndike and Hagen's Cognitive Abilities Tests (10:66) with minor changes in spellings and systems of measurement. The author of the manual for the Canadian version states the items are based on content familiar to children, although some items (e.g., caribou, Aesop fables, lumberman, Halloween, ketchup, and nickel) would not be appropriate to non-Canadians or non-North Americans and thus care should be taken when administering to those with other than a North American cultural background. There are few changes from the earlier edition: Some new items and "new art" are included.

The test developers claim the test assesses many abilities such as comprehension of oral English, following directions, holding material in short-term memory, scanning stimuli to obtain specific or general information, assessing general information and verbal concepts, comparing stimuli, classifying familiar objects, and using quantitative and spatial relationships. There is diagnostic information at the battery level (for Verbal, Quantitative, and Non-Verbal levels) but there are no diagnostics at either the test level or item level, or related to the above abilities. The test is not speeded but would take at least 2 hours of a child's time over two or three sessions. For this time investment, the test user obtains information on three scales (Verbal, Quantitative, and Non-Verbal) and an overall score. This is far from acceptable. The test has little use for anyone but the researcher. Too much is asked of the children for so little return.

Following the trend of many recent tests, the CCAT is a thinly disguised IQ test that merely does not highlight the term "IQ." The use of an IQ is frowned upon, so instead "standard age scores" are derived. These standard age scores are scaled to a mean of 100 with a standard deviation of 16, and are interpretable irrespective of age. These standard age scores can be converted to percentile ranks (which can lead to so many problems of interpretation), and to national stanine scores, both by age and grade.

The instructions are clear, although they require good listening skills. The level of oral comprehension required to understand the instruction at the lower levels may be too high for many examinees.

The Canadian sampling is excellent and the estimates of reliability are high. There are, however, no estimates of stability (despite the fact the manual includes data from which such estimates could have been derived) and the section on validity is weak. The correlations between the scales are presented but there are no factor analyses, no multitrait-multimethod analyses, and little conceptual analysis.

I performed a factor analysis on the data provided in the manual. There was most support for a single general factor for the grade 1, 3, 7, and 11 matrices. When a second factor was requested, this general factor split into verbal and quantitative factors but the correlation between them was very high (.64, .69, .72, .68 for each grade level, respectively). There was little support for a nonverbal factor separate from the quantitative factor.

The relationship between the CCAT and the Canadian Tests of Basic Skills and the Henmon-Nelson Ability Test (Canadian version) is very high. This relationship probably reflects the general ability assessed by all three batteries. It would have been useful to be convinced that the test assesses achievement rather than a general ability.

Altogether, this test does not reflect good measurement practice in the 1990s, requires too much time relative to the return of information, needs a good dose of modern measurement procedures, and given the availability of so many alternatives it probably will be used by few. If users desire to use the battery they could use the Verbal scale and probably would derive as much information compared to using the whole battery.

The test could be improved if the developers provided a computerized version using adaptive testing as this would cut the administration time, diagnostics could be added at the item or subtest level, and more acceptable equating across levels could be achieved.

[62]

The Candidate Profile Record.

Purpose: Constructed to predict successful performance in clerical positions.
Population: Applicants for clerical positions.
Publication Dates: 1982–89.
Scores: Total score only.
Administration: Group.
Price Data: Available from publisher.
Time: (30–45) minutes.
Authors: Richardson, Bellows, Henry & Co., Inc.
Publisher: Richardson, Bellows, Henry & Co., Inc.

Review of The Candidate Profile Record by F. MARION ASCHE, Professor of Education, Virginia Polytechnic Institute and State University, Blacksburg, VA:

The Candidate Profile Record (CPR) is an "autobiographical questionnaire designed for use in the prediction of successful performance in non-exempt clerical positions" (p. 1). It has 105 items and is not timed but typically requires 30–45 minutes for individual or group administration. It is based on some 10 years of continuing validity research with participating organizations (banks) and was developed based on the observation that competencies required for success in clerical and customer contact occupations apparently exceed those measured by typical general aptitude and clerical skills tests.

An extensive Technical Report details the large-samples, multiple-replication study conducted to refine the CPR and provide evidence of criterion-related validity which would meet EEOC guidelines. This study was also used to determine if autobiographical questionnaire scores could predict job performance across secretarial and clerical classifications with significantly lower impact than that produced by the use of traditional general aptitude tests. (Impact defined as irrelevant score variation associated with race or gender.) The research included four consortium groups of banks with several hundred locations and a total of over 37,000 respondents on one or more phases of the study. Three instruments were developed: (*a*) the Job Requirements Questionnaire (JRQ), to determine the duty requirements of each specific job classification as well as to determine the extent to which the same underlying abilities were necessary to successfully perform clerical duties, regardless of differences in job tasks; (*b*) the Non-Supervisory Performance Evaluation Record (PER) based on the JRQ and designed to serve as the criterion instrument; and (*c*) The Candidate Profile Record (CPR). The JRQ was produced in three forms for Teller/Customer Service job classifications, for Processing/Verifying classifications and for Secretarial/Clerical classifications. The same 32 ability statements were included on all three forms but each had unique task statements. The PER includes only the more general ability statements, not specific job tasks.

The CPR was used, along with the RBH Test of Learning Ability, Form STR, and the Minnesota Clerical Test (MCT) as multiple predictors of ratings on the criterion measure (PER) by the employee's immediate supervisor, and when feasible, by a second supervisor having adequate knowledge of the employee's performance. The experimental CPR was administered to applicants and new hires before advising them of the hiring decision and was not scored at that time or used in the hiring decision. Those hired were rated on the PER at the end of their probationary period or their termination, whichever occurred first. A total of 37,524 incumbents in Groups 1 through 4 completed the JRQ in one of its three forms. The PER was subsequently completed by 5,869 immediate superiors and 3,309 second raters.

Item analysis and item weighting procedures were used with Group 1 data to assess item validities. The original experimental CPR was subsequently shortened. Item weights and validities were then tested across the three remaining independent samples. The final CPR and scoring system were thus the result of repeated evaluations of the relationship between item responses and the Rater 1 criterion. The final step was to sum the resulting item weights to compute a total CPR score for all cases in all samples and evaluate its score distributions and validity along with those of the other experimental predictors (the RBH Test of Learning Ability and the Minnesota Clerical Test).

The two a priori design criteria of low impact and job relatedness (criterion-related validity) were addressed by examining mean CPR score differences of subgroups, intercorrelations, and correlations of CPR scores with job performance as rated on the PER in comparison with the other instruments for the total sample and within subgroups. The CPR evidenced substantially lower score differences between gender and racial subgroups than the general aptitude measure (RBH). CPR scores were relatively independent of the MCT and had a moderate relationship to the RBH. CPR score relationships to job performance were quite consistent across subgroups, indicating robust validity across geographic locations, gender, and ethnic groups.

A fairness analysis was conducted defining unfairness as the underprediction of actual job performance. Mean regression residual scores (obtained by subtracting actual performance scores from predicted scores) for each subgroup indicated a statistically significant overprediction for African-Americans, a slight overprediction for males (NS), and a slight underprediction (NS) for females. A monotonically increasing CPR–job performance relationship was clearly demonstrated for the total sample (the higher the score on the CPR, the greater the proportion of employees being rated as average or above in performance). Regression analyses which assessed the criterion-related validity of the CPR in conjunction with the MCT, the RBH, and all three instruments indicated decreased score validities when either the MCT, RBH, or both were used.

Because the research presented was based on clerical occupations in the bank setting only, it is not clear that validity generalization may be extended to other institutional settings. There was only one statement in all materials provided that mentioned that the CPR is designed to supplement, not replace normal interview, reference checks, and other procedures. Also, the Administrators Guide may be misleading in a very important area. It is implied that an *individual's* probability of success can be directly interpreted from his or her score on the CPR. Because no confidence band is provided for such predictions, the user may be led to assume that group results apply without error to the individual. Current materials provide very little information regarding how CPR items were developed. Reliability data were provided only for the PER (mean correlations of performance ratings by Rater 1 and Rater 2 for each of the sample groups). This reviewer did not locate reliability estimates for the CPR or JRQ. The fairly consistent correlations of the CPR with the PER across samples, however, provides an indirect estimate of the reliability of the CPR.

The CPR and its related instruments designed to assess job tasks/abilities and job performance represent a unique contribution to the field of clerical testing. The underlying theory that actual job performance is a reflection of underlying abilities and personal characteristics that generalize across specific job titles and go beyond those generally measured by traditional clerical performance and general ability tests appears to be supported by the evidence provided. The availability of site or job classification task and ability analyses as a part of the overall system should be considered an advantage in terms of judging appropriateness to new settings and continuing assessment of validity generalization. The availability of site-scored answer sheets and reusable CPR booklets helps make costs of administration reasonable.

Review of The Candidate Profile Record by GEORGE C. THORNTON III, Professor of Psychology, Colorado State University, Ft. Collins, CO:

The Candidate Profile Record (CPR) is a 105-item autobiographical inventory designed to measure competencies beyond basic aptitudes to perform clerical and customer service jobs. It was developed primarily for banking positions, but a companion job analysis instrument can be used to determine if the CPR is appropriate in other settings.

The development of the CPR represents the best and the worst aspects of the empirical test construction method using criterion keying. The "best aspects" are represented by a well-run study with four consortia, job analyses in 30 organizations, pooled responses for nearly 6,000 employees, and extensive performance ratings and turnover data. Item analyses identified biographical information that showed repeated differentiation between performance levels. The unit-weighted composite of valid items was found to be related to performance in independent samples. Correlation coefficients and an easy-to-read expectancy table demonstrate criterion validity (*r*s are approximately .30) for ethnic and gender groups. The CPR was found to be more highly related to the criteria than tests of learning ability and clerical speed and accuracy.

The "worst aspects" are represented by the fact that no theory of constructs underlying effective job performance is offered and, although the manual authors say the CPR measures basic competencies such as ability to communicate and to get along with others, there is no description of the attributes measured by the inventory. No construct validity evidence for the CPR is presented.

The background information covers school performance, early work experiences, self-descriptions of confidence and talkativeness, saving and spending patterns, and self-evaluations of skills. Some items may be considered invasions of privacy (e.g., expulsion from school, whether you have a bank account, and how many nights you go out) and other items may be quite transparent (e.g., how self-confident are you, and would you like to work with customers). It would be helpful to know what effects dissimulation, faking, or social desirability response sets have on reports of these background variables and the predictive validity of the test.

The answer sheet can be hand scored or adapted for computer scanning and scoring. A well-written administrator's guide, a detailed technical report, and a succinct executive summary are provided.

No normative data are provided beyond the means and standard deviations for groups from the developmental samples. These data are helpful, but norms for other subgroups (e.g., geographical regions, urban/rural residence) would be informative. Furthermore, no reliability estimates are presented for the CPR.

Adverse impact, differential validity, and discrimination (fairness) were investigated, but the implications of the findings are not fully discussed. Results showed no differential validity among ethnic or gender subgroups, but whites scored approximately one-half standard deviation (*SD*) higher on the CPR than African and Hispanic Americans, and whites received performance ratings approximately one-third *SD* higher and were involuntarily terminated less frequently than blacks. Regression analyses using formulae from the total sample showed that African American performance was actually overpredicted. Thus, the manual concludes that a single expectancy table is appropriate for all applicants.

What is left unstated is the important warning that the lower means on the CPR for minorities may result in adverse impact against African and Hispanic Americans. The 5- or 6-point deficit in raw scores would typically move minorities to a lower-level converted score. Whether this difference would result in adverse impact would be a function of the cutoff score used by any individual organization.

The results also suggest the CPR was not able to achieve the most important objective of causing "substantially lower impact than that produced by the use of traditional general aptitude tests" (Technical Report, p. 1). Whereas African Americans scored .40 *SD* lower than whites on the CPR, they scored 1.11 *SD* lower on the learning ability test, .38 lower on the names test, and .18 lower on the numbers tests. Thus, it would appear the CPR will produce lower adverse impact in comparison with one test, but higher adverse impact in comparison with two other tests.

In summary, the CPR was carefully developed using a large data pool collected from diverse banks. It provides a unique instrument to gather background information found to be predictive of performance and turnover. Although differential validity was not found, and the CPR was statistically fair in predicting success for ethnic and sex subgroups, adverse impact may still exist because, on average, minorities score approximately one-third standard deviation lower than whites. Organizations should examine the content of the biographical information to determine if any questions might be objectionable to their applicants.

[63]

CAP Assessment of Writing.

Purpose: Designed to measure "students' writing abilities through the writing and assessment of actual student essays."

Population: Grades 3–4, 5–6, 7–8, 9–10, 11–12.

Publication Dates: 1988–91.

Scores, 5: 6-point rating scale used for holistic scoring (Total) and for diagnostic scoring (Content, Organization, Usage and Sentence Structure, Mechanics).

Administration: Group.

Levels, 5: Elementary 1, Elementary 2, Secondary 1, Secondary 2, Secondary 3.

Price Data, 1993: $44 per 35 test booklets (specify level) and manual ('88, 7 pages); $5.25 per student for holistic scoring; $7.90 per student for holistic and diagnostic scoring.

Time: 40 minutes.

Comments: Part of Comprehensive Assessment Program; customized (unnormed) test available for Elementary and Adult levels.

Authors: John W. Wick, Louis A. Gatta, and Thomas Valentin.

Publisher: American College Testing Program.

Review of the CAP Assessment of Writing by RUTH JOHNSON, Professor of Linguistics, Southern Illinois University at Carbondale, Carbondale, IL:

The CAP Assessment of Writing (CAP) claims to measure students' writing abilities through the assessment of student essays and to provide "a standardized assessment of student writing on an objective scoring basis" (p. 1), with both norm-referenced and criterion-referenced information. Unfortunately, this information is not provided by the test authors or publishers. Student progress in writing can be measured, according to the CAP test manual, from grades 7 through 12 in a reliable manner.

The CAP utilizes a single student response booklet for each grade level; each booklet offers a choice of prompts, descriptive, narrative, expository, or persuasive in nature. No rhetorical mode is fixed, however. The test administrator decides whether one or more prompts are to be used for each administration of the test. Directions for administering the test are clear. The test authors/publishers provide no information as to the construction of the test—validity, reliability, or norms. Because of the lack of these data, the most that can be said of the test is, in considering face validity, it compares favorably to tests similar to it, such as the Comprehensive Tests of Basic Skills (CTBS; T4:623).

Review of the CAP Assessment of Writing by DALE P. SCANNELL, Professor of Education, Indiana University and Purdue University at Indianapolis, Indianapolis, IN:

During the past decade the assessment of student ability in written expression has increasingly relied on the scoring of examinee compositions. Most publishers of standardized achievement tests have provided optional writing tests as supplements to the battery which includes a multiple-choice test on written composition. This test is one of those supplements.

Several features of this test are interesting and attractive. At each level of the test, a choice of prompts is provided. Schools can decide whether to allow examinees a free choice among the options or whether to specify the option for all examinees. Thus, if for some reason the school believes it is important for the prompt to be narrative or persuasive, the appropriate choice can be selected. This virtue, however, has its drawbacks. Comparability of scores is always an issue, and particularly troublesome with free response test formats. One could wish the authors had provided some information on this question. More on this will be presented below.

Another attractive feature of the test is the scale for the scoring. This test uses a 6-point scale ranging from *excellent* to *seriously deficient* and also provides four categories for essays that cannot be scored. Related to this, the publisher provides, in addition to holistic scoring, diagnostic scoring on four standard components of good writing.

Prospective users of this writing test might be troubled by several features of this instrument. First, it seems that the essays must be scored by the publisher. The brief document provided by the publisher does not indicate how schools can elect to score their own essays. No reference is made to scoring protocols, training of scorers, or other information that might be useful to schools that like the approach represented in this instrument but who cannot afford to have the essays scored external to the school.

The second major weakness is the lack of any information about the quality of the information obtained from essays written to the prompts provided in this test. One might like to know what the distribution of scores was when the test was administered to a representative sample; in the absence of norms, this information would be extremely helpful in the interpretation of results. One might like to know what evidence exists that the 6-point scale produces reliable scores.

The quality of the prompts for this test is acceptable; the directions for administering the tests are satisfactory. The absence of a local scoring option limits the usefulness of the test, and the absence of technical data is troublesome. This reviewer finds nothing about this test that would make it stand out over the similar available tests.

[64]

Career Beliefs Inventory.

Purpose: Designed to assist people to identify career beliefs that may influence their career goals.
Population: Junior high school and over.
Publication Date: 1991.
Acronym: CBI.
Scores, 26: Administrative Index, Employment Status, Career Plans, Acceptance of Uncertainty, Openness, Achievement, College Education, Intrinsic Satisfaction, Peer Equality, Structured Work Environment, Control, Responsibility, Approval of Others, Self-Other Comparisons, Occupation/College Variation, Career Path Flexibility, Post-Training Transition, Job Experimentation, Relocation, Improving Self, Persisting While Uncertain, Taking Risks, Learning Job Skills, Negotiating/Searching, Overcoming Obstacles, Working Hard.
Administration: Group.
Price Data, 1992: $30 per 25 test booklets; $40 per 10 prepaid answer sheets (price includes scoring by publisher); $30 per manual (46 pages); $32 per specimen set.
Time: Administration time not reported.
Author: John D. Krumboltz.
Publisher: Consulting Psychologists Press, Inc.

TEST REFERENCES

1. McAuliffe, G. J. (1991). Assessing and treating barriers to decision making in career classes. *Career Development Quarterly, 40*, 82-92.
2. Niles, S. G., & Sowa, C. J. (1992). Mapping the nomological network of career self-efficacy. *Career Development Quarterly, 41*, 13-21.
3. Fuqua, D. R., & Newman, J. L. (1994). An evaluation of the Career Beliefs Inventory. *Journal of Counseling and Development, 72*, 429-430.
4. Krumboltz, J. D. (1994). Potential value of the Career Beliefs Inventory. *Journal of Counseling and Development, 72*, 432-433.
5. Krumboltz, J. D. (1994). The Career Beliefs Inventory. *Journal of Counseling and Development, 72*, 424-428.
6. Naylor, F. D., & Krumboltz, J. D. (1994). The independence of aptitudes, interests, and career beliefs. *Career Development Quarterly, 43*, 152-160.
7. Walsh, W. B. (1994). The Career Beliefs Inventory: Reactions to Krumboltz. *Journal of Counseling and Development, 72*, 431.
8. Watkins, C. E., Jr. (1994). Thinking about "Tests and Assessment" and the Career Beliefs Inventory. *Journal of Counseling and Development, 72*, 421-423.
9. Walsh, B. D. (1995). The Career Beliefs Inventory: A review and critique. *Measurement and Evaluation in Counseling and Development, 28*, 61-64.

Review of the Career Beliefs Inventory by DAVID L. BOLTON, Assistant Professor for Education, West Chester University, West Chester, PA:

The Career Beliefs Inventory (CBI) attempts to determine what beliefs may prevent individuals from reaching their career goals. It differs from other career guidance tools, which tend to look at the vocational interests of the person being counseled. An assessment of career beliefs is important when conducting career counseling. The test manual makes that point convincingly.

The Inventory covers 25 scales, divided into five categories. These categories are described as covering the beliefs that affect career choice. The 25 scales were developed based on about a thousand beliefs, reported over an 8-year period, that blocked individuals from reaching their career goals. Although the scales seem logical as possible factors related to career beliefs, there is little evidence provided by the author that the scales are distinctly different. In the manual section on validity, the author reports a factor analysis in which four factors are reported and named. The factor analysis seems to contradict the structure of the inventory and one is left wondering which to believe. Just looking at the items that comprise the scales, it appears that some scales would be highly related.

My general impression after reading the manual is the author views the Inventory as the beginning of a discussion rather than a definitive measurement of the person being counseled (and rightfully so). This is reinforced by the fact that many of the scales have very few items. Ten of the scales have only two items and only three scales have more than five items. Consequently, the reliabilities for some of the scales tend to be low. Although, as the author indicates, the test-retest and Cronbach-alpha reliabilities for the scales are satisfactory, any interpretation of the scales would be questionable.

The issue of reliability of the scales is of most concern with regards to assessing the validity of the instrument. In attempting to establish construct validity, the author attempts to correlate Inventory scores with other measures related to vocational selection. In doing so, he is trying to show the CBI is distinct from other instruments. For example, the author correlates each of the CBI's 25 scales with the various scales of the Strong Interest Inventory. After doing so, only 2.97% of the correlations were greater than an absolute value of .26 and were significantly different than zero at the .01 level. The author concludes the measures are assessing two different things. However, the low correlations may be simply due to the low reliabilities of the 25 scales coupled with a measure of unreliability of the scales on the Strong Inventory. In fact, one might expect to find reasonable correlations between the CBI and the Strong. For example, one could expect the correlations between the CBI's Taking Risk or Negotiating/Searching scales and the Strong's Introversion-Extroversion Scale. There are other similar examples in the manual. In general, the author seems to exhibit a shotgun approach to establishing construct validity; not hypothesizing specific interrelationships between variables, but correlating all 25 scales with scales from other instruments, hoping that there are no correlations between them and explaining away the correlations that are significant. Construct validity should be attempted in a more systematic fashion with specific hypotheses.

In assessing concurrent validity, the author correlates the scales with self-ratings of job satisfaction. Most coefficients are not significant. The significant correlations tend to be low, generally in the low to mid-20s. Despite the low correlations, the author tries to draw conclusions from these data. Most of the relationships explain no more than 6% of the variance, thus making interpretations likely to be misleading.

The attempts to establish validity seem like overkill considering the purpose of the instrument. The CBI is a tool to start a discussion. As the author points out, the preliminary interpretation of the scales should be viewed as tentative. As such, the best form of validity might be the testimony of the users. The author indicates the CBI has a successful history of use. Although perhaps true, it is difficult to assess the author's assertion as evidence of validity.

The norms are based on a sample of over 7,500 people in the United States and Australia. Those in the norming group from the United States come from a variety of states. Norms are provided for eight different groups broken down by sex, employment status, and maturity level (adult, college student, school student), with varying numbers for each group. The author does not claim the norming group is representative of any particular population.

The manual is easy to read. The instructions on the use of the instrument are somewhat skimpy. Only one case study is provided and one has the impression that it was selected because it was simple. It is not clear if this is a typical case. Because the CBI is to be a starting point for a discussion, it is important that more instruction be provided to the user of the test. I would not want to use the instrument solely on the basis of this one case study. This section of the manual requires considerable work.

Another concern regards scoring. Scoring must be done by a scoring service. Because the answers provided on the CBI serve as a basis for a discussion, it makes sense to discuss the answers immediately so individuals can explain their responses. A handscoring option would be very useful.

Although the CBI may be helpful for vocational counseling, a counselor with knowledge of the 25 scales could address the same issues without using the CBI. As such, knowledge of the 25 scales may be more important than the use of the instrument itself.

Review of the Career Beliefs Inventory by ROBERT M. GUION, Distinguished University Professor Emeritus, Bowling Green State University, Bowling Green, OH:

The Career Beliefs Inventory (CBI) is more an interview aid than a measurement tool. There are 26 "scales," 10 with as few as two items and none (except an "Administrative Index" designed to identify careless or otherwise "inaccurate" responses) with more than eight. The scales are scored, but the scores are signals to help vocational counselors explore with their clients any assumptions or beliefs that may be interfering with career development. Innumerable specific beliefs might prevent appropriate career decisions, but the scales offer generalities in which the more specific beliefs might fit. Low or moderate scores suggest areas to search during an interview. For example, a low score on "Approval of Others" might stem from the client's efforts to please a parent, a spouse, or some other person—or it might be a generalized search for approval. There are only two items for the Approval scale, one a statement that approval is deemed necessary and the other a reverse statement proclaiming that it is not. In neither case does the inventory itself look to see whose approval is or is not wanted; that, if the score is in the warning range, is left for the interview to ferret out. The CBI may serve a useful purpose, and the user (or reviewer) should not fault the CBI for not serving some other purpose.

The manual does not say which of the 96 items fit individual scales. A statement that the respondent would not move to some regions of the country, even with a "terrific" job offer, is not hard to place in the Relocation group; other items are not as certainly assigned. This may explain why answer sheets are purchased only with prepaid scoring. Sending off answer sheets for scoring elsewhere, however, seems an unnecessary interference with the counseling process. Hand scoring would be tiresome but not difficult. The response to each item uses the traditional 5-point scale from *strongly agree* to *strongly disagree*, direction of scale values depending on whether the item is positively or negatively worded. Hand scoring is feasible, could be used immediately and perhaps even in collaboration with the client, and would be much cheaper. Use of the scoring service is feasible and practical for groups in school guidance programs, but the CBI seems especially useful for counseling people who are out of school—perhaps unemployed (or about to be, as in an outplacement counseling setting) or employed but seeking a change. Waiting for scoring by the publisher seems undesirable in such cases. Further, the CBI does not provide any particular precision in measurement, thus, appears not to warrant an elaborate scoring procedure.

Habit is sometimes a terrible thing. Habit decrees that all tests and inventories be treated as devices for measuring more or less well-defined constructs with reasonable precision. Typically, that means giving the constructs names and definitions, writing items to fit, determining internal consistencies, and finding evidence of validity—preferably of construct validity. The CBI manual follows the habit. The results are not very impressive, but most of them have only limited relevance to the purpose of this particular inventory, anyway. Test-retest reliability estimates are probably relevant—a belief that inhibits effective career planning today should do so later unless something intervenes. Such reliability estimates are reported for three samples. The largest coefficient reported was for the high school sample, with a one-month interval, on the Career Plans scale, and this largest coefficient was a mere .74. Indeed, only three of the 78 coefficients reported reach .70, and nine were less than .40. If the CBI were used to make decisions about individuals, these would be appalling coefficients—but that is not its purpose.

The score on each scale is the average of the response values, multiplied by 10. If all item responses within a scale are 5s, the mean is 5 and the scale score is 50. According to the manual, a score below 40 represents uncertainty about the belief represented by high scores on the scale and a topic for probing in the interview. The appropriate use of the scores is, therefore, more like criterion-referenced than norm-referenced interpretations of test scores, yet true to psychometric habit, tables of norms are provided.

Habitual psychometric thought demands scales should be internally consistent. Coefficient alphas were reported for employed adults (male, female, and combined data), unemployed adults, and four student groups differing in age levels. For such small scales, these would not be expected to be very high—and they were not. A two-item Career Plans scale (whether decisions are firm or still open to change) had alphas ranging from .69 to .84, and alphas for three other scales were fairly consistently in the .70s; beyond these, the items defining the various scales seemed not to be remarkably internally consistent, although the manual author says the reliabilities "are deemed quite satisfactory" (p. 17). I do not deem them so, yet I do not deem the issue very important, either. If the inventory is used as a basis for a counselor's decision about the directions of needed probing, individual items may prove just as useful as the set of items, whether sets are internally consistent or not.

Similarly, several pieces of information are given that purport to be relevant to construct validity. The constructs themselves are not defined conceptually, so the question of construct validity is hard to pin down. Evidence of construct validity comes essentially in two forms: evidence that the measure can, in fact, be interpreted as reflecting the intended construct, and evidence that alternative interpretations are not plausible. In the case of the CBI, the first evidence of validity is that the inventory asks people what they believe: "Asking people to report their beliefs is the most straightforward way of discovering them" (p. 18). I happen to be predisposed to accept this, but it is not inherently persuasive for those who are not. Some concurrent validity evidence reports that some scale scores are correlated at least .20 with measures of satisfaction in some of the eight groups, although the reason for being impressed by the fact is not clear. Evidence explicitly directed to the construct validity question is mainly disconfirmatory; that is, these scales do not systematically correlate significantly with scales other than anxiety on other ability, interest, or personality measures. Some factor analytic data are presented, for reasons not entirely clear.

The point is that no case is made in the manual for evaluating any of the CBI scales as measures of important, continuous variables; to the contrary, the case made is that the scales are to be used as triggers for giving direction to the counseling process. No predictions, no irrevocable decisions, no nomothetic relationships are postulated making position on scale very important. What is important is whether counselors find the use of this inventory helpful in their efforts to help clients achieve some insight into the beliefs or assumptions that might stand in the way of sound career decisions. For this limited and individualistic purpose, the CBI can be useful, although the degree of usefulness may depend more on the skills of the counselor than on the psychometric properties of this instrument.

[65]

Caregiver's School Readiness Inventory.

Purpose: Constructed to predict a preschool child's success in school.
Population: Ages 3-11 to 5-10.
Publication Date: 1989.
Acronym: CSRI.
Scores: Total score only.
Administration: Individual.
Price Data, 1990: $12.50 per 200 rating forms; $6.50 per manual (36 pages); $10.50 per specimen set.
Time: [2–3] minutes.
Comments: Ratings by parents.
Author: Marvin L. Simner.
Publisher: Phylmar Associates.

Review of the Caregiver's School Readiness Inventory by ELAINE CLARK, Associate Professor of Educational Psychology, University of Utah, Salt Lake City, UT:

The Caregiver's School Readiness Inventory (CSRI) is a screening instrument intended to identify prekindergarten children who are at risk for later academic problems, and need further assessment. The author states that the CSRI is "primarily for children not able to be screened using more conventional screening devices" (p. 22), but does not go on to explain what this means. The CSRI consists of three items that were selected on the basis of their ability to discriminate children who experience failure in first or second grade (i.e., are retained, receive remedial instruction, or are placed in special education) from those who do not. Using a Likert-type scale, parents are asked to (*a*) estimate the number of age-appropriate books that are available in the home, (*b*) estimate the number of alphabetic characters the child recognizes, and (*c*) predict how well the child will perform at the end of first grade compared to peers.

The standardization of the CSRI was conducted between 1982 and 1984 in 11 public elementary schools in lower and middle income areas of London, Ontario. The sample, which consists of 321 children between the ages of 49 and 70 months, was divided into three groups, two senior kindergarten groups, ages 59 to 70 months, and one junior kindergarten group, ages 49 to 58 months (a footnote explaining the terms, junior and senior kindergarten, would have been helpful). The procedures for selecting the sample were not described in the manual; however, there was a brief description of the sample. There were slightly more males than females, each child was fluent in English, and all were in age-appropriate grades. For further information about the sample's characteristics, test users are referred to another publication. This information was requested from the author, who graciously sent a description of 581 children rather than the anticipated 321. Apparently, the CSRI sample was drawn from this larger sample of children who served as subjects for the standardization of the Teacher School Readiness Inventory (387), a measure developed by the same author. Although the socioeconomic range appears suitable, it is difficult to extrapolate this information. Without further information, generalizability from this small and relatively undefined sample is questionable.

Reliability was studied by randomly selecting 54 of the children's parents and asking them to respond a second time, 4 to 5 months later, to the CSRI. The reliability coefficients for Item 1 was .89; Item 2, .86; Item 3, .78; and total score, .92. Although there is little question about the adequacy of these coefficients, unfortunately, no other reliability data were reported, not even internal consistency.

Predictive validity was evaluated by comparing the CSRI to final report card marks and performance on standardized tests of reading and math achievement across a 3-year period. Although there was a 40% to 54% attrition rate, the stability of group mean scores from one time to the next suggests minimal impact on the data. On average, the CSRI accounted for only 25% of the variance for final marks, and 40% for achievement. Although it is not unexpected to find lower correlations with final marks given the number of factors that these include (e.g., compliance and social skills), the sizeable amount of variance in the achievement scores that was unaccounted for by the CSRI was unexpected. It was also surprising to find that the CSRI did not predict reading achievement much better than math (percentages of variance accounted for were 25% and 18%, respectively). Given the nature of the items, the CSRI would be expected to do a better job at predicting reading. Perhaps, the items are not predicting what they appear to be. Item 1 that pertains to numbers of books available to the child may be a powerful predictor; however, it may be serving more as an indirect measure of socioeconomic status. Further examination of the CSRI may show that it discriminates best children who are above average intelligence from those who are below, rather than readers from nonreaders. Item 1, therefore, may not be a very powerful predictor, especially if rote learning, or some other factor (e.g., watching Sesame Street) is influencing alphabet knowledge. Why Item 3, parent expectation, predicts later performance may be due to a number of factors, including self-fulfilling prophecy and parent ability to accurately assess their child's learning potential (research, however, suggests parents overestimate this).

As one would expect, the CSRI is easy to administer and requires little time. The manual provides specific instructions for administration, including time of year (mid to late fall of either the junior or senior kindergarten). An interviewer administers and scores the inventory. Scoring consists of adding the scores on the three items. The possible range of scores is 3 to 22, with 14 and below being the cutoff. Scores are interpreted in terms of "at-risk odds" (i.e., odds for a score of 14 is 1 to 1, that is, 1 of 2 children who get this score will be a false positive). The author spent considerable time explaining how to interpret the CSRI score and gave helpful examples. The CSRI's average hit rate for predicting academic problems in the standardization sample was 75%. This is higher than most screening tests whose hit rates hover around 50%. The average false negative rate of 25%, however, seems high, leaving a relatively large number of children with serious academic problems unidentified. Although the CSRI may have appeal because it takes only a few minutes to administer, this time savings could be more than made up for by the excessive amount of follow-up testing on students who do not warrant it. The false positive rate for two of the groups was 26%, and 5% for the third. Unfortunately, test users must rely on the cutoffs because scores cannot be converted to standard scores and percentiles are not available. Given the fact that differences in curriculum and grading standards could affect the meaning of the CSRI cutoff score of 14, test users are encouraged to develop local norms. Even though rather precise instructions are given as to how to conduct a norming study, this may be asking too much of test users. Test users who do not appreciate the potential high cost of such an inexpensive inventory (e.g., conducting follow-up testing on large numbers of "false positive" children), may resort to using the published cutoff score.

In conclusion, the CSRI certainly cannot be faulted for being too lengthy, nor can it be faulted for being irrelevant in terms of its relationship to school performance. The author demonstrated that the three-question CSRI asked some of the right questions to parents to predict later learning problems in the CSRI standardization sample. What is not clear is how good a prediction one would get from the CSRI if it were administered to a more homogeneous group of youngsters, the population prekindergarten screeners are typically used with. The author seems to be asking a lot of test users, especially those looking for a simple device, to conduct a local norming study before any cross-validation. Until further empirical support is provided, test users looking for a prekindergarten screening device that can be given in a relatively short amount of time, 15 or 20 minutes, may wish to consider another, such as the Lollipop Test (Chew, 1987; T4:1477). Of course, it is possible that using any screener, unlike more direct testing procedures, may reach a point of diminishing returns in terms of predicting school failure, even in the first couple of years of schooling when most failures occur.

REVIEWER'S REFERENCE

Chew, A. L., & Morris, J. D. (1987). Investigation of the Lollipop Test as a pre-kindergarten screening instrument. *Educational and Psychological Measurement, 47*, 467-471.

Review of the Caregiver's School Readiness Inventory by KEVIN MENEFEE, Assistant Professor in Special Education and Communication Disorders, University of Nebraska-Lincoln, Lincoln, NE:

The developer of the Caregiver's School Readiness Inventory (CSRI) describes it as "an alternative screening instrument that could be used in situations where it is difficult to employ more traditional screening measures" (manual, p. 4), such as a standardized individual psychometric screening test or teacher observation checklist. The inventory is designed, as the name implies, for the caregivers of preschool or beginning kindergarten children, and is intended, as nearly as I can determine, "to identify children who are at risk for failure before they enter school" (p. 1), apparently to facilitate their placement "in a properly designed preschool compensatory education program" (p. 1).

The inventory was developed in 11 public elementary schools in "lower and middle income areas" (p. 12) of a mid-sized city in Ontario, Canada. Subjects initially included 321 children enrolled in the Ontario system of junior or senior kindergartens. The inventory is directed towards children from 3-11 to 5-10 years of age. The inventory itself consists solely of three questions, asking the caregiver to estimate: (*a*) the number of age-appropriate books available to the child in the home, (*b*) the number of capital letters the child could name upon sight, and (*c*) the child's anticipated success in reading at the end of the first grade. The developer cites his own review of research literature linking these three factors to later school success. They state that these questions were selected from a larger pool, but the other items added no improvement in accuracy as a screening device.

Psychometrically, the CSRI has a number of serious problems that limit its usefulness. The original sample of preschoolers and kindergartners was followed for a 3-year period to compare their initial CSRI score to academic outcome. Nearly half of the original subjects were lost before final data collections, and the author was unable to determine how this might have affected the final results. By the end of the study, the original CSRI scores showed very modest correlations with the outcome variables (classroom grades and standardized test scores). These correlations were mostly in the range of $r = .45$ to $r = .55$, which, although statistically significant, provide a poor basis for prediction of outcome on an individual basis. The author developed a cutoff score to predict school failure, but based upon the obvious limitations of the sample, the "norms" cannot be safely generalized to other populations. To his credit, the author emphasizes this point and includes some guidelines for developing a local cutoff score. The author claims to have identified 75% of the subjects who later experienced school failure using this cutoff score, but examination of his figures reveals that this occurred at the cost of misidentifying an equal or greater number of children who did not fail (the author employed an extremely dubious procedure of omitting children with average grades of "C" from the final analysis, claiming that their academic outcome was "ambiguous," and thereby greatly decreasing the number of these misidentified "false positives"). Most significantly, his claim of an overall "hit rate" of 78% accurate prediction is actually identical to the "base rate" accuracy of prediction with this sample; because about 22% of the original sample experienced school failure (by the author's criteria), predicting 100% school success would have yielded a "hit rate" of 78% without bothering to administer any predictive measures at all.

From the examination of the CSRI manual, it was not clear to me precisely how the inventory developer envisioned this instrument to be employed by schools in their identification of young children with special needs. I could conceive of its use as part of a community-wide screening effort, for instance, as a component of a mass mailing to help locate potentially at-risk children who could then be invited to participate in further screening and evaluation. I cannot imagine this instrument actually being used as a substitute for an individual evaluation to "assess" a child for special placement, and presume that the developer did not intend it and is not promoting it for that purpose; the manual needs to be clearer on this point.

[66]

CERAD (Consortium to Establish a Registry for Alzheimer's Disease) Assessment Battery.

Purpose: "To develop brief, standardized instruments for the assessment of patients with probable Alzheimer's disease."

Population: Patients with mild to moderate dementia.
Publication Date: 1987.
Acronym: CERAD.
Scores: Information gathered in 19 areas: Demographic, Drug Inventory, Informant History (Clinical, Blessed Dementia Rating Scale), Subject History (Assessment of Insight, Short Blessed Test, Depression and Calculation and Language), Examinations (Physical, Neurological), Laboratory Studies, Diagnostic Impression, Neuropsychological Battery (Neuropsychology Battery Status, Verbal Fluency Categories, Boston Naming Test, Mini-Mental State Exam, Word List Memory, Constructional Praxis, Word List Recall, Word List Recognition).
Administration: Individual.
Restricted Distribution: Current use only with permission of CERAD Steering Committee.
Price Data: Price information available from publisher.
Foreign Language Editions: Forms available in French and Spanish.
Time: [50–70] minutes.
Comments: Manual title is *Instruction Manual for Assessment of Patient and Control Subjects Entered into the CERAD Study*.
Author: Consortium to Establish a Registry for Alzheimer's Disease, Albert Heyman (Principal Investigator).
Publisher: CERAD Administrative CORE.

TEST REFERENCES

1. Rothlind, J. C., Bylsma, F. W., Peyser, C., Folstein, S. E., & Brandt, J. (1993). Cognitive and motor correlates of everyday functioning in early Huntington's disease. *The Journal of Nervous and Mental Disease, 181*, 194-199.

Review of the CERAD (Consortium to Establish a Registry for Alzheimer's Disease) Assessment Battery by FRANK M. BERNT, Associate Professor, Department of Education and Health Services, St. Joseph's University, Philadelphia, PA:

The CERAD assessments represent an effort to provide standardized, uniform methods for evaluating patients with Alzheimer's Disease (AD). These instruments comprise four different components: (*a*) a clinical battery to be used by a physician for diagnosing the dementia and for staging its severity; (*b*) neuropsychological tests to identify differences in cognitive functions between patients with AD and normal elderly controls, and also to track deterioration over time in patients with AD; (*c*) a neuropathology protocol designed to provide a similar universal standard for diagnosing AD based on the pathoanatomic changes in the brain at autopsy (Mirra et al., 1991); and (*d*) a neuroimaging component developed to obtain uniform assessments of MR images of the brain (Davis et al., 1992). The first two components are usually combined in a single entry packet and have been described in detail (Morris et al., 1989); the latter two were developed very recently and will not be discussed here.

Use of the CERAD instrument was initially limited to participants in the CERAD project, but it is now being used in many other research projects. Potential users are provided with videotaped demonstrations of CERAD administration and with an instruction manual; sites are approved for use of the CERAD instrument only after taped assessments by trainees are reviewed and judged to be satisfactory by the chairs of the CERAD Clinical and Neuropsychological Task Forces. All participants in the CERAD project are kept abreast of current developments by means of a monthly newsletter. The result is a centralized, coordinated research effort, which is more effective than isolated investigation efforts.

Once examiners have been trained, administration of the CERAD Assessment Battery is apparently very straightforward. Initial validation studies have yielded high interrater reliability coefficients (ranging from .92 to 1.00) across centers. Although authors intend for the CERAD instrument to be administered by experienced physicians and psychometricians, it seems that certain portions of it could be easily administered by trained non-physicians or ancillary personnel.

Discussion of the reliability and validity of the instrument in the manual is detailed and balanced, weighing both the strengths and peculiarities of the instrument. Initial validation studies are based upon large case (AD) and normal control samples drawn from a broad geographic cross section of patients. Both cases and controls were (and continue to be) subject to exclusion criteria in order to minimize confounding factors and the occurrence of non-AD illnesses known to impair cognitive function (e.g., alcoholism, vascular dementia).

Authors acknowledge that initial validation samples were composed almost exclusively of middle-class white adults who were well educated. More recent studies of less educated whites from lower socioeconomic brackets have suggested that certain demographic variables (most notably, education) are associated with performance on cognitive tests and, therefore, require close scrutiny (Ganguli et al., 1991). The authors have also reported the effects of age, gender, and education on mental testing (Welsh et al., 1992a). Further replicative studies using minority subjects are needed.

The clinical evaluation is designed to be conducted by a physician for diagnostic purposes; it is administered independently from the neuropsychological component. The aim of the clinical component is to "furnish experienced clinicians with the minimum information necessary to make a confident diagnosis of probable AD" (manual, p. 7). It accomplishes this effectively by including several well-established brief measures of AD-related functioning: the Short Blessed Test or Blessed Orientation-Memory-Concentration test (BOMC; Katzman et al., 1983) which categorizes patients as without dementia, probable AD, or possible AD; and a modified, Blessed Dementia Rating Scale (BDRS; Blessed, Tomlinson, & Roth,

1968) which assesses changes in the patient's activities of daily living based upon an interview with a close relative of the patient. Each of these scales has been found to be correlated to histopathological markers of AD (Blessed, Tomlinson, & Roth, 1968; Katzman, et al., 1983). Little or no information is available on the effectiveness of these scales in discriminating between AD and non-AD patients confirmed through autopsy. Thus far, only 12 of the 79 patients autopsied had postmortem diagnoses other than AD (Heyman et al., 1992). For the most part, the authors' initial report makes rather general statements about association and discriminatory power without providing sufficient quantitative data to allow the reader to judge.

In addition to the above scales, the clinical battery includes demographic information, inquiry into selected chronic disorders, use of medications, depressive symptomatology, history, and physical and neurological examination relevant to the assessment of AD. Little is said about these sections in either the manual or in related literature. Future discussions of the CERAD would strengthen its case by articulating in more detail precisely what function these additional sections of the clinical battery do or might serve.

The neuropsychological battery consists of seven often used instruments, which assess memory, language, praxis, and general cognitive function. Its intended aim is to identify the various domains of impairment of mental function at entry and to track the course of deteriorating cognitive function in Alzheimer's patients. The Mini-Mental States Exam (MMSE; Folstein, Folstein, & McHugh, 1975), the best known of these, has been found to discriminate between AD and non-AD subjects (Cockrell & Folstein, 1988) and to be highly correlated with the BOMC (Fillenbaum, Heyman, Wilkinson, & Haynes, 1987). There is, then, some overlap between the clinical and neuropsychological batteries; the authors argue that this redundancy is in part due to the design of the CERAD study, which requires that some parts of the CERAD be done independently. In particular, the CERAD clinical evaluation is done by the physician without any knowledge of the data obtained from the neuropsychological component. The argument is sensible if the entire CERAD instrument is not used on every patient. However, if both batteries are administered to a single patient—even if at different times by different examiners—it is difficult to understand why information from the first battery could not provide data for the neuropsychological portion of the CERAD, rather than readministering identical (or nearly identical) items. Although diagnostic and research functions are distinct, the fact remains that a common core of data underlies them both.

Test-retest reliability estimates for the seven neuropsychological subtests after one month were generally satisfactory (.68 or higher) for diagnosed Alzheimer's patients, with the exception of the Word List Recall, where there was a floor effect, and Word List Recognition scales, where there was a ceiling effect.

One of the desirable features of the neuropsychological assessments is the diversity of difficulty levels among and within its subtests. The Boston Naming Test, for example, contains both high and low frequency objects to avoid ceiling or floor effects. The Word List Recall test, on the other hand, which involves delayed recall, demonstrates a rapid floor effect for Alzheimer's patients, thus serving to discriminate very effectively between mild AD patients and controls but not between various levels of AD functioning (Welsh, Butters, Hughes, Mohs, & Heyman, 1991). To a lesser extent, other scales (e.g., praxis, fluency) discriminate among the stages of AD itself (Welsh, Butters, Hughes, Mohs, & Heyman, 1992b). As a result, the seven subscales apparently provide a sensitive measure of differences in cognitive function over time. Again, inclusion in the manual of inferential statistics rather than simply listing means and standard deviations would strengthen the authors' case.

Moderate to high intercorrelations among the seven subtests suggest that the neuropsychological battery contains a number of redundancies. The authors argue that this is necessary in order to retain certain well-established instruments in their original forms. The MMSE, for example, is given in the standard manner even though some areas, such as drawings, are included elsewhere. Any one of the subscales (several of which are highly correlated) effectively discriminates between cases and controls, whereas none contributes additional discriminatory power once a first subtest has been entered in the analysis. Although it is not clear that anything is gained by including so many separate interrelated subtests at entry, recent findings suggest that such inclusion may provide an advantage in efforts to track the disease (Welsh et al., 1992b).

A principal components factor analysis revealed that the seven subtests loaded upon three factors: memory, language, and praxis. The authors may want to consider reviewing items within specific instruments to weed out redundancies which could be responsible for intercorrelations. For example, the MMSE contains items that clearly "belong" in the Constructional Praxis, Boston Naming, and Word Recall scales; whereas both the BOMC (from the Clinical Battery) and the MMSE contain items (in some cases, identical) regarding orientation to time and place. A fine-grained item-by-item analysis might allow for integration of items across subtests; weeding out the redundancy that occurs between specific scales would create a briefer and more elegant instrument.

In summary, the CERAD shows great promise and, at this point in its development, achieves all of its objectives but one. It is not as brief as it could be, but rather is cumbersome and unwieldy in the number of subtests it includes. It is very possible that elimination of redundant items might shorten it without sacrificing either diagnostic power or sensitivity to changes in cognitive performance. Such modifications would require some coordination of the two components, which are currently administered independently. In any case, this sin seems very forgivable and corrigible, in the face of the instrument's many other virtues.

REVIEWER'S REFERENCES

Blessed, G., Tomlinson, B. E., & Roth, M. (1968). The association between quantitative measures of dementia and of senile change in the cerebral grey matter of elderly subjects. *British Journal of Psychiatry, 114*, 797-811.

Folstein, M. P., Folstein, S. E., & McHugh, P. R. (1975). "Mini-mental State": A practical method for grading the cognitive state of patients for the clinician. *Journal of Psychiatry Research, 12*, 189-198.

Katzman, R., Brown, T., Fuld, P., Peck, A., Schechter, R., & Schimmel, H. (1983). Validation of a short orientation-memory-concentration test of cognitive impairment. *American Journal of Psychiatry, 140*, 734-739.

Fillenbaum, G. G., Heyman, A., Wilkinson, W. E., & Haynes, C. S. (1987). Comparison of two screening tests in Alzheimer's disease: The correlation and reliability of the Mini-Mental State Examination and the Modified Blessed Test. *Archives of Neurology, 44*, 924-927.

Cockrell, J. R., & Folstein, M. F. (1988). Mini-Mental State Examination (MMSE). *Psychopharmacology Bulletin, 24*, 689-691.

Morris, J. C., Mohs, R. C., Hughes, J. D., VanBelle, G., Fillenbaum, G. et al. (1989). The Consortium to Establish a Registry for Alzheimer's Disease (CERAD). Part 1: Clinical and neuropsychological assessment of Alzheimer's disease. *Neurology, 39*, 1159-1165.

Ganguli, M., Ratcliff, G., Huff, F. J., Belle, S., Kancel, M. J., Fischer, L., Seaberg, E. C., & Kuller, L. H. (1991). Effects of age, gender, and education on cognitive tests in a rural elderly community sample: Norms from the Monongahela Valley Independent Elders Survey. *Neuroepidemiology, 10*, 42-52.

Mirra, S. S., Heyman, A., McKeel, D., Sumi, S. M., Crain, B. J., Brownlee, L. M. et al. (1991). The Consortium to Establish a Registry for Alzheimer's Disease (CERAD). Part II: Standardization of the neuropathologic assessment of Alzheimer's disease. *Neurology, 41*, 479-486.

Welsh, K., Butters, N., Hughes, J., Mohs, R., & Heyman, A. (1991). Detection of abnormal memory decline in mild cases of Alzheimer's disease using CERAD neuropsychological measures. *Archives of Neurology, 48*, 278-281.

Davis, P. C., Gray, L., Albert, M., Wilkinson, W., Hughes, J., Heyman, A., et al. (1992). The Consortium to Establish a Registry for Alzheimer's Disease (CERAD). Part III: Reliability of a standardized MRI evaluation of Alzheimer's disease. *Neurology, 42*, 1676-1680.

Heyman, A., Fillenbaum, G., Mirra, S., & participating neuropathologists. (1992). Clinical misdiagnosis of Alzheimer's disease: A review of CERAD autopsy findings. *Annals of Neurology, 32*, 270-271.

Welsh, K., Butters, N., Beekly, D., Fillenbaum, G., Mohs, R., & Heyman, A. (1992a). Performances of the normal elderly on the CERAD battery. *Annals of Neurology, 32*, 244.

Welsh, K., Butters, N., Hughes, J., Mohs, R. C., & Heyman, A. (1992b). Detection and staging of dementia in Alzheimer's disease: Use of the neuropsychological measures developed for the Consortium to Establish a Registry for Alzheimer's Disease. *Archives of Neurology, 49*, 448-452.

Review of the CERAD (Consortium to Establish a Registry for Alzheimer's Disease) Assessment Battery by GABRIELLE STUTMAN, Adjunct Assistant Professor of Psychology, Bronx Community College/CUNY, Bronx, NY:

This test battery attempts a brief, uniform, and reliable evaluation of the severity and progress of deterioration of Alzheimer's Disease (AD) patients. Divided into two parts, a Clinical Assessment Battery (30–40 minutes) and a Neuropsychological Assessment Battery (20–30 minutes), it is potentially of use in structuring appropriate patient care, family counseling, epidemiologic studies, therapeutic trials, and multicenter investigations. The sample cases were differentially diagnosed as having AD (eligibility requirements specified an absence of other potentially dementing conditions, including Major Affective Disorders) prior to the validation studies of the instrument. Therefore, it is most appropriate for use by experienced clinicians and neuropsychologists as a measure of severity when a differential diagnosis of AD has already been made based on established criteria. Once the differential diagnosis has been made, the Clinical Assessment section of the battery might be used alone to make a confident diagnosis of probable AD. The battery has not been validated for differential diagnosis of AD versus other dementias. Because established diagnostic criteria for AD are exclusionary, and the category is residual, the construct validity of a unitary entity "AD" is questionable. Researchers are aware of many types of AD, some of which may be hereditary (St. George-Hyslop et al., 1987), some of which may be generated by early life events such as head injury (Roberts, 1988), and some of which may be generated by toxins such as aluminum (Neustatler, 1982) to name only a few possible causal agents. The AD category is, however, pragmatically validated by the relatively unitary constellation and course of physical and psychological symptoms. CERAD's registry may eventually be of help in creating a pool of information from which different kinds of AD may be discriminated.

Within the pragmatically derived category of AD, this battery does fully sample the universe of relevant behavior, and because the battery consists primarily of tests or portions of tests already in use, much of the content has already been validated and the instruments are familiar to the experienced practitioner. In addition, it provides good concurrent discrimination between levels of severity along several different dimensions. Global dementia severity is staged in accord with the Clinical Dementia Rating (CDR) scale (Berg, 1988), which ranges from CDR 0 (none) to 3 (severe dementia). But, because cases with very mild or severe cognitive impairment were excluded from study, the extremes of the scale await further validation. A 1-year follow-up indicates that the battery is sensitive to a fairly broad range of progression of the illness in midrange cases. However, sample cases have not been studied for a sufficient period of time to assess the extent to which this instrument may be able to predict the course of AD, especially in mild or severe cases. Measures of predictive ability, therefore, also await further research. Because the sample group was drawn from a well-educated, middle class, community dwelling, and white population, differential assessment and prediction—the effects of selection bias—are also unknown.

Rigorous standardization procedures for, and simplicity of, administration of the battery has insured a highly reliable instrument. Interrater reliability was no lower than .92. Test-retest (1 month) reliability is also reported to be statistically significant.

Significant correlations between the neuropsychological tests suggest that some of those tests may be superfluous. A factor analysis showed that three factors (memory, language, and praxis) account for 72% of the total variation. The results of a linear discriminant analysis suggest that once a single neuropsychological test is included in the discriminant severity function, the remaining tests provide little discriminatory power. In fact, the Short Blessed Test (a brief Clinical Assessment measure, easily administered) may be used to predict performance on the neuropsychological measures. This may be desirable because brevity is often an important factor in gaining reliable data from this population.

In summary, the CERAD Clinical Assessment Battery fills a need for a standardized, easily administered, brief, and reliable instrument for evaluating patients with AD. The Neuropsychological Assessment Battery, however, may prove needlessly redundant for the clinician who is not involved in research that specifically targets this dimension. Further investigation is needed to extend the validated range of severity, to explore the effects of selection bias, and to measure predictive validity more fully. However, CERAD's formation of a registry based upon a unitary assessment tool is of great value, and the potential usefulness of contributing one's data to the bank cannot be overestimated. Even the neuropsychological information, which appears to be redundant at this time, may later provide a key to important discriminations between different AD types. The use of this battery as a research tool is, therefore, highly recommended. The Clinical Assessment Battery by itself is also a reliable, brief, and easily administered instrument for assessment of severity.

REVIEWER'S REFERENCES

Neustatler, P. (1982). Aluminum tie to Alzheimer's? Intake of metal now an issue. *Medical Tribune, 23*(9), pp. 1, 12.

St. George-Hyslop, P. H., Tanzi, R. E., Polinsky, R. J., et al. (1987). The genetic defect causing familial Alzheimer's disease maps on chromosome 21. *Science, 235*, 885-890.

Berg, L. (1988). Clinical Dementia Rating (CDR). *Psychopharmacology Bulletin, 24*, 637-639.

Roberts, G. W. (1988, December 24). Immunocytochemistry of neurofibrillary tangles in dementia pugilistica and Alzheimer's disease: Evidence for common genesis. *The Lancet*, 1456-1458.

[67]

Charteris Reading Test.

Purpose: Measures reading achievement.
Population: Ages 10–13.
Publication Date: 1985.
Scores: Total score only.
Administration: Group.
Price Data, 1994: £9.99 per 20 test booklets; £5.50 per manual (15 pages); £5.99 per specimen set.
Time: (60) minutes.
Author: Moray House Institute of Education, Edinburgh.
Publisher: Hodder & Stoughton Educational [England].

Review of the Charteris Reading Test by CLEBORNE D. MADDUX, Professor and Chairman of Curriculum and Instruction, University of Nevada, Reno, Reno, NV:

The Charteris Reading Test is a group-administered, norm-referenced reading test intended for use in England, Wales, and Scotland. Test materials include a brief, clearly written test manual, and a 16-page consumable workbook that serves as combination student test booklet and record form.

The test consists of six reading passages, described as reflective of the reading commonly done in British schools by children, ages 10 to 13, who are in transition from primary to secondary school. Two of the passages are narrative/fiction, two are passages from environmental studies, and two are opinion pieces.

The test does not incorporate basal or ceiling procedures, and every examinee is instructed to read all the passages and to attempt to answer all 100 reading comprehension questions. No standardized instructions to students are included, but examiners are instructed they may elect to give practice in entering responses, that they should tell the students to fill out the demographic data on the front cover, and that students are to be given up to 60 minutes to complete the test. In addition, test administrators are urged to tell examinees when 10 and 40 minutes have passed, to do as much of the test as possible, to move quickly on to the next item rather than spending excessive time on difficult items, and to check their work if they finish before the 60 minutes elapses.

The 100 questions are distributed as follows: 12 after the first passage, 15 after the second, 21 after the third, 16 after the fourth, 17 after the fifth, and 19 after the sixth. The questions are a mixture of true/false, multiple choice, sequencing items, and, for the last three passages, items in which the examinee writes a word from the passage that means the same as a stimulus word or phrase. The test contains a wide variety of items and concepts that are culture-specific to the three target U.K. countries of England, Scotland, and Wales.

To score the test, the examiner first enters a table to convert the child's chronological age in years and months to one of twelve 3-month age bands. The total number of correct answers on the test is then determined, and a third table is entered with this raw score and the appropriate age band. The spot where the appropriate age band intersects the raw score reveals the child's reading quotient. These quotients are normalized standard scores with a mean of 100 and a standard deviation of 15.

NORMATIVE DATA. The test was standardized on a sample of 5,044 children from state schools, 2,511 from Scotland and 2,533 from England and Wales. In both cases, stratified samples were drawn using geographic area as the stratifying variable.

No information was provided on how children were selected for the sample, except to say the only criterion for inclusion was date of birth and sex. No information is given concerning who administered and scored the tests. Similarly, no data are provided on SES or ethnicity of those in the standardization sample.

Disabled and gifted children may have been excluded from the sample because neither special schools that serve children with reading problems nor those serving children with very high reading ability were included. This is a particular problem because the manual authors advise that children who receive very low quotients may need special consideration, and that the test is a good screening device to find those who may need to be referred for psychological services. Similarly, the authors assert those with very high scores may also require special attention. Thus, the publishers appear to be recommending the test be used with groups possibly underrepresented or excluded from the standardization sample.

RELIABILITY. The only reliability information is a statement the Kuder-Richardson formula was used to calculate KR20 coefficients for the overall test and for boys and girls separately in both Scotland and in England and Wales. The manual asserts that all coefficients are reported as.94.

VALIDITY. Very little information is given concerning validity, and what is available must be gleaned from various sections of the manual. There is no discussion of content validity, except the assertion the six passages reflect the type of reading done in school by children between the ages of 10 and 13. There is no evidence to substantiate this assertion, and no information given as to how the passages were selected or written. No information is provided concerning concurrent or predictive validity.

SUMMARY. The test is easy to administer and score, and the manual is clear and easy to read and understand. Standardization was completed with a large sample, but description of standardization procedures is inadequate. No information is given concerning how subjects were selected. Internal reliability appears adequate, but validity is completely unknown and is not addressed in the manual. The culture-specific nature of many items in the test limits its usefulness to Scotland and England or Wales. The test does employ basal and ceiling levels, creating a potential of boredom for advanced readers and frustration for poorer ones. No standardized administration script is provided.

Until these deficiencies are rectified, particularly the lack of validity data, the test must be regarded as experimental and of little value.

Review of the Charteris Reading Test by PATRICIA H. WHEELER, President, EREAPA Associates, Livermore, CA:

The Manual of Instructions describes the Charteris Reading Test as a test of reading achievement that provides "feedback to the teacher on the attainment in reading of children not only in day to day work but also over the whole primary to secondary transfer period" (outside back cover). Designed for children age 10 to 13 years, the test consists of six passages: two narrative-fiction, two environmental studies, and two journalistic sections dealing with opinions. Between 12 and 21 questions follow each passage for a total of 100 questions. The test yields a single total score. Children are allowed up to 60 minutes to complete the 100 items.

Although the test is group administered, the manual contains no specific directions for the test administrator to read to the students. The general guidelines that are provided can lead to extreme variations in the directions and amount of encouragement provided to students; thus, the test cannot be considered to have standardized test administrations. The manual should include specific directions for the test administrator to read aloud as well as suggested strategies for preparing students who are inexperienced with taking tests. The statement "the teacher should give the children practice in entering responses before the test is attempted" is included in the manual (p. 4), but no practice tests or suggested activities are provided.

Several obvious and correctable problems in layout and scoring undermine the test's usefulness. The test booklet has the passages on the left-hand pages with questions on the facing page. This layout could be disadvantageous to left-handed students. Students enter their responses in the test booklets, rendering them nonreusable booklets. Response methods include circling the answer, ranking five items, filling in blanks, and underlining. However, the manual provides no directions for scoring the tests. A gray bar down the side of each page with responses contains a number and line corresponding to each item, usually lined up with the position of the item on the page. A page total line is at the end of each page except for page 11. Page totals do not correspond to totals for each passage. It is not clear if the scorer should enter the response or a number (1 if right, 0 if wrong) or a check mark for correct responses. The only available scoring information is a list of correct answers.

The scoring process is excessively time-consuming and costly compared to other approaches, nonstandardized, lacking in quality control procedures, and fraught with opportunities for errors. Given the age of the students, they should be able to enter their answers for each question on the right edge of each page or on a separate answer document. The scorers could then use a scoring key on heavy-stock paper with correct answers lined up next to the responses on the page or an overlay stencil. Scorers could then check each correct response and count the number of check marks. To reduce the possibility of errors in adding up page totals, the front cover of the test booklet should have a set of boxes (one for each page), arranged vertically to reduce the likelihood of errors in addition, as well as spaces that a second scorer could use for double-checking the scoring. This would encourage some quality control efforts. The scoring process is one area of weakness that can be strengthened easily to ensure more efficient and accurate scoring.

The raw score converts to a reading quotient scale, with a mean of 100 and a standard deviation of 15. The similarity to the intelligence quotient (IQ) scale could easily lead to misinterpretation of results. The age bands are given in 3-month intervals and shown as 10:00 to 10:02, 10:03 to 10:05, etc. Such bands can easily lead to confusion as to whether they represent decimals (dividing the year into tenths) or months (dividing the year into twelfths). Although students enter their date of birth on the front cover, no conversion table is provided to allow easy determination of the age band, or the age expressed in numbers of years and months. The upper right corner of the front cover has spaces for the child's raw score and quotient. Because the age is critical in going from raw score to quotient, a space for age band should also be included, making it easier to verify conversion of date of birth to age band, and of raw score and age band to quotient.

Although the manual contains norms for some 5,000 children in England/Wales and Scotland, information on when the norming administrations took place, or who gave the tests, and what preparation they and the students had is not provided. Normative data based on the standardization sample include quotients for each test score and age band. Because the quotients are scaled scores, one can estimate percentile ranks, but none are given. Median scores for boys, for girls, and for all children are shown by the 12 age bands for each of the six passages for England/Wales and for Scotland. The scores go to two decimal places, implying more precision of the data than warranted, given that samples ranged from 72 to 139 children. However, no table contains median total raw scores for these groups. If the medians for each passage are totaled, they provide a median total raw score for each group. When compared to a quotient of 100 for the same group, these may differ by up to 3 or more points. Such difference may be due to rounding or to smoothing procedures.

No information on test validity is provided. The test is described as "six passages . . . which are designed to represent the kind of material currently read at the top of the primary school and in the early years of secondary schooling" (back cover), but there is no evidence to support this statement. No correlations between performance on this test and other indicators of reading performance are reported. Scores do tend to increase with age, from a median of 33 for age band 1 to 51 for age band 12 for England/Wales, and from a median of 36 for age band 1 to 57 for age band 12 for Scotland (based on the raw score corresponding to a quotient of 100). Such increases may be due however, to factors other than reading achievement.

Reliability data in the manual are scant. Based on Kuder-Richardson Formula 20 for boys and girls separately and combined and for England/Wales and for Scotland, "(i)n all cases the reliability coefficients were found to be 0.94" (p. 9). This is a reasonable value for a test of this type and with test takers of this age group. The manual lacks any data about quality control procedures and accuracy of the scoring process, difficulty level of the items, or speededness of the test. Based on 62 multiple-choice items for which we can determine a chance-level score, a child randomly guessing and responding to all 62 of these items would be expected to earn a raw score of 19.5. Assuming some do slightly better than random guessing and respond correctly to some of the open-ended or ranking items, their raw scores might approach the median raw scores of the youngest age groups (33 and 36). The test appears to be quite difficult for the younger children. If the test is designed to identify, as stated on the back cover of the manual, "individual children or groups of children who are seriously below the norm of the age group, and who have special needs which require to be met if the children are to benefit from later teaching," then this test may be too difficult to differentiate such children adequately, especially among the younger ones. A test this difficult can be quite frustrating to the child. The difficulty level of the test items and reading passages, and the adequacy of the one-hour time limit for children ages 10–13 years should be discussed in the manual.

The Charteris Reading Test does include a variety of types of reading passages and item formats. It includes items that measure literal comprehension and vocabulary as well as ones measuring higher-order skills, such as inferring what happened after the story. However, in some cases, the items require knowledge beyond what is presented in the passage and could be answered correctly without even reading the passage. Given the lack of validity information, standardized administration procedures, scoring and quality control steps, and technical data, this test should be used with caution and should not play a substantive role in any decision about promoting a child to the next grade level or redesigning the reading instructional services provided to a child.

[68]

Checklist for Child Abuse Evaluation.

Purpose: "Provides a standard format for evaluating abuse in children and adolescents."

Population: Children and adolescents.
Publication Dates: 1988–90.
Acronym: CCAE.
Scores: 24 sections: Identification and Case Description, The Child's Status, Accuracy of Allegations by the Reporter, Interview with the Child (Physical/Behavioral Observations, Disclosure, Emotional Abuse, Sexual Abuse, Physical Abuse, Neglect), Events Witnessed or Reported by Others (Neglect, Emotional Abuse, Sexual Abuse, Physical Abuse), The Child's Psychological Status, History and Observed/Reported Characteristics of the Accused, Credibility of the Child—Observed/Reported, Competence of the Child—Observed/Reported, Conclusions (Consistency of Other Information, Allegation Motives, Substantiation of Allegations, Competence of the Child as a Witness, Level of Stress Experienced by the Child, Protection of the Child), Treatment Recommendations.
Administration: Individual.
Price Data, 1994: $43 per complete kit including manual ('90, 19 pages), and 10 checklists; $11 per manual; $36 per 10 checklists; $75 per 25 checklists.
Time: Untimed.
Author: Joseph Petty.
Publisher: Psychological Assessment Resources, Inc.

Review of the Checklist for Child Abuse Evaluation by DENISE M. DeZOLT, Coordinator of Field Experiences and Adjunct Assistant Professor, University of Rhode Island, Kingston, RI:

The Checklist for Child Abuse Evaluation (CCAE) is a structured survey designed to facilitate evaluation of alleged child and adolescent emotional, sexual, and physical abuse and/or neglect. Its intended uses include: (*a*) providing a standard, comprehensive approach to evaluation of child abuse/neglect for both practice and research; (*b*) coordinating data from multiple sources (e.g., law enforcement, medical, therapist) and informants (e.g., child, reporter) involved in the evaluation; and (*c*) guiding evaluation training and report writing.

The CCAE relies on self-report data, often retrospective, provided by the child or by reporters and witnesses of alleged abuse/neglect. It consists of 264 items across 24 sections that are scored by checking the appropriate response option(s). Selection of sections to be used is contingent upon the reason for referral. It is recommended that sections on emotional abuse and identification and case description are completed in all cases. Sections include items that range from basic demographic information to evaluator ratings of the presence of psycho-social adjustment difficulties. Other sections examine the nature, extent, duration, and circumstances of abuse, and items in these sections are representative of the continuum of abuse and neglect. Information about the credibility and competence of the child or adolescent as a reporter and as a potential participant in the judicial process is included. The evaluator is provided with sections for drawing conclusions about allegations, current level of child stress, the protective needs of the child, and recommendations for treatment. Many of the 264 items require the subjective opinion of the evaluator, particularly in domains where standards or cultural norms may vary. For example, a child's dress may be described as too large or of an earlier generation, the assumption being that these may be indicators of problems. When viewed in the context of the child's social milieu, however, this same attire may be consistent with current fashion trends. Consider also the response item "Child was not encouraged to practice social etiquette" in the section examining neglect of social development. It is unclear from the item what constitutes social etiquette, and whose standards are to be used.

The manual author provides an overview of the CCAE and general guidelines for its use. The issue of posing leading questions is discussed briefly, and includes a caveat that such questions be avoided. The evaluator is advised to use the vocabulary of the child rather than the technical wording in the checklist. Because no specific details are provided regarding appropriate techniques for obtaining the responses, evaluators should be professionals with expertise in the areas of abuse and neglect. Evaluators with limited expertise inadvertently may contaminate important information in an effort to cover the numerous CCAE items. Although one purpose of this instrument is to serve as a training device, the manual does not contain specific information on how to accomplish training using the instrument.

The author clearly states this checklist is not a psychological test. Thus, no scales or scores are provided, nor are any technical data reported in the manual. Despite the lack of psychometric support, the checklist contains a conclusion section wherein the evaluator is able to draw conclusions with varying degrees of certainty (+95, +75, +50%) about substantiation of alleged abuse. With no empirical base to support these percentages, it is unclear exactly what these degrees of certainty represent and how they were derived. Preliminary support for item selection is provided from the clinical and abuse literature.

In summary, the CCAE may be a useful organizational tool when used primarily by professionals with expertise in diagnosis, evaluation, and treatment of child abuse. For example, it might best be used by members of a multidisciplinary child abuse and neglect team (including psychological, medical, legal, law enforcement, and child protection service providers) to reduce redundancy in data collection and to insure that essential data are not missing. Thus, it would serve as a central record of information derived from multiple sources and measures rather than a measure in itself. Given the lack of technical data regarding reliability and validity of the CCAE, extreme caution is imperative when drawing conclusions from data obtained and when making recommendations.

Review of the Checklist for Child Abuse Evaluation by JANICE G. WILLIAMS, Associate Professor of Psychology, Clemson University, Clemson, SC:

The Checklist for Child Abuse Evaluation (CCAE) provides a comprehensive format for documenting the results of a child abuse assessment. The assessment of physical, sexual, and emotional abuse is a topic of concern to many professionals in legal, educational, and clinical settings. The 264-item CCAE offers a framework for a detailed summary of the findings of an evaluation, from basic identifying information to treatment recommendations. Information about the child, the alleged abuser, and the abuse reporter are included. Appropriate use of the CCAE would entail conducting an evaluation and documenting those results on the checklist.

The manual author states the CCAE is not a test. It provides none of the usual information on test development, reliability, validity, or norms that might be expected. No strategy is given for acquiring the information listed on the CCAE. The user is cautioned about the use of leading questions and cautioned against letting the checklist guide the interview with the child. In the absence of specific guidelines for conducting the interview, there is high potential for misuse of the CCAE. As the results of a child abuse evaluation are likely to have legal consequences, proper collection of information is particularly important.

No empirical or theoretical rationale is given for item selection. Had the author used some model for creating the checklist, such as O'Donohue and Elliott's (1991), potential users would be better able to judge how well the CCAE would fit with their assessment strategies. Test development information would also help to address content validity, which would be valuable data about a checklist instrument. Inspection of the measure suggests that it is very thorough in addressing areas that might be covered in an evaluation, but documentation of content validity would strengthen the CCAE considerably.

Clearly, reliability is a critical issue in the use of an instrument such as the CCAE. Interscorer reliability would be particularly important for evaluating the merits of the CCAE. Although, as the manual author states, there are no scores on the checklist, each endorsement represents a judgment that may be made differently by different evaluators. Information about whether the CCAE can be used reliably by different examiners is necessary to evaluate its utility, but has not been addressed by the author.

In its current form, it would be inappropriate to estimate the validity of the CCAE for identifying child abuse. Because there is no standard way of obtaining the information recorded on the document, the conclusions sections of the CCAE serve as a means of conveying a decision, rather than a method for reaching a decision. The manual author cautions that the evaluation should be multimethod and includes a list for endorsing the methods that were used. The publisher (Psychological Assessment Resources, 1993) suggests that using the CCAE "will also enhance the possibility of providing legally sound conclusions" (catalogue, p. 72). Without examining the validity of the instrument, the basis for this statement is unclear.

STRENGTHS. The strength of the CCAE is its comprehensiveness. It provides a format for examining the extensiveness and intensiveness of an evaluation. The publisher states in the catalogue that the checklist can be used for preparation of reports and as a standard file document. It appears well suited to these purposes. It may also be useful in enhancing communication among the many professionals involved in a child abuse evaluation. The manual author asserts very clearly the CCAE is appropriate for use only by professionals with training in assessment of child abuse.

WEAKNESSES. The weakness of the CCAE is its author's lack of attention to technical standards. Although claims are made that the CCAE is not a test, it is packaged and presented in the PAR catalogue as though it is a test. Certainly there are psychometric standards applicable to the instrument. Its lack of reliability and validity information will likely reduce it acceptability in legal settings. There is a great potential for misuse of the CCAE, particularly as it appears to provide an outline for a thorough child abuse evaluation.

SUMMARY. The CCAE is a comprehensive checklist for documenting the results of a child abuse evaluation. It provides a format for communicating findings regarding physical, emotional, and sexual abuse, drawing conclusions about the likelihood that abuse occurred, and making recommendations. The lack of psychometric data on the CCAE makes its utility unclear. Individuals with experience in assessing child abuse may find the CCAE useful for summarizing findings and communicating with other professionals. It does not provide a method for assessing child abuse or for deciding whether abuse has occurred.

REVIEWER'S REFERENCES

O'Donohue, W. T., & Elliott, A. N. (1991). A model for the clinical assessment of the sexually abused child. *Behavioral Assessment*, *13*, 325-339.

Psychological Assessment Resources. (1993). *Summer 1993 update: Catalogue of professional testing resources.* Odessa, FL: Author.

[69]

Checklist of Adaptive Living Skills.

Purpose: "A criterion-referenced measure of adaptive living skills and a tool for program planning."
Population: Infants to adults.
Publication Date: 1991.
Acronym: CALS.

Scores: 4 areas: Personal Living Skills, Home Living Skills, Community Living Skills, Employment Skills; and 24 subscales: Socialization, Eating, Grooming, Toileting, Dressing, Health Care, Sexuality, Clothing Care, Meal Planning and Preparation, Home Cleaning and Organization, Home Maintenance, Home Safety, Home Leisure, Social Interaction, Mobility and Travel, Time Management, Money Management and Shopping, Cómmunity Safety, Community Leisure, Community Participation, Job Search, Job Performance and Attitudes, Employee Relations, Job Safety.
Administration: Individual.
Price Data, 1991: $65 per examiner's manual (63 pages) and 25 checklists; $45 per 25 checklists.
Time: [60] minutes
Comments: "Designed to be completed by a respondent who has had the opportunity to observe the learner in natural environments for a period of three or more months"; conceptually and statistically linked to two normative measures of adaptive behavior: Scales of Independent Behavior (SIB; 10:321) and Inventory for Client and Agency Planning (ICAP; 10:152); companion publication is the Adaptive Living Skills Curriculum.
Authors: Lanny E. Morreau and Robert H. Bruininks.
Publisher: The Riverside Publishing Company.

Review of the Checklist of Adaptive Living Skills by PATRICIA A. BACHELOR, Professor of Psychology, California State University, Long Beach, CA:

The Checklist of Adaptive Living Skills (CALS), an individually administered measure of adaptive living skills, comprises approximately 800 specific behaviors related to personal independence, self-care, and adaptive functioning in work, leisure, community, and residential environments. These 800 behaviors are categorized into four broad domains of living skills (Personal, Home, Community, and Employment), which are further divided into 24 specific skills modules. The CALS is appropriate for use with individuals, with and without disabilities, from various socioeconomic status levels, and of ages ranging from infancy to mature adulthood. It can be used to monitor program progress, develop training objectives, and/or determine mastery of skills in a variety of educational, residential, rehabilitation, and other human service settings. The CALS has been psychometrically tied to the Scales of Independent Behavior (SIB; T4:2335) and the Inventory for Client and Agency Planning (ICAP; T4:1260) as well as the Adaptive Living Skills Curriculum (ALSC; Bruininks, Morreau, Gilman, & Anderson, 1991). Consequently, the CALS can be used in conjunction with these instruments to provide an assessment-instruction-evaluation system tailored to individual needs or it can be used independently to assess independent living skills in a criterion-related manner. The technical manner contains concise explanations and graphic (flowchart) presentations of these applications as well as the procedures for converting scores on the companion scales into CALS item screening ranges.

Instructions for the administration of the checklist and planning and evaluation worksheets are clearly described in the CALS test booklet. Respondents assessing an examinee on any or all of the skill modules should have had the opportunity to observe the examinee in a natural environment for at least 3 months. Consultations with others who know the examinee well are permitted, if needed. Instructions for assessing a skill as *independent* are that the examinee "must perform the task *well* (with good quality), *most of the time* (75% or more), *when needed*, and *without being asked or reminded to do it*" (manual, p. 18).

TEST DEVELOPMENT. Items were generated from a review of the research on adaptive behavior. The preliminary conceptualization was revised based on criticisms of several researchers and practitioners in the field. Items within skill modules were arranged in order of progressive difficulty and then reviewed by an independent panel of experts and special education practitioners. Based on their feedback, items were reordered and revised as appropriate. The initial field-tested version of the CALS consisted of 1,271 items. The process by which approximately 500 items were subsequently eliminated was not described in the manual.

STANDARDIZATION SAMPLE. The standardization sample comprised 627 subjects from Illinois, Minnesota, Michigan, Montana, Texas, Utah, Vermont, and California. Ages of the subjects ranged from infancy to over 40; 45% were females and 55% were males; approximately half of the sample consisted of persons without disabilities and the remaining half consisted of persons with disabilities from a variety of service settings. I found the lack of breakdowns by respondents' age, SES, type of disability, service setting, and state to be troublesome. These omissions are problematic to external validity interpretation and prevent a sufficient appraisal of the suitable use of this instrument. The next version of the CALS should provide an ample description of the demographics of standardization samples and a discussion of the sampling design plus participation rates in the standardization study. These data should be presented with enough detail to permit an evaluation of the appropriateness of the study. Skill module means and standard errors of measurement for various age groups would provide a helpful frame of reference.

RELIABILITY. Internal consistency estimates of reliability were reported for persons with and without disabilities for the 24 skill modules. Reported Cronbach alpha coefficients for the 213 persons without disabilities ranged from .74 to .99 with 19 of these coefficients in the .90s. Split-half reliabilities ranged from .67 to .98 with the majority of coefficients in the .90s. For persons with disabilities (n = 287), the reported coefficients ranged from .79 to .97. Nineteen coefficients were in the .90s. Split-half reliabilities ranged from .65 to .95 with a majority of coefficients in the .80s and the .90s. These data sufficiently demonstrate the internal consistency of the 24 skill modules for the samples of persons with and without disabilities.

Unfortunately, interrater reliability was not assessed. Significant congruence between raters would seem to be the most compelling, and appropriate, data to support a claim of consistency of measurement for an instrument of this type.

VALIDITY. The authors relied extensively on prior research to establish an accepted conceptualization of adaptive living skills from which items were constructed, revised, and refined based on extensive feedback from experts in the field. These efforts resulted in critical domains and skills which comprise the 24 modules of the CALS. Claims of the content validity of the 24 modules were supported by providing evidence that researchers and practitioners in the field judged the skills assessed by the CALS to be important for successful and adaptive living in home, community, and employment settings.

The assertion of criterion-related validity of 22 of the 24 skill modules is based on correlations between the CALS skill module score with four other measures of adaptive behavior—the SIB total and cluster scores, and the ICAP total and cluster scores. The correlations ranged from .56 to.94 for 213 persons without disabilities and from .56 to .86 for 150 persons with disabilities. The majority of the correlations, in both samples, exceeded .73. The magnitude of these correlations could be indicative of moderate to high validity if one considers the SIB and ICAP to be appropriate criteria of adaptive behavior. I would prefer a more traditional and independent appraisal of the criterion of adaptive behavior. It is hoped this appraisal would take the form of evaluations by expert judges or assessments by experienced social service workers rather than another checklist.

Evidence offered in support of construct validity was correlations (ranging from .49 to .92) between 13 skill modules from three domains, selected on the expectation of a developmental sequence of skill acquisition, and the chronological age of 213 persons without disabilities. These correlations are indicative of a developmental sequence in those skill modules.

SUMMARY. The CALS is an easily administered assessment of self-care and personal independence for persons, with and without disabilities, from infancy to adulthood. Due in large part to extensive field testing, it is appropriate for use in residential, work, community, and leisure environments. The technical manual is concise, clearly written, and well organized. Information is presented in a logical manner with graphic and visual displays that enhance the textual material. Claims of internal consistency, construct validity, and content validity were substantiated. However, the lack of an adequate description of the demographics of the standardization samples prevents a meaningful discussion of examinee appropriateness. A determination of interrater reliability and criterion-related validity using independent judgements/measures precludes an enthusiastic endorsement of the psychometric quality of this instrument. Hence, in its current form, the CALS should be used as a descriptive tool of adaptive living skills.

REVIEWER'S REFERENCE

Bruininks, R. H., Morreau, L. E., Gilman, C. J., & Anderson, J. L. (1991). *Manual for the Adaptive Living Skills Curriculum*. Allen, TX: DLM.

Review of the Checklist of Adaptive Living Skills by JAMES P. VAN HANEGHAN, Assistant Professor of Educational Psychology, Counseling, and Special Education, Northern Illinois University, DeKalb, IL:

Over the past 30 years, adaptive behavior measures have become an important tool in the diagnosis and treatment of developmental disabilities. Normative measures are useful in diagnosing whether someone has an adaptive behavior deficit, but criterion-based assessments are needed to determine where that deficit lies and how it can be treated. This is the rationale for the development of the Checklist of Adaptive Living Skills (CALS), a criterion-based rather than normative measure of adaptive behavior. The CALS was designed with program planning and training in mind. The goal was to link the measurement of adaptive behavior in various domains directly to instructional objectives. A companion curriculum to the CALS, the Adaptive Living Skills Curriculum (ALSC) is indexed directly to CALS items. Hence, if a client cannot carry out a particular skill, the ALSC is a methodology for training a particular behavior.

The CALS is linked to two normative tests of adaptive behavior developed by Bruininks (one of the CALS authors) and several of his colleagues: The Scales of Independent Behavior (SIB; Bruininks, Woodcock, Weatherman, & Hill, 1984; see T4:2335) and the Inventory for Client and Agency Planning (ICAP; Bruininks, Hill, Weatherman, & Woodcock, 1986; see T4:1260). These two scales are equated with the items on the CALS to provide a starting point for evaluating particular adaptive behavior strengths and weaknesses. Thus, one use of the CALS is as a tool to help identify specific weaknesses in adaptive behavior based on concerns raised by normative measures that only sample items from a domain. The CALS can be used on its own, but the administration of 784 items is rather time consuming. Additionally, the large amount of information obtained from the CALS might be overwhelming without additional information about client strengths and weaknesses.

The items on the CALS span four different areas: Personal Living Skills, Home Living Skills, Community Living Skills, and Employment Skills. The 24 subareas fall into one of these four domains.

As noted above, the CALS can be administered in its entirety, or parts of the CALS can be administered based on scores from the ICAP, SIB, or other observations of adaptive behavior. Like other adaptive behavior measures, the CALS is administered to an informant familiar with the client. The authors also point out that not every individual is aware of all aspects of a client's adaptive behavior. Hence, the authors allow for the possibility of using multiple informants to respond to different areas. The starting item for any particular part of the CALS depends upon SIB or ICAP scores in conceptually similar domains. For example, the starting point for CALS items in the Employment Skills area is based on the Community Living scores from the ICAP or SIB.

Items within a domain are listed on the CALS in their order of difficulty as derived by the authors. An individual is given credit for having a particular skill described in an item, if he or she performs that skill at least 75% of the time. In addition to scoring whether an individual performed the item independently, items can be scored to indicate whether an individual can perform the item with a prompt. A mark is placed next to an item to indicate whether the individual can carry out the item with a gestural, verbal, or physical prompt. Hence, there are three possible scores: independent performance, performance with a prompt, or nonperformance. Respondents are asked to continue to answer items in a particular domain until there are 10 consecutive items in an area that the learner cannot perform.

The checklist test booklet contains a cover page to mark demographic information about the client and to record respondents. Additional pages provide places for converting ICAP or SIB scores, a space to mark where respondents should start, instructions for the respondents, and the items themselves. Finally, the booklet contains planning and evaluation worksheets to use in designing specific educational programs based on CALS results and the ALSC. The items themselves are grouped and numbered by overall category, subcategory of skill, and item number. For example, the item "Asks simple questions of others" is Item 1.1.15. The first "1" indicates that it is a Personal Living skill, the second "1" indicates that it is a socialization item, and the "15" indicates that it is Item "15" for that subskill. There is room in each test booklet to place the results of three assessments. Hence, trainers and other professionals can track changes in adaptive behavior with the CALS.

Development of items for the CALS was carried out with a great deal of rigor. The initial pool of items was developed based on an analysis of the literature on adaptive behavior. These items were given a preliminary ordering by the authors and then altered based on feedback from various professionals and parents who deal with individuals with developmental disabilities. The 1,271 items were then field tested by dividing them into parcels to be administered to part of the sample of individuals involved in a field test of the scale. The 784 items retained, their order of presentation, and their difficulty were determined based on Rasch techniques, professional judgment, and practical concerns.

The sample for the field test consisted of 627 individuals from eight states. Ages ranged from infancy to 40 years, and approximately half of the sample were disabled. There is very little additional information about the sample, although given that the CALS is a criterion-based measure and does not yield normative scores, we may be more concerned about the scaleability of the items than we are about the nature of the sample.

Rasch models were also used to equate the CALS items to SIB and ICAP scores. Thus, appropriate statistical procedures were used to identify where on a particular CALS domain someone would likely fall. The test manual provides tables for translating scores on the SIB and ICAP to starting points for CALS domains.

Like many other adaptive behavior measures, the CALS results are only as good as the reliability and validity of reports given by respondents (Salvia & Ysseldyke, 1991). This is especially true for the CALS, because decisions about program planning and training are going to be based on CALS responses. Yet, there is very little evidence provided in the manual concerning the reliability of respondents. Nor are any data reported on how well the items reliably portray a learner's actual behavior. In addition, there are no test-retest reliabilities described in the CALS manual to indicate whether a particular respondent is consistent over time in how he or she rates the performance of an individual. Test-retest reliabilities are important for the CALS because the users will be interested in tracking change over time. If respondents do not respond consistently to the items or have different ideas about what independent performance is, it may be difficult to interpret what score changes mean. The only form of reliability reported in the manual is internal consistency reliability. The authors report Cronbach alpha and split-half reliability coefficients for each of the 24 subareas from the scale. Most of the alphas reported for samples of disabled and nondisabled individuals are high, with only 5 out of the 24 subareas showing alphas below .90. The split-half coefficients are not quite as high, but generally show reasonable internal consistency in the subareas tested. Hence, although internal consistency reliabilities are reasonable, evidence for other forms of reliability are not reported in the manual.

In terms of validity, there is evidence of criterion-based validity, construct validity, and content validity. The CALS relates moderately to highly with ICAP and SIB scores, previously standardized measures of adaptive behavior. In addition, there is evidence for the validity of the modules in that success is moderately related to chronological age. The construct of adaptive behavior shows both developmental and experiential components. Moderate correlations with chronological age suggest that these two components are present in the CALS. Content validity evidence comes from the authors identifying the items and areas on the test from the literature on adaptive behavior.

One piece of validity evidence that would be helpful would be evidence of changes in CALS items with training in a particular area, either with the ALSC or some other program. Because an important use of the CALS is in conjunction with the ALSC or other training, its success in this role would be very important to prospective users.

In summary, the CALS has a great deal of potential as a criterion-based measure of adaptive behavior. Its strengths are its linkage to normative measures and its linkage to the ALSC, a curriculum for training adaptive behavior. Its linkage with normative measures allows trainers to pinpoint potential domains and items for instruction. Its linkage with the ALSC provides them with direct ways of training these skills. Given additional reliability evidence for the CALS, it may prove to be a very useful tool for trainers of developmentally disabled individuals.

REVIEWER'S REFERENCES

Bruininks, R. H., Woodcock, R. W., Weatherman, R. F., & Hill, B. K. (1984). Scales of Independent Behavior. Allen, TX: DLM.

Bruininks, R. H., Hill, B. K., Weatherman, R. F., & Woodcock, R. W. (1986). Inventory for Client and Agency Planning. Allen, TX: DLM.

Salvia, J., & Ysseldyke, J. E. (1991). *Assessment* (5th ed.). Boston: Houghton Mifflin Company.

[70]

The Child "At Risk" for Drug Abuse Rating Scale.

Purpose: "Seeks to assess risk factors for later drug abuse."
Population: Preschool–grade 6.
Publication Date: 1990.
Acronym: DARS.
Scores, 4: Developmental History, Family Relations, Child Behavior Pattern, Total.
Administration: Individual.
Price Data, 1990: $11 per manual (20 pages); $25 per program with diskette.
Time: (15) minutes.
Comments: Program designed to run on PC XT-like computer with a minimum of 256K of memory.
Author: Russell N. Cassel.
Publisher: Psychologists and Educators, Inc.

Review of The Child "At Risk" for Drug Abuse Rating Scale by ERNEST A. BAUER, Research, Evaluation and Testing Consultant, Oakland Schools, Waterford, MI:

The Child "At Risk" for Drug Abuse Rating Scale (DARS) "seeks to assess risk factors for later drug abuse" (p. 3). The "manual" presents a series of largely unsubstantiated assertions ("Timing of corrective action in relation to hazards from development and family relations is the most critical for fostering success"), circular arguments ("Drug abuse and deviant behavior are so closely allied, that when one predicts for one, it serves as an equally valid prediction for the other. It is not conceivable that one could be involved in drug abuse, and still not be involved in deviant behavior"), seemingly pointless analogies ("By the same logic, one would not say that a person born with a crippled hand is unable to type"), and philosophical meanderings ("The best way to deal with any problem, to be sure, is to prevent it from happening"). At one point, under the side-head "Drug Using Society," the reader is asked, "Could you be this kind of role model as a parent?" On page 15, the manual completely loses the at-risk for drug abuse theme and begins discussing language disorder clinics and never returns to the original theme. Two poems are printed on the inside and outside of the back cover, "Myself," and "Cocaine," respectively.

The "rating scale" is administered via a microcomputer. The approach is archaic, the entry redundant and irritating. Putting this rating scale on a microcomputer did nothing to improve it.

The rating scale contains 60 items that reflect developmental history, family relations, and behavior pattern. Each area is represented by 20 yes-no questions. Many of the "items" are standard sociological questions about family structure and relationships (divorce, separation, abuse, etc.) and developmental items about complications at delivery, development of bladder and bowel control, walking, talking, etc. Others seem idiosyncratic. "Were child's teeth scrubbed regularly?" "Did mother often hug and even kiss child?" "Did child dislike father?"

Several items try to deal with both school age and preschool age children in a unique way. For example, "Did child dislike school, if under 6 dislike home?" "Did child fail kindergarten or 1st grade? (retained in grade) if under 6, did child fight going to sleep?" "Does child fail to complete homework for school, or if under 6, refuse to play by self?" "Does child dislike arithmetic, if under 6, refuse to play with other children?" The user has entered the child's age, the computer program could easily ask the appropriate question, but, more importantly, one is left wondering if these alternative questions are "equivalent." "Six different levels of at risk for drug abuse serve as the norm reference, ranging from 'low risk level' to 'Crisis State'" (pp. 6-7). There may be some kind of "norms," because the scales are reported as "T-like" scores that range from approximately 10 through 100. This reviewer entered fake data that reached these extremes; however, the scale on the margin of the computer generated report ranges from 20 to 80. The program offers reports that purport to use general, female, male, "professional," and "Hispanic" norms, although neither the professional nor the Hispanic norms would function on the disk the reviewer received. There are absolutely no data about the norm groups or the distributions of scores. One cannot tell if there are age or grade norms within the sets of norms offered. There is no information about how the bounds of the "six at risk levels" were determined. There is no mention of reliability. There are no data about predictive or concurrent validity. There is not a single correlation coefficient or other descriptive statistic in the entire "manual." In short, there appears to be absolutely no attempt to assure potential users that the collection of items has any psychometric properties whatsoever.

The author describes the current version as "experimental." Given the complete lack of information available about the psychometric characteristics of the rating scale, it should not be used in its present form.

Review of The Child "At Risk" for Drug Abuse Rating Scale by RICHARD B. STUART, Professor Emeritus, Department of Psychiatry and Behavioral Sciences, School of Medicine, University of Washington, Seattle, WA:

The Child "At Risk" for Drug Abuse Rating Scale (DARS) is a risk assessment tool intended for use by adults who are interested in assessing the risk of drug use by school-age children, essentially in kindergarten through sixth grade. It contains 60 true/false items accessible on a 5.25-inch floppy drive which can be run on XT or later model IBM-compatible computers. The questions pertain to various aspects of the parents' demographic characteristics (e.g., married at time of child's birth, prison records, etc.), the circumstances of the subject child's delivery (e.g., prematurity) and development (e.g., walking, toilet training landmarks), aspects of the child's habit patterns (e.g., nailbiting), and aspects of the child's interaction with each parent during early developmental years (e.g., hugged by father and/or mother). Most of the answers to these questions require data from the parent who, along with professionals, are the intended users of this instrument. The 60 items are equally divided between three subscales: Developmental History, Family Relations, and Behavioral Pattern, although the specific items assigned to each category are not identified. A printout in the form of a histogram provided a "t-like score" (p. 20) description of the level of risk in the three categories, as well as yielding an overall risk rating. Risks are assigned one of six levels, from low through "crisis state," although the cutoff points for three of the levels are somewhat overlapping.

The manual stipulates that this instrument (published in 1990) is in "experimental form" (p. 5). As such, it must be assessed as an instrument in process rather than as a finished tool. A great many flaws mar the DARS, all of which would require correction before its use can be recommended.

The 20-page typescript manual is flawed by a great many omissions. After a cursory review of the nature of preventive programming, the manual identifies "gateway drugs" including coffee, cigarettes, tea, and chocolate as well as marijuana, which is identified as a "hard-core" drug. Drugs are dichotomized between stimulants and depressants, with hallucinogens presumably, but not explicitly, classified in one of these categories. As an even more serious omission, alcohol is not mentioned in this manual.

As is true throughout this manual, research findings are not cited to justify the inclusion or exclusion of various risk factors, or the weights, if any, assigned to each factor. Those for whom psychodiagnosis is a concern will find difficulty with the author's discussion of "character disorders," not in Axis II terms as one might expect, but in such categories as "disturbed home conditions" and "inability to use leisure time." In addition, the utility of assignment to one of the six risk levels is compromised by the fact that the highly general action recommendations suffer from considerable overlap.

The manual contains no data pertaining to the statistical stability or clinical utility of the DARS. Data are not presented to support the factorial independence of the three clusters of risk factors. Alpha coefficients are not presented to support the internal consistency of each class of risk factors. Neither test-retest and related forms of reliability nor validity (as in demonstrating the accuracy with which subsequent drug use is predicted by the risk levels assigned) are addressed as a means of assessing the coherence of the subscales.

The absence of appropriate statistical evaluation is sufficient reason to discourage use of the DARS. But other problems should be mentioned. The manual contains undocumented lists of apparent signs of drug abuse, a great many of which might as likely be symptoms of physical or psychological illness, posing the risk that serious physical illnesses might be overlooked. In addition, parents are perhaps the primary end-users of this product. Equipped with this apparently professional diagnostic information, they may take useful preventive steps. But they are also at risk of taking highly unproductive actions based upon inferences with unproven diagnostic or therapeutic value. For example, although the manual stipulates that risk level does not equate with use level, this qualification is apt to be overlooked by concerned parents. Because of the fact that access to the DARS is unrestricted, great care should have been taken to guard against misinterpretation by nonprofessionals, a risk that appears high in this instrument.

The manual does not contain explanations for the use of the software, requiring either considerable computer sophistication or concerted attempts to reach the author to obtain instructions. Although the disk is essentially user friendly once the program is accessed, it does contain a few bugs (e.g., drives must be designated as A, B, or C, not A:, B:, or C: per instructions, and the program also fails to reject data on subjects who fall outside the age spectrum of the program).

In conclusion, it is strongly advised that use of the DARS be restricted to efforts to evaluate its statistical properties and clinical utilities. Its use in educational or drug treatment programs is unwarranted due to its highly speculative nature.

[71]

Child Care Inventory.

Purpose: Developed to evaluate child care programs in order to improve program effectiveness or to determine the level of program implementation.
Population: Child care programs.
Publication Date: 1986.
Scores: 11 performance areas: Classroom Arrangement, Safety, Curriculum, Interacting, Scheduling, Child Assessment, Health, Special Needs, Parent Involvement, Outdoor Play, Infant Programs.
Administration: Individual.
Price Data, 1992: $19.95 per complete kit including test booklet and manual (32 pages); $9.95 per test booklet; $10.95 per manual.
Time: Administration time not reported.
Authors: Martha S. Abbott-Shim and Annette M. Sibley.
Publisher: Humanics Publishing Group.

Review of the Child Care Inventory by LISA G. BISCHOFF, Assistant Professor of Education and School Psychology, Indiana State University, Terre Haute, IN.

The Child Care Inventory (CCI) is a checklist designed to provide formative and summative evaluation of child care programs serving infants and children in daycare, preschool, and kindergarten settings. Potential users of the CCI, according to the authors, include directors, teachers, and aides in childcare settings, as well as consultants, curriculum specialists, licensing officials, and training directors involved with child care.

The CCI consists of a test book and an administration manual. The test book contains observation checklists and inventory profile sheets through which data are collected and visually displayed. The administration manual defines terminology and describes methods for determining the purposes of evaluation, establishing reliability among observers, collecting and summarizing data, and providing recommendations based on results. The administration manual also provides an outline for reporting the results of program evaluation and for developing a program improvement plan.

Administration of the CCI involves collecting data through direct observation, review of records, and interviews in order to document the occurrence or nonoccurrence of specific classroom indicators (e.g., talking to infants) deemed to be important in fulfilling specific child care goals (e.g., provider initiates positive interactions with the infant). Specific instructions regarding data collection and scoring of occurrence versus nonoccurrence are provided in the administration manual. Following data collection, area scores by classroom and program are computed by dividing the total number of indicators observed by the total number of indicators possible for each area. Area scores may then be visually displayed on inventory profile sheets provided in the test book. The number of observations required for the CCI varies depending on the purpose of evaluation (i.e., formative versus summative evaluation). Observation of a sample of classrooms may be used rather than observation in all classrooms if necessary. The number of observers required for the CCI is not stated in the manual. However, the manual does state that, "Whenever two or more observers will be collecting information, it is important that they are consistent in their use of the Inventory and their interpretation of the Inventory terminology" (p. 22). Procedures for establishing interrater reliability are documented in the manual.

The CCI provides area scores by classroom and by program for each of 11 performance areas including Classroom Arrangement, Safety, Curriculum, Interacting, Scheduling, Child Assessment, Health, Special Needs, Parent Involvement, Outdoor Play, and Infant Programs. Area scores are graphed on inventory profile sheets provided in the test manual. The inventory profile sheet designates criterion levels for low (less than 50%), moderate (50% to 74%), and high (75% to 100%) numbers of indicators observed in each area. The method for determining these criteria is not included in the administration manual. Although the authors do state that "interpretation of scores as low or high, weak or strong, is a discretionary decision and should be based on the values and goals of the individual child care program" (p. 27), information provided concerning program evaluation results defines weaknesses as "Performance Area scores that fall within the low level" and strengths as "Performance Area scores that fall within the high level" (p. 29).

The strength of the CCI lies in the detailed instructions for collecting, recording, and reporting data, the operational definitions provided for terms used in checklists, the attention to establishing reliability among observers, and the focus upon providing recommendations and developing plans for improvement. In contrast to these strengths are weaknesses related to a lack of information concerning test construction, reliability, and validity.

Information concerning test construction is not included in the CCI administration manual. Although reference to Head Start, Child Development Associated (CDA), and National Association for the Education of Young Children (NAEYC) standards is made in the foreword to the administration manual, and the authors indicate that "descriptive statements and indicators reflect values which have been derived from daycare and child development literature and professional expertise" (p. 10), no references are cited to indicate specific sources of information. Furthermore, information concerning development of checklist items, performance areas, and scores is not provided in the manual.

Information concerning validity is not included in the CCI administration manual. Although the instrument appears to have "face validity," no evidence of content-related, criterion-related, or construct-related validity is provided by the authors.

Interrater reliability for the CCI was calculated by computing the occurrence agreement (total agreement divided by total observations [agreement plus nonagreement plus nonoccurrence]). Observers in a training project achieved 94% agreement according to the authors. Information on the number of observers and the number of observations upon which this reliability figure is based is not provided in the manual.

In conclusion, the Child Care Inventory provides an evaluation instrument for child care classrooms and programs serving infants and children. The materials provided described procedures fully and forms employed in data collection and presentation are designed for ease of use and understanding. Although the content of CCI items and performance areas appears to provide an adequate sample of the domain of interest, information concerning validity is absent from the administration manual. Furthermore, information regarding test construction is also absent and information regarding reliability is scant. This instrument may provide child care providers and evaluators with a method of performing both summative and formative evaluation programs. However, because the reliability and validity of the instrument has not been adequately researched, and because the construction of the instrument is not fully defined, this instrument should be used with caution.

Review of the Child Care Inventory by ANNETTE M. IVERSON, Assistant Professor of Educational Psychology and Foundations, University of Northern Iowa, Cedar Falls, IA:

The Child Care Inventory is a checklist that was initially developed to assess the overall performance of Title XX day care centers. Subsequently, the Inventory has been used to measure the quality of care provided to young children in numerous other day care settings. The authors suggest that potential uses include needs assessment for staff development, program review, and data for reports for funding agencies and boards of directors.

The Child Care Inventory is a checklist of 92 items that are either present consistently (checked "yes") or present inconsistently or not at all (checked "no"). An entire chapter lists definitions of terms to aid in scoring items. The items are grouped into 11 categories that focus on concrete, observable components of the educational program: Classroom Arrangement, Safety, Curriculum, Interacting, Scheduling, Child Assessment, Health, Special Needs, Parent Involvement, Outdoor Play, and Infant Program. In a 1985 letter contained in the Foreword of the manual, Robert C. Granger suggested that the Inventory categories overlap with Head Start, CDA, and NAEYC's standards. However, the authors do not make these claims themselves.

The Inventory administration manual reports one study of the psychometric properties of the instrument. Specifically, "Observers participated in twelve hours of training . . . and they achieved a . . . (94%) agreement" (p. iv). The number of observers and settings observed and on which scores there was agreement is unknown. Additional evidence of reliability and validity are woefully lacking. The scale is a criterion-referenced assessment tool and, hence, no norms are available. Individual item scores, subscale scores, and total score are best interpreted in a criterion-referenced manner (i.e., What percent of the total number of items was checked "yes"?). A rating scale that yields scores resulting in a range of unacceptable to acceptable quality of care would be potentially more useful in formative evaluation and program evaluation and planning than a simple yes/no checklist.

The authors have been conscientious in presenting basic training in the skills needed to complete a checklist via observation, interviewing, and review of records methodology. The manual has several good chapters on training personnel in both formative and summative evaluation, data collection methods and observation recording procedures, interviewing skills, establishing reliability among observers, issues to consider when designing a schedule for data collection, scoring the protocol and graphing results, and using the evaluation results.

Although the Child Care Inventory may be well conceived and constructed, there is no evidence to support it as a reliable and valid measure of day care environments. Additional research to establish the psychometric properties of the Inventory is needed before this instrument can be recommended for widespread evaluation of day care environments or as a psychometrically sound addition to an ecological assessment plan. In the meantime, users should consider other instruments that offer more evidence of reliability and validity such as the Early Childhood Environment Rating Scale (Harms & Clifford, 1980; T4:833).

REVIEWER'S REFERENCE

Harms, T., & Clifford, R. M. (1980). Early Childhood Environment Rating Scale. New York: Teachers College Press.

[72]

Child Neuropsychological Questionnaire.

Purpose: Developed to evaluate children suspected of having brain dysfunctions.
Population: Children.
Publication Date: 1978.
Acronym: CNQ.
Scores: Overall evaluation of neuropsychological impairment.
Administration: Individual.
Price Data, 1995: $30 per complete kit including manual (6 pages) and 50 questionnaires.
Time: Administration time not reported.
Author: Fernando Melendez.
Publisher: Psychological Assessment Resources, Inc.

Review of the Child Neuropsychological Questionnaire by ROBERT A. BORNSTEIN, Professor and Associate Chairman, Department of Psychiatry, The Ohio State University, Columbus, OH:

This 42-item questionnaire is designed to be part of an overall evaluation. It is "of little value if used alone, or if answered in simple yes or no fashion," and "is useful only as part of a very extensive battery" (manual, p. 1). The manual is extremely brief and provides a short introduction to the development of the questionnaire as well as a description for the rationale of item inclusion.

As with the Adult Neuropsychological Questionnaire (19), item selection is based largely on the author's personal experience. The manual author suggests the aim is to "try to make a three-way differentiation between entities that generally show very similar signs and symptoms; childhood schizophrenia, abnormal electrical functions, and posterior fossa neoplasms" (p. 1). This is a curious selection of diagnostic entities, and overlooks the more common disorders such as a learning disability or Attention Deficit Disorder.

The manual contains no reliability or validity data. The age range of children for whom this questionnaire is intended is not stated. For older children and adolescents, the questionnaire could be administered in part or in whole directly to the patient, whereas other items would be addressed primarily to the parents.

The questionnaire suffers to some extent by lack of organization and unclear guidance regarding the applicability of items. Some items are more reflective of problems associated with early childhood, whereas others are associated with later childhood. The appropriateness or inappropriateness of these behaviors is likely to vary with age, although this is not reflected in any way in the questionnaire manual. The manual also does not include a statement as to who the proposed user of the instrument would be. Experienced clinicians or child neuropsychologists would be unlikely to use this instrument. On the other hand, general clinicians, students, and non-neuropsychologists would likely need specific guidance for the interpretation of responses to these various questions.

The lack of age-based validity data for the items included in this questionnaire is particularly problematic. The organization of items is haphazard with questions about school history, developmental history, and specific symptoms interspersed throughout the questionnaire.

Similarly, some of the offered interpretations or explanations of items seem overly broad and uncritical. For example, the explanation for Item 6 "does your child get along well with other children?" suggests that "children who later develop psychiatric problems seldom have a normal history of peer socialization" (p. 2). Although this may be true of patients with more severe psychiatric disorders, this cannot be asserted in relation to the majority of childhood psychiatric disorders. Furthermore, many children have an initial period of apparent normal socialization and interaction and develop symptoms later in childhood and adolescence. This type of uncritical overgeneralization is misleading, particularly if this questionnaire is intended for use by non-neuropsychologists or general clinicians. In the absence of any clear data showing a relationship between this questionnaire and subsequent diagnostic evaluations, it is unclear how this questionnaire actually contributes to clinical evaluation or management of patients.

Review of the Child Neuropsychological Questionnaire by JAMES C. REED, Director of Psychology, St. Luke's Hospital, New Bedford, MA:

The Child Neuropsychological Questionnaire consists of 42 items; 7 require narration and 35 require only a yes/no. The questions cover pre-, peri-, and postnatal problems, developmental milestones, medical events, psychosocial development, and educational history. The questions are not grouped by categories, and some of them are factual whereas others require answers that are subjective (e.g., Question 4 "Did your child go to kindergarten?"; Question 21 "Does your child's memory seemed to have changed, recently?"). The questions cover the standard information that should be obtained in a diagnostic interview that is directed toward a child's psychiatric or neuropsychological problems. As a questionnaire it is subject to the same limitations that befall any short yes/no screening device. In the manual Melendez warns that the questionnaire is of little value if used alone, and he states that the questionnaire is designed as a set of points of inquiry. The purpose is to "try to make a three-way differentiation between entities that generally show very similar signs and symptoms: childhood schizophrenia, abnormal electrical functions, and posterior fossa neoplasms" (manual, p. 1).

The rationale for each of the questions and suggestions concerning the possible diagnostic significance of each item and the type of follow-up that might be needed are provided in the manual. The manual author states that the questionnaire would be useful only as part of a battery that would include neuropsychological testing and pediatric neurological examinations.

It is difficult to fault the questionnaire. At the same time, it is difficult to praise it. One who has had experience in evaluating children will take a history that covers the areas itemized in the questionnaire. An experienced clinician is unlikely to benefit from or need the questionnaire. The questionnaire could be used as a teaching device to train students and to alert them to the possible significance of various behaviors and the reasons for pursuing diverse areas of inquiry.

The problem of differential diagnosis in pediatric neuropsychology is extremely complex. It is unlikely this questionnaire would make a unique contribution in resolving the complexities. I would not recommend the Child Neuropsychological Questionnaire to a colleague, but if one chooses to get information that is pertinent through the use of this instrument as opposed to some other procedure, it is a matter of personal preference.

[73]

Children's Apperceptive Story-Telling Test.

Purpose: "Identification of social, emotional, and/or behavioral problems in children."
Population: Ages 6–13.
Publication Date: 1989.
Acronym: CAST.
Scores: 19 scores and 9 indicators: Adaptive Thematic (Instrumentality, Interpersonal Cooperation, Affiliation, Positive Affect), Nonadaptive Thematic (Inadequacy, Alienation, Interpersonal Conflict, Limits, Negative Affect), Adaptive Problem-Solving (Positive Preoperational, Positive Operational), Nonadaptive Problem-Solving (Refusal, Unresolved, Negative Preoperational, Negative Operational), Factor Profile (Adaptive, Nonadaptive, Immature, Uninvested), Thematic Indicators (Sexual Abuse, Substance Abuse, Divorce, Hypothetical Thought, Emotionality, Self-Validation), Life Tasks (Family, Peer, School).
Administration: Individual.
Price Data, 1994: $109 per complete kit including 31 picture cards; 50 record/scoring forms, and manual ('89, 290 pages); $49 per set of 31 picture cards; $29 per 50 record/scoring forms; $34 per manual.
Time: (20–40) minutes.
Comments: Orally administered.
Author: Mary F. Schneider.
Publisher: PRO-ED, Inc.

Review of the Children's Apperceptive Story-Telling Test by EDWARD ARONOW, Associate Professor of Psychology, Montclair State College, Upper Montclair, NJ:

Dr. Mary F. Schneider has done yeoman's service in developing a psychometrically sound apperceptive test, the Children's Apperceptive Story-Telling Test (CAST), that is appropriate for use in clinical and school settings, with multi-ethnic characters appearing in the cards. The stimuli are in color and are quite contemporary, giving this test advantages over its chief competitor, the Children's Apperception Test (CAT; T4:444).

The test manual is well organized and well written. There is a good historical overview of the use of apperceptive techniques in assessment. As Dr. Schneider notes, the main projective instruments that have historically been used in psychological testing involve inkblots, stories, and picture drawings. The original and continued popular Thematic Apperception Test (TAT; T4:2824) designed by Henry Murray at the Harvard Psychological Clinic has pictures that are black and white, somewhat out of date, and strongly suggestive of emotional themes that make it difficult to judge whether the story originates from the stimulus or from personality aspects of the subject. The same is true of the CAT. In addition, the psychometric basis of the TAT and the CAT is deficient.

The design of the CAST takes into account research that has been done previously on apperceptive techniques. For example, the cards emphasize moderate ambiguity because this has been shown to give the best results. The somber tone of the TAT is avoided. Further, the cards are in color because color has been shown to add to the productivity of subjects with attention deficit disorder.

Some test users may be disappointed by the Adlerian theoretical substructure for this test. Adlerian psychologists, educators, and mental health practitioners are certainly in a distinct minority. However, it could also be noted that Adlerian theory has a strong commonsense orientation and also strongly emphasizes social aspects of functioning, which is quite relevant to apperceptive techniques.

The author indicates the CAST has four principal uses: identification of social, emotional, and/or behavioral problems in children; intervention planning; documentation of therapeutic change; and research. The test consists of 17 cards that are administered to all subjects. Three cards are given to everyone; 14 cards have male and female versions. The test is designed for subjects ages 6 to 13. Evaluation is carried out in terms of the main Adlerian spheres of interaction (i.e., the family, peers, and the school). The instructions used with the test are very precise, including follow-up ("prompt") questions. Responses to the cards are then scored according to thematic scales, problem-solving scales, and thematic indicators.

The thematic scales are as follows: Instrumentality, Interpersonal Cooperation, Affiliation, Positive Affect, Inadequacy, Alienation, Interpersonal Conflict,

Limits, and Negative Affect. The problem-solving scales are as follows: Positive Preoperational problem solving, Positive Operational problem solving, Refusal, Unresolved, Negative Preoperational problem solving, and Negative Operational problem solving. The thematic indicators are as follows: Sexual Abuse, Substance Abuse, Divorce, Hypothetical Thought, Emotionality, and Self Validation.

All of these scales and thematic indicators are well defined, and extensive scoring examples are provided. The raw scores for the thematic scales and the problem-solving scales are converted into *T*-Scores that are depicted in graphic form on the CAST profile. Scores for four factors are also obtained; the Adaptive factor, the Non-adaptive factor, the Immature factor, and the Uninvested factor. Confidence bands are also provided for the various scales and factors based on the imperfect reliability of the instrument.

The author reports data pertaining to the reliability of the instrument in terms of interrater, test-retest, split half, and coefficient alpha. Interrater reliability appears quite good. Test-retest coefficients are also on the high side, although the applicability of test-retest reliability to psychological tests in general and projective techniques in particular is questionable. Internal consistency reliability is also quite good. The coefficients reported certainly compare quite favorably with reliability coefficients of other projective techniques and other apperceptive techniques in particular.

Data are also reported pertaining to the validity of the instrument. This is reported as it should be in terms of content validity, construct validity, and criterion-related validity. Data are presented that are supportive in all respects.

The standardization sample for the CAST consisted of 876 children residing in 16 states. The standardization sample was selected to be representative of the U.S. population as described in the 1980 U.S. Census reports in terms of age, gender, race, parent education, geographic location, and community size. The sample was drawn from four geographic regions defined by the 1980 Census: the Northeast, the North Central, the South, and the West. The students in the standardization sample attended both public and private schools. In addition to these 876 typical children, 322 behavior-disordered students were tested.

In short, the CAST represents the most serious and psychometrically sound effort thus far to develop an apperceptive story-telling technique for use with children. The fly in the ointment, of course, is the time requirement of the test. As reported by the author, administration takes 20 to 40 minutes, scoring takes approximately 30 minutes, and 20 to 30 minutes are required for interpretation. Many clinical, consulting, or school psychologists may be unwilling to invest such time in an apperceptive technique. This might result in the apperceptive technique taking up more of the examiner's time than the typical intelligence test. Objective tests likewise provide psychometric soundness, but require very little in terms of time from the examiner. Dr. Schneider recommends tape recording test productions and transcribing them afterwards, which would further add to the time demands of this instrument.

Nonetheless, the CAST is strongly recommended for use in preference to the CAT because of the greater neutrality of the stimuli presented, the modernity of the pictures, the use of color, and the use of White, African-American, Hispanic, and Asian children in the test stimuli. However, it seems likely that such use of the technique will be in the idiographic rather than the nomothetic manner, as has traditionally been the case, with examiners relying on clinical sense rather than scores for interpretation. The author herself obliquely suggests at one point that the technique can be used in this way. For research purposes, of course, the CAST represents a psychometrically sound apperceptive technique unparalleled by other approaches.

Review of the Children's Apperceptive Story-Telling Test by MARTIN J. WIESE, Licensed Psychologist, Educational Service Unit No. 6, Milford, NE:

The Children's Apperceptive Story-Telling Test (CAST) was developed for use in schools and clinical settings with children ranging in age from 6 to 13 years. Designed to assess social, emotional, and behavioral concerns and provide information regarding the child's functioning in the family, with peers, and at school, the CAST may be used as a formal diagnostic instrument or informally during an interview with the child.

As with other instruments of its type (e.g., Thematic Apperception Test [T4:2824], Children's Apperception Test [T4:444], and Tell-Me-A-Story [T4:2716], the respondent is asked to generate stories freely for each of the 17 picture cards presented. Unlike the aforementioned tests, interpretation of the CAST is based upon the Individual Psychology principle of Alfred Adler.

Proponents of Adler's Individual Psychology view individuals as social beings with goal-directed drives to "belong." As a result, each person is directed toward goals that are in accord with his or her social interests or life style. In other words, the total person and that person's behavior are considered within the broader context of the social milieu.

This conceptualization of human functioning also views cognition as primary; feelings and actions are subservient to thoughts. In theory, the developing child's experiences, social interactions, and observations of others come to fit into a consistent, coherent thought pattern and eventually create a relatively stable scheme of apperceptions within the child.

The CAST reflects the sociological components of Adlerian psychology by eliciting apperceptive material associated with several major life-task contexts (family, peers, and school). The apperceptive stimulus materials of the CAST serve as a screen on which the child projects his or her own ideas. Themes of social interest or belonging are deduced by the stories elicited from children. The thematic material may then be classified as adaptive (positive) or nonadaptive (negative) in nature and broken down into nine Thematic scales. Similarly, the child's problem-solving style may be classified as adaptive or nonadaptive on six Problem-Solving scales.

In addition to the Thematic scales and Problem-Solving scales, the CAST also allows the evaluator to determine the frequency with which the child's stories contain thematic indicators such as sexual abuse, substance abuse, divorce, hypothetical thought (the child's ability to generate alternative stories or endings), emotionality, and self-validation (events described in the child's story actually happened).

The set of 31 stimulus cards consists of 3 cards that are administered to both boys and girls. The remaining 14 pairs of cards are designed with separate male and female versions and only one card from each pair is administered depending on the child's gender. The cards themselves are color drawings that reflect contemporary figures in contexts of modern problems. Test administration time is estimated to be 20 to 40 minutes and the test author states that scoring will require 30 minutes, with an additional 20–30 minutes for interpretation.

Tape recording of the respondent's stories is encouraged and was the method used during standardization. It is recommended that scoring of the child's responses not be attempted during the test administration session due to the complexity of the scoring criteria. The manual contains standardized directions and includes a series of five prompt questions to be asked by the examiner following presentation of each card.

Scoring is based on the words, phrases, and sentences used by the child to reflect particular themes, which are representative of the child's values, feelings, and beliefs. After scoring the Thematic Scales, Thematic Indicators, and Problem-Solving Scales, three Life Tasks (family, peer, and school) for each story are identified and are recorded on the optional Life Task Sociogram.

The manual authors provide tables to convert raw scores from each scale to *T*-Scores and four factor scores (Adaptive, Nonadaptive, Immature, and Uninvested). Confidence intervals for each of the scale scores can be calculated and plotted on a profile sheet. The examiner may analyze the obtained scores through quantitative analysis, utilizing the psychometric properties of the test, and through qualitative analysis of the child's responses, the Thematic Indicators, and behavioral observations. The manual contains numerous helpful scoring examples, appendices with common scoring terms and problem-solving examples, and an extensive case study to assist the examiner in mastering scoring procedures and interpretation.

The manual authors also provide detailed information regarding development and standardization. Standardized on a nationally representative sample of 876 school children residing in 16 states, the norm group sample was constructed to reflect the demographic characteristics of the U.S. population as described in the 1980 Census. About 7% of the sample consisted of children receiving special education services due to learning difficulties in the regular classroom setting. In addition to the standardization sample, a comparison group of 322 behavior-disordered students was tested to establish validity.

The author made a considerable effort to describe psychometric properties of the instrument and demonstrate its stability and validity. A discriminant function analysis between the scores of the behavior-disordered sample and the scores of 322 subjects randomly selected from the standardization sample provides evidence of construct validity. The analysis correctly classified 73% of the behavior-disordered sample and 80% of the standardization sample and demonstrated that the CAST discriminated between the two groups. Similarly, independent *t*-tests also showed significant differences between the two groups on 13 of the 15 scales.

The content validity and criterion-related validity of the CAST are also adequately addressed in the manual. Content validity was established by having practicing psychologists rate each stimulus card for the ability to elicit thematic content related to each of the scales. Criterion-related validity was established by correlating the scores from the CAST with the adaptive and clinical scales of the Roberts Apperception Test for Children (RATC). The resulting correlation between the CAST scores and the RATC scores indicated moderate relationships (most correlation coefficients ranged from .65 to .55) and provided sufficient evidence for the concurrent validity of the CAST.

Test reliability was assessed with interrater reliability, test-retest, split-half, and coefficient alpha. Interrater reliability was quite high with the medians of reliability coefficients for all 15 scales in the .90 range. An examination of test-retest reliability found the four factor scores, with a median reliability coefficient of .90, as more reliable than individual scale scores. Coefficient alpha, a measure of the internal consistency of a test, was calculated for three age levels, 6 to 8, 9 to 11, and 12 to 13 years. With the exception of the Immature Factor score at the 12–13 age level, coefficient alpha ranged from .90 to .93 for the four factors, indicating good internal consistency.

In summary, the CAST successfully meets its objective to be a valid, reliable, theory-based, objectively scored apperceptive instrument, supported by a nationally standardized representative sample of children, ages 6 through 13. The CAST has demonstrated good validity and reliability with school-aged behavior-disordered children and appears to be an adequate diagnostic instrument designed to assess a wide range of social, emotional, and behavioral adjustment issues. Hypotheses generated by the CAST Profile may also be useful to the examiner in developing therapeutic interventions relevant to the child's family life, peer relations, and school environment.

[74]

Children's Articulation Test.

Purpose: Designed to "assess child's ability to produce consonants, vowels and diphthongs in an in-depth relationship to other consonants and vowels."
Population: Ages 3–11.
Publication Date: 1989.
Acronym: CAT.
Scores, 7: Medial Vowels/Diphthongs, Final Consonants, Initiating Consonants, Abutting Consonants, Abutting Consonants and Vowels/Diphthongs, Connected Speech, Language Concepts.
Administration: Individual.
Price Data, 1991: $29.95 per test; $5 per 25 scoring sheets.
Time: [15] minutes.
Author: George S. Haspiel.
Publisher: Dragon Press.

Review of the Children's Articulation Test by KATHRYN W. KENNEY, Director, Kenney Associates, Certified Speech-Language Pathologists, Gilbert, AZ:

The Children's Articulation Test (CAT) consists of a scoring sheet and a 4-inch by 8-inch combined stimulus book/test manual. The test stimuli include 72 line drawings in a flip-book format. The line drawings are cartoon like and easily recognizable for the most part. Each is accompanied by the printed form of the target word which is appropriate for older children who are proficient readers. The protocol is designed to obtain productions of consonants in initial and final position of single words with a CVC syllable shape, in abutting context across word boundaries (CVC#CVC), and in connected speech. Vowel productions are obtained in single words (CVC), across word boundaries in word initial position (CVC#VC), and in connected speech. The remaining stimuli are purported to provide information on "language concepts." The items require reading the 26 letters of the alphabet in random order, identifying the numerals 1 to 10 in random order, answering questions about the names of people in a family, the names of shapes, and discriminating between shapes and letters based upon size dimensions.

The author's stated purpose is to sample a "child's production of all consonants in all phonemic contexts and any vowel/diphthong distortion" (p. i) in order to "serve as a guide to frugal, efficient treatment" (p. i). The need for a test of this design or the population for which is was intended is never specified. The CAT cannot be used as a diagnostic or screening test of articulation because normative data are not provided. Without the necessary normative data the most appropriate use of the CAT would be as a criterion-referenced test when coupled with information provided on phoneme acquisition in normally developing children (Prather, Hedrick, & Kern, 1975). When used in this manner the CAT could be described as a protocol for obtaining a phonemic inventory. As such it adds little to our knowledge base in phonological development or disorders.

The appropriateness of appending "language concepts" tasks to a test of articulation is questionable. The selection of the tasks is never addressed nor is their validity as a measure of language development among children ranging from 3 to 11 years of age. The items do not even correspond with the author's vaguely stated purpose of the test.

The author briefly addresses critical information concerning test construction, test administration, and scoring. In the description of the protocol it was indicated that the test stimuli were controlled for syllable shape and word boundary. Syllable shape is called "test pattern" and word boundary is shown by the joining of two words in the test pattern. This is the extent of the discussion on test construction. Furthermore, the rationale for the need to control these variables is never stated. The stimuli selected include easily depicted nouns, many of which are included in lists of vocabulary suitable for preschool children. Although specifics regarding the method of test construction are lacking, the comprehensive nature of the test protocol could be regarded as a strength if additional information about the test design, validity, and reliability were available. The CAT was designed to obtain consonant and vowel productions in several speaking situations including single words, abutting word pairs, and connected speech. Other test protocols are not specifically designed to accomplish this. The Goldman-Fristoe (Goldman & Fristoe, 1986) Sounds-in-Words and Sounds-in-Sentences Subtests assess speech productions in single words and in a story-retell format, but not in abutting contexts. A Screening Deep Test of Articulation (McDonald, 1976) samples speech in word initial, word final, and abutting contexts but not in conversation.

The manual provides the most information on test administration. Instructions are provided on how to use the flip book to elicit responses. It is a little awkward to read the instructions while practicing test administration because both instructions and stimuli are in the same book. The instructions on how to score responses are provided on the scoring sheet which indicates that errors should be recorded as substitutions, omissions, or distortions. No rationale is given for the use of this type of scoring system.

A serious shortcoming in the CAT is a lack of information on validity, reliability, and normative data. None are provided. The purchaser of the CAT is obtaining a test protocol, stimulus materials, and a scoring sheet. A clinician interested in obtaining a standardized instrument of articulation skills will need to purchase another instrument.

SUMMARY. The CAT could be useful as a protocol for obtaining information about consonant and vowel productions in a variety of speaking contexts. Little or no information is provided on test construction, validity, or reliability, making the CAT a poor selection as a diagnostic or screening test of articulation. Better choices would be the Goldman-Fristoe Test of Articulation (10:126) or the McDonald Screening Deep Test of Articulation (10:328), although these tests also have shortcomings.

REVIEWER'S REFERENCES

Goldman, R., & Fristoe, M. (1986). The Goldman-Fristoe Test of Articulation. Circle Pines, MN: American Guidance Service, Inc.

McDonald, E. T. (1976). A Screening Deep Test of Articulation. Tucson, AZ: Communication Skill Builders, Inc.

Prather, E., Hedrick, D., & Kern, C. (1975). Articulation development in children aged two to four years. *Journal of Speech and Hearing Disorders*, *40*, 179-191.

Review of the Children's Articulation Test by LAWRENCE J. TURTON, Professor of Speech-Language Pathology, Indiana University of Pennsylvania, Indiana, PA:

The Children's Articulation Test (CAT) is one more example of the misuse of the word "test." According to the manual, it is an all-purpose instrument that will allow a clinician to assess articulation in a standard three-item approach plus coarticulation plus language, fluency, and voice. It is in reality a simplistic screening device that relies solely on the professional knowledge base of its user. The manual is devoid of any data on reliability, validity, normative data, and standards for decision making.

The stimuli are cartoon-type images that are appealing to children and have the added bonus of the printed word to help the older child label the picture. But there is no evidence these items are age-appropriate, free of cultural bias, or discriminating for phonological disorders. The author makes unsubstantiated claims about "a phonological analysis of the child's production" (p. 1) of speech sounds but never describes how it is to be done.

This reviewer finds no reason to recommend this instrument. It is weak in terms of psychoeducational standards, phonological theory, and clinical applications. Authors and publishers should refrain from marketing stimuli like the CAT. Perhaps, however, only professional discretion in the market place will deter the proliferation of similar "tests."

[75]

Children's Attention and Adjustment Survey.

Purpose: "Designed to measure the diagnostic criteria of inattention, impulsivity, hyperactivity, and aggressiveness or conduct problems."
Population: Grades K–5.
Publication Date: 1990.
Acronym: CAAS.
Scores, 7: Inattention, Impulsivity, ADD, Hyperactivity, ADHD, Conduct Problems, DSM III-R ADHD.
Administration: Individual.
Editions, 2: School, Home.
Price Data, 1993: $30 per 25 self-scorable booklets (select School or Home form); $15 per 25 scoring profiles; $25 per manual (75 pages); $90 per starter set including manual and 25 each of Home Form, School Form, and Scoring Profile.
Time: (2–5) minutes.
Comments: Ratings by teacher or parent.
Authors: Nadine Lambert, Carolyn Hartsough, and Jonathan Sandoval.
Publisher: American Guidance Service, Inc.

TEST REFERENCES

1. Cotugno, A. J. (1993). The diagnosis of Attention Deficit Hyperactivity Disorder (ADHD) in community mental health centers: Where and when. *Psychology in the Schools*, *30*, 338-344.

Review of the Children's Attention and Adjustment Survey by CLAIRE B. ERNHART, Professor of Psychiatry, Case Western Reserve University and MetroHealth Medical Center, Cleveland, OH:

The Children's Attention and Adjustment Survey (CAAS), developed to document symptoms of attention deficit hyperactivity disorder (ADHD), was devised as part of the authors' longitudinal study of the contributions of biological, familial, health, and temperament characteristics to the development of hyperactive symptoms, particularly as these symptoms culminate in medical intervention. Reading the manual for this test is difficult because the psychometric work was an integral part of the longitudinal study. The authors weave some of their theoretical interpretations and the procedures of the overall study into the manual. This tends to interfere with presentation of the psychometric data.

The instrument consists of 31 items, with slightly different wording in two versions, called Home and School, for parent and teacher use, respectively. The items were derived from descriptions of hyperactivity in a number of articles, which are cited as the sources for the items. In addition to differentiating hyperactive from control children, it was expected that the identified behaviors would be sensitive to stimulant medication.

A four-level rating (*not at all*, *a little*, *quite a bit*, and *very much*, scored 1–4) was used for each item. After factor analyses, slightly different patterns of items from each of the two scales were classified into four nonoverlapping scales: Inattention, Impulsivity,

Hyperactivity, and Conduct Problems. (Some items retained are not scored on any scale.) Nonindependent composites are identified as Attention Deficit Disorder (ADD), Attention Deficit Hyperactivity Disorder (ADHD), and DSM III-R Attention Deficit Hyperactivity Disorder. The ADD composite score is the sum of the Inattention and Impulsivity scores; the ADHD composite is the sum of the Inattention, Impulsivity, and Hyperactivity scores. The DSM III-R ADHD score includes only the seven items from these scales listed in the DSM III-R criteria.

Evaluation of the standardization process apparently requires knowledge of the longitudinal study. This problem is most apparent as one seeks descriptions of the children involved. There were 3,674 assessments made at grades 1 through 5 of children recruited from schools in the greater San Francisco area. This total, however, may have included repeated measures on the same children over time. Some of these children were identified as hyperactive through the use of multiple criteria; several tables provide an N for the hyperactive group of 129. Another group, called the Proportional Sample, consisted of 121 boys and 62 girls. It was stated that this sample was used for studies of the structure, reliability, and validity of the CAAS scales. The specific sample used in some analyses is not specified (nor is whether or not it included the hyperactive group). Where sample sizes are given the discrepancies are not explained.

The Inattention, Impulsivity, and Hyperactivity scales each include from three to six items. Standard score conversions were provided for each scale based on a mean of 100 and a standard deviation of 15. (The sample size in this determination is not clear.) Given the small number of items and the extreme skewness of the distributions, these standard scores should not be relied upon. For example, the Impulsivity scale, with three items in the School Form, yields a standard score of 102 for its lowest possible raw score because 54% of a "representative sample" scored at this level. Furthermore, increments in standard scores with increments in raw scores are not smooth. Because they have more items, the composite scores are more reliable.

Alpha reliabilities and intercorrelations for the School Form were based on $N = 5{,}020$. Alphas ranged from .78 for Impulsivity to .94 for the longer ADHD scale. Test-retest reliabilities over 3 years ($N = 139$) ranged from .32 to .44. Data for only 135 children were used for similar analyses of the Home Form. These data yielded alphas from .40 for the Impulsivity scale to .82 for the ADD scale. The correlations between corresponding subscales of the School and Home Forms ranged from .04 for the Impulsivity scale to .34 for the Inattention scale ($N = 178$.) In a 3-year follow-up dataset ($N = 135$), the correlations between corresponding subscales ranged from .17 for the Impulsivity scale to .30 for the Conduct Problems scale. Differences between parent and teacher ratings of these behaviors are not uncommon, but they pose a major problem if these instruments are to be used diagnostically.

Norms, cutoff scores, and presumably other analyses were not differentiated by age, grade, or sex. It was stated there were no age differences. It may be that sample sizes were too small to demonstrate statistical significance. (The frequencies in each grade for girls in the Proportional Sample ranged from 7 to 13.) It was also stated there were only a few small differences between boys and girls, but other tables document significant correlations of sex and scores.

The content of the items appears valid; it is certainly consistent with much of what is written about ADHD. Given uncertainties about sample sizes and definitions of some terms and categories, it is difficult to assess the validity data provided. Use of cutoff scores yields a large number of false positives when evaluated with the data provided. The authors suggest that the false positive rate could be reduced by using a second criterion, "age of onset of symptoms."

This instrument may yield interesting findings in the authors' longitudinal study. Is it useful otherwise? The individual scales are too short to be more than crudely indicative of the dimensions. The ADHD scale might be effective as a screening instrument. Administration time is brief. Teachers could evaluate entire classes to identify children for further evaluation, but it would then be necessary to eliminate the false positives. Parents waiting in a clinic could complete the Home Form along with registration forms. As a screening device, the CAAS might identify children in need of follow-up assessment.

Because the Child Behavior Checklist (Achenbach & Edelbrock, 1988; 11:64) is well known, psychometrically well documented for use by parents and teachers, and has a well-written manual, it will probably continue to be the instrument of choice for most clinicians and researchers. The CAAS is not a strong competitor.

REVIEWER'S REFERENCE

Achenbach, T. M., & Edelbrock, C. (1988). Child Behavior Checklist. Burlington, VT: T. M. Achenbach.

Review of the Children's Attention and Adjustment Survey by STEPHEN L. KOFFLER, Managing Director, Center for Occupational and Professional Assessment, Educational Testing Service, Princeton, NJ:

The Children's Attention and Adjustment Survey (CAAS) is a rating scale system designed to evaluate behaviors related to hyperactivity in children, specifically the condition referred to as attention deficit hyperactivity disorder (ADHD) in the third revision of the American Psychiatric Association's (1987) *Diagnostic and Statistical Manual of Mental Disorders* (DSM III-R).

The scores from the CAAS can be used to (*a*) obtain a profile of a child from the perspective of both parents and teachers with respect to four critical symptoms associated with ADHD (Inattention, Impulsivity, Hyperactivity, and Conduct Problems); (*b*) determine the status of a child with respect to attention deficit disorder (ADD) or attention deficit hyperactivity disorder (ADHD); and (*c*) apply criterion scores to ratings in order to screen for further medical and psychological evaluation.

The CAAS is composed of two 31-item forms—the Home Form that is completed by a parent or other adult familiar with the child's behavior at home and the School Form that is completed by a classroom teacher or teacher's aide. Each form takes about 2 to 5 minutes to complete and the items are scored on a 4-point scale (*not at all characteristic, a little characteristic, quite a bit characteristic*, and *very much characteristic*). The items were selected based on a review of the literature on behaviors associated with characteristics of hyperactive children.

OVERALL EVALUATION. The CAAS is a very thoughtfully developed instrument. The manual is very detailed and the authors provide thorough research-based rationale and support for their approaches, decisions, and conclusions, using literature reviews and especially their own studies (the CAAS has been in development since the early 1970s when the authors began a longitudinal study of hyperactive children). There is also extensive material provided about score interpretation.

SCALES. Scales were developed and standard scores are reported for the four symptoms. The number of items in each scale is small—ranging from 3–8 for the School Form and 4–6 for the Home Form. In addition, combined scores can also be calculated for ADD and ADHD and a seventh score can be obtained for DSM III-R ADHD. The four symptom scales were developed based on a factor analysis of the items in each form. Three of the four scales on the School Form and Home Form are comparable, but not identical, in terms of items. The fourth scale (Impulsivity) includes completely different sets of items for each form.

An apparent problem with the CAAS is that some of the 31 items do not contribute to any scale. Based on the factor analysis, four items did not meet the selection criteria for inclusion in any scale for either form. In addition, four other items were included in a scale only for the School Form or for the Home Form Thus, some items in each form are not used for any scale, and it is not clear why they are included in the CAAS.

NORMS. The standardization sample for the School Form consisted of over 4,000 kindergarten to 5th grade children in public, private, and parochial elementary schools in Alameda and Contra Costa counties in California, who were involved in the authors' studies of the prevalence of hyperactivity. The standardization sample for the Home Form included children aged 6 through 14+ years who participated as control subjects in the authors' study and were never considered to be hyperactive. This latter sample was expanded to be representative of the elementary school children on whom the School Form was standardized. The standardization sample size for the Home Form was 183, far fewer than that for the School Form.

The characteristics of the standardization samples are clearly documented. There is no indication, however, that the students in the norm group are representative of a larger population. Thus, if there is something systematic about the children in the standardization samples, the generalizability of the data beyond the selected schools in California may be questionable.

Norm-referenced data are provided for each of the seven scales for the School Form and Home Form, including raw score to standard score conversions and standard scores to percentiles and stanines. The manual authors state that scaled score distributions are provided by age for the School Form. However, only one table (presumably combined across ages) is provided in the manual. For the Home Form, there were no age differences, so a single set of norms is provided (based on the 183 children in the sample). A child whose score is "not at all characteristic" for each of the three items in the Impulsivity scale would be at the 56th percentile on that scale.

The maximum raw score for each scale translates to a scaled score of 145, the highest possible scaled score. Such a translation is possible if the scale was developed with that restriction. However, the manual does not provide sufficient information about the derivation or meaning of the scaled scores and percentile ranks. In addition, the small number of items in each of the four symptom scales has an effect on the shape of the percentile distribution.

Cutoff scores are provided for both forms in order to use the scores in a criterion-referenced sense for diagnostic purposes. The cutoff score for each scale appears to have been set at the scaled score corresponding to a raw score that is one standard deviation above the raw score mean. More information is needed to describe the rationale behind the actual selection of the cutoff scores although validity related data are provided to show their appropriateness in terms of classification.

VALIDITY. Considerable construct-related and content-related evidence is provided regarding the rationale behind and process of item and scale selection. Also thorough, research-based discussions of other validity evidence are provide. The manual authors discuss a series of validity studies including: (*a*) the relationship of the CAAS scale scores/profile of physician-diagnosed hyperactive children to the data from the standardization samples; (*b*) the relationship of the CAAS scale score with external criteria, such as teacher and peer ratings of aggressiveness; teacher, parent, and psychologist ratings of hyperactivity; and cognitive test scores on measures of attentiveness, intelligence, and achievement; and (*c*) the proportions of each of these subject groups within the criterion range on the CAAS scales.

The intercorrelations range from .36 to .60 for the four Home Form symptom scales and from .67 to .74 for the School Form scales. As the authors note, the high correlations for the School Form question the independence of the four factors despite the care that they took to obtain the highest internal consistency and to eliminate items that shared variance with two or more factors. The authors, characteristic of the thoroughness they exhibit throughout the manual, provide the results of differential validity studies conducted to investigate this issue and to show support for maintaining the four scales.

RELIABILITY. The alpha reliabilities for the four symptom scales ranged from .78 (Impulsivity) to .92 (Conduct Problems) for the School Form and from .75 (Hyperactivity) to .81 (Inattention) for the Home Form. The manual also provides information about the relationship between the School Form and the Home Form and test-retest correlations over a 3-year period. The authors report factor analytic and alpha reliability studies of both forms. They assert their results indicate structural consistency across the scales. These findings contrast with the results of others who showed differences in the dimensions on School and Home scales.

SUMMARY. The CAAS has much to recommend it, even though there are some apparent problems/questions about certain aspects of the instrument. The CAAS was carefully and thoughtfully conceived and developed and includes a manual that is very detailed about all aspects of the instrument and provides clear information for users. As the authors note, the CAAS should not be the sole information source for a diagnosis or decision about an individual; however, it should provide considerable useful input for that diagnosis or decision.

REVIEWER'S REFERENCE

American Psychiatric Association. (1987). *Diagnostic and statistical manual of mental disorders—revised* (3rd ed.). Washington, DC: Author.

[76]

Children's Auditory Verbal Learning Test-2.

Purpose: Constructed to assess the presence and severity of learning and memory impairment in children.
Population: Ages 6-6 to 17-11.
Publication Dates: 1988–93.
Acronym: CAVLT-2.
Scores, 7: Immediate Memory Span, Level of Learning, Interference Trial, Immediate Recall, Delayed Recall, Recognition Accuracy, Total Intrusions.
Administration: Individual.
Price Data, 1995: $66 per complete kit including 25 test booklets and manual ('93, 68 pages); $29 per 25 test booklets; $40 per manual.
Time: (25–30) minutes.
Comments: Orally administered.
Author: Jack L. Talley.
Publisher: Psychological Assessment Resources, Inc.

Review of the Children's Auditory Verbal Learning Test-2 by JOHN O. ANDERSON, Associate Professor, Faculty of Education, University of Victoria, Victoria, British Columbia, Canada:

The Children's Auditory Verbal Learning Test-2 (CAVLT-2) is designed to be a norm-referenced test of auditory verbal learning of children from the ages of 6 years 6 months to 17 years 11 months who may have learning and memory impairment. This is an individually administered test consisting of three word lists, two consisting of 16 words and the third consisting of 32 words, from *normal* vocabulary: two for recall and one for recognition. The manual points out that the test is to be interpreted only by those with training in clinical psychology, neuropsychology, or school psychology.

The test is presented by the administrator reading a list of words to the child and requiring the child to recall as many words as possible from a particular list. First, the Learning List is read to the child five times; after each reading the child is asked to recall as many words as possible. Then the Interference List is read once and the child is asked to recall as many words as possible from the Interference List. Next, the child is asked to recall as many words as possible from the first list, the Learning List. Then the child is given a 15- to 20-minute rest period after which he or she is asked to recall as many words as possible from the Learning List. Finally, the administrator reads the Recognition List, which consists of all of the words on the Learning List, some of the words from the Interference List, and some new words. The child is asked to identify those words from the Learning List as they are read out. The administration of the CAVLT-2 requires approximately 30 minutes. A script of instructions is provided in the manual for the test administrator. The administrator records student responses on a single-use response and scoring form.

The scoring of the CAVLT-2 is based upon the number of correctly recalled or recognized words and the number of incorrect words *recalled*. Some rules are provided in regard to the correctness of words such as that plurals in the form of an additional "s" or "es" are considered correct whereas word changes (*feet* for *foot*) are incorrect. Seven scores are produced: Immediate Memory Span, Level of Learning, Interference Trial, Immediate Recall, Delayed Recall, Recognition Accuracy, and Total Intrusions. For interpretation of results the raw scores are converted to standard scores with a mean of 100 and standard deviation of 15.

Norms tables are provided for each year of age from 6 years 6 months through 17 years 11 months. The norms are based on a total of 444 children and 151 normal adolescents. Neither the population from which the children were drawn nor the sampling procedures are well described. This should cause some concern about the meaningfulness of the norms tables. Because the test is intended for children of ages 6.5 to 12, this means that the norms for each age are based on only approximately 54 children. The test is designed to identify children with impairment—according to the manual the lowest scoring 2% of the distribution (those scoring at or below a standard score of 70). So the norm groups would have only one or two of these students within each age level. This does not speak well for the norming of this test.

Another issue related to the norm group is the claim that the CAVLT-2 is unbiased in regard to race and sex. This claim is supported by statistical analyses which are briefly reported in the manual. There were no significant effects due to either sex or race with the exception of a sex difference on one scale which accounted for less than 1% of variance. However, the claim of no racial bias is not well founded given that the norm group consisted of only 58 African American children in total (10% of sample).

The manual provides guidance for the interpretation of results by means of some case studies, which consist of illustrative score profiles with interpretive comment including possible diagnoses. The presentation of interpretive comment is cautious, alerting the user to be conscious of alternative interpretations and to cross-check results with other sources of information about the child.

The manual also provides a discussion of the design parameters of test development and this is well supported by references to the research literature. Further, the research that was conducted into evaluating the word lists, the estimation of measurement error, and the convergent and discriminant validities of the CAVLT-2 are described in the manual.

In summary, the CAVLT-2 is a relatively straightforward test of verbal recall and recognition of auditory information, administered individually, and easily scored. However, the norms provided appear to be based on a sample of convenience rather than one representative of a described target population.

Review of the Children's Auditory Verbal Learning Test-2 by SHERWYN MORREALE, Director, Center for Excellence in Oral Communication, University of Colorado at Colorado Springs, Colorado Springs, CO, and RAY FENTON, Supervisor of Assessment and Evaluation, Anchorage School District, Anchorage, AK:

The Children's Auditory Verbal Learning Test-2 (CAVLT-2) examines the ability of a student or client to recall a list of 16 common words. There are five initial learning trials in which the examiner reads through the list of 16 words and the examinee endeavors to recall the words. The same process is repeated for each of the first five trials. Then, a second "interference list" of 16 other words is presented and the examinee is asked to recall that list. Next, the examinee is asked to recall the original or first list again. After a 15- to 20-minute delay, the examinee is asked again to recall the initial list, one last time. Finally, the examiner reads a 32-word list that includes the 16 original words from the first list, half the words from the interference list, and words not previously presented, and asks the examinee to indicate by a "yes" or "no" if each word was included in the initial word list.

The CAVLT-2 is essentially a test of list learning. Scores provide some insight into the extent that an individual has short and longer term retention of common words. The ability to recall such words or terms has a demonstrated relationship to general mental ability and learning ability even though the task is quite different from most school and classroom activities.

During administration, the examiner notes the words recalled by the examinee on the test booklet and counts the number of correct words and incorrect words that are recalled. Scores generated are based on the number of correctly stated or recognized words. Scores include: Immediate Memory Span (Trial 1 + Interference); Level of Learning (Trial 3 + Trial 4 + Trial 5); Recognition Accuracy (32 - errors in recall on the recognition trial); and Total Intrusions (Total of incorrect from all trials except the recognition trial). Raw scores are converted to percentile and normalized standard scores using tables included in the administrative manual. The test booklet allows standard scores to be recorded on a Summary Score Profile Chart and Learning Curve Profile which serve as the basis for interpretation.

The manual accompanying the test is clear and easy to understand. It includes a general introduction to the utility of the test, descriptions of materials, directions for administration and scoring, and detailed information on the norming sample and procedures. The information presented shows that standard methods were used in test construction and norming. Evidence is included of both convergent and discriminant validity (manual, pp. 29-31).

The CAVLT-2 is similar in form to the adult Auditory Memory Span Test (T4:231) and Auditory Sequential Memory Test (T4:233) and has similar uses and limitations. The CAVLT-2 has clear value when evaluating individuals where specific types of temporal lobe dysfunction are suspected. It has less value as a measure of overall learning, whereas a content-related measure such as the Woodcock-Johnson Psycho-Educational Battery, Revised (Woodcock & Johnson, 1991; 415) or a more general ability measure such as the Wechsler Intelligence Scale for Children—Third Edition (WISC-III; Wechsler, 1991; 412) would have more value in assessing academic attainment or potential.

The CAVLT-2 should be given consideration when the situation calls for a specialized test of recall or learning. The procedures are clear and the test is well constructed.

REVIEWER'S REFERENCES

Wechsler, D. (1991). Wechsler Intelligence Scale for Children—Third Edition. San Antonio, TX: The Psychological Corporation.

Woodcock, R. W., & Johnson, M. B. (1991). Woodcock-Johnson Psycho-Educational Battery, Revised. Chicago: The Riverside Publishing Co.

[77]

Children's Depression Scale [Second Research Edition].

Purpose: Constructed to assess childhood depression.
Population: Ages 9–16.
Publication Dates: 1978–87.
Acronym: CDS.
Scores, 10: Depressive (Affective Response, Social Problems, Self Esteem, Preoccupation with Sickness, Guilt, Miscellaneous, Total), Positive (Pleasure and Enjoyment, Miscellaneous, Total).
Administration: Individual.
Forms, 3: Child, Parent (Boys, Girls).
Price Data, 1994: $155 per complete kit including set of cards, 25 questionnaires for each sex, 50 record forms, and manual ('87, 55 pages); $26 per set of cards; $10 per 10 questionnaires (select Boys or Girls); $10 per 10 record forms; $32 per manual.
Foreign Language Edition: Australian Edition available from Australian Council for Educational Research, Ltd.
Time: Administration time not reported.
Comments: Questionnaire titles are Parent's Questionnaire [Parents of Boys, Parents of Girls].
Authors: Moshe Lang and Miriam Tisher.
Publisher: Consulting Psychologists Press, Inc.
Cross References: See T4:451 (13 references); for reviews by Howard M. Knoff and F. E. Sterling of an earlier Australian Edition, see 9:220; see also T3:397 (1 reference).

TEST REFERENCES

1. Glyshaw, K., Cohen, L. H., & Towbes, L. C. (1989). Coping strategies and psychological distress: Prospective analyses of early and middle adolescents. *American Journal of Community Psychology*, *17*, 607-624.

2. Wolchik, S. A., Ruehlman, L. S., Braver, S. L., & Sandler, I. N. (1989). Social support of children of divorce: Direct and stress buffering effects. *American Journal of Community Psychology*, *17*, 485-501.

3. Bernstein, G. A., & Garfinkel, B. D. (1992). The Visual Analogue Scale for Anxiety—Revised: Psychometric properties. *Journal of Anxiety Disorders*, *6*, 223-239.

4. Patton, W., & Burnett, P. C. (1993). The Children's Depression Scale: Assessment of factor structure with data from a normal adolescent population. *Adolescence*, *28*, 315-324.

Review of the Children's Depression Scale [Second Research Edition] by COLLIE WYATT CONOLEY, Associate Professor of Educational Psychology, University of Nebraska-Lincoln, Lincoln, NE:

The Children's Depression Scale (CDS) [Second Research Edition] has only two rather superficial changes from the previous instrument and is accompanied by the same test manual as the previously reviewed Australian Edition of the CDS (9:220). One change in the CDS [Second Research Edition] is stacking the answer cards rather than placing the answers in one of five boxes labeled from "Very Wrong" to "Very Right." The other change is the color coding of the question cards that the children read.

Because the test manual has not been updated, please see the previous reviews (Knoff, 1985; Sterling, 1985) for a thorough evaluation of the manual. Perhaps the most significant issue about the manual is that the "CDS should not be used independently for individual diagnosis" (Publisher's Forward in the test manual). However, the CDS record form and manual encourage the categorization of the individual using the CDS. The user of the CDS is unwisely encouraged by the authors to use the CDS to evaluate an individual child's depression by two pages of examples in the manual and specific space on the report form. There are decile tables and report forms based upon a sample size of 37 children (22 boys and 15 girls). There is a similar parent form norm table based upon 37 adult responses. These sample sizes are too small and probably too homogeneous to be trusted.

Similarly, the manual and report form encourage the normative interpretation of the subscales. No factor analysis is presented to substantiate the usefulness of the subscales.

Since 1983 (the date of the CDS manual's construction) there have been several studies involving the instrument. Two articles should be examined by the reader: Tisher, Lang-Takac, and Lang (1992), and Kazdin (1987). Tisher, Lang-Takac, and Lang (1992), the two authors of the CDS along with a colleague, reviewed the investigations of the CDS that should have been incorporated into the current test manual. Although the information in the 1992 article is helpful and does bolster the support of the CDS, many details were left out, probably because of space considerations—another good reason to rewrite the research information in greater depth in the test manual.

Kazdin (1987) conducted a good investigation of the CDS. He evaluated the measure to be of moderate validity and attaining an acceptable level of reliability.

The extant literature provides mixed results about the importance of age, sex, socioeconomic status, and country of residence. There are indications that depression scores inflate as children become pubescent (Tisher, Lang-Takac, & Lang, 1992). Generally, more studies indicated that adolescent girls score higher than adolescent boys. It seemed for every demographic correlate there was a contrary finding, however. The need for a well-thought-out study to norm the CDS is imperative.

Coefficient alpha internal consistency reliability estimates range from .82 to .95 (Tisher, Lang-Takac, & Lang, 1992) with coefficients of .90 and above most common. Only two measures of test-retest reliability were found. After 7 to 10 days Tonkin and Hudson (1981) found a correlation of .74 for 9–13-year-old Australian children. Comunian (1989) found a correlation of .88 after 3 weeks for 50 Italian youths aged 15 to 17 years. Although internal consistency appears good, the test-retest reliability is moderate to low-moderate.

The criterion validity of the CDS was supported by seven studies identified by Tisher, Lang-Takac, and Lang (1992). All of the studies in the literature found the CDS able to distinguish the depressed group from nondepressed groups.

Convergent/discriminant validity has also been investigated in the literature (Tisher, Lang-Takac, & Lang, 1992). Three studies correlated the CDS with the Children's Depression Inventory (Kovacs, 1981) Correlations were reported as .48 (Kazdin, 1987), .76 (Knight, Hensley, & Waters, 1988), and .84 (Rotundo & Hensley, 1985). Several other measures of well-being have been found to have moderate correlations with the CDS.

Factor analytic studies provide mixed support for the existence of two distinct scales, the Depression Scale and the Positive Scale. The Positive Scale's purpose in a depression inventory was to test for the possibility of a respondent's response set, and to provide information on an individual's ability to experience pleasure. Two factor analytic studies (Bath & Middleton, 1985; Rotundo & Hensley, 1985) support the P and D Scales, whereas Tonkin and Hudson (1981) found only one factor. No factor analysis or item analysis information was uncovered in the literature to support the six subscales. The subscales are grouped only by face validity.

The Parent CDS form asks the parent(s) to rate the child's depression. Generally, the validity of the parents' rating is mixed but lower confidence is expressed in parents' ratings. The discriminant ability of the Parent CDS appeared to be weaker. Several studies found the Parent form less able to discriminate between groups of children than the Child form (Rotundo & Hensley, 1985; Fine, Moretti, Haley, & Marriage, 1984; Moretti, Fine, Haley, & Marriage, 1985).

In comparing the level of depression identified in the children, the parents' scores were lower than the children's in the Lang and Tisher (1978) study. However, Kazdin (1987) found the parents' scores higher than the children's. This difference could be that Kazdin's sample was inpatient whereas Lang and Tisher's was not. Or it could indicate the differences between countries, or the instability of the measure.

The CDS appears to be promising as a measure of depression. However, several serious concerns need to be addressed. Tisher, Lang-Takac, and Lang (1992) suggest that the subscales need revision and reduction in number. They also suggest that some items should be discarded. The former suggestion appears clear from the literature. The latter must be based upon private data. No indication was given as to which items should be eliminated. Beyond the suggested revisions, a careful development of norms is imperative. Although the CDS child form has the potential to provide a valid and reliable measure for diagnosing the extent of depression for an individual child, that day has not yet arrived. However, there is considerable support for using the CDS child form in large group research.

REVIEWER'S REFERENCES

Lang, M., & Tisher, M. (1978). Children's Depression Scale: Research Edition. Melbourne: The Australian Council for Educational Research Limited.

Kovacs, M. (1981). Rating scales to assess depression in school age children. *Journal Acta Paedopsychiatrica, 46*, 305-315.

Tonkin, G., & Hudson, A. (1981). The Children's Depression Scale: Some further psychometric data. *Australian Council for Educational Research Bulletin for Psychologists, 30*, 11-18.

Fine, S., Moretti, M., Haley, G., & Marriage, K. (1984). Depressive disorder in children and adolescents: Dysthymic disorder and the use of self-rating scales in assessment. *Child Psychiatry and Human Development, 14*(4), 223-229.

Bath, H. I., & Middleton, M. R. (1985). The Children's Depression Scale: Psychometric properties and factor structure. *Australian Journal of Psychology, 37*(1), 81-88.

Knoff, H. W. (1985). [Review of the Children's Depression Scale]. In J. V. Mitchell, Jr. (Ed.), *The ninth mental measurements yearbook* (pp. 317-318). Lincoln, NE: Buros Institute of Mental Measurements.

Moretti, M. M., Fine, S., Haley, G., & Marriage, K. (1985). Childhood and adolescent depression: Child-report versus parent-report information. *Journal of the American Academy of Child Psychiatry, 24*(3), 298-302.

Rotundo, N., & Hensley, V. R. (1985). The Children's Depression Scale: A study of its validity. *Journal of Child Psychology and Psychiatry, 26*(6), 917-927.

Sterling, F. E. (1985). [Review of the Children's Depression Scale]. In J. V. Mitchell, Jr. (Ed.), *The ninth mental measurements yearbook* (pp. 318-321). Lincoln, NE: Buros Institute of Mental Measurements.

Kazdin, A. E. (1987). Children's Depression Scale: Validation with child psychiatric inpatients. *Journal of Child Psychology and Psychiatry, 28*(10), 29-41.

Knight, D., Hensley, V. R., & Waters, B. (1988). Validation of the Children's Depression Scale and the Children's Depression Inventory in a prepubertal sample. *Journal of Child Psychology and Psychiatry, 19*(6), 853-863.

Comunian, A. L. (1989). Some characteristics of relations among depression, anxiety, and self-efficacy. *Perceptual and Motor Skills, 69*, 755-764.

Tisher, M., Lang-Takac, E., & Lang, M. (1992). The Children's Depression Scale: Review of Australian and overseas experience. *Australian Journal of Psychology, 44*(1), 27-35.

Review of the Children's Depression Scale [Second Research Edition] by HARRISON G. GOUGH, Professor of Psychology, Emeritus, University of California, Berkeley, Berkeley, CA:

The Children's Depression Scale (CDS) is a 66-item measure developed in Australia. The current manual was published there in 1983, and reprinted in the United States in 1987 when the test was introduced in this country. For testing children, the items are on separate cards, which the child sorts into one of five categories: Very Wrong, Wrong, Don't know or not sure, Right, and Very Right. Scoring weights of 1, 2, 3, 4, and 5 are assigned to each category. The items, printed in a foldover questionnaire, can also be given to parents or other adults qualified to describe the child. The same response categories and weights are used with the observers' form.

The 66 items are intended to cover six facets of childhood depression: (*a*) negative affect, (*b*) low self-esteem, (*c*) anergy and anhedonia, (*d*) somatic complaints, (*e*) preoccupation with death or illness, and (*f*) difficulties in the management of aggression. Forty-eight of the items are negatively phrased to indicate worries or problems, and 18 are positively phrased. A "Total D Score" is based on the summed weights for the 48 negative items, and a "Total P Score" is based on the summed weights for the positive items.

In addition, there are eight rational subscales, including Affective Responses (AR), Social Problems (SP), Self-Esteem (SE), Preoccupation with own sickness and death (SD), Guilt (GL), Miscellaneous D items (MD), Pleasure and Enjoyment (PE), and Miscellaneous P items (MP). Intercorrelations among these subscales as reported in the manual are rather high. Excluding the two miscellaneous scales, the range is from .30 to .87 with a median of .66. A factor analysis of the items might well produce fewer subscales, with less redundancy.

There is also appreciable redundancy within the 66 items, in regard to content. Here are some examples: "Often school makes me miserable" and "Often my schoolwork makes me miserable"; "Often I feel that I am no use to anyone" and "Often I feel I'm not worth much"; and "Often I wake up during the night" and "I sleep like a log and never wake up during the night." Item versus total score correlations, and/or factor analysis at the item level would undoubtedly identify items that could be dropped from the measure without loss of internal homogeneity and coverage.

The only statement on reliability was the report of an alpha coefficient of .96 for the 48 D items, as computed from the protocols of 226 children and parents, pooled. What is needed, as a minimum, is a set of internal consistency coefficients for the two major scales and the eight subscales, on children's protocols along, and on parents' protocols alone. The most meaningful figure on reliability now given in the manual is the correlation of .56 between the Total D and P scales, for a sample of 96. This would give a reliability coefficient of .69, for a total score based on the sum of the D and P scales, should such an overall total score be proposed. An overall total score, whether based on the first factor in the item matrix, or on the combination of the D and P scales, would be a useful measure.

Validational evidence comes from several sources. One source resides in the content of the items, all of which clearly have something to do with feelings of depression, dysphoria, and pessimism on one side, or assertions of happiness and satisfaction on the other. An observant clinician, going over the items, would find information useful in working with the child.

A second source of validation information comes from correlations of the D score with scales from what is described as "The IPAT test." From the names of the scales, it appears that this was the 16PF (Cattell, Eber, & Tatsuoka, 1970) or one of its surrogates. Unfortunately, none of the 16PF scales or higher-order factors focuses directly on depression, which means that the correlations are not directly pertinent to the key question. Badly needed in any new manual for the CDS are correlations with other tests widely used in the study of depression and other forms of psychopathology in children, such as the Minnesota Multiphasic Personality Inventory—Adolescent (MMPI-A; Archer, 1992;238), the Child Behavior Check List and Child Behavior Profile (Achenbach & Edelbrock, 1983, 1987; T4:433), the Hopelessness Scale for Children (Kazdin, Rodgers, & Colbus, 1986), and the Personality Inventory for Children (Lachar, 1982, 1990; T4:1998).

A third source is the observed agreement between classification of children as depressed or not by a clinician and classification by the CDS. Forty children were classified by raters into 35 who were "unhappy" and 5 who were "happy" or indeterminant. This gives a baseline of .875 (35/40) for any other method of diagnosing. The CDS classification put 28 children in the "unhappy" category and 12 in the "happy" or indeterminant cell. Of these 12, only 5 were also called "happy" or indeterminant by the clinicians. The resulting hit rate of .825 (33/40) was actually lower than the baseline.

The CDS appears to be a reasonably good collection of items on depression among children that is badly in need of a psychometric tune-up, linkage to other tests frequently used with children, American norms (if use in the United States is to be continued), and better validation data than are now available.

REVIEWER'S REFERENCES

Cattell, R. B., Eber, H. W., & Tatsuoka, M. M. (1970). *Handbook for the Sixteen Personality Factor Questionnaire*. Champaign, IL: Institute for Personality and Ability Testing.

Lachar, D. (1982). *Personality Inventory for Children: Revised format supplement*. Los Angeles: Western Psychological Services.

Achenbach, T. M., & Edelbrock, C. (1983). *Manual for the Child Behavior Check List and Revised Child Behavior Profile*. Burlington, VT: Thomas M. Achenbach.

Kazdin, A. E., Rodgers, A., & Colbus, D. (1986). The Hopelessness Scale for Children: Psychometric characteristics and concurrent validity. *Journal of Consulting and Clinical Psychology*, *54*, 241-245.

Achenbach, T. M., & Edelbrock, C. (1987). *Manual for the Youth Self-Report and Profile*. Burlington, VT: Thomas M. Achenbach.

Lachar, D. (1990). Objective assessment of child and adolescent personality: The Personality Inventory for Children (PIC). In C. R. Reynolds & R. W. Kamphaus (Eds.), *Handbook of psychological and educational assessment of children* (Vol. 2, pp. 298-323). New York: Guilford Press.

Archer, R. P. (1992). *MMPI-A: Assessing adolescent psychopathology*. Hillsdale, NJ: Lawrence Erlbaum Associates.

[78]

Children's Inventory of Self-Esteem.
Purpose: Constructed to measure self-esteem.
Population: Ages 5–12.
Publication Dates: 1987–90.
Acronym: CISE.
Scores, 15: Passive, Aggressive, and Total scores for each of the following scales: Belonging, Exceptionality, Control, Ideals, Total.
Administration: Group or individual.
Price Data, 1994: $40 per complete kit including 10 reusable inventories, 50 answer sheets, 25 profile/strategy booklets, and manual ('90, 25 pages).
Time: (10) minutes.
Comments: Ratings by parents and teachers.
Author: Richard A. Campbell.
Publisher: Brougham Press.

Review of the Children's Inventory of Self-Esteem by KATHY E. GREEN, Associate Professor of Education, University of Denver, Denver, CO:

The Children's Inventory of Self-Esteem (CISE) is a relatively new test (copyright 1987–90) designed to provide information about four areas of self-esteem, their relative strength, and the child's coping mechanisms. It is intended for use by psychologists and other clinicians. Also provided are suggestions for clinicians in interviewing the child's parents and teacher, and information for parents about how to promote stronger self-esteem. The measure consists of 64 brief behavioral statements to be marked dichotomously as descriptive or not descriptive of the child. A significant adult (parent and/or teacher) completes the form. There is a version for boys, for girls, and a unisex version—which differ only in pronoun use. Administration and scoring takes 10–15 minutes and may be done individually or in groups. The CISE is not designed to be normative, thus there are no tables of average scores. Ten scales and 15 different scores can be generated assessing Belonging, Exceptionality, Control, Ideals, and Total self-esteem, and a Passive versus Aggressive subscale for each of the five components. Each behavior that is marked as true of the child is given one point, with higher scores indicating lower self-esteem. The clinician interprets test results, and can provide a booklet to parents listing suggestions to enhance self-esteem in each of the four areas. The manual is directed to clinicians, with 7 of 22 pages devoted to suggestions and descriptions of CISE use with clients.

Although the manual is written understandably, it provides very little information other than how to score the test and examples of test interpretation. No information is provided about the theoretical rationale of the measure; no information is provided regarding reliability; no information is provided regarding validity, or any technical aspect of measure development. Self-esteem and its subscales are neither defined nor differentiated. Because no norms are provided, it is difficult to use the measure diagnostically. It is suggested that children with high scores be offered counseling, but what is a "high" score? The author offers no guidelines. Because no validation information is available, it is not possible to tell the extent to which a self-esteem score would correlate with, for example, a measure of neurological impairment or other conditions that might result in some of the same behaviors.

Evaluation of behavioral descriptions on the CISE are provided by parents and teachers, rather than by the child. Self-ratings and inferred self-ratings provided by others are both conceptually and empirically distinct. In one respect, self-esteem is of a fundamentally private nature making behavioral observation insufficient as its sole reflection. And, behavior may be influenced by situational context and constraints and by developmental level as well as by self-esteem. Evaluation of self-esteem only by parents and teachers and not by the child may miss an important aspect of the construct—that is, how does the child feel about his/her coping and what is important to that child? A measure that includes *both* other- and self-perceptions may be more appropriate.

Finally, the CISE is listed as appropriate for use with children between ages 5 and 12. Each behavioral description agreed with earns one point. But at different ages, it may be developmentally appropriate to display some of the listed behaviors. The child may have low self-esteem if he/she does not behave that way. The author may have considered developmental level in instrument construction, but there is no mention of it in the manual and no accommodation for it in scoring.

In summary, the author of the CISE seems to have clear notions of the aspects of self-esteem he wants to assess and clearly wishes to have a measure easily used by clinicians with prescriptive advice attached. The measure is behaviorally oriented, and easily understood, administered, and scored. But lacking are any conceptual rationale for its development, evidence that it actually measures self-esteem or how well it does so, basis for interpretation of scores derived from its use, consideration of the child's developmental level, and consideration of the child's perspective. At this stage, the measure should be used only experimentally.

Review of the Children's Inventory of Self-Esteem by NICHOLAS A. VACC, Professor and Chairperson, Department of Counselor Education, University of North Carolina at Greensboro, Greensboro, NC:

The Children's Inventory of Self-Esteem (CISE), designed for use with children between 5 and 12 years of age, is available in three forms: one that avoids gender references and one each for boys and girls. The instrument measures a child's self-esteem by reporting scores for Belonging (B), Exceptionalities (E), Control (C), Ideals (I), and Total (T). Within each of the areas assessed there are 10 scales, resulting in a total of 15 different scores obtained for the CISE. The Belonging scale measures a child's sense of being part of something and being connected to his/her social environment. The Exceptionality scale is associated with a child's sense of uniqueness from others. The Control scale is reported to assess a child's sense of control, power, and influence over his/her life. The Ideals scale measures a child's sense of purpose, values, and models in his/her life. The Total score is the summative evaluation of a child's self-esteem. The author of the CISE purports that, in essence, the subscales are the components of self-esteem (i.e., belonging, exceptionalities, control, and ideals) and collectively yield a total measure of self-esteem. Also, the instrument measures a child's coping mechanism (Passive or Aggressive).

The CISE is designed for use by counselors, social workers, and school and clinical psychologists. It is an objectively scored paper-and-pencil test comprising 64 items which are completed by a significant adult in the child's life (e.g., parent, teacher, or someone else closely associated with the child). Administration time is approximately 10 minutes, and scoring takes approximately 2–5 minutes. The instrument is accompanied with an interpretation sheet that provides intervention strategies for helping to change a child's level of self-esteem. The instrument also includes a profile page which affords a visual representation of the scores. If multiple assessments are conducted for a child, space is included for up to four scores (e.g., instrument completion by the mother, father, teacher, and principal).

Embedded in the instrument's development is the author's point of view that children strive to fulfill their unmet needs through passive and/or aggressive strategies. The instrument interpretation is framed with a paradigm of children who take no direct action or avoid situations versus children who take aggressive actions to accomplish their goals by not considering the needs of others. The author reports the CISE was designed primarily as a practitioner's tool for use by clinicians in working with parents, teachers, and the child. As reported in the manual, a clinician can derive inferences for causes of the child's low self-esteem based on the results of the CISE. Often clinicians find information helpful that is reported from someone who can observe a child in his/her environment; these inferred ratings of self-esteem through observed behavior, however, are not comparable to those obtained through a child's self-report.

The author warns that the instrument should not be used for labeling. Rather, it should be used for understanding children. The major focus of the manual is to provide information about administering the CISE (i.e., time requirements, age levels, and instructions); scoring the scales of Belonging, Exceptionality, Control, Ideas, Total, and Passive/Aggressive; and interpreting the results (i.e., identifying a child with low-esteem, what can be done for a child, and working with adults). Missing, however, is information supporting the validity of the instrument. Although the instrument has been available since 1987, the manual is devoid of normative data and empirical psychometric data that evaluate the CISE's validity and reliability. Norms are not included, and there is no presentation of data or literature concerning (*a*) factors that may have contributed to the selection of subscales of belonging, exceptionalities, control, and ideals or (*b*) the author's suggestions that children strive to fulfill their unmet needs through passive and/or aggressive strategies.

In summary, the major problems with the CISE seem to be (*a*) vague and incomplete information concerning its technical development and (*b*) a lack of references to support its use. Aiding clinicians with an easy-to-use, time efficient instrument for identifying and remediating problems concerning a child's self-esteem is a good idea, but the CISE needs further development before it can be recommended. More information is needed concerning the constructs (B, E, C, I, T, and passive and/or aggressive coping), norms, reliability, and validity. Until more empirical data are available, the value of the instrument is highly questionable.

The author indicated that the CISE is intended as a practitioner's tool rather than a normative instrument. However, regardless of whether an instrument is designed for clinical practitioners or other uses, the test developer has an obligation to (*a*) address issues that document an instrument's value and (*b*) provide information that will assist in the interpretation of the test's results. It is unfortunate that the manual does not document empirically the author's claim of the CISE's utility. Also, the CISE's value for counseling has not been empirically documented by the author. Without evidence to support the conclusions reported in the manual, a user of the CISE is operating on "faith."

[79]

Chronicle Career Quest®.

Purpose: Designed to "help individuals identify careers related to personal interests and preferences."
Publication Dates: 1989–93.
Acronym: CCQ.
Scores: 12 G.O.E. clusters: Artistic, Scientific, Plants and Animals, Protective, Mechanical, Industrial, Business Detail, Selling, Accommodating, Humanitarian, Leading Influencing, Physical Performing.
Administration: Group or individual.
Forms, 2: S and L.

Price Data, 1994: $3.50 per specimen set including 1 each Form S and L, Interest Inventory, Interpretation Guide ('93, 20 pages), Administrator's Guide ('92, 20 pages), and Career Paths; $8 per 100 Occupational Profiles; $5.50 per 50 summary sheets; $4 per 50 Career Paths Chart; $10 per Technical Manual ('92, 30 pages); $12 per Career Crosswalk.
Time: (10–15) minutes for Interest Inventory (Form S and Form L); (10–15) minutes for Interpretation Guide (Form S and Form L); (20–45) minutes for Career Paths (Form S); (180–240) minutes for Career Paths (Form L).
Author: Chronicle Guidance Publications, Inc.
Publisher: Chronicle Guidance Publications, Inc.

a) FORM S.
Population: Grades 7–10.
Price Data: $40.50 per kit including 25 Interest Inventories, 25 Interpretation Guides, and Administrator's Guide; $18.75 per 25 reusable Career Paths (Form S).

b) FORM L.
Population: Grades 9–16 and adult.
Price Data: $59.50 per kit of 25 Interest Inventories, 25 Interpretation Guides, and Administrator's Guide; $20.75 per 25 reusable Career Paths (Form L).

Review of the Chronicle Career Quest® by LARRY G. DANIEL, Associate Professor of Educational Leadership and Research, University of Southern Mississippi, Hattiesburg, MS:

The Chronicle Career Quest® (CCQ) is a group-administered career guidance instrument that includes three major components: an Interest Inventory, a self-scoring Interpretation Guide, and a Career Paths Occupational Profile. Both short (Form S) and long (Form L) forms of the instrument are available. The instrument presents examinees with a number of occupational "activities" (i.e., items) to which examinees indicate their degree of interest. The occupational activities are categorized across 12 broad interest areas. This categorization is consistent with a structuring of occupations used by the United States Employment Service in its *Guide for Occupational Exploration*.

Form S includes nine items across each of the 12 interest areas for a total of 108 items, Form L includes 12 items across each of the 12 interest areas for a total of 144 items. The Form S items are identical to items included in Form L, with an occasional minor wording change. Form L simply includes three additional items for each interest area not included in Form S. The response format across the two forms varies slightly. Form S uses the dichotomous response options *like* (L) and *dislike* (D). Form L uses a three-option format of *uninteresting* (U), *interesting* (I), and *very interesting* (VI).

According to the CCQ's technical manual, Form S is intended for use with students in grades 7 through 9; Form L is intended for use with students in grades 10 through 12. However, the accompanying administrator's guide suggests that Form S may be used with students as late as grade 10 if occupational awareness, motivation, and/or reading level are somewhat low. Moreover, Form L may be used with students as early as grade 9 if they have at least some occupational awareness. Form L is also recommended for use with college students and other prevocational adults.

Once the Interest Inventory is completed, students are directed to complete the Interpretation Guide. The instrument may be easily scored by the examiner or by the average student. Students then use the 12 interest area scores to determine the several interest areas that represent their major occupational interests, and are referred to a listing of job titles included in the Interpretation Guide that are consistent with their interest areas. Students now proceed to the third component of the instrument, the Career Paths Occupational Profile. In this phase, they select one or more of the jobs included in the Occupational Guide listing to research further. The completed Occupational Profile includes descriptive information about such things as duties associated with the job, training requirements, salary, hours, and opportunities for advancement. All this information may be useful in assisting the student in making a career choice.

The technical manual includes information about reliability and validity studies of the Interest Inventory component of the CCQ. These data are based on responses of 1,554 examinees for Form S and 1,329 examinees for Form L. In general, the samples for these studies included a fair representation of males and females across several different geographic regions of the United States, as well as wide diversity in ethnicity generally reflective of percentages in the actual American population. Internal consistency reliabilities for the full scale of both forms were in the mid-.90s. Interest subscale reliabilities for Form L were in the .80 range, with a few subscales as low as the mid-.70s, and a few as high as .90. Alphas for subscale scores for Form S average in the mid-.70s, and range in value from .58 to.87. Content validity of the items was addressed by comparing the selected items to occupational categories as delineated by the *Guide for Occupational Exploration*. The instrument's construct validity was addressed by examining intercorrelations among the 12 interest area subscale scores across several administrations of the instrument using different samples. In general, these correlations were consistent with models hypothesized by Holland, thus supporting the validity of the interest inventory.

On the whole, the CCQ is a defensible system for assisting students in determining career opportunities. Each occupational activity (item) is rated in isolation of all others. Hence, unlike other similar instruments (e.g., Career Directions Inventory [10:44]; Kuder Occupational Interest Survey [10:167]), the CCQ yields scores that reflect *absolute* opinions about each occupational activity rather than *comparative* assessment of activities. The Career Paths Occupational Profile that ultimately results from the completion of the Interest Inventory is a logical process that allows the student to critically examine multiple facets of a given occupation. The various documents associated with the three components of the instrument are well organized and written generally at an appropriate level for middle and high school students. Another nice feature is the color coding of the three component documents across each form of the instrument (white for Form S and blue for Form L). This helps the administrator or the examinee to avoid selecting the wrong accompanying documents when moving from one phase of the CCQ process to the next.

The CCQ is not without its shortcomings, however. One questionable feature in the presentation of the Interest Inventory is the intentional grouping together of all items relative to each interest area. This procedure for ordering of the items may encourage response set. On the other hand, this procedure facilitates ease of scoring. As a solution, the authors might consider randomly arranging the items to discourage response set along with designing a computer program to sort and regroup the items into meaningful categorizations for scoring purposes.

The number of response options is also problematic. Generally, by allowing for greater response variance, a test developer increases the reliability of test items. This trend is demonstrated in the reliability data presented in the technical manual for Form S as compared to Form L. Subscale reliability coefficients for Form S, which allows for only two response options, were noticeably lower than those for Form L, which allows for three response options. The authors might even consider using additional scale steps with either of the forms to allow for even greater response variance.

An additional problem relative to reliability is the absence of studies of equivalence or stability of the Interest Inventory. Considering that the age ranges for the two forms of the instrument overlap, investigation of the equivalence of the forms across a given sample would add to the knowledge of the instrument's psychometric properties. Moreover, stability of the instrument determined by two administrations of the instrument across a relatively short interval would indicate the degree to which factors relative to a given testing occasion affect scores on the instrument.

Finally, several typographical and other related proofreading errors were noted in the text of the technical manual. Although these are by no means major flaws, they do cause some confusion in interpreting the technical information presented in the text. The authors may wish to further review and edit the technical manual to correct these errors.

Despite the aforementioned problems, the CCQ is a promising tool for educational personnel desiring to direct their students toward occupational choices. When used in conjunction with other sources of information about students, the CCQ serves well both to direct students toward appropriate interest areas and to educate students on various careers.

Review of the Chronicle Career Quest® by DONALD THOMPSON, Professor of Counseling Psychology, School of Education, The University of Connecticut, Storrs, CT:

Chronicle Guidance Publications is one of America's oldest and best known publishers of career education/development materials. The Chronicle Occupational Briefs series, Career Profile Guide, and the C-LECT computer-based career guidance system represent early and respected entries in their respective areas of career development resource materials.

The Chronicle Career Quest Interest Inventory (CQII) was first published in 1987. The current version has only minor differences in content, but since 1987 the publisher has completed reliability and validity studies and has added normative data. The technical manual that now accompanies the test package indicates a 1992 publication date. There are two forms of the Inventory. Form S is for use with students in grades 7–10, and Form L is for those in grades 9 through adult.

The CQII can be considered from two different perspectives, each of which can lead to different conclusions regarding the value of this measure. From one perspective, the CQII can be viewed as a part of a larger career exploration program for which the primary purpose is "to help users explore their interests as they seem to relate to occupations" (Administrator's Guide, p. 2). In this context, there are five primary components to the program including the CQII, Interpretation Guide, Career Crosswalk, Career Paths, and Reports to Parents. From a second perspective, the CQII can be examined strictly as a vocational interest inventory. This review will examine both roles.

The Interest Inventory is structured around the 12 interest areas that are used in the U.S. Department of Labor publication, *Guide for Occupational Exploration (G.O.E.)*. For each interest area, the respondent indicates whether they *Like* or *Dislike* (Form S), or find *Very Interesting, Interesting*, or *Uninteresting* (Form L), a series of job-related activities (e.g., Grow crops or raise farm animals). On Form S, there are nine activities for each area, whereas Form L provides 12 activities for each interest area. The inventory can be administered individually or in groups and takes about 15 minutes. The instructions and the administration and scoring processes are simple and quickly accomplished. However, there are discrepancies in the instructions for taking and scoring the inventory. Although they may appear to be minor, I believe that inconsistent terminology could cause confusion for some test takers. An example of the problem is found on Form S, where the instructions for completing the inventory state "2. If you would not like to do this activity, put an X in the D (Dislike) box. If you would like this activity, put an L (Like) in the L (Like) box." Scoring instructions in the CQ Interpretation Guide instruct the user to count the number of checkmarks in the L boxes for each scale. Because the earlier instructions said nothing about checkmarks, this would appear to be an error by the publisher. A similar inconsistency in terminology also appears in Form L, where the user is instructed to place an X in the boxes, and then later told to count the checkmarks.

A description of the development of the activities lists that make up the 12 scales is contained in the technical manual; however, this description does not indicate explicitly where the items came from, but it leaves the impression the initial pool of items was assembled by a group of experts using the *G.O.E.* as the principal source for the occupational activities. The initial item pool was then reduced and refined using several sophisticated statistical analyses.

In reviewing the activities listed for each scale, it is apparent that many of the activities represent specific job tasks that would be carried out by a worker in a particular occupation (e.g., test metals to learn how strong they are). Although it might seem the simplest and most direct manner to establish a person's interests is to simply ask, many empirical studies suggest that direct questioning is often an unreliable, inconsistent, and perhaps invalid method of determining occupational interests. This is a particular problem with younger test subjects because they lack the necessary experience and/or knowledge to know if they would like or dislike particular occupational tasks. Although many activities listed on the inventory are such that even younger students would have some personal experience with them (e.g., work with chemicals in a chemistry lab), many other activities are likely to be rather obscure for most students taking the inventory (e.g., use a radiation machine to treat hospital patients). I suspect very few 7th to 10th graders understand enough about the nature of this activity to determine whether they would like or dislike it. It is possible that students will respond to these items based on either inadequate or erroneous information.

The demographic data reported for the norm sample in the technical manual show good diversity in terms of geographic location, ethnicity, and sex. However, the manual authors provide very limited information about how the samples were drawn, and no information about the school sites other than the states from which samples were drawn. No indication is given whether the samples were drawn randomly from large representative groups at each site, or if intact class groups were used. The publisher supplied additional data regarding the norm samples that indicate the school sites were generally representative of American schools, but were somewhat skewed to urban schools or loosely defined "suburban" schools which have much higher minority percentages than would characterize the U.S. population as a whole. Few rural school sites were used as part of the sample. These factors seem to account for the overrepresentation of African American and Hispanic persons in the sample. No further information regarding how the samples were drawn at each site was provided except for a statement about on-site coordinators, preferably school counselors, who will be responsible for identifying an in-school sample.

The only instance of reliability data reported for the CQII is Cronbach's alpha. This form of reliability establishes only whether the individual scales are internally consistent. The alpha coefficients reported show a range of .58 to .95 for Form S, and .74 to .96 for Form L on the 12 interest areas. No test-retest reliability to determine the stability over time of the scale scores is reported.

For interest inventories, two primary techniques are used to establish validity. Empirical or criterion-related validity techniques determine whether the test can effectively predict future behavior or performance on a similar well-validated measure. The other primary type is construct validity (sometimes called homogeneous). The CQII reports only construct validity data, and the focus of the examination of the construct is on the internal consistency of each scale. To establish the construct validity, the publisher subjected scores from the 12 subscales to a factor analysis and discarded all items that did not meet a minimum factor loading requirement. In essence, this established that each item on the scale was strongly related to the other items on the scale, and therefore the items were all related to the same construct. This is a common practice in instrument development and is an empirically acceptable technique. In the absence of other data that establish exactly what the scale is measuring, it may have limited utility. The intercorrelation matrix of scale scores does show generally low to moderate correlations between the 12 scales, suggesting they are in fact measuring different dimensions.

It may seem a minor issue, but I was concerned about the fact the technical manual had two errors among the citations listed in the text. In one case, a reference was used in the text and not listed in the References, and in another, the citation had a discrepant date with the Reference page.

In summary, the Chronicle Career Quest is a good tool for initiating career exploration when it is used in conjunction with the other materials provided as part of the package, and with the direct assistance of a counselor or career development specialist. The major advantages of the CQ include tight integration with other Chronicle career resource materials, low cost, and quick and easy administration and scoring. The psychometric characteristics of this measure, although perhaps adequate for a counseling or career development tool, do not meet the more rigorous standards one should expect from a standardized interest inventory that would be used to help young people make occupational choices. The reliability data are limited, and consist of only a measure of internal consistency and there are no indications that an individual's scores would have stability over time. More importantly, there is no empirical evidence regarding the effectiveness of this measure as a predictor of occupational satisfaction or success.

[80]

CID Preschool Performance Scale.

Purpose: Designed to measure the intelligence of hearing-impaired and language-impaired children.
Population: Hearing- and language-impaired and normal children ages 2 to 5-5.
Publication Date: 1984.
Scores, 7: Manual Planning, Manual Dexterity, Form Perception, Perceptual-Motor Skills, Preschool Skills, Part/Whole Relations, Total.
Administration: Individual.
Price Data, 1994: $750 per complete kit including manipulatives for subtests, manual (29 pages), and 30 recording booklets; $25 per manual; $30 per 30 recording booklets.
Time: (40) minutes.
Comments: Adaptation of the Randall's Island Performance Series.
Authors: Ann E. Geers, Helen S. Lane, and Central Institute for the Deaf.
Publisher: Stoelting Co.

Review of the CID Preschool Performance Scale by BRUCE A. BRACKEN, Professor of Psychology, The University of Memphis, Memphis, TN:

The Central Institute for the Deaf (CID) Preschool Performance Scale was designed as a nonverbal measure of intelligence for children between the ages of 2-0 and 5-5 years. The scale is composed of six subtests that were derived from the Randall's Island Performance Series (Poull, 1931), a series of tasks intended as measures of intellectual functioning for use with mentally retarded children who were assessed at the Randall Island Institution in New York City.

Ostensibly, the scale was normed on 978 children who had been administered the Randall's Island Performance Series between 1965 and 1980. There is no description of the normative sample's characteristics (e.g., race, reason for referral, socioeconomic status, geographic representation), except age, gender, and child's hearing level. In essence, the sample is one of convenience, drawn from existing files from a single site in New York. Also, because the so-called norms were selected from existing cases dating back as far as 1965, the sample is outdated and ranges between 14 and 29 years in age. In fact, collection of the normative data spanned a 15-year period, and, arguably, the norms were outdated when the last case was gathered. Yet, the scale was not published for another 4 full years (i.e., 1984)!

The test manual authors provide virtually no information about item development, subtest structure, or theoretical underpinnings. The instrument appears to be largely atheoretical and is little more than a reanalysis and an unspecified restructuring of items from the Randall's Island Performance Series. The subtest names and tasks are historically fascinating and well dated (e.g., Montessori Cylinders, Pintner Two Figure Board, Wallin Pegs, Decroly Picture Matching, Seguin Formboard, Knox Cubes, Binet Drawings and Paper Folding, Stutsman Puzzles). As such, the scale is a historical relic; the stimulus materials are as dated as the names imply, with outdated stimulus pictures and objects.

In terms of technical adequacy, the manual authors cite minimal evidence, and that which is presented does not engender much confidence in the instrument. No measure of internal consistency is reported in the manual, but the test-retest coefficient for the overall IQ (over a 4-month to 3-years 5-month interval) was .71 for 92 children. No mean score comparison between pretest and post-test was presented and no stability coefficients were presented for the six subtests.

As evidence of validity, the manual authors report correlations between chronological age and CID test performance for each of the six subtests (range = .52 to .64). No age correlations were presented for overall IQ. A predictive validity study comparing the CID with the Wechsler Intelligence Scale for Children—Revised (WISC-R) is presented in the examiner's manual (n = 112). The study authors report a correlation of .485 between the CID overall IQ and the WISC-R Performance IQ (PIQ). No subscale correlations were presented, and no mean score comparisons were made between the average CID and PIQ. The scale evidences weak subtest floors at the youngest age level but improved floors beyond this lowest level. All of the subtests, except Form Perception and Manual Dexterity, have ceilings that exceed two standard deviations at all age levels.

No information is provided covering how the test should be interpreted, how the scores should be used, what the examiner should do when subtest administrations are accidentally spoiled, or similar such situations. Also, no examiner qualifications or level of training necessary to successfully use the instrument is described. In fact, the 29-page CID manual reveals very little information, other than the directions for administering the six subtests.

Given the instrument's dated and poorly defined normative sample, its outdated stimulus materials, and the absence of relevant information presented in the manual about theoretical underpinnings, technical adequacy, and interpretative guidelines, I would suggest that this instrument is no longer suitable for clinical practice. I can think of no justifiable reason why this instrument should be used, especially when one considers the alternatives that exist.

REVIEWER'S REFERENCE

Poull, L. E. (1931). *The Randall's Island performance series*. New York: Columbia University Press.

Review of the CID Preschool Performance Scale by ALBERT C. OOSTERHOF, Professor of Educational Research, Florida State University, Tallahassee, FL:

The Central Institute for the Deaf (CID) Preschool Performance Scale is an adaptation of the Randall's Island Performance Series. The latter is a test battery designed to measure the intelligence of mentally retarded preschool children at Randall's Island in New York City. The Randall's Series was developed in 1931 and is no longer available. The Central Institute for the Deaf (CID) acquired the copyright for the Randall's Series, and modified the test mostly by revising directions used during its administrations. The intent of the CID adaptation was to create an intelligence measure that could be used with young children who had hearing impairments. The adaptation involved redeveloping the instructions to the examinees so that the instrument can be administered without verbal directions.

The instruction manual to this test is well organized and clearly written. The introduction provides a background to this test and a limited discussion of the instrument's reliability and validity. Then separate chapters describe how to administer tasks associated with each of the scale's six subscales. The nonverbal directions to each task are well thought out and easy to understand. Optional verbal directions are also provided.

The manual also contains tables for deriving scaled scores for each of the six subtests. Separate tables are provided for different age groups, with each table spanning a range of 6 months. The scaled scores are said to have means and standard deviations of 10 and 3 respectively. The standardization sample, however, is inadequately described for one to know to which population these scales will generalize. The manual authors state only that norms are based on 978 children between ages 2 and 5½ years, containing approximately equal numbers of boys versus girls and hearing-impaired versus normal-hearing children. Interestingly, scaled scores for two of the subtests, Manual Dexterity and Preschool Skills, do not increase consistently with age. Children in the 2½- to 3-year age group scored higher than children in the next older age group.

Although a table is also provided for converting the sum of a child's six scaled scores to a deviation IQ score, these IQ scores are of no use. The norms are based on an inadequately described sample, and no meaningful evidence that the test provides a valid measure of intelligence is offered.

Evidence that this test measures intelligence is limited to two points. First, the performance tasks included in the test are those of the Randall's Island Performance Series. The Randall's Series, however, was developed in 1931 and does not take advantage of advances in psychology since that time. Also, the Randall's Series is no longer available. The developers of the Preschool Performance Scale should, but do not, assume responsibility for conveying evidence of validity that may generalize to the present instrument.

The correlation between scores on the Preschool Performance Scale and scores on the Wechsler Intelligence Scale for Children—Revised (WISC-R) provides the second evidence of validity. A correlation of .485 with the Wechsler scales was reported for a subsample of 112 children. This suggests, however, that only 24% of the variability in scores on the CID instrument is associated with variability of scores on the WISC-R. Also, no indication is given as to how the 112 children included in the validation study were selected from the 978 children in the standardization sample. Nor is evidence given that the WISC-R is an appropriate criterion variable for the present instrument or for the hearing-impaired population for which the Preschool Performance Scale is designed.

Evidence of reliability is quite weak. A test-retest reliability coefficient of .71 is reported. Children included in this reliability study are described only as being those at CID who had taken the test twice. For purposes of estimating test-retest reliability, these children are combined into a single group even though the interval between the child's test and retest ranged from 4 months to 3½ years. In addition to providing a more controlled study of the instrument's stability, the test developers should establish estimates of internal consistency.

In conclusion, unless the developers of the CID Preschool Performance Scale provide a more careful description of their norm group, users at other sites cannot meaningfully use the scaled scores. Evidence of validity presented in the manual is extremely limited. Essentially no evidence is presented that the Preschool Performance Scale measures the intelligence of children with hearing impairments. Instead of trying to establish this instrument as a measure of intelligence, the developers might better concentrate on helping the user interpret the performance of children on the various specific tasks they are asked to perform. These tasks as well as the nonverbal directions to the children are carefully described in the manual.

[81]

Clinical Rating Scale.

Purpose: Designed to type marital and family systems and identify intervention targets.

Population: Couples and families.
Publication Dates: 1980–1990.
Acronym: CRS.
Scores: 3 ratings (Cohesion, Change, Communication) yielding Family System Type.
Administration: Group.
Price Data, 1990: $5 per manual (includes unlimited copying privileges).
Time: Administration time not reported.
Author: David H. Olson.
Publisher: Family Social Science.

TEST REFERENCES

1. Olson, D. H. (1991). Commentary: Three-dimensional (3-D) circumplex model and revised scoring of FACES III. *Family Process, 30*, 74-79.
2. Seelig, W. R., Goldman-Hall, B. J., & Jerrell, J. M. (1992). In-home treatment of families with seriously disturbed adolescents in crisis. *Family Process, 31*, 135-149.
3. Cluff, R. B., & Hicks, M. W. (1994). Rejoinder: Superstition also survives: Seeing is not always believing. *Family Process, 33*, 479-482.
4. Olson, D. H. (1994). Commentary: Curvilinearity survives: The world is not flat. *Family Process, 33*, 471-478.

Review of the Clinical Rating Scale by STUART N. HART, Associate Professor of Counseling and Educational Psychology, Indiana University-Purdue University at Indianapolis, Indianapolis, IN:

The Clinical Rating Scale (CRS) is an instrument, based on the Circumplex Model, for the clinical assessment of families. Through its use the clinician is to be helped to "describe the type of marital and family system and also identify what characteristics might be most useful to focus on in terms of intervention" (manual, p. 1).

The manual for the CRS is incomplete and inadequate. The psychometric properties of the CRS are not adequately clarified. The manual contains brief and superficial description of the circumplex model and somewhat ambiguous directions for administration and scoring. Guidance for interpretation and application of findings is not given. Some information on reliability is provided (discussed below), but validity and normative data are not mentioned. The 1993 manual includes seven pages of material in addition to the title page: two pages of instructions, three pages of tables detailing the categories and subcategories of the three major dimensions of the scale, one page (actually about one-third page) dealing with one reliability study, and a page of references. An insert in the 1993 manual, originally printed within the 1992 manual, presents a diagram of the 16 subtypes of the circumplex model and a "family profile" to plot results. It is not possible to understand, appreciate, or evaluate the CRS based on the material provided in the manual; one must investigate the literature associated with the model and instrument to even begin to do so.

The CRS is intended to provide "an opportunity for clinicians and families to classify a family into the Circumplex Model derived from their observations of a family based on clinical interview or interaction tasks" (Thomas & Olson, 1993). The Circumplex Model postulates that the dimensions of Family Cohesion and Flexibility (originally called "adaptability"), mediated by the Family Communication, clarify major differences between families that function in healthy and unhealthy ways. "Family cohesion is defined as the 'emotional bonding that family members have toward one another,'" and "family adaptability is defined as 'the ability of a marital or family system to change its power structure, role relationships, and relationship rules in response to situational and developmental stress'" (Thomas & Olson, 1993). The three major scales of the CRS deal with these dimensions through attention to subscales: (*a*) Family Cohesion includes six subscales: emotional bonding, family involvement, marital relationship, parent-child relationship, internal boundaries, and external boundaries; (*b*) Family Flexibility includes five subscales: leadership, discipline, negotiation, roles, and rules; and (*c*) Family Communication includes six subscales: listener's skills, speaker's skills, self-disclosure, clarity, continuity/tracking, and respect and regard. Additionally, the authors suggest that to be able to adequately describe some families it may be necessary to consider the special characteristics of individuals emotionally separated from the rest of the family who they label "disengaged individuals" (i.e., mother, father, child[ren]) and/or an enmeshed subsystem of "coalitions" (i.e., mother-son, mother-daughter, father-son, father-daughter, son-daughter, same sex siblings).

Clinical assessment using the CRS, according to the authors, requires evaluating a couple or family "in terms of each of the concepts for each dimension" (p. 1) and can be conducted through a semistructured interview. Although "no specific clinical techniques or format" (p. 1) are recommended, it is suggested that the couple or family be encouraged to discuss with each other how they would handle issues such as time, space, or discipline; and that they be asked to describe a typical week's daily routines, conflict, and decision making. Four categories, each with 2 scale points, are provided for evaluation for two of the dimensions: Cohesion (i.e., disengaged, separated, connected, enmeshed) and Flexibility (i.e., rigid, structured, flexible, and chaotic). Scale points number from 1–8 across these categories. Three evaluation categories, each with 2 scale points, are provided for the dimension of communication: low, facilitating, and high; with scale points numbered 1–6 across these categories.

The preparation recommended for doing a clinical assessment is to "review all the concepts and descriptions on the rating scale for cohesion, flexibility (change), and communication" (manual, p. 1). Although not further clarified in the manual, in the judgment of this reviewer, to adequately apply this instrument a clinician would have to complete training similar to that demanded by the author for raters to develop sufficiently high interrater reliability; review all available literature on the Circumplex Model and the CRS; view movies and/or tapes presenting families exhibiting various cohesion, flexibility and communication characteristics and apply the instrument in making judgments; and discuss ratings, particularly difficult or conflicting ratings, with other raters. As described by Thomas and Olson (1993) this process appeared to require substantially more than 8 hours, including review and evaluation of 20–25 families.

The process for scoring and interpreting the CRS as presented in the manual is quite ambiguous. After completing the interview the clinician is to "carefully read the descriptions for each concept and select the scale value that is most relevant for that couple or family as a unit" (p. 1). Rather than summing the subscale ratings, the clinician is told to produce a "global rating" based on "an overall evaluation or gestalt" for each of the three major dimensions. The process is further complicated by the fact that (*a*) some subcategories include subdivisions that do not represent unitary dimensions, and may not covary in predictable ways (e.g., Cohesion subcategory "family involvement" includes both interaction and affective responsiveness; Communication subcategory "listener's skills" includes both empathy and attentive listening); (*b*) little guidance is provided for the possibility that quite dramatic differences may exist in the characteristics of members of a family; and (*c*) the assumed curvilinear nature of the cohesion and flexibility scales, which has been questioned (Fristad, 1989) may create confusion (i.e., global judgments are to fall along a very low to very high continuum, which doesn't reinforce the curvilinear notion). An extended preparation process with a feedback loop is likely to be required to support confidence and accuracy in achieving this goal.

Interpretations appear to emphasize determining through the global judgment whether the family is functioning in the balanced range (i.e., flexibly or structurally separated and/or connected), midrange (i.e., flexibly or structurally disengaged and/or enmeshed, rigidly or chaotically separated and/or connected), or extreme range (i.e., rigidly or chaotically disengaged and/or enmeshed). The Communication Scale and The Coalitions and Disengaged Individuals: Cohesion Subscale are available to encourage consideration of the manner in which these facilitate or mediate the global ratings for Cohesion and Flexibility dimensions. The only guidance provided by the manual toward applying findings toward intervention, a major stated goal, is found in titles and descriptions of references (see particularly, Olson, Russell, & Sprenkle, 1989).

Interrater agreement and correlation coefficients, and internal consistency reliability coefficients produced through one study of 192 families are provided in the manual. Interrater agreement (within 1 scale point for 8-point scale on global ratings) percentages range from 91 to 97; the interrater correlations range from .75 to .86, and the internal consistency alpha coefficients range from .94 to .97. These are all quite good. Consistency over time, assessment-reassessment reliability results, were not reported in the manual or other sources considered. If the CRS is to be used to guide and to monitor intervention, assessment-reassessment reliability must be determined.

Although no validity study information is presented in the manual, in another source Thomas and Olson (1993) cite factor analysis research supporting the conceptual base for the CRS; a series of previously conducted studies supporting the discriminant power of the FACES (I, II, III) self-report measure applying the Circumplex Model; and recent research with the CRS indicating effectiveness in discrimination between problem/clinical families and control groups. In the recent research using the CRS, clinical/problem group families tended to be judged as extreme on cohesion and flexibility as separate and combined factors, whereas control group families tended to be judged as balanced; and control families and families rated as balanced on cohesion and/or flexibility were found to be significantly more likely to have good communication than were clinical/problem families and those rated as extreme, respectively. It is important to note, however, that the procedure used in the Thomas and Olson (1993) research for applying the CRS required rigorous preparation of evaluators and evaluation of the video tapes of family behavior carrying out structured interaction and discussion tasks, none of which are required or encouraged for application in the CRS manual. The authors of this study recognized the instrument is most appropriate for two-parent families (e.g., the Cohesion subscale marital relations item presumes a two-parent family) and that gender differences for single-mother families may require differential coding of the flexibility subscales. The curvilinear relationship between family functioning and cohesion/flexibility was supported by the Thomas and Olson findings. This attribute deserves further study in light of the strong criticism it has received (Beavers & Voeller, 1983; Fristad, 1989).

The CRS has shown some promise for assisting clinicians and therapists in describing family characteristics associated with important family dimensions. The information provided in the manual for this instrument does not do justice to the years of work that have been devoted to refining the Circumplex Model and to translating it into an assessment tool; it simply does not provide sufficient information for judging the adequacy, usefulness, or proper application and interpretation of the CRS. Interested parties must pursue this information in journal articles and book chapters. It is strongly recommended the authors remedy this situation. Additionally, it is important to note that family assessment is considered to have generally "lagged behind the development of family therapy and concepts" (Fristad, 1989). Those interested in family assessment of the nature discussed here are advised to review carefully the debates and competing models and instruments associated with this topic (Beavers & Voeller, 1983; Fristad, 1989; Green, Kolevzon, & Vosler, 1985a, 1985b).

REVIEWER'S REFERENCES

Beavers, W. R., & Voeller, M. N. (1983). Family models: Comparing and contrasting the Olson Circumplex Model with the Beavers Systems Model. *Family Process, 22,* 85-98.

Green, R. B., Kolevzon, M. S., & Vosler, N. R. (1985a). The Beavers-Timberlawn Model of family competence, and the Circumplex Model of family adaptability and cohesion: Separate, but equal? *Family Process, 24,* 385-398.

Green, R. G., Kolevzon, M. S., & Vosler, N. R. (1985b). Rejoinder: Extending the dialogue and the original study. *Family Process, 24,* 405-408.

Fristad, M. A. (1989). A comparison of the McMaster and Circumplex family assessment instruments. *Journal of Marital and Family Therapy, 15,* 259-269.

Olson, D. H., Russell, C. S., & Sprenkle, D. H. (Eds.). (1989). *Circumplex Model: Systemic assessment and treatment of families.* New York: Haworth Press.

Thomas, V., & Olson, D. H. (1993). Problem families and the Circumplex Model: Observational assessment using the Clinical Rating Scale (CRS). *Journal of Marital and Family Therapy, 19,* 159-175.

Review of the Clinical Rating Scale by STEVEN W. LEE, Associate Professor of Educational Psychology and Research, University of Kansas, Lawrence, KS, and ERIC ROBINSON, Certified School Psychologist, Omaha, NE:

The Clinical Rating Scale (CRS) for the Circumplex Model (CM) of Marital and Family Systems was developed to assist family therapists in describing both problem and nonproblem families. There are three primary dimensions of the CRS: couple and family cohesion, couple and family adaptability (change), and family communication. Couples or families are rated on items within each dimension as well as an independent global rating for each dimension. All item and global ratings are to be done by an evaluator (i.e., therapist) after interviewing a couple or family.

All items on the couple and family cohesion dimension are assessed on the range from extremely low cohesion (disengaged) to extremely high cohesion (enmeshed) (Thomas & Olson, 1993). Items on the couple and family adaptability dimension are evaluated on a range of *extremely rigid* to *extremely chaotic*. The third dimension features family communication items that are rated on level of facilitativeness (low versus high). It is posited that the level of facilitativeness (for a family or couple) as noted on this scale is related to movement on the two other primary dimensions.

The manual indicates that a clinical interview with the couple or family unit should be used to elicit the information needed to complete the CRS. Olson states, "Before doing a clinical assessment of a couple or family, the therapist or interviewer should review all the concepts and descriptions on the rating scale for cohesion, adaptability (change) and communication" (manual, p. 1). There is no specific clinical format recommended for the interview or any specific training required to use the CRS. Instead the author gives examples of issues to investigate that include how daily routines are handled with the family and general issues such as time and space. After the interview has been completed, the evaluator is directed to "carefully read the descriptions for each item (concept) and select the scale value that is most relevant for that couple or family as a unit" (manual, p. 1). According to the manual, a global rating, based on an overall evaluation, should be made for each of the three dimensions, and this classification should be based on how the couple or family functions as a group. If one or more persons appears to function differently from the rest of the family, the therapist can complete a checklist from the Coalitions and Disengaged Individuals: Cohesion Subscale (CDI), which is presented in the manual. The directions are unclear as to how "disengaged" a person must be in order to use the checklist.

Information in the manual is vague on how an examiner incorporates the information from the CRS into the Circumplex Model. Olson states, "The global rating should be based on an overall evaluation or gestalt rather than a sum of the sub-scale ratings" (manual, p. 1). Yet he does not elucidate how this should be accomplished. Additionally, the manual contains no information on approaches for intervention.

Reliability information presented in the manual is limited to a single interrater reliability study using a sample of 192 families. There are no demographic data nor any indication of randomization of the sample. In the manual, Olson indicated an alpha reliability of .95 for Cohesion, .94 for Adaptability, and .97 for Communication. Interrater agreement between two raters used in this analysis was 95% for Cohesion, 91% for Adaptability, and 97% for Communication (agreement was defined as within one scale point of global ratings). No specific information was provided on the amount of training (if any) that was provided for the raters, or how the families were interviewed.

Thomas and Olson (1993) attempted to assess the reliability and validity of the CRS with a sample of 182 families (324 parents, 298 children) from an upper midwest metropolitan area. One hundred and twenty two of the families were divided into three separate clinical (problem) groups, and the remaining 60 families were no-problem, controls. All families participated in a $1^1/_2$-hour session where they completed a variety of tasks including a 30-minute Family Interaction Tasks (FIT), which was videotaped. The FIT consists of seven tasks, which included discussion tasks such as having parents describe a typical evening, spending $100 as a family, and family and couple strengths. The FIT videotapes were used to determine reliability. Interrater reliability (Pearson correlations) were .83 for Cohesion, .75 for Adaptability, and .86 for Communication. Alpha (Cronbach) scores indicated .95 for Cohesion, .94 for Adaptability, and .97 for Communication. These results appear to indicate adequate interrater reliability when using the FIT; however, interrater reliability using the clinical interview was not evaluated in this study.

To assess construct validity of the CRS, a factor analysis (varimax rotation) was done using all CRS subscale items and an analysis of the ability of the CRS to correctly classify "clinical" and "non-clinical" families was conducted. The factor analysis was based on the rater's mean scores for Global Cohesion, Global Adaptability, Global Communication, and all 16 subscale items. The Global Cohesion scale and three of the six subscales loaded exclusively on Factor 1 (Cohesion). Global Adaptability and all five Adaptability subscale items loaded exclusively on Factor 2 (Adaptability), and Global Communication and all five Communication subscale items loaded exclusively on Factor 3 (Communication). In general, the factor loadings of the CRS was congruent with the theoretical construction of the instrument.

Thomas and Olson (1993) presented information on the ability of the CRS to discriminate accurately between problem or clinical and nonclinical families. The CRS Cohesion dimension reportedly did differentiate between the control and clinical families. However, an analysis of the classification rate showed that 34% of the clinical families were found to be "balanced" on the Cohesion dimension. Similar results were found on the Adaptability dimension.

In summary, the Clinical Rating Scale (CRS) was developed to assist therapists in describing both problem and nonproblem families in relation to the Circumplex Model of Marital and Family Systems (CM). The author indicates the therapist should complete a clinical interview and use the CRS to determine how the family functions in relation to the three domains of Cohesiveness, Adaptability, and Communication. The manual does not contain a specific format for interviewing families and is vague on how to use the information once the CRS is completed. The manual author provides a single reliability study, with no demographic information, and no validity studies. Thomas and Olson (1993) evaluated the interrater reliability and construct validity using the CRS, yet did not use the interview format as described in the manual, instead using independent raters who viewed videotapes of family interactions. The authors report adequate interrater reliability and construct validity across the three dimensions. Thomas and Olson (1993) found significant differences between problem families (clinical) and the nonproblem families (control); however, a variety of methodological problems with this study and a lack of corroborating validity data relegates the CRS for use only as an informal instrument to assist family therapists.

REVIEWER'S REFERENCE

Thomas, V., & Olson, D. H. (1993). Problem families and the Circumplex Model: Observational assessment using the Clinical Rating Scale (CRS). *The Journal of Marital and Family Therapy, 19*, 159-175.

[82]

Clinical Support System Battery.

Purpose: "Designed for use with the potential school dropout student, and/or with chemical dependency rehabilitation programs."
Population: High school–adult.
Publication Dates: 1990–91.
Administration: Individual.
Time: Administration time not reported.
Comments: May be used with or without biofeedback equipment. Programs designed as a companion piece to the initial Life Style Analysis Test.
Author: Russell N. Cassel.
Publisher: Psychologists and Educators, Inc.

a) LIFE STYLE ANALYSIS TEST.
Purpose: To assess one's degree of wellness in relation to one's emotional stress.
Acronym: LFSTYLE.
Scores, 10: Positive Life Style (Self-Esteem, Satisfaction, Assertiveness, Involvement, Total Ego Strength), Negative Life Style (Loneliness, Anxiety, Health Worry, Depression, Total Stress Load).
Price Data, 1990: $11 per manual ('90, 38 pages); $25 per program diskette; $11 per added diskette.

b) NEURAL FUNCTIONING ASSESSMENT.
Purpose: To assess anxiety level.
Scores, 5: Relax, Disproof [guided imagery dissonance profile], Neural [neural personality cluster], Emote [unconscious need presence], Riskage [estimated coronary age].
Price Data: $11 per manual ('91, 36 pages); $25 per program diskette; $11 per added diskette.
Comments: Requires TRI-BI-SENSOR with 4 biofeedback units (price data available from publisher).

c) THE NEED GRATIFICATION ASSESSMENT TEST.
Purpose: "To assess level of need status."
Scores, 12: Home and Family, Religion and Inner Development, Affiliation and Social, Law and Security, School and Learning, Romance and Psychosexual, Sports and Risk Taking, Health and Safety, Travel and Relaxation, Aesthetic and Beauty, Money and Productivity, Survival and Pollution.
Price Data: $11 per manual ('90, 11 pages); $25 per program diskette; $11 per added diskette.

d) THE IDENTITY STATUS TEST.
Purpose: Assesses perception of "to love and to be loved."
Scores, 7: Intimate and Private, Heart and Soul, Committed Fully, Personal Acceptance, Compassion and Forgiveness, Romanticism, Total.
Price Data: $11 per manual ('91, 16 pages); $25 per program diskette; $11 per added diskette.

e) THE INDEPENDENCE VERSUS REGRESSION TEST.
Purpose: Assesses perception of unlicensed freedom in relation to perception of exaggerated constraints.
Scores, 8: Freedoms (Coping Style, Conforming, Sympathetic, Locus of Control), Constraints (Rationalization, Regression, Repression, Escapist).
Price Data: $11 per manual ('91, 14 pages); $25 per program diskette; $11 per added diskette.
f) THE COSMIC CONSCIOUSNESS TEST.
Purpose: Measures freedom to "escape earthly bounds and achieve cosmic consciousness."
Scores, 7: Mutuality and Synergy, Spirituality and Love, Loyalty and Pride, Caring and Commitment, Depersonalization and Reward, Parent/Child Role, Total.
Price Data: $11 per manual ('90, 7 pages); $15 per program diskette; $11 per added diskette.

Review of the Clinical Support System Battery by WILLIAM L. CURLETTE, Professor of Counseling and Psychological Services, Professor of Educational Policy Studies, and Director of the Educational Research Bureau, Georgia State University, Atlanta, GA:

The Clinical Support System Battery by Russell N. Cassel consists of a series of computerized tests to assess aspects of an individual's holistic health status. Actually, there are six different batteries of tests within the Clinical Support System, all of which relate to the underlying theme of holistic health. These batteries are Life Style Analysis, Neural Functioning Assessment, Need Gratification Assessment, Identity Status, Independence versus Regression, and Cosmic Consciousness. Given the extensive number of tests and subtests in each battery, the reader is referred to the listing that accompanies this review for the names of tests and subtests within a battery. Each battery is described in its own manual and also discussed in an overall manual for the Clinical Support System.

To obtain an understanding of this system, consider the first battery listed in the Clinical Support System, the Life Style Analysis Battery consisting of two tests: Positive Life Style and Negative Life Style. The four subtests for the Positive Life Style Test (Self-Esteem, Satisfaction, Assertiveness, and Involvement) are combined to yield a total score for Positive Life Style, described as "Ego Strength to handle problems" (Life Style Analysis Test manual, p. 1). It is suggested that this score be compared with the Negative Life Style Test score that measures "stress load being carried" (Life Style Analysis Test manual, p. 1). The Negative Life Style test also is the sum of four other subtests (Loneliness, Anxiety, Health Worry [or Negative Attitude], and Depression). Each of these subtests as well as the two test scores are reported as "T-like score" ranging from 20 to 80 with a mean of 50 on a one-page computer generated profile report for the examinee. Percent correct scores are also printed on the report below the bar representing the normalized *T*-scores. For the *T*-scores or percent correct scores, no standard errors of measurement are presented. When discussing the use of this battery with drug abusers, Cassel (Life Style Analysis Test manual, p. 3) says that "Whenever the Stress Load is greater than Ego Strength, a significant at risk is depicted." In contrast, "An ideal life style is where the ego strength is two times or more than as much as the stress load" (Life Style Analysis Test manual, Figure 1, p. 35).

Besides having an examinee answer questions presented on the computer screen, three of the "Holistic Health" modules obtain data from an examinee through biofeedback devices (electromyograph, galvanic skin response, peripheral temperature, and pulse rate). These three modules are dissonance assessment using guided imagery and neural personality cluster, assessment of self-control in relaxation, and non-dominant brain need-presence assessment.

To illustrate how a module is used, consider the non-dominant need-presence assessment (EMOTE) module in the Need Gratification Battery. The EMOTE module employs "from one to four different biofeedback instruments interfaced with a computer to measure neural functions in response to your bodily changes in connection with view of the 96 slides" (Neural Harmony Essential for Global Functioning manual, p. 32). The examinee responds to each slide on a scale of 1 to 10 depending on its appeal. The 96 slides cover 12 different areas of life (e.g., Home and Family, Religion and Inner Development, Survival and Pollution) during a 16-minute period. These assess need-presence in the "non-dominant" or unconscious brain areas. The examinee also responds to 20 true/false items on each of the same 12 areas of life in order to assess the needs in the conscious person or "dominant" brain. Contrasting the biofeedback data with the test data on the 12 life areas provides an indication of the disparity between conscious and unconscious need-presence. Not addressed in the manual is research on a possible order effect for presentation of the slides; however, the manual does note that EMOTE is still considered to be experimental.

The theory underlying the Clinical Support System Battery is based on the concept of wellness in contrast to fighting sickness. A fundamental aspect of this concept is the idea of "global functioning" and the connection of one's mind and body (psychoneroimunology). Furthermore, according to Cassel, "The notion underlying the holistic series is that no person is ever living as well as it is possible to live, and that the six different programs provide guidance for improved quality of life and greater life expectancy" (The Identity Status Test manual, p. 7). Although the number of references supporting the theory and tests in the seven manuals range from 9 to 51, more specific linking of the existing literature with the particular choice of tests or subtests in the various batteries is needed.

The development, administration, and interpretation of the six different batteries share many common features. Even though the manuals cite studies which support the general notion of measuring particular aspects of health, there is a lack of tables of specifications and/or outlines to operationally define the areas measured. Furthermore, there is no information on how the items were generated. Interjudge agreement studies regarding the placement of items on scales are not reported. The factor analyses which are reported appear to have factored the subtests as variables and consequently do not show loadings for items on scales. Incidentally, in one instance where the cutoff value for the eigenvalues in the factor analyses are reported, it was .5 (Neural Harmony Essential for Global Functioning manual, p. 8). This value is much lower than the recommended value of 1 in the literature.

Construct validity is obtained by using the group difference approach. Cassel correctly states that the "Validity begins with determining the discerning power of a psychological instrument" (Neural Harmony Essential for Global Functioning manual, p. 13). To validate the batteries, therapy and no-therapy groups are compared using discriminant analyses. Cassel points out that individuals who spend money and time for health services present "prima facie evidence of 'non-wellness'" (The Life Style Analysis Test manual, p. 6) leaving the wellness group to be defined by default. Not procuring health services could be due to factors such as lack of disposable income, lack of knowledge regarding symptoms, and non-availability of transportation. Hence, it may have been better to obtain additional information to more clearly define both the therapy and the no-therapy groups.

In addition to the problem of group definition, the reporting of the discriminant analyses is incomplete. Missing are statistics usually reported related to how well the discriminant function separated the groups, such as Bartlett's Chi-Squared for the overall model, discriminant function coefficients, and partial Wilks' Lambdas for each variable in the model. When hit-miss classification tables are reported, it is not clear whether the calibration samples were reclassified tending to result in a slight overestimation of the proportion of correct classifications or whether another procedure such as the holdout sample or jackknife technique was employed.

Essentially, the group difference approach reported in most of the manuals amounts to t-tests for the subtest means of the therapy and no-therapy groups. The results are often statistically significant lending some validity to the subtests, conditional to some extent on the quality of the therapy and no-therapy group definitions.

In regard to risk, one interesting possibility presented in the Life Style Analysis Battery is using the notion that an ideal profile has a Positive Life Style score at least twice the Negative Life Style score. By analogy, the physical body has many redundancies and strengths beyond what is normally required in everyday life. Perhaps then, the usual statement in the stress literature of resources just exceeding stressors as not inducing the stress response needs elaboration. A contribution of Cassel is that he has moved us in the direction of wanting more resources, although the 2:1 ratio as a minimum may need additional justification.

As an aside, it may be noted that when concerned with risk, the statistical analysis often seen in the medical journals is logistic regression. For the two-group problem, both discriminant analysis and logistic regression can be computed but interpretation of results may differ (Hosmer & Lemeshow, 1989). A difference between the analyses is that in logistic regression the coefficients provide an estimate of the log odds adjusting for other variables in the model and may approximate a quantity called the relative risk.

Missing from the manuals is criterion-related validity information which shows the correlations of the tests or subtests in the Clinical Support System with other measures of similar constructs. For example, correlations of Cassel's measure of depression could be reported with other measures of depression such as the Beck Depression Inventory (T4:268). Also, the usefulness of tests in the Cosmic Consciousness Battery could be shown by correlations with other variables or their incremental validity in a regression equation.

Reliability is supported by test/retest correlations, subtest intercorrelations, and subtest with test correlations. For the Life Style Analysis scale, the test and subtest test/retest correlations for the no-therapy group (n = 143) ranged from .86 to .54, whereas for the therapy group (n = 78) they varied from .81 to .22. The manuals for the other scales did not report test/retest reliability. There are no KR-20s, KR-21s, or coefficient alphas given in the manuals for internal consistency reliability. Furthermore, there are no standard errors of measurement reported in the manuals or presented in the profile reports to aid in score interpretation.

The intercorrelation of the subtests is discussed from the viewpoint of factorial validity which, according to Cassel, "is a quasi-reliability measure; since it deals with the structure of the instrument" (The Life Style Analysis manual, p. 9). The intercorrelations of most subtests seem to be in line with what is to be expected—low to moderate correlations within a battery. Furthermore, reliability is discussed in terms of the number of behaviors (items) sought. For many subtests, the number of true/false items is 25, which typically is more than sufficient to measure most constructs.

There is no research reported in the manuals on item bias. More specifically, there are no statistical analyses for item bias or sensitivity reviews of the items for possible ethnic or gender differences.

The issue of various groups responding differently to items on the test is handled by using different norm groups. Various norm groups are available in the computer programs for the different batteries to help interpret an examinee's scores. For example, the Life Style Analysis Battery first asks the person scoring the profile to select between the Adult Norm and the Youth Norm (under 22 years of age). Then the person scoring the profile selects from among the General Norm, Female Norm, or Male Norm. Frequently, norms and data analyses involve samples from the United States, New Zealand, and Australia. Most manuals do include *t*-tests for mean differences of males and females on many of the tests and subtests for various data sets. For some tests and subtests there are statistically significant differences.

The administration of the true/false items in a test is done on the computer with one item appearing on the screen at a time. The software, written in the BASIC computer language, ran without problems. It can be copied over to a hard disk and executed from there. The user is given the choice of from which drive to execute the program and on which drive to store the results. The programs do not require very much storage space if copied over to a hard drive. The Clinical Support System disk used 319 K bytes and the largest space requirement for any of the six separate disks for each of the batteries was 287 K bytes.

The items are presented on the screen in white characters against a black background. The same set of items is presented to every examinee. Although the initial screen of instructions tells the respondent how to go back and change an answer (down arrow key), this instruction does not appear on each screen and a respondent may forget how to go back and change answers. The program does not store changes regarding the drives and they must be entered each time at startup. There are no provisions to skip items or to exit the battery early and save item responses.

Two practical concerns for using any test are the amount of time required to administer the test and its reading level. On both accounts the Clinical Support System appears good. Typically a battery has between 120 and 200 items and takes about 20 minutes to administer. According to the SMOG reading formula, the first 100 words in the items at the beginning of the Life Style Analysis Battery were at approximately the 7th grade reading level.

In summary, the strengths of the instrument are that it furthers support for some newer ideas such as a higher ratio of resources to stressors, measuring cosmic consciousness, and biofeedback related to 12 life situations. It also provides ease of administration and immediate profile generation. However, the Clinical Support System could be improved by reporting standard errors of measurement and concurrent validity studies with other instruments designed to measure similar constructs. Overall, this test battery represents a starting point in the assessment of holistic health.

REVIEWER'S REFERENCE

Hosmer, D. W., Jr., & Lemeshow, S. (1989). *Applied logistic regression.* New York: John Wiley & Sons.

Review of the Clinical Support System Battery by MARY LOU KELLEY, Professor of Psychology, Louisiana State University, Louisiana State University Medical Center, Baton Rouge, LA:

The Clinical Support System is intended for assessing the lifestyle and health-related behavior of adolescents and adults. The battery consists of six computer-administered multiple-choice tests assessing a variety of personality traits that the author purports are related to health from a holistic perspective. Using the author's descriptors, the battery includes tests measuring ego strength, neural functioning, need gratification, identity status, balance of control, and cosmic consciousness. The test packet consists of a manual providing an overview of the battery and separate manuals for each of the tests. The tests are on 5.25-inch PC format floppy computer disks, which present individual items and which print a profile subsequent to administration. Unfortunately, when I attempted to complete one of the tests, which contained over 170 items, I encountered a "fatal flaw," which prevented the scoring of my test responses. A message instructed me to contact the author in California and listed two numbers, which apparently identified the nature of the "fatal flaw."

The author provides an overview of the test battery and its intended uses. The battery is very ambitious and creative and attempts to incorporate numerous psychodynamic and psychological tenets into the test content. For example, the Life Style Analysis Test measures ego strength, defined by the author as the "ability to cope with problems in one's life space" (Life Style Analysis Test manual, p. 2) and compares ego strength to the individual's perceived stress load. Thus, the lifestyle test compares positive and negative areas of one's life. The Positive Life Style component (ego strength), consists of four separate components (Self-Esteem, Satisfaction, Involvement, Assertiveness) each containing 25 true/false items. The Negative Life Style component (stress load), also consists of four components measuring Loneliness, Anxiety, Negative Attitude, and Depression. The other tests of the battery are also centered around various broad concepts with item selection apparently based on the author's intuition.

The author makes a very substantial effort to explain the philosophy and scholarly foundation of the constructs measured and to relate test purposes to a psychological theory perceived as important to health maintenance. Each test in the battery is accompanied by a fairly extensive explanatory manual. In spite of the author's ambitious efforts, the descriptions are highly jargonistic and esoteric. For example, the Cosmic Consciousness Test manual relates the test to tenets of transpersonal psychology and "is intended for use with persons who desire to escape the worldly bonds and soar into the heavens in mind and in spirit" (The Life Style Analysis Test manual, p. 2). Furthermore, some constructs for which there is a substantial literature are defined in an idiosyncratic manner without apparent consideration for other research. For example, the author states that "A comparison of the ego strength and stress load present serves as an effective means for depicting the 'TYPE-A Proneness' of an individual. Where the stress load of an individual is high in comparison to one's ego strength, TYPE-A proneness is the more likely to be present" (The Life Style Analysis Test manual, p. 2). The author cites his own research almost exclusively in support of this assertion.

Reliability data are provided for only some of the many constructs measured. Where reliability is addressed, the rationales and data presented are neither clear nor impressive. Measures of internal consistency (e.g., inter-item correlations) are not presented for any test. The author does provide data on the factor structure of each test in the battery as well as data on its use with clinical and nonclinical samples. Each test apparently is normed on male and female samples. However, very little information is provided on the standardization sample or the norming process. Moreover, data are not presented on the relationship of any of the tests to any external criterion other than sex, age, marital status, and therapy/nontherapy status.

In summary, the Clinical Support System is an ambitious effort aimed as assessing the author's theory of psychological factors related to health maintenance. In the absence of a thorough rewrite of the manual and the inclusion of extensive reliability and validity data documenting the psychometric soundness and criterion-related validity of the battery, I cannot recommend its use for any applied purpose. Further, anyone who intends to conduct research on the tests must contend with reading manuals that are heavy on theory and light on practical information about test administration and interpretation.

[83]

Cognitive Observation Guide.

Purpose: Constructed as "a criterion-referenced measure of sensorimotor intelligence."
Population: Birth to 2 years of age.
Publication Dates: 1981–87.
Acronym: COG.
Scores: Item scores only in 3 domains: Causal Deduction, Object Permanence, Symbolic Representation.
Administration: Individual.
Price Data: Not available.
Time: Administration time not reported.
Comments: Ratings by professional.
Authors: Gilbert M. Foley and Marilyn H. Appel.
Publisher: Communication Skill Builders.
[The publisher advised in April 1994 that this test is now out of print—Ed.]

Review of the Cognitive Observation Guide by BRUCE A. BRACKEN, Professor of Psychology, The University of Memphis, Memphis, TN:

The Cognitive Observation Guide (COG) was designed as a criterion-referenced measure of sensorimotor intelligence for the assessment of strengths and weaknesses in normal and developmentally delayed children between birth and 2 years. The scale is founded theoretically on Piaget's conceptualization of cognitive development. The COG is represented developmentally and structurally by *phases, domains, concepts*, and *items*. Six developmental phases (i.e., age levels) are represented in the instrument, which range from Phase I (0 to 1 month) to Phase VI (18 to 24 months). Within each phase the authors sampled three content domains, including: Causal Deduction (i.e., Intentionality and Causality), Object Permanence (i.e., Visual/Spatial Relationships and Object Concept), and Symbolic Representation (i.e., Sequencing, Imitation, and Representation). Two or three concepts are assessed within each of the three domains, and each concept is represented by three items or behavioral observations.

In addition to being theoretically grounded, the instrument is unique because it permits the examiner to use any of three administration formats (i.e., Naturalistic Observations, Structured Play, and formal Test Administration). Such administration flexibility allows examiners to note and record behaviors well beyond the confines of the standard formal assessment paradigm with which many young children are unfamiliar and uncomfortable.

The examiner's manual is brief, yet well written and easily read. The administration and scoring procedures are easily followed and are detailed sufficiently well in the manual. Also, the manual includes a sample case study to demonstrate the practical nature and utility of the instrument.

Unfortunately, the COG manual does not contain a considerable amount of information necessary when selecting an instrument for use. Piaget's 1958 conceptualization of cognitive development is described only in passing, with little reference to work or theoretical adaptations made since 1958. The authors report the items were derived from relevant literature, but specific scale content is not supported by individual references. The authors' casual reference to content validity and the review of a single "well known authority on Piagetian theory" (manual, p. 15) is the only support provided for the extent to which the instrument is true to its theoretical underpinnings.

The authors report fairly strong evidence of interrater agreement, which attests to the scale's objective scoring system and ease of administration; however, no evidence is provided about short-term stability, concurrent validity, criterion-related validity, or more importantly, evidence of age progression in children's performance on the scale. Also, no evidence of predictive validity is presented in the manual. Furthermore, although the scale allows for flexible administration, there is no evidence in the examiner's manual regarding the comparability of children's performances across the three possible administration formats or "alternate-forms."

Another serious limitation of the COG is related to scale interpretation and suggestions for remediation of deficient behaviors. Although the scale was designed to identify infants' cognitive strengths and weaknesses, there is no section in the manual that addresses how to make these interpretations. Equally important is the lack of information that informs the examiner of what to do once a child's strengths and weaknesses have been identified. Without knowledge of how to interpret the instrument or how to translate children's COG performance into meaningful remedial plans, the instrument is seriously limited.

Although the COG is brief, easily administered, and theoretically interesting, it fails to provide convincing information about its theoretical fidelity, technical adequacy (e.g., stability, alternate-forms reliability, evidence of age progression), interpretation, or what to do with children's cognitive strengths or weaknesses once they have been identified. This instrument could be useful in developmental research, but it is far too limited to warrant its use in clinical settings as advocated in the examiner's manual.

Review of the Cognitive Observation Guide by JAMES C. REED, Director of Psychology, St. Luke's Hospital, New Bedford, MA:

The purpose of the Cognitive Observation Guide (COG) is to provide a scale of sensorimotor intelligence in infants from birth to 2 years of age. Sensorimotor intelligence is criterion referenced and defined in a framework of Piagetian theory.

The scale is organized into items, concepts, domains, and phases. There are six phases and three domains. Phases are defined by chronological age in months, 0–1, 1–4, 4–8, 8–12, 12–18, and 18–24. The domains are defined in terms of concepts of cognitive development: Domain I, cause and effect relationships and intentionality behavior; Domain II, spatial relationships and knowledge of people and objects as permanence; Domain III, time and sequence, imitations, and symbolic representation. The concepts are defined by items. For example, Phase III (4–8 months) Domain I, the Intentionality concept is defined by three items, the child (*a*) hits, shakes, and bangs object; (*b*) smiles to mirror; (*c*) retrieves bottle/pacifier. As another example, Phase VI (18–24 months) Domain III, the Imitation concept is defined by (child) (*a*) performs vivid imitations, (*b*) pretends with objects, (*c*) uses body as a model.

Is this observation guide a test of intelligence? No, at least not in the traditional sense. The authors state "When a *diagnosis* of cognitive level is required, a standardized instrument must be administered, . . . the items . . . have not been normed on either a particular or exceptional population of children" (manual, p. 14).

TEST ADMINISTRATION. There are three ways to administer the test that have varying degrees of structure:

1. *Naturalistic observation*, over an extended period of time the child's spontaneous play interactions are recorded provided they meet criteria established in the scale. The observation period should not exceed 2 weeks according to recommendations of the authors.

2. *Structured play*, the manual provides a suggested list of 45 items (selected for their entertainment value for children), and in a play situation the behaviors can be encouraged, observed, and recorded.

3. *Test administration*, the evaluation should follow a sequence of items outlined in the scale, presenting the conditions presented in a structured manner using the suggested materials. Again, the test administration should not exceed two sessions over the course of 2 days.

ITEM SCORING. Following each item is a box. The item is scored blank (behavior not observed or not mastered), slash mark (behavior partially mastered), X or R (behavior mastered or reported). The behaviors are stated with sufficient clarity, and illustrations are provided so that an intelligent examiner should be able to evaluate a specific item without much difficulty. A blank box is evaluated as zero, a slash mark is .5, and an X or R receives a weight of one. The total score is obtained by summing the marks and dividing by 108 (item total), which indicates percentage mastery. A table is provided listing the percentage mastery for the six phases (e.g., mastery level between 23% and 42% represents Phase 3 or development at the chronological age 3–8-month level).

TEST RELIABILITY. Reliability was determined by amount of agreement among observers or raters. Six experienced and trained raters observed five video tapes of the COG in its test administration format. The sample was a cross-sectional sample of five handicapped infants of age 5 to 24 months. For Phases 2 through 5 the average interrater reliability coefficient was .935. An index of internal consistency was calculated for the six raters on each child, and the indices ranged from .73 to .94. The coefficient .73 was for one child. By dropping a low score the average index of internal consistency was .86. These are acceptable coefficients, but the reliability of this scale will depend upon having a trained administrator and a cooperative child.

TEST VALIDITY. The validity is content validity. The items, the concepts, the domains, and phases were derived from the literature. The initial review was completed by a well-known authority on Piagetian theory. The scale was evaluated for "its overall usability, taxonomic structure and classification of items, content validity, concept clarity and ordinality" (manual, p. 15). The concepts and items were sent to three independent experts in the field of infant development and a criterion level of 67% congruence among the raters' responses was used to retain items within their respective concepts, domains, and phases. In other words, the validity of the items was determined by the judgment of experts.

USE OF THE COG. The scoring sheet provides for a behavioral analysis not only in terms of level of development, but also in terms of areas of strengths and weaknesses. The scoring sheet facilitates the recording of observations made at different points in time; thus, a child may be observed at age 2 months and again at 6 months and the amount of improvement or change that he or she has made can be easily recorded. Within a domain, cognitive/behavioral weaknesses may be identified, and it would be possible to develop remedial programs centered to ameliorate or promote a given behavior.

The manual includes a case report of a 10-month-old infant referred because of developmental delays. His COG profile indicated that he was deficient in items that require essential motor activity. He appeared to have neurologically based weakness, so recommendations derived from his profile were made that were intended to help the youngster overcome his difficulties.

The manual contains a succinct (five pages double spaced) presentation of Piaget's theory of child and intellectual development. The COG is based on this theory, and the COG could serve as an "*instructional tool* to orient students . . . to the Piagetian perspective on infant cognitive development" (manual, p. 6). However, one need not be a Piagetian to use this instrument. The scale is sufficiently objective and the behaviors sufficiently well defined so that any specialist in child development can employ the instrument. The scale will provide an objective means of specifying those behaviors a child has achieved, those partially mastered, and those behaviors absent or deficient. Depending upon the ingenuity of the evaluator and/or therapist, a therapeutic program can be developed.

CAVEAT. Whether or not behavioral programs can hasten the development of the central nervous system is a question outside the domain of this test and this review. Persons in child development and early childhood therapy may find the instrument useful as a means of identifying behaviors and planning intervention programs. However, this test, as is true of any test used with infants, will require a skilled examiner who knows how to motivate and elicit cooperation from an infant whose emotions, behaviors, actions, and reactions are concentered entirely to self.

[84]

College Major Interest Inventory.

Purpose: Designed "to identify the academic majors that best match a student's pattern of interests."
Population: High school and college students.
Publication Date: 1990.
Acronym: CMII.
Scores: 135 scale scores: 6 Educational Area Interest Scales (Mechanical-Technical, Rational-Scientific, Aesthetic-Cultural, Social-Personal, Business-Management, Clerical-Data), 33 Educational Cluster Scales (Accounting, Administration, Agriculture, Art, Athletics, Biological Science, Clerical, Creative Writing, Dramatics, Engineering, Finance, Journalism, Laboratory Work, Language-Literature, Mathematics, Mechanical Activities, Medical Service, Military Activities, Music, Outdoors, Philosophy, Physical Science, Political Science, Public Speaking, Recreation, Religious Activities, Sales, Science Writing, Social Science, Social Service, Teaching, Technical Design, Technical Skills), 12 Personal Characteristics Scales (Accurate, Analytical, Coordinated, Creative, Helpful, Industrious, Organized, Outdoors-Oriented, Practical, Risk-Taker, Scholarly, Theoretical), 13 School and College Scales (Agriculture, Architecture, Arts & Sciences, Business, Education, Engineering, Journalism, Law, Medicine, Music, Nursing, Pharmacy, Vocational-Technical), 65 Academic Major Scales (Anthropology, Applied Math, Architecture, Biology-Environmental/Population/Organismic, Biology-Molecular/Cellular/Developmental, Business-Accounting, Business-Administration, Business-Finance, Business-General [Female Only], Business-International, Business-Management, Business-Marketing, Business-Real Estate, Chemistry, Communications, Computer Science, Conservation Education, Counseling, Distributive Studies, Economics, Education-Elementary, Education-Secondary, Engineering [Female only], Engineering-Aerospace, Engineering-Architectural, Engineering-Chemical, Engineering-Civil, Engineering-Design Economics, Engineering-Electrical, Engineering-Mechanical, Engineering-Physics, English Literature, Environmental Design, Fine Arts-B.A. Degree, Fine Arts-B.F.A. Degree, French, Geography, Geology, History, Individually Structured, International Affairs, Journalism-Advertising, Journalism-General, Journalism-News Editing, Law, Law Enforcement, Mathematics, Medical Technician, Medicine, Music, Nursing, Pharmacy, Philosophy, Physical Education, Physical Therapy, Physics, Political Science, Psychology, Public Administration, Recreation, Religious Studies, Sociology, Spanish, Speech Disorders, Theater), 5 Academic Achievement Interest Scales (Business, Social Science, Humanities, Natural Science, Engineering), Educational Level Interest Scale.

Administration: Group.
Price Data, 1992: $48 per 10 prepaid test booklets/answer sheets; $28 per manual (75 pages); $29 per specimen set.
Time: (35–45) minutes.
Comments: Formerly the Colorado Educational Interest Inventory; separate reports created for men and women students.
Authors: Robert D. Whetstone and Ronald G. Taylor.
Publisher: Consulting Psychologists Press, Inc.

TEST REFERENCES

1. Brown, N. W. (1994). Cognitive, interest, and personality variables predicting first-semester GPA. *Psychological Reports, 74*, 605-606.

Review of the College Major Interest Inventory by NORMAN FREDMAN, Professor and Coordinator, Counselor Education Programs, Queens College, City University of New York, Flushing, NY:

The theory behind the College Major Interest Inventory (CMII) is that students will more likely persist in college if they take courses that match their academic attitudes, interests, values, and goals. Developed by the late Robert Whetstone and his colleague and successor, Ronald Taylor, the CMII (formerly the Colorado Educational Interest Inventory) focuses on the educational rather than the vocational objectives of students. Geared primarily to students from grade 10 through college sophomores, the CMII compares student educational interest patterns with those of 17- to 19-year-old students primarily from Colorado who have declared an academic major, completed at least half their academic course work, and attained a passing GPA.

The CMII booklet contains 399 items. The student responds *Like, Indifferent*, or *Dislike* to Section I: Course Titles (185 items), Section II: Educational Experiences (48 items), and Section III: Instructor Characteristics (47 items). Section IV: Personal Preferences is subdivided into four groups of 10 items each. Students rank their Goals, Virtues, Values, and Life Styles. Section V: Educational Preferences (40 items) requires choosing between various educational opportunities and experiences. Section VI: Educational Self-Concept (39 items) requires self-evaluation of strengths and weaknesses.

Certain items that might be empirically valuable are insensitive to the respondent's or others' feelings. In this category I would place student evaluations of the following instructor characteristics: "234. Foreign accent," and "244. Over 55 years old."

The printout is organized according to Holland's RIASEC model. The CMII uses more meaningful terms than Holland: Mechanical-Technical instead of Realistic; Rational-Scientific instead of Investigative; Aesthetic-Cultural instead of Artistic; Social-Personal instead of Social; Business-Management instead of Enterprising; and Clerical-Data instead of Conventional. No mention is made, however, of the hexagon theory in the printout. These six Educational Area Interest (EAI) Scales are not reported in relation to each other despite the fact that intercorrelations between EAI Scales are consistent with the hexagon model: Adjacent Scales correlations range from .33 to .65; opposite Scales correlations range from .00 to .41. Indeed, the six EAI Scales' correlations with the equivalent Strong Interest Inventory (SII) themes that follow the same model range from .72 to .86.

Although the same printout is used for males and females, separate norms were necessary for each sex. Approximately 75% of the men-in-general and 80% of the women-in-general reference groups were drawn from the University of Colorado. The remainder come from technical schools, Kansas State University, and the Air Force Academy. The fact that a large number of out-of-state students are enrolled at the University of Colorado hardly justifies characterizing the reference groups as "representative of students in general" (p. 6). Equal numbers representing each Academic Major were used to constitute the student-in-general norm group. Thus, there were as many females majoring in mathematics in the norm group as there were females majoring in elementary education.

In addition to the six EAI Scales the CMII reports 33 Educational Cluster Scales (ECS) to help identify the type of educational experiences a student might like regardless of major; 12 Personal Characteristic Scales; 13 School and College Scales; and 63 Academic Major Scales (AMS) for men (65 for women, of which 25 are based on men students). Five Academic Interest scales and one Educational Interest scale are roughly comparable to the Strong's Academic Comfort Scale. Unlike the Strong, the CMII considers the unique interest pattern of business majors separately. The "Self Report" sections report personal preferences, academic attitudes, and self-estimates. Scales that measure response sets and random and rare responses require the manual for interpretation.

Except for the Self Report sections, the printout records percentile scores in five groupings: Really Like (80–99), Like (60–79), Average (40–59), Dislike (20–39), and Really Dislike (1–19). As is unfortunately true of personality inventories in general, confidence bands are not reported. On four occasions the manual lists means and standard deviations of percentiles—a meaningless statistic.

The "balanced scale method" was developed for the AMS. Items were selected not only because they discriminated between the specific academic major and same-sex students-in-general, but also because the items were marked in the same direction by students in that major ("high commonality"). In addition, the like-dislike response ratio was considered in order to lessen the bias in favor of the like response. A response set can interfere with the interpretation of the other scales. The computer printout, however, will warn about the very systematic pattern.

Though test-retest reliability is reported for 30-day and 9-month intervals, no internal consistency data are reported in the otherwise thorough manual. The median 1-month test-retest reliability for the EAI Scales was .90; for the other scales the medians were between .86 and .88. The median 9-month test-retest reliability for the EAI Scales was .77; for the other scales the medians were slightly lower.

The classification system of "Direct" and "Indirect" hits developed by McArthur (1954) was used to estimate concurrent and predictive validity. The percentage of Excellent and Good "Direct" hits that estimated concurrent validity ranged from a high of 79% for minority males to a low of 70% for nonminority females on the EAI Scales. The percentage of Excellent and Good "Direct" hits for those still enrolled 3 years later ranged from a high of 85% for minority females to a low of 67% for nonminority females. Similar ranges of "Direct Hits" were reported for Educational Cluster Scales and School and College Scales; lower percentage of "Direct" hits were reported for AMS.

Concurrent validity for AMS was also estimated by correlating AMS scores with Strong Occupational Scales. Sometimes the correlations were impressive (CMII Chemical Engineering Major correlates .76 with SII Chemist). Sometimes the correlations were not impressive (CMII Business Administration Graduate School Major correlates .27 with SII Banker). Sometimes the correlations were bewildering (CMII Business-Finance major correlates .58 with SII Female Police Officer).

The Academic Achievement Interest Scales predict GPA as well as traditional predictors. Multiple correlations of .43 result when using high school rank and SAT scores to predict GPA. When AAIS is added, the R rises to .52. However, this insight cannot be used by college admissions officers; the AAIS, like the rest of the Inventory, is fakable.

The Kuder Occupational Interest Survey (T4:1375) has a well-established College Majors Scale and uses the same triadic items for that scale that it uses to measure vocational interests. Users of the Strong Interest Inventory (374) may find the L-I-D format and the Holland themes of the CMII comfortable despite the fact that the CMII uses different items and a much more limited norm group. One hopes that a more representative norm group will replace the one presently used.

REVIEWER'S REFERENCE

McArthur, C. (1954). Long-term validity of the Strong Interest Test in two subcultures. *The Journal of Applied Psychology, 38*, 346-353.

Review of the College Major Interest Inventory by RICK LINDSKOG, Director of School Psychology Program and Associate Professor of Psychology and Counseling, Pittsburg State University, Pittsburg, KS:

The College Major Interest Inventory (CMII; previously known as the Colorado Educational Interest Inventory) was developed to assist students and counselors at the late secondary and early college level in making educational decisions. The authors point out that often these educational decisions are made in the absence of student experience and data. The test is intended to be self-administered with the supervision of a qualified testing professional. The objective is to provide valid and reliable information based on educational data as opposed to vocational interest inventories, personality ratings, and aptitude tests.

The CMII student booklet contains 399 items which comprise six categories: Course Titles (185 items), Educational Experiences (48 items), Instructor Characteristics (47 items), Personal Preferences (40 items), Educational Preferences (40 items), and Educational Self-Concept (39 items).

Examinees respond to the first 280 items using a *Like*, *Indifferent/Cannot Decide*, or *Dislike* scale. Items 281 to 320 are responded to using a scale of *most* or *least* liked, and Items 321 to 360 according to *left* and *right* column preferences, Items 361–388 are based on *Yes*, *?*, or *No* and Items 389 to 399 are responded to by *A*, *B*, or *C*, to indicate the item's similarity to the examinee. Because of the complexity inherent in scoring these areas into a number of scales, it is necessary to computer score the file. The policy of Consulting Psychologists Press is to score response sheets within 24-hours and ship results with 48 hours. Separate scores are created for men and women, and for some scales (e.g., Nursing) there are only norms for females, and for some scores (e.g., Engineering) there are only norms for men.

Scores are reported as *Really Like, Like, Average, Dislike*, and *Really Dislike* for the following scales: Educational Area Interest, Educational Cluster, Personal Characteristics, School and College Scales.

Scores are reported as *Excellent Choice, Like, Indifferent, Dislike*, and *Active Reject* for the Academic Major Scales.

All profile scores are reported in percentile scores, from high to low. All areas have an average at the 50th percentile rank with the exception of the Academic Major Scale, which uses the 90th percentile as an average.

A brief explanation of each score area is as follows:

EDUCATIONAL AREA INTEREST SCALES. This set of scales is derived from all 399 CMII items. It expresses stated interest in six areas: Mechanical-Technical, Rational Scientific, Aesthetic-Cultural, Social-Personal, Business-Management, and Clerical-Data.

The 30-day and 9-month reliability studies indicate excellent short-term and acceptable long-term reliability. Intercorrelations between pairs of the scales indicates the scales are drawn from different domains.

The relationship between the six CMII areas and the Strong General Occupational Themes (52 to 74 present common variances) indicates adequate concurrent validity of this scale. Another validity resource, which rates "direct" and "indirect" hits (developed by McArthur, 1954) was used to measure concurrent and predictive validity. For example, a student who was majoring in any business area and had a high score in Business was counted a direct hit. The Educational Area Interest Scales were effective in predicting the academic major areas selected by students.

EDUCATIONAL CLUSTER SCALES. This set of 33 scales reflects a student's interest in highly intercorrelated items. These general areas are good indicators of a specific emphasis within a specific major. Samples of these scales are: Accounting, Creative Writing, Recreation, Sales, and Technical Skills.

Intercorrelations for both genders are low, indicating relative independence. As with the prior scale, the 30-day was more reliable than the 9-month reliability studies, and both are adequate.

Correlations between the CMII and similarly named Strong Basic Interests Scales are positive and seem logical.

PERSONAL CHARACTERISTIC SCALES. These 12 highly homogeneous scales are categorized as: Accurate, Analytical, Coordinated, Creative, Helpful, Industrious, Organized, Outdoors Oriented, Practical, Risk-Taker, Scholarly, and Theoretical.

The reliability on this scale was lower, especially for the 9-month retest. The authors speculate the lower scores may reflect student changes in their first year at school due to "personal self-evaluation."

There were few data offered as validity for the Personal Characteristic Scale. This scale was cited as having "very good research potential."

These 12 Personal Characteristics Scales describe how students view themselves and as such are useful in a broad way to students and advisors in that they describe typical ways in which the students perform.

THE SCHOOLS AND COLLEGES SCALES (e.g., Agriculture, Business, Law, Pharmacy, Vocational Technical). These indicate which of the 13 major academic curricula the student finds most interesting.

The short-term (30-day) reliability was good, and as with the prior scale, the 9-month reliability was inadequate, perhaps reflecting changes as a result of being in college.

Validity evidence for this scale was provided by how well it predicted academic areas. The "Hit-Miss" method provides adequate support for predictive validity, according to the authors.

ACADEMIC MAJOR SCALES. The Academic Major Scales are, according to the authors, the most important of the CMII scales. The names of the scales align with typical major labels found at colleges and universities. The Academic Major Scales measure interest only, not ability. This scale was developed on the basis of response patterns of students who were successful as college seniors in a major named by the scale. Hence, a high score in a specific major indicates a response pattern similar to that of a person who successfully completed most of a major. The scores are reported in terms of *Excellent Choice, Like, Indifferent, Dislike*, and *Active Reject*. Those familiar with the Strong Interest Inventory (Occupational Scales) (374) will note similarities of construction.

Adequate reliability for this scale is indicated by the 30-day and 9-month statistics. As in previous scales, the 9-month was lower but adequate. The concurrent validity evidence was provided by determining the group's overlap with the reference sample. The data indicate that the scales separate the criterion groups from the original reference groups. Concurrent validity was further evaluated by referencing similar titles on the Strong. The correlations seemed "logically and intuitively correct" (p. 44) according to the authors.

The Achievement Interest Scales give information about two areas. Achievement Interest gives information about predicting student's first year GPA, and Educational Level Interest is intended to be a measure of a student's interest in attaining a certain level of postsecondary education.

In addition, there are several Response Scales that detect things such as confusion, incomplete protocols, rare responses, and response consistency.

The manual is well organized and easily digested, although I felt that the three examples discussed in the "Interpretation" chapter were of limited value. A didactic approach beyond the basics provided in scale descriptions would have helped.

In general, the CMII does offer a direct approach to a complicated retention issue facing most universities today—selection of a major. This is a complicated issue not addressed by most advisors (they work with students who have ostensibly selected a major), nor is this issue addressed directly by the wide variety of interest inventories available. I was impressed with two scales—the Academic Major Scale and the Academic Achievement Interest Scale—the former because of the valuable specific information provided the student and advisor and the latter because of the prospect of predicting GPA. (This scale, in conjunction with ACTs and SATs and high school rank, predicts first year GPA at the .50 to .52 level for all freshmen.)

The populations used to derive the various scales were drawn from 17- to 19-year-old high school and college students (over 20,000) over a period of several years. The data were drawn primarily at the University of Colorado at Boulder and the authors consider the data to be representative of students elsewhere because approximately one-third of the U.C.B. students are from out of state. The authors point out that students from 203 universities and 39 states are included in the norm group. Lack of representation in the norm group is a considerable problem in using the CMII, and I take issue with the authors' position that the CMII reference groups are "considered to be representative of students in general" (p. 6).

The reliability and validity data have been mentioned briefly for each scale. In general, the reliability and validity seem acceptable for this type of instrument, but there are no data regarding internal consistency. The "hit rate" validation procedure is an acceptable method to use for the authors' purposes. The authors' persistent use of percentile ranks diminishes somewhat the value of the scores (as compared to mean and standard deviation). Other limits include the 10th grade reading level and significant cost.

In sum, this instrument is unique in that it uses educational interests to predict educational decisions. There is evidence to support its predictive validity for first year GPA and major selection. No doubt many universities and colleges would find that quite useful given the high attrition rate of most freshman classes. The instrument norming did not include a nationally representative sample of that population, and the manual lacks sufficient technical data to draw conclusions about internal consistency and number of items on the many subscales that comprise this instrument. However, the uniqueness and predictive validity should make the CMII a useful tool for students and advisors.

REVIEWER'S REFERENCE

McArthur, C. (1954). Long-term validity of the Strong Interest Test in two subcultures. *The Journal of Applied Psychology, 38*, 346-353.

[85]

Collis-Romberg Mathematical Problem Solving Profiles.

Purpose: Assesses student progress through a variety of mathematical problem-solving skills.
Population: Ages 9–13, 13–17.
Publication Date: 1992.
Scores, 6: Number, Algebra, Space, Measurement, Chance and Data, Total.
Administration: Group.
Levels, 2: Junior, Senior.
Price Data, 1994: $99 per complete set including profiles A and B, and manual (72 pages); $35 per manual.
Time: (40–50) minutes.
Comments: Junior version (Ages 9–13) uses Parts A to C of each question; Senior version (Ages 13–17) uses Parts A to D of each question.
Authors: K. F. Collis and T. A. Romberg.
Publisher: The Australian Council for Educational Research Limited [Australia].

Review of the Collis-Romberg Mathematical Problem Solving Profiles by JOHN W. FLEENOR, Research Scientist, Center for Creative Leadership, Greensboro, NC:

The Collis-Romberg Mathematical Problem Solving Profiles were designed to diagnose a student's performance on five topics related to problem solving: Number, Algebra, Space, Measurement, and Chance and Data (probability). The Profiles consist of four elements: (*a*) the assessment items, (*b*) diagnostic forms for recording individual and group information, (*c*) guidelines for using the Profiles, and (*d*) suggestions for further teaching based on the student's performance. The instrument is a content-referenced test, rather than a norm-referenced test (e.g., an achievement test). In developing the Profiles, the authors applied recent advances in the understanding of the cognitive abilities required for problem solving. Items for two parallel forms were written using a structural taxonomy developed by the authors called the Structure of Observed Learning (SOLO).

ADMINISTRATION AND SCORING. The Collis-Romberg Mathematical Problem Solving Profiles contain the items for both the Junior and Senior versions of the test. The test user is allowed to create separate versions of the instrument by photocopying the appropriate pages and assembling them in the correct order. Forty minutes should be allowed for the Junior version and 50 minutes for the Senior version; however, the test is not timed. The Profiles may be administered in a group setting. The format and print quality of the test booklets are good.

All items are in a restricted-response format, where the student must produce the correct response. The items are what the authors call "superitems," groups of questions that refer to a single stem, usually a graph, a table, or a paragraph. The Profiles are hand-scored using answer keys in the manual. The answer keys indicate the exact answers to the items, or alternative solutions when more than one correct answer is possible.

In addition to counting the number of correct responses, the administrator also classifies the responses into the SOLO taxonomy. Within the superitems, each question measures an increasing level of complexity based on the taxonomy. A correct response to a question is classified according to the level of ability reflected by that question. The levels within the SOLO taxonomy are: (*a*) Unistructural, (*b*) Multistructural, (*c*) Relational, and (*d*) Extended Abstract. Unistructural questions, for example, elicit the use of one obvious piece of information coming directly from the stem. At the highest level of the taxonomy, Extended Abstract questions elicit the use of an abstract general principle or hypothesis derived from the information in the stem. SOLO levels for the five problem-solving topics are determined by the highest level of functioning for each topic. The most frequently occurring level becomes the overall SOLO level. The diagnostic form allows the administrator to produce a graphic representation of the SOLO level for each problem-solving topic.

RELIABILITY. The Profiles are constructed in such a way that internal consistency measures, such as Cronbach's alpha, probably are not appropriate. Because the questions within a superitem involve the interpretation of a single stem, they are not truly independent items. No evidence of test-retest or alternate forms reliability is presented in the manual, although these indices of reliability could be calculated using the raw scores from the five problem-solving topics.

VALIDITY. The five content areas of the Collis-Romberg Mathematical Problem Solving Profiles are based on the National Assessment of Educational Progress conducted in 1978. The content validity of the test items was judged by 20 Wisconsin school teachers and two indices of agreement among the teachers were calculated. The level of agreement among the teachers was acceptable. The items were then administered to a small sample of students to test expectations regarding the SOLO levels at the various grade levels, and the students' comprehension of the content of the items. Based on this information, items were rewritten when necessary.

Guttman Scalogram analyses were conducted to determine the extent to which the pattern of responses for each superitem was hierarchical and cumulative. Separate samples of students at ages 9, 11, 13, and 17 were used in these analyses. Each sample contained approximately 300 students from a central Wisconsin school district. Results indicated that, in general, the questions within the superitems appeared to form Guttman scales. Additional analyses were conducted to determine if students at each age level could be clustered into groups reflecting the SOLO levels. The results of a maximum hierarchical clustering procedure indicated that a majority of students were correctly classified. No evidence of criterion-related validity is presented in the manual.

CONCLUSION. The Collis-Romberg Mathematical Problem Solving Profiles appear to be a well-constructed test in terms of content validity. However, the profiles share the technical problems characteristic of content-referenced tests, especially in regard to the measurement of the reliability and validity of these instruments. The Profiles are a recently developed test, and the authors indicate that further research on the instrument is being conducted. Evidence of the reliability and validity of the instrument is limited to internal analyses conducted during the test development process. The Profiles cannot be recommended without reservation, therefore, until further information regarding the psychometric properties of the instrument is available.

The technical manual is well written and contains excellent instructions for administering and scoring the instrument. Some of the information regarding the SOLO taxonomy, however, may be difficult for less experienced users to understand.

Review of the Collis-Romberg Mathematical Problem Solving Profiles by JUDITH A. MONSAAS, Visiting Associate Professor of Educational Studies, Emory University, Atlanta, GA:

The Collis-Romberg Mathematical Problem Solving Profiles are designed to assess the problem-solving skills of students from 9 to 17 years of age. There are two versions of the profiles, a Junior version appropriate for children ages 9 to 13 and a Senior version for ages 13 through 17, and two forms of the test (Profile A and Profile B). Each profile contains five main items or "superitems" similar to those we are accustomed to seeing in reading comprehension tests. Each of these has a stem describing a certain set of conditions and three or four questions associated with the stem. Students taking the junior version of the test answer only the first three questions and those taking the senior version answer all four questions for each superitem. Each question represents a different level of the SOLO (Structure of Learned Outcomes) taxonomy (Biggs & Collis, 1982). This taxonomy includes four levels: Unistructural, Multistructural, Relational, and Extended Abstract. The Extended Abstract questions are answered only by students taking the Senior version.

Each superitem measures a different content area in math. The five areas are Number, Algebra, Space, Measurement, and Chance and Data. (A sixth topic area labeled "Unfamiliar" and including problems not taught in school was deleted from the final version presumably because of low agreement as to what belongs in this subarea.) A two-dimensional matrix including the content areas and the taxonomic levels constitutes the profile. Thus, at a glance, a teacher can see the level at which an individual student is operating by content area and overall. Instructions are provided for creating a class profile as well. This information could be especially useful for classroom instruction.

The test can be given in a single session and requires a minimum of 40 minutes for the Junior version and 50 minutes for the Senior version. The authors state that more time may be given if necessary, but this may be difficult with the fixed schedule in many secondary schools. The instructions for administering and scoring the profiles are very simple and straightforward as are the instructions for interpreting the profiles. An additional feature that is especially useful is a section including instructional recommendations for each topic and SOLO level. These suggestions can be used with individual students or entire classes. Many of the suggested activities are from the Mathematics Curriculum and Teaching Program (Lovitt & Clarke, 1988) published by the Canberra Curriculum Development Center, which may pose some difficulty for users in the United States. Otherwise the suggestions are quite good and clearly would encourage the use of problem-solving skills in the classroom.

The technical data are mixed. There are no normative data. This is defensible with a diagnostic test. The absence of reliability data is of more concern. Validity data suggest that range restriction is not a problem for most of the age levels, so it is not clear why reliability data are not provided. Given the test has only one item for each taxonomic level within each topic area this is potentially of concern. Some estimate of parallel forms reliability would also be of use to those researchers who may wish to use these profiles for pre and post assessment. (There are few tests that appear to measure mathematical problem-solving skills as well as this one does.)

The strength of this test is in the area of construct validity. The rationale for the development of the superitems and the use of the SOLO taxonomy are sound. The item development stage is clearly spelled out including the development of the item pool and the procedure for establishing the content validity of the items. A sample of 20 classroom teachers of students in grades 4, 7, and 12 in Wisconsin judged the items on the content, reasoning levels, and the appropriateness for students at their grade level. Light's coefficient for nominal agreement on each category was calculated. Agreement for the content categories ranged from .48 for variables (Algebra) to .82 for statistics (Chance and Data). Teacher agreement for cognitive levels was mostly in the .40s using a different taxonomy (Blooms?) than the SOLO taxonomy. Teachers' ratings of the appropriateness of the items for their students supported the developmental nature of the profiles and the taxonomy. The 12th grade teachers felt that almost all of the items were appropriate for their students, whereas the 4th grade teachers generally felt that fewer of the higher level items were appropriate for their students.

In addition to teacher data, the items were pilot tested on a sample of approximately 300 students at each of the following age levels: 9, 11, 13, and 17. The pattern of correct responses supported the SOLO taxonomy as did the Guttman Scalogram analysis. One major concern of mine is the evidence provided is all related to scale development. No data are reported on the final version of the profiles. Given that the content labels were modified, presumably based on this data, and the taxonomy used in the final version was changed, this appears to be a serious weakness.

In summary, this test is innovative and clearly answers the demand for a tool to assess a student's competence in true mathematical problem solving. It is well designed and based on a cognitive model appropriate for measuring mathematical problem solving. The test development process is sound and appears to support the construct validity of the test. Evidence supporting the test's reliability and validity evidence supporting the final version of the test would further support the test's use as a mathematical problem-solving diagnostic tool.

REVIEWER'S REFERENCES

Biggs, J. B., & Collis, K. F. (1982). *Evaluating the quality of learning: The SOLO taxonomy (structure of the observed learned outcomes).* New York: Academic Press.

Lovitt, C., & Clarke, D. (1988). *Mathematics curriculum and teaching program* (vols. 1-2). Canberra, Australia: Curriculum Development Centre.

[86]

Communication Abilities Diagnostic Test.

Purpose: Constructed to assess language development.
Population: Ages 3-0 to 9-11.
Publication Date: 1990.
Acronym: CADeT.
Scores: 6 subscores: Words, Structure, Grammar, Meaning, Pragmatics, Comprehension, plus 4 composite scores: Semantics, Syntax, Language Expression, Total Language.
Administration: Individual.
Price Data, 1991: $148.98 per complete kit; $49.98 per set of 2 story books; $34.98 per game board/cards/pieces; $15.99 per 12 record forms; $24.99 per examiner's manual (155 pages); $15 per technical manual (36 pages).
Time: (30–45) minutes.
Authors: Elizabeth B. Johnston and Andrew V. Johnston.
Publisher: The Riverside Publishing Co.

Review of the Communication Abilities Diagnostic Test by WILLIAM O. HAYNES, Professor of Communication Disorders, Auburn University, Auburn University, AL:

The Communication Abilities Diagnostic Test (CADeT) presents an unusual departure from most language tests especially in terms of its variety of sampling tasks and two methods of scoring (criterion and norm referenced). Most tests of language involve just a single response mode and provide for only norm-based scoring. Several positive aspects of the CADeT are especially noteworthy. First, the sampling of language takes place in three different modes. A storytelling task involves the child alternating turns with the examiner. Both the child and examiner have different picture stimuli for their stories, and as the examiner models sentences about one set of pictures, the child is to produce similar utterances about his or her stimuli. This results in sentences produced by the child that are of a similar grammatical arrangement to the adult models, yet with slight differences in the actors, attributes, or objects. This sampling mode is most adapted to assessment of syntactic and semantic abilities. A second sampling scenario involves a board game in which the child and adult jointly construct rules and talk about the picture stimuli. A variety of opportunities for the child to exhibit pragmatic functions are incorporated into the game scenario (e.g., asking for help, making choices, giving directions, predicting outcomes, speculating, etc.). Additionally, the responses during the game can be analyzed for length and semantic/grammatical errors. A third sampling is a "conversation" during which the examiner incorporates a series of 17 questions about the game.

This part of the sampling is designed to tap accuracy of comprehension and responsiveness in conversation. Through a combination of the three sampling modes, the examiner gains insight into the semantic, syntactic, and pragmatic domains.

A second positive feature of the CADeT is the opportunity to score a child's performance for norm-referenced as well as criterion-referenced comparisons. The former allows the examiner to determine if a child's language performance represents a clinically significant delay in communication development compared to a standardization sample. A total language score as well as subscores in the domains of semantics, syntax, and pragmatics are among the available standardized measures.

The criterion-referenced scores allow the examiner to make recommendations regarding treatment goals and characterize the child's performance in various domains in developmental space. A real strength of this test is the many examples of scoring conventions and many practice drills for examiners to use in developing their reliability in scoring.

The development and standardization of the CADeT are detailed in a technical manual. The standardization population was 928 children between the ages of 3 and 9 years with over 100 children at each age group. Thus, the number of subjects for standardization appears adequate. The sample was drawn from 63 different sites in the United States and represents northeastern, north central, southern, and western areas (however, over one-third of the subjects were from the west). The sample is also relatively balanced for sex. Several different cultural groups are represented in the sample (African-American, Hispanic, White, and Other); however, the group was predominantly White. Because the actual percentages of minority groups in the CADeT sample were less than current census figures, the authors used a statistical weighting system to approximate U.S. Census figures. The authors clearly indicate several times in the manuals that norms may not be appropriate for populations differing from the standardization sample and recommend the construction of local norms in these cases. About 3% of the sample were described as language-impaired children.

The CADeT provides two types of standard scores. One standard score (Mean = 10; *SD* = 3) is used in the interpretation of the individual components of language (e.g., Syntax, Semantics, Pragmatics). The other standard score (Mean = 100; *SD* = 15) is used in the interpretation of the Total Language score. The test also provides tables for percentile ranks so raw scores can be converted. Additionally, a table for developing confidence intervals based on standard error of measurement data is provided.

The test appears to have adequate internal consistency. This was analyzed with split-half reliability coefficients (generally >.80) and coefficient alpha. Test-retest reliability was analyzed with a relatively small sample of only 22 subjects limited to children at ages 4, 5, and 8. The coefficients ranged from .42 to .90 suggesting considerable variability in the stability among the different types of scores. The interrater agreement ranged from .37 to .99 with the area of grammar receiving the lowest coefficients.

Overall, the developers have attended to traditional psychometric issues related to reliability and the CADeT was shown to be acceptable on most measures. Some limitations, however, should be noted in terms of interrater agreement on grammar and the age ranges sampled for test-retest reliability.

The authors address the issue of validity in several ways. First, the authors engaged children between the ages of 5 and 8 years in a conversation to determine if the targets sampled in the CADeT also appeared with similar frequencies in spontaneous interactions. Unfortunately, the authors did not provide any data on the conversational sample in terms of length or elicitation method. Also, the comparison examined only the occurrence of specific language targets in both sample types. This shows only that more targets are present in the elicited condition than in the spontaneous sample, which could easily have been predicted. For validity purposes, it would have been interesting to determine if the errors in the spontaneous sample were similar to the errors that occurred on the CADeT.

Concurrent validity was computed on comparisons with the Test of Language Development (TOLD; Newcomer & Hammill, 1982); or TOLD-2 (Newcomer & Hammill, 1988). The sample size (*N* = 11) was, however, inadequate and prevents any meaningful interpretation. Comparisons were also done between the CADeT and the Bankson-Bernthal Test of Phonology (BBTOP; Bankson & Bernthal, 1990). Low correlations were found on phonological production scores. Higher correlations between word naming on the two measures were reported. Predictive validity studies using raw scores suggest the CADeT tended to produce more false negatives than false positives. This was not found when using normed scores. The accuracy of classifrication was 74% with the normed scores.

The construct validity of the CADeT was evaluated by showing relationships among the various domains on the instrument and factor analysis of the scores to determine the factor structure of the test. The results of these analyses support its validity at least as well as other language tests of a similar type.

Standardized language tests or approaches to elicit standardized samples all suffer from some distance between the actual use of communication skills in legitimate interactions and the communication used to accomplish the tasks used on the instrument. For example, there are no data provided as to the occurrence of specific types of errors in spontaneous conversations as compared to their occurrence on evaluation tasks. The authors say the CADeT is a "standardized language sample" (manual, p. 4) rather than a standardized test. This "standardization" of a language sample, however, results in a fair degree of distortion of real communication on a conversational level. Although the authors have made a real attempt to use tasks that are ecologically valid, there is still an element of artificiality in the test.

For example, the stories are essentially a delayed imitation task with only a very limited alteration in the child's sentence production. Perhaps the use of nominative modeling would have added to the ecological validity and resulted in similar grammatical forms with more disparate lexical items. The game, although interesting to children, results in a highly stilted interaction about specific pictures and single sentence productions. The "conversation" portion of the test sounds like a spontaneous interaction; however, it results in little more than single word and phrasal responses to questions in a rather formal question-and-answer format.

Thus, the notion of "validity" must be measured by more than statistical methods, and using the metric of ecological validity, the CADeT is similar to other tests that fall short of this goal. These limitations, however, should not detract from the fact that the CADeT does provide varied tasks to sample language, a scoring system that gives both norm-referenced and criterion-referenced scores and does provide an interesting assessment format for children. The test is recommended as a useful adjunct to spontaneous communication sampling and analysis.

REVIEWER'S REFERENCES

Newcomer, P. L., & Hammill, D. D. (1982). Test of Language Development: Primary. Austin, TX: PRO-ED, Inc.

Newcomer, P. L., & Hammill, D. D. (1988). Test of Language Development-2: Primary. Austin, TX: PRO-ED, Inc.

Bankson, N. W., & Bernthal, J. E. (1990). Bankson-Bernthal Test of Phonology. San Antonio, TX: Special Press.

Review of the Communication Abilities Diagnostic Test by DAVID A. SHAPIRO, Associate Professor of Communication Disorders, Department of Human Services, College of Education and Psychology, Western Carolina University, Cullowhee, NC:

Originally published as a doctoral dissertation at the University of Cincinnati, the Communication Abilities Diagnostic Test (CADeT) is a complex measure of language development for children ages 3 to 9 years. The components include an examiner's manual containing directions for administration, scoring, and interpretation, normative data, and mastery criteria; two picture books with parallel stories; a game board with cards, markers, and dice; record forms for transcribing and scoring the child's responses used in the norm-referenced test; criterion score forms for scoring the child's responses used in the criterion-referenced test; a technical manual addressing the model, development, standardization, and technical characteristics; and a carrying case. According to the authors, the CADeT is most sensitive to the language growth of children aged 3 to 5 years, and can be administered in 30 to 45 minutes. This reviewer found the administration time to be longer, and the time necessary for adequate preparation and training for administration, scoring, and interpretation to be substantial. The CADeT probes three areas of language—Semantics, Syntax, and Pragmatics—as well as recall and comprehension of spoken language with separate scores for each. Total Language scores are computed for classification or placement purposes. Raw scores are converted into percentile ranks and standard scores.

The CADeT samples language in three different contexts: stories, game, and conversation. Although the authors describe the contexts as naturalistic, this reviewer found the sampling contexts and methodologies to be artificially structured yet diversified. All responses are recorded verbatim for later scoring and analysis. In the stories context, two sets of parallel picture books are used whereby the examiner tells a story about one set of pictures and directs the child to tell a parallel story about the other set. The pictures in both books are colorful, appealing, and without distraction. Practice pictures and a practice story precede the test stories in order to train the child to the test format. The authors caution against encouraging imitation, preferring prompts such as "What is he doing?" or "What is happening?" to remain more "spontaneous." Although the caution is appropriate, the prompts and overall procedures encourage more elicitation (especially because the structure of the prompts provides the structure of the child's response) than spontaneous conversation.

Only the first test story ("A Day at the Beach") is used to obtain a normed score. This reviewer is concerned that a cultural or experiential interference exists in that many children have never seen the beach or experienced the activities being discussed. The other four stories are used to obtain criterion-referenced scores.

The game is played to create an opportunity to record pragmatic observations. Guidelines for making and recording judgments in the area of pragmatics include 34 questions about the child's performance during the stories, game, and conversation. The authors advise that the answers to the questions should be based on direct observation of the child's behavior, yet describe the method for evaluating the child's responses for pragmatics as subjective. An improvement, one that would effectively reduce the subjectivity of examiners' judgments, would be to include a space to record the direct observations that justify the judgments.

The conversation is structured by a series of 17 questions about the game and the stories. Again intending a spontaneous conversation, the questions provide a high degree of structure to the verbal interaction. According to the authors, the CADeT measures Semantics (rules governing communication of meaning) in the stories and game, Syntax (rules governing structural organization and relationships) in the stories and game, and Pragmatics (rules governing appropriate use of language with communicative contexts) in all three contexts.

Although the authors indicated the examiner's manual "contains all the directions necessary for learning to administer, score, and interpret the CADeT" (p. 3), adequate preparation for these processes requires a commitment on the part of the examiner and a working knowledge of standardized testing procedures and language sampling and analysis procedures. Directions for administering the test are complex. The step-by-step summary provided at the end of the directions is most useful. The authors should be credited for their recognition of the limitations of traditional standardized tests and their efforts to design a method of sampling and analyzing more conversational language behavior in a variety of communicative contexts. They refer to the CADeT as a standardized language sample, rather than a standardized test of language. The language behaviors that are scored necessarily reflect the inherent bias of the authors, as does the sampling format. The procedures are intended to achieve a more natural interaction between the examiner and child, yet do so with a relatively high degree of structure. That structure may facilitate conversationally meaningful interaction with a child for some examiners, yet may inhibit such interaction for others. There is no replacement for an examiner's ability to talk with a child.

Instructions for scoring the samples are given to obtain norm-referenced and criterion-referenced scores. To achieve norm-referenced scores, the story responses are scored on the bases of count of words, added structures, structure of the sentence(s), grammatical errors, meaning contributed to the child's story, consistency of perspective, and sentence modality and discourse form. Game responses are scored on count of words, grammatical errors, meaning appropriateness, and sentence modality and discourse form. Conversational responses are scored on responsiveness and accuracy. Guidelines and training protocols are provided for scoring each sampling context. As indicated, the preparation and scoring are complex and time-consuming. Frequent references to previous and later sections in the examiner's manual adds to the complexity. Training beyond that provided in the manual may prove necessary. The authors suggest that "Depending on how closely your scoring matches the model, either review this chapter again or practice on a sample you have obtained from administering CADeT" (p. 12).

Instructions are given to sum scores to compute raw scores, to convert those scores to normed scores, to compute a Total Language score and convert it to a normed score, and to express all scores in terms of confidence intervals. The CADeT reports three types of scores: raw scores, composite scores, and normed scores. Six raw scores are reported: Words, Structure, Grammar, Meaning, Pragmatics, and Comprehension. Four composite scores are reported: Semantics, Syntax, Language Expression, and Total Language. Each score is explained in the examiner's manual. Briefly, raw scores are computed by summing the points awarded to the child's response. Composite scores are computed by converting raw scores or sums of other composite scores to normed scores (standard scores) and summing those normed scores. The CADeT reports scores for two different dimensions of language, comprehension and expression, as well as a "global language score" reflecting overall performance. Extensive instructions are given for filling in the summary box on the cover of the record form, for reporting and interpreting standard scores and percentile ranks, and for establishing confidence intervals for interpreting scores.

Guidelines and sample protocols are given also for obtaining criterion-referenced scores in the story, game, and conversation contexts for semantics, syntax, and pragmatics. Unlike the summary scores provided for norm-referenced information, criterion-referenced scores address specific targets in each area. These targets include 34 pragmatic behaviors, 19 semantic relationships, and 40 syntactic constructions. Scoring these targets requires the examiner to analyze a set of responses from one or two stories, the game, and a brief conversation. The story responses contain most of the opportunities to score semantic and syntactic targets; the game responses provide most to score the pragmatic targets. Criterion-referenced scoring requires analysis of the child's responses to "A Day at the Beach" and one of the four other stories appropriate to the child's age on the basis of graduated semantic and syntactic complexity. Because no more than two stories are needed, reproduction masters are provided instead of printed forms. Recording and charting the criterion-referenced scores are done on the criterion score form, which can be used for any of the stories. The form provides space to record the occurrence of correct and incorrect use of all 93 targets. Definitions are given for the targets, and a method for recording and scoring is provided. The method is extremely complex yet well outlined, and requires substantial preparation and a related knowledge base. Additional instructions for criterion-referenced scoring of game and conversation responses are provided. Guidelines are given for interpreting criterion-referenced scores including how to display the scores for the individual targets, compare those scores to criteria based on performance of children sampled with the CADeT, and summarize a child's performance on each of the language components. Suggestions and cautions for interpreting these scores are provided, as are guidelines for planning interactive, experience-based intervention based on the CADeT results. Numerous tables are contained within the appendices of the examiner's manual and address Standard Scores, Percentile Ranks, and Supplementary Percentile Ranks; Criteria by Target; Percentile Ranks of Targets Mastered; and Percentages.

A separate technical manual contains information regarding the theoretical and research base, development and standardization, reliability, and validity. The authors indicate the test is grounded in theory and research that form the basis of current knowledge of language development. Although specific references are included and occasionally discussed, the construct (i.e., theoretical framework) upon which this test is based could be made more explicit. Furthermore, because of the importance of the information contained in the technical manual to prospective test users, the examiner's manual and technical manual should be integrated into one document. It is possible in the current organization for examiners to make decisions for selection and/or use of the CADeT without reviewing the technical manual. This would be unfortunate given the importance of agreement between the authors' and test users' assumptions about learning, language development, and intervention, and informed judgment by examiners regarding the appropriateness of the test for specific children.

The CADeT was developed on the basis of administration to 645 children between 3 and 9 years of age (577: 89.5% language normal; 68: 10.5% language impaired). Age criteria were established for Semantics, Syntax, and Pragmatics on the basis of field trials of 453 children. The reported data indicate that relatively few children aged 3, 4, 5, and 9 years (i.e., 24, 25, 48, and 34, respectively) were included for this field testing. The authors justified the small sample size for the 9-year-olds only by reporting that "no additional 9-year-olds were drawn from the standardization sample because no growth was observed for most of the targets between ages 8 and 9. The norm-referenced scoring of CADeT also indicated little or no growth from age 8 to 9 on the aspects of language measured" (technical manual, p. 11). The CADeT was standardized in 63 sites on 881 normally developing children and 47 language-impaired children between the ages of 3 and 9 years. Data provided for the standardization suggest the children studied were, after a statistical weighting for racial proportions, representative of a sample of the U.S.A. population. Factors considered included region of the country (the west was overrepresented and the other three regions were underrepresented), age, sex, race, and Spanish origin. Normative tables were constructed for six scores: Semantics, Syntax, Pragmatics, Language Comprehension, Language Expression, and Total Language. Percentile ranks were computed from frequency distributions of raw scores, and converted to normalized standard scores with a mean of 10 and a standard deviation of 3. The resulting standard scores for certain combinations were then summed to obtain composite standard scores. The procedures that were utilized for constructing the normative tables including composite scores were described in adequate detail.

Evidence of reliability, or consistency of results, was presented from the perspectives of internal consistency (how the performance on different parts of the score relate to overall language), stability (how the performance on the test changes over time), interrater reliability (how much agreement there is between different examiners' judgments), and standard error of measurement (how the test's reliability is reflected when reporting performance). Split-half reliability coefficients for Words, Grammar, and Meaning scores in both Stories (plus Structure) and Game by age revealed 29 between .81 and .96, and 20 between .31 and .78. Most of the coefficients falling below .80 were for Grammar in all age groups. Coefficient alpha for scores by age revealed all above .80 for Pragmatics (mean, .86) and all but one below .80 for Comprehension (mean, .76). Stratified alpha for scores by age were higher for the two composites made up of more parts (Language Expression mean, .91; Total Language mean, .93) than for Semantics (mean, .80) and Syntax (mean, .53). Coefficient alpha for mastery summary scores by age were computed for Pragmatics (from .76 to .98), Semantics (.59 to .84), and Syntax (.80 to .91). Finally, correlations between scores on the practice story and test story by age were computed (Words, .64 to .75; Structure, .46 to .64; Grammar, .00 to .66; Meaning, .48 to .70). These data reveal a fair degree of internal consistency. Test-retest correlations on 22 children aged 4, 5, and 8 were computed for Semantics (.65), Syntax (.42), Pragmatics (.68), Language Comprehension (.59), Language Expression (.90), and Total Language (.73), revealing a fair degree of stability. Twelve raters who scored batches of protocols from all ages revealed 78% to 92% agreement for the Stories scores, 52% to 92% agreement for the Game scores, and correlations from .37 to .99, thus indicating a fair degree of interrater agreement. The authors adequately discussed using the standard error of measurement for norm- and criterion-referenced scores, and comparing criterion-referenced scores from repeated administrations.

Evidence of validity, or the extent to which the test measures what it purports to measure, was presented for content validity, criterion validity (concurrent and predictive), and construct validity. Content validity was supported by making reference to the theoretical and research base for content selection and scoring format. As noted earlier, the underlying construct could have been addressed more directly. Concurrent validity seemed inadequately supported by providing correlations for 11 children between the standard scores on the CADeT and one other language test and one phonology test (i.e., a content area not sampled by the CADeT). Predictive validity was adequately supported by providing evidence of a series of discriminant analyses. Construct validity was adequately supported by providing evidence for developmental increases in CADeT scores, relationships among part scores, relationship between norm-referenced and criterion-referenced scores, and factor analysis of CADeT scores.

In summary, the CADeT is a complex and standardized method of collecting and analyzing a language sample in three predetermined and structured contexts. Examiners will need to be committed to study and learn the methodology, which assumes substantial practice and a thorough knowledge base in language development and intervention. The test's organization is complex and the evidence for reliability and validity is fair. Examiners can expect a tremendous amount of norm-referenced and criterion-referenced data for each child evaluated. According to the authors, "the scores one obtains depend not so much on the child's performance as the depth with which an examiner wishes to analyze and evaluate the responses" (technical manual, p. 2). With this caution, the CADeT is a welcomed departure from traditional language tests and should prove to be a valuable part of a comprehensive plan for evaluating language development of young children.

[87]

Community College Student Experiences Questionnaire.

Purpose: To measure the quality of effort community college students invest in using the college resources provided for their learning and development and to relate this to their estimate of progress toward educational goals.
Population: Community college students.
Publication Dates: 1990–92.
Acronym: CCSEQ.
Scores: Responses noted in 9 areas: Background, Work, Family, College Program, College Courses, College Activities, Estimate of Gains, College Environment, Additional Questions.
Administration: Group.
Price Data, 1993: \$.75 per questionnaire; \$1.50 per questionnaire processing; \$70 tape/disk fee (including student responses, scores, and a summary report of the results); \$11 per test manual and comparative data ('92, 95 pages).
Time: 20(30) minutes.
Authors: Jack Friedlander, C. Robert Pace, and Penny W. Lehman.
Publisher: UCLA Center for the Study of Evaluation.

Review of the Community College Student Experiences Questionnaire by CHARLES HOUSTON, Director of Research and Planning, Virginia Western Community College, Roanoke, VA:

The Community College Student Experiences Questionnaire (CCSEQ) is a student survey that focuses on four aspects of community college students and their college experiences:

1. Background. Who are the students and why are they at the college?
2. Quality of Effort: What do they do at the college, or more specifically, how extensively and productively do they use the facilities and opportunities the college provides?
3. College Environment. What are some of their impressions about the college?
4. Gains/Progress: What progress do they think they have made toward important goals?

The development and framework of the CCSEQ resulted from Jack Friedlander's professional focus in community colleges and his previous research experiences with C. Robert Pace's College Student Experiences Questionnaire (CSEQ; T4:588). Friedlander noted that the diverse characteristics, aims, experiences, and outcomes of community college students required expanding certain aspects of the CSEQ questionnaire. In 1985, he constructed and pilot tested at Napa Community College (CA) a new questionnaire, which was proposed to evaluate several constructs similar to the CSEQ. In Spring 1989, the Center for the Study of Evaluation (CSE) at UCLA prepared a "try-out" edition of this new questionnaire requesting participating community colleges to make any revisions and/or suggestions. These efforts resulted in the first published edition of the CCSEQ in 1990 including a final published edition that demonstrated that the "quality of effort" construct was applicable to community college students. The CSE at UCLA now serves as the administrative and financial base for both the CSEQ and the CCSEQ.

CONTENT OF THE CCSEQ. The first three sections of the CCSEQ are background questions (i.e., age; gender; ethnicity; hours per week spent working on a job, studying, and on campus; grades, number of credits taken; effect of job and family responsibilities on college work; reason for attending college; courses taken; and vocational concentration). These background variables can facilitate the comparison of specific subgroup's responses to other CCSEQ questions.

The fourth section of the CCSEQ contains 83 items grouped into 12 topics: (*a*) course activities, (*b*) library activities, (*c*) faculty, (*d*) student acquaintances, (*e*) art, music, and theater activities, (*f*) writing activities, (*g*) science activities, (*h*) vocational skills, (*i*) clubs and organizations, (*j*) athletics activities, (*k*) counseling and career planning, and (*l*) learning and study skills. These first 10 groups of activity items require the student to select one of the following responses: (1) *never*, (2) *occasionally*, (3) *often*, or (4) *very often*. The Counseling and Career Planning section requires (1) yes or (2) no responses and the Learning and Study Skill sections ask students whether they have received *none*, *some*, or *a lot* of instruction in each of these skills.

The fifth section asks students to report how much they have gained or made progress toward a series of 23 educational goals. Students indicate their progress toward each goal by selecting (1) *very little*, (2) *some*, (3) *quite a bit*, and (4) *very much*. (The CCSEQ: Test Manual and Comparative Data noted five responses include *none*, which represents leaving the response blank.)

The final section asks seven items about the College Environment including an index of satisfaction and an assessment of the campus environment regarding student interactions, interactions with faculty/support staff, and value of course work.

The last page of the CCSEQ also provides space for 16 locally developed questions in which the college can either ask students about additional aspects of the college or use additional questions to identify subgroups of students. A student identification number can also be requested on this final page.

PSYCHOMETRIC PROPERTIES OF THE CCSEQ. Although the authors have indicated that the CCSEQ is too new for establishing norming data, major efforts have been made to provide descriptive and analytical statistics including means, standard deviations, skewness/kurtosis, reliability coefficients, factor analyses, inter-item correlations by scale, and other comparative data. The three samples used for comparative purposes were: the total students sample (n = 7,683); the transfer sample (n = 4,024); and the vocational sample (n = 1,607). In addition, several suggested uses for the information gained from the CCSEQ included: assessing institutional effectiveness, compiling information for an accreditation self-study, evaluating general education programs, measuring student involvement, improving instructional programs and student support services, and comparing the experiences of students with students of other schools.

REVIEWER'S COMMENTS. The costs associated with using the CCSEQ include: Tape/Disk Fee: $150.00; Purchase of CCSEQ: $.75 per copy of the CCSEQ; and Processing Fee: $1.50 per completed questionnaire. Although these fees are very reasonable, each college must weigh the cost/benefits for these types of projects. Few college staff will be able to design and complete a similar study without greatly exceeding these costs; however, the college administration and faculty must discern the specific values of knowing whether or not its students have discussed their "school performance, difficulties, or personal problems with an instructor" (test form, p. 3). If findings from these types of studies can play a crucial role in the way a college's faculty and administration thinks about teaching and learning, then they should proceed immediately with these research activities. If the results are to be shelved with other student outcome assessment reports, then the value of this type of study is questionable. Bridging the cultural diversity gaps of community college students will be faced by many community colleges in the 1990s. In summary, the CCSEQ properly used can provide insights into assisting community colleges to address the diverse issues of the late 20th century. In any case, the readers should discern the positives and negatives of the CSEQ before experimenting with the CCSEQ.

Review of the Community College Student Experiences Questionnaire by ROSEMARY E. SUTTON, Associate Professor, and HINSDALE BERNARD, Assistant Professor, College of Education, Cleveland State University, Cleveland, OH:

In the wake of increasing demands for monitoring the quality of education provided by institutions of higher education, multifaceted self-report assessment instruments such as the Community College Student Experiences Questionnaire (CCSEQ) are in demand. The CCSEQ solicits information on students' backgrounds, status in college, coursework, college activities, estimate of gains, and their college environment.

The background section focuses on items related to age, gender, ethnicity, work, and family. The section on students' status in college addresses issues of load, grades, and time spent preparing for classes. The section on coursework focuses on the content of courses taken (e.g., social sciences, foreign languages, English composition) and the kind of the degree or diploma desired.

The majority of the questionnaire asks the students about their participation in a variety of college activities. The extent of this participation in eight areas (Course Activities; Library Activities; Faculty; Student Acquaintances; Art, Music, and Theater Activities; Writing Activities; Science Activities; Vocational Skills) is labeled Quality of Effort. The authors argue that Quality of Effort is an important dimension because what students gain from their college experience depends largely on their input. This input is measured by items such as, "Did additional reading on topics that were introduced and discussed in class" (Course Activities subscale) and "Completed an experiment/project using scientific methods" (Science Activities subscale). Possible responses are based on a 4-point Likert scale that ranges from *never* to *very often*.

An additional four areas of college activities are assessed but are not considered part of the Quality of

Effort dimension. These areas are: Clubs and Organizations; Athletic Activities; Counseling and Career Planning; and Learning and Study Skills. Examples of items are "Read or asked about a student club or organization" and "Read information about a 4-year college or university that you were interested in attending."

The Estimate of Gains section contains 23 items which ask students to assess, on a 4-point scale ranging from *very little* to *very much*, their perceptions of their growth in academic or personal goals. Examples of these goals are "Writing clearly and effectively" and "Understanding myself—my abilities and interests." The final section (seven items) assesses satisfaction with the college environment with questions such as "Do you feel this college is a stimulating and often exciting place to be?"

USES OF THE CCSEQ. The authors claim that the CCSEQ can be used for assessing institutional effectiveness; accreditation and self-study; evaluating general education, transfer, and vocational programs; measuring student interest, impressions, and satisfaction; and devising ways of improving student involvement. However, although the Quality of Effort subscales do identify the students' perceptions about their involvement in a variety of activities, the questionnaire does not ask for specific reasons for the level of involvement. For example, students are asked how frequently they used the library (e.g., "Used the library as a quiet place to read or study materials you brought with you") but not about how convenient or comfortable the library is (e.g., Are the library hours convenient? Do you feel safe walking to the library at night? How well does the heating/air conditioning work?). Thus, reasons for low involvement in library use (or any other area) cannot be identified and addressed.

NORMS. Because this instrument is new, norms are not available. The manual does provide, however, descriptive and psychometric data on the CCSEQ based on over 7,500 students including both transfer and vocation students. Demographics of this sample are provided, and the 24 community colleges which were sampled are listed. Unfortunately, this listing does not contain state identifications so it is not easy to determine how regionally representative these data are.

RELIABILITY. The manual accompanying the questionnaire clearly presents for the eight Quality of Effort subscales Cronbach's alpha values ranging from .83 to .94. No reliability indices are provided for the other sections of the CCSEQ. Although indices such as Cronbach's alpha are not appropriate, test-retest reliability should have been presented for the entire questionnaire. This omission is particularly serious for the Estimate of Gains section because the authors argue that the relationships between Quality of Effort subscales and Estimate of Gains items support their theory that effort is related to progress toward achieving important educational goals.

VALIDITY. In order to lend support to the underlying structure of the CCSEQ, three factor analyses were performed on each Quality of Effort subscale and in each case the one-factor solution was more appropriate than the two- and three-factor models. The factor loadings ranged from .46 to.91, providing further evidence that the subscales are unidimensional. These factor loadings and the Cronbach alpha indices may be artificially inflated, however, because of the physical layout of the questionnaire. The questionnaire is divided into subsections containing similar items worded in the same direction. This makes the instrument easy to read and complete but may result in a response set bias.

Unfortunately, the manual provides little clear information about validity beyond the factor analyses. The theoretical basis for this instrument, Quality of Effort, is not elaborated and substantiated. The authors may have omitted this because the CCSEQ is a modification of the widely used College Student Experiences Questionnaire (CSEQ), a questionnaire that measures quality of effort in 4-year colleges and universities. However, data supporting the CCSEQ should stand on their own. In addition, no data are provided that compare sections of this instrument with any other related instrument or student behavior. For example, Quality of Effort subscales could be compared with well-known motivation questionnaires or some Estimate of Gains items could be compared to actual classroom performance (e.g., the item "Writing clearly and effectively" could be compared with grades on written assignments).

The authors do provide data to support their notion that Quality of Effort is related to progress toward achieving important educational goals. To do this they correlated the 23 individual items of the Estimate of Gains section with the eight Quality of Effort scales. Moderate to high correlations were reported for logically related items and subscales. For example, the correlation between the Quality of Effort subscale, science activities, and the Estimate of Gains item "Understanding the role of science and technology in society" was .59. The relationships between the scales and corresponding items do provide evidence of validity; however, stronger evidence requires examining relationships between scales (or items) within the CCSEQ and some other questionnaire or behavioral index, rather than only examining these internal correlations.

CONCLUSION. Community colleges in search of an instrument to assist with self-study of institutional effectiveness may select the CCSEQ because it provides a variety of information, takes only 20–30 minutes to administer, and is scored by a professional testing organization that provides a variety of reports. Users must be cautioned, however, that the reliability and validity evidence is limited. In addition, although the CCSEQ does provide a multidimensional profile of the institution and student quality of effort, it is not intended to generate data that may suggest specific institutional modifications. For example, an item in the faculty subscale is, "Made an appointment to meet with an instructor in his/her office" but even if students state *never* or *occasionally* this instrument does not solicit possible reasons for the responses. For example, students may not see faculty members because they do not need one-to-one attention, and/or the office hours of the instructor may be inconvenient, and/or the instructors may be unfriendly and intimidating, etc. Identifying such reasons is necessary if an institution wishes to remedy a problem; therefore, community colleges seeking to become more responsive to their students cannot rely solely on data from the CCSEQ.

[88]

Comprehensive Assessment of Symptoms and History.

Purpose: "Designed as a structured interview and recording instrument for documenting the signs, symptoms, and history of subjects evaluated in research studies of the major psychoses and affective disorders."
Population: Psychiatric patients.
Publication Date: 1987.
Acronym: CASH.
Scores: Interview divided into 3 major sections: Present State (Sociodemographic Data, Evaluation of Current Condition, Psychotic Syndrome, Manic Syndrome, Major Depressive Syndrome, Treatment, Cognitive Assessment, Global Assessment Scale, Diagnosis for Current Episode), Past History (History of Onset and Hospitalization, Past Symptoms of Psychosis, Characterization of Course, Past Symptoms of Affective Disorder), Lifetime History (History of Somatic Therapy, Alcoholism, Drug Use and Abuse and Dependence, Modified Premorbid Adjustment Scale, Premorbid or Intermorbid Personality, Functioning During Past Five Years, Global Assessment Scale, Diagnosis for Lifetime).
Administration: Individual.
Price Data: Available from publisher.
Time: [60–180] minutes.
Comments: The CASH is one component of a modular assessment battery available from the publisher.
Author: Nancy C. Andreasen.
Publisher: Nancy C. Andreasen.

TEST REFERENCES

1. Andreasen, N. C., Flaum, M., Swayze, V. W., II, Tyrrell, G., & Arndt, S. (1990). Positive and negative symptoms in schizophrenia. *Archives of General Psychiatry, 47*, 615-621.

2. Andreasen, N. C., Swayze, V. W., II, Flaum, M., Yates, W. R., Arndt, S., & McChesney, C. (1990). Ventricular enlargement in schizophrenia evaluated with computed tomographic scanning. *Archives of General Psychiatry, 47*, 1008-1015.

3. Swayze, V. W., II, Andreasen, N. C., Alliger, R. J., Ehrhardt, J. C., & Yuh, W. T. C. (1990). Structural brain abnormalities in bipolar affective disorder. *Archives of General Psychiatry, 47*, 1054-1059.

4. Crowe, R. R., Black, D. W., Wesner, R., Andreasen, N. C., Cookman, A., & Roby, J. (1991). Lack of linkage to chromosome 5q11-q13 markers in six schizophrenia pedigrees. *Archives of General Psychiatry, 48*, 357-361.

5. Andreasen, N. C., Flaum, M., & Arndt, S. (1992). The Comprehensive Assessment of Symptoms and History (CASH): An instrument for assessing diagnosis and psychopathology. *Archives of General Psychiatry, 49*, 615-623.

6. Andreasen, N. C., Rezai, K., Alliger, R., Swayze, V. W., II, Flaum, M., Kirchner, P., Cohen, G., & O'Leary, D. S. (1992). Hypofrontality in neuroleptic-naive patients and in patients with chronic schizophrenia. *Archives of General Psychiatry, 49*, 943-958.

7. Wang, Z. W., Black, D., Andreasen, N. C., & Crowe, R. R. (1993). A linkage study of chromosome 11q in schizophrenia. *Archives of General Psychiatry, 50*, 212-223.

8. Wang, Z. W., Black, D., Andreasen, N., & Crowe, R. R. (1993). Pseudoautosomal locus for schizophrenia excluded in 12 pedigrees. *Archives of General Psychiatry, 50*, 199-204.

9. Amador, X. F., Flaum, M., Andreasen, N. C., Strauss, D. H., Yule, S. A., Clark, S. C., & Gorman, J. M. (1994). Awareness of illness in schizophrenia and schizoaffective and mood disorders. *Archives of General Psychiatry, 51*, 826-836.

10. Chen, E. Y. H., Wilkins, A. J., & McKenna, P. J. (1994). Semantic memory is both impaired and anomalous in schizophrenia. *Psychological Medicine, 24*, 193-202.

11. Gupta, S., Andreasen, N. C., Arndt, S., Flaum, M., Schultz, S. K., Hubbard, W. C., & Smith, M. (1995). Neurological soft signs in neuroleptic-naive and neuroleptic-treated schizophrenic patients and in normal comparison subjects. *American Journal of Psychiatry, 152*, 191-196.

12. Persico, A. M., Wang, Z. W., Black, D. W., Andreasen, N. C., Uhl, G. R., & Crowe, R. R. (1995). Exclusion of close linkage of the dopamine transporter gene with schizophrenia spectrum disorders. *American Journal of Psychiatry, 152*, 134-136.

Review of the Comprehensive Assessment of Symptoms and History by PATRICIA A. BACHELOR, Professor of Psychology, California State University, Long Beach, CA:

The Comprehensive Assessment of Symptoms and History (CASH) is a structured interview and data-capturing instrument of research subjects' signs, symptoms, and history of major affective disorders and psychoses. The extensive scope of descriptions included in this instrument enables researchers to examine the social, biological, cognitive, and psychological correlates of behavior and use a variety of criteria to determine diagnoses. Approximately 1,000 questions spanning 150 pages may be used to probe subjects about a current relevant illness, focusing on detailed descriptions of the course of illness. Data can also be obtained from past records and/or other sources. The examiner should have experience with psychiatric patients and should practice using the CASH. Training manuals and tapes are available upon request.

The CASH interview consists of three sections: Present State (sociodemographic data is included), Past History, and Lifetime History. Content assessed within the Present State section includes positive and negative psychotic symptoms, laterality, cognitive functioning, depressive symptoms, and mania. The overall severity of symptoms is given a global rating as well. Within the Past History section, previous episodes of affective and psychotic disorders, and any interrelationships, are explored in an attempt to characterize the course of illness over time. Additional information useful in describing a patient such as other disorders, history of treatment, premorbid functioning, and psychosocial functioning are recorded within the Lifetime History section.

Each section of the CASH is introduced with a clear presentation of the purpose of the section. Items are often defined and probes suggested. Most items are scored on a 6-point Likert-type scale with well-defined anchor points. For the most part, inquiry and interview items are grouped together as are observationally based items.

No technical manual accompanied the CASH test booklet. The test booklet did not contain any information on reliability, validity, or test development, nor did it contain normative data. This is out of compliance with the *Standards for Educational and Psychological Testing* (AERA, APA, & NCME, 1985). Upon requesting materials which would describe the psychometric properties of the CASH, I was sent two reprints. The data in one of those articles provided the quantitative information used in this review.

RELIABILITY. Prospective subjects for the reliability study were patients who had consecutive acute-care admissions to the University of Iowa (Iowa City) Psychiatric Hospital. Subjects were selected if mood or psychotic symptoms were the presenting problem. Thirty subjects so identified participated in the study. Diagnostic categories of the subjects were presented but no other descriptive or demographic information was provided. The opportunistic character of the sample calls into question examinee comparability and external validity interpretation.

A crossover design was used to estimate the reliability of the CASH. Subjects were first interviewed by two raters, one conducted the CASH and the other rater observed and clarified questions at the conclusion of the interview. The following day, within 24 hours, another interview with the CASH was conducted by a third rater. All raters had access to patients' medical records and scored the CASH independently. Eight raters, each with at least one year of experience with the CASH, participated in the study. Thus, the assessment of interrater reliability is embedded within an assessment of test-retest reliability. Given this design, the estimates of test-retest and interrater reliability as measured by intraclass r coefficients on several summary ratings were of adequate magnitude to warrant claims of consistency of measurement. Half of the test-retest intraclass correlations were greater than or equal to .65 and 75% of the intraclass correlations assessing interrater reliability were equal to or greater than .65.

VALIDITY. Validity studies are ongoing. It is hoped that evidence supportive of the claims of accurate symptom reporting will be forthcoming. Two preliminary studies were mentioned in Andreasen, Flaum, & Arndt (1992) but unfortunately were not referenced. Vague statements about these studies failed to reveal which type of validity was assessed or to provide any description of subjects. Intraclass correlations were reported but the lack of supporting detail about the validity study and the data derived from it calls into question the legitimacy of the conclusion of validity. Particularly problematic was that one study used a "consensus" CASH to serve as a criterion. This reviewer would suggest that an independent assessment, such as expert ratings, would be preferable psychometrically.

SUMMARY. The CASH is an individually administered structured interview that is extensive in its coverage of signs, symptoms, and history of research subjects' psychoses and affective disorders. Over 1,000 questions are contained in the test booklet which is divided into the Present State, Past History, and Lifetime History sections. Each section of the CASH contains introductory comments, instructions for administration, suggested probes, and anchor points. No technical manual was provided. The information on the psychometric properties and standardization sample was reported in a single research article. Claims of validity are premature but there is modest support for assertions of interrater and test-retest reliability of selected summary ratings. The author should prepare a technical manual containing a complete presentation of psychometric and normative data to accompany the CASH which conforms to the *Standards for Educational and Psychological Testing* (AERA, APA, & NCME, 1985). Consequently, in its current state, the CASH should be considered experimental and its use be limited to a data collection instrument in research settings.

REVIEWER'S REFERENCES

American Educational Research Association, American Psychological Association, & National Council on Measurement in Education. (1985). *Standards for educational and psychological testing*. Washington, DC: American Psychological Association, Inc.

Andreasen, N. C., Flaum, M., & Arndt, S. (1992). The comprehensive assessment of symptoms and history (CASH). *Archives of General Psychiatry, 49*, 615-623.

Review of the Comprehensive Assessment of Symptoms and History by BARBARA J. KAPLAN, Psychologist, Western New York Institute for the Psychotherapies, Orchard Park, NY:

The Comprehensive Assessment of Symptoms and History (CASH) is one of a group of interview schedules produced by the Mental Health Clinical Research Center, this one originating with the group at the University of Iowa College of Medicine. The interviews are those used in ongoing studies of individuals with schizophrenia and affective disorders, and the CASH appears likely to replace such instruments as Spitzer, Endicott, and Robin's (1978) Schedule of Affective Disorders and Schizophrenia—Lifetime Version (SADS-L). What the CASH adds to many other instruments is some systematic information on the somatic, social, and cognitive domains. This knowledge may serve as a valuable supplement to the symptoms and course of the illness as they are usually assessed.

The CASH itself includes sections to record information on the present episode and past history of the current disorder. Data are also included on the lifetime course of illness and the history of treatment with psychopharmacological substances, drug use and abuse adjustment, and personality dysfunction.

The psychometric properties of the instrument have been largely overlooked. Training manuals and tapes are available "on request," and these materials allow interviewers to learn how to negotiate the lengthy interview format. The instrument, however, is not one that can be used reliably with these materials alone. To begin with, the CASH does not include within it the basis for screening for the disorders it assesses. This work must be done prior to using the CASH. In addition, because this interview has been developed as part of the research protocol with patients already identified with schizophrenia or affective disorders, no information is available on the extent to which the interview itself discriminates these disorders from other overlapping diagnoses that reflect less serious psychopathology. In short, the CASH cannot and should not be used to make these diagnoses.

The CASH is an interview that runs about 150 pages and depending on the complexity of the syndrome and its history, might take several hours to administer. It allows the interviewer to code the presence and duration of symptoms as well as the severity of stressors that may have led to the onset of an episode.

The test itself provides no information as to the number of people on whom it has been standardized, selection of the research participants already used, or the reliability of the diagnoses generated compared to other diagnostic instruments available. The authors do indicate that users of the CASH can make diagnoses consistent with other diagnostic schemes such as the *DSM-III-R* (American Psychiatric Association, 1987). The principal author of the CASH, Nancy Andreasen, was part of the *DSM-IV* (American Psychiatric Association, 1994) Task Force so one can expect the CASH to be consistent with more recent diagnostic standards. Because of the current practice of updating diagnostic standards, this flexibility is a strength of the interview, but it also suggests that those using the CASH must possess considerable expertise in working with severely affected psychiatric populations. What the CASH does very well is to provide a *comprehensive* survey of symptoms and correlates of the disorders it assesses. Because of this strength, it can be a valuable part of the diagnostic workup or research protocol.

This is not an instrument to be used by clinicians or researchers who are still in training. Its reliability appears to depend on considerable preexisting knowledge of the disorders and the population they affect. The CASH may prove a valuable tool in expanding our knowledge of the linkages between psychopathology and the realms of social, cognitive, and biological functioning. The instrument is not appropriate, however, for most clinical settings.

REVIEWER'S REFERENCES

Spitzer, R. L., Endicott, J., & Robins, E. (1978). Schedule of Affective Disorders and Schizophrenia—Lifetime Version (SADS-L). New York: Biometrics Research, New York State Psychiatric Institute.

American Psychiatric Association. (1987). *Diagnostic and statistical manual of mental disorders, third edition—revised* (DSM-III-R). Washington, DC: American Psychiatric Association.

American Psychiatric Association (1994). *Diagnostic and statistical manual of mental disorders, fourth edition* (DSM-IV). Washington, DC: American Psychiatric Association.

[89]

Comprehensive Test of Visual Functioning.

Purpose: Designed to identify and differentiate type of visual perceptual dysfunction.

Population: Ages 8 and over.

Publication Date: 1990.

Acronym: CTVF.

Scores, 9: Visual/Letter Integration, Visual/Writing Integration, Nonverbal Visual Closure, Nonverbal Visual Reasoning/Memory, Spatial Orientation/Memory/Motor, Spatial Orientation/Motor, Visual Design/Motor, Visual Design/Memory/Motor, Total.

Administration: Individual.

Price Data, 1992: $79 per complete kit including manual (64 pages), stimulus cards/easel, and stimulus items; $18 per manual; $35 per examiner's directions and scoring protocol (18 pages); $22.50 per 25 examinee test booklets; $22.50 per stimulus cards/easel.

Time: (25) minutes.

Comments: "Norm-referenced"; includes 4 additional subtests (Visual Acuity, Visual Processing/Figure-Ground, Visual Tracking, Reading Word Analysis) which do not contribute to the overall visual performance quotient.

Authors: Sue L. Larson, Evelyn Buethe, and Gary J. Vitali.

Publisher: Slosson Educational Publications, Inc.

Review of the Comprehensive Test of Visual Functioning by STEPHEN R. HOOPER, Associate Professor of Psychiatry, University of North Carolina School of Medicine, Chapel Hill, NC:

According to the authors, the Comprehensive Test of Visual Functioning (CTVF) was designed to address several key problems in the assessment domain. These include the relative dearth of instruments designed to assess visual functions in a comprehensive and efficient manner, the usefulness of data for educational and clinical programming, and the availability of such procedures to a variety of professionals.

The materials are simple, but relatively durable, and should present few problems to their users. The test booklet is quite long (i.e., 18 pages), but fairly detailed in terms of providing the examiner with information regarding the materials needed, directions, scoring criteria, and special notations. The test also is "user-friendly," and test consumers with modest amounts of experience should have little difficulty learning the administration and scoring of this test. The testing time as stated in the manual (i.e., 25 minutes) is reasonably accurate, although this time clearly will increase with more severely involved patients.

The CTVF was designed to be used by a "diversity of professionals" (manual, p. 3), and the manual authors mention no restrictions on who should use this test. They do note, however, that the CTVF should not be used to make specific diagnoses without the inclusion of other diagnostic information. The test manual is brief, but written in a satisfactory manner; however, an errata sheet is provided because of a sizable number of errors in the manual. Three case studies also are provided, but the data tend to be presented in a unidimensional fashion and are not integrated with other information about the patients.

The CTVF was "designed as a general measure of visual functioning predicated on a neuropsychological model" (manual, p. 4). Although constructs of holistic and simultaneous processing are alluded to, no clear theoretical model is described. Further, even the constructs described are a mixture of constructs (e.g., Visual Design/Memory/Motor), thus raising questions regarding how to interpret obtained results. The test does include three screening subtests (i.e., Visual Acuity, Visual Processing/Figure Ground, Visual Tracking), two of which provide guidance to the examiner as to whether testing with the CTVF should continue. This is a nice feature typically not included in many psychological or educational tests.

The statistical properties of the CTVF are unrefined and quite poor. The manual authors state that a large pool of potential items were secured at the outset of test development but, outside of using consensus of opinion for item inclusion, there are no data describing how items were developed or selected for inclusion. There are no data presented in the manual related to item-total correlations, difficulty levels, or subsequent placement of the items within a specific subtest. For example, the Nonverbal Visual Closure subtest consists of incomplete drawings of 10 common objects (e.g., boy, turtle, owl), and the individual is asked to identify the object. It is unclear how these items were selected or how the items were placed in the subtest. In addition, some of the subtests are based on faulty reasoning, and this will cloud their ultimate clinical utility. As an example, the examinee is not permitted to sound out the words orally on the Visual/Letter Integration subtest but, rather, is encouraged to decode the word via visual methods. Most decoding strategies tend to be phonological, or a combination of phonological and orthographic methods, and not to consider these factors only serves to cloud the interpretation of the findings. In fact, outside of the actual visual recognition involved, the task actually may be a phonologically based task or, at best, one that taps into visual memory.

Information pertaining to the reliability of the CTVF also was quite meager. Interrater reliability was reported for the Total Visual Functioning standard score and the Visual/Writing Integration subtest. Using three raters, two of whom were blind to the status of the examinees, reliability coefficients ranged from .89 to .94 on the Visual/Writing Integration subtest, and from .95 to .97 for the Total Visual Functioning score. No interrater reliabilities were reported for any of the other subtests, although these would have been helpful given that there are other subtests having a high degree of subjectivity in the scoring (e.g., Visual Design/Motor, Visual Design/Memory/Motor, Spatial Orientation/Memory/Motor, Spatial Orientation/Motor subtests). A single alpha coefficient of .80 was generated, apparently for the Total Visual Functioning score; however, no internal consistency estimates are presented for any of the subtests. No temporal stability support was presented.

Given the lack of reliability, the validity of the CTVF is in question. The manual authors describe a process whereby face validity was established by having experts concur with item selection, although few details are provided. (This attempt might be better conceptualized as a content validity procedure. There is little importance to face validity.) The intercorrelations of the subtests also were quite high, suggesting the possibility of undue redundancy between the subtests. Factorial validity, arguably presented within the context of test reliability, apparently generated two factors. Outside of a modest narrative description, however, few data are provided on these findings (e.g., the loading of each subtest on the factors, what rotations were used, etc.). No concurrent or predictive validity data were presented.

Discriminant validity findings were described showing the utility of the CTVF to distinguish between a normal group and two disabled groups. The two disabled groups did not differ on the Total Visual Functioning score. Similarly, the Total Visual Functioning score was able to distinguish between five different age groups, although the developmental significance of this finding was not described. In fact, few details are presented with respect to these two studies (e.g., what variables might have been covaried to change these results; standard deviations, ranges, comparison of these groups across the subtests), again, making the results difficult to evaluate with respect to the clinical utility of the CTVF.

A brief discussion of test sensitivity and specificity is provided, but no data are presented with respect to this issue. Further, "the authors believe that persons with standard scores one standard deviation below the mean or greater should be failed and referred on for more definitive testing." This guideline takes into account only a normative interpretation of the data, as opposed to an ipsative interpretation. It does not state what "more definitive testing" should be conducted—especially if this is a comprehensive test of visual functioning.

Normative data are provided in the form of scaled scores for each subtest, and the average sum of scaled scores is presented for nine age bands. It is not clear from what populations these data were obtained, population characteristics, or the size of the normative sample. Further, from the tables provided, it appears there are ceiling effects on the tasks, with only one subtest allowing scores to fluctuate upwards as much as two standard deviations (i.e., Spatial Orientation/Memory/Motor).

In summary, the CTVF was designed to be a comprehensive measure of visual processes. Although well intended, the test does not appear to meet the stated goals in the manual. Basic test development standards are not described in detail, and the few psychometric properties that are presented appear tenable at best. Also, without a well-developed theoretical model to guide the test, its interpretation appears limited. In fact, even the case studies described in the manual do little to support its use in educational and clinical programming efforts. With many of the psychometric properties being poor or unknown, this test should not be used in clinical or research arenas beyond attempting to obtain a structured observation of an individual's visual-perceptual functioning on the tasks provided.

Review of the Comprehensive Test of Visual Functioning by DOUGLAS J. McRAE, Educational Measurement Specialist, Private Consultant, Monterey, CA:

PURPOSE. The purpose of the Comprehensive Test of Visual Functioning (CTVF) is to provide a general measure of visual functioning in order potentially to identify "at risk" individuals, age 8 and above.

DESCRIPTION. The CTVF consists of 12 subtests (8 of which contribute to a numerical scorc) mcasuring various facets of visual functioning. The manual authors state the CTVF may be administered in 25 minutes or less. The first four subtests (Visual Acuity, Visual Processing, Visual Tracking, and Reading Word Analysis) are scored pass-fail only and are used to establish a minimal level of visual/cognitive functioning for the remaining subtests to be administered and scored validly. The remaining eight subtests (Visual/Letter Integration, Visual/Writing Integration, Nonverbal Visual Closure, Nonverbal Visual Reasoning/Memory, Spatial Orientation/Memory/Motor, Spatial Orientation/Motor, Visual Design/Motor, and Visual Design/Memory/Motor) each yield a raw score and a scale score derived from norms tables. The scale scores are then summed to yield a Total Visual Functioning Standard Score that has pass-fail points identified for each of five age levels (8, 9–11, 12, 13–15, and 16–up).

RATIONALE. The CTVF is predicated on a neuropsychological model that assumes that visual perception involves a holistic and simultaneous visual scanning. The CTVF detects visual problems by nature of dysfunction rather than anatomical site of lesion. Initially a large pool of tasks were developed from the clinical experience and expertise of the authors. This pool was winnowed to 11 tasks via field testing. A factor analytic study revealed that 3 of the 11 tasks had positive loadings on a second factor judged not to measure the visual functioning construct. These 3 tasks were discarded, yielding the 8 numerically scored subtests.

TECHNICAL INFORMATION. Seven pages in the manual are devoted to development/technical information. The section labeled "Reliability" was instead a description of the factor analytic study that led to the selection of the eight subtests measuring a single visual functioning construct. Minimal data were presented to document interrater reliability, based on a sample size of only 20. There was no description of the norms sample or documentation for derivation of scale scores. No empirical evidence was provided for the setting of pass-fail scores; rather it was simply stated that in the authors' judgment persons with standard scores one standard deviation below the mean or greater should be failed. No description was provided on the size or composition of the group upon which the means and standard deviations were based. One validity study was presented documenting that the CTVF does indeed distinguish between individuals with known visual disorders and individuals with normal visual functioning. In general, the technical information provided did not support the use of the CTVF for detailed screening purposes, particularly for scores close to the pass-fail cut points.

EVALUATION. The strength of the CTVF is in the clinical experience, expertise, and insight the authors bring to the development of tasks and scoring rubrics. The CTVF may well yield interesting and valuable diagnostic information for an experienced clinician, via the detailed raw information available from most of the subtests. As a very global screening device, undoubtedly the instrument accurately classifies individuals appropriately for an acceptable percentage of administrations. However, the technical information supporting the test does not justify its use for other than very global screening purposes and for data gathering to support subjective clinical judgments.

[90]

Conflict Management Appraisal.

Purpose: "Designed to provide information about the various ways people react to and try to manage the differences between themselves and others."

Population: Adults.

Publication Date: 1986.

Acronym: CMA.

Scores, 20: 5 conflict management styles (9/1 Win-Lose, 1/9 Yield-Lose, 1/1 Lose-Leave, 5/5 Compromise, 9/9 Synergistic) for each of 4 contexts (Personal Orientation, Interpersonal Relationships, Small Group Relationships, Intergroup Relationships).
Administration: Individual.
Price Data, 1992: $6.95 per instrument.
Time: (30) minutes.
Comments: Adaptation of the Conflict Management Survey (91); to be used in conjunction with the Conflict Management Survey; ratings by person well acquainted with subject.
Author: Jay Hall.
Publisher: Teleometrics International.

Review of the Conflict Management Appraisal by WILLIAM L. CURLETTE, Professor of Counseling and Psychological Services, Professor of Educational Policy Studies, and Director of the Educational Research Bureau, Georgia State University, Atlanta, GA:

The purpose of the Conflict Management Appraisal (CMA) by Jay Hall is to obtain information from a rater about how an associate of the rater handles conflict. The term associate "refers to the person about whom you (i.e., the rater) are answering questions—whether that person is a co-worker, a personal or social acquaintance, or a family member" (manual, p. 1). The associate is rated on 60 different items concerning conflict using a 10-point scale for each item. These ratings may be compared to self-ratings obtained on the CMA's companion instrument, the Conflict Management Survey (CMS; 91). Thus, the CMA provides additional data to support or question a person's self-rating.

The Conflict Management Appraisal is a booklet that contains an overview, test taking instructions, the 60 test-rating items, and a sealed section that is opened after raw scores are totaled. The 11 pages in the sealed portion have sections labeled instructions for completing the scoring, the dynamics of conflict, a summary of style rationales, research and a theoretical ideal order of preference, and developmental information. The booklet is formatted nicely and looks attractive.

Conflict is broadly defined from "feeling tones which characterize a particular encounter all the way to outright warfare" (manual, p. i). A theory alluded to supports five styles of conflict management. The model postulates that "conflict dynamics are simply a very natural part of human interaction whose 'meanings' are imposed by the parties to the particular conflict" (manual, p. 14). More specifically, conflict is seen as having two dimensions: concern for personal goals and concern for the relationship.

In the nomenclature of this instrument, the five different styles for handling conflict are named with both numbers and a descriptive word. The five styles, starting with the most desirable, are named: 9/9 for Synergistic, 5/5 for Compromise, 1/9 for Yield-Lose, 9/1 for Win-Lose, and 1/1 for Lose-Leave. The first number in the pair represents degree of concern for personal goals and the second number represents the degree of concern for the relationship. Larger numbers indicate more concern. The CMA produces one overall style score, based on 12 items, for each of the five styles.

The 12 items for any overall style score are evenly distributed across four contexts: Personal Orientation, Interpersonal Relationships, Small Group Relationships, and Intergroup Relationships. Within a context, three conflict situations are presented. In each conflict situation, one of the five items listed under a situation is keyed to be scored on one of the five styles.

For instance, one situation asks the rater to assess the associate's "personal credo" concerning conflict using five one-sentence quotations from the world's literature as the five items. The rater first assigns one item as completely characteristic and another item as completely uncharacteristic of the associate along a 10-point scale. The highest and lowest values selected for these items become endpoints for the assignment of numbers to the other three items. It is unclear if a scale point (taking values from 1 to 10) can be used more than once because the CMA booklet is silent on this possibility.

Apparently, the rater may score the instrument, which gives an opportunity to learn which items are keyed to a style and interpretations of the scores. Thus, scoring the instrument appears to have some instructional value.

Across the four contexts, raw scores are summed to obtain total raw scores on the five styles. Actually, a subtotal raw score is obtained, as an intermediate step, on each one of the five styles within the four contexts. These intermediate subtotal style scores for each context are plotted on four graphs representing the four contexts. On these Context Graphs, areas are labeled "stronger than desirable" and "weaker than desirable" but no rationale for these areas is provided. There are no overall scores computed for the four contexts.

The total raw scores on the five styles are converted to *T*-scores by employing a conversion table. It is not stated whether or not the *T*-scores have been normalized. Then the *T*-scores are rank ordered and differences between adjacent scores are computed. The style with the largest *T*-score is possibly the perceived dominant conflict management style. Whether there is a dominant style or a clear ordering of other styles depends on the magnitude of the *T*-score differences. Without explanation, a less than 10-point *T*-score difference is considered indicative of "low style strength." Moreover, standard errors of measurement are needed to help interpret these differences.

The developmental information section which includes instrument design, reliability/validity, and norms is covered in a scant six paragraphs. Simply stated, reliability indices computed on the CMA are described in only one sentence: "Testing for internal consistency of the CMA, an item analysis yielded a mean Cronbach Alpha of .81; the median Alpha was .85" (manual, p. 20). Nevertheless, these summary values are good, although reliabilities for each style score should be reported. The CMA booklet does indicate that the CMA has construct and concurrent validities similar to the CMS.

The background of the test developer plays a role in content validity. The author, Jay Hall, has an experiential base in management for developing the test as exemplified by two books: *The Executive Trap: How to Play Your Personal Best on the Golf Course and on the Job* (1992), and *The Competence Process: Managing for Commitment and Creativity* (1980).

Because the CMA booklet did not have a reference list, computerized searches were done on PsycLit, ERIC, ABI/Inform, and Dissertation Abstracts International using the term "conflict management appraisal." No citations were found using the name of the test. However, searching the author's name "Jay Hall," produced many citations, including 14 references in Dissertation Abstracts International alone. The abstracts typically referred to other tests developed by Hall such as the Styles of Leadership Survey, co-authored with Williams (Sniderman, 1993; Joo, 1991; Burnett, 1989); Conflict Management Survey (Hale, 1990); and the Organization Competence Index (Thornberry, 1987).

Due to the lack of a separate technical manual, many issues are either not addressed or receive little attention, such as the following: a statement of purpose which identifies uses of the test supported by the publisher, a description of the user norm group, item bias research, interrater agreement, research on placement of items on scales, interscale correlations, instructions concerning the degree to which ratings are confidential, validity studies, buyer qualifications, and a listing of references from the literature. However, based on the literature review, there appears to be research which may address one or more of these concerns but it is not summarized in the CMA booklet. Also, guidelines for selecting the raters probably should be stated in the CMA booklet to help standardize the data gathering process.

Furthermore, a practical concern which could limit the use of the CMA is its reading level. The readability index for the first 100 words of the CMA test, according to RightWriter Version 3.1, is 12.5. This suggests, based on this limited sample, that raters probably need slightly more than a 12th grade reading level.

In summary, the strengths of the CMA are that the booklet has a nice format, it is interesting to read the situations and items, and the interpretation material is thought provoking. It could provide stimulus material for discussions in seminars or workshops centering on topics such as team building, enhancing employee relations, or family counseling. The weaknesses emanate from lack of a technical manual. It would be helpful to have standard errors of measurement and validity studies to aid in score interpretation. How do scores from the CMA relate to its companion instrument, the CMS? In general, more information needs to be reported for various aspects of the Conflict Management Appraisal so that the meaning of the scores will be clearer.

REVIEWER'S REFERENCES

Hall, J. (1980). *The competence process: Managing for commitment and creativity*. The Woodlands, TX: Teleometrics International.

Thornberry, D. (1987). The relationship between organizational competence and leadership styles in an urban school district (Doctoral dissertation, Wayne State University, 1986). *Dissertation Abstracts International, 47*, 4262A.

Burnett, J. N. (1989). An assessment of the administrative leadership style of the executives of Baptist boards and institutions of the Brazilian Baptist Convention and related state Baptist conventions as perceived by themselves and their associates (Doctoral dissertation, Southwestern Baptist Theological Seminary, 1988). *Dissertation Abstracts International, 50*, 462A.

Hale, L. (1990). The confronting leader (Doctoral dissertation, Dallas Theological Seminary, 1989). *Dissertation Abstracts International, 51*, 893A.

Joo, S. (1991). An analytical study of the leadership style of Korean Baptist pastors serving in Seoul as related to their self-esteem (Doctoral dissertation, Southwestern Baptist Theological Seminary, 1990). *Dissertation Abstracts International, 52*, 957A.

Hall, J. (1992). *The executive trap: How to play your personal best on the golf course and on the job*. New York: Simon & Schuster.

Sniderman, R. (1993). Leadership styles of school leaders and their relationship to thinking styles via brain preference (Doctoral dissertation, Wayne State University, 1992). *Dissertation Abstracts International, 54* 396A.

Review of the Conflict Management Appraisal by DAVID N. DIXON, Professor and Chair of Counseling Psychology, Ball State University, Muncie, IN:

The Conflict Management Appraisal is one of a long line of instruments authored by Jay Hall, Ph.D. and published by Teleometrics International. These instruments share in common a lack of psychometric information and negative reviews by *Mental Measurements Yearbook* (MMY) reviewers. Based on review of the current instrument and previous *MMY* reviews of their instruments, the purposes of *MMY* reviews to "stimulate higher professional standards of test construction and to impel test authors and publishers to present more detailed information on the construction, validity, reliability, norms, etc." have not shaped the professional behaviors of the author or the publisher.

The Conflict Management Appraisal is said to be based on theory, although no references to the literature are included in the booklet. This instrument defines styles of conflict management along two dimensions: (*a*) the context within which the conflict occurs (elsewhere described as the concern for relationship) and (*b*) the personal relevance of the issues involved in the conflict (concern for personal goals). Characteristic conflict management styles are defined by a number code for these two dimensions. Also of relevance is style strength as indicated by difference scores among the various styles.

Casual reading of the booklet reveals a sense of "face validity" to the instrument, but closer examination reveals many flaws. First, the reading level of the questionnaire is complex. No information is given on reading level, but it is advanced in vocabulary and the sentences and statements are complex and sometimes confusing. For example, the responses for the first item (I.A.) use fragmented quotations from literature, which require understanding of phrases such as "We should do by our cunning as we do by our courage . . . always have it ready to defend ourselves, never to offend others," and "The race is not to the swift, nor the battle to the strong . . . whosoever shall smite thee on the right cheek, turn to him the other also" (test booklet, p. 2). The rater is asked to rank order such phrases as applying to the person being rated, a complex reading task. Second, the rater is told that there are no right or wrong answers and that conflict is neither good nor bad; however, the reader later discovers that research "findings suggest an ideal ordering of style preferences" (p. 18) and the scores of the associate being rated are eventually compared to the ideal order. Third, the reader is told that differences between the dominant and backup conflict style of less than or more than 10 points have different meanings. With differences more than 10 point the person "will resist moving into the backup style" (p. 19) and with differences of less than 10 the person will quickly "move to the backup style when the individual is under stress" (p. 19). No information is given on how the difference of 10 points was chosen as the cutoff; validity research is needed to support the use of difference scores. Finally, the reliability, validity, and norms information is totally inadequate. No description of the size or demographics of the norm group is given. Likewise, reliability coefficients for the five conflict management modes are reported, but no information about the size and demographics of the group(s) used to calculate reliability estimates are given. To support the Conflict Management Appraisal, a test manual needs to be developed. I am not optimistic this will occur.

The conclusion to this review reads as those of previous tests by Jay Hall and Telemetrics International. In the *Ninth Mental Measurements Yearbook* the Incentive Management Index (9:501), the Leadership Appraisal Survey (9:598), and the NASA Moon Survival Task (9:740) were reported as having no data on reliability and validity. Reviews of the Power Management Inventory (9:967) concluded with it being an interesting instrument which required much more research; that the authors probably published prematurely; and that it needs further research before it will be ready for use. In the *Tenth Mental Measurements Yearbook*, the Management Appraisal Survey (10:182) was reviewed as "in dire need of a manual" and another reviewer stated "no student in my undergraduate class on tests and measurements, and certainly no graduate student in my class . . . would pass the course if he or she turned in such a deficient report of test construction efforts and data to support the instrument." Of another instrument, the Personal Opinion Matrix (10:276), the reviewer stated that "Client organizations should demand that management consulting firms use only those assessment instruments that have demonstrated acceptable psychometric characteristics and are accompanied by comprehensive technical manuals." In the *Eleventh Mental Measurements Yearbook*, a review of the Managerial Competence Index (11:224) concluded "this instrument should not be used for any purpose other than basic research." About the Team Process Diagnostic (11:416) a reviewer stated "the lack of supportive evidence and empirical research for the many claims and materials presented raise serious doubts."

The Conflict Management Appraisal takes its place alongside a list of instruments that should not have been published, and certainly not used for purposes other than research until more fully developed. I am not optimistic this will occur. Even though the purposes of the *MMY* in stimulating progress in test construction and in impelling progress toward higher professional standards of test construction seem lost on the author and publisher, the purpose of the *MMY* to provide test users with appraisals of test materials for their guidance in selecting and using tests can still be realized. Do not use this test until it is greatly improved.

[91]

Conflict Management Survey.

Purpose: "Designed to provide information about the various ways people react to and try to manage the differences between themselves and others."

Population: Adults.

Publication Dates: 1969–86.

Acronym: CMS.

Scores, 20: 5 conflict management styles (9/1 Win-Lose, 1/9 Yield-Lose, 1/1 Lose-Leave, 5/5 Compromise, 9/9 Synergistic) for each of 4 contexts (Personal Orientation, Interpersonal Relationships, Small Group Relationships, Intergroup Relationships).

Administration: Group.

Price Data, 1990: $6.95 per instrument.

Time: Administration time not reported.

Comments: Self-ratings.

Author: Jay Hall.

Publisher: Teleometrics International.

Cross References: For a review by Frank J. Landy, see 8:1173 (2 references).

Review of the Conflict Management Survey by FREDERICK BESSAI, Professor of Education, University of Regina, Regina, Saskatchewan, Canada:

The Conflict Management Survey is a 60-item instrument designed to assess the individual's typical reactions to conflict and conflict situations. Conflict responses in four contexts are assessed. These are Personal Orientation, Interpersonal, Small Group, and Intergroup Relationships. There are 15 items for each context. These items in turn are made up of five possible reactions or solutions to three situations in each context. The examinee rates each solution or reaction on a 10-point scale ranging from *completely uncharacteristic* (1) to *completely characteristic* (10) of himself or herself. The underlying rationale is a model that posits two orthogonal axes of concern which are scaled from 1–9. The first is a minimal to maximal concern for personal goals and the second is a similarly scaled concern for relationships. This gives way to four quadrants identified by scalar positions as 9/9 (Synergistic), 9/1 (Win-Lose), 1/1 (Lose-Lose), and 1/9 (Yield-Lose). The compromising individuals are rated as 5/5 because they are not at the extremes of either scale.

The survey is self-scored and raw scores are converted to *T*-scores which in turn are combined and by a method of differences between rank-ordered scores a context score is derived. Instructions are given on how to interpret these context scores.

The items appear well written and carefully organized. The language is simple and clear. Many items are written in the first person so the reader can easily understand the behavior being described. There are clear instructions for taking and scoring the survey. The latter is a bit complicated, however, and requires a careful reading and close adherence to the instructions. Norms based on 1,308 respondents are provided but the descriptions of the norming sample are very scant. There is no information on age, gender, or proportions which came from the various groups such as managers, law enforcement personnel, trainers, and labor contract negotiators. Adequate information on reliability is also lacking. Split-half coefficients ranging from .70 to .87 are reported for the five styles. There is virtually no information on validity and only very scant detail on research findings. Individual differences between *T*-score means of various organizational groups are reported in a final table, which is left for the reader to interpret. Numbers from each of the eight subgroups are all that is given.

The survey can be recommended for individual study and self-exploration but a good deal of research is still needed to establish some of the psychometric properties, particularly its construct validity. The underlying theoretical basis appears sound and further study may well show that the survey has some validity. Further norming is also needed before it can be recommended for general use by various kinds of organizations and by researchers to assess conflict management styles.

Review of the Conflict Management Survey by DOUGLAS J. McRAE, Educational Measurement Specialist, Private Consultant, Monterey, CA:

PURPOSE. The Conflict Management Survey (CMS) is designed to provide a client with information about his or her approach to managing conflict.

DESCRIPTION. The CMS consists of a single 28-page booklet that includes the survey itself, self-scoring directions including all necessary tables and graphs, interpretive material, and development/technical information. The survey consists of four potential conflict contexts (Personal Orientation, Interpersonal Relationships, Small Group Relationships, and Intergroup Relationships), each with three conflict scenarios. For each scenario, the survey taker responds by rating five alternatives on a scale from 1 (*Completely Uncharacteristic*) to 10 (*Completely Characteristic*) based on the survey taker's own practices. Thus, the CMS has 60 score points (4 contexts x 3 scenarios x 5 alternatives).

The CMS is scored by accumulating the raw rating values for the response alternative associated with each of five conflict management styles (1/9, 9/9, 5/5, 1/1, and 9/1 where the first number reflects concern for personal goals and the second number reflects concern for relationships). The raw scores are then converted to *T*-scores, difference scores between styles are computed, and results plotted to reveal weaker than desirable and stronger than desirable styles for each of the four conflict contexts.

The interpretation section of the CMS presents a model of conflict management based on two dimensions: concern for personal goals and concern for relationships. Each of the five identified styles is described, and flexibility of use of style is discussed. A theoretically ideal order of preference for conflict management style is also given. The survey taker is led through several exercises designed to interpret individual scores and to adapt one's own behavior in conflict situations to potentially more fruitful approaches.

RATIONALE. The CMS is primarily theoretically rather than empirically based. A two-dimensional model for conflict management is described, and the response alternatives from each scenario are assigned to each conflict management style on a priori grounds. Conversions to *T*-scores then adjust the survey taker's scores based on normative comparisons. However, the survey itself and the interpretation of the scores are based primarily on the two-dimensional model, placing the survey taker on the dimensions of concern for personal goals and concern for relationships.

TECHNICAL INFORMATION. The CMS booklet devotes only half a page to developmental information, with only a few sentences each on reliability/validity and description of the norms as the basis for *T*-scores. It is not mentioned that results may well differ considerably should the makeup of the norms group change; the norms group is only described as consisting of 1,300 individuals the greatest proportion of whom are persons from management positions in large organizations. Additional data are provided on average conflict management style scores for roughly 700 individuals from eight different organization types.

EVALUATION. The CMS is a potentially useful instrument for situations where descriptive-only, discussion-starting data on conflict management style are needed. The instrument itself is theoretically based, with very little empirical support. The validity, reliability, and normative information are weak. The instrument should not be used to contribute to either individual or group decisions regarding conflict management style. However, as a discussion starter for individuals or organizations desiring a focus on conflict management behaviors, it may serve a useful role.

[92]

Content Mastery Examinations for Educators.

Purpose: "Designed for use in licensing teachers, counselors, administrators, and reading and media specialists. Basic Skills also designed for use at entrance to college of education."
Population: Teachers, school administrators, and other educational specialists; Basic Skills also for entrants to colleges of education.
Publication Date: 1991.
Acronym: CMEE.
Administration: Group.
Parts: 24 tests.
Restricted Distribution: Distribution restricted; details may be obtained from publisher.
Price Data: Available from publisher.
Time: (120–180) minutes per test.
Comments: "Criterion-referenced."
Authors: IOX Assessment Associates.
Publisher: National Computer Systems [Iowa City, IA].

a) ADMINISTRATION AND SUPERVISION.
Scores: 10 content areas: School Law, Educational Finance, Collective Bargaining, Personnel Practices for Professional Staff, Student Personnel Services, Student Assessment and Program Evaluation, Curriculum, Public School Governance and School Community Relations, Leadership, Operational Management and Computer Technology.

b) ART EDUCATION.
Scores: 5 content areas: Art History, Art Community, Technical Aspects of Production, Visual Elements and Principles, Aesthetic Issues.

c) BASIC SKILLS.
Scores: 9 content areas: Reading (Vocabulary/Word Recognition, Reading Comprehension, Reference Selection and Usage), Writing (Writing Assignment, Standard American English Conventions), Math (Number Concepts and Operations, Measurement, Geometry, Statistics).

d) BIOLOGY.
Scores: 10 content areas: Introduction to Biology, The Basis of Life, Cell Structure and Functions, Microscopic and Submicroscopic Forms of Life, Plants, Animals, Developmental Biology, Genetics, Evolution, Ecology and Conservation.

e) BUSINESS EDUCATION.
Scores: 8 content areas: Equipment Operation, Business Communications, Economics, Basic Finance, Business and Consumer Law, Business Management, Career Development and Planning, Marketing Education.

f) CHEMISTRY.
Scores: 14 content areas: Fundamental Chemical Concepts and Basic Laboratory Tools and Techniques, Atomic Theory, The Periodic Table, States of Matter, Solutions, Bonding, Stoichiometry, Thermochemistry, Reaction Rates, Equilibrium, Oxidation Reduction and Electrochemistry, Nuclear Chemistry, Organic Chemistry, Current Chemical/Societal Problems.

g) EARLY CHILDHOOD EDUCATION.
Scores: 10 content areas: Early Childhood Development, Early Childhood Programs, Children with Special Needs, Language Arts, Reading, Visual and Performing Arts, Social Studies, Mathematics, Science, Physical Education and Health.

h) EARTH AND SPACE SCIENCE.
Scores: 11 content areas: Basic Earth Materials, Agents of Change, Earth Structure and Geological Processes, Geologic History, Ocean Structure, Ocean Shores and Floors, The Atmosphere, Weather, The Universe, The Solar System, Stars.

i) ELEMENTARY EDUCATION.
Scores: 8 content areas: Language Arts, Reading, Visual and Performing Arts, Social Studies, Mathematics, Science, Physical Education and Health, Special Education.

j) ENGLISH.
Scores: 3 content areas: Language Knowledge and Skills, Composition Knowledge and Skills, Literary Knowledge and Skills.

k) FRENCH.
Scores: 5 content areas: Grammar, Vocabulary, Reading Comprehension, Aural/Oral Communication, Culture.

l) HEALTH EDUCATION.
Scores: 10 content areas: Health in the United States, Physical Growth and Development, Mental and Emotional Health, Sexuality, Fitness, Substance Use and Abuse, Nutrition, Community and Environmental Health, Wellness and Disease, Consumer Health and Safety.

m) HOME ECONOMICS.
Scores: 7 content areas: Management, Child Development/Care/Guidance, Clothing and Textiles, Consumer Education, Food and Nutrition, Family Relationships, Housing and Home Furnishings.

n) MATHEMATICS.
Scores: 8 content areas: Algebra, Functions, Geometry from a Synthetic Perspective, Geometry from an Algebraic Perspective, Trigonometry, Statistics and Probability, Discrete Mathematics, Calculus.

o) MUSIC.

Scores: 7 content areas: Style Characteristics, Representative Composers, Representative Musical Forms, Music Notation, Elements of Music, Rehearsal Preparations and Procedures, Listening.

p) PEDAGOGY.

Scores: 7 content areas: Student Characteristics, Learning Theories, Planning, Classroom Management, Instructional Methods, Principles of Effective Instruction, Assessment/Evaluation/Working with Parents.

q) PHYSICAL EDUCATION.

Scores: 8 content areas: Physical Development, Motor Learning, Biomechanics and Kinesiology, Exercise Physiology, Psychosocial Development, Humanities, Legal Issues, Components of a Balanced Physical Education Program.

r) PHYSICS.

Scores: 5 content areas: Mechanics, Heat, Wave Motion, Electricity and Magnetism, Modern Physics.

s) READING SPECIALIST.

Scores: 8 content areas: Foundations of Reading and Basic Instructional Approaches, Word Recognition, Comprehension, Reading Across the Curriculum, Affective Aspects of Reading Instruction, Teaching Students with Special Needs, Assessment, Classroom Organization/Program Administration/Resources.

t) SCHOOL GUIDANCE AND COUNSELING.

Scores: 8 content areas: Human Growth and Development, Technical Aspects of Counseling, Individual and Group Assessment, Legal and Ethical Issues in Counseling, Referral and Community Resources, Life-Style and Career Planning, The Counselor as Consultant, The Counselor as Psychological Helper.

u) SCHOOL LIBRARY MEDIA SPECIALIST.

Scores: 5 content areas: Professionalism, Collection Management, Organization of the Library, Administration, Roles of the Library Media Specialist.

v) SOCIAL STUDIES.

Scores: 5 content areas: World History, United States History, Government, Geography, Social Science Theory.

w) SPANISH.

Scores: 5 content areas: Grammar, Vocabulary, Reading Comprehension, Culture, Aural/Oral Communication.

x) SPECIAL EDUCATION.

Scores: 9 content areas: Legal Requirements of PL 94-142, Classification and Characteristics of Disorders, Assessment, Individual Behavior Management, Instruction, Working with the Community, Class Behavior Management, Consultation/Collaboration, Paraprofessional Management.

Review of the Content Mastery Examinations for Educators by SUSAN M. BROOKHART, Assistant Professor of Education, Duquesne University, Pittsburgh, PA:

The Content Mastery Examinations for Educators (CMEE) include 24 tests: an entry level Basic Skills Test for candidates for teacher preparation, a general test of Pedagogy, two elementary education tests (K–3 and K–8), 15 tests in secondary education content areas, and 5 tests for specialty areas (Administration/Supervision, Library Media, Reading Specialist, School Guidance and Counseling, and Special Education). The chief purpose for which the CMEE tests were designed is to provide data for use in certification (licensure) of teachers, counselors, administrators, and reading and media specialists. Applicant screening and program improvement for teacher education are two additional potential uses the manual identifies. Drawing conclusions about teachers' instructional effectiveness would be a potential misuse. The manual also points out that using CMEE tests to determine experienced teachers' content mastery would be inappropriate because the tests were designed for beginning teachers.

The CMEE structure and purpose resemble those of the NTE Programs (T4:1825), a test series from Educational Testing Service (ETS). The NTE is being phased out and replaced with the Praxis Series (T4:2062). The CMEE structure and purposes resemble Praxis I (Academic Skills Assessments) and Praxis II (Subject Assessments). The major difference between CMEE and the ETS competition is that CMEE tests were developed and are scored in a criterion-referenced (as opposed to norm-referenced) manner. CMEE claims two other differences: (*a*) building bias detection into the test development process from the beginning, and (*b*) performing an extensive national validation so that states do not have to do local validation studies.

Because CMEE tests are criterion referenced, domain definition and content validity studies were of great importance. The content validation process was quite thorough and is carefully reported. Over 860 educators were involved in studies addressing content validity, job relatedness, and potential bias. The membership of the content and bias review panels was diverse.

The small number of minority examinees in the field testing process precluded an empirical investigation of bias. This is especially unfortunate because CMEE claims to have done a more thorough bias review during item development than the competition. ETS does studies of differential item functioning and can revise items accordingly. CMEE tests are demonstrably free of bias in content; the next revision of the manual should include evidence of freedom from bias in effects as well.

Because of the extensive work of the CMEE national content review panels, the claim is made that state officials need not conduct local validation studies to support the use of these tests. This is true for content validation. However, states are involved in setting the passing scores. States that choose to use the CMEE for licensure purchase the services of consultants who help each state convene a panel to set the passing standards with a modified Angoff procedure. Empirical validation of those cut scores is, however, still a question, as is reliability in the sense of decision consistency at those scores. The reviewer talked with one of the consultants who facilitates the state panels. The consultant said that the cut scores are set within 2 weeks after the first test administration, so that state panelists can be informed by data from examinees in their own state who, unlike the field test examinees, took the tests under high-stakes conditions. Consequential validity concerns, like state shortages in some content areas or the percent of minority candidates who might be licensed, can be considered in setting the cut scores. Decision consistency and accuracy can be estimated at that time, too. These panels are very important but somewhat contrary to the advantages implied in advertising no local validation studies are needed. The test developers would do well to perform some studies of decision consistency, using the passing scores the content and bias review panels recommended and some data from a high-stakes administration. This important aspect of test quality should then be reported in the CMEE Technical Manual.

Examinees are given the content outline upon which their test is based, offering them an opportunity to study relevant material. This is in keeping with the criterion-referenced nature of the test. The content outlines are indeed much more detailed than the content outlines in the ETS materials for examinees. Preparing for these criterion-referenced CMEE tests would be a more focused activity than preparing for the Praxis I and II exams from their "Tests at a Glance" booklets. An additional advantage to the examinee is that the mean scores for criterion-referenced tests are higher than for norm-referenced tests, so examinees are likely to experience the feeling that they were expected to know some content, studied it, and can demonstrate it. This is consistent with using the CMEE for licensure.

This reviewer looked at content outlines for Basic Skills, Pedagogy, English, Social Studies, Biology, and Music. Some of the relative emphases in the CMEE Pedagogy content outline are curious. For example, "Performance Assessment" is a subcategory under "Informal Assessment." Overall, however, these six content outlines are clear, thorough (16–25 pages long), and well organized. These long content outlines do indeed direct a student's preparation to the material on the test.

Another validity issue is the narrowing effect on teacher education curricula, as a consequence of test use, when a state adopts a content mastery test for licensure. This is a sticky wicket for the field of education because the state, not the profession, grants the license. Content mastery is clearly a necessary but not sufficient condition for licensure. States require evidence of students' teaching skills as well as their content mastery before granting a teaching certificate (licensure). If there were consensus about both content mastery and teaching skills sufficient for a beginning teacher, the phenomenon of teaching to external tests would not be a problem. In practice, there is no consensus, and only the content mastery exams are external. Teaching skill at the time of licensure is generally certified by the fact that the candidate successfully completed a student teaching experience. This measure is internal to the teacher education program and is subject to expected institutional pressures to help students succeed.

CMEE test items are all multiple choice, except for a writing sample in the Basic Skills test. The medium is paper and pencil, with the exception of some audiotape-based multiple-choice questions in Music, some videotape-based questions in Pedagogy, some slide-based questions in Art Education, and listening and speaking sections in French and Spanish. Calculators are used in the Mathematics, Physics, and Chemistry tests. Each item begins with a context description. The items and writing prompts are well written and clear; the contexts are helpful if sometimes sketchy. ("You are teaching a lesson about [*content area*]. You ask your students to explain [*concept from the content area*]. Which of the following is the best student response?")

There are about 100 multiple-choice items per exam, with four options each. There are 5 to 14 sections in the content outline for each exam. The shortest subtests have only five items; there are 17 five-item subtests among the 24 examinations, 7 of them on the Chemistry exam. The longest subtests has 45 items (the Mechanics section of the Physics exam).

Examinees receive a scale score for each exam, so that forms can be adjusted for slight differences in difficulty between forms. The results of the pass/fail decision are also reported. For each section of the content outline, a check mark indicates "Additional Study Recommended," defined as 60% or fewer items on the subtest answered correctly. This allows for interpretation that the test manual describes as "improvement-oriented." State and institutional summaries of these results are also generated.

When the purpose of the CMEE exams is to identify mastery for licensure, an examinee who failed a section would know where to concentrate study for another try. But the examinee would not ordinarily wish to use a high-stakes test for diagnosis. The diagnostic information would be a useful feature if the tests were used for their secondary purposes, admissions screening and/or program improvement for teacher education. The small number of items in many subtests, used to index large chunks of material in the content outline, mean that the diagnosis can only be in general terms. In the five-item subtests, missing more than one item would lead to a recommendation for additional study. The small sample of items relative to the domain of content does make for an efficient sample if what is needed is a mastery/nonmastery decision.

The exams were field tested in two forms. Twenty-five linking items were included in the field test of each examination. Reliability was established by examining equivalence, between the alternate forms of each exam, of (*a*) content and (*b*) overall and within-section mean difficulty levels and overall and within-section mean point-biserial coefficients. This way of conceptualizing reliability is consistent with the criterion-referenced purpose of presenting equivalent challenges to examinees across forms. Overall mean difficulty (p) for the 24 tests ranged from .56 to .77 (median = .70). For no exam did the mean difficulty differ by more than .002 between forms. Overall mean discrimination (point-biserial r) for the 24 tests ranged from .25 to .45 (median = .31). For no exam did the mean discrimination differ by more than .008 between forms. These values demonstrate appropriate levels of difficulty and consistency of challenge.

Field test sample sizes varied from 43 (Spanish) to 990 (Pedagogy), with a median of 86.5. Four tests (Pedagogy, Basic Skills, Elementary Education K–8, and Early Childhood K–3) were field tested with 545 or more students each. There were nine tests (French, Home Economics, Reading Specialist, Health Education, School Library Media Specialist, Business Education, Earth and Space Science, Physics, and Spanish) field tested with 58 or fewer students. The large number of field tests with small sample sizes is unfortunate. On the nine tests where about 50 students took two forms (25 each), p values would change by about .04 for each examinee.

In sum, this reviewer agrees in principle that certification and licensure exams should be criterion-referenced. However, the CMEE tests would need to report some empirical evidence for mastery/nonmastery decision consistency and for lack of differential item functioning before this reviewer would be comfortable recommending these tests for state use in licensing educators. This reviewer can recommend their use in admissions screening and program evaluation in teacher education if the program faculty from a content area agrees on the content outline as defining important program achievement outcomes. In this way, the content outlines would not drive instruction because they constitute an external criterion but because prior internal agreement made them part of program design.

Review of the Content Mastery Examinations for Educators by PATRICIA H. WHEELER, President, EREAPA Associates, Livermore, CA:

The Content Mastery Examinations for Educators (CMEE) are a series of 24 tests covering basic skills (reading, writing, mathematics); pedagogy; subject-matter knowledge in 18 fields; and content tests for school administrators, counselors, reading specialists, and library media specialists. They are described as "criterion-referenced" tests for use in licensing educators. They were designed to assess subject-matter knowledge mastery and skills within an educational context, not to measure content pedagogy, as pointed out in the publication *CMEE Development and Validation Process*.

Each test has 100 multiple-choice items (plus an essay in the basic skills test) and requires 2 to 3 hours. There are two forms for each test, compiled through psychometric equating based on overall and within-section mean difficulty levels (p-values) and point-biserial correlations. Stimulus materials used for the items include narratives, audio tapes, video tapes, and pictorial slides. Tests are administered through statewide programs on specified dates and at designated test centers. Examinee registration services are provided by NCS. The 1994 cost to the candidate is $45 per test. Provisions, such as large-print or Braille versions, are offered for disabled students.

The content outlines for the 24 tests were developed by IOX Assessment Associates specialists and educators, starting in the fall of 1988. Content determination panels reviewed the outlines to judge if the content was "truly necessary for satisfactory performance by a beginning educator in the field assessed" (technical manual, p. 19) and by university teacher educators for examinee opportunity to learn the content. These panels consisted of 15 educators per test, two-thirds of whom were considered to be exemplary and experienced teachers. The content outlines are 15–25 pages long and have between 5 and 14 major content domains for each test. However, the content outlines do not indicate how important each of the domains are for licensing, and how much emphasis should be given to a domain or category as reflected by the number of items on the test.

The items, which were developed by IOX staff and content consultants, were based on the content outlines. The pool of about 300 items per test underwent judgmental reviews by two panels of educators, a content review and a bias review. Across all 24 tests, there were 507 content panelists, 91% of whom were white, and 310 educators for the bias review, 76% of whom were African American. It is not clear if the bias reviewers had special training or expertise in doing bias reviews, or were simply basing judgments on their own experiences.

Reporting of test results is done at the individual and state levels, and is available for institutions. Each examinee receives an Individual Profile, which shows personal data, the individual's scaled score, the passing scaled score, the pass/fail status, and, for each content area or skills category, whether additional study is needed. There is space on the report for customized text, should the state desire to have such information reported on the Individual Profile. The reports to the state include an alphabetic score roster and a state summary report that shows the mean scaled score, the passing score, the number and percent of examinees who passed and who failed, and, for the content areas, the number and percent of examinees who need additional study.

The standardization sample included 26 teacher-training institutions, 12 in California (10 of these in Southern California) and 8 in the southeast (Alabama, Georgia, Mississippi, South Carolina, Virginia). Additional information on the sample's composition and distributions of scores for each test are not provided. Mean *r*-biserials and mean *p*-values by section within each test and the correlations between the 25 linking items common to the two alternate forms for each test are shown in the CMEE Technical Manual. No reliability data are given for the full test (e.g., split-half). Standard error of measurement values should be provided because such data are helpful in counseling candidates who do not pass and in setting passing scores for licensure.

There are no data on test speededness to determine if candidates are able to complete all items within the designated time limits. Because the test items are written in an educational context, they are longer than more traditional multiple-choice items. For example, instead of asking "Which notes are in a C-major, but not a natural C-minor, scale?" the item might say "You ask a student to play a C-major scale and then a natural C-minor scale on the flute. Which notes will the student play for the first scale, but not the second scale?" This increases the face validity of the item (i.e., makes it appear more appropriate for teacher licensure), but adds to the time required without providing additional information about the candidate's knowledge of the difference between the two scales.

The content outlines and items were reviewed by thousands of educators throughout the United States, according to the CMEE Overview. However, the number of reviewers for each test is considerably lower. Information on the ethnic composition, state, and occupation for the content determination panels (the 15 educators for each test who reviewed the content outlines) is provided across all tests and for each test. The national content and bias review panels, who judged the items in their respective subject areas, ranged from 7 reviewers for the physics bias panel to 29 reviewers for the mathematics content panel. No additional data are given on the composition of each of these panels.

The CMEE Overview states that "Because of this national validation process, it is not necessary for state officials to perform local validation studies" (p. 2). The assumption that the national review by the content and bias panels is generalizable to any state should be viewed with caution. All state users should conduct a validation study as part of the process of determining whether or not this program is appropriate for their teacher licensure candidates, and if it is aligned with their state's curriculum frameworks and educational policies.

Throughout the materials, the terms "adequate," "successful," and "satisfactory" performance of candidates are used interchangeably. If this test is for licensure, the focus should be on "minimally acceptable" performance. Adequate or satisfactory performance levels are used for completing a course or graduating from a program. Successful performance should be the focus for such purposes as hiring, promoting, or granting awards.

The national content and bias review panel members were asked, "What is the percentage of 100–150 items (from the CMEE item pool you just reviewed) that an individual would need to answer correctly in order to display the knowledge and skills necessary for satisfactory performance as a beginning content-area teacher?" (technical manual, p. 47). Mean percentage correct values are reported for each panel for each test in the CMEE Technical Manual as "Passing Standards Recommended During the National Item Review." Across tests they range from 66% to 83%. The largest difference in means between the two groups is for the Music test, 69.4 and 81.1. This is a questionable manner for setting cut scores and a poor example for states. Each state should conduct its own standard setting study, employing a method that meets current professional, technical, and legal guidelines. NCS does provide technical assistance to states for such studies.

Two key issues in setting licensure standards are the impact on certain groups of candidates (e.g., gender, ethnicity), and supply and demand of new teachers. No distributions of scores are provided, based on the standardization sample or on examinees tested within a state (only the percent pass/fail). Although the CMEE is called a criterion-referenced test, such data should be provided, especially in the regions around likely cut scores. The impact of various cut score levels cannot be adequately addressed by policymakers, given the data available to them.

The CMEE provides an option for states seeking alternatives to other national programs, and some flexibility for each state in terms of test content, administration, and reporting. However, such flexibility can compromise the security of the tests and make it more difficult for candidates who live in other states to become licensed in the user state. The involvement of large numbers of educators, especially teachers, in the review of the content outlines and items is a good feature of this program. The test booklets and materials are well formatted and easy to use. The provision of more data in the CMEE Technical Manual would strengthen the program.

[93]

Continuous Visual Memory Test.

Purpose: Assesses visual memory.
Population: Ages 18–70+.
Publication Dates: 1983–88.
Acronym: CVMT.
Scores, 6: Acquisition (Hits, False Alarms, d-Prime, Total), Delayed Recognition, Visual Discrimination.
Administration: Individual.
Price Data, 1995: $73 per complete kit including manual ('88, 19 pages), stimulus cards, and 50 scoring forms; $11 per manual; $21 per 50 scoring forms; $44 per stimulus cards.
Time: (45–50) minutes.
Authors: Donald E. Trahan and Glenn J. Larrabee.
Publisher: Psychological Assessment Resources, Inc.
Cross References: See T4:642 (4 references).

TEST REFERENCES

1. Trueblood, W., & Schmidt, M. (1993). Malingering and other validity considerations in the neuropsychological evaluation of mild head injury. *Journal of Clinical and Experimental Neuropsychology, 15*, 578-590.

2. Gold, M., Adair, J. C., Jacobs, D. H., & Heilman, K. M. (1995). Right-left confusion in Gerstmann's Syndrome: A model of body centered spatial orientation. *Cortex, 31*, 267-283.

Review of the Continuous Visual Memory Test by NANCY B. BOLOGNA, Assistant Professor of Psychiatry, Louisiana State University School of Medicine, New Orleans, LA:

The Continuous Visual Memory Test (CVMT) is a measure of visual recognition memory acquisition and retention. The test is divided into three phases. The first two are the Acquisition of visual recognition memories and the Delayed Recognition of those images. A final task, Visual Discrimination of target images from those used as distractors, provides confirmation that performance deficits measured in the first two tasks are a function of recognition memory and not gross perceptual abnormalities.

There are seven target images to be acquired. Each is a complex design which is low in meaningfulness, such that a verbal label cannot be readily generated. Target images are presented, one at a time, for a 2-second period, randomly interspersed with nontarget images, in seven blocks of trials. Each block contains 16 trials: 7 target images repeated in each block and 9 nonrepeating distractors. Distractors in each block include seven images matched to target images for structural characteristics and complexity, and two general distractors that are not structurally similar to any of the target images. At each trial, the subject must respond "old" if the image is a target image and has been seen in a previous trial, or "new" if the image is a distractor and has not been seen before. After the seven blocks of trials have been completed, there is a 30-minute delay followed by the Delayed Recognition task. This is unanticipated by subjects. For the Delayed Recognition task, each target image is presented on a page of multiple images. The images include the target and its specific distractors. The subject's task is to recognize the target image, which was seen seven times during the previous task.

ADMINISTRATION. The CVMT is always administered individually. Because of the standardized 2-second exposure time for each image, care must be taken to avoid interruptions during testing. The CVMT can be administered in 45–50 minutes, including the 30-minute period before the Delayed Recognition task. Subjects are not informed of the delayed task, and can use the 30-minute waiting period to participate in a clinical interview, or to complete other unrelated tasks or questionnaires.

The book of images has an annoying flaw. Greater than 120 heavy-weight pages are bound with a plastic spine that does not allow easy page flipping. Having to stop at least once midway through administration to flatten the pages is problematic, given the requirement of only a 2-second inspection period for each page.

SCORING. Several scores are provided for the acquisition task. First, total number of correct responses is summed. In addition, each response of "old" is scored according to signal-detection theory as a hit (when a repeated image is correctly recognized) or false alarm (when a distractor is labeled "old"). D-prime, a measure of sensitivity, is derived from the numbers of hits and false alarms obtained, via a table with simple instructions. The Delayed Recognition task is simply scored as the number of correct identifications of the target images. Normative tables are provided to transform raw scores into percentiles for four age ranges: 18–29 years, 30–49 years, 50–69 years, and 70 years and older.

The standardization sample for the CVMT is reported as 310 healthy adults (ages 18–29, n = 83; ages 30–49, n = 139; ages 50–69, n = 58; ages 70 and older, n = 30) who were screened to rule out neurological disease, major psychiatric illness, and mental deficiency. The manual does not contain details of the screening procedure. The demographic characteristics of the sample by age group are provided along with details of the nonsignificant score differences associated with gender and education.

RELIABILITY AND VALIDITY. Split-half reliability coefficients for responses to the target images and the distractors are reported from two groups of subjects (25 patients with histories of closed head trauma, and 25 normal adults matched for age and gender). Coefficients indicate that although the distractor images show high inter-item reliability (.98 and .90 for the normal and head trauma groups, respectively), target images may not be uniformly responded to by normal subjects (.80 for the normal group and .98 for the head trauma group). In practice, this suggests that recognition of some target images may be easier or harder to acquire than others.

Test-retest reliability was assessed with a sample of 12 normal adults who were each tested twice with a 7-day interval. Coefficients for the total number correct, d-Prime, and Delayed Recognition score were .85, .80, and .76, respectively.

Construct validity was examined via principal factor and maximum likelihood factor analyses of CVMT scores and scores from "several other common measures of intellectual function" (manual, p. 11) in a study of 92 normal adults aged 18–61 years. Only commonalities between scores from the CVMT and the Wechsler Memory Scale are reported in the manual. Results suggest the immediate recognition scores from the CVMT measure general cognitive ability and visual encoding strategy. The Delayed Recognition score measures visual memory, similarly to the Wechsler Memory Scale Delayed Visual Recognition.

Several other studies, reported in the manual, have evaluated patients with various neurological disorders and known memory deficits. Although the numbers are not reported, results suggest the Delayed Recognition score of the CVMT can accurately demonstrate neurological deficits in some patient populations. The manual authors caution test users to be conservative in interpreting results from adults older than 60 years. This is an important caveat because the validation studies focused on younger adults and normal elderly subjects exhibit much variability in Delayed Recognition scores, which have a restricted range of 8 points total (a score of 3 or more is significantly better than chance). In addition, the relatively low test-retest reliability (.76) of the delayed recall task indicates that normal performance may be quite variable. The manual contains an acknowledgment of a considerable overlap between the lower end of a neurologically normal population and the higher end of an impaired population.

SUMMARY. The CVMT is a quick, easy-to-administer instrument that measures general cognitive ability as related to visual encoding in a recognition paradigm. The delayed recall test is a good index of visual memory, and may be useful in the clinical assessment of neurological impairment in individuals no older than 60 years. The immediate recognition task is particularly well suited for measurements of visual encoding and acquisition of visual memories because it provides measures of hits, false alarms, and d-Prime. The well-designed distractor items and the balanced blocks also allow analyses of hits and false alarms across trial blocks.

Review of the Continuous Visual Memory Test by STEPHEN F. DAVIS, Professor of Psychology, Emporia State University, Emporia, KS:

The Continuous Visual Memory Test (CVMT) is based on two assumptions: (*a*) memory deficits are often symptomatic of functional and organic brain syndromes, and (*b*) the Atkinson-Shiffrin stage theory or sequence of memory processing (i.e., sensory memory—>short-term—> long-term memory) is correct. It is correctly argued that the type of assessment conducted may depend on the *type* of memory being assessed. For example, the assessment of verbal memory differs from the assessment of visual/nonverbal memory.

Due to the use of visual stimuli that may be encoded with verbal cues and long exposure times allowing verbal labeling to occur, current tests of visual memory may not measure just visual memory. Although Kimura's Recurring Figures Test (Kimura, 1963) has incorporated desirable features for assessing visual memory, the authors of the CVMT suggest it lacks a delay procedure necessary to make a distinction between acquisition and retention deficits. The CVMT was developed to correct this deficiency.

In its construction the CVMT was designed to incorporate five basic features inherent in an optimal test of visual memory: (*a*) a recognition memory format; (*b*) use of complex, ambiguous designs not easily susceptible to verbal labeling; (*c*) large numbers of stimuli; (*d*) limited exposure time to each stimulus (less than 3 seconds); and (*e*) a delayed recognition task. The CVMT consists of three tasks: Acquisition (testing recognition memory), Delayed Recognition (conducted after a 30-minute delay), and Visual Discrimination (which distinguishes visual discrimination deficits from visual memory problems). A Professional Manual, 137 spiral-bound stimulus cards, and a four-page scoring form comprise the CVMT testing materials.

The CVMT has been validated and norms established for adults 18 years and older. Although normative data are provided for ages 18–91, the authors express caution when interpreting scores for subjects older than 80 because of the small number in the sample for that age group. Because the majority of the subjects in the normative sample had completed high school, caution also is expressed for testing individuals who have not attained this educational level. Split-half reliabilities, ranging from .80 to .98, are reported for a group of 25 head trauma patients and a group of 25 matched normals. Test-retest reliabilities, ranging from .76 to .85, were obtained from a sample of 12 neurologically normal adults.

Construct validity was examined in 92 neurologically normal adults by investigating the relationships between the CVMT and other measures of intellectual functioning, as well as visual and verbal memory. Although specific factor-analytic results are not provided, the authors indicate that "The CVMT d-Prime score loaded on a general cognitive factor and showed no significant verbal cognitive or verbal memory associations" (manual, p. 11). Likewise, the CVMT Delayed Recognition Task and the Wechsler Delayed Visual Reproduction Task defined a clear visual memory factor. Validity also was investigated by testing patients known to have a high rate of memory impairment, especially those having right hemisphere lesions that result in the impairment of visual memory. Although such descriptions of validity are appreciated, including the results of these analyses would strengthen this material.

Even though the CVMT can be administered to a wide age range of adults, there are some restrictions of its use. The authors indicate that the CVMT may not be appropriate for use with individuals with severe aphasia, individuals with severe comprehension problems, individuals with severe perception problems, and individuals with severe psychiatric problems. However, patients with nonfluent dysphasia but intact language comprehension have no trouble with the CVMT.

The CVMT features ease of administration; the instructions are clear and comprehensible. No specific testing facilities, other than a comfortable room that is free from distractions, are needed. Administration requires 45–50 minutes (including the 30-minute wait for the Delayed Recognition Test). The CVMT is to be completed in one session. If a battery of tests is being administered, additional tests can be given during the 30-minute waiting period.

Scoring the CVMT, at least for the Acquisition component, is largely derived from signal detection theory. Thus, one records the number of "hits": (saying *old* to a recurring stimulus) and "false alarms" (saying *old* to a new stimulus). In addition to hits and false alarms, a "d-Prime" score and a "Total score" also are calculated. The d-Prime score represents signal strength and provides an overall measure of memory sensitivity. Although some calculation is required to derive d-Prime, the formula is clear and not difficult to follow. The Total Score is calculated by combining the number of hits with the number of correct recognitions of new items. Delayed Recognition and Visual Discrimination scores are determined by recording the number of correct responses (0–7) for each test.

Although the CVMT can be administered and scored by individuals who are not professionally trained, interpretation of the CVMT "requires professional training in clinical, experimental, or neuropsychology" (manual, p. 5). The three brief case studies presented to illustrate the interpretive use of the CVMT suggest that training in just experimental psychology may not provide a sufficient background. Although these case studies are informative, they are quite brief. Hence, expansions and/or additions would be welcomed.

Normative tables for four age groups (18–29, 30–49, 50–69, and 70+) are presented. Each table contains percentile scores. Because previous data failed to reveal gender differences, separate tables for men and women are not provided. For the assessment of overall performance, the authors recommend the use of the d-Prime, Total, and Delayed Recognition Task scores. It is noted that even though the d-Prime and Total scores provide similar information, the Total score is preferred in "cases where one value may fall above the cutoff and the other below" (p. 9) and when extreme values are present. Scores on the Delayed Recognition Task are used to discriminate between acquisition and retrieval deficits; they reliably distinguish "normal from neurologically impaired individuals up to age 60" (p. 9).

The CVMT appears capable of achieving the stated goal of assessing visual memory without incurring the risk of involving verbal memory processes. The reliability measures and reported validity support the appropriateness and effectiveness of this instrument.

There are, however, some minor flaws. First, although the Professional manual is quite clear concerning the instructions to be given to the subjects, specifications for the positioning and actual manipulation of the visual stimuli are not provided. The stimulus cards are contained in a spiral-bound booklet and it would be helpful to know exactly how the booklet is to be positioned in front of the subject (i.e., laying flat, standing on edge, etc.). Second, specific plans for the 30-minute delay session should be formulated prior to testing; subjects may not be comfortable just sitting and waiting during this period. These minor problems notwithstanding, the CVMT appears capable of making a significant contribution to the battery of assessment devices used by clinicians and neuropsychologists.

REVIEWER'S REFERENCE

Kimura, D. (1963). Right temporal lobe damage. *Archives of Neurology, 8*, 264-271.

[94]

Cooper-Farran Behavioral Rating Scales.

Purpose: Designed to assess social and cognitive skills.
Population: Kindergartners.
Publication Date: 1991.
Acronym: CFBRS.
Scores, 2: Interpersonal Skills, Work-Related Skills.
Administration: Individual.
Price Data, 1991: $7 per 25 test forms; $5 per 25 scoring sheets; $17 per manual (44 pages); $18 per specimen set.
Time: (10–20) minutes.
Comments: Ratings by teacher.
Authors: David H. Cooper and Dale C. Farran.
Publisher: Clinical Psychology Publishing Co., Inc.
Cross References: See T4:643 (1 reference).

TEST REFERENCES

1. Speece, D. L., & Cooper, D. H. (1990). Ontogeny of school failure: Classification of first-grade children. *American Educational Research Journal, 27*, 119-140.

Review of the Cooper-Farran Behavioral Rating Scales by FRANCIS X. ARCHAMBAULT, JR., Professor and Department Head, Department of Educational Psychology, The University of Connecticut, Storrs, CT, and DIANE GOLDSMITH, Director, Transition & Women's Programs, Manchester Community Technical College, Manchester, CT:

The Cooper-Farran Behavioral Rating Scales (CFBRS) is an easy-to-use experimental instrument designed to give educational practitioners and researchers a quantitative assessment of the social-cognitive development of kindergarten students. It is intended to be used by classroom teachers for screening children for potential behavior problems, by special service personnel to help them determine referred students' status with regard to various cognitive and behavioral handicaps, and by researchers interested in assessing the impact of the kindergarten curriculum.

The 37 items that comprise the instrument are designed to assess children's classroom behaviors on two scales: a 21-item Interpersonal Skills Scale and a 16-item Work Related Skills Scale. The instrument requires teachers or teacher aides to rate student behaviors, after a minimum of one month's observation of that student's classroom experience, on a 7-point Likert scale, which is anchored at points 1, 3, 5, and 7. Approximately 10 to 20 minutes per student are needed to complete the ratings (not including scoring).

The manual contains instructions and examples on how to rate, score, and interpret the results. The manual authors also rightly warn users to interpret scores cautiously because the instrument has not yet been adequately standardized. The authors also caution that "the CFBRS should be conservatively interpreted and always considered in concert with other psychoeducational data and clinical judgement" (manual, p. 15). Subscale standard scores for females and males and bounds for the 68%, 85%, 90%, and 95% confidence intervals are provided in the manual. However, the manual has very little information on the theory supporting the instrument, other than the authors' concern that the instrument be "congruent with the perceived needs of those for whose use it is intended" (p. 4). The absence of a strong theoretical rationale reduces one's ability to attach meaning to the behaviors measured and, thus, to effectively remediate problems that may lead to school failure.

Most of the items comprising the CFBRS were developed in two studies, not conducted by the authors, which asked kindergarten teachers to list behaviors they thought were critical for success in kindergarten and other behaviors they found to be most troublesome. These 36 behaviors were then pilot tested with 46 educators and graduate students to assess content validity. On the basis of this trial a number of items were rewritten and three new items were added. The revised 39-item scale was then tested with 37 practicing kindergarten teachers who rated the behaviors of two students, one they considered well adjusted and another maladjusted. On 38 of the 39 items, differences between the two groups of students exceeded one standard deviation; on 30 items, differences exceeded two standard deviations. Although the authors claim that these findings support the items' discriminant validity, one wonders whether any bias was introduced by having the teachers supply the criterion measure.

Two large-sample field trials were also conducted on the instrument on a total of 1,490 kindergartners. One study was done in two school districts in North Carolina; the second was conducted in public and private schools in Hawaii. Data from these trials were used to assess reliability and establish norms. Intrarater and interrater reliabilities were calculated from the North Carolina data. Eighteen of the 30 teachers participating in this study rated 443 children on two occasions separated by 8 weeks. Teachers and teacher aides also independently rated some of these youngsters (number not given). Test-retest reliabilities on individual items ranged from .49 to .80 with 22 items above .70. Interrater reliability ranged from .31 to .68 with 24 of the items above .50. A number of these reliabilities are quite low, and it is not clear why they are presented at all because item reliabilities are likely to be lower than scale reliabilities as well as less meaningful, assuming that scale scores rather than item scores are to be interpreted. In fact, the interrater reliabilities for the scale scores were reported as .78 for Interpersonal Skills and .79 for Work-Related Skills, both reasonably high levels of agreement. No test-retest reliabilities are provided for the scales.

Turning now to validity, the content validity of the CFBRS was established by choosing behaviors reported as important in the literature, by having over 100 educators review these behaviors for their appropriateness, by rewriting items that were ambiguous, and by having reviewers comment on the use of the anchors and the item rating process. The procedures followed here were appropriate. Concerning construct validity, the authors report the results of an exploratory factor analysis that uncovered two factors which accounted for 89% of the variance. The solution proposed produces the 21-item Interpersonal Skills Scale and the 16-item Work-Related Skills Scale, and both have alpha coefficients greater than .90. However, 7 of the 21 Interpersonal Skills items and 10 of the 16 Work-Related Skills items load .30 or above on the "other" scales leading one to question whether a single-factor interpretation is more appropriate. Additional evidence on this issue is needed. However, the authors do provide data to suggest the Work-Related Skills Scale is more predictive of school failure than the Interpersonal Skills Scale. They also provide correlations between the CFBRS and another behavioral screening instrument and the Wechsler Preschool and Primary Scales of Intelligence, which offer some additional evidence for the Scales.

By way of summary, the Cooper-Farran Behavioral Rating Scales gives kindergarten teachers an opportunity to rate their students on behaviors that have been judged to be important for school success or likely to be indicative of school problems so that those at risk for school failure may be discovered and remedies found. As suggested by the authors, the current version of the instrument must be used with caution and only in concert with other psychoeducational data and clinical judgement. Further, the norms that are provided must be interpreted cautiously in light of the insufficient standardization. Acknowledging these shortcomings, the instrument holds some promise of being a useful tool for school practitioners and researchers. Before widespread use, however, additional data on the instrument's reliability and validity would be required. Also required would be additional details on the theory which supports the particular set of items included on the scales and the manner in which test results are to be interpreted given that theory.

Review of the Cooper-Farran Behavioral Rating Scales by ANTHONY W. PAOLITTO, Assistant Professor of Education, School Psychology Program, Tufts University, Medford, MA:

The Cooper-Farran Behavioral Rating Scales (CFBRS) were developed to assess kindergarten children's overt classroom behaviors, relevant to both their work habits and developing socializations with peers and adults. The authors purport the usefulness of their instrument as both a screening device for potential problematic behaviors and as a contributor to more formal diagnostic evaluations, yielding results with prescriptive utility.

The Cooper-Farran Behavioral Rating Scales contain a total of 37 items in the form of neutrally worded behavior "stems" to which a rater responds by circling one number of a 7-point summated rating scale. The points are representative of a bipolar continuum, utilizing four different descriptive behaviors related to the stem, with three additional points serving as midpoints to the descriptors. Two subscales (Interpersonal Skills and Work-Related Skills) derived from the total items of the CFBRS are utilized for normative comparisons and interpretations. Polarity of half of the items in the total scale have been reversed to guard against the effects of response set. The scale is primarily intended for use by kindergarten teachers or their aides who are familiar with the student's classroom performance. Raters respond to their impressions of a child's recent behaviors or performances in general, thus specific periods to observe the child are not necessary, nor are skills in systematic observation.

Guidelines for completing the CFBRS record form are clear and direct; examples are provided, and the rating form itself is well laid out in regard to rating points lining up with their behavioral descriptors. However, a potential area of confusion exists relative to subjective interpretation of rating instructions: The form does not mention that ratings are to be based on current or most recent behaviors, as indicated in the manual. Thus, a child who has exhibited variable behaviors with regard to a particular stem might be rated by teachers according to their subjective summation of the student's behavior over time, rather than their most recent impressions.

The CFBRS is hand scored, with raw score ratings from the record form transferred to a score sheet. After transforming some scores to account for their reversal of polarity, raw scores are added yielding totals for each of the two subscales, from which standard scores and confidence intervals are derived. Although transcribing raw scores to the subscale column is not a task prone to error, extra spacing between each item or clusters of items would make scoring quicker and more efficient, especially when scoring several forms one after the other, as with kindergarten screenings. Both administration and scoring of an individual kindergarten student can usually be completed in under a half-hour.

The authors appropriately caution the current standardization of the CFBRS lends itself to conservative interpretations of results, recognizing that ongoing improvements from the original sample are warranted, while encouraging the development of more localized norms to utilize the CFBRS for group comparisons. The standardization data presented include ratings from a total of 1,490 kindergarten students drawn from four separate sites: two in North Carolina and two in Hawaii. Each child was rated by his or her kindergarten teacher, initially in the fall and then later in the spring of the same school year, yielding norms for both periods. Data concerning parents' socioeconomic status, the numbers of boys or girls, race or ethnicity, or students considered at risk for educational problems are only casually mentioned without any descriptive data provided. Additionally, there is no differentiation or mention of students who may have had prior preschool experiences before entering kindergarten, information which would undoubtedly be useful for comparison and analysis of children's scores on the CFBRS.

Item stems for the CFBRS were developed by soliciting from a sample of kindergarten teachers behaviors they viewed as both critical for kindergarten success and problematic. Results of this process appear to be documented in two unpublished manuscripts; however, specific details reporting the number of teachers involved or further characteristics of this sample are not provided in the manual. Procedures for pilot testing and large-scale field-based trials are described. Although the details and scope of this testing are limited, appropriate procedures appear to have been utilized to assist in establishing content validity for the CFBRS; factor analytic studies which adequately confirm the two scale model are also presented. Several analyses are presented in the manual supporting construct validity with moderate to high coefficients reported; however, small samples or limited descriptions of these comparisons are provided.

The authors employed intraclass correlations to report stability and interrater coefficients in order to estimate for true differences among subjects and account for variability between raters or rating occurrences. Although intraclass correlations can result in more conservative estimates of reliability, the stability coefficients for the CFBRS should still generally be considered moderate: 14 of the 37 items were below .70, and all but one were below .80. Subscale and total scale stability coefficients are not provided. Interrater reliability coefficients for individual items ranged from .31 to .68, which the authors contend should be superseded by the two subscale scores which are actually used for interpreting the CFBRS (.78 Interpersonal Skills; .79 Work-Related Skills). This assertion, however, is contrary to two sample case studies the authors utilize in the Interpretation section of the manual, where they provide several examples of single items being employed to describe individual students' strengths and weaknesses.

In summary, if the CFBRS is evaluated for its utility in screening kindergarten students' social and work-oriented skills, while also providing a vehicle to establish local norms to compare individual students, its use could certainly be encouraged. Caution should be exercised in utilizing the CFBRS beyond this current scope of application, especially in placement decisions, considering the restrictions of its standardization sample. The authors acknowledge some of the CFBRS limitations, and, in fact, encourage cautious interpretation while the CFBRS is in the process of ongoing standardization studies and research. The CFBRS is easy to use, score, and interpret, and is appropriate for a number of kindergarten applications. In addition to its facility as a screening instrument, kindergarten teachers may use the scale to monitor the progress of individual students over repeated administrations. Moreover, as significant variability of school-related development is common at the kindergarten level, the fall and spring norms provided by the CFBRS enhance its utility.

[95]

Coping Resources Inventory.

Purpose: Developed to assess a person's resources for coping with stress.
Population: High school and over.
Publication Dates: 1987–88.
Acronym: CRI.
Scores, 6: Cognitive, Social, Emotional, Spiritual/Philosophical, Physical, Total.
Administration: Group.
Price Data, 1992: $10 per 25 test booklets; $49 per 10 prepaid answer sheets; $28 per 50 not prepaid answer sheets; $36 per set of scoring stencils; $16 per 50 profiles; $12 per manual ('88, 30 pages); $13 per specimen set.
Time: (10) minutes.
Comments: For research use only.
Authors: Allen L. Hammer and M. Susan Marting.
Publisher: Consulting Psychologists Press, Inc.
Cross References: See T4:649 (2 references).

TEST REFERENCES

1. Coleman, M. R. (1992). A comparison of how gifted/LD and average/LD boys cope with school frustration. *Journal for the Education of the Gifted, 15*, 239-265.

Review of the Coping Resources Inventory by ROGER A. BOOTHROYD, Research Scientist, Bureau of Evaluation and Services Research, New York State Office of Mental Health, Albany, NY:

DESCRIPTION. The Coping Resources Inventory (CRI) is a 60-item measure designed to assess the internal resources people possess that relate to their capacity to handle stress. The items on the CRI are grouped into five domains: Cognitive, Social, Emotional, Spiritual/Philosophical, and Physical. These domains were established on the basis of the authors' experience in conducting stress programs, their work with clients, and through consultation with content experts. In excess of 150 items were constructed initially and reduced to 60 through a number of pilot studies. The authors carefully distinguish coping resources defined as the "precursors of behavior" from coping strategies defined as how people react to stressors. The CRI can be administered to individuals or groups and takes approximately 10 minutes to complete.

SCORING AND INTERPRETATION. Hand-scoring templates can be used to score the CRI; computer scoring is available from Consulting Psychologists Press. Normative data were collected on approximately 750 students and adults in a series of separate studies. Raw scores on each scale are converted to standard scores with a mean of 50 and a standard deviation of 10. Separate conversion tables are provided for men and women because of gender differences in coping resources. CRI scores can be interpreted ipsatively, whereby an individual's strong and weak resources are identified, or normatively, where an individual's profile is compared to other individuals.

RELIABILITY. The range and median item-to-scale correlations are reported for each domain. The median item-to-scale correlations range from .37 to .46 for the five scales. Separate alpha reliabilities are provided for each scale by norming subgroups and are generally in the .70s and .80s on individual subscales and in the .90s for total score. The internal consistency estimates of two of the subscales (Cognitive and Physical), however, vary from sample to sample. The alphas on the Physical scale, for example, range from .56 on a sample of high school students to .83 on a sample of college students. Estimates of test/retest reliability (over a 6-week interval) on the scales range from .60 to .73 but were derived from a limited sample of 115 high school students.

VALIDITY. Interscale correlations are provided for the total sample and separately for males and females. The total sample correlations suggest the independence of the five CRI domains is somewhat questionable. Correlations among the Cognitive, Social, and Emotional scales are high (.60 to .69) suggesting a fair amount of overlap among these constructs. Although the authors recommend treating these scales as distinct until additional data are available, I have reservations regarding the use of ipsative interpretations that infer an individual is weak or strong in specific domains when the independence of these domains is questionable.

Some evidence of predictive and construct validity is provided. The CRI total resource score was found to be a significant *incremental* predictor of stress symptoms in a study by Elkind (1981). A multitrait-multimethod procedure was used to examine CRI scores with simple self-ratings of coping resources. The correlations for the same traits across methods (i.e., convergent validity coefficients) ranged from .61 for the Spiritual/Philosophical to .80 for the Physical scale. With the exception of the Social scale, the validity coefficients exceeded the correlations found in the two heterotrait/heteromethod and heterotrait/monomethod triangles (i.e., discriminant validity).

Means and standard deviations are provided on each scale for males and females. Gender differences were found on the CRI, with women scoring significantly higher than men on the Social, Emotional, Spiritual/Philosophical, and Total Resources scores and significantly lower on the Physical scale.

The authors summarize a number of studies that provide further evidence of the CRI's validity. For example, healthy college students had significantly higher scores than ill college students on each CRI dimension with the exception of the Emotional scale. Other studies examined the coping resources of cardiac and pulmonary rehabilitation patients, stress center clients, counseling center clients, college student resident advisors, and high school peer counselors. The CRI scales are correlated with a number of other measures and demographic variables.

COMMENTARY. The manual is well written and contains clear directions regarding administration, scoring, and interpretation. The authors include practical information such as how to estimate scale scores when missing responses are present, complete with appropriate cautions. The manual also contains a concise summary of the development of the CRI.

Data on reliability and validity are provided and clearly summarized. Although authors present a theoretical basis for distinguishing between coping resources and coping strategies, jointly administering measures of both to a sample of people would allow an empirical assessment regarding the extent to which these two constructs differ. Given the high correlations among some of the subscales, however, the authors would be well advised to factor analyze the items as a means of empirically establishing structure and dimensionality of the CRI.

As acknowledged by the authors, the norms as well as the reliability and validity estimates tend to be based on small and homogeneous groups of subjects. High school and college students comprise a substantial proportion of the individuals on which the CRI was normed and with the exception of gender, little background information is provided. Although the authors have begun to examine gender differences, it seems likely that cultural and socioeconomic differences may also be related to shaping the internal resources that individuals can draw on when dealing with stress and should subsequently be examined.

In conclusion, at the present time the CRI seems best suited as a global measure of the internal resources individuals use when faced with stressful situations. The authors have used a variety of means to examine the validity of the measure and will likely continue to conduct further studies in this area. Caution is advised, however, when comparing and interpreting individuals' relative strengths and weaknesses given the high interscale correlations among several of the domains, particularly if one wishes to use these scores to develop specific intervention strategies or techniques to assist individuals in coping with stress.

REVIEWER'S REFERENCE

Elkind, D. (1981). *The hurried child.* Reading, MA: Addison-Wesley.

Review of the Coping Resources Inventory by LARRY COCHRAN, Professor of Counseling Psychology, Faculty of Education, The University of British Columbia, Vancouver, British Columbia, Canada:

The Coping Resources Inventory (CRI) is a test of coping resources, designed to assess a person's strengths and weaknesses for managing stress. A coping resource is an adaptive capacity that enables persons to manage stress more effectively, experiencing fewer and less intense symptoms, and recovering faster. It is not what a person does under stress, but an enduring capacity that precedes behavior. From a review of literature and personal experience in working with groups and individuals, the authors identified five coping resources that are amenable to counseling. These resources were termed Cognitive (a positive sense of self, others, and life generally), Social (extent to which one is embedded in a supportive network of people), Emotional (ability to accept and express affect), Spiritual/Philosophical (extent to which one is guided by an enduring and harmonious set of values), and Physical (degree of health-promoting behaviors that enhance physical well-being).

Through consultation, clinical experience, published research, and other tests, over 150 items were initially generated. In a series of pilot studies and one large sample of 300, items were excluded on the basis of low item-scale correlations and narrow range of responses. For the large sample, all 60 of the retained items correlated at or over .30 with their respective scales. Each item describes a characteristic of living such as "I have plenty of energy." For each item, individuals are instructed to mark the response that "best describes you in the last six months," using a 4-point frequency scale that ranges from *never or rarely* to *always or nearly always*. Raw scores are summed and converted into standard scores, using separate tables for males and females. The norm groups were composed of 327 male and 401 female high school students, college students, and adults. Because of the inadequate size and lack of diversity of their norm groups, the authors advise extreme caution in making normative interpretations.

Across different samples, the internal consistency of scales ranged from moderate to good, with alpha coefficients tending to rise with the age of the sample. For the total test, alpha coefficients were consistently strong (.89 to .93). Over a 6-week interval, scale stability ranged from .60 to .78 for high school students, and would probably increase with older groups.

No factor analytic studies have been conducted to examine the internal structure of the test, although a few strong intercorrelations among scales were reported. For example, the correlation between Social and Emotional was .80 in one study and .69 for the total norm group. For this test, the reluctance of the authors to combine scales without further evidence seems justified. As the test now stands, the scales have a definite content and are reasonably clear for interpretation. And there is good reason why, for instance, Social would be expected to correlate rather strongly with Emotional. Namely, it would seem that the expression of affect would partially depend upon a supportive network willing to listen. In this regard, the results of a multitrait-multimethod procedure, using the CRI and self-ratings for the five scales, were generally supportive, indicating convergence (higher correlations between different measures of the same coping resource) and divergence (lower correlations for other comparisons). The exception was the Social scale. Although future work might lead to a combination of scales, the present separation of the five scales seems warranted.

In one predictive study, the CRI and life events accounted for an impressive degree of variance in stress symptoms (46%). In several studies, the CRI was used to discriminate successfully between groups such as healthy and ill college students. Studies of concurrent validity were encouraging. The CRI scales correlated significantly with expected variables such as depression and distress, although there were some discrepant findings such as a lack of relationship between the emotional scale and a measure of emotional discharge. Thus far, correlational studies have demonstrated the relevance of CRI scales to symptoms of stress. However, the scales have not as yet been systematically correlated with tests that might confirm their meaning (for example, comparing the Spiritual/Philosophical scale with perhaps the Purpose of Life Test [T4:2169] or another relevant instrument). Comparisons with the Myers-Briggs Type Indicator (T4:1702) provided a fruitful beginning, but more needs to be done.

Overall, the CRI is a promising instrument for research, program evaluation, and counseling practice. For counseling practice in particular, it is well designed, useful, and easy to translate into work with individuals and groups. The scales reflect coping resources that can be improved through counseling and include resources that are not covered in other tests. Although the authors argue appropriately for caution in using results to make decisions about individuals, they are perhaps too cautious. The ordinary use of test information in counseling is to work with individuals. The test results facilitate an exploration of the person's life, drawing in various forms of evidence to confirm or challenge particular scores. As a stimulant for examining the coping resources of an individual or group, the CRI seems well conceived for broad and fruitful exploration to guide counseling efforts.

[96]

Coping With Stress.

Purpose: Constructed as a self-assessment tool to identify sources of stress and responses to stress.
Population: Adults.
Publication Date: 1989.
Scores, 9: Reaction to Stress (Obsessive, Hysteria, Anxiety, Phobia, Total, Normal), Adjustment to Stress (Healthy, Unhealthy), Sources of Stress.
Administration: Group.
Price Data, 1993: $60 per complete kit including 20 test folders, 20 response sheets, and 20 interpretation sheets.
Time: [20] minutes administration; [10] minutes scoring; [30] minutes interpretation.
Comments: Self-administered, self-scored.
Author: Training House, Inc.
Publisher: Training House, Inc.

Review of Coping With Stress by BERT W. WESTBROOK, Professor of Psychology, North Carolina State University, Raleigh, NC, and SUZANNE MARKEL-FOX, Post Doctoral Fellow, Center for Mental Health Policies and Services Research, University of Pennsylvania, Philadelphia, PA:

Coping With Stress was constructed as a self-assessment tool to identify sources of stress and responses to stress. The publisher claims that the exercise "will help you to understand the different types of responses to stress, how they distribute in your personality, what kinds of situations are most stressful, and how able you are to deal with stress" (from the face sheet of the instrument). Unfortunately, the questionnaire and interpretation sheet are all that are actually provided for the test-taker or administrator. This is a serious oversight, but this is not the first time that Training House has produced a self-administered and self-scored instrument. The list includes packages such as the Personal Style Assessment (T4:1990); the Self-Awareness Profile (T4:2406); the Communication Response Style: Assessment (T4:597); the Survey of Organizational Climate (T4:2656); the Management Style Inventory (T4:1519); and the Managerial Assessment of Proficiency MAP (T4:1528). Reviews of these instruments in the *Mental Measurements Yearbooks* have invariably drawn attention to the lack of manual or reliability and validity information. Most have adequate face validity and are simple to administer. Concerns about how their self-scoring system could "encourage cheating" (Norris, 1991), and about the lack of theoretical grounding of the instruments have been raised. Some reviewers have gone so far as to compare the Training Houses' products to "parlor games" (Stone, 1992) and "horoscopes" (Osberg, 1992). The same kind of concern must be raised at this time.

ADMINISTRATION AND SCORING. Coping With Stress can be completed in a group or individually, because it is both self-administered and self-scored. The instructions are printed on the first sheet under the subheading "A Self-Assessment Exercise." After a brief overview of the physiological reactions to stress and a paragraph on clinical terms, the test-taker is directed to answer "candidly," to then tally the responses and finally, to "read the Interpretation Sheet that explains the implications of your scores." Coping With Stress purports to measure the following: Reaction to Stress (Obsessive, Hysteria, Anxiety, Phobia, Total Score, Normal), Adjustment to Stress (Healthy, Unhealthy), and Sources of Stress. There is one form of this self-assessment exercise, provided on carbonless self-copy paper. This format allows the test taker to circle the desired response and when finished, to lift the first sheet and calculate his or her total score from the weighted scores on the copy.

There is no information about the theory behind the development of this questionnaire, how the items were selected, nor any information about how norms were established. Sixty questions are separated into three sections: (*a*) How do you feel about potentially stressful events or situations? (*b*) How do you react to potential stressors? and (*c*) What life stress events have occurred for you in the past year? Items are scored on a 4-point scale, ranging from "+++ = 'strong fit'" to "o = 'never.'" Scores are calculated and interpreted by the test-taker, based on the "Interpretation Sheet," which consists of a four-page key, bibliography, and list of suggestions for dealing with stress.

TECHNICAL CONSIDERATIONS. No statistical item analysis, method of validation, or further information about validity or reliability are provided. Although face validity may be adequate, Coping With Stress fails to follow the basic guidelines of the *Standards for Educational and Psychological Testing* (AERA, APA, & NCME, 1985). There is no test manual, and neither validity nor reliability data. The interpretation sheet suggests that, if one obtains a score of less than 20 on six selected items, the "remaining scores will have little validity" (p. 1). Unfortunately, the test publisher does not reveal the basis for this statement.

There are several assumptions on this checklist that are not validated, such as the above statement regarding a score of less than 20. The statement that "Any total above 10 indicates the presence of neurotic behavior" (p. 1) is not validated, either. It may be unprofessional to circulate an instrument that would lead individuals to classify themselves as "neurotic" without the aid of a counselor. The wording of items may lead to confusion, as well, both in what items do not mention (such as exercise as a way to deal with stress), and the terms used (such as choices of behaviors used to "forget" stress, a set of behaviors labeled "healthy" under "coping"). The terse classification and description system proposed in Coping With Stress should be eliminated, or at least moderated. As it now stands, this questionnaire sounds like the "armchair psychologist" one would expect to find in a popular magazine.

OVERALL CRITIQUE. Coping With Stress does not meet the requirements of the *Standards for Educational and Psychological Testing* (AERA, APA, & NCME, 1985). There was no technical manual provided; the face sheet of the questionnaire was the extent of technical information available. The authors offered no validity or reliability information nor any reporting of normative data. Coping With Stress can be a dangerous tool because there are too many ambiguous items, which may lead an individual to accept an erroneous psychiatric diagnosis. A self-report instrument that does not require the presence of a counselor for interpretation is inappropriate and counter to good psychological practice.

REVIEWER'S REFERENCES

American Educational Research Association, American Psychological Association, & National Council on Measurement in Education. (1985). *Standards for educational and psychological testing.* Washington, DC: American Psychological Association, Inc.

Norris, J. (1992). [Review of the Communication Response Style: Assessment]. In J. J. Kramer & J. C. Conoley (Eds.), *The eleventh mental measure-*

ments yearbook (pp. 207-209). Lincoln, NE: Buros Institute of Mental Measurements.

Osberg, T. M. (1992). [Review of the Self-Awareness Profile]. In J. J. Kramer & J. C. Conoley (Eds.), *The eleventh mental measurements yearbook* (pp. 806-807). Lincoln, NE: Buros Institute of Mental Measurements.

Stone, G. L. (1992). [Review of the Personal Style Assessment]. In J. J. Kramer & J. C. Conoley (Eds.), *The eleventh mental measurements yearbook* (pp. 666-667). Lincoln, NE: Buros Institute of Mental Measurements.

[97]

CPF [Second Edition].

Purpose: "To assess extroversion and preference for social contact."
Population: Ages 16–adult.
Publication Dates: 1954–92.
Acronym: CPF.
Scores, 3: Validity Scores (Uncertainty, Good Impression), Total Extroversion.
Administration: Group or individual.
Price Data, 1994: $14 per specimen set including manual ('92, 10 pages), 3 test booklets, and scoring key; $21 per 20 test booklets; $10 per manual.
Time: (5–10) minutes.
Comments: Previously listed as a subtest of the Employee Attitude Series of the Job-Tests Program (T3:1219).
Author: Samuel E. Krug.
Publisher: Industrial Psychology International Ltd.

Review of the CPF [Contact Personality Factor, Second Edition] by MICHAEL R. HARWELL, Associate Professor of Psychology and Education, University of Pittsburgh, Pittsburgh, PA:

The Contact Personality Factor (CPF) test is intended to assess "extroversion" and preference for social contact, information that, according to the manual, is often needed for job selection, career counseling, or understanding an individual's social orientation (manual, p. 1). The current CPF is a revision of the 1954 original test and contains 40 self-report items, each of which is answered by an examinee marking "Generally True," "Uncertain," or "Generally False." Responses are then scored using a stencil. The test also contains two validity scales. According to the manual, the Good Impression (GI) scale indicates the extent to which examinees may be faking their responses, and is assessed using 6 (of the 40) items which, if answered in a socially desirable way, invalidates the CPF score for an examinee. (A score of 5 on this scale suggests that test results should be interpreted cautiously.) The Uncertainty (U) scale reflects the total number of times an examinee chooses this option, with a U score greater than 19 invalidating the test and U scores of 16–19 raising the possibility of excessive defensiveness. No evidence is offered to justify these cutoffs and interpretations of the GI and U scales. The manual states that the CPF generally requires 5–10 minutes, although there is no time limit, and that it can be administered individually or in groups to examinees at least 16 years old. Directions for administration appear on the first page of the test booklet.

USABILITY. The test form contains explicit instructions for administering and responding (e.g., examinees are instructed to refrain from relying on the Uncertain response category, and to answer every question). The manual offers evidence that the reading demands of the CPF are satisfied by examinees with at least a sixth grade reading proficiency.

SCORING. The scoring system for the CPF is based on summing the keyed response for each of the 34 items (the 6 items comprising the GI scale are omitted). Each item is dichotomously scored and each keyed response is worth one point. Thus, the theoretical range of CPF raw scores is 0–34, with higher scores reflecting greater extraversion and preference for social contact. (Note that this scoring system means that items are weighted equally.) No explanation, theoretical or empirical, is offered for the selection of keyed options used to score the test. The manual suggests handling omitted items by adjusting the total score based on the answered items (e.g., if one item was omitted and the examinee's raw score was 20, the adjusted score would be 20 x 34/33 = 21). This procedures is said to be appropriate when, at most, three to four answers are missing although no rationale or evidence to support this recommendation is provided. Nor is there any guidance offered when the adjusted score is not an integer (e.g., 21.5). These concerns are aggravated by the fact that 12% of the examinees in the norming sample for the revised CPF had to be dropped because of missing data. If the experience in norming the revised CPF is indicative of what users can expect, questions about the recommended adjustment take on a troubling importance.

Tabled percentiles and stanines are provided for the CPF raw scores (although, interestingly enough, not for the GI or U scale scores). A detailed description of the interpretation accompanying an examinee's percentile or stanine is provided. For example, the interpretation of a percentile score between 77–88 is that "People who score at this level will usually become bored with paperwork or machine assignments" (p. 3). These explanations are easy to follow although, again, no theoretical or empirical evidence is offered to support the selection of the intervals (e.g., 77–88) or the interpretations. Nor is any attention paid to the possibility that the measurement of extraversion and social preference may be influenced by demographic variables (e.g., gender, race, age, socioeconomic status) which, if true, would presumably influence the interpretations of CPF scores. If this is not the case it should be clearly documented in the manual. A table allowing scores on the first edition of the test to be converted to their second edition equivalent is also presented (whether this is a good idea is not discussed—it probably is not).

NORMS. The norms for the revised CPF are based on a sample (N = 569) of high school seniors. The manual reports that 44% of the respondents were male, that the age of examinees in the sample ranged from 15–21 years, and that 86% of the respondents were white, 10% were black, and 4% represented other minorities. The respondents were also asked questions about how clear and understandable the questions were and whether they were easy or difficult to follow. These percentages are reported for each of the three response categories. Surprisingly, the responses to these questions by gender and race are not reported. Nor is any detailed information provided about the age distribution in the sample, where the respondents were from, whether they came from the same high school, how the 569 came to be respondents, or whether there were differences in CPF scores between demographic groups. Another troubling aspect of the reported norming information is that 15–21-year-olds were used in the sample, but the manual states that the test can be used for examinees older than 21, even though this group was not represented in the norming sample. Similarly, the test is recommended for examinees 16 or older, whereas the norming sample contained an unspecified number of 15-year-olds.

Technical work developing the norms relied on the Rasch model in item response theory (IRT). The manual provides a brief description of IRT and explains that, using the Rasch model, it is possible to describe the probability that an examinee will endorse an item in terms of the difference between an examinee's level of extraversion (what is usually called an ability estimate in IRT but here represents the examinee's level of extraversion) and the descriptive level of the item (known as the difficulty parameter in IRT). Thus, an item that describes very extraverted behavior is, according to the manual, more likely to be endorsed by a highly extraverted examinee than by one who is introverted. The manual also points out that using an IRT model to develop norms lessens their dependency on the composition of the norming sample. This means that the resulting norms are (assuming the Rasch model is correct) applicable to any random sample of examinees from the same population. However, this does *not* mean that the norms can be generalized across various demographic variables.

The need to assess the assumptions of the Rasch model is also emphasized in the manual, with unidimensionality of the item set specifically mentioned, although no evidence is provided that the items satisfy this assumption. Evidence of model-data fit is provided in the form of a chi-square goodness-of-fit test (*which* chi-square test of fit—there are many—is not mentioned) for each CPF item using the data of 498 of the 569 high school students (71/569 = 12% of these students had missing data). Four of the 36 items showed a lack of fit, and standard practice would be to investigate these items more closely, perhaps revising and repiloting them. There is no mention of this being done for the CPF, and apparently the misfitting items were used in the process of generating norms. The manual also states that some of the items are new and some were taken from the original CPF. It would be helpful to know which are the newer versus older items on the revised CPF (e.g., were the four misfitting items from the original CPF, the revised CPF, or both?).

RELIABILITY. Cronbach's coefficient alpha was used to assess reliability. Initially, a pilot sample of undergraduates (N = 331) was used, with half of these students being randomly assigned the revised version of the CPF (the other half received the original version). The internal consistency of the revised 34-item CPF was .89. Unfortunately, no information about the demographics of the 331 undergraduates is provided, or how items for the revised CPF which showed problems were dealt with. The piloted version of the CPF was then administered to the 569 high school seniors mentioned above, which produced alpha = .89. (Most statistics in the manual, such as reliabilities, correlations, etc., are reported to three or four decimal places, a sophomoric practice that should be avoided in future editions; two decimal places is sufficient.) It would also have been useful to report the reliability by gender and, where sample sizes permitted, by race, for the norming sample. The reliability of the GI and U scales for the 569 students was .65 and .89, respectively. Estimated standard errors of measurement for the CPF total score and the validity scales are not reported.

VALIDITY. The primary evidence of the validity of the revised CPF are correlations between it and various scales of the Adult Personality Inventory (API), a self-report inventory containing several scales (one of which is Extroversion), which purports to assess personality characteristics. (The author of the revised CPF also authored the API—in the future it would be better to use an additional test unconnected with the CPF's author to provide validity evidence.) Correlations between the CPF and the API Extroversion scale based on a sample of college students (N = 149) are offered as evidence of construct validity. (No information about this sample of students is provided.) For example, the correlation between the CPF and the Extroverted scale of the API is given as .5221, along with an explanation of this scale. In conjunction with the .5221 correlation, the manual states that "Again, this indicates that the CPF is measuring what it says it measures" (manual, p. 4). This phrasing is unfortunate and may mislead some users. The use of the word "indicates" implies a result that is incontrovertible, which is clearly not the case; "suggests" would have been more appropriate because it is possible that neither scale measures what it is purported to measure. Nor is a correlation of .5221 incontestable evidence of validity (27% of the variance in the CPF and Extroversion scale is shared and 73% is unexplained). Another troubling aspect of the validity evidence is the statement in the manual that several studies have confirmed that CPF scores correlate with job performance, providing evidence of criterion validity. (Correlations from two such studies based on sample sizes of 35 and 21 are reported.) However, references for these studies are not given, and it is unclear whether the reported evidence of criterion validity is for the original (1954) CPF or the revised version. At the very least, the reporting in this section of the manual is inexcusably sloppy.

SUMMARY. The task of the revised CPF is to assess extraversion and social contact and there is evidence that it partially succeeds. The revised version is easy to use, easy to score, and offers evidence of its reliability and, to some extent, its validity. The Good Impression index is particularly useful for a test of this nature. Unfortunately, there is precious little demographic information about the examinees in the norming sample, no explanation of why a test normed on 15–21-year-olds is appropriate for older examinees, no rationale provided for the recommended procedure for adjusting scores for omitted items, and no standard errors of measurement reported. Finally, there is no theoretical rationale provided for the interpretations associated with various CPF percentile and stanine scores. The revised CPF is, as the manual states, an improvement over the original version. Unfortunately, the absence of information about the norming groups, and some fuzziness in the explanation of the psychometric properties of the test, make it more difficult for users to judge its theoretical and empirical merits than it should be. It is hoped the next edition will clarify these deficiencies and allow this test to be recommended in a relatively unconditional way. Until then, users should be especially wary of adopting the substantive interpretations for various scores beyond the group used to norm the test (i.e., primarily white high school seniors 15–21 years of age).

Review of the CPF [Contact Personality Factor, Second Edition] by ALLEN K. HESS, Professor and Department Head, Department of Psychology, School of Sciences, Auburn University at Montgomery, Montgomery, AL:

A MEASURE UNTO ITSELF. The CPF is a version of a 1954 measure derived from Cattell's theory and test series. The 40-item 1992 edition is designed to gauge extraversion and preference for social contact in people 16 years of age and older who have at least a sixth grade reading level. Thirty-four items are used to derive a raw score with a table provided to convert raw scores to percentile and stanine norms. The measure is purportedly "useful when knowledge of [preference for social contact or extraversion] is necessary for job selection, career counseling or understanding an individual's social orientation" (manual, p. 1). The CPF has Good Impression (GI, six items) and Uncertainty (U) scales to measure test-taking attitude. The latter scale reflects the number of times a person opts for the "Uncertainty" response rather than the "Generally True" or "Generally False" options. The items are easily understood and face valid (e.g., "I like warm, friendly people" and "I would rather be a machinist than a salesperson").

PSYCHOMETRIC PROPERTIES. The manual provides a novel interpretation of Cronbach's alpha; to wit, "If different questions were asked, would the test results be the same? Ideally, a test score should generalize well beyond the specific set of items if the score is to be very useful. This aspect of test reliability is commonly described as 'internal consistency' and by a statistic known as 'Cronbach's alpha'" (manual, p. 4). The alpha coefficients of .89 for the CPF and .65 and .89 for GI and U are indicative of respectable coherence between items on the respective scales. Test retest reliability is defined, too, but no test-retest studies are reported.

Two validity studies are presented. The first correlates the CPF with cooperativeness (.31), work quantity (.53), work quality (.61), dependability (.45), and leadership ability (.58) as rated by 35 supervisors. No information is given as to whether the raters were "blind" or had access to the CPF scores, nor was any mention made of whether one person was rated by all raters, or all raters rated different individuals, or some raters rated some of the same persons as did other raters. Nor was any performance or actual behavior assessed.

The second study correlates the CPF with Krug's Adult Personality Inventory (API). The API portrays high CPF scorers as Extroverted (.52), Adjusted (.34), Disciplined (.30), but not Creative (-.39). They are Caring (.37), Assertive (.52), and not Nonconforming (-.36). A third set of API scales finds high CPF scorers to be Structured (.49), Social (.39), and Competitive (.32). No other validity data are presented. Finally, the author conducted a one-parameter Rasch items-response analysis which shows the items to be scaled from 1.71 to -.95, implying unidimensionality.

CONCLUSIONS. If someone is seeking an easily administered and readable extraversion scale with reasonably high internal coherence, but one that lacks test-retest or other reliability studies, the CPF may be suitable. If one seeks an easily scored measure of social dominance, but one that lacks any behavioral or performance based criterion studies, the CPF may prove desirable. The personality researcher and assessor may find this single dimension scale less satisfying than such well-validated measures as the Revised NEO Personality Inventory (NEO-PI-R; 330), an excellent measure of the "Big Five" or five-factor model of personality, which includes extraversion and much more. Measures other than the CPF may provide a richer data set and are embedded in a matrix of theory and research that the industrial psychologist may find more useful in personnel selection and career counseling than the CPF. The CPF (by the way, it stands for Contact Personality Factor, which is not revealed in the test or manual) seems not related to its parent theory and series of tests, the Cattell. It seems as a measure unto itself.

REVIEWER'S REFERENCE

Krug, S. E. (1984). *Adult Personality Inventory manual*. Champaign, IL: Institute for Personality and Ability Testing.

[98]

Critical Reasoning Tests.

Purpose: Assesses intellectual skills needed for a managerial level post.
Population: Prospective managers.
Publication Date: 1992.
Acronym: CRT.
Administration: Group.
Price Data: Available from publisher.
Authors: Pauline Smith and Chris Whetton.
Publisher: NFER-Nelson Publishing Co., Ltd. [England].

a) VERBAL TEST.
Purpose: "Assesses how well a candidate can cope with different reasoning tasks."
Scores: Total score only.
Time: (28–33) minutes.

b) NUMERICAL TEST.
Purpose: "Assesses how well the candidate interprets numerical information."
Scores: Total score only.
Time: (30–35) minutes.

Review of the Critical Reasoning Tests by TIMOTHY Z. KEITH, Professor of Psychology, Alfred University, Alfred, NY:

The Critical Reasoning Tests (CRT) are designed to aid in the selection of management trainees and managers in a variety of businesses. The CRT does so by assessing test takers' ability to use verbal and numerical data to make decisions and evaluations similar to those one might be asked to make as a junior or middle-level manager.

The authors contend that a fundamental part of the job that managers perform—regardless of the specifics of their company—is diagnosis, including the gathering of relevant information, evaluation of that information, problem specification, generation of strategies, and strategy selection. This process, they argue, is closely related to that of critical thinking, requiring skills such as being able to analyze information, evaluate evidence, and plan a course of action. The CRT is designed to assess these important management skills.

The CRT includes a 56-item Verbal test and a 30-item Numerical test. Both use multiple choice, and are group administered, generally as a set, in about 70 to 80 minutes. Both tests involve the activities of a fictitious British company (Hardiman's Ltd.) that produces gardening tools.

The Verbal test has three sections. In the Analysis section, examinees are given two pages summarizing Hardiman's employee policies and social club. Examinees then decide whether each of 14 statements is implied by the company policies, contradicts the policies, or if it is impossible to tell from the policies if the statement is correct or incorrect. In Evaluation, a belief of a new manager is paired with a statement providing additional information; the examinee must decide whether the new information supports, goes against, or has no bearing on the belief (14 questions). In Assumptions, the examinee must decide, by reading statements made by other employees, whether or not that employee has taken information for granted (made assumptions). It is not clear whether the authors believe being able to determine when assumptions have been made is the most important aspect of critical thinking, but the Assumptions section is twice as long (28 questions) as either of the other Verbal sections, and is thus weighted more heavily in scoring.

The Numerical test has only one section, but includes a variety of items of the type a manager might be required to perform on a daily basis: interpreting charts, making decisions based on numerical information, calculated areas in manufacturing, and comparing costs. All items have as one choice the option "can't tell from this data" [*sic*] in an effort to determine if examinees know when more data are needed. Because the questions dealing with money use pounds, the Numerical test, in particular, will not be useful outside the United Kingdom.

Test materials include a Verbal and Numerical test booklet, separate answer sheets, an information card for the Verbal tests, instructions for administration, and the user's guide. The materials are attractive and easy to use. The user's guide is fairly complete, well written, and easy to understand. The development of the test, including the development and testing of items and two item trials, is well described.

The CRT was standardized in 1990 and 1991 on two samples from Great Britain: about 350 students from FE colleges and 143 managers and trainees in one company. Thus, the norms apply only to Great Britain. Even within Britain, however, the norms are inadequate. The college sampling seems somewhat haphazard, with colleges choosing students to test stratified only on courses of study. The management sample, drawn from only one company, is too narrow. Test users may compare scores to either norm group; raw scores are converted to percentiles based on the norm group chosen, and may also be converted to *T* scores. Unfortunately, no extensions of the *T* scores are provided above the 99th or below the 1st percentile.

Reliability information is limited to internal consistency reliability, reported separately for the two samples. Reliability estimates are fairly low; internal consistencies (KR20) of .67 and .78 are reported for the total Verbal scale for the college and management samples, respectively, with estimates of .65 and .77 for the Numerical test. Verbal test section reliabilities ranged from .32 to .73; the authors correctly caution against using the section scores by themselves. The manual provides a good discussion of reliability, the standard error of measurement, and the importance of using the *SEM* and the standard error of difference in interpreting scores. If all users follow the advice of the manual—using the standard error of difference to decide if two applicants' scores are significantly different, and not interpreting insignificant differences—then the low reliabilities are not a problem. It seems doubtful that all users will follow such advice, however, but will instead interpret smaller differences. Therefore, the reliabilities of the CRT are troublesome.

Validity evidence is limited, as well, and only includes information concerning the relation between the CRT and school examination results and coursework. Even this limited information is poorly presented. For example, the manual shows significant CRT differences for students who have passed different numbers of examinations (O-level passes); the correlation between the CRT and number of passes would provide more valuable information.

Additional information concerning both convergent and discriminant validity is badly needed. There is no evidence that the CRT is related to other measures of critical reasoning, such as test scores or even employers' ratings. At the same time, it is just as unclear whether the CRT measures something above and beyond what is measured by traditional measures of aptitude and achievement. Both concurrent and predictive studies of the validity of this instrument are needed before it can be recommended as a method of selecting managers.

SUMMARY. The Critical Reasoning Tests are an intriguing attempt to aid employers in the selection of managers and management trainees. Unfortunately, the CRT does not fulfill this purpose, at least in its present form. At bare minimum the CRT publishers need to provide evidence that the test measures critical reasoning (construct validity), that the test can aid in selecting good managers (predictive validity), and that the test measures skills that are not measured with more common, better standardized instruments (discriminant validity). Broader, better defined norms are needed within the UK, and additional norms are needed before the test can be used outside the UK. At present, the test can only be recommended for research purposes within the UK.

Review of the Critical Reasoning Tests by HAROLD TAKOOSHIAN, Associate Professor of Psychology, Fordham University, New York, NY:

The Critical Reasoning Tests (CRT) are designed for pre-employment screening of management-level candidates—ranging from floor supervisors to middle-managers and upper executives. It is a speeded, group test presented in two parts, yielding a Verbal and a Numerical score. In both parts, the test taker is put into the role of a manager within a fictitious engineering firm called Hardiman's, Ltd. In the Verbal test, a two-page "Information card" details Hardiman's personnel policies, and one has 20 minutes to complete 28 items requiring quick yet thorough analysis of this complex information. The Numerical test presents detailed data on Hardiman's operations in some half-dozen diverse formats (a table, graph, pie chart, airline schedule), and one has 25 minutes to extract the answers to 30 questions. In both tests, the questions require thoughtful analysis more than simple recognition, so few test takers find sufficient time to complete all the items, and the ceiling for the tests remains high for even the most able examinees. Overall, the CRT requires about 70 minutes, plus another 20–30 minutes for practice items and breaks.

The underlying premise of the CRT is that our "academic intelligence" in schoolwork differs from our real-life "practical intelligence" needed to perform managerial tasks. Whereas the typical cognitive ability test is more academic in tone, the CRT is distinguished by its use of realistic industrial questions in measuring our verbal and numerical prowess. The content of the CRT does indeed resemble the "in-basket" exercises so often used in managerial selection by industrial assessment centers (Cascio, 1991).

NORMS. Unfortunately, despite the sedulous efforts of the coauthors, the CRT normative group is admittedly limited in several ways—353 students in 16 English colleges (62% male, 15% minority blacks or Asians), and 143 managers in an English retail chain (92% male, 2% minority). Such norms hardly seem representative of British, much less U.S. management candidates.

RELIABILITY. With no alternate forms nor test-retest data, the one indicator of reliability is KR-20 estimates of internal consistency. These KR-20 coefficients seem sufficiently high for the 353 college students on both the Verbal scale (.67) and the Numerical scale (.65), and even higher for the 143 managers (.78 and .77, respectively). These reliability estimates seem high, even when taking into account the artificial inflation of the KR-20 estimates whenever a test is speeded, as the CRT is.

VALIDITY. Ideally, the criterion for this sort of test is later job performance. Sadly, "such evidence is not yet available" from the publisher (manual, p. 41). There is as yet no independent literature on the CRT, nor on similar earlier tests by this publisher, such as the Reading Ability Series (11:324). Instead, the CRT manual focuses exclusively on concurrent validity within its student sample, using ANOVA (but not correlations) to compare the mean CRT scores for various levels of British school performance. This school data uniformly supports the CRT as a valid measure of cognitive ability. Still, a sad irony is apparent here. The CRT manual starts out by emphasizing "that 'academic intelligence' and 'practical intelligence' are not very closely related" (manual, p. 1), yet concludes by using school grades as the sole validator so far of its two measures of the "practical intelligence" that managers need. In fact, the CRT manual solicits local validation data from test users, acknowledging what remains most needed here—information on how CRT scores correlate with current and future job performance of managers across a variety of private and public organizations. Equally needed are some comparative data on whether, indeed, the later job performance of managers who completed the CRT and some more established ability test (such as the Wonderlic, or the Flanagan Industrial Tests) is better predicted by the CRT.

STRENGTHS. The CRT stands out on at least two points. First, its packaging is first-rate. A sturdy plastic pouch holds the durable, reusable large-print question booklets, and the carbon-paper answer sheets could not be easier to score, taking just seconds per applicant. Second, the 57-page manual is squarely aimed at human resource administrators with little or no training in psychometrics. It lucidly defines and explains all its psychometric terminology, and offers practical suggestions on test administration and interpretation. The manual does not skimp on detail, and is refreshingly frank in pointing out to users the limitations of its test.

LIMITATIONS. Like the half-dozen other cognitive ability tests developed by this British publisher, the CRT is simply inappropriate for U.S. usage in its current form, in at least three ways. First, it is laced throughout with uniquely English phrasing that would distract if not stymie American test-takers—biros, £, Ltd., arrears, sixth-form pupils, etc. Second, the norms are entirely British, with no attempt at U.S. data. Finally, the results of the CRT seem to fall short of the "fairness" standards set by U.S. law. The CRT found significant differences of up to two *SEM*s (standard errors of measurement) between minority and majority applicants, which likely violates the four-fifths rule and other fairness guidelines regulating U.S. Industry. (There is no significant gender difference in total scores.)

SUMMARY. In general, cognitive ability tests surpass other predictors of employee performance—such as interviews, biodata, school grades, and personality tests (Hunter & Hunter, 1984). The CRT is based on the reasonable premise that using management-related questions will further boost an ability test's accuracy in predicting managerial job performance. The CRT will be a useful test if it garners evidence to support this premise. So far it has not. Meanwhile, industrial test users should consider the many established general ability tests that continue to offer solid track records in predicting the performance of new employees in general, including managers—tests like the Wonderlic (T4:2972), the Employee Aptitude Survey (T4:894; yielding 10 scores in 60 minutes), and the Guilford-Zimmerman Aptitude Survey (T4:1115; 6 scores), to name a few.

REVIEWER'S REFERENCES

Hunter, J. E., & Hunter, R. F. (1984). Validity and utility of alternative predictors of job performance. *Psychological Bulletin, 96*, 72-98.

Cascio, W. F. (1991). *Applied psychology in personnel management* (4th ed.). Englewood Cliffs, NJ: Prentice-Hall.

[99]

Cultural Literacy Test.

Purpose: Designed to assess "general knowledge in the humanities, social sciences, and sciences."
Population: Grades 11–12.
Publication Date: 1989.
Scores, 4: Humanities, Social Sciences, Sciences, Composite; plus "criterion-referenced" scores for 23 objective areas.
Administration: Group.
Editions, 3: Machine-scorable (A, B), hand-scorable (Survey Edition B).
Price Data, 1991: $135 per complete machine-scorable test kit including 35 test booklets, 35 student report folders, administration and interpretation manual (30 pages), and materials needed for machine scoring; $42.30 per 35 Survey Edition reusable test booklets including administration and interpretation manual; $42.30 per 35 Survey Edition answer sheets including directions for administration and 35 student report folders; $6.90 per 35 student report folders; $6 per Guide to Cultural Literacy; $2.10 per administrator's summary (21 pages).
Time: 50 minutes.
Author: Cultural Literacy Foundation.
Publisher: The Riverside Publishing Co.
Cross References: See T4:698 (2 references).

Review of the Cultural Literacy Test by JERRY S. GILMER, Assistant Research Scientist, College of Medicine, The University of Iowa, Iowa City, IA:

The Cultural Literacy Test (CLT) is a test of general knowledge of subject matter in the three areas of Humanities, Social Sciences, and Sciences. The CLT was developed by the Cultural Literacy Foundation, a private, not-for-profit organization dedicated to the advancement of education, and supported by the National Endowment for the Humanities. The test is intended for high school juniors or seniors and purports to measure their level of cultural literacy as defined by Hirsch in *Cultural Literacy, What Every American Needs to Know* (Hirsch, 1987): "To be culturally literate is to possess the basic information needed to thrive in the modern world." Indeed, the entire philosophical underpinnings of the CLT are based on *Cultural Literacy, What Every American Needs to Know* and *The Dictionary of Cultural Literacy* (Hirsch, Kett, & Trefil, 1988).

The CLT is a test of factual information with the important qualifier that the facts tested have been rigorously selected to relate to cultural literacy, as defined in the supporting materials. According to the Manual for Administration and Interpretation, "A literate reader, writer, or speaker has knowledge of a large body of specific information—the same information that other literate people in the culture know. This body of shared information is 'cultural literacy'" (p. 3), and schools must "provide students with this body of shared cultural information" (p. 3). Much of this body of "shared cultural information" was originally listed in the appendix to *Cultural Literacy, What Every American Needs to Know* as "What Literate Americans Know" and was subsequently expanded and published with extensive discussion in *The Dictionary of Cultural Literacy*.

This body of knowledge has been categorized by the Cultural Literacy Foundation into the three areas of Humanities, Social Sciences, and Sciences which are further divided into 23 subcontent areas. The CLT corresponds directly to these 23 areas with five items covering each area for a total of 115 items. Parallel Forms A and B have been developed in machine-scorable booklets for administration in grades 11 and 12. Actual testing time is 50 minutes. In addition to the books *Cultural Literacy* and *The Dictionary*, the two machine-scorable forms, and the Manual for Administration and Interpretation, other available material includes individual report folders for each student, an Administrator's Summary containing general information about the test and a sample test, and a Guide to Cultural Literacy containing references for students to increase their knowledge in the relevant subject areas. Also available is a version of Form B in a nonscorable booklet with a separate Easy-Score Answer Sheet.

Local percentile ranks and national percentile ranks based on a national standardization sample of students in grades 11 and 12 in 1988, are reported to school teachers and students for the composite and each of the three areas of Humanities, Social Sciences, and Sciences. In addition, individual students' raw scores and national and local raw score averages are reported to teachers for each of the 23 subcontent areas.

The Manual for Administration and Interpretation contains technical data and other information related to each of the test forms, the standardization and sampling procedures, and reliability and validity. In general, Forms A and B appear to be reasonably parallel, but a 4.54 difference in the Social Sciences means between A and B is unexplained and, perhaps, not of practical importance because scores and norms are reported *by form*. The KR-20 reliability indices for the Humanities, Social Sciences, Sciences, and Composite scores are all greater than .82, with the Composite reliabilities being .95 and .94 for Form A and B, respectively.

The discussion of validity of the CLT is weak in the manual and the supporting tables comparing the CLT to four well-known standardized tests of achievement and ability tend to raise questions concerning the intended comparisons rather than answer questions. For example, why were these specific tests selected for validity comparisons and what do the results really show? The correlations between the CLT and the other tests are generally between .40 and .70 and could be interpreted to suggest that either the CLT measures something different than the other tests, or it does not, or both! Also, some of the Form A correlations with other tests are sufficiently different from some of the Form B correlations with the same tests to warrant additional questions concerning the parallelism of the two forms.

Prospective users of the CLT may wish to consider at least three basic issues during their decision-making process. All of these issues directly pertain to the validity of the CLT. The first of these relates to the proposed construct. Is there actually a construct of cultural literacy and is it reasonable and meaningful to try to define it? Is the proposed definition of cultural literacy—being in possession of basic information—reasonable? Strong arguments in support of the construct and its definition, as well as the philosophical foundations, are presented in *Cultural Literacy* and *The Dictionary*. Prospective users will want to be familiar with these discussions. In the absence of direct scientific evidence relating to construct validity, the test developers state in the Administrator's Summary: "The primary evidence for the validity of the *Cultural Literacy Test* comes from its close relationship to the construct of cultural literacy, as defined by the authors, and from the acceptance of this construct by various reviewers, educators, and the general public" (p. 8).

The second basic issue prospective users should consider relates to the alignment of the CLT with the construct of cultural literacy. Does the test actually measure cultural literacy as defined? Do test scores directly reflect students' levels of cultural literacy? Evidence in support of these issues does exist in the very direct alignment of the test with the 23 subcontent categories and also in the discussions of test development procedures in the Manual for Administration and Interpretation. One of the obvious concerns, however, is the degree to which five fact-based test items represent very broad content domains like The Bible and Physical Sciences and Mathematics. When a student correctly answers only one out of five specific questions about World Geography, for example, can a reliable and valid interpretation be made about the overall level of knowledge this student possesses in the broad area of World Geography? Based on the reliabilities reported in the Manual for Administration and Interpretation and the Spearman/Brown formula for estimating the reliability of a modified-length test, the reliabilities of the scores for the 23 five-item clusters would be between .40 and .50. These reliability estimates would necessarily limit generalizations to the broad content domains.

The third issue of concern for prospective users relates to the predictive ability of the CLT. What is the relationship between test performance and thriving in the modern world? At present, there appears to be no psychometric evidence either supporting or refuting a relationship between performance on the CLT and functioning in the world. The correlations between the CLT and other achievement and ability measures reported in the manual suggest a slight to moderate relationship between the CLT and functioning in the world to the extent these other measures relate to functioning in the world, but this evidence is indirect, at best.

In addition to these general but important concerns about the CLT, there are specific points regarding the actual use of the test that need additional clarification. For example, the Manual for Administration and Interpretation indicates that the "questions students miss can serve to point them toward learning about the subject matter of the test question" (p. 16). Although this is obviously true, it is unclear if either students or the teachers receive any information about exactly which items each student missed. In any event, even if students do some research in the areas of the missed items, they would not necessarily significantly increase their knowledge in the particular subcontent area beyond the specific content of the missed items.

Another point regarding test use pertains to the proposition in the manual that the "test will monitor students' progress in attaining essential knowledge" (p. 5). Exactly how this monitoring function will be fulfilled is unclear, however, when the test is for administration to high school juniors and seniors; the time available for remediation and additional follow-up is so limited as to render such activities virtually ineffective, particularly when such activities must compete with all the other demands on the educational system.

The principles underlying the CLT are laudable and the test aims toward fulfilling lofty goals. The issues and concerns discussed here, particularly regarding validity, may, however, limit the application and potential effectiveness of the test in the schools and ultimately, in society.

REVIEWER'S REFERENCES

Hirsch, E. D., Jr. (1987). *Cultural literacy, what every American needs to know.* Boston: Houghton Mifflin Company.

Hirsch, E. D., Jr., Kett, J. F., & Trefil, J. (1988). *The dictionary of cultural literacy.* Boston: Houghton Mifflin Company.

Review of the Cultural Literacy Test by ARLEN R. GULLICKSON, Professor and Chief of Staff for The Evaluation Center, Western Michigan University, Kalamazoo, MI:

The publishers of the Cultural Literacy Test present cultural literacy as general knowledge of subject matter in three topic areas: Humanities, Social Science, and Sciences (including mathematics). This test apparently is intended as a stimulus to increase the cultural literacy of students. Although the test may serve that purpose, it is at best a crude measure of cultural literacy. Disappointingly, the test's supporting literature strongly advocates improving student literacy and communication skills;-yet close study suggests the quality of the test is overstated, and the test development process has failed to meet reasonable standards for measuring such literacy. Five specific areas of concern are addressed.

VALIDITY. Both test content and supporting research are inadequate. The test is a vocabulary measure in 3 main content areas (Humanities, Social Science, and Sciences) and 23 subcontent (or objectives) areas, with five items representing each objective. For example, all of the content for the disciplines of physical science and mathematics is addressed through five items. Similarly, all of fine arts is assessed through five items. Although the criteria used in selecting vocabulary items seem appropriate, the limited number of terms used in each area makes the test prone to large sampling errors in measurement of any student's knowledge of an objective. Thus, the test provides only the crudest of measures for individual objectives. Those same concerns carry over to the three main content areas. For example, cultural literacy in the sciences is measured by a total of 25 items covering physical science, mathematics, earth sciences, life sciences, medicine and health, and technology.

The primary-research-based argument for the test's validity is built around correlations with aptitude measures. The importance of these correlations is not clear, especially given the argument that cultural literacy is a requisite for all students. Additionally, the correlations between the cultural literacy test and aptitude measures are as high as the test's correlations with achievement measures. This suggests the test is as much a measure of aptitude as a measure of achievement in cultural literacy.

CRITERION REFERENCED. The test is purveyed as a criterion-referenced test. A student who takes this test is presented with normed scores for the three topic areas and a composite across the three areas. Additionally, raw scores are presented for each of the 23 objectives that comprise the topic areas. These scores are represented as being criterion referenced though no criterion, aside from norms, is provided.

This representation gives credibility to the importance of the raw scores and may well mislead teachers and students regarding the actual literacy of the student in any targeted area.

TEST RELIABILITY. The test provides two forms that are reported to be parallel (equivalent). Yet, no correlative evidence is provided to support this argument. Instead, the author argues for equivalence based on commonality of scores for the two tests. The means across forms for the three main subareas do suggest comparability. However, this comparability is more a matter of perception than reality. Scores on the sets of five-item objectives, which make up the test, vary substantially for the two forms. Those differences across objectives tend to average out, giving the appearance that the tests are the same. The best measure of equivalence across forms, correlation between Form A and Form B, is not provided.

Equivalence across forms probably is not a problem if the teacher administers only one form to all students. However, if Form A is administered to some students and Form B to others, and then the teacher tries to interpret objectives scores, substantial differences due to test differences are likely to be viewed as differences in cultural literacy.

Cultural literacy as described must be a stable trait at least across a brief span of time. Thus, the two primary measures of reliability that should be provided are (*a*) equivalence across forms noted previously and (*b*) test-retest. Neither measure is provided to the user. Instead, only internal consistency (KR 20) is reported for the respective forms.

Internal consistency gives an inflated perspective of the test's capabilities and should be viewed as an upper bound on test reliability. Those coefficients show that only composite scores can possibly meet minimum requirements for individual interpretation. On this basis alone, then, it can be argued that subtest and objective scores should be interpreted only for groups such as a class of students.

NORMS. The "national" norms are based on the testing of students in 33 high schools or school districts across 18 states, with fewer than 3,000 students used in the norming of each form. Thus, results of the test are *not* representative of broad reaches of the U.S. For example, no students were included from the northern tier of states stretching from Wisconsin to Idaho. As such, the norms do not provide a strong reference group for score interpretation.

SECURITY. Substantial rhetoric is given to the importance of test security, and test security is given as the reason the test is administered in machine-scorable booklets. Yet, except for minimal precautions in the way the test is scored, no special security is given to the test. Given the nature of the test, it seems likely that the teacher could learn the test and, if he or she so desired, could quickly and easily teach to the test. Such cheating probably is not a serious problem, but certainly test security falls far short of optimum.

CONCLUSION. The test may serve as a reasonable measure in addressing the issue of cultural literacy for research purposes. However, much remains to be done to improve its capabilities and to firmly establish present claims about the test. As such, it should *not* be used in its present form to direct individual student improvement in cultural literacy.

[100]

Culture-Free Self-Esteem Inventories, Second Edition.

Purpose: Provides a measure of self-esteem and a monitoring of treatment progress.
Population: Grades 2–9, ages 16–65.
Publication Dates: 1981–92.
Acronym: CFSEI-2.
Administration: Group.
Forms, 2: Forms A and B for children grades 2–9, and Form AD for adults ages 16 to 65.
Price Data, 1994: $104 per complete kit including examiner's manual ('92, 84 pages), 50 Form A, 50 Form B, 50 Form AD, scoring acetate, and administration audiocassette; $33 per examiner's manual; $6 per scoring acetate; $14 per administration audiocassette.
Foreign Language Editions: All CFSEI-2 forms and the administration audiocassette are available in Spanish.
Comments: Previous edition entitled Culture-Free Self-Esteem Inventories for Children and Adults; derivative entitled North American Depression Inventories for Children and Adults.
Author: James Battle.
Publisher: PRO-ED, Inc.

a) FORM A.
Population: Grades 2–9.
Scores, 6: General Self-Esteem, Social/Peer-Related Self-Esteem, Academic/School-Related Self-Esteem, Parental/Home-Related Self-Esteem, Lie Subtest, Total.
Price Data: $19 per 50 Form A.
Time: (15–20) minutes.

b) FORM B.
Population: Grades 2–9.
Scores, 6: Same as for *a* above.
Price Data: $19 per 50 Form B.
Time: (5–10) minutes.

c) FORM AD.
Population: Ages 16–65.
Scores, 5: General Self-Esteem, Social/Peer-Related Self-Esteem, Personal Self-Esteem, Lie Subtest, Total.
Price Data: $19 per 50 Form AD.
Time: (15–20) minutes.

Cross References: See T4:700 (9 references); for reviews by Gerald R. Adams and Janet Morgan Riggs of the original edition, see 9:291 (1 reference); see also T3:644 (1 reference). For reviews by Patricia A. Bachelor and Michael G. Kavan of the North American Depression Inventories for Children and Adults, see 11:265 (1 reference).

TEST REFERENCES

1. Slaughter, D. T., Lindsey, R. W., Nakagawa, K., & Kuehne, V. S. (1989). Who gets involved? Head Start mothers as persons. *Journal of Negro Education, 58,* 16-29.

2. Doglin, K. G., Meyer, L., & Schwartz, J. (1991). Effects of gender, target's gender, topic, and self-esteem on disclosure to best and midling friends. *Sex Roles, 25,* 311-329.

3. Grimmell, D., & Stern, G. S. (1992). The relationship between gender role ideals and psychological well-being. *Sex Roles, 27,* 487-497.

4. Kalliopuska, M. (1992). Attitudes towards health, health behavior, and personality factors among school students very high on empathy. *Psychological Reports, 70,* 1119-1122.

5. Carroll, J. L., & Buhrow, M. (1994). Concurrent validity of the Culture-Free Self-Esteem Inventories and physical health in college students. *Psychological Reports, 74,* 553-554.

6. Brooke, S. L. (1995). Critical analysis of the Culture-Free Self-Esteem Inventories. *Measurement and Evaluation in Counseling and Development, 27,* 248-252.

7. Mustane, B. B., & Wilson, F. R. (1995). An exploration of the internal consistency of the Kurtines Autonomy Scale. *Measurement and Evaluation in Counseling and Development, 27,* 211-226.

Review of the Culture-Free Self-Esteem Inventories, Second Edition by MICHAEL G. KAVAN, Director of Behavioral Sciences and Associate Professor of Family Practice, Creighton University School of Medicine, Omaha, NE:

The Culture-Free Self-Esteem Inventories, Second Edition (CFSEI-2) are a set of three self-report instruments designed to measure "an individual's perception of self" (p. 3). This is accomplished by assessing general self-esteem and several self-esteem components. The author defines self-esteem as the "perception the individual possesses of his or her worth" (p. 3). He notes that once established, self-worth tends to be fairly stable and resistant to change. The "culture free" designation is based on the author's contention that items were chosen that were "least sensitive to change, one culture to another" (p. 8). A study by Yamamoto, Soliman, Parsons, and Davies (1987), which did not use the CFSEI or CFSEI-2, is cited as partial support for this contention. The CFSEI-2 comprises the same items as the previously published CFSEI (see 9:291 for review); however, it has a new publisher and an expanded manual that includes updated psychometric data.

ADMINISTRATION AND SCORING. The CFSEI-2 includes three forms (A, B, AD) that may be administered to individuals and groups by psychologists, psychiatrists, counselors, and teachers. Group administration of Forms A and B is not recommended for children below grade 2. All forms may be administered orally to young children and to persons with a reading disability or visual impairment. A prerecorded cassette tape is also available for oral administration. Although the CFSEI-2 was standardized in the English language and the manual is published in English only, protocols for each form as well as cassette tapes are available in French and Spanish.

Directions for each form request the respondent to make a check mark in the "yes" or "no" column according to how "you usually feel" (p. 4). Administration time ranges from 10 to 20 minutes.

An acetate template is then placed over the answer sheet in order to obtain a total raw score reflecting high self-esteem. In addition, separate raw scores may be obtained for each of the subtests (Forms A and B: General Self-Esteem, Social Self-Esteem, Academic Self-Esteem, Parent-Related Self-Esteem; Form AD: General Self-Esteem, Social Self-Esteem, Personal Self-Esteem). Each form also provides a lie score (i.e., measure of defensiveness). Raw scores are then converted to percentiles and *t*-scores. Raw scores for total self-esteem and the various subtests may then be used to classify the respondent according to the following categories: very low, low, intermediate, high, and very high self-esteem.

RELIABILITY. The manual contains information on reliability studies conducted for the original CFSEI. Test-retest reliability for Form A for 198 elementary school children (grades 3–6) ranged from .81 to .89 for total score and from .26 to .76 for various subtests over an unspecified time interval. Test-retest reliability for 117 junior high students (grades 7–9) ranged from .88 to .96 with subtest correlations ranging from .67 to .89 (no time interval given). Two-year test-retest correlation(s) ranged from .41 (Parental) to .65 (Total) for 75 boys and girls enrolled in the Edmonton, Alberta school system and was .74 for 33 students enrolled in grade 6. For Form B, test-retest data over an unspecified time period for 110 children in grades 3 to 6 ranged from .79 to .92 for the total score; subtest test-retest reliability ranged from .49 to .80. The correlation between Forms A and B was .86 for a sample of children in grades 5 and 6 (n = 160). Test-retest reliability for Form AD was .81 for a sample of 127 students enrolled in an educational psychology course over an unspecified time period. Internal consistency (Kr20) ranged from .66 to .76 for Form A when administered to 117 children in grades 7–9 and .54 to .78 (n = 85) for Form AD (no sample description provided).

VALIDITY. Although much of the validity data provided within the manual were obtained for the original CFSEI, several additional validity studies are cited for the CFSEI-2. In particular, concurrent validity data are provided comparing the relationship between the CFSEI-2 and depression, anxiety, academic achievement, attention-deficit hyperactivity disorder, and employment. The correlation between the CFSEI-2 and the North American Depression Inventories for Children and Adults (NADI), a derivative of the CFSEI-2, was -.73 for children in grades 2–6 (n = 676), -.72 for children in grades 7–9 (n = 302), and -.74 for adults (ages 15 and older) (n = 249). The author also completed studies examining the relationship between the CFSEI-2 and the Relative Anxiety Scales for Children and Adults (RAS), a scale developed by Battle. Correlations between the CFSEI-2 and the RAS were -.68 for children grades

2–6 (n = 433), -.73 for children in grades 7–9 (n = 365), and -.77 for adults (ages 15 and older) (n = 309). No supplementary information is provided on these groups. The author notes that these correlations support "acceptable validity" for the CFSEI-2, NADI, and RAS. Whereas numerous studies have demonstrated the association between self-esteem and depression/anxiety, the causal link between self-esteem and these disorders has not been clearly established (Robson, 1988).

Additional studies are cited within the manual to support the relationship between the CFSEI-2 and other disorders. For example, the author cites an unpublished doctoral dissertation that reports a significant relationship between scores obtained on "two depression inventories" and the CFSEI-2 for 620 students enrolled in grades 4 through 6. A published study is cited to support a significant relationship between the CFSEI-2 and depression in "learning disabled junior high school students" (p. 27). In addition, support is provided for the relationship between the CFSEI-2 and academic achievement in 716 junior high school students as measured by year-end final grades. The author also completed a study in which children with Attention-Deficit Hyperactivity Disorder earned lower self-esteem scores than those without this disorder. Finally, the author reports on 40 adults whose scores on the CFSEI-2 increased after participating in a comprehensive employment training program. Limited data are provided within the manual regarding samples used for these studies. Seven case studies are also presented within the manual along with brief descriptions of several programs that focus on raising the self-esteem of their participants.

NORMS. The manual provides normative data consisting of means, standard deviations, percentiles, and t-scores for total scores and subscale scores for elementary school students (n = 1,679) and junior high school students (n = 873) for Form A, and for elementary school students (n = 116) for Form B. Only percentiles and t-scores for junior high school students (n = 274) are given for Form B. Means, standard deviations, percentile ranks, and t-score values are also provided for total scores and subscale scores for adults (n = 585) for Form AD. Data are also supplied for the Lie subscale for Form A (elementary and junior high school students) and Form AD (high school students and adults). Limited demographic data are presented on these groups and no normative data are provided on culturally diverse groups.

SUMMARY. The CFSEI-2 is an easily administered and scored self-report measure of self-esteem in children and adults. For the most part, it is the same instrument as that published in 1981 (save for a new format, publisher, and expanded validity data within the manual). The CFSEI-2 is one of many attempts to develop a reliable and valid instrument to assess self-esteem. Reliability appears adequate. Validity, however, is comprised mainly of concurrent associations with depression and anxiety, an association that may be due to overlap of item content between these measures. The author also provides little evidence to support the "culture free" status of these inventories. Despite these problems, the author should be commended for developing an instrument that breaks down the broad concept of self-esteem into more precise elements. In doing this, the present strength of the CFSEI-2 may not necessarily be in its clinical utility, but instead in its ability to generate additional research, and thus, assist in defining more precisely the construct of self-esteem.

REVIEWER'S REFERFENCES

Yamamoto, K., Soliman, A., Parsons, J., & Davies, O. L. (1987). Voices in unison: Stressful events in the lives of children in six countries. *Journal of Child Psychology and Psychiatry, 28*, 855-864.

Robson, P. J. (1988). Self-esteem: A psychiatric view. *British Journal of Psychiatry, 153*, 6-15.

Review of the Culture-Free Self-Esteem Inventories, Second Edition by MICHAEL J. SUBKOVIAK, Professor of Educational Psychology, University of Wisconsin-Madison, Madison, WI:

The Culture-Free Self-Esteem Inventories, Second Edition (CFSEI-2) are designed to assess the perception an individual possesses of his or her own self-worth. Examinees (adults or children) answer yes or no to a series of questions about their thoughts, feelings, or behavior. Raw scores are computed by counting the number of responses indicative of positive self-concept and are then converted to percentiles and T-scores. A total self-esteem score can be derived as well as a profile of subtest scores (General Self-Esteem, Social Self-Esteem, etc.). There is also a Lie Subtest designed to detect social desirability response patterns. Administration and scoring are straightforward, but interpretation of scores should be attempted only by "someone knowledgeable in measurement, psychology of adjustment, and perceptual psychology" (p. 7). Furthermore, authors of other self-esteem inventories caution that such scores should be combined with information from other sources and should not be the sole basis of decision making.

The items on the current Forms A, B, and AD of the CFSEI-2 are identical to those on the first edition of the instrument, formerly titled the Culture-Free Self-Esteem Inventories for Children and Adults and previously reviewed in the *Ninth Mental Measurements Yearbook*. Unfortunately, two significant limitations identified in the *Ninth Mental Measurements Yearbook* have not been corrected. First, there is no evidence whatsoever that the CFSEI-2 is culture free. No statistical analysis to determine if CFSEI-2 items perform differently across various cultures has apparently ever been performed. The fact that the instrument has been translated into French, Spanish, or other languages in no way guarantees that examinees having different cultural orientations will respond in the same way to CFSEI-2 items. In fact, some differential item functioning across various cultures is quite likely. Thus, "Culture-Free" is a misnomer misleading to potential users. Second, as was the case for the first edition of the instrument, the normative samples for the CFSEI-2 are not described in terms of ethnic composition, socioeconomic status, and other important characteristics. Many of the standardization samples appear to have been drawn from districts in Western Canada. As such, the norm tables provided in the manual appear to have limited generalizability. This requires potential users to develop their own local norms.

The reliability of a scale is directly related to the number of items on the scale. Thus, total self-esteem scores on the CFSEI-2 are more reliable than the subtest scores (General Self-Esteem, Social Self-Esteem, etc.). For example, test-retest reliability coefficients for total scores on the 60-item Form A are generally high, ranging from .81–.96 for grades 3–9, whereas coefficients for the 5–10-item subtests are generally lower, ranging from .26–.89. Similarly, the reliability of total scores on Forms B (30 items) and AD (40 items) is generally adequate, whereas subtest reliabilities are more variable.

The authors (p. 5) suggest the CFSEI-2 may be used for three purposes: (*a*) as a "screening device to identify individuals who may be in need of psychological assistance," (*b*) as a "measure of change resulting from intervention," and (*c*) as a means of identifying specific areas of weakness or strength within an individual's profile of subtest scores. The instrument seems to be more valid for some of these purposes than for others. First, use of CFSEI-2 total scores to identify individuals with exceptionally low or high self-esteem appears justified in light of their high reliability, but subtest scores cannot be used in this way with the same degree of confidence. Unfortunately, the authors do not recommend particular cutoffs (e.g., 16th and 84th percentiles) for identifying exceptionally low or exceptionally high self-esteem scores. Second, a treatment group's *average* change in self-esteem could be assessed validly using the CFSEI-2. However, an individual's change over time cannot be assessed with the same degree of confidence because individual change scores are often quite unreliable, especially subtest scores. Third, analysis of an individual's profile of subtest scores to identify particular areas of weakness or strength is somewhat risky for the same reason—differences between an individual's subtest scores tend to be unreliable. In spite of certain limitations noted above, there is adequate evidence of construct validity as indicated by significant correlations between CFSEI-2 total scores and other measures: self-esteem (.71 to .82); perceived ability (.70); teachers' ratings (.36); and depression (-.55 to -.75). In contrast, the CFSEI-2 is generally uncorrelated with intelligence measures.

In summary, the CFSEI-2 is designed to assess an individual's self-esteem in particular areas and overall. There is no evidence that the CFSEI-2 is "Culture-Free," in spite of the use of this term in the instrument's title. Also, the norm groups are not well described and appear to lack generalizability. Reliability and construct validity of CFSEI-2 total scores are adequate. As such, total scores can be used with some degree of confidence to identify individuals with unusually low or high self-esteem, or to measure change in a group's average self-esteem. Other inventories for assessing self-concept, which may be of interest, include: Coopersmith's Self-Esteem Inventories (T4:647), Harter's Self-Perception Profile for Children, Piers-Harris Children's Self-Concept Scale (T4:2030), and Boersma-Chapman Perception of Ability Scale for Students (282).

[101]

Degrees of Reading Power.
Publication Dates: 1979–91.
Acronym: DRP.
Scores: Total score only.
Administration: Group.
Price Data, 1994: $13.35 per 30 NCS answer sheets; $12.25 per set of scoring keys (select level and form); $24.75 per Primary/Standard teacher's manual ('89, 112 pages); $31.25 per Advanced teacher's manual ('90, 98 pages); $15.75 per 5 test administration manuals (select Primary, Standard, or Advanced); $21 per Primary/Standard norms booklet ('88, 45 pages); $27 per *DRP: An Effectiveness Measure in Reading* ('87, 200 pages); $13 per norms update technical report ('89, 23 pages); $22.50 per validity and reliability technical report (select Primary or Advanced).
Time: (45–50) minutes (untimed).
Comments: Practice tests may be used to select appropriate test form for student; also provides readability analysis of instructional material in print.
Author: Touchstone Applied Science Associates (TASA), Inc.
Publisher: Touchstone Applied Science Associates (TASA), Inc.

a) PRIMARY.
Purpose: Constructed to measure "how well students are able to construct meaning from prose material."
Population: Grades 1–3.
Forms, 2: E, F.
Price Data: $75 per 30 machine-scorable test booklets (select form); $8.25 per 30 practice booklets.

b) STANDARD.
Purpose: Same as *a* above.
Population: Grades 3–5, 5–8, 8–12 and over.
Forms, 2: E, F.
Levels, 3: 3, 5, 7.

Price Data: $53.50 per 30 test booklets (select level and form); $10.50 per 30 practice booklets (select Level 5 or 7); $13.25 per 30 NCS answer sheets.

c) ADVANCED.

Purpose: Constructed to measure "how well students are able to reason with text."

Population: Grades 6–9, 9–12 and over.

Forms, 2: R, S.

Levels, 2: 2, 4.

Price Data: $64 per 30 test booklets (select level and form); $13.75 per 30 practice booklets; $13.25 per 30 NCS answer sheets.

Cross References: See T4:726 (14 references); for reviews of an earlier form by Roger Bruning and Gerald S. Hanna, see 9:305 (1 reference).

TEST REFERENCES

1. Barr, R., & Sadow, M. W. (1989). Influence of basal programs on fourth-grade reading instruction. *Reading Research Quarterly*, *24*, 44-71.

2. Carver, R. P. (1990). Rescaling the Degrees of Reading Power test to provide valid scores for selecting materials at the instructional level. *Journal of Reading Behavior*, *22*, 1-18.

3. Baumann, J. F., Seifert-Kessell, N., & Jones, L. A. (1992). Effect of think-aloud instruction on elementary students' comprehension monitoring abilities. *Journal of Reading Behavior*, *24*, 143-172.

4. Carver, R. P. (1992). What do standardized tests of reading comprehension measure in terms of efficiency, accuracy, and rate? *Reading Research Quarterly*, *27*, 347-359.

5. Simpson, M. L., & Nist, S. L. (1992). Toward defining a comprehensive assessment model for college reading. *Journal of Reading*, *35*, 452-458.

6. Truesdell, L. A., & Abramson, T. (1992). Academic behavior and grades of mainstreamed students with mild disabilities. *Exceptional Children*, *58*, 392-398.

7. Horn, C., Bruning, R., Schraw, G., Curry, E., & Katkanant, C. (1993). Paths to success in the college classroom. *Contemporary Educational Psychology*, *18*, 464-478.

8. Spires, H. A., Huntley-Johnston, L., & Huffman, L. E. (1993). Developing a critical stance toward text through reading, writing, and speaking. *Journal of Reading*, *37*, 114-115.

9. Fox, S. D. (1994). Metacognitive strategies in a college world literature course. *American Annals of the Deaf*, *139*, 506-511.

Review of the Degrees of Reading Power by DARREL N. CAULLEY, Senior Lecturer, Graduate School of Education, La Trobe University, Bundoora, Australia, ELAINE FURNISS, UNICEF, Hanoi, Vietnam, and MICHAEL McNAMARA, Graduate School of Education, La Trobe University, Bundoora, Australia:

The Degrees of Reading Power (DRP) program is designed to monitor students' progress towards specific reading goals. These are reported as follows:

Goal 1: Students will demonstrate the ability to understand the surface meaning of increasingly more difficult textual material.

Goal 2: Students will demonstrate the ability to reason, that is, to analyze, evaluate, and extend the ideas that are presented in increasingly more difficult textual material (Ivens & Koslin, 1991). The DRP is also designed to provide a measure for school accountability (teacher's manual, p. 1) in that it tests students' ability to construct meaning from text as it is being read, a generalizable requisite for all subject areas.

The DRP program has three components:

1. *Tests to measure comprehension of English prose*. The DRP tests are organized in three levels: Primary, Standard, and Advanced. The Primary and Standard levels are intended to measure students' progress in achieving the first of the goals listed above. The Advanced level is designed to measure progress in achieving the second.

Each test at the Primary and Standard levels consists of a number of informational prose passages, either reports or explanations, interspersed with seven blank spaces, to indicate a missing word. For each missing word, five possible responses are provided, and the student must choose the plausible response in terms of the whole paragraph. At the Advanced level, passages are followed by five possible sentences that can be used to fill sentence length spaces that are interspersed in the passage.

The test authors are sensitive to criticisms of tests that have traps for students (for example, a deliberately attractive distractor) or tests that favor students with extensive prior knowledge of the topic covered by the test item. Accordingly, they have attempted to ensure that each test requires no more or less than understanding of the passage for successful completion. The possible responses supplied for each gap all make sense if the sentence is read alone. Therefore, reference to the surrounding text is required. In the Primary and Standard tests, none of the word options occur infrequently in everyday prose. Possible responses are selected so that no more than one of the options could be chosen as a sensible answer. Because of the deliberately restricted nature of the tests (they are not what has been called "objective referenced tests," where test items are organized to test achievement on specific and discrete instructional objectives), and because the test designers have taken into account the criticisms from the literature they should be applauded for their sensitivity to current reading theory. They, in fact, claim credit for better performance on the DRP tests by students from a non-English-speaking background (teacher's manual, p. 6), emphasizing the tests are untimed and that they have the features listed above.

The scores gained on the DRP are calibrated on a continuous scale. Achievement is described in terms of "DRP units" (teacher's manual, p. 9). Ambitiously, the designers have linked this scale to scales of the readability of text materials, thus linking these test scores directly to probable success in reading on particular texts at a given level, which is equivalent to the DRP independent level gained by the student.

2. *Readability analyses of instructional materials*. Three books comprise this section of the DRP program, although the existence of a software program, MicRA-DRP is also described. The books are: *Readability of Textbooks, 8th Edition*; *Readability of Textbooks in Series, 8th Edition*; *Readability of Literature and Popular Titles, Volume 1*.

The DRP provides new ways of thinking about the difficulty of text by working out the most difficult level of text that students are able to read at independent, instructional, and frustration levels, and providing DRP scores from 15–100 for the three levels. These scores can be equated with the DRP level assigned to a particular book from the readability analyses suggested above.

However, there are problems with a view of readability that continues to see text difficulty as residing completely within the text and not in the reader's understanding of the field or familiarity with reading the text. Although the writers state that a reader's background knowledge contributes to prose difficulty (teacher's manual, p. 7), this criterion is not used in assessing text difficulty. DRP Readability is measured using the Bormuth mean cloze readability formula in which values relate to letters in a passage, words in a passage, Dale Long List words on a passage, and sentences in a passage. Although Bormuth acknowledges that the readability formula does not adequately ensure that students have read the text, so that comprehension is not adequately assessed, a number of other criticisms can be lodged. The use of this formula excludes important text level sources of passage difficulty including the genre of the piece and the differences that appear normally because of the specific character of the text form (e.g., the degree of nominalization within a text which is defined as a report). Other features such as topicality, cohesion, and referencing are omitted. Surface features such as layout of information in a double-page spread are also ignored. One might ask what proportion of readability is actually carried by those surface feature criteria used as measures of readability in these tests. The assertion that readability of a text is static is certainly open to debate.

3. *Support materials and services*. These materials are outlined in an accompanying catalogue. The instructional support services outlined from page 59 onwards in the 1991 catalogue including the edited book, *Reading, Thinking and Concept Development: Strategies for the Classroom* are quite interesting. It is certainly encouraging to see that the writers of this test are sensitive to the needs of teachers in providing general professional development in the area of literacy.

The package includes detailed accompanying volumes; four technical documents relating to norms, validity, and reliability; and a detailed explanation of the approaches taken in the test. The *DRP: An Effectiveness Measure in Reading* includes a number of studies that are accounts of interesting related research studies.

RELIABILITY AND VALIDITY. The tests have both high internal consistency reliability and high alternate form test-retest reliability. The standard errors of measurement are acceptably low. Evidence is presented that the tests centered on the abilities of a group of students are sufficiently sensitive to detect a gain in reading achievement over 5 months of instruction.

The evidence of convergent validity presented may be interpreted to mean that the tests measure reading comprehension. The discriminant validity evidence presented shows the tests do *not* measure every verbal ability, and that they are more related to verbal than to so-called nonverbal abilities.

GENERAL COMMENT. The use of any test such as the DRP for more than survey purposes in a large school population is open to question. Although the tests give an indication of which level of text relative to another a student is able to read in a particular manner (i.e., independently, with assistance, or at frustration level), the large dependence on readability measures for placing students with classroom texts is somewhat flawed, given the arguments about the simplistic nature of such measures as outlined above.

REVIEWER'S REFERENCE

Ivens, S. H., & Koslin, B. L. (1991). *Demands for reading literacy require new accountability methods: Report 91.1. New York: Touchstone Applied Science Associates, Inc.*

Review of the Degrees of Reading Power by LAWRENCE H. CROSS, Associate Professor of Educational Research and Measurement, Virginia Polytechnic Institute and State University, Blacksburg, VA:

Nearly 30 years ago, Glaser (1963) coined the term "criterion-referenced measures" to describe tests that would provide "explicit information as to what the individual can or cannot do" (p. 519). The Degrees of Reading Power (DRP) tests epitomize the type of test envisioned by Glaser in that all three forms (Primary, Standard, and Advanced) were designed to yield scores directly interpretable in terms of the readability level of prose that an examinee should be expected to read with a specified level of comprehension. Number-right scores are converted to a common scale called DRP units that index the difficulty levels of text students can be expected to read. DRP units are also used to index the readability of text materials. For example, a DRP score of 56 implies that a student could be expected to read, with 75% comprehension, the *Prince and the Pauper*, which also has a DRP index of 56. The test publisher makes available (at a price) catalogs and software that can be used to determine DRP ratings for textbooks and works of popular literature. Clearly, such criterion-referenced interpretations are much more meaningful for students, parents, teachers, and legislators than are stanines, grade-equivalent scores, or other norm-referenced scores.

Not only are the score interpretations afforded by these tests compelling, but the tests use novel and elegantly simple item types that almost anyone would perceive as credible measures of reading comprehension. All three forms of the DRP contain specially written passages ordered in difficulty. For the Primary and Standard forms, carefully selected words have been deleted from the passages, and the examinee is to identify the missing word. A multiple-choice format is used wherein each word offered as a choice is chosen to be "semantically plausible and syntactically correct" (technical manual, p. 12) within the context of the sentence containing the missing word. Information contained in the surrounding text is needed to select the correct choice with confidence, but it seems that some choices are less plausible than others for some items. The Primary DRP test, designed for grades 1–3, contains 14 three-sentence paragraphs followed by four longer passages, each containing approximately 325 words. A single word has been deleted from each of the three sentence paragraphs, and seven words have been deleted from each of the longer passages. Accordingly, there are 42 items in the Primary DRP.

The Standard DRP test consists of ten 250–300-word passages from which seven words per passage have been deleted, for a total of 70 items. Forms are available for three difficulty levels, appropriate for grades 3–5, 5–8, and 8–12.

The Advance DRP is somewhat different from the other two. It contains eight 250–300-word passages of increasing difficulty, but rather than identify missing words, examinees identify which of five statements is consistent with propositions presented within and across paragraphs making up each passage. There are three items for each of the eight passages for a total of 24 items. Forms are available for two difficulty levels, appropriate for grades 6–9 and 9–12.

The publishers describe the Primary and Standard DRP tests as measures of "ability to make inferences concerning the surface meaning of messages in English prose" (technical manual, p. 13), and the Advanced DRP test is described as a measure of "ability to integrate and manipulate propositions over increasing amounts of text" (teacher's manual, p. 40). Indeed, the tests have considerable face validity as authentic measures of reading comprehension.

The technical manual for the Standard DRP is based on older, longer forms, no longer available, and technical data for the new Standard forms were not provided for this review. Rather than recount the conventional indicators of reliability and validity reported for these older forms, the readers is directed to previous *MMY* reviews of the Standard DRP test by Bruning (1985; 9:305) and Hanna (1985; 9:305).

Very little information is available concerning the reliability and validity of number-right scores for the newer Primary and Advanced forms. KR-20 estimates ranging between .92 and .94 are reported for the 49-item Primary DRP administered to second and third grade samples. Alternate forms reliability estimates for the same samples ranged from .87 to .90. Reliability estimates are not reported for operational forms of the Advanced DRP, but KR-20 estimates averaged across twenty two 18-item calibration forms was .82 for students in grades 6 through 12. When .82 is entered into the Spearman-Brown prophecy formula, a coefficient of .86 is estimated for the 24-item operational forms.

Number-right scores from the Advanced DRP correlated .66 with the PSAT verbal scores and .56 with PSAT math scores for a sample of 234 tenth graders. No other evidence of criterion-related validity is reported for the Advanced DRP forms, and no correlational validity data are reported for the Primary DRP.

Although additional evidence of reliability and validity should be reported for current forms of all three DRP tests, the technical issues of greatest concern have to do with the adequacy of the DRP scale, rather than with the adequacy of the number-right scores.

As noted above, number-right scores are converted to a common scale called DRP units. In order to convert number-right scores to the DRP scale, two somewhat controversial methodologies were employed. The first is the Rasch measurement model used to obtain ability estimates that are theoretically independent of the items or forms on which they are based. The second is the use of the Bormuth (1969) procedure used to scale text difficulty. As noted by Stoker (1987) in his review of the DRP,

> Not all measurement specialists accept Rasch model scaling, which underlies the DRP scales. Neither do all reading specialists accept Bormuth's method for analyzing text difficulty. (p. 125)

Issues associated with using the Bormuth procedure to index text difficulty have been debated extensively in the reading literature and in previous reviews of the DRP and will not be addressed here. However, previous reviews have barely addressed the implications for using the Rasch model to place scores from these tests on a common DRP scale.

There are at least two concerns associated with using the Rasch model for these tests. The first has to do with whether the abilities measured by the DRP tests are unidimensional as required by the Rasch model. The generally high internal consistency reliability coefficients reported for the various forms and levels of these tests tend to support the notion that the ability measured *within* the levels of these tests is unidimensional. However, as noted above, even the publisher characterizes the ability measured by the Advanced level tests as being different from that measured by the Primary and Standard DRP tests. Moreover, the technical manual authors report the median correlation between 22 calibration forms of the Standard and Advanced DRP tests as being only .58. This coefficient is interpreted as indicating "there is a fair degree of independence between the capabilities assessed by the two tasks" (technical manual, p. 25). If this is so, what basis is there for placing ability estimates from the Advanced DRP on the same ability scale as the Primary and Standard DRP tests using the Rasch model?

A second, and perhaps a more important reason to be concerned with the applicability of the Rasch model to data from these tests has to do with the potential effect of guessing behavior. In order for the Rasch model to provide ability estimates that are independent of the test items on which they are based, it must be assumed that the probability of success on any item is a function only of item difficulty and examinee ability. Success due to guessing is not a part of the model. However, the potential for guessing on these multiple-choice tests is great. Each form of the DRP tests includes passages representing a wide range of reading levels, and when students encounter passages beyond their reading level, the potential for guessing increases. Thus, one might suspect misfitting items due to guessing.

The technical manuals for each of the three DRP tests present data attesting to the fit of the item data to the Rasch model, but it is difficult to evaluate these data because only the means and standard deviations of the item mean-square fit statistics have been reported. Although the means equal the expected values (1.0), the standard deviations (in the range of .2 to .5) suggest that there are more than a few items within these forms with divergent fit statistics. Lack of fit was acknowledged for five items across four old forms of the Standard DRP, but a misfitting item was defined as a mean square fit greater than 2.0, which is quite a liberal standard. The lack of fit for these items was attributed to guessing.

However, guessing may pose a greater threat to valid score interpretations for current and future administration of these tests than for the administrations reported in the technical manuals. At issue is the extent to which students are motivated to guess. Ordinarily, this should not matter, because any test directions should advise examinees concerning guessing. Unfortunately, the DRP test directions are silent as to the advisability of guessing. If we assume the students who were administered the tests reported in the technical manuals were under no particular pressure to do well, guessing may not have been prevalent, and the Rasch item fit statistics would be relatively unaffected by guessing. However, these test are described as a new breed of "effectiveness measures" (technical manual, p. 1) and are being used in many "high stakes" (test catalog, p. 9) applications. When these tests are used to determine eligibility for promotion, graduation, or student teaching, it could be argued that it is unethical *not* to advise students to guess when unsure of the answers to questions on these tests (Frary, 1988). Of course, to encourage guessing is antithetical to the Rasch model. In any event, it seems reasonable to expect that guessing will be more prevalent when DRP tests are administered in high stakes settings, than when administered in no fault field trials. If so, DRP scores calibrated on no fault test performances will tend to provide overestimates of ability when applied to high stakes test performances.

An indication of the potential effect guessing may have on DRP scores can be seen in normative data reported for 1981–82 and again in 1987–88. Both norming studies were limited to scores obtained in New York state, but these were weighted to reflect national distributions for ethnicity and percentage of students on free lunch programs. If the DRP scores from these two norming studies are to be believed, there has been a silent revolution in reading ability, especially among our nation's elementary school children. Between 1982 and 1988, DRP score increases (at the 75% comprehension level) were in the range of 8 to 10 DRP units for grades 3 through 6. Lesser, but meaningful increases were observed for all but 12th graders. To offer a criterion-referenced interpretation of an 8-point gain, consider a typical fifth grade student in 1982 for whom *Johnny Appleseed*, with a DRP rating of 46, is at the appropriate instructional level (75% comprehension rate). By 1988, *To Kill a Mocking Bird*, with a DRP rating of 54, would be appropriate instructional level reading material for a typical fifth grader. Such dramatic increases go well beyond the Lake Woebegone effect given notoriety by Cannell (1988). The publisher suggests these dramatic increases are in accord with a national trend of increasing tests scores. As Linn, Graue, and Sanders (1990) note, however, there is reason to question whether recent increases in norm-referenced test scores really reflect increases in student achievement. An equally plausible explanation for the dramatic gains noted in the DRP scores is that the motivation to guess has changed on these tests between 1982 and 1988 as these tests have become institutionalized in New York state.

Perhaps the major question to be answered before the DRP tests can be recommended as "effectiveness measures" (technical manual, p. 1), is what effect did guessing have on DRP score calibrations, and how might guessing distort these estimates when these tests are adopted in high stakes settings. If these tests are to be used only for instructional decisions, it may be acceptable to ignore the role of guessing and hope students will not respond to items for which they cannot answer with confidence. If used in high stakes settings, examinees ethically must be advised to guess, and what effect this will have on the validity of the DRP score interpretations is unknown.

In summary, these tests have the potential to fulfill the promise of criterion-referenced tests envisioned by Glaser nearly 30 years ago, but whether such score interpretations are warranted is still an open question in this reviewer's opinion.

REVIEWER'S REFERENCES

Glaser, R. (1963). Instructional technology and the measurement of learning outcomes: Some questions. *American Psychologist, 18*, 519-521.

Bormuth, J. R. (1969). *Development of readability analyses*. (Contract No. OEG-3-7-070052-0326). Washington, DC: U.S. Department of Health, Education, and Welfare, Office of Education.

Bruning, R. (1985). [Review of Degrees of Reading Power.] In J. V. Mitchell, Jr. (Ed.), *The ninth mental measurements yearbook* (pp. 443-444). Lincoln, NE: Buros Institute of Mental Measurements.

Hanna, G. S. (1985). [Review of Degrees of Reading Power.] In J. V. Mitchell, Jr. (Ed.), *The ninth mental measurements yearbook* (pp. 444-447). Lincoln, NE: Buros Institute of Mental Measurements.

Stoker, H. (1987). [Review of Degrees of Reading Power.] In D. J. Keyser & R. C. Sweetland (Eds.), *Test Critiques*, (Vol. VI, pp. 120-126). Kansas City, MO: Test Corporation of America.

Cannell, J. J. (1988). Nationally normed elementary achievement testing in America's public schools: How all 50 states are above the national average. *Educational Measurement: Issues and Practice*, 7(2), 5-9.

Frary, R. B. (1988). Formula scoring of multiple-choice tests (correction for guessing). *Educational Measurement: Issues and Practice*, 7(2), 33-38.

Linn, R. L., Graue, M. E., & Sanders, N. M. (1990). Comparing state and district test results to national norms: The validity of claims that "Everyone is above average." *Educational measurement: Issues and practice*, 9(3), 5-14.

[102]

Dental Admission Test.

Purpose: "Designed to measure general academic achievement, comprehension of scientific information, and perceptual ability."
Population: Dental school applicants.
Publication Dates: 1946–91.
Acronym: DAT.
Scores, 8: Natural Sciences (Biology, General Chemistry, Organic Chemistry, Total), Reading Comprehension, Quantitative Reasoning, Perceptual Ability, Total.
Administration: Group.
Price Data: Available from publisher.
Time: 235(330) minutes in 2 sessions.
Comments: Formerly called Dental Aptitude Testing Program; test administered 2 times annually (April, October) at centers established by publisher.
Author: Department of Testing Services.
Publisher: American Dental Association.
Cross References: For reviews by Henry M. Cherrick and Linda M. DuBois, see 9:308; see also T3:673 (2 references); for reviews by Robert L. Linn and Christine H. McGuire of an earlier edition, see 8:1085 (7 references); see also T2:2337 (8 references), 7:1091 (28 references), 5:916 (6 references), and 4:788 (2 references).

Review of the Dental Admission Test by JANET BALDWIN, Assistant Director, GED Testing Program, Washington, DC:

The Dental Admissions Test (DAT), conducted by the American Dental Association, is required of all applicants for admission to dental schools. Dental schools consider DAT test scores along with other information such as collegiate records and references in making admission decisions. Successful participation in the DAT program requires completion of at least one year of college, which should include courses in biology and in general and organic chemistry. The DAT is administered two times a year (April/October) and consists of four tests which take about 4 and a half hours to complete.

The format of the DAT includes a series of multiple-choice tests that include a Survey of the Natural Sciences (SNS), which measures undergraduate-level achievement in biology (40 items), general chemistry (30 items), and organic chemistry (30 items); a 50-item Quantitative Reasoning Test (QRT), which measures knowledge of basic mathematics and algebra; a 50-item Reading Comprehension Test (RCT), based on reading passages in dental, basic, or clinical science not covered in an undergraduate curriculum; and a 75-item Perceptual Ability Test (PAT), which includes five sets of perceptual tasks that measure ability to recognize two- and three-dimensional visual patterns.

The 1989–1990 user's manual noted several changes from previous versions of the DAT. In 1988, the standard score scale used to report the results of the test was changed from the -1 to 9 scale that was used since the test began to the new 1 to 30 scale. This change represents a major revision in the standard score scale from one based on a norm-referenced, true-score psychometric model, to an ability-referenced scale based on the Rasch psychometric model (Rasch, 1960, 1980; Wright, 1977; Wright & Stone, 1979). As noted in supporting documentation provided by the publisher (Smith, Kramer, & Kubiak, 1988), this model provides a way to compare the abilities of different applicant cohorts over time and over test forms, thereby improving the measurement properties and utility of the test scores. For example, the new scale permits both norm-referenced and criterion-referenced interpretations.

Also introduced in 1988 was the DAT Supplemental Score Report (SSR), which was designed to help admissions committees evaluate the quality of the standard scores relative to various examinee response patterns. Studies (Smith, Kramer, & Kubiak, 1990) conducted by the test developers indicated that there are examinees for whom the standard scores on the DAT may misrepresent their abilities due to the presence of measurement disturbances such as guessing, test anxiety, excessive cautiousness, cheating, or language skills unrelated to ability. As some of these disturbances may be due to the speeded nature of the tests, it is useful to ask whether the tests are too speeded for valid measurement of the abilities of some examinees or, more fundamentally, whether the ability to work quickly is an important criterion for dental school admission. To address such concerns, the test developers provide a useful description of how to interpret various score patterns on the DAT's Quantitative Reasoning Test. However, the format of these SSRs is numerically dense. Therefore, some training may be required to make effective use of these reports.

Other changes noted in the manual include increasing the number of reading passages on the RCT from one passage with 50 items to three passages, each with 16 to 17 items. In 1990, the QRT was to have been reduced in length from 50 to 40 items, containing 10 fewer applied mathematics items. Validation studies of the PAT (Kramer, Kubiak, & Smith, 1989) found multidimensionality in the data. This finding led to the appropriate suggestion that DAT transcripts should no longer include a single PAT score but rather separate scores for each of the five subtests—Angles, Apertures, Cubes, Orthographic Projections, and Form Development. This change was planned for the Spring 1990 tests, although no mention is made of the change in the 1991–1992 manual.

RELIABILITY. The only type of reliability information reported in the user's manual is internal consistency reliability coefficients (KR20). The reliability coefficients of the four tests used in the October 1989 administration ranged from .79 to .92. Reliability coefficients for the Survey of the Natural Sciences subtest scores were provided only for tests administered in 1988, not in 1989. A more notable omission is the absence of reliability coefficients for the Perceptual Ability Test subtest scores, as these are not reported for 1988 or 1989. No alternate form reliabilities or estimates of stability over time are provided for any of these scores.

VALIDITY. The DAT Program provides substantial documentation of the validity of the tests. In addition, the user's manual describes the content of the DAT, test construction and scoring procedures, and summaries of research studies on the tests. Both predictive and content validity evidence is included in support of the DAT. DAT Academic Average scores (the arithmetic mean of the QRT, RCT, Biology, General Chemistry, and Organic Chemistry standard scores) were found to be significantly and positively correlated with freshman dental grades by 100% of dental schools. However, correlations of these scores with dental first-year grades ranged between a l01 of .146 (Technic) and a high of .457 (Freshman GPA). A multiple regression using the individual DAT test scores—QRT, RCT, Biology, General Chemistry, Organic Chemistry, and PAT—resulted in better prediction of freshman GPA (Multiple R = .575) than did the Academic Average scores (Multiple R = .457). Multiple regression using individual DAT scores, predental GPA, and predental science GPA result in the best combination of predictors for first-year GPA (Multiple R = .700). PAT scores had the strongest relationship to technic course and preclinical operative technic performance (.346 and .315, respectively).

In summary, the test developers provide evidence of good internal consistency and considerable information in support of the predictive value of the DAT scores. Moreover, previous shortcomings—such as the absence of procedures for equating scores across cohorts and test forms—have been addressed with the new ability-referenced standard score scale. In light of the test developers' concerns about the influence of measurement disturbances on test scores, the introduction of the SSRs and the considerable amount of technical documentation on the DAT should facilitate the interpretation of scores.

REVIEWER'S REFERENCES

Rasch, G. (1960, 1980). *Probabilistic models for some intelligence and attainment tests.* Chicago: University of Chicago Press.

Wright, B. D. (1977). Solving measurement problems with the Rasch model. *Journal of Educational Measurement, 14,* 97-116.

Wright, B. D., & Stone, M. H. (1979). *Best test design.* Chicago: MESA Press.

Smith, R. M., Kramer, G. A., & Kubiak, A. T. (1988). Revision of Dental Admission Test standard score scale. *Journal of Dental Education, 52*(10), 548-553.

Kramer, G. A., Kubiak, A. T., & Smith, R. M. (1989). Construct and predictive validities of the Perceptual Ability Test. *Journal of Dental Education, 53*(2), 119-125.

Smith, R. M., Kramer, G. A., & Kubiak, A. T. (1990). Incidence of measurement disturbances in the Dental Admissions Quantitative Reasoning Test. *Journal of Dental Education, 54*(6), 314-318.

Review of the Dental Admission Test by JERRY S. GILMER, Assistant Research Scientist, College of Medicine, The University of Iowa, Iowa City, IA:

The Dental Admission Test (DAT) is sponsored and developed by the Council on Dental Education of the American Dental Association (ADA) and has been administered on a national basis since 1950. The test is administered in April and October each year at numerous testing sites in the U.S. and foreign countries. Much of the DAT is designed to measure academic achievement, with one subtest designed to measure perceptual ability. The test is used by dental schools to assist with admissions. Support materials related to the DAT appropriately point out that, along with test scores, other factors such as previous academic performance should be considered when making admissions decisions. The support materials also indicate that successful performance on the DAT is generally related to completion of college courses in biology and general and organic chemistry. The four subtests of the DAT, along with a fifth section containing pretest items, require one-half day for administration. Each of the five test sections is separately timed and there is a mandatory 15-minute rest period after the first 2 hours and 20 minutes of testing.

The Survey of Natural Sciences Test contains 100 items with 40 covering basic first-year biology, 30 items in general chemistry, and 30 items in organic chemistry. The Quantitative Reasoning Test contains 30 mathematical problems and 10 items (reduced from 20) in applied mathematics. The Reading Comprehension Test consists of three reading passages with 16 or 17 items related to each passage. The Perceptual Ability Test (PAT) contains 90 items (75 scored and 15 experimental) and is not designed to measure any of the traditional achievement areas such as verbal, scientific, or quantitative reasoning. The

PAT covers two-dimensional and three-dimensional problems in angle discrimination, block counting, form development, and object visualization—areas which the ADA believes are important in measuring one's ability to perceive small differences, which is, in turn, related to the development of fine manual dexterity, an attribute important to the practice of dentistry.

Eight scores are reported for the DAT: one for each of the Quantitative Reasoning, Reading Comprehension, and Perceptual Ability tests, and four for the Survey of Natural Sciences—biology, general chemistry, organic chemistry, and total science. The eighth score is an Academic Average which is the average of the quantitative reasoning, reading comprehension, perceptual ability, biology, and the general and organic chemistry tests.

The DAT preparation materials available to candidates include a small information booklet that contains a content description of each test along with application procedures and an application form. The preparation materials also include a booklet of sample items from the four tests along with answers. The Manual for Administration is written clearly and should be effective in establishing uniform administration procedures across all testing sites.

Of several changes in the DAT program in recent years, one of the most significant is the use of test score equating techniques. Test equating provides for scale comparability across testing dates. For example, with appropriate test equating it is safe to assume that a person with a score of 20 on a test has more of the trait tested than a person with a score of 15, regardless of which version of the test each person took and provided the test content specifications have not changed dramatically. In conjunction with test equating, the ADA also instituted a totally different score scale for the DAT; the new scale ranges from 1 to 30 and is based on the Rasch testing model primarily as it is presented in *Best Test Design* (Wright & Stone, 1979). Test equating and the use of an interval-type scale are major improvements in the DAT program over the purely norm-based -1 to 9 scale used previously. Because of the Rasch common-item equating used for the DAT, the structure of the tests required some changes; all tests now contain a small set of items (an anchor test) which was used in previous versions of the DAT. In addition, the Reading Comprehension Test was changed from one reading passage to three passages to allow for the reuse of items. This anchor test is the key to linking the score scales in the equating process.

The extensive series of reports prepared each year present a large amount of psychometric data and other information regarding the tests. These reports present acceptable reliability indices, correlations, and other additional evidence of test validation and contain no evidence of any major problems resulting from the conversion to the new score scale. Data appear to be comparable to similar data obtained prior to the scale conversion. Validity evidence is presented based on correlations between the DAT and dental school grades and performance on national boards.

The DAT is supported by an effective research program. Some recent or ongoing projects include an examination of gender-related differential item functioning in the quantitative reasoning test (which resulted in a reduction of the number of applied mathematics items), a study of the dimensionality of the perceptual ability test, an investigation of the cognitive behaviors assessed by the test items and consideration of pretesting problem-solving and higher-order-thinking items and examining how these thinking items are related to predictive validity.

One type of information that does not appear to be included in all of these reports, however, is data related to the issue of the fit of the Rasch model to the data. Fit indices are routinely included as output from the commonly used computer scaling and calibration programs and such information would be a valuable contribution to a DAT technical manual, which is also not available at this time. In addition to the issue of model fit, the technical manual should also present additional information on scale homogeneity, details of equating, and other psychometric concerns. The DAT would also benefit from a broader research program related to gender and minority issues; minority concerns, specifically, do not appear to be well documented. Despite these issues, however, the DAT is a well-developed, extensively researched, and strongly supported program. The transition to an equated score scale represents a major and significant improvement over the previous, norm-based, scale. The DAT remains a worthy predictor of dental school performance and an appropriate factor in dental school admissions decisions.

REVIEWER'S REFERENCE

Wright, B. D., & Stone, M. H. (1979). *Best test design*. Chicago: MESA Press.

[103]

Denver II.
Purpose: Designed to screen for developmental delays.
Population: Birth to age 6.
Publication Dates: 1967–90.
Scores: Item scores in 4 areas (Personal-Social, Fine Motor-Adaptive, Language, Gross Motor) and 5 test behavior ratings (Typical, Compliance, Interest in Surroundings, Fearfulness, Attention Span).
Administration: Individual.
Price Data, 1994: $58 per complete package; $33 per test kit; $15 per 100 test forms; $210 per training videotape (rental price $90); $17 per training manual ('90, 50 pages); $19 per technical manual ('90, 91 pages).
Time: (10–15) minutes for abbreviated version; (20–25) minutes for entire test.

Comments: Revision of the Denver Developmental Screening Test.
Authors: W. K. Frankenburg, Josiah Dodds, Phillip Archer, Beverly Bresnick, Patrick Maschka, Norma Edelman, and Howard Shapiro.
Publisher: Denver Developmental Materials, Inc.
Cross References: See T4:740 (18 references).

TEST REFERENCES

1. Newth, S. J., & Corbett, J. (1993). Behaviour and emotional problems in three-year-old children of Asian parentage. *Journal of Child Psychology and Psychiatry and Allied Disciplines, 34*, 333-352.

2. Nellis, L., & Gridley, B. E. (1994). Review of the Bayley Scales of Infant Development—Second Edition. *Journal of School Psychology, 32*, 201-209.

3. Bowin, M. J., Green, S. D. R., Davies, A. G., Giordani, B., Mokili, J. K. L., & Cutting, W. A. M. (1995). A preliminary evaluation of the cognitive and motor effects of pediatric HIV infection in Zairian children. *Health Psychology, 14*, 13-21.

Review of the Denver II by SELMA HUGHES, Professor, Department of Psychology and Special Education, East Texas State University, Commerce, TX:

The Denver II is a revision of the Denver Developmental Screening Test (DDST) first published in 1967 to screen for potential developmental problems in young children between birth and 6 years of age. It is an individually administered test that takes about 20 minutes to complete and is used to assess a child's performance on various age-appropriate tasks. The authors point out that it is not an IQ test, neither is it a definitive predictor of future adaptive or intellectual ability.

There are 125 items on the Denver II compared to 105 items on the DDST. The items are organized into four domains of development: Personal-Social, Fine Motor-Adaptive, Language, and Gross Motor. Within each domain items are arranged in approximate chronological order according to the ages at which most children can be expected to perform them.

The test kit consists of a pad of test forms, screening manual, technical manual, and the materials required for screening (which are in a small zippered bag). The materials are the same as for the DDST with the addition of a cup, doll, and bottle. The test forms are one-page (8.5-inch x 11-inch) sheets, which show the age across the top and bottom in monthly intervals to 24 months, then by 3-month intervals to 6 years. The scale is easier to read than on the DDST and is similar to the periodicity schedule suggested for checkups by the American Academy of Pediatrics.

Each of the 125 items is represented on the form by a bar that spans the ages at which 25%, 50%, 75%, and 90% of the standardization sample passed that item. This feature of the test is one that has endeared it to users because it enables one to see at a glance how the child compares to other children of the same age.

The screening manual contains clear criteria for scoring and fewer items (31%) are passed by report than on the DDST where nearly half (48%) could be by report. The child's age is calculated (with an adjustment for prematurity until 2 years of age) and shown as a line on the test form. Each item that is intersected by the age line determines the starting point of the test. Items are scored as Pass, Fail, No Opportunity, and Refusal and a letter notation shown on the bar. Three items to the left of the age line must be passed in each of the four domains or additional items administered. Three items are given to the right of the age line (to determine strengths) and testing continued until three items are failed in each domain.

A child can pass, fail, or refuse an item on which the age line falls between the 25th and 75th percentile, and the child's development will be considered normal. If the child fails an item where the age line passes between the 75th and 90th percentile, a "Caution" is scored. Items the child fails or refuses to the left of the age line are shown as "Delays."

Precise criteria are given for determining the child's development as Normal, Questionable, or Abnormal, based on the number of Delays and Cautions. This is helpful to users in interpreting the test, although the use of non-normative scores is rated as unacceptable by test reviewers (e.g., Hammill, Brown, & Bryant, 1989).

TECHNICAL ASPECTS. The Denver II has been restandardized on a sample of 2,096 children with slightly more females than males which approximates the percentage nationwide. The demographic characteristics of the sample approximate the distribution of the population of Colorado. Consequently, there is an overrepresentation of Hispanic infants, an underrepresentation of Black infants, and a disproportionate representation of infants from Anglo mothers with more than 12 years of education, when compared with the population of the United States. An appendix provides normative data for individual items in which one or more subgroups differed significantly from the composite.

The technical manual contains a detailed description of how the 125 items were derived from the pool of potential items and ample statistical evidence is provided to show the norms are current age norms. The reliability of the test in terms of interrater reliability and test stability is positive and high.

The validity of the Denver II rests upon its standardization (i.e., it simply presents the age at which children in Colorado are able to do a variety of tasks). There is no mention of concurrent validity because the authors point out there are no tests in some of the areas tapped by the Denver II.

The crucial question is how sensitive and specific the test is in identifying children who need further diagnostic study, assessment, and intervention. The authors do not address this but, no doubt, critical users in many countries will provide the answer (the DDST was used in more than 54 countries). Yet, as

Messick (1980) points out, validity is not a matter of all or nothing but a matter of degree. One may question whether a test could be developed that would be simultaneously culturally sensitive and valid across all cultures.

SUMMARY. The Denver II like its predecessor the DDST is a standardized, easily administered, and simply scored measure of development in infants and preschoolers. Like its predecessor it has a number of psychometric weaknesses, yet these are offset by the appeal of the test to health providers because of the ease of use and practicality (Walker, Bonner, & Milling, 1984). It fulfills an important role as a developmental screening instrument for both practical and research purposes. The test's value rests with the expertise and sensitivity of users. The authors are to be commended for emphasizing training and the periodic training evaluation of those who use the Denver II, and cautioning users against well-intentioned but inaccurate ways of interpreting the Denver II.

REVIEWER'S REFERENCES

Messick, S. (1980). Test validity and the ethics of assessment. *American Psychologist, 35*, 1012-1027.

Walker, C. E., Bonner, B., & Milling, L. (1984). Denver Developmental Screening Test. In D. J. Keyser & R. C. Sweetland (Eds.), *Test critiques* (Vol. 1; pp. 239-251). Kansas City, MO: Test Corporation of America.

Hammill, D. D., Brown, L., & Bryant, B. R. (1989). *A consumer's guide to tests in print*. Austin, TX: PRO-ED, Inc.

Review of the Denver II by PAT MIRENDA, Director of Research and Training, CBI Consultants, Ltd., Vancouver, British Columbia, Canada:

The Denver II is a 1990 revision of one of the most commonly used developmental screening tests. Like its predecessor, the Denver II is easy to administer, requires only a short period of time, and is comprehensive in scope. The revision includes a scale for rating the child's behavioral characteristics during the test, in areas such as compliance, alertness, fearfulness, attention span, and typical behavior. It now utilizes an age scale that is similar to the American Academy of Pediatrics' suggested periodicity schedule for health maintenance visits, to facilitate use of the Denver II in conjunction with these visits. It is meant to be used only as a screening instrument, not as a substitute for general intelligence, language, or other aptitude tests.

The revision was undertaken to address some of the limitations of the original test. Items that were difficult to administer or interpret were either deleted or revised with new directions for the examiner. Several new language items were created, and new personal-social items were also included for children between $4^1/_2$ and 6 years of age. These two changes resulted in the addition of 20 items to the Denver II, mostly in the language area. Only 39 (31%) of these items may be scored by report, compared to 50 (48%) of the items in the original test. This may strengthen the test without adding substantially to its complexity.

In addition to the item changes in the test, a number of important changes that affect test interpretation were also made. The age norms at which 25%, 50%, 75%, and 90% of children in the normative sample performed each item were updated from 1967. Systematic sampling procedures were utilized to construct a normative sample representing diversity in four subgroups: (*a*) gender; (*b*) ethnic group (Hispanic, African-American, Anglo); (*c*) maternal education level (less than 12 grades completed, 12 grades completed, 13 or more years completed); and (*d*) place of residence (rural, semi-rural, and urban). A total of 2,096 children were included in the final sample. Because the sample was drawn exclusively from Colorado, an analysis was also conducted to compare the Colorado composite 90% norms with theoretical U.S. norms (based on U.S. Census data). There were no clinically significant differences between these two groups, suggesting the norms are applicable to children across the United States. However, 17 items had significantly different norms for one or more subgroups when compared to the composite norms. For example, the item "names 4 colors" was passed, on the average, by 90% of all sample children aged 4 years 9 months. However, an additional 5.9 months was required, on the average, for the item to be passed by children whose mothers completed less than 12 grades of school. This difference was significant at $p<.10$. Although 17 items affected in this way were included in the test, data are provided in the technical manual to help diagnosticians interpret the findings for children who may be delayed in development. This is a nice addition to the Denver II, and enhances it applicability to children from diverse backgrounds.

Several types of reliability scores are included in the technical manual. The mean interrater reliability between trained examiners and trained observers was 99.7%. Test-retest reliability scores were obtained twice: once, on the same day, 5–10 minutes after the first test, with different examiners; and second, 7–10 days after the first test, with the same examiner. The mean score for the short interval (5–10-minute) test-retest was 90.8%, and mean score for the long interval (7–10-day) test was 89.0%. The kappa statistic (k) (Fleiss, 1981) was calculated for the interrater and long interval test-retest data, to determine if agreement was better than chance. All of the items included in the final version of the Denver II had excellent interrater agreement ($k \geq .75$). Sixty-three items in the final version had excellent long interval test-retest agreement ($k \geq .75$), 25 items had fair to good agreement ($k \geq .40 < .75$), and 19 items had poor agreement ($k > 0 < .40$). Overall, these scores suggest the Denver II is a reliable screening test when administered by trained examiners who conform to the screening protocols provided in the technical manual.

No concurrent validity scores are provided for the Denver II, and the rationale for this is discussed in detail on page 18 of the technical manual. The authors provide three main arguments against the appropriateness of validity measures for the test: (*a*) Some of the tasks of the Denver II are in areas where there are no well-standardized tests for comparison; (*b*) no single diagnostic test taps all of the areas of development covered by the Denver II, so obtaining correlations with existing tests is not possible; and (*c*) the Denver II does not presume unitary constructs in the individual, such as general intelligence. The authors suggest that, beyond face validity, the only way to establish the validity of the Denver II is to determine how valuable the test is in identifying children who need further diagnostic study, assessment, and intervention. They provide a number of guidelines regarding how to make these determinations in the context of a community screening program that utilizes the Denver II, as well as example screening data from Oklahoma, Tennessee, and Michigan.

Overall, the Denver II represents a significant improvement over the 1969 version of the test. The improvements make it easier to administer and allow for more individualized interpretation of the results. In addition, examiners can be more comfortable than previously that the normative scores are drawn from a culturally diverse sample that at least approximates the experiences and background of the children with whom it is used.

REVIEWER'S REFERENCE

Fleiss, J. L. (1981). *Statistical methods for rates and proportions* (2nd ed.). NY: John Wiley and Sons.

[104]

Determining Needs in Your Youth Ministry.

Purpose: Constructed to identify potential needs, problems, or concerns of youth in order to develop relevant programs.
Population: Junior and senior high church groups.
Publication Date: 1987.
Scores: Item scores only.
Administration: Group.
Price Data: Not available.
Time: (60) minutes.
Authors: Peter L. Benson and Dorothy L. Williams.
Publisher: Group Publishing, Inc.
[The publisher advised in December 1993 that this test is now out of print—Ed.]

Review of Determining Needs in Your Youth Ministry by SUSAN L. CROWLEY, Assistant Professor of Psychology, Utah State University, Logan, UT:

Determining Needs in Your Youth Ministry is a survey instrument designed to give ministry leaders "a well-rounded picture of your junior and senior highers' hurts, fears, worries, and interests" (manual, p. 6). It was developed to serve as a guide to youth program operators as they target teenagers' concerns. The survey is intended to help church leaders avoid the "chicken little syndrome," which is defined as basing decisions and programs on limited data and being overly reactive to isolated crises. The authors suggest this survey will provide ministry leaders with useful data about their teenagers, rather than potentially inaccurate or arbitrary assumptions.

The survey subtitle "a do-it-yourself research kit," sums up the tenor of the instrument. The single volume contains all the required information, introductory letters, and instructions to conduct the survey, tally and interpret results, and give feedback about the outcome. One of the major strengths of the instrument is the detail with which material is presented. The authors are incredibly explicit in their instructions and suggestions. For instance, in the chapter on administering the survey, the authors include the number of people that should be on the "steering committee," suggestions for publicizing the survey (e.g., the theme of "Our Puzzling Youth Group"), an informational letter to parents, and the structure for the survey administration meeting, including crowdbreaking exercises and an opening prayer. Clearly, almost any adult could follow the manual and conduct the survey successfully.

DESCRIPTION OF THE MEASURE. The survey itself consists of 160 questions divided into 16 areas. The sections encompass a broad range of potential teenage concerns (e.g., family, friends, future, school, self-esteem, relationships, values, and general worries) and attitudes toward the church and their faith (e.g., what I want from my church, how well is my church doing). The manual includes multiple copies of the survey as well as answer sheets, tally sheets, and summary sheets; permission is granted to photocopy all material. Chapters cover the administration, interpretation of results, reporting of results, and exploring the results in youth group meetings. In each section, the user is taken through the process step-by-step. Although this level of detail may be initially helpful, the manual becomes repetitive as several group meetings are described, all following a similar format. It might have been more helpful to outline a general strategy for holding group meetings and give multiple suggestions for crowdbreaking exercises, discussion strategies, and worksheets.

The survey form itself is easy to read, with complete instructions printed on the first page. Questions have a variety of response options including 3-, 5-, or 9-point Likert-type scales, true/false, and right/wrong. Subjects respond by circling their answers on a separate answer sheet printed with the initials of the response choices (e.g., "V S N" for Very important, Somewhat important, and Not important).

SCORING AND INTERPRETATION. Data are tallied (on the tally sheet) and then summarized (on the summary sheet). The data summary uses percentages based simply on the number of teenagers responding in a given manner to the questions. Percentages for each response option on every question can be calculated. However, to avoid becoming overwhelmed by the data, the authors have structured the summary sheet so that only percentages for the response option(s) they judged most important for each question are calculated. The authors have collapsed the data in some cases (e.g., *strongly agree* and *agree*) to promote comparisons of those who respond in a broadly positive or negative way. The basis on which questions were selected and/or collapsed is not explained.

Information for interpretation of the results is included on the summary sheet. After a space where the percentage for a questions is written, the appropriate statement appears. For instance, on the question about parental freedom the summary sheet reads "_______ % agree or strongly agree with the statement, 'I wish my parents would give me more freedom.'"

The authors warn repeatedly against allowing personal bias to color the interpretation of the data, either over- or underinterpreting the results. They encourage users to listen to the data (p. 24) and identify the interpretation of results as the most demanding part of the process. Yet there is limited information presented as to *how* this is to be accomplished. There are no normative data to suggest what percentages might be expected and so what constitutes a problem. If 1% of the teenagers report they do not like themselves is that a problem? What if it is 10%, or 25%, or 50%? A reference point for what is extreme, or atypical, would be helpful.

TECHNICAL INFORMATION. The manual provides no technical information regarding the survey. The survey sections target areas that have good face validity, but there is little else to suggest they are of greater importance to teenagers than other areas that might have been included. The items also have good face validity, but no other supporting validity data are provided. The number of items in each section varies from 5 to 24, although a psychometric rationale for this is absent. For every item the authors presumably excluded many others, and no explanation is presented for how such decisions were made.

At several points in the text, the authors allude to other research conducted by the Search Institute on teenagers' thoughts and beliefs (e.g., "Search Institute's national survey revealed . . ." p. 23; "Search institute's research has shown . . ." p. 22). Yet this information is not included in the manual, nor is a reference given. One might guess, given the referents to other research, that those are the data on which the survey was based, but this is purely speculative. Although the lack of psychometric rigor (or presentation of this information) may be intended to make the survey more user friendly, it nevertheless would have been a marked improvement for the authors to include information about prior research or the history and development of the survey *somewhere* in the manual (perhaps marked "for those interested"). Minimally, a reference to this information would be desirable. After all, the psychometric integrity of a measure and its approachability to a lay population need not be at odds.

SUMMARY. Determining Needs in Your Youth Ministry is a lay-person's guide to performing a survey. Other than face validity, there is no psychometric information on which to assess the merits of this instrument. The authors present the nuts and bolts of administration, scoring, feedback sessions, and group discussions in detail such that they could be easily followed by an adult. Interpretation of the results is compromised by the lack of normative data. Although the instrument is designed to replace "arbitrary assumptions" with "hard data" (manual, p. 5), the lack of normative information means the "hard data" is rather "soft" and one set of inaccurate assumptions may be replaced by another set. Yet, this survey may be a good starting point for ministry leaders who want to get better information about the teenagers in their youth groups. Clearly, however, data from this instrument will be best used qualitatively, rather than quantitatively.

Review of Determining Needs in Your Youth Ministry by DIANNA L. NEWMAN, Associate Professor of Educational Theory and Practice, University at Albany/State University of New York, Albany, NY:

Determining Needs in Your Youth Ministry was written by Benson and Williams for Search Institute and is a kit published in the form of a book that provides tools for conducting needs analysis for programmatic growth for those working in youth ministry. The goal appears to be the increased involvement of youth, parents, and congregation in the needs analysis, followed by a series of meetings that will gradually increase participation and activity.

The book consists of three sections. The first contains detailed instructions for conducting the survey(s). The second section has detailed instructions for follow-up activities for both parents and youth. The third section contains multiple (20) copies of the actual survey and response sheet with one copy of a detailed tally sheet and summary sheet. Permission to reproduce is acknowledged on several figures in the first two sections as well as the survey and supplemental materials.

The primary needs analysis survey, to be given to youth, consists of 16 subparts, totaling 162 questions. Questions solicit youths' attitudes or opinions on life goals; perceptions of self, family, school, and friends; areas of personal stress including sexual relationships, alcohol and drug use, and family problems; availability and use of resources for dealing with stress; and the local church's role in the respondent's life. The majority of questions utilize Likert-type responses ranging from three to five options. The authors recommend that approximately one hour be allocated to taking the survey. Each test booklet consists of six pages with a separate response sheet. As indicated above, the book contains 20 perforated copies of the booklet and answer sheet, with permission to reproduce more if required. The test booklet and answer sheet appear to be easy to use and at the appropriate level for 7th–12th graders with average or above average reading ability; youth with lower reading levels may find the instrument too difficult and/or too lengthy. No information is provided on how to adapt the test or the answer sheet for youth with disabilities. The manual authors indicate that not all sections of the test need to be given; selection of appropriate sections is left to the user.

No reliability or validity information is available for the instrument. No information is presented on how the items were developed, piloted, or validated. No information is presented on how users can provide their own psychometric properties.

Examination of the survey instructions, questions, and manual indicate that interpretation of questions and responses depend on the cultural and socioeconomic background of the church ministry. A review of test items indicates that most reflect traditional middle class Caucasian cultural values. Both questions and responses assume that respondents are part of a two-parent family, with both parents involved in the child's upbringing. There are no responses appropriate for youth from blended, single-parent, or group-home families. The instrument lacks any questions pertaining to youth with disabilities or instructions on how to include youth with disabilities in the needs analysis. Many of the questions pertaining to faith and involvement of the church are stated in a socially acceptable manner, biasing the responses in favor of the church unless respondents are actively discussing the concepts.

In-depth instructions for scoring the survey are provided in the manual. Overall, the use of the tally sheet and its accompanying directions appears to be cumbersome, making the task of scoring more difficult than necessary. Responses could be obtained more easily using an enlarged answer sheet or a separate piece of paper. The summary sheet is user friendly, presenting prehighlighted responses. Users should be aware, however, that this may limit, if not bias, the interpretation of responses. Use of the summary sheet also requires some reference to the test booklet as symbols (e.g., V, S, N) are used but not included on a key. Many users may prefer to develop their own scoring sheet and develop their own tables for interpretation.

In summary, the survey lacks many of the appropriate psychometric properties that should be present for consequential decision making. The real value of the book appears to be the authors' pre and post survey plans for including youth, parents, and other members of the congregation in planning the youth ministry. The book/instrument would be used best by urban or suburban middle class congregations with a moderately active youth group or a youth group that is ready to be formed. The materials would be difficult to use with inactive youth, youth with disabilities, or youth with varying cultural values.

[105]

Detroit Tests of Learning Aptitude—Adult.

Purpose: Designed to identify strengths and weaknesses in mental abilities and to identify examinees who are markedly deficient in general mental ability.
Population: Ages 16-0 and over.
Publication Date: 1991.
Acronym: DTLA-A.
Scores, 20: 12 subtest scores: Word Opposites, Story Sequences, Sentence Imitation, Reversed Letters, Mathematical Problems, Design Sequences, Basic Information, Quantitative Relations, Word Sequences, Design Reproduction, Symbolic Relations, Form Assembly and 8 composite scores (Linguistic Verbal, Linguistic Nonverbal, Attention-Enhanced, Attention-Reduced, Motor-Enhanced, Motor-Reduced, General Mental Ability, Optimal).
Administration: Individual.
Price Data, 1994: $209 per complete kit including picture book 1, picture book 2, 25 response forms, 25 examiner record booklets, 25 profile/summary forms, and manual (120 pages); $44 per picture book 1; $19 per picture book 2; $18 per 25 response forms; $39 per 25 examiner record booklets; $18 per 25 profile/summary forms; $32 per manual; $98 per microcomputer scoring and report system software (Apple or IBM).
Time: (90–150) minutes.
Comments: Upward extension of the Detroit Tests of Learning Aptitude (Second Edition) (10:85) and (Third Edition) (107).
Authors: Donald D. Hammill and Bryan R. Bryant.
Publisher: PRO-ED, Inc.

Review of the Detroit Tests of Learning Aptitude—Adult by THOMAS E. DINERO, Associate Professor of Evaluation and Measurement, Kent State University, Kent, OH:

The Detroit Tests of Learning Aptitude—Adult (DTLA-A) is a battery of 12 tests intended to measure developed mental abilities in adults ranging in age from 16 to 79 years. According to the manual, "results can be used to estimate general cognitive functioning (intelligence), predict future success (aptitude), or show mastery of particular content and skills (achievement)" (p. 6). The tests overlap in intention and content with those of the Detroit Tests of Learning Aptitude (107) which has a 50-year history. The subtests are: Word Opposites (WO), Story Sequences (SS), Sentence Imitation (SI), Reversed Letters (RL),

Mathematical Problems (MP), Design Sequences (DS), Basic Information (BI), Quantitative Relations (QR), Word Sequences (WS), Design Reproduction (DR), Symbolic Relations (SR), and Form Assembly (FA).

In the manual the authors present an elaborate history and description of intelligence as a tested construct, presenting both sides of the unifactorial versus multifactorial issue. They finally settle on a compromise for their instrument that is rather consistent with Wechsler, Cattell, and Horn's fluid and crystallized intelligences, Das's simultaneous and successive processing, and Jensen's associative and cognitive levels. This conceptualization allows the formation and interpretation of a variety of composite scores simultaneously with individual scaled subtest scores and a total General Mental Ability Quotient.

The test materials include a manual, two booklets, manipulatives, and six dice with rune-like patterns. The package is well produced. The tests are designed for individual administration by trained examiners and can take up to $2^1/_2$ hours over two administrations. The timing is flexible because not all subtests are timed. Although scoring of some subtests is straightforward, scoring for others involves examiner judgment or coding of rank order responses.

A wide variety of normalized and standardized subtest scales is available ranging from those for the 12 subtests to composites intended to reflect the linguistic domain (Verbal Quotient and Nonverbal Quotient), an attentional domain (Attention-Enhanced Quotient and an Attention-Reduced Quotient), a motoric domain (Motor-Enhanced Quotient and Motor-Reduced Quotient), and a variety of theoretical composites.

The tests were normed on 1,254 adults residing in 31 states. The norming group reflects the racial, ethnic, gender, residence, and geography of the United States very well.

There is a discussion of internal consistency and temporal reliability (called time sampling) in the manual. Although Cronbach's alpha coefficients are as low as .66 for one of the subtests, all the composites had internal consistency alphas above .89 on samples of 50 subjects within each of six age ranges. Test-retest reliabilities over a 2-week interval determined from a sample of 28 White and 2 Black examinees ranged from .67 on the Story Sequence to .88 on the Mathematical Problems. Because of their length, the reliabilities of the composites were correspondingly higher.

The discussion of the tests' validities is a more complex, and less clear-cut, issue. The authors present lengthy rationales for the inclusion of each of the subtests (usually based on historical and contemporary precedent and logical argument) under the guise of content validity. There is little or no justification for the actual content of the tests themselves. This is the weakest aspect of the battery. The Story Sequences, for example, contain pictures involving taking out garbage (where one of the frames includes what appears to be a garage full of tied plastic garbage bags), television repair, an excursion to a laundromat, and a visit by a male to a barbershop. The pictures contain simple line drawings with minimal detail. The sequences do not appear to be organized in any logical cause-and-effect pattern but instead in a pattern that might be clear only to people who have actually had the experiences depicted.

Other content issues may be more serious. "Mathematical Problems," for instance, includes knowledge of algebra, number series (same as in Quantitative Relations), recollection of the Pythagorean Theorem, and knowledge of Roman numerals. "Basic Information" ranges from "What dairy product would you buy in a grocery store?" and "What are Zeus, Apollo, and Mercury?" to "'La Cucaracha' was the marching song of what famous Mexican revolutionary?" This latter item may be an attempt at multiculturalism, but, if so, it would certainly be clearer to a bilingual person if it were rephrased. To the authors' credit, in the numerical sequences where more than one answer is possible, all are given (with the exception of one the reviewer found). Most of the other tests are content free. This reviewer is not arguing with the concept of "basic information" but with the idea that anyone has yet determined what basic *means* within our complex culture.

Also under the rubric of content validity the authors discuss item analysis, including the typical true score theory, item difficulties, and discrimination indices. This reviewer does not want to debate this approach, but does want to point out several weaknesses in the data. First, they use Anastasi's criteria for acceptable (statistically significant point biserial correlations of .2 or .3 for discrimination coefficients and, for item difficulties, percentages correct ranging from 15 to 85 and centering on 50). Although all of their point biserial correlations exceed .2, none of them exceeds .71, and many are in the .30s and .40s. They describe the coefficients as meeting the criterion, which they do, but the examiner who avoids the actual data may be using a series which does not meet his or her own criteria. The item difficulties range from the .30s to the .90s (with 12 of them exceeding 1.00!).

To establish criterion-related validity, two studies were done, resulting in correlations ranging from nonsignificant to .92 corrected for attenuation with subscales of the Scholastic Abilities Test for Adults (SATA), the Wechsler Adult Intelligence Scale—Revised (WAIS-R), and the Woodcock-Johnson Psycho-Educational Battery (WJ-R).

The authors' arguments for construct validity are tenuous. First, they refer to the same item discriminations used for defending content validity when they discuss construct validity. Although information on item discriminations could be useful in both contexts, within the same test such discussion blurs the distinction between the two test criteria. Such a blur may be appropriate if one assumes that construct validity subsumes all other types, but should be explained by the authors.

In addition, the authors report a confusing study of the factor structure. A first analysis revealed one factor with eigenvalue greater than one (no value recorded) and an unexplained subsequent analysis using Promax rotation of four factors. The authors recommend a one factor interpretation, quite inconsistent with the profusion of subtests described elsewhere in the manual.

The authors state that the "DTLA-A was built to minimize cultural and social bias" (p. 80), but that the battery does have "a decided bias regarding the English language" (p. 80). The authors could certainly have reduced this bias by simplifying some of the instructions (eliminating the words "cue" and "quantitative problems," for instance), which tend to seem stilted. However, reducing language bias in a vocabulary test seems paradoxical even if the inclusion of such a test is not.

The test manual is quite long with some organizational problems. The authors present a complex and internally inconsistent style, at one point discussing a Promax rotation and at another giving detailed instructions on how to calculate an examinee's exact (to the day) age. Their inconsistency also appears in the theoretical rationale for the tests and the wide variety of content included. For example, sometimes an aptitude is a "capacity" as in musical aptitude. In other contexts aptitude seems to mean intelligence and/or achievement (as in "many people consider a good vocabulary to be one of the many aptitudes necessary for success in life in general,") (p. 3). One gets the impression the authors have adopted Anastasi's term "developed ability" both to avoid any genetic-environmental debate and to allow a wide variety of content into their battery. They also show inconsistency in their use of "prorated" composite quotients (if a subtest is missing, calculate the quotient anyway but don't interpret it clinically).

In conclusion, the DTLA-A appears to rely greatly on its association with the DTLA which has credibility because of its longevity. The authors have done a massive job in organizing materials and research. The manual deserves study by anyone hoping to use the tests for clinical or research purposes. At this writing, it is recommended the tests be used only as the authors recommended in their discussion of discrepancy scores or in much needed validation studies. Readers requiring a strong measure of intelligence are urged to consider the Wechsler Intelligence Scale for Children, Third Edition (WISC-III; 412). Questions concerning the construct validity will have to be answered with further analyses such as structural equation modeling and/or some variation of hierarchical factor analysis, a methodology which would have been consistent with the authors' theoretical discussion.

Review of the Detroit Tests of Learning Aptitude—Adult by CYNTHIA ANN DRUVA-ROUSH, Assistant Director, Evaluation and Examination Service, The University of Iowa, Iowa City, IA:

The Detroit Tests of Learning Aptitude—Adult (DTLA-A) is a series of 12 subtests designed to assess the mental abilities of individuals 16 years of age and over. Eight composite scores are provided.

A number of theoretically based indices are reported as well: (*a*) Cattell and Horn's Model of Fluid and Crystallized Intelligence, (*b*) Jensen's Model composed of the Associative Level and Cognitive Level of processing, (*c*) Das's Model of Simultaneous and Successive Processing, and (*d*) Wechsler's Model defining a Verbal Scale and a Performance Scale.

The stated purpose of the DTLA-A is to: (*a*) determine strengths and weakness among developed mental abilities, (*b*) "identify older adolescents and adults who are significantly below their peers in important abilities," (*c*) "make predictions about future performance," and (*d*) "serve as a measurement device in research studies investigating aptitude, intelligence, and cognitive behavior" (p. 14).

The 12 DTLA-A subtests are administered on an individual basis within a $1^1/_2$- to $2^1/_2$-hour testing period. The manual provides explicit standardized administration procedures. Items within a subtest are to be presented until the individual fails a predetermined number of consecutive items. Detailed scoring procedures are provided complete with well-developed examples. Raw scores for each test are converted to standard scores which are then converted into several composite quotients. An interpretation is provided for each subtest and composite. Subtests are grouped into four contrasting "intra-ability" (p. 44) quotients (e.g., verbal and nonverbal, attention-enhanced and attention-reduced). A discrepancy analysis is proposed to examine whether pairs of contrasting test scores are statistically different, indicating to an educational psychologist the need to examine a possible source for the discrepancy in an individual's scores. Sufficient caution in interpreting and presenting test results is provided.

The battery of tests was normed using a group of 1,254 persons residing in 31 states. The sampling procedures involved a two-stage sampling scheme. A random sample of test administrators was chosen who then chose a purposive, nonrandom sample of 10 to 30 individuals whose demographic makeup matched that of their community. Raw score means and standard deviations were developed at 1-year intervals from ages 16 to 29, and at decade intervals thereafter. Both standard scores and percentiles were developed. Reliability was examined by sampling 500 protocols from the normative sample. The subtest coefficient alphas across the various ages range from .66 to .97. All but one of the composite coefficient alphas is above .90. Test-retest reliability was measured by administering the test to 30 individuals and then administering it again after 2 weeks. (It was assumed the same form was used as no mention is made of multiple forms.) The test-retest reliability coefficients range from .67 (Story Sequences) to .88 for the subtests and .72 to .95 for the composites. (Tables 6.2 and 6.3 in the manual are reversed in order.)

Evidence for content validity is established essentially through comparison of each subtest's content in comparison to a listing of behaviors usually measured by tests of aptitude and intelligence. No detailed table of specifications for the various aspects of intelligence is ever provided. Only a comparison of their content with other measures of intelligence is made. In the comparison with Salvia and Ysseldyke's classification system (1981), the higher processing of generalization and induction are missing. A detailed discussion of the rationale for the items and the format for each subscale is provided.

In the construction of the subtests, the pool of items was first administered to 100 people. A point biserial correlation discrimination index of .3 was arbitrarily selected to serve as the minimum level of acceptability for items to be retained on the experimental version of the subtest. Items distributed between 15% and 85% in difficulty were considered acceptable. Based upon the results of the administration of the first experimental version, a second experimental version was created and administered to 120 individuals. Items meeting the above criteria were used in the final version of the DTLA-A. Based upon samples of 50 from each group in the normative sample, median discrimination indices range from .30 to .71 and item difficulties from .24 to .95. (Table 7.4 in the manual has DR and FA subtest difficulty values greater than 1.00.)

Evidence for criterion validity was established by correlating results of the DTLA-A with the Wechsler Adult Intelligence Scale—Revised (WAIS-R) and Part 1 of the revised Woodcock-Johnson Psycho-Educational Battery (WJ-R) for 28 individuals. A second group of 40 individuals was administered the DTLA-A, the Scholastic Abilities Test for Adults (SATA), and the vocabulary and picture completion portion of the WAIS-R. A median correlation of .52 is reported. More helpful than a table of these correlations between the DTLA-A and other intelligence tests would have been a breakdown into a multitrait-multimethod matrix (Campbell & Fiske, 1959). A discussion as to how the various subscales related to other subscales assessing the same construct on other tests would seem essential. The authors of the battery fail to state or show why the DTLA-A is a better measure of intelligent behavior than other batteries (e.g., WAIS).

Evidence for construct validity was provided through examination of several research questions that pertain to the constructs presumed to be measured by the test battery. A weak argument is provided that because the intelligence scales fail to increase significantly with age, there is age differentiation. In their discussion of interrelationships among DTLA-A values, only 140 individuals from the normative sample were chosen. No explanation is given for not studying the entire normative group. Some discussion is provided as to the range of correlation values of subscales with the overall index (.40–.73). Again, a better discussion would have used a multitrait-multimethod matrix to lend evidence for convergent and divergent validity. A median correlation of.49 (rather low) was reported for a sample of 28 individuals between the DTLA-A and various measures of the Woodcock Johnson Achievement Test (Part 2 of the WJPB), the Nelson-Denny Reading Test, the Diagnostic Spelling Potential Test, the Wide Range Achievement Test—Revised (WRAT-R), and the SATA Achievement Test. Why these specific achievement tests are chosen is not explained. Why not American College Testing Assessment scores? A principal components factor analysis was performed. A single factor was found. A second analysis using Promax rotation was performed. Four factors emerged with eigenvalues greater than one. The interpretation of the four factors defined by the second analysis is not adequate. The manual simply summarizes that the test has a general factor only.

REVIEWER'S REFERENCES

Campbell, D. T., & Fiske, D. W. (1959). Convergent and discriminant validation by the multitrait-multimethod matrix. *Psychological Bulletin*, *56*, 81-105.

Salvia, J., & Ysseldyke, J. E. (1991). *Assessment* (5th ed.). Boston: Houghton Mifflin.

[106]

Detroit Tests of Learning Aptitude—Primary, Second Edition.

Purpose: Constructed to identify strengths and weaknesses in mental abilities and to identify "children who are markedly deficient in general mental ability."

Population: Ages 3–9.

Publication Dates: 1986–91.

Acronym: DTLA-P:2.

Scores, 7: Linguistic (Verbal, Nonverbal), Attentional (Enhanced, Reduced), Motoric (Enhanced, Reduced), General Mental Ability.

Administration: Individual.

Price Data, 1994: $119 per complete kit including picture book, 25 response forms, 25 profile/examiner record forms, and manual ('91, 106 pages); $39 per picture

book; $23 per 25 response forms; $29 per 25 profile/examiner record forms; $32 per manual; $98 per microcomputer scoring and report system software (Apple or IBM).
Time: (15–45) minutes.
Comments: Downward extension of the Detroit Tests of Learning Aptitude (Second Edition) (10:85) and (Third Edition (107).
Authors: Donald D. Hammill and Bryan R. Bryant.
Publisher: PRO-ED, Inc.
Cross References: For reviews of an earlier edition by Cathy F. Telzrow and Stanley F. Vasa, see 10:84 (1 reference).

TEST REFERENCES

1. Minshew, N. J., Goldstein, G., Taylor, H. G., & Siegel, D. J. (1994). Academic achievement in high functioning autistic individuals. *Journal of Clinical and Experimental Neuropsychology, 16,* 261-270.

Review of the Detroit Tests of Learning Aptitude—Primary, Second Edition by TERRY A. ACKERMAN, Associate Professor of Educational Psychology, University of Illinois, Champaign, IL:

The Detroit Tests of Learning Aptitude—Primary, Second Edition (DTLA-P:2) is a battery of tests of general mental ability for children between the ages of 3 and 9 years. It is designed to determine strengths and weaknesses among developed mental abilities, identify children who are below their peers in important abilities, predict future performance, and serve as a research instrument. The test, which is individually administered, consists of 100 dichotomously scored items that are classified into 16 different tasks: the ability to (*a*) articulate speech sounds, (*b*) match semantic concepts, (*c*) reproduce designs, (*d*) repeat digits, (*e*) draw a figure of a person, (*f*) sequence letters, (*g*) follow directions that involve manual dexterity, (*h*) sequence pictured objects, (*i*) follow oral directions, (*j*) identify fragmented pictures, (*k*) repeat sentences, (*l*) solve visual abstract reasoning problems, (*m*) call upon visual discrimination skills, (*n*) produce antonyms, (*o*) repeat a series of unrelated words, and (*p*) identify pictured objects. These skills are subdivided into three cognitive domains, each composed of two subtests: a Linguistic domain (with Verbal and Nonverbal subtests), an Attention domain (with Attention-Enhanced and Attention-Reduced subtests), and a Motoric domain (with Motor-Enhanced and Motor-Reduced subtests). Each item contributes to one subtest score in each domain as well as the total score, called the General Mental Ability (GMA) score.

Administration time ranges from 15 to 45 minutes. Each examinee begins the test at an entry point corresponding to his or her chronological age (e.g., a 3-year-old would begin the test at Item 1; 4-year-olds begin at Item 25). Testing continues until eight consecutive items are missed. Based upon the examinee's correct responses, examiners attempt to establish basal and ceiling points. All items below the basal point, although they may not all have been administered, are scored as correct. Likewise, all items above the ceiling point are scored as incorrect. It could be a problem to locate either the basal or ceiling point precisely for young examinees with short attention spans.

The authors recommend examiners have formal training in assessment. Because of the many different types of tasks, it is imperative that examiners acquaint themselves thoroughly with the administration directions. During testing the examiner fills in a formatted score sheet and is encouraged to write any anecdotal records that may aid score interpretation. For young children, examinee-examiner interaction could have a large impact on the results.

A software scoring package, DTLA-P:2 Software Scoring and Reporting, has been developed for both Apple and IBM-compatible computers. The user inputs demographic information about the examinee as well as item (or subtest) raw scores. The program then produces the appropriate percentile, standardized, and age equivalent scores. Standard scores use the same scale as the Wechsler IQ quotients: mean and standard deviation of 100 and 15, respectively. Two report forms are available, a short form and a long form. The long form is more complete, providing a detailed description of the various subtests as well as interpretation of examinee scores.

The DTLA-P:2 was normed on 2,095 students from 36 states. The stratified sample selection procedures were designed to parallel the U.S. Bureau of the Census' 1985 report according to race, ethnicity, gender, type of residence, and geographic location. It appears the test creators did a very thorough job in identifying a representative national norm population. Tables containing the percentages of the various subgroups are included in the manual.

Two types of reliability coefficients are reported: internal consistency and stability. In the first type, coefficient alpha values are presented for each subtest and the GMA for each age level. The most consistent subtest is the Verbal subtest, with coefficients ranging from .87 (age 3) to .94 (age 8). The least consistent subtest was the Motor-Enhanced subtest, with coefficients ranging from .82 (age 3) to .91 (age 8). Stability coefficients for a one-week period between administrations were all quite high, ranging from .89 (Attention-Enhanced subtest) to .95 (Motor-Enhanced and Motor-Reduced subtests). Standard errors of measurement are also listed for each subtest and the GMA at each age level.

As evidence of content validity, the authors display an interesting table of specifications in which the 16 item types are classified according to Salvia and Ysseldyke's (1988) classification scheme. The authors also classify the items according to several different theories of intellect, including those proposed by Cattell (1963) and Wechsler (1974). For inclusion on the final form, items had to fall within a p-value range of .15 to .85 and have point biserial coefficients greater than .3. Tables showing median point biserial and median item difficulty values are given for each subtest by age group.

The authors cite several studies as evidence of criterion-related validity. Using different groups of examinees, researchers gathered correlational evidence demonstrating the relationship between the DTLA-P:2 and other intelligence tests, including the Detroit Test of Learning Aptitude (DTLA-2), the Wechsler Intelligence Scale for Children—Revised (WISC-R), the Peabody Picture Inventory Test—Revised (PPVT-R), the Woodcock-Johnson Psycho-Educational Battery (WJPB), the Scholastic Aptitude Scale (SAS), and the Kaufman Assessment Battery for Children (K-ABC) for each subtest and the GMA. The coefficients are very acceptable, demonstrating perhaps the highest degree of linear relationship with the WJPB (coefficients range from .79 to .87) and the DTLA-2 (coefficients range from .52 to .93) and the lowest with the SAS (coefficients range from <.31 to .65).

Evidence of construct validity is presented using several approaches. According to the first, age differentiation, scores increase with age. A second approach was to examine the intersubtest correlations with age partialled out. The reported correlations range from .80 to .93, suggesting that all subtests, no matter how different the task, involve measuring the g-factor. Because each item contributes to three different subtest scores, the values of the coefficients should be expected to be high. A third approach was to correlate DTLA-P:2 results with measures of school achievement. Correlational evidence is provided between the DTLA-P:2 and several standardized achievement tests, including the SRA achievement series (SRA), the California Achievement Tests (CAT), the Metropolitan Readiness Tests (MRT), and the Iowa Test of Basic Skills (ITBS). The coefficients, for the most part, lend strong support that the skills being assessed by the DTLA-P:2 are related to the skills being measured by the widely used school achievement tests. Another piece of construct validity evidence shows that the DTLA-P:2 provides results similar to those of the WISC-R, (i.e., it can distinguish between examinees with normal IQs and examinees classified as below average in mental ability).

Evidence that the DTLA-P:2 does not contain any items that are gender or ethnically biased is also reported using delta plots. Although the authors' attempts to test for bias should be lauded, their methodology is somewhat outdated. The plot for the white-nonwhite values suggests a rather curious result: The nonwhite delta values are consistently greater than their white counterparts. This is not commented on, nor is it immediately evident because the scales of the axes for the graph are not the same. Because the delta method takes into account only difficulty differences and does not consider discrimination differences, a better approach to examine item bias is to use either the Mantel-Haenszel procedure (Holland & Thayer, 1988) or the Simultaneous Item Bias (SIB) procedure (Shealy & Stout, 1993).

In summary, I think the authors of the DTLA-P:2 did a very complete job. The norming procedures are well explained, and the reliability and validity evidence is quite thorough. It would be helpful to see a confirmatory factor analysis result demonstrating the subtests' scores are indeed measuring unique skills or traits. Because of the high cost of testing, it is necessary for test authors to furnish ample evidence of the quality of their tests so that practitioners can find the test that best matches their needs. The DTLA-P:2 authors have done this.

REVIEWER'S REFERENCES

Cattell, R. B. (1963). Theory of fluid and crystallized intelligence. *Journal of Educational Psychology, 54*, 1-22.

Wechsler, D. (1974). Wechsler Intelligence Scale for Children—Revised. San Antonio, TX: Psychological Corp.

Holland, P. W., & Thayer, D. T. (1988). Differential item performance and the Mantel-Haenszel procedure. In H. Wainer & H. I. Braun (Eds.), *Test Validity* (pp. 129-145). Hillsdale, NJ: Erlbaum.

Salvia, J., & Ysseldyke, J. E. (1988). *Assessment in special and remedial education* (4th ed.). Boston: Houghton Mifflin Co.

Shealy, R., & Stout, W. (1993). An item response theory model for test bias. In H. Wainer & P. Holland (Eds.), *Differential item functioning, theory and practice*. Hillsdale, NJ: Erlbaum.

Review of the Detroit Tests of Learning Aptitude—Primary, Second Edition by ROBERT T. WILLIAMS, Professor and Director, Student Literacy Corps, Colorado State University, Fort Collins, CO:

The Detroit Tests of Learning Aptitude—Primary, Second Edition (DTLA-P:2) follows in the tradition of the Detroit Tests of Learning Aptitude (DTLA) developed by Baker and Leland (1935) and the Detroit Tests of Learning Aptitude—Second Edition (DTLA-2) revised by Hammill (1985). The DTLA-P:2 is a revision of the Detroit Tests of Learning Aptitude—Primary (DTLA-P; Hammill & Bryan, 1986) and is designed for children ages 3 through 9 years. It is presented as a test that measures a variety of developmental abilities. The manual authors present different uses for the test. On page 5, the authors say: "Depending on the orientation or needs of the test user, DTLA-P:2 results can be used to estimate general cognitive functioning (intelligence), predict future success (aptitude), or show mastery of particular content and skills (achievement)." Later, on page 9, the authors say "The present version of the DTLA-P [the DTLA-P:2] has four principal uses: (a) to determine strengths and weaknesses among developed mental abilities, (b) to identify children who are significantly below their peers in important abilities, (c) to make predictions about future performance, and (d) to serve as a measurement device in research studies investigating aptitude, intelligence, and cognitive behavior." Although these two sets of uses are not mutually exclusive, they confuse this reviewer and distract from an otherwise well-developed, readable test and manual.

The DTLA-P:2 Examiner's Manual, Profile/Examiner Response Form, Examinee Response Form, and Picture Book are each well developed and readable. The Examiner's Manual is well organized and presented. It offers an overview of mental ability testing that is exemplary in its clarity. It is well written in style and language readable by educators and diagnosticians with a basic understanding of evaluation and measurement.

The DTLA-P:2 contains 100 items (a reduction of 30 items from the previous edition) arranged in increasing difficulty that the authors maintain sample 15 different behaviors they describe in the manual. These 100 items are grouped to yield a total score (*g*) and six subtest scores in three domains: Verbal and Nonverbal subtests within the Linguistic Domain, Attention-Enhanced and Attention-Reduced subtests within the Attentional Domain, and Motor-Enhanced and Motor-Reduced subtests within the Motoric Domain.

Directions for administering and scoring each of the 100 items are in both the Examiner's Manual and the Profile/Examiner Record Form. The directions are clear and easy to follow. Administration of the tests requires facility and attention to whether an item is associated with the Picture Book, the Response Form, on only the Profile/Examiner Record Form. The 100 items are arranged in order of difficulty, not by item or task type. This arrangement causes a task shift from item to item. This arrangement was of concern of Telzrow (1989) in her review of the DTLA-P. This reviewer does not share her concern. The test is untimed, with the guideline that it would take 15 to 45 minutes to administer, depending upon the child's age and ability. The test uses recommended age entry points and establishes basal and ceiling levels. These features are positive aspects of wide range testing. The shift in task type from item to item may serve to maintain examinee attention across a span of items varying in task type and difficulty.

Scores (raw scores, standard scores [mean = 100, *SD* = 15], percentiles, and age equivalents are available for a General Mental Ability (*g* or total score) and the six subtests, but not for the three domains. The manual contains a detailed discussion of what the subtests mean. In her review of the DTLA-P, Telzrow (1989) cited some inadequate directions for administration and scoring directions: For digit sequences the directions did not state whether one drops the voice or not at the end of the sequence; in the current DTLA-P:2 this is still not stated. Also, Telzrow (1989) found scoring for Design Reproduction items insufficient; the current DTLA-P:2 guidelines for scoring Design Reproduction give one quality figure and three examples of scored reproductions; there are still no descriptive criteria. There are good descriptive criteria in the DTLA-2 (Hammill, 1985); the DTLA-P:2 should offer such guidelines.

The technical characteristics of the test are completely and clearly discussed in the manual. The sampling procedure of this test is a textbook case in stratified, proportional sampling. The randomness of the sample is not discussed. The total sample of 2,095 subjects from 36 states is an excellent representation of the population characteristics based upon the 1990 U.S. Census data. The complete representation of stratification by age and geographic region, gender, race, and residence allows for relatively small numbers at each age level (low of 122 at age 3; high of 456 at age 6).

Reliability, standard error of measurement, and validity are clearly discussed and presented in readable tables. The authors establish the case for "Results based on tests having reliabilities of less than .80 should not be used" (manual, p. 32). The test-retest and stability reliability coefficients for DTLA-P:2 scores all approach or exceed .80; Attention Enhanced has a test-retest reliability of.79; all others exceed .80. The discussion and explanation with examples, of the standard error of measurement (*SEM*) is outstanding. *SEM* for the General Mental Ability score is between 3 and 5 points, depending on the age level, and the *SEM* for the subtest scores ranges from 4 to 7. These are relatively small. Content validity is well discussed and is adequate. Criterion related validity is not as adequate; it is based upon studies of exceptional populations, geographically intact populations, and/or small sample size.

Construct validity is good. There is a careful discussion and explanation. Of special note is the authors' discussion of "Controlling for Bias" (p. 48). Although this element is not often addressed by test developers, it should be of growing concern to test users. The authors note the DTLA-P:2 "has a decided bias regarding the English language" (manual, p. 48). The authors used delta scores (with citations of Jensen, 1980, and Slosson, Nicholson, & Hibpshman, 1990) to empirically investigate the DTLA-P:2 for bias. Two studies were conducted; the first checked for gender bias, the second for race bias. In the first study, delta values for males and females were found to have a correlation of .99; there is little to no gender bias. In the second study, delta values for nonwhites and whites were found to have a correlation of .98; there is no apparent race bias.

The Examiner's Manual contains an excellent chapter on "Interpreting the Results of the DTLA-

P:2" that is both a guide for interpreting this test and a set of principles for interpreting any test. The chapter includes a detailed explanation of the Profile/Examiner Record Form, an explanation of the use of the optional DTLA-P:2 Software Scoring and Reporting System (a copy of which was not available to this reviewer; see Bryant, 1991), and a section of reporting and interpreting the test scores (raw scores, percentiles, standard scores, and age equivalents). Of special note are the understandable sections "What do the Test Scores Measure" including an explanation of the General Mental Abilities Quotient and the Domain Quotients, the significance of differences between and among scores, "Caution in Interpreting Test Results," and "Sharing the Test Results."

In summary, the DTLA-P:2 carries on the Detroit Tests of Learning Aptitude tradition of careful, clearly articulated, well-written manual and test materials. The manual is a textbook in the development, scoring, use, and interpretation of tests. Standardization sample, test-retest and stability reliability, standard error of measurement, and content and construct validity are good. The criterion validity is weak. This reviewer finds the test useful for determining the strengths and weaknesses among mental abilities (intelligence) and identifying children who are significantly below their age peers in important abilities. This reviewer questions the usefulness of this test alone in making predictions about future performance (aptitude) and in showing mastery of a particular content and skills (achievement). Used conscientiously with other measures and observations, the DTLA-P:2 could be a valuable tool for the perceptive diagnostician.

REVIEWER'S REFERENCES

Baker, H. J., & Leland, B. (1935). Detroit Tests of Learning Aptitude. Austin, TX: PRO-ED.

Jensen, A. R. (1980). *Bias in mental testing*. New York: Free Press.

Hammill, D. D. (1985). Detroit Tests of Learning Aptitude—Second Edition. Austin, TX: PRO-ED.

Hammill, D. D., & Bryant, B. R. (1986). Detroit Tests of Learning Aptitude—Primary. Austin, TX: PRO-ED.

Telzrow, C. F. (1989). [Review of the Detroit Tests of Learning Aptitude—Primary.] In J. J. Kramer, & J. C. Conoley (Eds.), *The tenth mental measurements yearbook* (pp. 231-233). Lincoln, NE: Buros Institute of Mental Measurements.

Slosson, R. L., Nicholson, C. L., & Hibpshman, T. H. (1990). Slosson Intelligence Test for Children and Adults. East Aurora, NY: Slosson.

Bryant, B. R. (1991). DTLA-P:2 Software Scoring and Report System. Austin, TX: PRO-ED.

[107]

Detroit Tests of Learning Aptitude, Third Edition.

Purpose: Designed to measure "general intelligence and discrete ability areas."
Population: Ages 6-0 to 17-11.
Publication Dates: 1935–91.
Acronym: DTLA-3.
Scores: 11 subtest scores: Word Opposites, Design Sequences, Sentence Imitation, Reversed Letters, Story Construction, Design Reproduction, Basic Information, Symbolic Relations, Word Sequences, Story Sequences, Picture Fragments; and 16 composite scores: General Mental Ability Composite, Optimal Level Composite, Domain Composites (Verbal, Nonverbal, Attention-Enhanced, Attention-Reduced, Motor-Enhanced, Motor-Reduced), Theoretical Composites (Fluid Intelligence, Crystallized Intelligence, Associative Level, Cognitive Level, Simultaneous Processing, Successive Processing, Verbal Scale, Performance Scale).
Administration: Individual.
Price Data, 1994: $198 per complete kit; $34 per 25 examiner record booklets; $18 per 25 response forms; $18 per 25 Profile/Summary forms; $44 per Picture Book 1 (for Design Sequences, Story Construction, Design Reproduction, Symbolic Relations); $16 per Picture Book 2 (for Story Sequences); $14 per Picture Fragments Flipbook; $32 per examiner's manual ('91, 151 pages); $98 per software scoring and report system (specify Apple or IBM).
Time: (50–120) minutes.
Author: Donald D. Hammill.
Publisher: PRO-ED, Inc.
Cross References: See T4:752 (7 references); for reviews by Arthur B. Silverstein and Joan Silverstein of an earlier edition, see 10:85 (15 references); see also 9:320 (11 references) and T3:691 (20 references); for a review by Arthur B. Silverstein of an earlier edition, see 8:213 (14 references); see also T2:493 (3 references) and 7:406 (10 references); for a review by F. L. Wells, see 3:275 (1 reference); for reviews by Anne Anastasi and Henry Feinburg and an excerpted review by D. A. Worcester (with S. M. Corey), see 1:1058.

TEST REFERENCES

1. Kraker, M. J. (1993). Learning to write: Children's use of notation. *Reading Research and Instruction*, *32*(2), 55-75.

2. Zentall, S. S., Harper, G. W., & Stormont-Spurgin, M. (1993). Children with hyperactivity and their organizational abilities. *Journal of Educational Research*, *87*, 112-118.

3. Gaulin, C. A., & Campbell, T. F. (1994). Procedure for assessing verbal working memory in normal school-age children: Some preliminary data. *Perceptual and Motor Skills*, *79*, 55-64.

4. Goldstein, G., Minshew, N. J., & Siegel, D. J. (1994). Age differences in academic achievement in high-functioning autistic individuals. *Journal of Clinical and Experimental Neuropsychology*, *16*, 671-680.

Review of the Detroit Tests of Learning Aptitude, Third Edition by WILLIAM A. MEHRENS, Professor of Educational Measurement, Michigan State University, East Lansing, MI:

The Detroit Tests of Learning Aptitude was first published in 1935, revised in 1985, and again in 1991. This edition (the DTLA-3) has 11 subtests and 16 composites. Six of the current subtests are the same as ones in the 1985 edition.

Reviews of the previous edition raised several critical points. They raised questions about the overall length of time the test took, the lack of clear statements in the manual about the qualifications of the test administrators, and minimal stability data. Some of the concerns have been addressed in the current revision, but those mentioned in the previous sentence should have been addressed more thoroughly. Additional concerns I would raise relate to the theory and the construct validity for the theory (is the test measuring *g*, specific aptitudes, or both), the norms, the scaling of the composites, and some of the suggested interpretations.

The testing time is estimated to vary from 50 minutes to 2 hours, sometimes necessitating administration over several sessions. This seems like a practical limitation of this test compared to other individually administered tests of aptitude (intelligence).

The manual author states that examiners "should have some formal training in assessment," that "supervised practice . . . is also desirable," and that the examiner should "practice administering the test no fewer than three times" (p. 15). These statements are not forceful enough. This test is at least as hard to administer as other individual tests. Some subtests have entry points, basals and ceilings that vary across the different subtests. Some of the subtests require professional judgment in scoring. There simply should be stronger statements in the manual regarding administrator qualifications.

The internal consistency reliabilities of the subtests and composites are sufficiently high (averaging across ages the subtest reliabilities range from .77 to .94 and the composite reliabilities range from .89 to .96). However, the data on stability are quite sparse. The data come from 34 children ages 6 through 16 who were tested twice within a 2-week period. The scores were converted to standard scores before correlating the two sets of scores. Test-retest reliabilities ranged from .75 to .96 for the subtests and from .81 to .96 for the composites. Although the numbers themselves are high enough, the limited data and the short time interval leave questions about the stability reliability.

The manual author discusses various theoretical contributions to mental ability testing. In one summary statement the author, like Wechsler, notes the pervasive influence of general intelligence; but also recognizes that "the measurement of specific abilities . . . is useful in *generating reliable measures of g* [italics added]" (p. 8). At another place in the manual the author states that "all of the composite scores estimate general mental ability" (p. 11). Which of the 16 composites is the best estimate, and of what use are the others if they are inferior estimates of the same general mental ability? This problem is noted, but in a confusing manner. The author asserts the General Mental Ability Composite (composed of the sum of the standard scores of all 11 subtests) is for most people "probably the best estimate of g" (p. 11), that the Optimal Level Composite (composed of the four highest subtest standard scores) is "the best estimate of a person's overall 'potential.' . . . 'potential' means the highest level of performance that an individual is capable of when the inhibiting influences of his or her deficits are disregarded" (p. 12). This statement regarding "potential" cannot be true because random errors of measurement go in both directions!

In discussing the differences between other components the author makes some incorrect statements. For example, in contrasting the Attention-Enhanced Quotient (AEQ) and the Attention-Reduced Quotient (ARQ) the author suggests that a superiority of ARQ over AEQ is seen more often than the reverse. How could this be if the two are normed on the same population and standard scores comprise the composites? Then it is argued that "where the purpose of testing is to estimate general ability, the larger quotient should be accepted" (p. 49). Again, how about positive error of measurement? The same types of statements are made in contrasting the Motor-Enhanced Quotient and the Motor-Reduced Quotient.

In the construct validity section it is suggested that because all the composites measure general mental ability they should intercorrelate (they do), and that because the components measure similar, yet discrete, traits a factor analysis should support the constructs. However, the factor analysis performed does *not* support the constructs. A principal components method produces only a single factor. A Promax rotation produced four factors, one of which was called "Residual (difficult to interpret)" (p. 85).

The norms for this third edition are based on a total of 2,587 examinees, but 1,532 of these students were tested in 1984 on the DTLA-2 and these students were used as part of the norm group for six of the subtests that had not changed in this revision. The remaining five subtests were normed on 1,055 individuals from 12 different age groups. The sample was quite representative of the demographic characteristics of the nation although the data for the five subtests with the reduced sample size are not described separately.

The composite quotients (scores with means of 100 and supposedly standard deviations of 15) are formed by adding the appropriate subtest standard scores and converting them to quotients. However, the manual author assumes the variances of all the composites with the same number of subtests are equal. This is not the case. The intercorrelations between subtests range from .01 to .76, so computing the variance of the composites in the traditional fashion would produce different variances and consequently different sums would correspond to different quotients. Although I have not computed the variances of the different sums to see if this makes a practical difference, the manual should contain information regarding these computations.

My major reservation about the composites is with respect to the suggested interpretation of the Optimal Level Composite (the sum of the four highest subtest scores). To convert this sum to a composite quotient and to convert this into a percentile presents very misleading information. An example in which an individual's 4 highest percentiles (out of 11) were 75, 75, 63, and 63 is contained in the manual. When the standard scores were converted to a composite quotient (110) and this, in turn, converted to a percentile, it was 75. To suggest that this quotient (or percentile) gives a *relative ranking* of the best estimate of the individual's potential strains credulity. If this sort of score is to be used at all, at the very least it should be normed based on the actual distribution of the sums of the four highest subtests for each individual in the sample.

In conclusion, the DTLA-3 is a partial revision of its predecessor. It takes more time to administer than many of its counterparts. The norming is minimal, there is insufficient data on stability-reliability, the factor analysis does not support construct validity, the assumption of equal variances in the formation of the composite quotients is wrong and may have some practical impact, and the interpretations of the composites (especially the Optimal Level Composite) are open to question.

Review of the Detroit Tests of Learning Aptitude, Third Edition by G. MICHAEL POTEAT, Associate Professor of Psychology, East Carolina University, Greenville, NC:

The Detroit Tests of Learning Aptitude, Third Edition (DTLA-3) is a revision of the second edition published in 1984 (DTLA-2). The DTLA-3 is, however, considerably different from the DTLA-2. The current edition includes 3 new subtests and 3 subtests included on the DTLA-2 have been dropped. A number of other revisions have been made, and the DTLA-3 should be regarded as essentially a new test. The DTLA-3 consists of a battery of 11 subtests designed to measure an individual's "developed abilities" in both the verbal and nonverbal domains. The 11 subtests are labeled: Word Opposites (WO), Design Sequences (DS), Sentence Imitation (SI), Reversed Letters (RL), Story Construction (SC), Design Reproduction (DR), Basic Information (BI), Symbolic Relations (SR), Word Sequences (WS), Story Sequences (SS), and Picture Fragments (PF). Basic Information, Story Sequences, and Picture Fragments are new subtests. The remaining subtests were included on the DTLA-2 but two (Reversed Letters and Design Sequences) have been substantially revised. Norms are provided for subjects from 6 to 17 years of age. The DTLA-3 is described as having four principal uses: (*a*) the identification of strengths and weaknesses in developed mental ability, (*b*) the identification of children who are functioning below their peers, (*c*) the prediction of future performance, and (*d*) the measurement of cognitive behavior in research.

In addition to subtests standard scores, a number of Domain Composite scores may be calculated. The most useful of these is the General Mental Ability Composite based on all 11 subtests and described as the best estimate of *g*. A second is the Optimal Level Composite based on the four subtests on which an individual obtains the highest standard scores. Three other domains are divided into divergent composites. These include a Linguistic Domain (a Verbal Composite and a Nonverbal Composite), an Attention Domain (an Attention-Enhanced Composite and an Attention-Reduced Composite), and a Motor Domain (a Motor-Enhanced Composite and a Motor-Reduced Composite).

The 11 subtests are used repeatedly for the different domains (e.g., Design Sequences is included as part of the Nonverbal Composite, the Attention-Enhanced Composite, and the Motor-Enhanced Composite). It is also possible to calculate composites based on the models developed by Cattell and Horn (fluid and crystallized abilities), Jensen (associative and cognitive abilities), Das (simultaneous and successive processing), and Wechsler (verbal and performance abilities). This last composite is redundant with the Linguistic Domain.

The DTLA-3 can be administered by psychologists, educators, speech pathologists, and other professionals with "formal training in assessment" (p. 15). Administration of the test is adequately covered in the examiner's manual. Basal and/or ceiling levels are obtained for seven of the subtests; all items on the remaining subtests are administered to all subjects. Overall, the administration and scoring procedures are straightforward if the guidelines provided in the manual are followed. Story Construction will require practice in scoring before an examiner will be competent. The use of a tape recorder is suggested for initial administration. Test instructions could be better organized and the use of three different record booklets (response, examiner record, and profile/summary) is awkward. Testing time is estimated to range from 50 minutes to 2 hours.

The DTLA-3 is described in the manual and protocol as being normed on a total of 2,587 subjects from 36 states. Nonetheless, 1,532 of these subjects were actually part of the DTLA-2 standardization sample collected in 1984. An additional 1,055 subjects were administered the DTLA-3 in 1989 and 1990. The 1984 data from the 6 subtests common to the two editions was combined with the data obtained using the DTLA-3. The specifics of how these two sets of data were combined to obtain the published norms are not provided. The demographic characteristics presented for the normative sample closely match those of the U.S. population, but the demographics of the 1,055 subjects administered the full battery of subtests are not provided separately. The norms yield standard scores (with a mean of 10 and a standard deviation of 3) and percentiles for each of the 11 subtests. Sums of the subtests' standard scores can then be converted to quotients (with a mean of 100 and standard deviation of 15) for the various domains. Percentile ranks and age equivalents are also furnished.

Two measures of reliability are reported. Coefficient alphas based on 600 subjects are reported for each of the subtests and composites. The alphas range from .77 to .94 for the 11 subtests, and from .89 to .96 for the composites. With the exception of Picture Fragments, all of the measures of internal consistency are very satisfactory (above *r* of .80). Test-retest stability, based on 34 subjects, was assessed across a 2-week period and all of the subtests and composites were relatively stable.

Content, criterion-related, and construct validity are all addressed in some detail. Approximately seven pages of the manual are devoted to the rationale for the content of the subtests. Item analysis was also used to eliminate "bad" items based on item discrimination and difficulty levels. Criterion-related validity evidence is presented in the form of correlations between the six DTLA-2 subtests retained on the DTLA-3 and the Wechsler Intelligence Scale for Children—Revised (WISC-R) and the Peabody Picture Vocabulary Test—Revised (PPVT-R). Correlations between the DTLA-3 and the Kaufman Assessment Battery for Children, Woodcock-Johnson Psycho-Educational Battery—Revised, and other measures of aptitude and achievement are also provided. Overall, the correlations are significant and suggest that the DTLA-3 is related to both intelligence (or general academic ability) and to academic achievement. Evidence for construct validity is demonstrated by age-related differences reflecting developmental changes in the underlying abilities being measured, and by the correlations with other tests designed to measure similar constructs. An unrotated factor analysis of the 11 subtests resulted in one general factor. A Promax rotation resulted in four factors labeled sequential memory for words (SI and WS), general visual intelligence (RL, DR, and SR), conceptual verbal ability (SC, BI, and PF), and a residual (difficult to interpret) factor.

The DTLA-3 can be recommended with some reservations. First, the demographics of the normative sample are not satisfactorily presented. Second, the published qualifications for examiners should be reconsidered. The difficulty of interpreting the DTLA-3 should limit its use to those individuals who have graduate training in psychological or educational assessment and a working knowledge of psychometrics. Third, the factor structure of the test does not support the routine use of any of the domain scores except for the General Mental Ability Composite. The psychometrically naive examiner may choose to calculate the various domain scores and use these for comparisons, which are simply statistically unwarranted. The DTLA-3 does offer the knowledgeable examiner some worthwhile scales for examining various abilities in learning disabled or neurological impaired subjects. These data should, however, be interpreted with caution. In summary, the DTLA-3 can be recommended as a serviceable assessment of general academic ability for use as an ancillary instrument, but it should not be regarded as a substitute for some of the better developed measures of intelligence (e.g., the WISC-III [412]). It also provides some potential valuable information about diverse abilities.

[108]

Developing Skills Checklist.

Purpose: Designed to measure skills and behaviors that children typically develop between prekindergarten and the end of kindergarten.
Population: Ages 4–6.8.
Publication Date: 1990.
Acronym: DSC.
Scores: 9 scales: Mathematical Concepts and Operations, Language, Memory, Auditory, Print Concepts, Motor, Visual, Writing and Drawing Concepts, Social-Emotional.
Administration: Individual.
Price Data, 1995: $239 per complete kit; $9.50 per 50 Writing and Drawing books; $26.50 per 50 Social-Emotional Observational Records; $26.50 per 50 score sheets (specify Hand-Recording or Machine-Scoring); $26.50 per 50 Parent Conference Forms; $2.50 per Class record book; $50 per set of 3 DSC item books; $6.25 per A Day at School; $13.50 per Administration and score interpretation manual; $9.75 per Concepts of Print and Writing administration manual; $9.75 per Social-Emotional Administration manual; $11 per norms book and technical manual (90 pages); $28.50 per training video; $20 per 5 replacement bunnies; $2.42 per student scoring service available from publisher; $124 per La Lista test kit.
Foreign Language Editions: Spanish adaptation entitled Lista de Destrezas en Desarrollo (La Lista) available as an all-in-Spanish supplement to the DSC. English DSC kit is also required in order to administer La Lista.
Time: (10–15) minutes per session (untimed).
Authors: CTB Macmillan/McGraw-Hill.
Publisher: CTB Macmillan/McGraw-Hill.

TEST REFERENCES

1. Orth, L. C., & Martin, R. P. (1994). Interactive effects of student temperament and instruction method on classroom behavior and achievement. *Journal of School Psychology, 32*, 149-166.
2. Whitehurst, G. J., Epstein, J. N., Angell, A. L., Payne, A. C., Crone, D. A., & Fisher, J. E. (1994). Outcomes of an emergent literacy intervention in head start. *Journal of Educational Psychology, 86*, 542-555.

Review of the Developing Skills Checklist by ELAINE CLARK, Associate Professor of Educational Psychology, University of Utah, Salt Lake City, UT:

The Developing Skills Checklist (DSC) is a component of the CTB Early Childhood System that was developed to assist in instructional planning for young children. Specifically, the DSC is an individually administered test of prereading and mathematic skill, fine and gross motor development, printing and writing, and social and emotional development. Like similar tests of early child learning, the DSC places more emphasis on direct testing; however, unlike many others, input from teachers and parents is sought by way of classroom observations and a home behavior checklist.

The DSC can be administered by teachers or trained aides in less than an hour. Stations can be set up to facilitate the testing of several children by more than one examiner, or a single examiner can administer the test to a particular child. The test can be scored by machine, or easily by hand. Norms for the Mathematical Concepts and Operations, Language, Memory, auditory function, printing and writing, and prereading scales can be found in the Norms Book and Technical Bulletin, but not easily. The test user must scan through numerous table listings, 61 to be exact, to locate this information. Once the norms are found, the test user will be pleased to find norms for both age (from 4 years, 0 months to 6 years, 8 months, reported at 2-month increments) and time of year (spring prekindergarten, fall kindergarten, winter kindergarten, and spring kindergarten). In addition to these normative data, descriptive statistics are given for each scale, and item difficulties, based on the national norming sample, are provided for each item. There are no normative data, however, for the Visual and Motor scales (not even descriptive statistics were provided for the Home Inventory, but then, other than a sample of the Home Inventory in the administration manual, the inventory was never found).

The procedures used for test development appear adequate, and include efforts to reduce content bias and sample widely across a full range of skills and behaviors that typically develop between prekindergarten and the end of the kindergarten year. The standardization and norming studies for the DSC took place during the fall of 1988 and the winter and spring of 1989. The normative sample is large (N = 3,985) and seems to be fairly representative of the U.S. population. The sample consists of almost equal numbers of males and females, and the expected proportion of whites and nonwhites. The DSC was stratified on the basis of school size, type of community, socioeconomic status, and geographic region. Percentages of the sample enrolled in special education programs are provided.

Reliability data, in the form of standard error of measurement and internal consistency (KR20), are adequate for most scales (i.e., KR20s ranged between .81 and .95 for all scales except Visual, the mean of which was .69). Unfortunately no information can be found on test-retest reliability. This is unfortunate because stability data may help with the interpretation of other test data (e.g., changes in interitem correlation coefficients across time, such as a .48 correlation between Language scale and prereading total during prekindergarten and .70 during fall kindergarten).

Given the fact the primary purpose of the DSC is instructional planning, not screening and diagnosis, information about content validity is critical. Adequate attention was paid to the content validity of the DSC, consequently, the tasks measure basic skills and behaviors that children in the early years of school typically display. Construct validity of the DSC was examined by comparing the DSC with the Early School Assessment (ESA), another component of the CTB Early Childhood System. Evidence of construct validity was weak. Considerable variance was unaccounted for, and correlations between the DSC and ESA scales showed little discrimination. Until further comparative data are available, it will remain unclear as to whether the lack of discriminant validity is a function of the test itself or lack of skill differentiation at this age. No data on predictive validity were included in the technical manual; however, the author indicated that predictive validity studies were planned for spring of 1990 and 1991. It will be interesting to see what the nature of the predictions are, and how well the DSC can predict future performance. There is some question, however, as to whether the DSC has an adequate ceiling for this. A rather sizeable group of the normative sample approximate the maximum score on a number of the DSC scales. A low ceiling also poses a threat to the test's use in instructional design. It is unclear what the curriculum would look like for children who get all the answers correct, which appears to be the case for most of the sample.

The testing materials are adequate, however, not terribly engaging for a young child. Most of the manipulative materials are red or blue, but a marked improvement over the colorless pictures in the testing booklets. The DSC Administration and Score Interpretation Manual provides sufficient information about standard test procedures and specific test instructions; however, this information is not easily found due to the manual's poor organization. The same can be said of the Norms Book and Technical Bulletin; that is, most of the expected technical information is present, but test users will be frustrated by trying to find it. Inconsistencies in the technical manual are also a problem (e.g., sample numbers for various demographic characteristics do not match). Two supplemental manuals are provided, one for administering the Social-Emotional Observational Record, and the other for the Print and Writing Concepts Scale. When these manuals are located, which by the way will not be easy because they are printed on the same paper as the test protocols and in the same blue and black ink, users will discover that much of the information is redundant. It would have been more convenient to include any information found exclusively in these manuals (e.g., directions for administering and scoring the Print and Writing Concept scale) in the DSC Administration and Score Interpretation Manual. Similarly, the hard-to-find Writing and Drawing Book, which is nothing more than two blank pieces of paper with space for examiner notes, could also have been included in the main recording protocol. The separate recording forms for the Social-Emotional observations and home report, however, are needed because teachers must retain the observation protocol for recording behaviors and parents are given the Home Inventory to complete.

In conclusion, the DSC shares many of the strengths and weaknesses of other developmental tests. On the positive side is its practical application. The DSC, though an individually administered test, can be given by a classroom teacher in a reasonable period of time. However, given the poor organization of the manuals and look-alike protocols (both annoying aspects of the test), administering and scoring the DSC may take more time initially than do other measures. Another plus for the DSC is the breadth of item content and inclusion of data from the child, teacher, and parents. One of the more negative aspects of the DSC, however, is its low ceiling. A test with broader difficulty range would be preferred, and is critical if used for any purpose other than instructional planning.

Review of the Developing Skills Checklist by CLAIRE B. ERNHART, Professor of Psychiatry, Case Western Reserve University and MetroHealth Medical Center, Cleveland, OH:

The Developing Skills Checklist (DSC) is primarily a criterion-referenced test designed to assist preschool and kindergarten teachers as they plan programs to aid individual children in meeting curriculum requirements. The areas covered are prereading and mathematics skills, social and emotional skills, fine and gross motor development, and print and writing concepts. The content of the items is closely related to the classroom activities through which children master kindergarten skills. The coverage is comprehensive. The activities and materials are attractive.

Although details of the standardization are not provided in the Preliminary Edition of the Norms Book and Technical Bulletin, the psychometric procedures that are described reflect knowledge of sampling methods and pretesting of items. A national probability sample of about 6,000 children of ages 48 to 80 months enrolled in prekindergarten and kindergarten provided the normative data. Data are classified by 3-month age groupings and by four time-of-year categories. Time-of-year refers to spring of a prekindergarten year and fall, winter, and spring of kindergarten. Criterion-related scoring methods are useful in evaluating the progress of a child through these stages of early education.

Examiner training is limited to administering the DSC to an adult before working with children; the DSC is designed to be used by teachers. The scoring materials, spread through several manuals, lack detailed instructions about further questioning or the scoring of unusual responses. Scoring and transferring scores to record sheets is tedious. Mastery of the scoring and coding system takes considerable effort. For example, both the manual and the Norms Book and Technical Bulletin refer to a scale called "Prereading Total." It is, however, only by referral to the score sheet that one learns this is the sum of the Language, Memory, Visual, Auditory, and Print Concepts scales. No guidance regarding the use of this norm-referenced score is given. This score is not part of the criterion-referenced cutoff procedures.

Time for administration is not given, but it would probably be about 1 hour per child. The manual authors suggest that four portions of the test might be given at round robin stations, with children rotating across stations with 10 minutes per station in an area such as a gym. Additional writing and drawing work may be administered to an entire class in one sitting. Information used for the Social-Emotional Record results from a limited number of behaviorally recorded observations at other times. The merits of the round robin method, as opposed to individual administration, were not assessed. It may present problems both in terms of developing rapport with some children and because of the distractions associated with the moving about of other children.

Very little information about the construction of the scales in terms of assignment of items to scales or scales to the Prereading Total, mentioned above, is given. The Mathematical Concepts and Operations scale is not included in the Prereading Total, yet this scale correlates more highly with the Prereading Total than does the Language scale, which is a component.

Also, little information is provided regarding the collection of reliability and validity data. KR20 coefficients for seven scales consisting of 16 to 116 items are reasonable (range from .64 to .95). Associated standard errors of measurement are also provided.

Because this is primarily a criterion-referenced test, content validity is emphasized. A reasonable level of construct validity is demonstrated through intercorrelations of the scales within the DSC. Correlations between DSC scales and similarly labeled scales of the Early School Assessment (standardized for the end of kindergarten or beginning of first grade) are not usually higher than the correlations for differently named scales. The Bulletin states that follow-through studies are being conducted to assess predictive validity.

Criterion-referenced proficiency criteria were established through an unspecified combination of judgment and statistical analysis. For each of 34 objectives in six scales, cut scores are provided to indicate whether or not performance is consistently observed and, hence, whether further instruction toward the objective is indicated or whether the child is ready to undertake more difficult activities in the domain. Scoring and evaluation of the Writing and Drawing Concepts and Social-Emotional scales require more interpretation in order to judge a child's progress.

Normative scores are provided in percentiles for age and time of year, stanines, and a normal curve equivalent. (The mean of the normal curve equivalent is apparently 50, the standard deviation is not given.) Even for the youngest children, most distributions are negatively skewed. The instrument is thus more suitable for describing the needs of children requiring further instruction than for identifying children who might benefit from an enrichment program.

The DSC is a professionally constructed instrument that should prove useful in assisting teachers to plan instruction for individual children. Users must be willing to cope, however, with the various manuals and to relate the scales to actual classroom activities. Although it is not a diagnostic test, norms provided by the DSC can be used to identify children to be referred for detailed assessments. The normative data might also be used in global manner for the evaluation of educational programs for this age range. It is not designed as a school readiness test.

[109]

Developmental Assessment of Life Experiences [1986 Edition].

Purpose: Developed to assess motor, intellectual, and adaptive skills of disabled persons.
Population: Individuals in developmental settings.
Publication Dates: 1974–86.
Acronym: D.A.L.E. System.
Administration: Individual.
Price Data, 1990: $10.50 per complete set; $3.50 per Level I inventory; $3.50 per Level II inventory; $5 per manual ('86, 54 pages).
Time: Administration time not reported.
Authors: Gertrude A. Barber, John P. Mannino, and Robert J. Will.
Publisher: The Barber Center Press, Inc.

a) LEVEL I.
Scores: 5 categories: Sensory Motor, Language, Self-Help, Cognition Skills, Socialization.

b) LEVEL II.
Scores: 5 categories: Personal Hygiene, Personal Management, Communications, Residence/Home Management, Community Access.

Cross References: For a review by Frank M. Gresham of an earlier edition, see 9:295.

Review of the Developmental Assessment of Life Experiences [1986 Edition] by MARTIN E. BLOCK, Assistant Professor of Education, and LINDA K. BUNKER, Professor and Associate Dean of Education, University of Virginia, Charlottesville, VA:

GENERAL INFORMATION. The Developmental Assessment of Life Experiences (D.A.L.E. System) is a criterion-referenced assessment tool designed to measure home living and community skills in individuals with disabilities, including persons with severe disabilities. Results from the D.A.L.E. System can be used to prioritize goals and objectives and to develop individualized programs for a wide age range, including school-age through adulthood, but it appears to be most applicable to older school-age students and adults. The system can be used in a variety of settings including public schools, small community residences, and larger residential facilities. With minimal training, the system can be administered by a variety of personnel working with individuals with disabilities. The authors suggest that examiners go through some formal training before attempting to administer the D.A.L.E. System although the system assesses functional living skills and no special equipment is needed other than the materials that are used by the individual client throughout the day.

CONTENT. The D.A.L.E. System includes two separate inventories that reflect general principles of normalization and cover a wide range of self-care and community living skills. Each inventory includes general priority areas, subscales, and individual items which are listed hierarchically. Level I is designed for individuals with severe disabilities and includes the following priority areas and subscales (examples of subscales noted in parentheses): Sensory Motor (e.g., gross-motor, fine-motor, perception), Language (e.g., receptive and expressive language), Self-Help (e.g., feeding, dressing, toileting), Cognition Skills (e.g., attention span, time and number concepts), and Socialization (e.g., social relations, self-concept). Many items on the Sensory Motor and Cognition subscales are not age-appropriate or functional for older students or adults. Level II is designed for "higher level" clients and includes the following subscales: Personal Hygiene (e.g., toileting, bathing, grooming), Personal Management (e.g., meal time, clothing care, personal scheduling), Communications (e.g., verbal skills, telephone skills, writing/reading skills), Residence/Home Maintenance (general housekeeping, outdoor maintenance), and Community Access (e.g., mobility, use of public transportation, shopping skills, money concepts). Other functional living items can be added by staff to further individualize assessment. One of the things lacking within each subscale is the application of items to specific settings. For example, the subscale of "shopping" describes general shopping/purchasing behaviors but does not delineate specific shopping skills that are needed in specific venues such as a grocery store versus a fast food restaurant (see e.g., Freagon, Wheeler, McDannel, Brankin, & Costello, 1983).

SCORING SYSTEM. The D.A.L.E. System was developed at the Gertrude A. Barber Center Residential Services Division (Erie, PA) and utilizes formal observations supplemented by reports from care providers to measure functional living skills. Testing procedures are presented in the therapist manual. The authors noted that the D.A.L.E. System does not rely on standardized procedures but rather presents a systematic approach to observation, assessment, and program planning with illustrative examples presented in the instruction manual. The criterion-referenced rating system includes both quantitative and qualitative components. Information about the development and validation of the rating systems was not provided in the instruction manual. The quantitative component (ratings of 1–3) focuses on "how often" an individual performs a particular skill, and the qualitative component (rating of a–c) focuses on "how well" the skill is performed. Functional competency is defined as the proficiency level of the general (normal) community for a particular skill and is assigned a quantitative rating of "3" (demonstrates skill almost all of the time [9/10 time] and a qualitative ration of "c" (good approximation of desired behavior with few, if any, reminders). The qualitative rating system is somewhat vague and open to uneven interpretation, which can affect reliability, although no reliability data were reported in the instructional manual. The authors noted this and suggested training in using the qualitative rating system to assess competence. Both quantitative and qualitative data are utilized in a graphing system in which baseline data and progress can be charted. Graphs are included for (*a*) subscales, (*b*) priority area, and (*c*) the full inventory.

SUMMARY. The D.A.L.E. System is a relatively easy-to-administer, criterion-referenced scale that measures functional living skills in individuals with mild to severe disabilities. It can provide the examiner a quick inventory of an individual's functional domestic and home living skills. However, the D.A.L.E. System scoring system, particularly the qualitative rating system, is somewhat suspect because there is no report of how the scoring criteria were created. In addition, there is virtually no validation or reliability information, and the subscales describe general situations rather than specific settings. Still, the D.A.L.E. System can be a useful instrument for special education teachers working with students being transitioned into the community as well as direct care workers working with young adults. A similar tool but one that is more specific to various functional settings is the Individual Student Community Life Skill Profile System for Severely Handicapped Students (Freagon et al., 1983).

REVIEWER'S REFERENCE

Freagon, S., Wheeler, J., McDannel, K., Brankin, G., & Costello, D. (1983). Individual Student Community Life Skill Profile System for Severely Handicapped Students. DeKalb, IL: DeKalb County Special Education Association.

Review of the Developmental Assessment of Life Experiences [1986 Edition] by ELIZABETH L. JONES, Assistant Professor of Psychology, Western Kentucky University, Bowling Green, KY:

The Developmental Assessment of Life Experiences (D.A.L.E. System) is an instrument for which the stated purpose is to facilitate the habilitation of persons with mental retardation. This is an assessment system that is criterion-referenced and uses a mastery testing approach to the assessment of "skills" or "skills of daily living in the community" (manual, p. 11). The D.A.L.E. System is for use by staff working in institutional, group home, transitional, day care, and daily living programs. The manual states that this instrument is "not a test utilizing standardized procedures, but rather a systemized approach to observation, planning, programming and assessment" (p. 9). The authors propose that the system be used for program planning in one of four ways: (*a*) identifying goals/objectives for program planning, (*b*) designing Individual Habilitation Plans, (*c*) charting an individual's progress, and (*d*) evaluating an individual's progress.

The present edition of the D.A.L.E. System is the fifth edition (1986). The following is a brief description of the changes made in the fifth edition. The current revision added some areas under some subdomains and separated some items within one subdomain into two subdomains. For example, Hearing was added to the Language Skills area and Dressing Skills and Undressing skills were separated. Items were added to some domains. In addition, a record-keeping system of charts and bar graphs was introduced (B. Skirzynski, personal communication, June 20, 1994).

This edition (1986) of the D.A.L.E. System has not addressed the psychometric concerns expressed in the previous review of an earlier edition (Gresham, 1985). The reader is referred to this review for a thorough analysis of the psychometric shortcomings of the D.A.L.E. System. The following provides the reader a brief summary of some of these shortcomings. The instrument lacks empirical evidence of reliability and validity. This is just as important for criterion measures as for norm-referenced measures. It also lacks evidence to substantiate consistency in measurement and evidence that it does assess a definable domain(s) (construct validity). The authors provide a vague rationale for the system in the statement that the "inventory items reflect some of the general principles of normalization which tend to foster a normative life style in most communities" (p. 9). However, the manual provides no evidence to support this statement. There is no substantiation for the hierarchical sequencing (scaling) of the items other than the statement that "[t]he items also tend to represent an orderly progression with each sub-scale, highlighting significant 'benchmark' skills" (p. 12). Additionally, the system provides no empirical documentation or logical rationale for the system's stated purpose. Thus, the authors failed to provide any evidence of adherence to recommended practices for test construction.

The manual is lacking in many areas. Although the manual provides a general overview of the instrument and its use, it fails to provide the user with a thorough conceptualization of the system. Specific definitions of the domains and subscales are not provided. The domains and subscales are generally referred to as "skills," or "skills of daily living in the community" (p. 11). The manual provides no information about revisions made in this fifth edition. Further, the manual provides only limited empirical support as no references are more current than 1977. A summary of the scoring procedures and scoring examples are presented in the manual. However, scoring of some items might be problematic as some items appear to need further clarification. For example, providing examples may enhance the consistency of such ratings as: "Uses small appliances," "Responds to questions," and "Cleans ears." The manual provides an explanation and examples of the scoring and charting system. However, the manual never describes the appropriate use and interpretation of the scores and charts. Because no empirical evidence of validity or reliability is provided for the system, this omission is considered to be unconscionable. In all, the manual fails to provide the user with the necessary background, rationale, and specificity with which to implement the described system.

Over and beyond the lack of evidence for sound test construction is the lack of evidence of treatment validity. The intent of the D.A.L.E. System is to plan an individual's habilitation program and to evaluate an individual's progress in such a program. As described in the manual, program effectiveness can be measured by the development of new skills. Therefore, the charts and bar graphs can serve as a "visual reference to the success (or lack of success) of our programming efforts" (p. 32). The authors provide no empirical evidence to show that the instrument is useful for this purpose.

The D.A.L.E. System does not provide any evidence to show that it was developed with recommended standards for test construction and publication (American Educational Research Association, American Psychological Association, & National Council on Measurement in Education, 1985). Therefore, the use of this assessment system as recommended by the authors is not supported. This system may be considered as a collection of skills that appear to have face validity. At best this is a rough inventory of skills that might be consulted when creating individual treatment plans.

REVIEWER'S REFERENCES

American Educational Research Association, American Psychological Association, & National Council on Measurement in Education. (1985). *Standards for educational and psychological testing*. Washington, DC: American Psychological Association, Inc.

Gresham, F. (1985). [Review of the D.A.L.E. System: Developmental Assessment of Life Experiences.] In J. V. Mitchell, Jr. (Ed.), *The ninth mental measurements yearbook* (pp. 428-430). Lincoln, NE: The Buros Institute of Mental Measurements.

[110]

Developmental Indicators for the Assessment of Learning—Revised/AGS Edition.

Purpose: Constructed as a screening instrument to identify children with potential developmental problems and children who appear to be developing in an advanced manner.
Population: Ages 2-0 to 5-11.
Publication Dates: 1983–90.
Acronym: DIAL-R.
Scores, 4: Motor, Concepts, Language, Total.
Subtests, 3: Motor, Concepts, Language.
Administration: Individual.
Price Data, 1993: $249.95 per complete kit including area subtests for motor, concepts, and language areas, set of administrative forms (100 cutting cards, 50 record booklets), 50 parent information forms, training packet, and manual ('90, 148 pages); $119.95 per upgrade packet including set of administrative forms, 50 parent information forms, training packet, and manual; $34.40 per set of administrative forms; $17.45 per 50 Parent-Child Activity forms; $8.95 per set of 3 operator's handbooks.
Time: (20–30) minutes.
Comments: Updated edition of the 1983 revision of the Developmental Indicators for the Assessment of Learning.
Authors: Carol Mardell-Czudnowski and Dorothea S. Goldenberg.
Publisher: American Guidance Service.
Cross References: See T4:762 (6 references); for reviews by David W. Barnett and G. Michael Poteat of an earlier version, see 10:89 (6 references); see also 9:326 (1 reference) and T3:696 (2 references); for reviews by J. Jeffrey Grill and James J. McCarthy of an earlier edition, see 8:428 (3 references).

TEST REFERENCES

1. Strom, R., Johnson, A., Strom, S., & Strom, P. (1992). Designing curriculum for parents of gifted children. *Journal for the Education of the Gifted*, *15*, 182-200.

Review of the Developmental Indicators for the Assessment of Learning—Revised/AGS Edition by DARRELL L. SABERS, Professor of Educational Psychology, University of Arizona, Tucson, AZ:

The Developmental Indicators for the Assessment of Learning—Revised/AGS Edition (DIAL-R) differs only slightly from the original DIAL-R. First, the norms are new, although the newness comes from the analysis of previous data rather than from a different sample of respondents. Second, these new norms result in different cutoff levels for the three descriptions that can be made about a child as a result of DIAL-R screening: (*a*) Potential Problem, (*b*) OK, or (*c*) Potential Advanced. A new manual was developed to report these changes. The other components remain the same as in the previous DIAL-R except for materials for training examiners. The authors' attempt to respond to earlier reviewers of the DIAL-R seems indicated by the statement, "DIAL-R users should keep in mind that all previous reviews of the DIAL-R must be tempered by the information presented in this manual" (p. 1). However, the descriptions of the DIAL-R in previous *MMY* reviews are still relevant.

The cutoff levels are changed, so the validity studies reported in the manual may not be valid for judging the use of the AGS edition. Validity studies may have included decisions based on previous cutoff levels. The manual includes many cautions about interpreting the validity data because of this change.

The original DIAL was inadequately normed because the sample was obtained only in the state of Illinois. The DIAL-R was standardized on a more widespread sample, although there is still a limitation: Only two sites from each of four regions of the country were used. Minorities were deliberately oversampled for the purpose of providing minority norms as well as Caucasian norms. The initial DIAL-R norms were based on a subsample of 1,861 students adjusted to match the 1980 U.S. Census. The effect of the AGS analysis was to weight these minority data and the Caucasian data in proper proportion to the U.S. Census data. In the AGS edition, the Angoff and Robertson procedure for developing norms was used for the three samples for which norms are presented: Minority, Caucasian, and Census.

Because there were no alterations to the DIAL-R test in the AGS edition, only the data resulting from the scoring will be different from the previous edition of the DIAL-R. Thus, any previously known advantages or disadvantages of the DIAL-R that do not pertain to norms and cutoff levels remain relevant. Poteat (1989) cautioned, "It is recommended the norms be used with caution because of the lack of information on the recruitment of subjects, the possible effects of the truncation procedure, the small number of standardization sites, and the failure to stratify by socioeconomic status" (p. 248). Only the second of these four points could be corrected in the AGS analysis.

There are a few remaining concerns over the original standardization of the DIAL-R that the reanalysis of the data could not correct. The term "minority" is not defined beyond indicating that these students were not classified as Caucasian. Hispanics were classified according to indication of race; that is, whether they indicated that they were Caucasian or minority. There was an attempt to stratify sites by urban and rural, but that was not very successful. Some additional data were obtained to increase the numbers of children in rural sites. Both the urban-rural and the Caucasian-minority stratifications are problems whether the minority norms or total norms are used.

The manual includes many cautions about misinterpretation of data and misuse of the test. However, although standard errors of measurement are reported, the issue of error of measurement is almost ignored. All cutoff points are exact for each of the three indicator areas (Language, Concepts, and Motor) and for the total score with no suggestion that the error of measurement in each area should be considered. For example, for the earliest age a total score of 3 indicates a Potential Problem whereas a score of 4 means OK.

The authors emphasize the importance of "ecological validity"; that is, an "authentic" setting for preschool assessment is required for the DIAL-R. This authenticity is achieved by having the child tested by three operators at different places in a large open room. The desired authenticity of the setting may be achieved for a child with some preschool experience, but could introduce fear for the child who has had no previous experience in such a setting. The examiner may want assurance that such a setting is realistic for the child who has had few experiences with a group of children, or a potential user may wonder why there are no provisions or norms for the DIAL-R when used in a regular one-on-one testing situation. No evidence is found in the manual to address these concerns. This reviewer suggests caution when using the DIAL-R with children with differing degrees of familiarity with preschool experiences.

The predictive validity evidence for the DIAL-R consists of studies where the criterion measures were tests. One expects predictive validity to be measured with criteria other than test scores. Another oversight is that one operator must measure a distance of 5 feet to set the conditions for testing, but is not provided with a string or tape of that length.

There are obvious strengths of the DIAL-R which deserve mention. Training materials are available for providing instruction to the operators who will cooperate in the testing situation (the DIAL-R must be administered by a team for the norms to be valid, but many reviewers question the validity of the norms anyway). Separate written tests (two parallel forms) over each area and overall are included so that the examiners can check their progress in learning how to administer the DIAL-R prior to conducting the assessment of children.

The dials used to present some of the stimuli in each area are attractive to children. One child tested enjoyed turning the dial herself, and said later, "Let's play the game again."

One small child (age 3) had difficulty manipulating the large sorting chips. Her mother commented that, "You could see what her preschool emphasizes by her performance on the test." If one agrees that the DIAL-R has content validity for a preschool curriculum, it may be easy to recommend the DIAL-R as an achievement test for preschoolers.

The use of the test to assess children locally does not require national norms. The serious reservations of this reviewer about the norms, the use of cutoff scores, and the restricted definition of authentic setting should not be seen as serious limitations when the test is used for preschool assessment. The important concern is the degree to which the content of the DIAL-R is considered relevant to the preschool curriculum. With apologies to the late Will Rogers, "I never showed the DIAL-R to anyone who didn't like it."

REVIEWER'S REFERENCE

Poteat, G. M. (1989). [Review of The Developmental Indicators for the Assessment of Learning—Revised.] In J. C. Conoley & J. J. Kramer (Eds.), *The tenth mental measurements yearbook* (pp. 246-248). Lincoln, NE: Buros Institute of Mental Measurements.

Review of the Developmental Indicators for the Assessment of Learning—Revised/AGS Edition by SCOTT SPREAT, Administrator of Clinical Services, The Woods Schools, Langhorne, PA:

The DIAL-R (Developmental Indicators for the Assessment of Learning) is an individually administered screening test. It is designed to identify youngsters who may need more intensive diagnostic assessment of their learning abilities. The manual identifies four clinical applications of the DIAL-R. They are the identification of (*a*) children with potential problems, (*b*) potentially advanced children, (*c*) children who may be "at risk," and (*d*) individual strengths and weaknesses in order to plan instruction. The DIAL-R is an untimed assessment of conceptual, motor, and language abilities of children from the ages of 2-0 to 5-11 years.

The DIAL-R is a revision of the earlier Diagnostic Indicators for the Assessment of Learning (1975). The initial version was revised in 1983; the current version was produced in 1990 and primarily represents an effort at renorming the instrument. Other changes included providing a wider range of cutoff points, a more complete explanation of the norm sample, and expanded psychometric support data.

ADMINISTRATION. The DIAL-R consists of three separate screening areas (Language, Motor, and Concepts). Each area has a total of eight items, and these items are divided into tasks that sample typical developmental behaviors of preschool children.

The DIAL-R is administered by a team of three adults, each of whom is responsible for one of the areas. In addition, each team has a coordinator. Children progress from one area to the next, so at any given time three children may be under evaluation. The manual did not explain the rationale for the use of three or four persons to administer this test. With appropriate training, I can see no reason why a single person could not administer the entire test. It would appear the administration procedures complicate a relatively straightforward assessment process. Administration instructions are clear and easy to follow.

NORM GROUP. The DIAL-R was normed in 1983, and these norming data were reanalyzed for this 1990 version of the DIAL-R. The norm group was 2,227 children selected from eight representative metropolitan areas across the country. The Caucasian norm group included 1,220 children, and the minority norm group included 1,007 children. These two groups were combined and weighted according to the 1980 U.S. Census to create a census-based norm group. Thus, three norm tables are presented in the manual: Caucasian, Minority, and Census Group. Each norm table is divided in 3-month intervals from 2 years through 5 years 11 months. Cutoff scores are defined in terms of various standard deviations in the performance of the norm group.

Considerable information is provided about the various properties of the norm groups. These include sex, age, geographic region, father's age and education, mother's age and education, race, and primary language. In contrast, little information is presented on the actual recruitment process. For a test for school-age children, this issue might be of less significance because recruiting would probably be done in schools where there is an equal probability of selection. It would have been instructive for the authors to present information that explained how representativeness of the sample was ensured. The manual suggests a possible overrepresentation of children whose parents suspect some sort of problem.

RELIABILITY. Data are presented on both test-retest and internal consistency data. Test-retest data were collected on 65 individuals with about one month between administrations. The obtained correlation coefficients would be considered acceptable for the Concept area and the Total DIAL-R score (.90 and .87 respectively); however, the coefficients for both Motor and Language failed to exceed a barely minimal threshold of .80. Only the DIAL-R Total Score achieved an acceptable level of internal consistency. A Cronbach's alpha of .86 was obtained. Internal consistency estimates for the three subscales did not exceed .80. No data are provided on interrater reliability, even though rater judgement would seem to be a possible source of bias for this test. No reliability data are presented on the behavioral observations.

Related to the modest reliability for subscales, the standard errors of measurement are relatively large. Consider the situation of a 4-year, 4-month-old child who achieves the mean score on the Motor subscale. According to the reported standard error of measurement, the 68% confidence interval for this score of 20.1 would vary from 17.4 to 22.8. Thus, we know that the average score is somewhere between the 25th and 69th percentile.

Given the above findings on reliability, only the Total Score of the DIAL-R can be recommended for use with individual students. Subscale scores are adequate for research purposes, but are likely to introduce too much error into any screening process.

VALIDITY. The authors appropriately caution that the reported validity studies were done using previous versions of the norms rather than the reanalyzed 1990 norms. Studies that were based on the correlation of DIAL-R total scores or subscale scores are unaffected by the reanalysis; however, studies reporting sensitivity or overall agreement would not apply to the new version.

A number of validity studies are reported in the manual. In many cases, insufficient information is presented about the study to enable a consumer to evaluate it, but the authors have included the full references for these studies allowing interested consumers to obtain the original source.

Construct validity was reported in terms of the correlation of the DIAL-R Total score with age and with the Learning Accomplishment Profile. As noted in the manual, scores on a developmental scale should correlate with age, and the reported correlation of .98 between age and DIAL-R Total score confirms this. This high correlation also suggests the reliability of the scale may actually be higher than reported. Correlations with various subscales of the Learning Accomplishment Profile suggest that in common areas, the two scales are measuring the same basic constructs. Earlier factor analytic work is no longer reported in the manual.

Although the DIAL-R is not considered an intelligence test, concurrent validity was demonstrated via a comparison of the DIAL-R and the Stanford-Binet Intelligence Scale (Form L–M) for identifying children at extreme ends of the skill development continuum. This comparison was done using the 1990 norms and it revealed the DIAL-R was fairly efficient in identifying children with potential problems; however, it was less satisfactory in identifying children in the potential advanced category.

Concurrent validity was also assessed by correlating the DIAL-R scores with conceptually similar scores on the Kaufman Assessment Battery for Children (K-ABC). Total Score, Motor, and Concepts all achieved moderate correlations with various K-ABC subscales. It is probable the reliabilities of the two instruments limited the obtained correlations.

A variety of information was presented on predictive validity, or the extent to which scores on the DIAL-R are related to some subsequent measure of performance. The DIAL-R was strongly related to subsequent scores on the Metropolitan Readiness Test and a variety of teacher ratings. Less strong, but still significant correlations were reported with the Clymer-Barrett Readiness test and the Stanford Reading Test. The DIAL-R was also reported to predict kindergarten performance with high accuracy, but actual data were not presented.

In addition to the above information, the manual presented validity data on criterion validity, ecological validity, cross-cultural studies, and face validity. The manual also invites continuing research on the psychometric properties of the scale.

There are some concerns with the reliability of the instrument, and it is probably reasonable to limit the use of the subscale scores to research purposes. Only the Total score has sufficient reliability to justify its use with individual children. The validity data suggest the scale is adequate for the purpose for which it was designed. Additional information on the recruitment of the norm sample would be appreciated, and the administration procedure could probably be simplified. Neither of these latter issues are of great significance.

[111]

Developmental Test of Visual-Motor Integration [Third Revision].

Purpose: Constructed to screen for visual-motor problems.
Publication Dates: 1967–89.
Acronym: VMI.
Scores: Total score only.
Administration: Group.
Price Data, 1994: $20.42 per manual ('89, 112 pages).
Time: Administration time not reported.
Authors: Keith E. Beery and Norman A. Buktenica (tests).
Publisher: Modern Curriculum Press.

a) SHORT FORM.
Population: Ages 3–8.
Price Data: $41.12 per 25 test booklets.

b) LONG FORM.
Population: Ages 3–18.
Price Data: $57.13 per 25 test booklets.

Cross References: See 9:329 (15 references) and T3:701 (57 references); for reviews of an earlier version by Donald A. Leton and James A. Rice, see 8:870 (24 references); see also T2:1875 (6 references); for a review by Brad S. Chissom, see 7:867 (5 references).

TEST REFERENCES

1. Carr, S. H. (1989). Louisiana's criteria of eligibility for occupational therapy services in the public school system. *The American Journal of Occupational Therapy, 43*, 503-506.

2. Mantzicopoulos, D., Morrison, D. C., Hinshaw, S. P., & Carte, E. T. (1989). Nonpromotion in kindergarten: The role of cognitive, perceptual, visual-motor, behavioral, achievement, socioeconomic, and demographic characteristics. *American Educational Research Journal, 26*, 107-121.

3. Oliver, C. E. (1990). A sensorimotor program for improving writing readiness skills in elementary-age children. *The American Journal of Occupational Therapy, 44*, 111-116.

4. Tompkins, C. A., Holland, A. L., Ratcliff, G., Costello, A., Leahy, L. F., & Cowell, V. (1990). Predicting cognitive recovery from closed head-injury in children and adolescents. *Brain and Cognition, 13*, 86-97.

5. Cermak, S. A., & Murray, E. A. (1991). The validity of the constructional subtests of the Sensory Integration and Praxis tests. *The American Journal of Occupational Therapy, 45*, 539-543.

6. Greenberg, M. T., Speltz, M. L., Derlyen, M., & Endriga, M. C. (1991). Attachment security in preschoolers with and without externalizing behavior problems: A replication. *Development and Psychopathology, 3*, 413-430.

7. Kleinman, B. L., & Stalcup, A. (1991). The effect of graded craft activities on visuomotor integration in an inpatient child psychiatry population. *The American Journal of Occupational Therapy, 45*, 324-330.

8. Kinghorn, J. (1992). Upper extremity functional changes following selective posterior rhizotomy in children with cerebral palsy. *The American Journal of Occupational Therapy*, *46*, 502-507.
9. Shapiro, M. E. (1992). Application of the Allen Cognitive Level Test in assessing cognitive level functioning of emotionally distrubed boys. *The American Journal of Occupational Therapy*, *46*, 514-520.
10. Wilson, B., Pollock, N., Kaplan, B. J., Law, M., & Faris, P. (1992). Reliability and construct validity of the clinical observations of motor and postural skills. *The American Journal of Occupational Therapy*, *46*, 775-783.
11. Brown, R. T., Buchanan, I., Doepke, K., Eckman, J. R., Baldwin, K., Goonan, B., & Schoenherr, S. (1993). Cognitive and academic functioning in children with sickle-cell disease. *Journal of Clinical Child Psychology*, *22*, 207-218.
12. Cotugno, A. J. (1993). The diagnosis of Attention Deficit Hyperactivity Disorder (ADHD) in community mental health centers: Where and when. *Psychology in the Schools*, *30*, 338-344.
13. Exner, C. E. (1993). Content validity of the In-hand Manipulation Test. *The American Journal of Occupational Therapy*, *47*, 505-513.
14. Farrell, W. J., & Muik, E. A. (1993). Computer applications that streamline test scoring and other procedures in occupational therapy. *The American Journal of Occupational Therapy*, *47*, 462-465.
15. Friedrich, W. N., Shurtleff, D. B., & Shaeffer, J. (1993). Cognitive abilities and lipomyelomeningocele. *Psychological Reports*, *73*, 467-470.
16. Korkman, M., & Peltomaa, A. K. (1993). Preventive treatment of dyslexia by a preschool training program for children with language impairments. *Journal of Clinical Child Psychology*, *22*, 277-287.
17. May, D. C., & Kundert, D. K. (1993). Pre-first placements: How common and how informed? *Psychology in the Schools*, *30*, 161-167.
18. Roth, M., McCaul, E., & Barnes, K. (1993). Who becomes an "at-risk" student? The predictive value of a kindergarten screening battery. *Exceptional Children*, *59*, 348-358.
19. Taylor, H. G., Barry, C. T., & Schatschneider, C. (1993). School-age consequences of *haemophilus influenzae* Type b meningitis. *Journal of Clinical Child Psychology*, *22*, 196-206.
20. Tseng, M. H., & Cermak, S. A. (1993). The influence of ergonomic factors and perceptual-motor abilities on handwriting performance. *The American Journal of Occupational Therapy*, *47*, 919-926.
21. Blennerhassett, L., Strohmeier, S. J., & Hibbett, C. (1994). Criterion-related validity of Raven's Progressive Matrices with deaf residential school students. *American Annals of the Deaf*, *139*, 104-110.
22. Goldstein, D. J., & Britt, T. W., Jr. (1994). Visual-motor coordination and intelligence as predictors of reading, mathematics, and written language ability. *Perceptual and Motor Skills*, *78*, 819-823.
23. McCormick, C. E., Stoner, S. B., & Duncan, S. (1994). Kindergarten predictors of first-grade reading achievement: A regular classroom example. *Psychological Reports*, *74*, 403-407.
24. Yeates, K. O., & Mortensen, M. E. (1994). Acute and chronic neuropsychological consequences of mercury vapor poisoning in two early adolescents. *Journal of Clinical and Experimental Neuropsychology*, *16*, 209-222.
25. Zelkowitz, P., Papageorgiou, A., Zelazo, P. R., & Weiss, M. J. S. (1995). Behavioral adjustment in very low and normal birth weight children. *Journal of Clinical Child Psychology*, *24*, 21-30.

Review of the Developmental Test of Visual-Motor Integration [Third Edition] by DARRELL L. SABERS, Professor of Educational Psychology, University of Arizona, Tucson, AZ:

The "third revision" of the Developmental Test of Visual-Motor Integration (VMI) is not a revision in the usual use of the term. Only the scoring system, manual, and norms have been changed from previous editions. The same 24 items have been used since 1964 when the test was known as the Developmental Form Sequence. Because the VMI has remained essentially the same test through the ensuing years, the comments in previous *Mental Measurement Yearbook* reviews remain relevant to this revision.

There are two reasons why a user might prefer the latest VMI to a previous edition: A different scoring system and new norms. However, this revision is questionable in both aspects.

The scoring system retains the dichotomous nature of scoring items used in previous editions, but instead of awarding 1 point per item, weights of 2, 3, and 4 points are awarded for correct responses to more difficult items. Abundant examples of scored responses demonstrate some arbitrary decisions regarding the application of the scoring criteria. A very sloppy line approximating a vertical line is acceptable as a substitute for a straight vertical line in Item 1 (worth 1 point), but a missed intersection on Item 22 results in a score of 0 rather and 4. Thus, because the items are scored dichotomously, a slight drawing error may result in a loss of 4 points, whereas the inability to draw a straight line was previously ignored. A lack of a "good corner" on Item 20 results in a score of 0 but a score of 4 was assigned on Item 22 to a response with nearly the same error.

Because "weighted scores and scores based on the original scoring guidelines correlate almost perfectly at .98" (p. 25) there is little justification for applying weighted scoring. In addition, it is psychometrically unsound to assign different weights to highly intercorrelated dichotomously scored items. If dichotomous scoring were not used, it might be defensible to assign item scores ranging from 1 to 4. Beery indicates that partial scoring is not allowed because "such scoring would make inappropriate use of the VMI norms" (p. 25). The current norms are, however, already questionable.

It is not clear how the norm tables for the third revision were developed. The norm group appears to consist of the original 1,030 records from a 1964 sample from Illinois (which appear to be called the 1967 U.S. norms), 2,060 from California in 1981 (which, combined with the original data, were considered to be the 1982 norms), and 2,734 from several eastern, northern, and southern states in 1988. Because the 1988 results were not significantly different from earlier samples, all three groups were combined to form the 1989 VMI norms. The merging of the three groups casts doubts about these norms.

The similarity of the three data sets is surprising for several reasons. Bracken (1992) suggests that it is well known that a gradual increase in intelligence results in differences in test scores as a result of standardization dates. How can the VMI be so unrelated to intelligence that it does not show growth? The reason for no growth could easily be that one of the groups included in these norms fails to represent the U.S. norms at the date tested. If that is the reason, which group and what effect there is on the total norms should be known before credibility can be given to the norms presented in this manual.

Another problem is that there is one set of norms to be used for three types of administration: individual, stopping after three consecutive errors; individual, complete test; and group. The manual does not present the examiner with the necessary information for valid use of the VMI scores.

There is nothing in the manual describing how the data based on number-correct scoring were combined with the weighted scores to produce the norms included in this edition. The user should not have to guess how these data were combined or how the performances of the three groups were compared prior to the creation of the present norms. Because the scoring criteria are more explicit in the third revision than in previous editions, why would a user expect that the earlier scores are now valid?

Previous *MMY* reviewers have questioned the lack of evidence regarding validity for the VMI. There remains inadequate description of the construct that is being measured by the test. However, because the "primary purpose of the VMI is to help prevent learning and behavioral problems through early screening identification" (p. 8), predictive validity might appear to be the type of evidence most needed. Some evidence is cited regarding the prediction of achievement; none is cited regarding behavioral problems.

The VMI might be viewed as an achievement test measuring how well the child can draw geometric figures. Achievement tests often are not justified on the basis of construct validity, and there is reason to remediate weaknesses found on achievement tests if the content is judged important. Beery does present some suggestions on remediation, and asks, "Would these children achieve more fully and easily if their visual-motor weaknesses were remediated? And the related question remains: How can such weaknesses best be remediated?" (p. 18). Beery's position on remediation is more reasonably taken when using an achievement test than an IQ test, and his questions are especially appropriate when the test covers skills considered to be prerequisite for future learning.

The VMI cannot be recommended as a measure of intelligence, and the present norms are suspect for the purpose of deriving normative scores for the construct of visual-motor integration. As a test of achievement in copying geometric figures, the lack of adequate description for the norms is a minor problem. For use as an achievement test, the relevancy of the VMI's content needs to be judged according to the user's purpose. Regardless of the testing purpose, there is no obvious advantage in using the third revision over previous editions.

REVIEWER'S REFERENCE

Bracken, B. A. (1992). The interpretation of tests. In M. Zeidner & R. Most (Eds.), *Psychological testing: An inside view* (pp. 119-156). Palo Alto: Consulting Psychologists Press.

Review of the Developmental Test of Visual-Motor Integration [Third Edition] by JAMES E. YSSELDYKE, Professor of Educational Psychology, Director of National Center on Educational Outcomes, University of Minnesota, Minneapolis, MN:

The Developmental Test of Visual-Motor Integration (VMI) is designed to assess the extent to which children can integrate visual and motor skills as evidenced by copying a set of 24 geometric designs. The author indicates the "primary purpose of the VMI is to help prevent learning and behavioral problems through early screening identification" (p. 8). The test is rooted in the assumptions that adequate visual-motor integration is a necessary prerequisite to school success, that when it is absent it should be remediated, and that successful remediation of difficulties will enable students to be successful in school and/or overcome learning and behavior problems. There is no evidence in the manual that such assumptions are firmly grounded, nor is such evidence present in the professional literature. The VMI is best viewed as a 24-item measure of children's skill in copying geometric designs. Children are asked to copy the designs, and their efforts are scored pass-fail.

The 1989 version of the test is an update on earlier versions. The items have remained the same throughout revisions of the test, but scoring procedures have changed. Scoring range was expanded from 1–24 to 1–50, and items were weighted in terms of their developmental difficulty. The author argues that in spite of the changes, technical data for earlier versions of the test still apply to the 1989 edition.

The VMI was originally standardized on 1,030 children in Illinois. In 1981 the test was cross-validated with groups of children from California. Then, in 1988 the test was again cross-validated with students from several eastern, northern, and southern states. There are minimal data on the make-up of the norm group, and no description of the cross-tabulations for the standardization samples, so those who use the test to make norm-referenced interpretations are comparing those they assess to an unknown group. The test should be used with caution in making norm-referenced comparisons.

Reliability of the VMI is based on a set of investigations of interscorer, internal consistency, and test-retest reliability of the measure by others who have used the scale since its inception. Interscorer reliabilities ranged from .58 to .99 with a median of .93. Test-retest reliabilities ranged from .63 to .92, whereas split-half reliabilities ranged from .66 to .93. The samples on whom the reliabilities were obtained are not described.

Beery reports correlations of performance on the VMI with measures of handwriting, readiness, chronological age, and performance on other tests like the Bender Visual Motor Gestalt Test. These relationships do not establish evidence the test measures what the author says it measures. Evidence for predictive validity is mixed, with some investigators finding moderately strong correlations between performance on this test and later achievement, others reporting little relationship.

SUMMARY. The VMI can be used to provide assessors with information on how well students copy geometric designs. It provides a larger behavior sample than tests like the Bender Visual Motor Gestalt Test (11:40) and the Memory-for-Designs Test (9:694). It has better reliability than those measures, though indices of reliability are on unspecified samples. The standardization sample is not described, so norm-referenced use of the test should be avoided.

[112]

Developmental Test of Visual Perception, Second Edition.

Purpose: Measures visual-perceptual and visual-motor abilities.
Population: Ages 4-0 to 10-11.
Publication Dates: 1961–93.
Acronym: DTVP-2.
Scores, 8: Motor-Reduced Visual Perception (Position in Space, Figure Ground, Visual Closure, Form Constancy), Visual-Motor Integration (Eye-Hand Coordination, Copying, Spatial Relations, Visual-Motor Speed), General Visual Perception.
Administration: Individual.
Price Data, 1994: $124 per complete kit including examiner's manual ('93, 73 pages), picture book, 25 profile/examiner record forms, and 25 response booklets; $29 per examiner's manual; $32 per picture book; $18 per 25 profile/examiner record forms; $49 per 25 response booklets; $79 per IBM score system; $89 per Macintosh score system.
Time: (35–45) minutes.
Comments: 1993 revision of the Marianne Frostig Developmental Test of Visual Perception (DTVP).
Authors: Donald D. Hammill, Nils A. Pearson, and Judith K. Voress.
Publisher: PRO-ED, Inc.
Cross References: See T4:767 (2 references); for reviews by Richard E. Darnell and David A. Sabatino of the earlier edition, see 9:650 (4 references); see also T3:1371 (25 references), 8:882 (72 references), and T2:1921 (43 references); for reviews by Brad S. Chissom, Newell C. Kephart, and Lester Mann, see 7:871 (117 references); for reviews by James M. Anderson and Mary C. Austin, see 6:553 (7 references).

TEST REFERENCES

1. Laucht, M., Esser, G., & Schmidt, M. H. (1994). Contrasting infant predictors of later cognitive functioning. *Journal of Child Psychology and Psychiatry and Allied Disciplines, 35*, 649-662.

Review of the Developmental Test of Visual Perception, Second Edition by NANCY B. BOLOGNA, Assistant Professor of Psychiatry, Louisiana State University School of Medicine, New Orleans, LA:

The Developmental Test of Visual Perception, Second Edition (DTVP-2) is a recent revision of the original test developed by Marianne Frostig and coworkers in 1961. This revision provides a well-organized manual that begins with a theoretical model of visual perception and the rationale for testing the development of this ability.

Within the structure of this test, perception refers to "those brain operations that involve interpreting and organizing the *physical* elements of a stimulus rather than the sensory or symbolic aspects of a stimulus" (examiner's manual, p. 2). Therefore, like the original test developed by Frostig and co-workers, the DTVP-2 does not provide measures of sensory or cognitive ability. Eight subtests in the DTVP-2 that measure each of four specific types of visual perception (Form Constancy, Figure-Ground, Position in Space, and Spatial Relations) have been chosen based on Frostig's original work. Within each type of perceptual ability, there are subtests denoted "motor reduced" or "motor enhanced" to provide a further diagnostic distinction. There are two motor reduced subtests of Form Constancy and no motor enhanced subtest of Position in Space.

ADMINISTRATION. The entire test takes from 30 to 60 minutes to administer. The test is always administered individually and is not suitable for group administration. According to the manual, because the instructions for each subtest are brief and easily translated into gestures, the test can be administered to non-English-speaking children or those who are hearing impaired. Although this may be true regarding administering the test, no norms are provided for these special populations.

Each subtest begins with Item 1 and continues until a criterion number of errors has been reached (except for subtests 1 and 7 in which all items are administered). Instructions to be given orally are presented clearly in capital letters in the examiner's manual. Responses are entered into a test booklet that is well designed and easy to use.

SCORING. The manual includes clear scoring instructions, scoring examples, and specific criteria for each item or subtest as appropriate. Norms are provided for ages 4 years, 0 months through 10 years, 11 months at 6-month intervals. Raw scores for each subtest are converted into standard scores and percentiles. Standard scores are combined to yield two composite factor scores: Motor-Reduced Visual Perception and Visual-Motor Integration, and a general composite score: General Visual Perception. Test materials include a Profile/Examiner Record Form on which individual item performance can be noted, along with subtest and composite scores. A profile can be generated with a graphic display clearly marking normal ranges. Space is provided on this form for entry of other test results. There are sections provided to note other test data and administration conditions (such as noise level, interruptions, distractions, etc.).

RELIABILITY AND VALIDITY. The manual provided with the DTVP-2 contains a description of the history of this instrument's development. According to the manual author, the original DTVP was immediately popular until a substantial body of literature was reviewed (Hammill & Wiederholt, 1973) that questioned the reliabilities and independence of the subtests. A later article in *A Consumer's Guide to Tests in Print* (Hammill, Brown, & Bryant, 1992), gave a rating of "unacceptable" to the DTVP in the areas of reliability, validity, and normative data. The current edition, the DTVP-2, was developed to address these problems. It is interesting to note the first author of the DTVP-2 is also the first author in the critiques noted above.

The DTVP-2 manual describes seven areas that have been changed or improved since the original instrument was published:

1. Reliability for the subtests was increased to acceptable levels.

2. Ample evidence of content, criterion-related, and construct validity was provided.

3. Factorial validity analysis was undertaken to strengthen the test's validity.

4. Studies showing an absence of racial, gender, and handedness bias were performed.

5. Normative data are now based on a large, stratified sample whose characteristics are demographically similar to those for the 1990 census school-aged population.

6. Two new composite scores (motor-reduced visual perception and visual-motor integration) were developed to facilitate diagnosis.

7. The ages at which the test can be administered were extended to include 10-year-olds. (examiner's manual, p. viii)

The manual has dedicated one chapter each to the description of the new normative sample, and reliability and validity studies. The normative sample includes 1,972 children who were tested between February and June 1992. Tables are provided with the demographic characteristics of the sample and the stratification by age of geographic region, gender, race, and residence (rural vs. urban).

Three forms of reliability are reported. Cronbach's alpha was measured for a subset of 100 protocols randomly drawn from each age group (at 1-year intervals) of the normative data base. No reliability coefficient for any subtest at any age is lower than .80. Averaged across all ages, the eight subtest reliability coefficients range from .83 to.95. As expected, the three composite scores have somewhat stronger internal consistency. No composite score coefficient at any age is below .93. The alpha coefficients of the General Visual Perception score (a composite of all subtests) for the seven age groups range from .96 to .98. Test-retest reliability was assessed in a set of 88 students from a single location ranging in age from 4 through 10 years, who were tested twice with a 2-week interval between test administrations. Because the sample was evaluated as a whole, the effects of age were partialed out statistically. The stability coefficients (test-retest with age effects partialed out) range from .71 to .86 across the eight subtests, and from .89 to .93 for the composite scores. Interrater reliability was also assessed from this sample of 88 protocols. In each case, two independent individuals scored each test given. The resulting reliability coefficients range from .87 to .94 across the subtests, and .95 to.97 for the composite scores.

The manual author provides an impressive description of the content, criterion-related, and construct validity of each subtest and composite score of the DTVP-2. Multiple tables illustrate the intercorrelations across subtests and ages, correlations between subtests and composites of the DTVP-2 with scores from the National Teacher Assessment and Referral Scales, and correlations with the Wechsler Intelligence Scale for Children—Revised. The results of factor analyses are provided to support the validity of the composite scores. Perhaps the weakest link is the section on group differentiation, in which discriminant validity is approached by testing a sample of 49 children diagnosed as "neurologically impaired," "autistic," or "cerebral palsied" (p. 33) for comparison to the normative sample. No details are provided regarding specifics of this group. Clearly additional work must be done to provide details on pathology related performance before this instrument can be considered useful in assessing special populations. However, this comparison does provide some evidence that the test can be used to index "normal" performance.

SUMMARY. This is an impressive revision of a previously weak instrument. The DTVP-2 manual suggests four principal uses for this test: "(a) to document the presence and degree of visual-perceptual or visual-motor difficulties in individual children, (b) to identify candidates for referral, (c) to verify the effectiveness of these intervention programs, and (d) to serve as a research tool" (p. 6). Unfortunately, as the manual authors acknowledge, the diagnosis and treatment of visual-perceptual deficits have not always been found to be a useful adjunct to the treatment of educational difficulties. As such, there may be little clinical demand for this well-honed tool. For developmental researchers seeking clear quantifiable indices of visual perception, however, this may become the instrument of choice.

REVIEWER'S REFERENCES

Hammill, D. D., & Wiederholt, J. L. (1973). Review of the Frostig Visual Perception Test and the related training programs. In L. Mann & D. A. Sabatino (Eds.), *The first review of special education* (vol. 1, pp. 33-48). Philadelphia, PA; JSE Press.

Hammill, D. D., Brown, L., & Bryant, B. R. (1992). *A consumer's guide to tests in print* (2nd ed.). Austin, TX: PRO-ED.

Review of the Developmental Test of Visual Perception, Second Edition by GERALD TINDAL, Associate Profes-

sor of Special Education, University of Oregon, Eugene, OR:

The Developmental Test of Visual Perception (DTVP-2) is a well-organized, single-construct test designed to provide normatively based performance estimates on eight visual tasks:

1. Eye-Hand Coordination: drawing lines within a specified band width between two points.
2. Position in Space: comparing a figure with geometric objects to five similar objects, four of which are rotated/displayed in different formation/position.
3. Copying: drawing lines to reflect a model geometric object.
4. Figure Ground: identifying geometric objects enmeshed in the model from five separated and displayed below the model.
5. Spatial Relations: drawing lines between points within an area that has many points (a dot-to-dot-like task to match a model).
6. Visual Closure: selecting one of five incomplete drawings that would match a model above, were it drawn completely.
7. Visual Motor Speed: repetitively drawing four lines within two shapes (displayed in two sizes—large and small): a cross (x) within a small box and parallel lines (=) within a large circle.
8. Form Constancy: selecting a figure modeled above from within five more complex figures displayed below that have the model figure embedded within them.

These eight subtests are arranged to provide separate subscores as well as three different combined scores: General Visual Perception (average of all 8), Motor-Reduced Visual Perception (subtests 2, 4, 6, 8), and Visual-Motor Integration (also referred to as Motor-Enhanced and composed of subtests 1, 3, 5, 7). The manual and all accompanying booklets (including a response booklet, picture booklet, and record form) are well designed and easy to follow. Very complete information is provided about the test in particular and testing more generally. The materials are clear, both for the respondent and the examiner. Administration and scoring procedures are very easy to follow and are well documented. The only serious problem arises in the description provided by the authors for prorating scores to calculate combined subtotals when individual subtests are not taken, a procedure which is not justified and should be avoided. Furthermore, the following issues should be noted when attending to the normative sample, reliability, and validity data.

NORMATIVE SAMPLE. The test is based on a minimal sample of approximately 2,000 students across ages 4 through 10 (inclusive) distributed in 12 states, although the sample reflects many of the national census data regarding race, ethnicity, gender, residence, geographic area, and handedness. Nevertheless, the original sample from which the norm was based is selectively sampled: "Normative data collection sites were selected in a relatively random manner by using the PROD-ED customer file to locate professionals who had purchased tests of visual perception or visual motor integration within the past three years" (p. 29). The number of students at each age range from 100 to 467 (median of about 300). Scores are reported for age equivalence in spite of strong proscriptions by the professional community, based on the argument that practitioners use them. Users of this test should be encouraged to avoid such scores and write the publishers advising them not to print them, particularly given the selective and limited sampling of the norm group.

RELIABILITY. All major types of reliability are considered and tables are used to display coefficients for each type. Generally, the data reflect a very reliable instrument, particularly with combined scores of perception and integration. Reliability of content sampling is addressed by documenting internal consistency and is quite adequate. Stability coefficients are based on a study of 88 students across the entire age range (4–10), spuriously increasing the results; consequently, when age is partialed out, virtually all stability coefficients are unacceptable, ranging from .71 to .86 for individual subtests (with all but two coefficients in the .70s range). The reliability of the combined test scores is adequate. Although the authors partial out the influence of content sampling, this procedure is not justified and the net effect is to inflate the individual subtest coefficients. Interscorer reliability coefficients are all quite high, which is likely a function of the clarity in scoring procedures. In summary, the subtests have consistency in the individual items and can be scored consistently, but may not be stable, a serious problem with this type of measure.

VALIDITY. In the manual, the authors present very complete information about validity, including content, criterion, and construct. Content validity is oriented to a description of tasks, comparing them to other tests purportedly measuring similar constructs. Ironically, under the sections on criterion validity, two findings are noteworthy:

1. "Students' performance on the DTVP-2 subtests has little to do with school skills as seen by their teachers" (p. 42).
2. Of the 44 coefficients between subtests on the DTVP-2 and the Comprehensive Test of Basic Skills (CTBS; CTB/McGraw-Hill, 1989), 41 were not significant; the other 3 were low (educationally insignificant).

Such findings, when taken together, reflect the difficulty the authors eventually have in defining and establishing construct validity. For example, further criterion-related validity is provided by interrelating the DTVP-2 with the Wechsler Intelligence Scale for

Children—Revised (WISC-R; Wechsler, 1974); the results reflect a high relationship with the performance but not the verbal subscales. Furthermore, the DTVP-2 subtests are both intercorrelated and a factor analysis is presented, confirming the two major combined scores (perception and motor-integration). Finally, changes in performance are noted across the entire age range.

Nevertheless, the measure is not anchored to anything other than other tests, which may or may not be predictive of performance in school (work or activity) environments. Construct validity, when viewed from Messick's (1989) vantage of decision making and both evidential and consequential basis, is basically unsupported. Therefore, users of this test should be cautious when making interpretations. Although the authors discount specific uses of the test (planning school interventions and conducting subtest profile analysis), the manner in which the results are summarized and analyzed lead to such uses. For example, the recording form is designed to compare performance levels across the subtests. And a section of the manual contains information on making clinical judgments.

This test may be useful, at best, in determining three total scores: General Visual Perception, Motor-Reduced Visual Perception, and Visual-Motor Integration. These scores, however, may have nothing to do with performance in any functional environment in which children ages 4–10 are involved. The test is best used only for two of the four purposes noted by the authors: (*a*) for "documenting the presence and degree of visual perceptual deficits in children" and (*b*) "as a research tool, especially [for] investigators who wish to use standardized instruments to study visual perceptual processes" (p. 6). The other two purposes are not yet warranted: (*a*) for referral to other professionals and enrollment in remedial programs, and (*b*) to show the "effects of special training programs designed to correct visual perceptual and visual-motor problems" (p. 6).

REVIEWER'S REFERENCES

Wechsler, D. (1974). Wechsler Intelligence Scale for Children—Revised (WISC-R). San Antonio, TX: The Psychological Corporation.

CTB/McGraw-Hill. (1989). Comprehensive Test of Basic Skills. Monterey, CA: Author.

Messick, S. (1989). Validity. In R. Linn (Ed.), *Educational measurement* (pp. 13-104). New York: Macmillan.

[113]

The Devine Inventory.

Purpose: Designed to assist "in the selection, deployment and development of individuals" in job settings.
Population: Employees and prospective employees.
Publication Date: 1989.
Scores, 3: Problem Solving, Self Description, Personal Choices.
Administration: Group or individual.
Price Data, 1991: $1.75 per reusable booklet; $12.50 per 25 response forms.
Time: Administration time not reported.
Author: Donald W. Devine.
Publisher: Donald W. Devine & Associates.

Review of The Devine Inventory by PHILIP BENSON, Associate Professor of Management, New Mexico State University, Las Cruces, NM:

The Devine Inventory is a relatively new (1989) measure of characteristics deemed important in the performance of various jobs. The particular population intended for the inventory is not well defined, and is presumably most occupational groups. The supporting material suggests the inventory was developed through critical incidents from "service, manufacturing and other industries," implying the measure is intended to have general applicability.

The inventory is organized into three major categories: Problem Solving, Self Description, and Personal Choices. These areas have 56, 22, and 99 items, respectively, for a total of 177 items. All items dealing with Problem Solving or with Personal Choices appear to be of a forced-choice format, in that the test taker is required to choose one of two statements as "best" describing the respondent. The Self Description items require the test taker to rate, on a 0 through 9 scale, the extent to which the item is of great importance to the individual.

The supporting material for the Devine Inventory includes a list of 33 "behavior definitions" that are presumably measured by the inventory. These would appear to be the "scales" reported, but too little supporting information is given to properly assess these definitions. Examples of the behaviors listed include aggressiveness, decisiveness, mobility, and emotional composure.

These same 33 behaviors are listed on a second questionnaire, to be completed by a supervisor or other person familiar with the organizational environment for the job in question. Each of the 33 behaviors is rated twice, once for "ranges" (i.e., the range of behavior that is desired in each area, rated as 0–2, 1–3, 2–4, and so forth up to 7–9, with high scores indicating a strong need for the behavior in question) and once for "priorities" (a ranking from 1 to 33 of the importance of the behavior in the particular job and organizational context). The instructions indicate this information is used in developing reports that are useful to the organization using the inventory.

Very little information is given regarding the reliability and validity of the Devine Inventory. Although no formal manual was included, a three-page typed description of "The Development of the Devine Inventory" was provided. The author of this document states the "Devine Inventory validation is done in order to maximize the content and construct validity of the instrument." However, too little information is given to assess the veracity of this claim.

The items in the inventory were taken from a group of "at least thirteen thousand" critical incidents of highly positive and highly negative job behaviors in a wide variety of occupational settings. Although the documentation suggests that this ensures that the inventory measures the "actual content of jobs," it is not clear what content of what jobs is represented.

A table is given with correlation coefficients between the Devine Inventory and relevant scales on the Edwards Personal Preference Schedule (EPPS). The descriptive material suggests this is a measure of the construct validity of the Devine Inventory, although the table lists the correlations as "reliability" measures. Correlations listed range from .48 to .83, but no information is given on the sample used or its size, and no indication is given as to precisely what is being correlated with what. The descriptive material indicates the "equivalent scales on the two instruments correlated high enough to be statistically significant (p is less than .05) on the majority of scales." In addition, it is noted that three separate studies are currently underway in three different organizations to relate the Devine Inventory scales to performance appraisal measures of employees.

It is not unusual for reviewers in *The Mental Measurements Yearbooks* to suggest that relatively new measures are best viewed as experimental only. However, in this case I find that the Devine Inventory should not even be viewed as experimental. Far too little information is available to evaluate the inventory, its intended purpose, or the populations where it may be useful.

For example, assuming that the two scales are truly forced-choice in format, how were they developed? Are the "a" and "b" answers matched in any meaningful way (usually social desirability), and thus useful in distinguishing two important dimensions of behavior, or are they merely two different items that are matched haphazardly? What items relate to which scales of the Devine Inventory? What jobs and organizations were used to develop the critical incidents, and how were the 13,000 such incidents reduced to the present inventory? Just what do the correlations with the EPPS scales mean, and what do they represent?

Until many such questions can be answered, the Devine Inventory should not even be considered as experimental or preliminary in its nature. Too little has been documented to date to even offer the measure for sale.

Review of The Devine Inventory by WILLIAM L. DEATON, Professor and Dean, School of Education, Auburn University at Montgomery, Montgomery, AL:

The Devine Inventory is a package containing a booklet of 177 items, a brochure of ranges and priorities of job behavior requirements, a response form, two pages of behavioral definitions appropriate to the inventory, and a brief description of how the instrument was developed. The assessment materials are attractive and instructions are easy to follow. Apparently, employers describe the desired strengths and importance of behaviors required in a particular position and prospective employees respond to the 177 items; a report is then generated that seeks to match prospects with positions. A sample report is available from the author upon request.

Three areas are used to present the items. Problem Solving consists of 56 items each with two choices that describe what the prospective employee does or would prefer to do when solving a problem. Twenty-two items are presented under the Self Description section. Respondents are instructed to indicate the importance of statements on a scale from 0 to 9. Personal Choices presents pairs of statements that require a choice. Because only scores from the Self Description and Personal Choices sections are evident from the response form, this review will focus on those.

Based upon the information presented in the materials, one score is obtained for each individual from the single item in the Self Description section and a similar score is produced from choices of nine keyed responses for items in the Personal Choices section. These scores are Recognition, Dominance, Gregariousness, Structure, Kinship, Utilitarian Focus, Intimacy, Negotiating, Follow Through, Energy, Order, Mobility, Potential, Hard Worker, Judgment, Aggressiveness, Loyalty, Change, Thinking, and Quiescence. The author and publisher explained that the two other scores (X and Z) assess Trusting.

The inventory was developed through a critical incident study of "at least thirteen thousand examples of highly positive and highly negative actual job behaviors . . . gathered on a wide variety of occupations in service, manufacturing and other industries . . . recorded by supervisors in order to reflect the actual content of jobs . . . (and) the actual vocabulary used by the supervisors were retained in the development of the items . . . Thus, the items in the Devine Inventory do measure actual content of jobs" (The Development of the Devine Inventory, p. 1). These statements are made to substantiate the claim that the inventory was developed "to maximize the content and construct validity" (p. 1). A table of correlations (Pearson product-moment correlation coefficients?) is contained in the material to establish the construct validity of the inventory as "the extent that relevant scales on this instrument are similar to those on the Edwards Personal Preference Schedule" (p. 1). Values in the table, labeled "Reliability," range from .83 to .48. The undated paper indicates that three separate studies are being conducted to determine the predictive validity of the inventory.

The Devine Inventory awaits well-planned and complete studies to provide thorough information on validity, reliability, item analyses, score (scale) structure, interdependence of scores, and score interpretation. When, and if, sufficient supporting data are provided, some employers may consider this instrument for use in job settings. This instrument *looks* good. Unfortunately, good looks is not one of the criteria of the *Standards for Educational and Psychological Testing* (AERA, APA, & NCME, 1985).

REVIEWER'S REFERENCE

American Educational Research Association, American Psychological Association, & National Council on Measurement in Education (1985). *Standards for educational and psychological testing*. Washington, DC: American Psychological Association, Inc.

[114]

Diagnostic Achievement Battery, Second Edition.

Purpose: "To assess children's abilities in listening, speaking, reading, writing, and mathematics."
Population: Ages 6-0 to 14-11.
Publication Dates: 1984–90.
Acronym: DAB-2.
Scores, 20: Spoken Language (Listening [Sentence Completion, Characteristics], Speaking [Synonyms, Grammatic Completion]), Written Language (Reading [Reading Comprehension,Alphabet/Word Knowledge], Writing [Punctuation, Spelling, Capitalization, Writing Composition]), Mathematics (Math Calculation, Math Reasoning), Total Achievement.
Administration: Individual.
Price Data, 1994: $119 per complete kit; $29 per student booklet; $34 per 25 profile/answer sheets; $29 per 25 student worksheets; $31 per manual ('90, 99 pages); $79 per computer scoring system (specify IBM or Apple).
Time: (60–120) minutes.
Authors: Phyllis L. Newcomer and Dolores Curtis (student booklet).
Publisher: PRO-ED, Inc.
Cross References: For a review by William J. Webster of the original edition, see 9:333.

TEST REFERENCES

1. Cooper, D. H., & Speece, D. L. (1990). Maintaining at-risk children in regular education settings: Initial effects of individual differences and classroom environments. *Exceptional Children*, 57, 117-126.

2. Speece, D. L., & Cooper, D. H. (1990). Ontogeny of school failure: Classification of first-grade children. *American Educational Research Journal*, 27, 119-140.

Review of the Diagnostic Achievement Battery, Second Edition by JEAN-JACQUES BERNIER, Full Professor, and MARTINE HÉBERT, Assistant Professor, Department of Measurement and Evaluation, University Laval, Quebec, Canada:

The Diagnostic Achievement Battery, Second Edition (DAB-2) is a standardized individual test used to assess children's abilities in listening, speaking, reading, writing and mathematics. The DAB-2 is designed for use with children between the ages of 6-0 and 14-11 and provides 3 construct scores (Spoken Language, Written Language, and Mathematics), 5 component scores (Listening, Speaking, Reading, Writing, and Mathematics) and 12 subtest scores. The Second Edition retains eight subtests of the first DAB published in 1984 (Sentence Completion, Characteristics, Synonyms, Grammatic Completion, Alphabet/Word Knowledge, Spelling, Math Calculation, and Math Reasoning). Two subtests were changed in administration as well as in scoring format (Capitalization and Punctuation). One subtest (Reading Comprehension) was altered slightly by changing a few items. One new subtest (Writing Composition) provides a score based on writing vocabulary and content maturity and replaces the Written Vocabulary subtest in the original edition.

According to the author, the DAB-2 is intended to accomplish four goals: (*a*) identify those pupils who are significantly below their peers in the area of spoken language (listening and speaking), written language (reading and writing), and mathematics; (*b*) determine a child's strengths and weaknesses; (*c*) document pupils' progress in achievement areas as a consequence of specific intervention programs; and (*d*) serve as a measurement instrument in research in the area of academic achievement.

The test development model reflects principles such as reviewing commonly used curricula and teaching programs, the representativeness of the skills measured on the basis of achievement areas delimited by P.L. 94-192, as well as empirical validation of items by using item difficulty and discrimination indices.

The DAB-2 is a standardized norm-referenced test. The standardization sample included 2,623 students from 40 different states tested in 1988–89. The sample was representative of the national population in terms of sex, residence, race, and ethnicity variables as well as geographic distribution. The administration and scoring instructions presented in the examiner's manual are clearly written and make it easy to use this instrument and interpret the different scores obtained. Raw scores may be converted into percentiles, standard scores (M = 10, SD = 3), grade equivalents, and composite scores (M = 100, SD = 15). Tables providing minimal differences between subtest scores and composite scores to achieve a significant difference (.05 level) are included, permitting a discrepancy analysis by contrasting test scores within and across domains. Also, the examiner who wishes to engage in further assessment can find additional references in the manual.

Testing time may vary from 1 to 2 hours. Although the subtests have no time limits, entry, basal, and ceiling points are offered for most subtests. The individual format of the DAB-2 permits a greater variety of item and response format than what is available in group-administered tests. The instructions provided on the profile/answer form and the student worksheet are easy to follow and respond to the suggestions of test users of the first edition.

DAB-2 subtests and composite scores present acceptable reliabilities. Internal consistency measures based on alpha coefficients range from the .70s to the .90s for the subtests scores with the great majority reaching or exceeding .80 and from .83 to .99 for the composite scores. The author reports acceptable stability coefficients. However, one must specify that these coefficients were based on the first edition of the DAB and were obtained from a sample of only 34 children with a 2-week interval. For the DAB-2, only subtests that were changed dramatically (Capitalization and Punctuation) and the new Writing Composition were submitted to test-retest reliability analysis. The coefficient obtained with a sample of 52 students and a 1-week interval suggests that scores are stable over time.

With regards to the criterion validity, DAB-2 subtests and composite scores were correlated with the Wide Range Achievement Test—Revised (WRAT-R) and the Detroit Tests of Learning Aptitude—School Edition (DTLA-SE) in a sample of 45 students from grades 1 through 6. Analysis of the correlation coefficients obtained does not provide strong evidence of criterion validity for every type of scores. In some cases, it appears that different subtests measure different aspects of the same skill.

Substantial evidence for construct validity is presented and supports the author's pretention for this hypothesis. Indeed, performance on the DAB-2 subtests is significantly related to chronological age and grade level, the subtests intercorrelation coefficients as well as the correlation with scholastic aptitude tests are sufficiently high, and the test has been shown to discriminate between "regular" and learning-disabled pupils.

One criticism is the author does not provide sufficient information concerning the new Writing Composition subtest. Although the data from this subtest are not amenable to standard analysis, it would be of interest to provide some information (for example, mean across different age groups).

In summary, the DAB-2 is a well-designed individual diagnostic test. The addition of information concerning the administration instructions and the new studies improving norms, reliability, and validity make this instrument an excellent tool.

Review of the Diagnostic Achievement Battery, Second Edition by RIC BROWN, Acting Director, University Grants and Research Office, California State University, Fresno, Fresno, CA:

The author describes the Diagnostic Achievement Battery, Second Edition (DAB-2) as a standardized achievement test to assess abilities in listening, speaking, reading, writing, and mathematics. The need expressed for this individual test stemmed from the reported problems with group tests and their inability to diagnose effectively specific weaknesses in children. The author contends that although other individual tests (e.g., Woodcock Reading Mastery Test, KeyMath Diagnostic Arithmetic Test—Revised) are more specific and others (Peabody Individual Achievement Test—Revised, Test of Adolescent Language-2) are more comprehensive, no other test examines the variety of skills related to P.L. 94-192 as does the DAB-2.

The purposes of the DAB-2 as described by the author are to (*a*) identify students who are below their peers in areas of spoken language (listening and speaking), written language (reading and writing), and mathematics who may benefit from remedial assistance; (*b*) determine specific area strengths and weaknesses; (*c*) document progress in specific areas as a result of intervention; and, (*d*) serve as a measurement device of academic achievement.

The DAB-2 was developed around three major constructs, subsuming five major components composed from 12 subtests. The test manual provides a detailed description of each of the following constructs listed with its respective components and tests: Spoken Language (Listening—Story Comprehension, Characteristics; Speaking—Synonyms, Grammatical Completion); Written Language (Reading—Comprehension, Alphabet/Word Knowledge; Writing—Punctuation, Spelling, Capitalization, Writing Composition); Mathematics (Mathematics—Calculation, Reasoning). A score for each subtest can be calculated and various subtests can be combined to produce composite scores and construct scores.

For those familiar with the 1983 version of the DAB, the author indicates that eight subtests remain unchanged. Reading Comprehension was altered by changing a few questions and Writing Composition replaced Written Vocabulary. Two subtests (Capitalization and Punctuation) were noted to be significantly altered.

Many tables are presented to support the reliability and validity of the test, although most of the data are from very small, convenience samples. Although the author reports 2,623 children tested between the ages of 6 and 14 are included for norming of the DAB-2, data reported for validity and reliability are based upon small samples as well as from a 1982–83 testing. For example, for item selection, 100 students from (apparently) one city were used for item difficulty and item discrimination statistics.

In terms of reliability, 50 tests for each 1-year age interval yielded alpha coefficients (internal consistency) of .70 to .98 for all subtests. Test-retest (2 weeks) reliability is reported for 34 Delaware children in 1981 for the DAB and 52 students in Los Angeles (for three subtests) with 1-week time interval for the DAB-2. Acceptable coefficients, all greater than .80, were found. For validity support, small samples of 46 students from Pennsylvania in 1982 and 45 students in Texas in 1989 were given the DAB and DAB-2 respectively, with a variety of similar tests (e.g., Wide Range Achievement Test, Woodcock Reading Mastery Test). Subtest correlations ranged from .36 to .81. Although what is presented in terms of reliability and validity is encouraging, the data are on very small, convenience samples and must be interpreted with caution.

Norms (means) for each subtest are presented for each age from 6 to 14 based on the selected sample of 2,623 children from 40 states. The subjects were obtained by asking previous users of the original DAB and other users of the publisher's tests to give 20 to 30 DAB-2 tests. Although clearly not a random sample, the demographics of the selected sample do match the 1985 Statistical Abstracts for the general population of the U.S.

Specific instructions for administration using a student booklet and a profile/answer form are provided in the examiner's manual. Although there are no set time limits, a range from 1 to 2 hours is recommended. For each age, an entry point on each subtest is specified (to avoid easier items as older children are tested) and five consecutive incorrect answers stop the testing session for a subtest. Specific examples are given for each subtest in terms of the entry point and the ceiling.

The profile/answer form provided makes determining the subtest and composite scores very simple by providing a workspace and computation grid. Space is also provided for some examinee information including results of other similar tests the child may have taken. The conversion of raw scores (number of items correct) on each subtest forms the basis for developing what the author refers to as standard scores (each subtest distribution has 20 points and is normed by age with a mean of 10 and a standard deviation of 3). These scores are then combined to form a total score which is then converted (by use of a table) to what the author calls quotients. Although not specifically stated, these quotient scores give the appearance of an IQ test distribution. A variety of tables are provided to produce these scores as well as provide percentiles and the ubiquitous grade equivalents (with the appropriate caveat that they not be used).

SUMMARY. Although the test is called a diagnostic battery, very little text is devoted to interpretation. Some cautions are given regarding test use as well as a 3-point process to discuss the results with others.

It is not clear what the unique contribution of this test is relative to other group or individual academic achievement tests. The subtests seem to measure common constructs and the questions are fairly standard (e.g., read a sentence or two and answer questions regarding theme, sentence completion items, synonym word lists, verbal spelling and verbal math problems). Additionally, the DAB-2 has a problem in terms of the adequacy and representativeness of the norm group. This test has norms that are now 4 years old and are based on a nonrandom group of children. Further, for a user to know that a particular child in a particular state is below the mean of some selected norm group belies the concept of diagnostic assessment.

[115]

Diagnostic Assessments of Reading.

Purpose: Constructed to assess skills in reading and language.
Population: Grades 1–12.
Publication Date: 1992.
Acronym: DAR.
Scores: Mastery level scores in 6 areas: Word Recognition, Word Analysis, Oral Reading, Silent Reading Comprehension, Spelling, Word Meaning.
Administration: Individual.
Price Data, 1992: $150 per complete kit including testing materials listed below plus teaching strategies materials; $12 per student book; $15 per 15 student record booklets; $30 per response record with directions for administration; $6 per manual (33 pages).
Time: (20–30) minutes.
Authors: Florence G. Roswell and Jeanne S. Chall.
Publisher: The Riverside Publishing Co.

Review of the Diagnostic Assessments of Reading by KEVIN D. CREHAN, Associate Professor of Educational Psychology, University of Nevada, Las Vegas, Las Vegas, NV:

DESCRIPTION. The Diagnostic Assessments of Reading (DAR) is an individually administered multilevel-multiscale system for determining areas of reading and language proficiency and weakness. The DAR is the assessment part of a package designed to diagnose reading difficulties and assist in the development of remedial instructional programs. The six areas of reading and language assessed are Word Recognition (WR), Word Analysis (WA), Oral Reading (OR), Silent Reading Comprehension (SRC), Spelling (SP), and Word Meaning (WM). Mastery tests within each of these areas, except SR, are provided for Beginning Levels 1-1 and 1-2 and Primary Levels 2 and 3. The Word Analysis mastery tests are skipped if the examinee scores at Level 4 or higher on the Word Recognition test. The Word Analysis mastery tests include scales measuring Consonant Sounds, Consonant Blends, Short Vowel Sounds, Rule of Silent E, Vowel Digraphs, Diphthongs, Vowels with R, and Polysyllabic Words. Prereading measures of Naming Capital Letters, Naming Lower Case Letters, Matching Letters, and Matching Words are also included. Mastery tests for all areas except WA are provided as follows: Intermediate, Levels 4 through 8; and Advanced, Levels 9/10 and 11/12. Directions for administration and scoring are clear and should lead to efficient use (administration time is 20–30 minutes) and acceptable objectivity in scoring by the classroom teacher.

Results of testing an individual student are summarized on the DAR Interpretive Profile which displays mastery level attained for WR, WA, OR, SRC, SP, and WM. A mastery check list is provided for the sub-areas of WA if used. Performance on the DAR is evaluated for strengths and weaknesses leading to selection of appropriate Trial Teaching Strategies (TTS) which are part of the total package accompanying the DAR. Case studies for prototypical DAR profiles are provided to aid in using the TTS. Ultimately, a program of remedial instruction is developed based on the student's DAR profile and teacher judgment of performance on the TTS exercises.

BACKGROUND. The rationale for the development of the DAR instruments is based on Carroll's (1977) theory of three components underlying reading comprehension: language, cognition, and reading skills. Reading comprehension is explained by the development and relative strengths in these areas. An additional basis for the DAR is a state developmental theory, presented by DAR coauthor Jeanne S. Chall in 1979 and as subsequently elaborated (Chall, 1983). The authors believe that assessment of the components of reading and language skills and direct instruction in deficit areas are more useful than attempting to identify and remedy the supposed underlying causes of reading difficulty.

RELIABILITY AND VALIDITY. An unpublished preliminary technical note provided by the publisher presents some results of a pilot testing in 1989 and a validation study in 1990–1991. The pilot, or tryout, study observed 1,664 students in grades 1 through 8 with sample sizes ranging from 90 to 318 per grade. Students who were judged by teachers to be reading at grade level were selected to participate in the study. The vocabulary subtest of the Gates-MacGinitie Reading Tests (GMRT) was used as an anchor for two preliminary forms of the DAR. Students were tested at and out of grade level on one of two pilot forms of the DAR. The results of this pilot were used to develop the final form of the test, using reading passages and test items with the "best statistical characteristics" from the two pilot tests. The actual item selection process was not described. Means scores of the pilot sample were generally comparable to the GMRT standardization sample scores, but were somewhat less variable. Correlations among DAR subtest scores and GMRT vocabulary scores were moderate and varied over grade. The highest correspondence between DAR subtests and the GMRT vocabulary score was for the WR subtests, with an average correlation of .61 over grade levels 2 through 8 (range .24 to .80). Correlations could be attenuated due to the relatively lower variability of the tryout sample compared to the national standardization sample to the GMRT.

A nominal validation study was conducted during the 1990–91 school year in grades 1 through 12, with a sample of 1,216 students judged by their teachers as achieving below potential in reading. Sample sizes ranged from 10 to 185 per grade. Smaller sample sizes at grades 9/10 and 11/12 were combined in the data summarization. Again, the GMRT was used for comparison. Students were first tested on the GMRT, then administered the DAR and given the TTS exercises. Two subsequent administrations of the GMRT were conducted but the results of these testings were omitted from the report. Not surprisingly, the validation sample, selected as underachieving, had lower scores on the GMRT than the national standardization sample for this test. Correlations among the GMRT vocabulary and comprehension subtests and the highest mastery level attained on the DAR subscores were moderate in aggregate. A pattern of higher correlations between highest DAR mastery level and GMRT Vocabulary as compared to GMRT Comprehension was evidenced over grades. Surprisingly, this was true even for correlations between DAR mastery level in SRC and the GMRT Vocabulary. Seven of the nine levels had higher correlations between GMRT Vocabulary and DAR SRC than for GMRT Comprehension and DAR SRC.

Several tables of item statistics and descriptive statistics were provided for the validation sample. These tables, especially those reporting percentile ranks, need careful interpretation, given the nature (nominal underachievers) and sizes of the samples involved in the study.

SUMMARY. The DAR and TTS assessment and teaching materials demonstrate considerable thought and effort in preparation and production. It is likely the materials will be valuable to teachers attempting to develop remedial reading programs for individuals and small groups. However, more evidence must be developed and reported to support the psychometric quality and instructional utility of the package. The preliminary technical report does not report the reliability of results for either the pilot study or the validation study. Reliability of results might be inferred from correlations of DAR subtests with GMRT scores but more direct evidence is desired. Evidence related to concurrent/construct validity of the DAR and the GMRT does not fit consistently what would be expected. One would expect that two nominal measures of reading comprehension would correlate higher than would a measure of vocabulary and a measure of comprehension. Perhaps this apparent anomaly is attributable to the nature of the two score distributions involved in the correlation. The DAR SCR score is a relatively gross measure of mastery with a change in one level (one point) conceivably equivalent to a year's growth in reading comprehension, whereas the GMRT Comprehension normative score is on a more refined scale.

Additional studies of DAR score reliability should be conducted to determine the stability and consistency of the mastery level decisions as well as to establish further evidence of validity.

REVIEWER'S REFERENCES

Carroll, J. B. (1977). Developmental parameters of reading comprehension. In J. T. Guthrie (Ed.), *Cognition, curriculum, and comprehension* (pp. 1-15). Newark, DE: International Reading Association.

Chall, J. S. (1983). *Stages of reading development*. New York: McGraw-Hill Book Company.

Review of the Diagnostic Assessments of Reading by GENE SCHWARTING, Project Director of Early Childhood Special Education, Omaha Public Schools, Omaha, NE:

For a number of years, attempts have been made to develop assessment tools with related educational programs to work towards remediation of those specific areas of relative weakness as noted in the obtained test profile for each individual. The Diagnostic Assessments of Reading with Trial Teaching Strategies (DARTTS) package is yet another effort, focusing on the area of reading. The goal is ambitious, as the instrument purports to serve this purpose for grades 1 through 12.

The Diagnostic Assessment of Reading (DAR) measures skills in six areas of reading: Word Recognition (used to determine student placement into all but one of the other scales), Word Analysis (containing eight regular and four prereading subtests), Oral Reading, Silent Reading Comprehension, Spelling, and Word Meaning. Objectives indicated by the authors include the assessment of relative strengths in reading and language, determination of the areas in which further instruction is needed, and the provision of feedback to students regarding skills and needs. Materials include a teacher's manual, a student book, student record booklets, and response records with directions for administration.

Trial Teaching Strategies (TTS) consists of a series of short lessons that may be utilized to follow up on the DAR through a diagnostic teaching approach. Materials include a teacher's manual, record booklets, 10 envelopes with stimulus cards, and six storybooks.

All materials are well designed, although they are not sufficiently colorful to appeal to younger children. Directions are clear, but do require study prior to administration due to complexity with regards to sequence and variability of the levels of mastery from one task to another.

A concern is the manual's lack of psychometric information regarding the DAR—nowhere in the manual is there information on background or development of the instrument, the credentials of the authors, norming, reliability, validity, or relationships with other assessment instruments or reading curricula. A request to the publisher for such information elicited a response which noted the authors have substantial experience in the diagnosis and treatment of reading disorders as well as in administration of programs for such purposes. Norming was conducted in 1990–91 on 1,216 students, grades 1 through 12, who were also administered the 1989 Gates-MacGinitie Reading Tests. Unfortunately, information as to the geographical location, sex, race, socioeconomic status, and selection process for the subjects was not provided.

Correlations among the DAR and Gates subtests vary widely, with some comparisons (such as Word Recognition with Vocabulary and Silent Reading Comprehension with Comprehension) being significantly lower than anticipated (in the .50 to .70 range). Intercorrelations of the various DAR subtests are sometimes quite high, raising the question of whether they actually measure different skills. Measures of reliability were not provided.

In summary, the Diagnostic Assessments of Reading with Trial Teaching Strategies (DARTTS) package appears to be an adequate tool for assessing and teaching reading skills. However, prospective users should be provided additional information in the manual. Without normative data, concern exists as to the applicability of the instrument for a school population.

[116]

Diagnostic Mathematics Profiles.

Purpose: Constructed to diagnose problems in addition, subtraction, multiplication, and division.
Population: Australian school years 3–6.
Publication Date: 1990.
Scores: Item scores only.
Administration: Group or individual.
Parts, 4: Addition, Subtraction, Multiplication, Division.
Price Data, 1994: A$37.50 per test package including 30 copies of each part; $14.50 per manual (23 pages).
Time: Administration time not reported.
Author: Brian Doig.
Publisher: Australian Council for Educational Research Ltd. [Australia].

Review of the Diagnostic Mathematics Profile by JOHN M. ENGER, Professor of Education, Arkansas State University, Jonesboro, AR:

The Diagnostic Mathematics Profile is a series of four tests on whole numbers. There is one test on each of the arithmetic operations: Addition, Subtraction, Multiplication, and Division. The tests are from Australia where they were copyrighted in 1990. Each of the four tests consists of 20 items. Each test is related to a set of objectives: 8 objectives in Addition, 8 in Subtraction, 12 in Multiplication, and 7 in Division. The objectives are quite specific in describing the number of digits in the numbers and whether or not regrouping is a part of the arithmetic operation. The tests are said to be appropriate for assessing children from Year 3 to Year 6 (in the Australian system).

The publisher claims a unique feature of the Diagnostic Mathematics Profile is the DIAMAP, a handy visual guide to interpret children's performance in regard to the hierarchy of the objectives being tested. A class analysis chart is also provided to record student performance by objective being tested.

In a very limited tryout, the four tests in the Diagnostic Mathematics Profile appeared to work well, and in the manner described in the teacher's manual. Students in grades 2 through 4 were administered these tests by their teacher. It generally took the children about 20 minutes to complete each test. [The children seemed intrigued to find the test they had taken was from Australia.] The scores recorded on the DIAMAP were quite consistent with how the teacher had anticipated each student would perform. This analysis was made using a separate, independent teacher appraisal of student performance on the objectives being tested.

In comparison with other mathematics tests commonly used for diagnosis, several favorable features of the tests in the Diagnostic Mathematics profile were: (*a*) the number of items dedicated solely to whole numbers; and (*b*) the shorter time it took to administer the tests. The tests would be very useful for instructional diagnosis and very helpful for initial placement of students. However, in comparison with other tests commonly used for mathematics diagnosis, a feature lacking in the tests in the Diagnostic Mathematics Profile was a standard score (such as an NCE, normal curve equivalent score) to report the results. Reporting a standard score such as the NCE would be helpful for using these tests in a Chapter 1 program.

Other concerns in using the tests from the Diagnostic Mathematics Profile include the limited number of items, generally two and sometimes three, used to test mastery of each objective. Also, in selecting a test, the user would expect more information from the publisher on reliability, validity, and normative data.

Overall, the Diagnostic Mathematics Profile with the accompanying DIAMAP worked as the publisher suggested. The tests were easy to administer and score; the results were also easy to plot and interpret on the DIAMAP. These tests are most useful for diagnosing problems an elementary student may have in the addition, subtraction, multiplication, and division of whole numbers.

Review of the Diagnostic Mathematics Profile by ARLEN R. GULLICKSON, Professor and Chief of Staff for The Evaluation Center, Western Michigan University, Kalamazoo, MI:

The Diagnostic Mathematics Profile is a collection of four tests for instructional use in the elementary classroom (Australian Years 3–6). Its purpose is to help the teacher determine the extent to which students have mastered basic skills in addition, subtraction, multiplication, or division, and to provide diagnostic information when the student has not mastered the tested skill.

The tests, developed in Australia, are neither normed nor standardized, though the tests appear to be carefully developed. The tests are not timed, and teachers are encouraged to give students sufficient time to complete a test, though test taking can be stopped if the student is having substantial difficulty. Each test comprises 20 items carefully organized by topic (objective) and arranged in a hierarchical fashion with easier items presented first and more difficult items last.

The publishers encourage the teacher to employ the test in ways that seem most sensible. For example, teachers' reuse of the tests is encouraged, with a time lapse between, so that students do not remember individual items. Teachers are even encouraged to allow students to start the test at some point after the beginning, if the teacher is confident the students understand and can properly complete one or more of the objective sets.

The scoring schemes presented with the test make the test unique and desirable. Two separate schemes are provided. The first serves evaluation of individuals; the second serves evaluation of the larger group. The individual score reporting scheme is presented on the back page of the student's test booklet. Each item is shown on this page, with items completed correctly being marked in the left "column" and incorrect items in the right column. Objectives are presented in "rows" with the first low skill items in the bottom row of the page. This presentation format allows both the teacher and student to see which items have been worked correctly and to identify those particular basic skills that still need to be learned. This scoring presentation is to be used by the teacher in concert with the actual work of the student to make diagnostic decisions. The group scoring scheme (class chart) provides a table in which the teacher profiles objectives for the group. Each row of the table depicts a specific student, and each column depicts an objective. The value reported in each cell is the number of items the student got correct for a specific objective. That arrangement makes it easy for the teacher to quickly determine which, if any, of the objectives are causing problems for the group as a whole. That strategy has good potential for directing instruction to clarify problems common to the class.

There are several potential problems with the test profile. First, each test objective is covered by very few items, never more than four, typically two, and as few as one. Therefore, individuals may be misdiagnosed if a test is relied on too heavily. Second, test items are likely to be remembered; thus, a test probably will not serve well for retesting purposes, particularly where teachers retest within a week or two. However, the blueprints for the tests are clearly evident in the scoring and reporting formats. Thus, teachers can construct comparable tests to use alongside these tests in instruction.

Despite their minor shortcomings, this group of tests is a welcome addition to the classroom. The tests are not geared to a specific textbook and can be used in a variety of situations from standard instructional role to providing special assistance in situations where a student is falling behind. Perhaps most importantly, the Diagnostic Mathematics Profile provides a clear lesson on how tests can be organized and presented to directly facilitate instruction.

[117]

Differential Aptitude Tests—Computerized Adaptive Edition.

Purpose: A system of computer programs that measures the "abilities of examinees for the purpose of educational and vocational guidance."
Population: Grades 8–12.
Publication Date: 1987.
Acronym: DAT Adaptive.
Scores, 8: Verbal Reasoning, Numerical Ability, Total, Abstract Reasoning, Clerical Speed and Accuracy, Mechanical Reasoning, Space Relations, Spelling, and Language Usage.
Administration: Individual.
Price Data, 1994: FOR APPLE COMPUTERS: $54.50 per examination kit including user's manual (103 pages), demonstration diskettes A and C, orientation booklet, score report folder, sample individual report, and product summary; $145.50 per start-up package including diskette A, reusable diskette B/C, reusable user's manual, diskette jacket/waiting list form, 10 orientation booklets, and 10 score report folders, $75 per replenishment package including diskette A, diskette jacket/waiting list form, 10 orientation booklets, and 10 score report folders; FOR IBM COMPUTERS: $54.50 per examination kit including demonstration disks 1 and 2, guide to the demonstration software, orientation booklet, score report folder, orientation booklet score report folder, sample individual report, and product summary; $145.50 per 10-use start-up package available in 5.25-inch or 3.5-inch diskettes including user's manual, disks 1, 2, and 3, disk jacket/waiting list form, 10 orientation booklets, and 10 score report folders; $303.50 per 35-use start-up package in 5.25-inch or 3.5-inch diskettes including same accessories as 10-use start-up package with 35 orientation booklets and 35 score report folders; $75 per 10-use replenishment package in 5.25-inch or 3.5-inch diskettes including disk 1, disk jacket/waiting list form, 10 orientation booklets, and 10 score report folders; $30.50 each for disk 2 and disk 3; $25.50 per administrator handbook; $20.50 per counselor's manual.
Time: (90) minutes.
Comments: Computer requirements: Apple (IIc, IIe, and II+, Franklin Ace 1000, and Laser 128; 64K memory, two drives; monochrome or color monitor); IBM (PC, XT, AT, PS/1, and compatibles; 256K memory; two disk drives; two 5.25-inch or 3.5-inch floppy, or one 5.25-inch and one 3.5-inch floppy; monitor with graphic capability, a Hercules or color graphics [CGA, EGA] card); contains the Differential Aptitude Tests (DAT) and the optional Career Planning Questionnaire; adaptive selection of test items from the traditional DAT (118).
Author: The Psychological Corporation.
Publisher: The Psychological Corporation.

Review of Differential Aptitude Tests—Computerized Adaptive Edition by STEVEN L. WISE, Associate Professor of Educational Psychology, University of Nebraska-Lincoln, Lincoln, NE:

The Differential Aptitude Tests—Computerized Adaptive Edition (DAT-Adaptive) is a computer-administered version of the DAT, which is an aptitude battery that has been widely used in a paper-and-pencil format for many years. The DAT was designed to measure the abilities of students in grades 8–12 for the purposes of educational and vocational guidance. Development of the DAT has been well documented, and the DAT norms were based on a carefully chosen, nationally representative standardization sample. Moreover, the reliabilities of the eight subtests are acceptable, and an impressive body of validity evidence has accumulated.

The DAT-Adaptive Examination Kit contains two 5.25-inch demonstration disks and five items of documentation, including a software guide, a sample individual report, a score report interpretation folder, an orientation booklet for students, and a user's manual for test administrators. Notably absent from the test materials was information regarding the technical aspects of the adaptive test, such as type of item response theory model used, size of the item pool for each subtest, type of item selection algorithm used, the ability estimation method used, and the criteria used for termination of a subtest. The DAT-Adaptive test materials contain several statements that the test difficulty is adapted to each student and that number of administered test items is reduced by half, relative to the conventional DAT. This information, however, is vague and inadequate for a potential user who wishes to understand any of the technical characteristics of the adaptive version.

The DAT-Adaptive, which can be administered via either Apple II or DOS-based IBM-compatible microcomputers, requires only 256K of memory (IBM version), which suggests that the DAT-Adaptive can be used with many available microcomputers. Although this may have been true in the mid-1980s when the DAT-Adaptive was developed, it is far less true in the mid-1990s where Macintosh and Windows operating systems have become increasingly common. I contacted The Psychological Corporation regarding this matter, and was informed by a technical consultant that the DAT-Adaptive was not available in Macintosh or Windows versions, nor are there any current plans to develop such versions. This restricts the usefulness of the DAT-Adaptive, particularly the Apple version, because it requires computer hardware and operating systems that some schools may no longer possess. In addition, the practice of running the DAT-

Adaptive from floppy disks is obsolete in the 1990s. Virtually all microcomputers sold in recent years contain internal hard disks, which are extremely useful in efficiently administering adaptive tests. I found the DAT-Adaptive, with its frequent disk accesses, to be very slow by current standards.

In running the demonstration program (Apple version), I found the item presentation to be adequate. Responding to an item, however, is a bit awkward, as a student cannot simply select an option. Instead, the student must respond "no" to Option A to highlight Option B, "no" to Option B to highlight Option C, and so on. Thus, if the student wanted to choose Option E for a particular item, he or she must first answer "no" to Options A, B, C, and D before Option E can be chosen. This style of item responding is likely to be annoying to some students.

Although the conventional DAT is established and well studied, the conversion of any test to an adaptive version raises a number of technical and psychometric questions that require attention. The developers of an adaptive test have a responsibility to provide a user with both technical information regarding the workings of the adaptive test and psychometric information regarding the reliability and validity of the adaptive test and comparability between scores obtained from the adaptive and conventional versions. Until such information is provided, potential users of the DAT-Adaptive should be cautious in adopting this test.

It is therefore difficult to recommend the DAT-Adaptive in its present form. My overall impression of the DAT-Adaptive is that, although it was once a state-of-the-art example of adaptive testing, it has suffered from neglect. It is hoped that new versions of the DAT-Adaptive will be developed that take advantage of current computer capabilities, and that potential users will be provided adequate technical and psychometric information.

[118]

Differential Aptitude Tests, Fifth Edition.

Purpose: "Designed to measure students' ability to learn or to succeed in a number of different areas."
Population: Grades 7–9, grades 10–12 and adults.
Publication Dates: 1947–92.
Acronym: DAT.
Scores: 9 tests (Verbal Reasoning, Numerical Reasoning, Abstract Reasoning, Perceptual Speed and Accuracy [Part 1, Part 2], Mechanical Reasoning, Space Relations, Spelling, Language Usage) and Total Scholastic Aptitude.
Administration: Group.
Levels, 2: 1, 2.
Price Data, 1994: $37.50 per 25 Form C partial battery test booklets (Levels 1 or 2) including Directions for Administering ('90, 47 pages); $81.50 per 25 Form C complete battery test booklets (Levels 1 or 2) including Directions for Administering; $63.50 per 100 Type 1 machine-scorable answer documents with DAT (Levels 1 or 2, Form C), $96 per 100 Type 1 machine-scorable answer documents with DAT (Levels 1 or 2, Form C) and Level 1 or Level 2 Career Interest Inventory; $82 per Type 2 machine-scorable answer documents with 100 Perceptual Speed and Accuracy—Part 1 answer sheets and DAT (Levels 1 and 2, Form C); $43 per Ready-Score answer documents with 25 Perceptual Speed and Accuracy—Part 1 answer sheets, Profile Your DAT scores pamphlet, and Levels 1 or 2 of Form C; $21.50 per norms booklet (Fall or Spring); $21.50 per Using the DAT with Adults; $17.50 per 25 Practice Tests including a practice test for the Career Interest Inventory and Directions; $74.50 per Guide to Careers Student Workbook; $12 per 25 Exploring Aptitudes: An Introduction to the Differential Aptitude Tests; $12 per 25 Using Test Results for Decision-Making; $21.50 per Technical Manual ('92, 192 pages); $3 per Directions for Practice Test; $4.50 per Directions for Administering; price information for scoring and reporting services available from publisher.
Time: 156(206) minutes.
Comments: 2 forms (C, D) per level; partial battery includes only 2 subtests (Verbal Reasoning and Numerical Reasoning); can be used in conjunction with Career Interest Inventory (T4:396).
Authors: G. K. Bennett, H. G. Seashore, and A. G. Wesman.
Publisher: The Psychological Corporation.
Cross References: See T4:802 (31 references); for reviews of Forms V and W by Ronald K. Hambleton and Daryl Sander, see 9:352 (19 references); see also T3:732 (26 references); for reviews by Thomas J. Bouchard, Jr., and Robert L. Linn and an excerpted review by Gerald S. Hanna of earlier forms, see 8:485 (56 references); see also T2:1069 (64 references); for a review by M. Y. Quereshi and an excerpted review by Jack C. Merwin of earlier forms, see 7:673 (139 references); for reviews by J. A. Keats and Richard E. Schutz, see 6:767 (52 references); for reviews by John B. Carroll and Norman Frederiksen, see 5:605 (49 references); for reviews by Harold Bechtoldt, Ralph F. Berdie, and Lloyd G. Humphreys, see 4:711 (27 references); for an excerpted review, see 3:620.

TEST REFERENCES

1. Westbrook, B. W., Sanford, E., Gilleland, K., Fleenor, J., & Merwin, G. (1988). Career maturity in grade 9: The relationship between accuracy of self-appraisal and ability to appraise the career-relevant capabilities of others. *Journal of Vocational Behavior*, *32*, 269-283.

2. Henly, S. J., Klebe, K. J., McBride, J. R., & Cudek, R. (1989). Adaptive and conventional versions of the DAT: The first complete test battery comparison. *Applied Psychological Measurement*, *13*, 363-371.

3. Sparrow, J. (1989). The utility of PAQ in relating job behaviours to traits. *Journal of Occupational Psychology*, *62*, 151-162.

4. Benbow, C. P., & Minor, L. L. (1990). Cognitive profiles of verbally and mathematically precocious students: Implications for identification of the gifted. *Gifted Child Quarterly*, *34*, 21-26.

5. Guttman, R., Epstein, E. E., Amir, M., & Guttman, L. (1990). A structural theory of spatial abilities. *Applied Psychological Measurement*, *14*, 217-236.

6. Hampson, E. (1990). Variations in sex-related cognitive abilities across the menstrual cycle. *Brain and Cognition*, *14*, 26-43.

7. Sowell, E. J., Zeigler, A. J., Bergwall, L., & Cartwright, R. M. (1990). Identification and description of mathematically gifted students: A review of empirical research. *Gifted Child Quarterly*, *34*, 147-154.

8. BouJaoude, S. B. (1992). The relationship between students' learning strategies and the change in their misunderstandings during a high school chemistry course. *Journal of Research in Science Teaching*, *29*, 687-699.

9. Luthar, S. S., Zigler, E., & Goldstein, D. (1992). Psychosocial adjustment among intellectually gifted adolescents: The role of cognitive-developmental and experimental factors. *Journal of Child Psychology and Psychiatry and Allied Disciplines*, *33*, 361-373.

10. Keig, P. F., & Rubba, P. A. (1993). Translation of representations of the structure of matter and its relationship to reasoning, gender, spatial reasoning, and specific prior knowledge. *Journal of Research in Science Teaching, 30,* 883-903.

11. Lawton, C. A. (1993). Contextual factors affecting errors in proportional reasoning. *Journal for Research in Mathematics Education, 24,* 460-466.

12. Luthar, S. S., & Quinlan, D. M. (1993). Parental images in two cultures: A study of women in India and American. *Journal of Cross-Cultural Psychology, 24,* 186-202.

13. Schmitt, N., Cortina, J. M., & Whitney, D. J. (1993). Appropriateness fit and criterion-related validity. *Applied Psychological Measurement, 17,* 143-150.

14. Campion, M. A., Campion, J. E., & Hudson, J. D., Jr. (1994). Structured interviewing: A note on incremental validity and alternative question types. *Journal of Applied Psychology, 79,* 998-1002.

15. Hayes, Z. L., & Waller, T. G. (1994). Gender differences in adult readers: A process perspective. *Canadian Journal of Behavioural Science, 26,* 421-437.

16. Liberatore Cavallo, A. M., & Schafer, L. E. (1994). Relationships between students' meaningful learning orientation and their understanding of genetics topics. *Journal of Research in Science Teaching, 31,* 393-418.

Review of the Differential Aptitude Tests, Fifth Edition by KEITH HATTRUP, Assistant Professor of Psychology, New York University, New York, NY:

The latest revision of the Differential Aptitude Tests represents a significant improvement in a well-established battery of aptitude tests used in educational counseling and personnel assessment. With the exception of the Perceptual Speed and Accuracy (PSA) measure (previously named Clerical Speed and Accuracy), completely new items have been provided in two parallel forms for each of two levels (grades 7–9 and grades 10–12). Overall testing time has also been shortened by reducing the length of some of the tests. The Verbal Reasoning, Numerical Reasoning (previously Numerical Ability), Abstract Reasoning, Spelling, and Language Usage tests now each contain 40 items. Mechanical Reasoning consists of 60 items, Space Relations includes 50, and PSA has 100 items. The new items are of the same type, and are intended to measure the same constructs as previous editions.

Expanded normative information has been provided for both Fall and Spring administrations. The DAT also comes with a variety of materials included in a revised career planning kit, including the Career Interest Inventory and the Guide to Careers Student Workbook. In the revision, the authors have responded to many of the criticisms regarding item content and available normative information provided by previous reviewers. The battery continues to represent high professional and scientific standards and remains among the best of its kind. Nevertheless, there remain a number of weaknesses pointed out by previous reviewers, and a few new observations can be offered as suggestions for future improvements.

Rather than measuring conceptually independent factors, the DAT is purported to measure broader aptitudes that should have relevance to the domains of educational and occupational tasks. Hence, each of the subtests probably assesses several common and unique factors. In fact, the high correlations among the tests support the notion that a general factor, *g*, underlies performance on each of the measures. The PSA measure appears most unique given its lower correlations with the other measures. Despite substantial overlap among the tests, differences in the correlations among DAT subtests and scores on achievement subtests and grades in various courses provide some support for the differential validity of tests for different criteria. In many cases Verbal Reasoning (VR) correlated highest with verbal achievement scores, whereas Numerical Reasoning (NR) correlated highest with math scores. However, no direct evidence is provided of the significance of differences in correlations or regression equations involving different subtest-criterion combinations, or of the incremental contribution of subtests in the prediction of various criteria. Discriminant function analyses of possible differential score profiles among relevant criterion groups are also not presented. The longstanding criticism that several subtests of the DAT may not be sufficiently *differential* remains. Test users may find that the prediction of overall academic GPA or job proficiency may not be improved by adding tests after using a composite of a small subset of the tests, such as VR + NR. Much more research needs to be directed to the differential and incremental validity of the subtests for prediction of valid educational and occupational criteria.

Although there is a lack of evidence of differential or incremental validity, substantial support is offered for the tests' reliability and validity. Despite the reduction in test length, internal consistencies remain high, ranging from .80 to .95 across tests and samples. Alternate-forms reliabilities were computed by correlating scores on the two new forms, C and D. These values ranged from .73 to .90, with a median of .83. Correlations are also presented between scores on Form C and scores on Form V from the Fourth Edition. Although the authors claim that these values provide evidence of the criterion-related validity of the Fifth Edition, the correlations are probably more appropriately considered alternate-form reliabilities. Most of these correlations are in the 70s and low 80s; however, the values for the PSA measure range only from .49 to .57. The results generally support the notion that scores are stable over different operationalizations of item content.

Evidence of the tests' validities consists primarily of correlations with other aptitude tests and standardized high school achievement tests. Many of the correlations with aptitude tests are quite high. For example, the VR + NR composite correlated on average .72 with composite scores on the ACT, .76 with the ASVAB Academic Ability composite, .68 with SAT Verbal, and .77 with SAT Math. This provides support for the inference that the DAT measures aptitudes that have been conceptualized and measured in similar ways by other authors. Correlations with achievement test scores are also very high. For example, VR + NR correlated on average .85 with total battery scores from the California Achievement Tests. A graphic summary of correlations of DAT scores with grades in high school English, math, science, and social studies is also provided in an appendix. Over one-half of the correlations are in the .30 to .60 range. Hence, substantial evidence of the tests' predictive validity for high school achievement is provided. It is unfortunate, however, that data are not provided regarding the validity of the DAT as a predictor of job performance, despite very widespread use of the battery in personnel selection.

A significant limitation to the evidence provided regarding test-criterion relationships has to do with the manner in which validity information is presented. Separate correlations are provided for different samples taking the same DAT-criterion combinations, resulting in a large number of tables with very similar information. This causes two problems. First, although the level of detail and the large number of samples are to be commended, the great number of entries without any summary tables makes interpretation of the results difficult. Second, many of the sample-specific correlations are based on small *n*s, often as small as 16 to 30 cases. Although the authors are careful to call attention to the role of sample size in interpreting correlational results, they fail to address the impact of sampling error using modern statistical techniques. Specifically, meta-analytic techniques should have been applied to the data presented in the technical manual to ascertain the average relationship between scores across settings, and the impact of sampling error and other statistical artifacts on variance in the observed correlations (Hunter & Schmidt, 1990). Previous research with the General Aptitude Test Battery suggest that aptitude-criterion correlations are quite stable across jobs of similar complexity, even when error-prone measures of job performance, such as supervisory ratings, are used (e.g., Hunter & Hunter, 1984). The authors' neglect of meta-analytic research is also apparent in their recommended emphasis on local validation research by users of the DAT. Although local validation is often of value, results of such local efforts may be seriously misleading unless sample sizes are large and representative. The authors are not incorrect in emphasizing continued local validation; however, they neglect to address the extent to which correlations computed with DAT scores generalize across samples and settings.

Several previous reviewers have criticized the Language Usage (LU) and Mechanical Reasoning (MR) tests for containing items that may be biased against women. For the Fifth Edition of the DAT, a careful study of sex, race, ethnic, and regional bias was performed. Experts in the field of education were asked to screen items for stereotypic, offensive, or demeaning content, and for content that may have different meanings across regions of the U.S. The numbers of male and female figures depicted in the MR test were also balanced. Mantel-Haenzel and Rasch analyses were then performed to identify items of unequal difficulty across African Americans versus Whites, Hispanics versus Whites, and females versus males who were matched in terms of overall performance on the subtests. Consistent with recommendations in the literature (e.g., Humphreys, 1986), items showing differences in favor of one group were balanced out by items showing differences in favor of the contrasting group. The creators of the current revision are to be commended for their careful attention to issues of bias in testing. Left unexplored, however, is the question of whether DAT items show unequal relationships with their corresponding latent constructs across groups, and whether DAT subtest scores predict criterion performance differentially across groups. Differences of these types would require further revision of item content.

Substantial improvements have been made to the normative information provided with the DAT. The practice of deriving Spring norms from interpolations from the Fall data has been abandoned in the new edition. Approximately 100,000 students participated in the Fall standardization, and approximately 70,000 participated in the Spring standardization. Proportionate representation of geographic regions, socioeconomic status, urbanicites, ethnicities, and nonpublic schools was accomplished with only trivial differences from nation-wide school enrollment statistics in both standardization samples. Separate norms are provided for males and females in each grade for each test level and form and for both Fall and Spring administrations. Raw scores may be readily converted to percentile ranks and stanines within each norm table. Percentile ranks are no longer collapsed into 23 categories, a practice that had drawn criticism from previous reviewers. In addition, scaled scores are provided which are scale and sample free, meaning that derived scale scores can be compared across levels and forms of the same measure, and across examinees of different ages and grades. A table is also provided for converting raw scores from Fourth Edition Forms V and W to equivalent raw scores on Form C or D.

Individual score reports include raw scores, percentile ranks and stanines for males and females, and 90% confidence bands around same-sex percentiles. The national percentile bands are based on the standard errors of measurement and are plotted graphically on a normalized scale. This represents an improvement over the previous practice of drawing bands .5 inches on either side of examinees' observed percentiles. A special form may also be used by examinees to graph their profile of stanine scores across the eight tests. Examinees may also receive a computer-generated interpretation of their responses to the Career Interest Inventory (CII) with their individual score reports. Norms are not provided for the CII, however. The Guide to Careers Student Workbook contains a wealth of information and exercises to help students explore work values, hobbies, interests, and career options.

It cannot be overemphasized that the DAT and CII may only provide a partial view of a student's likelihood of success and satisfaction in various careers. The CII, for example, consists of a series of questions asking examinees to indicate their preferences for various job and educational activities, such as "Work in a gas station" or "Design computer programs." Hence, examinees may respond based on their preconceptions or attitudes about the likability of tasks with which they may have limited experience. Alternative methods of career exploration often request participants to begin by rating their values for various job-related rewards, and then direct participants to additional information about careers that are consistent with those general values. Hence, test takers, administrators, and counselors must be urged to supplement the DAT and CII with additional sources of information. The Guide to Careers Student Workbook provides many relevant exercises in this context.

SUMMARY. Like previous editions, the Fifth Edition of the DAT represents an excellent battery of tests that will continue to be of value for educational and personnel assessment. Particularly impressive are the ongoing efforts to revise and develop the battery in light of new developments in test theory and in response to reviewers' concerns. Careful attention to issues of test bias and expanded normative information represent the most significant improvements in the newest revision. The most serious weakness of the battery continues to be the lack of evidence of differential validity for different criteria, and incremental validity of specific subtests in prediction contexts. It is also unfortunate that evidence of the DAT's validity as a predictor of job performance is still absent in the latest revision. Users of the test in personnel selection contexts would benefit from more thorough normative information and validity evidence in future revisions of the DAT.

REVIEWER'S REFERENCES

Hunter, J. E., & Hunter, R. F. (1984). Validity and utility of alternative predictors of job performance. *Psychological Bulletin, 96*, 72-98.

Humphreys, L. G. (1986). An analysis and evaluation of test and item bias in the prediction context. *Journal of Applied Psychology, 71*, 327-333.

Hunter, J. E., & Schmidt, F. L. (1990). *Methods of meta-analysis: Correcting error and bias in research findings*. Newbury Park, CA: Sage.

Review of the Differential Aptitude Tests, Fifth Edition by NEAL SCHMITT, Professor of Psychology and Management, Michigan State University, East Lansing, MI:

The fifth edition of the Differential Aptitude Tests (DAT) includes a number of innovations which should enhance the usefulness of this multi-aptitude test battery, especially when it is used as a vehicle for career counseling with high school students. First, there are now two aptitude batteries: Level 1 is designed for use with 7th, 8th, and 9th grade students; Level 2 should be used for students in the last 3 years of high school. All items in both batteries are revisions or replacements of items in the previous editions. There are also two forms (C and D) of each level of the test. Data are presented in the manual that allow for equating test scores across forms and with scores on earlier editions of the test.

The test materials now include a Practice Test that students can use as a means of becoming familiar with the types of test items and time requirements for the various subtests. Perhaps the most significant change in this edition of the test is the addition of the Career Interest Inventory with items that assess students' interests in activities related to 15 different occupational groups. Along with the Career Inventory and an accompanying manual, the publisher provides *Guide to Careers* and *Guide to a Career Portfolio*, both of which are labeled student workbooks although the latter is meant as a guide for counselors using these materials. These materials include information on the 15 occupational groups and directions as to how one would access information in the various volumes on careers published by the U.S. Department of labor. A major portion of these two Guides is devoted to directions on how to do a self-analysis of career interests and capabilities. Both students and career counselors should find these Guides helpful.

This edition of the DAT includes extensive norm tables for 84,000 fall and spring participants in testing. The norm group very closely matches the composition of all U.S. high school students with respect to ethnicity, geographic region, socioeconomic status, and urbanicity (rural, suburban, and urban). Internal consistency reliabilities of the various subtests are all in the high .80s or .90s; alternate forms reliability of all the subtests including the speeded Clerical Speed and Accuracy Test are between .73 and the .90s.

There are some areas in which I would hope this battery and perhaps others like it could be improved. First, one of the strengths of the DAT is the wealth of information collected on previous versions of the test and the fact that the current version is highly correlated and linked to the fourth edition of the test. It also seems to me that this may be one of its most significant weaknesses as well. Are these the most important knowledge, skills, and abilities in today's workplace? The manual states that the test developers looked at the skills required today in deciding how to revise the test, but no changes in the constructs measured were made. Certainly, one would expect that verbal and numerical skills would be important, but the SCANs work, which is heavily used in the career materials described above, suggests that other constructs be measured in a modern inventory. That this may be a problem is even more likely when one looks at the similarity of the items in individual subtests; for example, all the items in the Verbal Reasoning test are analogies. There are also Spelling and Language Usage subtests, but what about reading comprehension and actual writing? At least a serious look at the constructs measured in this inventory would seem advisable in light of today's work world.

A second problem mentioned in previous reviews of the DAT is the lack of discriminant validity between the eight subtests. With the exception of the Perceptual Speed and Accuracy test, all of the subscales are highly intercorrelated (.50 to .75). If one wants only a general index of the person's academic ability, this is fine; if the scores on the subtests are to be used in some diagnostic sense, this level of intercorrelation makes statements about students' relative strengths and weaknesses highly questionable. No mention of this fact or any discussion of the standard error of difference between test scores is provided in the manual.

A third problem relates to the lack of external validity data. There are a large number of studies that relate DAT scores to grades and these validities are very high. However, I am not sure they are particularly relevant. If this instrument is used to make predictions about probable success in college or in jobs, then the manual should present correlations with indices of college and job success. No such validity data are presented for this edition of the test. I think it is actually more important that we see correlations with job success than college success for two reasons. Many other instruments are used to make predictions about college success and are probably better designed to do so (e.g., the ceiling of other tests is likely to be higher allowing for discrimination at higher levels of ability). Second, the level of difficulty of all the tests and the nonacademic nature of some of the subscales suggests that the DAT may be most applicable for a high school student who may not be considering further education, at least not education at a traditional 4-year institution. Thus, data regarding predictors of job success seem particularly desirable.

Fourth, the manual presents separate norms for men and women and justifies these separate norms appropriately, I think. However, it seems to me that equally good arguments could be raised for the presentation of separate norms for different ethnic groups. The manual describes several means by which the test developers sought to minimize ethnic group differences in scores on this version of the DAT. These efforts certainly are laudatory, but we are not given any information as to whether there remain subgroup differences on these tests. This is important information for both counseling and selection uses of this battery. One must also note that use of separate norms in any selection applications of this test are likely to produce legal difficulties given the passage of the Civil Rights Act of 1991 is usually interpreted as prohibiting such "score adjustments."

Finally, it should be noted that many of the convergent validities (correlations with measures of similar constructs from other test batteries) are based on very small samples (in a large number of cases less than 30). It seems that some attempt to aggregate these findings should have been made. On the whole, however, these data strongly support the notion that the DAT measures correlate highly with alternate measures of similar constructs.

SUMMARY. The fifth edition of the DAT along with the new Career Interest Inventory is likely to be more useful as a counseling tool than previous versions of the DAT, because of the more holistic view these materials take with respect to the assessment of a student's capabilities and interests. Moreover, the normative data, the tests' reliabilities and standard errors, and the evidence for convergent validity all indicate that this was a carefully developed instrument that should provide useful information. However, I believe that the publisher should at least reconsider the nature of the constructs measured in the DAT, that data regarding subgroup differences in test scores should be provided, and that limitations in the interpretations of subtest score differences should be noted and explained in the manual.

[119]

Differential Aptitude Tests for Personnel and Career Assessment.

Purpose: Designed to measure ability to learn in eight aptitude areas.
Population: Adult.
Publication Dates: 1972–91.
Acronym: DAT for PCA.
Scores, 8: General Cognitive Abilities Tests (Verbal Reasoning, Numerical Ability, Total), Perceptual Abilities Tests (Abstract Reasoning, Mechanical Reasoning, Space Relations), Clerical and Language Tests (Spelling, Language Usage, Clerical Speed and Accuracy).
Administration: Group.
Price Data, 1994: $78 per 25 General Cognitive Abilities Battery tests; $98 per 25 Perceptual Abilities Battery tests; $78 per 25 Clerical/Language Battery tests; $48 per 25 tests (select Verbal Reasoning, Numerical Reasoning, Abstract Reasoning, Spelling, Language Usage, or Clerical Speed and Accuracy); $74 per 25 tests (select Mechanical Reasoning or Space Relations); $38 per 25 ready-score answer sheets (select battery); $25 per 50 General Cognitive Abilities Battery hand-scorable answer sheets; $25 per 50 Perceptual Abilities Battery or Clerical/Language Battery hand-scorable answer sheets; $25 per 50 specific test hand-scorable answer sheets (select test); $21 per set of General Cognitive Abilities Battery scoring keys; $21 per set of Perceptual Abilities Battery or Clerical/Language Battery scoring keys; $15 per set of scoring keys for specific tests (select test); $28 per directions for

administering (includes norms); $28 per technical manual; $40 per examination kit.
Time: 114(144) minutes.
Comments: Abbreviated form of the Differential Aptitude Tests, Form V/W (118).
Authors: George K. Bennett, Harold G. Seashore, and Alexander G. Wesman.
Publisher: The Psychological Corporation.

Review of the Differential Aptitude Tests for Personnel and Career Assessment by VICTOR L. WILLSON, Professor of Educational Psychology, Texas A&M University, College Station, TX:

The Differential Aptitude Tests for Personnel and Career Assessment (DAT for PCA) is a short form of the Differential Aptitude Tests Forms V/W, the 1980 revision of this long-lived battery. It consists of eight tests grouped into three areas. The DAT for PCA is intended for use in adult assessment for hiring, a departure from the long use of the DAT in high school guidance. The Form V tests were shortened (except for Clerical Speed and Accuracy), repackaged, and renormed to produce the DAT for PCA. Administration time and number of items were reduced by about one-third for all tests, with a few tests shortened more and a few less.

The DAT authors' orientation toward aptitudes emphasizes the individual's ability to acquire knowledge through training. The eight aptitudes represented as being measured on the DAT for PCA are Verbal Reasoning, Numerical Ability, Abstract Reasoning, Clerical Speed and Accuracy, Mechanical Reasoning, Space Relations, Spelling, and Language Usage. This is indeed a mixed set of aptitudes; the authors contend they provide information about many areas of mental activity, and this reviewer does not contradict them. The issue of relative importance and complexity of the aptitudes is of concern, however, as is the issue of trainability. This is relevant to construct validity, one of several validity concerns to be discussed.

The shortened tests of the DAT for PCA were all constructed from the items of Form V of the DAT using the norm sample of grade 12 males and females, intended to represent an adult population. The new tests were targeted to have difficulties at or above .6; for most tests the empirical difficulties were generally somewhat lower, indicating the tests were a bit more difficult than expected. Items were avoided that increased existing male-female differences on various tests. The authors reported also that culturally transparent items were sought; this is particularly important with worldwide use of the DAT and presumably of the DAT for PCA. Reliabilities for each subtest were predicted using Spearman-Brown estimation; all reliabilities for an independent sample of grade 10–12 males were between .88 and .94, typically about .04 below the original test. These values are acceptably high for use in decisions about individuals, although it is appropriate to caution users that no single test or score is usually adequate to make significant decisions about selection of an individual.

The norm sample for the DAT for PCA consisted of the grade 12 males and females in the DAT Form V standardization sample, and all reference to selection of the entire norm sample occurs in the DAT Administrator's Handbook for Forms V/W, not in the technical manual for the DAT for PCA. This requires purchasing that Handbook if a user wishes to learn details about the norm sample. Even in that case, the norm sample for Form V included students at various grades. The logical leap from the grade 12 norm sample to adult applicants for industrial and business positions is great, and use of the norms would be questionable without the inclusion by the authors of extensive concurrent validity information about adults in various occupations. As it is, the norms give only a scale for which to separate test takers. Unless the applicant pool for a position consists largely of recent high school graduates, interpretation of percentile or stanine scores is limited to use as standard scores indicating relatively low or high performance. Although many different trades and occupations are listed, even more are needed if one is to have a good sense of how the various tests function in the work situations.

Norm tables are given for males, females, and combined samples grouped into 23 separate percentile and stanine bands. The authors appropriately limited the intervals to avoid overinterpretation of small differences. The tables are easy to read and convert from raw scores to percentiles and stanines. Gender differences do exist, primarily for Mechanical Reasoning and Space Relations (males score higher), and for Spelling, Language Usage, and Clerical Speed and Accuracy (females score higher). Overall, however, a male at the median for males on all tests will score about 233, a female 227 for her group. The combined norms indicate a 227 for median performance across the tests slightly favoring males. Because the test is not typically used as a summed score, users will generally be aware of the gender differences as they apply the norms.

The technical manual also suggests profile interpretation, both for between and within person comparisons. Unfortunately, this use is not well documented. No profile characteristics are presented that might lead one to conclude that someone possesses significantly higher verbal ability than numerical. The use of mean raw scores means and standard deviations is insufficient to interpret profiles. Some individual intelligence and personality tests provide distributions of profiles, and the authors would be well served to include such validity information for various occupations if they wish to promote profile interpretation.

Validity information on the DAT for PCA is presented in sections devoted to construct and criterion (concurrent and predictive) validities. Under construct validation correlations with the ASVAB (Armed Services Vocational Aptitude Battery) tests were suitably large in magnitude and displayed differential degree of relationship consistent with the type of test. A factor analysis of the DAT and ASVAB tests further supported some separation of the tests into verbal/reasoning, mechanical-science, language, and clerical speed. Although the authors used varimax rotation, it is clear from the structure matrix given that the reasoning, mechanics, and language factors are intercorrelated. Thus, one should not assume the DAT for PCA tests measure independently the three factors discussed in the beginning of the manual.

The construct validity of the DAT for PCA also has much to do with the theoretical basis for the test. As mentioned earlier, the DAT does not represent one particular theoretical approach to intelligence, and perhaps it no longer represents any current theory well. The tests are a mix of clearly school-related topics, experience, verbal and nonverbal analogical reasoning, nonverbal spatial ability, and perception. It is important for users to realize these are not equally trainable, and it is somewhat misleading to suggest that all scores indicate trainability. Only direct studies showing training gains differentially related to DAT for PCA test scores would provide such evidence. Further, the gender differences in tests such as Mechanical Reasoning have clearly been linked over the years to different educational and learning experiences, whereas the gender difference in Space Relations has been resistant to training. A better discussion of these issues is needed to orient users to the potentials for the DAT for PCA tests.

The criterion-related validities reported for various occupation groups are the most useful part of the reported research, along with the means for various tests in different occupations presented with the norms. The criteria include grades in courses in high school, grades and rankings in courses in the armed services, supervisors' ratings of performance, and in a few cases indicators from actual job performance. Not all tests appear with all occupation groups because employers may use only some tests. Correlations tend to be in the .1–.4 range, with grades often correlating quite a bit higher than performance ratings. Nevertheless, the range of validities and generally high magnitude are impressive. Again, it is difficult to ascertain differential validity across the incomplete selection of occupations and tests, and this remains the difficulty in deciding about which tests to use for a given situation. The Spelling, Language Usage, and Clerical Speed and Accuracy tests have the least occupational information.

Employee selection, career counseling, and ability to benefit, the latter a term specifically used in federal training program evaluation are discussed in a brief section at the end of the technical manual. Although the employee section is very brief, it may be assumed that companies employing such tests will be cognizant of the federal guidelines for use and local validation for tests such as the DAT for PCA. It would be useful at least to indicate the issues for the users who may not be aware of important guidelines.

The section on career counseling, containing no information on counseling use with adults, is so abbreviated the authors should place cautions stating they do not provide any evidence for use of the DAT for PCA in a counseling setting. Much research has been conducted on the DAT in the high school counseling setting but there does not appear to be a similar body of research for this test in the industrial and business setting. Until such research is reported the authors should place cautionary statements about the test's use.

Finally, the ability-to-benefit use of the test is intended to allow it to compete in federal training programs that screen applicants for entry. These tests are typically very low level, or they have low floors. No data are presented on this use, but I believe they have sufficient ease to be usable for this purpose.

Overall the DAT for PCA exhibits excellent criterion-related validity for use as a general screening test for employment with young adults. There is no evidence that it can be suitably used for reentry of older adults. All tests can be improved, and the authors are encouraged to continue work on this worthy test battery.

Review of the Differential Aptitude Tests for Personnel and Career Assessment by HILDA WING, Personnel Psychologist, Federal Aviation Administration, Washington, DC:

The Psychological Corporation has repackaged the venerable Differential Aptitude Tests (DAT), Forms V/W, for Personnel and Career Assessment (DAT for PCA). The seven ability tests have been shortened by about one-third (Clerical Speed and Accuracy is unchanged) and the battery of eight tests has been divided into three booklets, both to facilitate ease of administration of the separate tests as well as to reflect three more general ability constructs used in personnel assessment: General Cognitive, Perceptual, and Clerical and Language.

The parent DAT has a rich and extensive history that, although primarily reflecting use for guidance with high school populations, also includes extensive use with adults for employment selection and placement. To the extent this repackaged, shorter version can tap into that history, as well as being easier for employers to use, the DAT for PCA will provide healthy competition for popular batteries such as the Flanagan Aptitude Classification Tests (FACT; T4:988), published by Science Research Associates/

London House; the Employee Aptitude Survey (EAS; T4:894), published by Psychological Services, Inc.; the USES General Aptitude Test Battery (GATB; T4:2868); and the Armed Services Vocational Aptitude Battery (ASVAB; T4:196). Indeed, the technical manual compares DAT content, structure, and data against both the GATB and the ASVAB.

The major concern I have about this "new" battery is that virtually all of the necessary documentation is via analogy to either the parent DAT or to these other batteries. Recent directions in personnel selection, particularly the wide-spread acceptance of validity generalization, suggest the information provided for the shorter version of the DAT will be adequate. Standard 3.17 of the *Standards for Educational and Psychological Testing* (American Educational Research Association, American Psychological Association, & National Council on Measurement in Education, 1985) reads: "If a short form of a test is prepared by reducing the number of items or organizing portions of a test into a separate form, empirical data or a theoretical rationale should be provided to estimate the reliability of each short form and its correlation with the standard form (Primary)." The technical manual for the DAT for PCA contains a theoretical rationale that most professionals would find acceptable. However, some practitioners are likely to have some hesitation about operational use without first collecting their own evidence.

The packaging to produce the DAT for PCA is designed, according to the technical manual, to match the GATB factors. But do they? The DAT Perceptual Abilities (Mechanical Reasoning, Space Relations, Abstract Reasoning) cover more territory than does the GATB Spatial. They are also different from the ASVAB Technical Information factor composed of General Science, Auto and Shop Information, Mechanical Comprehension, and Electronics Information. The DAT Clerical Abilities include Language Usage, present in neither the GATB nor the ASVAB. The DAT for PCA, because it includes a different mix of tests, may be more useful for some occupations than either the GATB or the ASVAB. I will grant this last assertion may not be supportable by validity generalization research. (For example, see Schmidt, 1993.) The absence of data specifically from the DAT for PCA makes all such inferences hypothetical at the present time.

The test assembly and normative data used to develop and evaluate the DAT for PCA were from grade 12 students in the 1982 parent DAT standardization. Again, generalization to adults is reasonable but empirical verification would provide a stronger defense. The reliabilities for the shorter subtests were estimated with Kuder-Richardson Formula 20, on the basis of the same historical samples, again with no empirical corroboration from a sample more reflective of the intended population of test takers.

Extensive validity documentation is provided. The construct validity of the DAT for PCA, as suggested above, is supported by correlational data of the parent DAT with the GATB, the ASVAB, and college admissions tests. There is also an extensive table of criterion-related validity coefficients, presumably again using the parent DAT, but there are no citations to identify the origin of these coefficients. This table begs for its own validity generalization analyses. A second table contains normative "old" DAT data for many occupational samples, with estimated means (but not standard deviations) for the DAT for PCA.

The DAT for PCA, as must any newcomer to the employment scene, faces a familiar dilemma: Recommendation for use depends on experience, and experience is not possible without being used in the first place. Obtaining validation data in employment settings has become both more costly as well as (because of validity generalization efforts) perhaps less necessary. Thus, the professional judgment to use the DAT for PCA, relying on the evidence form the parent DAT, could be accepted as reasonable. My concern is the DAT for PCA can also be expected to share the characteristic of adverse impact against protected groups that virtually all such cognitive batteries have repeatedly demonstrated. (See Wing, 1980.) This puts the user at risk for legal action. Here, the technical manual does not include sufficient information, in my opinion, to justify the use of the DAT for PCA in adult assessment. For example, there is no mention of the 1978 *Uniform Guidelines on Employee Selection Procedures*, in which the requirement of job analytic information as the basis for test choice and use is mandatory. Nor is consideration given to more recent research (e.g., Campbell, McCloy, Oppler, & Sager, 1993) focusing on the characteristics of the criteria, in criterion-related validity. Although the school norms show possible differential performance by gender, there is no reference to performance by members of other protected groups such as African-American and Hispanics. More material could provide the essential information for defensible employment selection as well as for more effective career counseling.

The DAT for PCA could be a major player in employment selection and career counseling, a potential that can be realized as technical support tailored to these ends is systematically collected and provided to potential users.

REVIEWER'S REFERENCES

Uniform guidelines on employee selection procedures, Section 3, D. (1978). *Federal Register, 43*, (166), 38297.

Wing, H. (1980). Profiles of cognitive ability of different racial/ethnic and sex groups on a multiple abilities test battery. *Journal of Applied Psychology, 65*, 289-298.

American Educational Research Association, American Psychological Association, & National Council on Measurement in Education. (1985). *Standards for educational and psychological testing*. Washington, DC: American Psychological Association, Inc.

Campbell, J. P., McCloy, R. A., Oppler, S. H., & Sager, C. E. (1993). A theory of performance. In N. Schmitt, W. C. Borman, & Associates, *Personnel selection in organizations* (pp. 35-70). San Francisco: Jossey-Bass.

Schmidt, F. L. (1993). Personnel psychology at the cutting edge. In N. Schmitt, W. C. Borman, & Associates, *Personnel selection in organizations* (pp. 497-515). San Francisco: Jossey-Bass.

[120]

Differential Test of Conduct and Emotional Problems.

Purpose: "Designed to effect differentiations between conduct problem, emotionally disturbed and noninvolved populations."
Population: Grades K–12.
Publication Dates: 1990–91.
Acronym: DT/CEP.
Scores, 2: Emotional Disturbance Scale, Conduct Problem Scale.
Administration: Group.
Price Data, 1991: $50 per complete set including manual ('90, 58 pages), score forms, and scoring template; $16 per 50 score forms.
Time: (15–20) minutes.
Comments: Ratings by teachers.
Author: Edward J. Kelly.
Publisher: Slosson Educational Publications, Inc.
Cross References: See T4:804 (1 reference).

Review of the Differential Test of Conduct and Emotional Problems by RICHARD BROZOVICH, Director, Psychology and Learning Clinic, Oakland Schools, Waterford, MI:

The Differential Test of Conduct and Emotional Problems (DT/CEP) is a test with a mission. In addition to its function as a tool for psychometric assessment, in the author's words: "This manual (for the DT/CEP) was not written simply to describe a test. Rather, its rationales and purposes seek to transform current thinking about the identification and diagnosis of, and programming for, conduct problem and emotionally disturbed students in public school settings" (p. 47). It is important to recognize the author's purpose in devising the scale because this purpose influences the format for the scale and the author's suggestions for interpreting the scale.

To the author's credit he is direct and open about the mission of the test. His opinion regarding PL 94-142 and the social maladjustment exclusionary clause for emotional impairment is similar to Slenkovich (1992); that is, most students with acting-out behavior disorders are socially maladjusted and thus ought be excluded from special education services for the emotionally impaired. This is a controversial issue. The *School Psychology Review* [1992, *21*(1)] contains comments on both sides of this issue and would be useful background reading for anyone planning to use this scale.

The DT/CEP standardization procedures are not adequate to support the use of its norms with a general population. All the students in the sample were from one large metropolitan area. The manual author presents no data regarding the possible impact of geographic area and/or urban/rural setting upon scores. Another standardization problem was the use of required subject (English or Mathematics) teachers to do the ratings in grades 9–12. This procedure resulted in a few teachers having a major effect on the results obtained at the high school level. Also, one can only wonder if other subject matter teachers or teachers with a different internal standard for behavior would perceive and rate students in a similar way.

Data presented in the manual show some puzzling findings that may reflect problems in the standardization procedures. For example, in Table 23 data are presented for conduct problem scores by sex, ethnic group, and school level. Analysis of this table indicates that in high school, African-American females have a mean score much lower than any other ethnic group but for all previous grade-level groupings they had the highest score on this scale. In the same table, the number of African-American students rated at the elementary level is 4, whereas the numbers at other grade levels range from 33–45. No explanation is offered for this striking discrepancy. Data in Table 25 show similar unexplained anomalies among scores for Hispanic and African-American females at different grade levels on the Emotional Disturbance Scale.

The manual author does not present sufficient data to evaluate some of the standardization information. Means and variance data are reported in some tables without reporting sample sizes. In some instances the summary statistics reported for various groupings are based on *N*s of less than 10. This is a dubious practice, especially when the data are based on an underlying distribution where the median score is zero and the variances far exceed the mean scores. Also puzzling is the author's advice to use combined groups on norms for both scales despite the reported finding of significant main effect differences among subgroup means on the Conduct Problem Scale and significant interaction effects on the Emotional Disturbance Scale.

The internal consistency of the two scales based on split-half correlations of results from the standardization sample was adequate for a screening instrument (Conduct Problems = .92 and Emotional Disturbance = .81). The discussion in the manual of test/retest stability reports a single study apparently conducted by the author. The method in this study combined two distinct groups of students of about equal number (one group "mildly handicapped," the other in regular education), a procedure likely to inflate variance and hence generate a high reliability estimate. Due to this atypical sampling procedure, it is felt that the obtained stability estimates (.91 and .85) are grossly inflated and should not be accepted as reflecting the stability of the score for typical applications. Support for this opinion is suggested by the author's finding that long-term stability (approximately 100 days) for the Emotional Disturbance Scale exceeds the internal-consistency estimate, a highly unusual result.

Validity data reported in the manual consist of various studies conducted by the author verifying the scale's ability to differentiate between conduct problem (acting-out) and emotionally disturbed (internalized problems) students. The author presents some impressive data regarding the scale's ability to identify students nominated by professional teams as conduct disordered or emotionally disturbed. Unfortunately, the professional teams doing the nominations used written differential criteria based on the author's philosophical and theoretical position. These criteria are then used in the scale items to discriminate between Conduct Problems and Emotional Disturbance, making this study more a reflection of interrater reliability than construct validity. Other validity studies indicate that the DT/CEP is able to discriminate the author's defined groups better than other scales, confirming the scale does a good job of sorting students along a continuum of acting-out/internalized behaviors.

Some cause for concern regarding the scale's construct validity is generated by data that show a general trend for moderate to high correlations with other teacher rating scales, moderate or low correlations with parent rating scales, and low or no correlation with self-rating scales. This is particularly disconcerting because it is the author's contention that "Emotionally disturbed students either directly or subtly express internalized self-concept and self-esteem problems in affectively self-devaluing ways" (p. 2). Based on this theoretical position it seems fair to predict that the Emotional Disturbance Scale would correlate with self-ratings on self-concept and personality scales. Studies reported in the manual suggest no such relationship.

Because of flaws in standardization procedures and lack of evidence to establish test/retest reliability or construct validity, the DT/CEP is not recommended for use as a screening instrument. Evaluating students for the presence of Conduct Problems and/or Emotional Disturbance, even at the level of screening, calls for caution regarding one's purpose and extreme care in the selection of instruments.

For the purpose of obtaining teacher perceptions of students along the dimension of acting-out/internalizing behaviors, the Teacher's Report Form of the Child Behavior Checklist (Achenbach & Edelbrock, 1986; T4:433) is a well-standardized instrument that has demonstrated adequate reliability and validity.

REVIEWER'S REFERENCES

Achenbach, T. M., & Edelbrock, C. S. (1986). Teacher's Report Form. Burlington, VT: T. M. Achenbach.

Slenkovich, J. E. (1992). Can the language "social maladjustment" in the SED definition be ignored? *School Psychology Review, 21*(1), 21-22.

Review of the Differential Test of Conduct and Emotional Problems by ALIDA S. WESTMAN, Professor of Psychology, Eastern Michigan University, Ypsilanti, MI:

The purpose of the Differential Test of Conduct and Emotional Problems (DT/CEP) is to help school personnel screen kindergarten through 12th grade pupils for emotional or conduct problems. Another intent of the DT/CEP is to differentiate troubled pupils from normal ones. In this regard it is important to note that many disorders, such as identity problems, eating disturbances, drug effects, Attention-Deficit Hyperactivity Disorder, etc., are not identified by the DT/CEP.

The 28 scored items of the Conduct Problem (CP) Scale and the 30 scored items of the Emotional Disturbance (ED) Scale are quite clear. The CP items are analogous to the criteria for Conduct and for Oppositional Defiant Disorders of the *DSM-III-R* (American Psychiatric Association, 1987). The ED items reflect various emotional disturbances. The scales are shorter than the number of items might indicate, because content is repeated.

The manual contains important warnings. Evaluators should know the youngster well. If school personnel do not know an answer, they are to leave the item blank. There also is a warning not to rate a youngster shortly after misbehavior.

Although respondents are warned against bias, the scales are not written to minimize response bias. There are only three true items on the two scales combined and the scales and weights of the items are written out to the left of the items on the questionnaire.

Scoring would be easier if a template were available to put on top of the answers with the 2-point items colored differently from the 1-point items. Then summing each scale would be simplified.

The DT/CEP may not tap school personnel's expertise. Only true or false responses are allowed. No written comments are permitted, not even at the end of the scale.

The 2,367 standardization group appears representative of the U.S. population in terms of ethnic composition (Caucasian, Black, Hispanic, Asian, other) and sex at each educational level (Primary, Elementary, Jr. High, High School). The Clark County School District in Nevada, which includes Las Vegas, was sampled randomly. Unfortunately this meant that there were fewer than 19 "Asian" or "Other" males at each educational level. Representativeness of females in the sample is not reported.

RELIABILITY. Two split-half calculations yielded a respectable correlation of .81 or better. One test-retest correlation was computed but not with a sample of the standardizing population, but with a group of 100 mild ED, CP, and LD elementary children and 109 regular children. The reliabilities of this atypical sample were .85 (ED) and .91 (CP).

ITEM ANALYSIS. Item analysis used scores above and below scale means and in the top or bottom 27% of the standardization group and of a group of 172 severely emotionally handicapped pupils, as well as a combination of these indices. This led to five items being eliminated from scoring on the two scales and to nine items in each of the two scales being given 2-point weight. The result was good discrimination between high scorers on the two scales.

VALIDITY. Teachers designated a group of severely handicapped elementary and secondary pupils as having conduct (77 boys and 15 girls) or emotional problems (62 boys and 18 girls). Their CP and ED scores were analyzed. The resultant *F*-test is not well described. The severely emotionally handicapped could be categorized well using the CP and ED scores. Their CP and ED scores also were correlated with a few other tests. At the secondary level, the CP and ED scores correlated well with the relevant scales of the Louisville Behavioral Checklist but not meaningfully with the Tennessee Self-Concept Scale. Similarly, correlations with the Sixteen Personality Factor Questionnaire (16PF) were low or nonsignificant. At the elementary level, conduct problems correlated with lower Lie scale scores, whereas there was no correlation with anxiety scores on the Revised Children's Manifest Anxiety Scale. There was no correlation with the Piers-Harris Children's Self-Concept Scale subtests and only a very low correlation with the Myers-Briggs' Thinking-Feeling scale and ED scores. On the Revised Behavior Problem Checklist, pupils with more conduct problems in elementary school scored higher on Conduct Disorder and Socialized Aggression, whereas emotionally disturbed pupils had higher Anxiety-Withdrawal and Psychotic Behavior scores. Correlations with the Selected Personality Inventory for Children were more modest. The much respected Child Behavior Checklist was not used. The standardization population was not sampled for any of these studies.

SUMMARY. This test holds some promise if a school wants only a simple screening device to distinguish between conduct problems and some emotional problems. If more extensive emotional screening is desired, then another instrument (e.g., Achenbach & Edelbrock, 1986) is a better option.

REVIEWER'S REFERENCES

Achenbach, T. M., & Edelbrock, C. (1986). Manual for the Teacher's Report Form and Teacher Version of the Child Behavior Profile. Burlington, VT: Thomas M. Achenbach.

American Psychiatric Association. (1987). *Diagnostic and statistical manual of mental disorders (DSM-III-R)*. Washington DC: American Psychiatric Association.

[121]

Digital Finger Tapping Test.

Purpose: Constructed to measure "psychomotor performance as an element in neuropsychological functioning."

Population: Individuals with potential cortical damage or impairment.

Publication Date: 1985.

Acronym: DFTT.

Scores, 2: Right Hand, Left Hand.

Administration: Individual.

Price Data: Not available.

Time: (10) minutes for administration, scoring, and interpretation; 10 seconds per trial.

Authors: Allen D. Brandon and Thomas L. Bennett.

Publisher: Western Psychological Services.

[The publisher advised in January 1994 that this test is now out of print—Ed.]

Review of the Digital Finger Tapping Test by KEVIN J. McCARTHY, Ph.D. Candidate, Associate in Psychology Department, E. Hunt Correctional Center, St. Gabriel, LA, and PENELOPE W. DRALLE, Associate Professor of Psychiatry, Louisiana State University School of Medicine, New Orleans, LA:

The Digital Finger Tapping Test (DFTT) is available from Western Psychological Services (WPS) and consists of an administration manual and an electronic tapping device incorporating "a tapping-key and a self-contained timer, which automatically begins timing with the first depression of the tapping key" (manual, p. 2). The device is a lightweight, black box and is powered by a 9-volt battery. Its appearance is similar to a remote control unit for a TV or garage door opener. The display window for the tapper is visible both to the subject and the examiner and remains blank until the end of 10 seconds. It then indicates the number of taps for that interval and does not record any additional taps after the 10-second period. The DFTT is portable and adaptable for testing in a number of situations. The self-contained timer is a feature designed to reduce examiner error and thereby increase the accuracy in measuring individual performance.

The manual provides an adequate description of standardized instructions to be used with each client. Further, record forms are provided for recording individual performance scores. The manual contains specific instructions to the subject and directs the examiner in a clear, unambiguous fashion.

The normative data collected on the digital finger tapper (PY-2) and on the manual key-driven device included in the standard Halstead-Reitan Neuropsychological Test Battery (T4:1119) are on 80 introductory psychology students at Colorado State University between the ages of 18 and 20. Subjects were screened for non-righthandedness and previous brain injury.

The manual notes that "both males and females showed significantly faster rates of tapping regardless of whether their dominant or nondominant hand was used" (manual, p. 7) on the DFTT. Furthermore, males obtained significantly faster rates than females within an average increment in rate for the DFTT of 5.76 taps per 10 seconds faster than the standard manual tapper. In conjunction with the differences, the authors acknowledge that the "norms typically used for the manual apparatus (e.g., Russell, Neuringer, & Goldstein, 1970) cannot be used" (manual, p. 7). The manual does note that "the average standard deviations of rates obtained between these instruments were comparable (DFTT = 5.33, manual = 5.10)" (manual, p. 6). Further, they noted that "observed differences in tapping rate by instrument and sex were significant ($p<.05$)" (manual, pp. 6–7). The manual also notes that "finger tapping scores are significantly affected by several factors including the sex of the individual, educational level, emotional state, and prior test experience" (manual, p. 9). The factors addressed in the normative study are gender and dominance. Because the data provided by the normative sample represent a narrow range, the DFTT should be used with caution. The manual notes,

> Based on the fact that standard deviations are similar across both instruments, and, on the average, there is more than a 5-point advantage using the DFTT, we recommend the widely used Russell et al. (1970) norms be increased 5 points when using the DFTT to evaluate level of impairment in adults. Using a 5-point increment would be analogous to data-smoothing techniques frequently used in the development of test norms to prevent an overreliance on the uniqueness of a given data sample. (manual, p. 8)

The authors suggest that use of such technique is justified on the basis of statistical propriety.

Certainly, the electronic version of the test presents an instrument worth consideration if only for the enhanced accuracy of measurement. Its introduction at this time seems premature based upon the limited normative data available to evaluate its effectiveness as a neuropsychological test instrument. In a research setting, the DFTT may enhance the clinician's evaluation of fine-motor speed. Its use in a clinical setting using the Halstead-Reitan established norms and cutoffs even with the adjustment for speed is questionable at this time.

As indicated in the manual, a difference of just several taps can have a significant impact on the tapping score. When standardized cutting scores are used, these differences can lead to misinterpretation of the clinical data. Also, as noted in the manual, co-factors including gender, age, educational level, emotional state, and prior test experience variably impact performance.

The DFTT manual (WPS Catalog #W-206B) seems to be consistent since its publication in 1985, but the actual tapping test/timer/stop watch has changed significantly over the same period of time. The tapping device sent for review is WPS W-277 and is different from the DFTT apparatuses listed in the 1988–89 catalog, the 1991–92 catalog, and the device WPS PY-2 used in the normative study. None of the instruments involved have the same dimensions, the same configurations, nor the same standard functions. When inquiry was made regarding this discrepancy to Western Psychological Services we were assured by the company spokesperson that the manual was appropriate for use with the W-277 instrument.

It would appear the authors of this instrument have sought to develop an electronic version of the finger tapper using existing reliability and validity data. The manual notes, "A review of the reliability and validity of this standard instrument would go beyond the scope of this brief administration manual" (manual, p. 10). By incorporating general references to Reitan's work and referring the reader to standard neuropsychological literature on the Halstead-Reitan Neuropsychological Test Battery, it would appear the publishers are attempting to enhance the credibility and clinical usefulness of their device by utilizing statistical evaluations of a different instrument. Evaluation of the DFTT as a distinct instrument should include reliability and validity data in light of its inherent differences from the standard finger tapper. Additionally, it should be noted the tappers may have different levels of tension and are obviously postured at different angles, suggesting substantial difference in function. As the authors noted, "The developmental use of the digital finger tapping test (DFTT) as a clinical and research instrument was based on the knowledge that even minimal error . . . can have a major influence on the resulting finger tapping score" (manual, pp. 2–3). Certainly, variations in basic function contribute to the standard error of measurement. As the authors note, "Misinterpretation of several finger taps in a 10-second interval can have critical implications" (manual, p. 2). Additional normative studies incorporating age and organic factors in addition to instrument and sex would enhance the clinical usefulness of this instrument.

Although the DFTT is likely to be an effective and valuable research instrument, deficiencies in reliability, validity, and normative studies curtail its current clinical usefulness. Neuropsychological assessment incorporating the manual Halstead-Reitan tapper, when used in conjunction with appropriate norms, is likely to provide the most relevant data for clinical evaluation.

REVIEWER'S REFERENCE

Russell, E. W., Neuringer, C., & Goldstein, G. (1970). *Assessment of brain damage: A neuropsychological key approach*. New York: Wiley.

Review of the Digital Finger Tapping Test by AGNES E. SHINE, Assistant Professor of Educational Psychology, Mississippi State University, Mississippi State, MS:

The Digital Finger Tapping Test (DFTT) is an individually administered test of psychomotor speed. The manual states the DFTT was "developed to minimize examiner error in timing" (manual, p. 2). The DFTT is similar to other finger tapping tests in administration and scoring. The major procedural difference is the inclusion of an electronic test/counter/timer device. This is an advantage since accurate timing is, obviously, a key measure in the assessment of psychomotor speed. The DFTT requires the examinee to tap with the index finger of the dominant hand for five 10-second trials. After a brief rest, the same procedures are followed for the nondominant hand. If the range of scores for each hand across the trials is within 5 points, the test is terminated for the hand and scored. If the range of scores is larger than 5 points, additional trials are administered with a maximum of 10 trials per hand. Scoring the test is very simple. The test protocol is clearly written and easy to use.

The manual of the DFTT is quite brief and information usually found in test manuals is incomplete or missing. The manual does not indicate who can administer the test or what type of professional preparation is needed to administer and interpret the test. Noticeably missing from the manual is a clear indication for whom the test is appropriate and for what age levels. The standardization sample is restricted to 80 (40 males and 40 females) subjects enrolled in an introductory psychology course at Colorado State University. Because the manual states that the test can be used in the prediction of cerebral dysfunction, a wider random stratified sample including different age ranges and subjects with known impairment should have been included in the sample. The limited sample used in the standardization of the DFTT severely limits the utility of the test.

Specific validity and reliability data for the DFTT were not reported in the manual. Instead, the authors discussed the psychometric properties of other finger tapping tests (e.g., Halstead Finger Oscillation Test).

The test authors made a point of describing the procedures used during the standardization of the test. Each subject was administered the DFTT using the electric apparatus and a manual apparatus used in other similar tests. The authors found the subjects were significantly faster on the electronic apparatus and that males outperformed females. Based on this finding the test authors cautioned using traditional finger tapping norms. Instead, the authors recommended using their own norms. These norms consisted of adding 5 points to the widely used Russell impairment norms (Russell, Neuringer, & Goldstein, 1970). Although the authors indicated the norms could be used when making an estimate of the level of impairment, it was suggested that more research was needed.

The authors discussed several factors that may affect finger tapping scores such as gender differences, educational level, and prior test experience. One important aspect the authors failed to mention was the difference in scores may have been due to the physical structure of the apparatus used. For example, on the electric apparatus the tapping key must be depressed .13 inches. On the manual apparatus the tapping key must be depressed .50 inches. It should also be noted that for the electric apparatus 80 grams of pressure was needed to change the counter whereas 400 grams of pressure was needed to change the counter on the manual apparatus. Given the difference in the physical requirements of the task, it is unclear whether or not the tasks are equivalent. Therefore, fatigue may be a greater factor on the manual apparatus trials whereas less energy may be needed to complete the finger tapping trials on the DFTT, thus resulting in higher finger tapping scores.

The authors should be applauded for their introduction of an electric apparatus in measuring finger tapping speed, ease of scoring, and test protocol. Although the DFTT is appealing to those in clinical practice, a number of issues must be addressed in the manual before recommending the DFTT for wide use in the prediction of cerebral dysfunction. Specifically, a larger standardization sample is indicated. The sample should include normal as well as neuropsychologically impaired individuals. Validity and reliability studies should be included in the test manual. Norms and cutoff scores should be generated for impaired and nonimpaired performance. Adherence to test development standards would most certainly allow the DFTT to contribute to the improvement of practice in the area of measuring finger tapping speed. At present, based on the information provided in the test manual, the DFTT should be used with extreme caution.

REVIEWER'S REFERENCE

Russell, E. W., Neuringer, C., & Goldstein, G. (1970). *Assessment of brain damage: A neuropsychological key approach.* New York: Wiley.

[122]

Dissociative Experiences Scale.

Purpose: "Developed to serve as a clinical tool to help identify patients with dissociative psychopathology and as a research tool to provide a means of quantifying dissociative experiences."
Population: Late adolescent–adult.
Publication Dates: 1986.
Acronym: DES.
Scores: Total score only.
Administration: Group or individual.
Price Data, 1992: $2 per DES manual (24 pages); $1 per DES.
Foreign Language Editions: Available in French, Spanish, Italian, Dutch, Hindi, Cambodian, Czech, Swedish, Norwegian, Japanese, and Hebrew.
Time: [10] minutes.
Comments: Self-report inventory; translation also in progress for version of the DES in German.
Authors: Eve Bernstein Carlson and Frank W. Putnam.
Publisher: Eve Bernstein Carlson (the author).
Cross References: See T4:809 (1 reference).

TEST REFERENCES

1. Gabel, S. (1989). Dreams as a possible reflection of a dissociated self-monitoring system. *The Journal of Nervous and Mental Disease, 177,* 560-568.

2. Armstrong, J. G., & Loewenstein, R. J. (1990). Characteristics of patients with multiple personality and dissociative disorders on psychological testing. *The Journal of Nervous and Mental Disease*, *178*, 448-454.

3. Goff, D. C., Brotman, A. W., Kindlon, D., Waites, M., & Amico, E. (1991). The delusion of possession in chronically psychotic patients. *The Journal of Nervous and Mental Disease*, *179*, 567-571.

4. Miller, D. A. F., McCluskey-Fawcett, K., & Irving, L. M. (1993). The relationship between childhood sexual abuse and subsequent onset of bulimia nervosa. *Child Abuse & Neglect*, *17*, 305-314.

5. Spanos, N. P., Arango, M., & deGroot, H. P. (1993). Context as a moderator in relationships between attribute variables and hypnotizability. *Personality and Social Psychology Bulletin*, *19*, 71-77.

6. Coons, P. M. (1994). Confirmation of childhood abuse in child and adolescent cases of multiple personality disorder and dissociative disorder not otherwise specified. *The Journal of Nervous and Mental Disease*, *182*, 461-464.

7. Covino, N. A., Jimerson, D. C., Wolfe, B. E., Franko, D. L., & Frankel, F. H. (1994). Hypnotizability, dissociation and bulimia nervosa. *Journal of Abnormal Psychology*, *103*, 455-459.

8. Leavitt, F. (1994). Clinical correlates of alleged satanic abuse and less controversial sexual molestation. *Child Abuse & Neglect*, *18*, 387-392.

9. Ross, C. A. (1994). Comentary on positive associations between dichotic listening errors, complex partial epileptic-like signs, and paranormal beliefs. *The Journal of Nervous and Mental Disease*, *182*, 56-58.

10. Saxe, G. N., Chinman, G., Berkowitz, R., Hall, K., Lieberg, G., Schwartz, J., & van derk Kolk, B. (1994). Somatization in patients with dissociative disorders. *American Journal of Psychiatry*, *151*, 1329-1334.

11. Shearer, S. L. (1994). Dissociative phenomena in women with borderline personality disorder. *American Journal of Psychiatry*, *151*, 1324-1328.

12. Shearer, S. L. (1994). Phenomenology of self-injury among inpatient women with borderline personality disorder. *The Journal of Nervous and Mental Disease*, *182*, 524-526.

13. Sno, H. N., Schalken, H. F. A., de Jonghe, F., & Koeter, M. W. J. (1994). The Inventory for Déjà Vu Experiences Assessment: Development, utility, reliability, and validity. *The Journal of Nervous and Mental Disease*, *182*, 27-33.

14. Bremner, J. D., Randall, P., Scott, T. M., Bronen, R. A., Seibyl, J. D., Southwick, S. M., Delaney, R. C., McCarthy, G., Charney, D. S., & Innis, R. B. (1995). MRI-based measurment of hippocampal volume in patients with combat-related posttraumatic stress disorder. *American Journal of Psychiatry*, *152*, 973-981.

15. Mann, B. J. (1995). The North Carolina Dissociation Index: A measure of dissociation using items from the MMPI-2. *Journal of Personality Assessment*, *64*, 349-359.

16. Rauschenberger, S. L., & Lynn, S. J. (1995). Fantasy proneness, DSM-III-R Axis I psychopathology, and dissociation. *Journal of Abnormal Psychology*, *104*, 373-380.

Review of the Dissociative Experiences Scale by SAMUEL JUNI, Professor, Department of Applied Psychology, New York University, New York, NY:

This review is based on the Dissociative Experiences Scale (DES), the manual, the basic paper on the development of the scale (Bernstein & Putnam, 1986), and a perusal of dozens of papers on the scale culled from the literature, many written by the test author and her colleagues. References will be made in this review to some of these papers.

Creating a scale is a process of several steps. First is the "bread and butter" stage where theory and conceptualization are hammered out to design a structure for the scale. Second, the "nuts and bolts" of the test format, as well as item characteristics and nuances, are spelled out. Next, test integrity is determined empirically or through statistical methods. Finally, the domain of the scale and prescriptions for its use are spelled out to the professional consumer.

The DES fares fairly well with the third of these steps. The "bread and butter" of conceptualization lacks in scholarship, the "nuts and bolts" of test format and item construction is haphazard, and the prescription for test use is lacking in uniformity and consistency.

CONCEPTUALIZATION. In establishing the conceptual basis of the notion of dissociation, Bernstein demarcates the dissociative disorders detailed in the *DSM-III*: amnesia, fugues, depersonalization, and multiple personality. Reading the description of the DES in the original paper, uneasiness is warranted: "The DES score is an index of the number of different types of dissociative experiences and the frequency of each experience" (p. 731). Despite the differential content and features of these categories, the DES lumps them all into one score. Such an amalgamation is all the more questionable in view of the fact (cited by the author) that the overwhelming majority of dissociative experiences are categorized as falling into the depersonalization category.

Some of the items suggest a notion of dissociation which, although literally correct, belies the conceptual rationale of the scale. I was miffed by discovering that being absorbed in a movie to the point of disregarding the activity in the seats around you (Item 17) ranks with blatant indices of disintegration. I do not believe that such an adaptive phenomenon is unusual. Indeed, it would be impossible to carry on a normal conversation in a restaurant or cocktail party or on a city street without it.

There was one item which grated on me personally. I happen to have an anonymous/typical/familiar face; hardly a week goes by when I am not (mis)recognized as being "so-and-so." I was dumbfounded to discover that my facial makeup is indicative of dissociation. Item 6 catalogs being approached by unfamiliar people who call you by another name as a dissociative experience.

Besides the above noted problems of inclusion, there is also the issue of exclusion in the test conceptualization. The manual authors state explicitly that the concepts of dissociation of moods and impulses are excluded from the DES, in order to avoid overlap with the general category of affective disorders. It is not at all certain that the differential category alluded to here is a real dichotomy or one of classificatory convenience. One may well suspect that, in fact, expedience has won out over analysis and conceptualization.

FORMAT. The test format leaves much to be desired. The notion of using self-report to measure clinical dissociation is enigmatic. Self-reporting of aberrant psychological phenomena requires a certain degree of introspective and integrative capacity by the respondent. This is a peculiar attribute of an instrument that measures the very degree of integrative capacity of the respondent, and spells the potential for recursive confounding of measurement. As an illustrative clinical example, seeing oneself in the mirror and failing to recognize oneself (Item 11) may well occur often to an individual, but his or her ability to report that this often occurs is contingent on the integrative realization that something is amiss here. Indeed, a dissociative patient may well see the stranger in the mirror and blissfully proceed after saying "hello," with never a clue that dissociation was manifest.

The DES is presented as a measure of "trait" rather than "state." Although defensible psychometrically, based on test-retest statistical findings, there is no precaution in the actual test vis-a-vis this concern. Instructions to the respondent merely caution that items refer to times when the person is not under the influence of alcohol or drugs. If the trait/state issue is of concern, why not include a time frame as a reference? Why leave such potentially crucial factors to the post-mortem statistical reliability analyses?

The original test version features a 100-mm response line for each item, requiring the respondent to mark an "X" on the spot representing the percentage of occurrence between 0 and 100. This response mode presumes precise graphomotor and eye-hand coordination, and a concise understanding by the respondent of the correspondence between graph and temporal/ratio continua. Although not recommended as a response format even for professionals, it is totally inappropriate for untrained respondents—let alone clinical subjects.

The alternate form (DES-II) offered by the authors features a printed series of percentage options (ranging from 0 to 100, by tens) for each item. The respondent is directed to circle one of the numbers. This form avoids the graphic guesswork necessary in the original form.

The format of the items is fraught with problems and inconsistencies. One gets the distinct impression of inattention to content validity, a trend not at all uncommon in tests that stress statistical factor analytic techniques over basic structural foundations.

It is unfortunate that differential item weightings were not considered in the test construction. One wonders if any criteria of severity were used as guidelines in item collection. Consider, for example, Item 21 which refers to people who talk to themselves when alone. Is the degree of dissociation of such behavior indeed on par with that inherent in not recognizing family members (Item 8) or hearing voices inside the head (Item 27)? What happened to content validation?

All items begin with the introductory sentence which states that some people have a specific experience, and then proceeds to ask the respondents to indicate their own behavior in that domain. Giving this kind of empirical information on test items, regardless of the issue of information accuracy, is peculiar. The rationale of beginning items with such "facts" is not developed by the author. I wonder if this is a neat method of avoiding the sexist form of the singular pronoun in direct third person descriptions.

The introductory item wordings often fluctuate between the following:

Some people have the experience . . .

Some people have the experience of sometimes . . .

Some people sometimes have the experience . . .

Some people have the experience of finding . . .

Some people find . . .

Why these variations? Are they differentially formulated per the specific item contents? Again, one suspects the pattern is merely random, due to the inattention to the "nuts and bolts" of the test. In fact, no test can ever fully achieve its goals when the basics are haphazardly assembled.

Some items qualify their questions with the word "sometimes" whereas others do not. This variation is bound to have direct influence on percentage ratings, because an unqualified statement rated on a percent occurrence has a different perceived frequency than a temporally qualified item rated on frequency. (Mathematically, a percentage of a percentage yields less than a percentage of unity. "Sometimes" is an implicit percentage.)

Some items refer to "sudden" realizations of dissociation, whereas others do not. There is no explanation in the DES literature for such a differential based on content or expected durations of the realizations of dissociative experience.

Poor diction and punctuation make some items difficult to understand. Commas are shunned by the author. I counted one 34-word item sentence with not a comma in sight. Such inadequacies decrease item reliability.

Some items refer to various dissociative elements, concatenated by the "and" or "or" conjunctives. Consider the following items, for example:

6. Some people sometimes find that they are approached by people that they do not know who call them by another name or insist that they have met them before.

7. Some people sometimes have the experience of feeling as though they are standing next to themselves or watching themselves do something and they actually see themselves as if they were looking at another person.

In view of some of the above-noted item attributes, it is not surprising that research on the reading level of the DES has demonstrated that 43% of the items require at least a high school education (Paolo, Ryan, Dunn, & VanFleet, 1993).

Besides the linguistic-based confusion with conjunctives there is at least one case where "apples and oranges" are presented as units, expecting a uniform reaction from the respondent. Item 17 asks if the respondent ever becomes so absorbed while watching television or a movie that he or she is unaware of other events. It is simply wrong to lump the experience at a movie with that of watching television. The total sensory input at the former (darkness, screen size, nonfamiliar surroundings or distractions) totally differentiates the two vis-a-vis the likelihood of disregarding other aspects of the surroundings.

Although items generally ask for personal evaluations of experience, there are exceptions. Item 8 reads: "Some people are told that they sometimes do not recognize friends or family members." Because this represents a dual-level item (the respondent's and the person who may tell the respondent of such events) is the respondent expected to rate how often he or she is told about this behavior, or is the respondent expected to indicate how often such behavior occurs? Similar problems arise in Item 10 (being accused of lying by others) and (to some extent) in Item 6 (being called a different name by others). As a rule, it is not suitable to mix several items stressing others' behaviors into a scale which is basically self-reflective.

Some items feature straightforward descriptions of behaviors and some offer examples. Moreover, some offer one example, whereas others offer several. It is not at all clear to me why only specific items rate examples. Furthermore, items with examples enhance response sets that either restrict the respondent to focus only on the examples, or deflect the true intention of the item.

PSYCHOMETRICS. The strength of the test is in its statistical validation. Psychometrically, the test is presented as a single score computed by averaging the responses to the 28 items. Factor analysis further suggests three main factors: (*a*) amnesia, (*b*) absorption and imaginative involvement, and (*c*) depersonalization and derealization. Limiting factor loadings to .45 or above, no one item loads on more than one factor. It is unfortunate that these categories are not quite congruent with the *DSM-III* categories cited in the rationale for the scale.

The scoring of the DES calls for the measurement of the "X" spot on the continuum to the nearest 5%. The rationale for this rounding is not developed. In the DES-II, the respondent is directed to circle 1 of 11 percentages ranging from 0 to 100. Here, too, the logic of offering these particular options is not developed. One wonders if these were thought out at all.

The primary validation studies with the DES feature Spearman rank-order correlations of the instrument with age and socioeconomic status. Item-total correlations also use this statistic. Why the Pearsonian correlation was not used is unclear, although it is doubtful that this would have made any significant difference in the results. In fact, the manual now recommends the use of parametric statistics for validation studies.

In general, research shows good test-retest reliability as well as internal consistency, although there are some rough edges debated in the literature (e.g., Sanders, 1992; Wiener, 1992). The use of internal consistency as evidence of construct validity by the test author is weak but convergent validity with other semirelated tests (Frischholz, et al., 1991) is quite impressive. The many papers published that have used the DES do put the test in the forefront in the field, and buttress its status as a psychometrically sound instrument.

TEST USE. The DES is presented as being designed for respondents over age 18. No other limitations are presented for the DES. (It is noted, however, that the DES-II was developed on data from a nonclinical sample only.) I am leery of the multiple language forms that are being offered by the test author. Offering simple translations of tests without due regard for cultural relativism borders on the injudicious.

I am somewhat suspicious of the findings (reported in the manual) discounting any correlations of the DES with age, race, gender, education, and socioeconomic status. Age is intuitively related to dissociation, in view of the prevalence of such mechanisms in adolescence. I am incredulous about the negative race findings. There is quite a discrepancy across various ethnic cultures vis-a-vis frequency and tolerance of dissociative experiences. For example, nonclinical Hispanics and Africans, in some American subgroups, speak openly of contact with spirits and communication with the dead.

The differential aspects of dissociative experience in normals versus the pathological are touched upon often in the DES literature. However, all in all, the final categorization of the instrument vis-a-vis its intended population is muddled. The manual is clear that dissociation has "different meanings across clinical and non-clinical populations" (p. 4). The original validation paper summarizes findings of transient feelings of depersonalization in normal subjects which range from 8.5% to 70%, depending on definitions, methodology, and age. The congruence of the DES scores of schizophrenics and adolescents presents a serious challenge to the exact formulation of the use of the instrument.

In the validation paper, the authors conclude the DES "has proven useful as a screening test for major dissociative psychopathology . . . . Although not intended as a diagnostic instrument, this scale will serve as a useful research tool and dissociative screening device" (Bernstein & Putnam, 1986, p. 732). Such statements are inconsistent with the way the DES is referenced in the literature, leaving the critical test consumer confused and mystified.

If the test is to be used for screening, the issue of cutoff scores is paramount. Various cutoffs are offered in the literature, with 30% seeming to be the most reasonable, albeit equivocal. In addition, the very methodology of using the DES as a screening device to detect patients with high risk for dissociative disorders has been questioned (Leibowitz, 1992).

CONCLUSION. Dissociation as a construct is a phenomenon that spans normal and aberrant functioning. The DES purports to measure a major portion of the construct, excluding affective manifestations. Test and items formats are analyzed as problematic. Psychometric attributes are summarized as being solid, especially in view of the sizeable validity literature for the scale. The clinical/diagnostic use of the instrument is seen as not being well defined vis-a-vis cutoff criteria and classification.

REVIEWER'S REFERENCES

Bernstein, E. M., & Putnam, F. W. (1986). Development, reliability, and validity of a dissociation scale. *Journal of Nervous and Mental Disease, 174,* 727-735.

Frischholz, E. J., Braun, B. G., Sachs, R. G., Schwartz, D. R., Lewis, J., Shaeffer, D., Westergaard, R., & Pasquotto, J. (1991). Construct validity of the Dissociative Experiences Scale (DES): I. The relationship between the DES and other self-report measures of DES. *Dissociation Progress in the Dissociative Disorders, 4,* 185-188.

Leibowitz, M. R. (1992). Dissociative Experiences Scale. *American Journal of Psychiatry, 149,* 719.

Paolo, A. M., Ryan, J. J., Dunn, G. E., & VanFleet, J. (1993). Reading level of the Dissociative Experiences Scale. *Journal of Clinical Psychology, 49,* 209-211.

Sanders, B. (1992). "The Dissociative Experiences Scale": Reply. *American Journal of Psychiatry, 149,* 144.

Wiener, A. (1992). The Dissociative Experiences Scale. *American Journal of Psychiatry, 149,* 143.

Review of the Dissociative Experiences Scale by NIELS G. WALLER, Associate Professor of Psychology, University of California, Davis, Davis, CA:

At the turn of the century, dissociation was one of the most widely studied topics in psychopathology research. *The Journal of Abnormal Psychology* (1906) contained no less than 11 articles on dissociation, double consciousness, personality disintegration, and hypnosis in its premier issue. Two years later it published one of the earliest autobiographical accounts of multiple personality disorder (B.C.A., 1908). The field's auspicious beginning would not last, however. Classical behaviorism—with its disdain for mental events—was lurking around the corner, and interest in dissociation waned for more than five decades.

Recently, there has been a renaissance in dissociation research (Spiegel & Cardeña, 1991). Clinicians have rediscovered the link between dissociative experiences and early childhood sexual abuse, Multiple Personality Disorder (MPD), Posttraumatic Stress Disorder (PTSD), eating disorders, and other clinical syndromes. Several of these clinicians, moreover, have developed questionnaires that are specifically designed to tap dissociative experiences. The most popular and well validated of these questionnaires is the Dissociative Experiences Scale (DES).

The DES is a brief self-report questionnaire designed to identify patients with dissociative psychopathology and to provide a means of quantifying dissociative experiences. Content for the scale's 28 items was garnered from extensive interviews with dissociative patients and from consultations with clinical experts. The scale taps a broad range of dissociative experiences including disturbances in memory, identity, and cognition, and feelings of derealization, depersonalization, absorption, and imaginative involvement.

The DES comes in two forms: the original DES and the DES II. Both versions use the same items, but they differ in their item formats. The DES in its original format uses a visual analogue scale (Oborne & Clarke, 1975; Remington, Tyrer, Newson-Smith, & Cicchetti, 1979) that requires examinees to mark their responses along a numerically anchored 100-millimeter line. Item responses range from 0%, "This never happens to you," to 100%, "This always happens to you." Subjects are asked to determine the "degree the experience described in the question applies to you and mark the line with a vertical slash at the appropriate place" (DES cover sheet). The position of the slash is recorded to the nearest 5 millimeters. The DES II uses a more convenient 11-point Likert scale. On both versions subjects are instructed to ignore drug- or alcohol-related experiences when marking their answers. Total scores are obtained by averaging the 28 item scores.

The DES can be purchased with an accompanying manual for a mere dollar. This is quite a bargain because the scale can be xeroxed an unlimited number of times for either clinical or research purposes. The manual is a compendium of psychometrically informative text and tables that should be consulted by potential users of the scale. It contains useful information on norms, reliability, validity, structure (via factor analysis), and use of cutoff scores for classification. Norms are presented for both clinical and nonclinical samples including subgroups with anxiety disorder, affective disorder, eating disorders, schizophrenia, borderline personality disorder, PTSD, dissociative disorders, and multiple personality. Scale means or medians are reported for each diagnostic group. Unfortunately, this table is poorly labeled in the manual and it is not clear which numbers refer to means or medians. Because DES scores are highly skewed in many clinical and nonclinical subgroups, the scale means and medians can differ markedly from one another. No other descriptive statistics are reported. The manual would be strengthened if it also reported standard deviations, interquartile ranges, skewness, and kurtosis coefficients for the scale. Additional information concerning item functioning, such as item endorsement frequencies in clinical and nonclinical samples, would also be informative.

Reliability findings from six studies are also reported in the manual. The weighted means of the test-retest and internal consistency reliabilities from these studies are .85 and .93, respectively. These figures indicate that the DES yields reliable scores in many assessment contexts. Two points concerning this conclusion warrant comment, however. First, readers are not told how long the inter-testing intervals were in the test-retest studies. Without this information it is difficult to evaluate the reliability coefficients. Second, the authors of the DES suggest in a later section of the manual that the scale measures *three* dissociation factors. If this were true it would vitiate the use of an internal consistency index, such as Cronbach's alpha, as a lower-bound reliability estimate.

Heretofore, two published studies have examined the DES factor structure (Fischer & Elnitsky, 1990; Ross, Joshi, & Currie, 1991). Both studies used nonpsychiatric subjects, and consequently their results may not generalize to clinical populations. Nevertheless, their findings warrant scrutiny because one study (Fischer & Elnitsky, 1990) advocated a one-factor model, whereas the other study (Ross, Joshi, & Currie, 1991) advocated a three-factor model. The three factors were labeled (*a*) absorption-imaginative involvement, (*b*) activities of dissociated states and, (*c*) depersonalization-derealization. Carlson and Putnam, the authors of the DES, indicated in a personal communication that they also previously endorsed a modified version of the three-factor model.

Ross, Joshi, and Currie (1991), the original defenders of the three-factor model, arrived at their findings by performing a principal components analysis, followed by varimax rotation, on the DES interitem correlation matrix. There are two reasons why this procedure may have yielded biased results. First, the DES items are notably skewed in nonclinical and many clinical samples, and Pearson correlations are adversely affected by variable skewness (Carrol, 1961; Tobin, 1958). Moreover, a principal components or common factor analysis of skewed data oftentimes produces spurious factors (Muthén, 1989).

What is a reviewer to do if he questions previous factor analytic findings that are cited in a questionnaire's manual? Telephone the authors, of course, and ask to look at the original data. When I spoke with Dr. Carlson she kindly offered to send me more than 1,500 protocols so that I could reanalyze the DES using methods designed for censored (i.e., highly skewed) variables (Muthén, 1989). The results of this analysis supported my initial suspicion. A general dissociation factor runs through the DES item pool. Amnestic dissociation and derealization factors *can* be identified in the item pool (the absorption factor is subsumed by the general factor), but they cannot reliably be measured. The general factor variance invariably swamps any group factor variance in unit-weighted factor scales. That is my take on the DES factor structure. Other investigators will undoubtedly disagree with me, so my advice is to be cautious when interpreting DES factor scores.

The DES has galvanized research on dissociative experiences in both clinical and nonclinical populations. The scale is easily administered, it provides reliable scores, and it has established validity in many assessment situations. For these reasons, if you are looking for a valid measure of dissociative experiences, you should associate with *dis* [sic] scale.

REVIEWER'S REFERENCES

B.C.A. (1908). My life as a dissociated personality. *The Journal of Abnormal Psychology*, *3*, 240-260.

Tobin, J. (1958). Estimation of relationships for limited dependent variables. *Econometrica*, *26*, 24-36.

Carroll, J. B. (1961). The nature of the data, or how to choose a correlation coefficient. *Psychometrika*, *26*, 347-372.

Oborne, D. J., & Clarke, M. J. (1975). Questionnaire surveys of passenger comfort. *Applied Ergonomics*, *6*, 97-103.

Remington, M., Tyrer, P. J., Newson-Smith, J., & Cicchetti, D. V. (1979). Comparative reliability of categorical and analogue rating scales in the assessment of psychiatric symptomatology. *Psychological Medicine*, *9*, 765-770.

Bernstein, E. M., & Putnam, F. W. (1986). Development, reliability, and validity of a dissociation scale. *Journal of Nervous and Mental Disease*, *174*, 727-735.

Muthén, B. O. (1989). Tobit factor analysis. *British Journal of Mathematical and Statistical Psychology*, *42*, 241-250.

Fischer, D. G., & Elnitsky, S. (1990). A factor analytic study of two scales measuring dissociation. *American Journal of Clinical Hypnosis*, *32*, 201-207.

Ross, C. A., Joshi, S., & Currie, R. (1991). Dissociative experiences in the general population: A factor analysis. *Hospital and Community Psychiatry*, *42*, 297-301.

Spiegel, D., & Cardeña, E. (1991). Disintegrated experience: The dissociative disorders revisited. *Journal of Abnormal Psychology*, *100*, 366-378.

[123]

Diversity Awareness Profile.

Purpose: "Designed to assist people in becoming aware of ways in which they discriminate against, judge, or isolate others."
Population: Employees or managers.
Publication Date: 1991.
Acronym: DAP.
Scores: Total score only.
Administration: Group.
Forms, 2: Employee, Manager.
Price Data, 1991: $3.95 each for (1–50 copies); $3.75 each for (51–100) copies; $3.55 each for (101–300) copies; $3.35 each for (301 or more) copies.
Time: (90) minutes.
Author: Karen Grote.
Publisher: Pfeiffer & Company International Publishers.

Review of the Diversity Awareness Profile by DONALD B. POPE-DAVIS, Associate Professor, Department of Counseling and Personnel Services, University of Maryland, College Park, MD, and JONATHAN G. DINGS, Graduate Student, Measurement and Statistics Program, University of Iowa, Iowa City, IA:

The Diversity Awareness Profile (DAP) employs a self-report format in which participants rate 40 items using a 4-point Likert scale of 1 = *almost never,* 2 = *seldom,* 3 = *usually,* and 4 = *almost always,* to describe how often they act in accordance with a specified discriminatory behavior. Because the purpose of this instrument is made clear to the participant in its instructions and the scoring mechanism (i.e., adding up scores on each item, with higher scores being indicative of less frequent discriminatory behavior) is quite obvious, it is important to be able to detect respondents who are answering the questions in a socially desirable manner. The DAP provides no means for such detection, and, in fact, may encourage socially desirable responding by removing any genuine assurance of anonymity in asking the participant to write their name on the instructions page. The absence of any validity-related evidence demonstrating a low correlation between DAP scores and an acceptable measure of socially desirable responding only increases the level of concern over social desirability, whereas the lack of any normative data or quantitative information about reliability or validity raises serious questions as to what the DAP measures.

If the DAP is used solely to begin discussions or a training session related to discrimination in the workplace, concerns with item content are probably paramount to the issues raised above. Development of the items from discriminatory behaviors described by persons of color, women, and others "in more than a hundred focus groups and in one-on-one interviews over a three year period" (as noted in the two-page DAP Trainer's Notes) provides some evidence of content-related validity. Although DAP item content is apparently related to discrimination, the presence of multiple clauses, jargon (e.g., "personal comfort zone") and verbs stated in other-than-behavioral terms is problematic. There are a number of circumstances under which it is difficult to say how a participant should respond to the question, "How often do I accept and reinforce the fact that not everyone has to act or look a certain way to be successful in or valuable to my organization?" For the person who accepts but does not reinforce this fact, it is difficult to answer this question unambiguously, even if the person has a clear idea of what it means to reinforce a fact. And, how about the person who "usually" accepts but only "seldom" reinforces the fact? The conjunction of "act or look a certain way" in the latter half of the question causes a similar difficulty, compounding the ambiguity already present in the item. Thus, it is rather problematic for one person to interpret another's response to this item. This same item also illustrates the seeming property of not being based entirely on a behavior, because acceptance appears to indicate a state of belief rather than an action.

Ambiguous items would be less problematic if the purpose of the test were to serve as a basis for discussion of the items themselves, but such a limited use is suggested neither in the instrument nor in the Trainer's Notes. The instrument provides a system of interpreting scores, in which the participant is classified as a "Perpetuator," "Avoider," "Change Agent," or "Fighter" on the basis of total score, and a two-paragraph interpretation is provided for each. Although a minor caveat for this classification scheme is provided by the inclusion of a "Naive Offender" category, said to be potentially applicable at any score level, the selection of cut points for the four categories appears somewhat arbitrary. It would be reassuring to be provided with some evidence validating the interpretations given to each of these categories.

On the positive side, the DAP does include a useful set of discussion questions for the trainer, and is ready for use without additional materials. Completing the 40 items probably should require less than one-third of the one-and-one-half hours listed as time for use, with the remainder of a session being devoted to discussion. The availability of separate forms for managers and employees is appropriate because the topic of discriminatory behavior is probably not as readily discussed in groups comprising both managers and employees, and because this allows inclusion of a few items in each version which are tailored to each group.

The DAP could improve its item format by including "Always" and "Never" options because the frequency with which one undertakes behaviors described in some items can indeed be always or never. Inclusion of reverse-scored items would make the DAP less sensitive to response sets other than socially desirable responding, such as simply marking high responses. The name "profile" could stand to be changed to something more appropriate to an instrument yielding a single score. However, any such changes in item format or scoring would come at a cost to the primary strength of the DAP: simplicity of administration and scoring.

It is unclear whether the DAP should be commended for the spirit of the severe advice it offers managers who fall into the "perpetuator" category, or censured for offering such harsh advice on the basis of a self-report and no other information.

Although the concerns noted above are substantive, this instrument can undoubtedly be used in its intended manner, especially if the trainer employing the instrument is cognizant of its potential shortcomings and can make efforts to address socially desirable responding concerns with participants.

Review of the Diversity Awareness Profile by GARGI ROYSIRCAR SODOWSKY, Associate Professor of Educational Psychology, University of Nebraska-Lincoln, Lincoln, NE:

The two measures, Diversity Awareness Profile and Manager's Version Diversity Awareness Profile (DAP), purport to measure similar diversity-oriented sensitivity, but do not have identical item content. Although each measure has 40 items, 8 items in both measures that carry the same numbering system have different wordings. In addition, each measure has 5 unique items. The reason for such content differences is not known. The differences are not owing to a different conceptualization about the diversity of work attitudes and behaviors of workers versus managers because the general DAP has items relating to policy-related matters that a manager has more opportunities to address and change.

There are no reverse scaled items that could control for content-dependent response sets. Therefore, it is questionable whether scores in the higher ranges are not influenced by cultural social desirability. Also, because the measures (*a*) do not control for cultural social desirability, and because no research provides evidence that (*b*) the diversity awareness construct being measured is independent of social desirability, it will be difficult to discriminate between respondents who are genuinely sensitive and those who are faking good..

The 4-point Likert scale may not have equal interval units. There is not much difference semantically between *usually* (3 points) and *almost always* (4 points) and between *seldom* (2 points) and *almost never* (1 point). On the other hand, there is considerable semantic difference and distance between *seldom* and *usually*, but only a 1-point difference is assigned between these two descriptors. Either the Likert scale range needs to be increased or the descriptors need to be changed.

The interpretive categories "Naive Offender," "Perpetuator," "Avoider," "Change Agent," and "Fighter" are created in an a priori method. No research evidence is provided to demonstrate that these categories are derived from empirical criterion groups. The range of scores of each category is not shown to be statistically different from the range of scores of the preceding category and the following category. Attitudinal overlap could be expected between "a perpetuator" and "an avoider" and between "a change agent" and "a fighter." Thus, the categories seem to be judgmental labeling, especially in the case of the term "fighter." A respondent who is most diversity-oriented may also be paranoid and "on the lookout for prejudice when nothing has indicated that prejudice exists" (p. 6). On the other hand, the author does not address the issue that "a change agent" may not be aware of racism and value biases at a deeply personal, affective level, but instead may be operating from a defensive intellectual level, focusing on others, institutions, and politics of oppression rather than being introspective of, for example, one's own racial consciousness. The interpretation of the category "naive offender" seems most confusing. A score range is not assigned to this category. Therefore, a respondent with the highest possible score (checking off *almost always* for all items—that is a fighter) may be a naive offender just as any other categorized person. Because the naive offender cannot be identified in measurement terms, all other categories become invalid.

Naive people, by definition, cannot be expected to do what they are asked to do—"give some serious thought to the types of behavior that indicate bias and prejudice" (p. 5). Contrary to the author's understanding, naive people cannot change attitudes and behavior just because they solicit feedback from colleagues. Perhaps only significant environmental changes, social events, personal critical incidents, and life exposure could gradually influence changes in naive racist cognitions and behaviors.

The author says in the Trainer's Notes, a two-page leaflet, that the DAP "is based on information gathered in more than a hundred focus groups and in one-on-one interviews over a three-year period with members of protected classes" (Trainer's Notes, p. 1). However, the author provides no data to show the criterion-related validity of findings obtained from the focus groups or the content validity of the items derived from interviews with minority individuals. The items generated from minority interviews should have been examined by diversity experts, and the interrater reliability of the experts' categorization of scores as certain types of attitudes could have been examined. The DAP does not have a manual containing normative data or other types of score information such as standard scores and means and standard deviations. The lack of such measurement information also suggests why, at the basic conceptual level, there is a confusion about the differences between the experiences of legally protected classes in the United States and those of perceived minorities, such as overweight people. Thus, the construct validity of the DAP is in question. The use of an over-inclusive and diluted construct of minority raises another related question. Who should be the respondents of this instrument?

On the positive side, the printed measure is attractive, easy to read, and portable. Information about terms, instructions, the self-scoring format, a figure illustrating the diversity awareness spectrum of scores, and accompanying brief interpretive explanations will appeal to respondents because of the features of time efficiency and simplicity. For the same reasons organizations may be tempted to use the DAP for staff development purposes. However, users are cautioned about the limited meaningfulness of the DAP score categories and about the usefulness of the DAP for planning sustained interventions to change prejudiced attitudes and behaviors. At best, the DAP could be used as an "ice-breaker" to start discussions in a diversity workshop.

[124]

Draw A Person: Screening Procedure for Emotional Disturbance.
Purpose: Designed to screen for children who may have emotional disorders.
Population: Ages 6–17.
Publication Date: 1991.
Acronym: DAP:SPED.
Scores: Total score only.
Administration: Group.

Price Data, 1992: $59 per complete kit including 25 record forms and manual (77 pages); $28 per 25 record forms; $29 per manual.
Time: 15(20) minutes.
Authors: Jack A. Naglieri, Timothy J. McNeish, and Achilles N. Bardos.
Publisher: PRO-ED, Inc.

TEST REFERENCES

1. Briccetti, K. A. (1994). Emotional indicators of deaf children on the Draw-A-Person Test. *American Annals of the Deaf, 139,* 500-505.
2. Clark, A. J. (1995). Projective techniques in the counseling process. *Journal of Counseling and Development, 73,* 311-316.

Review of the Draw A Person: Screening Procedure for Emotional Disturbance by MERITH COSDEN, Associate Professor, Counseling/Clinical/School Psychology, Department of Education, University of California, Santa Barbara, CA:

The Draw A Person: Screening Procedure for Emotional Disturbance (DAP:SPED) is a formal system of administering and scoring human figure drawings to screen children for emotional problems. Practitioners can detect children who are "at risk" of having an emotional disturbance by comparing the scores obtained on their figure drawings with the scores from the normative sample.

The DAP:SPED was developed by the same author of the Draw A Person: A Quantitative Scoring System (Naglieri, 1988; 11:114) which is designed to screen for cognitive deficits. The same basic protocol is used in each assessment system, with different scoring criteria used to provide the information needed in each domain.

The test relies on a pattern of administering human figure drawings that was first used by Harris (1963) called the Goodenough-Harris Draw A Person test. A child is asked to create three drawings: a woman, a man, and a picture of themselves. The use of three pictures, and, in particular, the use of the self-drawing, was considered experimental in the Goodenough-Harris system. The three drawings are used in both the DAP:SPED and the Draw A Person: A Quantitative Scoring System, although little support has been provided for use of the three figures.

The criteria used for scoring the DAP:SPED were developed systematically. A standardization sample of 2,260, 5–17-year-old students was drawn to be representative of U.S. geographic regions, gender, ethnicity, and socioeconomic status. This is part of the same sample used to standardize the Draw A Person: A Quantitative Scoring System. Preliminary scoring criteria were generated from prior studies of the use of figure drawings to expose emotional disturbance. These scoring criteria were tested on a small sample of subjects and modified several times to assure that the descriptors could be coded reliably. The modified criteria were then applied to the drawings of the larger standardization sample. The system is designed to detect behavior that occurs infrequently in the normative population; only items that occurred in less than 16% of the standardization sample were kept in the final coding system. Emotional disturbance is not detected from any one type of response in this system; rather, it is screened through observation of a large number of unusual responses thought to reflect emotional problems.

Through the standardization procedure it was found that subjects did not vary in their responses to the three types of figures. Thus, each picture is scored by the same criteria, and scores are summed to provide an indication of the client's needs. This suggests the three different types of pictures may not be needed for the protocol. Little variation in scores was found as a function of age. Scores are clustered by ages 6–8, 9–12, and 13–17. Significant sex differences were obtained, however. As a result, norms are presented separately by sex for each of the age groups. Raw scores, summed across the three pictures, are converted to T scores with a mean of 50 and a standard deviation of 10. T scores of 55 and over are considered appropriate for further evaluation, whereas scores of 65 and above are considered strong indicators of the need for additional assessment.

Reliability of the DAP:SPED is relatively high. The two studies in the manual on intrarater reliability (the same rater scoring each drawing twice) and interrater reliability (different raters scoring the same drawings) found reliability correlations in the .8 to .9 range. One study on the stability of test scores over a 1-week period found slightly lower correlations between scores, $r = .67$; students' scores were not significantly different across test periods, however, indicating that the scores were relatively stable.

Four studies on the validity of the DAP:SPED, none independently published at the time of this review, are presented in the manual. In each study, the scores of a group of children who have been diagnosed with a range of emotional problems are compared with the scores of a group of individuals without known diagnoses but who are otherwise matched to the clinical group by age and sex. In each instance, the diagnosed group had significantly higher scores on the DAP:SPED than did the control group. Using a cutoff score of 55 or more the studies were able to accurately classify children at conventional levels of statistical significance; however, the numbers of children accurately classified, as well as those who would be misclassified under this system, were not reported.

Although the DAP:SPED appears straightforward in its conception and purpose, I have several concerns about its utility. The test makes certain assumptions about the nature of emotional disturbance. Among them, that emotional problems can be generically assessed, that all types of emotional problems will be screened through the items on the test, and that emotional disturbance is more effectively screened through the presence of a number of unusual items rather than one or two specific criteria. The manual does not provide strong support for these assumptions.

In determining whether the DAP:SPED is a useful screening device one has to justify the time expended in administering and scoring the test with the benefits obtained. To what extent is this screening tool able to accurately capture emotional disturbance? And is it more effective and less intrusive than other screening tools? The available research on this instrument does not adequately address the number of false positives or false negatives likely to occur from use of this tool. This concern aside, the context in which the DAP:SPED is used is seen as critical to its utility. If the DAP:SPED is administered to a broad group of children who have not been identified with special needs, it may be useful in detecting some students who are at risk for or experiencing emotional problems. On the other hand, if the DAP:SPED is part of a screening battery for a child who teachers or counselors have already identified as needing some help, it appears less likely that it would provide significant additional information.

In sum, children's drawings are easily administered and clinically interesting, thus tempting to use for screening and assessment. However, the actual contribution of these procedures to the screening process remains unclear. The DAP:SPED does not provide specific information with regard to the type of emotional disturbance children are experiencing, nor is it clear that it is sensitive to all types of emotional disturbance. For children already identified by teachers or parents as experiencing some emotional problems, this instrument may not add substantively to their understanding of the child. For broad screening purposes, however, the DAP:SPED may yield useful information not otherwise available.

REVIEWER'S REFERENCES

Harris, D. B. (1963). *Children's drawings as measures of intellectual maturity*. New York: Harcourt, Brace & World.

Naglieri, J. A. (1988). Draw A Person: A Quantitative Scoring System. San Antonio, TX: The Psychological Corporation.

Review of the Draw A Person: Screening Procedure for Emotional Disturbance by GALE M. MORRISON, Associate Professor of Education, Graduate School of Education, University of California, Santa Barbara, CA:

The stated goal of the Draw A Person: Screening Procedure for Emotional Disturbance (DAP:SPED) is to "provide a screening measure to aid in the identification of children and adolescents who may have emotional or, as termed by some, behavioral disorders" (p. 3). The rationale for their approach to measurement is based on what the authors consider shortcomings of existing projective human figure drawing systems. Thus, their emphasis is on easy and objective scoring, recent national norms, differentiation between disturbed and normal populations, reliability, and provision of the ability to score for cognitive functioning (as measured by a separate system, not included in this review).

The test development procedures were clearly described. The initial pool of items was chosen for previously documented clinical significance; the final set of items was chosen for item contributions to the reliability (item-total correlations) and validity (infrequency of occurrence in a normal sample). The clinical and substantive significance of projective tests is not emphasized beyond the initial selection of items. The authors deliberately chose the number of emotional indicators in drawings as their sole index of emotional disturbance. Interpretations of the meaning of the drawings are *not* included. Although this approach perhaps gives less interesting information, it facilitates the creation of an instrument that is psychometrically sound as well as easily and objectively quantified.

The manual authors provide a clear description of the scoring system. Templates are provided for the scoring of figure size and placement on the page. Sample drawings and a delineation of corresponding scores for training purposes are provided. The record form is clear and efficient.

Standardization procedures included the selection of a large sample that represented factors of age, gender, geographic region, ethnicity, and household income. A weakness in the description of the standardization procedures is that the authors failed to describe how these subjects were chosen. Also, in terms of representativeness, no information was given on the inclusion or exclusion of children with handicaps. Test users are left uninformed about the extent to which the standardization sample is representative of a range of abilities. Therefore, norms are provided for what is assumed to be a normal sample. Because the DAP:SPED is a screening instrument for emotional disturbance, it would be interesting to be able to compare scores to a sample of children and adolescents with emotional disturbances as well. Such norms are not provided.

The scoring that resulted in the normative data was completed by "approximately 20 raters" (p. 7) of undisclosed background. Test authors should be more exact in their description of this aspect of the standardization procedures.

Documentation of validity relies primarily on four studies (done by the test authors) that document the ability of this instrument to discriminate between emotionally disturbed and normal populations. These studies lend support to the fact that scores on the DAP:SPED can discriminate between disturbed and nondisturbed children and adolescents. The screening function of the instrument would be more convincingly validated by comparing the scores on the DAP:SPED with other screening instruments such as teacher, parent, or child behavior and/or emotional adjustment rating scales or behavioral observations by teachers and other school support personnel. These other measures are more closely aligned with the function of screening at the prereferral stage (rather than post-identification) for children and adolescents experiencing emotional and behavioral difficulties.

The authors also note the lack of correlation of the DAP:SPED scores with a measure of intelligence as evidence of validity. Because one of the intended purposes of this instrument was to provide an instrument that lends itself to assessment of cognitive functioning (specifically, the Draw A Person: A Quantitative Scoring System or the DAP:QSS) and because the same standardization sample was used, information concerning validity also could have been easily gleaned by comparing the DAP:QSS and the DAP:SPED. The test user is left wondering why such information was not presented.

Information about internal consistency, test-retest stability, and inter- and intrarater reliability was presented. Although the case for inter- and intrarater reliability was based on a limited number of raters, the reliability indices, in general, were acceptable considering the screening function of the instrument. The authors appropriately emphasized the importance of using standard error of measurement (*SEM*) in developing confidence intervals and provided detailed information for determining these confidence intervals.

Cutoff scores are provided. The description of the process of determining these scores is vague. However, the authors do urge that appropriate caution be used in the use of these cutoff scores.

The test authors provide the appropriate cautions about the function and scope of the instrument as a screening instrument, emphasizing the importance of gathering additional information about children or adolescents who get scores that indicate further evaluation is needed. However, the authors could have discussed the implications of the widespread use of this instrument in a school setting, where children or adolescents potentially could be identified when they might not otherwise be having significant difficulties with school. The consequences for the individual students, as well as the school system, of referring false positives for further evaluation should be discussed.

In summary, the DAP:SPED has been constructed for the purpose of screening children and adolescents for emotional disturbance. Appropriate cautions were given by the authors about using the instrument beyond its screening function. Administration and scoring procedures are objective, easy, and clear. The DAP:SPED manual includes recent national norms for age and sex groups of a "normal" sample. Addition of norms for a sample of emotionally disturbed children and adolescents would add an additional perspective for test users. Although somewhat limited in scope and size, studies completed by the authors have established initial validity and reliability. Their validity argument would be improved by comparisons with other instruments that are known indicators of emotional and behavioral disturbance.

[125]

Driver Risk Inventory.

Purpose: "Designed for DUI/DWI offender risk assessment."
Population: Convicted DUI and DWI offenders.
Publication Dates: 1986–92.
Acronym: DRI.
Scores: Behaviors/characteristics relevant to DUI offenders in 5 areas: Validity, Alcohol, Drugs, Driver Risk, Stress Coping Abilities.
Administration: Individual or group.
Price Data, 1992: $5 to $6 per test; other price data available from publisher.
Time: (30–35) minutes.
Comments: Self-administered, computer-scored test.
Author: Behavior Data Systems, Ltd.
Publisher: Behavior Data Systems, Ltd.

Review of the Driver Risk Inventory by FRANK GRESHAM, Professor and Director, School of Psychology Program, University of California, Riverside, Riverside, CA:

The Driver Risk Inventory (DRI) is a computer-administered, computer-scored, and computer-interpreted self-report instrument designed for use with individuals convicted of Driving While Intoxicated (DWI) or Driving Under the Influence (DUI). The DRI comprises 139 items and requires 25 minutes to complete. It is typically administered on IBM-compatible computers, but can be administered in test booklet format. Regardless of administration mode, it is computer scored and interpreted. The DRI is written on a 6th grade reading level and is available in both English and Spanish.

STANDARDIZATION SAMPLE AND NORMS. The technical manual published in 1992 by Behavior Data Systems, Ltd. is unclear as to who the DRI was standardized on, how many subjects were in the standardization sample, what states were involved in the standardization, and the demographic breakdown of the standardization sample. According to the manual, the DRI database is being continually expanded and is updated annually. This, however, is no excuse for not providing a clear description of the most currently available standardization data. In short, one does not know from reading the manual exactly upon whom the DRI was standardized.

SCALES AND SCORES. The DRI comprises five scales: (*a*) Truthfulness, which is a validity scale designed to identify self-protective, recalcitrant, and guarded individuals trying to conceal information; (*b*) Alcohol, which is a measure of alcohol proneness and alcohol-related problems; (*c*) Drugs, which is a measure of drug-abuse related problems; (*d*) Driver Risk, which is a measure of driver risk independent of that person's involvement with alcohol or drugs; and (*e*) Stress Quotient, which is a measure of the respondent's ability to cope with stress.

Scores on each scale are reported as percentile ranks and are assigned "risk levels" or "risk classification ranges." Four ranges are presented for each scale: (*a*) Low Risk, 0 to 39th percentile; (*b*) Medium Risk, 40th to 69th percentile; (*c*) Problem Risk, 70th to 89th percentile; and (*d*) Severe Problem Risk, 90th to 100th percentile. Scores on four of the scales (Alcohol, Drugs, Driver Risk, and Stress Quotient) are corrected by their correlations with the Validity Scale to yield "truth-corrected" scores.

RELIABILITY AND VALIDITY DATA. The manual provides evidence for internal consistency and interrater reliabilities. Coefficient alphas based on several studies consistently are in the .70 to .90 range with a median coefficient alpha of .81. Interrater agreement based on the correlations between DRI scales and independent DWI examiners ranged from .02 (Stress Coping Abilities) to .63 (Alcohol) with a median coefficient of .44.

Validity data are based on correlations between the DRI and various other scales and measures such as the MMPI MacAndrews Scale, number of moving violations, blood alcohol content at time of arrest, Michigan Alcohol Screening Test (MAST), Mortimer-Finkins Interview, and the Substance Abuse Questionnaire. Some of the validity coefficients, although significant, are extremely low (e.g., .05 to .15) and achieved statistical significance because of extremely large sample sizes (*N*s = 480 to 1,487).

SUMMARY. The DRI represents a convenient computerized approach to screening drivers who may be at risk for future DWI/DUI offenses. The technical manual is unclearly written, "scattered," and poorly documented. Tables of data are presented without any apparent organization and often lack clear description of the samples upon which the data are based. At present, the validity data in the manual are not convincing and users should be cautious in using the DRI to make important decisions regarding driver risk.

[126]

Dropout Prediction & Prevention.

Purpose: Developed to identify students at risk for dropping out of school.
Population: Grades 9–12.
Publication Date: 1990.
Acronym: DPP.
Scores: Total score only.
Administration: Individual.
Price Data, 1991: $4 per 25 scales (select High School Form or Experimental Form for 8th Grade); $15 per manual (93 pages); $15.50 per specimen set.
Time: [5] minutes.
Comments: Scale information obtained from student cumulative records.
Authors: Clarence E. Nichols and Rochelle E. Nichols.
Publisher: Clinical Psychology Publishing Co., Inc.

Review of the Dropout Prediction & Prevention by IRVIN J. LEHMANN, Professor of Measurement, Michigan State University, East Lansing, MI:

To predict school dropouts and develop a program of remediation would, without a doubt, be a major boon to American education. This was the intent of the Dropout Prediction & Prevention (DPP) instrument.

After undertaking a careful review of the literature on school dropouts, instrument authors Nichols and Nichols concluded that available instruments were unsuitable for a variety of reasons: "they were too cumbersome, had a low predictor value, did not include enough predictor factors, were too expensive and time-consuming to administer, or because the necessary information was too difficult to obtain or was not available" (manual, p. 15). I am sympathetic to the difficulties associated with instrument development, but the above assertions create concern regarding how the DPP has been validated.

The DPP does not appear to be based on a particular theory; rather, the instrument builds on some previous research in the area. The test authors suggest that an acceptable prediction instrument has to satisfy the following criteria: (*a*) easy to administer and score; (*b*) based on data already collected (that is, no interviews or tests); (*c*) short; and, (*d*) accurate. No doubt, by accurate, the authors meant valid. The DPP is short, can gather the data needed from existing files, and is relatively simple to administer and score. But, is it valid?

Nichols and Nichols describe the feasibility study they undertook to identify potential dropout factors. The sample consisted of only 50 students (25 dropouts and 25 graduates). The composite instrument was developed on only 20 students (10 dropouts and 10 graduates). Although identifying the perfect number needed to support instrument development is difficult, this sample appears grossly inadequate.

Insufficient information is provided regarding the representativeness of the sample. The authors suggest their sample was drawn from a pool comparable to the U.S. Census with some exceptions. Regrettably, the exceptions were not described.

From an original pool of 20 items, the final instrument consists of five items: (1) days absent, (2) years repeated, (3) G.P.A., (4) alternative school, and (5) number of parents in the home. A weight was assigned to the type of response for each variable and the total weighted score (each weighted score is called a scaled score which is *not* correct or conventional usage of the term). Those students having a total scaled score of 5 or more are identified as potential dropouts.

Although Nichols and Nichols used regression analysis to identify the five variables making up the scale (there were actually six, but parental education was deleted because of the availability or reliability of this information in the students' files), they do not provide a regression equation. This is an oversight.

One might also raise the question why regression analysis appears to have been used to identify those factors/items that make up the scale. Why wasn't discriminant function analysis used to identify those items that differentiate between students who graduate and those who drop out? Computing a multiple R will only provide information as to the contribution particular variables make in predicting a criterion.

Finally, I do not understand why z-scores were computed for five predictor variables. There might be a good reason but the reader is left in the dark as to their purpose.

The essential type of validity evidence needed for an instrument such as the DPP is *predictive* validity, which for the DPP, are data that show the instrument (*a*) permits users to make better decisions with the data than the best decision one could make without DPP data, and (*b*) the cost of testing and faulty decisions.

The value of any test, and especially those claiming predictive power, is dependent upon the difference between the cost of testing and how much is saved in the cost of errors (for the DPP, it would be either predicting a dropout when one would not have occurred but *more* damaging would be the error where the potential dropout would *not* be identified, that is, a false negative). Because the DPP's major purpose is not only identifying potential dropouts but also the program developed to identify and counsel such students, it is essential that false negatives be minimized. Again, the question to be answered is whether or not the DPP has a smaller number of false negatives than would be made without using the data it provides. Only careful long-term research will supply information about incremental validity gains through use of the DPP.

Any instrument claiming predictive validity must be cross validated. Although I am not completely satisfied with the cross-validation sample, primarily because of its small size and lack of representativeness, the authors used proper procedures to attempt a cross validation.

In summary, the DPP *may* be a promising instrument but more research is needed with larger and more representative samples. Until then, potential users should be very careful in making decisions about who should and should not enter a dropout prevention program based on results of this approach. The program, per se, seems quite reasonable but its success in preventing dropouts is not well documented.

Review of the Dropout Prediction & Prevention by *BERT W. WESTBROOK, Professor of Psychology, North Carolina State University, Raleigh, NC and SUZANNE MARKEL-FOX, Post Doctoral Fellow, Center for Mental Health Policies and Services Research, University of Pennsylvania, Philadelphia, PA:*

The Dropout Prediction & Prevention (DPP) was developed to facilitate the school counselor's task in identifying and tracking students who are at risk for dropout but who may fall between the extremes of those with very poor attendance and behavior, and those who are successful in school. The DPP, which purports to measure the risk of student dropout from elementary (8th grade) or secondary school, was designed to be part of a global dropout prevention program. The accompanying booklet describes model preventive programs in detail.

The DPP has two forms, a Dropout Prediction Profile for High School Students, and experimental Dropout Prediction Profile for 8th-graders. The factors to be entered on the high school form include attendance (days absent last full year), years repeated (number of years not promoted), grade-point average, alternative school (any behavior placement), and parents in home (one- or two-parent home). On the 8th-grade experimental form, the items are the same except for alternative school, for which behavior problems (causes classroom disturbance) is substituted. Data are entered on the DPP from existing school records. This can be accomplished by the school counselor or a reliable office assistant who is not a student, because some of the information may be sensitive (e.g., number of parents in the home, previous placements for behavior problems). The booklet authors suggest that some of these data are already computerized in many school districts and that a minor modification of the school system software would allow for automatic data entry.

DEVELOPMENT OF THE INSTRUMENT. The authors generated the items on the DPP based on their experience with students who had performed poorly in school or who had dropped out. Then, randomly selected records of 25 each of graduates and dropouts were used in a feasibility study of the instrument. The variables included "attendance, years repeated, over age, grades, suspensions, behavior placements, standardized test scores, sibling dropout, and delinquency" (manual, p. 23). The rationale for the item choice and the scoring and weights attributed to scores was not described, and the data from this administration are not reported. There was no mention of any theoretical basis for the item choice or the structure of the DPP.

Results from the study of 50 individuals were reportedly analyzed (no details of this analysis were provided) and 20 items which included "all sources of student information that had any potential for influencing dropout behavior" (manual, p. 23) were tested on another set of records, from 10 graduates and 10 dropouts. Lack of detail makes it impossible for the reader to understand what constituted a "successful trial" of the initial instrument, nor why items were expanded from 9 to 20. Again, no results for the 20 subjects are reported, so it is impossible to evaluate the goodness of the predictors which were eventually selected.

Validation and cross validation of the items judged to be the best predictors of dropping out was reportedly performed on a sample of 400 student records, 200 of which represented graduates and 200 dropouts. Stepwise regression procedures identified the six most discriminating items (R^2>.68), five of which were chosen for inclusion on the instrument. The sixth variable, parent education, although adequately productive, was not included because of inconsistent availability of the information. However, the authors report a fair degree of overlap in predictions based on the use of the DPP (Figure 2, manual, p. 26); the rejection of the parent education variable because of inconsistency of results with a small sample might have been a premature decision.

ADMINISTRATION AND SCORING. Raw scores are entered in the appropriate column and then scaled by means of a weighting scale which is conveniently placed in the right-most column on the same single sheet used for all data entry. Each item is weighted separately and then all weights are summed to yield a cumulative total score. This weighting process appears rather arbitrary. For example, a student who has repeated three grades, missed more than 80 days, maintains a grade point average of 1, has been placed in an alternative setting, and who has only one parent in the home, would receive a weighted score of 11. Yet another student with less than 21 absences, a grade point average of 2, no history of alternative placements and both parents in the home, but who has repeated twice, would receive a score of 4, which would not meet the criteria for dropout risk.

Scaled scores are derived from weighted raw scores and the cumulative total renders a single arbitrary cutting score: either graduate (scaled score of 0 to 4) or not graduate (any score over 5). The DPP authors discuss the incremental validity of modified cutting scores, and recommend that administrators with particular budgetary or personnel limitations may wish to use that flexibility. "As the horizontal axis moves toward the top of the chart, the school administrator will improve his or her prediction of graduates; however, error in predicting dropouts will increase. In terms of saving education dollars, the higher the axis the greater the savings, because fewer dropouts are identified for prevention programs" (manual, p. 32).

TECHNICAL CONSIDERATIONS. The sample of student records used for developing the normative scores for the DPP came from one high school in a medium-sized city in south-central Pennsylvania. The high school served 1,297 students, 75.8% of whom were African-American, 18.2% Euro-American, and 6% Hispanic and "other." The 200 graduates came from the graduating class of 1982. The 200 dropouts came from the same school, but had dropped out over a period of 4 years. The authors do not describe the racial composition of the groups nor how the 200 students from each group were selected.

Stepwise regression analysis was used to select the final five items, after which one-half of the sample was cross validated. Dropout prediction scores were correlated with the dichotomous criterion (graduated or dropped out). The authors described the findings from their multiple regression as discriminative but did not report convergent and discriminant validity studies. The items on the DPP were tested using records from students who graduated in 1982 or who had dropped out of school over a 4-year period including 1982. The authors did not repeat the analyses performed on the first group, which makes it difficult to determine whether the five variables retained are indeed the best predictors. Records were randomized and data obtained from them were analyzed using stepwise multiple regression.

Means, standard deviations, and range of variables are not reported. This is an egregious oversight; variability can determine whether the variable is likely to be rejected based on regression analysis. This is particularly important in the present example, because the population upon which this instrument was tested is very unusual. Minority groups are overrepresented, students were absent frequently (mean = 37 days), had a mean retention record of nearly one year of school, and a mean of one parent in the home.

OVERALL CRITIQUE. The DPP is easy to complete and the booklet offers many helpful recommendations for local development and implementation of dropout prevention programs, as well as problems to avoid. Used in conjunction with a Student Information Management System, the DPP could generate risk profiles at a relatively low cost. The DPP could also be used as part of a training program for future counselors, special education teachers, and dropout prevention coordinators.

The DPP uses information readily available in most school systems, and should significantly reduce the time involved in identifying students potentially at risk for school dropout. The authors include detailed recommendations for developing aggressive dropout prevention programs, based on their own experience. Some of the resources they identified include academic skills improvement programs, alternative school programs, school and community recreation programs, counseling, employment, and programs that address the students' special interests and needs. The booklet includes a practical guide for establishing and maintaining a prevention program. Successful prevention programs from across the United States are also reviewed, and the elements of a good prevention program are covered in some detail. For this reason, the DPP may be a good tool for a school board or planning committee which is preparing to develop and budget for a dropout prevention program.

Unfortunately, however, the development and presentation of this instrument do not meet the requirements of the *Standards for Educational and Psychological Testing* (AERA, APA, & NCME, 1985). There was no technical manual provided; in its place was a booklet that included practical application considerations and incomplete information about the test's statistical properties. The authors offered no validity or reliability information aside from the inadequately reported validity studies conducted in the development of the instrument. The sample of student records used for development and validation of the final instrument may not be representative of the high school population at large. In addition, because the school district where these students were served offered a variety of alternatives to standard high school education, including a vocational-technical facility, the district may not be representative of school districts in general across the United States. This instrument was developed and tested exclusively from school records, without any student contact.

The 25% dropout rate reported by various governmental and educational agencies underscores the need for a dropout prediction instrument. However, because two items alone (years repeated, grade point average) accounted for 61% of the variance in rates of graduation reported by the test developers, further carefully designed validity studies should be conducted for this instrument to be a worthwhile investment for school districts and social agencies.

Care should be taken to use the DPP in conjunction with personal student/family contact. The Dropout Prediction Profile (DPP) appears to be a concise and easy-to-use instrument that can draw upon data already available to the school counselor. Used as part of an overall prediction and prevention program, as proposed by the developers of the instrument, this profile may be a practical screening tool. In its current form, however, it should not be considered a measuring instrument.

Overall, the development procedures for this instrument were atheoretical and lacking in sound methodological analysis. The DPP may be a good starting point for development of a dropout prevention counseling program, but its validity and reliability remain to be demonstrated. It would not be wise to base placement decisions on scores generated by this checklist.

REVIEWER'S REFERENCE

American Educational Research Association, American Psychological Association, & National Council on Measurement in Education. (1985). *Standards for educational and psychological testing*. Washington, DC: American Psychological Association, Inc.

[127]

Early School Assessment.

Purpose: Designed to measure prereading and mathematics skills.
Population: End of prekindergarten to middle of kindergarten, middle of kindergarten to beginning of grade 1.
Publication Date: 1990.
Acronym: ESA.
Scores, 7: Prereading (Language, Visual [also used in Mathematics total], Auditory, Memory, Total), Mathematics Concepts and Operations (Visual [also used in Prereading total], Total).
Administration: Group.
Levels, 2: 1, 2.
Price Data: Price data available from publisher for test materials including: complete testing kit including 35 machine- or hand-scorable test booklets (select level), 35 practice books, scoring key, class record sheet for hand scoring, and examiner's manual (81 pages, select level); 35 parent conference forms (select level); teacher's guide (51 pages, select level); preliminary norms book; preliminary technical bulletin; test organizer; scoring service available from publisher.
Time: 229 (Level 2) to 239 (Level 1) minutes over 8 sessions.
Authors: CTB MacMillan/McGraw-Hill.
Publisher: CTB MacMillan/McGraw-Hill.

Review of the Early School Assessment by SONYA BLIXT, Professor of Evaluation and Measurement, and CHRISTINE F. STRAUSS, Graduate Assistant in Evaluation and Measurement, Kent State University, Kent, OH:

The Early School Assessment (ESA) measures prereading and math skills as an aid in determining the formal training needs for children in the early years of school. The ESA is group administered and is presented to children as an enjoyable game in story format. Although the main purpose of the ESA is to guide instructional planning, the authors indicate that it can also be used to identify children who qualify for federally funded programs.

Objective Performance Indexes (OPI) serve as criterion-referenced scores in determining each child's level of proficiency in a specific area. Based on the number of correct responses for each scale, children are categorized as proficient, in need of continuing instruction, or in need of introduction to the topic. Suggestions for at-home activities matched to the OPI are provided to aid parents in helping their children develop these skills. Furthermore, the distracters for each item were chosen based upon common errors made in answering the item. Thus, incorrect answers further aid the teacher in diagnosing the type of instruction needed for the child. Although the three diagnostic categories are helpful in determining the level of instruction necessary for each student, there is no rationale provided in the test manuals that justifies the criteria used for determining these specific cut scores.

Scoring can be done either by hand or machine. The test booklet provides norm-referenced scale scores, national percentile ranks, stanines, and normal curve equivalents by grade level and time of year (fall, winter, spring). The norming group is a sample of approximately 23,000 prekindergarten, kindergarten, and first-grade children from diverse school districts, geographic areas, socioeconomic levels, and ethnic backgrounds. The norms tables are easy to read and understand, although several readings of the description of the sampling methods left the reviewers unclear about the procedures used.

The manual provides the theoretical rationale for the development of the objectives of the instrument, as well as the instructions for use of the test. The instructions booklet, though clearly written, permits the teacher to determine the time of the test, the number of breaks to give to the children, and the duration of these breaks. Such lack of standardization in the administration of the test causes reservation regarding the interpretation of the norm-referenced scores. Comparisons to other children's performance are not meaningful if standard procedures are not implemented in the instructions given to each group of children.

ITEM SELECTION. A pilot study was conducted using 1,200 items. Items were selected based upon established content criteria, and were tested for gender and cultural bias, using both item reviewers and empirical tests. Biased items were revised or eliminated, according to the requirements of McGraw-Hill's *Guidelines for Bias-Free Publishing* (1983).

Scaling was based on a three-parameter IRT model using items from the California Achievement Test (CAT) Form E to ensure adequate ability ranges in the items. It is not clear why the three-parameter IRT model was used. This is the least stable of the IRT models and difficulty and discrimination indices may interact causing a scale score to be difficult to interpret.

VALIDITY. It is important to establish the predictive validity of the ESA in estimating achievement, that is, does, in fact, proficiency on the Prereading Total scale predict reading achievement in the early grades? The technical manual authors state that predictive validity studies are in progress and the results will be supplied in the final technical report.

In an attempt to establish concurrent validity, the ESA was correlated with the Developing Skills Checklist (DSC). The DSC measures a fuller range of skills than does the ESA, though no reliability or validity information on this instrument is available. The Prereading Total scale on both instruments correlated between .67 and .76. The Total Mathematics scale of the ESA correlated between .59 and .73 with the Mathematical Concepts and Operations scale of the DSC. However, the ESA Total Mathematics scale had similar correlations with the Memory scale of the DSC (.57 to .71), and even *higher* correlations with the DSC Prereading Total (.62 to .74). It is therefore difficult to know what the Total Mathematics scale of the ESA is measuring. The correlations between the other scales of the ESA (e.g., Visual, Memory, Language) and their DSC analogues ranged from .32 to .70. The intercorrelations among all subscales of the ESA range from .52 to .94. Despite these moderate to high correlations, the use of an established instrument, rather than the DSC, would have been preferable in demonstrating concurrent validity. It would then be clearer what constructs are being measured by the ESA scales.

RELIABILITY. Internal consistency reliability (KR20) is reported for each scale of the ESA. In Level 1, the Prereading and Mathematics Totals have reliabilities ranging from .90 to .93. The other scales range from .69 (Language) to .87 (Mathematical Concepts and Operations). The lower reliability for the Language scale seems reasonable when considering that it is based on only 21 items, as opposed to the larger pool of items composing the Prereading (86 items) and Mathematics (54 items) Totals. The Prereading Total scale and the Mathematics Total scale have internal consistency reliabilities ranging from .89 to .93 in Level 2 of the ESA. The reliabilities of the shorter scales range from .73 (Memory) to .90 (Auditory; Mathematical Concepts and Operations).

Test-retest reliability was established using a 2-week interval between the pre- and posttests. The reliability for Level 1 ranges from .67 (Language) to .91 (Prereading Total and Mathematics Total). Level 2 reliabilities ranged from .76 (Visual) to .91 (Prereading Total). Overall, the internal consistency and temporal stability of the scales were acceptable for this type of instrument.

SUMMARY. Two positive features of the test materials are the clear instructions for use of the norms tables and the suggestion of at-home activities that correspond to the proficiency level of each child. However, the timing of the test is under the discretion of the examiner. This lack of standardization weakens the comparisons to other groups of children.

It is apparent that much time and effort went into the item selection process. Items were tested for bias and calibrated using an established instrument (CAT). However, the interpretation of the scale scores may be ambiguous because of the scaling method used. Although the reliabilities are adequate, the concurrent validity was estimated using an instrument (DSC) that has not been established as measuring what it purports to measure. In summary, the ESA may be useful in guiding classroom instruction, but one should hesitate using it for diagnostic purposes without further evidence of cut-score criteria and predictive validity information.

REVIEWER'S REFERENCE

McGraw-Hill Book Co. (1983). *Guidelines for bias-free publishing*. New York: the author.

Review of the Early School Assessment by HERBERT C. RUDMAN, Professor of Measurement and Quantitative Methods, Department of Counseling, Educational Psychology and Special Education, Michigan State University, East Lansing, MI:

The Early School Assessment series (ESA) is one part of a multi-faceted assessment program that attempts to meet the varying perceptions of what is important in early childhood education. Views of preschool and kindergarten programs differ among preschool educators. Some would emphasize developing a child's social, emotional, cognitive, and psychomotor skills. Others would advocate a narrower view of preparing children for formal instruction in reading, mathematics, and language. The CTB Early Childhood System presents a four-component program that attempts to encompass the scope of views of what is important in the earliest years of education. The system includes the ESA (a two-level series of group-administered tests of prereading and mathematics skills), the Developing Skills Checklist (which includes assessments of social and emotional skills, fine and gross motor development, and print and writing concepts; 108), a Primary Test of Cognitive Skills (a group administered scholastic aptitude test that measures memory, verbal, spatial, and conceptual abilities; 307), and *Play, Learn and Grow! Instructional Activities for Kindergarten and First Grade* (a set of software and literature-based instructional activities linked to the objectives reflected by the ESA and Developing Skills Checklist). Only the first of these, The Early School Assessment (ESA), is reviewed here.

TEST CONTENT. The content measured by the ESA is similar to that measured by other standardized tests given at similar grade levels (the end of the prekindergarten through the beginning of first grade). There are some interesting approaches to the testing of some of the concepts (notably listening comprehension and following directions), but on the whole the ESA is a good though not remarkable measure of early school achievement. In a questionable attempt to personalize the characters used in the test items, children who will be taking the test are introduced to the characters a few days before the test is administered. A story is read to the children entitled, "Meet Our Friends." After the story is read, the children are given a picture to color that includes five children, two rabbits, and a puppy. When the test is given a few days later, the examiner begins by naming the eight characters. Presumably the children will remember those names. However, as one gets into the tests themselves, these names and character recognition play almost no role in the testing process. Although a laudable attempt to reduce test anxiety, no evidence is presented to indicate that it does.

Unlike the Stanford Early School Achievement Test (SESAT; T4:2557), its closest multi-subject competitor, the Early School Assessment does not reflect an important part of the early school curriculum: the environment. Although the ESA will satisfy those who view early childhood curriculums as preparation for the structured academic programs that follow in grades 1–12, it falls short by not dealing with the social and natural environments that are part of kindergarten programs: community, the family, transportation, plants, animals, weather. On the other hand, it does offer a more balanced set of materials which meet the needs of those varying views of what should comprise an early childhood curriculum.

The Teacher's Guides for both levels of the ESA are very well written and should be helpful, especially, for new teachers. The guides include the theoretical basis for the Early School Assessment (a succinct and clear discussion), a section on test interpretation (which unfortunately does not clearly explain the guessing parameter, which results in varying derived scores from a given raw score), and sections dealing with the instructional objectives sampled and examples of the items that reflect those objectives. On the whole, the Teacher's Guide is an important part of the ESA and should not be ignored by those who will administer and use the tests. Ancillary materials also include the Norms Book, Technical Bulletin, and the Examiner's Manual.

TECHNICAL ASPECTS. The norms booklet is clearly written for teachers as are other components accompanying the ESA. The scores used include raw scores and such criterion-referenced scores as percent correct and proficiency criteria labeled: "+" (continue instruction at the same level), and "-" (reteach material). Norm-referenced scores used include scale scores (equal interval scales which serve as the basis for translating raw scores into percentile ranks, stanines, and normal curve equivalents). Demographic data appear to be comprehensive in terms of the variables one would normally consider (school type, system size, geographic region, ethnic group membership, SES, gender, and program followed). However, one cannot tell from these descriptions how representative they actually are when compared to U.S. Census data. This is a significant omission that will, perhaps, be addressed in subsequent editions. If these national norms are to have external validity they need more than descriptive categories and percents in each category. The user making judgments about the validity of conclusions to be applied to the local sample needs to know how well this "national" sample fits the national population parameters.

The Technical Bulletin accompanying the ESA needs the most modification of all of the ancillary materials provided. It suffers from brevity and leaves this reviewer with a feeling of tentativeness of the topics covered and the data presented. The opening paragraph speaks of a nationally representative sample of private and public schools surveyed for data on curricular trends and the like but no evidence is presented in the bulletin of the basis of that representativeness. "Popular basal text series" were analyzed, but given the early school nature of the material reviewed, what text books are to be found at the prekindergarten and kindergarten levels? None of these are noted in any of the accompanying ancillary materials.

Important facets of test construction are handled well in the Technical Bulletin with some exceptions. The three-parameter Item Response Theory model is fairly well explained although the notation for equations is sparse. The paragraphs dealing with bias review need considerable elaboration. Differential item functioning between ethnic and racial groups ought not to be treated globally. There is considerable variance within these groups as well as between groups. To state that items were deleted from a test because of differential functioning without an explanation of whether the deleted items affected the validity of the test is a mistake that should be addressed. A statement is made in the text of the Technical Bulletin (p. 7) that "one simply cannot conclude that Spanish-speaking children are illiterate if they fail an English test, *since it is probable that they are literate in Spanish*" (italics added). No evidence is given for this assumption. Of course, if one does not speak a second language they can hardly be judged illiterate, but it does not follow that they are literate in the language they do speak. This kind of an observation does not belong in a technical bulletin without supporting data.

The validity statements within the Technical Bulletin appear to be weak. Content validity is supported by lists of curricular objectives without detailed explanations of sources for these objectives. Predictive validity is acknowledged to be tentative until longitudinal studies can be completed, and evidence for construct validity is given as intercorrelations between two components of the same Early Childhood System (i.e., ESA scales and the Developing Skills Checklist). Because both tests were published and developed within the same publishing company, it is not surprising that intercorrelations are moderately high. The presentation of evidence for construct validity would better be served by correlating results with an established test or tests from a different source such as the Stanford Early School Achievement Test.

Reliabilities are moderately high, given the age level of the standardization population, but when compared to the SESAT they are somewhat lower in comparable subtests. Test-retest reliability coefficients for separate scales range from a low of .67 (Language) to a high of .86 (Mathematical Concepts and Operations; Visual) for ESA Level 1, and .76 (Visual) to .86 (Auditory) for ESA Level 2. Total Prereading and Mathematics coefficients were .91 (Level 1). For Level 2, the Prereading Total coefficient was .91, and for Mathematics Total, the coefficient was .88.

Intercorrelations between scales should be relatively low if diagnostic-like decisions are going to be made about relative proficiencies in various content areas. The intercorrelations for ESA Levels 1 and 2 were consistently higher than for SESAT Levels 1 and 2. Caution should be exercised when drawing differences between subscale results.

SUMMARY. The Early School Assessment component of CTB's Early Childhood System incorporates a multidimensional approach to assessing children in prekindergarten through the beginning of first grade. It incorporates tests, checklists, and instructional components into one assessment system. In that sense it provides teachers a comprehensive tool for working with children ages 4 and 5.

The one component, the Early School Assessment, under review here is a good test featuring some imaginative approaches to listening skills, math concepts, and language. The coverage of a preschool and kindergarten curriculum is limited by the exclusion of social and natural environment. Although pictures of animals and social situations abound, the concepts measured have little to do with the pictured situations and dwell on distinctions between large and small, most and least, thin and thick, and the like. The social concept of "family" is not addressed even though a picture may show such a grouping.

Despite limitations, the ESA deserves consideration by early childhood educators who are attempting to wed the contrasting views of early childhood education as furthering the development of children, and those who view this period as one preparing them for more formal instruction.

[128]

Early Speech Perception Test.

Purpose: "Developed to obtain increasingly more accurate information about speech discrimination skills as the profoundly hearing-impaired child's verbal abilities develop."

Publication Date: 1990.

Acronym: ESP.

Administration: Individual.

Price Data, 1992: $150 per ESP kit including manual (32 pages), scoring forms, box of toys, full-color picture cards, and audio cassette tape; $50 per Macintosh computer diskette; $25 per randomization audiotape.

Time: (15–20) minutes.

Comments: Information available from publisher regarding specialized hardware and software equipment necessary for administering the computerized version of the ESP test battery.

Authors: Jean S. Moog and Anne E. Geers.
Publisher: Central Institute for the Deaf.
a) ESP STANDARD VERSION.
Population: Ages 6–15.
Scores, 4: Pattern Perception, Spondee Identification, Monosyllable Identification, Total.
Price Data: $3 per 25 standard version scoring forms.
b) ESP LOW-VERBAL VERSON.
Population: Ages 3–6.
Scores, 4: Pattern Perception Test, Word Identification Test (Spondee Identification, Monosyllable Identification), Total.
Price Data: $3 per 25 low-verbal version scoring forms.

Review of the Early Speech Perception Test by ARLENE E. CARNEY, Associate Professor of Communication Disorders, University of Minnesota, Minneapolis, MN:

The Early Speech Perception (ESP) Test was developed to assess aspects of the listening skills of young children with profound hearing losses. This is an important goal for two reasons: (*a*) these children are fitted with sensory aids, such as hearing aids and cochlear implants, that should enhance their listening skills; and (*b*) the majority of tests available for auditory skill testing for children with hearing losses focus on the recognition of words that vary only in phonetic or phonemic content or on the understanding of connected phrases and sentences. The ESP Standard Version is directed at school-aged children between 6 and 15 years of age. The ESP Low-Verbal Version is directed at younger children with poorer vocabulary skills between 3 and 6 years of age. The premise underlying the test is that there is a known hierarchy of speech perception skills observed in children with hearing losses. Specifically, the test assumes that a child listener with hearing loss necessarily moves from being unable to perceive differences in the prosodic patterns of words (e.g., number of syllables and stress pattern of the syllables) to pattern perception to higher levels of actual word recognition for monosyllabic and bisyllabic words. This hierarchy used in the two versions of the ESP is supported by research from the authors of the test (Geers & Moog, 1988, 1989), and that of other investigators (Erber, 1982; Erber & Alencewicz, 1976). The authors specifically recommend that the results of the ESP battery can be used to formulate objectives for auditory training and to test progress in speech perception ability over time. No specific examples of either application are provided for the prospective test user, however. Further, as the test is now constructed, progress can only be observed in a child listener when he or she moves to a different category of perception (1 through 4). There is no way to monitor progress continuously within a given category in the present form of the test, either the Standard or the Low-Verbal Version.

The ESP Standard Version uses picture representations of target words; the ESP Low-Verbal Version uses object representations of target words. Both sets of stimuli, pictures and objects, are generally well conceived and represented. However, among the objects for testing in the Low-Verbal Version of the ESP, there are size discrepancies among certain sets of items that may provide distracting to a young child. For example, one could choose a set of four items for pattern perception testing in the Low-Verbal Version that included: boot (monosyllable), baby (trochee—two-syllable word with the first syllable stressed and the second syllable unstressed), airplane (spondee—bisyllable with two stressed syllables, and ice cream cone (a three-syllable word complex). In this set, the largest object is the baby, followed by the ice cream cone, airplane, and finally the boot. This size discrepancy problem is a difficult one for any object test and is not a serious drawback to the use of the objects on the Low-Verbal Version of the ESP.

The authors present a clear set of instructions for training and familiarization for both versions of the test, as well as for test administration and scoring. The instructions for use of the audiotaped and computerized versions (on a Macintosh) of the test are also specific and complete. The authors have provided information that allows even live-voice presentations of the test to be performed with as great a precision as possible.

The test manual provides information about test-retest reliability and validity. For both types of measures, only a small number of participants was used in the calculation (23 for the ESP Standard Version for reliability, 24 for the ESP Low-Verbal Version for reliability, 30 for the validity version). The small number of participants is somewhat understandable because profound hearing loss is a low-incidence disorder. Nevertheless, because the results of both versions of the ESP are presented in categorical rather than continuos fashion, the reliability and validity data would have been enhanced and strengthened by the presence of a large number of participants across the age range of the test.

In summary, the two versions of the ESP meet a need in the assessment area of listening skills in young children with hearing loss. The ESP has tasks that can be carried out by young children and contains stimuli that are highly recognizable words. Clear directions are provided for administration and scoring of the test. Nevertheless, the interpretation of performance of young children with hearing loss may be hindered somewhat by the strong adherence to a categorical model that only examines listening skill in four discrete categories and by limited data on test-retest reliability and validity.

REVIEWER'S REFERENCES

Erber, N. P., & Alencewicz, C. M. (1976). Audiologic evaluation of deaf children. *Journal of Speech and Hearing Disorders, 41*, 256-267.

Erber, N. P. (1982). *Auditory training*. Washington, DC: Alexander Graham Bell Association for the Deaf.

Geers, A. E., & Moog, J. S. (1988). Predicting long-term benefits of cochlear implants in profoundly hearing-impaired children. *American Journal of Otology, 9*, 169-176.

Geers, A. E., & Moog, J. S. (1989). Evaluating speech perception skills: Tools for measuring benefit of cochlear implants, tactile aids, and hearing aids. In E. Owens & D. Kessler (Eds.), *Cochlear implants in children* (pp. 227-256). Boston: College Hill Press.

[129]

Early Years Easy Screen.

Purpose: Constructed to screen for strengths and weaknesses in the areas of physical and cognitive development.
Population: Ages 4–5.
Publication Date: 1991.
Acronym: EYES.
Scores, 6: Level of Performance in 6 areas: Pencil Coordination, Active Body, Number, Oral Language, Visual Reading, Auditory Reading.
Administration: Group.
Price Data: Available from publisher.
Time: (160–194) minutes over several sessions.
Comments: Other test materials (e.g., bean bag, beads) must be supplied by examiner.
Authors: Joan Clerehugh, Kim Hart, Rosalind Pither, Kay Rider, and Kate Turner.
Publisher: NFER-Nelson Publishing Co., Ltd. [England].

Review of the Early Years Easy Screen by MARTIN J. WIESE, Licensed Psychologist, Educational Service Unit No. 6, Milford, NE:

The Early Years Easy Screen (EYES) is designed to identify potential learning difficulties in early childhood. The test authors selected and designed items to meet the assessment requirements of the National Curriculum of Great Britain. Under the National Curriculum, teachers must make detailed records of achievement, with assessment compulsory at age 7.

Dissatisfied with the use of time-consuming, lengthy, developmental checklists, the authors designed the EYES as a whole-class, criterion-referenced, screening measure used to observe and record children's development in six skill areas: Pencil Coordination, Active Body, Number, Oral Language, Visual Reading, and Auditory Reading. The EYES is intended to provide a formative profile of early childhood physical and cognitive skills of children and to identify areas of strengths and weakness, thus enabling the teacher to develop individual curriculum plans.

Administration of the six modules is done over several sessions. There are five items or tasks within each module and each item takes only a short time to administer, the maximum length of time being about 5 minutes per task. Four record forms (Group Observation Working Sheet, Individual Record Sheet, Individual Profile, and Group Record Sheet) are photocopied from the teacher's guide for use by the examiner.

Module 1, Pencil Coordination, assesses five areas: figure copying, pencil control, figure completion, copying, and draw a person. All are desk-top activities that require the use of a worksheet and pencil.

The Active Body Skills module contains five tasks that examination coordination and fine and gross motor control, including cutting, marching, jumping, hopping, and skipping. Number Skills includes activities to document sorting, matching, and number language skills.

Module 4, Oral Language, examines expressive language skills and language comprehension. The final two modules, Visual Reading and Auditory Reading, require the examiner to observe and record readiness for visual reading skills and the development of auditory skills supportive of reading readiness.

The five tasks within each module are administered in one session when possible. The Group Observation Worksheet is used to record group observations while working through each module. These observations are then transferred to the Individual Record Sheets and finally the Individual Profile sheets. With the Profile, the examiner indicates the child's current level of performance (developing, emerging, and mastered) in each skill area based on the number of activities successfully mastered in each area. If it is determined that a child has not mastered a particular task, the teacher's guide suggests follow-up activities to help the teacher improve the child's skills.

Although the teacher's guide provides four case studies to demonstrate the use and interpretation of the EYES, it lacks substantial information about test construction and development. It is reported that the EYES went through a series of revisions over the course of 5 years before resulting in its present form but it is not apparent how the items/tasks were selected. The guide also fails to provide a rationale to support a decision that a skill is emerging, developing, or mastered based upon the number of tasks completed.

Because it is a criterion-referenced test and seeks to determine whether children have reached a preestablished level of functioning, no normative data are available. The teacher's guide also lacks any evidence for reliability or validity of the EYES as an assessment instrument.

From a cross-cultural perspective, the EYES is designed to assess the skills of children from a specific geographical location (Great Britain); therefore, some items do not generalize well for use in the United States. For example, the use of the words "lorry" for "truck" and "pram" for "carriage" would most likely confuse an American child. In addition, the auditory skills module requires children to identify various recorded sounds including an ambulance siren with a characteristic European high pitch to low pitch change rather than the more familiar American wailing siren.

In its present form the EYES is useful only to a limited audience in Great Britain who seek to document children's specific skills in order to meet the requirements of a National Curriculum. With this purpose in mind, the EYES may provide some useful information on what should be taught to each child and it allows the teacher to make repeated observations to document a child's development in several skill areas.

[130]

Eating Disorder Inventory-2.

Purpose: Constructed as a self-report measure of psychological features commonly associated with anorexia nervosa and bulimia nervosa.
Population: Ages 12 and over.
Publication Dates: 1984–91.
Acronym: EDI.
Scores, 11: Drive for Thinness, Bulimia, Body Dissatisfaction, Ineffectiveness, Perfectionism, Interpersonal Distrust, Interoceptive Awareness, Maturity Fears, Asceticism (provisional), Impulse Regulation (provisional), Social Insecurity (provisional).
Administration: Group or individual.
Price Data, 1994: $73 per complete kit including 25 item booklets, 25 symptom checklists, 25 answer sheets, 25 profile forms, and manual ('91, 74 pages); $16 per 25 item booklets; $16 per 25 symptom checklists; $16 per 25 answer sheets; $10 per 25 profile forms; $20 per manual.
Time: (20) minutes.
Comments: Computer version available.
Author: David M. Garner.
Publisher: Psychological Assessment Resources, Inc.
Cross References: For a review of an earlier edition by Cabrini S. Swassing, see 10:100 (16 references).

TEST REFERENCES

1. Dolan, B. M., Evans, C., & Lacey, J. H. (1989). Family composition and social class in bulimia: A catchment area study of a clinical and a comparison group. *The Journal of Nervous and Mental Disease*, *177*, 267-272.

2. Yager, J., Landsverk, J., & Edelstein, C. K. (1989). Help seeking and satisfaction with care in 641 women with eating disorders: I. Patterns of utilization, attributed change, and perceived efficacy of treatment. *The Journal of Nervous and Mental Disease*, *177*, 632-637.

3. Dacey, C. M., Nelson, W. M., III, Clark, V. F., & Aikman, K. G. (1991). Bulimia and body image dissatisfaction in adolescence. *Child Psychiatry and Human Development*, *21*, 179-184.

4. Paxton, S. J., & Sculthorpe, A. (1991). Disordered eating and sex role characteristics in young women: Implications for sociocultural theories of disturbed eating. *Sex Roles*, *24*, 587-598.

5. Reed, D. L., Thompson, J. K., Brannick, M. T., & Sacco, W. P. (1991). Development and validation of the Physical Appearance State and Trait Anxiety Scale (PASTAS). *Journal of Anxiety Disorders*, *5*, 323-332.

6. Thornton, B., Leo, R., & Alberg, K. (1991). Gender role typing, the superwoman ideal, and the potential for eating disorders. *Sex Roles*, *25*, 469-484.

7. Mizes, J. S. (1992). The body image detection device versus subjective measures of weight dissatisfaction: A validity comparison. *Addictive Behaviors*, *17*, 125-136.

8. Raciti, M., & Hendrick, S. S. (1992). Relationships between eating disorder characteristics and love and sex attitudes. *Sex Roles*, *27*, 553-564.

9. Taub, D. E., & Blinde, E. M. (1992). Eating disorders among adolescent female athletes: Influence of athletic participation and sports team membership. *Adolescence*, *27*, 833-848.

10. Berman, K., Lam, R. W., & Goldner, E. M. (1993). Eating attitudes in seasonal affective disorder and bulimia nervosa. *Journal of Affective Disorders*, *29*, 219-225.

11. Davis, C., & Fox, J. (1993). Excessive exercise and weight preoccupation in women. *Addictive Behaviors*, *18*, 201-211.

12. Davis, C., Brauer, H., & Ratusny, D. (1993). Behavioral frequency and psychological commitment: Necessary concepts in the study of excessive exercising. *Journal of Behavioral Medicine*, *16*, 611-628.

13. George, M. S., Brewerton, T. D., & Harden, R. N. (1993). Bulimia nervosa in outpatients with migraine: A pilot study. *The Journal of Nervous and Mental Disease*, *181*, 704-706.

14. Gettelman, T. E., & Thompson, J. K. (1993). Actual differences and stereotypical perceptions in body image and eating disturbance: A comparison of male and female heterosexual and homosexual samples. *Sex Roles*, *29*, 545-562.

15. Grubb, H. J., Sellers, M. I., & Waligroski, K. (1993). Factors related to depression and eating disorders: Self-esteem, body image, and attractiveness. *Psychological Reports*, *72*, 1003-1010.

16. Rutherford, J., McGuffin, P., Katz, R. J., & Murray, R. M. (1993). Genetic influences on eating attitudes in a normal female twin population. *Psychological Medicine*, *23*, 425-436.

17. Silverstein, B., Perlick, D., Clauson, J., & McKoy, E. (1993). Depression combined with somatic symptomatology among adolescent females who report concerns regarding maternal achievement. *Sex Roles*, *28*, 637-653.

18. Brookings, J. B., & Wilson, J. F. (1994). Personality and family-environment predictors of self-reported eating attitudes and behaviors. *Journal of Personality Assessment*, *63*, 313-326.

19. Herkov, M. J., Greer, R. A., Blau, B. I., McGuire, J. M., & Eaker, D. (1994). Bulimia: An empirical analysis of psychodynamic theory. *Psychological Reports*, *75*, 51-56.

20. Kinzl, J. F., Traweger, C., Guenther, V., & Biebl, W. (1994). Family background and sexual abuse associated with eating disorders. *American Journal of Psychiatry*, *151*, 1127-1131.

21. Klingenspor, B. (1994). Gender identity and bulimic eating behavior. *Sex Roles 31*, 407-431.

22. Laquantra, T. A., & Clopton, J. R. (1994). Characteristics of alexithymia and eating disorders in college women. *Addictive Behaviors*, *19*, 373-380.

23. Olmsted, M. P., Kaplan, A. S., & Rockert, W. (1994). Rate and prediction of relapse in bulimia nervosa. *American Journal of Psychiatry*, *151*, 738-743.

24. Parker, R. M., Lambert, M. J., & Burlingame, G. M. (1994). Psychological features of female runners presenting with pathological weight control behaviors. *Journal of Sport and Exercise Psychology*, *16*, 119-134.

25. Schaaf, K. K., & McCanne, T. R. (1994). Childhood abuse, body image disturbance, and eating disorders. *Child Abuse & Neglect*, *18*, 607-615.

26. Stice, E., Schupak-Neuberg, E., Shaw, H. E., & Stein, R. I. (1994). Relation of media exposure to eating disorder symptomatology: An examination of mediating mechanisms. *Journal of Abnormal Psychology*, *103*, 836-840.

27. Strauman, T. J., & Glenberg, A. M. (1994). Self-concept and body-image disturbance: Which self-beliefs predict body size overestimation? *Cognitive Therapy and Research*, *18*, 105-125.

28. Baran, S. A., Weltzin, T. E., & Kaye, W. H. (1995). Low discharge weight and outcome in anxorexia nervosa. *American Journal of Psychiatry*, *152*, 1070-1072.

29. Brennan, K. A., & Shaver, P. R. (1995). Dimensions of adult attachment, affect regulation, and romantic relationship functioning. *Personality and Social Psychology Bulletin*, *21*, 267-283.

30. Gleaves, D. H., Williamson, D. A., Eberenz, K. P., Sebastian, S. B., & Barker, S. E. (1995). Clarifying body-image disturbance: Analysis of a multidimensional model using structural modeling. *Journal of Personality Assessment*, *64*, 478-493.

31. Gleaves, D. H., & Eberenz, K. P. (1995). Validating a multidimensional model of the psychopathology of bulimia nervosa. *Journal of Clinical Psychology*, *51*, 181-189.

32. Harris, S. M. (1995). Family, self, and sociocultural contributions to body-image attitudes of African-American women. *Psychology of Women Quarterly*, *19*, 129-145.

33. Leon, G. R., Fulkerson, J. A., Perry, C. L., & Early-Zald, M. B. (1995). Prospective analysis of personality and behavioral vulnerabilities and gender influences in the later development of disordered eating. *Journal of Abnormal Psychology*, *104*, 140-149.

34. Macdiarmid, J. I., & Hetherington, M. M. (1995). Mood modulation by food: An explortion of affect and cravings in "chocolate addicts." *British Journal of Clinical Psychology*, *34*, 129-138.

35. Mallinckrodt, B., McCreary, B. A., & Robertson, A. K. (1995). Co-occurrence of eating disorders and incest: The role of attachment, family environment, and social competencies. *Journal of Counseling Psychology*, *42*, 178-186.

36. Mintz, L. B., Kashubeck, S., & Tracy, L. S. (1995). Relations among parental alcoholism, eating disorders, and substance abuse in nonclinical college women: Additional evidence against the uniformity myth. *Journal of Counseling Psychology*, *42*, 65-70.

37. Rubenstein, C. S., Altemus, M., Pigott, T. A., Hess, A., & Murray, D. L. (1995). Symptom overlap between OCD and bulimia nervosa. *Journal of Anxiety Disorders*, *9*, 1-9.

38. Thiel, A., Broocks, A., Ohlmeier, M., Jacoby, J. E., & Schussler, G. (1995). Obsessive-compulsive disorder among patients with anorexia nervosa and bulimia nervosa. *American Journal of Psychiatry*, *152*, 72-75.

Review of the Eating Disorder Inventory-2 by PHILIP ASH, Director, Ash, Blackstone and Cates, Blacksburg, VA:

The Eating Disorder Inventory-2 (EDI-2) is an expanded version of the Eating Disorder Inventory (EDI) introduced in 1984. It is a self-report measure of symptoms usually associated with anorexia nervosa (AN) and bulimia nervosa (BN). The EDI-2 retains the 64 items (grouped into eight scales) of the EDI and adds 27 new items in three provisional scales: Asceticism, Impulse Regulation, and Social Insecurity. The Inventory takes about 20 minutes to complete.

The EDI-2 package also includes the EDI Symptom Checklist (EDI-SC), a structured self-report form soliciting current and historical information about the client's eating-related and menstrual history. Users are advised to administer the EDI-SC along with the EDI-2 in clinical settings and other circumstances where detailed specific symptom occurrence and frequency are required. The EDI-SC takes about 10 minutes to complete.

The EDI-2 is supported by a very good manual that includes a 250+ items reference list, reflecting the growing volume of EDI and eating disorders research. Most of the data reported, however, derive from research limited to the original EDI scales.

Descriptive age and weight data are reported for groups of patients ($N = 782$) who took the original scales, later patient groups that took all 11 scales ($N = 107$), and a female college comparison group ($N = 205$). Eating disorder patients are divided into three subgroups: Anorexia Nervosa Restrictors (AN-R; $N = 129$); Anorexia Nervosa Bulimics (AN-B; $N = 103$); and Bulimia Nervosa (BN; $N = 657$). The 205-person Female College Comparison group mean age was 19.9 years. The eating disorder groups were somewhat older (AN-R, 22.8 yrs; AN-B, 23.9 yrs; BN, 23.4 yrs). Although the age differences were statistically significant, their implications for assessing the scale scores are not clear. Bulimia patients weighed (present weight as percent of average) as much as female college students (99.6% of average); anorexic patients weighed about a third less.

Percentile rank norms are provided for the 11 scales for the eating disorder patients combined, for each of the three eating disorder diagnostic groups, and a sample of nonpatient college females, for nonpatient college males, high school boys, high school girls, 11- to 18-year-old females (broken down into age subgroups) and, for the new scales, for a mixed male-female college student group.

Two sets of internal consistency reliability estimates for the original eight scales for the eating disorder samples yielded coefficients of .8 or higher. Estimates for nonpatient female comparison groups also yielded high coefficients, with about a third of the coefficients scattering below .80. The internal consistency of the scales is further demonstrated by item-total correlations for each of the 11 scales for the eating disorder group, ANs, and a female college sample. Item-total correlations are uniformly high, as is to be expected from the fairly high internal consistency reliability estimates. The item-total correlations are included, incorrectly I believe, in the discussion of validity. Neither test reliability estimates nor item-total coefficients speak to item or test validity.

Three test-retest studies for nonpatient (students, staff nurses) samples over intervals of 1 week, 3 weeks, and 1 year showed, for the 1 or 3-week interval, coefficients generally of .8 or higher. For the 1-year interval, over the eight scales the median was .57. Such shrinkage is to be expected. Test-retest data on eating disorder patients would also be desirable.

Three factor analyses substantially confirm the eight-scale structure of the original EDI for eating abuse patient samples; another study, however, on three nonpatient samples, yielded a three-factor solution into which most of the original scales collapsed. Apparently the meanings of the traits and constructs measured differ for eating disorder patients and for normals.

Data on the original eight-scale Inventory's validity for a variety of purposes is fairly extensive. The original development of the EDI involved item selection on the basis of a contrasted group's (patients versus female college student normals) design, which was followed by comparing clinicians' judgments with self-report patient profiles. For the provisional scales, mean differences between the eating disorders patients and the nonpatient college females were significant. Correlations between clinician ratings or other independent criteria and scores for these scales do not yet appear to be available. A degree of convergent validity is demonstrated by correlations between the original EDI scales and two other eating disorder scales—EAT-26 (Garner, Olmsted, Bohr, & Garfinkel, 1982) and the Restraint scale (Herman & Polivy, 1975). Scores on the EDI correlated substantially with the scores yielded by both. Correlations between EDI scales and other personality instruments also yielded many positive correlations (from about -.08 to .76) indicating that the constructs measured by the EDI involve to some degree other personality characteristics not unique to eating disorders. Finally, a number of treatment outcome studies have shown that, particularly for those with good posttreatment outcomes, there tend to be significant intraindividual score changes in the favorable direction.

The manual author distinguishes between the formal diagnosis of an eating disorder and assessment of the severity of the symptomology that is frequently associated with it. The EDI should not be used alone, but as a first step in symptom-severity assessment. To establish the diagnosis, a clinical interview to determine if the client meets criteria for an eating disorder diagnosis as set forth in the *Diagnostic and Statistical Manual of Mental Disorders-III—Revised* (American Psychiatric Association, 1987), or the *International Classification of Diseases* (World Health Organization, 1987) should be undertaken.

Overall, the EDI-2 is a significant contribution to the assessment of eating disorders. The growing volume of research bespeaks its perceived usefulness. Although external validity is limited primarily to comparisons with college-age females, the EDI-2 can help expand clinical knowledge about eating disorders and associated personality attributes. Its use is recommended in that context.

REVIEWER'S REFERENCES

Herman, C. P., & Polivy, J. (1975). Anxiety, restraint and eating behavior. *Journal of Abnormal Psychology, 84*, 666-672.

Garner, D. M., Olmsted, M. P., Bohr, Y., & Garfinkel, P. E. (1982). The Eating Attitudes Test: Psychometric features and clinical correlates. *Psychological Medicine, 12*, 871-878.

American Psychiatric Association. (1987). *Diagnostic and statistical manual of mental disorders* (revised 3rd ed.). Washington, DC: American Psychiatric Association.

World Health Organization (WHO), Division of Mental Health. (1987). *International classification of diseases-10 (ICD-10)*. Geneva, Switzerland: WHO.

Review of the Eating Disorder Inventory-2 by STEVEN SCHINKE, Professor, Columbia University School of Social Work, New York, NY:

The Eating Disorder Inventory (EDI-2) is a self-report measure of symptoms frequently related to anorexia nervosa or bulimia nervosa. As such, the EDI-2 was designed as an aid to forming a diagnosis and not as the exclusive basis for making a diagnosis. The original inventory consisted of three subscales assessing attitudes and behaviors concerning eating, weight, and shape (Drive for Thinness, Bulimia, Body Dissatisfaction), and five subscales tapping more generalized organizing constructs or psychological traits clinically relevant to eating disorders (Ineffectiveness, Perfectionism, Interpersonal Distrust, Interoceptive Awareness, Maturity Fears). The latest version of the Eating Disorder Inventory (the EDI-2) includes 27 more items tapping three new constructs: Asceticism, Impulse Regulation, and Social Insecurity.

The EDI-2 provides clinical information regarding the psychological and behavioral dimensions of eating disorders. The original subscales show appropriate content, criterion, convergent, and discriminant validity. Further, many of the findings from these earlier validation studies have been replicated by new research. The psychometric properties of the instrument are sound and the constructs measure symptom domains that have clinical utility.

The authors of the measure have evidence the EDI-2 is sensitive to clinical change and that it can play a valuable role in clinical evaluations of eating disorder patients. More research is needed to determine the clinical utility and predictive validity of the new subscales measuring Impulse Regulation and Social Insecurity.

Internal consistency reliability coefficients for the EDI-2 scales are between .44 and .93. Test-retest reliability for EDIs administered one week apart to 70 student and staff nurses revealed coefficients of .79 to .95 for all subscales except Interoceptive Awareness. After 3 weeks, test-retest reliabilities for 70 nonpatient university undergraduates were all above .80, excluding Maturity Fears.

Psychiatrists, psychologists, and social workers who work with young women or men who are suspected or known to have eating disorders would benefit from using the EDI-2. For suspected eating disorders cases, the measure is useful for gathering information with current and historical diagnostic relevance. For known eating disorders cases, the measure can monitor constructs over treatment and deliver outcome data. Reliability and validity scores for the EDI-2 are good. The authors are careful to point out the limitations of the EDI-2. These limitations are mainly due to the instrument's reliance on self-report. Overall, the EDI-2 is an excellent clinical tool for assessing eating disorders.

[131]

Eby Gifted Behavior Index.

Purpose: Designed to identify students for gifted programming based on the use of gifted behaviors.
Population: Elementary and high school and college students.
Publication Date: 1989.
Scores, 8: General, Verbal, Math/Science/Problem-Solving, Musical, Visual/Spatial, Social/Leadership, Mechanical/Technical/Inventiveness, Product Rating.
Administration: Individual.
Price Data, 1991: $24.95 per complete kit including manual (16 pages).
Time: Administration time not reported.
Comments: Ratings by teachers; checklists may be used separately.
Author: Judy W. Eby.
Publisher: United/DOK Publishers.

Review of the Eby Gifted Behavior Index by LISA A. BLOOM, Assistant Professor of Special Education, Western Carolina University, Cullowhee, NC:

The Eby Gifted Behavior Index (EGBI) was developed by the author "to allow classroom teachers to observe and evaluate the extent to which [gifted] behaviors are used and demonstrated by students in six different content and talent areas" (manual, p. 1).

It consists of a product rating scale that provides criteria for the evaluation of original works produced by students and seven gifted behavior checklists designed to identify gifted behavioral processes in general and in six talent fields: Verbal, Math/Science/Problem-Solving, Musical, Visual/Spatial, Social/Leadership, and Mechanical/Technical/Inventiveness.

The Product Rating Scale consists of 10 criteria for rating a target student product such as a written work or piece of artwork. Each criterion is to be rated on a scale from 1 to 5. The manual suggests that items be rated by examining a student product and observing the student in the process of creating the product or questioning the student about the process used to create the product. No sample questions are offered. Specific guidelines for completing the scale are not provided and rating criteria are subject to user judgment. The items for the Product Rating Scale are vague and intentionally generic so that any type of product can be evaluated. For example, the first criteria, perceptiveness, is defined as "Distinction between the important and unimportant elements of the topic or issue; Perception and use of subtle and mature patterns, connections and relationships" (Product Rating Scale, p. 1).

The gifted behavior checklists for the talent areas each consist of 10 gifted behavior descriptors. The general checklist consists of 20 items. Like the Product Rating Scale, the user is asked to rate student behavior on items in the seven checklists on a scale from 1–5. Ratings are based on observations of students. Again, detailed directions for completing the scale are not provided. Some of the descriptors such as "States mechanical goal and plans for reaching it" are more observable than others, for example "Understands the relationships of parts to the whole" (Mechanical/Technical/Inventiveness Checklist).

The product checklist and behavior checklists are scored by totaling the ratings from each criteria. Each behavior checklist also has a space for describing recent products seen by the rater. A sample student matrix for summarizing results is provided. The matrix is, however, confusing. The directions for completing the matrix allude to weighting scores and combining them with scores on other measures but no instructions for doing so are provided. Ranges of scores to use in considering students for gifted programs are recommended but are not empirically based.

Information on the reliability of the EGBI is not provided. Because of the subjective nature of the scoring procedures and the items, reliability may be a problem.

Albeit limited, the author does provide information on content and criterion-related validity. First, the author reports that content validity was established by having teachers with 5 or more years of experience teaching gifted students review the instruments. Revisions were made on each form until the teachers reached consensus. Second, criterion-related validity was established via a study with a small sample of 20 students from elementary school, high school, and college. Products from these students were rated by independent judges. These ratings were compared with the process and product ratings made by teachers using the EGBI. The teachers' ratings had an average correlation of +.46 with the independent judges' ratings. This study involved only two of the six talent areas, art and writing.

The author's rationale for developing this instrument is included in the manual. The author cites literature to support her view of gifted behavior as developmental and observable rather than unchanging. Although this notion can be supported by current literature, this instrument fails to provide a psychometrically sound instrument for identifying giftedness.

The EGBI is easy to administer despite the number of subjective judgments required. It also appears to be easy to score with the exception of the matrix. Because it is relatively easy to use, this instrument may be useful as a way to encourage teachers to look for signs of giftedness other than high grades. However, because of its weak psychometric properties, the EGBI would be an inappropriate tool for screening, eligibility decisions, or evaluation of gifted students.

Review of the Eby Gifted Behavior Index by JEFFREY K. SMITH, Professor of Educational Psychology, Rutgers, the State University, New Brunswick, NJ:

The Eby Gifted Behavior Index is a set of rating scales designed for classroom teachers to use in the assessment of student selection to gifted programs. No lower or upper bounds are given for age or grade level, but a validity study suggests the scales may be used from elementary school through college. The same set of scales is used for all students. There are seven scales for rating what the author calls gifted behavior. Six concern subject areas and a seventh is an overall rating (listed above). An eighth scale can be used for rating a product generated by a student. The seven behavior rating scales consist of 20 five-point Likert-type items. Two items are written for each of 10 behavioral variables that are argued to serve as the basis for the operational definition of gifted behavior. The 10 behavioral variables are: Perceptiveness, Active interaction with the environment, Reflectiveness, Persistence, Independence, Goal orientation, Originality, Productivity, Self-evaluation, and Communication of findings. Each of the six subject matter scales ask roughly the same set of questions, but slant them toward the content of interest, and the general scale poses the same statements fairly broadly. The Product Rating Scale uses just 10 Likert-type items. These items are basically summaries of the items in the general rating scale.

The strength of the materials reviewed for this assessment probably lies in the items themselves. They seem a fairly thorough delineation of a mainstream view of the desirable gifted child. That is, giftedness is portrayed here as the ability to find an important problem; work on it diligently, enthusiastically, and independently; generate new ideas for the problem and evaluate them; see the project through to a timely and high quality solution; and communicate one's ideas effectively. This conceptualization probably represents what many if not most educators want in gifted children and thereby meets a certain demand. Because the scales are summated and total scores are used, the whole package is necessary to be considered gifted. The student who daydreams, has trouble completing work, or does not communicate well may be out of luck no matter how creative or original his or her ideas are. This is a problem endemic to programs and identifying procedures; we want our gems polished, not in the rough. The child who consistently produces 3s and 4s on the scales will do better than a child producing 1s and 5s. The administration manual provides ranges for children's performance and suggests who should and should not be in special programming. No data are presented to substantiate these claims. The administration manual also argues that the approach taken here is different from others in part because it views gifted behavior as developmental and the current view is that giftedness is static. This is not an accurate depiction of the field nor is there anything about this measure that is inherently more developmental than other measures.

No reliability data of any type are presented for the scales. This is a particular problem for a measure that relies heavily upon teachers' impressions of students. There is a small validity section that presents generally positive results from a criterion-related study in the areas of art and writing at the elementary, high school, and college levels. Means and standard deviations are not presented for the study; only correlations can be evaluated.

The Eby Gifted Behavior Index contains a reasonable set of Likert-type items for quantifying behaviors associated with giftedness. The technical data provided are quite inadequate and the writing in the administration manual substantially oversells the measure. In the absence of more substantial documentation it is not possible to recommend this measure for use in schools.

[132]

ECOScales.
Purpose: Designed "for assessing the interactive and communicative skills of preconversational children and their adult caregivers."
Population: Delayed child-significant adult dyads.
Publication Date: 1989.
Scores: Ratings on behaviors in 5 areas of competencies: Becoming Play Partners, Becoming Turntaking Partners, Becoming Communicating Partners, Becoming Language Partners, Becoming Conversation Partners.
Administration: Individual.
Price Data, 1991: $48.99 per complete kit including 24 ECOScales forms, 24 practice plans and records, and manual (141 pages); $15.93 per 24 ECOScales forms; $14.94 per 24 practice plans and records; $19.95 per manual.
Time: [10–30] minutes.
Comments: Ratings by professional based on observations and interview.
Authors: James D. MacDonald, Yvonne Gillette, and Thomas A. Hutchinson (manual).
Publisher: The Riverside Publishing Co.

Review of the ECOScales by ALLEN JACK EDWARDS, Professor of Psychology, Southwest Missouri State University, Springfield, MO:

The Ecological Communication (ECO) Scales are based on a model that proposes assessment of interaction and conversation between children and adults (in dyadic relationships). The data recorded from observation of the dyad may be used for describing the child's performance level. This result permits program planning where performance shows deficiencies and subsequent monitoring of progress. The Scales may be used on a single instance or multiple occasions. If communication training is needed, additional volumes may be purchased to assist in the effort. Because the purpose of this review is to judge the qualities of the test alone, only the ECOScales will be considered.

As the authors point out (p. 93 of the manual), the ECOScales are not, strictly speaking, a test. Indeed, they also state the manual is not a test manual (p. v). These statements are valid because the intent is much more than to measure the degree (or presence) of a behavior at a point in time. The "score" attained is to serve as a guide to develop means of helping adults and children (who are "delayed" in communication) become more functional both as social interacters and in communication. The authors are to be commended for their forthright description of purposes and rationale at the same time they employ standard reliability and validity criteria within the limits to which they apply to the scales. These "limits" deal principally with situations where inferences are made about dyadic interactions, and decisions arrived at based on those inferences (p. 93).

The scale evolved through several channels. There was the usual literature review, several parent-child interaction studies, and longitudinal programs developed for clinical intervention with parent and child. There are 40 behaviors rated on a scale of 1 (low) to 9 (high) by the observer. These are classified into five categories (Play, Turntaking, Communicating,

Language, and Conversation). The result represents what is called the Competencies Profile. Within each category, there is one (or more) behavior used to plot an Interaction Profile (Interactive Goals, Child Goals, Adult Strategies, and Problems). Thus, the 40 items serve both for assessment and for potential intervention. A Practice Plan and Record is provided both for recording parent interactions and objectives. The ECOScales form may be used to record multiple observations for the same dyad.

VALIDITY. One evidence of validity for the scales involved videotape samples made at different times in the process, yielding five observations. There was no significant change between the two observations before treatment, significant change during treatment, with maintenance of gains in the post-treatment phase of one month. The authors state that these results testify to the effectiveness of ECO intervention as well as the validity of the Scales in measuring both status and change. Although one might wish a longer period than one month post-treatment, the data are supportive of the claims.

Concurrent validity was computed by comparison to an index of a child's language development based on an interview with the parent or other significant person in the life of the child (Receptive-Expressive Emergent Language Scale: For the Measurement of Language Skills in Infancy [REEL], Bzoch & League, 1979; reviewed in 8:956 and revision reviewed 323). The REEL was administered before treatment, with the mean indices correlated with means from "selected" (not specified) Interaction ratings and Competency ratings during the pretreatment, treatment, and post conditions. Thirty of 40 coefficients met the minimum criterion (r = .40 or greater) on the Interaction scales; 34 of 40 on the Competencies scales.

The authors also have presented data about intercorrelations on both Competencies and Interactions. The results indicate that relationships for the same scale on two occasions are lower than between different scales on a single occasion. Thus, the correlation for Language at Time 1 and Language at Time 2 is lower, for example, than between Language at Time 1 and Conversation at Time 1. This would indicate, where the divergence is large enough, that changes are occurring in Language competence that influence the degree of relationship. The authors table these values and imply that the results are pertinent to demonstrating validity for the *treatment* (i.e., intervention directed at Language competence, in this example). However, they do not present analyses which would justify that other than chance variables are responsible.

Overall, the evidence for validity—though explicitly presented—is marginal.

RELIABILITY. Four sources are presented to indicate reliability of the Scales. First is interjudge agreement, using two raters trained specifically to rate behaviors to a criterion developed for the program. Videotape segments of dyadic relationships were used in the experimental condition, with the raters compared for percent agreement between ratings. Unfortunately, details of the results are published in a separate volume, not available to this reviewer.

A second expression of reliability is described by the authors as "stability." They follow the procedures usually employed: correlation of performance over time when change is not expected (test-retest). The larger the coefficient under these circumstances, the greater the probability the test has adequate consistency to warrant its use. Comparing pretreatment conditions, during which change would not be expected, they report coefficients (rs) that support the position of stability. Of the nine rs, eight are statistically significant, but range in magnitude only from .47 to .86. Although test-retest coefficients may be attenuated by various factors (depending in part upon time interval between testings), the values reported are not very impressive.

Of greater concern is the interpretation of results for the one-month period between the end of treatment and follow-up. Here, rs were statistically significant in seven of nine comparisons, with a range from .31 to .72. Generally, these values were lower than the pretreatment coefficients. The point may be made that there was apparently less stability for this latter period than for the former. Without stating so explicitly, the authors leave the impression this suggests that the treatment effects continue to exert positive effects. Such may be the case, but there are other possible reasons, and any conclusion should be guarded considering that four of the nine comparisons favor pretreatment "low" stability over post-treatment.

Cronbach's alpha (a method of estimating the average of all possible split-half comparisons within a test) was used to compute internal consistency. The values are reported for the pretreatment and post-treatment evaluations separately, and in most cases are in the .80s and .90s, signifying good to excellent reliability.

Finally, the standard error of measurement (an estimate of the limits around an obtained score within which repeated measurements would yield scores) was computed using the results of Cronbach's alpha. These values are tabled, with the authors suggesting that any obtained score be considered in terms of a 95% probability level (about 2 *SEm*s generally).

Overall, reliability would seem to be fair to good.

EVALUATION. From a conventional measurement viewpoint, the ECOScales must be considered marginal in meeting criteria of adequacy. Whether it should be considered a "test" at all, and consequently whether the accepted measurement principles are appropriate, is debatable.

REVIEWER'S REFERENCE

Bzoch, K. R., & League, R. (1970). The Receptive-Expressive Emergent Language Scale: For the Measurement of Language Skills in Infancy. Gainesville, FL: The Tree of Life Press.

Review of the ECOScales by CATHY TELZROW, Psychologist and Director, Educational Assessment Project, Cuyahoga Special Education Service Center, Cleveland, OH:

The ECOScales incorporates an ecological approach to the assessment of children's social communication. Designed primarily for use with populations of young children who are nonverbal or who have significant disorders in interactive communication, the ECOScales results in a description of the behavior of both the target child and the adult communication partner. Unlike traditional, norm-referenced tests that provide a measure of a child's relative performance but typically offer few insights regarding remediation, the ECOScales is designed as an intervention planning tool. Thus, the instrument not only identifies the competencies and deficits of the target child's communication, but also analyzes the interactive ecology of the dyadic relationship.

The ECOScales is the assessment component of a comprehensive model of communication enhancement for persons with developmental disabilities. Other components mentioned in the ECOScales manual include a developmental guide that describes the author's model; a case book, designed to illustrate application of the models in intervention settings; and video resources illustrating the effects of these interventions in a pre-post treatment format.

The ECOScales employs structured observation and interview to assess five broad competencies: social play, turn taking, communication, language, and conversation. The ECOScales manual describes each of these competencies in detail, offering important distinctions among the apparently similar dimensions of communication, language, and conversation. As is clearly evident from this list of competencies, the authors emphasize the social interactive and pragmatic aspects of communication rather than the phonological, syntactical, or semantic characteristics common to traditional language-based assessments.

The ECOScales manual provides cursory guidelines for structuring assessment observations. These guidelines include a brief description of the context (e.g., play with people only, play with people and objects/toys), sample instructions, and possible objects/toys to be used during observations. In addition, the manual provides guidelines about conducting a "post observation validity check" (querying the adult regarding the generalizability of the behaviors observed) and an interview to further assess the communication dyad. In the judgment of this reviewer, these guidelines are vague and incomplete, particularly for practitioners without a strong foundation in both social-interactive communication and ecological assessment. Although sample interview questions are included in the manual's appendix, the authors caution that these are offered "as guides to discovering what the adult knows and feels about the child's social and communicative skills" (p. 124), and should be used only to supplement observations. Finally, the ECOScales incorporates a "trainability" assessment, perhaps best conceptualized as assessment for intervention planning. Once again, the authors offer general guidelines for conducting this portion of the assessment, but note, "because your success in assessing trainability will depend on your skills in interacting and communicating with children, there is no set regimen for this process" (p. 15).

The ECOScales scoring employs clinician ratings determined from the observations and interviews described above. True to their ecological philosophy, ratings are assigned to adult communicative strategies and the interactive process as well as to specific child characteristics. The instructions direct the observer to assign ratings from 1 to 9 to each of the ECOScale behaviors. General guidelines for assigning numerical ratings are offered, but these require interpretation of evaluative terms such as "poor," "inappropriate," "fair," and "almost appropriate." Furthermore, these descriptors are assigned to pairs of ratings, thus offering observers no means of differentiating between a rating of 1 or 2, 3 or 4, etc. Scores can be summarized on two profiles, one organized by the five communicative competencies, and one according to the interactive element (i.e., interactive goals, child goals, adult strategies, and problems). The latter profile, in particular, is helpful in directing ecologically based interventions. Finally, total ratings from each of the four interaction scales and each of the five competencies can be recorded on a summary table to facilitate repeated measurements as part of a treatment program.

Evaluating the technical properties of a non-normative assessment measure, particularly one that utilizes an ecological approach, is extraordinarily complex. The ECOScales manual includes a chapter that provides a thorough, scholarly discussion of this topic. Item selection was directed by the literature, by the authors' work in clinical and research settings, and by peer reviews in teaching and clinical contexts. Conclusions regarding the validity of the ECOScales are derived from a single study involving 25 parent-child dyads in which a 34-item version of the instrument was used before, during, and following intervention. Results of this treatment-effects study offer support for the construct validity of the instrument (i.e., sensitive to treatment effects). Concurrent validity is indicated by moderately high correlations with the Receptive-Expressive Emergent Language Scale (REEL; Bzoch & League, 1970) for this population across several administrations. Interrater agreement figures are reported as one measure of reliability; when compared with criterion ratings performed by one of the ECOScales developers, average percentage agreements ranged from approximately 81 to 93. Internal consistency reliability coefficients ranged from the low 70s to the high 90s.

In summary, the ECOScales offers a systematic means of conducting ecological assessments of the communication of persons who are nonverbal or who have significant interactive deficits. The measure has a strong foundation in both research and clinical practice. The manual is not sufficiently explicit regarding the conditions for structuring and recording observations for the novice clinician; thus, use of this procedure is best reserved for individuals who have training and experience in social-interactive communication, in clinical interviewing, and in ecological assessment. When employed by such individuals, the ECOScales offers a unique system for describing the present context of interaction, for helping to target and structure ecological interventions, and for monitoring progress over time.

REVIEWER'S REFERENCE

Bzoch, K. R., & League, R. (1970). The Receptive-Expressive Emergent Language Scale: For the Measurement of Language Skills in Infancy. Gainesville, FL: The Tree of Life Press.

[133]

Edinburgh Picture Test.

Purpose: To assess reasoning ability in young children.
Population: Ages 6-6 to 8-3.
Publication Dates: 1985–91.
Scores, 6: Doesn't Belong, Classification, Reversed Similarities, Analogies, Sequences, Total.
Administration: Group.
Price Data, 1994: £5.25 per specimen set; £8.99 per 20 test booklets; £4.99 per manual (1988, 15 pages).
Time: (30–60) minutes.
Author: Godfrey Thomson Unit, University of Edinburgh.
Publisher: Hodder & Stoughton Educational [England].

Review of the Edinburgh Picture Test by CAROLE M. KRAUTHAMER, Assistant Professor of Psychology, Trenton State College, Trenton, NJ:

The Edinburgh Picture Test is composed of five subtests for children from 6 years and 6 months old to 8 years and 3 months old. In its manual the test is described as an updated version of an outdated test to measure cognitive processes and as a test of verbal reasoning. Perhaps its claim for modernity resides with the authors' (the Godfrey Thomson Unit, University of Edinburgh) declaration they had abandoned its earlier items which were considered inappropriate because of their sex or culture bias, and those items "likely to depend on very specific knowledge or experience" (manual, p. 3). The test manual does not contain a definition or explanation of any of these au courant concepts and leaves the reader uninformed with respect to the rationale for eliminating specific previous items. Worse, readers are also uninformed concerning the selection process for items included in the test currently being reviewed. The 100 items that were redrawn, albeit with some new ideas, need not be psychometric exemplars when one recalls that these 100 items were pretested on children in Edinburgh, Scotland only.

The five 10-item subscales provide only a limited sampling of children's skills. Though means and standard deviations are given for the total scores, there are no similar data reported for each of the subtests. Data to clarify the validity of the test are absent. No concurrent or predictive validity data are presented by the test developers. Despite its claim to measure the same cognitive processes as verbal reasoning tests, the appeal of the pictures, and the easy use for teachers, the test's authors have not substantiated what the test measures. In spite of the test's claim to distinguish children with "some form of mental handicap" (manual, p. 3), data to clarify the validity of the test are absent.

Data used in the reliability estimates are not specifically stated. It would be worthwhile to know whether the reliability was estimated using a raw score total. Reliability estimates using internal consistency were high. Reliability estimates using a time interval between two testings are not reported. Data concerning reliability and errors of measurement were for a one-time-only testing situation; moreover, using the standard errors of measurement to assess the accuracy of the obtained scores should be discouraged. Although the reported reliability estimates for the test are based on internal consistency, there is a tendency to interpret them as if they have value for prediction and interpretation of obtained scores. Predictions and interpretations of predicted performance should be kept to a minimum. Finally, the manual includes conversion tables for raw scores; the use of conversion tables for raw scores implies a precision of measurement that is not warranted by the reliability and validity of the data; a range of scores was not reported.

The Edinburgh Picture Test may have some appeal to testers because of its stated gender and cultural fairness and because of the flexibility contained in its administration guidelines. This flexibility is likely grounded in a concern for promoting optimal performance, but allowing different testing times for different children invites confounding halo effects and impossible interpretation problems.

In conclusion, the Edinburgh Picture Test does not provide supportive data to demonstrate that it is an updated, fairer test than the Moray Test on which it is based; the test authors err in assuming that pictures, per se, will permit the avoidance of the problems of written language in tests for young people;

there is no evidence that these particular pictures, themselves, are bias free, although the use of drawings, not narratives, tempts the expectation. Likewise, belief in the test's possibilities for distinguishing children ages 6-6 to 8-3 with "mental handicaps" and/or its ability to help in "selection procedures . . . if non-native English speakers are involved" (manual, p. 3) does not seem to be justified.

Review of the Edinburgh Picture Test by BRUCE G. ROGERS, Professor of Educational Psychology and Foundations, University of Northern Iowa, Cedar Falls, IA:

The Edinburgh Picture Test was designed by its authors to be a test of reasoning ability for children 6 years 6 months to 8 years 3 months old. The authors expected that it would measure the same mental constructs as verbal reasoning tests, with children who had not yet developed the skill of reading printed materials. The intended principal use is to serve as a screening device for the identification of children with mental handicaps.

DEVELOPMENT. This test is a major revision of an older test, the Moray House Picture Tests, first published in 1944 and reviewed in the *Fourth Mental Measurements Yearbook*. The authors of the manual state that of the seven subscales in that test, the five that functioned best were retained. This probably was the case, but users could have more confidence in the test development process if the authors were to give a theoretical justification for determining which subscales were discarded or included. The inclusion or exclusion of items within each scale was determined by examining the difficulty and discrimination indices and by interpreting the results of a cluster analysis. Items were eliminated if they showed sex bias. Although five subscales were used, the authors state the test was designed to produce a reliable overall score rather than distinct subscores. Thus, the total score reliability index is given but no values are given for the subtests.

DESCRIPTION OF THE SUBTESTS. Each subtest has a similar format consisting of two practice problems, followed by 10 test items. The pictures are simple line drawings, neatly drawn. The child responds by putting a line through one of the pictures with a pencil, and is told that a change can be made by erasing a mistake. The pictures are arranged on the page attractively.

The first subtest, entitled Doesn't Belong, presents the child with six pictures, five of which are the same in some way. The student is directed to determine how the five are the same and then select the sixth picture which is different from the others. The pictures are of familiar objects, such as fruits, flowers, and furniture.

The second subtest, Classification, is in a modified multiple-choice format. The child is presented with a set of five rows of pictures, each row containing three pictures that are the same in some way. The child is then presented with another picture and asked to find the row in which it belongs.

The third subtest, Reversed Similarities, contains items in which the student is presented with a simple line drawing and then asked to choose, in a multiple-choice format, the reversed image of that drawing.

In the fourth subtest, Analogies, the child is first presented with a pair of pictures that go together in some way. A single picture is then presented and the child is asked to choose, from a set of five pictures, the picture that will complete the analogy.

In the fifth and final subtest, Sequences, each item contains five pictures which can be arranged in a sequence (e.g., smallest to largest). The child is to decide the proper order of the arrangement and then identify the first and last pictures.

To score the test, the examiner uses the answer key in the manual. One point is awarded for each correct item in each of the five subtests. The subtest scores are then added up to obtain a total score, with a maximum of 50 points. Using the conversion chart in the manual, the total test score and the child's age in months are entered to obtain a Reasoning Quotient (RQ), which is interpreted as a normally distributed standard score with a mean of 100 and a standard deviation of 15.

STANDARDIZATION AND NORMS. The test was standardized using data from four areas in England and Scotland, with a total of about 10,000 subjects. These data were subdivided by age in months, for ages 6 and 7, and then the total scores were converted into Reasoning Quotients (RQ). The conversion chart in the manual was created from these data. In the standardization, the average score of the girls was found to be about one-half of a raw score point higher than the average score of the boys. Because this is equivalent to less than a one-point difference in the RQ scores, it was not deemed necessary to have separate norm tables for boys and girls. The authors believe the test "may be used with some confidence throughout the country" (manual, p. 11), because the data showed that "there was less variation in [these results] than is seen in verbal reasoning results from the same [areas] at a higher age" (p. 11). Unfortunately, no data are presented to demonstrate this relationship. No other information is given by the authors to substantiate the use of these norms with other groups. An examination of the ERIC index did not indicate any studies using this test in the United States.

RELIABILITY AND VALIDITY. In the standardization sample, the internal consistency of the test was estimated, using a modification of the well-known Kuder-Richardson formula 21 (KR 21), to be .91, which is comparable to other standardized tests of mental reasoning. This results in a standard error of about 5 RQ points. No further data on reliability are given. The topic of validity is not discussed in the test manual. Correspondence with the publisher indicated that no additional information, beyond that in the manual accompanying the test, had been provided by the authors for distribution by the publisher.

MANUAL. As mentioned above, a manual of instructions, containing 15 pages, is provided with the test. The manual contains clear instructions for administering and scoring the test. However, there is a lack of both discussion of the proper interpretation of the scores, and references to interpretive guides provided. No other supporting materials are provided by the publishers.

CONCLUSION. The Edinburgh Picture Test was designed to be a nonverbal test of reasoning ability to screen children, at ages 6-6 through 8-3, who may exhibit mental handicaps. It was developed as a major revision of older materials, but no information is provided for the construct validity of the test. Although the names of the subtests are names that commonly appear in other measures of reasoning ability, there is no evidence to substantiate the inference that the subtests actually measure the named constructs. Each user must judge, by examination of the test items, the validity of the scales. It would be very useful to potential users if appropriate evidence for construct validity could be presented and discussed in subsequent editions of the manual. An examination of the actual items does suggest a certain degree of face validity, in that a certain amount of reasoning ability is required for the selection of the correct answers. The fact that previous versions of the test have been used by thousands of children is also a positive feature that suggests that the search for validity evidence may be fruitful. Therefore, this test seems to warrant further study to substantiate its construct validity. Until then, practitioners should be very cautious before administering the test to make actual decisions about the identification of children with mental handicaps.

[134]

Emotional and Behavior Problem Scale.

Purpose: "Developed to contribute to the early identification and service delivery for students with behavior disorders/emotional disturbance."
Population: Ages 4.5–21.
Publication Date: 1989.
Acronym: EBPS.
Scores, 12: Theoretical (Learning, Interpersonal Relations, Inappropriate Behavior Under Normal Circumstances, Unhappiness/Depression, Physical Symptoms/Fears, Total); Empirical (Social Aggression/Conduct Disorder, Social-Emotional Withdrawal/Depression, Learning/Comprehension Disorder, Avoidance/Unresponsiveness, Aggressive/Self-Destructive, Total).
Administration: Individual.
Price Data, 1993: $57 per complete kit including technical manual (47 pages), 50 rating forms, and IEP and intervention manual (205 pages); $10 per technical manual; $25 per 50 rating forms; $22 per IEP and intervention manual; $12 per computerized quick score (IBM or Apple II); $149 per computerized IEP and intervention manual (IBM or Apple II).
Time: (15) minutes.
Comments: Ratings by teachers.
Author: Frederick Wright.
Publisher: Hawthorne Educational Services, Inc.

Review of the Emotional and Behavior Problem Scale by J. JEFFREY GRILL, Coordinator, Ingram State Community College, Deatsville, AL:

The Emotional and Behavior Problem Scale (EBPS) is intended to be used to identify students who may be classified as emotionally disturbed or behaviorally disordered. The scale consists of 58 statements of inappropriate or problem behaviors, and a set of seven quantifiers, numerical ratings indicating frequency of occurrence and ranging from 1—*not in my presence*, to 7—*more than once an hour*, one of which must be ascribed to each statement as the rater considers one student.

The statements, divided into five subscales, represent elements of the U.S. federal government's definition of emotional disturbance/behavior disorders. The subscales are Learning—12 items (referring to an inability to learn, which cannot be explained by intellectual, sensory, or health factors); Interpersonal Relations—12 items (an inability to build or maintain satisfactory relationships with peers and teachers); Inappropriate Behavior—18 items (inappropriate types of behavior or feelings under normal circumstances); Unhappiness/Depression—9 items (a general pervasive mood of unhappiness or depression); and Physical Symptoms/Fears—7 items (a tendency to develop physical symptoms or fears associated with personal or school problems). The federal definition specifies that one or more of these characteristics must be exhibited by a student over a long period of time, to a marked extent, and must adversely affect educational performance in order for the student to meet criteria for this classification. The EBPS addresses only the "to a marked extent" criterion.

The EBPS may be completed in about 15 minutes by anyone familiar with the student's behavior. The rater simply writes one of the seven quantifiers beside each statement. Within each subscale, ratings are totaled to obtain a raw score. Raw scores are converted to standard scores (with a mean of 10 and a standard deviation of 3) by using the appropriate conversion table. Standard scores are totaled and converted to a percentile score that represents the entire scale. This scoring procedure for the "theoretical interpretation" of the EBPS is also used for an alternate, "empirical interpretation" derived from a regrouping of the items into five differently named subscales: Social Aggression/Conduct Disorder, 21 items; Social-Emotional

Withdrawal/Depression, 13 items; Learning/Comprehension Disorder, 6 items; Avoidance/Unresponsiveness, 11 items; and Aggressive/Self-Destructive, 7 items. This regrouping of items is based on one of several factor analyses, and is intended to represent a more "clinical" view of a student's behavior.

The EBPS includes a 200+ page IEP and Intervention Manual, which offers one or more goals, several objectives, and numerous interventions for each of the 58 behaviors identified in the scale. It also includes an appendix of forms, behavioral contracts, lists of reinforcers, and suggestions.

Protocols are simple and easy to use. One 11 x 17-inch folded sheet provides space for demographic information, nine considerations for rating the student, space for plotting standard scores, the items (arranged as theoretical subscales), the quantifiers, and spaces for ratings, raw scores, and standard scores. A separate sheet is used for the empirical subscales arrangement.

Simplicity and ease of use is a strength of the EBPS, but its only strength. Individual items, the writing in the manual, the norms, and some technical characteristics are seriously flawed. Many items, although stated as observable behaviors, are open to broad interpretations. Rating Item 6, "Does not remain on task" seems a function of the nature of the task, and of the rater's criterion. Seven items use the word "inappropriate," but this word may elicit highly subjective ratings. Items 54, "Moves about unnecessarily," and 55, "Engages in nervous habits," are especially interesting. When does a student's movement become unnecessary? Are nervous habits (such as biting fingernails, twirling hair, chewing pencils), which may easily occur more than once an hour in some situations, really indicators of disturbed or disordered behavior?

The manual contains inconsistencies, strained, unclear writing, unsupported statements, and grammatical errors. On page 5, the norm sample is said to include 3,188 students from 4.5 to 21.0 years of age, but on page 8, the total is shown as 2,988, ranging in age from 4.5 to only 20 years. Raw score conversion tables include pupils up to age 20 years.

The norm sample roughly approximates the national population on sex, race, urban/rural residence, geographic region, and parent's occupation variables, but is not adequately described. Normative data were collected from identified behaviorally disordered and regular education students, but nowhere is the number of behaviorally disordered students, or their distribution throughout the sample given. Norms for three age groups, 4.5–11, 12–14, and 15–20 years are provided separately for males and females, but do not indicate how many students are included in each. Standard scores should range from 0–20, but never exceed 13. Percentile scores (not ranks) are wrongly described, and inaccurately include scores of 100 (an impossibility). A composite standard score would be more appropriate for the comparisons with the norm group that the author suggests for the percentile score. No descriptive data (e.g., years of experience, age, sex, special or general education placement, or level of instruction) on the 867 teachers who conducted the norm group ratings are provided.

Reported coefficients for three types of reliability seem adequate, but are not adequately reported. Essentially no student or rater characteristics are given for the test-retest reliabilities (which range from .87 to .93), nor for interrater reliabilities (which range from .83 to .91). No reliabilities, including internal consistency, are reported by the sex and age groups given in the norm tables.

Discussion of validity covers content, construct, and criterion-related validity, and all are poorly done. Content validity evidences no field testing of items prior to norming. The point biserial correlation, used to determine each item's discriminating power, was incorrectly used. Construct validity rests on several factor analyses, the results of which suggest a reduction in number of items and subscales, neither of which was done. Indeed, these results are used to support a set of five "empirical" subscales, conveniently parallel to the theoretical set. Diagnostic validity is discussed as an aspect of a principal components analysis, and includes comparison of two sets of "regular" with behaviorally disordered students. Mean raw score differences between groups are said to be significant, but no means are presented. Criterion-related validity is briefly and poorly described.

The section on interpretation and use of scale results and of the IEP and Intervention Manual is poorly written, inaccurate, and dangerous, in that some recommended actions would clearly violate federal law that applies to the education of students with disabilities.

SUMMARY. The EBPS is inadequate for any purpose. Inconsistencies, inadequacies, and errors throughout the manual intensify the problems with the subjective items, which the author claims are objective. Space limitations prohibit inclusion of a complete delineation of all the problems inherent in this scale. Avoid the EBPS.

Review of the Emotional and Behavior Problem Scale by ROBERT C. REINEHR, Associate Professor of Psychology, Southwestern University, Georgetown, TX:

The primary purpose of the Emotional and Behavior Problem Scale (EBPS) is to provide educators with an objective method of identifying students who meet governmental guidelines for behavioral disorder. It is to be completed by educators who have had an opportunity to observe the student; usually teachers or aides who work directly with the student in instructional situations.

The scale consists of 58 items designed to describe the student's behavior relative to the five behavioral domains in the federal definition of behaviorally disordered students. Factor analysis of the responses to these items yielded five additional scales. There are thus two "interpretations" possible from the EBPS: a "theoretical" interpretation based on the relationship of the items to the federal definition and an "empirical" interpretation based on the five subscales derived from factor analysis.

For each interpretation, the raw score for the appropriate subscale is converted to a standard score with a mean of 10 and a standard deviation of 3 by the use of tables provided in the manual. Separate tables are provided for the calculation of male and female standard scores, as well as for three different age ranges. In both interpretations, scores of more than one standard deviation below the mean are viewed as indications of an area of serious behavior problems. Each subscale is viewed as independent of all others, and educators are not required to include all subscales in an evaluation. In addition to the subscale scores, a percentile score is calculated for each interpretation by summing the subscale standard scores and comparing this summary score to scores obtained by the students in the standardization sample.

Normative data were gathered from teacher ratings of 2,988 behaviorally disordered and regular students, ages 4.5 to 21, with from 117 (age 16) to 392 (age 12) students in each age group. Ratings were done by 867 different teachers, ranging from 30 raters for students aged 15 to 92 raters for students aged 7.

A random sample of 201 students chosen from the normative population was retested 30 days after the initial rating. Test-retest reliabilities for the various subtests ranged from .87 to .93, with a mean of .90 for the theoretical interpretation subtests and .91 for the empirical interpretation subtests. Interrater reliability coefficients based on a subsample of 277 students ranged from .84–.91 for the various age groups.

In addition to some limited item analysis and factor analysis information presented as evidence of content and construct validity, the manual provides two types of criterion validity information. A comparison of scores obtained by 57 behaviorally disordered students on the Behavior Evaluation Scale (BES) and on the theoretical interpretation of the EBPS yielded correlations ranging from .59–.68, suggesting that the instruments are assessing similar dimensions. Data are also presented comparing the EBPS subscale standard scores of behaviorally disordered male students with those of regular students. Behaviorally disturbed male students scored significantly lower than regular students on all subscales of the EBPS. No data are given for female students.

Test-retest reliabilities and interrater reliabilities are generally satisfactory. The limited validation information presented suggests that the EBPS may be valuable in the identification of students with behavioral disturbance, although important technical information is missing from the manual. No evidence is presented to support the claim that each subscale in the theoretical interpretation is independent of others, for example, and the factor analysis data suggest that this is not the case. Neither is there any information regarding the rate of false positives or false negatives when the EBPS is used as a classification tool. More information is needed concerning the composition of the standardization sample, differences found between male and female students, differences between age groups, and the statistical characteristics of the various subscales.

The manual is clearly intended primarily for the use of educators rather than researchers, and the user-oriented portion of the manual is adequate, although the organization could be improved. The EBPS was designed for a specific purpose: to aid in the identification of behaviorally disturbed students, as defined by governmental eligibility criteria. The scale shows considerable promise with respect to the standardization of this evaluation procedure, providing a reasonably reliable instrument for the recording of student behavior and some normative information allowing the comparison of that behavior with the behavior of regular students. More technical information is required before the EBPS may be recommended as an instrument for diagnosis or classification, however.

[135]

The Employability Inventory.

Purpose: A self-assessment instrument to assess job seeking and job keeping skills.
Population: Prospective employees.
Publication Date: 1987.
Scores: Item scores only.
Administration: Group.
Forms, 2: Card deck; computer software.
Price Data, 1993: $12.75 per card deck version; $79.99 per software package (specify IBM 5.25, IBM 3.5, or Apple 5.25); $99 per Windows software package.
Time: Administration time not reported.
Authors: John D. Hartz, Merle Stephey, Donald Steel, and Susan Kosmo.
Publisher: Education Associates, Inc.

Review of The Employability Inventory by JEFFREY JENKINS, Attorney, Narvaez & Jenkins, P.A., Albuquerque, NM:

The Employability Inventory (EI) is an instrument for assessing job-seeking and job-keeping skills. Rather than providing a measure of an individual's job skills, the EI takes the user through an exploration of the user's knowledge about the world of work, including the process of finding and interviewing for jobs and the skills needed to function and succeed in the workplace. Through a series of 68 items and two booklets, the user learns effective tools useful in searching for and holding a job.

The EI consists of a three-ring binder that contains 68 multiple-choice items, computer diskettes, and two booklets, *Successful Transitions: A Guide Through the Employment Process* and *Seven Steps to Employment*. The first booklet offers a fairly basic yet thorough overview of career exploration, with such chapters as "Establishing Employment and Life Goals," "Finding Job Openings," and "Before You Accept the Job." The second booklet provides concrete suggestions for finding a job: "Developing Your Resume" and "Acting on Job Leads." The first 34 of the items involve job search skills. Items 35–68 address situations in the work place, and skills necessary for success in the work setting. Each of the items is presented on an 8.5-inch x 5.5-inch card, and most items have four answer choices. The reverse side of each card contains the "best" answer, along with an explanation as to why it is best and the other choices are not. Many of the answers also reference specific pages of either of the two booklets, directing the user to additional information on the content area addressed by the item. The first card of the item set contains brief instructions for responding to the items, directing the user to simply select the "most appropriate response" among the choices. The instructions note that:

> There is no single correct response. The appropriate action may depend on the individual, that person's skills, and the supply and demand for workers in that field. Not necessarily having a single "right" answer was intended. The items were designed based on real-life experiences of workers. As you will find out for yourself, there is not always a perfectly "right" way to act in every situation. Sometimes the only courses of action available create value conflicts. We ask you to keep this in mind when you go out to obtain work and when you meet frustrations during the early periods on the job. (cover card)

In addition to the item cards, users can work through the items via computer software. The software is unembellished, if not somewhat dated, and does nothing more than present each item and prompt the user for the correct response. After two false responses (with accompanying discordant music), the program shows the best answer with its explanation. A correct response is accompanied by a pleasant melody.

The EI does not provide for written responses to be recorded, and no procedures for scoring the items are given. Users are to work through the items and review the explanation of the best answer as they go along. This process is consistent with the educational, rather than evaluative, nature of the instrument.

Both the job-searching and job-keeping items are informative, practical situations involving employment, which require a what-to-do type of response. For example, one job-search item states: "Julie is interviewing for a job as a beginning sales agent. The interviewer begins by saying to her, 'Tell me about yourself.' How should Julie begin? What should she talk about?" One of the job-keeping items presents a typical workplace scenario: "Emily's supervisor is responsible for preparing an annual evaluation for all his employees. Her ratings were considerably lower than she felt she deserved. As a result, her salary increase is less than she thought it should be. What should Emily do?" Items such as these allow users to examine their knowledge of appropriate responses to various job or job search situations and learn effective means of dealing with such situations.

No information is provided regarding the reliability or validity of the EI. The user instructions state that the items "were designed based on real-life experiences of workers" (cover card), but no description of the design process is given. It would be helpful to have such a description, including some discussion of the content validity of the inventory. Content validity appears to be adequate by a review of the items, but it is unclear whether this is true without some documentation of the manner in which the items were constructed. Reporting of reliability coefficients is unnecessary and inappropriate for an unscored instrument of this type. Given the apparent purpose of the instrument in helping users to a better understanding of job searching and the work environment rather than assessing the skills and abilities of users, it is less crucial that the technical characteristics for educational or psychological measures be documented for this instrument.

The EI has utility in allowing users to explore their knowledge of the employment setting and the job search process. The instrument is easy to use in both the software and paper forms, and the items generally reflect "real life" situations that are for the most part informative and, at times, entertaining. The accompanying booklets are also useful in helping the user to examine all facets of the job search process. Although the EI is not particularly ambitious in its approach to career information, it does provide a useful overview of the basics for any user.

Review of The Employability Inventory by PAUL M. MUCHINSKY, Joseph M. Bryan Distinguished Professor of Business, University of North Carolina, Greensboro, NC:

The publisher describes the purpose of The Employability Inventory to assist those who are seeking employment, going from one job to another, or transitioning from school to job. The inventory is accompanied by two resource books: *Successful Transitions: A Guide Through the Employment Process* and *Seven Steps to Employment*. I hold the books and the overall intent of the publisher's effort in much higher regard than I do the inventory.

The inventory consists of 68 5-inch x 8-inch cards printed on thick paper. The first 34 cards are devoted to job seeking and the next 34 cards are devoted to job keeping. Each of the two sets of cards is printed on paper of a different color. On the front of each card is a problem situation facing a job applicant or employee, followed by four possible courses of action. On the back of the card is the "correct" answer, "best" answer, or a rank ordering of the answers in terms of desirability. There is one cover card which explains, "The appropriate action [to the problem situation] may depend on the individual, that person's skills and the supply and demand for workers in that field" (cover card).

The best way I can explain to the reader my concerns about this inventory is to present a sample question:

> Zeke has worked at the plant only two weeks. His coworkers, led by Al, are constantly needling him and playing "dirty tricks" on him, like hiding his lunch bucket, his coat and things like that. He's had it. What should Zeke do?
>
> 1. Report Al and his friends to the foreman and the union steward.
>
> 2. Grin and bear it. It's probably customary treatment of a new worker.
>
> 3. Smack Al in the mouth the next time he says or does something.
>
> 4. Retaliate with some tricks of his own on Al. (Item 44)

The back of this card informs us that the best answer is #2, followed by a brief rationale (being good-natured would cause the least friction for a new employee). The other 67 cards are similar to this one. There is no way to ascertain how the "best" answers are determined from among those presented, or if even the best possible answer is among those presented for consideration. However, the notion that there *is* a single best answer contradicts the statement that the most "appropriate action" (cover card) depends on several contingency factors.

I believe the value of the inventory would manifest itself in the following way. It is probably most useful for the population of individuals who are new to the job market. The inventory presents very realistic problem employment situations of which the user might not be aware. The four alternatives represent four possible courses of action, upon which the user could reflect in considering his or her own response to the situation. Thus, the inventory could serve to expand the repertoire of response alternatives to potential employment problems, and compel the user to formulate his or her own manner of behavior in such situations. I would not pay much attention to the alleged best or correct response in guiding the user's judgment.

The two books (172 and 75 pages in length, respectively) are excellent. They both contain very practical information on how to complete a resume, conduct oneself in a job interview, get job leads, etc. Nowhere in either book could I find reference to The Employability Inventory. On the back of some of the cards reference is made to the books for further information about the problem situation represented on the card. There could have been a clearer and more direct association between the books and the inventory. The books are not in any way a substitute for a manual, which leaves the user of the inventory in a quandary as to what exactly one does with it, and how it relates to the books. I am of the opinion that the two books represent the stronger parts of the package, and that The Employability Inventory was developed as an afterthought by people whose primary area of expertise was not psychological assessment.

My copy of the card deck became dog-eared after a few readings—the quality of the paper could be better. A computer software version of the inventory is also available. The inventory is untimed and there is no scoring. There is no manual. No information is available on validity, reliability, norms, or limits of the inventory. Although I believe that any device that reduces unemployment has practical and social significance, the lack of fundamental psychometric information regarding the inventory is enough to make me feel like Zeke—very frustrated.

[136]

Employee Effectiveness Profile.

Purpose: "Designed to assist managers in identifying the overall effectiveness of individual employees."
Population: Managers.
Publication Date: 1986.
Scores: Total score only.
Administration: Individual.
Price Data, 1992: $7.95 each (1–25 profiles) (24 pages); $3.95 each (1–50 short forms); quantity discounts available.
Time: No time limit.
Author: J. William Pfeiffer.
Publisher: Pfeiffer & Company International Publishers.

Review of the Employee Effectiveness Profile by LAWRENCE M. ALEAMONI, Professor of Educational Psychology, University of Arizona, Tucson, AZ:

The purpose of the Employee Effectiveness Profile is laudable. It is designed to assist managers in identifying the overall effectiveness of individual employees in determining the optimal levels of "coaching" for those employees. The respondents are managers rating each of their employees on a 20-item questionnaire.

The Employee Effectiveness Profile questionnaire employs a 6-point response scale, ranging from *strongly disagree* to *strongly agree* that appears to fit each of the 20 items. However, 4 of the items appear to have other problems. Item 5, "Does his or her current job in at least an above-average manner," should be more explicit with regard to what "above-average" means.

Item 12, "Has and uses good interpersonal skills," and Item 14, "Has the capacity to grow and keep up with added responsibilities," are double-barreled in that they are asking the respondent to attend to more than one point. Finally, Item 15, "Would be difficult to replace with someone else who could do his or her job equally well," does not fit with the other 19 items in terms of providing useful diagnostic information.

In the "Interpreting Employee Effectiveness" part of the manual, the author points out how two previous models, the Product-Analysis Model of the Boston Consulting Group and the Employee-Performance-Analysis Model developed by George Odiorne (the "father" of management by objectives), were used to develop his Productivity-Potential Model. Although this is an interesting discussion, no evidence was provided to indicate the Productivity-Potential Model is any better than the previous two.

The section following the presentation of the Productivity-Potential Model entitled "Managers and the Marginal Employee" makes claims about ineffective management of marginal employees without providing substantiating evidence. For example, "A common reason for this ineffective management practice is the 'savior syndrome'—the belief of managers that they can make a difference where others have failed" (manual, p. 8). In fact, only two references are cited in the entire manual.

In the "Scoring the Employee Effectiveness Profile" section, two categories (productivity and potential) are presented into which particular item scores are to be entered. In the Short Form version a third category (traits) is presented to account for the five items not included in the first two. However, no information is provided on how these categories were determined either logically or statistically. In fact, there is no evidence provided on the reliability of the entire questionnaire, the three categories, or the items.

In the section "Graphing the Score," the productivity and potential axes are erroneously referred to as "boxes" in the manual but correctly referred to in the Short Form version.

In the "Action Guidelines" section, the Employee Effectiveness Profile Matrix is divided into the six categories of the proposed model: star, workhorse, marginal, trainee, problem child, and deadwood. These six categories, however, all appear to be based on cliches and anecdotal evidence and *not* on empirical or consensual evidence. Each of the six categories is then presented with specific suggestions for "Typical Managerial Response" and "Recommended Managerial Response," such as "A desirable goal for most Trainees is one to two hours of the manager's time *per day* for the first two weeks and one-half to one hour per day for the next two weeks" (p. 14). However, no evidence is provided to substantiate the claimed basis for and effect of the responses.

In the "Employee Traits" section several unsubstantiated claims are made regarding high positive correlations between the trait scores and productivity and potential scores.

The "Legal Considerations" section appears to be the only one that provides documentation for suggestions made to deal with employees. The subsection "Suspension and Investigation Before Dismissal" contains an excellent list of thoughtful questions to consider before recommending employee dismissal.

In summary, although the Employee Effectiveness Profile appears to be a well thought out system for managers to use, the manual contains very little information on the development, reliability, and validity of the questionnaire. The manual also contains little to no substantiation for any of the claims made regarding the Productivity-Potential Model and its actual or potential effectiveness.

Review of the Employee Effectiveness Profile by DANIEL E. VOGLER, Associate Professor of Education, Virginia Tech, Blacksburg, VA:

The Employee Effectiveness Profile provides a means of assessing an employee's overall effectiveness. The Productivity-Potential Model of this profile is a logical extension of The Product-Analysis Model developed by the Boston Consulting Group and the Employee-Performance-Analysis Model developed by George Odiorne. A graph score falls into a matrix with six categories: (*a*) deadwood, (*b*) trainee, (*c*) problem child, (*d*) marginal, (*e*) workhorse, or (*f*) star. The category then becomes the infrastructure to develop an action plan for working with the employee.

The instrument includes 20 items. A 0-to-5 rating scale with a verbal interpretation ranging from *strongly disagree* to *strong agree* is provided for each item. Ten of the items relate to the construct of *productivity*. Five of the items relate to the construct of *potential*. The remaining five items relate to the construct of *traits*. The aggregated ratings of the *productivity* items and the aggregated ratings of the *potential* items are used to plot the category of the employee for the matrix described above. The *traits* items are not used to plot an employee's effectiveness because of legal implications. The ratings can be completed in less than 20 minutes.

The author indicates that the Employee Effectiveness Profile was designed for use by managers to identify the overall effectiveness of individuals. The author also suggests that it can be used to obtain "upward perceptions" by an employee from supervisors, "downward perceptions" by an employee from subordinates, and "peer perceptions" by an employee from peers. No data were provided on reliability, validity, or norm groups. Thus, it is impossible to make any statistically based inferences regarding these dimensions of the profile.

Nonetheless, the instrument and the attendant manual generate confidence in its utility. The instrument items are void of jargon, the response options make sense, the directions for plotting the scores are clear and simple, and the manual is concise with ample illustrations. It is easy to visualize an employee and make the necessary judgments regarding that person.

The aggregate responses are then used to place the employee into one of the six categories listed above. The category descriptions are common sense in nature. It is easy to picture an employee who falls into any one of the categories. Indeed, it is almost impossible not to associate a person from your past with each category. Suggestions are offered to create an action plan. The action plan is structured around three main elements: (*a*) conclusions, (*b*) action to be taken, and (*c*) 90-day follow-up. Managerial responses are provided in the manual. Use of the instrument and the action plan provide structure for an effective formative evaluation approach of an employee.

The manual also includes a section on legal considerations. The creditability of this section is enhanced as the author has a jurist doctorate. He provides helpful information related to the orientation, appraisal, discipline, suspension, and dismissal of an employee.

Notwithstanding the inherent problems of no validity, reliability, and norm data, the instrument should be carefully studied to determine if it is appropriate for the organizational climate and specific job description characteristics of the employee. For instance, is the instrument appropriate for the autocratic, participatory, and collaborative climates? Further, does the instrument account for the differences among skilled, nonskilled, and professional employees? Finally, does the specific occupation such as a service, manufacturing, or marketing make any difference?

In summary, The Employee Effectiveness Profile is a commonsense approach to assessing an employee's overall effectiveness. The results of the profile positions a manager to develop an action plan for working with the employee. The approach is formative. Caution should be exercised by the user to make sure that the instrument is appropriate for the particular employee and employment situation. Users who prefer tests with known psychometric characteristics will not choose this test, however, because supporting data are not available.

[137]

Employee Reliability Inventory.

Purpose: Designed to be used as a preemployment instrument assessing a number of different dimensions of reliable and productive work behavior.
Population: Prospective employees.
Publication Dates: 1986–93.
Acronym: ERI.
Scores, 7: Freedom from Disruptive Alcohol and Substance Use, Emotional Maturity, Conscientiousness, Trustworthiness, Long Term Job Commitment, Safe Job Performance, Courtesy.
Administration: Group.
Price Data, 1992: $14 or less (volume discounts available) per questionnaire including User's Manual ('93, 52 pages), Addendum for Courtesy Scale ('93, 7 pages), all documentation, training, toll-free (or in-house computer) scoring, technical support, and consultation; $55 per Americans With Disabilities Act Kit including User's Manual Addendum ('92, 19 pages), Audio version, Braille version, and Large Print version.
Special Editions: Braille, Large Print, and Audio versions available.
Time: (12–15) minutes.
Author: Gerald L. Borofsky.
Publisher: Bay State Psychological Associates, Inc.; distributed by Wonderlic Personnel Test, Inc.
Cross References: See T4:899 (2 references).

TEST REFERENCES

1. Borofsky, G. L., & Wagner, J. (1993). Termination for cause and job tenure: The contribution of a pre-employment screening inventory. *Psychological Reports*, *72*, 591-599.
2. Borofsky, G. L., Bielema, M., & Hoffman, J. (1993). Accidents, turnover, and use of a preemployment screening inventory. *Psychological Reports*, *73*, 1067-1076.
3. Borofsky, G. L., & Watson, R. (1994). Prediction of early voluntary turnover and job performance: The contribution of a preemployment screening inventory. *Psychological Reports*, *74*, 819-826.

Review of the Employee Reliability Inventory by ROBERT M. GUION, Distinguished University Professor Emeritus, Bowling Green State University, Bowling Green, OH:

Unreliable employees, unlike unreliable tests, are not necessarily undependable. Only dependable unwanted behavior is predictable. Reliability testing differs from integrity testing. The Employee Reliability Inventory (ERI) has a broader concept of unreliability. Integrity (Trustworthiness) is only one of its seven scales.

ERI development began with a pool of more than 500 items, each judged relevant to the general idea of reliable (or unreliable) behavior. Item responses of one group of people, some hospitalized for alcohol or drug treatment and some found guilty of theft, were compared to those of another group with no such history. Stepwise discriminant function analysis eliminated all but 81 items. Why so many? Perhaps because criteria were stringent, or because surviving items capitalized on chance. In any case, the survivors formed a single scale, labeled R.

Eventually, the R scale was replaced by six scales, and a seventh—Courtesy—was added later. All are based on discriminant functions analysis of the same 81 true-false items, differing only in the groups distinguished. Scores, based on the discriminant equations, are reported as "zone scores." Four zones are apparently equal intervals on the basic score distribution; each zone has been divided into two intervals, so scores are reported in eight score categories. Normative data for each scale consist of the percentage of more than 43,000 job applicants (60,000 for the Courtesy scale) whose scores fall in each category. With so much data, different norms could be provided for various subgroups (based on ethnicity, sex, age, etc.). It would be useful to know if score distributions differ appreciably from one such group to another.

Test-retest reliability estimates for the six older scales range from .79 to .97 with intervals of 5 to 9 days. The Courtesy scale has a lower test-retest coefficient, .68, with 7- to 21-day intervals. These are based on small samples and brief time intervals; I would prefer stronger evidence of score stability. Internal consistencies, estimated by three LISREL indices, are acceptable, but the scales are far from unidimensional. An undated factor analytic report provided by the author shows three or four factors for most scales.

Original validity evidence was based on group comparisons of sometimes rather extreme groups. For each scale, two groups (reliable and unreliable) were identified and discriminant functions computed. The equations were then applied to cross validation groups; validity is the percentage of correct classifications in the cross validation groups. Specifically:

A, Freedom from Disruptive Alcohol and Substance use: 53 (29) people being admitted to hospital treatment for alcohol or substance use, versus 58 (15) people with security clearance; 84% correct classifications. [Numbers in parentheses are those in cross-validation samples and are the ones used in computing percentages of correct classifications.]

E, Emotional maturity: 35 (14) people being admitted to a private hospital (no Axis I disorders) because of inability "to perform effectively on the job and in their personal lives due to the presence of maladaptive personality traits" (manual, p. 26), versus 56 (17) job applicants with Top Secret security clearances; 84% correct classifications.

F, Conscientiousness: 10 (9) people fired within 30 days, versus 77 (93) who stayed more than 30 days; 84% correct classifications.

H, Trustworthiness: 19 (10) people found guilty of theft, versus 54 (19) job applicants with Top Secret security clearances; 90% correct classifications.

Q, Long Term Job Commitment: 22 (17) people who quit (not fired) within 30 days, versus 104 (66) who did not; 76% correct classifications.

S, Safe Job Performance: 14 (5) people who had a significant on-the-job accident in the first 4 months of employment, versus 45 (21) who did not; 85% correct classifications.

C, Courtesy: 81 (14) hotel employees in 32 departments rated as *best* in each department on an 8-point definition of courtesy, versus 31 (2) rated *poorest* in each department; 75% correct classifications.

In short, validations were marred by small primary samples, use of extreme groups, and *very* small cross validation samples. Equally troublesome is that some comparison groups do not seem to fit the scale labels. Is 30 days without quitting an acceptable sign of *long term* commitment? Is getting fired within 30 days a sign of deficiency in conscientiousness, or is it a sign of incompetence?

Necessary information is often missing. Procedures for rating and grouping some hotel employees were not described at all. From information available, we can surmise that many hotel employees were excluded from the study because we can assume that most departments had numerous employees between the best and the poorest; we can surmise, but we are not told.

More seriously, procedures and decision rules for classifying cross validation scores are not reported. Again, consider the C scale. Cross validation was based on 16 people; 14 good guys (87.5%) and only two identified as "less courteous." Classifying everyone as a good guy (100%) would have been as close to the mark as the classifications based on scale scores (75%), yet the conclusion reported is that the scale is "effective in differentiating individuals who performed on the job in a courteous manner, from those who did not" (p. 2).

Further validity evidence continues to accumulate. Borofsky (1992) used 13 items in a self-report questionnaire as criteria and six groups of people varying in expected likelihood of reliable or unreliable behavior (e.g., patients in hospitals, general job applicants, job applicants with Top Secret security clearances). The validation design is clever but not satisfying. It consisted of one-way analyses of variance testing for significantly different group means but with no measure of effect size.

Borofsky and Wagner (1993) reported a significant chi square, finding that significantly more people were employed more than 30 days when the ERI was used than when it was not. When I recomputed chi square with complete data (including those terminated), the significance evaporated.

There are other disappointments. I would have liked a more integrated discussion of validity than the discrete treatments of content, construct, and criterion-related evidence. Adverse impact ratios mean little without specifying selection ratios. A training program for users is available but not evaluated. Several ERI versions motivated by the Americans with Disabilities Act (ADA) have been created (audiotape, Braille, large print, and even a piece of paper with a large T and a large F on it to be pointed at by people who have trouble expressing themselves verbally), but the problem of interpreting nonstandard scores is ignored. To be fair, these disappointments are nearly universal; the ADA accommodation problem seems especially intractable. Others, however, are avoidable. For example, considering reliability and low scale intercorrelations, discriminant validity could be argued; a counter consideration would argue that the different scales have similar correlates. Together, these considerations could lead to useful suggestions for validity-relevant research.

Perhaps some of these disappointments stem from the fact that the user's manual is not intended to be a technical manual. Such a manual is badly needed. It is hard, however, to decide whether the disappointments stem from sparing nontechnical readers or from psychometric naiveté.

I do not want to seem too negative. The author and his colleagues have recognized a number of problems in the potential misuse of the inventory and have spoken against them clearly. They have also been more positive than most in providing helpful features like user training, an interview, and the ADA kit. But these features remain unevaluated.

In general, the ERI is not technically well supported. There is indeed evidence of validity, but it is not compelling evidence. But is must also be said that none of the evidence argues against its use. The evidence is weak, but it is not negative. It can be used, but users need healthy skepticism leading them to search for information supporting the inferences they draw.

REVIEWER'S REFERENCES

Borofsky, G. L. (1992). Assessing the likelihood of reliable workplace behavior: Further contributions to the validation of the Employee Reliability Inventory. *Psychological Reports, 70*, 563-592.

Borofsky, G. L., & Wagner, J. (1993). Termination for cause and job tenure: The contribution of a pre-employment screening inventory. *Psychological Reports,* 72, 591-599.

Review of the Employee Reliability Inventory by LAWRENCE M. RUDNER, Director ERIC Clearinghouse on Assessment and Evaluation, The Catholic University of America, Washington, DC:

The Employee Reliability Inventory (ERI) is a well-documented and well-supported instrument that can be used to help employers screen job candidates as part of a company's pre-employment selection program. The ERI is a self-administered, true-false type questionnaire consisting of 81 statements written at the sixth-grade reading level. The results provide estimates of the likelihood the candidate would work reliably and productively with regard to six behavioral-psychological traits: (A) Freedom from Disruptive Alcohol and Substance Use, (E) Emotional Maturity, (F) Conscientiousness, (H) Trustworthiness, (Q) Long Term Job Commitment, and (S) Safe Job Performance. Properly used, the instrument appears to be well suited for companies concerned with production deviance, property deviance, and unplanned turnover.

The user's manual, training materials, and the documentation in support of the validity of the ERI left this reviewer impressed by the company's integrity and commitment to assuring appropriate and fair test use. For example, the company clearly recommends the ERI results should be used as part of a larger screening program. Potential problems identified by the ERI should be followed up with interviews and other verification activities aimed at developing information that will either clarify, confirm, or question the ERI results. They provide a manual complete with sample questions to help guide the interviewer. They repeatedly emphasize that employment decisions should be based on all information collected during the selection process. They also repeatedly emphasize the ERI should not be used with employees after they have been hired. The ERI was not developed for that purpose and there is no evidence that the ERI is valid for that purpose.

Users are provided with clear, explicit instructions on how to administer the ERI, how to use it as part of a screening program, how to safeguard the rights of test takers, and limitations to the use of the ERI. The publishers have an ERI Americans with Disabilities Act (ADA) kit to assist in assessing individuals with impaired sensory, manual, or speaking skills. Several pages are devoted to principles of test use. Several pages are devoted to reviewing the test results in the context of an overall employee selection program. The documentation clearly states how the test was developed. An ongoing research program provides insight into the field use of the ERI.

TEST DEVELOPMENT. The 81 items in the ERI were selected from an initial pool of 500 items based on discriminant function analysis. The items selected were those that best separated (*a*) a group of people with impaired on-the-job performance due to a pattern of substance use and a control group of people with no history of impaired on-the-job performance and (*b*) a group of people who have been found guilty of theft offenses and the control group. Sample sizes were relatively small—a total of 117 individuals. Nevertheless, a cross validation with a different sample correctly classified 90% of the cases.

The original ERI produced a single scale. The current ERI uses the same items but provides six scale scores that were also derived from discriminant function analysis. For each scale, groups were obtained with clearly defined reliable and unreliable behavior—individuals who had just been found guilty of theft offenses versus individuals with top security clearance, individuals who have been fired within 30 days of hire versus those who neither quit nor were fired within 30 days of hire, etc. Again, the sample sizes where low—the unreliable groups had between 10 and 53 subjects.

VALIDITY. Evidence contained in the user's manual and several journal articles attests to the validity of the instrument. The evidence in support of the validity of the ERI in the user's manual is based on accuracy of classifications for the scale development samples and for new cross-validation samples. The percent of correct classifications was typically high, in the 80–90% range. Unfortunately the samples were again quite small (as low as 5 in one group), and the nature of classification errors was not specified.

Stronger evidence of validity is emerging from a series of studies using the ERI. In the largest study, Borofsky (1992a) categorized six groups of people into one continuum of a low to high likelihood of behaving in a reliable fashion. Group sizes ranged from 104 to 3,863. The mean scores on each of the scales progressed as expected. Other studies have demonstrated the effectiveness of the ERI in particular locations. In one study, Borofsky and Smith (1993) noted a sharp decline in the number of employees who had accidents, hours lost due to accidents, unauthorized absences, and disciplinary actions after one company began using the ERI as part of its employee selection process. In another study (Borofsky & Wagner, 1993), 5.3% of the 247 employees hired using the ERI were fired for cause within 30 days of hire compared to 8.2% of the 190 employees hired without the ERI. These later two results are very impressive.

RELIABILITY. The test-retest reliability reported in the manual is quite high—ranging from .78 on the Q scale to .97 on the H scale. However, only 24 people were included in that sample and there is no information regarding their representativeness. More compelling evidence the scales provide consistent results can be found in the appendix to a prepublication manuscript by the test's author (Borofsky, 1992b). The goodness of fit statistics for the scales' ranges were typically in the .88 to .94 range based on a sample of 43,762 examinees.

ADVERSE IMPACT. Adverse impact should always be a concern in employment selection. Based on a sample of 1,350 examinees, there was no adverse impact for any scale, by race, gender, or age based on the four-fifths rule of thumb contained in the *Uniform Guidelines* (Bureau of National Affairs, 1979). Unfortunately, again, there is no information in the manual with regard to how this sample was obtained.

FAKING GOOD. The questions on the ERI appear to be the type of questions that would be susceptible to response distortion—examinees responding according to what they think would make them look better rather than providing an accurate self-description. There are several arguments that this is not a significant factor on the ERI. First, the items selected for the ERI from the larger item pool were the ones that best differentiated reliable and unreliable workers. These are the items that work best. Second, corrections for response distortion are built into the scaling. Third, the correlations between each of the ERI Scale scores with the 16PF Motivational Distortion Scale and the MMPI Lie Scale are extremely low (<.10).

SCALES. Scores are reported in terms of four zones numbered 1 to 4 and two subzones, numbered A and B. Thus, each scale is divided into eight intervals. The use of intervals is a commendable approach. This, in effect, accounts for some of the error associated with any score and it encourages better test use. Data, based on 43,000 examinees, identifying the percent of all examinees falling within each zone for each scale are provided in the manual.

SCORING. The scale scores on the ERI are based on a proprietary discriminant function. Several options are available to the test administrator for obtaining the zone scores for each scale. The answer sheets can be scored in house using a special scoring template. The item scores are then phoned into the publisher. The publishers enter user data into their computer and provide users with the results immediately. Another option is to score the results entirely in house using IBM-PC software provided by the publisher. A third option is to mail the raw answer sheets to the publisher. Upon arrival the results are scored and phoned to the user. A fourth option, to be used on a limited basis, is to fax answer sheets to the publisher.

SUMMARY. The ERI has the potential to greatly improve hiring decisions when employers are concerned with employee reliability and ongoing productivity. Preliminary field-based results have been quite promising. In the few documented situations, turnover rate, hours lost due to accidents, unauthorized absences, and the number of disciplinary actions have gone down dramatically. The publisher appears to be committed to appropriate test use and offers a great deal of written and telephone support. Because the test was developed and validated on small samples, this reviewer strongly suggests that local validity studies be conducted wherever the test is adopted.

REVIEWER'S REFERENCES

Bureau of National Affairs, Inc. (1979). *Uniform guidelines on employee selection procedures*. Washington, DC: BNA Education Systems.

Borofsky, G. L. (1992a). Assessing the likelihood of reliable workplace behavior: Further contributions to the validation of the Employee Reliability Inventory. *Psychological Reports, 70*, 563-592.

Borofsky, G. L. (1992b). *Assessing the likelihood of reliable workplace behavior*. Unpublished manuscript.

Borofsky, G. L., & Smith, M. (1993). Reductions in turnover, accidents, and absenteeism: The contribution of a preemployment screening inventory. *Journal of Clinical Psychology, 49*, 109-116.

Borofsky, G. L., & Wagner, J. (1993). Termination for cause and job tenure: The contribution of a pre-employment screening inventory. *Psychological Reports, 72*, 591-599.

[138]

Endler Multidimensional Anxiety Scales.

Purpose: Developed to assess state and trait anxiety and the respondent's perception of threat in the immediate situation.

Population: Ages 15 and over.

Publication Date: 1991.

Acronym: EMAS.

Administration: Group.

Price Data, 1995: $80 per complete kit including 10 EMAS-S AutoScore test forms, 10 EMAS-T/EMAS-P

AutoScore test forms, 2 EMAS-S prepaid answer sheets, 2 EMAS-T/EMAS-P prepaid answer sheets, and manual; $22.50 per 25 test forms (select EMAS-S or EMAS-T/EMAS-P); $10.50 per prepaid test report answer sheets (select EMAS-S or EMAS-T/EMAS-P); $45 per manual; $150 per IBM microcomputer edition.
Time: (25) minutes.
Comments: Tests may be used separately.
Authors: Norman S. Endler, Jean M. Edwards, and Romeo Vitelli.
Publisher: Western Psychological Services.

a) EMAS-STATE.
Acronym: EMAS-S.
Scores, 3: Cognitive-Worry, Autonomic-Emotional, Total.

b) EMAS-TRAIT.
Acronym: EMAS-T.
Scores, 4: Social Evaluation, Physical Danger, Ambiguous, Daily Routines.

c) EMAS-PERCEPTION.
Acronym: EMAS-P.
Scores: Item scores only.

Cross References: See T4:905 (7 references).

TEST REFERENCES

1. Cox, B. J., Endler, N. S., & Swinson, R. P. (1991). Clinical and nonclinical panic attacks: An empirical test of a panic-anxiety continuum. *Journal of Anxiety Disorders*, *5*, 21-34.

2. Clewes, J. L., & Endler, N. S. (1994). State-trait anxiety and the experience of elective surgery in children. *Canadian Journal of Behavioural Science*, *26*, 183-198.

Review of the Endler Multidimensional Anxiety Scales by DEBORAH L. BANDALOS, Assistant Professor of Educational Psychology, University of Nebraska-Lincoln, Lincoln, NE:

The development of the Endler Multidimensional Anxiety Scales (EMAS) was based on an interaction model of anxiety, which specifies that increases in levels of state anxiety are the result of interactions between levels of trait anxiety and the degree of threat perceived in the situation. The EMAS, therefore, consists of three parts: The EMAS-S, measuring state anxiety; the EMAS-T, measuring trait anxiety; and the EMAS-P, measuring the degree to which a threat is perceived. All three instruments consist of Likert-type items. The EMAS-S contains 20 items, 10 that were developed to measure an Autonomic-Emotional (AE) dimension, and 10 that were designed to be indicators of a Cognitive-Worry (CW) dimension. The EMAS-T is divided into four sections, each designed to measure the amount of anxiety felt in one of four situations: Social Evaluation, Physical Danger, Ambiguous Situations, or Daily Routines. The same set of 15 items is administered for each of the four situations. The EMAS-P requires the respondent to rate the degree the situation is perceived to be socially evaluative, physically dangerous, ambiguous, or a daily routine, and also asks the degree to which the respondent feels threatened in the current situation. The EMAS-P consists of only one item for each of the five situations plus three open-ended questions.

Data are presented for five standardization samples: American and Canadian undergraduates and adults, and Canadian adolescents. The two American samples were both from the same areas of Ohio and New York, and the Canadian samples were mostly from Toronto. This rather limited geographical representation makes generalization to other areas difficult, especially as no information regarding ethnic or economic status is given. All norms are given separately for males and females within each sample. Although these breakdowns are useful, I would like to have seen norms provided for the combined groups as well, particularly for scales on which no gender differences were found.

The authors are to be commended for the thoroughness of the test manual. The interpretation and use of the EMAS are carefully detailed, with the appropriate caveats included. Handscoring procedures are described that yield both scale scores and profiles. Conversion tables for obtaining *T*-scores are given by gender for each norm group, although given the limitations of these groups the user may want to develop local norms. The manual also contains detailed sections on the history and development of the EMAS, and has a comprehensive section on its psychometric properties.

Estimates of the internal consistency reliability, as measured by coefficient alpha, for both the EMAS-S and EMAS-T are quite acceptable, ranging from .78 to .94 for the EMAS-S and from .82 to .96 for the EMAS-T in the various norm groups. Throughout the manual, statistical results are reported by gender for each of the norm groups. Although this completeness is commendable, the small size of some of the norm groups brings into question the stability of some of these results.

Test-retest reliability estimates are also given although these are quite low. This is not surprising, as the authors point out, given the reactive theory of anxiety on which this instrument is based. In light of this, it is difficult to see why they were reported at all.

Evidence of validity is presented in three areas: content, criterion-related, and construct. Because the suggested uses of the instrument are to make diagnostic and treatment decisions and to conduct empirical studies of anxiety, I will concentrate on the two latter types of validity.

Strong evidence of concurrent validity for the EMAS-S is presented in the form of correlations with the state scale of the State-Trait Anxiety Inventory (STAI). These range from .68 (for 87 males) to .75 (for 125 females). Correlations between the four EMAS-T dimensions and the trait form of the STAI were somewhat lower, ranging from .07 for the EMAS Physical Danger scale to .65 for the Social Evaluation scale. The smaller magnitude of these correlations is not surprising, given that the STAI does not include specifically the four dimensions of the EMAS-T.

The remainder of the evidence given under the heading of criterion-related validity could more correctly be interpreted as evidence of construct validity. This evidence consisted of studies reporting correlations of the EMAS scales with measures of constructs such as depression, locus of control, neuroticism, and fear of success. The amount of information presented is overwhelming, but little attempt is made to imbed these relationships within any theoretical framework. The result is a laundry list of apparently unrelated studies from which it is difficult to determine the answer to the fundamental question of whether this instrument is measuring what it was designed to measure. This section would have been much easier to interpret if the authors had first presented their theories regarding how anxiety should relate to the other constructs, and then reported whether the evidence supported these theories.

Factor analyses of the EMAS-S items appear to support the presence of the AE and CW dimensions. These analyses would have benefited from larger sample sizes in some cases, as they were done by gender within each norm group, with sample sizes as low as 49 for the 20 items. Also, a varimax rotation, which results in uncorrelated factors, was used in spite of the fact that the correlation between the two factors was reported to be about .7. Use of an oblique rotation may have resulted in a more interpretable solution.

The interaction theory of the relationship between state and trait anxiety was examined in a number of studies, the majority of which supported this theory. However, because many of these studies used measures other than the EMAS instruments to measure anxiety, the use of these studies in validating those instruments is limited.

In sum, the EMAS-S and EMAS-T are very reliable instruments that are accompanied by an excellent manual. I would recommend its use with the following caveats. The norm groups, although fairly large, appear to be limited in geographical and ethnic diversity. Users may find it worthwhile to establish local norms. Although much work has been done is establishing construct validity, the evidence is not entirely satisfactory for the various reasons discussed above. More careful study examining the interaction theory of anxiety as well as more attention to the results of the factor analytic studies would be of benefit in strengthening the evidence in this important area.

Review of the Endler Multidimensional Anxiety Scales by STEVEN D. SPANER, Associate Professor of Educational Psychology, Department of Behavioral Studies, School of Education, University of Missouri-Saint Louis, Saint Louis, MO:

The Endler Multidimensional Anxiety Scales (EMAS) deserves praise for adherence to the highest standards for reporting general and technical information. The manual that accompanies the EMAS addresses all the relevant information required to review the instrument: the theoretical basis for the instrument, description of the scales, administration and scoring instructions with examples, graphical score plotting and interpretation with examples, case study presentations, description of the standardization processes with appropriate statistical summaries of the norm samples, and, most laudatory, extensive and complete presentation of reliability and validity evidence.

The EMAS is an integration of two of the most commonly used models for describing anxiety: indigenous, trait anxiety and situational, state anxiety. The authors have designed the EMAS to assess both forms of anxiety plus an added element of the individual's perception of stress press. These three views of anxiety form the basis for a theoretical model of interacting elements in the formation and explanation of the anxiety experience. The authors, fortunately, do not leave it there; they demonstrate a good-faith effort to examine construct validation through several studies of their own as well as those of a few other researchers. However, the authors' conclusion, "The EMAS has proven to be a reliable and valid test instrument for the clinical and experimental measurement of the multiple dimensions of state and trait anxiety" (manual, p. 57), is an overstatement and, at best, an ambitious desire.

PRACTICAL EVALUATION. The EMAS is quick and easy to administer. EMAS test items and directions are on AutoScore™ Forms eliminating the necessity of an exam booklet. The AutoScore™ Forms record a carbon impression onto a set of prearranged ratings that reflect reversed items. Scale scores are derived by simple addition of the circled numbers. Although this is an efficient and recording-error-preventative system, the score form packets are low in durability and thicker and weightier than machine-scorable forms. The publishers should consider using the more light-weight and durable, pressure-sensitive copy paper (e.g., credit card receipt copies). The machine-scorable forms (not included in the specimen kit) are a single sheet form. The EMAS-T and EMAS-P AutoScore™ Forms are back-to-back. Again, these are efficient but prone to oversight and omission if examinees are not individually monitored and directed to turn the form over.

Scoring of the EMAS is simple and easy. Profile charts for "eyeball interpretation" are easy to prepare. The manual identifies response patterns indicative of *faking bad* or malingering, and *faking good*, or providing the socially desirable responses. The authors' sensitivity to these psychometric contaminants is admirable, but no explanation or justification is given for the asymmetrical cutoffs suggested: above 97% and below 15%.

EMAS items are reportedly written at the eighth-grade level. Because Minnesota Multiphasic Personality Inventory (MMPI) items are written at the sixth-grade level and the daily newspaper is written at the fourth-grade level, this higher language level seems to limit the applicable population for the EMAS. There are 15 EMAS-T items and 20 EMAS-S items. These item sets are both limited and simplistic in their assessment. Common indicators of high stress are not queried (e.g., sleep disorders, eating disorders, increased alcohol and tobacco consumption, frequent urination, idiosyncratic avoidance behaviors). Item revision may be in order.

TECHNICAL EVALUATION. Description of norm samples consists of sample size by gender and geographic location of the convenience sample (country, city, and school); age ranges are listed for convenience samples (but not by gender). Descriptive statistics (*M, SD,* and *SEM*) are presented for each of the convenience samples plus two undescribed samples of Canadian psychiatric outpatients and Canadian soldiers (all males, no explanation). Although the overall norm sample size would be adequate for a randomly selected norm sample, the use of specific sites of convenience challenges the representativeness of the "five population groups on which the EMAS was standardized: U.S. adults, Canadian adults, U.S. undergraduates, Canadian undergraduates, and Canadian adolescents" (p. 39).

Norm score conversions are limited to *T*-scores and percentile ranks. Of considerable irritation is the perpetuation of the confusion between *percentiles* and *percentile ranks*. All the norm tables are mislabeled and text statements misstated. The columns labeled *percentile* are actually *percentile ranks* of the raw scores (or percentiles)! It is unforgivable for professionals to let these confusing statements go to press even if the concepts are equally confused among practitioners.

The manual offers a clear presentation of the concept of standard error of measurement and its use in the interpretation of individual scores, changes in scores, and profiles of score. The authors even raise the level of sophistication of the discussion to caution the user against the use of confidence intervals (CIs) with obtained scores (presumably due to the regression effect of unreliable measures, but not labeled as such in the discussion). Unfortunately, the authors fail to offer one of the corrective approaches: CIs built around the *estimated true score* (Salvia & Ysseldyke, 1995).

The authors present a full complement of reliability and validity correlations, indices, and study results. The internal consistency reliabilities are represented by coefficient alphas and support the authors' conclusion of "very good internal consistency reliability" (p. 43). The test-retest reliabilities are a different story, however. The time intervals between repeat testings ranged from 2 to 4 weeks. The test-retest reliabilities (lowest = .50 and highest = .79) are characterized by the authors as evidence that the EMAS "remained relatively stable over time" (p. 45). Yet, if a clinician were to wait 4 weeks before beginning therapy with a client whose EMAS-T Social Evaluation scale score (average r_{xx} = .70) had warranted a particular intervention she or he could be taking an unwarranted action 50% of the time. And, if the therapy were premised on the EMAS-T Daily Routines scale score (r_{xx} = .50) the intervention could be unwarranted as high as 75% of the time. High test-retest reliability is critical for such decisions.

The validity presentations for the EMAS begin to build a rich and deep picture of just what the instrument does measure and what are the interrelationships and interactions of the trait, state, and perceptive field dimensions of anxiety. Table 33 (p. 67) of the manual is a superior conclusion to the validity section. This table concisely summarizes the empirical research evidence the authors have assembled (through 1983) bearing on the interaction model of anxiety. It is here that the EMAS should be left (for the time being): in the hands of the validity researchers. The EMAS is not suitable for clinical or diagnostic use. And, because the validity evidence collected to date is neither complete nor definitive, consideration of some revisions may be warranted integrating some of the more recently confirmed salient markers of anxiety. But, the EMAS is unique in its field and offers many exciting opportunities for psychometric as well as psychological/psychiatric research. The concluding section of the manual, "Future Directions in Validity Research," recognizes several areas.

REVIEWER'S REFERENCE

Salvia, J., & Ysseldyke, J. (1995). *Assessment* (6th ed.). Boston: Houghton Mifflin Co.

[139]

Enhanced ACT Assessment.

Purpose: "To help students develop postsecondary plans."
Population: Grades 10–12.
Publication Dates: 1959–92.
Administration: Group.
Price Data: Available from publisher.
Time: 175 (190) minutes.
Comments: Tests administered 5 times per year (February, April, June, October, December) at centers established by the publisher; previous version entitled ACT Assessment Program (9:43).
Author: American College Testing.
Publisher: American College Testing.

a) ACT ENGLISH TEST.
Purpose: "Measures the student's understanding of the conventions of standard written English."
Scores, 3: Usage/Mechanics, Rhetorical Skills, Total.
Time: 45 minutes.

b) ACT MATHEMATICS TEST.

Purpose: Measures reasoning and mathematical skills.
Scores, 4: Pre-Algebra/Elementary Algebra, Algebra/Coordinate Geometry, Plane Geometry/Trigonometry, Total.
Time: 60 minutes.
c) ACT READING TEST.
Purpose: "Measures reading comprehension as a product of skill in referring and reasoning."
Scores, 3: Social Studies/Sciences, Arts/Literature, Total.
Time: 35 minutes.
d) ACT SCIENCE REASONING TEST.
Purpose: "Measures the interpretation, analysis evaluation, reasoning, and problem solving skills required in the natural sciences."
Scores: Total score only.
Time: 35 minutes.

Cross References: See T4:913 (71 references); for reviews by Lewis R. Aiken and Edward Kifer of the ACT Assessment Program, see 9:42 (27 references); see also T3:76 (76 references); for a review by John R. Hills, see 8:469 (208 references); see also T2:1044 (97 references); for a review by Wimburn L. Wallace of an earlier program, see 7:330 (265 references); for reviews by Max D. Engelhart and Warren G. Findley and an excerpted review by David V. Tiedeman, see 6:1 (14 references).

TEST REFERENCES

1. Barnett, J. E., & Seefeldt, R. W. (1989). Read something once, why read it again?: Repetitive reading and recall. *Journal of Reading Behavior*, *21*, 351-360.

2. Woodruff, D. J., & Sawyer, R. L. (1989). Estimating measures of pass-fail reliability from parallel half-tests. *Applied Psychological Measurement*, *13*, 33-43.

3. Nist, S. L., Mealey, D. L., Simpson, M. L., & Kroc, R. (1990). Measuring the affective and cognitive growth of regularly admitted and developmental studies students using the Learning and Study Strategies Inventory (LASSI). *Reading Research and Instruction*, *30*(1), 44-49.

4. Boggiano, A. K., Barrett, M., Silvern, L., & Gallo, S. (1991). Predicting emotional concomitants of learned helplessness: The role of motivational orientation. *Sex Roles*, *25*, 577-593.

5. Callahan, C. M. (1991). An update on gifted females. *Journal for the Education of the Gifted*, *14*, 284-311.

6. Cardoza, D. (1991). College attendance and persistance among Hispanic women: An examination of some contributing factors. *Sex Roles*, *24*, 133-147.

7. Harris, D. J. (1991). Effects of passage and item scrambling of equating relationships. *Applied Psychological Measurement*, *15*, 247-256.

8. McMurray, M. A., Beisenherz, P., & Thompson, B. (1991). Reliability and concurrent validity of a measure of critical thinking skills in biology. *Journal of Research in Science Teaching*, *28*, 183-192.

9. Reckase, M. D., & McKinley, R. L. (1991). The discriminating power of items that measure more than one dimension. *Applied Psychological Measurement*, *15*, 361-373.

10. Wedman, J. M., & Moutray, C. (1991). The effect of training on the questions preservice teachers ask during literature discussions. *Reading Research and Instruction*, *30*(2), 62-70.

11. Hodge, E. A., Palmer, B. C., & Scott, D. (1992). Metacognitive training in cooperative groups on the reading comprehension and vocabulary of at-risk college students. *College Student Journal*, *26*, 440-448.

12. Miller, L. D. (1992). Teacher benefits from using impromptu writing prompts in algebra classes. *Journal for Research in Mathematics Education*, *23*, 329-340.

13. Sanacore, J. (1992). Encouraging the lifetime reading habit. *Journal of Reading*, *35*, 474-477.

14. Schwartz, M. D. (1992). Study sessions and higher grades: Questioning the causal link. *College Student Journal*, *26*, 292-299.

15. Simpson, M. L., & Nist, S. L. (1992). Toward defining a comprehensive assessment model for college reading. *Journal of Reading*, *35*, 452-458.

16. Skipper, C. E. (1992). Instructional preference of academically talented preservice teachers. *College Student Journal*, *26*, 274-280.

17. Berenbaum, H., & McGrew, J. (1993). Familial resemblance of schizotypic traits. *Psychological Medicine*, *23*, 327-333.

18. Bliss, L. B., & Mueller, R. J. (1993). An instrument for the assessment of study behaviors of college students. *Reading Research and Instruction*, *32*(4), 46-52.

19. Colangelo, N., Kerr, B., Christensen, P., & Maxey, J. (1993). A comparison of gifted underachievers and gifted high achievers. *Gifted Child Quarterly*, *37*, 155-160.

20. Cooksey, R. W. (1993). The problem of multidimensionality in course scores and course choices in the production of a single year 12 tertiary entrance score. *Australian Journal of Education*, *37*, 26-45.

21. Duchein, M. A., & Mealey, D. L. (1993). Remembrance of books past...long past: Glimpses into aliteracy. *Reading Research and Instruction*, *33*, 13-28.

22. Frazier, D. W. (1993). Transfer of college developmental reading students' textmarking strategies. *Journal of Reading Behavior*, *25*, 17-41.

23. Larrick, R. D., Nisbett, R. E., & Morgan, J. N. (1993). Who uses the cost-benefit rules of choice? Implications for the normative status of microeconomic theory. *Organizational Behavior and Human Decision Processes*, *56*, 331-347.

24. Mouw, J. T., & Khanna, R. K. (1993). Prediction of academic success: A review of the literature and some recommendations. *College Student Journal*, *27*, 328-336.

25. Woehr, D. J., & Cavell, T. A. (1993). Self-report measures of ability, effort, and nonacademic activity as predictors of introductory psychology test scores. *Teaching of Psychology*, *20*, 156-160.

26. Ackerman, T. A. (1994). Using multidimensional item response theory to understand what items and tests are measuring. *Applied Measurement in Education*, *7*, 255-278.

27. Johnson, P. J., Goldsmith, T. E., & Teague, K. W. (1994). Locus of predictive advantage in pathfinder-based representations of classroom knowledge. *Journal of Educational Psychology*, *86*, 617-626.

28. Rech, J. F., & Harrington, J. S. (1994). An examination of variables related to mathematics achievement among economically disadvantaged students. *College Student Journal*, *28*, 452-455.

29. Stein, K. F. (1994). Complexity of the self-schema and responses to disconfirming feedback. *Cognitive Therapy and Research*, *18*, 161-178.

30. Williams, J. E. (1994). Gender differences in high school students' efficacy-expectation/performance discrepancies across four subject matter domains. *Psychology in the Schools*, *31*, 232-237.

31. Wilson, J. S., Stocking, V. B., & Goldstein, D. (1994). Gender differences in motivations for course selection: Academically talented students in an intensive summer program. *Sex Roles*, *31*, 349-367.

32. Benton, S. L., Corkill, A. J., Sharp, J. M., Downey, R. G., & Khramtsova, I. (1995). Knowledge, interest, and narrative writing. *Journal of Educational Psychology*, *87*, 66-79.

33. Brodnick, R. J., & Ree, M. J. (1995). A structural model of academic performance, socioeconomic status, and Spearman's *g*. *Educational and Psychological Measurement*, *55*, 583-594.

34. House, J. D. (1995). Noncognitive predictors of achievement in introductory college mathematics. *Journal of College Student Development*, *36*, 171-181.

35. Jurden, F. H. (1995). Individual differences in working memory and complex cognition. *Journal of Educational Psychology*, *87*, 93-102.

Review of the Enhanced ACT Assessment by A. HARRY PASSOW, Professor Emeritus of Education, Teachers College, Columbia University, New York, NY:

The ACT Assessment Program was designed in the late 1950s in response to the perceived needs of institutions of higher education for "meaningful and objective data on which to base decisions about" (Preliminary Technical Manual, p. 2) the growing college-bound student population. The main purposes of the ACT Assessment Program are "to help students develop postsecondary plans and to help postsecondary education institutions develop programs suited to the needs and characteristics of their applicants" (Preliminary Technical Manual, p. 1). In addition to its use in the college admissions programs, ACT Assessment data are also used by student financial aid agencies, by state departments for identifying state scholars, and recently, by various state and federal agencies in their overall evaluation and planning activities.

The *Enhanced* ACT Assessment was introduced in October 1989 in response to changes in the high school curriculum and to the expectations regarding the skills and knowledge that students need for college success. To make these changes, ACT consulted with high school and college teachers, curriculum specialists, and subject content experts; studied the numerous critiques driving school reform; examined state curricula; and reviewed widely used school and college textbooks.

Based on the findings from this review process, the contents of the four ACT tests were revised and enhanced—greater emphasis on rhetorical skills in measuring writing proficiency, more advanced math items, a new reading test featuring inferential and reasoning skills, and a test assessing science reasoning. The Enhanced ACT Assessment now provides subscores in English, Mathematics, and Reading. A third of the items on the ACT Interest Inventory were replaced or revised. Other components of the ACT Assessment are basically unchanged.

The Enhanced ACT Assessment Program consists of four tests of educational development and three "Noncognitive Components"—a High School Course/Grade Information questionnaire, the ACT Interest Inventory, and a Student Profile Section. The latter components are completed by the student as part of the registration process.

The four tests of educational development include: (*a*) a 75-item English Test covering six elements of effective writing and yielding subscores in Usage/Mechanics (40 items) and Rhetorical Skills (35 items); (*b*) a 60-item Mathematics Test providing subscores in pre-algebra/elementary algebra (24 items), intermediate algebra/coordinate geometry (18 items), and plane geometry/trigonometry (18 items); (*c*) a 40-item Reading Test measuring "comprehension as a product of skill in referring and reasoning" (pp. 5-6) with subscores in Social Studies/Sciences (20 items) and Arts/Literature reading skills; and (*d*) a 40-item Science Reasoning Test that conveys science information in three different formats: representation (15 items), research summaries (18 items), and conflicting viewpoints (7 items)—and yields a single score.

The ACT Assessment is basically a college aptitude test—"a measure of how well [the student] can perform the skills necessary for college work" (p. 3). The tests consist of multiple-choice items, the format of choice for large-scale testing programs. The ACT Assessment tests themselves are secure tests and are not available for review.

The ACT Assessment Program administers several new test forms each year, taking about $2^1/_2$ years to produce each form. The test development process appears to follow psychometrically sound procedures throughout. The information provided in three technical manuals is reassuring in that the processes used in preparing this large-scale college aptitude test program appear to have been carried out competently.

The ACT Assessment Program Technical Manual (1988) contains comprehensive information on the procedures used in the test development; the norming, scaling, and equating of the instruments; and the validity and reliability data. The Preliminary Technical Manual (October 1989) contains much the same kind of information concerning the new Enhanced ACT Assessment Program introduced at that time but without the research data from pre-1989 studies. The Supplement to the Preliminary Technical Manual (December 1991) updates the 1989 manual and has information about the tests and their users, demographic characteristics of the 1991 high school graduating class and the norms they provided, and a summary of the technical characteristics.

According to the technical manuals studies are regularly undertaken regarding such questions as the predictive validity of the tests for college performance and the performance of various populations (e.g., male/female, minority/white, and handicapped).

Two publications—*Preparing for the ACT Assessment* and *Sample Test Booklet and Answer Sheet*—are available to students. The former provides information the student needs to have in preparing for the test—test-taking strategies, what to expect, taking and scoring the practice test, and completing registration. The latter publication makes it possible for the student to take a complete sample test, timing and scoring it.

The *ACT Assessment Test Preparation Reference Manual for Teachers and Counselors* is a practical and informative document that contains "information that can be used by teachers and counselors to help their students prepare for taking" the test (p. 9). Guidance is provided to prepare students who need assistance with taking the test. The *ACT Assessment User Handbook* authors provide school and college personnel with comprehensive information about the construction and use of the program in a less technical fashion than found in the manuals.

The 1988 ACT Assessment Program Technical Manual, the last "pre-enhanced" ACT Assessment Program technical document, has a review of a number of research studies dealing with the content, criterion, construct, and predictive validity as well as the reliability of the Tests of Educational Development and the ACT Interest Inventory. The preliminary technical manuals for the Enhanced ACT Assessment (1989 and 1991) do not yet have the same quality and quantity of research available. Validity issues regarding assessment of students' educational development, assistance to students and officials making college admissions decisions, and aid in making course placement decisions are mentioned. Presumably the enhanced versions have the same high validity and reliability as did the earlier tests and inventory.

The ACT Assessment Program is subject to the same controversies as its counterpart, the College Board Program, including questions about its predictive value, its actual contribution to the admissions process, its equity for diverse populations, etc. These widely debated issues surrounding both programs are obviously not readily resolved nor are they likely to be in the near future.

The Enhanced ACT Assessment Program is technically well designed, well constructed, well administered, and well studied. Although there will be modifications made in response to the ongoing controversies, college aptitude tests apparently will endure in the foreseeable future. As long as they do, the ACT Assessment Program will continue to fill a need that students, schools, and colleges have for a program that is perceived as providing real assistance in college admissions decisions. Moreover, if all parties make full use of all of the information generated from both the noncognitive components and the test of educational development, the Enhanced ACT Assessment Program will provide a valuable counseling tool that will augment the value of the tremendous investment that college assessment programs involve.

Review of the Enhanced ACT Assessment by JAMES S. TERWILLIGER, Professor of Educational Psychology, University of Minnesota, Minneapolis, MN:

GENERAL OVERVIEW. The original ACT Assessment Program was initiated in 1959 to serve the needs of colleges and universities in both admissions and placement decisions concerning prospective students. The ACT Program has grown from a modest testing service used primarily in the midwest and plains states to a truly national program. In 1993, between 1.4 and 1.5 million college applicants took the ACT tests on the five national testing dates. The ACT program is the most commonly employed college testing program in 28 states.

The ACT Assessment Program consists of four components: (*a*) four tests of educational development, (*b*) the High School Course/Grade Information questionnaire, (*c*) the ACT Interest Inventory, and (*d*) the Student Profile Section. The last three components (referred to as the "non-cognitive components" in ACT brochures) are intended to provide a broader spectrum of data than is available from the four tests alone. In particular, data from the High School Course/Grade Information are reported to colleges as part of the College Report, the ACT Interest Inventory results (based upon Holland's World-of-Work Map) are reported on individual Student Reports for discussion with counselors and advisors, and information from the Student Profile Section (educational plans, extracurricular plans, major accomplishments, etc.) is reported in various combinations on reports that go to the student, the student's high school and prospective colleges.

The ACT program provides a comprehensive set of high quality materials. A booklet to assist examinees prepare for the ACT contains many helpful hints for taking the tests and presents an extensive sample of items of the types included in each test. User handbooks and reference manuals for teachers and counselors are very thorough and clearly written. More technical information is provided in two manuals: a Preliminary Technical Manual published in 1989 and a Supplement to the Preliminary Technical manual published in 1991. Hereafter, these will be referred to simply as the 1989 Manual and the 1991 Supplement.

The most prominent component of the ACT is the battery of four tests of educational development. The tests are curriculum based as defined by major areas of instruction in American secondary schools and colleges. According to the 1989 Manual, "student preparedness for college is best assessed by measuring, as directly as possible, the academic skills that the student will need to perform college-level work" (p. 3). Prior to 1989, the ACT tests consisted of: English Usage (75 items, 40 minutes), Mathematics Usage (40 items, 50 minutes), Social Studies Reading (52 items, 35 minutes), and Natural Sciences Reading (52 items, 35 minutes).

REVISIONS IN THE ACT TESTS. In October 1989, the Enhanced ACT Assessment was introduced in response to changes both in the school curricula and in expectations held by colleges concerning skills and knowledge essential for academic success at the postsecondary level. The major changes were to drop the Social Studies and Natural Sciences Reading Tests and to replace them with two new tests: Reading and Science Reasoning. In addition, subtest scores were added to the English and Math Tests. Detailed descriptions of the new tests are available in the 1989 Manual.

ACT NORMS. Due to the extensive modifications in the ACT tests, it was necessary to develop completely new technical data for users. This required a series of norming studies. The 1989 Manual contains the following statements concerning the score scale on the Enhanced ACT:

The scale is new. Scores on the Enhanced ACT and the original ACT are *not* directly comparable.

The score range is 1–36 on the four main tests and the composite and 1–18 for the subscores.

The test means are 18 and subscore means are 9 for 12th graders who plan to attend college.

The standard error of measurement (*SEM*) is approximately 2 points for each test and 1 point for the composite.

Data presented on a nationally representative sample used for scaling the enhanced ACT in 1988 reveal the scale means stated above were realized (within .01) for all tests. However, data subsequently presented on a much larger sample of ACT "users" in a 1991

Supplement reveal that actual ACT users tend to have systematically higher scores than those initially reported. The means on the four tests and the composite are all in the 20 to 21 range. The subscore means range from 10 to 11. Also, it should be noted that all test (and subtest) score distributions exhibit a definite positive skew.

RELIABILITY AND VALIDITY. Reliability data provided in the 1989 Manual indicate that three of the test scores have reliabilities between .88 and .93. The Science Reasoning Test has a reliability of .79. The *SEM*s for the English and Mathematics Tests are both 1.50 whereas those for the Reading and Science Reasoning Tests are slightly larger than 2.0. The subscore reliabilities range from a low of.55 (Intermediate Algebra/Coordinate Geometry) to a high of.86 (English Usage/Mechanics). Obviously, considerable caution should be taken in making interpretations of the Intermediate Algebra subscore in view of its low reliability and the correspondingly high *SEM* (1.84).

Both the 1989 Manual and the 1991 Supplement contain detailed plots of the *SEM* as a function of true scores on each test. Generally speaking, the *SEM* is reasonably constant except at the higher end of the score scale (>30) where the *SEM* becomes much smaller. This is attributed to a truncation of scores near the top, which avoids gaps at the upper end of the raw-to-scale score conversion tables.

Validity evidence presented in the 1989 Manual relies primarily on content validity rationales. It is argued that, "Detailed test specifications have been developed to ensure that the test content is representative of current high school and university curricula" (p. 42). The absence of correlations (or expectancy tables) relating test scores to college grades is somewhat surprising. Results of placement studies at six postsecondary institutions in which ACT scores (or subscores) were correlated with grades in specific freshman courses are reported in the 1991 Supplement. As one would expect, the results are highly variable ranging from an r of .12 between English scores and grades in English Composition to an r of .59 between Intermediate Algebra/Coordinate Geometry subscores and grades in Honors Calculus. Future research designed to "more directly address admission issues than correlational analyses do" (p. 18) is promised in the 1991 Supplement. Additional data should be most welcome to colleges that employ the ACT for admissions purposes.

The 1989 Manual contains correlations among the ACT tests. When corrected for unreliability, correlations among the scores for college-bound students are uncomfortably high. The disattenuated correlations among the tests range from a low of .70 (Reading and Mathematics) to a high of .89 (Reading and Science Reasoning). Although the authors state these correlations "are sufficiently below 1.0 to suggest that the tests are measuring skills that are at least somewhat distinct, statistically" (p. 44), it is highly likely the four tests all share a large general factor which loads most heavily on the Reading and English tests. This conjecture is supported by data in the manuals that show the Reading and English tests carry higher effective weights than do the other two tests in defining the variability in Composite scores.

SUMMARY. The Enhanced ACT Assessment presents a clear philosophic contrast to the SAT (College Board SAT I Reasoning Test; T4:564). The emphasis upon school-based learning with a total of seven subscores in addition to the four test scores provides a potentially rich basis for both admissions and placement decisions. The tables of specifications for the tests reflect great care in the design of the tests. However, at present, there is no compelling body of empirical evidence to suggest the additional data provided by the ACT result in superior admissions decisions. Perhaps studies in the near future undertaken by the staff of ACT and other researchers will provide such evidence.

[140]

Entrance Examination for Schools of Nursing [RN Entrance Examination].

Purpose: Constructed to assess academic achievement for use in selection and placement of students.
Population: Applicants to schools of registered nursing.
Publication Dates: 1938–91.
Acronym: RNEE.
Scores, 6: Verbal Ability, Numerical Ability, Life Sciences, Physical Sciences, Reading Skill, Total.
Administration: Group.
Restricted Distribution: Distribution restricted and test administered at licensed testing centers; details may be obtained from publisher.
Price Data: Available from publisher.
Time: 160(175) minutes.
Comments: Title on test is RN Entrance Examination for Schools of Nursing.
Author: The Psychological Corporation.
Publisher: The Psychological Corporation.
Cross References: For reviews by Carolyn Dawson and Christine H. McGuire, see 8:1121; see also T2:2379 (1 reference), 7:1115 (3 references), and 6:1156 (2 references).

Review of the Entrance Examination for Schools of Nursing [RN Entrance Examination] by ANITA S. TESH, Assistant Professor, School of Nursing, University of North Carolina at Greensboro, Greensboro, NC:

Schools of registered nursing exist in a variety of educational settings (e.g., universities, hospitals, and community colleges) and serve students from diverse educational backgrounds. In recent years many schools have experienced an increase in applications from nontraditional, older, and second-degree students. Currently, many schools are unable to admit all applicants who meet their minimum qualifications, and find selecting among applicants with heterogeneous backgrounds and qualification to be difficult. The RN Entrance Examination (RNEE) is intended to provide "a means of comparing and evaluating applicants from diverse educational backgrounds by offering a uniform measure of academic performance for use in the admission process" (The Psychological Corporation, 1987, p. 4).

The RNEE consists of five timed scales addressing Verbal Ability, Numerical Ability, Life Sciences, Physical Sciences, and Reading Skill. Scales are composed of 40 to 50 multiple-choice items, each item having four answer choices. Passages from the natural and social sciences precede the questions in the Reading Skill scale. Results are reported as scaled scores and percentile scores. A total score is provided in addition to scores for each scale. A Candidate Information Booklet available to applicants contains test-taking strategies and sample questions.

The Verbal and Numerical Ability scales assess knowledge that examinees could have acquired in a variety of educational and work settings, such as vocabulary and basic arithmetic operations. The Life Sciences and Physical Sciences scales, however, assess knowledge that appears dependent on specific educational preparation, such as the ability to recognize formulae for isomers of organic compounds and to interpret the ionization energy of ions. Such content may discriminate against nontraditional students. Conversely, some items of the Reading Skill scale assess information that some examinees are likely to know without reading the assigned passage, thus testing knowledge rather than reading skill.

ADMINISTRATION, SCORING, AND FEES. The RNEE is designed for on-site group or individual administration by the schools of nursing. Group administration at designated testing centers is also available. The RNEE is scored by the publisher. The test fee is $20 per applicant, with additional fees for hand scoring and reporting of scores to additional schools.

TEST MANUAL. No technical manual is available for the RNEE (Personal communication, M. L. Wall, Project Director, The Psychological Corporation, 1992). The *Guide for Admissions Officers* (The Psychological Corporation, 1987) contains some of the information deemed primary in the *Standards for Educational and Psychological Testing* (AERA, APA, & NCME, 1985), but lacks other primary information. The *Guide* includes guidance on use and interpretation of test scores. It contains only vague information on test development. No information is provided regarding use of the test with the handicapped or with linguistic minorities. Qualifications for test administrators and conditions for administration are not discussed, although conditions for administration can be inferred from the Manual of Directions for Examiners. No information is available on validity and reliability under different testing conditions, or on the effects of coaching or retaking the test.

NORMS. Test results are provided as norm-referenced percentile ranks, comparing applicants' scores to a norm group of 6,834 applicants to 134 schools of nursing in 1984 and 1985 (The Psychological Corporation, 1987). Because the composition of the pool of applicants to schools of nursing has changed dramatically since 1985, these percentile ranks may be misleading. The types of nursing programs represented in the norm group are not described.

RELIABILITY. Although disclosing information on the reliability of a test is deemed primary by the *Standards for Educational and Psychological Testing* (AERA, APA, & NCME, 1985), no information on reliability of the RNEE is provided. Use of the test in the absence of information on its reliability is imprudent.

VALIDITY. According to the Guide for Admissions Officers (The Psychological Corporation, 1987) the content validity of the RNEE was established by nursing educators and is reviewed periodically. Composition of the panels of experts and review processes are not described.

Because the RNEE is intended for use in selecting applicants for admission to schools of nursing, predictive criterion-related evidence of validity is of primary concern. According to the test publisher, the median correlation between RNEE scores and first-year nursing grade-point averages (GPA) reported by schools using the RNEE is .42. The median correlations between RNEE scores and RN licensure examination scores is reported as .49 (The Psychological Corporation, 1987, p. 11). Because the RNEE scores used in these studies presumably suffer from restriction of range (i.e., not all applicants were admitted), and there is often little variance in the GPA of student nurses, these correlations provide some support for use of the RNEE as a part of admissions decisions. In one small-scale study done at an associate-degree program the ability of the RNEE to predict GPA and performance on the licensure examination surpassed that of the American College Testing (ACT) Program; in a study done at a diploma program it surpassed the Scholastic Aptitude Test (SAT) in predicting GPA (The Psychological Corporation, 1984, pp. 11–12).

Some uses beyond admission testing, such as evaluation of curricular needs, is suggested in the Guide. The validity of such uses is not discussed.

CONCLUSIONS. The RNEE provides information that is potentially useful in selecting among applicants to schools of nursing. Little information is provided on the psychometric properties of the RNEE. Potential test users should carefully assess the reliability and validity of the test for their program *before* making admissions decisions based on test results. Potential users should keep in mind that scores on some RNEE subtests may be dependent on certain educational experiences. Potential users must also assess whether the RNEE provides useful information beyond that which they already have on applicants, such as GPAs and scores on the ACT or SAT.

The RNEE is similar in cost and content map to the NLN Pre-Admission Examination for Schools of Nursing-RN (Rubens, 1991). More information is provided for the Pre-Admission Examination for Schools of Nursing-RN regarding test development, norms for programs of different types, reliability, and validity (Rubens, 1991). The findings in at least one study (Breyer, 1985) suggests slightly higher correlation between the Pre-Admission Examination for Schools of Nursing-RN and first-year GPA than is reported for the RNEE.

The *Standards for Educational and Psychological Testing* (AERA, APA, & NCME, 1985, p. 54) stress that decisions that have a major impact on a person's life, such as admissions decisions, should never be based solely on the results of a single test. Professionals responsible for making admissions decisions for schools of nursing must keep this canon in mind, as they select from an increasingly heterogeneous applicant pool.

REVIEWER'S REFERENCES

American Educational Research Association, American Psychological Association, & National Council on Measurement in Education. (1985). *Standards for educational and psychological testing*. Washington, DC: American Psychological Association, Inc.

Breyer, F. J. (1985). *NLN's Pre-Admission Examination-RN: A validation study*. New York: National League for Nursing.

The Psychological Corporation. (1987). *Guide for admissions officers: Entrance Examination for Schools of Nursing*. San Antonio, TX: Author.

Rubens, Y. A. (1991). NLN Pre-Admission Examination for Schools of Nursing. New York: National League for Nursing.

Review of the Entrance Examination for Schools of Nursing [RN Entrance Examination] by LARRY WEBER, Professor of Education, Virginia Tech, Blacksburg, VA:

The Entrance Examination for Schools of Nursing (RNEE) is designed for use by nursing schools to measure their applicants' achievement in subject areas deemed important for success in nursing programs. The RNEE consists of five subtests: Verbal Ability consists of vocabulary items requiring examinees to identify synonyms and antonyms; Numerical Ability measures skills in arithmetic, algebra, and geometry; Life Sciences contains questions focusing on the biological sciences; Physical Sciences concerns knowledge about chemistry and physics; and Reading Skill tests the ability to comprehend passages from the natural and social sciences. The RNEE emphasizes the "hard sciences" and noticeably absent from the exam are questions from subject areas concerning the behavioral sciences and business administration (management), topics that are becoming more important in the nursing field.

The questions in the exam are straightforward. Many are factual but the Numerical Ability subtest is problem oriented and the Physical Sciences subtest contains items that require the examinee to apply knowledge. They are similar to those found on other types of aptitude examinations. A noted shortcoming in the Reading Skill subtest is that some of the passages contain information that may be already known to some examinees and, as such, not be a good measure of their reading ability. The passages on heart disease and conditioning exhibit this kind of problem.

It is alleged that the RNEE is a uniform measure of academic performance and that it provides a basis for comparing and evaluating nursing school applicants from diverse backgrounds. The questions in the examination are contributed by nursing professionals and educators. They are edited and categorized by the professional staff at the Psychological Corporation. Proficiency in the five areas of academic achievement tested on the RNEE was established by nursing educators as prerequisites for entering nursing students. Its content is reviewed periodically by the Psychological Corporation staff and nursing educators. No evidence of the identities, qualifications, or affiliations of the nursing educators was given in the test materials, however.

The RNEE is a secure test, meaning that its content is carefully guarded and considered to be confidential. The likelihood that examinees may have had access to the exam is reduced, under such circumstances. The directions for administering the exam seem unusually thorough and structured, with little opportunity existing for variation in its presentation. The Psychological Corporation seems to have anticipated the various problems that might be associated with administering the test.

The RNEE is administered under two modes. It may be taken by individual applicants as an unscheduled exam, on site, at a nursing school. For a large number of applicants it is given at testing centers, in the United States and Canada, on dates published by the Psychological Corporation.

The norm groups for the RNEE consisted of 6,834 applicants to RN programs, who were tested between the Fall of 1984 and the Spring of 1985. The examinees were applicants to 134 schools that used the test. No information about the makeup of the nursing schools in the norm group is provided. That is, the percent of schools that are hospital affiliated diploma schools, associate degree granting institutions, or baccalaureate degree schools is not given. This might present a problem if the norm group is overrepresented by one type of institution, and a school contemplating using the exam is another type.

"To avoid confusion" raw scores on the RNEE are converted to scaled scores, using a system based on a median (50 %ile) score of 200. Scores usually range from 100–300. The scaled scores can be used to compare two applicants' performance on a specific subtest. However, they may *not* be used to make comparisons across subtests. Selected percentile ranks for selected scaled scores are also provided.

An examinee receives an individual score report and may designate that an official transcript of the report be sent to one school. (Additional score reports may be requested by the applicant for a fee.) In addition to a set of official school transcripts, a nursing school receives a roster of scores for all its applicants. The roster includes the date of testing and scaled and percentile scores for the five subtests and the composite.

Although no evidence about the reliability of the RNEE was provided, information on two types of validity is presented. The first concerns content validity and the data consist of two sentences, which essentially state that the test's content was established by nursing educators. Evidence about the RNEE's predictive validity is more complete, but still deficient, and possibly dated. One validity report, which included six schools using the RNEE's composite score to predict first year nursing GPA, showed correlations ranging between .38 to .61 (median = .42). It also showed that the overall correlation between the RNEE and licensure exam scores was .49. The Psychological Corporation's claim of strong support of the ability of the RNEE to predict success is, based on these data, somewhat exaggerated.

More recent studies (1985) contrasted the RNEE's predictive ability with the ACT and SAT examination programs. In both, comparisons between the ability of the various test scores (RNEE vs. ACT; RNEE vs. SAT) to predict nursing GPAs were made. The RNEE was better in each study. The RNEE was also superior to pre-nursing-college GPA in predicting cumulative nursing GPA; and superior to the ACT composite score and pre-nursing-college GPA in predicting board scores. The validity coefficients for the studies, between RNEE total scores and GPA, were .58 and .30; between the RNEE total scores and board scores it was .58.

In summary, the RNEE is an established examination, having been in use since the 1940s. It is designed to be used by schools of nursing for screening applicants seeking admission to their programs. In reviewing the test several deficiencies about it were noted. Major questions concerned the lack of definitive evidence about the technical characteristics of the exam (i.e., normative data, information on reliability, and the adequacy of content validity). Also noted was the fact that the studies on predictive validity are dated and few in number. However, they did provide some evidence about the value of the RNEE as an admission tool to be used by schools of nursing. Finally, because of the absence of information about the makeup of types of school constituting the norm group, individual schools using the exam would probably be well advised to develop normative data based upon their own applicants and their success in that particular nursing program.

[141]

Entrance Examination for Schools of Practical/Vocational Nursing.

Purpose: "Designed to measure achievement in areas critical for success in the basic practical/vocational nursing curriculum."
Population: Applicants to practical/vocational nursing schools.
Publication Dates: 1942–91.
Acronym: PNEE.
Scores, 5: Verbal Ability, Numerical Ability, Science, Reading Skill, Total.
Administration: Group.
Restricted Distribution: Distribution restricted and test administered at licensed testing centers; details may be obtained from publisher.
Price Data: Available from publisher.
Time: 180(195) minutes.
Author: The Psychological Corporation.
Publisher: The Psychological Corporation.
Cross References: See 7:1116 (2 references).

Review of the Entrance Examination for Schools of Practical/Vocational Nursing by GEORGE ENGELHARD, JR., Associate Professor of Educational Studies, Emory University, Atlanta, GA:

The Entrance Examination for Schools of Practical/Vocational Nursing (PNEE) is an instrument designed to aid in the selection decisions of practical/vocational nursing schools that typically offer 2-year programs leading to an associates degree. The PNEE was originally developed in the 1940s, and has been revised several times over the intervening years; this is the first review of the PNEE in a *Mental Measurements Yearbook*. The PNEE is designed to measure the academic skills that are believed to be necessary for success in a practical/vocational nursing course of study. The PNEE consists of 255 multiple-choice items in the content areas of Verbal Ability (75 items), Numerical Ability (60 items), Science (75 items), and Reading Skill (45 items). The Guide for Admissions Officers (Guide) serves as a technical manual for the PNEE.

The internal consistency of the items included in the PNEE is quite high. On Form 7, KR20 coefficients range from .87 for Reading Skill to .95 for Verbal Ability, whereas the KR20 coefficients for Form 8 range from .90 for Reading Skill and Science to .94 for Verbal Ability. The KR20 coefficients for total scores are .97 for both forms. Standard errors of measurement are included by form for each of the subtests, as well as for the total scores. A nice description of how to interpret the standard errors of measurement is also included in the Guide. No evidence is provided regarding the stability of the scores on the PNEE over varying time periods. An even more troublesome omission is the absence of any alternate form reliability coefficients for the subtests and the total instrument. Information on the correlations between scores obtained on Forms 7 and 8 should be provided in a revision of the Guide. The two forms vary in difficulty with a total score mean of 145.1 (*SD* = 39.9) on Form 7, and a total mean score of 129.9 (*SD* = 36.1) on Form 8. It is disturbing that no information is provided regarding how scores are equated on the two forms. If the forms are not equated, then decisions about candidates may depend on whether they happen to take the easy (Form 7) or hard (Form 8) forms of the PNEE.

In order to obtain evidence regarding the content validity of the PNEE, the items included in the instrument are periodically reviewed by the test publisher and nursing program educators. No further details are provided regarding how these content validity studies are conducted. It would be helpful to have additional information about these studies, such as how often this activity takes place, how the participants are selected, and what procedures are used.

Evidence in support of the predictive validity of the PNEE is provided in terms of correlations of PNEE scores with cumulative grade-point averages obtained in nursing courses, scores on licensure examinations developed by state boards, and scores from the National League of Nursing Achievement Tests. The evidence presented in support of the predictive validity of the PNEE is obtained from five studies completed since 1980. It is not clear why these particular studies, which reflect different practical/vocation nursing schools, were selected. Do these schools have the best predictive validity coefficients or were these the worst? The correlations between PNEE scores and cumulative nursing GPAs are quite good with a range of .30 to .57; correlations between PNEE total scores and state board scores range from .37 to .76. It is difficult to interpret the value of this information without more detail regarding how these schools were selected. The descriptions of the five studies are too brief to provide the potential test user with enough detail to critically evaluate the studies. For example, a range of correlations is reported for the NLN Achievement Tests (6 tests) without describing what content areas were measured by these six tests.

It is also important to consider the consequential validity of tests that are used for admission decisions. Users of the PNEE should examine the differential predictive validity of the scores including differences in the admission rates for candidates from different social categories (e.g., gender, social class, and race/ethnicity). The Guide provides sound advice to users of the PNEE when it suggests that schools examine the validity of the scores for their particular pool of candidates. Given the limited resources of some schools, a short and specific set of suggestions on how to design and evaluate these validity studies would be a useful addition.

Examinee scores are reported as raw scores and percentile ranks for each of the subtests and the total test. The score reports provide a nice description of how to interpret percentile ranks, but the reports do not include the number of items in each subtest. This information may be helpful to some examinees so that they can determine the percentage of items that they answered correctly in each content area. The norm group used to develop these percentile ranks consists of 6,500 examinees tested between the fall of 1984 and the spring of 1985 who applied to 134 schools using the PNEE. No further details are provided regarding the demographic composition of the norm group. More details about the norm group should be provided.

In summary, decisions regarding admission to nursing schools should be based on a variety of criteria. As with other multiple-choice examinations, the user must carefully consider the strengths and limitations of this method of assessment. The PNEE reflects sound professional test development strategies, and should be useful as one of several criteria that can be used for screening candidates for admission to schools of practical/vocational nursing. Individual programs and schools should examine the predictive validity of the PNEE for their particular pool of candidates, and also the predictive validity of other criteria (e.g., grade-point average in high school, professional recommendations, and candidate interviews) that are used for decisions regarding admissions.

Review of the Entrance Examination for Schools of Practical/Vocational Nursing by JAMES W. PINKNEY, Professor of Counseling and Adult Education, East Carolina University, Greenville, NC:

The Entrance Examination for Schools of Practical/Vocational Nursing (PNEE) is intended to be used as part of the information on which decisions to admit or not admit candidates are made by practical and vocational nursing schools. There are apparently four forms of the PNEE but only Form 7A was reviewed. The manual for examiners lists Forms 7A, 7B, 7C, and 7D, whereas the user's manual notes that "two different forms" (Form 7 and Form 8) are in current use. There is no information available in the manual about the comparability of the forms. The question of how many forms exist and the degree to which they are interchangeable or comparable is never addressed in any of the material available for review.

The PNEE consists of five parts: Verbal Ability (assessed by 75 synonym items), Numerical Ability

(60 basic arithmetic items), Science (75 recall items from chemistry, biology, and physics), Reading Skill (45 items based on three reading passages of science material), and an unlabeled fifth section that consists of 30 antonym items and 20 analogies. The assumption that this last section is part of the assessment of Verbal Ability cannot be made because the manual indicates only four sections and specifies that Verbal Ability consists of 75 items (see above). The possibility exists that Section 5 is part of a new version that is being piloted by the publisher. Both the confusion over the number of forms and the intent of Section 5 may be explained by the dates of the materials reviewed. The manual was copyrighted in 1987, the actual PNEE instrument in 1990, the examiner's manual in 1991, and the candidate booklet in 1991. Anyone considering this instrument should be very careful about the dates of the materials provided. The manual needs to be revised to conform with the current forms of the instrument.

A strong point for the PNEE is the candidate information booklet. It provides information in a clear and thorough fashion. The test taker's options and responsibilities are covered and include accommodations for the disabled, testing center rules, and how the test is scored. An interesting option of the PNEE is that a person taking it can, during the examination, request that no score be calculated. A person finding that he or she was not ready can elect to have no reported outcome of taking the PNEE. This option might be important for nursing candidates who have been out of education for an extended period. The procedure for the "no score option" is simply to fill in a circle on the answer sheet.

The manual for examiners is also well done. It is thorough, precise, and discusses potential problems, exam preparations, follow-up procedures, and suggested answers to frequent questions from examinees. It emphasizes security and clearly outlines what to do when problems arise that might compromise the PNEE. Verbatim instructions are provided for administration and for timing the sections of the PNEE. A 12-point checklist covers completing the examiner's report and returning the exams for scoring. Score reports to an admissions officer are promised within 5 working days of receipt of the answer sheet by the publisher. The candidates may expect to receive a score report in about 4 weeks.

The manual for the PNEE offers the potential user confusion rather than help. Copyrighted in 1987, it was written for an earlier version of the PNEE quite different from the current Form 7A being reviewed. The manual discusses and presents data for a PNEE of four sections totaling 255 items. Form 7A has five sections and 305 items copyrighted in 1990. Given that the data reported for reliability and validity are for an earlier version, what is presented is both skimpy and confusing for an instrument "in use since the 1940's."

The 6,500 applicants who took the PNEE in 1984–85 are reported to be the norm group, but no raw scores or percentile ranks are given. The explanation for this is that each school and program will determine what scores mean for their particular applicants. This may be true, but it does not excuse the publisher from making comparative information available. The utility of a 10-year-old norm group is suspect even if the current PNEE was not a longer, more complicated edition than the one used and presumably normed in 1984–85.

Related problems occur when reliability is considered. Impressive coefficients are reported (.87 to .95 for section scores and .97 for the total score), but for the PNEE used in 1985–86. No information is provided on the current version, and assuming that reliability translates without change to a newer version of an instrument is suspect. It is more reasonable to assume one of two unpleasant possibilities: Either more recent data are available but not as supportive of the current version, or no effort has been made to assess the reliability of the present PNEE.

The manual claims content validity based on periodic review of the items by nursing program educators. No other information is given about content validity. Predictive validity is based on moderate correlations between PNEE scores and outcome variables such as state board scores, cumulative grade point averages, and achievement tests related to nursing. Only five studies are reported (with correlations between .13 and .76). It is difficult to believe that only 5 nursing schools out of over 100 have assessed the predictability of the PNEE over the last 15 years, and selective reporting seems likely. Again, the assumption is made that data on earlier versions apply to the present version.

In summary, the manual for the PNEE is poorly done and was prepared for earlier versions of the instrument. No data on the current version's reliability or validity are presented, even though there have been extensive changes in the PNEE. Neither raw scores nor percentile ranks of any kind are provided. The discrepancies between the manual and the instrument, the lack of data on the current version of the PNEE, and the use of outdated information all argue against using this instrument. Both extreme caution and an awareness of the critical necessity of local norms are needed by the potential user who is considering the PNEE as part of the admissions process for a nursing program.

[142]

Erhardt Developmental Prehension Assessment.

Purpose: Designed "for charting the prehensile development . . . of the child who is delayed or abnormal or both."

Population: Children with cerebral palsy (spastic, athetoid, or mixed) from birth to adolescence.
Publication Dates: 1982–89.
Acronym: EDPA.
Scores: 3 areas: Involuntary Hand-Arm Patterns (Positional-Reflexive), Voluntary Movements (Cognitively Directed), Pre-Writing Skills.
Administration: Individual.
Price Data, 1993: $10 per 5 Erhardt Developmental Prehension Assessment booklets ('89, 20 pages); $35 per Developmental Hand Dysfunction manual ('89, 151 pages).
Time: Administration time not reported.
Comments: Research base and reliability information included in text entitled *Developmental Hand Dysfunction, Theory, Assessment, and Treatment.*
Author: Rhoda P. Erhardt.
Publisher: Therapy Skill Builders.

TEST REFERENCES

1. Exner, C. E. (1993). Content validity of the In-hand Manipulation Test. *The American Journal of Occupational Therapy, 47*, 505-513.

Review of the Erhardt Developmental Prehension Assessment by MARTIN E. BLOCK, Assistant Professor of Education, and LINDA K. BUNKER, Professor and Associate Dean of Education, University of Virginia, Charlottesville, VA:

INTRODUCTION. The Erhardt Developmental Prehension Assessment (EDPA) is a norm-referenced assessment tool designed to measure fine motor development in children from birth to 15 months of age as well as older children with delayed prehensile development. In addition, the tool includes a developmental evaluation of prewriting skills for children 1 year to 6 years of age.

Erhardt explained that she developed the EDPA because pediatric occupational therapists had no tools for evaluating normal and abnormal hand function in infants. The EDPA is based on Erhardt's Theory of Inappropriate Prehensile Patterns, which builds on the works of Gesell (Gesell & Amatruda, 1961) and Halverson (1931) as well as the Bobaths' (1967) neurodevelopmental approach. In essence, Erhardt proposed that abnormal prehensile patterns are manifestations of normal patterns (primary developmentally inappropriate patterns) or a combination of normal patterns (secondary developmentally inappropriate patterns) that appear at inappropriate times. For example, she noted that fisting is normal for a 1-month-old but not normal (i.e., represents a prehensile delay) for a 3-year-old. Thus, the quality of prehensile movement and whether or not certain prehensile patterns represent hand dysfunction can be measured using a developmental approach.

The EDPA is designed to be individually administered by trained pediatric occupational therapists, but it also can be used by other therapists (e.g., physical therapists) and special education teachers working with young children with suspected developmental hand dysfunction.

TEST CONTENT AND INSTRUCTIONS. The EDPA manual was published in Erhardt's text: *Developmental Hand Dysfunction: Theory, Assessment, Treatment* (Erhardt, 1989) and includes (*a*) an introductory section with three case studies describing children with varying disabilities which affect hand function, (*b*) a theoretical rationale for the development of Erhardt's Theory of Developmental Hand Dysfunction, (*c*) a description of the development of the EDPA as well as instructions for administering the EDPA, and (*d*) an extensive review of ways of taking results from the EDPA and developing individual treatment plans. The case studies in the introductory section as well as in the treatment section are excellent and provide clear examples of how the EDPA can be used in evaluation and treatment. The theoretical section is a little long and somewhat difficult to follow.

Directions for administering and scoring the EDPA are very limited both in the manual (test booklet) and the original book. Pictures plus narrative explain the components of each skill to be observed, and a material list is provided. However, no information is given as to how to position or elicit the behaviors, how to present materials, how long one should wait before moving on to a new behavior, effects of immediate environment, or how behavioral state might affect appearance and intensity of behaviors. Such procedures would be helpful for assessment specialists as well as for other educators and parents.

Scoring uses a 4-point scale ranging from a "+" (all pattern components present) to a "-" (no pattern components present). Examples of scoring are provided in both the instruction section and the treament sections. Information related to specific scoring criteria is quite limited. For example, a "±" indicates "emerging or abnormal pattern not well-integrated" and a "II" indicates "transitional pattern replaced by more mature patterns." No information is given as to what defines either of these scores. The lack of clear criteria negatively impacts both test-retest and interrater reliability of the EDPA.

The EDPA includes three sections: Section 1 focuses on "primarily involuntary arm-hand patterns" (Positional-Reflexive); Section 2 focuses on "primarily voluntary movements" (Cognitively Directed); and Section 3 focuses on Pre-Writing skills. Sections 1 and 2 are divided into several "developmental sequence clusters" with items listed hierarchically by month from fetal through 7 to 15 months (the ceiling level varies for each particular cluster). Section 1 includes the following clusters: (*a*) arms at rest and during body play (supine); (*b*) arms at rest and during head raising (prone); (*c*) asymmetrical tonic neck reflex; (*d*) grasping reactions; (*e*) placing responses; and (*f*) avoiding responses. Section 2 includes the following clusters: (*a*) arms on approach (supine); (*b*) arms on approach (prone); (*c*) arms on approach (sitting); (*d*) grasp of dowel; (*e*) grasp of cube; (*f*) grasp of pellet; (*g*) manipulation skills; (*h*) release of dowel or cube; and (*i*) release of pellet. Section 3 has two skill clusters with items listed hierarchically every 6 months to a year and one-half: (*a*) pencil grasp and (*b*) drawings that depict actual prehensile behaviors accompany each skill within clusters. These pictures are excellent and make the EDPA relatively easy to use by persons other than pediatric occupational therapists (e.g., special education teachers and parents). A summary score sheet in the back of the EDPA can be used to present graphically an infant's developmental profile.

PSYCHOMETRIC PROPERTIES. Erhardt's book contains information on test construction and validation and specifies that the EDPA was originally developed in 1977 from fine motor development norms found in nine different research studies. Items and time sequences were chosen that had a 50% or greater agreement and scoring was based on Gesell's developmental schedules. The test was revised and expanded in 1981 and pictures were included to describe behaviors in all skill clusters. The EDPA was "informally field tested" in 1982 by the author and several occupational and physical therapists in the midwest. Thus, content validity appears to be based on the author's review of literature and informal field testing. No specific validation studies have been conducted, and even the author suggests that statistical evidence for construct validity is needed. There is no information as to the EDPA's predictive validity or what Erhardt called "discriminant validity," the ability of the test to discriminate between groups of children.

Interrater reliability was tested in a study conducted by Erhardt, Beatty, and Hertsgaard (1981). They found that percent agreements ranged from 70.8 to 94.5 and that intraclass correlations ranged from .418 to .853 ($p<.001$). No other reliability tests were conducted, and Erhardt noted that test-retest reliability studies are needed. In fact, Erhardt noted that "Since the EDPA was a compilation of test items from published evaluation scales and child development literature, it could not be considered a standardized assessment tool with established validity and reliability" (p. 242). Thus, validity and reliability of the EDPA is suspect at best. Although the test appears to have logical or face validity, without statistical analysis its usefulness is questionable.

COMPARABLE TESTS. The EDPA is virtually the only test available that specifically examines prehensile development. Other tests such as the Peabody Developmental Motor Scales (Folio & Fewell, 1983; T4: 1943), Bayley Scales of Infant Development (Bayley, 1969; T4:266), Gesell Developmental Schedules (Gesell & Amatruda, 1969), and Developmental Programming for Infants and Young Children (Schafer & Moersch, 1980), to name a few, contain sections on fine motor development, but none are as extensive as the EDPA. In addition, the EDPA is the only assessment tool that presents pictures of normal prehensile patterns to aid in assessment, and is the only assessment tool that includes an extensive guide for developing remedial programs for children with hand dysfunction. Still, limited validity and reliability should caution the consumer.

SUMMARY. In summary, the EDPA is one of the few, if not the only, developmental test on the market that specifically examines fine motor development in infants and young children. Erhardt has taken the works of other researchers and melded their ideas into a theory of inappropriate prehensile development that is used as the basis for the EDPA. The assessment is easy to administer, and the pictures are excellent guides to observation. More specific information on how to administer the EDPA and guidelines regarding such ancillary factors as behavior state and environment would enhance the reliability. In addition, the EDPA's limited validity and reliability evidence should raise a red flag to practitioners wishing to use the EDPA. Still, the EDPA appears to fill a unique niche in developmental assessment, and, with the above cautions, we recommend the EDPA for pediatric occupational therapists as well as others working with young children who have fine motor delays.

REVIEWERS' REFERENCES

Bobath, B. (1967). The very early treatment of cerebral palsy. *Developmental Medicine and Child Neurology, 9*, 373-390.

Halverson, H. M. (1931). An experimental study of prehension in infants by means of systematic cinema records. *Genetic Psychologic Monographs, 10*, 107-286.

Gesell, A., & Amatruda, C. S. (1969). *Developmental diagnosis*. New York: Harper & Row.

Erhardt, R. P., Beatty, P. A., & Hersgaard, D. M. (1981). A developmental prehension assessment for handicapped children. *American Journal of Occupational Therapy, 35*, 237-242.

Schafer, D. S., & Moersch, M. S. (1981). *Developmental programming for infants and young children: Early intervention developmental profile*. Ann Arbor: University of Michigan Press.

Folio, M. R., & Fewell, R. (1983). Peabody Developmental Motor Scales. Allen, TX: DLM Teaching Resources.

Erhardt, R. P. (1989). *Developmental hand dysfunction: Theory, assessment, treatment*. Tucson, AZ: Therapy Skill Builders.

Bayley, N. (1993). *Manual for the Bayley Scales of Infant Development, Second Edition*. San Antonio, TX: The Psychological Corporation.

Review of the Erhardt Developmental Prehension Assessment by GERALD TINDAL, Associate Professor of Special Education, University of Oregon, Eugene, OR:

The Erhardt Developmental Prehension Assessment (EDPA) provides a data collection system for scaling three types of hand movements: (*a*) primarily involuntary arm-hand movements, (*b*) mostly voluntary movements, and (*c*) prewriting skills. The scale for measuring development is by successive months for the two former areas (ranging from fetal to 12 and 15 months, respectively) and years in the last area (ranging from 1 to 6 years). The 18 subscales (listed in the test description) are presented in developmental sequence clusters for both left and right hands.

The scoring card and protocol sheets (developmental sequence clusters) provide the test administrator pictures and text descriptions of various hand positions and arm/upper body movements and positions. A score and summary sheet are presented at the end of the protocols. The test administrator is required to assemble the materials for some of the subtests (i.e., dowels, cubes, containers, pellets, etc.). The basic assessment procedure is summarized as simply:

1. Present the stimuli and/or observe the child.
2. Record the pattern component scores, lowest levels first.

The scoring key requires the administrator to code the response into the following categories: (*a*) well-integrated, (*b*) pattern not present, (*c*) emerging, and (*d*) transitional pattern replaced by more mature patterns. The appropriate developmental levels are then recorded using a normative chart on the score sheet.

The test is accompanied by a book that contains considerable text on the theoretical rationale using three case studies of children and an architect, a synthesized theory of prehension, a developmental prehension assessment system, and finally, recommendations for treatment. Most referenced professional work in the manual is quite old, ranging from the mid-1930s to the early 1980s. The basic theoretical approach of the test is Piagetian, although a complex mix of medical and therapeutic perspectives are intermingled. The book contains a plethora of pictures of children and adults in black and white photographs that serve little purpose.

The only significant chapter of note for the actual assessment protocol is the Evaluation of the EDPA (chapter 7), where the only technical information on the instrument is presented. In this chapter, Bloom's taxonomy is used as the basis for evaluating the instrument. Validity is poorly described as the test's ability to discriminate among subgroups of children. Reliability is addressed as interscorer and decision-making (also referred to as consistency or dependability of the instrument). Although a number of questions are specifically asked that would address some (albeit incomplete) aspects of validity, the author finally summarizes the most complete technical information of this assessment device by stating that "informal feedback reports indicate that the EDPA is extremely appropriate for children with developmental delays or dysfunction" (p. 69). Scant reliability information is presented with some actual coefficients. It is not reported, however, with whom the instrument was used and when or how (either testers or those tested). The intervention recommendations are equally specious.

In summary, the EDPA is a highly speculative instrument designed to integrate a complex theory of motor development focused exclusively on grasping and arm-hand movements. The instrument provides an outdated and rich mix of speculation and medical-therapeutic perspectives and is most noteworthy in its lack of any serious technical information supporting it. It is unlikely this instrument is useful for more than structured clinical observations; the normative levels are of unknown integrity; the stages are questionable in breadth and application. Finally, the implications of performance (summarized in developmental time) are lacking in credibility.

[143]

Erhardt Developmental Vision Assessment.

Purpose: Designed to assess visual-motor development.
Population: All ages.
Publication Dates: 1982–90.
Acronym: EDVA.
Scores: Item scores only.
Administration: Individual.
Price Data, 1993: $10 per 5 assessment booklets; $39 per Developmental Visual Dysfunction book ('90, 222 pages).
Time: Administration time not reported.
Comments: Administered with the help of an assistant; ratings by therapist; short screening form for visual assessment also available.
Author: Rhoda P. Erhardt.
Publisher: Therapy Skill Builders.

Review of the Erhardt Developmental Vision Assessment by DEBORAH ERICKSON, Associate Professor of Education, Niagara University, Niagara University, NY:

The test was originally developed to assess the motor components of vision, specifically related to "eye-hand linkage." The test is a 16-page booklet that comes with a clear and concise 210-page manual describing development of visual processes including possible dysfunctions. The description of the test includes the assessment of development of primary involuntary visual patterns such as the pupillary response, Doll's Eye Response, and the eyelid reflexes. The primary voluntary eye movement section describes the assessment of localization, fixation, ocular pursuit, and gaze shift. The test directions are complex and require a thorough knowledge of these visual processes. Most professionals in the area of assessment will need to attend a training workshop before being competent to administer this test.

The test booklet directions allow objects used in the testing to be selected from the local environment. There is potential difficulty in using objects from the local environment rather than from a standardized test kit. For example, one professional's interpretation of "large moving target" defined in the booklet as "bigger than examiner's hand" may be a softball whereas another professional's interpretation may be a beach ball. Again, to be competent to administer this test, the professional must attend a training workshop. The manual also recommends that accurate administration and scoring of the test is facilitated by an assistant or through the use of a video tape recording of the testing session.

The test examines developmental levels from fetal through 6 months of age. However, this test was designed mainly to assess multiply handicapped children. The test can be used to assess visual functioning in an attempt to understand how visual anomalies can affect a child's development of intellectual, academic, and social performance.

The manual does not discuss standardization procedures. The author refers to the test as a nonstandardized assessment tool that examines the "whole" child in terms of the difference between actual developmental levels demonstrated by the subject versus their own potential level of development. Four theoretical models (medical, educational, developmental, and functional) are used as a framework to illustrate an assessment and management process that can facilitate achievement of the potential level of development in an individual student. Concrete examples describe a transdisciplinary management system for multiply handicapped children that enlists the cooperation of a variety of professionals, paraprofessionals, and family members (e.g., therapists, teachers, psychologists, eyecare specialists, and physicians). Examples incorporating visual goals and objectives into the total Individualized Education Plan are discussed. Three thoroughly explained and illustrated case examples are interwoven throughout the test manual.

Evidence for construct validity for the test is provided throughout the manual. However, as the test author candidly admits, further research is needed to provide statistical evidence of construct validity. The test attempts to include all visual behaviors observed in the normal developmental process from fetal through 6 months of age. Therefore, content validity is not an issue. Discriminant validity is not demonstrated in the manual. The test author, again, admits that further research is needed to determine if the test discriminates between groups of children.

I believe the test is entering a new frontier in assessment. Assessing a multiply handicapped (or any handicapped) student by attempting to relate the diagnostic assessment directly to curriculum design and facilitation of the individual child's potential development, rather than just comparing the child's abilities to other children's scores is what assessment should accomplish. Therefore, concurrent validity is not easy to demonstrate. Possible options could have included correlating optometric/ophthalmologic assessments of early childhood visual functioning to this test. Predictive validity is also difficult to demonstrate with this type of test. Therefore, the test reviewer believes the test author described the relevant validation procedures available at the present time. However, further research is needed within this area to determine if assessment of the early motor components of vision can be related to later intellectual, academic, and social development, especially in multiply handicapped individuals.

The test manual section on reliability of the test is weak. The author reported interrater reliability to be 80.9%, defined as the average percent of agreement between the 20 raters attending a 5-day training workshop and the test author. Again, the test author candidly admitted that test-retest reliability studies are needed before the Erhardt Developmental Vision Assessment (EDVA) can be considered reliable.

In summary, the EDVA test manual does not give enough research support to fulfill the requirements of a well-constructed standardized test. However, the EDVA assessment process, with its potential for the development of an effective transdisciplinary management team and useful individualized educational plans is a positive contribution to the field of assessment. Further research on this test and its appropriate uses would yield valuable information for the future use of the test and for the future of other diagnostic tests attempting to break the barriers between assessment and curriculum development.

[144]

Evaluating Movement and Posture Disorganization in Dyspraxic Children.

Purpose: Designed to determine and analyze the normal and disorganized components of movement and posture.
Population: Learning disabled children ages 5 and above.
Publication Date: 1989.
Scores, 2: Total Quality Performance, Total Problem Performance.
Subtests, 10: Supine to Stand, Supine to Flexion Hold, Prone Reach, Alternating Prone Reach, Kneel Walk Forward and Back, Alternating One Foot Kneel, Alternating Half Kneel-Stand, One Foot Balance, Squat Pick-up, Unilateral/Bilateral Toss.
Administration: Individual.
Price Data, 1991: $89 per 5 manuals (52 pages) and analysis of movement and posture disorganization (VHS videotape); $16.95 per 5 manuals.
Time: Administration time not reported.
Comments: "Criteria-referenced" test; full-color videotape (30 minutes) shows examples of normal and disorganized movement responses for each subtest.
Author: W. Michael Magrun.
Publisher: Therapy Skill Builders.

Review of Evaluating Movement and Posture Disorganization in Dyspraxic Children by RANDY W. KAMPHAUS, Associate Professor of Educational Psychology, University of Georgia, Athens, GA:

A few sentences from the preface of the manual sum up well the strengths and weaknesses of the instrument. According to the manual, this is a "criteria-based referenced test for the evaluation of quality movement components and disorganized compensations. The test is designed to be used for evaluating incoordination or dyspraxia in learning disabled children who demonstrate soft neurological signs of motor clumsiness. The test criteria are based on subjective analysis of normal movement and postural components" (p. ii).

The first stated objective to develop a criteria-referenced test of motor movements seems to be the most clearly met of the test development objectives. The authors seemingly expended considerable effort in developing subtests and scoring criteria. The videotape is extremely helpful in this regard allowing examiners to develop a detailed understanding of a child's motor behavior.

The second objective regarding the assessment of dyspraxia in learning-disabled children is not supported by any information in the test manual. The manual does not include any validity evidence demonstrating the ability of this measure to differentiate learning-disabled children from other populations of exceptional children or among subtypes of learning disabilities. Most importantly, epidemiological data on the frequency of motor difficulties among learning disabled children are not presented in the manual. Hence, there is no compelling reason given for why children with learning disabilities should be the intended audience. This statement leads to many questions. Why not use this test with dyspraxic children with other etiologies such as traumatic injuries? According to the *Standards for Educational and Psychological Testing* (AERA, APA, & NCME, 1985), validity evidence should be presented for various interpretations of an assessment device. No validity evidence supporting use of the measure with learning-disabled children is given. This central premise regarding the utility of the measure with learning-disabled children is therefore highly questionable.

A similarly questionable test development practice is the development of test criteria that are based on subjective analysis. Subjective analysis or the use of content experts to define content domains and design item blueprints is a common and wise practice for many test development activities. There is no information in this manual, however, to suggest that any content input was provided by individuals other than the test author. Although the advantages of criteria referencing are extolled in the manual, the specific methods for devising this referencing are not provided. Most importantly, the degree to which the items, subtests, and scoring criteria are supported by experts in the field is not known.

Several aspects of the scale are laudable. The differentiation between level and quality of performance is an important distinction that is often not available in assessment instruments. Although the administration of the scoring instrument at first appears difficult to master, the videotape is extremely helpful. In fact, it is absolutely crucial for proper examiner training.

Although not pretending to be a norm-referenced measure, the instrument should show some evidence of reliability. At the very least, an estimate of interrater or interscorer reliability would be appropriate.

The manual, at times, is difficult to comprehend, and often seems to use "technobabble" that hinders direct communication with the reader. Language in the manual could also be identified as sexist as is indicated in the following quote: "Movement and posture are man's demonstrative tools" (p. 1).

In summary, in many ways the concept of this scale is a good one. One can see how the subtests are designed to assess qualitative aspects of motor behavior. The execution, however, of the test development goals is so suspect as to make the test unusable without some evidence of reliability and validity. The notion that this test is applicable to learning-disabled children above and beyond other populations is not supported in any way in the test manual. This test is in conflict with the *Test Standards* in that sufficient validation is not provided for even the most basic interpretation(s) of the measure. The test cannot be used with confidence until such evidence becomes available.

REVIEWER'S REFERENCE

American Educational Research Association, American Psychological Association, & National Council on Measurement in Education. (1985). *Standards for educational and psychological testing*. Washington, DC: American Psychological Association, Inc.

Review of Evaluating Movement and Posture Disorganization in Dyspraxic Children by BARBARA A. ROTHLISBERG, Associate Professor of Psychology in Educational Psychology and School Psychology I Program Director, Ball State University, Muncie, IN:

Dyspraxia, or impairment in the production of voluntary movement, is a less comprehensive dysfunction than its "parent" disorder, apraxia. The term apraxia evolved from the concept that certain voluntary motor acts had associated with them higher mental functions. Thus, voluntary motor behaviors are the result of a mental representation of the behavior and the consequent observed motor sequence the representation evokes (Luria, 1980). Given the complexity and variety of motor functions, different forms of apraxia have been proposed, ranging from those focusing on gross to fine motor sequences of movement. Typically, evaluations of apraxic behavior concentrate on the individual's ability to reproduce or imitate a series of learned movements of the face and limbs, including gestures and the use of common tools (Lezak, 1983). In situations of equivocal neurological involvement, dyspraxic behavior has been defined by the impairment, but not total loss, of motor fluency.

Evaluating Movement and Posture Disorganization in Dyspraxic Children presents itself as a criteria-based format from which teachers, psychologists, and other health professionals can gather insights into the movement patterns of dyspraxic children (including the learning disabled) and thereby provide a more integrated therapy program. The 10 subtests (e.g., Supine to Stand, Supine to Flexion Hold, etc.), developed based on subjective analysis of motor clumsiness, are designed to provide the observer with the "parameters necessary for skilled performance" (manual, p. 4). Normal 6-year-old children are claimed to be able to easily perform each of the developmental movement sequences. An accompanying videotape (*Analysis of Movement and Posture Disorganization*) offers examples of both skilled and disorganized motor performances.

The administrative procedure for each of the subtests is probably the easiest part of the evaluative process. The clinician or therapist simply demonstrates the motor sequence for the child and then asks the child to imitate the movements. Three attempts may be made by the examinee to determine whether performance improves or declines with practice. The therapist has the option of computing subtest scores based on the average of all trials or of counting only one of the attempts. Given the nature of the subtests (i.e., the analysis of motor sequences), it is suggested in the manual that the child's performance be videotaped for more careful analysis.

To score each subtest, the therapist must evaluate the quality of the child's reproduction based on the subjective evaluation of his/her starting position, movement initiation, transitional phase, and final position. This will be a difficult process for those individuals unfamiliar both with movement disorders and with the terminology common to occupational or physiological therapists (e.g., flexion, hyperextension, anterior, etc.). Movements are to be separated and quantified for each subtest into two lists: quality of performance and problem performance. The checklists consist of sets of movement criteria which the test author suggests are standards of adequate performance. Quality performance criteria are intended to allow the clinician to determine which components of the movement sequence the child has successfully completed. Successes are noted by placing a "Y" (yes) next to the appropriate criterion listed. An "N" (no) indicates that all or some portion of that criterion is immature. If an "N" appears on the quality checklist, the clinician then refers to the problem performance list, where movement components or criterion are further subdivided into subcomponents. The presence of difficulty, as detailed on the problem performance list, suggests what aspect of the given subtest will demand remediation.

Components of movement on the quality performance list are awarded up to one point for successful production; partial credit is awarded if only selected subcomponents have been mastered. For example, on Subtest 1: Supine to Stand, Criterion 6 on the quality performance list is "Are child's arms relaxed and hands open?" If "no" is answered, the therapist refers to the problem performance list which breaks down Criterion 6 into 6a "Are elbows flexed?" and 6b "Are hands fisted?" If the child shows only one of the problems, he/she is awarded ".5" for partial difficulty on the problem list); if both problem criterion are presented, "0" points are awarded on the quality performance list with the "1" point appearing on the problem performance list. Each criterion can have assigned to it a different number of subcomponents and each subcomponent is worth a fraction of one point based on the number of subcomponents present. Likewise, subtests vary in the number of quality performance criteria involved. For instance, Unilateral/Bilateral Ball Toss lists only 3 quality performance criteria whereas Alternating Prone Reach offers 16 criteria. In addition, therapists are encouraged to modify the criteria for the subtests to meet their particular needs. A scoring example for Subtest 1 is given in the manual to help clarify the complicated scoring procedure.

Although the evaluation system supposedly is appropriate for a wide audience, it appeared to this reviewer to be specialized for therapists well versed in movement disorders. The quality and performance lists employ terms that would have little meaning to nonprofessionals. For example, "Does R foot show dorsiflex or toes used for push off?" (Problem list-5e for Subtest 7: Alternating Half Kneel-Stand) or "Does child lean over L and abduct R leg?" (Problem list-5a for Subtest 8: One Foot Balance) obviously include specialized vocabulary. Use of the video to clarify understanding of movement sequences is limited by the marginal quality of the filming and the lack of explanation of scoring procedures.

The intent of the convoluted scoring system is to make it possible for the clinician to obtain a total quality score (TQS)—the sum of all points and partial points earned for performance—and a total problem score (TPS)—the sum of all total and partial points given on the problem performance list. A "percent of disorganization for each subtest" can then be computed by dividing the TPS for each subtest by the maximum possible score (MS) for that subtest. A cumulative percentage of disorganization can also be determined by dividing the cumulative TPS by the cumulative MS. Such a scoring procedure is claimed to offer the clinician a mechanism through which improvements in performance can be documented and reviewed, but may only confuse the teacher or therapist uninitiated to this type of assessment. Even those individuals who may believe they understand the scoring may be at a loss as to the benefits such movement information provides.

Unfortunately, the lack of evident rationale for Evaluating Movement and Posture Disorganization in Dyspraxic Children creates difficulties for the user in his/her attempts to determine if the evaluation system is set on a strong theoretical or experiential base. No background information on the construct of dyspraxia is provided nor is it explained how the 10 subtests were derived as key areas for evaluation and treatment. A brief introductory narrative on the evaluation system makes only oblique references to quality of movement and the "postural control and a delicate balance of dissociated integration" (manual, p. 1) needed for each motor sequence. Although neuropsychology texts may stress the fine motor aspects of apraxia in evaluation of motor skill (see, for example, Lezak, 1983 or Luria, 1980) the subtests included in this measure seemed to focus only upon gross motor incoordination and balance and did not even acknowledge fine motor activities! Thus, the association of dyspraxic behavior to specific learning disabilities was never explored—leaving the reviewer to wonder about the long term utility of such a system.

Without a knowledge base from which to judge the components of the evaluation system, the user must take on faith the claims of the system's author. No norms or references established the claim that average 6-year-olds can complete the motor sequences; no checks on the reliability or the validity for the subtests were offered. In addition, no direction was given to aid in planning any remedial strategy. Given the fact the measure suggests itself as appropriate for and benefiting teachers and psychologists in their understanding of dyspraxic children, such oversights severely curtail the type of information this instrument can provide to someone not specifically trained in the evaluation of movement disorders. Indeed, it is questionable what purpose would be served by using the scoring criteria unless one had an extensive occupational therapy background.

In summary, Evaluating Movement and Posture Disorganization in Dyspraxic Children may be a reasonable scoring system for occupational therapists who are well versed in the terminology and knowledge base of their discipline, but of extremely restricted benefit to teachers, psychologists, and other health care workers who have limited experience with gross motor skill development. Lack of both a conceptual knowledge base and the documented utility of the evaluation criteria make the instrument of questionable value to the clinical community at-large in rehabilitating dyspraxic children.

REVIEWER'S REFERENCES

Luria, A. R. (1980). *Higher cortical functions in man* (2nd ed.). New York: Basic Books.

Lezak, M. D. (1983). *Neuropsychological assessment* (2nd ed.). New York: Oxford University Press.

[145]

Evaluating the Participant's Employability Skills.

Purpose: "To evaluate the participant's overall understanding of the employment process."
Population: Individuals seeking employment.
Publication Dates: 1984–89.
Administration: Group.
Manual: No manual.
Price Data, 1992: $89.99 per Apple or IBM diskette including both pre- and post-tests; $105 per Windows version.
Time: [45–60] minutes.
Author: Education Associates, Inc.
Publisher: Education Associates, Inc.

a) PRE-EVALUATING THE PARTICIPANT'S EMPLOYABILITY SKILLS.
Scores: Total score only.
Price Data: $.79 per pre-test.

b) POST-EVALUATING THE PARTICIPANT'S EMPLOYABILITY SKILLS.
Scores: Total score only.
Price Data: $.79 per post-test.

Review of the Evaluating the Participant's Employability Skills by DEBRA NEUBERT, Associate Professor of Special Education, University of Maryland at College Park, College Park, MD:

Evaluating the Participant's Employability Skills (Pretest and Posttest) reportedly assists in understanding individuals' knowledge of the employment process. Both the pretest and posttest are available in a six-page printed format or on a diskette for use on a computer. Each test consists of three parts: 15 multiple-choice questions, 20 true-and-false questions, and 15 open-ended questions. An answer key is available for each test. There is, however, no manual or information regarding test construction, technical adequacy, readability level, or targeted populations.

Although the administration time for this test is not reported, it could probably be given during a 30–45 minute session provided the participant is able to read and capable of responding to more traditional question-and-answer formats. Because there is no information regarding content specification and sequencing of items, it is difficult to determine if this test does indeed measure knowledge of the employment process. In my view, there is too much variability in content difficulty of the items (e.g., "in order to keep your job, you should try to become chummy with the boss" to "what is the difference between required deductions and optional deductions?"). Before administration of this test, it would seem important to record an individual's previous work history and achievement skills; this information would definitely impact on a participant's ability to answer the questions. In addition, the correct responses listed on the answer key to some items are debatable and again, could vary depending on a participant's previous work history and cultural background.

The only directions for scoring include a statement at the beginning of each section of the test concerning the number of points for true-false answers, multiple-choice answers, and open-ended questions. Based on a possible score of 100 points, the examiner enters the participant's total score on the first page of the test and then compares it to four "Recommended Grading Levels" to determine knowledge of the employment process. Participants scoring 90–100 points are reported to have a thorough knowledge of how to get and keep a job, 80–89 points indicates a basic understanding of how to get and keep a job, 70–79 points indicates additional training is needed, and individuals scoring below 70 points are targeted as needing intensive training. Recommendations concerning the type of intervention program or strategies that might assist a participant who scores below 79 are not included. Most importantly, information concerning the equivalency of the Employability Skills Pretest and Posttest is not available. Without information regarding the reliability of the two tests, it would be difficult to assess if a change in pre- and posttest scores was due to the effectiveness of an intervention or to the difference in the tests.

If the computer version of this test is used, the participant is informed if their response is correct after each true-false and multiple-choice question. At the end of each of these sections, the total of correct responses is displayed. To complete the open-ended section of the test, the participant is instructed to print out the test questions and write out the answers. This part of the test is then scored by the administrator with the answer key.

Given this test was copyrighted in 1984 and there is no information regarding the development of the test, the technical adequacy of the test, or field test studies, this reviewer cannot recommend use of the Employability Skills Pre- and Posttest.

Review of the Evaluating the Participant's Employability Skills by LELAND C. ZLOMKE, Director of Clinical Psychology, and SUSAN F. ADAMS, Intensive Treatment Service Unit Manager, Beatrice State Developmental Center, Beatrice, NE:

The Evaluating the Participant's Employability Skills (EPES) package, according to the author, was developed to assist in the evaluation of individual participant knowledge of the employment process and need for further training. The EPES comprises a pre- and posttest, both of which require participants to answer multiple-choice, true-false, and short answer questions regarding the process of acquiring and maintaining employment (e.g., resumé development, interview skills, job search techniques). It is assumed, because no administration manual is provided, there is a training intervention designed to improve identified employability skills. Apparently the training is delivered to participants between the pre- and posttest. The EPES attempts to provide a general raw score or "grading level" to evaluate individual participant's "knowledge of how to get and keep a job" (Pretest, p. 1).

GENERAL DESCRIPTION. The evaluation package contains two options for testing. The first option includes hard copy, paper-and-pencil protocols, and answer keys for both the pre- and posttests. A second option is provided for computer-assisted testing. For this option two 3.5-inch diskettes are provided along with basic instructions for initiating the program on personal computers. The computer-assisted testing and scoring is a nice option and is one of the few strengths of these instruments.

The tests apparently are to be administered individually within a group setting using either the paper-and-pencil protocols or via the personal computer presented format. Administration time is not specified. Scoring is completed for the multiple-choice and true-false questions through the computer program or by following the provided hand-scoring keys. The short answer questions are hand scored awarding points according to global descriptions of expected content for each question. General content expected for each of the short answer questions is globally provided in the scoring keys. The total raw score is obtained by summing the multiple-choice, true/false, and short answer points. This total raw score is then compared to a recommended grading scale. This scale divides scores into four levels proceeding through "intensive training needed, additional training needed, basic understanding of how to get and keep a job, and through [*sic*; thorough] knowledge of how to get and keep a job" (Pretest, p. 3). The procedures used to develop the cutoff scores between levels are not reported.

TECHNICAL ADEQUACY. The EPES provides no development or administration manual. Thus, information regarding these tests' normative data, standardized administration procedures, test development, and psychometric properties is not available. In view of the lack of any psychometric data, a review of these tests as criterion-referenced instruments was attempted. According to Hambleton and Eignor (1978), in order for any criterion-referenced test to be useful several major pieces of information must be present. This information includes: purpose, population, and rationale for the test; test item generation and selection data; test administration information; psychometric details regarding validity and reliability; cutoff score development; test score interpretation guidelines; and options for reporting test score information. None of the above information is available in the EPES package. In addition to the total lack of adequate test development procedures for the EPES, there is no reported attention to the examination of the equivalency of the pre- and posttests. Indeed upon review the pre- and posttests do not consistently measure similar information.

SUMMARY. The EPES pre- and posttests are poor instruments. The instruments violate nearly every accepted standard for test construction. Unless the authors provide a manual specifying essential information as required in the *Standards for Educational and Psychological Testing* (AERA, APA, & NCME, 1985), the consumer is advised to choose alternative means to assess employability skills. Information generated by the EPES should be used as purely anecdotal. These instruments are at best based on some specific employability training curriculum and meant to measure the participant's learning through their exposure to the presentation of the curriculum. Unfortunately, the EPES pre- and posttests are not constructed well enough to serve as a valid indicator of learning even for that purpose. Based upon an informal survey of professionals in the job training area no instruments are currently being used to assess the type of information examined by the EPES. If no instruments are indeed available assessing employability skills the EPES may be a very small first step. However, the EPES cannot be recommended for use beyond the collection of anecdotal information.

REVIEWER'S REFERFENCES

Hambleton, R. K., & Eignor, D. R. (1976). Guidelines for evaluating criterion-referenced tests and test manuals. *Journal of Educational Measurement, 15*, 321-327.

American Educational Research Association, American Psychological Association, & National Council on Measurement in Education. (1985). *Standards for educational and psychological testing*. Washington, DC: American Psychological Association, Inc.

[146]

Executive Profile Survey.

Purpose: Constructed to assess "self-attitudes, self-beliefs, and value patterns" needed for executive-level jobs.
Population: Prospective executives.
Publication Dates: 1947–83.
Scores: 11 dimensions: Ambitious, Assertive, Enthusiastic, Creative, Spontaneous, Self-Focused, Considerate, Open-Minded, Relaxed, Practical, Systematic.
Administration: Group or individual.
Price Data, 1992: $20 per 25 reusable test booklets; $12.50 per manual ('83, 82 pages); $24.60 per introductory kit.
Time: (60) minutes.
Comments: Self-administered; manual title is Perspectives on the Executive Personality.
Authors: Virgil R. Lang and Samuel E. Krug (manual).
Publisher: Institute for Personality and Ability Testing, Inc.
Cross References: For a review by William I. Sauser, Jr., see 9:401.

Review of the Executive Profile Survey by S. DAVID KRISKA, Personnel Psychologist, City of Columbus, Columbus, OH:

The Executive Profile Survey (EPS) measures 11 dimensions related to the occupational self-concept of top-level executives. The EPS is theoretically based on David Riesman's (*The Lonely Crowd*) inner/other-directed orientations, Erich Fromm's (*Man for Himself*) descriptions of marketing, hoarding, receptive, and exploitive orientations, and Charles Morris's (*Varieties of Human Values*) identification of 13 distinctive life styles.

The 11 profile dimensions on which the EPS is scored are entitled: Ambitious, Assertive, Enthusiastic, Creative, Spontaneous, Self-Focused, Considerate, Open-Minded, Relaxed, Practical, and Systematic. In addition, there are two validity scales to identify faking good and responding randomly. The 94 items on the EPS are usually answered within a hour and with minimal supervision.

The first section includes 13 paragraphs test takers must read and judge whether they like or dislike the lifestyle described in the passage. The second section includes 33 statements and test takers decide how well each describes themselves. The last section includes 48 adjectives test takers judge as either true or false about themselves.

The response forms are scored by the publisher and the results report, including percentile scores and descriptions of high scores for each dimension, is quickly returned to the user. The user must establish his or her credentials with IPAT (the publisher) prior to obtaining the EPS. The development of the EPS spanned more than 10 years and included the testing of approximately 2,000 executives from a variety of businesses. The current form was published in 1978.

Factor analytic results support the development of the 11 dimensions and provide construct validity evidence. A comparison involving the 1,768 executives surveyed in 1966 and again in 1972 resulted in factor congruence statistics ranging from .61 to .88. The users' manual also includes scale reliabilities that range from .81 to .90. The validity evidence presented in the users' manual also includes several pages of correlations with scales of the 16PF, California Psychological Inventory (CPI), Edwards Personal Preference Schedule, and the Adjective Checklist. In general, the correlations are as expected in terms of signs of correlations, pattern of significant correlations, and magnitude of correlations. Many of the correlations between scales of the EPS and scales of other instruments are greater than .40 and range up to .71 for the EPS Systematic dimension with the Self-Description Inventory Orderly dimension. Further validity evidence is provided by a multiple discriminant function analysis of almost 2,000 executives. This analysis shows that the EPS differentiated executives from 29 different occupations. For example, an executive from a giant advertising agency has a profile different from that of a president of a large bank. The users' manual also includes correlations of EPS scales with job performance of bank presidents. The performance indicators include measures of responsibility, income, and tenure. All of the EPS scales, except the Relaxed dimension, correlate significantly with at least one of the performance indicators.

The data base for the EPS is based on 1,992 male executives surveyed between 1966 and 1976. The sampling plan itself was carefully executed and includes individuals from all 50 states. Although carefully conducted, the sampling is cause for concern. The data base for score reporting norms includes information that is over 20 years old, and is lacking in race and sex information. A user concerned about glass ceilings needs to obtain more information about this instrument than is contained in the manual. Moreover, because only executives are included in the sample, evidence of how well the EPS distinguishes executives from other professionals is lacking. The manual does include results showing executives respond differently than college students, but the obvious confounding with age makes these results less useful than a comparison of similarly aged people.

In summary, the EPS is a useful instrument for examining an individual's personality. The construct validity evidence regarding the 11 dimensions is sound. However, although the EPS promotional literature claims it can be used to select an individual with executive abilities, the users' manual does not present the results to support the claim.

Review of the Executive Profile Survey by GREGORY J. MARCHANT, Associate Professor of Educational Psychology, Ball State University, Muncie, IN:

The Executive Profile Survey is a well-developed instrument designed to yield scores on 11 dimensions relative to successful executives. The instrument is composed of three parts. The first part contains 13 short paragraphs describing life styles, which the respondent must rate on a 1 to 7 scale of desirability. The second part of the instrument requires basically a yes, no, or uncertain response to 33 statements. In the third part, the respondent must decide how applicable 48 adjectives are on a 7-point scale. The 94-item questionnaire usually takes less than one hour to complete, and the results are computer scored and a computer-generated report is processed by the company.

The social psychological basis for the instrument rests in the 1950s. The original 69-item questionnaire was designed and pilot tested in 1961, and in 1966 the responses from 666 executives were factor analyzed. Eleven of the 17 factors produced by the 1966 study and a 1972 analysis demonstrated clear matches and were used as dimensions. The dimensions for the instrument are factor scores obtained by multiplying each item by its factor weight for each factor. For the latest version of the instrument (1983) the names of the 11 dimensions were changed from the 1978 version, but the scales and their scoring remain the same. The 11 dimensions are: Ambitious, Assertive, Enthusiastic, Creative, Spontaneous, Self-Focused, Considerate, Open-Minded, Relaxed, Practical, and Systematic. The dimensions have demonstrated good reliability (consistency estimates >.81).

A major study using the instrument was conducted in 1972. This study included Fortune 500 chief executive officers (n = 90), newspaper editors (n = 145), executives with a Harvard MBA (n = 114), college and university presidents (n = 173), and business school deans (n = 42). Some small studies were conducted between 1972 and 1974, and the instrument was revised again for a study conducted in 1978. For the 1978 study, 25 items were added to provide two validity and verification scales. A computer program was created to conduct a sophisticated analysis of each individual's responses relative to the 2,000 executives accumulated in the data base. The validity scales allow for a test of faking perceived good characteristics and the computer analysis adjusts for this.

Some validity estimates such as correlations with other instruments are presented in the manual; however, the ultimate validity of the instrument would rest in its ability to discern the characteristics of successful executives from unsuccessful ones or even from a nonexecutive sample. Although some relations between the dimensions and income and number of exployees were reported, no study using the instrument was identified in the manual or by a computer literature search that clearly distinguished "successful" executives.

The way in which the respondents' results are interpreted are unclear and problematic. The respondent's raw score on each dimension is converted to a percentile rank based on the total executive sample. For example, an individual could score at the 69th percentile on the Considerate dimension. The score is above "average," but is it high enough or too high? The computer report would probably describe the individual as "high" on the dimension, but how high is too high? Can an executive be too considerate? (See Kaplan, 1990 for a discussion of taking ambition to extremes to the point of being counterproductive.) One would need to consult the manual for assistance. There one could find tables of information for comparison based on subsamples. For instance, based on the 1966 data from presidents of banks with deposits between $100,000,000 and $500,000,000 the respondent would be too considerate compared to the 26th percentile rank of the sample (n = 129). However, the individual would be just considerate enough based on the 1972 data from presidents of banks with deposits between $9,000,000 and $10,000,000 ($n$ = 129). Percentile ranks on dimensions changed by as much as 25 from the 1966 data to the 1972 data for the same sample category. This suggests that interpretation of an individual's score represents an effort to hit a moving target based on occupational setting, company, sex, time, and perhaps many other variables.

The change in the previously mentioned scores points to another problem in using the current version of the instrument. If a percentile rank on a dimension can change by as much as 25 over a 6-year period, what could have happened after more than 20 years? Ross and Unwalla (1988) found that characteristics associated with upward mobility have changed in recent years based on a comparison of 1952 and 1982 survey data on corporate executives. It is quite likely that the characteristics of successful executives have changed over the last 20 years and this change has not been reflected in the instrument.

In summary, the personality of an executive can play a major role in the success or failure of a business (McCarthy, 1992). The Executive Profile Survey is a well-documented instrument designed to assess characteristics of executives along 11 dimensions. However, the instrument uses constructs established over 20 years ago and compares individuals to a sample of successful executives most of whom were surveyed over 20 years ago. There appear to be many variables influencing the desirability of a particular score on a dimension such that it would be difficult to make personnel judgements based on the information from the instrument. Further research using the instrument on an updated data set is recommended.

REVIEWER'S REFERENCES

Ross, J. E., & Unwalla, D. (1988). Making it to the top: A 30-year perspective. *Personnel*, *65*(4), 70-78.

Kaplan, R. E. (1990). The expansive executive: How the drive to mastery helps and hinders organizations. *Human Resource Management*, *29*(3), 307-326.

McCarthy, J. L. (1992, January). Special skills needed to spearhead a turnaround. *American Banker*, *157*(11), 6.

[147]

Expressive One-Word Picture Vocabulary Test, Revised.

Purpose: To obtain an estimate of a child's verbal intelligence.
Population: Ages 2–12, 12–16.
Publication Dates: 1979–90.
Acronym: EOWPVT.
Scores: Total score only.
Levels, 2: [Lower Level], Upper-Extension.
Price Data, 1994: $10 per 25 remedial checklists.
Time: (10–15) minutes per level.
Comments: Spanish form available.
Author: Morrison F. Gardner.
Publisher: Academic Therapy Publications.

a) [LOWER LEVEL].
Population: Ages 2–12.
Publication Dates: 1979–90.
Administration: Individual.
Price Data: $75 per test kit including test plates, 25 English record forms, and manual ('90, 88 pages); $20 per 25 English record forms; $10 per 25 Spanish record forms; $35 per test plates; $17 per manual; $17 per specimen set including manual and sample form.

b) UPPER-EXTENSION.
Population: Ages 12–16.
Publication Date: 1983.
Administration: Individual and group.
Price Data: $68 per test kit including test plates, 50 English record forms, and manual (39 pages); $20 per 50 English record forms; $10 per 25 Spanish record forms; $10 per 50 group administration forms; $30 per test plates; $15 per manual; $15 per specimen set including manual and sample form.

Cross References: See T4:946 (23 references); for reviews by Jack A. Cummings and Gilbert M. Spivack of the Lower Level, see 9:403 (2 references).

TEST REFERENCES

1. Tompkins, C. A., Holland, A. L., Ratcliff, G., Costello, A., Leahy, L. F., & Cowell, V. (1990). Predicting cognitive recovery from closed head-injury in children and adolescents. *Brain and Cognition*, *13*, 86-97.

2. Alessandri, S. M. (1991). Play and social behavior in maltreated preschoolers. *Development and Psychopathology*, *3*, 191-205.

3. Brown, R. T., Buchanan, I., Doepke, K., Eckman, J. R., Baldwin, K., Goonan, B., & Schoenherr, S. (1993). Cognitive and academic functioning in children with sickle-cell disease. *Journal of Clinical Child Psychology*, *22*, 207-218.

4. Arnold, D. H., Lonigan, C. J., Whitehurst, G. J., & Epstein, J. N. (1994). Accelerating language development through picture book reading: Replication and extension to a videotape training format. *Journal of Educational Psychology*, *86*, 235-243.

5. Vázquez, C. A. (1994). Brief report: A multitask controlled evaluation of facilitated communication. *Journal of Autism and Developmental Disorders*, *24*, 369-379.

6. Whitehurst, G. J., Epstein, J. N., Angell, A. L., Payne, A. C., Crone, D. A., & Fisher, J. E. (1994). Outcomes of an emergent literacy intervention in head start. *Journal of Educational Psychology*, *86*, 542-555.

Review of the Expressive One-Word Picture Vocabulary Test, Revised by GREGORY J. CIZEK, Associate Professor of Educational Research and Measurement, University of Toledo, Toledo, OH:

The Expressive One-Word Picture Vocabulary Test, Revised (EOWPVT-R) is an updated version of the EOWPVT (Gardner, 1979) and is intended for use with children of age 2 to 12 years. An "Upper Extension" of the original EOWPVT is available for assessing the expressive vocabulary of children of ages 12 to 16 years and a booklet of *Remedial Activities to Enhance Expressive and Receptive Vocabulary* (Gardner, 1989) is available to assist in planning interventions for children with weakness in these areas. For this review, only the EOWPVT-R was evaluated.

PURPOSE. The EOWPVT-R maintains the same purpose as the original which, according to the manual, is "to obtain a basal estimate of a child's verbal intelligence" (manual, p. 1). It is also stated that the test provides valuable information about speech defects, learning disorders, bilingual fluency in English, auditory processing, and auditory-visual-verbal association ability. However, the test appears to best serve the purpose of measuring expressive vocabulary. No information is provided to substantiate the claim that the test measures the more global construct of verbal intelligence, or to support inferences about speech defects, learning disorders, etc. In fact, one substantial weakness of the EOWPVT-R is the skimpy and dated information on the theoretical grounding of the instrument—shortcomings that were identified in reviews of the previous version (see Altepeter, 1983).

ADMINISTRATION AND FORMAT. The manual indicates that the EOWPVT-R can be administered by a wide variety of personnel, including "physicians, psychologists, teachers, counselors, social workers, learning specialists, speech therapists, optometrists, principals and other professionals" (p. 14). However, the manual suggests that it would be advisable—and, I think, necessary—for examiners to have some training in the administration and interpretation of educational and psychological tests.

Administration instructions begin with a description of the importance of conducive testing conditions and examiner rapport with the examinee. The test itself consists of 100 black-and-white line drawings of common objects or collections of objects. To administer the test, the examiner presents pictures one at a time to an individual child who is told by the examiner: "I want you to look at some pictures and I want you to tell me the name of each picture or pictures." Four practice pictures are provided with the EOWPVT-R to familiarize the child with the task.

The manual cautions that testing should be terminated for children "who do not really understand the reason for the testing" (p.11). It seems likely that complete understanding of the task could be a common problem for younger children taking the EOWPVT-R. In a trial administration of the test to a 5-year-old child, I found the directions were somewhat misleading and adversely affected the child's performance, because the task changes for some of the prompts and the nature of the change is not highlighted to examinees.

Specifically, most of the prompts contain a picture of a single object. Having been shown these pictures the student learns that the task is to name the object shown in the prompt. However, because some of the prompts contain a collection of objects, the directions to "tell me the name of the picture or pictures" can induce the child to name each pictured object, rather than providing the correct response which is a generalized category name to which the objects belong (e.g., the correct response for the prompt showing an ant, bee, grasshopper, and beetle is "bugs" or "insects"). In other cases the salient aspect of the prompt is difficult to discern. For example, in one prompt the only difference between the correct response, "smoke," and the incorrect response, "chimney," is that the drawing portrays the smoke as darker than the chimney from which it is rising.

The test is begun by administering one of the pictures corresponding to the child's chronological age. If an error is made identifying the picture, the examiner selects pictures at a lower chronological age until the child responds correctly to eight consecutive prompts; this point is termed the child's "basal level." The examiner then continues showing more advanced prompts until the child makes six consecutive incorrect responses; a point called the child's "ceiling level." The manual indicates that the test is not speeded and that examinees should be allowed enough time to formulate a response to each prompt; testing time should be adapted to the age of the child, with more time allowed for younger students than for older students who tend to respond more quickly.

All responses are recorded by the examiner on an easy-to-use response sheet. Directions for marking responses are clear, and admissible correct answers are listed for each picture. However, admissible correct responses seem limited; for example, "PC" is unacceptable as a response to the picture of a computer. For some children, the inadmissibility of certain synonyms or slang expressions could serve to attenuate the accuracy of intended inferences.

SCORING AND REPORTING. A child's raw score is computed by summing all correct responses below the ceiling level. All items below the basal level are counted as correct responses. Raw scores can be converted to Age Equivalent Scores, Standard Scores, Scaled Scores, Percentiles, and Stanines, using tables provided in the manual. Test users are provided with accurate descriptions of these scores and assistance in interpreting them.

REVISIONS. Many of the revisions to the original Expressive One-Word Picture Vocabulary Test were undertaken to address format problems and outdated picture prompts. For example, in the EOWPVT-R pictures are presented one per page in a larger format, with tinting on the reverse side of each plate to improve visibility. Further, outdated pictures have been deleted, replaced, or revised.

NORMING. The norms for the EOWPVT-R have also been revised. A sample of 1,118 children ages 2 years to 11 years 11 months was selected from children residing in the San Francisco Bay area. The sample consisted of 49% males and 51% females and the number of male and female children at each age range (e.g., 2 years to 2 years 11 months) is provided. The manual indicates that the sample included children from parochial schools, private schools, public schools, and nursery schools. Very young children were tested in a home or office setting.

Unfortunately, other critical information about the norming sample is omitted from the manual. For example, numbers of children from each educational setting are not provided, nor is information on indicators of socioeconomic status or ethnicity. Accordingly, users of the EOWPVT-R cannot be confident that the reported norms are necessarily relevant.

RELIABILITY. Indices of internal consistency (KR-20) and standard errors of measurement are reported for each age level tested and succinct explanations of the meanings of these indices are provided. Reliability estimates are high for a test of this length, ranging from .84 to .92, with a median coefficient of .90. Unfortunately, the internal consistency estimates are the only reliability evidence provided. An estimate of score stability (i.e., test-retest reliability) seems to be of greater interest to users of this test.

VALIDITY. Some useful information is provided about the validity of inferences based upon a child's score on the EOWPVT-R. For example, a section on content validity indicates that items in the EOWPVT-R "were selected to represent a common core of English words" (p. 27). However, it is also noted that the core vocabulary was restricted to single words "which could be illustrated without ambiguity" (p. 27), resulting in an unknown influence on the content validity of the test.

A section on criterion-related validity provides correlations between the EOWPVT-R and other tests of vocabulary, perceptual skills, and general ability. Generally, the correlations are moderate; as would be expected, they are higher between the EOWPVT-R and other tests of expressive and receptive vocabulary, and lower between the EOWPVT-R and more dissimilar constructs. Also, as one would expect, scores on the EOWPVT-R are highly related to both age and grade, and unrelated to gender. However, the EOWPVT-R correlates more strongly with a test of general cognitive ability (r = .69 with the Wechsler Preschool and Primary Scale of Intelligence—Revised, Wechsler, 1989) than with other measures of expressive or receptive vocabulary.

RECOMMENDATIONS AND CAUTIONS. Overall, the changes made to the EOWPVT-R maintain the usefulness of the test as a quick assessment of a child's receptive vocabulary that is easy to administer and score. Some information about the reliability, validity, and norming sample is provided in the manual, though not enough to meet the legitimate expectations of concerned test users.

Major problems identified in previous *Mental Measurements Yearbook* reviews of the test persist (see Cummings, 1985). For example, although the test is intended as a measure of expressive vocabulary, little construct validity evidence is provided; the test's theoretical grounding is still weak. None of the several independent studies of the EOWPVT are cited or reviewed. No evidence is provided to differentiate between the use of the test to measure expressive vocabulary and verbal intelligence, the latter representing a substantially more complex construct.

No information is provided in the manual to document any judgmental or statistical investigations of potential differential item functioning. As noted earlier, the norming study sampled only children from the San Francisco Bay area. Although the test is claimed to be suitable for Spanish-speaking children, no validity evidence is provided for this use; the manual cautions that scoring responses on the Spanish version is necessarily subjective. Information on the stability of the EOWPVT-R scores is lacking.

Overall, the EOWPVT-R represents an improvement over the previous version in terms of the quality and currency of the illustrations and in ease of administration. The revision does not, however, represent a substantial improvement in psychometric propriety. The EOWPVT-R is best suited for use as a brief screening measure of a child's expressive vocabulary. It should not be used solely as an assessment of general verbal intelligence. The conclusion of an earlier review of the EOWPVT that "the technical superiority of the Peabody Picture Vocabulary Test—Revised is overshadowing" (Cummings, 1985, p. 566) still seems appropriate.

REVIEWER'S REFERENCES

Gardner, M. F. (1979). *Expressive One-Word Picture Vocabulary Test: Manual and form.* Novato, CA: Academic Therapy Publications.

Altepeter, T. (1983). A discussion of the Expressive One-Word Picture Vocabulary Test. *School Psychology Review, 12*(1), 106-109.

Cummings, J. A. (1985). [Review of the Expressive One-Word Picture Vocabulary Test.] In J. V. Mitchell, Jr. (Ed.), *The ninth mental measurements yearbook* (pp. 564-566). Lincoln, NE: Buros Institute of Mental Measurements.

Gardner, M. F. (1989). *Remedial activities to enhance expressive and receptive activities: Booklet of general information and remedial activities.* San Francisco: Health Publishing.

Wechsler, D. (1989). Wechsler Preschool and Primary Scale of Intelligence—Revised. San Antonio, TX: The Psychological Corporation.

Review of the Expressive One-Word Picture Vocabulary Test, Revised by LARRY B. GRANTHAM, Associate Professor of Counselor Education, Western Carolina University, Cullowhee, NC:

The Expressive One-Word Picture Vocabulary Test, Revised (EOWPVT-R) was published in 1990 to replace the original version which first appeared in 1979. The purpose of the EOWPVT-R is unchanged from that of the original edition, "to obtain a basal estimate of a child's verbal intelligence by means of a child's acquired one-word expressive picture vocabulary" (manual, p. 1). The author indicates the test is also valuable in providing information about speech defects, possible learning disorders, a bilingual child's fluency in English, auditory processing, and auditory-visual-verbal association ability.

As with the first edition, the EOWPVT-R claims to be useful in determining "readiness for kindergarten, for grouping children in nursery school programs, and as an excellent instrument for pediatricians to use to determine a young child's expressive language functioning based on formal testing" (manual, p. 2). The revised edition offers quick scoring and easy use by teachers, principals, optometrists, physicians, speech therapists, psychologists, social workers, learning specialists, and counselors; is designed for children ages 2 to 12 years; and is offered in both English and Spanish.

Changes in the revised edition include new standardizations and norms, a reduction in the number of plates (from 110 to 100) and an enlargement of the plate size to 7 inches x 8.25 inches. Pictures on the reverse side of the plates have been eliminated. The plates have been revised to "1) update some of the pictures, 2) delete some of the pictures, 3) replace some of the pictures with other similar pictures within the same category, 4) attain more likeness to the pictures of the objects, things, and persons, and 5) maintain greater proportion of the pictures of objects, things, and persons" (p. 16).

The individual score form format has been changed in size to 8.5 inches x 11 inches, and the number of forms in English is now 50 per package instead of 25. The Spanish score forms continue to be available at 25 per package. New items have been included and older, dated items have been deleted. An item analysis has been calculated along with new norms and standardization. The larger plate size is certainly an improvement over the first edition, although picture quality could still be improved on some of the plates.

The revised form was administered to 1,118 children ages 2 to 12 years of age in the San Francisco, California area. Included in the revision were all the 110 items of the original Expressive One-Word Picture Vocabulary Test (1979) and an additional 33 new items. In an attempt to be culture fair the author made every effort "to avoid using words and pictures that could have a cultural, racial or sex bias, or which would contain acronyms or bilingual idiosyncrasies" (p. 8). The attempt was also made "to include words that were, for the most part, common to all geographic areas of the United States and, to some extent, to other countries, as well as words common to various occupations with which a child would be familiar" (p. 8). There is no explanation in the test manual as to how this was accomplished so the user has to accept the author's statement that it was done. The revision was standardized on a sample in a limited geographic area, which seems to contradict the effort to use words common to all geographic areas of the U.S.

The norms of the EOWPVT-R have been revised to include Age Equivalents, Standard Scores, Scaled Scores, Percentiles, and Stanines. Language standard score intervals have been reduced from 6 months to 2 months between chronological age groups. Administration time of the test can vary from 7 minutes for young children to 15 minutes for children who are older and who respond to all the test items. Directions for administering this power test are clear for persons who have some previous experience or training in formal appraisal. This reviewer would prefer more specific directions including seating arrangement and the method of presentation of the plates to go along with the examiner's statements in the general directions. Standardizing the administration of the test would eliminate ambiguities in scoring and strengthen validity and reliability.

To begin the test, the examiner determines the child's chronological age and locates the appropriate beginning plate number from a table in the manual. The child is required to give a one-word response to each item presented. A basal is determined when the child gives eight consecutive correct responses, and the ceiling is established with six consecutive incorrect responses. Scoring is easily accomplished by determining the raw score in the individual score form and using the tables in the manual to determine the derived scores. Reliability is estimated by using the Kuder-Richardson formula (KR-20) for each 1-year age level from age 2-0 to age 11-11. The range of reliability coefficients is from .84 to .92 with a median of .90. This range of values would seem to indicate adequate reliability for the test; however, there appears to be a need for additional support for reliability such as test-retest information. This would certainly strengthen the author's claims of the accuracy of the test. Content validity evidence was collected as the EOWPVT-R was developed. The final form includes items which "represent a common core of English words which could be illustrated without ambiguity" (p. 27). Criterion validity evidence is presented through the correlations of EOWPVT-R scaled scores with the subtests and full scale of the Wechsler Preschool and primary Scale of Intelligence—Revised (WPPSI-R; .36 to .69 for children ages 4 and 5), the WPPSI-R vocabulary subtest (.48 for children ages 5 and 6), the Peabody Picture Vocabulary Test—Revised (PPVT-R) involving children in all the ranges (.59), the Detroit Test of Learning Abilities (DTLA) subtest on Word Opposites (.49), the Test of Auditory-Perceptual Skills (TAPS) with five subtests administered to children ages 4 and 5 years (range from .19 to .52), as well as the Receptive One-Word Picture Vocabulary Test (.61).

In summary, the EOWPVT-R appears to be strengthened as a screening instrument for expressive vocabulary with the additional criterion-related studies presented in the manual. There continues to be a need for more norming studies from wider geographical areas. This weakness along with the obvious strengths of some of the more established tests such as the PPVT-R suggests that the EOWPVT-R would not be a first choice for everyday use.

[148]

The Extended Merrill-Palmer Scale.

Purpose: Assesses the content, semantic or figural, and process, production or evaluation, of thinking in young children.

Population: Ages 3–5.

Publication Date: 1978.
Scores: 4 Dimensions: Semantic Production, Figural Production, Semantic Evaluation, Figural Evaluation.
Administration: Individual.
Price Data, 1994: $500 per complete kit; $25 per 50 scoring forms (ages 36–47 mo., 48–59 mo., or 60–71 mo.); $45 per manual (142 pages); $75 per 50 task record forms.
Time: (45) minutes.
Comments: The Extended Merrill-Palmer Scale may be used either independently of, or in conjunction with the original Merrill-Palmer Scale (T4:1614).
Authors: Rachael Stutsman Ball, Philip Merrifield, and Leland H. Stott.
Publisher: Stoelting Co.

Review of The Extended Merrill-Palmer Scale by SCOTT W. BROWN, Professor of Educational Psychology, University of Connecticut, Storrs, CT:

The Extended Merrill-Palmer Scale consists of 16 separate tasks each designed to measure one of four separate dimensions of intelligence in children ages 3 through 5 years, and is a significant revision from the 1931 Merrill-Palmer Scale of Mental Tests. The Extended version is based on Guilford's (1967) model of intelligence and is designed to yield four separate measures rather than a composite intelligence score. The four measures represent four distinct types of thinking across two different dimensions: content or mode, and process or operation. The four scales are Semantic Production, Figural Production, Semantic Evaluation, and Figural Evaluation.

The Extended Merrill-Palmer Scale contains a different configuration of tasks than the earlier version of the scale. Through the process of factor analyses, the field testing of new tasks and further examination of several of the original tasks, the Extended Scale consists of 16 separate tasks. Each dimension is measured by four separate tasks.

Semantic Production is measured by Actions, Agents, Food Naming, and Round Things. These tasks require the child to use language or other familiar ways of communicating to produce a variety of responses to verbal prompts. A certain level of knowledge is assumed regarding common objects and ideas, which appear age appropriate. The score is influenced by the number and quality of the responses to the prompts.

Figural Production is measured by Ambiguous Forms, Block Sorting, Dot Joining, and Design Production. These tasks require the child to manipulate a pencil, a crayon, sets of blocks, or cards in response to verbal and visual prompts. This score is influenced by the child's perceptual skills.

Semantic Evaluation is measured by Pie Completion, Directions, Word Meaning, and Stick Manipulation. The child is required to use language or other means of communication to make judgments regarding actions, statements, or configurations. The authors are aware these tests appear to be strongly influenced by spatial ability because of the use of terms such as "behind" or "under," but argue that such terms provide semantic content and therefore, are semantic in nature. This score appears to be influenced by both semantic abilities, judgment and decision making, and to some extent perceptual organization skills.

Figural Evaluation is measured by Copying, Little Pink Tower, Three-Cube Pyramid, and Six-Cube Pyramid. The scale requires the child to use a writing instrument or manipulate objects in response to instructions concerning relative spatial relations. The goal is for the child to match a specific spatial arrangement. These tests appears to be influenced by the child's perceptual skills and psychomotor abilities.

Actual scoring of the responses of the children during testing appears clear. The manual provided several samples of the scoring system with suggestions for determining the quality of the child's response. Scores of the Extended Scale are in the form of percentiles and stanines for each individual dimension. No standard scores on an interval scale are provided. A rationale is provided for the use of weights for the scale scores. These weights adjust the raw scores of each scale to be of the same range, minimizing the impact of varying numbers of items and scoring mechanisms within and across scales.

The norms of the scale were developed based on the responses of 1,124 children aged 3 to 5 years with approximately 200 each for each 6-month interval. Although tables are provided in the manual detailing the results of the responses by the normative sample, no detail beyond gender and age is provided about the sample. Normative tables are provided in 6-month intervals portraying intercorrelations among the scales and the percentile conversions.

The scale's validity was determined based on the factor loadings for the unweighted normalized scale scores. The authors interpreted the average task-scale correlation as a coefficient relevant to construct validity. Coefficients ranging from .57 to .67 are reported for intercorrelations across the different age groups, providing support for the validity of the individual scales. The structure of the four scales was established through factor analysis. Although the authors acknowledge the results of the intercorrelations among the separate scales were too large to indicate statistical independence, they do argue that the four separate scales should be used independently and that the factor analysis results support the contention of construct validity.

The reliability estimates are based on the Spearman-Brown Prophecy formula for each of the 6-month age groups. The reliability estimates ranged between .54 and .81. Although the lower bound of this range is unacceptable, the majority of the reliability estimates were approximately .75. No test-retest estimates were reported in the manual.

The manual is complete and detailed in the description of the development of the Extended Scale, the technical aspects, the scoring system, and numerous sample profiles and case studies to assist the test administrator in the interpretation of the child's responses. The manual was published in 1978 and contains few references of research results employing the Extended Scale.

The Extended Merrill-Palmer Scale is an improvement over the earlier version providing detailed assessments of four separate dimensions of children's thinking. The scale requires approximately 45 minutes to administer, is easy to administer and score, appears sufficiently engaging to hold the attention of young children, and has a strong theoretical foundation. It has the potential for providing important information about a child's thinking but it has an extremely limited age range, does not make accommodations for children with handicaps, and provides only stanines and percentiles, rather than a standard interval score.

REVIEWER'S REFERENCE

Guilford, J. P. (1967). *The nature of human intelligence*. New York, McGraw Hill Co.

Review of The Extended Merrill-Palmer Scale by ALBERT C. OOSTERHOF, Professor of Educational Research, Florida State University, Tallahassee, FL:

The Extended Merrill-Palmer Scale is an individually administered intelligence test designed for children of ages 3 to 5 years. The present scale, published in 1978, is not a new instrument. The Extended Scale is an adaptation of the original Merrill-Palmer Scale that was published in 1931.

Construction of the present scale is based on the notion that intelligence consists of a series of factors rather than a general of "g" factor. Consequently, the Extended Scale produces a set of scores and no overall measure of intelligence. The four scores correspond to four components from Guilford's structure of the intellect judged relevant to a preschool child's limited experience and maturation.

The four components can be visualized as four cells within a 2 by 2 contingency table. Within this table, rows represent modalities, consisting of meanings (Semantic) and forms (Figural). Semantic modality involves verbal tasks such as knowing meanings of words, following directions, and expressing ideas. Figural modality pertains to problems that involve shapes, colors, and visual patterns. Columns within the 2 by 2 table represent two thinking processes, productive and evaluative. Productive thinking requires generating a series of ideas in response to a task. Evaluative thinking demands selecting the most appropriate among a series of possible responses. Within the Extended Merrill-Palmer Scale, these components are referred to as dimensions.

Each of the four dimensions is measured by 4 of the 16 subtests that comprise the Extended Scale. One test associated with figural production, for example, requires the child to list all the names of foods that come to mind. A second subtest in this dimension then asks the child to name as many examples as possible of things that share a common quality, such as things that run, things that bite, and things that melt.

Administering the Extended Merrill-Palmer Scale will require careful training and experience. For the most part, the tasks a child is asked to perform are straightforward. However, directions that are to be given the child and conditions under which a task is to begin and stop cannot be quickly ascertained from the Instruction Manual. Also, a child's actions must be scored quickly, and the examiner must remember what the child said so no credit is given for repeated responses. Standards associated with a correct response are not always obvious. Procedures for assuring that a child is cooperative and highly motivated are not well standardized.

A child's scores on The Extended Merrill-Palmer Scale are expressed as percentiles. The Instruction manual contains a scoring scheme for combining performance on the subtests. This aggregate score is converted to a scaled score and then a percentile rank for each of the four dimensions.

Essentially no help is provided for interpreting the percentile scores. Norms are based on the performance of approximately 1,100 children, but no description of this reference group is given other than its breakdown by age and gender. No guidelines are given for interpreting patterns among the four dimensions. Percentile ranks are presented in a manner that confuses them with percentage scores.

The manual includes what it refers to as "case studies" for 26 children. Each of these studies, however, consists only of a photocopy of the scoring sheet used to compute percentiles and a one- or two-paragraph description of the child's background. These are not meaningful case studies in a traditional sense. Interpretative statements within case studies that explain the child's performance on the test are very general. A typical statement is "With this kind of ability he should be independent and self-reliant and capable of doing things for himself." No evidence is provided that justifies even these basic interpretations.

Reliability and validity evidence provided in the manual is limited. Estimates of interval consistency for each dimension are derived by first finding the average correlation among the four subtests associated with the dimension and then using the Spearman-Brown formula to adjust this average coefficient to a test four times the length. These adjusted coefficients generally are in the .70s. In a separate study, 10 children were retested after a period of 12 to 31 months, and substantial changes in relative performance were noted. This information does not provide an adequate basis for determining the stability of scores.

Furthermore, information regarding the representativeness of these 10 children is not provide other than that included in the case studies. No information is provided as to interrater reliability.

Brief summaries of prior studies that provided the basis for selecting tasks included in The Extended Merrill-Palmer Sale are in the manual. Project reports from the early 1970s are cited, and these reports, if available, may provide further clarification. Other than the brief summaries in the manual, no evidence is provided as to the construct being measured by the present instrument. No evidence is provided as to how scores on this instrument relate to other measures of achievement or aptitude. The potential user will find little assistance in determining what The Extended Merrill-Palmer Scale measures, and no guidance in how to interpret or use the profile of scores resulting from this instrument.

[149]

Facial Action Coding System.

Purpose: Constructed to assess facial movements or expressions.
Population: Adults.
Publication Date: 1978.
Acronym: FACS.
Scores, 4: Upper Face, Lower Face, Head/Eye Position, Full Face.
Administration: Individual.
Price Data, 1992: $290 per complete kit including 500 scoring sheets, 146 illustrative facial photographs, VHS videocassette, manual (341 pages), and investigator's guide (111 pages); $16 per 100 scoring sheets; $64 per VHS videocasette; $12 per investigator's guide no. 1; $20 per investigator's guide no. 2; $275 per training film (16mm).
Time: Administration time not reported.
Authors: Paul Ekman and Wallace V. Friesen.
Publisher: Consulting Psychologists Press, Inc.
Cross References: See T4:952 (11 references).

TEST REFERENCES

1. Weddell, R. A. (1989). Recognition memory for emotional facial expressions in patients with focal cerebral lesions. *Brain and Cognition*, *11*, 1-17.

2. Berenbaum, H. (1992). Posed facial expressions of emotion in schizophrenia and depression. *Psychological Medicine*, *22*, 929-937.

3. Matsumoto, D. (1992). American-Japanese cultural differences in the recognition of universal facial expressions. *Journal of Cross-Cultural Psychology*, *23*, 72-84.

4. Krehbiel, D., & Lewis, P. T. (1994). An observational emphasis in undergraduate psychology laboratories. *Teaching of Psychology*, *21*, 45-48.

5. Weddell, R. A. (1994). Effects of subcortical lesion site on human emotional behavior. *Brain and Cognition*, *25*, 161-193.

6. Gosselin, P., Kirouac, G., & Doré, F. Y. (1995). Components and recognition of facial expression in the communication of emotion by actors. *Journal of Personality and Social Psychology*, *68*, 83-96.

7. LaFrance, M., & Hecht, M. A. (1995). Why smiles generate leniency. *Personality and Social Psychology Bulletin*, *21*, 207-214.

Review of the Facial Action Coding System by KATHRYN M. BENES, Director of Counseling Services, Catholic Social Services, Lincoln, NE:

The Facial Action Coding System (FACS) was developed as a comprehensive method of objectively describing facial action based on anatomical analysis. The authors point out that "most research on facial behavior has not measured the face itself, but instead measured the information that observers were able to infer from the fact" (p. 1). In contrast, the FACS serves as a research tool to aid in collecting facial movement independent of data interpretation. Observers code the smallest visible units of muscular activity, called Action Units (AU); however, no meaning is assigned the AUs. Although the authors believe the FACS accounts for all visible facial movement, they stress that the FACS "is in the experimental stage of development" and "is not complete, final, nor proven" (Preface).

The Investigator's Guide (Part 1) states that the FACS consists of: (*a*) a manual (*b*) illustrations (e.g., photographs, videotape, 8mm cartridges); (*c*) scoring sheets; (*d*) practice items along with correct responses; (*e*) norms on learners' progress; (*f*) computer programs; (*g*) final test of scoring; and (*h*) a two-part investigator's guide. It is important to note this reviewer did not examine the illustrations presented on 8mm cartridges, the practice items or correct responses to those items, norms for learners progress, computer programs, the final test of scoring, or Part II of the Investigator's Guide.

The manual is a 370-page self-instruction text that provides a detailed description of terminology, explicit definitions for AUs, and scoring procedures. Although the manual, in combination with the illustration media, practice tests, and scoring materials provide a comprehensive system for training observers, the Investigator's Guide (Part I) serves as a highly technical resource for the researcher. The Investigator's Guide (Part I) presents the rationale for the development of the FACS, measures of reliability, requirement for behavioral records, training procedures, and materials required in order to use the FACS. The authors have gone to great lengths to provide a detailed description of the genesis and subsequent research of the FACS.

Although the Investigator's Guide (Part I) reports that the FACS can be learned by nonscientifically trained individuals, all coders described in the Investigator's Guide (Part I) appeared to have some degree of scientific training. Information presented in the Investigator's Guide (Part I) related to coder training and measures of reliability describe the coders as seven persons who were previously unfamiliar with the FACS. Of the seven persons, only six completed training. The six remaining individuals were described as two bachelor's level research assistants, two doctoral candidates, a post-doctoral fellow, and an associate professor. The authors report they had "minimal contact" with the trainees during instruction and that "working about half-time it took five weeks for them [the trainees] to complete the FACS instructional procedure" (p. 22). Not only is the coder training time intensive, coding the facial behaviors is also a highly technical process. Kaiser and Wehrle (1992) report that obtaining an accurate description of 1 minute of videotaped facial behavior is estimated to take 5 hours depending on the complexity of the facial action.

Measures of reliability of the FACS were based on the six individuals previously described who learned the FACS as a group during a 2-month period. Reliability measures were computed separately for 34 events based on (*a*) identification of any of the 44 AUs, singly or in combination; (*b*) intensity of the action for 5 of the 44 AUs; (*c*) determination of unilateral or bilateral presence of any AU; (*d*) coding of head and eye position during an observed facial movement, and (*e*) level of agreement following arbitration of coder discrepancies. Agreement among individual trainees and agreement between each of the six trainees and an "expert" (one of the authors) was calculated for all descriptive codes. The authors report a mean ratio of .822 across all coders (six) and all events scored (34) when scoring was compared to experts, and intercoder agreement was .756. Ekman and Friesen (1982) report that comparable reliabilities have been achieved with subsequent studies.

The FACS was designed to measure any facial movement, therefore the validity of the FACS requires that each AU measures the *type* and *intensity* (for some AUs) of the behavior it purports to measure. Ekman and Friesen (1982) report one study where trained volunteers were videotaped while performing various *types* of requested facial actions. The videotaped records were scored by coders who had no knowledge of the requested actions. Using the FACS, the coders were able to distinguish accurately among the *types* of facial actions. In another study reported by Ekman and Friesen, they utilized EMG to measure electrical activity in the different muscular regions of the face. They indicate that the FACS could accurately differentiate among the various *types* of facial actions. Measures of *intensity* were also found to be valid with FACS *intensity* scores highly correlated to EMG readings (Pearson $R = .85$).

In summary, the FACS is a highly complex research tool that holds great promise for investigators interested in the study of human ethnology. It is meritorious that the authors have chosen to develop a method of description without assigning meaning to the AUs. Therefore, the FACS can be used in an exploratory or confirmatory manner without a priori hypotheses. Although it may not be necessary for coders to have the qualifications of those reported in the Investigator's Guide (Part I), it is important for those considering using the FACS to realize that coders must be relatively sophisticated in their ability to score accurately very complex data sets. The overall reliability scores are remarkable given the complexity of the FACS. Whether or not other investigators can attain similar levels of reliability will be revealed in future studies.

REVIEWER'S REFERENCES

Ekman, P., & Friesen, W. V. (1982). Measuring facial movement with the Facial Action Coding System. In P. Ekman (Ed.), *Emotions in the human face* (pp. 178-211). Cambridge: Cambridge University Press.

Kaiser, S., & Wehrle, T. (1992). Automated coding of facial behavior in human-computer interactions with FACS. *Journal of Nonverbal Behavior, 16*, 67-84.

Review of the Facial Action Coding System by THOMAS F. DONLON, Director, Office of Test Development and Research, Thomas Edison State College, Trenton, NJ:

The Facial Action Coding System (FACS) is a somewhat different entry in a work devoted to "mental" measurement. The materials provided to this reviewer constitute a complex system for coding facial expressions in terms of Action Units (AUs), which are essentially different facial movements or positions that are controlled by individual muscles or combinations of muscles. As stated by the authors: "Our primary goal in developing the Facial Action Coding System (FACS) was to develop a *comprehensive* system which could distinguish all possible visually distinguishable facial movements" (p. 2). The materials offer an avenue for training persons to apply the system, largely by practicing with sizable photographic and video material. The appraisals are based entirely on what is visible. Essentially, what is offered is a taxonomic system.

Although the system is basically a tool or instrument for securing descriptions in the service of conducting studies in any relevant area, an underlying goal of assessing emotional states is clearly reflected in the writing. Thus, towards the end of the last of the two booklets that comprise the Investigator's Manual, there are "Suggestions About Using the FACS," and here it is noted that "some of those using FACS will be interested in converting the AU descriptive scores into emotions" (p. 141). This is followed by Table 11-1, listing six major emotions (surprise, fear, happy, sadness, disgust, and anger) and their parallel AUs. The authors cautiously acknowledge that "Ideally there should be various sources of evidence to demonstrate that an AU combination is a sign of an emotion . . . . There is evidence for each entry, but it is partial" (p. 141). Whatever this evidence is, it is not presented, other than photographically.

Elsewhere, in justifying the elaborateness of the system, the authors note: "If we wish to learn all the facial actions which signal emotion . . . then a method such as FACS is needed" (p. 17). But essentially, there is no effort to demonstrate that the system can be successfully used to assess emotion. All of the effort is in presenting the system, defining the AUs and the combinations of AUs, and working toward reliable descriptions of facial states by using the system.

The authors note that "FACS is in the experimental stage of development" (first page of Preface). Writing in 1978, they stated that: "Six people have learned FACS" (p. 16). Although this review comes considerably later, it seems doubtful that many persons have made the investment to master the system, for it required about 100 hours for the system to be learned.

The authors note that "FACS is an unavoidably expensive package" (Preface), and they have developed the Guide in order to give prospective users "an opportunity to find out something about FACS at a minimal cost" (Preface). But the first five chapters of the Guide, separately bound in order to effect this purpose, have virtually no photographic information at all. This reviewer, privy to the extensive photographic materials in the manual, felt that a potential user should be given specific examples of facial expressions, AUs, the underlying musculature, and how the experts coded the observation. In facial taxonomy, as elsewhere, a picture is worth a thousand words.

Scoring reliability was assessed by a very simple index that established the proportion of all of the uses of any AU by either of two observers that is based on uses of AUs that reflected agreement. Thus, if Observer A coded a give facial expression as 1 + 2 + 3, while Observer B coded it as 1 + 2, the proportion attributable to AUs in common was 4 out of 5 = .80. Using this index, the average coefficient of agreement among all possible pairings of the six persons studied with the two expert raters was .82.

The authors write that "If two coders disagreed about only one AU and agreed about one AU, they would earn a ratio of.50" (p. 24). This ratio would reflect a situation where one says "it's 1 + 2," and the other says "it's 1 + 3." The total of all uses of any AU is 4, the proportion that reflects uses of a common AU is .5. But, contrary to what the authors suggest, the coders in such a situation have actually disagreed about *two* AUs: one coder thought AU 1 was involved, whereas the other did not, and one coder thought that AU 3 was involved, whereas the other did not. Thus, the simple index does its job of reassuring the user that a substantial level of agreement may be reached among users of the system, but some better means of assessing agreement will be needed. There will be a need to make distinctions that the authors are not presently making. This seems particularly likely when users attempt to establish correlates between observers' reports of AUs and internal emotional states. The discussion of reliability is limited to demonstrations of interrater agreement. There are no data on intrarater agreement for ratings prepared on the same stimulus material at different times.

The authors provided three computer programs to assist users: one to verify that no internally inconsistent errors have been made in using the system, one to summarize scores across coders, assessing agreement, and one to evaluate codings against some benchmark or standard. These were Fortran IV programs anticipating punch cards and other features of the then world of computing. The pro

[151]

Family Environment Scale, Second Edition.

Purpose: Developed to "measure the social-environmental characteristics of all types of families."
Population: Family members.
Publication Dates: 1974–86.
Acronym: FES.
Scores, 10: Cohesion, Expressiveness, Conflict, Independence, Achievement Orientation, Intellectual-Cultural Orientation, Active-Recreational Orientation, Moral-Religious Emphasis, Organization, Control.
Administration: Group.
Editions, 3: Real (R), Ideal (I), Expectations (E).
Price Data, 1992: $15 per 25 Form R test booklets; $16 per 25 test booklets (select Form I or Form E); $10 per 50 answer sheets; $15 per 25 self-scorable answer sheets; $7 per set of scoring stencils; $8 per 50 profiles; $80 per prepaid narrative; $15 per 25 interpretive report forms; $13 per manual ('86, 68 pages); $19 per specimen set.
Time: [15–20] minutes.
Comments: A part of the Social Climate Scales (T4:2495).
Authors: Rudolf H. Moos and Bernice S. Moos (manual).
Publisher: Consulting Psychologists Press, Inc.
Cross References: See T4:961 (136 references); for reviews by Nancy A. Busch-Rossnagel and Nadine M. Lambert of an earlier edition, see 9:408 (18 references); see also T3:872 (14 references); for a review by Philip H. Dreyer, see 8:557 (4 references). For a review of the Social Climate Series, see 8:681.

TEST REFERENCES

1. Christensen, A. J., Turner, C. W., Slaughter, J. R., & Holman, J. M., Jr. (1989). Perceived family support as a moderator of psychological well-being in end-stage renal disease. *Journal of Behavioral Medicine, 12*, 249-265.

2. Wallander, J. L., & Varni, J. W. (1989). Social support and adjustment in chronically ill and handicapped children. *American Journal of Community Psychology, 17*, 185-201.

3. Abbott, D. A., Berry, M., & Meredith, W. H. (1990). Religious belief and practice: A potential asset in helping families. *Family Relations, 39*, 443-448.

4. Falconer, C. W., Wilson, K. G., & Falconer, J. (1990). A psychometric investigation of gender-tilted families: Implications for family therapy. *Family Relations, 39*, 8-13.

5. Friedman, S. (1990). Assessing the marital environment of agoraphobics. *Journal of Anxiety Disorders, 4*, 335-340.

6. Goelman, H., Shapiro, E., & Pence, A. R. (1990). Family environment and family day care. *Family Relations, 39*, 14-19.

7. Jackson, J. L., Calhoun, K. S., Amick, A. E., Maddever, H. M., & Habif, V. L. (1990). Young adult women who report childhood intrafamilial sexual abuse: Subsequent adjustment. *Archives of Sexual Behavior, 19*, 211-221.

8. Landsman, I. S., Baum, C. G., Arnkoff, D. B., Craig, M. J., Lynch, I., Copes, W. S., & Champion, H. R. (1990). The psychosocial consequences of traumatic injury. *Journal of Behavioral Medicine, 13*, 561-581.

9. Moos, R. H. (1990). Depressed outpatients' life contexts, amount of treatment, and treatment outcome. *The Journal of Nervous and Mental Disease, 178*, 105-112.

Errata for *The Twelfth Mental Measurements Yearbook*, beginning on page 382, conclusion of reviews for Test 149.

The authors provided three computer programs to assist users: one to verify that no internally inconsistent errors have been made in using the system, one to summarize scores across coders, assessing agreement, and one to evaluate codings against some benchmark or standard. These were Fortran IV programs anticipating punch cards and other features of the then world of computing. The programs seem useful and, if needed, easily adapted to the modern computing environment.

Although the system is complex and detailed, users should be able to adapt it to their particular needs, declining to use some dimensions of it while retaining others. The authors are sensitive to this possibility, noting "investigators may wish to . . . more selectively score only certain AUs or AU combinations" (p. 17).

The FACS is a major and serious effort to develop a taxonomic system at a very high level of comprehensiveness. It appears to require a considerable investment in training on the part of users, but to then offer a variety of flexible applications. Although no data are offered to demonstrate that it is especially relevant to the assessment of emotional states via facial actions, or superior to other systems for this purpose, the FACS will require serious consideration by investigators working in this area.

[150]

Family Apperception Test.

Purpose: Designed to assess family system variables.
Population: Ages 6 and over.
Publication Dates: 1985–91.
Acronym: FAT.
Scores, 35 to 40: Obvious Conflict (Family Conflict*, Marital Conflict*, Other Conflict, Absence of Conflict), Conflict Resolution (Positive Resolution, Negative or No Resolution*), Limit Setting (Appropriate/Compliance, Appropriate/Noncompliance*, Inappropriate/Compliance*, Inappropriate/Noncompliance*), Quality of Relationships (Mother=Ally, Father=Ally, Sibling=Ally, Spouse=Ally, Other=Ally, Mother=Stressor*, Father=Stressor*, Sibling=Stressor*, Spouse=Stressor*, Other=Stressor), Boundaries (Enmeshment*, Disengagement*, Mother/Child Coalition*, Father/Child Coalition*, Other Adult/Child Coalition*, Open System, Closed System*), Dysfunctional Circularity*, Abusive Remarks (Physical Abuse*, Sexual Abuse*, Neglect/Abandonment*, Substance Abuse*), Unusual Responses*, Refusals, Total Dysfunctional Index (total of scores with *) plus 5 optional Emotional Tone

scores: Sadness/Depression, Anger/Hostility, Worry/Anxiety, Happiness/Satisfaction, Other.
Administration: Individual.
Price Data, 1995: $125 per complete kit including set of test pictures, 100 scoring sheets, and manual ('91, 36 pages); $62.50 per set of test pictures; $19.50 per 100 scoring sheets; $45 per manual.
Time: (30–35) minutes.
Comments: Projective test.
Authors: Alexander Julian, III, Wayne M. Sotile, Susan E. Henry, and Mary O. Sotile.
Publisher: Western Psychological Services.

Review of the Family Apperception Test by MARK J. BENSON, Associate Professor of Family and Child Development, Virginia Polytechnic Institute and State University, Blacksburg, VA:

The Family Apperception Test (FAT) is a projective storytelling measure modeled after the Thematic Apperception Test (TAT; Murray, 1943; T4:2824). Like the TAT, the FAT consists of series of stimulus cards about which the respondent tells a story including the feelings and thoughts of the characters. The FAT joins a number of apperception tests that emulate the TAT including the Children's Apperception Test (T4:444) and the Senior Apperception Test (T4:2429; Bellak, 1986), the Roberts Apperception Test (McArthur & Roberts, 1982; T4:2285), and the Michigan Picture Test—Revised (Hutt, 1980).

The FAT is a sound measure according to three basic criteria for evaluating storytelling projectives. These three criteria include the strength of the theoretical rationale, the evocativeness of the stimulus cards, and the reliability and validity of the coding schemes.

Several family system perspectives provide the theoretical basis for the test. Although the theoretical scope could be wider, the theories cited include the major family system thinkers such as Bowen, Minuchin, Haley, and several contemporary strategic theorists. These theoretical perspectives provide the basis for several scoring categories including boundaries, limit setting, and dysfunctional circularity. The attention to the theoretical underpinnings and the use of theory in developing some of the scoring categories are important strengths of the FAT.

Despite the attention to theory, the authors fail to link theory with the purpose of the test. The purpose of the FAT is to "bridge the historical gap between individual and family assessment" (p. 1). Actually, the FAT can assess only individual perceptions about family contexts. The manual authors further claim the FAT "allows family systems hypotheses to be systematically generated from the assessment of a single family member" (p. 7). This assertion is also unjustified. Like other storytelling projectives, the FAT ultimately provides only data at the individual level. The manual should include statements indicating the FAT accesses a sample of perceptual and verbal data from an individual.

The quality of the verbal data generated by the FAT lies in the capacity of the stimulus cards to evoke a variety of family projections. Although other storytelling projectives can generate family data, the FAT is unique in eliciting family perceptions for most of the 21 pictures. Moreover, the responses to the FAT stimulus cards are fairly diverse across examinees. Most of the FAT cards, however, are less ambiguous than the typical TAT card. Because of the limited ambiguity, some cards tend to elicit descriptions rather than stories.

Stimulus cards 5, 7, 11, and 12 are more ambiguous than the others. A study reported in the manual indicates these four cards discriminated effectively between clinical and nonclinical children on scores in the conflict category (Table 6, $N = 44$). A follow-up study reported in the manual indicated these four pictures were nearly as effective as the entire set of 21 pictures in discriminating between clinical and nonclinical children (Tables 8 and 9, $N = 56$). Clinicians may find this FAT Short Form of four cards to be a valuable supplement to data derived from other measures such as the TAT.

The codings within the FAT categories provide the basis for evaluating its reliability and validity. The reliability and validity data derive from five masters theses conducted at Wake Forest University in 1987 and 1988. These five studies were based on a sample of 187 children aged 6 to 15. Each of the studies uses a subsample ranging from 44 to 83 of the children. The basis for selection of subsamples is omitted from the manual.

Two subsamples reported in the manual ($N = 44$ and $N = 83$) provide data on interjudge agreement across the coding categories. The degree of agreement is good for several categories including obvious conflict, conflict resolution, open versus closed system, and quality of relationship. There is low interjudge agreement, however, for the remaining categories. Clarification of the rating criteria or development of additional categories could increase the number of reliable scoring categories. In addition, evaluating the test-retest reliability and the split-half reliability of the measure would help to strengthen confidence in the use of the quantitative ratings.

Validity data based on two subsamples (N = 44 and N = 56) drawn from the primary sample (N = 187) are reported. The findings indicate that many of the scoring categories discriminated between clinical and nonclinical children. Several scoring categories that would be expected to differentiate between clinical and nonclinical respondents, however, failed to show significant differences.

Because only some of the FAT scoring categories meet acceptable standards for reliability and validity, further development of scoring categories is needed. Expanding the theoretical base to include more family system theories would generate additional constructs for scoring. The broad field of family systems theories offers an ample supply of constructs for conceptualizing additional scoring categories with sufficient interjudge agreement. Additional reliable codings would increase the interpretive value of individual FAT protocols.

Although norms for the FAT are absent, this is a problem shared by other storytelling projectives as well. Clinicians are most likely to use such story projectives for hypothesis generation. In fact, the use of these measures for differential diagnosis is discouraged (Ryan, 1984).

In summary, the FAT is a valuable addition to the field of story projectives tests. The use of some family systems theories in developing the scoring is a particular strength of the test. Broadening the theoretical base to include other family systems theories holds the potential for increasing the number of reliable and valid scoring categories. The evidence in support of the validity of the Short Form FAT suggests these four stimulus cards may be particularly valuable to clinicians seeking to supplement TAT assessment with family stimulus cards.

REVIEWER'S REFERENCES

Murray, H. A. (1943). *Thematic Apperception Test manual.* Cambridge: Harvard University.

Hutt, M. L. (1980). The Michigan Picture Test—Revised. New York: Grune & Stratton.

McArthur, D. S., & Roberts, G. E. (1982). Roberts Apperception Test For Children. Los Angeles: Western Psychological Services.

Ryan, R. M. (1984). Thematic Apperception Test. In D. J. Keyser & R. C. Sweetland (Eds.), *Test critiques compendium: Reviews of major tests from the Test Critiques Series* (pp. 517-532). Kansas City, MO: Test Corporation of America.

Bellak, L. (1986). *The T.A.T., C.A.T. and S.A.T. in clinical use* (4th ed.). Orlando, FL: Grune & Stratton.

Review of the Family Apperception Test by MERITH COSDEN, Associate Professor of Counseling/Clinical/School Psychology, Department of Education, University of California, Santa Barbara, CA:

The Family Apperception Test (FAT) is a relatively new addition to the domain of picture apperception tests. This review will address the design and psychometric properties of the test and its relationship to other commonly used picture apperception tests such as the Thematic Apperception Test (TAT; T4:2824) and the Children's Apperception Test (CAT; T4:444).

The manual authors do not indicate how the cards to be used in the test were selected. That is, the process by which important family events were sampled and then depicted through drawings is not described.

The scoring categories were developed to reflect family interaction issues related to different models of family therapy systems. Thus, cards are scored for the presence of family or marital conflict, quality of relationships with family members, and boundaries, among other things. Although the manual authors provide examples of the types of responses that would receive each score, they do not provide nonexamples, nor describe how to decide between scoring categories.

Normative data are not presented. The authors state that normative data were being collected at the time the manual was published. It would have been advisable for the authors to wait to publish the test until after these norms were developed, as interpretation of test results is impeded by their absence.

General guidelines for interpretation of scoring patterns are provided. Results also may be interpreted on the basis of one's clinical judgment. Several case studies are provided using these approaches. No data are presented to validate these procedures, however. It is not evident whether basing one's interpretation of test results on the quantitative scoring criteria is any more effective than basing the interpretation on clinical judgment. It is also not clear how the information obtained through use of this test is significantly different from that obtained through other aspects of a clinical assessment. There are no data to support use of this instrument over a strong clinical interview or other type of projective device.

Currently, there are no published studies on the reliability or validity of the FAT. One needs to rely on the manual for this information. The supportive data provided in the manual are based on five unpublished masters theses.

Interrater reliability was assessed in two of these studies. Reliability coefficients are provided through kappas. Although this is an appropriate statistical measure, it may be difficult for some readers to interpret the outcomes. For example, although the authors state the kappas are very strong, the kappa values themselves are not compelling, ranging, for the most part, from fair to moderate. Only scores of conflict and conflict resolution reflect superior levels of interrater agreement. Other measures of test reliability, such as the internal consistency of the test items, and the stability of test scores over time, are not available.

The validity of the FAT was assessed in three studies. In each of these studies the author addressed the ability of the test to distinguish between students served through a clinic and those without known clinical problems. In the first of these (Lundquist, 1987, as cited in the 1988 FAT test manual) only scores for conflict differentiated between clinic and nonclinic child samples. Further, differences in conflict scores were obtained on only four out of the full set of cards.

In a second study (Buchanon, 1987, as cited in the 1988 FAT test manual) 11 out of 34 minor scoring categories were reported as significantly different between a clinic and a nonclinic sample of children. Although a MANOVA was conducted to control for experiment-wise error rates, the MANOVA itself is not reported. It is unclear, also, whether the reported differences were obtained on all or just some of the cards.

In the final study (Eaton, 1988, as cited in the 1988 FAT test manual) 30 scoring categories (some were combined from the prior studies) and a total dysfunction score were compared across clinic and nonclinic samples. Subjects ranged in age from 8 to 16. Between-group differences were obtained on 19 of the scoring categories, indicating the clinic sample reported more conflictual relationships than the control sample.

Thus, the only validity studies on the FAT assess its ability to differentiate clinic from nonclinic samples of children. There are no data to support its use for assessment of patterns of family dysfunction. This is a major limitation. Further, only some of the scores, and only some of the cards, have been found to differentiate clinic from nonclinic samples. These problems should have been addressed during the development of the scoring system, with a final scoring system reflecting only those items that successfully differentiate clients and reflect their specific needs. Finally, it should be noted that all of the reliability and validity studies were conducted with children. Although the authors suggest the test can be used with children and adults, the validity of the test for assessing adults' problems was not reported.

The authors, in developing this test, designed both a scoring system and a set of cards. They do not make a strong argument as to why their cards are preferable to those used in the TAT or CAT. The authors state the FAT cards draw for material related to family issues, but so do many of the cards on the older picture apperception tests. The questions asked during administration of the FAT are similar to those asked during administration of the other picture apperception tests. I wonder if the FAT scoring system could be used with either the TAT or CAT cards. These have a history of clinical use.

There are also some conceptual problems related to the use of this projective instrument as an assessment tool within a family systems approach to treatment. First, the test is not based on any one systems theory. Second, and more important, the test is both administered and scored individually, with little consideration for how that information could or should be used with the family. There is no discussion of how to use the test with multiple family members, or even whether multiple family members should respond to the same cards or share their responses.

In sum, neither the utility of the FAT nor its advantage over other clinical devices appear compelling. The test does not have strong psychometric properties. Although interrater reliability of parts of the coding system is adequate, other types of reliability are not assessed, and studies on the validity of the test provide limited support. The manual lacks detail in areas of scoring and interpretation. This is particularly problematic as there are no other published studies on the test instrument. It is not apparent how the information obtained through the FAT differs from that which could be obtained through clinical interviews. Finally, there is also an underlying conceptual problem with using the FAT in its designated manner for assisting in family systems approaches to therapy. There is a need for better conceptualization of how to collect and use projective information so that it will be useful to those working within family systems approaches.

10. Shapiro, J., & Tittle, K. (1990). Maternal adaption to child disability in a Hispanic population. *Family Relations, 39,* 179-185.

11. Cornell, D. G., Callahan, C. M., & Loyd, B. H. (1991). Socioemotional adjustment of adolescent girls enrolled in a residential acceleration program. *Gifted Child Quarterly, 35,* 58-66.

12. Dadds, M., Smith, M., Webber, Y., & Robinson, A. (1991). An exploration of family and individual profiles following father-daughter incest. *Child Abuse & Neglect, 15,* 575-586.

13. Ingersoll-Dayton, B., & Neal, M. B. (1991). Grandparents in family therapy: A clinical research study. *Family Relations, 40,* 264-271.

14. Seltzer, G. B., Begun, A., Seltzer, M. M., & Krauss, M. W. (1991). Adults with mental retardation and their aging mothers: Impacts of siblings. *Family Relations, 40,* 310-317.

15. West, S. G., Sandler, I., Pillow, D. R., Baca, L., & Gersten, J. C. (1991). The use of structural equation modeling in a generative research: Toward the design of a preventative intervention of bereaved children. *American Journal of Community Psychology, 19,* 459-480.

16. Alessandri, S. M. (1992). Effects of maternal work status in single-parent families on children's perception of self and family and school achievement. *Journal of Experimental Child Psychology, 54,* 417-433.

17. Bederman, J., Faraone, S. V., Keenan, K., Benjamin, J., Krifcher, B., Moore, C., Sprich-Buckminster, S., Ugaglia, K., Jellinek, M. S., Steingard, R., Spencer, T., Norman, D., Kolodny, R., Kraus, I., Perrin, J., Keller, M. B., & Tsuang, M. T. (1992). Further evidence for family-genetic risk factors in attention deficit hyperactivity disorder: Patterns of comorbidity in probands and relatives in psychiatrically and pediatrically referred samples. *Archives of General Psychiatry, 49,* 728-738.

18. Brunson, J. A. (1992). Perceived family environment of Black adolescent alcohol users and nonusers. *The Journal of Black Psychology, 18*(2), 37-46.

19. Christensen, A. J., Smith, T. W., Turner, C. W., Holman, J. M., Jr., Gregory, M. C., & Rich, M. A. (1992). Family support, physical impairment, and adherence in hemodialysis: An investigation of main and buffering effects. *Journal of Behavioral Medicine, 15,* 313-325.

20. Cole, P. M., Woolger, C., Power, T. G., & Smith, K. D. (1992). Parenting difficulties among adult survivors of father-daughter incest. *Child Abuse & Neglect, 16,* 239-249.

21. Deal, J. E., Wampler, K. S., & Halverson, C. F., Jr. (1992). The importance of similarity in the marital relationship. *Family Process, 31,* 369-382.

22. Hardesty, P. H., & Hirsch, B. J. (1992). Summer and school-term youth employment: Ecological and longitudinal analyses. *Psychological Reports, 71,* 595-606.

23. Henderson, D., & Vandenberg, B. (1992). Factors influencing adjustment in the families of autistic children. *Psychological Reports, 71,* 167-171.

24. Holdnack, J. A. (1992). The long-term effects of parental divorce on family relationships and the effects on adult children's self-concept. *Journal of Divorce & Remarriage, 18*(3/4), 137-155.

25. Hops, H., & Seeley, J. R. (1992). Parent participation in studies of family interaction: Methodological and substantive considerations. *Behavioral Assessment, 14,* 229-243.

26. Martin, J. A., & Elmer, E. (1992). Battered children grown up: A follow-up study of individuals severely maltreated as children. *Child Abuse & Neglect, 16,* 75-87.

27. Sandler, I. N., West, S. G., Baca, L., Pillow, D. R., Gersten, J. C., Rogosch, F., Virdin, L., Beals, J., Reynolds, K. D., Kallgren, C., Tein, J. Y., Kriege, G., Cole, E., & Ramirez, R. (1992). Linking empirically based theory and evaluation: The family bereavement program. *American Journal of Community Psychology, 20,* 491-521.

28. Solomon, Z., Waysman, M., Levy, G., Fried, B., Mikulincer, M., Benbenishty, R., Florian, V., & Bleich, A. (1992). From front line to home front: A study of secondary traumatization. *Family Process, 31,* 289-302.

29. Stone, M. K., & Hutchinson, R. L. (1992). Familial conflict and attitudes toward marriage: A psychological wholeness perspective. *Journal of Divorce & Remarriage, 18*(3/4), 79-91.

30. Timko, C., Stovel, K. W., Moos, R. H., & Miller, J. J. (1992). Adaptation to juvenile rheumatic disease: A controlled evaluation of functional disability with a one-year follow-up. *Health Psychology, 11,* 67-76.

31. Benedict, L. W., & Zautra, A. J. (1993). Family environmental characteristics as risk factors for childhood sexual abuse. *Journal of Clinical Child Psychology, 22,* 365-374.

32. Bloom, B. L., & Naar, S. (1993). Self-report measures of family functioning: Extensions of a factorial analysis. *Family Process, 33,* 203-216.

33. Casella, A., & Kearins, J. (1993). Cross-cultural comparison of family environments of Anglo-Australians, Italian-Australians, and southern Italians. *Psychological Reports, 72,* 1051-1057.

34. Chernen, L., & Friedman, S. (1993). Treating the personality disordered agoraphobic patient with individual and marital therapy. *Journal of Anxiety Disorders, 7,* 163-177.

35. Gehring, T. M., & Marti, D. (1993). The Family System Test: Differences in perception of family structures between nonclinical and clinical children. *Journal of Child Psychology and Psychiatry and Allied Disciplines, 34,* 363-377.

36. Kurtz, L., & Derevensky, J. L. (1993). The effects of divorce on perceived self-efficacy and behavioral control in elementary school children. *Journal of Divorce & Remarriage, 20*(3/4), 75-94.

37. Leonard, H. L., Swedo, S. E., Lenane, M. C., Rettew, D. C., Hamburger, S. D., Bartko, J. J., & Rapoport, J. L. (1993). A 2- to 7-year follow-up study of 54 obsessive-compulsive children and adolescents. *Archives of General Psychiatry, 50,* 429-439.

38. Mahabeer, M. (1993). Correlations between mothers' and children's self-esteem and perceived familial relationships among intact, widowed, and divorced families. *Psychological Reports, 73,* 483-489.

39. Markland, S. R., & Nelson, E. S. (1993). The relationship between family conflict and the identity of young adults. *Journal of Divorce & Remarriage, 20*(3/4), 193-209.

40. Nelson, W. L., Hughes, H. M., Handal, P., Katz, B., & Searight, H. R. (1993). The relationship of family structure and family conflict to adjustment in young adult college students. *Adolescence, 28,* 29-40.

41. Pruett, C. L., Calsyn, R. J., & Jensen, F. M. (1993). Social support received by children in stepmother, stepfather, and intact families. *Journal of Divorce & Remarriage, 19*(3/4), 165-179.

42. Sallis, J. F., Nader, P. R., Broyles, S. L., Berry, C. C., Elder, J. P., McKenzie, T. L., & Nelson, J. A. (1993). Correlates of physical activity at home in Mexican-American and Anglo-American preschool children. *Health Psychology, 12,* 390-398.

43. Seltzer, M. M., Krauss, M. W, & Tsunematsu, N. (1993). Adults with Down syndrome and their aging mothers: Diagnostic group differences. *American Journal on Mental Retardation, 97,* 496-508.

44. Thompson, R. J., Merritt, K. A., Keith, B. R., Murphy, L. B., & Johndrow, D. A. (1993). The role of maternal stress and family functioning in maternal distress and mother-reported and child-reported psychological adjustment of nonreferred children. *Journal of Clinical Child Psychology, 22,* 78-84.

45. Turner, R. A., Irwin, C. E., Jr., Tschann, J. M., & Millstein, S. G. (1993). Autonomy, relatedness, and the initiation of health risk behaviors in early adolescence. *Health Psychology, 12,* 200-208.

46. Brookings, J. B., & Wilson, J. F. (1994). Personality and family-environment predictors of self-reported eating attitudes and behaviors. *Journal of Personality Assessment, 63,* 313-326.

47. Christensen, A. J., Wiebe, J. S., Smith, T. W., & Turner, C. W. (1994). Predictors of survival among hemodialysis patients: Effect of perceived family support. *Health Psychology, 13,* 521-525.

48. Felker, K. R., & Stivers, C. (1994). The relationship of gender and family environment to eating disorder risk in adolescents. *Adolescence, 29,* 821-834.

49. Fukunishi, I., Ichikawa, M., Ichikawa, T., & Matsuzawa, K. (1994). Effect of family group psychotherapy on alcoholic families. *Psychological Reports, 74,* 568-570.

50. Greene, R. C., Jr., & Plank, R. E. (1994). The short-form Family Environment Scale: Testing a different response format. *Psychological Reports, 74,* 451-464.

51. Grolnick, W. S., & Slowiaczek, M. L. (1994). Parents' involvement in children's schooling: A multidimensional conceptualization and motivational model. *Child Development, 65,* 237-252.

52. Henry, B., Moffitt, T. E., Caspi, A., Langley, J., & Silva, P. A. (1994). On the "remembrance of things past": A longitudinal evaluation of the retrospective method. *Psychological Assessment, 6,* 92-101.

53. Jaderlund, N. S., & Waldron, H. B. (1994). Mood states associated with induced defensiveness. *Journal of College Student Development, 35,* 128-134.

54. Kurtz, L., & Derevensky, J. L. (1994). Family configuration and maternal employment: Effects on family environment and children's outcomes. *Journal of Divorce & Remarriage, 22*(1/2), 137-154.

55. Lakey, B., & Dickinson, L. G. (1994). Antecedents of perceived support: Is perceived family environment generalized to new social relationships? *Cognitive Therapy and Research, 18,* 39-53.

56. Levy-Shiff, R., Einat, G., Har-Even, D., Mogilner, M., Mogilner, S., Lerman, M., & Krikler, R. (1994). Emotional and behavioral adjustment in children born prematurely. *Journal of Clinical Child Psychology, 23,* 323-333.

57. McCullough, J. D., McCune, K. J., Kaye, A. L., Braith, J. A., Friend, R., Roberts, W. C., Belyea-Caldwell, S., Norris, S. L. W., & Hampton, C. (1994). Comparison of community dysthymia sample at screening with a matched group of nondepressed community controls. *The Journal of Nervous and Mental Disease, 182,* 402-407.

58. McCullough, J. D., McCune, K. J., Kaye, A. L., Braith, J. A., Friend, R., Roberts, W. C., Belyea-Caldwell, S., Norris, S. L. W., & Hampton, C. (1994). One-year prospective replication study of an untreated sample of community dysthymia subjects. *The Journal of Nervous and Mental Disease, 182,* 396-401.

59. Muench, D. M., & Landrum, R. E. (1994). Family dynamics and attitudes toward marriage. *The Journal of Psychology, 128*, 425-431.
60. Naidoo, P., & Pillay, Y. G. (1994). Correlations among general stress, family environment, psychological distress, and pain experience. *Perceptual and Motor Skills, 78*, 1291-1296.
61. Smith, T., & Rotatori, A. F. (1994). Relation of adult supervision to academic and social development of fifth and sixth graders. *Psychological Reports, 75*, 1261-1262.
62. Vostanis, P., Nicholls, J., & Harrington, R. (1994). Maternal expressed emotion in conduct and emotional disorders of childhood. *Journal of Child Psychology and Psychiatry and Allied Disciplines, 35*, 365-376.
63. Yeatman, F. F., Bogart, C. J., Geer, F. A., & Sirridge, S. T. (1994). Children of Alcoholics Test: Internal consistency, factor structure, and relationship to measures of family environment. *Journal of Clinical Psychology, 50*, 931-936.
64. Braungart-Rieker, J., Rende, R. D., Plomin, R., DeFries, J. C., & Fulker, D. W. (1995). Genetic mediation of longitudinal associations between family environment and childhood behavior problems. *Development and Psychopathology, 7*, 233-245.
65. Faraone, S. V., Biederman, J., Chen, W. J., Milberger, S., Warburton, R., & Tsuang, M. T. Genetic heterogeneity in attention-deficit hyperactivity disorder (ADHD): Gender, psychiatric comorbidity, and maternal ADHD. *Journal of Abnormal Psychology, 104*, 334-345.
66. Felner, R. D., Brand, S., DuBois, D. L., Adan, A. M., Mulhall, P. F., & Evans, E. G. (1995). Socioeconomic disadvantage, proximal environmental experiences, and socioemotional and academic adjustment in early adolescence: Investigation of a mediated effects model. *Child Development, 66*, 774-792.
67. Fletcher, J. M., Brookshire, B. L., Landry, S. H., Bohan, T. P., Davidson, K. C., Francis, D. J., Thompson, N. M., & Miner, M. E. (1995). Behavioral adjustment of children with hydrocephalus: Relationships with etiology, neurological, and family stress. *Journal of Pediatric Psychology, 20*, 109-125.
68. Gidcyz, C. A., Hanson, K., & Layman, M. J. (1995). A prospective analysis of the relationships among sexual assault experiences. *Psychology of Women Quarterly, 19*, 5-29.
69. Gillis, J. S., & Mubbashar, M. H. (1995). Risk factors for drug abuse in Pakistan: A replication. *Psychological Reports, 76*, 99-108.
70. Gotlib, I. H., Lewinsohn, P. M., & Seeley, J. R. (1995). Symptoms versus a diagnosis of depression: Differences in psychosocial functioning. *Journal of Consulting and Clinical Psychology, 63*, 90-100.
71. Hur, Y., & Bouchard, T. J., Jr. (1995). Genetic influences on perceptions of childhood family environment: A reared apart twin study. *Child Development, 66*, 330-345.
72. Mallinckrodt, B., McCreary, B. A., & Robertson, A. K. (1995). Co-occurrence of eating disorders and incest: The role of attachment, family environment, and social competencies. *Journal of Counseling Psychology, 42*, 178-186.
73. Plomin, R. (1995). Genetics and children's experiences in the family. *Journal of Child Psychology and Psychiatry and Allied Disciplines, 36*, 33-68.
74. Snell, W. E., Jr., Gum, S., Shuck, R. L., Mosley, J. A., & Hite, T. L. (1995). The Clinical Anger Scale: Preliminary reliability and validity. *Journal of Clinical Psychology, 51*, 215-226.
75. Toro, P. A., Bellavia, C. W., Daeschler, C. V., Owens, B. J., Wall, D. D., Passero, J. M., & Thomas, D. M. (1995). Distinguishing homelessness from poverty: A comparative study. *Journal of Consulting and Clinical Psychology, 63*, 280-289.
76. Trief, P. M., Carnrike, C. L. M., Jr., & Drudge, O. (1995). Chronic pain and depression: Is social support relevant. *Psychological Reports, 76*, 227-236.

Review of the Family Environment Scale, Second Edition by JULIE A. ALLISON, Assistant Professor of Psychology, Pittsburg State University, Pittsburg, KS:

The Family Environment Scale, Second Edition (FES) was developed to measure social and environmental characteristics of families. The scale is based on a three-dimensional conceptualization of families. Each dimension includes related subscales. The Relationship dimension includes measurements of Cohesion, Expressiveness, and Conflict. The Personal Growth dimension involves assessments of Independence, Achievement Orientation, Intellectual-Cultural Orientation, Active-Recreational Orientation, and Moral-Religious Emphasis. The System Maintenance dimension includes Organization and Control measures. Scores for each of these 10 subscales are derived to create an overall profile of family environment. Based on these scores, families are then grouped into one of three family environment typologies (which generally reflect the three underlying dimensions of the scale), based on their most salient characteristics. A measure of Family Incongruence may also be derived in order to examine the extent to which family members may agree or disagree about their family climate. Additionally, three separate forms of the FES are available that correspondingly measure different aspects of these dimensions. The Real Form (Form R) measures people's perceptions of their actual family environments. In contrast, the Ideal Form (Form I) rewords items to assess individuals' perceptions of their ideal family environment, whereas the Expectations Form (Form E) instructs respondents to indicate what they expect a family environment will be like under, for example, anticipated family changes.

Each of the subscales is represented by nine brief statements concerning family climate. Respondents are asked to make a dichotomous judgement about whether the statement is true or false about their family, resulting in 90-item scales. Inclusion of items into the FES was based on five psychometric criteria: "The overall item split should be as close to 50–50 as possible to avoid items characteristic only of unusual families" (p. 19), items should correlate more highly with their own subscale than any other, "each of the subscales should have an approximately equal number of items scored true and scored false" (p. 19), "the subscales should have low to moderate intercorrelations" (p. 19), and "each item (and each subscale) should discriminate among families" (p. 19). Each of these criteria was met in subsamples of a variety of different families. Internal consistency for each of the subscales ranged from moderately low (.61) to moderately high (.78). Additionally, acceptable evidence for test-retest reliability, and construct and discriminant validity has been found. Normative data on the Form R subscales are available from a total of 1,625 different families (1,125 normal, 500 distressed), each of which came from a variety of sources. Normative data for Form I are available, but based on only 281 families, and should therefore be considered tentative.

Research applications of the FES are many and varied. The FES has been used to describe and compare different types of families (e.g., variations in family profile in abusive families), and to aid in the understanding of how different family social climates may develop (e.g., the effects of parental occupations, child-rearing attitudes and practices). The FES has also succeeded in aiding the understanding of how family environment may influence a family's successful adaptation to life transitions and crises. It has been included in studies investigating how family climate may affect children and their personal and social growth, as well as the psychosocial and health-related impact of family climate on adults. Finally, researchers have used the FES to help predict and measure treatment outcomes of psychiatric and alcoholic patients.

The FES is a viable approach to the study of family systems. Although the instrument should not be considered a comprehensive approach because of its primarily social nature, it would be a valuable complementary tool to researchers and practitioners alike.

Review of the Family Environment Scale, Second Edition by BRENDA H. LOYD, Professor of Education, University of Virginia, Charlottesville, VA:

The Family Environment Scale, Second Edition (FES) is a 90-item paper and pencil instrument that measures perceptions of family structure, orientation, and interactions. The 90 items are used to produce 10 subscales, representative of three domains of family environment. The three subscales of Cohesion, Expressiveness, and Conflict represent the Relationship domain. The six subscales of Independence, Achievement Orientation, Intellectual-Cultural Orientation, Active-Recreational Orientation, and Moral-Religious Emphasis represent the Personal Growth domain. The two subscales of Organization and Control represent the System Maintenance domain.

There are three different forms of the scale. Form R, the Real Form, is the form on which the normative data were gathered; this form receives the greatest emphasis and fullest interpretation in the test manual. Directions for the Real Form ask an individual to decide which of the statements are true of his or her family and which statements are false. Form I, the Ideal Form, presents the same statements as Form R but uses future tense instead of present tense verbs. For the Ideal Form, individuals are asked to decide which statements are true of an ideal family and which are false. Form E, the Expectations form, presents the same statements as Form I, but asks an individual to decide what his or her family will be like and to determine which statements are true or false for this future family.

The administration and scoring of the instrument are, in general, clear and simple. The raw scores on the 10 subscales are computed in an efficient, straightforward manner. Calculating standard scores from raw scores is accomplished through a conversion table for Form R subscale scores. However, the mathematical derivation of the standard scores from raw scores is not clearly described in the manual and conversion tables are not provided for Form E and Form I. A Family Incongruence Score, derived from administration of the scale to more than one member of a family, is more difficult to compute, and a detailed example is provided in the manual. Standard scores corresponding to the Family Incongruence Scores are also presented in a conversion table; however, the derivation of these standard scores is not presented in the test manual.

RELIABILITY. Internal consistency reliability estimates for the Form R subscales range from .61 to .78. Intercorrelations among these 10 subscales range from -.53 to .45. These data suggest that the scales are measuring relatively distinct characteristics of family environment and with reasonable consistency. Although the internal consistency estimates are reasonable and the subscales could be used for determining differences between groups, for an individual's score the standard error of measurement should be taken into account. Scores for two individuals would need to differ by approximately 3 raw score points on most subscales to be sure that the difference was not due to measurement error. Similarly, when evaluating a profile, small differences should not be overinterpreted.

Estimates of Form R subscale stability across time are provided. Test-retest reliabilities for 2-month, 3-month, and 12-month intervals range from .52 to .91. These estimates suggest that the scale is reasonably stable across these time intervals. These stability estimates are based on samples of 47, 35, and 241 respectively. Within these samples, multiple members of a family are measured suggesting that the stability estimates, which are larger than the estimates of internal consistency, may be inflated due to dependence of individuals within the samples.

Estimates of reliability, stability, and intercorrelations for Form E subscales, Form R subscales, and for the Family Incongruence Score are not provided in the test manual.

VALIDITY. The face and content validity of the instrument are supported by clear statements about family situations that relate to subscale domains. Most statements refer to "family members"; this could refer to traditional or nontraditional family situations. In a few items, references to the Bible, bowling, Little League, lectures, plays, and concerts may suggest a middle-class orientation.

Evidence of construct validity is presented in the manual through comparative descriptions of distressed and normal family samples; comparisons of parent responses with those of their adolescent children; descriptions of responses by families with two members, three members, four members, five members, and six or more members; and descriptions of families with a single parent, of minority families, and of older families.

Additional validity evidence is provided in the manual through summaries or references to approximately 150 additional research studies. These studies help delineate the strengths and weaknesses of the scale. For example, the factor structure of the domains and subscales has been examined in 14 studies and the results of those studies have suggested considerable variation in the number and nature of the underlying dimensions.

SUMMARY. The Family Environment Scale is a well-constructed measure of family social structure that allows for multiple perspectives and for consideration of multiple aspects of the family system. The psychometric properties are sufficient to make this a valid instrument for group research. The FES is reasonable for clinical use with an individual or family if attention is restricted to interpretation of differences that are larger than the standard error of measurement. Caution is suggested in interpreting profiles without additional evidence to support the interpretation. Additional caution is suggested when families are nontraditional or from non-majority cultures.

[152]

Figurative Language Interpretation Test.
Purpose: Designed to assess comprehension of figurative language (simile, metaphor, hyperbole, and personification), "which is integral to language development and reading comprehension."
Population: Grades 4–10.
Publication Date: 1991.
Acronym: FLIT.
Scores: Total score only.
Administration: Group or individual.
Forms, 2: A, B.
Price Data, 1991: $45 per test kit including manual (32 pages), 25 each of Forms A and B, 50 answer sheets, and scoring template; $15 per specimen set.
Time: Less than (60) minutes.
Author: Barbara C. Palmer.
Publisher: Academic Therapy Publications.

Review of the Figurative Language Interpretation Test by GABRIEL M. DELLA-PIANA, Director of Evaluation, El Paso Collaborative for Academic Excellence, University of Texas at El Paso, El Paso, TX:

The Figurative Language Interpretation Test (FLIT) consists of two 25-item parts and two forms. The task in Part I is to select from among four alternatives the "most common meaning" of a given figure of speech such as, "To have *a heart of gold.*" The task in Part II is to choose the meaning of a figure of speech "as it is used in [a given] sentence." For example, "Mary was loved by all for she had *a heart of gold.*"

The author designed the test for grades 4 through 10, as "a norm-referenced diagnostic test which examines a student's ability to comprehend frequently used types of figurative language such as simile, metaphor, hyperbole, and personification" and to provide equivalent forms that "can be used to pre- and post-test a student's comprehension of figurative language" (manual, p. 6).

The content for the test should presumably come from a defined domain of "frequently used" figurative language of types indicated in the purpose. Where the author obtained the content is specified (basal readers, trade books, dictionaries of quotations and phrase and fable, newspapers, and magazines). However, no clear domain specification parameters are given nor any procedures for selecting content from the sources indicated.

Test items were written to be at or below the 5th grade readability level based on a published core vocabulary. However, how readability actually enters into performance was not examined. The final test of 100 items used for Form A (Parts I and II) and Form B (Parts I and II) consists of the same 100 items used in the pilot version except that an item analysis was used to "improve" the items. How the item analysis was used or what improvement consisted of was not specified. Thus, as far as content selection and item development is concerned one has little help in determining what kind of comprehension is tapped and in what way the test is diagnostic.

The item appropriateness for the range of grades indicated (grades 4 through 10) is not directly discussed although some data are presented on item difficulties at each grade level (manual, p. 28). One wonders how many items were as difficult as .06 or as easy as .91 at the 4th grade level. Or indeed how many items were very easy (the range is .80 to .98 across all grade levels) or very difficult (the range is .06 to .29 across all grade levels).

Reliabilities (Kuder-Richardson 20) reported for grade 4 are .67 and .74 for alternative forms and overall reliability over all grades was .85 and .84 for alternative forms (manual, p. 29). However, it is surprising to find no evidence of reliability for diagnostic purposes because the test was presumably designed to be "diagnostic" with respect to comprehension of different types of figurative language. In any case the authors should discuss what the observed reliabilities suggest with respect to intended test use and what additional data the user must provide.

The test items are intended to call upon ability to recognize the meanings of figurative language phrases in isolation and in context. For test takers not acquainted with the term "figure of speech" the instructions are not likely to help in understanding the test task. For example, the instructions for Part I simply ask the test taker to "Choose the most common meaning for each figure of speech." But no explanation of figure of speech is given. It is true the examples might help, but no feedback on student performance on the examples is suggested nor any check to see if the test takers understand the task. I have already noted the test has no item selection nor scoring for "different types" of figures of speech. What of the "no context" (Part I) versus "context" (Part II) implied in the two sections of the test? Do the following "example items" provide a "context" for interpretation? "Mary was loved by all for she had *a heart of gold.*" "Joe asked them to *give it to him straight.*" It seems unlikely the context helps here. Although some of the actual items do provide a helpful context for interpretation, others do not. It would be interesting to compare item analysis data for such items.

Validity has, of course, already been discussed above. The author claims that "construct validity" is supported in part by correlations with the total reading score on a standardized achievement test. This is a strange validity strategy considering the fact there was an attempt to limit the effect of reading ability by writing items that were at a 5th grade readability level (unless the intent was to demonstrate a low correlation with the total reading score on a standardized test). The author also claims that construct validity is supported in part by comparison with the content and format of similar instruments, but no discussion of this comparison is included. Content selection representing "common usage" was also considered evidence of construct validity. However, there is no definition or supporting evidence for "common usage" other than noting the selection sources (not selection rules). Usage might be expected to vary across grades 4 to 10. There is no specified selection of content for the intended diagnostic uses of the test (presumably for "context" versus "no context" and for different types of figurative language), and the standardization sample (379 students in grades 4–10 in northern Florida) leaves much to be desired with respect to supporting inferences from normative comparisons.

All that said with respect to the work yet to be done in test development, the author's suggestions in the "Interpretation" section of the manual (p. 14) seem to be a helpful guide for the teacher as test user. The test is suggested as a way of getting at "prior knowledge" of figurative language and for identifying particular kinds of figurative language (hyperbole, metaphor, simile, personification). On the latter use the teacher must be willing to go through the items to identify the types. Thus, used informally as suggested, the classroom teacher may find the test useful if she or he is willing to carry the interpretive load for which the manual gives less help than one would hope.

Review of the Figurative Language Interpretation Test by BIKKAR S. RANDHAWA, Professor of Educational Psychology, University of Saskatchewan, Saskatoon, Canada:

This test was designed to assess comprehension of frequently used types of figurative language such as hyperbole, metaphor, personification, and simile. Understanding and using figurative language are important components of language development. The Figurative Language Interpretation Test (FLIT) assesses only the ability to understand figurative language. Contrary to the inference in the manual, the FLIT does not assess the ability to use figurative language because an examinee is never provided the opportunity to demonstrate the use of this ability in written or spoken samples. Authentic assessment of the use of figurative language can be made only through written and spoken expression.

A rationale for the development of the FLIT is that it focuses specifically on the ability to comprehend and use frequently used figurative language, allowing "educators to determine the level of instruction needed" (p. 5). It is argued that this ability is an important factor in reading comprehension. Many reading comprehension tests assess figurative language comprehension to varying degrees but the FLIT assesses this ability exclusively. The development of this test is premised on the finding that figurative language is a major source of comprehension breakdown. Further, figurative language is seen as an important vehicle for thinking and expressive processes. Despite the importance of figurative language, the FLIT author suggests that other than a few examples of the most common types of figurative language, very little direct instruction is provided in this area. The author of the FLIT is hoping the diagnostic information yielded by this test and the teaching strategies provided in the manual will correct the limited instructional emphasis on figurative language. I think the FLIT should not play the advocacy role for instruction of figurative language in language arts classrooms. This role properly belongs to curriculum committees and professional organizations.

The manual describes the sources of items for the test. Although the FLIT is designed to assess the ability to comprehend frequently used types of figurative language, the manual does not provide a listing of the items in various categories. This limits the diagnostic value of the test. What does "most common meaning for each figure of speech" mean? There is no information available on the frequency counts of the similes, metaphors, hyperboles, and personifications that became the basis of selection of the items. I think categorized information of this kind would be required for a test to be useful for diagnostic instructional purposes. In its current form only item performance of an examinee is available for analysis.

The items on the two forms of the test supposedly were written at or below the 5th grade readability level. The test is intended to be used for assessing the figurative language development of students from grades 4 through 10. I find it difficult to accept the claim that this test is appropriate for such a large age range. The normative and other data are based on a very small number of cases at various grade (N =

42 to 67) and age (N = 7 to 34) levels. The numbers make using the test as a normative device quite suspect. The normative samples are not sufficiently representative to warrant proper interpretation of the norms even in Florida because the 400 students who were tested were from northern Florida, with 379 students completing both forms of the FLIT.

This test is at best a preliminary version. Validity evidence is inadequate. Data that are provided are on very small samples and cannot be regarded as robust and useful for making defensible interpretations.

Two forms of the test are presented in parallel structure, with two parts of 25 items each. The first part consists of items that assess the comprehension of figurative language expressions out of context and each item stem contains the word "means." This repetitive and boring format could be improved by using improved directions for this part.

In summary, the FLIT is not properly standardized. The validity evidence is based on very small and nonrepresentative samples. Claims regarding the appropriateness of this test for diagnostic purposes in a large grade range, 4th to 10th, are not substantiated. For a wider use of this test, validity evidence and norms on large representative samples are required. Also, frequency counts of the item pool and of the common usage of the various types of the figurative language are needed for this test to serve a diagnostic instructional function. This version of the test, I think, is only a preliminary one. Marketing it, in this form, was premature.

[153]

Fleishman Job Analysis Survey.

Purpose: "A means for analyzing the knowledge, skills and abilities needed to perform jobs."
Population: Adults.
Publication Date: 1992.
Acronym: F-JAS.
Scores, 72: 52 Abilities Scales: Cognitive (Oral Comprehension, Written Comprehension, Oral Expression, Written Expression, Fluency of Ideas, Originality, Memorization, Problem Sensitivity, Mathematical Reasoning, Number Facility, Deductive Reasoning, Inductive Reasoning, Information Ordering, Category Flexibility, Speed of Closure, Flexibility of Closure, Spatial Orientation, Visualization, Perceptual Speed, Selective Attention, Time Sharing), Psychomotor (Control Precision, Multilimb Coordination, Response Orientation, Rate Control, Reaction Time, Arm-Hand Steadiness, Manual Dexterity, Finger Dexterity, Wrist-Finger Speed, Speed of Limb Movement), Physical (Static Strength, Explosive Strength, Dynamic Strength, Trunk Strength, Extent Flexibility, Dynamic Flexibility, Gross Body Coordination, Gross Body Equilibrium, Stamina), Sensory/Perceptual (Near Vision, Far Vision, Visual Color Discrimination, Night Vision, Peripheral Vision, Depth Perception, Glare Sensitivity, Hearing Sensitivity, Auditory Attention, Sound Localization, Speech Recognition, Speech Clarity); 9 Interactive/Social Scales (Persuasion, Social Sensitivity, Oral Fact Finding, Oral Defense, Resistance to Premature Judgement, Persistence, Resilience, Behavior Flexibility, Sales Interest); 11 Knowledge/Skills Scales (Electrical/Electronic Knowledge, Mechanical Knowledge, Knowledge of Tools and Uses, Map Reading, Drafting, Reading Plans, Driving, Typing, Shorthand, Spelling, Grammar).
Administration: Group.
Levels, 3: Job-Level Analysis, Job Dimension-Level Analysis, Task-Level Analysis.
Price Data, 1992: $35 per sampler set including test booklet, answer sheet, and administrator's guide (34 pages); $75 per 5 reusable test booklets; $25 per 25 self-scorable answer sheets; $10 per 20 tally sheets; $25 per administrator's guide; $45 per Handbook of Human Abilities (132 pages).
Time: (40) minutes.
Comments: Previously referred to as the Task Assessment Scales, Ability Requirement Scales, Manual for the Ability Requirement Scales (MARS); Handbook of Human Abilities contains ability definitions, tasks, jobs, and test descriptions.
Authors: Edwin A. Fleishman and Maureen E. Reilly.
Publisher: Consulting Psychologists Press, Inc.

Review of the Fleishman Job Analysis Survey by JEFFREY S. RAIN, Assistant Professor and Chairman, Industrial/Organizational Psychology Program, Florida Tech, Melbourne, FL:

The Fleishman Job Analysis Scale (F-JAS) and the accompanying abilities manual and administrative guide are offered as a method for determining the knowledge, skills, and abilities (KSAs) required to perform jobs. The foundation of the F-JAS is, in large part, the *Handbook of Human Abilities*. Herein lies one of the major strengths of this instrument, that is, as a compendium of abilities. The Handbook and the resulting F-JAS represent several decades of research beginning with physical and psychomotor abilities (Fleishman, 1975).

Not surprisingly, the 52 scales used to determine the importance of psychomotor, cognitive, physical, and sensory-perceptual abilities are the best developed of the F-JAS. In addition to being well researched, the Handbook contains a list of published tests specifically designed to assess many of the abilities found to be important in successful job performance. The Interpersonal/Social and Knowledge/Skills scales hold promise of rounding out the scope of the survey. However, these scales do not have the strong foundation of the first 52 scales. Future editions of the Handbook also will include, I hope, a list of published tests that assess abilities covered by these newer scales.

The F-JAS places a substantial amount of information in the hands of the user. More responsibility on the part of the instrument's user is therefore assumed. Two issues related to the experience and/or expertise of the user may limit the utility of the F-JAS. First, the F-JAS was not designed as a complete job analysis instrument, particularly if used beyond the job level. The F-JAS does not generate a job task or dimension list. Therefore, a greater burden is placed on any existing job task analysis if the F-JAS is used at the dimension level or task level. At the task level, the more clearly the job is defined prior to use with the F-JAS, the more likely the resulting KSAs will be comprehensive.

Second, the required expertise of the raters or the administrator may vary with the level at which the F-JAS is used. At the job level, the subject matter experts completing the scales must be familiar enough with the job's dimensions and tasks to systematically cover all requisite KSAs. These experts may be asked to rate the abilities without having the dimension and tasks in front of them as they might with a job task analysis. With complex jobs, inexperienced incumbents may overlook specific dimensions or tasks, resulting in missed KSAs. The authors do present research indicating good agreement between raters even when inexperienced raters were included (Reilly & Zink, 1980; 1981). Nevertheless, as the authors indicate, the job knowledge of the rater is critical.

A hidden value of the F-JAS may emerge as the Americans with Disabilities Act receives more attention. If the intent of the F-JAS administrator is to link KSAs to the essential functions of a job, the F-JAS will likely provide two additional advantages. The F-JAS and Handbook may suggest specific tests or information allowing for reasonable accommodations not only for testing issues, but in redesigning components of the job. Further, it may pinpoint more legally defensible links of the KSAs to essential job tasks and functions.

Reliability studies indicate strong support for the agreement among raters. Agreement between types of raters, such as between supervisors and job incumbents was lower than agreement within rater type, but was still well in the mid to upper .80s. To achieve acceptable levels of reliability, the authors suggest that 20–30 job experts provide the ability ratings.

Evidence of substantial internal and external validity is presented. Predictive validity is demonstrated by linking ratings of individual's abilities and job performance. No data were included that compared the F-JAS to other job analysis methods. Unfortunately, the lack of comparison data is endemic to job analysis research, not only to the F-JAS (for some comparison information see Levine, 1983).

One limitation of the reliability and validity analyses is that they were based almost exclusively with the psychomotor, cognitive, physical, and sensory-perceptual abilities. The reliability and validity of the Interpersonal/Social and Knowledge/Skills scales should be evaluated.

Normative data are not extensive. Three appendices provide data on a very narrow selection of jobs and dimensions within those jobs. Although the authors suggest referring to the bibliography for additional information, ideally the normative data would be available with the F-JAS. The F-JAS may develop into a more norm-based taxonomic tool as more data are collected.

On the purely practical side, the instrument itself is simple and easy to use. The Rating Scale Booklet presents a definition of each scale, how the dimension is different from other abilities, and a behaviorally anchored rating scale. Aside from a misplaced anchor for Near Vision, the Rating Scale Booklet explains the abilities in a manner facilitating any type of rater's discrimination between abilities. This is especially helpful because discrimination between abilities is often difficult for subject matter experts not accustomed to thinking in job analysis terms.

From the administrator's viewpoint, the F-JAS is equally easy to use. Step-by-step instructions are provided for each of the three levels: job, dimension, and task. Tallying results is also simple, although it is left up to the administrator to determine how to use the ratings. For example, at what rated level is a KSA no longer important to a job? The answer may need to be left to the administrator, but could be facilitated with improved job-specific norms.

Overall, the F-JAS provides a comprehensive framework for identifying knowledge, skills, and abilities. The F-JAS simplifies one of the more difficult job analysis tasks: linking KSAs to job, dimension, and task level information. As the normative base increases and more research is conducted on the Interpersonal/Social and Knowledge/Skills scales, the F-JAS's value should increase. The usefulness of the F-JAS may ultimately depend on the expertise of administrator, experience of subject matter experts, and thoroughness of job task analysis or job description information. However, this is a criticism inherent to almost all job analysis methods.

REVIEWER'S REFERENCES

Fleishman, E. A. (1975). Toward a taxonomy of human performance. *American Psychologist, 30*, 1127-1149.

Reilly, R. R., & Zink, D. L. (1980; 1981). *Analysis of four inside craft jobs* (AT&T Research Reports). American Telephone and Telegraph, Inc.

Levine, E. L. (1983). *Everything you always wanted to know about job analysis*. Tampa, FL: Mariner Pub. Co.

Review of the Fleishman Job Analysis Survey by ROSS E. TRAUB, Professor of Measurement, Evaluation, and Computer Application, The Ontario Institute for Studies in Education, Toronto, Ontario, Canada:

Starting from the definition of an ability as "a relatively enduring general trait or capacity that is related to performance in a variety of tasks" (*Administrator's Guide to the F-JAS*, hereafter referred to as AG, pp. 1–2), the authors of the Fleishman Job Analysis Survey (F-JAS) presuppose that analysts can identify the abilities persons need to perform jobs successfully. They also presuppose this knowledge will somehow inform and facilitate the recruiting, selecting, training, and evaluating of personnel.

The F-JAS is an excellent resource, given the aforementioned presuppositions. Its 72 scales, 52 of which are in final form and 20 of which represent domains "still under development" (AG, p. 2), span the gamut of human abilities defined and refined in the psychometric research of the past century. A companion publication, *Handbook of Human Abilities*, includes for each ability a list of standardized tests available for use in assessing the capabilities of job applicants or job incumbents.

The scale definitions provided in the *Rating Scale Booklet for the F-JAS* and the *Handbook of Human Abilities* are extraordinarily clear. For example, "Time Sharing," the meaning of which was not immediately obvious from the label, is defined as "the ability to shift back and forth between two or more sources of information. The information can be in the form of speech, signals, sounds, touch, or other sources." Also included for each ability are descriptions of how it differs from other, more-or-less closely related abilities ("Time Sharing: involves using information from more than one source" whereas "Selective Attention: Involves concentrating on relevant information and filtering out distracting material").

The amount of each ability required to perform a job is rated on a 7-point scale. Statements of "definition-clarification" (AG, p. 12) are provided for the extremes of each scale. In addition, each ability scale is anchored to selected jobs judged by panels of experts to require particular amounts of the ability (e.g., a little more than 6 of the 7 units on the Time Sharing scale is what the experts judge to be required of air traffic controllers, a little less than 5 units for "monitor[ing] several teletypes at the same time in a newsroom," and only about 3 units for "[w]atch[ing] street signs while driving at 30 miles per hour").

RELIABILITY. How reliable are the ratings that judges provide of jobs using the F-JAS? The instructions for administering the instrument cover, among other things, the crucial matters of selecting and training raters. According to an extensive body of research summarized in the AG, these instructions are effective in producing ratings possessed of relatively high interrater reliability, with coefficients reported to lie for the most part in the range of .7 to .9 for a wide variety of jobs. Coefficients this size are reported regardless of whether the raters being compared are from the same category of persons (job incumbents or job supervisors or job analysts) or from different categories.

Despite the apparently high level of interrater agreement reported for the F-JAS, a cautionary note must be sounded. It is not clear that all the coefficients reported in AG are appropriate for assessing interrater reliability. For example, Table 1 (AG, p. 13) contains coefficients said to reflect agreement between raters of different types (job incumbents, supervisors, analysts) on the "Relative Rank Orders of the 19 Abilities for Each Job Category." No explanation is provided for why only 19 (of 52 or 72) abilities were involved in the study of each of 15 occupation categories. More important, rank-order coefficients of correlation ignore the metric information in job ratings, yet this metric information would seem an important outcome of job assessment; otherwise, why bother anchoring each rating scale in the F-JAS to the amounts of ability required to perform particular jobs? (The latter feature of the F-JAS has already been noted.)

What appears to be needed is a generalizability study (Shavelson & Webb, 1991) of the F-JAS. Such a study would yield a matrix of data for each job considered in the investigation, with raters and F-JAS scales defining the dimensions of the matrix. This would provide the information needed to assess interrater agreement in judging a particular job. A further question is how well judges can use the scales of the F-JAS to distinguish among the ability requirements of different jobs. This question could be addressed by a study in which several jobs were considered simultaneously, with the data collected forming a cube and making it possible to estimate several additional and informative components of variance for F-JAS ratings.

VALIDITY. Evidence of validity is provided under three headings—internal, external, and predictive validity. Included as evidence of internal validity are (*a*) a description of the process by which the F-JAS abilities were identified—references to several factor analytic studies have been included here, (*b*) several references to demonstrations that the proportion of tasks in a job that can be related to F-JAS scales is much closer to 1 than to 0, and (*c*) a single reference to a demonstration that the abilities one would expect a priori to be important for a type of job are in fact judged important by analysts. Evidence of external validity includes the citation of several studies demonstrating "that the same ability profile emerges across job sites for a particular job" (AG, p. 16).

As persuasive as the foregoing validity evidence is, what a prospective user needs to know is whether or not an F-JAS analysis will produce information useful in selecting and training job applicants and evaluating job incumbents. This issue is addressed to a limited extent in AG through brief reference to two types of predictive validity evidence. The first type of evidence derives from a study in which 38 job tasks apparently were the units of observation in a multiple-regression analysis, the criterion variable being mean performance (over 400 individuals) of the job tasks and the predictor variables being mean F-JAS ratings (over job analysts) of the job tasks, the latter for an unspecified number of abilities. The resulting multiple correlation was relatively high (.64) (but note that the number of observations on which the correlation is based, namely 38, is relatively small). The second type of predictive validity evidence consists of research showing that scores on ability tests chosen on the basis of an F-JAS job analysis correlated significantly with ratings of job performance.

UNRESOLVED PROBLEMS. It is one thing to know that an F-JAS analysis will identify the abilities needed to do a job, it is quite another to know how much of the ability is required. The job anchors provided for F-JAS scales are inadequate for this purpose because neither the anchor jobs nor the points on an F-JAS scale are equated to the scales of the ability tests that could be used to assess a job applicant's or a job incumbent's capabilities. For example, the test score representing an amount of ability equal to a Level 6 F-JAS job requirement in the ability is a matter presumably left to individual personnel officers to resolve, something they might do by building up job-related norms for a test of each relevant ability.

Another problem to be confronted by users who plan to base training programs on the results of an F-JAS job analysis is that the 72 abilities identified in the instrument vary considerably in the degree to which one can expect to enhance capabilities through training. For example, training could very well be expected to increase a person's "Social Sensitivity." On the other hand, such abilities as "Far Vision," "Finger Dexterity," and even "Originality" seem very much less amenable, on the face of the matter at any rate, to improvement through training.

CONCLUSION. The F-JAS is an excellent instrument of its kind. It is highly usable, with clear definitions of 72 important abilities, and with rating scales that are very well anchored, both by descriptions and by reference to jobs judged to demand specified amounts of the abilities. Usability is enhanced by a list, for each ability, of standardized tests that can be used to measure it. But these tests are not equated to the rating scales, so users will be unable to tell from a job analysis how high job applicants should score in order to satisfy the ability requirement for a job.

A final point: Users of the F-JAS might all too easily fall into the trap of presuming that successful job performance is almost certain provided applicants possess the requisite amounts of the abilities identified in a job analysis. This presumption is unlikely to be valid for most jobs. Successful job performance is almost certainly more than the sum of its constituent abilities, and evaluations of job performance will almost certainly involve factors other than those tapped by the F-JAS.

REVIEWER'S REFERENCE

Shavelson, R. J., & Webb, N. M. (1991). *Generalizability theory: A primer*. Newbury Park, CA: Sage Publications.

[154]

Frenchay Dysarthria Assessment.

Purpose: Developed to diagnose dysarthria.
Population: Ages 12 and over.
Publication Date: 1983.
Scores, 11: Reflex, Respiration, Lips, Jaw, Palate, Laryngeal, Tongue, Intelligibility, Rate, Sensation, Associated Factors.
Administration: Individual.
Price Data, 1994: $34 per complete kit including examiner's manual (59 pages) and scoring form; $19 per 25 scoring forms.
Time: [20] minutes.
Comments: Tongue depressor, stop watch, tape recorder, glass of water, and word cards needed for administration.
Author: Pamela M. Enderby.
Publisher: PRO-ED, Inc.
Cross References: See T4:1007 (2 references).

Review of the Frenchay Dysarthria Assessment by STEVEN B. LEDER, Associate Professor of Surgery, Yale University School of Medicine, New Haven, CT:

The Frenchay Dysarthria Assessment's purpose is to assess dysarthric patterns across five neurological conditions (i.e., upper motor neuron lesions, mixed upper and lower motor neuron lesions, extrapyramidal disorders, cerebellar dysfunction, and lower motor neuron lesions). A test procedure manual provides an introduction and background information, description, normal data, interjudge reliability, validity, and instructions. Eight major sections are employed in the assessment: Reflex, Respiration, Lips, Jaw, Palate, Laryngeal, Tongue, and Intelligibility. A profile rating sheet that incorporates the major sections also includes subtests for each of the sections to be rated, influencing factors, a rating scale, and response form for a written summary and recommendations. Patterns of responses based on a 9-point rating scale are derived from observation of the patient's second attempt at clinician initiated tasks.

Dysarthria comprises a group of speech disorders resulting from disturbances in muscular control due to damage to the central or peripheral nervous system, with some degree of weakness, slowness, incoordination, or altered muscle tone that influences and characterizes the speech production mechanism (Darley, Aronson, & Brown, 1975). As a result, much more useful information can be obtained from observation of speech tasks than of isolated nonspeech tasks associated with specific structures involved in oromotor skills. For example, it is not necessary to assess independently tongue mobility in nonspeech tasks and then reassess these same basic movements during isolated word and connected speech tasks. Only the latter is necessary, thus making testing quicker and more directly related to rehabilitation strategies.

The test manual contains instructions that are clear and concise. Scoring directions are provided that result in a profile or pattern of responses. A discrepancy appears regarding the rating scale. The manual states that a 9-point scale is used to score the patient's response for each subtest. However, inspection of the rating sheet reveals that only 8 boxes are available for scoring responses (1 = *normal* to 8 = *no function*). In addition, the detailed grade for each subtest is specific to that subtest and has five choices (a–e). Using a 9-point scale for five choices on each subtest is a difficult task for the examiner.

A drawback to the test is that no individual section score or overall score is obtained. The examiner must rely on visualization of the profile on the rating sheet (i.e., the test gives patterns of dysarthria but no severity score). It is not known which areas are significantly different. It would be more valuable to derive significant differences between the five neurological disorders on the different sections and subtests based upon the test severity rating within each diagnostic category.

A number of problems arise regarding the sample population on which the test is normed. Why did the normal population not score 100% on all nonspeech and speech tasks? How did the author account for the variation in severity of dysarthria across the neurological subjects? The author stated (manual, p. 16) that, "The mean scores can be misleading, however; therefore, careful examination of the standard deviations is necessary to understand the characteristics of each group." However, no actual standard deviations were provided, forcing the reader to "eyeball" the profiles for approximate standard deviations.

A criticism of the test is that nondysarthric areas are assessed, and people may form the erroneous conclusions that these areas are of importance in the differential diagnosis of dysarthria. Under the major section titled Reflex, dysphagia is assessed in a rudimentary fashion and it is unclear how swallowing relates to dysarthria as defined above. Under the Influencing Factors area of the rating sheet, hearing, sight, teeth, language, mood, and posture also do not relate to dysarthria.

In conclusion, the Frenchay Dysarthria Assessment can provide the beginning clinician with a systematic descriptive system to assess dysarthria. Unfortunately, some of the information collected is irrelevant to dysarthria, other information is collected on nonspeech tasks that may not correlate with speech production skills, and no individual subtest or overall numerical rating is generated.

REVIEWER'S REFERENCE

Darley, F. L., Aronson, A. E., & Brown, J. R. (1975). *Motor speech disorders*. Philadelphia: W. B. Saunders.

Review of the Frenchay Dysarthria Assessment by MALCOLM R. McNEIL, Professor and Co-chair, Department of Communication and Director of Communication Science & Disorders, University of Pittsburgh, Pittsburgh, PA:

The goals for the construction of the Frenchay Dysarthria Assessment (FDA) were to provide a test for dysarthria that: (*a*) was a guide to treatment; (*b*) was sensitive to change in patient behavior; (*c*) was efficient and easy to administer; (*d*) would require minimal training to achieve high reliability; (*e*) was easy to communicate to other medical professionals; and (*f*) was standardized in terms of established test-retest, intrajudge, interjudge reliabilities, and in terms of reference data for normal and pathological populations. The explicit purpose of the FDA was to provide speech pathologists with a means to categorically diagnose individuals with dysarthria according to lesion location (Upper Motor Neurone [UMN], Lower Motor Neurone [LMN], Mixed Upper and Lower Motor Neurone [M], Extrapyramidal [E], and Cerebellar [C]).

CONSTRUCT VALIDITY. The theoretical existence of the discrete anatomical or behavioral (dysarthric) categories was not discussed or justified in the test manual. No theoretical discussion or justification was provided that the 11 areas evaluated, the specific tasks utilized, the specific behaviors observed, or the means of describing or quantifying the behaviors on the FDA are appropriate for any of the state purposes. The FDA was presented essentially without construct validity. Reference to other theoretical frameworks as a rationale for the FDA such as the Mayo Clinic Diagnostic Classification System (Darley, Aronson, & Brown, 1969), however, can be found in other publications about the test by its author (Enderby, 1980, 1983).

CONTENT VALIDITY. The FDA consists of eight major sections and a section on "influencing factors" such as hearing, sight, teeth, language, mood, posture, movement rate, and oral sensation. Although not explicitly stated in the test manual, the justification for the evaluation of these areas appears to be derived from a survey undertaken by the author in which she reviewed the written summaries from clinical evaluations conducted by nine speech pathologists. From this, the common trends in topics and subheadings reported were summarized and became the sections of FDA targeted for examination. The resultant categories are: oral reflexes, respiration, lips, jaw, palate, vocal cords, tongue, intelligibility, posture, and rate of speech. The 29 observations/tasks include: cough; swallow; dribble/drool; respiration at rest and in speech; lips at rest; speed of lip movement; lip seal; alternate motion rate of the lips; lips in speech; jaw at rest and in speech; velopharyngeal leakage (termed palate) during vegetative functions, and repetitive non-nasal speech sounds, and during alternating nasal/non-nasal speech sounds, sustained vowel (termed laryngeal time); pitch range; vocal intensity or loudness; voice quality in speech; tongue at rest; tongue during rapid protrusion/retraction; tongue elevation; tongue lateralization; tongue diadochokinetic rate;

tongue movement in conversation; intelligibility for single word, sentence reading, and elicited conversational speech.

The scoring (termed grading) for each of the tasks/observations is based on a 5-point equal appearing interval scale, with the score assigned by subjective evaluations of specific behaviors. The clinician is required to translate the 5-point scale into a 9-point scale of severity for graphing and later profile analysis. In addition to the subjective assignment of values to each of the 29 observations, there remain serious questions about the intervality of several of the scales. Although the scales are used for pattern analysis in making the differential diagnosis, numerical values were assigned in order to compute the discriminant function and the reliability analyses. Only the second attempt at all tasks is scored, the first being used for practice.

Although the FDA manual does not include an explicit discussion of its content validity, most of the targets of evaluation and the tasks used to elicit behavior are routinely found on other oral-motor assessment procedures (e.g., The Dworkin-Culatta Oral Mechanism Examination, Dworkin & Culatta, 1980; and The Oral Mechanism Screening Examination, St. Louis & Ruscello, 1981). The evaluation of speech intelligibility is routinely utilized for the full assessment of dysarthria and other sensorimotor speech disorders (e.g., the Assessment of Intelligibility of Dysarthric Speech; Yorkston & Beukelman, 1981). The evaluation of swallowing on the FDA involves making similar observations and judgments as found in such tests as the BELZ Dysphagia Scale (Longstreth, 1986) and the Fleming Index of Dysphagia (Fleming & Waver, 1987).

The instructions given the patient for eliciting the specific behavior to be judged are generally vague and subject to a variety of interpretations across administrators. For example, the instructions to the test administrator for evaluating lip seal for the second task is to have the patient produce /P/ 10 times. There is no control of the vowel produced or the rate of productions, both variables that could have substantive effects on whether the patient performs the task with (*a*) a good lip seal, (*b*) occasional air leakage, (*c*) auditory weakness, or (*d*) and (*e*) without auditory representation (the description used for two ratings for this task).

SOCIAL VALIDITY. A measure of the social validity of the FDA was generated by comparing the author's written descriptions of 112 patients' FDA scores to clinicians' impressions of these patients. It was reported that of the 112 tests analyzed, 89.3% "were found accurate by the patient's therapist" (manual, p. 22). Although this method of "clinically" validating the FDA has some appeal, there is a confounding variable in that the same clinicians who assessed the patients were those who judged the adequacy of the author's interpretation. These data provide only the weakest of evidence for the clinical validation of the FDA.

CONCURRENT VALIDITY. No concurrent validity evidence was reported for the FDA.

PREDICTIVE VALIDITY. The validity of the FDA to predict patient group based on lesion location was evaluated by performing two separate discriminant analyses. The first analysis was conducted on 30 UMN, 10 LMN, 13 M, 18 E, and 14 C lesioned patients. It is not stated which variables were entered into the analysis, the alpha level chosen, how each subject was verified to have the specific lesion that was assumed, who verified the lesion location, or that the subjects were even dysarthric. High percentages of correct category assignment were achieved across all groups (i.e., UMN = 83%, LMN = 100%, M = 92%, E = 89%, C = 100%) and for all subjects combined (90.6%). It is not, however, possible to assign any degree of confidence to these predictions because it is not known if the diagnosis was made independent of the speech characteristics (except for the cerebellar group) on which they were later classified. In addition, the variables that were likely entered into the discriminant analysis (those 29 variable that are rated) were too numerous given the small number of subjects in each group. This likely resulted in statistical shrinkage and may have inflated the percentage of group members who were correctly identified.

The second discriminant analysis was conducted on an unspecified group (with respect to lesion location) of 22 individuals with dysarthria. Subjects were assigned to all categories from this analysis; however, there is no discussion of how or if the diagnosis was verified, leaving the assignment from the discriminant analysis essentially uninterpretable. In addition, no statistical data were provided for either of these analyses.

NORMATIVE SAMPLE. The FDA was administered to 194 normal healthy adults ranging in age from 15 to 97 years. Of the 15- to 59-year-old ($N = 175$) subjects, 94.6% received a score of 9 (presumably on all 29 variables rated) and 4.6% achieved a score of 8. Less than 1% scored a 7 or lower (presumably on any of the 29 variables). It was reported that overall, the lowest total score achieved by any of these subjects was 172 of 180 total possible points. It is unknown how 180 total points are derived from this test. Nearly 91% of the older group (60 to 97 years; $N = 37$) scored all 9s and 8.95% scored an 8. These results indicate that overall, independent of age, the FDA is insensitive to any possible effects of normal aging on the speech motor control and, therefore, should serve as a valid measure with which to detect dysarthria. This was not, however, verified by the test's authors.

A study by Wallace (1991) reported that overall performance on the FDA was not significantly different for four groups ($N = 10$ for each group of ages 50–59, 60–69, 70–79, and 80–89) of normal subjects. Using the *FDA Computer Differential Analysis* (Enderby & Rowarth, 1983), Wallace reported that 80% of the normal subjects were designated as having performance characteristics of dysarthria and the remaining 20% were designated as normal. Whether this represents a sensitivity of the FDA to the effects of aging or an extremely high false positive classification of dysarthria remains unanswered. The finding does, however, invite extreme caution in judging the test's validity for the main purpose for which it was constructed (classification of dysarthria). It also suggest that a great deal of research is needed before it can be used confidently for this clinical purpose.

Means and standard deviations are provided for 30 UMN, 10 LMN, 13 M, 18 E, and 14 C groups on the 9-point equal appearing interval scale for all 29 observations/tasks. It is suggested that these means and standard deviations, across the 29 categories that are rated, are to be used to differentiate the groups. Descriptive guidelines are offered for this perceptually based pattern evaluation of the graphs. The author suggests that a differential pattern is detectable across diagnostic groups. If the discriminant analysis were appropriately verified and shown to provide a valid pattern analysis this observation could be justified. In general, the sample sizes used in the validation study are too small. The distribution of scores for the samples are not provided. The normative data on these pathological populations are, therefore, not adequate to serve as a reference base against which other dysarthric subjects can be compared.

RELIABILITY.

Test-retest. The FDA does not report test-retest reliability; however, Wallace (1991) reported no significant difference in scores (the exact scores entered into the analyses were not reported) for eight normal subjects tested one week apart on the FDA. She also reported no difference in the impaired versus unimpaired classification of the subjects between the two tests. Although these data do support test-retest reliability for normal aging adults, they may not be generalized to test-retest reliability estimates for pathological populations.

Interjudge. Eight speech-language pathologists who were unfamiliar with the FDA received 3 hours of training in the test procedure and then scored 113 video taped, and three live FDAs. The 113 subjects examined were reported to present a broad range of types and degrees of dysarthria. Although it is not reported which scores or combinations of scores were entered into the analysis, and no significance values were reported, interjudge correlation coefficients were all high and ranged between .79 and .92. This suggests that with training, judges can become reliable scorers of the FDA. There is no report of the interjudge reliability for test administration.

Intrajudge. No within-judge scoring or administration reliability was reported in the FDA manual.

SUMMARY.

Strengths. A potentially positive attribute of the test's administration procedures is that the second trial of each task is the one scored for later analysis. Although not discussed or justified in the test manual, the majority of tasks utilized in the FDA are quite similar to those routinely used in tests and informal clinical protocols for the assessment of dysarthria.

Weaknesses. The FDA is presented without an adequately developed theoretical construct. The phenomenon that the test attempts to assess (dysarthria) is inadequately defined by the test's author. The content validity of the test is not justified in the test manual; however, the areas evaluated and tasks used to elicit the behaviors are, for the most part, similar to those found in other tests that attempt to assess similar functions in persons with sensorimotor speech disorders. The most obvious exception to this generalization is the inclusion of the assessment of coughing, swallowing, and drooling, as their relevance to dysarthria per se has not been justified. The impairment in any of these functions, therefore, does not by itself signal a motor speech impairment yet it is rated as such and included into the overall profile of dysarthria. The validity of the scoring system in terms of its interval properties has not been established, making judgments about patient severity from the derived ratings highly suspect. The relationship of the 5-point rating scale to the 9-point scale is not explained in the test manual. The instructions to the patients and the guidelines for assigning ratings is inadequately specified in the test manual leading to the probability of poor interjudge and intrajudge reliabilities without specific training by the author, which is not available.

The measure of "clinical validity" discussed in the test manual is at best weak evidence for its concurrent validity. The data provided as support for the classification of patients based upon lesion location are not interpretable given apparent experimental, including statistical, limitations in the study. In general, insufficient data are provided with which to judge the validity and reliability data that are presented in support of the FDA.

Although the sample size for normal control subjects is reasonable for establishing reference data, the relevant biographical variables for selection and description were not reported. For example, there is no indication that the subjects were in fact normal in ways that are relevant for these particular tasks. Further, evidence from a study by Wallace (1991) contradicts the data reported in the FDA on normal subjects' clear differential performance from dysarthric subjects.

Test-retest reliability was not reported for pathological subjects although data reported by Wallace (1991) suggest that it may be reliable for normal subjects. Although no intrajudge reliability was reported, it appears that acceptable levels of interjudge reliability can be achieved with 3 hours of training. No reliabilities for test administration were reported.

Overall, there is insufficient evidence that the FDA has achieved five of the six goals for which it was constructed (i.e., as a guide to treatment, to measure patient change, require minimal training to achieve high reliability, be easy to communicate to other professionals and have sufficiently high reliabilities and presented with appropriate normal and pathological reference data). Only the goal of ease and efficiency of administration might be judged to have been achieved. This, however, would be important only if the validity and reliability of the FDA were clearly established. In addition, there is insufficient evidence that the FDA can be confidently used to diagnose differentially the dysarthrias according to the lesion-location category system for which it was designed. In its current state of development, the FDA cannot be recommended for use for any purpose that one might wish to assess a person with dysarthria. It does serve as a structured set of tasks/observations of behaviors commonly assessed in persons with dysarthria and is no worse than other self-designed or "informal" protocols that are frequently used clinically.

REVIEWER'S REFERENCES

Darley, F. L., Aronson, A. E., & Brown, J. (1969). Differential diagnostic patterns of dysarthria. *Journal of Speech and Hearing Research, 12*, 246-269.

Dworkin, J., & Culatta, R. (1980). Dworkin-Culatta Oral Mechanism Examination. Nicholasville, KY: Edgewood Press.

Enderby, P. (1980). Frenchay dysarthria assessment. *The British Journal of Disorders of Communication, 15*, 165-173.

St. Louis, K., & Ruscello, D. (1981). The Oral Mechanism Screening Examination. Baltimore: University Park Press.

Yorkston, K. M., & Beukelman, D. R. (1981). Assessment of Intelligibility of Dysarthric Speech. Tigard, OR: C. C. Publications, Inc.

Enderby, P. (1983). The standardized assessment of dysarthria is possible. In W. R. Berry (Ed.), *Clinical dysarthria* (pp. 109-119). San Diego: College-Hill Press.

Enderby, P. M., & Roworth, M. (1983). *College-Hill Press user's guide for Frenchay Dysarthria Assessment computer differential analysis*. San Diego: College-Hill Press.

Longstreth, D. (1986, November). *The BELZ dysphagia scale.* Paper presented to the annual convention of the American-Speech-Language-Hearing Association, Detroit, MI.

Fleming, S., & Waver, A. (1987). Index of dysphagia: A tool for identifying deglutition problems. *Dysphagia, 1*, 206-208.

Wallace, G. L. (1991). Assessment of oral peripheral structure and function in normal aging individuals with the Frenchay. *Journal of Communication Disorders, 24*, 101-109.

[155]

Functional Needs Assessment.

Purpose: Designed to provide an integrated, systematic method for assessment, treatment planning, clinical program designing, and progress monitoring.
Population: Chronic psychiatric patients.
Publication Date: 1990.
Acronym: FNA.
Scores, 26: Physical Ability, Receptive Communication, Expressive Communication, Place Orientation, Time Orientation, Personal Knowledge, Numerical Concepts, Toileting Skills, Bathing Skills, Personal Hygiene, Dressing Skills, Dining Skills, Safety and Prevention, Care of Living Quarters, Kitchen Skills, Laundry Skills, Community Mobility, Food Preparation, Money Management, Shopping and Purchasing, Participation in Treatment, Task Skills, Prevocational Skills, Social Etiquette, Planning and Decision Making, Leisure Skills.
Administration: Individual.
Price Data, 1991: $49 per complete kit including 20 assessment forms and manual (95 pages); $24.95 per 10 assessment forms.
Time: (60) minutes.
Comments: Ratings by therapist using "criterion-referenced" assessment.
Author: Lynn Blewett Dombrowski.
Publisher: Therapy Skill Builders.

Review of the Functional Needs Assessment by JOHN R. GRAHAM, Professor and Chair, Department of Psychology, Kent State University, Kent, OH:

The Functional Needs Assessment (FNA) was designed to provide occupational therapists with a framework for guiding chronic psychiatric patients toward optimum functioning. The FNA is really more of a program than it is a test. The program involves the assessment of 26 functional components. The resulting assessment is used to develop an occupational therapy program and to monitor changes as the treatment program progresses.

The assessment part of the program involves having an occupational therapist determine if a patient is able to perform each of 130 specific activities (e.g., "can walk unassisted"; "is able to prepare a simple, uncooked meal"). For each item 5 points are awarded if the patient is able to perform the specified behavior and no points if the behavior cannot be performed. Whenever possible, ratings are to be based on direct observation of relevant behaviors, but when therapists have not been able to observe the relevant behaviors, they are advised to rely on "staff knowledge" to complete the items. For some items raters are to make passive observations of ongoing behavior; for other items raters ask patients to do specific things (e.g., lift a box from a table to the floor). The FNA manual contains instruction sheets needed for some items (e.g., simplified job application form) and lists a large number of materials needed but not provided for some of the items (e.g., clean cloth, dirty cloth, photographs of people engaged in leisure activities).

A score for each of the 26 functional areas is obtained by summing the points awarded for the five items in that area and dividing the sum by 5. A total score is obtained by summing points awarded for all 130 items. An average functional level score is determined by dividing the total score by 26. These average scores are assigned subjectively determined labels indicating functional capacity levels (Prebasic, Basic, Preintermediate, Intermediate, Advanced).

Scores on the 26 functional components are rationally grouped into six treatment areas (Verbal Communication, Self-Care Skills, Nutritional Management, Community Skills, Prevocational Skills, Preplacement Skills) to determine each patient's clinical program needs. Suggestions are made in the FNA manual for designing and implementing interventions in the various treatment areas.

In each booklet monitoring worksheets are provided to permit therapists to keep track of changes in functioning in each of the treatment areas as the treatment program progresses. It is suggested in the FNA manual that these data can be used to demonstrate the effectiveness of treatment programs.

The FNA manual does not contain the basic psychometric information needed to evaluate the instrument. The items and the scales into which items are grouped seem to have been selected based on clinical experience. There are no data indicating that the items selected are representative of the various behavioral domains they are intended to represent or that the groupings into the 26 functional components are appropriate. No data are reported concerning the reliability with which points can be awarded for the FNA items. This is an especially important concern because many of the behaviors to be evaluated are complex and rely on the judgment of the persons completing the FNA. No information is presented to support the assignment of labels for various scores to indicate levels of functioning. No data are reported concerning the FNA performance of a representative group of patients.

The FNA manual author reports several kinds of data related to the validity of the FNA. For example, the author reports that the scores of 83 patients improved over the course of occupational therapy. However, no extra test data were provided concerning changes in relevant behavior of the patients. Data also were presented for 108 patients who were discharged to settings involving different levels of supervision. As expected, patients discharged to the settings involving the least amount of supervision had obtained the highest FNA scores prior to discharge. These data are difficult to interpret, because it is likely that discharge decisions were based, at least in part, on FNA scores.

In summary, the FNA may be of interest to occupational therapists who work with chronic psychiatric patients. It provides a framework for organizing the various behaviors involved in occupational therapy programs. However, the absence of appropriate information concerning the development, reliability, and validity of the FNA scores makes it impossible for this reviewer to recommend the instrument for research or routine clinical use.

Review of the Functional Needs Assessment by PETER F. MERENDA, Professor Emeritus of Psychology and Statistics, University of Rhode Island, Kingston, RI:

The Functional Needs Assessment (FNA) is offered by the authors to be a program, "designed to provide therapists with a framework for guiding their patients toward optimum functioning" (manual, p. 1). It is not, therefore, the usual type of psychometric instrument that is typical of those reviewed in a volume of the *MMY* series. This fact, however, does not excuse the test author and her contributing authors or this reviewer from attending to the principles of good scale construction that serve to provide sound psychometric properties of instruments developed for measuring and evaluating aspects of human behavior. Evidence of such properties is required to support the claim made in the Introduction of the FNA manual that through the program clinicians *can* show that occupational therapy interventions contribute significantly to patient progress toward independent functioning. In order to avoid the usual caveats that are present in the field of assessment, such claims are expected to be supported by convincing empirical data provided through well-designed and controlled developmental and applied research studies. Unfortunately, both for the authors and the potential users of the program, this does not appear to be the case.

As stated by the authors, the Functional Needs Assessment program consists of: (*a*) an assessment comprising 26 functional components; (*b*) a set of goals and objectives emanating from the assessment; and (*c*) evaluation of the program. They go on to say that the 26 components are all neurologically based and developmentally sequenced into five progressive skill levels. Although the authors' professional experience and clinical intuition might be envisioned by themselves and others as sufficient for producing the adequate paradigm necessary for sound construction of instruments, a fatal flaw exists. These subjective judgments, no matter how reasonable, are not accompanied by any objective data, nor by sound methodologies for producing them.

Reviewers of tests for the *MMY*s are entreated by the editors of the series to include among the criteria for their critiques, the *Standards for Educational and Psychological Testing* (AERA, APA, & NCME, 1985). It would be expected by reviewers that test authors do likewise, especially at the early stages of design and development of their instruments. The main content of the critique that is to follow deals with issues and principles set forth in that document, and with sound practices in psychometrics, research design, and basic statistics.

The FNA program purports to provide a comprehensive, performance-based evaluation that is theory based and one that can demonstrate the effectiveness of treatment intervention for chronic psychiatric patients. However, there is not—as there should be—any postulation, description, or explanation of the underlying theoretical model. Further, attempts at demonstrating the effectiveness of the program are neither scientifically sound nor impressive or convincing. In fact, the weak attempts at simple statistical analyses are fraught with errors both of commission and omission.

The authors begin their attempt at scientific reporting by describing the target population for the FNA program by citing a brief hospitalization history of two "typical" patients. In doing so there arises in each case both the problem of generalizing from an isolated instance and that of negative instance.

With reference to the development of the FNA, it is stated that it was designed as a criterion-referenced instrument. No details of the construction process are given, but from what is said, it becomes clearly evident that its development did not include the analysis of empirical data derived from carefully designed research studies. A trial run with the instrument being developed was made with only 12 patients on whom subjective judgments were given by some unidentified clinician who classified them into low-, medium-, and high-functioning categories. The validity of such a procedure is highly questionable without any rigorous controls.

In examining what is reported further by the authors regarding the field testing of the FNA, several serious errors are noted. A study was conducted to determine the variability in time to administer the assessment by experienced and new evaluators. It was concluded that similar results were obtained at the first site where the data are based on 907 patients and at the second site involving 29 patients. In fact, the results are highly dissimilar! The first distribution is highly negatively skewed with a range of 15–105 minutes; the second, is markedly positively skewed with a range of 20–90 minutes. This statement asserting the similarity between the two distributions serves to mislead the naive reader and to confuse the astute potential user.

The field testing was obviously conducted on samples which are erroneously referred to as *populations*. Hence, the few data that are reported apply only to the specific samples, as defined, and cannot legitimately be generalized to other populations. This fact also invalidates what little statistical analyses (e.g., *t*-tests) that have been performed on data yielded by the assessment. Statistical inference is based on samples, whereas parameters are merely descriptive of population characteristics. Also, the authors note that although the program was designed for the purpose of assessing a chronic psychiatric patient population, theirs is substantially imbalanced (36%) with geriatric patients. They go on to say that due to this bias it is, therefore, possible to use the instrument effectively with a geriatric psychiatric patient population. They do so without first questioning whether they had done their field testing on appropriate patients or, more importantly, providing potential users with the necessary cautions regarding the questionable practice of applying the program to either type of patient.

There are categories of functional needs that the authors call "components" comprising the assessment instrument. Evaluation of each patient's current status and progress is accomplished by an evaluator's judgment of whether or not the patient can successfully perform the functions included in each category. Although many of these functions appear quite simple and clear on the surface, sound test construction principles require some evidence of interrater reliability. Evidently such analyses have never been performed on the "items" of the FNA.

The items on the instrument are dichotomously scored, the 2-point response categories being "yes" or "no." However, instead of scoring the items in the usual manner, 0/1, the authors have created a 0/5 scoring system. They explain that they find patients, "to be more impressed by the 'larger' number" (p. 31), and that fact also appears to motivate them to participate. What they do not seem to realize is that although for some purposes this approach may not present much of a problem (because a constant is involved) the practice does create a situation in which there are gaps in the distribution of scores. For many purposes, especially for statistical analyses, distributions that are not continuous, but are treated as if interval measures are involved, violate an important underlying assumption.

Perhaps the authors do realize what has just been said above or they have encountered a problem or two. Perhaps for that reason, they have resorted to a system of average scores (total score/26). This is a questionable practice, however. It assumes that all the 26 components are highly correlated with each other and are, therefore, merely measuring different aspects of the same general construct. This may be true, but without empirical demonstration, it is merely an assumption. Empirical data to support the practice are required.

An extensive bibliography (48 citations) is presented at the end of the manual. However, it is difficult to understand its pertinence to the construction and use of the FNA. A briefer list of references would have sufficed and been more meaningful. With appropriate references a potential user and/or critic could have gained some insight into the theory, rationale, and ultimate purpose of the assessment.

In summary, this reviewer finds many faults with the Functional Needs Assessment instrument and program with very little to recommend its adoption and use. Little or no consideration appears to have been given to sound psychometric principles and to the current APA *Standards* (AERA, APA, & NCME, 1985). The authors are encouraged to review and study this critique and to seek out a well-qualified psychometrician as a consultant to their project for developing a sound assessment instrument.

REVIEWER'S REFERENCE

American Educational Research Association, American Psychological Association, & National Council on Measurement in Education. (1985). *Standards for Educational and Psychological Testing*. Washington, DC: American Psychological Association, Inc.

[156]

Functional Performance Record.

Purpose: "For recording the observable actions and behaviours of people whose physical, social or psychological functioning is impaired."

Population: Individuals of all ages with disabilities.

Publication Date: 1989.

Acronym: FPR.

Scores: 27 topic areas: Activity Level, Aggression, Attention Span, Domestic/Survival Skills, Dressing Female/Male, Feeding, Fits and Faints, Hearing, Incontinence, Memory, Mobility, Motor Co-ordination and Loss of Balance, Movement of Limbs and Trunk, Number Skills, Personal Hygiene, Personal Safety, Reading Skills, Social Behaviour, Socially Unacceptable Behaviour, Speech and Language Reception, Speech and Language Production, Toileting, Touch, Temperature and Hypothermia, Transportation, Vision, Writing Skills.

Administration: Individual.

Price Data, 1992: £51.75 per administration manual (33 pages); £19 per 5 checklists; £155.25 per administration set diskette; £103.50 per client diskette; £747.50 per database software pack.

Time: Untimed.

Author: David J. Mulhall.

Publisher: NFER-Nelson Publishing Co., Ltd. [England].

Review of the Functional Performance Record by DELWYN L. HARNISCH, Associate Professor of Educational Psychology, University of Illinois at Urbana-Champaign, Champaign, IL:

NATURE OF THE INSTRUMENT. The Functional Performance Record (FPR) is a "clinical instrument for recording the observable actions and behaviors of people whose physical, social, and psychological functioning is impaired" (Introduction, p. viii). It can also be used in planning services for people with disabilities, in setting standards for the services provided, in monitoring the progress of functional performance obtained by people with disabilities, and in related research and evaluation studies. The author pointed out that the FPR was nondiagnostic in the sense that it was not designed to account for why people behave as they do, and that the FPR was nonrestrictive in that it provided only numerical and descriptive information on a client's functioning. This information can be utilized by a wide variety of concerned parties in a number of different ways.

The FPR is an attempt towards providing a systematic and objective picture of people with an array of problems ranging from learning difficulties to geriatric and physical difficulties. The goal of the FPR is to filter out the recorder's subjective impressions and to standardize, to an extent, the recording and description of the client's functional performance so that inter- and intra-client comparison would be possible.

GENERAL DESCRIPTION OF THE INSTRUMENT. The FPR includes more than 600 items divided into 27 topics or areas of functioning. The care provider observes the client, then completes all or part of the instrument using simple numeric codes. The numeric codes are used to categorize the nominal data. They were not meant to be nor should they be interpreted as quantitative measures. For example, in the Activity Level Section, 1 = no supervision needed; 3 = responsive to supervision; 5 = unresponsive to supervision; 7 = incapable, regardless of supervision; 9 = not applicable; 0 = unknown. Some users may tend to use 2 if they feel the client's situation is somewhere between "no supervision needed" and "responsive to supervision." This, however, is an invalid use of the instrument. The user should use the code as given, and uncertainties may be addressed by putting down a brief note beside the relevant numeric code.

The percentage deficit is the score used in the FPR that measures the functional performance at the time of observation and recording. It is the ratio of the observed level of deficit to the maximum possible deficit, expressed as a percentage. Specifically, the response codes are translated to weights. The observed deficit is the summation of the weights of all observed items except for those coded "not applicable" or "unknown." The maximum deficit is the summation of maximum weights for the corresponding items. The user can compute the deficit score by hand, but the process is time-consuming and tedious. The deficit score can be easily obtained by using the software called the Individual Client Disk supplied along with the instrument. Therefore, it is suggested the software be used. Another advantage of using the software is that the user can get what the author calls *deficit range,* which is similar to a confidence interval of the percentage deficit. The software also provides a graphical representation of the percentage deficit on the chosen items.

INSTRUMENT CONTENT AND ITEM TYPE. The complete FPR instrument contains over 600 survey type questions divided into 27 areas of functioning: Activity Level (e.g., how active on domestic tasks); Aggression (e.g., break/damage property); Attention Span (e.g., average concentration on group recreation); Domestic/Survival Skills (e.g., budget money, preparing drinks); Dressing (female—items that she was able to put on); Dressing (male—items that he was able to put on); Feeding (e.g., how the client manages eating and drinking); Fits and Faints (e.g., epilepsy); Hearing; Incontinence (e.g., frequency of incontinence); Memory (e.g., how reliable is the memory); Mobility; Motor Coordination and Loss of Balance (e.g., picking up objects); Movement of Limbs and Trunk; Number Skills (e.g., telling time); Personal Hygiene (e.g., washing hands); Personal Safety (e.g., amount of help needed in using stove); Reading Skills (e.g., being able to recognize general words); Social Behavior (e.g., relating to others); Socially Unacceptable Behavior (e.g., begging/cadging); Speech and Language Production (e.g., stammer); Speech and Language Reception (e.g., degree of language reception in different settings); Toileting; Touch, Temperature, and Hypothermia; Transportation; Vision; and Writing skills. Although the user may choose to use the complete form, it is more likely that only parts of the instrument will be used. For example, to create a profile of an individual with a learning difficulty, the user may select Attention Span, Domestic/Survival Skills, Dressing, Feeding, Memory, Mobility, Motor Coordination, Personal Hygiene, Personal Safety, Social Behavior, Toileting, and Transportation. To ensure reliable and comprehensible inter- or intra-person comparison, the same part or parts should be administered to the individuals whose functional performance is to be compared or to the same individual over a period of time.

INSTRUMENT ADMINISTRATION AND SCORING. Due to the nature of the instrument, the FPR is administered on an individual basis. The user is provided with a 46-page booklet. A check-box is placed at the end of each question, which is to be filled out by the care provider after detailed observation of the client or discussion with the spouse, parents, and other care providers. No special training is required for using the FPR. Expertise in the relevant field, however, would be very helpful in making the observations of the client's functional performance. The author provides basic definitions and explanations of the topics included in the instrument that can serve as a quick reference in case of uncertainty.

The FPR requires 1 to 2 hours to complete, depending on how many parts are selected for use. Every response is associated with a number or code that is used as a representation of the response. The codes are nonconsecutive odd numbers intended to reflect the fact that these numbers are merely identifiers, and to facilitate checking the accuracy of recorded responses. Any even number is excluded as an invalid response.

Scoring is actually a process of computing the percentage deficit (d) which is a measure of dependency. According to test specifications, the higher the percentage deficit score, the more dependent an individual is. The scoring software can be used on an IBM or 100%-IBM-compatible machine. It is easy to use and offers three options in producing results: the *descriptive* result is actually a list of items that serves as a quick reference to the client's functioning; the *quantitative* results weight the response codes to produce numerical scores including percentage deficit and deficit range; the *graphical* results simply present the numerical results in a bar chart format intended to give an immediate visual impression of the client's functional performance.

RELIABILITY. The author supplied some evidence of interrater reliability. In determining the extent to which different observers tended to agree, the author chose to consider three aspects. The first is the extent to which different observers choose the same topics to record in reference to particular clients. This type of interrater reliability was reported to be no less than .625 between two raters for 11 of the 12 residents. The second type of reliability considered was the similarity between the percentage values derived from the various questions, with at least two observers using the same topics in reference to the same 7-day period. The correlation of the deficit scores for the same 12 residents observed by the same caretakers as in the earlier example was reported to be at least .85 (one correlation per resident). The third aspect involved comparing the responses to individual items by different observers once agreement had been reached about topics. Twelve of the 17 kappa values were .70 or more over a 7-day period.

The instrument appears to be criterion-referenced, as no normative data are available. For criterion-referenced tests or instruments, data on validity and concurrent reliability are usually provided. The author of the FPR, however, supplied neither validity nor concurrent reliability data.

OVERVIEW. The FPR attempts a systematic description of the functional performance of individuals with physical, psychological, or social problems based on observations and standardized recording. The common language represented by the numerical codes is designed to reduce confusion so that communication among professionals from different disciplines would be possible. This would, in turn, facilitate better services for individuals with disabilities. The computer software supplied along with the instrument provides a means to assemble and consolidate the data derived from the observations. Simple descriptive information and graphical representation can be obtained from the computer-generated results. The percentage deficit is a value that is similar to a composite score of an individual's performance on a certain area of functioning.

One serious limitation of the instrument is that psychometric data regarding the FPR are limited. Coefficients are derived from a very small sample in one location using only two raters. The lower bound of reliability was often omitted. Therefore, it is difficult for the user to evaluate the instrument based on the available data. Compared with other behavioral instruments of similar nature, the reliability reported for the FPR is relative low (e.g., Dirks, 1985; Lee, 1992). For example, the Community Living Skills Screening Test (9:252) that purports to assess the skills that developmentally disabled clients will need for living in noninstitutional settings has an interobserver reliability of .79 to .92 (Dirks, 1985).

Although the instrument appears to be criterion referenced, no evidence regarding validity is given. It is critical that content validity be investigated in instruments such as the FPR. In addition, the predictive validity and treatment validity of the instrument must be investigated.

The deficit score calculation procedure does not provide any means for handling data coded as "Unknown" or "Not applicable." Such data are automatically dropped whenever encountered. This procedure introduces some potentially systematic bias into the final obtained scores. For example, the client with fewer unknown or not applicable items could have a deficit score different from that of a client with more unknown or not applicable items although they have similar levels of dependency. The scores may be unduly affected by observer expertise, time, or knowledge.

On the whole, the FPR is deficient, from the psychometric perspective, as a criterion-referenced measure of functional performance for persons with dependency problems. The instrument has no validity data. The reliability data supplied by the author are both limited and confusing. The main value of the FPR lies in that it provides a way to describe and record in a standard and systematic fashion an individual's functional performance and to monitor that individual's changing functional performance over a certain period of time. It is not recommended, however, to use the FPR alone in making comparisons of several people's functioning or to make decisions on such comparisons.

REVIEWER'S REFERENCES

Dirks, J. (1985). [Review of the Community Living Skills Screening Test, Second Edition]. In J. V. Mitchell, Jr. (Ed.), *The ninth mental measurements yearbook* (Vol. I, pp. 372-373). Lincoln, NE: The Buros Institute of Mental Measurements.

Lee, S. W. (1992). [Review of the Survey of Functional Adaptive Behavior]. In J. J. Kramer & J. C. Conoley (Eds.), *The eleventh mental measurements yearbook* (pp. 900-901). Lincoln, NE: The Buros Institute of Mental Measurements.

Review of the Functional Performance Record by DEBORAH D. ROMAN, Director, Neuropsychology Laboratory, PM & R and Neurosurgery Departments, University of Minnesota, Minneapolis, MN:

The Functional Performance Record (FPR) surveys functional capacity as inferred by observable behavior. It is intended for use with physically, socially, or psychologically disabled individuals and may be especially appropriate as a means of determining treatment and placement needs.

Twenty-seven functional areas, comprising cognitive, academic, physical, and adaptive living skills are assessed. In most instances only some of the 27 topic areas will be assessed, depending on the particular needs and circumstances of the patient. Specific guidelines for choosing topical areas are not provided. Altogether, there are 600 items that are most often scored on a 6-point scale. Scores are based on the amount of assistance required, the degree of impairment, or the frequency of a given behavior. Items were selected based on discussions with various health care professionals and presumably reflect their views regarding the importance of various behaviors. Anyone familiar with the client may complete the FPR. Administration time is 1 to 2 hours.

The test yields descriptive summaries as well as quantitative results for each item in the form of percentage of deficit (the ratio of the observed deficit to the maximum possible deficit). In addition, a percentage deficit can be calculated for each topic area. Using the software package, these results can be printed out in summary tables or bar graphs.

The author suggests that FPR results can be used to measure change in client status across time, plan services, determine placement needs, and provide facility managers with statistics needed to determine health care resource allotment. Further, the author proposes the FPR can be employed to provide a data base for regional registers.

The validity of the FPR is not addressed in the manual. The author appears to have relied on face validity in selecting test items. This may be defensible in the assessment of readily observable behaviors, such as mobility or adaptive living skills, but not in the evaluation of higher mental functions, such as memory.

There are several sources of concern regarding the validity of the FPR. First, a single rater may have insufficient opportunity to note all relevant behaviors during the recommended 1-week observation period. Second, raters will vary in professional training and may not have the clinical acumen needed to appreciate the relevance of all behaviors. Third, sole reliance on manifest behavior in making inferences about internal states is ill-advised; using these techniques alone, the risk of making an erroneous inference seems great. For example, a patient's failure to retain information may lead a rater to conclude that memory is impaired when in fact the difficulty is due to hearing loss, poor attention, or depression. Incorrect inferences could lead to ineffectual treatment interventions, faulty prognostications, and inappropriate placements.

Interrater reliability was assessed using two independent raters, employed in a hostel for chronic psychiatric patients. They were first asked to identify relevant problem areas (select the pertinent FPR topic domains) for 12 patients. There was an 80% overall agreement in the topics chosen. The correlations between the two rating sets on percentage deficits were .85 or better. These preliminary reports are encouraging, but further study using a larger number of raters and different patient populations is warranted. The item-by-item interrater correlations, using the kappa statistic, were less impressive. Four of the 17 comparisons were below 50% agreement and the remaining 12 values were 70% or more. Serial use of the FPR in making inferences about change would have to be undertaken with caution, particularly if different raters were used.

Some of the language used in the manual is antiquated and may be perceived as pejorative. For instance, in one of the case examples an unmarried woman is referred to as a "spinster."

As a measure of adaptive living skills, the FPR is in some ways comparable to the AAMR Adaptive Behavior Scale (T4:1) and the Vineland Adaptive Behavior Scales (T4:2882). Of the three, the Vineland has the most to recommend it. It has the advantages of covering several domains (Communication, Daily Living, Socialization, and Motor Skills) in greater detail, very good test-retest reliability, and norms for both the normal population and special populations (including emotionally disturbed, physically handicapped, and mentally retarded populations). The Adaptive Behavior Scale covers many of the same behavioral domains as the FPR but is specifically designed for use with the mentally retarded and provides norms only for that population.

Cognitive abilities and academic achievement skills would be more appropriately assessed using standardized, adequately normed individually administered batteries (such as the Wechsler Scales, Woodcock-Johnson, etc.).

In conclusion, the FPR has merit as a means of identifying behavioral problems and physical limitations and appraising adaptive living skills but does not compare favorably with existing adaptive behavior measures. It is not an appropriate measure of cognitive abilities and, for this purpose, should be used only in conjunction with individually administered cognitive tests of proven validity. Further study of the validity and reliability of the instrument is needed.

[157]

Functional Time Estimation Questionnaire.

Purpose: To provide "an overview of children's abilities to estimate time correctly."
Population: Ages 7–11.
Publication Date: 1990.
Acronym: FTEQ.
Scores: Total score only.
Administration: Group or individual.
Price Data, 1991: $40 per complete kit including 25 tests and manual ('90, 47 pages); $20 per 25 tests; $17 per manual; $17 per specimen set including 1 test and manual.
Time: (30–35) minutes.
Comments: FTEQ is the seventh version of the Dodd Test of Time Estimation.
Authors: John M. Dodd, Larry Burd, and John R. Cook.
Publisher: Academic Therapy Publications.
Cross References: See T4:1018 (1 reference).

Review of the Functional Time Estimation Questionnaire by DEBORAH COLLINS, Deputy Director, Center for Survey Research, Virginia Polytechnic Institute and State University, Blacksburg, VA:

The Functional Time Estimation Questionnaire (FTEQ) is a paper-and-pencil instrument (which may be administered orally) proposed to assess time-estimation skills of school children, to study time-estimating skills of individuals and groups, and to identify deficits for remediation. The current 46-item scale evolved from the 1979 version of the Dodd Test of Time Estimation, with several preliminary versions administered to American Indian, learning disabled, and emotionally disturbed children. Items retained in the FTEQ attempt to measure time-estimation skills across three broad domains: general time estimation; intermediate term time estimation; and time estimation of short-term, personal events. According to the authors, problems in time estimation may be associated with cultural and developmental differences as well as various psychological or psychiatric problems. Proper assessment of time-estimation abilities should enable teachers and parents to understand better the particular needs of those children with time-estimation deficiencies and to plan activities/strategies for strengthening these skills.

The authors state the primary normative population for the test is middle-class, Caucasian students from rural cultures. Two other populations are also included: Native American Indian students from a reservation in North Dakota and suburban students from Euclid, Ohio. In all, six school sites were selected, five of which were located in small to medium-sized communities in North Dakota and Minnesota, with one of the five being the Fort Yates Indian Reservation in North Dakota. The sixth school was the suburban site in Ohio. Normative data are not presented by these three population groups; rather, the final standardization sample of 1,221 students includes all students tested across the six sites. Consequently, the American Indian population comprises 17% of the standardization sample and the suburban Ohio students make up 23% of the sample. The sample so constructed hardly represents middle-class, rural students. Given the authors' interest in using the FTEQ to study various target groups (e.g., Native American Indians, learning disabled, emotionally disturbed, public school elementary students), it may be that test users should be encouraged to collect and develop local norms for use with specific populations.

Normative data based on the sample described above revealed no significant differences between rural and suburban students; however, differences were determined between males and females. Consequently, raw score to standard score conversions are presented by age/grade for males and females separately. Reliability measures focused primarily on internal consistency using split-half reliability (Spearman-Brown coefficient = .92) and Kuder-Richardson 20 (KR20 = .91) measures. Although these measures fall within acceptable reliability ranges, the authors should have also reported test-retest reliability measures in that they recommend use of the test for reassessment of students' estimation skills in the event of initial low scores.

Factor analysis was used to confirm measurement of time estimation across the three underlying construct domains of general time estimation, intermediate time estimation, and short-term time estimation of personal events. Although the scale may successfully assess estimation skills across these domains, calculation of subscale scores for these areas are not included in test results. To the extent the authors propose use of this test to identify deficits for remediation, development of subscale scores and accompanying norms would be useful in identifying the area(s) of estimation deficit requiring treatment or training. Test users are directed to consult the factor analysis information for specific items related to each domain and assess problem areas from there. Unfortunately, the items as numbered and labeled in the technical manual do not correspond to the items as presented on the FTEQ instrument. Additionally, there are 14 items not accounted for in the factor analysis information—how do teachers assess time-estimation deficits for items not falling within the three construct domains?

Regression analysis was employed to check for age differentiation. Theoretically, time-estimation ability increases progressively with age and establishment of this relationship corroborated the FTEQ's measurement of the construct. Attempts to fit the data using a linear regression model resulted in the development of separate models for males versus females. The authors might have reviewed their item pool for gender-free references. At least one item is particularly male oriented: "How long does it take to grow a beard?" not to mention inappropriate as a time estimator of "personal events" (p. 20). Additional items referring to scouts, baking cakes, and vacuuming may also be construed as more or less gender oriented and warrant closer investigation.

In summary, the FTEQ authors should improve the normative data used to standardize test results. Also, to the extent that the instrument is developed to address special populations, the authors should develop separate norms for specific populations and/or encourage the development of local norms to provide proper interpretation of results. The current item pool needs further refinement. Removal of gender-related items and clarification of items not found to measure time estimation within the primary construct domains needs to be considered. Finally, the FTEQ manual does not include a final version of the instrument and a complete set of instructions. A separate instrument was provided this reviewer, which did not correspond to the description of items (per the factor analysis information), the description of scoring codes or Canadian items, or the description of administration directions outlined in the manual.

Review of the Functional Time Estimation Questionnaire by RICHARD E. HARDING, Senior Vice President, Gallup, Inc., Lincoln, NE:

The Functional Time Estimation Questionnaire (FTEQ) is a 46-item (U.S. version) or 53-item (Canadian version) instrument designed to help professionals identify children who are having difficulty in estimating time requirements for various day-to-day activities.

Based on a factor analytic study three scales were identified. These three areas involve time estimation factors such as general time estimation skills, which are longer term periods; that is, seasons of the year, etc., a second factor that is of an intermediate length measured in hours, and a third factor that is very short term, usually measured in minutes. From this, the authors identify three uses for the FTEQ. They are: "To evaluate time estimating skills of public school children. . . an instrument to study time estimating skills of individuals or groups . . . as a tool to identify deficits that can be targeted for remediation" (manual, p. 8).

The authors do an excellent job in relating the structure of the FTEQ to a theory of time estimation. The authors feel the FTEQ does actually fill a gap in studying time-estimation deficiencies in children. And indeed, the authors indicate this current instrument is the seventh version of the original Dodd test of time estimation developed in 1979. The authors provide an excellent reference list with regard to past thought on time estimation, as well as current thought; and very importantly, the work they have completed in developing this test that has the potential to further knowledge in this area.

Time-estimation skills are important in school-age children as they complete various activities according to a schedule. Children who are deficient in time estimation may have difficulties completing exact activities according to a time schedule because they severely underestimate the amount of time needed to complete these tasks and, at the end, have to rush through the project to even come close to getting it done on time.

The authors do an excellent job studying various samples of children to help establish reliability and validity estimates of the test. For example, the current test was developed after administering several versions of the test to more than 3,800 school-age children.

Included in these samples were Native American children, learning disabled children, and emotionally disturbed children. The current age ranges for this test were from 7 years through 11 years of age. According to the authors the socioeconomic class of the normative population was primarily middle-class Caucasian students from a rural culture. Additionally, Native American children who came from a reservation in North Dakota were studied, as well as a third group from a suburb of Cleveland, Ohio.

The authors provide a very good but brief discourse on the importance of time-estimating skills with regard to developmental issues. They explore cultural differences, the influences time-estimating skills have on learning, neuropsychiatric factors, and a relationship to sleeping and time estimation.

SAMPLE. The test was standardized on 1,221 elementary school students between the ages of 6 years and 13 years, 2 months. Of the sample, 51% were male, with a mean age of 9 years, 6 months. The remaining females had a mean age of 9 years, 5 months. According to the authors, the one-month difference between males and females in age was not significant. The sample included six schools from rural and suburban areas, five of which were located in small and medium-sized North Dakota and Minnesota communities. Native American students comprise 17.4% of the total sample; the remaining sixth school was in a suburban community near Cleveland, which represented 22.8% of the total sample. Students were reported to be representative of a wide range of social and economic backgrounds.

The authors indicate that, from a 58-item pool, the core 46-item scale was developed. The items were selected because of a strong positive correlation to total test score and a strong negative correlation to age in months. Specifically, an item-to-total correlation of .29 or greater, coupled with a significant negatively correlated item-to-age were utilized to retain items. The authors do not indicate whether or not the item-to-total correlation was corrected for part-to-whole overlap; however, they do indicate the Pearson product moment correlation was used.

NORMS. It is interesting to note that no differences were found with regard to mean test scores among the six schools or between rural and suburban students. However, the authors used an analysis of covariance procedure to partial out the effects of age and found a significant difference between males and females. And, through regression analysis, it was shown the differences between male and female test scores do actually covary with changing age levels. Raw test scores for each of the age categories and grade levels were converted to a "t" score. Additionally, different tables are reported for male and female children.

RELIABILITY. The internal consistency of the test was examined in a number of ways. The first was the split-half reliability. The Pearson product moment coefficient was .84. The Spearman-Brown formula yields a split-half reliability of .92. The coefficient alpha estimate was .91.

The authors indicate, and rightly so, these reliability estimates are acceptable. Reliability estimates were also provided by male and female students according to age and grade levels. For males, the reliability estimates range from .78 for 11-year-olds to .87 for 8-year-olds. By grade, for males, the range of reliability was .75 for first and fourth graders to .84 for second graders. Appropriately, standard errors of measurement are also reported. For females, the range of reliability was from .79 for 11-year-olds to .84 for 9-year-olds. For females by grade level, the range was from .76 for first and fifth graders to .83 for fourth graders.

CONSTRUCT VALIDITY. The authors report two efforts in this area. The first was to take the 46 test items through a principal components factor analysis. The authors report using a varimax rotation.

Three factors were identified, which involve general time estimation, intermediate time estimation, and short-term time estimation. The proportion of test item variance accounted for by the three factors was 90.8%. The three factors account for (respectively) 34.6%, 32.7%, and 23.6% of the variance.

A second analysis to evaluate construct validity was a regression analysis. The authors report a -.64 correlation of total test score to age for males and a -.70 for females. Utilizing the regression approach, the null hypothesis of no linear relationship was rejected. Additionally, the authors found a different prediction equation for males, as opposed to females. Thus, the interaction of age and gender was partialed out and evaluated.

ADMINISTRATION OF THE FTEQ. Administration of the FTEQ requires the teacher to read each of the questions or items to the children. There are very easy to score answer sheets available, and the authors report that usually not more than 30 seconds is required to answer any given item. They do allow for the teacher to read the item to the subject more than once if the child does not seem to understand. They have also made allowances for children who are unable to write, as they may respond by nodding or using another response system.

The authors have also included case histories in a teaching time-estimation skills chapter. This reviewer found that section to be extremely helpful and informative as, once the teacher has identified a problem with any given child in time estimation, here are some ideas in methods the teacher can use to help the child develop in this area.

SUMMARY. In summary, the FTEQ appears to have great potential in helping professionals assess time-estimation deficiencies in children and then actually provide developmental activities to help children improve in these areas. And because there is a Canadian series of questions, the authors make an excellent suggestion in asking the help of any teacher or practitioner who works with Canadian students to contact the authors to help them develop norms for Canadian students. All things considered, the FTEQ is an appealing instrument that is very easy to administer and to score and has relatively sound psychometric properties.

[158]

General Clerical Test.

Purpose: Developed to assess clerical speed and accuracy, numerical skills, and language-related skills.
Population: Clerical applicants and workers.
Publication Dates: 1972–88.
Acronym: GCT.
Scores, 4: Clerical, Numerical, Verbal, Total.
Administration: Group.
Price Data, 1994: $96 per 25 Clerical/Numerical/Verbal test booklets; $62 per 25 Clerical/Numerical test booklets; $62 per 25 Verbal test booklets; $350 per 100 Clerical/Numerical/Verbal test booklets; $220 per 100 Clerical/Numerical test booklets; $220 per 100 Verbal only test booklets; $30 per set of handscoring keys; $30 per manual ('88, 68 pages); $32 per examination kit.
Time: 46(51) minutes.
Author: The Psychological Corporation.
Publisher: The Psychological Corporation.

Review of the General Clerical Test by DIANNA L. NEWMAN, Associate Professor of Educational Theory and Practice, University at Albany/State University of New York, Albany, NY:

The General Clerical Test: 1988 Revision is a nine-part right/wrong test assessing skills related to general clerical and office management activities. Originally developed in the 1930s, revised in 1969, and renormed again in 1972, the 1988 version differs little in actual format or content from the original versions. Major changes include updating type format, revising prices in math problems, changes in the scoring key, and providing new validation studies.

The main test consists of nine parts, summing to three subscores labeled Clerical, Numerical, and Verbal. Two short forms of the instrument are available, the first containing only the Clerical subcomponent, the second containing the Clerical and Numerical subcomponents. The section questions are identical across the three versions. No alternative forms of any version have been developed. According to the publisher's manual, the test may be used to predict success in jobs requiring applications of the three specific areas, the suitability of a given job for a particular applicant, or in assigning an inexperienced person to appropriate work. Suggested users include personnel departments of businesses, industry, and government organizations, employment agencies, school and training institutions, and human resource consultants. Total test time requires a minimum of an hour, and due to the number of tests and abbreviated testing times, constant attendance of the test examiner. Scoring and interpretation may be completed by the local examiner using publisher provided scoring keys and norms.

Changes found in the 1988 test and manual reflect attempts to update cultural social validity, correct deficits of the 1972 version, and increase the breadth of validation and use. The first set of changes reflects superficial modifications of the test such as changing state abbreviations to match those currently used by the postal system and changing prices to reflect the current economy. Numerical values of test parts were also changed from the Roman to Arabic system. According to the manual, these changes do not affect the scoring or validation of the instrument. Cosmetic changes that may have affected face validity of the instrument include modernizing the type face and changing the cover of the test to reflect a more generic occupation classification. Prior versions of the test used the title "General Clerical Test" on the cover; the 1988 version uses the term "GCT" on the cover, and uses the term Subtest C instead of Clerical Test. These changes are in response to comments from users indicating that some respondents and interpreters were biased by the use of the term "clerical," which no longer matched some job titles or descriptions. Validity studies provided by the publishers indicate that the 1972 and 1988 versions of the test are equivalent. The third change, modification of the scoring key, was based on recommendations of previous reviews and user comments, making the test more user friendly. Other changes in the manual from the 1972 version to the 1988 version include the addition of several new reliability and validity studies.

The test consists of nine parts summing to three subscores. The first section, Clerical, consists of two parts and reflects speed and accuracy on perceptual tasks. The Numerical section contains three parts reflecting computation, reasoning, and error location. The Verbal component consists of four sections addressing spelling, grammar, vocabulary, and reading comprehension. A separate test booklet for each examinee presents all items and includes blank pages for mathematical calculations. All items have one correct answer and responses are entered directly onto the test booklet. Oral and written directions are provided for all sections of the test; oral directions correspond to the written and are included in the examiner's manual. For the most part, directions are clear and easy to follow; however, users should be aware that because of the number of test parts and the need for separate directions for each part, constant attention on the part of the test examiner is required. According to the publisher, the improved scoring key is easier to use than the 1972 fan method; however, a copy of the scoring key was not available for review. To score the test, raw values are obtained for each of the nine sections and then combined to form the three subscores. The test publishers advise, in several places, that individual part scores not be used, as no percentiles or validation data are available for them. Extensive tables are available to convert raw scores to percentiles for each of the three subscores and for converting total scores. These tables reflect various levels or functions of clerical/office work. The publishers also advise users to create their own local norms if appropriate.

The section on norms for the 1988 version does an adequate job of explaining what normative data are and to what purpose they should be used. This section of the manual, and the section on validity, would be excellent material for instructors to take into the classroom as hands-on applications of test theory and development. Table 4 in the 1988 version summarizes norms developed since the 1972 version. These include norms for paralegal students, community college trainees, customer service applicants, clerical/service positions in public utilities, blue collar and management trainee positions, and multiple levels of clerical tasks in industry, government, and university settings. It should be noted that in most cases the norms reflect scores of white females. Scores reflective of male respondents are included in blue collar, utility, and management trainee positions. No separate gender-based norms are available.

Because no alternate forms of the test are available, test-retest reliability is the only form of consistency provided. A significant change in the procedure of estimating test reliability did occur with the 1988 version. Prior versions used a 1-month time period between testing; the current version utilized a 2-week time period. Examination of this information indicates a one-half standard deviation gain of scores over the 2-week time period. Earlier data, where testing took place over longer time periods, indicate less gain. The publishers suggest that any future efforts do not use the 2-week period but use a time period exceeding 4 weeks.

Extensive information on validity of the test, as well as an excellent test history, are available. Both can be used to provide the user with a broad overview of the test and its potential uses. This section also includes good explanations and examples of various types of validity including content, criterion-related, concurrent, contrasted groups, and correlations with other tests. Correlations provide reasonable evidence of validity, but users must be aware of the fact that not all types of validity evidence are available for all populations. As a consequence, some interpretations of the results are limited. Validation information from prior manuals is available in the appendices. Again, users must take care when using prior norms because this information is dated and may not reflect cultural/social changes in what constitutes a clerical position.

In summary, the 1988 Revised Manual of the General Clerical Test is an excellent example of what manuals should provide test users. The in-depth presentation of different norms, the efforts at validation, and the continued updates are laudable. Readers should note, however, that the reliability of the test may be questionable and that they may wish to establish their own local norms based on their organization's definition of what constitutes a clerical position. The new norms do broaden the definition to include many of the current changes; however, schools and training institutions may still have difficulty determining which norms are appropriate for their students.

Review of the General Clerical Test by ALFRED L. SMITH, JR., Personnel Psychologist, Federal Aviation Administration, Washington, DC:

The General Clerical Test (GCT), published by the Psychological Corporation, is purported to be a comprehensive ability test used for predicting success in an array of jobs, especially those that involve computation and grammar. The GCT comprises nine content areas that make up three subtest scores. The Clerical Subtest (C) includes two types of items, checking and alphabetizing, with the scoring based on both speed and accuracy. Checking exercises involve identifying errors by comparing a "Copy" list of names, addresses, and dollar amounts to an "Original" list. In the alphabetizing exercise, the individual sorts a list of names to appropriate "drawers." The Numerical Subtest (N) contains items covering computation, error location, and arithmetic reasoning. Error location involves finding the wrong number in tables of rows and columns. The Verbal Subtest (V) includes spelling, reading comprehension, vocabulary, and grammar. The Total score is an estimate of general cognitive ability required for many jobs as it correlated highly with several tests of mental abilities.

The test is easy to administer and score. The manual provides clear instructions. It may be a little long (about an hour), but the user has the option of only giving parts of the test. The manual provides sound information for users who are not experts in psychometrics, such as personnel officers, in that it presents good information about norming, validity, and reliability.

The test has been in circulation for 50 years. The 1988 Revision contains very few modifications from the 1972 Revision, which, in turn, was little modified from the 1950 version. In both of these revisions, the publisher claims the very modest changes were "superficial," just enough to modernize the style and format rather than change the content. Some of the changes noted were emphasis on using the acronym GCT, use of nonclerical terms such as "found" instead of "filed," and the renaming of subtests with letters only to address concerns for "users employing the test with higher level, non-clerical occupational groups" (manual, p. 3). Data presented to test the equivalency of old and new versions indicate both versions are equivalent.

Updated validation studies support earlier findings of modes validity in terms of overall supervisor ratings for employees and higher validity in terms of grades among students. Validity coefficients were much higher for relationships between ratings on verbal and numerical tasks and respective subtest scores. Although the test is more valid in the educational setting than in industry, this may in part be due, as the manual indicates, to restriction in range for predictor or criterion scores. In any event, local validation is recommended.

In his review of the 1972 Revision, Cranny (1978, 8:1033) noted the lack of information about development and selection of the items and evidence that the instrument measures abilities that actually are related to clerical job tasks. In the 1988 manual, results of a factor analysis are given to support the use of the three subtest scores. Additional information relating to content validity is essentially secondhand, citing an extensive project from the U.S. Office of Personnel Management that examined a variety of clerical tests. The publisher concludes that the test items reflect abilities commonly held to predict success in clerical jobs without real empirical backup specific to this test. Still another concern noted by Cranny (1978, 8:1033) is the lack of any alternate form of the test. Given continued evidence from the reliability studies that considerable improvement in scores is noted on retesting, there remains a need for an alternate form.

Norms have been upgraded for the 1988 version. In his earlier review, Cranny (1978, 8:1033) pointed out a potential need for separate norms for males and females and racial/ethnic groups. In the present revision, only general norms are given. Separate norms are provided for various samples, but all are predominantly white females, again raising the question of their applicability with male and/or minority examinees. The presentation of the norms, however, may confuse and frustrate the user. All the norms are presented in a single Table 4. It was only after careful scrutiny that this reviewer determined that there were norms for management trainee and supervisory positions. Given the suggestion, and even encouragement, in the manual that users should consider the test for other positions as well, there should be separate tables for various job categories and more explicit directions to the appropriate norms. Norms from 1972 and 1950 are included in an appendix with only a mild warning that it is best to use the most recent norms, or, preferably, local norms.

This test has been used for decades with little or no change. Familiarity with the test may be its best advantage in some settings. It may be most appropriately used in educational rather than actual employment settings. It will continue to need better norms, especially if being used for selection in nonclerical occupations. Users are strongly encouraged to develop and use their own local norms. In some settings, it may have an advantage of providing assessment of specific clerical ability while at the same time providing an estimate of general mental ability, eliminating the need for more than one test.

REVIEWER'S REFERENCE

Cranny, C. J. (1978). [Review of the General Clerical Test.] In O. K. Buros (Ed.), *The eighth mental measurements yearbook* (pp. 1652-1653). Highland Park, NJ: Gryphon Press.

[159]

General Health Questionnaire.

Purpose: Designed to screen for nonpsychotic psychiatric disorders.
Population: Adolescents to adults.
Publication Dates: 1969–88.
Scores: Total scores only for GHQ-60 and GHQ-30; Total and scale scores for GHQ-28: Somatic Symptoms, Anxiety/Insomnia, Social Dysfunction, Severe Depression.
Administration: Group.
Forms, 3: GHQ-60, GHQ-30 (short form), GHQ-28 (research form).
Price Data, 1992: £7.50 per 25 GHQ-28 or GHQ-30 questionnaires (select form); £11.25 per 25 GHQ-60 questionnaires; £34.50 per user's guide.
Time: [3–8] minutes.
Comments: Self-administered.
Authors: David Goldberg and Paul Williams (user's guide).
Publisher: NFER-Nelson Publishing Co., Ltd. [England].
Cross References: See T4:1028 (183 references); for a review by John D. Black, see 9:434 (50 references); see also T3:941 (34 references) and 8:565 (15 references).

TEST REFERENCES

1. Benjamin, R. S., Costello, E. J., & Warren, M. (1990). Anxiety disorders in a pediatric sample. *Journal of Anxiety Disorders, 4*, 293-316.

2. Clegg, C., & Wall, T. (1990). The relationship between simplified jobs and mental health: A replication study. *Journal of Occupational Psychology, 63*, 289-266.

3. Isaksson, K. (1990). A longitudinal study of the relationship between frequent job change and psychological well-being. *Journal of Occupational Psychology, 63*, 297-308.

4. Leana, C. R., & Feldman, D. C. (1990). Gender differences in responses to unemployment. *Journal of Vocational Behavior, 38*, 65-77.

5. Power, K. G., Simpson, R. J., Swanson, V., & Wallace, L. A. (1990). A controlled comparison of cognitive-behavioral therapy, diazepam, and placebo, alone and in combination, for the treatment of generalised anxiety disorder. *Journal of Anxiety Disorders, 4*, 267-292.

6. Starkstein, S. E., Preziosi, T. J., Bolduc, P. L., & Robinson, R. G. (1990). Depression in Parkinson's disease. *The Journal of Nervous and Mental Disease, 178*, 27-31.

7. Ullah, P. (1990). The association between income, financial strain and psychological well-being among unemployed youth. *Journal of Occupational Psychology, 63*, 317-330.

8. Asen, K., Berkowitz, R., Cooklin, A., Leff, J., Loader, P., Piper, R., & Rein, L. (1991). Family therapy outcome research: A trial for families, therapists, and researchers. *Family Process, 30*, 3-20.

9. Kalimo, R., & Vouri, J. (1991). Work factors and health: The predictive role of pre-employment experiences. *Journal of Occupational Psychology, 64*, 97-115.

10. Kelloway, E. K., & Barling, J. (1991). Job characteristics, role stress and mental health. *Journal of Occupational Psychology, 64*, 291-304.

11. Lund, H. G., Beck, P., Eplov, L., Jennum, P., & Wildschiodtz, G. (1991). An epidemiological study of REM latency and psychiatric disorders. *Journal of Affective Disorders, 23*, 107-112.

12. Parkes, K. R. (1991). Locus of control as moderator: An explanation for additive versus interactive findings in the demand-discretion model of work stress? *British Journal of Psychology, 82*, 291-312.

13. Redman, S., Webb, G. R., Hennrikus, D. J., Gordon, J. J., & Sanson-Fisher, R. W. (1991). The effects of gender on diagnosis of psychological disturbance. *Journal of Behavioral Medicine, 14*, 527-540.

14. van den Brink, W., Leenstra, A., Ormel, J., & van de Willige, G. (1991). Mental health intervention programs in primary care: Their scientific basis. *Journal of Affective Disorders, 21*, 273-284.

15. Firth-Cozens, J. (1992). The role of early family experiences in the perception of organizational stress: Fusing clinical and organizational perspectives. *Journal of Occupational and Organizational Psychology, 65*, 61-75.

16. Fisher, N., & Jacoby, R. (1992). Psychiatric morbidity in bus crews following violent assault: A follow-up study. *Psychological Medicine, 22*, 685-693.

17. Gentile, J., Cicchetti, D., O'Brien, R. A., & Rogosch, F. A. (1992). Functional deficits in the self and depression in widows. *Development and Psychopathology, 4*, 323-339.

18. Harding, L., & Sewel, J. (1992). Psychological health and employment status in an island community. *Journal of Occupational and Organizational Psychology, 65*, 269-275.

19. Heeren, T. J., van Hemert, A. M., Lagaay, A. M., & Rooymans, H. G. (1992). The general population prevalence of non-organic psychiatric disorders in subjects aged 85 years and older. *Psychological Medicine, 22*, 733-738.

20. Koeter, M. W. J. (1992). Validity of the GHQ and SCL anxiety and depression scales: A comparative study. *Journal of Affective Disorders, 24*, 271-280.

21. Lewis, G. (1992). Dimensions of neurosis. *Psychological Medicine, 22*, 1011-1018.

22. Parkes, K. R. (1992). Mental health in the oil industry: A comparative study of onshore and offshore employees. *Psychological Medicine, 22*, 997-1009.

23. Romanoski, A. J., Folstein, M. F., Nestadt, G., Chahal, R., Merchant, A., Brown, C. H., Gruenberg, E. M., & McHugh, P. R. (1992). The epidemiology of psychiatrist-ascertained depression and DSM-III depressive disorders. *Psychological Medicine, 22*, 629-655.

24. Romans, S. E., & McPherson, H. M. (1992). The social networks of bipolar affective disorder patients. *Journal of Affective Disorders, 25*, 221-228.

25. Shek, D. T. L. (1992). Meaning in life and psychological well-being: An empirical study using the Chinese version of the Purpose in Life Questionnaire. *The Journal of Genetic Psychology, 153*, 185-200.

26. Stanfeld, S. A., Sharp, D. S., Gallacher, J. E. J., & Yarnell, J. W. G. (1992). A population survey of ischaemic heart disease and minor psychiatric disorder in men. *Psychological Medicine, 22*, 939-949.

27. Stansfeld, S. A., & Marmot, M. G. (1992). Social class and minor psychiatric disorder in British civil servants: A validated screening survey using the General Health Questionnaire. *Psychological Medicine, 22*, 739-749.

28. Stewart, D. A., Stein, A., Forrest, G. C., & Clark, D. M. (1992). Psychosocial adjustment in siblings of children with chronic life-threatening illness: A research note. *Journal of Child Psychology and Psychiatry and Allied Disciplines, 33*, 779-784.

29. Vaillant, G. E., Roston, D., & McHugo, G. J. (1992). An intriguing association between ancestral mortality and male affective disorder. *Archives of General Psychiatry, 49*, 709-715.

30. Whelan, C. T. (1992). The role of income, life-style deprivation and financial strain in mediating the impact of unemployment on psychological distress: Evidence from the Republic of Ireland. *Journal of Occupational and Organizational Psychology, 65*, 331-344.

31. Anderson, J., Huppert, F., & Rose, G. (1993). Normality, deviance and minor psychiatric morbidity in the community: A population-based approach to General Health Questionnaire data in the health and lifestyle survey. *Psychological Medicine, 23*, 475-485.

32. Andrews, G., Page, A. C., & Neilson, M. (1993). Sending your teenagers away: Controlled stress decreases neurotic vulnerability. *Archives of General Psychiatry, 50*, 585-589.

33. Berg, I., Butler, A., Franklin, J., Hayes, H., Lucas, C., & Sims, R. (1993). DSM-III-R disorders, social factors and management of school attendance problems in the normal population. *Journal of Child Psychology and Psychiatry and Allied Disciplines, 34*, 1187-1203.

34. Braithwaite, V., & Devine, C. (1993). Life satisfaction and adjustment of children of alcoholics: The effects of parental drinking, family disorganization and survival roles. *British Journal of Clinical Psychology, 32*, 417-429.

35. Capner, M., & Caltabiano, M. L. (1993). Factors affecting the progression towards burnout: A comparison of professional and volunteer counsellors. *Psychological Reports, 73*, 555-561.

36. Chay, Y. W. (1993). Social support, individual differences and well-being: A study of small business entrepreneurs and employees. *Journal of Occupational and Organizational Psychology, 66*, 285-302.

37. Coyle, A. (1993). A study of psychological well-being among gay men using the GHQ-30. *British Journal of Clinical Psychology, 32*, 218-220.

38. Cramer, D., & Kupshik, G. (1993). Effect of rational and irrational statements on intensity and "inappropriateness"of emotional distress and irrational beliefs in psychotherapy patients. *British Journal of Clinical Psychology, 32*, 319-325.

39. Dorman, A., O'Connor, A., Hardiman, E., Freyne, A., & O'Neil, H. (1993). Psychiatric morbidity in sentenced HIV-positive prisoners. *British Journal of Psychiatry, 163*, 802-805.

40. Dossetor, D. R., Nicol, A. R., & Stretch, D. D. (1993). Hostel-based respite care for adolescents with developmental retardation: The need for "normalized" respite resources. *Journal of Child Psychology and Psychiatry and Allied Disciplines, 34*, 391-412.

41. Goldberg, D. P., Jenkins, L., Millar, T., & Faragher, E. B. (1993). The ability of trainee general practitioners to identify psychological distress among their patients. *Psychological Medicine, 23*, 185-193.

42. Griffiths, T. C., Myers, D. H., & Talbot, A. W. (1993). A study of the validity of the scaled version of the General Health Questionnaire in paralysed spinally injured out-patients. *Psychological Medicine, 23*, 497-504.

43. Joseph, S., Yule, W., Williams, R., & Andrews, B. (1993). Crisis support in the aftermath of disaster: A longitudinal perspective. *British Journal of Clinical Psychology, 32*, 177-185.

44. Joseph, S., Yule, W., Williams, R., & Hodgkinson, P. (1993). The herald of free enterprise disaster: Measuring post-traumatic symptoms 30 months on. *British Journal of Clinical Psychology, 32*, 327-331.

45. Martin, J., Anderson, J., Romans, S., Mullen, P., & O'Shea, M. (1993). Asking about child sexual abuse: Methodological implications of a two stage survey. *Child Abuse & Neglect, 17*, 383-392.

46. Mullen, P. E., Martin, J. L., Anderson, J. C., Romans, S. E., & Herbison, G. P. (1993). Childhood sexual abuse and mental health in adult life. *British Journal of Psychiatry, 163*, 721-732.

47. Ormel, J., Oldehinkel, T., Brilman, E., & Brink, W. (1993). Outcome of depression and anxiety in primary care: A three-wave $3^1/_2$-year study of psychopathology and disability. *Archives of General Psychiatry, 51*, 759-766.

48. Orner, R. J., Lynch, T., & Seed, P. (1993). Long-term traumatic stress reactions in British Falklands War veterans. *British Journal of Clinical Psychology, 32*, 457-459.

49. Roman, S. E., Walton, V. A., McNoe, B., Herbison, G. P., & Mullen, P. E. (1993). Otago Women's Health Survey 30-month follow-up I: Onset patterns of non-psychotic disorder. *British Journal of Psychiatry, 163*, 733-738.

50. Romans, S. E., Walton, V. A., McNoe, B., Herbison, G. P., & Mullen, P. E. (1993). Otago Women's Health Survey 30-month follow-up II: Remission patterns of non-psychotic psychiatric disorder. *British Journal of Psychiatry, 163*, 739-746.

51. Shams, M. (1993). Social support and psychological well-being among unemployed British Asian men. *Social Behavior and Personality, 21*, 175-186.

52. Stanfeld, S. A., Sharp, D. S., Gallacher, J., & Babisch, W. (1993). Road traffic noise, noise sensitivity and psychological disorder. *Psychological Medicine, 23*, 977-985.

53. Abiodun, O. A. (1994). A validity study of the Hospital Anxiety and Depression Scale in general hospital units and a community sample in Nigeria. *British Journal of Psychiatry, 165*, 669-672.

54. Barton, J. (1994). Choosing to work at night: A moderating influence on individual tolerance to shift work. *Journal of Applied Psychology, 79*, 449-454.

55. Basoglu, M., Paker, M., Paker, O., Ozmen, E., Marks, I., Incesu, C., Sahin, D., & Sarimurat, N. (1994). Psychological effects of torture: A comparison of tortured with nontortured political activists in Turkey. *American Journal of Psychiatry, 151*, 76-81.

56. Bell, R. C., Low, L. H., Jackson, H. J., Dudgeon, P. L., Copolov, D. L., & Singh, B. S. (1994). Latent trait modelling of symptoms of schizophrenia. *Psychological Medicine, 24*, 335-345.

57. Brooker, C., Falloon, I., Butterworth, A., Goldberg, D., Graham-Hole, V., & Hillier, V. (1994). The outcome of training community psychiatric nurses to deliver psychosocial intervention. *British Journal of Psychiatry, 165*, 222-230.

58. Craig, T. K. J., Drake, H., Mills, K., & Boardman, A. P. (1994). The south London somatisation study: II. Influence of stressful life events, and secondary gain. *British Journal of Psychiatry, 165*, 248-258.

59. Deahl, M. P., Gillham, A. B., Thomas, J., Searle, M. M., & Srinivasan, M. (1994). Psychological sequele following the Gulf War. *British Journal of Psychiatry, 165*, 60-65.

60. Epstein, R. S., Fullerton, C. S., & Ursano, R. J. (1994). Factor analysis of the General Health Questionnaire. *Psychological Reports, 75*, 979-983.

61. Goreje, O., Omigbodun, O. O., Gater, R., Acha, R. A., Ikuesan, B. A., & Morris, J. (1994). Psychiatric disorders in a paediatric primary care clinic. *British Journal of Psychiatry, 165*, 527-530.

62. Gournay, K., & Brooking, J. (1994). Community psychiatric nurses in primary health care. *British Journal of Psychiatry, 165*, 231-238.

63. Hantz, P., Caradoc-Davies, G., Caradoc-Davies, T., Weatherall, M., & Dixon, G. (1994). Depression in Parkinson's disease. *The American Journal of Psychiatry, 151*, 1010-1014.

64. Lewis, G., & Booth, M. (1994). Are cities bad for your mental health? *Psychological Medicine, 24*, 913-915.

65. Liaw, F., & Brooks-Gunn, J. (1994). Cumulative familial risks and low-birthweight children's cognitive and behavioral development. *Journal of Clinical Child Psychology, 23*, 360-372.

66. Malla, A. K., & Norman, R. M. G. (1994). Prodromal symptoms in schizophrenia. *British Journal of Psychiatry, 164*, 487-493.

67. Ohaeri, J. U., & Odejide, O. A. (1994). Somatization symptoms among patients using primary health care facilities in a rural community in Nigeria. *American Journal of Psychiatry, 151*, 728-731.

68. Power, M. J., Katz, R., McGuffin, P., Duggan, C. F., Lam, D., & Beck, A. T. (1994). The Dysfunctional Attitude Scale (DAS). A comparison of Forms A and B and proposals for a new subscaled version. *Journal of Research in Personality, 28*, 263-276.

69. Pushkar Gold, D., Franz, E., Reis, M., & Senneville, C. (1994). The influence of emotional awareness and expressiveness on care-giving burden and health complaints of men and women. *Sex Roles, 31*, 205-224.

70. Samuels, J. F., Nestadt, G., Romanoski, A. J., Fólstein, M. F., & McHugh, P. R. (1994). DSM-III personality disorders in the community. *The American Journal of Psychiatry, 151*, 1055-1062.

71. Schrader, G. (1994). Natural history of chronic depression: Predictors of change in severity over time. *Journal of Affective Disorders, 32*, 219-222.

72. Shams, M., & Jackson, P. R. (1994). The impact of unemployment on the psychological well-being of British Asians. *Psychological Medicine, 24*, 347-355.

73. Simon, G. E., Vonkorff, M., & Durham, M. L. (1994). Predictors of outpatient mental health utilization by primary care patients in a health maintenance organization. *American Journal of Psychiatry, 151*, 908-913.

74. Thompson, J., Chung, M. C., & Rosser, R. (1994). The marchioness disaster: Preliminary report of psychological effects. *British Journal of Clinical Psychology, 33*, 75-77.

75. Turrina, C., Caruso, R., Este, R., Lucchi, F., Fazzari, G., Dewey, M. E., & Ermentini, A. (1994). Affective disorders among elderly general practice patients. *British Journal of Psychiatry, 165*, 533-537.

76. Welch, S. L., & Fairburn, C. G. (1994). Sexual abuse and bulimia nervosa: Three integrated case control comparisons. *American Journal of Psychiatry, 151*, 402-407.

77. Zinbarg, R. E., Barlow, D. H., Liebowitz, M., Street, L., Broadhead, E., Katon, W., Roy-Byrne, P., Lepine, J., Teherani, M., Richards, J., Brantley, P. J., & Kraemer, H. (1994). The DSM-IV field trial for mixed anxiety-depression. *American Journal of Psychiatry, 151*, 1153-1162.

78. Eckhardt, M. J., Stapleton, J. M., Rawlings, R. R., Davis, E. Z., & Grodin, D. M. (1995). Neuropsychological functioning in detoxified alcoholics between 18 and 35 years of age. *American Journal of Psychiatry, 152*, 53-59.

79. Pini, S., Piccinelli, M., & Zimmermann-Tansella, C. (1995). Social problems as factors affecting medical consultation: A comparison between general practice attenders and community probands with emotional distress. *Psychological Medicine, 25*, 33-41.

80. Shek, D. T. L., & Tsang, S. K. M. (1995). Reliability and factor structure of the Chinese GHQ-30 for parents with preschool mentally handicapped children. *Journal of Clinical Psychology, 51*, 227-234.

81. Siegert, R. J., & Chi-Ying Chung, R. (1995). Dimensions of distress: A cross-cultural factor replication. *Journal of Cross-Cultural Psychology, 26*, 169-175.

82. Silove, D., Harris, M., Morgan, A., Boyce, P., Manicavasagar, V., Hadzi-Pavlovic, A., & Wilhelm, K. (1995). Is early separation anxiety a specific precursor of panic disorder-agoraphobia? A community study. *Psychological Medicine, 25*, 405-411.

83. Simon, G., Ormel, J., von Korff, M., & Barlow, W. (1995). Health care costs associated with depressive and anxiety disorders in primary care. *American Journal of Psychiatry, 152*, 352-357.

84. Totterdell, P., Spelton, E., Smith, L., Barton, J., & Folkard, S. (1995). Recovery from work shifts: How long does it take? *Journal of Applied Psychology, 80*, 43-57.

85. van Hemert, A. M., den Heijer, M., Vorstenbosch, M., & Bolk, J. H. (1995). Detecting psychiatric disorders in medical practice using the General Health Questionnaire. *Psychological Medicine, 25*, 165-170.

86. Verhaak, P. F. M. (1995). Determinants of the help-seeking process: Goldberg and Huzley's first level and first filter. *Psychological Medicine, 25*, 95-104.

87. Walsh, J., Joseph, S., & Lewis, C. A. (1995). Internal reliability and convergent validity of the Depression-Happiness Scale with the General Health Questionnaire in an employed adult sample. *Psychological Reports, 76*, 137-138.

88. Wanberg, C. R. (1995). A longitudinal study of the effects of unemployment and quality of reemployment. *Journal of Vocational Behavior, 46*, 50-54.

Review of the General Health Questionnaire by STEVEN G. LoBELLO, Associate Professor of Psychology, Auburn University at Montgomery, Montgomery, AL:

The General Health Questionnaires (Forms GHQ-30 and GHQ-28) are brief, paper-and-pencil inventories that are designed to detect psychiatric illness. (There is also a 60-item and a 12-item version of the GHQ.) The authors of the tests make no claim that the tests will aid in the differential diagnosis of various psychiatric disorders. Rather, the purpose of the tests is to distinguish people with some form of psychological disturbance from those who are relatively healthy. The assumption is that, although mental disorders may manifest themselves with a wide range of symptoms, there is an underlying commonality to all of these states. This common denominator is the disruption in the performance of daily life activities and the experience of subjective distress.

The GHQ-30 is a 30-item questionnaire that asks subjects to respond to questions about recent symptoms or changes in behavior (e.g., HAVE YOU RECENTLY: been having restless, disturbed nights? felt capable of making decisions about things? felt constantly under strain?). The subject circles one of four responses to each question that best describes recent experiences. The responses can be scored either as a 4-point Likert scale, or as a bimodal scale where endorsing either of the two response alternatives that deny problems receives a 0 score, and endorsing either of the two responses that affirm difficulties receives a score of 1 point. The GHQ-30 yields a single score, for which threshold scores of 4 or 5 (bimodal scoring) would indicate probable psychiatric disorder. (Threshold scores established by determining modal values are reported in 31 validity studies.) The authors also note that these threshold scores may not be applicable to specific populations, and recommend consulting some of the many validity studies on the GHQ in the literature.

The GHQ-28 is similar in format to the GHQ-30, but has four subscales (Somatic Symptoms, Anxiety and Insomnia, Social Dysfunction, and Severe Depression) developed by principal components analysis and varimax rotation. Each scale consists of seven items and the sum of these scale scores can be used in the same manner as the total score on the GHQ-30. Scores of 4 or 5 (bimodal scoring) also serve as thresholds on the GHQ-28 (modal values from 16 validity studies). The GHQ-30 and GHQ-28 are not recommended for use with children, but the authors state that several research studies have successfully utilized the scales with adolescents. A specific appropriate age range is not provided.

Temporal stability studies of the GHQ scales introduce special problems and considerations. Specifically, if a scale is designed to measure transient phenomena, to what degree does the test-retest coefficient reflect change in state or unreliability of the scale? To avoid this problem, the authors conducted a study of psychiatric patients whose conditions had not improved over a period of 6 months. A stability coefficient of .75 is reported for patients who rated their conditions as unchanged. A coefficient of .51 was obtained for patients whose physicians made retrospective judgments about their lack of improvement. These results are difficult to interpret because the manual does not specify which version of the GHQ was used in this study. Independent studies of the internal consistency of the GHQ-30 have yielded Cronbach's alphas ranging from .84 to .93. Split-half reliability is reported to be .95, although again, the particular form of the GHQ used to establish this value is not given.

Validity of the GHQ-30 and GHQ-28 is supported by numerous studies investigating the specificity (probability that a "true normal" will be correctly identified) and sensitivity (probability that a "true abnormal" case will be correctly identified) of each scale across a variety of cultures. The median specificity of the GHQ-28 is .82 and the median sensitivity is .86. For the GHQ-30, the values are .80 for specificity and .81 for sensitivity. Again, summarizing the data from various research studies, the authors report that the median correlation between the GHQ-30 and various psychiatric interview measures is .59; for the GHQ-28 and similar measures, the coefficient is .76.

The manual is impressive in its coverage of statistical properties of the scales. Independent research conducted around the world is liberally cited and discussed. The only major shortcoming is the occasional failure to specify which version of the GHQ is being discussed when validity and reliability data are presented. Also, the GHQ scales originated in England, and some of the terminology in the manual may be unfamiliar to American readers. The same may be said of some of the scale items. The authors point out that the scales were originally designed for use in London, but that researchers from many diverse cultures have translated them into 38 languages and that the cross-cultural studies have been generally favorable. Moreover, the manual includes the item analysis statistics for the original pool of 140 items and test users are encouraged to substitute equivalent items for those that may be difficult to understand in a given locale. Formal norms tables are also absent from the manual, but many studies of (some) large samples are cited.

The GHQ scales have value as brief, economical screening tools in clinical and research settings. The scales could be easily administered and scored by paraprofessional or clinic support staff, and may be completed by patients in a waiting room setting. For physicians, the scales would have utility in detecting psychiatric disorders that may require referral for specialized assessment and treatment. In research, the GHQ tests could be used as screens for pathology when "normal" populations are desired. The GHQ-28 is something of a puzzle. Why construct a multiscale version of an instrument when its main purpose is to serve as a *general* indicator of psychopathology? For screening tests, more precise assessment would be completed during a second stage with those individuals who exceeded the threshold score on the GHQ. The authors state that the GHQ-28 is "increasing in popularity," but fail to give a rationale for developing this version in the first place.

Despite the few objections noted above, the GHQ scales have been the focus of a large amount of research over the 25 or so years since development. The scales should be considered by anyone desiring rapid, accurate determination of general psychiatric status.

Review of the General Health Questionnaire by CECIL R. REYNOLDS, Professor of Educational Psychology, Texas A&M University, College Station, TX:

The General Health Questionnaire (GHQ) is a self-administered questionnaire designed to detect nonpsychotic, psychiatric disorders in medical and other nonpsychiatric community settings. The authors propose that it may be used with adolescents and adults of any age and contend that the GHQ detects inability to carry out normal functions and the appearance of new and distressing phenomena. They caution the test is not diagnostic but may be used to screen for acute conditions. It is supposedly applicable to uses by a wide variety of professionals including physicians, psychiatrists, psychologists, and counselors. Administration time is proposed as 3 to 8 minutes depending upon whether the full-length 60-item questionnaire is used, or briefer 30-item, 28-item, or 12-item versions are used.

The questionnaire consists of 60 questions all beginning with the phrase "Have you recently" followed by a stem such as "been getting any pains in your head?" The respondent then circles one of the four following answers: *Not at all*, *No more than usual*, *Rather more than usual*, or *Much more than usual*. Although proposed for use with adolescents or adults at any age, some of the wording seems archaic and it is doubtful that adolescents would be able to respond reliably or validly to Question 2, "Have you recently been feeling in need of a good tonic?" The reading level is not specifically assessed and varies substantially from item to item. My informal appraisal indicates a reading level of approximately eighth grade based on the vocabulary of the items.

An extensive manual provided with the GHQ reviews many years of research and does so quite thoroughly. A substantial amount of valuable information is contained in the manual that would be of interest to many psychologists and others who might have an interest in using a device such as the GHQ. When restricted to its originally intended purpose, detecting psychiatric disorders among respondents in nonpsychiatric settings, such as when seeing their primary care physician, the GHQ items and format appear to be quite useful. Reliability and validity data are appropriately derived and presented although most of the data come from research published over approximately the last 30 years. Thorough reviews of this literature indicate good reliability for the 60-item version but far less satisfactory psychometric characteristics are apparent for the short forms. I do not recommend the short forms for use due to their psychometric inadequacies and the remainder of the commentary in this review applies to the full-length, 60-item form.

Although advertising material for the GHQ refers to scaled scores that may be used to bring light to changes in the condition of a patient, the GHQ does not, in fact, yield any scaled or otherwise specifically standardized scores. There is no standardization sample as traditionally defined. Rather, cut scores or so-called threshold scores are used to determine the presence or absence of psychiatric illness. These cut scores are based upon numerous studies reviewed thoroughly in the manual and appear to be appropriately derived. The authors are to be commended for their thorough review of the research literature and the preparation of such a thorough manual. At times, however, the authors go beyond their own cautionary statements and seem to promote the GHQ for use in a variety of settings for which it is not appropriate, such as the psychiatric population being seen by psychiatrists or psychologists. It does not appear to be useful in this context but certainly could be useful to a general medical practitioner in an attempt to determine when psychiatric referrals were appropriate. The GHQ serves this purpose well by providing a clear, objective, quantified basis for making such decisions and would enable the general practitioner to be much more adept at detecting potential psychiatric problems. Beyond this use, the GHQ is not supported.

The greatest problem in practical application of the GHQ is its presentation in the manual despite the thoroughness of this effort. The determination of the threshold score is quite complex as given in the manual and few medical providers are likely to go to the trouble to make the necessary calculations. Based on the thousands of subjects used in the various studies reviewed in the manual, the authors could certainly have derived *T*-scores and could have done so for multiple samples varying by demographic level or even medical presentation. The derivation of such scores would have enhanced greatly the practical use of the GHQ and made it available to far more practitioners. As it stands, use of the GHQ is simply too abstruse for the typical medical practitioner, most of whom will not understand the concepts discussed in the manual related to the psychometric nature of the scale and the determination of the best threshold score to apply.

The authors are nevertheless to be commended for the amount of information provided in the manual and the development of this work. It would be a benefit to the profession if appropriate psychometricians were consulted to enable the development of a manual with more applied information along with appropriate scaling techniques. In the absence of such an effort, the promise of the GHQ is likely to go largely unfulfilled.

[160]

General Management In-Basket.

Purpose: "Designed to assess supervisory/managerial skills independent of any particular job classification; may be used for selection and/or career development."
Population: Supervisors and managers.
Publication Dates: 1986–94.
Acronym: GMIB.
Scores, 5: Leadership Style and Practices, Handling Priorities and Sensitive Situations, Managing Conflict, Organizational Practices/Management Control, Total.
Administration: Group.
Forms, 4: Private and public sector forms include Standard Version, Police Versions, Fire Versions, and Engineer Version.
Restricted Distribution: Clients must pay a one-time overhead/sign-up fee of $150–$300.
Price Data, 1993: $75 per candidate for rental/scoring and bar chart; $70 per optional GMIB Feedback Report.
Time: 165 (175) minutes.
Author: Richard C. Joines.
Publisher: Management & Personnel Systems, Inc.

Review of the General Management In-Basket by S. DAVID KRISKA, Personnel Psychologist, City of Columbus, Columbus, OH:

The General Management In-Basket (GMIB) is a 15-item examination that is published in a standard form with three variations designed specifically for fire, police, and engineering. The test can be used to select supervisors and managers in a variety of settings including government and private sector employment. The time limit ranges from 2.5 to 3 hours depending upon the form being used. The candidate assumes the role of the director of a division of an organization, and responds by analyzing the supervisory or management issue involved in each of the 15 items, indicating what action should be taken to resolve the item, and writing a memo or letter, if appropriate. Each of the items is a self-contained problem and the test taker does not need to identify issues that cross problems as is done in many in-basket tests. Even though the GMIB is thought of as a power test, many examinees do not complete all 15 items in the allotted time.

Many of the GMIB items were developed to test the application of management theory to practice. High scores on the test will result from applying concepts advanced by McGregor's Theory Y, participative management, and situational leadership. The GMIB author notes that the proper handling of some items is based more on the application of theory to the problem rather than the judgment of subject matter experts or assessors. The author properly advises the potential user that the GMIB is not appropriate for an organization that desires autocratic leadership. The items deal with supervisory and management issues that include employee motivation and morale, managing organizational conflict, implementation of new procedures, dealing with personnel external to the organization, delegation, performance problems, staff development and growth, work organization and efficiency, and group dynamics and team efforts.

Performance on the GMIB can be reported according to a variety of norms. There are norms for public and private sector organizations, job type, size of organization, and level of job. As of the writing of this review, the total data base includes approximately 3,000 examinees. In selecting result reports, the user may select a bar chart format that shows performance on four factors and the total score. An alternative format provides detailed text information about performance on each of the four factors along with suggestions for training.

The scoring of the GMIB is performed by the publisher and guidelines for grading are proprietary. The author states that there are specific guides for scoring each of the items and 4 or 5 points can be earned on each of the items. The guides for grading the item include the goal for the item, an analysis of the issues, and behaviorally anchored rating scales. The 5-point items are those items considered critical. In order to preserve test security, strict procedures must be followed for using the test and returning response booklets to the publisher for scoring.

The psychometric characteristics of the GMIB are quite satisfactory. Interrater reliability studies show the reliability of a single rater grading the entire in-basket to range from .87 to .95 with these high reliabilities presumably being a function of the detailed scoring guides. The internal consistency of the test is examined by review of the 15-item total test correlations. The correlations range from .37 to .52. In a criterion-related validity study including 578 employees of a public sector organization, the GMIB author reported validity coefficients ranging from .28 to.34 when correlating the GMIB total score with overall job performance. After correcting the coefficients for criterion unreliability, the estimated validity of the GMIB ranged from .35 to .44 for the prediction of overall job performance. The author also notes other studies that demonstrate the reliability and validity of the instrument.

A factor analysis of the 365 individuals in the original validation sample resulted in the following four factors: Leadership Style and Practice, Handling Priorities and Sensitive Situations, Managing Conflict/Interpersonal Insight, and Organizational Practices/Management Control. These factors are used to report scores to candidates and serve as the basis for the text report of candidate performance. The textual reports of candidate performance are generated without compromising test security.

A test user today must be aware of cultural factors related to test results. In a personal communication, the author reports less than a one standard deviation difference between White, Hispanic, Asian, and African American test takers. (For Whites, mean = 19.12, n = 2,837; for Asians, mean = 18.25, n = 91; for Hispanics, mean = 16.40, n = 236; for African Americans, mean = 14.38, n = 434; *s.d.* = 7.64.) A comparison of males and females shows women scoring slightly higher than men. (For men, mean = 18.10, n = 3,070; for females, mean = 19.55, n = 946.)

This review would not be complete without addressing two reservations I have about the GMIB. My greatest concern is about the large volumes of text contained in the test even though the items are clearly written and easily understood. Although I would not hesitate to use this test for most management jobs, I would not use it for a supervisory job with minimal reading demands. The amount of material that must be comprehended makes the test inappropriate for jobs that are primarily hands-on. My other concern about the GMIB is the format of the technical manual. The author provides technical information in the form of an update of a paper read at the 19th International Congress on the Assessment Center Method. A clearly identified users' manual would be preferred.

In summary, the GMIB is a sound test of management skills. Most users will be employers selecting management staff and in some cases supervisory personnel. The results will be informative to the candidates, and their acceptance of the test should be favorable. The psychometric properties of the test show it to be a carefully developed examination that can be used with confidence in many selection situations.

Review of the General Management In-Basket by WILLIAM J. WALDRON, Administrator, Employee Assessment, Tampa Electric Company, Tampa, FL:

INTRODUCTION. The General Management In-Basket (GMIB) is an instrument designed by Management & Personnel Systems (MPS) in the late 1980s to assess common management skills independent of job or occupation. It is presented by the authors as useful in both selection and development contexts.

In-basket methods have long been associated with the *assessment center* method (Thornton, 1992). A distinguishing feature of the assessment center is the use of situational exercises: tests simulating important aspects of the job for which participants are being considered, or for which their skills will be developed. These exercises or "simulations" require more complex responses from examinees than the typical standardized paper-and-pencil test. Such methods have the advantage of high candidate acceptance; the fidelity of the test situation to actual work behavior should also lead to improved predictive validity—which has, in fact, generally been demonstrated by the assessment center method. However, the complex and relatively nonstandardized nature of participant responses in simulation exercises makes reliable scoring difficult. There is, in fact, a vast literature on the assessment center method addressing scoring and construct validity issues. The authors of the GMIB set out to develop an instrument that retains the advantages of the simulation exercise, while using a more structured (and reliable) scoring method.

In the GMIB, as in the typical in-basket exercise, participants are placed in the role of a newly appointed manager. Background information about the position and the organization is provided in written form for the participants to review. They are informed that they have available a fixed amount of time (2 hours and 45 minutes, in this case) in the office alone, to review the in-basket of the previous position incumbent and deal with its items (letters, memos, notes, phone messages) and the issues contained therein. The GMIB contains 15 items; for each item, a response sheet is provided on which the participants must describe the management issues involved in the item and what action they plan to address. On items for which participants believe immediate action is necessary, they are asked to write the actual memos or letters to handle them. This unique approach provides a more detailed and consistent basis for evaluating participant performance on all items than the typical in-basket, where only the actual memos or letters would be available (and nothing at all on items where a participant decided only to defer action).

After administration of the exercise, the participants' materials are sent to MPS for scoring. Written results reports are returned by the publisher within a matter of a few days.

PSYCHOMETRIC EVIDENCE. As noted, the GMIB is scored by the publisher, and the scoring "key" is not available to the test user. Partly because of this, no technical manual is currently available—although MPS plans to complete one in the near future. The publisher does provide very specific and clear administration instructions, as well as a research report containing a good deal of psychometric and other information about the instrument.

The items on the GMIB were written to reflect a participative and situational style of leadership, as well as commonly accepted principles of sound management practice. Using written scoring guidance, participant performance on each item is scored on a 0 through 4 scale (for three especially important items, a 0–5-point scale is used), and a total score is derived for each participant as the sum of the item scores. In addition, each participant receives scores on four performance factors. These factors were derived through principal components analysis. A single rater assigns item scores. The rationale for this is based on results of interrater reliability studies showing support for this practice (single rater reliabilities ranging from .87 to .95 for total test score in four separate studies, and a mean single item reliability of .87 in the study with the largest N).

The publisher describes a number of criterion-related research studies that have been conducted on the GMIB. In these studies, which used a concurrent design and were conducted largely in the public sector, solid validity evidence was found. In the largest of these studies, an estimated true correlation of .41 was found between GMIB scores and a composite of immediate supervisor ratings across six performance dimensions; a corresponding correlation of .44 was found with second-level supervisor ratings. Relationships with the individual performance dimension ratings show the GMIB typically demonstrating the highest correlations with Written Communication and Planning and Organizing, as might be expected. Perhaps a bit surprisingly, strong correlations with ratings of Oral Communication were also found.

A number of studies are very briefly described in which the GMIB was demonstrated to correlate very highly with other simulation exercises and results of full-scale assessment centers.

CRITIQUE. As noted above, the psychometric quality of the instrument certainly meets commonly accepted professional standards. However, additional data would be useful in order to more fully evaluate the instrument. A complete technical manual should definitely be a priority for the publisher. Included in such a manual should be the following:

1. More detailed information about the test development process (i.e., how items were written to match the publisher's theory of management, and how the item pool was refined to the final 15 items).

2. Additional information about test fairness and adverse impact against legally protected groups. The authors note that no evidence of differential prediction by race/ethnicity was found in the one study with a large enough minority sample to address it—no statistical data are provided, however. No information at all is provided about the relative validity of the GMIB for females and males. No information is provided on potential adverse impact of the GMIB with regard to protected groups—that is, mean score differences across groups. Even if the test does, in

fact, fail to demonstrate any differential prediction, these data are still important when evaluating competing instruments.

3. More information regarding the normative sample on which reported scores are based. The results provided by the publisher give scores (total and for each of the four factors) reported as percentile ranks "in the GMIB data base," but do not provide any information about the makeup of this data base. The reports otherwise are very clear; detailed performance information and career development suggestions are provided as an extra-cost option for the test user. The publisher provides clear interpretive guidance for using the results report, written in terms understandable by managers—not just testing specialists.

MPS has attempted to address face validity—an important factor—by tailoring the standard GMIB for a number of job types (e.g., police and fire). No information is provided, however, on how these alternate forms were developed, or on their statistical equivalence to the standard version of the test.

Although it is clear that the GMIB demonstrates significant predictive validity when used as a selection device, those interested in using it as a developmental or career guidance tool would benefit from further information. The developmental suggestions provided in the (optional) GMIB career development report appear to be quite useful and generally applicable. Using the GMIB for development would be enhanced, however, by a more detailed presentation of the results of studies relating it to other types of simulation exercises. For example, how do the four GMIB factors relate to more traditional assessment dimensions (such as leadership, planning and organizing, interpersonal sensitivity, etc.)? Future research might also examine the relationship of GMIB total and factor scores to those obtained on other instruments commonly used in management selection (i.e., common cognitive and personality tests). This would not only benefit those who desire to use the GMIB as a developmental tool, but also those interested in using other instruments in conjunction with the GMIB as part of an assessment center or a more complex selection or developmental battery.

SUMMARY. The above criticisms and suggestions for improvement should be kept in perspective—the fact remains that the General Management In-Basket is a unique instrument that fills an important need. Many organizations are flattening their structures these days—thereby simultaneously increasing the demands upon the remaining managers and greatly expanding the pool of potential management candidates from lower levels. The identification and screening of managers is more critical than ever, yet budget tightening means that many organizations cannot afford a full "assessment center" approach. In comparison to assessment centers, the GMIB provides a similar level of validity at significantly lower cost. In comparison to cognitive or personality tests which might be used in management selection, the GMIB provides superior candidate acceptability. Although a more detailed technical manual is needed, the publisher has demonstrated a commitment to a continuing research program using the instrument. In short, the GMIB should be seriously examined by any organization interested in improving the identification and selection of its management talent.

REVIEWER'S REFERENCE

Thornton, G. C., III. (1992). *Assessment centers in human resource management.* Reading, MA: Addison-Wesley.

[161]

The Gesell Child Developmental Age Scale.

Purpose: Designed to determine in which of the 10 Gesell early development periods a child is presently functioning.
Population: Ages 2–10.
Publication Date: 1990.
Acronym: GCDAS.
Scores, 11: Developmental Patterns (Bladder and Bowel Control, Parallel Play, Speech and Sentences, Analogies and Numbers, Sociability and Play, Monopolizes Situation, Ethical Sense, Competitive, Self Motivation and Reasonableness, Loyalty and Hero Worship), Total Developmental Age.
Administration: Individual.
Price Data, 1990: $11 per manual (16 pages); $25 per diskette with program.
Time: Administration time not reported.
Comments: GCDAS program uses a PCXT or AT like computer with 256K memory; separate ratings by mother, teacher, therapist.
Author: Russell N. Cassel.
Publisher: Psychologists and Educators, Inc.

TEST REFERENCES

1. Hecht, B. F., Levine, H. G., & Mastergeorge, A. B. (1993). Conversational roles of children with developmental delays and their mothers in natural and semi-structured situations. *American Journal on Mental Retardation*, 97, 419-429.

Review of The Gesell Child Developmental Age Scale by WILLIAM STEVE LANG, Assistant Professor of Measurement and Research, University of South Florida at St. Petersburg, St. Petersburg, FL:

The Gesell Child Developmental Age Scale (GCDAS) by Russell Cassel is an interesting attempt to create an instrument based on the well-known work of Arnold Gesell describing the behavior of children from birth to age 10 in detail. Psychologist Cassel has revived Gesell's 1940 stage theory and has introduced a descriptive tool to measure the developmental age of a child. Gesell proposed 12 stages from birth to age 10. Each state was discerned by observation and analysis of movies of children. Gesell sought behaviors that were common across cultures and defined linear development. The GCDAS proposes to measure the range of child development from 18 to

120 months covering the top 10 of Gesell's 12 stages. As Cassel says, the GCDAS "is designed to standardize ten of Gesell stages (two first Gesell stages are eliminated) in a computerized scale where mothers can quickly and easily make comparisons between the Gesell development levels and the actual age of their child or children" (manual, p. 4).

In order to use the GCDAS, a mother, teacher, or clinician would simply respond "yes" or "no" to a set of descriptive items as presented on a computer screen. Cassel suggests that more than one observer is appropriate and that the scale can be completed with the child present or from memory. He cautions that parents may inflate the child's true score so that a neutral observer is desirable. Each of the 10 developmental stages is represented by 20 statements. Each profile of a child covers the 5 stages (100 questions) around their chronological age. The computer produces a score chart with the child's actual age graphically compared to each observer's rating and the average rating of multiple raters. Each item is worth 5 points, which results in a scaled score from 0 to 1,200.

The manual author states that the GCDAS "is in experimental form, with an overall plan to validate the critical items selected against first typical individuals, and later against persons with varied learning, developmental, or behavioral problems (a process now well underway" (manual, p. 4). Currently, there is no empirical evidence of validity or reliability suggested in the manual or literature. Without evidence, the argument that the GCDAS measures Gesell's stages appropriately and accurately is speculative at best. Criterion-related validity is essential for a measure of this type.

There are several other concerns about this scale the author should address for minimal acceptability. First, there needs to be some assurance the 20 items properly reflect the proposed developmental scales. Second, the multiplication of each item by 5 points seems unnecessary unless having a 1,200-point scale has some unstated value. Third, the interrater reliability should be assessed. Similarly, comparisons for "rating from memory" to "ratings while observing" are necessary.

As a basic underlying construct, this instrument depends on behaviors identified by Gesell. In many cases, Gesell and his co-workers performed professional, clandestine observations and careful analysis of films and movies to distinguish the child's defined development. There is reason to suspect that high inference items from casual observers (like parents or teachers) with the subject present would not result in the recognition of the item behavior. Most raters would have no trouble with "Knows right from left," but items such as "Evidence of reasonableness" or "Beginning self criticism period" would cause judgment difficulty for many who tried to use the instrument without specific training or examples. The manual and directions are inadequate for these items.

Even though the computerized scoring is convenient and the use of Gesell's developmental research has promise, the experimental edition of the GCDAS is still not refined enough for serious assessment use. There simply is no current evidence of reliability or validity, and there are no sample data or preliminary item analysis to support the profiles resulting from its scores. There are potential problems with high inference items, interrater reliability, and construct validity. Parents and teachers wanting assessment of children would be advised to use currently proven instruments specific for ability and achievement. Researchers interested in the Gesell stages might consider the GCDAS as long as they are willing to report the validity and reliability for their particular applications.

Review of The Gesell Child Developmental Age Scale by HOI K. SUEN, Professor of Educational Psychology, The Pennsylvania State University, University Park, PA:

Based on the work of Arnold Gesell on child development (e.g., Gesell, Ilg, Learned, & Ames, 1943), the Gesell Child Developmental Age Scale (GCDAS) is a computerized assessment tool designed to obtain information to contrast a child's Gesell age against the child's chronological age. The instrument includes a 5.25-inch floppy diskette and a 16-page written manual. The computer program is available only on 5.25-inch floppy diskettes and requires an IBM-compatible computer for execution. Results of assessment are accessible only through a printer and cannot be obtained on screen.

Essentially, the GCDAS contains a file of 240 behavioral checklist items taken from the works of Arnold Gesell. When rating a child, the program requests a set of basic demographic information and then selects 100 items from the 240. It appears that item selection is based on the chronological age of the child. The 100 items are presented on screen one at a time. As each item appears on the monitor screen, the rater is to respond by entering "1" if the statement about the child is more true than it is false and by entering "2" if the statement is more false than it is true. After all 100 items have been administered, one can proceed to rate a different child, rate the same child with a different rater, exit the program, or print a profile on a printer. Up to three raters may be used to rate the same child. The three potential raters include a parent, a teacher, and a psychologist. The necessary qualifications of the psychologist are not specified. The resulting profile contains a graphic depiction of the chronological age of the child, the Gesell age based on the ratings of each rater, and the average Gesell age across all the raters used. In addition, a standard text description of the general characteristics of the particular Gesell age of the child is provided.

Psychometrically, this scale can be described best as being at an experimental stage of development as no psychometric information is available. The author suggested that the Gesell Child Developmental Age Scale "is designed to standardize ten of the Gesell stages" (manual, p. 4). It is not clear what "standardize" means in this case as the usual norming, scaling, reliability, and validity information are not available. Consequently, there is no information on the expected standard error of measurement, nor accuracy of classifications, nor any other aspects of validity. However, should such analyses be conducted, there is a fair chance that results could be favorable. First, the items are selected from the original items developed, and presumably tested, by Gesell. Thus, these can be expected to have sound evidence of validity, consistent with Gesell's child development theory. The pooling of scores from raters can also be expected to optimize the reliability and validity of the average score. Unfortunately, these speculations cannot be confirmed until data are available for such analyses. Furthermore, because the items were selected from Gesell's work several decades ago, there is a need to examine these items to determine if some of them may be dated.

A major advantage of this program is its minimal hardware requirements. The diskette on which the program is provided contains 22 files occupying only about 240K disk memory. Thus, if one wishes to transfer the files to a hard disk, the disk memory requirement is minimal. The 22 files include a compiled program file, an executable program file, and a number of text files. When executed, it can be estimated that the program will take only a little over 100K RAM. It is, however, required that a printer be available as results of assessment can be accessed only through a printer.

The program is generally user friendly. However, a few improvements would be useful to facilitate its use. For example, a child's data file is identified by the initials of the child only. As a result, two children who happen to have the same initials would be treated as the same child with only a single profile for this "combined" child. With the creation of multiple files in this program, a means of distinguishing between different children with the same initials is needed. For another example, raters are required to enter a rater number. The program apparently treats 1 as a parent, 2 as a teacher, and 3 as a psychologist. Unfortunately, this is not explained anywhere in the program or the manual. Additionally, fathers are not distinguished from mothers and the program can accommodate only one parent. One other area that needs modification is the absence of a termination key. It would be useful for a user not familiar with DOS commands if a termination key is built into the program so that a rater can restart the ratings after making an error without having to finish the sequence. As it is now, one has to use a DOS control key sequence to interrupt or terminate the program.

REVIEWER'S REFERENCE

Gesell, A., Ilg, F. L., Learned, J., & Ames, L. B. (1943). *Infant and child in the culture of today*. New York: Harper and Brothers Publishers.

[162]

Gifted Evaluation Scale.

Purpose: A means to "document the five characteristics of giftedness in the federal definition: intellectual, creative, specific academic, leadership ability, or in the performing and visual arts."
Population: Ages 4.5–19.
Publication Dates: 1987–90.
Acronym: GES.
Scores, 7: 5 subscales (Intellectual, Creativity, Specific Academic Aptitude, Leadership Ability, Performing and Visual Arts), Quotient Score, Percentile Score.
Administration: Individual.
Price Data, 1993: $60 per complete kit including GES technical manual ('87, 40 pages); 50 GES rating forms, and Gifted Intervention Manual ('90, 107 pages); $28 per 50 rating forms.
Time: (15–20) minutes.
Comments: Ratings by teachers; manual title is Gifted Intervention Manual.
Authors: Stephen B. McCarney and Diana Henage (manual).
Publisher: Hawthorne Educational Services, Inc.

TEST REFERENCES

1. Levinson, E. M., & Folino, L. (1994). Correlations of scores on the Gifted Evaluation Scale with those on WISC-III and Kaufman Brief Intelligence Test for students referred for gifted evaluation. *Psychological Reports*, 74, 419-424.

Review of the Gifted Evaluation Scale by CAROLYN M. CALLAHAN, Professor, Curry School of Education, University of Virginia, Charlottesville, VA:

Giftedness has been defined in the Gifted and Talented Children's Act of 1978. These same premises guided the development of the Gifted Evaluation Scale (GES). The definition is based on the notion there are five relatively independent areas that might be recognized as areas of giftedness. The items on the GES are described as resulting from the recommendations of "educational diagnosticians and educators of the gifted" (manual, p. 5) as to the behavioral indicators of these dimensions. However, the details regarding the qualifications of these individuals are not provided. Further, the resulting instrument and its psychometric properties described in the manual suggest that it measures one underlying construct that is not clearly identifiable.

The manual author describes five subscales corresponding to the five dimensions of the definition, but the factor loadings presented suggest the factors are not independent. The item/total correlations support internal consistency of the subscales, but the high correlations among the subscales raises questions about the independence of the subscales in measuring separate constructs.

The construct validity of the GES is also difficult to ascertain given the problems with the definition of the sample (no data were provided on how students in the sample were identified as gifted or on what dimensions of giftedness they had been identified). Although the academic and intellectual subscale correlated significantly with Wechsler Intelligence Scale for Children—Revised (WISC-R) and System of Multicultural Pluralistic Assessment (SOMPA) scores, correlations of the WISC-R with the subscale of Creativity were also significant and no data were provided to indicate whether the Academic or Intellectual subscale correlated more strongly with the WISC-R than did the Leadership and Performing and Visual Arts scales. No data were provided to support the construct validity of the Performing and Visual Arts, Creativity, or Leadership subscales through concurrent or predictive, discriminant or convergent validity studies. No data were provided concerning the relationship of those scales with other indicators of talent in those areas. Claims of diagnostic validity based on the correlations with the WISC-R are not explained.

The discussion of validity also presumes there is a single construct "giftedness" when the statement is made, "Considering that the subscales of the GES were all designed to measure *the* [emphasis added] construct of giftedness, then the subscales should correlate to a level of significance" (p. 20). This statement violates the premises of the definition and use of the subscales as indicators of separate talent areas. The resultant overall quotient and percentile score further violate the assumptions of the definition upon which the instrument is based.

The items on the instrument and its scoring are at times inconsistent with claims in the manual. For example, the first item on the instrument asks the teacher (or other rater) to declare whether the student consistently scores high on aptitude or intelligence measures. In contrast is a statement in the manual, "On-going performance observation and reporting, such as the GES, have unlimited potential compared to the more limited formal testing situations which tend to measure intelligence and achievement only and are notoriously biased against minorities and culturally different" (p. 5). No data are given to indicate this instrument is any less culturally biased than the instruments that are criticized. Further, the use of scores on standardized tests and grades as a basis for rating are likely to give double weight to such indicators of ability in screening and placement protocols.

Norms are only vaguely described as derived from a sample of typical and gifted students. The criterion for the selection of teachers ("unselected sample") is vague and there was no apparent check of the "random selection" (p. 10) of the students they rated. The criterion for labeling the "gifted" in the norming group is not specified. Empirical data justifying or explaining the grouping of the norming sample for the standardization tables are not provided.

One underlying assumption of this or any other rating scale based on the observation of student performance is that the rater (teacher) has provided opportunities for the behavior to occur. No attention is given in the manual to assuring that such opportunities are provided to the students who are to be rated or to taking into account halo effects and generosity or leniency errors.

Although the reliability and internal consistencies of the subscales of the Gifted Evaluation Scale meet standards established in the measurement field, the lack of clear evidence of the validity of the subscales or total scale and inappropriate combining of subscale scores into an overall indicator of giftedness combine to make it impossible to recommend its use.

Review of the Gifted Evaluation Scale by ROSS E. TRAUB, Professor of Measurement, Evaluation, and Computer Application, The Ontario Institute for Studies in Education, Toronto, Ontario, Canada:

The Gifted Evaluation Scale (GES) is intended for use in identifying students who are gifted in some significant way. This having been done, the Gifted Intervention Manual is available as a guide to the development of educational programs for the chosen students.

The case for the GES, as made in the GES Technical Manual (GTM), includes a reference to the Gifted and Talented Children's Act, passed by the U.S. Congress in 1978. Five dimensions of talent are defined in the Act: general intellectual, general creative, specific academic, leadership, and the arts, both performing and visual. The GES was designed to assess giftedness along these dimensions.

Applying the GES involves having someone—usually a teacher—rate a student on 48 items each keyed to one of the five dimensions. The behaviors that are rated range from the objectively verifiable (e.g., whether or not the student achieved IQ scores of 130 or more on standardized intelligence tests) to the highly subjective (e.g., "Demonstrates significant knowledge," "Enjoys working toward goals," "Demonstrates superior artistic abilities"). The scale for rating a behavior has five categories, ordered in terms of the consistency with which the behavior occurs. The categories range from no demonstration of the behavior whatsoever (perfect negative consistency, Category 1), through inconsistent displays (Category 3) to demonstrations at every opportunity (perfect positive consistency, Category 5). Category 2 refers to "developing the behavior" (test booklet, p. 2), and seems off the scale.

Although designed for a worthy purpose, the GES is seriously flawed. In addition to the already noted subjectivity-of-judgement and rating-scale problems are flaws associated with the evidence presented regarding the instrument's validity, reliability, and norms.

VALIDITY. Content and construct aspects of validity are discussed in the GTM. As regards content validity, reference is made to "a careful literature review" and to "input from 37 diagnosticians and educational personnel" (p. 16). The former yielded 53 behavior scales, and the latter reduced the number of scales to 49. A further item was discarded, but the GTM includes no explanation. Readers must judge for themselves how well the 48 GES items represent the domain of giftedness.

Several kinds of construct validity evidence are reported in the GTM. One kind consists of coefficients of correlation between GES scores and scores on the Wechsler Intelligence Scale for Children—Revised (WISC-R) and the System of Multicultural Pluralistic Assessment (SOMPA). These are called criterion validity coefficients, but no argument is advanced for why either the WISC-R or SOMPA should be regarded as a criterion for the GES. Scores on the three instruments were obtained for 157 students, ranging in age from 4.5 to more than 18 years and all identified somehow as being gifted. GES scores increase with age—see the norms tables in the GTM—so the coefficients of correlation were presumably computed using standard scores on the GES scales. (The GTM authors do not confirm this.) The correlation coefficients were about .6 between scores on either the WISC-R or the SOMPA and scores on the Intellectual, Creativity, and specific Academic Aptitude dimensions of the GES. Scores on the Leadership and Performing Arts dimensions of the GES correlated about .4 with scores on the SOMPA. It is concluded, without justification, that these coefficients "exceeded the levels of [acceptable coefficients of correlation] (.30 to .35) considered necessary" (GTM, p. 20). We might ask what these coefficients would have been had the range of ability not been restricted by the inclusion of gifted students only in the sample.

As further evidence of construct validity, the GES ratings for the norming sample were factor analyzed in an attempt to show the instrument assesses five distinct dimensions. On the evidence, however, the scales of the GES appear to assess only a single dimension. This analysis revealed one extremely dominant eigen root, and the coefficients of the varimax rotation of the four-factor orthogonal model reported in the GTM (Table 3, p. 13) do not come close to defining an independent clustering of scales by dimensions. The four-factor model was chosen on the basis of the eigen-roots-greater-than-one rule. Had choice of model been based on design, it would have included five factors. No comparisons of different models, with one, four, or five factors, are provided.

The intercorrelations reported among the five GES dimensions (subscales) also indicate their lack of separation. The smallest of these 10 coefficients was .71 (Intellectual and Arts dimensions), with 8 coefficients greater than .78, and the largest greater than .90. Clearly, if the GES does not measure just a single dimension, then it is tapping one very strong general dimension and several very weak subsidiary dimensions.

Also reported as evidence of construct validity is a comparison of the ratings for "132 randomly selected students from the normative sample . . . to [the ratings for] a corresponding group of identified gifted students who were receiving gifted program services in 11 [of the] school districts [that participated] in the standardization activity" (GTM, p. 20). No information is provided as to how the two groups of students were matched. Regardless of their sex, the younger gifted-program participants received higher average GES ratings on all five subscales than students from the normative sample, and, again regardless of their sex, the older gifted-program participants received higher average GES ratings on three subscales—Intellectual, Creativity, and Specific Academic Aptitude—than students from the normative sample. No explanation is provided for the disparity in results for the younger and the older students.

RELIABILITY. Internal consistency (alpha) coefficients were calculated for GES subscales using the data from the norming sample. These coefficients were all larger than .90. Test-retest reliability was estimated for a randomly selected group of 107 students from the norming sample, each rated a second time. The single coefficient reported—.91—pertains, presumably, either to the sum of subscale standard scores or to the corresponding quotient score. Separate interrater reliability coefficients are reported for each of 14 age groups. I read (GTM, p. 16) that 25 students were chosen for each age group from the standardization sample, but I also read that a total of 302 students were rated twice; this number should be 350 if all 14 age groups included 25 students, as claimed. In any case, the 14 interrater reliability coefficients that are reported all equal or exceed .90. I am again left to presume that these coefficients pertain either to summed standard scores or to quotient scores.

The alpha coefficients and the test-retest reliability coefficient, although impressively large, cannot be taken at face value. Lower values of the alpha coefficients can be expected for groups of students all the same age. Also, the internal consistency of the ratings must be biased high because in most instances the same person will have rated a student on all 48 GES items. Both the factors that biased the alpha coefficients in an upward direction will have similarly biased the test-retest reliability coefficient.

The interrater reliability coefficients, however, are unaffected by heterogeneous age grouping. Moreover, the two raters of each student apparently worked independently, so there should be no upward bias in these coefficients, which are impressively large.

NORMS. The norming sample was drawn from only 26 states, and involved only 569 teachers rating randomly selected students from their classes. Inasmuch as the ratings of 2,276 students were used to produce the norms, it appears that every teacher rated four students. There must, therefore, be less variability in these norms than would be present if 2,276 randomly chosen students had each been judged by a different rater. Given the unrepresentative nature of the sample vis-à-vis U.S. Census data (see GTM, Table 2, p. 11) on the variable of parental occupation, plus the omission of a number of states from the sample, it seems inappropriate to conclude "that the [norming] results are accurate" (GTM, p. 11).

Users of the GES are to judge students for giftedness as follows: "If the student scores one or more standard deviations above the norm on one or more of the subscales of Intellectual, Creativity, or Academic Aptitude, a decision as to the student's giftedness can be made on that basis. *The student need not score one or more standard deviations above the mean on all five subscales in order to be recognized as gifted*" (GTM, p. 30). This is interesting for the reason that the claim is advanced in the GTM that only 3% to 5% of students are gifted. (Sisk, 1981, is cited for support.) GES users, however, are encouraged to include more than 15% of students in the gifted category!

CONCLUSION. The GES was developed to serve an important purpose. But the instrument probably does not serve this purpose well. The evidence of validity is dubious, the evidence of reliability is flawed, and the norms seem unlikely to represent any known population. What is more, we are encouraged by the authors to think of one in every six students as gifted. Were giftedness as common as this, the concept would be meaningless.

REVIEWER'S REFERENCE

Sisk, D. A. (1981). Educational planning for the gifted and talented. In J. M. Kauffman & D. P. Hallahan (Eds.), *Handbook of special education* (pp. 441-458). Englewood Cliffs, NJ: Prentice Hall, Inc.

[163]

The Gifted Program Evaluation Survey.

Purpose: Constructed to evaluate the effectiveness of a gifted program as perceived by parents, teachers, students, and administrators.
Population: Gifted and talented programs.
Publication Date: 1991.
Scores: Item scores only.
Administration: Individual.
Forms, 4: Parent, Teacher, Student, Administrator.
Price Data, 1991: $24.95 per evaluation kit consisting of manual/forms (42 pages).
Time: Administration time not reported.
Author: Richard Lahey.
Publisher: United/DOK Publishers.

Review of the Gifted Program Evaluation Survey by DAVID W. BARNETT, Professor of School Psychology, University of Cincinnati, and RITA M. BARNETT, Teacher, and LOIS NICHOLS, Teacher of Gifted and Talented, Oak Hills Local School District, Cincinnati, OH:

The Gifted Program Evaluation Survey is an assessment instrument that was developed to help determine the strengths and weaknesses of gifted and talented programs in the schools. Survey questions were based on a 7-year longitudinal evaluation of a school district's gifted and talented program. The survey is designed to gather information from parents of gifted children, students in the gifted program, teachers who have identified gifted and talented children in their classrooms, and administrators involved directly with program implementation.

The instrument consists of three parts. Part I is an anonymous questionnaire (33 items for parents, 37 for students, 40 for teachers, and 41 for administrators) with five possible responses (ranging from *Strongly Agree* to *Strongly Disagree*). Items include global ratings of the overall program and policy (i.e., grading, "pull out" characteristics, etc.), interactions between the gifted program and regular classrooms, reactions associated with factors such as self-esteem, relationships with peers, and specific ratings pertaining to a number of dimensions such as critical skills, creativity, problem solving, and leadership. Part II is a narrative form used to ascertain suggestions, problems, and benefits. Part III is optional and allows for open-ended individual or small-group consultation or discussion. Strategies for implementation are suggested for each part of the evaluation.

After survey responses are collected, the author suggests that responses to Part I for each category be converted to percentages, and that bar graphs be used to show the information. However, the format may be unwieldy (the number of graphs would be 151). Furthermore, the content of questions and item numbers between teacher, parent, and child questionnaires do not correspond, making the identification of patterns labor intensive. (However, teacher and administration forms are similar.) In order to compare and contrast responses among parents, teachers, and students, questions that are similar in content should be grouped, but recommendations to equate questions are not given.

For Part II, the narrative, the author recommends that a summarizing paragraph for each question should be written (seven for parents, eight for students, four for teachers, and four for administrators) to include the issues and concerns repeated most often. From the summarizing paragraphs, strengths and weaknesses of the program are identified and recommendations are made that include strategies for implementation.

For the submission of results, a booklet format is suggested with graphic representation on the left side of a page and the evaluator's summary of data and recommendations on the right side. Sessions should be held to share information and recommendations with stakeholders. The author also stresses the importance of follow-up sessions to insure that desired changes have been implemented and that evaluation occurs as an ongoing process.

Overall, the Evaluation Survey requires further development. Educational programs need strong evaluation procedures either to justify or expand programs. Only some of the basics of program evaluation are addressed (i.e., multiple raters, synthesis, and reporting) by this survey. It would be helpful to include sections on the basics of evaluation design from planning programs and initiating programs (i.e., goals, models of service delivery) to the challenges of evaluating existing or mature programs (i.e., the differences between formative and summative evaluation). Using principles of evaluation design, the author could communicate where the Survey fits into an overall plan. Basic to the integrity of a program evaluation is assessing whether the desired program is actually carried out in practice in a manner consistent with stated program philosophy, theory, and goals. This crucial factor is not addressed by the present evaluation system. In many cases, programs deviate greatly from plans and intentions.

The Survey is based on ratings that frequently have low to modest correlations with observed behavior. A concern is the potential biases of gifted and talented personnel conducting evaluations. Many questions are framed in ways that would lead to socially desirable responses. Some questions may lead to conclusions that would be difficult to validate even through rigorous experimental design (i.e., "High ability students seem to be better problem solvers and critical thinkers because of the TAG [talented and gifted] experience"). Furthermore, many districts would be interested in cost-outcome procedures not addressed by this evaluation process.

Documentation for technical adequacy is not addressed. Information pertaining to background review and strategies for item selection (an issue of content validity) are not included. Evaluation strategies should include an analysis of instruments and selection procedures for TAG programs. These facets of design may result in considerable problems resulting from basic decision reliability and validity issues. Also, the author does not provide details concerning the number of surveys distributed and the number returned. Methods to determine the representativeness and adequacy of survey results would be critical before considering the need for program changes.

Despite these concerns, the content and process of the evaluation procedures will be of great interest to districts. The most useful function may be to provide a look into a district's significant local efforts related to program evaluation. The criticisms relate not so much to the Survey itself, but to the need for more attention to the basics of evaluation design as a context.

Review of the Gifted Program Evaluation Survey by STEPHEN H. IVENS, Vice President, Research & Development, Touchstone Applied Science Associates, Brewster, NY:

Questionnaires to be completed by various parties at interest can be an important component of a program evaluation. The Gifted Program Evaluation Survey is a handbook that consists of a series of such questionnaires designed to be administered to parents, students, teachers, and administrators to assess their perceptions of a school district's program for gifted and talented students. In addition to the questionnaires, the handbook contains chapters that discuss strategies for implementation, and for compiling, organizing, categorizing, and analyzing the data. Each questionnaire consists of approximately 40 items with 5-point, *strongly agree* to *strongly disagree*, Likert-response options. In addition, each questionnaire contains a section with free response items. The items are consistently well-written and integrated across the four questionnaires.

Although the publishers state these questionnaires are "a generic version" of a longitudinal evaluation conducted at a specific school district in New York, the term "generic" appears to be a misnomer. All items in the questionnaires refer specifically to the "TAG" program, an acronym for "Talented and Gifted Program." As a result, the items may not be applicable for talented and gifted programs, in general. For example, items such as "I would have liked TAG to have started in the lower grades," "I would have liked TAG classes in the high school," and "My regular classroom teachers did not like me leaving class for TAG" are not consistent with the "generic version" claim of the publisher.

Although it is not likely that many schools could use the questionnaires in The Gifted Program Evaluation Survey as published, this handbook does serve as a useful model for those who wish to design their own program evaluation instruments. Although helpful suggestions are provided for analyzing and presenting the results from the questionnaires, no technical information is provided.

In summary, The Gifted Program Evaluation Survey is a pretentious title for what is, at best, a useful model for school personnel who want to develop their own instruments to assess the perceptions of parents, students, teachers, and administrators as part of a program evaluation.

[164]

The Golombok Rust Inventory of Marital State.
Purpose: Constructed to assess the overall quality of the relationship between married or cohabiting heterosexual couples.
Population: Married or unmarried heterosexual couples living together.
Publication Date: 1988.
Acronym: GRIMS.
Scores: Total score only.
Administration: Group.
Price Data, 1992: £46 per complete kit including 20 record forms and manual (31 pages); £28.75 per 20 record forms.
Time: [10–15] minutes.
Authors: John Rust, Ian Bennun, Michael Crowe, and Susan Golombok.
Publisher: NFER-Nelson Publishing Co., Ltd. [England].
Cross References: See T4:1047 (1 reference).

TEST REFERENCES

1. Golombok, S., Cook, R., Bish, A., & Murray, C. (1995). Families created by the new reproductive technologies: Quality of parenting and social and emotional development of the children. *Child Development, 66,* 285-298.

Review of the Golombok Rust Inventory of Marital State by MICHAEL J. SPORAKOWSKI, Professor of Family and Child Development, Virginia Polytechnic Institute and State University, Blacksburg, VA:

The Golombok Rust Inventory of Marital Status (GRIMS) is a 28-item marital inventory that is very relationship focused with an heavy emphasis on the outcomes of that relationship for the individual responding to the items. Although the word marital appears in its title, it could be equally appropriate for nonmarital, cohabiting relationships. The manual accompanying the instrument appears very complete and well designed. The authors have developed the inventory for clinical purposes using input from practitioners, therapists, counselors, and clients. The GRIMS appears psychometrically sound and would seem to be simple to administer and score.

The manual contains sections on: Aims, applications, and scope; a comprehensive, though brief, review of marital discord and its treatment; a commentary on assessing the marital state; issues of construction, reliability, validity, and sex differences; the relationship of this scale with one the authors developed for assessing sexual functioning; and, administrative related topics—refusal to answer, lying, sampling, and scoring instructions.

The authors give solid evidence of their appreciation of the field of marital assessment in their discussions and judicious use of references. I was troubled, however, by the authors' intimation of cultural biases in scales such as Spanier's Dyadic Adjustment Scale (11:117), yet they did not address that issue regarding their instrument.

Data presented regarding reliability and validity appear sound. Reliability was assessed using both split-half and Cronbach's alpha methods and ranged from .81 to .94 across several groups. It was similar for men and women (.91 and .87 respectively, in one comparison). Validity beyond content and face was indicated primarily in ability of the inventory to differentiate between separating couples, those in marital therapy or experiencing clinical marital problems, and couples experiencing sexual problems. After treatment scores changed significantly in positive directions.

Scoring of the inventory is simple and straightforward. Interpretation is based on the total score and a simple chart with statements ranging from "very severe problems" to "very good." It was not clear to this reviewer from whence those categories were derived. Normative data based on larger *N*s for diverse groups are necessary.

The GRIMS offers a useful alternative for relationship assessment. With more widespread clinical and research use and additional comparisons with related instruments the Golombok Rust Inventory of Marital State could prove to be a viable alternate, if not primary tool, in assessing and treating marital or relationship dysfunction.

Review of the Golombok Rust Inventory of Marital State by RICHARD M. WOLF, Professor of Psychology and Education, Teachers College, Columbia University, New York, NY:

The Golombok Rust Inventory of Marital State (GRIMS) is a 28-item self-report questionnaire intended to assess the overall quality of the relationship between a man and a woman who are married or living together. All items are presented in a Likert scale format with the four response categories ranging from *Strongly Agree* to *Strongly Disagree*. A single total scale is obtained. The instrument was developed in England and all data pertaining to it were gathered on samples in that country.

The motivation for developing this instrument was to have a simple measure that could be easily administered and scored. The intended use of the instrument is for researchers either to assess the efficacy of different forms of therapy or to investigate the impact of social, psychological, medical, or other factors on a relationship. It is also intended to be used to obtain a quick assessment of the severity of a marital problem.

The authors developed the instrument on the basis of several surveys of marital problems in England and in consultation with specialists in the field of marital counseling. A plan for an instrument was developed consisting of eight content dimensions of marriage (e.g., interests shared, communication, sex) and five areas in which these might be manifested (e.g., beliefs, behaviors, attitudes) resulting in a 40-cell test plan. One hundred and eighty three items were developed initially to measure all cells of the test plan but through tryouts and factor analysis, this was eventually reduced to 28 items measuring a single factor. Evidence supporting the cohesiveness of the scale is a set of substantial and positive item-remainder correlations presented in the test manual.

As with many newly developed scales, evidence for validity is spotty. Therapists rated couples in the clinical group used for tryout as to type of problem (primarily marital, primarily sexual, and no problem). Analyses of variance revealed significant differences between the three groups for both males and females. The actual differences were about three quarters of a standard deviation. However, because this was the group on which the instrument was developed, the results can only be regarded as suggestive.

Other analyses were carried out on the standardization group. This standardization sample is not representative of any population. Two groups comprise the sample. The first was made up of 80 couples presenting themselves as clients at a number of Marriage Guidance Clinics at several locations in England. The second consisted of attenders at a general practitioner's clinic in central London. The results of these studies of group differences, although in the expected direction, are hardly definitive.

Unfortunately, although the authors acknowledge the existence of other instruments in this area such as the Locke-Wallace Marital Adjustment Test (Locke & Wallace, 1957) and the Dyadic Adjustment Scale (ll:117), they do not supply evidence showing relationships of these measures with their instrument. This is unfortunate because the items in the GRIMS appear to be pertinent to U.S. culture.

Evidence for reliability of the scales is based on internal consistency estimates from the two subgroups used in the so-called standardization. Coefficient alphas for these subgroups ranged from .85 to .92. Split-half reliabilities ranged from .81 to .94. Taken together, the reliability of the instrument was .91 for men and .87 for women.

A notable problem with this instrument is its standardization and the interpretation of scores. On the basis of the very weak standardization process, raw scores were transformed into what the authors call "pseudo-stanine" scores. Interpretations range from "very good" for a score of 2 to "very severe problems" for a score of 9. These appear to be, at best, judgmentally determined and, at worst, impressionistic. I suggest that potential users confine their use of the instrument to the raw scores and to note relative changes as a result of therapy or group differences.

SUMMARY. The Golombok Rust Inventory of Marital State is a short, easily administered and scored self-report questionnaire assessing the general state of a marital relationship. The items are simple and straightforward. The instrument shows acceptable levels of reliability although evidence for validity is tenuous. The standardization process is questionable and score interpretation is a problem. However, the instrument may be serviceable in comparative studies. The use of the instrument to estimate effects of marital counseling is possible but probably should be used in conjunction with other available instruments.

REVIEWER'S REFERENCE

Locke, H. J., & Wallace, K. M. (1957). Short marital adjustment and prediction tests: Their reliability and validity. *Marriage and Family Living, 21*, 251-255.

[165]

Graded Word Spelling Test.

Purpose: Designed to measure spelling achievement.
Population: Ages 6-0 to adult.
Publication Date: 1977.
Scores: Total words correct.
Administration: Group.
Price Data, 1994: £5.25 per test booklet/manual (15 pages).
Time: (20–30) minutes.
Author: P. E. Vernon.
Publisher: Hodder & Stoughton Educational [England].

TEST REFERENCES

1. Hatcher, P. J., Hulme, C., & Ellis, A. W. (1994). Ameliorating early reading failure by integrating the teaching of reading and phonological skills: The phonological linkage hypothesis. *Child Development, 65*, 41-57.
2. McManus, I. C. (1995). Familial sinistrality: The utility of calculating exact genotype probabilities for individuals. *Cortex, 31*, 3-24.
3. Stothard, S. E., & Holme, C. (1995). A comparison of phonological skills in children with reading comprehension difficulties and children with decoding difficulties. *Journal of Child Psychology and Psychiatry and Allied Disciplines, 36*, 399-408.

Review of the Graded Word Spelling Test by CAROL E. WESTBY, Senior Research Associate, Training and Technical Assistance Unit, University of New Mexico Medical School, Albuquerque, NM:

The Graded Word Spelling Test was originally published in Great Britain in 1977 and standardized on 3,313 students in England and 1,909 students in Canada. It was designed to assist teachers in knowing how their students' spelling capabilities compared to recent norms. The test consists of 80 words selected from the Macmillan Spelling Series and graded in order of difficulty for British and Canadian students, with approximately six words for each age group from 6-0 to 18-0 years of age. Words were selected that were not difficult to enunciate clearly, that showed regular rises from one age group to the next, and that were equally familiar to English and Canadian students. Specific instructions are provided for presenting the words. The examiner is to say the word, read the sentence provided in the manual containing the word, and then repeat the word. Guidelines are provided for selecting the set of words to be used for group or individual testing at each grade level. Scoring is based on the total number of words spelled correctly. The author recommends adjusting scores for students who score very high or very low. This is because the test may not include sufficient difficult words for good spellers to reach their limit or because poor spellers would almost certainly have failed some of the easier words that were not given. Guidelines are given for adjusting the scores of good spellers who make nine or fewer errors and the scores of poor spellers who spell nine or fewer words correctly.

A split-half reliability of .94 is reported. No information is provided on test-retest reliability or on test validity. Spelling quotients between 70 and 130 (in 5-point steps) are provided in 2-month intervals for students from 6-0 to 17-6+ years. Separate norms are provided for English and Canadian children between ages 5-5 to 7-5 because English children had earlier school entries and earlier and more exposure to spelling. The differences between the two groups were not significant after age 7-5.

The date of the original standardization (1975) and the standardization population probably limit the usefulness of the Graded Word Spelling Test in the United States. The test, which takes 20–30 minutes to administer, may provide a quick way for English and Canadian teachers to determine how their students compare to the norms. With limited information on test reliability and validity, however, caution is warranted in interpreting test scores. The words were not chosen to represent any specific spelling patterns or rules. As a result, the test would not be useful in diagnosing the nature of a student's spelling difficulty or providing guidelines for remediating spelling difficulties.

[166]

Gray Oral Reading Tests, Third Edition.

Purpose: Designed to be "an objective measure of growth in oral reading and an aid in the diagnosis of reading difficulties."
Population: Ages 7-0 to 18-11.
Publication Dates: 1967–92.
Acronym: GORT-3.
Scores, 3: Passage, Comprehension, Oral Reading Quotient.
Administration: Group.
Price Data, 1994: $109 per complete kit including 25 Form A Profile/Examiner record forms and 25 Form B Profile/Examiner record forms; $29 per student book; $29 per 25 Profile/Examiner record forms; $31 per examiner's manual ('92, 71 pages); $79 per Apple or IBM Software Scoring and Report System.
Time: (15–30) minutes.
Authors: J. Lee Wiederholt and Brian R. Bryant.
Publisher: PRO-ED, Inc.
Cross References: For reviews by Julia A. Hickman and Robert J. Tierney, see 10:131 (15 references).

TEST REFERENCES

1. Chase, C. H., & Tallal, P. (1990). A developmental, interactive activation model of the Word Superiority Effect. *Journal of Experimental Child Psychology, 49*, 448-487.

2. Gilger, J. W., Pennington, B. F., Green, P., Smith, S. M., & Smith, S. D. (1992). Reading disability, immune disorders and non-right-handedness: Twin and family studies of their relations. *Neuropsychologia, 30*, 209-227.

3. Kushch, A., Gross-Glenn, K., Jallad, B., Lubs, H., Robin, M., Feldman, E., & Duara, R. (1993). Temporal lobe surface area measurements on MRI in normal and dyslexic readers. *Neuropsychologia, 31*, 811-821.

4. Ackerman, P. T., Dykman, R. A., & Ogesby, D. M. (1994). Visual event-related potentials of dyslexic children to rhyming and nonrhyming stimuli. *Journal of Clinical and Experimental Neuropsychology, 16*, 138-154.

5. Bolton, P., MacDonald, H., Pickles, A., Rios, P., Goode, S., Crowson, M., Bailey, A., & Rutter, M. (1994). A case-control family history study of autism. *Journal of Child Psychology and Psychiatry and Allied Disciplines, 35*, 877-900.

Review of the Gray Oral Reading Tests, Third Edition by JOHN D. KING, Professor of Special Education and Educational Administration, The University of Texas at Austin, Austin, TX:

The Gray Oral Reading Tests (GORT-3) is the third edition of this standardized measure of oral reading proficiency. It was originally published in 1967. The first revision (GORT-R) came out in 1986. Like its predecessors, the aims for this edition are to compare reading proficiency of students who are significantly below their peers, identify which students may benefit from interventions, aid in determining particular reading strengths and weaknesses, document students' progress following intervention, and serve as a measurement device in reading research. It retains the same 13 progressively more difficult reading passages of the GORT-R, each followed by five comprehension questions. The authors estimate it should take from 15 to 30 minutes to administer individually.

The GORT-3 seeks to improve upon previous versions in the following ways: (*a*) by providing a larger, stratified, normative sample whose demographic characteristics closely approximate 1990 U.S. Census data; (*b*) by providing new reliability and validity data; (*c*) by simplifying scoring; and (*d*) by providing standardized Rate and Accuracy scores in addition to the composite Passage score, Comprehension score, and Oral Reading Quotient of the GORT-R. Percentile scores and grade equivalents are provided. The provision of alternate forms allows for pre- and posttest comparisons to assess intervention effects. In addition, the GORT-3 allows for sophisticated analysis of errors in reading.

NORMS. "The GORT-3 was standardized on 1,485 children residing in 18 states" (p. 31). All but 226 of these comprised part of the normative sample for the GORT-R. The remainder of the cases were tested in 1990 on the GORT-3. Information is presented and compared to 1990 national census data for sex, residence (urban or rural), race (Black, White, other), ethnicity (American Indian, Hispanic, Asian, other), and geographic area. Data for geographic region, gender, and race are stratified by age. The predominant use of the GORT-R standardization sample seems justified because both administration procedures and the reading passages are identical for the two versions. "A comparison of the percentages demonstrates that, on the whole, the sample is nationally representative" (p. 31). However, tables or normative scores for subtests and composites are not stratified for race, ethnicity, or SES; nor does the Examiners' Manual state that performance differences between these groups are insignificant. Therefore, the appropriateness of the GORT-3 for nonwhite or low SES populations is unknown.

RELIABILITY. Two forms of reliability data are reported. Cronbach's coefficient alpha for internal consistency was calculated using 600 protocols, 50 from each age group 6–17, selected at random from the normative sample. All but 1 of 96 coefficients reported attain .80, whereas 54 attain .90. Standard Error of Measurement for each of the subtest standard scores and Oral Reading Quotient is provided. Test-retest reliability data were "taken from 100 randomly selected protocols of students who participated in the GORT-3 standardization" (p. 35). The Comprehension Score is sufficiently unreliable to warrant considerable caution when interpreting test-retest scores.

VALIDITY. Information is provided for content, criterion-related, and construct validity. Content validity is supported by "a detailed rationale for the structure and content of the passages and comprehension questions" (p. 37). This rationale is clear, plausible, and relies on recent theories of reading. Item analysis procedures were also employed in selection of comprehension questions. Coefficients of discrimination are reported and, for the most part, easily achieve generally accepted standards.

Criterion-related validity data are reported showing correlations between GORT-3 scores and several other measures of reading ability. These include Form C of the Formal Reading Inventory (n = 30), Iowa Tests of Educational Development Vocabulary and Total Reading scores (n = 108), teacher ratings in grades 3, 4, and 5 (n = 37), Reading scores from the California Achievement Test (n = 74), the Reading subtest of the Screening Children for Related Early Educational Needs (n = 34), reading subtests of the Diagnostic Achievement Battery—Second Edition (n = 34), and the Gray Oral Reading Tests—Diagnostic (n = 34). Significant correlations ranged from .22 to .89. Seven of the 180 failed to reach significance. In general, however, correlations were moderately strong suggesting that the GORT-3 does measure what it intends to measure but is not so similar to the other measures as to be redundant.

Construct validity data are reported in terms of relationship to age, subtest intercorrelations, relationship to other language scores, relationship to other achievement test scores, relationship to intelligence, ability to differentiate between groups of children identified as having reading deficiencies and those who do not, and item discrimination. Again, on the whole, the data presented suggest the GORT-3 is both a sufficiently reliable and valid instrument for its stated purposes.

STRENGTHS. The GORT-3 appears to achieve most of its stated goals for the revision. The standardization sample is not much larger, but the information on demographic characteristics supports its close match with population percentages. New reliability and validity data are provided in considerable detail. Convenient charts in the examiner's booklet make determining Rate, Accuracy, and hence, Passage scores much simpler than with the GORT-R. The Examiner's Manual is generally very good. It defines and discusses the author's viewpoints on the nature of reading and factors affecting proficiency. Administration instructions are clear. Production quality is high. The authors provide a good discussion of and guidance for interpreting test scores, seeking further assessment, and/or planning interventions. Furthermore, the manual provides explanations of the psychometric principles involved which should aid those with relatively little psychometric expertise to make appropriate interpretations of test scores.

LIMITATIONS. The GORT-3 appears to have two primary limitations. Although scoring is indeed simpler than before, the necessity of keeping track of separate basal and ceiling criteria for Passage and Comprehension scores makes it complicated to determine when to discontinue testing. A more serious limitation is the omission of normative data stratified along race/ethnicity/SES lines. Although great care was given ensuring the standardization sample closely approximates national census data, this does not ensure that normative interpretation of test scores is appropriate across categories. No data are reported in the manual to address this issue.

SUMMARY. The GORT-3 appears to be a generally successful revision of this standardized measure of oral reading proficiency. It is easier to use than previous editions and provides more detailed information concerning the standardization sample and the psychometric properties of the test. It is sufficiently reliable and valid to use for its stated purpose. However, some aspects of test administration remain complex. Furthermore, the lack of norms for interpretation of test scores by nonmajority-group students renders the appropriateness of the GORT-3 for these populations unknown.

Review of the Gray Oral Reading Tests, Third Edition by DEBORAH KING KUNDERT, Associate Professor of Educational Psychology and Statistics, University at Albany, State University of New York, Albany, NY:

The Gray Oral Reading Tests, Third Edition (GORT-3) is described by the authors to be "a means of evaluating oral reading speed and accuracy while accounting for comprehension abilities" (p. 4). This current edition follows two previous versions of the test (1967 and 1986). The general purposes of the GORT-3 include: identifying students who are significantly below peers in oral reading proficiency and who may profit from supplemental help, determining the particular kinds of reading strengths and weaknesses that the individual possesses, documenting student's progress in reading as a consequence of special intervention programs, and a measurement device in investigations where researchers are studying the reading abilities of school-age students. In the main, reviewers of previous editions of the GORT (e.g., McLoughlin & Lewis, 1990; Salvia & Ysseldyke, 1991) have indicated that the test is acceptable.

When comparing the GORT-R to the GORT-3, only minor changes are noted; the GORT-3 provides separate scores for rate and accuracy, whereas the GORT-R provided scores for rate and accuracy combined. Furthermore, the passages and comprehension questions on the GORT-3 are identical to those on the GORT-R. Salvia and Ysseldyke (1995) stated that "test users would have been better served by the publication of modified test protocols and a brief supplement to the GORT-R manual (including separate standard scores and percentiles for rate and accuracy, and better described norms, and better descriptions of the test's reliability)" (p. 469).

The GORT-3 is appropriate for students ages 7–18, and has two alternate forms (A and B), which each contain 13 passages of increasing difficulty. Each passage is followed by five comprehension questions. Scores derived from this measure include scaled scores ($M = 10$, $SD = 3$) for the subtests (rate, accuracy, Passage score, Comprehension score), and standard scores ($M = 100$, $SD = 15$) for the Oral Reading Quotient, and percentile ranks and grade equivalents.

According to the authors, the GORT-3 yields clinical information regarding: oral reading rate and accuracy (student's ability to read passages orally with speed and accuracy), oral reading comprehension (student's responses to orally presented multiple-choice questions), total reading ability (combination of student's performance on the Passage score and Comprehension score to yield an overall index of the student's reading ability), and miscues (an analysis of oral reading miscues as a judgment of the student's use of comprehension strategies in reading). This is an individually administered, norm-referenced test, and typical administration time varies from 15 to 30 minutes. Specific basal and ceiling rules are used on all subtests.

In developing the GORT-3, the authors made a number of changes based on reviews of the previous editions. These included: increasing the normative sample size, stratifying the norm sample, comparing the norm sample to the 1990 Census, adding new reliability and validity data, providing new rate and accuracy scores, and providing separate basals and ceilings for the Passage score and Comprehension score. The authors also included six basic rules for reliable administration (e.g., familiarity with the manual, establishing rapport, administer in distraction-free environment).

The norming sample consisted of 1,485 students from 18 states, with data collected in two phases. The first phase was in 1985 with testing completed using the GORT-R; the second phase was in 1990 with 226 students tested using the GORT-3. The norm sampling procedures resulted in a representative, national sample in terms of gender, residence, race, ethnicity, and geographic area. It was noted by this reviewer that sample sizes were inconsistent across the different ages (i.e., $n = 175$ for age 9, and $n = 73$ for age 18). This norming sample appears to meet the first three changes that the authors attempted based on previous reviews of the test.

In the manual, the authors provide information regarding the reliability of the GORT-3. Specifically, they cited internal consistency (Cronbach's alpha) estimates of .87–.93 for the subtests, and .96–.97 for the Oral Reading Quotient based on a random sample of 600 protocols (50 at each age level). Alternate form reliability information is also provided, based on 100 randomly selected protocols. These estimates range from $n = .62$ (Comprehension score) to .82 (Rate and Passage score). The authors also include information regarding the standard error of measurement of the GORT-3. Across all of the age levels, the *SEM* for the subtests is 1, and the *SEM* for the Oral Reading Quotient is 3. In the main, it seems to me that the authors provide adequate evidence of the reliability of the GORT-3.

Evidence of content validity, criterion-validity, and construct validity is also provided in the test manual. When evaluating the validity of the GORT-3, test users should note that some studies use the GORT-R rather than the GORT-3. The authors stated that validity data regarding the GORT-R Passage score, Comprehension score, and Oral Reading Quotient "can be applied to the GORT-3 because the two versions correlate so highly with one another" (manual, p. 36). This relationship was based on 100 randomly selected protocols. In terms of content validity, the authors presented a detailed rationale for the structure and content of the passages and comprehension questions. Text structure is used by the authors to refer to the vocabulary level and the interest in the topic. Passages were reportedly developed by a professional writer who controlled for word density, word length, sentence length, sentence complexity, and topic coherence. The authors stated that stories were adapted from the 1967 GORT, selected from topics of interest to students, or based on fables, current events, or unusual situations. A variety of comprehension question types were used (literal, inferential, critical, and affective), as well as passage-dependent and passage-independent questions. Item analysis was completed using 600 randomly selected protocols.

Concurrent criterion-related validity was also examined for the GORT-3. Three studies were reported which used the GORT-3 in combination with group achievement tests (Iowa Tests of Educational Development, the California Achievement Test, the Gray Oral Reading Tests—Diagnostic, Screening Children for Related Early Educational Needs, and the Diagnostic Achievement Battery-2) with subjects of various ages (grades 2–12). The median correlation between the GORT-3 and these criterion measures was .57.

Evidence of construct validity is also provided in the test manual. The authors present the constructs and the related testable questions of the GORT-3. Data are presented regarding the correlations of the GORT-3 and: Age (Form A median r = .81), subtest intercorrelations (Form A median r = .68), other language scores (median r = .57), other achievement tests (median r = .55), and intelligence (median r = .58). Evidence of group differentiation (good readers versus problem readers) is reported in the summaries of three studies. Based on these, the authors concluded that there is "considerable support for the ability of the GORT-3 to discriminate among groups of readers" (manual, p. 43). The user is cautioned that these results are based on two studies with small samples (≤25). On page 38, the authors cite Wallace and Larsen (1991); the correct citation for this work is Wallace, Larsen, and Elksnin (1992).

The authors provide nine pages in the manual for a discussion of the interpretation of the GORT-3; this would seem to be a rather limited coverage of such an important topic. Adjective ratings are provided for the standard scores. The authors further note the importance of identifying individual relative strengths and weaknesses through the use of discrepancy analyses. Formulas and a table provide the minimum difference scores for each form. In addition, the procedures for analyzing oral reading miscues are provided with appropriate caution from the authors regarding the idiosyncratic nature of miscue patterns (i.e., miscues are a function of complex interactions among several factors). No tables are presented with the average number of miscues by age level to assist in interpretation.

In a previous review of the GORT-R, Salvia and Ysseldyke (1991) noted difficulties in scoring the test. In the GORT-3 manual, the authors present limited information regarding examiner qualifications. Specifically, they state that examiners using this measure "should have some formal training in assessment . . . . Supervised practice in using reading tests is also desirable" (manual, p. 7). The authors further state that prospective examiners should "consult local school policies, state regulations, and professional organizations regarding the use of tests" (p. 7). It would seem to me that extensive practice with the miscue notation system would be necessary for examiners to have the required level of proficiency to use the GORT-3 in an efficient and appropriate manner.

In reviewing the educational and psychological literature through data-based searches, I noted that the GORT-R has been cited in eight journal articles; two of these were reviews of the GORT-R. Furthermore, when test usage surveys were reviewed, some decline in popularity of the GORT-R was noted. Specifically, in 1981, Goh, Teslow, and Fuller found that the GORT-R was the second most commonly used reading test (#1=Woodcock Reading Mastery Tests), whereas in 1992, Hutton, Dubes, and Muir noted that the GORT-R was the third most commonly used reading test (#1=Test of Reading Comprehension—Revised, and #2=Woodcock Reading Mastery Tests).

Overall, it would appear that the GORT-3 may be an appropriate measure to use when examining oral reading and comprehension; it seems to serve a limited role in reading assessment. The authors were responsive to reviews of the previous version. They are to be commended for the updated and expanded standardization sample, as well as the reliability estimates, and the somewhat tentative validity conclusions. Further research is needed on the interpretation of the scores from this measure for individual students.

REVIEWER'S REFERENCES

Goh, D. S., Teslow, C. J., & Fuller, G. B. (1981). The practice of psychological assessment among school psychologists. *Professional Psychology, 12*, 696-706.

McLoughlin, J. A., & Lewis, R. B. (1990). *Assessing special students.* Columbus, OH: Merrill.

Salvia, J., & Ysseldyke, J. E. (1991). *Assessment in special and remedial education* (5th ed.). Boston: Houghton-Mifflin.

Hutton, J. B., Dubes, R., & Muir, S. (1992). Assessment practices of school psychologists: Ten years later. *School Psychology Review, 21*, 271-284.

Wallace, G., Larsen, S., & Elksnin, L. K. (1992). *Educational assessment of learning problems: Testing for teaching* (2nd ed.). Boston: Allyn & Bacon.

Salvia, J., & Ysseldyke, J. E. (1995). *Assessment* (6th ed.). Boston: Houghton Mifflin Company.

[167]

Gregorc Style Delineator.

Purpose: "Designed to aid an individual to recognize and identify the channels through which he/she receives and expresses information."

Population: Adults.

Publication Dates: 1982–90.

Scores, 4: Concrete Sequential score, Abstract Sequential score, Abstract Random score, Concrete Random score.

Administration: Group.

Price Data, 1993: $42.95 per sample set including *An Adult's Guide to Style* ('82, 74 pages), *Inside Styles: Beyond the Basics* ('85, 285 pages), the Gregorc Style Delineator, and a one-page synopsis of the manual; $15.95 per technical manual ('82, 46 pages); $42.50 per 25 instrument packets or $24.95 per 10 instrument packets including guidelines for group administration; $9.95 per audiocas-

sette on careful use; $14.95 per *An Adult's Guide to Style;* $29.95 per *Inside Style: Beyond the Basics.*
Time: 3(5) minutes.
Comments: Self-assessment instrument.
Author: Anthony F. Gregorc.
Publisher: Gregorc Associates, Inc.
Cross References: See T4:1086 (2 references).

TEST REFERENCES

1. O'Brien, T. P. (1991). Relationships among selected characteristics of college students and cognitive style preferences. *College Student Journal, 25*, 492-500.

2. O'Brien, T. P., & Wilkinson, N. C. (1992). Cognitive styles and performance on the national council of state boards of nursing licensure examination. *College Student Journal, 26*, 156-161.

3. O'Brien, T. P. (1994). Cognitive learning styles and academic achievement in secondary education. *Journal of Research and Development in Education, 28*, 11-21.

Review of the Gregorc Style Delineator by STEPHEN L. BENTON, Professor of Educational Psychology, Kansas State University, Manhattan, KS:

The Gregorc Style Delineator (GSD), a self-report noncognitive inventory, assists in identifying dominant styles of processing information. Styles vary among two dimensions: perception (abstract vs. concrete) and sequence (sequential vs. random). The GSD seems closely related to the Gregorc Transaction Ability Inventory (TAI), the Kolb Learning Style Inventory (LSI; T4:1438) and the Kirton Adaption-Innovation Inventory (KAI; T4:1364). The GSD's sequential and random styles correlate with the KAI's adaptor and innovator types (Joniak & Isaksen, 1988).

Researchers have questioned the reliability and validity of the GSD (e.g., Joniak & Isaksen, 1988; O'Brien, 1990). The GSD test manual and accompanying audiotapes do little to dispel such concern.

TEST DEVELOPMENT. The test author took a phenomenological rather than an empirical approach to test development. He presented the words used in the original TAI to 60 adults employed in private industry. The 60 adults then apparently selected 40 words they considered expressive of the four styles. How the adults selected the words is unclear. In addition, no information is provided about the sampling methodology.

The 40 words fall within four combinations of the two dimensions of style: Concrete Sequential (CS), Abstract Sequential (AS), Abstract Random (AR), and Concrete Random (CR). Respondents must rank order words within each of 10 sets, by assigning the numbers 1 (least descriptive of self) to 4 (most descriptive of self). Ranks assigned to each of the 10 words that characterize a particular style (i.e., CS, AS, AR, CR) are then summed to yield four subscale scores. Subscale scores ranging from 27–40 are considered "high," those ranging from 16–26 are considered "intermediate," and those ranging from 10–15 are considered "low." The ranges were not derived empirically.

RELIABILITY. Some evidence exists for subscale internal consistency and stability, although no standard errors of measurement are reported. One hundred and ten adults completed the GSD twice across intervals ranging in time from 6 hours to 8 weeks. Again, the sampling methodology was not described. Measures of stability ranged from .85 to .88 for the four subscales. Standardized alpha coefficients ranged from .89 to .93. Joniak and Isaksen (1988), however, reported alpha coefficients ranging from .23 to.66, and O'Brien (1990) found values ranging from .51 to .64. Therefore, reliability is suspect. Further research should employ representative samples (clearly defined) and alternative forms of the test.

VALIDITY. The 40 words on the GSD lack parallelism. For example, Set 2 contains the words *perfectionist, research, colorful,* and *risk-taker*. This mixture of adjectives and nouns is common throughout all 10 sets. Furthermore, the ratio of adjectives to nouns varies from one subscale to another. The author claims that this arrangement reduces "linear processing," which this reviewer interpreted as response set or social desirability. In spite of this concern, the author selected words having only positive connotations (e.g., nonjudgmental, insightful, and creative) and arranged words within a scale all in the same row (i.e., CS first row, AS second row, etc.), factors which are likely to affect response set.

The ipsative scale also presents problems. In ranking a word as 4, a respondent must at the same time assign lower ranks to the other three words. Using the words above as examples, this eliminates the possibility that one could equally describe herself as a perfectionist, a researcher, and a risk-taker. In addition, because the total score summing across all subscales is the same for all respondents, the scores do not reflect intensity of a style relative to others. Therefore, it is questionable whether having a higher score on one subscale relative to others indicates a dominant style.

No empirical evidence is presented for construct validity. Joniak and Isaksen (1988) found no evidence to support the four constructs of CS, AS, AR, and CR. Only 4–6 words loaded on each of the four factors in their study, and only the AR and CR subscales were uncorrelated. O'Brien (1990) conducted a confirmatory factor analysis using LISREL 7 and found a moderate relationship between the CS and AS subscales, thus giving support to the sequence dimension. He found no correlation between the AR and CR subsales, however.

The author attempted to establish criterion-related validity. One hundred and ten adults completed the GSD and also responded to a list of 40 words theoretically attributed to individuals who have a dominant style. (Although the author claims a study of predictive validity, the two instruments were actually administered on the same occasion.) Neither the sampling method nor the method of selecting the 40 words were described. Although moderate correlations are reported between the GSD subscales and the subscales derived from the word list, criterion-related validity is still suspect. The author apparently chose the criterion (the 40-word list) more for its availability than for some carefully reasoned hypothesis. Ideally, a criterion should reflect respondents' standing on some criterion other than one closely related to the original test. In addition, no evidence is presented to support the construct validity of the 40-word list.

NORMATIVE DATA. No normative data are reported. The author claims that normative data cannot be obtained from the general population because he cannot be sure that everyone would use the same reference point (self). This begs the question as to whether respondents actually *do* use the same reference point. And if they do not, then what are the implications for validity?

OTHER CONSIDERATIONS. Some confusion exists about administration time limit. Although the directions in the manual specify 4 minutes, the audiotape presentation suggests 3 minutes. Also, some information in the audiotape is misleading. For example, the author claims that the GSD is a "very powerful research-based self-assessment system" and that it is "mandatory for mental health to maximize your dominant trait." These statements are unfounded. Finally, in the accompanying manual, *Inside Styles: Beyond the Basics*, the author claims the concept of style is not taught in undergraduate classes because "Many educational psychology departments . . . use behavioral psychology as their base and sole tenets" (p. 59). A more likely explanation is that students' knowledge, learning strategies, and interests are more important predictors of academic success than is style.

REVIEWER'S REFERENCES

Joniak, A. J., & Isaksen, S. G. (1988). The Gregorc Style Delineator: Internal consistency and its relationship to Kirton's adaptive-innovative distinction. *Educational and Psychological Measurement, 48*, 1043-1049.

O'Brien, T. P. (1990). Construct validation of the Gregorc Style Delineator: An application of LISREL 7. *Educational and Psychological Measurement, 50*, 631-636.

Review of the Gregorc Style Delineator by TRENTON R. FERRO, Assistant Professor of Adult and Community Education, Indiana University of Pennsylvania, Indiana, PA:

Subtitled "A Self-assessment Instrument for Adults," the Gregorc Style Delineator "was specifically designed to aid an individual to recognize and identify the channels through which he/she receives and expresses information efficiently, economically, and effectively" (technical manual, p. 1). It consists of a word matrix, similar in format and design to that of Kolb (1985), composed of 10 sets of four terms each which must be ranked from "4" ("the word in each set which is the best and most powerful descriptor of your SELF [sic]") to "1" ("the word which is the least descriptive of your SELF [sic]"). The numbers so assigned are summed to provide four scores representing four mediation channels: Concrete Sequential (CS), Abstract Sequential (AS), Abstract Random (AR), and Concrete Random (CR). Scores between 27 and 40 points indicate dominant styles or mediation channels, scores between 16 and 26 are considered intermediate, and scores between 10 and 15 indicate low styles or channels. These scores are then graphed on a Style Profile "designed to illustrate polar oppositions of Concrete Sequential/Abstract Random and Concrete Random/Abstract Sequential" (technical manual, p. 6). Connecting the four points on the two axes provides a four-sided figure that graphically illustrates a person's dominant, intermediate, and low styles or channels.

The instrument was developed on the basis of research using the phenomenological method and relates to the work of Jung (1971). Because of the brevity of Gregorc's treatment, those not familiar with phenomenology will have trouble following the discussion. These readers are referred to Spiegelberg (1982) and Stanage (1987) for fuller descriptions of the methodology of phenomenology and its application to the study of adults. Data collected from interviews with more than 400 individuals were used in the development of the instrument design, including the operational and theoretical definitions of the four channels that are cited in the manual by Gregorc in attesting to the construct validity of the instrument.

The Gregorc Style Delineator and its predecessor, the Transaction Ability Inventory (Gregorc, 1978), have attracted considerable attention and study. No fewer than 45 dissertations written between 1980 and 1991 have been based on this instrument or have used it as a means of data collection. Participants in this reviewer's classes and workshops have responded favorably to the instrument and its descriptions of the four channels or styles, thereby establishing its face validity. In their survey of learning style instruments for adults, James and Blank (1993) assess as "moderate" the evidence of validity, the evidence of reliability, and the strength of the research base and assess as "strong" the overall usability of the instrument (p. 52).

On the other hand, several studies raise questions concerning the extent of the reliability and validity of this instrument. Gregorc reports reliability (alpha) coefficients ranging from .89 for the AS scale to .93 for the AR scale and predictive validity correlations ranging from .55 for the CR scale to .76 on the AS scale. Sewall (1986) notes that the reliability coefficients may be spuriously high. Because "the words which comprise a scale are all in the same row . . . an individual could consciously or unconsciously bias the results by consistently ranking the words in a particular row either high or low" (p. 47). O'Brien

(1990) found alpha coefficients of .64 for CS, .51 for AS, .61 for AR, and .63 for CR. "Although within an acceptable range, these were substantially lower than the internal-consistency estimates reported by Gregorc" (p. 634). According to O'Brien, "high error terms, low squared multiple correlations, unacceptable total coefficients of determination and chi-square statistics are manifested which did not support [the] construct (dimensional) validity for the measured population" (pp. 635-636).

A study of Joniak and Isaksen (1988) provides several related conclusions. First, an examination of the correlations between the Style Indicator and the Kirton Adaption-Innovation Inventory suggest that "only the S[equential]-R[andom] dimension was potent in describing the differences among subjects with respect to Kirton's [1977] theory" (p. 1048). Because the Style Delineator was intended to define styles, the four subscales should be uncorrelated. Third, the alpha coefficients found by Joniak and Isaksen (1988) range from .23 to .66 in contrast to the .89 to .93 reported in the technical manual by Gregorc.

In spite of the concerns raised by these studies, the Gregorc Style Delineator should prove serviceable if used according to its proclaimed purpose, as a self-assessment instrument. Facilitators of adult learning can use it as well to gain better understanding of, and insight into, the preferred learning channels of their participants. However, until further research is conducted, as has been promised by the developer of this instrument, this Style Indicator should not be relied on for predictive or diagnostic purposes. As a final note, the time estimate of 3–5 minutes for completing the Style Indicator is the recommended time for rank ordering the items in the word matrix. Reading the directions, scoring, graphing scores on the Style Profile, and completing the self-assessment may take as much as 30 minutes.

REVIEWER'S REFERENCES

Jung, C. G. (1971). Psychological types. In H. Read, M. Fordham, G. Adler, & W. McGuire (Eds.), *Collected works of C. G. Jung* (R. F. C. Hull, Trans.). Princeton, NJ: Princeton University Press.

Kirton, M. J. (1977). Research edition: Kirton Adaption-Innovation Inventory [KAI]. London: National Federation for Education Research.

Gregorc, A. F. (1978). Transaction Ability Inventory. Columbia, CT: Gregorc Associates.

Spiegelberg, H. (1982). *The phenomenological movements: A historical introduction* (3rd ed.). The Hague: Martinus Nijhoff.

Kolb, D. A. (1985). Learning Style Inventory. Boston: McBer.

Sewall, T. J. (1986). *The measurement of learning style: A critique of four assessment tools*. Green Bay, WI: University of Wisconsin Green Bay, Wisconsin Assessment Center.

Stanage, S. M. (1987). *Adult education and phenomenological research: New directions for theory, practice, and research*. Malabar, FL: Robert E. Krieger.

Joniak, A. J., & Isaksen, S. G. (1988). The Gregorc Style Delineator: Internal consistency and its relationship to Kirton's adaptive-innovative distinction. *Educational and Psychological Measurement, 48*, 1043-1049.

O'Brien, T. P. (1990). Construct validation of the Gregorc Style Delineator: An application of LISREL 7. *Educational and Psychological Measurement, 50*, 631-636.

James, W. B., & Blank, W. E. (1993). Review and critique of available learning-style instruments for adults. In D. D. Flannery (Ed.), *Applying cognitive learning theory to adult learning* (pp. 47-57). San Francisco: Jossey-Bass.

[168]

The Grief Experience Inventory.

Purpose: Intended as a "multidimensional measure of grief which is sensitive to the longitudinal evolution of the process of bereavement."

Population: Bereaved adults.

Publication Dates: 1975–85.

Acronym: GEI.

Scores, 15 to 18: 3 validity scales (Denial, Atypical Responses, Social Desirability), 9 clinical scales (Despair, Anger/Hostility, Guilt [Form A only], Social Isolation, Loss of Control, Rumination [Form A only], Depersonalization [Form A only], Somatization, Death Anxiety), 6 research scales (Sleep Disturbance, Appetite, Loss of Vigor, Physical Symptoms, Optimism/Despair, Dependency).

Administration: Group.

Forms, 2: A (Death), B (Non-death).

Price Data, 1990: $22 per 25 reusable test booklets; $13 per scoring key; $15 per 50 answer sheets; $21 per 50 profiles; $14 per manual ('85, 31 pages); $14.50 per specimen set.

Time: (20–30) minutes.

Authors: Catherine M. Sanders, Paul A. Mauger, and Paschal N. Strong, Jr.

Publisher: Consulting Psychologists Press, Inc.

[The publisher advised in May 1992 that this test is now out of print—Ed.]

Review of The Grief Experience Inventory by JAYNE E. STAKE, Professor of Psychology, University of Missouri-St. Louis, St. Louis, MO:

The Grief Experience Inventory (GEI) comprises 135 true/false items, each of which is designated for one of 18 subscales. Norms for the GEI were based on 693 respondents who had recently experienced the death of a close relative. The GEI includes three validity scales, nine clinical scales, and six research scales not recommended for clinical use. The validity scales are: (*a*) naive defensiveness (Denial scale); (*b*) random, confused, or exaggerated responding (Atypical Response scale); and (*c*) responding in stereotyped bereavement patterns (Social Desirability scale). The Atypical Response scale is composed of items endorsed by less than 25% of the normative sample. The Social Desirability scale includes items that distinguished between responses obtained under standard instructions and responses obtained under instructions to give socially desirable responses. The GEI manual provides no information about the development of the Denial scale. Contrary to statements in the manual, the Denial scale has a substantial correlation (-.52) with one of the clinical scales, Death Anxiety. The validity scales may have value as measures of response set specific to the grief experience. However, because the meaning of high scores on the validity measures has not been explored, validity scores should be interpreted very cautiously. The test user will be on safer ground with the Minnesota Multiphasic Personality

Inventory-2 (MMPI; T4:1645) or other established response set measures until more is known about the construct validity of the GEI response set scales.

The GEI was constructed from an earlier Q-sort measure of 180 items. Content for these items was derived from previous studies of the grief experience. Each item was converted to a true/false format and then tested in a sample of 135 bereaved individuals. Items on the clinical scales were retained if they (*a*) correlated less than .30 with the Denial Scale, (*b*) correlated .30 or higher with other items on the scale for which they were intended, and (*c*) correlated higher with their intended target scale than with nontarget scales. The selected items were not cross validated in a second sample.

The test authors claim in the manual that this process of item analysis resulted in scales that each measure one trait or behavior. However, items within scales do not have homogeneous content. For example, items on the Despair scale refer to physical sensations in the limbs, restlessness, apathy, depression, and religious faith. Internal consistency estimates confirm the diversity of intrascale item content. Six of the nine clinical scales have alpha coefficients below .70, which is often recommended as a minimum value for application to research and below the often recommended minimum value for clinical use. The alpha coefficients for the validity scales (.34–.59) and research scales (.23–.68) are even lower.

Three factor analyses of GEI scale scores were undertaken. The first two included the nine clinical and three validity scales. These analyses revealed that all clinical scales had substantial factor loadings on a single factor. This primary factor, which accounted for over 70% of the common variance in two samples of bereaved individuals, was apparently a general factor of intensity of the grief experience. In the third analysis, scores from the GEI and MMPI clinical and validity scales were factor analyzed together. All clinical GEI scales had their highest factor loading on one primary factor, and none of the MMPI scales had their highest loading on this factor. The outcomes of these factor analyses indicate that all GEI clinical scales reflect, in part, a common grief factor that is distinct from pathology measured by the MMPI scales. Furthermore, a group of 107 individuals who were not bereaved scored significantly lower on all GEI clinical grief scales than bereaved individuals. This finding, and the results of the factor analyses, provide evidence that the GEI successfully discriminates between grieving and nongrieving respondents.

Despite this support for the validity of the GEI as a global measure of the bereavement response, there is very little evidence to justify the use of nine separate measures of the grief reaction. The authors did not use factor analysis as a means of determining the number of scales to include in their measure nor the items to include in each scale. Moreover, no factor analysis has been reported for the 135 selected test items. To justify the inclusion of nine clinical scales, a confirmatory factor analysis should have been undertaken. Given the poor internal consistency values and heterogeneous content of the GEI scales, it is unlikely that a nine-factor structure would be confirmed. Until the authors can demonstrate empirically that each scale represents a distinct component of the bereavement experience, we do not know that individual scale scores represent meaningful distinctions between aspects of the grieving process.

In summary, there is evidence that the GEI reflects the general level of distress associated with the grieving process and that it can differentiate this distress from psychopathology. However, there is no confirming evidence that the nine clinical scales measure distinct aspects of the grieving process or that the labels attached to the scales accurately represent the range of scale content. Because total GEI scores appear to provide some information of the depth of the grieving experience, they may be of some value in a clinical setting. However, the meaning of individual scale scores and interscale variations has not been established, and this information should not be used in making clinical judgments until more is known about the scale scores.

A non-death version of the GEI was created by eliminating items that refer to a specific death. The 104 remaining items are intended to measure reactions to significant losses, such as divorce and separation. The norms provided for the non-death version were based on the responses of 127 respondents who had suffered a recent significant loss. No other psychometric information was provided in the test manual. Hence, the value of this measure for understanding reactions to non-death losses has not been tested, and better known instruments, such as the Beck Depression Inventory (T4:268), are recommended for measuring the impact of non-death losses.

[169]

Grooved Pegboard Test.

Purpose: To assess manipulative dexterity.
Population: Ages 5 to 8-12, 9 to 14-12, 15 to adult.
Publication Date: 1989.
Scores, 3: Total Time, Number of "Drops," Total Pegs Correctly Placed.
Administration: Individual.
Price Data, 1991: $80 per Grooved Pegboard; $26.50 per 30 replacement pegs.
Time: Trial discontinued after 5 minutes.
Comments: Ages 5 to 8-12 only complete first two rows of the Pegboard.
Author: Ronald Trites (manual).
Publisher: Lafayette Instrument.
Cross References: See T4:1089 (2 references).

TEST REFERENCES

1. Tompkins, C. A., Holland, A. L., Ratcliff, G., Costello, A., Leahy, L. F., & Cowell, V. (1990). Predicting cognitive recovery from closed head-injury in children and adolescents. *Brain and Cognition, 13*, 86-97.

2. Casey, J. E., Rourke, B. P., & Picard, E. M. (1991). Syndrome of nonverbal learning disabilities: Age differences in neuropsychological, academic, and socioemotional functioning. *Development and Psychopathology, 3*, 329-345.

3. Heinze, H., Münte, T. F., Gobiet, W., Niemann, H., & Ruff, R. M. (1992). Parallel and serial visual search after closed head injury: Electrophysiological evidence for perceptual dysfunctions. *Neuropsychologia, 30*, 495-514.

4. Chouinard, M. J., & Braun, C. M. J. (1993). A meta-analysis of the relative sensitivity of neuropsychological screening tests. *Journal of Clinical and Experimental Neuropsychology, 15*, 591-607.

5. Ryan, C. M., & Williams, T. M. (1993). Effects of insulin-dependent diabetes on learning and memory efficiency in adults. *Journal of Clinical and Experimental Neuropsychology, 15*, 685-700.

6. Taylor, H. G., Barry, C. T., & Schatschneider, C. (1993). School-age consequences of *haemophilus influenzae* Type b meningitis. *Journal of Clinical Child Psychology, 22*, 196-206.

7. Brookshire, B. L., Butler, I. J., Ewing-Cobbs, L., & Fletcher, J. M. (1994). Neuropsychological characteristics of children with Tourette syndrome: Evidence for a nonverbal learning disability. *Journal of Clinical and Experimental Neuropsychology, 16*, 289-302.

8. Damos, D. L., & Parker, E. S. (1994). High false alarm rates on a vigilance task may indicate recreational drug use. *Journal of Clinical and Experimental Neuropsychology, 16*, 713-722.

9. DCCT Research Group. (1994). A screening algorithm to identify clinically significant changes in neuropsychological functions in the diabetes control and complications trial. *Journal of Clinical and Experimental Neuropsychology, 16*, 303-316.

10. Heaton, R., Paulsen, J. S., McAdams, L. A., Kuck, J., Zisook, S., Braff, D., Hams, J., & Jeste, D. V. (1994). Neuropsychological deficits in schizophrenics: Relationships to age, chronicity, and dementia. *Archives of General Psychiatry, 51*, 469-476.

11. Kemeny, M. E., Werner, H., Taylor, S. E., Schneider, S., Visscher, B., & Fahey, J. L. (1994). Repeated bereavement, depressed mood, and immune parameters in HIV seropositive and seronegative gay men. *Health Psychology, 13*, 14-24.

12. Podraza, A. M., Bornstein, R. A., Whitacre, C. C., Para, M. F., Fass, R. J., Rice, R. R., & Nasrallah, H. A. (1994). Neuropsychological performance and CD4 levels in HIV-1 asymptomatic infection. *Journal of Clinical and Experimental Neuropsychology, 16*, 777-783.

13. Yeates, K. O., & Mortensen, M. E. (1994). Acute and chronic neuropsychological consequences of mercury vapor poisoning in two early adolescents. *Journal of Clinical and Experimental Neuropsychology, 16*, 209-222.

14. Manjiriona, J., & Prior, M. (1995). Comparison of Asperger Syndrome and high-functioning autistic children on a test of motor impairment. *Journal of Autism and Developmental Disorders, 25*, 23-39.

Review of the Grooved Pegboard Test by RODERICK K. MAHURIN, Assistant Professor of Psychiatry, University of Texas Health Science Center, San Antonio, TX, and ERIN McCLURE, Research Associate, Department of Psychiatry, University of Texas Health Science Center, San Antonio, TX:

PURPOSE. The Grooved Pegboard Test (GPT) is a brief, portable measure of finger dexterity. It is commonly used as a component of the Wisconsin Motor Steadiness Battery (Matthews & Klove, 1964), as well as the extended Halstead Reitan Neuropsychological Test Battery (HRNB) (Reitan & Davison, 1974). Uses of the GPT may be subdivided into two broad categories: (*a*) measurement of finger dexterity, and (*b*) inference of brain dysfunction from test performance. The first use is more applicable to occupational or rehabilitation settings where fine-motor coordination is important as a predictor of job performance or as an indicator of everyday functional abilities. The second application is more frequently encountered in clinical evaluations, in which discrepancies from age-adjusted normative scores are hypothesized to relate to lateralized cerebral dysfunction.

MATERIALS AND ADMINISTRATION. The GPT consists of 25 ridged pegs and a 10-centimeter-square metal board containing a five-by-five array of randomly slotted holes. Each peg must be lifted from the storage well and manipulated to fit into a hole. The subject is instructed to fill in the holes row-by-row. Subjects aged 9 years through adult complete one trial of the entire board with each hand. Children aged 5 years to 8 years fill only the first two rows using each hand.

Directions for administering the test are brief and easy to follow. Including instructions, the GPT requires approximately 5 minutes to complete for both hands. No specialized training is required to administer the test; however, interpretation is best undertaken by individuals with appropriate experience. As cautioned in the test manual, scores obtained from the GPT are diagnostically meaningful "only within the context of an extensive sampling of medical, cognitive, motor, sensory, and personality factors" (p. 3).

The manual describes three scores for each hand: (*a*) time required to complete the trial, (*b*) the number of times the subject drops any pegs, and (*c*) the number of pegs correctly placed in the holes. The utility of the third score is unclear, as the task necessitates that the subjects fill all holes. The three scores can be summed to obtain a composite measure of time and errors based on "age curve reference scores" provided in the manual.

RELIABILITY. Little information is available regarding the reliability of the GPT, and no data are provided in the manual. Knights and Moule (1968) presented evidence of test-retest reliability within a clinical trial of 40 children aged 8 to 15 years referred for assessment of suspected neurological dysfunction and tested before and after a 6-week trial of methylphenidate. Reliability coefficients for completion time were .80 and .81 for preferred and nonpreferred hands, respectively. For number of errors much lower coefficients were obtained (preferred hand: $r = 20$; nonpreferred hand: $r = .21$); however, this may reflect either the limited range of error scores, or the effects of the pharmacological trial itself. Standard reliability studies with normal subjects across diverse age groups are lacking.

VALIDITY. Several studies have been performed that address the concurrent validity of the GPT in children. Two of these are mentioned in the manual; however, they are not listed as sources of validation for the instrument. One of these studies indicated that the GPT adequately discriminated normal children from those with "suspected neurological dysfunction." The other study presented evidence that head injured children ($n = 100$) and children with "minimal cerebral dysfunction" (n = 44) performed more poorly than normal controls matched for age (n = 44). Recent research by Knights, Ivan et al. (1991) indicated that the GPT successfully discriminated severely impaired head-injured children from those with mild and moderate injuries. Francis, Fletcher, Rourke, and York (1992) studied GPT performance in a mixed clinical sample of learning disabled children (n = 722), and found support for a distinction between a primary simple motor factor (e.g., finger tapping and grip strength) and a complex motor factor that included the GPT.

The manual cites several validation studies for adult populations. One revealed significantly slower GPT scores for patients with multiple sclerosis than for control patients with other central nervous system impairment (Matthews, Cleeland, & Hopper, 1970). Haaland and Delaney (1981) reported impaired GPT performance following unilateral hemispheric stroke or brain tumor. In a factor analytic study of motor skills in dementia, Mahurin and Inbody (1989) found the GPT to load on a Visual-Motor factor (with such tasks as Rotary Pursuit, Finger Tapping [Reitan & Wolfson, 1985] and the Purdue Pegboard [Purdue Research Foundation, 1948]) significantly discriminated dementia patients from normal controls.

There is limited information available regarding the incremental validity of the GPT over other common measures of visual-motor dexterity, such as the Finger Tapping Test, the Purdue Pegboard Test, the Pin Test (Satz & D'Elia, 1989), or the Nine-Hole Pegboard Test (Mathiowetz, Weber, Kashman, & Volland, 1985). In general, validity data that equal or exceed that of the GPT are available for all of these tests.

NORMATIVE DATA. The normative data provided in the manual are limited. Although means and standard deviations for test completion time are provided for males and females aged 5 years to 60+ years, they are compiled from several studies and no information is given regarding the size of the samples, or such crucial sample characteristics as IQ, socioeconomic status, educational level, or ethnicity of subjects. Separate norms are not provided for the number of drops or the number or pegs correctly placed. Instead, error scores are included in the composite age-curve reference scores.

Knights and Moule (1968) published additional normative data for children aged 5 to 14 years (n = 184); these data have since been updated and revised (Knights & Norwood, 1980). A further set of norms for children aged 9 to 15 years (n = 106) is presented in Klonoff and Low (1974). Comprehensive adult norms (n = 475; age 20 to 80 years) are presented in a compendium of normative data for the HRNB and supplementary tests (Heaton, Grant, & Matthews, 1991). This data set allows direct comparison of standard scores on the GPT with other neuropsychological tests normed on a common reference group. Bornstein (1985) also published normative information based on 365 normal adults ranging in age from 18 to 69 years. As with the Heaton et al. norms, significant age effects were found for the GPT (r = .58), as were both gender and education effects. Females obtained somewhat better scores than males, and subjects with a high school education or greater performed better than those without. In contrast to the Finger Tapping Test, in which a 10% difference is common between preferred and nonpreferred hands (Reitan & Wolfson, 1985), between-hand performance on the GPT often differs by only a few seconds; therefore, a finding of no difference between the hands may not be clinically significant.

CONCLUSIONS. In summary, the GPT is a convenient measure of fine visual-motor coordination and finger dexterity for both children and adults. However, comprehensive reliability and validity data are not readily available, and the manual is limited in this regard. There is also little empirical evidence for the instrument's incremental validity for either occupational or clinical prediction over that of other fine-motor tests. Nevertheless, the complex visual-spatial demands of the test suggest that it may provide additional sensitivity to subtle brain impairment. Recent publications provide normative data beyond that given in the manual, and these references should be consulted to assist in clinical interpretation of GPT scores.

REVIEWER'S REFERENCES

Purdue Research Foundation. (1948). *Examiners manual for the Purdue Pegboard.* Chicago: Science Research Associates.

Matthews, C. G., & Klove, H. (1964). *Instruction manual for the Adult Neuropsychological Test Battery.* Madison, WI: University of Wisconsin Medical School.

Knights, R. M., & Moule, A. D. (1968). Normative data on the Motor Steadiness Battery for children. *Perceptual and Motor Skills, 26,* 643-650.

Matthews, C. G., Cleeland, C. S., & Hopper, C. L. (1970). Neuropsychological patterns in multiple sclerosis. *Diseases of the Nervous System, 31,* 161-170.

Klonoff, H., & Low, M. (1974). Disordered brain function in young children and early adolescents: Neuropsychological and electroencephalographic correlates. In R. M. Reitan & L. A. Davison (Eds.), *Clinical neuropsychology: Current status and applications* (pp. 121-178). Washington, DC: V. H. Winston & Sons.

Reitan, R. M., & Davison, L. A. (1974). *Clinical neuropsychology: Current status and applications* (Appendix). Washington, DC: V. H. Winston & Sons.

Knights, R. M., & Norwood, J. (1980). *Revised smoothed normative data on the Neuropsychological Test Battery for Children.* Ottawa, Canada: Author.

Haaland, K. Y., & Delaney, H. D. (1981). Motor deficits after left or right hemisphere damage due to stroke or tumor. *Neuropsychologia, 19,* 17-27.

Bornstein, R. A. (1985). Normative data on selected neuropsychological measures from a nonclinical sample. *Journal of Clinical Psychology, 41,* 651-659.

Mathiowetz, V., Weber, K., Kashman, N., & Volland, G. (1985). Adult norms for the Nine Hole Peg Test of finger dexterity. *Occupational Therapy Journal of Research, 5,* 24-38.

Reitan, R. M., & Wolfson, D. (1985). *The Halstead-Reitan Neuropsychological Test Battery: Theory and clinical interpretation.* Tucson: Neuropsychology Press.

Mahurin, R. K., & Inbody, S. B. (1989). Psychomotor assessment of the older patient. *Clinics in Geriatric Medicine, 5,* 499-518.

Satz, P., & D'Elia, L. (1989). *Manual: The Pin Test.* Odessa, FL: Psychological Assessment Resources.

Heaton, R. K., Grant, I., & Matthews, C. G. (1991). Comprehensive norms for an expanded Halstead-Reitan Battery: Demographic corrections, research findings, and clinical applications. Odessa, FL: Psychological Assessment Resources.

Knights, R. M., Ivan, L. P., Ventureyra, E. C. G., Bentivoglio, C., Stoddart, C., Winogron, W., & Bawden, H. N. (1991). The effects of head injury in children on neuropsychological and behavioral functioning. *Brain Injury*, 5, 339-351.

Francis, D. J., Fletcher, J. M., Rourke, B. P., & York, M. J. (1992). A five-factor model for motor, psychomotor, and visual-spatial tests used in the neuropsychological assessment of children. *Journal of Clinical and Experimental Neuropsychology*, 14, 625-637.

Review of the Grooved Pegboard Test by RICHARD K. STRATTON, Associate Professor of Education, Division of Health and Physical Education, Virginia Polytechnic Institute & State University, Blacksburg, VA:

The instructions for administration for the Grooved Pegboard Test are generally well written and contain sufficiently detailed descriptions of the administration and scoring procedures with one notable exception. The test requires that the "dominant/nondominant" hands be used but does not suggest how this dominance be determined. It seems likely the test actually refers to the preferred hand rather than the dominant hand. Regardless, there should be standardized directions for identifying the hand designations.

The scoring system and norms reported in the manual are not consistent and also problematic. The norms for the Kiddie (poor choice of subject descriptor) and Adolescents are based on time only with no penalty added for drops. The Adult norms use a scoring formula that adds together time, drops, and number of pegs inserted. This formula penalizes subjects who place the most pegs in the board during the test. It would make more sense to add together time, drops, and holes *not* filled to arrive at a total score. A more fundamental question is why are different scoring formulas being used? The age-score curves included in the manual are of extremely poor quality and virtually useless for interpreting the derived scores.

The instrument itself is physically well constructed and would appear to hold up well with repeated usage. Extra pegs are included, which should minimize any problem that might result from the test administrator needing to remove already inserted pegs to replace pegs that might be dropped on the floor. (The test set I reviewed had one defective peg.)

The instructions for interpretation of test scores provide several suggestions for developing local norms when using the test for personnel selection. Following these procedures is critical to maintain validity when using the test for this purpose.

[170]

Group Diagnostic Reading Aptitude and Achievement Tests, Intermediate Form.

Purpose: Designed to assess reading achievement and to diagnose reading problems.
Population: Grades 3–9.
Publication Date: [Orig. 1937].
Scores, 13: Achievement [Reading (Paragraph Understanding, Speed, Word Discrimination), Arithmetic, Spelling], Diagnostic [Word Discrimination Errors, Visual (Letter Memory, Form Memory), Auditory (Letter Memory, Discrimination and Orientation), Motor (Copying Text, Cross Out Letters), Language-Vocabulary].
Administration: Group.
Price Data, 1992: $.27 per book; $5.50 per set of visual test cards; $2.20 per set of norms.
Time: (40) minutes (includes both timed and untimed tests).
Authors: Marion Monroe and Eva Edith Sherman.
Publisher: C. H. Nevins Printing Co.

Review of the Group Diagnostic Reading Aptitude and Achievement Tests, Intermediate Form by DEBORAH KING KUNDERT, Associate Professor of Educational Psychology and Statistics, University at Albany, State University of New York, Albany, NY:

According to the authors, the Group Diagnostic Reading Aptitude and Achievement Tests, Intermediate Form (GDRAAT) is a series of group-administered tests designed to assess reading achievement and to diagnose reading problems in students enrolled in grades 3–9. Materials that were made available for this review included: intermediate form protocol, Visual Test stimulus cards, a 12-page scoring sheet, and Directions to Examiner. This measure contains a series of 14 subtests which are divided into two parts: Part 1—Achievement Tests (Reading Tests [Paragraph Understanding, Speed of Reading, and Word Discrimination], Arithmetic Computation, and Spelling), and Part 2—Aptitude Tests (Visual Tests [Letter Memory, Form Memory], Auditory Tests [Letter, Discrimination and Orientation], Motor Tests [Copying Text, Crossing Out Letters], and a Language Test [Vocabulary]). Scores that are obtained from these measures include grade equivalent scores on the Paragraph Understanding and Reading Speed subtests, and percentiles on the Word Discrimination and aptitude subtests.

The publisher indicated that the two-page Directions to Examiner serves as the test manual. Examination of this document indicates that these are directions for administration and general comments (e.g., "Be very careful that the children start and stop promptly on this test"). No information was provided regarding the standardization group, reliability, or validity of this instrument.

An analysis of each subtest included in this measure was conducted to determine the stimuli presented to and the required response from the students. In the Paragraph Understanding subtest, the students are to read a question, then read a short paragraph (ranging from 2–11 lines), and then circle the one word that answers the initial question; time limit for this is 7 minutes. The Reading Speed subtest requires the students to read a sentence and then do what was requested (e.g., underline the tree) in 90 seconds. For the Word Discrimination subtests, the student is presented with three sentences in a group and is instructed to select the correct sentence (separate subtest for vowels, consonants, reversals, and additions/omissions); time limit 2 minutes for each subtest. On the Arithmetic subtest the student is given a page of 30 computations to complete in 5 minutes. The required operation for each item is written in parentheses; operation signs are included for 20 of the items. For the Spelling subtest, the examiner dictates a word, and the student writes the word in the blank space in a sentence. The Visual Tests examine memory for nonsense letter sequences (e.g., ag) and for abstract designs. For the Auditory Tests, the examiner first spells aloud the letters of nonsense words and then students must write as many of the letters as they can remember. The second part of this subtest involves discrimination and orientation. Students are presented with 25 rows each containing 4 Xs. The examiner says a word, and then the students are to circle the X that represents the position of the target word. The Motor Tests include two parts: Copying Text and Crossing Out Letters. The copying section presents the students with a seven-line short story and the students must copy it in the provided space in 90 seconds. For cross out, the students are presented with a paragraph of nonsense words, and are directed that they are to cross out the *a* in every other word in 60 seconds. The final subtest is Vocabulary. Students are presented with pairs of words, the examiner reads the pairs aloud, and then the students must select the pair that makes the best sense.

Scoring rules are included on the protocol for each subtest. In general, these criteria seem straightforward. All students in grades 3–9 begin the subtests at the beginning; there are no basal or ceiling rules. It would seem likely that students with reading difficulties might become frustrated with such a format. Interpretation guidelines are provided to the user in the 12-page scoring sheet. To interpret the achievement subtests, the authors instruct the examiner to plot the child's grade, mental age, and subtest scores (grade equivalent or percentile), and then proceed through a series of questions (i.e., is reading achievement up to grade, up to mental age, and does the child fall low in one special type of reading, does the child perform especially high in one area, is spelling at about the same level as reading, and is arithmetic higher than reading?). After these questions, the authors provide a one-paragraph summary stating what student types would be classified as remedial students (i.e., "children needing remedial work in reading are those whose reading achievements fall below mental age or below arithmetic," and "children who are reading up to mental age but below grade are not regarded as remedial cases, but are slow learners who need easy reading material," (scoring sheet, p. 4). No citations are provided to support diagnoses using these criteria.

Likewise, interpretation summaries are presented for the diagnostic and aptitude tests. For example, if the word discrimination score is low, the student's errors should be analyzed to determine specific difficulties (i.e., vowels, consonants, reversals, additions, and omissions). Depending on the area of difficulty, broader interventions are suggested (e.g., for vowel and consonant errors, "a systematic review of phonics is helpful," and for reversals, "word tracing while saying the word aloud slowly is helpful," (scoring sheet, p. 4). Again, no citations are included to substantiate the interpretations and interventions offered by the authors.

Evidence of the psychometric properties of the GDRAAT is lacking. The publisher, when contacted by this reviewer, indicated no information on reliability or validity was available. No information was provided for the selection of items for this measure. For example, the inclusion of visual tests as aptitude tests (predictors of reading ability) is questionable (e.g., Sattler, 1988). Furthermore, in examining these materials, I noted the lack of documentation or citations for the interpretations that were presented by the authors. For example, do all remedial reading programs use the authors' criteria for placement in remedial reading, and what is the source of the general principles of remedial work?

In summary, the GDRAAT purports to assess reading achievement and to diagnose reading problems. The use of a group-administered test to diagnose reading problems is suspect; in-depth, individual techniques as part of a comprehensive evaluation of reading skills are recommended (Salvia & Ysseldyke, 1995). The lack of information on item selection procedures, item ordering criteria, no basal and ceiling rules, norming/standardization, reliability, and validity preclude the use of this measure. It is unclear how this test might aid in determining student performance level and identifying areas of reading difficulty in any meaningful manner.

REVIEWER'S REFERENCES

Sattler, J. M. (1988). *Assessment of children* (3rd ed.). San Diego: Jerome M. Sattler, Publisher.

Salvia, J., & Ysseldyke, J. E. (1995). *Assessment* (6th ed.). Boston: Houghton Mifflin Company.

Review of the Group Diagnostic Reading Aptitude and Achievement Tests, Intermediate Form by MARGARET R. ROGERS, Assistant Professor of School Psychology, University of Maryland-College Park, College Park, MD:

The Group Diagnostic Reading Aptitude and Achievement Tests, Intermediate Form is designed for use with individuals age 8 to 15+. The test kit contains a protocol, stimulus cards, instructions to the examiner (one page double sided), and a 12-page "scoring sheet," which includes an answer key, normative information, interpretive guidelines, and instructions for remediation. Curiously, no information is included in the test kit that describes the purpose of the instrument. Although the title leads one to believe that it is a diagnostic instrument to be used in the assessment of reading abilities, one surmises by reviewing the contents of the kit that the test was designed as a screening device to assess reading comprehension, spelling, arithmetic computation, visual discrimination, visual motor, memory for letters, and auditory comprehension skills.

ADMINISTRATION. Testing begins with the Achievement subtests (reading comprehension, spelling, arithmetic computation) and ends with the Aptitude subtests. Altogether, there are 15 subtests each yielding a separate raw score. The "scoring sheet" allows users to convert subtest raw scores into grade scores, and in the case of the Aptitude subtests, raw scores are also converted into percentiles (based on age and grade). Score transformations are also listed on the protocol after each subtest so that users can obtain a quick index of performance without referring to the scoring sheet. The front page of the protocol is designed to be completed by the test user and contains an educational profile (requires computation of chronological age, mental age) and a diagnostic profile (scores are plotted to reflect "inferior," "average," or "superior" functioning). These labels, along with language used throughout the test items, suggest that the instrument is quite dated.

Directions to the examiner about proper test administration are sparse and although a minor inconvenience, ill-placed. Some of the directions are provided on the "instructions to the examiner" sheet whereas others, in particular the amount of time each subtest is allotted, are found only on the protocol. The scoring sheet does not describe examiner qualifications and training needed in the use of the scale. The scoring sheet also does not discuss how to use the instrument with limited-English-proficiency individuals or with bilingual persons.

PRACTICAL EVALUATION. Qualitatively, testing materials are simple and stark. The test, including the stimulus cards, presents visual stimuli in black typeset on a white background. The paragraphs and questions that comprise the Paragraph Understanding subtest (reading comprehension) contain errors in spelling and capitalization. Also, when taking the Paragraph Understanding subtest, the format of the testing is confusing. Each item within this subtest consists of a paragraph, a corresponding question, and a set of multiple-choice responses. But, the typical sequence in which one reads the paragraph first then reads the question is reversed so that the question precedes the paragraph. This irregular sequencing configuration is distracting to the test taker.

The scoring sheet contains interpretive guidelines that include recommendations for remediation. Although the inclusion of interpretation guides is a laudable feature, the contents of these guidelines are simplistic and suggest a cookbook approach to remediation. Possible causes of problems on a subtest are listed with a corresponding remedy and the recommended interventions tend to emphasize kinesthetic approaches to skill remediation.

TECHNICAL EVALUATION. Although the test is a norm-referenced instrument, no information is provided about the standardization sample. Without such information, it is not possible to tell whether the instrument was designed to be used with a locally or nationally representative group of people. Also absent is a discussion of the steps taken to ensure that items are not biased. Further, no information is provided on the construction, norms, reliability, and validity of the scale.

SUMMARY. The overall impression of the Group Diagnostic Reading Aptitude and Achievement Tests, Intermediate Form is of an out-of-date, outmoded instrument that fails to provide basic technical information needed to evaluate its usefulness. Before this instrument could be recommended for use in either clinical or research contexts, it would need to undergo a complete revision with special attention devoted to item construction, norming procedures, providing evidence of reliability and validity, and revising the manual. Information is also needed about for whom the instrument is appropriate (e.g., in terms of race, ethnicity, language, sex, SES, etc.) and when and for what reason the scale should be used.

[171]

Group Reading Test, Third Edition.

Purpose: Measures early and intermediate reading skills.
Population: Ages 6-4 to 11-11 and 8-0 to 11-11 below average.
Publication Dates: 1968–91.
Acronym: GRT.
Scores: Total score only.
Administration: Group.
Price Data, 1994: £3.75 per 20 Form A; £3.75 per 20 Form B; £5.50 per manual; £3.25 per template A or template B; £5.99 per specimen set.
Time: (13) minutes.
Author: Dennis Young.
Publisher: Hodder & Stoughton Educational [England].
Cross References: See T4:1102 (4 references); for reviews by Patrick Groff and Douglas A. Pidgeon of the Second Edition, see 9:458 (1 reference); for a review by Ralph D. Dutch of the original edition, see 8:729.

TEST REFERENCES

1. McArdle, P., O'Brien, G., & Kolvin, I. (1995). Hyperactivity: Prevalence and relationship with conduct disorder. *Journal of Child Psychology and Psychiatry and Allied Disciplines*, *36*, 279-303.

Review of the Group Reading Test, Third Edition by WILLIAM R. MERZ, SR., Professor and Coordinator, School Psychology Training Program, California State University, Sacramento, CA:

The Group Reading Test, Third Edition (GRT) is designed to assess the word reading skills of children from 6-4 to 11-11 years old. It consists of two sections, a word reading section and a sentence reading section. In the word reading section, the child circles the word in a list of three to five nouns that represents a stimulus picture. In the sentence reading section, the child circles a word in a list of five to six words that best completes a sentence stem. Administration time for the two sections is 13 minutes with the word reading section containing 15 items, and the sentence reading section containing 30 items.

This instrument was developed for British schools with children "in the last term of the infants' stage, the first year . . . of the junior stage, and older, below-average juniors" (manual, p. 1). Roughly, in American schools that equates to the end of first grade through the beginning of third grade. The test was published for the first time in 1968, revised for the first time in 1980, and revised a second time in 1989. Its longevity probably indicates its usefulness in schools in the United Kingdom. A similar test by the same author, the Spelling and Reading Tests, is available for children in what would equate in American schools to third through fifth grade.

The author claims that the method of item construction controlled for the effects of differences in vocabulary, general knowledge, and intelligence, although the methodology used to accomplish this is not described. Unfortunately, cultural effects cannot be controlled so that the vocabulary load appropriate for children in British infant and junior levels may not be appropriate for children in American primary grades.

The test is hand scored and yields a total raw score that is converted to a quotient, which the author labels a standard score. Although the magnitudes of the mean and the standard deviation of the quotient distributions are not reported, it appears that the mean for the first grade students is 100, and the standard deviation is 15. The distribution seems to be truncated for children 8 years old and older because their maximum standard scores range from 88 to 96 rather than the 120 to 130 for younger children.

The author provides a brief rationale for the test in the first part of the test manual. There are short sections on administration, marking, and using the norms tables, as well. Another short section on the use of test scores in teaching presents the author's views on using tests to help select reading material and improve instruction. Comments to teachers on assisting children with reading difficulties are included in the manual, too.

Technical information is provided in a section titled "Construction and Investigations." That section includes descriptions of item construction and selection, efficiency of instructions, establishing the time limit, scoring, standardization, validity, reliability, and practice effects. In the discussion of item analysis the author indicates that probits were used to describe item difficulty and discrimination, something not usually done in American test construction. He also states that items showing strong gender bias were eliminated without reporting the method for determining bias. The efficacy of test directions was assessed with children during the item trials. Time limits are based on experience with the two earlier editions of the test. In grading, no credit is given past the 10th error; this decision is based on empirical evidence that aims at maximizing test reliability. Norms were established on 2,585 children from 6-4 to 11-11; there were 1,272 boys and 1,313 girls. A common norm was constructed with the scores of boys and girls being given equal weight. No further description of the norm group is presented. Although content-related evidence of validity and criterion-related evidence of validity are discussed; construct-related evidence is not presented. Reliability is discussed in terms of standard errors of estimate, standard errors of measurement, differences between test and retest scores, and reliability of reading ages, quotients, and gains. This information is presented in a way a little different from the way American test authors and publishers present their findings on the reliability of the scores generated from test performance; however, the information is clear and logical.

Three questions address whether or not a test is appropriate for general use. First, do the test content and scores relate to the questions being asked of the quantitative results? Second, has the test been constructed in such a way that results are generalizable; that is, does the author offer adequate information on reliability and validity? Third, are the test results interpretable; that is, are there norms or criteria by which performance on the test may be judged?

In the case of the GRT, the answer to the first question depends on the definition of reading in the primary grades. If reading is defined as word identification, then the test assesses that skill and answers a question about a child's skill in identifying nouns for which pictures are presented and identifying words in the context of an incomplete sentence. The second question is answered with evidence that the content addresses the question and that scores obtained correlate with the results of other tests. Evidence that the scores are reliable is presented with the caveat that reliability of individual scores declines for children older than 8.5 years. The third question dealing with interpretability is addressed minimally because the description of the standardization group is restricted to age and school placement and does not report any other demographics.

Utilizing a test out of its cultural context is always problematic. This GRT is designed for British children in schools in the United Kingdom. Whether or not it assesses the same skills taught in the curriculum of American schools or school districts requires careful critical analysis. Certainly the norm group is quite different from one found in American first and second grades. The manual presents information about the test in a straightforward manner; yet, there is a paucity of information about the norm group. It is clear that the quotients for children over 8 years old are quite skewed; one would expect that. How maximum scores in the high 80s and low 90s are derived for the older children when maximum scores for younger children exceed 120 is not explained. There are technical gaps in the information presented on reliability, too. The usual Pearson Product-Moment correlation coefficients are not presented. Rather, standard errors and differences between test and retest scores are presented, as are average gains for retest on parallel forms. That is valuable, useful information. Nevertheless, as useful as this test has been found in the United Kingdom, it is probably not appropriate for general use in American schools.

Review of the Group Reading Test, Third Edition by DIANE J. SAWYER, Murfree Professor of Dyslexic Studies, Middle Tennessee State University, Murfreesboro, TN:

The Group Reading Test (GRT) was developed for use in British infant and junior schools. The author specifically states that the optimum period in which to use this test is the last term of infant school and the first term of junior school. In the United States, this appears to be equivalent to the end of first grade or the beginning of second. Raw scores may be converted to standard scores (quotients) that are tied to the age equivalents 6 years 4 months (6:4) to 8 years 11 months (8:11) for average students, and extended to 11 years 11 months (11:11) for below-average students.

The GRT consists of two parts. In Part One children are asked to circle the appropriate word label, from among three to five printed words, for a pictured object appearing in the same box. Three examples are provided to familiarize children with the task. Fifteen test items are provided for children to complete independently in a 4-minute period. Some pictures and word labels are not culture free. For example, a double decker bus is pictured, the word "shop" is given to pair with a store front, the word "lid" is paired with a trash can cover, the word "tap" is paired with a picture of a water faucet. Also, the drawing of a doll looks more like a young child.

Part Two consists of sentence stems followed by five to six words from which to select and circle the appropriate completer word (e.g., We read—up books the is can). Three sample items are followed by 30 test items to be completed in 9 minutes. Many of the vocabulary terms and choices are sophisticated for typical 7-year-olds (e.g., Usual means—notion, nostril, noteworthy, normal, novel, number). Two forms of the test (A and B) are available to use either simultaneously, so as to discourage copying within the group, or for follow-up testing at some future time within the recommended school term.

The stated purpose of the GRT is to assist teachers in obtaining a general measure of reading, in the group setting, that may then be followed up, as needed, with additional individual testing to guide instructional adjustments for children whose progress is unsatisfactory. Some detailed suggestions for follow-up testing are provided in the section of the manual titled "From Testing to Teaching."

The 45-item GRT yields one raw score that may then be converted to a standard score (quotient) computed for the age groups 6 years 4 months through 8 years 11 months (Table 1). These standard scores were also extrapolated (Table 2) to estimate the performance of older (up to age 11:11), below-average students. The author states that the standard scores presented in the third edition are based upon GRT test score distributions accumulated over 4 years from a sample of schools whose populations were collectively representative of "national norms" (manual, p. 13).

The discussion of how the GRT quotients were actually established is confusing. However, it appears that 2,585 children in the last term of infant school were tested in May/June using the GRT. A common table of standard scores was constructed and then, using an adjustment for age, estimates of expected scores at subsequent ages were calculated. No mention is made of studies to assess the validity of the expected scores as calculated.

The author makes a reasonable claim for content validity by arguing that the GRT tasks reflect real classroom reading tasks for the targeted age group. Although the picture-word matching task reflects early concern for decoding skills, the sentence reading task reflects the concern that beginning readers learn to read for meaning.

Concurrent validity was assessed by correlating GRT results with those obtained from other reading tests administered at the same time. Scores obtained for 80 students on the GRT, the Neale Analyses of Reading Ability, and the Vernon Graded Word Reading Test yielded correlations of.82 to .93 for comprehension and .61 and .82 for word recognition. These are within the acceptable range.

The author chose not to provide evidence of predictive validity due to the belief that the principal value of the GRT rests in its potential to inform immediate instructional practices.

Estimates of reliability of the GRT might have been produced for several samples, but coefficients were not reported in all instances. A standard error of estimate (for predicting Form A from Form B or vice versa) of about 3 raw score points was calculated for a sample of 100 seven-year-olds who took both Forms A and B. From this same sample an alternate form reliability coefficient of .945 was produced. The standard error of measurement calculated for this sample was approximately 2.5 raw score points. Mean test-retest differences for a sample of 886 students was 2.37 raw score points. The author reports that the reading age/quotient scale is reliable up to age 8:5 and that the reliability progressively decreases thereafter.

The GRT was originally developed in 1968 and remains essentially unchanged. In the third edition only "the tables of quotients have been reorganized" (manual, p. 1) and a section on the use of the results has been expanded. Views on the nature of appropriate testing in the primary grades have changed considerably in recent years. Standardized, norm-referenced tests that are independent of instructional experiences provided offer little to help teachers restructure instruction. Teachers know which children are struggling with reading at the end of the first grade. A low score on the GRT offers no insight into where, for any given child, the reading process is breaking down. It does not seem efficient or reasonable to administer any test simply to provide "backing" for information in cumulative folders (manual, p. 1) or for teacher judgment. In my opinion, the GRT serves no valid purpose in first grade classrooms of the 1990s.

[172]

Group Styles Inventory.

Purpose: Designed to "assess the particular style or styles of your work group following a simulated or real problem-solving session or meeting."
Population: Group members.
Publication Date: 1990.
Acronym: GSI.
Scores: 12 styles in 3 general clusters: Constructive (Achievement, Self-Actualizing, Humanistic-Encouraging, Affiliative), Passive/Defensive (Approval, Conventional, Dependent, Avoidance), Aggressive/Defensive (Oppositional, Power, Competitive, Perfectionistic).
Administration: Group.
Price Data: Price information for test materials including Participant Guide (50 pages) and Leader's Guide (72 pages) available from publisher.
Time: [10–15] minutes.
Authors: Robert A. Cooke and Clayton J. Lafferty.
Publisher: Human Synergistics, Inc.

Review of the Group Styles Inventory by LAWRENCE M. ALEAMONI, Professor of Educational Psychology, University of Arizona, Tucson, AZ:

The Group Styles Inventory (GSI) is designed to facilitate team building and improve group processes by first assessing the particular style or styles of a work group following a simulated or real problem-solving session. The GSI is claimed to be useful for analyzing the styles of planning committees, project teams, coordinating committees, task forces, boards of directors, and quality or safety circles as well as other types of groups where members interact to solve problems or make decisions.

The Leader's Guide is a 72-page document that contains seven sections: Introduction to the Group Styles Inventory, Understanding the GSI, The 12 Group Styles, Using the GSI with a Simulation, Using the GSI with an Emphasis on Group Outcomes, Group Summary, and Research Appendix.

In the section "Introduction to the Group Styles Inventory" claims are made that the GSI is capable of demonstrating how individual behavior can affect group processes and how group processes can affect individual behavior. It is also claimed the GSI can be used by organization leaders to change patterns of behavior within groups in a direction consistent with overall cultural change efforts. However, no empirical evidence is provided to support any of these assertions.

The GSI contains 72 statements with a 5-point response scale for each item consisting of *Not at all, To a slight extent, To a moderate extent, To a great extent, To a very great extent.* This scale does not represent a balanced continuum from negative to positive and, therefore, does not satisfy the requirements of an interval or quasi-interval scale. This means that calculating arithmetic averages and using scores for correlation purposes will be highly suspect.

In the section "Understanding the GSI," it is claimed the GSI measures 12 distinct patterns of group interaction, which can be organized into three general clusters: Constructive, Passive/Defensive, and Aggressive/Defensive. In order to determine if the 12 patterns and three general clusters were the result of empirical analysis the Section "Research Appendix" was perused. Under the heading "Development of the GSI" is the statement, "the GSI was developed on the basis of research" and "field testing confirmed that the GSI was a valuable tool for team building and could readily be built into various types of training and development programs" (Leader's Guide, p. 71). However, no supporting data, analysis, description of studies or cited references were provided.

In the section devoted to reliability and validity, it is reported the data base used to assess the statistical reliability and validity of GSI-I included 1,000 respondents representing 184 different groups; 104 groups had completed a Human Synergistic Simulation and 80 had been working on an actual organizational problem. It is further reported that statistical analysis of the data indicated "that the GSI-I was a valid and reliable instrument for measuring the styles of problem-solving groups. More specifically, the results of our analyses show that the 12 scales were generally reliable (internal consistency, reliability), factored into three general 'clusters' of styles as intended (construct or factor validity) and effectively distinguished between effective vs. ineffective groups (criterion-related validity)" (p. 71). However, nowhere in this appendix was any *actual evidence* of studies or citations of studies provided to substantiate any of these claims. In fact, the only validity data reported indicates that respondent scores on the seven group outcomes are based on subjective evaluations but are still considered valid and meaningful. To support this claim they report a correlation of .29 between the scores on the Quality of Solution Item and the actual performance of groups (as subsequently measured by their Team Scores) on Human Synergistics' simulations. Such a correlation cannot possibly justify the concluding statement in the Research Appendix, "These findings indicate that group members generally are able to accurately evaluate their team's performance" (p. 72).

In summary, the idea of providing an instrument and system to assess group problem-solving styles and then use the information to facilitate improvement is excellent. The Leader's and Participant Guides present a very attractive, well-organized, and compelling format for accomplishing such objectives. However, the complete lack of supporting evidence and empirical research for the many claims, materials, and processes presented raise serious doubts about the claims as well as the utility of the Group Styles Inventory.

Review of the Group Styles Inventory by BERT A. GOLDMAN, Professor of Education, University of North Carolina at Greensboro, Greensboro, NC:

Authors Robert Cooke and Clayton Lafferty have not only developed an inventory purporting to measure patterns of group behavior, they have developed an entire program and array of materials to enable participants to learn about their individual behavior as members of a group, their interaction within the group, and their organization's effect upon their group's behavior and direction.

In addition to the Group Styles Inventory (GSI), the array of materials consists of the Leader's Guide, the Participant Guide, Human Synergistics' business simulations, Human Synergistics' survival simulations, Human Synergistics' Life Styles Inventory, and the Organizational Culture Inventory.

The GSI Leader's Guide is a nicely formatted manual with index tables that provides detailed instructions for using the GSI, requiring an estimated 6 hours; but this would be 6 hours after one has mastered an understanding of all of the concepts, all of the materials, and the entire administration process. This reviewer has no idea how long such mastery would take.

The GSI consists of 72 statements divided evenly among 12 group styles, which in turn are divided evenly among three general clusters. One must master an understanding of each of the 12 group styles and the three general clusters in order to use the GSI in conjunction with all of the other materials including what is called the Group Styles Circumplex upon which the group's GSI scores are plotted.

The GSI purports to measure patterns of behaviors that emerge when people work together. Consequently, it is not an instrument designed for administration to one person, but instead it is intended for administration to a group of people who work together either temporarily or permanently to solve problems and/or make decisions.

Interpretation of each of the 12 group styles presented in the Leader's Guide is intended to contain a general description of the style, a list of the inventory items measuring the style, a description of the kind of activity groups so classified are likely to display, research findings pertaining to the style, and suggestions for influencing what is referred to as a constructive group style and minimizing what is referred to as a defensive group style. These descriptions are said to be based upon observations and statistical data from 184 different groups totaling 1,000 members all of whom completed the GSI after working on a simulations problem or on an actual organizational problem. No description of these 1,000 people or how they were selected is given, nor are any of the statistical data provided. Further, the research findings presented with each style description are not documented. The reader is told nothing about how these research findings were gathered.

The process for converting raw scores to percentiles is based upon the norms developed from the same 1,000 people mentioned previously for whom no information is given. Further, authors of the research appendix of the manual indicate the reliability and validity of the first version of the GSI, the GSI-I, was apparently determined from a data base obtained from those same 1,000 people. The manual authors go on to say that these data indicated the GSI-I was a valid and reliable instrument. In addition, the manual authors state that (*a*) the 12 scales were generally reliable (which the authors equate with internal consistency); (*b*) these 12 scales factored into three general clusters of styles (which is equated with construct or factor validity); and (*c*) the scales effectively distinguished between effective versus ineffective groups (which is equated with criterion-related validity). All of the foregoing was presented without offering a single shred of statistical evidence.

Although the GSI-I is described as sufficiently reliable and valid, the GSI-II was developed to further strengthen reliability, predictive power, and usefulness for group process and team-building programs. The authors state the six items measuring each of the group styles are strongly associated with one another, are distinct from the items measuring the other 11 styles, and are strongly related to group outcomes such as the quality of acceptance of solutions. Once again there is not a shred of evidence given to support this information.

Along with a request for demographic information on the back of the GSI is a request for response to a list of seven group outcomes. Validity for respondents' scores on these seven group outcomes is presented by one example in the form of a significant correlation ($r = .29$) between the scores on the Quality of Solution items and performance of a sample of 95 groups working on simulations. In addition, a significant correlation ($r = .40$) between this group's scores on the Quality of Solution item and the percentage of improvement score on subsequent problem-solving simulations is offered as further proof of validity presented by the one example. These two correlations are the only statistical data presented in the entire manual (Leader's Guide) and they provide statistical information concerning the validity of only one item of a seven-item supplement to the GSI. No evidence supporting validity of the other six items is presented, nor is any information provided concerning the 95 groups upon whom the two correlations were determined.

In summary, the idea of measuring patterns of behaviors that emerge when people work together in order to facilitate team building and improve group processes is intriguing. The array of materials including the Group Styles Inventory developed by Robert Cooke and Clayton Lafferty through the Human Synergistics Corporation to accomplish this task are also intriguing. The Inventory along with the Leader's and the Participant Guides are produced in very clear and appealing formats and indeed the Inventory may well be valid and reliable. However, no statistical evidence is presented to support claims for validity and reliability. Further, no information is given to describe the norming population. And, finally, in addition to the approximate 6 hours indicated to conduct the simulation, administer the instrument, score, record, and explain the results, there is an unspecified amount of time it must take for someone to become proficient in conducting the entire program. Given the lack of information concerning norms, validity, and reliability, and the tremendous amount of time the entire procedure consumes, one should proceed very cautiously in making a decision to use the Group Styles Inventory.

[173]

Group Tests of Musical Abilities.

Purpose: Developed to measure an individual's musical ability level.
Population: Ages 7–14.
Publication Date: 1988.
Scores, 2: Pitch, Pulse.
Administration: Group.
Price Data, 1992: £28.75 per starter pack including cassette tape, 25 answer sheets, and manual (25 pages); £10.95 per cassette tape; £7.50 per 25 answer sheets; £10.35 per manual.
Time: [15–20] minutes.
Comments: A good quality audiocassette player is needed to administer test.
Author: Janet Mills.
Publisher: NFER-Nelson Publishing Co., Ltd. [England].

Review of the Group Tests of Musical Abilities by J. DAVID BOYLE, Professor and Chairman, Department of Music Education and Music Therapy, School of Music, University of Miami, Coral Gables, FL:

DESCRIPTION, ADMINISTRATION, AND SCORING OF TESTS. The Group Tests of Musical Abilities include two tests, a Pitch Test and a Pulse Test. As the author of the tests notes, the Pitch Test has similarities to the pitch subtests of the Seashore Measures of Musical Talents (Seashore, Lewis, & Saetveit, 1960) and the Measures of Musical Abilities (Bentley, 1966), but with some differences. Essentially, the Pitch Test uses two sine-wave stimulus tones for each item, and the testing task is to indicate which of the two tones is higher in pitch (1 or 2); if the respondent hears no difference in the pitch of the two tones, a "nought or nothing sign" (presumably a zero) should be indicated. Only 20 of the 24 items are to be scored, numbers 4 through 23. Each of these 20 items does have a pitch difference of at least $^1/_{10}$ of a semitone; however, one of the three example items and two of the four items which are not scored have no pitch difference between the two stimulus tones.

The Pulse Test is similar to the Rhythm Test of the Drake Musical Aptitude Tests (Drake, 1957) in that the testing task is to continue counting silently the number of pulses after hearing the first four pulses counted aloud in synchronization with a metronome. The tempo of the 10 test items ranges from M.M. = 42 to M.M. = 120. (Note for nonmusicians: M.M. = Maëlzel's Metronome; it is a tempo indication—e.g., M.M. = 120 means the tempo is 120 beats per minute.) Upon hearing a signal tone, the respondent writes down the number last counted silently. In scoring, the respondent gets 2 points for each item answered correctly, 1 point for a "near miss" (±1 count), and no points for any other number.

The test should be easily administered within the time frame suggested by the author. All directions, sample items, and test items are on the cassette tape. The tape is of good quality, the directions are clear, and the answer sheet appears easy to use. The British accent of the female voice on the tape is pleasant and should not be distracting for American children. However, a test administrator would have to explain that a "nought or nothing sign" is a zero.

The manual, which is called a Teacher's Guide, includes keys for scoring both the Pitch Test and the Pulse Test. No provisions are made for machine scoring, apparently because hand scoring of the tests is a relatively quick and simple matter.

NORMATIVE AND TECHNICAL DATA. The norms for the Pitch Test and the Pulse Test are based on separate samples. The normative sample for the Pitch Test included 1,715 children ranging in age from 6 through 16 and was drawn from intact mixed ability classes from 22 Oxfordshire LEA schools in the U.K. Because of some technical limitations with the original tape for the Pulse Test, a new normative sample was necessary for it. Drawn from essentially the same population, this sample included 839 children ranging in age from 7 through 14.

The manual provides limited norms for children ages 7 through 14. Rather than converting raw scores to standard scores or providing percentile ranks for the respective raw scores at each age level, the manual provides the score ranges for the top 10% and top 50% of the normative groups at each age level.

The manual provides two types of reliability data, internal reliability and test-retest, both of which are lower than what one might desire. Reliabilities for the Pitch Test range from .43 for test-retest data to .70 for corrected split-halves data to .72 for data based on Horst's modification of Cronbach's coefficient alpha. Reliabilities for the Pulse Test include coefficients of .52 for test-retest and .81 for corrected split-halves.

The author maintains that the tests have validity as a predictor of potential for instrumental performance, although no empirical validity coefficients are provided. The case for predictive validity is based on statistically significant differences in the scores of students who have achieved a certain success in instrumental performance (i.e., students who have passed any graded performance examination on an instrument) and the remainder of the sample. Similar data from a smaller sample of students attending a specialist music school corroborated this finding and yielded additional data indicating that successful instrumentalists score higher than less successful instrumentalists.

USES OF TEST DATA. The test author has sought to provide a practical and usable group test for teachers to use in conjunction with their personal observations in making decisions about the nature of musical experiences to be provided to children. The manual provides for two types of interpretations of test data. Stage one interpretations focus on finding out more about children's musical abilities, are based primarily on the number of errors each child makes, and are intended to provide guidance regarding (*a*) children who score high but otherwise might not have been predicted to do so and (*b*) children who did not score in the top 10%.

The second stage analysis focuses on the *nature* of each child's errors and seeks to diagnose *why* a child scored poorly. Other than "naive errors" related to test taking, the manual identifies two basic types of pitch errors: (*a*) failure to detect pitch differences and (*b*) confusion over which of two stimulus tones was higher. Errors on the Pulse Test reflected either counting too fast or too slow.

CONCLUDING OBSERVATIONS. Essentially the Group Tests of Musical Abilities is a traditional and limited approach to gathering data relevant to children's musical abilities. It might be argued that these tests are subject to the same validity concerns that have plagued the Seashore and other such tests throughout the history of music testing. Furthermore, one might raise concerns about the relatively low reliability coefficients for the tests. However, if one accepts the premise that data relative to pitch discrimination and pulse maintenance abilities are relevant objective data to be considered in conjunction with other information, both objective and subjective, when making decisions regarding children's learning experiences and opportunities in music, the low reliabilities become much less of a concern. Viewed from this perspective, the tests may be seen as providing additional objective data to teachers and parents seeking to make enlightened decisions regarding children's musical potentials, experiences, and opportunities.

REVIEWER'S REFERENCES

Drake, R. M. (1957). Drake Musical Aptitude Tests. Chicago: Science Research Associates.

Seashore, C. E., Lewis, D., & Saetveit, J. (1960). Seashore Measures of Musical Talents. New York: The Psychological Corporation.

Bentley, A. (1966). Measures of Musical Abilities. London: George G. Harrap & Co. Ltd.

Review of the Group Tests of Musical Abilities by ANNABEL J. COHEN, Assistant Professor of Psychology, University of Prince Edward Island, Charlottetown, Prince Edward Island, Canada:

The Group Tests of Musical Abilities is one of at least a dozen published musical aptitude tests that contain a sound recording. Among its positive features are its relative recency of development, clear manual, and simplicity of use with groups of children.

It consists of a 20-item Pitch Test and 10-item Pulse Test and is designed for two main groups of users: class teachers concerned with children's total music education and specialist instrument teachers concerned mainly with the performance component of children's music education. In its use of a written response, its avoidance of conventional instrument timbres, and its minimal use of musical terms, the test does to some extent meet the claim of being unbiased with respect to past training and ability to sing. Nevertheless, this conflicts with the claim of validity with respect to achievement on a musical instrument. Indeed, our own testing of 84 children in a Charlottetown elementary and junior high school revealed higher scores on those children in band or music classes. Thus, as a test of pure musical aptitude, this one falls short as do others (e.g., Seashore Measures of Musical Talents; 9:1088), and it must be recognized that children who have access to musical training will have an advantage on this test.

THE PITCH TEST. The Pitch Test measures the ability to discriminate small differences in the pitch of pairs of pure tones separated by from .75 to .10 semitones. Recorded instructions first explain the terms high and low with respect to pitch. Mills claims that "It is necessary to include some difficult examples so that the children understand that they must listen very carefully and regard any difference in pitch, no matter how slight, as significant" (teacher's guide, p. 4). This rationale might make more sense if the items were not presented in a graduated order of difficulty. If difficulty increases with trial number, children may only begin to attend later rather than throughout the test. Indeed, an analysis of our Charlottetown results for the seven levels of difficulty suggested that some listeners "tune in" to the task on the more difficult later trials.

THE PULSE TEST. This test concerns the ability to maintain a steady beat. For each item, a steady count of up to 4 is presented and synchronized with a metronome. The children are to continue counting in silence until they hear a signal tone. At that point, they stop counting and write down the last number they counted.

ADMINISTRATION. The author claims that the children enjoy both tasks. The children typically do not get lost and they complete the test. The instructions are very clear and allow for good standardization of procedure, enabling anyone to administer the test. In our administration of the test to children as young as 10 years of age, there were no difficulties encountered, although errors in early (easy) trials revealed that some children required more than the three unscored practice trials to settle in to the test.

INTERPRETATION. There are two stages in the interpretation of the children's scores on each of the tests. The first considers the total scores on each test and the second concerns an error analysis. The second stage may be necessitated only for diagnosing specific problems of children with low scores.

Tables are provided for each age from 7 to 14 years, which show the scores achieved by 10% and 50% of children previously tested. For example, for the Pitch Test, 50% of children of age 7 score 8 or above and 10% score 12 or above; 50% of children age 14 score 11 or above and 10% score 16 or above.

It is likely that there is more information in the results of both tests that could indicate the most sensitive ears. It is unfortunate that the author did not delve farther into her analysis and presentation of norms, although this does help to keep the exposition simple.

One concern is the provision of a "same" option in the Pitch Test when, in fact, in all cases one tone is higher than another and the "same" answer is never correct except on the third (easy) practice trial (gearing the child up for future same examples). Whereas it is true that the "same" response probably helps to distinguish those children who truly can hear differences from those who cannot and may contribute to the function of the test norms, more impressionable children might be biased by this option.

Test-retest reliability seems relatively low for 137 students retested after 14 weeks. Mills claims that the test can be given again, but recommends not doing so more than once a year. Age norms reveal continuing positive development for the Pitch Test but there is an interesting small decline in the Pulse Test for children of ages 13–14 whose low 50% norm is below that for children of ages 11–12. The internal reliability seems reasonable given the paucity of test items (20 for Pitch and 10 for Pulse) for the split-half test that was used. The external validity measures are based on small samples of students in music courses compared with students who are not so involved in music. Significantly different mean scores for musician and non-musician children were obtained but the Pitch Test was more sensitive than the Pulse Test in this regard. In our own tests of Charlottetown children, much higher scores for the students in high school music classes were evident. It was also only music students who scored 100% on the test.

Wilson, Wales, and Pattison (1994) in Australia used information from the Mills' test to characterize the participants in their investigations of the mental representation of tonality and meter in 80 children aged 7 and 9, finding the two grades to fall within Mills' predicted norms. The Mills' scores also significantly correlated with degree of musical training of the children, even at this young age when training in many cases was less than one year. Such use of the Mills' Test in the context of a research study also provides additional information about the validity of the Mills' Test. In the particular case of Wilson et al. (1994), performance on the Pitch Test significantly correlated with an overall score on experimental tasks entailing sensitivity to tonality whereas performance on the Pulse Test correlated significantly with an overall score on experimental tasks entailing sensitivity to rhythm. Correlations between Pitch Test and rhythm tasks and Pulse Test and tonality tasks were not significant supporting Mills' implication of the independence of these two components of musical aptitude.

In summary, the use of this test in the public school would seem to be a good use of class time. It may be helpful in alerting parents to children with exceptionally good hearing and time perception. Although it is not mentioned by the author, certainly children who are hard of hearing would have difficulty on the Pitch Test and this result might alert the teacher to such a problem. The test can also educate children about sound at the same time as it tests their auditory skills.

The author mentions the advantage of recent technology (i.e., cassette tape players). Nevertheless, tape players are giving way to digital media and recorded tapes may give way to interactive computerized testing, which ultimately would be more efficient and would provide more sensitive measures of pitch and pulse perception. As it stands, this simple test contains even more information about children than Mills describes. There may be both more and less than meets the eye in this test. I would not hesitate to recommend it for its value to children and to regular classroom and music teachers. The extent to which this test is truly a measure of music aptitude rather than a test of hearing sensitivity (which to some extent sets the potential for musical development) remains debatable. The test could also be helpful for psychology researchers who wish to screen listeners for music perception experiments.

REVIEWER'S REFERENCE

Wilson, S. J., Wales, R. J., & Pattison, P. (1994). The representation of tonality and meter in children aged 7 and 9. In I. Deliege (Ed.), *Proceedings of the 3rd International Conference on Music Perception and Cognition* (pp. 151-152). Liège, Belgium: University of Liège.

[174]

The Guilford-Zimmerman Interest Inventory.

Purpose: A vocational interest measure.
Population: College and adults.
Publication Dates: 1962–89.
Acronym: GZII.
Scores, 10: Natural, Mechanical, Scientific, Creative, Literary, Artistic, Service, Enterprising, Leadership, Clerical.
Administration: Group.
Price Data, 1992: $16 per 25 test booklets; $28 per 25 self-scorable answer sheets; $22 per 25 report forms; $29 per manual ('89, 15 pages); $30 per specimen set.
Time: (20–30) minutes.
Comments: Self-report and self-scorable.
Authors: Joan S. Guilford and Wayne S. Zimmerman.
Publisher: Consulting Psychologists Press, Inc.
Cross References: For information regarding a previous edition, see T3:1045. See also T2:2185 (7 references); for a review by Kenneth B. Hoyt, see 6:1057.

Review of The Guilford-Zimmerman Interest Inventory by BRUCE H. BISKIN, Senior Psychometrician, American Institute of Certified Public Accountants, Jersey City, NJ:

The Guilford-Zimmerman Interest Inventory (GZII) is intended to be "a short yet comprehensive and reliable instrument for measuring interests" (manual, p. 1). It comprises 150 items, grouped equally into 10 scales. The manual suggests these scales relate closely to Holland's (1973) general occupational themes (GOTs), reporting substantial correlations between the GZII scales and the GOTs as measured by the Strong Interest Inventory (SII). There is not a strict correspondence between the two sets of measures; however, several GZII scales have notable correlations with two GOTs and four of the six GOTs have large correlations with 2–3 GZII scales. The manual authors describe in detail the GZII scales and generally the item content fits with the scale descriptions. GZII items are activity statements (e.g., "Work in the outdoors") to which respondents are asked to mark their degree of like or dislike on the answer sheet (*definite* to *some/slight*). This results in items scores from 0 to 3 and scale scores from 0 to 45.

SCALE DEVELOPMENT. The GZII was developed through reducing an initial 450-item pool to 150 by selecting the 15 most discriminating items for each scale. A "trained psychometrician" then classified correctly all but five items, which were revised for clarity. Although the manual contains a description of this process as supporting "face validity," depending on the qualifications of the psychometrician, it might better be described as supporting the GZII's content validity.

QUALITY OF TEST MATERIALS. All materials are printed in black on nonreflective white paper and I found them generally easy to read and use. Included with the manual is a photocopy of a one-page March 1990 "Erratum." This sheet identifies printing errors for seven correlations contained in three different tables. As of August 1993, the corrected manual had not yet been reprinted. I suggest the publisher reprint the manual when possible—a user easily can misplace a loose page of errata. Three years is a long time to leave such errors unchanged. Test users should transfer the corrections directly to the manual themselves to minimize the risk of losing the errata. (Note: I found two additional errors. In Table 2, the median score on Clerical for "females" in 1989 should be "11," as identified from the profile form, not "5." On page 7, the manual reports a factor analysis that gives two loadings for the Leadership scale on the third factor.)

ADMINISTRATION, SCORING, AND NORMS. The GZII is self-administering and self-scoring. Accurate scoring requires modest computational skills. Scoring accuracy could be enhanced by machine scoring, which apparently is currently not available.

I am particularly concerned with the adequacy of the GZII's norms. The original 1962 norms—reported separately for men and women—reflect the responses of about 800 college freshmen. Though the norm group may have been adequate in 1962 for college and university users wishing to limit their inferences to college freshmen, the manual does not detail the norm groups' demographic features. Despite the apparently greater diversity of the 1989 norm groups, the manual describes them only as consisting of "233 adults residing in northern California" (p. 5). Other than gender, the manual contains no other descriptive information about the 1989 norm groups. The actual number of men and women is uncertain because the number of males is reported as either 97 or 107 and the number of females as either 118 or 126. The manual contains no evidence to support the adequacy of either the size or representativeness of the norm groups. Thus, I would advise the user to ignore the reported norms and, if desired, develop local norms.

RELIABILITY AND VALIDITY. No reliability estimates for the original 1962 norms are reported although high item-total score correlations—in the original 450-item pool—for the 150 retained items are reported. This presentation of information is difficult to evaluate and does not allow the user to estimate standard errors of measurement, limiting its value. For the 1989 norm groups, coefficients alpha were high for 15-item scales, ranging from .89 to .96, suggesting homogeneous item content. The manual contains no test-retest correlations, so there is no way to estimate score consistency over time.

The manual reports three pieces of validity evidence: (*a*) factor analysis of the scales comprising the original 450-item pool, (*b*) scale intercorrelations for each gender norm and the combined norms, and (*c*) correlations with the Strong Interest Inventory (SII) for "273 adults." However, the manual reports sparse interpretation of these data. For the factor analysis, neither the analytic method nor the type of rotation are identified. Also, the manual does not describe the sample of test takers whose scores were factor analyzed. Finally, the manual does not explain why the final 150-item version of the GZII was not factor analyzed. Thus, the usefulness of the factor analysis results is questionable.

For the second set of validity evidence, the manual authors state only that "a number of scales tend to cluster together (e.g., the Leadership and Enterprising scales and the Artistic and Literary scales)" (p. 10). The correlations among the scales make sense, except those involving the Creative scale. The Creative scale correlations, and my evaluation of the Creative scale item content, suggests the scale measures aspects of creativity related primarily to scientific, literary, and artistic interests. This suggests the authors did not meet their objective to "keep the Creative scale as independent as possible of the other interest categories" (p. 4). The Creative scale's reported correlations with the SII Investigative and Artistic GOT scales (r = .48 and .45, respectively) are much larger than those with the other SII GOT scales (Realistic: r = .25; other Creative/SII correlations are near zero). When the GZII is next revised, the publisher should consider including items that reflect creativity in all interest areas (e.g., "Finding innovative ways to help others solve problems" (p. 10) might reflect a creative aspect of Service). Alternatively, consideration could be given to narrowing its interpretation or even dropping the scale from the GZII.

No evidence of criterion-related validity for the GZII is offered, despite 27 years between its original publication in 1962 and its renorming in 1989. This is disappointing because there has been extensive validation of inferences that can be made from interest measures such as the SII, including inferences about choice and satisfaction in educational and occupational fields (Hansen & Campbell, 1985). If there is similar evidence for GZII inferences, the publisher should report it in the manual.

CONCLUSIONS. Inadequate norms, lack of evidence for score stability, and the scantness of validity evidence limit the GZII's usefulness in career, job, and personal counseling. Until research confirms the GZII's promise as an interest measure, counselors should ignore the normative data and focus on the scales' rank order. Further, this use of the scores should be limited to helping clients identify options to explore. The GZII should not be used to make normative statements about clients' interests. Counselors wishing to make normative interpretations of interests would be better advised to use the longer and more complex SII (T4:2581), which has available a wealth of documentation for interpreting scores (Hansen, 1992; Hansen & Campbell, 1985). Optionally, if counselors wish to use an interest measure shorter and less detailed than the SII for screening, they should consider the Self-Directed Search (T4:2414) or Vocational Preference Inventory (T4:2910).

REVIEWER'S REFERENCES

Holland, J. L. (1973). *Making vocational choices: A theory of careers.* Englewood Cliffs, NJ: Prentice Hall.

Hansen, J. C., & Campbell, D. P. (1985). *The manual for the SVIB-SII* (4th ed.). Stanford, CA: Stanford University Press.

Hansen, J. C. (1992). *User's guide for the Strong Interest Inventory.* Palo Alto, CA: Consulting Psychologists Press.

Review of The Guilford-Zimmerman Interest Inventory by GARY L. MARCO, Executive Director, College Board Statistical Analysis, Educational Testing Service, Princeton, NJ:

This inventory is a 150-item instrument intended to measure interest in 10 areas (15 items each) related to vocational and avocational preferences. Like the 1962–63 version of the inventory, it consists of 150 items, but the names of two scales have been changed (Mercantile to Enterprising and Aesthetic to Artistic) to reflect modern usage. In the new instrument, the inventory developers eliminated the overlap between the Creative scale and the other scales.

INVENTORY DEVELOPMENT. The inventory consists of the 150 most discriminating items from the 450-item experimental version that was given to 800 college freshmen in 1962. Although the items are brief and generally unambiguous in meaning, there are a few items that could be worded more clearly to avoid misinterpretations. For example, Item 1, "Live in the country," can be interpreted differently depending on whether an examinee lives in a large city or on a farm in a rural area. Item 54, "Adopt an unconventional approach to life," can also be interpreted in various ways.

ADMINISTRATION. Appropriate for groups as well as individuals, the inventory, although administered with no time limits, takes about 20 minutes to complete. Thus, this instrument may be completed in considerably less time than other interest measures such as the Kuder Preference Record and the Strong Vocational Interest Blank. Examinees indicate their interest in the 15 items constituting each of the 10 scales by responding in one of four categories: *definite dislike*, *no interest or mild dislike*, *some interest or slight like*, and *definite like*.

SCORING. Each item is scored on a 0-to-3 scale: 0 = *definite dislike*, . . . 3 = *definite like*. The total score for a scale is simply the sum of the item scores. The self-scoring answer sheet is easy to use and cleverly set up to allow the examinee to tally the number of items in each of the four item-response categories and then apply the category weight. Because it is easy to make an arithmetic error in scoring the inventory, as an additional scoring instruction the examinee should be told to make sure there are a total of 15 tallies, the number of items representing each scale, before proceeding to the multiplication step.

SCORE INTERPRETATION. The score report facilitates the translation of raw scores to percentile ranks by plotting. The middle 50% and middle 80% of the male and female norm groups are indicated on the plot, thus making it easy to determine how unusual an examinee's scores are. To prevent clerical error, the instructions should tell the examinee to make sure his or her x's are plotted on the bar corresponding to the correct gender group. Clerical error could also be diminished if the Artistic and Literary scales and the Leadership and Enterprising scales were ordered the same way on the score report and the answer sheet.

The score profile can be interpreted in both normative and ipsative ways. The normative interpretation by itself could provide a misleading picture of an examinee's interests and could lead to poor educational and occupational planning decisions. The difference between the two interpretations is particularly notable for the Clerical scale because scores on this scale are so low relative to scores on the other scales. A response of *no interest or mild dislike* to each item on the Clerical scale would result in a score of 15, which translates into a male percentile rank of 70 and a female percentile rank of 66! A percentile rank of 70 falls into the moderately high range for males—despite the fact that the examinee has no interest or even a mild dislike for clerical activities! If only percentile rank scores were interpreted, this important fact would be missed.

NORMS, RELIABILITY, AND VALIDITY. The normative data are based on only 233 adults from northern California and thus are very limited. More information about the sample in terms of age, occupation, etc., would help the user evaluate the adequacy of the sample. The score distributions from samples this small are likely to vary considerably from sample to sample; yet the manual places considerable interpretive value on the norms. Broader norms should be collected at the first opportunity.

The inventory manual has very little information on reliability and validity. Alpha reliability coefficients are reported by gender without any discussion. It would be helpful to the unsophisticated user for the manual to say that such coefficients are internal consistency estimates of reliability, not test-retest estimates, and thus do not take into consideration day-to-day fluctuations in performance.

The manual contains scale intercorrelations by gender, but says little about what they mean except to note that some of the scales cluster together. Of course, the sample sizes are small and the sampling variation large, thus making it difficult to interpret the data. Perhaps the main conclusion one can draw from the intercorrelations is that each of the scales may be fairly independent of one another. If data were available on a larger sample, a confirmatory factor analysis would be informative.

The manual contains no validity information concerning the primary use of the inventory—guidance and counseling. Information about how people in the various occupations score on the inventory would be very helpful to the counselor in trying to judge how the scores relate to occupational satisfaction.

The manual as a whole seems not to have been carefully written and edited. An erratum sheet dated March 1990 notes seven errors in three of the four intercorrelation tables. Furthermore, there are some inconsistencies in the sample sizes reported in the manual for the 1989 group in the text, Figure 1, and Tables 4 and 5. Finally, Table 3 is misplaced in the section providing technical data rather than in the previous section where it belongs. Further research is needed to provide additional technical data on the inventory.

SUMMARY. The main strengths of this instrument are that it can be self-administered and self-scored and provides in 20 minutes a profile of 10 interest scales. Although the instrument seems to be well developed (from a larger pool of 450 items) and to provide reliable measurement, the lack of technical data on large samples limits its use at the individual level. Until such data are collected and the norms and validity better established, the instrument's value lies primarily in research and as a means of describing the interests of groups of people.

[175]

Hall Occupational Orientation Inventory.

Purpose: Designed to help individuals understand their values, needs, interests, and preferred life-styles, and how these relate to career goals and future educational plans.
Population: Grades 3–7, 8–16 and adults, low-literate adults, junior high students–adults.
Publication Dates: 1968–89.
Administration: Group or individual.
Price Data, 1993: $28.30 per 20 inventory booklets; $20.60 per 20 interpretive folders; $20.60 per 20 response sheets; $15.50 per Hall Career Education Reader; $15.50 per counselor's manual ('76, 54 pages); $25 per specimen set (specify Intermediate, Young Adult/College, or Adult Basic form; $21.50 without manual); $92.50 per 20 Form II self-interpretive folders; $15.50 per Form II professional manual; $32 per Form II specimen set ($22.95 without manual).
Time: (30–60) minutes.
Authors: L. G. Hall, R. B. Tarrier (manual), and D. L. Shappel (manual).
Publisher: Scholastic Testing Service, Inc.

a) INTERMEDIATE FORM.
Population: Grades 3–7.
Publication Dates: 1968–76.
Scores, 22: Free Choice, Chance Game, Effort to Learn, Belonging, Being Safe, Goals, Being Important, Being Yourself, Being Proud, Order, Working Alone, Working with Your Hands, Working with People, Places, Ready to Learn, Rewards, Physical Fitness, The World Around You, Others, Skills, Use of Time, Being on Guard.

b) YOUNG ADULT/COLLEGE FORM.
Population: Grades 8–16 and adults.
Publication Dates: 1968–88.
Scores, 22: Creativity-Independence, Risk, Information-Knowledge, Belongingness, Security, Aspiration, Esteem, Self-Actualization, Personal Satisfaction, Routine-Dependence, Data Orientation, Things Orientation, People Orientation, Location Concern, Aptitude Concern, Monetary Concern, Physical Abilities Concern, Environment Concern, Co-worker Concern, Qualifications Concern, Time Concern, Deciding-Influencing.

c) ADULT BASIC FORM.
Population: Low-literate adults.
Publication Dates: 1968–76.
Scores, 22: Same as for *b* above.

d) FORM II.
Population: Junior high students–adults.
Scores, 15: Creativity-Independence, Information-Knowledge, Belongingness, Security, Aspiration, Esteem, Self-Actualization, Personal Satisfaction, Routine-Dependence, People-Social-Accommodating, Data-Information, Things-Physical, People-Business-Influencing, Ideas-Scientific, Aesthetics-Arts.

Cross References: See T3:1051 (4 references); for reviews by Robert H. Dolliver and Austin C. Frank, see 8:1003 (5 references); see also T2:2187 (3 references); for a review by Donald G. Zytowski of the original edition, see 7:104 (4 references).

TEST REFERENCES

1. Cochran, L. (1986). Harmonious values as a basis for occupational preference. *Journal of Vocational Behavior*, *29*, 17-26.

Review of the Hall Occupational Orientation Inventory by GREGORY SCHRAW, Assistant Professor of Educational Psychology, University of Nebraska-Lincoln, Lincoln, NE:

The Hall Occupational Orientation Inventory is a self-administered, self-scored, and self-interpreted inventory designed to promote reflective evaluation of one's occupational needs and interests. The adult version consists of 15 major scales, six of which assess differing job interests, and nine which measure needs and values important to the test taker. The 150-item adult inventory can be completed in roughly 30 to 40 minutes. However, a thorough reading of the self-interpretive digest, scoring, and interpreting the test requires at least several additional hours.

The test is grounded in the humanist tradition most closely associated with Maslow's theory of motivation and is based on a four-stage developmental model of career choice modeled loosely after Kohlberg. The four stages include subjective external authority, objective external authority, subjective internal authority, and shaping, autonomy, and self-empowerment. Thus, career choice development progresses from an external to internal locus of control. No information is given regarding the normal developmental sequence through the four hypothesized stages.

The complete adult version of the Hall includes a test booklet, a scoring manual, and optional professional and counselor's manuals. As suggested above, interpretation may be very time-consuming, although the test's author would no doubt consider this a positive attribute of the test. One potential interpretive problem is that the test taker must evaluate 15 separate scales. Another is that the interpretation manual has few suggestions about interpreting one's total score profile. Thus, although individual scales appear to be interpretable by most adults without difficulty, coming to a consensus on one's total profile may be quite difficult. This is true especially for test takers in the lower stages of the four-stage model described above. Indeed, the author of the professional manual that accompanies the adult version recommends group interpretive sessions for such individuals.

Given the Hall is a self-administered test, a special emphasis is placed on its "explorational validity" by its author. No predictive validity evidence is given, nor is there any discussion of the instrument's construct validity other than a very brief description of its factor structure. Limited information is provided on its reliability as well. One study with 525 high school and college students found its test-retest reliability at a 60-day interval to average .81. Split-half reliabilities using the same sample averaged .92. No parallel version of the inventory is available.

The strengths of the Hall include: (*a*) It is self-administered and scored; (*b*) it is nonthreatening; (*c*) it is guided by a clear theoretical framework; (*d*) it provides the examinee with a variety of information, including needs, values, and career interest scales; and (*e*) it encourages self-reflection on the meaning of one's score profile. Its major weaknesses include: (*a*) A lack of comparative information to other occupational inventories; (*b*) a lack of information regarding its reliability and validity; and (*c*) the responsibility for interpretation is placed totally on the test taker's shoulders.

Overall, I believe the advantages of the Hall outweigh its disadvantages. Encouraging test takers to think for themselves regarding their occupational interests and talents may be more helpful than even highly reliable and valid information provided by someone else. Thus, the Hall's effectiveness must be determined by the degree to which it promotes critical self-examination of one's inventory profile. Examinees who invest time and effort to consider its results carefully will no doubt benefit from the Hall in a way that is less likely to occur following a standardized, other-administered inventory. Failure to invest time and effort will lead in most instances to little gain. Mature individuals who are seeking a framework from which they may evaluate their career interests should be encouraged to complete the Hall. Individuals with less maturity should complete the Hall only when assisted by a vocational counselor who can facilitate an interpretation of its scales. In this case, an alternative occupational inventory with proven construct and predictive validity may be more appropriate.

Review of the Hall Occupational Orientation Inventory by HILDA WING, Personnel Psychologist, Federal Aviation Administration, Washington, DC:

"A personality test for jobs" is a reasonable description of the Hall Occupational Orientation Inventory. The seeker indicates to what extent the job characteristic presented by each sentence (150 for Form II, 220 for the Young Adult/College Form) is a fitting self-description, by rating from *Most Desirable* through *Not Important* to *Very Undesirable*. Self-scoring response sheets are available. The purpose of completing these inventories is to explore one's own values and needs, to relate them to one's life and career goals, to "stay in touch with your inner self."

The forms share the majority of items in common for nine of the Value/Needs scales: Creativity-Independence, Information-Knowledge, Belongingness, Security, Aspiration, Esteem, Self-Actualization, Personal Satisfaction, and Routine-Dependence. The Young Adult Form includes the Risk scale as a Value/Need whereas Form II includes the Risk scale as a Work-Style Preference. Form II has six Career Interest scales that could be but have not been related to the six Holland themes. For example, Hall's People-Social-Accommodating could be linked with Holland's Social, Data-Information with Clerical, Things-Physical with Realistic, People-Business-Influencing with Enterprising, Ideas-Scientific with Investigative, Aesthetics-Arts with Artistic. The Young Adult Form includes only three Job Characteristics scales, traceable to Fine's Functional Job Analysis (Fine, 1988): Data Orientation, Things Orientation, and People Orientation. Finally, the two forms share Work-Style Preferences (Form II) or Worker Traits (Young Adult), as follows: Geographic Location or Location Concern, Workplace or Environment Concern, Pay $$$ or Monetary Concern, Co-Worker Concern, Time (Work Schedule) Concern, Risk (a Value/Need in the Young Adult Form), Abilities or Aptitude and Physical Abilities Concern, and Qualifications Concern. The Young Adult form also includes the Worker trait of Deciding-Influencing.

This is an interesting and comprehensive set of characteristics, for people and for jobs, to consider. Are the potential respondents likely to be knowledgeable enough about themselves to obtain useful information? How might one determine if a specific job opportunity had the desired characteristics? Some of the attributes to evaluate seem more part of organizational cultures than of jobs or occupations. This does not make them any the less valuable. Are there clusters or subsets of these characteristics that typify certain jobs or occupations? Such information could be very useful.

Both forms have self-interpretive brochures. The brochure for the Young Adult Form is shorter, the instructions appear to be easier to follow, and there is less information about jobs and job groups.

The Professional Manual for Form II contains technical documentation appropriate for both forms. The purpose of the instrument is for counseling, for personal exploration, to develop self-awareness, "rather than scientific measurement and predictive devices for individuals" (Professional Manual, Preface). Are these mutually conflicting goals? The author's choice of purpose is legitimate, but any choice requires the appropriate information for responsible use, such as the description of what the instruments measure, and how well. Such information should also be related to recent research in industrial-organizational psychology on the importance of personality factors on the job, by, for example, Borman and Motowidlo (1993) and Hough (1988).

The theoretical background of the inventories, according to the author, is personality-need theory, initially stated by Abraham Maslow, adapted to occupational choice by Anne Roe, and tied to the U.S. Department of Labor's *Guide for Occupational Exploration*. This latter work is the primary reference cited in linking Hall's effort to the research literature in occupational interest and choice. Hall proposes the inventory assists individuals "to experience a controlled confrontation with himself or herself" (Counselor's Manual, p. 7) which should alert the reader not to expect certain kinds of data support, such as subsequent occupational selection and attrition. I believe this thoughtful and provocative approach deserves the extensive documentation required, but not presented here, to support the author's assertions.

Reliability coefficients are provided after a preliminary (and gratuitous) caveat about the changing, dynamic character of the personality variables being assessed. Alpha coefficients of internal consistency for high school and college students have medians in the low .90s for the 15 Values/Needs and Career Interests, indicating quite acceptable homogeneity. Test-retest coefficients are not quite as high, with greater stability from older and male examinees. The inventories are or will be in use in several foreign countries, but no further details were provided in the manual.

Given the purpose of this type of inventory, much of the desired validity evidence might have to be of the "smiley face" variety (i.e., a subjective assessment of the respondent's impression of the test). The documentation provided does not appear to meet these standards. The author asserts that many people (undifferentiated further) have stated their approval of the inventory. People find the complete set of items adequately comprehensive, not unsurprising but undocumented. Three studies with tantalizing but preliminary findings are described: (*a*) A follow-up study showed that people who found work in jobs with characteristics previously rated as undesirable to them were unhappy whereas those in jobs with desirable characteristics were happy; (*b*) pre-post studies showed that taking the inventory enhanced self-awareness; (*c*) mean scores from the majority of the 15 Hall scale scores differentiate 21 occupational groups from workers-in-general.

What is perhaps most frustrating is the inclusion of an extensive bibliography and reference section at the end of the manual, with most references not cited in the manual's text. What was the contribution of each of these references to the development and possible use of these inventories?

Other assertions are made without the citation of supporting data. For example: Inventory administration requires minimal counselor assistance. Individuals completing the inventory experience increases in self-awareness. (Do they also make more effective occupational choices?) The selection of items for the inventories was data-driven.

Although the scale scores are not normed and are designed to be used idiographically, the person who selects this instrument, as well as those to whom it is administered, would be better served by having systematic information about the scores earned by different kinds and types of people. Otherwise it is difficult to distinguish the Hall Inventories from the pop psychology scales found in the Sunday supplements or popular magazines.

The inventory does not limit occupations by gender or race, but does ask for preferences for working with older or younger people, with people of different races and ethnicity, unfortunately without further elaboration. Everyone has preferences, but it would be unwise to attempt to implement some of them explicitly in the workplace. For example, a young person with a strong preference for working with others of the same sex, age, and ethnicity appears to be headed for certain disappointment as more and more organizations proclaim the positive contributions of diversity.

The materials I received did not include enough of what I consider to be necessary for adequately informed use. Today's requirements include sensitivity to the quality of the empirical support for the assertions made in the technical manual about human behavior, attitudes, feelings, and values. These inventories appear promising, and should produce the research evidence that would be necessary for responsible use.

REVIEWER'S REFERENCES

Fine, S. A. (1988). Functional job analysis. In S. Gael (Ed.), *The job analysis handbook for business, industry, and government* (pp. 1019-1035). New York: John Wiley & Sons.

Hough, L. (1988, April). *Personality assessment for selection and placement decisions*. Workshop presented at Third Annual Conference of the Society for Industrial and Organizational Psychology, Dallas, TX.

Borman, W. C., & Motowidlo, S. J. (1993). Expanding the criterion domain to include elements of contextual performance. In N. Schmitt, W. C. Borman, & Associates, (Eds.), *Personnel selection in organizations* (pp. 71-98). San Francisco: Jossey-Bass.

[176]

Halstead Russell Neuropsychological Evaluation System.

Purpose: Provides "comprehensive measures of the functions relevant to neuropsychological assessment."
Population: Neuropsychological patients.
Publication Date: 1993.
Acronym: HRNES.
Scores, 3: Percent Impaired Score, Average Index Score, Lateralization Key.
Administration: Individual.
Price Data, 1993: $450 per complete kit including manual (99 pages), 10 recording booklets, and 3.5-inch IBM unlimited use microcomputer disk; $49.50 per 10 recording booklets; $52 per manual; $395 per unlimited use microcomputer disk.
Time: Administration time not reported.
Comments: HRNES computer program compiles raw scores from up to 22 tests, corrects them for age and education, and converts them to scaled scores; includes unlimited use disk.
Authors: Elbert W. Russell and Regina I. Starkey.
Publisher: Western Psychological Services.

TEST REFERENCES

1. DCCT Research Group. (1994). A screening algorithm to identify clinically significant changes in neuropsychological functions in the diabetes control and complications trial. *Journal of Clinical and Experimental Neuropsychology, 16*, 303-316.

Review of the Halstead Russell Neuropsychological Evaluation System by RODERICK K. MAHURIN, Assistant Professor of Psychiatry, University of Texas Health Science Center, San Antonio, TX:

DESCRIPTION. The Halstead Russell Neuropsychological Evaluation System (HRNES) is an integrated neuropsychological test battery and software system for scoring, reporting, and profiling clinically obtained data. The program accepts raw scores from a variety of measures included in the HRNES battery, and transforms them into uniform scale scores corrected for age and education. The battery covers a broad range of cognitive abilities and, by inference, their associated brain functions. By facilitating comparisons among multiple measures, the scoring system is designed to aid the user in clinical interpretation of neuropsychological deficits.

Many of the individual tests that comprise the HRNES battery will be familiar to neuropsychologists. The core set is from the original battery pioneered by Halstead (Halstead, 1947; Reitan & Wolfson, 1993); others are drawn from widely used clinical instruments, or from newer tests specifically developed by Russell to expand the Halstead battery. The HRNES includes the following 22 tests: Lateral Dominance Examination Parts 1 and 2 (including Grip Strength), Trail Making Test, Wechsler Memory Scale (WMS; Logical Memory and Visual Reproduction subtests), Index Finger Tapping Test, Tactual Performance Test, Halstead Category Test, Speech Perception Test, Rhythm Test, Perceptual Disorders Examination, Aphasia Screening Test, Miami Selective Learning Test, H-Words Test, HRNES Analogies Test, Peabody Picture Vocabulary Test—Revised, Boston Naming Test, Grooved Pegboard Test, Gestalt Identification Test, Design Fluency Test, Corsi Board, Wide Range Achievement Test—Revised, and the Wechsler Adult Intelligence Scale (WAIS). The user can enter scores from either the revised or original versions of the WMS and the WAIS. Taken together, the tests cover a broad range of cognitive abilities including executive control, abstract reasoning, language, verbal and spatial memory, psychomotor function, visual and somatosensory perception, and spatial localization.

MATERIALS. The HRNES package contains a single IBM-compatible diskette (3.5-inch or 5.25-inch), manual, and 10 data recording sheets. System requirements include an IBM-compatible computer (80286 processor or higher), one megabyte of free hard disk space, and Microsoft Windows 3.1 or above. Older computers, or DOS systems not running the Windows environment cannot use the program. Currently the software is not available for the Apple Macintosh line of computers.

Installation of the program onto the computer is straightforward, with system adjustments, directory setup, and copying of files to the hard drive done automatically. There are no hardware interfaces or access codes required; however, the program can be installed on only a single computer at a time. Although initially released on a fee-per-use basis, the program now allows for unlimited use. This is a welcome departure from many commercial scoring programs that charge the user for each use of the software. A user's guide is contained on the program disk. This clearly written 11-page guide, which can be printed out, describes installation, maintenance, and information on various aspects of program use.

The 99-page manual provides a thorough overview of the HRNES, including directions for administration and scoring of each of the tests, description of psychometric properties, and several chapters on the theoretical basis and use of the HRNES in clinical assessment. Appendices include a useful listing of sources for test materials incorporated in the HRNES, as well as scoring criteria for selected tests in the battery (WMS Logical Memory subtest, Tactual Performance Test, and Cross Drawing). A listing of 86 references relating to the development and theoretical background of the HRNES and many of its component tests is included in the manual. In addition, a full printout of results from a sample case is reproduced at the end of the manual, with annotations describing the various portions of the report.

PROGRAM USE. The opening screens of the program request administration information and the client's demographic data, including name, age, education, gender, handedness, and premorbid IQ scores (if available). The user then decides whether or not to have the program correct raw scores for age and education (most users will probably opt for corrected scores). The next screen consists of a menu of all 22 tests in the HRNES. Selection of a test (by mouse click or keyboard) brings up the data entry screen for that test alone, lessening possible confusion between tests. The program screens are laid out in a manner corresponding to that of the test score recording booklet, greatly facilitating data entry. All screens are uncluttered and clearly arranged. Drop-down menus accessible by keyboard or mouse are implemented in standard Windows fashion. Using standard Windows conventions, context-sensitive on-line help is also available from most screens. A mouse, the tab key, or arrow keys are used for menu choices and movement between fields for entering scores. The program traps mistakes in data entry (e.g., out of range values) and provides on-screen explanatory messages.

Once the user has entered all raw scores for a particular test, the program returns to the main test menu, and indicates the test has been scored. An important feature of the system is that the user does not need to enter all tests in the HRNES for the program to calculate standardized scores. Thus, any combination of tests may be given in a battery, and normative scores and profiles for just those tests can be obtained. Additionally, a Score Averaging module allows for comparison of any test (or group of tests) with any other selected group of tests in the battery, a useful feature for analyzing patterns of performance. Each test has the further convention of two additional choices, "Could not do" (CND) and "Not given" (NG). Once entered, a file can be accessed at a later time either for reprinting or modification of data entry.

OUTPUT. The HRNES Test Report immediately can be printed out, or results can be exported as an ASCII "flat text" data file. The Report is divided into a Summary Section, a Profiles Section, and an Evaluation Record. The Summary Section prints summary indices based on scores from 10 Index Tests demonstrated to be sensitive to brain damage (Category, Trail Making Part B, Finger Tapping, Digit Symbol, Tactual Performance Time and Memory, Speech Perception, Block Design, Aphasia Screening, and Perceptual Disorders). In keeping with the Halstead tradition, the program calculates an Average Impairment Scale (AIS) based on the mean scores of the 10 Index Tests. However, unlike the scoring used in the Halstead-style Impairment Index, the AIS is scaled to the same metric as all other tests in the HRNES (i.e., a mean of 100 and standard deviation of 10). Scores above 95 are described as normal, 90–95 indicates borderline impairment, 80–89 indicates mild impairment, 70–79 indicates moderate impairment, 60–69 indicates severe impairment, and scores below 60 indicate profound impairment. A Percent Impaired score is also calculated, which is simply the percentage of the 10 Index Tests with scores below their respective cut-points for suspected brain damage. In addition, the program calculates a Lateralization Index, indicating the degree to which impairment is lateralized to one or the other cerebral hemisphere. The bulk of the Summary Section of the report consists of tabulations of corrected and uncorrected scores for each test and corresponding HRNES scale scores.

The Profiles section of the report provides well-organized graphic representations of standardized test scores in each of six neuropsychological domains: Executive, Cognitive, Language, Memory, Motor, and Perception. Because the system references all test profiles to the common standardization scale, test performance can be compared directly either within or across domains. Because of the complex nature of neuropsychological assessment, many of the tests are represented across several domains of functioning. Scaling extends from 55 (profound impairment) to 110 (above normal), and each profile has labels (Normal, Borderline, Mild, Moderate, Severe, and Profound) to anchor performance to probable clinical implications. Clinicians may find this portion of the report quite useful in integrating and interpreting a client's overall test performance. The final sections include an Evaluation Record, which lists all raw scores entered into the program from the client's protocol, Score Averaging results (if chosen to be calculated), and free-form Notes that may be entered at any time during data entry.

STANDARDIZATION. The HRNES accommodates neuropsychologists who use a fixed battery of tests, as well as those who select specific testing materials according to a client's presenting problems. The program greatly simplifies the task of integrating these diverse tests (which frequently had been developed and normed on different populations) by offering direct comparability of performance on any test or group of tests within the battery. This integration of the program is based on two elements: (*a*) "coordinated norming," in which all of the tests in the battery were simultaneously normed on the same standardization sample; and (*b*) "reference scale norming," in which a score from any one test is referenced on an equivalent standard scale to any other test in the battery.

These two key aspects of the scoring program are well described in the manual. Reference scale norming uses the subject's own performance on the AIS as a standardized reference, and through linear regression adjusts all other tests in the battery to a scale based on this metric. This procedure creates scores that are comparable at all levels of impairment. The result is conversion of raw scores into age- and education- (or premorbid IQ) adjusted standard scores with a mean of 100 and a standard deviation of 10. All standard scores are scaled in the same direction, so that a higher score always means better performance (i.e., "attainment" scores rather than "error" scores). Adoption of this convention is, in itself, a worthwhile feature, as would be attested to by many clinicians who have tried to interpret a summary table of tests scaled in opposing directions. The range of scores will be familiar to clinicians experienced with other intelligence and ability tests, and is broad enough to allow for avoidance of floor effects in test performance. It is unclear, however, if all of the tests (e.g., the sensory-perceptual examination) actually follow a normal distribution in the normative sample, and how deviations would affect the transformation to the standardized scoring system.

The standardization sample for the HRNES consisted of 576 brain-damaged individuals and a comparison group of 200 non-brain-damaged subjects. The brain-damaged group was drawn from patients in two Veterans Administration hospitals, and comprise a group with a variety of clinical diagnoses. The authors do not provide sufficient detail about how the presence or lateralization of brain damage was independently verified (e.g., whether neuroimaging was obtained in all cases), although apparently all patients received a neurological examination and follow-up review of case records. Scores from patients are grouped into right, left, or diffuse damage for comparison with the normative sample.

The comparison group, from which the HRNES norms were derived, consisted of VA patients who had "initially been suspected of having neurological conditions, but whose neurological examinations yielded negative findings" (manual, p. 27). Patients with schizophrenia, severe depression, or systemic vascular disease were excluded from this group. Subjects in this "negative neurological sample" typically were diagnosed as "neurotic" with memory or somatic complaints, and personality disorder, often with episodic explosive behavior. No patient in this group received a diagnosis of central nervous system pathology. However, further information regarding diagnostic criteria and procedures is not provided. Due to the nature of the VA population, women are underrepresented in this sample (12% female), as are ethnic minorities (6% African American; representation of other minorities, such as Hispanic or Asian American, is not explicitly documented).

This rather unusual normative group is defended on two grounds: (*a*) the clinician will most likely be referred similar patients for whom the clinical question is whether or not actual brain damage is present, and (*b*) "there is every reason to believe that such individuals constitute a substantial proportion of the normal population" (manual, p. 32). In support of this choice of a "negative neurological" normative group, data comparing the HRNES norms for Halstead tests with those obtained from four other published normative samples are included in the manual. In fact, the HRNES norms appear to be close to those derived from the nonmedical samples, with no strong evidence for systematic bias in scores one way or the other. Nevertheless, the current HRNES norms should be cross-validated on a non-VA, nonmedical sample drawn in a systematic manner from the community before they can comfortably be accepted as representing true "normative" performance on these tests.

RELIABILITY AND VALIDITY. Because of their wide usage, many of the tests in the HRNES have undergone separate published evaluation of their psychometric properties. The transformation of these tests into a different metric should not affect their reliabilities. A table of inter-test correlations for selected tests and a list of sources containing test-retest reliability studies is provided. Validity of the HRNES is supported by tables showing mean and standard deviations scores for brain-damaged and normative samples for each of the tests in the battery. All but a few of these between-group comparisons are significant at the $p<.001$ level. The authors also present evidence for the discriminant validity of the cut-point scores on selected HRNES tests by comparing brain-damaged subjects to members of the normative group. These data show generally high correct classification rates, ranging from 86% for the AIS and 83% for Percent Impaired, and from 64% to 83% for the various subtests themselves. It should be noted that tests more recently added to the battery are not well represented in these comparison tables, and consist of information from far fewer subjects (e.g., only 32 control and 84 brain-damaged subjects for the Miami Selective Learning Test). An additional table contains means and standard deviations for Right-, Left-, and Diffuse-Brain-Damaged groups. Analyses of variance are used to compare the groups. However, the manual does not contain evidence for the validity of the Lateralization Index (e.g., a classification table). Given current models of brain functioning that stress interconnected multiregional processing of information and the multifactorial nature of many neuropsychological tests, one suspects that, except in cases of focal motor or sensory impairment, the Lateralization Index would be among the least valid of the summary measures.

CAUTIONS. As with use of any computer-automated scoring system, the user of the HRNES must observe several cautions. First, the clinician must ascertain how closely his or her own clinical population matches the clinical and normative samples of VA patients on which the HRNES was validated. Second, the clinician must adhere to the same administration and scoring procedures for each test as those employed in development of the HRNES (some of which vary slightly from standard conventions). Third, the clinician should attempt to ascertain the accuracy and validity of the normative tables and lookup algorithms used in the program. Due to the proprietary nature of commercially available computer-scoring programs, such information often is not made available either to end-users or test reviewers. This is less of a concern with the HRNES than with many other commercial tests because Russell has published extensively regarding his development and modifications to the Halstead battery, including both his techniques for normative sampling and specific clinical applications (e.g., Russell, 1984; Russell, 1987; Russell, Neuringer, & Goldstein, 1970). Nevertheless, a printed version of the normative tables, such as that provided by Heaton, Grant, & Matthews (1991), would be welcome in order to verify the program's accuracy.

CONCLUSIONS. How would a practicing neuropsychologist benefit from this program? First, the time saving as compared with looking up scores manually in separate normative tables may be up to 20 minutes per test session. Second, assuming the program's algorithms are accurate, the automated lookup procedures should provide error-free conversion of raw scores to standard scores. Third, all scores are standardized and referenced to the same scaling, allowing for direct comparisons among various tests in the battery. Finally, the printout itself provides an easily readable, neatly laid-out summary of scores in both graphic and tabular formats, aiding in the interpretation of overall test performance.

Few neuropsychologists would disagree with the need to make scoring, organizing, and interpreting test scores more manageable and efficient. Laboriously looking up individual scores in normative tables is both time-consuming and error prone. However, it should be emphasized that the HRNES leaves integration of the obtained test profile in the hands of the clinician. Proper interpretation of neuropsychological test performance requires specialized clinical and theoretical training. Nevertheless, the HRNES and kindred programs represent the future of neuropsychological scoring procedures. Given the advantages of computer-based scoring systems, it would not be surprising within a few years to see such programs in the offices of many clinical neuropsychologists.

In summary, the HRNES provides a professionally developed, easily used software package for scoring and profiling of many popular neuropsychological tests. The program functions very well, and the clearly organized output can add to the efficiency and interpretive confidence of the experienced clinician. The program will be less attractive to potential users who do not wish to switch to the Windows operating environment, who use a majority of neuropsychological tests not included in the HRNES, or who do not feel comfortable with the adequacy of the "non-neurological" normative base provided by the system. These users should evaluate other computer-based scoring systems to see if they meet the standards set by the HRNES.

REVIEWER'S REFERENCES

Halstead, W. C. (1947). *Brain and intelligence.* Chicago: The University of Chicago Press.

Russell, E. W., Neuringer, C., & Goldstein, G. (1970). *Assessment of brain damage: A neuropsychological approach.* New York: Wiley-Interscience.

Russell, E. W. (1984). Theory and developments of pattern analysis methods related to the Halstead-Reitan battery. In P. E. Logue & J. M. Schear (Eds.), *Clinical neuropsychology: A multidisciplinary approach* (pp. 50-98). Springfield, IL: Thomas.

Russell, E. W. (1987). A reference scale method for constructing neuropsychological test batteries. *Journal of Clinical and Experimental Neuropsychology, 9,* 376-392.

Heaton, R. K., Grant, I., & Matthews, C. G. (1991). *Comprehensive norms for an expanded Halstead-Reitan battery.* Odessa, FL: Psychological Assessment Resources, Inc.

Reitan, R. M., & Wolfson, D. (1993). *The Halstead-Reitan Neuropsychological Test Battery: Theory and clinical interpretation* (2nd ed.). Tucson, AZ: Neuropsychology Press.

Review of the Halstead Russell Neuropsychological Evaluation System by PAUL RETZLAFF, Associate Professor of Psychology, University of Northern Colorado, Greeley, CO:

This type of product really does not lend itself to traditional test review. In actuality, the product is not a new test that must be critiqued as to psychometrics, but a data base delivery system. As such, this review will focus upon the selection of tests for inclusion in the Halstead Russell Neuropsychological Evaluation System (HRNES), the quality of the norming process, and the utility of the software delivery system.

TESTS. In its simplest form the HRNES is a group of tasks and norms that is a superset of the Halstead-Reitan Neuropsychological Test Battery (T4:1119). It includes many of the tasks or constructs often added to the Halstead by neuropsychologists in order to "flesh out" the results of the battery. Such additional tasks include the Wide Range Achievement Test, Peabody Picture Vocabulary Test, Boston Naming Test, Grooved Pegboard, and Wechsler Memory Scale (WMS) as well as several specifically designed for the battery such as the Miami Selective Learning Test. The HRNES is, however, also a fairly complex system of neuropsychological theory, operationalization, and application which can be viewed as a comprehensive system of neuropsychological practice.

The selection of domains of interests and the tests to operationalize those domains within neuropsychology is often more akin to intuition than to science. Although many neuropsychology batteries use beloved tests and then attempt to define the domains assessed, the HRNES tests were, for the most part, primarily chosen on the basis of the cognitive functions of interest and as such the tail is not wagging the dog. The domains are hierarchically nested. The general domains include executive, cognitive reasoning, language, memory, motor, and perception functions. Under each of these are subdomains. For example, under motor function, the subdomains of pure motor speed, strength, complex motor, and psychomotor speed reside. Each of these subdomains is operationalized by one or more tests within the battery. For example, psychomotor speed is operationalized by Trails time score and the WAIS-R Digit Symbol score. There is also an omnibus Average Index Score, which is the linear combination of the major Halstead tasks.

Although some may argue with the specifics of the general domains, the organization of the subdomains, or the selection of the specific tasks, there are no serious mistakes or omissions. At each choice point there would probably be more agreement than disagreement among neuropsychologists.

NORMS. Discussion of the quality of the norms must include the subject sample, the norming procedures, and the referencing theory applied.

The 776 subjects included 576 "brain damaged" patients and 200 "normals." The data were collected at two VA hospitals between 1968 and 1989. Herein perhaps lies one of the double-edged swords of data collection. There is obvious tradition and hard work manifest in these data but there is also the curse of time. One must wonder how many of the subjects were given the WAIS rather than the WAIS-R. Also, it is unfortunate that perhaps the more recently published WMS-R or California Verbal Learning Test could not have been included.

There is also the problem of collecting large scale norms for women while working in a VA hospital. Although sex has not been shown to be a significant covariate on most tasks, having only one "brain damaged" female in the norming of the left-handed handwriting speed task is a problem. To be fair, most of the tasks have at least 50 women although it appears from the manual that only 24 of these were "normal" comparisons.

This leads to the second area of interest, that of the norming technique. In neuropsychology it has long been understood that variables such as age and education must be accounted for in order to interpret test data properly. In theory this requires large-scale norming studies that include a large number of subjects within each cell of interest (e.g., males between 55 and 65 years of age with less than 12 years of education). Due to various practical limitations, it is becoming fashionable in neuropsychology to collect data from a number of subjects and then use regression techniques to smooth, interpolate, and extrapolate data across all combinations of these variables. These techniques usually do a good job of modeling the means and standard deviations of the cells but have unknown impact on the tails of skewed distributions. As a neuropsychologist looking for significant decrement in performance, the data of interest are not the means but the tails of the distribution. I fear there is no way to properly norm neuropsychology batteries without collecting huge stratified samples.

This leads to the final norming point, the referencing theory. The HRNES, like all neuropsychology batteries and the vast majority of individual tests, references an individual's score to the mean. This is norm referencing and answers the question "How far is this subject from the mean?" Although for some constructs and in some situations such as intelligence in schools this is appropriate, there are other domains within neuropsychology, such as language ability, for which this is inappropriate. Are patients aphasic if they are 2 standard deviations below the mean on a language task? What neuropsychology needs to do is map the level of function for each domain that is indicative of pathology and use this as a cut score. This would be a criterion-referencing approach and specifically a behavioral-referencing approach. In general, the HRNES suggests identical levels of pathology given identical distances from the mean. There is some novel mapping of the pathology of each test against the omnibus Average Index Score but this is yet to be tested.

This also leads to questions of sampling. Although somewhat unclear in the manual, the HRNES seems to have taken a middle ground in its use of 200 "normals" for the initial distribution work and 576 "brain damaged" subjects for some of the pathology mapping. From a positive perspective, the pool encompasses all levels of function. From a negative, it is hard to know whether the plotting of your patient is against "normal" or "brain-damaged" subjects.

DELIVERY SYSTEM. The software can be divided into two parts, the input and the output. The user input interface is based on Windows and as such is fairly friendly. It is necessary to set the patient record with things like name and examiner prior to use. At that point a window can be pulled down with each test available for data entry. This allows the user to quickly input data for the tests given without walking through the unneeded tests. The input could be more user friendly with on-screen messages as to what is required next.

The output is excellent but too lengthy at times. Output can be sent to the printer or to an ASCII file. When sent to an ASCII file it is immediately loaded into a notepad for editing and viewing on the screen. The output is based upon the assumption that the user will be giving a comprehensive battery from the available HRNES tests. As such, it will always output five or six pages even if only one test was given. The output includes the tests given, the raw score, the age and education corrected raw score, and the HRNES scales score (Russell, 1994). The tests are also presented under the domains and subdomains of the evaluation theory and the scores are plotted across a "normal" to "profound deficit" anchoring system. It allows for easy comparison across tests.

What is missing in the software is a quick "look up" function where one could quickly input a score and see what the corrected and scaled scores were. If the "system" is used as a soup-to-nuts evaluation, this is unnecessary but many neuropsychologists will want to use only a subset of the tests and norms.

SUMMARY. The HRNES is a major improvement over the use of differing norm sets across all tests used by a neuropsychologist. The tests selected for inclusion in the HRNES encompass many of those used by neuropsychologists regardless of orientation. The norming system is sophisticated but suffers many of the problems encountered by other data base sets. Finally, the software system is fairly friendly and the output is straightforward and useful. The recent change to an unlimited software use system is very welcome and should make the HRNES more widely used and available. The other Halstead superset norming system is Heaton's (Heaton, Grant, & Matthews, 1991), which is similar to the HRNES in terms of psychometrics. The HRNES probably is more idiosyncratic and complex in theory but more comprehensive as an evaluation system.

REVIEWER'S REFERENCES

Heaton, R. K., Grant, I., & Matthews, C. G. (1991). *Comprehensive norms for an expanded Halstead-Reitan battery*. Odessa, FL: Psychological Assessment Resources, Inc.

Russell, E. W. (1994). The cognitive-metric, fixed battery approach to neuropsychological assessment. In R. Vanderploeg (Ed.), *Clinician's guide to neuropsychological assessment* (pp. 211-258). Hillsdale, NJ: Lawrence Erlbaum Associates.

[177]

The Hare Psychopathy Checklist—Revised.

Purpose: "Designed to assess psychopathic (antisocial) personality disorders in forensic populations."
Population: Prison inmates.
Publication Dates: 1990–91.
Acronym: PCL-R.
Scores, 3: Factor 1, Factor 2, Total.
Administration: Individual.
Price Data, 1993: $250 per complete kit including manual ('91, 77 pages), 1 rating booklet, 25 QuikScore™ forms, and 25 interview guides; $100 per manual; $40 per rating booklet; $50 per 25 QuikScore™ forms; $100 per 25 interview guides.
Time: (90–180) minutes.
Comments: Time includes interview and review of available collateral information; Factor 1 description: Selfish, callous, and remorseless use of others; Factor 2 description: Chronically unstable and antisocial lifestyle, social deviance.
Author: Robert D. Hare.
Publisher: Multi-Health Systems, Inc.
Cross References: See T4:1127 (3 references).

TEST REFERENCES

1. Patrick, C. J., & Iacono, W. G. (1989). Psychopathy, threat, and polygraph test accuracy. *Journal of Applied Psychology, 74*, 347-355.
2. Gacono, C. B., & Meloy, J. R. (1991). A Rorschach investigation of attachment and anxiety in antisocial personality disorder. *The Journal of Nervous and Mental Disease, 179*, 546-552.
3. Becker, J. V., & Quinsey, V. L. (1993). Assessing suspected child molestors. *Child Abuse & Neglect, 17*, 169-174.
4. Patrick, C. J., Cuthbert, B. N., & Lang, P. J. (1994). Emotion in the criminal psychopath: Fear image processing. *Journal of Abnormal Psychology, 103*, 523-534.
5. Levenson, M. R., Kiehl, K. A., & Fitzpatrick, C. M. (1995). Assessing psychopathic attributes in a noninstitutionalized population. *Journal of Personality and Social Psychology, 68*, 151-158.

Review of The Hare Psychopathy Checklist—Revised by SOLOMON M. FULERO, Professor and Chair of Psychology, Sinclair College, Dayton, OH:

The Hare Psychopathy Checklist—Revised (PCL-R) is a rating scale for the assessment of psychopathy in male forensic populations. As noted in the manual, the behaviors and personality traits associated with "psychopathy" have been well-described by Cleckley (1976) and include superficial charm and good intelligence; absence of delusions and other signs of irrational thinking; absence of nervousness or neurotic manifestations; unreliability, untruthfulness, and insincerity; lack of remorse or shame; inadequately motivated antisocial behavior; poor judgment and failure to learn from experience; pathologic egocentricity and incapacity for love; general poverty in major affective relations; specific loss of insight; unresponsiveness in general interpersonal relations; fantastic and uninviting behavior with drink and sometimes without; suicide rarely carried out; sex life impersonal, trivial, and poorly integrated; and failure to follow any life plan. Like all personality disorders, psychopathy has an early onset, is characteristic of the individual's long-term functioning, and results in social dysfunction or disability (see also Hare, 1993).

Although many see psychopathy as synonymous with the DSM-IV classification of Antisocial Personality Disorder (APD), several authors have objected that DSM focuses solely on antisocial behavior, on the assumption that clinicians cannot validly or reliably assess interpersonal or affective characteristics (Hare, 1983; Hare, Hart, & Harpur, 1991; Rogers & Dion, 1991). Indeed, dissatisfaction with the DSM-III classification of APD was one of the major motivations for the original PCL (Hare, 1980). In addition, self-report inventories such as the Minnesota Multiphasic Personality Inventory-2 (MMPI-2), the Millon Clinical Multiaxial Inventory—II (MCMI-II), and the California Psychological Inventory (CPI) were believed to be inadequate as assessment tools for psychopathy, due to three problems: (*a*) They require cooperation from test takers and are, therefore, susceptible to distortion; (*b*) they fail to assess the interpersonal/affective characteristics of psychopathy adequately; and (*c*) they do not correlate well with each other and with clinical diagnoses of psychopathy (Hare, 1985; Hart, Forth, & Hare, 1991; Harpur, Hare, & Hakstian, 1989).

The original PCL contained 22 items. The scale became extremely popular since its publication in 1980, and an impressive and consistent body of research began to accumulate relating PCL scores to a variety of other measures, including violence and violent recidivism in offenders, even mentally disordered offenders (Conacher & Quinsey, 1992; Hare & Hart, 1993; Harris, Rice, & Cormier, 1991; Harris, Rice, & Quinsey, 1993; Forth, Hart, & Hare, 1990) as well as differences in various cognitive, linguistic, and affective measures (see Hare, 1993 for a review).

However, as the popularity of the PCL grew, Hare began to see the need for more explicit scoring instructions than were given with the original scale. At the same time, two items were deleted, and several item descriptions were modified. As noted in the manual, the correlation between total score on the PCL and the PCL-R is .88, although when one corrects or attenuates for the inherent unreliability of the scales, the correlation is found to lie between .95 and 1.0 (Hare, Harpur, Hakstian, Forth, Hart, & Newman, 1990). Factor analysis has revealed a stable two-factor structure, which is the same as that for the PCL (see also Harpur, Hakstian, & Hare, 1988; Harpur, Hare, & Hakstian, 1989). The first factor contains the interpersonal/affective traits and is titled by the authors "selfish, callous, and remorseless use of other" (p. 38). Eight of the items load .40 or above on this factor. The second contains the impulsive and antisocial behavioral characteristics, and is titled "chronically unstable, antisocial, and socially deviant lifestyle" (p. 38). Nine of the items loaded above .40 on this factor. The two factors correlate about .5 with each other.

The PCL-R manual emphasizes that in clinical settings, those using the scale should: (*a*) possess an advanced degree such as a Ph.D., Ed.D., or M.D.; (*b*) be registered or licensed; (*c*) have experience with forensic populations; (*d*) limit the use of the PCL-R to those populations in which it has been fully validated, meaning adult male forensic populations; and (*e*) insure that they have adequate training and experience in the use of the PCL-R. Hare also recommends that wherever possible, the PCL-R scores of two independent raters be averaged so as to increase the reliability of the assessment.

The assessment procedure using the PCL-R "typically consists of an interview and a review of available collateral information" (p. 5). An Interview and Information Schedule form is provided for this. The authors estimate that the interview takes about 90–120 minutes, and the collateral review another 60 minutes. After this is completed, each of the 20 PCL-R items is rated using a 3-point scale: 2 if the item applies to the individual, 1 if it applies to a "certain extent, but not the degree required for a score of 2," or a 0 if the item does not apply to the individual. Extensive item descriptions are given in the manual and the PCL-R Rating Booklet to assist the scorer. In the case where there is insufficient interview or collateral information to score an item, up to five items can be omitted without invalidating total scores. Scoring of each item yields a score on one of the two factors, as well as a total score. Raw scores can then be converted to percentile rank scores, and compared to scores of male prison inmates or male forensic patients, as appropriate. The manual notes that although the PCL-R provides a dimensional score rather than a categorical diagnosis (i.e., a psychopath, yes or no), often such categorical diagnoses may be required. The manual recommends that a cutoff score of 30 or higher be used to classify individuals as psychopaths. In prior research (Hare, 1985), this has been found to yield an overall hit rate of .85, a sensitivity of .72, a specificity of .93, and a kappa of .67. All are acceptably high.

There is no doubt that the PCL-R is the "state of the art" in this area, both clinically and in research use. Presently, the use of this scale is limited to males who are in either prison or forensic settings. Still, in "risk assessment" diagnostic situations where the question is the likelihood of success or failure of such a person, mentally disordered or not, on a status such as probation or parole, or some other form of conditional release, the PCL-R is likely to become the standard instrument.

REVIEWER'S REFERENCES

Cleckley, H. M. (1976). *The mask of sanity: An attempt to clarify some issues about the so-called psychopathic personality* (5th ed.). St. Louis, MO: Mosby.

Hare, R. D. (1980). A research scale for the assessment of psychopathy in criminal populations. *Personality and Individual Differences, 3*, 35-42.

Hare, R. D. (1983). Diagnosis of antisocial personality disorder in two prison populations. *American Journal of Psychiatry, 140*, 887-890.

Hare, R. D. (1985). A comparison of procedures for the assessment of psychopathy. *Journal of Consulting and Clinical Psychology, 53*, 7-16.

Harpur, T. J., Hakstian, A. R., & Hare, R. D. (1988). Factor structure of the Psychopathy Checklist. *Journal of Consulting and Clinical Psychology, 56*, 741-747.

Harpur, T. J., Hare, R. D., & Hakstian, A. R. (1989). A two-factor conceptualization of psychopathy: Construct validity and assessment implications. *Psychological Assessment, 1*, 6-17.

Forth, A. E., Hart, S. D., & Hare, R. D. (1990). Assessment of psychopathy in male young offenders. *Psychological Assessment, 2*, 342-344.

Hare, R. D., Harpur, T. J., Hakstian, A. R., Forth, A. E., Hart, S. D., & Newman, J. P. (1990). The Revised Psychopathy Checklist: Reliability and factor structure. *Psychological Assessment, 2*, 338-341.

Hare, R. D., Hart, S. D., & Harpur, T. J. (1991). Psychopathy and the DSM-IV criteria for antisocial personality disorder. *Journal of Abnormal Psychology, 100*, 391-398.

Harris, G. T., Rice, M. E., & Cormier, C. A. (1991). Psychopathy and violent recidivism. *Law and Human Behavior, 15*, 625-637.

Hart, S. D., Forth, A. E., & Hare, R. D. (1991). The MCMI-II as a measure of psychopathy. *Journal of Personality Disorders, 5*, 318-327.

Rogers, R., & Dion, K. (1991). Rethinking the DSM-III-R diagnosis of antisocial personality disorder. *Bulletin of the American Academy of Psychiatry and Law, 19*, 21-31.

Conacher, G. N., & Quinsey, V. L. (1992). Predictably dangerous psychopaths. *The Lancet, 340*, 794.

Hare, R. D. (1993). *Without conscience: The disturbing world of the psychopaths among us*. New York: Simon & Shuster.

Hare, R. D., & Hart, S. D. (1993). Psychopathy, mental disorder, and crime. In S. Hodgins (Ed.), *Mental disorder and crime* (pp. 104-115). Newbury Park, CA: Sage.

Harris, G. T., Rice, M. E., & Quinsey, V. L. (1993). Violent recidivism of mentally disordered offenders: The development of a statistical prediction instrument. *Criminal Justice and Behavior, 20*, 315-335.

Review of The Hare Psychopathy Checklist—Revised by GERALD L. STONE, Professor of Counseling Psychology and Director, University Counseling Service, The University of Iowa, Iowa City, IA:

The Hare Psychopathy Checklist—Revised has evolved from the conceptual work of Cleckley on psychopathy (1976) and the global clinical ratings of personality and behavior consistent with Cleckley's work. The more immediate predecessors were attempts to objectify, operationalize, and quantify Cleckley's conceptualization. One such attempt to develop Cleckley criteria was by Hare and later by Hare and his colleagues, resulting in the Psychopathy Checklist (PCL). The 22-item PCL was developed in 1980 as a research scale. A mimeographed manual provided rudimentary scoring instructions for the 3-point scale used (0 indicates characteristic was not present or does not apply; 1 indicates uncertainty; and 2 indicates it was definitely present or applied). Initial statistical work and subsequent research were reported, providing evidence that the PCL was a useful and valid measure of psychopathy in a male prison population.

Experience with the PCL led to revisions and fine-tuning. The 1985 draft deleted two items (drug or alcohol abuse and previous diagnosis as a psychopathy). Some items were changed slightly and item descriptions and scoring procedures were given more specifications. Evidence regarding the reliability and validity of the draft version was collected. After the manual of the draft version was disseminated, further fine-tuning of the item descriptions and scoring criteria resulted in the 1990 version (PCL-R). It was reported that the PCL and its various versions measure the same construct.

A user-friendly manual is available that includes a conceptual and historical introduction and an administration section covering units on use, assessment procedures, scoring, and item descriptions. Psychometric data were also provided in six chapters and an appendix.

The assessment procedure is typically composed of two components: interview and collateral review. The recommended interview protocol is contained in Part I of the Interview and Information Schedule (included in the PCL-R kit), a semistructured interview that elicits the material and interpersonal style information for clinical judgments required by the PCL-R. The 90- to 120-minute interview covers educational, occupational, family, marital, and criminal history.

Part II of the Interview and Information Schedule provides for a collateral review of records to enhance the credibility of the material and interpersonal information obtained during the interview. If there are ample records available, the collateral review can provide primary data for scoring. A collateral review typically takes 60 minutes, depending on the extent of available records. It should also be mentioned that valid PCL-R ratings can be made solely on the basis of collateral information if there is sufficient information available. Furthermore, PCL-R ratings should not be made in the absence of adequate collateral information.

PCL-R ratings should reflect prototypicality, that is, a person's typical functioning, on the average, throughout life. Each of the 20 PCL-R items (largely, characteristics of a psychopathy listed by Cleckley—impulsivity, pathological lying) are rated using a 3-point ordinal scale, based on the degree of match between the personality/behavior of the person and the item description in the manual (2 = Yes, 1 = Maybe, 0 = No). The QuikScore Form (also included in the PCL-R kit) is a self-scoring form that records the ratings for all 20 items and provides a scoring grid for the three scores: Factor 1 (selfish, callous, and remorseless use of others), Factor 2 (chronically unstable and antisocial lifestyle), and Total Score. Percentile ranks for each of these three scores are provided on the Profile Form, which is on the back of the QuikScore Form.

The psychometric data presented argue for a reasonable level of confidence in the reliability, factor structure, validity, and usefulness of the measure. The normative data are not as multicultural, racially, and gender diverse, nor as longitudinally based as hoped. Most of the data are about white males in prison settings, primarily in Canada. The data for arguing that the findings derived from the PCL and PCL-R are interchangeable are based on a modest sample (N = 122) and need replication.

In summary, the PCL-R is a promising measure with many attractive attributes including a conceptualization, research-based development, user-friendly manual, and objective scoring format for making clinical judgments. The limitations are really a challenge to users for further research to refine the criteria (e.g., What is an adequate collateral information base? How useful for clinical purposes is making 20 global ratings versus one global rating?) and to replicate the usefulness of the measure for diverse groups of people, including persons in society who are not in prisons or forensic medical settings. It will be interesting to see the results of the AXIS II Work Group of the DSM-IV Task Force that is using items based on the PCL-R in its field trials.

REVIEWER'S REFERENCE

Cleckley, H. M. (1976). *The mask of sanity: An attempt to clarify some issues about the so-called psychopathic personality* (5th ed.). St. Louis, MO: Mosby.

[178]

The Harrington-O'Shea Career Decision-Making System Revised.

Purpose: An interest inventory that provides an assessment of career interests, job choices, school subjects, future plans, values, and abilities.
Population: Grade 7 and over.
Publication Dates: 1976–93.
Acronym: CDM-R.
Administration: Group or individual.
Price Data: Available from publisher.
Foreign Language Edition: Hand-scored version of original CDM also available in Spanish.
Authors: Thomas F. Harrington and Arthur J. O'Shea.
Publisher: American Guidance Service, Inc.

a) LEVEL I.
Publication Date: 1992.
Scores: 6 scores: Crafts, Scientific, The Arts, Social, Business, Office Operations, used to identify occupational areas from among 18 career clusters: Manual, Skilled Crafts, Technical, Math-Science, Medical-Dental, Literary, Art, Music, Entertainment, Customer Service, Personal Service, Social Service, Education, Sales, Management, Legal, Clerical, Data Analysis.
Time: (20–25) minutes.
Comments: Hand-scored.

b) LEVEL 2.
Publication Dates: 1976–92.
Scores: Same as *a* above and questions in 5 areas: Job Choices, School Subjects, Future Plans, Values, Abilities.
Time: (30–35) minutes.
Comments: Hand-scored edition and machine-scored edition (group summary reports available for machine-

scored edition); computer option available through Guidance Information System® (Houghton-Mifflin).

Cross References: See T4:1128 (1 reference); for a review by Caroline Manuele-Adkins of an earlier edition, see 10:136 (1 reference); see also T3:1054 (3 references); for a review by Carl G. Willis of an earlier edition, see 8:1004.

Review of The Harrington-O'Shea Career Decision-Making System Revised by DEBRA NEUBERT, Associate Professor of Special Education, University of Maryland at College Park, College Park, MD:

The Harrington-O'Shea Career Decision-Making System Revised (CDM-R) is designed to survey interests, abilities, job values, and school subject preferences, and to promote career exploration and decision making. Individuals identify areas of interest within six career clusters which are renamed Holland codes (RIASEC model). The CDM-R was revised in 1991 and is available in two levels.

The CDM-R Level 1, the new version of the CDM, is reported to be most appropriate to use as a planning tool with younger students (grades 7–12) or with those who have reading and learning difficulties. Written at a fourth grade reading level, the stated purpose is to provide directions for career exploration and planning while providing basic occupational information. The 96-item interest survey and interpretation section are contained in one booklet.

Participants handscore the interest survey to identify their two highest career areas of interest. The interpretation section includes a two-page job chart for each of the six career areas. Using the job charts, participants circle job titles of interest, school subjects of interest, job values of importance, and abilities they possess. Job titles include minimum training required, opportunities for employment, and the first three digits of the *Dictionary of Occupational Titles* (DOT) number, which enhances the career exploration process. The final step includes prioritizing choices from the job charts in a summary profile. Although the directions are easy to follow and the terms are well defined, individuals with reading or learning difficulties may require assistance to complete the job chart section due to the overwhelming amount of information included.

The CDM-R Level 2, which is similar to the original CDM, is written at a seventh grade reading level. It is reported to be most useful for high school students and adults making choices regarding college major, career training, or occupation. This level is available in hand-scored English and Spanish versions (12 pages) and an English machine-scored version (8-page reusable booklet). The survey booklet combines self-report of job choices, preferred school subjects, future plans, values, and abilities with a 120-item interest inventory. A separate interpretive folder includes a summary profile (which identifies choices from the survey booklet) along with a career cluster chart that includes 18 career clusters. Participants circle job titles and school subjects of interest, job values of importance, and abilities they possess and compare these to their choices on the summary profile. The job chart also relates the 18 career clusters to the Guide to Occupational Exploration (GOE) work groups to further enhance the career exploration process.

There are many interest inventories on the market. The inclusion of occupational information and suggestions for furthering the career exploration process make the CDM-R especially attractive. In addition, the *CDM-R Career Videos: Tour of Your Tomorrow* are also available to enhance the career exploration process. The two videos provide realistic, up-to-date views of workers in both traditional and nontraditional roles in the six career areas. Workers discuss skills needed for their jobs, how their personality pattern fits a career area, and the importance of lifelong learning. Because many of the occupations depicted require advanced training and/or college preparation, additional information regarding a wider range of entry level jobs in the six career areas may be needed for the younger viewer or for those with learning difficulties.

The CDM-R manual is excellent. Step-by-step instructions regarding the administration, scoring, and interpretation of the inventory are in the first several chapters. A discussion of the underlying rationale and development of the original CDM instrument is also included. The manual contains evidence for the validity and reliability of the original CDM which is reviewed by Manuele-Adkins (1989) and Willis (1978). Little additional information regarding reliability is presented for the revised levels of the CDM-R. Coefficient alpha reliabilities for the CDM-R interest scales range from .88–.93 for the Level 1 and from .92–.95 for the Level 2. Test-retest correlations are reported only for the CDM-R Level 1 and ranged from .74–.87. This information should be interpreted with caution because the instrument was administered to 45 unemployed adults and the target population for the Level 1 instrument is younger students or those with learning difficulties. Evidence is also presented regarding the equivalency of the CDM and the CDM-R.

Additional normative data for the CDM-R Level 1 and 2 include junior and senior high school students from regular and special education. Although the sample is representative of various groups (by grade, age, sex), the small number of subjects (less than 100) in grades 6, 9, 10, 11, and 12 for the CDM-R Level 1 make these normative data questionable (Sattler, 1988). Finally, efforts to eliminate sex bias continue in the CDM-R. Gender neutral occupational titles are used in the CDM-R booklets. Males and females use the same survey form and raw scores are used to explore interest areas.

In summary, the CDM-R appears to be a well-developed instrument that combines identification of interests and preferences along with varied occupational information. The development of the two levels of the CDM-R should meet the needs of diverse individuals who are at various stages in the career decision-making process. The interpretation section of the CDM-R contains some advantages in terms of occupational information and self-exploration that are not found in other interest inventories.

REVIEWER'S REFERENCES

Willis, C. G. (1978). [Review of The Harrington-O'Shea System for Career Decision-Making.] In O. K. Buros (Ed.), *The eighth mental measurements yearbook* (pp. 1584-1585). Highland Park, NJ: Gryphon Press.

Sattler, J. M. (1988). *Assessment of children* (3rd ed.). San Diego, CA: J. M. Sattler.

Manuele-Adkins, C. (1989). [Review of The Harrington-O'Shea Career Decision-Making System.] In J. C. Conoley & J. J. Kramer (Eds.), *The tenth mental measurements yearbook* (pp. 344-345). Lincoln, NE: Buros Institute of Mental Measurements.

Review of The Harrington-O'Shea Career Decision-Making System Revised by MARCIA B. SHAFFER, School Psychologist (Retired), Lancaster, NY:

Level 2 of The Harrington-O'Shea Career Decision-Making System Revised (CDM-R) has been around for several years, and is already a reputable instrument. Level 1 is a questionnaire concerning desired activities. Level 2 items tap job choices, school subject preferences, future plans, values, abilities, and interests. Both levels are suitable for use with individuals from about age 12 (seventh grade) to adults. The levels differ in format, however. Level 1 is described as being written for fourth grade readers and above, and is less complicated than Level 2, which is written for a base of seventh grade reading. Both involve the same six occupational areas.

The six scores, with their 18 career clusters, cover a majority of the vocational choices for which a subject might like to plan. It should be noted that the choices are ones that require specific personality traits, skills, and training. There are no descriptions of the work encompassed by such necessary jobs as driving a truck, waiting table, or collecting rubbish.

The time allotted in the identifying data for using the system is somewhat misleading. It appears to include only the administration of the questionnaires. That is the beginning, but not the meat, of the system. Considerably more time is needed to show the career videos and to discuss the job potentials and the personality characteristics related to each of the six score types. These are significant parts of the test, and may, in this reviewer's opinion, consume as much as another 2 hours—hours well spent.

This test is meticulous in detail. The manual contains, in addition to excellent statistical tables, information about the historical development of the test; the respected research and theories on which the system is founded; recent confirming studies by the authors on the test itself; data on the six groups of vocational possibilities; and suggestions to counselors for interpreting questionnaire results.

Not mentioned in the identifying data are the career videos. They are organized by vocational sections, but within the segments they hop from one job description to another and back again. This makes for an interesting dramatic effect, but might be obfuscating to an adolescent viewer. Certainly some seventh or eighth graders (and some adults of limited vocabulary and experience) would be bewildered by the lack of definitive order. The videos are very useful, however, and they present one particularly important lesson: Work can be a pleasure and a source of great individual satisfaction.

The CDM-R, in both of its levels, should be helpful to anyone involved in vocational guidance. It is well researched and has a respectable theoretical foundation. The hand scoring, mentioned in the identifying data, is no problem; it can even be done by the subject. The videos, despite their possible confusing effect, are highly informative. The manual contains many ideas to give the counselor confidence in employing the system. All in all, the CDM-R has many advantages.

[179]

Hay Aptitude Test Battery.

Purpose: "Helps select applicants with the ability to deal accurately with numerical and alphabetical detail and the ability to work with numbers."
Population: Applicants for clerical and plant positions.
Publication Dates: 1947–88.
Scores, 3: Number Perception, Name Finding, Number Series Completion.
Administration: Group.
Price Data, 1991: $100 per 25 complete batteries; $30 per 25 warm-up tests; $40 per 25 of any other test.
Time: 13(30) minutes.
Comments: Cassette tape available for administration.
Author: Edward N. Hay.
Publisher: E. F. Wonderlic Personnel Test, Inc.

a) THE WARM-UP TEST I.
Time: 1(3) minutes.
b) NUMBER PERCEPTION TEST.
Forms, 2: A, B.
Time: 4(9) minutes.
c) NAME FINDING TEST.
Time: 4(9) minutes.
d) NUMBER SERIES COMPLETION TEST.
Time: 4(9) minutes.

Cross References: For a review by Robert P. Vecchio of an earlier edition, see 9:470; see also T2:2132 (2 references) and 5:849 (2 references); for reviews by Reign H. Bittner and Edward E. Cureton, see 4:725 (8 references).

Review of the Hay Aptitude Test Battery by SUE M. LEGG, Associate Director, Office of Instructional Resources, University of Florida, Gainesville, FL:

The Hay Aptitude Test Battery is designed as a selection instrument for clerical job applicants "with the ability to deal accurately with numerical and alphabetical detail and the ability to work with numbers," according to the test manual (p. 3). These skills are deemed vital for a range of occupations from bookkeepers to stockroom clerks. The tests consist of a 1-minute low-level general knowledge test and three 4-minute tests that require applicants to recognize distinctions among similar names, rearranged numbers, and to recognize patterns in number series.

The structure of the test limits its usefulness. The general knowledge test is offered as a practice test, but this test gives practice only in taking a timed test. It does not prepare the examinee for the scanning skills required in the alphabetic and numerical recognition tests. A scoring key is provided for the practice test, and evidence of predictive validity based on 21 employees' supervisor ratings was presented. Correlations of the scores of the practice test are included in a table of intercorrelations with the other three tests and the Wonderlic Personnel Test. Yet, the practice test is the only one that has no score interpretation section in the manual. This ambiguity in purpose could lead to inappropriate use of the test score.

Another limitation of the test design is its low level of difficulty. The manual cautions that test score differences are important between applicants scoring between the 35th and 50th percentiles but not between applicants at the high end of the range. It is likely that these tests are best used to screen out incompetent applicants rather than to differentiate between applicants with varying degrees of competence in clerical skills. This is an important point because the median scores tend to represent slightly more than one-half of the items, but improvement in scores beyond this level may be more a function of speed than of accuracy. The degree to which high levels of speed in name or number recognition are important clerical skills is not clear.

The degree to which these tests are valid indicators of general clerical skills is uncertain. The manual states the tests represent skills in many jobs; indeed accuracy is important. Whether or not number and letter recognition are adequate indicators of accuracy is not documented. The validity evidence provided includes chi-square analyses and correlations of scores and salary, performance ratings, and typing volume. No details of these studies are given beyond the number of cases for each position. The sample sizes ranged from 39 for bookkeepers to 140 for clerical-bank. Moreover, the rationale for including salary as a criterion implies that higher paid clerks are more accurate. This assumption may not be true. Higher paid workers may be better organizers or supervisors or may only have been employed longer.

The extent to which these tests represent a "job sample" as stated in the manual is not explicated. No task analyses data are provided. Nor are there any instructions to the test administrator about the possible limitations of these tests for selecting applicants beyond a discussion of possible disparities between test scores and applicants' prior experience.

The Hay Aptitude Test Battery may be a useful screening device to identify applicants with problems in discriminating among letters or numbers. It may also help identify applicants who can do clerical tasks accurately. The test does not give direct evidence that it predicts spelling or typing skills or the many other skills that are required to be an effective clerical employee. If it is used, it should be done with a clear understanding of the requirements of the job and the degree to which these particular measures of speed and accuracy are related to success in particular positions.

Review of the Hay Aptitude Test Battery by M. DAVID MILLER, Associate Professor of Foundations of Education, University of Florida, Gainesville, FL:

The Hay Aptitude Test Battery is designed to help in the selection of job applicants into positions (particularly clerical workers) requiring the ability to work accurately with numerical and alphabetical detail. The manual claims the tests have been proven valid for plant jobs and operating positions as well.

The test battery consists of four tests with high face validity for measuring detail aptitude. The tests are speeded tests composed of simple activities.

The Warm-Up Test 1 consists of 20 simple information items with a 1-minute time limit. The purpose of the test is to familiarize applicants with the testing procedures and to reduce anxiety. The other tests are each timed for 4 minutes and are more focused on detail rather than information. The Number Perception Test consists of 200 pairs of numbers which the applicant identifies as the same or different. The Number Series Completion Test consists of 30 number sequences for which the applicant must complete the last two numbers. The Name Finding Test consists of 32 names which need to be identified from a list of 128 names. Each test includes clear and simple directions, as well as practice exercises to familiarize applicants with the tasks. In addition, the Name Finding Test, which has 32 names on one side of the sheet and the list of 128 names on the reverse side, is available for both right-handed and left-handed applicants.

Although the test battery appears reasonable for job selection of clerical workers and others, the psychometric evidence does not support the inferences made with the test. Many of the problems identified in a review of an earlier edition of the test battery by Vecchio (1985) continue to plague the exam. Psychometric evidence is lacking, or weak, in the areas of reliability, validity, norms, and standards.

RELIABILITY. No reliabilities are reported for the Warm-Up Test 1 nor the Number Perception Test.

Given the intended purpose of the Warm-Up Test 1, not reporting the reliability is not as serious of a limitation as for the Number Perception Test. High split-half reliabilities are reported for the Name Finding Test (.94) and the Number Series Completion Test (.94). However, as pointed out by Vecchio (1985) and the measurement literature (e.g., Anastasi, 1988), split-half reliabilities are spuriously high for speeded tests. A more appropriate form of reliability with a speeded test would be alternate form or test-retest.

VALIDITY. Several pieces of evidence in support of the validity of the tests are reported. However, problems with these data limit their usefulness. First, a study of the Warm-Up Test 1 as a predictor of overall job performance is reported. Besides the ethical issues in using tests in a way unknown to the applicant (see Vecchio, 1985), the study can be faulted in two ways: The expected values for the chi-square are too small with the small sample size ($N = 21$), and the test was given under nonstandardized conditions (i.e., as an untimed "power test").

Second, several studies are reported as providing evidence of criterion-related validity. Although these studies could provide a reasonable basis for the use of the test battery, not enough information is provided to assess the adequacy of the criteria used or the specific procedures of the studies. In addition, no references are provided for the studies. According to Standard 10.3 of the *Standards for Educational and Psychological Testing* (AERA, APA, & NCME, 1985), "the rationale for criterion relevance should be made explicit. It should include a description of the job in question and of the judgements used to determine relevance" (p. 60). Vecchio (1985) also points to a published account of the failure of the Number Perception Test to correlate with supervisor ratings, raising the question of the representativeness of the reported results (all reported studies show reasonable levels of criterion-related validity).

The correlations of the tests with each other and the Wonderlic Personnel Test are also reported. No interpretations of these correlations are given. Only three correlations were of moderate size with two of them involving the Warm-Up Test 1 (a test ostensibly used to reduce anxiety). The three correlations were between the Warm-Up Test 1 and the Wonderlic Personnel Test (.55), the Warm-Up Test 1 and the Number Series Test (.55), and the Wonderlic Personnel Test and the Number Series Test (.54).

Subpopulation differences on the test battery are reported for gender and education level. Not surprisingly, higher education is related to higher scores. The relationship with gender, which should be seen as problematic when hiring applicants, is found only on the Number Series Test with males scoring higher. Ethnic differences, which should be examined, are not.

Finally, each of the tests is reported as being "job related" and the tasks are being "similar to those required in a 'job sample.'" No evidence is provided for these claims nor is the "job sample" described. Again, providing no evidence for these claims clearly violates Standards 10.5 and 10.6 of the *Standards for Educational and Psychological Testing* (AERA, APA, & NCME, 1985) dealing with the content-related validity of the exam.

NORMS AND STANDARDS. Norms and suggested cutoffs are provided. The norms appear to be based on a convenience sample (past users of the test battery who have returned the results) with potentially mixed occupations. In violation of Standard 4.4 of the *Standards for Educational and Psychological Testing* (AERA, APA, & NCME, 1985), insufficient detail is provided to judge the appropriateness of the norms.

Similarly, the basis for the cutoffs suggested is not clearly explained (Standard 10.9). It is unclear who set the cutoffs, how they were set, and for what job classifications. On the other hand, the test manual emphasizes that the cutoffs are only "suggested" and companies may need to set their own standards.

In summary, the Hay Aptitude Test Battery is a series of tests that show good face validity in measuring detail aptitude. However, the psychometric information available may not justify its use. On the other hand, the *Standards for Educational and Psychological Testing* (AERA, APA, & NCME, 1985) emphasize the role of the test user in examining the particular uses and interpretations of the test. The Hay Aptitude Test Battery may be psychometrically sound, but insufficient evidence (or inadequate documentation of the evidence) leads to the need for further study to justify its use in personnel selection.

REVIEWER'S REFERENCES

American Educational Research Association, American Psychological Association, & National Council on Measurement in Education. (1985). *Standards for educational and psychological testing*. Washington, DC: American Psychological Association, Inc.

Vecchio, R. P. (1985). [Review of the Hay Aptitude Test Battery]. In J. V. Mitchell, Jr. (Ed.), *The ninth mental measurements yearbook* (pp. 651-652). Lincoln, NE: Buros Institute of Mental Measurements.

Anastasi, A. (1988). *Psychological testing* (6th ed.). New York: Macmillan Publishing.

[180]

Henmon-Nelson Ability Test, Canadian Edition.

Purpose: "Designed to measure those aspects of cognitive ability which are important for success in academic work and in similar endeavors outside the classroom."

Population: Grades 3–6, 6–9, 9–12.

Publication Dates: 1957–90.

Scores: Total score only.

Administration: Group.

Price Data, 1994: $49.45 per 35 reusable or consumable test booklets (specify level); $37.45 per 100 answer sheets (hand/machine scorable); $10.45 per scoring mask (all levels); $10 per examiner's manual ('90, 44 pages); $8.95 per 10 class record sheets; $12.45 per examination kit.

Time: (30) minutes.

Comments: Adapted from the 1973 U.S. edition of the test (The Henmon-Nelson Tests of Mental Ability, 3:1073).

Authors: Tom A. Lamke, M. J. Nelson, and Joseph L. French.
Publisher: Nelson Canada [Canada].
Cross References: See T3:1073 (13 references); for a review by Eric F. Gardner, see 8:190 (14 references); see also T2:391 (52 references); for a review by Norman E. Wallen and an excerpted review by John O. Crites of an earlier edition, see 6:462 (11 references); for reviews by D. Welty Lefever and Leona E. Tyler and an excerpted review by Laurance F. Shaffer, see 5:342 (14 references); for a review by H. M. Fowler, see 4:299 (25 references); for reviews by Anne Anastasi, August Dvorak, Howard Easley, and J. P. Guilford and an excerpted review by Francis N. Maxfield, see 2:1398.

Review of the Henmon-Nelson Ability Test, Canadian Edition by JOHN O. ANDERSON, Associate Professor, Faculty of Education, University of Victoria, Victoria, British Columbia, Canada:

The Henmon-Nelson Ability Test is intended to measure cognitive ability related to academic success for Canadian students in grades 3 to 12. As such it is not an index of academic achievement but is an index of academic aptitude or potential. The test is essentially the U.S. version with norms tables based on a sample of Canadian students and minor modifications to the items.

The Henmon-Nelson Ability Test consists of three levels: grades 3 to 6, 6 to 9, and 9 to 12. Each level consists of 90 multiple-choice items measuring student ability in tasks associated with problems with numbers, graphical representations, and words (e.g., synonyms and sentence completion). The items are ordered by difficulty (*p*-values presumably) so that the student will be required to respond to an eclectic ordering of item types: for example, a number problem then identification of a synonym and then perhaps a graphic relations-type task. The Henmon-Nelson yields a single score for the student based upon summing the number of correct responses. An interesting characteristic of the test is that each of the three levels of the test has exactly the same scoring key.

The tests can be obtained as either reusable booklets for use with a separate answer sheet or as *consumable* booklets. In both formats, the 90 items are printed in a horizontal format which gives the booklets a very crowded, text-dense appearance. Given that the students, regardless of level, are given 30 minutes to complete the test it would seem that speed would be a major factor in determining overall performance particularly with younger children. This concern about test speededness is reinforced by the low completion rates of the norm group reported in the examiner's manual (Table 6.2).

The norms are based on the responses of English-speaking students from 48 schools from across Canada. On average there were 772 students per grade administered the test, the number of students per grade varied from 457 in grade 3 to 1,410 in grade 7. It appears that test administration was conducted sometime during the 1988–89 school year but it is unclear exactly when, and if all schools completed the test in the same time interval. This can have some influence on the interpretation of grade-related scores. Tables are provided to transform raw scores into both grade- and age-based stanines and percentiles and into standard age scores (mean = 100, *sd* = 16). The examiner's manual explains the scoring of the test and the use of the norms tables clearly with appropriate cautions. The score conversion tables are straightforward and well laid out for each level of the test.

The issue of validity is discussed briefly in terms of content, construct, and criterion-related validity largely on the basis of work done on early versions (U.S.) of the test but no references to this work are provided. These studies suggest the test is valid in terms of relevant content, correlation to other respected tests of cognitive ability, and correlation to academic performance. In addition, a study was conducted as part of the development of this Canadian Edition by correlating Henmon-Nelson scores to those of the Verbal component of the Canadian Cognitive Abilities Test (CCAT) for samples of students in grades 4, 7, and 10. The correlations ranged from .78 to .84, suggesting concurrent validity to the Verbal component of the CCAT.

The examiner's manual does not offer any references to relevant research literature and is rather light on details about test and item characteristics. It would be informative and an aid to score interpretation to provide test score distributions and item statistics, particularly item difficulty and omission rates. Further, in order to engender confidence in using scores from the Henmon-Nelson Ability Test to make judgements about students, the manual should provide information regarding differences in test performance based on gender and cultural background of respondent, and on the format of the test booklet used (separate answer sheet versus consumable booklet).

In conclusion, the Henmon-Nelson Ability Test provides a quick, easily administered and scored test of student performance related to aspects of language usage, spatial relations, and numeracy. However, the single score derived from responses to this diverse item set is not easily interpretable in relation to academic performance. Academic performance is generally considered in terms of specific abilities and skills such as numerical problem solving, word knowledge, pictorial analogies, and the like. A score derived from responses to an amalgam of item types, which the Henmon-Nelson provides, does not seem well suited for informing instructionally related decisions. A test which provides more task specific information, such as the aforementioned CCAT would likely be more informative.

Review of the Henmon-Nelson Ability Test, Canadian Edition by DAVID J. BATESON, Associate Professor of Mathematics and Science Education and the Educational Measurement Research Group, University of British Columbia, Vancouver, British Columbia, Canada:

The items for all three levels (grades 3–6, grades 6–9, and grades 9–12) of the Canadian edition of the Henmon-Nelson Ability Test are derived directly from the 1973 U.S. edition. They have been "Canadianized" by metricating and changing contexts (state/province, governor/premier), and have also been updated so that money questions reflect more modern prices. The 90 items in each of the levels lead to a single general cognitive ability or academic aptitude score that can be reported as a Standard Age Score (SAS, mean of 100, standard deviation of 16) along with percentile rank and stanine of the SAS, or percentile rank (or stanine) of the raw score by grade within the level.

From a psychometric point of view, the tests appear to more than meet presently acceptable standards. The examiner's manual is a well-written document that provides accurate, understandable, and, therefore, useful discussions and cautions for the user. Administration and "hand" scoring are fast and simple, and there appears to be little chance for examiner transcription or addition errors to occur. The reported KR20 reliability coefficients are quite acceptable for a test of this kind, ranging from .90 to .96, depending on the level and grade. The authors recognize the potential problem of speededness, with 90 items to be completed in 30 minutes, and present arguments and evidence regarding the issue. The problem is temporized by having the items ordered in increasing difficulty. Correlation coefficients between the same grades using different levels of the test, although satisfactory, are not as high as one might expect. The fact that content between the levels is, at times, considerably different may explain this situation. For example, there are 15 symbolic analogies at Level 3–6, eight at Level 6–9, and none at Level 9–12. Validity evidence provided shows appropriately high correlations with the Canadian Cognitive Abilities Test, Form 7.

There may be two potential problems with these instruments. First, the tests come in two formats, the consumable Clapp-Young self-marking forms, which have been successfully used in the U.S. editions for many years, and reusable forms with accompanying machine-scorable answer sheets. The manual provides different administration and scoring instructions for the two formats, but then ceases to differentiate between the formats. Unfortunately, the authors provide no evidence that results would be equivalent regardless of format. Based on experience, I would predict that results from the different formats would not be equivalent, particularly at the lower grade levels. This is particularly cause for concern because the format used for the reliability, validity, and norming studies is not reported.

The second problem is connected with sampling. Although the document does an excellent job in presenting the sampling framework and schools used for the norming study, this presentation draws attention to a possible bias in the sample. At all three levels of the test, approximately two-thirds of the items depend on English language verbal abilities. Performance on these items can be greatly influenced by a student having English as a second language, a situation applying to a growing number of Canadian students. Because "English as a Second Language" students were not appropriately represented in the sample, the norms may not be appropriate.

In summary, the Henmon-Nelson provides a quick, inexpensive, and usable result for those wishing an undifferentiated gross score of academic aptitude or general cognitive ability. Caution with respect to the test utility and normative interpretations should be used in the case of students for whom English is a second language.

[181]

High School Career-Course Planner.

Purpose: Designed "to develop a high school course plan that is consistent with self-assessed career goals."
Population: Grades 8 and 9.
Publication Dates: 1983–90.
Acronym: HSCCP.
Scores: Total score only.
Administration: Group.
Price Data, 1992: $.50 per HSCCP folder and User's Guide ('90, 4 pages); $2 per Job-O dictionary; $16.50 per Occupational Outlook Handbook; $89.95 per HSCCP computer program.
Time: (50) minutes; (5–8) minutes for computer version.
Comments: Computer version also available.
Author: CFKR Career Materials, Inc.
Publisher: CFKR Career Materials, Inc.

Review of the High School Career-Course Planner by MARY HENNING-STOUT, Associate Professor of Counseling Psychology, Lewis & Clark College, Portland, OR:

The High School Career-Course Planner (HSCCP) was developed as a counseling and teaching tool for working with students in 8th, 9th, and 10th grades to aid their identification of career interests and related high school courses. The packet of materials forwarded to the purchaser of the HSCCP includes a four-page record form and a four-page user's guide (both 8.5 x 11 inches). Multiple record forms may be ordered for group administration. Computer administration is also available.

INSTRUMENT CONSTRUCTION. When I began my review of these materials, I elected to approach the record form without reading the user's guide. This, I reasoned, was the way a student respondent would likely face this instrument. I read the brief introduction at the top of the first page and prepared to "follow all directions." The first task was to rate my interest in nine different occupational interest areas (A-1) using 1 to indicate high interest, 2 to indicate some interest, and 3 to indicate low interest. Almost from the beginning, I anticipated confusion with some of the multiple stems composing each area descriptor. For example, the first stem reads "work with tools . . . work with your hands . . . operate machines in an office . . . fix things . . . build things using blueprints . . . design machinery or buildings . . . work with plants and animals . . . use mechanical skills." Students who like working with their hands and being with animals, but who do not like to fix things, trouble with plants, or design machines or buildings might have difficulty answering. Perhaps they would respond with "2" (some interest). As I read on, however, it seemed that many of the stems would have led to "2" responses: for students who like to express themselves artistically but do not like to perform, for students who want to work with people in a caring and helping way but do not feel comfortable with the power implied in the stem "influence people's lives." The authors' intent with constructing these stems in this fashion is not clarified in the user's guide. There is also no explanation of the decision to provide only three response options. The use of so few response options seems to limit accurate expression of fine gradations in preference for clusters of occupations interest stems.

The user's guide author indicates the occupational areas in this section, referred to in the guide as "assessment variables," were "worded and coded to intercorrelate with the *Holland-RAISEC* personality and work environment types" (p. 4). To find out more about this source and about other assessment construction issues I will discuss later, I contacted CFKR Career Materials, the organization that produces and markets the HSCCP. According to the CFKR representative, they have none of the sources used for developing the assessment variables (occupational interest areas) available for consumers. There is also no additional information available on the construction of the occupational areas. The use of the term "intercorrelate" seems not to indicate statistical procedure but the judgement of the test developers.

The inside pages of the HSCCP are a place for students to record their responses to the occupational interest items for comparison with 16 job areas selected from the *Occupational Outlook Handbook* and the *Guide for Occupational Exploration*, both produced by the Department of Labor and available through CFKR. There is no explanation in the user's guide of the procedures through which these two sources determine job clusters.

During my first review of the instrument itself, I became quite confused with the instructions to respondents provided at the top of page 2. I understood that respondents would record their responses from the first page but was completely unclear on what to do with those numbers and the rows of numbers beside each of the job clusters. Even after reviewing the user's guide, I continued unclear on how respondents would complete the form. This seems a primary weakness of the instrument.

However, according to their literature and the comments of the CFKR representative, the developers of the HSCCP have marketed hundreds of thousands of these forms over the past two decades. Someone must be figuring out how to use them.

PSYCHOMETRIC PROPERTIES. On the back page of the user's guide is a brief reference to the face validity of the instrument, "the results fit in with dreams, aspirations, and realistic personal appraisals" (p. 4) of the respondents. There is an additional brief statement that "a matching score of 6 or more usually provides a cluster that has high validity for decision-making" (p. 4). I interpret this to indicate that when a student successfully uses her or his interest scores to enter the center pages of the HSCCP, a score of 6 or more can be taken as a good indication of job interest. There is, however, no additional indication of the validity data available to support this statement.

My conversation with the CFKR representative revealed no additional insight into the psychometric foundations of the HSCCP. The first paragraph of the user's guide invites inquiries from consumers who want "specific information regarding validity and reliability, and field testing results" (p. 4). When I called, I was told there were no written materials on the reliability and validity of the instrument, but received a fax from the CFKR representative including a brief comment on the content validity of the *JOB-O Professional Manual*, which may be related to the HSCCP in its use of nine occupational interest variables. Also included in the fax was a quote from one of the owners of CFKR: "This product has been sold since 1969—reliability based on customer satisfaction—it does what it is promoted to do."

SUMMARY. Based on my review of the instrument and its supporting materials, it is difficult to recommend the HSCCP. The intent of the instrument seems sound. The delivery on that intent is lacking. The HSCCP would be strengthened with clearer instructions, clearer stems, a wider range of response options, and substantially expanded explanation of its construction and proven record. The reported use of the HSCCP by more than 200,000 students indicates there is interest in such an instrument—one that focuses practically on linking student occupational interests with high school courses. The documentation available on the HSCCP leaves questions as to the extent to which this instrument responds effectively to the need for career-linked course planning for high school students.

Review of the High School Career-Course Planner by JAMES W. PINKNEY, Professor of Counseling and Adult Education, East Carolina University, Greenville, NC:

The High School Career-Course Planner (HSCCP) is designed to help 8th, 9th, and 10th grade students combine career awareness and career exploration with course planning for their high school coursework. The HSCCP uses students' self-ratings of *high, some* and *low* interest on nine items to provide a basis for course selection in high school. In the first six items the student rates his or her level of interest in each of Holland's six career environments. The last three items rate interest in working at a "high level of responsibility" with data, people, or things (the worker functions of the *Dictionary of Occupational Titles*). The four-page user's guide outlines a four-step process for using the HSCCP with students. The user's guide author states the reading level of the HSCCP is appropriate for "over 90% of 8th grade students" (p. 3).

The self-rating of the items is followed by a comparison of the ratings with the interest profiles of 16 occupational groups. Each group is represented by approximately 15 job titles, suggested courses to take in high school, and a brief statement about typical job entry requirements. Occupational groups are selected that have the highest "score," or number of matches between a student's self-ratings and the profile values given for each occupational group. The educational and entry requirements of the selected groups or titles are then explored and related to high school courses available to the student. The last page of the HSCCP is a 4-year planning guide for required and elective high school courses. The simplicity of the HSCCP, self-rating followed by counting matches with the values assigned to each item for an occupational group, is noted in the user's guide as a quality of the HSCCP that many users find attractive.

Evidence of the validity and reliability of the HSCCP is lacking. Several references in the guide to field testing are of questionable value (at best) to the prospective user because the implied results of field testing are not substantiated. A call to the publisher resulted in an observation that the HSCCP has heuristic value and face validity because it does what it claims—gets middle school students to use career information in planning their high school courses. The guide author does state that the HSCCP has been used by over 200,000 students and extensively field tested, but no data concerning the field testing, validity, or reliability are reported. The absence of data may reflect the brevity of the HSCCP—nine relative independent ratings can, at best, provide only a sketchy and questionable basis for planning and decision making.

The statement "A matching score of 6 or more usually provides a cluster that has validity for decision-making" (p. 4) is unsupported and highly questionable given the scoring procedure of the HSCCP. Scoring is a matter of counting matches between student ratings on the nine items and the values assigned to an occupational group for the items. The Holland work environment item considered most important for an occupational group (indicated by highlighting on the consumable form) is weighted to count as three matches. In general, this weighted item would occur first in Holland's three-letter code for occupations in the group. For example, the engineering and science group has the science and math item (investigative occupations) highlighted whereas the education group has the helping people item (social occupations) highlighted. Obviously, a "score" of 6 means a student could match the profile on only four of the nine items. Given the simplistic rating system of the HSCCP (high, some, or low interest), it is intuitively difficult to see where fewer than half of the item ratings matching a profile is a valid basis for decision making.

This issue is further complicated by the fact the profiles for the occupational groups are not exclusive. Identical profiles are given for the following pairs of occupational groups: Transportation with Industrial Production, Engineering & Science with Computer & Electronic Technology, and Mechanical with Construction. Some students would likely find this confusing, discouraging, or contradictory without intervention by a teacher, counselor, or parent. The user's guide does encourage adult support of the students as they use the HSCCP, and this would be critical with younger or less capable students. Both the abstract purpose of the HSCCP and the multistep process involved would suggest that many, if not most, students are going to need help to use the HSCCP and its results. To some extent the utility and benefits of the HSCCP will depend on the quality of the support provided throughout the process of relating career issues to high school course selection.

Potential users of the HSCCP might do well to think of it not as an "instrument" or "test" but rather as a structuring tool for subsequent interaction with students, or as a guide to help students with career awareness. The HSCCP does provide a process that helps students, counselors, teachers, and parents know more about a student's career awareness, career thinking, and career exploration. Being able to focus that information on the process of selecting high school courses would encourage the student to see the relationships between education, career planning, and job entry at an earlier age than might otherwise happen. Quite clearly, however, this potential gain means the HSCCP will require more one-to-one interaction rather than less for overworked teachers and counselors.

It is encouraging to see a career-oriented task that does not focus first on job titles but rather on the student's self-perceptions of his or her career-related interests. This seems more appropriate than starting career exploration from a job title focus, especially for a younger age group. The HSCCP presents career-related interests as important when selecting high school courses, but it does not expect or encourage final career decisions. In fact, prior to filling out the course planner on the last page the student is given several intermediate steps to take if more information is needed (i.e., "visit a career center" and "visit someone on-the-job").

In summary, the HSCCP has little support to recommend its use. Certainly using it for research purposes is out of the question, and using it in group situations is problematic. Its most appropriate use at this time would appear to be with individual students where the test giver will have an opportunity to follow up with the student after the HSCCP is completed. There are some options to be considered for the HSCCP and its targeted age group of 8th, 9th, and 10th graders. The computer program "DISCOVER for Junior High Schools" would provide similar information for course planning. The Judgement of Occupational Behavior—Orientation (JOB-O; 200) shares some of the psychometric short-comings of the HSCCP, but uses job titles to generate similar information for this age group as well as high school students.

[182]

The Hooper Visual Organization Test.

Purpose: Measures an individual's ability to organize visual stimuli.
Population: Ages 13 and over.
Publication Dates: 1957–83.
Acronym: VOT.
Scores: Total score only.
Administration: Group or individual.
Price Data, 1995: $180 per complete kit; $16.50 per 25 test booklets; $30 per reusable test pictures booklet; $12.50 per scoring key; $19.50 per 100 answer sheets; $37.50 per manual ('83, 39 pages).
Time: (10–15) minutes.
Author: H. Elston Hooper.
Publisher: Western Psychological Services.
Cross References: See T4:1174 (28 references), T3:1109 (6 references), T2:1216 (5 references), and P:111 (7 references); for reviews by Ralph M. Reitan and Otfried Spreen of an earlier edition, see 6:116 (4 references).

TEST REFERENCES

1. Jongbloed, L., Stacey, S., & Brighton, C. (1989). Stroke rehabilitation: Sensorimotor integrative treatment versus functional treatment. *The American Journal of Occupational Therapy, 43*, 391-397.

2. Benke, T. (1993). Two forms of apraxia in Alzheimer's disease. *Cortex, 29*, 715-725.

3. Chouinard, M. J., & Braun, C. M. J. (1993). A meta-analysis of the relative sensitivity of neuropsychological screening tests. *Journal of Clinical and Experimental Neuropsychology, 15*, 591-607.

4. Crockett, D. J. (1993). Cross-validation of WAIS-R prototypical patterns of intellectual functioning using neuropsychological test scores. *Journal of Clinical and Experimental Neuropsychology, 15*, 903-920.

5. Anderson, S. W., & Rizzo, M. (1994). Hallucinations following occipital lobe damage: A pathological activation of visual representations. *Journal of Clinical and Experimental Neuropsychology, 16*, 651-663.

6. Palmer, B. W., Boone, K. B., Chang, L., Lee, A., & Black, S. (1994). Cognitive deficits and personality patterns in maternally versus paternally inherited myotonic dystrophy. *Journal of Clinical and Experimental Neuropsychology, 16*, 784-795.

7. Faraone, S. V., Seidman, L. J., Kremen, W. S., Pepple, J. R., Lyons, M. J., & Tsuang, M. T. (1995). Neuropsychological functioning among the nonpsychotic relatives of schizophrenic patients: A diagnostic efficiency analysis. *Journal of Abnormal Psychology, 104*, 286-304.

Review of the Hooper Visual Organization Test by KATHY E. GREEN, Associate Professor of Education, University of Denver, Denver, CO:

The Hooper Visual Organization Test (VOT) consists of 30 line drawings depicting common objects cut into pieces and rearranged. The subject's task is to name the objects verbally or in writing. The VOT was designed as a brief instrument to be used in screening for deficits in organization of visual stimuli, in creating a visual "Gestalt." The VOT was originally intended for use in identifying people with neurological impairment associated with organic brain pathology. The test can be administered and scored, individually or in groups, in under 15 minutes. There is no time limit per item but subjects are instructed to work as fast as they can. The test score is the total number of correct responses, with partial credit given for some responses. The total raw score can be interpreted directly or converted to a corrected score which is adjusted for the subject's age and educational level. The manual author also suggests that item responses be interpreted qualitatively but no data are yet available to ground this interpretation.

The VOT manual (1983 edition) is generally well organized and well written, clearly presenting information on scoring, reliability, and validity. The manual contains tables of scores that are adjusted for age and education. As the manual author states, significant positive correlations between VOT score and IQ have also been found. This relationship has not been controlled for in adjusting scores, possibly because education indirectly reflects IQ and educational level is used to adjust VOT scores. Tamkin and Jacobsen (1984) found that IQ was more strongly related to VOT score than was education. They suggested the VOT score be adjusted for age and IQ rather than age and education. Of course, IQ scores are not as easily obtainable as age and education, making it less practical to require IQ estimates for use of the VOT as a screening test. The suggestion in the manual is to restrict use of the VOT to those persons with IQs above a certain level, which requires an estimated IQ. Subsequent versions of the manual might benefit from provision of tables of IQ-adjusted scores, especially for persons with IQs lower than 75. Also, in view of the fact that the VOT is used as a visual-perceptual measure, it is surprising that no mention is made of any gender-related differences.

A second welcome addition to a future manual would be information about item analyses and item functioning as well as information regarding test and item bias. Although the VOT is constructed to provide a total score, researchers have used shortened versions of the measure. Item difficulty, be it expressed as *p*-values or logits, would be useful in guiding item selection for shortened versions and would be interesting. The VOT is clearly a language-dependent measure, so information regarding the effects of language and cultural test and item bias would also be useful.

A variety of corrected split-half reliability coefficients were calculated for the VOT. Reliability of the VOT for the original nonclinical sample was .82; reliability for a sample of psychiatric inpatients was .78, and .80 for a mixed group of neurologically impaired, psychologically disturbed, and normative medical patients and hospital employees. Lezak (1982) found test-retest reliabilities of .77 to .92 for a small nonclinical sample. Future analyses of VOT scores using item response theory could provide score-specific estimated standard errors that may prove more useful in application than reliability coefficients.

Validity of the VOT has been addressed in greater depth than has reliability. Conceptually, because language plays a part in the VOT, it is clearly not a pure measure of visual organization. To make it so, the response format could be changed to multiple choice or a form not requiring language use.

Two factorial validity studies have found the VOT to define a visual-perceptual factor, similar to measures such as Wechsler Adult Intelligence Scale (WAIS) performance subtests and Halstead-Reitan subtests. Criterion-related validation studies have sought to assess the ability of the VOT to discriminate neurologically impaired from psychologically disturbed from nonclinical groups. More recent applications have gone further afield. Groups characterized by alcoholism, stroke, early Parkinson's, multiple sclerosis, bipolar disorders, memory impairment, and criminal psychopathology have been given the VOT along with comparison groups, generally with null results. The initial validation study found significantly lower scores for the neurologically impaired group with 21% misclassification for this group (and 0% misclassification for the nonorganic group). This study has been criticized on grounds of its failure to control for age, IQ, and other confounding variables. Results of a second early validation study are confusing because the VOT was part of the screening battery. A third study failed to control for IQ. A fourth study found significant differences between normal and neurologically impaired groups, with a 19% misclassification rate for the neurologically impaired group, and somewhat higher misclassification rates for the other groups.

Using the cutoff point suggested in the manual, a study by Wang (1977) resulted in a 43% misclassification rate, whereas a study by Boyd (1981) resulted in 85% misclassification for brain-impaired subjects. Optimal adjustment of the cutoff scores in both studies reduced misclassification for the impaired group to, respectively, 17% and 32.5%. These studies yield results of significantly lower mean VOT scores for neurologically impaired groups but of considerable overlap between the distributions of impaired and normative groups. These studies have maximized power to detect differences by using groups of equal size, providing a base correct classification rate of 50%. The predictive power of the test for a prevalence rate for brain damage of less than 33%–50% is not known.

Evidence for concurrent and discriminant validity is scant. One study found no incremental predictive value in use of the VOT when the WAIS, Benton Visual Retention Test, and Porteus Mazes formed the basic test battery. Another study found the VOT to increase correct classification when the Benton and the Weigl Color-Form Sorting Test were used as the basic battery (Tamkin & Kunce, 1985).

The validity evidence reviewed in the manual and provided by several studies conducted since 1983 suggests VOT scores to be substantially lower for neurologically impaired subjects than for nonimpaired subjects. Favoring use of the VOT are its brevity, ease of administration and scoring, adequate reliability, and evidence of ability of VOT scores to discriminate at a gross level among neurologically impaired and nonclinical groups. Limiting the use of the VOT is lack of information in several areas, a limitation true of some of the other less well-developed neuropsychological measures. Lacking are item analysis and item functioning information, alternate forms, a computerized version, adequate information regarding cultural bias, and evidence of the utility of VOT scores in identifying the locus of lesion. Also of concern are the test's language dependence, a floor effect, and confounding of scores with IQ (and possibly gender). Of greatest concern are issues of construct validity and diagnostic utility. There seems to be little reason to prefer the VOT to measures such as WAIS subtests or parts of the Halstead-Reitan, for which much more information is available. A study comparing the utility of the VOT to these measures as a screening device is needed.

REVIEWER'S REFERENCES

Wang, P. L. (1977). Visual organization ability in brain-damaged adults. *Perceptual and Motor Skills*, *45*, 723-728.

Boyd, J. L. (1981). A validity study of the Hooper Visual Organization Test. *Journal of Consulting and Clinical Psychology*, *49*, 15-19.

Lezak, M. D. (1982). *The test-retest stability and reliability of some tests commonly used in neuropsychological assessment.* Presented at the fifth European conference of the International Neuropsychological Society, Deauville, France.

Tamkin, A. S., & Jacobsen, R. (1984). Age-related norms for the Hooper Visual Organization Test. *Journal of Clinical Psychology*, *40*, 1459-1463.

Tamkin, A. S., & Kunce, J. T. (1985). A comparison of three neuropsychological tests: The Weigl, Hooper, and Benton. *Journal of Clinical Psychology*, *41*, 660-664.

Review of the Hooper Visual Organization Test by WILFRED G. VAN GORP, Associate Professor in Residence and Director, Neuropsychology Assessment Laboratory, UCLA School of Medicine, Department of Psychiatry and Biobehavioral Sciences and Interim Chief, Psychology Service, Department of Veterans Affairs Medical Center, West Los Angeles, CA:

The Hooper Visual Organization Test (VOT) is a well-known neuropsychological test which has been in use for over 40 years. It consists of 30 line drawings of common objects, which have been "cut" into pieces and arranged such that the respondent must visually integrate them and state what the object would be if the pieces were reassembled. A total raw score is computed by summing the number correct (with half-point credit available for 11 items). From tables in the manual, this raw score may then be converted into a corrected raw score and *T*-score, taking into account the respondent's age and education. The derived *T*-scores must be interpreted with caution, however, until contemporary validation studies are conducted, because these norms are based upon a sample of exclusively male veteran patients obtained approximately 30 years ago (Mason & Ganzler, 1964).

The test manual author suggests two primary uses for the VOT: (*a*) as a screening test for central nervous system dysfunction; and (*b*) as a research measure to quantify a respondent's ability to integrate visual information. As noted by some neuropsychologists (Rathbun & Smith, 1982), many clinicians use the VOT to assess visuospatial function in patients suspected of having these deficits associated with a unilateral brain injury.

The test manual has been greatly improved from its original version. It contains a complete review of the literature on the VOT, including reliability and validity data and a thorough and honest discussion of the strengths and weaknesses of the test. Another strength of the manual is the inclusion of norms allowing for adjustments to the total raw score based upon the respondent's age and education, in light of data from several studies indicating a significant association between age and intelligence on the VOT score. Given the probable curvilinear relationship between VOT performance and age (with older subjects performing significantly worse), clinicians evaluating older individuals should avoid use of the test with those aged 70 and over because raw score conversion data are available only for individuals up to age 69.

SCREENING INSTRUMENT. Despite a number of validity studies on the VOT, which have appeared since the VOT was first introduced, very little has changed to suggest a different analysis than one offered three decades ago. Reitan (1965) concluded that "there is not yet sufficient evidence to recommend the Hooper VOT as an instrument with special promise for detecting the psychological effects of brain lesions" (p. 116).

Although several studies have shown that "brain damaged" subjects perform worse than normal controls on the VOT, a number of studies have reported unacceptably low hit rates using the recommended cutoff scores by Hooper. In at least two studies, the hit rates barely exceeded chance based upon the base rate of brain injury in the sample studied (e.g., Boyd, 1981; see response by Woodward, 1982; Tamkin & Kunce, 1985). When used as part of a neuropsychological screening battery, at least two other studies found the addition of the VOT to contribute no significant gain in classification of patients (Sterne, 1973; Jackson & Culbertson, 1977). Sterne found the addition of the Trail Making Test (especially Part B), in contrast, to significantly improve the detection rate of subjects with "brain damage."

Although few professionals view "brain damage" as a unitary concept, there are legitimate occasions in which a cost-effective but reliable means of screening for those with various types of cognitive impairment is needed. For this purpose, the VOT appears less useful than other measures (such as the Trail Making Test), as it lacks sufficient sensitivity to detect those with brain dysfunction.

THE VOT AS A MEASURE OF SPATIAL PROCESSING. It has been argued (Rathbun & Smith, 1982) the VOT can assist in assessing patients with lateralized unilateral brain dysfunction because a decrease in spatial cognitive abilities is often associated with right hemisphere damage. The two studies that examined this question both found the VOT *not* to be differentially sensitive to right versus left hemisphere lesions (Wang, 1977; Boyd, 1981). As such, possibly because of the naming component which is part of the VOT, this test has not been shown to be useful in specifically measuring spatial processing per se, or in showing a discrimination in performance of those with right versus left hemisphere lesions.

In summary, despite a much improved test manual and appropriate corrections for age and education, the low sensitivity as a screening measure and the inability of the VOT to differentiate those with left versus right hemisphere lesions require considerable caution before deciding to use the VOT in standard neuropsychological practice.

REVIEWER'S REFERENCES

Mason, C. F., & Ganzler, H. (1964). Adult norms for the Shipley Institute of Living Scale and Hooper Visual Organization Test based on age and education. *Journal of Gerontology, 19*, 419-424.

Reitan, R. M. (1965). [Review of the Hooper Visual Organization Test.] In O. K. Buros (Ed.), *The sixth mental measurements yearbook* (pp. 244-245). Highland Park, NJ: Gryphon Press.

Sterne, D. M. (1973). The Hooper Visual Organization Test and the Trail Making Tests as discriminants of brain injury. *Journal of Clinical Psychology, 29*, 212-213.

Jackson, R. E., & Culbertson, W. C. (1977). The Elizur Test of Psycho-organicity and the Hooper Visual Organization Test as measures of childhood neurological impairment. *Journal of Clinical Psychology, 33*, 213-214.

Wang, P. L. (1977). Visual organization ability in brain-damaged adults. *Perceptual and Motor Skills, 45*, 723-728.

Boyd, J. L. (1981). A validity study of the Hooper Visual Organization Test. *Journal of Consulting and Clinical Psychology, 49,* 15-19.
Rathbun, J., & Smith, A. (1982). Comment on the validity of Boyd's validation study of the Hooper Visual Organization Test. *Journal of Consulting and Clinical Psychology, 50,* 281-283.
Woodward, C. A. (1982). The Hooper Visual Organization Test: A case against its use in neuropsychological assessment. *Journal of Consulting and Clinical Psychology, 50,* 286-288.
Tamkin, A. S., & Kunce, J. T. (1985). A comparison of three neuropsychological tests: The Weigl, Hooper and Benton. *Journal of Clinical Psychology, 41,* 660-664.

[183]

The Hundred Pictures Naming Test.

Purpose: "A confrontation naming test designed to evaluate rapid naming ability."
Population: Ages 4-6 to 11-11.
Publication Date: 1992.
Acronym: HPNT.
Scores, 3: Error, Accuracy, Time.
Administration: Individual.
Price Data, 1992: $195 per complete kit including manual (84 pages), test book, and 25 response forms; $10 per 25 response forms.
Time: (6) minutes.
Authors: John P. Fisher and Jennifer M. Glenister.
Publisher: Australian Council for Educational Research Ltd. [Australia].

Review of The Hundred Pictures Naming Test by JEFFREY A. ATLAS, Deputy Chief Psychologist and Assistant Clinical Professor, Bronx Children's Psychiatric Center, Albert Einstein College of Medicine, Bronx, NY:

The Hundred Pictures Naming Test (HPNT) is introduced in its test manual as "a confrontation naming test designed to evaluate rapid naming ability across age groups" (manual, p. 1). Given this stated purpose, the HPNT seems to qualify as a "test," and a valuable one, for "preparatory" (preschooler) boys and girls aged 5 to $6^1/_2$, a grouping that constituted roughly 66% of the test reference group of 275 children. The remaining group cells have too few children to provide truly normative data, but may be suggestive in screening subjects who may have language disability or in evaluating recovery of function after brain injury.

The manual and test plates are attractively packaged and sturdy (except for the cardboard test container which will likely be discarded after several uses), but a bit overpriced at $195 for a test with restricted norms and limited generalizability. My sample package contained repeats of the manual pages 1–6 and test plate 18. These are minor distractors that I hope do not reflect overall quality control.

The reference group has nearly equal sex distribution, satisfactory city-suburban-country stratification (64%, 25%, and 11%), but scant socioeconomic information. The fact the test was developed in Australia seems not to have resulted in much content sampling bias. Preliminary inspection for test items that might prompt minor concern suggest "unicorn" and "rake" are words that may be absent from the linguistic environment of preschoolers living in cinder-block projects in New York City, and "koala" and "crown" reflect Australian versus other English-language nationality locales.

The mean "accuracy" score for the reference group was 74.34 (sd = 15.67), with a range of 23 to 98. These numbers comprise expectable figures for a 100-item examination and the linearity of increased test scores by age was impressive, permitting some normative evaluation, especially for preschoolers. Useful indicators for evaluating poor test performance, with some error categories indicating the need for speech therapy, some response categories indicating psychological intervention (e.g., for Selective Mutism), and overall poor lexicon indicating language remediation. The inclusion of 31 speech-language problem youngsters in the reference group provides suggestive screening norms but the low sample number and uneven linearity of scores limits the usefulness of the HPNT as a test for this group. Similarly, the division of the reference group into English First, English Main(ly), and English Only is helpful in qualitative assessment of performance but inadequate in providing test norms.

A useful aspect of the HPNT may be as a monitor of recovery of function after brain injury. Test-retest data (r = .98, after about 1 month for a bit over a fifth of the reference pool) and interrater reliability (r = .97 using a little over a tenth of the pool) furnish adequate criteria for retest using the HPNT. A sample protocol in the manual illustrates 6-year-old Warren's notable improvements in accuracy and significant error reduction, reflecting good recovery of function approximately 7 months following brain injury suffered in a car accident.

In summary, The Hundred Pictures Naming Test offers a useful test of English-only preschoolers' expressive speech accuracy, of recovery of speech function in some aphasias, and a screening device for psychological, environmental, and second-language interferences. As such it represents itself as a useful addition to the armamentarium of speech-language pathologists, early childhood educators, and in a more limited way, English-as-Second-Language instructors.

Review of The Hundred Pictures Naming Test by STEPHEN JURS, Professor of Educational Psychology, Research, and Social Foundations, College of Education and Allied Professions, University of Toledo, Toledo, OH:

The Hundred Pictures Naming Test (HPNT) consists of 100 line drawings of noun objects that are meant to be familiar to both children and adults. The test provides a quick, quantifiable assessment of a person's ability to name familiar things. The HPNT is intended to assess word retrieval through a timed, confrontational naming task. Examinees have up to 5 seconds to respond to each drawing. The drawings are uncluttered, large, and of high quality. The test was developed in Australia, but the pictures are relevant to most developed countries. The content is certainly appropriate for examinees in the United States. The sturdy construction of the bound set of pictures is easy to use and will last through many, many test administrations.

The test is intended for use "by speech pathologists, psychologists, special educators, English-as-a-Second-Language (ESL) teachers, classroom teachers, and other professionals investigating child, adolescent, and adult language" (manual, p. 1). It is unlikely that many classroom teachers would ever use the test, but it could be very useful to the other intended audiences. The HPNT could be an important measure in research about word retrieval and its relation to language. Because this is a new test, we will have to wait to see whether this potential is realized.

The authors identify the competitors as the Boston Naming Test, the Renfrew Word Finding Vocabulary Scale, and the Expressive One-Word Picture Vocabulary Test. The HPNT differs from these tests in that it does not order the words by difficulty level and examinees are to confront each of the 100 words. It is meant to be a measure of word retrieval, not word knowledge. All of the objects pictured are intended to be familiar to persons 8 years of age or older. Thus, the test will be to some extent a measure of vocabulary for examinees whose vocabulary is less than that of an average 8-year-old.

Items were carefully selected in that over 90% of the answers are single words and over half are of one syllable. Items cover nine semantic themes, including objects such as animals, tools, and clothing. The range of consonant and vowel phonemes is well described.

Examiners must be trained in how to administer the items and score the responses within the 5-second-per-picture time limit. There is ample time for an examinee who makes few errors, but it could be challenging for one with many errors because the examiner must not only record how many seconds elapse before the response, but also any misarticulated responses. Self-corrections must be listed. The authors suggest the session be tape recorded for later transcription to the answer sheet. This is probably prudent advice in every case.

A key element in the test administration is strict adherence to the time limits. A timer is required but it is unclear whether the time should be visible to the examinee. The timer runs from the first picture to the last picture to get a measure of total test time. Because there are 100 drawings done in 6 minutes, it would be helpful to determine what proportion of the variance in the times might be due to differences in the examiners rather than in the examinees.

There are several scores reported. An Accuracy score indicates how many of the 100 objects were correctly named. The Time is the number of seconds required to complete the test. Correct responses include variants of the keyed response, delayed rather than immediate responses, and self-corrected responses. Errors include giving the wrong name, giving no name within the 5-second interval, recognizing the object but not being able to name it, and not knowing the object.

Sample response sheets are provided along with narrative interpretations for a variety of examinees. Follow-up procedures that can be used with examinees allow for clarification of responses which, in turn, allows for a richer interpretation of the scores.

The manual contains norms from the "HPNT reference group," which consists of 275 children from the Melbourne suburbs and county Victoria in Australia. About 40% were from recent immigrant or low socioeconomic backgrounds. Ages ranged from 4 years 6 months to 11 years 11 months, but most were between 5 and 8 years old. The reference group is well described but the relevance to other settings may be questioned. Users of the test may get better information from an appraisal of the answer sheets than from a comparison with this set of norms.

Test-retest reliability coefficients for the accuracy scores with $n = 25$ at 4 weeks and $n = 23$ at 5 weeks were both .97. The mean completion time for the retest was 43 seconds faster than on the first test. That is a substantial decrease on a test of 6 minutes at most. The testing time is clearly affected by practice on this test.

The HPNT has been carefully constructed and the authors may eventually develop norms for various age groups of normal and special education populations in and beyond Australia. Until then users should remember the usefulness of this new test has yet to be demonstrated. However, researchers interested in the relationship between confrontational naming and language should consider using The Hundred Pictures Naming Test.

[184]

Hutchins Behavior Inventory.

Purpose: Designed to assess "the interaction of thoughts, feelings, and actions."
Population: High school and over.
Publication Date: 1992.
Acronym: HBI.
Scores, 8: Thinking, Feeling, Acting, Comparison (Thinking-Feeling, Feeling-Acting, Acting-Thinking), Characteristic (Thinking, Feeling, Acting).
Administration: Group.
Price Data, 1992: $45 per 25 tests/answer sheets; $18 per manual (44 pages); $19 per sampler set.
Time: (10–15) minutes.
Authors: David E. Hutchins and Ralph O. Mueller.
Publisher: Consulting Psychologists Press, Inc.
Cross References: See T4:1193 (1 reference).

Review of the Hutchins Behavior Inventory by ISADORE NEWMAN, Professor and Associate Director for the Institute of Life-Span Development and Gerontology, The University of Akron, and Adjunct Professor of Psychiatry, N.E. Ohio Universities College of Medicine, Akron, OH:

PURPOSE OF THE INSTRUMENT. The Hutchins Behavioral Inventory (HBI) was designed to assess an individual's Thoughts (T), Feelings (F), and Actions (A), and the TFA interactions in specific situations. It is based upon the assumption that virtually all behavior can be explained by these components and their interactions. Hutchins and Mueller (the authors) believe their scale is reflective of the positions of theorists such as Ellis, Meichenbaum, Lazarus, Krumboltz, Glasser, and others. It is their contention that the three components measured by this instrument are behaviors over which every individual has some form of control and, therefore, the information derived from this instrument is helpful in diagnosing individual problems, designing intervention strategies, and communicating with clients and other professionals. The authors suggest their instrument is not only appropriate for counseling and psychotherapy but also in many problem-solving and goal-setting situations, as well as for identifying and resolving interpersonal conflicts. The authors further suggest that for the above reasons, this instrument is also potentially useful with groups, organizations, businesses, and industry.

DESCRIPTION OF THE SCORING. The authors present a very clear and easy method for scoring and present several examples to aid in test interpretation of this 75-item forced-choice instrument, which takes approximately 15 minutes. The scale produces three sets of scores: the frequency with which the subject chose a Thinking, Feeling, Acting item; comparison scores produce a relation score for each individual by comparing their actions scores to their thinking scores; their feeling scores to their action scores; and their thinking scores to their feelings scores based upon 25 word pairs, which produces scores ranging from 0–25. The third set of scores is derived from the Characteristics subscales. The purpose of these is to provide more information about the subject's functioning in specific situations, related to their thinking, feeling, and action.

TECHNICAL DATA. The authors present reliability, validity, and some normative data in support of the scales. Test-retest reliability is presented for 7, 14, and 28 days. The test apparently has sufficient test-retest reliability for group prediction on all scales except possibly the Thinking Characteristic Scale (Tc), after 28 days (r = .57). As a rule of thumb, one would want at least a .8 reliability coefficient for individual prediction. The 7-day reliability coefficient, as reported in Table 4.1 in the manual, demonstrates this level of .8 is met for both the TFA scales but misses this criterion for the Characteristics Scales (Tc = .77; Fc = .73, Ac = .68). Virtually none of the scales meet this criterion of .8 for the 14 or 28 days, which is probably acceptable, if one assumes that individuals will change somewhat over time.

The reliability coefficients were based upon one study by Wheeler (1986), who tested 245 males and 344 females, with a mean age of 20 and fewer than 5% minority. It would have been desirable to present separate tables of reliability for males and females.

Another estimate of reliability was done by Mueller, Hutchins, and Vogler (1990) using confirmatory factor analysis to estimate common factor reliability (similar to the concept of internal consistency). They tested 178 students; 94 males and 78 females provided usable responses with an age range of 19–24. They noted that this common factor reliability estimate was estimated after controlling for gender, social economic status, and situation effects. The appropriateness of this approach would be based upon the assumption of no interaction, even though there is no indication they tested for interaction. Personal conversation with Mueller confirmed that interactions were tested and found not to be significant. These statistical results can be found in the dissertation by Mueller (1987).

The factor reliability estimates, presented in Table 4.2 of the manual, indicate the Acting component had the lowest common factor reliability estimate (r = .58), with the other components tending to have higher reliability estimates than were produced by the corresponding test-retest reliabilities. These lower estimates on the Action component may be due to the possibility the items making up this component were not as homogeneous in making up the underlying construct as were the items for the other two components.

There is an inconsistency between Table 4.3 and the text. In the table the TF comparison scores negatively correlated with the Myers-Briggs TF score (-.35), whereas in the text it is a positive .35. The authors indicate this is a typographical error and the positive .35 is correct.

The major validity estimates reported were convergent validity and discriminant validity, as supported by the intercorrelation of the HBI subscales, the intercorrelation of the HBI subscales with the Strong Interest Inventory, and the intercorrelation with the Myers-Briggs, as well as the Adjective Checklist with the HBI Comparison subscales. The other major estimate of validity was a confirmatory factor analysis by Mueller, Hutchins, and Vogler (1990) indicating the data fit the theoretical model well.

It appears from the manual there were three studies supporting reliability (Wheeler, 1986; Mueller, 1987; and Mueller et al., 1990), and four estimates of validity (Wheeler, 1986; Hawkins, 1988; Mueller, 1987; and Mueller et al., 1990). The authors indicate their belief that this instrument has sufficient data to support its use for research purposes. I would concur, but would suggest the following is needed. On the structural equation model that was used to test for goodness of fit, I would like to see some shrinkage estimates to have some estimate of the stability of these relationships. The indication there is a significant difference in gender for the Feeling Component would support the potential value of establishing separate norms and reliabilities for males and females. It would also be useful to have item and scale norms, means and standard deviations, standard error of measurement and/ or standard errors of estimates for each separate study, as well as correlations between items and subscales and items and total scores. Also, additional validity estimates such as predictive validity and known group validity (with hit rates). I see this lack as a shortcoming, based upon how the authors indicate this instrument can or should be used. One additional concern is that the norming sample is somewhat smaller than one would expect.

Overall, I see this instrument as a very useful research tool dealing with a very meaningful concept that appears in the educational psychology literature, and which heretofore has not had any effective methods of evaluation. The use of this instrument as a research tool is consistent with the authors' intentions as identified in the introduction and with the titling of the manual as a research edition.

REVIEWER'S REFERENCES

Wheeler, H. W., Jr. (1986). The reliability and validity of ipsative and normative forms of the Hutchins Behavior Inventory (Doctoral Dissertation, Virginia Polytechnic Institute and State University, 1986). *Dissertation Abstracts International*, 47, 4072A.

Mueller, R. O. (1987). The effects of gender, socioeconomic status, and situation specificity on thinking, feeling, and acting (Doctoral Dissertation, Virginia Polytechnic Institute and State University, 1987). *Dissertation Abstracts International*, 48, 1441A-1442A.

Hawkins, R. E. (1988). The assessment of behavior patterns, personality characteristics and theoretical orientations for master's level counseling students (Doctoral Dissertation, Virginia Polytechnic Institute and State University, 1988). *Dissertation Abstracts International*, 49, 1373A.

Mueller, R. O., Hutchins, D. E., & Vogler, D. E. (1990). Validity and reliability of the Hutchins Behavior Inventory: A confirmatory maximum likelihood analysis. *Journal of Measurement and Evaluation in Counseling and Development*, 22(4), 203-214.

Review of the Hutchins Behavior Inventory by WILLIAM D. SCHAFER, Associate Professor of Educational Measurement, Statistics, and Evaluation, University of Maryland, College Park, MD:

The Hutchins Behavior Inventory (HBI) consists of 75 forced-choice items and is intended to assess three components of behavior in a specific situation: thoughts, feelings, and actions. It is designed to be used with normal adolescents and adults with a reading level of 10th grade or higher. The test may be taken on one side of a machine-scorable answer sheet. There is space on the other side for identification and demographic information. The test begins with a space for the examinee to write a brief description of a situation that is supposed to have been agreed to by the examinee and the examiner. Each item presents a pair of adjectives and the examinee is to choose which is more characteristic of his or her behavior in the situation. The examinee also indicates whether the selected adjective is somewhat, moderately, or very characteristic.

The HBI is based, in part, on the theoretical principles that thoughts, feelings, and actions exist as poles of three dimensions of behavior, that they interact with and affect each other, that they must be evaluated in one specific situation or set of related contexts, and that persons whose behavioral components are more characteristic of them demonstrate more consistent and perhaps more predictable behavior. Each pole can characterize behavior that is advantageous or disadvantageous.

The HBI items are based on the responses of 277 university students who were asked to compile adjectives that describe a thinking, a feeling, and an acting person. From those lists, five nonredundant words were chosen for each characterization. This resulted in five thinking adjectives, five feeling adjectives, and five acting adjectives. The word pairs that form the items on the HBI consist of each adjective paired with all 10 adjectives of the other two types. That yields 25 thinking-feeling pairs, 25 thinking-acting pairs, and 25 feeling-acting pairs to form what are three subscales of the 75 items on the instrument.

Three scorings are derived. The first yields three scores that range from zero to 50, called TFA scores. Each is the number of (T)hinking, (F)eeling, or (A)cting adjectives selected. As the manual authors note, the usefulness of these scores is limited because they are ipsative. The other scorings are nonipsative.

The second scoring results in three scores that are called comparison scores. These range from zero to 25 and each is the number of adjectives of a given pole selected from the relevant 25-item subscale. For example, a large score on the Thinking-Feeling (Tf) dimension is interpreted to indicate relative dominance of thinking over feeling. The other dimensions are noted (Fa) for Feeling-Acting and (At) for Acting-Thinking. A large score is defined as 18–25, and a score of 0–7 indicates dominance of the opposite pole. Scores of 8–17 may indicate either balanced integration or ambivalence.

The third scoring results in characteristic scores. These are three scores based on the somewhat (1), moderate (2), or very (3) responses of the examinee. The thinking characteristic score (Tc) is the average response for the thinking adjectives selected. The other two are similarly derived and are called feeling characteristic (Fc) and acting characteristic (Ac) scores. They range from 1 to 3 (but a score is arbitrarily set at zero if no adjective of that type was selected).

The manual describes a graphic to interpret the comparison scores. An equilateral triangle has as its vertices the three behavioral components: Thinking,

Feeling, and Acting. The three sides correspond to the three dimensions and three equally spaced circles are placed on each side. Each comparison score is categorized by whether a pole is dominant and if so, which one. The examinee's position on each side of the triangle is plotted and the three plotted circles connected by straight lines to form an inner triangle. Although 27 patterns are possible, the manual has a description of eight primary configurations: the three in which only one pole is dominant, the three in which a pair of poles are dominant, one in which no pole is dominant, and one in which each pole is dominant (of which there are two subtypes). Possible advantages and disadvantages (called payoffs and tradeoffs) of each of these are noted.

The manual authors describe eight cases chosen to represent the eight primary configurations. This is an attractive feature. The cases illustrate the desirable practice of interpreting test scores in the context of other information about the person.

Test-retest reliability was evaluated for a sample of undergraduate students over 1 (N = 104), 2 (N = 68), and 4 (N = 229) weeks. The TFA score reliabilities ranged between .70 and .86. The comparison score reliabilities were from .71 to .84 and the characteristic score reliabilities were from .57 to .77.

The comparison and characteristic score reliabilities were further evaluated, along with construct validity, in a confirmatory factor analysis using data from 172 student resident assistants. The model postulated three correlated latent constructs (Thinking, Feeling, Acting), each contributing to variance of the relevant two comparison scores and the relevant characteristic score. The three comparison score common-factor reliability estimates were .93 for Tf, .94 for Fa, and .58 for At. The characteristic score reliabilities were .89 for Tc, .70 for Fc, and .72 for Ac. This same study further evaluated the effects of situations (the HBI was completed for two different situations), gender, and socioeconomic status on the constructs. Statistically, only situations affected thinking and acting and only gender affected feeling.

There appears to be considerable overlap among the constructs. Based on the data in the manual, the observed correlations among the factors were all strong and positive: .7 between Thinking and Feeling, .9 between Thinking and Acting, and .7 between Feeling and Acting. The theoretical implications of this finding are not described in the manual and should be explored. Although the manual authors do suggest that thinking, feeling, and acting components of behavior should be related intrinsically, the argument is not persuasive. For example, there is no discussion of whether the relationship should be direct or inverse, or strong or weak, or even why a strong, direct relationship was observed.

Concurrent and divergent validity was evaluated in one study through correlations of the HBI scales with those on the Strong Interest Inventory (SII; N = 128) and the Myers-Briggs Type Indicator (MBTI; N = 134). Only the HBI comparison scores are described here because the TFA scores are ipsative and not recommended for analysis. These comments are based on a table in the manual. For the HBI At scores, the strongest SII correlation was .19 with Enterprising scores and the strongest MBTI correlation was -.30 with Extroversion-Introversion scores (the manual authors do not comment on the latter, perhaps because it was unexpected). For the HBI Tf scores, the strongest SII correlation was .19 with Realistic scores and the strongest MBTI correlation was -.35 with Thinking-Feeling scores (the latter appears in the text as .35 and is taken to indicate convergent validity; there is clearly a typo). For the HBI Fa scores, the strongest SII correlation was -.21 with Realistic scores and the strongest MBTI correlation was .32 with Thinking-Feeling scores. All other correlations appear to be at chance levels. Although they are from only one study, more complete analyses of these findings should be undertaken before they are interpreted as support of the construct validity of the HBI.

The same study also evaluated the correlations of the three HBI comparison scores (N = 583). As expected, all were negative and statistically significant. The correlation between At and Tf was -.30; the correlation between At and Fa was -.25; and the correlation between Tf and Fa was -.69.

One other study is described. Eighty graduate counseling students were classified by HBI triads. Those within the group for which the Acting and Thinking poles were dominant were found to differ from the other two bipolar and tripolar types on the Achievement, Dominance, Nurturance, Self-Confidence, and Succorance Adjective Check List (ACL) scales and to prefer more behavioral approaches to counseling.

The manual authors emphasize that at this time the HBI should be regarded as a research instrument. That caution is appropriate. There are very few available studies about its reliability and validity. No norms exist, which means that all comparisons are between raw scores on scales that have unknown characteristics. Interpretation, whether for individuals or groups, should be performed very cautiously if at all until these issues have been addressed.

[185]

Imagery and Disease.

Purpose: Constructed to evaluate the process of disease using a combination of guided imagery, relaxation, patient drawings, and structured interview.

Publication Dates: 1978–84.

Administration: Individual.

Price Data, 1994: $20.50 per handbook ('84, 261 pages).

Time: Administration time not reported.
Comments: Previous edition entitled Imagery of Cancer (9:499).
Authors: Jeanne Achterberg and G. Frank Lawlis.
Publisher: Institute for Personality and Ability Testing, Inc.

a) IMAGE-CA.
Population: Cancer patients.
Scores, 14: Disease Dimensions (Vividness of Cancer Cells, Activity of the Cancer Cells, Strength of Cancer Cells), The Body's Defenses (Vividness of White Blood Cells, Activity of White Blood Cells, Numerosity of White Blood Cells, Size of White Blood Cells, Strength of White Blood Cells), Treatment (Vividness of Treatment, Effectiveness of Treatment), General Characteristics of the Imagery (Symbolism, Overall Strength of Imagery, Estimated Regularity of Imagery, Clinical Judgment).

b) IMAGE-SP.
Population: Spinal pain patients.
Scores, 2: Affective, Prediction of Treatment Response.

c) IMAGE-DB.
Population: Diabetic patients.
Scores, 16: Vividness of the Pancreas, Activity of the Pancreas, Strength of the Pancreas, Size of the Pancreas, Vividness of the Beta Cells, Activity of the Beta Cells, Numerosity of the Beta Cells, Size of Beta Cells, Strength of the Beta Cells, Vividness of the Insulin, Quantity of Insulin, Effectiveness of the Insulin, Symbolization Versus Realism, Overall Strength of Imagery, Overall Regularity of the Positive Image, Clinical Impressions.

Review of Imagery and Disease by RAOUL A. ARREOLA, Director of Educational Technology, The University of Tennessee, Memphis, TN:

PURPOSE OF THE INSTRUMENT. The Imagery and Disease evaluation instrument is described by its authors Jeanne Achterberg and G. Frank Lawlis as a diagnostic tool for behavioral medicine. Briefly, behavioral medicine is based on the premise that a person's health, and thus responsiveness to treatment for disease, can be affected by a person's state of mind. Imagery and Disease is based on findings in the literature correlating physiological functioning with the psychological act of imagery. The literature on the physiological effects of the mental imagery process is reviewed in some detail in the manual for Imagery and Disease. The emergence of a new discipline within medicine called "psychoneuroimmunology" is cited from the apparently considerable experimental evidence for the role of the brain in the immune response. Imagery and Disease was created in response to this medical interest in the role imagination (of the patient) plays in the diagnosis and responsiveness to treatment of a disease.

First published in 1978, and then again in 1984, by the Institute for Personality and Ability Testing, Inc., Imagery and Disease is composed of three different tools: PART I: IMAGE-CA; PART II: IMAGE-SP; and PART III: IMAGE-DB. These parts of the tool are intended to provide information on which diagnostic predictions may be made concerning a patient's responsiveness to treatment for (*a*) cancer (CA), (*b*) spinal pain (SP), and (*c*) diabetes mellitus (DB).

All three parts of Imagery and Disease are essentially projective in nature and are clearly intended to be used as a supplement to a clinician's generally accepted medical or psychological diagnostic techniques. As measurement instruments they leave much to be desired from certain technical perspectives described below. However, in the hands of clinical specialists in the diagnosis and treatment of the diseases involved, they may provide an additional avenue of communication between physician and patient which may be of value in and of itself.

PART-I: IMAGE-CA: INTRODUCTION. The IMAGE-CA was developed in response to a need by practitioners for a better understanding of the psychological components of cancer. The objectives for the design of the IMAGE-CA were to (*a*) form a closer communication link between physician and patient, (*b*) assist the patient to participate in the rehabilitation process, and (*c*) allow the physician to anticipate the course of the disease.

ADMINISTRATION. Administration of the IMAGE-CA, as well as the other parts of Imagery and Disease, includes (*a*) listening to a relaxation and guided imagery tape, (*b*) drawing the visualizations, and (*c*) a structured interview. The relaxation and guided imagery tape is a specially scripted audio tape designed to both induce a relaxed state and provide information as to the basic components of the disease. After listening to the tape the patient is then requested to draw on a letter-sized piece of typewriter paper a picture which contains three elements: (*a*) their tumors (or disease, or cancer) as they picture it in their mind's eye; (*b*) their body's defense against the tumor, or white blood cells; and (*c*) their treatment, if any is being received. After having completed the drawing, the patient is asked to discuss these three factors in the form of a structured interview. The authors note that because this is a projective instrument, the skill of the administrator is a major determinant of the amount of clinical information obtained. The authors also note that under no circumstances should the testing take place before a close rapport has been established. The patient's responses to the structured interview are recorded on an Interview Record.

SCORING. The IMAGE-CA results in scores on 14 dimensions (items) related to the patient's responses to the interview questions and the drawing: Vividness of the cancer cell; Activity of the cancer cell; Strength of the cancer cell; Vividness of the white blood cell;

Activity of the white blood cell; Relative comparison of numbers of cancer cells to white blood cells; Relative comparison of the size of cancer cells to white blood cells; Strength of the white blood cell; Vividness of the medical treatment (radiation, chemotherapy, surgery, etc.); Effectiveness of the medical treatment; Concreteness vs. symbolism; Overall strength of imagery, the emotional investment the patient projects to his drawing; Estimated regularity of the number of times per day the patient thinks of his disease in the described way; A clinical opinion by the examiner as to the prognosis for the disease.

Scores for each of the 14 dimensions (items) are produced by using a 5-point scale, the points of which are defined differently for different dimensions (items). From a measurement perspective many of the 5-point scales are flawed in that the anchor points are poorly defined and the scale itself is unbalanced, inconsistent, or both. For example, the rating scale for dimension 1, Vividness of Cancer Cell assigns a value of 1 to *very unclear*, a 2 to *somewhat unclear*, a 3 to *moderately vivid*, a 4 to *quite vivid*, and a 5 to *maximally vivid*. Also, the reliability of the dimension scores is questionable given that each is derived from a single item.

The authors recommend that only experienced examiners who have administered the IMAGE-CA at least 50 times complete Item 14. Item 14 asks the examiner to: "Score imagery on basis of how you would predict it related to disease from a clinical standpoint, i.e., '5' would indicate it predicted complete recovery, a '1' would predict a poor prognosis or death" (manual, p. 28).

Further, the authors note: "As with any projective instrument, the skill of the administrator is a major determinant of the amount of clinical information that is obtained" (manual, p. 35).

The manual contains descriptions of how to score each dimension with sample drawings and excerpts from interview transcripts as examples. However, generally only extreme examples are given. That is, an example of a drawing that would be given a rating of "1" or a description that would warrant a "5" rating are provided. No consistent attempt is made to provide guidelines for discriminating among rating values other than at the extreme ends of the scale.

In determining a patient's overall score, the examiner must combine the ratings of each of the 14 dimensions by (*a*) transforming each raw rating into a weighted score, (*b*) summing the weighted scores, and (*c*) transforming the weighted sum to an overall standard score by means of a table provided. The determination of dimension weights and the normalization procedure used in constructing the table is, at best, methodologically questionable. Rather than go into depth here pointing out the various methodological flaws in the procedure prescribed for the computation of the final score, it is best to quote the authors' own disclaimer as to the usefulness of the score:

> It is mandatory that the clinician keep in mind that the usefulness of this instrument may be justified on a broader perspective than "a score." For example, the content and descriptive terminology may be of greater assistance in facilitating communication between doctor and patient, or greater understanding within the patient, than a quantifiable status. Moreover, the dynamic understanding of relating to another person's concerns about their disease is the goal of this technique, and the score is merely a method of condensing the dimensions to one continuum. (manual, p. 84)

After the dimension scores are weighted and reported on a normalized 10-point scale, the authors conclude by noting that a precise score discrimination is not possible and recommend that the scores be interpreted into one of just three categories: poor prognosis, expected prognosis, or excellent prognosis. Because the competent clinician should be able to make this level of prognosis without the instrument, its value is called into question.

RELIABILITY AND VALIDITY. Two judges were used in the initial reliability study with 58 patients. The reported results yielded a significant concordance ($Chi^2 = 607.23, p<.0001$). Validity of the instrument was determined by conducting a multiple regression analysis on 2-month follow-up data based on objective medical criteria: death, evidence of new tumor growth and degenerative disease, stabilized condition, evidence of reduction in existing tumor(s) and positive process, and evidence of complete absence of tumor(s) or diseases. Two separate regression analyses were computed. The first analysis utilized 13 dimensions, omitting the clinical judgment scale (Dimension 14). Multiple regressions were also conducted using the clinical experience dimension (Dimension 14). Even though both predictions were statistically significant, the impact of clinical experience is reflected in a 25% increase in the variance coefficient.

The validity coefficients were reported as follows: Concurrent Disease Process with clinical judgment: $R = .76$ (R adj. $= .71$); Two-month follow-up without clinical judgment (Dimension 14): $R = .53$ (R adj. $= .50$); Two-month follow-up with clinical judgment (Dimension 14): $R = .78$ (R adj. $= .76$).

CONCLUSION. Because the response scales on which the data used in conducting the reliability and validity analyses are methodologically flawed, the results of these analyses are called into question. Although the administration of the IMAGE-CA may prove useful in increasing the communication between physician and patient, taken purely as a measurement instrument its value is questionable. However, taken as part of an overall diagnostic effort on the part of a physician or clinician expert in the diagnosis of cancer, the IMAGE-CA may provide additional insights that may be of value in helping the patient through the rehabilitative process. As the authors themselves note in their description of the reliability and validity studies:

> Statistical analyses do not reflect the intuition so extremely helpful in determining a patient's investment in his or her own health. The fact that a person's score might be 98 is not a condemnation to an early grave. The health professional is encouraged to use the statistical description to provide a frame of reference for decisions in therapy, but not as the basis for an absolute judgment of heath outcome. (manual, p. 125)

PART II: IMAGE-SP: INTRODUCTION. The IMAGE-SP is intended to use imagery as a tool in assisting the physician or clinician to assess more accurately the location and subjective severity of pain in a patient.

ADMINISTRATION. As with the PART I: IMAGE-CA, the IMAGE-SP relies on a structured interview to solicit information from the patient concerning his or her pain symptoms, methods of pain management, images and feelings about the pain symptoms, attitudes toward the setting where the injury took place, the family's responses, etc. Although no relaxation and imagery tape is used with the IMAGE-SP, it is expected that the examiner will establish a rapport with the patient so as to facilitate disclosure and open communication. A Response Sheet is provided for the structured interview which, in addition to asking for standard demographic information such as name, age, occupation, also asks for information including how the injury occurred, when the pain started, when the pain occurs, and what relieves the pain. The Response Sheet can be used to address several aspects of the social setting that may impede progress including (*a*) pending litigation, (*b*) role in the family, (*c*) duration of chronic pain, (*d*) work history information, (*e*) medical or social complications, and (*f*) any previous treatment failures. The examiner is asked to indicate whether any of these problems are present and whether they are believed to be critical to recovery.

After completing the structured interview, the patient is given a piece of paper on which a symmetrical human figure is outlined. The patient is asked to draw his or her pain on the areas involved, and to indicate the quality of the pain using specific notation. Also on the sheet is a 5-inch line that serves to record perceived percentage of pain in the back versus the legs. The figure drawing is constructed to allow a grid of half-inch squares to be placed over the drawing, yielding a way of quantifying the amount of space the person has invested in pain.

SCORING. There are two methods prescribed for scoring the pain drawing. One determines the affective components of pain and the other method predicts treatment response.

The first method specifies that 2 points be given to pain described in several specific sites such as circumferential thigh pain, or bilateral tibual pain. An extra point is to be given for pain that is dramatized in specific ways such as drawing a circle around a specific pain area, or additional notes written about the pain in a certain area. A typical patient's affective score is indicated to be zero, meaning that none of the affective or psychological aspects are incorporated in the pain symptom. A score of 3 or more is described as indicating evidence of significant psychological influence. The second method of scoring involves overlaying a grid of half-inch squares on the drawing and counting the number of squares that contain any mark or notation representing pain.

According to the authors, in practice the total obtained score for the IMAGE-SP ranges from 1–55, with the average being 10. The critical cutoff score indicating a significant behavioral component to pain is reported as 15.

RELIABILITY AND VALIDITY. An interrater reliability of .85 is reported (two raters, 125 subjects). The grid-counting scoring system resulted in a consistency measure of .97 as reported on a study employing 318 subjects. The precise statistical procedure used in determining these reliability values is not indicated.

The validity of the IMAGE-SP, based on the grid-counting scoring method, was determined by correlating physicians' ratings of the outcome of surgical and rehabilitation procedures (i.e., 1 = poor composite outcome, 2 = average outcome, and 3 = excellent outcome) with the number of squares marked on the grid. Based on an $N = 318$, a statistically significant association between outcome rating and grid score was found ($X^2 = 73.06, p<.001$).

CONCLUSION. The authors of the IMAGE-SP make it clear that the primary purpose of the instrument is to serve as a communication enhancement tool between patient and physician. They recommend that the IMAGE-SP not be used in isolation but that it be used within a battery of other tests intended to determine the physiological, neurological, and psychological condition of the patient relative to the spinal pain problem.

PART III: IMAGE-DB: INTRODUCTION. The IMAGE-DB instrument is designed to elicit the patient's knowledge of and response to diabetes mellitus. In addition, the authors indicate that it was constructed to "inform and redirect false notions about the disease and its impact" (manual, p. 205).

ADMINISTRATION. As with the IMAGE-CA, the IMAGE-DB is administered by first asking the patient to listen to a 20-minute relaxation tape, draw images of the disease, and participate in a structured interview. The specifically scripted tape is designed to encourage the patient to relax as well as to provide information concerning the disease of diabetes and the mechanisms within the body that it affects. After completing the tape, the patient is asked to draw three pictures: (*a*) a drawing of how the patient views his or her pancreas; (*b*) a drawing indicating how the patient sees his or her beta cells working to produce insulin; and (*c*) a drawing indicating how the patient sees the insulin working. Typically the patient is given a piece of letter-sized typewriter paper and a pencil with which to make the drawings. Crayons, marking pens, or paints may also be used, depending upon the patient.

SCORING. A structured interview, using a scoring sheet, results in 16 dimension (item) scores relative to the imagery drawings—four for the drawing of the pancreas, five for the drawing of the beta cells, three for the drawing of the insulin, and four for a general evaluation of the drawings taken altogether. The specific dimensions are: Pancreas: Vividness, Activity, Strength, Size (relative to body); Beta Cells (insulin-producing cells): Vividness, Activity, Numerosity, Size (relative to pancreas), Strength; Insulin: Vividness, Quantity (relative to amount of sugar in blood), Effectiveness; General: How Symbolistic is Visualization vs. How Concrete, Overall Strength of Imagery vs. Weakness, Estimated Regularity of Positive Image, Clinical Impressions.

Scores for each of the 16 dimensions (items) are produced by using a 5-point scale, the points of which are defined differently for different dimensions (items). From a measurement perspective many of the 5-point scales are flawed in that the anchor points are poorly defined and the scale itself is unbalanced. For example, the rating scale for Dimension 1, Vividness of Pancreas assigns a value of 1 to *very unclear*, a 2 to *somewhat unclear*, a 3 to *moderately vivid*, a 4 to *quite vivid*, and a 5 to *maximally vivid*. The reliability of the dimension scores is questionable given that each is derived from a single item.

Item 16, Clinical Impressions, asks the clinician to provide an overall rating of how well it is felt the patient will be doing in the future in terms of personality and motivational factors, as well as physical health. Thus, Item 16 prompts a general evaluation, which the instrument as a whole is intended to provide. Adding the data from this item to the others to produce the total score would appear to rather beg the question of the entire instrument.

The manual contains descriptions of how to score each dimension with sample drawings and excerpts from interview transcripts as examples. However, generally only extreme examples are given. That is, an example of a drawing that would be given a rating of "1" or a description that would warrant a "5" rating are provided. Only a few guidelines for discriminating among rating values other than at the ends of the scale are provided.

In determining a patient's overall score, the examiner must combine the ratings of each of the 16 dimensions by (*a*) summing the raw scores, and (*b*) transforming the raw sum to an overall standard score by means of a table provided. The standard score is based on a normalized distribution with a mean of 5.5 and a standard deviation of 2.0. The converted scores are grouped into five descriptor categories: Very Low, Lower Than Average, Average, Greater Than Average, and Very High. Although these categories are not explained in the manual, it is assumed that they refer to the probability that the patient will respond positively to treatment for diabetes mellitus.

RELIABILITY. Reliability, as internal consistency, yielded an alpha coefficient of .97. Interrater reliability coefficients between two raters on two samples are reported at .82 and .94 respectively. The sample size reported is 72. However, it is not clear if two samples of 72 were employed or whether the 72 subjects reported are the sum of two smaller samples.

VALIDITY. The authors report that the validity of the IMAGE-DB, in terms of the relation of the score to the quality of life, could not be determined. However, the IMAGE-DB score was found to be negatively correlated (r = -.53) with blood glucose levels (sample size = 45). This finding is in keeping with literature citing a relationship between stress and blood glucose levels.

CONCLUSION. The three parts of Imagery and Disease, PART I: IMAGE-CA, PART II: IMAGE-SP, and PART III: IMAGE-DB are not measurement instruments in the generally accepted sense of the word. They are seriously flawed in their construction as rating instruments. As projective tests they are weak in that the interpretation guidelines are incomplete and, at times, cryptic. The score computations employ a unique, if not inappropriate, application of statistics. However, used as the authors repeatedly recommend, that is, as part of a larger, comprehensive clinical diagnosis and treatment procedure, there is no doubt that the instruments can be of some use. In my opinion the primary, if not sole, value of these instruments is to provide a means by which the physician makes a serious, consistent effort to get to know the patient and his or her condition better. The fact that the physician must spend up to an hour with the patient finding out how he or she feels, not only about the disease condition, but about those factors in the patient's life that may affect their recovery, is, in itself, of great value. If used for this purpose, and not for generating "scores" that will later be interpreted in isolation, the Imagery and Disease instruments may be a worthwhile addition to the physician's little black bag.

Review of Imagery and Disease by FRANK M. BERNT, Associate Professor, Department of Education and Health Services, St. Joseph's University, Philadelphia, PA:

The stated objectives of the Image-CA [CA, cancer] and, by implication, of its two more recent applications (Image-DB [DB, diabetes mellitus] and Image-SP [SP, spinal pain]), are three: to provide a closer communication link between physician and patient; to assist the patient in participating in the rehabilitation process through education about the disease process and through developing some level of control over autonomic processes; and to allow the physician to evaluate and to anticipate the course of the disease. In addition to being diagnostic, the instruments are intended also to provide a means for communicating with and for educating patients.

Of the three versions of the Image instrument, those for diabetes and cancer patients are similar in structure; the Image-SP, developed for spinal pain patients, shares common features with the McGill Pain Questionnaire (Melzak, 1975) and is very different from the other two; it will be discussed separately near the end of this review.

IMAGE-CA AND IMAGE-DB. For both the Image-CA and the Image-DB, administration involves three phases. First, the patient listens to a 12-minute audiotape intended to both relax and to educate him or her about the imaging process. The patient is then instructed to draw three pictures depicting how he or she visualizes the disease. Cancer patients (completing the Image-CA) are instructed to draw (*a*) the tumor; (*b*) the body's defenses (white blood cells); and (*c*) how their treatment (if they are receiving any) is working. Diabetes patients (completing the Image-DB) are asked to draw (*a*) the pancreas; (*b*) how beta cells work to produce insulin; and (*c*) how the insulin works. Generally, a pencil and typing paper are used; however, interesting (if very tentative) results have been obtained using color crayons (Trestman, 1981). For both instruments, the final phase involves a structured interview, during which the patient is asked to describe what has been drawn and to verbalize additional feelings and beliefs about the disease in question.

Using both patient drawings and interviews, the physician then rates the patient on a number of dimensions using a 5-point rating scale. There are 14 dimensions for the Image-CA and 16 for the Image-DB. For both instruments, the dimensions address such issues as clarity and vividness of imagery, relative activity of disease process versus healthy body functioning, strength or effectiveness of treatment, and the examiner's clinical judgment regarding prognosis.

Scoring for the two scales differs slightly. For the Image-CA, each subscale is given a different weight, ranging from 1 (e.g., cancer cell vividness) to 14 (clinical judgment). The importance of the clinical judgment dimension is discussed briefly below. Authors recommend that novice scorers (who have completed fewer than 50 supervised administrations) should use only the first 13 dimensions of the Image-CA; different weights are presented in the manual to allow for this. For the Image-DB, all 16 dimensions are weighted equally. In both cases, the end result is a single overall score which, when translated into a sten score, represents the patient's expected prognosis. The patient's prognosis is determined by referring to a table dividing the 10 sten scores into five prognosis categories (extremely lower, slightly lower, average, etc.). There is no indication that individual dimension scores can or should be treated as subscales in either case. Although an exploratory factor analysis has suggested that the Image-CA may be multidimensional rather than unidimensional in character (Trestman, 1981), the issue of dimensionality has not been further investigated.

Evidence for the validity and reliability of the above-mentioned instruments is generally poorly presented and less than adequate. Norms and validation data are based upon very small samples for both tests. Descriptions on the demographic characteristics of these samples are too sparse to allow the reader to determine what target populations are being represented. Although obtained interrater reliability estimates (ranging from .60 to .95 for Image-CA; from .82 to .94 for Image-DB) and internal consistency estimates (.97 for the Image-DB) are promising, further replication is needed using larger and more carefully constructed samples. In addition, the manual is excessively sparse in its inclusion of statistical tables and descriptions of validation procedures (e.g., the level of training possessed by clinicians used in determining interrater reliability).

With regard to concurrent and predictive validity, two multiple regression analyses were performed with Image-CA data using either the first 13 or all 14 dimensions (the 14th being clinical judgment) as predictor variables and using concurrent disease process and 2-month follow-up health status as criterion variables. Apparently, weights for each dimension were determined according to these results, although their stability is highly questionable given the small sizes of the validation samples (*N*s range from 21 to 48). The authors report that, when clinical judgment is included among the predictors, roughly 50% of the variance in both concurrent and future disease process can be accounted for; however, when clinical judgment is omitted as a predictor variable, predictive strength drops to 25%. Apparently, clinical intuition—which comes only after very extensive training—accounts for as much of the explained variance as do the remaining dimensions of the scale.

To further support the concurrent validity of the Image-CA, the authors present zero-order correlations from two separate studies. Roughly 200 low-to-moderate (out of more than 900 possible) correlations are reported; presentation and interpretation of these results are confusing and highly speculative. The potential user is referred to a related article (Achterberg & Lawlis, 1979) that explores these data using canonical analysis. Results suggested three factors underlying intercorrelations: resignation, nondirected struggle, and purposeful treatment.

There is less evidence for the validity of the Image-DB. The total score was found to be moderately correlated with glucose blood levels ($r = -.53$), suggesting that subjects rated high for imagery aptitude possess lower levels of variability in urine and blood sugar (Stevens, 1983). Other efforts to establish either concurrent or predictive validity have not been successful.

The authors report several experimental studies aimed at establishing a cause-effect relationship between the use of imagery and physiological changes. Carefully controlled studies provided tentative evidence to suggest the use of directed imagery can influence neutrophil function (Rider & Achterberg, 1989), providing preliminary support for the use of the Image-CA as an educational tool. It is reasonable to suspect the same advantage might obtain for the Image-DB, although there is no evidence to date to support such a hope.

IMAGE-SP. The Image-SP consists of an interview schedule or response sheet, a pain drawing, and a pain summary sheet. The interview begins with gathering information related to patient background, work history, nature of pain (cause, duration, means of relief, etc.), and family/social factors. The patient is then instructed to relax; at the clinician's discretion, a relaxation tape (similar to those used for the Image-CA and Image-DB) is available for use in facilitating this state. After imagining his or her pain, the patient is instructed to "map" the extent and type of that pain (e.g., aching, burning, pins and needles) using a Pain Drawing Sheet, consisting of front and back body profiles superimposed on a 15 X 16 grid of half-inch squares. This sheet also contains spaces for indicating what percentage of the overall pain occurs in one's back and in one's legs, as well as a visual analogues scale. It yields two scores: an Affective score, which indicates the "psychological aspect" of pain, and a Prediction of Treatment Response score. The Affective scale is calculated using a Pain Drawing Summary Sheet, that involves identifying any reported pain which "does not follow any known neurological pathway" (e.g., total leg pain, bilateral tibial, anterior ankle). A score of 3 or more (out of 24 possible points) indicates "evidence of significant psychological influence." Apparently, the Prediction of Treatment Response score is obtained by counting the number of half-inch squares containing pain symbols; the more squares filled in, the poorer the prognosis. Instructions for scoring are very brief and sometimes unclear; normative data are presented in a single paragraph, with no description of sample characteristics. Several case studies are presented for purposes of illustration. Generally, the treatment and description of the Image-SP is much too brief to allow the reader to administer and to score it with confidence, and it leaves many questions unanswered; for example, the purpose and scoring of the visual analogue scale and the importance of different pain qualities.

There is some support for the interrater reliability of the Image-SP; authors report estimates of .85 and .97 for the Affective and Prediction of Treatment Response scales, respectively (although again, no details concerning either sample characteristics or scorer experience are provided). Results of efforts to establish criterion-related validity provide tentative support for the second scale: High scores were associated with abnormal MMPI profiles, failure to return to work, and poor response to spinal pain rehabilitation. Once again, description of research procedures and vague presentation of results demands the reader base judgement upon faith as much as upon empirical confirmation.

The authors offer the Image-SP as an alternative to the McGill Pain Questionnaire (MPQ; Melzack, 1975), a widely accepted and well-established instrument they dismiss with two brief comments about readability and bias and without fully considering its virtues. Having carefully considered both instruments (see Bernt, 1991 for a full review of the MPQ), this reviewer strongly recommends consideration of the MPQ rather than the Image-SP as a measure of spinal pain; it has been carefully validated in more than a dozen languages and is based upon an explicit and articulate model of pain perception. In contrast, the theoretical basis for the Image-SP is cursory and superficial at best—a three-page discussion of a very complicated subject for measurement.

The Image-SP lacks the projective character of the Image-CA and Image-DB; it is incongruous with its two counterparts in being strictly spatial and quantitative, rather than projective or verbally descriptive, in its character. As such, its inclusion as one of three "imagery instruments" seems unwarranted, conflating the related but clearly distinct issues of pain and disease.

In summary, the three Image instruments are innovative in their methods and aims, but fall well short of acceptable standards in their development and application. Scoring instructions are not clear; validity and reliability data are minimal and in most cases lack rigor both in how studies were conducted and in how data are presented. One would expect that, by now, further validation studies would have been conducted and that more supportive data—if any exist—would have been incorporated into the manual.

The promise of the Image-CA and Image-DB instruments seems to lie in their potential as tools for communication and education. Inasmuch as the manual contains a wealth of patients' descriptions and images of their diseases, these instruments may also provide a very useful method of investigating what such illnesses mean to the patients experiencing them. Such understanding may also assist the patient in unlearning counterproductive ways of thinking about disease. Accordingly, the first and second objectives stated at the beginning of this review may be within the reach of the Image instruments; at present, a great deal more careful work is required before their diagnostic or predictive value can be affirmed.

REVIEWER'S REFERENCES

Melzack, R. (1975). The McGill Pain Questionnaire: Major properties and scoring methods. *Pain*, *1*, 277-299.

Achterberg, J., & Lawlis, G. F. (1979). A canonical analysis of blood chemistry variables related to psychological measures of cancer patients. *Multivariate Experimental Clinical Research*, *4*, 1-10.

Trestman, R. L. (1981). *Imagery, coping, and physiological variables in adult cancer patients*. Unpublished doctoral dissertation, University of Tennessee, Knoxville.

Stevens, L. (1983). *An intervention study of imagery with diabetes mellitus*. Unpublished doctoral dissertation, North Texas State University, Denton, TX.

Rider, M. S., & Achterberg, J. (1989). Effect of music-assisted imagery on neutrophils and lymphocytes. *Biofeedback and Self Regulation*, *14*(3), 247-257.

Bernt, F. M. (1991). [Review of the McGill Pain Questionnaire.] In D. J. Keyser & R. C. Sweetland (Eds.), *Test Critiques* (Vol. 8, pp. 402-412). Austin, TX: PRO-ED, Inc.

[186]

Impact Message Inventory, Research Edition.

Purpose: "Designed to measure . . . interpersonal style."
Population: College.
Publication Dates: 1975–87.
Acronym: IMI.
Scores, 15: Dominant, Competitive, Hostile, Mistrustful, Detached, Inhibited, Submissive, Succorant, Abasive, Deferent, Agreeable, Nurturant, Affiliative, Sociable, Exhibitionistic.
Administration: Group.
Forms, 2: Male Targets, Female Targets.
Price Data, 1992: $17 per 25 test booklets (select Male or Female); $14 per 50 answer sheets; $15 per manual ('87, 60 pages); $16 per specimen set.
Time: [15] minutes.
Comments: Self-report inventory.
Author: Donald J. Kiesler.
Publisher: Consulting Psychologists Press, Inc.
Cross References: See T4:1205 (13 references); for reviews by Fred H. Borgen and Stanley R. Strong of an earlier edition, see 9:500 (1 reference); see also T3:1130 (1 reference).

TEST REFERENCES

1. Hoyt, W. T. (1994). Development and awareness of reputations in newly formed groups: A social relations analysis. *Personality and Social Psychology Bulletin*, *20*, 464-472.

2. McCullough, J. D., McCune, K. J., Kaye, A. L., Braith, J. A., Friend, R., Roberts, W. C., Belyea-Caldwell, S., Norris, S. L. W., & Hampton, C. (1994). Comparison of community dysthymia sample at screening with a matched group of nondepressed community controls. *The Journal of Nervous and Mental Disease*, *182*, 402-407.

3. McCullough, J. D., McCune, K. J., Kaye, A. L., Braith, J. A., Friend, R., Roberts, W. C., Belyea-Caldwell, S., Norris, S. L. W., & Hampton, C. (1994). One-year prospective replication study of an untreated sample of community dysthymia subjects. *The Journal of Nervous and Mental Disease*, *182*, 396-401.

4. Tan, J. C. H., & Stoppard, J. M. (1994). Gender and reactions to dysphoric individuals. *Cognitive Therapy and Research*, *18*, 211-224.

Review of the Impact Message Inventory, Research Edition by STEPHEN L. BENTON, Professor of Educational Psychology, Kansas State University, Manhattan, KS:

The Impact Message Inventory (IMI) measures the interpersonal style of a target person as experienced by others. Respondents who are familiar with the target person describe their feelings, actions, and perceptions about that person. They respond to 90 statements, each having a 4-point scale that indicates the extent to which the target person evokes feelings, actions, or perceptions (where 1 = *not at all*, 2 = *somewhat*, 3 = *moderately so*, and 4 = *very much so*). Male and female forms are included. Similar instruments might include the Interpersonal Check List (T4:1252), the Interpersonal Behavior Inventory (Lorr & McNair, 1967), and the Interpersonal Adjective Scales (Wiggins, 1981), although the author cautions that the IMI differs significantly from these.

TEST DEVELOPMENT. To develop the 90 statements, the author initially wrote 15 paragraph descriptions of "pure" interpersonal styles based on items from Lorr and McNair's (1967) Interpersonal Behavior Inventory. No information is provided about the validity of those 15 paragraph descriptions. He then gave the 15 descriptions to six members of his research team and directed them to write free-response convert reactions to each description using the sentence stem, "He makes me feel. . . ." It is unclear why he did not select a more representative sample from the general population for this task. Through group consensus, the team agreed on 259 responses that were descriptive of one or more of the 15 interpersonal styles. The author then assigned 451 undergraduates (method of selection not described) randomly to 1 of 15 paragraph description groups. The students responded to each of the 259 statements using a 4-point scale to indicate the degree to which a statement accurately described their reactions to the paragraph description. For each of the 15 interpersonal styles, the six statements with the highest mean ratings were selected. The decision to select six items each seemed arbitrary.

RELIABILITY. Correlations of each item with the item total (minus the particular item score) yielded coefficients ranging from .57 to .99 in the sample of 451 undergraduates. The magnitude of these correlations is astounding, with mean subscale correlations ranging from .80 to.99. However, the author acknowledged that those coefficients reflect internal consistency of the IMI for the 15 paragraph descriptions, not actual target persons. It is more difficult to assess the internal consistency of the IMI for a target person because of error variance attributable to differences among target persons, respondents, and the interactions between target persons and respondents. Measures of stability also would be confounded because test-retest differences might reflect changes in the relationship between the interactants.

Given the high item-total correlations, why did the author not use factor analysis to reduce the number of items on the test? A worthy goal would be to reduce the number of items while still maintaining adequate internal consistency.

The author attempted to establish some reliability through an intact-sample actor study. The actors (target persons) consisted of late adolescent and adult psychiatric patients of both sexes. The respondents were clinical psychology trainees who each completed an IMI on a patient after an intake session. Kuder-Richardson coefficients ranged from .54 to .798 for the 15 subscales.

Employing a homogeneous-sample actor design, Reagan (1978, 1979) identified groups of undergraduates who varied in assertiveness. She then videotaped them in experimental sessions, and observers filled out IMIs on each subject. Ebel intraclass coefficients for the extent of observer agreement ranged from .12 to .82 with a mean of .65 for scale scores. In a similar study, Nelson (1983) also found that certain observer pairs were more consistent than others.

The reliability of the IMI remains a complex issue. The author correctly advises users to rely more on the four cluster scores (described below) than on the individual scale scores because of the small number of items associated with the latter. However, potential users should be aware of the numerous sources of error variance that contribute to both cluster and scale scores.

VALIDITY. Principal components analysis (varimax rotation) revealed three factors from the sample of 451 undergraduates. Nonetheless, the author recommends calculating four factor or cluster scores. Analyses performed on scores from a sample of psychiatric patients yielded a different factor structure. Therefore, users should interpret cluster scores cautiously.

Gender differences may affect respondent scores. Male respondents respond more strongly to the Submissive, Succorance-seeking, and Abasive subscales than do female respondents. Males also score higher on the Mistrust subscale when rating female targets, whereas female respondents have greater Mistrust for male targets. Male respondents also score higher on Agreeableness and Nurturance when rating male targets than when rating female targets.

NORMATIVE DATA. No normative data exist.

SUMMARY. The dyadic nature of the IMI presents problems for reliability, validity, and normative data. Further research must be done on live interactants before I would recommend its use for clinical decisions.

REVIEWER'S REFERENCES

Lorr, M., & McNair, D. (1967). The Interpersonal Behavior Inventory: Form 4. Washington, DC: Catholic University of America.

Reagan, S. A. (1978). *The Impact Message Inventory: An interpersonal measure of assertive behavior*. Unpublished master's thesis, Virginia Commonwealth University, Richmond, VA.

Reagan, S. A. (1979). The interpersonal and behavioral dimensions of assertive refusal. *Dissertation Abstracts International, 40*, 5416-B. (University Microfilms No. DEM80-11255)

Wiggins, J. S. (1981). Revised Interpersonal Adjective Scales. Vancouver: University of British Columbia.

Nelson, A. P. (1983). Rigidity in the interpersonal functioning of psychiatric patients and normals. *Dissertation Abstracts International, 44*, 2902-B. (University Microfilms No. DA83-26839)

Review of the Impact Message Inventory, Research Edition by STEVEN G. LoBELLO, Associate Professor of Psychology, Auburn University at Montgomery, Montgomery, AL:

The Impact Message Inventory (IMI) is a paper-and-pencil instrument that is designed to measure the "interpersonal consequences" that an individual's behavior has on an observer. The inventory consists of 90 items and 15 interpersonal categories or scales (e.g., Dominant, Competitive, Agreeable); the items are also grouped into sets of 30 under three different sentence stems. Each grouping of 30 items makes up a category of response type that the authors have labeled Direct Feelings, Action Tendencies, and Perceived Evoking Messages. An example of the sentence stems is, "When I am with this person he (or she) makes me feel . . ." (examples of items used to complete the sentence stems are uneasy, admired, cold, I could ask her to do anything).

Separate forms are available for male and female "targets" and the items on each form are identical except for pronouns. Responses are made on a separate answer sheet using a 4-point Likert scale, where 1 = *not at all* and 4 = *very much so*. First introduced in the 1970s, the IMI was designed to measure the 15 interpersonal styles of Leary (1957) and to be consistent with the circumplex dimensions of Lorr and McNair's (1967) Interpersonal Behavior Inventory (both studies cited in test manual).

In the manual, it is emphasized that the IMI is neither a self-report inventory nor a systematic rating of some other's behavior. It is a transactional inventory that attempts to measure the impact of one person's behavior on another. As such, some unique problems attend to such issues as establishing score stability and norms, which are discussed later.

The IMI is intended for use with late adolescents and adults in the "normal, psychoneurotic, and personality disorder range" (manual, p. 16). Originally cast as a method of evaluating therapist-client relationships, there is potential utility in the IMI for studying husband-wife, parent-adolescent, employer-employee, and other dyadic interactions. Scoring is relatively straightforward: The average score on the six items of each interpersonal scale provides the scores for these dimensions. Twelve of the component scale scores can then be used to calculate four Cluster scores (Dominant, Hostile, Submissive, Friendly). As mentioned above, three subscales can also be obtained by separately scoring items that measure direct feelings, action tendency, or perceived evoking messages. It is not recommended that this be done at the level of the interpersonal scales, because each scale has only two items from each domain.

The problem with establishing traditional norms for the IMI is that consideration must be given not only to the characteristics of the actor, but also the characteristics of the observer. At a very basic level, one example of this dilemma would be seen if same-gender and cross-gender ratings of an actor's behavior were to differ. Racial, age, and personality differences between actor and observer makes the construction of a definitive normative group (or normative subgroups) a difficult undertaking. When one considers that the nature of the interaction would also figure into the development of norms, the problems associated with this task increase exponentially. The original "norms" of the IMI were developed by having undergraduate students respond to written descriptions of "pure" interpersonal behaviors based on the items of the Interpersonal Behavior Inventory (Lorr & McNair, 1967). The means and standard deviations derived from this sample for each scale are provided in the manual, but these are of limited usefulness because they are based on undergraduates' responses to written descriptions of behavior. Moreover, the unique variance attributable to the interaction between actor and observer may not be adequately accounted for in these norms.

The IMI manual points out that ipsative scoring may be more sensible for some research and counseling applications. The recommended procedure is to routinely conduct ipsative *and* normative analysis, a practice that has been criticized elsewhere (Anastasi, 1988). Beyond this advice, the IMI manual includes a table listing 38 studies that have generated information about various subject groups that may be helpful to researchers.

The 15 IMI scales are not all independent. Scale intercorrelations utilizing Q coefficients reveal values ranging from .00 to .95. Internal consistency for the individual scales ranges from .80 to .99, using the method of averaging correlations between item and sum (minus the particular item). In an earlier review, Borgen (1985) commented that this method of estimating reliability was "certain to give inflated values" (p. 679). The final chapter of the IMI manual is a summary of many studies that have used the IMI as a measure, and that provide some evidence as to its validity. Score stability is also difficult to assess. If two people interact on two different occasions, the second rating will be influenced not only by the passage of time, but also by the nature of the first encounter.

The Impact Message Inventory is not a typical personality test and it does not lend itself to conventional psychometric analysis. It would be much neater to be able to evaluate the IMI from this conventional perspective, but the difficulties of satisfying these demands are acknowledged and adequately explained in the manual. The instrument is labeled a Research Edition, which implies that it may not be developed to the point where it can be recommended for everyday clinical use. However, practitioners may wish to use the IMI as an adjunctive measure in counseling marital partners in distress, for example, or in any setting where informal study of transactional impacts is desired.

REVIEWER'S REFERENCES

Lorr, M., & McNair, D. (1967). The Interpersonal Behavior Inventory: Form 4. Washington, DC: Catholic University of America.

Borgen, F. H. (1985). [Review of the Impact Message Inventory: Form II.] In J. V. Mitchell, Jr. (Ed.), *The ninth mental measurements yearbook* (pp. 678-679). Lincoln, NE: Buros Institute of Mental Measurements.

Anastasi, A. (1988). *Psychological testing* (6th ed.). New York: Macmillan Publishing.

[187]

Individualized Criterion Referenced Testing.

Purpose: "Designed to measure student achievement against a specific set of math and reading objectives."
Publication Dates: 1973–90.
Acronym: ICRT.
Administration: Individual or group.
Price Data: Price information available from publisher for test material including technical manual ('90, 81 pages), teacher's guide for Reading ('90, 87 pages), and teacher's guide for Math ('90, 79 pages).
Time: Administration time not reported.
Comments: Designed to be taken at the student's functional level rather than grade level; each student takes 5 booklets measuring 40 objectives; each test booklet contains 16 items measuring 8 objectives; computer scoring with 10-day turnaround available from publisher; administration time varies with individual students.
Authors: Wanda M. Richardson, Deanna Thompson, Jo Riffe, and Anna Mae Callaway.
Publisher: Educational Development Corporation.

a) ICRT MATH.
Population: Grades 1, 2, 3, 4, 5, 6, 7, 8, 9.
Acronym: ICRTM.
Scores: Total score only.
Comments: Skills are tested in six strands: Whole Number Operations, Measurement, Decimal-Percent, Fractions, Geometry, Special Topics; criterion and norm-referenced scores.

b) ICRT READING.
Population: Grades 1, 2, 3, 4, 5, 6, 7, 8.
Acronym: ICRTR.
Scores: Total score only.
Comments: Skills are tested in four strands: Phonetic Analysis, Structural Analysis, Word Function, Comprehension; criterion and norm-referenced scores.

Cross References: For a review of ICRTM by Jane Dass, see 8:275; for reviews of ICRTR by Ruth N. Hartley and Martin Kling, see 8:764.

Review of the Individualized Criterion Referenced Testing by SHERRY K. BAIN, Visiting Assistant Professor of Psychology, University of Southern Mississippi, Hattiesburg, MS:

DESCRIPTION. The Individualized Criterion Referenced Testing (ICRT) was originally published in 1973. Since that time several updates have been performed, including renorming and the addition of items covering higher order thinking skills in reading comprehension and math problem solving.

TEST ADMINISTRATION AND USEFULNESS. This test offers several conveniences for prospective users. Test booklets are reusable, reducing expenses. Booklets at sequenced difficulty levels allow for test tailoring for individual students. The test is untimed and can be administered over several days, with students working at their own pace.

The publisher's scored result formats provide potentially useful information, linking test mastery to basal reader levels, and correlating nonmastered objectives to available instructional resources. Information on the documented success of interventions based upon ICRT evaluations is not offered.

A parallel form of the test, labeled Benchmark is available and recommended by the authors for use in interim testing during instructional intervention. Although items are said to measure the same objectives as the standard test booklets, no alternate form reliability information is offered for the Benchmark test.

STANDARDIZATION, RELIABILITY, AND VALIDITY. The ICRT originally provided only criterion-referenced results. In response to demands from users and Chapter 1 reporting regulations, normative data (percentile scores and normal curve equivalents) were provided in 1979. The ICRT updated its standardization for the current revision in spring and fall, 1989, testing 30,000 subjects. The technical manual authors compare the normative group with published census and educational statistics from 1973 and 1976, respectively. Proportions by geographic area and ethnic group appear to match closely, but comparison to more recent census data would lend more credibility to the information.

For the normative testing, students sitting for the fall test were administered test booklets for the previous grade level to avoid frustration, especially for entering first graders. Ability estimates and average ability were based upon the spring results, and fall score distributions were recentered lower on the achievement scale. Internal consistency reliabilities (Kuder-Richardson Formula 20) for normative testing of both reading and math fell above .90.

Content validity was studied in fall 1979 using a panel of expert consultants. The consultants were asked to judge objectives for appropriateness, clarity, and sequencing correctness; to judge test items for whether each reflected its matching objective; and to judge for technical soundness (e.g., ambiguous statements). Following this study, the authors reported they modified deficient objectives and items. Since then, 289 additional math items and 386 additional reading items were field tested and included in the current testing form (Form C). Content validation of revised items and additions is not reported in the technical manual and is necessary to judge the validity of the present test form.

The technical manual authors report two reliability studies, both using decision-consistency methods. Although the ICRT has a trichotomous criterion standard, based upon mastery, partial mastery, or nonmastery of each objective, decision-consistency studies were based upon dichotomous standards with partial mastery classified as nonmastery. In the first study, using 1978 and 1979 normative data and methodology developed by Subkoviak (1976), the authors reported that 80% of the students were consistently classified for more than 98% of the objectives. The authors noted that Subkoviak's method can result in overestimates for short tests, such as those represented by ICRT test booklets. The second reliability study, for the ICRT Reading only, was carried out by Byars (1979) using Huynh's (1976) statistical method. This study resulted in an average level of consistency of classifications across reading objectives of approximately 70%, a more conservative value than reported above. Both reliability studies were carried out on the test booklets developed before 1979. No reliability studies on updated booklets are reported.

Concurrent validity was examined, also using the 1978–79 normative data. Correlations for ICRT math and reading subtests ranged from .67 to .84 compared to results of the Metropolitan Achievement Test. Again, concurrent validity for the newly normed test edition is not reported.

SUMMARY AND RECOMMENDATIONS. The publishers have made several efforts to improve the ICRT since first publication. Although the present technical manual contains information on reliability and validity, data are based predominantly upon the previous test forms and the 1978–79 normative sample. For proper evaluation of the current form, with its item additions, updates, and normative sample, new studies on reliability and validity should be carried out. Because the test now provides normative data, standard test-retest reliability information should definitely be presented. For the renormed test, only internal consistency reliability data are listed in the technical manual. Decision-consistency reliability is helpful but applies only to the criterion-referenced use and not to normative reporting and interpretations. Other desirable information not included in the technical manual are data on ethnic or racial bias, especially important when test data are used in a normative manner. A construct validity study should also be considered because objectives fall into content domains.

The Teacher's Guide contains no information on the use or interpretation of normative scores; test publishers should include a section or supplement addressing this. Particularly important would be the advantages or limitations of interpreting normative test data based upon relatively homogeneous test items.

The ICRT appears to be well designed administratively, and may be useful as an objective-linked test, offering information about related basal reading levels and available instructional material. Suggestions are that potential users carefully examine individual objectives to determine if there is an adequate match with the local curriculum. Updated validity and reliability information are lacking, and users should be extremely cautious in using the normative information for interpretation.

REVIEWER'S REFERENCES

Huynh, H. (1976). On the reliability of decisions in domain-referenced testing. *Journal of Educational Measurement, 13*, 253-264.

Subkoviak, M. J. (1976). Estimating reliability from a single administration of a criterion-referenced test. *Journal of Educational Measurement, 13*, 265-276.

Byars, A. G. (1979). Performance indices of the "Individualized Criterion Referenced Tests." *A report from the Office of Evaluation and Research*. Charleston, SC: Charleston Public Schools.

Review of the Individualized Criterion Referenced Testing by RICK LINDSKOG, Director of School Psychology Program and Associate Professor of Psychology and Counseling, Pittsburg State University, Pittsburg, KS:

The Individualized Criterion Referenced Testing (ICRT) is intended to be as the name implies, a comprehensive criterion-referenced testing system for grades K–8 in the areas of reading and math. Norm-referenced scores are also provided.

Both reading and math tests are accomplished by evaluating groups of students according to specific ability levels. As such, it is recommended the teacher obtain information on each child's reading and math levels to determine the correct entry levels for math and reading. The Reading test has a bank of 38 booklets (344 objectives) and the Math test has a bank of 51 booklets (384 objectives). In order to assess skill levels adequately (i.e., already mastered, needs to review, and needs to learn), each pupil is tested with five levels of booklets in reading and five in math. As noted, the levels are determined by the child's current estimated instructional level.

There is no time limit for test administration, and the manual authors specify the ICRT is intended to be a power test. In that all students will be tested with 5 booklets in each area, it is necessary for teachers to plan activities for students who complete their books rapidly and who must, therefore, wait for others to finish. Because each pupil will use 10 booklets from the 99 available, and the teacher must prepare and fill out multiple forms and transcribe the data onto a computer-bubble scoring format, considerable planning and organization are required. Older students can directly fill in the answer sheet, which will be computer scored.

All completed tests are then sent to the Educational Development Corporation for computer scoring. A hand-scoring template is available, but the computer-scoring service provides processing, printing, and shipping of the test results.

The results are transmitted in criterion-referenced and normative forms for both the math and reading areas. The norm-referenced administrative summary contains scale scores, grade equivalents, percentile ranks, and normal curve equivalencies (NCEs). The criterion-referenced format contains the total number of objectives in each booklet and the total number of objectives mastered. Where pre- and posttest data are submitted, the report includes matched scores and the average gains. The *number* of students and *percent* of students by quartile are also provided.

The administrative report describes pupil performance by class, building, and district. Domain objectives are listed by domain area by indicating a mastery level: mastered, needs review, or needs to be learned.

The instructional grouping (by domain/objective) report summarizes which pupils need to review or learn an objective. For example, in the domain of Geometry, Billy L., Sara H., and Jane P. all need to review identifying the diameter of a circle. This report groups students by specific deficit area.

The individual student summary is a report which outlines, item by item, which objectives have been mastered, which objectives need review, and which objectives need to be learned. All objectives are keyed to instructional material codes so that a teacher may reference appropriate instructional materials.

The manual authors indicate that in 1972 and 1973 over 80,000 students in grades K–8 participated in the development of the ICRT, and the instrument has been periodically updated. The most recent efforts were in 1979 and 1989. Only grouped data were provided in the technical manual.

In 1979 committees of content specialists judged the instrument on the basis of appropriateness, clarity, sequencing, alignment with objectives, and technical soundness of the reading objectives. The specialists found that 93.5% to 95.8% of the items met these standards. The agreement for math objectives was somewhat lower ranging from 83.1% to 98.4%. Objectives were revised on the basis of these data.

The reliability of the ICRT Reading and Math scores was determined using a method developed by Subkoviak (1976) for single administration criterion-referenced instruments. The authors note "one shortcoming of Subkoviak's method is that with short tests it will produce estimates of decision consistency which are substantial overestimates of those which would be obtained from a test-retest or a parallel-form reliability study" (teacher's guide, p. 12). The results indicated that for 98% of the objectives, slightly more than 80% of pupils would be consistently classified as master or nonmaster. This estimate is, however, positively influenced by statistical artifact. These data were computed from 1978–1979 data, however, and the authors state that "it is expected that the reliabilities of the reorganized and improved test booklets would be in the same range" (p. 12). In another study, which used a more complex method developed by Huynh (1976), Byars (1979) found mastery/nonmastery classifications were at the 70% level for reading objectives only.

The norming of the test aligns with 1976 demographics, and provides for four geographic regions and ethnicity (Black, Hispanic, White, and other). These norms are obviously outdated and there was a significant level of estimation in deriving the ethnic representation.

Tables provided in the manual convert raw scores to percentile ranks and normal curve equivalents (NCE) scores. The tables are based on a fall date of October 15 and a spring date of May 12. A formula is provided to adjust a score for early or late administration dates. The norming took place in the spring and fall of 1989. The sample population adequately aligned with 1976 data from the National Center for Educational Statistics of Public and Secondary Schools. However, the same characteristics were matched for four regions and ethnicity (Black, Hispanic, White, and other). There are also scaled scores available, and NCE scores are available as well.

Concurrent validity with the Metropolitan Achievement Test was studied during the 1979 norming study. For grades 2–8 in both fall and spring the reading area demonstrated correlations varying from .70 to .84, and for the math area from .67 to .82.

SUMMARY. The ICRT is an adequate instrument to measure reading and math skills of elementary school-age students. The instrument has extensively documented information regarding the propriety of its domains and individual items. The reliability data are outdated (as are the norms) and overworked. The instrument is quite complicated to use; extensive organizational planning must be done to administer this instrument in a meaningful way. One major obstacle to using this test is the necessity of the teacher transcribing data to computer sheets; in a large class this would amount to a considerable time commitment. Although hand-scoring plates are provided, the instrument data really require the purchase of the publisher's computer scoring services. The materials provided offered no software for local use.

I conclude this instrument would require a broad commitment of the entire system to using this assessment and its computerized scoring/reporting system. This extensive commitment, along with the aforementioned weaknesses in the technical base, lead this reviewer to recommend prospective purchasers to explore the myriad of curriculum-based assessment alternatives delineated in the *School Psychology Review* (vol. 18(3), 1989, Rosenfield & Shinn). The current emphasis on outcomes better aligns with measurement systems such as those presented in the above-mentioned *School Psychology Review*.

Those districts without in-house expertise to establish and maintain program evaluation may wish to purchase a system like the ICRT.

REVIEWER'S REFERENCES

Huynh, H. (1976). On the reliability of decision in domain-referenced testing. *Journal of Educational Measurement, 13*, 253-264.

Subkoviak, M. J. (1976). Estimating reliability from a single administration of the criterion-referenced test. *Journal of Educational Measurement, 13*, 265-276.

Byars, A. G. (1979). Performance indices of the "Individualized Criterion Referenced Tests." *A report from the Office of Evaluation and Research*. Charleston, SC: Charleston Public Schools.

Rosenfield, S., & Shinn, M. R. (Eds.). (1989). Mini-series on curriculum-based assessment. *School Psychology Review, 18*(3).

[188]

Infant/Toddler Environment Rating Scale.

Purpose: Developed to assess "the quality of center-based child care for children up to 30 months of age."
Population: Infant/toddler day care centers.
Publication Date: 1990.
Acronym: ITERS.
Scores, 8: Furnishings and Display for Children, Listening and Talking, Personal Care Routines, Learning Activities, Interaction, Program Structure, Adult Needs, Total.
Administration: Individual.
Price Data, 1993: $8.95 per rating scale; $7.95 per 30 scoring sheets.
Time: (120) minutes to observe and rate.
Comments: Adaptation of the Early Childhood Environment Rating Scales (9:365) and the Family Day Care Rating Scale (T4:960).
Authors: Thelma Harms, Debby Cryer, and Richard M. Clifford.
Publisher: Teachers College Press.

Review of the Infant/Toddler Environment Rating Scale by NORMAN A. CONSTANTINE, Senior Associate, Far West Laboratory for Educational Research and Development, San Francisco, CA:

The Infant/Toddler Environment Rating Scale (ITERS) completes a triad of rating scales designed to measure the quality of early childhood day care across different age groups and settings. Derived from the Early Childhood Environment Rating Scale (ECERS, T4:833) and also related to the Family Day Care Rating Scale (FDCRS, T4:960), the ITERS employs items developed or revised specifically for infant and toddler group care (covering ages birth through 30 months).

The ITERS consists of 35 items grouped into the seven categories of Furnishings and Display for Children, Personal Care Routines, Listening and Talking, Learning Activities, Interaction, Program

Structure, and Adult Needs. Each category contains from two to nine items. Each item is rated on a 7-point scale with detailed criteria at 1 (inadequate), 3 (minimal), 5 (good), and 7 (excellent). The ITERS is advertised as being comprehensive in coverage yet easy to use. The authors recommend its use by caregiving staff as a self-assessment, by directors and supervisors as a program quality measure for program planning, by agency staff for monitoring, and in research.

The items and a scoring sheet are published in a booklet together with three pages of background and instructions. A video training tape (Harms & Cryer, 1991) is now available from the publisher, although this was not mentioned in the published instrument booklet. An unpublished research report describing the reliability and validity study is available from a separate source (Clifford et al., 1989).

The booklet provides an explicit algorithm for assigning item ratings at the four anchor points and at the three points between anchors. This is useful, although these instructions could be clearer and some specific examples would help. Administration of the scale will require both on-site observation and interviewing of staff. The authors suggest that 2 hours be allocated for observation by an outside observer. This assumes good familiarity with the detailed item criteria, as well as efficient scheduling to be able to observe during any 2-hour period all or most of the various activities that are to be rated. The score sheet provides space for subscale totals, but no instructions are provided on how to compare scores across subscales, which are based on varying numbers of items. The user must infer that each subscale score should be divided by the number of items in the subscale. No norms are provided, nor is any guidance in interpreting and using the results.

RELIABILITY. A comprehensive reliability and validity study was conducted prior to publication of the test. Unfortunately, the short summary provided in the instrument booklet is inadequate and does not do justice to this work. To obtain a copy of the unpublished study required four phone calls over 3 weeks. This is more effort than is reasonable to expect from a potential test user. Interpretation of results of this study is somewhat hampered by the restricted range of quality found in the 30 classrooms observed by two observers each. Of the 60 observations reported, 75% yielded average item scores below "minimal," with only one observation averaging at or above the "good" criteria for individual items. Reliability estimates might differ with a wider sample, possibly but not necessarily in the direction of larger estimates.

Exact agreement on individual items between both members of observer pairs was disappointing, ranging from 25% to 77% of observers agreeing for each item. Only 12 of the 35 items yielded exact observer agreements for more than half of the classes observed. Somewhat more reassuring were the agreements within plus or minus one point, ranging from 53% to 100% of the classrooms (observation pairs). Twenty-nine of the 35 items yielded agreement within one point for at least 70% of the classrooms. Spearman rank order interrater correlations for individual items ranged from .34 to 1.0, whereas subscale correlations ranged from .58 to .89, and the full scale correlation was .84.

The total score test-retest correlation over 3–4 weeks was .79, with subscale correlations ranging from .58 to .82. The total score coefficient alpha was .83, and ranged on the subscales from lows of .26 and .41 to a high of .79. The authors of the reliability study appropriately recommend that the two internally inconsistent subscales (Program Structure and Adult Needs) not be used in research (however, this caution never made it into the instrument booklet).

VALIDITY. No effort was spared in demonstrating the excellent content validity of this instrument. These analyses were based on a comprehensive cross-instrument review against eight sets of quality standards and other rating scales, together with item importance ratings by an impressive national panel. The only complaint here is that the cross-instrument matrix was not provided with the reliability report.

The case for criterion-related validity was not as well made. The authors relied on agreements between the ITERS and experts' judgements on gross classifications of six classrooms into either high or low quality. Future research should attend more thoroughly to construct validity. One way this could be accomplished would be to investigate whether the ITERS is sensitive to changes in program quality as a result of training or programmatic structural changes. Interscale correlations also should be calculated and evaluated to see whether the separate subscales are indeed providing distinct information.

SUMMARY. The ITERS provides a comprehensive structured checklist of quality criteria for infant and toddler group care programs. It should serve well when used in a criterion-referenced manner for three of its four recommended uses: program self assessment, program quality monitoring, and program planning. Its recommended use as a research measure, however, should be approached cautiously until further work is done to better establish its psychometric properties and construct validity.

All potential users should consult the reliability and validity study report to make their own judgements for their own particular needs. This study should be made available directly from the publisher. Although the video training tape was not reviewed, it is available from the publisher and should be considered as a supplement to the brief instructions provided in the instrument booklet.

REVIEWER'S REFERENCES

Clifford, R. M., Russell, S., Fleming, J., Peisner, E., Harms, T., & Cryer, D. (1989). *Infant/Toddler Environment Rating Scale, Reliability and Validity Studies*. Chapel Hill, NC: Frank Porter Graham Child Development Center, University of North Carolina.

Harms, R. M., & Cryer, D. (1991). Video observation training package for the Infant/Toddler Environment Rating Scale. New York: Teachers College Press.

Review of the Infant/Toddler Environment Rating Scale by ANNETTE M. IVERSON, Assistant Professor of Educational Psychology and Foundations, University of Northern Iowa, Cedar Falls, IA:

By 1989, half of the infants in the United States had employed mothers (Clarke-Stewart, 1989). Infant/toddler day care is now the norm rather than the exception. Although many question the effects of nonparental care for those under the age of 3, research suggests that high-quality care does not adversely affect development. Thus, there is a need to define and measure high quality care.

The Infant/Toddler Environment Rating Scale (ITERS) is a rating scale for day care environments and is an adaptation of the Early Childhood Environment Rating Scale (ECERS; T4:833), a rating scale for center-based settings, and of the Family Day Care Rating Scale (FDCRS; T4:960), a rating scale designed to provide users with an environmental assessment of day care homes. Although all three instruments are environmental rating scales, the ITERS was developed specifically for assessing the quality of group care for infants/toddlers up to 30 months of age. Potential uses include self-evaluation by care providers, supervision and monitoring by agency staff, and research and program evaluation.

The ITERS has 35 items grouped into seven categories that focus on the physical and psychological attributes of the setting. The rating scale represents an attempt at ecological assessment by covering setting appearance and contents, setting operation, and setting opportunities as recommended by Hiltonsmith and Keller (1983).

A number of studies of the psychometric properties of the ITERS have been conducted and a complete description is contained in Clifford et al. (1989). The scale is a criterion-referenced assessment tool and, hence, no norms are available. Individual item scores, subscale scores, and total score are best interpreted in a criterion-referenced manner (i.e., What level of competency, based on a range of descriptive terms from 1 = inadequate to 7 = excellent, does the day care environment exhibit?).

The manual describes the development and rationale of the ITERS and demonstrates how each ITERS item matches at least one of the six competency goals of the *CDA Competency Standards* (Child Development Asssociate, 1984). Ratings of items are based on observation and interview; instructions for using the test are accordingly thorough. Items are operationally defined, as are the odd-numbered ratings (i.e., 1, 3, 5, and 7). The scale includes additional items to assess the environment of children with disabilities.

Interrater reliability and internal consistency are reported for a wide variety of 30 day care centers in North Carolina. Interrater reliability on the overall scale was .84; the subscales ranged from .58 to .89 (Spearman's correlation coefficient). Internal consistency was also high (Cronbach's alpha = .83) for the overall scale but subscale scores varied substantially. Test-retest reliability was based on a 3–4-week interval in 18 of the centers, yielding Spearman's correlation coefficients of .79 on the overall scale and ranging from .58 to .76 on the individual subscales. Given proper observer training, the ITERS overall scale score can be a reliable measure of infant/toddler day care environments.

Content-related evidence of validity included an item-by-item comparison of the ITERS with seven other infant/toddler program assessment instruments. An average of 82% of the ITERS items were included in the other instruments, suggesting that the ITERS not only provides a valid measure of the quality of infant/toddler environments but also has items not covered by any of the other seven instruments. Content-related evidence of validity was also based on the ratings of importance that five nationally recognized experts assigned to each ITERS item for the provision of high quality care. Using a 5-point Likert-type scale (1 = low to 5 = high), the overall mean rating was 4.3. Individual item means ranged from 3.0–5.0 and 86% of the ratings were 4 or 5. Further evidence of the content validity of the ITERS is observed in the authors' preparation of items that match the six CDA goals.

Criterion-related evidence of validity is supported by a study that compared experts' sorting of 12 classrooms into high and low quality groups to ITERS scores' ability to sort into the same groups. An overall agreement rate of 83% was attained.

Weaknesses of the instrument include the lack of guidance in the manual for (*a*) following accepted practices in observation (e.g., Observe on a routine day), (*b*) interpretation of scores, and (*c*) recommendations for improving environments based on ITERS results. Hints are offered, however, on the order in which to observe items, how to be a considerate observer, and how to phrase questions during the interview portion of the assessment.

Harms and colleagues have again carefully developed a promising assessment tool, this one for infant/toddler day care environments. Although the items have been developed on the basis of professionals' judgments of face value, they are not carelessly conceived. Furthermore, the ITERS is not a yes/no checklist that limits qualitative data to be obtained. Instead, several levels of acceptable quality are possible through the 7-point rating scale procedure. Additional research to establish construct-related evidence of validity is needed before this instrument can be recommended for widespread evaluation of infant/toddler day care environments or as a psychometrically sound addition to an ecological assessment plan. Final determination of validity depends on a wide range of studies documenting the ability of the scale to discriminate among quality of environments and the relation of quality to child development outcomes.

REVIEWER'S REFERENCES

Hiltonsmith, R. W., & Keller, H. R. (1983). What happened to the setting in person-setting assessment? *Professional Psychology: Research and Practice, 14*, 419-434.

Child Development Associate National Credentialing Program. (1984). *CDA competency standards for infant/toddler caregivers*. Washington, DC: Author.

Clarke-Stewart, K. A. (1989). Infant day care: Maligned or malignant? *American Psychologist, 44*, 266-273.

Clifford, R. M., Russell, S., Fleming, J., Peisner, E., Harms, T., & Cryer, D. (1989). *Infant/Toddler Environment Rating Scale, Reliability and Validity Studies*. Chapel Hill, NC: Frank Porter Graham Child Development Center, University of North Carolina.

[189]

Inquiry Mode Questionnaire: A Measure of How You Think and Make Decisions.

Purpose: Developed to measure "individual preferences in the way people think."
Population: Business and industry.
Publication Dates: 1977–89.
Acronym: INQ.
Scores, 5: Synthesist, Idealist, Pragmatist, Analyst, Realist.
Administration: Group or individual.
Price Data: Not available.
Time: (20) minutes.
Comments: Manual title is *INQ Styles of Thinking*.
Authors: Allen F. Harrison and Robert M. Bramson.
Publisher: INQ Educational Materials Inc. [No reply from publisher; status unknown.]

TEST REFERENCES

1. Kienholz, A., Hayes, P., Mishra, R. K., & Engel, J. (1993). Further validation of the revised Inquiry Mode Questionnaire. *Psychological Reports, 72*, 779-784.
2. Huang, J., & Chao, L. (1994). Japanese college students' thinking styles. *Psychological Reports, 75*, 143-146.
3. Huang, J., & Sisco, B. R. (1994). Thinking styles of Chinese and American adult students in higher education: A comparative study. *Psychological Reports, 74*, 475-480.

Review of the Inquiry Mode Questionnaire: A Measure of How You Think and Make Decisions by PHILIP BENSON, Associate Professor of Management, New Mexico State University, Las Cruces, NM:

The Inquiry Mode Questionnaire (InQ) is a self-report measure designed to assess the manner in which an individual solves problems, or the "thinking strategies" that are most typically employed when an individual approaches a problem, collects and evaluates data relevant to the problem, orders the data to address the problem, and reaches a conclusion. The authors suggest that individuals approach reality in different ways, and thus draw different conclusions, provide different approaches to implementation of plans, and thereby operate in very different modes in solving problems.

The theory underlying the InQ suggests that these individual differences are *not* personality-based styles, but are thinking modes or styles of cognition. We develop these styles early in life, and then tend to show clear preferences for one approach (or a very few approaches) in most situations. The Administration and Interpretation Manual (the manual) for the InQ suggests that half of us almost always think in a single way, and about an additional third of us will alternate between two preferred styles. Thus, only a relatively small percentage of people use a diverse set of approaches to problem solving.

The InQ measures five such cognitive styles, and these approaches to problem solving thus form the core of the measure. These include:

THE SYNTHESIST. This thinking style is characterized primarily by an integrative viewpoint. This individual sees relationships between opposites, and uses conflict to reach synthesis. Speculative arguments are often preferred, and such individuals tend to dislike simplistic and fact-centered arguments. Indeed, facts are only of value when interpreted, and it is the abstract quality of data which is relevant.

THE IDEALIST. This thinking mode is characterized as assimilative, and such individuals tend toward the "big picture" or holistic thinking. Such individuals focus heavily on process, and downplay the value of facts. They also function best without structure, but may tend to overlook details.

THE PRAGMATIST. This style of thinking is characterized by an emphasis on effectiveness: Use whatever facts, values, or solutions that work. Keep decision-making groups active and moving toward outcomes that resolve immediate problems. However, such individuals may place too great an emphasis on expedience and fail to deal with the long-term implications of the solutions they generate.

THE ANALYST. This style of thinking is typified by people who look for the "one best solution" to a given problem. There is an emphasis on formal logic and analysis, as well as an emphasis on theory as the basis for decisions. Data are seen as useful to the extent that they support theory, and such individuals function best in relatively structured environments. However, data that fail to support a theoretical perspective may be ignored, and aspects of reality that cannot be quantified may be given insufficient consideration.

THE REALIST. This thinking style is characterized by an extreme emphasis on facts and data, those things that can be directly perceived. A Realist would likely reject the "subjective" and "theoretical" viewpoints of Synthesists and Analysts, but does share with Pragmatists an emphasis on solutions that are immediately workable. They are good at simplifying a problem, but may be too results oriented.

Because about 35% of individuals are argued to be typified by combinations of two thinking styles, the manual discusses such people (who are termed Combination Dominant). The most common such individuals are the Idealist-Analyst, the Analyst-Realist, and the Synthesist-Idealist, although all other combinations are seen as possible.

The theoretical background to the InQ is heavily drawn from the work of individuals such as C. West Churchman, Ian Mitroff, Jerome Bruner, George A. Kelly, and George S. Klein. Sources for such influence are given in the manual, along with substantial discussion of the five basic types. The authors assume that the styles are based in the physiology of the brain, and may have both genetic and learned aspects. In either case, the styles develop early in life.

The questionnaire consists of 18 items, each with five response choices. Each item presents a statement with optional endings. The five endings correspond to each of the five thinking styles, such that a preference for one particular style will tend to inflate the resulting scale score. For each item, the respondent must rank order each of the choices from *most like you* (5) to *least like you* (1), and the numbers are then totaled across all 18 items to get resulting scale scores. The sum of all responses is thus 270, or 15 total points for each of 18 separate items. The scores on any scale can range from 18 (1 point for each item) to 90 (5 points for each item). It is suggested in the manual that scores of 60 or more indicate a "marked preference" for the style in question, scores of 66 or more indicate a "strong preference" for the style, and scores of 72 or more indicate a "very strong preference, or a commitment" to a particular style. At the low end, scores of 48 or less indicate a "marked disinclination," scores of 42 or less indicate a "strong disinclination," and scores of 36 or less indicate a "virtual disregard" for a particular style. The manual states that these levels represent scores that are about one, two, or three standard deviations above or below the mean.

Scores are placed in a profile, and about half of all respondents show clear preference for a single style. Some profiles (about 35%) show two peaks, and about 2% show a preference for three styles. About 13% of respondents show "flat" profiles, with no peaks or valleys outside of the approximate first standard deviation.

Technical details are very sketchy in the manual, consisting of three pages of tables, with no explanatory text to go with them. An additional three pages give occupational norm profiles for a total of 14 occupational groups. These data are not sufficient to support the measures in a technical sense.

The research notes begin with percentages of people who score high (60 or more) or low (48 or less) for each of the five styles, based on samples of 727 and 651 respondents, respectively. The specific respondents are not clearly identified. Additionally, mean differences between men and women are given for the five scales, based on an unidentified sample of 646 respondents (the numbers of men and women are not given). The manual concludes that there are no gender-based differences in mean scores, and although "eyeballing" the data given suggests strongly that this is true, no technical information is given to support the claim.

The remaining tables in the research notes are almost uninterpretable. The first gives a "correlational item analysis," the second a "Likert item analysis," the third a set of "Spearman rank correlation coefficients for test-retest subtest scores," and the fourth a "cross-tabulation of profile types with a measure of profile stability" (pp. 66–67). Absent any textual description of these tables, they provide very little clue as to what they support or fail to support regarding the InQ. However, a published journal article (Bruvold, Parlette, Bramson, & Bramson, 1983) gives the same tables, with a description of their development. The tables in fact are relevant and useful, but more of the information must be included in the manual. The following discussion will draw heavily from Bruvold et al. (1983).

Item analyses were done two ways. First, each item was correlated with its relevant scale score, although this was done with the contribution of each item to the scale score left intact, resulting in a very slight inflation of these correlations. Of 90 correlations computed, all but 5 were significant at $p<.001$. Additionally, the top 25% and bottom 25% of scorers on each subtest were identified, and mean differences were computed for the relevant subtest scores. Again, the vast majority (82 of 90 comparisons) were significant at $p<.001$. This suggests some degree of internal consistency among subtest or scale score items.

Reliability was assessed two ways. First, test-retest reliability was evaluated for a sample of 63 students from three universities, measured at 6-week intervals. The resulting five reliabilities attained values from .61 to .75, with a median of .65. These reliabilities seem marginal, although not low enough to rule out the use of the InQ.

Reliability was also assessed for profiles. Scores for each of the 63 respondents were converted to rank orders; the highest subtest score was ranked as one, the second as two, etc., for each of 63 profiles, on each of two administrations. Spearman rank correlations were then computed for all respondents. Of 63 correlations, all were greater than .10, seven were perfect (1.00), and the median was .75. In addition, further analyses showed that the unreliable profiles were primarily those that were relatively flat, without peaks and valleys (defined as all subtest raw scores being in the range of 45 to 65). Taken in total, these data suggest adequate but not overwhelming support for the reliability of the InQ.

The manual also gives profiles based on samples of workers in specific occupational groups. In total, 14 such profiles are included, with sample sizes ranging from 15 to 389. Again, far too little detail is given in the manual, and this discussion draws in part from Bruvold et al. (1983). The published article includes six profiles, many with smaller samples, and thus likely based on preliminary data.

The major conclusion to be drawn from these analyses is that the InQ does indeed yield different profiles across different occupational groups. Unfortunately, the sample sizes are in most cases too small, and the occupational classifications are too general (e.g., "Engineers" or "Administrators") to allow for much to be concluded. In addition, the manual is very confusing in this regard; all profiles in the scoring instructions and other sections are given in raw scores, whereas the vertical axis used in the occupational norm profiles is based on standard scores. Thus, it is very difficult for some users to see how these norms apply to actual raw scores, severely limiting the usefulness of these data as true norms.

Much of the manual is given to suggestions for use of the InQ in training or organization development activities. Many of the suggestions seem interesting, but research supporting the usefulness of the activities would do much to support the value of the InQ.

Overall, the InQ is worthy of further research. The manual is not adequate from a technical standpoint, but the theory underlying the measure is interesting, and further research would be useful. Its actual value in training or counseling employees is not documented in the supporting material for the measure.

REVIEWER'S REFERENCE

Bruvold, W. H., Parlette, N., Bramson, R. M., & Bramson, S. J. (1983). An investigation of the item characteristics, reliability, and validity of the Inquiry Mode Questionnaire. *Educational and Psychological Measurement, 43*, 483-493.

Review of the Inquiry Mode Questionnaire: A Measure of How You Think and Make Decisions by TAMELA YELLAND, Psychologist, Veterans Administration, Anaheim Vet Center, Anaheim, CA:

The Inquiry Mode Questionnaire (InQ) is targeted to business and industry and is designed to measure thinking styles along five dimensions: Synthesist, Idealist, Pragmatist, Analyst, and Realist. It is purported to enable people to discover their own and other people's ways of thinking. It is suggested for use in team building, to improve supervisor effectiveness in dealing with subordinates, and to aid in selection, hiring, and project assignment.

The test is self-administered and scored, and interpretation is apparently facilitated by trained staff in a business seminar or educational setting. The measure is made up of 18 questions and respondents are asked to rank the responses from 5–1 as *most like you* to *least like you* respectively. Each item places the respondent in hypothetical situations such as "When I begin work on a group project, what is most important to me is:" and asks him or her to rank order the five responses given. The last page of the test provides the respondent with scoring instructions and a scoring grid. On the grid raw scores are summed and categorized into the five thinking styles. The test directions and scoring are well organized, concise, and easy to follow.

Several important items were lacking in the manual. The theory behind the development of the five styles is not described in the manual or journal article about the test (although the authors refer to another publication in which the theory is stated). There is no discussion of other models such as the Janis and Mann decision model which also has five approaches to problem solving. There is no provision for detection of invalid records, nor is there a means to detect the influence of social desirability in the responses. Information about the psychometric properties of the test were also not clearly described in the manual. The majority of this information is found in Bruvold, Parlette, Bramson, and Bramson (1983).

Several "norms" are given for various occupations in the form of mean profiles. These are based on the results of 460 cases obtained in 1978 and 1979 as part of the item analysis of the test. No descriptive statistics are provided beyond the means and standard deviations for each "occupational group" making interpretation and generalization impossible. The means are standardized so that ready comparison to the raw scores is prohibited.

The interpretation of the results is based on the assumption that profiles will include at least one scale with a standard score above 60. Brief interpretations are given for profiles with one or two marked thinking style preferences. Each of the style preferences is described in terms of characteristics, strengths, and liabilities. Unfortunately, the authors have found a relatively large percentage (13%) of the profiles are "flat" with no scale score over 60. Very little information is given on the flat profile, pointing to the need for further research.

The development of the test items was accomplished by a "series of group meetings in which the proposed versions were compared and consensus was reached." We are not told who the judges were or their qualifications. There is also no mention of the rationale for choosing a hypothetical decision format for tapping thinking styles. Would a behavioral task with raters provide a more objective and accurate analysis of the person's decision making and interaction in group problem solving? Such a format may avoid the unaddressed problems of validity and social desirability biases, as well as provide the opportunity for feedback on behaviors.

Item analysis consisted of correlating single items with overall subtest score. Here the items all correlated positively and all but five showed statistical significance, but the highest coefficient was .50 and the analysis included auto-correlation because the item being analyzed was included in the subtest score. Similar results were found from comparing the highest and lowest means of each subtest in a *t*-test of significant differences, with only four additional items lacking significance.

Test-retest reliability was investigated with 63 college students who were tested at a 6-week interval. The correlation coefficients ranged from .61 to .75. The reliability of the score profiles was examined with Spearman rank difference coefficients, with 30% of coefficients below .60. The authors note that the flat profiles made up the majority of the weaker coefficients, again pointing to the need for further refinement of the scale. The authors note this level of reliability does not support the interpretation of single subtest scores for individuals, but state that the profile reliability is substantial enough to support interpretation of profiles. Indeed, the profiles may be stable over time, but with the ipsative measurement, the use of college students as subjects, and the high rate of flat profiles which evade interpretation, the wisdom of interpreting profiles for use in business is questionable.

Validity of the test is based on the occupational classifications of the profiles. The sample was made up of 460 "professionals" in 1978–1979. No other data are given about the subjects or the statistical results beyond means and standard deviations for each occupational group. Apparently differentiation among the occupations was successful enough to distinguish occupational groups, but without any statistical or demographic data, the means given are meaningless. This attempt at differential prediction could be taken a lot farther and provide substantial results. Criterion-related validity could be established if the profiles predicted occupation or effectiveness in actual group problem-solving tasks.

A preliminary factor analysis was performed but little is known of the results. The author notes that a quartimax rotation procedure found a five-dimensional factorial structure. Again, with further work validity evidence could be strengthened through establishing the dimensions and aligning the test with the components of each factor.

To conclude, the InQ holds both promise and appeal as a measure of thinking styles for many uses in business and industry. The authors are encouraged to continue refining the instrument and its psychometric properties. However, the use of the test at this time is cautioned against because of the limited reliability and validity data.

REVIEWER'S REFERENCE

Bruvold, W. H., Parlette, N., Bramson, R. M., & Bramson, S. J. (1983). An investigation of the item characteristics, reliability, and validity of the Inquiry Mode Questionnaire. *Educational and Psychological Measurement, 43*, 483-493.

[190]

Instructional Leadership Evaluation and Development Program (I*LEAD*).

Population: School climates and leadership.
Publication Dates: 1985–88.
Acronym: I*LEAD*.
Administration: Individual or group.
Price Data: Available from publisher.
Time: Administration time varies with form.
Authors: Larry A. Braskamp (School Climate Inventories, School Administrator Assessment Survey), Martin L. Maehr (same material as above), and MetriTech, Inc. (manual and Instructional Leadership Inventory).
Publisher: MetriTech, Inc.

a) SCHOOL CLIMATE INVENTORY (FORM T).
Purpose: "Designed to assess instructional leadership behavior, job satisfaction and commitment, and school culture or climate from the teachers' perspective."
Scores, 12: Instructional Leadership (Defines Mission, Manages Curriculum, Supervises Teaching, Monitors Student Progress, Promotes Instructional Climate), Climate (Satisfaction, Commitment, Strength, Accomplishment, Recognition, Power, Affiliation).
Comments: Ratings by teachers.

b) SCHOOL CLIMATE INVENTORY (FORM S).
Purpose: "Designed to assess school climate from the student perspective."
Scores, 5: Strength of Climate, Accomplishment, Recognition, Power, Affiliation.
Comments: Ratings by students in grades 3–12.

c) SCHOOL ADMINISTRATOR ASSESSMENT SURVEY.
Purpose: "Designed to simultaneously assess the person, the job, and the culture or climate of the setting in which the person works."
Scores, 19: Personal Incentive (Accomplishment, Recognition, Power, Affiliation), Self-Concept (Self-Reliance, Self-Esteem, Goal-Directedness), Job Opportunity (Accomplishment, Recognition, Power, Affiliation, Advancement), Organizational Culture (Accomplishment, Recognition, Power, Affiliation, Satisfaction, Strength of Culture, Commitment).
Comments: Adaptation of SPECTRUM; self-ratings by principals.

d) INSTRUCTIONAL LEADERSHIP INVENTORY.
Purpose: "Designed to assess instructional leadership behavior."
Scores, 8: Instructional Leadership (Defines Mission, Manages Curriculum, Supervises Teaching, Monitors Student Progress, Promotes Instructional Climate), Contextual (Staff, School, Community).
Comments: Self-ratings by principals.

Cross References: See T4:1240 (1 reference).

*Review of the Instructional Leadership Evaluation and Development Assessment Program (*ILEAD*) by DAVID L. BOLTON, Assistant Professor of Education, West Chester University, West Chester, PA:*

The Instructional Leadership Evaluation and Development (I*LEAD*) Assessment Program consists of a series of four instruments designed to assess school climate resulting from the activities and beliefs of the principal of the school. Two of the instruments, the Instructional Leadership Inventory (ILI) and the School Administrator Assessment Survey (SAAS) are self-report measures administered to the principal of the school. Whereas the ILI asks the principal to report on his or her instructional leadership behavior (as well as perception of the staff, school, and community), the SAAS attempts to determine why the principal behaves in this manner through determination of his or her values. The Instructional Climate Inventories (ICI) attempt to measure a principal's instructional leadership behavior (Form T) and the school climate (Forms T and S) through the perspective of the teachers (Form T) and the students (Form S).

The authors have done extensive work in developing and validating the *ILEAD*. The development process is based in instructional leadership and organizational theory, attempting to measure both effective instructional leadership behaviors and the values of the organization. The *ILEAD* is a direct extension of the research in those areas.

In assessing the validity of the *ILEAD*, the authors correlated related scales from different instruments. For example, they correlated superintendents' ratings of principals' instructional leadership behavior with principals' self-report data. For all such studies, the correlations tended to be low to moderate. This is not surprising because one is dealing with perceptions from different individuals. These differing perceptions should perhaps be viewed as separate constructs rather than two measures of the same construct.

Also, the authors correlated scores on the *ILEAD* with external measures of the same construct. For example, in validating the ILI the authors correlate it with the Principal Instructional Management Rating Scale (PIMRS), another measure of instructional leadership behavior. In doing so, they correlated all 10 scales of the PIMRS with the 5 leadership inventory scales. The resulting correlations vary between .21 and .88 with the majority being above .50. Because not all scales of the PIMRS may logically correlate with the ILI scales, it is not clear which correlations should be high and which should be low. Multiple correlations were also calculated, with all but one being higher than .58. By including all scales in the calculations though, the authors may be capitalizing upon chance. Eliminating unrelated scales would reduce the multiple correlation somewhat.

The authors use other methods of assessing the construct validity of the instruments, such as testing expected differences between groups. In general, the rigor in assessing the validity of the instrument is exemplary and the cumulative evidence of this research tends to support the construct validity of the *ILEAD*.

Two cautions must be noted. Because the instrument is self-report, caution must be exercised when interpreting the scores. Principals might, for example, indicate that they are engaged in certain instructional activities when they are not, in order to look good. Alternatively, teachers might not be willing to be honest in reporting if there may be negative consequences for them. Although this was not the case in the research conducted by the authors, it might happen in a school with a negative climate. In determining the school climate, the principal, although an influence, is not the only or even, perhaps, the most important influence. School board and community play a significant role. For a complete picture of a school climate, an assessment should be made of these factors also. This need was acknowledged by the authors in their manual and will, perhaps, be addressed at a later time.

In assessing the reliability of all four instruments, the authors consistently use coefficient alpha and generally report high reliability coefficients, in the 70s and 80s. Given the self-report format of the instrument it would make more sense to use the test-retest method of determining reliability. Individuals may be internally consistent in their responses for one administration, but mood and other personal factors will cause the reliability estimates to decrease.

In assessing the reliability of the SCI-Form S, the authors estimate both individual student reliability as well as school level reliability. For this instrument, school level reliability is more important because the instrument averages scores across students and teachers. For the SCI-Form S, the authors provide a table with reliability estimates for differing numbers of students. In the table, reliabilities ranged from .65 to .86 for 25 students and from .77 to .92 for 50 students. Although from the research reports it is apparent the authors followed the same procedure for SCI-Form T, there were no tables provided in the manual.

Information regarding the norms was difficult to find (the best place to find the information is in the accompanying research reports) and was not as complete as it should be. The description of the norming group for the ILI was 242 Illinois principals. Although not stated, it is presumed the norms for the SCI-Form S were derived from the final pilot study group consisting of 3,056 students sampled equally from grades 3 through 12 (norms are provided for each grade separately in research reports). The norming group for the SAAS consisted of 505 elementary, middle school, or junior high and high school principals from Illinois. Better descriptions of the norming groups are provided for the SCI-Form T. The norms were developed on the basis of 515 teachers from Illinois and Nebraska, with 33% elementary school, 14% junior high, and 53% high school teachers (separate norms are provided for each level in research reports).

The fact the norming groups are from the Midwest might be of concern to those living in other parts of the country. A more nationally representative norming group or regional norms are needed. At a minimum a better description of the norming group, and their corresponding schools, is needed.

The documentation of the instruments is extensive including a thick manual and two research reports. Although quite explicit, it requires a lot of reading and is not well ordered. Some of the material in the research reports should be placed in the manual itself. A much better introduction should be provided at the beginning of the manual. In general, the manual should be reordered to improve clarity.

One thing lacking in the manual is an explanation on how to use the information provided by the instruments. Because a user is obtaining so much information from the four instruments, it is important to understand how to interpret it. As an example, there is no indication of what to do when teachers and students or teachers and principals differ in their assessment of school climate. Some information is provided in the research reports about how the authors used the instruments. It is not extensive. Until a better explanation is provided, users should be aware that they will have to figure out how to best use the information for their purposes.

The *ILEAD* comes with four diskettes for use in analyzing data from the four instruments and printing out reports. Although the programs are straightforward and easy to run, they do not allow for flexibility in usage. For example, the reports must be printed out and cannot be viewed on the screen. Also, there appears no way of entering local norming data. They do, however, allow for importing the data from scanners. The reports are easy to understand once one has read the explanation in the manual.

Overall, the development of the *ILEAD* is an important and significant step in assessing instructional leadership. It is a rather sophisticated instrument that will require effort on the part of those using it to collect and use the information. It is not for users who want to have a quick check of school climate. More research should be done using the *ILEAD* in order to understand how to best use the information provided by the instrument.

*Review of the Instructional Leadership Evaluation and Development Program (I*LEAD*) by DONNA L. SUNDRE, Associate Assessment Specialist/Associate Professor of Psychology, James Madison University, Harrisonburg, VA:*

GENERAL INFORMATION. The Instructional Leadership Evaluation and Development (*ILEAD*) Program was designed to provide information from multiple perspectives concerning the instructional leadership, job satisfaction and commitment, and school culture or climate of an educational setting. The *ILEAD* Program consists of four instruments intended to assess various dimensions of an educational setting. Two instruments provide individually based assessments: the School Administrator Assessment Survey (SAAS) and the Instructional Leadership Inventory (ILI). Reports for these instruments are generated on the basis of a single individual's responses. The other two instruments provide group-based information: the Instructional Climate Inventory for Teachers, Form T (ICI-T), and a parallel instrument designed for students, Form S (ICI-S). Additional program materials include a set of four IBM microcomputer software programs to facilitate data entry, scoring, analysis of data, and report generation.

PRACTICAL EVALUATION. The instrument materials are durable, with the exception of the student form, which is not intended to be reused. Administration of the instruments appears relatively easy and efficient.

Review of the item content for the four instruments reveals a number of concerns. The intended student population for the Instructional Climate Inventory Form S (ICI-S) is listed as 3rd to 12th graders; a single instrument designed for such a span of age levels presents a difficult challenge. The item content of the student form includes items with constructs and vocabulary inappropriate for students in the lower levels. For example, "Competition among students in this school is very high," or items addressing concepts such as "loyalty," "trust," "talented," and a few others may provide data of questionable worth. Children in the early school years are concrete thinkers and abstract notions such as loyalty and talent may be beyond many children in 3rd or 4th grades. Within the technical development portion of the program manual, the authors state that some early grade students may have difficulty reading items, and the items may be read to them. However, it is doubtful that reading the items would overcome the vocabulary and conceptual difficulties, despite the fact that listening comprehension for children at this age tends to be higher than reading comprehension.

Problems related to item composition may also be present in both of the administrative instruments: The School Administrator Survey (SAAS) and the Instructional Leadership Inventory (ILI). Both instruments appear to be heavily loaded with socially desirable items that may contribute to response bias and weaken score validity.

The software programs and instructions are provided in a durable *ILEAD* Report Generation Programs User Manual that is clearly written. Each page in the manual is reinforced along the three-ring binding to enhance the durability, a thoughtful addition. Data entry procedures include excellent data validation opportunities throughout each data entry screen *and* record. For example, out of range responses are not accepted when data are manually entered. All programs also allow for data entry from machine-scannable forms, a definite plus. When the reports are run, the program will inform the user if out of range responses are encountered from scanned data. Standard item response coding is used (i.e., A = 1, B = 2, etc.), which facilitates scannable data entry with a variety of opscan forms; however, it would be helpful for the authors to state specifically the data file format required rather than repeatedly referring users to "review the sample data set on program disk for an example of the appropriate format."

TECHNICAL EVALUATION. A common complaint of potential users trying to assess the merits of a particular test, or in this case an inventory, is the lack of accessible and understandable information concerning norming groups, reliability, and validity evidence. This all too familiar pattern is repeated with these instruments. For example, interpretive/statistical manuals are included for each of the instruments and report generation programs; however, the test construction, reliability, and validity evidence are reported to be presented in separate technical reports. This reviewer requested this information from the publisher and it is included as supplementary information for each instrument.

Separate norms, reliability, and validity evidence are required for review of each instrument and will be described in turn for each of the four instructional leadership assessment programs: the School Administrator Assessment Survey (SAAS); the Instructional Leadership Inventory (ILI); the Instructional Climate Inventory for Teachers, Form T (ICI-T); and the Instructional Climate Inventory for Students, Form S (ICI-S).

School Administrator Assessment Survey (SAAS)

GENERAL DESCRIPTION AND SCALES. The School Administrator Assessment Survey consists of 200 self-report items used to form 19 scales. Four broad incentives: (*a*) Accomplishment; (*b*) Recognition; (*c*) Power; and (*d*) Affiliation are measured at different levels forming three sets of scales: (*a*) the Personal Incentive (PI) scales; (*b*) the Job Opportunity (JO) scales; and (*c*) the Organizational Culture scales. The Job Opportunity scales also include a score for a scale called Advancement. The four elements were identified in the Theory of Personal Investment (Maehr & Braskamp, 1986) and are used to measure the personal values, the individual's perception of opportunity for fulfillment of the four incentives, and the underlying values of the administrator's school district. Three Self-Concept scales are included: (*a*) Self-Reliance; (*b*) Self-Esteem; and (*c*) Goal-Directedness, as well as three other independent measures: (*a*) Satisfaction; (*b*) Strength of Culture; and (*c*) Commitment. This instrument is a direct adaptation of SPECTRUM (Braskamp & Maehr, 1985; 366), which was originally designed for organizational culture assessments. The developmental procedures for SPECTRUM are reported within the Interpretive Manual as well as a separate Technical Report #1 containing information on the construction and validation of the SAAS. The development procedures for the SPECTRUM appear to have been quite thorough. The adaptations for the School Administrator Assessment Survey were based upon item context modifications and continued refinements by Suddarth (1987) and Stonehouse (1987).

NORMS. The norming sample is described as a random selection of 600 Illinois principals from elementary, middle or junior high, and high schools. Only 239, or 40% of the original sample responded; no mention is made of potential response biases. This norming group was combined with an elementary principal sample collected by Suddarth (1987) after review indicated minimal differences on scale profiles. This group of 505 principals is considered a "more representative norm base for use in the Illinois program" (p. 12).

RELIABILITY. The reliability information presented appears to be from the SPECTRUM development studies, not from school administrators or principals from Illinois or elsewhere. In fact, the more recent interpretive/statistical manual for the SAAS received upon request by this reviewer is apparently adapted from the Braskamp and Maehr (1985) SPECTRUM manual. Although the internal consistencies appear more than adequate, the reliability estimates really should emanate from samples appropriate for current intended use. In addition, test-retest reliability estimates would also be very helpful to evaluate the stability of the instrument over at least short periods of time.

VALIDITY. No specific validity section appears in the psychometric characteristics section of the manual; however, a great deal of comparative findings of the school administrator sample with the original SPECTRUM data base are provided. Results of analyses of variance indicated that many of the mean scale scores for the principal sample were significantly different from those in the SPECTRUM norming group. These results confirmed the need for the development of separate norming groups upon which to derive school administrator *T* scores. These data apparently did not contribute to validation evidence. The scale intercorrelations for the SAAS norming group are provided but no interpretation on theoretical grounds is provided. The Technical Report #1 referred to earlier contains essentially the very same information included in the interpretive/statistical manual that accompanies the instrument. This was very disappointing. It would seem that a great deal of reliability and validity evidence would be available for this instrument given its extended use in the state of Illinois and at least two doctoral dissertations (Stonehouse, 1987; Suddarth, 1987) that relied heavily on it. In a separate article, Krug (1989) describes a study that demonstrated the ability of the SAAS to explain or predict significant variance in the dimensions assessed by the ILI. He reported that an average of 25% of the total variance in ILI dimensions was explained by the SAAS.

Instructional Leadership Inventory (ILI)

GENERAL DESCRIPTION AND SCALES. This inventory consists of 100 short, multiple-choice items that assess the following five broad, yet related, categories of instructional leadership: (*a*) Defines Mission, (*b*) Manages Curriculum, (*c*) Supervises Teaching, (*d*) Monitors Student Progress, and (*e*) Promotes Instructional Climate. These categories were developed upon dimensions of instructional leadership identified by researchers (Kroeze, 1984; Murphy, 1988; Rogus, 1983) in the instructional leadership literature. The authors note that a single general factor appears to be present; this impression is supported by the fairly strong positive correlations reported among the five dimensions (i.e., between .52 and .74). These correlations call into question whether these separate categories carry much meaning for interpretive objectives. Administration of the instrument requires about 20–30 minutes.

Despite the high intercorrelations, the interpretive/statistical manual contains cogent descriptions of each of the scales with descriptions of high and low scoring profiles and sample items. It should be noted the intent of these scales has been to identify and measure "practices and characteristics of administrators that are associated with measurable improvements in student achievement" (p. 1 of interpretive/statistical manual for the Instructional Leadership Inventory). Some administrators perceive their role as that of a school manager rather than as an instructional leader, staff motivator, or mentor. Such administrators, although being very efficient and effective in a wide variety of domains, would not be expected to score highly on these scales. In fact, on the basis of the profile descriptions, these scales should discriminate between administrative managers and instructional leaders.

The instrument also includes three contextual scales that assess the administrator's perception of factors related to staff, students, and the community; these scales are thought to be helpful for interpretation of scores on the five leadership dimensions. The authors have also included four experimental scales that parallel the Personal Incentive (PI) scales included in the SAAS inventory measuring: (*a*) Accomplishment, (*b*) Recognition, (*c*) Power, and (*d*) Affiliation. The supplemental materials sent to this reviewer upon request do not include descriptions of the experimental scales, so they may have been deleted.

NORMS. Norms are derived from the responses of 242 Illinois principals. The sampling plan included proportional representation of administrators at the elementary and secondary school levels as exist in the state of Illinois. No other information regarding the norms is provided in the interpretive/statistical manual. Although the manual suggests the instrument is intended for all administrators active in instructional leadership (including associate principals, department heads, etc.), only principals have been included in the norming group thus far.

RELIABILITY. The only reliability evidence provided in the interpretive/statistical manual supported the internal consistency of the items contributing to each scale. The lowest alpha coefficient reported was .74 for Manages Instruction and the highest, .89, was for the Staff contextual scale. These coefficients provide strong evidence of the homogeneity of items within scales. This conclusion is entirely expected when a large general factor is evident across all of the items. Other forms of reliability evidence would be important to determine if scores on the scale might be stable over at least short periods of time, or perhaps with different raters assessing an administrator's instructional leadership qualities.

VALIDITY. In an effort to collect scale validity evidence, the 242 principals used in the norming study were requested to also complete Hallinger's (1984) Principal Instructional Management Rating Scale (PIMRS), which also purports to assess instructional leadership. The PIMRS consists of 10 subscales assessing a wide variety of instructional leadership areas similar to those assessed with the ILI. The correlations among the scale scores provide some evidence of convergence between them. Several pairs of scales one would expect to be most highly related do result in very high positive correlations. For example, the correlation between the ILI Define Mission scale and the PIMRS Communicate School Goals is .78; Manage Curriculum and Coordinate Curriculum have a correlation of .87; the relationship between the two scales that measure Monitor Student Progress is .85. These are the highest correlations found in the table and provide strong evidence the scales are measuring the same thing. There is substantial variance shared between the two instruments and higher correlations observed for scales that should be highly related.

A pilot study conducted to assess the relationship between superintendent PIMRS item ratings of principals with the same principals' self-ratings using the ILI scale scores is also reported as validity evidence. A number of statistically significant correlations between PIMRS item ratings provided by superintendents and principal self-report ILI scale scores emerged. However, not knowing the number of items comprising the PIMRS and its 10 scales, the presentation of 16 significant items is not compelling validity information. Further, the use of less reliable single PIMRS items rather than scale scores seems inappropriate in a comparison with ILI scale scores.

The supplemental technical materials requested and later received by this reviewer were largely a disappointment. Although the interpretive/statistical manual for the ILI originally received indicated that "Test construction, reliability, and validity evidence is presented in a separate technical report" (p. 1), the supplementary material is entirely composed of the same material included in the original, with the exception that the technical development of the ILI portion of the original document (p. 4–10) has been labeled Technical Report #2 and consists of pages 2C-1–2C-7.

Fortunately, Krug (1989) and Krug, Ahadi, and Scott (1991) report on their research covering the PIMRS and the ILI. This work suggests some evidence of discrimination by the ILI on relevant behaviors of instructional leaders and provides some fascinating evidence regarding the importance of principal belief systems (in contrast to discrete behaviors) in identifying effective instructional leaders.

Instructional Climate Inventory for Teachers (ICI-Form T)

GENERAL DESCRIPTION AND SCALES. The ICI-T is designed to gather teacher perceptions of school climate; it consists of 108 brief, multiple-choice statements. The inventory comprises 12 separate scales related to three general domains: (*a*) Instructional Leadership, (*b*) Satisfaction and Commitment, and (*c*) Climate. Five Instructional Leadership Dimension scales were developed specifically for the *ILEAD* Programs: (*a*) Defines Mission, (*b*) Manages Curriculum, (*c*) Supervises Teaching, (*d*) Monitors Student Progress, and (*e*) Promotes Instructional Climate. These scales are also included in the ILI, which gathers data from the school administrator perspective. The remaining seven scales were adapted from the SPECTRUM (Braskamp & Maehr, 1985) organizational settings instruments. Two scales assess: (*a*) Satisfaction and (*b*) Commitment, and the remaining five are intended to assess instructional climate: (*a*) Strength of Climate, (*b*) Accomplishment, (*c*) Recognition, (*d*) Power, and (*e*) Affiliation. The items are listed in several places within the manual and sample inventory report forms, appear straightforward, and were developed or modified from the original SPECTRUM series with care. Administration of the instrument does not appear problematic and should require about 20–30 minutes.

NORMS. The ICI-T was originally normed with 515 teachers. No information is provided concerning the population from which the sample was drawn, sampling methods, or participation rates in the brief (nine-page) interpretive/statistical manual. The 515 Illinois and Nebraska teacher responses are broken down by level of school setting: elementary (170 respondents, or 33% of the sample); junior high or middle (72 respondents, or 14% of the sample); and high school (273 respondents, or 53% of the sample). If the school type is left blank, default norms are provided; however, there is no mention of how these default norms are generated or composed. On the information thus far provided, neither the original norming group nor the default norms can be properly evaluated, should be considered "user group" norms, and should be used with caution.

RELIABILITY. Only coefficient alphas, or scale internal consistencies are provided; these appear more than adequate, with the possible exception of the Power subscale, which boasts an alpha of only .69. All other scales have internal consistencies in the mid to high .80s. A separate column reports the seven SPECTRUM scale internal consistencies for 339 adult respondents from a variety of work settings; these reliabilities appear adequate, again, with the exception of the Power subscale (alpha = .51). A puzzling feature of the table is the footnote that reliabilities for teachers are based on the results from a sample of only 101 teachers. This reviewer cannot help but wonder why the reliabilities are not based on the 515 teachers included in the norming group.

No temporal stability coefficients are provided; these would be very useful for the evaluation of the instrument, even over relatively brief periods of time. Of course, test-retest reliabilities require multiple administrations of the instrument to at least a subset of the original sample, an inconvenient burden for many, but a necessary characteristic for instruments purporting to measure stable constructs. The supplementary technical information sent by the publisher (Technical Report #3), provides the same information as that provided in the original interpretive/statistical manual.

A very interesting study by Krug, Ahadi, and Scott (1991) describes some important potential sources of systematic error in teacher ratings of instructional climate. Several significant and troubling differences in ICI-T ratings were found in their study; the demographic variables they included all showed some significant differences in instructional climate ratings; school level, gender, age of teacher, ethnicity, years of teaching experience, and highest educational degree. Krug et al. recommended aggregated teacher responses over sufficient numbers to achieve sufficient interrater reliability. Their work is highly recommended reading for potential users.

VALIDITY. Essentially no validity evidence is provided. Mention is made that SPECTRUM scales were previously validated and extensively researched; however, if inferences are to be made with different populations for different purposes, the Instructional Climate Inventory for Teachers and all associated scales must be validated. Within the supplementary reports sent to this reviewer (Technical Report #3), initial validity studies in which 8–25% of the variation in scale scores was found to be attributable to differences between schools as reported. Alas, no references were provided, and no other mention of this study was found within the materials originally provided or later requested. A separate article by Krug (1989) also mentions these preliminary studies but did not elaborate any further than the information provided in the original MetriTech, Inc. manual.

Instructional Climate Inventory for Students (ICI-Form S)

GENERAL DESCRIPTION AND SCALES. The ICI-S is a very short 20-item multiple-choice instrument comprising six scales: (*a*) Commitment, (*b*) Strength of Climate, (*c*) Accomplishment, (*d*) Recognition, (*e*) Power, and (*f*) Affiliation. These scales parallel those in the ICI-T, and as with that instrument, all of these scales, and the items comprising them, were drawn and revised from the SPECTRUM (Braskamp & Maehr, 1985) organizational culture instruments. The quantity and precision of information provided concerning the technical quality of the scales is much better for the ICI-S than that provided for the ICI-T. The developmental process is briefly but well described across two stages with independent samples drawn for both.

NORMS. The norming group for the current form on the instrument is composed of 3,056 students. Approximately equal numbers of students from each of the 3–12 grade levels were included in the sampling plan. Grade level effects were found that warrant the use of grade level norms in the scoring of the instrument. This is an important finding, and in essence renders the norming groups much smaller than that reported for potential users at a given grade level. As with the ICI-T, if no grade code is selected, the scoring program will employ default norms, though these are not defined. No other details are provided concerning the norms.

RELIABILITY. Both student level and aggregated level reliabilities are provided, and both appear more than adequate. Internal consistencies range from a low of .66 for Recognition and a high of .82 for both Accomplishment and Commitment. The Total instrument boasts a .90 alpha coefficient. As with the ICI-T, reliabilities that would provide evidence for the stability of responses over time are not provided and would be very helpful. For the class, grade, or school reliabilities, the scales appear quite reliable even with groups as small as 25, and the reliabilities increase as expected with groups of 50, 75, and 100. The pooling of scores across students, classes, grades, or schools is the more typical application of the instrument, and the intraclass correlations provide fairly solid evidence of the consistency, or generalizability, of aggregated scores.

VALIDITY. An impressive inclusion for the ICI-S is a section devoted to validity. According to the manual, "the fundamental utility of these scales for guiding a development program designed to improve the school's instructional climate rests on the ability of these scales to discriminate among schools with differing cultures" (p. 5). Two empirical studies, one using five elementary schools and the other three high schools, were conducted to provide such evidence. The results indicated significant differences across grade levels, supporting the earlier decision to use grade level specific norms. In the elementary school study, five of the seven significance tests (they included a total score), indicated significant differences across schools, and all seven tests in the high school study were significant. Nine of the 14 school-by-grade interactions were significant. Potential users of the inventory would want an answer to the fundamental questions of whether the observed scale score differences among the elementary and high schools were indicative of true school climate differences as measured by other indicators. Evidence that provided a theoretical linkage between demographic or historical differences of the school populations and scale scores would have been welcome but are not included.

An unpublished study in which the Instructional Climate Inventory was administered along with measures of student motivation and achievement is mentioned in the MetriTech manual. The results were said to have "established the relevance of these climate factors as an antecedent of motivation and school achievement" (p. 3). Again, very intriguing results are presented without sufficient information to ascertain whether the conclusions made are warranted. The test developers conclude the results of the ICI-S "conform to theoretical expectations and identify reliable differences in various aspects of school climate" (p. 10); however, readers and potential users of the inventory may not agree with this conclusion on the basis of the evidence thus far provided.

SUMMARY EVALUATION. Although the *ILEAD* programs offer great promise, there are many questions that should be answered regarding the utility and psychometric strength of the instruments at this time. All manuals and materials related to *ILEAD* need to be more carefully integrated and updated. For example, the Instructional Climate Inventory is referred to as the School Climate Inventory in the title to the interpretive/statistical manual. Articles referenced in bibliographies are listed as in press when they are clearly published now. Norms, reliability, and especially validity evidence all must be expanded and updated for the current instruments with the current intended population more carefully sampled and described. Of critical importance is the incorporation of the Krug (1989) and Krug, Ahadi, and Scott (1991) works into the MetricTech, Inc. user manuals. Some of the psychometric evidence reported is still "borrowed" from the SPECTRUM instruments, and the validity evidence is largely missing from materials provided by the test publisher and distributor. This is not to say that such evidence does not exist; it does.

These instruments have been broadly used, particularly in the state of Illinois. The two previously cited articles (Krug, 1989; Krug, Ahadi, & Scott, 1991) provide a very useful and integrated presentation of the *ILEAD* program, the four instruments comprising the inventory, and the role they are playing in a systematic research program that seeks to increase our understanding of the structure and dynamic of school leadership behaviors, school climate, teacher and student motivation, and achievement. Krug (1989) stressed the importance of precise measurement, particularly in the construction of complex models and made a strong case for the *ILEAD* inventory. Potential users of the *ILEAD* program will need to search beyond the materials currently available in the test publisher's manuals and other materials; unfortunately, the strength of the case for the *ILEAD* program is not detailed there sufficiently.

REVIEWER'S REFERENCES

Rogus, J. F. (1983). How principals can strengthen school performance. *NASSP Bulletin, 67*, 1-7.

Hallinger, P. (1984). Principal Instructional Management Rating Scale. New York: Leading Development Associates.

Kroeze, D. J. (1984). Effective principals as instructional leaders: New directions for research. *Administrator's Notebook, 30*, 1-4.

Braskamp, L. A., & Maehr, M. L. (1985). SPECTRUM: An Organizational Development Tool. Champaign, IL: MetriTech, Inc.

Maehr, M. L., & Braskamp, L. A. (1986). *The motivation factor: A theory of personal investment*. Lexington, MA: Lexington Books.

Suddarth, E. (1987). *Personal investment theory of motivation applied to elementary principals*. Unpublished doctoral dissertation, Southern Illinois University, Carbondale, IL.

Stonehouse, N. (1987). *A comparative investigation of personal incentives, perceived opportunities, and organizational culture among administrative and teaching staffs in elementary and secondary education*. Unpublished doctoral dissertation. University of Nebraska, Lincoln, NE.

MetriTech, Inc. (1988). *ILEAD report generation programs: User manual*. Champaign, IL: MetriTech, Inc.

Murphy, J. (1988, April). *Methodological, measurement, and conceptual problems in the study of instructional leadership*. Paper presented at the annual meeting of the American Educational Research Association, New Orleans, LA.

Krug, S. E. (1989). Leadership and learning: A measurement-based approach for analyzing school effectiveness and developing effective school leaders. In C. Ames & M. L. Maehr (Eds.), *Advances in motivation and achievement: Motivation enhancing environments* (vol. 6; pp. 249-277). Greenwich, CT: JAI Press.

Krug, S. E., Ahadi, S. A., & Scott, C. K. (1991). Current issues and research findings in the study of school leadership. In P. W. Thurston & P. P. Zodhiates (Eds.), *Advances in educational administration: An annual series of analytical essays and critical reviews: School leadership* (vol. 2; pp. 241-260). Greenwich, CT: JAI Press.

[191]

Integrated Literature and Language Arts Portfolio Program.

Purpose: "To assess students' reading and language arts proficiency."
Population: Grades 2–8.
Publication Date: 1991.
Scores, 7 to 9: Prior Knowledge/Predicting Content, Reading Strategies, Vocabulary, Constructing Meaning (Literal, Analytical, Extended), Feature Scores (Responsiveness to Task, Development and Organization, Language Use) or 1 Holistic Score.
Administration: Group.
Levels: 2 forms for each of 8 levels.
Price Data, 1992: $39 per 25 Student Activity Booklets including Directions for Administration and 1 Class Record Form (specify form and level); $5.40 per Student Activity Booklet Scoring Guide (specify form and level); $9 per Local Scoring Leader's Handbook (23 pages); $27.90 per 25 Student Portfolio Folders; $9 per 25 Individual Observation Check Lists; $4.20 per Teacher's Directions (specify form and level); $12 per 25 Class Record Forms levels 2–8; $15 per Technical manual (64 pages).
Time: Three 45-minute sessions.
Author: Nambury Raju.
Publisher: The Riverside Publishing Co.

Review of the Integrated Literature and Language Arts Portfolio Program by STEVE GRAHAM, Professor of Special Education, University of Maryland, College Park, MD:

The Integrated Literature and Language Arts Portfolio Program (ILALAPP) is used to assess interest and experiences in reading, overall reading ability, and proficiency in other language arts activities (most notably writing) in the context of reading and listening experiences. The instrument was designed to be used as part of a student's evaluation portfolio in grades 2 through 8, and the author is to be commended for addressing how this goal is accomplished. Clear guidelines for developing a portfolio approach to evaluation, student portfolio folders, and teaching implications for hypotheses drawn from the ILALAPP and other portfolio assessments are provided.

The ILALAPP is administered in three 45-minute sessions on 3 separate days. On the first day, students complete a survey designed to assess preferences and experiences in reading. Next, they listen to a work of fiction, respond to questions before and after listening to the selection, and complete a writing activity in response to the selection presented. During the remaining two sessions, reading is tested using the same format. Session two focuses on fiction and session three on nonfiction. Teachers can also complete an individual observation checklist that assesses a student's attitude toward and proficiency in reading and other language arts tasks. Directions for administering the ILALAPP are clear and easy to follow.

There are two forms, A and B, of the test at each grade level. The reading and listening materials for both forms present a wide range of genres and topics while offering a balanced picture of a multicultural society. With the exception of some of the materials at grades 2, 3, and 7, the readability of reading selections at each grade level for the two forms appears to be comparable and at the correct grade level. No information, however, is presented on the readability of the listening selections.

Detailed instructions for scoring the test at each grade level are provided. Some of the questions administered before or after listening or reading are easy to score, involving a single correct answer. Many of the questions, however, allow for diverse thinking and, therefore, require some interpretation on the part of the scorer. Examples of acceptable responses are included in the scoring guide presented with each test.

Students' responses to questions yield five different scores: Prior Knowledge/Predicting Content, Reading Strategies, Vocabulary, Constructing Literal Meaning, and Constructing Analytical Meaning (use text information and prior knowledge to interpret text). The five categories are not mutually exclusive and a single response may contribute to two different scores (e.g., Reading Strategies and Constructing Analytical Meaning). A chart is provided that identifies what specific reading strategies, including the activation of prior knowledge and predicting content, are assessed by relevant questions at each grade level. It is important to note that questions generally assess students' prompted, not independent, use of the target strategies.

Scores in a sixth category, Constructing Extended Meaning, are obtained from students' responses to the writing activities at the end of each session. Students' papers are scored either by rating separate features (Responsiveness to the Task, Development and Organization, and Language Use) or by rating the overall effectiveness of the response. Detailed guidelines for scoring students' writing at each grade level are provided through the inclusion of scoring rubrics that define the relevant characteristic of each score and anchor papers that illustrate specific scores and the reasoning behind them.

A chart is provided for converting the raw scores in each category to percent of possible points correct. It should be noted that scoring is time-consuming, requiring 15 minutes or more for each student. Scoring can be done by groups of teachers at the school or district level, and the author provided helpful guidelines for accomplishing this task.

No psychometric data were available for Form B of the ILALAPP, the individual observation checklist, or the survey on preferences and experiences in Forms A and B. In addition, information on the construction of the instrument was incomplete. Normative data and evidence of reliability and validity, however, were presented for Form A. This test was administered to a diverse group of 3,987 students in grades 2 through 8 in five states. Summary statistics for approximately 300 randomly selected students at each grade level revealed that approximately 70% to 80% of the points possible on the test were scored by students at each grade level. Because of the possibility of ceiling effects, the use of Form A to assess progress over time is not recommended, as the test may underestimate the degree of student improvement. Although trained raters demonstrated a high degree of reliability in scoring the ILALAPP (correlations mostly in the .90s), it is not clear if normal users of the test would obtain an equivalent level of reliability. Finally, alpha coefficients and a generalizability index were modest, reflecting both rater error and examinee error, and raising questions about using the results from Form A to make decisions about individual children.

In summary, the ILALAPP represents an ambitious alternative for assessing reading and language arts. Noteworthy aspects of the instrument include guidelines for developing a portfolio approach to evaluation, recommendations for teaching based on the resulting assessment data, clear administration and scoring guidelines, and the assessment of a wide range of reading and language arts skills including attitudes, experiences, reading and listening levels, reading strategies, and writing. Nonetheless, considerable caution must be exercised when using the ILALAPP, as the psychometric qualities of the instrument have yet to be adequately established.

Review of the Integrated Literature and Language Arts Portfolio Program by REBECCA J. KOPRIVA, Associate Professor of Educational Measurement, California State University, Fresno, Fresno, CA:

Riverside's Integrated Literature and Language Arts Program consists of two assessment booklets, Forms A and B, per grade, for grades 2–8, as well as an Observation Checklist for each grade. A Teacher's Directions booklet and a Student Activity Booklet Scoring Guide (for teachers) booklet accompanies each assessment booklet. Other materials, such as a Local Scoring Leader's Handbook for school or district scoring, are optional.

Each assessment booklet consists of student activities for 3 days of testing (about 45 minutes per day). Each booklet begins with prior knowledge and experience items. Day 1 consists of a listening passage, and short answer items, selected response items, and an open-ended response item, each of which corresponds to the listening passage. Days 2 and 3 consist of a reading passage and the same kinds of items as noted above, with each item corresponding to the passage of the day. The three types of passages per booklet are categorized as a listening passage, a narrative passage, and an expository passage. Category scores aggregated across three days of activities are available from assessment booklet student data.

NORMATIVE INFORMATION. All technical information is for Form A only. Psychometric analyses were "currently planned for Form B" (manual, p. 1) as of publication in 1991. As of 1995 when this review is written there appear to be no analyses for Form B, which is very problematic. Analyses and standardization data regarding the Observation Checklists are also reported to be "in progress" as of 1991, but the data were not forthcoming for this evaluation.

From 16 public school districts and 1 Catholic district (an *n* of 3,987 students), Riverside researchers randomly selected intact classrooms so that standardization data were generated on approximately 300 students at each grade level, grades 2–8. Unfortunately, general demographic data were reported only for the 3,987 students. No information was reported in the technical manual for the members of the standardizations study. Although the Riverside researchers report that the results of the study should not be considered to be nationally representative, it is unclear of whom the data are representative.

Passages were selected and items were written. It was not stated that there was any field testing done to determine how well the items were measuring what was intended. A rationale was given under content validity about the types of features and holistic scores desired, and an explanation of the latent dimensions or categories was provided. However, no empirical evidence was presented to confirm that these methods of scoring yielded what was intended. Also, there were no bias studies done, which I think is problematic.

The following category scores were given for each student based on data aggregated across the 3 days. Prior Knowledge/Predicting Content, Reading Strategies, Vocabulary, Constructing Meaning/Literal, Constructing Meaning/Analytical, and Constructing Meaning/Extended (from the responses to the open-ended items). Constructing Meaning/Extended can be scored holistically or a score can be derived for each of three features. The three features are: Responsiveness to Task, Development and Organization of the response, and Language Use in the response. The rubric for scoring the open-ended items is generic, meaning it is not passage specific.

Data presented in the technical manual give means and mean percents of scores for each category, each day, at each level for the Form A assessments. Means, mean percents, standard deviations, and other descriptive information were given for the aggregated sets of category scores over the 3 days, per level. This appears to be a useful way to present a sense of central tendency and variability.

RELIABILITY. Alpha coefficients, interrater coefficients, and generalizability coefficients were computed. These are appropriate statistics for these types of data. Because there was no mention of the type or how much training the raters had received, it is not clear how representative were the interrater coefficients. The generalizability coefficients demonstrated that adding raters did not produce large gains in consistency; however, these results are not clear in light of the training issue.

No procedures were specified in the technical manual, the teacher scoring guide, or in the leader's handbook, regarding calibration of scorers or procedures to detect and deter drift. These are known to be important issues in ensuring accuracy of scoring.

VALIDITY. The authors explained which sources helped to shape the performances that were valued in this program, that is, the California curriculum frameworks, and the types of evidence valued by Michigan, Pennsylvania, Illinois, and Arizona state education agencies. From this input the categories were shaped. Because there was no empirical confirmation of these categories, it is not clear whether they were fully captured in this assessment program.

Authentic literature was chosen from specified recommended lists. Specified readability formulas were applied for grade appropriateness. The advantages and limits of using the recommended lists and readability formulas were clearly explained.

The teacher materials appeared to be somewhat useful, but they were too sketchy. Limited space was provided to explain how these types of assessments fit in with desired curriculum reforms. There is little discussion of how the teacher should use the data produced from the observation checklists. No training and only limited text were devoted to ensuring that teachers were scoring and interpreting the same concepts that were intended by the publishers. Unfortunately, the leader's handbook also did not address these issues, but was mostly limited to logistical and procedural tips.

SUMMARY. The Integrated Literature and Language Arts Portfolio Program does not appear to be an actual portfolio program. Rather it is a series of on-demand assessments, mostly short answer and selected response, with observation checklists provided as supplementary materials. The authors demonstrate a demand from teachers, districts, and states for performance assessment, and their categories appear to extend consistently from what is wanted in the field. Empirical support is limited for demonstrating that these items measure adequately what is intended, or to whom the standardization study data can reasonably be generalized.

[192]

Intrex Questionnaires.

Purpose: Designed to measure the patient's perceptions of self and others, based on trait x state x situational philosophy and Structural Analysis of Social Behavior (SASB).

Population: Psychiatric patients and normals.

Publication Dates: 1980–88.

Scores: Pattern Coefficient scores in each of 3 areas (2 equivalent forms): Interpersonal Transitive-Focus on Other, Interpersonal Intransitive-Focus on Self, Intrapsychic Introjection; 7 subtests: Introject (Best, Worst), He/I Present Tense (Best/Worst), She/I Present Tense (Best/Worst), He/I Past Tense (Best/Worst), She/I Past Tense (Best/Worst), Mother with Father/Father with Mother Present Tense (Best/Worst), Mother with Father/Father with Mother Past Tense (Best/Worst).

Administration: Group or individual.

Restricted Distribution: Clinical users must meet degree requirements and attend workshop on clinical uses of SASB conducted by various sponsors.
Price Data, 1991: $1 per clinical patient for short form or long form; no charge for research use of long form; $.10 for research use of short form; $20 per short form manual ('88, 106 pages); $20 per patient for profile processing by publisher; $50 per set of 5 IBM software programs for research use.
Time: (1) hour for complete battery, short form.
Author: Lorna Smith Benjamin.
Publisher: Intrex Interpersonal Institute, Inc.
Cross References: See T4:1258 (2 references).

Review of the Intrex Questionnaires by SCOTT T. MEIER, Associate Professor of Counseling and Educational Psychology, State University of New York at Buffalo, Buffalo, NY:

Lorna Smith Benjamin's Structural Analysis of Social Behavior (SASB; 1974, 1984) is an interpersonal model of human behavior based on a long history of theory building and empirical research. The SASB is perhaps best known for its use in interpersonal diagnosis (McLemore & Benjamin, 1979) as an important conceptual alternative to the medical model followed by the *Diagnostic and Statistical Manual* (DSM-V). Clearly, the strength of Benjamin's SASB lies in its history of challenging and expanding accepted beliefs about psychiatric diagnosis.

The methodology of the SASB includes a system for coding videotapes of interpersonal behavior and the long- and short-form Intrex Questionnaires. I reviewed the short-form here. The product of the questionnaires is a profile that describes respondents' transactions with others and self in terms of three basic dimensions: focus on other/self, love-hate, and enmeshment-differentiation. Additionally, a profile with pattern coefficients can be obtained to group item responses statistically into factors labeled attack, control, and conflict. Respondents rate self and others (including mother, father, and their relationship), at their "best" and "worst," on items tapping the basic dimensions. Relationship qualities are assumed to be potentially different across relationships and within each relationship over time. Sample items include "I like her and tried to see her point of view even if we disagreed," "He trustingly depended on her, willingly took in what she offered," and "Without considering what might happen, I murderously attacked him in the worst way possible."

The SASB provides information about social relationships and their presumed impact on an individual's self-concept. Thus, in the manual Benjamin suggests that the questionnaire can be usefully applied in psychotherapy to create psychotherapy goals at the beginning of therapy or rerate the items during therapy to document progress. The questionnaire is not intended as an objective evaluation of the individual, but as "subjective reports generated for the stimulation and guidance of psychotherapy when there is a collaborative relationship between the rater and the therapist" (manual, p. 8). Benjamin also suggests that the questionnaire be employed to help clients learn about their interactive patterns and the history and purposes of such patterns.

Benjamin indicates that the items can be completed by seriously disturbed persons (including those with thought disorders), but that responses must be honest. No measure of social desirability or biased responding is included. Benjamin discourages use of the questionnaire with respondents who are defensive and unable to form a collaborative relationship with the test administrator or therapist.

Although a technical section exists, data regarding reliability and validity are scattered throughout the manual. The manual needs to be reorganized so that technical information is presented in a more traditional format. Part of the problem may result from a philosophy that appears to relegate psychometric principles to a secondary status. For example, the manual states that "In the case of the Intrex reports . . . where the purpose is collaborative enhancement of interpersonal learning during psychotherapy, such technical mastery of principles of psychological testing is not required" (p. 10). SASB studies clearly emphasize theory and statistical testing of theory over psychometric evaluations.

Basic psychometric data are available in the manual, and reliability and validity estimates appear to be about average for these types of self-reports. Benjamin reported test-retest reliability estimates for a one-month period with college students: .90 for ratings of significant other at best, .67 for relationship with significant other at worst, .84 for memory of relationship with mother, and .89 for memory of relationship with father. As Benjamin notes, ratings of relationship at worst appear considerably less stable than ratings of relationship at best. These estimates, however, are based upon sample sizes of less than 20. Some validity support is provided through factor analytic results and differences between clinical groups. However, the manual contains little data about predictive validity. Further work examining predictive validity and the construct validity of the separate dimensions would be useful.

Benjamin and colleagues have clearly made considerable efforts in their theory building, methodology, and research program to significantly extend knowledge about interpersonal perceptions and behavior. To be fair, the SASB appears to be a system that requires considerable training to be applied usefully. Videotapes and workshops are offered to enable professionals to gain proficiency in the SASB approach. Nevertheless, the structure and language of the SASB Short Form User's manual is moderately disorganized, very clinically oriented, and largely idiosyncratic to the SASB. Better organization in terms of separating psychometric data and terminology from clinical data and SASB terminology would significantly improve the questionnaires' accessibility to non-SASB adherents.

REVIEWER'S REFERENCES

Benjamin, L. S. (1974). Structural analysis of social behavior. *Psychological Review, 81*, 392-425.

McLemore, C. W., & Benjamin, L. S. (1979). Whatever happened to interpersonal diagnosis? A psychosocial alternative to DSM-III. *American Psychologist, 34*, 17-34.

Benjamin, L. S. (1984). Principles of prediction using Structural Analysis of Social Behavior. In R. A. Zucker, J. Aronoff, & A. I. Rabin (Eds.), *Personality and the prediction of behavior*. Orlando: Academic Press.

[193]

Inventory of Perceptual Skills.

Purpose: "Assesses visual and auditory perceptual skills."
Population: Ages 5–10.
Publication Date: 1983.
Acronym: IPS.
Scores, 11: Visual Perception Skills (Visual Discrimination, Visual Memory, Object Recognition, Visual-Motor Coordination, Total), Auditory Perception Skills (Auditory Discrimination, Auditory Memory, Auditory Sequencing, Auditory Blending, Total), Total.
Administration: Individual.
Price Data, 1994: $45 per complete kit including manual (16 pages), stimulus cards, student workbook, and record books; $20 per 10 student record books; $15 per manual; $15 per stimulus cards; $6 per student workbook.
Time: (15) minutes.
Author: Donald R. O'Dell.
Publisher: Stoelting Co.

Review of the Inventory of Perceptual Skills by DONNA SPIKER, Clinical Assistant Professor of Psychiatry and Behavioral Sciences, Stanford University, Stanford, CA:

The Inventory of Perceptual Skills is an instrument used to evaluate visual and auditory perceptual skills in eight areas. The manual author states this instrument was developed in Oregon to assist special education teachers, and has been used there since 1979. It is recommended for use by "teachers, aides, or specialists to individual students" (manual, p. 1) to be used: (*a*) as a pre- and post-test for measuring progress in the perceptual areas identified, (*b*) as a screening device to identify problem areas, and (*c*) as an aid in instructional planning. The 16-page manual consists of very brief instructions about administration of the inventory, a copy of the form (seven pages), an example of the scoring summary from a sample student, and six pages of suggested activities for teachers to use in the classroom to promote skills in the perceptual areas tapped by the inventory. The inventory also comes with an 18-page workbook to be used with the students in the classroom; the workbook contains items that are highly similar to those on the inventory to give students practice with the perceptual areas identified.

Although the materials contained in this scale may be useful for classroom teachers in identifying specific visual and auditory perceptual skills (e.g., Visual Memory, Auditory Blending, Auditory Sequencing), and many useful suggestions for classroom activities that are creative and interesting ways to stimulate perceptual skills are in the manual, this instrument must not be construed as either a test or a screening instrument. There is no information in the manual about the actual development of the scale, the populations sampled, or normative data, and no reliability or validity data of any kind are presented.

The data form identifies the scoring for the Visual Perception Skills and the Auditory Perception Skills based on total scores of 1–10 as very low, 11–24 as low, 27–33 as low average, and 34–39 as average, with similar categorical totals which combine visual and auditory scores. There are, however, no empirical data in the manual to determine how these categorical determinations were derived. Without adequate empirical data and population characteristics for either normative or well-defined special samples, such categorical characterizations are meaningless and misleading. To qualify as a test or screening instrument, indices of test-retest reliability, interrater reliability, and convergent and predictive validity must be made available so users can assess the adequacy of this inventory. Thus, this instrument must be clearly identified and used as a classroom teaching aid, but *not* as a test or screening instrument in a psychometric sense. One of the misleading features of this inventory, that is sometimes missed by users with minimal or no psychometric training, is to assume that the separate skill areas identified are well validated as distinct skills. No data are presented to support this assumption. Furthermore, without normative data, users cannot assume that the scores obtained for the eight skill areas are comparable, an assumption made by the scoring system which treats the total scores in each area as equivalent.

There are a number of well-validated tests and scales to assess visual perceptual and auditory perceptual skills, and which should be administered by a trained psychologist or speech pathologist. These include some entire scales or subtests from the Developmental Test of Visual-Motor Integration (111), the Kaufman Assessment Battery for Children (T4:1343), the Wechsler Intelligence Scale for Children, Third Edition (412), the Wechsler Preschool and Primary Scale of Intelligence—Revised (T4:2941), and the Stanford-Binet Intelligence Scale, Fourth Edition (T4:2553) among others.

Review of the Inventory of Perceptual Skills by LOGAN WRIGHT, Associate Professor of Psychology, and TIM ECK and NATASHA GWARTNEY, Graduate Students, University of Central Oklahoma, Edmond, OK:

The purpose of the Inventory of Perceptual Skills (IPS) is the assessment of visual and auditory perceptual skills for special education students from 5 to 10 years of age. The suggested applications for the instrument include screening students for areas of poor perception, performing pre- and post-intervention comparisons, and aiding in educational planning. Materials include an instructor's manual, stimulus cards, and a student manual.

The IPS provides scores for 11 measures including Visual Discrimination, Visual Memory, Object Recognition, Visual-Motor Coordination, Total Visual Perception Skills, Auditory Discrimination, Auditory Memory, Auditory Sequencing, Auditory Blending, Total Auditory Perception Skills, and Total Auditory and Visual Perception Skills. However, no factor analytic or other rationale is given for the selection of these components or the exclusion of others.

The IPS manual author states that "no special training is required" for administration, and that "when there is a question concerning a correct response, the student should be given the benefit of the doubt" (manual, p. 1). Thus, standardization of administration and scoring is minimal. This in turn could impact the reliability and therefore the validity of the instrument.

The IPS classification scheme employs four categories: very low, low, low average, and average. However, an inconsistency exists in the scoring, in that a perfect score on the visual measures still results with the subject's placement in the "average" group. No explanation is provided for this scoring method. Therefore, the classification categories warrant further definition before the IPS is broadly accepted as a tool for academic assessment.

After completion of an initial test, students are supposed to undertake exercises in the student manual and then retake the test in order to assess improvement. However, whether improvement can be attributed to test-taking practice effects or actual changes in the subjects' perceptual abilities is not readily discernible. The Inventory's section on Visual Memory employs familiar shapes. A more valid test of visual memory might be achieved by employing some shapes with which the typical subject is *un*familiar. Given the fact that the validity of these exercises is unknown, teachers may wish to deliberate at length before spending large amounts of valuable class time on the workbook exercises.

The 11-measure IPS has not been subjected to either reliability or validity studies. Thus, the value of the IPS as a criterion measure for either research or clinical/educational judgements is questionable. However, the IPS *is* simple to administer and score. It is relatively economical, and does not make any explicit claims to predictive validity.

Further explanation (than is currently provided in the manual) of the rationale underlying the construction and utilization of the IPS would be of benefit.

Used solely as an instructional tool for special education students, the IPS may provide useful information. However, more research is needed to assess the reliability and validity of the IPS, and to provide other forms of psychometric refinement. Until then, the use of the IPS for classification or placement of students should be discouraged.

The release of the IPS for commercial distribution at this time may be premature.

[194]

Inwald Personality Inventory [Revised].

Purpose: "To aid public safety/law enforcement and security agencies in selecting new officers."
Population: Public safety, security and law enforcement applicants (post-conditional job offer only).
Publication Dates: 1980–92.
Acronym: IPI.
Scores, 26: Guardedness, Externalized Behavior Measures (Actions [Alcohol, Drugs, Driving Violations, Job Difficulties, Trouble with the Law and Society, Absence Abuse], Attitudes [Substance Abuse, Antisocial Attitudes, Hyperactivity, Rigid Type, Type A]), Internalized Conflict Measures (Illness Concerns, Treatment Programs, Anxiety, Phobic Personality, Obsessive Personality, Depression, Loner, Unusual Experiences/Thoughts), Interpersonal Conflict Measures (Lack of Assertiveness, Interpersonal Difficulties, Undue Suspiciousness, Family Conflicts, Sexual Concerns, Spouse/Mate Conflicts.
Administration: Group.
Price Data, 1993: $60 per complete starter kit including test booklet, 3 computer-scorable answer sheets, and manual ('92, 78 pages); $2 per test booklet; $2.50 per 10 Scantron/standard answer sheets; $3 per 10 Sentry answer sheets; $15 per manual; scoring service offered by publisher at $10–$12.75 per test; (all prices may be adjusted for volume discounts).
Time: (30–45) minutes.
Author: Robin Inwald.
Publisher: Hilson Research, Inc.
Cross References: See T4:1275 (1 reference); for reviews of an earlier edition by Samuel Juni and Niels G. Waller, see 11:183 (2 references); for reviews of an earlier edition by Brian Bolton and Jon D. Swartz, see 9:530.

Review of the Inwald Personality Inventory [Revised] by BRIAN BOLTON, University Professor, Arkansas Research and Training Center in Vocational Rehabilitation, University of Arkansas, Fayetteville, AR:

Recent allegations of police corruption; unwarranted use of force, including brutality and murder; and other forms of misbehavior have brought to public attention the importance of careful selection of police officer candidates. The Inwald Personality Inventory (IPI) was developed 12 years ago for the express purpose of improving the effectiveness of the law enforcement officer selection process. After a decade of experience in candidate evaluation and the accumulation of considerable evidence for predictive validity, it is appropriate now to rereview the IPI.

My first review of the IPI was published in the *Ninth Mental Measurements Yearbook* (Bolton, 1985). Since then the IPI computer report has been expanded and the IPI technical manual has been revised, with the results of recent validity studies added, along with other changes. For the convenience of readers who would like to refer to the original review, the psychometric issues are addressed below in the same order as in the first review. However, the current review can also be read independently of the initial review.

The IPI booklet and the scored scales have not been modified. The 26 scales are grouped into five types of measures: Validity (i.e., Guardedness), Acting-Out Behavior (e.g., Drugs, Trouble with the Law and Society), Attitudes and Temperament (e.g., Hyperactivity, Rigid Type), Internalized Conflict (e.g., Anxiety, Obsessive Personality), and Interpersonal Conflict (e.g., Interpersonal Difficulties, Family Conflicts).

Dr. Inwald did not explain how she selected or developed the 26 scales, except to say that the scales were designed using a "common sense" approach to the measurement of behavioral patterns relevant to successful performance in a stressful occupation. She generated the 310 IPI items from a review of over 2,500 pre-employment interviews with public safety officer candidates. No specific guidelines were followed; the author simply depended on her "best judgment" to identify the items for the inventory.

Several comments about the construction of the IPI are warranted. First, because Dr. Inwald is a psychologist, it must be assumed that she relied, in part, on the results of several decades of personality assessment research to develop the IPI scales. And although it is true that the rational (or deductive) approach to test construction has been demonstrated to be as effective as sophisticated statistical strategies, this does not relieve test authors of the responsibility for providing an outline of the instrument development plan.

I am sure that Dr. Inwald had a tentative map of the behavioral domain that she wanted to measure firmly in mind when she initiated work on the IPI, but that plan should have been made explicit for users. What was the specific rationale for the various scales? Where did the ideas for the scales originate? At the very least, the manual should include a table showing the items that are keyed on each of the 26 scales. This information would provide literal (content) definitions of the scales.

The data presented in the manual do not permit an accurate evaluation of the dimensionality of the IPI. Tabled factor analytic results include fewer than half of the 26 scales. These incomplete data suggest that one factor accounts for about 60% of the variability in the IPI scales. This finding is not unreasonable, considering the relatively high proportion of multiply keyed items (i.e., more than half of the items are scored on two or more scales). With all of the data that have been collected, there is really no excuse for not publishing a definitive factor analysis of the IPI.

The IPI can be scored only by the publisher. The computer-generated IPI report includes six sections. The narrative section provides one brief interpretive paragraph for each of the 26 scales. These are previously prepared or "canned" statements that correspond to score intervals on the scales. The author repeatedly cautions users not to quote these interpretive statements in psychological reports. The second section lists "critical items" for follow-up evaluation and converts the total to a standard score. It was not explained how the critical responses were identified; presumably, the author's clinical judgment was the criterion applied.

The third section of the IPI report presents a statistical prediction of the risk rating (low, moderate, high) assigned by a psychologist after conducting a comprehensive assessment based on other tests and an interview. The fourth section includes statistical predictions of four performance criteria: tardiness, absences, disciplinary actions, and termination. The fifth section is a standard normative profile of the 26 scale scores in a graphical form. The final section contains a printout of the examinee's responses to the 310 items.

The description of the IPI computer report contains a statement that separate norms for males and females are used, but a short section at the end of the manual indicates that a combined norm group is employed. The current normative sample is apparently composed of 1,512 male and 873 female public safety officer applicants. No other demographic information is provided. An analysis of the recommended decision rule for designating "high risk" candidates identified equal proportions of males and females in the normative sample. Interestingly, an earlier study of sex difference found IPI results consistent with "stereotypical behavior patterns of males and females" (manual, p. 44).

Although the normative sample is not adequately described, the normative data tabled in the manual suggest that females and minority candidates may be overrepresented. Without presenting any supporting data, the author indicates in a short sentence that "National norms on the IPI have remained stable over the past decade, with the exception of the DV (Driving Violations) scale" (p. 12). Considering the enormous amount of data that have been collected during the last 12 years, it should be a straightforward task to construct a large normative sample that is representative in terms of sex, race, age, location, position, and other relevant demographic variables. This information should be detailed in the manual.

The only reliability statistics presented for the IPI scales are the original figures. Median test-retest coefficients with a 6- to 8-week interval for male and female correction officer candidates were .72 and .70, respectively. Almost all coefficients were between .60 and .80. Four of the scales are rather short, with just three, five, six, and eight items. Although the reported reliabilities for the IPI scales are adequate, it should be noted that the coefficients would be somewhat higher with a more appropriate interval of 1 to 2 weeks.

The strongest feature of the IPI is the program of ongoing validation research. Since 1982, two dozen studies of the predictive validity of the IPI have been carried out. The typical investigation of law enforcement officer candidates compared the IPI with the MMPI (Minnesota Multiphasic Personality Inventory) in predicting a variety of performance criteria. The outcomes usually analyzed were termination and disciplinary reviews, with lateness, absences, and supervisory ratings often included. Various other criteria were also studied, such as psychologists' risk ratings, derelictions, results of urinalysis, psychiatric illness, and examination scores.

The outcomes were typically assessed between 6 and 12 months after the IPI was administered, but two investigators obtained follow-up data on hired candidates 5 and 7 years later. The research samples included police officer applicants, correction officer candidates, government security personnel applicants, and candidates for other law enforcement positions. Samples were divided by sex and occasionally separated by race/ethnicity (White, Black, Hispanic). The results of cross-validated statistical analyses demonstrated that the IPI consistently predicted the performance criteria more accurately than the MMPI, but that the two instruments in combination produced the most accurate predictions.

The latter result is consistent with the findings of a redundancy analysis of the IPI and MMPI. These two instruments have a rather small overlap, suggesting that the IPI generally measures nonpathological characteristics and behavior patterns. It is unfortunate the results of the validity investigations are presented only in nonstandardized abstracts in the manual. A tabulation consisting of the samples, procedures, and findings of each study, with an overall statistical integration, would be an excellent way to summarize the predictive validity of the IPI. Ironically, the manual does include a nice summary table for a dozen "selected" predictive studies that is not referred to in the validity section!

The final section of the manual contains a discussion of the implications of the Americans with Disabilities Act when using the IPI as a psychological screening instrument. Two issues are critical: the IPI has empirically documented job-relatedness and it has never been recommended for use in diagnosing specific mental disorders. After reviewing the opinions of several professional organizations, the author concluded that the IPI can be appropriately used in the assessment of police officer candidates, but should be administered only after a conditional job offer has been made.

SUMMARY. The IPI was developed to assist psychologists in the assessment of police officer candidates. The revised IPI has an expanded computer report and is supported by additional validity evidence. The manual does not present the rationale for the development of the instrument, nor is the normative sample adequately described. The manual is poorly organized and should be revised again. During the past decade two dozen studies of the predictive validity of the IPI against a variety of outcome criteria have been conducted. The research results support the value of the IPI in assessing the suitability of law enforcement officer applicants. Despite the deficiencies noted above, it can be concluded that the IPI has been demonstrated to be useful for its intended application.

REVIEWER'S REFERENCE

Bolton, B. (1985). [Review of the Inwald Personality Inventory]. In J. V. Mitchell, Jr. (Ed.), *The ninth mental measurements yearbook* (pp. 711-713). Lincoln, NE: Buros Institute of Mental Measurements.

Review of the Inwald Personality Inventory [Revised] by RICHARD I. LANYON, Professor of Psychology, Arizona State University, Tempe, AZ:

This is the third *MMY* review for the Inwald Personality Inventory (IPI), and it is occasioned by the appearance of the revised edition of the manual in 1992. The IPI is a 310-item, 26-scale, true/false inventory intended "to aid public safety/law enforcement agencies in selecting new officers who will be able to satisfy job requirements" (technical manual, p. 2). Scoring is available only through Hilson Research, Inc., by mailing back the answer sheet or by computer linkage. A computerized narrative report is provided to the user; however, the manual author warns the user not to utilize statements from the report unless independent information has been obtained to verify the accuracy of the statements.

The manual author states the IPI scales were designed "to measure specific behavioral patterns or characteristics judged appropriate and necessary in the evaluation of a job candidate's 'suitability' to perform in a stressful occupation" (p. 5). Representative examples of scale names include Rigid Type, Alcohol, Job Difficulties, Phobic Personality, Depression, and Undue Suspiciousness. The manual author points out that the bars on the computer-generated profile graph are divided into three areas: Externalized Behavior Measures, Internalized Conflict Measures, and Interpersonal Conflict Measures. In fact, they are divided into four areas, plus the Guardedness scale as a fifth area, and the computerized narrative is also divided into four areas. Eight sets of norms for males and eight for females, with sample sizes ranging from 15 to more than 2,000 are presented. It is not indicated which normative group or groups are used in the preparation of the computerized report, or if they differ according to the person being tested.

The test itself appears to be basically unchanged from its original publication in 1982. Its development at that time employed procedures that have been obsolete for many years. Essentially, there was no development at all. On the basis of clinical experience with employment interviewing, items were written and fitted, using the author's "best judgment," into scale categories that were apparently also created subjectively. The extensive available technology of test construction appears to have been completely ignored. The essential components of this technology, as demonstrated in the development of tests such as the NEO Personality Inventory (Costa & McCrae, 1986; 330) and the Personality Assessment Inventory (Morey, 1991; 290), include the formulation of concepts based on a systematic plan, development of a definition and universe of content for each concept, preparation of items that map each universe, and psychometric procedures that include the computation of item reliabilities, skewness, relationship to social desirability, item correlations within each preliminary scale and with other scales, and exploratory and/or confirmatory factor analyses. The purpose of this tedious but necessary work is, of course, to build into each scale the potential for the greatest possible validity in practical use. Indeed, each step contributes to the potential for predictive accuracy in a unique way.

The use of no more than common sense in putting a test together practically guarantees a low ceiling on predictive accuracy, and the validity research reported in the manual confirms this expectation. An overall analysis of reported studies that give cross-validated figures for predicting job success show an overall hit rate of only about 60%. A further difficulty is that most of the studies use discriminant function analyses, which yield the "statistically best" prediction. It is unlikely that either the computerized narrative report or the test user's subjective analysis of the profile could achieve even this level of accuracy.

Examination of the several exploratory factor analyses presented in the manual indicates that a single factor consistently accounts for about two thirds of the common variance in the IPI scales. This factor is represented by the scales Rigid Type, Type "A," and Undue Suspiciousness. The second factor represents substance abuse/impulsiveness/hyperactivity, and the content of the third factor varies among the analyses. However, the relatively few studies listing the actual scales that carry the greatest predictive power for job success versus failure show that two entirely different concepts are relied on to make these predictions: a "mental health problems" concept and a "previous legal and job difficulties" concept. Thus, it is likely that a test assessing the latter concepts, developed in a methodologically adequate manner, would have better success than the IPI in making relevant predictions in the public safety personnel area.

The major difficulties with the IPI and the 1982 manual, as identified in Bolton's (1985) review, remain in the 1992 edition. In addition to those discussed above, the computer-generated report has no demonstrated empirical basis, and the manual author instructs the user to all but disregard it. Thus, there appears to be no supportable reason to continue offering it. Also, the profile form incorrectly displays a zero through 100 range for the *T*-scores that represent each scale, giving the impression that they are percentiles.

OVERVIEW. Although the manual emphasizes that the IPI is to be used as only one of a number of sources of information in making a personnel decision, it is difficult to believe that enough useful information is added by such low hit rates to justifying using it. It is commendable that a significant amount of research has been done on the ability of the IPI to make useful predictions, and those data give the beginnings of an empirical basis for understanding what predictors might be most relevant. Thus, a partial foundation is laid for a new and properly constructed instrument that would be potentially useful.

REVIEWER'S REFERENCES

Bolton, B. (1985). [Review of the Inwald Personality Inventory.] In J. V. Mitchell, Jr. (Ed.), *The ninth mental measurements yearbook* (pp. 711-713). Lincoln, NE: Buros Institute of Mental Measurements.

Costa, P. T., Jr., & McCrae, R. R. (1986). *NEO Personality Inventory: Manual*. Odessa, FL: Psychological Assessment Resources.

Morey, C. C. (1991). *Personality Assessment Inventory: Manual*. Odessa, FL: Psychological Assessment Resources.

[195]

Iowa Algebra Aptitude Test, Fourth Edition.

Purpose: "To assess student readiness for Algebra I."
Population: Grades 7–8.
Publication Dates: 1931–93.
Acronym: IAAT.
Scores, 5: Interpreting Mathematical Information, Translating to Symbols, Finding Relationships, Using Symbols, Total.
Administration: Group.
Price Data, 1993: $48 per 25 test booklets Form 1 or 2; $4.50 per Directions for Administration ('93, 13 pages); $24 per 25 self-scoring answer sheets; $66 per 100 computer-scored answer sheets; $18 per 25 class record sheets; $15 per Manual for Test Use and Interpretation ('93, 26 pages); $18 per 25 report to parents and students; $1,200 per scanning and scoring system; $18 per examination kit.
Time: (50) minutes.
Authors: Harold L. Schoen, Timothy N. Ansley, H. D. Hoover, Beverly S. Rich, Sheila I. Barron, and Robert

A. Bye. (Earlier edition by Harry A. Greene and Darrell Sabers).

Publisher: The Riverside Publishing Co.

Cross References: See T2:681 (7 references); for reviews by W. L. Bashaw and Cyril J. Hoyt, and an excerpted review by Russell A. Chadbourn of an earlier edition, see 7:*505* (8 references); for reviews by Harold Gulliken and Emma Spaney of an earlier edition, see 4:393; for a review by David Segel, see 3:327 (2 references); for reviews by Richard M. Drake and M. W. Richardson, see 2:1441 (1 reference).

Review of the Iowa Algebra Aptitude Test, Fourth Edition by JOHN W. FLEENOR, Research Scientist, Center for Creative Leadership, Greensboro, NC:

The first edition of the Iowa Algebra Aptitude Test (IAAT) was published in 1931. Revised editions of the test were published in 1942 and 1967. The two revisions received generally positive reviews in the *Mental Measurements Yearbooks*. The Fourth Edition of the IAAT represents a major revision in which the test content was revised following standards set by the National Council of Teachers of Mathematics (NCTM). According to the authors, the content of the test was brought in line with current thinking in math education in areas such as (*a*) symbolism and language, (*b*) applications of algebra, (*c*) interpretation of graphs, and (*d*) emphasis on problem solving rather than computation. Using the NCTM standards as a guide, the authors developed two equivalent forms of the test, each having 63 items and four parts. The items were developed using standard psychometric procedures (e.g., item discrimination and difficulty). The authors indicate that all the items on the Fourth Edition of the IAAT were newly developed; however, some of these items are similar to items on the Third Edition.

ADMINISTRATION AND SCORING. The IAAT is a speeded test with a total completion time of 36 minutes. The four subtests are timed separately. All items are in a four-alternative multiple-choice format. Several items have "not given" or "not enough information to tell" as alternatives. The test is administered in a group setting. Scoring can be completed by hand using self-scoring answer sheets, or answer sheets can be scanned and scored by NCS scanning equipment and software sold by the publisher. The format and print quality of the test booklets and answer sheets are excellent.

The IAAT yields five raw scores (four subtest scores plus a total score). Total scores are presented as four types of derived scores: (*a*) standard scores ($M = 150$, $SD = 15$), (*b*) percentile ranks, (*c*) stanines, and (*d*) normal curve equivalents ($M = 50$, $SD = 21.06$). Normal curve equivalents are useful for comparing IAAT scores with scores from similar measures. Tables for converting the raw scores to derived scores are in the technical manual. The raw and derived scores are recorded in spaces provided on the answer sheets. A class record sheet also is included.

The authors stress that IAAT scores must be interpreted in the context of other information regarding a student's mathematical abilities (e.g., teacher observations and recommendations).

NORMS. The test was standardized on a national sample of approximately 8,000 7th and 8th grade students from 98 public and private schools in the U.S. Normative data, however, are reported only for the 8th graders ($n = 5{,}359$). Sampling was stratified by geographic region, district enrollment, and socioeconomic status. There were approximately equal numbers of males and females in the sample.

RELIABILITY. Internal consistency reliabilities (KR20) were estimated using four subsamples of the standardization sample. The subsamples were separated by test form and grade level. Internal consistency reliabilities of the four subtests ranged from .67 to .84 with a median of .77. The reliabilities of the total scores were .90 or higher. The intercorrelations of the subtests ranged from .50 to .68 with a median of .57. Standard errors of measurement for various standard score levels also are presented in the manual. For example, for a standard score of 150, the standard error of measurement is 4.8.

No evidence of test-retest or alternate forms reliability is presented in the manual. The reliabilities of the difference scores among the four subtests are presented; however, the meaningfulness and the usefulness of these coefficients for the test user is not apparent. Additionally, because the IAAT is a timed test, any estimate of reliability must be interpreted with caution. The manual does not indicate what percentage of students complete all the items on each subtest.

VALIDITY. The authors indicate that content validity for the IAAT was assured by using the NCTM standards to develop the test items, and by using subject matter experts to evaluate the content and possible bias of the items. Each user, however, must determine if the test is appropriate for the intended application. The authors report that a test of gender bias of the IAAT indicated that the test did not yield biased predictions of success in algebra for either males or females.

As evidence of criterion-related validity, the authors report correlations between IAAT total scores and exam scores and grades from two semesters of Algebra I ($n = 825$). The uncorrected correlation coefficients ranged from .45 to .69. The authors also present correlations of the IAAT total scores with scores from the math sections of the Iowa Tests of Basic Skills (ITBS) ($r = .69$) and the Iowa Tests of Educational Development (ITED) ($r = .48$).

As additional evidence of criterion-related validity, multiple regressions were conducted using IAAT total scores and ITBS math scores as predictors and Algebra I exam scores and grades as criteria. The IAAT scores were found to add significantly to the power of the ITBS scores to predict success in Algebra I.

CONCLUSION. The IAAT appears to demonstrate acceptable levels of internal consistency reliability and criterion-related validity. Some evidence of test-retest and alternate forms reliability is necessary, however, before the test can be recommended without reservation. Because this edition of the IAAT was only recently published, one hopes that additional reliability and validity studies are being conducted.

The revised content of the items and the subtests seems to be an improvement over the Third Edition. However, two of the revised subtests, Interpreting Mathematical Information and Translating to Symbols, are similar in some ways to subtests from the earlier edition.

The technical manual is well written, and it presents much useful information for the test user. The test package also contains an administrator's manual with verbatim instructions for administering the test. Additionally, the normative sample used for the Fourth Edition appears to be more representative than the sample used in the earlier editions.

Review of the Iowa Algebra Aptitude Test, Fourth Edition by JUDITH A. MONSAAS, Visiting Associate Professor of Educational Studies, Emory University, Atlanta, GA:

The Fourth Edition of the Iowa Algebra Aptitude Test (IAAT) is designed to assist educators in making placement decisions for 7th and 8th grade students entering the secondary mathematics curriculum. There are two forms (Forms 1 and 2) and four subtests (Interpreting Mathematical Information, Translating to Symbols, Finding Relationships, and Using Symbols). The content reflects a considerable change from the Third Edition published in 1967. This current edition uses the *Curriculum and Evaluation Standards for School Mathematics* from the National Council of Teachers of Mathematics (1989) as a guide to bring the test content in line with the math curricular recommendations. Additionally, the authors claim to have used cognitive research in Algebra to guide the test construction.

BOOKLETS AND MATERIALS. The test booklets are well designed and clearly written. The graphics are attractive and the items are read easily and well spaced. Bashaw (1972) had found some of the items in the Third Edition "cramped." The test appears to do a good job of testing the understanding of concepts rather than computational skills. Further, one can see the authors' efforts to make the problems "real life," especially in the first subtest. Each subtest begins with clear directions and a brief section entitled "How to Use the Skills Tested." This includes a description of how the skills in this subtest are relevant/important in everyday life. For example, the section on "Interpreting Mathematical Information" ties the importance of reading mathematical/technical information to the problems that many adults have programming a VCR.

Manuals and score reports are attractive and clearly written. Educators should have no difficulty administering the test after a careful reading of the administrators manual. The score reports for parents report raw scores and percentiles by subtest and total test and explain clearly how to interpret the scores. In all, the tests, manuals, and score reports reflect the quality that we have come to expect from the professionals at Iowa/Riverside.

NORMS. The norms in the Fourth Edition of the IAAT seem to be an improvement over those of the Third Edition. Bashaw (1972) felt that the national norms in the earlier edition were poorly identified. The current norms include 7th and 8th grade students from 88 public schools in 38 states plus a nonpublic school sample gathered in 1991. Unfortunately, the norm data are reported only for 8th graders because the 7th grade sample used volunteers and thus did not constitute a representative sample. In fact, the 7th grade group performed better than the 8th grade group. The norms were not reported for 7th graders—a limitation for a test measuring a construct on which one would expect 7th and 8th graders to differ. The 8th grade sample was compared to the national population on several demographic variables. Unweighted samples were adequate and the weighted samples were good in terms of geographic region, district size, and socioeconomic status. One weakness was the racial/ethnic representativeness of the sample. Blacks were considerably underrepresented (8.3% in the sample vs. 16.1% in the population) and weighting did little to correct this (9.4% Blacks in the weighted sample). In all, the 8th grade norms seem to be more representative than those of earlier editions but there is still room for improvement.

RELIABILITY. Reliability estimates were obtained using information from the grade 7 and 8 norm groups although it is not clear if the entire standardization sample was used. KR20s reveal good subtest reliability coefficients ranging from .67 to .84 and total test reliability over .90 for both forms of the test. Notably missing is any test-retest or equivalent forms reliability.

VALIDITY. The strength of the test is in the careful adherence to the *NCTM Standards* (1989) in the development of the IAAT. The procedure for development included careful review of current texts and the mathematics educational research literature, careful item review and field testing, and content review by mathematics educators. The authors note that despite the care involved in the development of the IAAT, users should review the test carefully to insure that it is appropriate for their particular application. The test was reviewed for gender bias but no mention was made of any attempt to check for racial/ethnic bias.

Criterion-related validity studies reveal that the IAAT does a good job of predicting 9th grade Algebra grades and test scores. IAAT scores were also significantly related to ITBS Mathematics Total scores (r = .69) and ITED Quantitative Thinking scores (r = .48). The authors also noted that multiple regression analyses demonstrated "that the IAAT composite scores did indeed significantly add to the prediction of success in Algebra 1" (Manual for Test Use and Administration, p. 14). This writer would like to see the statistical estimates to support these results. Given the sample size of 825, a relative small increase in prediction could be statistically significant, but of little substantive significance.

No data on construct validity were provided in the manual. This is of some concern because the authors indicate that they used the latest cognitive research in Algebra in the test's development. Some description of how this research was used and evidence that students had to use the cognitive skills assessed by the test would have strengthened this claim.

In summary, this test appears to be well constructed. The quality of the materials is very professional. The technical characteristics are adequate although 7th grade norms and equivalent forms reliability would seem important additions. In all, the test would seem to help in making secondary Algebra placement decisions, especially in programs emphasizing *NCTM Standards* (1989). As with any test, users should review all materials to ensure appropriateness for their particular situation.

REVIEWER'S REFERENCES

Bashaw, W. L. (1972). [Review of the Iowa Algebra Aptitude Tests—Third Edition]. In O. K. Buros (Ed.), *The seventh mental measurements yearbook* (pp. 899-900). Highland Park, NJ: The Gryphon Press.

National Council of Teachers of Mathematics. (1989). *Curriculum and evaluation standards for school mathematics*. Reston, VA: Author.

[196]

Iowa's Severity Rating Scales for Speech and Language Impairments.

Purpose: Intended to provide a system to transform results of speech and language assessments into severity of impairment scores.
Population: Pupils of all ages served in the school.
Publication Dates: 1978–86.
Scores: 5 ratings: Language Severity, Articulation Severity, Voice Severity, Fluency Severity, Combined Severity.
Administration: Individual.
Price Data: Not available.
Time: Administration time not reported.
Comments: Revision of Iowa's Severity Rating Scale for Communication Disabilities.
Author: Iowa Department of Education.
Publisher: PRO-ED, Inc.
[The publisher advised in June 1993 that this test is now out of print.—Ed.]

Review of Iowa's Severity Rating Scales for Speech and Language Impairments by AIMÉE LANGLOIS, Professor of Child Development, Humboldt State University, Arcata, CA:

SYNOPSIS. The Iowa's Severity Rating Scales for Speech and Language Impairments (SRS) is designed for speech-language pathologists to rate their school-age patients' Articulation, Language, Voice, and Fluency on a 5-point severity continuum from 0 to 4. The authors identify specific scoring criteria for the scales in the following manner: 0 and 1 = adequate speech and language, 2 and 3 = speech and language deviations, 4 = speech and language disorders. Clinicians are enjoined to use these criteria to rate each of the above speech and language parameters for their patients following an assessment; it is suggested that severity ratings be based on test results, informal observations, and history information. In addition, the authors indicate that SRS criteria can be used to document patient changes when a program of therapy is completed. Scoring criteria are provided respectively for the parameters of Articulation, Language, Voice, and Fluency; instructions are also given for determining both specific severity ratings for each parameter and the overall severity of a patient's speech and language skills.

CRITIQUE. The authors provide a cogent description of the pitfalls of labeling and classifying individuals with speech and language disorders. They view the SRS as "an attempt to make labeling a meaningful step" (manual, p. 13), in the diagnostic and therapeutic process. However, the authors do not explain clearly how much more meaningful a label is when a severity rating of 0 to 4 is tied to it. They simply state the "the severity of any deficit must first be determined" presumably following "the appraisal of a speech and language difference" (p. 17), an assertion that some might consider debatable. In addition, the rationale presented for determining the overall severity rating—a process which does not reflect the mathematical computation of the four parameter ratings—is lost on this reader.

The authors rightfully caution clinicians throughout the SRS manual to "exercise sound professional clinical judgement" (p. 25) and to consider diagnostic and a host of other factors when making clinical decisions and assigning a severity rating. Some of the factors listed include age, attending behavior, stimulability, consistency of errors, and the home environment. However, the criteria provided for rating each speech and language parameter do not take into account many of the numerous factors listed in the manual. Moreover, the distinction between speech and language deviations (ratings of 2 and 3) and disorders (rating of 4) emphasized at the beginning of the manual is not provided; these terms are not even used in the descriptions of characteristics to consider to determine the severity of each parameter. For example, the Articulation scale assigns scores on the basis of intelligibility, types of errors, and appropriateness of sound development (phonological processes and phoneme development) without attention to what may be considered articulatory deviations and disorders. In the case of Language, the authors state that "criteria developed for the [scale] addresses [sic] syntax, semantics, pragmatics, and morphology" (p. 65). However, a closer look reveals that only the language component of pragmatics is rated.

Other weaknesses of the SRS include but are not limited to the absence of reliability and validity information. Although reference is made to "a year of study and a year of field testing" (foreword) no information is provided about the data gathered during that period of time. The authors' assertion that the "system also has the advantage of allowing one to measure progress over time" (p. 23) must be demonstrated with test-retest reliability data. The manual does provide case histories with which readers can train themselves; it is, however, unknown whether clinicians with different levels of training and experience would rate the patients described in these case histories as reliably as the authors. The sole reliance on "perceptual judgements of voice" (p. 95) to rate the severity of phonatory disturbances also demands documentation of interrater reliability not to mention a determination of the validity of such an approach.

The value and validity of the SRS are deemed questionable in light of other factors such as: the absence of content and concurrent validity, the fact that "severity ratings are not directly translatable into intervention strategies" (p. 24), the exclusion of information about the structure-function of the oral mechanism, and the lack of consideration for aspects of second language learning for the articulation and language scales. On the Fluency scale severity ratings pertain only to the problem of stuttering to the exclusion of fluency disturbances seen in other disorders such as cluttering and apraxia of speech. In addition, ratings of 3 and 4 on the Fluency scale do not appear to reflect obvious distinctions.

SUMMARY. The SRS is a tool that speech-language pathologists should use with caution to rate the severity of their patients' communicative disorders. Its strength lies in the authors' repeated recommendation that therapists use sound clinical judgement based on test results, informal observations, and history information when making decisions about initiating and terminating treatment; to support their point the authors provide valuable lists of factors to consider to aid in the decision-making process. In this light assigning a severity rating to a speech and/or language impairment is seen as superfluous. Furthermore, in the absence of reliability and validity data the usefulness of the SRS as a clinical tool is yet to be determined.

[197]

Is This Autism? A Checklist of Behaviours and Skills for Children Showing Autistic Features.

Purpose: Designed to indicate the presence of autistic features in each area in order to develop educational and therapeutic programs.

Population: Ages 2–8.

Publication Date: 1987.

Scores: Item scores only in 8 areas: General Observations, Attention Control, Sensory Function, Non-Verbal Symbolic Function, Concept Formation, Sequencing and Rhythmic Abilities, Speech and Language, Educational Attainments and Intelligence.

Administration: Individual.

Price Data, 1992: £32.20 per complete kit including handbook (31 pages); £18.70 per 10 checklists.

Time: Untimed.

Comments: Other test materials (e.g., Playdo, cubes) must be supplied by examiner.

Authors: Maureen Aarons and Tessa Gittens.

Publisher: NFER-Nelson Publishing Co., Ltd. [England].

Review of Is This Autism? A Checklist of Behaviours and Skills for Children Showing Autistic Features by WILLIAM M. BART, Professor of Educational Psychology, University of Minnesota, Minneapolis, MN:

The authors of this Checklist are speech therapists and contend that autism can be placed on a deficit continuum with social, educational, and linguistic features. With that underlying assumption in mind, they recommend against using the Checklist to determine whether a child is autistic or not. Rather, they hold the Checklist can be used to identify behaviors and attributes among children that are related to autism. They also contend that the Checklist could be useful for practitioners who work with a wide range of handicapped children who manifest various autistic features.

The handbook for the Checklist attests to the scholarship of the authors, as a substantial body of relevant research on autism is reviewed. A case is made for each of the eight sections in the checklist: General Observations, Attention Control, Sensory Function, Non-Verbal Symbolic Function, Concept Formation, Sequencing and Rhythmic Abilities, Speech and Language, and Educational Attainments and Intelligence. The Checklist is clearly rooted in disciplined inquiry.

The Checklist is intended for use with children who are 2–8 years of age. For some parts in the Checklist, an observer would indicate whether a child manifests a certain type of behavior or not. For other parts in the Checklist, the observer describes certain skills and behavior patterns of the child being assessed. Thus, certain parts of the Checklist require short answers such as one-word responses and other parts of the Checklist require longer answers in the form of sentences and even paragraphs. Both the various parts of the Checklist and the responses to the parts are quite varied in their form.

One reason for the variety of parts of the Checklist is that it is eclectic and composed of parts of other tests and measurement devices. For example, the recommended method of assessing classification and sorting skills and behaviors entails usage of vocabulary cards from another testing instrument. The Checklist is not self-sufficient, but requires usage of parts of other tests.

The Checklist is also intended to guide treatment of child subjects. In the summary part of each Checklist section, there is room for an observer to suggest goals for the subject regarding the behaviors and skills associated with that Checklist section. From a consideration of such goals, the observer could then consider a treatment to facilitate the attainment of those goals.

The scoring of the items in the Checklist is somewhat elusive. The authors recommend using a scoring code with three levels: (*a*) the first level relates to the subject manifesting some understanding of the task without completing the task; (*b*) the second level relates to the subject earnestly attempting to complete the task with some success; and (*c*) the third level relates to the subject completing the task successfully. However, even with such a scoring code, it seems that the predominant scoring system being recommended with the Checklist is a qualitative one, as the observer considers the various items in one of the sections in the Checklist along with the responses to the items and then renders a holistic judgment in the summary part of the Checklist section as to the degree to which the subject manifests autistically related behaviors and skills associated with that section in the Checklist.

In addition to the vagueness of the scoring procedure used with the Checklist, there is the paucity of description regarding the psychometric properties of the Checklist. No information is provided as to reliability or validity, although an argument could be made in support of the content validity of the Checklist. This Checklist lacks an array of necessary data to support its reliability and validity.

In general, the Checklist is essentially a qualitative instrument that may likely be of help to individuals interested in assessing children for skills and behaviors that are related to autism.

Review of Is This Autism? A Checklist of Behaviours and Skills for Children Showing Autistic Features by DOREEN WARD FAIRBANK, Adjunct Assistant Professor of Psychology, Meredith College, Raleigh, NC:

Is This Autism? A Checklist of Behaviours and Skills for Children Showing Autistic Features was designed initially for speech therapists to gather information on children (ages 2–8 years) with suspected autistic features. The authors have attempted to revise the instrument to be relevant to any professional group concerned with the care, assessment, or treatment of young children with autistic characteristics or behaviors. The information obtained is intended to provide a pattern of relative strengths and weaknesses rather than a statistical comparison with normal peers. The authors base this approach on their observations that children with autism "may develop skills unevenly, omit some stages or appear not to follow the usual developmental order" (manual, p. 6). It is these unstable areas of emerging skills and the relationship between the various aspects of development that the Checklist aims to identify. A clear strength of Is This Autism? is that it provides a systematic method of collecting and organizing information across areas of social, educational, and language development and could serve as the basis of a comprehensive individual needs assessment.

Is This Autism? consists of a handbook and a Checklist of Behaviours and Skills for Children Showing Autistic Features. Aarons and Gittens (the authors) divided the Checklist into eight sections that are intended to represent a developmental approach and order: General Observations, Attention Control, Sensory Function, Non-Verbal Symbolic Function, Concept Formation, Sequencing and Rhythmic Abilities, Speech and Language, and Educational Attainments and Intelligence.

The handbook that accompanies Is This Autism? contains a short history and excellent summary of autism. Commentary in the handbook is cross referenced to items in the Checklist and provides information on research findings, theoretical concepts, and clinical observations underlying each question as well as examples and specifications for response criteria. In principle, these item-by-item specifications should enhance the consistency of administration of Is This Autism? by professionals.

A major limitation of Is This Autism? is that the instrument (Checklist and handbook) is not self-contained with respect to providing all the information and materials necessary for administration. Several additional instruments and texts are needed to administer the checklist, including Lowe and Costello's "Symbolic Play Test" for Section IV, and the "Derbyshire Language Scale," "Test of Recognition of Grammar (TROG)," and "Reynell Developmental Language Scales" for Section VII. In addition, users are advised to be "thoroughly familiar" with Cooper, Moodley, & Reynell's (1978) text titled "Helping Language Development," because Sections II, IV, and V are influenced by this work.

The instrument also does not contain the equipment needed to complete the test, such as unifix cubes, Logiblocs, and John Horniman Outline Vocabulary Cards. Although the handbook lists the equipment needed for each item as well as the names and addresses of suppliers, all are located in Great Britain and may be of limited accessibility to some potential users in North America.

Most importantly, the handbook authors do not provide any information on the interrater and test-retest reliability of the instrument, nor on the validity of the instrument as a measure to detect and describe autistic characteristics and features in young children. Information on the specificity and sensitivity of the items in the instrument for detecting behavioral excesses and deficits associated with autism is needed. It would be helpful to know, for example, how well the items in this instrument correspond with information obtained from other instruments with known psychometric properties, such as The Autism Screening Instrument for Educational Planning (ASIEP; T4:235) by Krug, Arick, and Almond.

More space is needed on the Checklist for recording observations and qualitative information, such as descriptions of appearance and behavior. Also, the procedures for administering the instrument are not completely clear. In particular, Appendix I could provide more information about how to use the recommended scoring codes. The authors do not specify the items for which the codes are intended. Although they do not specify how to score a task the child does not attempt, I assume this would be coded "0."

Instructions for administering some items are insufficient, especially for items that are general and potentially subjective, such as "Does the child show any signs of neurological abnormality?"

The instrument could also benefit from specifying in greater detail the potential sources of information for each of the eight sections. Across sections it appears that both sources and methods for obtaining information vary considerably (e.g., interview with parent, observation of child, abstraction of information from medical or educational records, interview with teachers, administration of performance test to child, etc.). The level of training required for examiners to administer this instrument is also unspecified.

If this instrument is to be marketed in North America, then the section at the end on case management considerations should be expanded or revised. To be of use to educators and service providers in North America, regulations, legislation, and service and support agencies relevant to the countries of North America should be included.

The specific aims of Is This Autism? are to help the "user decide *what* to look at, how to *interpret* the information, and how to *use* it appropriately, so that teaching or therapy is designed to be realistic and relevant to the child's needs" (handbook, p. 1). The Checklist varies regarding how successful it is in achieving each of these objectives. Is This Autism? is likely to be most successful in describing developmental deficits, and could serve as a useful starting point for developing a comprehensive needs assessment for individuals with autistic features. However, the utility of the instrument for providing guidance for educational and treatment planning is much less certain and should be determined empirically.

[198]

Jenkins Non-Verbal Test, 1986 Revision.

Purpose: Designed to measure general reasoning ability based on nonverbal material.
Population: Australian years 3–8.
Publication Dates: 1986–89.
Scores: Total score only.
Administration: Group.
Price Data, 1994: A$5 per reusable test booklet; $4.50 per 10 answer sheets; $4.10 per scoring key; $16.70 per manual ('89, 30 pages); $26 per specimen set.
Time: 25(40) minutes.
Comments: Adaptation of the Scale of Non-Verbal Ability; intended to be used in conjunction with verbal general ability measures.
Author: M. de Lemos.
Publisher: Australian Council for Educational Research Ltd. [Australia].

Review of the Jenkins Non-Verbal Test, 1986 Revision by ROGER A. BOOTHROYD, Research Scientist, Bureau of Evaluation and Services Research, New York State Office of Mental Health, Albany, NY:

DESCRIPTION. The Jenkins Non-Verbal Test (JNVT) consists of 75 diagrammatic items intended to assess the general ability of children in years 3 through 8 in the Australian school system. The JNVT is appropriate for group administration. Testing takes 25 minutes with an additional 15 minutes being required for completing the information section, directions, and practice problems. The 75 items are grouped into five 15-item subtests and the items in each subtest are arranged in increasing order of difficulty. Two subtests are based on the principle of classification, two on identification of serial order, and the fifth on diagrammatic analogies.

The current version of the JNVT is based on an adaptation of the original Non-Verbal Test designed by J. W. Jenkins in 1947. According to the author, the primary changes in the current version of the test are the introduction of machine-scorable answer sheets, the elimination of a few poorly discriminating items, redrawing of the figures, and the restandardization of the JNVT in conjunction with the Standard Progressive Matrices (SPM; Raven, Court, & Raven, 1988).

The manual contains specific test administration guidelines and directions which include a script to be read to students as part of the test administering procedures. As noted by Nitko (1983), although tests such as the JNVT emphasize "nonverbal responses, verbal ability or language ability are definitely not irrelevant to success on these tests. Directions to examinees are usually oral, requiring examinees to carry a large aural-verbal load" (p. 22). This is certainly relevant for the JNVT.

The use of the JNVT test for non-Australian children is questionable. The norms were developed with Australian children, and the equivalence, if any, between year level and grade level is unclear.

ITEM CONSTRUCTION AND SELECTION. Issues of particular interest with nonverbal tests concern the construction and selection of items. From a review of items in the test booklet it is evident that the items differ on a number of dimensions including, among others, shape, size, shading, directionality, complexity, and abstractness. The number of dimensions on which these items differ raises questions such as: How were items originally developed? Was faceting used? On what basis were items selected for inclusion? How representative are the items on the test to the domain of all possible items? What is the domain of items?

The manual provides the reader with little information to answer any of these questions. No information on item development and construction is provided. Although the author indicates that "A few items which were not discriminating well were omitted from the test, and the figures were redrawn" (manual, p. 2), item discriminations are not provided even though they were presumably examined. Furthermore, the basis on which items were redrawn is not explained. Do the redrawn items offer better discriminating power than the items they replaced? The user of this test is left only to assume that is the case.

The issue of content validity is an important one. What is the theoretical and/or empirical rationale for including items based on the principles of classification, serial order, and analogies? More importantly, why these specific items? The inclusion of an explanation of the procedures and rationale used in item construction and selection is strongly encouraged by this reviewer.

NORMS. The JNVT was normed in 1986 in conjunction with the SPM. A two-stage sampling procedure was used, sampling first schools and then students within schools. Schools were selected proportionally, by state, and "State, Catholic and other independent schools were included in the sample according to their representation in the total population" (p. 8). A total of 91 schools and 2,634 students were sampled. Although information on student gender, language background, ethnicity, and socioeconomic status was collected and analyzed during standardization, no information was provided regarding the extent to which the norming sample was representative of the population.

Raw scores can be directly converted to percentiles, standard scores, or stanines. Norms are provided by year level. Although not specified by the author, year level appears to be analogous to grade level as the average age for students in Year 3 is 8 years, 10 months which would approximate the average age of American students in the third grade. For Years 3 to 6, norms are based only on the sample of students who took the JNVT first because students who took the JNVT after the SPM obtained consistently higher scores than students taking the JNVT first. Years 7 and 8 are based on the total sample of students tested. Descriptive statistics for the total sample and for students taking the JNVT first are presented for each year level.

Gender differences, favoring females, were present for all students collectively, and for students in grades 4, 7, and 8. Significant differences favoring English-speaking students were found in Years 3 and 4. Among English-speaking students, socioeconomic status (SES) differences were detected with students from higher SES families (as determined by father's occupation) performing significantly better. No SES differences were present, however, among students from non-English-speaking families.

RELIABILITY. The only reliability information provided is the KR-21 estimate of internal consistency calculated at each year level. The KR-21 estimates are quite consistent across year levels, ranging from .91 to .94. Given that this test is an adaptation of a measure originally developed in 1947, it is surprising to this reviewer that the test/retest reliability of this measure has never been examined. An examination of the stability of this measure is recommended.

VALIDITY. The correlation of students' scores on the JNVT with both timed and untimed versions of the SPM serve as the primary validity evidence. Correlations between these two measures ranged from .52 to .73 at various year levels. Given that the JNVT is a timed test, it is not surprising that correlations were generally higher with the timed as opposed to the untimed version of the SPM. The correlations of JNVT and SPM scores were similar for boys and girls. JNVT and SPM correlations were similar for English and non-English speakers, although the correlation for the timed version was .78, much higher than the untimed version (.65) among non-English speakers.

Modest correlations were found between students' JNVT scores and teachers' assessment of English, mathematics, and scholastic ability. These correlations ranged from .41 to .57 across year level.

COMMENTARY. The most serious concern of this reviewer is the limited information available on item construction, reliability, and validity for a test that was first developed over 25 years ago. The manual does indicate that it is an interim manual for use until publication of the final manual. Given that this is the 1986 revision with a 1989 copyright, it seems unlikely that the final manual will be forthcoming any time soon.

As previously mentioned, the appropriateness of the JNVT test for non-Australian children is unknown. The degree to which JNVT year levels correspond to grade levels is also uncertain. For this reviewer, the JNVT has too many unanswered questions for a measure with such a long history. If the Australian Council for Educational Research considers the JNVT to be a useful measure of general ability and is truly interested in promoting its use, information on the development and further validation is needed.

REVIEWER'S REFERENCES

Nitko, A. J. (1983). *Educational tests and measurements: An introduction.* New York: Harcourt Brace Jovanovich, Inc.

Raven, J. C., Court, J. H., & Raven, J. (1988). *Manual for Raven's Progressive Matrices and Vocabulary Scales: Section 3 Standard Progressive Matrices.* London: H. K. Lewis & Company, Limited.

Review of the Jenkins Non-Verbal Test, 1986 Revision by W. GRANT WILLIS, Associate Professor of Psychology, University of Rhode Island, Kingston, RI:

The 1986 revision of the Jenkins Non-Verbal Test is adapted from a scale that originally was published in 1947 and 2 years later was normed on a sample of Australian children. The revised version comprises five subtests of 15 figural items each, which are diagrammed in shades of black, white, and gray, and are based on principles of classification, identification of serial order, and solution of analogies. The test is group administered, responses are recorded on optical-mark-reader sheets, and examinees are permitted only 25 minutes to complete the 75 items.

The test manual is described as an "interim manual," which was prepared to permit the use of the test until the final manual is published. This final manual reportedly will provide more detailed technical information about the standardization study. As described in the current manual, the standardization data were collected in 1986 from 2,634 Australian students enrolled in Years 3 (*M* age = 8 years, 10 months) through 8 (*M* age = 13 years, 11 months). Schools selected for participation apparently were stratified according to size and state, and 10 students then were randomly selected from each of these schools at each of six year levels. The test was co-normed with the Standard Progressive Matrices, and order of test presentation was counterbalanced. Statistical analyses showed significant practice effects on scores for the Jenkins Non-Verbal Test when it was administered second for Years 3 through 6. There were no practice effects at Years 7 and 8, but the author speculates that the reason for this is due to a ceiling effect. Thus, although the sampling procedure resulted in between 418 and 467 students at each school-year level, norms are based on only the 183 to 194 students in Years 3 through 6 who completed the Jenkins Non-Verbal Test first, contrasted with 467 and 463 students in Years 7 and 8, respectively, for whom first versus second test administrations were collapsed.

Besides effects due to initial administration of the Standard Progressive Matrices, test scores also were affected by gender, language background, and socioeconomic level. Even so, separate norms are not provided according to these variables. The test author argues that these mean differences do not necessarily indicate bias because there is little evidence of differential validity according to these variables. This argument essentially involves the concept of slope bias and would be more convincing in the presence of stronger criteria than those that were used in the concurrent validity studies reported in the manual.

The manual reports that at lower age levels, raw test-score distributions are positively skewed, but given ceiling effects at upper age levels, distributions become increasingly negatively skewed. In fact, the author cautions against using the test in situations requiring discrimination between relatively older students of above-average ability. Tables for converting raw scores to percentiles, stanines, and standard scores ($M = 100$, $SD = 15$) are presented, despite the noticeably absent explanation about normalizing these skewed distributions. Although it is possible to transform raw scores from a skewed distribution into standardized scores, associated percentiles cannot be derived from a normal curve as a perusal of this test's norms tables would suggest. The author does advise test users to use the norms tables and interpret the derived scores with caution, but the specific warnings refer to test reliability, validity, and confidentiality, rather than to the issue of how the norms were derived.

Reliability data for the Jenkins Non-Verbal Test are limited to internal-consistency estimates reported by year level. These estimates are good, ranging from .91 to .94, and standard errors of measurement are presented ranging from 3.32 to 4.02. There is no discussion of the stability of the test scores, although they clearly were influenced by an initial administration of the Standard Progressive Matrices.

Finally, validity data are relatively weak. There is no discussion of construct, content, or predictive validity. Evidence of the test's concurrent validity includes correlations with (*a*) scores for timed and untimed versions of the Standard Progressive Matrices according to year level (*r*s = .52 to .73), gender (*r*s = .70 to .76), and language background (*r*s = .65 to .78); (*b*) 5-point Likert-scale teacher ratings in English, Mathematics, and Scholastic Ability according to year level (*r*s = .41 to.57), gender (*r*s = .46 to .51), and language background (*r*s = .43 to .52); and (*c*) scores on three group-administered school aptitude/achievement tests according to year level (*r*s = .34 to .71).

In summary, the 1986 edition of the Jenkins Non-Verbal Test was normed on a large number of Australian students, who are differentiated on the basis of its scores according to gender, language background, socioeconomic level, and previous administration of another nonverbal aptitude test. Raw-score distributions are skewed, and even though standard scores and percentiles are presented in norms tables, these distributions apparently were not normalized. Internal-consistency estimates are respectable, but the test lacks convincing validity evidence. I would not recommend the use of this test for its stated purpose of measuring general reasoning ability based on nonverbal material.

[199]

Job Descriptive Index and Retirement Descriptive Index.

Administration: Group or individual.
Price Data, 1993: $25 (plus $5 shipping and handling) per bound photocopy of out-of-print book *The Measurement of Satisfaction in Work and Retirement* ('75, 193 pages).
Time: [10–15] minutes per Index.
Authors: Patricia C. Smith, Lorne M. Kendall, and Charles L. Hulin.
Publisher: Bowling Green State University.

a) JOB DESCRIPTIVE INDEX [REVISED 1987].
Purpose: Designed to measure satisfaction with facets of the job and global job satisfaction (i.e., Job in General [JIG] Scale).
Population: Employees.
Publication Dates: 1969–90.
Acronym: JDI.
Scores, 6: Work on Present Job, Present Pay, Opportunities for Promotion, Supervision, People on Your Present Job (Co-Workers), Job in General.
Price Data: $42 (plus $5 shipping and handling) per 100 Revised JDI test booklets; $5 per set of hand-scoring keys; $25 (plus $5 shipping and handling) per User's Manual ('90, 147 pages) for the Job Descriptive Index and Job in General Scales (including hand-scoring key).

b) RETIREMENT DESCRIPTIVE INDEX [REVISED 1993].
Purpose: Designed to measure satisfaction with facets of retirement and global retirement satisfaction (i.e., Retirement in General [RIG] Scale).
Population: Retirees.
Publication Dates: 1969–93.
Acronym: RDI.
Scores, 5: Present Work and Activities, Financial Situation, Present Health, People You Associate With, Retirement in General.
Price Data: $34 (plus $5 shipping and handling) per 100 Revised RDI test booklets; $5 per set of hand-scoring keys.

Cross References: See T4:1312 (63 references); for reviews of an earlier edition by John O. Crites and Barbara A. Kerr of the Job Descriptive Index, see 9:550 (49 references).

TEST REFERENCES

1. Morrow, P. C., & McElroy, J. C. (1987). Work commitment and job satisfaction over three career stages. *Journal of Vocational Behavior, 30*, 330-346.
2. Stout, S. K., Slocum, J. W., Jr., & Cron, W. L. (1987). Career transitions of supervisors and subordinates. *Journal of Vocational Behavior, 30*, 124-137.
3. Ironson, G. H., Smith, P. C., Brannick, M. T., Gibson, W. M., & Paul, K. B. (1989). Construction of a job in general scale: A comparison of global, composite, and specific measures. *Journal of Applied Psychology, 74*, 193-200.
4. Kacmar, K. M., & Ferris, G. R. (1989). Theoretical and methodological considerations in the age-job satisfaction relationship. *Journal of Applied Psychology, 74*, 201-207.
5. Keller, R. T. (1989). A test of the path-goal theory of leadership with need for clarity as a moderator in research and development organizations. *Journal of Applied Psychology, 74*, 208-212.
6. Levin, I., & Stokes, J. P. (1989). Dispositional approach to job satisfaction: Role of negative affectivity. *Journal of Applied Psychology, 74*, 752-758.
7. Roznowski, M. (1989). Examination of the measurement properties of the Job Descriptive Index with experimental items. *Journal of Applied Psychology, 74*, 805-814.
8. Smither, J. W., Collins, H., & Buck, R. (1989). When ratee satisfaction influences performance evaluations: A case of illusory correlation. *Journal of Applied Psychology, 74*, 599-605.
9. Tait, M., Padgett, M. Y., & Baldwin, T. T. (1989). Job and life satisfaction: A reevaluation of the strength of the relationship and gender effects as a function of the date of the study. *Journal of Applied Psychology, 74*, 502-507.
10. Bliss, J. R., Konet, R. J., & Tarter, C. J. (1990). Leadership style and effectiveness in secondary school departments. *The High School Journal, 74*, 38-46.
11. Hanisch, K. A., & Hulin, C. L. (1990). Job attitudes and organizational withdrawal: An examination of retirement and other voluntary withdrawal behaviors. *Journal of Vocational Behavior, 37*, 60-78.
12. McGinnis, S. K., & Morrow, P. C. (1990). Job attitudes among full- and part-time employees. *Journal of Vocational Behavior, 36*, 82-96.
13. Meir, E. I., Melamed, S., & Abu-Freha, A. (1990). Vocational, avocational, and skill utilization congruences and their relationship with well-being in two cultures. *Journal of Vocational Behavior, 36*, 153-165.
14. Roznowski, M., & Hanisch, K. A. (1990). Building systematic heterogeneity into work attitudes and behavior measures. *Journal of Vocational Behavior, 36*, 361-375.
15. Bagozzi, R. P., Yi, Y., & Phillips, L. W. (1991). Assessing construct validity in organizational research. *Administrative Science Quarterly, 36*, 421-458.
16. Bedeian, A. G., Ferris, G. R., & Kacmar, K. M. (1992). Age, tenure, and job satisfaction: A tale of two perspectives. *Journal of Vocational Behavior, 40*, 33-48.
17. Schell, B. H., Paine-Mantha, V. A., & Morrison, K. (1992). Stress-coping styles and personality descriptors of ice arena workers: Indicators of "victims" or "copers" of on-the-job stressors? *Journal of Vocational Behavior, 41*, 270-281.
18. Judge, T. A., & Hulin, C. L. (1993). Job satisfaction as a reflection of disposition: A multiple source causal analysis. *Organizational Behavior and Human Decision Processes, 56*, 388-421.
19. Mallam, U., & Eddy, J. P. (1993). A study of polytechnic faculty turnover at selected Nigerian institutions. *College Student Journal, 27*, 523-524.
20. Watson, D., & Slack, A. K. (1993). General factors of affective temperament and their relation to job satisfaction over time. *Organizational Behavior and Human Decision Processes, 54*, 181-202.
21. Edwards, J. R. (1994). The study of congruence in organizational behavior research: Critique and a proposed alternative. *Organizational Behavior and Human Decision Processes, 58*, 51-100.
22. Jacobs, K. (1994). Flow and the occupational therapy practitioner. *The American Journal of Occupational Therapy, 48*, 989-996.
23. Morrow, P. C., McElroy, J. C., & Elliott, S. M. (1994). The effect of preference for work status, schedule, and shift on work-related attitudes. *Journal of Vocational Behavior, 45*, 202-222.
24. Morrow, P. C., McElroy, J. C., & Phillips, C. M. (1994). Sexual harrassment behaviors and work related perceptions and attitudes. *Journal of Vocational Behavior, 45*, 295-309.
25. Necowitz, L. B., & Roznowski, M. (1994). Negative affectivity and job satisfaction: Cognitive processes underlying the relationship and effects on employee behaviors. *Journal of Vocational Behavior, 45*, 270-294.
26. Okolo, R. E., & Eddy, J. P. (1994). A job satisfaction study of faculty at historically Black colleges and universities in Texas. *College Student Journal, 28*, 345-346.
27. Riggs, M. L., & Knight, P. A. (1994). The impact of perceived group success-failure on motivational beliefs and attitudes: A causal model. *Journal of Applied Psychology, 79*, 755-766.
28. Smart, R., & Peterson, C. (1994). Stability versus transition in women's career development: A test of Levinson's theory. *Journal of Vocational Behavior, 45*, 241-260.
29. Wanberg, C. R. (1994). A longitudinal study of the effects of unemployment and quality of reemployment. *Journal of Vocational Behavior, 46*, 40-54.
30. Meir, E. I., Melamed, S., & Dinur, C. (1995). The benefits of congruence. *Career Development Quarterly, 43*, 257-266.

31. Melamed, S., Ben-Avi, I., Luz, J., & Green, M. S. (1995). Objective and subjective work monotony: Effects on job satisfaction, psychological distress, and absenteeism in blue-collar workers. *Journal of Applied Psychology, 80*, 29-42.
32. Norman, P., & Bonnett, C. (1995). Managers' intentions to be assessed for national vocational qualifications: An application of the theory of planned behavior. *Social Behavior and Personality, 23*, 59-68.
33. Wanberg, C. R. (1995). A longitudinal study of the effects of unemployment and quality of reemployment. *Journal of Vocational Behavior, 46*, 50-54.

Review of the Job Descriptive Index and Retirement Descriptive Index by CHARLES K. PARSONS, Professor of Organizational Behavior, Georgia Institute of Technology, Atlanta, GA:

The Job Descriptive Index (JDI), Job in General (JIG), and Retirement Descriptive Index (RDI) are intended to assess the affective reactions of individuals to their jobs and retirement. The JDI and RDI were initially developed in the 1960s. The JDI is a widely used measure that has been reviewed in an earlier edition of the *Mental Measurements Yearbook* (Crites, 1985; Kerr, 1985). A revised version of the JDI was completed in 1985. The JIG was reported in Ironson, Smith, Brannick, Gibson, and Paul in 1989. The current review will comment on the revision of the JDI completed in 1985, the JIG, and the user's manual for the JDI and JIG published in 1990 (Balzer et al., 1990).

Using a total of 72 items, the JDI assesses satisfaction with five facets of job satisfaction: work itself (18 items), promotional opportunities (9 items), supervision (18 items), co-workers (18 items), and pay (9 items). The Job in General scale (JIG) consists of 18 items. The assessments are based on individuals rating adjectives or adjective phrases as being descriptive or not descriptive of their jobs. The rating is done on a 3-point scale of yes (Y), no (N), or cannot decide (?).

The format of the JDI and JIG is straightforward and easily understandable by individuals with a wide range of reading abilities. The authors report that the JDI and JIG can be completed in about 5 minutes by most employees. My personal experience with the scales would support this estimate. Scoring can be done either by hand or by computer. The publishers provide hand-scoring sheets to be used by the person who administers the scales. Interpretation of JDI scores is supported by norms that are based on large samples of individuals. The norms are presented separately for men and women, different educational levels, and different tenure levels. The educational norms and tenure norms are based on men.

The psychometric data on the JDI and JIG are impressive. The development of the original JDI, published in 1969 (Smith, Kendall, & Hulin, 1969), contains extensive information on item development, item selection, response format alternatives, and so on. It also contains reports on construct and criterion-related validity. The revised version of the JDI and JIG were based on Item Response Theory (Lord, 1980) and resulted in changing 11 items across four facets of the JDI. Internal consistencies of the JDI have remained high (averaging .88 across the five facet scales). The internal consistency of the JIG was reported to be consistently above .90.

Construct validity of the JIG was supported by its high correlations with other existing, well-documented measures of general job satisfaction. Further validity evidence was gathered in an investigation of employees of an electrical utility facility. The authors (Ironson et al., 1989) found moderately high correlations with variables such as intention to leave the organization, life satisfaction, and identification with the work organization. In this work, the JIG scale was administered following the JDI. It is quite possible that the JDI facet-scales set the psychological context in which the JIG items are interpreted. Further work is needed to see if the JIG, when administered alone, will have similar validity.

The user's manual provided for this review provides an excellent summary of the development of the instruments, their appropriate use, and interpretation. The authors do a commendable job in describing the conceptual framework in which their instrument assesses job satisfaction. It goes on to provide an overview of appropriate survey administration practices. This section of the manual will be particularly helpful to users who are relatively new to survey administration procedures. Issues of project scope, overall survey design, and administration are presented. Administering and using large-scale surveys in work organizations is substantially different than the administration of instruments to individuals or small groups.

One of the primary strengths of the JDI is the normative statistics available on which to interpret results. The authors provide both numerical tables and graphical norms. They provide figure templates that represent median and quartile information on which users can plot the results from their surveys to allow easy distributional comparisons.

The authors provide guidelines on appropriate interpretation of subgroup data within a given organization. This allows the user to identify strengths and weaknesses in the management of people in the organization. Finally, the authors provide useful guidelines on follow-up procedures to the interpretation of survey results.

The authors of the JDI have taken the position that the JDI should be used only to interpret satisfaction with each of the five facets. The scores should not be combined into a composite score and interpreted as general job satisfaction. The facet level scores are typically correlated at a low to moderate level, but not high enough to support a strong general factor. The need for a measure of general job satisfaction in the JDI format led to the development of the JIG. Because of the recent development of this instrument, normative information was not available at the time of the publication of the user's manual. I would hope that norms similar to those for the JDI will be available soon for the JIG.

The JDI is a very popular measure of job satisfaction, but it does have a disadvantage. The recommended format is one scale per page. This yields six pages of questionnaire dedicated to the assessment of job satisfaction. Although the time requirement is not ominous, it does impact the administration of other measures simply due to questionnaire length constraints. The Minnesota Satisfaction Questionnaire (Weiss, Dawis, England, & Lofquist, 1967; T4:1649) is an alternative, shorter measure that has also had a great deal of psychometric evaluation and provides an assessment of intrinsic satisfaction, extrinsic satisfaction, and overall job satisfaction. A simple, nonverbal measure of overall job satisfaction is the Faces Scales (Kunin, 1955) that is appropriate for populations with low reading ability. For further information from outside reviewers of the Job Descriptive Index, interested readers are encouraged to consult Price and Mueller (1986) and Kinicki, Schriesheim, and Carson (1994).

REVIEWER'S REFERENCES

Kunin, T. (1955). The construction of a new type of attitude measure. *Personnel Psychology, 8*, 65-77.

Weiss, D. J., Dawis, R. V., England, G. W., & Lofquist, L. H. (1967). *Manual for the Minnesota Satisfaction Questionnaire*. Minneapolis, MN: Vocational Psychology Research, University of Minnesota.

Smith, P. C., Kendall, L. M., & Hulin, C. L. (1969). *The measurement of satisfaction in work and retirement: A strategy for the study of attitudes*. Chicago: Rand McNally.

Lord, F. M. (1980). *Applications of item response theory to practical testing problems*. Hillsdale, NJ: Lawrence Erlbaum Associates.

Price, J. L., & Mueller, C. W. (1986). *Handbook of organizational measurement*. Marshfield, MA: Pitman Publishing, Inc.

Crites, J. O. (1985). [Review of the Job Descriptive Index.] In J. V. Mitchell, Jr. (Ed.), *The ninth mental measurements yearbook* (pp. 753-754). Lincoln, NE: The Buros Institute of Mental Measurements.

Ironson, G. H., Smith, P. C., Bannick, M. T., Gibson, W. M., & Paul, K. B. (1989). Construction of a Job in General scale: A comparison of global, composite, and specific measures. *Journal of Applied Psychology, 74*, 193-200.

Kerr, B. A. (1985). [Review of the Job Descriptive Index.] In J. V. Mitchell, Jr. (Ed.), *The ninth mental measurements yearbook* (pp. 754-756). Lincoln, NE: The Buros Institute of Mental Measurements.

Balzer, W. K., Smith, P. C., Kravitz, D. A., Lovell, S. E., Paul, K. B., Reilly, B. A., & Reilly, C. E. (1990). *Users' Manual for the Job Descriptive Index (JDI) and the Job In General (JIG) scales*. Bowling Green, OH: Bowling Green University.

Kinicki, A. J., Schriesheim, C. A., & Carson, K. P. (1994). *The construct validity of the Job Descriptive Index (JDI): Review, critique, and analysis*. Unpublished Manuscript, Dept. of Management, Arizona State University.

Review of the Job Descriptive Index and Retirement Descriptive Index by NORMAN D. SUNDBERG, Professor Emeritus, Department of Psychology, University of Oregon, Eugene, OR:

The Job Descriptive Index (JDI) and the Retirement Descriptive Index (RDI) are separate tests but will be reviewed together. Both were developed with similar methods by Patricia Cain Smith and her associates, first at Cornell and later at Bowling Green State University. Of the two tests, much more attention has been given to the JDI, and it will be reviewed first.

In organizational psychology, job satisfaction is the most frequently studied job attitude and the JDI is its most frequently used measure (O'Reilly, 1991). The JDI has been translated into many languages since its inception in 1959 (Smith, Kendall, & Hulin, 1969). An extensive and reader-friendly manual (Balzer & Smith, 1990) includes the JDI, revised in the mid-1980s, and the new Job In General (JIG). The JIG is added to the end of the JDI form. If the JIG is used by itself, the authors warn that users should recognize that the validation research is based on the JIG immediately following the JDI.

The JDI and JIG use a very simple answering form—lists of 9 or 18 terms on several small sheets to which the respondent answers "Yes," "No," or "?" to words similar to these: Interesting, unfair, no chance for promotion, hard-working, or desirable. This reviewer's impression is the words would be readily readable to most workers, and positives and negatives are roughly balanced. The scoring is also simple: Favorable choices count 3 points, and omissions or questions count 1 point. Scoring can be done by hand or by machine. The JDI, JIG, and RDI are copyrighted, and Patricia Smith (personal communication, September 16, 1993) urges potential users to write or call for more information at the Department of Psychology, Bowling Green State University, Bowling Green, OH 43403 (419/372-8247).

Response sets or test-taking attitudes should be considered because the items are obvious and appear to be easily fakable. The subject is asked to describe the job, not give feelings about it, but it is assumed the person is revealing his or her attitudes in the process. It would be interesting to experiment with different instructions, such as asking "What most people would say" or "Express your feelings as if you wanted the job very much" or "Answer as if you wanted to give a bad picture of your boss." In a personal communication (September 16, 1993), Dr. Smith has indicated that she and her colleagues had investigated various aspects of test-taking attitudes, including a Lie scale, but have found them to be of little utility; she indicated that "If honest answers are to be obtained, respondents have to believe that their answers will not affect them adversely," and maintaining confidentiality is essential.

The subject can quickly (in 5–10 minutes) produce descriptions of six aspects of his or her job: Work on the Present Job, Present Pay, Opportunities for Promotion, Supervision, Coworkers, and Job in General (JIG). The authors indicate the first five are facets of job satisfaction based on factor analytic studies. (Some investigators have found a different number of factors, e.g., Yeager, 1981). They warn the five facets should not be summed to get a general satisfaction score, because they cover aspects of jobs which are only moderately correlated. The last part, JIG, is designed to cover broader, longer range attitudes toward one's job. The authors make a strong argument, based on studies, that there is a need for reports of satisfaction about both detailed job areas and general job satisfaction.

The JDI and JIG are to be used for revealing strong and weak points within and across organizations, not across individuals, and the responses are to be anonymous and/or confidential. What the consultant or manager of the organization obtains is a set of scores for a division or the whole company. The scores can be used in two major ways—to compare with general norms or to compare one division with another within the organization. Informally, tallies of particular item responses might give clues to problems. The user's manual contains an excellent introduction to job satisfaction and the test itself. Percentage norms for the five JDI areas and the JIG are included. The breakdowns are by gender, length of job tenure, and education. The manual authors warn the user must take into account contextual matters such as the history and state of the economy of the organization and the community. Interestingly, job satisfaction is often higher in depressed areas than in affluent areas; the authors explain that the frames of reference or general adaptation levels of the respondents affect results.

The JDI and JIG have been subjected to many studies over the years, including a large number not by the authors themselves. In general the authors of the manual are attentive and thorough about test construction methods (including use of item response theory for the revision), and present considerable information on reliability, validity, and norms. For example, the JIG shows coefficient alphas between .91 and .95 with samples totalling over 3,000; convergent validities with ratings, the Brayfield-Rothe scale, and the Faces scale range from .66 to .80; and variable predictive validity is shown against a variety of measures in a study of a specific organization (Ironson, Smith, Brannick, Gibson, & Paul, 1989). Much more detail is available in the manual and in references. There are gender differences; women tend to give higher satisfaction scores than men. Users are advised to use separate norms available at nonprofessional levels but male norms with professional women. In a review, Leong and Vaux (1992) cover research extensively; they conclude that the JDI is an excellent measure of job satisfaction but have a few criticisms, including comments about possible confusion in scoring and underrepresentation of some items or areas, such as intrinsic job rewards and satisfaction with benefits.

The Retirement Descriptive Index is similar to the JDI but much less developed. Information is scattered in a 1969 book (Smith, Kendall, & Hulin, 1969), and there is no updated manual or report. Obviously the RDI needs more work on it, and the authors ask for data from users. This reviewer was supplied with somewhat confusing materials about the RDI; for instance, in one place instructions were to double the score on Finances and in another the score on Health (the latter being the appropriate one). A revision of the RDI is under way and will be available in the near future with instructions and scoring keys, and a manual is in preparation (personal communication, P. C. Smith, September 16, 1993).

Somewhat paralleling the JDI, the RDI aims to measure satisfaction in retirement in several different areas: Present Work and Activities, Financial Situation, Present Health, and People You Associate With. These facets have only low to moderate correlations, and there is no "retirement in general" scale. Keeping these area scores separate makes good sense; for example, a retired person may be satisfied with finances but very unhappy about health. Like the JDI, the RDI scales have either 9 or 18 terms, and the answering and scoring methods are the same. Smith, Kendall, and Hulin (1969) report general support for validity from a factor analysis of the RDI and many additional variables with 631 male retirees from 20 plants. Health is the most important contributor to outside indicators of general satisfaction. Norms are presented for almost 600 male and 240 female retirees at various age levels. Ratings of satisfaction in retirement are at about the same level as ratings of those still working, but one must recognize the ratings are affected greatly by changing expectations after retirement. As the number of elderly people in the population and the corresponding need to understand this immense human resource grows, it seems likely that there will be increasing use of the RDI.

In conclusion, for those wishing to study organizational job satisfaction, the JDI presents an impressive measure, well researched, and documented. For those wishing to study satisfaction with retirement, the RDI constitutes a good research possibility that needs more work and a good manual.

REVIEWER'S REFERENCES

Smith, P. C., Kendall, L. M., & Hulin, C. L. (1969). *The measurement of satisfaction in work and retirement*. Chicago: Rand McNally. (Reprinted by Bowling Green University in 1975)

Yeager, S. J. (1981). Dimensionality of the Job Descriptive Index. *Academy of Management Journal, 24*, 205-212.

Ironson, G. H., Smith, P. C., Brannick, M. T., Gibson, W. M., & Paul, K. B. (1989). Construction of a Job In General scale: A comparison of global, composite and specific measures. *Journal of Applied Psychology, 74*, 193-200.

Balzer, W. K., & Smith, P. C. (1990). *Users' manual for the Job Descriptive Index (JDI) and the Job In General (JIG) scales*. Bowling Green, OH: Bowling Green University.

O'Reilly, C. A. (1991). Organizational behavior: Where we've been, where we're going. *Annual Review of Psychology, 42*, 427-458.

Cranny, C. J., Smith, P. C., & Stone, E. F. (1992). *Job satisfaction: How people feel about their jobs and how it affects performance*. New York: Lexington Books.

Leong, F. T. L., & Vaux, A. (1992). [Review of the Job Descriptive Index.] In D. J. Keyser & R. C. Sweetland (Eds.), *Test critiques* (vol. 9; pp. 319-334). Austin, TX: PRO-ED, Inc.

[200]

JOB-O.

Purpose: "To facilitate self-awareness, career-awareness, and career exploration."

Publication Dates: 1981–92.

Administration: Group.

Price Data, 1992: $1.65 per test booklet; $.30 per answer folder; $4.95 per administration (Professional) manual ('85, 20 pages).

Comments: Also known as Judgement of Occupational Behavior-Orientation.

Authors: Arthur Cutler, Francis Ferry, Robert Kauk, and Robert Robinett.

Publisher: CFKR Career Materials, Inc.

a) JOB-O (ELEMENTARY).

Population: Grades 4–7.

Scores: 6 ratings: Mechanical/Construction/Agriculture, Scientific/Technical, Creative/Artistic, Social/Legal/Educational, Managers/Sales, Administrative Support.

Time: Administration time not reported.

b) JOB-O.

Population: Junior high school through adult.

Scores, 8: Education, Interest, Inclusion, Control, Affection, Physical Activity, Hands/Tools/Machinery, Problem-Solving, Creative-Ideas.

Foreign Language Editions: Spanish and Vietnamese test booklets and answer sheets available.

Time: (60–65) minutes.

Price Data: $89.95 per Apple or IBM software.

c) JOB-O A (ADVANCED).

Population: Grades 10–12 and adult.

Scores, 16: Occupational Interest, Training Time, Reasoning Skills, Mathematical Skills, Language Skills, Working with Data, Working with People, Working with Things, Working Conditions, Physical Demands, Leadership, Helping People, Problem-Solving, Initiative, Team Work, Public Contact.

Price Data: $99.95 per IBM software.

Time: [50–55] minutes.

Comments: May be self-administered.

Cross References: For a review by James W. Pinkney of an earlier edition, see 10:160; for a review by Bruce J. Eberhardt of an earlier edition, see 9:560.

Review of the JOB-O by F. MARION ASCHE, Professor of Education, Virginia Polytechnic Institute and State University, Blacksburg, VA:

The original Judgement of Occupational Behavior-Orientation (JOB-O) was designed as a career interest inventory in 1970. Since that time, it has undergone several minor revisions and two additional versions have been added. The JOB-O A (Advanced Version, Career Decision Making) was first copyrighted in 1988 and is designed to be used with adults and persons who have previously taken the JOB-O. The JOB-O E (Elementary, Career Awareness) was introduced in 1989 and is designed for use with students in grades 4–6. The revised JOB-O (Career Exploration) is recommended for students in grades 7 through 10. The format of all three instruments is similar, consisting of a reusable booklet and a consumable answer folder. This review focuses on the JOB-O but includes descriptions of how basic features are modified in the other two versions.

The JOB-O is presented as a career assessment inventory in which the user is asked to make self-assessments about nine career-relevant variables and then to compare these estimates with the "requirements" of 120 selected jobs. Because the labor market is enormously complex, the 120 occupations selected for inclusion are those which account for a large percentage of employment in this society and which show promise of being in demand over the next decade. Other criteria for inclusion of particular job titles were that jobs requiring all levels of education are included and that each of the eight broad career clusters covered by the JOB-O are represented.

The JOB-O first asks the respondent to estimate how long he or she wants to go to school (go to work right out of high school, attend community college or special school, go through a 4-year or more college program). The second variable asks respondents to select, from the eight job clusters provided, the one or two in which they have the greatest interest. For each grouping, the cluster is named (e.g., Performing Arts, Design, Communications Occupations) and several specific job titles are listed. Variables 3 through 5 are based on the FIRO-B (inclusion, control, and affection). Variable 6 deals with desired level of physical demands (based on the *Dictionary of Occupational Titles* estimates of physical demands of jobs). Variables 7 through 9 deal with the extent to which the respondent wishes to work with hands-tools-machinery, problem solving, and creativity-ideas. Variables 3 through 9 are estimated on a 3-point scale (*usually or often, sometimes or occasionally,* and *seldom or rarely*).

After completing the self-estimates on each of the nine variables, the respondent is asked to compare responses with those provided for the 120 job titles, writing the number of matches for each job title in the space provided. The respondent is asked to consider all job titles for which there are five or more matches, then to choose the three that are most interesting and to enter basic information (from the response folder) for these three including number employed, percent of growth, job outlook, average earnings (high, medium, low), kind of training, years of training, and related jobs. The respondent is finally asked to pick the one job title he or she likes best for further research using such resources as the *Occupational Outlook Handbook*, visiting a career resource center, talking to a counselor, etc.

The JOB-O A differs from the JOB-O in a number of ways although the basic approach of self-estimates and matching is the same. Eighteen variables are self-appraised including interests (direct estimate rather than picking job clusters); training time; reasoning skills; mathematical skills and language skills; desire to work with data, people, and things; working conditions (inside, outside, or both); physical demands of job (light, medium, heavy); and eight areas of personal skills including leadership, helping people, problem-solving, initiative, team work, public contact, manual dexterity, and physical stamina. Responses are not direct self-assessments but rather statements of preference for jobs having or requiring varying levels of each of the variables. Matching is a bit different with the JOB-O A in that the respondent matches his or her responses with 24 job clusters rather than with 120 specific job titles (with a listing of several examples of specific jobs within each cluster provided for reference). The job research section is similar but with greater emphasis on making a specific career decision.

The JOB-O E is a much simplified version of the basic JOB-O which focuses on interests only. Six broad job clusters which parallel Holland's typology and the *Guide for Occupational Exploration* interest areas are included for investigation. The respondent is asked to rate his or her degree of interest in each as high, some, or low after reading a limited amount of information about jobs in each cluster. The stated purpose of the JOB-O E is to increase the student's self awareness and career awareness.

The JOB-O instruments have a number of desirable characteristics. They are straightforward, have "face validity," should be relatively easy for most individuals to complete and score, and appear to be useful for individual and group career exploration. A Spanish version of the JOB-O is available as is a computer version of the JOB-O A. The information provided on the included occupations is concise and useful.

There are also, however, a number of shortcomings and potential problems with the JOB-O series. Although the authors claim that almost five million persons have taken the JOB-O, there are no data reported on characteristics of this sample such as gender, ethnicity, age, etc. There is no way to tell whether the instrument responses relate to such variables in a way that might promote continued occupational stereotyping. The "Professional Manual" is severely lacking in technical detail. There are essentially no reliability data provided (one 1973 test-retest correlation of selected occupations) and only one study related to concurrent validity is cited. The validity study was also conducted in 1973 and compared responses with those on the Kuder Occupational Interest Survey (Form DD) using a chi-square test to determine there was no significant difference in responses. No information on sample size or characteristics is provided for either study and neither study appears to have been published. Evidence of content validity consists of the rather usual statements regarding rational judgement by experts but no detail as to how items were selected or sampled is provided.

Although the authors state that "no claim is made for predictive validity" they go on to state that data are available for a 10-year study and that it is "hoped that a study will be completed in the future" (p. 7). It would seem that if the primary purpose of the JOB-O is to assist students in matching their interests (and to a limited extent, abilities) to potential future careers, evidence of predictive validity is absolutely essential. How else can one judge whether or not taking the JOB-O is helpful or misleading to individuals in their career exploration? Unfortunately, although the authors include cautions in the JOB-O booklet itself that the instrument does not measure ability and that it is an exploratory instrument to "help you compare your interests with the 120 major job titles in the world of work" (p. 2), the manual authors suggest that for high-school, college, and adult levels, it can be used for making job decisions. In fact, the final page of the answer insert is labeled "It's Decision-Making Time."

Consider the following from the Users Guide, "Any teacher, counselor, teacher aide, or career technician with the usual degree of professional competence can administer JOB-O without specific professional training" (p. 3). The important difference between administering the JOB-O and assisting students in interpreting the results is not explained. Inadequate attention is paid to the problems of self-assessment and to the lack of information on measured aptitudes or abilities of respondents. These problems are similar to those cited by both Eberhardt (1985) and Pinkney (1989) in earlier reviews of the JOB-O. It is particularly disturbing that earlier criticisms and the obvious weaknesses of the test manual have not been addressed.

On a more philosophical level, there is one additional area of concern that deserves mention. The theoretical rationale for the JOB-O and other instruments of this type lies in the "matching model" originally proposed by Frank Parsons in the early 1900s, an approach that still is a mainstay of much vocational guidance practice. The basic premise is the probability of career success and satisfaction is maximized when the individual chooses a career in which his or her interests and abilities most nearly match the modal interests and abilities of incumbents. The user must be the judge of the viability of this model but should be aware that there is a great deal of variability in the interests and abilities of individuals who are successful and satisfied within any broad cluster of occupations. Because there is substantial within-group variability, there is necessarily a great deal of overlap among occupations and groupings. It is therefore somewhat misleading to imply that averages of incumbents are "requirements" although they may constitute best estimates in the statistical sense.

CONCLUSION. The authors have addressed an important area of need—career awareness and exploration. The use of occupational clusters to simplify the complex world of work makes sense and the importance of interests in job success and satisfaction is widely recognized. The intuitive appeal and simplicity of the JOB-O, however, tend to mask its technical shortcomings and make its misuse by uninformed individuals more likely. Individuals who take the JOB-O should be assisted with interpretation of results by practitioners with specific career/vocational guidance preparation and should be cautioned against premature foreclosure in occupational or educational decision making based on such limited information.

REVIEWER'S REFERENCES

Eberhardt, B. J. (1985). [Review of Judgement of Occupational Behavior-Orientation]. In J. V. Mitchell, Jr. (Ed.), *The ninth mental measurements yearbook* (pp. 767-769). Lincoln, NE: Buros Institute of Mental Measurements.

Pinkney, J. W. (1989). [Review of JOB-O, 1985-1995]. In J. C. Conoley & J. J. Kramer (Eds.), *The tenth mental measurements yearbook* (pp. 409-410). Lincoln, NE: Buros Institute of Mental Measurements.

Review of the JOB-O by LAWRENCE H. CROSS, Associate Professor of Educational Research and Measurement, Virginia Polytechnic Institute and State University, Blacksburg, VA:

The original JOB-O was designed as a career interest inventory that ostensibly can provide a process for career development at three levels: career awareness, career-exploration, and career-decision making. In 1989, the authors of the JOB-O introduced an elementary version (JOB-O E) that emphasizes career awareness for students in grades 4–6 and an advanced version (JOB-O A) that emphasizes career decision making for older students and adults. Because the original JOB-O has been in use for approximately 20 years and has been the object of reviews in two previous editions of the *Mental Measurements Yearbook*, this review will focus on the two new versions.

The assessment booklet for the elementary version is devoted almost entirely to two-page descriptions of six job clusters called job groups. After reading each two-page description, students are instructed to record on a consumable answer sheet whether they have "high," "some," or "low" interest in each job group (cluster). The description of each job group lists four major occupations with single sentence descriptions of the type of work associated with each. This is followed by a list of five interests people in a job group presumably have in common. For example, users learn that "LEGAL WORKERS work in the field of LAW" and "they are interested in making friends and keeping them" (p. 10). The adjacent page lists approximately 20 job titles along with a one-sentence characterization of the associated work. For example, a "SECURITIES BROKER—sells a variety of stocks and bonds of all kinds." Students are directed to ask their teachers to help pronounce the names of jobs new to them, but one has to wonder how much understanding 4th graders will gain if their teacher pronounces securities broker. Nonetheless, after recording their level of interest in each job group, children are instructed to write the titles of three of the jobs they like best in each job group. Career exploration is then addressed by directing the students to select one job they like best in each of two job groups and respond to questions about these jobs using the descriptions contained in the JOB-O E booklet.

If not frustrated by having to make choices with limited information, students in 4th through 7th grades may find the JOB-O E an interesting career awareness activity. I fear they may find it a little laborious as a career exploration exercise. The authors appear to take career decision making at this age a bit more seriously than seems warranted, as indicated by the title of the last page in the assessment booklet: "ADDITIONAL THINGS TO THINK ABOUT WHEN MAKING *FINAL* CAREER DECISIONS" (p. 17, emphasis added).

The advanced version (JOB-O A) is much more elaborate than the elementary version. The first part of the instrument is devoted to self-assessment of user "interests and skills," which are then matched to "jobs with similar skill and job requirements." Whereas the standard JOB-O assesses "interests and skills" with 9 questions, the advanced version asks 18 questions. It should be noted that two different editions were provided for this review, and only the one with the most recent publication date (1990) is reviewed here, even though there appear to be fewer problems with the older edition. Initially, the respondents review a list of nine occupational interest areas (clusters) and select the one area they like best. The only information provided to inform this key decision is a one-sentence description of the presumed interests of people in each occupational area. It is noteworthy that interests in occupational areas are requested, rather than interests that might be related to occupational areas.

The next seven questions are poorly worded and could introduce serious problems of interpretation. For example, the second question asks, "How long do you want to prepare for a job?" (p. 5). A better phrasing might be: How many years are you willing to prepare for a job? The next three questions concern the reasoning, mathematical, and language skills the respondent will "bring to a job." Curiously, the stem of each question asks what skill level he or she would *like* to bring to the job. Because most people surely would like to bring advanced level skills to the job, what reason would there be to select the other response options? These items are followed by another three questions that ask about the "skill level that best meets your desire to work with DATA, PEOPLE, and THINGS" (p. 7). The problem with the items thus introduced is that the response options are not mutually exclusive. In one item, the descriptor "operate things" is given for both Options 1 and 2, and for another item the descriptors "teach" and "train" are used for two different options. If the items used to assess "interests and skills" are flawed, the resulting job-matches must also be flawed.

As noted in the user's guide, "The general goal of the JOB-O A is to match the user's interests and skills with the work activities and requirements that will be found on the job." To achieve this goal, respondents are directed to compare their answers to the 18 "interests and skills" questions with response profiles to the same items that presumably represent the skills and interests of workers in various jobs. The JOB-O A booklet provides profiles for 24 job groups, and for three illustrative job titles within each job group. For each job group and job title, respondents are instructed to count the number of matches they have across the 18 variables but to count 3 points for matches on the first two variables. To compare profiles with 24 job groups, and with 72 job titles, across the 18 variables, requires 1,728 comparisons! Clearly identifying job-matches is a tedious undertaking, which is further complicated by the fact that the answer sheet does not provide spaces to record the number of matches for job titles within job groups.

The last page of the answer sheet is headed: "Make a career decision!" (p. 16). Here respondents are directed to list up to seven jobs they like most, and to "choose three that you want to research further to make a good career decision." The respondent is then instructed to consult the *Occupational Outlook Handbook* and other references to find information about the jobs selected for exploration.

To the extent these instruments provide valid "job matches," they can potentially facilitate career exploration by directing attention to jobs compatible with interests. Of course, mismatches could have the unfortunate consequence of misdirecting career exploration and leading to poor career decisions. Incredibly, no empirical evidence is offered to support the validity of (*a*) the profiles of skills and interests "required" for the various jobs, (*b*) the choice of variables used to assess skills and interests, or (*c*) the inference that greater job satisfaction or job success will result if people pursue jobs which closely match their interests and skills as measured by the JOB-O instruments. Authors of the Professional Manual state the selection and coding of the variables was based on a "rational judgmental procedure" rather than on quantitative relationships, and "no claim is made for predictive validity." Although rational judgements may have provided a starting point for developing the JOB-O instruments, it is noteworthy that after nearly 20 years, no empirical evidence has been presented to substantiate the face validity claims made for an instrument that reportedly has been administered to almost five million people.

In light of the logical deficiencies noted above for the assessment items and in the absence of empirical evidence to support the validity of the resulting job-matches, none of these instruments should be taken seriously, except perhaps for increasing awareness of job titles. To base career decisions on any of them would be "Risky Business" at best.

[201]

Job Seeking Skills Assessment.

Purpose: "For assessing clients' ability to complete a job application form and participate in the employment interview, and to serve as a guide for integrating the results into program planning."
Population: Vocational rehabilitation clients.
Publication Date: 1988.
Acronym: JSSA.
Scores, 2: Job Application, Employment Interview.
Administration: Group.
Price Data, 1994: $10 per manual (96 pages).
Time: Administration time not reported.
Comments: Designed as a component of the Diagnostic Employability Profile (DEP).
Authors: Suki Hinman, Bob Means, Sandra Parkerson, and Betty Odendahl.
Publisher: Arkansas Research & Training Center in Vocational Rehabilitation.

Review of the Job Seeking Skills Assessment by PAUL M. MUCHINSKY, Joseph M. Bryan Distinguished Professor of Business, University of North Carolina, Greensboro, NC:

The stated purpose of the Job Seeking Skills Assessment (JSSA) is "for assessing clients' ability to complete a job application form and participate in the employment interview, and to serve as a guide for integrating the results into program planning" (p. 3). The intended population is vocational rehabilitation clients who wish to improve their job-finding skills. Although I have a few minor criticisms of the assessment, my overall opinion of the JSSA is highly positive.

In the preface of the manual the reader is told the JSSA is one component of the Diagnostic Employability Profile (DEP), also developed by one of the authors of the JSSA. However, the authors state that although they prefer the JSSA be used in conjunction with the DEP, it can also be used as a free-standing assessment. I did not receive any other material to review besides the JSSA, and I would have preferred examining how this assessment fits into the total DEP evaluation. Nevertheless, the JSSA is sufficiently well developed and described that it can be reviewed as a separate entity.

The JSSA consists of two assessments, one dealing with the best way to complete a job application form, and the second dealing with the best way to conduct oneself in the employment interview. The assessments are presented within a well-developed and user-friendly manual (i.e., there is no separate test or answer sheet). The rationale behind the JSSA is if vocationally disabled individuals want to be employed, they must first appear employable.

The first assessment consists of a series of scoring criteria for completing a job application. A job application form, which appears to be highly typical of employment applications in general, is presented in the manual. In a group context individuals complete the application. The administrator is also instructed to unobtrusively record the amount of time needed to complete the application. The completed application is scored on the basis of five criteria: neatness/legibility; spelling; completeness; whether the applicant used printing versus long-hand writing to complete the application; and following directions/accuracy. The manual contains detailed instructions for the scoring of the application, with points deducted for misspellings, sloppiness, omissions, etc. The score on the application is used to guide coaching and training—its purpose is diagnostic. For example, certain training would be used if most of the errors were for misspellings, whereas another approach might be used to address problems of legibility.

The second assessment consists of evaluating a candidate's performance in a mock employment interview. Use of a videotape camera with a zoom lens is recommended. The manual contains scripts for both the interviewer and candidate to follow. A 33-factor checklist with scoring weights is presented as a means to evaluate the interview performance. Each factor is scored on either a 2-point (present/absent) or 3-point scale. For example, did the candidate shake the interviewer's hand on arrival (yes/no). And for the posture and body position factor, 2 points are awarded for proper posture, 1 point for occasional slouching, and 0 points for poor posture. Other factors include composure, manner of speech, grooming, and eye contact. Again, the emphasis is on using the interview evaluation for diagnostic and coaching reasons, providing a basis for improving the candidate's performance in employment interviews. The manual also includes advice on how to set up the camera including distance and position. In general the manual is very well written and contains both clear instructions and usable reference material.

In arriving at a judgment of the JSSA, it should clearly be noted that this is not your typical "test." Its function is solely to guide skill enhancement, and is not used for prediction or classification purposes. No validity or reliability data are presented in the manual, but their absence does not detract from the assessment's usability. I would like to know more about the origin of the five criteria for scoring the application, assessments of inter- and intra-rater reliability, and whether the criteria are differentially important in evaluating job applications by employers. Although nothing is stated directly as to why they were selected, the five criteria certainly seem reasonable to me. Similarly, I have no reason to question the comprehensiveness of the 33 factors used to evaluate the employment interview. However, I do have minor concerns about the clarity of some of the levels of the factors (e.g., the difference between "good enthusiasm" [2 points] and "some enthusiasm" [1 point]). The authors devote several pages in the manual to the results of published empirical research describing the development of the JSSA. Although I consider this level of empirical undergirding to be somewhat thin, it does give the interested reader an avenue to pursue the developmental process of the JSSA. No information is presented on the ultimate question of whether the JSSA actually helps vocationally disabled individuals in gaining employment.

Although most certainly the JSSA is not a psychometric *tour de force*, it more than adequately addressees the issues for which it was intended. I give it a clear thumbs up.

Review of the Job Seeking Skills Assessment by WILLIAM I. SAUSER, JR., Associate Vice President for Extension and Professor of Educational Foundations, Leadership, and Technology, Auburn University, Auburn, AL:

In preparing their clients to succeed in the workplace, vocational rehabilitation specialists must be mindful of the following:

> The hiring process often involves a series of decisions on the part of the employer, including a screening based on written applications, an interview, and subsequent decision by personnel to refer or not refer an applicant to the department with an opening, and final disposition by the person responsible for supervising the vacant position. To get a job, the job-seeker and the counselor must influence each decision in the job-seeker's favor. Preparation in job-seeking skills can help a person describe personal abilities favorably, convey enthusiasm about the job, and explain why disability will not interfere with productivity. (Zadny, 1979, p. 77)

Because vocational rehabilitation clients often have poor job-seeking skills, providing training for them in how to complete application blanks and how to perform in job interviews is part of the recommended standard methodology to be followed by vocational rehabilitation specialists (Rubin & Roessler, 1983, p. 191; Power, 1984, p. 11).

The Job Seeking Skills Assessment (JSSA) is designed to help determine whether vocational rehabilitation clients possess the necessary job-seeking skills to succeed in gaining employment. It consists of a standardized job application blank to be filled out by the client, plus a standardized script for a 5-minute employment interview. Although the JSSA was developed to serve as one component of the Diagnostic Employability Profile (DEP), its authors state clearly that it can be used independently of the other parts of the DEP, or as part of another comprehensive assessment system. Furthermore, they note that the two components of the JSSA may be used independently of one another at the option of the assessor.

The JSSA manual contains detailed instructions in how to prepare for, administer, and score the JSSA components. Scored samples are provided, as are blank forms, conveniently perforated, so that they "can easily be removed and used as masters for photocopying your own supply" (p. 72). The manual also contains instructions for videotaping the interview (optional), debriefing the clients, interpreting performance on the JSSA, and report writing. The JSSA assessment results are intended to provide guidance to clients in improving their ability to seek jobs in the economic marketplace. Presumably they may also be used as diagnostic tools for planning personalized training programs, or as program evaluation devices.

Both components of the JSSA (the application blank and the employment interview) possess considerable face validity. They were also designed to assure content validity: Relevant literature was reviewed, existing application blanks were obtained and examined, a pool of interview questions was developed and pilot-tested, and the two components were assembled, reviewed by experts, and subjected to several norming studies.

The application blank was administered to 152 "job ready" clients at a comprehensive rehabilitation facility. Twenty-five blanks were scored independently by one of the test developers and two other raters; proportion of agreement with the expert's scores was .96 and .95 respectively. The mean time to completion of the blank for the 152 clients was 20 minutes, although the standard protocol considers a 15-minute maximum "optimal." The vast majority of clients performed very poorly on the instrument: "need for improvement" judgments were rendered for each of the six major components of the blank—they ranged from 71% (on the signature block) to 100% (on education/military history). No external validation estimates were provided.

Two normative studies were performed with the standardized interview protocol, using 94 and 32 vocational training clients respectively. No reliability estimates were provided for either sample. Again, the clients performed very poorly in terms of both quantitative and qualitative scores. No estimates of external validity were provided.

Clearly, the limited research reviewed above is not enough to establish the psychometric quality of the JSSA. The instrument may have promise, but considerable research is needed before the JSSA can be accepted as a standard instrument for professional use. Interrater and test-retest reliabilities must be established, criterion-related validity studies must be performed, and norms must be formulated using much broader samples.

Two things about the JSSA particularly bother me. First, the manual contains detailed instructions for calculating a large number of quantitative scores for both components—as well as numerous qualitative scores—yet instructs assessors virtually to ignore these scores and interpret instrument results based on clinical judgment! The manual authors state: "Knowing that Bill, Judy and Sam all scored 76% on the job application form is about as useful as not knowing that Bill, Judy and Sam all scored 76% on the job application form. The scores have little meaning aside from the constellation of skills, deficits, wants, motivations, knowledge, and other factors which constitute a unique person" (p. 47). Why calculate this plethora of scores if they are meaningless?

My second major concern relates to a conscious decision on the part of the test developers noted on page 65 of the manual: "The application blank selected, like the majority of those reviewed, includes items that, according to current labor law, should be excluded. However, since it appears to be common practice in the private sector to retain such potentially discriminatory items, and job seekers are therefore likely to encounter them, we opted for realism." Items of concern include date of birth, height, weight, hair color, eye color, marital status, number of children, civic and fraternal activities, and the egregious "list any physical defects." Even in the name of realism, I oppose the inclusion of these items in the JSSA lest they be somehow construed as having the blessing of rehabilitation professionals.

In summary, the JSSA is an interesting and potentially useful standardized application blank and interview protocol designed to assess job-seeking skills of vocational rehabilitation clients. In my opinion, it is in a very early stage of development, and requires considerable normative work and establishment of reliability, validity, and utility before it can be accepted for professional use. The authors are encouraged to continue work with the JSSA, because it could fill an important niche in vocational assessment, particularly with clients of rehabilitation facilities. Special attention should be devoted to the utility of the many scores generated by the assessment device, and to the advisability of including legally questionable items on the standardized application blank.

REVIEWER'S REFERENCES

Zadny, J. J. (1979). Planning for job placement. In D. Vandergoot & J. D. Worrall (Eds.), *Placement in rehabilitation: A career development perspective* (pp. 71-82). Baltimore: University Park Press.

Rubin, S. E., & Roessler, R. T. (1983). *Foundations of the vocational rehabilitation process* (2nd ed.). Baltimore: University Park Press.

Power, P. W. (1984). *A guide to vocational assessment*. Baltimore: University Park Press.

[202]

Johnston Informal Reading Inventory.

Purpose: "To assess the reading comprehension of junior and senior high school students."
Population: Grades 7–12.
Publication Date: 1982.
Acronym: JIRI.
Scores, 2: Vocabulary Screening, Reading Comprehension.
Administration: Group or individual.
Price Data, 1992: $9.95 per complete set including manual (106 pages) and Forms C, B, and L.
Time: (20) minutes.
Comments: Forms B and C are approximately parallel and Form L is longer; "high-interest materials utilized."
Author: Michael C. Johnston.
Publisher: Educational Publications.

Review of the Johnston Informal Reading Inventory by MARGARET R. ROGERS, Assistant Professor of School Psychology, University of Maryland-College Park, College Park, MD:

The Johnston Informal Reading Inventory (JIRI), designed for use with individuals from junior high school age to adults, is an informal reading scale that assesses understanding of antonyms and synonyms, and silent reading comprehension skills. The test author states that his primary motivation in constructing the test was to produce a more practical, flexible, and interesting assessment device than traditional informal reading inventories. To enhance practicality and flexibility, the test can be group or individually administered, and test results are purported to be useful for diagnostic as well as placement purposes. To enhance interest level, the author adapted portions of stories from already published sources (e.g., magazines, short stories, and novels) for inclusion in the test as narrative passages.

The JIRI consists of three types of tasks: word opposites, word synonyms, and graded narrative passages. Test users are instructed to begin a test administration with the Word Opposites Test, then use the resulting word opposite "strength" score to determine entry level into the narrative passages. The test author does not include evidence of any empirical support for the "strength" score. Without such information, the applicability of this scoring procedure is questionable. The manual is also not clear about the role that the Synonyms Test plays in the assessment process.

Following the administration and scoring of the Word Opposites Test, the narrative passages are administered. The JIRI contains three forms of passages: parallel Forms B and C, and Form L. The author recommends that test users employ Form B to assess reading comprehension and gauge reading placement level, then use Form L after Form B to "verify" placement level, and Form C as a post-teaching measure. The three forms each contain nine graded passages. The passages begin with simple stories and progress to more complex narratives. Each passage is followed by a series of short answer, weighted questions that require written responses. Questions assess comprehension in five areas: main idea, detail, vocabulary, cause-effect, and inference. Although the manual is helpful in providing examples of correct answers to every question, it does an inadequate job of indicating how many points to allot to correct/incorrect answers. In addition, no evidence for the difficulty levels of the passages or questions are offered, the author describes the weighting of the questions as "subjective," invites test users to create their own weighting system if the proposed system is unacceptable, and recommends that testing be discontinued once a 60% frustration level is established but does not describe his rationale for determining the 60% cutoff. Thus, throughout the JIRI the scoring procedures lack both clarity and a sound empirical foundation.

The test author briefly notes that the instrument underwent 6 years of development and field testing (including item analysis) but fails to fully describe and document the scope of procedures that comprised these activities. Also notable by its absence is the lack of theoretical and empirical support that would lend credence to the concept of reading comprehension as operationalized in this scale. Despite the emphasis on employing "high interest" passages to assess comprehension, there is no discussion of the procedures used to establish the content validity of the scale.

In fact, the content validity of the scale appears to be seriously compromised. The author asserts that the JIRI is suited equally well for males as well as females, yet in 19 of the 27 stories males are the dominant or only characters. Of the 11 stories that refer to females, the narratives describe the females in either marginal roles as girlfriends, mothers, or grandmothers or portray them as helpless victims, cooks, or "mean ugly" teachers. Adding to these sexist images are themes involving beatings and death (certain and uncertain). In 12 of the 27 narratives, verbal and physical assaults, as well as themes of sexual harassment, are depicted. These images do not enhance the interest level of the stories for this female reviewer and instead, are quite disturbing. I would expect that these themes would inhibit rather than enhance motivation for many potential test takers. I also question how relevant and appropriate these themes are to the contemporary curricula of the targeted audience.

Also, although the scale is made up of parallel Forms B and C there is no discussion of alternate form reliability. In fact, no evidence is provided in the manual that supports the reliability or validity of the instrument, no information is provided regarding examiner qualifications, and the manual does not discuss the appropriateness of using the instrument with linguistically diverse or exceptional populations. Despite the fact that the test is advertised as addressing "a wide range of ethnic and cultural background," evidence of sensitivity to diversity is lacking. Given the number of years the author devoted to the development of the instrument, it seems a serious oversight not to document and publish the development, construction, and field testing efforts more completely.

The JIRI also suffers from logistical problems vis-á-vis the group administration procedures. As students complete a passage, they are instructed to turn their responses in to the test administrator who then scores and makes a decision about the need to continue or terminate testing for each individual student. The author suggests that in one class period, test administrators can usually administer two to four passages to each student. In a class with many students, it would seem practically impossible for a single teacher to simultaneously (*a*) administer the test, (*b*) read and score the short answer questions of each student, (*c*) make decisions about continuing or stopping testing for each student, and (*d*) successfully manage the classroom. Also, the amount of time the test takes to administer is not consistently reported in the manual. Initially, testing time is reported as 20 minutes. Subsequently, the manual states that test users should plan to devote two to three class periods for each administration.

Finally, the manual contains a number of editorial mistakes that could have been easily corrected with careful proofreading. Spacing problems exist (words run into each other) and there are punctuation errors.

Overall, in my opinion, the JIRI suffers from a number of substantial flaws that preclude recommending using the scale over teacher made IRIs that are linked to actual curricula. The test manual lacks clarity, scoring procedures are loose and unsubstantiated, and test development and construction procedures as well as reliability and validity data are not reported. Furthermore, the premise that serves as the basis for the test (to produce "high interest" narratives) appears to be seriously undermined by the preponderance of narratives in which females are depicted in marginal roles and themes of verbal and physical assault are represented.

Review of the Johnston Informal Reading Inventory by CLAUDIA R. WRIGHT, *Associate Professor of Educational Psychology, California State University, Long Beach, CA:*

The Johnston Informal Reading Inventory (JIRI) is viewed by the author as providing an assessment of a student's reading comprehension attained during silent reading. The primary purpose of the instrument is to provide an estimate of a student's highest reading level range. It is suggested that this reading level estimate can be used as an informal placement index for identifying classroom reading materials of appropriate levels of difficulty for each student. Use of the JIRI is predicated on the assumption that a teacher's instructional program includes "high-interest" reading materials, typically narratives. Although the instrument was originally designed to serve students at the secondary level, the author indicates that the JIRI has been successfully applied at junior high school through adult levels (including community college and adult education classes).

The JIRI is made up of the JIRI Word Opposites Test, the JIRI Synonyms Test, three groups of reading comprehension passages (Forms B, C, and L), and three groups of reading comprehension question sheets corresponding to each of the three forms. Answer keys are provided for all tests. The JIRI Word Opposites Test is a group-administered, self-scored test yielding a vocabulary strength level score (Level 3 through 10) that is used to identify the appropriate entry reading level for each student. Administration of this test is recommended to identify the beginning level of reading passage that will be used in subsequent testing. Consisting of words selected from a listing of possible target words from each of the passages (across forms and readability levels) the Word Opposites Test is organized in terms of eight reading levels. Appropriate procedures and types of analyses are reported to have been employed in the development of the final form of the test. No statistical data, however, are reported. The JIRI Synonyms Test (Level 3 through Level 9) is considered to be useful for follow-up testing for those students who have difficulty with the Word Opposites Test.

The 27 reading comprehension passages were selected from novels and magazine articles reflecting diverse ethnic and cultural backgrounds, and were considered to be of interest to adolescents and young adults, males and females, with topics ranging from adventure and mystery, science and sports, to personal problems confronting children at home, in school, and in relationships to others. Nine reading passages, each coded with a corresponding reading level (2nd through 10th), are provided for each of the three forms. The B and C forms are reported by the author to be approximately parallel to one another in that, overall, the readings for both forms share the same range of reading difficulty and length of passage (250 to 700 words). Form L is made up of nine passages, each of a length of 700 words or more. The author indicates that Form B is typically used to provide an initial measure of a student's reading level for placement purposes (identification of appropriate reading materials) with Form L serving as a second estimate to verify placement and Form C providing reading passages and questions employed as a post measure.

Corresponding to each passage for each form is a reading comprehension test made up of seven or nine questions about the readings. Students continue to read subsequent passages and answer corresponding questions until they score below 60% on items for two consecutive reading levels. Although no statistical information is provided regarding the readability levels of the JIRI passages, the author notes that Fry's revised readability formula (Fry, 1977) was employed to evaluate each passage. No correlational data are offered, however, to support the claim of parallel forms.

Because no oral reading is required on the part of the student for this assessment (although a teacher/test administrator may elect to include oral reading as part of the procedure), passages coded by readability level can be easily administered to individuals or to small or large groups of students with the test administrator tracking test materials for individual students in all testing conditions. Detailed test administration directions, student instructions, along with evaluation guidelines and follow-up procedures are provided. Helpful summary charts are also included.

In summary, the JIRI appears to be a time-efficient and relatively inexpensive instrument for estimating a student's reading level. Much attention has been directed toward establishing face and content validities. The primary limitation of this instrument is that no documentation of the psychometric properties is included in the manual for test users seeking information regarding the reliability and validity characteristics of the various JIRI tests or concerning the JIRI's placement success relative to that of other measures of reading comprehension. It would be most useful if validation efforts had been undertaken examining the relationship between standing on the JIRI and performance on other informal reading inventories (IRIs) and standardized reading tests, as well as other criterion-related (behavior-based) variables.

REVIEWER'S REFERENCE

Fry, E. (1977). Fry's readability graph: Clarifications, validity, and extension to level 17. *Journal of Reading*, *21*, 242-252.

[203]

Jordan Left-Right Reversal Test (1990 Edition).

Purpose: Constructed "to measure letter and number reversals in the area of visual receptive functioning."
Population: Ages 5–12.
Publication Dates: 1973–90.
Scores: Total score only.
Administration: Individual or group.
Levels: 2 overlapping levels (ages 5–12, 9–12) in a single booklet.
Price Data, 1994: $60 per complete kit including 50 test forms, 50 laterality checklists, 50 remedial checklists, and manual ('90, 64 pages); $20 per 50 test forms; $10 per 50 laterality checklists; $10 per 50 remedial checklists; $17 per manual; $17 per specimen set.
Time: (20) minutes.
Comments: "Norm-referenced."
Author: Brian T. Jordan.
Publisher: Academic Therapy Publications.
Cross References: See T4:1326 (4 references); for reviews by Mary S. Poplin and Joseph Torgesen, see 9:557; see also T3:1224 (2 references); for reviews by Barbara K. Keogh and Richard J. Reisboard, and excerpted reviews by Alex Bannatyne and Alan Krichev, see 8:434 (5 references).

TEST REFERENCES

1. Jordan, B. T., & Jordan, S. G. (1990). Jordan Left-Right Reversal Test: An analysis of visual reversals in children and significance for reading problems. *Child Psychiatry and Human Development*, *21*, 65-73.

Review of the Jordan Left-Right Reversal Test (1990 Edition) by CHRISTINE W. BURNS, Assistant Professor of Educational Psychology, University of Utah, Salt Lake City, UT:

The Jordan Left-Right Reversal Test was designed to measure letter and number reversals in children ages 5 through 12 years. The test may be administered individually or to large groups. Different testing instructions are given for age groups 5, 6 through 8, and 9 through 12. Children ages 5 through 8 are required to identify letters and numbers that are written in reversed form. Children 5 years of age are provided with a visual demonstration by the examiner to facilitate comprehension of the task. The instructions for 5-year-olds require an understanding of the basic concepts of "same" and "backward." In addition to identifying letter reversals, children ages 9 to 12 are asked to identify letter reversals in words and reversed words presented in sentences.

The test was standardized on more than 3,000 children ages 5 through 12, in average classroom settings. Ten percent of the sample was of nonwhite racial backgrounds. The author states that care was taken to include all socioeconomic levels; however, specific data regarding sample size and characteristics are not available in the test manual. No known cases of children with mental retardation (IQ below 80), emotional disturbances, or learning disabilities were included in the normative group.

Test-retest reliabilities were reported for a sample of 99 children with a 1-week interval between testing. Reliability estimates were calculated for four age levels. They ranged from .60 for the 5-year age level to .94 for ages 10 and 11. The test has acceptable reliability for ages 7 through 11; however, caution should be exercised when evaluating young children because of the lower reliability with this age group.

The test manual provides little evidence for the validity of this instrument. Evidence for content validity was provided by including only those letters, whole words, and numbers that presented a clear reversal when reproduced in a left-right position (e.g., R, was, 4). Concurrent validity evidence was provided using "a representative sample of children ages six through twelve" (manual, p. 48). These children were administered the Reversal Test, the Bender Gestalt Test, and the Wide Range Achievement Test (WRAT). The data were analyzed using a *t*-test. The author concluded that the Jordan Left-Right Reversal Test shows substantial validity because children diagnosed with reading disability scored significantly higher than normal children. No sample size is given for this validation study. The author identified his reading-disabled sample with an outdated test; the WRAT is now in its third edition. Furthermore, the WRAT was never intended to be used to diagnose reading disabilities, but rather was intended as a screener. Comparisons of the Jordan scores between learning-disabled children and normal children revealed significant differences. These results are in the expected direction; however, what they mean for the interpretation of the Jordan test is not clear. There is no attempt in the manual to incorporate current research to assist test users with an understanding of the meaning of letter and number reversals in children and their relationship to reading disabilities. For each test level and each gender, developmental ages and percentiles are reported. All scores below the 50th percentile are statistically in the abnormal range according to the test author. It is unclear how the author determined that percentile scores below 50 would be considered deviant or abnormal and warrant remediation. The manual devotes a chapter to remediation of letter and number reversals; however, no research data were cited to support this type of instruction to be effective in improving basic academic skills.

In summary, the Jordan Left-Right Reversal Test is an easily administered test of letter and word reversals in children. However, the validity data provided are inadequate to support the use of this test either as a screening instrument or as part of a diagnostic battery for learning disabilities. There is no evidence to support that this test makes a unique contribution to the diagnosis of learning disabilities.

Review of the Jordan Left-Right Reversal Test (1990 Edition) by JEFFREY H. SNOW, Neuropsychologist, Capital Rehabilitation Hospital, Tallahassee, FL:

This test is designed to assess visual reversal of letters, numbers, and words for children 5 years of age and older. The author points out that visual reversals are not unusual for preschool children, although the persistence of this characteristic is often associated with reading difficulties. The author further indicates that investigation into reading disabilities suggests that symptoms of visual reversals have a "neurological basis" (manual, p. 11). This test was designed because of a need for a standardized assessment of visual reversals. The manual indicates this standardized assessment should prove useful in terms of adding to diagnostic batteries for learning disabilities, early identification of potential learning difficulties, and remedial training for children who evidence reversal disorders.

The test comprises two sections (Level I and Level II). Level I is administered to children 5 through 8 years of age, and Levels I and II are administered to children 9 years of age and older. Level I consists of single letters and numbers presented in either correct or reversed orientation. Level II consists of words presented in correct or reversed orientation and complete sentences which contain a reversed word. Specific directions are provided for Level I, although no directions are listed in the manual for Level II. Each level is scored for number of errors; with an error constituting reversed test symbols that were not marked or correctly oriented symbols that were marked as reversed.

Sketchy information is provided concerning the test construction and standardization. For Level I, it is indicated that a panel of judges selected only letters and symbols that would present a clear-cut reversal, and that ambiguous letters were not selected. A description is provided for the content of Level II, but no detail is given pertaining to selection of the words or construction of the sentences. The manual reports the test was standardized using a sample of 3,000 children from regular education classes ages 5 through 12. The author indicates that care was taken to include all socioeconomic levels, and that 10% of the sample was nonwhite. Mentally retarded, emotionally disturbed, and learning-disabled children were excluded from the normative group. No detail is given as to number of males and females within the normative sample or where the sample was drawn. Although the manual reports that care was taken to include all socioeconomic levels, specific breakdown as to the SES characteristics of the sample is not provided.

The manual does list results of statistical analyses of normative data. For Level I, a two-factor analysis of variance was conducted to investigate age and sex effects. Significant main effects for sex and age were found. In general, the results indicated that younger children made more reversal errors and boys of all ages scored more errors than girls. The author concludes that these data suggest developmental skills associated with correct visual directionality are not correlated in a step-wise manner with chronological age. He felt that the data do indicate that even with younger children, necessary developmental skills for correct visual orientation are reasonably intact. An analysis of variance was run for Level II, with the results again indicating a significant age and sex effect. As with Level I, younger subjects made more errors than older subjects and boys committed more errors than girls.

To score the instrument, errors are summed; this value can then be converted to either a Developmental Age or percentile. Norms are provided for children ages 5-0 to 12-6. The Developmental Ages were derived by plotting median raw scores for each 6-month age level against a midpoint of the chronological age interval. The developmental ages were then determined by locating the chronological age which corresponded to the raw score on the developmental curve. Percentiles were derived based on distributions of raw error scores and corresponding cumulative percentages for each 6-month age level.

Limited information concerning reliability and validity are reported in the test manual. Test-retest reliability coefficients for a sample of 99 children using a 2-week interval are reported. Coefficients ranged from a low of .60 at the 5-year level to a high of .94 at the 7-year and 10- and 11-year levels. The reliability coefficient across all age groups is .90. The manual reports evidence of content validity was based on the fact that only letters, whole words, and numbers were chosen that present a clear reversal when reproduced in a left-right position. The manual then reports a study consisting of 220 children between the ages of 6 and 12 who were identified as learning disabled. Test scores for these children were then compared with normal children in the same age ranges. Significant differences are reported at all levels. Another study is reported in which children between the ages of 6 and 12 were chosen and classified based on scores from the Wide Range Achievement Test. The children were placed into groups considered "average readers" and those considered as "below average readers." All children were administered the reversal test as well as the Bender-Gestalt. Comparing average and below average readers, significant differences were found; the "below average readers" committed a higher average frequency of errors than the "average readers."

Other sections are provided within the test manual. Case histories are listed which provide results of various psychological tests and list brief summaries and recommendations. The manual also contains a section on Remediation of Reversals, which provides specific activities for various age levels.

I recommend that potential users of this test should be cautious. Very little information is provided concerning the composition of the standardization sample, making generalizability problematic. Although reliability coefficients appear adequate, there are several concerns in this area. The test-retest interval was only 1 week, which makes practice effect a definite consideration. It is also noted that as children get older, they tend to make very few errors on this measure. Therefore, inflated reliability coefficients may be the case particularly for older children as near perfect to perfect performance was probably obtained on both assessments. The validity data are sketchy, as the relationship between this measure and other tests is not established. It is difficult to ascertain if this test is assessing a relatively discrete construct, or is merely tying into more global type assessments of visual discrimination and/or basic reading recognition. In this regard, it would add little to use this test in a comprehensive assessment of learning difficulties. In general, further research with this measure is clearly warranted. Data concerning the measure's relationship with other measures, as well as more appropriate reliability indices would allow for a more educated decision concerning use of this test.

[204]

Kaufman Adolescent and Adult Intelligence Test.

Purpose: Designed as a "measure of general intelligence."
Population: Ages 11 to 85+.
Publication Date: 1993.
Acronym: KAIT.
Scores, 9 to 14: Crystallized Scale (Definitions, Auditory Comprehension, Double Meanings, Famous Faces [alternate subtest], Total), Fluid Scale (Rebus Learning, Logical Steps, Mystery Codes, Memory for Block Designs [alternate subtest], Total), Measures of Delayed Recall [optional] (Rebus Delayed Recall, Auditory Delayed Recall), Mental Status [supplementary subtest], Total.
Administration: Individual.
Price Data, 1994: $495 per complete kit; $40 per record set including 25 each, record booklets and mystery code booklets; $40 per manual (161 pages); $135 per KAIT Assist (IBM); $79 per KAIT training video.
Time: (58–73) minutes for Core Battery; (83–102) minutes for Expanded Battery.
Authors: Alan S. Kaufman and Nadeen L. Kaufman.
Publisher: American Guidance Service, Inc.
Cross References: See T4:1342 (1 reference).

TEST REFERENCES

1. Kaufman, A. S. (1993). Joint exploratory factor analysis of the Kaufman Assessment Battery for Children and the Kaufman Adolescent and Adult Intelligence Test for 11- and 12-year-olds. *Journal of Clinical Child Psychology*, *22*, 355-364.

2. Brown, D. T. (1994). Review of the Kaufman Adolescent and Adult Intelligence Test (KAIT). *Journal of School Psychology*, *32*, 85-99.

3. Chen, T-H., Kaufman, A. S., & Kaufman, J. C. (1994). Examining the interaction of age x race pretraining to Black-White differences at ages 15 to 93 on six Horn abilities assessed by K-FAST, K-SNAP, and KAIT subtests. *Perceptual and Motor Skills*, *79*, 1683-1690.

4. Kaufman, J. C., McLean, J. E., Kaufman, A. S., & Kaufman, N. L. (1994). White-Black and White-Hispanic differences on fluid and crystalized abilities by age across the 11- to 94-year range. *Psychological Reports*, *75*, 1279-1288.

5. Shaughnessy, M. F., & Moore, J. N. (1994). The KAIT with developmental students, honor students, and freshmen. *Psychology in the Schools*, *31*, 286-287.

6. Kaufman, A. S., Kaufman, J. C., & McLean, J. E. (1995). Factor structure of the Kaufman Adolescent and Adult Intelligence Test (KAIT) for Whites, African Americans, and Hispanics. *Educational and Psychological Measurement*, *55*, 365-376.

Review of the Kaufman Adolescent and Adult Intelligence Test by DAWN P. FLANAGAN, Assistant Professor of Psychology, St. John's University, Jamaica, NY:

GENERAL DESCRIPTION. The Kaufman Adolescent and Adult Intelligence Test (KAIT) is an individually administered intelligence test battery designed for individuals from age 11 to 85+. It is composed of three intelligence scales: Fluid (Gf), Crystallized (Gc), and Composite Intelligence. The three KAIT scales yield standard IQs that have a mean of 100 and a standard deviation of 15. The subtests that comprise the Fluid Scale of the KAIT include Rebus Learning (a task that involves paired-associative learning), Logical Steps (a task that involves deductive reasoning), and Mystery Codes (a task that involves both inductive and deductive reasoning). The Crystallized Scale also contains three subtests: Definitions, Auditory Comprehension, and Double Meanings. The Definitions subtest measures lexical knowledge and requires the individual to synthesize clues to arrive at a correct solution. Auditory Comprehension measures listening ability and requires memory for meaningful material. The Double Meanings subtest measures lexical knowledge, involves inductive reasoning, and requires the individual to integrate stimuli that are seemingly disparate in meaning. These six subtests comprise the Core Battery of the KAIT and, together, yield the Composite IQ, an index of general intelligence.

The Expanded Battery of the KAIT consists of the six Core Battery subtests plus the following additional subtests: (*a*) Memory for Block Designs—an alternate subtest for the Fluid Scale that involves visual memory, analysis, and synthesis; (*b*) Famous Faces—an alternate subtest for the Crystallized Scale that assesses an individual's general factual knowledge and involves long-term retrieval as well as integration of facts and concepts; and (*c*) Rebus Delayed Recall and Auditory Delayed Recall—two memory subtests that may be used with Rebus Learning and Auditory Comprehension to make comparisons between immediate and delayed memory. Because, according to the test manual, all KAIT subtests (Core and Expanded Battery) were constructed following Piaget's stage of formal operations and Luria and Golden's conception of planning ability, they require high level though processes for success. [For more detailed descriptions of the KAIT subtests and their underlying cognitive abilities see Kaufman and Horn (in press), Kaufman and Kaufman (1995), and McGrew (1995)].

In addition to the subtests on the Core and Expanded Batteries, the KAIT contains a Mental Status subtest. This subtest is composed of 10 items that are designed to assess attention and orientation in time and space. Performance on the Mental Status subtest is classified into one of three categories: Average, Below Average, or Lower Extreme. The category of Lower Extreme is subdivided into Mild, Moderate, and Severe Deficit for individuals between the ages of 55 and 85+ years. According to Kaufman and Kaufman (the test authors), a valid assessment of intellectual functioning may not be possible using the KAIT Core Battery (or any other intelligence test for that matter) for individuals who are classified as Lower Extreme-Moderate or Lower Extreme-Severe on the Mental Status subtest. In this instance, the Kaufmans suggest administration of the Famous Faces subtest only. However, because the 10 individuals in the standardization sample (aged 55+) who scored in the Lower Extreme on the Mental Status subtest obtained an average IQ Composite of 73.5, the Core Battery may yield some clinically useful information about these individuals. Overall, the KAIT subtest materials are well constructed, innovative, and stimulating to examinees.

THEORETICAL MODEL. The theoretical model underlying the KAIT is Horn and Cattell's (1966, 1967) *original* Fluid-Crystallized theory of intelligence. In this early conception, intelligence was viewed as a dichotomy and measured typically by tasks that required an individual to solve novel problems through reasoning (fluid ability) or to solve problems that depended on accumulated knowledge, general life experiences, and acculturation for success (crystallized ability). Moreover, when intelligence was conceived as a dichotomy, an individual's performance on tasks designed to measure fluid ability was influenced by short-term acquisition, long-term storage and retrieval, response speed and so on. However, recent refinements to the Fluid-Crystallized theory by Horn and his colleagues have resulted in a multiple theory of intelligence that is referred to as *modern Gf-Gc* theory. In this modern conception of intelligence, short-tern memory (Gsm), long-term retrieval (Glr), speed of processing (Gs), visual processing (Gv), and auditory processing (Ga) as well as other cognitive abilities and processes are measured separately, resulting in a "purer" measure of fluid ability (Horn, 1991).

Kaufman and Kaufman chose to have the KAIT reflect the Gf-Gc *dichotomy* (rather than the multiple theory) because they do not believe that the clinical information provided by purer measures of ability is as valuable as information provided by less pure (or mixed) measures (manual, p. 12). The Kaufmans' viewpoint, however, appears to be based on their own clinical experience and not empirical evidence. The differential clinical utility of pure versus mixed measures of ability notwithstanding, the KAIT, one of the newest measures of cognitive functioning in the field of intellectual assessment, appears to be based on an old theory. That is, the KAIT must be interpreted from a two-factor theoretical perspective—a view not held by major proponents of Gf-Gc theory (Horn and Cattell) for almost three decades (Woodcock, 1993) and not supported by scientific evidence. For example, several recent reviews of the extant factor analytic research on human intelligence over the past 40–50 years (e.g., Carroll, 1993) have demonstrated support for a multiple-factor theory of intelligence rather than a simplistic two-factor conceptualization. Because the KAIT was not intended to be interpreted from a multiple intelligence theoretical model, such as modern Gf-Gc theory, this type of interpretation should not be made in the absence of supporting empirical evidence. In this regard, it is important to note that recent studies (e.g., Kaufman & Horn, in press) have demonstrated the utility of the KAIT's broad Fluid and Crystallized IQs within the context of *current* Gf-Gc research (i.e., age-related progressions of Gf and Gc).

STANDARDIZATION. The KAIT was standardized on 2,000 individuals between the ages of 11 and 85+ years. The sample spanned 13 age levels, contained at least 125 individuals at each level, and closely approximated U.S. population estimates for 1990 (cf., U.S. Census data, 1988) on most demographic variables including gender, socioeconomic status (examinee or parental education levels), and race or ethnic group. The sample contained a slight (6.8%) underrepresentation of subjects from the Northeast and overrepresentation (6%) of subjects from the West. Overall, when evaluated against the criteria set forth by Hammill, Brown, and Bryant (1992), the KAIT standardization sample is exemplary.

RELIABILITY. The KAIT has high internal consistency reliability coefficients for the Fluid, Crystallized, and Composite IQ scales (i.e., ≤.90). Test-retest reliability coefficients (mean = 31 days) for the IQ scales are also good, ranging from .87 (Fluid IQ Scale) to .97 (Crystallized IQ Scale). As expected, internal consistency and test-retest reliability coefficients are lower for the KAIT subtests. Although internal consistency reliability coefficients exceed .80 for all KAIT subtests with the exception of Memory for Block Design (.79) and Auditory Delayed Recall (.71), most of these subtests have averaged test-retest reliability coefficients that fall below .80. In general, the KAIT IQ scales are sufficiently reliable for making judgments regarding an individual's performance in two separate domains of cognitive functioning (Fluid and Crystallized) as well as in general intellectual ability. The KAIT subtests, however, should not be interpreted separately or be used to make diagnostic or screening decisions. Rather, these subtests may be used in conjunction with other data to form hypotheses about an individual's cognitive strengths and weaknesses (see manual, chapter 6).

VALIDITY. The KAIT manual presents extensive information on the content, construct, criterion-related, and diagnostic validity of this instrument. The construct validity evidence of the KAIT includes age trend analyses, intercorrelations of KAIT IQs and subtests, correlations with other intelligence tests, exploratory and confirmatory factor analyses of the KAIT subtests, and joint factor analyses of the KAIT and Wechsler subtests. In general, age trend data revealed that the Fluid and Crystallized IQs increased and decreased according to patterns predicted by the Horn-Cattell theory of intelligence (see also Kaufman & Horn, in press). The studies reported in the manual provide support for a two-factor (Gf/Gc) interpretation of the KAIT and demonstrate that this instrument is a good measure of global intellectual functioning. Confirmatory factor analyses showed that a two-factor Fluid-Crystallized model emerged consistently across the age range of the KAIT. Studies conducted subsequent to the publication of the KAIT showed that a two-factor (Gf/Gc) solution emerged in separate white, African-American, and Hispanic subgroups of the standardization sample (see Kaufman & Kaufman, 1995). In addition, results of joint factor analyses showed that the KAIT Crystallized and Wechsler Verbal subtests measure the same construct (labeled *Crystallized/Verbal*) and KAIT Fluid and Wechsler Performance subtests measure different constructs, labeled *Fluid* and *Perceptual Organization*, respectively. Finally, studies reported in the manual demonstrate that many KAIT subtests (particularly those included on the Expanded Battery) discriminate between control samples and samples of individuals with neurological impairment and Alzheimer's-type dementia. The results of these and more recent studies conducted with clinical samples (e.g., depressed patients) provide support for the KAIT Expanded Battery as a useful supplemental measure in neuropsychological assessment (see Kaufman & Kaufman, 1995).

Although the data presented in the manual appear to support the Fluid-Crystallized dichotomy underlying the KAIT, these data must be viewed cautiously. The manual does not provide evidence that convinced this reviewer that the KAIT Fluid Scale is actually a good measure of fluid ability. That is, the KAIT was not correlated or factor analyzed with a comprehensive array of empirically validated Gf-Gc marker variables that included a well-validated measure of fluid ability, such as the Woodcock-Johnson Psycho-Educational Battery—Revised (WJ-R) (see Flanagan, Alfonso, & Flanagan, 1994, for a discussion). The fact that the KAIT Fluid subtests are relatively distinct from the Wechsler Performance subtests does not necessarily mean that they measure what they purport to measure (i.e., fluid ability). For example, results of a comprehensive task analysis revealed that Rebus Learning (a subtest on the KAIT Fluid Scale) is most likely a measure of Glr, associative memory in particular (McGrew, 1995). This classification is consistent with Woodcock's (1990) finding that the WJ-R Visual-Auditory Learning test (the very test from which Rebus Learning was adapted) is a measure of Glr, although Kaufman and Horn (in press) consider Rebus Learning to be a mixed measure of Gf and Gc abilities. In addition, McGrew's (1995) task analysis suggests that Memory for Block Designs, the KAIT's alternate Fluid subtest, is most likely a mixed measure of short-term visual memory (Gsm) and Gv. This task analysis also suggested that some KAIT Crystallized subtests may involve fluid reasoning (e.g., Double Meanings). Thus, many KAIT subtests appear to be mixed measures of two or more Gf-Gc abilities. Although Kaufman and Kaufman did not set out to develop "pure" tests of Gf and Gc abilities, additional studies are needed to determine exactly which Gf-Gc abilities underlie the KAIT subtests. These types of studies (e.g., joint factor analyses that include good marker tests that span a broad range of cognitive abilities) would provide empirical support for interpreting the KAIT from contemporary theory and research (Flanagan & McGrew, 1995).

CONCLUSIONS. The KAIT is a well-standardized test of general intellectual functioning that was developed specifically for adolescents and adults (11–85+ years). The integration of the developmental (Piaget), neuropsychological (Luria), and experimental-cognitive (Horn-Cattell) models that underlie the KAIT permits interpretation from well-researched theories. The KAIT is easy to administer and score and contains test materials that are well constructed, easy to manipulate, and stimulating to examinees. The KAIT yields highly reliable Fluid, Crystallized, and Composite IQs across the age span of the test. The manual is well organized; provides thorough instructions related to administration, scoring, and interpretation; and contains detailed information about the technical characteristics of the instrument. With the exception of the WJ-R, the KAIT appears to be the only other intelligence battery having *more than one* test measuring fluid ability (i.e., Logical Steps and Mystery Codes), which would allow for an adequate assessment of this construct (McGrew, 1995). However, additional construct validity studies seem warranted before inferences can be made about an individual's Fluid Intelligence as measured by *all* of the KAIT's purported fluid subtests. Once researchers gain a clearer understanding of the Gf-Gc abilities that underlie the KAIT, it is likely that its utility as a clinical and research tool will be realized more fully.

The KAIT is a viable alternative to the Wechsler Scales as a measure of general intellectual functioning. Also, there is preliminary support for using the KAIT Fluid Scale to supplement the information provided by the Wechsler Scales. Alternatively, the Wechsler Performance Scale may be used to provide additional information (e.g., Gv) about the cognitive abilities of an individual who was assessed with the KAIT. Although other instruments appear to assess a wider range of Gf-Gc abilities than the KAIT (e.g., WJ-R), future research will show how the KAIT can augment the information provided by existing intelligence test batteries as the field begins to move toward a cross-battery approach to intellectual assessment (McGrew, 1995). Finally, the mounting diagnostic validity evidence for the KAIT (see Kaufman & Kaufman, 1995) demonstrates its potential utility for making differential diagnoses.

REVIEWER'S REFERENCES

Horn, J. L., & Cattell, R. B. (1966). Refinement and test of the theory of fluid and crystallized general intelligences. *Journal of Educational Psychology, 57*, 253-270.

Horn, J. L., & Cattell, R. B. (1967). Age differences in fluid and crystallized intelligence. *Acta Psychologica, 26*, 107-129.

Woodcock, R. W. (1990). Theoretical foundations of the WJ-R measures of cognitive ability. *Journal of Psychoeducational Assessment, 8*, 231-258.

Horn, J. L. (1991). Measurement of intellectual capabilities: A review of theory. In K. S. McGrew, J. K. Werder, & R. W. Woodcock, *Woodcock-Johnson technical manual: A reference on theory and current research* (pp. 197-246). Chicago: Riverside.

Hammill, D. D., Brown, L., & Bryant, B. R. (1992). *A consumer's guide to tests in print* (2nd ed.). Austin, TX: PRO-ED.

Carroll, J. B. (1993). *Human cognitive abilities: A survey of factor analytic studies*. New York: Cambridge.

Woodcock, R. W. (1993). An information processing view of *Gf-Gc* theory. In B. A. Bracken & R. S. McCallum (Eds.), *Journal of Psychoeducational Assessment monograph series, advances in psychoeducational assessment: Woodcock-Johnson Psycho-Educational Battery—Revised* (pp. 80-102). Cordova, TN: The Psychological Corporation.

Flanagan, D. P., Alfonso, V. C., & Flanagan. R. (1994). A review of the Kaufman Adolescent and Adult Intelligence Test: An advancement in cognitive assessment? *School Psychology Review, 23*, 512-525.

Kaufman, A. S., & Kaufman, N. L. (1995). The Kaufman Adolescent and Adult Intelligence Test (KAIT). In D. P. Flanagan, J. L. Genshaft, & P. L. Harrison, *Beyond traditional intellectual assessment: Contemporary and emerging theories, tests, and issues*. New York: Guilford. Manuscript in preparation.

McGrew, K. S. (1995). Analysis of the major intelligence batteries according to a proposed comprehensive framework of human cognitive and knowledge abilities. In D. P. Flanagan, J. L. Genshaft, and P. L. Harrison, *Beyond traditional intellectual assessment: Contemporary and emerging theories, tests, and issues*. New York: Guilford. Manuscript in preparation.

Flanagan, D. P., & McGrew, K. S. (1995). The field of intellectual assessment: A current perspective. *The School Psychologist, 49*, 7-14.

Kaufman, A. S., & Horn, J. L. (in press). Age changes on tests of fluid and crystallized ability for women and men of the Kaufman Adolescent and Adult Intelligence Test (KAIT) at ages 17 to 94 years. *Archives of Clinical Neuropsychology*.

Review of the Kaufman Adolescent and Adult Intelligence Test by TIMOTHY Z. KEITH, Professor of Psychology, Alfred University, Alfred, NY:

The Kaufman Adolescent and Adult Intelligence Test (KAIT) is an individually administered test of intelligence for adolescents and adults ages 11 to 85 years and older. In addition to assessing general intelligence, the scale is designed to assess crystallized and fluid intelligence, and can also be used to assess memory skills and general mental status.

The core battery of the KAIT includes six subtests, three of which are designed to assess fluid intelligence and three of which are designed to assess crystallized intelligence. In the Definitions subtest (part of the Crystallized scale) examinees are shown a word with blanks inserted for some of its letters and are told the definition (or some other clue) of the word. From these two clues the examinees are to provide the missing word. In Rebus Learning (Fluid) examinees learn an increasing number of rebuses and read "sentences" made up of those rebuses. For Logical Steps (Fluid) examinees are shown how different people or objects relate to one another and then are required to make conclusions about the placement of other objects. For example, in an early item examinees are shown a series of steps. Examinees are told and shown that Cindy is on step four, Ann is one step below Bob, Bob is two steps below Cindy, and Ann is four steps below Dave. Examinees are to figure out which step Dave is on. Examinees listen to news stories for the Auditory Comprehension subtest (Crystallized) and then answer questions derived from those news stories. In Mystery Codes (Fluid) examinees are shown pictures that vary on several dimensions and codes that correspond to those pictures. Examinees then have to figure out the code that goes with a final picture. Two sets of word clues are presented in the Double Meanings (Crystallized) subtest; examinees think of one word that fits both sets of clues.

The expanded battery includes two measures of delayed recall. For the subtest Rebus Delayed Recall, examinees are asked to read sentences using the rebuses learned in the Rebus Learning Test. In Auditory Delayed Recall examinees are asked questions about the news stories used in the Auditory Comprehension subtest. The expanded battery also includes an alternate subtest for both the Crystallized and Fluid scales, to be used if a subtest is spoiled or is inappropriate for a particular examinee. Memory for Block Designs is the alternate for the Fluid scale. Examinees are given six blocks with a different pattern on each side and are presented with a six-block stimulus for 5 seconds. The stimulus is then removed and examinees have 45 seconds to reproduce the stimulus. For the alternate subtest for the Crystallized scale—Famous Faces—examinees are asked to identify the famous people shown in photographs.

A final subtest in the expanded battery is Mental Status. Mental Status includes 10 very basic questions designed to "assess attention and orientation to the world" (p. 7). The mental status subtest is designed to produce descriptive categories for examinees who are too low-functioning to be assessed with the full KAIT. According to the manual, the core battery can be given in about an hour, whereas the expanded battery requires approximately an hour and a half.

For all subtests, raw scores are converted to subtest scale scores (M = 10, SD = 3). Subtest scaled scores for the core battery (including an alternate subtest if one is to be substituted for one of the core batteries subtests) are added together and converted to Crystallized, Fluid, and Composite IQs (M = 100, SD = 15). Subtests from the expanded battery may also be converted to scaled scores, although they are not used in the calculation of IQs. Instead, they may be compared in profile form to other subtest scaled scores. The mental status subtest is used to obtain descriptive categories (average, below average, lower extreme). The manual includes extensive information on scoring the KAIT and interpreting the scores obtained from the test. The approach to interpretation is logical, cautious, and follows the recommendations developed by A. Kaufman elsewhere (e.g., 1979). The manual also includes extensive description of the abilities and development of each subtest, a resource that should be helpful in interpretation.

The primary KAIT materials include two easels that include most of the stimuli, directions, and scoring criteria for the Core battery (Easel 1) and the expanded battery (Easel 2). Additional materials include the blocks used in Memory for Block Designs, a tape for use with the Auditory Comprehension subtest, the manual, an item booklet for Mystery Codes, and the individual test records. The 159-page manual is well organized and complete. The authors explain the theoretical and clinical rationale for the scale; there is extensive information on administration, scoring, and interpretation; and there is considerable attention devoted to the development, standardization, and reliability and validity of the scale. The materials are attractive, well organized, and easy to use.

There is considerable detail concerning the development of the KAIT in the manual. In the introduction and rationale chapters of the manual the authors explain that the KAIT is based on Horn and Cattell's theory of fluid and crystallized intelligence, Piaget's stage of formal operations, and Golden and Luria's notion of planning ability. It would appear that the fluid and crystallized intelligence orientation was the *guiding force* for the development of the scale because the test is organized to obtain fluid and crystallized scores. However, the chapter on development makes it clear that the decision of the theoretical model was made, at least partially, after the fact: "The final decision on a theoretical model was delayed until standardization" (p. 68). Thus, it seems likely that the KAIT would adhere to the *Gf-Gc* model less completely than a scale designed explicitly to assess fluid and crystallized intelligence.

Beyond this post hoc choice of a guiding theory, the KAIT appears to be well developed and well standardized. The original item pool included almost 2,500 items and over 30 subtests, which were reduced to a battery of 16 subtests following an analysis of national tryout data. The KAIT was standardized between 1988 and 1991 on a national sample of 2,000 adults and adolescents ages 11 to over 85 (the test was actually standardized on approximately 2,600 individuals, but 2,000 were used to create the norms). The subtests and items were also reduced during and after the standardization. With a few exceptions, the standardization sample appears to be representative of the U.S. population based on gender, geographic region, socioeconomic status, and ethnic group. In sum, the standardization appears very well done, and the detail reported in the manual is exceptional.

The manual presents extensive information concerning the reliability and validity of the KAIT. Split-half reliabilities are presented for all subtests for all age groups, and most appear quite adequate (the reliabilities for 11–12-year-olds are generally lower than for other ages, however). Average internal consistency reliabilities range from .79 for the Memory for Block Designs subtest to .93 for Rebus Learning. Coefficients for the intelligence scales were above .90 for all age groups, with average coefficients of.95 for the Crystallized and Fluid scores and .97 for the Composite score. The manual also presents test-retest reliabilities (approximately 1-month interval) for 153 adolescents and adults in three age groups. Test-retest reliabilities appear quite adequate for overall scores; reliabilities for Crystallized and Composite scales were all above .90, although Fluid scale reliabilities range from .85 to.90. Reliabilities for subtest scores were much more variable and range from .63 (average reliability) for the Auditory Delayed Recall subtest to .95 for Definitions. Most were in the .70s to low .80s.

There is also extensive information concerning the validity of the KAIT, including graphs of the age progression of scores, exploratory factor analyses of the KAIT and the KAIT along with other measures of intelligence, confirmatory factor analyses of the KAIT, and correlations with other tests. Briefly, the information presented suggests that KAIT scores show a developmental progression similar to what might be expected if the tests measured crystallized and fluid intelligence. Exploratory and confirmatory factor analyses suggest that the KAIT does indeed measure two factors similar in structure to the organization of the test. The crystallized factor is similar to the verbal factor found for the Wechsler tests, whereas the fluid scale (as expected) appears relatively distinct from a Wechsler perceptual organization factor. Multi-sample confirmatory factor analyses suggest that the KAIT does indeed measure the same abilities across its age span. In correlations with other tests, the Crystallized scale appears to correlate well with other measures of crystallized ability, but the Fluid scale does not always behave in the manner that would be predicted if it were indeed a measure of fluid intelligence.

Despite the extensive validity information, additional information concerning the validity of the KAIT is needed. The KAIT is designed to measure crystallized and fluid intelligence. However, the final decision to base the test on *Gf-Gc* theory was not made until the test was standardized, and thus the test is less theoretically driven than it might have been had these constructs guided item and subtest development from the start. In addition, the KAIT uses a fairly old version of the continuously developed *Gf-Gc* theory of Horn and Cattell. The KAIT purports to measure only fluid and crystallized abilities, whereas in its modern form *Gf-Gc* theory postulates six to eight general factors *in addition to* fluid and crystallized intelligence. Many of the KAIT subtests are speeded (they have fairly strict time limits) and thus mingle level with speed factors (cf., Carroll, 1993). In addition, many of the subtests also require memory abilities. Indeed, among the Fluid subtests, two are speeded (Logical Steps, Mystery Codes) and two require memory abilities (Rebus Learning, Memory for Block Designs). In modern *Gf-Gc* theory many of the subtests used here would be placed partially or totally on other factors. Rebus learning, for example, may be seen more as a measure of long-term storage and retrieval (*Glr*; e.g., Woodcock, 1990) or general memory and learning (*Gy*; Carroll, 1993, ch. 15) rather than fluid intelligence.

At present, the evidence presented in the manual suggests the KAIT provides a good measure of intelligence for adolescents and adults. However, it is unclear whether the tests measure fluid and crystallized intelligence or some other abilities. Given these questions, what is needed is *strong* evidence that the KAIT does indeed measure fluid and crystallized intelligence. Scores on the KAIT should be correlated with scores from other tests, such as the Woodcock-Johnson Psycho-Educational Battery—Revised (415), specifically designed to assess fluid and crystallized intelligence and the other general abilities in the Horn-Cattell model (cf., Flanagan, Alfonso, & Flanagan, 1994). Until further validity evidence is presented concerning the nature of the constructs measured by the KAIT, examiners should interpret scores on the separate subscales cautiously.

SUMMARY. The Kaufman Adolescent and Adult Intelligence Test is an individually administered test of intelligence for adolescents and adults ages 11 through adulthood. The tasks included are interesting and many of them are novel in their approach to the measurement of intelligence; they should retain the interest of most adolescents and adults. The test appears to be well standardized and have good reliability to fulfill its purposes. The test seems to provide a good measure of general intelligence. It is unclear, however, the extent to which the test measures crystallized, and especially fluid, intelligence. In comparison with other measures, the KAIT appears to have a firmer grounding in research and theory than the Wechsler Adult Intelligence Scale—Revised (T4:2937) but lacks the WAIS-R's clinical lore. The Woodcock-Johnson Psycho-Educational Battery—Revised (415), on the other hand, should provide a stronger theoretical basis than does the KAIT.

REVIEWER'S REFERENCES

Kaufman, A. S. (1979). *Intelligent testing with the WISC-R*. New York: Wiley.

Woodcock, R. W. (1990). Theoretical foundations of the WJ-R measures of cognitive ability. *Journal of Psychoeducational Assessment, 8*, 231-258.

Carroll, J. B. (1993). *Human cognitive abilities: A survey of factor-analytic studies*. New York: Cambridge University Press.

Flanagan, D. P., Alfonso, V. C., & Flanagan, R. (1994). Review of the Kaufman Adolescent and Adult Intelligence Test: Advancement in cognitive assessment? *School Psychology Review, 23*, 512-525.

[205]

Kaufman Brief Intelligence Test.

Purpose: Intended as a brief measure of verbal and nonverbal intelligence.
Population: Ages 4–90.
Publication Date: 1990.
Acronym: K-BIT.
Scores, 3: Vocabulary, Matrices, IQ Composite.
Subtests, 2: Vocabulary (including Part A, Expressive Vocabulary and Part B, Definitions) and Matrices.
Administration: Individual.
Price Data, 1993: $99.95 per complete kit including easel, manual (123 pages), and 25 individual test records; $24.95 per 25 individual test records; $26.95 per manual.
Time: (15–30) minutes.
Comments: Definitions task not administered to children ages 4–7 years; examiners are encouraged to teach individuals, using teaching items, how to solve the kinds of items included in both subtests.
Authors: Alan S. Kaufman and Nadeen L. Kaufman.
Publisher: American Guidance Service.
Cross References: See T4:1344 (4 references).

TEST REFERENCES

1. Parker, L. D. (1993). The Kaufman Brief Intelligence Test: An introduction and review. *Measurement and Evaluation in Counseling and Development*, *26*, 152-156.

2. Prewett, P. N., & McCaffery, L. K. (1993). A comparison of the Kaufman Brief Intelligence Test (K-BIT) with the Stanford-Binet, a two-subtest short form, and the Kaufman Test of Educational Achievement (K-TEA) Brief Form. *Psychology in the Schools*, *30*, 299-304.

3. Childers, J. S., Durham, T. W., & Wilson, S. (1994). Relation of performance on the Kaufman Brief Intelligence Test with the Peabody Picture Vocabulary Test—Revised among preschool children. *Perceptual and Motor Skills*, *79*, 1195-1199.

4. Kramer, A. F., Humphrey, D. G., Larish, J. F., Logan, G. D., & Strayer, D. L. (1994). Aging and inhibition: Beyond a unitary view of inhibitory processing in attention. *Psychology and Aging*, *9*, 491-512.

5. Levinson, E. M., & Folino, L. (1994). Correlations of scores on the Gifted Evaluation Scale with those on WISC-III and Kaufman Brief Intelligence Test for students referred for gifted evaluation. *Psychological Reports*, *74*, 419-424.

6. Meador, K. S. (1994). The effect of synectics training on gifted and nongifted kindergarten students. *Journal for the Education of the Gifted*, *18*, 55-73.

7. Canivez, G. L. (1995). Validity of the Kaufman Brief Intelligence Test: Comparisons with the Wechsler Intelligence Scale for Children—Third Edition. *Assessment*, *2*, 101-111.

8. Prewett, P. N. (1995). A comparison of two screening tests (the Matrix Analogies Test—Short Form and the Kaufman Brief Intelligence Test) with the WISC-III. *Psychological Assessment*, *7*, 69-72.

9. Taverne, A., & Sheridan, S. M. (1995). Parent training in interactive book reading: An investigation of its effects with families at risk. *School Psychology Quarterly*, *10*, 41-64.

Review of the Kaufman Brief Intelligence Test by M. DAVID MILLER, Associate Professor of Foundations of Education, University of Florida, Gainesville, FL:

The Kaufman Brief Intelligence Test (K-BIT) is an individually administered measure of intelligence. The K-BIT can be administered in 15–30 minutes for ages 4 to 90. The test is composed of two subtests measuring verbal or crystallized thinking (Expressive Vocabulary and Definitions) and nonverbal or fluid thinking (Matrices). The Vocabulary subtest measures verbal knowledge through pictures (Expressive Vocabulary) and definitions. The Matrices subtest measures the ability of subjects to perceive relationships and complete analogies through pictures or abstract designs. In addition, overall IQ is measured through the K-BIT IQ Composite.

For each subtest and the composite, age-based standard scores are provided with a mean of 100 and a standard deviation of 15. In this way scores are on a common metric with other intelligence scales (e.g., the Wechsler scales) and achievement tests (e.g., Wide Range Achievement Test—Revised, Peabody Individual Achievement Test—Revised, and the Kaufman Test of Educational Achievement).

Although the K-BIT is scaled as the Wechsler instruments, the authors caution that a test user should not assume "the K-BIT may substitute for a comprehensive measure of a child's or adult's intelligence" (p. 1). Instead, the K-BIT is designed for use in situations where a complete intelligence screening is not necessary such as an initial or large scale screening for more in-depth evaluation, a screening for job placement or hiring, or for research purposes. The K-BIT is intended to be a brief intelligence measure that is reliable, valid, well normed, and can be administered by personnel without sophisticated psychometric backgrounds. Test administration and scoring directions are clear and simple to follow, but the authors caution that greater psychometrtic sophistication is needed for score interpretation.

DEVELOPMENT. The K-BIT was developed in conjunction with the Kaufman Adolescent and Adult Intelligence Test (KAIT) and the AGS Early Screening Profiles. In addition, the norms for the K-BIT and KAIT overlap making scores directly comparable. After initial screening with the K-BIT, a more complete intelligence profile with comparable results can be obtained from the KAIT for ages 11 to 90. Similarly, more information can be gained for younger subjects on the AGS Early Screening Profiles which is appropriate for ages 2 to 6.

NORMS. Norms are based on a national sample of 2,022 subjects ranging in age from 4 to 92. Although the sample is not random, subjects were tested at 60 sites representing 29 states. The actual sample size met or exceeded the target sample size at most age levels, with sample size decreasing with age level. For example, 100 subjects were targeted for each age from 4 to 10. In contrast, older subjects were combined into broader groups with similar targeted sample sizes (i.e., ages 20–34 [$N = 200$], ages 34–54 [$N = 150$], and ages 55-90 [$N = 100$]). Given the steady decline in composite IQ and performance IQ after age 20 (e.g., see pp. 194-197 in Kaufman, 1990), the adequacy of the norms for older subjects seems questionable. Sample sizes are adequate for subjects under age 20.

The sample was stratified by sex, geographic region, socioeconomic status, and race or ethnicity. The sample matched the U.S. population on gender, race, and ethnicity. However, the Northeast region of the country was slightly underrepresented. In addition, examinees or parents of examinees with some college (1–3 years) or technical school were slightly overrepresented.

Norms were developed using state-of-the-art procedures as proposed in Angoff and Robertson (1987). The smoothing and normalizing procedures led to some small differences in the standard scale across ages. As a result, caution needs to be exercised in making comparisons across ages. For example, a subject who is one standard deviation above the mean on the Matrices subtest at age 4 ($M = 99.1$, $s = 16.3$) would have a standard score of 115.4. A comparable subject (one standard deviation above the mean) at age 5 ($M = 96.9$, $s = 13.1$) would score 110.0. Thus, a mean difference between two groups might be interpreted as significant when it could be attributed to a difference in scales.

Scores are reported in six ways: standard scores ($M = 100$, $s = 15$), percentile rank, normal curve equivalents, stanines, or in descriptive categories. The latter scores are developed to "reflect in words the approximate distance from the group mean" (manual, p. 40). For example, the middle 50% of the scores are "average" whereas the bottom 2.2% are "lower extreme."

RELIABILITY. Split-half reliabilities are reported by age level for each subtest and the composite. The reliabilities across age level were high for the Vocabulary subtest (.89–.98) and the K-BIT IQ Composite (.88–.98). Reliabilities were lower, but acceptable for the Matrices subtest (.74–.95). On the other hand, assuming that items above (below) the last (first) item attempted are correct (incorrect) could lead to a spuriously high reliability estimate. As a result, test-retest reliabilities may give more appropriate estimates. Test-retest reliabilities, which are reported for wider age ranges, are comparable to the split-half reliabilities for the Vocabulary subtest (.86–.97), the Matrices subtest (.80–.92), and the K-BIT IQ Composite (.92–.95).

In addition to the reliability coefficients, the standard error of measurement (*SEM*) is reported to assist in the interpretation of individual scores on each subtest and the composite. The *SEM* by age level ranges from about 2 to 5 on the composite and the Vocabulary subtest. On the Matrices subtest, the *SEM* ranges from about 3 to 7. For each subtest and the composite, the *SEM* was lower for older subjects. Further simplifying features for test users are the tabled multiples of the *SEM* which are used in estimating "Bands of Error" in the score reports. Tabled values include 68%, 85%, 90%, 95%, and 99% confidence levels, with the manual recommending a 90% confidence level.

Finally, tabled values are also used to compare differences between subtests. Using the standard error of the difference, the magnitude of the difference between the Vocabulary subtest and the Matrices subtest can be compared against a tabled value to determine significance at the .05 or .01 level. These two features on the score report should be useful in score interpretation.

VALIDITY. Many of the suggested uses of the K-BIT (e.g., initial screening, hiring and promotion, measurement across time) are not addressed through validation studies. Studies more closely linked to particular uses of the K-BIT should be done. The construct validity of the K-BIT is examined in the test manual. The construct validity of the K-BIT is in part addressed through the initial selection of subtests that are good measures of general intelligence. The Vocabulary subtest is a typical measure of verbal intelligence, based on the Binet-Wechsler tradition whereas the Matrices subtest has a foundation in the Raven's Progressive Matrices.

Using data collected in national tryouts, classical item analysis, Rasch one-parameter latent trait analysis, and item bias analysis (see Holland & Thayer, 1988) were completed. Based on these analyses, the K-BIT seems to be psychometrically sound. Additional studies are reported to examine the construct validity of the test both internally and externally. The internal studies show a reasonable correlation of the two subtests at each age level (.38 to .75) and the expected growth patterns on tasks and subtests across ages. Externally the K-BIT is correlated with a series of measures of intelligence and achievement. The combined evidence from the correlations show that the K-BIT has moderate to high correlations with other intelligence tests and moderate correlations with the achievement tests.

SUMMARY. The K-BIT is a well-constructed brief test for measuring intelligence. State of the art procedures have been used in norming and measuring reliability and validity. The combined evidence, which is fairly extensive, points to a psychometrically sound measure of verbal, nonverbal, and composite intelligence. Caution should be exercised in interpreting standard scores for older subjects (ages 20–90) because of the use of small *N*s in the norming. In addition, further validation of the K-BIT is needed for the potential uses listed in the manual.

REVIEWER'S REFERENCES

Angoff, W. H., & Robertson, G. J. (1987). A procedure for standardizing individually administered tests, normed by age or grade level. *Applied Psychological Measurement*, *11*, 33-46.

Holland, P. W., & Thayer, D. T. (1988). Differential item performance and the Mantel-Haenszel procedure. In H. Wainer & H. I. Braun (Eds.), *Test validity* (pp. 129-145). Hillsdale, NJ: Lawrence Erlbaum.

Kaufman, A. S. (1990). *Assessing adolescent and adult intelligence*. Boston: Allyn and Bacon.

Review of the Kaufman Brief Intelligence Test by JOHN W. YOUNG, Assistant Professor of Educational

Statistics and Measurement, Rutgers University, New Brunswick, NJ:

The Kaufman Brief Intelligence Test (K-BIT) is an individually administered measure of verbal and nonverbal intelligence appropriate for ages 4 to 90 years. The K-BIT is intended for those circumstances, such as a large-scale screening of students or patients, in which a brief measure of intelligence will suffice. The test is easy to administer and may be given by appropriately trained technicians or paraprofessionals. Total testing time is approximately 15 to 30 minutes and tends to be shortest for young children and longest for adults. The K-BIT consists of two subtests: Vocabulary (composed of Part A, Expressive Vocabulary and Part B, Definitions) and Matrices.

The K-BIT was developed to meet the needs of professionals for a brief, self-contained, and adequately normed test of both verbal and nonverbal abilities. Presently, many intelligence measures are inadequate for situations when testing time is limited. Administering only some of the subtests from a comprehensive intelligence test can yield misleading results. Research has shown that an individual will earn quite different scores on a two-subtest short form of a longer test as compared to scores earned when the subtests are embedded in the longer test battery (Thompson, Howard, & Anderson, 1986). In comparison, K-BIT norms are based on the administration of both subtests that comprise the whole test.

K-BIT SUBTESTS. Subtest 1, Vocabulary, is an 82-item measure of verbal ability that requires the examinee to respond orally. Part A, Expressive Vocabulary (45 items), administered to all examinees, requires the individual to name a pictured object such as a lamp or a calendar. Part B, Definitions (37 items), for examinees 8 years and older, requires the individual to provide the word that fits two clues: a phrase description and a partial spelling of the word. The Vocabulary subtest measures a person's language development and his or her level of verbal concept formation.

Subtest 2, Matrices, is a 48-item measure of nonverbal ability using several item types involving visual stimuli, both concrete (persons and objects) and abstract (designs and symbols). All items are multiple choice and require the examinee to either select one of five alternatives that goes best with a stimulus picture or to choose one of six or eight options to solve a 2x2 or 3x3 matrix of pictures or patterns.

The Vocabulary subtest is intended to measure crystallized intelligence, the type of learning and problem solving that derives directly from formal schooling and cultural experiences. In contrast, the Matrices subtest measures fluid intelligence, the type involved in novel problem situations and is assumed to be less culture-bound. Collectively, the two subtests yield a more complete assessment of an individual's level of intelligence than either subtest alone.

SCORES. All items are scored 0 (incorrect) or 1 (correct). Raw scores are converted to standard scores (M = 100, SD = 15) for each subtest using one of 53 age group conversion tables. The two subtest scores are also combined to yield an IQ Composite Score.

STANDARDIZATION. The K-BIT is normed on 2,022 subjects ages 4 to 90 years tested during 1988–89. The sample was stratified on the basis of age, sex, geographic region, socioeconomic status (examinee or parental education level), and race to match U.S. Census 1990 projections, if available, or 1985 estimates if projected figures were unavailable. The normative sample appears to be representative of the contiguous U.S. population on all combinations of the stratification variables.

RELIABILITY. Split-half reliability coefficients were computed for several age categories in the norming sample. For the subtests, coefficients range from .74 to .98 with means of .93 for the Vocabulary subtest and .88 for the Matrices subtest. For the IQ Composite, the split-half reliability ranges from .88 for age 5 to .98 for ages 55–90 with a mean of .94. Test-retest reliability coefficients were computed for a sample of 232 examinees, ages 5 to 89, based on a retest interval of 12 to 145 days (mean interval = 21 days). The coefficients for the four age groups in the sample have a mean of .94 for the Vocabulary subtest, .85 for the Matrices subtest, and .94 for the IQ Composite.

VALIDITY. Test validity was established in a three-stage process: selection of the subtests, item analysis, and internal and external test analysis. Use of the Vocabulary and Matrices subtests is cited as a logical choice because of the corresponding dichotomy on other measures of intelligence such as the Verbal/Performance split on the Wechsler tests and the crystallized/fluid distinction on the Stanford-Binet. Over 300 items were pretested on a sample of 1,058 examinees in 1986–87. Based on several item analysis methods, the original item pool was trimmed to the current form of the K-BIT. As evidence of construct validity, changes in raw scores on the subtests are shown to reflect growth patterns often found in developmental studies of intelligence. Mean raw scores on the Vocabulary subtest increase steadily through early adulthood, peak in middle age, and then decline gradually. In contrast, mean raw scores on the Matrices subtest peak in early adulthood and then decline steadily and rapidly through the adult years. Results from numerous concurrent validity studies are included which show the correlation of K-BIT scores with established intelligence tests and school achievement tests.

COMMENTS ON THE K-BIT. The K-BIT is a well-normed, standardized, individual intelligence test that appears to be useful when testing time is limited and only a gross measure of intellectual functioning is required. The authors of the K-BIT have developed other psychometric instruments including the Kaufman Assessment Battery for Children (K-ABC; T4:1343), the Kaufman Adolescent and Adult Intelligence Test (KAIT; 204), and the Kaufman Test of Educational Achievement (K-TEA; T4:1348). Test administrators will find the K-BIT a welcomed addition to these other tests. Although the authors state the K-BIT can be administered by other than highly trained professionals, this practice should be discouraged as the probability of test misuse increases greatly. Overall, the K-BIT has many good qualities to recommend its use.

REVIEWER'S REFERENCE

Thompson, A. P., Howard, D., & Anderson, J. (1986). Two- and four-subtest short forms of the WAIS-R: Validity in a psychiatric sample. *Canadian Journal of Behavioral Science, 18*, 287-293.

[206]

Kaufman Survey of Early Academic and Language Skills.

Purpose: A measure of children's language, preacademic skills, and articulation.
Population: 3-0 to 6-11.
Publication Date: 1993.
Acronym: K-SEALS.
Scores, 8: Vocabulary, Numbers/Letters and Words, Articulation Survey, Early Academic and Language Skills Composite, Language Scales (Expressive Skills, Receptive Skills), Early Academic Scales (Number Skills, Letter and Word Skills).
Subtests, 3: Vocabulary, Numbers/Letters and Words, Articulation Survey.
Administration: Individual.
Price Data, 1993: $140 per complete kit including manual (109 pages), presentation easel, and 25 record booklets; $18 per 25 record booklets.
Time: (15–25) minutes.
Comments: The Early Academic Scales can be interpreted only for ages 5-0 to 6-11.
Authors: Alan S. Kaufman and Nadeen L. Kaufman.
Publisher: American Guidance Service, Inc.

Review of the Kaufman Survey of Early Academic and Language Skills by PHILLIP L. ACKERMAN, Professor of Psychology, University of Minnesota, Minneapolis, MN:

The Kaufman Survey of Early Academic and Language Skills (K-SEALS) is described by the authors as a measure of language, prearticulation skills, and articulation. It is an expanded version of the AGS Early Screening Profiles (24) published in 1990. The test is aimed at a broad array of uses from assessment in day care centers and schools to clinical situations. According to the authors, the test "provides a good contrast to tests that measure young children's so called intellectual potential" (manual, p. 1). The aim is to provide a test that is "more in tune with the curriculum used for intervention or enrichment programs" (p. 1) than are intelligence tests.

RELIABILITY/VALIDITY. The K-SEALS is composed of three subtests (Vocabulary, Numbers/Letters and Words, and Articulation Survey). The first two tests are split to make up two Language Scales (Expressive Skills and Receptive Skills) and two Early Academic Scales (for use only with children aged 5-0 to 6-11). An overall composite is also computed. Test-retest reliabilities are only provided for a small sample ($N = 81$) with a wide range of age 3-0 to 6-10. The reported values are respectable, ranging from .94 (for the total composite) to .87 for the Vocabulary subtest, though age heterogeneity may have inflated the reliability estimates above what would be expected for single age groups. For the validation sample ($N = 995$), the three subtests show a range of intercorrelations from .47 to .67, with the Expressive Skills and Receptive Skills composites showing intercorrelations from .81 to .91, suggesting little differential validity for these two measures. The authors acknowledge that, given the low correlations between the Vocabulary and the Numbers/Letters and Words subtests, it is common to find statistically significant differences between an individual's scores—and they caution that only very large differences should be interpreted. The lack of differentiation among the composites, and the lack of meaningful differences among the subtests, suggests that the overall composite is the only generally useful score. The manual presents a wide variety of concurrent and predictive validity information. Given large disparities of sample sizes and characteristics for the various studies, it is difficult to get a complete picture of the discriminant and convergent validity of the instrument, but a few features stand out. Of foremost importance are the K-SEALS composite correlations with the Kaufman Assessment Battery for Children (K-ABC) and the Stanford-Binet, which are in the neighborhood of .80. Such high correlations suggest that the K-SEALS is a rather good measure of intelligence, despite the goals of the constructors to differentiate the K-SEALS from these other standard tests. The K-SEALS composite score also correlates well with teacher ratings of ability, typically in the neighborhood of $r = .60$. For the Articulation Survey, only age differentiation is shown, and no correlational validations were presented. In addition, given the inherent ceiling effects (3-year-olds can be expected to pass 70% of the items) of the Articulation Survey, it could only be useful for the broadest categorical descriptions. A major shortcoming of the instrument and manual is the lack of any validational data that support differential interventions on the basis of relative differences between scores and composites.

NORMS. Norms are adequate, especially for this new instrument. The primary norms consisted of a diverse sample across age, gender, race/ethnic, and geographic groups, with a total size of 1,000 children. The manual presents norms by age (in 6-month increments). However, although the manual presents a comprehensive description of the sampling procedures and demographic breakdown of the examinees, no data are presented that describe gender and race/ethnic group differences in scores for either the individual subtests or for the composite scores.

ADMINISTRATION INTERPRETATION. Instructions to the examiner are clear and complete. Administration is simple and straightforward, as is preparing the raw score summary information. Computation of standard scores and confidence intervals is a bit more complex, and requires that the examiner collate information from several tables in the manual's appendix. Thankfully, the authors have instructed the examiner how to indicate whether various score differences are statistically significant, an especially important procedure given the general lack of differential validity of the various scales and composites. The manual takes great pains to explain how such differences should be interpreted (or not interpreted), given the fact that 30% of the examinees in the standardization sample 3-0 to 5-11 age groups had statistically significant differences between the Vocabulary and the Numbers/Letters and Words subtests. The Report to Parents is generally clear and thorough, though it tends to overemphasize the importance of the comparisons of score differences (e.g., "As important as this overview, however, is a comparison of your child's performance on certain skill areas" [p. 50]). Such an expression is unabashedly Thurstonian in emphasizing an individual's relative strengths and weaknesses, but it is unwarranted for this test.

SUMMARY. As a short general intelligence test for children ranging in ages from 3 to 6 years, the K-SEALS is remarkably reliable and valid. However, the overarching rationale presented for the test regarding the differentiation between expressive and receptive skills is likely to be useful only in the most extreme of cases. The test generally has little to offer in the domains of differential diagnosis and intervention, especially in the absence of specific validation for such purposes. It does *not* as claimed by the authors, "[provide] a good contrast to tests . . . [of] so-called intellectual potential" (p. 1).

Review of the Kaufman Survey of Early Academic and Language Skills by LAURIE FORD, Assistant Professor of Psychology, University of South Carolina, Columbia, SC, and KERRI TURK, Graduate Student, Department of Educational Psychology, Texas A&M University, College Station, TX:

The Kaufman Survey of Early Academic and Language Skills (K-SEALS) is an individually administered measure of children's language, both expressive and receptive, preacademic skills (knowledge of numbers, number concepts, letters, and words), and articulation. The K-SEALS is an expanded version of the language area of the AGS Early Screening Profiles (Cognitive/Language Profile) (24). The K-SEALS is normed for use with children 3 years 0 months to 6 years 11 months. The authors report an administration time of 15 to 25 minutes. The complete K-SEALS kit includes (*a*) a manual that includes both administration/scoring and technical information, (*b*) an easel booklet, and (*c*) 25 individual test records.

The authors report that the K-SEALS was developed for use in speech/language evaluations and other types of assessment that require measurement of a young child's language skills and/or preacademic development. They refer to the instrument as a "survey" of young children's language development. However, it is unclear in the manual as to whether the K-SEALS primary use is that of a screening measure or a diagnostic measure. The K-SEALS consists of three separate subtests: Vocabulary; Numbers/Letters and Words; and Articulation Survey. Items on both the Vocabulary and the Numbers/Letters and Words subtests comprise two language scales: the Expressive Skills Scale and the Receptive Skills Scale. The Numbers/Letters and Words subtest is further organized into two early academic scales for children 5-0 to 6-11: Number Skills Scale and Letter and Word Skills Scale. The Vocabulary and the Numbers/Letters and Words subtests are combined to produce the Early Academic and Language Skills Composite.

The Vocabulary subtest Expressive and Receptive components assess both nouns and verbs. The authors report that the four types of items comprising the Vocabulary subtest add to the task's linguistic diversity. They report that vocabulary tests are well known as excellent measures of *g* (or general intelligence) and good predictors of early school success. In reference to the Numbers/Letters and Words subtest, the authors point to the understanding of these and other basic quantitative concepts as necessary for success in the primary grades. We caution the user not to overinterpret scores on these subtests as predictors of future academic especially in the case of young children from culturally and linguistically diverse backgrounds and those children with less rich early home environments.

As with other individually administered assessment instruments developed by Drs. Kaufman, the K-SEALS was designed to be easily administered by a variety of professionals working with young children. The instrument may be administered and scored easily by those familiar with standardized assessment of young children and it is time efficient. The test provides information regarding a child's functioning in a variety of language areas (e.g., expressive, receptive, and articulation) and preacademic areas (e.g., number and letter recognition). Although the instrument provides scores in a variety of areas and is easily scored, some caution must be taken in interpreting test results due to the limited item coverage in all areas. We recommend that the instrument is best used as a screening measure or as a part of a comprehensive language battery. Although Vocabulary and Numbers/Letters and Words subtests may be easily interpreted by non-speech professionals (e.g., school psychologists, early childhood educators) experienced with norm-referenced assessment, the Articulation Survey administration, scoring, and interpretation is likely to be a challenge for professionals not formally trained in the assessment of articulation difficulties.

The test has the normal limitations of a flip-easel format with young children in that it may be difficult to engage the children in the tasks. This may be a particular challenge for children with attention and concentration difficulties. However, the authors have made an attempt to make this test more engaging to young children through the use of color pictures on many of the items. Despite their efforts, however, the average examiner is likely to have difficulty engaging children who demonstrate more challenging test behaviors and more severe delays—children typically referred for early intervention programming—on the K-SEALS tasks. However, we see the use of a "flip-easel" format as a critique of most standardized preschool assessment tools currently commercially available. Young children are typically not accustomed to sitting at a table and pointing to pictures. These are highly unnatural activities for young children and are difficult for most. Similar screening information is likely to be more accurately obtained through systematic observation of the young child in natural environments and with objects with which they are more familiar. Efforts must be made to evaluate the skills of young children in a manner that is more representative of the activities they engage in on a daily basis. Users of this test are encouraged to observe children in their natural environments and use this information in conjunction with the information obtained from this screening tool before a formal referral for additional testing is made.

The general technical properties of the instrument are addressed thoroughly in the manual. The manual is well organized and easy to read. Detailed descriptions of the standardization sample, data collection procedures, and norm development are provided. However, at times the author makes assumptions regarding the readers' understanding of complex statistical procedures used in the standardization of the instrument. It appears that although children with identified delays or disabilities were not systematically sampled, some were included in the standardized sample. However, details of the number of children with delays and/or disabilities are not included in the manual. Given the children with delays and/or disabilities are likely to be one of the primary populations for this test, this lack of detail and the omission of separate validation studies of children with developmental delays and/or identified disabilities should be remedied. Further, given the flip-easel format, it is likely this test may be administered to individuals with motor impairments. The authors report that subjects with "physical problems" (p. 55) were excluded from the standardization sample. This is of concern. Also, considering the attention given to the psychometric problems of standardized tests with culturally diverse populations, we would like to see studies specifically addressing the technical properties of the tool with culturally and linguistically diverse young children.

In summary, the K-SEALS appears to be a well-developed norm-referenced assessment tool for use by speech-language personnel. The test appears to have its best utility as a screening tool. Non-speech-language personnel are likely to experience difficulty with the administration and scoring of the articulation tests and all examiners may have difficulty engaging children with more challenging test behaviors. Some caution should be used when interpreting results of children with developmental delays, disabilities, and/or from culturally/linguistically diverse backgrounds.

[207]

Kindergarten Readiness Test.

Purpose: Determines the readiness of children to begin kindergarten.
Population: Ages 4–6.
Publication Date: 1988.
Acronym: KRT.
Scores: Total score only.
Administration: Individual.
Price Data, 1992: $69 per complete kit; $16 per manual (39 pages); $35 per 25 test booklets; $6 per 25 performance grid sheets; $6 per 25 letter to parent; $6 per 25 scoring interpretation; $14 per stimulus items.
Time: (15) minutes.
Authors: Sue L. Larson and Gary J. Vitali.
Publisher: Slosson Educational Publications, Inc.

Review of the Kindergarten Readiness Test by MICHAEL D. BECK, President, BETA, Inc., Pleasantville, NY:

The Kindergarten Readiness Test (KRT) is an individually administered assessment of various developmental achievements purported to relate to a child's readiness for kindergarten.

FORMAT AND ADMINISTRATION. The KRT is administered using a 33-page test booklet, the format of which is generally open and clear. Test directions are acceptable, although additional information concerning appropriate prompting on specific items would be desirable.

The KRT is composed of an assortment of 25 tasks plus a scored set of examiner observations during testing. The test is untimed, although the manual states that it can be administered in 15–20 minutes. Given a moderately "ready" age-5 child, this estimate appears to be on the low side.

Test content is described on the Performance Grid as assessing five general skill areas: awareness of one's environment, reasoning, numerical awareness, fine-motor coordination, and auditory attention span. The manual, however, lists the content as being grouped into *seven* areas, most of which overlap with the above five. Whichever breakdown applies, the large majority of the items assess the environmental awareness and the motor coordination areas. The skill areas are judgment-based categorizations rather than a content taxonomy that guided test item development or a skills clustering derived from empirical data.

The construct of interest, "kindergarten readiness," was defined essentially by developing items similar to those contained on a broad set of previously published instruments for this age range. These reference sources range from the Stanford-Binet and Wechsler Preschool and Primary Scale of Intelligence (WPPSI) through the Bender-Gestalt, Vineland Social Maturity Scale, and Developmental Test of Visual-Motor Integration. Given the lack of a theoretical grounding for KRT content, and the miscellany of reference products that purport to assess essentially no common constructs, the absence of any validity evidence in the manual is especially disconcerting.

Item sequence is described as being based on an "orderly progression of skills" (manual, p. 6), but is rather disorganized, both in terms of content and difficulty. For example, a separate task (#5) involves crediting a child for correctly holding a pencil for drawing; each of the four preceding tasks require the child to draw, making this distinct task unnecessary. Normative item difficulty values indicate very difficult tasks (#4, 8, 9D, and 12) early in the test and several extremely easy tasks (#14, 21, and 23) toward the end of the test. Typical item sequencing procedures would indicate a different arrangement.

On the whole, both test item quality and administration procedures are acceptable. The content coverage may or may not adequately represent "kindergarten readiness," depending on the local program. Prospective users should carefully review KRT content vis-á-vis that of competing commercial products.

ANCILLARY TEST MATERIALS. Separately packaged letters to parents and General Performance Grids are not recommended by this reviewer. The letter to parents is not well written, containing several long, unclear statements, unsupportable claims, and even a sentence fragment. School personnel can undoubtedly develop a far more professional and informative communication device. The Performance Grid is an attempt to provide a skills-based interpretation for the KRT. Although the manual states that this breakdown "indicate[s] task performance weaknesses" (p. 1), the test content is not sufficiently comprehensive to yield much useful diagnostic information. The post-facto task categorization into the five overlapping skill areas and the very limited coverage of three of the five areas make use of this grid ill-advised.

The Scoring Interpretation sheet (in fact, simply a record of the child's raw score and equivalent percent-correct value) may be functional for experienced test users, but should *not* be given to parents as recommended in the manual—certainly not without a personal interpretation by a trained professional. Labels on this sheet such as "above average" and "questionable readiness" are of dubious soundness (see technical data below). Even the straightforward percent-correct value is ambiguously labeled as "percent of correct scored responses" (p. 33), which is unclear. KRT users would be well advised to develop their own score-reporting forms.

The KRT manual contains a short description of the test's development and purported uses, copies of the score sheets and ancillary forms, a brief assortment of garbled technical data (see below), and examples for the several tasks for which the scoring requires examiner judgment. These latter rubrics are clear and well presented. Very little interpretive information is provided in the manual, an unfortunate omission given the purpose of the KRT.

TECHNICAL DATA. The serious flaws and inadequacies with all of the technical underpinnings of the KRT are my most serious reservations about the instrument. The KRT is essentially a criterion-referenced test, interpretation of which is described improperly in norm-referenced terms. That is, almost the entire interpretive foundation for the KRT is simply the total percent-correct value. There are two significant problems with this scheme:

1. The KRT skill outline and, more critically, the target construct are weakly described and less adequately defended.

2. Interpretive suggestions for the test naively and inexcusably intermix norm-referenced and criterion-referenced score interpretations. For example, the Summary of scores describes the percent-correct score (purely the raw score divided by the number possible X 100 to convert to a percent) as a "percentile." Such a blatant mislabeling of a basic metric gives great pause concerning any of the technical procedures used in developing the KRT.

Most serious among the multitude of psychometric inadequacies summarized in the manual are: an imprecise calculation of the median score (based on grouped-interval data), naive and improper labeling of various statistical tests (e.g., "upper-tailed tests of variance" [p. 8] to describe *t*-tests and interpreting nonsignificant change in group means as indicative of test-retest reliability), totally improper application of chi square procedures to assess relationships between KRT scores and teacher ratings, unexplained and indefensible merging of data for ages 4 through 6 in norming, and justification of curious double-weighting of five tasks "to compensate, somewhat, for bias in the norms" (p. 8). The technical data that accompany the KRT are, simply stated, inadequate.

SUMMARY. The KRT is best characterized as an experimental assessment. The manual provides no indication that the instrument provides a sufficiently reliable indication of a young child's readiness for kindergarten. Prospective users must assess for themselves whether the content coverage of the KRT adequately samples from the range of activities that best predict success in their local kindergarten programs. Users must further develop their own local descriptors of performance levels and/or cutoffs based on a period of local use of the test. Under no circumstances should KRT normative data be relied upon until the publisher provides a more sound description of the data already available and/or collects more data and reports such in a professionally acceptable form. This reviewer would discourage use of the KRT in its current form for the screening of young children prior to their entrance into kindergarten.

Review of the Kindergarten Readiness Test by ROSEMARY E. SUTTON, Associate Professor, and CATHARINE C. KNIGHT, Visiting Assistant Professor, College of Education, Cleveland State University, Cleveland, OH:

The purpose of the Kindergarten Readiness Test (KRT) is to answer the question "Is this child ready to begin school?" This test is designed to be used by early childhood education professionals as a general screening tool for late-4-, 5-, and 6-year-olds. The test is norm referenced; children are considered ready to enter school if they score at the 63rd percentile or above. The 26 tasks that comprise the test were selected by the authors after reviewing a number of early childhood cognitive and social measures and consulting with early childhood professionals. The authors classified the tasks into five skill areas: Understanding, Awareness, and Interactions with One's Environment; Judgment and Reasoning In Problem Solving; Numerical Awareness; Visual and Fine-Motor-Coordination; Auditory Attention Span and Concentration.

The authors present data purported to assess interrater and test-retest reliability. However, in assessing interrater reliability, different children were evaluated by different evaluators rather than having more than one evaluator assess the same child. This process renders the data meaningless. It is not clear from the manual how the authors assessed test-retest reliability; however, it is clear that they did not correlate the performance of the same students over time. Hence, these data are also meaningless. A more subtle but significant issue is that test-retest reliability is not appropriate to assess characteristics that are assumed to develop at different rates in different children. Test-retest reliability, which is assessed by comparing rank-orderings from one time to another, assumes that the constructs are stable over time.

Current formulations of validity require that a variety of evidence be provided by the test developer (Messick, 1989; Shepard, 1993). The authors do provide three kinds of data to give evidence of validity. Evidence of concurrent validity was sought by comparing children's scores on the KRT with the School Readiness Survey (Jordan & Massey, 1967). Unfortunately, rather than providing a correlation, the authors reported only mean differences, which are irrelevant.

Evidence of predictive validity was sought by comparing children's scores on the KRT with the ratings from their kindergarten teacher halfway through the school year. We were unable to understand the data as presented in both text and table and consequently believe that school personnel would encounter similar difficulty. Evidence of construct validity of any developmental assessment should include data indicating that older children score at more advanced developmental levels than do younger children. Data showing that 5-year-olds score at a higher level than do 4-year-olds is clearly presented.

The samples of children upon which the norms, reliability, and validity evidence are based were all drawn from Nebraska, Kansas, Iowa, and Minnesota. These samples are highly unrepresentative of children nationwide, in part because less than 5% of the norming sample was minority. Another point of concern with the KRT is that the authors make no attempt to discriminate this developmental assessment from an intelligence test. In fact, the authors state that several well-known intelligence tests were reviewed in the development of this test. The concept of school readiness is based upon a maturational model, and discriminant validity evidence, which distinguishes this model from a psychometric intelligence one, is essential.

Any test used for educational placement decisions must show differential validity evidence: "Groups must be better off in their respective treatments than they would have been without the test-based placement" (Shepard, 1993, p. 441). This means, for any kindergarten readiness test, children deemed not ready for regular one-year kindergarten must be better off than in alternative settings (e.g., transitional, kindergarten retention). Recent reviews of the literature (Shepard, 1989) indicate no benefit for placement in these alternative settings, consequently questioning the utility of widespread use of kindergarten readiness tests.

Despite the questionable utility of most kindergarten readiness assessments, their use is mandated in some states and school districts. We recommend where school personnel operate under such mandates the KRT *not* be used. The reliability and validity evidence is inadequate and the normative sample is highly restrictive. In addition, there are a number of other concerns: The content of several items is problematic (e.g., children are asked to count dots from bottom left to top right, instead of top left to bottom right which mirrors the reading process in English); the directions of a number of items are convoluted; and the authors' recommended letter to parents is confusing and misleading.

REVIEWER'S REFERENCES

Jordan, F. L., & Massey, J. (1967). School Readiness Survey. Palo Alto, CA: Consulting Psychologists Press, Inc.

Messick, S. (1989). Validity. In R. L. Linn (Ed.), *Educational measurement* (3rd ed.; pp. 13-103). New York: MacMillan.

Shepard, L. A. (1989). A review of research on kindergarten retention. In L. A. Shepard & M. L. Smith (Eds.), *Flunking grades: Research and policies on retention* (pp. 64-78). New York: Falmer Press.

Shepard, L. A. (1993). Evaluating test validity. In L. Darling-Hammond (Ed.), *Review of research in education* (vol. 19; pp. 405-450). Washington, DC: American Educational Research Association.

[208]

Kolbe Conative Index.
Purpose: Constructed to measure "instinctive talent."
Population: Adults.
Publication Dates: 1987–91.
Acronym: KCI.
Scores: Degree of Intensity in 4 Action Modes (Fact Finder, Follow Thru, Quick Start, Implementor).
Administration: Group or individual.
Restricted Distribution: Available only to Certified Kolbe Consultants who must attend a 3-day seminar and complete an extended training program.
Price Data: Available from publisher.
Time: (25) minutes.
Comments: Untimed and self-administered.
Author: Kathy Kolbe.
Publisher: KolbeConcepts, Inc.

Review of the Kolbe Conative Index by COLLIE WYATT CONOLEY, Associate Professor of Educational Psychology, University of Nebraska-Lincoln, Lincoln, NE:

The Kolbe Conative Index (KCI) is a self-report assessment for describing and predicting performance. The assessment is based upon four "instincts" that define the creative abilities of every person: instinct to probe, pattern, innovate, and demonstrate. The author assumes that these instincts are strengths innate to every person. The instincts are associated with four patterns of behaviors contributing to success in specific jobs. The four behavior patterns are subscales of the KCI: Fact Finder, Follow Through, Quick Start, and Implementor. The theoretical or empirical basis of the instincts or subscales was not revealed. If two subscale scores are high, the scales are combined. There may be a total of 17 descriptions of performance, which includes one that has no high scores (the mediator or facilitator).

The KCI is used to determine the characteristics of success in a specific job. Then the KCI is used to identify individuals who fit those characteristics. The process appears well thought out.

The KCI consists of 36 items, each having four response options. Examinees make a forced-choice selection of two of the four responses. One response is specified as the least likely behavior and one response is the most likely to behave in the specified manner. The KCI uses ipsative scoring.

To use the KCI a person must be trained and receive continuing education from the Kolbe company. The description of the training and continuing education appears thorough. The KCI is scored, analyzed, and reported via computer. There was no formal test manual available for review. However, a booklet entitled "Statistical Analysis of the Kolbe Conative Index" (1994) and a book, *Pure Instinct* by Kathy Kolbe (1993) were the sources for the review. Although it appears that a great deal of effort has gone into developing and testing the KCI, the documentation is lacking.

The development of the KCI items is somewhat vague. However, it appears that the KCI was purposefully constructed to remove items that correlated with either an unspecified intelligence measure, the Wonderlic Personnel Test, or an unspecified social desirability measure. This process reduced the item set from the original 200, down to 44 items. In an unspecified manner, 36 items of the 44 were retained.

The KCI developers investigate gender, age, race, and national origin bias. The variables are encouraging; however, details of the data collection and analysis are missing.

A factor analysis was said to exist but no results were supplied. Reliability based upon internal consistency was reported as existing but not given. Test-retest reliability over 8 to 15 months was moderate (.69 to .85, $n = 70$). Another test-retest study (Kolbe, 1993) reported that 43 unspecified persons were drawn from an unspecified pool, in an unspecified manner. The time lag was unspecified also. Only 4% of the persons changed assessed behavioral labels.

Construct validity evidence is provided via several tables demonstrating the fit between profiles of individuals in occupations and the theorized profiles. The tables provide percentile scores probably representing the proportion of people scoring in the category. There were no means or standard deviations supplied. The tables appeared to support construct validity.

Several studies are mentioned that support criterion-based validity. In a study conducted at the University of Chicago Graduate School of Business, the professors were somehow used to determine the KCI scores for successful students. Of 600 incoming students all of the students not fitting the characteristics failed to complete the program. The number of students who were identified as not fitting was not specified. The way of defining a misfit was not specified.

The number of students identified as fitting who did not complete the program was unspecified.

A problem with the validity studies was the lack of detail in the information. It appears that the KCI has strengths in validity. However, the lack of information leaves a large degree of discomfort in evaluating the KCI.

Sometimes the information about the KCI appears inaccurate. For example, "The scores are normally distributed across the general population with a mean of 5 and a standard deviation of 1" (p. 305, Kolbe, 1993). It is also stated that scores between 0 and 3 are 20% of the population, scores between 3 and 7 represent 60% of the population, and scores between 7 and 10 represent 20% of the population (p. 305, Kolbe, 1993). These two ways of interpreting the numbers cannot both be accurate.

A study investigating gender, age, and race bias also demonstrated faulty logic (p. 37, Statistical Analysis of the Kolbe Conative Index, 1994). This study sought to show that if means are not significantly different at the .0125 level of significance, they can be considered the same. This was indicated in the statement "In all cases the means can be shown to be significantly similar. . . . Since the instrument result is four interdependent scores, the test of significance for each replication of the analysis is divided by four, i.e., an alpha = 0.05, and will result in a criterion of acceptance on each Mode when the Prob > F is greater than or equal to 0.0125" (p. 37, Statistical Analysis of the Kolbe Conative Index, 1994).

If the data supplied can be trusted, the KCI appears strong. The KCI appears to be effective in avoiding gender, age, and race bias. The reliability appears to be moderate. The validity appears good. There are some important concerns about the presentation of information. The lack of detail of the studies substantiating the KCI make it difficult to feel entirely comfortable with the validity and reliability conclusions. Also the logic of the analysis at times appears flawed. The data presented, however, do support the use of the KCI.

REVIEWER'S REFERENCES

Kolbe, K. (1993). *Pure instinct: Business' untapped resource.* New York: Times Books.

Statistical Analysis of the Kolbe Conative Index. (1994, January). Phoenix, AZ: KolbeConcepts, Inc.

Review of the Kolbe Conative Index by FRANK GRESHAM, Professor and Director, School Psychology Program, University of California, Riverside, Riverside, CA:

It is not often that one encounters a "test" that violates virtually every standard (primary, secondary, and conditional) specified in the *Standards for Educational and Psychological Testing* (American Educational Research Association, American Psychological Association, & National Council on Measurement in Education, 1985). The Kolbe Conative Index (KCI) holds this dubious distinction. Touted as a measure of "instinctive talent," the KCI seeks to identify four action modes in individuals. These action modes or "modes of operation" (M.O.) are: (*a*) Fact Finder, which is a mode through which a person is a pragmatist, prober, arbitrator, or realist; (*b*) Follow Thru, which is a mode of a planner, designer, theorist, systematizer, or pattern maker; (*c*) Quick Start, which is a mode of a catalyst, generalist, innovator, entrepreneur, or promoter; and (*d*) Implementer, which is a mode of a manufacturer, molder, builder, weaver, or handler.

The KCI seeks to measure these action modes through the use of a 36-item scale in which respondents designate the items that are *Most Like* and *Least Like* themselves. There is also a six-item attitude scale on which respondents specify agreement or disagreement on a 10-point Likert-type scale. According to the KCI materials, *conation* is an "instinctive drive" or "instinctive way of striving." The four modes of operation, therefore, are viewed as instincts and, thus, are not learned.

The psychological sophistication underlying the KCI and its purported measurement perhaps is exceeded by that of a middle school student completing a 4-week study of introductory psychology. The KCI represents some of the worst of pop psychology, is simple-minded and inane, and bears closer correspondence to horoscopes and mood rings than to anything remotely resembling a psychological measure. An example of an interpretation from the KCI materials is instructive. The following interpretation was made from the KCI results: "Your KCI result shows your Natural Advantage is that of an: INNOVATOR. Your conative creativity is intuitive, visionary, and highly original. You have a knack for finding alternatives and discovering unique ways to get things done" (sample, p. 1).

There are absolutely no standardization, reliability, validity, or research data in the materials provided to this reviewer regarding the psychometric adequacy of the KCI. Perhaps the most offensive part of the KCI is the so-called "Professional Opportunities" presented in the materials. According to these materials, "Only those who successfully complete the certification process are entitled to use the Kolbe Concept technology. . . . Interested persons from all fields and professions are encouraged to apply for training and certification in the administration, interpretation, and application of the Kolbe Concept" (p. 1).

According to these materials, one achieves Kolbe Conative Consultant Status for a mere fee of $4,200.00 to cover tuition costs and curriculum materials. This, of course, is important because once licensed, only the Kolbe Consultants may administer, interpret, and apply the Kolbe Concept products to individuals and managers in their client organizations. If the $4,200.00

fee is a little steep, one can always opt for the Conative Specialist Status for a fee of $3,600.00, which allows them to apply the Kolbe Concept *only within their own organizations*.

In summary, the KCI does not appear to be a psychological measure of anything, but rather it seems to be a marketing device to make money for its originator. The idea of the KCI measuring "instinctive modes of responding," of which there are *only four*, is laughable and sad at the same time. There is no way that the KCI should ever see the light of day in the area of vocational or any other serious form of psychological assessment.

REVIEWER'S REFERENCE

American Educational Research Association, American Psychological Association, & National Council on Measurement in Education. (1985). *Standards for educational and psychological testing*. Washington, DC: American Psychological Association, Inc.

[209]

Kuder General Interest Survey, Form E.

Purpose: Constructed to assess "broad interest areas" related to occupational choices.
Population: Grades 6–12.
Publication Dates: 1963–91.
Scores, 11: Outdoor, Mechanical, Computational, Scientific, Persuasive, Artistic, Literary, Musical, Social Service, Clerical, Verification.
Administration: Group.
Price Data, 1994: $49.35 per complete hand-scored kit including 25 consumable booklets, 25 interpretive leaflets, and instructions for administration; $44.85 per complete locally machine-scored kit including same materials above; $79.30 per CTB machine-scored kit including materials above plus 2 answer sheet return envelopes, 2 scoring control cards, and complete scoring; $15.25 per 25 punch pins and backboards; $22 per 100 punch pins; $40 per 100 backboards; $11.95 per Job and College Major Charts; $5.60 per manual ('88, 48 pages); $7.40 per specimen set; information regarding microcomputer administration and scoring available from publisher.
Time: [45–60] minutes.
Comments: Extension of the Kuder vocational interest inventories series.
Author: G. Frederic Kuder.
Publisher: CTB MacMillan/McGraw-Hill.
Cross References: See T3:1269 (4 references); see also 8:1009 (16 references); for reviews of an earlier edition by Barbara A. Kirk, Paul R. Lohnes, and John N. McCall, and excerpted reviews by T. R. Husek and Robert F. Stahmann, see 7:1024 (8 references).

Review of the Kuder General Interest Survey, Form E by MARK POPE, President, Career Decisions, San Francisco, CA:

The Kuder General Interest Survey (KGIS), Form E is a lower extension of Frederic Kuder's measures of vocational interests. These measures evolved from a need to measure vocational interests at the junior high school level. In order to accomplish this task, the publishers of the KGIS have made a substantial attempt to design the inventory for this population. The KGIS attempts to avoid the use of concepts about which the individual's knowledge may change considerably, such as specific occupational titles, restrict the vocabulary used in the survey to a 6th grade reading level, use a larger number of items on each scale to enhance reliability because the responses of younger people tend to be slightly less reliable, and report scores on broad interest areas rather than on specific occupations as done by the Kuder Occupational Interest Survey (10:167). The broad interest areas for which scores are reported include: Outdoor, Mechanical, Computational, Scientific, Persuasive, Artistic, Literary, Musical, Social Service, and Clerical.

The version reviewed here was the self-scorable version although two other versions are available, both requiring computer scoring. The materials for the self-scorable version of the KGIS include a preliminary edition (1988) of a general manual; a 42-page consumable booklet that includes the test taker instructions, question booklet, self-scorable answer sheet, profile sheet, and interpretive report form; a memorandum of instructions for the test administration; an $8^1/_2$ by 11 inch sheet of white corrugated cardboard; and a stainless steel, pointed punch pin. No other materials are supplied with the KGIS.

The preliminary edition of the general manual is a 45-page booklet containing three sections (general, interpretive, and technical) along with two substantial appendices and a references list concerning the KGIS. The general section begins with a subsection on why vocational interests are measured at all followed by an overview of the KGIS, a list and description of the scales, a narrative on the development of the KGIS, and ends with a how-to subsection on its use in guidance and counseling. The interpretive section contains specific detailed information on the use and interpretation of the KGIS. The technical section consists of information on the history and construction of Kuder's inventories in general and the KGIS in particular along with the development of the 1988 norms, the raw-to-percentile-score conversion tables, scale intercorrelations, and reliability and validity data.

Two substantial appendices are also included that consist of background on the Kuder interest inventories (Appendix A) along with a sample interpretive counseling session (Appendix B). Appendix A puts the KGIS in a historical perspective with the development of the other Kuder inventories. Appendix B also is very helpful to the counselor who is preparing for an interpretive session with a student/client.

An important issue for junior high school or high school students and their parents might be the stability of vocational interests over time. If interests change substantially, the interpretation of scores received on any career interest measure would be affected. The publishers of the KGIS discuss the stability of interests in younger people, citing specific research using both the KGIS and the Kuder Preference Record.

The response format used in the KGIS is the forced-choice triad which consists of three activities. The test takers are instructed to mark the one they like most and the one they like least.

In both popular press and professional literature, interest inventories have received scrutiny for their use of separate sex norms. The publishers have responded to this in the manual with a section on the use of separate sex normative data and a disclaimer regarding innate biological sex differences versus environmentally provoked sex differences.

The current version of the KGIS was restandardized in 1987. In the technical section, the publishers note the changes from the 1963 to 1987 standardizations. They conclude the changes seen in these scores reflect the changes in sex role stereotypes that occurred over that period of time.

An issue that deserves attention is the use of the KGIS in multicultural settings. In the preliminary manual no summary demographic data were included from the 1987 restandardization other than general geographic, sex, and educational data. The publishers did state there were data for 11,550 students of the 13,007 students in the restandardization sample. Ethnic, racial, and economic status data, however, were not included in this preliminary general manual. Such data were requested by this reviewer; however, the data could not be located. This situation is intolerable for a major psychological inventory. Data should be available and saved as historical reference if for no other reason.

The 42-page consumable, combined administration/questions/answer/profile/interpretive form contains very detailed and user-friendly instructions that enable the test taker easily to complete the administration and scoring process almost unaided by a counselor/test administrator. In this self-scorable format (as with any self-scorable format with large numbers of items) there is, however, substantial room for error, but because of the peculiar format of this inventory, errors are particularly possible.

For example, the response format requires the test taker to place the piece of white corrugated cardboard in front of page 35 and then to use the punch pin to punch holes through the answer sheet (four sheets of paper). I know people have been doing this for a long time (I took the self-scorable version of the Kuder Preference Record in 1968 using this same unique format), but much manual dexterity, detail orientation, and concentration is required to consistently push that awkward little steel needle through four sheets of paper and to consistently hit that little hole for "M" (most like) or "L" (least like). An examinee might wish for a good set of callouses on the appropriate fingers because the test taker is required to punch two holes for each of 168 items with a little steel needle. A "push pin" like those found on most bulletin boards might be a better ergonomic design.

Another example of a potential source of error is in the scoring. First, the instructions in the consumable booklet are not very explicit concerning how to open the answer sheet section to begin the scoring. The scoring is very tedious. Scorers must find the starting place for each scale and then follow the circles and lines, counting the punched holes, until they reach the end place. Four of the six pages have two different scales on the page creating possible confusion. The beginning place for scoring Scales 5 and 6 is the same item. As scoring progresses for Scales 5 and 6 it is not easy to differentiate between them. The publisher has included research that verifies the increased error rate for the self-scored version.

The profile sheet, included in the consumable booklet, has two separate sex differentiated profiles on the same side of the sheet of paper. Although this placement is very useful for counseling (i.e., the counselor does not have to flip the page over to enable the test taker to see the other profile) the resulting profiles are too close together to read easily and accurately. Also, the boxes where raw scores are to be written are too small for double digit numbers.

In a major change, the 1987 profile sheet does have a place for test takers to calculate their Holland (RIASEC) code. This enables comparison across other career interest inventories which generate the same coding (Strong Interest Inventory, Self-Directed Search, Vocational Preference Inventory, etc.). Although the data used to justify this procedure and the mathematic calculation used to arrive at the scores are somewhat suspect, the resultant code when used cautiously as an estimate of the RIASEC model can be useful in career exploration for the individual student/client. The method, rationale, and justification for this conversion are included in the interpretive and technical sections of the general manual.

There are several reasons to recommend use of the KGIS with junior high and high school students and with adults who require a measure with a low reading level. The Kuder interest inventories have a long and respected place in the history of career interest measurement. The modest cost and availability of hand-scored results make the KGIS a good instrument to be used in financially strapped school districts. The manual contains substantial statistical data along with some interpretive information; however, an update with additional normative demographic data should be published soon. Of the major hand- or self-scorable career interest inventories (Self-Directed Search [10:330], Vocational Preference Inventory [10:382], Career Occupational Preference System [T4:399;

T4:400; T4:401]), the KGIS should be chosen for use with junior high school students who want to get a Holland (RIASEC) code to aid in career exploration. The KGIS is useful with computerized career information systems.

Review of the Kuder General Interest Survey, Form E by DONALD THOMPSON, Professor of Counseling Psychology, School of Education, The University of Connecticut, Storrs, CT:

The Kuder Interest Inventory series began in 1939. The longevity of the series in the competitive world of commercial test publishing indicates the authors and publishers have been doing something right. With over a half century of existence, the Kuder inventories have been the subject of extensive empirical study. This research base provides considerable evidence regarding the utility of these measures.

The Kuder General Interest Survey (KGIS-Form E) represents the third generation of Kuder tests, and was built on a foundation established by its predecessors. There is considerable debate among psychometrists regarding the methods used to validate the Kuder inventories and the interpretation of the meaning of the volumes of research. The KGIS was first published in 1963, with subsequent revisions in 1976 and 1988. The current version has only minor differences in content, but since 1975, the publisher and other researchers have completed additional reliability and validity studies and new normative data have been added. The general manual that accompanies the test package contains the following statement: "The basic purpose of the surveys is to stimulate career exploration and suggest career possibilities—to open up options, rather than limit them. Because the General Interest Survey suggests broad interest areas to be explored, it is better suited to the guidance of younger people" (p. 4). This statement and other information in the manual suggests the publisher views the KGIS as a tool that is appropriately used as a part of a systematic and comprehensive career exploration program rather than as a stand-alone measure of occupational interests.

The KGIS is available in three different scoring versions. The self-scored version uses the punch pin method for recording answers and can be self-scored by the test taker. The other two forms are computer scored (one is mailed to the publisher and the other is locally scored on a microcomputer at the user site). For the computer-scored versions, the test is taken with paper and pencil and then scanned into the computer, and both computer-scored versions provide a comprehensive narrative report. The specimen set for the self-scored version used for this review includes a consumable test booklet with the survey, an answer pad, profile sheet, and interpretive guide; a memorandum of instructions; and a general manual that includes administration, counseling, interpretation, and technical information.

The same form of the KGIS is used for grades 6 through 12; however, separate norms are provided for grades 6–8 and 9–12. The average testing time is between 45 minutes and 1 hour, and administration can be done individually or in groups. The inventory contains 168 items written at the 6th grade reading level. Each item contains three possible alternative activities and the testee is required to choose the *most liked* and *least liked* from each triad by using a punch pin to perforate a small circle adjacent to the activity. The KGIS is structured around 10 vocational interest areas (scales) and one verification scale. The verification scale provides an estimate of whether the testee has responded sincerely and correctly, whereas the vocational scales provide percentile scores for the testee in comparison to the norm group. The 10 vocational scales are Outdoor, Mechanical, Computational, Scientific, Persuasive, Artistic, Literary, Musical, Social Service, and Clerical. The instructions, administration, and scoring processes are relatively simple and quickly accomplished. Based on my experience with the scoring and interpretation, however, there can be problems for younger students and low level readers that may cause significant scoring errors. Research reported in the manual also points out this possibility. Based on the description of the development of the activities statements, it appears that item content for the KGIS has remained the same through the three revisions, and many of the items were taken directly from the Kuder Form C. The revision of Form C to the KGIS in 1964 involved simplifying the language of some activities statements, adding some new ones, and the addition of new norms in the 1988 version. A review of the activities listed for each scale indicates there has been a concerted effort to avoid using terminology that suggests specific job tasks and occupational titles. Most of the activities are ones that many youngsters (especially middle class) will have experienced and therefore should understand.

The reported norms show good diversity in terms of geographic location, grade level, and sex; however, it is troubling that no indication of ethnic or racial composition of the sample is provided. Also, there is no information regarding how the samples were drawn. The description does indicate the samples were drawn from "45 cities" (p. 23), leading to the possible conclusion that no rural areas were included as sample sites. In addition, there is no indication whether the samples were drawn randomly from large representative groups at each site, or if intact class groups were used.

The reliability data reported are test-retest over a 2-week period. Correlations range in the 70s and 80s and are acceptable for this type of measure. Generally, the higher the grade level of the respondent, the higher the test-retest reliability. Also, the KGIS manual author reports stability indices in the .40 to .60 range for scores on Kuder Form C over a 4-year period. No measures of internal consistency are reported in the manual.

For interest inventories, there are two principal types of validity. Empirical or criterion-related validity examines if the test can effectively predict future behavior or performance on a similar well-validated measure. The other principal type is construct validity (sometimes called homogeneous). The manual author indicates the KGIS vocational scales have been compared to similar scales of both the California Occupational Preference System (COPS) and the Vocational Preference Inventory (VPI). The correlations indicate moderate concurrent validity with the scales of these measures.

The intercorrelation matrix of KGIS vocational scale scores indicates generally low to moderate relationships between and among the 10 scales, suggesting they are, in fact, measuring different constructs.

Earlier reviewers have criticized the KGIS for: (*a*) having a middle-class bias and a limited number of items to which persons from underrepresented groups might relate; (*b*) variations in both the logically expected and unexpected correlations between vocational scales; (*c*) the validity data regarding predictiveness with later occupational satisfaction and/or success are inadequate; and (*d*) test-retest reliability data do not provide confidence in the long-term stability of scores. The present examination of the KGIS indicates that criticisms *a*, *b*, and *c* continue to be problem areas. Criticism *d* appears to have been addressed adequately in the current revision.

This reviewer noted several areas where improvements could be made. First, the antiquated punch pin method for recording answers should be eliminated (other inventories such as the COPS have developed much improved methods for self-scoring). Also, the interpretation process for the self-scored version is not as simple and easy as suggested and will take considerable involvement of a professional. I would not recommend purchase of the self-scored version. The computer-scored versions will save time and money in the long run and provide more accurate scoring and a good interpretive report.

There are several improved features that make this edition of the KGIS a more useful tool for initiating career exploration. The addition of Holland's RIASEC code conversions to the interpretation sheet make the results profile easier to interpret and it is simpler to locate career resource materials that are keyed to the RIASEC system. Also, the verification scale is a particularly attractive feature of this inventory, because faking and response sets are common problems with interest and personality inventories. The 1988 norms have provided more comprehensive comparison data and provide a much needed correction regarding the changing preferences for certain career areas.

In summary, the KGIS could be a valuable tool for initiating career exploration when it is used with youngsters of middle school age and with the direct supervision of a counselor or other staff member. Major advantages of the KGIS include its unambiguous language; its long history of use; and it is inexpensive, quick, and easy to administer. Because there is no empirical evidence regarding the effectiveness of this measure as a predictor of future occupational satisfaction or success, the KGIS should not be used to help clients make specific career choices and, therefore, is not recommended as a stand-alone interest measure. Also, its use should be confined to younger students, and then primarily for initiating a broad exploration of career interests.

[210]

Language Assessment Scales—Oral.

Purpose: Designed to "measure those English and language skills necessary for functioning in a mainstream academic environment."
Population: Grades 1–6, 7–12.
Publication Dates: 1987–91.
Acronym: LAS-O.
Scores, 6: Vocabulary, Listening Comprehension, Story Retelling, Minimal Sound Pairs, Phonemes, Total.
Administration: Individual.
Forms, 2: C, D.
Parts, 2: Oral Language (for Level 1 & 2), Pronunciation (for grades 2–12).
Price Data, 1992: $34.55 per test review kits including administration manual, scoring and interpretation manual, student test booklet or multicopy scoresheet, and cue picture booklet along with a test reviewer's guide (specify level and form); $21 per 50 scoresheets; $23.75 per reusable cue picture booklet; $13.50 per audiocassette (specify level and form); $16.50 per administration manual (specify level); $18.35 per scoring and interpretation manual (specify level); $8.95 per technical manual ('91, 144 pages).
Foreign Language Edition: Spanish edition ('90) available.
Time: [15] minutes.
Authors: Edward A. DeAvila and Sharon E. Duncan.
Publisher: CTB Macmillan/McGraw-Hill.
Comments: Language Proficiency Score also incorporates Language Assessment Scales, Reading and Writing (211).
Cross References: For a review of the Language Assessment Scales by Lyn Haber, see 9:584 (1 reference).

TEST REFERENCES

1. Medina, M., Jr., & Escamilla, K. (1992). English acquisition by fluent- and limited-Spanish-proficient Mexican Americans in a 3-year maintenance bilingual program. *Hispanic Journal of Behavioral Sciences, 14,* 252-267.
2. Medina, M., Jr., & Escamilla, K. (1994). Language acquisition and gender for limited-language-proficient Mexican Americans in a maintenance bilingual program. *Hispanic Journal of Behavioral Sciences, 16,* 422-437.

Review of the Language Assessment Scales—Oral by NATALIE L. HEDBERG, Professor of Communication

Disorders and Speech Science, University of Colorado, Boulder, CO:

According to the authors, the Language Assessment Scales—Oral (LAS-O) "is intended for use as a screening device to produce placement and reclassification information" for language-minority students (Administration Manual, p. 2). It contains both discrete-point and integrative tasks in its two forms. The Short Form measures vocabulary and discourse comprehension and production with measures of aural discrimination and pronunciation added in the Long Form. There are two levels of the test, one for grades 1 to 6 and the second for grades 7 to 12. The LAS-O is part of a battery of tests available for assessing oral and written language proficiency in English and Spanish across the ages 4 to adult. First used in 1976, the measure has been expanded with the most recent addition published in 1990. This review is based on the 1990 materials.

The formats for Levels 1 and 2 are the same with Cue Picture Books containing stimuli for the Vocabulary, Listening Comprehension, and Story Retelling subtests. Level 1 Vocabulary assesses concrete nouns and action verbs. For the nouns, four black-and-white drawings depict school scenes with the 10 objects to be labeled, such as a flag and a typewriter, shown in color. The examiner points to the pictured object and asks the student to name it. Several of the objects appear difficult to identify. Level 2 Vocabulary replaces concrete nouns with opposite words presented on audiotape. For the verbs, 10 one-color single pictures clearly represent a person engaged in an action such as eating or singing. The examiner asks the student to tell what the person is doing. No explanation is given for using 75% of the same verb items on Levels 1 and 2.

The Listening Comprehension subtests present a multicolored picture of a scene, such as a girl selecting lunch items in a school cafeteria, while the student listens to an audiotaped recording of a conversation between two persons shown in the picture. (Different scenes are presented for the two levels.) Following the conversation, 10 questions are presented on the audiotape to which the student must answer "yes" or "no." Both the Comprehension tasks and the Story Retelling tasks, to be described next, simulate the use of language in real-life contexts, a definite strength of these measures. However, it is important to note that both tasks entail heavy auditory memory loads, that in spite of visual support may confound language and memory factors.

At each level of the Story Retelling task the examiner selects one of four sets of four pictures, each set showing a sequence of events, and an audiotaped story about the events depicted for the student to listen to. Stories at Levels 1 and 2 contain approximately 150 and 175 words respectively. The student must retell the story, which is both written down and audiotaped by the examiner. The story retelling is rated holistically on the same 6-point scale for both levels. The scale takes into account both the correctness of grammatical and vocabulary usage and the amount and sequencing of story details, with greater weight seemingly placed on correct language use. Explicit instructions are given for scoring the Story Retelling and for establishing interrater reliability for this measure. On both the Short and Long Forms the Story Retelling score is weighted as 50% of the Total Score according to the authors' determination of its "theoretical and empirical importance" (manual, p. 23). Although the Scoring and Interpretation manual references this point to an earlier publication by the authors, the Technical Report does not discuss the determination of subtest weightings.

The Pronunciation component, included in the Long Form, consists of the Minimal Sound Pairs and the Phonemes subtests. Minimal Sound Pairs assesses auditory discrimination of the phonemes "shown to cause the most difficulty" for students learning English as their second language. The student listens to a taped production of 35 word pairs, 30 of which differ on a single phoneme in different word positions such as "feed-field" and "wish-witch," and reports whether they sound the "same" or "different." On the Phonemes subscale the student must repeat 35 audiotaped words, phrases, and short sentences such as "Girl Scout badges" with one targeted phoneme in various positions.

Either hand or computerized tabulation, plotting of student profiles based on percent correct weighted scores for each subscale, and determination of English fluency level can be carried out. A table for conversion of the Total Score to normal curve equivalent (NCE) scores is also provided "to establish a normative index to simplify comparisons" (Scoring and Interpretation Manual, p. 24). However, it is important to note that "placement information" is based on the nonnormative percent correct score rather than the NCE normative scores. An Observation Form to be completed by someone other than the examiner is included for use with students whose LAS-O Total scores fall within the standard error of measurement of the cutoff point between the levels of proficient and nonproficient English speaker. The authors claim that this procedure reduces placement errors by as much as 50%.

The LAS-O manuals provide clear instructions for administering, scoring, and profiling test results using percentage of correct items for each test section. Unfortunately, the inadequacy of the standardization procedures described in the LAS-O Technical Report, as discussed below, calls into question the validity of the normal curve equivalent scores even if they were used for interpreting test results. Herein lies a serious weakness in using this measure for the stated purpose of placement of language-minority students.

The authors describe in considerable but confusing detail a national "try-out" sample of approximately 3,600 students tested at five primary sites. Some sites were not represented at all grades or even both test levels. Additional variability in the sample was also apparent at the two test levels. Twenty-five percent of "minority" versus "mainstream" students were included at Level 1 compared to 60% at Level 2. There was also a discrepancy in oral proficiency level with 282 limited proficiency students at Level 1 and 925 at Level 2. Although the authors stated that missing data caused at least some of the variability, more careful selection of the reference sample would have increased the usefulness of the sample data.

The data reported in the Technical Report were not adequate to support reliability and validity. Internal consistency statistics were included for all subtests except Story Retelling; however, there was no control for the effects of age resulting in inflated coefficients. There was also insufficient evidence of test validity. Additionally, the Technical Report has many errors, such as in the procedures used to create the Total scores where the formula for weighting of the Total scores differs from that given in the Scoring and Interpretation manual. In discussing these concerns with the first author of the LAS-O, he concurred that there were significant limitations in the Technical Report.

In summary, the LAS-O testing materials appear satisfactory for use in situations where normative comparisons are not required. However, the technical characteristics of the measure are inadequate as presented.

Review of the Language Assessment Scales—Oral by PAMELA S. TIDWELL, Assistant Professor of Psychology, Auburn University at Montgomery, Montgomery, AL:

The Language Assessment Scales—Oral (LAS-O) is a battery of scales that are designed to assess whether or not language minority students have the oral language skills that are necessary for success in monolingual classrooms. There are two versions of the scale, a version that measures English language skills and a version that measures Spanish language skills. The English version comes in two alternative forms (C and D), and the Spanish version has only one form. The actual test battery includes an administration manual, a scoring manual, and a draft of a technical manual. It also includes an answer booklet, a student profile sheet, and a booklet of pictures and cassette tapes that are used to administer the test.

According to the authors of the LAS-O, this test is designed to measure the four major aspects of language (phonology, the lexicon, syntax, and pragmatics), and both language production and comprehension abilities. It employs five subscales to do so. These five subscales can be sorted into one of two components of the LAS-O, the Oral Language component and the Pronunciation component. The Oral Language component is made up of the Vocabulary, Listening Comprehension, and Story Retelling subscales. The Pronunciation component is made up of the Minimal Sound Pairs and Phonemes subscales. There are two levels of the LAS-O oral component, Level 1 and Level 2. The Level 1 oral component is designed for use with students in grades 1–6, whereas the Level 2 oral component is designed for use with students in grades 7–12. There is only one level of the LAS-O pronunciation component. It is designed for use with students in grades 2–12. Either level of the oral component can be given alone or in conjunction with the pronunciation component. When the oral component of the LAS-O is given alone, it is referred to as the LAS-O Short Form. When it is given in conjunction with the pronunciation component, it is referred to as the LAS-O Long Form. The Short Form of the LAS-O yields seven indices, one for each subscale (for a total of three subscale scores) a total LAS-O score, a normal curve equivalency score, a language proficiency level (levels range from 1-low to 5-high), and a language proficiency category (fluent, limited or, non-English speaker). The LAS-O Long Form yields all of the scores listed above, and it also yields two additional scores, one for each of the pronunciation subscales. Thus, the LAS-O Long Form yields nine indices.

The LAS-O is designed for individual administration. Specific instructions for each subscale are printed in both the answer booklet and the administration manual. The picture booklet that is a part of the test battery is used to administer the Vocabulary subscale; cassette tapes are used to administer all of the other subscales. Administering the Short Form takes at least 15 minutes; administering the Long Form takes at least 25 minutes.

Most of the subscales can be scored during administration of the test. These subscale scores are entered into a formula that produces the total LAS-O score. Then, the total LAS-O score can be used to identify the corresponding language proficiency level and category. The LAS-O total score, the language proficiency level, and the language proficiency category can be computed by the scorer or by computer. However, computer calculation requires a special program called LASBASE.

Administration and scoring of the LAS-O is not terribly complicated. However, both processes have their limitations. One problem with the administration of this test concerns the answer booklet and the administration manual which occasionally give two differently worded sets of instructions for the same subscale. Which set of instructions should the administrator read to the student before reading the subscale items, the set in the answer booklet or the set in the administration manual? Other administration problems are specific to certain subscales. For example, during the administration of the Vocabulary subscale, the administrator has to point to objects in picture drawings so that the child can provide names for these objects. Some of the to-be-named items are hard to find because they are small and/or because they are in black and white like most of the other objects in the drawings. This problem could be solved if the drawings were larger and if all of the to-be-named objects were in color. Other problems exist with the subscales that are administered by playing the tapes. For some of these subscales, it is permissible to replay some of the items for the student. However, replaying these individual items is somewhat difficult because it is often impossible to rewind the tape back to the exact starting point of the item to be replayed. Another problem arises during the administration of the Story Retelling subscale in that the administrator is required to write down exactly what the child is saying as he or she retells the story. At the same time, the administrator may also have to prompt the child for responses.

As stated above, the LAS-O scoring procedures also have their difficulties. One problem in scoring some of the subscales is that the scorer must make subjective judgments. For example, scoring the Vocabulary scale might sometimes require the scorer to decide if a word given by the student is an appropriate referent for an object. During the Phonemes subscale the administrator has to judge whether or not the student's pronunciation of a phoneme would be misunderstood or make the student a target of ridicule from others. Another scoring difficulty concerns the scoring of the Story Retelling subscale. This subscale has to be scored by at least two people who have completed a scorer training exercise. If the scores of these two do not agree, a third person scores the Story Retelling subscale responses. This third person assigns the final score.

Another scoring issue concerns the way in which the LAS-O total score is calculated. The LAS-O total score is calculated by entering the subscale scale scores into a formula that weights all of the subscales equally, except for the Story Retelling subscale. The Story Retelling subscale is weighted more than four times any other subscale in the total score formula for the Long Form. The authors claim that this subscale is weighted more heavily because it is of more theoretical importance than the other subscales. However, they fail to explain sufficiently why it is of special theoretical importance.

Technically speaking, the norm group (or what the technical manual calls the try-out sample) contains both English majority and minority students from various areas of the country. The relevant characteristics of this group are presented in the technical manual. However, there is no mention of how this sample was obtained. Data in the technical manual show that most of the subscales of the test have high Cronbach's alphas and high to moderate correlations with the total score. Also, correlations between the Long and Short Forms and correlations between the C and D forms are .90 and above. Test scores on the LAS-O also correlated highly with the linguistic proficiency ratings of students made by their teachers.

However, this technical data does point out that there are certain problems with the LAS-O. One of the most notable problems has to do with some of the items that were selected for inclusion on the test. In the technical manual, the authors state that one of the criteria for dropping an item from the test was an item-to-subscale correlation below .30. They do admit that they kept a few items in the test that fell below this criteria. However, an examination of the item-to-subscale correlations indicates that they actually kept more than a few. Most of the items below the criterion that they kept were on the Minimal Sound Pairs subscale. They claim that they kept these items on the test because of their theoretical importance, but do not explain why these items are theoretically important. Another technical problem with this test has to do with the low reliability of one of the subscales, Listening Comprehension. Although most of the subscales have high reliability indices, the reliability coefficient for the Level 2 Listening Comprehension subscale is relatively low. Another issue related to the Listening Comprehension subscale is whether or not it measures just language skills. A close examination of this subscale leads one to believe that performance on this subscale is probably also reflecting the memory ability of the student.

Other problems with the technical data for this test are more general. For example, the technical manual relies too much on descriptive statistics and too little on inferential statistics. When inferential statistics are reported, they usually are not reported in much detail. For example, the technical manual reports that *t*-tests comparing the scores of limited speakers to fluent speakers were all significant, but the direction of the significance is not mentioned. Another major problem with this test battery is with the technical manual itself. It is replete with errors (e.g., typos, references to tables that are not there or that do not contain what the text says that they should contain, mistitled tables, incomplete tables) and is rather poorly written. Because of these problems, it was often difficult to evaluate the technical merits of this test. Also, certain psychometric terms are discussed in the manual in a confusing way. For example, the manual discusses the value of having an interval measurement scale over a ratio measurement scale, whereas most statistics books point out that it is the ratio scale that is the more advantageous of the two. Also, one of the chapters in the technical manual is titled "Discriminant Validity," yet none of the statistics reported in this chapter attempt to show that the LAS-O is dissimilar to various measures that do not assess language skills.

In summary, the LAS-O is a test that does seem to produce scores that are reliable and valid measures of language skills in language minority students. However, it does have its problems. It is up to the potential user of this test to decide whether or not the merits of the test outweigh its problems. It would be easier for the potential user to make this decision if a better technical manual for this test was available.

[211]

Language Assessment Scales, Reading and Writing.

Purpose: Designed to measure "English language skills in reading and writing necessary for functioning in a mainstream academic environment."
Population: Language-minority students in grades 2–3, 4–6, 7–11.
Publication Date: 1988.
Acronym: LAW R/W.
Scores, 3: Reading, Writing, Total.
Administration: Group.
Levels, 3: 1, 2, 3.
Forms, 2: A, B.
Price Data, 1992: $83.30 per 35 Level 1 test booklets and examiner's manual (67 pages); $35.70 per 35 Level 2 or Level 3 Reading test booklets and Reading/Writing examiner's manual (Level 2, 79 pages; Level 3, 73 pages); $27.30 per 35 Level 2 or Level 3 Writing test booklets; $21.50 per 50 CompuScan answer sheets (select Level 2 or 3); $74.50 per 9 Level 1 scoring stencils; $10.35 per set of scoring stencils (select Level 2 or 3); $7.95 per examiner's manual (select level); $11.20 per technical report (98 pages); $54 per training kit.
Time: (50–75) minutes for Level 1; (49–87) minutes for Level 2; (53–86) minutes for Level 3.
Comments: May be used in conjunction with LAS Oral (210).
Authors: Sharon E. Duncan and Edward A. DeAvila.
Publisher: CTB Macmillan/McGraw-Hill.

Review of the Language Assessment Scales, Reading and Writing by C. DALE CARPENTER, Professor of Special Education, Western Carolina University, Cullowhee, NC:

The Language Assessment Scales, Reading and Writing (LAS R/W) is intended to assess the functioning of language minority pupils in reading and writing. The purpose is to measure competence to succeed in a mainstream class and cutoff points are set to aid in entry and exit decisions for students in special programs for English as a Second Language (ESL). This instrument follows the introduction of Language Assessment Scales, Oral (LAS Oral; 210) and is meant to be used in conjunction with the LAS Oral.

The approach used follows a probabilistic model. The aim is to predict the point at which language minority students would achieve proficiency comparable to that of students in mainstream classes succeeding at the 40th percentile rank level or better. It is not designed to measure higher level skills with accuracy. Although the LAS R/W is used with the LAS Oral to arrive at a Language Proficiency Index, the LAS R/W must be evaluated for its own qualities because it may be used alone.

Each level has two forms and contains four measures of reading—mechanics and usage, vocabulary, fluency, and reading comprehension—and two to three measures of written expression—sentence completion, sentence writing, and essay writing. All use multiple-choice items except for three writing subtests. The three writing subtests are used to elicit sentences (or endings for sentences) and a story. The content and format are appropriate. The authors are to be commended for using an open-ended format for the writing subtests as they better tap written expression than would all multiple-choice items. They should also be commended for including a passage to be read with accompanying comprehension questions for reading comprehension. Other formats included on some tests do not adequately measure comprehension.

The number of items on the LAS R/W is small. Only 10 or 15 items are used for multiple-choice items. For reading comprehension, there is one story and 10 multiple-choice items. For story writing, students write only one story. Students write five sentences in sentence writing.

TECHNICAL ADEQUACY. The small number of items may be one of the factors contributing to relatively low (about half are less than .80) reliability coefficients for internal consistency on many of the subtests. Forms A and B correlate highly with each other for adequate alternate form reliability. Although the need for interrater reliability is stressed, it is not reported based on the criteria available for the writing measures.

Validity is addressed in several ways. Form A and Form B predict three levels of proficiency with efficiency for reading, writing, and reading and writing combined. As might be expected, proficiency in writing does not predict proficiency in reading nor does proficiency in reading predict proficiency in writing. Scores on the LAS R/W correlate highly with scores on the California Test of Basic Skills (CTBS) and with teacher classifications of student proficiency. Unfortunately, solid evidence to show that the LAS R/W will predict success in mainstream classes is not strong. Nevertheless, evidence is presented in the Technical Report which supports validity of the LAS R/W.

The norm sample included almost 4,000 pupils in grades 1 through 12. Pupils came from the Southwest,

Northeast, Midwest, and Hawaii. Approximately twice as many language minority as language majority students were included. The home language of participants included English, Spanish, Chinese, Vietnamese, Tagalog, Japanese, Arabic, and Native American. No information about the socioeconomic status of the pupils is provided.

SUMMARY. The LAS R/W is a valuable complement to the LAS Oral. The design appears appropriate to assist in making entry and exit decisions from ESL programs although evidence does not clearly justify using the LAS R/W alone or even in combination with the LAS Oral to make such decisions. The LAS R/W is simple to administer but scoring the non-multiple-choice portions requires training, and interscorer reliability has not been established. The LAS R/W appears to fill a need and further validity data would help to establish its place in the field. If practitioners want an instrument to predict success in mainstream classes or to decide eligibility for ESL programs, the LAS R/W in conjunction with the LAS Oral may be helpful, but users cannot feel confident that decisions based on these instruments would be better than teacher judgement or other available instruments. Both low reliability and less than adequate validity contribute to lack of confidence for this use. If the LAS R/W is to be used with any student to measure reading and writing achievement, it has problems due to the small number of items and lack of sensitivity at the upper ranges of performance. The design of the instrument makes it promising, however, as a screening measure.

Review of the Language Assessment Scales, Reading and Writing by THOMAS W. GUYETTE, Assistant Professor of Speech Pathology, University of Illinois at Chicago, Chicago, IL:

The purpose of this test is to measure "those English language skills in reading and writing necessary for functioning in a mainstream academic environment" (p. 2). The authors emphasize that this is not an achievement test but rather a test used to make decisions about placement and reclassification of language minority students. The test can be used in conjunction with the Language Assessment Scales: Oral (210) in order to obtain a more complete picture of language skills.

The Language Assessment Scales, Reading and Writing comes with 12 different test forms. First, there are separate test forms for the two language modalities (i.e., Reading and Writing). Second, there are separate test forms for each of three educational levels (Form 1, 2, 3). Form 1 is appropriate for grades 2 and 3. Form 2 is appropriate for grades 4–6. Form 3 is appropriate for grades 7–9+. Third, there is an alternate form for each of the above domains.

Test content areas include receptive and expressive vocabulary, fluency, reading for information, mechanics and usage, finishing sentences, and short essay writing. Not all educational levels include all content areas. The Vocabulary section is composed of 10 items that measure the student's ability to match pictures to words. The Fluency section measures the student's ability to fill in a missing word in a sentence. In the Reading For Information section the student reads a paragraph and responds to 10 true-false questions regarding the content of the paragraph. The Mechanics and Usage section is composed of 15 items that test skills in areas such as punctuation and grammatical usage. The Finishing Sentences section is composed of 5 items that measure the student's ability to finish or complete a sentence correctly. In the "What's Happening?" section an action picture is used to elicit a one-sentence written response.

The documentation accompanying the test provides adequate instructions to prepare administrators, students, and proctors to give or take the exam. There is also a description of precautions to be taken during test administration. The authors suggest that the test be administered in two 45–55-minute sections.

Scoring is unambiguous for Sections 1 through 4. However, the scoring of Sections 5 and 6 involves examiner judgement using a 4-point rating scale. The manual provides descriptions of each point on the scale. To further reduce the ambiguity there are numerous sample responses and discussions of scoring for each section. The authors describe a procedure for testing reliability between raters. They suggest that raters strive for 90% agreement.

Once a raw score is obtained it is converted to a standardized score using the appropriate tables. A standardized score can be obtained for the Reading section, the Writing section, and the combined Total. The interpretation of the standardized score is facilitated by the Competency Level Tables that allow interpretation of the standardized score into one of the following categories: Non-Reader, Limited Reader, Competent Reader.

A separate manual is provided for the validity and reliability data. Reliability and validity data were collected from students in the Northeast, Midwest, Southwest, and the Pacific. There were approximately 3,969 completed tests with 2,504 fluent-English speakers, 1,221 limited-English speakers, and 36 non-English speakers. Home languages of subjects were Spanish, English, Chinese, Vietnamese, Tagalog, Arabic, Japanese, and Native American.

Several different measures of test reliability are presented. Reliability quotients are presented for each subscale. Alpha values were calculated within each subscale for Forms A and B across the three educational levels. Values ranged from r = .6492 to .9064 with the majority of values in the .7 and .8 range. These data suggest the internal consistency of the test subscales is adequate. In an attempt to increase the reliability of placement decisions, the authors provide limited information on the standard error of measurement. Confidence interval bandwidths are provided for those scores that fall near the cutoff between language competent and language limited and between language limited and nonliterate. If the student scores within the category confidence intervals then it is suggested that placement should be considered provisional. I did not find information on test-retest reliability or interrater reliability regarding the scoring of certain items.

Several different measures of alternate form validity are presented. First, the authors present correlations between the subscales on Forms A and B. The majority of correlations are greater than $r = .8$ except in those subscales involving less objective scoring. The authors also present information on the agreement of placement decisions based on Forms A and B. Presenting cross-tabulations across three categories (competent, limited, non-reader/writer) the authors demonstrate agreement of 80–90% when classifying students into the end categories (competent and non-reader/writer) but exhibit only 60–70% agreement in the "limited" category.

Two studies of concurrent validity are also presented. In the first, the classification of students based on the Language Assessment Scales (LAS) is compared with the classification of students based on the results of a standardized test of basic skills. Correlations between the two tests are in the .8 to .9 range. Cross-tabulation data indicate 92% agreement on the classification of these students. In a second study, classification of students based on the Language Assessment Scales is compared to a classification system used by a school district to classify students learning English as a second language. Although there is a linear relationship between the two classification systems, the percent agreement between the two systems is only 65.66%.

In summary, the LAS is a screening test designed to produce placement information for language minority students. Generally the manual provides adequate information about test rationale, administration, scoring, and interpretation. Information on test reliability and validity is adequate.

[212]

Leader Behavior Analysis II.

Purpose: Developed to assess leadership style.
Population: Middle and upper level managers.
Publication Date: 1991.
Acronym: LBAII.
Scores, 6: Style Flexibility, Style Effectiveness, Directing Style, Coaching Style, Supporting Style, Delegating Style.
Administration: Group.
Editions, 2: Self, Other.
Price Data, 1990: $29.50 per complete kit including 1 LBAII-Self instrument, 8 LBAII-Other instruments, data summary sheet, and scoring instructions; $2.95 per instrument (select Self or Other).
Time: [15–20] minutes.
Comments: Ratings by employees and self-ratings.
Authors: Drea Zigarmi, Douglas Forsyth, Kenneth Blanchard, and Ronald Hambleton (tests).
Publisher: Blanchard Training & Development, Inc.

Review of the Leader Behavior Analysis II by H. JOHN BERNARDIN, University Research Professor, and DONNA K. COOKE, Assistant Professor, College of Business, Florida Atlantic University, Boca Raton, FL:

The Leader Behavior Analysis II (LBAII) instruments are designed to measure perceived leadership style from the perspective of either the leader him or herself or subordinates to the leader. Currently, there are two main versions. The LBAII Self assesses self-perceived leadership style and the LBAII Other assesses perceptions of a manager's leadership style. There are also Self and Other versions written specifically for sales force managers. The revised version of the Situational Leadership theory is the basis for the LBAII and application of its principles are expected to result in increased satisfaction and organizational effectiveness (Hersey & Blanchard, 1982; Blanchard, Zigarmi, & Zigarmi, 1985). Recent research on the original theory of situational leadership has not been favorable (Blank, Weitzel, & Green, 1990).

Two types of managerial behavior, Directive and Supportive, are dichotomized (high and low) to produce four LBAII styles. Style 1 (S1) = high Direction/low Support, Style 2 (S2) = high Direction/high Support, Style 3 (S3) = low Direction/high Support, and Style 4 (S4) = low Direction/low Support. The technical manual reports that the instruments have been edited to eliminate gender and race biases. However, for the LBAII Self there were gender differences on the S2 and S3 dimensions. Tests of racial/ethnic differences were not reported. The instruments are available in 14 translations with norms provided by the distributors.

Each LBAII version has 20 items. Each item is a description of a situation requiring the selection of one of four behavioral responses. One weakness in this methodology is that there are only four possible behavioral alternatives for each situation, none of which may resemble the actual or anticipated behavior of the manager. No options are available for selecting alternative responses. Little discussion is presented in the manual to explain either how the authors arrived at the four alternative behaviors per situation or the extent to which the situations were representative of important, leadership situations. As an alternative, Fiedler (1967) presented considerable data and research to justify the three contingency factors captured in his contingency theory of leadership.

As reported in the manual for the LBAII, most users employ only the Self version prior to a training program. Few studies have compared Self and Other scores, despite considerable research illustrating the lack of validity in self-assessments and showing discrepancies in self and significant other assessments to be moderators of several measures of unit and group effectiveness (e.g., Atwater & Yammarino, 1992).

Scoring for the LBAII is done by the respondent and is rather complicated. The derivation of the "Flexibility" score is a measure of the degree to which the four styles are selected with equal frequency. The other score, style "Effectiveness," is computed by comparing the selected style to the recommended style. Effectiveness is described as the more important of the two scores. For each item the behavioral styles are rated excellent, good, fair, and poor. The excellent style is weighted 4, the good style is weighted 3, and the fair and poor styles are weighted 1 each. The empirical justification for the magnitude of the weights of the behavioral responses and the unit-weights across items is not given in the manual.

The lengthy manual is written for the non-researcher. Although there is some redeeming value, the manual is generally not well organized and the reader must use the Table of Contents and the List of Tables in order to gather information. The manual provides a poor introduction to the LBAII and the explicit purpose for the instrument is not presented. Although the changes in the situational leadership model prompted the new instruments, a clear delineation of the differences in the old and new situational models is not presented. The authors assume familiarity with two previous works, one of which does not appear in the reference list. Although mean Flexibility and Effectiveness scores, standard deviations, and sample sizes are presented for the Self version from 13 studies, very little data are available for the Other version. Research clearly shows that follower-derived leadership scores are much more valid than self-assessments of leadership style. More normative data are needed on both instruments. Because these are instruments for use in applied settings, it is expected that there would be attention paid to helping the user to improve the Effectiveness score. The only guidance given is to review the descriptions of the prescribed behaviors in the questionnaire. There is no description of what key elements in the situation would call for a particular management style. The user appears to be none the wiser from using the instrument.

Because the manual is apparently designed for non-researchers, the authors attempt to explain technical terms such as reliability and validity. They describe their strategy of estimating concurrent criterion-related validity as "prediction." This could be very misleading, particularly to their non-researcher audience, and the footnote does not clarify the distinction. Overall, the manual is disorganized and poorly written, in spite of the summary of the computer readability analysis results.

The internal consistency reliability of the LBAII Other's dimensions were calculated in three studies. The alphas of S1 and S4 were typically in the .80s. S2 and S3 have lower reliabilities, generally in the .70s. Only one study reported alphas for the Self scale. They were .51, .45, .56, and .42 for S1, S2, S3, and S4, respectively. the alphas for the sales manager versions range from .29 to .82, with S2 tending to be the most unreliable. These estimates are low for scales of this nature, although the authors consider them to be "extremely good" (for Other) and "adequate" (for Self).

More than 60 pages are devoted to establishing the validity of the LBAII Other against Wilson's Multi-Level Management Survey (MLMS) because the MLMS measures the Directive and Supportive constructs. Considering the numerous leader behavior instruments, other more widely known and better established operationalizations of related constructs should have been included. Worth noting was an unpublished dissertation cited in the manual in which the author correlated the LBAII to Consideration and Initiating Structure from the Leader Behavior Description Questionnaire (LBDQ). The correlation coefficients, though small (e.g., .07, .12), were all in the correct direction and significant at the .05 or better level.

The LBAII's predictive validity was tested against eight MLMS subscales which served as the dependent variables. They measured, for example, the follower's satisfaction with factors such as climate and commitment. One would have reasonably expected the effectiveness criteria to include measures of output, because increased output is thought to be a benefit of using the LBAII prescriptions. The independent variables of the ANOVA with the MLMS were the four style scales, plus the Flexibility and the Effectiveness scales. Out of the eight analyses, Flexibility was never a significant variable, and Effectiveness was not a significant variable in five. This is disappointing because Effectiveness is supposed to be the most important score. The six scores failed to explain variance in work involvement and commitment. It is possible that the ipsative nature of the style scales disqualifies them from use in an ANOVA.

In summary, the authors have not demonstrated that the LBAII fulfills its purpose to measure Directive and Supportive styles. The instrument appears to be of limited use to both researchers and practitioners due to the relatively poor reliabilities and the failure to justify the situations presented. Further research to establish construct validity is needed and the authors of the instrument admirably offer free use of the instruments for research purposes. Without a clearer understanding of the relationship between instrument scores and the new situational theory, it is difficult for researchers to assess validity and virtually impossible for users to understand how to improve Effectiveness scores.

Vecchio (1987) has argued that the LBDQ-XII and the Leader Opinion Questionnaire (a self-assessment instrument) (Stogdill & Coons, 1957) are more widely accepted (and researched) measures of task (i.e., initiating structure) and relationship (i.e., consideration) leadership style. Other instruments which have more substantive research trails are the Managerial Style Questionnaire (MSQ; 10:185) from McBer and Company, the Management Skills Profile (MSP) from Personnel Decisions Incorporated (Davis, Hellervik, & Sheard, 1989), and the Team Evaluation and Management Systems (TEAMS; Edwards, 1990). Both self and "significant other" assessments are available for the MSQ, the MSP, and TEAMS. Normative data for the MSP are more extensive than for the LBAII of the MSQ and excellent training materials are available as an adjunct to the MSP.

REVIEWERS' REFERENCES

Stogdill, R. M., & Coons, A. E. (Eds.) (1957). *Leader behavior: Its description and measurement.* (Research Monograph No. 88). Columbus, OH: Ohio State University, Bureau of Business Research.

Fiedler, F. E. (1967). *A theory of leadership effectiveness.* New York: McGraw-Hill Book Co.

Hersey, P., & Blanchard, K. (1982). *Management of organizational behavior.* Englewood Cliffs, NJ: Prentice-Hall.

Blanchard, K., Zigarmi, P., & Zigarmi, D. (1985). *Leadership and the one minute manager.* New York: William Morrow.

Vecchio, R. P. (1987). Situational leadership theory: An examination of a prescriptive theory. *Journal of Applied Psychology, 72,* 444-451.

Davis, B. L., Hellervik, L. W., & Sheard, J. L. (Eds.) (1989). *Successful manager's handbook.* Minneapolis: Personnel Decisions, Inc.

Blank, W., Weitzel, J. R., & Green, S. G. (1990). A test of the situational leadership theory. *Personnel Psychology, 43,* 579-597.

Edwards, M. R. (1990). Assessment: Implementation strategies for multiple rater systems. *Personnel Journal, 21*(6), 130-139.

Atwater, L. E., & Yammarino, F. J. (1992). Does self-other agreement on leadership perceptions moderate the validity of leadership and performance predictions? *Personnel Psychology, 45,* 141-164.

Review of the Leader Behavior Analysis II by SHARON McNEELY, Associate Professor of Educational Foundations, Northeastern Illinois University, Chicago, IL:

The Leader Behavior Analysis II (LBAII) comes in two forms, the Self, and the Other, both designed to provide perceptions of leadership style by having the respondent choose one of four leader decisions in 20 "typical" job situations. The authors' Validity and Reliability Study booklet reports this update of the original Leadership Behavior Analysis (LBA) is supposed to present "generic" situations that try to achieve business realism while eliminating gender and race biases as much as possible.

The Self form of the test has the respondent assume that he/she is the leader and is to choose the decision that "would most closely describe your behavior in the situation presented." The Other form allows the name of the leader to be inserted, with the respondent then describing this person's behavior. According to the study, the Self form yields six different scores, two primary: the Effectiveness, and the Flexibility Scores; and four secondary style scores. The Effectiveness Score is meant to represent how effective the respondent is in certain situations, whereas the Flexibility Score indicates how often the respondent used a different style to solve the situations.

The authors present correlations showing that the LBAII is statistically and conceptually related to the Multi-Level Management Survey (MLMS; Wilson, 1981). The MLMS is used for construct validity studies. These studies do not lend full support to the Flexibility construct. However, the authors explain these findings by arguing the managers should be able to use more than one leadership style to solve management problems. To their credit they do assert the score "may not be an important psychometric measure of the general concept of Leadership in comparison to the MLMS" (p. 27). The predictive validity studies also do not lend consistent support to the LBAII.

The four leadership styles have also been redefined from the LBA, based on two types of observable and verifiable managerial behaviors: Directive and Supportive. The definitions of these styles assume the extremes of high or low can be applied to each behavior. The lack of a middle ground for each behavior is somewhat troublesome, and may help explain why there is consistent correlation with most of the MLMS' 15 subscale scores, in that the LBAII may not be measuring anything different than the MLMS scales. In this case, the 15 scales of the MLMS may be more effective for use in labeling behaviors and providing feedback to managers concerning specific strengths, weaknesses, and desired behaviors than information gleaned from the LBAII.

Reported studies on the internal consistency of the LBAII show moderate correlations (.43–.60 for Self, .54–.86 for Other). Further, 5 of the 20 items do not fit within the Rasch model for unidimensionality, and only one test-retest reliability study has been done yielding a .72 stability coefficient on Flexibility scores.

Although an experienced manager may focus on a few key words in select orders to complete the survey in a short time, the LBAII has an untimed administration that could take well over an hour for the careful reader or new manager to complete. The choices for each item usually contain much of the same wording in different order, and severely limit the possible choices of action for the respondent. Not only are the responses very similar, but they also appear redundantly across most of the situations. This could lead to sloppy reading and haphazard responding with corresponding threats to reliability and validity.

The authors described the prompts as business-appropriate situations. The situations are, however, redundant, with recurrences of employees not doing their tasks, groups not functioning effectively, and the manager missing something important. The authors contend that the situations also are free of gender bias. Twelve of the 20 situations identify either the male or female employee. However, the six male versions appear in the first 11 items. Four of the six female versions occur in the last 7 items. Females are presented as "new" employees in one-half of these situations, compared to only one of six for the males. Although statistical analysis may not support discrimination between male and female managers, more studies need to be done on this area.

In summary, although the LBAII may be better suited to use in today's business environment than the LBA, its use of six scales, lack of adequate reliability, inconsistent construct validity, possible gender-presentation biases, and possible unlimited time for administration lead me to rate it as only a fair instrument, at best.

The LBAII should not be used in isolation for making any decisions about respondents or their leaders. The MLMS (11:471) provides more varied and useful information to businesses, and may be more appropriate for use despite its age.

REVIEWER'S REFERENCE

Wilson, C. L. (1981). Survey of Management Practices (Form SMP-SE). New Canaan, CT: Clark Wilson Publishing.

[213]

Leadership Practices Inventory [Pfeiffer & Company International Publishers].

Purpose: Designed to provide ratings of five leadership behaviors.
Population: Managers.
Publication Dates: 1990–92.
Acronym: LPI.
Scores, 5: Challenging the Process, Inspiring a Shared Vision, Enabling Others to Act, Modeling the Way, Encouraging the Heart.
Administration: Group.
Editions, 2: Self, Other.
Price Data, 1991: $29.95 per trainer's package including LPI: Self-Assessment booklet and inventory, LPI: Other inventory, technical manual ('92, 31 pages) and trainer's manual ('90, 39 pages); $8.95 per LPI: Self-Assessment booklet and inventory; $3.95 per LPI: Other inventory; $195 per IBM-PC (or compatible) scoring software.
Time: Administration time not reported.
Comments: Scale for ratings by employees and for self-ratings.
Authors: James M. Kouzes and Barry Z. Posner.
Publisher: Pfeiffer & Company International Publishers.
Cross References: See T4:1411 (2 references).

Review of the Leadership Practices Inventory by FREDERICK T. L. LEONG, Assistant Professor of Psychology, The Ohio State University, Columbus, OH:

The Leadership Practices Inventory (LPI), developed by James M. Kouzes and Barry Z. Posner, is based on five leadership practices believed to be common among successful leaders. These five practices include: Challenging the Process, Inspiring a Shared Vision, Enabling Others to Act, Modeling the Way, and Encouraging the Heart. Each of these five practices are in turn divided into two components, which Kouzes and Posner (1987) describe as the 10 commitments of leadership.

The LPI was developed based on a series of case studies in which over 1,100 managers were asked detailed questions about their personal best experiences as leaders. From these case studies the five leadership practices were identified and items were written to tap into the five dimensions. The final LPI consists of 30 items in 5-point Likert format. There are six items for each of the five practices. There are two versions of the LPI—the LPI Self-Assessment version and the LPI Observer version.

The internal consistency estimates of the LPI-Self range from .70 to .85. The LPI-Observer has generally higher internal consistency with estimates ranging from .81 to .92. A test-retest reliability study based on a convenience sample of 157 MBA students yielded retest estimates ranging from .93 to.95 for the five leadership practices. Studies of gender differences found there were no significant differences between males and females across a set of different studies. Similarly, cross-cultural studies with the LPI have found few significant differences across the various ethnic and cultural groups such as African-, Hispanic-, and Asian-Americans, as well as the French and British.

A principal factor analysis of the 30 items resulted in five factors with all the items loading in the appropriate dimension. The five factors accounted for 60.2% of the variance. All five factors were interpretable in terms of the five practices: challenging, inspiring, enabling, modeling, and encouraging. The stability of the factors was also tested across different subsamples and in these various factor analyses the factor structure remained stable across samples totaling 36,000 subjects.

In terms of the construct validity of the LPI, a study examining the relationship between the LPI and managerial effectiveness found strong evidence for the discriminant validity of the LPI. Using a Leadership Effectiveness Scale developed for this study, it was found the five practices were significantly related to subordinates' rating of managerial effectiveness. The Leadership Effectiveness Scale contained six Likert-type questions. These questions asked the raters to evaluate their managers with regard to meeting the job-related needs of subordinates, building a committed work group, having an influence on upper management, their degree of satisfaction with the leadership provided by the manager, belief that the manager's leadership practices are appropriate, and feelings of empowerment. The coefficient alpha for the Leadership Effectiveness Scale was .98 and a test-retest reliability based on 57 MBA students was .96. Using a multiple regression the five component practices of the LPI significantly predicted the Leadership Effectiveness Scale (F = 318.9, $p<.0001$ adjusted R^2 = .756). In the same study, discriminant functions were used to discriminate between those scoring high and low on the LPI and approximately 93% of the known cases were classified correctly in the discriminant function.

A series of other studies continued to provide evidence of the validity of the LPI. For example, Smith (1991) examined the relationship between the leadership practices on the LPI and how these impacted job satisfaction, organizational commitment, and productivity of employees. Using 41 managers in two medium-size hospitals, Smith (1991) found positive and significant correlations between each of the leadership behaviors and the three outcome variables. Stepwise regression found that Modeling the Way accounted for the greatest amount of variance in productivity and Enabling Others to Act explained the greatest amount of variance around both job satisfaction and organizational commitment.

Further evidence for the discriminant validity of the LPI is provided in the study by Stoner-Zemel (1988; cited in Posner & Kouzes, 1992). In this study the LPI was used as an operationalization of visionary leadership, whereas traditional leadership was assessed with the Leader Behavior Analysis (Blanchard, Hambleton, Zigarmi, & Forsyth, 1991). Respondents completed the excellent organizational practices index created to measure perceptions of characteristics typical of peak performing organizations. These scales included assessment of productivity, performance, team effectiveness and alignment, empowerment, commitment, and inspiration. Employees who rated their supervisors strong in visionary leadership (LPI) reported significantly high scores on the excellent organizational practices index regardless whether that supervisor was high or low in traditional leadership (management skills).

Although much of the empirical research supports the LPI, there are several problems related to some of the supporting evidence. First, the examination of potential social desirability effects (Posner & Kouzes, 1988) on the LPI with the Marlowe-Crowne scale revealed no significant correlations. Yet, this relationship was examined on a select sample of only 30 middle-level managers and the statistical significance of correlations is highly dependent on sample size. With a sample size of 30 and a critical value of $p<.01$, it would take an $r>.44$ to be statistically significant. It would seem worthwhile to conduct additional studies of the potential social desirability effects of the LPI with larger and diverse samples. This research is especially important given that the LPI-Self and LPI-Observer versions tend to produce different results. Second, there is a need for further research to examine the differential results when the LPI-Self and LPI-Observer versions are used as well as their complex interactions. For example, in the original validation study, much of the evidence for the predictive and discriminant validity of the LPI was based on the LPI-Observer version only. Future research to examine the relative validity of the LPI-Self version is needed. We need to know if the LPI-Self version, relative to the LPI-Observer version, provides the same level of discriminant and predictive validity with regard to the typical outcomes used in the various studies. Depending on the nature of the differences found between the LPI-Self and the LPI-Observer versions, it is possible differential recommendations about their use may have to be formulated.

Third, more research is needed on the validity of the LPI that goes beyond concurrent validity with other self-rating measures. A multi-trait multi-method (MTMM) methodology would seem quite valuable. Finally, there is the perennial "criterion problem" in leadership research (see Austin & Villanova, 1992, for a recent discussion) and this applies equally to the LPI as to other measures of leadership styles; namely, what is a good leader and how do we recognize one? According to the LPI model, a good leader is one who engages in five specific leadership practices. Are leaders who engage in this set of practices better or more effective leaders? Better and more effective than what (differential validity question)? Better and more effective at what (criterion problem)? According to whose perspectives (another part of the criterion problem)?

In conclusion, the Leadership Practices Inventory is a promising new empirical measure of a conceptual leadership framework developed by Kouzes and Posner (1987). There is good evidence to support the reliability and validity of the LPI. The conceptual scheme on which the LPI is based is elegant and the test items have excellent face validity as well as psychometric validity. Factor analyses and multiple regressions provide strong support for both the structural and concurrent validity of the LPI. Although the LPI seems to be a promising and valid measure of leadership practices, there is room for further research to examine the differential validity and utility of the LPI, especially relative to the Self and Observer versions and to the criterion problem.

REVIEWER'S REFERENCES

Blanchard, K. H., Hambleton, R. K., Zigarmi, D., & Forsyth, F. (1981). Leader Behavior Analysis. Escondido, CA: Blanchard Training and Development.

Kouzes, J. M., & Posner, B. Z. (1987). *The leadership challenge: How to get extraordinary things done in organizations.* San Francisco: Jossey-Bass.

Posner, B. Z., & Kouzes, J. M. (1988). Development and validation of the Leadership Practices Inventory. *Educational and Psychological Measurement, 48*, 483-496.

Stoner-Zemel, M. J. (1988). *Visionary leadership management and high performance work units: An analysis of workers' perceptions*. Unpublished doctoral dissertation, University of Massachusetts, Amherst.

Smith, D. K. (1991). *The impact of leadership behaviors upon job satisfaction productivity and organizational commitment of followers*. Unpublished doctoral dissertation, Seattle University.

Austin, J. T., & Villanova, P. (1992). The criterion problem: 1917-1992. *Journal of Applied Psychology, 77,* 836-874.

Posner, B. C., & Kouzes, J. M. (1992). *Psychometric properties of the Leadership Practices Inventory*. San Diego, CA: Pfeiffer & Company.

Review of the Leadership Practices Inventory by MARY A. LEWIS, Manager, Human Resources, PPG Architectural Finishes, Pittsburgh, PA:

The Leadership Practices Inventory (LPI) is a 30-item multiple-choice questionnaire designed to measure five empirically developed leadership scales, with six items per scale. The two versions of the LPI, Self and Other, may be self-scored using comprehensive directions in the Self-Assessment and Analysis Manual. PC scoring software is also available. There is also a Trainer's Manual that is intended to support a half to full day training session built around the LPI, and a reference book with more theoretical and developmental suggestions (Kouzes & Posner, 1987).

The LPI was developed through a multi-year study in which over 1,100 managers responded to a 12-page "personal best" survey. Behavioral statements from their responses were content analyzed and sorted through several iterations of category labels to generate the items in the survey. After several developmental iterations, the LPI was administered to over 2,100 managers and their subordinates. The data from this sample were factor analyzed and measures of internal consistency were calculated, leading to the final instrument. Reliability and validity of the final version of the LPI were estimated based on an additional 2,876 managers and subordinates.

The LPI has five leadership practices scales: Challenging the Process, Inspiring a Shared Vision, Enabling Others to Act, Modeling the Way, and Encouraging the Heart. Internal reliabilities ranged from .70 to .85 for the Self version of the LPI and from .81 to .92 for the Other version, with test-retest reliabilities of .93 to .95. In addition, there were significant relationships between performance on the LPI and subordinates' assessment of their leader's effectiveness. There were also significant relationships between the LPI scales and job satisfaction, organization commitment, and productivity (Smith, 1991).

Initial studies found no difference in LPI scores across a number of Western cultures, and found two significant differences between men and women. Women score significantly higher than men on Encouraging the Heart and Modeling the Way (Posner & Kouzes, 1992). I recommend that individuals interested in cross-cultural and gender studies read the Posner and Kouzes review of 13 studies of the LPI.

The LPI is one of the most extensively researched management development tools I have encountered. It is a model of sound research design from its initial development and refinement through subsequent concurrent validity studies. The instrument and instructions are easy to read and follow, and the trainer's guide is logical and clear. I highly recommend it as a developmental tool for new and experienced managers.

REVIEWER'S REFERENCES

Kouzes, J. M., & Posner, B. Z. (1987). *The leadership challenge*. San Francisco: Jossey-Bass.

Smith, D. K. (1991). *The impact of leadership behaviors upon job satisfaction, productivity and organizational commitment of followers*. Unpublished doctoral dissertation, Seattle University.

Posner, B. Z., & Kouzes, J. M. (1992). *Psychometric properties of the Leadership Practices Inventory*. San Diego: Pfeiffer & Company.

[214]

Learning Disability Evaluation Scale.

Purpose: Designed as a measure of learning disabilities.
Population: Ages 4.5–19.
Publication Dates: 1983–91.
Acronym: LDES.
Scores, 8: Listening, Thinking, Speaking, Reading, Writing, Spelling, Mathematical Calculations, Learning Quotient.
Administration: Individual.
Price Data, 1993: $129 per complete kit including pre-referral learning problem checklist form, pre-referral intervention strategies documentation, technical manual ('83, 52 pages), rating form, Parent's Guide to Learning Disabilities ('91, 200 pages), and learning disability intervention manual ('89, 217 pages); $25 per 50 pre-referral learning problem checklist forms; $25 per 50 pre-referral intervention strategies documentation; $12 per manual; $30 per 50 rating forms; $22 per learning disability intervention manual; $15 per Parent's Guide to Learning Disabilities; $12 per computerized quick score (Apple II); $149 per computerized version of learning disability intervention manual (Apple II).
Time: (20) minutes.
Comments: Ratings by teacher.
Authors: Stephen B. McCarney and Angela Marie Bauer (intervention manuals).
Publisher: Hawthorne Educational Services, Inc.

Review of the Learning Disability Evaluation Scale by GLEN P. AYLWARD, Professor of Pediatrics, Psychiatry and Behavioral and Social Sciences, Southern Illinois University School of Medicine, Springfield, IL:

The Learning Disability Evaluation Scale (LDES) is an observational instrument designed to enable educators to distinguish areas of learning problems in their students. Overt, problematic behaviors are identified without making suppositions as to underlying etiologies. The primary utility of the LDES is that it provides useful information for referral and the subsequent diagnostic process.

The LDES consists of 88 behavioral items corresponding to the diagnostic nomenclature of PL 94-142. The readily observable classroom behaviors are considered characteristic of learning disabilities. The rater (teacher) quantifies a specific behavioral description such as "does not remember math facts" using an ordinal scale: 1 = *rarely or never*, 2 = *inconsistently*, and 3 = *all or most of the time*. Items are grouped into seven areas: Listening, Thinking, Speaking, Reading, Writing, Spelling, and Mathematical Calculations. The number of items in each area ranges from 7 (e.g., Listening) to 20 (Mathematical Calculations). Raw scores are converted into standard scores using 13 conversion tables grouped by age (M = 10, SD = 3). Standard scores range from 0 to 17, depending on age and subscale; as a result, minimum and maximum scores vary. The Learning Quotient is produced by adding the subscale standard scores and converting the sum (M = 100, SD = 15). Learning Quotients range from 47–132, with much variability in regard to floors and ceilings, again depending on age (e.g., Learning Quotients in the 4.5–6.0 year age grouping are particularly higher than any other age). An LDES Profile is provided, allowing for visual representation of the student's performance in all areas. Scores in the shaded area are indicative of below average functioning. Guidelines are provided for raters, and the LDES requires 20 minutes to complete.

A Pre-Referral Learning Problem Checklist, a Pre-Referral Intervention Strategies Documentation page, and a Learning Disability Intervention Manual are included. It is not specified as to how the Pre-Referral Learning Problem Checklist fits into the screening procedure. The Learning Disability Intervention Manual contains *goal statements*, *objectives*, and *interventions*. These correspond to specific behavioral descriptors listed in the LDES. For example, if the Listening area is deemed deficient, three possible goal statements are provided, from four to eight objectives are furnished to address specific behaviors, and intervention strategies for each behavioral description are delineated (ranging from 29–46 suggestions). Other educational aids such as a Reinforcer Survey, Point Record, Contracts, and a Schedule of Daily Events are found in the Appendix.

Initially, 62 educational diagnosticians and special educators were polled to identify indicators commonly found in children with learning disabilities. This procedure produced an item pool of 97 behaviors that was reduced to 89 items. These were then grouped into the seven areas listed previously, based on the items' face validity.

The LDES was field tested by 162 K–12 classroom teachers; each teacher rated four randomly selected children and also rated a student previously identified as having academic difficulties. Although the first group of students was considered "typical," this group may have contained "exceptional" students as well.

Four analyses were performed on 216 sets of responses: (*a*) a principal components analysis with varimax rotation of interitem correlations for the entire LDES, (*b*) a principal components analysis of each of the seven logically defined subscales, (*c*) item analysis of each subscale, and (*d*) determination of the reliability of each subscale. The first principal components analysis yielded 13 factors with eigenvalues >1.0. The skree plot indicated one dominant factor and three common factors: processing verbal material, mathematical skills, and mental processing. One item was dropped because it did not load on any factor, leaving a final pool of 88 items. The amount of variance accounted for was not indicated in the manual.

The standardization sample of 1,666 students is geographically representative: 414 teachers rated these students, who were grouped into 13 age levels, from 4.5 to 18+ years. There were 96–161 students per age grouping. The same analyses outlined with the pilot LDES were applied. The skree plot indicated one dominant factor with four additional factors; the first three were similar to those obtained in field testing, whereas the fourth factor was spoken communication, and the fifth involved mechanical writing. The author supports the seven subscale model even though Spelling, Writing, and Reading all load on the first factor.

Loadings of the variables assigned to the seven a priori ("logically defined") subscales range from .40 to .88. Correlations between the seven LDES subscales range from .43 to .86. Mathematical calculations routinely had the lowest correlations with other subscales. Principal components analysis of subscales generated one or two factors for each subscale, suggesting that several subscales could be reduced further. The modal response on the LDES was "1" (*rarely or never*), with no item having over an 85% response for this quantifier. Coefficient alpha reliabilities ranged from .88 to .97. Test-retest reliability was r = .98; interrater reliability ranged from .96–.98 for all age levels. Criterion-related validity was established by comparing the LDES to the Wechsler Intelligence Scale for Children—Revised (WISC-R), Peabody Individual Achievement Test (PIAT), and the Woodcock Reading Mastery Tests. Only four LDES subscales were used in the WISC-R comparison (the rationale was not provided), with correlations ranging from .46 to .63. Correlations between the LDES and corresponding PIAT subtests ranged from .39–.63; between the LDES and Woodcock, .59–.65. Construct validity was measured by comparing 92 "learning disabled" students (selection criteria not specified) to 92 regular education controls; the mean Learning Quotient for the former group was 22 points lower (M = 76 and 98, respectively).

The LDES is particularly useful as the first step in the workup of a student who is experiencing learning problems. Rather than provide a diagnosis, the LDES is a screen for potential problems. Information gleaned from the LDES could specify areas needing further evaluation, facilitate discussion between parents and professionals, and help quantify the efficacy of intervention. The intervention manual may prove useful in development of the student's IEP, and in providing educators with specific intervention techniques.

The diagnostic utility of the LDES may be overstated in the manual. Psychometric terms are sometimes used too liberally (e.g., "The values of the reliability of the subscales were all uniformly high, indicating that the instrument consistently measures what it purports to measure" [p. 18]), and information such as variance accounted for in factor analyses or the reasons why certain subscales were deleted in analyses is lacking. Because elementary teachers observe their students in a wider variety of situations than do junior or senior high school educators, the LDES is more applicable to the former group (particularly because no items should be left blank). The requirement that *all* items must be completed is procedurally difficult.

In summary, the LDES is a package that appears particularly useful in the initial workup of elementary and middle-school children who experience academic difficulty. The instrument also is applicable in development of IEPs and intervention strategies. However, professionals using the LDES should be certain this is a component of the evaluation procedure and that the findings in regard to learning disabilities are considered "indicative" and not "definitive."

Review of the Learning Disability Evaluation Scale by SCOTT W. BROWN, Professor of Educational Psychology, University of Connecticut, Storrs, CT:

The Learning Disability Evaluation Scale (LDES) is an observation system designed to gather systematic observational data from teachers. The LDES was designed to respond to a need expressed by teachers and diagnostic personnel for an instrument that would provide a comprehensive reporting mechanism based on the classroom environment where learning difficulties are most evident. It is designed for students aged 4.5 to 19 years and according the manual, conforms to the most commonly accepted definition of learning disabilities (USOE, 1968) by including subscales that represent the intent of the definition of learning disability used by Public Law 94-142 and most states. The seven subscales are: Listening, Thinking, Speaking, Reading, Writing, Spelling, and Mathematical Calculations.

The subscales, based on 88 items, are designed to assess specific skills and abilities. The number of items within each scale range between 7 (Listening and Spelling) and 20 (Mathematical Calculations). Items are scored on a 3-point system: *Rarely or Never*, *nconsistently*, and *All or Most of the Time*, for scores of 1, 2, and 3, respectively. Items focus on specific behaviors exhibited by the child during observations, such as "Omits, adds, substitutes, or reverses letters, words or sounds when reading" (Reading), and "Has difficulty solving math word problems" (Mathematical Calculations). The authors claim the items of the LDES were selected because they are relevant to the classroom environment, may be observed by teachers, and are related to commonly employed definitions of learning disabilities.

The norms for the LDES are based on data from 1,666 children aged 4.5 to 18+ years from 19 different states and 71 different school districts. The manual contains information that clearly relates the breakdown of the normative sample with the population at large, demonstrating the representativeness of the sample. The normative data were collected by 414 different teachers. The data from the normative sample were used to develop the estimates of reliability, validity, and standard score tables.

The LDES provides scaled scores and a Learning Quotient, which is an overall score based on performance on the seven subscales. The standard scores range from 0 to 20, with a mean of 10 and a standard deviation of 3. The Learning Quotient is calculated by summing the standard scores for the subscales and comparing the total standard score to the appropriate age table. Learning Quotients are also standard scores and have a mean of 100 and a standard deviation of 15. Tables are presented for each children aged 4.5 to 18+ years in one year increments, except for the first interval of 4.5 to 6.0 years of age.

Three types of validity are reported for the LDES: Content, Criterion-Related, and Construct. Content validity is reported based on the creation of an item pool related to the direct observation of learning-disabled students' performance, a careful review of the literature, and the participation of 62 educational diagnosticians and special education personnel. The criterion-related validity is presented in the form of correlations ranging between .39 and .65 between the Listening, Thinking, Reading, Spelling, and Mathematical Calculation subscales and the total scores of the Wechsler Intelligence Scale for Children—Revised, the Peabody Individual Achievement Test, and The Woodcock Reading Mastery Tests, for a total of 71 children between 4.5 and 18+ years of age. In each case, the correlations were statistically significant, supporting the contention that the LDES and the three stated criterion were measuring similar, but not identical, dimensions. Construct validity was assessed through the examination of 92 students randomly selected from the normative sample compared to a corresponding sample of 92 identified learning-disabled students. The mean Learning Quotient of the learning-disabled students was 76 compared to a mean of 98 for the randomly selected regular education students. The differences between the two groups were statistically different at the p<.001 level for all the subscales and the Learning Quotient. Median point biserial correlations for the seven subscales are reported as ranging between .41 (Writing) and .73 (Listening). Intercorrelations among the seven scores ranged from .43 to .86, with the majority in the .70s, suggesting the scales are highly interrelated. Factor analyses are also reported as supporting the existence of seven separate subscales.

Interestingly, no discussion is included of a discriminate function analysis conducted on the identified Learning Disabled students and the subsample of regular education students in an attempt to use the subscales or Learning Quotient to accurately predict the group membership. This analysis appears to be specifically appropriate and important in assessing the value of the LDES.

Test-retest reliability estimates were based on 93 students representing the 13 age levels rated twice, 30 days apart. A correlation of .98 between the two testings indicates a high degree of stability over time. Internal reliability estimates of the seven subscales employing the Kuder-Richardson Formula 20 ranged between .88 and .94, the very good range. The manual also contains interrater reliability estimates for teachers across all age levels ranging between .96 and .98, indicating the high degree of agreement among teacher raters.

The manual of the LDES is complete and well written. It contains a description of the foundation of the LDES and the procedures for administration, scoring, and interpretation. There is also an additional manual, *The Learning Disability Intervention manual* that contains specific interventions and suggestions for teachers and other professionals working with learning-disabled students based on each of the 88 LDES items.

The LDES provides a standardized observation instrument for screening learning-disabled students to be employed by teachers, those most familiar with the student and the classroom environment. The norms are well defined, the validity and reliability estimates are within the acceptable range, the administration procedures are clear, and the scoring system is sound. Although the process for identifying a student as learning disabled should involve multiple sources of information, I recommend the LDES for teachers looking for a screening device for learning-disabled students.

REVIEWER'S REFERENCE

U.S. Office of Education. (1968). *First annual report of national Advisory Committee on Handicapped Children*. Washington, DC: U.S. Department of Health, Education, & Welfare.

[215]

Learning Efficiency Test-II (1992 Revision).

Purpose: "Yields information about a person's preferred modality for learning and provides insights about the impact of interference on memory storage and retrieval, and the kinds of metacognitive strategies used during learning."
Population: Ages 5–75.
Publication Dates: 1981–92.
Acronym: LET-II.
Scores, 15: Visual Ordered Recall (Immediate Recall, Short Term Recall, Long Term Recall) Visual Unordered Recall (Immediate Recall, Short Term Recall, Long Term Recall), Auditory Ordered Recall (Immediate Recall, Short Term Recall, Long Term Recall), Auditory Unordered Recall (Immediate Recall, Short Term Recall, Long Term Recall), Total Visual Memory, Total Auditory Memory, Global Memory.
Administration: Individual.
Price Data, 1992: $60 per test kit including manual ('92, 159 pages), stimulus cards, and 50 record forms; $25 per specimen set including manual and sample forms.
Time: (10–15) minutes.
Author: Raymond E. Webster.
Publisher: Academic Therapy Publications.
Cross References: For a review by Robert G. Harrington of an earlier form, see 9:601.

Review of the Learning Efficiency Test-II (1992 Revision) by ALICE J. CORKILL, Assistant Professor of Counseling and Educational Psychology, University of Nevada, Las Vegas, NV:

The Learning Efficiency Test-II (LET-II), a revision of the Learning Efficiency Test (LET; 9:601), is an individually administered, diagnostic test appropriate for use with individuals from age 5 through adult who do not have mental disabilities or are not hearing impaired or deaf. It is designed to determine how efficiently one processes and retains visual and auditory input. The test was designed to identify the information processing characteristics that impede learning. The deficits are identified as auditory, visual, retention of ordered information, retention of unordered information, and perhaps, number of items retained.

The test manual provides a brief review of the literature pertaining to the relationship between information processing ability (short-term memory deficits) and learning disabilities. A brief report of research using the LET suggests that under certain circumstances it does an adequate job of identifying individuals who would benefit from special education services. Compelling evidence of the relationship between the type of information processing tasks used on the LET-II and classroom performance in reading and math is in very short supply.

The LET-II measures ordered and nonordered retention of visual and auditory input in three time frames: (*a*) immediate, no interference; (*b*) short-term memory, brief delay with an interference task (counting by ones between specified numbers 10 places apart); and (*c*) long-term memory, another brief delay with a different interference task (repeating a 6–9 word sentence). The LET-II author claims the interference tasks used approximate typical classroom interference. In addition, the test is described as identifying the student's (*a*) learning style, (*b*) immediate memory capacity, (*c*) short term memory capacity, and (*d*) transfer ability between short and long term memory.

The learning style is apparently identified as either auditory or visual. Immediate and short term memory capacity are identified by how many stimulus items are recalled immediately or after a brief delay with minimal interference. Whether transfer from short to long term memory is being measured is debatable. The time required for each interference task, whether counting 10 places or repeating a 6–9-word sentence is less than 10 seconds for an adult and 10, perhaps 15, seconds for a kindergarten student. Whether a delay as short as 20 seconds (from presentation of stimulus materials to long term recall) actually measures transfer ability between short and long term memory is doubtful.

The input is in the form of nonrhyming consonant strings as short as two letters and as long as nine. The upper limit of nine letters was selected based on research that suggests the average adult can retain about seven items plus or minus two in short term memory. Thus, the nine-letter string should adequately assess the full range of short term memory.

Serial strings were constructed by randomly selecting from a list of 11 nonrhyming, phonetically nonconfusable consonants. Nonrhyming consonants were selected rather than digits to reduce the potential effect of guessing (i.e., only 9 digits as possible stimulus materials as opposed to 26 letters). Further, letters recalled out of order allegedly represent sequential memory problems rather than reflecting selection from a restricted response domain (i.e., digits). The stimulus materials used in the LET-II are the same as in the LET.

No new reliability studies have been conducted since the 1981 publication date of the LET. For the LET, 40 secondary students with learning and behavior problems were used in order to determine test-retest reliability. The interval between administrations ranged from 1 to 6 weeks with a mean test interval of 3.68 weeks. Test-retest reliability coefficients ranged from .81 to .97. An informal reliability study involving 55 students with learning disabilities reports test-retest reliability coefficients ranging from .71 to .86 with a median of .80. Given the time span between publication of the LET and the LET-II and that the test materials for the LET and the LET-II are identical, an in-depth study of reliability using larger samples of subjects at a variety of age levels could have been conducted.

The LET-II was standardized on a sample of 1,126 subjects between the ages of 5 years, 0 months and 85 years, 4 months (average *n* at each age group = 53.62; smallest group: 55–59 years, *n* = 25; largest group: 17–19 years, *n* = 113). Students, who were enrolled in public schools, were randomly selected for participation provided they were functioning at grade level or higher and had not been referred for special education services. Adults were recruited from community or social agencies. Adults were screened and were required to obtain a standard score higher than 85 on the Peabody Picture Vocabulary Test. Further, students with organically or physically based learning problems or with behavioral or emotional problems were excluded from the standardization sample. Adults with obvious physical or sensory impairments were also excluded. The sample was 53.73% female and reports 66.43% Caucasian and 33.57% African American. No differences in performance were found between males and females. As a result, one set of norms appropriate for both males and females is provided. The test manual author states that a "broad range of socio-economic backgrounds" (p. 29) were represented but no specific information is provided. Further, no information concerning where, geographically, the subjects came from is reported. The incomplete information made available suggests caution in using this instrument.

Directions for administering the test are clearly described. Directions for scoring are somewhat less clear but can be understood by closely examining a provided example. Scaled scores are obtained for immediate, short term, and long term recall on both the visual and auditory modality subtests and for ordered and unordered recall. This results in six scores for each modality. The scaled scores are based on the length of the longest string recalled correctly at immediate recall. One point is given for each correct letter recalled. Thus, scores can range from 0 to 9. Tables are provided for converting raw scores to standard scores. Although the test manual states the youngest examinee at age 5.0, conversion information for 5-year-old examinees is not provided. As was cited in the review of the LET (Harrington, 1985), the limited range of raw scores (0–9) results in potentially inadequate discriminating ability.

Standard scores have been added to the LET-II. These standard scores were deemed necessary in order for the LET-II to serve as a tool for qualifying a student for special education services. Standard scores are computed by summing total numbers of letters recalled correctly under immediate, short term, and long term recall—both ordered and unordered by modality. The summed raw scores are converted to standard scores using provided tables. These standard scores appear to have a mean of 100 and a standard deviation of 15 so they may be compared to intelligence test scores. The summed raw scores for visual (the Visual Modality Factor) and auditory (the Auditory Modality Factor) modality subtests are added together resulting in a Global Memory Factor. This sum is converted to a standard score using provided tables. Although no tables were available for subjects age 5.0 for scales scores, subjects age 5.0 are included in the standard score conversion tables. Standard scores may be converted to percentile ranks using provided tables. The standard error of measurement was reported as problematic for the LET but is less so for the LET-II. Whether this is due to greater precision in the conversion from raw to scaled or standard scores (which is possible, given the larger norming sample) or differences in how percentile ranks are acquired, for example, is not clear.

Assessment of content validity of the LET-II is not different from that of the LET given the use of identical stimulus materials. Construct validity was examined by comparing correlation matrices between groups of average students, students with emotional disabilities, students with learning disabilities, students with mental disabilities, and slow learners (it is unclear what qualifies someone as a "slow learner"). The manual author suggests that inconsistent patterns of intercorrelations on scores on both subtests indicate different information processing abilities between modalities. No substantiating research is cited. Further claims include that students with learning or mental disabilities and slow learners show impaired recall for each time frame and subtest when compared to students of average ability or students with emotional disabilities. Even a brief perusal of the means and standard deviations of these groups shows differences in recall ranging no greater than 2.22 items (this for auditory modality, ordered recall, short term memory). The average difference in recall scores at immediate recall was 1.04; at short term, 1.28; at long term 1.24; with an overall average difference in recall of 1.19 items. Although reported as statistically significant differences across the board, a question of practical significance arises. The differences as presented are not convincing.

Predictive validity was addressed via stepwise multiple regression using the same groups in the diagnostic validity study. The LET-II and the LET-II plus WISC-R (Wechsler Intelligence Scale for Children—Revised) scores were used to predict actual reading and math scores. For the LET-II alone, correlations with reading achievement for other than average students range from .282 to .558. When the WISC-R is included, the correlations range from .605 to .676. For mathematics achievement—LET-II only: .410 to .613; LET-II + WISC-R: .596 to .682. Correlations for average students although reported as significant ($p<.01$) are so low as to be inconsequential. Of the four groups of students with disabilities, the LET-II alone shows greatest potential predictive ability for students with mental disabilities. There is, however, no information about whether inclusion of the LET-II enhances the predictive ability of the WISC-R. It is likely that the contribution to prediction of the LET-II is insignificant when added to the WISC-R. The LET-II does appear to show some predictive ability, but just as with the LET, limited information about the sample precludes generalizability.

Evidence of construct validity was addressed via factor analysis using five age groupings from the norming sample. The factor analysis resulted in a two-factor solution. One factor was identified as Global Memory; the other as Modality. All 12 scores of the LET-II (6 scores for each modality) load at a satisfactory level on the Global Memory Factor for each age group. In addition, for each age group there are positive and negative loadings consistent with modality for each subtest. That is, on the Modality Factor, the factor loadings are consistently positive for one modality and negative for the other by appropriate modality subtest. The findings were consistent regardless of age level.

Guidelines for interpreting the test results are available in the manual. An individual's score can be interpreted in as many as four ways: (*a*) comparison to norm group, (*b*) examination of scaled scores for identifying specific modality strengths and weaknesses, (*c*) use of standard scores as a measure of cognitive functioning, and (*d*) determining the strategies used to retain the serial strings. With the exception of determining strategies, the interpretation relies on the actual test scores. In order to determine the strategies someone uses to retain the serial strings, the examiner is supposed to listen for whispered rehearsal, watch for lip movement, listen to how the stimulus materials are reported, and so on. These procedures may or may not actually aid in examining retention strategies. Suggested strategies for remediation are included. As with the LET, some of the suggestions are questionable.

SUMMARY. As it stands, it appears that little has changed since the publication of the LET. Although 12 years have passed between publication of the LET and the LET-II, insufficient reliability and validity information is available. The major strength of this instrument lies in ease of administration and time to administer (roughly 15 minutes). It could be used as a preliminary examination of information processing difficulties, but given the problems with reliability and validity it should be viewed as supplemental to other, more well-established instruments designed to identify individuals with learning or mental disabilities.

REVIEWER'S REFERENCE

Harrington, R. G. (1985). [Review of the Learning Efficiency Test]. In J. V. Mitchell, Jr. (Ed.), *The ninth mental measurements yearbook* (pp. 832-833). Lincoln, NE: Buros Institute of Mental Measurements.

Review of the Learning Efficiency Test-II (1992 Revision) by GREGORY SCHRAW, Assistant Professor of

Educational Psychology, University of Nebraska-Lincoln, Lincoln, NE:

The Learning Efficiency Test-II is a norm-referenced, individually administered test of visual and auditory memory appropriate for individuals from 5 to 75 years of age. The purpose of the test is to provide diagnostic information regarding memory capacity and possible impairment. This information may be used by diagnosticians to isolate problems with retention due to modality (visual vs. auditory), type of memory (sensory vs. short-term vs. long-term), or fidelity of recall (ordered vs. nonordered).

The test consists of two main batteries, visual and auditory memory, with each battery consisting of six subtests measuring ordered and unordered recall in immediate, short term, and long term memory. Each of the 12 total subtests may be compared directly using standard scores.

A concise yet thorough description of the LET-II's theoretical underpinnings is provided in the test manual. The test is based on the two-store model of memory that proposes information is processed sequentially in discrete memory systems which include sensory, short term, and long term stores. The effects of interference on memory and how interference is assessed using the LET-II are described as well.

The LET-II can be administered and scored in 10 to 20 minutes depending upon the memory skill shown by the examinee. In both the visual and auditory tests, individuals are provided random letter strings that are repeated immediately or after completing an interference task such as counting number strings or repeating unrelated sentences. Individuals begin with two-letter strings and proceed to longer strings until two consecutive errors are committed on the test of immediate memory. Only nonrhyming consonants are included in the LET-II (e.g., F, H, P, X) because rhyming consonants (e.g., B, C, G, T) are known to interfere with reading-disabled students' recall.

Scoring and interpretation are especially easy. Raw scores may be converted to standard scores or compared to developmental norms using conversion tables included in the Appendices. The manual also includes an extensive interpretation section that discusses a variety of diagnostic errors and provides several illustrative case studies. A special section on remediation strategies has been added to the revised version as well. The remediation section provides a number of helpful suggestions and references of special usefulness to practitioners.

Norms for the LET-II are based on a combined sample of roughly 1,150 examinees at all age levels. Unfortunately, neither test-retest or split-half reliabilities are reported for the LET-II. In contrast, test-retest reliabilities for the LET (1981) ranged from .71 to .86 (median of .80). A predictive validity study found the LET-II correlated with teacher ratings of achievement between .28 and .61 across several different groups of academically disadvantaged students. Correlations with observed reading ability approached .50 in most cases. A factor-analytic study of the LET-II's construct validity reported two factors: a *global memory* factor on which all 12 subtests loaded, and a *modality* factor which distinguished between the auditory and visual subtests.

The strengths of the LET-II include (*a*) easy administration and scoring, (*b*) a high degree of face validity, (*c*) statistically significant predictive validity, and (*d*) a clearly written and informative manual. There are no substantial weaknesses that limit its use.

As noted above, additional reliability data on the LET-II would be helpful, although there was no evidence from the LET that reliability was ever a concern for this instrument. Second, a parallel form of the instrument, which currently is not available, would be helpful for follow-up testing following a lengthy intervention.

Overall, the LET-II provides a quick, reliable way (on the basis of test-retest data) to assess memory capacity and specific problems with memory storage. The main advantage of the LET-II is that it enables the test giver to isolate retention problems with respect to modality and type of memory store. The ability to identify specific problems quickly and accurately should greatly facilitate remediation. Its use for testing memory storage among all age groups is recommended without reservation.

[216]

Learning Inventory of Kindergarten Experiences.

Purpose: Developed to screen for kindergarten readiness.
Population: Beginning kindergarten.
Publication Date: 1988.
Acronym: LIKE.
Scores: Item scores only in 4 areas: Motor, Language, Preacademic, Prereading.
Administration: Individual.
Price Data, 1990: $175 per complete kit including paper supplies (50 record sheets, 50 summary sheets, 5 grid summary sheets, pads of 50 circles, squares, and geometric shapes, strips and squares of colored paper, 10 letter cards, 6 numeral cards, 18 picture cards), test manual (42 pages), and instruction manual (14 pages); $50 per set of paper supplies; $25 per 50 record sheets; $20 per set of manuals.
Time: Administration time not reported.
Authors: Nathaniel O. Owings, Paulette E. Mills, and Cynthia Best O'Dell.
Publisher: University of Washington Press.

Review of the Learning Inventory of Kindergarten Experiences by DOUGLAS A. PENFIELD, Professor of Education, Graduate School of Education, Rutgers University, New Brunswick, NJ:

The Learning Inventory of Kindergarten Experiences (LIKE) is a norm-referenced screening procedure designed to measure the skill development of kindergarten children. The authors suggest that it can also be used to "aid the teacher in curriculum planning" and "to detect potential handicapping conditions" (manual, p. 7). The LIKE is composed of a collection of items believed to be correlated with future academic success. Some items were taken from existing kindergarten screening procedures and then modified to meet current test needs. The authors have acknowledged that a number of items were selected from the Madison Public Schools Kindergarten Screening tool and the Miller-Yoder Language Comprehension Test (Clinical Edition).

The LIKE is broken into five subtests defined as (*a*) gross motor, (*b*) fine motor, (*c*) conceptual, (*d*) comprehension, and (*e*) academic/production. Test items are developmentally sequenced within each subtest. Assuming a small number of practice trials, new examiners should have little trouble in administering the instrument. The authors suggest the test can be administered in 30 minutes or less. This time estimate is heavily dependent upon the skill of the examiner in presenting the questions and the receptiveness of the child.

Materials needed to carry out the assessment are many and varied (see LIKE description above). They are packaged in ziploc type bags and assembled with other test information in a handy carrying case. Directions for administering the LIKE are very explicit and should be followed precisely. An Instruction Manual, consisting of the test questions, procedures to be followed when administering the questions, and scoring methodology, provides a detailed outline of the testing process. Other pertinent information regarding the LIKE can be found in the Interpretation Manual.

When scoring, one point is awarded for each question answered correctly. In most instances, there is more than one question associated with a test item. Points are summed within an item and then across items to produce a subtest total score. The expected total subtest score of a child "at or below the 30th percentile" and "at or above the 50th percentile" (manual, p. 15) is presented for comparative purposes. Subtest percentile rank norms are displayed in tabular form for the variables age (5, $5^1/_2$, 6), school type (rural, urban), and sex (female, male). These tables tend to be somewhat difficult to comprehend, especially the ones displaying the percentile distributions for school type and sex by subtest, and they should definitely be reformatted. Simple examples in the text illustrating the use of the norms tables would also be beneficial. Please note that there is a minor error in the Interpretation Manual which should be readily apparent to an examiner. On page 15, one of the scoring categories is labeled "Scores at or below the 50th percentile" instead of "Scores at or above the 50th percentile." A display grid and screening record sheet allow the examiner to record the response of each child to each item on the test. This consolidation of test information should aid teachers when setting objectives for the purpose of remediation.

A K-R 20 reliability coefficient, computed on a sample of 364 children, was reported to be .92. The sample was composed of incoming kindergarten children drawn from both an urban and rural setting. The authors address the question of validity by discussing content, predictive, and concurrent validity. Content validity was assessed by comparing the structure of the test items with the abilities inherent in a normal kindergarten population. Expected age norms for each test item as well as an associated reference are presented. With respect to predictive and concurrent validity, there is no evidence of either at the present time. An item analysis was also performed on the test items. Question difficulty levels and biserial correlations between the question score and the total test score are reported for the sample of 364 entering kindergarten children. The authors regard biserial correlations above .2 as indicative of a useful question. Only a small number of questions fell below this benchmark.

To some, the scope of the LIKE may appear somewhat limited as a preacademic assessment tool. Regardless, the authors have attempted to focus their attention on those skills suggestive of future academic growth. Given the attention span of a child and the time allotted for testing, the LIKE represents a good cross-section of test items useful in screening kindergarten children.

Review of the Learning Inventory of Kindergarten Experiences by DONNA WITTMER, Assistant Professor of Education, University of Colorado at Denver, Denver, CO:

The Learning Inventory of Kindergarten Experiences (LIKE) covers four primary areas including Motor, Language, Preacademic, and Prereading resulting in five subtest areas: gross motor, fine motor, conceptual–aural/oral, comprehension, and academic/production. These are typical areas covered for a kindergarten readiness test. Items were selected from other procedures that have proven to be predictive of later academic skills. Process skills such as classification, conservation, and seriation are included. However, areas such as eye-hand coordination, visual-perceptual skills, recognizing rhythm patterns, visual matching skills, tactile skills, motor behavior memory skills, verbal memory skills, attending/task-order skills, and social interaction skills are not covered. Broad areas such as sensory integration, discrimination, and attending/responding are not included. This assessment taps academic knowledge acquired, such as knowledge of names of colors and shapes, alphabet recognition, and number recognition rather than focusing primarily on skills needed to learn academics and function well in school (e.g., matching, visual-perceptual, and motor behavior memory skills). Thus, this assessment seems less culturally sensitive than one would hope to find in a kindergarten readiness assessment.

The LIKE does not assess a critical area that has been found to be highly related to school success, social skills. The authors state that social skills "cannot be adequately evaluated in the manner presented here" (manual, p. 8). Because this is an assessment that is *not* designed to be given over time, the authors did not think that social skills could be assessed adequately given that the child is going to be tested only once. However, a parent questionnaire on social skills would have at least tapped into this vital area. This assessment also does not include any type of parent questionnaire or opportunity for parents to validate the findings.

The authors state they do not condone the use of the LIKE to "screen" children out of kindergarten. One large school district has used the LIKE to rule on whether children who are underage for kindergarten should be allowed to enter. In order to enter kindergarten, the underage children must be above the 50th percentile. The basic purpose of the test, then, is "(1) to identify certain key preacademic abilities in beginning kindergarten children; (2) to aid the teacher in curriculum planning . . . and (3) to detect potential handicapping conditions in beginning kindergarten children" (p. 7). The areas of children's needs and strengths are being identified so that teachers and parents can plan a more appropriate program for the kindergarten children. Given the stated purposes of the assessment, the authors would have ensured ecological validity if the assessment had been designed to be given over time, as a program assessment. Designed as it is, it invites a misuse of the test by professionals who would "screen" children out of kindergarten by saying they are not "ready" based on a one-time kindergarten "readiness" test.

This assessment is designed for teachers to administer together with help from a speech/language pathologist. The assessment is easy to administer with few materials required. The materials needed are included in a small blue case that is very easy to carry. The test is designed to be given to children individually. Professionals must exercise care in the administration of this test by making sure that children are familiar with the person administering the test and that testing conditions are as comfortable and familiar as possible. Three types of responses are recorded: right answer, wrong answer, and don't know/no response.

The statistical information on the test is scanty. Although the publication date is 1988, the normed sample was obtained in 1977. The LIKE was given to 364 children who were just entering kindergarten in the fall of 1977. Most of the children in the normed sample (285) were enrolled in the Bozeman School system, an urban setting, whereas 79 children were enrolled in the neighboring rural Gallatin Valley Schools. The normed sample, then, is not representative of race and socioeconomic groups in the United States. The children ranged in age from 5 to 6 years. Percentile ranks were determined for raw scores based on this population. Validity and reliability issues are not addressed well. Concurrent and predictive validity studies have not been completed.

In summary, I would not recommend this kindergarten "readiness" test for several reasons. The standardization sample is not adequate and the items tap academic knowledge more than processing skills. Also, although the authors advocate using the test as a curriculum-based assessment with a major purpose being to design a curriculum program for the child, testing is not done over time, social skills are not assessed, and parent input is nil.

[217]

Learning Style Profile.

Purpose: Designed to evaluate student learning style as the basis for student advisement and placement, instructional strategy, and the evaluation of learning.
Population: Grades 6–12.
Publication Dates: 1986–90.
Acronym: LSP.
Scores, 23: Cognitive Skills (Analytic, Spatial, Discrimination, Categorizing, Sequential Processing, Memory), Perceptual Responses (Visual, Auditory, Emotive), Persistence Orientation, Verbal Risk Orientation, Study and Instructional Preferences (Verbal-Spatial, Manipulative, Study Time [Early Morning, Late Morning, Afternoon, Evening], Grouping, Posture, Mobility, Sound, Lighting, Temperature).
Administration: Group.
Price Data: Price information available from publisher for materials including Technical Manual ('88, 105 pages).
Time: (50–60) minutes.
Authors: James W. Keefe (test, Handbook II), John S. Monk (test), Charles A. Letteri (test, Handbook I), Marlin Languis (test), Rita Dunn (test), John M. Jenkins (Handbook I), and Patricia Rosenlund (Handbook I).
Publisher: National Association of Secondary School Principals.
Cross References: See T4:1433 (1 reference).

TEST REFERENCES

1. Vaidya, S. R. (1994). Diagnostic assessments and consideration of learning styles and lows of control characteristics—How do they impact teaching and learning? *College Student Journal*, *27*, 159-162.

Review of the Learning Style Profile by SONYA BLIXT, Professor of Evaluation and Measurement, and JAMES A. JONES, Doctoral Candidate and Graduate Assistant in Evaluation and Measurement, Kent State University, Kent, OH:

According to the examiner's manual, the Learning Style Profile (LSP) is designed to be given within a 50-minute period, but is not timed. Part of the test is printed upside down on the backs of the pages. After examinees complete 108 of the 126 multiple-choice items, they must turn the test booklet upside down to finish the remaining items. These last items differ from the previous ones in that a drawing is shown as an initial stimulus, then each subsequent page contains a drawing for which the examinee needs to determine if it is a match with the initial drawing without turning back. Printing this portion of the LSP upside down on the backs of pages was done presumedly to conserve paper, but this produces an unnecessary distraction for examinees.

Scoring the LSP can be accomplished by hand or computer. Although not difficult to hand score, it would be quite time consuming because there are several scales and for some items, responses are given different weights. The raw score is converted to a *T*-score, and then a corresponding "X" is placed in one of three categories: one standard deviation or more below the mean, within plus or minus one standard deviation of the mean, and one standard deviation or more above the mean. The LSP uses varying labels for these categories depending on the subscales (weak, average, and strong; low, average, and high; and high, neutral, and high for the bi-polar subscales). In addition to subscale scores, a consistency score is also computed for the preferential questions to give an indication of the potential validity of the profile for the student. When hand scored, the norms provided by the examiner's manual are not broken down by sex, race, or grade. If computer scored, separate norms are used, but the examiner's manual indicates differences in scores generated by the two methods are not notable.

The technical manual appears well documented, but had some interesting omissions. The final version of the LSP was normed on a sample of 4,871 students enrolled in grades 6 through 12 from approximately 40 schools randomly selected by zip code. Not explained, however, was how the students were selected once the schools were identified. In comparing the numbers of students and schools, clearly not all the students from grades 6 through 12 were used from a given zip code, but no information was provided as to what additional selection procedures were used.

The coefficient alphas, test-retest (10-day), and test-retest (30-day) reliability coefficients as well as tables providing descriptive statistics for the items comprising the subscale are provided in the technical manual for most of the items. Brief summaries of some attempts to establish validity are also given. More information regarding the standard error of measurement and potential group differences between the scores for sex, race, or grade levels would be useful, however.

The internal consistency coefficients of the subscales ranged from .47 to .76 with an average coefficient alpha of .61. The examiner's manual attributed this low average reliability to the small number of items that comprise each subscale. The range of items was from 2 to 20 with 5 items comprising the typical scale. Tripling the length of the subscales from 5 items to 15 would produce a theoretical increase in the internal consistency reliability from .61 to .82 based on the Spearman-Brown Prophecy formula. The three subscales of the LSP with 20 items, however, had an average coefficient alpha of only .49, so number of items alone may not be the reason for the LSP's low internal consistency. The test-retest coefficient for a 10-day time period ranged from .36 to .82 with an average coefficient of .62. For the 30-day time period, the range increased to .21 to .76 with an average coefficient of .47.

The examiner's and technical manuals discussed the content, concurrent, and construct validity of the LSP. The content validity of the LSP was judged by a task force assembled by the test developers. The concurrent validity was assessed by correlating the subscales of the LSP with other tests that purport to measure a similar construct. For the majority of the subscales this meant correlating the LSP with the Learning Style Inventory (T4:1432), which also suffers from low reliability and questionable validity. Overall, the correlations between the subscales ranged from a low of .15 to a high of .71 with a mean of correlation of .51. The construct validity was assessed by examination of the first and second order factor structure of the LSP and did not incorporate any criteria external to the test that would enhance credibility.

The LSP handbooks describe how the test items assess the various areas and give some suggestions for incorporating a given subscale area into curriculum. The assumption communicated in these manuals is that the LSP will identify the strengths and weaknesses in learning style of an individual or classroom. The teacher could then conceivably use the suggestions in the handbooks to enhance the effectiveness of classroom instruction. Given the low reliabilities and questionable validity of many of the subscales of the LSP, this assumption seems unwarranted.

The LSP manuals describe the test as a first-level diagnostic tool that can be used to modify curriculum. The instability of the subscale scores would make this practice inadvisable. Although the manual includes warnings against overinterpretation of the subscale scores, the inclusion of the handbooks provides additional temptation. Even if the LSP were used only as a screening device, the manuals are not clear as to what follow-up testing would be appropriate. In summary, the addition of the LSP to the already full testing agenda of the typical school is not justified.

Review of the Learning Style Profile by PHILIP NAGY, Associate Professor of Measurement, Evaluation, and Computer Applications, The Ontario Institute for Studies in Education, Toronto, Ontario, Canada:

The Learning Style Profile (LSP) attempts to use research on cognitive style and learning style, mostly from the period 1950–1975, to develop a group-administered screening test. It also incorporates scales designed to assess study preferences such as for time of day, lighting, and temperature. The test booklet, examiner's and technical manuals, and two handbooks on developing skills and accommodating preferences represent a massive undertaking, for which the authors should be commended. However, the product is not commensurate with the effort.

As the authors point out, psychologists lost interest in this field of cognitive styles just as practitioners took it up. There were reasons for this loss of interest, despite much conceptual (e.g., Messick, 1970) and empirical (e.g., Messick & French, 1975) effort. The root difficulty 20 years ago was a failure to assess cognitive style accurately enough to legitimate individual rather than group average scores. Attempts to find aptitude-treatment type interactions met with little success. This lack of evidence of educational import was attributed by some to these reliability problems, whereas others expressed more fundamental doubts about the underlying theory. Meanwhile, and since then, isolated reports of remarkable success with individuals fueled hope for useful clinical applications at the classroom level—a hope that downplayed the fact that the clinical successes were often with learning-disabled and in some cases brain-damaged populations. The problems in moving from laboratory to classroom have not been overcome in the Learning Style Profile.

The test booklet contains 126 items. Although not labelled as preliminary, the LSP bears the marks of a work-in-progress: a few errors and inconsistencies, some replacement pages, and one scale conceded to be still experimental. This is not a criticism. The profile is untimed, but aimed at requiring one class period. Most of the items (there are a few unscored distractors and experimental items) are divided, by hand or using machine-scorable answer sheets, into 23 subscale scores: 6 skills, 3 perceptual responses (Visual, Auditory, Emotive), 2 orientations (Persistence and Verbal Risk), and 12 preferences. There is also a consistency score for the preferences. My comments are mostly directed at the skills, perceptual responses, and orientations, rather than the preferences. Little can be said about preference questions that ask, for example, what time of day a student prefers to study, except to wonder if such information requires the expense of a standardized test.

Raw subscale scores are converted to *T*-scores (mean 50, standard deviation 10) and plotted on a one-page profile sheet. Hand scoring uses a single norming table, but computer scoring "simultaneously adjusts for sex, grade and race" (examiners manual, p. 10). Some detail on how this is done, and how much difference it makes, would improve the manual; many cells in the sex-by-grade-by-race breakdown are tiny.

There are strong points to this package. These must be stated before further criticisms.

First, the profile and its subtests are rooted in the literature and based on a theoretical framework. There is an information-processing framework for the entire package, and a literature outlining the history of each subtest. The manual provides good summaries of this literature.

Second, the development steps are outlined, and reliability and validity evidence clearly presented. Most subscales have internal consistency and test-retest evidence, and many have construct validity evidence. For example, the Analytic Skill subscale has been validated against its parent Group Embedded Figures Test.

Third, the authors present strong factor analytic evidence for the integrity and independence of the subscales. Analysis of all but two subscale scores supported four large groups, cognitive, study preference, perceptual response, and instructional preference, with only a little overlap. This evidence is probably as clear as can be expected of such elusive constructs (compare, for example, Messick & French, 1975).

Fourth, the authors offer sound advice on cautious interpretation of the profile data. Users are cautioned, and prompted by the profile form, to focus on scores more than one standard deviation from the mean; these individuals "are more likely to be governed by the element of style" (examiner's manual, p. 14).

Fifth, we are cautioned that this is only a screening device, and references are given to individual diagnostic instruments for most subscales. As well, the authors admit that some scales may be "contextually sensitive" (examiner's manual, p. 6). One quibble is that much of this information is buried in a long technical manual, and does not appear in the much simplified examiner's manual.

Sixth, the authors discuss the augmentational versus adaptational issue, that is, whether to retrain the child to cope with the existing learning environment, or to change the learning environment rather than train the child. The compromise position, practiced in the two accompanying handbooks, is that "Augmentation is more suited to cognitive style 'growth'; adaptation to affective and physiological style 'matching'" (technical manual, p. 7).

In short, this package is a major contribution to research in a difficult area. This does not make it, unfortunately, a viable standardized test, or even a useful screening instrument. What are the problems?

First, the norming is unsystematic. The authors used (in round numbers) a probability sample of 4,900 for all but one scale, but apparently added another sample of convenience (initial purchasers) of about 3,800. In addition, undescribed samples were used for other aspects of the validation: about 3,900 to validate a replacement scale, 483 for test-retest studies, and three samples of 100 for different validity studies. In fairness, data are provided to investigate how important grade, sex, and race differences might be, and the authors offer to supply a data tape for further investigation. However, better sampling and clearer definitions (e.g., geographical regions) would have helped. Failing that, a comparison between the probability sample and the large sample of convenience might have served to set this issue aside.

Second, there are reliability problems, both for internal consistency and stability over time. The Analytic Skill subscale has a Cronbach's alpha of .56, the median for the non-preference subscales. This is as good as figures from 20 years ago, but it still gives unacceptably wide confidence intervals for individual scores. For example, an observed score of 3, on a 5-item test, has a 95% confidence interval between 1 and 5 (.63 and 5.37 before rounding), from a weak to a strong rating. Even as a screening device, this is of dubious value. And this problem does not disappear for even the longest (20-item) subtests. In addition, despite claims of "relatively stable characteristics," 30-day test-retest reliabilities are largely below .50. These figures are somewhat attenuated by low internal consistency, but still raise the question of whether these variables, even accurately measured, are stable enough over time to be of practical value (see Gardner, 1973).

Third, there are problems with the underlying rationale. The profile uses an information-processing model that includes six phases and six operations. In conjunction with these operations, several cognitive style "controls" are posited: analyzing, comparing, focusing, scanning, searching, sharpening, narrowing, and categorizing. The model is global enough to be untestable, and thus speculative at best. The authors have been thorough in furnishing references on the antecedents of the subscales, but provide none supporting the relationship between cognitive controls and operations. I infer the project team hopes that use of the profile will provide data to support its theoretical foundation. This is laudable for a research program, but not for a commercially available test.

Fourth, there are difficulties linking the definitions of some subscales with their content. For example, the Categorization subscale tests how narrow or wide people perceive categories to be. The authors connect the narrow view with "intrinsic (denotative)" (technical manual, p. 29) properties, and the broad with "imputed (connotative)" (p. 29) meanings. This may be so, but the theory then goes on to link the narrow view with "greater *skill*" (p. 29, emphasis added) in categorization. This is not supportable. More on this test will be mentioned in connection with the next problem.

Fifth, there are difficulties with some items and instructions. In the Categorization subscale, knowledge of the world impinges on validity. For example, Questions 17 and 18 give the length of the average whale, and then ask for guesses on the length of the longest whale and shortest whale respectively. Choices nearest the mean are scored best, but the biologically correct answers are far more extreme than these "best" answers. Similar problems exist for most of the items in this subscale.

As another example, the Memory skill items present a moderately complex cartoon drawing of a robot (later repeated with a bird and turtle) on a single page with the instructions "Study the picture below carefully. You will need to remember what it looks like. You will not be able to turn back to see it again" (test, p. 21). The next page shows a similar (possibly identical) picture, and asks if it is the same or different. The instructions are repeated on this second page, and another robot appears, with the same questions, on the third (and fourth, fifth, and sixth) page. The problem is that there is no opportunity to see two figures side by side, to learn the level of detail required for the observation. Nor is there any feedback for respondents to see if they are on the right wavelength. Thus, it becomes a stressful guessing game. Coupled with the two-choice nature of the response, this subscale is highly suspect.

Finally, the most serious problem with this profile is the lack of evidence that the subscales have any relationship to learning or instruction. For example, in the Analytic skills subscale, subjects have to recognize the presence or absence of moderately complex shapes in even more complex visual patterns. The handbook exercises link this skill to other analytic skills, such as the ability to write specific directions, produce a flowchart, or follow steps in a "scientific method." In the light of what is now known about the difficulty of skill transfer (Perkins & Salomon, 1989; Brown, Collins, & Duguid, 1989) even between cognitive contexts, this rationale has little currency.

In summary, this profile is an ambitious report on an intriguing research project. The documentation has established that the skills assessed by the subscales are unequivocably independent of each other. It has added to the validity evidence for many constructs from the cognitive style research of the 1950–1975 period. It has avoided the problem of treating people near the mean of a scale as if they were at the extreme, and has offered appropriate cautions about the difference between a screening device and a clinical instrument. And it has dealt with the problem of changing the child versus changing the environment. However, it has not improved the reliability difficulties of 20 years ago, and thus the scores of individuals remain suspect. There are also unsupportable inferential leaps from theory to subscale design, and a lack of evidence for the educational benefits of using this instrument. As the authors themselves state many times in the manual "no concurrent or predictive validity studies have yet been conducted" (technical manual pp. 21, 25, 30, etc.). As a research enterprise, I recommend this project; as a diagnostic kit for applied classroom use, I cannot.

REVIEWER'S REFERENCES

Messick, S. (1970). The criterion problem in the evaluation of instruction: Assessing possible, not just probable, intended outcomes. In M. C. Wittrock & D. E. Wiley (Eds.), *The evaluation of instruction: Issues and problems* (pp. 183-202). New York: Holt, Rinehart & Winston, Inc.

Gardner, R. W. (1973). Reliability of group-test scores for cognitive controls and intellectual abilities over a one-year period. *Perceptual and Motor Skills, 36*, 753-754.

Messick, S., & French, J. W. (1975). Dimensions of cognitive closure. *Multivariate Behavioral Research, 10*, 3-16.

Brown, J. S., Collins, A., & Duguid, P. (1989). Situated cognition and the culture of learning. *Educational Researcher, 18*(1), 32-42.

Perkins, D. N., & Salomon, G. (1989). Are cognitive skills context-bound? *Educational Researcher, 18*(1), 16-25.

[218]

Learning Styles Inventory [Piney Mountain Press, Inc.].

Purpose: Designed to identify learning needs of students.
Population: Students and adults.
Publication Date: 1988.
Scores: 9 subtopics in 2 areas: Learning (Auditory Language, Visual Language, Auditory Numerical, Visual Numerical, Auditory-Visual-Kinesthetic), Working (Group Learner, Individual Learner, Oral Expressive, Written Expressive).
Administration: Individual or group.
Price Data, 1990: $395 per complete kit including instructor guide, software, video, and 100 response sheets; $1,095 per Learning Styles Inventory Media Kit with Chatsworth Card Reader.
Time: [11] minutes.
Author: Piney Mountain Press, Inc.
Publisher: Piney Mountain Press, Inc.

Review of the Learning Styles Inventory [Piney Mountain Press, Inc.] by KEVIN D. CREHAN, Associate Professor of Educational Psychology, University of Nevada, Las Vegas, Las Vegas, NV:

DESCRIPTION. The instrument under review is an audio-visual/computer formatted adaptation of an unpublished learning styles inventory (LSI) developed by Babich, Burdine, Albright, and Randol at the Center for Innovative Teaching Experiences, Wichita Public Schools (Babich & Randol, 1976). The original instrument was derived from Hill's (1971; 1976) model and instrument, the Cognitive Style Interest Inventory. This is a 27-scale inventory conceptualizing learning styles as based on instructional preference (Curry, 1987). The authors selected 9 of Hill's 27 constructs, grouped into three areas, for inclusion in their instrument:

I. LEARNING-INFORMATION GATHERING/RECEIVING.

1. *Auditory Language*: The way a student hears words; processing spoken language.

2. *Visual Language*: The way a student sees words; processing written language.

3. *Auditory Numerical*: The way a student hears numbers; processing spoken numerical values.

4. *Visual Numerical*: The way a student sees numbers; processing written numerical values.

5. *Auditory-Visual-Kinesthetic*: The way a student learns by doing or involvement. Emphasizing the experiencing or manipulative learning style which is almost always accompanied by either auditory stimuli, visual stimuli, or a combination of both.

II. WORKING-SOCIAL WORK CONDITIONS.

1. *Group Learner*: A student who likes to work with at least one other person when there is important work to be done.

2. *Individual Learner*. A student who works and thinks best alone. This student is usually a self-starter and frequently finds working with other students distracting.

III. EXPRESSIVENESS PREFERENCE.

1. *Oral Expressive*: A student who prefers to say what he knows. Usually answers or explanations are better given orally; however, some students may indicate this preference simply because they are too lazy to write things down.

2. *Written Expressive*: A student who prefers to write down answers or explanations. Students who exhibit a reflective cognitive learning style may prefer this method.

Each of the nine subscales consists of five items that are answered on a 4-point scale from *most like me* to *least like me*.

DEVELOPMENT. The development of the LSI is described by Babich and Randol (1976). A two-phase process wherein a 106-item pool of 10 to 14 items per subscale was culled to yield the 45-item final version of the LSI is described. In phase one, the 106-item pool was piloted with a small sample of junior high school students (N = 166). Based on item-subscale score correlations 5 to 8 items per subscale were retained for further study. In phase two, the retained items were randomly assigned to one or more of three test forms and administered to a total sample of 2,229 junior high school students with samples of 625, 1,181, and 423 responding to each form.

The final version of the LSI was based on a selection of the subscale item set from the form with the highest split-half reliability for seven of the subscales and on item-total correlations for the remaining two subscales (Auditory Numerical and Expressive Oral). Median odd-even split-half reliabilities, for the seven subscales selected on that basis, range from .64 to .76. Reliabilities for the two subscales selected on the basis of item-total correlation were not estimated but, based on the data provided, are probably in the same range. No interscale correlations are reported.

Other than means and standard deviations of the subsamples, no normative data are reported. This is surprising because, in the absence of normative data, the manual authors provide score classifications of major, minor, and negligible for each of the nine learning style subscales and, additionally, provide prescriptive interpretations.

EVALUATION. Literature searches and personal communications with the publisher and the first author of the developmental study yielded no subsequent sources of evidence related to the instrument's reliability or validity. A concluding comment in the report on the LSI's construction (Babich & Randol, 1976) suggests that "The instrument reported at the present state of developing is in its infancy." It seems that this statement still obtains. Other than the appearance of content relevant items and ease of administration, there is little to recommend the usefulness of the LSI.

RECOMMENDATION. A potentially useful source of information on alternate measures is Curry's (1987) review of 21 instruments designed to measure cognitive or learning style.

REVIEWER'S REFERENCES

Hill, J. S., & Nunney, D. N. (1971). *Personalized education programs utilizing cognitive style mapping.* Bloomfield Hills, MI: Oakland Community College.

Babich, A. M., & Randol, P. (1976). *Learning Styles Inventory reliability report.* Wichita, KS: Wichita Public Schools.

Hill, J. S. (1976). Cognitive Style Interest Inventory. Bloomfield Hills, MI: Oakland Community College.

Curry, L. (1987). *Integrating concepts of cognitive or learning style: A review with attention to psychometric standards.* Ontario, Canada: Canadian College of Health Service Executives.

Review of the Learning Styles Inventory [Piney Mountain Press, Inc.] by MARK H. FUGATE, Assistant Professor of School Psychology, Alfred University, Alfred, NY:

The Learning Styles Inventory (LSI) was designed to provide teachers with information that can be used to understand and accommodate the "unique learning styles" of their students. The LSI is a self-report measure that can be administered through a variety of methods. Individual or group administrations of the LSI can be conducted using paper and pencil, a filmstrip, an audio cassette, a video tape, or an IBM/Apple computer. The publisher claims the various audio-visual administration methods facilitate administration and scoring, eliminate problems that may arise from use of a teacher-generated script, may be more appealing to students who demonstrate a variety of learning styles, and may be more motivating to students.

Scores obtained from the LSI provide information about individual student learning style preferences across three main areas: Learning, Working, and Reporting. Within these main areas there are nine subtopics. In the area of Learning preferences for Auditory Language, Visual Language, Auditory Numerical, Visual Numerical, and Auditory-Visual-Kinesthetic styles of learning are explored. In the Working area individual preference for group or individual learning experiences are examined. Finally, student preferences for Oral or Written Expression are measured in the Reporting area.

The LSI contains five questions for each of the nine subtopics for a total of 45 questions. Students are required to rate their comparability to each statement using a 4-point Likert scale. Responses are used to determine students' major, minor, or negligible learning style preferences across the nine subtopics.

The primary manual for administration, scoring, and interpretation of the LSI is the Learning Styles Inventory Media Kit. This manual provides a brief overview of the LSI, directions for administration of the LSI for all of the various media venues, and guidelines for basic interpretation of LSI results. Generally, the material presented in this manual is well organized and clearly presented. Similarly, the directions for administration and scoring are easy to follow. However, the guidelines for interpretation and individual decision making are rather basic. The usefulness of the LSI Media Kit would be enhanced if additional information were provided regarding the practical utility of test results.

The most glaring weakness of the LSI Media Kit is the failure of the publisher to provide any technical information regarding the reliability or validity of the LSI. It is possible that such information does not exist. Some technical information surrounding the development of the LSI is available from the publisher in the Learning Styles Inventory Reliability Report. According to the LSI Reliability Report the current version of the LSI was developed in the mid 1970s from three alternate forms which were administered to 2,229 seventh, eighth, and ninth grade students enrolled in a single school district. The "reliability" data provided in this manual primarily consist of correlation coefficients between the individual test items and the nine subtopic "constructs." The closest this information may come to a report of reliability is that it provides a sense of the internal consistency within each of the subtopic areas. Data pertaining to the consistency of LSI scores and profiles are missing. Although test-retest correlation coefficients might be preferable, it may be at least possible to provide alternate forms reliability data. Given the potential problems related to obtaining consistent self-report data from children and adolescents, it would seem imperative that this type of reliability information be reported.

Beyond the lack of reliability data there are several other areas in which the information provided in the

LSI Reliability Report is found wanting. There is no information on how cutoff scores for major, minor, or negligible learning preferences were determined. Although mean scores and standard deviations are provided for each item and subtopic area, it is not readily apparent how this information was used to determine preference ratings. The appropriate ages or grades of students covered by the LSI are not provided. The grade range of the norming sample was quite restricted, yet there is no caution the LSI is most appropriate for junior high students, or for any other group of students.

There is also an absence of information regarding the validity of the LSI. Inasmuch as self-report instruments such as the LSI do not provide a direct measure of ability, evidence of concurrent criterion-related validity is vital. It is necessary the publisher demonstrate, for instance, that the self-report of auditory learning preferences is related to a measured strength in this area. It is also important that a demonstration of the treatment utility of the LSI be presented. Both LSI manuals claim this instrument was developed to determine the learning style preferences of students, and that once these preferences are determined, this information can be used to more effectively teach these students. No evidence is presented to suggest that when individual student instruction is adjusted to reflect learning style preferences, as measured by the LSI, that positive changes in academic achievement occur. The LSI was first developed almost 18 years ago. There has been ample time to study the educational utility of this instrument.

The LSI was designed to determine the learning style preferences of individual students, so that teachers could use this information to help improve student educational outcomes. Toward this end the LSI seems to be generally well designed and may ultimately have some value. However, the norming sample is dated and unrepresentative. Also, given the absence of data regarding the reliability and validity of this instrument it is difficult to endorse the use of this measure.

[219]

Leatherman Leadership Questionnaire [Revised].

Purpose: "To aid in selecting leaders, providing specific feedback to participants on their leadership knowledge for career counseling, conducting accurate needs analysis, and screening for assessment centers or giving pre/post assessment feedback."
Population: Managers, supervisors, team leaders, and potential leaders.
Publication Dates: 1987–92.
Acronym: LLQ.
Scores, 28: Assigning Work, Career Counseling, Coaching Employees, Oral Communication, Managing Change, Handling Employee Complaints, Dealing with Employee Conflicts, Counseling Employees, Helping an Employee Make Decisions, Delegating, Taking Disciplinary Action, Handling Emotional Situations, Setting Goals/Planning with Employees, Handling Employee Grievances, Conducting Employee Meetings, Giving Positive Feedback, Negotiating, Conducting Performance Appraisals, Establishing Performance Standards, Persuading/Influencing Employees, Making Presentations to Employees, Problem Solving with Employees, Conducting Selection Interviews, Team Building, Conducting Termination Interviews, Helping an Employee Manage Time, One-on-One Training, Total.
Subtests, 2: May be administered in separate parts.
Administration: Group.
Price Data, 1992: $1,500 per administrator's kit including administrator's manual ('92, 52 pages), overhead transparencies, 10 sets of reusable questionnaire booklets, and 10 sets of answer sheets with scoring service; $65 per additional answer sheets and scoring service including development manual ('92, 347 pages); $55 per additional answer sheets and scoring service; $20 per additional sets of questionnaire booklets; $1 each for "confidential service" (participant's scoring sheet sealed in an envelope), $100 per extra administrator's kit; testing materials and service will be provided without charge for qualified, not-for-profit college or university research.
Time: (300–325) minutes for battery; (150–165) minutes per part.
Comments: Complete test administered in 2 parts; machine scored by publisher.
Author: Richard W. Leatherman.
Publisher: International Training Consultants, Inc.
Cross References: For reviews by Walter Katkovsky and William D. Porterfield of an earlier edition, see 11:205.

Review of the Leatherman Leadership Questionnaire [Revised] by JEFFREY S. RAIN, Assistant Professor and Chairman, Industrial/Organizational Psychology Program, Florida Tech, Melbourne, FL:

The Leatherman Leadership Questionnaire [Revised] (LLQ) was designed to be a knowledge-based paper-and-pencil alternative to the assessment center that could be used to select leaders, define leadership training needs, and provide career counseling information. Although the LLQ has been revised and improved since its 1990 review, several serious limitations remain, most notably in the area of concurrent validity. Reporting that over 500 organizations have purchased the LLQ (Administrative Guide, p. 15) and the acknowledgment of a 5,000-person normative base by a previous reviewer would suggest that data are available to address these issues.

Considerable effort was expended in developing the tasks and behaviors that form the LLQ items. A panel of industry experts and an independent sample of seven sites ($N = 229$) rated the importance of each task. The behaviors also were rated by the industry panel. What remains unclear is whether the behaviors within each task are stable and, in fact, relate to the task they are to describe. Factor analysis would be instructive in demonstrating the singular structure of the LLQ and the link between behavior and task. Reliability of the behavioral items within each task could also be presented. Both the factor analysis and task reliability would be helpful in determining the ability of the LLQ to be used for training and developmental feedback of specific leadership knowledge and skills. Factor analysis may begin to answer questions raised by Katkovsky (1992) regarding the LLQ's construct validity. Correlations with other measures could be used to demonstrate construct convergence and divergence.

Administratively, the LLQ is easy to give. Specific instructions are provided along with viewgraphs to aid in presenting the test. No special training is need to administer it. The instrument may be given in two parts, which is an advantage because it takes up to 5 hours to complete. Scoring is conducted by the publisher and results are fed back individually and in aggregate form. Items are scored dichotomously. If scoring allowed for partial credit for answers finer discrimination among individuals might be possible.

A new addition to the LLQ is the Development Manual. The Development Manual is designed as a study guide to facilitate an individual's development after being assessed with the LLQ. Each behavior under the 27 tasks is discussed and specific suggestions of how to perform the behaviors are presented.

"International" norm comparisons are included as part of the feedback on test scores, though it appears that the norms are based on everyone who has taken the LLQ. No information is given to reflect what is meant by "international." Breakdowns by ethnicity and gender should be presented for fairness analysis and norms. Normative information with respect to age, level within the organization, and industry would be helpful. Further normative information would allow for general cutoff scores for varying supervisory levels.

Internal consistency reliability is a strong point for the LLQ. For the combined validity samples ($N = 301$), the KR-20 analysis yielded .9657 for the entire instrument demonstrating its excellent consistency overall. Reliability for each dimension was not reported nor was test-retest reliability. Reliability at the task level may be more important than overall reliability. The task level is how the LLQ may be best used, particularly when relying on the Developmental Manual for identifying training needs or providing individual career counseling. Also, considering the tasks are weighted in determining an overall score, it would be important to know if the most reliable tasks carried the greatest weight.

In our litigious society, organizations often put the question of fairness before questions about reliability and validity. Whereas several concurrent validity studies have been added to the LLQ Research Report since the 1990 review, no data are presented with the materials regarding potential adverse impact. The studies included do indicate high concurrent validity when the LLQ is compared with overall ratings from assessment center scores and rankings, performance appraisal ratings, and other leadership or supervision measures. The average sample size from the 14 validity studies cited is 30 subjects (median is about 21 subjects). Scarce other information is provided with these validity studies, such as gender/ethnic breakdown or any details about the criterion.

As the LLQ measures 27 important leadership tasks, comparisons between the tasks and dimensions of the assessment centers and performance ratings would be instructive as to its construct validity. This type of analysis may have to wait for a larger sample size to be conducted adequately.

The construct validity was further questioned by an earlier reviewer (Katkovsky, 1992). Katkovsky suggested that the analysis of variance (ANOVA) test reported between groups of supervisors rating task importance questioned the underlying assumption of the LLQ, namely whether the essential tasks of leadership were identified. The same criticism remains. An ANOVA ($F = 2.4$, $p = .0216$) indicated that the raters, in fact, did not agree on the importance of the leadership tasks. Other information is provided that graphically depicts the task ratings from each group and comparison to other studies that ranked importance of similar leadership tasks. Eyeballing the task ratings is not a substitute for a statistical analysis. Further, if a subjective analysis is used, the depicted comparison of rankings with other studies' ranks show little agreement.

The Leatherman Leadership Questionnaire may be a good measure of leadership knowledge, capable of selecting leaders, aiding career counseling, and identifying training needs. The research studies are pointing in that direction. However, numerous questions remain unanswered. Before conclusions can be made, additional validation work is needed.

REVIEWER'S REFERENCE

Katkovsky, W. (1992). [Review of the Leatherman Leadership Questionnaire]. In J. J. Kramer & J. C. Conoley (Eds.), *The eleventh mental measurements yearbook* (pp. 465-466). Lincoln, NE: Buros Institute of Mental Measurements.

Review of the Leatherman Leadership Questionnaire [Revised] by LAWRENCE M. RUDNER, Director, ERIC Clearinghouse on Assessment and Evaluation, The Catholic University of America, Washington, DC:

Preparing written critiques of tests typically involves a significant amount of detective work. Almost all of the publishers of tests I have examined have included exaggerated claims and hidden critical information. In almost every case, I had to search for critical information and carefully think about that which was presented. The documentation for the Leatherman Leadership Questionnaire (LLQ) is the other extreme. By far, it is the most thoroughly and honestly documented instrument this reviewer has ever seen. In addition, the publisher provides wonderful post-administration support. Other publishers would do well to replicate this approach.

The LLQ seeks to provide a comprehensive, objective assessment of an individual's knowledge concerning 27 leadership tasks, such as Assigning Work, Managing Change, Performance Appraisal, and Individual Training. The LLQ assessment of knowledge is quite distinct from the usual assessment of leadership which asks people to rate perceived behavior or perceived skill. This orientation makes the test well suited to a variety of assessment situations. It can be used as a selection instrument, training tool, or when administered to a group of managers, as the basis for a needs assessment or for program evaluation.

Users of the LLQ should keep in mind that knowing the optimal behavior given key leadership tasks does not mean that an individual will perform accordingly. Factors such as organizational climate, assigned responsibilities, perceived roles, and available time will affect performance. Nonetheless, this reviewer believes knowledge of what to do is a prerequisite for good leadership.

CONTENT VALIDITY. The primary question in evaluating the LLQ is whether the skills assessed on the LLQ actually reflect leadership (i.e., is the LLQ content valid). The 99-page LLQ Research Report shows that the LLQ was developed using textbook procedures. The developers started with a detailed analysis of over 400 related existing measures, noting strengths, format, and content. They then focused on 2 key industry studies, 4 training modules, 6 articles by authors of note, and 13 needs assessment instruments. Thirty-six well-defined leadership tasks that were cited frequently in this literature formed the initial task pool. The Report provides a table mapping each task to this related literature.

A well-qualified panel of experts then rated the importance of each task. Behaviors reflective of each important task were then identified. An appendix identifies sources of these behaviors by each task. The expert panel then rated the importance and congruence of the behaviors to the tasks. Items were written and the expert panel rated the importance, clarity, and congruence of the items to the behaviors. The items were then pilot tested and revised. The final set of tasks were reviewed by 229 experts in seven additional panels representing different client groups. The eight panels consistently rated each task as either very important or critically important.

The developmental process clearly demonstrates the LLQ assesses widely accepted and well-documented leadership skills and that each task of the LLQ has accompanying evidence that it is content valid.

RELIABILITY. As part of the developmental process, the second version of the LLQ was administered to 301 subjects in nine groups. The KR-20 reliabilities ranged from .9054 to .9905, with an average of .9657. Deleting a few items with low item-test and item-task correlations raised the composite reliability to .9706. Task reliabilities on the final form ranged from .47 for helping an employee make decisions to .83 for conducting selection interviews. These task reliabilities are quite acceptable given the relatively small number of items within each task. Nonetheless, prudence dictates careful analysis and consideration of individual task scores, especially if they are to be the basis for helping to make high-stakes decisions.

CRITERION RELATED VALIDITY. The research report summarizes 14 criterion-related correlation studies. Because the LLQ is designed to measure knowledge as opposed to perceived behavior, we would expect less than perfect correlations. Knowledge about what to do in different situations does not mean the appropriate behavior will be exhibited. Similarly, exhibiting a behavior can be due to instinct rather than knowledge. Correlations will also be attenuated by lack of reliability in the criterion measure, reduced variance in the group being assessed, relatively small sample sizes, and by the fact that the LLQ is designed to be a lower cost alternative. Further, the weighing of the tasks in the LLQ is not the same as the weights that are inherent in these other measures. To this reviewer, correlations of .4 or above with these criteria would be acceptable, .6 or above would be outstanding.

In 9 of the 10 studies using time-consuming and costly assessment center results as the criterion the correlations were above .40, 7 had correlations above .60, and 5 had correlations above .70. When in-basket exercises were used as the criterion, the correlations were .43 and .71. When performance appraisals were the criterion, the correlation was .35. The correlation of the LLQ with the Supervisory Practices Test by M. Bruce was .41 and .77 and the correlation of the LLQ with the How Supervise? test by File and Remmer was .60. These correlations are quite exceptional. It should be noted, however, that seven of these studies had sample sizes under 20 people. Although this is to be expected when assessing managers, most of these validation studies had small samples from test validation and generalizability viewpoints.

TEST ADMINISTRATION. Administration of the LLQ is quite easy. The test is composed of 339 multiple-choice questions divided into two parts. Examinees are given answer forms and examination booklets. The administrator is given an extensive collection of overhead transparencies and an annotated notebook for group presentation. The LLQ is untimed and typically takes between 3 and 5 hours to complete.

REPORTS. Reports are provided for both the organization and the individual examinees. The organizational report lists each task and the scores of the group on that task. This provides a handy tool for identifying staff strengths and remediation needs. The individual reports provide task and total scores for the individual, the group taking the test, and everyone who has taken the test to date (currently 23,000 individuals). Task and total percentile scores are also computed for the individual and group, based on this normative group. In addition, norms are also available for a large number of industries. Accompanying the individual results is a glossy 12-page booklet which provides an explanation and answers numerous questions. This booklet provides realistic answers to typical real-life questions.

The total score on the LLQ reflects the weights assigned by the test publisher. Although the weights reflect the judgements of 229 experts from eight different groups, they may not reflect what is important in your organization. This limitation should be kept in mind when evaluating total scores.

FOLLOW-UP SUPPORT. One of the major strengths of the LLQ is the LLQ Development Manual. This massive 350-page manual is intended to be used by examinees as a way of helping them identify positive behaviors (i.e., strengthening their knowledge on the tasks with low scores). Each chapter examines one of the 27 tasks measured by the LLQ. Each task is divided into behaviors that are typical of the task. Each of these behaviors is then discussed in detail. At times some of the discussion is obvious and trivial. But most of the time, the discussions are informative, clear, and insightful. This manual and the references used in the content development provide an excellent basis for staff improvement.

SUMMARY. Based on reading the technical documentation, examining the items, and reviewing the support materials, I can highly recommend the Leatherman Leadership Questionnaire to any organization interested in improving the quality of its managers. The instrument provides detailed information concerning the most important leadership tasks. It was developed using the most sound of procedures. The documentation provides compelling evidence that the test does what the publishers claim. The supporting material is outstanding.

[220]

The Leisure Diagnostic Battery.

Purpose: Developed to assess leisure functioning.
Population: Ages 9–18, adult.
Publication Date: 1987.
Administration: Group.
Levels, 2: Version A, Version B.
Price Data, 1991: $19.95 per manual ('87, 102 pages).
Time: (30–60) minutes.
Authors: Peter A. Witt and Gary D. Ellis.
Publisher: American Alliance for Health, Physical Education, Recreation, and Dance.

a) SHORT FORM.

Scores, 6: Perceived Leisure (Competence, Control), Leisure Needs, Depth of Involvement in Leisure Experiences, Playfulness, Total.

b) LONG FORM.

Scores, 6 to 9: Same as for *a* above plus 3 optional scores: Barriers to Leisure Involvement Scale, Leisure Preference Inventory, Knowledge of Leisure Opportunities Test.

Review of the Leisure Diagnostic Battery by E. THOMAS DOWD, Professor and Director of Counseling Psychology, Kent State University, Kent, OH:

INTRODUCTION. The Leisure Diagnostic Battery (LDB) was constructed by the authors to assess leisure functioning along several dimensions with a variety of handicapped and nonhandicapped individuals. It is actually a collection of tests. There are both long and short forms as well as separate forms for adolescents (ages 9 through 18) and adults and two different response formats.

The long forms consist of two sections each. Section 1 consists of 95 questions arranged in five subscales: Leisure Competence, Leisure Control, Leisure Needs, Depth of Involvement, and Playfulness, which together are considered to measure the construct of Perceived Freedom in Leisure. Section 2, given only if the score on Section 1 identifies a problem, consists of 112 items arranged in three subscales: Barriers to Leisure, Knowledge of Leisure Opportunities, and Leisure Preferences. Long Form Version A (adolescents) uses a 3-point Likert scale for most subscales; *Doesn't sound like me*, *Sounds a little like me*, and *Sounds like me*. Long Form Version C (adults) uses a 5-point Likert scale, ranging from *Strongly disagree* to *Strongly agree*. No reason is given for the change in response format. The last two subscales use multiple-choice and forced-choice responses, respectively. Version B Long Form was originally designed for mentally retarded individuals, but the authors were not satisfied with its psychometric properties and have not released this version.

The short forms were developed later and consist of 25 items taken from the first five scales, Perceived Freedom in Leisure. Version A is for adolescents and Version B is for adults. In both the long and short forms, the adolescent and adult versions differ only in the wording of some items.

CONCEPTUALIZATION. The LDB is based on a psychological, rather than an activities, conception of leisure. Leisure is defined as a high degree of perceived freedom to engage in activities out of intrinsic motivation, rather than external constraint. Intrinsic motivation is said to arise from a self-serving attributional pattern, in which involvement in leisure activities is attributed to internal and stable factors. In contrast, the self-degenerative pattern, leading to extrinsic motivation and learned helplessness, is said to arise from the attribution of engagement in leisure activities to external and unstable factors. Thus, the authors argue that perceived freedom and learned helplessness represent opposite ends of a continuum of "leisurability." Although attribution theory may be oversimplified in this model, this is a fairly sophisticated view of leisure and a distinct improvement over the older model that defined specific activities as leisure and others as nonleisure.

The individual items were developed over a period of time according to the theoretical domains mentioned earlier. The process appears to have been extremely thorough. Unfortunately, although the authors state the conceptual structure of the test was reviewed by over 30 people knowledgeable in the social psychology of leisure, they do not state who or how many individuals actually wrote the items. This is important because the use of few authors of test items can have a constraining effect on the range and scope of items generated. Likewise, the authors state the scales were checked for readability but do not say how this was done.

RELIABILITY. Existing reliability data, although quite good, are incomplete. The authors imply that additional data are being collected. Internal consistency reliabilities for Long Form Version A, which are much more extensive than test-retest, consistently range in the .80s and .90s. Test-retest reliabilities are mostly in the .70s and .80s, with a few in the .60s and one in the .50s. Unfortunately, no reliability data have yet been collected for Long Form Version C. The authors state they expect it to be about the same, but differences might occur because Version A uses a 3-point response scale whereas Version C uses a 5-point response scale. This means that no reliability data exist for the adult test in the long form, although strangely enough there are reliability data for adults in the short form version.

Internal consistency reliabilities of the short forms are comparable with those of the long forms, ranging from .83 to.94. No test-retest reliability data have been collected for the short forms.

VALIDITY. Convergent, predictive, and discriminant validity data are provided for Long Form Version A. All seem generally good. Predictive and discriminant validity data are provided for the Short Form Versions A and B, again generally supportive. The manual has sections on the nature of reliability and validity. Content, predictive, and construct validity are presented in the manual, but are not covered completely by scale development efforts.

NORMS. Although no national norms yet exist for this instrument, the authors present numerous data sets from specific populations on which the test has been normed. A valuable aspect of the normative samples is that some consist of individuals with a variety of handicapping conditions. The authors provide an excellent discussion of the interpretation of the test scores, and appropriately advocate that local norms be developed by users. Appendix A gives detailed directions on how to do this. Test users should have little difficulty interpreting these scores meaningfully.

FACTOR ANALYSIS. This, in my view, is the most problematic aspect of this instrument and one that implicates its construction. The authors hypothesized that a single factor from the first five subscales would exist, which they subsequently found and labeled "Perceived Freedom." They seem, throughout the manual, to imply that the total score of the first five subscales should be used. But if this is true, why identify or use the subscales at all? In fact, the authors appear not to do so, stating in the interpretation guidelines that users might obtain some useful information from the subscale scores. This concern is exacerbated by the lack of an intercorrelation matrix indicating how the subscales correlate with each other. Thus, the user does not even know if the subscales represent discrete concepts at all.

The manual is very thorough and detailed. Not only are there extensive presentations of normative data, reliability, validity, and interpretation, but also detailed directions for administration. It would be difficult for the user to go wrong! The manual is written for the novice, which might offend some sophisticated users, but which is preferable to an overly technical manual.

In summary, this is a well-constructed instrument, with a sound theoretical rationale and impressive psychometric properties. I would encourage the authors to continue the collection of reliability and validity data for the other versions and to provide intercorrelations among the subscales. Perhaps some rationale for the difference in response format between the adolescent and adult forms might be given. I suspect the authors thought the 3-point scale might be more understandable to an adolescent population. In view, however, of the lack of reliability data on the adult long form, I am concerned about the possible impact of such a format change.

Review of the Leisure Diagnostic Battery by ELLEN WEISSINGER, Associate Professor of Educational Psychology, University of Nebraska-Lincoln, Lincoln, NE:

The Leisure Diagnostic Battery (LDB) is a collection of instruments designed to assess current level of leisure functioning and to identify constraints that may inhibit leisure functioning. The instruments were developed for use with orthopedically handicapped adolescents in rehabilitation settings, but the authors state the battery is appropriate for educable mentally retarded persons and nonhandicapped populations. A revised version with slightly modified item wording is offered for adults. Both long (95 items) and short

(25 items) forms of the adolescent and adult versions are available.

The long forms of the LDB consist of two sections. The first includes five scales: Perceived Leisure Competence, Perceived Leisure Control, Leisure Needs, Depth of Involvement in Leisure Experiences, and Playfulness. A 3-point response format (*doesn't sound like me* to *sounds a lot like me*) is provided for adolescents and a 5-point format (*strongly agree* to *strongly disagree*) for adults. Scores on these first five scales can be summed to a total score, which is referred to as "Perceived Freedom in Leisure."

If the results of the Perceived Freedom in Leisure battery suggest deficiencies in one or more areas of leisure functioning, the second section of scales is then administered. These three instruments (Barriers to Leisure Involvement Scale, Knowledge of Leisure Opportunities Test, Leisure Preference Inventory) identify specific problems with leisure functioning. For both adolescents and adults, the Barriers scale is scored on the same 3- and 5-point formats as the Perceived Freedom in Leisure scales. The Leisure Opportunities Test utilizes a multiple-choice format; the Leisure Preference Inventory, a forced-choice format. The authors estimate that the long form takes approximately 30 minutes to complete. The short form of the adolescent and adult versions of the LDB consists of 25 items from the competence, control, needs, and involvement scales of the long form. A single, total score results from the short form.

The test manual describes in detail the procedures used to define conceptually and operationally the constructs represented by each scale. Initial pools of items were written based on applicable theoretical and empirical literature. Based on pilot data from 200 adolescents (52% male, mostly white, mean age = 13.2), final items were selected using item-total and interitem correlations and factor loadings. Items for the short forms were selected from the long forms based on item-total correlation coefficients.

The test manual presents internal consistency reliability data from five datasets (total n = 897) for the adolescent long form. Alpha coefficients for individual scales ranged from .75 to .90 and total score alphas were from .87 to .89. Two-week test-retest correlations for the adolescent long form were .54 and .90 for two datasets (total n = 137). No reliability data were offered for the adult long form. Alpha coefficients for the adolescent short form ranged from .83 to .94 across eight data sets (total n = 575). Alphas for the adult short form ranged from .88 to .94 across six data sets (total n = 1,405). Temporal stability data were not offered for either version of the short form.

As evidence of convergent validity, the authors present factor analyses from seven datasets (total n = 982) for the adolescent long form verifying the five scales that contribute to the total score do load on a common underlying factor for six of the datasets. This factor is presumed to be Perceived Freedom in Leisure, though no convergent validity data are offered that directly justify this presumption. As evidence of discriminant validity, the authors correlate LDB long form scale scores with age and gender. These data generally followed the hypothesized pattern of nonsignificant correlations. The authors also present several analyses of hypothesized score differences between various disabled and nondisabled groups as evidence of discriminant validity. Finally, the authors correlate scores on the Perceived Freedom scales with scores on the Barriers scale, Knowledge test, and Preferences Inventory. These correlations, which generally followed hypothesized trends, were offered as evidence the perceived freedom scales predict scores on the scales that indicate leisure constraints.

For the adolescent and adult versions of the short form, validity data similar to those presented for the long form were offered. In addition, evidence of construct validity was provided by correlating short form scores with other measures of theoretically related constructs. These correlations generally follow the predicted pattern of hypothesized relationships with such constructs as life satisfaction (.43), self-esteem (.39), self-concept (.22), and leisure satisfaction (.81).

The test manual is logically organized and clearly written. Extensive background information on scale development is offered. A brief primer on psychometric language and concepts is included. Sections that concern procedures for administering and scoring the battery are thorough and easily understood. The section that deals with normative interpretation lacks any national norms, but instructs the user in four methods for local or institutional norming. A bibliography is attached.

In general, the LDB appears to demonstrate psychometric qualities that are sufficient to justify its use as an assessment battery. Internal consistency data support the existence of unitary constructs. Temporal stability data suggest constructs that are relatively stable over a 2-week period. Validity data suggest that constructs presumed to be measured by the LDB scales generally follow hypothesized patterns of relationships. However, additional construct validation is required before the theoretical definitions of measured constructs are fully understood. It is also necessary to have additional data concerning the ability of the LDB scales to predict observable external variables related to leisure functioning. The establishment of this degree of predictive validity is essential for instruments intended as diagnostic tools in clinical settings. Finally, the establishment of more extensive normative data would seem to be necessary in order to make the LDB fully useful as a diagnostic tool. Even with these limitations, the LDB is clearly the most sophisticated and sound measurement battery available for assessing leisure behavior.

[221]

Life Experiences Checklist.

Purpose: Designed to assess a client's quality of life.
Population: Adults.
Publication Date: 1990.
Acronym: LEC.
Scores, 6: Home, Leisure, Relationships, Freedom, Opportunities, Total.
Administration: Individual.
Price Data, 1990: L28.75 per complete set; L17.25 per 25 checklists.
Time: (10) minutes.
Author: Alastair Ager.
Publisher: NFER-Nelson Publishing Co., Ltd. [England].

Review of the Life Experiences Checklist by JUDITH CONGER, Professor of Psychology and Director of Clinical Training, Purdue University, West Lafayette, IN:

DESCRIPTION AND APPLICATION. The Life Experiences Checklist (LEC) is designed to assess the "quality of life" through the endorsement (or nonendorsement) of a broad range of experiences, events, and activities. In addition, a space is provided on the answer sheets for comments that a respondent might want to make. The focus is on the range and number of activities that an individual experiences, rather than on subjective perceptions of well-being, although there is an obvious connection between them. The checklist is composed of five broad areas: Home, Leisure, Relationships, Freedom, and Opportunities, each of which contains 10 items (Total items = 50). It is an easily administered and easily scored instrument. The checklist can be completed by an individual or by a rater on the person's behalf, through either direct administration or an interview format. The author cautions relating scores obtained in different formats; however, a correlation of .80 is reported between information gleaned through a subject versus an informant interview based on a study cited in the manual.

The author sees the applications of the LEC as falling into four broad areas: quality assurance, program planning, individual therapy, and staff training. The instrument appears to be most applicable to longer term client care or monitoring where there has been resettlement from institutional to community care or resettlement within institutional or community facilities in which care givers actually have some control in planning and intervening. The LEC, however, could be used to assess quality of life of an individual, as well as to assess the quality of life provided by a particular setting or living arrangement by assessing multiple respondents. Used in this way, it could provide some estimate of quality assurance. Further, specific areas could be explored and used for client or programmatic interventions if an individual has a particularly low endorsement in a subarea thought to be important for the person's overall welfare. For example, a very low endorsement in the leisure area might suggest some modifications in the overall program or lifestyle of an individual. In that regard the instrument aids in a more holistic approach and might suggest environmental or organizational interventions influencing the individual and/or programmatic level.

PSYCHOMETRIC CHARACTERISTICS. The basic normative sampling was done on 410 individuals in the general population in Great Britain. Norms are provided on the answer sheet and are broken down into percentage of respondents who endorsed a particular item by subsamples of urban, suburban, rural, as well as the combined sample, thereby attempting to provide a more relevant comparison sample for the individual. A perusal, however, indicates very similar response patterns across these samples for many of the items, although there is some variation on a few. Thus, although this is an appealing idea, in reality there is less discrimination than one might want. Further, the respondents are described as "householders" with little other description of the sample in the manual as regards demographics such as sex, age, ethnicity, education, etc. There is no information as to how the sample was drawn from the general population further masking possible biases, although there are references to studies on the LEC where information was obtained and those studies might contain more specific details. Additional information is reported in the manual for other populations such as undergraduates, medical students, psychology students, and clients of various types, although in the latter case the *N*s are often quite meager. Finally, data are also presented in terms of centile equivalents for subscale scores; however, because the distributions are different (and skewed) for each subscale, a score of 5 on the Home scale places one at the 6th percentile, a score of 5 on the Leisure scale places one at the 48th percentile. This can be misleading and lead to misinterpretation, as the author notes.

There are several studies reported dealing with various types of reliability. A total test-retest reliability of .93 is reported with a sample of 20 students using an "agreement index" score with subsection scores ranging from .91 to .96. Further, there was an informant-rater correlation of .80 based on 10 subjects with learning difficulties, as well as an interrater correlation of.80 that appears to be based on 10 subjects, although it is not clear if this sample of 10 represents the same learning-impaired subjects or not. Expanded reliability data, particularly with the subscale scores using larger samples, including the general population, are needed. Further, internal consistency estimates on the subscale scores might be useful in ascertaining the homogeneity of each area subscore.

There are some validity data reported indicating, for example, that the LEC is positively related to staff-client ratio (r = .36) and negatively related to the number of clients on a ward (r = -.36). Further, the LEC was correlated with a list of social and demographic factors with a range of correlations between -.19 (more than three dependent children) and -.36 (social class). Although it is suggestive that social and economic variables are negatively related to Life Experiences, most of the relationships are rather modest, albeit statistically significant due to the large N. Validity coefficients are often modest and a construct such as this may gain validational strength through its modest associations with other variables. Still, data bearing directly on the relationship between the LEC with other quality of life measures would be useful. This approach could provide stronger validational evidence for this measure.

In summary, the LEC appears to be an interesting, easily administered, and potentially useful instrument which is in need of further psychometric investigation. As such, in my opinion it is still in the development phase and ought to be considered "experimental." In the future, the author may want to consider some kind of transformation which would allow conversion into a more "standard" type score for subscales so that comparisons across subareas can be made more easily. A major drawback of the LEC for U.S. users is that it appears to be entirely normed on a British population.

[222]

Life Styles Inventory.

Purpose: Designed to assess an individual's thinking and behavioral styles.

Population: Adults.

Publication Dates: 1973–90.

Acronym: LSI.

Administration: Individual.

Price Data: Price data for test materials including Leader's Guide ('89, 211 pages), Self-Development Guide ('89, 75 pages), and Description by Others Self-Development Guide ('90, 123 pages) available from publisher.

Time: (20–25) minutes.

Author: J. Clayton Lafferty.

Publisher: Human Synergistics, Inc.

a) LSI1: LIFE STYLES INVENTORY (SELF DESCRIPTION).

Scores, 12: Constructive Styles (Achievement, Self-Actualizing, Humanistic-Encouraging, Affiliative), Passive/Defensive Styles (Approval, Conventional, Dependent, Avoidance), Aggressive/Defensive Styles (Oppositional, Power, Competitive, Perfectionistic).

b) LSI2: LIFE STYLES INVENTORY (DESCRIPTION BY OTHERS).

Scores, 12: Same as for *a* above.

Comments: Administered to manager and 4 or 5 others.

Cross References: See T4:1459 (6 references); for reviews by Henry M. Cherrick and Linda M. DuBois, see 9:620 (1 reference).

Review of the Life Styles Inventory by GREGORY J. BOYLE, Associate Professor of Psychology, Bond University, Gold Coast, Queensland, Australia:

The Life Styles Inventory (LSI) is a 240-item questionnaire purported to measure 12 different thinking styles. The instrument comprises two forms: self-descriptions (LSI1) or description by others (LSI2) of an individual's characteristic interpersonal styles (comprising his/her attitudes, behaviors, and reactions). The LSI is based on Maslow's (1954) conceptual model of lower- and higher-order needs and is intended to provide insights into the behavioral effects of thinking patterns, which would enable individuals to modify their existing styles of thought.

Preparation of the LSI materials has been comprehensive. Not only are there separate forms, and a scorer's worksheet containing detailed instructions on steps involved in calculating an individual's raw scores, but in addition, a profile summary form in which cards summarizing the characteristics of each thinking style, along with suggestions for improving one's interactions with others, provide a practical benefit to the individual. This is a very positive feature of the LSI. There are comprehensive self-development guides for both versions of the instrument. Most personality questionnaires measure an individual's characteristic traits, but few actually provide accompanying suggestions on ways in which to improve on one's weaknesses. By seeing how they think about themselves and how they are perceived by others, individuals may choose to modify their self-concepts in an effort to improve their interpersonal and behavioral effectiveness. The LSI can also be used as part of an organization's management development program to improve the success and efficiency of its members. A comprehensive leader's guide is provided for this purpose.

The psychometric properties of the LSI have been addressed in several research articles included in the leader's guide. Results of these studies, however, suggest the LSI may require substantial improvements both in terms of its reliability and validity.

Reliability has been assessed via Cronbach's alpha coefficient, and also split-half coefficients. These internal consistency estimates range from .80 to .88 (median .85), and from .82 to .91 (median .85), respectively. No information is provided on the homogeneity of items, so it is not clear whether the LSI scales have redundant items (due to item overlap) and are therefore narrow measures of the particular constructs (cf. Boyle, 1991). Unfortunately, no test-retest reliability coefficients are reported, so the user has no knowledge of either the dependability (immediate retest) or the longer term stability of the instrument over various intervals of time (cf. Boyle, 1987). Interrater reliability coefficients (along the same-style, different-rater diagonal) range from .16 to .32 (mean .24), suggesting that reliability between raters is inadequate.

In one of the research reports, the self/others correlations reported for the three derived factors range from .20 to .32, so that over 90% of the variance is not explained. In another report, they range from .16 to .32 (median .24). Self-ratings are quite discrepant with observers' ratings, which also differ considerably among raters themselves. Consequently, despite the optimistic interpretations given in the research reports, it appears highly likely that the LSI scales are unreliable.

Correlations between the 12 LSI scales, although significant in many instances, are in the main quite trivial, indicating relatively low commonality. There is no apparent recognition of the critically important distinction between statistical significance and practical or conceptual meaningfulness (cf. Boyle, 1985). Most of the correlations are only "significant" because of the large sample sizes employed. This does not seem to be recognized as a statistical artifact in the research articles accompanying the LSI. Multiple regression results show virtually no predictive variance for numerous criterion variables. For example, in one of the research reports, an R^2 of .07 for a regression with life styles (omitting life events) is reported as being statistically significant (using a sample size of 1,000 subjects), but it is clearly trivial in magnitude, failing to account for 93% of the variance.

Exploratory factor analyses of the scale intercorrelations have been reported. In each instance, a somewhat inappropriate "Little Jiffy" procedure has been employed. This procedure is known to produce invalid factor solutions (Gorsuch, 1983; McDonald, 1985). Even the three pseudo-higher-order factors reported do not fully support the postulated four-factor structure. In addition, cluster analysis of the scale intercorrelations is reported. Apart from being a weaker procedure statistically, cluster analysis provides only a superficial approximation to the more appropriate factor analytic procedures, and elucidates only "surface traits" rather than "source traits" (cf. Cattell, 1978). Moreover, both factor analysis and cluster analysis of the LSI scale intercorrelations assume that the scales are reliable and valid in the first place.

The construct validity of the 12 separate LSI scales needs to be verified. The LSI scales are based primarily on Maslow's (1954) theoretical postulations, and are not derived from empirical investigations. Cross-validation of the LSI scale structure must be regarded as an urgent issue to be resolved. Unless the scales can be shown to be construct valid, then research findings premised on the existing scale structure may serve merely to conflate theory, rather than resolve issues and discriminate between competing hypotheses. Factor analyses of item-parcel intercorrelations (more reliable than for single items) using appropriate factor analytic methodology would enable the factor validity of each scale to be assessed. More importantly, confirmatory factor analyses should be carried out, for example, via Lisrel (Jöreskog & Sörbom, 1989) on item (or preferably, on item-parcel) intercorrelations to test the goodness-of-fit of the proposed 12-factor model.

Nevertheless, the LSI is one of the few instruments currently available for promoting changes among members of organizations. It would appear to be creatively conceived, and to be a very useful tool in management/leadership training for stimulating self-awareness of one's thinking styles and the effects of one's interactions on others. Clearly though, more sophisticated research into the psychometric properties of the LSI needs to be undertaken, and modifications to item content and/or scale structure may be required. Although the LSI would appear to be potentially a very useful instrument for fostering the personal development of individuals within organizations, its use at present cannot be recommended unequivocally until these more basic issues pertaining to its psychometric reliability and validity can be clarified.

REVIEWER'S REFERENCES

Maslow, A. H. (1954). *Motivation and personality*. New York: Harper & Row.

Cattell, R. B. (1978). *The scientific use of factor analysis in behavioral and life sciences*. New York: Plenum.

Gorsuch, R. L. (1983). *Factor analysis* (2nd ed.). Hillsdale, NJ: Erlbaum.

Boyle, G. J. (1985). Self-report measures of depression: Some psychometric considerations. *British Journal of Clinical Psychology, 24*, 45-59.

McDonald, R. P. (1985). *Factor analysis and related methods*. Hillsdale, NJ: Erlbaum.

Boyle, G. J. (1987). Review of the (1985) "Standards for educational and psychological testing: AERA, APA, and NCME." *Australian Journal of Psychology, 39*, 235-237.

Jöreskog, K. G., & Sörbom, D. (1989). *Lisrel 7: A guide to the program and applications* (2nd ed.). Chicago: SPSS Inc.

Boyle, G. J. (1991). Does item homogeneity indicate internal consistency or item redundancy in psychometric scales? *Personality and Individual Differences, 12*, 291-294.

Review of the Life Styles Inventory by PATRICIA SCHOENRADE, Associate Professor of Psychology, William Jewel College, Liberty, MO:

The Life Styles Inventory (LSI), developed by J. Clayton Lafferty, assesses "thinking patterns and self-concept" (Leader's Guide, p. 7) and is intended for the assessment of individuals primarily in an organizational context. The instrument consists of 240 descriptive words and phrases. The items refer to personality characteristics and to cognitive-behavioral patterns. The primary measure (LSI1) employs the individual's own self-rating, whereas a second level (LSI2) employs ratings by several others who know the individual well. The Leader's Guide stresses the goals "Awareness, Acceptance, and Action, (p. 11)"; the intent is that the respondent recognize both strengths and weaknesses in current patterns, become receptive to the feedback the instrument provides, and take action on those areas where a need for change is suggested.

The 12 scales that comprise the instrument are subdivided into three groups: Constructive Styles

(Achievement, Self-Actualizing, Humanistic-Encouraging, and Affiliative), Passive/Defensive Styles (Approval, Conventional, Dependent, and Avoidance), and Aggressive/Defensive Styles (Oppositional, Power, Competitive, and Perfectionistic). The divisions appear conceptually reasonable. The respondent receives a score (0–40) on each of the 12 scales. A clock-graph presentation aids the respondent in visualizing the relationships of the scales to each other and of obtained scores to those of normative samples. Though it may appear complex at first glance, the LSI is fairly easy to complete; an NCR form facilitates translation of responses to scores and to the profile.

The authors provide in-depth supporting materials for the trainer, manager, or other organizer of a self-development program. The program will require a commitment of preparation time on the part of the leader; the extensive Leader's Guide offers virtually all information the leader will need for preparation. Among the features in the Leader's Guide are detailed descriptions of the meaning of profiles, scripts and examples for introducing the instrument, suggestions for assisting respondents in processing feedback, answers to questions, and copy for transparencies. The information presented is generally clear and understandable. Information on norms, reliability, and validity is presented both in a simplified summary form and in copies of original research reports.

The goal of self-development through use of the LSI is further underscored by the provision of two Self-Development Guides (one for LSI1 and one for LSI2). The Self-Development Guides offer detailed understanding of the scale scores and their potential implications for organizational and managerial effectiveness. They suggest the implications of change in each of the 12 areas and recommend specific exercises for change. Although the exercises are at times quite general or somewhat vague, most users will find something helpful among them. Taken in its entirety, the self-development program may seem overwhelming, but in smaller units it has the potential to prove enjoyable as well as enlightening. Inclusion of comic-strip examples throughout the guide aids the user in processing feedback in a nondefensive manner.

Norms are provided for each of the 12 scales based on a sample of over 9,000 adults. These normative data were apparently gathered from results returned by program leaders—the authors request such information—and thorough demographic information is provided for this sample. Because it is unclear from the descriptions what percentage of users respond to the request for return information, there may be a question as to the representativeness of the sample. The relative ease of supplying the return results moderates this concern. The normative data are important, as they are used in the conversion to the final profile to allow the respondent to identify a score as high, medium, or low.

The authors supply three studies that address the reliability of the 12 scale scores (for the LSI1). These reveal good internal consistency, with coefficient alphas ranging from .78 to .88 (all but one reach at least .80) and split-half reliabilities ranging from .90 to .95. Unfortunately, no data are presented to address test-retest reliability. The Leader's Guide discusses the problem that "changes between the two testing occasions can occur within an individual that will produce changes in his/her scores" and so "reliability will be lower for reasons independent of the instrument" (p. 34). This logic is supported by the description of the LSI profile as a "snapshot of how he or she is thinking and behaving right now" (p. 23). Yet if individuals are encouraged to undertake self-development on the basis of scores, a certain consistency of styles would seem to be assumed. Further consideration of the test-retest reliability issue is warranted.

The level of fact validity is appropriate to the purpose. The tone of self-descriptors is readily apparent, yet the intermingling of groups of adjectives on several scales mediates the inclination to present oneself as having a particular profile. The effectiveness of the LSI1 depends on the respondent's willingness to self-report honestly, which in turn is to some degree a function of the context and the leader's role.

Data presented to address construct validity are generally encouraging. The scale scores appear to relate to each other very much as predicted (for example, adjacent scales on the clock-chart correlate most strongly), and the interrelationship of the scales supports the logic of Maslow's conception of higher-order versus lower-order needs, a logic underlying the measure. Relationships of the major groupings to such variables as managerial function, other-reported managerial effectiveness, and other-reported quality of relationships suggest that these categories have some ability to predict relevant managerial behaviors. The causal direction of this relationship and the parallel power of the individual scales are not yet clear.

Though predictive validity largely remains to be explored, results provided in the appendix to the Leader's Guide are promising. The three major life style groupings have demonstrated relationships with physiological health (including some stress-related symptoms) and problem solving. Low but significant correlations with instances of medical problems have been observed for many of the scales. Again, users must exercise caution in inferring causal relationships from these results.

A caution to those considering the use of the LSI2 (in which five others who know the respondent provide ratings) is that most of the supporting research presented in the manual has been conducted on the LSI1. The appendix includes one study in which a "fairly high" degree of agreement was found among raters, with eta-squares from .33 to .47. Agreement of self-reports with others' descriptions was somewhat lower, with correlations ranging from .16 to .32. Given that perceptions are the focus, self and other ratings would not be expected to agree in all cases. Indeed, the author provides interpretations for areas of disagreement with labels such as "blind spot" and "unrecognized strength." The author is appropriately cautious regarding the LSI2, encouraging the user to regard it as a "thought starter."

The manager or group leader considering the use of the LSI must be prepared to commit adequate time for preparation and guidance, and must keep in mind the limitations of measures of direct, face-valid, self-report measures. Within these parameters, it can provide a useful means of encouraging developing professionals to consider personal style and its relevance to quality of work and advancement.

[223]

Listening Comprehension Test.

Purpose: To estimate a student's ability to comprehend orally presented basic English structures.
Population: Nonnative speakers of English who wish to pursue academic work at universities where English is the medium of instruction.
Publication Date: 1986.
Acronym: LCT.
Scores: Total score only.
Administration: Group.
Forms, 3: 4, 5, 6 (equivalent forms).
Price Data, 1993: $46 per complete kit including 20 test booklets, 3 scoring stencils, 100 answer sheets, cassette tape, and manual (17 pages); $5 per 20 test booklets; $6 per scoring stencils; $5 per 100 answer sheets; $12 per cassette; $6 per manual; no charge for specimen set.
Time: 15(20) minutes.
Comments: Created for use as one of the component tests of the Michigan English Language Assessment Battery.
Authors: H. Koba, M. Spaan, and L. Strowe.
Publisher: English Language Institute, The University of Michigan.

Review of the Listening Comprehension Test by JAMES DEAN BROWN, Associate Professor of Applied Linguistics, Department of English as a Second Language, University of Hawaii at Manoa, Honolulu, HI:

The English Language Institute Listening Comprehension Test (LCT) is a 15-minute cassette-recorded listening test for English-as-a-Second-Language (ESL) students. The students listen to sentence-length statements and select the best responses from three options in written multiple-choice format. The LCT was first developed in 1972. The current version is published by the English Language Institute (ELI) of The University of Michigan and is designed to measure "a student's ability to comprehend basic English structures orally presented" (manual, p. 1). As such, the LCT tests only sentence-level listening comprehension.

Forms 4, 5, and 6 are currently available to educational institutions and researchers. These three forms share a common test booklet, but are based on different portions of the cassette tape. Each form has 45 items that test 15 basic structures with three items for each structure.

The manual authors clearly label and describe the 15 structures (with plenty of examples) and indicate which items test each structure. A tape script for each of the forms, a brief description of the development process, and directions (for administering, scoring, and interpreting the test) are also provided. All of these elements are clear and concise. In addition, the manual includes technical information on norms, reliability, and validity.

The norms reported in the manual are based on a total of 1,486 ESL students who took the University of Michigan battery of tests during 1983. The descriptive statistics (based on subsamples of 515, 450, and 521 for each of the three forms) indicate that Forms 4, 5, and 6 are reasonably parallel with very similar raw score means (36.13, 37.14, and 37.40), and standard deviations (5.78, 5.22, and 5.31). However, there is no indication of equal covariances or correlations with an outside measure.

A reliability estimate of .796 is reported for the LCT. This estimate is based on the Kuder-Richardson Formula 21 and appears to be calculated from the mean and standard deviation for the three forms combined. The manual does not report reliability estimates for the three forms separately. However, based on the raw score descriptive statistics, the K-R 21 estimates for Forms 4, 5, and 6 turn out to be .805, .773, and .794, respectively. These reliability estimates cannot be considered high for this type and length of test.

The validity of the LCT is defended using the content and criterion-related validity strategies. According to the manual authors, the performance domain for which the LCT is content valid is "aural comprehension and grammatical structures" (manual, p. 12). The grammar points on the LCT were selected on the basis of the grammar books (from 1958 and 1971) that served as core texts in the ELI "at the time" (presumably in 1972 when the test was first developed).

The criterion-related (concurrent) validity arguments are based on correlations with other listening tests at the University of Michigan (i.e., the MTAC [Michigan Test of Aural Comprehension] and Forms AA, BB, and CC of the MELAB [Michigan English Language Assessment Battery]) as criterion measures. The correlation coefficients found between the LCT (apparently with the scores on the three forms combined) and each of these four criterion measures (based on subsamples of 107, 216, 178, and 269, respectively) indicate only moderate degrees of relationship: .755, .636, .673, and .761, respectively. The coefficients of determination, or the squared values of these correlations coefficients can be directly interpreted as the proportion of overlapping variance between the pairs of measures involved: .570, .404, .453, and .579, respectively. Thus, the results reported in the manual indicate only 40% to 58% overlap between the LCT and the criterion measures. Because the correlations with the grammar, vocabulary, and reading subtests on the MTELP (Michigan Test of English Language Proficiency, yet another University of Michigan test) are only slightly lower (.650, .401, and .540, respectively), this concurrent validity argument is not very convincing.

In defense of the LCT, it does include useful scoring masks and an audio cassette that has good sound quality. In addition, the strategy of using a single test booklet and three versions of the audio stimuli on one cassette to produce three forms of a listening comprehension test is clever and efficient.

However, in general, although the norms for the LCT are clearly explained and the test is easy to administer and score, the reliability is not high and the validity arguments are weak. Even if the validity arguments were much stronger, the LCT would be appropriate only in ESL settings where grammar-translation approaches and structural syllabuses are still being applied. Such settings are dwindling in number because ESL teachers' options have expanded well beyond the limited view that aural comprehension should be taught through grammatical structures.

In its day, the LCT may have been adequate, but in most ESL programs that day has passed.

Review of the Listening Comprehension Test by PHYLLIS KUEHN, Associate Professor of Educational Research, Measurement, and Statistics, California State University, Fresno, Fresno, CA:

The three forms of this test were designed to be used as a component of the Michigan English proficiency battery for assessing the English academic language skills of adult non-native speakers who wish to study in undergraduate or graduate programs taught in English. The manual authors describe the tests as aural grammar tests. Each test form has 45 short, orally presented sentences or questions designed to test comprehension of basic English structures (a tape is provided), but all three tests use the same set of 45 three-option multiple-choice answers. Presumably, this design was aimed at efficiency, but the result is at the expense of some naturalness of language. Test users who intend to use the three forms in repeated administrations should consider the influence of practice on obtained scores.

Although the three forms were designed to be parallel (using the same grammatical structures), no information about the method of equating is provided. Mean difficulties and discrimination indices are reported only for pretest versions of the three forms. One cannot assume the mean difficulties are the same for the published version of the tests. The sampling method and sample characteristics of the pretest subjects and a subsequent sample of the 269 students who were administered the final version of the test in 1972 were not described. This latter group's scores were used to scale the Listening Comprehension Test (LCT) on the Michigan 0–100-point scale. No report of the subsequent checks done after 1972 on the equivalency of the forms or the adequacy of the scaling are reported.

The manual authors warn test users of a ceiling effect. Advanced students may find the test too easy. This issue may make the test of questionable value for assessment of students applying for admission to academic programs, the population for whom the test was developed. No guidelines or suggestions are given to test users for developing local norms or cut scores.

The characteristics of the 1,486 test-takers in the norm group are not described, leaving a test user with no way of interpreting what the percentile ranks reported for the whole group might mean. Percentile ranks are also reported for five language subgroups in this sample (Arabic, Chinese, Other Asian, Romance, All Other Languages) with no explanation or recommendation to test users what these group score differences might mean, how or whether to interpret individual's scores by language group norms, or what the subgroups' characteristics are.

A somewhat low KR 21 reliability is reported (.796) for the three forms together. No separate reliability estimates are reported (and therefore no separate standard errors of measurement for the three test forms are reported).

The validity evidence provided is not sufficient to support inferences from the test scores about academic listening comprehension proficiency. Evidence of content validity comes apparently from two grammar books (published 1958 and 1971) that were in use at the Michigan English Language Institute at the time the tests were developed (1972). However, no data are provided that the grammatical structures tested are a representative sample of the content of the books. In addition, no information is offered that the structures tested are those found typically in the academic listening tasks required in postsecondary educational settings.

Evidence of concurrent validity is offered by the presentation of correlations from small subgroups for whom other Michigan English proficiency subtest scores are available. The method of sampling these subgroups and their characteristics are not reported. Correlations for the listening tests with four other Michigan listening tests range from .636 to .761, not high enough to claim equivalency and thus not providing sufficient evidence to conclude concurrent validity. The correlation with the Michigan grammar subtest was .650. This finding is not convincing evidence the tests are measuring the same content. No evidence of the relationship between scores and success in academic settings (predictive validity) is provided.

The answer choices are brief and require minimal reading skills or vocabulary knowledge. The questions also require little vocabulary knowledge (correlations reported were lowest with the Michigan vocabulary subtest, $r = .401$). Although this design may have the advantage of requiring minimal reading skills or vocabulary knowledge, and thus not be confounding measurement of listening comprehension with reading ability, the question of the purpose of the tests and the construct they are designed to measure should be considered. The tests were developed to provide assessments that would allow inferences about English academic listening proficiency to be made. The conceptual framework implied by the test design is that academic listening proficiency is related only to successful recognition of the grammatical structures in the short utterances presented. This orientation is, perhaps, reflective of an era when language testing was certainly less focused on communicative competence and naturalistic approaches to assessment.

In summary, inferences made from scores should be limited only to recognition of basic structures in English. Other inferences regarding academic listening proficiency are not supported by the validity evidence presented.

[224]

LOTE Reading and Listening Tests.

Purpose: Designed to assess achievement in a foreign language.
Population: Secondary school students in their second year of learning another language.
Publication Dates: 1990–91.
Scores, 2: Listening, Reading.
Administration: Group.
Editions, 3: French, Japanese, Modern Greek.
Price Data, 1990: A$25 per test pack including 10 test booklets, 10 magazines, photocopy master for answer/profile sheet, and score key (select French, Japanese, or Modern Greek); A$12 per cassette (select French, Japanese, or Modern Greek); A$25 per manual ('91, 23 pages); A$30 per specimen set (select French, Japanese, or Modern Greek).
Time: 42(50) minutes.
Comments: Cassette recorder necessary for administration.
Author: Susan A. Zammit.
Publisher: Australian Council for Educational Research Ltd. [Australia].

Review of the LOTE Reading and Listening Tests by JOHN HATTIE, Professor of Education, The University of North Carolina, Greensboro, NC:

The LOTE (Language Other Than English) Reading and Listening Tests aim to assess reading and listening skills of secondary school students who are in their second year of learning French, Japanese, or Modern Greek. The tests, which are intended to be diagnostic rather than placement tests, provide an estimate of the student's reading and/or listening skills and help identify each student's and the class' areas of strengths and weakness. The Reading tests involve using a magazine and the prerecorded Listening test is provided on a cassette tape with instructions in English.

Although splendidly packaged, the tests must be considered only at the research stage of development. There is no examiner's manual and no information on standardization, test calibration, reliability, or validity. In all, this test cannot be used.

The test author claimed that as the tests are diagnostic neither an examiner's manual nor information on standardization were printed. There is a teacher's manual that outlines a profile score and an associated interpretation of the level of difficulty. The test author supplied this reviewer with data that appear to be based on reasonable sample sizes, items calibrated using the one-parameter item response model, coefficient alphas, and some fit-statistics. The test author indicated that this information may be included in further versions of the test manual.

Based on information from the author, it appears that sample sizes ranged from 437 (Greek) to 1,912 (French). Reading means ranged from 15.39 (Japanese) to 20.21 (French) and Listening means ranged from 8.39 (Greek) to 12.0 (French). Difficulty levels ranged from .67 (French Reading) to.80 (Japanese Listening) with point-biserial indicators from .34 (French Reading) to .48 (Greek Reading). Reliabilities were lowest for Japanese Listening (.50) and highest for Greek Reading (.89).

Although the items have excellent discrimination they tend to be a little too easy. The estimates of reliability for the Listening Tests are below publishable standard, and the Japanese Listening test cannot be considered dependable. The variability in the discriminations indicate that a one-parameter model may not be the best method for deriving the profile scales.

These data indicate these tests have potential, but they cannot be used to make dependable diagnostic decisions until an examiner's manual is provided that includes information on the dependability and validity of the test. The tests should be used, at best, only as a research tool.

Review of the LOTE Reading and Listening Tests by IAN C. PALMER, Program Officer for English and Orientation, Latin American Scholarship Program of American Universities, Harvard University, Cambridge, MA:

The *purpose* of the LOTE (Languages Other Than English) Reading and Listening Tests is to evaluate secondary school students' reading and listening skills in French, Japanese, or Modern Greek. One form is available for each skill in each language. A 20-page teacher's manual contains explanations of test administration, scoring, and interpretation of results. The manual provides an answer key but no tapescripts. The series is aimed at students in the equivalent of grades 8 to 10 who are at the start of their second year of learning another language. Although not based on any particular curriculum or text, the series follows the Statement of Suggested Syllabus for Stage 1 of the Australian Language Levels Guidelines.

The Reading test varies in length (30 questions in the French version, 25 for Greek, and 19 for Japanese) but in each case 30 minutes is allowed for the test administration. Students base their answers on the information given in the target language in a four-page magazine, including letters from pen-friends, lost-dog announcements, daily activities on a tour, and the like. The questions, and many of the answers, are in English. In the French test, five of the questions are true/false and the rest are multiple choice. Both the magazine and the test book are clear, interesting, and attractively illustrated.

The Listening test is short (12 minutes), with 17 questions in the French version and 12 for Japanese and Greek. The instructions are given very clearly in English, and the voices heard on the tape speak in a realistic way, just a little slower than normal conversational speed. Each item is spoken twice. The content focuses on greetings, making purchases, asking for directions, and expressing feelings. In the Japanese version social context is important, as in the question that asks the student to choose the appropriate response to a situation from the four spoken choices. The standard procedure would be to conduct the Listening test immediately following the Reading test.

In the French version some questions are of dubious value: Reading question 23 asks the student to complete the sentence, "Alain a ________ ________ cassé." The correct answer is given as Answer (C), "un bras," but Answer (A), "une jambe," is factually possible but impossible grammatically. Listening Question 6 asks how much the new baby weighs; common sense alone would allow the student to eliminate two of the choices. However, the overall validity of the questions is good. The language used is realistic and includes contemporary French borrowings from English (T-shirt, grill, shopping). The student is likely to be engaged throughout, and there are some extra unscored activities for those who finish early.

The key to the test's usefulness is ostensibly the diagnostic scoring procedure. The answer sheet, a two-sided 8-inch by 12-inch card, includes a profile, to be completed by the teacher on the basis of the student's answers. Four levels of proficiency are designated: Preliminary (no mastery of introductory elements of the target language); 1 (understanding of some everyday words and simple greetings, distinguishing sounds, etc.); 2 (understanding of a range of expressions, identifying simple information); and 3 (ability to draw conclusions). The levels are not uniformly described across the three languages, and no attempt is made to correlate the levels with any instructional response.

The profile is completed by circling the numbers of questions answered correctly then drawing a line on a vertical scale at the total number of questions answered correctly. In the French Listening test, for example, seven of the questions typify Level 1 proficiency, six Level 2, and four Level 3. A student scoring nine correct would be assigned to Level 1, even if she had answered some of the more difficult questions correctly, because she did not exhibit 70% mastery of the Level 2 questions. The author of the test suggests a procedure for obtaining a class profile by arranging the answer sheets from highest to lowest; this would enable the teacher to determine which questions the class found most troublesome (perhaps due to unfamiliarity with vocabulary items).

The test is diagnostic only to the extent that it helps the teacher identify the questions most often missed. It does not relate these to any particular skill: This task is left to the teacher. Furthermore, the descriptions of Levels 2 and 3 seem to confuse linguistic descriptors ("can understand a range of everyday words and phrases") with cognitive skills (can "draw conclusions from several pieces of written information").

The interpretation section of the manual raises (and answers) several questions about the test. The author correctly believes that it is better to separate the Listening and Reading profiles, as these skills may develop at different rates. The last question and answer are quoted in their entirety to give a flavor of the LOTE Tests' author's respect for the teacher's judgment and avoidance of any overstated claims for this modest but useful instrument.

> [Question] 5 How do I know if this test is suitable for my students?—Answer: The best way is for each teacher to work through the questions in each test to evaluate how appropriate and suitable the questions are for the students and to what extent the test matches the teacher's objectives. (p. 18)

The reviewer believes this to be a highly practical test series for a specific purpose, which, in spite of a lack of a statistical corpus or theoretical underpinning, appears to fill a real need and invites the test user to evaluate its usefulness on its merits.

[225]

Management Development Profile.

Purpose: Provides field managers with feedback on their managerial skills and suggestions on how to improve those skills.

Population: Managers.
Publication Dates: 1988–91.
Scores, 18: Tasks (Staffing, Training, Counseling, Appraisal, Sales Support, Sales Motivation, Management Development, Business Management), Skills (Interpersonal Relations, Communication, Adaptability, Problem Solving, Planning, Delegation and Time Management), Attributes (Integrity and Loyalty, Stress Tolerance, Achievement Motivation, Self-Improvement).
Administration: Group.
Price Data, 1993: $40 per Administrator's Manual ('89, 40 pages); $110 per profile; $275 per enhanced version including extended feedback report and results for each of the 92 items in the questionnaire.
Time: Administration time not reported.
Comments: Profiles scored by publisher.
Authors: James O. Mitchel (administrator's guide) and LIMRA International.
Publisher: Life Insurance Marketing and Research Association, Inc.
[The publisher advised in December 1994 that this test is now out of print. It has been replaced by SkillScan for Management Development which will be reviewed in a future *MMY*—Ed.]

Review of the Management Development Profile by RICHARD M. WOLF, Professor of Psychology and Education, Teachers College, Columbia University, New York, NY:

The Management Development Profile is a 92-item questionnaire to be completed by managers in the insurance industry, their subordinates, and the manager's boss. All respondents complete the same questionnaire, focusing on the manager. The instrument was developed under the auspices of the Life Insurance Marketing and Research Association. The intended use of the instrument is to provide information to managers for the purpose of self-improvement and not for appraisal. The instrument was developed on the basis of a survey of 600 field managers in 150 companies. On the basis of the information provided, eight major activities were identified that required 14 skills and abilities. One hundred and one (101) managerial tasks, skills, and attributes were then produced and administered to over 200 managers from 10 companies that participated in a pilot test of the instrument along with 1,200 of their bosses and subordinates. The resulting information was used to produce the final version of the instrument, which consists of scores on 18 dimensions.

The instrument is administered on a form that can be optically scanned and a computer-generated report produced for the individual manager. The report provides scores on the 18 dimensions for the manager, his or her subordinates, and boss for each dimension. The individual report form provides suggestions for improvement on dimensions where scores are low.

The issue of validity is not specifically addressed in the manual. The initial survey provided a basis for the identification of the dimensions to be studies. The data for the norm group, consisting of responses from managers, subordinates, and bosses were subjected to a factor analysis. These results are presented in the manual. However, they are quite problematic. For example, the first factor that was identified showed high loadings on 19 items but only 6 of these items were included in the first dimension score, Interpersonal Relations. Other discrepancies exist between the factor analysis results and the dimensions. In fact, 10 of the 18 dimensions contain a different number of items than were identified in the factor analysis. Something is clearly amiss. There is no other information supplied regarding validity.

Coefficient alpha reliabilities are presented in the manual. These range from .70 to .92 with a median of .86. These are remarkably high considering that the dimension scores consist of from three to seven items. Inspection of the items indicates that, within each dimension, they are rather redundant. This will tend to yield high internal consistency reliability coefficients.

The norm group for the instrument consisted of 210 managers, 137 bosses, and 1,100 subordinates. No explanation of how the group was selected is provided nor is it clear what this sample is supposed to represent. It is also questionable whether response data from the three groups should have been combined into a single set of norms. At this time the instrument should not be used with managers outside of the life insurance industry until there is evidence to support such use. Its use within the life insurance industry is even open to question.

SUMMARY. The Management Development Profile is an instrument developed for self-study by managers in the life insurance industry. It consists of a 92-item questionnaire that is completed by a manager, his or her subordinates, and boss. Evidence to support its use even in the life insurance industry is weak. There is little evidence of validity and what evidence is presented has been largely ignored in the development of the 18 dimensions for which scores are obtained. The scales are fairly reliable, but this appears to be largely a function of the use of redundant items. The norm group is sizable (1,447) but there is no description of how they were selected. Furthermore, data from managers, subordinates, and superordinates were combined into a single norm group. This instrument suffers from a number of deficiencies that make its use, even as an instrument for self-study in the life insurance industry, questionable.

[226]

Management Inventory on Leadership, Motivation and Decision-Making.
Purpose: Designed for use in the training and selection of managers.
Population: Managers and manager trainees.

Publication Date: 1991.
Acronym: MILMD.
Scores: Total score only.
Administration: Group.
Price Data, 1991: $30 per 20 test and answer booklets; $2 per Instructor Manual ('91, 8 pages); $5 per Review Set including one test, one answer booklet, and Instructor Manual.
Time: (15–20) minutes.
Author: Donald L. Kirkpatrick.
Publisher: Donald L. Kirkpatrick.

Review of the Management Inventory on Leadership, Motivation and Decision-Making by KEVIN R. MURPHY, Professor of Psychology, Colorado State University, Fort Collins, CO:

The Management Inventory on Leadership, Motivation and Decision-Making (MILMD) is a 59-item attitude survey designed to assess beliefs and attitudes about several aspects of leadership. The first section includes 55 items representing statements about leadership, motivation, or decision making (e.g., "Leaders are born, not made"); respondents are asked whether they agree or disagree with each statement. The second section describes four decision-making approaches (e.g., manager makes decisions without input from subordinates), and asks the respondent to indicate the frequency (described in terms of percentages) with which they have used each strategy in the past, and the frequency with each one should be used in the future.

Scores on the first section of the MILMD are obtained by comparing the respondent's answer to the "correct" answer, as defined by the author of the inventory. For example, the author asserts that it is possible to teach people many of the characteristics of a leader, and that the "correct" answer to the statement "leaders are born, not make" is, therefore, to disagree. The total number of "incorrect" answers (i.e., answers in which the respondent's beliefs differ from those of the author of the inventory) is subtracted from 55 to obtain the total score on this portion of the inventory. As noted in the Instructor's Manual for this inventory, the "correct" answers represent the author's opinion (but are often backed by research findings), and some of the "correct" responses may be open to debate. The manual contains a brief rationale for many of the "correct" answers, but very few references to the specific research that supports the "correct" response are provided. Thus, the total score on this section of the inventory should be interpreted as the extent to which the respondent agrees with the (well-informed) opinion of the author of this inventory; this score does not necessarily indicate the soundness of the respondent's opinions.

The Instructor's Manual contains norms that are based on small samples of supervisors, human resource consultants, and human resource professionals in organizations. On average, members of these three groups agreed with the author of the inventory on between 83% and 89% of the items. Presumably, higher scores indicate more well-informed views regarding leadership, motivation, and decision making, but no evidence is presented to support the validity of this interpretation.

There is no formal scoring system for the second section of the MILMD. The manual author lists seven factors that should be taken into account in evaluating the appropriateness of each decision style (e.g., the urgency of the decision, the desire of subordinates to participate), but little explicit guidance is given in evaluating the allocation of past or future decisions to each category, or to possible discrepancies in past and future decision styles.

The most common use of the MILMD is to stimulate lively, practical discussion in a training program; cassette tapes are available from the author describing the use of this inventory in structuring and stimulating group discussions about leadership. The Instructor's Manual also has claims that the MILMD can be used to determine training needs, to assist in the selection of managers, and to evaluate the effectiveness of training programs, but no evidence is presented to substantiate these claims. The professional standards that govern the development and use of psychological tests and inventories (e.g., *Standards for Educational and Psychological Testing* [AERA, APA, & NCME, 1985]) make it clear that evidence of the validity of an instrument for purposes such as personnel selection or training evaluation must be presented before a test can be recommended for these purposes. At the present time, there is no evidence of the validity or usefulness of this inventory for purposes such as selecting managers for a managerial training programs, or for evaluating managerial training, and the inventory should, therefore, not be used for these purposes. The set of inventory items might serve as a useful stimulus for lively discussion because many of the items reflect widely held but incorrect beliefs about leadership and motivation. But there is at present no evidence that scores on this instrument tell us anything useful about the respondent's knowledge of or attitudes toward leadership, motivation, or decision making. Given the potential for misuse of an unvalidated instrument of this type, extreme caution should be observed in using the MILMD; scores on this instrument should not in any circumstances be used to make decisions about either individuals or training programs.

REVIEWER'S REFERENCE

American Educational Research Association, American Psychological Association, & National Council on Measurement in Education. (1985). *Standards for educational and psychological testing*. Washington, DC: American Psychological Association, Inc.

Review of the Management Inventory on Leadership, Motivation and Decision-Making by EUGENE P.

SHEEHAN, Associate Professor of Psychology, University of Northern Colorado, Greeley, CO:

According to the author, D. L. Kirkpatrick, the Management Inventory on Leadership, Motivation and Decision-Making (MILMD) is an attempt to help users define leadership and to help managers recognize that they should behave as leaders. To do this the inventory measures opinions on behaviors related to leadership, motivation, and decision making. The author recommends the inventory be employed in training programs to determine training needs, to stimulate discussion in training groups, and to evaluate the effectiveness of training programs.

There are two sections to the MILMD. The first section contains 55 agree-disagree items: 20 dealing with leadership, 25 with motivation, and 10 with decision making. In the second section, the author describes four approaches to decision making, from autocratic to participative. Respondents provide the percentage of times they have used each decision-making approach in the past and the percentage of times they believe they should use each approach in the future. The instrument is attractively designed with clear and easily followed instructions. It is self-scored and includes an answer booklet and an optional cassette tape that describes the development and uses of the inventory.

Upon completion of the instrument, respondents are provided with an answer booklet. This booklet contains the author's reasons or rationales why an agree or disagree response to each of the 55 items is "correct." It also contains a description of seven factors (organization culture, decision urgency, scope of the decision, need for acceptance, subordinate attitudes, subordinate qualifications, and employee desire to participate) that managers should consider in evaluating their approach to decision making. The answer booklet is to be used to facilitate discussion as test takers compare their answers with each other and with Kirkpatrick's answers.

The combination of the inventory, answer booklet, and cassette may be effective in causing managers to reflect on their leadership-related behaviors and in provoking discussion. However, some problems exist. For example, Kirkpatrick points out in the manual that the correctness of each response is a matter of debate. Kirkpatrick's definitions of leadership and motivation are not shared by all theorists and practitioners. However, such controversy with respect to the answers is not revealed in the answer booklet. A naive reader of this booklet might regard the author's opinions alone as "correct." Related to this, respondents who are unaware of or whose definitions differ from Kirkpatrick's will probably get several items "wrong."

Another problem pertains to differences in the type of answers provided in the answer booklet. Some answers have a rationale that is based on research. However, some of this research, for example Herzberg's, is controversial. Other rationales rely on test-taking acumen. For example, one should disagree with the statement "a decision made by employees is always better than one made by their manager" because of the presence of the word always. Other agree-disagree items have rather simplistic answer rationales including making sense, being evident to all, and "this item speaks for itself." As psychologists we should be wary of the perils of common sense. Such simplistic statements are not helpful when educating managers. The ambiguity pertaining to the information included in the answer booklet leads me to question the quality of discussion this inventory might provoke.

The inventory is designed as a learning tool, not a standardized test. Kirkpatrick does not present any data on item analysis, reliability, or validity. Kirkpatrick rightly warns against using inventory total scores in a selection process without validity data. The author also fails to provide information on item selection or instrument construction. The meaningfulness of the test scores is compromised by the absence of construct validity data.

The only psychometric data in the manual are a set of norms. These norms are based on small populations: 35 supervisors, 16 HRD consultants/educators, and 15 HRD professionals in organizations, for a total population of 66. The normative data are rudimentary, providing only average scores and ranges on the 55 agree-disagree items for each group. On the approaches to decision-making question, the author provides average responses (percentages) and ranges for each of the four approaches by each of the three norm groups.

Throughout the instrument Kirkpatrick uses the less common, although correct, spelling for employee: employe. In the manual the author indicates that previous reviewers of the inventory had recommended changing to the more traditional spelling. He also suggests that those who administer the inventory inform participants the word employe is not misspelled. I agree with the suggestion to use the more common spelling as the employe spelling interfered with my reading of the inventory and apparently others may be similarly affected. The employe spelling seems to be an affectation that detracts from the inventory.

Overall, the MILMD is an interesting device to provoke discussion in a training group. However, due to both the issues surrounding the correctness of items and the absence of psychometric data, I question the quality of any such discussion and I recommend against using this inventory to determine training needs or to evaluate the effectiveness of a training program.

[227]

Management Styles Inventory.
Purpose: Assesses individual management style under a variety of conditions.
Population: Adults.
Publication Dates: 1964–90.
Scores, 5: Philosophy, Planning and Goal Setting, Implementation, Performance Evaluation, Total.
Administration: Group.
Price Data, 1993: $6.95 per inventory.
Time: Untimed.
Comments: Self-administered survey.
Authors: Jay Hall, Jerry B. Harvey, and Martha S. Williams.
Publisher: Teleometrics International.

Review of the Management Styles Inventory by RALPH F. DARR, JR., Professor of Education, Department of Educational Foundations and Leadership, The University of Akron, Akron, OH:

The Management Styles Inventory published by Teleometrics International is a self-assessment instrument designed to provide the respondent with information about the way she or he manages, or would manage, under a variety of conditions. The inventory is composed of 12 questions organized into four categories: Concerning a philosophy of management, Concerning planning and goal setting, Concerning implementation, and Concerning performance evaluation. Under each category, three situations are presented. Altogether 12 situations are assessed. For each of the 12 situations, five possible alternatives are presented, making a total of 60 management alternatives to which the respondent is to react. The five alternatives are different for each of the 12 situations. The respondent reads all five alternatives to the situation presented, then rates each of the five alternatives on a 10-point scale that ranges from 10 points for *Completely Characteristic* to zero (0) for *Completely Uncharacteristic*.

In the Philosophy area, the authors deal with (*a*) the conflict between the needs of the individual employee (people) versus needs of organization (productivity), (*b*) the supervisor/subordinate relationship, and (*c*) the manager's notions about handling his or her employee evaluation functions. The Planning and Goal Setting section deals with (*a*) the manager's role in planning his or her unit's activities, (*b*) the manager's role in the training of personnel to get the identified goals accomplished, and (*c*) the manager's role in budget development and allocation. Implementation items assess the respondent's attitude toward the manager's role (*a*) during the implementation phase, (*b*) in delegating responsibility for implementation, and (*c*) in hiring and promoting personnel to get plans executed. Under Performance Evaluation, the authors deal with (*a*) the procedures that the manager uses to evaluate the performance of subordinates, (*b*) treating subordinates' errors, and (*c*) how the manager handles his or her negative feelings toward subordinates.

SCORING. The instrument can be self-scored. After responding to all 60 alternatives across the 12 situations, the respondent converts letters on each of the 12 scales to numerical values. These are then entered on the scoring form into one of five positions for each of the four areas of concern: Philosophy, Planning and Goal Setting, Implementation, and Performance Evaluation. The five columns represent five styles of management: Developer, Manipulator, Taskmaster, Comforter, and Regulator. Raw scores for each of the five management styles are than converted to *T*-scores by use of a conversion table. By comparing *T*-scores for each of five management styles, the respondent can first determine his or her dominant management style and then identify likely alternate styles if the primary style is not effective.

The authors suggest that the magnitude of the difference between first and second rank indicates the individual's flexibility in using various management styles. The greater the magnitude the lower the flexibility. The component score tables enable the respondent to identify which leadership style he or she manifests for each of the four areas of management concern: Philosophy, Planning, Implementing, and Evaluating. Overall management style can then be compared to style in each of the four areas (e.g., is the respondent's philosophy congruent with his or her identified management style?).

In the materials accompanying the scoring protocol, the authors provide a lengthy discussion of each of the five management styles. Each style is discussed in terms of how it balances care for people against unit productivity. It is the authors' hypothesis that only one management style, The Developer, which puts emphasis upon both productivity and people, can be effective over the long run. All other styles are flawed. The Taskmaster emphasizes productivity at the expense of people. The Comforter puts emphasis on employee satisfaction at the expense of productivity. The Regulator spends most of his or her time trying to control people and productivity, thus obtaining very little employee satisfaction or productivity for the energy expended. The Manipulator obtains only moderate performance and moderate employee satisfaction. This type of manager focuses on compromise while sending messages to employees that they should exercise responsibility yet keeping a tight rein on them. Each management style is discussed in terms of its characteristics, its effect on people and productivity, and in some cases the situations that often lead a manager to adopt that particular style.

CRITIQUE. The *T*-score tables are based on data from 12,809 "managers from business, industry, government, and service organizations" (p. 9). The current instrument was developed from Jay Hall's study of "over 18,000 managers." Minimal evidence of reliability and no evidence of criterion-related validity are provided. Careful perusal of the 12 questions and 60 alternatives suggests there is considerable face validity to this instrument. None of the questions or alternatives seem contrived or implausible. The raw score transpositions initially are somewhat difficult to plot and interpret, but the extra effort required for insightful interpretation of the results is worth it. Regardless of the management style or the style with which the individual becomes identified, respondents may learn something enlightening about themselves and how they relate to their fellow workers.

Review of the Management Styles Inventory by CHARLES K. PARSONS, Professor of Organizational Behavior, Georgia Institute of Technology, Atlanta, GA:

The Management Styles Inventory (MSI) is intended to assess managerial beliefs and behaviors that are related to important outcomes such as achievement. Its conceptual basis is similar to the "grid theory" of Blake and Mouton (1964) in that the two primary dimensions are performance-orientation and people-orientation resulting in the interpretation of five possible styles.

The instrument is a self-report description of feelings and behaviors. The individual reads 12 managerial situations. For each one, the respondent rates each of five possible responses on a 10-point scale that is anchored by *completely uncharacteristic* and *completely characteristic*. The set of 60 ratings (five response to each of 12 situations) is self-scored by having the respondent enter the ratings into a series of tables. The ratings are then totaled and converted to *T*-scores, resulting in the identification of the predominant style. Difference scores between the style scores are also computed and interpreted as reflecting how easily the individual can shift between styles when the predominant style is not working. Finally, the respondent is asked to enter the ratings in a different set of tables in order to yield profiles on the four components of style which are Philosophies of Management, Planning and Goal Setting, Implementation of Plans, and Performance Evaluation.

Overall, I believe the scoring procedures are quite complicated. This complexity might occasionally lead to confusion and errors. Furthermore, the required reading level appears to be fairly high, but there is no guidance on appropriate educational levels in the test booklet/manual. Given the complexity of the instrument and its scoring, I am surprised the authors do not provide further guidance on appropriate usage.

Based on a discussion with a representative of the test publishing company, the MSI appears to reflect mainly a cosmetic change from the Styles of Management Inventory (SMI), which is distributed by the same company and was reviewed by Korman (1978) in the *Mental Measurements Yearbook* series. The items, response format, and scoring are the same, but the resulting styles are given different names. Several related instruments by the same author and publisher, all based on the "grid theory," have also been reviewed (Bernardin, 1989; Thornton, 1989; Geisinger, 1992). These reviewers all questioned the usefulness of the "grid theory" as well as the limited information on development and validation of the instruments.

The psychometric evidence cited by Bernardin is the same as that cited in the current instrument. The authors report a median coefficient of stability of .72 with no description of sample or time interval. The authors go on to report the instrument discriminates between high-, average-, and low-achieving managers. The study upon which this was based is reported in Hall's (1988) edited book of readings.

In a concurrent validity study of 1,878 managers, the author reports an association between managerial style and managerial achievement where achievement is defined as organization level attained, corrected for age. No statistics were presented concerning statistical significance. In the test booklet, the authors claim the MSI has been found to be predictive of career achievement. The cited study provides evidence of concurrent but not predictive validity. The manual authors also report a significant canonical correlation between the MSI and the MMPI (Minnesota Multiphasic Inventory) and interpret this as construct validity evidence. Without knowledge of the theoretical rationale or the specific findings concerning which subscales of the MMPI were highly weighted on the canonical functions, this statistic is impossible to interpret.

Beyond the lack of psychometric evidence, I am also troubled by the labels for the five styles: Comforter, Developer, Regulator, Taskmaster, and Manipulator. There is no evidence the labels are anything more than catchy, value-laden terms the author has contrived. There is substantial interpretation that goes with each style label, but I question the basis of interpretation. For example, individuals who achieve score patterns that represent moderate levels of people-orientation and moderate levels of performance orientation are labeled "Manipulators" and told they are "less than honest and above board." It goes on to say that "Perhaps the most unfortunate aspect of this style for the manager is that its manipulative qualities also tend to be self-deluding." This is pretty strong stuff based on a self-report instrument of unknown validity.

The authors do provide some industry-specific norms in the test booklet. The sample sizes available for these industrial samples are respectable, ranging from 158 to 3,253. If sample sizes are sufficient, I would urge the authors to provide norms broken down by gender, functional specialty, and organizational level.

CONCLUSION. The MSI appears to be little more than a renamed instrument that has been criticized earlier (Korman, 1978) and belongs to a family of instruments that has been criticized (Bernardin, 1989; Thornton, 1989; Geisinger, 1992). The current reviewer shares the concerns of the earlier reviewers on this set of instruments. Alternative instruments to the MSI are available. As Geisinger suggested, I would recommend the Leader Behavior Description Questionnaire, Form XII (Stogdill, 1963; 9:596) or the Managerial Practices Survey (Yukl, Wall, & Lepsinger, 1990).

REVIEWER'S REFERENCES

Stogdill, R. M. (1963). *Manual for the Leader Behavior Description Questionnaire—Form XII.* Columbus, OH: Bureau of Business Research, Ohio State University.

Blake, R. R., & Mouton, J. S. (1964). *The managerial grid: Strategic new insights into a proven system for increasing organization productivity and individual effectiveness, plus a revealing examination of how your managerial style can affect your mental and physical health.* Houston: Gulf Publishing Co.

Korman, A. K. (1978). [Review of Styles of Leadership and Management.] In O. K. Buros (Ed.), *The eighth mental measurements yearbook* (p. 1763). Highland Park, NJ: The Gryphon Press.

Hall, J. (1988). To achieve or not: The manager's choice. In J. Hall (Ed.), *Models for management: The structure of competence* (2nd ed.) (pp. 497-519). The Woodlands, TX: Woodstead Press. (Reprinted from *California Management Review*, 1976, *18*, 4).

Bernardin, H. J. (1989). [Review of the Managerial Competence Index.] In J. C. Conoley & J. J. Kramer (Eds.), *The tenth mental measurements yearbook* (pp. 458-459). Lincoln, NE: The Buros Institute of Mental Measurements.

Thornton, G. C., III. (1989). [Review of the Managerial Competence Index.] In J. C. Conoley & J. J. Kramer (Eds.), *The tenth mental measurements yearbook* (pp. 459-460). Lincoln, NE: The Buros Institute of Mental Measurements.

Yukl, G., Wall, S., & Lepsinger, R. (1990). Preliminary report on the validation of the Managerial Practices Survey. In K. E. Clark & M. B. Clark (Eds.), *Measures of leadership* (pp. 223-237). West Orange, NJ: Leadership Library of America.

Geisinger, K. F. (1992). [Review of the Managerial Competence Index.] In J. J. Kramer & J. C. Conoley (Eds.), *The eleventh mental measurements yearbook* (pp. 502-503). Lincoln, NE: The Buros Institute of Mental Measurements.

[228]

Manager Style Appraisal.

Purpose: A measure of managerial style.
Population: Adults.
Publication Dates: 1967–90.
Scores, 5: Philosophy, Planning and Goal Setting, Implementation, Performance Evaluation, Total.
Administration: Group.
Price Data, 1993: $6.95 per survey.
Time: Untimed.
Comments: Self-administered survey.
Authors: Jay Hall, Jerry B. Harvey, and Martha S. Williams.
Publisher: Teleometrics International.

Review of the Manager Style Appraisal by KENNETH N. ANCHOR, Dean, School of Health and Human Services, and Professor, Senior University, Center for Disability Studies, Nashville, TN:

Time and economic constraints placed upon consultants often leave them confronting the same problem that produces stress for a grocery store owner: too many products to choose from and too little shelf space to display them. The plethora of recently published tests makes it increasingly difficult for psychologists to stay familiar with new ones and allocate time for mastering revised versions of tests on which they were initially trained and continue using in their practices. The Manager Style Appraisal (MSA) is an instrument that has considerable merit and deserves serious consideration for organizational consulting.

The Manager Style Appraisal is not the first of its kind but it has succeeded in blending and consolidating many of the better methods initiated previously for assessing management styles and leadership effectiveness. The MSA is one member of a family of test instruments from the same publisher (Teleometrics International) that appears to specialize in instruments for organizations.

Organizations that seek to become stronger value input from personnel at all levels regarding quality of supervision or management. The MSA, revised in 1990, is administered to employees and asks them to review 60 management strategies in clusters of five according to 12 separate realistic situations. Data are organized around four themes: Philosophy of Management, Planning and Goal Setting, Implementation, and Performance Evaluation. With each of the 12 situations, the subject is asked to rate his or her manager according to which of the five options is "completely characteristic" and which one is "completely uncharacteristic" of that manager.

This concise, equal-appearing interval scale affords each manager the opportunity to rate himself or herself along the same dimensions—and then use worksheets (provided) to discover where there is agreement or disagreement with subordinates' perceptions.

The booklet is well laid out and the overall test is efficient, versatile, and carefully crafted. Reliability and validity are not described in great detail but referred to as being at acceptable levels.

The test booklet contains a scoring form for the individual to complete and lucid explanatory information regarding the five management styles the model employs: task master, comforter, regulator, manipulator and integrated style. The theoretical underpinning is based upon what is termed the "style parallax model" which examines the extent to which priority is placed upon either people or performance by the manager. The model goes beyond mere pigeonholing by establishing another category for the situational manager or "tap dancer," which is less consistent and cohesive than the other management styles.

This measure has several appealing features. It is easily administered and scored. The items are constructed with gender-neutral wording. Content is neither intimidating nor overwhelming to the literate respondent. The scale lends itself to training and prevention such that ineffective supervisors can be identified and helped before widespread morale problems develop. The MSA lends itself to exploration of critical incident analysis with the supervisor's boss and/or consultant. The descriptive material that explains the scale helps to demystify the interpretation of test data. Graphics presented are a helpful guide to understanding and applying the results. Moreover, the items are not readily transparent—and consequently are less likely to be answered in the socially desirable or politically correct direction by those with a high need for social approval.

Certain limitations should not be overlooked. Some of the response options are quite detailed and require a somewhat higher degree of literacy and concentration than some other scales (e.g., checklist methods and basic employee attitude survey formats). Uninterested rank-and-file employees may not feel sufficiently invested in the process to give serious or thoughtful responses (a generic problem). The naive or unsophisticated respondent may perceive items as unnecessarily technical. A relatively high degree of concentration and attention is required and distractions or noise should be minimized. In an era of rampant litigiousness, labels such as "task master" and "manipulator" may have potentially unfavorable implications and could be misused in certain circumstances.

The booklet itself might do well to supplement certain information. Despite a normative basis of roughly 24,000 supervisor ratings obtained with the MSA, greater detail is needed explaining the number of organizations represented and age distribution of participants. A caution should be provided to participants that perceptions of a manager may not equate with actual performance (i.e., much the same way that physicians with the best bedside manner are not necessarily the finest surgeons). For balance and thoroughness not only should input from managers' subordinates be examined but also that of the manager's own supervisor(s) and peers.

In summary, the MSA has many attractive features enabling it to be used with little disruption in a wide range of organizational settings. The test is compact, allowing for individual or group administration. As test construction technology has become more sophisticated in recent years, this sensible measure appears to be well designed. The scoring system is straightforward and easily mastered. Margin for scoring error appears slim. The style parallax model of people/performance issues successfully encompasses the data generated by this assessment tool. If systematically administered on a regular basis, it probably provides a useful benchmark to determine improvement in overall supervisory effectiveness as well as trust, confidence and respect toward supervisory personnel. Unlike many other instruments, it allows for the supervisor to rate him/herself independently and to ascertain how congruent self-ratings are with those produced by subordinates.

At a recent conference of the American Board of Medical Psychotherapists and Psychodiagnosticians several themes were identified as predictive of career success: adaptability, interpersonal skills and perceptiveness, self-discipline, resources for coping with stress, time management, initiative, effective problem solving and negotiation skills. Data generated by the MSA are illuminating on most of these topics.

It is well established that the larger sample of data one obtains, the sounder one's conclusion. In most consulting projects I have encountered during the past two decades, it would be extraordinarily rare to find a single instrument (even when accompanied by an interview) to address all referral questions. As useful as the MSA is it would fit well within a battery of measures and, in turn, bolster the consultant's confidence in his or her conclusions. Even those consultants who have a favorite "all purpose" scale would probably want to collect their own substantial normative pool of data before using this tool on a regular basis.

Review of the Manager Style Appraisal by CLAUDIA J. MORNER, Associate University Librarian for Access Services, Boston College, Chestnut Hill, MA:

This 60-item instrument provides a mechanism for managers to learn their employees' view of their style of management, with scores for five kinds of managers: developer, manipulator, taskmaster, comforter, and regulator. A companion measure, Management Styles Inventory (not reviewed), is a self-appraisal instrument for managers. Using both instruments is intended to provide a realistic two-dimensional measure of a person's management style and an opportunity for improving manager/employee communication. This is the fourth edition of the instrument which was first published in 1967. Based on the 30-year-old managerial grid theory (Blake & Mouton, 1964), this instrument's purpose is to measure managers on both people and performance criteria.

The content of the instrument focuses on four areas of management: Philosophy, Planning and Goal Setting, Implementation, and Performance Evaluation. Employees are given descriptions of management behavior and asked to rank on a scale from 10 (completely characteristic) to 1 (completely uncharacteristic) how much these behaviors describe their manager. An example of a manager's behavior in the evaluation section is one on how a manager reacts to mistakes made on the job. "Because it is only natural for some mistakes to occur, [my manager] tries to avoid emphasizing those which do happen unless they call the attention of superiors to the department." Items are clustered in groups of five, with one scale per group. Each of the five items in the cluster represents one of the types of managers described above.

After employees have completed the instrument, managers have the option of allowing the employees to continue to score the results and learn the managerial type of their supervisor, or the manager can collect the booklets and score the results privately. The scoring system gives individual raw scores for five managerial types: Developer, Manipulator, Taskmaster, Comforter, Regulator. A table is provided to convert raw scores to norms using *T*-scores. These *T*-scores were based on data from 24,000 persons rating their immediate supervisor.

The *T*-scores for each category (Developer, Manipulator, etc.) are ranked to show the manager's preferred style. These *T*-scores can be subtracted from each other to show how likely a manager is to move away from a preferred style to a backup. A chart for computing subscores for each managerial area, such as planning, performance evaluation, etc., are given to provide additional data from the instrument. These charts have shaded areas which show the desired range of scores for each aspect of management. If a manager's score falls below the range the chart indicates the manager has less than desirable use of the style and a score above the desirable range shows a more than desirable reliance on the given style. Therefore, a manager might find that he or she is weaker than desirable in planning, average for philosophy, and stronger than desirable in implementation and evaluation. For further interpretation, a table gives norms for the five types of managers in nine different kinds of organizations, such as manufacturing, sales and marketing, and human service. A bibliography for further reading is composed entirely of books and chapters by one of the authors.

A number of problems were cited in reviews (Bernardin, 1989; Thornton, 1989) of an earlier instrument similar to this one from the same publisher. Most of these problems still exist in the current instrument. A primary concern is the lack of a manual. Without a manual an opportunity to provide detailed information such as on reliability and validity and helpful advise on using the instrument is lost. It is important for employees taking this instrument to understand how the results will be handled. People can be very reluctant to provide honest responses if they think their answers might be used against them. There is no mention of confidentiality or advice in helping those administering the instrument to understand the issues and make wise decisions before launching the project. Because the main purpose for using this kind of instrument is to gather objective information that can be used to open up a dialogue between an employee and the manager to foster better understanding, the lack of guidance from the authors on ways to use the results, such as possible scripts or ideas about appropriate settings and techniques for developing the best dialogue, is unfortunate.

Real information about norms, validity, and reliability is also needed to better judge the instrument. It appears that some additional data have been included in this edition, but the information is included in the instrument packet and written for the employee to understand how to interpret the scores, and therefore, the test lacks technical and specific data on how norms, and reliability and validity data were obtained. For example, the authors say that the "instrument discriminates between high, average, and achieving manager" (p. 15), but no explanation was offered about what that means or how the discrimination was determined.

In a future edition the authors should consider reformatting the items so that they are easier to read. Although the instructions for marking answers are clear, the layout of text is very dense and may be hard for some employees to follow. This layout with 14 to 20 words per line is too long to be easily read; the one-column format is dense.

Improvements to this edition over the past include more information about interpreting the scores, the removal of sexist language, and a chart of norms for various occupations.

For companies or organizations that are interested in what employees think of their managers' styles, a better choice would be the Myers-Briggs Type Indicator (MBTI; 9:739 and 10:206) or the Leader Behavior Descriptive Questionnaire, Form 12 (9:596). Both are better instruments for this kind of two-way discussion when taken by both individuals, not just the manager, and it gives people a common language to understand the personality differences found in the workplace which lead to different perceptions, responses, and behaviors. This reviewer has used both instruments and found the MBTI a superior instrument for fostering managerial/employee communication.

REVIEWER'S REFERENCE

Blake, R. R., & Mouton, J. S. (1964). *The managerial grid: Key orientations for achieving production through people*. Houston, TX: Gulf Publishing Company.

Bernardin, H. J. (1989). [Review of the Management Appraisal Survey.] In J. C. Conoley & J. J. Kramer (Eds.), *The tenth mental measurements yearbook* (pp. 458-459). Lincoln, NE: Buros Institute of Mental Measurements.

Thornton, G. C., III. (1989). [Review of the Management Appraisal Survey.] In J. C. Conoley & J. J. Kramer (Eds.), *The tenth mental measurements yearbook* (pp. 459-460). Lincoln, NE: Buros Institute of Mental Measurements.

[229]

Memory Assessment Scales.

Purpose: Developed to assess areas of cognitive function that are involved in memory.
Population: Ages 18 and over.
Publication Date: 1991.
Acronym: MAS.
Scores, 16: Short-Term Memory (Verbal Span, Visual Span, Total), List Acquisition, Delayed List Recall, Delayed Prose Recall, Global Memory Scale (Verbal Memory [List Recall, Immediate Prose Recall, Total], Visual Memory [Visual Reproduction, Immediate Visual Recognition, Total], Total), Delayed Visual Recognition, Names-Faces (Immediate, Delayed) and 7 Verbal Process

scores: Total Intrusions, List Clustering (Acquisition, Recall, Delayed Recall), Cued List Recall (Recall, Delayed Recall), List Recognition.
Administration: Individual.
Price Data, 1994: $199 per complete kit including stimulus card set, 25 record forms, manual (131 pages), and attache case; $171 per kit minus attache case; $95 per stimulus card set; $38 per 25 record forms; $45 per manual.
Time: [40–45] minutes.
Author: J. Michael Williams.
Publisher: Psychological Assessment Resources, Inc.

Review of the Memory Assessment Scales by RONALD A. BERK, Professor, School of Nursing, The Johns Hopkins University, Baltimore, MD:

The Memory Assessment Scales (MAS) is an individually administered battery of tasks that are designed to measure memory functions in normal and clinical populations. Three areas of cognitive functioning are assessed: "(a) attention, concentration, and short-term memory; (b) learning and immediate memory; and (c) memory following a delay" (manual, p. 3). For each area, separate verbal and nonverbal tasks are used to measure material-specific (verbal versus visual-spatial) memory abilities. Both recall and recognition formats are used.

The MAS consists of 12 subtests based on seven memory tasks. Five of the subtests involve the repeated assessment of retention of information. These subtests yield 16 scores: 12 subtest scores plus a Short-term Memory Summary score, Verbal Memory Summary score, Visual Memory Summary score, and Global Memory score.

The research on amnesic disorder was the primary source for both the theoretical models of memory function and the tasks developed for the MAS. The assessment procedures used in these studies of memory disorder provided an item pool from which tasks on the MAS were selected or modified. Although descriptions of the content from which the tasks were generated are given for each area or subscale, no content domain specifications are presented to display the relationship between the content in each area and the task distribution or coverage. Also, no evidence of content-related validity is reported from any panel of experts. Such evidence is essential to determine the match of the tasks to their respective content and the representativeness of the task distribution. Further, the content of the tasks does not reflect the possible ethnic and cultural diversity of the intended population of test takers. This is particularly evident in the Names-Faces and Delayed Names-Faces Recall Subscales where the 10 faces (six women, four men) are all Caucasian, selected from the yearbook of a local high school, and their names were chosen from the local phone book to be "generally familiar names" (p. 44).

A major consideration in the design of the MAS was to balance the number of tasks against the realistic time constraints of the usual clinical setting. This translates into the maximum number of important tasks that can be administered within one hour. Although administration time can vary with the skills of the test taker, the author's goal seems to have been attained.

Administration and scoring of the MAS can be performed by individuals not formally trained in neuropsychology or clinical psychology. A trained person with a background in psychological testing may serve as an examiner. Training in administration and scoring should be provided by a qualified psychologist. Interpretation of the scores should not be attempted without a firm understanding of psychological theories and principles of memory functioning.

The standardized procedures for administration are clearly explained in the manual. Directions to be read to each test taker are presented in sufficient detail so the test taker can respond appropriately to the tasks. No sample materials or practice questions are provided.

The scoring procedures to be applied to the MAS Record Form are described in the manual. The step-by-step computation of scores for each subscale, conversion to standard scores, computation of summary scale scores, and plotting of the MAS subscale profile are presented in a simple straightforward manner with sample data. The standard score scale for the subscales has a mean of 10 and standard deviation of 3; the summary scores are scaled with a mean of 100 and standard deviation of 15. The scoring criteria for the drawings in the Visual Reproduction Subscale are clearly defined, with interexaminer generalizability (reliability) coefficients based on naive and experienced examiners exceeding .95. The guidelines for interpretation of all of the scores in terms of age and education norms and in comparison to WAIS-R (Wechsler Adult Intelligence Scale—Revised) Full Scale IQ are clinically meaningful, with several illustrative case examples. The clinical evaluations interpreted from the normalized scores are intended to focus on a person's functional level of cognitive ability and the diagnosis of memory disorder resulting from brain illness or injury.

The normative sample from which 19 tables of normative scores are derived consisted of 843 adult volunteers without a history of neurological disease or chronic substance abuse. It included 361 men and 482 women who were 18 to 90 years of age. A stratified random subsample of 467 was selected from the 843 to reflect the U.S. population distribution by age and gender and by age and education. No profiles of the demographic characteristics for the total sample as well as the census-matched subsample were presented. Such information is necessary to understand the norms and to determine their appropriateness for the wide range of individuals who will take the MAS. Normative scores are presented only by age, age and gender, and age and education. Difference scores are also reported between the Global Memory Scale and WAIS-R Full Scale IQ, between all pairs of MAS subscales, and between pairs of MAS summary scores. They are based on the standard error of a difference score at the .05 level of significance.

Despite the rigor demonstrated in the computation of the normative scores, the partitioning of the sample into age subgroups of approximately 38 subjects each undermines the stability of the estimated scores. The polynomial regression analyses used in the continuous norming procedure can yield biased estimates of the scores with such small samples. Although the age-decade and age-education norms provide useful structures for interpretation, the instability of those norms due to inadequate sample sizes belies their usefulness. Aggregating the age categories differently to assure larger samples would have been more desirable.

The technical adequacy of the MAS was reported via several reliability and validity studies. As far as reliability evidence, generalizability coefficients were computed to assess score stability (test-retest) over 6 months based on a sample of 30 adults. The coefficients ranged from .70 to .95. The most unstable subscales were Verbal Span, Visual Span, List Acquisition, List Recall, and Immediate Visual Recognition. Given the small sample size used for these analyses, those estimates should be regarded as tentative. Generalizability coefficients were also reported for the Visual Reproduction task to determine interexaminer reliability, noted previously. Again, very small samples of subjects' drawings (5 to 10) were used in the analyses of variance.

Construct-related validity evidence was reported in terms of an intercorrelation matrix of subscale scores, factor analyses using normal ($n = 471$) and neurologically impaired ($n = 52$) samples, and comparisons of criterion group performance based on patients with dementia ($n = 34$), closed-head trauma ($n = 37$), left hemisphere lesion ($n = 16$), and right hemisphere lesion ($n = 23$). These types of evidence were appropriate and informative; however, the sample sizes in these studies question the importance assigned to the results in their interpretation. No caveats were given by the author to acknowledge these limitations. One type of validity evidence not studied is the concurrent validity of MAS scores with those of alternative memory scales. Such evidence would furnish insight into the measurement of the memory disorder construct.

In summary, the MAS is a systematically developed clinical tool to assess memory functions. Its design, scoring, and interpretation procedures are meaningful and clearly explained. Despite these assets, there are several technical weaknesses: (*a*) no content-related validity evidence, (*b*) norms estimated from inadequate and possibly biased samples, and (*c*) reliability and validity studies that report and interpret results beyond the scope of the limited samples used for the analyses. Although the MAS is a potentially useful instrument, clinicians should exhibit caution in interpreting the scores and should regard the results as preliminary until these technical problems can be corrected.

Review of the Memory Assessment Scales by JOHN W. YOUNG, Assistant Professor of Educational Statistics and Measurement, Rutgers University, New Brunswick, NJ:

The Memory Assessment Scales (MAS) is an individually administered battery of tasks developed to assess a variety of memory functions in normal and clinical populations. The MAS has been standardized and validated for use with adults ages 18 to 90. The major functions measured by the MAS include: verbal and nonverbal learning and immediate memory; verbal and nonverbal attention, concentration, and short-term memory; and memory for verbal and nonverbal material following delay. In addition, measures of recognition, intrusions during verbal learning recall, and retrieval strategies are also available. The MAS was designed with consideration of the constraints faced by many test administrators: the possibility of bedside administration, the need for easily transportable test materials, and the need for simple scoring procedures. Norms that enable the comparison of an individual's results with several target groups are an important feature of the MAS.

The MAS consists of 12 subtests based on seven memory tasks. Five of the subtests assess the retention of information learned in an earlier subtest. These subtests measure memory functioning following brief or extended delay. Total testing time is approximately one hour.

MAS SUBTESTS. The 12 MAS subtests in order of presentation are as follows: (*a*) List Learning: an auditory verbal learning task that requires the subject to recall a list of 12 common words; (*b*) Prose Memory: an auditory verbal prose recall task that requires the subject to recall a short story; (*c*) List Recall: requires the subject to recall the words presented in the List Learning subtest; (*d*) Verbal Span: a short-term auditory memory task that requires the subject to repeat increasingly longer series of numbers; (*e*) Visual Span: a nonverbal analogue of the Verbal Span subtest; (*f*) Visual Recognition: measures recognition memory for geometric designs; (*g*) Visual Reproduction: requires the subject to reproduce a geometric design; (*h*) Names-Faces: measures the ability to associate names with faces; (*i*) Delayed List Recall: requires the subject to recall the words presented in the List Learning subtest; (*j*) Delayed Prose Memory: requires the subject to recall the short story from the

Prose Memory subtest; (*k*) Delayed Visual Recognition: subject is presented with 20 geometric designs and required to identify those 10 which were presented earlier in the Visual Recognition subtest; (*l*) Delayed Names-Faces Recall: requires the subject to recognize the correct names of individuals in photographs from the Names-Faces subtest.

SCORES. Detailed scoring procedures for each of the subtests are provided. Subtest raw scores are converted to standard scores ($M = 10$, $SD = 3$) using one of the age group conversion tables. In addition to the 12 subtest scores, the MAS provides three Summary Scale scores: Short-Term Memory, Verbal Memory, and Visual Memory. A measure of general memory ability, the Global Memory Scale score, is computed from the Verbal and Visual Memory Summary scores. Examinee responses, subtest and summary scores, and a subtest profile can be recorded on the MAS record form.

STANDARDIZATION. The MAS is normed on 843 adults, ranging in age from 18 to 90 years, who do not have a history of neurological disease. A stratified sample of 467 subjects, a subset of the original sample of 843, was selected to match the distribution of the U.S. population based on Census Bureau projections for 1995, classified by age and gender and by age and educational level. The normative sample closely matches the projected population values when compared on the stratification variables.

RELIABILITY. Test-retest reliability for the MAS was estimated using generalizability theory because traditional reliability coefficients are not appropriate for repeated administrations of the same task. A complete discussion of generalizability theory can be found in Cronbach, Gleser, Nanda, & Rajaratnam (1972). Generalizability coefficients can be interpreted in a similar fashion as traditional reliability coefficients. Generalizability coefficients for the subtests range from .70 to .95 with a mean of .85; for the Summary Scales, coefficients ranged from .86 to .92 with a mean of .90; for the Global Memory Scale, coefficients ranged from .94 to .95 with a mean of .95. These coefficients fall within the range of acceptable values.

VALIDITY. The validity of the MAS was established using three types of studies: convergent and discriminant validity, factorial validity, and group differentiation. The convergent and discriminant validity of the MAS was examined by correlating subtest scores from 677 normative subjects. Tests of short-term memory are predicted to correlate highly with each other but only low to moderately with tests of either verbal or visual memory. The same would be expected of verbal or visual memory tests and their relation to the two other categories of tests. The pattern of correlation results reported generally support these predictions. Factor analyses were performed on MAS subtest scores for two samples of adults: 471 normals and 52 neurologically impaired. Construct validity of the MAS was tested using marker variables computed from combinations of WAIS-R (Wechsler Adult Intelligence Scale—Revised) subtest scores. MAS subtests were expected to load on the same factor as the marker variable that theoretically measured similar constructs. Factor analytic results reported appear to support the use of three separate Summary Scale scores. Validity of the MAS was also examined by comparing the scores of the 843 normal subjects in the normative sample with the scores of 110 impaired individuals. Impaired subjects were one of four types: dementia, left-hemisphere lesion, right-hemisphere lesion, and closed-head trauma. The pattern of scores for these groups on the Summary Scales and the Global Memory Scale are reported to be consistent with studies of these disorders.

COMMENTS ON THE MAS. The MAS appears to be a valid, reliable, and comprehensive measure of memory functioning appropriate for normal and impaired populations. Although standardization of the test appears adequate, further norming with a larger sample and conducting additional validity studies would strengthen the applicability of this instrument. The test manual is detailed but clearly written and is suitable for both novice and experienced administrators. The section on the interpretation of scores and subtest profiles can provide highly useful information when developing clinical diagnoses.

REVIEWER'S REFERENCE

Cronbach, L. J., Gleser, G. C., Nanda, H., & Rajaratnam, N. (1972). *The dependability of behavioral measurements: Theory of generalizability for scores and profiles*. New York: Wiley.

[230]

Menstrual Distress Questionnaire.

Purpose: Designed as "a self-report inventory for use in the diagnosis and treatment of premenstrual and menstrual distress."
Population: Women who experience strong to severe premenstrual or menstrual distress.
Publication Dates: 1968–91.
Acronym: MDQ.
Scores, 8: Pain, Water Retention, Autonomic Reactions, Negative Affect, Impaired Concentration, Behavior Change, Arousal, Control.
Administration: Group or individual.
Forms, 3: Form C, Form T, Short Form T.
Price Data, 1993: $110 per complete kit; $25 per 10 Form C questionnaires; $80 per 50 Form T questionnaires; $17.50 per Form C prepaid test report answer sheet; $99.50 per 50 Form T prepaid test report answer sheets; $57.50 per manual ('91, 124 pages); $220 per IBM microcomputer edition for Form C.
Time: (15) minutes for Form C; (5) minutes for Form T or Short Form T.
Author: Rudolph H. Moos.
Publisher: Western Psychological Services.
Cross References: See 9:695 (6 references) and T3:1466 (4 references).

TEST REFERENCES

1. Amodel, N., & Nelson-Gray, R. O. (1989). Reactions of dysmenorrheic and nondysmenorrheic women to experimentally induces pain through the menstrual cycle. *Journal of Behavioral Medicine*, *12*, 373-385.
2. Hedlund, M. A., & Chambless, D. L. (1990). Sex differences and menstrual cycle effects in aversive conditioning: A comparison of premenstrual and intermenstrual women with men. *Journal of Anxiety Disorders*, *4*, 221-231.
3. Heilbrun, A. B., Jr., Friedberg, L., Wydra, D., & Worobow, A. L. (1990). The female role and menstrual distress. *Psychology of Women Quarterly*, *14*, 403-417.
4. Richardson, J. T. E. (1990). Questionnaire studies of paramenstrual symptoms. *Psychology of Women Quarterly*, *14*, 15-42.
5. Gallant, S. J., Hamilton, J. A., Popiel, D. A., Morokoff, P. J., & Chakraborty, P. K. (1991). Daily moods and symptoms: Effects of awareness of study focus, gender, menstrual-cycle phase, and day of the week. *Health Psychology*, *10*, 180-189.
6. Morse, C. A., Dennerstein, L., Farrell, E., & Varnavides, R. (1991). A comparison of hormone therapy, coping skills training, and relaxation for the relief of premenstrual syndrome. *Journal of Behavioral Medicine*, *14*, 469-489.
7. Klebanov, P. K., & Jemmott, J. B. III. (1992). Effects of expectations and bodily sensations on self-reports of premenstrual symptoms. *Psychology of Women Quarterly*, *16*, 289-310.
8. Lindner, H., & Kirkby, R. J. (1992). Premenstrual symptoms: The role of irrational thinking. *Psychological Reports*, *71*, 247-252.
9. Chrisler, J. C., Johnston, I. K., Champagne, N. M., & Preston, K. E. (1994). Menstrual joy: The construct and its consequences. *Psychology of Women Quarterly*, *18*, 375-387.
10. Veeninga, A. T. (1994). The relationship between late luteal phase dysphoric disorder and anxiety disorders (1994). *Journal of Anxiety Disorders*, *8*, 207-215.
11. Whitehead, W. E. (1994). Assessing the effects of stress on physical symptoms. *Health Psychology*, *13*, 99-102.
12. Choi, P. Y. L., & Salmon, P. (1995). How do women cope with menstrual cycle changes? *British Journal of Clinical Psychology*, *34*, 139-151.

Review of the Menstrual Distress Questionnaire by JENNIFER J. FAGER, Assistant Professor of Teacher Education, University of New Hampshire at Manchester, Manchester, NH:

The Menstrual Distress Questionnaire (MDQ) "is a 47-item self-report inventory for use in the diagnosis and treatment of premenstrual and menstrual symptoms" (p. 1). The questionnaire developer designed the instrument to "distinguish cyclical from noncyclical changes in physical symptoms, mood and behavior, and arousal" (p. 1). These changes in symptoms are examined during three phases of the menstrual cycle: four days before menstrual flow, during menstrual flow, and the remainder of the cycle. The questionnaire is also designed to identify the type and intensity of symptoms experienced during each phase of the menstrual cycle, and as an aid in identifying the effect of specific interventions administered by clinicians and researchers.

The Menstrual Distress Questionnaire includes three forms. Form C (Cycle), which includes the 47 self-report items, was designed to measure symptoms experienced during each of the three stages of the menstrual cycle. Women completing Form C use a rating scale of zero (*No experience or symptom*) to four (*Present, Severe*) to rate the severity of symptoms listed on the form based upon their menstrual cycles in general. Form T (Today), using the same 47 items and rating scales as Form C, examines symptoms experienced during the menstrual cycle. In addition, Short Form T consists of the first 22 items and the first four scales of Form T.

The MDQ includes statements representing eight scales; these eight scales include three somatic scales: Pain, Water Retention, and Autonomic Reactions. The three scales that tap mood and behavioral changes include Negative Affect, Impaired Concentration, and Behavior Change. Of the two remaining scales, one measures arousal and the other is a control scale or a scale measuring symptoms not traditionally associated with menstrual cycles. The scales are used on all forms to examine symptoms before, during, and between menstrual cycles.

The results provided by the forms are designed for different uses. Form C is designed for use in the screening process of menstrual symptoms and is used to identify actual menstrual problems. Form T is to be used for diagnosis, treatment, and research applications and provides a detailed, concurrent record of cyclical changes in symptom severity when used every other day for one or two cycles. The Short Form T is used if one is not interested in monitoring changes in the Impaired Concentration, Behavior Change, Arousal, and Control scales.

Each of three forms of the MDQ have three options in scoring. The forms can be hand scored from results on the AutoScore Form. Other scoring options include a computer-scannable mail-in answer sheet or a microcomputer program. Each patient who takes the MDQ is provided with a report from each form. Form C provides patients with a score profile, an analysis of symptom significance, charted results, and a display of item responses. In addition to the information provided from the scoring of Form C, Form T provides the patient with an overview of treatment options. These results allow the patient and clinician to determine the best procedures for treating the identified menstrual problems.

In order to establish content validity the instrument developer conducted a review of the research and assessment procedures to examine menstrual cycle symptoms. The 47 symptoms that appear on the MDQ were the result of the gathering of information from several sources. The procedure included collecting information via an open-ended questionnaire given to women, symptoms identified in the review of research, and a list from the Blatt Menopausal Index. The instrument developer also included symptoms to tap feelings of excitement and well-being as well as control symptoms or symptoms not usually associated with menstrual cycles. The questionnaire developer did not provide complete data on the women involved in the instrument development procedures nor did he identify the source of the items not found in the literature but included on the questionnaire.

The MDQ was piloted on 839 women to establish reliability and validity criteria. A factor analysis provided the author with the eight scales mentioned earlier. Internal consistencies for the initial sample varied from .89 to.53 using the Kuder-Richardson Formula 20. Additional data on the internal consistencies are provided based on previous research in the field completed by researchers other than the author.

The questionnaire developer suggests in the preface to the manual that the MDQ has been used for over 20 years in research of menstrual cycles and symptoms. Difficulties arise in analyzing the reliability of the instrument, however, due to the lack of information provided on the standardization sample. Although the author provides basic demographic information on the sample such as age, education, and marital status, it is unclear from the manual where and when the sample was obtained. It is also unclear from the information provided in the manual whether or not the psychometric data were completed for the current publication data or for the initial conceptualization of the instrument used over two decades ago.

The manual that accompanies the MDQ is a complete review of the research that incorporates research data into the description of the questionnaire. This information, although useful to researchers, is cumbersome for clinicians. This is particularly true in the sections of the manual related to test development and use. I would recommend a separation of the research from the initial instrument development information of clarification of how the research has aided in the instrument development for the MDQ user.

The reference list and annotated bibliography included in the manual provide researchers interested in menstrual symptom research with many resources for further investigation. Chapter 6 of the manual reviews the literature in treatment of perimenstrual distress providing ample opportunity for researchers and clinicians to seek additional information in treating patients. As a resource manual it is invaluable.

The MDQ provides the patient, the clinician, and the researcher with extensive information on menstrual symptoms. The reports provided from an analysis of results from both Form C and Form T are thorough in their examination when scored by computer. Hand scoring is laborious and may be complicated for clinicians working under time constraints. The printouts provided from the computer-scored forms are easy to read and interpret. Sample reports are included in the manual to aid in interpreting results.

If the problems associated with clarification of the manual are rectified, the Menstrual Distress Questionnaire will be a useful tool for clinicians working with patients experiencing menstrual difficulties. As it now stands the MDQ is helpful to researchers in menstrual distress; however, additional information should be provided regarding the development of the instrument.

Review of the Menstrual Distress Questionnaire by DONNA L. SUNDRE, Associate Assessment Specialist/Assistant Professor of Psychology, James Madison University, Harrisonburg, VA:

GENERAL INFORMATION. The Menstrual Distress Questionnaire (MDQ) and its manual represent over 25 years of research and instrument development focusing on understanding the physical and psychological fluctuations associated with the menstrual cycle. An expanding base of literature has indicated a renewed interest in women's health issues and evidence for the linkage of perimenstrual symptoms to a variety of health risks (Logue & Moos, 1986). Designed to provide clinicians with a standard method for diagnosing and treating premenstrual and menstrual symptoms and researchers with measures for exploring perimenstrual symptoms, treatments, and etiological theories, the MDQ is a 47-item self-report inventory, which can be group or individually administered. The 47 items provide a listing of common symptoms and feelings associated with menstruation. Subjects are requested to indicate the presence and severity of the symptoms and feelings using a 5-point scale (0 = *No experience of symptom*; 4 = *Present, severe*). The MDQ is composed of eight scales; three measure somatic symptoms: Pain, Water Retention, and Autonomic Reactions. Three scales assess mood and behavioral changes: Negative Affect, Impaired Concentration, and Behavior Change. One of the two remaining scales measures Arousal, and the other is a Control scale designed to assess the extent to which symptoms not typically associated with the menstrual cycle are reported.

Three forms are available. Form C (Cycle) is administered once and intended to estimate severity of symptoms at the three stages of the most recent menstrual cycle: most recent flow, four days before flow, and the remainder of the cycle. Form T (Today) assesses the presence and severity of the 47 symptoms on the day of administration. Short Form T consists of the first 22 symptoms of Form T comprising the first four scales.

PRACTICAL EVALUATION. The self-report instruments, although not attractive or particularly durable, are straightforward, and the directions easy to understand. All three forms can be administered in any of three ways: with computer-scannable mail-in answer sheets, via microcomputer, or using a carboned answer sheet (AutoScore Form). Administration should be relatively uncomplicated and require no more than 15 minutes with literate subjects. Scoring procedures are, of course, related to the administration method selected, and should meet most needs with immediate results available using microcomputer administration or the carboned answer sheets. Users can hand score the AutoScore Forms and individual profiles can be generated by carefully following the instructions provided. The scannable answer sheets can be mailed to the publisher where they will be scanned, scored, and interpreted. The computer report is promised to be mailed out within one working day. Although many individuals would be qualified to administer this instrument, the author is careful to advise that users should be familiar with the MDQ interpretation guidelines, psychometric properties, and limitations included in the manual.

The manual is well written, fairly well organized, and includes a very helpful annotated bibliography of 1985–1989 related research. It provides clear instructions for the administration of the instruments and care is taken to mention the importance of completing all items, building rapport with the respondent, and ensuring the confidentiality of responses. Hand-scoring procedures are also carefully described, including how to handle missing data and how much missing data can be reasonably tolerated.

Technical Evaluation.

NORMS. The original norming sample of 839 women is in one paragraph of the manual described as "representative" and in the next as "homogeneous." This is puzzling because the intended target population with whom potential users of the inventory would wish to compare scores would not necessarily be limited to a homogeneous sample of younger (Mean = 25.2 years), highly educated (Mean = 15.2 years), recently married (Mean = 2.7 years) women with over half (56%) having no children. More disturbing is the lack of description of the sampling design and participation rates to evaluate the nature, adequacy, and appropriateness of the intended norming group. The tables included in Appendix A have combined data from the original sample of 839 with 1,542 observations from a multitude of undescribed samples obtained by other investigators to form means and standard deviations for Form C scales. Appendix A also presents a sample of 399 responses used to form means and standard deviations for Form T scales. No subgroup norms are reported; this is unfortunate because the characteristics of the menstrual cycle are known to vary with factors such as age (Logue & Moos, 1986).

A number of additional and potentially important limitations to the original norms must be mentioned. The original norming group was not presented a current version of the MDQ. The norming sample was asked to respond to Form A, a questionnaire similar to the current Form C (Cycle), which has been modified in the following ways: The items have been reordered; the rating scale has been changed from 1 to 6 to the current 0- to 4-point scale; and the premenstrual phase duration has been reduced from the week prior to menstrual flow to 4 days prior to menstrual onset. The impact of such contextual effects is unknown; however, Appendix B in the manual presents raw score to *T*-score conversions for the 0–4-point scale with exactly the same *n*s reported in Appendix A using the original Form A 1–6-point scale and other modifications described above. More information concerning the creation of the norms is required.

It would also appear that scores generated from pencil-and-paper instruments are to be considered parallel with microcomputer presented scores. Considerable effort was spent exploring and describing the lack of differences resulting in questionnaire versus interview responses; however, similar attention has not been addressed to questionnaire versus microcomputer administration of the inventory. No data providing evidence of comparability have been provided. Without assurance that the two modes of score generation are equated, the reliability and validity of the scores may also be variant. Thus, generalizing reliability and validity evidence from the original sample to data collected using computer administration is not advisable at this time.

RELIABILITY. All MDQ scales were developed through factor analysis, therefore measures of internal consistency should be adequate. For the most part, the scales comprise homogeneous items, and the factor structure seems to be stable across varied samples and menstrual cycle stages. Of further interest, preliminary studies addressing symptom reports across menstrual cycles for premenstrual, menstrual, and intermenstrual phases resulted in moderate to high positive correlations. These results suggest good intercycle reliability in subject reports for each of the three cycle phases and are encouraging. However, the sample was very small ($n = 15$) and not described. A curiosity relates to the presentation of KR-20 internal consistencies, a common method for estimating the consistency of responses that can be scored as right or wrong, for scales comprising items measured on the 0- to 4-point metric. An additional puzzle relates to the rather high correlations of the subscale factors derived using varimax rotation, which generally results in orthogonal or independent factors. The subscale factors appear to be related to one another. The manual also includes data from a variety of research studies, some using adaptations of the MDQ, to demonstrate internal consistency with less information than that provided regarding the original norming sample.

VALIDITY. The most crucial psychometric property of any measurement is validity, and this reviewer was disappointed in the implicit rather than explicit treatment given to the validity of measurement throughout the manual. A section devoted to all aspects of validity was expected in the first chapter, which included a section on psychometric properties. Immediately following the descriptions of evidence for scale internal consistency and intercycle consistency, some validity evidence was expected. It is not that such evidence does not exist; it is spread throughout the manual without explicit referral to it as such. The author may contend that much of the following chapters describe validity evidence; this is true, but for the sake of the reader it should have been summarized briefly in the psychometric properties section with referrals to other chapters of the manual. The stability of the factor structure is prerequisite to validity evidence, and the correlations between factors suggest that although the scales are related, unique variance is accounted for by each. This is the critical issue: What is the variance attributable to? Although the author suggests the variance is not due to memory or order effects, the truly critical issue remains unanswered in this section and potential readers must search several additional chapters to locate and evaluate the potential validity of the instrument for intended purposes.

SUMMARY EVALUATION. Despite the criticisms mentioned above, the MDQ has much to offer. The MDQ and various adaptations have been widely used in the published research. Now that the instrument is commercially distributed, the research published using the MDQ may be easier to interpret because adaptations will be allowed only by the publisher. The development of a truly representative norming group and subgroup norms may be forthcoming.

The MDQ compares favorably to other available instruments. For example, the Premenstrual Assessment Form (PAF) (Halbreich & Endicott, 1982), which examines only premenstrual physical, mood, and behavior changes, has two forms which allow retrospective (previous three cycles) and concurrent (daily) symptom assessments. Comparisons of MDQ and PAF prevalence rates are discrepant, with about twice as many women reporting premenstrual symptoms with the PAF; however, severe symptom reports (about 3%) are similar for both inventories. The conclusion drawn by Logue and Moos (1986) was that research indicates that women tend to report greater symptomology on retrospective assessments and the greater prevalence rates generated by the PAF are a function of retrospective reports across *three* cycles. The same authors point out fairly consistent results from the two MDQ forms, although the retrospective Form C (Cycle) version, consistent with other research findings, does result in slightly higher reports of mild symptomology than the concurrent Form T (Today). Moos does suggest the use of Form C for screening and repeated administrations across cycles of Form T for more accurate and detailed profiles.

Although the MDQ materials, and particularly the computerized reports, are expensive, the information provided is elaborate. For women experiencing severe perimenstrual distress, the research generated from this instrument represents both a source for understanding the phenomenon and a means to assist their clinicians in arriving at appropriate diagnoses and prescribing effective treatments.

REVIEWER'S REFERENCE

Halbreich, U., & Endicott, J. (1982). Classification of premenstrual syndromes. In R. Friedman (Ed.), *Behavior and the menstrual cycle*. New York: Marcel Dekker.

Logue, C. M., & Moos, R. H. (1986). Perimenstrual symptoms: Prevalence and risk factors. *Psychosomatic Medicine*, *48*, 388-414.

[231]

Metaphon.

Purpose: Designed to be "a complete assessment and therapy programme for children with phonological disorders."
Population: Ages 3.5–7.
Publication Date: 1990.
Scores: Total score only.
Administration: Individual.
Parts, 4: Screening, Probing, Intervention, Monitoring.
Price Data, 1990: £201.25 per complete set; £28.75 per manual (48 pages); £23 per 25 screening forms; £28.75 per 10 probe record books; £40.25 per screening picture book; £74.75 per probe picture book; £34.50 per set of monitoring pictures.
Time: (15) minutes.
Authors: Elizabeth Dean, Janet Howell, Ann Hill, and Daphne Waters.
Publisher: NFER-Nelson Publishing Co., Ltd. [England].

Review of the Metaphon by ALLAN O. DIEFENDORF, Associate Professor, KATHY KESSLER, Clinical Lecturer, and MICHAEL K. WYNNE, Associate Professor, Department of Otolaryngology, Indiana University School of Medicine, Indianapolis, IN:

According to its authors, the Metaphon approach "provides a theoretical basis for the remediation of phonological disorder in children" (manual, p. 1) ages 3.5 to 7 years of age. The authors have adopted the practice of using the generally accepted term, phonological disorder, to refer to those children whose predominant problem is one of establishing the sound contrasts of their native language. A lengthy rationale is provided for the development of this approach, including a general review of phonological theory and phonological process analysis of speech. The authors contend that therapeutic approaches to date have focused upon a child's *discrimination* and *production* of speech sounds rather than upon the child's metaphonological skills (an underlying rule system). The major thrusts of the Metaphon approach to the remediation of phonological disorders, therefore, are to assist phonologically disordered children in exploring their sound systems and the *rules* of those systems, in using repair strategies during breakdowns in communication, and in making communicative attempts effective by utilizing the knowledge the children have gained regarding how speech production influences meaning.

The skills necessary to address phonological disorders in children are numerous, requiring the specific training in phonological theory that only speech-language pathologists receive. Inasmuch as training programs differ in their emphasis upon phonological theory, it is clear that phonological process analysis is not intended to be undertaken by an inexperienced clinician. The clinician conducting such diagnostic evaluations and subsequent therapies must be skilled in listening to and transcribing subtle deviations in speech production, determining which deviations are developmental in nature, prioritizing those processes deemed to be disordered, and developing therapy activities that reduce the frequency of occurrence of these processes ultimately resulting in increased speech intelligibility.

The Metaphon Resource Pack (MRP) consists of four major components: a screening device, a procedure for in-depth probing of the specific process(es) identified in the screening, a monitoring procedure, and a two-phase therapy approach with suggested activities. In developing the screening procedure, the authors focused on 13 "simplifying phonological processes" (p. 10) they deemed to occur most frequently; this inherently limits the clinician in describing the large number of possible phonological processes known to be demonstrated by phonologically disordered children. Unless the clinician is very skilled in recognizing additional phonological processes through observation of the child's conversational speech, it is likely that important processes will be overlooked. In the child demonstrating subtle phonological processes, the clinician may find the MRP screening ineffective. The MRP screening and Process Specific Probes may be useful with only a select group of children, and may not be applicable for the broad range and variability of phonologically disordered children encountered in speech-language pathology practices.

The vocabulary chosen for both the MRP screening device, monitoring procedure, and process Specific Probes include items that appear to be within the standard British dialect of English, but are less familiar to speakers of General American English. In addition, the line drawings used to represent the target items do not correspond with the most familiar representations known to the American English speaker. For example, a cargo van is used to represent the word *van*, rather than the passenger vehicle most children would recognize. The word *path* refers to a sidewalk leading up to a house, rather than a footpath through a woods, jumping rope is called "skipping" rope, and *jelly* is the target associated with a picture of what appears to be a jello mold. Stimuli included in the monitoring procedure include words such as *thistle* and *yacht*, words not common in the receptive vocabulary of young children in the United States and Canada. Although these differences in dialect and vocabulary may seem insignificant, the lack of familiarity of these words in their respective contexts will necessitate elicitation of the stimuli through imitation rather than spontaneous production.

The study conducted to determine the efficacy of the Metaphon approach to phonological therapy was acknowledged by its authors to be "preliminary" and the results "tentative"; however, only 13 subjects were used in the study. Although the design of the study was explained, the results of the study were not fully addressed. There was no discussion regarding any form of standardization. The authors did not indicate if further study would be explored or if modifications to the program were under way, in spite of the fact that their results were acknowledged to be "unexpected." Assumptions regarding the efficacy of the Metaphon approach were made based on very limited information. A reader of the Metaphon manual may conclude that its authors have created a program in which they firmly believe, and are intent upon bringing it into the clinical armamentarium, in spite of minimal research findings substantiating their claims of effectiveness.

In spite of the limitations of the assessment, monitoring procedures, and the efficacy study described above, the clinician addressing phonological disorders in children should find the tenets and techniques for the Metaphon approach to remediation useful. Focusing on developing metaphonological skills rather than emphasizing only the accuracy of speech sound production helps eliminate the self-consciousness and reticence to participate often encountered when working with phonologically disordered children. Teaching speech sound production as a tool for effective communication and transmission of meaning focuses on the pragmatic reasons why children must correct their speech sound production, even if they are too young to understand such rationales if presented didactically. The therapy approach espoused by the Metaphon authors allows children to experience natural, real world consequences of phonological speech errors by emphasizing transmission of meaning as the primary goal of speaking.

Several changes to the existing Metaphon approach should be considered to eliminate the fundamental problems of using this tool. First, the diversity of blatant and subtle phonological disorders children demonstrate coupled with the varied dialects of English spoken throughout the world may preclude the Metaphon from addressing the variety of phonological disorders observed in children. The potential for false negative results using the MRP may exist unless the number of phonological processes evaluated is expanded. Secondly, the application of this approach to speakers of dialects other than standard British English should be considered in the modification of stimulus items and line drawing depictions for those stimuli. Finally, an efficacy study should evaluate the program's effectiveness with a larger number of phonologically disordered children of varying cultural and dialectal backgrounds to determine its application within the broad range of phonologically disordered speakers of English.

[232]

Metropolitan Achievement Tests, Seventh Edition.

Purpose: Designed to measure the achievement of students in the major skill and content areas of the school curriculum.
Publication Dates: 1931–93.
Acronym: MAT7.
Administration: Group.
Forms, 2: S, T (secure form).
Restricted Distribution: Distribution restricted to accredited schools and school districts; Form T available by special arrangement only.
Price Data, 1994: $62.50 per complete battery (Levels Primary 1, Primary 2, Elementary 1) including 25 hand-scorable test booklets, one directions for administering, and one class record; $52 per basic battery (Levels Preprimer, Primer) including 25 hand-scorable test booklets, one directions for administering, and one class record; $57 per basic battery (Levels Primary 1, Primary 2); $62.50 per complete battery (Levels Elementary 1 through Secondary 4) including 25 hand-scorable test booklets and one directions for administering; $57 per basic battery (does not include social studies and science) (Levels Elementary 1 through Secondary 4) including 25 hand-scorable test booklets and one directions for administering; $83 per Type 1 complete battery (Levels Primary 1, Primary 2, Elementary 1) including 25 machine-scorable test booklets and one directions for administering; $78 per Type 1 basic battery (Levels Preprimer through Elementary 1) including 25 machine-scorable test booklets and one directions for administering; $95.50 per Type 2 complete battery (Levels Primary 1, Primary 2, Elementary 1) including 25 machine-scorable test booklets and one directions for administering; $90.50 per Type 2 basic battery (Levels Preprimer and Primer) including 25 machine-scorable test booklets and one directions for administering; $31 per 25 writing test booklets and one directions for administering (Levels Primary 1 through Secondary 3/4); $88.50 per stencil keys for hand-scorable, Type 1, and Type 2 test booklets (Levels Preprimer through Elementary 1); $21.50 per set of translucent overlay keys for Type 1 and Type 2 answer documents; $21 per set of response keys (Levels Preprimer through Secondary 4); $10.50 per practice tests (Levels Preprimer through Intermediate 2/3/4) including 25 practice tests and one directions for administering; $50 per 100 Type 1 machine-scorable answer sheets (Levels Elementary 1/2 through Secondary 1/2/3/4); $62.50 per 100 Type 2 machine-scorable answer sheets (Levels Elementary 1/2 through Secondary 1/2/3/4); $7.50 per directions for administering; $4.50 per directions for administering practice tests; $15 per directions for administering writing test; $36.50 per norms booklet; $36.50 per technical manual ('93, 199 pages); $45 per writing test manual; $29 per writing test technical data and norms booklet; $12 per teacher's manual for interpreting; $18.50 per compendium of instructional objectives; $17 per *Strategies for Instruction: A Handbook of Performance Activities*; $4 per class record; $3.50 per MAT7 bookmark; $15.50 per 25 parent pretest folders; $15.50 per examination kit (Levels Preprimer through Intermediate 4) including one Type 1 basic battery booklet for Preprimer and Primer, Type 1 complete battery booklet for Primary 1 and Primary 2, either hand-scorable or reusable complete battery booklet (Levels Elementary 1 through Intermediate 4), directions for administering, practice test, practice test directions, and Type 1 answer document (Levels Elementary 1 through Intermediate 4) (Examination kits for preview purposes only).
Foreign Language Edition: Parent pretest folders available in Spanish.
Comments: Information regarding numerous customized and package scoring and reporting services available from publisher.
Author: The Psychological Corporation.
Publisher: The Psychological Corporation.

a) ACHIEVEMENT TESTS.

1) *Preprimer.*
Population: Grades K.0–K.5.
Scores, 4: Prereading, Mathematics, Language, Basic Battery.
Time: (90–100) minutes.

2) *Primer.*
Population: Grades K.5–1.5.
Scores, 4: Same as for Preprimer.
Time: (100–110) minutes.

3) *Primary 1.*
Population: Grades 1.5–2.5.
Scores, 12: Word Recognition, Reading Vocabulary, Reading Comprehension, Total Reading, Concepts and Problem Solving, Procedures, Total Mathematics, Language, Science, Social Studies, Basic Battery, Complete Battery.
Time: (215–225) minutes.

4) *Primary 2.*
Population: Grades 2.5–3.5.
Scores, 12: Same as for Primary 1.
Time: Same as for Primary 1.

5) *Elementary 1.*
Population: Grades 3.5–4.5.
Scores, 11: Same as for Primary 1 minus Word Recognition.
Time: (225–235) minutes.

6) *Elementary 2.*
Population: Grades 4.5–5.5.
Scores, 11: Same as for Elementary 1.
Time: Same as for Elementary 1.

7) *Intermediate 1.*
Population: Grades 5.5–6.5.
Scores, 11: Same as for Elementary 1.
Time: (245–255) minutes.

8) *Intermediate 2.*
Population: Grades 6.5–7.5.
Scores, 11: Same as for Elementary 1.
Time: Same as for Intermediate 1.

9) *Intermediate 3.*
Population: Grades 7.5–8.5.
Scores, 11: Same as for Elementary 1.
Time: Same as for Intermediate 1.

10) *Intermediate 4.*
Population: Grades 8.5–9.5.
Scores, 11: Same as for Elementary 1.
Time: Same as for Intermediate 1.

11) *Secondary 1.*

Population: Grade 9.
Scores, 9: Reading Vocabulary, Reading Comprehension, Total Reading, Mathematics, Language, Science, Social Studies, Basic Battery, Complete Battery.
Time: (220–230) minutes.
12) *Secondary 2.*
Population: Grade 10.
Scores, 9: Same as for Secondary 1.
Time: Same as for Secondary 1.
13) *Secondary 3.*
Population: Grade 11.
Scores, 9: Same as for Secondary 1.
Time: Same as for Secondary 1.
14) *Secondary 4.*
Population: Grade 12.
Scores, 9: Same as for Secondary 1.
Time: Same as for Secondary 1.

b) WRITING TESTS.
Purpose: Provides a reliable, norm-referenced measure of student writing abilities from a free-response assessment.
Population: Grades 1.5–12.
Scores: Total score only (holistic scoring); 6 scores: Content Development, Organizational Strategies, Word Choice, Sentence Formation, Usage, Writing Mechanics (analytic scoring).
Time: 45 (55) minutes.

Cross References: See T4:1618 (31 references); for reviews of an earlier edition by Anthony J. Nitko and Bruce G. Rogers, see 10:200 (44 references); for reviews by Edward H. Haertel and Robert L. Linn, see 9:699 (30 references); see also T3:1473 (89 references); for reviews by Norman E. Gronlund and Richard M. Wolf and an excerpted review by Joseph A. Wingard and Peter M. Bentler of an earlier edition, see 8:22 (41 references); see also T2:22 (20 references) and 7:14 (25 references); for reviews by Henry S. Dyer and Warren G. Findley of an earlier edition, see 6:16 (16 references); for a review by Warren G. Findley, see 4:18 (10 references); see also 3:13 (7 references); for reviews by E. V. Pullias and Hugh B. Wood, see 2:1189 (3 references); for reviews by Jack W. Dunlap, Charles W. Odell, and Richard Ledgerwood, see 1:874. For reviews of subtests, see 8:283 (1 review), 8:732 (2 reviews), 6:627 (2 reviews), 6:797 (1 review), 6:877 (2 reviews), 6:970 (2 reviews), 4:416 (1 review); 4:543 (2 reviews), 2:1458.1 (2 reviews), 2:1551 (1 review), 1:892 (2 reviews), and 1:1105 (2 reviews).

TEST REFERENCES

1. Canney, G. (1989). Metropolitan Achievement Tests (MAT6) reading diagnostic tests. *Journal of Reading, 33,* 148-150.
2. Dillon, D. R. (1989). Showing them that I want them to learn and that I care about who they are: A microethnography of the social organization of a secondary low-track English-reading classroom. *American Educational Research Journal, 26,* 227-259.
3. Swanson, H. L. (1989). The effects of central processing strategies on learning disabled, mildly retarded, average, and gifted children's elaborative encoding abilities. *Journal of Experimental Child Psychology, 47,* 370-397.
4. White, T. G., Power, M. A., & White, S. (1989). Morphological analysis: Implications for teaching and understanding vocabulary growth. *Reading Research Quarterly, 24,* 283-304.
5. Cunningham, A. E. (1990). Explicit versus implicit instruction in phonemic awareness. *Journal of Experimental Child Psychology, 50,* 429-444.
6. McKeown, M. G., & Beck, I. L. (1990). The assessment and characterization of young learners' knowledge of a topic in history. *American Educational Research Journal, 27,* 688-726.
7. Miller, P. H., & DeMarie-Dreblow, D. (1990). Social-cognitive correlates of children's understanding of displaced aggression. *Journal of Experimental Child Psychology, 49,* 488-504.
8. Miller, S. D., & Smith, D. E. P. (1990). Relations among oral reading, silent reading and listening comprehension of students at differing competency levels. *Reading Research and Instruction, 29*(2), 73-84.
9. Sowell, E. J., Zeigler, A. J., Bergwall, L., & Cartwright, R. M. (1990). Identification and description of mathematically gifted students: A review of empirical research. *Gifted Child Quarterly, 34,* 147-154.
10. Toth, L. S., & Baker, S. R. (1990). The relationship of creativity and instructional style preferences to overachievement and underachievement in a sample of public school children. *Journal of Creative Behavior, 24,* 190-198.
11. Barnhart, J. E. (1991). Criterion-related validity of interpretations of children's performance on emergent literacy tasks. *Journal of Reading Behavior, 23,* 425-444.
12. Beck, I. L., McKeown, M. G., Sinatra, G. M., & Loxterman, J. A. (1991). Revising social studies text from a text-processing perspective: Evidence of improved comprehensibility. *Reading Research Quarterly, 26,* 251-276.
13. Greenwood, C. R. (1991). Longitudinal analysis of time, engagement, and achievement in at-risk versus non-risk students. *Exceptional Children, 57,* 521-535.
14. Groller, K. L., Kender, J. P., & Honeyman, D. S. (1991). Does instruction on metacognitive strategies help high school students use advance organizers? *Journal of Reading, 34,* 470-475.
15. McCabe, P. P., Margolis, H., & Mackie, B. (1991). The consistency of reading disabled students' instructional levels as determined by the Metropolitan Achievement Test and the Ekwall Informal Reading Inventory. *Reading Research and Instruction, 30*(3), 53-62.
16. Purcell-Gates, V., & Dahl, K. L. (1991). Low-SES children's success and failure at early literacy learning in skills-based classrooms. *Journal of Reading Behavior, 23,* 1-34.
17. Wineburg, S. S. (1991). On the reading of historical texts: Notes on the breach between school and academy. *American Educational Research Journal, 28,* 495-519.
18. Armour-Thomas, E. (1992). Assessment in the service of thinking and learning for low achieving students. *The High School Journal, 75,* 99-104.
19. DuPont, S. (1992). The effectiveness of creative drama as an instructional strategy to enhance the reading comprehension skills of fifth-grade remedial readers. *Reading Research and Instruction, 31*(3), 41-52.
20. McCormick, S. (1992). Disabled readers' erroneous responses to inferential comprehension questions: Description and analysis. *Reading Research Quarterly, 27,* 55-77.
21. McKeown, M. G., Beck, I. L., Sinatra, G. M., & Loxterman, J. A. (1992). The contribution of prior knowledge and coherent text to comprehension. *Reading Research Quarterly, 27,* 79-93.
22. Payne, B. D., & Manning, B. H. (1992). Basal reader instruction: Effects of comprehension monitoring training on reading comprehension, strategy use and attitude. *Reading Research and Instruction, 32*(1), 29-38.
23. Romance, N. R., & Vitale, M. R. (1992). A curriculum strategy that expands time for in-depth elementary science instruction by using science-based reading strategies: Effects of a year-long study in grade four. *Journal of Research in Science Teaching, 29,* 545-554.
24. Greenwood, C. R., Terry, B., Utley, C. A., Montagna, D., & Walker, D. (1993). Achievement, placement, and services: Middle school benefits of classwide peer tutoring used at the elementary school. *School Psychology Review, 22,* 497-516.
25. Hollingsworth, M., & Woodward, J. (1993). Integrated learning: Explicit strategies and their role in problem-solving instruction for students with learning disabilities. *Exceptional Children, 59,* 444-455.
26. Jenkins, J. R., & Jewell, M. (1993). Examining the validity of two measures for formative teaching: Reading aloud and maze. *Exceptional Children, 59,* 421-432.
27. Kibby, M. W. (1993). What reading teachers should know about reading proficiency in the U.S. *Journal of Reading, 37,* 28-40.
28. Lupkowski-Shoplik, A. E., & Assouline, S. G. (1993). Identifying mathematically talented elementary students: Using the lower level of the SSAT. *Gifted Child Quarterly, 37,* 118-123.
29. Dennebaum, J. M., & Kulberg, J. M. (1994). Kindergarten retention and transition classrooms: Their relationship to achievement. *Psychology in the Schools, 31,* 5-12.
30. Gagné, F. (1994). Are teachers really poor talent detectors? Comments on Pegnato and Birch's (1959) study of the effectiveness and efficiency of various identification techniques. *Gifted Child Quarterly, 38,* 124-126.
31. Hayes, Z. L., & Waller, T. G. (1994). Gender differences in adult readers: A process perspective. *Canadian Journal of Behavioural Science, 26,* 421-437.
32. House, E. R., & Lapan, S. (1994). Evaluation of programs for disadvantaged gifted students. *Journal for the Education of the Gifted, 17,* 441-466.

33. Jenkins, J. R., Jewell, M., Leicester, N., O'Connor, R. E., Jenkins, L. M., & Troutner, N. M. (1994). Accomodations for individual differences without classroom ability groups: An experiment in school restructuring. *Exceptional Children, 60*, 344-358.

34. Loxterman, J. A., Beck, I. L., & McKeown, M. G. (1994). The effects of thinking aloud during reading on students' comprehension of more or less coherent text. *Reading Research Quarterly, 29*, 353-367.

35. Rekrut, M. D. (1994). Teaching to learn: Strategy utilization through peer tutoring. *The High School Journal, 76*, 304-314.

36. Whang, P. A., & Hancock, G. R. (1994). Motivations and mathematics achievement: Comparisons between Asian-American and non-Asian students. *Contemporary Educational Psychology, 19*, 302-322.

37. Brannigan, G. G., Aabye, S. M., Baker, L. A., & Ryan, G. T. (1995). Further validation of the qualitative scoring system for the modified Bender-Gestalt Test. *Psychology in the Schools, 32*, 24-26.

Review of the Metropolitan Achievement Tests, Seventh Edition by CARMEN J. FINLEY, Research Psychologist, Santa Rosa, CA:

The Seventh Edition of the Metropolitan Achievement Test (MAT7) continues to be a strong competitor among achievement test batteries, as it has been over a number of decades. Originally published in the 1930s, the current version is vastly different from the earlier versions and does differ somewhat from its predecessor, the MAT6. There has been an extensive updating of content and all items are new. The general rationale provided by the publisher states that the decision for a revision at this time is based on:

1. Changes in the school curriculum.
2. Changes in assessment trends and methods.
3. The need for updated testing materials, normative information, and interpretive materials.

A major change has been in going from 8 testing levels, each of which contains more than one grade (from grade 5 on, any given level is designed for two or more grades), to 14 levels (two preschool and one each for grades 1 through 12). Another change in MAT7 over MAT6 is the discontinuation of the Diagnostic Battery, apparently from lack of demand. A shortened form has recently been added that tests Reading, Mathematics, and Language in 90 minutes. There is also an abbreviated form that provides shortened versions of all the tests in the full length battery. A separate Writing test for grades 1 through 12, with two forms at every grade, is also available. Some of the supplemental materials available with MAT6 have been discontinued due to little demand: Pre-test and Post-test Workshop Kits (which train staff to administer the tests), a Basal Textbook Resource Guide, the Test Coordinator's Handbook, and an Administrator's Guide. However, some of the features contained in these materials have been incorporated into other current supporting materials.

The development of this edition faithfully followed standard procedures of test development starting with a review and analysis of recent editions of major textbook series in every subject area covered by test batteries. Attention was also given to recent state and district school curricula and educational objectives and to trends indicated by national professional organizations (International Reading Association, National Council of Teachers of Mathematics, National Council of Teachers of English, National Science Teachers' Association, American Association for the Advancement of Science, and National Council for the Social Studies). An impressive 10-page bibliographical review of textbooks and instructional materials is presented in Appendix 1 of the technical manual. Based on this review and analysis, emphasis was given to creating items with greater appeal and to including more items designed to assess higher-order thinking skills.

TEST SPECIFICATIONS, ITEM DEVELOPMENT, AND TRYOUT FORMS. Test specifications were developed for 14 levels, 2 kindergarten levels and grades 1 through 12, designating content, objectives, and items to be included in two parallel forms. All items were to be newly written and to be classified not only as to content, but also as belonging to a cognitive objective—knowledge, comprehension, or thinking skills. As is customary, more items were initially developed than needed in the final forms and special attention was given to new item types that were being developed. (Item writers were, for the most part, independent consultants who contracted with the test publisher. They were primarily teachers and former teachers, usually free-lance writers with various specialties. Approximately three times as many items were written as were tried out.) Small local pilot studies were conducted prior to the national tryouts to allow for continual revision and refinement based on student performance and comments of both teachers and students. Tryout booklets containing about 22,500 items across 14 levels were assembled into 132 packets.

NATIONAL TRYOUTS. Specific research questions of the national item tryout program stated by the publisher included:

1. How difficult is each item for students at the intended grade level?
2. How well does each item work to separate high-scoring students from low-scoring students?
3. Does each item get progressively easier for students in the next higher grade?
4. How are the response choices for each item working?

Teacher reaction was also solicited concerning appropriateness of the objectives; overall difficulty of the tests; design clarity, and format; appeal of the booklets; and interest level of test content.

Administration of the tryout booklets took place between February 15 and March 1, 1991, with approximately 750 students participating at each grade level. In addition, each student took a subset of the MAT6 for purposes of equating and scaling the old and new editions.

Participating school districts were selected to be representative of the national school population with stratification variables consisting of socioeconomic status, urban/suburban/rural status, and geographic region. A total of 197 districts from 39 states and the District of Columbia participated and included about 136,000 students.

A special advisory panel consisting of seven African Americans, four Hispanics, two Asians, and a representative of women's issues was assembled to review tryout results. Their charge was to identify and suggest changes for any items that might reflect ethnic, gender, socioeconomic, cultural, or regional bias or stereotyping.

DEVELOPMENT OF FINAL FORMS. The selection of items to be included in the final tests was based on six criteria, as stated by the publisher:

1. Appropriate content fit to the test blueprint.

2. Appropriate difficulty for the intended grade and increase or decrease in difficulty for adjacent lower or higher grades.

3. Good discrimination between high scorers and lower scorers.

4. Appropriate clarity and interest.

5. Absence of bias according to advisory panel and statistical procedures.

6. Good spread of students choosing each distractor.

Special attention was given to the balance of cognitive skills across forms. In general, with grade progression, the number of items classified as knowledge/recognition decreased, whereas the number of items classified as requiring understanding or thinking skills increased. For example, in Reading for the first four levels (Preprimer through Primary 2), the percent of knowledge/recognition items ranged from 67% to 100%, whereas items measuring understanding ranged from 0 to 26% and those measuring thinking skills ranged from 0 to 11%. In contrast, at the upper four levels (Secondary 1 through Secondary 4), the percent of knowledge/recognition items ranged from 41% to 51% whereas items measuring understanding ranged from 26% to 34% and those measuring thinking skills ranged from 22% to 25%. The figures for mathematics are even more striking. At the lower levels, the knowledge/recognition items ranged from 13% to 30%, understanding ranged from 52% to 66%, and thinking skills ranged from 10% to 21%. At the upper levels, no items were classified as strictly knowledge/recognition items, 44% to 48% required understanding, and 52% to 56% required thinking skills. Scope and sequence for all levels is clearly presented in the technical manual.

STANDARDIZATION AND EQUATING. Spring standardization data involving 100,000 students in 300 school districts were collected between April 1 and April 30, 1992. An additional 50,000 students participated in the equating programs. Fall standardization data were collected between October 5 and October 31 with another 79,000 students participating. All students were also administered the Otis-Lennon School Ability Test to ensure comparability across levels and forms. In addition, special substudies were conducted involving the use of separate answer sheets for third-grade students and for students using calculators when taking the Mathematics tests. Separate norms are available for students using calculators in the Mathematics tests. An additional substudy was made to compare MAT7 and NAEP (National Assessment of Educational Progress) performance at selected grades in the areas of Reading, Mathematics, Science, and Social Studies.

School districts that participated in the standardization studies were a randomly selected sample based on the same stratification variables as the item tryouts with the addition of ethnicity and type of school, public versus nonpublic. The publisher used a "five-wave" sampling procedure that involved pulling five separate nationally representative samples. Participation from everyone in each group or "wave" was solicited. When a school in one group declined to participate, a school having the same characteristics in another group was selected instead. This procedure was used to avoid "lack of first choice" (manual, p. 28) bias. The School District Fifth County Summary Tape, a recompilation of the 1980 U.S. Census data by school district, provided the information for selection based on the chosen variables. The 1990 U.S. Census data, available in August 1992, were used to weight standardization samples "when necessary" (p. 28).

NORMS. The MAT7 provides various types of derived scores. They include scales scores, percentile ranks and stanines, normal curve equivalents, grade equivalents, achievement/ability comparisons, functional reading levels, content cluster performance categories, proficiency statements at the high school grades, and predicted SAT and ACT performance ranges.

Functional reading levels are criterion-referenced scores that place a pupil's performance into three categories: Instructional Reading Level, Independent Reading Level, and Frustration Reading Level. The Instructional Level is the level at which a student can succeed in the classroom. The Independent Level is the level of material a student can easily read on his own, and the Frustration Level reflects the place at which he will have difficulty reading with comprehension.

Content cluster analysis attempts to identify a student's strengths and weaknesses in specific objectives within a content area. For example, some of the clusters under Concepts and Problem Solving for Intermediate 2 (grade 6) include: numeration, number theory, measurement, geometry, estimation, statistics and probability, and strategies in problem solving. One of the inherent problems in cluster analysis is that in many cases a cluster does not contain many items. Those just cited have been three and six items per cluster. Estimation, for example, contains just three items. Much depends on whether a given student knows just one, or two, or all three of the items. And it is conceivable that a student who fails all three might have succeeded on all of them if given different items that measure this same cluster. This is why cluster scores are less stable (i.e., less reliable) than subtest scores or any scores that contain a greater number of items. Some of the clusters contain many more items, over 30 items in some cases (for example, the knowledge cluster under the Language subtest for this level). The user who ventures into cluster analysis needs to be aware of how many items each cluster contains.

VALIDITY AND RELIABILITY. Content validity, or the extent to which the test items reflect an appropriate sampling of the goals of instruction, is thoroughly demonstrated and presented in the MAT7 Compendium of Instructional Objectives. This 116-page publication clearly delineates the scope and sequence by content area across all battery levels and is contained in two booklets, one for Form S and one for Form T. Extensive tables classify each test item according to the objective measured and the cognitive process measured (knowledge/recognition, understanding, thinking) for each level and give behavioral descriptors for most objectives. Items are also classified across content areas delineating those that measure thinking skills and research skills to form the basis for a separate reporting in these two areas.

The publisher reports completion rates by subtest ranging from 72% for Reading Comprehension, Primary 1, Form S, to 100% for various subtests at several levels. However, for students taking Intermediate 1 and higher levels, completion rates are in the high 80% to 90% range and generally increase with grade level. Tables of *p*-values, the percent of students who correctly answer an item, are given by subtest and level. Mean *p*-values are also presented for subtests and total scores.

The extent to which an item is functional in separating high and low scoring students, where "good" students tend to pass and "poor" students tend to fail, is expressed by biserial correlation coefficients. The publisher gives this information in the form of tables of median biserials by subtest across levels. Growth over time is shown by the increase in mean scaled scores and is portrayed graphically for Total Reading, Total Mathematics, Language, Science, and Social Studies. Correlations between MAT6 and MAT7 are quite high with only a few subtests dropping below .70: Language, Preprimer and Primer; Procedures, Science and Social Studies, Level 1; Science, Level 2; Reading Vocabulary, Levels 4, 6, 8, and 9; and Science, Level 11.

As evidence of construct validity, the publisher gives correlations between MAT7 and the Otis-Lennon School Ability Test (OLSAT), Sixth Edition. These generally show a substantial relationship between most of the MAT7 subtests and the OLSAT. Finally, to demonstrate the continuity of MAT7 across levels, correlations between adjacent levels of the test battery are given. Most subtests are at least .70 or better except at the lower levels.

Reliability, or the extent to which a test yields consistent results, is indicated using three approaches. Kuder-Richardson formula #20, Kuder-Richardson formula #21, and alternate-forms correlations and standard errors were all calculated and are quite acceptable.

TEACHER'S MANUALS. A Teacher's Manual for Interpreting test results is a well-selected mix of what the test is designed to measure in scope and sequence, factors to consider when interpreting performance, and tips for teaching. It also explains the various kinds of scores using nontechnical and easily understandable language. It makes brief mention of achievement/ability comparisons, content cluster performance indicators, instructional reading levels, independent reading levels, frustration reading levels, proficiency statements, predicted SAT and ACT performance ranges, and research skills and thinking skills. A section on interpreting MAT7 results gives good sturdy guidelines such as always ask "why," don't emphasize small difference in scores, interpret in light of other factors, etc., and discusses factors affecting achievement and the evaluation of group and individual performance. Another section discusses how to use test results mentioning the misuse of test results in promotion and retention of students, grading students, teacher evaluation, and comparison of different tests, as well as the proper use of test results in establishing instructional priorities and grouping for instruction. The manual concludes with a substantial section on strategies for using test results and includes worksheets for developing instructional priorities.

SCORING SERVICES. An impressively wide array of scoring services is offered. The first level of reporting is the test results for each student by class, school, or district. Any combination of the following scores may be selected for each test total and battery total: raw score, scaled score, national percentile rank-stanine, national NCE, grade equivalents. Reports with objective-based information are available at the individual, class, school, and district level. There are also reports designed for administrators, superintendents, school boards, and parents. The report for parents includes a bar graph and a written summary of the student's standing, called proficiency information.

Various statistical summaries are also available. An item analysis by grade lists the percent answering each item correctly (*p*-value) for the class/school/district, or the school/district, or district only. For easy comparison the national *p*-values are listed as well as district values, and significant differences between the national and local values are flagged. Cluster summaries are also included. Other statistical services include local norms conversion tables; frequency distributions by grade, school, or district; and student data tapes. The publisher also offers pre/post test evaluation, a learner outcome/proficiency reporting service that allows districts to redefine MAT7 items to their own objectives. School districts that score their own tests must make a licensing agreement with the publisher.

CONCERNS: MAT7 AS COMPARED WITH MAT6. Nitko (1989), in his review of MAT6, commented:

> A presumed advantage of using a multilevel battery is its potential for out-of-level testing (i.e., administering a test at a level that is closer to a student's functional level of educational development than is the student's actual grade placement). It would be difficult to recommend out-of-level testing with the MAT6 because of practical considerations stemming from the tests' design. First, there are no validated locator tests available . . . Second, the discrete nature of many of the objectives for a level make it difficult to test comparable material with easier items. Third, if out-of-level testing were to be done on a wide scale, students would need to be removed from their normal classroom locations. (p. 511)

Nitko was speaking about a battery with eight levels. The MAT7 has 14 levels. Unless there has been a tremendous realignment of students actually placed in the grade where they function best, one would expect the creation of additional levels to compound the problem. Representatives of the publisher, however, claim that construction and scaling practically eliminate the need for out-of-level testing. Their expectations are that no child at a given grade level will meet with total failure, nor will any child who passes all items on the test fail to be adequately measured. It will be interesting to see, under normal conditions of classroom use, if this is actually true.

Nitko was also concerned, especially with high school students, that there was not adequate measurement of higher order thinking skills. This problem has been remedied not only at the secondary level, but at the lower levels as well.

This reviewer of the MAT6 was also concerned about cluster analysis:

> Some important reliability information is not provided. The authors encourage cluster analyses interpretations, but provide little help about the extent to which teachers are likely to be misled because of measurement error when they use cluster scores as indicators of skill mastery. (Nitko, 1989, p. 514)

The MAT7 does provide standard errors of measurement by cluster (pages 84–112 in the spring technical manual). However, only a brief cautionary statement is made in the teacher's manual to the effect that the reliability of scores at the cluster level is lower than scores at the test level due to the smaller number of items. This will probably have little meaning for the average educator who does not have a basic understanding of reliability. A fuller discussion and some concrete examples would enhance this section.

SUMMARY. In summary, the MAT7 is a well-constructed achievement test battery. The developers have succeeded in achieving their primary mission of updating their materials to be better aligned with changes in the school curriculum, in assessment trends and methods, and in providing normative information and interpretive materials. I was especially impressed that much of the technical material was presented in fairly understandable terms, which should be readily understood by users.

REVIEWER'S REFERENCE

Nitko, A. J. (1989). [Review of the Metropolitan Achievement Test, Sixth Edition]. In J. C. Conoley & J. J. Kramer (Eds.), *The tenth mental measurements yearbook* (pp. 510-515). Lincoln, NE: Buros Institute of Mental Measurements.

Review of the Metropolitan Achievement Tests, Seventh Edition by RONALD K. HAMBLETON, Professor of Education and Psychology, University of Massachusetts at Amherst, Amherst, MA:

A standardized school achievement test battery in its seventh edition is obviously meeting the assessment needs of many administrators, teachers, and students. The Metropolitan Achievement Tests (MAT) have now been in use for over 60 years. According to the publisher, the MAT has considerable value to school administrators and teachers for (*a*) assessing the level of individual student performance in relation to a "national consensus curriculum" (technical manual, p. 11); (*b*) determining the current status of school achievement at the district and the school level and for special groups; and (*c*) answering questions about the district and school curricula and measuring change from one grade to the next, and from one year to the next.

The publisher was clear about four inappropriate uses of the MAT. These inappropriate uses include promotion and retention of students, grading of students, teacher evaluations, and comparison of results from different tests. Clear explanations of the reasons for various misuses of the MAT are especially significant at a time when the misuses of educational tests appear to be widespread and the misuses are undermining the positive uses of assessments such as the MAT.

As per the practice over seven editions, each new edition of the MAT is revised by the publisher to respond to (*a*) changes in the school curriculum; (*b*) the need for up-to-date testing materials, norms, and interpretative material; and (*c*) changes in assessment trends and methods. The publisher must surely have found the preparation of the seventh edition of the MAT (referred to as the MAT7) difficult because the educational reform movement in the United States is having a profound effect on school curricula and assessment practices. For example, the emphasis today on the teaching of higher-level thinking skills and the expanded use of performance assessments has led to questions being raised about the validity of multiple-choice items in educational assessments. The MAT is an all-multiple-choice test in the major subject areas. But the publisher states:

> In fact, there remains nothing more appropriate for high stakes testing programs than the multiple-choice batteries that not only have the breadth of content coverage necessary for valid assessment, but also provide the normative information, efficiency and accuracy of scoring, and timeliness of reporting of results that are so critical in these programs. (Technical Manual, 1993, p. 11)

The publisher may be correct in its claims, but a statement like the one above runs counter to popular trends in assessment practices.

The validity of the multiple-choice item format for assessing many important school outcomes has been seriously challenged by many educators. Evidence (not simply claims) to show that the multiple-choice item format can provide valid assessments of many higher-level thinking skills would be one approach to responding to these criticisms. Another important piece of evidence from the publisher would be evidence that showed that the multiple-choice item format does not undermine the instructional efforts of teachers. The results from a survey of teachers, or possibly a summary of pertinent research in the assessment literature could provide useful evidence to support the publisher's claims.

BASIC DESCRIPTION. The seventh edition of the MAT consists of 14 levels from Preprimer at the kindergarten level to Secondary 4 for high school seniors. Three parallel forms are available at each level, and within each subject area, all forms and levels are linked to a common reporting scale. Reading, Mathematics, and Language skills are assessed at all 14 levels. Social Studies and Science are included in all but the two lowest levels of the test battery. There is also a Writing test for students in grades 1 to 12 along with scoring instructions, national norms, and useful advice for improving student writing. Finally, there are "Short Forms" of the MAT to assess achievement in Reading, Mathematics, and Language for grades 1 to 11.

TEST DEVELOPMENT. The preparation of test specifications for the MAT seems especially well done. Considerable care and thought appears to have gone into the development of test specifications with careful reviews of textbook series and instructional materials. The Teacher's Manual for Interpreting lays out in considerable detail the scope and sequence of test content across grades. In addition, for each test item in the MAT, the objective measured by the test item is reported as well as its expected cognitive level. As noted by the publisher, the detailed information on the objectives measured in the MAT provides an excellent basis for school districts to match the contents of the MAT against their own curricula and make informed decisions about the suitability of the MAT for their own purposes.

Item development and review with the MAT7 appears to be fairly standard for the construction of standardized achievement tests. Considerable effort went into item writing and review and field testing. The combination of both local and national field tests (on samples of 750) undoubtedly contributed to the quality of test items in the final test battery. More information on the number of item writers and reviewers and their qualifications would be useful, however.

The item statistics play an important role in test development. Item difficulties are presented in great detail in 25 tables in the technical manual. Disappointingly, only the median item biserials (item discrimination indexes) for each subtest are reported. This is unfortunate because the range of item biserials or even better, the item biserials themselves, provide an indirect basis for judging the fit of the Rasch model to test items in the MAT7. The fit of the Rasch model to MAT data is important because of the central role of the Rasch model in test score equating.

The reason for the interest in the spread of the item biserial correlations is that the Rasch model makes the assumption that all items within a subject area have identical item discrimination indices. If the spread of item biserials is substantial, the Rasch model may provide a less than satisfactory fit to the test data. The result could be improper test and form equating. Failure to provide information on model fit or the variability of the item discrimination indices (i.e., item biserials) are omissions from the technical manual that complicate the test review process and raise questions for measurement specialists.

Because the publishers of the other major standardized achievement tests either use classical methods in item analysis and equating, or item response models with additional item parameters to account for variations in item discrimination and guessing (i.e., the two- and three-parameter logistic models), it seems especially important for the MAT publisher to address fully in the technical manual (*a*) the utility of the Rasch model with the MAT, (*b*) model fit statistics, and (*c*) how items that assessed appropriate content but were not fit well by the Rasch model were handled. Information on the consequences of retaining any misfitting items would also assist reviewers.

A comment was made in the technical manual that the:

> MAT7 was planned not only to include new kinds of enhanced multiple-choice items that would stretch the limits of prewritten-response achievement tests, but also to include a greater number of items assessing higher-order thinking skills than has ever been on this kind of test before. (p. 12)

It would have been helpful had the publisher drawn attention to these new types of items in the tests, or at least described the characteristics of these "enhanced multiple-choice items" (technical manual, p. 12). With respect to the point about the higher level thinking skills, the Compendium of Instructional Objectives provides an indication of the skills measured by the items as well as the expected cognitive levels.

As part of the test battery development process, two steps were taken to eliminate bias in the items: There was an advisory panel review and empirical work using the Mantel-Haenszel procedure was carried out. Both procedures are essential, but better documentation of how these procedures were carried out would have been helpful. For example, with respect to the advisory panel, what specific questions were reviewers asked to answer in reviewing the tests? Were they asked to identify vocabulary, topics and contents of passages, and technical terminology, which may have place members of minority groups, males or females, or persons living in particular regions of the country at a disadvantage when taking the tests? Such a list of questions would have been helpful in a review of the procedure.

With respect to the Mantel-Haenszel procedure, details such as the sizes of the majority and minority groups, choice of significance levels, the size of the group ability score differences, the size of score group intervals used in the matching, etc., are essential for evaluating the suitability of the procedure used to identify potentially biased test items. To say in the technical manual that "all items from the tryout were analyzed according to the Mantel-Haenszel procedures" (p. 19) is to communicate only in the most general way about the nature of the analyses. For example, if the sample sizes used in the analyses were fairly small, there would be little statistical power to detect potentially biased items. With very large samples, many items might be detected, including large numbers reflecting practically insignificant performance differences in the groups of interest. Also, it is well known that the Mantel-Haenszel procedure is not effective in detecting nonuniform item bias. Were any steps taken to detect nonuniform bias?

The publisher was correct in noting the central importance of studies to detect potentially biased test items. Biased test items lower test validity and test acceptability. More thorough descriptions of the procedures, therefore, would have been useful in the technical manual. Also, item bias statistics could have been reported alongside item difficulty and discrimination indices, to add additional evidence of their importance.

TEST ADMINISTRATION. The Directions for Administering appeared to be very thorough and clearly presented. The directions for each level described the test developers, provided a useful introduction to the MAT7, answered common questions of teachers, and provided both general and specific directions for test administration. The availability of practice materials and detailed lists of factors to consider before, during and after testing will enhance the validity of the assessment process. The experience of the test publisher was clearly evident in the Directions for Administering. This part of the MAT7 appeared to be especially well handled.

HORIZONTAL AND VERTICAL EQUATING. The equating of multiple forms at each level of the MAT7 and then linking the forms at each level in each subject area to a common scale involves the choice of an item response model (IRT), evidence that the model fits the test data, the choice of an equating design, and evidence of how the design was actually applied. Unfortunately, other than a statement of the equating design, no other results are reported in the technical manual. The same statement is true for the equating of the MAT6 to the MAT7.

How well does the Rasch model fit the test data? Do the fits in any way depend on the grade level or subject matter? For example, one might speculate that the tests for high school students would be more multidimensional than the tests for elementary school students because of the diversity of content at the higher grade levels. It is not even clear from the section on equating that an IRT model was used. Possibly classical equating was done. Such a fundamental question needs to be addressed in the technical manual.

Whether a classical or an IRT model was used in equating, the results of plots of item statistics obtained at grade level and one grade lower should have been summarized along with the method of handling items that appeared to be outliers. Such plots and summaries of plots are needed to understand how well the test form equating was done. Horizontal equating of forms (especially when they are carefully matched) is straightforward and choice of equating design is not likely to be too consequential. This is not the situation with vertical equating and choice of method and design are critical. Also, there is evidence in the measurement literature to suggest that vertically equating achievement tests can be problematic, in part because of the effects of instruction on item statistics.

TEST SCORE NORMING. The method for norming the MAT is described in some detail in the technical manual and in the Multilevel Norms Book. About 180,000 students at grades K to 12 participated in the fall and spring norming study in 1992. One of the interesting features of the norming study was the administration of NAEP (National Assessment of Educational Progress) assessment material at several grades. This provides a basis for comparing the comparability of the MAT7 and NAEP national samples. Unfortunately, the findings were not reported in the technical manual. Such a comparison would be especially interesting because NAEP sampling procedures are unusually good and involve randomly selecting students from within classrooms. It seemed unusual to mention the point about NAEP and then fail to provide results of the comparisons.

Two statistics that would be useful to know about the MAT samples are (*a*) the percent of schools in the norming samples that were current users of the MAT and (*b*) the percent of schools that declined an invitation to participate in the norming study. Both statistics provide important information about the validity of the samples used in test score norming.

Demographic characteristics of the samples drawn appeared to closely match national statistics on demographic variables such as geographic region, SES status, urbanicity, ethnicity, and nonpublic schools. And, when the matches were less than ideal, weights were used. In addition, the publisher reported the breakdown of the samples in terms of handicapping conditions. This was a useful addition to the descriptions of the test norming samples.

The norms tables for converting test scores to scaled scores are clear, though some practitioners will find the sheer volume of tables confusing. Still, little more can be done when there are 14 levels, three forms per level, and five subject areas.

Standard errors of measurement are reported in the norms book on the test score scales. These may be confusing because readers are informed that the test score metric is not very useful for interpreting scores. It would be useful to report the errors of measurement at each scaled score point, something that is possible when IRT models such as the Rasch model are used.

RELIABILITY OF MAT7 SCORES. Forty-five tables in the technical manual provide information about score reliability. KR-20, KR-21, and/or parallel-form reliability estimates along with the corresponding standard errors of measurement are available in the technical manual for all of the scores included in the score reports. Perhaps there is a good reason, but no reason was given for reporting both KR-20 and KR-21 values. The effect of reporting both is that the appendices are considerably lengthened and some confusion may result among users about which of the two statistics is the most useful when clearly the KR-20 is the more useful of the two. The only virtue of the KR-21 over the KR-20 is computational and this virtue is of no consequence to users of the MAT.

About the only surprising finding in the myriad of reliability statistics was that the KR-20 and parallel-form reliabilities for the Science and Social Studies scores at the lower grade levels tended to drop below .80, and sometimes substantially below .80. Though all of the appropriate reliability estimates are in the table for review, perhaps some mention of this pattern of findings would have been useful.

VALIDITY OF MAT7 SCORES. Validity evidence to support score inferences from standardized achievement test batteries often comes in three forms: content validity, concurrent validity, and construct validity. As the publisher notes, the ultimate content validity evidence is not something the test publisher can provide but rather must be determined by individual school districts (or state education agencies). They must determine the extent to which test content lines up with their district's (or state's) curricula. The Compendium of Instructional Objectives is an excellent document to assist users or potential users in completing such a review. It would have been helpful, however, to see compiled evidence from reviewers that the MAT7 test items did, in fact, measure the objectives to which they were matched by the publisher. Item-objective congruence is an important component of a content validity study and can be carried out by the publisher.

With respect to concurrent validity, there is evidence in the technical manual about the high relationship between the MAT6 and MAT7. This evidence suggests there have not been any substantial changes in the two versions, hence any validity evidence compiled for the MAT6 can be reasonably extended to the new MAT7. But such a finding seems to challenge the validity of other statements in the technical manual about the significance of new item formats and the assessment of higher-level cognitive skills.

The technical manual also contains some very useful correlations between the MAT and SAT, ACT, PSAT, and the P-ACT+. These correlations should be of special interest to high school students and their guidance counselors. The availability of these correlations could be used as one of the motivators for high school students taking the MAT7 administration seriously. A prediction of performance on college admissions tests will be of interest to many high school students. It would have been of interest to see some additional correlations between MAT scores and school grades.

Construct validity evidence reported in the technical manual came in several forms. For example, item difficulties reported at several grade levels showed that what the various tests were measuring was influenced by schooling and that the placement of the items into the tests was acceptable. The high biserial correlations show that the items are discriminating between high- and low-scoring students, and this evidence supports the validity of MAT scores to the extent that the test scores are a proxy for real school achievement. Again, it would have been useful to see correlations between MAT scores and school grades.

Intercorrelations among the MAT subtest scores and the Otis Lennon School Ability Test scores tended to be higher than might be desirable. In part, what these high correlations reflect is a capability to take multiple-choice tests as well as motivation to perform on the tests, regardless of content. I would be interested in seeing additional evidence that the enhanced multiple-choice items and/or the test items to measure higher level thinking are, in fact, performing as expected. Also, because of the central role of test validity evidence, more than one page of text in the technical manual should have been used in explaining the validity results in nine appendices.

SCORE INTERPRETATIONS. The Teacher's Manual for Interpreting should be very helpful for teachers. Consider, for example, the manual for Intermediate Levels 1/2/3/4. The manual is divided into five sections. In the first section, the contents of the test battery are described in considerable detail. For each content area, a clear description of how the appropriate content was distributed across the levels of the test battery is provided. Details on how the content is measured are provided. Also, factors to consider when interpreting scores are provided along with tips for teaching.

The second section contains definitions of the various scores that appear in the reports such as percentile ranks, stanines, grade equivalent scores, etc. The material in this section is informative and clear. The third section provides readers with a plan for reading through the test results. Such points as general considerations, factors affecting performance, and suggestions on the steps to take in working through the plethora of material that is provided will be invaluable for administrators and teachers. In the fourth section, suggestions are made for using the scores in establishing instructional priorities and grouping, as well as emphasis on how not to use the scores from the MAT. Here, valuable information is provided. In a final section, some excellent strategies are offered for using the test results.

All of the material in these manuals is valuable for teachers. They need to understand about the sequencing of content; they need to know the characteristics of the various scores reported and the strengths and weaknesses of these scores; and they certainly will benefit from strategies for working through the score reports and using the information correctly. Of course, the big question is whether or not teachers will take the time to read this valuable manual. At the Intermediate Level, this manual is 72 pages long with minimal use of graphics, boxes highlighting main points, tables, and figures to help readers. The information is technically sound but I think more could be done to make the document readable by teachers.

CONCLUDING REMARKS. The Metropolitan Achievement Tests have been very popular standardized achievement tests, and the seventh edition of these tests appears to be of the same high quality as previous editions. The content specifications for the tests appear to have been carefully and thoroughly researched and the technical characteristics, or at least those characteristics that can be evaluated with the technical manual and the teacher's manuals, are excellent. The Psychological Corporation is an experienced test publisher with a long tradition of excellence in developing test specifications, preparing tests, norming and equating tests, etc.

On the other hand, the technical documentation to evaluate several significant aspects of the MAT is incomplete. Item bias studies as noted by the publisher are important to conduct, but few details on the nature of these studies were provided nor were details included on the way in which the Mantel-Haenszel procedure was carried out. Details on horizontal and vertical equating were missing except for a brief outline of the design. The Rasch model played a central role in the scaling and equating, but no details on fit were provided. One indirect way to assess fit was to look at the distribution of the item biserial correlations but only the medians were provided, this despite the fact that all of the item p-values were reported. Not even a measure of spread of r-values was provided. None of these omissions suggest that there are major problems, but from the perspective of a technical review, these omissions are serious and make it impossible to adequately review the MAT. In sum, the presence of more technical information in the technical manual would be desirable. Interested users should not need to go back to the publisher for basic results on item bias studies, scale construction, and equating.

One final point needs to be made. Standardized achievement tests are receiving considerable criticism from many policy-makers and educators because they seem to be "out of step" with the educational reform movement. That may or may not be true. Certainly to the extent that standardized achievement tests only use multiple-choice items, test publishers are going to need to demonstrate that their multiple-choice tests can measure many of the important higher-level cognitive skills. One way that test publishers might respond to these concerns is to expand the amount of validity evidence that they collect and report.

[233]

Metropolitan Readiness Tests, Fifth Edition.

Purpose: Assesses basic and advanced skills important in beginning reading and mathematics.
Population: Prekindergarten through grade 1.
Publication Dates: 1933–86.
Acronym: MRT.
Administration: Group.
Price Data, 1994: $26 per examination kit including test booklet, directions for administering, class record, parent-teacher conference report, practice booklet for each level, Early School Inventory—Developmental (ESI-D), and Early School Inventory—Preliteracy (ESI-P); $309 per machine-scorable version and $281.50 per hand-scorable version for each level of the complete Metropolitan Readiness Assessment Program (MRAP) starter package

including same materials as examination kit plus 35 practice booklets and scoring sheets, 35 self-scoring checklists for ESI-D, 35 self-scoring sheets for ESI-P, 35 parent-teacher conference reports, norms booklet, manual for interpreting, ESI manual for interpretation and use, and handbook of skill development activities; $80 per 35 hand-scorable test booklets with directions for administering, class records, and scoring sheets (specify level); $137 per 35 machine-scorable test booklets and copy sheets with directions for administering, information for evaluating copying sheets, accessory documents, and order for scoring service (specify level); $38.50 per set of keys for hand-scoring test booklets (specify level); $18.50 per set of keys for hand scoring diagonally marked test booklets (specify level); $175 per IBM (5.25-inch diskette) or Apple (5.25-inch diskette) version of MRT scoring assistant; $18.50 per norms booklet ('86, 63 pages); $18.50 each per manual for interpreting ('86, 43 pages for Level 1; '86, 41 pages for Level 2); $7 each per directions for administering ('86, 38 pages each for Level 1 and Level 2); $38.50 for each level of parent-teacher conference reports; $6 per copy of Level 1 or Level 2 class records; $9 per 5 MRT skills records including one copy each of the auditory, visual, language, quantitative, and preliteracy skill record forms.
Foreign Language Edition: Spanish version (MRT Español, 1990) available.
Time: (90) minutes per level; (15) minutes for the practice booklet for each level.
Comments: Both levels include an optional copy sheet for assessing eye-hand coordination; may be given in conjunction with Early Screening Inventory (T4:844).
Authors: Joanne R. Nurss and Mary E. McGauvran.
Publisher: The Psychological Corporation.

a) LEVEL 1.

Population: Beginning and middle of kindergarten.
Scores: 6 tests (Auditory Memory, Beginning Consonants, Letter Recognition, Visual Matching, School Language and Listening, Quantitative Language) in 3 skill areas (Auditory, Visual, Language), plus Pre-Reading Composite.

b) LEVEL 2.

Population: Middle and end of kindergarten and beginning of grade one.
Scores: 8 tests (Beginning Consonants, Sound-Letter Correspondence, Visual Matching, Finding Patterns, School Language, Listening, Quantitative Concepts, Quantitative Operations) in 4 skill areas (Auditory, Visual, Language, Quantitative), plus Total Battery Composite.

Cross References: See T4:1619 (35 references); for a review of an earlier edition by Michael M. Ravitch, see 9:700 (11 references); see also T3:1479 (73 references), 8:802 (111 references), and T2:1716 (55 references); for reviews by Robert Dykstra and Harry Singer of an earlier edition, see 7:757 (124 references); for a review by Eric F. Gardner and an excerpted review by Fay Griffith, see 4:570 (3 references); for a review by Irving H. Anderson, see 3:518 (5 references); for a review by W. J. Osburn, see 2:1552 (10 references).

TEST REFERENCES

1. Cunningham, A. E. (1990). Explicit versus implicit instruction in phonemic awareness. *Journal of Experimental Child Psychology, 50*, 429-444.
2. Juel, C. (1990). Effects of reading group assignment on reading development in first and second grade. *Journal of Reading Behavior, 22*, 233-254.
3. Neuman, S. B., & Soundy, C. (1991). The effects of "storybook partnerships" on young children's conceptions of stories. *Yearbook of National Reading Conference, 40*, 141-147.
4. May, D. C., & Kundert, D. K. (1993). Pre-first placements: How common and how informed? *Psychology in the Schools, 30*, 161-167.
5. Schoen, M. J., & Nagle, R. J. (1994). Prediction of school readiness from kindergarten temperament scores. *Journal of School Psychology, 32*, 135-147.

Review of the Metropolitan Readiness Tests, Fifth Edition by LINDA MABRY, Assistant Professor of Counseling and Educational Psychology, College of Education, Indiana University, Bloomington, IN:

Although the Metropolitan Readiness Tests, Fifth Edition reveal some commendable efforts, the tests also demonstrate some important difficulties in assessing the abilities of preschoolers, difficulties that have resulted in the prohibition by some states of standardized testing of young children. For this review, the MRT Levels 1 and 2 were analyzed. A Spanish-language version was not reviewed. Level 1 is intended to assess school—particularly reading—readiness at the end of prekindergarten and at the beginning and middle of kindergarten. Its six subtests address Auditory Memory, Visual Matching, School Language and Listening, Beginning Consonants, Letter Recognition, and Quantitative Language. The eight subtests of Level 2, for the middle and end of kindergarten and for the beginning of grade 1, are intended to address Beginning Consonants, Sound-Letter Correspondence, Visual Matching, Finding Patterns, School Language, Listening, Quantitative Concepts, and Quantitative Operations. The instruments are described as developmentally appropriate tests of ability.

Whether the tests are truly diagnostic of reading ability is questionable on at least two grounds. First, the skills tested may correlate with reading (e.g., Letter Recognition), but the correlation between test items and reading is not obvious. Second, the subtests clearly imply a theory of reading as a conglomeration of specific subskills which, in the era of constructivism and whole language approaches to reading instruction, is outdated.

The obsolescence of the tests is also evident from their age. Originally developed in 1933 and updated at approximately 15-year intervals, pilot testing of the edition reviewed was done in 1984 and norming in 1985–86 based on 1980 U.S. Census data. In the 10–14 years since, education has become somewhat more culturally sensitive than these test items reflect, although item review reportedly included bias checking.

Validity and reliability evidence are conventional but insufficient. Validity was reportedly addressed in three ways. First, two *predictive validity* studies in 1985–86 matched the performances on MRT Level

2 of small samples of students with their later performances on the Metropolitan Achievement Tests Form L and on the Stanford Achievement Test Form E. Second, performances on subtests was compared to overall performances on the tests, a matter of internal consistency, *not* validity. Third, to pursue *content validity*, an "extensive review of the literature was conducted prior to the test's development to provide evidence that the tests are assessing those skills that are important to early learning" (norms booklet, p. 36). Problems with this approach are: A review of the literature prior to 1984 is antique; the nature of the effort, if any, to match tests or test items to the literature is undescribed; and the construct of "early learning" does not directly correlate with the construct of "reading readiness." *Construct validity* was completely neglected.

Claims of reliability largely depended upon the internal consistency of items calculated by the Kuder-Richardson 20 formula. Internal consistency of items, although popular with test developers and easy to achieve, is far removed from common understanding of reliability as consistency among a testee's performances on equivalent tests. Test-retest reliability, which better matches the concept, was done with a small sample of students at 2-week intervals in 1985 but appears faulty; 152 students were tested but 233 retested.

Tests may be hand- or machine-scored. Both present difficulties. Handscoring involves the completion of a form for each child tested and of three class summary forms. Of the latter, raw scores are recorded on one form and could be used diagnostically to identify students needing instruction in tested skills, but doing so would be difficult because of the format of the record sheet. On the other two forms, content-referenced and norm-referenced information is derived from tables in the norms booklet and used to rank students. This might easily lead to premature labeling by ability of young children and long-term disadvantages to individuals. The process of handscoring would require re-recording of much data, redundancy that suggests part of the process might be neglected in many instances. However, if not, the process would probably ensure that teachers acquire some understanding of the distinctions between content-referenced scores (+ for proficient, check mark for continuing to learn, - for instruction needed) and norm-referenced percentiles and stanines. (There is also mention of scaled scores and normal curve equivalents [NCE].) Machine-generated reports would offer no such assurance of understanding; moreover, the type of results reported, listed at the top of each of these forms along with much other information, might be easily overlooked. Because very few teachers are trained in measurement or assessment, most could not be expected to understand why a student whose performance was "average" on a norm-referenced form might be listed as "needs instruction" on a content-referenced form (sample forms include examples of such discrepancies). The redundancy of both hand- and machine-generated record sheets might lessen teacher attention given to each form and increase confusion about meanings. Laudably, teachers are exhorted to compare test results with their observations and knowledge of students' backgrounds and contexts.

Parent-teacher conference reports offer content-referenced results of subtests and a list of home activities. However, confusion regarding class summary forms might be introduced during and might complicate, parent-teacher conferences. Also, the home activities are didactic, academic, and specific without suggesting the possibility of adaptive variations.

Information for administrators suggests using test results for personnel hiring aligned with student needs, for school accountability by listing numbers of students performing in each stanine for each subtest, and for curriculum study. This suggests that it is the norm-referenced data that are useful to schools and, even more problematic, that schools need to match curricula to tests for public credibility. The latter is one of the most widely bemoaned countereducational effects of standardized testing today. Also, a single paragraph defining and describing measurement errors (± 1 stanine) is clearly written but brief and hidden on page 34 of the Manuals for Interpreting.

To both begin and conclude with reference to the impact on children, it is difficult to imagine a group of no more than 15 preschoolers not "peeking" at the pictures in the items until after the teacher reads the prompt, filling in bubbles, and erasing corrections fully and neatly. It is easy to imagine they would be confused by the items (e.g., auditory memory items in which eight line drawings are grouped and regrouped for different items). A 4-year-old with no experience with standardized tests might easily be confused by line after line of these regroupings.

Although developers of the MRT have exercised the conventional strategies in constructing their test and offered the usual caveats to users, these are insufficient. The test is outdated, passé in terms of learning theory, technically inadequate, confusing to targeted audiences, and likely detrimental to children and schools.

Review of the Metropolitan Readiness Tests, Fifth Edition by GARY STONER, Associate Professor of School Psychology, University of Oregon, Eugene, OR:

The Metropolitan Readiness Tests (MRT), Fifth Edition are the primary assessment tools of the Metropolitan Readiness Assessment Program (MRAP). The MRAP is intended for use in evaluating the general development and prereading skills of students at the prekindergarten, kindergarten, and grade 1 levels of schooling. The MRT consists of Level 1 and Level 2 versions (also available in a Spanish translation) with accompanying practice materials, and with technical manuals describing test development, norms, and methods of interpreting test results. The MRAP consists of the MRT, plus supplementary materials including two inventories of child development (i.e., physical, cognitive, language, social-emotional) based on teacher observations, forms for summarizing and organizing assessment data for all children in a classroom, forms for presenting assessment information and instructional recommendations to parents, and forms for assessing children's skills at copying the printed letters of their own names.

PURPOSE AND CONTENT. The basic purpose of the MRT to measure the prereading skills of children has been the same since its inception in 1933. According to the MRT technical information, the tests reflect "the current thinking of experts in the fields of child development and reading," and test content was selected "after extensive research to determine the types of measures that are most relevant to Pre-Kindergarten and Kindergarten pre-reading skill development" (norms booklet, p. 8). Unfortunately, neither the experts involved, nor the research reviewed is specifically identified. Users and potential users of future editions of the MRT would be well served by such information, assuming it would lead to a better understanding of the rationale behind the development and content of the tests. Level 1 of the MRT is organized around Auditory, Visual, and Language Skill Areas, further divided into subtests named Auditory Memory, Beginning Consonants, Letter Recognition, Visual Matching, School Language and Listening, and Quantitative Language. Level 2 is organized around Auditory, Visual, Language, and Quantitative Skill Areas, with subtests named Beginning Consonants, Sound-Letter Correspondence, Visual Matching, Finding Patterns, School Language, Listening, Quantitative Concepts, and Quantitative Operations.

ADMINISTRATION, SCORING, AND INTERPRETATION. The subtests of the MRT Level 1 and Level 2 are designed to be administered by classroom teachers in seven and five sittings, respectively, with each subtest administration requiring between 9 and 25 minutes time excluding distribution and collection of materials. Administration is designed to occur in groups of 10 or fewer prekindergarten children, or 15 or fewer children at the kindergarten and grade 1 levels. The directions provided to teachers are clear and well written, and provide for teaching children how to take the MRT via pretesting practice materials. Directions and forms for scoring, summarizing, and interpreting completed tests are similarly well written, clear, and user friendly.

Users of the MRT are encouraged to summarize the test performance of individual children in two ways. First, individual subtest performance can be classified into one of three categories: (*a*) the child is proficient in this skill, (*b*) the child is in the process of learning this skill and instruction should continue, and (*c*) the child needs further instruction in this skill or its prerequisites. Next, Skill Area and Pre-Reading Composite scores can be compared with national norms to yield percentile rankings and stanine scores. Based on these classifications and comparisons, users are encouraged to make educational decisions such as evaluating the efficacy of curricula in use, grouping children for instruction, and identifying specific skills that need to be taught to individuals and/or groups of children. In the latter area, specific instructional recommendations are made in the summary parent report forms and in an available teacher's handbook. Data or research studies in support of using the MRT for these purposes are conspicuous in their absence, and the test authors should caution users in this regard.

TECHNICAL ADEQUACY. Evidence for reliability and well-developed national norms are the technical adequacy strong points of the MRT. For example, 2-week test-retest reliability coefficients for Skill Area scores are in the .74–.88 range. Evidence also is provided for internal consistency of the tests with Skill Area reliability coefficients generally above .80. With respect to MRT norms, the test developers are to be commended for their extensive efforts in developing norms representative of the United States population based on the 1980 U.S. Census.

In contrast to the evidence for reliability and available norms, evidence for the validity of the MRT is relatively weak. As noted previously, evidence for content validity is based on expert opinion. It is likely, however, that current expert perspectives on prereading skills predictive of success for beginning readers would differ from those informing development of the MRT. For example, Adams's (1990) review and integration of the research on beginning reading suggests indirectly that the skills tapped by several MRT subtests (e.g., Auditory Memory, Visual Matching, Finding Patterns), despite their intuitive appeal, may have relatively little to do with learning to read for beginning readers.

The primary evidence provided for the criterion-related validity of the MRT are those correlations between Level 2 MRT scores and scores obtained approximately 6 months later on the Metropolitan Achievement Test (range of obtained correlations with various summary scores was .54 to .65) and on the Stanford Achievement Test (range of obtained correlations with various summary scores was .68 to .83). More appropriate validity evidence, given the goal of assessing prereading skills and the construct of "readiness" to learn or benefit from instruction, would be data to suggest that children who perform differentially on the MRT benefit differentially from similar instruction in a prereading or reading curriculum. Pursuit of such evidence for the *utility* (see Hayes, Nelson, & Jarret, 1987) of the MRT is the logical next step in this instrument's development.

CONCLUSIONS. The Metropolitan Readiness Tests (MRT), Fifth Edition materials are well written and user friendly. However, the purported usefulness of the tests for making educational decisions about curricula and instruction are unsubstantiated. In the absence of further research and data, current use of the MRT should be limited to screening decisions to determine which children in a classroom might benefit from further assessment or from ongoing monitoring of their skill development.

REVIEWER'S REFERENCES

Hayes, S. C., Nelson, R. O., & Jarret, R. O. (1987). The treatment utility of assessment: A functional approach to evaluating assessment quality. *American Psychologist, 42,* 963-974.

Adams, M. J. (1990). *Beginning to read: Thinking and learning about print.* Cambridge, MA: Massachusetts Institute of Technology.

[234]

Meyer-Kendall Assessment Survey.

Purpose: Constructed to assess work-related personality style.
Population: Business employees and job applicants.
Publication Dates: 1986–91.
Acronym: MKAS.
Scores, 12: Objectivity, Social Desirability Bias, Dominance, Extraversion, People Concerns, Attention to Detail, Anxiety, Stability, Psychosomatic Tendencies, Determination, Achievement Motivation, Independence.
Administration: Group or individual.
Price Data, 1990: $195 per complete kit including 5 assessment sheets, 1 pre-assessment sheet, and manual ('91, 72 pages); $35 per assessment sheet (price includes scoring and report by publisher); $7.50 per pre-assessment sheet; $24.50 per manual.
Time: (15–20) minutes.
Authors: Henry D. Meyer and Edward L. Kendall.
Publisher: Western Psychological Services.

Review of the Meyer-Kendall Assessment Survey by MARK H. DANIEL, Senior Scientist, American Guidance Service, Circle Pines, MN:

The Meyer-Kendall Assessment Survey (MKAS) is a self-report measure of 10 personal attributes thought to be important for success in business management. According to its authors (one a corporate psychologist and the other the president of a management consulting firm), the MKAS "was designed to fill the need for a business-oriented personality inventory" (p. 47). Thus, it is a normal-range instrument for adults that is intended for use in career and out-placement counseling, personnel work, and research.

Despite its 1991 copyright date, the MKAS is not a new instrument. It evolved from the Employee Questionnaire (EQ) of World War II, and it is almost identical to the EQ-C developed by Meyer in 1958. The present version was created in 1980 by rephrasing the brief "yes/no" items of the EQ-C from first-person to second-person (e.g., "You are inclined to put off making decisions"). Although it may take some time to get used to this second-person format, the authors report no difference in score levels between the two versions. It appears the norms as well as all statistical analyses reported in the manual are based on data from the EQ-C, that is, the version written in the first person.

The MKAS may be scored only be sending completed forms to the publisher. The resulting computer-generated report provides *T* scores and percentiles on the 10 personal attributes and on two response tendencies (Objectivity and Social Desirability Bias), each of which reflects the person's tendency to give a favorable self-report.

There are no higher-order composite scores, but the 10 attribute scales are clustered into four groups: Interpersonal Style (Dominance, Extraversion, and People Concerns); Detail Interest (Attention to Detail); Psychological Characteristics (Anxiety, Stability, and Psychosomatic Tendencies); and Motivational Levels (Determination, Achievement Motivation, and Independence). These groupings seem reasonable on content grounds, although without knowing the item composition of each scale it is difficult to judge. Factor analyses reported in the manual show the Psychological Characteristics scales belong to a common factor but the other groupings consist of scales drawn from several factors.

TECHNICAL CHARACTERISTICS. Norms are based on 187 applicants for managerial positions, of whom 91% were males; no data are provided on age, race/ethnicity, region, or type of industry. In view of the large amount of data collected over the years for the EQ-C and the MKAS, it is puzzling that this relatively small group is the only norm group available. The rationale presented in the manual for using this norm group is not very persuasive. Data purporting to show that this group's scores are close to those of a group of 2,300 miscellaneous employees are presented, although if one does some calculations one finds that on 6 of the 10 personal attribute scales the means differ by one-third to almost one-half of a standard deviation; furthermore, several of the standard deviations differ markedly. A third group of 644 corporate managers differs from the norm group on several of the scales (higher on Determination, Achievement Motivation, and Psychosomatic Tendencies and lower on Anxiety). These data do not explain why the sample of 187 applicants should be the sole norm group. No rational bias for selecting this group is offered in the manual. One or more larger or better-defined groups might provide more valuable information to the user.

The ancestor of the MKAS, the Employee Questionnaire, developed its scales by empirical keying. That is, each scale was made up of items that differentiated between people known to be high or low on the target attribute. In the course of several revisions new scales were added and others were dropped, and items were subjected to additional types of statistical analysis. Nevertheless, the low internal-consistency reliabilities of the MKAS show that these scales have not been developed to have homogeneous content. In the norm sample, coefficient alpha for the 10 personal-attribute scales ranges from .18 to .63 with a median of .45. These results raise concern about whether the scales measure distinct constructs. In particular, three of the scales—People Concerns, Anxiety, and Stability—each have three or four correlations with other scales that are near the theoretical maximum, given their reliabilities. More generally, the low level of internal consistency precludes high scale specificity and calls into question the meaningfulness of profile analysis. The high test-retest reliabilities, averaging .78 for a sample of 39 business students (2-week interval), unfortunately do not provide evidence of scale distinctiveness.

Validation data provide some support for scale interpretability. Correlations with the Guilford-Zimmerman Temperament Survey (GZTS) in the norm sample provide convergent validity for the Extraversion scale (r = .79 with GZTS Sociability) and the Dominance scale (r = .70 with Ascendance). These are the two MKAS scales with internal-consistency reliabilities above .6. The three Psychological Characteristics scales (Anxiety, Stability, and Psychosomatic Tendencies) each have their highest correlation with the GZTS Emotional Stability scale, and although the correlations are only in the .50s, these are respectable given the low reliabilities of these MKAS scales.

Other criterion-related validation comes from several studies that compared the score patterns of individuals at varying levels of management, correlated scale scores with job ratings or sales success, or examined the scores of rapidly promoted managers. Only brief narrative summaries of these studies are provided in the manual. Results suggest that upper-level managers score relatively high in Dominance, Stability, and Independence and relatively low in Attention to Detail and Anxiety. The consistency of these findings with prior research supports these scales' construct validity. Interestingly, Attention to Detail correlates positively with rated job performance, as do Dominance, Objectivity, Extraversion, and Achievement Motivation.

SCORE REPORT. The computer-generated report provides extensive analyses in addition to the profile of scale *T* scores and percentiles. There are two validity indexes, one based on a combination of the number of highly frequent and highly infrequent responses, and the other sensitive to patterned responding. Two graphs depict the probability that the individual belongs to one of four empirically derived occupational groups (from a cluster analysis of the norm sample) and to one of five hypothetical, "prototypical" groups (executive, supervisor, technical, staff, and sales professional). These probabilities are sophisticated and require some study to be interpreted properly; the manual appropriately cautions users who are unfamiliar with the underlying technical concepts to ignore these graphs, although the report itself does not contain this warning.

An unusual feature of the MKAS is the optional Pre-Assessment Worksheet (PAW) on which the test user may describe the ideal score range on each MKAS scale for the position of interest. The user may submit one or more PAWs along with completed MKAS forms for scoring. The resulting report for each examinee gives a numerical index of similarity to the ideal profile and indicates which scales contributed most to dissimilarity, enabling the user to judge the importance of these discrepancies. This system appears to give the user control over the influence that each scale will have on the similarity index: By specifying a wide score range, the user can make it unlikely for individuals to fall outside the range, thereby minimizing the scale's influence.

Both the several forms of profile analysis described above and the verbal narrative included in the report place considerable weight on the individual scales. In light of the scales' low reliabilities, this may be inappropriate. The narrative discusses individual *T* scores without reference to their (often sizable) standard errors. One portion of the report alludes to this problem by saying that "the Determination scale should be interpreted in relation to the other scales, since by itself it has relatively low reliability" (p. 24). However, how information from the other scales can help interpret a scale whose alpha coefficient is .18 is not obvious.

SUMMARY. The MKAS score report offers a number of useful aids to interpretation, but the technical properties of the scales are a weak foundation for this sophisticated structure. Some of the scales appear to be valid measures of dimensions that are known to be relevant to business management, but for others there are little data to support interpretation; and the very low reliabilities of some scales undermine their use in pattern analysis. Several other instruments, such as the GZTS (9:460) and the Gordon Personal Profile and Inventory (10:128), assess similar sets of dimensions more reliably and with greater evidence of validity.

Review of the Meyer-Kendall Assessment Survey by GREGORY H. DOBBINS, Associate Professor of Management, The University of Tennessee at Knoxville, Knoxville, TN:

The Meyer-Kendall Assessment Survey (MKAS) is an omnibus personality instrument designed to assess constructs predictive of work performance. It differs from other personality measures (e.g., California Psychological Inventory [CPI], Gough, 1987) in that the items were specifically designed for a work context.

The 12 constructs assessed by the MKAS are consistent with those assessed with other personality instruments, although there are three scales (Determination, Achievement Motivation, and Independence) that are particularly relevant for work settings. Each of the constructs is clearly defined, although several of the scales are multidimensional. For example, the People Concerns scale assesses tact, empathy, and tolerance for others. Although empathy and tolerance for others are conceptually similar, an individual may be empathic, but not tolerant. Indeed the CPI contains separate scales to assess empathy and tolerance. Similarly, Attention to Detail is purported to measure preference for involvement with details and the ability to delegate responsibility. Although these two areas are conceptually related, there are differences between them (e.g., an individual with low preference for details may still not delegate).

ADMINISTRATION PROCEDURES. The MKAS is very short by personality test standards. Applicants are asked to indicate whether each of the 105 statements describes them or does not describe them. The statements are clearly written and unambiguous. Although the reading level of the instrument is not presented in the technical manual, the vocabulary and content of the scale items should be readable by most applicants.

The MKAS contains a pre-assessment worksheet that asks the organization to indicate the range of values that would be acceptable on each of the 12 scales. This serves as a formal mechanism to insure that the organization considers the temperament needed for the position. In addition, completing the pre-assessment worksheet should focus attention on the extent to which the applicant matches the organization's definition of an acceptable candidate.

The MKAS is scored by sending completed answer sheets to Western Psychological Services. The computer-generated interpretations are very thorough and clear. An overview of the instrument and its limitations are described. *T*-scores and a paragraph interpretation are presented for each scale. However, all scale interpretations appear to be independent (i.e., interpretations on one scale are not affected by performance levels on the other scales). Configural interpretations are not presented.

The computer-generated reports also indicate the extent to which the applicant matches one of four personality groups (Type I–sociable and people-oriented; Type II–typical; Type III–dependent and distressed, and Type IV–introverted) and five occupational groups (executives, supervisors, technical, staff, and sales professionals). Finally, the report provides a probability estimate that the person matches the prototype specified by the organization in the preassessment worksheet.

PSYCHOMETRIC CHARACTERISTICS OF THE MKAS. The technical manual indicates that "The most compelling evidence for the validity of the MKAS comes from its successful use in assessing more than 3,000 supervisors, salespeople, managers, professionals, and job applicants" (p. 47). However, close scrutiny of the reliability and validity of the MKAS raises some serious concerns. First, the scales generally have poor reliability. Test-retest reliabilities for the various scales averaged .78 over 2 weeks and .51 over 2 years. Coefficient alphas range from .18 to .67 for the 12 scales. These findings suggest that either the individual items are unreliable, there are too few items per scale, or that the constructs assessed with each MKAS scale are multidimensional. As was noted earlier, the MKAS is remarkably short for a comprehensive personality inventory and some of the scales do appear to be multidimensional.

Some validation work has been conducted with the MKAS. Several studies (e.g., Meyer & Fredian, 1959; Meyer & Pressel, 1954) have compared employees at different levels (e.g., factory and office workers, corporate officers, and general managers) and have shown that the groups score differently on some of the MKAS scales (e.g., stability, dominance, attention to detail, anxiety). Other research has evaluated the construct validity of the MKAS. Some of this work has focused on the discriminant validity of the MKAS scales. The scales show remarkably low levels of intercorrelations, especially for a self-report personality instrument. These small correlations may be a function of the low reliabilities for some of the MKAS scales.

The relationship between the MKAS and other personality instruments has also been examined. When the MKAS was correlated with the Guilford-Zimmerman Temperament Survey (GZTS; Guilford & Zimmerman, 1949), a large number of statistically significant relationships were revealed. Some of these relationships were supportive of the construct validity of MKAS scales. For example, Ascendance on the GZTS is correlated .70 with Dominance on the MKAS. However, there are also a large number of uninterpretable correlations between the GZTS and MKAS. Once again, this may reflect the low reliabilities of some of the MKAS scales.

There has been limited investigation of the criterion-related validity of the MKAS. Attention to detail and objectivity were significantly related to sales success in a study described in the technical manual. Other criterion-related validity studies are alluded to in the technical manual, but are not clearly presented.

Furthermore, the validity of the scoring procedure and the inferences generated by the computerized scoring procedure have not been examined. Thus, it is not clear that an applicant who is identified as having a 90% chance of matching the manager prototype will actually be more effective as a manager than an applicant who is identified as having a 40% chance of matching the manager prototype. Clearly, such investigations are critical and must be examined in future research.

There have also been few studies examining the test fairness of the MKAS. In fact, two of the three normative groups referenced in the technical manual are almost all male (91%) and the sex composition of the third group is not presented. Similarly, little research has examined the use, reliability, and validity of the MKAS with women and minorities.

In summary, the psychometric characteristics of the MKAS must be considered questionable at best. The scales do not appear to be reliable and there has been limited work examining the constructs being assessed. Perhaps most distressing is the lack of evidence concerning the effectiveness of predictions made with the MKAS. The predictive validity of the inventory is the most essential ingredient for organizations that are using it. Unfortunately, data relevant for this issue are missing at the present time.

SUMMARY. There are two potential advantages associated with the MKAS. First, it was designed to assess work-related aspects of personality. Hence, it was not imported from clinical or counseling psychology. Second, the pre-assessment worksheet of the MKAS asks the organization to describe the characteristics of an acceptable applicant and an algorithm determines how well each candidate matches the profile. This should insure that the organization thinks about the temperament that is needed for the job prior to selecting a candidate.

Unfortunately, there are serious psychometric limitations with the MKAS. The reliabilities of the scales are very low. In addition, limited construct and criterion-related validation research has been conducted on the MKAS. Furthermore, given the reliabilities of the MKAS scales, I am not very optimistic that the MKAS can do a good job predicting job performance.

The MKAS may turn out to be a very effective instrument for selecting employees in work settings. However, given the lack of evidence to support its use and its current psychometric characteristics, I would not recommend that it be used by organizations at the present time. There are more rigorously developed personality instruments (such as the CPI [11:54]) that can be easily adopted to work-related settings. Given the rejuvenation of personality as a predictor of job performance in work settings, perhaps the MKAS and other personality inventories will be investigated more carefully in the future.

REVIEWER'S REFERENCES

Guilford, J. P., & Zimmerman, W. S. (1949). Guilford-Zimmerman Temperament Survey. Orange, CA: Sheridan Psychological Services.

Meyer, H. D., & Pressel, G. L. (1954). Personality test scores in the management hierarchy. *Journal of Applied Psychology*, *38*, 73-80.

Meyer, H. D., & Fredian, A. J. (1959). Personality test scores in the management hierarchy: Revisited. *Journal of Applied Psychology*, *43*, 212-220.

Gough, H. G. (1987). California Psychological Inventory. Palo Alto, CA: Consulting Psychologists Press.

[235]

Miller Analogies Test.

Purpose: Constructed to assess mental ability for use in selecting graduate students.
Population: Applicants for graduate schools.
Publication Dates: 1926–92.
Acronym: MAT.
Scores: Total score only.
Administration: Group.
Restricted Distribution: Distribution restricted and test administered at licensed testing centers; details may be obtained from publisher.
Price Data: Available from publisher.
Time: 50(55) minutes.
Author: W. S. Miller (test).
Publisher: The Psychological Corporation.
Cross References: See T4:1630 (1 reference) and T3:1486 (16 references); see also 8:192 (31 references), T2:404 (15 references), and 7:363 (57 references); for reviews by Lloyd G. Humphreys, William B. Schrader, and Warren W. Willingham, see 6:472 (26 references); for a review by John T. Dailey, see 5:352 (28 references); for reviews by J. P. Guilford and Cart I. Hovland, see 4:304 (16 references).

TEST REFERENCES

1. Wade, S. E., Trathen, W., & Schraw, G. (1990). An analysis of spontaneous study strategies. *Reading Research Quarterly*, *24*, 147-166.

2. Shore, T. H. (1992). Subtle gender bias in the assessment of managerial potential. *Sex Roles*, *27*, 499-515.

Review of the Miller Analogies Test by ROBERT B. FRARY, Professor and Director, Office of Measurement and Research Services, Virginia Polytechnic Institute and State University, Blacksburg, VA:

The Miller Analogies Test (MAT), now in its seventh decade, continues in its role as "a high-level mental ability test requiring the solution of problems stated as analogies" (1994 Technical Manual, p. 4). Scores from the MAT have been used for a variety of purposes but mostly in connection with admission to graduate programs as an alternative to the Graduate Record Examinations (T4:1076). The MAT can be scored on site, which can greatly expedite the admission decision-making process. The seven available forms of the MAT permit retesting of candidates. The analogies can be categorized into 14 relationship categories, such as similarity, subordination, completion, and part-whole. The subject matter contained in the analogies is quite varied, ranging from literature-philosophy to mathematics and the physical sciences. Thus, the MAT would appear to measure adequacy of educational background as well as problem-solving ability.

Given the MAT's longevity, it has been reviewed many times. In addition to the earlier *Mental Measurements Yearbook* reviews listed above, Geisinger (1984) provides an extensive description of the MAT and commentary on its use. There is a substantial consensus among the various reviewers to the effect that the MAT is well constructed (with respect to content) and yields scores with good reliability. However, previous reviewers found problems with the norming of MAT scores and with the methodology for equating its forms. Also, they found the evidence of MAT score validity presented in its technical manual to be inadequate. A completely rewritten technical manual was published in 1994, and it would appear that little has changed in these regards, except for some improvement in norming.

New norming data are based on all domestic 1991–92 examinees who took the MAT for the first time. One table combines intended majors into conglomerate categories such as business, education, and natural science and contains percentile ranks for scores within the categories using 5-point intervals. All of these categories contain respectable numbers except perhaps engineering, for which only 434 examinees were available. Education had over 86,000. These norms suffer from lack of specificity, especially in disciplines as diverse as the natural sciences or humanities. Also doctoral and master's-level candidates are combined. Another table gives the percentages of examinees within 10-point score ranges for each distinct major with more than 50 candidates. Many of these majors contain substantial numbers of examinees, but a number contain fewer than 100. Nevertheless, this information is definitely an improvement over what was available in the previous technical manual, although, as is the case for the conglomerate categories, doctoral and master's-level candidates are combined. And, of course, the norms relate only to applicants who elected to take the MAT, not to all students anticipating graduate study.

The 1981 technical manual provided over 40 correlations between MAT scores and graduate grade-point averages (GPAs). This presentation was criticized for its failure to specify the circumstances underlying each coefficient (homogeneity of the groups, difficulty of the courses of study, etc.). The new technical manual simply aggregates data collected in 1992 from over 50 graduate departments that had at least eight students with MAT scores, undergraduate GPAs, and first-year graduate GPAs. The reader is left in the dark concerning the number and characteristics of the universities involved, the subject areas of the departments, the total number of students involved, and the time period represented by the data. The correlation between MAT scores and first-year graduate GPA is only .23. The multiple correlation using undergraduate GPA and MAT scores to predict first-year graduate GPA is .37, whereas the correlation between undergraduate GPA and graduate GPA is .29. The technical manual contains a warning that the data may not be representative of all graduate departments and points out likely restriction in range of both predictor and criterion due to selection and graduate school grading practices. In other words, accepting the validity of the MAT for informing graduate school admission decisions has to be more or less an act of faith.

A new section in the 1994 technical manual contains data concerning score changes upon retaking the MAT. Because a lower-than-expected score would likely be the motivating factor for a substantial proportion of the retests, it is not surprising the average score difference is positive (about 5–6 points). This fairly small mean difference remained remarkably constant across time between the initial and subsequent testing (presumably with a different form). The correlation between the scores from the two testings, a sort of hybrid test-retest/parallel-form reliability coefficient, was only .73, much lower than the KR-20s of over .9 reported for the various forms of the MAT. This discrepancy no doubt reflects variation in the time differences between testings as well as content differences between forms. The extent to which coaching may lead to score improvement is not mentioned.

In the 1981 technical manual, the methodology for establishing parallel forms was not described with any degree of precision, and the same is true for 1994. However, in the new technical manual, data on form comparability are given for 1991–92 examinees. Means across forms range from 44.4 (Form R17) to 48.5 (Form V21). The difference of 4.1 between these means is about the size of the standard error of measurement, which varies only slightly across forms. Regardless, candidates should certainly prefer to take Form V21, which appears to be meaningfully more easy than some of the others. Given the current state-of-the-art in test equating, one should expect better from the publisher.

Summary statistics for 1991–92 examinees by gender and by ethnicity for each of the seven forms and for all forms combined are available in the 1994 technical manual. This information could potentially be useful, but, if there is a group x form interaction of meaningful size, one could never spot it in the welter of figures provided, and the manual authors never even mention the possibility. One wonders whether group x form analyses of variance have been done.

Compared to the 1981 edition, the 1994 technical manual contains considerably more verbiage concerning interpretation of scores. Much of this is appropriately cautionary (e.g., don't have fixed cut point for admission, look at a variety of evidence reflecting each candidate's adequacy, consider the standard error of measurement, remember that the norms are based on self-selected examinees).

Another new publication for the MAT is the Candidate Information Booklet, published in 1991. In addition to general information, it contains a 1988–90 version of the conglomerate group norms referred to above with appropriate cautionary advice concerning interpretation. Excellent advice concerning test taking strategies for the MAT is provided, especially concerning guessing. (The MAT is scored number right.) Candidates are encouraged to eliminate options prior to guessing and to guess even if completely baffled. However, when examinees actually take the test, the instructions are less emphatic: "If you are not sure of an answer mark the response you think is correct" (1991 Manual of Directions for Examinees, p. 19).

Given the MAT's low predictive power, it seems likely that its continued use will be justified as a handy means of checking whether candidates are endowed with levels of mental capacity or functioning judged to be adequate for the subject matter at hand. For example, with MAT scores in hand, one could quickly eliminate extremely low scorers and perhaps spend considerably less time on the other qualifications of candidates with very high scores. Purists would probably denounce such usage, but, if practiced conservatively, it is *very* unlikely to cause inappropriate or unfair admissions decisions.

REVIEWER'S REFERENCE

Geisinger, K. F. (1985). [Review of the Miller Analogies Test.] In D. J. Keyser & R. C. Sweetland (Eds.), *Test critiques* (vol. 4; pp. 414-424). Kansas City, MO: Test Corporation of America.

Review of the Miller Analogies Test by STEPHEN H. IVENS, Vice President, Research & Development, Touchstone Applied Science Associates, Brewster, NY:

Applicants to graduate school may be required to take either the Miller Analogies Test (MAT) or the Graduate Record Examination (GRE; T4:1076). The MAT, developed by W. S. Miller at the University of Minnesota in 1926, is a mental ability test designed to differentiate among high-ability applicants. There is no question that, over the last 60 years, the MAT has done well what it was designed to do. Whether this differentiation is related to performance in graduate school is a questions of predictive validity, which will be discussed later.

The MAT consists of 100 multiple-choice items presented in the format of an analogy with four response options. The content of the items may be classified into one of nine categories: language usage, mathematics, physical sciences, biological sciences, social sciences, history, literature-philosophy, fine arts, and general information. The publisher states that "An applicant to graduate school will typically have been exposed to much, if not all, of the information necessary to complete each analogy" (manual, p. 4). As many examinees will attest, exposure to the necessary information is not a sufficient condition for successfully completing the analogies on the MAT. The cognitive complexity of the items is due, in large part, to the nature of the relationship among the word pairs. Because of the 50-minute time limit, examinees may select the first plausible response option. Those who do not carefully consider each response option do so at their own peril.

The Candidate Information Booklet is an excellent document for prospective test takers. Information on applying to take the test, testing center procedures, and scoring and reporting of test results is clearly presented. The analogy item type is described in detail, and specific test-taking strategies are provided. Candidates are presented with 17 example items with detailed explanations for the correct answers. In addition, 50 sample items with annotated answers provide ample opportunity to become familiar with the MAT. The publisher is to be commended for the clarity and thoroughness of this publication.

The Candidate Information Booklet includes information to prospective examinees that "fluency in the English language, a broad knowledge of literature, philosophy, history, science, mathematics, and fine arts, and the ability to reason out relationships may contribute to performance on the MAT" (p. 17). Although a minor point, the use of the auxiliary verb "may" is most curious. If the aforementioned factors do not contribute to performance on the MAT, what does?

A Guide For Controlled Testing Centers and Directions for Examiners are clear, prescriptive, and detailed publications. From the admission of examinees, to seating arrangements, to the assignment of appropriate test forms, nothing is left to chance. To ensure a level playing field for all examinees, this is as it should be.

Test results are reported in terms of a raw score, a percentile based on the intended major of the candidate, and a percentile based on the general population of MAT examinees. Scores from earlier administrations are reported if earned within the previous 5 years. The percentiles are derived from the performance of self-selected, first-time test takers who took the MAT between January 1, 1990 and December 31, 1992. Technically, these reference group data are not norms, and the publisher correctly cautions users that the percentiles may not be representative of all graduate school applicants. Similar cautions, however, are not as clearly stated in materials for examinees.

The publications referenced above are excellent. There is no ambiguity regarding the intended audience. Regrettably, this is not the case for the publication entitled Miller Analogies Test Technical Manual—A Guide to Interpretation. The stated purpose of this publication is to "help university deans, faculty, and other administrators responsible for graduate admissions use Miller Analogies Test scores to aid in their decision-making processes" (p. 3). Although it may fulfill this purpose, the publication is disappointing as a technical manual. This is particularly surprising in light of the Willingham (1965) review in *The Sixth Mental Measurements Yearbook* of an earlier edition of the MAT technical manual.

The "technical manual" reports average K-R_{20} reliability coefficients between .90 and .94 for the 7 current forms of the MAT. The reliability of the instruments is quite acceptable but no evidence of the equivalence of scores across the seven forms is provided. The manual authors simply state that "If the characteristics of the [old and new form] are similar, the forms are considered to be comparable" (p. 28). Comparable does not necessarily mean equivalent, and the publisher is remiss in not providing empirical evidence on this issue. The manual, surprisingly, does not address the issues of possible race, ethnic, and/or gender bias except through uninterpreted tables.

The concept of content validity is discussed, but no evidence of content validity is presented. One correlation matrix based on aggregated data from over 50 graduate schools/departments is presented as evidence of predictive validity. The correlation between MAT and graduate GPA is .23, between undergraduate GPA and graduate GPA is .29, and the multiple correlation of MAT and undergraduate GPA with graduate GPA is .37. The resulting incremental validity for the MAT over undergraduate GPA, therefore, is .08.

Grade inflation, restriction in range, and inconsistencies in grading practices both within and across schools and departments make graduate GPA a less than ideal criterion variable to predict. Coupled with restriction in range in MAT scores due to explicit or implicit selection, modest incremental validity coefficients for the MAT are not unexpected. The publisher appears to exacerbate the difficulties in predicting graduate GPA by aggregating data across 50 graduate schools/departments. Ultimately, each institution that requires MAT scores as part of the admissions process is responsible for assessing the utility of the instrument for this purpose. The MAT would have been better served, however, if the publisher had disaggregated the data and displayed predictive validity coefficients separately by school/department.

In summary, the MAT is an excellent instrument for differentiating among high-ability students. Although it is reasonable to assume that MAT scores will contribute useful information to the graduate school application process, the onus of confirming this assumption rests with each school/department that requires the submission of MAT scores.

REVIEWER'S REFERENCE

Willingham, W. W. [Review of the Miller Analogies Test.] In O. K. Buros (Ed.), *The sixth mental measurements yearbook* (pp. 749-750). Highland Park, NJ: Gryphon Press.

[236]

Millon Adolescent Clinical Inventory.

Purpose: Designed to assess "an adolescent's personality, along with self-reported concerns and clinical syndromes."
Population: Ages 13–19.
Publication Date: 1993.
Acronym: MACI.
Scores: 27 scales: Personality Patterns (Introversive, Inhibited, Doleful, Submissive, Dramatizing, Egotistic, Unruly, Forceful, Conforming, Oppositional, Self-Demeaning, Borderline Tendency), Expressed Concerns (Identify Diffusion, Self-Devaluation, Body Disapproval, Sexual Discomfort, Peer Insecurity, Social Insensitivity, Family Discord, Childhood Abuse), Clinical Syndromes (Eating Dysfunctions, Substance Abuse Proneness, Delinquent Predisposition, Impulsive Propensity, Anxious Feelings, Depressive Affect, Suicidal Tendency), and 3 Modifying Indices (Disclosure, Desirability, Debasement).
Administration: Individual or group.
Price Data, 1994: $80 per Mail-In Preview Package; $80 per MICROTEST Q Preview Package; $18.60 per Prepaid Interpretive mail-in answer sheet; $18.60 per Prepaid Hispanic Interpretive mail-in answer sheet; $11 per prepaid Profile mail-in answer sheet; $11 per Prepaid Hispanic profile mail-in answer sheet; $12 per 25 MICROTEST Q answer sheets; $12 per 25 Hispanic MICROTEST Q answer sheets; $17.60 per Interpretive MICROTEST Q Administrations; $10 per Profile MICROTEST Q administrations; $41.50 per audio cassette (specify English or Hispanic); $23 per 10 handscoring test booklets; $32 per manual (123 pages); $200 per handscoring starter kit including manual, handscoring user's guide, 10 test booklets, 50 handscoring answer sheets, 50 handscoring work sheets, and 50 profile forms and handscoring keys; $100 per handscoring reorder kit including 50 handscoring answer sheets, 50 worksheets, and 50 profile sheets.
Time: (30) minutes.
Comments: Self-report personality inventory replacing the Millon Adolescent Personality Inventory (9:707); available in paper-and-pencil and on-line administration; MICROTEST Q, mail-in scoring, and handscoring available.
Authors: Theodore Millon with Carrie Millon and Roger Davis.
Publisher: NCS Assessments.
Cross References: See T4:1633 (14 references); for reviews by Douglas T. Brown and Thomas A. Widiger of the Millon Adolescent Personality Inventory, see 9:707.

TEST REFERENCES

1. Knoff, H. M., & Paez, D. (1992). Investigating the relationship between the Millon Adolescent Personality Inventory and the Personality Inventory for Children with a sample of learning disabled adolescents. *Psychological Reports, 70,* 775-785.

2. Hart, L. R. (1993). Diagnosis of disruptive behavior disorders using the Millon Adolescent Personality Inventory. *Psychological Reports, 73,* 895-914.

3. Burnett, K. F., & Kleiman, M. E. (1994). Psychological characteristics of adolescent steroid users. *Adolescence, 29,* 81-89.

4. Pantle, M. L., Barger, C. G., Hamilton, M. C., Thornton, S. S., & Piersma, H. L. (1994). Persistent MAP Scale 6 elevations after inpatient treatment. *Journal of Personality Assessment, 63*, 327-337.

5. Siemen, J. R., Warrington, C. A., & Mangano, E. L. (1994). Comparison of the Millon Adolescent Personality Inventory and the Suicide Ideation Questionnaire-Junior with an adolescent inpatient sample. *Psychological Reports, 75*, 947-950.

6. Craig, R. J., & Olson, R. E. (1995). MCMI-II profiles and typologies for patients seen in marital therapy. *Psychological Reports, 76*, 163-170.

Review of the Millon Adolescent Clinical Inventory by PAUL RETZLAFF, Associate Professor of Psychology, University of Northern Colorado, Greeley, CO:

The Millon Adolescent Clinical Inventory (MACI) is a revision of the Millon Adolescent Personality Inventory (MAPI) (see MMY 9:707). The change in name is indicative of the very major revision that was undertaken. For the most part the changes are appropriate, useful, and welcome.

The MACI has 27 content scales and 4 response bias scales. It is intended for "disturbed" adolescents who have come to the attention of clinical professionals. It is not appropriate for screening or for the assessment of "normal" personality. The 160 sixth grade reading level items should be finished by most adolescents in 20 minutes.

The Personality Patterns scales (Introversive, Inhibited, Doleful, Submissive, Dramatizing, Egotistic, Unruly, Forceful, Conforming, Oppositional, Self-Demeaning, and Borderline Tendency) parallel the DSM-III-R/IV personality disorders in the order of their presentation in the Millon Clinical Multiaxial Inventory-II (MCMI-II/III) (see MMY 11:239). Specifically, Introversive is viewed as an adolescent equivalent of Schizoid, Inhibited as Avoidant, Doleful as Depressive, etc. The MACI includes a number of patterns/disorders that were not included in the MAPI including Doleful (Depressive), Forceful (Sadistic), Self-Demeaning (Self-Defeating), and Borderline Tendencies.

The expressed Concerns scales include Identity Diffusion, Self-Devaluation, Body Disapproval, Sexual Discomfort, Peer Insecurity, Social Insensitivity, Family Discord, and Childhood Abuse. Here Academic Confidence has been dropped from the MAPI and Childhood Abuse has been added. Also, the scale names have been changed to reflect high scores on the domains appropriately. For example, Self Concept has been changed to Identity Diffusion and Body Comfort to Body Disapproval.

The last section of the test has been changed from Behavioral Correlates to Clinical Syndromes. These include Eating Dysfunctions, Substance-Abuse Proneness, Delinquent Predisposition, Impulsive Propensity, Anxious Feelings, Depressive Affect, and Suicidal Tendency. Most of these are new to the MACI and represent the more clinical focus of this instrument. The inclusion of the Anxiety and Depression scales are of particular clinical importance.

The response bias scales are referred to as Modifying Indices and include Reliability, Disclosure, Desirability, and Debasement. The Reliability scale is a low level screen to determine if the patient could or did read the items. The first of the two items is, "I have not seen a car in the last ten years." With the typical motivational problems of an adolescent in treatment this is an important screen and, perhaps, three or four items should have been included. The Disclosure scale is similar to the Disclosure scale on the MCMI-II/III. It represents a linear combination of scale scores that are indicative of over- or under-reporting psychopathology. It should be fairly effective (Retzlaff, Sheehan, & Fiel, 1991). The final two indices are Desirability and Debasement. These, unfortunately, did not enjoy the very sophisticated domain construction model that the rest of the test did.

The construction of the test followed the domain theory construction model. It included face-valid pools of initial items, internal structural-statistical methods, and, finally, external empirical keying. As such, it encompasses most of the traditional methods of construction and should have high reliabilities and strong (cross) validities. The initial item pool was 331 items including the MAPI item set and newly written items. These items faced subsamples of a total subject pool of 1,017. After item-total homogeneity procedures, final validities were against clinician judgments. The Base Rate scores represent this underlying criterion referencing. On the basis of these construction procedures, items are weighted in the scoring of the test. This has been shown to be unnecessary (Retzlaff, Sheehan, & Lorr, 1990).

The Cronbach alpha reliabilities are excellent, ranging from .73 to .91. Most of these internal consistencies are in the .80s. The correlations against clinician judgments are not impressive and are largely between .10 and the .20s. They do not seem much worse though than the interrater reliability kappa statistics in the field trials of the DSMs. Finally, from a psychometric perspective, the interscale, intercorrelation matrix has far too many scales correlating with each other in the .70s. There seems to be a lack of specificity of the scales above and beyond what should be clinically expected.

This lack of scale specificity is the largest problem with the MACI and is a manifestation of the largest construction problem with the test. The 160 items are insufficient to score the 30 (Disclosure is a formula) scales. Indeed, the 160 items are keyed 923 times. Each item, on average, is keyed on six scales. As part of this problem, each scale has too many items keyed to it with most scales having 30 or more items out of the 160. To correct this, the test should have more items, fewer scales, and/or fewer items per scale. The intent was noble but so few items cannot be stretched that far.

The computer scoring and interpretation of the MACI is easy to use. The MACI is one of the first tests on National Computer System's new "Q" platform for Microsoft Windows. The software can be loaded on any number of computers and security is maintained by a small firmware devise inserted in the printer port. There are a number of input, output, and utility options. The interpretations are informative and clinically useful. There should be a Macintosh version though.

The problems of too few items for too many scales aside, this is a good test. It includes personality variables mapped to DSM personality disorders, expressed concerns appropriate to adolescents, and clinical syndromes of significance. No other test even attempts this. In practice, the test works and works much better than the MAPI. There is no better test available.

REVIEWER'S REFERENCES

Retzlaff, P., Sheehan, E., & Lorr, M. (1990). MCMI-II scoring: Weighted and unweighted algorithms. *Journal of Personality Assessment, 55*, 219-223.

Retzlaff, P., Sheehan, E., & Fiel, A. (1991). MCMI-II report style and bias: Profile and validity scales analysis. *Journal of Personality Assessment, 56*, 466-477.

Review of the Millon Adolescent Clinical Inventory by RICHARD B. STUART, Professor Emeritus, Department of Psychiatry and Behavioral Sciences, School of Medicine, University of Washington, Seattle, WA:

The Millon Adolescent Clinical Inventory (MACI) is a revision of the Millon Adolescent Inventory (MAI), developed in 1974, and the Millon Adolescent Personality Inventory (MAPI), developed in 1982, which is identical to its predecessor in item content, but differs in its norms and intended uses. The original MAPI was written in two forms: the MAPI-C, designed for use by mental health workers assessing teenagers who exhibited emotional or behavioral disorders and who were in a diagnostic or treatment setting at the time of testing; and the MAPI-G, designed for use by guidance personnel in school settings in their efforts to determine which students would benefit from further psychological assessment. The MACI was developed to serve both purposes, taking advantage of suggestions from those who had used its predecessors for a decade, to make it more reflective of developments in its guiding theory, and to make it more consonant with recent developments in DSM-IV. In addition to adding new personality scales and weighting items differently, the MACI retains only 49 items used in its predecessors, adding 111 new ones.

The MACI consists of 160 items which are scored to yield 12 Personality scales, 8 Expressed Concerns scales, 7 Clinical Syndrome scales, and 4 modifying indices (Disclosure, Desirability, Debasement, and Reliability). From 2 to 48 items comprise each scale. Although not all items are used equally, a total of 923 items are included in the 32 varied scales, an average of 5.77 applications per item. Although Millon has surely anticipated this problem, there is a risk that adolescents who carelessly answer a few items may bias their scale scores in several areas. The justification, however, for this multiple use of items is its contribution to the brevity of the MACI.

The MACI is available in two pencil-and-paper formats, one for handscoring and one for computer scoring, as well as in English and Spanish audiocassettes. Its items are written at a sixth grade reading level and were easily comprehended by the adolescents to whom I administered the MACI as a test. Test administration took an average of 30 minutes, in contrast to the 20 minutes stipulated in the manual. Computer scoring can be done either on-site or by mailing protocols to NCS Assessments. The manual contains instructions for handscoring, with the admonition that this is a very complex process. The complexity stems from the need for the test scorer to make base rate transformations of raw scores, and then to adjust these scores for the age of the adolescent, as well as further adjustments for disclosure, anxiety/depression, desirability/debasement, and denial/complaint. In effect, the MACI cannot be handscored in an efficient manner, although those who intend to use it extensively are well advised to handscore at least a few protocols in order to better understand the ways in which subjects' responses are used.

Millon did not use projectable or population proportionate samples to establish norms for the MACI. Instead, norms were developed from a primary sample of 579 adolescents and two cross-validation samples of 139 and 194 each. Subjects in these three groups were subsequently pooled in a combined sample for the development of norms. All of the subjects were in treatment programs. Adolescents who were not identified as patients were not included in the normative sample, thus limiting the utility of the MACI for use as a screening tool with general adolescent populations. The three samples were 78.8% white, somewhat limiting the applicability of the norms to populations of nonwhite adolescents. An even more serious limitation stemming from the validating sample is the fact that although the test is recommended for use by adolescents ages 13–19, 18-year-olds comprised only 3.2%, and 19-year-olds only .03% of the development and cross-validating samples. At this time use of the MACI with 18- and 19-year-olds is ill-advised. If the MACI enjoys the wide use of its sister adult measure, the Millon Clinical Multiaxial Inventory-II (MCMI-II; T4:1635), Millon will surely be able to fill in the demographic gaps in his normative sample, enhancing the validity of using the MACI with the broader range of adolescents for which it was intended.

Items were selected for inclusion in the scales using the very careful criteria one has come to expect of Millon. Base rates were then developed for each item through an unfortunately arcane process which is difficult to follow in the manual. The value of this type of item weighting has not necessarily been established, and the process potentially threatens the validity of conclusions drawn from the MACI. Given the importance of base rates in scoring the MACI, its use with groups not included in its development should be undertaken with caution.

Reliability of the MACI is estimated in terms of its internal consistency, with alphas ranging between .73 and .91 for the various scales. Test-retest reliability was found to range from .57 to .92 when the test was readministered at 3- to 7-day intervals with two of the samples. Given the fact that only two state-dependent scales, Introversive and Peer Insecurity, fell below the very satisfactory range of .70 to .90, responses to the MACI can be accepted as quite stable over short intervals. Data on test-retest scores across a longer interval of perhaps 2 months would lend greater confidence in the reliability of the MACI with a population which, by definition, experiences very rapid change.

The content validity of the MACI is somewhat assured by its congruence with the underlying theory of personality, which has been well developed in the writings of its creator. Its concurrent validity was assessed first by contrasting its results with the judgments of the clinicians through whom the validation samples were created. The resulting correlations tended to be generally modest. Of 49 comparisons in two samples, only five exceeded the level of .35. Responses to the MACI were intercorrelated with a range of other measures including the Beck Depression Inventory (BDI), Beck Hopelessness Scale (BHS), Beck Anxiety Inventory (BAI), and Eating Disorder Inventory. Because sample sizes are unknown, it is not possible to determine the clinical significance of these statistical correlations. In a number of instances, many scales of the MACI correlated above the moderate level of .25 with responses to the other measures. For example, 20 of its 27 scales had such correlations with total scores of the BDI and BHS, and 16 of its scales correlated at this level with the BAI. In the array of correlations presented in the manual it is possible to pinpoint some which support the interinstrument validity of the MACI (e.g., correlations of .75 and .88 respectively between the Eating Dysfunction Scale of the MACI and the Drive for Thinness and Body Dissatisfaction measures on the Eating Disorder Inventory-2, or correlations of .59 between the Depressive Affect Scale of the MACI and both the BDI and the BHS). But it is also possible to find some discordant associations. For example, the correlation between the Body Disapproval scale of the MACI and a bulimia measure was only .25 and the correlation between the Peer Insecurity Scale of the MACI and a measure of social insecurity was -.02. These correlation charts should be taken as a starting point for examining the relationship between the MACI and other measures. It remains to be seen whether the instrument redundantly overlaps other tests or correlates highly enough with other measures to offer a meaningful overview of their results through administration of a single instrument.

Printouts of responses include a cover sheet, a histographic display of scale scores, an average of six pages of narrative, and a complete list of respondents' answers. The responses of NCS was quick and flawlessly accurate in the test protocols. Clinicians are very likely to find its list of Axis I and II entities to be a very useful source of diagnostic hypotheses, although one major presenting problem was not detected in one of the protocols studied for this review. Those who use the MACI extensively may be disturbed by the amount of boiler-plate redundancy across printouts. It seems that as much as 75% of the word-count was identical across protocols. This is a necessary characteristic of computer-scored instruments in which different responses to a small number of items trigger prepared blocks of text. Presenting the ideographic information in bold type would help to minimize this problem. Clinicians may also be uneasy about the forcefulness with which some of the conclusions and treatment recommendations are expressed. In general, these recommendations go beyond assessment per se and one aspect of the development of the MACI assessed respondents' ability to benefit from varied treatment approaches. If these printouts were placed in an adolescent's school file, nonpsychologists who have not been trained to use test results to formulate rather than validate diagnostic hypotheses, might construe their contents as firm conclusions rather than as suggestive diagnostic impressions. Clinicians may also regret the fact that contrary to the manual's assertion that the MACI assesses adolescents' strengths and weaknesses, the printouts generated make few if any strength-oriented statements, leaving therapists to infer assets from the absence of pathological indications.

In summary, although the MACI has a 20-year history, it is best to regard its present iteration to be a new instrument. It holds great promise for use as a screening instrument to assess a broad spectrum of adolescent problems, and as a means of generating DSM-IV diagnostic categories in clinical settings. Confidence in these uses, however, must await validating studies by clinicians working independently of Millon.

[237]

Minnesota Manual Dexterity Test.

Purpose: "Measures capacity for simple but rapid eye-hand-finger movement."

Population: Ages 13–adult.
Publication Date: [Undated].
Scores: Total time for each of two tests.
Administration: Group.
Tests, 2: Placing Test, Turning Test.
Price Data, 1991: $150 per test; $2.25 per replacement wooden cylinders; $10 per 50 record blanks.
Time: Administration time not reported.
Author: Lafayette Instrument.
Publisher: Lafayette Instrument.

Review of the Minnesota Manual Dexterity Test by DEBORAH ERICKSON, Associate Professor of Education, Niagara University, Niagara University, NY:

The manual states that the Minnesota Manual Dexterity Test was previously referred to as the Minnesota Rate of Manipulation Test and The Placing and Turning Test. According to the seven-page, poorly photocopied manual, the place and turn parts of the test are administered sequentially. The Placing Test measures the speed of gross hand movements and the Turning Test measures the speed of fine-motor finger movements. The tests are designed to be administered on an individual basis and projected to be completed in about 15 minutes. The test board and corresponding pegs are sturdy and designed to last.

The test is described as useful in determining the speed of an individual performing tasks such as filling containers with pharmaceutical pills and capsules, packing materials, stuffing envelopes, wrapping food articles, etc.

Directions for administration of the tests are clear and precise. However, the rest of the manual is inadequate. Validity and reliability of the test are not discussed. The standardization procedure is vague, although there is reference to standards developed on 3,000 randomly sampled cases obtained from a population of 10,000 tested cases. There is a statement in the standards section that the Place Test and the Turn Test "correlation . . . in 500 cases is claimed to be .47" (manual, p. 4). No further explanation is offered. No differences between gender were found.

Interpretation of the norms based upon the conversion tables is extremely confusing. The tables are described to be "standardized on the basis of ten-quartiles making it convenient to convert each quartile range to a percentile placement basis, where each 10 percent is equivalent to one quartile range" (manual, p. 4). I wondered if the test author meant deciles instead of quartiles.

Further, the test author explains that percentile ratings are sometimes exaggerated at both ends of the scale but intimates this is not very important because developing local norms may be better than using the norms from the manual. A quote from the manual regarding scoring and interpretation captures the essence of the interpretive norms section: "As in the case of traveling by rail or automobile, the speed itself may be the more important factor rather than the percentage of automobiles or trains which are traveling at that speed" (manual, p. 4).

In summary, it is not clear from the manual that this test can be used in a standardized manner to assess the speed of gross hand movements or the speed of fine-motor finger movements. There is no proof the test assesses what it claims to measure because the manual does not contain any validity and reliability studies. In addition, the interpretative norms section does not appear to be statistically sound. Therefore, users must use caution when comparing their test results to the given norms on manual dexterity. If the Place and Turn Tests were to be used, local norms should be developed. An alternative test, with reviews that also question the accuracy of the norms, is the USES General Aptitude Test Battery (T4:2868), which has a place and turn subtest along with a finger dexterity board.

Review of the Minnesota Manual Dexterity Test by ALIDA S. WESTMAN, Professor of Psychology, Eastern Michigan University, Ypsilanti, MI:

This test was designed to provide employers with a means to measure "native speed capacity of simple but rapid eye hand coordination . . . . Precision of eye hand coordination is not an important factor, but merely the speed of gross hand and arm movements. It is therefore an ideal test for semi-skilled operations such as wrapping of food articles, packing of components and similar articles in envelopes, and in filling containers with pharmaceutical pills & capsules. It is also applicable to many clerical operations such as sorting checks or addressing cards" (manual, p. 1).

The test has two parts. Both use the same thin ($^3/_{16}$-inch) board. It is 33$^3/_4$ inches long and consists of three flexibly connected sections to permit folding up the board. There are four rows of 15 1$^1/_2$-inch holes into which cylinders are to be put.

In the Placing task, the person tested pushes the board with the cylinders in it at least 12 inches away, lifts the board off while leaving the cylinders in place, puts the board in front of the cylinders so the holes are in line with the cylinders, and puts the cylinders into the board as fast as possible with only one hand, from right to left, column by column and in mirror-image order, so that the bottom cylinder is put in the top hole and the top cylinder in the bottom hole. Following a practice trial there are four timed trials that are summed to give a raw score.

The second task is the Turning task and involves both hands. Testing begins with the top row. The left hand picks up the right-most cylinder, turns it, and the right hand puts it back into the hole. The person first does the whole top row, then reverses hands for the next row and moves to the right. The last two rows repeat the first two. There again are one practice trial and four timed trials.

Tables allow for transforming raw scores on each task to percentile rank, a percent placement within a quartile range, and a 6-point verbal descriptive scale ranging from *extremely fast* to *extremely slow*.

EVALUATION. Giving the test is difficult because the instructions are not clear. Is the person tested to be seated or standing? If seated the test crosses the midline of the body, and this is difficult for some people to do. Also, how to score when a cylinder is not completely placed into a hole is not explained. For the Placement task, is taking off the board part of the timed trials? If so, the board's size and lack of rigidity make it difficult to remove, especially because the board is at least a foot away and the cylinders fit snugly.

The recommended testing condition is problematic. "The most representative results are obtained from this test when competition enters the picture. Therefore, the best procedure is to have at least two persons tested at the same time" (manual, p. 1). The person tested has to time, record, and sum time spent. A competitive situation threatens accuracy. To time the trials, the person tested has to listen to the examiner count off seconds. Even assuming motivation to be honest, this is very difficult to do for individuals who give themselves verbal instructions as they work. Verbal instructions may be more likely in the Placement task, because producing mirror images rather than directly copying the order onto the board is more difficult, especially for individuals who may have special learning problems (Gladstone, Best, & Davidson, 1989).

Given the test's purpose, other difficulties are apparent. On the job, tasks are done in whatever way seems easier. For this reason it is unclear why only one hand may be used in the Placement task, instead of using both hands, or changing hands at the midline of the body. Similarly, it may be easier to scan and work from left to right in the direction we normally read than from right to left. On the Turning task, for individuals who show strong hand preference, two of the rows are more difficult to do and take longer, and this hand combination would not be used on the job. Furthermore, the instructions when a cylinder is dropped on the floor are for the examiner to "say 'Let it go' and pick it up at the end of the trial" (manual, p. 3). On the job it is likely to take time to retrieve lost material. To test for speed in stuffing envelopes and sorting checks, the cylinders are too large and rigid. Such jobs require finger skills and not only gross hand and arm movements.

No reliability or validity data are provided. The norm group is not described. No sex differences were found, and no reference is made to age differences. Yet prior research with pegboards showed women to be consistently faster and for speed to decrease with age (Agnew, Bolla-Wilson, Kawas, & Bleecker, 1988).

The two tasks are meant to show "native speed capacity" (p. 1), but practice effects and strategies probably have significant effects (Sherwood & Canabal, 1988), for example, in how high the blocks are lifted.

SUMMARY. Currently, the Minnesota Manual Dexterity Test is a poorly designed test, lacking in data to support its use. The authors should reconsider the purpose for which their test is designed, clarify instructions and norms, and do reliability and validity studies.

REVIEWER'S REFERENCES

Agnew, J., Bolla-Wilson, K., Kawas, C. H., & Bleecker, M. L. (1988). Purdue Pegboard age and sex norms for people 40 years old and older. *Developmental Neuropsychology, 4*, 29-35.

Sherwood, D. E., & Canabal, M. Y. (1988). The effect of practice on the control of sequential and simultaneous actions. *Human Performance, 1*, 237-260.

Gladstone, M., Best, C. T., & Davidson, R. J. (1989). Anomalous bimanual coordination among dyslexic boys. *Developmental Psychology, 25*, 236-246.

[238]

Minnesota Multiphasic Personality Inventory—Adolescent.

Purpose: Designed for use with adolescents to assess a number of the major patterns of personality and emotional disorders.

Population: Ages 14–18.

Publication Date: 1992.

Acronym: MMPI-A.

Scores, 68: 16 Basic Scales [6 Validity Scales (Cannot Say (?), Lie, Infrequency, Defensiveness, Variable Response Inconsistency, True Response Inconsistency); 10 Clinical Scales (Hypochondriasis, Depression, Hysteria, Psychopathic Deviate, Masculinity-Femininity, Paranoia, Psychasthenia, Schizophrenia, Hypomania, Social Introversion); 28 Harris-Lingoes Subscales (Subjective Depression, Psychomotor Retardation, Physical Malfunctioning, Mental Dullness, Brooding, Denial of Social Anxiety, Need for Affection, Lassitude-Malaise, Somatic Complaints, Inhibition of Aggression, Familial Discord, Authority Problems, Social Imperturbability, Social Alienation, Self-Alienation, Persecutory Ideas, Poignancy, Naivete, Social Alienation, Emotional Alienation, Lack of Ego Mastery-Cognitive, Lack of Ego Mastery-Conative, Lack of Ego Mastery-Defective Inhibition, Bizarre Sensory Experiences, Amorality, Psychomotor Acceleration, Imperturbability, Ego Inflation); 3 Si Subscales (Shyness/Self-Consciousness, Social Avoidance, Alienation); 15 Adolescent Content Scales (Anxiety, Obsessiveness, Depression, Health Concerns, Alienation, Bizarre Mentation, Anger, Cynicism, Conduct Problems, Low Self-Esteem, Low Aspirations, Social Discomfort, Family Problems, School Problems, Negative Treatment Indicators); 6 Supplementary Scales (Anxiety, Repression, MacAndrew Alcoholism Scale, Alcohol/Drug Problem Acknowledgment, Alcohol/Drug Problem Proneness, Immaturity).

Administration: Group.

Price Data, 1992: Microtest Reports ($20 per Adolescent Interpretive System, $14 per Extended Score Report, $8 per Basic Service Profile); Prepaid Mail-In Reports ($21 per Adolescent Interpretive System; $15 per Extended Score Report; $9 per Basic Service Profile); $40 per manual; $15 per Adolescent Interpretive System User's Guide; $25 per 10 softcover test booklets; $25 per hardcover test booklet; $75 per audiocassette; $60 per 100 Content/Supplementary Scales Profile Forms; $60 per 100 Harris-Lingoes Subscales Profile Forms; $50 per Basic Scales answer keys; $50 per Content/Supplementary Scales answer keys; $50 per Harris-Lingoes Subscales answer keys; $385 per hand-scoring starter kit including manual, test booklets, Basic Scales keys, Harris-Lingoes Subscales keys, Content/Supplementary Scale keys, 100 hand-scoring answer sheets, 100 Basic Scale Profile Forms, Harris-Lingoes Profile Forms, 100 Content/Supplementary Profile Forms.
Time: Administration time not reported.
Comments: May be administered by audiocassette or microcomputer.
Authors: James N. Butcher, Carolyn L. Williams, John R. Graham, Beverly Kaemmer, Robert P. Archer (manual); Auke Tellegen (manual), Yossef S. Ben-Porath (manual), S. R. Hathaway (test booklet), and J. C. McKinley (test booklet).
Publisher: University of Minnesota Press (distributed by National Computer Systems).
Cross References: See T4:1646 (4 references).

TEST REFERENCES

1. Gurrera, R. J. (1990). Some biological and behavioral features associated with clinical personality types. *The Journal of Nervous and Mental Disease, 178*, 556-566.
2. Archer, R. P., & Gordon, R. (1994). Psychometric stability of MMPI-A item modification. *Journal of Personality Assessment, 62*, 416-426.
3. Archer, R. P., & Krishnamurthy, R. (1994). A structural summary approach for the MMPI-A: Development and empirical correlates. *Journal of Personality Assessment, 63*, 554-573.
4. Phelps, L. (1994). MMPI-2 and MMPI-A computerized interpretation: An adjunct to quality mental health service. *Measurement and Evaluation in Counseling and Development, 27*, 186-189.

Review of the Minnesota Multiphasic Personality Inventory—Adolescent by CHARLES D. CLAIBORN, Professor, Division of Psychology in Education, Arizona State University, Tempe, AZ:

Nearly 50 years after the development of the Minnesota Multiphasic Personality Inventory (MMPI), years during which it became without doubt the most widely used inventory for assessing psychopathology, the MMPI was extensively revised and restandardized as the MMPI-2 (T4:1645). The MMPI-2, like its predecessor, was designed for use with adults. More recently, a second, largely parallel inventory, the Minnesota Multiphasic Personality—Adolescent (MMPI-A), was designed for use with adolescents, ages 14 to 18. Given its parallel development and structure, the MMPI-A shares many strengths and a few weaknesses with the MMPI-2; however, it has a number of unique features as well, as appropriate to its intended use with adolescents.

The development of the MMPI-A so resembles that of the MMPI-2 and is so clearly described in the MMPI-A Manual for Administration, Scoring, and Interpretation that a few comments about it will suffice here. First, the normative sample is admirably diverse and, with a few acknowledged exceptions, probably representative of the adolescent population of the United States. Adolescent norms are essential because adolescents tend to score higher on the MMPI than adults and, if adult norms are used, adolescents may appear more disturbed than they actually are. The clinical sample is less representative than the normative sample: All are from settings in Minneapolis, and the majority are from drug and alcohol treatment. Further work with other, specific clinical samples will strengthen the empirical base of the inventory.

Second, many items from the MMPI and MMPI-2 have been reworded for or omitted entirely from the MMPI-A, and items unique to the MMPI-A have been added (see Appendix E of the manual). The language of MMPI-A items is generally suitable for contemporary adolescents, and item content appropriately reflects adolescent personality and psychopathology. The length of the inventory has been shortened, as well, to 478 items (compared with the MMPI's 566 items), and some of the validity scales and all of the basic clinical scales may be completed in the first 350 items. Length changes, like item changes, make the MMPI-A more accessible to adolescents than the MMPI.

Third, MMPI-A developers employed uniform, rather than linear, *T* scores for most of the basic clinical scales (Scales 1 to 4 and 6 to 9) and all of the content scales. Uniform *T* scores, an innovation carried over from the MMPI-2, preserve the positively skewed distributions of these scales but at the same time correct for differential skewness across scales, so that the percentile scores of the different scales are comparable.

User qualifications, administration, and scoring of the inventory are clearly described in the manual. A large part of the manual is devoted to conceptual and psychometric information about each scale and guidelines for scale interpretation. Although users will, of course, consult research reports and texts in making interpretations, the overview to interpretation provided in the manual is excellent. In addition to the text descriptions of the scales, Tables 12 and 24 of the manual contain general interpretive guidelines for the basic clinical and content scales, respectively. These guidelines include cutoff scores for high (or "clinically significant") and moderate evaluations on the scales and describe the degree of confidence one might have in interpretations at each elevation. The clear and uniform guidelines provided in these tables make MMPI-A interpretation more straightforward than interpretation of the original MMPI. Nevertheless, interpretation is still a complex process.

Throughout the text suggestions for interpretation are specific, appropriately tentative and flexible, and empirically based. The tables in Appendix D of the manual, which contain specific behavioral correlates of the validity and basic clinical scales for the normative and clinical samples, are particularly helpful in interpreting those scales. Table 23 in the text has similar information for the content scales but in narrative, rather than statistical, form. Finally, the manual contains two extended case illustrations that are extremely helpful in demonstrating the interpretive process and highlighting features of the inventory. (The only unfortunate aspect of the case illustrations is that although we learn that Joyce, the subject of Case 1, is "attractive," we never discover how Scott, in Case 2, rates on this variable.)

Like the MMPI-2, the MMPI-A has four sets of scales: validity scales, basic clinical scales (several of which have subscales to aid in their interpretation), content scales, and supplementary scales. The authors of the MMPI-A manual helpfully point out the relation between MMPI-A scales and their MMPI-2 and MMPI counterparts, both in terms of the items they comprise and the personality constructs they measure. With respect to validity, the K scale of the MMPI-A is not used as a correction factor for some of the basic clinical scales, as it is with adults, and indeed is hardly interpretable for adolescents. Otherwise, the validity scales of the MMPI-A feature the innovations found in the MMPI-2. The F scale is divided into subscales, F_1 and F_2, that appear in the first and second halves of the inventory, respectively. F_1 may thus serve as a validity indicator for the basic clinical scales, and F_2 for the content and supplementary scales. The old problem with F—that it may indicate validity problems (exaggeration of symptoms) or serious disturbance—remains; however, helpful suggestions for sorting this out are contained in the manual. The MMPI-A also contains the valuable response set indicators, VRIN (Variable Response Inconsistency) and the TRIN (True Response Inconsistency), which assess indiscriminate and acquiescent/nonacquiescent responding, respectively. The use of these indicators in interpreting the traditional validity scales, particularly F, is well demonstrated in the manual.

The basic clinical scales, despite the wealth of information they provide about client symptomatology, are the most problematic for the inventory. Because they are intended to measure multifaceted psychopathological constructs and because they were developed for this purpose using an empirical criterion method, the clinical scales range widely in internal consistency. Alpha coefficients for the 10 clinical scales are presented in Table 14 of the manual, by sample (normative and clinical) and gender. Of the 40 alpha coefficients, 17 (43%) range from .75 to .91; 18 (45%) range from .55 to .68; and the remaining 5 (13%) range from .35 to .53. Internal consistencies like these make scale interpretation difficult, but the use of the Harris-Lingoes subscales in interpreting Scales 2, 3, 4, 6, 8, and 9 and the Si subscales for interpreting Scale 0 ameliorates this problem somewhat.

Intercorrelations among the clinical scales range widely, as well, from .00 to .85 in the normative sample, as reported in Table C-1 in Appendix C of the manual. There is considerable overlap in what the scales measure. Factor analysis of the clinical and validity scales supports this notion, with a familiar (within the MMPI family) four-factor solution: The first factor, described as "general maladjustment," includes positive loadings by Scales 1 to 4 and 6 to 9, which are the clinical scales most concerned with psychopathology. Scale 9 also loads positively on the second factor, "overcontrol," which is otherwise influenced by the validity scales. The third and fourth factors are represented by Scales 0 and 5, respectively; these are the two clinical scales less concerned with psychopathology. The intercorrelation and factor analytic data simply confirm that interpretation of the clinical scales is going to be a complicated affair.

The clinical scales have retained the labels given to their original MMPI counterparts. This is unfortunate because some of the labels (Hypomania, Psychasthenia) are archaic and others (Hysteria, Psychopathic Deviate) are offensive. A better approach might have been to retain only the scale numbers, because these are widely used and recognized, and to have used the more accurate of the scale labels, such as Depression, only within the scale descriptions. The authors of the manual have actually done this to some extent, for example, in their description of Scale 7 as "originally designed to measure psychasthenia, a neurotic syndrome most closely related to the currently used category of obsessive-compulsive disorder" (p. 48).

The biggest mystery—and interpretive problem—among the clinical scales is Scale 5, which purports to measure Masculinity-Femininity. Why is this scale in the inventory? How is it to be interpreted? Unlike the other clinical scales, with the possible exception of Scale 0, Scale 5 has nothing to do with psychopathology, nor indeed personality. It is an interest measure, and its scores address the clinically (and otherwise) uninteresting question of whether one has stereotypically masculine or feminine interests. The interpretation of the scale is understandably troublesome. It has the lowest internal consistency of the clinical scales, ranging from .35 to .44 in the normative and clinical samples, and the scale correlates are few and contradictory across studies. In addition, interpretive descriptors have nothing explicitly to do with gender or gender identity. The MMPI-A's developers themselves seem puzzled about this scale, as evidence by the odd, inappropriately causal statement in the manual, "Having Scale 5 as the highest scale . . . seems to have an inhibitory effect on acting-out behaviors in both genders" (p. 47). The developers have a challenge ahead of them if they hope to justify the retention of Scale 5 in the inventory.

The content scales and the new supplementary scales represent probably the most important innovation of the MMPI-A. The content scales were developed using the "rational and statistical" approach that was used for the MMPI-A and that is described in Table 20 of the manual. They have generally higher and less variable internal consistencies than the basic clinical scales. Many of the content scales have MMPI-2 counterparts, though some are unique to the MMPI-A. Even when conceptually similar scales are found on both instruments, they may share only a portion of their items; for example, the Adolescent—Family Problems scale of the MMPI-A has only 15 of its 35 items in common with the Family Problems scale of the MMPI-2. Table 23 of the manual contains information on the relation between the content scales of the MMPI-A and MMPI-2, as well as interpretive information for the MMPI-A scales.

The content scales measure constructs relevant to adolescent symptomatology—for example, anger, low self-esteem, and school problems—and assess symptomatology more specifically and straightforwardly than the basic clinical scales do. The constructs measured by the content scales seem to be more unitary than those measured by the clinical scales, and the content scales themselves seem more homogeneous than the clinical scales. The content scales are clinically interesting in their own right, given the range of symptoms they cover, and they are likely to be helpful, as well, in interpreting the clinical scales.

The MMPI-A contains three unique supplementary scales in addition to supplementary scales found in the MMPI-2. The unique scales measure acknowledgment of alcohol and drug problems, likelihood of having alcohol and drug problems, and (in an unusual step for an MMPI) a theoretically based construct of psychological maturity. Like the content scales, the supplementary scales are clearly relevant to understanding adolescent development and symptomatology; they are interesting in themselves and as adjuncts to clinical scale interpretation.

In conclusion, the MMPI-A is an impressive inventory, sure to become a preeminent tool for assessing adolescent psychopathology. Its flaws are relatively minor, correctable, and enormously outweighted by the strengths of the inventory. Clearly, the MMPI-A was developed with a great deal of care, expertise, and sensitivity to the problems of adolescents and the needs of practitioners who work with them. Practitioners will find MMPI-A materials easy to use, and they may satisfy themselves that despite the complexities involved in interpretation (complexities hardly surprising given the nature of adolescent behavior itself), the considerable and expanding empirical base of the inventory will support their efforts.

Review of the Minnesota Multiphasic Personality Inventory—Adolescent by RICHARD I. LANYON, Professor of Psychology, Arizona State University, Tempe, AZ:

The Minnesota Multiphasic Personality Inventory—Adolescent (MMPI-A), published in 1992, is a revision of the MMPI for use with adolescents of age 14 through 18. It can be considered as parallel to the MMPI-2 (T4:1645), the revision of the MMPI for adults, that was published in 1989. Previous authors have documented the need for these revisions, or restandardizations, of the MMPI: the lack of nationally representative norms; the presence of obsolete and otherwise objectionable items; the lack of percentile equivalence of the *T*-scores for the clinical scales; and, particularly for adolescents, the lack of item content and scales to assess problems of specific relevance to this population.

DEVELOPMENT. The challenge faced in producing both the MMPI-2 and the MMPI-A was to keep them similar enough to the MMPI so that its vast collection of empirical findings would also apply to the new tests, while correcting as many as possible of the deficiencies. This goal is judged to have been achieved for the MMPI-2 (Archer, 1992), and it is this reviewer's opinion that it has also been achieved for the MMPI-A. Because the MMPI-2 was done first, most of the technical and policy decisions that needed to be made in regard to the MMPI-A had already been worked through, and the basic strategy for revision was the same. An experimental Form TX was created with 704 items: the 550 MMPI items, plus the 58 new items written for the MMPI-2 (to expand the item pool for treatment compliance, attitudes toward self-change, amenability to therapy, alcohol and drug use, eating problems, and suicide potential), plus 96 items specific to adolescence (in the areas of identity formation, negative peer-group influence, school and teachers, relationships with parents and families, and sexuality).

The end-product is a test for which the format is virtually identical to that of the MMPI-2. There are the original three "validity" scales (L, F, and K) and three new ones (F_2, VRIN, and TRIN), the original 10 basic scales, 15 new content scales, and 6 supplementary scales. All the items on the basic scales appear in the first 350 of the 478 items.

NORMS. Credit is due to the seminal work of Marks, Seeman, and Haller (1974), who discovered that separate adolescent norms were needed for the MMPI, and that omitting the K-correction resulted in better validities. To develop norms for the MMPI-A, subjects were obtained through schools in eight states (California, Minnesota, New York, North Carolina, Ohio, Pennsylvania, Virginia, and Washington), with the goal of obtaining a balanced sample of subjects according to geographic region, urban-rural residence, and ethnic background. These balances were satisfactorily achieved; however, like the MMPI-2, the MMPI-A normative sample is quite heavily skewed in the direction of higher education and occupational level. The significance of these imbalances, although minimized in the manual, is unknown at the present time. The intended age range for the MMPI-A is 14–18, although bright, mature 12- and 13-year-olds can also be tested, and 18-year-olds who have completed high school should be given the MMPI-2.

SUPPLEMENTARY SCALES. Of the six supplementary scales, A (Anxiety), R (Repression), and MAC-R (Alcoholism) are revised and shortened versions of the corresponding MMPI scales. Three additional scales are included: ACK (Alcohol/Drug Problem Acknowledgment), PRO (Alcohol/Drug Problem Proneness), and IMM (Immaturity). These scales focus specifically on adolescents, and each was constructed using a different series of psychometric steps. The manual includes somewhat variable test-retest reliabilities for these scales.

CONTENT SCALES. Based on the premise of the primacy of content in underpinning the validity of personality assessment devices, and on the success of the Wiggins' (1966) content scales for the MMPI, a great deal of effort was expended in developing and validating a set of 15 content scales for the MMPI-A. This work is documented in a separate, book-length report (Williams, Butcher, Ben-Porath, & Graham, 1992). Although the scale constructs partially overlap with those of the 15 MMPI-2 content scales, the item sets are different in all cases.

VALIDITY. Although the procedures used in the original development of the MMPI were technically advanced for their time, they are simplistic by today's standards. Specifically, state-of-the-art test construction technology involves the use of many psychometric steps in the development and final selection of the items. All of these steps are geared toward ensuring that the scale will be valid for its intended uses; in other words, they can be viewed as procedures for *building into* an instrument the foundation for its validity. Scales that are not based on such work are simply collections of items, whose validity is more-or-less unknown and must be established entirely through subsequent research. Although such research is also necessary for state-of-the-art scales, it is much more likely to be successful because of the extensive item development procedures.

As with other tests of its era, the original MMPI could be considered valid only to the extent that it was supported by subsequent empirical research. Fortunately, there is a huge quantity of such work, presented in many sources, including landmark works by Lachar (1974) and Marks, Seeman, and Haller (1974). Thus, to the extent that the MMPI-A retains the essence of the MMPI, the basic clinical scales come complete with demonstrated validity.

The validity of the 15 new content scales must be examined separately. Fortunately for MMPI-A users, the development of these scales involved extensive psychometric procedures, and although experts might disagree as to a particular strategy or sequence of steps, there can be no doubt that the potential of these scales for clinical utility is very high. Initial research toward the establishment of external validity for the content scales is presented in the volumes by Butcher and Williams (1992) and Williams et al. (1992), and is summarized in the manual. Thus, the future of the MMPI-A as an empirically valid device seems assured.

OVERVIEW. How wise was it to expend such a huge amount of time and energy in "cleaning up" the MMPI for more satisfactory use with adolescents, rather than simply building a new test? The answer, as with the MMPI-2, is that the life of the MMPI has thereby been enhanced and significantly extended, and it is a safe prediction that further empirical validity studies will appear rather quickly to facilitate the adaptation of the existing MMPI adolescent interpretive research for use with the MMPI-A. Overall, in surveying the available test instruments for assessing psychopathology in adolescents, the MMPI-A would appear to have no serious competition.

REVIEWER'S REFERENCES

Wiggins, J. S. (1966). Substantive dimensions of self-report in the MMPI item pool. *Psychological Monographs, 80*(20, Whole No. 630).

Lachar, D. (1974). *The MMPI: Clinical assessment and automated interpretation*. Los Angeles: Western Psychological Services.

Marks, P. A., Seeman, W., & Haller, D. L. (1974). *The actuarial use of the MMPI with adolescents and adults*. Baltimore: Williams and Wilkins.

Archer, R. P. (1992). [Review of the Minnesota Multiphasic Personality Inventory-2.] In J. J. Kramer & J. C. Conoley (Eds.), *The eleventh mental measurements yearbook* (pp. 558-562). Lincoln, NE: Buros Institute of Mental Measurements.

Butcher, J. N., & Williams, C. L. (1992). *Essentials of MMPI-2 and MMPI-A interpretation*. Minneapolis: University of Minnesota Press.

Williams, C. L., Butcher, J. N., Ben-Porath, Y. S., & Graham, J. R. (1992). *MMPI-A content scales: Assessing psychopathology in adolescents*. Minneapolis: University of Minnesota Press.

[239]

Modern Occupational Skills Tests.

Purpose: Developed to assess skills in checking, numeracy, verbal skills, and office administration skills for use in "recruitment, selection and development of clerical and related staff."

Population: Potential and current office employees.

Publication Dates: 1989–90.

Acronym: MOST.

Scores: Total score only for each test.

Administration: Group.

Editions, 2: British, Australian.

Price Data, 1992: £21.85 per administration pack including task inventory, 10 question and answer booklets, 10 profile sheets, 10 test taker's guides, scoring key, test record sheet, and administration and scoring instructions (select area); £54.05 per reference set including one each of question and answer booklets and test taker's guides, a profile sheet, task inventory, administration and scoring instructions, and user's guides ('89 and '90, 77 pages).
Authors: Charles Johnson, Steve Blinkhorn, Robert Wood, and Jonathan Hall.
Publisher: NFER-Nelson Publishing Co., Ltd. [England].
Foreign Adaptation: Australian Edition available from Australian Council for Educational Research Ltd. [Australia].

a) NUMERICAL ESTIMATION.
Time: 12 minutes.
b) NUMERICAL AWARENESS.
Time: 8 minutes.
c) NUMERICAL CHECKING.
Time: 8 minutes.
d) TECHNICAL CHECKING.
Time: 12 minutes.
e) WORD MEANINGS.
Time: 12 minutes.
f) VERBAL CHECKING.
Time: 8 minutes.
g) DECISION MAKING.
Time: 15 minutes.
h) SPELLING AND GRAMMAR.
Time: 8 minutes.
i) FILING.
Time: 12 minutes.

Review of the Modern Occupational Skills Tests by JOSEPH C. CIECHALSKI, Associate Professor of Counselor Education and Adult Education, East Carolina University, Greenville, NC:

The Modern Occupational Skills Tests (MOST) were designed for use in the recruitment, selection, and development of clerical, administrative, and stores personnel, junior managers, and other related occupations. The authors claim that although a large number of good clerical test batteries exist, a new British clerical and office skills test was necessary because the current tests were either American or in need of updating.

Two editions of the MOST are published. There are Australian and British editions. Both editions consist of the following nine tests: Verbal, Numerical, and Technical Checking, Numerical Awareness, Numerical Estimation, Spelling and Grammar, Word Meaning, Filing, and Decision Making. The nine tests may be grouped into four skill areas: checking, numerical, verbal skills, and office administration. Differences in the two editions are found where currency and distance problems are included. For example, dollars and miles are used on the Australian edition and pounds and kilometers on the British edition.

ADMINISTRATION AND SCORING. The tests are easy to administer. In addition to the instructions in the User's Guide, each test has a separate administration instruction sheet. Each instruction sheet has been laminated to prevent wear and tear. Time limits for each test range from 8 to 15 minutes.

No one takes all nine MOST tests, rather a preliminary Task Inventory is used to determine which tests to select. The Task Inventory includes directions for using the inventory and identifies 19 tasks along with the test(s) that assess each task. Tests within each of the four skill areas are identified by subject matter and levels of difficulty. The authors suggest that no more than four tests be selected. If more than four tests are selected, those tests identified as higher level on the Task Inventory are used. For example, if the Technical Checking tests was selected, one would not use the Verbal or Numerical Checking tests because the Technical Checking test includes both verbal and numerical checking.

A Test Taker's Guide is available for each of the nine tests. It provides individuals with information about the test session including time limits for each test and sample test items.

Scores are totaled for each test only. In fact, examiners are urged not to combine the scores from separate tests. No separate answer sheets are included. Responses to each item are made in the test booklet. The MOST is hand scored and the answer keys are easy to use. The keys correspond to the responses in the test booklet. Specific directions for scoring each test are included in the User's Guide. A Profile Sheet may be used to identify an individual's strengths and weaknesses.

Although conversion tables exist for transforming raw scores to percentiles, *T*-scores, stens, and stanines, the authors state that, "The best way of comparing individuals is to examine their raw scores and decide whether differences in these scores can be meaningfully interpreted as real differences in ability" (p. 30). A table describing the significance of raw score differences may be found in the manual.

NORMS AND STANDARDIZATION. The norming population consisted of 1,048 school students and 814 college students. No more than 50 students were tested in any one school or college. The norms are described in separate tables according to number of schools and colleges sampled, by geographical area, age, ethnic origins, sex, academic levels, qualifications, and job aspirations. Norming data from the occupational sample are not included in the construction of norms; however, data from the occupational sample are included in the subgroup statistical tables.

RELIABILITY. The authors believe that you cannot speak of the reliability of a test because reliabilities are very sensitive to the size of the score range. Therefore, they emphasize the use of the standard error of measurement which remains constant and aids in the interpretation of an individual's scores. To support their claim of the standard error of measurement's consistency, the authors report the reliability coefficients of .86 and .75 and standard errors of 2.62 and 2.31 respectively for the educational and occupational samples. Table 18 in the manual contains the standard errors of measurement for the educational and occupational samples for each of the nine tests. Test-retest correlations would have been helpful to document the reliability of the MOST over time.

Intercorrelations among the nine tests of the MOST are reported in three separate tables for the educational sample, students with two O levels or less, and the work sample. The correlations range from a low of -.06 between the Technical Checking test using students with two O levels or less to a high of .80 between the Decision Making test and the Verbal Checking test using the educational sample.

VALIDITY. Validation data using samples of individuals either applying for, training in, or working in clerical occupations were selected from different organizations. A description of each sample may be found in 13 tables. Because the sample sizes in many cases were small (N<15), the differences among organizations must be viewed with caution. I agree with the authors that additional follow-up studies are needed to establish the predictive validity of the MOST among the different organizations.

To establish concurrent validity, the Word Meanings, Verbal Checking, Numerical Awareness, and Decision Making tests were correlated with the Verbal, Numerical, and Perceptual tests of the AH3 (acronym not defined in the manual) using 32 job applicants for junior clerical jobs. The correlations range from a low of .25 between the Verbal Checking and AH3-Numerical to a high of .81 between Numerical Awareness and AH3-Numerical. Correlations using the other five tests of the MOST with the AH3 would be useful.

SUMMARY. The MOST is easy to administer and score. Selection of tests to administer is simplified by using the Task Inventory. Identifying an individual's relative strengths and weaknesses may be easily found using the Profile Sheet. However, until additional studies are conducted to establish the predictive validity and reliability of the MOST for individuals applying for, training in, and working in clerical occupations, I suggest that the results be used with considerable caution.

Review of the Modern Occupational Skills Tests by BIKKAR S. RANDHAWA, Professor of Educational Psychology, University of Saskatchewan, Saskatoon, Canada:

The Modern Occupational Skills Tests (MOST) are a set, not a battery, of nine tests. The reason for this distinction is that these tests are designed in such a way that a prospective or current employer can choose those tests that are appropriate for the specific skills required of an office employee. The manual for the MOST provides appropriate advice on choosing relevant tests for a particular selection or promotion decision. It is a laudable characteristic of this series that it discourages overassessing, and it advises the user to determine clearly what specific skills an employee requires to do the job, and to avoid testing for some higher-level skills that would rarely be required to do the job well.

The task inventory of this series categorizes the nine tests into three levels, three tests at each level. Highest level tests are Numerical Estimation, Technical Checking, and Decision Making. Numerical Awareness, Word Meaning, and Spelling and Grammar are medium level tests. Lowest level tests are Numerical Checking, Verbal Checking, and Filing. This categorization is based supposedly on the difficulty of the tests within each skill domain. Our examination of the item difficulties of the items in the tests does not bear this out. Perhaps a more rigorous empirical basis could be derived from hierarchical factor or cluster analysis.

The test questions in this series are authentic; that is, they pertain to real-life situations. The goal to be authentic and objective seems to have resulted in cumbersome test formats in a few tests. For example, in the Word Meaning test, the list of alternatives in each case is too long. Precious time may be wasted in a speed and accuracy test.

Despite a few cumbersome formats, I commend the authenticity of the questions in the MOST. Two tests in particular, Numerical Awareness and Numerical Estimation, consist of items that are scored for 2 points for a correct solution. The formats of these tests could have been simplified if only one answer was required for each item. In the Numerical Awareness test, the examinee is required to find and to correct errors in calculations. Each item has a series of calculations based on the correct information on which each calculation is based. One calculation in each series and the total are incorrect. But the total in each item is correct, if the incorrect calculation for a component is not corrected. Thus, the correct ultimate total changes by as much as the incorrect calculation is corrected. Examinees discovering this to be the case during practice examples may not show any higher level skill than simply changing the total by that constant amount. Requiring only one error, either in a component or the total, in each item to be found and corrected would force error detection in the total as well.

The Numerical Estimation test could be improved in format by reducing the number of response options in the actual test questions to five and requiring the examinee to pick the number closest to the real answer. Estimation skill can be tested this way, but the redundant estimate is eliminated.

These kinds of changes in format would not destroy the authentic nature of the test questions in these tests, but would have the added advantage that more items could be completed in the allowed time. An additional advantage will be the consistent and comparable information for all the tests provided in the item analysis tables. As it stands now, these two numerical tests have their item difficulties in the range 0 to 2. This format defies standard interpretation.

The standardization (educational) sample came from randomly selected schools and colleges in England. From the sampled 35 schools and 35 colleges, 28 of the schools and 22 of the colleges allowed their students to be tested. No more than 50 students were tested in any school or college. It is not clear how those students from a school or college who were tested were selected for participation in testing. From the age distribution of the sample, evidently 82.9% of the sample was 17 years of age or younger, 11% was 18 years old, 3.6% was 19 years old, and the remaining 2.5% was older than 19 years. The User's Guide (p. 19) reports that 1,048 school pupils and 814 college students, a total of 1,862, were tested, but Table 3 lists 1,668 individuals and Tables 2, 4, 5, 6, and 7 list from 1,866 to 1,870 subjects. No explanation for these discrepancies is offered.

Schools and colleges agreeing to participate in the standardization of MOS tests were randomly assigned to 1 of 12 subsamples with each subsample taking three of the nine tests in the series. The order of the tests for administration for each trial site was randomized, thus eliminating the systematic fatigue and boredom effects. This strategy of test administration produced between 558 and 711 examinees taking a test in the series, enough data points for establishing norms for the combined group for each test. Among the reliability estimates available, only Cronbach's coefficient alpha reliability estimate for each test is given. As items in all tests, except Numerical Estimation, are arranged in sections with up to 10 items sharing the common question material, interdependencies among items could affect psychometric properties of these tests. Another source that could inflate the reliability estimate of these tests is the speededness of these tests. Evidence of the extent of this influence is not available. Also, we do not see evidence of the average number of items completed in the time allowed for each test.

Percentile norms and scale statistics, mean, standard deviation, minimum and maximum scores, and standard error of measurement for the tests are available. For the educational subgroups, the provision of descriptive statistics adds a positive feature. To aid in interpreting difference scores on each test, a minimum reliable score difference for each test is conveniently available in a table in the User's Guide. For those who prefer other norms, such as *T*-scores, stens, and stanines, conversion of percentiles to these is provided in a table. Suggestions for combining test scores, when desired, by changing the raw scores to standardized scores are clear, and it should alleviate the possibility of misuse of percentiles or standard scores for such purposes.

For the validation of the tests of the MOST, data were collected from 13 samples, with sample size in these ranging from 4 to 33 individuals. Supervisors of the sample employees rated them on individual tasks in the Task Inventory for speed, accuracy, and quality of performance on simple scales. Also, each individual was given one or more MOS tests. Employers used the Task Inventory to make decisions to use specific tests relevant for an individual employee. Because these individual occupational samples were small, descriptive statistics for the MOS tests by sample are given. In these tables corresponding statistics for the relevant standardization subsample and the total occupational sample also are provided.

Concurrent validity results by test are summarized. Validity evidence is provided in terms of multiple correlation and analysis of variance results for testing the effects of work experience, educational level, and the interaction of these two for each MOS test.

The User's Guide provides evidence (albeit weak) of construct validity in terms of intercorrelations of four of the MOS tests (Word Meaning, Verbal Checking, Numerical Checking, and Decision Making), with three subtests of the AH3 (Heim, Watts, & Simmonds, 1974), Verbal, Numerical, and Perceptual, based on a sample of 32 job applicants for junior clerical jobs. Although a recognition of the limitation of the sample size used is made, this matrix of intercorrelations is used to infer convergent validity and discriminant validity evidence. If such evidence is deemed appropriate, why is no evidence given for the other three tests? Are these tests not appropriate for use for the purpose for which they were developed?

Under the heading of construct validity, correlations among MOS tests are provided for the educational sample, for the students in the educational sample with the two O levels or less, and for the work (I assume the occupational) sample. These three correlation matrices show that correlations between pairs of tests vary as a function of both the size and type of sample. This is not unique evidence for MOS tests, but rather a well-known phenomenon in the statistical literature. Consequently, this evidence is not necessary.

The test bias issue is critically discussed and evidence of differential performance by gender and ethnicity is provided for the educational sample. Users are well advised to read this section in the User's Guide to decide for themselves how such a sensitive issue should be handled in their specific context.

The Australian Council for Educational Research (ACER) adapted the MOST for use in Australia. Our examination of the adaptation shows that test items and examples that had British currency (pound and pence), weight, distance, and postal codes in their content were changed. All except two MOS tests, Spelling and Grammar and Word Meaning, were changed. The User's Guide for this adaptation is the same as the British edition, only the name of the publisher is changed. Because norms and other evidence are not specific to the Australian situation, the assumption that educational qualifications of the trainees and prospective employees in the two countries are similar should be tested. Consequently, users must be careful in using the norms. I think skills tapped by the tests in the series may be appropriate for clerical and office workers in most English-speaking nations. However, users in other countries should have their national or local norms for proper interpretation of results. Also, it is valuable to get as much local validity evidence as possible to understand the nature and issues surrounding the use of these tests.

In conclusion, MOS tests are well designed to measure appropriate skills of clerical and other office personnel. The provision of a Test Taker's Guide for each test in this series is a positive step toward moderating test bias. The validity evidence on these tests for the educational and occupational samples is adequate for users to decide the potential utility of the intended measures for their specific decisional contexts. Although only minor changes to the examples and test content in most of the tests in the series have been made for the Australian adaptation, that does not preclude the necessity of validity evidence and norms. Therefore, Australian users should exercise caution without such important test information.

REVIEWER'S REFERENCE

Heim, A. W., Watts, K. P., & Simmonds, V. (1974). AH2/AH3 manual. Windsor, UK: NFER-Nelson Publishing Company Ltd.

[240]

Modified Vygotsky Concept Formation Test.

Purpose: "Measures an individual's ability to think in abstract concepts."

Population: Older children and adolescents and adults.

Publication Dates: 1940–84.

Scores, 2: Convergent Thinking, Divergent Thinking.

Administration: Individual.

Price Data, 1994: $195 per Kasanin-Hanfmann test kit; $25 per modified manual ('84, 75 pages); $25 per 30 record forms.

Time: (30) minutes.

Comments: Modified manual used in conjunction with Kasanin-Hanfmann Concept Formation Test (Vigotsky Test) (T3:1239).

Author: Paul L. Wang (modified manual).

Publisher: Stoelting Co.

Cross References: For information on the Kasanin-Hanfmann Concept Formation Test, see also T3:1239 (1 reference), T2:1140 (9 references), P:47 (7 references), and 6:78 (11 references); for a review of an earlier edition by Kate Levine Kogan (with William S. Kogan), see 4:35 (8 references); for a review of an earlier edition by O. L. Zangwill, see 3:27 (21 references).

Review of the Modified Vygotsky Concept Formation Test by KATHRYN A. HESS, Research Associate, Montgomery, AL:

WHEN IS A "TECHNIQUE" A "TEST"? Psychology is blessed with a variety of ways to understand people. Sometimes one methodology evolves into another form. For example, Binet developed a set of standardized interactions, which eventually were scored and normed, evolving from an interview method to the heritable Stanford-Binet Intelligence Test. Rorschach experimented with inkblots as a way to understand people's mental representations. His efforts led others to develop standardized administration and scoring procedures, and to develop normative data, to the point where computerized interpretations are available. More pertinent to the Modified Vygotsky Concept Formation Test (MVCFT) are Luria's and Goldstein's approaches to neuropsychological assessment. Although Luria's genius fueled the genesis and development of his flexible set of tasks by which he qualitatively assessed and localized brain dysfunction, his tasks only approached the definition of tests with the work of Christiansen (1975) and Golden, Purisch, and Hammeke (1985). Goldstein's theory and assessment of the abstract attitude reached its pinnacle in the Goldstein and Scheerer (1951) monograph, which offered insightful techniques but were bereft of empirical support.

In 1934 Vygotsky described his technique as a way of studying concept formation ability in schizophrenics. The Hanfmann-Kasanin administration, developed in 1942, as well as the 1984 modifications developed by Wang are described in the manual.

Wang has made a number of administrative revisions in the MVCFT. These include the following: (*a*) identified four sets of problems with the subject solving one set at a time, (*b*) provided feedback in a standardized manner, (*c*) developed a coding system to analyze subject's problem-solving approach, (*d*) added a measure of divergent thinking, and (*e*) simplified the scoring system producing an objective quantifying method. Wang wrote in the Preface that he had tested more than 300 subjects with the MVCFT and that it was now ready for "trial usage in both clinical and research fields" (manual, 1984).

Subjects taking the MVCFT are asked to sort 22 blocks of different colors, sizes, widths, and heights into sets according to two of the dimensions while ignoring the other characteristics. The MVCFT provides an observation of an individual's problem-solving approach and their ability to learn from errors in a structured setting. Quantitative information such as numbers and types of errors, distribution of errors across trials, and the subject's ability to verbalize principles used in solving the task and ability to create additional ways of categorizing test materials can be obtained from the MVCFT.

Although Wang has attempted to simplify the administration and to quantify the scoring, both the administration and scoring remain complex processes requiring training in giving specific instructions and in the exact recording of all responses and verbalization. A six-page recording form has been developed to assist the examiner in administering the test and in recording and scoring its responses. Over two-thirds of the manual consists of the scoring of 10 case samples. These are necessary to review in order to learn to accurately score perseveration errors and to demonstrate findings on a variety of pathologies. The cases presented range from "normal subjects" to head injury and encephalitis patients. Although Wang reports that he found the technique useful in the study of mental retardation and schizophrenia, case demonstrations of neither were presented.

RELIABILITY AND VALIDITY. The manual presents no information on reliability or validity and no normative data are presented. A review of the literature reveals no publications using the MVCFT.

CONCLUSIONS. In the tradition of the Binet, Rorschach, Goldstein, and Luria, the Vygotsky was developed as a technique to be used by a talented clinician. The Vygotsky was to measure abstract reasoning, particularly the lack thereof in schizophrenic, retarded, and organically dysfunctional people. Wang helped make the technique even more amenable to clinical use but with no norms, no studies showing abstract reasoning deficits in patient groups, no other validity studies, no cutting scores, nor any other features of a psychometrically sound test, the MVCFT, as a test, is stillborn.

REVIEWER'S REFERENCES

Goldstein, K., & Scheerer, M. (1951). *Tests for abstract and concrete thinking*. New York: Psychological Corporation.

Christensen, A. L. (1975). *Luria's neuropsychological investigation: Test, manual, and test cards*. New York: Spectrum.

Golden, C. J., Purisch, A. D., & Hammeke, T. A. (1985). Luria-Nebraska Neuropsychological Battery: Forms I and II. Western Psychological Service.

Review of the Modified Vygotsky Concept Formation Test by GREGORY SCHRAW, Assistant Professor of Educational Psychology, University of Nebraska-Lincoln, Lincoln, NE:

The Modified Vygotsky Concept Formation Test is based on a test first used by Lev Vygotsky (1934) to examine the cognitive reasoning skills of schizophrenics. Vygotsky's initial test was modified by Hanfmann and Kasanin (1942) and, in turn, modified further by Paul Wang (1984). The test consists of 22 different blocks that vary on four dimensions (i.e., shape, color, height, and width). Each block belongs to one of four mutually exclusive groups based on two shared dimensions. For example, the large orange circle and large blue square belong to the LAG group because they are high and wide. The short white triangle and short green square belong to the BIK group because they are short and wide. Each block has its group label written on its bottom.

The test is administered by a trained examiner to a single examinee. There are two modes of testing. When used as a test of *convergent thinking*, the blocks are arranged randomly with their labels down. A sample block (i.e., cue) is then shown to the examinee, who is asked to guess which other blocks belong to the same group. The examiner provides feedback after each choice. Correct choices and errors are noted and examinees are encouraged to describe their mental processes while making their selections. After three consecutive errors, the examiner identifies another block that belongs to the target group, and the test continues. Test administration requires roughly 15 minutes to 1 hour, although no specific limits are provided in the manual.

When used as a test of *divergent thinking*, the examinee is asked to sort the blocks into meaningful categories based on a single dimension of his or her choosing. This is repeated as many times as necessary provided the categories are meaningful. The manual states that eight sortings are possible. Test administration requires from 5 to 20 minutes.

Both the convergent and divergent forms of the test are scored using scoring forms provided in the test manual. Four kinds of information are used in the convergent test: total errors, perseverative errors, the number of cues provided by the examiner, and principles described by the examinee during testing. The total error score includes all errors made during the entire test, which consists of four trials (one for each of the four groups). A perseverative error occurs when three consecutive errors based on a single irrelevant dimension (e.g., color) are made. Principles are transcribed verbal statements made by the examinee. An analogous scoring sheet is available for the divergent test. Some categorization schemes receive more points than others, although no rationale for this scoring system is provided.

Unfortunately, the test has a number of interpretative difficulties. One is the total absence of information about the reliability and validity of the test. The manual indicates that the test was normed on 300 individuals with psychiatric disorders at a hospital in Toronto, Ontario, Canada; however, no information is given about this sample, how these individuals performed, or how performance on the test was related to other cognitive and affective phenomena. A second problem is lack of specificity regarding the test's target population and purpose. Although the test can be administered to anyone, it is unclear how normal and impaired examinees differ and what kind of information these differences provide to the examiner. Presumably, the test is most useful for individuals with schizophrenic and frontal lobe disorders. A third problem is that the test is atheoretical. No linkages are made to contemporary Vygotskian theory or other classic studies of concept formation such as Bruner, Goodnow, and Austin (1956). A fourth problem is the absence of interpretative norms in the test manual. Assuming the test is administered successfully, the examiner must determine what these results mean without additional information. One serious limitation of this situation is that identical profiles could be interpreted in different ways by two examiners. A fifth problem is that no guidelines are given for the scoring or interpretation of verbal statements made during the testing phase. A sixth problem is that time factors are not discussed in the test manual. This is potentially a major oversight due to the well-documented trade-off between information-processing speed and accuracy (Meyer, Irwin, Osman, & Kounios, 1988). Hypothetically, one examinee could be highly accurate, yet require considerably more time to complete the test than a less accurate, yet speedier examinee. How trade-offs between speed and accuracy affect test performance and interpretation are open to question.

It is difficult to recommend the use of this test given the major problems outlined above. It may be helpful as an informal diagnostic instrument when used in conjunction with other concept formation tasks, especially those that depend on visual concept formation. However, I cannot imagine how this test can be used in a reliable and valid manner to assess concept formation ability outside this limited context. For the test to provide truly useful information, it must specify much more clearly its target population, its reliability and validity, performance norms, the interpretation of individual performance with respect to these norms, speed-accuracy trade-offs, and what these findings mean within the context of a well-articulated theoretical framework. Without this information, the Modified Vygotsky Concept Formation Test provides little more than a subjective screening instrument.

REVIEWER'S REFERENCES

Vygotsky, L. (1934). Thought in schizophrenia. *Archives of Neurology and Psychiatry, 31*, 1063-1077.

Hanfmann, E., & Kasanin, J. (1942). Conceptual thinking in schizophrenia. *Nervous and Mental Disease*, Monograph 67.

Bruner, J. S., Goodnow, J. J., & Austin, G. A. (1956). *A study of thinking*. New York: John Wiley & Sons.

Meyer, D. E., Irwin, D. E., Osman, A. M., & Kounios, J. (1988). The dynamics of cognition and action: Mental processes inferred from speed-accuracy decomposition. *Psychological Review, 95*, 183-237.

[241]

Monitoring Basic Skills Progress.

Purpose: "Designed to monitor students' acquisition of basic skills in one of three academic areas" using curriculum-based measurements.

Publication Date: 1990.

Acronym: MBSP.

Scores: Total score only for each test (Basic Math, Basic Reading, Basic Spelling).

Administration: Individual.

Price Data, 1994: $279 per complete program; $109 per math program including 3 diskettes and manual (61 pages); $19 per book of math blackline masters; $98 per reading program including 5 diskettes and manual (72 pages); $98 per spelling program including 3 diskettes and manual (118 pages).

Comments: Apple II microcomputer required for administration.

Authors: Lynn S. Fuchs, Carol Hamlett, and Douglas Fuchs.

Publisher: PRO-ED, Inc.

a) BASIC MATH.

Population: Grades 1–6.

Time: 3 minutes.

b) BASIC READING.

Population: Grades 1–7.

Time: 2.5 minutes.

c) BASIC SPELLING.

Population: Grades 1–6.

Time: (3) minutes.

Comments: Orally administered.

Review of Monitoring Basic Skills Progress by JOSEPH C. WITT, Professor of Psychology, and KEVIN M. JONES, Research Associate, Louisiana State University, Baton Rouge, LA:

Monitoring Basic Skills Progress (MBSP) is a computer software package that facilitates the use of curriculum-based measurement (CBM) for educational decision making. The MBSP employs standardized fluency measures in each of the basic skills areas of reading, spelling, and math. Each MBSP software program (Basic Reading, Basic Spelling, and Basic Math) automatically administers one of 30 brief alternate-form tests at the designated grade level. The computer scores the tests and provides feedback in the form of performance graphs and skills analyses. The tests are administered frequently across baseline and treatment conditions.

The MBSP is not a traditional norm-referenced instrument, but an idiographic approach to determining performance levels and enhancing instruction through direct and frequent measurement. The MBSP can be used by teachers to monitor a student's performance toward long-term goals derived from ongoing assessment. Graphs provide visual feedback, which can be used to modify these goals or make instructional changes.

The Basic Reading program utilizes a modified cloze procedure wherein the child is exposed to a story with the seventh word deleted from the text and replaced with a blank. Using the cursor and return key, the child selects one of three choices to complete each blank. The total score reflects the number of correct choices within a 2.5-minute time limit. Alternate form reliability of Basic Reading overall scores is good, ranging from .86–.92 for two forms at 1-week intervals, and .94–.96 for aggregated forms. Criterion-related validity is supported, with correlations between the Basic Reading scores and criterion and norm-referenced reading tests ranging from .56–.85. The highest correlations were obtained when comparing Basic Reading scores with oral reading fluency measures.

The Basic Spelling program requires an examiner to dictate a list of 20 words in isolation while the child attempts to spell each word on the computer screen. The test session is ended after 20 words or 3 minutes (a maximum of 15 seconds per word is allowed), whichever comes first. The total score reflects the total number of correct letter sequences. The computer can also generate a skills analysis, which lists the child's mastery of 24 phonetic spelling errors. Alternate form reliability of Basic Spelling scores is excellent, ranging from .90–.93 for two forms of 1-week intervals, and .97–.98 for aggregated forms. Criterion-related validity is supported, with correlations between the Basic Spelling scores and criterion and norm-referenced reading tests ranging from .76–.95. The highest correlation was obtained when comparing the Basic Spelling scores of a nonhandicapped population (N = 227) with standardized spelling tests.

The Basic Math program employs a standardized paper-and-pencil math test which is completed within a time limit specified for each grade. After completion, students transfer their responses to the computer screen. The total score reflects the total number of digits correct. After scoring the test, the computer can generate a skills analysis, which lists the child's mastery of 49 math objectives across six grade levels. Alternate form reliability of Basic Math scores is excellent, ranging from .90–.93 for two forms at 1-week intervals, and .97–.98 for aggregated forms. Content validity of the Basic Math program was investigated by obtaining favorable acceptability ratings from educators in four school districts. Criterion-related validity is supported by moderate correlations (.66–.67) between the Basic Math scores and norm-referenced math calculation tests. Much higher correlations, ranging from .78–.83, were obtained when comparing the Basic Math scores with criterion-referenced tests that utilized similar fluency measures.

In summary, the MBSP represents a blatant disregard for the traditional model of achievement testing where the goal has been to obtain a single estimate of a child's ability on a small sample from the universe of educational objectives, and compare this estimate against a large normative group. Instead, the MBSP is designed to obtain frequent estimates of a child's performance on a large number of objectives, and to compare these estimates against individualized goals. Given the choice between very little information at one point in time, and much information across time, we believe the MBSP represents all that is good about current educational assessment technology. Some positive features of the MBSP are its emphasis on ambitious goal setting and instructionally relevant error analyses. Perhaps the most important use of the MBSP, however, is related to the sensitivity of direct and frequent measurements of academic behavior. While monitoring basic skills across different treatments educators may determine instructional variables which are functionally related to achievement gains.

Potential weaknesses of the MBSP are related to the inferences derived from assessment data. Although the MBSP authors offer standardized procedures for incorporating the local curriculum, we believe that most educators will probably ignore this burdensome task, and use MBSP measurement stimuli. Consequently, there may be some discrepancy between MBSP objectives and the student's local curriculum. Second, because the decisions regarding instructional levels and goal establishment are somewhat subjective, examiners and students may have to endure some initial errors in placement and goal-setting decisions. Finally, there is a need to determine the equivalency of computer-assisted CBM and the more familiar method utilizing paper-and-pencil tasks. In light of the scarce resources among public school systems (e.g., computer labs), there should be some investigation to justify the added investment. Relatedly, there may be a need to determine teachers' acceptability of this approach. There is not much evidence that educators have embraced the data-based approach of CBM technology. An instrument such as the MBSP, which usurps a large share of teaching responsibilities, may be seen as threatening to teachers who are comfortable with what they may perceive as a more humanistic approach to education.

[242]

The Mother-Child Relationship Evaluation, 1980 Edition.

Purpose: Designed to measure "attitudes by which mothers relate to their children."
Population: Mothers.
Publication Dates: 1961–80.
Acronym: MCRE.
Scores, 4: Acceptance, Overprotection, Overindulgence, Rejection.
Administration: Group.
Price Data, 1993: $35 per complete kit; $16.50 per 25 test forms; $19.50 per manual ('80, 16 pages).
Time: [25–30] minutes.
Comments: Experimental form.
Author: Robert M. Roth.
Publisher: Western Psychological Services.
Cross References: See T4:1671 (2 references); for information regarding an earlier edition, see P:174; for re-

views by John Elderkin Bell and Dale B. Harris of an earlier edition, see 6:146.

[Note: The following reviews are based on materials available in 1992. In February 1994 the publisher advised that this instrument is being replaced by the Parent-Child Relationship Inventory.—Ed.]

TEST REFERENCES

1. Mahabeer, M. (1993). Correlations between mothers' and children's self-esteem and perceived familial relationships among intact, widowed, and divorced families. *Psychological Reports*, *73*, 483-489.

Review of the Mother-Child Relationship Evaluation, 1980 Edition by BETH DOLL, Assistant Professor of School Psychology, University of Colorado at Denver, Denver, CO:

Despite its title, the Mother-Child Relationship Evaluation (MCRE) does not assess a relationship. Instead, it is a questionnaire sampling a mother's attitudes towards children and the role of parent. Items have been written to form four scales representing maternal attitudes of Acceptance, Overprotection, Overindulgence, and Rejection. Only one of these scales, Acceptance, assesses positive parent beliefs. The majority of the questions describe inappropriate maternal attitudes, diminishing the utility of the scales for identifying strong parenting skills that could provide the foundation for intervention.

The questionnaire is outdated in several respects. It presumes the mother is the caretaking parent and uses the words "mother" and "parents" interchangeably; fathers are never mentioned in the scale or the manual. Items frequently refer to the child as "it" as in "A child is not at fault when it does something wrong" (p. 3, test form). In some instances, items describe parenting behaviors that were discouraged in the past, but have since come to be accepted parenting practices. For example, an item assessing maternal overindulgence describes the practice of lying next to one's child to settle him or her to sleep. Although several decades ago child therapists considered this to be inappropriate parenting, the practice might be seen today as evidence of a nurturing parent-child relationship. Finally, the format of the mother's response sheet is confusing, requiring that letters be circled in one of 20 columns on the page.

The MCRE manual does not provide the psychometric data necessary to justify its use in any applied setting. Estimates of the scales' internal consistency range from .41 to.57, insufficient for a clinical instrument. No information is available on the stability of the scores over time. Description of the MCRE's validity is scanty. A single short paragraph reports that scores on the three negative scales (Overprotection, Overindulgence, and Rejection) show negative correlations with the one positive scale (Acceptance). Additional validity analyses are required to establish that scores from the four scales relate in a meaningful way to independent measures of mother attitude. Factor analytic studies are necessary to establish that items on the four scales do, in fact, assess distinct dimensions of parental attitudes, and that each item has been assigned to the appropriate scale.

Tables that provide users with percentiles and *t*-scores for each scale are deceptive because this is not, in fact, a standardized measure. Instead, these descriptive statistics are based on an experimental population of 80 middle-class mothers. Insufficient information is provided about the family composition of these mothers; and, major changes have occurred in families with children since the scales were first published. The norms are not likely to reflect the differing home environments of single-parents, teenage mothers, mothers from social/ethnic minorities, or low-income mothers. Although the manual states that the MCRE is not a refined clinical measure, it still encourages clinical interpretation of the scales by providing a graphic score profile and sample case interpretations. Scale descriptions and sample interpretations utilize provocative language such as "hostility" and "lack of ego strength" in referring to the mother, and "psychopathic reactions" and "counter hostility" in referring to the child. This level of interpretation is unjustified given the limited reliability and validity information provided about the scores.

Better measures exist for evaluating parent-child relationships. The Parenting Stress Index (PSI; Abidin, 1986; T4:1933) is a research instrument that assesses dysfunctional parent-child relationships. The PSI has adequate reliability and strong validity, although, like the MCRE, it lacks representative norms (Doll, 1989). Alternatively, observations of mother-child behavior during problem-solving situations have provided useful research measures of parent-child relationships and are currently being evaluated as a clinical tool (Pianta, Smith, & Reeve, 1991).

The MCRE is not recommended for use in applied settings. Its reliability and validity are insufficient to justify its use in making important decisions about parents and children, and the normative information provided is not adequate for use with present day families. As a research instrument, the questionnaire would require considerable revision in order to recognize the diversity of families and cultures, the role of fathers in childrearing, and revised knowledge about child-parent relationships. Users are advised to consider alternative measures of parental attitudes.

REVIEWER'S REFERENCES

Abidin, R. R. (1986). Parenting Stress Index. Charlottesville, VA: Pediatric Psychology Press.

Doll, E. J. (1989). [Review of Parenting Stress Index, 2nd ed.]. *Professional School Psychology*, *4*, 307-312.

Pianta, R. C., Smith, N., & Reeve, R. E. (1991). Observing mother and child behavior in a problem-solving situation at school entry: Relations with classroom adjustment. *School Psychology Quarterly*, *6*, 1-15.

Review of the Mother-Child Relationship Evaluation, 1980 Edition by NORMAN FREDMAN, Professor and Coordinator, Counselor Education Programs, Queens College, City University of New York, Flushing, NY:

The Mother-Child Relationship Evaluation, 1980 Edition, is virtually identical to the 1961 experimental form. Criticisms by John Elderkin Bell (1965) and Dale B. Harris (1965) in *The Sixth Mental Measurements Yearbook* are still applicable.

About a third of a century ago, Robert Roth gathered 80 volunteer PTA mothers, 25 to 35 years of age, who resided in the same middle-class community. That remains the norm group. No fathers, no minorities, no sample representative of the nation's parents. Would even the same PTA mothers, or their daughters, give the same responses today when ideas of childrearing have so radically changed?

The conceptual framework remains the work of P. M. Symonds and Marian Fitz-Simons from the 1940s. There are four 12-item subscales for the inventory, one of Acceptance and three specific expressions of nonacceptance: Overprotection, Overindulgence, and Rejection. Mothers are asked to record the strength of their agreement with each of the 48 items using a 5-point Likert scale. The raw scores can be converted into *T*-scores or percentile equivalents and then plotted on a separate profile sheet. The manual states, "If three or four scales are relatively high and of similar magnitude (i.e., in the same quartile) the mother's attitudes towards her child can be considered as confused" (p. 4).

Barbara Whitman and Robert Zachary (1986) evaluated the factor structure of the inventory. They found that eight of the 48 items failed to correlate uniquely with the a priori scales. They discovered four different factors: Factor I corresponded to Acceptance; Factor II reflected a need to exert firm parental control; Factor III related to the original scales of Overindulgence and Overprotection; Factor IV concerned a willingness to seek outside help with problems in childrearing. These four factors, however, accounted for only 33% of the total variance.

Intercorrelations of the scales remained similar to the original findings. The Acceptance scale correlated negatively (-.38 to -.53) with each of the other three, which intercorrelated positively (.43 to .54) among themselves. Whitman and Zachary found no significant response differences between fathers and mothers.

Many items may measure different constructs than the a priori subscales indicate. Some items ("Children cannot choose the proper food for themselves"; "A child needs more than two medical examinations each year") might depend on the age of the child. Six times the item is phrased, "My child"; the remaining times it is phrased "children" or "child." Thus, the attitude elicited is not consistent across items. The results of Whitman and Zachary's research suggest the need for both revision and renorming of the instrument.

The directions to the mother who responds to the items state: "Keep in mind the child for whom you are seeking help" (p. 1, test form). This seems to indicate that the inventory is intended for clinical use. Robert Roth's italicized warning is at the beginning of the manual: "It is emphasized that the MCRE is primarily exploratory and experimental, rather than a refined clinical measurement" (p. 1). Perhaps, like the Surgeon General's warning, this caveat can be placed on each profile sheet to warn judges and mental health personnel.

REVIEWER'S REFERENCES

Bell, J. E. (1965). [Review of The Mother-Child Relationship Evaluation.] In O. K. Buros (Ed.), *The sixth mental measurements yearbook* (pp. 319-320). Highland Park, NJ: Gryphon Press.

Harris, D. B. (1965). [Review of The Mother-Child Relationship Evaluation.] In O. K. Buros (Ed.), *The sixth mental measurements yearbook* (p. 320). Highland Park, NJ: Gryphon Press.

Whitman, B., & Zachary, R. A. (1986). Factor structure of the Mother-Child Relationship Evaluation. *Educational and Psychological Measurement, 46*(1), 135-141.

[243]

Mother/Infant Communication Screening.

Purpose: Constructed to screen for problems in mother-infant communication.

Population: Mother-infant dyads with infants under 1 year old.

Publication Date: 1989.

Acronym: MICS.

Scores, 3–6: Language and Synchrony plus 1–4 activity scores (Distress, Feeding, Play/Neutral State, Rest), Total.

Administration: Individual.

Price Data: Not available.

Time: Administration time not reported.

Comments: Ratings by professionals.

Author: Catherine B. Raack.

Publisher: Communication Skill Builders.

[The publisher advised in April 1994 that this test is now out of print—Ed.]

Review of the Mother-Infant Communication Screening by ROBERT W. HILTONSMITH, Associate Professor of Psychology, Radford University, Radford, VA:

OVERVIEW. The Mother-Infant Communication Screening (MICS) is described by the author as a screening measure "designed to indicate if a mother-infant dyad may be at risk for a threatening disorder of mother-infant communication" (manual, pp. 36–37). The MICS is to be completed retrospectively following any 10-minute or longer information-gathering interview with a mother and her infant of less than one year of age. The screening can be completed by any professional trained in conducting interviews. The professional ranks the mother-infant dyad in "language and synchrony" and also in one or more areas that best characterized the nature of the infant's activity during the interview: Distress, Feeding, Play/Neutral State, or Rest. Following scoring, what the author refers to as "screening failures" may be referred to agencies or individuals for intervention.

TEST MATERIALS AND PROCEDURES. The MICS consists of a 55-page manual and an 8-page screening form. The manual, despite its attractive cover, appears to be an informal compendium of several different sources of information about the scale that do not always dovetail neatly, and even are printed in different typefaces. The screening form, on the other hand, looks very professional and is attractively organized and printed. The test manual author devotes three pages to an overview of the MICS, and then provides a fairly lengthy discussion of research and theory that provide the underpinnings for the development of the screening measure. The author stresses that mother-infant communication is a constantly changing process that is built on three major components: mutuality, reciprocity, and synchronicity. The author also includes an informative discussion of maternal and infant variables that contribute to disordered mother-infant dyads and the importance of feeding as an overall indicator of general patterns of maternal interaction with her child. This latter emphasis on feeding and nutrition presumably is related to the fact that the MICS was developed in two WIC (Women, Infants, and Children) clinics in Illinois. Unfortunately, other links between the reviewed literature and the development of the MICS are not as clear. It would have been helpful for the author to describe more precisely how MICS items are derived from this important literature.

The procedures for administering and scoring the MICS, though seemingly straightforward, could be presented more clearly. For example, the critical cutoff score of 3.0 is noted in a single sentence at the end of the "Why" section that is actually devoted to discussing why disorders of mother-infant communication are important to assess. No mention of cutoff scores is made later in the "How" section, which describes how to administer and score the MICS. Here, the author discusses how to compute a Language and Synchrony score and one or more Activity scores, and from these a Total score. But after being told to "record this score," the user is left without additional guidance, except for the 3.0 cutoff score mentioned in an earlier section. According to the author, mother-infant dyads receiving scores under 3.0 are screening failures and "may be referred to agencies or individuals that may complete the medical and/or therapeutic picture." It is unclear what this might entail or what interventions would be suggested. There also is no information presented about how this cutoff score was determined.

An additional area of ambiguity in the procedures relates to the role of siblings and the father. The directions note that the MICS may be administered to any mother-infant dyad "as long as only the mother and the infant are present and the infant is one year old or less." But in the next sentence, the author states that "the other siblings may also be present." The author then goes on to say that the "MICS should not be administered if the father is present" (p. 36). In the earlier literature review section of the manual, the author provides a practical rationale for not including the father. Yet the MICS screening form makes no mention of excluding father, and 21 of the 24 questions ask about the "parent" (the other 3 specifically ask about the mother). One of the pictures on the screening form even shows a father feeding his infant child as the mother looks over his shoulder.

NORMS AND STANDARDIZATION. The manual gives a short description of the development of the MICS. Questions chosen were "observable aspects and components of mother-infant communication which were well documented in the literature as the most basic and critical ingredients for positive mother-infant communication" (p. 38). Fifteen mother-infant pairs were videotaped in their homes in routine caretaking activities, and a list of 80 behaviors was developed. Subsequently, 30 mother-infant dyads were observed in two WIC clinics in Illinois to determine "which of the 80 observable behaviors would be most likely to be observed in a ten minute interview." Another 50 dyads were observed to "further describe and verbally qualify the mother-infant interactions." Last, "an additional 40 dyads were observed to add the 'not observed' category, to further examine interrater reliability, and to compare the MICS scores with the qualifying factors for WIC." These observation procedures were completed by the same four speech and language pathologists.

RELIABILITY. All 24 MICS items are scored on a 1–5 scale. During the pilot study, the four participating speech and language therapists rotated roles as interviewer and observer. The average interrater differences was .327 with a range of 0–1 and a standard deviation of .260. No other reliability data are reported.

VALIDITY. No validity data are reported. Because this is a screening measure, the lack of criterion-related validity information (both concurrent and predictive) is a serious shortcoming. No information is presented about how mother-infant dyads scoring below the cutoff score differ from those scoring above, either presently or over the long term.

SUMMARY. The MICS is a brief screening instrument for mothers and infants below one year of age that purports to describe and document critical interactive behaviors for the purpose of identifying a potential high-risk situation. The measure is easy to administer and the screening protocol is attractive and clear. The author herself notes that the instrument is not a comprehensive assessment, nor does it have "conclusive predictive ability." In the absence of representative norms and more detailed information about reliability and validity, it is difficult to tell just what this measure is screening. Additional research directed at the issue of validity, perhaps by correlating the MICS with a more established measure such as the Parent-Child Early Relational Assessment (Clark, 1985), is essential before this instrument can be recommended for widespread use.

REVIEWER'S REFERENCE

Clark, R. (1985). *The Parent-Child Early Relational Assessment*. (Available from Roseanne Clark, Ph.D., Department of Psychiatry, University of Wisconsin Medical School, 600 Highland Avenue, Madison, WI 53792).

Review of the Mother/Infant Communication Screening by WILLIAM STEVE LANG, Assistant Professor of Measurement and Research, University of South Florida at St. Petersburg, St. Petersburg, FL:

The Mother/Infant Communication Screening (MICS) was designed "to indicate if a mother-infant dyad may be at risk for a threatening disorder of mother-infant communication." The intent of the instrument is to locate at-risk mother-infant relationships with children less than one year old. In this case, the infants might be at risk of having or developing a wide range of organic and nonorganic problems with a general description as "failure to thrive." According to the MICS manual, both the infant and the mother may suffer as a result of communication disorder. The infant is threatened emotionally, socially, nutritionally, and intellectually, whereas the mother's risks are to her self-esteem and the normal maternal role. The MICS is intended to be a short, observational tool to be used as part of any interview process with the mother and child present. The author states that "The MICS was not designed as an assessment" (manual, p. ii). In other words, the scale is supposed to indicate a need for further screening or investigation, but not to compare to any given norm or standard. In brief, a screening "failure" on the MICS would be a clue to referral.

The MICS is appropriate, according to the author, for professionals "trained to conduct interviews for the purpose of acquiring unbiased, objective information on behalf of the client" (manual, p. 37). In practice, typical users would be dietitians, nurses, speech therapists, social workers, medical doctors, or psychologists who work with new mothers and their children. Fathers are specifically excluded from the instrument and should not be present during its administration. The author of the MICS claims this is not sexist, but a result of the fact that mothers are almost exclusively the early caretaker with the at-risk population and also the subject of the maternal research which led to the instrument development.

The MICS was constructed from the author's synthesis of literature on mother-infant communication and the projected consequences and correlates of poor relationships in the early years of life. The author makes a compelling and complete argument in the first two-thirds of the manual that there is research to support the development of an observational instrument to detect this communication process. The reference list is extensive and current, although the author admits that correlates of future developmental problems do not suggest cause.

The instrument was developed by observing mother-infant communication samples to gather a pool of behaviors for which to look, classifying those behaviors as constructs (mutuality, reciprocity, synchronicity), and creating scales to rate those behaviors in specific situations (Language, Distress, Feeding, Play/Neutral, Rest). The sample used for development were 130 mother-infant pairs in a cluster sample from two clinics in Illinois. The end product is a set of 24 items in five subsets. Each item is designed as a 5-point Likert scale to rate observation of a behavior. For example:

"Did the parent praise the child?"

1. Very Negative comments (e.g., "Your spit makes me sick").
2. Made Negative comments (e.g., "Man, I can't believe you're wet again").
3. Rare or no praising.
4. Praised at least a few times.
5. Praised several times. (Question 4, p. 36)

According to the manual author, a score is obtained by simply using the items or subscales that are appropriate to a situation and averaging the items observed. If the average is less than 3.0 on the 5.0 scale, a referral or investigation is warranted. The manual author states that interrater differences on the scale averaged .327 on the 130 sample observations. There are no reliability or criterion-validity investigations described in the manual. There are no norms or explanations of construct validity, factor analyses, or explanations as to the legitimacy of averaging different items for subscores or totals.

In all areas, this instrument lacks critical psychometric data. Simply stating the scale is not to be used for assessment docs not make sense if the items return a number that is used for status determination (referral vs. nonreferral). That is assessment! With so few items and a very short situational observation, it is the obligation of the scale author to demonstrate the MICS results in better referral screening than any trained professional might achieve through anecdotal watching. Usually observation, few items, short administration, nonstandardized administration, and rapidly developing infants all are reliability problems in measurement. Because the MICS has all those characteristics, it is likely that any given score is simply not accurate as a predictive instrument.

Other weaknesses in development of the instrument include the initial sample from one population in Illinois. Certainly the question of generalizability to other groups is evident. The manual author suggests the administrator of the instrument should be sensitive to special cultural and individual differences, but the items themselves do not reflect such cultural fairness. A warning in the manual to avoid the Halo effect is not sufficient for demonstrating cultural fairness when the instrument target is clearly including minority and cross-cultural clients.

In summary, the MICS should not be given serious use at the current time for screening or referral on the basis of its results. Possibly, the validity and reliability of the instrument could be determined, but that is not evident now. The weakness of the instructions, scoring, number of items, and development sample outweigh the construct argument of the author. If used at all, it would be more of an anecdotal record than a scored device. The MICS needs research to validate its construction and psychometric properties before being used for screening as the manual and title suggest.

[244]

Motivation Analysis Test.

Purpose: Constructed to measure "a person's interests, drives, and the strengths of his sentiment and value systems."

Population: High school seniors and adults.

Publication Dates: 1959–82.

Acronym: MAT.

Scores, 45: 4 Motivation scores (Unintegrated, Integrated, Total Motivation, Conflict) for each of 5 Drives (Mating, Assertiveness, Fear, Narcism-Comfort, Pugnacity-Sadism) and each of 5 Sentiment Structures (Superego, Self-Sentiment, Career, Home-Parental, Sweetheart-Spouse), plus 5 Special scores (Total Integration, Total Personal Interest, Total Conflict, Autism-Optimism, Information-Intelligence).

Administration: Group or individual.

Price Data, 1994: $30 per 25 test booklets; $12.75 per 25 machine-scorable answer sheets; $12.75 per 50 hand-scorable answer sheets; $17.25 per set of 4 scoring stencils; $15 per handbook/manual ('70, 108 pages); $29.60 per hand scoring introductory kit; $24.75 per computer interpretation introductory kit.

Time: (50–60) minutes.

Comments: Test book title is MAT.

Authors: Raymond B. Cattell, John L. Horn, Arthur B. Sweney, and John A. Radcliffe.

Publisher: Institute for Personality and Ability Testing, Inc.

Cross References: See T4:1674 (6 references) and T3:1538 (3 references); see also 8:627 (31 references) and T2:1291 (13 references); for reviews by Henry A. Alker and Andrew L. Comrey, and an excerpted review by Gilbert E. Mazer of the 1964 test, see 7:110 (18 references); see also P:175 (6 references).

Review of the Motivation Analysis Test by JAMES T. AUSTIN, Assistant Professor of Psychology, The Ohio State University, Columbus, OH:

The Motivation Analysis Test (MAT) was developed within a psychometric/individual differences perspective on motivation, a topic more closely associated with experimental-manipulative approaches (Cofer & Appley, 1964). A related instrument derived from the framework is the School Motivation Analysis Test (SMAT; T4:2362), which pertains to the narrower domain of academics. On first inspection, the MAT has several positive features. First, it was developed iteratively within a conceptual framework to assess the "dynamic calculus" theory proposed by R. B. Cattell (1959a, 1959b, 1985) and various coworkers (e.g., Boyle, 1988; Horn, 1966). These researchers, guided by Cattell's work, distinguished *ability, dynamic* (motivational), and *personality-temperament* trait constructs that span the domain of individual differences or person variables. Ability traits are inferred from performance differences between individuals on tasks that differ in complexity; dynamic variables likewise, but from differences on tasks that vary in incentives; temperament variables are defined as the residual when ability, dynamic, and error variance have been subtracted from total variance (believed to be less related to the external situation). Cattell has presented researchers with significant instrumentation for the assessment of each of these domains, including the 16PF, Culture Fair Intelligence Test, and the scale under review here. Madsen (1968), in a metatheoretical review, classified the dynamic calculus as "an almost deductive, constructive, mostly molar, neutral-formal, dynamic, and mainly statistical theory" (p. 250). Methodologically, *factor analytic techniques* (including estimation, rotation, guidelines, and development of various specification equations), *variance component estimation and purification* (i.e., isolation by partialling vehicle [measure] effects and ipsatization), and the *operational measurement of conflict* are major contributions to psychological instrumentation (cf. Sells, 1959). However, the thesis of this review is that the failure of the developers and publishers of the MAT to update their conceptions and database has negated an excellent start that promised to provide a complementary approach to experimental-manipulative operations; such a combined approach fits well with current views of construct validation as increasing understanding of concepts (Messick, 1989).

As opposed to ability, personality, and interest measures, which assume stability over time, the MAT assesses 2 motivational components and 10 structure factors identified and replicated in Cattell's research program. The two motivational components, defined as generalized modes of motive expression, are *Integrated* and *Unintegrated*. These higher-order factors represent conscious-cognitive-socialized control and partially conscious-impulsive control, respectively. Further, objective item formats (corresponding to maximum performance, or T-data) rather than scales or checklists (corresponding to typical performance, or Q-data) are used to assess the two motivational components (Uses, 48 items; Estimates, 56 items; summed to assess the Unintegrated Component; Paired Words, 48 items; Information, 56 items; summed to assess the Integrated Component). Only the Paired Words portion is timed. Optional measures include GSR after frustration, systolic blood pressure, and reaction time (although these methods are listed and not described in the documentation). Dynamic structure factors correspond to motives and when analyzed as a whole are roughly analogous to the physical concept of energy. The factors are subdivided into ergs, or primary drives, and sentiments, or learned drives. Five ergs are assessed by the MAT, specifically Fear, Narcism, Mating, Pugnacity, and Assertiveness. Five sentiments are assessed: Career, Home-Parental, Superego, Self, and Sweetheart-Spouse. Similarities to Freud's theory of psychoanalysis are marked (cf. Boyle, 1988; Madsen, 1968), with the major differences existing in the increased number of specific constructs hypothesized, and the empirical research program associated with the dynamic calculus.

The documentation combines in one location a Handbook and an Individual Assessment Manual. The Handbook dated 1964, takes up 62 pages and comprises introductory materials, summaries of reliability and validity, directions for administration, scoring, and interpretation, a bibliography, and three appendices. The Manual dated 1969, takes up 47 pages and includes a brief description of how the four measurement formats operate, materials on interpretation of integrated, unintegrated, conflict, and total summary scores, some general precautions for clinical usage, and motivational patterns of special groups. The references in both sources are dated relative to recent work on the theory (Boyle, 1988; Cattell, 1985; Dielman & Krug, 1977; Sweney, Anton, & Cattell, 1986). Positive features I noticed include a worked example that provides a sample MAT protocol on one side and a dynamic structure profile and quick AVS method scoring worksheet on the opposite side. However, the scoring procedures themselves appear complex when completed by hand, which could contribute to scoring errors. A sample MAT Test Report contains an initial disclaimer about stability; broad dynamic patterns for total interest, expectation, fulfillment, and frustration (sten [standard ten] and percent); Unintegrated scores across the 10 structure factors (sten and percent); Integrated scores across the 10 structure factors (sten and percent); total motivation scores derived from combining Integrated and Unintegrated scores for each factor; conflict or frustration scores for each factor (sten and percent); raw score and sten score summaries by subtest across the 10 structure factors; and item responses (optional). The documentation contains no details about this report, which appears to be computer generated.

Supporting evidence presented in the Handbook pertains to various reliability estimates and to concept (construct) validity, or correlations with latent factors. I applaud the reporting of multiple reliability estimates, including dependability, coefficient alpha, and stability, together with detailed information on data collection and samples. I am unsure whether the dependability coefficients refer to generalizability theory, however, because the Handbook refers to them as short-term retest coefficient. Given the domain of interest and provision of caveats to test users, the moderate values are acceptable but suggest future development priorities (i.e., adding items, assessing sensitivity to experimental manipulations). Validity evidence presented in the Handbook is less compelling, because it pertains only to "factorial" rather than to construct validity. Bolton (1987) reviewed additional evidence in his evaluation, but because Bolton's review preceded many of these articles they could not have been cited. However, if clinical or counseling use of the instrument is recommended then such validity evidence is required. Further, examination of the factor structure using confirmatory and multiple sample methods, as discussed by various authors in Nesselroade and Cattell (1988), would provide much stronger evidence for factorial validity.

SUMMARY. This instrument represented an unusual approach to the assessment of motivation when it was first developed (1950–1975). Various reviewers since that time, both in this series and others, have categorized it as a research instrument with promise (Alker, 1972; Comrey, 1972). As I stated at the beginning of this review, however, my thesis is that an impressive start has fallen on hard times in terms of updating and expansion. Specific critiques of the MAT are fairly well known and have been repeated so often that it is surprising that they have not been addressed by the test publisher. For example, Boyle's (1988) recent review of the conceptual framework noted that only 5 of 16 hypothesized ergs and 5 of 27 sentiments are assessed by the MAT. Additionally, Boyle noted enough evidence for a third higher-order component, labeled an impulsive conflict dimension, that it should be strongly considered in updating the MAT. Further, Horn (1966) listed some 68 T-data methods of measurement, and Cattell (1980) described nearly 100. Of these, only 4 are used to assess the U-I (Unintegrated-Integrated) components. Further construct validation research examining relations of the MAT with other instruments purporting to assess motivation, investigating its fit with ability and temperament-personality constructs, and extending the MAT to match the theory more closely would be useful. In defense of Cattell, he has disagreed with many of the traditional formulations of reliability and validity, so much so that he has offered alternative formulations (e.g., consistency to subsume various type of reliability; Cattell, 1964).

However, current evidence bearing on his alternatives is lacking in the test manual and handbook. Additionally, I noticed an instance of what might be considered sexist interpretation in the Individual Assessment Manual, specifically in the discussion of the Career score. There the author indicated that "too high a score for a female may therefore indicate masculine strivings and suggest sex role confusion" (p. 6). Given that significant problems exist with gender stereotyping and test interpretation (cf. Selkow, 1984), such advice should be checked empirically and either supported or deleted. This advice is suggestive of the lack of updating of the instrument and its associated documentation. Finally, all this is not to say that the theory itself could not use some modification. Primarily, much of motivation theory has shifted its focus recently toward a renewed consideration of volition (Howard & Conway, 1986), goals (Kanfer, 1992; Locke & Latham, 1990; Pervin, 1989), and motive patterns (McClelland, 1987). Although Cattell's work is replete with references to goals, he uses the term somewhat differently than the authors cited above. In addition, integrative approaches that combine motivation, personality, and cognition appear increasingly popular and useful (e.g., Hamilton, 1983; Kanfer, Ackerman, & Cudeck, 1989). Therefore, I hope that the developers modernize this instrument, especially the interpretive sections of the manual, and provide additional validity evidence and updated norms. Failure to do so will nullify the excellent and comprehensive foundation initiated by Cattell.

REVIEWER'S REFERENCES

Cattell, R. B. (1959a). The dynamic calculus: Concepts and crucial experiments. In M. R. Jones (Ed.), *Nebraska symposium on motivation 1959* (pp. 84-137). Lincoln: University of Nebraska Press.

Cattell, R. B. (1959b). Foundations of personality measurement theory in multivariate experiment. In B. M. Bass & I. A. Berg (Eds.), *Objective approaches to personality measurement* (pp. 42-65). Princeton, NJ: Van Nostrand.

Sells, S. B. (1959). Structural measurement of personality and motivation: A review of contributions of Raymond B. Cattell. *Journal of Clinical Psychology, 15*, 3-21.

Cattell, R. B. (1964). Validity and reliability: A proposed more basic set of concepts. *Journal of Educational Psychology, 55*, 1-22.

Cofer, C. N., & Appley, M. H. (1964). *Motivation: Theory and research*. New York: Wiley.

Horn, J. L. (1966). Motivation and dynamic calculus concepts from multivariate experiment. In R. B. Cattell (Ed.), *Handbook of multivariate experimental psychology*. (pp. 611-641). Chicago: Rand McNally.

Madsen, K. B. (1968). *Theories of motivation: A comparative study of modern theories of motivation*. Kent, OH: Kent State University Press.

Alker, H. A. (1972). [Review of the Motivation Analysis Test.] In O. K. Buros (Ed.), *The seventh mental measurements yearbook* (pp. 266-267). Highland Park, NJ: Gryphon Press.

Comrey, A. L. (1972). [Review of the Motivation Analysis Test.] In O. K. Buros (Ed.), *The seventh mental measurements yearbook* (pp. 267-269). Highland Park, NJ: Gryphon Press.

Dielman, T. E., & Krug, S. E. (1977). Trait description and measurement in motivation and dynamic structure. In R. B. Cattell & R. M. Dreger (Eds.), *Handbook of modern personality theory* (pp. 117-138). Washington, DC: Hemisphere.

Cattell, R. B. (1980). *Personality and learning theory* (2 vols.). New York: Springer.

Hamilton, V. (1983). *The cognitive structures and processes of human motivation and personality*. New York: Wiley.

Selkow, P. (1984). *Assessing sex bias in testing: A review of the issues and evaluations of 74 psychological and educational tests*. Westport, CT: Greenwood Press.

Cattell, R. B. (1985). *Human motivation and the dynamic calculus*. New York: Praeger Press.

Howard, G. S., & Conway, C. G. (1986). Can there be an empirical science of volitional action? *American Psychologist, 41*, 1241-1251.

Sweney, A. B., Anton, M. T., & Cattell, R. B. (1986). Evaluating motivation structure, conflict, and adjustment. In R. B. Cattell & R. C. Johnson (Eds.), *Functional psychological testing: Principles and instruments* (pp. 288-315). New York: Brunner/Mazel.

Bolton, B. (1987). Motivation analysis test. In D. J. Keyser & R. C. Sweetland (Eds.), *Test critiques VI* (pp. 359-368). Kansas City, MO: Test Corporation of America.

McClelland, D. C. (1987). *Human motivation*. Cambridge, England: Cambridge University Press.

Boyle, G. J. (1988). Elucidation of motivation structure by dynamic calculus. In J. R. Nesselroade & R. B. Cattell (Eds.), *Handbook of multivariate experimental psychology* (2nd ed.; pp. 737-787). New York: Plenum.

Nesselroade, J. R., & Cattell, R. B. (1988). *Handbook of multivariate experimental psychology* (2nd ed.). New York: Plenum.

Kanfer, R., Ackerman, P. L., & Cudeck, R. (Eds.). (1989). *Abilities, motivation, and methodology*. Hillsdale, NJ: Erlbaum.

Messick, S. (1989). Validity. In R. L. Linn (Ed.), *Educational measurement* (3rd ed.; pp. 13-103). New York: Macmillan.

Pervin, L. A. (ed.). (1989). *Goal concepts in personality and social psychology*. Hillsdale, NJ: Erlbaum.

Locke, E. A., & Latham, G. P. (1990). *A theory of goal setting and task performance*. Englewood Cliffs, NJ: Prentice-Hall.

Kanfer, R. (1992). Work motivation: New directions for theory and research. In C. L. Cooper & I. T. Robertson (Eds.), *Review of industrial and organizational psychology 1992* (pp. 1-53). Chichester, England: Wiley.

Review of the Motivation Analysis Test by JAMES C. CARMER, Clinical Psychologist, Lincoln, NE:

The Motivation Analysis Test (MAT) is a self-report device that combines a variety of assessment methodologies in the construction of an understanding of some fundamental personality characteristics of the test subject. The MAT has been carefully developed to have relevance to both the vocational/educational setting and the clinical setting. The authors suggest that use of the MAT as part of a complete testing battery can contributes to the understanding of an individual's clinical and vocational/educational test results.

Test administration can be conducted individually or in groups and is estimated to take about one hour. Instructions for the MAT are read aloud as the test subject reads along. The MAT consists of four different tasks. The Uses subtest involves the test subject choosing from two alternative completions of sentence stems pertaining to the subject's judgment of which is a better use of the resource mentioned in the stem. The Estimates subtest consists of choices rating the perceived veracity of or making estimates related to ambiguous and speculative statements. The Paired Words subtest is a forced-choice word association task. Lastly, the Information subtest is a test of basic knowledge in which guessing is encouraged. All sections contribute to scores on 10 factors considered by the authors to represent a stable and thorough sampling of fundamental drives and needs. Five of these factors are considered to be ergs, or needs for emotional expression built into human nature, and the other five factors are considered to be sentiments, or attitude aggregates, which build up through one's life experiences and reflect an individual's acculturation.

Because of the wish fulfillment aspects of the section tasks, responses to the Uses and Estimates subtests result in scores considered to represent the Unintegrated, or unconscious strength of the individual's motivations related to each of the 10 factors. Because the tasks involved in the Paired Word and Information subtests are considered to reflect educational, developmental, and socially shaped motivations, scores on these subtests represent the Integrated, or socially influenced strength of the individual's motivations related to each of the 10 factors. In addition to sten [standard ten] scores for unintegrated and integrated strength of motivations related to the 10 different factors, a total motivation sten score is derived, which reflects the amount of motivational energy related to each factor. Finally, a conflict sten score is derived that reflects the degree of contrast between unintegrated and integrated levels of motivation for each factor. Scoring is done with stencils and a profile form, or by mailing the answer sheet to IPAT, who will return a brief report of the resulting profiles. A sample report is included with the test packet.

The manual is extremely thorough in its explanation of the development of the test items, scales, and standardization. The development process of the scoring procedures is presented in great detail, including the explanation of factor analyses used in the development of the scoring procedure. The authors report multiple indications of acceptable levels of reliability. Concept (construct) validity is demonstrated through high correlations of estimated factor scores with multiple correlations of the factor scores. The manual's discussion of MAT validity is complex, and explores the concept of circumstantial validity.

Included as a part of the manual is a separate document, *Individual Assessment with the Motivation Analysis Test*, that makes suggestions for clinical interpretation of the MAT scales and includes composite profiles for several different groups. The authors state several general cautions about test interpretation that apply well to the interpretation of all psychological tests.

The MAT is an elegantly conceived instrument in its construction and scale development. Scores on the MAT scales are particularly rich in that they are derived from performance on two different kinds of tasks. It is clear that the MAT is integrated conceptually with the 16PF and the larger body of personality factor research. The authors invite ongoing collaboration in the further refinement of the MAT.

The MAT is similar in structure to the School Motivation Analysis Test (SMAT; T4:2362), which is standardized for 11- to 17-year-olds. The authors cite SMAT scale correlations with school performance ranging from -.33 to.44 as evidence for the predictive capability of the MAT, because it is based on a similar structure. However, the correlations reported account for only very small portions of variability and therefore do not support the MAT's predictive value for the individual.

The MAT's standardization group was predominately young adults. The MAT needs expanded normative data to include a more representative age range. Further, although the MAT's relevance to a factor theory of personality is clear, the developmental aspects of this theory of personality have not been clearly elucidated. Such a developmental framework could aid in the interpretation of the variability inherent in assessments of motivation.

The *Individual Assessment with the Motivation Analysis Test* portion of the manual included composite profiles comparing an identified group with average performances. These composite comparisons yielded very few obvious differences that would aid in profile analysis. A more informative analysis of these composite profiles is needed to demonstrate the discriminative power of the MAT. The clinical usefulness of the MAT is limited presently.

The manual is in dire need of revision in order to more effectively integrate discussions of the theoretical basis and statistical properties of the MAT with the possible interpretation of MAT test results. The MAT has grown out of a wealth of research and theoretical work pertaining to personality dynamics, but the literature review has not been updated since the early 1970s. Although the authors conceive of the MAT as expanding the usefulness of vocational assessment instruments, no studies are reported investigating the relationship of the MAT to standard vocational assessment instruments. Because a substantial portion of vocational testing attempts to measure interest levels, it would seem that the MAT could contribute to the understanding of the dynamic relationships among interest, motivation, and behavior.

Most importantly, though, the manual needs revision because the *Individual Assessment with the Motivation Analysis Test* section contains sweeping generalizations that are not only inaccurate, but also blatantly sexist and racist. For example, the following statements are from a section discussing the career scale:

> Females are usually somewhat lower [in their scores on the career scale than males], and this indicates the degree to which they subordinate the career role to the role of being a woman. Too high a score for a female may therefore indicate masculine strivings and suggest sex role confusion. (p. 6)

After explaining that the mating scale "measures heterosexual interest directed toward the sexual act itself" (p. 9), the following statements are included in the discussion:

> Low integrated scores indicate inhibitions in this area, and if accompanied by low tension, a general indifference to it

[sex] would be suggested. This is likely to occur in mother-dominated boys such as may be found within the Irish subculture in this country. This combination would understandably be desirable for young men entering the priesthood. (p. 9)

Individual Assessment with the Motivation Analysis Test contains further statements that reflect both misunderstanding of and prejudice against homosexuality.

The MAT is an elegantly conceived and developed assessment device potentially useful in personality factor research. In my opinion, clinicians seeking an analysis of drives and conflicts related to treatment planning would be better served by Measures of Psychosocial Development (T4:1593), an instrument whose integration with Erik Erikson's theory of psychological development enables it to offer relevant clinical discrimination.

[245]

Motivational Patterns Inventory.

Purpose: "Designed to help members of an organization explore dominant motivations that can affect the way they contribute to the success of that organization."
Population: Organizational members.
Publication Date: 1990.
Scores, 3: Farmer, Hunter, Shepherd.
Administration: Group.
Price Data, 1990: $7.95 per inventory (33 pages) including administrator's guide (2 pages).
Time: Administration time not reported.
Comments: Self-scored.
Authors: Richard E. Byrd and William R. Neher.
Publisher: Pfeiffer & Company International Publishers.

Review of the Motivational Patterns Inventory by LARRY G. DANIEL, Associate Professor of Educational Leadership and Research, University of Southern Mississippi, Hattiesburg, MS:

In recent years, theorists have come to value metaphorical thinking in describing and understanding organizational behavior. However, few paper-and-pencil, group-administered instruments are available to measure constructs associated with these metaphorical theories. The Motivational Patterns Inventory is an interesting effort toward designing such an instrument consistent with the authors' theory of personal and organizational value systems. Their theory suggests that human motivational patterns within organizations can be understood using three competing metaphorical stances. Based on three of the earliest human occupations, these stances are the Farmer, the Hunter, and the Shepherd. In a narrative interpretation included in the test booklet, the authors describe these orientations as follows: "*Farmers* value quality, technical competence, and constant attention to the details of the work. *Hunters* value competition, objective goal achievement, power, and recognition. *Shepherds* value cooperation, teamwork, and involvement with people" (p. 13). The authors further posit that most organizations are biased toward one of the three orientations as an "archetypal pattern."

The instrument's 20 ipsative items are developed to measure the individual's work value system against these three competing value orientations. Each item stem presents a brief statement relative to organizational behavior followed by three response options, each representing one of the three value orientations. Responses are indicated by circling a symbol next to the alternative that examinees feel best describes their opinion on the item. Two response columns are provided, allowing examinees to record both a first and a second choice response to the item. Boxes are provided at the bottom of each physical page of the inventory for summing the symbols marked on that page. The instructions for completing the instrument are clearly presented and easy to follow; however, an illustration of the response format would have been useful.

The instrument is packaged in an attractive 31-page booklet, which includes a brief introduction to the instrument, instructions, the 20 inventory items, a presentation of the authors' theoretical ideas underlying the instrument (titled "Interpretation"), instructions for self-scoring, and worksheets for examinees to specify strengths, potential conflicts, and an "action plan" for future consideration consistent with their assessed value orientation. The text of the test booklet is easy to read, although some of the theoretical explanations are overly obvious (e.g., "Hunters probably feel most at home in a hunter organization," p. 26).

The instrument appears to be potentially of use to organizational consultants who conduct workshops with members of various organizations relative to organizational communication and/or goal setting. Instructions included in the test booklet direct the examinees, once completing and scoring the inventory items, to try to predict the motivational patterns of various colleagues. This activity could lead naturally to small group discussion relative to organizational problems that might result from individuals' motivational differences.

The theoretical ideas underlying the instrument are nicely presented and, although somewhat oversimplified, are appealing from an intuitive viewpoint; however, considering the vast array of extant literature on organizational cultures and metaphorical explanations of organizational behavior, it is interesting that the authors fail to reference any of this literature. By the same token, their own Farmer-Hunter-Shepherd theory needs further articulation. The explanation of the theory included in the test booklet is adequate for understanding the instrument, but a fuller discussion, including a review of relevant literature and an explanation for how the inventory items were developed, should be included in a separate treatise.

At least four factors relative to the instrument's format are problematic. First, examinees are requested to provide responses to several demographic items prior to their completing the inventory items; however, no explanation for why this information is needed is provided. The inclusion of these items in the instrument is especially questionable considering the self-scoring and self-interpretation features of the instrument, prompting the user to wonder who will utilize the data from these items. A second problem has to do with the use of the symbols in recording response options. Although the symbols allow for easy scoring of the instrument, they may also tend to sway the responses of the examinees resulting in response set. For example, if an examinee were to mark the "heart" response for the first several items, there might be a tendency for the examinee to continue to mark responses associated with the heart symbol without carefully considering the content of the items. A third problem has to do with the content of the items. Some items are too specific to fit well with a wide array of organizational settings in which the instrument may be administered. For instance, there seems to be a bias toward organizations focusing on sales or customer service in several of the items. Finally, there are problems with a matrix presented by the authors for determining the score for a given subscale when the examinee has responded to a given orientation one or more times as a "second choice." Although the matrix is easy to use, there is no explanation provided as to how the resulting scores were determined.

Beyond these problems with the format of the instrument is the more substantial problem of the instrument's psychometric integrity. Information on the instrument's psychometric properties is limited to a single paragraph (p. 22) in which the authors state the instrument is primarily educational in intent and, therefore, is not useful for purposes of personnel placement. No evidence of reliability is presented, and the only statement about the instrument's validity regards its face validity.

Even though the instrument is designed primarily as a teaching tool, the absence of data to support its reliability and validity is nevertheless a major concern. Quantitative measurement tends to legitimate a concept (Pedhazur & Schmelkin, 1991). Hence, despite the authors' disclaimers as to the instrument's predictive validity, an analysis of individuals' scores on the Motivational Patterns Inventory may result in a supervisor, consciously or unconsciously, forming judgments about the work habits of various workers. Moreover, because users may see the instrument as a means for determining organizational concerns, its lack of validity may result in inappropriately defined areas of concern. As Crandall (1973, p. 52) has noted, "the casual generation of new scales is professionally irresponsible."

In sum, the Motivational Patterns Inventory has potential as a viable measure of the value orientation of persons within an organization. The theories underlying its construction need to be more clearly articulated. Methods for recording responses could be improved to increase the likelihood of examinees' thoughtfulness in their responses, and the logic underlying the scoring procedures needs to be explained. Studies to determine evidence of its measurement integrity across various samples need to be conducted. With these improvements, the Motivational Patterns Inventory has the promise of becoming a solid research tool. In its present form, it is useful at best only as an information gathering tool to prompt discussions within organizations.

REVIEWER'S REFERENCES

Crandall, R. (1973). The measurement of self-esteem and related constructs. In J. P. Robinson & P. R. Shaver (Eds.), *Measures of social psychological attitudes* (rev. ed.; pp. 45-167). Ann Arbor, MI: Institute for Social Research.

Pedhazur, E. J., & Schmelkin, L. P. (1991). *Measurement, design, and analysis: An integrated approach.* (student ed.). Hillsdale, NJ: Lawrence Erlbaum Associates.

Review of the Motivational Patterns Inventory by BARBARA A. REILLY, Assistant Professor of Management, Georgia State University, Atlanta, GA:

The Motivational Patterns Inventory is a 20-item measure of feelings and values that people hold about work and work orientations. Each item forces a choice among three responses and it is possible to endorse two responses, provided that the responses are marked in such a manner that superior and subordinate importance are noted. An example item follows: "Which of the following words describes you best in meetings?" and the responses include: "Cooperative, Analytical, Assertive." The individual chooses the response most accurate for himself or herself. Individuals also have the option of selecting a second response in situations in which a second answer is nearly as accurate as the first. The inventory takes about 10 minutes to complete and about 10 minutes to hand score. The scoring sheet and instructions are extremely straightforward and easy to follow. The scoring outcome provides the test taker with three scores reflecting the person's motivational pattern (Farmer, Hunter, or Shepherd) and his or her orientation toward a dominant pattern (the highest score). According to the inventory, "*Farmers* value quality, technical competence, and constant attention to the details of the work. *Hunters* value competition, objective goal achievement, power, and recognition. *Shepherds* value cooperation, teamwork, and involvement with people" (manual, p. 13).

The strengths of the inventory include the use of very clear and concise responses and the relative ease of administration and scoring. Similar personality measures often take much longer to administer and score effectively. Another strength is that each inventory comes with all the necessary scoring and interpretation materials, thus allowing the test taker to hand score, interpret, and retain his or her inventory for future reference.

The weaknesses of the inventory revolve around two factors: the test itself and the interpretation. None of the weaknesses preclude the use of the inventory outright, but they should be considered carefully. With respect to the test itself, the scoring is facilitated by circling symbols next to the desired responses. However, some symbols have connotations which would make them more or less desirable than others (a heart, for example). It is unknown whether response patterns are altered by the desire to seek or avoid these value laden symbols. In addition, test takers tally the number of symbols endorsed, page by page for three consecutive pages. One could argue that having tallied page one, a test taker might differentially respond to pages two and three either maintaining consistency or seeking diversity. There are two weaknesses related to the interpretation of the test. The first has to do with the situation where a test taker has two or three equally dominant patterns. This is given very little attention relative to the likelihood of occurrence. The majority of the interpretive material is focused on the dominant pattern theme. However, of the subjects that I tested in the process of preparing this review, only one had a dominant pattern. The others had two or three equally dominant patterns. Another interpretive weakness involves the test taker's ability to understand how their particular pattern fits in with their organization culture. The inference is made that once a test taker understands his or her pattern the test taker should reflect on how his or her pattern fits with an organization's culture. It is my belief that this leap might be difficult for some and impossible for others.

With respect to reliability, validity, and normative data these are not reported with the declaration that "the intent of this inventory is educational. It is not designed, per se, for personnel selection and placement" (p. 22). Although I agree that less evidence is needed for a purely educational measure, I do feel that some data related to reliability and norms would be helpful. Most traditional validity information is not relevant given the intended use.

This inventory is best used to facilitate general discussions of motivations and motivational conflicts. An additional use is as a backdrop to discussions of organizational values and organizational cultures. This inventory would be misused by anyone seeking to use it for any type of selection or placement, to address developmental needs, or any use that stresses the benefit of being one pattern over another.

[246]

Multidimensional Self Concept Scale.

Purpose: Designed to provide a multidimensional assessment of self concept in clinical and research settings.

Population: Grades 5–12.

Publication Date: 1992.

Acronym: MSCS.

Scores, 7: Social, Competence, Affect, Academic, Family, Physical, Total.

Administration: Group.

Price Data, 1994: $64 per complete set; $39 per 50 record booklets; $27 per examiner's manual (82 pages).

Time: (20) minutes.

Author: Bruce A. Bracken.

Publisher: PRO-ED, Inc.

Cross References: See T4:1682 (1 reference).

TEST REFERENCES

1. Rotatori, A. F. (1994). Multidimensional Self Concept Scale. *Measurement and Evaluation in Counseling and Development, 26*, 265-268.

Review of the Multidimensional Self Concept Scale by FRANCIS X. ARCHAMBAULT, JR., Professor and Department Head, Department of Educational Psychology, University of Connecticut, Storrs, CT:

The Multidimensional Self Concept Scale (MSCS), a relatively recent addition to the testing literature, conceives of self-concept as an interactive, environmental-behavioral construct organized according to behavioral principles. The MSCS assumes that individuals' self-concepts are learned evaluations of themselves that are "based upon their [past] successes and failures, reinforcement histories, and the ways others react to them and interact with them" (manual, p. 4). Because the MSCS is behaviorally based, its author considers self-concept to be a stand-alone construct rather than a part of a larger "self-system," as self-concept is conceived by Harter (1982) and other cognitivists. Thus, the term "self concept" is not hyphenated in MSCS materials, as it would be in these other contexts.

The MSCS is based on a hierarchical model of self-concept (Shavelson, Hubner, & Stanton, 1976) that presumes the six dimensions that comprise the model (i.e., Social, Competence, Affect, Academic, Family, and Physical) are moderately correlated and of approximately equal importance. These dimensions are among those most frequently cited in the literature and are generally similar to those assessed by other popular multidimensional scales, such as Harter's Self-Perception Profile for Children (Harter, 1985), which does not include a Family scale, the Tennessee Self-Concept Scale (Roid & Fitts, 1988), which does not include an Academic scale, and the Self-Description Questionnaire-III (Marsh & O'Neill, 1984), which does not include a Competence scale but measures 13 self-concept facets, including one general self-concept, three academic self-concepts, and nine non-academic self-concepts.

The MSCS is designed for use in both research and clinical settings, unlike other self-concept instruments developed largely as research tools. In a clinical setting the MSCS can be used either as a screening device or a comprehensive diagnostic tool. The subscales can be administered together or separately and can be used in conjunction with other objective or subjective measures to produce a more comprehensive assessment than afforded by the MSCS alone. Bracken's advice that assessment within each of the six MSCS contexts can be accomplished best in a multiple-measure, multiple-source format that uses more than one instrument and more than one data sources (e.g., parents, teachers, child, etc.) is on target. The chart in the appendix of the examiner's manual that lists common psychoeducational instruments that assess one or more of the MSCS dimensions will help the clinician achieve this goal.

Norm-referenced (i.e., comparing an individual's performance against that of a norming group) and ipsative (i.e., comparing an individual's performance on a particular scale with his/her overall performance on the instrument, as described by Bracken, not to be confused with ipsative scoring systems) interpretations of test results are available. These in combination with practical advice on the possible meaning of scores will also help the clinician uncover examinee strengths and weaknesses.

The examiner's manual is generally well written and easy to follow, but perhaps due to the instrument's comparative newness, it is not as detailed or comprehensive as the manuals accompanying some of the more established self-concept measures cited above. Despite this shortcoming, as well as the availability of a greater number of studies supporting the use of instruments such as the Self-Description Questionnaire, the Tennessee Self-Concept Scale, the Self-Perception Profile For Children, and the Piers-Harris Children's Self-Concept scales, it should be noted that the MSCS was standardized on a much larger and more nationally representative sample than these more well-established competitors and that on most technical grounds it compares favorably with them, at least on the basis of data available at this time. Internal consistency (coefficient alpha) for the total scale derived from the sample of 2,501 students in grades 5–12 comprising the overall standardization sample was .98; alphas for the six subscales ranged from .87 to .97. For the separate grades, total scale alphas were .97 to .99 and subscale alphas ranged from .85 to .97. Given these high reliabilities, which are explainable in part by the large number of items comprising the scales, it is not surprising that the standard errors of measurement for the total scale and the subscales are quite low. Test-retest reliability, which was based on a much smaller sample of 37 students and a 4-week interval, was found to be .90 for the total scale and .73 to .81 for the subscales. Despite these encouraging findings, however, more data on the instrument's test-retest reliability derived from larger samples and for different intervals of time is required.

Turning now to validity, the manual includes descriptions of several small-scale studies which investigated the relationship between MSCS scores and scores obtained on other self-concept measures. Bracken calls these concurrent validity studies, but they appear to get at the construct validity of the scale. In the first study, conducted with 32 fifth graders and 33 sixth graders, substantial correlations were found between the MSCS scales and the Coopersmith Total Scale (correlations ranging from .57 to .73) and the Piers-Harris subscales (correlations ranging from .66 to .77 for theoretically similar scales). In two other studies, sizable correlations were found between the MSCS and two multidimensional self-concept instruments developed by Marsh, the Self-Description Questionnaire-II (correlations ranging from about .40 to .74 for similar scales for a sample of 35 subjects of unspecified age). The results of these three studies all suggest that the MSCS measures aspect of one's self-concept that are similar to those assessed by competing instruments. Data from two "contrasted groups" studies, as well as a discriminant validity study in which MSCS scores were compared to scores on the Assessment of Interpersonal Relations, also developed by Bracken, provide additional evidence about the validity of the scale. However, Bracken's claims that separate and distinct factors are assessed by the MSCS, which are grounded in Kaufman's (1979) contention that any subtest or scale that has more specific variance than error variance has sufficient specificity to justify its unique contribution to the total test, are not convincing. What is needed to convince this reviewer that the scales are distinct are the results of confirmatory factor analyses such as those performed by Marsh and others in support of the Self-Description Questionnaire. In the course of these analyses the developers might also investigate whether the number of items per scale can be reduced without affecting the technical quality of the instrument. If so, some redundancy in the items might be eliminated.

In summary, the Multidimensional Self Concept Scale is attractive on a number of grounds. It rests on a sound theoretical base, it is easy to administer and score, it provides a wealth of information for both research and clinical applications, it was normed on a large sample drawn from various parts of the country, it has very good internal consistency and stability measures of reliability, and it correlates well with other measures of the same construct. The major shortcoming of the instrument is that there is insufficient evidence concerning its dimensionality. Nonetheless, the MSCS is clearly worthy of serious consideration by those wishing to assess the self-concept of youth in grades 5 through 12.

REVIEWER'S REFERENCES

Shavelson, R. J., Hubner, J. J., & Stanton, G. C. (1976). Self-concept validation of construct interpretations. *Review of Educational Research, 46,* 407-441.

Kaufman, A. S. (1979). *Intelligent testing with the WISC-R*. New York: Wiley.
Harter, S. (1982). The Perceived Competence Scale for Children. *Child Development, 53*, 87-97.
Marsh, H. W., & O'Neill, R. (1984). Self Description Questionnaire III: The construct validity of multidimensional self-concept ratings by late adolescents. *Journal of Educational Measurement, 21*, 153-174.
Harter, S. (1985). Self-Perception Profile for Children. Denver: University of Denver.
Roid, G. H., & Fitts, W. H. (1988). Tennessee Self-Concept Scale. Los Angeles: Western Psychological Services.

Review of the Multidimensional Self Concept Scale by W. GRANT WILLIS, Associate Professor of Psychology, University of Rhode Island, Kingston, RI:

The Multidimensional Self Concept Scale (MSCS) is an objective self-report instrument that comprises 150 items, each of which is rated on a 4-point Likert-type scale. It was written at a third-grade reading level; examiners are permitted to explain words in the test, but it is not recommended for individuals who read below a fourth-grade level. Items are worded positively and negatively in order to avoid response bias. In addition to a composite measure of self concept, the MSCS provides an assessment of six dimensions, or environmental contexts.

Self concept is defined in the test manual as "a multidimensional and context-dependent learned behavioral pattern that reflects an individual's evaluation of past behaviors and experiences, influences an individual's current behaviors, and predicts an individual's future behaviors" (manual, p. 10). This reciprocal environment-behavior (versus a cognitive) model is clearly described and illustrated in the manual, and supporting empirical literature is cited. Theoretically, the MSCS is well grounded and this bodes well for its content validity. In addition to a thorough explanation of the author's perspective of self concept as a hierarchically structured, multifaceted, and reciprocally determined behavioral construct, a two-perspectives (i.e., personal and other) by four-standards (i.e., absolute, ipsative, comparative, and ideal) matrix is proposed as the basis for the evaluation process inherent in the acquisition of self concept.

The manual provides a clear description of the development and standardization of the MSCS. Its six subscales were based on previous theoretical and empirical work, and items were evaluated through two item-tryout procedures and a 180-item field test. Based on empirical analyses of these data, test length was reduced to 25 items per scale. These items then were administered to a standardization sample of 2,501 individuals enrolled in grades 5 through 12. The sample characteristics closely matched 1990 U.S. Census data according to gender, race, and ethnicity. Geographic region also was considered, but the Northeastern region of the U.S. was underrepresented (sample =6.9%, population = 20.2%) and the Southern region of the U.S. was overrepresented (sample = 52.5%, population = 35%). Additionally, although grades 5 through 12 were all well represented (*n*s = 228 to 447), 5th graders of lower ages and 12th graders of higher ages were not. Here, sample sizes ranged from 265 to 371 for children and youth between ages 10 and 17 years, but were considerably lower for 9-year-olds (n = 25), 18-year-olds (n = 93), and 19-year-olds (n = 11). Analyses of raw scores by demographic variables, however, showed no significant effects, and reported correlations between raw scores and chronological age were negligible (*r*s = -.11 to .07).

These results suggest that MSCS scores are unlikely to be influenced systematically by age, race, gender, or region of the country, and, therefore, norms were collapsed across all demographic variables. Appropriately for a skewed distribution, raw scores first were converted to percentile ranks and percentile ranks then were converted to standard scores (M = 100, SD = 15). The author suggests that using this common metric permits easy comparisons with scores from other instruments. Some test users probably would benefit from an explicit warning that in addition to common metrics, comparisons among test scores require other information (e.g., reliability data) as well.

Administration, scoring, and prorating procedures are clearly described in the manual, and a detailed guide for interpreting the MSCS from normative and ipsative approaches follows. The author suggests that each MSCS scale can be interpreted independently as well as in combination with other MSCS scales, and presents data on the specific variances associated with each scale to support this practice. Specificities are described as either "ample" or "adequate" for all subtests and a footnote explains how these labels were operationally defined. It probably would have been helpful for less psychometrically sophisticated test users to know that subtests with "adequate" degrees of specificity require greater interpretive caution than those with "ample" degrees. Beyond the normative and ipsative interpretation of scale scores, the author asserts that item clusters can provide valuable information. In the absence of any empirical support for this claim, however, clinicians probably should avoid this potentially unreliable avenue of interpretation. The manual's chapter on interpretation concludes with a well-organized and clinically useful section on the ecological improvement of self concept.

Psychometrically, the MSCS improves substantially on other popular measures of self concept. Internal consistency estimates range from .87 on the Competency Scale to .98 on the Total Scale (all other scales are .90 and higher), and standard errors of measurement based on these data are presented at four levels of confidence. A 4-week test-retest of 37 eighth graders showed stability coefficients that ranged from .73 for the Affect Scale to .90 for the Total Scale. Neither the subscale nor total-test mean scores changed significantly over the test-retest interval.

The manual also reports several validity studies with the newly developed MSCS, and more recent factor-analytic findings are available from the author. Convergent and divergent validity are demonstrated through reported correlations between MSCS scores and scores on the Assessment of Interpersonal Relations, Coopersmith Self-Esteem Inventory, Piers-Harris Self-Concept Scale, and Self-Description Questionnaire (SDQ) (Forms I and II). Correlations between the Total Scale score for the MSCS and the Total Scales for the latter three measures of self concept ranged from .69 (on the SDQ-I; n = 43) to .85 (on the Piers-Harris; n = 65). Convergent validity coefficients between MSCS subscales and theoretically similar subscales on the other instruments ranged from .29 (between the MSCS Academic Scale and the SDQ-I Math scale; n = 43) to.82 (between the MSCS Social Scale and the SDQ-I Peer Relations Scale; n = 43). Divergent validity coefficients between MSCS subscales and theoretically dissimilar subscales ranged from .02 (between the MSCS Family Scale and the SDQ-II Opposite-Sex Relations Scale; n = 38) to .77 (between the MSCS Competence Scale and the Piers-Harris Anxiety Scale; n = 65).

The manual also reports two studies comparing control groups with students identified as (*a*) having low self-concepts reported in psychological records and (*b*) in need of further assessment on the basis of a screening test for emotional disturbance. In the first study (n = 49) significant differences were found on three scales (i.e., Social, Competence, and Total); in the second study, significant differences were found on one scale (i.e., Affect). Thus, some external validity evidence has begun to accrue, but further study is warranted.

Finally, to support the construct validity of the MSCS, a five-instrument factor analysis is noted in the manual and is available from the author. Here, a conjoint analysis (principal factor with orthogonal rotation; n = 221) of the Coopersmith, Piers-Harris, Self-Esteem Index, Tennessee Self Concept Scale, and the MSCS supported a global self concept factor and the six dimensions corresponding to the subscales of the MSCS. With the exception of the MSCS Competence Scale, all MSCS subscales showed highest significant loadings (ranging from .55 for Affect to .81 for Family) on their respective factors. Given the nonsignificant factor loading (.29) of the MSCS Competence Scale on the Competence factor and other findings indicating that the Competence Scale shows the lowest proportion of specific variance (.17), the highest proportion of common variance (.70), and the lowest internal consistency (.87), clinicians might wish to avoid the independent interpretation of that subscale.

In summary, the MSCS is a theoretically well-grounded instrument with excellent psychometric characteristics. The manual is clear and addresses issues in sufficient detail for test users to make informed decisions about its utility. Additional external validation evidence is warranted, but the newly developed MSCS already improves substantially on other currently available measures of self-concept. My only reservation would be to reiterate the author's warning that the Competence Scale should be interpreted cautiously if used as an independent measure. With this minor caveat, I would recommend its use for the clinical and research purposes identified by its author.

[Note: The author of this test makes a distinction between self concept (not hyphenated) and self-concept (hyphenated). This has been carried over in this review.—Ed.]

[247]

Multifactor Leadership Questionnaire.

Purpose: Designed to "capture the broadest range of leadership behaviors while differentiating ineffective from effective leaders."
Population: Managers.
Publication Date: 1990.
Acronym: MLQ.
Scores: 10 factors: Transformational Leadership (Charisma, Inspiration, Intellectual Stimulation, Individualized Consideration), Transactional Leadership (Contingent Reward, Management-by-Exception), Nonleadership (Laissez-Faire), Outcome Factors (Satisfaction with the Leader, Individual and Group Effectiveness, Extra Effort by Followers).
Administration: Group.
Price Data, 1992: $60 per leader package including 9 Rater Forms, 1 self-rater form, 10 confidentiality envelopes, 1 return mailing envelope, and instruction sheet; $30 per manual (69 pages); $32 per examination materials including manual and 1 self-rater form.
Time: (15) minutes.
Comments: Questionnaire has two forms: Self-Rating Form, Rater Form; part of the Transformational Leadership Development Program.
Authors: Bernard M. Bass and Bruce J. Avolio.
Publisher: Consulting Psychologists Press, Inc.
Cross References: See T4:1684 (5 references).

TEST REFERENCES

1. Howell, J. M., & Higgins, C. A. (1990). Champions of technological innovation. *Administrative Science Quarterly*, *35*, 317-341.

2. Deluga, R. J., & Souza, J. (1991). The effects of transformational and transactional leadership styles on the influencing behaviour of subordinate police officers. *Journal of Occupational Psychology*, *64*, 49-55.

3. Komives, S. R. (1991). The relationship of same- and cross-gender work pairs to staff performance and supervisor leadership in residence hall units. *Sex Roles*, *24*, 355-363.

4. Howell, J. M., & Avolio, B. J. (1993). Transformational leadership, transactional leadership, locus of control, and support for innovation: Key predictors of consolidated-business-unit performance. *Journal of Applied Psychology*, *78*, 891-902.

5. Tepper, B. J., & Percy, P. M. (1994). Structural validity of the Multifactor Leadership Questionnaire. *Educational and Psychological Measurement*, *54*, 734-744.

Review of the Multifactor Leadership Questionnaire by FREDERICK BESSAI, Professor of Education, University of Regina, Regina, Saskatchewan, Canada:

The Multifactor Leadership Questionnaire, Self-Rating Form, is an 80-item instrument designed to measure the 10 factors of leadership listed above and the leader's perceptions of his or her effectiveness. An optional section to gather detailed biographical information on the leader is included. In all, the first 70 items measure the leadership factors and the last 10 assess the rater's perceptions of outcomes. It is available in two forms: self-rating, in which a leader rates him or herself and a rater form, in which a leader is rated by colleagues and supervisees.

Generally, the authors are to be commended on a carefully constructed instrument and on a report consisting of a detailed profile of the leader that is explained in the manual and accompanying brochure. The manual provides detailed information on the development of the scales and their psychometric properties, the profile, and even a chapter on future research. The theoretical basis of the scales is clearly explained and ample evidence of construct validity including the factor structure is provided. One of the major strengths of the questionnaire seems to be the empirical support it provides for the new paradigm of leadership that distinguishes between transactional and transformational leadership.

Alpha reliability coefficients for the self-rating form range from .60 to .92. The authors are careful to point out that self-ratings tend to be higher and also more consistent than ratings by others and indeed they recommend that the former be used for research purposes. Test-retest reliabilities over a 6-month period for the factor scales range from .44 to .74 for the self-rating form. These appear adequate, especially because the authors mention that the 33 managers used in this particular study had some individual training between the two testings.

Norms are presented in the form of scale means and standard deviations based on data from 251 leaders and 1,006 followers or supervisees. The standard errors of measurement for each scale are also given in these tables. Although the identity of the corporations that provided the norming data must remain anonymous a few more general details on the type of corporation or organization would be helpful.

Although the manual contains much useful research information, it is not as well organized as it could be and in places is difficult to follow. The section on normative information in which the reader expects to find the norms for different kinds of settings contains tables of intercorrelations for different kinds of self-ratings and supervisee ratings and a discussion of these data. A further section on intercorrelations follows. The next chapter on description, interpretation, and use does contain organizational norms but reference is made to Tables 1A and 1B of which there are two sets and the table numbers are in small print below other information. The accompanying brochure also has organizational norm Tables 1A and 1B with different norms and no information on this norming sample is given. Presumably the norms in the brochure are to be used by a coordinator or are presented as examples of what a potential user can expect to receive from the publisher because all scoring services are done by the publisher.

All in all, it appears to be an adequate test with good construct validity, adequate reliability, and a strong research base. Corporate users would be well advised to engage the services of a test consultant or coordinator who can assist with the test administration and present and interpret the results as they relate to a given context and a specific setting. The manual contains a lot of information useful to theoreticians and researchers who are concerned with describing and measuring leadership behavior and leadership outcomes, but is of little use to a corporation or organization seeking a valid and thorough assessment of its leaders. A short non-technical guide outlining what the test measures and what information it can provide about leadership behavior and the outcomes would be helpful in promoting the use of the test. The test can be recommended for use by corporations and other organizations and is strongly recommended for research uses.

Review of the Multifactor Leadership Questionnaire by JEAN POWELL KIRNAN, Associate Professor of Psychology, Trenton State College, and BROOKE SNYDER, Research Assistant, Trenton State College, Trenton, NJ:

The Multifactor Leadership Questionnaire (MLQ) is the measurement tool of the Transformational Leadership Development program (TLDP) and as such measures the constructs of transformational leadership, transactional leadership, and non-leadership. The MLQ differs from earlier measures of leadership style in that it is designed to be used at all levels of leadership. This includes low to high levels in the organization, as well as both formal and informal leadership positions. It is most appropriately used in training and organizational development.

Earlier research into leadership had identified leaders who recognize the needs of followers and arrange rewards for their efforts. The transformational leader, on the other hand, goes beyond this simple exchange process by raising the followers' level of awareness, and emphasizing self and group development and maturity. Thus, the goals and rewards under a transformational leader are self-development of the followers or transformation.

The development of the MLQ began with a review of the theoretical literature on leadership and responses of 70 senior executives to open-ended surveys. This process yielded 142 leadership behaviors. Eleven graduate students in a leadership seminar sorted these behaviors into transformational, transactional, or undecided. A total of 73 items that had demonstrated a large percent of agreement were selected. A subsequent factor analysis of data from 176 senior military officers yielded seven factors: the four transformational factors of Charisma, Inspiration, Intellectual Stimulation, and Individualized Consideration; the two transactional factors of Contingent Reward and Management by Exception; and the nonleadership factor, Laissez-Faire. These findings were later supported in a second factor analysis. Three outcomes are also identified although their origin is unclear as they are not a part of the factor analysis: Extra Effort, Effectiveness, and Satisfaction.

The MLQ consists of 80 items that are self-contained on an optically scannable answer sheet. There are two forms available, the self-rating form and the rater form. These are identical except for minor variations in wording. The majority of the items (70) consist of leadership behaviors that the respondent rates on a 5-point Likert-type scale ranging from zero *Not at all* to 4 *Frequently, if not always*. Immediately to the left of each statement, the respondent can record his/her response. Items 71 to 74 rate the effectiveness of the leader in various areas on a similar 5-point scale where zero indicates *Not effective* and 4 indicates *Extremely effective*. The final six items assess satisfaction, position in company, education, and perception of the accuracy of the questionnaire. Additionally, optional descriptive information is requested regarding the individual and the organization.

The MLQ contains a separate section immediately preceding the items that requires the respondent to mark the statement that "best applies" according to the individual's perspective when answering the questionnaire. The respondent indicates if he or she: (*a*) reports directly to the person he/she is rating; (*b*) is a peer or co-worker of the person he/she is rating; (*c*) is rating the person who reports directly to him/her; (*d*) is a client or customer of the person he/she is rating; or (*e*) other. It is unclear how this section should be used. No information is presented in the manual about this section. Indeed, many of the items in the MLQ do not appear easily answered from the perspective of clients, peers, or superiors. For example, clients would not be able to respond to items dealing with the leader's ability to motivate one to do their job or provide feedback on job performance.

The MLQ can be self-administered in a group or individual setting. Although the instrument is untimed, an average of 20 minutes is suggested for completion. Clear, detailed instructions and a sample item are on the answer sheet preceding the actual items. It is recommended that the respondents be able to read at the ninth grade level. To ensure confidentiality and anonymity among raters, three or more individuals are advised to evaluate any one leader.

The MLQ answer sheet is mailed to the publisher where it is optically scanned and results reported in a standard 24-page computer-generated profile. Feedback is presented on an organizational level, analyzing all leaders in an organization, and on an individual level focusing on a specific leader. The first two pages of the profile provide descriptions of the seven leadership factors and six outcome factors. No information is given about how the original three outcome factors were increased to six. The remainder of the profile consists of various tables referring to the organization and individual leader.

The first two of these tables offer mean ratings for the organization regarding both leadership factors and outcomes, not mentioning the individual leader, but focusing on the organization as a whole. Following these are a series of eight tables that depict the relationship between the leadership factors and the outcomes for the organization. These data are presented in graph format and are on an organizational level. The final data on the organizational level present correlations between leadership factors and outcomes. The manual suggests that a trained professional with knowledge of behavioral statistics interpret this table. Data reported here are subject to "source error of measurement" in that the same individuals rated both leadership factors and outcomes.

Not until page 13 does one find specific information about the leader being evaluated. Leader's results should be compared to other leaders in the same organization if the sample size is greater than 20. Otherwise, they should be compared to the normative database. Caution should be exercised when comparing a leader's profile with others in the same organization as indications of "high" or "low" are relative to this cohort group of leaders and not to a standard measure of leadership.

Differences between self-perceptions and others' (supervisees or colleagues) perception of leadership ability and effectiveness are presented. This allows the leader to gain a more realistic view of him/herself that provides a basis for the personal development plan. The manual states that a difference of .5 or greater "warrants attention." The last set of tables provides additional information on an item-by-item basis for each individual leader.

One should be cautious when interpreting the profile. The manual must be read and examined thoroughly and the interpreter should be well versed in the leadership model. Examples are provided in the manual to assist in the interpretation of each table.

An average of 3 hours, divided between two sessions, is necessary to review and discuss the information obtained in the profile. The first session should be used to provide feedback and explain the MLQ results to the leader. The second session should be used to set goals and specific behaviors for development as well as a self-exploratory exercise for the leader. A retest is advised after 6 months to measure change.

No instructions are provided as to how one can best use the interpretations. The profile points out the strengths and weaknesses of the leader but does not advise one how to act. A more concise written explanation might facilitate the interpretation of the profile by managers in the organization.

Whether using the rater form with supervisees or coworkers, the alpha reliability coefficients were all in an acceptable range of .77 to .95. However, in both the studies of the supervisees and the coworkers, the corresponding self-rating forms yielded dramatically lower alpha coefficients. These ranged from a low of .60 to a high of .98. The authors cite the difficulty in self-ratings (inflated nature) found in other research studies. Although the reliability of self-ratings is lower than ratings by supervisees and coworkers, they are higher in the MLQ than in other measures of leadership such as the Leader Behavior Analysis II which reports reliability for self in a range of .43 to .60 (McNeely, 1994). In all instances, the Management-by-Exception (MBE) and Laissez-Faire factors were among the lowest reliability estimates.

Test-retest reliability estimates were not as strong, ranging from .52 to .85 on the rater form and .44 to .74 on the self-rating form. The two measures were taken over a 6-month period during which the leaders participated in team development and individual training. The authors suggest that the lack of consistency over time may be reflective of a true developmental change and not a large error margin in the instrument. However, if the decrease in reliability is due to changes in scores as a result of training, the mean scores of the factors should increase from one time to the other. These data should be presented. A drop in reliability is indicative merely of change and one cannot assume its direction.

Four different normative tables are provided: Self-ratings of supervisor leaders (N = 251), supervisee ratings of those supervisors (N = 1,006), self-ratings of peer leaders (N = 169), and peer ratings of peer leaders (N = 474). The supervisor leader ratings were derived from individuals working in industrial organizations (high technology and manufacturing industries). It is not stated if the peer ratings were derived from the same organizations. In both cases, self-ratings were inflated relative to peer or supervisee ratings. Additionally, the authors cite differences in mean factor scale values in organizations that vary by structure (flat versus tall), age, and type. This suggests that the normative data would not be widely useful as it is reflective of such a specific industry type.

Validity is demonstrated in a number of ways: factor intercorrelations consistent with theory, correlations of self and supervisee ratings, correlations between supervisee ratings of leaders with supervisee ratings of outcomes, and correlations of supervisee ratings of leaders with external criteria.

Evidence of agreement with theory is presented in the high intercorrelations among the four transformational factors and lower correlations between the transformational and transactional factors. As predicted by theory, the transactional factor of Contingent Reward was moderately related to the transformational factors. As one would expect, self-ratings consistently produced lower intercorrelations as reflective of the lower reliability of these measures. The same general patterns appear when calculating intercorrelations for the supervisor being rated by supervisee versus self and peer leader being rated by peer versus self. Although the high intercorrelations among the four transformational factors may support theory, coefficients of .79 and .81 raise the concern that these are not unique factors.

Correlations between self-ratings and supervisees' ratings showed only three of the seven factors to be significantly related: Charisma, Individualized Consideration, and Contingent Reward. This raises the question of the utility of the self-ratings and suggests that self and peer ratings are measuring different factors.

Evidence of criterion-related validity is provided through the correlation of the seven factors (as rated by supervisees) with rated outcomes (as rated by supervisees). The four transformational factors correlated most highly with the three measures of organizational outcomes. Of the three transactional factors, Contingent Reward correlated positively, although to a lesser extent than the transformational factors. MBE tended to be low positive and Laissez-Faire was negatively related. The authors expressed concern that contamination and bias might exist in that a single source (the supervisee) rated both the leader and the outcomes. Statistical attempts were made to remove this source of bias using a criss-cross method where several supervisees rated one leader. In this situation, one supervisee's leader ratings were correlated with another supervisee's outcomes. The results of this analysis mirrored the above.

Criterion-related validity was also demonstrated through a correlation of the factors with external criteria. With subjects as diverse as MBA graduate students to Methodist ministers and U.S. Naval Academy graduates, a variety of soft and hard criteria have been found to correlate with more transformational and active transactional (high on Contingent Reward) leadership styles. The criteria included supervisors' ratings, promotion reports, financial outcomes, and church attendance. Although appearing to demonstrate validity, the studies are summarized and often relevant information such as sample size and the full range of correlation coefficients are not presented.

This type of validity demonstration is a strength of the MLQ as other leadership measures fail to show a relationship between score and outcomes (Bernardin & Cooke, 1994). A more complete discussion of these studies would add substantially to the manual.

The authors have identified two major areas for future research: improvement of the normative database and further investigation into the single source bias issue. These are the major weaknesses identified by these reviewers also. The MLQ stands apart from other measures of leadership in its sound psychometric properties. The complexity of the feedback report and current reliance on local organizational norms identify its greatest use as part of a leadership development program within an organization. A serious commitment to the Transformational Leadership Development Program is crucial for the MLQ to be a cost-effective investment at this time.

REVIEWERS' REFERENCES

Bernardin, J., & Cooke, D. K. (1994). [Review of the Leader Behavior Analysis II.] In J. C. Conoley & J. C. Impara (Eds.), *The supplement to the eleventh mental measurements yearbook* (pp. 131-133). Lincoln, NE: Buros Institute of Mental Measurements.

McNeely, S. (1994). [Review of the Leader Behavior Analysis II.] In J. C. Conoley & J. C. Impara (Eds.), *The supplement to the eleventh mental measurements yearbook* (pp. 133-134). Lincoln, NE: Buros Institute of Mental Measurements.

[248]

Multiphasic Environmental Assessment Procedure.

Purpose: Characterizes the "physical and social environments of residential care settings for older adults."
Population: Nursing home residents, residential care facilities, congregate apartments.
Publication Dates: 1979–92.
Acronym: MEAP.
Administration: Individual.
Time: [4–8] hours.
Comments: Administration time dependent on size and complexity of facility.
Authors: Rudolf H. Moos and Sonne Lemke.
Publisher: Center for Health Care Evaluation.

a) PHYSICAL AND ARCHITECTURAL FEATURES CHECKLIST.
Acronym: PAF.
Scores, 8: Community Accessibility, Physical Amenities, Social-Recreational Aids, Prosthetic Aids, Orientational Aids, Safety Features, Staff Facilities, Space Availability.
Price Data, 1994: $12 per test.

b) POLICY AND PROGRAM INFORMATION FORM.
Acronym: POLIF.
Scores, 9: Expectations for Functioning, Acceptance of Problem Behavior, Policy Choice, Resident Control, Policy Clarity, Provision for Privacy, Availability of Health Services, Availability of Daily Living Assistance, Availability of Social-Recreational Activities.
Price Data: $12 per test.

c) RESIDENT AND STAFF INFORMATION FORM.
Acronym: RESIF.
Scores, 6: Resident Social Resources, Resident Heterogeneity, Resident Functional Abilities, Resident Activity Level, Resident Activities in the Community, Staff Resources.
Price Data: $10 per test.

d) SHELTERED CARE ENVIRONMENT SCALE.
Acronym: SCES.
Scores, 7: Cohesion, Conflict, Independence, Self-Disclosure, Organization, Resident Influence, Physical Comfort.
Price Data: $9 per test.

e) RATING SCALE.
Acronym: RS.
Scores, 4: Physical Attractiveness, Environmental Diversity, Resident Functioning, Staff Functioning.
Price Data: $8 per test.

Cross References: See T4:1688 (4 references), 9:733 (1 reference), and T3:1546 (4 references).

Review of the Multiphasic Environmental Assessment Procedure by JULIAN FABRY, Counseling Psychologist, Omaha Psychiatric Institute, Omaha, NE:

The Multiphasic Environmental Assessment Procedure (MEAP) is a comprehensive evaluation procedure that can be utilized by clinicians to study the physical and social environments of group residential facilities for older adults. It was designed to assess Nursing Homes, Residential Care Facilities, and apartments arranged in groups for the benefit of older adults. The MEAP was developed to measure resident and staff characteristics, physical features, policies, and services, as well as the social climate of these residences. Five instruments compose the MEAP and these can be used individually, in combination, or all together in order to describe and possibly compare facilities with regard to the previously mentioned four domains.

The Resident and Staff Information Form (RSIF) can be used to characterize the residents and staff of a given facility. The Physical and Architectural Features Checklist (PAF) is concerned with the physical features of these facilities, and the Policy and Program Information Form (POLIF) is used to evaluate the policies and services provided within the residences. The Sheltered Care Environment Scale (SCES) is used to determine a residence's social climate. A Rating Scale is also available that assesses the physical environment as well as resident and staff functioning.

Each of the instruments used in the MEAP has a manual along with a User's Guide that introduces the clinician to the instruments in general. Guidelines for the general administration and scoring and particulars for each of the instruments involved in this comprehensive assessment are also available within not only the User's Guide but each individual manual. The forms, checklists, and rating scales are contained in each assessment's manual.

The Resident and Staff Information Form (RSIF) is an attempt to assess the background and personal characteristics of people living or working the particular facility under study. Records, interviews, and staff reports are used in obtaining information. The RSIF contains several subscales. The residents' Social Resources, their Heterogeneity, Functional Abilities, Activity Level, and Activities in the Community are the principal subscales contained within the RSIF along with the Staff Resources subscale. Each of these dimensions seems to be operationally defined in order to best serve the objectives of the overall assessment. The current version of this assessment is based on conceptual and empirical criteria. Specific information relating to the development of the RSIF is contained in the manual for that particular instrument.

The Physical and Architectural Features Checklist (PAF) is an attempt to assess the physical features both inside and outside the facility as well as space allowances and the structure's location within the community. These features are usually assessed through direct observation. Again, a manual is provided for this particular instrument. The manual contains the instrument and technical information related to its development, administration, and scoring. The Checklist has several subscales as well. The Community Accessibility to the facility and its services is one such subscale. The convenience and comfort of the physical features are contained in the Physical Amenities and Social-Recreational Aids subscales. The extent to which the facility provides a barrier-free environment, visual cues to orient the resident, and the presence of features for preventing accidents are all contained in the Prosthetic Aids, Orientational Aids, and Safety Features subscales. The extent to which the physical facilities aid the staff in maintaining and managing the facility as well as the number and size of communal areas within the residence are also measured in the subscales of Staff Facilities and Space Availability.

The Policy and Program Information Form (POLIF) is an attempt to measure the particular facility's policies as well as attempting to demonstrate how the facility is organized and the extent to which services are provided. This information is usually obtained from the facility administrator and staff reports. As with the previous two instruments, a blank form is contained in the manual to facilitate organizing the subscales, collecting information, administering, and scoring. The POLIF has nine subscales. The minimum capacity to perform daily living functions that are acceptable within the facility and the extent to which aggressive, destructive, or eccentric behaviors will be tolerated are contained within the Expectations for Functioning and Acceptance of Problem Behavior subscales. The extent to which the facility individualizes daily routines and whether the residents have a voice in the facility's administration and policy making are assessed through the Policy Choice and Resident Control subscales. The Policy Clarity subscale attempts to measure the institution's mechanisms for defining and communicating expected behaviors. The extent of privacy given to each resident is contained in the Provision for Privacy subscale. An attempt is also made to identify the availability of health services contained within the facility in addition to assistance that residents may need in tasks of daily living and the extent to which organized activities are available combine the last three subscales contained within the POLIF.

The Sheltered Care Environment Scale (SCES) is an attempt to assess the facility's social milieu from resident and staff reports. The amount of cohesion and conflict as well as independence and the extent of self-disclosure are contained in the various subscales of the SCES. The organization, the parameters of Residents' Influence, in addition to the Physical Comfort that is provided by the environment are all subscales contained in the SCES.

Finally, there is a Rating Scale that can be used to measure the physical environment along with resident and staff functioning. This information is usually obtained through direct observation. The extent to which the facility is clean and whether it is aesthetically appealing are characteristics that compose the Physical Attractiveness subscale in the Rating Scale. The diversity of stimulation provided by the physical environment is measured by the Environmental Diversity subscale, whereas the appearance, activity level, and interactions of the residents are contained in the Resident Functioning subscale. The Staff Functioning subscale measures the quality of interaction between staff and residents as well as the organization of the facility and the relationships between the various staff members.

As was previously indicated, the protocols, instructions for administration, scoring, and the development of each of the instruments contained in the MEAP are provided within the context of each individual manual and the User's Guide. Technical information regarding the reliability and to some extent the validity are also contained in the manuals. Test-retest reliability coefficients for each of the instruments is contained in the manual along with internal consistency coefficients and technical information concerning construct, concurrent, and discriminant validity.

The RESIF subscale internal consistency coefficients range from .56 to .95, whereas the test-retest correlations are between .68 and .99. The PAF subscales range from .62 to .84 for internal consistency and .61 to .95 for test-retest correlations. The POLIF subscales range from .69 to .89 for internal consistency and the test-retest correlations are between .72 and .96. The SCES subscales have internal consistency coefficients ranging from .44 to .79. Finally, the rating subscales have internal consistency coefficients that range from .67 to .82 and test-retest coefficients that range from .34 to .94. Interrater reliability coefficients for these subscales range from .29 to .90.

Although there are no delineated sections in the manual specifically devoted to validity, there appear to be a proliferation of studies describing various facilities and differentiating types from, not only the norms, but across residences, as well. The unique aspect of the MEAP is that several of the instruments allow for obtaining actual information about a facility and comparing it to a so-called ideal. Residents or staff complete two forms asking the same information and the results suggest proposed changes that would be preferred. Actual trends within selected types of facilities (e.g., nursing homes) have been determined as well as differences across types (e.g., nursing homes versus congregate apartment facilities). Several of the scales have been utilized in describing or making comparisons of various facilities throughout a variety of countries. The information thus obtained may be used in making comparisons to enrich interpretation.

The MEAP can be used by consultants, program evaluators, and other professionals to assess and learn more about particular facilities and how they work and to monitor changes in programs. The procedure can be used to describe a particular facility in comparison to normative data and can help with the identification of strengths and weaknesses relative to that particular environment's physical, social, and psychological climate. Comparisons can also be made between or among facilities that may be part of a network of public or private organizations. A comparison between what actually exists and the ideal for several of the scales can help to identify some of the discrepancies between a facility's characteristics and the resident's and staff's preferences.

The amount of information that needs to be collected is exhaustive. The authors have provided standardized protocols and work sheets for data collection in order to facilitate administering and scoring each of the instruments. The administration, scoring, and comparison of norms should be facilitated through the use of computer programming.

Overall, the MEAP attempts to provide an extensive comprehensive picture of residential facilities. It has been developed and refined over a number of years. The MEAP permits comparing various aspects of a facility to a normative sample to judge the effectiveness and efficiency of the day-to-day operations of various organizations and groups that maintain and provide for quality care.

Review of the Multiphasic Environmental Assessment Procedure by KENNETH SAKAUYE, Associate Professor of Clinical Psychiatry, LSU Medical School in New Orleans, New Orleans, LA:

DESCRIPTION OF THE INSTRUMENT. The Multiphasic Environmental Assessment Procedure (MEAP) was designed to help "describe and contrast facilities, monitor the outcome of program changes, and compare existing facilities with resident and staff preferences" (user's guide, p. i). It is based on four conceptual domains: resident and staff profiles, policies and services, physical and architectural features, and social climate.

The MEAP contains five parts: the Resident and Staff Information Form (RESIF), Physical and Architectural Features Checklist (PAF), the Policy and Program Information Form (POLIF), the Sheltered Care Environment Scale (SCES), and an overall Rating Scale (RS), which is similar to a global rating or impressions which overlaps other areas in content coverage. The instruments are designed to be used separately or together as no composite scoring system is available. Three scales (PAF, POLIF, and SCES) each have two forms: Form R measures the actual facility; Form I provides information on respondents' preferences and suggests areas where change may be desired. A large number of additional noncoded comments about the facilities are also collected for many areas to provide details for institutional profiles.

METHOD OF ADMINISTRATION. A variety of sources of information are required. The PAF and RS require direct observations and measurements. The POLIF requires registry sheets for services and interviews with an administrator. The RESIF requires a review of medical records, social histories, and staff records. The SCES requires interviews or questionnaires with staff and residents.

ESTIMATED TIME NEEDED TO COMPLETE THE MEAP. The PAF is estimated to take 2 hours, with a few minutes longer to complete the RS if done simultaneously. The POLIF is estimated to take 1 hour. The RESIF requires up to 3 hours per 100-resident facility. The SCES takes about 30 minutes for each questionnaire administration (which can be done in a group). A sixth grade reading level is required to complete a self-administered SCES questionnaire. To administer the ideal forms, people usually need 30 minutes for the SCES-I, 1 hour for the PAF-I, and 1 hour for the POLIF-I. Additional time is required for scoring.

CONTEXT OF DEVELOPMENT AND SUBSEQUENT USE. The current test replaces the original 1984 version that was revised to insure varied item distribution, balanced scoring direction (yes/no), and to improve internal consistency of each subscale. The differences from the original instrument are not described in detail in the manual, but reflect modifications based on the expanded normative data base.

The instrument has been widely used to determine how well a program is implemented compared to reference facilities. It has also been used to develop a topology of programs and services and compare discrepancies between actual and preferred programs. Further, it has been used to monitor intervention programs, to plan and improve facilities, to describe residential facilities for the elderly, to make cross cultural comparisons, and to evaluate psychiatric treatment programs.

SAMPLE. Normative data for the scales were obtained from two samples of facilities for older adults: 262 community facilities (135 nursing home, 60 residential care units, 67 apartment buildings), and 81 veterans facilities (57 nursing care units and 24).

SCORING. The questions generally entail a series of dichotomous choices (Yes or No) regarding the presence or absence of particular criteria, or ask for discrete nominal variables (numbers of residents meeting a certain criteria). A complicated handscoring worksheet has been developed for each form in order to calculate percentage scores and then convert to standard scores. A score of 100% indicates the total possible points on the subscale, and not a perfect facility. Standard scores with a mean of 50 and a standard deviation of 10 were derived to compare characteristics of one facility relative to others.

FORMAL TESTS OF RELIABILITY. Split half reliabilities were computed for comparable size facilities by comparing the scores of one-half of the respondents from the remainder. Nine- to 12-month test-retest reliability was computed for a subsample of homes. Stability is generally moderate on subscales (mean r values around .6). However, accuracy (validity) of ratings was not determined. Given the complexity of the information, heavy reliance on the impressions of those interviewed, lack of a single source of information, and ambiguity of some items, it seems likely that there are many random sources of measurement error that cannot be controlled.

FORMAL TESTS OF VALIDITY. Studies of validity are limited. Stein, Linn, and Stein (1987) showed adequate correlation between subscales and social workers' ratings of social climate. Timko and Moos (1989) report adequate predictive validity of resident functioning and community participation by MEAP subscales. The manual does not clarify theoretical factors underlying the subscales.

USABILITY. Despite its length, the scale seems remarkably simple to administer. Questions are sequenced in a logical manner in all scales. The RESIF, PAF, and POLIF items are well thought out and are generally unambiguous. Administrators from institutions have been reported to be cautious about having their facility evaluated with the MEAP, and this may be more limiting than the time needed for administration.

GENERAL COMMENTS AND RECOMMENDATIONS. The MEAP allows a comprehensive profile to be developed about a facility and can be very beneficial for planning and evaluation of system change. It is the most comprehensive and complete index for environmental assessment to date.

Its main weakness appears to be its assessment of social care. Studies on its concurrent validity are very limited, and at face value, items such as whether "residents hide their feelings from each other," or "sometimes criticize this place" would be expected to have a wide scatter and be almost impossible to rate as a dichotomous response. Random response biases will undoubtedly occur.

REVIEWER'S REFERENCES

Stein, S., Linn, M. W., & Stein, E. M. (1987). Patients and staff assess social climate of different quality nursing homes. *Comprehensive Gerontology, 1*, 41-46.

Timko, C., & Moos, R. H. (1989). Choice, control, and adaptation among elderly residents of sheltered care settings. *Journal of Applied Social Psychology, 19*, 636-655.

[249]

Murphy-Meisgeier Type Indicator for Children.

Purpose: Designed to assess "how an individual child best perceives and processes information and how that child prefers to interact socially and behaviorally with others."
Population: Grades 2–8.
Publication Date: 1987.
Acronym: MMTIC.
Scores, 4: Extraversion/Introversion, Sensing/Intuition, Thinking/Feeling, Judging/Perceiving.
Administration: Group.
Price Data, 1992: $19 per 25 test booklets; $48 per 10 answer sheets (prepaid for scoring by publisher); $24 per 50 answer sheets (not prepaid for scoring); $18 per set of scoring keys; $20 per 50 student profile sheets; $20 per 50 professional report forms; $16 per manual (45 pages); $18 per specimen set.
Time: (30) minutes.
Comments: Modeled after the Myers-Briggs Type Indicator (T4:1702).
Authors: Charles Meisgeier and Elizabeth Murphy.
Publisher: Consulting Psychologists Press, Inc.

Review of the Murphy-Meisgeier Type Indicator for Children by JOANNE JENSEN, Research Associate, and NORMAN A. CONSTANTINE, Senior Associate, Far West Laboratory for Educational Research and Development, San Francisco, CA:

The Murphy-Meisgeier Type Indicator for Children (MMTIC) is an extension to children of Isabel Briggs Myers' work on Jung's psychological type theory. Like the Myers-Briggs Type Indicator (MBTI; Briggs, Myers, & McCaulley, 1985; 9:739; 10:206), the MMTIC is a two-option forced-choice self-report instrument that can be administered to individuals or groups. Children are to indicate which response they like best, or the one that is most like them. The MMTIC is intended for use with children in grades 2 through 8. Its reported reading level is approximately grade 2.0. The authors note that the vocabulary has not been leveled for 7th and 8th grade students, and may be most appropriate for grades 3 through 6.

The MMTIC yields preference scores, psychological type, and dominant function (the function that is most preferred and first to develop). The instrument employs the same four bipolar dimensions as the MBTI: extroversion (E) vs. introversion (I), sensing (S) vs. intuition (N), thinking (T) vs. feeling (F), and judging (J) vs. perceiving (P). When children show no clear preference within a preference dimension, they are placed in the U-band (undetermined), and no preference score is assigned. The MMTIC is designed for identification of types and directions of preferences; it is not intended to be used as a normative instrument.

VALIDITY. The MMTIC is based on the well-developed type theory of the MBTI. Therefore, central to the validity argument for the MMTIC should be a clear analysis of the distributional and relational consistencies and inconsistencies between the two instruments. This is lacking. The authors mention in the Descriptive Statistics section of the manual that their children's distributions are "somewhat different from the distributions usually found in adult samples" (p. 24). The extent of these differences is not divulged, however. In fact, the children's overrepresentation of F over T is extreme compared to typical adult distribution. The authors' reference to a possible social desirability effect does not adequately explain this inconsistency, and their suggestion that it may be due to an interaction between type and cognitive development, if true, would argue against the instrument's validity as a measure of stable traits in children. Also troublesome is that on the E/I and T/F scales the proportions of children in the norm sample who fall into the undetermined category are greater than the proportions who are identified with preferences for introversion and thinking. The authors are unclear whether these figures accurately represent proportions of introversion and thinking preferences or are solely a function of the weights used to assign cut scores.

Results of concurrent validity analyses of the MMTIC with the Children's Personality Questionnaire based on 55 students from grades 3 through 5 are reported to parallel the relationship between the MBTI and the 16PF (for adults). Although these analyses do provide some validity support, the sample size is small for the number of variables (18) and types of analyses employed (multiple regression and canonical correlation). Correlations of an earlier version of the MMTIC with the Learning Preferences Inventory (LPI) and the Learning Pattern Assessment (LPA) are provided. The correlations with the LPI follow predictable patterns, but the authors found a "striking absence of correlations" (p. 33) between the LPA and the MMTIC. The LPA is designed to provide a measure of learning style based on temperament theory. Its scores are based on observer ratings rather than direct responses from the children. This might explain the absence of positive findings.

RELIABILITY. Internal consistency reliability estimates for the four preference scales range from .62–.72 within the full original sample and from .63–.75 within the full cross-validation sample. Estimates also are provided by gender and grade level. The authors report that "the coefficients in these tables support the conclusion that the reliability of MMTIC raw scores is consistent across grade level, gender, and reading level" (p. 24). However, the gender and gender/grade estimates range widely from .42 (for the thinking/feeling scale at grade 8 for males) to .81 (for thinking/feeling for grade 7 females).

Test/retest reliability coefficients are reported by reading level based on a 4- to 5-week interval. These values are low for the special education students (.35–.51), raising questions about the use of this instrument with this population. The estimates for students reading within one year above or below grade level range from .55–.78. In analyzing overall stability of preference classifications, it was found that 30% of the sample changed one preference and 6% changed two or more preferences over the 4- to 5-week intervals.

APPLICATIONS. The manual contains practical ideas on teaching and learning activities to be introduced into the classroom to accommodate student types. The goal of these teaching strategies is to address, but not to teach solely to, the student's dominant function. The applications reflect relatively simple accommodations that can be made in the classroom. Educators could beneficially put these recommendations in place even if they did not know their students' types. A stronger case could be made for the importance of the identification of a student's dominant function in the context of individualized instruction.

SUMMARY. The MMTIC is based on the extensive theoretical and empirical foundation of the MBTI for adults. The available evidence, however, does not yet provide sufficient support of the validity of this instrument for its intended use with children. In particular, the unexplained distributional differences between it and the MBTI, combined with the large proportions of undetermined preference types, require caution in the interpretation of its results by way of conventional type theory.

REVIEWER'S REFERENCE

Briggs, K. C., Myers, I. B., & McCaulley, M. H. (1985). Myers-Briggs Type Indicator. Palo Alto, CA: Consulting Psychologists Press.

Review of the Murphy-Meisgeier Type Indicator for Children by HOI K. SUEN, Professor of Educational Psychology, The Pennsylvania State University, University Park, PA:

Based on the concept of psychological types of Carl Jung and emulating the Myers-Briggs Type Indicator

(Myers & McCaulley, 1985; 10:206), the Murphy-Meisgeier Type Indicator for Children (MMTIC) is designed to classify a child into 1 of 16 psychological types. The intended population includes children from grade 2 through grade 8. The classification is based on the child's preferred orientation along four bipolar dimensions: extraversion-introversion, sensing-intuition, thinking-feeling, and judging-perceiving. The test consists of 70 two-option multiple-choice type items. For each item, a child is to select between two choices as to which is the preferred action. For example, a child is to choose between "you like doing" and "you like imagining." From the child's responses, four separate scores are derived, corresponding to the four dimensions. From these scores, the child's preferred orientation along each dimension is determined. The specific combination of the four preferred orientations of a child determines to which of 16 psychological types the child is to be classified.

Psychometrically, the outcomes of this assessment tool have been analyzed extensively. The results of these analyses by and large confirm the reliability and validity of the intended interpretation and use of the outcomes. The reliabilities of the preference scores (i.e., scores on each of the four orientation dimensions) are mostly low to marginally high, ranging between .34 and .81 for various scores and grade levels. These led to relatively large standard errors of measurement. Fortunately, these need not be detrimental as these scores are not used directly. Instead, they are used to classify individuals into regions. Preference orientations of individuals who score within one standard error of the midpoint of the scale are undetermined and, thus, not classified. These individuals are said to fall within a U-band. Thus, for the purpose of the bipolar classifications, the standard errors of measurement (i.e., reliabilities) have been accounted for by not classifying individuals within the U-band. To determine the width of the U-band, the same constant standard error estimate was used across different grade levels. Because the reliability estimates fluctuated across grade levels, it would have been more precise to have different U-bands for different grade levels. Again, this is a minor consideration.

Evidence of validity, primarily derived through criterion-related validation processes via correlational techniques, are not cogent, but adequate. The correlations are generally quite low, albeit statistically significant. These do not suggest deficiencies of the instrument; rather, they reflect the limitations of existing statistical validation methodologies and, as with most other instruments, the need for further and continuous accumulation of additional evidence. Overall, although the evidences are not cogent, the psychometric analyses for the Murphy-Meisgeier Type Indicator for Children are rigorous and of sufficient sophistication.

Whereas the conservative approach to classify only individuals falling outside of the U-band is sound and commendable, the resulting certainty of classification for these children is gained at the expense of the utility of the instrument for other children. Based on analyses results reported in the manual, a large number of individuals fell within the U-band for each of the four preference scales. Specifically, it can be deduced that more than one-third of the children can be expected to fall within the U-band on each scale and thus are of undetermined preference in orientation. This is not surprising and is consistent with the idea of maximizing discrimination between two bipolar groups as demonstrated by Kelley's (1939) 27% rule. Unfortunately, the utility of the instrument is severely reduced because it can be expected that the results for at least one-third of the children will be inconclusive.

The authors are quite explicit about the intended use of the test. In general, the information about psychological type in children is intended to contribute to a better understanding of a child. As with other instruments, validity is relative to intended use. No validation studies were reported for uses beyond those suggested by the authors. As such, if a user intends to use this instrument for other purposes such as placement or evaluation of counseling, the appropriateness of these specific uses must be validated locally.

Overall, the MMTIC is a well-designed and well-analyzed instrument with trustworthy outcomes. Psychometrically, it is adequate but evidence and estimates could be more cogent. When used, the results for a substantial portion of children may be inconclusive.

REVIEWER'S REFERENCES

Kelley, T. L. (1939). Selection of upper and lower groups for the validation of test items. *Journal of Educational Psychology*, *30*, 17-24.

Myers, I. B., & McCaulley, M. (1985). *Manual: A guide to the development and use of the Myers-Briggs Type Indicator*. Palo Alto, CA: Consulting Psychologists Press.

[250]

Music Achievement Tests 1, 2, 3, and 4.

Purpose: Constructed to measure musical achievement.
Publication Dates: 1968–86.
Acronym: MAT.
Administration: Group.
Price Data, 1987: $7.50 per record (select test); $22 per set of 4 records; $2 per administrative and scoring manual (select test); $5.50 per interpretive manual (select Tests 1 and 2 ['69, 143 pages] or Tests 3 and 4 ['70, 254 pages]).
Comments: Record player necessary for administration.
Author: Richard Colwell.
Publisher: MAT.

a) TEST I.
Population: Grades 3–12.
Scores, 4: Pitch Discrimination, Interval Discrimination, Meter Discrimination, Total.
Price Data: $5.75 per 35 answer sheets including hand-scoring template and class record sheet; $25 per

250 answer sheets including administrative and scoring manual ('68, 32 pages), hand-scoring template, and class record sheet.
Time: (18) minutes.
b) TEST 2.
Population: Grades 4–12.
Scores, 6: Major-Minor Mode Discrimination, Feeling for Tonal Center, Auditory-Visual Discrimination (Pitch, Rhythm, Total), Total.
Price Data: $7 per 35 answer sheets including same materials as *a* above; $31.50 per 250 answer sheets including administrative and scoring manual ('68, 36 pages), hand-scoring template, and class record sheet.
Time: (28) minutes.
c) TEST 3.
Population: Grades 4–12.
Scores, 5: Tonal Memory, Melody Recognition, Pitch Recognition, Instrument Recognition, Total.
Price Data: $6.50 per 35 answer sheets including same materials as *a* above; $28.50 per 250 answer sheets including administrative and scoring manual ('70, 32 pages), hand-scoring template, and class record sheet.
Time: (32) minutes.
d) TEST 4.
Population: Grades 5–12.
Scores, 7: Musical Style (Composers, Texture, Total), Auditory-Visual Discrimination, Chord Recognition, Cadence Recognition, Total.
Price Data: $6.50 per 35 answer sheets including same materials as *a* above; $28.50 per 250 answer sheets including administrative and scoring manual ('70, 32 pages), hand-scoring template, and class record sheet.
Time: (38) minutes.
Cross References: See T2:207 (5 references); for a review by Paul R. Lehman, see 7:248 (5 references).

TEST REFERENCES

1. Vispoel, W. D., & Coffman, D. D. (1994). Computerized-adaptive and self-adapted music listening tests: Psychometric features and motivational benefits. *Applied Measurement in Education*, 7, 25-51.

Review of the Music Achievement Tests 1, 2, 3, and 4 by J. DAVID BOYLE, Professor and Chairman, Department of Music Education and Music Therapy, School of Music, University of Miami, Coral Gables, FL:

DESCRIPTION OF TESTS. The Music Achievement Tests (MAT) include four tests, each of which has several subtests. All parts of the tests require responses to recorded tonal or musical stimuli and essentially involve one of three types of tasks: (*a*) aural discrimination, (*b*) aural recognition, or (*c*) aural-visual discrimination. Test 1 provides measures of (*a*) Pitch Discrimination in two contexts, one asking which of two successive tones is higher and the other asking which of three successive tones is lowest; (*b*) Interval Discrimination, also in two contexts, one asking whether a three-tone pattern moves scalewise or in leaps and the other asking whether the melody of a musical phrase generally moves scalewise or in leaps; and (*c*) Meter Discrimination, which asks whether a musical phrase moves in duple or triple meter. Test 2 provides measures of (*a*) Major-Minor Mode Discrimination in two contexts, chords only and musical phrases; (*b*) Feeling for Tonal Center, also in chords only and musical phrase contexts; and (*c*) Auditory-Visual Discrimination, part of which assesses auditory-visual Pitch discrimination and part of which assesses auditory-visual Rhythm discrimination.

Test 3 provides measures of (*a*) Tonal Memory, which involves identifying the tone of an arpeggiated chord that differs from the tones of a previously played block chord; (*b*) Melody Recognition, which first presents a melody alone and asks respondents to identify the voice (high, middle, or low) in which that melody occurs in a subsequent three-voice harmonization of that melody; (*c*) Pitch Recognition, which presents two notated pitches, the sound of the first pitch, and the sounds of three subsequent pitches, one of which respondents must designate as the second notated pitch; and (*d*) Instrument Recognition, which involves selecting the name of an orchestral instrument heard, some unaccompanied and some with orchestral accompaniment. Test 4 provides measures of (*a*) Musical Style, the first subtest of which asks respondents to select the names of probable composers for given recorded excerpts and the second subtest of which requires recognition of monophonic, homophonic, or polyphonic textures; (*b*) Auditory-Visual Discrimination, but with more difficult rhythms than were assessed in Test 1; (*c*) Chord Recognition, which requires matching one of three chords heard with a previously heard chord; and (*d*) Cadence Recognition, which requires determination of cadence type (full, half, or deceptive) for given musical phrases.

NORMATIVE AND TECHNICAL DATA. Responses of some 20,000 students ranging from grade 3 through high school provided the data for standardization of Tests 1 and 2; standardization data for Tests 3 and 4 were based on responses of some 9,000 students from grade 4 through high school. Both normative samples were selected to reflect representation of four geographic areas of the U.S. and a balance of students from three broad classifications of city size. Total test and subtest percentiles and standard scores for Tests 1 and 2 are provided for grades 3 through 8, for high school, and for combined grades 4 through 12. Total test and subtest percentiles and standard scores for Tests 3 and 4 are provided for grade level (4 through 12 for Test 3 and 5 through 12 for Test 4). Additional norms for combined grades 4–6, 7–9, and 10–12 and for students with piano experience and instrumental experience are available for tests 3 and 4.

Kuder-Richardson Formula 21 reliability coefficients are the only reliability data available for all parts of all tests. Ranges of the coefficients for the various grade levels for each of the four tests are as follows: Test 1—.84 to .92; Test 2—.80 to .97; Test 3—.46 to .90; Test 4—.81 to .88. Subtest ranges generally are much lower, and the subtests reliabilities for Tests 3 and 4 are lower than those for Tests 1 and 2. Notably low reliabilities are reported for the Composer and Cadence subtests of Test 4; their grade level reliability coefficients range respectively from .36 to .64 and from .25 to.46. The manual for Tests 3 and 4 contains reliability data for several other breakdowns of the norming group: (*a*) sex, (*b*) geographic area, (*c*) size of school system, and (*d*) musical participation (instrumental, choral, and general) and experience (piano and instrumental).

The manuals contain information on three types of validity data—content, criterion-related, and predictive. Data for the predictive validity, however, are too limited to be useful. Claims for content validity are based on the extent to which the tests' contents are believed to reflect certain basic instructional objectives common to nine basal music series and one MENC (Music Educators National Conference) curriculum guide that were published during the 1960s. Subsequent conferences between the test author and noted "elementary school music authorities" (p. 22, Test 1 and 2 manual) regarding the types of items being developed for the MAT substantiated the view the test content indeed reflected the content of those basic objectives. (Objectives related to performance and creativity, which did not lend themselves to groups measurement, were not considered for the MAT.) Tests 1 and 2 are based on objectives for grades 1 through 5; Tests 3 and 4 are based on objectives for grades 4 through 8.

Criterion-related validity claims are based on correlations between music teachers' selections of their "best five and poorest five" (p. 23, Test 1 and 2 manual) students and test scores for several of the trial versions of the MAT; correlations between teachers' selections and selected students' scores on the final form of the MAT were .92 (N = 1,893).

The manuals include item difficulty and item discrimination indices for every item in the MAT. Also, standard error of measurement data are provided. In all, the technical data provided in the manuals suggest that much care was taken in the development and standardization of the MAT. Further, the technical aspects of the recorded items, answer sheets, and administrative procedures reflect similar care and professionalism.

USES AND USABILITY OF THE MAT. The reviewer and his students have used various parts of the MAT on a number of occasions over the past 20 years, and it has proven to be easily administered, easily understood by students taking the tests, and useful for a variety of research and evaluation purposes. In this reviewer's opinion, the MAT is by far the most useful standardized music test on the market today. It provides measures of many achievement tasks that are relevant to music instruction in today's schools.

The fact that the MAT's content validity is based on its reflections of instructional objectives of elementary basal music series of the 1960s may be a concern to some test users; however, this reviewer examined the objectives of several basal music series published in the late 1980s (Silver Burdett's *World of Music*, 1988; Macmillan's *Music and You*, 1988; University of Hawaii's *Music, Comprehensive Musicianship Program*, 1986; and the Music Educators National Conference's *The School Music Program: Description and Standards*, 2nd ed., 1986) and found that, with a couple of exceptions, most aural recognition, aural discrimination, and aural-visual discrimination tasks measured by the MAT are still relevant to the instructional objectives of these series. In essence, curriculum in elementary music basal series has changed little since the development of the MAT, and the claim of content validity made at the time of test development is still warranted.

This is not to imply that this reviewer holds every aspect of the MAT in equally high regard. Some of the subtests appear much more useful than others, and at least two subtests of Test 3 seem less relevant than other subtests. Even though the technical data do not necessarily suggest it, the Tonal Memory subtest, which is different from all other tonal memory tasks on other music tests, and the Pitch Recognition subtest seem to be the least useful. Regardless, the MAT remains an important measurement tool for music teachers and researchers.

REVIEWER'S REFERENCES

Curriculum Research and Development Group. (1986). *Music: Comprehensive Musicianship Program* (K-8). Honolulu: University of Hawaii.

Music Educators National Conference. (1986). *The School Music Program: Description and Standards*. Reston, VA: Music Educators National Conference.

Music and You (K-8). (1988). New York: Macmillan Publishing Company.

World of Music (K-8). (1988). New York: Silver Burdett & Ginn, Inc.

Review of the Music Achievement Tests 1, 2, 3, and 4 by RUDOLF E. RADOCY, Professor of Music Education and Music Therapy, University of Kansas, Lawrence, KS:

PURPOSE. The Music Achievement Tests (MAT) measure auditory skills that Richard Colwell, employing the advice of nine other individuals active in music education during the 1960s, including professors, music supervisors, and publishers' representatives, believed to be important components of music achievement. The battery's content was based also on examination of the then most recent versions of elementary/junior high school general music series texts in use during MAT development; copyright dates ranged from 1963 through 1970. The manual for Tests 1 and 2 indicates a sixfold purpose: Evaluating mastery of basic auditory objectives, discovering students who might profit from instrumental instruction, yielding information with which to counsel students, providing data for use in program evaluation, showing students where they stand in relation to program objectives, and providing information for curriculum researchers.

TEST CONTENT. MAT Test 1 includes three parts. Pitch Discrimination includes two sections: In the first section, the student indicates whether a second tone sounds higher than, lower than, or the same as a first tone for 15 pairs. In the second section, the student hears 10 groups of three tones and indicates which one of the three sounds is the lowest in each group. The Interval Discrimination subtest includes 10 three-tone patterns in the first section and 18 phrases in the second section. In each case, the student indicates whether each tonal sequence moves in steps or skips ("leaps"), or if he or she is unsure. The Meter Discrimination subtest asks the student to classify 15 excerpts as duple or triple meter, or indicate uncertainty.

The second MAT test includes three parts, each of which has two subtests. In Major-Minor Mode Discrimination, the student classifies 15 chords as major or minor, and indicates whether each of 13 phrases is in major or minor, or changes within the phrase. The second part, Feeling for Tonal Center, includes subtests of cadences and phrases. In the cadences section, the student hears four-chord sequences and then indicates whether the first, second, third, or none of a set of three following tones was the tonic for each of 10 items. Similarly, in the phrases section the student notes which of three, if any, tones following each of 10 accompanied phrases was the tonic tone. In Auditory-Visual Discrimination, discrepancies exist between what the student sees in notation and what he or she hears. In the pitch section, the 12 items include measures where the discrepancy is in pitch; the 12-item rhythm section features measures discrepant in rhythm. In each case, the student indicates the measures that contain a discrepancy.

Test 3 includes four parts. Tonal Memory presents 20 block four-tone chords, each followed by the arpeggiated version. The student indicates whether any change occurs between the simultaneous and successive tone versions, and if it does, the number of altered tone. In Melody Recognition, the student indicates whether the melody in 20 items is in the highest, middle, or lowest voice, or if he or she is unsure. In Pitch Recognition, the student sees two printed notes for each of 20 items. He or she hears the first tone and then hears three more tones, from which he or she must identify which one, if any, is the notated second tone. The Instrument Recognition part includes two subtests: In a solo section, the student indicates what instrument of a choice of four plus "none" is playing each of 10 unaccompanied solo passages. In an accompanied section, the student makes a similar indication for each of five accompanied passages.

Four parts comprise Test 4. Musical Style includes two sections, the first of which requires the student to choose from four possibilities the likely composer of each of 20 excerpts. The second 20-item section requires indicating whether the musical texture is monophonic, homophonic, or polyphonic. The Auditory-Visual Discrimination part presents 14 four-measure phrases; the student follows notation and indicates each measure in which the notation is different from what he or she hears. (Discrepancy is always due to rhythm.) Chord Recognition includes 15 single chords, each followed by four others. The student indicates whether the first, second, third, or no chord is the same as the original, or if he or she is unsure. The final part, Cadence Recognition, includes 15 phrases; the student indicates whether each phrase ending comprises a full, half, or deceptive cadence.

NORMS. The four tests comprising the MAT were normed with national samples ranging from approximately 9,000 to 20,000 students. Percentile ranks and standard scores (mean = 500, standard deviation = 100) for different grade levels and combinations thereof are provided. For Tests 1 and 2, norms are presented for grade 3 through 8 individually, for high school, and for a 4–12 grade combination. The norms presented for Tests 3 and 4 are for individual grades 4 or 5 through 12 and for combinations of grades 4–6, 7–9, and 10–12. In addition, separate Tests 3 and 4 norms appear for students with experience in piano and in band and orchestra instruments for the various grade combinations. The manuals present detailed descriptions of the who, where, and when of the standardization groups.

RELIABILITY AND VALIDITY. For MAT Test 1, a reliability estimate for the total test across all grade levels of .88 by the KR21 method and .94 by the split-halves method is reported. For Test 2, a KR21 estimate of .92 is reported. Similar reliability estimates for Tests 3 and 4 based on all grade levels combined are not reported. KR21 estimates for total test scores and section scores for separate grade levels are provided. For Test 1, these figures range from a low of .557 (5th grade, Meter Discrimination) to a high of .921 (high school, total test). The reliability extremes for Test 2 range from .425 (4th grade, Feeling for Tonal Center) to .965 (high school, total test). The Test 3 range is from .427 (4th grade, Pitch Recognition) to .907 (12th grade, total test). Test 4 reliability estimates range from .254 (5th grade, Cadence Recognition) to .883 (12th grade, total test).

Content validity is based on the judgments of the experts with whom Colwell conferred and the content of the music series texts and several music education textbooks. Several studies are cited to show evidence of predictive validity regarding other evaluations of musical achievement.

OVERALL EVALUATION. The MATs have been available since 1970. The version inspected by this reviewer is identical to that of over 20 years ago. The only apparent difference, other than cost, is that the test is now available from a firm in Urbana, Illinois (home of the University of Illinois, Richard Colwell's former employer) rather than the Follett Educational Corporation. Many contemporary comments regarding the MAT could have been made 20 years ago, and vice versa.

The MATs are carefully constructed and normed. The manuals provide a wealth of information about development, administration, scoring, and interpretation. Colwell is careful to describe what the test is not (e.g., a measure of musical performance or aptitude) as well as what it purportedly is. The four tests are easy to administer and score; one would not have to be a musician to administer the tests and obtain scores.

The necessity for consulting two manuals may be annoying. In the interest of efficiency and eliminating redundancy, a manual encompassing all four tests could be assembled.

Although phonograph recordings remain an important component of most schools' musical resources, they are technologically obsolete. Cassette recordings, easier to manage and store, and compact discs, superior in quality and durability, might be more useful. (In fairness, the quality of the phonograph recordings is quite satisfactory.)

The decision to use the MAT is a matter of relevance to the curriculum in the school contemplating its use. The auditory skills which the battery tests are important musical skills, and they are all relevant in comprehensive music education. Students should be learning to listen analytically so that they may identify chord changes, modalities, cadences, meters, and textures. They should be sensitive to differences in pitch and timbre and to discrepancies between what is written and what is heard. Although some of the materials that inspired the test items may be outdated, the items themselves and the skills the items require remain contemporary. Of course, if a particular curriculum does not include the skills, or presents them in a substantively different way, the MAT may lack validity for that curriculum.

The MATs remain the best known standardized measure of musical achievement. They provide a basis for norm-referenced comparisons, among schools and school systems as well as with a large reference group. The passage of time inevitably calls into question the continuing representativeness of the norming groups.

In summary, although the MATs are not new, they may continue to be useful as a diagnostic measure and an individual achievement measure in school settings where the measured skills are deemed important. They also may be useful for comparing particular achievements of music programs that agree regarding the curricular relevance of the tested auditory skills.

[251]

Musical Aptitude Profile [1988 Revision].

Purpose: Designed to evaluate music aptitude.
Population: Grades 4–12.
Publication Dates: 1965–88.
Scores, 11: Tonal Imagery (Melody, Harmony, Total), Rhythm Imagery (Tempo, Meter, Total), Musical Sensitivity (Phrasing, Balance, Style, Total), Total.
Administration: Group.
Price Data, 1992: $330 per complete kit including 3 cassette tapes, 100 answer sheets, scoring stencils, 100 profiles, 100 record file folders, 2 class record sheets, and manual ('88, 151 pages); $69 per cassette (select T, R, S); $51 per 100 answer sheets; $16.50 per set of scoring stencils; $29.10 per 100 profiles; $88.50 per 100 record file folders; $28.50 per manual.
Time: 110 minutes.
Comments: Audiocassette recorder necessary for administration; parent-student report is entitled Musical Talent Profile.
Author: Edwin Gordon.
Publisher: The Riverside Publishing Co.
Cross References: See T4:1697 (2 references) and T3:1552 (4 references); see also 8:98 (25 references) and T2:209 (11 references); for reviews by Robert W. Lundin and John McLeish, see 7:249 (33 references).

Review of the Musical Aptitude Profile [1988 Revision] by ANNABEL J. COHEN, Assistant Professor of Psychology, University of Prince Edward Island, Charlottetown, Prince Edward Island, Canada:

Edwin Gordon's Musical Aptitude Profile (MAP) measures stabilized musical aptitude, a term coined by the author to reflect his belief that musical ability is fixed, or stabilized, by the age of 9 years. Stabilized ability has three basic and measurable factors: Tonal (T), Rhythmic (R), and Expressive/Aesthetic (S, sensitivity) audiation (i.e., auditory imagery). Such measures, he argues, can lead to better musical education for a child by directing music teachers and by informing parents about how well the child is likely to do in music.

The three basic factors are examined via subtests: T_1 Melody, T_2 Harmony, R_1 Tempo, R_2 Meter, S_1 Phrasing, S_2 Balance, and S_3 Style, each having between 30 and 40 items. The class time required is 2.5 hours—a minimum of three 50-minute segments—for all testing, plus a short session introducing the test and a final session discussing the results. The manual provides 11 separate standardized norms (seven subtests, the three factors, and a composite) for grade 4 to grade 12 inclusive based on over 12,500 students (including over 4,500 with musical training) from a national stratified sample developed for a broader and independent purpose in 1964–65. Separate norms are also provided for elementary, junior high, and senior high school music students. Though aptitude is stabilized, Gordon notes that test-taking skills may improve with age, and any test of aptitude is naturally contaminated by achievement; thus, norms vary systematically with age and training.

In the first publication of the MAP (1965), test materials were presented on reel-to-reel tape. In this second publication, there is a cassette tape for each of the three test components including, as before, explicit taped instructions so that no intervention from the test administrator is necessary on test days. Introducing the concepts of testing to the class and discussing the test outcomes are left to the discretion of the test administrator, though general guidelines are provided in the manual. The test structure is uniform and each item requires that the student compare two musical excerpts in a specific way depending on the particular test type. The excerpts, performed by professional string players in the early 1960s, represent a wide range of styles and modes, and were constructed with great care. All included test items were answered correctly by at least 58% of the test sample; item discrimination (item-total score correlation) always exceeds .20 and is generally higher.

As indicated in the manual, the MAP composites and subtest scores correlate with measures of music performance. Low intercorrelations between subtests reveal that the subtests measure different components of stabilized musical aptitude. In addition, the mean item difficulty (percent of students scoring correctly) increases with grade level and the mean discrimination index increases (although for neither measure is this true of each individual test item and indeed there are some large discrepancies). Split-halves reliability coefficients are above .90 for all composites for all grades.

SUBTEST DESCRIPTION. For the Melody subtest (T_1), the second excerpt on each test trial has more tones than the first. If removal of the extra tones results in the original, the student is to fill in the circle under the "like" column (marked L) and if not the circle under the "different" column (marked D). If the student is unsure, the column under "?" (in doubt) is to be filled in. For the Harmony test (T_2), each excerpt has two simultaneous parts. The student must decide whether the addition of tones in the lower part produces something like the original excerpt, again filling in the columns L, D, or ?. The rhythm tests have a more objective basis and require that the student state whether the second excerpt has the same tempo (R_1) or the same meter (R_2) by circling S, D, or ?. The sensitivity tests examine preference and knowledge of style conventions. For Phrasing (S_1) the student must state which of two performances of an excerpt makes the better "musical expression," circling 1, 2, or ?. For the Balance test (S_2), the student must choose which of two performances has the best ending. For the Style test (S_3), the two excerpts differ only in tempo and the excerpt with the best style must be selected. The "correct answers" for the sensitivity tests were determined prior to 1966 by a panel of at least 10 experts from a pool of 25 professional musicians. All items that passed this screening were administered in public schools and only those items passing the item difficulty and discrimination criteria were retained. From 500 items, only 90 were retained. In contrast to the tests of tonal and rhythmic imagery, which have a more objective right answer, the correctness of musical sensitivity answers is less clear. To give an extreme example, the proper tempo for music of a particular style may change from century to century, and styles of popular music commonly change in less than a decade. Whether the sensitivity norms from the 1960s apply to students 30 years or more later might be questioned.

1994 DATA. To address the issue partially, in 1994 the reviewer supervised administration of the MAP to 103 students in five band classes in high school in a small urban community: one grade 7 class, two grade 8 classes, and two grade 9 classes. For all but the grade 7 class, final band class grades from a previous year were available for comparison. Because the school operated on a 45-minute schedule, complete scores were obtained only for T_1, R_2, and S_1 and S_2. One class which had a double-period (1.5 hours) also completed T_2 and R_2. Missing data resulted from students leaving the room, omitting answers, talking to other students, and perseverating responses. Complete data were available for 55% of grade 7 students, 69% of grade 8 students, and 63% of grade 9 students. The problems in obtaining data suggest that administration of the test is not completely straightforward, although the regular music teacher was not the one to administer the test, as suggested by the manual.

The five separate classes produced mean raw scores which, with only one exception (Grade 7, R_1), fell within one standard deviation of the published junior high norms and showed the published developmental trend for individual grades. An external validity measure was less successful, but only one measure of student performance (final grade of the preceding year) was correlated with the various test performance scores. Evidence was provided for the continuing relevance of the 1965 norms with respect to item difficulty. For all grades considered both individually and together, scores on the items were correlated with the published norms for music students resulting in significant group correlations between .54 and .77. Lowest correlations for S_1 and S_2 (both were .54) may have resulted from either lower number of subjects and test items than for T and R tests or style change over the last decades.

SPECIFIC VERSUS GENERAL MUSICAL INTELLIGENCE. Gordon's view is akin to that of Gardner (1983) who argues for music as a separate intelligence. He claims that intelligence and MAP scores are weakly related, only as closely as intelligence and socioeconomic status (SES) (p. 79). Gordon's published correlations between SES and MAP test results ranging from .03 to .21 (Table 5, p. 25), are much lower than correlations between MAP test results and performance on various intelligence tests such as the Lorge-Thorndike or tests of educational development (e.g., Iowa Tests of Basic Skills with composites between .48 and .58; p. 80). Gordon accentuates the connection between MAP results and musical performance measures, which indeed can be higher (e.g., a correlation between Etude performance and MAP composite of .68; p. 86). Correlation with an achievement test, however, was .71 and with teachers' ratings, .35. From these data it is not clear how to draw strong conclusions regarding the independence of intelligence and musical aptitude.

USE OF THE TEST RESULTS. Gordon believes that ideally the student should receive the results of the MAP. Indeed, the student is to be introduced to the test, including the blank student-parent report in a separate session some time prior to testing. At the completion of all testing and scoring, the form is to be handed back to the student. More research is required on the psychological benefits and problems arising from providing students with their profiles. It is possible that if this were not handled appropriately, students who do poorly might become discouraged about music education. Other students who do well on the test might have an inflated sense of their abilities. In fact, it would be very difficult for a teacher to explain to the student what the test scores really mean. What we know is that the norms represent scores for over 10,000 students tested several decades ago, some other tests on smaller samples show that scores do not change much over time and with music training, that the test predicts future success in music and although musical aptitude cannot change, there are still techniques suggested in the manual that can help to improve performance of music.

One study shows that teacher's knowledge of test results facilitates learning but no studies are reported to show the benefits of the students' knowledge of the test results.

THE MANUAL. The manual of 146 pages is detailed and relatively easy to read. The bibliography is a bit of a puzzle. Much material is included which is not referred to in the manual but numerous studies mentioned in the manual are not referred to in the bibliography. For example, Gordon's *Jump Right In* is referenced in the text but not in the bibliography, Gordon's *Learning Sequences* is referenced in both, and Dailey's *Project Talent Monograph* and the critical Sandusky study among others seem unmentioned at all (but in fact, one can find the Dailey reference if one searches through all articles under the second author). Gordon's critique of "test constructors in the past" (p. 8) would be more meaningful if specific references were given. To be fair, Gordon refers the reader to several of his books for more information.

The manual appears to be accurate. However, this 1987 version introduces at least one numerical error: When describing the interpretation of standard error it is claimed that 19/10 of obtained scores fall within two standard errors (p. 63); 19/20 is meant. Differences between the two editions are minimal. It is disappointing that in such a detailed manual, the second edition provides no information about what has been changed from 1965. One might have assumed that the test materials were altered or that contemporary norms were obtained. The major change, however, is from the medium of reel-to-reel tape to cassette tape. Tables up to Table 23 are for the most part identical. In one case, third-year longitudinal data that became available in 1966 show higher predictive validity than the data originally reported from the first year of the study (e.g., a difference in grand composites of .15). Tables 24–31 (of 34 tables in total) are entirely new in the 1987 manual and strengthen the evidence for predictive and diagnostic validity of the MAP. It is a new study which suggests that teacher's knowledge of MAP results influences the student's musical proficiency (implying knowledge of MAP scores increases the teacher's efficiently). A new study also shows how the test has assisted predicting success in band classes when used in conjunction with Gordon's more recent Timbre Preference Test. Thus, the present manual provides a stronger argument for using the MAP than did the 1965 manual. For the most part, the manual is unchanged and this along with the unchanged tests themselves can also be regarded as a strength. Indeed, over the last 30 years the MAP has been successful and has provided evidence for stabilized musical intelligence.

SUMMARY. I have no hesitation in recommending to a school board the MAP as an investment in its musical education program. Testing time is long, at least three class periods and ideally five if the introduction and discussion sessions are carried out. But this time provides a teacher with new insight into his or her students' abilities and provides students with opportunities for training auditory skills. Perhaps surprisingly, the norms from the 1960s still seem to apply to the 1990s in spite of the changes in musical style and increased accessibility to music during this period. New norms, for Style tests (S) especially, would be welcomed. The test can be used to advantage by researchers in music education to indicate the equivalence of comparison and control groups with respect to stabilized musical intelligence (e.g., Azzara, 1993). If used wisely, the test is likely to contribute to Gordon's goal of increasing effective use of human potential.

REVIEWER'S REFERENCES

Gardner, H. (1983). *Frames of mind: The theory of multiple intelligences.* NY: Basic.

Azzara, C. D. (1993). Audiation-based improvisation techniques and elementary instrumental students' music achievement. *Journal of Research in Music Education, 41*, 328-342.

Review of the Musical Aptitude Profile [1988 Revision] by JAMES W. SHERBON, Professor of Music, Director of Graduate Studies in Music, School of Music, University of North Carolina at Greensboro, Greensboro, NC:

Over a span of almost three decades, the Musical Aptitude Profile (MAP) has served educators, psychologists, and researchers as the principal instrument within the field of standardized music aptitude tests. Gordon obviously has created a test that withstands the trials of time, study, and usage. Since its original publication in 1965, Gordon and other researchers have continued to study the effectiveness of the test from multiple perspectives, resulting in the establishment of substantial published documentation supporting its value in research and education. In addition to applications in schools, the MAP has been selected by researchers to serve as a primary instrument of measurement in studies where music aptitude is a factor.

The 1988 revision of the MAP appears to support the author's confidence in the overall strength of the original test package and its acceptance by the profession, as little more than cosmetic changes are present. The answer sheet, scoring masks, report and record forms, and tapes are essentially unchanged; however, the original open reel tapes have been converted to high quality cassette tapes and the plastic storing masks, which never quite fit the answer sheet, have been replaced with tagboard masks. As with the original test, machine-scoring service is available. There are some significant revisions in the 1988 manual, but a page-by-page comparison with the original publication is necessary to identify many of the changes.

The manual is one of the strengths of the test as it contains more than an adequate amount of information for the interested reader, including relevant studies, documentation, supportive material, explanations, and normative and statistical data. The layout is logical, convenient, and thorough—undoubtedly one of the most complete music test manuals on the market. The narrative is clear, basic, and contains information of value for both the professional and novice. The publisher has precisely converted the many pages of statistics and technical data from the original manual without noticeable error; the one glaring exception being on page 63 where 19/20 has been incorrectly transcribed to "19/10."

A significant revision throughout the manual is the insertion of Gordon's term "audiation," which does not appear in the 1965 publication. This word has become quite prevalent in the literature and is defined by Gordon: "Audiation, the basis of music aptitude, is the ability to hear music for which the sound is not physically present" (manual, p. 2). In addition, conclusive research on the MAP dealing primarily with longitudinal predictive and diagnostic validity, not available for publication in the original manual, is reported in the narrative. Gordon's (1967) classic longitudinal study, *A Three-Year Longitudinal Predictive Validity Study of the Musical Aptitude Profile*, is appropriately reported as well as two later longitudinal studies, *Fourth-Year and Fifth-Year Final Results of a Longitudinal Study of the Musical Achievement of Culturally Disadvantaged Students* (Gordon, 1975) and *Final Results of a Two-Year Longitudinal Predictive Validity Study of the Instrument Timbre Preference Test and the Musical Aptitude Profile* (Gordon, 1986). Significance herein point to conclusive evidence of the validity of the MAP. In fact, the MAP is the only test of its kind to receive such extensive longitudinal study supporting its validity.

In the revised manual, Gordon initiates an informative discussion on developmental and stabilized music aptitude stages. Research by Gordon on these stages of music aptitude employing the MAP, the Primary Measures of Music Audiation (T4:2099) and the Intermediate Measures of Music Audiation (T4:1249) is also cited. The inclusion of tabled statistical data from these studies provides supplementary and conclusive information on the strengths of the MAP not available in 1965. The bibliography has been extensively updated and includes current materials and studies while retaining a broad perspective across topics and years.

Although some critics may yet consider the MAP to lack strength in certain areas, Gordon provides reasonable justification in answer to at least four common concerns that have emerged through the years: test length, instruments used, validity of the "in doubt" (?) response, and establishment of correct answers for the Musical Sensitivity test. First, Gordon cites a study by Merrill Brown who concludes that the MAP cannot be shortened without sacrificing reliability (manual, p. 64). It is this reviewer's opinion, however, that regardless of Gordon's carefully worded instructions on administration in school classrooms, the test is self-limiting for use in a traditional school music program due to its length. In practicality, not many school schedules are conducive to three 50-minute testing sessions, and teachers and administrators are not easily convinced of values gained from test results versus time spent in testing. Second, a laconic justification for use of violin and cello is repeated from the original manual. Although additional study on instrument selection may be appropriate, there is little evidence in the literature or in practice supporting possible advantages from using other means of stimulus production. Therefore, violin and cello appear to be effective. Third, Gordon has provided adequate support for the "in doubt" response by reporting additional research in this area by Schleuter, Thayer, and Levendusky (manual, p. 78). A final concern emerging intermittently through the years regards the possibility of arbitrary procedures used in establishing correct answers for the Musical Sensitivity test. Gordon, however, presents new material that adequately supports his procedures for objectively determining item answers.

In summary, the MAP retains its stature as the best test of its kind in publication today. Gordon precisely states the rationale forming the foundation for the test and provides specific instructions on how scores should be interpreted and applied in educational environments. Gordon has provided an excellent instrument to measure music aptitude; however, users are well advised to take advantage of the comprehensiveness provided by the manual and stay within the application context Gordon specifies.

REVIEWER'S REFERENCES

Gordon, E. E. (1967). *A three-year longitudinal predictive validity study of the Musical Aptitude Profile*. Iowa City: The University of Iowa Press.

Gordon, E. E. (1975). Fourth-year and fifth-year final results of a longitudinal study of the musical achievement of culturally-disadvantaged students. *Experimental Research in the Psychology of Music: Studies in the Psychology of Music, 10*, 24-52.

Gordon, E. E. (1986). Final results of a two-year longitudinal predictive validity study of the Instrument Timbre Preference test and the Musical Aptitude Profile. *Bulletin of the Council for Research in Music Education, 89*, 8-17.

[252]

National Adult Reading Test, Second Edition.

Purpose: Developed to estimate "the premorbid intelligence levels of adult patients suspected of suffering from intellectual deterioration."
Population: Ages 20–70.
Publication Dates: 1982–91.
Acronym: NART.
Scores: Total score only.
Administration: Individual.
Price Data: Available from publisher.
Time: Administration time not reported.
Authors: Hazel E. Nelson and Jonathan Willison (manual).
Publisher: NFER-Nelson Publishing Co., Ltd. [England].
Cross References: See T4:1705 (80 references); for reviews by Kathryn H. Au and John M. Bradley of an earlier edition, see 9:741.

TEST REFERENCES

1. Kesner, R. P., Adelstein, T. B., & Crutcher, K. A. (1989). Equivalent spatial location memory deficits in rats with medial septum or hippocampal formation lesions and patients with dementia of the Alzheimer's type. *Brain and Cognition, 9*, 289-300.

2. Taylor, A. E., Saint-Cyr, J. A., & Lang, A. E. (1990). Memory and learning in early Parkinson's disease: Evidence for a "frontal lobe syndrome." *Brain and Cognition, 13*, 211-232.

3. Adelstein, T. B., Kesner, R. P., & Strassberg, D. S. (1992). Spatial recognition and spatial order memory in patients with dementia of the Alzheimer's type. *Neuropsychologia, 30*, 59-67.

4. Austin, M.-P., Ross, M., Murray, C., O'Carroll, R. E., Ebmeier, K. P., & Goodwin, G. M. (1992). Cognitive function in major depression. *Journal of Affective Disorders, 25*, 21-30.

5. David, A. S. (1992). Stroop effects within and between the cerebral hemispheres: Studies in normal and acallosals. *Neuropsychologia, 30*, 161-175.

6. Flint, J., & Goldstein, L. H. (1992). Familial calcification of the basal ganglia: A case report and review of the literature. *Psychological Medicine, 22*, 581-595.

7. McCarthy, R. A., & Warrington, E. K. (1992). Actors but not scripts: The dissociation of people and events in retrograde amnesia. *Neuropsychologia, 30*, 633-644.

8. Money, E. A., Kirk, R. C., & McNaughton, N. (1992). Alzheimer's dementia produces a loss of discrimination but no increase in rate of memory decay in delayed matching to sample. *Neuropsychologia, 30*, 133-143.

9. O'Carroll, R. E., Moffoot, A., Ebmeier, K. P., & Goodwin, G. M. (1992). Estimating pre-morbid intellectual ability in the alcoholic Korsakoff syndrome. *Psychological Medicine, 22*, 903-909.

10. Paller, K. A., Mayes, A. R., Thompson, K. M., Young, A. W., Roberts, J., & Meudell, P. R. (1992). Priming of face matching in amnesia. *Brain and Cognition, 18*, 46-59.

11. Sharpe, M. H. (1992). Auditory attention in early Parkinson's disease: An impairment in focused attention. *Neuropsychologia, 30*, 101-106.

12. Young, A. W., Robertson, I. H., Hellawell, D. J., DePauw, K. W., & Pentland, B. (1992). Cotard delusion after brain injury. *Psychological Medicine, 22*, 799-804.

13. Zipursky, R. B., Lim, K. O., Sullivan, E. V., Brown, B. W., & Pfefferbaum, A. (1992). Widespread cerebral gray matter volume deficits in schizophrenia. *Archives of General Psychiatry, 49*, 195-205.

14. Allen, H. I., Liddle, P. F., & Frith, C. D. (1993). Negative features, retrieval processes and verbal fluency in schizophrenia. *British Journal of Psychiatry, 163*, 769-775.

15. Baddeley, A., Emslie, H., & Nimmo-Smith, I. (1993). The Spot-the-Word Test: A robust estimate of verbal intelligence based on lexical decision. *British Journal of Clinical Psychology, 32*, 55-65.

16. Baker, G. A., Hanley, J. R., Jackson, H. F., Kimmance, S., & Slade, P. (1993). Detecting the faking of amnesia: Performance differences between simulators and patients with memory impairment. *Journal of Clinical and Experimental Neuropsychology, 15*, 668-684.

17. Clare, L., McKenna, P. J., Mortimer, A. M., & Baddeley, A. D. (1993). Memory in schizophrenia: What is impaired and what is preserved. *Neuropsychologia, 31*, 1225-1241.

18. Cockburn, J., & Smith, P. T. (1993). Correlates of everyday memory among residents of Part III homes. *British Journal of Clinical Psychology, 32*, 75-77.

19. Cooper, J. A., & Sagar, H. J. (1993). Incidental and intentional recall in Parkinson's disease: An account based on diminished attentional resources. *Journal of Clinical and Experimental Neuropsychology, 15*, 713-731.

20. David, A. S. (1993). Spatial and selective attention in the cerebral hemispheres in depression, mania, and schizophrenia. *Brain and Cognition, 23*, 166-180.

21. David, A. S. (1993). Callosal transfer in schizophrenia: Too much or too little? *Journal of Abnormal Psychology, 102*, 573-579.

22. David, A. S., & Lucas, P. A. (1993). Auditory-verbal hallucinations and the phonological loop: A cognitive neuropsychological study. *British Journal of Clinical Psychology, 32*, 431-441.

23. Egan, V. G., Chiswick, A., Brettle, R. P., & Goodwin, G. M. (1993). The Edinburgh cohort of HIV-positive drug users: The relationship between auditory P3 latency, cognitive function and self-rated mood. *Psychological Medicine, 23*, 613-622.

24. Gooding, P. A., van Eijk, R., Mayes, A. R., & Meudell, P. (1993). Preserved pattern completion priming for novel, abstract geometric shapes in amnesics of several aetiologies. *Neuropsychologia, 31*, 789-810.

25. Harvey, I., Ron, M. A., DuBoulay, G., Wicks, D., Lewis, S. W., & Murray, R. M. (1993). Reduction of cortical volume in schizophrenia on magnetic resonance imaging. *Psychological Medicine, 23*, 591-604.

26. Huppert, F. A., & Beardsall, L. (1993). Prospective memory impairment as an early indicator of dementia. *Journal of Clinical and Experimental Neuropsychology, 15*, 805-821.

27. Mayes, A. R., Downes, J. J., Shoqeirat, M., Hall, C., & Sagar, H. J. (1993). Encoding ability is preserved in amnesia: Evidence from a direct test of encoding. *Neuropsychologia, 31*, 745-759.

28. O'Carroll, R. E., Murray, C., Austin, M.-P., Ebmeier, K. P., & Goodwin, G. M. (1993). Proactive interference and the neuropsychology of schizophrenia. *British Journal of Clinical Psychology, 32*, 353-356.

29. Roxborough, H., Muir, W. J., Blackwood, D. H. R., Walker, M. T., & Blackburn, I. M. (1993). Neuropsychological and P300 abnormalities in schizophrenics and their relatives. *Psychological Medicine, 23*, 305-314.

30. van den Broek, M. D., Bradshaw, C. M., & Szabadi, E. (1993). Utility of the modified Wisconsin Card Sorting Test in neuropsychological assessment. *British Journal of Clinical Psychology, 32*, 333-343.

31. Wilson, B. A., & Davidoff, J. (1993). Partial recovery from visual object agnosia: A 10 year follow-up study. *Cortex, 29*, 529-542.

32. Alderdice, F. A., McGuinness, C., & Brown, K. (1994). Identification of subtypes of problem drinkers based on neuropsychological performance. *British Journal of Clinical Psychology, 33*, 483-498.

33. Archer, J., Hay, D. C., & Young, A. W. (1994). Movement, face processing and schizophrenia: Evidence of a differential deficit in expression analysis. *British Journal of Clinical Psychology*, *33*, 517-528.

34. Beardsall, L., & Huppert, F. A. (1994). Improvement in NART word reading in demented and normal older persons using the Cambridge Contextual Reading Test. *Journal of Clinical and Experimental Neuropsychology*, *16*, 232-242.

35. Bolton, P., MacDonald, H., Pickles, A., Rios, P., Goode, S., Crowson, M., Bailey, A., & Rutter, M. (1994). A case-control family history study of autism. *Journal of Child Psychology and Psychiatry and Allied Disciplines*, *35*, 877-900.

36. Boyle, G. J., Ward, J., & Steindl, S. R. (1994). Psychometric properties of Russell's short form of the Booklet Category Test. *Perceptual and Motor Skills*, *79*, 128-130.

37. Breen, K., & Warrington, E. K. (1994). A study of anomia: Evidence for a distinction between nominal and propositional language. *Cortex*, *30*, 231-245.

38. Bullmore, E., Brammer, M., Harvey, I., Persaud, R., Murray, R., & Ron, M. (1994). Fractal analysis of the boundary between white matter and cerebral cortex in magnetic resonance images: A controlled study of schizophrenic and manic-depressive patients. *Psychological Medicine*, *24*, 771-781.

39. Burgess, A. P., Riccio, M., Jadresic, D., Pugh, K., Catalan, J., Hawkins, D. A., Baldeweg, T., Lovett, E., Gruzelier, J., & Thompson, C. (1994). A longitudinal study of the neuropsychiatric consequences of HIV-1 infection in gay men. I. Neuropsychological performance and neurological status at baseline and at 12-month follow-up. *Psychological Medicine*, *24*, 885-895.

40. Burke, J., Knight, R. G., & Partridge, F. M. (1994). Priming deficits in patients with dementia of the Alzheimer type. *Psychological Medicine*, *24*, 987-993.

41. Busatto, G. F., Costa, D. C., Ell, P. J., Pilowsky, L. S., David, A. S., & Kerwin, R. W. (1994). Regional cerebral flow (rCBF) in schizophrenia during verbal memory activation: A 99mTC-HMPAO single photon emission tomography (SPET) study. *Psychological Medicine*, *24*, 463-472.

42. Chen, E. Y. H., Wilkins, A. J., & McKenna, P. J. (1994). Semantic memory is both impaired and anomalous in schizophrenia. *Psychological Medicine*, *24*, 193-202.

43. Christensen, H., MacKinnon, A., Jorm, A. F., Henderson, A. S. Scott, L. R., & Korten, A. E. (1994). Age differences and interindividual variation in cognition in community-dwelling elderly. *Psychology and Aging*, *9*, 381-390.

44. Damos, D. L., & Parker, E. S. (1994). High false alarm rates on a vigilance task may indicate recreational drug use. *Journal of Clinical and Experimental Neuropsychology*, *16*, 713-722.

45. David, A. S. (1994). Thought echo reflects the activity of the phonological loop. *British Journal of Clinical Psychology*, *33*, 81-83.

46. Feinstein, A., Brown, R., & Ron, M. (1994). Effects of practice of serial tests of attention in healthy subjects. *Journal of Clinical and Experimental Neuropsychology*, *16*, 436-447.

47. Grunseit, A. C., Perdices, M., Dunbar, N., & Cooper, D. A. (1994). Neuropsychological function in asymptomatic HIV-1 infection: Methodological issues. *Journal of Clinical and Experimental Neuropsychology*, *16*, 898-910.

48. Harvey, I., Persaud, R., Ron, M. A., Baker, G., & Murray, R. M. (1994). Volumetric MRI measurements in bipolars compared with schizophrenics and healthy controls. *Psychological Medicine*, *24*, 689-699.

49. Harvey, M., Milner, A. D., & Roberts, R. C. (1994). Spatial bias in visually-guided reaching and bisection following right cerebral stroke. *Cortex*, *30*, 343-350.

50. Howard, L. A., Binks, M. G., Moore, A. P., & Playfer, J. R. (1994). How convincing is the evidence for cognitive slowing in Parkinson's disease. *Cortex*, *30*, 431-443.

51. Howard, R., Almeida, O., & Levy, R. (1994). Phenomenology, demography and diagnosis in late paraphrenia. *Psychological Medicine*, *24*, 397-410.

52. Jones, D. L., Bradshaw, J. L., Phillips, J. G., Iansek, R., Mattingley, J. B., & Bradshaw, J. A. (1994). Allocation of attention to programming of movement sequences in Parkinson's disease. *Journal of Clinical and Experimental Neuropsychology*, *16*, 117-128.

53. Jones, P. B., Harvey, I., Lewis, S. W., Toone, B. K., van Os, J., Williams, M., & Murray, R. M. (1994). Cerebral ventricle dimensions as risk factors for schizophrenia and effective psychosis: An epidemiological approach to analysis. *Psychological Medicine*, *24*, 995-1011.

54. Jorm, A. F. (1994). A short form of the Informant Questionnaire on Cognitive Decline in the Elderly (IQCODE): Development and cross-validation. *Psychological Medicine*, *24*, 145-153.

55. Jorm, A. F., Christensen, H., Henderson, A. S., Korten, A. E., MacKinnon, A. J., & Scott, R. (1994). Complaints of cognitive decline in the elderly: A comparison of reports by subjects and informants in a community survey. *Psychological Medicine*, *24*, 365-374.

56. Jorm, A. F., Henderson, A. S., Scott, R., MacKinnon, A. J., Korten, A. E., & Christensen, H. (1994). Do mental health surveys disturb? Further evidence. *Psychological Medicine*, *24*, 233-237.

57. Kopelman, M. D., Green, R. E. A., Guinan, E. M., Lewis, P. D. R., & Stanhope, N. (1994). The case of the amnesic intelligence officer. *Psychological Medicine*, *24*, 1037-1045.

58. Lyon, H. M., Kaney, S., & Bentall, R. P. (1994). The defensive function of persecutory delusions: Evidence from attribution tasks. *British Journal of Psychiatry*, *164*, 637-646.

59. McCreadie, R. G., Connolly, M. A., Williamson, D. J., Athawes, W. B., & Tilak-Singh, D. (1994). The Nithsdale schizophrenia surveys XII. "Neurodevelopmental" schizophrenia: A search for clinical correlates and putative aetiological factors. *British Journal of Psychiatry*, *165*, 340-346.

60. O'Carroll, R. E., Curran, S. M., Ross, M., Murray, C., Riddle, W., Moffoot, A. P. R., Ebmeier, K. P., & Goodwin, G. M. (1994). The differentiation of major depression from dementia of the Alzheimer type using within-subject neuropsychological discrepency analysis. *British Journal of Clinical Psychology*, *33*, 23-32.

61. O'Carroll, R., Egan, V., & MacKenzie, D. M. (1994). Assessing cognitive estimation. *British Journal of Clinical Psychology*, *33*, 193-197.

62. Paller, K. A., & Mayes, A. R. (1994). New association priming of word identification in normal and amnesic subjects. *Cortex*, *30*, 53-73.

63. Rifkin, L., Lewis, S., Jones, P., Toone, B., & Murray, R. (1994). Low birth weight and schizophrenia. *British Journal of Psychiatry*, *165*, 357-362.

64. Tata, P. R., Rollings, J., Collins, M., Pickering, A., & Jacobson, R. R. (1994). Lack of cognitive recovery following withdrawal from long-term benzodiazepine use. *Psychological Medicine*, *24*, 203-213.

65. van den Broek, M. D., & Bradshaw, C. M. (1994). Detection of acquired deficits in general intelligence using the National Adult Reading Test and Raven's Standard Progressive Matrices. *British Journal of Clinical Psychology*, *33*, 509-515.

66. Weddell, R. A. (1994). Effects of subcortical lesion site on human emotional behavior. *Brain and Cognition*, *25*, 161-193.

67. Wiggs, C. L., & Martin, A. (1994). Aging and feature-specific priming of familiar and novel stimuli. *Psychology and Aging*, *9*, 578-588.

68. Wilson, B. A. (1994). Syndromes of acquired dyslexia and patterns of recovery: A 6-to 10-year follow-up study of seven brain-injured people. *Journal of Clinical and Experimental Neuropsychology*, *16*, 354-371.

69. Christensen, H., Henderson, A. S., Jorm, A. F., MacKinnon, A. J., Scott, R., & Korten, A. E. (1995). ICD-10 mild cognitive disorder: Epidemiological evidence on its validity. *Psychological Medicine*, *25*, 105-120.

70. Cockburn, J. (1995). Task interruption in prospective memory: A frontal lobe function? *Cortex*, *31*, 87-97.

71. Law, W. A., Mapou, R. L., Roller, T. L., Martin, A., Nannis, E. D., & Temoshok, L. R. (1995). Reaction time slowing in HIV-1-infected individuals: Role of the preparatory interval. *Journal of Clinical and Experimental Neuropsychology*, *17*, 122-133.

72. Sahgal, A., McKeith, I. G., Galloway, P. H., Tasker, N., & Steckler, T. (1995). Do differences in visuospatial ability between senile dementias of the Alzheimer and Lewy body types reflect differences solely in mnemonic function? *Journal of Clinical and Experimental Neuropsychology*, *17*, 35-43.

73. Shaw, C., & Aggleton, J. P. (1995). Evidence for the independence of recognition and recency memory in amnesic subjects. *Cortex*, *31*, 57-71.

74. Slaghuis, W. L., & Bakker, V. J. (1995). Forward and backward visual masking of contour by light in positive- and negative-symptom schizophrenia. *Journal of Abnormal Psychology*, *104*, 41-54.

75. Tarbuck, A. F., & Paykel, E. S. (1995). Effects of major depression on the cognitive function of younger and older subjects. *Psychological Medicine*, *25*, 285-296.

76. Taylor, R., & O'Carroll, R. (1995). Cognitive estimation in neurological disorders. *British Journal of Clinical Psychology*, *34*, 223-228.

77. Upton, D., & Corcoran, R. (1995). The role of the right temporal lobe in card sorting: A case study. *Cortex*, *31*, 405-409.

Review of the National Adult Reading Test, Second Edition by JANET F. CARLSON, Assistant Professor of Counseling and Psychological Services, State University of New York at Oswego, Oswego, NY:

The National Adult Reading Test, Second Edition (NART) is an individually administered test of reading. It is intended to assess premorbid levels of intelligence in adults from 20 to 70 years of age who are suspected of suffering from dementia. It consists of 50 words printed in order of increasing difficulty. All words have irregular pronunciations so that they cannot be phonemically decoded. Thus, the subject can read them only if he or she recognizes them, and may remain unaware of errors made in guessing at the correct pronunciations by applying rules for regular words. The test authors suggest that this latter feature preserves rapport.

The rationale for developing a measure to assess past levels of intelligence is reviewed in the test manual. The test authors note that in assessing a patient suspected of having dementia, there is a clear need to establish the level of premorbid intelligence in order to ascertain whether a decline has occurred and to assess the extent of the loss, if present. On rare occasions, such patients have been tested previously and data are available to provide dependable measures of preexisting levels of intellectual abilities. More often, however, such data are not available.

Standardized tests of intelligence measure current cognitive capacities. Some portions of these tests are considered to be less susceptible to dementing processes than others. For example, vocabulary skills are regarded as among the "last to go" by many test givers. Thus, comparing scores on subtests tapping these skills to other subtest scores can provide an estimate of premorbid cognitive functioning. However, the test authors note the limitations of this type of discrepancy analysis, such as the variability in patterns of abilities that occur in the normal population.

Administration and scoring of the NART are described in the test manual and are straightforward. The test materials consist of a single word card or a small spiral-bound word booklet, a record form, and the test manual. The test taker is given the word card or word booklet and asked to read the words presented. The booklet format presents the words one to a page and in considerably larger print than the card format. It may be preferable for persons who are elderly or who have poor eyesight as well as for those who may become easily distracted or fatigued. The test giver records the words pronounced correctly. The test authors note that the actual errors made may be recorded as well, although no mechanism for analyzing these errors is provided. Test takers are encouraged to attempt all the words, but a ceiling of 14 incorrect pronunciations in 15 consecutive responses is used. Suggestions for addressing anxiety that may arise as the test taker meets with more and more difficult words are provided in the instructions for administration.

A total score is determined by counting the number of errors committed. By using the total score and one of three formulae provided in the test manual, one can estimate Full-Scale, Verbal, and Performance intelligence scores on the Wechsler Adult Intelligence Scale—Revised (WAIS-R). If fewer than 10 words are read correctly the procedures call for combining the results with those from another reading test, the Schonell Graded Word Reading Test. In this way, below average intelligence levels can be more accurately predicted than when the NART is used alone. It is not entirely clear from the test manual, however, if the Schonell scores are to be used with the second edition of the NART. No mention is made of these scores either in the text or in the tables contained in the second part of the manual—that dealing with restandardization of the NART.

The scores generated provide estimates of premorbid intellectual functioning, and can be compared to scores obtained currently on the WAIS-R. Thus, the discrepancy between the actual WAIS-R scores and the predicted (i.e., premorbid) WAIS-R scores can be determined and used to assess the extent of intellectual decline. The proportion of the normal population in whom discrepancies of various sizes occur are provided in tables in the appendix of the test manual. These values are intended to aid in the interpretation of score discrepancies obtained in a clinical population. Unfortunately, the interpretive guidelines are too broad to be of much use. Essentially, the guidelines state that discrepancies that occur in 35% of the normative population are not meaningful, and those that occur in 2% of the population are "strongly suggestive of intellectual deterioration" (manual, p. 3). That leaves a lot of room for uncertainty.

The second edition of the NART comprised a restandardization of the original 1982 version. No stimulus words or procedures from the original NART were changed although some consideration of doing so is vaguely noted in the test manual. The 50 stimulus words and selected subtests of the WAIS-R were administered to a group of subjects (N = 182). From these data, regression equations were extracted. The manner in which the restandardization sample was obtained is not specified in the test manual. Apparently, some participants were referred for intellectual or other type of evaluation, others were volunteers of some sort, still others were patients at a general hospital and it is most unclear how these individuals came to be part of the sample. Representativeness of the restandardization sample cannot be easily assessed as no information is provided concerning national distributions of the few demographics reported in the test manual as characterizing the sample.

The test authors report that 62 participants completed all 11 WAIS-R subtests and that for this subsample a correlation coefficient of .98 was obtained between the full and shortened versions of the WAIS-R. The regression equations are based on the shortened WAIS-R, which consisted of seven subtests including four Verbal subtests (Vocabulary, Digit Span, Arithmetic, and Similarities) and three Performance subtests (Picture Completion, Picture Arrangement, and Block Design). That the subtests used in this sample predict the full battery so well may be an exception rather than a rule, as implied by Wechsler's (1981) view that it "is inadvisable to undertake prorating a Verbal score if it is based on fewer than five Verbal tests, or a Performance score if it is based on fewer than four Performance tests. If either the Verbal or Performance score is based on too few tests . . . the Full Scale score should not be computed" (p. 88).

The rationale underlying the selection of subtests to include as part of the shortened version of the WAIS-R is not apparent. Particularly with regard to the Verbal portion, the choice of subtests appears poor, given that the goal here was to estimate component and full-scale IQs and not to gain clinically meaningful information about a particular patient. The shortened battery includes the two worst subtests (Digit Span and Arithmetic) as far as correlations between subtest scores and Verbal and Full-Scale IQs. Among the two Verbal subtests that were not administered is Information, a subtest which is second only to Vocabulary in terms of its correlation with both Verbal and Full-Scale IQs. If an empirically derived argument was used to guide subtest selection, it is not mentioned in the test manual as it should be.

The NART was standardized and restandardized in England. Demographic information relating to the standardization samples is presented in the test manual and is limited to sex, social class (categories of which are not explained in the test manual), and the range of ages (but not the distribution of ages within the samples). Only individuals whose first language was English and whose Verbal IQ/Performance IQ discrepancy was less than 5% were included in the study. It is not clear from the test manual why the 5% discrepancy exclusion criterion was used. The test authors suggest that large discrepancies may yield "clinically meaningless" (manual, p. 15) full scale IQs.

Overall, the presentation of technical information is insufficient. The *Standards for Educational and Psychological Testing* (American Educational Research Association, American Psychological Association, & National Council on Measurement in Education, 1985) note that test manuals should provide enough information on the technical properties of a test to permit a potential test user to evaluate the test's appropriateness for the user's intended purpose. The NART manual falls short of this goal.

Reliability is reported as high for split-half (.93), interscorer (.96–.98), and test-retest (.98). However, only references to reliability studies are presented in the test manual and no information about how these studies were conducted (e.g., sample sizes used, interval length, qualifications of scorers, and so forth) is provided. Hence, the potential user cannot evaluate the NART's reliability nor its suitability for a particular application.

Evidence in support of validity is similarly lacking. Validity is not addressed in the traditional manner. Several references to validation-type studies are contained in the test manual. For example, the test authors report the NART loads highly (.85) on *g*. At the conclusion of the section on validation, the test authors state that the evidence reviewed indicates that the NART may underestimate IQs in cases where dementia is more severe or those in which a pronounced language deficit is present. Bradley (1985) notes the "NART also greatly needs to be validated with dementia patients already having premorbid intelligence test information. Until such retro-predictive validity information is gathered, the use of the NART should probably be confined to research" (p. 1034).

In summary, the NART was developed to estimate premorbid intelligence in patients suspected of suffering from a dementing process. Although the need for such an instrument is apparent, the NART is lacking in several important ways. The rationale underlying numerous decisions made during test development and standardization is, perhaps, the most glaring problem. Other significant problems relate to the lack of information or clarity regarding standardization and restandardization samples, reliability, validity, and interpretation of test scores. At this point, the NART is best suited for research purposes, including those that may serve to strengthen the instrument itself, particularly in those areas noted to be weak.

REVIEWER'S REFERENCES

Wechsler, D. (1981). *Wechsler Adult Intelligence Scale—Revised manual.* San Antonio, TX: The Psychological Corporation.

American Educational Research Association, American Psychological Association, & National Council on Measurement in Education. (1985). *Standards for educational and psychological testing.* Washington, DC: American Psychological Association, Inc.

Bradley, J. M. (1985). [Review of the National Adult Reading Test.] In J. V. Mitchell, Jr. (Ed.), *The ninth mental measurements yearbook* (pp. 1033-1035). Lincoln, NE: Buros Institute of Mental Measurements.

[253]

National Police Officer Selection Test.

Purpose: Measures skills critical to the successful performance of entry-level officers.
Population: Police officer candidates.
Publication Dates: 1991–92.
Acronym: POST.
Partial Batteries: POST III or POST IV.
Administration: Group.
Restricted Distribution: Available to authorized police personnel only.
Price Data, 1992: $6 per administration guide ('91, 12 pages); $6 per interpretation guide ('91, 13 pages); $10 per examiner's manual ('92, 13 pages); $3.50 per study guide.
Comments: Test may be self-scored or scored by Stanard & Associates, Inc.
Authors: Stanard & Associates, Inc.
Publisher: Stanard & Associates, Inc.

a) POST III.

Scores, 4: Mathematics, Reading Comprehension, Grammar, Total.
Price Data: $20.50 per 1–250 POST III (scored by publisher); $12.50 per 1–250 POST III (self-scored).

Time: 66 (71) minutes.
b) POST IV.
Scores, 5: Mathematics, Reading Comprehension, Grammar, Incident Report Writing, Total.
Price Data: $22.50 per 1–250 POST IV (scored by publisher); $12.50 per 1–250 POST IV (self-scored).
Time: 83 (88) minutes.

Review of the National Police Officer Selection Test by JIM C. FORTUNE, Professor of Research and Evaluation, and ABBOT PACKARD, Research Assistant, Virginia Tech University, Blacksburg, VA:

INTRODUCTION AND GENERAL DESCRIPTION. The National Police Officer Selection Test was created to screen for the most qualified individuals seeking to become candidates of police training. It is a four-section test of basic skills in mathematics, reading, grammar, and report development, which was designed to measure component skills required in the normal line of duty for a police officer. The test is to be used in the selection of candidates rather than in the certification or licensing of officers.

Criteria for the quality of any employment test, whether the test is designed to be used for selection, promotion, licensure, or certification, include: linkage of content with the job, coverage of relevant content, reliability, administrative ease, and ability to produce results for which valid interpretations can be made. The linkage of content with the job is discerned through the comprehensiveness and rigor of the job analysis. Coverage of the content can be assessed in the thoroughness of the table of specifications. The reliability of the instrument is usually studied in a tryout of the instrument before its use. Administrative ease is reflected in the clarity of the administration instructions, the time requirements, and the scoring requirements. And the ability to yield valid results is determined by the recommended cut scores, validity studies, and technical manual. This review will address each.

REASON FOR THE TEST. A review of entry-level test materials initiated by Stanard & Associates in 1989 resulted in a decision to develop a new, nationally marketed, entry-level police officer selection test. In the review and in the literature are contained the evidence that police officer candidates without basic skills are likely not to pass the training program and if they do, are likely not to succeed in the law enforcement area.

THE JOB ANALYSIS. This test was developed through a job analysis based on a literature review, analysis of work samples, on-site observations at two academies, and a survey to identify the "basic skills necessary to perform successfully as a police officer" (p. 3). Descriptions of both methodology and results of the literature review, the analysis of work samples, and the on-site observations at two academies were not provided in detail in the technical report. The survey was performed using a three-part job analysis questionnaire. This questionnaire was designed to collect ratings of importance for 227 related police tasks grouped under the following topics: administration and record keeping, training, investigating, law enforcement, communications, public relations and counseling, apprehensions, special circumstances, safety precautions, routine activities, and traffic related tasks. The questionnaire also collected demographics and ratings of importance for 62 types of equipment. The questionnaire presented a list to which the respondents reacted. This form of questionnaire has several weaknesses, including: the potential of suggesting tasks of which the respondent would have never thought and the potential of respondents not having uniform levels for the rating scale categories.

Respondents for the survey were field training directors in all 50 states, with selection of representative departments from urban to county law enforcement agencies. The initial distribution was 1,000 questionnaires, 500 to county agencies and 500 to city agencies. Returns were from 68 counties and 183 cities for a 25.5% return rate. From these returns it was determined that four areas were needed for the police officer's job. They included the following: Mathematics, Reading Comprehension, Grammar, and Incident Report Writing. In the Mathematics subtest, the candidates were examined on their abilities to complete mathematical analyses that would be applied in several basic tasks in law enforcement, such as handling money, estimating value, and calculating time. In the Reading Comprehension subtest, the applicant is examined on the ability to understand the words and concepts found in a segment of the test related to the laws that will need to be enforced, rules of evidence, and other related reports. Grammar subtests examine the ability to carry out written communication and the Incident Report Writing subtests examines the candidates on their capability to write necessary police reports.

THE TABLE OF SPECIFICATIONS. The technical report suggests that a content validity ratio having number rating the item as essential minus the number rating the item as nonessential as the numerator and the total number doing the rating as the denominator was used to select content. A content validity ratio of .50 or greater was required for a statement to be included in the content matrix. No table of specifications showing number of items from a domain was used. Four subtests were developed, but in the absence of a table of specifications for each subtest, proportions of basic skills are not described. Content validity is enhanced in that items on the subtests have been written using materials taken from police files.

THE RELIABILITY. Reliability was calculated using KR-20 for the Mathematics, Reading Comprehension, and Grammar subtests and for the combination of the three. The coefficient alpha was used to estimate reliability for the Incident Report Writing subtest. Reported reliabilities are: Mathematics subtests, .72; Reading Comprehension, .58; Grammar subtest, .59; Incident Report Writing subtest, .80; and total of the first three subtests, .79. These reliabilities appear low for the task of making decisions that will affect career aspirations and employment of individuals.

ADMINISTRATIVE EASE. Administrative ease is reflected in the clarity of the administration instructions, the time requirements, and the scoring requirements. The Administration Guide that accompanies the exam is brief, clear, and easy to use. The experimental test was developed and given to 45 subjects to determine the actual time to allow most candidates to complete the test. There is also a self-scoring manual making it easy to identify correct items. Scoring of the Incident Report Writing subtests is a little more difficult. Number correct is converted by table for percentages, which are then subjected to a cut score of 70% or 80%.

VALIDITY. The experimental test that was developed to fix time requirements provided some information on content validity. A sample of individuals (N = 443) from several states participated and the results are presented in the technical report sent with the test kit. Included in the sample group were representation across gender, ethnicity, and different levels of educational attainments. One can question both the selection of the sample which is inadequately described and the representation of the sample to the population of law enforcement departments. The proportions of demographics are adequately described in the manual. Report of item content validity by type of department are printed in the technical report. A lower content validity ratio than desired was found in several areas (investigation, law enforcement communication, public relations and counseling, apprehensions) and suggests a closer look at item construction. The total test scores were found to be correlated with success in training. Items were studied for differential performance across gender, ethnicity, age, and different levels of educational attainments.

SUPPORTIVE TEST MATERIALS. The package received for review included: a technical report, two sample tests, a study guide, an administration guide, an interpretation guide, a scoring guide, and an order form. This package is constructed well to permit any department to make an informed decision possible for adoption. The study guide has been designed so as to effectively give the prospective candidate the opportunity to prepare to take the test by demonstrating test format, giving hints on taking the examination within time limits, and explaining how to mark answers. The administration guide contains an overview of the test and the procedures needed to administer the test. The interpretation guide explains the background for the test development, how the results are to be interpreted, and the options that departments may possibly use to establish minimum scores for qualification of their applicants. With the exception of the technical manual, the other manuals are well written.

REVIEWERS' COMMENTARY. Although the task analysis is somewhat suspect, all other evidence suggests that this examination will perform as it was proposed to do. There are cut score setting methods that should be employed with this test. The final line on the test is that it is an appropriate selection test that could be greatly improved with just a little additional polish and a better written technical manual. The examination is in an area where need is great. As a screening device, it appears useful. However, it lacks the comprehensive nature to be used alone as a selection tool.

Review of the National Police Officer Selection Test by KURT F. GEISINGER, Professor of Psychology and Dean, College of Arts and Sciences, State University of New York at Oswego, Oswego, NY:

This test is based upon an extensive job analysis performed by the publisher of the test: Stanard & Associates, a Chicago-based consulting firm. The test is not especially well described by the technical manual; more of the manual is spent depicting the job analysis, the justification for the test, and some rudimentary validation information.

The test is intended to aid in the selection of police officers and police officer candidates for positions in public settings. The test publishers themselves indicate the purpose in a somewhat more limited fashion; they state that its purpose is "to screen entry-level candidates for basic skills required in the field of law enforcement" (p. 1). The market for which this test is explicitly intended is cities, counties, and other jurisdictions that must make police officer selection decisions. The test would appear to be attractive on a superficial level for such settings; it is a relatively short, objective, and ostensibly fair and unbiased measure offered by a company with an extensive history of working with police agencies. This particular test, however, is flawed in its conception, as is noted below. Many aspects of the test and the job analysis results are justified in the manual "based on Stanard and Associates' experience and expertise" (p. 6). Such explanations are not especially convincing and one would have preferred empirical bases.

The test contains four tests broken into two parts: three objective tests and a short, written response test. The first three tests assess Mathematics, Reading Comprehension, and Grammar (which includes spelling). The fourth test concerns Incident Report Writing. It is reported that these tests were selected for use in the test based upon the results of the job analysis. As is demonstrated below, the job analysis was seriously flawed as those conducting it appear to have implicitly and preliminarily decided that these measures would compose the test. The primary justification for this assortment of tests is found in the technical manual. It is reported that an industrial psychologist visited 4 days of police training and "found that the basic skills of reading, writing, and mathematics were critical to success in the training academy, and that individuals without such skills were having trouble succeeding in training" (Stanard & Associates, 1991, p. 4).

The author of this review has professional experience that includes conducting about 10 job analyses for entry-level police work for large cities and populous states. My experience indicates the Mathematics and Grammar subtests are unlikely to be highly related to performance on the job for police officers. The level of Mathematics used by Police Officers is generally quite limited. Grammar and Spelling are simply not very important in report writing for police officers. Furthermore, due to educational differences among societal groups, such measures are likely to cause adverse impact on various minority or underrepresented groups (e.g., African-Americans, Hispanic-Americans, and Native Americans) without adding appreciably to the validity of the test.

Because the Incident Report Writing subtests involves scoring by human judges, the technical manual author suggests that some test administrators may wish to employ only the three objective subtests, although others would use all four. Throughout the analyses presented in the manual, therefore, the authors provided statistical information with the first three tests (Post III) and the entire test (Post IV).

The Mathematics subtest is composed of 20 mathematics multiple-choice questions; the Reading Comprehension subtest is composed of 25 multiple-choice and true-false questions; and the Grammar subtest is composed of 20 multiple-choice questions. (The Grammar subtest is reportedly a measure of English grammatical ability and spelling—two skills that are probably only marginally involved in police work.) If these three tests were used alone, the test would be shorter than most cognitive tests used to select police officers. It might be noted that it is extremely unusual to find true-false questions in a professionally developed selection test. It is not clear how many questions are in the Incident Report Writing subtest, although the maximum score is 50 points.

A great number of other skills and abilities are required for success as a police officer in addition to those assessed by this instrument. The test authors recognize this point to some extent. They report that some skills such as apprehending persons are also critical, but are either not amenable to paper-and-pencil testing or are learned in training (Stanard & Associates, 1991, p. 6). The latter of these grounds is acceptable under the *Uniform Guidelines* (Uniform Guidelines on Employee Selection Procedures, 1978). They are correct that a number of skills required by police officers are not easily assessed by paper-and-pencil means. However, others are, especially if a broader perspective on human skills and abilities is employed. For example, Fleishman's taxonomy of human abilities (e.g., Fleishman & Quaintance, 1984) has proven useful both in identifying skills and abilities required in police work and in guiding the construction of measures for this profession.

The test publishers report they set the time limits for the instrument by the use of a practice administration of the test to 45 police officers in Alabama. Such a procedure should be effective. However, additional information would be useful, such as the age and experience levels of the police officer sample, the educational background of this group, what the actual time limits are, and what portion of the sample finished the test.

ANALYTIC INFORMATION CONCERNING THE TEST. Stanard & Associates administered the test to a diverse sample of 443 prior to publishing the instrument. The sample is not especially comparable to those who will eventually take this examination. This sample was 80% male—probably an acceptable percentage given the fact the vast majority of those typically seeking police employment are male. The minority composition in the sample, however, is just under 10%, and therefore reflects an unacceptably small proportion in this heavily litigious employment setting. Furthermore, approximately 20% of the sample is older than 32 years; many police agencies continue to employ age limits of 29 or 30 years, where such limits are acceptable. This older portion of the sample provides little useful information and could potentially bias the results. The sample also appears to be more well educated than the typical police recruit population. Almost two-thirds of the sample comes from the Midwest and less than 1% comes from the East, another significant biasing of the sample. Finally, 40% of the pool were college students and another 21% were incumbent police officers. Students, of course, would be expected to excel on an educationally oriented test and may not accurately reflect the population of candidates for the examination. Incumbents would be helped to the extent that experience on the job might aid performance. In this writer's opinion, however, job experience is not likely to impact test performance positively in that some of the skills measured on the test are probably only minimally related to the position of police officer.

The reliability analyses presented in this section relate to analyses based on the above sample and are, therefore, subject to the appropriate cautions based on the above-cited limitations. The reliability estimates (coefficient alpha internal consistency coefficients and, in some cases, mathematically equivalent KR-20 internal consistency coefficients) are too low for this measure to be considered an acceptable selection measure. The internal consistency coefficients are .72, .58, .59, and .80 for the Mathematical, Reading Comprehension, Grammar, and Incident Report Writing subtests, respectively. The authors report the overall internal consistency reliability coefficient for the three objective subtests as .79. This index is rather low when compared to other measures used to screen police officers. The authors do not report an overall index, incorrectly believing that they cannot combine information from dichotomously scored and otherwise scored test items (Stanard & Associates, 1991, p. 20). One other statement also needs to be corrected; they state that "coefficients are internal consistency estimates of test-retest reliability" (p. 19). Internal consistency reliability coefficients capture different information than test-retest reliability coefficients (Anastasi, 1988) and should not be used to estimate the other.

The authors should be commended for performing Mantel-Haenszel DIF procedures to attempt to identify items biased against minorities and women. The analysis comparing the male and female samples is not faulted. However, not in keeping with the *Uniform Guidelines* (1978), they combined all the minority groups into a single pool. This ambiguous sample is unlikely to provide useful results. Furthermore, the small number of minorities involved (approximately 40) is too small to provide adequate generalizability. Finally, the authors report editing or eliminating items based upon these analyses in only very general ways; the test appears to be identical to the one pretested with this group. The results of these analyses are provided, but it is difficult to interpret them because no raw data are provided, only the results of the statistical significance tests.

The test publishers also present some advice regarding the setting of a passing score. It appears that they arbitrarily recommend the setting of a 70% standard for passing. At that point, 86% of their sample passed the test. The authors continue, stating "This means that if a department chose a 70% cutoff on each section of POST III, they might expect 86% of their applicants to pass" (Stanard & Associates, 1991, p. 27). This statement obviously is misleading; it asks test users to assume that their candidate population will be similar to the amorphous sample assembled by the publishers, a bad assumption. The authors proceed by suggesting that one can estimate the adverse impact ratio that one is likely to have in one's candidate population using their pretest sample. They employed the 4/5's rule found in the *Uniform Guidelines*. They report, "In general, 80% of the minority group should pass the selection procedure compared to the majority group . . . at a 70% cut-off score on each section of POST III, the ratio of the percentage of the Total Minority passing compared to the percentage of whites passing is 81%, therefore, no adverse impact occurs at this cutoff score" (Stanard & Associates, 1991, p. 28). Several criticisms of this statement are warranted. First, a negative impact indeed has occurred; it simply has not exceeded the 80% criterion mentioned in the *Uniform Guidelines* (1978). Second, this statement would appear frankly deceptive. They used the three-subtest POST III rather than the entire POST test. Had they used the entire test, the 80% figure would have been exceeded, although this index is found in tabular matter (Stanard & Associates, 1991, p. 35).

A criterion-related validation study also was performed using data from three settings, all in Iowa. The samples totaled only 123 individuals. The two larger groups who took the test were 67 recruits nearing the completion of their training at the Iowa law enforcement academy and 38 Department of Public Safety recruits near the completion of their training experience (Stanard & Associates, 1991, Appendix 2). The time that these two groups took the exam is not optimal; typically the test would be given prior to the onset of training. There would, therefore, be a time interval between the testing and the collection of the criterion measure. Such an interval could certainly lower the correlation by introducing "error variance" of various types. Furthermore, to the extent that training covers material both on the exam and in the criterion measure, it is likely to make individuals similar with respect to their two scores.

Another serious concern relates to their choice of a criterion measure—what they call a training score. They define this index as an "average cumulative score based on classroom and practical skills tests. An individual's average cumulative percent correct is used in determining success in training" (Stanard & Associates, 1991, Appendix 2). Clearly, trainability criteria are acceptable, but they are less relevant than measures of actual police job performance (Landy & Farr, 1983). It is much more important for a test to predict actual job success than success in training. Trainability criteria are much more likely to be predicted highly than on-the-job measures (Ghiselli, 1966).

ANALYTIC INFORMATION CONCERNING THE JOB ANALYSIS. The job analysis report appears both as an appendix to the test manual (Stanard & Associates, 1991) and as a stand-alone report (Stanard & Associates, Inc., 1990).

Stanard & Associates developed a job analysis questionnaire and administered it to representatives from some 1,000 police agencies. They attempted to make their sample representative by sending it to 20 police agencies of varying sizes from each of the 50 states. Such a strategy obviously overrepresents states with lower populations relative to populous states. Of these

1,000 surveys sent out, only 255 were returned, a low 25.5% return rate. No mention of follow-up procedures is made. It is also confusing that they report 28 responses from Iowa when only 20 questionnaires were supposed to be sent to each state. Only 75 of the 255 respondents reported they supervise day-to-day patrol activities and a number were training officers; the extent to which the respondents were informed about the nature of entry-level police work is questionable.

The job analysis questionnaire is flawed. It appears the test publisher used this questionnaire to justify the test that they had planned to build rather than to devise the test based upon the job analysis. In the first section of the job analysis, only three skill-related questions are asked of respondents. These three questions relate to "How important it is for patrol officers" (*a*) "to be able to read and interpret various types of reports," (*b*) "to possess good writing skills (legible writing, correct grammar, correct spelling," and (*c*) "to possess basic mathematical skills (addition, subtraction, multiplication, division)?" (manual, pp. 17-19). The second component of the job analysis questionnaire asked respondents to evaluate the criticality of approximately 200 tasks performed by police officers. A review of the results casts doubt on the validity of the selection. For example, only three "mathematically-oriented" job analysis tasks were seen as critical. These tasks are of the most minimal quantitative nature: diagramming crime and accident scenes, investigating traffic and off-road vehicle accidents, and administering roadside sobriety tests.

AN EVALUATION OF THIS INSTRUMENT. At the outset of this review, the test publisher's purpose for the instrument was provided: to screen for basic skills *required* in the field of law enforcement. Nothing that this writer has seen in the Stanard & Associates job analysis or elsewhere indicates that Mathematics skills (at least beyond simple addition), Grammar, and Spelling are required or even significant skills and abilities for police officers currently. Reading Comprehension is needed on the job. More information on how they set the reading level of police work at the 12th grade level would be useful, however. This test appears primarily to be a measure of educational background rather than one to assess cognitive skills required by police officers. As such, it is likely to lead to adverse impact against those groups underrepresented in advanced education and other advantages of society.

The reliability of the measure falls short of what is expected of a measure used to make important decisions affecting those who take it. The validity of the examination is probably primarily as a surrogate for educational background. The criterion-related validity study that was presented is faulted by only predicting a trainability criterion—one based upon other educationally oriented tests. Little content validation information is presented in the manual and the job analysis report. As part of the content validation effort, it would have been useful for the test authors to estimate the portion of the job that they assess with this measure. In this reviewer's opinion, that percentage would be low enough to limit the usefulness of the measure. Although the job analysis was inadequate, it was, nevertheless, a significant effort. It is, therefore, surprising that so little effort was made to match the critical job tasks with specific items and tests from the analysis. Too little information has been presented on how representatives of various minority groups perform on this examination. Much Title VII litigation has occurred in the past two decades related to police selection tests; to publish a new test for this purpose without such information appears misguided. To use it in an employment setting would be still more questionable.

REVIEWER'S REFERENCES

Ghiselli, E. E. (1966). *The validity of occupational aptitude tests*. New York: John Wiley & Sons.

Uniform Guidelines on Employee Selection Procedures. (1978). *Federal Register, 43*, No. 166, 38290-38309.

Landy, F. J., & Farr, J. L. (1983). *The measurement of work performance: Methods, theory, and applications*. Orlando, FL: Academic Press.

Fleishman, E. A., & Quaintance, M. K. (1984). *Taxonomies of human performance: The description of human tasks*. Orlando, FL: Academic Press.

Anastasi, A. (1988). *Psychological testing* (6th ed.). New York: Macmillan.

Stanard & Associates, Inc. (1990). *Job analysis report for the entry-level police tests*. Chicago: Stanard & Associates, Inc.

Stanard & Associates, Inc. (1991). *Report on the development and content validation of the National Police Officer Selection Test (POST)*. Chicago: Stanard & Associates, Inc.

[254]

NewGAP.

Purpose: Constructed to assess reading comprehension using Cloze technique.
Population: Grades 2–5.
Publication Date: 1990.
Scores: Total score only.
Administration: Group or individual.
Forms, 2: I, II.
Price Data, 1991: $45 per complete kit including 25 each Forms I/II, scoring template, and manual (39 pages); $22 per 50 test forms (25 each form); $5 per scoring template; $15 per manual; $15 per specimen set.
Time: 15(20) minutes.
Comments: "Norm-referenced."
Authors: John McLeod and Rita McLeod.
Publisher: Academic Therapy Publications.

Review of the NewGAP by TERRY A. ACKERMAN, Associate Professor of Educational Psychology, University of Illinois, Champaign, IL:

Historically, the NewGAP is an updated version of the GAP Test, which was originally developed in Australia in 1965 and later revised for use in Canada and the United Kingdom. Like its predecessors, the NewGAP is basically designed to measure the reading comprehension ability of students in grades 2 through

5 or older students suspected of having reading deficiency.

The NewGAP can be administered individually or to a group of students and has an administration time of 15 minutes. It employs the cloze technique (Taylor, 1953) in which examinees are given a passage with certain words missing and replaced with blanks. It is the task of the examinee to read through the text and determine which words are missing. However, for each blank there is only one *correct* word (and various misspellings thereof). (Examinees are specifically instructed not to worry about spelling.) The authors claim that for each blank, there is only one word that would capture the shade of meaning intended. Synonyms are counted as wrong responses. Such scoring is certainly debatable and may actually penalize students who are well read and have a large vocabulary. Practice examples are provided for examinees, but one wonders about how the cloze test format affects performance.

In the development process eight forms, each following a systematic pattern of word deletion, were pretested on 50 to 100 students in the 12th grade. No demographic information about the pretest group is presented. The decision as to which items would be deleted was based on the results of only the top 25 scorers. Words selected for deletion had to have been identified by 95% of the top scoring pretest examinees. The authors use an index of relative redundancy to help select which words to delete, but computation of this index is never explained.

Using the pretest results two final forms were created, each containing six passages, varying in length. The average number of words missing per passage is about 10. It would be helpful if the authors expanded upon the selection process for deciding the subject content for the passages. Likewise, some measure of the readability level of the passages seems to be warranted.

The technical manual provides several pages of technical information for the GAP test which is of no value for U.S. practitioners because it pertains to a different test than the NewGAP and results are based on data from Australia. Sadly, what information is provided about the NewGAP in the U.S. leaves a lot to be desired!

Raw scores can be converted to grade equivalent and reading age equivalent scores using norming tables. However, these tables have not been established using a nationally representative sample. Norms were established using 400 students in grades 2 through 5 in Marin County, California. Unfortunately, the manual does not describe how this pretest sample was chosen nor does it offer any demographic characteristics. This renders the norms table useless for any attempts to make valid comparisons (unless, of course, you live in Marin County).

Only corrected split-half reliability coefficients are provided for each form by grade. These range from .88 to .96 for Form 1 and from .93 to .97 for Form 2. Form 1 becomes increasingly less reliable with grade. No standard errors of measurement or evidence of internal consistency or stability are listed. Because there is a 15-minute time limit, the test may be speeded for some younger examinees. The authors do not comment on this, although if the test were speeded, the split-half coefficients would not be an appropriate measure of reliability.

Validation information is also quite sparse. Product-moment correlations between NewGAP results and CTBS Reading Comprehension scores are provided for each form by grade level. These correlations are corrected for attenuation and range from .77 to .85 for Form 1 and from .71 to.83 for Form 2. Ideally, uncorrected correlations should be reported with the respective reliabilities. If the test reliabilities were underestimated, attenuated correlations would be greatly inflated. No evidence of content validity or construct validity is discussed.

The technical manual also fails to provide any information concerning item bias. The authors need to demonstrate that the selected passages and the deleted words do not bias results against either gender or any ethnic group.

The paucity of technical information concerning the norming procedures, reliability, and validity of the NewGAP does not even meet the minimal criteria suggested in the *Standards for Educational and Psychological Testing* (AERA, APA, & NCME, 1985). Practitioners need such information to determine the quality of the instrument within their respective settings. Thus, I strongly urge practitioners to avoid the NewGAP until the authors provide more information about its quality.

REVIEWER'S REFERENCES

Taylor, W. L. (1953). "Cloze procedure". A new tool for measuring readability. *Journalism Quarterly*, *30*, 415-433.

American Educational Research Association, American Psychological Association, & National Council on Measurement in Education. (1985). *Standards for educational and psychological testing*. Washington, DC: American Psychological Association, Inc.

Review of the NewGAP by RUTH JOHNSON, Professor of Linguistics, Southern Illinois University at Carbondale, Carbondale, IL:

Citing reading as "the most important skill taught in schools" (manual, p. 1), the authors of the NewGAP present their battery of reading tests that utilize the cloze technique as testing comprehension as opposed to word recognition. The tests are also characterized as minimizing (*a*) interference of the test taker's flow of reading because most of the items deleted are function words (articles, pronouns, prepositions, and conjunctions); (*b*) not penalizing writing and spelling problems; and (*c*) ensuring that the test taker must be able to read contextual content words ("hard words," according to the test manual, p. 8) in order to complete the cloze.

Use of the cloze technique is justified based upon Taylor's (1953) experiment which showed a correlation between, on the one hand, scores on the cloze and scores on two recognized valid tests of reading comprehension and, on the other hand, the correlation between the comprehension tests themselves. The cloze itself as a reading test technique has been both highly praised and roundly criticized. One issue is the use of synonyms in scoring. Katz and Mullen (1981) concluded that cloze tests are valid measures of reading comprehension, with or without inclusion of synonyms in scoring, and that including synonyms in scoring did not increase construct validity. Green and Tomlinson (1983) found a high correlation between synonymic scoring and verbatim scoring. Another issue is the validity of the cloze. Shanahan and Kamil (1983) found that the cloze as a measure of reading comprehension had limited construct validity, which in turn slightly influenced its concurrent validity with other types of measures of comprehension. They stated that the cloze predicted best when within-sentence comprehension dominated and was less useful across sentence boundaries, a conclusion with which McKenna and Layton (1990) do not agree, stating that cloze scores reflect intersentential comprehension sufficiently to warrant continued use. The point of this is whether or not the NewGAP, as a cloze test, can be compared to reading tests that are of other types. If one accepts the concurrent validity of the cloze, the NewGAP authors offer statistics showing that their test correlates highly with, for example, the Comprehensive Test of Basic Skills (CTBS). The NewGAP also correlates with the Illinois Goal Assessment Program: Reading test.

The GAP was first developed for use in Australia, then Great Britain and Canada; the NewGAP was developed for the U.S. with completely different test items, using redundancy (meaning the deleted item is almost 100% unambiguous) and the proportion of fluent readers agreeing on the correct response. The NewGAP was standardized using data from tests administered to more than 400 students in grades 2–5 in California. The norming sample was divided into two samples matched for achievement in reading comprehension; each of the two forms of the NewGAP was normed on one matched, independent sample. Student performance on the NewGAP was compared with Stanford and CTBS scores to provide evidence of validity.

Reliabilities of the two forms were estimated by the split-half method, with Spearman-Brown correction. Reliabilities of the forms for grade 2 were .96 and .93; for grade 3, .93 and .97; for grade 4, .91 and .93; and for grade 5,.88 and .94, with the first figure for each grade representing the correlation for Form I and the second for Form II.

Validity of the NewGAP was estimated using product-moment correlation between NewGAP and CTBS Reading Comprehension scores, calculated for each grade level. For grade 2 the correlation was .81 and .83; for grade 3, .77 and .71; for grade 4, .85 and .76; and for grade 5, .84 and .80, with the first figure representing the correlation for Form I with CTBS and the second for Form II with CTBS.

The authors advise that "[g]reater reliability, and therefore greater validity may be obtained by administering both forms of NewGAP to the same students, e.g., on consecutive days" (p. 18). However, sometimes validity is a trade-off for reliability and vice versa (Brewer, personal communication, September 16, 1992); thus, one must decide whether or not one accepts the NewGAP claim because it is not explained further.

Norms are presented as Reading "Age Equivalents" and "Grade Equivalents"; no percentile rank equivalents are provided because, the authors state, "such implicit precision is not appropriate" (p. 18). The "achievement quotient," which is obtained by dividing the Reading Age Equivalent by the Actual Age, is defined as an approximate criterion for determining whether a student's reading comprehension achievement provides cause for concern and further diagnosis; the NewGAP is such an approximate criterion: A student whose reading achievement, as measured by the NewGAP, falls more than 15% below the norm is in need of individual diagnosis and help, according to the test manual.

The use of such a gatekeeper is justified because "[r]eading achievement . . . is less dependent on a specific curriculum [and] has a significant developmental component" (pp. 27–28); therefore, a student's reading ability can be translated into his or her "Reading Age." The authors caution about using grade equivalents to diagnose an individual due to insufficient consideration of age-within-grade effect. Grade equivalents are reliable measures of evaluation of the overall performance of classes or schools. Norm tables for each of the NewGAP forms (I and II) and for Forms I and II combined are provided as well as a table that includes cutoff scores for achievement/underachievement. This test is not a reliable measure for identifying gifted students because the only distinction made is for a student whose score falls below a set level. No interpretation of "exceptional" can be made if a student's score is very high. The test is best suited as a first screening for determining an individual's readiness for instruction at a particular level.

The test is straightforward in appearance and readily administered and scored. The results (test scores) are easily interpreted by teachers, curriculum planners, and parents. The test manuals are well written and easy to follow, providing clear directions for administration of the test.

REVIEWER'S REFERENCES

Taylor, W. L. (1953). "Cloze procedure": A new tool for measuring readability. *Journalism Quarterly*, *30*, 415-433.

Katz, I., & Mullen, T. P. (1981, October). *Construction and practicability of cloze procedures in diagnosis and establishing support programs in college reading.* Paper presented at the annual meeting of the Southwest Regional Conference of the International Reading Association, Tucson, AZ.

Green, D. R., & Tomlinson, M. (1983). The cloze procedure applied to a probability concepts test. *Journal of Research in Reading*, *6*(2), 103-118.

Shanahan, T., & Kamil, M. L. (1983, November). *Investigation of concurrent validity of cloze.* Paper presented at the annual meeting of the National Reading Conference, Austin, TX.

McKenna, M. C., & Layton, K. (1990). Concurrent validity of cloze as a measure of intersentential comprehension. *Journal of Educational Psychology*, *82*, 372-377.

[255]

NOCTI Teacher Occupational Competency Test: Child Care and Guidance.

Purpose: Designed to measure the individual's occupational competency in child care.

Population: Teachers and prospective teachers.

Publication Dates: 1988–90.

Scores, 12: 9 scores for Written part (Total and 8 subscores), 3 scores for Performance part (Process, Product, Total).

Parts, 2: Written, Performance.

Administration: Group.

Price Data: Price information available from publisher for test materials including Written test booklet ('88, 29 pages), Performance test booklet ('88, 10 pages), examiner's copy of Performance test ('88, 18 pages), manual for administering NOCTI TOCT Written tests ('94, 18 pages) and manual for administering NOCTI TOCT Performance tests ('94, 17 pages).

Time: (180) minutes for Written part; (240) minutes for Performance part.

Comments: Test administered at least twice a year at centers approved by publisher.

Author: National Occupational Competency Testing Institute.

Publisher: National Occupational Competency Testing Institute.

Cross References: For a review of the NOCTI program, see 8:1153 (6 references).

Review of the NOCTI Teacher Occupational Competency Test: Child Care and Guidance by PATRICIA B. KEITH, Assistant Professor of Psychology, Alfred University, Alfred, NY:

It is no surprise that the National Occupational Competency Testing Institute (NOCTI) has developed a vocational competency test that evaluates child care workers. For the last two decades social, economic, and political forces have influenced the structure of the American family. With the increase of single-parent and female-headed households and families shifting from one to two wage earners, it is obvious that there is a need for high quality child care providers.

NOCTI has developed a two-part test for child care and guidance workers (Test Code #081). The written portion includes 200 multiple-choice questions and is said to take 3 hours to complete. Test items measure child care service providers' knowledge about: infant-toddler, preschool, and young children's development and learning patterns (45% of the test); child and service provider behavioral interaction patterns (25% of the test items); health, safety, and Center management issues (25% of the test); and special needs (disability focus; 5% of the test). The content of many of the written test items appears to be more suited for a Center Administrator who has taken a number of courses in child development and administration, than for a child care service provider. The reading skill level of these questions is higher than one might also expect; many examinees may find the test difficult to complete. Additionally, the wording of stems and responses is awkward and could be easily misunderstood. Information about the scoring and interpretation of this portion of the test is not available.

The performance portion of the test requires a specially trained NOCTI evaluator to meet with the examinee for approximately 5 hours. During this period of time the examinee is required to: diaper a toddler, observe a toddler and write up a report, teach small and large groups of children, write daily lesson plans, and take part in examiner-examinee role play activities. The examinee is ranked on a 5-point scale (from extremely skilled worker to inept worker). The Performance portion of the test, although appearing to have suitable activities, appears excessively long. Furthermore, the use of the examiner as a role player and an evaluator of the activity may not be wise. I would have preferred the examiner function as an observer and have the examinee and another person perform the role-playing activities. Additionally, performance items the examiner does not think are applicable receive the highest rating (extremely skilled worker). A "not applicable" option would be appropriate for this portion of the test. The current scoring system may inflate the performance ranking of the child care provider.

NOCTI information about this test is limited and could lead one to question the integrity of the instrument. One NOCTI document shows means, standard deviations, and standard errors as percentages. No information is available about the norm group upon whom reliability coefficients were generated. Furthermore, different sample sizes (11, 27, 28, and 7) were used to calculate reliability coefficients for various portions of the test. Information about the validity of the instrument is not available. Available support materials, illustrating NOCTI's test development and revision procedures, are old and dated; it appears NOCTI is operating from a psychometric reference base of the mid 1970s.

Although there is a need to test child care service workers' knowledge and performance of duties, the NOCTI Child Care and Guidance test is not recommended. It is excessively long, does not have sufficient reliability, validity, and normative data, and requires a higher reading level, vocabulary, and knowledge base than may be appropriate for many child care workers.

Review of the NOCTI Teacher Occupational Competency Test: Child Care and Guidance by JEAN POWELL KIRNAN, Associate Professor of Psychology, Trenton State College, Trenton, NJ, and JENNIFER DeNICOLIS, Instructor, Temple University, Philadelphia, PA:

The National Occupational Competency Testing Institute (NOCTI) oversees the development and administration of competency tests for many different jobs and occupations such as plumbing, welding, auto mechanics, and architecture (Baldwin, 1978). Although the Child Care and Guidance test is a departure from the skilled trade tests traditionally sponsored by this organization, it is similar in format as it has both a paper-and-pencil knowledge component and a separate performance assessment. The publisher states the purpose of the instrument is to identify "competent workers" and should not be used to predict probabilities of success or aptitude to teach. The instrument may be used in certification or as a means of acquiring academic credit.

The performance section of the test is a collection of tasks that provide the examiner with the opportunity to judge the applicant's proficiency in caring for children. The materials required for these tasks are specified in the manual and must be prepared ahead of time in the child care facility where the applicant is tested. The following seven jobs constitute the performance component:

1. *Infant Diapering:* The applicant must successfully diaper an infant.

2. *Toddler Observation and Recording:* The applicant must observe a toddler for 20 minutes. After observing the toddler, the applicant must record information on the physical, intellectual, social, and emotional states of the child.

3. *Large Group Teaching:* Prior to the test date, the applicant must plan a teaching experience for more than eight children of preschool age that should include at least one story and one other activity. The examiner will observe the applicant carry out the lesson plan as well as review a written copy of the plan.

4. *Small Group Teaching:* Prior to the test date, the applicant must plan a teaching experience for a group of three to eight children. The examiner will observe the applicant carry out the lesson plan as well as review a written copy of the plan.

5. *Daily Program Plans:* The applicant is asked to prepare two full-day routines for two groups of children—infants and toddlers.

6. *Role Play Situation: Parent/Staff Relationship:* The examiner selects one role play from a group of four and observes how the applicant interacts with the individual chosen to play the part of a parent or staff member.

7. *Role Play Situation: Discipline:* The examiner selects one role play from a group of three and observes how the applicant interacts with the individual chosen to play the part of a child involved in a discipline situation.

The tasks assessed above represent a good variety of the skills and knowledge needed including safety, teaching, interpretation of behavior, and interaction with both children and adults. Although this breadth is a strength of the test, it is also a weakness. The length of time required for the performance component severely impacts on the utility of the instrument. According to the publisher, 240 minutes are required. This is in addition to the preparation time of the candidate.

Each of the seven tasks is scored by the examiner following the guidelines that appear on the scoring sheet provided by NOCTI. These guidelines provide for the scoring of "process" and "procedure" within each of the seven tasks. A rating scale of "A" through "E" is provided with maximum scores listed for each task. The subtasks are differentially weighted, which would seem reasonable. However, it is unclear how these weights were determined. Most disturbing is the instruction that if any one task is not applicable for the candidate, they are to receive an "A" rating. The potential for grossly exaggerated scores exists here. A different technique of proportional or other weighting scheme should be used.

The written portion of the Child Care and Guidance test assesses the candidate's knowledge of different areas of child care. The 200 multiple-choice items cover such areas as: Infant-Toddler Development, Infant-Toddler Learning, Preschool and Young Child Development, Preschool and Young Child Learning, Guiding Behavior, Health and Safety, Center Management, and Special Needs. As with the performance test, the written test is directed toward formal child care centers and not "in-home" care. This is apparent in two aspects: (*a*) reference in items to specific equipment (woodworking and housekeeping centers) and administrative issues (salary and physical set-up of a center); and (*b*) reliance on specific terminology such as the moro reflex or Maslow's hierarchy of needs. Individuals skilled in child care but who lack either experience in large care facilities or formal training may do poorly on the written test. The test is more suited to those facilities that require a good amount of education of their caregivers or training schools desirous of a cumulative knowledge exam.

Several items are developmental in nature and specify the age to be considered that is critical in determining the correct answer. However, not all items list age and this should be corrected. A few items contain ambiguous phrases (bursts of crying, group time) or the answers appear subjective (topics such as thumb-sucking). These should be modified to present clearer, more defensible questions. A few editing errors should be corrected.

The written test is designed for administration in a group setting in one of NOCTI's test centers. The instructional manual for the administration of NOCTI written tests contains tremendous detail and could serve as a model for any paper-and-pencil assessment. It includes materials needed, seating charts, verbatim instructions, and an irregularity report form.

Form A was provided for review. It is unclear if other forms exist or if retesting is allowed. This should be clarified as scores may increase with retesting.

The subscores and total score for both the written and performance measures are reported as percent correct by the candidate with corresponding center means and national means. Additionally, a candidate's total scores are depicted on a graph that places them relative to 68% of the center and national groups. It might be more meaningful to report the exact percentile that corresponds to each candidate's scores. Information is lacking regarding the center and national samples (i.e., sample size, age, experience level, educational level, geographic representation, date tested) that would aid in interpreting these scores. It is difficult to interpret the test scores meaningfully—indeed, at what score does one find the "competent worker" the instrument is intended to identify?

Personal communication with the publisher and supplemental materials received by these examiners shed some light on the construction, reliability, and validity of the instrument. This information should be fully documented in a technical manual available to all users.

Other NOCTI tests have reported small samples for reliability (Baldwin, 1978) and this remains a problem with the Child Care and Guidance test. Split-half coefficients were reported for the Written test as .89 (using KR-21) and .92 (using KR-20) utilizing a sample of 28. For the Performance test, alpha coefficients were reported separately for the process, product, and combined scores as .91, .91, and .96 based on a sample of 7. Again, no information was provided regarding the composition of the sample.

In constructing the instrument, over 150 critical competency areas were identified for the child care occupation. This would appear to have been done very carefully as the breadth and depth of the resulting 200 written items and the tasks in the performance test suggest a high level of content validity. However, detail on the number of people involved, who was involved, and actual techniques used (interview, observation, diary, etc.) should be cited.

Item analyses were conducted but relied on data from a sample of only 20 individuals. A committee of experts in the child care area revised items following this analysis and continues to review comments by examiners and examinees. Again, this suggests content validity in that a "panel of experts" is utilized in test development. More detail on the composition of this committee, and the actual tasks and procedures used should be provided. The instrument has clear face validity and appears quite content valid. A more detailed account of the steps in construction and ongoing validation would serve the users better than the informal documentation provided.

It would be helpful if the publisher would provide suggestions as to how one interprets the scores and combines them with each other and other selection information. One would certainly conduct an interview and reference checks prior to hiring child care givers and these data should be judged along with the results of this instrument.

Recent attempts at identifying selection tools in the child care field have concentrated on appropriate personality traits and the need to weed out individuals prone to abuse or neglect (Jones, Joy, & Martin, 1990; Mufson, 1986). The Child Care and Guidance test is unique in that it attempts to identify specific job knowledge and skills needed for proper child care.

In conclusion, the Child Care and Guidance test appears to make a unique contribution in the assessment of child caregivers. It is a thorough knowledge and performance measure aimed at a trained applicant population. The weaknesses of the instrument lie in the small sample sizes used in the reliability studies, the lack of formal documentation of the test's construction and psychometric properties, and the lack of clarity in score interpretation. These weaknesses can and should be addressed by the publisher.

REVIEWERS' REFERENCES

Baldwin, T. S. (1978). [Review of the National Occupational Competency Testing Program]. In O. K. Buros (Ed.), *The eighth mental measurements yearbook* (pp. 1732-1735). Highland Park, NJ: The Gryphon Press.

Mufson, D. W. (1986). Selecting child care workers for adolescents: The California Psychological Inventory. *Child Welfare, 65*, 83-88.

Jones, S. W., Joy, D. S., & Martin, S. L. (1990). A multidimensional approach for selecting child care workers. *Psychological Reports, 67*, 543-553.

[256]

NOCTI Teacher Occupational Competency Test: Mechanical Technology.

Purpose: Designed to measure the individual's occupational competency in mechanical technology.

Population: Teachers and prospective teachers.

Publication Dates: 1989–94.

Scores, 14: 11 scores for Written part (Total and 10 subscores), 3 scores for Performance part (Process, Product, Total).

Parts, 2: Written, Performance.
Administration: Group.
Price Data: Price information available from publisher for test materials including Written test booklet ('89, 23 pages), Performance test booklet ('89, 7 pages), examiner's copy of Performance test ('89, 16 pages), manual for administering NOCTI TOCT Written tests ('94, 18 pages) and manual for administering NOCTI TOCT Performance tests ('94, 17 pages).
Time: (180) minutes for Written part; (300) minutes for Performance part.
Comments: Test administered at least twice a year at centers approved by publisher.
Author: National Occupational Competency Testing Institute.
Publisher: National Occupational Competency Testing Institute.
Cross References: For a review of the NOCTI program, see 8:1153 (6 references).

Review of the NOCTI Teacher Occupational Competency Test: Mechanical Technology by BRUCE K. ALCORN, Director of Certification, Teachers College, Ball State University, Muncie, IN:

BACKGROUND. The Mechanical Technology Test (Form C) is part of a series of tests developed and administered by the National Occupational Competency Testing Institute (NOCTI) currently located at Ferris State University in Big Rapids, Michigan. The test series, also known as the NOCTI tests, were originally developed in 1973 through a U.S. Office of Education grant with the goal of developing objective measures of the technical competence of prospective teachers of industrial/technical education. Originally tests were developed for 23 major industrial occupations. Knowledge and skills are measured in each area with two separate instruments: a written test and a performance test. The tests are administered through controlled test centers located around the country and administered by Area Center Coordinators. These coordinators select and train the examiners for each of the occupational tests. The technical data (pertaining to norms and reliability) were published as part of the project's report for the U.S.O.E. grant in 1978. Although the industrial occupational education community seems to have accepted the content validity of the tests, it must be pointed out that the reliability data were based upon questionable sample sizes which ranged from 2 to 390 for individual tests. Subsequent reports appear to be absent from the public research literature. NOCTI exam development was positive in that actual performance measures were used in addition to paper-and-pencil tests. This feature, although positive, contributes to reliability problems that stem from questions about the standardization of performance test administration.

TECHNICAL TECHNOLOGY EXAM. This exam was originally developed for use only in Pennsylvania and the current form (C), published in 1989, is the result of a major revision also done specifically for Pennsylvania. The written test, lengthened to 180 items, measures knowledge in 10 areas deemed necessary for individuals teaching mechanical technology: Machine Shop, Mathematics, Metallurgy, Electricity, Strength of Materials, Fluid Mechanics, Thermodynamics, Computer, Physics, and Statics. The performance test measures skills by requiring the completion of seven "Jobs": Hydraulics, Computer Application, Electricity, Design, Strength of Materials, Machine Tool Operations, and Metallurgy. Both the process used and the product produced by the examinee are evaluated.

Two major questions must be raised about the NOCTI Mechanical Technology exam. First of all, reliability is still a question, if for no other reason than the small numbers of individuals who take this exam. The statistics for the original form were based upon a sample of only six and there is no reason to believe that this situation has improved much. In Indiana, for example, there are two separate license majors for industrial-related teaching assignments, one of which requires the passing of a National Teacher Exam Specialty Area exam and the other requires the passing of a NOCTI exam. Since 1985, when licensing exams were first required in Indiana, there have been less than a handful of teachers who have had to take a NOCTI exam and all of them have passed. Complicating matters is the difficulty of assuring standardization during the administration and scoring of the performance test. Not only is it difficult, if not impossible, to duplicate identically the test environment across test centers and from one administration to another, the scoring is very subjective. The process must be scored as it happens and it cannot be repeated once it happens. In addition, little guidance for scoring the performance test is contained in the manual. Therefore, the reliability and validity of the scoring is dependent to a large degree upon the thoroughness (or lack thereof) of the training of the examiners.

The second question that must be raised has to do with the content validity of the Mechanical Technology exam. Because it was developed and revised specifically for and in Pennsylvania, users in other states must analyze the knowledge and skills required by this exam to determine if it is applicable in their regions. Industrial/mechanical curricula across the nation are not standardized.

On the positive side, several issues should also be mentioned:

1. The measurement of occupational competency should include some performance measures and not rely solely upon paper-and-pencil tests. This exam does reach that objective.

2. Although the reliability of the test is questionable due to lack of sufficient data it has probably increased due to its increased length.

3. It probably has some content validity, at least in one state.

4. New norms are produced after each administration.

This test can be useful as long as the questions about reliability are taken into consideration and its content validity is acceptable to the user.

Review of the NOCTI Teacher Occupational Competency Test: Mechanical Technology by DAVID O. ANDERSON, Senior Measurement Statistician, Educational Testing Service, Princeton, NJ:

The NOCTI Teacher Occupational Competency Test: Mechanical Technology consists of a paper-and-pencil test and a performance test. The written test contains 180 four-option, multiple-choice questions covering the following content categories: Machine Shop (25 questions), Mathematics (25), Metallurgy (20), Electricity (20), Strength of Materials (15), Fluid Mechanics (15), Thermodynamics (15), Computer (15), Physics (15), and Statics (15). The performance test contains seven problem-solving tasks covering Hydraulics (estimated completion Time: 1 hour), Computer applications (45 minutes), Electricity (1 hour), Design (30 minutes), Strength of Materials (45 minutes), Machine Tool Operations (30 minutes), and Metallurgy (30 minutes). No time limit was stated for the written test; the performance test can be completed in approximately 5 hours. The multiple-choice answer sheet and performance rating form are sent to NOCTI for scoring and reporting.

The manuals accompanying the test booklets relate to both the written and performance tests and contain lists of materials and equipment needed for the tests, standardized administration directions, and solutions to the performance problems.

SCORING AND REPORTING. Responses to the multiple-choice questions are bubbled onto a General Purpose NCS Answer Sheet, which is then sent to NOCTI for scoring. No information is provided about the type and detail of written-test scores reported to score recipients.

Examinee performance on the problem-solving tasks is observed and then rated by the examiner for both process and product. Process assessment typically includes planning, method, accuracy, speed, and safety. Product assessment includes quality and completion of the task. The examiner awards several ratings for process and product for each task (the number of ratings varies across tasks). The alphabetic ratings range from A = extremely skilled worker to E = inept worker. The examiner is also asked to rate the examinee's overall performance and write a detailed overall impression of the examinee. This rating form is then sent to NOCTI for processing. At NOCTI these ratings are transformed into score points, with a total of 650 points available, 440 for Process and 210 for Product. Raw scores and percentage scores are computed for the examinee. Again, no information is provided about the type and detail of scores reported to score recipients.

VALIDITY AND RELIABILITY. The test materials appear to have face validity; however, no information is presented concerning job relevance, test development, suggested/required rater training, standardization of the rating scale, relationship between ratings and numeric scores, differential weighting of the content categories, establishment of regional or national norms, score interpretation, test-retest reliability, and criterion validity.

SUMMARY. This test could be an adequate device to measure teacher knowledge and competency on mechanical technology tasks; however, the lack of any technical information regarding job relevance, test development, score interpretation, and reliability data severely limits this test's usefulness.

[257]

NOCTI Teacher Occupational Competency Test: Microcomputer Repair.

Purpose: Designed to measure the individual's occupational competency in repairing microcomputers.
Population: Teachers and prospective teachers.
Publication Dates: 1988–94.
Scores, 15: 12 scores for Written part (Total and 11 subscores), 3 scores for Performance part (Process, Product, Total).
Parts, 2: Written, Performance.
Administration: Group.
Price Data: Price information available from publisher for test materials including Written test booklet ('93, 25 pages), Performance test booklet ('93, 26 pages), examiner's copy of Performance test ('93, 46 pages), manual for administering NOCTI TOCT Written tests ('94, 18 pages), and manual for administering NOCTI TOCT Performance tests ('94, 17 pages).
Time: (180) minutes for Written part; (250) minutes for Performance part.
Comments: Test administered at least twice a year at centers approved by publisher.
Author: National Occupational Competency Testing Institute.
Publisher: National Occupational Competency Testing Institute.
Cross References: For a review of the NOCTI program, see 8:1153 (6 references).

Review of the NOCTI Teacher Occupational Competency Test: Microcomputer Repair by KURT F. GEISINGER, Professor of Psychology and Dean, College of Arts and Sciences, State University of New York at Oswego, Oswego, NY:

This test is published by the National Occupational Competency Testing Institute (NOCTI) at Ferris State University and is one of the many certification examinations that they publish. Remarkably little documentation accompanies the test. A telephone call to the Coordinator of the Teacher Testing Services program at NOCTI indicated that the tests offered by this center are used to test teachers who provide instruction in vocational and technical educational programs. Among the areas covered by the NOCTI are appliance repair, brick masonry, cosmetology, and diesel engine repair. This particular test is used to assess teachers who teach skills for repairing microcomputers, obviously a rapidly changing and developing area. The test form is marked as Form A (1988); Form B (1993) is currently available, but was not available at the time of this review.

The test contains two parts: a Written test and a Performance test. The Written test is composed of 200 multiple-choice test questions. Examinees are allowed 3 hours to complete this examination. In advance of taking the examination, test takers are provided an informational page that describes the test plan. The eight areas covered on the test are each defined briefly and the percentages of the total test assigned to each of these areas are also provided. The areas and their percentage of the 200-item test follow: Safety, Hand Tools, D. C. Theory (17%); A.C. Theory (10%); Semiconductors (9%); Digital (12%); Flip Flops and Registers (6%); Encoders and Decoders, Counters, Multiplexer and Demultiplexer, A/D and D/A Converters (6%); Computer Maintenance—Fundamentals and Peripherals (25%); and Microprocessors (15%). Because no background information accompanies this test and there is no test manual, one cannot help wondering how these percentages were assigned to the eight areas. All 200 questions are of the multiple-choice variety and are grouped by their subdomain in the actual printing of the test (e.g., the 30 microprocessor questions are grouped together on the test under this heading). Many of the questions employ diagrams and graphs. They do not appear to require an unnecessarily high level of reading ability. The test is in the English language.

The 1988 Form A Performance test is composed of 10 "jobs." Four of these are required of all examinees and the remaining six subtests are grouped in three pairings; the test administrator selects one of the two from each pair. Thus, the examinee will take a total of seven subtests. (Only one criterion is provided for examiners to employ in deciding which of the subtests from each pair to select—which of the pieces of equipment they have at the testing center.) The four required tests include (*a*) construction of an RC controlled clock circuit, measuring pulse amplitude, pulse frequency, pulse width, and rise time using an oscilloscope; (*b*) determination of the value of an unknown inductor using specified equipment and components; (*c*) drawing, construction, and evaluation of a full wave bridge rectifier power supply; and (*d*) troubleshooting peripherals. The three pairs of performance subtests appear to relate to (*a*) gates (NAND and digital), (*b*) troubleshooting defective converter circuits, and (*c*) testing semiconductor or transistor amplifier circuits. Considerable electrical equipment is required by a testing center in order to administer the examination. A precise scoring key is provided in the examiner copy of the Performance Test. This key appears to be carefully developed; however, application of some of the rules would appear to require additional elaboration of the rules, which is not available in the documentation.

ANALYTIC INFORMATION. Remarkably little research has been reported by the test publishers. A telephone call to the test publisher yielded a small table that contained some summary information regarding the Written test; no information was then available for the Performance test. The paltry information provided by NOCTI includes a listing of the number of individuals who have taken the Written test, the mean of their Written test scores, the percentage equivalent for the mean, the standard deviation, the standard error of the mean (a generally useless piece of information in this instance), the Kuder-Richardson 20 and 21 (KR-20 and KR-21, respectively) estimates of internal consistency, and the standard error of the measure.

Only 11 individuals had taken the examination by the time its data were analyzed. The mean of the test was approximately 122.2 raw score points, or about 61% of the total possible. No information is provided as to whether scaling is employed to convert the raw scores to some index other than the percentages.

The KR-20 index of reliability is .835, an acceptable index, but one that is somewhat low for a 200-item multiple-choice test. The KR-21 index of .707 is rather low relative to the KR-20, indicating that there is a considerable range in terms of item difficulties of the items composing the test.

AN EVALUATION OF THIS INSTRUMENT. It is nearly impossible to evaluate an instrument about which so little information has been provided. Only 11 individuals were reported to have taken the Written portion of the test and it appears that only 7 took the Performance test at the time of the printing of the NOCTI information. Whether a test should be published and/or sold when only 11 individuals have taken the test is a dilemma that should have been faced by the test publisher and author. One can have little confidence in either the mean or the reliability coefficient for this reason.

That many of the items are dated may be one reason that the test has been used so infrequently. Any review of the items by one knowledgeable in microcomputers would quickly recognize the dated quality of the examination. For example, one item on the Written test asks information regarding the quality of print from different printers, but laser printers are not an option. Another question addresses single-sided 5.25-inch floppy disks, a technology that has largely disappeared. Test developers who build tests that ambitiously assess quickly changing domains either face the challenge of updating their instruments frequently or offering an examination that does not reflect current developments. In the case of this test, it may assess certain basic concepts and principles that are important to microcomputer repair; its specifics are certainly questionable, however.

The information provided by NOCTI is so paltry that it justifies the consideration of this test instrument in the general category of teacher-made tests rather than professionally developed tests. That only 11 individuals have taken the instrument and no validation information exists, yet it is available for use, places it in the category of teacher-made tests that are essentially unstudied at the time of their release. The basis supporting the use of the test is apparently content validity. Information as to whether a job analysis was performed, how percentages were assigned to each area of the test domain, and so on, should be addressed before the test is used. The test has been so infrequently administered since its copyright date of 1988, that one must question whether it even has a market to justify its use.

Review of the NOCTI Teacher Occupational Competency Test: Microcomputer Repair by DAVID O. HERMAN, Associate Education Officer, Office of Educational Research, New York City Board of Education, Brooklyn, NY:

The National Occupational Competency Testing Institute, or NOCTI, has developed and published assessments of occupational competence in nearly 60 areas, at a level of difficulty suitable for screening prospective teachers or granting credit toward degree programs. All of the assessments contain a written and a performance component and share other similarities in terms of the procedures used to develop them and monitor their use. The tests are prepared by committees of experts working with job-analysis data. The tests are published without norms or other psychometric data, which are developed only later on the basis of accumulated examinee records.

An overall review of the NOCTI program, referenced above, presents what appears to be a fair assessment of its strengths and weaknesses. The review is still much to the point, even though it dates from 1978. It should be required reading for anyone interested in using the tests today.

The Written test in Microcomputer Repair contains 200 four-choice objective questions that cover the field broadly, from safety and basic electronics to microprocessors and the servicing of hardware. The time limit is a generous 3 hours. Scores are reported as the percentage of items answered correctly within each of 11 subsections, as well as for the test as a whole. The score reports present normative data in the form of means and standard deviations of these percentage scores for whatever test records are in NOCTI's files at the time. No cut scores or other interpretive guidelines are offered.

The Performance test consists of 10 diagnosis and repair tasks that may vary from one testing site to another according to the equipment available locally. The total time permitted varies from 270 to 305 minutes, depending on which tasks are chosen. Performance of each task is scored by giving multiple ratings for Process (technique, use of materials, logic of procedures, checking completed work, and so forth), and for Product (correctness of diagnosis, accuracy of results, completeness of repair, and the like). A 5-point scale is used for each rating, and ranges from A (exceptionally competent worker) to E (incompetent worker). The examiners who assign the ratings are required to be experienced practitioners in the field, and properly so. All the same, the scale points are "unanchored" and may connote different levels of accomplishment to different raters.

The ratings are assigned numerical weights according to a scheme that impresses me as rational but complicated. The weighted ratings are summed to give a total numerical rating for each task that reflects both Process and Product. Score reports express the total rating for each task as a percentage of the maximum possible rating obtainable for that task. The reports also show analogous percentage figures for the total of all "product" ratings across all tasks, and for the grand total of all the ratings. As with the Written test, normative data are given on the score reports as means and standard deviations of these percentage scores. As is true of the Written test, users of the Performance test must decide for themselves how to interpret an individual's scores.

It was noted earlier that these NOCTI assessments are developed without the benefits of item analysis. Such analyses are carried out whenever sufficient data accumulate from the field. Form B of the Microcomputer Repair Test, which is the form under review, has a copyright date of 1993, and replaces Form A. Useful item and test data have not yet been gathered for Form B, for which recent norms were based on results from only six examinees (P. E. Rupe, personal communication, June 16, 1994). The norms issue, cited in reviews of other NOCTI instruments, is especially critical for tests that are infrequently used, as this one seems to be. This is because of the length of time that users must wait until a reasonable sample has accumulated for the generation of meaningful norms.

Because of the lack of formal item analysis, it is likely that the multiple-choice portion of the assessment includes material, as yet undetected, that is psychometrically marginal. (For starters, there are at least five very easy questions that novices in the world of computers should be able to answer correctly at sight. What place do these have on a test for selecting prospective teachers of microcomputer repair?)

The scope of the Written test appears both comprehensive and fair. The questions impress me as carefully worded and edited. The test itself has been clearly reproduced. The diagrams are generally easy to read, although the labels in two of them would benefit from larger lettering. The list of keyed options for the 200 multiple-choice questions reveals a preference for one of the response positions, and at one point in the test nine consecutive items are keyed for this response. Minor flaws like these should be easy to correct in future editions.

The coverage of the Performance test likewise seems adequate for its purpose. The principal criticism here is that scores obtained from different testing sites may not be fully comparable because the tasks presented will sometimes be different, and because some raters will be systematically more lenient or severe than others. NOCTI does make it a practice to study the test results from different sites to identify examiner effects of this kind, but obviously cannot do this until there are sufficient records on file (J. Bullington, personal communication, September 20, 1994).

In January 1991, NOCTI published KR-20 reliability estimates for 48 NOCTI Written tests; they varied from .72 to .97 (but 13 of the samples had 20 cases or fewer). For what it is worth, the reliability coefficient of Form A of the microcomputer repair test was given as .84 for a group of 11 examinees.

As far as one can tell, the reliability of the Performance part of the microcomputer repair test has not been studied. Granted, there are problems in estimating the internal consistency of a test whose content may shift. Within a single testing site, though, it should be feasible at least to study the relationship between ratings given to the same performance by two independent raters, and the results would be of interest. Much remains to be done to establish the measurement characteristics of this test, and to explore the kinds of generalizations one may reasonably make from its scores.

In summary, NOCTI gets good marks for its efforts to ensure the content validity of this test of microcomputer repair. On the other hand, the lack of meaningful norms for well-defined groups of examinees severely compromises the test's usefulness. Until they are provided, users must estimate for themselves what constitutes adequate performance. To be fair, examinees who receive very low percentage scores on both parts of the test almost certainly lack the knowledge and skill that teachers in the field need, and those with very high percentage scores probably have the needed grounding in knowledge and practice. But the scores of most examinees will be less extreme, and their meaning will be unclear. The reliability of the instrument must be taken on faith.

The test appears to have no direct competition.

[258]

Non-Reading Intelligence Tests, Levels 1–3.

Purpose: Measures "aspects of language and thinking that are not fully represented in the earlier stages of learning in reading and mathematics."
Population: Ages 6-4 to 8-3, 7-4 to 9-3, 8-4 to 10-11.
Publication Dates: 1989–92.
Acronym: NRIT.
Scores, 5: Total score for each of four subtests (A, B, C, D), Grand Total.
Administration: Group.
Levels: 3 overlapping levels.
Price Data, 1994: £5.99 per specimen set including manual ('89, 48 pages) and one copy each of the three test forms; £5.50 per manual; £3.99 per 20 Level 1 test sheets; £3.99 per 20 Level 2 or Level 3 test sheets; £5.50 per marking template.
Time: (60) minutes for Levels 1 and 2; (45–60) minutes for Level 3.
Comments: Incorporates the Non-Readers Intelligence Test (9:811) as Level 1 and the Oral Verbal Intelligence Test (8:197) as Level 3, along with a new intermediate test as Level 2.
Author: Dennis Young.
Publisher: Hodder & Stoughton Educational [England].
Cross References: See T4:1816 (1 reference). For a review by A. E. G. Pilliner of the Oral Verbal Intelligence Test, see 8:197; for reviews by Calvin O. Dyer and Steven I. Pfeiffer of the Non-Readers Intelligence Test, Third Edition, see 9:811.

Review of the Non-Reading Intelligence Tests, Levels 1–3 by CAROLE M. KRAUTHAMER, Assistant Professor of Psychology, Trenton State College, Trenton, NJ:

The Non-Reading Intelligence Tests (NRIT) is designed to collect a large array of information concerning school children's ability and experience. The NRIT author suggests the tests correct teachers' judgments, which he presumes are too strongly influenced by knowledge of the children's attainments. Additionally the Non-Reading Intelligence Tests distinguish themselves by offering to shed a new light on children for whom other intelligence tests would merely confirm teacher expectations. According to the NRIT manual the tests' oral administration and nonreading features permit poor readers at each of its three age levels to score better than on traditional measures of intelligence.

In addition to serious deficits in terms of evidence to support the tests' validity and reliability, the items appear inappropriate for any audience, but especially an American audience. English-speaking children, unfamiliar with the tests' language bias will be at a loss if their teachers administer the NRIT as an intelligence test, instead of as an example of a British vocabulary test.

The Non-Reading Intelligence Test was developed in three levels purportedly to assess intellectual capacity or intelligence in children in three age groups. The means and standard deviations for total test scores and subtest scores are not stated, nor is the range of raw scores obtained by the normative groups. The subjects used as normative are not described in detail and this absence of demographics makes comparability to similar age and/or grade groups in the United States and elsewhere not warranted or possible.

According to the manual, the tests have been successful in labeling children with "'specific learning difficulties', 'specific reading difficulties', 'specific reading retardation', etc." (p. 6). There are no definitions of these terms, nor is there any effort to establish how the Non-Reading Intelligence Tests manages to diagnose reading problems. Reliability for the total test scores was estimated in different ways, using both internal consistency and different forms. However, data were not given to verify the different forms were, indeed, alternate forms. Although the alternate forms are said to be described in more detail in previous material, these data should be described in this manual; no rationale for using different forms in estimating reliability is stated in this manual. The presentation to clarify the concepts of reliability and validity is not clearly presented. The text and the tables described in the text are not arranged for optimal clarity; for example, for the data in Table 6, the correlations are derived from data where quotients were used instead of raw scores; this procedure has the possibility of inflating the magnitude of the correlations. The use of quotients instead of raw scores is not fully justified by the author and remains unclear.

In summary, the true benefits of this test as an intelligence test are not apparent. Little information is provided regarding the criteria for selection of the items; no information is given with respect to criteria for inclusion of the content selected by the author. No linguistic modifications are recommended by the tests' author. Although written in the tradition of the intelligence movement, the NRIT does not help teachers or children with respect to the assessment of intelligence.

Review of the Non-Reading Intelligence Tests, Levels 1–3 by ESTHER E. DIAMOND, Educational and Psychological Consultant, Evanston, IL:

The Non-Reading Intelligence Tests (NRIT), Levels 1–3, were designed to help teachers in the primary grades to sample a wide background of a child's experience and ability, thereby making it possible to correct assessments of children that have been strongly influenced by the teacher's knowledge of their attainments. Intelligence test results, the author maintains, tend to confirm the teacher's judgments of a child's general ability, but potentially are most useful when they differ from the teacher's expectations, casting new light on the child.

The rationale for these nonverbal tests and their oral administration is that poor readers do poorly on tests that require reading, making it difficult to interpret the results clearly. Levels 1 to 3 of the NRIT now incorporate the original Non-Readers Intelligence Test, which has become Level 1 and restandardizd for use with infants and children in the first term of the junior school. NRIT Level 2 is a new intermediate level, suggested for use with children in the second and third terms and the first term of the second junior year. The original Oral Verbal Intelligence Test is now incorporated as NRIT Level 3, suggested for use from the beginning of the second term of the second junior year to the end of the third year for classes of normal ability range, as well as with children of less than average intelligence to age 13–11.

Standardization of all three tests is based on test results of the same schools over the period 1983 to 1986, thus eliminating one possible cause of differences between quotients. Schools were selected to be representative of national rather than local standards. Gender differences are minimal and, according to the author, "negligible for practical purposes" (p. 40). A 4-year follow-up of 75 children who had scored below 20 as infants found that children with scores below 14 had extreme learning difficulties over the next 4 years.

The NRIT is to be used for early identification of children who might have special educational needs (e.g., children with specific learning difficulties, specific reading retardation, or specific reading difficulties). These are judgments, says the author, that teachers often make on their own when a child is not performing as well as expected based on knowledge of his or her ability. Suspected underachievement, it is suggested, can be checked by comparing NRIT results with attainment quotients, using a table in the manual designed to help the teacher quantify the extent of underachievement.

The tests provide intelligence quotients for three chronological age groups: Level 1, for ages 6-4 to 8-3; Level 2, for ages 7-4 to 9-3; and Level 3, for ages 8-4 to 10-11 and ages 11-0 to 13-11. However, just why the tests can be considered intelligence tests and the IQs yielded can be considered measures of children's intelligence is never fully supported on a psychometric or a theoretical or conceptual basis. There is a brief reference to the "mutual dependence of language and thinking," and to "a higher correlation between language/thinking as measured by the NRIT tests and language in the reading mode" (p. 6). Nor is there any indication of awareness of the issues surrounding IQ measurement in the last two decades and that, especially in the United States, use of reported IQ in making educational (and employment) decisions about people has fallen from grace.

NRIT Level 1 contains four subtests: finding an object from a brief, orally read puzzle-like description of four objects; finding an object that is unlike the others in a group of four; analogies; and opposites. There is no explanation as to how or why these particular content areas were chosen. With guidance from the teacher/administrator, the children record their responses on a sheet on which the numbers of the items and the four letter options for each item appear. The administration instructions seem to be fairly straightforward, but the manual contains a startling admonition to the teacher: "Given this degree of care, a child's failure to follow the instructions can be taken as evidence of very low general ability and the urgent need for further investigation" (p. 7).

Levels 2 and 3 also have four subtests each: identifying an object presented orally as a puzzle; identifying the object that is not in the same category as the other three; analogies; and opposites. Items appear to be devoid of anything that might prove offensive to various groups. They might even prove to be fun or challenging or interesting to the children responding to them. The analogy items seem a bit difficult for young children, and tests like the Scholastic Aptitude Tests (T4:2351) are reconsidering their use, even with college-entrance students. Items written by the author were pretested by groups of 120 J1, J2, J3, and J4 children. Items were placed in order of relative difficulty and unsatisfactory distracters were eliminated. A provisional full test was then tried out with at least 1,100 children in groups J2 and J3 and standardized on a temporary basis. Percentages of success at each ability level were then found for samples of 50 papers each with total scores corresponding on the average to quotients of 75, 85, 100, 115, and 125 at age 9.2. Percentages were then adjusted for chance and each item graphed to show the facility level and discriminatory power. Intercorrelations between the subtests of Level 1 and Level 3 ranged from .59 to .72 for Level 1 and .54 to .70 for Level 3. In answer to the suggestion the subtesters might be testing the same factors, the manual author responds that even if that could be demonstrated there would still be justification for the four subtests because the various breaks in administration "all help to renew and sustain the children's interest to the end of testing" (p. 38).

How conflicts are resolved when more than one alternative can be supported as a right answer fits the NRIT conception of intelligence. Using as an example an item that asks for the alternative that is different from sparrow, plane, helicopter, and glider, the manual author points out that half of the 7-year-olds chose "sparrow" and the most intelligent infants, those with IQs about 130, chose "sparrow" 99 times out of 100. The reason they gave was the sparrow is alive, distinguishing it from the inanimate alternative choices. This is interpreted as a reflection of the children's "superior structure of meanings" (p. 39), the ability to recognize structural relations between categories. According to the manual, children who fail the item have a concept of sparrow that is more superficial and less integrated into wider categories. Instead of relying mainly on deduction, the author asserts the NRIT items ask questions in which the *meanings* of the words are essential to determining the correct answer. Furthermore, early NRIT quotients are increasingly correlated with later language achievement as tested by reading—implied as evidence of construct validity.

As principal evidence of validity, concurrent correlations with the Verbal sections of the Wechsler Intelligence Scale for Children (WISC) and with the Stanford Binet are cited. Additional evidence includes correlations with other tests, among them the Moray House Pictures Test, the English Picture Vocabulary Test, and Raven's Coloured Progressive Matrices. The .86 correlation with the Moray House Pictures Test reflects the basic similarity of the tasks ("i.e., the emphasis on perceiving and applying relationships"), according to the manual. Correlations with reading tests range from .69 to .80. Users are cautioned the validity data may be somewhat questionable because some of the items have been modified over time, but that nevertheless the data would "retain relevance as strong evidence of the validity of this *type* of test" (p. 42). Evidence is also offered of NRIT Level 1 and 2 as predictors of future mathematics and reading attainment.

Reliability data are reported as standard errors of measurement. Two-thirds of the IQs of top infants and first-term juniors fall within 4 points of the true quotients and within 3.5 points by J3. In general, then, 19 of 20 quotients can be expected to fall within 7 or 8 points of the true quotients. Evidence of stability and equivalence is also presented in the form of correlations, ranging from .79 to.85, between NRIT test quotients after one or more year intervals.

In summary, the NRIT fails to establish that it is a measure of intelligence. Psychometric or theoretical/conceptual support is missing. It does not, as claimed in the manual, measure a wide range of abilities. For example, math ability, which might have been measured pictorially, is not measured. Information about test construction and the rationale underlying the choice to tap the four areas tested is scant and scattered, with ambiguous references to early editions and other sources. The sections on validity and reliability are similarly vague and difficult to ferret out. The manual contains a table of critical attainment quotients at which and below which the worst achieving 5% of children will be found if the correlation between attainment and intelligence is below .58. Providing accompanying percentiles would have been helpful.

A better choice is the Test of Nonverbal Intelligence, Second Edition (TONI-2; 11:439), designed as a language-free measure to assess general intelligence through a series of abstract figural problem-solving items for children and adults, including aphasics and people with impaired linguistic skills. The TONI-2 serves much the same purpose as the NRIT purports and might be used in research with the NRIT or as a substitute until the NRIT has overcome many of the current criticisms. In the meantime, the NRIT should be used only as an experimental measure.

[259]

Non-Verbal Ability Tests.

Purpose: Designed to measure perceptual, conceptual, attention/concentration, and memory skills.
Population: Ages 8 and over.
Publication Dates: 1982–86.
Acronym: NAT.
Scores, 19: Matching Shape, Matching Direction, Categorization, Picture Completion, Embedded Figures, Figure Formation, Mazes, Sequencing, Picture Arrangement, Visual Search, Simple Key Test, Complex Key Test, Code Tracking I, Code Tracking II, Visual Recognition, Auditory Recognition, Auditory Recall, Visual Recall, Total.
Administration: Group or individual.
Price Data: Not available.
Time: (80–110) minutes.
Author: Helga A. H. Rowe.
Publisher: Australian Council for Educational Research Ltd. [Australia].
[The publisher advised in January 1994 that this test is now out of print—Ed.]

Review of the Non-Verbal Ability Tests by ROBERT F. McMORRIS, Professor of Educational Psychology and Statistics, State University of New York at Albany, Albany, NY:

Some ability tests come with toys. The Non-Verbal Ability Tests (NAT) does not. The first piece to emerge from the pouch containing the test, manuals, and keys was an almost 300-page book *Language-Free Evaluation of Cognitive Development*. Perhaps a self-evaluation for the user, as well as for the reviewer, is to comprehend enough of this book and the accompanying test and manual to decide whether to select the test, and, if so, to be able to interpret the results professionally. The book, then, becomes a verbal test for use of a nonverbal test.

THE TEST. The NAT has 18 subtests categorized on factor loadings into four categories, specifically: perceptual, conceptual, attention/concentration, and memory. The author considers the four memory tests optional, so the number of subtests could be shaved to 14. Minutes per subtest ranges from 1 to 15, with 2 minutes the mode. The author estimates total testing time for the first 14 subtests as about 70 minutes (for 12–13-year-olds) plus 25 to 40 minutes for the optional memory tests.

Some of the subtests are more intriguing, memorable, or potentially problematic than others. For example, Test #3 (Categorization) contains five pictures per item. The test taker is expected to infer the category and select the picture not included in the category. Not everyone will interpret the pictures and categories the same way. For example, a practice item presumably has the category of fruit, with the odd picture being a car, but if the test taker considers the car a lemon, no option may appear appropriate. More likely confusion would include classifying 5C as a domestic cat, where the category could be wild animals versus domestic, or as a panther, where the category could be felines versus the primate. Similarly, an individual might have trouble determining the identity of 12E, which would make the item rather difficult.

Test #4 (Picture Completion) contains 20 pictures, each with a missing part to be drawn in by the test taker. With only 3 minutes, the test taker had better seek the most obvious omission and sketch it very quickly. The tidy or compulsive need not apply. (Perhaps the game Pictionary would be good for coaching.) To illustrate, #2 would be better conceptualized as a cube than as a desk, and the picture in #4 would benefit from a door, another window, or chimney smoke, but the test taker would benefit from making a quick decision and quick execution. At least three items (11, 15, and 20) have cultural limitations.

Test #5 (Embedded Figures) involves the test taker tracing over the embedded figure in each of the three pictures per item. Often the figures are changed in direction, sometimes changed in size, and at least one seems to be missing altogether (#15). Such changing of direction and size would appear to make more formidable the task of responding to 22 items with three pictures each (i.e., 66 pictures) in the 6 minutes available. (How realistic is the task of locating the figure and tracing it in 5–6 seconds on the average?)

Especially if the (optional) memory subtests are to be given, the test administrator encounters some special demands in preparing for and conducting the testing. In addition to several booklets and stimulus materials, he or she will need a projector, transparencies, a cassette player, and two audio tapes. Some of the subtests (e.g., Auditory Recall and Auditory Recognition) would be particularly difficult to monitor in a group format, insuring students were keeping pace with the cassette and responding in the correct places on the record sheets.

NORMS. According to the author (technical supplement, pp. 2, 6), the test has not been normed. Nevertheless, she has provided scaled scores (mean = 100, standard deviation = 10) for each subtest, plus a form for displaying the scores graphically, plus procedures for summing those scores to obtain category and total scores. Further, she has provided a table for converting scaled scores to percentile ranks and stanines and has specified NAT scores corresponding to descriptive categories of Borderline, Deficient, and so on. The 14 age groups on which these scaled scores are based tended to be small and only slightly described.

RELIABILITY. Test-retest coefficients for the total score were provided based on four ethnic groups, with *n*s from 13 to 22. A 4-week interval was specified. Groups were at least as variable as "normal," that is, these groups had standard deviations ranging from 10 to 20, where the standard deviation for the score scale was set at 10. Means for three groups were about a standard deviation above the scale mean of 100, and had coefficients in the .70s; the mean for the remaining group on the first testing was about two standard deviations below the 100 but the group was so heterogeneous that the coefficient was .90. No further description of the groups (e.g., age, location, occupation) was given.

Kuder-Richardson 20s were also provided for 13 of the subtests. No description of the group on which these coefficients were based was included. Similarly, standard errors of measurement (*SEM*s) were given for the subtests, but with no group description. If the coefficients were based on the total group over the vast span of ages, the reliability estimates would likely be inflated, and, if those coefficients were used to estimate *SEM*s, the resulting intervals would likely be too small. No KR20s or *SEM*s are given for the total score or the four categories (e.g., conceptual).

A profile is provided with up to 18 subtests and four category scores. The reliability section, however, contains no mention of profile reliability or reliability of differences. Intercorrelations may be found (Tables B1–B3) albeit based on ill-defined and often tiny groups. Other sets of intercorrelations are given in Tables 12.4 to 12.7 in the book. (Chapter 11 in the book contains relevant discussion of profiles, and will be considered in the next section of the review.) The test user is urged to consider a dilemma: To what extent is this a single-construct test whose subtests measure *g*, and to what extent is any of the subtest reliability sufficiently independent of other subtests to encourage interpretation of a profile? Such a dilemma faces authors and interpreters alike for questions of reliability and validity.

VALIDITY. First, I have a question and a caution concerning nonverbal and language-free tests. Does the language-free or even nonverbal approach provide for more culture-fair testing? Obviously, the question is more profound than the accompanying response, but we note that determinants of behavior in cultures and the myriad of subcultures are so varied and subtle that a test taker may miss an item for reasons of which the interpreter may be unaware. (See Anastasi, 1988, pp. 359–360 for a brief discussion.) As with testing more generally, it tends to be easier and safer to interpret a successful rather than an unsuccessful performance.

Some information on criterion-related validity is provided. Summary is difficult given varied results with often small and only slightly described samples.

Rowe (the test author), in the accompanying book, has provided considerable and helpful information on intelligence, testing, and factor analysis. The very extensive reference list is limited, however, not only by the publication date (1986) but by containing few references later than 1982. The treatment of validity is at times atypical (e.g., "Construct validity is probably the most sophisticated form of content validity" [p. 136]), at times antiquated (e.g., referring to empirical and content validities), and at times modern, as when the use of the test for designing interventions is urged (e.g., "purposes [of assessment] . . . include the design of intervention procedures to meet individuals' needs that have been identified by means of testing" [p. 221]).

Given the construct validity orientation of this book, test users are not surprisingly assumed to be grounded in testing, basic statistics, cognition, and developmental psychology, as noted on the first page of the book. Emphasis on factor analysis is also consistent with the construct validity orientation. Principal component analyses were done for a large sample (ages 5 to 17+), for various smaller samples defined by age, and for retarded adult and aboriginal groups. (Recall this test is Australian.) Three-, four-, or five-factor solutions were judged most appropriate depending on the group. The first factor, *g*, ordinarily accounted for 30–40% of the variance, and, for each analysis, each test had a positive loading on the first factor.

Does performance relate to age? The author discusses the decline of scores with age found for those of us old enough to vote. She also includes two tables with correlations of subscores with age, with only the Mazes test showing negative correlation with age (*r*s = -.10 in one table and -.11 in the other). The mean correlations are .25 in one table and .27 in the other. Presumably the coefficients are based on individuals in the ages 5 to 17+ used for the large-sample factor analysis, but this reviewer has been unable to verify the source. Such correlations would appear reasonable for such a sample. Note, however, these correlations of subscores with age underline the danger of interpreting a factor analysis or a correlation matrix based on such an age-diverse sample. If the resulting variability in scores is excessive, the correlations in general would likely be exaggerated and misleading, as may be the statement that the first factor in the total-group factor analysis accounts for 49% of the variance. And any interpretation for the total group would be further confounded if the factor structure evolves over the age span tested.

This reviewer examined two sets of illustrative correlations to study further the relationships within age groups and comparison with the total group, specifically by looking at the correlations between two perceptual subtests (1 and 2) and between a perceptual and a conceptual subtest (1 and 5). For the 12 groups (age 7 through age 18+), median correlations for the subgroups by age were very close to the total-group correlations, that is, *r*s = .40 versus .38 for subtests 1 and 2, and .26 versus .25 for subtests 1 and 5. Admittedly, then, the expected exaggeration in the total-group correlations did not occur in these illustrations. There is some support for the subtest clusterings: Two perceptual tests agreed more with each other than one of them did with a conceptual test. The variability of the correlations is considerable, however; *r*s for subtests 1 with 2 range from .25 to .72, and *r*s for 1 with 5 range from -.23 to .74.

Given this instability among the correlations, interpreting a profile of scores becomes difficult at best. The manual contains directions on how to plot scaled scores for the subtests and the statement:

> The advantage of a NAT profile is that it provides a graphic representation of the candidate's strengths and weaknesses as indicated by his or her performance on the NAT subtests. However, caution is required in interpreting small differences between scaled scores obtained in any of the subtests.
>
> Chapter 11 of the monograph *Language-Free Evaluation of Cognitive Development* (Rowe, 1985) discusses this in detail. (p. 9; Note: Rowe [1985] should be Rowe [1986])

The discussion of profiles is indeed detailed, and three tables are provided that at first seem to be admirable steps toward considering profile reliability and construct validity issues. Given the serious concerns raised previously in this review regarding norms and reliability, however, the numbers are likely built on sand. To illustrate, the normative base necessary for the intended comparisons across scales has eluded the developer.

ALTERNATIVE TESTS. Among alternative tests to consider would be parts of the Stanford-Binet Intelligence Scale, Fourth Edition (T4:2553) and the Wechsler (T4:2937, T4:2938, T4:2939, T4:2940, and T4:2941) tests, where the norms and reliability data are more complete and supportive, and going beyond the manuals, considerable validity data may be found. Potential users of ability tests are urged to consult Sattler (1988).

IN SUMMARY. The NAT is quite an endeavor, with considerable thought, energy, and research going into its development. The research to support its interpretation is uneven, however, with considerable attention paid to theory and construct validity, including diagnostic suggestions, but with severe limitations in norms, reliability data, and even some of the validity data. For this reviewer, the acronym NAT could also be considered to indicate "Not Appropriate at this Time."

REVIEWER'S REFERENCES

Anastasi, A. (1988). *Psychological testing* (6th ed.). New York: Macmillan.
Sattler, J. M. (1988). *Assessment of children* (3rd ed.). San Diego: Jerome M. Sattler.

Review of the Non-Verbal Ability Tests by DOUGLAS K. SMITH, Professor of School Psychology, University of Wisconsin-River Falls, River Falls, WI:

The Non-Verbal Ability Tests (NAT) is a nonverbal, group-administered ability test. Subtests are organized into four areas: perceptual skills (Matching Shape, Matching Directions); conceptual skills (Categorization, Picture Completion, Embedded Figures, Figure Formation, Mazes, Sequencing, Picture Arrangement); attention/concentration (Visual Search, Simple Key Test, Complex Key Test, Code Tracking I, Code Tracking II); and memory (Visual Recognition, Auditory Recognition, Auditory Recall, Visual Recall). Practice items are provided for each subtest. Subtests with the exception of the memory subtests are timed (limits of 1 to 15 minutes). Subtest stimuli consist of drawings of geometric shapes, familiar objects, abstract designs, and mazes. The memory subtests are optional and use stimuli presented by overhead projector or cassette recorder. Their scores are not included in the overall NAT score. Instructions for subtest administration are clear and concise.

The theoretical bases of the NAT include the following premises: (*a*) individuals with similar levels of measured intelligence display varying patterns of cognitive strengths and weaknesses; (*b*) intellectual ability depends on the efficiency of the individual's information-processing capacity; and (*c*) intelligence is malleable. Thus, the NAT is a profile battery with an information-processing focus designed to provide both quantitative and qualitative information. The theoretical basis of the battery and of individual subtests is provided in the monograph, *Language-Free Evaluation of Cognitive Development*.

Although raw scores can be converted to scale scores, the NAT has not been normed. Scale scores are "based on the performance of 1135 individuals of different ages and background" (manual, p. 6). This sample consisted of students (ages 5 and older) in schools of New South Wales, Northern Territory, Victoria, and Queensland and adults from South Australia and Victoria. "'Gifted children' and institutionalized retarded adults" (p. 6) were also included in the sample. Major language groups represented included English, Greek, Italian, Spanish (Europe and South

America), Turkish, and Vietnamese. Additional details about the sample are not provided.

Raw scores are converted into scaled scores using tables arranged by 1-year age levels from 5 years to 18 years/adult. These scaled scores were generated for each subtest and age level by converting the raw scores into z-scores. The scaled score distribution for each subtest and age level was based on a mean of 100, standard deviation of 10.

Four groups of students (English, Greek, Italian, and Turkish) ages 12 to 16 years and ranging in group size from 13 to 22 were tested and retested after a 4-week interval. Test-retest reliability coefficients ranged from .71 to .90 for the subtests. Internal consistency estimates using the Kuder-Richardson formula 20 procedure ranged from .51 to .99 for the subtests with an average reliability estimate of .81 and a median estimate of .83.

Validity of the NAT was examined in a number of ways. The extensive data provide by the author in the monograph support the content/construct validity of the NAT. Factor analytic data support the presence of a general ability factor along with conceptual and perceptual factors. The attention factor emerged in five of the nine age group analyses. Concurrent validity of the NAT was examined by comparing scores on the NAT to other measures of ability such as the Wechsler Intelligence Scale for Children—Revised (WISC-R) with correlations in the low to moderate range (.19 to .59). Concurrent validity data are limited.

Although many technical aspects of the NAT are discussed in the NAT manual, technical supplement, and monograph, several issues remain to be addressed. Qualification of examiners, for example, are not indicated. Although profile analysis is recommended as an approach to interpreting test results, the NAT has not been normed so the reference group is the 1,135 individuals utilized in developing scaled scores. Detailed selection procedures for the 1,135 individuals in the reference group are not provided. Similarly, little information is provided on the try-out phase of the instrument.

The NAT appears to have strong face validity and to be a well-conceived measure of nonverbal ability. Unfortunately, the lack of norming severely limits the usefulness of the instrument. The lack of a normative base precludes the battery from being used in many assessment situations and relegates it to use in research settings. Although the NAT may well be a valid measure of nonverbal ability, this is speculative pending successful norming and standardization. The instrument does have potential and it is recommended that it be standardized.

[260]

Norris Educational Achievement Test.

Purpose: Designed to assess educational ability.
Publication Dates: 1991–92.
Acronym: NEAT.
Administration: Individual.
Forms, 2: A, B.
Price Data, 1995: $120 per complete kit including 10 test booklets, administration and scoring manual ('92, 234 pages), and technical manual ('92, 86 pages); $34.50 per 25 test booklets (select Form A or B); $65 per administration and scoring manual; $42.50 per technical manual.
Authors: Janet Switzer and Christian P. Gruber (manuals).
Publisher: Western Psychological Services.

a) READINESS.
Population: Ages 4-0 to 6-11.
Scores, 4: Fine Motor Coordination, Math Concepts, Letter, Total.
Time: (10–15) minutes.

b) ACHIEVEMENT.
Population: Ages 6-0 to 17-11.
Scores, 4–6: Word Recognition, Spelling, Arithmetic, Total plus 2 supplemental scores (Oral Reading and Comprehension, Written Language).
Time: (20–30) minutes for basic battery; (30–40) minutes for entire battery.

Review of the Norris Educational Achievement Test by A. HARRY PASSOW, Professor Emeritus of Education, Teachers College, Columbia University, New York, NY:

The Norris Educational Achievement Test (NEAT) is a set of individually administered tests intended to assist teachers, psychologists, and others in assessing a child's skills. The NEAT is also intended to teach changes in children's skills over time and to assist providers in making student placement decisions.

The NEAT consists of a standard battery of three achievement tests, two supplemental achievement tests, and a standard battery of three readiness tests, each in two forms. The author states the three NEAT Achievement tests "can be administered in under 30 minutes" (technical manual, p. 1) although two are untimed and 10 minutes are allowed for the third.

The three NEAT Achievement tests—Word Recognition, Spelling, and Arithmetic—provide an Overall Achievement composite scale. Two supplemental achievement tests, Oral Reading and Comprehension and Written Language, assess a student's ability to read aloud and recall material from a short passage and to write a brief expressive essay.

Tests of Fine Motor Coordination, Math Concepts, and Letters provide an Overall Readiness composite scale, intended to furnish a validated prediction of achievement skills. Norms are provided for both NEAT Readiness and NEAT Achievement for the sixth year (first grade) to enable adequate assessment, regardless of the child's level of functioning and the time of the year the test is administered.

The author states the format and standardization make the test appropriate for use with students ranging from prekindergarten (4 years old) to 12th grade (17 years, 11 months). In addition, the author suggests the test can be used with adults, although no adult norms were collected. The NEAT Readiness test can be used with students through age 6; the NEAT Achievement tests with 6-year-olds and up.

The "Introduction" to the 201+-page administration and scoring manual is intended for experienced NEAT users because "only brief instructions and the minimum information necessary for everyday use by those familiar with the NEAT" (manual, p. 1) are provided. Testers are referred to two chapters in the technical manual that furnish more extensive instructions for administering the tests. All first-time users are urged to read those chapters and all users are advised to review those materials periodically to ensure maintenance of standard testing procedures.

The administrative and scoring manual contains complete, step-by-step instructions for administering the tests—the materials needed, the directions to be given the student, the time allowed, actions to be taken, and all other necessary information. Detailed instructions for scoring each item of each of the tests are furnished. These directions and guidelines are sufficiently detailed so that the tester should have no difficulty administering and scoring the tests following standard procedures.

Norms are available for the NEAT Achievement tests by age and by grade. All tests are also normed to provide a standard score. Tables are provided for converting raw scores to standard scores.

The standardization sample and normative study are described in adequate detail. The NEAT was normed on a national sample of over 2,920 students, ranging in age from 4 years 0 months to 17 years 11 months and from prekindergarten to grade 12 and stratified by geographic region, ethnicity, parental education level, community type, and sex.

Statistical data presented by form, test, and age group indicate high internal consistency of both the NEAT Achievement and Readiness tests. Test-retest and form equivalence reliabilities are both high. Based on the analyses of concurrent validity (NEAT versus the WRAT-R [Wide Range Achievement Test—Revised] and the WISC-R [Wechsler Intelligence Scale for Children—Revised]) and construct validity, the NEAT has acceptable test validity. All correlations with the WRAT-R and the WISC-R are reported as significant at $p<.01$ or less.

The author asserts the NEAT Written Language test "employs a new and extensively developed approach to assessing students' writing skills" (p. 53), a holistic rating rather than the more conventional atomistic alternatives. The rationale, the design, normative and technical information, as well as reliability and validity data are presented to explain the development of the Written Language scales.

Efforts were made to avoid bias toward minority populations, particularly Blacks and Hispanics, by item analyses during test construction and inspection of test factor structures. The structural similarity of the NEAT Achievement test is reported as virtually identical for three ethnic groups—Whites, Blacks, and Hispanics with all correlations significant at $p<.01$ or less.

The Norris Educational Achievement Test is a relatively new test and there appear to be no reports of experience with or research regarding its use. The test seems to meet a need for a test of educational achievement that can be administered individually to a student for diagnosis and placement. The descriptive information and data in the technical manual suggest that it is well designed, tests important aspects of student basic skills, and is competently normed.

Review of the Norris Educational Achievement Test by MICHAEL S. TREVISAN, Assistant Professor of Educational Leadership and Counseling Psychology, Washington State University, Pullman, WA:

The Norris Educational Achievement Test (NEAT) "is a set of individually administered tests of educational ability" (technical manual, p. 1). It consists of a battery of achievement tests, two supplemental achievement tests, and a battery of "readiness" tests. The three achievement tests measure Word Recognition, Spelling, and Mathematics. The two supplemental tests measure Oral Reading and Comprehension, and Written Language. The readiness tests measure Fine Motor Coordination, Math Concepts, and Letters. Composite scores are available for both test batteries. Parallel forms exist for each. This is a new product, first being marketed in 1992.

NORMING. The tests are designed to be administered to students ages 4 years to 17 years and 11 months. The norming sample is based on 1,517 students taking Form A and 1,403 students taking Form B, both spanning the aforementioned age range. The sample was stratified by geographic region, ethnicity, parental educational level, community type, and sex. The adequacy of the sample sizes obtained for standardization of the NEAT are tenuous. The authors did attempt to realign the agreement between this sample and the U.S. population characteristics through corrective weights obtained through statistical analyses. This was done after data collection but before norms were created. Still, the artificial nature of this approach is suspect. Standard scores with a mean of 100 and a standard deviation of 15 are available, as well as age and grade norms. An excellent description of the strengths and limitations of the age and grade norms is provided in the technical manual. Interpretive categories based on standard score cutoffs are provided, which may prove useful when discussing a child's test results with her or his parents. Another feature of the NEAT is the provision to test adults. Although the test was not normed with adults, there are special directions and cautions should the need arise for testing of this type.

ADMINISTRATION AND SCORING. The authors recommend using the readiness tests for ages 4 years 0 months to 5 years 11 months. For students 6 years 0 months to 6 years 11 months, either the readiness tests or the achievement tests may be administered depending on the student. Guidelines are presented for this situation. For 7 years 0 months and older the achievement tests are to be given. The directions for administration are clear and easy to understand. Guidelines for establishing basal and ceiling scores are provided. The achievement battery can be administered in less than 30 minutes and the readiness test can be done in 10 to 15 minutes. All materials needed for test administration are supplied with purchase.

RELIABILITY. Reliability estimates for all portions of the NEAT are generally excellent. The internal consistency reliability coefficients range from a low of .81 to a high of .99 depending on the age and subtest. This is true for both forms. The readiness tests have internal consistency estimates ranging from .59–.96 with most coefficients at the high end of this range. These estimates are high, given the often unpredictable nature of childrens' behavior in a testing situation. Test-retest and alternate forms reliability estimates are also provided ranging in the .70s to .90s. All estimates are nicely tabled corresponding to subtest and form. In addition, the proper reliability evidence for the scoring of the writing assessment is provided. Because writing assessment is based on observation and judgment, additional reliability evidence over and above what is typically necessary for traditional forms of assessment is required. To this end, reliability evidence concerning rater consistency is presented. The authors have done a fine job of establishing the writing tasks and scoring criteria, enhancing the credibility and reliability of the assessment.

VALIDITY. Herein lies one of the critical weaknesses of this test. By title, the authors state the test to be an achievement test. Validity evidence for an achievement test must in part be content validity. It is not clear in any detail what the NEAT actually measures. Subtest titles like Word Recognition, Spelling, or Mathematics, for example, are not sufficient content validity evidence. Information concerning the objectives assessed is essential. On the other hand, if this is truly an ability test as the authors also claim, then evidence of predictive validity is necessary. Key decisions regarding students, especially whether or not a student will receive special education services, are often made in part with information provided from ability tests. Validity evidence must be provided to warrant these important decisions. Given the brief nature of this test and the time demands in schools and clinics, use of the NEAT will be enticing for educators and clinicians, despite the lack of validity evidence. Many may justify its use as a screening tool. However, there is no validity evidence to justify this use either. The authors have provided other validity evidence, such as correlations with the Wide Range Achievement Test (WRAT-R). These range from the .70s to .90s depending on the subtest. This is evidence that the NEAT and WRAT-R are measuring the same thing. That being the case, it would be possible to determine some content validity by inferring from the WRAT-R what the NEAT is measuring. However, it has never been entirely clear what the WRAT-R actually measures. There is some evidence of construct validity for the NEAT. Perhaps the most notable for the practitioner is the existence of an appropriate developmental trend. This is a necessary but not sufficient condition for construct validity, however (Anastasi, 1988). In short, validity is the Achilles Heel of the NEAT.

USEFULNESS. As a brief measure of educational ability (achievement?), the NEAT is clearly competing with the WRAT-R. The addition of a supplemental measure of expressive writing is a significant plus for the NEAT, considering the national push toward performance assessments. This addition may provide a complex, rich assessment of writing, often difficult to obtain with traditional forms of assessment and not found on the WRAT-R.

The authors wish to market this assessment for clinical purposes, especially to meet the needs of special educators who must qualify children for special education services under the constraints of measurement models adopted by states to meet the P.L. 94-142 mandate. The authors of the NEAT have conducted the necessary psychometric research to provide the interpretive information for three of these models. The first is the determination of statistically significant differences between standard scores of tests within the achievement or readiness battery. Significance levels of .10, .05, and .01 are provided. A statistically significant difference between the Mathematics and Word Recognition subtest, for example, is partial evidence for a learning disability in mathematics if the Mathematics standard score is much lower than the Word Recognition standard score. A second method supplied with the NEAT and widely used is the reliability-based standard error of measurement (*SEM*) method. The need for special education services is often defined as a significant discrepancy between an aptitude and an achievement measure. Differences between the NEAT and the WISC-R (Wechsler Intelligence Scale for Children—Revised), WISC-III, and Stanford-Binet Intelligence Scale are provided in *SEM* units and the aforementioned significance levels. The third method supplied with the NEAT is the regression method, and has been recommended as the method of choice (Reynolds, 1984/1985). This model takes into account the regression of aptitude on achievement. The authors have also supplied quality instructions for each method. The interpretative information on these three methods is a benefit the NEAT provides, that the WRAT-R does not. This psychometric addition is an advancement toward sound placement of children in special education programs.

CONCERNS. Although some controversy exists concerning the distinction between ability and achievement tests, some differentiation can be obtained by considering the stated purpose of a test and the validity evidence provided (Sax, 1989). As previously mentioned, the authors have not made this distinction by explanation or through validity evidence. The authors of the NEAT describe the tests as measures of educational ability but educational achievement is stated in the title. This contradiction will cause confusion among consumers and become a disservice to the educational community.

Another problem with the language describing these tests is the notion of a readiness test. There is mounting evidence that readiness tests are extremely inaccurate and based on inappropriate assumptions about child development (Shepard & Smith, 1986). At best a readiness test indicates where children need academic help as they enter and progress through school. Unfortunately, readiness tests are used as gatekeepers preventing children who do not score well enough from entering school. Readiness tests currently on the market have classification error rates approaching 50%. The authors of the NEAT have not provided any evidence regarding error rates associated with classifying students as ready or not ready. Another readiness test option for districts may serve to reinforce faulty testing policy.

SUMMARY. Given the brief nature of this test and the psychometric information needed to assist in the decision of whether or not to give special education services to children, the NEAT will probably be widely used and enjoy a large market share. It is recommended that a distinction be made concerning whether this test is an ability or achievement test and appropriate validity evidence be garnered. Also, a readiness test may do a disservice to consumers and potentially to children if, in fact, it is used as such. Although tremendous effort and skill is demonstrated by the authors in the technical manual regarding the norming of the NEAT, the adequacy of the sample sizes are suspect. Despite these shortcomings, the NEAT has the potential to become a solid alternative for educators, especially regarding special education placement decisions. Much of the work done to develop this test is truly an advancement over competing tests. Users of this test should be cautious, however. There is much psychometric work yet to be done.

REVIEWER'S REFERENCES

Reynolds, C. R. (1984/1985). Critical measurement issues in learning disabilities. *Journal of Special Education, 18*, 451-476.

Shepard, L. A., & Smith, M. L. (1986). Synthesis of research on school readiness and kindergarten retention. *Educational Leadership, 44*(3), 78-86.

Anastasi, A. (1988). *Psychological testing* (6th ed.). New York: Macmillan.

Sax, G. (1989). *Principles of educational and psychological measurement and evaluation* (3rd ed.). Belmont, CA: Wadsworth Pub. Co.

[261]

NPF [Second Edition].

Purpose: "To assess stress tolerance and overall adjustment."

Population: Ages 16–adult.

Publication Dates: 1955–92.

Acronym: NPF.

Scores, 3: Validity Scores (Uncertainty, Good Impression), Total Adjustment.

Administration: Group.

Price Data, 1994: $14 per specimen set including manual ('92, 10 pages), 3 test booklets, and scoring key; $21 per 20 test booklets; $10 per manual.

Time: (5–10) minutes.

Comments: Previously listed as a subtest of the Employee Attitude Series of the Job-Tests Program (T3:1219).

Author: Samuel E. Krug.

Publisher: Industrial Psychology International Ltd.

Review of the NPF [Neurotic Personality Factor, Second Edition] by CHARLES D. CLAIBORN, Professor, Division of Psychology in Education, Arizona State University, Tempe, AZ:

The second edition of the NPF, released in 1992, is a revised version of the 1955 edition. The language of items has been modified in a more contemporary direction, the response format has been simplified so that it is the same for each item, and the scoring has been changed to include only True and False, and not Uncertain, responses. Still, the second edition, like the first, is a puzzling instrument.

The puzzles begin with the name and purpose of the instrument. What does "NPF" stand for? The manual for the second edition does not say. What construct is measured by the instrument? According to the manual, the NPF measures "stress tolerance and overall adjustment" (p. 1), but this is not a satisfactory answer. For one thing, stress tolerance and overall adjustment are (at least) two constructs, yet the NPF yields only one score (leaving aside the validity scores). Furthermore, neither construct is defined. What does stress mean here? What kind of tolerance? Adjustment to what? No meaningful framework is given, theoretical or empirical, within which we can find answers to these questions. Thus, the relation of these constructs to particular domains of behavior or experience is unclear. This, in turn, makes inquiry into the construct validity of the instrument difficult.

The purpose of the NPF is also puzzling. The manual indicates that its possible uses include "job selection, career counseling, or understanding an individual's social orientation" (p. 1), but there is no description of its application in any of these areas. With respect to job selection, the instrument is put forth in the manual as an adjunct to ability measures, because "there are aspects of job performance that lie beyond the capacity of ability tests to predict" (p. 7). No support is given for this assertion, however plausible it may seem, and in any case, there is little indication of how the NPF might improve predictions in job performance. What few data there are on this question (reported on page 4 of the manual) are based on small samples and relate NPF scores to ratings of workers on a variety of characteristics, from leadership ability to cooperativeness.

In conclusion, we must remain skeptical of an instrument for which conceptual underpinnings and intended uses are so vague and untested. The NPF may be a fine measure of some personality construct, but we do not know what that construct is. The NPF may contribute importantly to job selection, over and above ability measures, but that remains to be seen.

Review of the NPF [Neurotic Personality Factor, Second Edition] by HOWARD M. KNOFF, Professor of School Psychology, Department of Psychological Foundations, University of South Florida, Tampa, FL:

The Neurotic Personality Factor (NPF) is a 40-item self-report scale developed "to assess the stress tolerance and overall adjustment" (p. 1) of adolescents and adults from 16 years of age and older. Organized with 34 items comprising the primary (or raw score) scale and six items comprising the Good Impression scale (one of the NPF's validity scales), the NPF's author claims that this tool can be used when assessments of stress tolerance and overall adjustment are necessary "for job selection, career counseling, or understanding an individual's social orientation" (manual, p. 1). The NPF recently has been updated and revalidated using 331 university undergraduates and 569 high school seniors. The NPF now has a readability level of between the 4th and the 7th grade (depending on the readability formula used), and it comes with a 10-page manual that details its development and psychometric properties.

Based on a review of the tool and its manual, the NPF has a number of psychometric and practical problems that preclude its use either in research (other than to improve or demonstrate its utility) or in the field. Among the most significant problems are the lack of (*a*) a sound norming group and process, (*b*) any type of construct validity, and (*c*) data reflecting test-retest reliability; and (*d*) the test's dependence on an unsupported use of Item Response Theory in the development of its stanine and percentile scores. There also is a great deal of critical information missing from the NPF manual such that it must be considered incomplete in its present form.

Beyond these broad concerns, a list of other problems with the NPF would have to include the following:

1. Nowhere in the manual or on the test forms is the NPF identified by name. Thus, there is no explanation as to why its given name, the Neurotic Personality Factor, is inconsistent with its stated goal of assessing stress tolerance and overall adjustment. Further, the author never defines "stress tolerance" nor "overall adjustment," thus the operationalized construct that the NPF purports to measure is unknown.

2. Nowhere in the manual is there a clear description of how the test items were updated and validated from a content (and other) validity perspective. No construct validity (via factor analysis) data are presented to demonstrate that the NPF items are measuring a single construct of personality, and thus, no item-to-factor correlations are reported to support the inclusion of the 34 items. In addition, no description concerning the selection of the six Good Impression items is offered, and again, there are no validity data provided to demonstrate that the Good Impression scale is truly a validity scale that measures and does what the author suggests.

3. Relative to scoring, the author states that a raw score of 6 on the Good Impression scale and more than 19 "Uncertain" responses on the total scale invalidates the NPF for an individual respondent. Yet, no data either from the new norming samples or from other clinical studies are presented to validate these assertions. Further, the author provides, without research or empirical verification, a number of style- and personality-oriented hypotheses (e.g., defensiveness, confusion, lack of cooperation) to explain the presence of more than 16 "uncertain" responses.

4. The NPF's updated norming process involved 331 university undergraduates and 569 high school seniors. Once again, there is virtually no demographic information on these students. For example, for the university sample, the manual reports no information on the geographic location of the university, the number of males and females, the students' ages and what year in college they were, the students' socioeconomic levels (SES) and Grade Point Averages (GPAs), and their racial distributions. For the high school sample, geographic, SES, mental health status, and GPA information was missing.

Significantly, it appears that the final NPF norms were derived from the high school sample of 569 seniors (manual, pp. 8–9). Given this, it must be demonstrated that the NPF norms can be generalized to other high school students across the country and other (adult) age groups. Further, it must be demonstrated that the construct of stress tolerance and adjustment purportedly assessed by the NPF is stable, once again, across the geographic and age boundaries of the new norms.

5. Beyond the information gaps in the norming sample, the statistical approach used to generate the new NPF norms appears questionable. According to the author, the simplest Item Response Theory (IRT) approach, a one-parameter Rasch model, which typically is used for ability measures, can be used to norm personality assessment tools. In using this model, it is assumed that each NPF item can be rated according to how much behavioral stability it describes, and that "(a)n item that describes very stable behavior . . . is much more likely to be endorsed by a highly adjusted person than a poorly adjusted person" (p. 9). Unfortunately, previous research studies using the Rasch model in this way are not cited, nor does the manual provide the statistical proof, through convergent and discriminant validity studies, of the relationship between the NPF items and stable behavior.

The manual does use the high school norming sample in some undefined way to generate an "IRT calibration" of the NPF items, and it concludes that the items do demonstrate their ability to predict stable versus unstable individuals. The author then transforms these calibration data into percentile norms that approximate a normal curve. Once again, it must be noted that the NPF norms are based on the high school senior sample, and that the percentile and stanines are derived from an untested (or, at least, unsupported) use of Item Response Theory.

6. Using the norms derived, the manual provides interpretive descriptions for each of the nine stanines (and corresponding percentile ranges). No information on how these descriptions were generated is provided, and no independent concurrent, convergent, or discriminant validity studies are reported.

7. Finally, the Psychometric Properties section of the NPF manual reports only internal consistency data for reliability, two studies that correlated the NPF with job performance ratings, and one concurrent validity study using the Adult Personality Inventory, another personality assessment tool developed by the NPF's author. The reliability and concurrent validity studies used the high school and university norming samples, respectively, whereas the two job performance studies appeared to be unpublished and provided no demographic data and no information on how the job performance ratings were obtained.

In summary, as a personality assessment tool, the NPF will have to address and resolve its many flaws before it can be comfortably used either for research or clinical practice. The lack of construct validity and factor analytic data is significant as there is no proof that the test measures what it purports to measure. Even though the norms are "updated," the absence of a random, stratified standardization sample spanning the ages advertised by the NPF is notable. Finally, the NPF manual is missing so much information and so many assumptions are reflected in the norming, scoring, and interpretation process, that one can only warn "the buyer to beware."

[262]

Nurse Aide Practice Test.

Purpose: Constructed "to assist nurse aides in preparing for the nurse aide competency evaluation, to inform candidates of their areas of strengths and weaknesses, and to assist with inservice curriculum planning."
Population: Nurse aides.
Publication Date: 1989.
Scores, 6: Basic Nursing Skills, Basic Restorative Services, Mental Health/Social Service Needs, Personal Care Skills, Resident Rights, Total.
Administration: Group.
Price Data, 1994: $30 per 10 test booklets.
Time: 90(95) minutes.
Author: The National Council of State Boards of Nursing, Inc.
Publisher: The Psychological Corporation.

Review of the Nurse Aide Practice Test by MICHAEL B. BUNCH, Vice President, Measurement Incorporated, Durham, NC:

The Nurse Aide Practice Test was developed by the National Council of State Boards of Nursing partly in response to the Nursing Home Reform Act of 1987. The act requires persons employed as nurse aides after July 1, 1989 to enroll in a nurse aide training program and then successfully complete a competency evaluation. Since passage of the act, several different evaluations have appeared. The Nurse Aide Practice Test, designed to measure the content of the federal curriculum guidelines from the Health Care Financing Administration, is intended to serve as a training tool for individuals preparing to take examinations supposedly on these same guidelines.

The Directions for Administering describe the background of the test and provide a verbatim script for test administrators to follow. The script permits the administrator to simulate a testing environment that should be close to that of the competency evaluation. This document contains a scoring key (subdivided into the five content areas listed above), appendices for converting number correct to percent correct, a sample individual score report, and a group summary report. All scoring is done by hand.

The test booklet contains simple instructions, two practice questions, 75 content questions, and a sample score report that the examinee or administrator completes. The relationships between individual test items and the associated content areas as described in the administration manual are generally quite clear.

To their credit, the authors note in the opening paragraph of the administration manual that the practice test is not intended to predict whether or not any candidate will pass any particular evaluation. Rather, the test is supposed to expose candidates to test content and instill self-confidence. These modest claims seem reasonable. It should be up to local administrators to determine whether the practice test has any practical value in helping candidates perform well on evaluations. These administrators would be well advised to examine the content of the practice test carefully to make sure its content does indeed match that of the local version of the evaluation and to interview test takers to determine whether or not the practice test instills self-confidence and actually helps in preparing for the evaluation. The authors could perform a great service by providing guidelines.

Review of the Nurse Aide Practice Test by JIM C. FORTUNE, Professor of Research and Evaluation, and ABBOT PACKARD, Research Assistant, Virginia Tech University, Blacksburg, VA:

INTRODUCTION AND GENERAL DESCRIPTION. When is a test not a test? That question becomes the prime consideration in the review of the Nurse Aide Practice Test. The test is designed like a test except for its lack of supporting information, yet the test is not designed to be used as a test. Instead, the test is to be used as a study preparation for the Nurse Aide Competency Evaluation (NACE). The design encompasses five main content areas of required knowledge with benefits of experience of test taking and assessment of the students' strengths and weaknesses. Should the rules and criteria for test quality apply in this case? We think so.

If the test is to emulate the NACE, then it should meet the minimum criteria for a licensure or certification test. These criteria include: linkage of content with the job, evidence of coverage of relevant content, reliability, administrative ease, and ability to produce results from which valid interpretations can be made. The linkage of content to the job is usually made through a job analysis. Coverage of content can be attested to by either panel review or through a table of specifications. The reliability of the instrument is usually studied in a tryout of the instrument before its use. Administrative ease is reflected in the clarity of the administration instructions, the time requirements, and the scoring requirements. The ability to yield valid results is determined by what can be concluded about the candidate's knowledge and the predictive ability of the scores produced by the test.

REASON FOR THE TEST. The Nurse Aide Practice Test was constructed for the specific purpose of preparing candidates for the Nurse Aide Competency Evaluation. The practice test is intended to reduce anxiety and to increase self-confidence. As a test, it can achieve the goal of giving a candidate a feel for taking the actual examination. If it is not developed totally as a test, then the information produced by it is suspect. Review materials suggest to us that the practice test is easier than the actual examination, so it can be expected to increase self-confidence, but its results could be misleading in that candidates could believe that they are better prepared for the actual examination than they are.

THE JOB ANALYSIS. There are no explanations of how the questions were developed—only the implication that the questions are similar to those found in the Nurse Aide Competency Evaluation Program (NACEP). The material suggests that the "actual weights or percentage of questions within the five main content areas on the NACEP are provided with the Evaluation Blueprint available from The Psychological Corporation" (p. 13).

THE TABLE OF SPECIFICATIONS. There is neither a table of specifications nor a report of a panel review of the content. Experience in taking the test suggests that much of the content is based on "common sense" and basic skills.

RELIABILITY. There is no report of reliability in the materials provided for review and a telephone call to The Psychological Corporation did not produce any evidence.

VALIDITY. The interpretation materials appear helpful and straightforward. Experience in test taking can be important and the test would perhaps flag those who clearly do not have a chance on the actual NACEP test. The test is well presented with similar content areas grouped together to aid in the interpretation of areas that may need work or are well understood. The scoring is intended to be done as a group to allow corrections to be made and concepts to be discussed with in the group.

SUPPORTIVE TEST MATERIALS. The materials that were included in the test kit were: the test booklet, which includes an Individual Score Report, and a booklet, Directions for Administration—with scoring key, individual score report, and group summary report. The directions for administration describe the benefits, contents, overview, general instructions, directions for administration and scoring, and interpretation of scores.

REVIEWERS' COMMENTARY. Although the practice test is not a standard way that candidates generally study for a certification or licensure examination, it is the role of the Nurse Aide Practice Test. The test can give a candidate experience in test taking and the simplicity of the content may help to reduce anxiety and build confidence. Given the lack of supportive evidence of quality test development and of measurement performance, it is felt that the information produced by the practice test could be misleading. Given that its goals are preparation for the competency evaluation, it is hard to understand why it is marketed only in booklets of 10.

Both of the reviewers took the test and felt both the ease and the relevance of the items were evident. The bottom line on the test is that it does have value as a practice examination, but that it could be greatly improved with the provision of psychometric evidence of appropriate test development and performance.

[263]

Occupational Aptitude Survey and Interest Schedule, Second Edition—Aptitude Survey.
Purpose: Designed to measure career development of students.
Population: Grades 8–12.
Publication Dates: 1983–91.
Acronym: OASIS-2 AS.
Scores, 6: General Ability, Verbal Aptitude, Numerical Aptitude, Spatial Aptitude, Perceptual Aptitude, Manual Dexterity.
Administration: Group.
Price Data, 1994: $98 per complete kit including 10 test booklets, 50 answer sheets, 50 profile sheets, and manual ('91, 38 pages); $29 per 10 test booklets; $28 per 50 answer sheets; $19 per 50 profile sheets; $26 per manual.
Time: 35(45) minutes.
Comments: May be used in conjunction with the OASIS-2 Interest Schedule (264).
Author: Randall M. Parker.
Publisher: PRO-ED, Inc.
Cross References: See T4:1862 (2 references); for reviews by Rodney L. Lowman and Kevin W. Mossholder of an earlier edition, see 10:243.

TEST REFERENCES

1. Levinson, E. M., Rafoth, B. A., & Lesnak, L. (1994). A criterion-related validity study of the OASIS-2 Interest Schedule. *Journal of Employment Counseling, 31,* 29-37.

2. Parker, R. M., & Schaller, J. (1994). Relationships among self-rated and psychometrically determined vocational aptitudes and interests. *Educational and Psychological Measurement, 54,* 155-159.

Review of the Occupational Aptitude Survey and Interest Schedule, Second Edition—Aptitude Survey by LAURA L. B. BARNES, Assistant Professor of Educational Research, Department of Applied Behavioral Studies, Oklahoma State University, Stillwater, OK:

The Occupational Aptitude Survey and Interest Schedule, Second Edition—Aptitude Survey (OASIS-2AS) is intended to provide students with information "regarding their relative strengths in several aptitude areas related to the world of work" (p. 1). The Aptitude Survey was developed basically as a shorter version of the U.S. Department of Labor General Aptitude Test Battery (GATB). Through factor analytic studies of the 12 GATB subtests, five factors were deemed to be responsible for a significant portion of test score variance. These five factors became the basis for developing the five subtests of the OASIS-2AS. The OASIS-2AS yields six scores: a General Ability score derived by summing raw scores from the Vocabulary and Computation subtests and five scores corresponding to each of the five subtests. Briefly, the subtests are: Vocabulary, which requires students to find two words that have the same or opposite meaning; Computation, which is composed of arithmetic problems; Spatial Relations, which requires students to visualize and compare objects; Word Comparison, which requires students to compare two names, letters, or numbers to see if they are the same or different; and Making Marks, which measures how quickly students can make marks in a square.

Test materials are easy to use and administration is straightforward. Hand scoring is easily accomplished and computer scoring is available. Separate answer sheets with somewhat different instructions are required for machine and hand scoring. Hand scoring takes about 3 to 5 minutes per examinee. Raw scores on each test are converted to percentiles and stanines by referring to the norms table in the Examiner's Manual. No formal training is required for administering and scoring the tests beyond that required to ensure that standardized conditions are maintained; however, the manual appropriately cautions that test interpretation should be done only by trained professionals. Score interpretation is facilitated by the inclusion of a table containing job titles organized according to the "minimum level of aptitude estimated to be needed to perform the work" (p. 30) and containing the *Dictionary of Occupational Titles* (DOT) and *Guide for Occupational Exploration* (GOE) codes for those jobs. The section in the manual on Interpreting Test Results provides guidelines and two case-study illustrations for interpreting test results to students.

According to the Examiner's Manual, the standardization sample of 1,505 cases from grades 8 through 12 was obtained from 13 states and reflects regional, gender, racial, and urban-suburban/rural characteristics similar to U.S. Census data. Presumably this refers to the 1980 Census, although the manual does not specifically state this, nor does the manual provide the dates for normative data collection. It must be inferred that the bulk of the standardization data were collected before 1983 (the date of the first edition of the OASIS), because the author states that the original norm group was retained and increased by 107 cases. Separate norms by grade are not provided based on statistical analyses indicating no significant differences among the grade levels. In fact, there was no pattern indicating that older students performed any better than younger students. Likewise, separate sex norms were eliminated; although females as a group scored significantly higher than males on the Computation subtest (p<.05), the 2.0 difference was within a 95% confidence band based on the standard error of measurement.

Internal consistency reliabilities are reported for Vocabulary, Computation, General Ability, and Spatial Relations (the latter as split-half coefficients) and alternate forms reliabilities are given for the two speeded tests: Making Marks and Word Comparison. These are reported separately by grade, and except for the General Ability composite, also by sex. Median reliabilities (adjusted for range restriction) across grades range from .78 to .90 and no difference between males and females is apparent in terms of measurement consistency. Two-week test-retest coefficients are reported for a combined group of junior and senior high students with coefficients ranging from .76 to .94. Generally, the highest reliabilities are reported for General Ability, Word Comparison, and Making Marks, and the lowest for Spatial Relations. The author states that these tests do not have high enough reliability to be used as a sole predictor of specific job performance but are sufficiently high for use within the context of vocational exploration. This reviewer agrees, but would point out further the lack of long-term stability data also severely limits the usefulness of these tests for predictive purposes. It should be noted also that characteristics of the examinee groups from which reliability estimates were obtained are not reported in the manual. Because reliability estimates are known to be population specific, potential users should be aware that reported reliabilities may not be obtained in all cases. Instructions for completing student profile sheets encourage appropriate consideration of measurement error in interpreting scores and score differences. Standard errors of measurement and standard errors of score differences are reported.

With respect to validity, the OASIS-2AS subtests have high correlations, mostly in the .80 range (with the lowest being .61), with their respective GATB factors. Lower correlations with the nonrelated GATB factors are presented as evidence for discriminant validity. Correlations between the OASIS-2AS subtests and Iowa Test of Educational Development (ITED) and SRA Achievement Series subtests also show expected patterns of correlations. Vocabulary and General Ability scores have correlations in the .57 to .77 range with the achievement subtests. Vocabulary has its strongest relationship with the Reading achievement subtests. Computation correlates moderately with SRA Math (.44) but higher with ITED Math (.64); correlations with other achievement subtests are in the .31 to .44 range. Spatial Relations shows its strongest correlations with SRA Math and Science subtests (.49 and .46, respectively). As expected, the two perceptual-motor subtests (Word Comparison and Making Marks) share the least in common with achievement subtests, particularly Making Marks which correlates negligibly with all ITED and SRA achievement subtests except for SRA Language ($r = .17$).

Statements that the tests should be used only in the context of stimulating occupational exploration are repeated throughout the manual. The author refrains from saying the tests are predictive of occupational success. However, the lack of claims for prediction do not eliminate the need for evidence of relationship between test performance and occupational criteria. After all, the scores have to be interpreted with respect to some criteria, and the inclusion of job titles grouped according to the "minimum level of aptitude estimated to be needed to perform the work" (p. 30) certainly implies a linkage between test performance and job performance. Although nearly two-thirds of the section on technical information comes under the heading of Validity, only one study used a relevant criterion (academic major in a community college) to examine this relationship. Results partially supported the occupational aptitude groupings. There is a definite need for further supportive documentation that how students perform on these tests is related to occupational criteria; specifically the validity of the occupational aptitude groupings must be examined.

Other studies cited as evidence of construct validity examined test performance in relation to learning styles and decisiveness in selecting a major, and investigated group differences among students with and without learning and emotional disabilities. References for these studies are given in the Examiner's Manual and should be of value to those working with special populations.

The Examiner's Manual contains a significant number of errors. Some readers may be confused by an error on page 13 where scores of 85, 75, 50, and so on are referred to as stanine scores. It is apparent these were intended to be percentile scores. On page 15 of the manual the following appears, "Criterion-related validity includes the subcategories of content- and criterion-related validity." Obviously, this should have read, ". . . the subcategories of concurrent and predictive validity." The title of Table 11 on page 23 claims to present validity coefficients between the OASIS subtests and 15 GATB factors and subtests, when in fact the table presents correlations for 7 GATB factors. Other similar types of confusing presentations in text and tables abound.

The OASIS-2AS appears to have promise as an instrument for assisting adolescents to begin a career search. Reliabilities are acceptably high for exploratory guidance purposes. This test is less time consuming to administer than some established instruments, yet the OASIS-2AS shows evidence for relationship with the GATB scales. However, there is a definite lack of evidence for occupation-specific criterion-related validity. Although there is some comfort in the substantial correlations of these scales with the GATB, it is incumbent upon the test developer to demonstrate the validity of the suggested score interpretations.

Review of the Occupational Aptitude Survey and Interest Schedule, Second Edition—Aptitude Survey by THOMAS E. DINERO, Associate Professor of Evaluation and Measurement, Kent State University, Kent, OH:

The Occupational Aptitude Survey and Interest Schedule, Second Edition—Aptitude Survey

(OASIS-2AS) was developed to assist secondary school students in "self-exploration, vocational exploration, and career development" (p. 1) while they are in the early stages of developing career goals. The feedback provided to the students by the instrument includes several aptitude areas selected so that their interpretation stimulates the "process of self-exploration and vocational exploration" (p. 2). The instrument was designed for students in grades 8 through 12.

The authors based the rationale of the profile on Anastasi's use of the term "developed abilities" in an effort to avoid the distinction between aptitude as an "intrinsic, relatively stable" (p. 2) ability and achievement as the effects of learning. They unabashedly credit the General Aptitude Test Battery (GATB) for the structure and development of the OASIS-2AS.

The OASIS-2AS comprises five paper-and-pencil subtests selected to parallel the GATB: Vocabulary, Computation, Word Comparison, Making Marks, and one test which is similar to the Differential Aptitude Test's (DAT) Space Relations and the GATB's Three-Dimensional Space, here called Spatial Relations. A sixth score, General Ability, is based on the raw scores of the Vocabulary and Computation subtests. The tests are timed and take a total of 35 minutes.

An extended section describes how the counselor can determine the standard scores available (percentile ranks and stanines) for the individual students. Information in the manual concerning the norming group indicates that scores on 1,505 8th through 12th grade students in 13 states comprised the initial data set. Quota and representative sampling were used to generate a sample which well matches the demographics of the United States. Norms are presented for the combined male and female samples because there were no statistically significant differences. The scores do not appear to be normally distributed.

Reliability information on the subtests includes Cronbach's alpha (for Vocabulary and Computation), split half (for Spatial Relations, because alphas are "negatively affected" by multifactorial tests), test-retest, and alternate form (Word Comparison and Making Marks) data. All reliabilities are above .70 for a group of 357 students at five grade levels. The authors should be commended for being selective in their use of reliability coefficients, but it is curious that a split half would be considered appropriate for a bifactorial test when an alpha would not. They then present Lord's estimates (Lord & Novick, 1968) of KR 20s for the General Ability test. Presenting these values for general ability (which might indeed by multifactorial) is inconsistent with their assertion that alpha might be affected because alpha and the KR20 are essentially the same. Internal consistency data on word comparison would have been a good addition but probably would have been high given the other information available.

Validity data on the OASIS-2AS appears to have been well conceptualized, but the potential user is warned to study the data before implementing any use. For example, the first five factors resulting from a principal axis factor analysis with varimax rotation accounted for only 73% of the variance. The authors present these results while writing of and discussing a five-factor and two-factor solution.

Item-total point biserials (not biserials) were calculated using a group of Texas students who may or may not have been part of the norming group. Most correlations were between .20 and .60.

Correlations of the separate subtests with their appropriate match on the GATB were evenly spread between .37 on the Manual Dexterity test to .84 on the Verbal. Data are also presented showing moderate validity coefficients with the three subtests of the Iowa Tests of Educational Development.

The OASIS-2AS is highly recommended for the intended, rather modest and useful, purpose of vocational counseling. If used for no other purpose, the tests can prompt a beginning dialogue specifically focusing on the entire profile of five subtest scores. School-based users are encouraged to supplement these data with portfolio style information from the students' school history or teacher-made tests that would add to the content validity of the data set. Researchers, particularly those who are familiar with the GATB, will find this test familiar and should be encouraged to help increase the factorial validity of this promising instrument.

REVIEWER'S REFERENCE

Lord, F. M., & Novick, M. R. (1968). *Statistical theories on mental test scores.* Reading, MA: Addison-Wesley Publishing Co.

[264]

Occupational Aptitude Survey and Interest Schedule, Second Edition—Interest Schedule.

Purpose: "Developed to assist students in grades 8–12 in self-exploration, vocational exploration, and career development."
Population: Grades 8–12.
Publication Dates: 1983–91.
Acronym: OASIS-2 IS.
Scores, 12: Artistic, Scientific, Nature, Protective, Mechanical, Industrial, Business Detail, Selling, Accommodating, Humanitarian, Leading-Influencing, Physical Performing.
Administration: Group.
Price Data, 1994: $98 per complete kit including examiner's manual ('91, 42 pages), 25 student test booklets, 50 hand-scorable answer sheets, 50 profile sheets, and 50 scoring forms; $26 per manual; $28 per 25 test booklets; $19 per 50 answer sheets; $19 per 50 profile sheets; $11 per 50 scoring forms.
Time: (30–45) minutes.
Comments: Intended to be used with Occupational Aptitude Survey and Interest Schedule, Second Edition—Aptitude Survey (263).

Author: Randall M. Parker.
Publisher: PRO-ED, Inc.
Cross References: See T4:1863 (2 references); for reviews by Christopher Borman and Ruth G. Thomas of an earlier edition, see 10:244 (1 reference).

Review of the Occupational Aptitude Survey and Interest Schedule, Second Edition—Interest Schedule by ROBERT J. MILLER, Associate Professor of Special Education, Mankato State University, Mankato, MN:

The Occupational Aptitude Survey and Interest Schedule, Second Edition—Interest Schedule (OASIS-2) has two components, an Aptitude Survey and an Interest Schedule. This is a review of the Interest Schedule portion of the OASIS-2. The Interest Schedule (OASIS-2 IS) is a vocational interest inventory designed "to assist 8th through 12th grade students in self-exploration, vocational exploration, and career development" (pp. 2-3). The information generated by completing the Interest Schedule is intended to be the basis on which students can explore realistic, systematic, and meaningful decisions about themselves and their futures. The OASIS-2 IS is not designed to predict the occupations that students should or will select in adult life.

This instrument consists of 240 items with each item assigned to 1 of 12 scales and each scale made up of 20 items. The 12 scales are: Artistic, Scientific, Nature, Protective, Mechanical, Industrial, Business Detail, Selling, Accommodating, Humanitarian, Leading-Influencing, and Physical Performing. Subjects answer the 240 items regarding their likes and dislikes including 120 occupational titles and 120 short statements describing job activities. The three-choice response options for the individual include: like (L), neutral (N), and dislike (D). Subjects read the occupational title or job description from the student booklet and fill in their corresponding answer on a student answer sheet.

The OASIS-2 IS is untimed and simple to administer. Most students can finish the IS in approximately 30 minutes. The manual author suggests a one-proctor-to-30-students ratio to be desirable for administration of the IS and also suggests the proctor should feel free to define words and explain terminology. The IS can be machine or hand scored. It will take between 3 and 5 minutes per student for the examiner to hand score and record the IS results.

A profile of high and low interest is created by converting the raw score to percentile and stanine equivalents. The norm group for this edition of the OASIS-2 IS has been expanded to 1,505 students in 8th through 12th grade. This norm group resides in 13 states and is representative of U.S. census data for region of the country in which the sample resides, as well as gender, race, domicile, and grade level.

Alpha and test-retest reliability were employed in the development of the OASIS-2 IS. Alpha reliability was based on a sample of 260 students grades 8, 10, and 12 as well as a sample of 177 males and females grades 8–12. Alpha coefficients ranged from .78 to .94 for the 260 students and coefficients ranged from .85 to .95 for the 177 students when grouped by sex. The test-retest reliability was based on a 2-week interval from a sample of 54 junior high and high school students for the 12 subscales. Test-retest reliability ranged from .66 to .91. Alpha coefficients indicate that the IS has adequate internal reliability. Test-retest reliability suggests the IS scales to be relatively stable over time.

The discussion of test validity provided in the test manual focused on the construct-related validity of the instrument. Factor analysis was completed on the 12 interest factors of the OASIS-2 IS from data on 1,221 junior high and high school students of both sexes as well as separate groups of males ($n = 551$), and females ($n = 558$). This principal component analysis indicated the 12 components extracted could be identified as corresponding to one of the IS scales. Evidence of content validity was suggested because the 120 items related to occupational titles and the 120 items related to job activities relate directly to the *Guide for Occupational Exploration* (Harrington & O'Shea, 1984). In addition, internal scale consistency values were computed for each of the 12 scales. Correlations ranged from .31 to .81 with the preponderance (108 or 45%) falling in the .60s. This information generally supports the internal consistency of the instrument. No attempt was made to provide evidence of predictive validity. This would seem to be appropriate as the scale is to be used as a vehicle for "vocational exploration and career development" (p. 2).

Issues of sex equity in test design were well addressed in the test manual. Test items use gender-neutral language and the same form of the test is used for males and females. Item-by-sex cross tabulations were computed for all test items on all 12 scales. Males were found to have significantly higher mean scores on 2 scales, Mechanical and Physical Performing. Females obtained significantly higher scores on 3 scales including Business Detail, Accommodating, and Humanitarian. As a result of these sex differences, separate male-female norms were prepared for these 5 scales. The remaining 7 scales are represented by total group norms only.

In conclusion, the OASIS-2 IS is a well-designed and well-researched interest inventory. It is easy to administer, score, and interpret. The OASIS-2 IS is a valuable tool for vocational exploration and career development activities for students of junior high and high school age. This reviewer recommends the use of the instrument.

REVIEWER'S REFERENCE

Harrington, T., & O'Shea, A. (1984). *Guide for occupational exploration* (2nd ed.). Circle Pines, MN: National Forum Foundation.

Review of the Occupational Aptitude Survey and Interest Schedule, Second Edition—Interest Schedule by DONALD G. ZYTOWSKI, Professor Emeritus of Psychology, Iowa State University, Ames, IA:

The Occupational Aptitude Survey and Interest Schedule, Second Edition—Interest Schedule (OASIS-2 IS) is the interest inventory half of a pair of aptitude and interest assessments that share a common norm group and similar profiles and scores intended to assist students in grades 8 through 12 in career exploration. It consists of 12 scales of 20 items, half occupational titles, and half job activities, to be marked "Like," "Neutral," or "Dislike." The present edition is a revision of a 1983 version that replaced four obsolete job title items and simplified the language of several of the job activities items.

The challenge for homogeneously scaled interest inventories like this one is to link validly their scores to the spectrum of occupational alternatives. The OASIS-2 IS neatly finesses this problem by extracting the items for each of its scales from the occupations and job descriptions from the 12 occupational groups of the Department of Labor's *Guide for Occupational Exploration*. This review will necessarily concentrate on how well this solution has been realized in the OASIS-2 IS.

It is generally accepted that the items in an interest inventory should be familiar to the inventory taker. I would question what knowledge 8th grade students have of jobs like "Sales Exhibitor" or "Packaging Machine Operator" or with activities such as "Teach undergraduate or graduate college courses." Another problem presents itself in how the job activities might be interpreted. For instance, job title items "Assembly Line Worker" and "General Laborer" are assigned to the Industrial scale with the job activity describing the jobs as directing and organizing assembly work. This description seems more associated with management functions that would load on the Leading-Influencing scale. Concerns like this suggest careful examination of the psychometrics presented in the manual.

The answer sheet is arranged so that scores for each scale are obtained by counting the number of Ls and Ns across the sheet in four sections, multiplying the Ls by 2 and summing. A separate profile sheet is used to convert total raw scores to percentiles and stanines, using data on three pages in the manual. This process requires reference to different tables depending on the scale in question. The manual author is silent on whether students may score their own inventories, but if they do, which seems likely, I would like to see some data on the frequency of arithmetic errors.

Giving Neutral responses a score of 1 makes possible some logical inconsistencies. For instance, endorsing only Ns on the items of the Selling scale results in a percentile rank of 80, the respondent never having indicated that he or she liked any of the jobs or activities. Perhaps the N response really represents "Not Disliked."

The OASIS-2 Interest Schedule was normed on 1,505 high school students carefully stratified on five variables. The sample appears to include the 1,398 who comprised the norm group of the 1983 edition plus another 107 cases who took the present edition. Although the impact may be small, the new edition is normed on a group who by and large did not take that edition. An unfortunate characterization in the racial distribution is the use of "Mongoloid" to describe students neither Black nor White. Hispanic is absent.

The inventory takes care to examine each scale for gender differences and provide separate sex norms where needed. In addition to percentile scores, users can convert raw scores to stanines, which by reason of their equal interval metric affords the probability of real differences between scale scores to be reported. This option is a desirable approach in a multiscale inventory that few other inventories address. The lack of age-related norms implies there were no differences of this kind. Data should be presented; other inventories provide separate norms for junior and senior high school levels.

A principal components factor analysis is presented in support of the inventory's construct validity. It yields 12 factors, with almost every scale loading .81 or higher on only one factor. The exceptions consist of a factor loading of.68 for Leading-Influencing, plus a .35 for Mechanical on one factor and .80 on the same factor that Industrial loads on. As the manual author notes, Mechanical and Industrial appear to be highly related. The amount of variance accounted for by each of the 12 factors and the total variance accounted for is not reported, nor is a matrix of intercorrelations that went into the analysis. I would prefer to look for myself.

Internal consistency of the scales varies within the respectable range of median coefficients of .86 to .94. The median stability of the 12 scales over a 2-week period is .81. These coefficients are comparable with those of the more well-established instruments in the field.

No studies of the convergent validity of the OASIS-2 IS with well-known inventories with like-named scales, such as Holland's Self-Directed Search (T4:2414), are presented. Several studies investigating relationships between the OASIS-2 IS and a measure of learning styles and differences among learning disabled and emotional disturbed students verge on irrelevant. Two studies of concurrent validity suggest that students in selected majors or programs of study get higher scores on related scales, but no data are revealed to support these conclusions. All of these studies appear to have used the 1983 edition.

The manual author gives general guidelines for interpretation, and in two illustrative cases strongly suggests that students should attend to the rank ordering of the scales on the basis of their stanine scores. Use of the percentile scores is not mentioned. As well, it would have been instructive to see a combined interpretation of the OASIS-2 IS with its sibling aptitude assessment.

In sum, the features of the OASIS-2 Interest Survey concerned with gender biases and the use of stanine scores to assess the reliability of differences in the profiled scores are exemplary. Reliability and content validity are quite good. There could be some question regarding norms, and evidence of relevant validity is largely absent. The OASIS-2 IS might be reasonably effective in applications such as identifying occupational groups that 8th or 9th graders might profitably explore, but should be used cautiously or not at all in higher order applications such as prioritizing alternatives or confirming tentative choices.

[265]

The Occupational Interests Explorer.
Purpose: Designed to assess "interest in several general fields of work and in a wide range of occupational activities."
Population: Ages 15 and over ("above average ability").
Publication Date: 1989.
Acronym: OIE.
Scores, 8: Interest Areas (Practical/Active, Enterprising/Persuasive, Scientific/Investigative, Clerical/Administrative, Artistic/Creative, Social/Supportive), Work Satisfactions (Intrinsic, Extrinsic).
Administration: Group.
Price Data: Not available.
Time: (20) minutes.
Comments: Revision of the Occupational Check List.
Author: Tony Crowley.
Publisher: Hobsons Publishing PLC [England].
Cross Reference: For a review by David G. Hawkridge of the Occupational Check List, see 8:1014.
[The publisher advised in January 1994 that this test is now out of print.—Ed.]

Review of The Occupational Interests Explorer by SAMI GULGOZ, Assistant Professor of Psychology, Koc University, Istanbul, Turkey:

The Occupational Interests Explorer is a test developed primarily for the use of career counselors in exploring the possibilities for a student in high school or college. It is composed of three parts. Part 1 endeavors to reveal the interest areas, Part 2 assesses the importance of intrinsic and extrinsic demands of jobs for the respondents, and Part 3 aims to acquire further information about the career expectations of the person.

The test is printed on a single durable sheet that is folded to make four pages. Purchasers are allowed to make photocopies of the test for use within a school or college. However, because some of the items are printed on the inside fold, there may be some minor difficulties in photocopying or using the test booklet. The instructions are clear and simple and should not cause any problems for test takers. The language of the test may be difficult for a few test takers and some may have difficulty with the British spelling of the words.

The first part includes 108 activities to which the test taker responds by circling a 2 (*I would like it*), a 1 (*I am not too sure*), or a 0 (*I am not interested*). This part also requires the respondent to pick 20 activities and then, among them select three that the respondent likes best. Finally, the respondent marks three activities that are definitely undesirable. In the second part, there are 20 satisfactions that one would derive from a job and the respondent needs to indicate the importance of each by circling a 2 (*very important*), a 1 (*quite important*), or a 0 (*not important*). In Part 3, there are three open-ended questions that are designed to aid the counselor get a better insight into the expectations of the respondent.

There is no need for sophisticated scoring equipment or templates. Rather, scoring is fairly straightforward and rapid. The examiner need not have any special qualifications or training. Part 1 produces scores in six interest areas: Practical/Active, Enterprising/Persuasive, Scientific/Investigative, Clerical/Administrative, Artistic/Creative, and Social/Supportive. Very little to no information exists in the manual about the interpretation of these scores or the information gathered in Part 3.

This interpretation problem is exacerbated with a lack of normative data. Although there are some guidelines about interpreting low and high scores, for instance, there is no reference to what constitutes a low or a high score. No information is provided about any standardization procedure or any procedures used to assess the reliability or validity of the Explorer. The manual author indicates the statements in Part 2 were selected from the results of extensive statistical analyses but provides no information about the nature of these analyses and their results.

To conclude, I find the Occupational Interest Explorer hardly a good choice without norms, reliability information, and validity support. It may allow the test taker to "explore" his or her own interests and to use the items as a checklist of alternative activities. However, I would not recommend the use of the test as part of a career counseling program.

Review of The Occupational Interests Explorer by JOSEPH G. LAW, JR., Associate Professor of Behavioral Studies, University of South Alabama, Mobile, AL:

The Occupational Interests Explorer is a revision of Tony Crowley's Occupational Check List and was developed for use in Great Britain.

Three sections comprise the test: interest areas and themes, work values, and career expectations. This instrument, like its predecessor, contains 108 items that assess interest areas and themes. The author notes in his 22-page manual that the interest areas and themes are based on work by Guilford and Holland. A review of the labels of the interest areas and their individual items shows similarity to John Holland's realistic, investigative, artistic, social, enterprising, and conventional categories.

This inventory has a number of interesting features and some strengths. It is a brief instrument that appears to have considerable face validity. Linking the items to a well-known theory such as that of John Holland should also enhance its value as a career counseling tool for professionals who use that system.

The section on work values is also a useful feature. This should contribute considerable insight and assist clients in understanding the rationale behind their career decisions.

The third section of open-ended questions is also very helpful in that it produces material for the trained counselor in assessing the career maturity, vocational identity, and decision-making styles of the client. Although the last part is not tied to a numerical system it should have clinical utility in counseling situations.

The inventory consists of a large sheet that is folded in help to produce four pages of items and a section at the end for summarizing the scores. Although the inventory itself is a large simple foldout sheet, it is somewhat cumbersome to score because the summary area is on the back of the form and requires flipping back and forth to tabulate scores.

The manual is attractively packaged and fairly easy to read. It also contains case studies and additional information to assist the counselor in utilizing this instrument. The test is fairly inexpensive. The author lists a restricted waiver of copyright in the manual so that potential users may duplicate it and use the inventory as long as a price is not charged for the service.

Hawkridge (1978) noted in a review of the Occupational Check List that its manual contained norms on 124 boys and girls. A statistical appendix containing reliability information was also in the predecessor's manual. Unfortunately, the manual for The Occupational Interest Explorer does not contain any information on the norm groups that may have been used to develop it. There is absolutely no information on internal consistency, test-retest reliability, validity, or sampling practices. There are no references in the manual to validity studies on the instrument. Issues such as use with minority groups or gender bias are not touched on either. The inventory was designed for use with adults and above average students, thus limiting the range of clients that can be assessed by it.

It certainly shows promise as a source of topics for group discussion, but career counselors should be cautioned about its use until further data are available on reliability, validity, and the existence of any gender or minority biases. Practitioners would be better served to use an instrument like John Holland's (1985) Vocational Preference Inventory (VPI; T4:2910). The manual for the VPI contains 28 pages of statistical data and 3 pages of references that enhance the scientific basis of its use for career counseling. This enables the counselor to make ethical and practical decisions about the validity of applying the instrument to a particular individual. Unfortunately, The Occupational Interests Explorer does not provide that necessary information.

REVIEWER'S REFERENCES

Hawkridge, D. G. (1978). [Review of the Occupational Check List.] In O. K. Buros (Ed.), *The eighth mental measurements yearbook* (pp. 1596-1597). Highland Park, NJ: The Gryphon Press.

Holland, J. L. (1985). *Vocational Preference Inventory: Professional manual.* Odessa, FL: Psychological Assessment Resources.

[266]

The Occupational Interests Surveyor.

Purpose: Constructed to measure "interest in five basic fields of work and five sources of job satisfaction."
Population: Students and adults with minimal educational qualifications.
Publication Dates: 1990–91.
Acronym: OIS.
Scores, 10: Interests (Outdoor, Facts, People, Machines, Hands), Satisfaction (Money, Security, Companionship, Working Conditions, Interest).
Administration: Group.
Price Data: Not available.
Time: (30–40) minutes.
Author: Tony Crowley.
Publisher: Hobsons Publishing PLC [England].
[The publisher advised in January 1994 that this test is now out of print.—Ed.]

Review of The Occupational Interests Surveyor by RICHARD A. WANTZ, Associate Professor of Human Services and Director of the Office for Counseling and Life Planning Services (OCLPS), and SUSAN K. SPILLE, Graduate Clinical Coordinator for the OCLPS, College of Education and Human Services, Wright State University, Dayton, OH:

The Occupational Interests Surveyor (OIS) represents about 25 years of research and development by Tony Crowley in England. The OIS was first published in 1967 as the Simplified Occupational Interest Blank. In 1970, it was published as the Crowley Occupational Interests Blank by the Career Research and Advisory Centre (CRAC). This inventory underwent a major revision in 1976 to comply with the Sex Discrimination Act, and was reviewed by David G. Hawkridge in the *Eighth Mental Measurements Yearbook* (1978). The OIS complements the Occupational Interests Explorer (265).

The OIS assesses "five basic fields of work and five sources of job satisfaction" (front cover) and focuses attention on clients' employment interests. The inventory has utility for individual and group career guidance and for monitoring career development. The questionnaire was designed for pupils from about the third grade through college and for adult guidance centers and enables respondents to gain insight into the reasons behind their preferences and career plans with emphasis on why they respond as they do. The OIS is not intended to match people to occupations or to provide users with instant solutions to their career decisions. The OIS takes from 30 to 40 minutes to complete.

The OIS is based on the rationale that (*a*) people are more motivated and satisfied working at occupations and tasks that interest them, and (*b*) those who select occupations consistent with their interests remain with the position longer and report more work satisfaction. The manual includes a discussion of the development of the OIS, rationale for the four parts of the questionnaire, and indirect evidence of validity.

The OIS answers document is a single 11-inch by 17-inch page folded to form four $8^1/_2$-inch by 11-inch pages and is included within the 25-page manual. The OIS is presented in four sections: Part 1 is ranking of short, simple job titles presented in a diamond-shaped grid containing 25 job titles arranged in rows of five. Each row has five job titles with each job representing one of five interest areas: "O" for Outdoor and active work; "F" for Facts in office, store, or paperwork; "P" for People in helping, persuading, and caring occupations; "M" for Machines in jobs requiring tools or machines; and "H" for Hands in artistic, light craft, or domestic work. Job titles in each row are rank ordered from 5 to 1. Scoring is accomplished by adding the scores in the five different rows of interests. Crowley justifies the use of job titles by referencing Holland's Vocational Preference Inventory. He reports job titles have been found to be a reliable and valid method of evaluating job interests. The OIS holds the premise that (*a*) stereotypes are generally correct in terms of the duties and demands made by each job, and (*b*) the titles of the OIS used are simple enough to be ranked without difficulty.

Part 2 is a checklist of 75 occupational activities that complement the five categories of job titles of Part 1. The descriptive activities are placed in three columns of five groups, which are scored across the page. The examinee is asked to score each activity, "How would you like to . . . ." as 2 points for *like to perform*, 1 point for *not too sure*, and zero points for *does not interest.* Totaling the activities across the page results in activities of preference. Crowley reports there is considerable agreement between the interest preferences of Parts 1 and 2 unless there are misinterpretations of job titles in Part 1, a lack of occupational awareness, misunderstanding of instruction, and/or indifference to completing the assessment. In addition to scoring the activities, the examinee is asked to select the 15 items of most interest and underline them. Of note is the manual's elaboration of the exercise in reviewing these activities. Each of the phrases contain a verb, an object, and an environment. This design permits a more extensive interpretation if the examinee is asked to identify the part of the underlined statement that most influenced their choice (i.e., the selections of environments may indicate the examinee's preference for the context of the work area rather than the job; selection of objects suggests a preference for working with items; and selection of verbs indicates concern with job activities). Samples of occupations using combinations of interest areas are provided in the manual.

Part 3 measures the relative importance of five sources of job satisfaction: Money, Security, Companionship, Working Conditions, and Interest in the job. It consists of a paired-choice exercise with each of the five areas represented by eight statement. Each examinee is asked to select their most important job satisfaction source within each pair. Scoring is done by totaling the choices in each column under headings of M, S, C, W, and I. The purpose of Part 3 is to enable students to consider what factors they *perceive* as important to job satisfaction. According to Crowley, research shows examinees responses to work values inventories may be less reliable than responses to work interests because of the lack of experience that students or young adults have with work-related satisfaction.

In Part 4, the final section of the Surveyor, the examinee is asked to complete an open-ended section and list three jobs they would like to do and three they would avoid. Completion of the first three parts of the inventory may improve awareness of job interest.

Weaknesses of the survey are the vague and culturally biased vocabulary of the occupational titles (i.e., examinees unfamiliar with the U.K. job titles may need explanation of "VUD operator," "Playleader," and "Window dresser"). the manual clarifies administration procedures but does not define occupational titles specific to the U.K. In addition, the manual references but does not clarify the U.K. National Vocational Qualification levels. Some examinees found the graphic presentation of Part 1 to be difficult to understand and score without individual instruction. Others found the placement of the directions to be awkward in that they are scattered around the page and not in order.

In summary, the OIS is recommended as a quick screening device for clients desiring occupations requiring less formal education. It offers insight to the clients' vocational preferences based on their interests and sources of job satisfaction. The questionnaire is easy to complete, economical (purchasers are granted permission to reproduce the questionnaire), and does not require electronic scanning or computer interpretation.

REVIEWER'S REFERENCE

Hawkridge, D. G. (1978). [Review of the Occupational Check List.] In O. K. Buros (Ed.), *The Eighth Mental Measurements Yearbook* (pp. 1596-1597). Highland Park, NJ: Gryphon Press.

[267]

Occupational Test Series—Basic Skills Tests.

Purpose: Designed for the "assessment of current levels of skill in comprehension, writing and dealing with numbers."
Population: New trainees and employees.
Publication Date: 1988.
Scores, 7: Literacy (Reading Comprehension and Information-Seeking, Writing [optional], Total), Numeracy (Calculating, Approximating, Problem-Solving, Total).
Administration: Group.
Price Data, 1992: £27.05 per Reference Set; £27.60 per 25 reusable Literacy Newspapers; £24.75 per Literacy Administration pack; £16.90 per Numeracy Administration pack; £15.85 per 25 reusable Numeracy Question Booklets.
Time: 35(45) minutes for Literacy Test (both sections); 20(30) minutes for Reading section of Literacy Test; (35) minutes for Numeracy Test.
Authors: Pauline Smith and Chris Whetton.
Publisher: NFER-Nelson Publishing Co., Ltd. [England].

Review of the Occupational Test Series—Basic Skills Tests by PHYLLIS KUEHN, Associate Professor of Educational Research, Measurement, and Statistics, California State University, Fresno, Fresno, CA:

This battery includes a two-part Literacy Test (Reading, 20 short-answer items; Writing, 5 tasks) and a three-part multiple-choice Numeracy Test (Calculating, 20 items; Approximating, 20 items; and Problems, 25 items). The Literacy Test uses a mock local newspaper, simulating authentic materials an adult might be expected to read, as the stimulus for both the Reading and Writing subtests. For testing adult basic literacy skills, this is certainly an excellent approach. Unfortunately, parts of the 10-page newspaper were printed with a dot matrix printer and did not reproduce well; some letters are difficult to recognize, making the reading task more complicated for low-level or nonnative English test takers.

The stated purposes of the tests are to identify individuals who may need remedial help or for use as part of a "low-level" job selection process. The tests were developed in England but probably should not be used in the United States for two reasons. First, differences in British vocabulary and spelling may obscure the meaning for most native and nonnative English-speaking U.S. readers. For example, test takers are required to find information about where to "join a coach" for a day trip to France. Second, the use of these tests in the U.S. for their second stated purpose, employee selection, would require a validity study, including some form of job analysis, to demonstrate the job relatedness of the tests for this purpose. Federal legislation and employment testing guidelines, as well as decades of court precedent related to employment test validity, must be considered when a test is used for employee selection. Although the test manual is well written and suggests methods test purchasers can use for standard setting and developing local norms, the suggestions would be unlikely to provide sufficient evidence of test validity for employee selection.

Scoring of the Reading section requires minimal judgments to be made about the short phrases or sentences that constitute the test takers' answers. The five Writing tasks can be scored as adequate or inadequate, or a more detailed full-scoring method can be used that requires the scorer to make a total of 28 judgments about the writing samples. This full-scoring scheme is problematic for several reasons. First, only 5 of the 28 points are awarded for "functional adequacy" (providing correct and sufficient detail), which should certainly be a major consideration. In contrast, handwriting adequacy is worth 4 points, and an additional 3 points are awarded for the formality and correctness of the salutation and closing of a mock letter. Handwriting and appropriate formality seem to be disproportionately weighted (7 points) relative to content correctness (5 points) in this scoring method. Second, test users are required to make judgments on the clarity and tone/style of the writing. Without extensive training, the reliability of such judgments is questionable. Third, users must judge whether a test taker's responses conform "to the grammatical rules which are universally accepted for the production of formal English" (p. 22). Fourth, spelling is judged as adequate or inadequate for three of the Writing tasks based on a scoring scheme that requires the test user to decide whether misspelled words are "easy" or "difficult." It is unlikely that most test purchasers will have the level of linguistic sophistication necessary to make these judgments reliably. Finally, for both Literacy test sections, 1 point is awarded for an answer judged adequate, and zero is awarded for inadequate or missing answers. A low total score thus may reflect slowness, lack of ability, and/or unwillingness to guess.

The Numeracy test is to be done without the use of a calculator. The first two sections require no reading. The third section (Problem-Solving), however, requires some reading and interpretation of recipes, histograms, maps, charts, rulers, and schedules to set up the problems to be solved. These are many of the same reading tasks required on the Literacy test and low scores, as the manual points out, may reflect low reading ability or low problem-solving ability. Test takers have six choices in the multiple-choice answer format. Item discrimination data are presented (point biserials) but evidence of the effectiveness of this large number of distractors is not discussed.

Percentile ranks from two norm groups are provided for interpretation of scores. However, these norms and the educational levels described in the manual are not useful for test users outside Great Britain and no equivalent U.S. educational levels or norms are provided.

KR 20 reliability estimates range from .81 for subtests to .96 for total test scores for the two norm groups. However, no information is given regarding interrater reliability on the Literacy test scoring. Much lower reliabilities could be expected from the untrained raters who purchase and score the tests. Besides the difficult scoring judgments already described, the reliability of scores may be affected by a number of factors test users are told to consider when interpreting score results. For example, users are told to consider the varying difficulty of literacy items (difficulties not given) when interpreting scores, to consider the number of items attempted by the test taker, to set their own cut scores, to consider the test taker's ethnic background when interpreting some answers, and to consider the type of job the test taker is applying for when scoring the answers. Unknown sources of unreliability will be introduced into scores by test users trying to consider all these factors when scoring responses and making a judgment of adequacy.

Scores from these tests may be valid for estimating general adult literacy and numeracy unrelated to performance of any particular job if evidence of score reliability can be established and appropriate norms can be developed by the test user. The knowledge, skills, and abilities required to perform particular jobs differ greatly, and scores on such global literacy and numeracy measures would not give information about the specific skills needed in a particular job setting. Without diagnostic or subskill information, a compensatory model of these skills is assumed. In other words, if reading a schedule is a critical skill for a particular job, but the test taker missed the items related to reading a schedule, a passing total score presumes that his other skills have compensated for this skill deficit.

In summary, these tests may be usable for low-stakes decisions about general levels of literacy and numeracy in a British-English context, but probably should not be used for employee selection. The tests should not be used for general literacy/numeracy assessment or for employee selection in the U.S.

Review of the Occupational Test Series—Basic Skills Tests by MARK POPE, President, Career Decisions, San Francisco, CA:

The Basic Skills Tests (BST) of the Occupational Test Series are two separate paper-and-pencil tests (Literacy and Numeracy) designed as easily administered screening instruments of the individual's current level of English comprehension and writing along with the ability to deal with numbers. The major use of the BST is for initial screening of new employees in situations where academic qualifications may not be available or possessed. The major purpose of the instrument is to select individuals who may need remedial help in the two skill areas; however, it also may be used as part of a low-level personnel selection instrument where these two skills areas are part of the job requirements. The tests were designed to assess the basic levels of literacy and numeracy, to use materials suitable for adults, to not use occupationally specific terminology or examples, and to be brief and easy to administer. The development was conducted by individuals at the National Foundation for Educational Research and was commissioned by NFER Nelson (the tests' publisher).

These two basic skills tests can be used separately as well as in conjunction with each other. The Literacy test is composed of two sections: Reading (Comprehension and Information-Seeking) and Writing (optional). The Writing section is described as optional and two different "Marking Guides" are included to score the Literacy test: a Limited one for use when only Reading is administered and a Full one for use when both Reading and Writing sections are used. The Numeracy test is composed of three sections: Calculating, Approximating, and Problem-Solving.

The format of the Reading section of the Literacy test includes having the test taker locate and read parts of a newspaper and then write brief answers to questions concerning what the person has read. In the Writing section the test taker has to perform writing tasks related to specified features in the newspaper. In the Calculating section of the Numeracy test the test taker must add, subtract, multiply, and divide using positive integers, decimals, fractions, and percentages. The Approximating section of the Numeracy test requires the test taker to work out approximate answers to difficult calculations. Finally, in the Problem-Solving section of the Numeracy test, the test taker must solve problems found in everyday life which are presented using graphs or text.

A standardized guide to a timed administration along with a more informal administration guide are included. These two different guides allow for both ipsative (for comparison with each individual) and normative (for comparison with other group scores published in the manual) interpretations.

The components of the BST include: a user's guide, an introduction and information sheet, a mock-up of a free community newspaper ("The Shelley Gazette: Your Community Newspaper"), administration instructions for the Literacy test (both for the "Full Test" and "Section 1 Only"), a question and answer booklet for the Literacy test, a scoring booklet

("Marking Guide") for each section of the Literacy test, administration instructions for the Numeracy section, a question booklet for the Numeracy test, an answer sheet for the Numeracy test, and a scoring key for the Numeracy test. All of the components are available in a "reference set" which comes in an attractive flexible vinyl duofold binder.

The BST user's guide is both a technical manual and an interpretation guide. It serves the purpose as a basic guide to the administration, scoring, and interpretation of the BST and as a manual regarding the development of the BST. The user's guide is divided into seven separate sections: an introduction; development which includes the technical development information and item analysis; administration and scoring; interpreting scores; supplementary information which includes the psychometric data on reliability and validity, along with the standardization method and sample; case studies which include data from a variety of English settings where the instruments have been used; and untimed administration guidelines. Three appendices are also included: item analysis statistics, a glossary of terms, and a references list.

The user's guide is clearly and elegantly organized using a variety of appropriate graphic presentation techniques. The information is presented with extensive basic historical and use information along with in-depth development information. For example, the mock-up of a community newspaper was analyzed for complexity using a statistical computer program that analyzes text and calculates the average sentence length, average number of syllables per word, number of complex words, and commonly used estimates of readability and reading age, such as the Fry Grade and the Mugford Reading Level. This detailed analysis was then used to revise the newspaper. Such specialized, thorough, detailed analyses are used throughout the development of these instruments. They are not, however, presented in the highly complicated language of the statistician; they are instead presented in readily understandable English sentences with the appropriate numbers presented in context.

Administration of the BST can be accomplished in three different ways: timed group, untimed group, and untimed individual. The test authors are also careful to state that only when the administration has been done in a way similar to that used with the normative groups, that is, a timed group, can comparisons be made with the published norms. Further, the authors delineate the very specific conditions under which a standardized administration is to be conducted, including the physical conditions, timing, materials, and more. The Literacy test (both sections) requires 10 minutes for instructions and practice with 35 minutes for actual test taking. When only the Reading section of the Literacy test is given, the actual test taking is 20 minutes. The Numeracy test requires 10 minutes for instructions and practice with 25 minutes for actual test taking. The process to administer both the Literacy test and the Numeracy test of the BST is outlined in the user's guide; however, step-by-step instructions for each different test are also included on two separate four-page "administration instructions," one sheet $11^5/_8$ inches by $16^1/_2$ inches of white paper folded in half (gives the standard British paper size of $8^1/_4$ by $11^5/_8$ inches).

The Literacy test's question and answer expendable booklet is eight pages in length on the standard size British paper. The front cover is a light gray, standard bond paper. The remainder of the pages are white. The 20 items in Section 1, the Comprehension section, are presented in a graphically appealing way with the questions presented inside of gray rectangular boxes on the left side of the page with a black outlined rectangular box next to it on the right side of the page for the test taker's response. Responses are to be written directly in the booklet. Only five items are included in Section 2, the Writing section, the format of which is a question presented in a gray rectangular box which extends across the width of the page, followed immediately by a black outlined rectangular box for the test taker's handwritten response. Also, the response box contains appropriate graphics, for example, one of the items requires the test taker to address an envelope and the response box has a stamp appropriately placed in the upper right corner. Scoring is done using two separate "marking guides" or scoring keys. The marking guide for Section 1 is printed on one side of a standard British size sheet of white paper and the marking guide for Section 2 consists of a four-page, folded guide. Printing is done in black ink on both.

The Numeracy test's question-only reusable booklet is 16 pages in length on the standard size British paper. Each page of the booklet is printed on white, standard bond paper with gray and black ink. There are three separately timed sections: Section 1, Calculations, 20 items, 5 minutes; Section 2, Approximations, 20 items, 5 minutes; Section 3, Problems, 25 items, 15 minutes. In the Numeracy sections six responses are supplied for each item. Answers are recorded on a separate, handscorable, two-sided sheet of paper printed in black and gray ink. Handscoring is accomplished using an easily readable, translucent plastic answer key printed in red ink. Raw scores are recorded directly on the answer sheet with spaces to record the confidence band, norm group used, percentile rank, and *T*-score also.

The questions booklet for the Literacy test is easily differentiated from the Numeracy test by having a light gray color on the cover along with the words "LITERACY" or "NUMERACY" presented in the largest typeface on the page and in bold print. Also, the items are clear and understandable with some of the items on both the Literacy test and the Numeracy test using idiomatic words or phrases of Great Britain ("look at the advert"; "School of Motoring"; "collection licenses").

Two groups provided the normative, standardizing data: 71 secondary schools (a Form Five sample, equivalent to high school senior year students) and 8 Youth Training Scheme centers (a technical schools sample). A large sample of secondary school students (N>1,500 for both BST tests) was selected using a multistage random method along with a smaller sample of trainees attending classes at the YTS centers (N = 336) who were selected using a nonrandom method.

Substantial evidence of reliability is reported. The section concerning reliability begins with three paragraphs that provide an overview of what reliability means in order to both familiarize the reader with what reliability means and to justify their decision to provide only internal consistency reliability data using the Kuder-Richardson 20 formula. KR20 scores ranged from .81 to .94 for secondary schools (a Form Five sample, equivalent to high school senior year students) and from .87 to .96 for Youth Training Schools (a technical schools sample). Overall and subscale intercorrelations were calculated using the Pearson product-moment correlation method with correlation coefficients ranging from .65 to .71 for the secondary schools sample and from .66 to .74 for the Youth Training schemes sample.

The user's guide contains a discussion of content-related validity, criterion-related validity (especially predictive), and "face" validity. No data, however, are provided concerning specific positions for which the BST might have some predictive validity for personnel selection. Instead, the authors substitute a general statement on validity and, when commenting on the evidence or predictive validity of the instrument, state that an example of this would be if the scores on the Literacy test were related to future success on a clerical training course. They follow this with a substantial section in the user's guide on how to use the instrument in determining the level of literacy and numeracy skill required for selection and then linking that to the level needed for a job. Also, they differentiate between a position analysis and local norms and provide a detailed guide to establishing local norms.

In summary, the BST has substantial reasons to recommend its use as a lower level aptitude screening instrument in England. In England, these tests could be very useful as many government-funded training programs are open to people regardless of academic achievement. Consequently, program administrators are expected to provide remedial help for their trainees with inadequate basic skills. These two tests can assist in the identification of these individuals in need of remedial education.

No data are presented to support their use in countries outside of Great Britain and, because of the idiomatic use of English, revisions would be necessary for such use in other native English-speaking countries. Further, although no data are provided concerning the positions for which the BST might have some predictive validity for personnel selection, a detailed discussion of a method for establishing specific cutoff scores is included.

The format of the BST appears to be a sound one, however, and much care has obviously gone into the development of these instruments.

[268]

Offer Self-Image Questionnaire, Revised.

Purpose: Designed to measure the self-image of adolescents.
Population: Ages 13–18.
Publication Dates: 1971–92.
Acronym: OSIQ-R.
Scores, 13: Emotional Tone, Impulse Control, Mental Health, Social Functioning, Family Functioning, Vocational Attitudes, Self-Confidence, Self-Reliance, Body Image, Sexuality, Ethical Values, Idealism, Total Self-Image.
Administration: Group or individual.
Price Data, 1995: $115 per complete kit including manual ('92, 75 pages), 2 reusable administration booklets, and 5 WPS Test Report prepaid mail-in answer sheets; $27.50 per 10 reusable administration booklets; $45 per manual; $14.50 per mail-in answer sheet; $225 per 25-use WPS Test Report IBM Microcomputer scoring disk; $15 per 100 answer sheets for use with Microcomputer disk; $9.50 per FAX scoring.
Time: [30–45] minutes.
Comments: Computer scored via disk or prepaid mail-in answer sheet.
Authors: Daniel Offer (test/manual), E. Ostrov (manual), K. I. Howard (manual), and S. Dolan (manual).
Publisher: Western Psychological Services.
Cross References: See T4:1877 (6 references); for reviews of an earlier edition by Robert Hogan and Roy P. Martin, see 9:855 (5 references); see also T3:1673 (1 reference) and 8:633 (10 references).

TEST REFERENCES

1. Cole, D. E., Protinsky, H. O., & Cross, L. H. (1992). An empirical investigation of adolescent suicidal ideation. *Adolescence, 27,* 813-818.

2. Stern, M., & Alvarez, A. (1992). Knowledge of child development and caretaking attitudes: A comparsion of pregnant, parenting, and nonpregnant adolescents. *Family Relations, 41,* 297-302.

3. Andrews, J. A., Lewinsohn, P. M., Hops, H., & Roberts, R. E. (1993). Psychometric properties of scales for the measurement of psychosocial variables associated with depression in adolescence. *Psychological Reports, 73,* 1019-1046.

4. Arnett, J., & Balle-Jensen, L. (1993). Cultural bases of risk behavior: Danish adolescents. *Child Development, 64,* 1842-1855.

5. Fine, S., Haley, G., Gilbert, M., & Forth, A. (1993). Self-image as a predictor of outcome in adolescent major depressive disorder. *Journal of Child Psychology and Psychiatry and Allied Disciplines, 34,* 1399-1407.

6. Howe, G. W., Feinstein, C., Reiss, D., Molock, S., & Berger, K. (1993). Adolescent adjustment to chronic physical disorders-1. Comparing neurological and non-neurological conditions. *Journal of Child Psychology and Psychiatry and Allied Disciplines, 34,* 1153-1176.

7. Smith, D. E., & Pike, L. B. (1994). Relationship between Jamaican adolescents' drinking partners and self-image: A cross-cultural perspective. *Adolescence, 29,* 429-437.

8. Craighead, W. E., Curry, J. F., & Ilardi, S. S. (1995). Relationship of Children's Depression Inventory factors to major depression among adolescents. *Psychological Assessment*, 7, 171-176.

9. Gillis, J. S., & Mubbashar, M. H. (1995). Risk factors for drug abuse in Pakistan: A replication. *Psychological Reports*, 76, 99-108.

Review of the Offer Self-Image Questionnaire, Revised by SARAH J. ALLEN, Assistant Professor of School Psychology, University of Cincinnati, Cincinnati, OH:

The Offer Self-Image Questionnaire, Revised (OSIQ-R) is a norm-referenced, self-report measure designed to evaluate adolescents' own view of themselves. Originating from an interest in the developmental psychology of average or "normal" adolescents, this self-image questionnaire is intended for use with youth 13 to 18 years of age. The authors suggest that it will be beneficial in work with both troubled and normal teenagers.

Premised on the notion that an individual can master some aspects of development while failing too adjust to another, the OSIQ-R is designed to evaluate self-image in multiple areas. Specifically, the 129-item test comprises 12 scales including Emotional Tone, Impulse Control, Mental Health, Social Functioning, Family Functioning, Vocational Attitudes, Self-Confidence, Self-Reliance, Body Image, Sexuality, Ethical Values, and Idealism. A Total Self-Image Scale score is derived by combining scores from 10 of these subscales.

Administration of the OSIQ-R is done using either paper-and-pencil or microcomputer disk options. Respondents are asked to read descriptive statements and then indicate how well each characterizes them using a 6-point Likert-type scale. Potential responses range from *describes me very well* to *does not describe me at all*. Some statements are gender specific and answered only when applicable to the respondent. Items from each of the 12 component scales comprising the OSIQ-R are presented in random order. In an attempt to reduce the risk of response bias, the wording of items is balanced to ask about both desirable and undesirable behavior. In addition, reverse scoring of some of the items is used.

All scoring of the OSIQ-R is done using a computer program available from the publisher. In addition to individual scale scores and the results of score transformations (e.g., *T*-scores), this computerized scoring procedure also provides the "automatic interpretation" of OSIQ-R results (manual, p. 55). Intended to reduce computation errors, this practice raises serious concerns related to the potential over- or misinterpretation of results.

The OSIQ-R is the most recent edition of an instrument that may be familiar to some readers; earlier editions of the Offer Self-Image Questionnaire were published in 1969 and 1979. Although the actual questionnaire was not changed substantially from earlier editions, several changes were made to the format of the OSIQ-R. For example, the names and reporting order (but not content) of scales were changed to reflect current practice. Also one item was deleted from the Mental Health subscale in order to increase the broad appeal of the instrument. The psychometric properties of the instrument were not affected by these changes.

A noted improvement to this edition of the OSIQ-R is the metric of the scaled score index was altered to conform with conventional practice, that is, a *T*-score with a mean of 50 and a standard deviation of 10. Previous editions of this instrument used an uncommon form of scale score (i.e., Mean = 50, *SD* = 15) that may have contributed to interpretation errors. Conversion formulas are provided in the manual for those who wish to compare scores from current and earlier versions of the instrument.

Unfortunately, some of the limitations associated with previous versions of the OSIQ-R are applicable to the 1992 edition also. For example, the construction and development of this instrument are poorly described in the manual and seemingly casual. The test items and scales appear to have been derived based on a review of theory, findings from empirical studies, and clinical experience without ever being verified with appropriate statistical analyses. The initial pool of items was piloted on an inadequate sample of 40 adolescent males (30 high school students and 10 psychiatric patients). Based on the results from that preliminary study, some items were rewritten and other replaced. Unfortunately, no further information is provided regarding the criteria for item retention or scale development.

Derived from 13 samples collected between 1980 and 1988, the normative sample was reported to include 964 adolescents. The demographic characteristics of the sample closely approximate those of a recent United States Census. Exceptions were noted to include a slight (4%) overrepresentation of whites as compared to other ethnic groups. Also the normative sample included an overrepresentation of adolescents whose parents had completed higher levels of education and an underrepresentation of youth reporting lower levels of parental education.

With regard to reliability, coefficient alpha values were reported for each OSIQ-R scale for age (i.e., younger vs. older) and gender groups. The internal consistency data for the Total Self-Image Scale were best; all coefficients were .90. Only six of the remaining 48 coefficients reported met or exceeded a .80 criterion; the median alpha coefficient for these scores was .69. The reliability coefficients for subscales of this instrument are relatively low based on conventional standards of practice and thus, the confidence placed in the results from some subscales must be tempered with a consideration of their accuracy.

Calculated from scale alpha reliabilities, the standard error of measurement for all OSIQ-R scales for reference groups based on age and gender also are available in the manual. However, these statistics are based on a confidence interval of only 68% and thus, also must be interpreted cautiously.

In terms of validity, a number of studies representing both the authors' own and independent research were reported in the manual. Preliminary evidence is provided to demonstrate construct validity. For example, data from the normative sample were submitted to factor analyses for the purpose of establishing construct validity. Results indicated that a 2-factor structure reliably emerged: one intraindividual self-image factor and the other more effected by societal image. Multiple studies were reported to show the correlation of the OSIQ-R with other personality tests. The results were judged to be supportive of construct validity.

A careful review of item content reveals several concerns that may limit the utility of this instrument with diverse populations. First, there appears to be reliance upon jargon or phrases that will be meaningful to members of some cultures or groups but may not generalize well to others. Examples include: "I 'lose my head' easily" (Item 8), "I would rather sit around and loaf off than work" (Item 45), and "Eye-for-an-eye and tooth-for-a-tooth does not apply for our society" (Item 115).

Secondly, the constructs underlying the subscales that comprise this instrument appear to reflect the values of a particular culture or segment of the population. For example, the manual indicates that the Sexuality subscale is intended to assess concerns with adolescents' feeling, attitudes, and behavior "toward the opposite sex" (manual, p. 5). Implicit in this description, the phrasing of some questions, scoring procedures, and interpretation of scores is the assumption that a straight or heterosexual orientation is "normal." Consideration will need to be given to this bias when determining the utility and interpretation of the scale with adolescents either uncertain of their own sexual orientation or identifying with another.

In summary, the Offer Self-Image Questionnaire, Revised is the most recent edition of a self-report measure designed to investigate self-image of adolescents 13 to 18 years of age. Despite the fact this instrument has existed for more than two decades and reportedly has been used in many studies, it is not one of the best tools available to either clinicians or researchers. In particular, a lack of attention to basic psychometric issues in the development of this instrument has limited the potential utility of the OSIQ-R. Caution should be used in the interpretation of any results derived from the test.

Review of the Offer Self-Image Questionnaire, Revised by MICHAEL FURLONG, Associate Professor, and MITCHELL KARNO, Doctoral Student, Graduate School of Education, University of California, Santa Barbara, Santa Barbara, CA:

CONTENT. The Offer Self-Image Questionnaire, Revised (OSIQ-R) is a self-report instrument designed to measure self-esteem and normal adjustment of youth 13 to 18 years of age. The OSIQ-R's predecessor, the OSIQ, was developed in 1962 to provide a reliable means of selecting a representative group of "normal" or adjusted adolescents from a broader pool of senior high school students. It has since been used frequently in research and has been administered to over 30,000 adolescents. The OSIQ-R represents the latest effort by Offer and his colleagues to tap the experiences and feelings of young people through a conventionally standardized, administered, and interpreted assessment tool.

The OSIQ-R comprises 12 scales that assess areas related to an adolescent's psychological well-being: Emotional Tone, Impulse Control, Mental Health, Social Functioning, Family Functioning, Vocational Attitudes, Self-Confidence, Self-Reliance, Body Image, Sexuality, Ethical Values, and Idealism. The OSIQ-R purports to measure the construct of "self-image." Although not specifically mentioned by the authors, this construct appears to be similar to "self-concept" in that it is meant to evaluate self-perceptions across multiple domains relevant to normal adolescent developmental tasks. This includes how adolescents negotiate their social environment (e.g., Family Functioning, Vocational Attitudes, Sexuality) as well as their development of personal values (e.g., Ethical Values and Idealism). In this sense, it is more similar to other multidimensional self-concept inventories such as the Tennessee Self-Concept Scale (T4:2723) than it is to omnibus personality measures. Furthermore, it examines self-image in a broad context and is dissimilar to self-concept instruments that focus on youth's self-perceptions as a student or the academic context of school. In fact, the OSIQ-R includes only a few items that have a primary school content, so it has limited application in psychoeducational assessments.

In general, high scores are considered to be more positive and reflective of sound self-image. One exception is the Sexuality subscale, which has negative interpretations at both ends of the score continuum—high scores indicate an unusually high level of sexual awareness and interest, and low scores indicate limited awareness or interest. One potential application of the OSIQ-R is to help identify youth who express attitudes associated with involvement or vulnerability to high-risk sexual behavior.

COMPARISON OF OSIQ AND OSIQ-R. There are several notable differences between the OSIQ-R and the OSIQ. The most obvious change is the renaming of the subscales to be more appropriate for clinical use and interpretation. This change was primarily cosmetic, however, because (*a*) only one item was deleted from the OSIQ, (*b*) no items were added, (*c*) no item wording was modified, and (*d*) the item composition of each subscale was unaltered. In addition, the OSIQ-R uses a *T*-score with a mean of 50 and a standard deviation of 10. This is an improvement over the OSIQ, which employed a *T*-score with an unconventional standard deviation of 15. Also, the OSIQ-R is scored by simply summing raw scores, whereas for the OSIQ-R, scores were summed and then divided by the number of subscale items (i.e., average score per item). The new method of computing subscale scores allows for simpler scoring and easier computation of the Response Bias and Completeness validity checks. The authors provide conversion formulas to compare scores from the older OSIQ with the newer OSIQ-R. Given the different norm sample between the two versions of the test, however, we can see no reason to support such cross-version score comparisons, other than limited research applications.

STRENGTHS. Much of the same praise that has been bestowed upon the OSIQ applies equally to the OSIQ-R. The OSIQ-R is oriented toward assessing self-image in normal, or psychologically adjusted adolescents. There are precious few assessment tools that are sensitive to individual differences among adolescents in this range of social and emotional functioning. The sensitivity of the OSIQ-R to these individual differences is enhanced by its use of a variety of different scales that probe multiple areas of normal functioning. Another strength of the OSIQ-R is the use of a 6-point Likert response scale ranging from *describes me very well* to *does not describe me at all*. This flexible and easy-to-use response code is an advantage over similar tests that often use a true/false response system. The OSIQ-R manual is written clearly and directions for use of the test are laid out succinctly. The test may be administered in a group format, and a broad range of computer scoring services are available. The user may find these to be a necessity because the manual does not contain normative tables.

CRITIQUE. It is helpful to evaluate how past criticisms of the OSIQ have been addressed in its revision. Hogan (1985) criticized the OSIQ manual for not providing validity data. Similarly, Adams (1986) stated that sufficient evidence of concurrent, construct, and predictive validity was not reported. In the OSIQ-R manual, the authors attempt to address this oversight by reporting results of studies that primarily focus on the OSIQ. Because the OSIQ and the OSIQ-R are virtually identical, it is likely that these validity data are applicable to the OSIQ-R, but similar studies are not reported for the new version. The authors report an adequate concurrent validity coefficient of .84 between the OSIQ (composite Self-Image) and the Tennessee Self-Concept Scale (composite Self-Esteem). Interestingly, the authors give a lot of attention to reporting concurrent validity between the OSIQ and clinical assessment measures (e.g., the Minnesota Multiphasic Personality Inventory [MMPI] and the Beck Depression Inventory [BDI]). Although moderate correlations were found, this detracted from an examination of the relationship between the OSIQ and other commonly used measures of self-concept, self-esteem, and self-adjustment. It is unclear whether the authors want the OSIQ-R to be based on a theoretical model of normal adolescent development or on one emphasizing psychopathology. Although the revised manual does contain validity information, evidence of the construct validity is not overwhelmingly convincing. The reported evidence for predictive validity of the OSIQ-R comes primarily from a single, all-male longitudinal study that effectively predicted "psychologically normal" functioning. However, without more detailed documentation of the subjects included in the sample and how "psychologically normal" functioning was operationalized, we have little means to evaluate the predictive validity of the OSIQ-R. Overall, the authors have made some improvement in reporting the validity of the OSIQ-R, which appears to be fair to good.

Martin's (1985) primary criticism of the OSIQ was the manual did not adequately describe the test's construction, and that poor item analysis subsequently resulted in low internal consistencies in the scales. In the OSIQ-R manual, the authors present information about test construction, stating that original questions came from literature based on adolescent psychology, development, and psychopathology. Yet half the subscales on the OSIQ-R have reliability coefficients about .70. Although test-retest reliability for the OSIQ-R normative sample is not reported, a stability coefficient of .73 for the total score after a 6-month period is reported in the manual.

Notwithstanding previous criticisms of the OSIQ, there are some notable issues about the OSIQ-R of which users should be aware. First, the standardization sample consists of only 964 adolescents. The small sample size and the limited geographic representation (primarily eastern seaboard states) negatively impacts the generalizablity of the reference group to adolescents elsewhere across the country. Also, the ethnic background of the reference group is broken down into White, Black, and Other, which is an inadequate means of reporting ethnicity—we are only told that the "Other" category represents 8% of the sample. Use of the OSIQ-R with adolescents whose ethnic background is other than African American or Caucasian is therefore cautioned, especially in regions with large numbers of ethnic minorities (e.g., California). For that matter, the inclusion of less than 100 African-American youth in the norm sample renders judgments based on standardized scores highly suspect for them. A second concern is that the wording of some of the test items is awkward (e.g., Item #79: "*I do not attend sexy shows*"). This problem may make it difficult for some respondents to answer items accurately. Other items are scored based on double-negative responses, which may lead to confusion.

SUMMARY. The OSIQ-R is one of the few instruments that assesses youth's general self-image. Nonetheless, one is left with basic questions about what the OSIQ-R actually measures. In their reviews of the OSIQ, Martin (1985) and Hogan (1985) refer to the test as a measure of "adjustment," whereas Adams (1986) states that the test also measures "self-esteem." The authors of the OSIQ-R indicate that it provides a "window into the feelings of adolescents" (manual, p. 1). These constructs certainly are related, but are they interchangeable? This coupled with the tendency to use the OSIQ, and now the OSIQ-R, in studies with clinical samples leads to confusion abut what the scale measures and its primary use. In addition, the computer scoring and interpretation service that is available contributes to this confusion by comparing a youth's pattern of scores to those from clinically diagnosed groups (e.g., single episode, major depression). The OSIQ-R is not presented as a diagnostic instrument, yet the computerized profile analysis suggests that it might be used as one. It is useful to keep in mind that low scores do not indicate the presence of psychopathology, although presumably a youth who obtains low scores on the OSIQ-R may be wrestling with experiences related to clinical symptoms. It would be useful if the authors provided some clarification about the OSIQ-R construct validity and address deficiencies in the test's norms.

REVIEWER'S REFERENCES

Hogan, R. (1985). [Review of the Offer Self-Image Questionnaire for Adolescents.] In J. V. Mitchell, Jr. (Ed.), *The ninth mental measurements yearbook* (pp. 1079-1080). Lincoln, NE: Buros Institute of Mental Measurements.

Martin, R. (1985). [Review of the Offer Self-Image Questionnaire for Adolescents.] In J. V. Mitchell, Jr. (Ed.), *The ninth mental measurements yearbook* (p. 1080). Lincoln, NE: Buros Institute of Mental Measurements.

Adams, G. (1986). Offer Self-Image Questionnaire for Adolescents. In D. J. Keyser & R. C., Sweetland (Eds.), *Test critiques* (vol. 5; pp. 297-302). Kansas City, MO: Test Corporation of America.

[269]

Optometry Admission Testing Program.

Purpose: "Designed to measure general academic ability and comprehension of scientific information."
Population: Optometry school applicants.
Publication Dates: 1987–93.
Acronym: OAT.
Scores, 8: Natural Sciences (Biology, General Chemistry, Organic Chemistry, Total), Reading Comprehension, Quantitative Reasoning, Physics, Academic Average.
Administration: Group.
Price Data: Available from publisher.
Time: 235(330) minutes in 2 sessions.
Comments: Supplants the Optometry College Admission Test.
Author: Optometry Admission Testing Program.
Publisher: Optometry Admission Testing Program.
Cross References: For a review by Penelope Kegel-Flom of the Optometry College Admission Test, see 8:1104 (3 references).

Review of the Optometry Admission Testing Program by ALAN C. BUGBEE, JR., Director of Educational Systems/Associate Professor of Psychology, The American College, Bryn Mawr, PA:

The Optometry Admission Test is an aptitude test designed to assess whether applicants possess the necessary prerequisite knowledge to enter optometry school and, from this, determine whether they can successfully complete the first year of optometry school. The Optometry Admission Test (OAT) is required by the 19 schools and colleges of optometry in the United States and Canada. It is administered in October and February at numerous sites in 47 states (although two of them, Alaska and South Dakota, are ad hoc), Puerto Rico, and Canada. For a fee ($67 according the material reviewed), a person may take the exam, have "official transcripts of scores" (Optometry Admission Testing Program ([OATP], 1990a, p. 6) sent to up to five optometry schools, have his or her pre-optometry advisor receive a copy, unless otherwise indicated by the test taker (OATP, 1990a, p. 10), and receive a personal copy of results. The examination consists of four different tests, collectively lasting about 4 hours. The four tests are Survey of Natural Science, Quantitative Reasoning, Reading Comprehension, and Physics.

The Survey of Natural Sciences is the longest test in the OAT, lasting 90 minutes. It is composed of sections on Biology (40 items), General Chemistry (30 items), and Organic Chemistry (30 items). This test is presented all at once, but questions on the general subjects are clustered together. The test taker receives a score for each subject area on this test.

The Reading Comprehension test is designed to assess the taker's ability to read, comprehend, analyze, and remember information. This section is 50 minutes long and comprises three passages, with 16 or 17 questions on each passage for a total of 50 questions overall. The convention of having three passages began in February 1990. Prior to this date, the Reading Comprehension test had one lengthy passage (about 4,000 words) and 50 questions. The sample provided for this review (OATP, 1989a) had only one reading passage. One score is given for this test.

The Quantitative Reasoning test is intended to measure the test taker's ability to "reason with numbers, to manipulate numerical relationships, and deal intelligently with quantitative materials" (OATP, 1989a, p. 1). It covers algebra, fractions, conversions, percentages, exponential notation, statistics, geometry, probability, and trigonometry in 30 questions on mathematics and 20 applied mathematical problems

(OATP, 1989b). Like the Reading Comprehension test, one score is reported. It is 45 minutes long.

The Physics test measures "areas covered in a two semester physics course" (OATP, 1989a, p. 1), including units and vectors, kinematics, statistics and dynamics, motion, energy, optics, thermodynamics, and nuclear physics (OATP, 1990a, pp. 2-3). It is 50 minutes long and contains 40 questions spread across the aforementioned array of topics in physics. A single score is reported for this test.

The scores are reported in a standard score form. The OAT utilizes a 200 to 400 scale with a mean of approximately 300 and a standard deviation of approximately 40. Because the OAT has no penalty for guessing, the raw score is computed by adding up the number of correct answers for each test.

In addition to the scores for Biology, General Chemistry, Organic Chemistry, Reading Comprehension, Quantitative Reasoning, and Physics, the OAT presents a Total Sciences score and an Academic Average Score. The Total Sciences score is composed of the subtest scores in the Natural Sciences test and the Physics test. The Academic Average score is a composite of the six individual test standard scores. This is done by summing the standard scores for each of the test scores and dividing by 6 (OATP, 1989a, p. 46). This is then rounded to the nearest 10-point interval (i.e., 293.7 would be converted to 290).

The reliability reported in the test taker's booklet for the OAT (OATP, 1990a, p. 3) is .80 for both the Reading Comprehension test and the Physics Test, .83 for the Quantitative Reasoning test, and .93 for the Survey of Natural Sciences tests as a group. No information is provided on the subtests within the Survey of Natural Sciences or on the composite Total Science score. No explanation is given on these reported reliabilities or their accompanying standard errors of measurement. It is not mentioned, for example, whether these standard errors are for the raw scores or the scaled scores, although from their size (Quantitative Reasoning 16.46, Reading Comprehension 19.17, Survey of Natural Sciences 11.62, Physics 19.57), they are almost certainly from the standard scores. Apparently, the OATP assumes that test takers either already know about reliability or do not care about it, so further information is unnecessary.

A more detailed report (OATP, 1989b) examined the reliability of the OAT for two administrations. The October 1988 administration (N = 1,194) had KR-20 reliabilities ranging from .77 to .86 on the six tests and .92 on the composite Total Science score. The February 1989 administration (N = 695) yielded KR-20 reliabilities from .79 to .86 for the six tests and .93 for the Total Science score.

The Optometry Admission Test began in March 1987, replacing the Optometry College Admission Test (see Kegel-Flom, 1978). Starting in March 1988, utilizing the Rasch model—a one parameter logistic model of Item Response Theory (see Suen, 1990, pp. 92-93; Hambleton & Swaminathan, 1985, pp. 39, 46-48; Wright, 1988), an ability-referenced scale was developed to equate current scores to the original March 1987 scores. This allowed a comparison of a current test taker with prior takers in addition to other current takers. In other words, with this method, the OAT was no longer restricted by its normative group.

No explanation was provided about why the Rasch model was selected for the OAT nor is any information provided on what studies, if any, were conducted on how well the OAT fulfills the assumptions of Item Response Theory, in general, or the Rasch model, in particular. This is unfortunate, as a very good report and explanation on the uses of IRT in conjunction with Classical testing is provided to users (Smith, 1990). This report, intended for the use of admissions officers, faculty, and committees, demonstrates the relationship between total standard scores, total raw scores, percentile ranks, and test item difficulty. It provides good examples of relationship of total test scores in Classical Theory with a test taker's probability of answering an item correctly given that test taker's underlying ability, a purpose of Item Response Theory. This is very refreshing and provides a good example for test developers and publishers to follow.

There are around 2,500 applicants to Optometry school every year (OATP, 1989a, p. 1), all of whom are required to take the OAT. The validity criterion for the OAT is, therefore, how well it predicts students' first year performance in optometry school. A study (OATP, 1990b) on the performance of students in their first year of optometry school compared its relationships with undergraduate grade point average (GPA), math-science GPA, and scores on the OAT. This study covers 14 schools and 1,026 students in academic year 1988–1989. Overall, it showed (pp. 10-11) that the OAT scores (apparently, all eight of them), in combination with the student's GPA in mathematics and science courses, were the best predictors of first year performance in optometry school.

Because schools of optometry are apparently different from one another in their curricula, this study examined relationships in terms of schools, as opposed to studying relationships overall. Therefore, the value of the OAT as a predictor of success in the first year of optometry education depends on to which school it is applied. This is consistent with the OAT's objective (Smith, 1990; OATP, 1988; OATP, 1989b) of helping schools establish their own criteria for selection of students for admission to their program. Viewed collectively, however, based on reported medians of correlations (OATP, 1990b), it seems that the Reading Comprehension Test has the weakest relationship with first year overall GPA in optometry school. The strongest relationship is between GPA and the Quantitative Reasoning Test score. From these tables, it is worth noting that the student's overall GPA and math-science GPA generally have very strong, if not the strongest, relationship with the first year optometry school GPA. Nonetheless, if it can be assumed that the current OAT is the same or very similar to the OAT used in this study, then it can be concluded that the OAT is a good, though moderate, predictor of first year performance in optometry school.

In summary, the Optometry Admission Test is a group of four general tests in reading, mathematics, natural sciences, and physics. These tests, which yield eight scores (Reading Comprehension, Physics, Quantitative Reasoning, Biology, General Chemistry, Organic Chemistry, Total Science, and Academic Average), are used in conjunction with undergraduate GPA, references from pre-optometry teachers, and interviews to select students for admission to optometry school. As a whole, the OAT is a good test. It accounts for a moderate proportion of grade variance in the first year of study in optometry and is adequately, though not exceptionally, reliable.

The OAT shines in its presentation of how the quality of a test item and a subject's performance on it relates to total test scores. That is, through a report provided to users, the OAT shows the relationship between the difficulty of an item, in the Item Response Theory (IRT) sense, and how this can be utilized in estimating whether an applicant can meet the criteria for admission at a particular school. Through this report, the OAT is providing valuable information to test users about this test theory, which is relatively new to end users and becoming more popular. Furthermore, unlike many explanations of IRT, it does not require a doctorate in psychometrics to use. This is most commendable, and, regrettably, rare.

REVIEWER'S REFERENCES

Kegel-Flom, P. (1978). Optometry College Admission Test. In O. K. Buros (Ed.), *The eighth mental measurements yearbook* (pp. 1702-1703). Highland Park, NJ: The Gryphon Press.

Hambleton, R. K., & Swaminathan, H. (1985). *Item response theory*. Boston: Kluwer-Nijhoff.

Optometry Admission Testing Program (1988). *A guide to the interpretation of the OAT response pattern score report*. Chicago: Author.

Wright, B. D. (1988). Rasch measurement models. In J. P. Keeves (Ed.), *Educational research, methodology, and measurement: An international handbook* (pp. 286-292). Oxford: Pergamon Press.

Optometry Admission Testing Program. (1989a). *Optometry Admission Test preparation materials*. Chicago: Author.

Optometry Admission Testing Program. (1989b). *User's manual*. Chicago: Author.

Optometry Admission Testing Program. (1990a). *Optometry admission testing program 1991*. Chicago: Author.

Optometry Admission Testing Program. (1990b). *Correlation study: OAT scores and prehealth gpa and first-year grades of 1988-1989*. (1989-1990 Report 1). Chicago: Author.

Smith, R. M. (1990). *Optometry Admission Testing Program: Variable maps*. (Technical Report 1990-1). Chicago: Optometry Admission Testing Program.

Suen, H. K. (1990). *Principles of test theories*. Hillsdale, NJ: Lawrence Erlbaum Associates.

Review of the Optometry Admission Testing Program by JAMES E. CARLSON, Director of Research, Educational Testing Service, Princeton, NJ:

The Optometry Admission Testing Program (OAT) appears to have been very carefully constructed. The psychometric procedures used in the development of the instrument and derivation of the reported scores also appear to be well conceived and executed. The OAT supplants the Optometry College Admission Test (OCAT) and its purpose is to provide standardized information about the abilities of candidates for optometry school, abilities that are demonstrably related to performance in such schools.

The OAT comprises four examinations: Survey of the Natural Sciences (40 biology items, 30 general chemistry items, and 30 organic chemistry items: 90-minute time limit), Reading Comprehension (50 items based on three reading passages), Quantitative Reasoning (50 items), and Physics (40 items). Standard scores are reported for Reading Comprehension, Quantitative Reasoning, the Survey of Natural Sciences, Biology, General Chemistry, Organic Chemistry, Physics, and Total Science. The Total Science score "is based on the raw scores for the 100 items from the Survey of the Natural Sciences and the 40 items from Physics" (manual, p. 1). A composite score, referred to as the Academic Average, and computed as the "average of the Quantitative Reasoning, Reading Comprehension, Biology, Inorganic and Organic Chemistry, and Physics standard scores" (manual, p. 2) is also reported. The OAT is administered under the auspices of the Association of Schools and Colleges of Optometry and all such schools in the United States and Canada currently require candidates to take it.

The Survey of the Natural Sciences is described as an achievement test with "content limited to those areas covered by an entire first-year course in biology general chemistry, and organic chemistry." The Reading Comprehension test "contains a passage typical of material that might be read in optometry school." The Quantitative Reasoning Test is described as measuring "the candidate's ability to reason with numbers, to manipulate numerical relationships, and deal intelligently with quantitative materials." The Physics instrument is described as an achievement test with content "limited to those areas covered in a two semester physics course" (preparation materials).

The standard scores for Quantitative Reasoning, Survey of Natural Sciences, Biology, General Chemistry, Organic Chemistry, Physics, and Total Science were equated using a Rasch Item Response Theory (IRT) model to the March 1987 test administration. That for Reading Comprehension "was set using the normal distribution method" (manual, p. 3). The standard score scales range from 200 to 400 with means of 300.

Supplemental Score Reports "designed to assist admission committees in evaluation the [sic] appropriateness of a [sic] examinee's standard score based on his/her response pattern" are also available. These are described in the document, *A Guide to the Interpretation of the OAT Response Pattern Score Report*.

Reliability information presented in the User's Manual cites KR-20 coefficients ranging from .77 to .92 for the October 1988 administration, and from .79 to .93 for the February 1989 administration.

A case is made for content validity in the User's Manual, based on "the expertise of the evaluations and judgments of the members of the test construction committees" (manual, p. 4). Distributions by gender and ethnicity are also reported. Distributions by other background variables are available in a report entitled *OAT Candidate General Information*. Distributions by gender and number of years of pre-optometry education are reported by undergraduate college, and accumulated by state, in a report entitled *Pre-optometry School Analysis of Fall 1988 and Spring 1989 Optometry Admission Test Participants*. Predictive validity studies are reported in the publication, *Correlation Study: OAT Scores and Prehealth GPAs and First-Year Grades of 1988-1989*.

The main criticism I have of the material I reviewed is that some of the explanations of psychometric/statistical procedures are not as clear as I would like to see, or are oversimplified or incorrect. In addition, several of the documents are badly in need of editing for grammar and consistency. An example can be seen above in the quotation from *A Guide to the Interpretation of the OAT Response Pattern Score Report*. As a second example, in the User's Manual one examination is referred to as both General Chemistry and Inorganic Chemistry. Many additional examples could be cited. For the most part the oversimplification and unclear explanations are those written for users and not for measurement professionals, and it is admittedly difficult to describe such procedures clearly without using jargon with which the users might not be familiar.

In the document, *Correlation Study: OAT Scores and Prehealth GPAs and First-Year Grades of 1988-1989* there are a number of statistical errors that should be corrected. Significance tests are cited for correlation coefficients without stating whether one- or two-tailed tests were conducted. A significant correlation is incorrectly described by the statement "there is 95 percent probability that the relations are not attributable to chance" (p. 2). The terms "Valid N" and "percent" require additional explanation. No data are reported to support the statement "the explained variance of first-year grades is higher for the OAT than for undergraduate GPAs" (p. 2). Multiple regression results are reported in conjunction with tables in which these results do not appear (they are reported in later tables). Median multiple correlation coefficients are described with the phrase "do not change significantly" (p. 10). Not only are there no significance tests reported to support this type of statement but, to my knowledge, no such significance test exists in the statistical literature. Finally, if the IRT and "normal distribution method" equating procedures and the response pattern score report methodology are to be understood by measurement experts, a technical manual containing much more detail than that presented in the reviewed material is necessary.

In summary, despite the few criticisms above, the OAT instrument and psychometric methodology used in its development are superior in quality. Documentation, however, could be vastly improved by thorough editing and preparation of a detailed technical manual.

[270]

Oral Language Evaluation, Second Edition.

Purpose: "An oral language measure, in both English and Spanish, designed to quickly assess or diagnose and prescribe instructional activities to help develop the student's oral language."
Population: Elementary students and older students requiring oral language training.
Publication Dates: 1977–85.
Scores: Language development in English and Spanish of bilingual and monolingual children on a 7-level continuum (Labeling, Basic Structures, Expanded Structures, Connected Structures, Simple/Concrete Discourse, Complex/Abstract Discourse, Combined Vocabulary/Concept and Background Development).
Administration: Individual.
Parts, 3: Part I (Assessment), Part II (Diagnosis), Part III (Prescription).
Price Data, 1986: $7.95 per teacher's manual ('85, 63 pages) including testing material on reproducible blackline originals.
Time: Administration time not reported.
Comments: Tape recorder necessary for administration of Part II.
Authors: Nicholas J. Silvaroli, Jann T. Skinner, and J. O. "Rocky" Maynes, Jr.
Publisher: EMC Publishing.
Cross References: See T3:1734 (1 reference).

Review of the Oral Language Evaluation, Second Edition by ROBERT B. FRARY, Professor and Director, Office of Measurement and Research Services, Virginia Polytechnic Institute and State University, Blacksburg, VA:

The Oral Language Evaluation is a paper-bound volume designated as a "teacher's manual" and includes testing materials. The instrument should be viewed mainly as a teaching aid, as it is designed for use within a classroom to determine the level of oral language training appropriate for individual students. About one-third of the manual is devoted to exercises and activities suitable for the various levels. Although the orientation is clearly toward elementary school, the manual could be used with older students.

The testing materials are provided in English and Spanish and may be used with monolingual and bilingual students. Of course, bilingual students might be tested in both languages. The exercises are provided only in English but would be simple to translate.

The manual authors specify two evaluation formats, "Assessment" and "Diagnosis." Diagnosis is the more formal. Four pictures are provided in the manual, each accompanied by a brief story in Spanish and in English. Two are selected by the teacher, who reads the story for each picture in the chosen language. The student is then asked to select one picture and describe or otherwise talk about it. The responses are tape recorded and later transcribed and assigned to one of seven fluency levels (see descriptive test entry above). Definitions of these levels are stated, and examples for each level are given for each picture in English and in Spanish. Sample forms for recording each student's outcome are provided. Assessment, in contrast, consists simply of using any interesting picture (selected by the teacher) to elicit an oral response from the student. The response (in whichever language) is then classified into one of three fluency levels corresponding to the two lowest, the next two higher, and the top three of the diagnosis levels. The exercises and activities are keyed to the diagnosis levels.

No norms and no data on reliability or validity are available. In fact, it would appear that no empirical studies have been done to evaluate the efficacy of the Oral Language Evaluation. Nevertheless, within the limited scope of its intended use, a teacher should be able to judge its effectiveness adequately based on student performance on the exercises and activities corresponding to the assigned diagnosis level. This effectiveness may vary according to the school setting and the teacher's own proclivities. In any case, little harm seems likely if one uses the Oral Language Evaluation for its intended purposes, and many teachers may find that it provides a useful structure for oral language training. Given the lack of empirical studies, it should *not* be used for other purposes, such as assignment of students to specific educational programs.

Review of the Oral Language Evaluation, Second Edition by IAN C. PALMER, Program Officer for English and Orientation, Latin American Scholarship Program of American Universities, Harvard University, Cambridge, MA:

The purpose of the Oral Language Evaluation (OLE) is to "assess (Part I) or diagnose (Part II) [a child's oral language proficiency in English or Spanish,] and prescribe (Part III) instructional activities to help develop the student's oral language" (manual, p. 10). This instrument is inexpensive and accessible to teachers with little or no language evaluation experience. It consists solely of a teacher's manual that includes reproducible pictures and response record forms.

The authors express very concisely the rationale for the development and use of this measure. With no widely agreed upon description available of language development, the authors base their methodology and descriptors on their experience in the field. They believe that the spoken word (the symbol for the "real thing" in the child's experience) precedes the written word, and also that fluent language use in speech is the prerequisite for fluent reading and the other activities that follow from that.

Since the U.S. Supreme Court's 1974 *Lau vs. Nichols* decision, courses in English have been required in the U.S. for language-minority students in order not to exclude them from public school education, making it necessary for teachers to identify these students and measure their proficiency in English. In response the authors present their seven-level model of the "language continuum": Level I: Labeling (no use of structures); II: Basic structures (sentence level); III: Expanded structures (answering: where, when?); IV: Connected structures (using: if, because); V: Simple, concrete discourse; VI: Complex, abstract discourse; VII: Combined vocabulary, concept, and background development.

Level I characterizes a nonspeaker of the target language (English or Spanish); Level VII represents a fluent speaker, in no need of specialized instruction, who nevertheless should continue language development activity.

Use of the OLE allows the teacher to *assess* (quickly) or *diagnose* (by a lengthier procedure) the student's level and then *prescribe* activities for the classroom. The use of the terms diagnosis and prescription suggest a medical analogy that may be useful in building confidence in this procedure among parents or the general public.

The Assessment procedure requires the student to choose one of the four pictures provided or others provided by the teacher and describe it or answer questions about it for 2 to 3 minutes. This allows the teacher to place the student in one of three approximate groupings: Levels I–II, II–IV, or V–VII. The authors remind users that both the oral description of a picture and the suggested question-and-answer procedure are not natural language situations and should therefore be approached cautiously, enhanced where possible by warm-up exercises and by using prompts that call for longer and more complex statements. They also emphasize that pronunciation errors are not crucial at this stage.

The Diagnosis procedure involves the use of the provided pictures, after a warm-up stage, but the student's response is recorded and transcribed onto a record form (provided). The response can then be compared with typical examples at each level (given in English and Spanish for all four pictures). The total number of words in the response should be recorded on the form. There is no correlation attempted between the number of words in a student's response and the OLE level, although this might be established through experimentation. The student is then described as, for example, "proficient at Level III" and, therefore, as needing instruction at Level IV. Four record forms are shown fully or partially completed in order to provide practice in this procedure. All four examples are, unfortunately, in English.

The Prescription stage amounts to a collection of exercises at the basic levels and suggestions for communicative activities at higher proficiency levels. The 85 ideas for pattern drills for Levels I–II start out at the most basic ("What's this?" "It's a ________.") and progress to a still elementary level ("Who knows where she is?" "I do. She is ________."). There are seven more pages of ideas for activities at the other levels. This stage occupies 18 pages of the manual and provides information which would be useful to a teacher with no training in ESL or other language instruction, but which would be of limited usefulness to experienced ESL professionals.

In fact, the OLE may well lose its usefulness altogether as more and more school districts, individual schools, and instructional staff become sensitized to the language issue that emerged in the 1970s and to the responses to this issue that the OLE itself pioneered. I hope the adjustment process to the presence of language-minority students is complete nationwide, and that as a result of this process, teachers and administrators know where to go for specialized expertise. To the extent that this becomes true, there will be less dependence on instruments that require no previous knowledge of language proficiency evaluation.

The OLE manual does not include any suggestions for further reading on language testing or language dominance issues. I recommend the OLE user at the very least consult *Reviews of English Language Proficiency Tests* (edited by J. C. Alderson, K. J. Krahnke, and C. W. Stansfield and published by TESOL in 1987) for reviews of other measures that address the situation for which the OLE is offered; examples include the Bilingual Syntax Measure (T4:298; a more expensive test kit available from the Psychological Corporation, San Antonio, Texas), the Language Assessment Battery (T4:1385; with placement and evaluation functions, by the New York City Board of Education), and the Quick Language Assessment Inventory (T4:2182; an inventory of home and school language exposure factors, from the Moreno Educational Company, San Diego, California).

Nonetheless, the OLE remains a significant and consciousness-raising resource for those institutions at which the language proficiency issue is not an overrriding one or for instructional staff who only occasionally meet with a language-minority student.

REVIEWER'S REFERENCE

Alderson, J. C., Krahnke, K. J., & Stansfield, C. W. (Eds.). (1987). *Reviews of English proficiency tests*. Washington, DC: TESOL, Inc.

[271]

Oral-Motor/Feeding Rating Scale.

Purpose: Constructed to assess "oral-motor movement/feeding dysfunction."
Population: Ages 1 and over.
Publication Date: 1990.
Scores: Item scores only.
Administration: Individual.
Price Data, 1991: $29.95 per complete kit including 25 progress charts and manual (26 pages); $15.95 per 25 progress charts.
Time: Administration time not reported.
Comments: Ratings by professional.
Author: Judy Michels Jelm.
Publisher: Therapy Skill Builders.

Review of the Oral-Motor/Feeding Rating Scale by GLEN E. RAY, Assistant Professor of Psychology, Auburn University at Montgomery, Montgomery, AL:

The Oral-Motor/Feeding Rating Scale (OMFRS) was constructed to "aid evaluators in assessing individuals with oral-motor movement/feeding dysfunction" (manual, p. 1). The suggested age range is wide, going from one year of age through the adult years. The test form has two sides. Side one is divided into five sections. Section I is identifying information (client's name, evaluator's name, etc.). Section II, the main section, rates three specific oral movements: lip/cheek area movements, tongue movements, and jaw movements for eight major feeding areas. These areas include Breast Feeding, Bottle Feeding, Spoon Feeding, Cup Drinking, Biting (soft cookie), Biting (hard cookie), Chewing, and Straw Drinking. Each specific oral movement is rated on a 6-point Likert-type scale ranging from 0 (*Within Normal Limits*) to 5 (*Abnormal and Atypical for more than 75% of observations*). In addition to numerical scores, evaluators are encouraged to document specific oral-motor feeding patterns observed while specific movements are being evaluated. Section III, Related Areas of Feeding Function, provides information about behaviors related to the feeding function areas in Section II. Section IV, Respiration/Phonation and Motor Functions (both optional), is provided for narrative elaborations of verbal and motor behaviors related to the eight major feeding function areas of Section II. Section V is simply a rating scale summary of Section II. Side two is divided into four sections and serves as a narrative review of side one. On this side, the evaluator develops a synopsis of the oral-motor movement patterns, related areas of feeding function, respiration/phonation, and motor functions. Side two concludes with both long-term and short-term goals for the client.

The test manual gives an adequate description of each OMFRS section including the purpose of each section. To assist the evaluator in describing normal and abnormal movement patterns, a glossary of commonly used terms is provided. The addition of this terminology not only facilitates ease and speed of administration, it will aid in the standardization of the large amount of narrative description used with this instrument.

Weaknesses of the OMFRS center around scoring, administration, and lack of information about psychometric properties. The OMFRS is an instrument based on behavior observations of the client by the evaluator. As such, the manual lacks instructions as to the type of observation method the evaluator is to use (e.g., event sampling) or how the evaluator is to arrive at a particular score while observing the client. For example, to score behaviors in Section II, the manual states that numerical ratings of specific feeding behavior represent percentages based on 10 trials per presentation. Are evaluators to use event sampling and simply mark down each time a problem behavior occurs and then tally them up at the end of 10 trials, convert this into a percentage, and then pick a numerical score to represent the percentage? Additionally, although numerical ratings are to be based on 10 trials per presentation no mention is given as to what constitutes a trial or where in the stream of behavior the 10 trials are to be taken. Without specific instructions standardizing how and what particular behaviors to observe, the instrument lacks objectivity. Further, the instrument form could be better tailored to a specific observation technique. As is, the evaluator has no space to mark, tally, and convert scores to percentages, all of which must be done to score a behavior in Section II.

A related scoring problem has to do with the coding of related behaviors in Section III. Here, the evaluator rates behaviors by using either a plus symbol (+) for normal behavior, a plus-minus symbol (±) for occasional problems, or a minus symbol (-) for consistent problems. However, no mention is made in the test manual or on the test form as to how the evaluator is to determine the difference between occasional and consistent behavior problems.

The instrument allows for the evaluator to serve as the feeder in the event that the primary caregiver or other familiar feeder is unable to attend the testing session. Although flexible, this option may interfere with the evaluator's ability to observe and rate problem behaviors objectively. The organization of the instrument is structured such that three different sections (II, III, and IV) are to be coded simultaneously. Further, these three sections have different scoring formats (numerical, symbolic, and narrative, respectively). Thus, administration of the OMFRS appears to be very demanding on the evaluator.

The OMFRS manual fails to include mention of any psychometric properties of the instrument. Although the author states that the construction of the instrument was in response to the need of countless individuals, it is unclear as to why or how the author developed this particular coding scheme. How were the eight major feeding areas and the three specific oral movements to be rated arrived at? Further, as a behavior observation technique, reliability of the coding scheme must be assessed. This appears to be one of the first tests of its kind, making comparisons to similar established instruments very difficult. However, conducting interrater reliability studies would provide a means for determining the replicability of the test results.

In summary, the OMFRS has potential in assisting professionals dealing with feeding dysfunctions. As one of the first of its kind, it is an important first step in the generation of a sound assessment instrument. As is, lack of standardization of administration and scoring, coupled with a complete lack of supporting psychometric properties, severely limits the widespread utility of this measure.

Review of the Oral-Motor/Feeding Rating Scale by DONNA SPIKER, Clinical Assistant Professor of Psychiatry and Behavioral Sciences, Stanford University, Stanford, CA:

The Oral-Motor/Feeding Rating Scale is an assessment instrument to be used to evaluate specific oral-motor dysfunctions related to feeding. The scale includes a 13-page manual and rating scale form, and can be used for individuals who are at least one year of age through adulthood. The manual states that evaluators using the scale should be "a trained professional familiar with oral-motor movement development and oral-motor movement function/dysfunction" (manual, p. 3) who should conduct at least two practice evaluations before using the scale in a formal administration situation. Presumably, suitably trained professionals would include speech and language specialists, occupational and physical therapists, and other medically trained professionals, but more specific training requirements are not elucidated in the manual. Ideally, the scale requires the evaluator to observe the individual while self-feeding or while being fed in the person's typical feeding environment at the usual feeding time. The person's primary feeder should be used for individuals who require assistance with feeding, and if relevant, individuals may be observed while self-feeding and again while being fed by the primary feeder (two separate forms are completed in this case).

The rating scale form consists of five sections: one for identifying information, one for ratings of oral-motor/feeding patterns in eight areas, and three sections used for written comments providing summaries of the observed movements, the special feeding considerations (e.g., need for adaptive equipment, position during feeding, food sensitivities). Spaces are also provided to note problem areas and to identify therapeutic goals for feeding programming. The core portion of the scale is the ratings of feeding movements and the special feeding needs and problems. For each feeding pattern (e.g., bottle feeding, spoon feeding, biting: soft cookie, chewing), the evaluator rates lip/cheek movement, tongue movement, and jaw movement on a 6-point scale rating from normal function (0) to abnormal and/or atypical movement patterns (5). The manual provides good descriptions of the movement abnormalities to be noted with consistent operational definitions that a trained professional should be able to apply. The manual also contains two sample illustrations of completed forms and several references that should be helpful for program planners.

The major problem with this instrument is that the manual contains no information on reliability or validity. Missing is all the information about how the scale was developed, characteristics of the populations sampled to develop the scale, and the empirical data on either normative or specific atypical populations. Without such basic background information in the manual, users must not present observed assessment results as if they are standardized; rather, results obtained using this instrument should be framed in terms of clinical observations. This problem is particularly important for users to heed if this scale is used with very young children with unspecified neurological problems or milder developmental difficulties. Without normative, well-validated information about the specific movements evaluated by this scale, including estimates of the reliability of the observational ratings, users cannot be confident about whether assessments with very young children, at least, represent normative immaturities or atypical dysfunctions. For more severely disabled youngsters and adults with obvious feeding difficulties, the scale can be useful because it does provide a systematic method of noting the specific movement dysfunctions and related feeding considerations needed for planning specific feeding interventions. When used for this purpose, administered by a properly trained professional, this scale can serve a useful observational and documentation function.

[272]

Organizational Culture Inventory.

Purpose: Designed to measure an organization's norms and expectations.
Population: Organizational members.
Publication Dates: 1987–89.
Acronym: OCI.
Scores: 12 culture styles: Constructive Cultures (Achievement, Self-Actualizing, Humanistic-Encouraging, Affiliative Styles), Passive/Defensive Cultures (Approval, Conventional, Dependent, Avoidance Style), Aggressive/Defensive Cultures (Oppositional, Power, Competitive, Perfectionistic).
Administration: Group or individual.
Price Data: Price information available from publisher for test materials including Leader's Guide ('89, 74 pages).
Time: [15–20] minutes.
Authors: Robert A. Cooke and J. Clayton Lafferty.
Publisher: Human Synergistics, Inc.

TEST REFERENCES

1. Cooke, R. A., & Szumal, J. L. (1993). Measuring normative beliefs and shared behavioral expectations in organizations: The reliability and validity of the Organizational Culture Inventory. *Psychological Reports, 72*, 1299-1330.

Review of the Organizational Culture Inventory by CHARLENE M. ALEXANDER, Assistant Professor of Counseling Psychology, Fordham University, New York, NY:

PURPOSE AND PSYCHOMETRIC EVALUATION. The Organizational Culture Inventory (OCI) shows some promise as an instrument for measuring the culture of an organization; however, much more research is needed before it can be used with any confidence for the purposes described in the manual. Of major concern is the absence of, and scant reference to, any validity or reliability data presented in the Leader's Guide. Reference is made throughout the manual to the Life Styles Inventory (LSI; 222), yet, no data are presented to describe this relationship. What the inventory developers report is that the instrument was used in a number of studies, "including one focusing on over 150 supermarkets for the Coca-Cola Retailers' Research Council and another involving sub-units of many diverse organizations in the Midwest. It is evident that the instrument has been tested extensively with respect to its reliability and validity and its appropriateness for organizational change and management development programs" (p. 1). Such statements are common throughout the manual, yet no corroborating evidence for these claims can be found. Concurrent validity evidence could have been provided by use of the Life Styles Inventory (Lafferty, 1990). Overall, more work is needed before claims of validity and reliability made in the manual can be substantiated.

STRUCTURE AND ADMINISTRATION. The OCI purports to measure 12 organization styles: Humanistic-Encouraging, Affiliative, Approval, Conventional, Dependent, Avoidance, Oppositional, Power, Competitive, Perfectionistic, Achievement, and Self-Actualizing. These styles are similar to those found in the LSI. The only exception being that whereas the LSI measures an individual's own thinking and behavior along these 12 styles, the OCI purports to measure the extent to which individuals in organizations *are expected* to think and behave along these dimensions. It is not clear from the information provided in the manual how the concept of what one believes *is expected* of himself or herself in an organization differs significantly from one's *own thinking* and behavior along these exact styles. Thus, in effect, the two inventories are rendered redundant if these differences cannot be determined.

The OCI is also thought to measure three types of organizational culture: (*a*) Constructive, (*b*) Passive/Defensive, and (*c*) Aggressive/Defensive cultures. Positive outcomes are thought to be related to Constructive cultures and negative outcomes to both Passive/Defensive and Aggressive/Defensive cultures. Although developers acknowledge that some organizations (e.g., accounting firms, because of their goals and tasks) need elements of Passive/Defensive and Aggressive/Defensive cultures, no strengths are reflected in the language used to describe them. The language should be changed to reflect positive aspects of defensive cultures.

Each of the 12 cultural styles measured by the OCI is further described in terms of the norms and expectations associated with them, as well as the environmental factors that lead to those norms and expectations. Outcomes associated with each style are also highlighted, yet no data are presented to verify these findings. Test developers reiterate, however, that "In general, the results reported are supported by relationships (correlations) that are statistically significant" (p. 23). (When results are reported that only approach statistical significance, qualifying words like "might" and "may" are used.) The authors assume a lack of sophistication on the part of users of the inventory, an assumption that may not be warranted.

Administration instructions for the inventory are also quite confusing. Respondents are requested to think about what it takes for themselves as well as "people like yourself" to fit in and meet expectations in your organization. It is difficult if not impossible to think simultaneously of one's own thinking about expected behaviors and that of one's peers. For each statement of organizational behavior, respondents are to indicate expected organizational behavior on a 5-point Likert scale anchored by (1) *Not at all* and (5) *To a very great extent* (e.g., "follow orders . . . even when they're wrong"). Additionally, no information regarding item development is provided in the manual.

SUMMARY. In summary, the OCI developers need to provide much more information regarding the inventory's validity and reliability instead of simply relying on leading statements provided in the manual. Careful distinctions should be made between the three organizational cultures described, specifically, distinctions between Passive/Defensive cultures and Aggressive/Defensive cultures are needed. As a self-report measure the inventory can be used as a starting point for organizations to make assessments of members' perception of the organization and the administrators' perception of the organizational culture. Any discrepancies can be helpful jumping off points for further discussion, organizational planning, and implementing action plans.

REVIEWER'S REFERENCE

Lafferty, J. C. (1990). Life Styles Inventory. Plymouth, MI: Human Synergistics.

Review of the Organizational Culture Inventory by GARGI ROYSIRCAR SODOWSKY, Associate Professor of Educational Psychology, University of Nebraska-Lincoln, Lincoln, NE:

The Organizational Culture Inventory (OCI) measures respondents' perceptions of work-related behavioral norms and expectations that are believed to be held collectively by the members of an organization. Thus, culture is given the operational definition of individualized reports of work styles and interactional values that are shared within an organization. It is important to caution that an individual's specific personality and phenomenological constructions could bias the individual's observations of an organization's culture. Measuring an individual's experiences of a culture versus studying a whole culture group need different assessment methodologies. Culture is a group-level phenomenon, and individuals are only one among many units that propagate and demonstrate a culture. Composite profiles based on average responses, although providing aggregate information about a sample of respondents, may not reflect a culture that is greater than the sum of its parts.

The authors state that in a "strong" culture, individual interpretations are "relatively small." What do the authors mean by "strong cultures"? For example, would White American society not be considered a strong culture group because individualistic interpretations are a common cultural style? Concomitantly, could there be an opposite "weak culture," and what would the characteristics of this culture be? These issues need to be addressed theoretically because of an implicit suggestion that the OCI should be used only in organizations with strong cultures.

The OCI, it is proposed, could be used to implement organizational development and changes. It is recommended for use in particular subunits or departments, which would allow for the identification of and discussion of "subcultures" within a larger organization. The authors seem to be taking liberty with anthropological and multicultural terms and diluting their meanings by associating "culture" and minority cultures with units and departments of a business organization, which is itself a reflection of a larger racial or cultural or nationality group.

One hundred and twenty statements measure 12 different cultural styles. The authors do not explain psychometrically how all dimensions could have the same number of items. The 12 styles are related to managerial philosophies that could be changed, if dysfunctional, by the leaders of an organization. Styles relatively similar to one another are placed next to each other in the profile sheet; styles that are more distinct and independent are placed further apart. The authors state that styles that are close to one another are likely to occur together, and styles that are distant from one another might not coincide. However, the notion that proximity reflects expected degree of association is not supported with evidence of interscale correlations or criterion-related findings. The positioning may have been done in an a priori manner.

Constructive styles consist of Achievement, Self-Actualizing, Humanistic-Encouraging, and Affiliative styles. Passive/Defensive styles consist of Approval, Conventional, Dependent, and Avoidance styles. Aggressive/Defensive styles consist of Perfectionistic, Competitive, Power, and Oppositional styles. These organizational styles are proposed to meet various needs of employees such as satisfaction needs, which are assumed to be the polar opposite of security needs, and people-orientation concerns, which are believed to be the polar opposite of task-orientation concerns. Higher order satisfaction needs are placed near the top of a circular profile, and lower-order security needs are placed at the bottom. Concern for people and concern for tasks are placed at the two opposite sides of the circular profile. Because the writing in the manual subscribes to some extent to popular psychology and to eclectic psychological views, the constructs mentioned previously are not substantively grounded in theory. The items of the Constructive styles may tend to elicit socially desirable responses because many respondents would like to perceive themselves and their organizations as being achieving and self-actualizing.

Scores can range from 10 to 50, and are plotted differently for each of the 12 styles because of differences in response distributions of the normative group along the 12 cultural styles. Raw total scores are converted to percentile scores. Scores are plotted around a "circumplex" or "clock" with 12 slivers representing the 12 styles. Within this clock there are six circles with one common center. The circles represent from inside out ascending percentile ranks. It is not explained why and how the 99th percentile rank indicates a raw score of 50 across all 12 styles, whereas lower percentile ranks have different raw scores for the different styles. It is not clear why the total scores of the 12 styles are labeled, for example, as "Total 7 O'Clock Position" or "Total 1 O'Clock Position." Such labeling appears to have no criterion meaning and may only be of metaphorical value to complete the image of the circumplex or clock. Similarly, it is not understood why the profile is circular in shape, which is different from the general appearance of profiles of psychological instruments.

Composite profiles can be generated in two different ways, depending on the objectives of the user. A group profile, based on averaging, could be drawn when making comparisons across groups or subunits. Or OCI scores of the various members could be plotted separately, showing the similarities and differences among members. According to the author, inconsistent individual profiles would indicate a weak organizational culture and consistent profiles would indicate a strong culture. The author states that key executives, who respond within their strongly socialized cultural framework, generally show positive profiles, whereas a group of lower ranking officers who respond in terms of global norms and not their specific organizational norms may have negative profiles. The authors suggest that this discrepancy could result in some important discussion among key-level people. Profiles can also be based on years in the organization, sex, age, education, or salary.

The authors provide minimal information on methodology, data analyses, and results. The norms of the OCI are based on the responses of 3,939 individuals selected from a larger population of respondents from different organizations. No information is provided about the procedures for the selection of the normative sample and about its characteristics. Principal components factor analysis with data from 604 subjects indicated three factors, People-Security, Satisfaction, and Task-Security, accounting for 65% of the variance. However, factor loadings of the 120 items on the three factors are not reported. Instead, factor loadings of each of the 12 subscales on the three factors are reported, making it appear as though the OCI was used as a 12-item instrument in the factor analysis. It is not known how the 12 subscales were derived. On the basis of the reported factor analysis findings, one may expect only three subscales. Data from another subgroup of 661 subjects indicated Cronbach alphas ranging between .67 and .92 for the 12 subscales, with the highest alphas for subscales that could elicit socially desirable norms and the lowest alphas for subscales suggestive of negative behaviors such as oppositional, dependence, and perfectionistic. The means scores of the Satisfaction styles are also higher than the scores for People-Security and Task-Security styles. Analysis of variance for the 12 styles by organizations indicated significant differences between organizations, implying, according to the authors' views, that there is consistency within organizations in members' perceptions of their respective organizational norms and expectations, as measured by the OCI.

The OCI has some attractive features. The Leader's Guide (which, however, is not a manual) and the instrument are attractive and have face validity. The instrument is printed on NCR (No Carbon Required) paper, so that respondents can score and profile their own results on the reverse side of the NCR sheet. Individual totals can be averaged quickly, enabling the generation of a composite profile for a group in a timely manner. The self-scoring provides immediate feedback on respondents' own perceptions of their organization's culture, thus facilitating from the initial stages an awareness of one's culture and of the changes required in that culture. Individuals can compare their respective OCI profiles with the group average profile to see whether their perceptions of organizational norms and expectations are consistent with a unit's average perception. However, if there is a significant discrepancy between the individual profile and the group profile, the accuracy of either profile cannot be established. The Leader's Guide provides directions for administering the OCI, with good examples of commonly asked questions. Instructions for scoring and profiling results are given in the inventory.

[273]

Orientation Test for Professional Accounting.

Purpose: Developed to measure "skills necessary for success in a business environment."
Population: Applicants for accounting positions.
Publication Dates: 1946–81.
Scores, 4: Verbal Skills (Vocabulary, Reading Comprehension), Quantitative Skills, Total.
Administration: Group.
Manual: No manual.
Price Data: Not available.
Time: 50(55) minutes.
Comments: Formerly called the AICPA Orientation Test for Professional Accounting; no longer affiliated with the AICPA.
Author: American Institute of Certified Public Accountants.
Publisher: The Psychological Corporation.
Cross References: For information on the AICPA programs see T2:2323 (7 references), 5:911 (6 references), and 4:787 (15 references).
[The publisher advised in March 1994 that this test is now out of print.—Ed.]

Review of the Orientation Test for Professional Accounting by BRUCE K. ALCORN, Director of Certification, Teachers College, Ball State University, Muncie, IN:

HISTORICAL BACKGROUND. This test has its origins in 1943 when a committee was appointed by the American Institute of Accountants "to investigate procedures for selecting and guiding into public accounting well qualified young people and to develop a program of selection" (Wood, 1948). The committee subsequently identified four major factors, which were conditions for success in the profession, three of which they felt could be objectively measured: "general intelligence . . . technical training . . . professional interests" (Wood, 1948). Their efforts resulted in the initiation of the American Institute of Accountants Testing Programs in 1946, which was administered by the Educational Records Bureau. Two programs were supported: One was aimed at college students and the other was for use with employees and job applicants. Although both programs used the Orientation Test plus one or two accounting achievement tests, only the college program included an interest test (Strong's Vocational Interest Blank for Men). The Orientation Test yielded a verbal score, a quantitative score, and a total score. This test was considered by the developers to be an intelligence test (test of general aptitude) slanted toward business situations. Although the Institute recognized the fact that general aptitude tests were already in existence, the Orientation Test was developed so they could have a "confidential test . . . which would be under the control of the Institute" and it was also hoped that such a test would do a better job of predicting success in accounting than existing instruments (Wood, 1948).

The American Institute of Accountants Testing Program was extensively used well into the 1960s and during that time a considerable amount of research was reported pertaining to its reliability and validity. Although the related research generally supported the reliability and validity of the several forms of the Achievement Tests and the reliability of the Orientation Test, the literature reported more questionable results for the validity of the Orientation Test. For example, in relation to predicting college grades, Hendrix concluded that, "If a single test is to be utilized in predicting grades in elementary accounting, 'ACE Psychological Exam,' and 'OSU Psychological Test' are preferable to the AIA Orientation Test" (Hendrix, 1953). When it comes to predicting success as an accountant, Frederick concluded (with 5 years of data) that the Orientation Test was not nearly as valid a predictor of job success as were the Achievement Tests (Frederick, 1957).

During the 1960s the use of the AIA tests started to decline, and that trend continued until its practical demise today. In fact, they are no longer affiliated with its founding accounting organization. Today's schools of business tend to rely on other measures directly or indirectly (e.g., course grades, college entrance exam scores, and performance on the CPA exam).

THE CURRENT ORIENTATION TEST. The most recent version of the test has a 1981 copyright. Like the original version, the 1981 form yields the following scores: Verbal Skills, Quantitative Skills, Total. The Verbal score is determined by performance on two subtests: a vocabulary test using business-related terms and a reading comprehension test using business-related texts. The Quantitative score is determined by the results of solving business-related mathematical problems. Total test time is 50 minutes.

The value of this test is questionable at best for several reasons: (*a*) No manual is available and therefore the availability of norms is unknown (if available they are probably out-dated); (*b*) the most recent version of the test is 12 years old (more recent technological advances, e.g., computers, are not apparent); and (*c*) there are other and more advanced ways to measure aptitude and at less cost to the user (indices of general aptitude are available via college entrance exams at both the undergraduate and graduate levels).

There is one situation in which the use of the Orientation Test might be helpful. If a firm employs a number of individuals who have only completed high school, and they have a policy of promoting promising employees from within, and they encourage such employees to seek further education, they might want to use an instrument such as this as one of several ways of identifying those individuals most likely to benefit from such education. The catch here is the need for norms!

REVIEWER'S REFERENCES

Wood, B. D., Traxler, A. E., & Nissley, W. W: (1948). College Accounting Testing Program. *Accounting Review, 23*, 63-83.

Hendrix, O. R. (1953). Predicting success in elementary accounting. *Journal of Applied Psychology, 37*, 75-77.

Frederick, M. L. (1957). Testing the tests. *Journal of Accounting, 103*, 42-47.

[274]

OSOT Perceptual Evaluation.

Purpose: Designed to identify perceptual impairment in adults.

Population: Adults.

Publication Date: 1991.

Scores, 19: Scanning, Spatial Neglect, Motor Planning, Copying 2 Dimensional Designs, Copying 3 Dimensional Designs, Body Puzzle, Draw-a-Person, Right/Left Discrimination, Clock, Peg Board, Draw-a-House, Shape Recognition, Colour Recognition, Size Recognition, Figure Ground Discrimination, Proprioception, Stereognosis R, Stereognosis L, Total.

Administration: Individual.

Price Data: Price information for test materials including manual (60 pages) available from publisher.

Time: Administration time not reported.

Authors: Pat Fisher, Marian Boys, and Claire Holzberg.

Publisher: Nelson Canada [Canada].

Review of the OSOT Perceptual Evaluation by RAOUL A. ARREOLA, Director of Educational Technology, The University of Tennessee, Memphis, TN:

INTRODUCTION. The Ontario Society of Occupational Therapists' (OSOT) Perceptual Evaluation is designed to be a practical assessment instrument for use by occupational therapists to identify perceptual impairment in adults. Utilizing 18 subtests, the OSOT Perceptual Evaluation battery is intended for use as a wide-range screening measure of perceptual dysfunction in several areas related to basic daily living skills. The manual indicates that the instrument may also be used to (*a*) provide information on the degree of impairment, (*b*) monitor change, and (*c*) measure the effects of treatment and/or spontaneous recovery, among brain-damaged adults. The instrument is not intended to be used in isolation, but rather as part of a total patient profile that includes professional assessments of the patient's motor, sensory, and cognitive status as determined in accordance with the professional standards and guidelines of practicing occupational therapists.

ADMINISTRATION. The OSOT Perceptual Evaluation is intended to be administered by a qualified occupational therapist. Several of the subtests appear to require some measure of psychological training to be scored correctly. In fact, a number of the subtests will be quite familiar to those accustomed to administering the Stanford Binet Intelligence Scale, the Wechsler Adult Intelligence Scale, or similar cognitive diagnostic instruments. A qualified psychologist should have little difficulty administering the instrument, if necessary, given some familiarity with the emotional and physiological needs and characteristics of brain-damaged adults.

The guidelines for administering the instrument make it clear that the person administering it should be able to make the patient comfortable and provide encouragement. Because the instrument is intended to be used with adults who have suffered brain damage, the directions instruct the person administering the instrument to take special care to be sensitive to the emotional needs of the patient. Specific instructions include recommendations to take "time to greet the patient, to smile, to listen, and to generally provide a supportive environment" (p. 9). Because the administration of the instrument may be part of the patient's total therapy, the therapist administering it is instructed to assist the patient in completing subtest tasks if desired, but only after scoring the unassisted performance of the patient.

A quiet environment with a table on which the testing materials may be placed is required for administration. The materials include paper and pencil for the patient, and such items as cards on which drawings, shapes, and colors are represented, blocks, discs, cut-out representations of a person, and three wire/ring devices. The person administering the instrument should sit at the table directly across from the patient and present the materials or objects to the patient as specified by the subtest directions. A screen or shield is required to keep the patient from seeing the preparation of certain of the subtests' objects such as the blocks in the Copying 3-Dimensional Designs subtest.

The timing of the administration of the 18 subtests is often open-ended with the clear intent of eliciting the patient's maximum performance. Only four subtests, Motor Planning, Figure Ground Discrimination, and Stereognosis (R) and (L), contain any reference to time in their directions. A weakness of the instrument is that the time considerations for each subtest are not clearly indicated and must be deduced from the short references to time that are embedded in the directions or scoring instructions. The implicit assumption is that the therapist will be able to judge how much time to give the patient in completing each of the subtest tasks. The directions indicate, however, that should the patient need the time, a second session may be conducted, although it is advised that the second session be scheduled as soon as possible after the first. In order to make meaningful use of the normative data provided, it is recommended that the instrument be administered in its entirety, rather than use its subtests in isolation.

SCORING AND SCORE INTERPRETATIONS. A 5-point scoring scale, using the numbers 0, 1, 2, 3, and 4, is defined and used with each of the subtests. This scale is defined in terms of representations of the ability of the patient to perform certain tasks requiring intact basic perceptual functioning. Each subtest places patients into one of the following categories in terms of the task required: 0 = *Unable to Perform*, 1 = *Severe Dysfunction*, 2 = *Moderate Dysfunction*, 3 = *Minimal Dysfunction*, and 4 = *Intact Perceptually for Basic Functioning*. Specific guidelines as to how to classify the performance of the patient in terms of these categories is presented for each subtest. In some cases, such as the Draw-A-House and Draw-A-Person subtests, detailed representations of examples of performance at each level of functioning (or dysfunction) are provided as a guide to scoring.

Scores for all subtests are recorded on a single score sheet provided. Because the results may be used in the overall therapy of the patient, space for brief comments is also provided on the score sheet for each subtest. The total score for the instrument is computed by simply summing all subtest scores. For the 18 subtests a total score of 72 is possible (4 x 18 = 72). Based on the results of the validation study comparing the performance of brain-damaged patients to normal unimpaired subjects, a series of cutoff scores have been set that indicate the final determination of patient impairment. Total scores of 40 and below indicate Severe Impairment, 41–50 Moderate Impairment, 51–60 Mild Impairment, and 61–69 Borderline (requires further testing). Subjects scoring 70 and above are considered normal.

A summary of the technical information from the published validation study is presented in the manual. The validation study used 80 patients, diagnosed as having a range of frequently seen brain damage or impairment, and 70 normal subjects, matched as to age, sex, and education. The summary includes means, standard deviations, and *t*-test results comparing patients to normal subjects. The validity of the instrument is supported by the finding of statistically significant differences between scores of brain-damaged patients and normal subjects on each of the subtests as well as the total instrument score. Although the standard error of measurement is not presented in the manual, evidence of the sensitivity of the instrument in classifying individuals to various levels of impairment is presented. The data indicate that subjects at or above the cutoff score of 70 have a 100% probability of NOT being impaired, whereas subjects at or below the cutoff score of 60 have a 100% probability of being impaired to some degree. The manual interprets scores of 61–69 as indicating the possibility of some impairment and that further assessment should be conducted. Estimates of the reliability of the instrument is reported at r = .90 (Cronbach's alpha coefficient).

Used as intended, that is, as a part of the total patient profile, the OSOT Perceptual Evaluation appears to be a valid, reliable, and useful diagnostic instrument.

[275]

PACE.

Purpose: Developed to identify learning deficits for use in pre-school screening, educational placement, and remediation planning.

Population: Ages 4–6.

Publication Dates: 1986–88.

Scores, 6: Motor Coordination, Sensory Integration, Auditory Memory, Discrimination, Attending/Responding, Social Interaction.

Administration: Individual or group.

Comments: Ratings by parents and teachers.

Authors: Lisa K. Barclay and James R. Barclay.

Publisher: MetriTech, Inc.

a) PACE.

Price Data, 1991: $17 per 50 individual record forms; $180 per software program for scoring (IBM version only) including manual ('88, 50 pages).

Time: Administration time not reported.

b) FAST PACE.

Price Data: $12.95 per 10 group record forms.

Time: (10–15) minutes.

Cross References: See T4:1915 (1 reference).

Review of the PACE by SCOTT SPREAT, Administrator of Clinical Services, The Woods Schools, Langhorne, PA:

The PACE is a third party rating scale that is designed to identify learning skill deficits in young children. It is a 68-item instrument that yields six scale scores. The six scale scores are Motor Coordination, Sensory Integration, Auditory Memory, Discrimination, Attending/Responding, and Social Interaction. The 68 items are rated as Satisfactory, Deficient, or Needs Improvement. Although no direct statements are made about scalability, it would appear that items within each of the six scales are developmentally sequenced, such that the more complex items come toward the end of the scale. The PACE also includes 10 items for parents, and a brief screening device called FAST PACE is also available.

Administration of the PACE is generally flexible. It can be administered to groups of students or to a single individual. It can be completed at a single session, or the evaluation may be spread over several days. No information is provided on the impact of these varying administration methods.

The PACE offers a computerized data analysis system. Performance scores are entered into the computer, and the system is able to generate both individual and group summary reports. The system is menu driven and easy to use. This same system will also generate prescriptive recommendations for the teacher.

NORMS. The norm group for the PACE consists of 1,285 children, ages 4 to 6. Data were collected from these individuals from 1976 to 1985. Approximately 80% of the norm group is 5 years old, a finding that tends to reflect the admissions policies of most kindergartens. An analysis of the male versus female performance on the PACE led the authors to conclude that a single norm group was satisfactory. Although male-female differences were evident on the PACE, the percentage of score variance attributable to sex was only about 3%. The authors seem justified in the election of a single norm group.

RELIABILITY. The test guide manual reports both test-retest and internal consistency reliability data. No interrater reliabilities were reported, although the administration process and the type of items would seem to invite interrater variation.

Test-retest data were collected on 31 children. The PACE was administered at the start and end of a school year, and the resultant scale scores were compared. A median Pearson product moment correlation of .73 indicated relatively impressive stability given the amount of time between ratings. Test-retest data collected over a shorter interval and without educational or developmental intervention would have been interesting. The calculation of a test-retest coefficient over a significantly shorter period of time would be likely to enhance the reported reliability.

Internal consistency estimates ranged from .47 to .99, with a median alpha coefficient of .78. The first three subscales (Motor Coordination, Sensory Integration, and Auditory Memory) seem particularly weak with respect to internal consistency, whereas the final three (Discrimination, Attending/Responding, and Social Interaction) are stronger. Psychometricians have debated about the criterion for acceptable internal consistency, with some suggesting that scales should have internal consistency in excess of .90 for use with individuals. Clearly, only two of the PACE subscales (Attending/Responding and Social Interaction) meet this lofty criterion. There are, however, mitigating factors that should be considered. The PACE was developed for and normed on a specific group. It is probably quite reasonable to expect this group to be relatively homogeneous with respect to performance on the PACE, and this homogeneity would be likely to force a limitation on the obtained internal consistency coefficient. Given the limited purpose of the PACE and with the provision that the PACE be part of a comprehensive assessment strategy, the obtained reliabilities seem acceptable. Nevertheless, one might suggest that an item analysis might improve the internal consistency of the first three subscales.

VALIDITY. The test manual offers some information on several types of validity. The most thorough work appears to have been done with respect to construct validity. Factor analytic work provided relatively sound support for four of the six subscales. The construction of the remaining subscales (Sensory Integration and Auditory Memory) did not receive appreciable support from the factor analytic research.

Some information is presented on predictive validity. The reported study suggests that the PACE was "highly effective in assessing students' readiness skills and in specifying effective intervention strategies to promote skill development" (p. 35). A second study suggested that the PACE identified training strategies that led to significant increases in performance on the PACE. Although both of these studies are relevant to the validation of the PACE, considerably more information about these studies would have been beneficial. With the information presented in the test manual, it is a bit difficult to evaluate the adequacy of the validational work.

A primary validity question would seem to be the relationship between PACE scores and achievement. The test manual describes a study in which PACE scores were found to be positively related to scores on the SRA achievement series test. These correlations ranged from .27 to .67. Although the sample size was under 70, these findings suggest that PACE ratings are related to achievement.

In addition to the full-length PACE, the test offers a brief screening scale called FAST PACE. FAST PACE consists of 18 of the PACE items. No information is provided on the rationale for selecting these 18 items. The correlations between PACE and FAST PACE scores are acceptable. It was also reported that FAST PACE tends to err in favor of false positives rather than false negatives. That is, FAST PACE would rather incorrectly suggest that a child has a need than fail to identify a need. This claim was supported in a sample of 391 children. Cross-validational data are presented, but never explained.

The PACE offers prescriptive suggestions as well as evaluative data. A computer program will generate a report containing programming recommendations for students with identified needs. Although the computer-generated prescriptive report is certainly helpful and easy to use, the user is not privy to the decision rules that lead to the specific recommendations, nor is the theoretical model supporting the recommendations ever specified. This reviewer generated several individual prescriptive reports and noted that recommendations tended to incorporate sound teaching strategies such as shaping and task analysis. It was not possible to determine if there was any integration of strengths and needs in making recommendations, or whether each identified need resulted in an independent recommendation. Although there is some controversy over the use of computer-generated test reports, it seems the PACE system would be a useful adjunct to the teaching/assessment process.

The PACE is a brief rating scale that addresses a number of areas that are related to learning, and it seems appropriate for use with kindergarten children. The reliability is generally acceptable; however, improvements in two scales would be appreciated. Additional validational work would be beneficial. The computerized report generator will make this scale an asset for teachers and parents.

Review of the PACE by DONNA WITTMER, Assistant Professor of Education, University of Colorado at Denver, Denver, CO:

The PACE, a computer-based instrument for assessing and developing learning skills, covers 12 primary areas of skill development including motor coordination, eye-hand coordination, small muscle coordination, visual-perceptual, rhythm pattern recognition, listening, visual matching, tactile, motor behavior memory, verbal memory, attending/task-order, and social interaction skills. These 12 areas are then presented in terms of six broad scales: Motor Coordination, Sensory Integration, Auditory Memory, Discrimination, Attending/Responding, and Social Interaction. Thus, this assessment evaluates skills that have been found through research to be related to school success. This assessment also taps academic knowledge acquired, such as knowledge of names of colors and shapes, but this is a very small part of the total assessment. Because the assessment emphasizes skills such as matching, visual-perceptual, and motor behavior memory skills, the assessment is less culturally bound than other available measures.

The PACE is inclusive of the primary areas of skill development including social skills. It has a 10-item parent questionnaire. Although very brief, this at least involves parents in the assessment process. To its credit this assessment is not designed to be used to "screen" children out of kindergarten, but rather to determine the needs of the children, so that teachers and parents can plan a more appropriate program for the kindergarten children.

This assessment is recommended for teachers or trained aides to use in the classroom after the child has entered kindergarten. The assessment is easy to administer with few materials required. A short "screening" version, FAST PACE, is available. Many items on the PACE seem as if they would be fun for the child taking the test. Area 11 (attending/task order skills) and Area 12 (social interaction skills) are to be rated based upon generalized observations of the child's behavior over time. This ensures ecological validity concerning these important areas of development. A number of items can be administered to a group of children easing the administration time. However, if a child does not do well, the child should be assessed individually. Also, professionals should exercise care in the administration of this test by making sure that children are familiar with the person administering the test and that testing conditions are as comfortable and familiar as possible.

I would question the basic philosophy of the assessment which, as stated by the authors, is to "meet the need for early identification and remediation of learning skill deficits in kindergarten children." I have concerns with the computer-written report that specifies whether the child was superior, above average, average, below average, or deficient in the six broad skill areas. Is it fair to say that 4-year-olds have "deficits" if they cannot copy a diamond or letters? The computer then generates "strategies for intervention" that focus on the areas of "deficit," giving activities to "remediate" these areas. This general philosophy seems contrary to IDEA (Individuals With Disabilities Education Act) which promotes the assessment of children's strengths and needs as opposed to the identification of "deficits" only. Those professionals who use the computer program should be aware that the assessment is based on a "deficit" model.

The normed samples could have been obtained with greater sophistication. The PACE is advertised to be directed at preschool and kindergarten-age children thus including norms for 4-, 5-, and 6-year-old children. However, only 2–3% of the standardization sample were 4-year-olds, whereas approximately 17% of the total sample of 1,285 children were 6 years old at the time of testing. The remainder of the sample was composed of 5-year-olds. An equal representation of the three age groups seems warranted. The standardization sample taps the south central region of the United States. The authors state that a "number of states are included" (p. 29); however, they do not specify how many states nor how many children in the sample were from these states. Also, the authors state that the sampling includes a "number of children who might be designated as culturally somewhat disadvantaged" (p. 29). What is the definition of "culturally somewhat disadvantaged"? Head Start children seem to have been included in the sample. The ratio of children from each socioeconomic group is not specified. This information is critical to the test users for interpretation of the assessment results.

Validity and reliability issues are addressed. When area scores were analyzed, three main higher-order factors were identified. The first represents a broad dimension of motor-perceptual coordination. The second factor combines the attending/responding area and the social skill area. The third broad factor that emerges was called the auditory-verbal memory factor.

Concurrent validity was studied by comparing SRA achievement series test scores for 39 boys and 29 girls to PACE scores for these children tested at the beginning of first grade. Correlations are reported to have ranged between .27 and .67 with a median value for the various scales. There were significant, high correlations between achievement in reading, language, and mathematics, and scores on the attending/responding and social skills scales. There are no predictive validity studies reported. Reliability studies were completed on a group of 31 Head Start children of kindergarten age at the beginning and end of a year. The median pre-post correlation across scales was .73. The median alpha coefficient for the six primary scales is .78 and the overall degree of internal consistency for the system is reported to be high.

In summary, this assessment is useful for determining strengths and needs of children who have entered kindergarten, so that teachers and parents can plan a more developmentally appropriate classroom and program for the child. However, professionals need to exercise caution when using the norms and when using the computer program printouts of intervention strategies that emphasize "deficits" of the child rather than building on strengths and interests that each child has.

[276]

PAR: Proficiency Assessment Report.
Purpose: Developed to identify proficiency in 22 abilities associated with effective management.
Population: Supervisors and managers.
Publication Date: 1989.
Scores: Item scores only.
Administration: Group or individual.
Manual: No manual.
Price Data, 1990: $20 per 20 inventories.
Time: (30) minutes.
Comments: Ratings by manager and self; administered prior to training program and then discussed in pairs.
Author: Training House, Inc.
Publisher: Training House, Inc.

Review of the PAR: Proficiency Assessment Report by STEPHEN F. DAVIS, Professor of Psychology, Emporia State University, Emporia, KS:

The PAR: Proficiency Assessment Report consists of four, 8.5-inch x 11-inch printed sides. The PAR can be administered individually or in groups. Although the time required for administration is not indicated, personal experience indicates this instrument can be completed within 15 minutes. There is no manual. Likewise, no norms or other relevant data are presented.

The intended use of the PAR is clearly stated: "This exercise is designed to help supervisors and managers determine their proficiency on a series of abilities commonly associated with effective management" (p. 1). The PAR allows *both* the supervisor and his or her "immediate boss" to rate the supervisor. The results of the PAR can be used for "training and development, and as a benchmark against which future improvement can be compared" (p. 1).

The PAR consists of 22 paragraphs; each paragraph describes a skills cluster. The respective skills clusters are: Managing in Perspective, Conducting Performance Reviews, Interacting Face to Face, Applying Transactional Analysis, Understanding Motivation, Interpreting Management Style, Training and Coaching Others, Listening Effectively, Running Effective Meetings, Writing to get Results, Career Planning, Conducting Selection Interviews, Setting Goals and Standards, Planning/Scheduling/Controlling, Negotiation, Administering Personnel Policies, Making Effective Presentations, Improving Productivity, Building Teamwork, Solving Problems, and Making Decisions.

The respondent is required to provide separate ratings of the Relevance and his or her Proficiency for each skills cluster. The ratings are made on a Likert-type scale that ranges from 5 (*extremely*) to 1 (*negligible*). The results are summarized by counting the number of unmarked boxes *between* ratings for each item. For example, responses of 5 (Relevance) and 2 (Proficiency) would be scored 7.

A score of 6 or more prompts concerns. Missing from the scoring/interpretation instructions, however, is consideration of those situations where a major discrepancy exists between the score of the supervisor and boss. One must assume that a score of 6 by either individual on any skill cluster is sufficient to warrant further discussion. Not surprisingly, "the need for training and development is greatest on those skills clusters that are ranked high on relevance and low on proficiency" (p. 4).

Although the PAR is completely lacking in reported norms and apparently has not been assessed for validity and reliability, it appears capable of serving several potentially useful functions. Perhaps its most beneficial function is to facilitate discussion between the supervisor and his or her immediate "boss." The strengths and weaknesses as perceived by the supervisor *and* the boss may be expressed in a low-threat, quantitative manner that can be approached through open dialogue. The presentation of the results and the ensuing dialogue can be used as the first steps in an effective program of development and training.

Such positive features and strengths notwithstanding, a close examination of this instrument suggests that the PAR may be biased toward the production of low Proficiency scores. Specifically, it appears that many of the 22 skills-cluster descriptions refer to specific abilities by name and/or require the respondent to be familiar with a certain procedure. Can it be assumed that these names, procedures, and the specified number of steps/activities will be familiar to all who complete the PAR?

For example, Skills Cluster 3 (Conducting Performance Reviews) refers to the "seven-step process for analyzing performance deficiencies" (p. 1), Skills Cluster 5 (Applying Transactional Analysis) refers to Transactional Analysis and "three ego states" (p. 2), Skills Cluster 6 (Understanding Motivation) assumes an in-depth understanding of motivational theories (e.g., Marlow, Herzberg, McGregor, and McClelland), and Skills Cluster 9 (Listening Effectively) assumes the respondent will know what "the ten guidelines (Dr. Ralph Nichols) to listening effectively" (p. 1) are.

At least seven similar problems could be cited for other skills clusters. If the respondent is not familiar with the specific names, techniques, terms, number of steps, etc. that are mentioned, then a bias toward a lower Proficiency rating may well be created. Although it is arguable that such interpretation problems will be revealed during the subsequent conference between the supervisor and the boss, it seems counterproductive to allow them to develop in the first place.

Other than its ability to initiate a meaningful and guided dialogue between a supervisor and his or her boss, the PAR really has little else to offer. Given the relatively low cost of administration, perhaps that outcome is sufficient.

Review of the PAR: Proficiency Assessment Report by S. ALVIN LEUNG, Associate Professor in Educational Psychology, University of Houston, Houston, TX:

The Proficiency Assessment Report (PAR) was developed as a method for supervisors or managers in an organizational setting to self-evaluate their management skills in a number of areas. The PAR can also be used by a supervisor to evaluate performance of a manager, or by employees who work under a supervisor to rate the effectiveness of the supervisor.

The PAR consists of 22 items, and each item represents a "skills cluster" related to the work of a manager or supervisor (e.g., managing time effectively, conducting performance reviews). A list of knowledge and behavior associated with each skills cluster is provided in each item. Each item has two parts. The first part is the Relevance scale. The respondent is asked to rate the relevance or importance of a skills cluster in his or her work environment. The second part is the Proficiency scale. The respondent is asked to rate his or her proficiency in the same skills cluster. A 5-point scale is used (1 = *negligible*, 5 = *extremely*). The PAR booklet does not provide instruction on what reference group the test taker is compared to when responding to the items. The PAR is designed for self-scoring. The respondent is asked to follow the instructions to obtain a score to determine if there is a need for further training in a skills cluster.

The PAR does not come with a user manual. The four-page test booklet does not contain information about the development of the instrument. No normative information is provided. There is no information about what type of organizations the PAR is designed for, and how the scores can be used to aid the test taker in career and professional development. Most importantly, no evidence is provided concerning the reliability and validity of the instrument. With all this critical information missing, the PAR is far from being an acceptable psychological instrument. It is clearly the ethical and professional responsibility of the test developer and publisher to ensure that, before a psychological test is published for general use, there is evidence to support the reliability and validity of the instrument. A user manual should be developed to provide technical information in the above areas.

The PAR can be used as a tool for self-assessment. It can also be used by employees who work under a manager, or by the boss of the manager to rate the latter. The test booklet includes a suggestion that the inventory can be "used as a basis for training and development, and as a benchmark against which future growth and improvement can be compared" (p. 1). This suggestion may lead organizations to use the PAR for purposes other than self-exploration, such as formal performance evaluation or personnel selection. Without appropriate normative information, and evidence of reliability and validity, the scores from the PAR may be misused. Organizations that use the PAR may not be aware of its limitations, and may make poor decisions about employee selection, promotion, and career development.

Each of the 22 skills clusters in the PAR is operationally defined by a number of knowledge or behavior areas associated with the skills cluster. Some of the knowledge and behavior areas are not clearly elaborated (e.g., "applying a seven-step process for analyzing performance deficiencies" in the "conducting performance review" skills cluster). Also, technical jargons used may not be familiar to the respondent (e.g., transactional analyses). The most critical flaw in the design of the PAR items is that there are multiple elements in the same item. One cannot tell to which knowledge and behavior the person is responding. For example, if the response to the Proficiency scale of an item is 3 (average) on the 5-point scale, one may interpret the respondent to view self or the target manager as being average in this skills cluster. The respondent may also perceive self or the target manager as highly proficient in some knowledge and behavior areas, but low in proficiency in others, resulting in an average rating. All of the above concerns confound the interpretation of the test scores and further reduce the utility of the PAR.

The scoring method used is arbitrary. For each item, the respondent is asked to compute a score indicating a need for training by "counting the unmarked boxes" between the two ratings. If the score is 6 or higher, a strong need for training is recommended. However, there is no explanation on how this cutoff number is determined. There is no research evidence to support that this recommendation is valid.

In conclusion, there is no evidence indicating that the PAR is a carefully constructed instrument, nor is there evidence to support that it is a reliable and valid instrument. Hence, the PAR may be an interesting self-exploration exercise for a manager, but it should not be used as a tool for employee evaluation, or as a basis of decisions about hiring and promotion in an organization.

[277]

Parallel Spelling Tests.

Purpose: To chart the progress of children at all levels of ability in spelling.
Population: Ages 6-4 to 12-11.
Publication Dates: 1983–92.
Scores: Total score only.
Administration: Group.
Price Data, 1994: £6.50 per test booklet/manual ('83, 41 pages).
Time: (15–25) minutes.
Comments: Teachers create tests from two banks of items, A and B.
Author: Dennis Young.
Publisher: Hodder & Stoughton Educational [England].

Review of the Parallel Spelling Tests by STEVEN R. SHAW, Assistant Professor of Psychology, and MARK E. SWERDLIK, Professor of Psychology, Illinois State University, Normal, IL:

The Parallel Spelling Tests (PST) are measures of oral spelling designed for use in the United Kingdom. Clearly, the spelling of the words, the grade levels used, and the phrasing used in the illustrative sentences make the PST inappropriate for use in the United States. The PST was designed for students from 6 to 13 years of age. Test A is designed for Infants, First-year Juniors, and Second-year Juniors (roughly equivalent to first, second, and third grades). Test B is designed for Upper Juniors and Secondary students (roughly equivalent to fourth, fifth, and sixth grades). The PST is designed so that for each level there are two banks of test items that are purported to be parallel. Thus, a pretest/posttest approach could be used to evaluate the effectiveness of an academic intervention related to spelling. However, no data are presented indicating that the two banks of items are parallel. The author of the PST recommends that it be used by regular and special education teachers, school and educational psychologists, and researchers. The author states other uses for the PST: (*a*) may be used by teachers as a screening instrument to determine which children may need to be referred to an educational specialist; (*b*) may be used as a system for evaluating the effectiveness of an intervention or treatment; (*c*) and may be used to assess progress in spelling as compared to other subjects, such as reading.

ADMINISTRATION AND SCORING. The starting point is determined by the age of the student. Discontinuation rules are unclear. The manual author states that testing should be discontinued of "those infants in a test group who are out of range of any possible success" (p. 4). To administer items, the examiner dictates each word, reads a sentence containing the word, and dictates the word again. Estimated time to administer the test is 20 minutes.

Raw scores are converted into spelling ages and spelling quotients. Spelling quotients are deviation standard scores with a mean of 100 and a standard deviation of 15. The author recommends spelling quotients over spelling ages, but the limitations of the spelling ages are discussed only briefly. Spelling ages are recommended for purposes of classifying students into spelling groupings. The author suggests that spelling ages correspond more directly to teachers' impressions of children's spelling ability than to children's actual ability. No data are presented to support this claim. The author also notes that considerable variation in percentile rankings exists across schools depending on socioeconomic conditions and other factors.

The PST manual author devotes a great deal of attention to the teaching of spelling, assessing spelling rather than handwriting, and examining the qualitative nature of spelling errors. This information may be helpful to teachers. As such, the PST appears to be a curriculum guide or a lesson in spelling pedagogy rather than a psychometrically sound test of spelling ability.

NORMATIVE DATA. The norming sample was drawn from 19 schools in England, "selected from knowledge of their children's ability to be collectively representative of national standards" (pp. 34-35). Only gender and median age of the sample were provided. It is not clear if this sample is representative of England.

Gender differences were noted with girls performing better than boys at many grade levels. However, these differences were not reflected in the tables.

RELIABILITY. Stability coefficients and corresponding Standard Errors of Measurement and Standard Errors of the Estimate were provided. Most stability coefficients were above .90. However, the lengths of the intervals between testings were not reported for many of the coefficients. One interval that was reported is a one-year interval for which a stability coefficient of .91 was found. No internal consistency data were presented.

VALIDITY. Ninety percent of the 576 words were drawn from one source (*A Study of the Vocabulary of*

Young Children, Burroughs, 1957). The relevance of this source is unclear other than it ensures that the words "are within the understanding of at least some 7-year-old children" (manual, p. 34). Words drawn from other unnamed sources were used to extend the range to the higher level of ability. The author states that the PST has satisfactory discriminating power when used with students from England. The author also states that dictated spelling relates to context spelling. However, no data were presented to support this assertion with the PST.

Data on concurrent validity correlating the PST with the Graded Spelling Test (Vernon, 1977), Diagnostic and Attainment Testing (Schonell & Schonell, 1950), the Standard Reading Test (Daniels & Diack, 1958), and the SPAR Spelling and Reading Tests (Young, 1976) are presented. All correlation coefficients were greater than .82 with most being greater than .90. However, the validity study samples upon which these correlations were computed were not described. In addition, no data were presented to support the validity of the PST for many of the purposes that the author recommends.

SUMMARY. The Parallel Spelling Tests is created exclusively for use in the schools of the United Kingdom. The PST is fast and efficient to administer and score. Creating parallel forms makes the PST less vulnerable to coaching and practice effects. However, only incomplete data are presented in determining whether the test banks are truly parallel forms. Moreover, the manual is poorly written, not well organized, and lacks vital technical data. Reliability and validity data are not complete. The spelling of some of the words (e.g., coloured, programme, behaviour) will be unfamiliar to many American children. Moreover, many of the sentences to be read along with the spelling words contain syntax or content unfamiliar to American readers (e.g., To reckon is to count or consider). This test is clearly inappropriate for American students. The lack of clear and convincing data supporting the author's stated uses of this test make the PST's use as a norm-referenced measure of spelling ability questionable in any country or culture.

REVIEWERS' REFERENCES

Schonell, F. J., & Schonell, F. E. (1950). *Diagnostic and attainment testing.* Scotland: Oliver & Boyd.

Burroughs, G. E. R. (1957). *A study of the vocabulary of young children.* Scotland: Oliver & Boyd.

Daniels, J. C., & Diack, H. (1958). *The standard reading test.* Chatto and Windus.

Young, D. (1976). SPAR Reading and Spelling Tests. London, England: Hodder & Stoughton.

Vernon, P. E. (1977). Graded Word Spelling Test. London, England: Hodder & Stoughton.

Review of the Parallel Spelling Tests by CLAUDIA R. WRIGHT, Associate Professor of Educational Psychology, California State University, Long Beach, CA:

The Parallel Spelling Tests (PST) A and B are graded-word type tests developed to provide norm-based assessments of spelling competence for students ranging in age from approximately 6.5 to 13 years, corresponding roughly to grades 2 through 7 in the United States. Although thorough test standardization procedures have been undertaken and documented, all normative data and reported evidence of the instrument's psychometric properties have been derived from test scores obtained from samples of children attending non-U.S. schools (probably Great Britain, but not specified).

The PST-A is made up of 276 item statements each comprising an item number, a target word to be spelled, a grammatical sentence containing the target word, and the target word restated. The items, organized by level of difficulty, are presented as 138 pairs clustered into 23 sections (6 pairs per section). Bank A yields 34-item tests for younger children (ages 6-4 through 7-11; grades 1–3); 40-item tests for students 7-0 through 8-11 years (grades 2–4); and 46-item tests for students 8-0 to 9-11 years (grades 3–5). The PST-B, is made up of 300 item statements organized into 25 sections of 6 pairs of items of increasing difficulty. This form was designed to provide 44-item tests for students 9-0 to 10-11 years (grades 4–6) and 50-item tests for those 10-0 to 12-11 years (grades 5–7). An advantage of the PST bank system constructed with word pairs matched for difficulty and discrimination levels is that a number of parallel tests without overlapping items can be generated.

A review of the spelling words in the first section of Bank A reveals nouns, verbs, or prepositions; in the second section, nouns, verbs, or adjectives; and so forth. Although no rationale is given for the specific patterns of parts of speech found in each section, the author reports that 90% of the items were selected from Burroughs' (1957) Lists 1 and 2 which are considered to provide "an unbiassed [sic] proportional representation of the common spelling structures" (manual, p. 34).

Test preparation instructions are clearly stated. Random selection of test items from each section is recommended but the author notes that specialists may build tests reflecting "some preferred set of spelling patterns . . . without invalidating the norms" (p. 4). Even the sentences can be modified "but the procedure (dictation of the word, sentence, diction of the word) must be adhered to" (p. 4). Although partial evidence in support of the equivalency of parallel forms generated from random selection of items can be found primarily in the author's discussion of test reliability, with all coefficients in the low to mid-.90s, no empirical evidence is provided supporting the other claims.

The language contained in the test manual and which is also apparent in some of the test items is standard British English. For example, the author uses the term "infants" throughout the manual when referring to students aged 6-4 to 7-11; whereas the closest corresponding designation among U.S. educators might be "early elementary" or "1st–3rd graders." Although not a widespread problem with this test, the conventional spelling of words should also be checked when constructing tests for U.S. students (e.g., programme vs. program). In addition, a review of items should be made to eliminate potential semantic ambiguity.

Detailed instructions and appropriate cautions are given for the administration of the spelling tests.

Two useful indexes, the "spelling age" and the "spelling quotient," provide for the comparison of students both across and within age groupings. Spelling age (ranging from 6 to 15) is considered to provide a practical index of a child's relative spelling ability when compared with the average test performance of students at various ages. Spelling ages are provided corresponding to possible total score values for each of the three test lengths (34, 40, or 46 words) for Bank A and for each of the two test lengths (44 or 50 words) for Bank B. Spelling quotients are standardized scores reflecting the relative position of children's performance of the same age (within a month).

RELIABILITY. Satisfactory test-retest reliability estimates (no time delay reported) are reported using parallel forms (.93 for 7-2 years; .96 for 8-2 years; and .94 each for 9-2, 10-2, and 11-2 years [all median ages]). A stability coefficient of .92 was obtained for a sample of 82 students tested at age 9-2 and again at 10-2.

PST NORMS. The samples used to generate normative data, which ranged in size from 421 to 1,008, were drawn from 19 schools between 1978 and 1982, and were reported to be representative of children's abilities in the country (probably Great Britain) in which the tests were administered. A comparison of age norms (spelling ages) derived from the PST-A and B with the Vernon Graded Word Spelling Test (norm differences of 0 to ±.2 years), with the Schonell Graded Word Spelling Test (norm differences ranging from .2 to .7, with the Schonell projecting the lower norm in all comparisons), with the Graded Spelling Test (no differences), and with the Richmond Tests of Basic Skills (no differences) yielded evidence of relatively high agreement between norms.

VALIDITY. Evidence of construct validity was obtained through correlations of the PST scores with each of the spelling tests just cited. Coefficients ranged from a low of .83 for the Richmond (a multiple-choice test for which the test taker identifies the misspelled word) to .91 or .92 for the remaining coefficients (graded-word type spelling tests).

Evidence of criterion-related validity was obtained between performance on the PST and essay spelling scores for a sample of 130 11-year-olds (r = .82). Other predictors of PST scores were examined including reading ability, mathematics, and intelligence tests. The most valid single predictor was reading ability for all age groups; (rs ranged from .81 to .83 (7-2 years), .90 to .91 (8-2 years), .74 to .75 (9-2 years), .84 to .86 (10-2 years), and .71 (11-2 years) (all median ages).

SUMMARY. The Parallel Spelling Tests A and B show promise as a valid and cost-efficient approach to the assessment of spelling for elementary and middle school students if one addresses the need to establish local norms and follows conventional procedures in item selection when constructing new forms of the test. The test manual includes test construction guidelines along with reliability and validity information. Also provided are several useful sections and appendices with detailed discussions covering the teaching of spelling, examining spelling errors, and assessing spelling in children's writings.

Currently, no data are available supporting the generalizability of the PST norms to the diverse subpopulations of children schooled in the U.S. Researchers might seek to validate the PST against appropriate spelling subscales of such tests as the Comprehensive Tests of Basic Skills, Fourth Edition (T4:623), the Test of Written Language-2 (T4:2804), or the Iowa Tests of Basic Skills, Form J (T4:1280), to name several, any of which are routinely employed as assessments in state-wide and district-wide testing programs.

REVIEWER'S REFERENCE

Burroughs, G. E. R. (1957). *A study of the vocabulary of young children*. Scotland: Oliver & Boyd.

[278]

Parent-Adolescent Communication Scale.

Purpose: Designed to assess "the views of adolescents and their parents regarding their perceptions and experience of communication with each other."

Population: Adolescents and their parents.

Publication Date: 1982.

Scores, 3: 2 subscale scores (Open Family Communication, Problems in Family Communication), Total Communication.

Administration: Group.

Price Data, 1990: $10 per manual (16 pages) including scale.

Time: Administration time not reported.

Authors: Howard Barnes and David H. Olson.

Publisher: Family Social Science.

Cross References: See T4:1930 (3 references).

TEST REFERENCES

1. Christopher, F. S., & Roosa, M. W. (1990). An evaluation of an adolescent pregnancy prevention program: Is "Just Say No" enough? *Family Relations*, *39*, 68-72.

2. Robsa, M. W., & Christopher, F. S. (1990). Evaluation of an abstinence-only adolescent pregnancy prevention program: A replication. *Family Relations*, *39*, 363-367.

3. Olson, D. H. (1991). Commentary: Three-dimensional (3-D) circumplex model and revised scoring of FACES III. *Family Process*, *30*, 74-79.

4. Brage, D., Meredith, W., & Woodward, J. (1993). Correlates of loneliness among midwestern adolescents. *Adolescence, 28,* 685-693.

5. Skopin, A. R., Newman, B. M., & McKenry, P. C. (1993). Influences on the quality of stepfather-adolescent relationships: Views of both family members. *Journal of Divorce & Remarriage, 19*(3/4), 181-196.

6. Knight, G. P., Virdin, L. M., & Roosa, M. (1994). Socialization and family correlates of mental health outcomes among Hispanic and Anglo American children: Consideration of cross-ethnic scalar equivalence. *Child Development, 65,* 212-224.

7. Stewart, E. R., McKenry, P. C., Rudd, N. M., & Gavazzi, S. M. (1994). Family processes as mediators of depressive symptomatology among rural adolescents. *Family Relations, 43,* 38-45.

Review of the Parent-Adolescent Communication Scale by ALLEN JACK EDWARDS, Professor of Psychology, Southwest Missouri State University, Springfield, MO:

The Parent-Adolescent Communication Scale was developed by Barnes and Olson with three purposes in mind. First, they desired a measure that would describe "communication" between parents and adolescents from different parent types. Although not specifically defined, the authors apparently use the term "communication" to mean verbal interaction between parent and child. Second, they wanted to disclose at least part of the diverse nature of experiences found among different families. Third, they wished to produce data from responses to the scale which would reflect the attitudes and feelings of the different family members (in this case, apparently, parent and child). Such goals are commendable and potentially useful to the family members and/or clinicians working with parent-adolescent problems. Unfortunately, the material presented in the so-called manual accompanying this scale offers only partial support for the first purpose, little support for the third, and no support for the second.

In fact, data to assure effective use of the scale for any purpose are scant, often confusing when present, and disturbingly absent where needed. A brief (almost two-page) review of literature is presented to indicate the importance of "communication" from several perspectives: family development and systems, cohesion and adaptability, spousal relationships, even marital problems. The authors make clear, however, that research efforts have suffered limitations. Studies are rarely comparable, and prior efforts to develop measures of communication have reflected interests and preferences of the test designer, further limiting comparisons. Despite this history of restricted success, Barnes and Olson decided to study, with a consequent scale from the results, communication from four directions: father and mother to adolescent; adolescent to mother and father. The outcome expresses the amount of openness within dyads, specific problems in communicating within dyads, and the degree of selectivity which occurs in verbal interaction.

METHOD. To accomplish their purposes, the authors began by surveying the literature for relevant variables. As a result, they crafted a pool of items (number not stated) to measure aspects of parent-adolescent interaction. Additional items (number and sources not stated) were obtained from other sources but reworded so as to be applicable to the dyadic relationship specified for this scale. From the total, 35 items were selected for pilot study. The items included were felt to measure both process and content of communication. Where necessary, they were apparently revised so that persons as young as age 12 could respond to them.

This pilot study used adolescents only as respondents; thus, no parent data were collected. A 5-point Likert scale (from *strongly disagree* to *strongly agree*) was the basis for the choices. This procedure remains in the present form of the scale. Their subjects came from four institutions (colleges and high schools) in Wisconsin and Minnesota. There were 433 participants in total, only 127 of whom were of high school age. They report that the "vast majority" were between 16 and 20 years of age.

STATISTICAL TREATMENT. The resulting data were factor analyzed and three factors were labeled: Open Family Communication, Problems in Family Communication, and Selective Family Communication. For the 20 items meeting statistical criteria, test-retest (4 to 5 weeks) reliability coefficients were computed.for each factor and for total. These values ranged from .78 for Factor I to .60 for the total scale. There is a troubling element, however, in the fact that the authors report 124 subjects from 12 different institutions but with test-retest *r*s based upon numbers ranging from 106 (for total scale) to 117 (for Problems in Family Communication). Missing cases are not mentioned, much less explained. In the same table of data, internal consistency (Cronbach's alpha) is reported for a sample of 433. Apparently these are the 433 adolescents mentioned before. Coefficients ranged from .92 for Open Family Communication to .72 for the total scale. The results for either estimate of reliability are only satisfactory, at best.

Whatever the details not included for the pilot study, the explanation and explication for the definitive scale that resulted and is currently marketed is even more mysterious and baffling. Factors II and III were collapsed into a second subscale. Because parent to adolescent measurement was the intent of the scale at this point, the authors state that a "larger study" was conducted and analyzed. This study is not described nor are any data cited. A factor analysis was conducted with a sample of 925. No description was provided.

RELIABILITY. Internal consistence (Cronbach's alpha) was computed for two samples (n = 925 and 916) and total (r = 1,841), although the characteristics of the samples are not given. The coefficients are good for Open Family Communication (r = .87) and the total scale (r = .88), and satisfactory for Problems in Family Communication (r = .78). No other data are given.

VALIDITY. No validity data are reported.

SCORING. Three scores result: one for each subscale and one for total. Only total scores are reported in raw score form (the possible range is 20 to 100) for fathers, mothers, and adolescents (for father and mother independently). The effective range of scores is 48 through 96, and they are tabled as percentiles. There is the confusing fact that sample size is inconsistent: There are 496 fathers, 502 mothers, but only 417 adolescents. As might be expected from prior comments, there is no explanation. There are no "norms" for the two subscales, but the authors give no reason for this omission.

OVERALL EVALUATION. Although the purposes cited by the authors seem both reasonable and potentially useful, supporting data to demonstrate such outcomes are lacking. Indeed, the descriptions of procedures, data collection, analysis, and use of results ranges from poor to nonexistent. Given such limited bases for recommendation, this reviewer sees no reason to use the Parent-Adolescent Communication Scale. It is of more than passing interest that most references predate 1980, and that the "manual" submitted with the scale was published in 1982 with apparently no updating since that time.

Review of the Parent-Adolescent Communication Scale by STEVEN IRA PFEIFFER, Director, Devereux Institute of Clinical Training & Research, Devon, PA:

INTRODUCTION. The Parent-Adolescent Communication Scale (PAC) was designed to assess the quality of parent-child communication. The 20-item scale is a self-report measure of perceived interpersonal communication that reflects one of the three major dimensions of Olson et al.'s Circumplex Model of Marital and Family Systems (Olson, McCubbin, Barnes et al., 1982; Olson, McCubbin, Barnes et al., 1983; Olson, Russell, & Sprenkle, 1980). The other two dimensions of the Circumplex Model are cohesion and adaptability, with communication viewed as the facilitating dimension (Barnes & Olson, 1985).

The scale consists of three almost identical forms. Two of the forms are completed by the adolescent (the Adolescent and Father Form and the Adolescent and Mother Form) and reflect the adolescent's perception of the openness of family communication (10 items) and problems in family communication (10 items). The Parent Form assesses each parent's perception of the quality of their interpersonal communication with their adolescent.

Each of three forms is printed on a single $8^1/_2$-inch x 11-inch sheet of white bond paper. The three forms do not include instructions, although the simple and straight-forward format makes it relatively easy for respondents to discern what is expected. Each of the 20 items is rated on a 5-point Likert-type scale ranging from 1 (*strongly disagree*) to 5 (*strongly agree*).

TECHNICAL QUALITIES AND APPLICATION/USES. The test items were generated based on a review of the literature, which included a revision of existing test items and the development of a new pool of items all designed to measure various aspects of parent-adolescent communication. Thirty-five items made up the initial instrument, which was piloted on 433 high school and college students from Minnesota and Wisconsin. On the basis of factor analysis, and theoretical and practical considerations, the final form of the PAC scale was reduced from 35 to 20 items and from three to two subscales. Selective Family Communication (Factor III in the pilot study) was consolidated with Factor II (Problems in Family Communication).

Internal consistency using Cronbach's alpha for a sample of 1,841 was .87 for Open Family Communication, .78 for Problems in Family Communication, and .88 for the total scale. No information on this sample is provided in the manual, and it can only be assumed that the sample was similar to the pilot study. No test-retest reliability is reported in the manual.

Support for the validity of the PAC scale is restricted to a factor analysis supporting a two-factor solution consistent with the authors' contention of two related but distinct components of interpersonal communication. However, the results of the factor analyses are not unequivocal, and there is support for the presence of three factors, two negative and one positive. Perhaps most telling is the omission of any content or criterion-related validity studies in the manual. This is particularly disappointing because the manual provides no evidence that the scale actually measures family communication, reflects family functioning, or predicts to the 16 family types of the Circumplex Model. Moreover, the authors provide no validity studies that support the veracity of the respondents' willingness to respond frankly and honestly to the scale. This is always a concern with self-report instruments, and it is particularly problematic if the PAC scale is used in a clinical setting with a client population that might be inclined to be less open or revealing.

The norms table reported in the manual is inadequate. There is no information on socioeconomic status, geographic representation, race/ethnicity, type of families, or type of community in which the families reside. The authors provide no information on profiles or cut scores that would be needed by the user to generate clinical hypotheses or to interpret obtained scores on the PAC. Similarly, the manual provides no explanation on when to use the two subscales and when to use the total scale score. Finally, the scoring of the scale is no simple matter, requiring a clerical manipulation of 10 of the 20 raw item scores.

SUMMARY. The PAC scale has promise as a clinical tool to better understand parent-adolescent communication. Considerably more work is required to establish its reliability and validity, however, before its use as a family interaction assessment or diagnostic measure.

REVIEWER'S REFERENCES

Olson, D. H., McCubbin, H. I., Barnes, H., Larsen, A., Muxen, M., & Wilson, M. (1982). *Family inventories: Inventories used in a national survey of families across the family life cycle*. St. Paul: Family Social Science, University of Minnesota.

Olson, D. H., McCubbin, H. I., Barnes, H., Larsen, A., Muxen, M., & Wilson, M. (1983). *Families: What makes them work*. Beverly Hills, CA: Sage.

Olson, D. H., Russell, C. S., & Sprenkle, D. H. (1983). Circumplex model of marital and family systems: VI. Theoretical update. *Family Process, 22*, 69-83.

Barnes, H. L., & Olson, D. H. (1985). Parent-adolescent communication and the circumplex model. *Child Development, 56*, 438-447.

[279]

Parent Awareness Skills Survey.

Purpose: Constructed to identify strengths and weaknesses in a parent's sensitivity to typical child care situations.

Population: Parents involved in custody decisions.

Publication Date: 1990.

Acronym: PASS.

Scores, 18: 6 categories (Awareness of Critical Issues, Awareness of Adequate Solutions, Awareness of Communicating in Understandable Terms, Awareness of Acknowledging Feelings, Awareness of the Importance of Relevant Aspects of a Child's Past History, Awareness of Feedback Data) for each of the following conditions (Spontaneous Level, Probe Level One, Probe Level Two).

Administration: Individual.

Price Data, 1994: $169 per complete kit including 6 PASS-BOOKS, 6 PASS scoring summaries, handbook and scoring guide, answer pens, updates, author contact number, and 3 years update service; $69 per 6 PASS-BOOKS.

Time: [30–60] minutes.

Comments: Orally administered.

Author: Barry Bricklin.

Publisher: Village Publishing, Inc.

Review of the Parent Awareness Skills Survey by LISA G. BISCHOFF, Assistant Professor of Education and School Psychology, Indiana State University, Terre Haute, IN:

The Parent Awareness Skills Survey (PASS) is an instrument designed to assess parent awareness of factors important in reacting to and dealing with typical child care problems. The PASS is designed for use with parents of children of all ages. According to the author, data generated through administration of the PASS may be used to determine relative strengths and weaknesses of parents, to compare responses provided by mothers and fathers, to form conclusions "as to whether the responses meet minimal standards of adequacy" (p. 6), and to "strengthen parental communication skills" (p. 6).

The PASS consists of an administration manual and a PASS-Book. The administration manual contains information regarding test content, administration procedures, and scoring procedures. The PASS-Book contains 18 "typical child care dilemmas, called 'situations'" (p. 3) to which a parent is asked to respond, as well as two "nonspecific" probe questions and six "specific" probe questions designed to further explore the parent's response to the first eight situations and to allow the parent to improve upon their initial response.

Administration of the PASS involves presenting each of 18 "situations" to a parent and then asking the parent to tell what they would do in that particular situation. After all 18 situations have been presented and parent responses have been recorded, probing questions are asked in order to ascertain issues a parent believes they should think about *before* deciding how to respond to a particular situation (Probe I) and *after* responding to the same situation (Probe II).

The PASS yields scores said to reflect parental awareness of (*a*) critical issues in child care situations; (*b*) the importance of selecting adequate intervention strategies; (*c*) the importance of speaking in language understandable to the child; (*d*) the desirability of acknowledging a child's feelings; (*e*) the importance of considering relevant aspects of a child's past history; and (*f*) the necessity of attending to feedback from the child to determine the child's understanding of a parental response. Scores are provided at three levels including a spontaneous level (initial responses), Probe I level, and Probe II level.

PASS responses are scored by assigning a rating of 0, 1, or 2 for each of the six areas, at each of the three levels listed above. Although general guidelines are provided to assist the evaluator in scoring responses, specific criteria are not included in the manual. The author suggests "the evaluator, by virtue of appropriate training in psychology and/or child-development, can apply his or her own standards in assigning the suggested scores" (p. 11). However, no guidelines are provided to indicate specific qualifications necessary to administer and interpret the PASS.

The author states the data obtained from administration of the PASS may be clinically useful in working with parents. However, specific information linking PASS data and scores with intervention strategies is not provided in the manual.

The author indicates the first version of the PASS was developed in 1975 and that the instrument has been modified since that time. No further information concerning test development is included in the manual.

Lack of information concerning validity and reliability is a serious limitation of the PASS. No information is included in the manual. Evidence supporting the validity of inferences concerning parent awareness skills constructed from PASS scores, and evidence supporting the reliability of scores is necessary before this instrument can be considered for clinical use.

In conclusion, although the PASS presents an interesting format for assessing parent awareness of factors important to consider in reacting to and dealing with typical childhood problems and may provide the clinician with relevant information for planning and implementing interventions with parents, the lack of information concerning test construction and psychometric properties of the PASS are serious limitations. Clinical use of this instrument should be approached with caution.

Review of the Parent Awareness Skills Survey by DEBRA E. COLE, Director of Partial Hospitalization, Virginia Treatment Center for Children, Medical College of Virginia, Richmond, VA:

The Parent Awareness Skills Survey (PASS) is a semistructured interview designed to assess a parent's awareness skills. The parent is asked to respond to 18 typical child-raising scenarios. The author explains that these responses alert the interviewer to the parent's level of awareness of salient and appropriate developmental issues in parenting. This scale is based on the premise that a parent's effectiveness is a function of his or her awareness of these issues.

The 18 predominately one-sentence situations cover parental dilemmas involving children ranging in age from $2^1/_2$ to 15 years. The interviewer ranks each response on a 3-point scale in six areas: (*a*) Critical Issues, (*b*) Adequate Solutions, (*c*) Understandable Terms, (*d*) Acknowledging Feelings, (*e*) Relevant History, and (*f*) Feedback Data. A score of 2 indicates a pronounced awareness of salient issues involved, a 1 denotes minimal awareness, and a 0 is given when a response indicates no awareness at all. Because critical issues and adequate solutions are seen as the most important areas, the manual contains a section with suggested acceptable responses for these two categories.

The child-raising scenarios are evaluated at three levels. The Spontaneous Level evaluates the respondent's uninterrupted initial response to each situation. Respondents are then given two opportunities to improve their scores. Probe Level One questions ask the respondents two nonspecific questions about each scenario which are again rated in each of the six areas specified above. Probe Level Two questions are more specific. These probes give six questions per scenario, each one addressing one of the six rating categories.

Scoring of the PASS is vague, relying on the "appropriate training in psychology and/or child-development" (p. 11) of the evaluator. The instrument is designed to discover relative strengths and weaknesses of parents examined. The author does stress the use of the same set of standards when scores between respondents are to be compared but offers no way to insure this is the case.

The PASS may be used in a number of shortened versions determined by the evaluator's needs and/or the adequacy of the respondent's spontaneous answers. According to the manual, the Spontaneous Level responses are more accurate indicators of the respondent's true behavioral predisposition.

The PASS is an attempt to bring some uniform standards to parental evaluations, particularly in custody decisions. The PASS may be a useful addition to a battery of tests because it does give an indicator of the parent's awareness of important child care issues. It may also be a useful tool to screen for inadequate parental awareness. Individual administrators are given wide latitude in scoring and length of interviewing. This gives some adaptability and flexibility to the use of the PASS.

Unfortunately, the author does not present supporting empirical data. The manual for the Parent Awareness Skills Survey provides none, and this omission severely limits the survey's usefulness. Although the scenarios have high face validity, no rationale is given for their election over others which might be seen as relevant and useful. No support is given for how awareness translates into adequate parenting—especially when difficult custody decisions are being made. The six basic areas used to rate answers appear relevant but no research is cited to support these as the six most critical areas to evaluate. The Spontaneous Probe Level One, and Probe Level Two system of scoring lacks empirical support as well.

The Parent Awareness Skills Survey is an interesting attempt to quantify an often complicated assessment process. Until the measure is better substantiated, however, it has limited usefulness to the evaluator for whom it has been designed.

[280]

Parent Perception of Child Profile.

Purpose: Designed to elicit a parent's knowledge and understanding of a child.
Population: Parents.
Publication Date: 1991.
Acronym: PPCP.
Scores, 13: Interpersonal Relations, Daily Routine, Health History, Developmental History, School History, Fears, Communication Style, Depth of Knowledge, Scope of Knowledge, Emotional Tone, Value/Philosophy, Areas Needing Attention, Recall.
Administration: Individual.
Price Data, 1994: $169 per comprehensive starting kit including directions ('91, 11 pages), 6 Q-books, 6 recall worksheets, 6 summary forms, "answer" pens (black), "other source" pens (red), author contact number, and three years update service; $69 per 6 Q-books; $109 per 12 Q-books.
Time: (60) minutes.
Comments: Self- or evaluator-administered.
Authors: Barry Bricklin and Gail Elliot.
Publisher: Village Publishing, Inc.

Review of the Parent Perception of Child Profile by ROBERT W. HILTONSMITH, Associate Professor of Psychology, Radford University, Radford, VA:

OVERVIEW AND USES. Human services professionals working in the area of child custody often must obtain specific information about parent-child interrelationships that may not be available from questionnaires and other assessment instruments devised with different purposes in mind. To address this need, Barry Bricklin has authored a series of scales, profiles, and related materials to gather data for custody hearings. The latest of these, coauthored with Gail Elliot, is the Parent Perception of Child Profile (PPCP). This instrument can be used to "elicit (an) extensive portrait of a parent's knowledge and understanding of a specific child" (manual, p. 2). Responses from the parent are gathered in eight categories, noted above in the descriptive entry for this instrument.

The PPCP can be either evaluator-administered or self-administered. No information is provided about the comparability of the obtained data for these two administration formats. This is a concern because the PPCP Summary calls for a judgment about parental depth of knowledge based on "the number of specific or 'supporting' details a respondent spontaneously provides" (manual, p. 9). How do we know that the number of these details would be the same if the parent completed the instrument verbally with an evaluator or individually in a paper-and-pencil format?

No details on administration time are provided, but it would appear that this instrument, if given in its entirety, would be time-consuming to complete. There are 121 questions, most of which require the parent to recall a very broad range of information about the child. Often these questions contain many subquestions, thereby increasing the actual length of the instrument. For example, one of the PPCP questions asks the parent to rate their child using a 5-point scale on 19 separate aspects of interpersonal relationships. Other questions ask for extremely specific information, such as a parental judgment about whether the child's "shoe-tying ability" is below average, average, or above average. Granted, the purpose of the PPCP is to assess the extent to which a parent really knows his or her child, but nonetheless the completion of the entire PPCP seems like a formidable task. It is possible that the PPCP's length may "wear down" some respondents, making it appear that their depth of knowledge about the child is not as extensive as it might actually be. The authors advise, however, that the evaluator can decide "on a case-by-case basis which PPCP items to administer and which to omit" (directions manual, p. 3).

Many items on the PPCP have a provision for gathering additional corroborative information from another source who is knowledgeable about the child. This is important "in cases where the Evaluator is highly concerned about the accuracy of a parent's perceptions" (pp. 3-4). Specifically, this information is useful when the real degree of genuine parental interest in the child and/or attentiveness is in question, and when the evaluator is afraid that the parent is "faking good" or "faking knowledge, caring, and concern" (pp. 3-4) to get custody of the child. The authors add that the need to gather corroborative information is at the discretion of the evaluator, and will vary from case to case.

In addition to the eight categories noted in the descriptive entry, the PPCP includes an Irritability Scale. Here, the respondent is asked how he or she would respond to 21 challenging situations with their child (e.g., the child teases others or is disobedient). Instead of providing a verbal answer, the respondent is asked to choose a number corresponding to one of five Likert-type categories, from *would not annoy me at all* to *angry enough to yell and hit*. The evaluator can then use the respondent's choices in this section "to red-flag areas where psychological assistance is needed." No specific guidelines or cutoff scores are offered, however.

Finally, the PPCP includes a series of recall questions. After the PPCP has been completed, the evaluator poses these recall questions to the respondent in cases where "the Evaluator suspects a respondent's interest in a child is not sincere" (p. 5). These questions ask the respondent to repeat the information they had provided earlier to certain questions on the PPCP. Presumably, parents or other respondents who simply guessed or made up their answers during the formal administration of the PPCP will be unable to recall accurately what they had said, thus exposing their possible lack of sincerity and genuine interest in the child. The PPCP manual suggests that when respondents are unable to recall 20 or more of the 39 recall questions, this "should be considered indicative of guessing [or impaired memory]" (p. 5). No validity data for this cutoff score are provided.

TEST MATERIALS. The PPCP includes an eight-page set of directions, a 27-page spiral-bound question book, a 4-page recall worksheet, and a 3-page summary form. All materials appear to be printed directly from a typewritten original. The directions are fairly specific; however, it appears that the authors intend this instrument to be flexible, and, therefore, many administration decisions (such as which items to administer) are left to the evaluator. There are very few concrete scoring guidelines for the scale. As noted earlier, there is a cutoff score for the recall questions. For the Summary Form, only general guidelines are offered for determining judgments about the respondent's accuracy, depth of knowledge, scope of knowledge, emotional tone, and value/philosophy toward children and child-rearing. After these judgments are made, the evaluator can assess the respondent's degree of "genuine interest" in the child by "look[ing] at the full array of PPCP scores and appraisals, including the Recall Score" (p. 10). The manual concludes by advising that "the higher the scores (other than the

Recall Score) the more the interest in, and knowledge of, the child" (p. 11). No numerical guidelines are offered to help make this judgment, however. Thus, it appears that the PPCP is to be used more in a clinical than a psychometric fashion.

NORMS AND STANDARDIZATION. None are provided. The PPCP directions allude to "parent in our sample" (p. 5) and "Scale data collected so far (N= 60)" (p. 6) but no other information is provided. Therefore, we have no data about how parents from different socioeconomic, educational, and cultural backgrounds might be expected to respond to the PPCP. We also have no data about the comparability of responses by fathers or mothers to the PPCP questions.

RELIABILITY. No reliability data are presented.

VALIDITY. No validity data are presented. It would be important to know what the summary judgments about accuracy, depth of knowledge, scope of knowledge, emotional tone, and value/philosophy mean. Do they have predictive validity in terms of making custody decisions? How do we know that the overall judgment contained in the final section of the Summary Worksheet actually predicts "interest in, and knowledge of, the child"?

SUMMARY. The PPCP is a potentially useful instrument for assessing a parent's knowledge of his or her child. It can be used in court custody cases where this kind of information is necessary for determining custody arrangements and resolving custody disputes. It appears that this instrument will take a substantial amount of time to administer, and the potential user must judge whether the information gained is worthwhile based on the necessary administration time. It might be possible to assess parental knowledge of a child through more efficient means, perhaps by administering a standard adaptive behavior measure. The PPCP includes little or no information on scoring, norms, reliability, or validity, and therefore can only be considered a clinical tool rather than a psychometric instrument.

Review of the Parent Perception of Child Profile by MARY LOU KELLEY, Professor of Psychology, Louisiana State University Medical Center, Baton Rouge, LA:

The Parent Perception of Child Profile (PPCP) is designed to obtain parents' perceptions of their children's behavior and development in eight domains: Interpersonal Relations, Daily Routines, Health History, Developmental History, School History, Fears, Personal Hygiene, and Communication Style. In addition, the Irritability Scale evaluates parental self-reported responses to a variety of anger-provoking situations. The Irritability Scale is intended to "red flag areas where psychological assistance is needed" (directions manual, p. 6).

A unique feature of the PPCP is the inclusion of a scale that requires parents to recall their responses given to a subset of the items at the conclusion of PPCP administration. The "recall" questions are used to assist in detecting parents who may be guessing or whose memory is impaired. According to the authors, the scale can be used to help identify parents whose interests in their children are insincere such as sometimes seen in adversarial custody disputes.

The PPCP is a 27-page booklet that elicits responses using a variety of response formats. Most items require a fill-in-the-blank response. For example, the parents are asked to identify specific hobbies and activities enjoyed by their children. One booklet is used to obtain parental perceptions of a single child. Multiple booklets are required to obtain perceptions from more than one parent or caretaker on more than one child.

Parental responses are obtained through evaluator or self-administration. During evaluator administration, the items are read and the answers are recorded by the evaluator in the response booklet. With some items, the booklet contains space for recording corroborative responses such as perceptions of teachers. Corroborative responses can be obtained in instances where parental accuracy is a concern.

The authors provide a manual that presents the directions for completing the PPCP and scoring guidelines. The manual also presents guidelines for interpreting scores such as the score obtained on the recall items. The directions are straightforward and the data summarization guidelines are relatively objective. In scoring the data, the interviewer evaluates the respondent's accuracy by comparing responses to other sources, depth and scope of knowledge, emotional tone, and values/philosophies expressed. Areas of special attention and degree of genuine parental interest are also determined. Although attempts were made to specify the procedures for deriving scores in each of the areas, the procedures rely heavily on clinical judgment.

The manual outlines specific purposes of the PPCP. The PPCP provides a structured way of obtaining parents' perceptions of their children and their attitudes towards many aspects of their children's lives. The questionnaire provides a framework for assessing the depth and accuracy of parental knowledge by comparing responses across informants. The authors believe an important use of the PPCP is to compare parental responses and parental recall in disputed custody situations where one parent may be acting out of insincere interests in the child.

The authors avoid calling the PPCP a test or even a questionnaire. They qualify their use of the word "scale" in reference to the Irritability Scale. The intended uses and directions generally are carefully worded and generally conceptualize the PPCP as an interview or self-report tool to aid in decision making about parental perceptions and knowledge. In fact, the authors carefully present data on the Recall scale and caution against inappropriate interpretations.

The PPCP appears to be a valuable tool in determining parental perceptions, especially in relation to custody disputes. The instrument might best be used as a structured interview that adds to the uniformity of data obtained in custody evaluations. The instrument appears to have good face validity and reflects the authors' clinical experience with and sensitivity to custody and other forensic issues involving children.

In spite of the clinical appeal of the PPCP, the instrument is limited in many respects and should be used with considerable caution. The PPCP lacks reliability and validity data and it is unclear how the items included in the booklet were chosen. It appears that clinical experience alone and not empirical methods guided item selection. Thus, the validity of the data obtained through using the PPCP is unsubstantiated.

Although the PPCP may be very useful for standardizing the clinical interview, the results obtained should be interpreted cautiously. It is important that the evaluator not overly interpret the data and be well aware of the limitations of information derived from the PPCP. The lack of validity and reliability suggests that any scores obtained from the instrument probably should not be used in report writing. Although cautiousness and conservatism should be employed in all test interpretation, it is especially important in tools used to aid in decisions regarding custody and other forensic issues related to parenting.

Thus, in an area that is very much lacking valid and reliable assessment instruments, the PPCP does, at least, represent an attempt at objectifying and standardizing data obtained from parents during clinical interviews. However, psychometric data on the instrument are minimal and, therefore, the validity of data derived from the PPCP is unknown.

[281]

Partner Relationship Inventory (Research Edition).

Purpose: "Designed to assess interactional, emotional, and sexual needs in a relationship and to point to areas of conflict."
Population: Married couples.
Publication Date: 1988.
Acronym: PRI.
Scores, 2: Interactional Needs, Emotional Needs.
Administration: Individual.
Forms, 3: Long Form, Form I (includes 2 alternate forms), Form II (includes 6 alternate forms).
Price Data, 1992: $18 per 25 Long Form test booklets; $15 per 25 self-scorable short form test booklets (select 1A or 1B); $14 per 25 scoring forms (select form); $22 per manual (30 pages); $23 per specimen set.
Time: (10–30) minutes.
Author: Carol Noll Hoskins.
Publisher: Consulting Psychologists Press, Inc.

Review of the Partner Relationship Inventory (Research Edition) by BRADLEY ELISON, Partial Hospitalization Program Team Leader, Virginia Treatment Center for Children, Virginia Commonwealth University, Richmond, VA:

The Partner Relationship Inventory (PRI) is a self-report measure designed to assess interactional and emotional needs in a relationship and to help couples identify areas in which their needs are perceived as being unmet. There are three forms of the PRI: the 80-item Long Form, Forms IA and IB (which are short forms derived from the original 80 items), and Form II (which includes items from the Long Form as well as new items designed to assess sexual needs in a relationship). In addition to the scores on the Interactional and Emotional Needs scales, the Long Form and Form I provide scores for eight categories of needs: agreement in thinking, communication, disagreement in behavior, perception of others feelings, companionship and sharing, emotional satisfaction, security, and recognition. Form II produces a combined Interactional/Emotional Needs score and a Sexual Needs score.

ADMINISTRATION, SCORING, AND INTERPRETATION. The 80 items of the PRI are presented in statement form and respondents are asked to rate each statement on a 4-point scale that includes *definitely feel, feel slightly, cannot decide*, and *definitely do not feel*. The asymmetry of the response options is not well justified in the manual and appears to bias responses in the positive direction. Scoring can be done using the available hand-scoring form, which is easy to understand and use.

The standardization of each form of the PRI is based on small convenience samples and the author appropriately cautions users that the norms are not representative of all couples and are only references for comparison. The author goes on to suggest that users establish local norms and/or interpret results by looking at item-by-item comparisons. No guidelines for the interpretation of individual item differences are provided. The only interpretive information derived from scores on the PRI is an assessment of the need for counseling. Cutoff scores indicating the need for counseling are set at the 70th percentile for the Interactional Needs scale and at the 60th percentile for the Emotional Needs scale. No rationale for these cutoff scores is provided and their derivation from nonrepresentative samples requires they be used with extreme caution.

THEORETICAL BACKGROUND AND DEVELOPMENT. The PRI grew out of a study by Matthews and Mihanovich (1963) that explored the frequency of specific problems in happily and unhappily married couples. Fifty items for the PRI were obtained from the Matthews and Mihanovich study and were classified into the eight categories mentioned above plus

Perception of Behavior. Additional items were added to expand the number of items per category to 10. No rationale for the development or selection of items is provided and the process for assigning items to categories is not described. Independent corroboration of item selection and category assignment is not provided. Field testing and factor analysis resulted in one category being dropped as a result of its loading in the factor analysis. No item analysis is reported and apparently no items were dropped or altered as a result of the field test. Form I was derived directly from the Long Form by ranking items according to their mean scores and dividing them into two roughly equal parts. Correlations between Form IA and IB are reported to be .94 for the Interaction Scale and .93 for the Emotional Needs scale.

Form II represents an attempt to incorporate a Sexual Needs scale in the PRI and to develop multiple forms of the inventory. For Form II a total of 31 sexual needs items were added to the 80 items of the Long Form and the resulting 111 items were administered to a sample of 212 subjects. Analysis of the responses was used to develop six alternate forms of Form II. The specifics of the tryout are not provided in the manual although it indicates that many revisions were necessary.

RELIABILITY AND VALIDITY. Reliability and validity data for the PRI are minimal. Much of the data that are available are suspect as they are derived from the same small samples used to field test and norm the instrument. Reliability coefficients for the PRI based on a test-retest comparison are reported to range from .26 to .95. The manual author does not provide a complete listing of the reliability data nor are the scales with the .26 and .95 reliability coefficients identified. Correlations between partner scores are reported for both the morning and evening administrations of the PRI and range from .49 to .58. Split-half reliability coefficients were determined for Forms IA and IB using the Spearman-Brown formula and range from .75 to .92. Although additional reliability data are needed and some of the reliability coefficients are low, the PRI appears to be a reliable instrument.

This reviewer found the statements making up the PRI to be good representations of the constructs they were designed to assess. The only independent validation of the PRI is a study correlating the PRI scales with the Locke Wallace Marital Adjustment Scale. This study produced correlations ranging from -.40 to -.75. The correlations were in the expected direction and are high enough to lend support for the validity of the instrument. An initial factor analysis of the PRI leads credibility to the assignment of the categories to two larger needs scales.

SUMMARY. The PRI seems to have potential as a useful tool in both clinical and research applications. In order for this potential to be realized a substantial amount of research and clarification is needed. The push to develop alternate forms appears to have overshadowed the need for well-planned and executed validation studies. Normative data relevant to a broader range of couple populations are needed and should include different ethnic groups, groups from different socioeconomic classes, and groups of non-married couples. The 4-point response format either should be revised to provide for a full range of negative and positive responses or justified in more detail. Rationale and evidence are also needed to support the cutoff scores used in interpretation of the PRI. Last but not least, the manual must be organized in a manner that helps the user differentiate data relevant to specific forms of the inventory.

REVIEWER'S REFERENCE

Mathews, V. D., & Mihanovich, C. S. (1963). New orientations on marital maladjustment. *Marriage and Family Living*, *25*, 300-304.

Review of the Partner Relationship Inventory (Research Edition) by STEPHEN OLEJNIK, Professor of Educational Psychology, University of Georgia, Athens, GA:

The Partner Relationship Inventory (PRI) is based on research findings first reported in the 1960s, which indicated that perceived unmet interactional and emotional needs are primary sources of conflict among couples. Multiple forms of the inventory are available and they are not gender dependent. A Long Form consists of 80 items with the Interactional Needs scale consisting of five categories (Agreement in Thinking, Communication, Disagreement in Behavior, Perception of the Other's Feelings, and Companionship and Sharing). The Emotional Needs scale consists of three categories (Emotional Satisfaction, Security, and Recognition). Each category contains 10 declarative statements soliciting the perceptions of the respondent's partner. Responses are made on a 4-point scale from *Definitely feel* to *Definitely do not feel*. Items are presented in a random order and to avoid response sets approximately half of the items are phrased in reverse form.

Form I consists of two alternate forms (IA and IB) each having 40 items selected from the Long Form. Finally, Form II was developed to facilitate the repeated measurement of respondents and consists of six alternative forms. Each form contains 33 items and a Sexual Needs scale is provided in addition to the Interactional and Emotional Needs scales.

Scoring of the inventory is easy and can be completed quickly by hand. One disadvantage of the scoring procedure, however, is that responses to the inventory must be transferred twice. First, responses on the inventory itself must be transferred to a scoring form that assigns item point values. The item point values are then recorded on a special grid that groups the items into categories to facilitate summing and the computation of category and total needs scores. Because this is done by hand, chances of recording errors are possible.

Interpretation of the Total Interactional Needs and Emotional Needs to the Long Form is based on the responses from 104 individuals (52 couples). First, second (median), and third quartiles are reported and the author suggests that individuals with scores above the 70th percentile for the Interactional Needs scale and above the 60th percentile for the Emotional Needs scale be considered as candidates for counseling. No rationale is provided for these guidelines nor is an explanation offered for the difference in criteria between scales. Characteristics of the distribution of the couples' discrepancy scores are not reported. Very little information is provided regarding demographics of the participating normative group.

Quartiles are also reported for the 52 couples on Form IA and IB. Interpretation of scores obtained on Form I is not offered. Means and standard deviations on the two Needs scales and the division points for the lower, middle, and upper thirds of each category are reported from a second study based on 336 respondents using Form I. The author suggests the division points be used to identify low, medium, and high conflict levels.

Form II is still under development and no guidance is provided regarding the interpretation of the Sexual Needs scale nor any of the six alternative forms.

Content validity is based on the opinions of two judges. No information is provided on the qualifications of these individuals other than their professional affiliation (educational psychology and marriage counseling). In terms of construct validity, appropriate negative correlations between each of the category scores and a marital adjustment scale are reported. Correlations with the Interactional and Emotional Needs scales, however, are not reported. Two other correlational studies are cited as providing evidence of convergent and divergent validity but no details are provided. Finally, the authors report the intercorrelation matrices for Form IA and Form IB and the results of a factor analysis based on category scores. Factor loadings support the two-factor model and the grouping of the categories. No details are given regarding the complete factor solution and it is not clear whether the solution is based on the Long Form, Form IA, or Form IB. Justification of the grouping of items into the eight categories is not provided. The author does not provide any evidence indicating that individuals having high scores on either of the Needs scales or any of the category scores are experiencing high conflict.

Reliability for the Long Form is based on the correlations between morning and evening administrations of each category. Individual correlations are not reported but are said to range between .26 and .95. Consistency for the Total Needs scale is not reported. Correlations between partners on the Interactional and Emotional Needs scales are reported for each of the two administrations and range between .49 and .58. The author does not report a measure for internal consistency for the Long Form.

Form IA and Form IB were developed by splitting the Long Form in half. Alternate forms reliability for each category was obtained by correlating the two halves from each administration of the inventory (morning and evening). For morning administration reliability estimates range between .55 and .90 and evening administration reliability estimates range between .68 and .88. The author also reports Spearman-Brown reliability for each administration of each category. Using the Spearman-Brown formula, I could not reproduce the reported values using the alternate forms correlations reported. The usefulness of these values is limited because they predict the reliability of the category scores if the number of items in a category is increased or decreased. A much better estimate of internal consistency could have been provided through coefficient alpha.

The research edition of the Partner Relationship Inventory will require considerably more research before its use can be justified in either a clinical or research setting. Scores on this instrument are virtually meaningless. A much larger and more representative sample of couples is needed. In addition, more evidence is needed to support the belief that high scores on this instrument truly do reflect conflict in a relationship. At best, responses to this inventory might be used by counselors to begin a discussion in a clinical setting. The author does caution users that this is a research edition and not to over interpret the responses. However, the Long Form and Form I have been available for some time and it appears that little new evidence has been gathered to support the validity and reliability of the instrument. Guidance for the interpretation of the responses focuses on the two Needs scales but the reliability and validity estimates provided apply to the category scores. Additional reliability and validity studies are needed for the Needs scales. Alternatively, guidance for the interpretation of the category scores are needed. Finally, the research studies supporting the theory on which the instrument is based were conducted more than 20 years ago. Because society has changed considerably since that time, more recent research is needed to provide current support for the theory.

[282]

Perception of Ability Scale for Students.

Purpose: "Designed to assess children's feelings about their academic abilities and school-related achievement."
Population: Grades 3–6.
Publication Date: 1992.
Acronym: PASS.

Scores, 7: General Ability, Math, Reading/Spelling, Penmanship and Neatness, School Satisfaction, Confidence, Total.
Administration: Group or individual.
Price Data, 1995: $72.50 per complete kit including manual (88 pages), 2 test report answer sheets, and 10 AUTOSCORE™ answer forms; $25 per 25 answer forms; $45 per manual; $9.50 per test report answer sheet.
Time: (15) minutes.
Comments: Self-report inventory.
Authors: Frederic J. Boersma and James W. Chapman.
Publisher: Western Psychological Services.
Cross References: See T4:1953 (1 reference).

Review of the Perception of Ability Scale for Students by MICHAEL R. HARWELL, Associate Professor of Psychology and Education, University of Pittsburgh, Pittsburgh, PA:

Many test reviewers seem to struggle to say something positive about a test. Fortunately, the Perception of Ability Scale for Students (PASS), a 70-item self-report instrument designed to assess perceptions of academic abilities and school-related achievement of children in grades 3–6, is not in this category. Rather, this instrument, which may be administered individually or in a group, is a sparkling example of test construction. Virtually all the guidelines for test construction presented in the *Standards for Educational and Psychological Testing* (AERA, APA, & NCME, 1985) have been attended to by the PASS authors. There is a clear description of the purposes of the test (to help identify high risk children, to aid in clinical assessment and to plan remedial intervention, to get children to talk about school and other concerns affecting their performance, and to monitor general program effects on school-related self-perceptions), the settings in which it can be appropriately used (regular and special education classes, counseling and psychological service facilities, residential treatment centers), and by whom (teachers, psychologists, counselors, social workers, and school officials). PASS offers easy-to-follow instructions for administering and scoring the test, and succinct and well-documented interpretations of scores. There are six subscales in the PASS, five of which were chosen to reflect school subject areas: Reading/Spelling, Math, and Penmanship, plus a subscale reflecting General Ability, School Satisfaction, and Confidence in academic abilities. Three validity indices are also embedded in the test, designed to assess response bias, inconsistency, and misrepresentation (faking), all of which are useful for a test of this sort. Aspects of the test manual that are particularly welcome include (*a*) an understanding of the importance of carefully documenting the test construction process, (*b*) consistent warnings against overinterpreting PASS scores, and (*c*) references for almost every topic covered, information which is too often missing from test manuals. There is also a chapter devoted to the clinical use of the PASS.

ADMINISTRATION. The breadth and depth of information about the PASS test produces a manual about 90 pages long. The manual authors state the PASS is easily and quickly administered, but this probably applies to experienced users. First time users should, as the manual suggests, carefully read the supporting documentation, a critical but time-consuming activity. Instructions for administering the PASS are clear and include sample response forms and explicit directions for administrators. (The manual emphasizes that the PASS test should be administered only under the supervision of a qualified psychologist.) Testing time is approximately 20 minutes, although there is no time limit. The response form should be relatively simple for examinees to use. The form consists of a place for demographic information and their Yes-No responses to the 70 items, which appear on a carbon copy used for scoring. Evidence that the reading proficiency required by examinees is consistent with that of second graders is provided, but the manual authors advise a test administrator to read the items aloud if there is any question about the ability of younger examinees to understand the test questions, or if examinees have special needs (e.g., LD children). Although the test is designed for children in grades 3–6, the authors state the PASS may be useful for second graders (to whom the questions should be read) and to students slightly beyond the sixth grade.

SCORING. The scoring system for the PASS is based on summing keyed responses to the 70 items. Each item is scored dichotomously and is worth 1 point. Thus, the theoretical range of PASS Full Scale total scores is 0–70 (high scores reflect a favorable academic self-concept). Subscale scores are also generated, most of which have a range of 0–12; the Confidence in Academic Ability subscale has a range of 0–10. The authors indicate that eight or more omitted items invalidates an examinee's test, and suggest that if the omissions are discovered before the examinee leaves the testing, to ask the examinee to respond to these items. No advice is offered for dealing with raw and subscale scores when a few items are omitted. Apparently the authors felt that a few omitted items do not seriously affect interpretations of total and subscale scales; if this is so, it would be helpful to state this explicitly in the manual. No rationale is offered for the cutoff of eight omitted items. Once an examinee's response is scored a profile can be created on the response form using transformed scores (e.g., *T*-scores) for each subscale and the Full Scale score. (The validity indices are also scored on the response form.) For example, an examinee with a *T*-score of 39 (% = 14) on the Perception of Math Ability scale has "below average perceptions of his ability to perform basic arithmetic operations. He indicates that he has difficulty working with numbers and completing math tasks in school. Overall, this student sees himself as having less ability in this area than most of his peers" (p. 15). One difference between the hand-scored and computer-scored forms (available from the publisher of PASS) is that an examinee's ethnicity is solicited only on the computer-scored response form.

Another welcome aspect of this test is the inclusion of validity indices. The Response Bias Index assesses acquiescence and negative response bias, and is computed by summing the number of Yes's chosen by an examinee (range = 0–70). According to the manual, if the number of Yes's exceeds 41 it probably indicates acquiescence, and if the number of Yes's is less than 19 it probably indicates a negative response bias. A table is included giving the percentage of examinees in the $N = 831$ normative sample having 13–49 Yes's. Thus, we learn that 2.8% of the normative sample had 19 or fewer Yes's and 2.2% had 41 or more Yes's. These cutoffs correspond to the 5% most extreme numbers of Yes's, which are treated as indexing an unusual response pattern.

The Inconsistency Index assesses the extent to which an examinee is responding randomly (range 0–15), with scores exceeding 4 (.7% of the normative sample) suggesting a random pattern of responses. The Misrepresentation Index scores range from 0–6 and reflect the social desirability of an examinee's responses, with scores greater than 4 (7.5% of the normative sample) suggesting that the examinee's responses are unlikely to be an accurate reflection of their perceptions. Unfortunately, there is no explanation of the selection of the cutoffs for the validity indices. This concern is mediated to some degree by the statement in the manual that especially high or low values of these indices do not automatically invalidate an examinee's responses (although such responses probably merit special attention).

Detailed instructions are provided for transforming raw scores to percentile, *T*-, or stanine scores (the response forms only use percentile and *T*-scores; the manual contains stanine equivalents), which is done separately for male and female examinees. Interpretations of transformed scores follow a process ascribed to Cattell (1950), in which a profile of statistically reliable deviations in an examinee's scale scores based on their mean score across all subscales is developed. The manual authors recommend finding the average *T*-score, and then drawing dashed lines corresponding to 10 points (1 standard deviation) above and below the average *T*-score. According to the manual, *T*-score differences exceeding 10 points (i.e., outside the dashed lines) are, in general, indicative of below or above average perceptions. For example, suppose an examinee has a Full Scale score of 60 and an average *T*-score of 63, placing the horizontal dashed lines at 73 and 53, and suppose that all subscale scores fell within these lines except School Satisfaction and Confidence in Academic Ability, which were $T = 42$ and 80, respectively. According to the manual, this examinee's perception of his or her general ability, math ability, reading/spelling ability, and penmanship/neatness would be identified as areas of strength, and satisfaction with school and confidence in their abilities as areas that may need attention. The authors emphasize that all score interpretations should be made in light of the estimated standard errors of measurement (*SEM*), and encourage the use of confidence intervals for Full Scale and subscale scores. (There is a nonstandard use of the term confidence interval, wherein, for example, the 68% confidence interval for a Full Scale scores is given as 3.35, where 3.35 is the *SEM*. What is meant is that the interval is computed as the Full Scale score ± 3.35. These confidence intervals also assume that the distribution of test scores are normally distributed, which is not mentioned in the manual.)

NORMS. In an early piloting of the PASS test, 143 items were administered to $N = 310$ children in grade 3 in Canada in 1976. Factor analysis and item difficulty and item discrimination (point biserial correlations) indices were used to pare the 143 items to 70. The description of the factor analyses will be too technical for someone with no training in this methodology. Information from the factor analyses was used to help identify subscales that generally agreed with the authors' groupings of items according to the five elementary school topics plus the Confidence in Academic Ability subscale. Next, the 70-item PASS was administered to $N = 642$ children from middle-income families in grades 3–6 in Canada. These data were also analyzed using item difficulty and discrimination indices and factor analysis. The results of these analyses are reported in the manual. (The two factor analyses showed good agreement.) Intercorrelations among subscales were also computed. The authors used the median correlation of a subscale with the remaining five subscales as evidence of scale independence. The authors state that "These low median correlations indicate that each subscale is quite independent" (p. 37). This statement may mislead some users. The smallest median correlation was .27 and the largest .39. These correlations do not indicate that the scales are independent, but that the overlap of information provided by the scales is modest.

Next, a normative sample from the United States consisting of $N = 831$ children from mostly middle-income families in grades 3–6 in Idaho, Oregon, and Washington was taken in 1988. Although the authors state the schools served a range of urban and rural communities, they also (wisely) remind users that data based on schools in Idaho, Oregon, and Washington may not easily generalize to other regions in the United

States. Gender differences in PASS scores have been frequently observed, and separate norms are presented for males and females. Interestingly, the overall difference between males and females in the N = 831 normative sample is reported to be significant (t = 3.91, p<.01), although, if an estimate of the size of the effect is computed using a squared point biserial correlation, we obtain $r^2_{pb} = t^2/(t^2 + N\text{-}2) = .018$, meaning that less than 2% of the variation in the PASS scores is attributable to gender. A particularly useful feature of the manual is that the percentage of males and females who responded to each item in a positive direction in the normative sample is reported, augmenting the normative information for the subscales. Of the 747 of the 831 children in the norming sample for whom ethnicity was available, 88% were White, 7% were Hispanic, 1.5% were Native American, 1.3% were Black, .7% were Asian, and 1.5% fell in the Other category. The authors deal with the lack of diversity in the norming sample by citing several studies that used the PASS and found no evidence of ethnic differences, although users are reminded that generalizing PASS scores to nonwhite examinees should be done very carefully. The authors encourage the development of local norms.

RELIABILITY. Detailed reliability information, including subscale reliabilities and *SEM*s, is presented in several tables. Cronbach's coefficient alpha was used to assess reliability. The pilot sample of N = 310 produced an alpha of .91 for the Full Scale, the sample of N = 642 Canadian 3rd–6th graders an alpha of .92, and the normative U.S.. sample an alpha = .93. Most of the subscales show alphas greater than .75, with the exception of the Confidence subscale, which produced a reliability of approximately .69 for the norming samples. The Full Scale *SEM* is approximately 3¹/₃ points, whereas the subscale *SEM*s are generally between 1.2–1.35. Both values suggest the accuracy of the test scores is high. The authors report test-retest correlations across three time periods (4–6 weeks, 1 year, 2 years) for various samples, including an LD sample of N = 51. Test-retest correlations for the 4–6-week period for N = 603 (out of 642) range between .71–.83 for the Full Scale and the subscales, between .55–.75 for the 1-year period for N = 932, and between .49–.67 for the 2-year period. The test-retest correlations of the LD sample are slightly lower.

VALIDITY. Evidence of content, criterion, and construct validity are reported in the manual, and, on the whole, the authors make a strong case for the validity of inferences associated with PASS scores. The thoroughness of the presentation of validity evidence in the manual is highly commendable, and serves as a model for what users of a test should *expect* to see in a test manual. The authors also point out that validation of the inferences made from PASS scores (or any test, for that matter) is an accretionary process occurring over time.

SUMMARY. The PASS test is intended to assess perceptions of academic ability and school-related achievement for children in grades 3–6, and the evidence presented in the manual makes a strong case that it succeeds. The documentation of theoretical and empirical evidence of the development, norming, and validation of PASS is, with only a few exceptions, exemplary. One is left with the impression of an instrument that rests on a solid theoretical and empirical foundation, making it easy to recommend. Perhaps the only thing that could be wished for is that the PASS authors will continue to try to develop norms based on more ethnically diverse samples. Not surprisingly, they promise in the manual to do so.

REVIEWER'S REFERENCES

American Educational Research Association, American Psychological Association, & National Council on Measurement in Education. (1985). *Standards for educational and psychological testing*. Washington, DC: American Psychological Association, Inc.

Cattell, R. B. (1950). *Personality*. New York: McGraw-Hill.

Review of the Perception of Ability Scale for Students by MICHAEL J. SUBKOVIAK, Professor of Educational Psychology, University of Wisconsin-Madison, Madison, WI:

The Perception of Ability Scale for Students (PASS) is a self-report inventory designed to assess a child's academic self-concept. The PASS is intended for grades 3 through 6 and consists of 70 declarative statements written at a second grade readability level, such as: "I am good at spelling"; "I like math"; and "I am a smart kid." The examinee responds either "Yes" or "No" to the statements by selecting the appropriate option on an answer sheet. Administration time is about 15–20 minutes.

Raw scores are computed by counting the number of responses indicative of positive self-concept and are then converted to percentiles, stanines, and *T*-scores. A total academic self-concept score can be derived as well as a profile of six subscale scores (General Ability, Math, Reading/Spelling, Penmanship/Neatness, School Satisfaction, Confidence). The availability of subscales for *specific* academic subjects, as well as for general academic areas, is unique and distinguishes this self-concept scale from others. Invalid response patterns may be detected via three measures: Inconsistency Index (detects random response patterns), Response Bias Index (detects acquiescence or negative response sets), and Misrepresentation Index (detects social desirability response set). The instrument can be administered and scored by teachers, and computerized scoring and reporting are also available. However, the authors caution that only trained professionals should interpret results and PASS scores should be "integrated with information from other sources" (p. 32).

The six PASS subscales were derived via principal components analysis of the intercorrelations among 143 pilot items administered to 310 grade 3 children. Seventy items with the highest factor loadings on the principal components (subscales) were selected for the final form of the PASS. However, some statisticians would question the accuracy of such factor loadings, based upon an analysis involving as many as 143 items and only 310 subjects. In fact, certain items do seem to belong on subscales *other than* those to which they were assigned on the basis of the factor loadings. For example, "I think my schoolwork is really good" is an item on the Math Ability subscale rather than the General Ability subscale, and there are other anomalies of this type. Furthermore, the fact that all subjects used in the principal components analyses were third graders somewhat limits direct generalization of results to other grade levels. Because the PASS is intended for grades 3–6, a more representative sample of subjects might have been employed during the item selection phase of instrument development.

The PASS was subsequently administered to a normative sample of 831 children in grades 3–6 attending nine schools in the Northwestern United States, and norm tables were derived for transforming raw scores to percentiles, stanines, and *T*-scores. Given the regional bias of this norm sample, the authors caution the norms "may have limited generalizability" (p. 38) and encourage users to develop local norms. Because females tend to score higher than males on the PASS, separate norm tables are provided for girls and for boys, as well as a combined group table. Although there also appear to be statistically significant mean differences in PASS scores across certain grade levels, separate grade level norms are *not* provided. Furthermore, the authors urge caution in comparing PASS scores for children from ethnic minorities with the normative sample, which is 88% white in its composition. Additional research is needed regarding the relative performance of various ethnic groups on the PASS.

The reliability of a scale is directly related to the number of items on the scale. Accordingly, internal consistency coefficients for the full 70-item PASS scale are high, ranging from .91–.93 for various reliability studies, whereas coefficients for the 10–12-item subscales are variable, ranging from .64–.86. Similarly, test-retest stability coefficients over 4–6 weeks, 1-year, and 2-year intervals were, respectively, .83, .72, .64 for the full scale and .71–.82, .55–.75, .49–.67 for the subscales. The Reading/Spelling subscale was the most reliable, whereas the Confidence subscale and the School Satisfaction subscale were less consistent and stable. Because subscale scores are less reliable, the authors (p. 25) recommended analysis of an individual's profile of subscores to identify a student's strengths and weaknesses should be undertaken with caution, due to the amount of random fluctuation in subscale scores. The suggested examination of an individual's responses to particular PASS items (pp. 28–32) is unwise for the same reason; the reliability of responses to a single item is extremely low (well below .10).

There are several suggested uses for the PASS: as a measure of change in academic self-concept following treatment programs, as a screening device for identifying exceptional children, or as a means of assessing an individual's relative strengths and weaknesses. The instrument appears to be more valid for certain of these purposes than for others. For instance, a treatment group's *average* change in academic self-concept could be assessed validly using the PASS. However, an individual's change over time cannot be assessed with the same degree of confidence because individual change scores are typically quite unreliable, especially subscale scores. As previously noted, the assessment of an individual's profile of subscale scores in order to identify particular strengths and weaknesses is somewhat risky for the same reason—differences between an individual's subscores tend to be unreliable. Use of PASS total scores to identify exceptional children appears justified in light of their high reliability, but the subscale scores cannot be used in this way with the same degree of confidence. The authors (p. 26) suggest use of the 16th and 84th percentiles, respectively, as cutoffs for identifying children with exceptionally low or exceptionally high self-concept. However, an exceptionally high score may be due to a social desirability response tendency. The Misrepresentation Index is designed to identify individuals responding in this way, but correlations of PASS scores with social desirability are *not* included among the various validity studies summarized in the manual. However, there is ample evidence of construct validity as indicated by positive correlations between the full PASS scale and other measures: academic self-concept (.48–.74); general self-concept (.25–.70); achievement expectations (.36–.67); grade-point average (.49–.57); achievement tests (.26–.49); teacher ratings (.40–.52); and parents' perceptions (.36). In contrast, the PASS is generally uncorrelated with intelligence measures.

In summary, the PASS is a self-report measure designed to assess a child's academic self-concept in specific subject areas and overall. Other inventories, such as Coopersmith's Self-Esteem Inventory (T4:647), Harter's Self-Perception Profile for Children, or the Piers-Harris Children's Self-Concept Scale (T4:2030), include an academic self-concept subscale but do not focus on particular subjects like reading or math. Standardization procedures are generally adequate and include the development of indices for detecting invalid response patterns, but the norms are unrepresentative. Other psychometric properties such as reliability and construct validity of PASS full scale scores are favorable. As such, full scale scores can be used with some degree of confidence to identify children having exceptionally high or low self-concept, or to assess change in a group's average self-concept.

[283]

Perception-Of-Relationships-Test.

Purpose: Constructed to measure the degree to which a child seeks psychological "closeness" with each parent; and the types of behaviors the child has had to develop to permit or accommodate interaction with each parent.
Population: Children age 3 and over.
Publication Dates: 1964–90.
Acronym: PORT.
Scores: No scores.
Administration: Individual.
Price Data, 1994: $169 per complete kit including 6 test/scoring booklets and handbook ('90, 179 pages); pens, eraser, updates, author contact number, and 3 years update service; $69 per 6 test/scoring booklets.
Time: [30] minutes.
Comments: Projective test for use in custody decisions.
Author: Barry Bricklin.
Publisher: Village Publishing, Inc.

Review of the Perception-Of-Relationships-Test by JANET F. CARLSON, Assistant Professor of Counseling and Psychological Services, State University of New York at Oswego, Oswego, NY:

The Perception-Of-Relationships-Test (PORT) is an individually administered projective test derived from human-figure-drawing techniques and intended to yield information regarding the degree of closeness a child feels or seeks with a given parent and the psychological price of sustaining that relationship. The test author suggests the scoring system indicates the parent best able to be the primary caretaking parent. It was developed for use with children from 3 years 2 months of age and up. The PORT consists of seven tasks, several of which have subtasks. The tasks require the child to draw his or her parents, family, and self in relation to others, or to indicate preferences of other subjects regarding their parents.

Administration and scoring guidelines are provided in the test manual. The test materials are conveniently organized in a spiral-bound test booklet. As well, a special pen and eraser are to be used and are included in the test materials. Some scores appear objective, but several depend on judgments (e.g., determining which parent has been drawn with a more pleasant or relaxed expression). Each task score indicates a preference of one parent over the other, so that the number of choices out of seven that favor one parent is used to judge which parent should be considered the best custodial parent. Interpretation of scores, too, often depends upon judgment rather than objective criteria.

The test author is careful to note the goal of the PORT is not to determine a winner and a loser where custody is at issue. Rather, the PORT's author purports the test is used most effectively to illuminate the nature of the relationships the child perceives to exist between him- or herself and each parent in order to arrive at a custody arrangement that maximizes the benefits of these relationships.

In addition to determining custodial advantages, the test author suggests that considerably more information can be gleaned from the data generated on the PORT. Much of this additional information takes the form of clinical intuition. Little empirical support for these propositions is provided in the test manual. Evidence cited in support of the clinical signs suggested by the test author to be associated with particular features of children's drawings is based primarily on individual case studies. The clinical expertise of the test user may influence the extent to which clinically meaningful conclusions are reached. Efforts to extract clinically relevant information may be successful but probably not because of the instrument. Rather, because of the skill of a particular clinician in using the PORT, meaningful information other than that pertaining to custody decisions may emerge.

The development of the PORT is incompletely described in the test manual. Because several references are made to standardization and to statistical data, the potential user is led to believe that norms exist or that comparison data from something resembling a standardization sample are contained in the test manual. They are not. In the section of the test manual in which test development and validation are described, the author notes that a variety of (largely unspecified) instruments believed to have the capacity to elucidate children's perceptions of relationships with their parents were administered to 30 children. Very little information is provided about these 30 children, except to imply that most were being seen in someone's private practice and that none were presently in the throes of divorce or custody proceedings. No demographic information is provided and the date of data collection is not noted, making an assessment of sample representativeness impossible. However, it would be exceedingly unlikely for such a small, nonrandom sample to reflect accurately the characteristics of the population for whom the instrument is intended.

The presentation of technical information is insufficient. The *Standards for Educational and Psychological Testing* (American Educational Research Association, American Psychological Association, & National Council on Measurement in Education, 1985) note that test manuals should provide enough information regarding the technical properties of a test to permit a potential test user to evaluate the test's appropriateness for the user's intended purpose. The PORT manual falls short of this goal. The section in the test manual concerning reliability begins with an argument that reliability cannot be expected of an instrument such as the PORT. "There are no reasons to expect the measurements reported here to exhibit any particular degree of stability, since they should vary in accordance with changes in the child's perceptions" (manual, p. 64). The test author proceeds to describe four sets of circumstances where it just so happened that retesting occurred. Given the sample sizes used (n = 8, 6, 10, and 2), the fact that these studies considered only the chosen parent decision rendered and did not consider statistically changes in task scores (although the test author notes that indeed there were shifts in scores), and that no other form of reliability (such as interrater or split-half) was addressed, it is apparent that reliability of the PORT has not been addressed adequately.

An enduring issue that permeates the PORT manual and leaves considerable doubt about the instrument's validity is the lack of base rate information. That is, the frequency with which mothers are chosen over fathers must be taken into account when considering the extent to which PORT findings corroborate court decisions or judgments made by experts. The test manual contains simple percent agreement figures on such matters and uses these figures as validation evidence. However, the appropriate statistic to use in situations where base rates must be taken into account is the kappa coefficient, because this statistic adjusts for base rate influences.

In summary, the PORT was developed to assist in custody decisions by accessing "gut level" perceptions of the child in question regarding his or her relationship with each parent, both in terms of the closeness experienced and desired, as well as the expenditure of psychological energy needed to sustain the relationship. Applications for an accurate, dependable instrument of this sort are apparent, but the PORT has serious flaws regarding its psychometric properties. These shortcomings might be less problematic if the PORT were presented strictly as a projective technique. The test author broaches the subjects of standardization, statistical data, validation, and reliability, however, and the PORT does not measure up favorably. At this point, the PORT is probably best suited for research purposes, including those that may address validation and reliability issues. For psychologists with considerable clinical experience and expertise, it may serve as a useful adjunctive source of interview data as might other projective measures for which little support of psychometric viability exists.

REVIEWER'S REFERENCE

American Educational Research Association, American Psychological Association, & National Council on Measurement in Education (1985). *Standards for educational and psychological testing*. Washington, DC: American Psychological Association, Inc.

Review of the Perception-of-Relationships-Test by JUDITH CONGER, Professor of Psychology and Director of Clinical Training, Purdue University, West Lafayette, IN:

According to the author, the Perception-of-Relationships-Test (PORT) is a drawing-based, projective test for children, ages 3 years 2 months and up, to assist in custody decision making. The PORT consists of seven tasks, five of which are drawings produced by the child. The sixth item is a picture of a horse placed between houses, labeled mom and dad, in which the child is required to draw a line to the preferred house. The seventh item is having a dream about mom or dad, and the child is required to tell the examiner about these dream(s). The scoring for the last item is somewhat less clear, although all items result in a choice of parent and these choices appears to be summed over the seven items. Additionally, there is a section that discusses the use of the PORT in the detection of physical and sexual abuse. The author feels the PORT shows "promise" in this regard and provides some guidelines that might suggest abuse. There is no empirical evidence to validate its use in this regard, although the author reports personal success.

There is an extensive scoring system for the drawings with a number of examples provided. In addition, there are case presentations, clinical anecdotes, and many suggestions to guide administration and special scoring for children under 4 years of age. The manual is written in a "chatty," informal style in which the author encourages suggestions and is supportive of research and input for the instrument. In addition, in the test manual that I received was a supplement (#8), which suggests that new material is periodically included and updated.

The development of the test was based on items gleaned from a panel of three mental health practitioners who observed an unspecified number of family interactions of parents and children. Additionally, standardized tasks were employed (e.g., solving math problems) and a checklist was used to indicate how many times the child looked at each parent, requested information, smiled, etc. The parents were *not* involved in custody disputes. The panel used the information from the observations to choose the preferred parent. Based on this procedure, although not clearly specified, a list of seven items emerged which best choose the preferred parent in a post-dictive fashion. These items were then applied to a sample of 30 new subjects in a predictive way where the items were compared with independent judgments as to the designated preferred parent. Further validation consisted of comparing the parental choice indicated by the PORT as compared with judgments in court where a 90% agreement was obtained. Further substantiation was based on the author's personal use of the instrument in 57 cases between 1964 and 1981 where small subsamples yielded strong agreement.

Although some basis for validity is found in the comparison between PORT-indicated and judicial custody outcomes, the validity support is meager. It is not clear these were independent events. There is little other validity evidence, particularly of an independent sort, and there are no reliability data. The test author feels that traditional views of reliability do not apply. Thus, there is no strong psychometric evidence supporting the use of this instrument. At best, it is an exploratory clinical tool to gather impressions. The impressions must be substantiated by other means.

To the author's credit, he recognizes the need for more research and actively solicits participation and data from others in the field. Although the author has devoted his own time and expense to the development of the PORT, it is in need of much more extensive psychometric investigation.

[284]

Perceptual-Motor Assessment for Children & Emotional/Behavioral Screening Program.

Purpose: "Designed for screening visual, auditory and haptic perception; fine and gross motor abilities; and perceptual memory in children."

Population: Ages 4-0–15-11.

Publication Date: 1988.

Acronym: P-MAC/ESP.

Scores, 12: 3 scores for the Perceptual Memory Task-Abbreviated (PMT-A): Spatial Relations, Auditory-Visual Colors Recognition, Auditory-Visual Colors Sequence; 3 scores for Haptic Visual Discrimination Test-Abbreviated (HVDT-A): Shape, Size, Texture; 6 scores for McCarron Assessment of Neuromuscular Development-Abbreviated (MAND-A): Beads in Box, Finger Tapping, Nut and Bolt, Hand Strength, Standing on One Foot, Finger-Nose-Finger.

Subtests, 3: PMT-A, HVDT-A, MAND-A.

Administration: Individual.

Price Data, 1994: $1,745 per P-MAC including P-MAC battery, computer program, manual (219 pages), 25 Protocol/Data Entry Forms, and 5 GEM volumes; $250 per ESP including 25 Behavioral Checklists for Students, computer program, and manual; $1,995 per combined P-MAC & ESP; $38.50 per each of 5 GEM volumes; $25 per 25 P-MAC Protocol/Data Entry Forms; $16.75 per 25 Behavioral Checklists for Students; $55 per P-MAC manual; $22.50 per separate ESP manual.

Time: (45) minutes.

Comments: P-MAC battery consists of selected subtests from the MAND, HVDT, and PMT; 5 age-specific volumes of Guides for Educational Management (GEM) that provide expanded recommendations and functional implications; computer software included; Behavioral Checklist for Students for ESP program.

Authors: Jack G. Dial (P-MAC and ESP), Lawrence McCarron (P-MAC), and Garry Amann (P-MAC and ESP).

Publisher: McCarron-Dial Systems.

Review of the Perceptual-Motor Assessment for Children by BARBARA A. ROTHLISBERG, Associate Professor of Psychology in Educational Psychology and School Psychology I Program Director, Ball State University, Muncie, IN, and RIK CARL D'AMATO, Professor and Director of Programs in School Psychology, Division of Professional Psychology, University of Northern Colorado, Greeley, CO:

The Perceptual-Motor Assessment for Children (P-MAC) is designed to screen the performance of 4- through 15-year-olds in visual, auditory, and haptic perception and memory as well as in fine and gross motor abilities. The P-MAC is packaged in a large case with related protocols, manual, computer-scoring disks, a brief Behavioral Checklist, and five Guides for Educational Management (GEMS) included. Materials are not well secured in the case; the majority of items dislodge themselves when the kit is transported. The resultant disarray increases administrative difficulty because test items must be rearranged before the measure can be used effectively.

Scoring and interpretation of P-MAC results are computer dependent. The system is designed to integrate not only the outcome of the perceptual-motor testing but ancillary data sources such as intellectual, achievement, adaptive, and emotional/behavioral measures, too. The computer analysis directly accesses the GEMS, a compilation of remedial or compensatory suggestions, to aid in educational programming. The GEMS are offered in a fashion that enables easy application to IEP development or rehabilitation goals. Although computer-generated scoring assists the professionals for whom the screener was fashioned (e.g., educator, physical/occupational therapist, or psychologist), the authors of the P-MAC caution that adherence to the standardized administration procedures outlined in the manual must be maintained. Likewise, the computerized interpretation of results should be evaluated in light of the clinician's review of the probable hypotheses causing score deviations to insure an accurate picture of the examinee's potential strengths and weaknesses.

Although the P-MAC is presented as a perceptual-motor screener, the information about the administration of the perceptual-motor tasks accounts for a minor portion of the manual; the bulk of the presentation and the computerized scoring and interpretive schemes hinge on the examiner's use of other assessment data to supplement the abbreviated perceptual-motor tasks included in the battery. Indeed, many of the components of the software system pay limited homage to the contribution of the subtests actually housed in the battery. For instance, the P-MAC can provide the examiner with results on up to 37 "traits" described as combinations of various test scores across several domains: intellectual/achievement, perceptual/motor, emotional/behavioral, and adaptive. Operational definitions and the derived weighting scheme for the measures used to develop scores for the traits were incompletely described in the manual. The supplemental instruments that contribute to these factors are well known to assessment specialists but have limited association with perceptual-motor performance itself (with the exception, of course, of the perceptual/motor factor).

The intellectual/achievement factor instrumentation includes measures such as the Wechsler Intelligence Scale for Children—Revised (WISC-R), the Peabody Individual Achievement Test (PIAT), and the Woodcock-Johnson Psycho-Educational Battery (W-J). Unfortunately, most of the instruments listed in this domain have since been revised (Kamphaus, 1993). No information is given as to how the new editions' scores would be equated to those of the older instruments. If no equating is available, the P-MAC's facility for accurately reflecting the trait information sought will be compromised because older instruments will risk providing a biased view of performance.

Information on the structure of the emotional/behavioral and adaptive factors available as part of the scoring and interpretation system was extremely limited. The emotional/behavioral factor relies on a single primary measure, the Behavioral Checklist for Students (BCS), whereas the adaptive factor depends primarily on the Street Survival Skills Questionnaire (SSSQ). Few psychometric data were provided for each, although the system software appears to maximize the amount of interpretive power the instruments provided. The lack of validity information was particularly troubling for the emotional/behavioral factor because the manual provides an Emotional/Behavioral Screening Program that can be used alone or in conjunction with the P-MAC. Twelve different disorders, including DSM III-R designations, can be diagnosed and included in the computerized report. Certainly, when determining emotional/behavioral status, a multifactored evaluation of the area is warranted. Here, the use of abbreviated formats on a number of dimensions and limited data on any one domain should demand caution because of the potential for identifying too many individuals as disturbed (Knoff, 1986).

In terms of the stated purpose of the instrument, the P-MAC is said to provide a reliable overview of motor and perceptual functioning within the 45-minute testing time. The rationale for this type of assessment is tied to the developmental perspective of Piaget and suggests that the availability of intact sensorimotor capacities contributes to normal cognitive development. The abbreviated measures selected for the P-MAC address three of the sensory systems available to the developing child or adolescent: visual, auditory, and haptic functioning. The Spatial Relations and the Auditory-Visual Recognition and Sequencing subtests were derived from the Perceptual Memory Task, whereas abbreviated forms of the Haptic Visual Discrimination Test (Right Shape, Size and Texture, Left Shape, Size and Texture) and the McCarron Assessment of Neuromuscular Development (Beads in Box, Finger Tapping, Nut and Bolt, Hand Strength, Standing on One Foot, and Finger-Nose-Finger) round out the subtests administered.

Unfortunately, the P-MAC's claim of reliable and valid perceptual-motor measurement must be taken on faith because extremely limited reference to the psychometric integrity of the selected subtests is given. The few correlations listed in the body of the manual did not indicate what type of correlation is represented (i.e., split-half, test-retest, etc.) or even whether the correlation is associated with the abbreviated subtest or its "parent" measure. Moreover, there is no specific information provided as to the developmental characteristics of the abbreviated test forms. Few data are furnished regarding the standardization sample used to establish the norms for the subtests used or the relation those subtests have to non-test behavior. The sparse information given is relegated to appendices and a list of references through which the psychometric information can be accessed. In reality, discussion in the P-MAC manual focuses on the time-efficient report writing functions of the computer system and the way in which it can integrate data from multiple measurement sources into psychometric goals. Given that the P-MAC is supposed to address perceptual-motor capability, the relatively limited attention paid to that component of the process is puzzling. Perhaps instead of calling the test Perceptual-Motor Assessment for Children, the P-MAC should more appropriately be named the Computerized Assessment System for Children, where it is clearly acknowledged that the intent of the system goes far beyond the simple subtests included in its battery.

Administration of the actual P-MAC subtests seems straightforward with fairly detailed instructions provided. The inclusion of photographs and diagrams in the manual helps the examiner to get a clearer sense of the setup of the various subtests. In addition, example scoring of some of the subtests helps to clarify item scoring criteria. It would appear that the nature of the subtests would be interesting or at the very least nonthreatening to examinees as they involve simple matching and manipulation tasks. Verbal requirements are kept to a minimum. As mentioned earlier, the inherent strengths of the various subtests for actual intervention with children could not be gauged due to the lack of normative information on the battery. It was interesting to note that it appears the subtests are given in the same manner to 4-year-olds as they are to 15-year-olds. For the most part, floor and ceiling levels for performance are not a factor because most subtests require that all items be administered. Subtests that mention discontinue rules are Spatial Relations, Auditory-Visual Colors, and the Haptic Visual Discrimination Test (Abbreviated). Psychometric data on conversion of subtest raw scores to standard scores were not available.

The GEMS are an interesting adjunct to the P-MAC because they afford a link between the assessment and intervention phase of the evaluation. These age-related recommendations offer skill definitions, then "functional implications" that suggest areas where the student may have difficulty (e.g., anticipating rewards, size discrimination). They then provide specific recommendations (e.g., allowing more time for tests, using concrete materials, or reducing the length of assignments). The layout of these interventions offers easy access for use in goal development. Although the assessment-intervention link is obviously critical, the clinical foundation of these recommendations (and lack of actuarial information) forces one to question the proven utility (and empirical base) of these intervention suggestions.

The P-MAC, then, presents something of an assessment conundrum for the examiner searching for a valid measure of perceptual-motor skill. Although designated as evaluating these functions, it attempts through its interpretive programming to integrate a diverse range of assessment data into a cohesive treatment plan. Such an undertaking is important and noteworthy; however, lack of appropriate normative data, key psychometric information, and information on treatment utility precludes one from recommending this test for general use. A better choice of a wide-band instrument that evaluates similar abilities is the Reitan-Indiana Neuropsychological Test Battery for Children or the Halstead-Reitan Neuropsychological Test Battery for Children (T4:1119) (see Hynd & Willis, 1988; Whitten, D'Amato, & Chittooran, 1992). Presently, the P-MAC could be recommended for research purposes, particularly in the area of relating student abilities to appropriate interventions.

REVIEWER'S REFERENCES

Hynd, G. W., & Willis, W. G. (1988). *Pediatric neuropsychology*. Orlando, FL: Grune & Stratton.

Whitten, J. C., D'Amato, R. C., & Chittooran, M. M. (1992). A neuropsychological approach to intervention. In R. C. D'Amato & B. A. Rothlisberg (Eds.), *Psychological perspectives on intervention: A case study approach to prescriptions for change* (pp. 112-136). New York: Longman.

Kamphaus, R. W. (1993). *Clinical assessment of children's intelligence*. Boston, MA: Allyn & Bacon.

Knoff, H. M. (Ed.). (1993). *The assessment of child and adolescent personality*. New York: Guilford Press.

Review of the Perceptual-Motor Assessment for Children and Emotional/Behavioral Screening Program by E. W. TESTUT, Associate Professor of Audiology, Department of Speech Pathology/Audiology, Ithaca College, Ithaca, NY:

INTRODUCTION AND OVERVIEW OF CONTENTS. The Perceptual-Motor Assessment for Children and Emotional/Behavioral Screening Program (P-MAC/ESP) is a computer interpretable means of screening, recording, and reporting the visual, auditory, and haptic perceptual abilities, fine and gross motor abilities, perceptual memory capabilities, emotional/behavioral concerns, and intellectual/achievement potential of children between the ages of 4 years and 15 years, 11 months. Its dual purpose is to assess the educational potential of individual children while streamlining the educational management process. The P-MAC/ESP consists of a manual, interpretive computer software, data entry forms, and the five-volume, age-specific Guides for Educational Management, that contain client-appropriate educational and other remediation strategies. Additionally, selected subtests from the McCarron Assessment of Neuromuscular Development—Abbreviated (MAND-A), the Haptic Visual Discrimination Test—Abbreviated (HVDT-A), and the Perceptual Motor Test—Abbreviated (PMT-A) are included.

PROGRAM OPERATION. The P-MAC/ESP is utilized by entering client data obtained from various tests and behavioral measures identified by or included within the P-MAC/ESP package or from other examiner selected evaluative measures. Meaningful data entry for the areas of intellectual and academic achievement, perceptual/motor analysis, and adaptive behavior, however, is only possible with data that can be expressed in standardized format (i.e., group mean and expressed standard deviation). In the emotional/behavioral domain, checklist observations, rather than standardized data, are utilized. Various "traits" are then assigned as operationally defined by P-MAC/ESP algorithms. All P-MAC/ESP algorithms are presented in the manual along with a detailed description of the significance (weight) attached to each factor in each algorithm. The authors report that the weight assigned each factor in each algorithm was determined according to published statistical findings. Relevant bibliographic references are provided, but a discussion of the statistical significance of the P-MAC/ESP or contributing algorithms is not provided. Clinician input is permitted, in fact encouraged, in all phases of P-MAC/ESP administration to provide client background information and to assist in interpreting evaluation results and recommended actions. Clinician input is accomplished by a mini-editor (i.e., limited-function word processor). Following the data collection, a formal evaluation report including educational implications and suggested educational treatment or modification can then be generated. Four possible P-MAC/ESP formal report formats are offered: (*a*) a Comprehensive Evaluation Report that includes all other report formats; (*b*) the Educational Analysis Report that aids in identifying primary educational problems while suggesting related clinical diagnoses other than educational; (*c*) the Classroom Report that is designed for the classroom teacher, covering pertinent demographic and background data along with areas identified as limiting to the individual client; and (*d*) the Report of Trait Scores that provides summary profiles, strengths, deficits, and standard scores for all of those traits that have been defined in the evaluation.

DISCUSSION. This reviewer was not provided with the Guides for Educational Management (GEM) or any of the three tests normally accompanying the P-MAC/ESP (i.e., the McCarron Assessment of Neuromuscular Development—Abbreviated [MAND-A], the Haptic Visual Discrimination Test—Abbreviated [HVDT-A], and the Perceptual Motor Test—Abbreviated [PMT-A]). It should also be mentioned that the program this reviewer worked with was said to be a prototype and not necessarily a final copy. The following discussion, therefore, focuses primarily on the operation of the program itself rather than the constituent tests.

The P-MAC/ESP has much to offer. Its primary strength is that it offers a means for streamlining the educational management of individual children. P-MAC/ESP reports identify (i.e., diagnose) problem areas, specify the implications the assessments have for the classroom, and provide suggested strategies for managing identified problem areas, while allowing for individualized narrative input. Additionally, the accompanying manual is thorough, providing detail regarding the design, operation, and implementation of the P-MAC/ESP, and providing detailed, readable information on running and troubleshooting the computer program. This reviewer, despite limited IBM or IBM-compatible experience, found the program to be logically developed, and the instructions, both on-screen and in the manual, easily followed. To summarize, an individual faced with having to evaluate school-aged children would find the P-MAC/ESP a detailed, organized, time-saving, professional tool.

The P-MAC/ESP is not without limitations. For example, although the use of menus made the program easily workable, cursor operation was cumbersome, requiring sequential movement through long lists of menu selections rather than permitting the user to jump directly to a desired choice. Similarly, the program, especially the mini-editor (i.e., narrative generator), utilized atypical key commands, at least when compared with other commercial programs and word processors with which this reviewer is familiar. Furthermore, reviewing previously computer-recorded narrative information required resaving to exit, an unnecessary and time-consuming step. In fact, it was not possible to review an entire client's report without printing the report or relying on one's memory while jumping from subsection to subsection, working subsection menus, and resaving subsection narratives along the way. In short, the P-MAC/ESP might be less cumbersome if: (*a*) a more logical command sequence (i.e., function key usage, <CONTROL> key plus alphanumeric key combination, and/or the use of arrows) were provided; (*b*) it were possible to merge "ASCII text files" from popular word processors; and (*c*) there were a means whereby complete reports could be viewed.

A separate concern was that the reports generated by the P-MAC/ESP gave the appearance of a computer-generated form letter. Large, open spaces between various topic areas, apparently where optional narrative data had not been selected, detracted from what otherwise gave the appearance of custom personalized reports. Another "form letter" characteristic was the appearance of grammatical errors, specifically number agreement. For example, "would predict in the following areas [*sic*]: reading." Finally, the printout program printed two copies of reports, when only one had been requested.

A general concern inherent in programs of this type is their use as de facto "expert systems." The authors do not claim that the P-MAC/ESP is an educational assessment expert system or that suggestions from the Guides for Educational Management are infallible or all encompassing. In fact, disclaimers appear in the final reports cautioning the reader not to substitute the report for a professional diagnosis. The nature of the P-MAC/ESP report, however, with its detailed descriptive data and treatment suggestions, coupled with the likelihood that those using the program would fail to evaluate the program algorithms, could result in the substitution of a P-MAC/ESP generated report for professional diagnosis. The P-MAC/ESP might, in other words, wind up being employed as an expert system and individuals using the P-MAC/ESP might limit their selection of tests and their narrative commentary to those that "fit the program."

SUMMARY AND CONCLUSIONS. The P-MAC/ESP provides a viable, efficient means for evaluating, recording, and reporting the educational readiness of children between the ages of 4 years and 15 years, 11 months. The usefulness of the P-MAC/ESP, however, is somewhat limited by its cumbersome nature and the degree to which it might be employed as an arbiter.

[285]

The Personal Communication Plan.

Purpose: Designed to "provide a subjective, descriptive analysis of a person's communication strengths and needs in their everyday environment."
Population: Ages 14 to adult with learning disabilities.
Publication Date: 1991.
Acronym: PCP.
Scores: Ratings in 5 sections: Background Information, Speech and Language Profile, Social Communication Skills, Environment, Shared Action Planning.

Administration: Individual.
Price Data: Available from publisher.
Time: Administration time not reported.
Authors: Alex Hitchings and Robert Spence.
Publisher: NFER-Nelson Publishing Co., Ltd. [England].

Review of The Personal Communication Plan by JANET NORRIS, Associate Professor of Communication Sciences and Disorders, Louisiana State University, Baton Rouge, LA:

The Personal Communication Plan for people with learning disabilities (PCP) is a functional assessment and planning system designed to ascertain the communicative strengths and needs of adults, age 16 and over, with disabilities in the context of everyday life and environmental situations. The term "learning disabilities" for this instrument is generic, and can include individuals with mild-to-severe disabilities. Four sections that assess home and environmental background, speech and language abilities, social communication skills, and the environment in which the individual is communicating comprise the PCP along with one additional section where the needs identified in the assessment sections are summarized and an action plan for intervention is generated. The PCP may be given in total, or selected sections of the assessment profile can be administered to meet specific needs. The purpose is to provide one instrument through which all of the relevant people in the life of a focal individual can work together systematically to assess, plan for, and monitor the communicative needs of that individual.

The goal of the PCP is to provide an assessment and intervention plan that will maximize the individual's independence and status in the community, and to normalize the individual's daily life and environment to as great an extent as possible. Administration of the PCP requires a lengthy process, rather than a discrete one-time measurement of skills or abilities. Conducting the assessment can take as little as 2 hours for a person whose personality and lifestyle are highly familiar to those involved in the evaluation, and as much as several weeks if many observations of the individual's communication skills must be conducted in a range of settings.

The process begins with a referral that identifies the need for an assessment of communicative functioning. An initial meeting is planned that includes all persons who spend significant time with or who have an important role in the focal person's life. These individuals complete the first section of the PCP, or Background Information, including the focal person's address, age, home environment (family home, hospital, residential home), occupation, major people in the environment, physical disabilities, cultural background, and interests and hobbies.

If the individual's daily living situation is unfamiliar, a series of interviews, home visits, and other data-gathering observations are planned and assigned to various group members. The data to be gathered for the second section, the Speech and Language Profile, include impressions of the vocabulary, syntax, fluency, articulation, volume, rate, and intonational characteristics used by the individual. These are rated as a strength or a need, relative to that person's abilities and relative to the context of use. For example, the person's vocabulary of available words may be rated as a strength, but the use of specific vocabulary to meet communication needs in the occupational setting may be ranked as a need. An in-depth evaluation of language use is conducted following the guidelines in Section 3, or Social Communication Skills. Thirty-three different behaviors, ranging from aspects of body language through conversational strategies, are each rated along a scale from 1 to 5. For each behavior, the individual's performance is rated relative to specified criteria, as in a rating of "1" for conversational relevancy if the focal person exhibits extreme difficulty in following the topic of the conversation, introducing irrelevancies or unrelated ideas; through a rating of "5" if the person can maintain and develop a topic effectively and appropriately.

Section 4 assesses the focal person's opportunities for communication, including participation in community functions and activities (Relationships), engagement in active decision making (Choice), positive recognition from peers and/or the community (Respect), changes or development observed in the recent past (Personal Skills), and the degree of independence and presence within the community (Community Presence). A series of questions guide observations in this section, as in "What other facilities would the focal person benefit from using?" or "What are the barriers to improving choice in the focal person's life?" At the completion of the data-gathering phase of the assessment process, the coordinator compiles the observations and the group meets to discuss the findings and generate an action plan.

In the Shared Action Plan (Section 5) the needs of the focal person are identified and prioritized. The group members agree on the future steps to be taken to either change the environment and/or provide training to the focal person to improve social-communicative functioning. The person(s) responsible for implementing and monitoring the goals are designated, and a time frame for accomplishing the goals is established. Finally, one or more review meetings are scheduled in which goals are evaluated and revised, as appropriate.

The PCP is a descriptive instrument and not a psychometric test, and so norms and standard scores are not established. The individual is not compared on any dimension to peers, but rather only relative to personal communicative functioning within the person's daily environment. Although some observations are judged according to a rating scale, these ratings also are supported with descriptive statements indicating what behaviors were exhibited that resulted in that score. To the extent the observations are typical of the focal person's performance in the specified context, this method of documentation adds reliability to the judgments and impressions specified by the rater. No measures of reliability or validity are reported for this instrument.

The Personal Communication Plan is a well-designed and systematic guide for conducting observations of communicative functioning in daily living situations. The questions and rating scales found throughout the PCP provide a structure for imposing purpose and organization on observations conducted in complex situations. The behavioral statements used to support ratings add descriptive power and objectivity to impressions, and increase the reliability of observations. The instrument would be strengthened by measurements of reliability and validity. For example, samples of representative interactions involving the focal person could be videotaped and rated twice by a single observer to establish intrarater reliability, and rated by several independent observers to measure interrater reliability. Reliability is particularly important because these observations are used as the basis for identifying goals and measuring progress or change. The entire intervention program established for the focal person is invalid if the observations from which it was derived do not accurately reflect the person's abilities.

Similarly, although the items on the PCP have intuitive appeal, validity measurement is necessary to determine if they, in fact, do accurately reflect communicative functioning in the focal person's environment. For example, individuals who interact on a daily basis with the focal person could be asked to select from a choice of several the profile of strengths and needs that corresponds to the focal person. If completion of the PCP does not result in a profile that accurately describes the focal person, then a tremendous investment in time and effort will have been expended to achieve invalid findings.

SUMMARY. The PCP represents a positive step toward creating a systematic method of assessing communicative abilities in context. It is comprehensive enough to consider a variety of factors, including those inherent to the individual and those present within the environment that interact to determine the individual's communicative competence. This comprehensive evaluation results in recommendations for providing training to the individual, but also for making changes within the environment that will enable the focal person to function more successfully. It is selective enough to examine a wide variety of behaviors using a limited number of questions. The PCP is flexible, so that parts of the instrument can be administered for specific purposes, or all of the sections can be given when conducting a comprehensive evaluation. Its primary weakness is the lack of support for the reliability and validity of the procedure.

[286]

Personal Experience Screening Questionnaire.
Purpose: "Designed as a brief screening tool to aid . . . in the identification of teenagers likely to need a drug abuse assessment referral."
Population: Adolescents.
Publication Date: 1991.
Acronym: PESQ.
Scores, 3: Infrequency, Defensiveness, Problem Severity.
Administration: Group.
Price Data, 1993: $70 per complete kit including 25 test forms and manual (30 pages); $29.50 per 25 test forms; $42.50 per manual.
Time: (10) minutes.
Author: Ken C. Winters.
Publisher: Western Psychological Services.

TEST REFERENCES

1. Winters, K. C. (1992). Development of an adolescent alcohol and other drug abuse screening scale: Personal Experience Screening Questionnaire. *Addictive Behaviors*, *17*, 479-490.

Review of the Personal Experience Screening Questionnaire by STUART N. HART, Associate Professor of Counseling and Educational Psychology, Indiana University-Purdue University at Indianapolis, Indianapolis, IN:

The primary general purpose set for the Personal Experience Screening Questionnaire (PESQ) was "to provide clinicians with a standardized self-report screening tool to assist in the identification of teenagers needing a drug abuse assessment referral" (p. 1). The author intended more specifically to provide a quick screening, standardized, adolescent-specific instrument, sensitive to alcohol and other drug abuse and to response distortion tendencies. To accomplish this the author produced the 40-item PESQ intended for youth 12 to 18 years of age and consisting of three subsections dealing with drug involvement problem severity, psychosocial problems, and personal drug history; and including items to assess faking bad and faking good response tendencies.

The manual for the PESQ is well developed and presents information in a clear and logical manner, which displays the respect of the author for the criteria of the *Standards for Educational and Psychological Testing* (AERA, APA, & NCME, 1985). The PESQ can be easily administered by a properly prepared and supervised technician or clerk and interpretations should be made or closely supervised by an appropriately trained professional. No time limit for completion of the PESQ is set but it is usually completed in approximately 10 minutes. Individual administration is preferred but group administration is indicated to be acceptable and was incorporated in addition to individual administration in the development of normative data. Required test materials include a two-sided PESQ "Auto-Score" form and a pencil. Examinees place their responses on the questionnaire/answer sheet, and the responses transfer to the scoring section on the examinee-inaccessible inside of the form. The instructions and items of the PESQ are at approximately the 4th grade reading level. By having an examinee read the instructions aloud the examiner can determine whether it will be necessary to read the items to the examinee.

The PESQ scores are organized to provide results for three scales labeled Problem Severity, Defensiveness, and Infrequency; and to provide information on two content areas labeled Psychosocial Indicators and Drug Use History. Part I of the PESQ contains 18 items that accumulate to give a global measure of Problem Severity indicating the extent to which the individual is psychologically and behaviorally involved with drugs. The items fall within subcategories exploring frequency of use of drugs under various conditions and behaviors associated with drug use and procurement. Part I also includes the three items of the Infrequency scale, to measure faking bad and dealing with extremely unlikely drug use behavior. All items of Part I are responded to on a 4-point scale (i.e., *never, once or twice, sometimes, often*). Part II of the instrument contains eight items that accumulate to provide information for the content area of Psychosocial Indicators covering "emotional distress, problems with thinking, and physical and sexual abuse" associated with adolescent drug use. Part II also includes the five items of the Defensiveness scale to measure faking-good response tendencies. All items of Part II require yes or no responses. Part III requests information about the respondent's Drug Use History by asking the frequency of use of various drugs during the last 12 months and provides seven response options ranging from never to over 40 times for alcoholic beverages and marijuana or hashish and once or more for a list of hard drugs; and additionally two questions are asked about the time when the person first got high or first used drugs regularly.

Scoring the PESQ is relatively easy, requiring only that simple instructions inside the response form be followed to accumulate totals for the three scales and two content areas. To guide interpretations cutoff scores and ranges are provided for the Problem Severity scale by age and sex subgroupings. Scores above specified points are labeled "red flag" to indicate the examinee may be in need of a referral and that a "more complete and reliable drug abuse assessment" (p. 10) is advised, or "green flag" to indicate a referral is probably not needed. The results for the Infrequency and Defensiveness scales are to be used to modify considerations of profile results, particularly for the Problem Severity scale. Scores above the red flag cutoffs for the faking-bad and faking-good scales suggest that the validity for the rest of the profile is in question and that caution is needed in interpreting results, whereas scores in the green flag range indicate "the profile is probably valid" (p. 10). Information contained in answers to specific questions on the three scales and from the two content areas provides the interpreter with opportunities to derive additional meaning. The author urges the interpreter be knowledgeable regarding drug abuse and interpretation of these tests in order to maximize the validity of the test.

The PESQ was developed through the Chemical Dependency Adolescent Assessment Project (CHDAAP), which was established in 1982 to develop "assessment tools to aid clinicians in the identification, referral, and treatment of teenagers suspected of drug abuse" (p. 11). The Problem Severity scale of the PESQ was developed by selecting unused items from the pool of items previously used to construct the Personal Involvement With Chemicals scale of the Personal Experience Inventory (PEI), a well-respected CHDAAP instrument meant for the clinical evaluation of drug abuse and treatment needs (see reviews of the PEI in *The Eleventh Mental Measurements Yearbook*; 11:284). These items were part of the set that had a high loading for a general drug abuse severity factor. The specific items selected for the Problem Severity scale of the PESQ met requirements of having Pearson product-moment correlations greater than .50 with the PEI Personal Involvement With Chemicals scale, and less than -.40 with the Marlowe-Crowne Social Desirability scale. The PESQ five faking-good Defensiveness scale items were derived from the Marlowe-Crowne Desirability Scale, whereas the three faking-bad, inattentive, or random responding Infrequency scale items and the content area items were derived from logical analyses of the PEI's psychosocial section and adapted from national survey instruments.

Reliability of the PESQ has been addressed only through internal consistency estimates for the Problem Severity scale thus far. The population sample employed for this purpose included 2,744 subjects from schools (n = 1,885), juvenile detention centers (n = 611), and drug clinics (n = 248). School and juvenile center populations completed questionnaires similar to the PESQ which included the 18 Problem Severity items whereas the drug clinic sample completed 203 items of the original PEI pool. Quite good alpha coefficients ranging from .90–.95 were produced across samples. Internal consistency measures were essentially the same regardless of the nature and length of the larger item pool within which the PESQ items were placed; and across male and female, white and nonwhite subjects. Test-retest reliability, stability over time, clearly needs to be addressed in future research.

Although it would be expected to be adequate on the basis of the very good to good test-retest results that have been found for the similar longer scale on the PEI, this is not sufficient evidence.

The content validity of the Problem Severity scale of the PESQ is clearly tied to the content validity of the PEI, which has been judged to be "quite adequate" (Toneatto, 1992). PESQ items were selected from the item pool used to construct the PEI. A "broad spectrum approach" (p. 17) to adolescent use problem severity guided the development of this pool, which included 10 scales produced by "statistical and rational approaches" (p. 17) derived from 24 content categories identified as relevant. A Pearson product-moment correlation of .94 was found for the relationship between the PESQ Problem Severity scale and PEI personal involvement with chemicals section of its problem severity scales. The items of the Defensiveness scale (adapted from the Marlowe-Crowne Social Desirability Scale) and of the Infrequency scale resulted from a review of empirical knowledge and from consultant advice. They appear to have adequate content validity but, as with all the items of the PESQ, the user must determine their relevance for the population and setting to which they will be applied.

The construct validity of the PESQ is also closely tied to the construct validity of the PEI Personal Involvement with Chemicals scale which has been found to best tap the core of its chemical severity section (Tucker, 1992). This fact, added to knowledge of the fairly high and significant correlations between the PEI and related measures (Toneatto, 1992), the high internal consistency found for the PESQ, and the ability of the PESQ to discriminate between those at various levels of drug abuse (see later section), indicates its construct validity is satisfactory.

Criterion validity, of greatest significance in determining the usefulness of a screening device, appears to be strong for the PESQ. The PESQ has been assessed for its criterion validity relative to distinguishing between treatment populations, current diagnoses, and counselor referrals. Individuals with drug treatment histories and with a clinical diagnosis of dependence were found to have significantly higher PESQ Problem Severity scale scores than those with no prior treatment histories and those with abuse but not dependence problems. Problem Severity scale scores for a drug clinic population were found to be significantly higher than those of juvenile offenders, which were in turn found to be significantly higher than those of a normal school population. Individuals from a school clinic sample referred by counselors for further drug abuse evaluations had significantly higher Problem Severity scale scores than those not referred for this purpose. A post hoc analysis of the relationships between the two response bias scales and the Problem Severity items produced correlations similar to those found for the response bias scales and the PEI Personal Involvement With Chemicals scale items.

The "red flag" criterion is inherently a criterion validity issue. It was developed through discriminant analysis applied to the first half of the school clinic sample in a cross validation procedure. The cut-point on the Problem Severity scale of 40T, one standard deviation below the drug clinic sample, was identified as optimal and found to correctly classify 88% of the initial school clinic sample (sensitivity .91, specificity .84) and 87% of the second half of the school clinic sample (sensitivity .88, specificity .85). This cut-point falls 1 $^1/_2$ standard deviations above the mean of the school sample and appears to be appropriate for differentiating those who do and do not need a more comprehensive drug abuse evaluation.

The PESQ, in particular its Problem Severity scale, appears to be a well-developed screening device, which should be quite useful for its intended purposes. Its psychometric properties are strong with the exception of the need to establish temporal stability and to clarify the validity and reliability of the area scores. The "red flag" cut-point provides a good guide to decisions about 12–18-year-old individuals who do and do not require more comprehensive evaluations. The practical and research application potentials of the instrument are promising.

REVIEWER'S REFERENCES

American Educational Research Association, American Psychological Association, & National Council on Measurement in Education. (1985). *Standards for educational and psychological testing*. Washington, DC: American Psychological Association.

Toneatto, T. (1992). [Review of the Personal Experience Inventory]. In J. J. Kramer & J. C. Conoley (Eds.), *The eleventh mental measurements yearbook* (pp. 660-661). Lincoln, NE; Buros Institute of Mental Measurements.

Tucker, J. A. (1992). [Review of the Personal Experience Inventory]. In J. J. Kramer & J. C. Conoley (Eds.), *The eleventh mental measurements yearbook* (pp. 661-663). Lincoln, NE; Buros Institute of Mental Measurements.

Review of the Personal Experience Screening Questionnaire by RICHARD W. JOHNSON, Adjunct Professor of Counseling Psychology and Associate Director of Counseling & Consultation Center, University of Wisconsin-Madison, Madison, WI:

The Personal Experience Screening Questionnaire (PESQ) serves as one of three instruments in a comprehensive assessment package created for adolescents suspected of drug abuse. The PESQ, a brief self-report inventory that can be completed in 10 minutes or less, should be administered first as a screening device to determine if a more thorough assessment needs to be undertaken. The other two instruments, the Personal Experiences Inventory (PEI; 11:284) and the Adolescent Diagnostic Interview (ADI; 16), are employed if scores on the PESQ suggest that alcohol or other drug abuse may be an issue.

The PESQ provides a broad range of information concerning the nature and the extent of drug use and related matters. It contains 40 items divided into five parts as follows: (*a*) a Problem Severity scale of 18 items with 4-point response options (*never, once or twice, sometimes, often*); (*b*) a Defensiveness scale of 5 items that measures "faking good"; (*c*) an Infrequency scale of 3 items that measures "faking bad" or careless or random responding; (*d*) 8 individual items that assess psychosocial concerns (emotional distress, problems with thinking, and physical and sexual abuse); and (*e*) 6 items that provide a history of drug usage.

In contrast with most drug assessment measures, the PESQ was constructed especially for adolescents. A number of the questions refer specifically to situations that involve teenagers (e.g., skipping school, making excuses to teachers or parents) but not other age groups. It differs from similar instruments by including validity scales to detect either denial or exaggeration of problems, both frequent concerns when assessing drug use by adolescents in institutional settings.

The instrument can be easily hand-scored by opening a seal on the test booklet that separates the answer sheet from a scoring guide inside the test booklet. In the course of using the PESQ with a client, we noted that one of the items on the Defensiveness scale (Item 29) was keyed in the wrong direction on the score sheet. Test users should check this item (one of only five items on the Defensiveness scale) to make sure that it is keyed correctly in their test booklet.

The PESQ has been normed on adolescents 12 to 18 years old in three settings: drug clinic assessment programs, juvenile detention centers, and public schools. The normative samples have been used to set cutoff scores ("red flags") for referral purposes. The cutoff scores vary somewhat depending on the age and sex of the respondents. However, very little information regarding the actual distribution of scores among the samples has been provided in the test manual. It would be helpful to know the means and standard deviations for all scales and the results of item analyses for the different norm groups. Additional normative data for minority groups are also needed.

The Problem Severity scale of the PESQ possesses high interitem consistency (alpha coefficients = .90 to .95) across different settings and types of clients. No attempt has been made to determine the interitem consistency of the Defensiveness or Infrequency scales because of their brevity. Information regarding the test-retest reliabilities for each scale also should be reported.

The PESQ derives much of its validity from studies conducted on the PEI. Factor analytic studies with the PEI revealed one large general factor that accounted for much of the variance in surveys of drug use among adolescents. This factor, severity of drug use, is measured by the Problem Severity scale of the PESQ. Scores on the Problem Severity scale correlate highly with the scale (Personal Involvement with Chemicals scale) on the PEI that measures this factor.

The most crucial question concerning the validity of the PESQ pertains to its effectiveness in detecting those adolescents in need of a comprehensive drug assessment program. Ideally, the instrument should identify those young people at risk for substance abuse at the same time that it rules out the dangers of addiction for others not at risk. In a cross-validation study reported in the test manual, the author successfully used the PESQ to select 88% of those students who needed additional drug assessment based on a variety of criteria (official records, collateral reports, and interview data) while eliminating 85% of those students who did not need such assessment. In other words, it proved to be both highly sensitive (few false negatives) and highly selective (few false positives). These results should be substantiated by research in other settings.

In conclusion, the PESQ presents a number of advantages as an assessment tool. It has been integrated with other drug assessment procedures as part of an ongoing research and treatment program. It is more comprehensive and less easily faked than other inventories designed specifically for adolescents such as the Adolescent Drinking Index (ADI; 17) or the Adolescent Alcohol Involvement Scale (AAIS; Mayer & Filstead, 1979). It can be conveniently administered, scored, and interpreted. Although the PESQ can benefit from further study as described above, research conducted thus far indicates that it is highly reliable and valid for the purpose for which it was designed. I recommend it as a screening instrument for assessing drug use among adolescents.

REVIEWER'S REFERENCE

Mayer, J., & Filstead, W. J. (1979). The adolescent alcohol involvement scale: An instrument for measuring adolescents' use and misuse of alcohol. *Journal of Studies on Alcohol*, *40*, 291-300.

[287]

Personal Inventory of Needs.

Purpose: Designed as a self-assessment tool to identify the strengths of basic needs.
Population: Employees.
Publication Date: 1990.
Scores, 3: Achievement, Affiliation, Power.
Administration: Group or individual.
Price Data, 1990: $60 per complete kit including 20 inventories, 20 response sheets, and 20 interpretation sheets.
Time: [30] minutes administration; [30] minutes interpretation.
Comments: Self-administered, self-scored; based on David McClelland's research at MIT.
Authors: Training House, Inc.
Publisher: Training House, Inc.

Review of the Personal Inventory of Needs by GARY J. DEAN, Associate Professor and Department Chairperson,

Department of Counseling, Adult Education, and Student Affairs, Indiana University of Pennsylvania, Indiana, PA:

GENERAL COMMENTS. The purpose of the Personal Inventory of Needs is to identify the strengths of basic needs of employees. This instrument is self-administered, scored, and interpreted. The format is self-report and the items are forced choice.

The instrument consists of an inventory, an answer sheet, and an interpretation guide. The inventory is a three-page booklet, A Self-Assessment Exercise, with directions on the first page and the inventory on the inside two pages. The answer sheet consists of two copies with a carbonless copy format. The interpretation booklet, Scoring and Interpretation Sheet, consists of four pages.

There are 20 items with three responses for each item. Respondents are to rank the three responses for each item: 3—"you most agree with this statement," 2–"you next most agree with this statement," and 1–"you least agree with this statement." The item responses consist of statements describing how an employee feels or thinks on an issue.

TECHNICAL INFORMATION. No technical data were provided by the publisher for this review. Therefore, comments on the validity and reliability of the instrument cannot be made.

ADMINISTRATION AND SCORING. Administration of the instrument is easy and straightforward. It takes 15 to 30 minutes to complete the instrument. The answer sheet provided is easy to complete. On the second page of the answer sheet each response is marked by a code: "ach" for the need for achievement, "aff" for the need for affiliation, and "pow" for the need for power. Respondents total their scores for each need. The total score is 120 with the points being divided among the three needs.

INTERPRETATION. According to the Scoring and Interpretation Sheet scores can range from a low of 20 to a high of 60 with an average score of 40 for each need. A score between 20 and 40 indicates below average strength of need and a score between 40 and 60 indicates above average strength of need. In the booklet it is stated: "Obviously, the question 'what is a good score?' is irrelevant. Different types of jobs, assignments, and organizations draw on different needs" (p. 1). Respondents are then left on their own to find meaning from the instrument. Without the availability of norms for different groups of employees, types of occupations, or organizational settings, the need strengths as measured by the instrument remain relatively meaningless.

A description of each need is provided in the Scoring and Interpretation Sheet. The descriptions are based on the work of Dr. David McClelland although no references to his work are provided. It is perceived that the intent of this format is for a user-friendly interpretation guide uncluttered with research. Nevertheless, because no technical or research information is provided, users are left to use their best judgment as to what the results of the instrument mean and how to use those results. For example, the following statement appears in the Scoring and Interpretation Sheet: "One needs to treat high achievers quite differently from high affiliators in a wide variety of organizational considerations: job assignments, methods used to reinforce behavior, pay and incentive programs, delegation of responsibility and authority, and so on" (p. 3). No further information or guidance is given.

CONCLUSION. The Personal Inventory of Needs is relatively easy to take and score. The format and procedures for use are clear. The greatest weakness of the instrument is in its interpretation. No validity or reliability data are provided by the publishers. There are no norms given for interpreting one's scores. The interpretation guide contains only a general description of each of the three types of needs measured by the instrument. No information is given as to how the results can be used, rather the good judgment of employees and managers is invoked. Because of the lack of information there is potential for misuse and abuse of this instrument. Managers could be doing a great disservice to employees and the organization by making potentially important personnel decisions based on the information provided by the instrument.

Review of the Personal Inventory of Needs by TRENTON R. FERRO, Assistant Professor of Adult and Community Education, Indiana University of Pennsylvania, Indiana, PA:

The complete set of materials is made up of three items. The first item is a "Self-Assessment Exercise" that includes one-half page of instructions and 10 sets of three statements to rank order: the statement with which the respondent most agrees is given a "3," the statement with which the respondent next most agrees is given a "2," and the statement with which the respondent least agrees is given a "1." The second item is a two-ply "Answer Sheet" on NCR paper. The first page is composed of 20 sets of three boxes into which are entered the respondent's rankings in response to the 20 sets of statements in the self-assessment exercise. The second page of the answer sheet provides the key for adding the numerical responses to develop "ach," "aff," and "pow" scores. The total of the three scores should be 120 points. The third item is a four-page "Scoring and Interpretation Sheet." There is no technical manual.

The instrument is intended to identify the relative strengths of "three needs that exist in each of us and that have a strong bearing on our effectiveness and our happiness at work." These are identified as the need to achieve, the need to affiliate, and the need for power. Each set of 20 items includes a statement intended to reflect one of these three needs. Adding the assigned ranking numbers of "3," "2," or "1" provides scores ranging between a possible high of 60, indicating the strongest possible need, and a possible low of 20, indicating the lowest possible need. A score of 40, the average, is cited as the demarcation between above average and below average need. Because the instrument has not been normed or standardized, the scores actually have little intrinsic meaning. They are primarily useful for comparing the. three scores, and the three needs depicted by them, on this instrument. Even then the scores are only relative.

According to the interpretation sheet the three categories of need are based on the motivational research of David McClelland and are related to levels of Maslow's hierarchy of human needs. The descriptions include lists of characteristics supported by research into these three orientations and the motivational factors related to each. There is a particular effort to depict high need for power in a positive light. Although the presentation of the needs to achieve and affiliate are more descriptive and objective in tone, the presentation for the need for power tends to be more apologetic.

The instrument is intended to be used strictly as a tool for self-assessment and self-understanding; it is descriptive, not prescriptive. The validity of the instrument is judged by the individual (face validity): "Do the descriptions arising from the use of this instrument make sense to me? Do they square with my self-perception? Do they help me better understand myself and how I perform?" Because the instrument is intended for individual insight and is not at all prescriptive, any other use (e.g., as a tool for job screening) is inappropriate and invalid.

Although the research of David McClelland and Maslow is mentioned, no references to their body of work are provided. Some individuals, and many facilitators who might want to use this instrument in group exploration settings, would want to develop a greater understanding of the theoretical background to the instrument and would benefit from the inclusion of such references. Furthermore, researchers should be provided with the evidence that supports the development of the three scales and the basis upon which the work of Maslow has been related to that of McClelland. The development of a technical manual should provide such material.

[288]

Personal Relationship Inventory.

Purpose: "Designed to assess one's capacity to love and engage in intimate interpersonal relationships."
Population: Ages 15 and over.
Publication Dates: 1988–91.
Acronym: PRI.
Scores, 13: Compassion, Friendship, Intimacy, Masculine/Feminine, Primitive Self, Psychological Adjustment, Romantic Love, Self-Respect, Sensitivity, Spirituality, Trust, Love Capacity (Total), Persona.
Administration: Group or individual.
Price Data, 1992: $9 per 5 test booklets; $18.50 per prepaid answer sheet for scoring by publisher; $2 per answer sheet (on-site scoring by computer); $18 per manual ('91, 91 pages); $4.50 per A Guide to Using The Love Factor; $499 per computer program for on-site processing.
Comments: Originally published as the Love Factor Inventory.
Time: (20-30) minutes.
Author: Ronald L. Mann.
Publisher: Behaviordyne, Inc.

Review of the Personal Relationship Inventory by BRADLEY ELISON, Partial Hospitalization Program Team Leader, Virginia Treatment Center for Children, Virginia Commonwealth University, Richmond, VA:

The Personal Relationship Inventory (PRI), previously entitled the Love Factor Inventory, is a 119-item self-report inventory "designed to assess one's capacity to love and engage in intimate personal relationships" (manual, p. 7). The PRI produces scores for 11 separate scales and a Total Capacity for Love score. The author has also included a Personal scale designed to identify respondents who attempt to present a false positive image. Each scale is made up of 10 items except the Personal scale, which has 9 items and the Total Love Capacity score, which is derived from scores on the other 11 scales.

ADMINISTRATION, SCORING, AND INTERPRETATION. The PRI items are presented as statements in a separate questionnaire booklet and respondents are asked to rate each statement on a 5-point Likert-type scale ranging from *absolutely agree* to *absolutely disagree*. Responses must be computer scored and can be recorded on a prepaid response form or, if the available computer package is purchased, can be directly entered into the computer by keyboard. The scored report provides a detailed description of the subject based on individual scale scores. If a subject is dissatisfied with his or her report, suggestions for personal change can be found in the interpretation guide. The authority for these suggestions is not provided and virtually no research is presented to support their inclusion in the interpretation of the PRI. Although it is suggested that a qualified professional be present for the interpretation of the PRI, the potential for misuse and misinterpretation is high. No information is provided concerning populations the PRI is intended for and there are no safeguards to ensure that users have the qualifications and/or professional help necessary to interpret their results.

THEORETICAL BACKGROUND AND DEVELOPMENT. Despite references in the manual to the great traditions in psychology and the qualities essential for an individual to behave in a consistent, balanced, and loving fashion, there is no clear line of reasoning or coherent theory base provided that explains the choice of constructs included in the PRI. A rational connection between each construct and one's capacity to love is provided, yet the relationships among the constructs and the degree to which they encompass the entire domain of love capacity is unexplored. The constructs tend to lack operational definitions and are described in a vague and circular manner. In some cases, separate constructs are defined in strikingly similar ways—Friendship and Intimacy both purport to measure one's ability to sustain close relationships—with little indication of what differentiates one from the other.

As in the selection of constructs, the author does not provide a clear description of the process used in item development and selection. Apparently items were assigned rationally to all scales and three postdoctoral psychologists with 5 or more years of experience corroborated the assignments. The final version of the inventory was derived from an item pool of 248 statements that were administered to 50 subjects from a Brugh Joy conference and 50 from a Unitarian church. An item analysis was performed and items with low item-to-total correlations were dropped. The sample was clearly one of convenience and no information on the representativeness of the sample is provided.

NORMATIVE INFORMATION. The PRI was standardized on a sample of 1,933 subjects that was weighted statistically to create a normative sample of 2,606 subjects. The author makes no attempt to establish the representativeness of the normative sample. Close scrutiny reveals that the sample was composed of approximately 43% prisoners, 23% students, and 17% mental health professionals with the remainder made up of small groups of subjects ranging from at-risk teens to Yogis. Generalization from this sample to the general public is unwarranted without specific evidence the sample is representative of the population being tested.

RELIABILITY AND VALIDITY. Reliability coefficients for internal consistency are provided for each of the subscales of the PRI with alpha levels ranging from .73 for the Spirituality scale to .83 for the Psychological Adjustment scale. No measure of internal consistency for the overall Love Capacity score is provided, and no test-retest reliability estimates are provided. The author does not establish standard errors of measurement for the PRI scales.

The validity of the various scales of the PRI rests on an elaborate network of rationalizations derived from a series of studies yielding weak to moderate correlations between the PRI and a variety of external variables. Statistically significant correlations are reported between some PRI scales and the Bennett Self-Esteem scale, some PRI scales and some scales of the Personal Orientation Inventory, and between the PRI scale and an independent rating of expected group scores. Discussion of the above relationships is not theory based nor does it reveal an attempt to test specific hypotheses about the PRI. Instead, simplistic post hoc rationalizations for findings are presented. Although solid evidence is provided in support of the homogeneous grouping of items for each scale, the discriminant and concurrent validity of the scales remains poorly established.

The most troublesome aspect of the attempts to validate the PRI scales is the lack of clarity in what the inventory purports to measure. Validity data are based on exploring the relationships between the PRI scales and measures of psychological functioning, self-esteem, and self-actualization. No coherent attempt is made to establish or produce a valid external measure of love capacity that might be correlated to the PRI Love Capacity score. The same criticism applies to the individual PRI scales. Few of the validation efforts reported in the manual provide any evidence relative to the specific constructs measured by each scale.

SUMMARY. As a measure of one's capacity for love the PRI lacks the theoretical and empirical foundation necessary to make it a good instrument. Validation data are insufficient to justify the detailed interpretive information provided in the computerized results readout and cautions for the casual user are too limited to prevent misinterpretation and misuse of the inventory. Clarification (including operational definitions) of the constructs being measured coupled with further research to validate the individual scales of the PRI is essential if the PRI is to become a useful psychological instrument.

Review of the Personal Relationship Inventory by WILLIAM K. WILKINSON, Assistant Professor of Counseling and Educational Psychology, New Mexico State University, Las Cruces, NM:

The Personal Relationship Inventory (PRI), originally entitled the Love Factor Inventory, is a 119-item self-report instrument constructed to measure a person's "capacity to love and engage in intimate interpersonal relationships" (manual, p. 7). Materials include a reusable questionnaire booklet, a scan-tron answer sheet, a brief user's guide, and a manual for scoring and interpretation. The inventory can be taken via paper and pencil or may be computer administered, with respondents answering each statement on a 5-point Likert-type scale (e.g., 1 = *Absolutely Agree*, 3 = *Neutral*, 5 = *Absolutely Disagree*). Scoring is accomplished either on site, by using appropriate scanning equipment and the PRI computer-scoring program, or complete protocols may be sent to Behaviordyne, Inc. for scoring and interpretation. The instrument is said to be appropriate for individuals with a high school education. Normative data are presented in terms of original sample size (N = 1,933) and weighted sample size (N = 2,631), with both samples described by gender, age, race, income, religion, marital status, and so on. Percentile scores are available for females and males for the 12 scales the instrument purportedly measures: Compassion, Friendship, Intimacy, Masculine/Feminine, Primitive Self, Psychological Adjustment, Romantic Love, Self-Respect, Sensitivity, Spirituality, Trust, and Love Capacity, plus a separate Persona scale. Reliability and validity data are included in the manual.

Overall, the PRI represents an admirable attempt to measure a diffuse and heretofore minimally developed construct, at least in terms of psychometrically sound assessment. Unfortunately, the PRI suffers from serious psychometric shortcomings.

First, and foremost, the meaning of the separate 12 factors the PRI supposedly measures is highly questionable. For example, because the intercorrelation of the scales was high, factor analysis (N = 688) of the 119 items revealed one significant factor, accounting for almost 53% of the total interitem variance. In other words, from a factor analytic perspective, the PRI appears to measure one dimension of love, not 12.

In addressing this concern, the author notes that items do show highest correlations with their home scales. Thus, it would seem self-evident that in the development of PRI scales, items correlating most highly with their home scale would be scored accordingly. Yet, the most perplexing aspect of the PRI was that items correlating highest with a particular scale were keyed (scored) on a different scale. For example, in reviewing the items correlating highest with the Compassion scale, *all* 10 were scored on a different scale. Thus, Item 61—"I hate to perspire" correlated .53 with the Compassion scale, yet is scored as a Primitive-Self item (r = .28). Item 41—"I like to share my feelings with those I love" correlates highest with Compassion (r = .28), but again, is keyed on the Intimacy scale (r = -.12). Such is the case for the remaining eight Compassion items. How can a Compassion scale be constructed when all its items correlate more strongly with any scale other than Compassion? Clearly, the meaning of the PRI scales is seriously called into question.

Still, the author reports internal consistency estimates (Cronbach's alpha) for the 12 scales, with these estimates ranging from .73 to .83. Although this evidence does speak to item sets as "internally reliable" within scales, it does not speak to the essential meaning, or validity of the scales. Further, knowing that Cronbach's alpha is higher for PRI scales than random item mixes does not bear upon the essential meaning of the scales.

Perhaps the difficulty in identifying a meaningful structure underlying the PRI is due to the nature of "love capacity," a construct inherently elusive and diffuse. Thus, PRI items were likewise vague (e.g., "I feel sacred realms of love and bliss," "I believe that the mystery of life is fully grasped as one learns to surrender to its many challenges"), reflecting the difficulty translating "love capacity" into self-report statements. Unfortunately, vague items are prone to individual interpretations, which increases error variance. The one-factor solution, which accounts for barely half the total item variance, is evidence of the intrinsic difficulty operationally defining love vis-a-vis self-report statements.

The second significant area of concern pertains to the normative sample. As indicated earlier, the author reports original and statistically weighted sample data. However, the rationale for weighting is unclear, and the exact weights are never provided. The effect of statistical weighting is to (*a*) artificially add cases to the normative sample, and (*b*) artificially redistribute the cases with respect to sample demographics. For example, the total number of original cases was 1,933, distributed by groups as 827 prison inmates, 328 professionals, 446 college students, and various other groups (e.g., unwed teen moms, psychotherapy outpatients) all with sample sizes less than 100. The weighted equivalent of the original sample produces 2,631 cases, distributed as 984 professionals, 892 college students, and 255 psychotherapy outpatients, with the inmate sample reduced to 74. Clearly, in the case of group affiliation, the author's desire is to statistically derive a more "appropriate" normative sample, one giving the PRI broader appeal. Yet, when other sample demographic characteristics are considered, such as gender and race, weighting increases the sample's disparity across gender and racial categories. And, because percentile ranks are provided only for gender, the weighted sample may do more harm than good. What would be more appropriate, and customary, is to report the percentile equivalents for the original sample groups, and let the test user decide which norms best apply.

The aforementioned concerns clearly reduce the meaning and utility of the PRI. Without knowing what dimensions of love the instrument measures (or whether the instrument adequately measures love at all), and, in light of the idiosyncratic sample-weighting procedure, the clinical and practical relevance of the PRI is dubious. Thus, in clinical and counseling situations, the use of the PRI cannot presently be recommended.

[289]

Personality Adjective Check List.

Purpose: "Developed primarily as a self-report instrument for measuring personality in normal adults."
Population: Ages 16–adult.
Publication Dates: 1987–91.
Acronym: PACL.
Scores, 9: Introversive, Inhibited, Cooperative, Sociable, Confident, Forceful, Respectful, Sensitive, PI (indicator of potential personality problems).

Administration: Group.
Price Data, 1993: $65 per start-up kit including manual (92 pages), scoring keys, 50 test sheets, and 50 profile sheets; $26 per introductory kit including manual, 1 test sheet, and 1 profile sheet; $25 per manual; $25 per 50 test sheets; $20 per 50 profile sheets; $10 per scoring key set; $395 per AutoPACL software with narrative interpretations; $195 per AutoPACL software basic program; $10 per AutoPACL demonstration program.
Time: (10–15) minutes.
Comments: Conceived as a tool for measuring the personality styles outlined by Theodore Millon among normal adults.
Author: Stephen Strack.
Publisher: 21st Century Assessment.
Cross References: See T4:1996 (3 references).

TEST REFERENCES

1. Merenda, P. F., & Fava, J. L. (1994). Role of behaviorally descriptive adjectives in description of personality. *Psychological Reports, 74,* 259-274.

Review of the Personality Adjective Check List by ALLEN K. HESS, Professor and Department Head, Department of Psychology, School of Sciences, Auburn University at Montgomery, Montgomery, AL:

Adjective checklists have a number of advantages that account for both their long history and profusion. Adjective checklists appear easy to construct, flexible in content and format, and seemingly cheap to construct, administer, score and interpret. Also, adjective checklists appear simple and face valid, amenable to use with less than fully literate populations and to use in describing others (as opposed to self-report only), and easily employed in research and clinical applications requiring repeated assessments (Masterson, 1975).

However, because adjective checklists are psychometric devices and used in research to address a theory's validity and used in clinical work to determine or embellish client depictions, checklists are subject to the same psychometric requirements of other tests and measurements. These requirements include one that is sometimes overlooked: to wit, the theoretical matrix from which the test is born and in which it is used. With this assumptive context specified, we can turn to examining the Personality Adjective Check List (PACL).

THE PACL'S BACKGROUND. Stephen Strack, the PACL's author, claims an intellectual heritage that includes Millon's research group, and an influence formed at the University of California-Berkeley by the Blocks, Craik, and Gough. The PACL, with 153 items, is an attempt at providing a quickly administered measure of the "normal form" of Millon's model of personality. As such, it consists of nine scales. Eight are basic personality "styles": Introversive (19 items), Inhibited (27 items), Cooperative (26 items), Sociable (21 items), Confident (22 items), Forceful (26 items), Respectful (21 items), and Sensitive (26 items). The ninth scale is an 11-item personality impairment (PI) scale composed of adjectives left when Millon's schizoid, cycloid, and paranoid personality adjective lists were decomposed in the course of Strack's item refinement. The careful reader will have added up more scale items than are total items on the PACL. More will be said below about the 46 overlapping items.

The manual provides an adequate basis for evaluation of the PACL. Yet its sequence seems peculiar in providing chapters on normative data, studies concerning threats to validity, such as response sets, and an interpretive guide before it presents the chapters on validity and reliability (and in that chapter validity precedes reliability). Psychometric properties are fundamental to know before using any measure.

RELIABILITY. Alpha coefficients for the nine scales (eight content scales plus the PI scale) range from .65 to .89, with an average of .81 over two samples of 859 male and female subjects indicating reasonable intrascale homogeneity. Test-retest coefficients range from .55 to .90, with samples tested at 1-, 2-, and 3-month intervals. This indicates good stability of scores over time. The chapter then provides scale intercorrelations, factorial, social desirability, and discriminant and convergent validity data. And herein, too, lies a major problem. With 30% of the items overlapping across scales, the intercorrelations are inflated creating a collinearity problem. Collinearity yields inflated factor eigenvalues. Because overlap varies from scale to scale (from 1 to 9 overlapping items in the scales, with the scales composed of from 6 to 21 adjective items), one cannot determine which correlations and factors are more or less compromised by collinearity. Millon (1987) and Strack (PACL manual, pp. 45–46) assert that because symptoms and syndromes are inherently correlative, it is natural for scales to correlate. This argument is specious (Hess, 1985); the enterprise of assessment, particularly differential diagnosis, is to distinguish between entities or taxons. Hence, nonoverlapping scales, and orthogonal rotations for factor analytic solutions are the order of the day for diagnostics.

VALIDITY. Items were created using a sound substantive and structural validity model. There is adequate convergent validity with some interesting biodata as well as some of the usual referent tests (California Personality Inventory, Interpersonal Adjective Inventory, Multiple Affect Adjective Checklist, 16 PF, Interpersonal Style Inventory), with one inventory strangely absent. The parent of the PACL is Millon's theory, yet the Millon Clinical Multiaxial Inventory (MCMI) was not included. It would be informing to see whether the two offspring of Millon (1969) share factor structures and are bipolar images of each other, one (PACL) anchoring a positive, normal pole, the other (MCMI) defining the pathological pole, as the author postulates. Instead, the factor structure is well defined by the five-factor (Big 5) model, with Factor 1 depicting neuroticism, Factor 2 showing agreeableness, and Factor 3 tapping intraversion-extraversion. Finally, the absence of data regarding externally anchored behaviors compromises both concurrent and predictive validity, moving the test one step back from being usefully applied in the field.

USING THE PACL. The PACL has been found resistant to random, favorable, and unfavorable response sets. A partial but practical solution was used to counter the distortion of scale scores due to number of adjectives checked. This solution provides conversion tables from raw to *T* scores for five groups of respondents, from those checking few adjectives to those checking many items.

Chapter 4 provides an interpretive guide, which is troublesome in the absence of external validity data. Four cases are presented. In Case 2, C.W. is called "stubbornly insistent," "punitive," "overly demonstrative," "shallow," and "somewhat impulsive and fickle." This is stated in the absence of any validity data and lapses toward the pathological terms belying the PACL's Millon heritage. In Case 3, B.W. is termed "people-oriented," "modest," "patient," "conscientious," "reliable," "warm," "nurturant," and "sympathetic," all of which is claimed "would serve her well in the social sciences and helping professions where a genuine interest in people and desire to care for others is needed" (manual, p. 33). This interpretation is kind and face valid, but one built on a stereotype and not on empirical foundations. Although the test user is warned not to use only the protocols and the automated computer interpretations to draw conclusions, the examples seem to be highly suggestive, if not outright determinative of the persons described, in the absence of any other data.

CONCLUSIONS. The PACL is an intriguing device in several respects. Foremost, it is designed to measure the positive aspects of Millon's eight-cell personality model but winds up as both a positive and pathological descriptor, best fitting the Big 5 model. Items were carefully crafted to fit in scales, then allowed to contaminate the scales via a 30% item-scale overlap. The reliability studies and correlations with other personality tests show a consistent and robust test that nonetheless lacks external criterion validity studies.

Thus, the PACL provides a theory-based attempt to map the positive poles of Millon's personality model but winds up in the Big 5 domain. The PACL needs research-based validity studies to empirically anchor the scales and descriptors before it can be used in applied work. Currently it could be used as an experimental device to provide an adjunct in describing personality in conjunction with more validated tests in a battery. One would have to be committed to the PACL or Millon's model to opt for this measure rather than the more established adjective checklists, which have empirical research foundation and are directly related to the Big 5.

REVIEWER'S REFERENCES

Millon, T. (1969). *Modern psychopathology*. Philadelphia: W. B. Saunders.

Masterson, S. (1975). The adjective checklist technique: A review and critique. In P. McReynolds (Ed.), *Advances in psychological assessment* (pp. 275-312). San Francisco: Jossey-Bass.

Hess, A. K. (1985). [Review of the Millon Clinical Multiaxial Inventory.] In J. V. Mitchell, Jr. (Ed.), *The ninth mental measurements yearbook* (pp. 984-986). Lincoln, NE: Buros Institute of Mental Measurements.

Millon, T. (1987). *Manual for the Millon Clinical Multiaxial Inventory-II* (2nd ed.). Minneapolis, MN: National Computer Systems.

Review of the Personality Adjective Check List by HOWARD M. KNOFF, Professor of School Psychology, Department of Psychological Foundations, University of South Florida, Tampa, FL:

The Personality Adjective Check List (PACL) is a 153-item objective personality scale designed to measure the "eight basic personality styles outlined by Theodore Millon (1969, 1983) for use with normal adults" (manual, p. 1). The PACL is organized into nine scales: eight scales reflecting Millon's basic personality styles—Introversive, Inhibited, Cooperative, Sociable, Confident, Forceful, Respectful, and Sensitive—and one scale that measures potential personality problems using items operationalizing Millon's Schizoid, Cycloid, and Paranoid personality styles. The PACL's author states that whereas Millon's personality assessment inventories (e.g., the Millon Clinical Multiaxial Inventory) focus on abnormal personality functioning and psychopathology, this checklist operationalizes Millon's theory for typical adults. In addition, the PACL's author cites seven distinguishing features of the tool: (*a*) It can provide a quick and comprehensive assessment; (*b*) it can be used as a self-report and a rating inventory; (*c*) its validity indices can identify biased protocols that should be disregarded; (*d*) it is a theory-based tool; (*e*) it has been sequentially developed and validated; (*f*) its development and standardization samples are culturally broad and extensive; and (*g*) computerized scoring and interpretation is available. The PACL was developed and validated using 1,189 men and 1,318 women accumulated primarily from college settings over a 6-year period (i.e., from 1980 to 1986). The sample came from across the United States, but it was not random and it had an overrepresentation of Hispanic and Asian individuals and an underrepresentation of Whites. The PACL was developed to evaluate high school graduates from 16 years of age and older, it requires reading skills at the eighth grade level, it can be completed in 10 to 15 minutes, and it comes with a 91-page manual that details its development and psychometric properties.

Based on a review of the tool and its manual, the PACL appears to be a personality assessment scale of some promise. Although much of its development has been empirically driven, there still are a number of psychometric, research, and practical problems that are troublesome. At this time, the PACL is recommended for research use but not for clinical use in the field. Among the most significant problems with the PACL are: (*a*) its lack of norms reflecting a random sample that is stratified especially by age, race, geography, and SES; (*b*) its need to externally validate, through research, the decision to present norms based on the number of adjectives checked on each scale; and (*c*) its need to more completely describe the research samples used in the scale's development and validation studies and presented in the manual such that external validation and replication can occur. To expand on these broad concerns and others, a list of other PACL weaknesses are discussed below.

1. The PACL was developed using a step-by-step, theory-driven process that operationalizes Millon's interpersonal/biopsychosocial theory of personality using single-word adjectives that respondents check off when they are descriptive of them. Although the test development process, involving the demonstration of substantive validity, structural validity, and external or convergent-discriminant validity appears conceptually sound, the PACL norms, as noted above, are based on individuals sampled across a 6-year time period primarily from unspecified college settings, with 10% of the sample coming from a number of unspecified businesses. Although the absence of SES data and stratification is notable, the median age of the sample (20 years old) also limits the generalizability of the norms to the degree that the author's assertion that the PACL can be used with normal adults must be questioned until empirical data demonstrate otherwise. All of this can be remediated through a restandardization of the tool using a random, stratified, national sample.

Regardless, the existing PACL norms are organized to correct for the number of adjectives checked by the respondent. The rationale given for this is that "in all tests where an individual is allowed to endorse as many items as he or she chooses, variance occurs in scores that is independent of the quality or characteristic being measured" (p. 17). Although this may be defensible from a test development perspective, this rationale seems to contradict the fact that the PACL's scales were developed such that the more adjectives a respondent checks off from a particular scale, the more the respondent should reflect the personality characteristics inherent in the scale. Indeed, the author states in the interpretation section of the manual that "it is important to remember that with increasing elevations above 50 (*T*-score), the likelihood that an individual will demonstrate the behaviors and characteristics represented by a given personality scale also increases" (p. 28). This contradiction needs to be resolved either theoretically or empirically.

As it stands now, however, respondents are separated, by gender, into one of five groups based on the total number of adjectives checked (e.g., for males: Group I: 0–22 items, Group II: 23–35, Group III: 36–55, Group IV: 56–73, and Group V: 74–153). Raw scores for each PACL scale are then entered into a *T*-score conversion table based on the respondent's gender and the Group designation. For the Cooperative scale, for example, this procedure generates *T*-scores of 69, 55, 45, 37, and 28 for males in Group 1, 2, 3, 4, and 5, respectively, who check off the same 10 adjectives. Somehow, this does not seem logical. From an empirical perspective, it would seem more logical if the author could externally demonstrate that males scoring this way on the Cooperative scale differ behaviorally or from some other facet of personality.

2. From an internal validity perspective, a PACL protocol can be invalidated due to too many or too few adjectives checked, randomly answered protocols, or protocols that reflect either "fake-good" or "fake-bad" response sets. Although the first validity check is based loosely on response means from the PACL's norm group, the decision rules for the latter two validity checks were generated using discriminant analyses from small and unspecified college samples of less than 75 students of each gender. The resulting regression equations are overly complex, may not generalize to individual respondents, and may not demonstrate the sensitivity needed for clinical use. All in all, it may be that, beyond too many or too few adjectives chosen, an internal validity check for a personality tool using single-work descriptors may be impossible.

3. Relative to interpretation, the PACL's author does a nice job of providing a step-by-step interpretive process that utilizes the standard error of measurement of each scale blocked by gender. The author then presents a table identifying the pairs of scales that are most frequently elevated based on the normative sample. The biggest potential problem in interpretation is when the data must be translated into functional descriptions of personality. For this, the author provides four brief case studies and paragraph-long descriptions of each of the PACL's nine scales based "on those presented by Millon [that] have been refined to reflect empirical information about the personalities as they exist in normal form" (p. 7). Unfortunately, the descriptions of the scales are not correlated with different *T*-score elevations, the empirical information referenced above is not described, and the construct and concurrent validation of the PACL is not complete nor helpful. In the end, the researcher or clinician is left without enough functional information (and validation) to responsibly interpret the PACL, thereby helping it to accomplish its original reason for existence.

4. Relative to the psychometric properties of the PACL, the manual does an excellent job of presenting intercorrelational, factor analytic, reliability (Cronbach's alpha and test-retest), and validity (convergent

and discriminant) data for the scale, and much of it looks quite impressive. Unfortunately, beyond those studies that used the flawed normative sample, most of the studies described do not provide sufficient information on the samples involved, the methodologies and data collection procedures used, and the potential generalizability of the results. Although some of this information may be available in the original articles referenced and cited in the manual, this again puts the responsibility on the researcher or clinician to independently seek out the sources needed to fully evaluate this scale.

In summary, despite the appearances above, I do believe the PACL is an interesting and potentially useful personality assessment tool that could become a "standard" in the field. In order to reach this potential, however, the PACL will need to address and resolve some of the weaknesses described above. This will necessitate a restandardization of the tool, and some more complete writing and description in the next manual. For now, I would not hesitate to use the PACL in research. At the present time, however, its clinical use is not recommended.

[290]

Personality Assessment Inventory.

Purpose: Designed to provide information relevant to clinical diagnosis, treatment planning, and screening for psychopathology.
Population: Ages 18–adult.
Publication Date: 1991.
Acronym: PAI.
Scores, 54: Inconsistency, Infrequency, Negative Impression, Positive Impression, Somatic Complaints (Conversion, Somatization, Health Concerns, Total), Anxiety (Cognitive, Affective, Physiological, Total), Anxiety-Related Disorders (Obsessive-Compulsive, Phobias, Traumatic Stress, Total), Depression (Cognitive, Affective, Physiological, Total), Mania (Activity Level, Grandiosity, Irritability, Total), Paranoia (Hypervigilance, Persecution, Resentment, Total), Schizophrenia (Psychotic Experiences, Social Detachment, Thought Disorder, Total), Borderline Features (Affective Instability, Identity Problems, Negative Relationships, Self-Harm, Total), Antisocial Features (Antisocial Behaviors, Egocentricity, Stimulus-Seeking, Total), Alcohol Problems, Drug Problems, Aggression (Aggressive Attitude, Verbal Aggression, Physical Aggression, Total), Suicidal Ideation, Stress, Nonsupport, Treatment Rejection, Dominance, Warmth, Total.
Administration: Individual or group.
Price Data, 1995: $135 per comprehensive kit including professional manual (193 pages), 2 reusable item booklets, 2 administration folios, 25 Form HS handscorable answer sheets, 25 adult profile forms, and 25 critical items forms; $30 per professional manual; $17 per reusable item booklet; $24 per 25 Form HS handscorable answer sheets; $15 per 25 profile forms; $17 per 25 critical items forms; $17 per administration folio.
Time: (40–50) minutes.
Comments: Self-report inventory of adult psychopathology.
Author: Leslie C. Morey.
Publisher: Psychological Assessment Resources, Inc.
Cross References: See T4:1997 (3 references).

TEST REFERENCES

1. Boyle, G. J., Ward, J., & Lennon, T. J. (1994). Personality Assessment Inventory: A confirmatory factor analysis. *Perceptual and Motor Skills, 79*, 1441-1442.

2. Schinka, J. A., Curtiss, G., & Mulloy, J. M. (1994). Personality variables and self-medication in substance abuse. *Journal of Personality Assessment, 63*, 413-422.

3. Alterman, A. I., Zaballero, A. R., Lin, M. M., Siddiqui, N., Brown, L. S., Jr., Rutherford, M. J., & McDermott, P. A. (1995). Personality Assessment Inventory (PAI) scores of lower-socioeconomic African American and Latino methadone maintenance patients. *Assessment, 2*, 91-100.

4. Bartelstone, J. H., & Trull, T. J. (1995). Personality, life events, and depression. *Journal of Personality Assessment, 64*, 279-294.

5. Deisinger, J. A. (1995). Exploring the factor structure of the Personality Assessment Inventory. *Assessment, 2*, 173-179.

6. Rogers, R., Flores, J., Ustad, K., & Sewell, K. W. (1995). Initial validation of the Personality Assessment Inventory—Spanish Version with clients from Mexican American communities. *Journal of Personality Assessment, 64*, 340-348.

7. Schinka, J. A. (1995). Personality Assessment Inventory scale characteristics and factor structure in the assessment of alcohol dependency. *Journal of Personality Assessment, 64*, 101-111.

8. Trull, T. J. (1995). Borderline personality disorder features in nonclinical young adults: I. Identification and validation. *Psychological Assessment, 7*, 33-41.

Review of the Personality Assessment Inventory by GREGORY J. BOYLE, Associate Professor of Psychology, Bond University, Gold Coast, Queensland, Australia:

The Personality Assessment Inventory (PAI) has been developed as a multidimensional alternative to the Minnesota Multiphasic Personality Inventory (MMPI) for assessing abnormal personality traits. According to Morey (manual, p. 5), the PAI was designed "to provide information relevant to clinical diagnoses, treatment planning and screening for psychopathology." The PAI is a self-report questionnaire consisting of 344 items (scored on a 4-point ordinal scale: F = False, Not At All True; ST = Slightly True; MT = Mainly True; VT = Very True). Some 22 nonoverlapping scales include 4 validity scales, 11 clinical scales, 5 treatment scales, and 2 interpersonal scales (10 scales are further subdivided into 31 conceptually distinct subscales). Most scales consist of 8, 12, or 24 items with an average grade 4 reading level. Validity scales measure response Inconsistency, Infrequency, Negative Impression, and Positive Impression. The clinical scales are Somatic Complaints, Anxiety, Anxiety-Related Disorders, Depression, Mania, Paranoia, Schizophrenia, Borderline Features, Antisocial Features, Alcohol Problems, and Drug Problems. Treatment scales are Aggression, Suicidal Ideation, Stress, Nonsupport, and Treatment Rejection. Interpersonal scales are Dominance and Warmth.

Psychopathological syndromes measured by the PAI were selected in view of contemporary nosology and diagnostic practice. Answers can be scored by hand (HS Answer Sheet), or optical scanning (SS Answer Sheet). Profile forms (Adults; College Students) allow quick conversion of raw scale scores into linear *T*-scores. A Critical Items Form provides specific information as to Delusions and Hallucinations, Potential for Self-Harm, Potential for Aggression, Substance Abuse, Potential Malingering, Unreliability/Resistance, and Traumatic Stressors. The test author recommends that positive responses to any critical items should be investigated further.

The PAI was developed in the USA for use with individuals aged 18 and older, using an adult normative standardization sample (stratified on gender, race, and age according to 1995 U.S. Census projections); adult clinical patients; and college students (all samples comprised at least 1,000 individuals). The PAI manual contains descriptive characteristics for each sample, including scale and subscale means and standard deviations by gender, race, and age, as well as detailed specimen profiles.

The PAI contains a number of items concerning sexual and bodily functions that may be objectionable to some individuals, such as Item 315 ("I have little interest in sex"), and Item 312 ("I frequently have diarrhea"). Item 40 ("My favorite poet is Raymond Kertezc") assumes specific knowledge.

Moderator variables (age and sex) appear to have some effects on the discriminative validity of PAI scales (Boyle & Lennon, 1994). For the normative group, differences in scale scores between males and females are negligible, except for the Antisocial and Alcohol Problems scales (higher incidence of antisocial disorder and alcoholism in males). Differences due to race are also small. Age is important, as younger individuals obtain higher scores on Anxiety, Paranoia, Borderline Features, and Antisocial Features. For adults aged 60 or over, mean scores generally are below those for the entire sample. Also, years of education are directly related to PAI scale scores, with more highly educated individuals usually obtaining lower mean scores.

Use of the pathognomic sign approach for the Schizophrenia scale may be problematic (cf. Newmark, Falk, Johns, Borer, & Forehand, 1976). The limited scope of the 12-item Alcohol Problems scale may not be sufficiently sensitive in view of the occurrence of distinct alcoholic subgroups (cf. Corbisiero & Reznikoff, 1991). The implicit assumption of comparability across scales may be unwarranted, as linear *T*-scores do not take account of differing distributions of scale scores.

The manual author suggests adequate scale and subscale reliabilities. Alpha coefficients of internal consistency for the 22 scales range from .45 to .90 (median .81); from .22 to .89 (median .82); and from .23 to .94 (median .86) for the normative, college, and clinical samples. Item homogeneity is low (median .22, .21, .29 respectively), so that item redundancy is minimal and breadth of measurement good, with most items within each scale contributing new information to the particular construct being measured (cf. Boyle, 1991).

Median alphas for Whites and Nonwhites are .77 and .78; for Men and Women .79 and .75; and for Under Age 40 vs. Age 40 and Over .79 and .75, respectively. Subscale median alphas are .71, .73, and .80 for the normative, college, and clinical samples, whereas median item homogeneities are .27, .28, and .35, respectively.

Test-retest reliabilities (retest interval 3–4 weeks) ranged from .31 to .92 (median .82). Low test-retest coefficients were obtained for Inconsistency (.31) and Infrequency (.48), two of the validity scales. Subscale test-retest reliabilities ranged from .68 to .85 (median .78). Boyle and Lennon (1994) reported test-retest coefficients (retest interval 28 days) for the PAI scales ranging from .62 to .86 (median .76), with several scales exhibiting inadequate stability (some less than .7). For trait scales, stabilities should be .8 or higher (cf. Boyle, 1985).

A short-form of 160 items is available, but the 22 scales have insufficient items (mean of 8 items/scale) to achieve adequate reliability. Application of the Spearman-Brown prophecy formula (Crocker & Algina, 1986) suggests that even an adequate stability coefficient of .8 would reduce to .65 for the 160-item version of the PAI. Consequently, use of the short form is not recommended.

Concurrent validity correlations of the PAI validity, clinical, treatment, and interpersonal scales with several other personality instruments (e.g., MMPI, STAI, Beck Scales, Wahler Physical Symptoms Inventory, Fear Survey Schedule) reveal many small to moderate coefficients, suggesting only relatively modest common variance. Exploratory factor analyses based on the scale and subscale intercorrelations for the standardization and clinical samples are methodologically questionable (using the inadequate "Little Jiffy" procedure—cf. McDonald, 1985). Consequently, the four higher-order personality trait factors reported are almost certainly inaccurate. The confirmatory factor analyses are apparently based on the same data sets ("standardization clinical subjects") used in the exploratory factor analyses (Breckler, 1990). Application of cluster analysis (using a subsample of only 300 clinical subjects) to discover modal profiles in clinical samples would be expected to yield unstable clusters (cf. Cuttance & Ecob, 1987, p. 243).

On the positive side, the PAI includes current items, and avoids colloquial and slang expressions. Items considered potentially biased (on gender, ethnic, economic, religious or other grounds) were excluded. Furthermore, the PAI manual is both comprehensive and informative. Detailed information is provided on psychometric issues, including reliability and concurrent validity data, for each of the scales and subscales across several samples. One notable exception is the lack of concurrent validity correlations between the PAI and the Clinical Analysis Questionnaire or CAQ

(Krug, 1980)—a factor analytically derived measure of abnormal personality dimensions.

Boyle and Lennon (1994) reported a significant multivariate main effect across normal, alcoholic, and schizophrenic groups after age and gender effects were partialled out, and significant differences between alcoholic and control groups, and between alcoholic and schizophrenic groups, supporting the discriminative validity of the new PAI instrument. Although the PAI may comprise too many scales with insufficient numbers of items for greatest practical utility, undoubtedly, it will serve a very useful role in both research and applied psychological applications.

Further studies into psychometric properties of the PAI instruments should be encouraged, especially into its construct validity and factor structure. It is important to know whether or not the existing scale and subscale structure of the instrument will stand up in the light of new confirmatory factor analyses, based on appropriately large and independent samples of normal and clinical adult populations (cf. Boyle, Ward, & Lennon, 1994). In addition, development of normative data for use of the PAI overseas (e.g., Australia or Britain) would greatly enhance the utility of the instrument. As compared with other multidimensional measures of abnormal personality such as the MMPI or CAQ, the PAI appears to make an exciting new contribution in its own right, pending further investigations along the lines suggested above.

REVIEWER'S REFERENCES

Newmark, C. S., Falk, R., Johns, N., Boren, R., & Forehand, R. (1976). Comparing traditional clinical procedures with four systems to diagnose schizophrenia. *Journal of Abnormal Psychology, 85*, 66-72.

Krug, S. E. (1980). *Clinical Analysis Questionnaire manual*. Champaign, IL: Institute for Personality and Ability Testing.

Boyle, G. J. (1985). Self-report measures of depression: Some psychometric considerations. *British Journal of Clinical Psychology, 24*, 45-59.

McDonald, R. P. (1985). *Factor analysis and related methods*. Hillsdale, NJ: Erlbaum.

Crocker, L., & Algina, J. (1986). *Introduction to classical and modern test theory*. Chicago: Holt, Rinehart & Winston.

Cuttance, P., & Ecob, R. (1987). *Structural modeling by example: Applications in educational, sociological, and behavioral research*. New York: Cambridge University Press.

Breckler, S. J. (1990). Applications of covariance structure modeling in psychology: Cause for concern? *Psychological Bulletin, 107*, 260-273.

Boyle, G. J. (1991). Does item homogeneity indicate internal consistency or item redundancy in psychometric scales? *Personality and Individual Differences, 12*, 291-294.

Corbisiero, J. R., & Reznikoff, M. (1991). The relationship between personality type and style of alcohol use. *Journal of Clinical Psychology, 47*, 291-298.

Boyle, G. J., & Lennon, T. J. (1994). Examination of the reliability and validity of the Personality Assessment Inventory. *Journal of Psychopathology and Behavioral Assessment, 16*, 173-187.

Boyle, G. J., Ward, J., & Lennon, T. J. (1994). Personality Assessment Inventory: A confirmatory factor analysis. *Perceptual and Motor Skills, 78*, 1441-1442.

Review of the Personality Assessment Inventory by MICHAEL G. KAVAN, Director of Behavioral Sciences and Associate Professor of Family Practice, Creighton University School of Medicine, Omaha, NE:

The Personality Assessment Inventory (PAI) is a self-administered, objective inventory designed to measure adult (ages 18 and over) personality. Specifically, it is meant to yield information related to the screening, diagnosis, and treatment planning for psychopathology. Three-hundred and forty-four items make up 22 nonoverlapping full scales (i.e., 4 validity, 11 clinical, 5 treatment, and 2 interpersonal scales). Ten of these full scales contain conceptually derived subscales that are meant to more completely cover each clinical construct and facilitate interpretation. The clinical syndromes measured by the PAI were selected based on their historical importance within the nosology of mental disorders and their current significance in diagnostic practice.

ADMINISTRATION AND SCORING. The PAI is designed to be administered to adults in either individual or group testing situations. A fourth grade reading level (Flesch-Kincaid) is necessary to complete the PAI. Upon administration, respondents are requested to first complete basic demographic information on the answer sheet and then to follow the directions within the test item booklet. Unlike many other objective personality inventories, the PAI does not use "true/false," "yes/no," or forced-choice response formats. Instead, it uses a 4-point Likert-type response format (i.e., *false, not at all true, slightly true, mainly true*, or *very true*). The inventory is available in English, Spanish, and audiotape versions. A software system for administration, scoring, and interpretation may also be purchased from the publisher. Answer sheets are available for both handscoring and optical scanning. Typical administration times range between 40–50 minutes.

In order to hand score the PAI one must peel away the top answer sheet to reveal a self-carbon page that has item scores (ranging from 0 to 3) for all 344 items. Items belonging to each full scale or subscale, which are designated by ruled and color-shaded boxes, are summed and transferred to a profile sheet. Although most of this is done with ease, some difficulty occurs in the calculation of the Inconsistency (ICN) scale because it requires one to determine the absolute value of the difference in scores for 10 pairs of items.

PAI full scale and subscale raw scores are then plotted onto the profile sheet and converted to linear *T*-scores. These scores may then be compared to both the standardization sample and a "representative *clinical* sample" (p. 11) that is noted by a blue profile line on the form. For the adult form, this blue profile line is two standard deviations above the mean for 1,246 patients selected from "a variety of clinical settings." Interpretation proceeds by using single scale interpretation and then examining the configuration or pattern of elevations. Cluster analysis was used to determine 10 modal profiles that can serve as a foundation for interpretation; however, assigning a particular profile to one of these groups is both complicated and laborious. Finally, 27 critical items, which are distributed across seven content areas, may be examined for further inquiry.

RELIABILITY. Internal consistency (coefficient alpha) values are presented within the manual for full scales and subscales for the census-matched normative sample (*N* = 1,000), college student sample (*N* = 1,051), and the clinical sample (*N* = 1,246). Median alphas for the 22 full scale scores for the three groups are .81 (range of .45 to.90), .82 (range .22 to .89), and .86 (range .23 to .94), respectively. Whereas most of these alphas are in the .70s to.90s range, coefficients for the Inconsistency (ICN) and Infrequency (INF) full scales tend to be low for each sample. The alpha ranges for the 31 subscales are .51 to .81 for the census sample, .57 to .85 for the college sample, and .55 to .89 for the clinical sample. Alpha coefficients for the full scales are also presented by race, gender, and age for the census-matched standardization sample.

Test-retest correlations for a community sample (*n* = 75) ranged from .29 to .94 for the full scales and from .67 to.90 for the subscales over a 24-day period. Test-retest correlations for a college sample (*n* = 80) ranged from .32 to .90 for the full scales and from .54 to .86 for the subscales over a 28-day period. Mean *T*-scores for the combined samples are also provided for the two administrations for full and subscale scores. Whereas most of the test-retest subscale correlations are respectable given their length, the ICN and INF full scale correlations are considerably lower (i.e., range is .31 to .48) for the combined sample.

Rogers, Flores, Ustad, and Sewell (1995) administered the English and Spanish versions of the PAI to monolingual and bilingual clients and found considerable variability in the correlations between the Spanish and English PAI validity scales. The mean correspondence correlation between these versions for the 11 full scales was *r* = .71. Slightly lower correlations existed between these versions on the five treatment and two interpersonal scales (mean *r* = .68). The median test-retest correlation was *r* = .58 for the validity scales and *r* = .78 for the clinical scales (median interval was 14 days).

VALIDITY. Extensive validity data are provided for the validity and clinical scales. For the validity scales, several subject samples and computer-generated responses were used to examine issues of random responding, impression management, and various item/response sets. In addition, correlational studies were performed using the four PAI validity scales and the L, F, and K scales of the Minnesota Multiphasic Personality Inventory (MMPI) and the Marlowe-Crowne Social Desirability scale to determine convergent and discriminant validity. The Negative Impression (NIM) and Positive Impression (PIM) scales demonstrated moderate correlations in the expected direction; however, the INF scale had negligible correlations with these measures and the ICN scale demonstrated only a weak, negative correlation with the Marlowe-Crowne. In another study, Rogers, Ornduff, and Sewell (1993) found that the NIM cutoff score (i.e., >8) was highly effective with feigned schizophrenia, marginally effective with feigned depression, and ineffective with feigned generalized anxiety disorder.

Data regarding scale intercorrelations, factor analyses, confirmatory factor analyses, and cluster analyses are presented within the manual. For most scales, small to moderate intercorrelations existed in the expected direction. Factor analyses have typically resulted in two to four factors being generated including: (*a*) subjective distress and affective disruption, (*b*) behavioral acting-out, (*c*) egocentricity and exploitiveness in interpersonal relationships, and (*d*) validity/carelessness (for the clinical groups) and social detachment/sensitivity (for normal subjects). As noted previously, 10 clusters emerged through the use of Ward's method of cluster analysis.

Convergent and discriminant validity data are also provided for three broad classes of disorders (i.e., neurotic [Somatic Complaints, Anxiety, Anxiety-Related Disorders, and Depression], psychotic [Mania, Paranoia, and Schizophrenia], and behavior disorder [Borderline Features, Antisocial Features, Alcohol Problems, and Drug Problems] scales). The manual also includes mean profiles for different diagnostic groups. In addition, correlations between PAI subscales and MMPI scales and subscales, NEO-PI scales, and other measures are included in the manual. Research by Schinka (1995) has also provided support for the generalizability of the PAI to a sample of mostly male alcohol-dependent inpatients.

NORMS. Means and standard deviations for full scales and subscales are available for the complete census-matched standardization (*n* = 1,000), clinical (*n* = 1,246), and college student (*n* = 1,051) samples. Projected U.S. Bureau of the Census projections for the year 1995 were used for the census-matched group. The clinical sample was recruited from 69 clinical sites and appears to be quite representative in its coverage of various diagnostic groups. The college student sample consists of psychology students in seven universities across the U.S. Means and standard deviations are presented for full scales and subscales by gender, race (i.e., whites, blacks, and "other"), age (i.e., 18–29, 30–49, 50–59, and 60+ years), and education level (i.e., 4–11, 12, 13–15, and 16+ years of education). For most scales, differences among the demographic groups are generally small.

SUMMARY. Overall the PAI is an impressive inventory. The manual contains clear and comprehensive discussions of scale development, reliability, and validity data. The inventory itself is relatively easy to use, score, and interpret. Some difficulty occurs in attempting to assign a respondent's profile to one of the modal profiles contained within the manual; however, the available software system can facilitate this process. Except for previously mentioned weaknesses associated with the validity scales, the instrument has decent reliability and validity. Unlike the MMPI-2 and Millon Clinical Multiaxial Inventory-II, the PAI contains nonoverlapping scales that enhance its discriminant validity. Its major flaw appears to be its relative novelty. As further research and clinical information are collected on the PAI, it should prove to be a worthy competitor to the MMPI-2, which remains the dominant objective personality inventory.

REVIEWER'S REFERENCES

Rogers, R. Ornduff, S. R., & Sewell, K. W. (1993). Feigning specific disorders: A study of the Personality Assessment Inventory (PAI). *Journal of Personality Assessment, 60*, 554-560.

Rogers, R., Flores, J., Ustad, K, & Sewell, K. W. (1995). Initial validation of the Personality Assessment Inventory—Spanish version with clients from Mexican American communities. *Journal of Personality Assessment, 64*, 340-348.

Schinka, J. A. (1995). Personality Assessment Inventory scale characteristics and factor structure in the assessment of alcohol dependency. *Journal of Personality Assessment, 64*, 101-111.

[291]

PERSONALYSIS®.

Purpose: Constructed "to inventory personality characteristics of individuals, work groups, and management teams to show how individuals need to be placed, motivated, and managed for maximum productivity."
Population: Leaders, employees, families, individuals.
Publication Dates: 1975–87.
Scores, 32: Preferred Style-Adult (Authoritative, Democratic, Structured, Self Directed), Communication Expectations-Parent (Direction, Involvement, Methodology, Input), Motivational Needs (Authority, Influence, Control, Understanding), Negative Parent (Coerce, Provoke, Resist, Reject), Negative Child (Hostile, Rebellious, Stubborn, Withdrawn); Act, Adapt, Analyze, and Assess scores for Preferred Style-Adult, Back-Up Style-Parent, and Functional Stress-Child.
Administration: Individual or group.
Price Data: Available from publisher.
Time: Untimed.
Comments: Self-administered.
Author: James R. Noland.
Publisher: Manatech, Management Technologies, Inc.

Review of the PERSONALYSIS by GEORGE ENGELHARD, JR., Associate Professor of Educational Studies, Emory University, Atlanta, GA:

The PERSONALYSIS is a self-report instrument developed by James R. Noland to measure individual differences in personality characteristics. The PERSONALYSIS consists of 85 forced-choice items that generally take 20 minutes for the examinee to fill out. A profile of 32 scores is generated for each examinee.

The theoretical basis for the PERSONALYSIS rests on a combination of a Jungian four-quadrant model with a transactional analysis model. The Jungian model is used to classify individuals into four personality types which are color coded; these types are as follows: Red = extroverted sensing type (action oriented, independent, authoritative style), Yellow = extroverted responsive type (socially oriented, group minded, democratic style), Green = introverted sensitive, feeling type (communication oriented, autonomous, bureaucratics style), and Blue = introverted impersonal type (analysis oriented, individualistic, self-directed style).

The PERSONALYSIS uses transactional analysis as the theoretical basis for classifying individuals in terms of three ego states or dimensions called Adult, Parent, and Child. These personality dimensions refer to (*a*) how a person would like to act based on reason (Adult dimension); (*b*) how a person perceives he or she "ought to" behave based on social conditioning (Parent dimension); and (*c*) the emotional aspects of behavior related to the basic needs, strong feelings, and motivational forces of a person (Child dimension).

The publisher recommends using the PERSONALYSIS as a part of the Personalysis Management System that can be used as a management tool for a variety of purposes within the workplace, such as human resource assessment and planning, placement and promotion, and conflict resolution. The PERSONALYSIS is also recommended as a tool for family counseling. A summary of research related to the reliability and validity of the PERSONALYSIS is provided in a technical manual entitled *PERSONALYSIS: Reliability and Validity*.

Score reports are attractive and very colorful. The scores of the 32 scales range from 0.0 (lowest intensity) to 6.0 (highest intensity) in .5 increments. Because of the ipsative nature of the PERSONALYSIS, the four personality type scores (Red, Yellow, Blue, and Green) always sum to 12.0 within an Ego state (Adult, Parent, or Child). According to the manual, "Scores within each Ego state can be compared with the scores of other profiles, making possible meaningful comparisons of individuals competing for job vacancies" (p. 3). No mention is made of the controversy in the personality assessment literature over the use of ipsative scores for comparing individuals or any of the other limitations of ipsative scoring (Aiken, 1989; Clemans, 1966). According to Horst (1965), "these measures [ipsative] do not purport to be comparable from one individual to another for a given attribute, but only for different measures of the same individual" (p. 291). Ipsative scores can be appropriately used for intraindividual comparisons, but are not recommended for comparing individuals because the scores do not have the same meaning across different examinees; a score of 3.0 for one individual does not have the same meaning as a score of 3.0 for a different individual.

The technical manual and the other supporting literature are very confusing. The technical manual does not provide clear evidence regarding the psychometric quality of the PERSONALYSIS for potential users. The manual is filled with ambiguous and contradictory information that may confuse rather than enlighten the reader about this instrument. For example, in the manual it is claimed the PERSONALYSIS "is very stable, demonstrating a high degree of reliability" (p. 10), and later it is stated the "PERSONALYSIS eschews the concept of consistency" (p. 11). If consistency is avoided, then how can reliable scores be obtained? No quantitative information is provided on the internal consistency of the scales or standard errors of measurement. No normative data are provided regarding the scores on the instrument. Even though this type of normative information may not be appropriate for ipsative scores, many of the recommended uses of the PERSONALYSIS involve comparing individuals and therefore this information should be available to users.

Evidence for the validity of the PERSONALYSIS is also amorphous. Content validity is dismissed as irrelevant because the PERSONALYSIS "does not test the knowledge, abilities, or related characteristics which are determined by a careful job analysis" (p. 11). If the personality characteristics measured by the PERSONALYSIS do not relate to the job, then why would the potential user need the PERSONALYSIS in the first place? Although several studies are reported in the manual as providing evidence for the concurrent and predictive validity of the PERSONALYSIS, these studies are not described in sufficient detail to evaluate the quality of the information provided. It also appears the scoring of the PERSONALYSIS has evolved over time and it is not clear how the results of these earlier studies relate to the current scoring system with its 32 scores. The discussion of construct validity is perhaps the most frustrating section in the technical manual. After a convoluted discussion, it is concluded that "usefulness" is the central aspect of validity. From this conclusion, it is argued the PERSONALYSIS is valid because clients have bought the instrument and continue to find it useful. Similar logic and arguments can be offered for the validity of other pseudoscientific procedures for assessing personality, such as astrology, palmistry, and phrenology.

Many questions can be raised concerning the ethics of personality assessment in general, as well as its application and validity for particular groups within specific work contexts. No evidence is provided regarding how the PERSONALYSIS functions for individuals in various social categories related to gender, race/ethnicity, social class, age, education, or nationality. It is important to consider the consequential validity of instruments that are used for occupational decisions, and potential users of the PERSONALYSIS should examine the differential predictive validity of the scores for employees from different social categories.

In summary, the PERSONALYSIS appears to be an integral part of management and counseling seminars conducted by the publisher of the instrument. It is unlikely that the PERSONALYSIS could be used by anyone without hiring consultants from the publisher to interpret the scores for them. The psychometric data presented for the intended uses of the PERSONALYSIS are quite weak, and do not meet current standards for reporting evidence regarding the reliability and validity of scores. Because the PERSONALYSIS is scored ipsatively, many of the individual comparisons recommended by the publisher may not be valid. The assessment of personality is an extremely complicated task, and the use of personality instruments in the workplace should be approached with extreme caution. There is very little empirical support provided for the recommended uses of the PERSONALYSIS within the workplace. Until stronger evidence is available, users of this instrument should use caution when making decisions based on PERSONALYSIS scores.

REVIEWER'S REFERENCES

Horst, P. (1965). *Factor analysis of data matrices*. New York: Holt, Rinehart and Winston, Inc.

Clemans, W. V. (1966). An analytical and empirical examination of some properties of ipsative measures. *Psychometric Monographs*, No. 14.

Aiken, L. R. (1989). *Assessment of Personality*. Boston: Allyn and Bacon.

Review of the PERSONALYSIS by L. ALAN WITT, Human Resources Manager, Barnett Banks, Inc., Jacksonville, FL:

PERSONALYSIS is advertised to address a wide range of on-the-job behaviors, including meeting organizational goals, communication, morale, personal and organizational focus, stress management, managing individual differences, conflict resolution, sales, teamwork, and planning. Implicit in the approach is that identification of certain components of an individual's personality provides a key to understanding an individual's needs and likely effectiveness in certain situations. Theoretically based on psychoanalytical perspectives of Freud, Jung, and Berne, PERSONALYSIS is designed to accomplish this by profiling individuals in terms of three ego states—the child (emotion), the parent (social conditioning), and the adult (reasoning)—and color-coded personality traits.

The instructions are straightforward. Administrations are likely to run smoothly, as items are clearly stated. The reference manual suggests that the instrument requires about 15–20 minutes to complete. Face validity as seen by managers is comparable to that of most personality instruments. Scoring is done by the publisher, and results are intended to be shared with the organization rather than only with the subject.

A handbook of reliability and validity are provided. Unfortunately, a convincing case was made for neither. Mention was made of a test-retest study done on 82 customer service trainees (all but 7 of whom were female) employed by a bank. The reliability assessment methods described were inconsistent with standard practices and thus difficult to interpret. The author suggested that PERSONALYSIS has yielded acceptable validity support. He mentioned a study examining relationships between PERSONALYSIS scores and 16PF scores and separate studies of participants in seminars of the sponsoring organization and of 108 members of Church of Christ congregations. Two validity studies were discussed in detail. One examined 105 Navy organization development consultants, 66 of whom were enlisted personnel. Performance criteria were performance ratings from superiors and peers. The second study was conducted on 144 students entering a U.S. Army course training staff organizational effectiveness officers. Although one could question various technical components of the studies, the bottom line is that a program of validation research assessing a sufficiently large and diverse group of workers was not presented. For example, church members and military organization development consultants are not representative of the population of workers.

A reference manual is provided for users. Unfortunately, interpretation is not straightforward. Phone support is available, so it is possible that all questions might be satisfactorily addressed.

The primary weakness of the PERSONALYSIS is also a strength. Many contemporary personality assessments developed for use in organizations are based on the "big five" personality traits or specific personality constructs identified through job analysis. Based on psychoanalytical perspectives, PERSONALYSIS is outside the mainstream of contemporary industrial psychology. As such, it might be difficult to defend in selection litigation or to integrate with organization development interventions. On the other hand, the psychoanalytical perspective—relatively rare in industrial settings—may add value beyond the standard fare. Indeed, PERSONALYSIS is probably among very few instruments that advertise a capability of capturing "hidden motivation" and also utility in assessing a plethora of at-work situations as well as family issues.

Overall, because PERSONALYSIS advertises utility in so many arenas, its effectiveness in any one area is questionable. Moreover, the cases for reliability and validity were not convincing.

[292]

Phelps Kindergarten Readiness Scale.

Purpose: Constructed to assess "the academic readiness of children preparatory to enrolling in kindergarten" or shortly after starting school.
Population: Pre-kindergarten and early kindergarten.
Publication Date: 1991.
Acronym: PKRS.
Scores, 4: Verbal Processing, Perceptual Processing, Auditory Processing, Total Readiness.
Administration: Individual.
Price Data: Available from publisher.
Time: (20) minutes.
Author: LeAdelle Phelps.
Publisher: Psychology Press Inc.

Review of the Phelps Kindergarten Readiness Scale by THERESA H. ELOFSON, Program Specialist, Chapter 1/Learning Assistance Program, Federal Way School District #210, Federal Way, WA:

The Phelps Kindergarten Readiness Scale (PKRS) is an instrument designed to evaluate three domains predictive of later school achievement. The three domains, Verbal Processing, Perceptual Processing, and Auditory Processing, although not all inclusive, are certainly a means of obtaining a general screening of kindergarten populations.

The test can usually be administered in 20 minutes and has clear directions and scoring procedures, thus enabling a variety of educational personnel to administer the scale. The manual does state that it must be administered by "a competent examiner who is familiar with testing procedures and scoring format" (p. 3). Items are scored by a "0" or a "1." The directions and scoring procedures are not difficult. An examiner should study the materials thoroughly because the decisions made by the examiner become more difficult in the Perceptual Motor subtest.

The Perceptual Motor subtest gives brief written descriptions of unacceptable responses in the Test Record Booklet. The responses to both Perceptual Processing subtests are recorded by the student in the Perceptual Processing Booklet. However, it is in Appendix A of the manual where actual examples of errors are illustrated for the Perceptual Motor subtest. It is imperative that the examiner study all three separate documents thoroughly because the ceiling on this subtest is three consecutive errors. There is no time during the test for the examiner to reflect on how to score the responses.

Testing procedures caution that "there be adequate rapport with the child before testing begins" (p. 3). Although this is a given when testing young children, an additional consideration to be included in these testing instructions is how the examiner should respond to each item after a response is given. Selected items have instructions to query the child further. items that do not have such instructions have no set response to encourage or not encourage the child's work. This is an important consideration with young children.

Materials for administering the PKRS include the listing of a stopwatch. Nowhere in the test itself is a stopwatch listed as necessary equipment. The Auditory Discrimination subtest does say "If the child does not respond to an item within a reasonable time . . ." (p. 7, test booklet). Test administrators should probably come to terms with their definition of reasonable time because a definition is not given. The stopwatch could be used for timing those responses.

Three subtests have space for "notes" in the Test Record Booklet. The utilitarian purposes for the notes in the Auditory Discrimination Subtest are not apparent. Notes that might be taken by the administrator would be just as useful, or perhaps more so, in other sections of the test.

Nowhere in the manual is it clearly stated how the items were initially chosen or constructed other than to say they were based on data from research studies. Information about these procedures would help an individual be more confident about the nature of this test.

If a readiness test is considered as a basis for improvement of instruction, the PKRS provides a list of remediation activities for each of the domains used in this test. Specific cautions and suggestions are included in the introduction to this chapter of the manual. As the author indicates, the suggestions are a starting point. The activities are very appropriate and adaptable to classroom work.

The manual indicates how to transform the raw sores into percentiles, standard scores, and stanines. There are no directions regarding the utility of these transformed scores. Chapter 5 gives three case studies as examples of follow-up for students who were identified as academically at-risk by the PKRS. Each of the case studies models different procedures. The case studies illustrate the creativity that could be employed in follow-up interventions.

The standardization sample consisted of 554 children from four states (three geographical areas of the United States). The variables of age, gender, ethnic group, and parent education (used as an indication of socioeconomic status) were designed to approximate the 1980 U.S. Census data. The distribution of the standardization sample was very similar to the U.S. Census data, with only parent education of the sample group being higher at all levels of education.

The Total Readiness Score was reported as a standard score having a mean of 100 and a standard deviation of 15. Evidence of validity focused on internal consistency, concurrent validity, and predictive validity. To examine concurrent validity, the PKRS and the Missouri Kindergarten Inventory of Developmental Skills (KIDS; T4:1656) were administered to 279 children. Correlation coefficients ranged from .26 to .75 and were significant at the .001 level. Three smaller studies were completed for predictive validity. In separate studies the Woodcock-Johnson Psycho-Educational Battery, Part Two: Tests of Achievement, the Otis-Lennon School Ability Test (1982 edition), and the Stanford Achievement Test (1982 edition) were correlated with the PKRS. The lowest correlations in these three studies were consistently in the Perceptual Processing Domain.

Reliability measures included the Kuder-Richardson 20 formula, with a caution regarding the inflated values that may be present. Test-retest reliability coefficients for a sample of 61 students ranged from .61 to .87 and a *t*-test for mean differences, computed for each domain and the total score, indicated no significant differences.

The Phelps Kindergarten Readiness Test is a simple-to-administer, individual test, supported by initial research. The materials are easy to use, with prior, careful study. The manual does have a brief, excellent list of remediation activities, which teachers will find helpful.

[293]

Philadelphia Head Injury Questionnaire.

Purpose: Developed for use in gathering the history of individuals with head injuries.
Population: Head trauma patients.
Publication Date: 1991.
Acronym: PHIQ.
Scores: No scores.
Administration: Individual.
Price Data, 1991: $17.50 per complete kit including 25 questionnaires and manual (2 pages).
Time: [20] minutes.
Authors: Lucille M. Curry, Richard G. Ivins, and Thomas L. Gowen.
Publisher: Western Psychological Services.

Review of the Philadelphia Head Injury Questionnaire by MARK ALBANESE, Associate Professor of Preventive Medicine and Education and Director, Office of Education Research and Development, The University of Wisconsin-Madison Medical School, Madison, WI:

The Philadelphia Head Injury Questionnaire (PHIQ) is a brief questionnaire designed to screen patients who have had a head injury for further investigation and making appropriate referrals. The instrument is based upon the developer's "extensive clinical experience in assessing victims of head trauma," (administration and use document, p. 1) and is composed of two pages of straightforward questions about the symptoms and complaints many people have following head injury. The authors recommend that users of the PHIQ have some background knowledge of head injury assessment and indicate that this knowledge is a valuable asset in interpreting the results of the instrument.

The form itself is divided into six sections: Identifying Information, Accident Information, Persistent Symptoms, Cognitive Aspects of Head Injury, Personality Changes, Pertinent Personal/Medical History, and Comments and/or Additional Information. The two-page document on Administration and Use gives the rationale for each of the six sections; however, there are no citations of literature. Individual items use simple language and are mostly in a yes/no format. The questionnaire may be self-administered, completed by a family member/significant other, or administered by an interviewer. The authors indicate that administration by a skilled interviewer generally elicits the most comprehensive and reliable data. The authors further suggest the reliability of the information obtained can also be significantly increased by asking a spouse or close relative to complete the PHIQ with respect to the injured person. The authors state that some patients may respond in a biased manner and that recognition of response biases depends upon clinical judgment and increases with time. Further, the nature of response biases may give important information to the examiner.

The instrument is simply an information collection form and there is no scoring mechanism. Interpretation relies strictly on clinical judgment. Consequently, there is no information on validity and reliability; however, the Administration and Use document alludes to administrative methods for increasing the reliability of the data.

The strengths of the PHIQ are its brevity and simplicity. The language used on the form is very straightforward and information collected seems to be appropriate to the intent to serve as a screening instrument.

The weaknesses of the PHIQ are primarily related to validity issues. There is no literature cited to support the validity of the instrument. Further, there are no data provided to support the use of the instrument for any of the applications for which it is recommended. The Administration and Use document indicates the credibility of the PHIQ relies exclusively on the extensive clinical experience of the authors. Curiously, the document provides no information on the authors' affiliation nor level of clinical experience. The only information provided about the authors is their academic degrees, Ph.D. and J.D.

The validity issue is important for two reasons. First, a screening instrument that omits important information or collects data in ways likely to miss information critical to appropriate referral can be very damaging. Patients may be inappropriately comforted that symptoms are not serious or, conversely, needlessly made to be concerned about a nonexistent or overstated problem. The former problem will result in patients failing to receive medical care they need; the latter will lead to unnecessary costs being incurred for followup.

The second validity issue has to do with use of the instrument in medical-legal settings as is recommended by the Administration and Use document. The potential for abuse of such an instrument in the high-stakes world of injury litigation is troubling. Even describing the instrument as simply a screening questionnaire does not disguise the potential for it to be entered as evidence in court. The fact that one of the authors possesses a law degree heightens this possibility. Under these circumstances it is incumbent on the authors to document the appropriateness of the instrument to its recommended use. This clearly has not been done for the PHIQ.

In summary, the PHIQ is a brief and simple questionnaire designed as a screening tool for assessing whether individuals who have received a head injury need further evaluation. No data are provided from the literature or from the authors regarding the instrument's validity or reliability. As a result, it is up to the user to determine whether the PHIQ serves a specific need.

Review of the Philadelphia Head Injury Questionnaire by WILLIAM W. DEARDORFF, Clinical Faculty, U.C.L.A. School of Medicine, Los Angeles, CA:

The Philadelphia Head Injury Questionnaire (PHIQ) was developed to "aid in documenting areas for further investigation and making appropriate referrals" (administration and use document, pg. 1) vis-a-vis clinical findings secondary to head trauma. It is a structured information and history gathering instrument designed to make a preliminary assessment of head injury. Areas of inquiry include identifying information, accident information, persistent symptoms, cognitive aspects of head injury, personality changes, and pertinent personal/medical history. Most questions are presented in a "yes-no" format. The PHIQ can be self-administered, completed by a family member, or in an interview format. The measure is not a neuropsychological instrument as the patient's performance is not directly assessed and there are no norms for comparing response.

The content of the PHIQ "is based upon the authors' extensive clinical experience in assessing victims of head trauma" (administration and use document, p. 1). The test manual is two pages in length and offers no information regarding test development and little information about test interpretation. It asserts that the PHIQ was developed for use by a wide variety of professionals who assess and treat head injuries, including neuropsychologists, neurologists, and attorneys. The manual authors state that users of the PHIQ should have some background knowledge of head injury assessment and that expertise in the use of the PHIQ and reliability will increase with practice. The authors warn that biased responding can occur (over- or underreporting of symptoms) and that recognition of this phenomenon increases with clinical experience.

No information or standardization data on any type of reliability or validity are presented. One must, therefore, assume that such studies have not been done. In addition, no data are presented which support the utility of the PHIQ in assessing symptoms of head injury. There is no indication the questionnaire can help differentiate between clinically significant and nonsignificant neurological dysfunction. Further, no information is available about false negative rates. This is a crucial issue in this patient population.

Until reliability, validity, specificity, and sensitivity studies of the PHIQ are completed, use of this questionnaire cannot be recommended as an aid to assessing head injury symptoms or making referrals.

[294]

Phonological Process Analysis.

Purpose: Constructed to assess speech by determining phonological patterns.
Population: Children ages 2–5 with phonological disability.
Publication Date: 1979.
Acronym: PPA.
Scores, 31: Proportion of Test Processes and Frequency of Nontest Processes scores for 16 phonological processes: Syllable Structure (Deletion of Final Consonants, Cluster Reduction, Weak Syllable Deletion [no Frequency of Nontest Process score], Glottal Replacement), Harmony (Labial Assimilation, Alveolar Assimilation, Velar Assimilation, Prevocalic Voicing, Final Consonant Devoicing), Feature Contrast (Stopping, Gliding of Fricatives, Affrication, Fronting, Denasalization, Gliding of Liquids, Vocalization).
Administration: Individual.
Price Data: Not available.
Time: (45–50) minutes.
Author: Frederick F. Weiner.
Publisher: PRO-ED, Inc.
[The publisher advised in January 1994 that this test is now out of print.—Ed.]

Review of the Phonological Process Analysis by JEFFREY A. ATLAS, Deputy Chief Psychologist and Assistant Clinical Professor, Bronx Children's Psychiatric Center, Albert Einstein College of Medicine, Bronx, NY, and DEBORAH H. ATLAS, Coordinator, Rehabilitation Speech Pathology, Mt. Sinai Medical Center, New York, NY:

The Phonological Process Analysis is a spiral-bound manual constituting an assessment procedure for determining phonological patterns in speech-disordered children aged 2–5. Originally published in 1979, the process analysis subsumes phonological categories of Syllable Structure, Harmony, and Feature Contrast. Its 136 criteria stimulus measures were selected as those best able to identify phonological disability in a sample of 100 language-disordered subjects, whose demographic characteristics are not further specified. Given the absence of true normative data, even for the subset of language-disordered children, the Phonological Process Analysis is best conceived of as an assessment procedure, loosely criterion referenced, enabling the speech-language pathologist to identify underlying patterns of phonological disability without sampling the entire universe of (English-language) phonemes. The procedure is most effective in this area and sensible in its attendant treatment recommendations. It is also successful in its secondary attempt to "predict" (delineate) associated and cross-category speech difficulty from specimen productions.

The manual is attractively packaged, giving clear instructions to the speech pathologist in eliciting two responses for each of two stimulus pictures, which as a couplet constitute an assessment item for a phonological measure, the 136 of which are distributed unevenly over the 16 categories. The number of assessment items sampled within the 16 categories varies from 6 to 8, except for 28 within the category of Cluster Reduction, which seems warranted given the multidimensionality of this category and its significant contributions to unintelligibility in language.

The item stimuli are droll and engaging, featuring as they do a balding, mustached, peripatetic "Uncle Fred" who observes, eats, skis, and even wears a dress (!), all in attempts to help the examiner elicit a delayed imitation of utterance (e.g., Uncle Fred is wearing a ________), and a sentence recall response (What is Uncle Fred doing?). A concern of the present reviewers was the Mean Length of Utterance comprised in even the first sentence recall (4), ranging to 10 under preliminary inspection which might confound the assessment of phonological processes in children as young as 2. Another factor which might dampen, but not necessarily confound, verbal (and secondarily, phonological) productivity, is the black-and-white format of the test stimuli. Colorizing of the test materials might be expected to enhance young children's engagement and the procedure's validity in eliciting speech competence.

The Phonological process Analysis provides "control items contrasts" composed of nonsense syllables in Place Harmony (Labial Assimilation, Alveolar Assimilation, Velar Assimilation) in order to differentiate potential additional within-category or cross-category processes. For example, in the contrast control "sɛtr," for the Labial Assimilation target "sweater," the sample respondent's "wɛo" was seen to predict (delineate) Consonant Reduction instead of Labial Assimilation by controlling for the enunciation of /w/. In this manner the underlying faulty phonological process is identified, permitting sample testing of other errors without universal testing of sounds.

In summary, the Phonological Process Analysis presents a useful assessment instrument in efficiently sampling disordered articulation in English-speaking children aged 2–5. It yields a portrait of phonology problems with implications for treatment prioritized according to normal language development. It constitutes a useful instrument in the test armamentarium of any pediatric speech-language pathologist. For more advanced practitioners, parts of the measure, for instance the Fronting items within Feature Contrast Processes, might be administered in lieu of the whole instrument to verify and further delineate the fronting process.

Review of the Phonological Process Analysis by KATHARINE G. BUTLER, Research Professor, Communication Sciences and Disorders, Syracuse University, Syracuse, NY:

The author of the Phonological Process Analysis (PPA) contends that the PPA is "an alternative to traditional articulation assessment" (manual, p. ix) but that the "PPA is not a test. It is not [to] be used to determine whether a speaker meets some basic standard" (p. ix). The author also points out that the responses to the PPA are obtained in an unnatural manner compared to spontaneous speech; however, he reports that because children examined with the instrument usually have unintelligible speech, a structured approach, even one that does not sample all possibilities, is more useful.

The brief introductory chapter credits Ingram's (1976) ground breaking work of the 1960s and 1970s. The 1979 manual for the PPA has not been updated and fails to reflect the current approaches of the mid-1990s (Hodson, 1994).

The phonological processes identified are those involved at the Syllable Structure level (i.e., Deletion of Final Consonants, Cluster Reduction, Weak Syllable Deletion, and Glottal Replacement) and Harmony process (i.e., Labial Assimilation, Alveolar Assimilation, Velar Assimilation, Prevocalic Voicing, and Final Consonant Devoicing, Manner Harmony and Syllable Harmony). The Feature Contrast processes addressed include Stopping, Affrication, Fronting, Gliding of Fricatives and Liquids, Vocalization, Denasalization, and Neutralization. Thus, 20 individual phonological processes are evaluated by having the child imitate the examiner, providing the verb and the object of a brief sentence. Assimilation requires the child to produce responses to nonsense word control items, a process many of the 2- and 3-year-olds tested by this reviewer found difficult to discriminate.

The authors suggest in the administration chapter that it is not necessary to complete the analysis and/or to examine every phonological process. Although 45–50 minutes are required to complete the assessment, considerable additional time is required to complete the analysis and preparation of the process profile. The profile is a one-page summary which provides considerable information to a child phonologist; however, to be used as a part of a speech-language assessment report, it would need additional explanatory statements to be meaningful to parents or teachers.

This individually administered instrument is not a test, as noted by the author; it also has no validity or reliability data. It may be useful in the hands of an experienced child phonologist who is interested in using a single spiral-bound document, with simple black-and-white plates (two per page), all cartoon-like sketches showing "Uncle Fred" engaged in a task. Interpretation of the PPA is encapsulated within four pages, with three being given over to specifying the conditions of each phonological process, and one to remediation on the basis of the phonological process analysis. Neither of these two objectives are met sufficiently well to be useful to beginning speech-language pathologists, although the scoring exemplars provided early on in the manual will be helpful.

More useful to many clinicians may be the Assessment of Phonological Processes—Revised (Hodson, 1986; T4:220), which addresses 30 error patterns and the Khan-Lewis Phonological Analysis (Khan & Lewis; 1986; T4:1356), which evaluates 15 processes. Both of these instruments represent more current approaches and provide more extensive documentation.

REVIEWER'S REFERENCES

Ingram, D. (1976). *Phonological disability in children*. New York: Elsevier.
Hodson, B. W. (1986). The Assessment of Phonological Processes—Revised. Austin, TX: PRO-ED, Inc.
Khan, L. M. L., & Lewis, N. P. (1986). Khan-Lewis Phonological Analysis. Circle Pines, MN: American Guidance Service.
Hodson, B. (1994). Helping individuals become intelligible, literate, and articulate: The role of phonology. *Topics in Language Disorders*. *14*(2), 1-16.

[295]

Picha-Seron Career Analysis.

Purpose: "Provides a description and analysis of an individual's workstyle and relates this workstyle to 178 selected technical, managerial and professional occupations (career profile and occupational profile) or to an in-depth workstyle analysis (personnel profile)."
Population: Middle school–adult.
Publication Dates: 1991–93.
Acronym: PSCA.
Administration: Individual or group.
Price Data, 1994: $1 per in-house generation of score reports; $3 per individual answer sheets and scoring (26+) if ICPS scores; $5 per individual answer sheets and scoring (1–25) if ICPS scores; $20 per manual ('93, 70 pages); $25 per Occupational Profile Handbook; $15 per Technical Report 1.
Time: [10–15] minutes.
Author: Merron S. Seron.
Publisher: International Career Planning Services, Inc.

a) PSCA-CAREER PROFILE.
Population: Middle school–secondary school.
Acronym: PSCA-CP.
Scores, 16: Workstyle Graph Interpretations (Dominance, Influence, Adaptance, Compliance), Occupational Strengths (Practical, Analytical, Creative, Service, Managerial, Supportive), Learning Styles (Cognitive Organization, Internality, Time Orientation), Occupational Scales (178).

b) PSCA-OCCUPATIONAL PROFILE.

Population: College–adult.
Acronym: PSCA-OP.
Scores, 18: Workstyle Graphs (Ideal Self, Pressure Self, Usual Self), other scores same as *a* above.
c) PSCA-PERSONNEL PROFILE.
Population: Adults.
Acronym: PSCA-PP.
Scores, 18: Verification Score, Workstyle Graphs (Ideal Self, Pressure Self, Usual Self), Workstyle Graph Interpretations (Dominance, Influence, Adaptance, Compliance), Strength of Occupational Area (Practical, Analytical, Creative, Service, Managerial, Supportive), Learning Styles (Internality, Cognitive Organization, Time Orientation), Major Workstyles.

Review of the Picha-Seron Career Analysis by MICHAEL B. BUNCH, Vice President, Measurement Incorporated, Durham, NC:

The Picha-Seron Career Analysis (PSCA) is based on the dynamic, situational theory of human behavior of W. M. Marston (1928; Marston, King, & Marston, 1931). The original instrument was developed by R. E. Picha (1981, 1990) and revised by Merron S. Seron in 1993. The theory and the instrument focus on four primary emotional traits: dominance, influence, adaptance, and compliance. In earlier publications, adaptance was referred to as stability.

The PSCA is primarily for use in vocational counseling and career exploration. The target audience ranges from junior high to retirement age. In the words of the author, "You should be who you are. You should do who you are" (manual, p. 2). The philosophy underlies most of the work on the instrument to date.

The PSCA yields descriptions and an analysis of individual workstyle and relates this workstyle to typical workstyle profiles of 178 selected job titles. The instrument consists of 24 sets of four short descriptions in a forced-choice format. The subject selects one description that is most like and one that is least like him or her. For example, one item contains the following four descriptions: Sure of self; Get along with others; Argue a lot; Easy going. From this set, the subject selects one description that is most similar and one that is least similar. If a subject selects more than one description in each category per item or leaves more than five items blank, no score is reported.

SCORES. Four scores are reported: Dominance (degree of control over the work environment—D); Influence (degree of influence over others in the workplace—I); Adaptance (degree of adaptation within the workplace—A), and Compliance (conformity to rules—C). Each is scored on a 0–20 scale.

From earlier work with over 500 job titles, Dr. Seron has extracted 178 job titles of interest. A nationwide team of consultants evaluated job analysis data over a period of several years to compile the ratings for each job title. Selected profiles were then empirically validated with samples of incumbents in several of the job titles. The PSCA was then administered to a sample of 1,554 individuals spanning the age range of interest. This sample makes up the general population against which subjects are compared.

Subjects typically receive three scores on each of the four traits: Ideal Self, Pressure Self, and Usual Self. Ideal Self and Pressure Self scores on each trait are calculated by applying a key to the 24 sets of scores. Each trait is keyed to one description in each item. Total scores for each trait are obtained by subtracting *L*s (least like) from *M*s (most like). These totals are then compared to general population scores to derive scores on the four trait scales (D, I, A, C). Tables of means and standard deviations (by sex) for transforming scores are supplied in an appendix to the manual. Usual Self scores are derived by averaging the scores on Ideal and Pressure Self.

Additional scores include Strength of Occupational Area (Practical, Analytical, Creative, Service, Managerial, Supportive) and Learning Style (Internality, Cognitive Organization, and Time Orientation). Weights used in calculating scores on these traits, along with explanations, are provide in the manual.

TECHNICAL DATA. The manual reports internal consistency (alpha) and test-retest coefficients for a sample of 1,554 subjects ranging in age from 17 to 68. Alpha is reported to be between .40 and .74 across the eight original scales (four scales each for Ideal and Pressure Self), with slightly higher coefficients for females than for males on most of the traits. Test-retest reliability coefficients (5 weeks) for those scales range from .52 to .75, with a median of.69. In contrast, Westbrook (1985) reported median test-retest reliability coefficients of .91 (2 weeks) to .64 (20 years) for the Strong-Vocational Interest Blank administered to men who were first tested at age 19 to 21.

The manual reports scale intercorrelations as well as correlation coefficients between PSCA scores and grade point average (GPA) and scores on related tests. Scale intercorrelations range from .00 (Pressure Dominance vs. Pressure Influence) to -.74 (Ideal Dominance vs. Ideal Adaptance). The median absolute value of scale intercorrelations is .44. Although the manual describes these intercorrelations as negligible, in 8 of 24 instances the traits share more than 25% common variance.

Correlations between PSCA scales and GPA (based on the same sample of 1,554) are virtually zero, providing support for the claim that scores on the PSCA are independent of grades. Correlations with other interest tests (Comrey Personality Inventory, Myers-Briggs Type Indicator, Leiter Scale, Hidden Figures Test) reported in the manual show a consistent pattern of shared variance with like traits. These correlations, taken together, provide reasonable evidence of construct validity.

Technical Report 1 summarizes the results of a factor analytic study of the PSCA scales. Three factors are interpreted and account for 100% of variance. The first factor, accounting for 66.8% of variance, seems stable (estimated alpha = .86), whereas the other two factors, accounting for a total of about 30% of variance (unrotated), would actually yield negative alpha coefficients.

SUMMARY. The PSCA seems to be well founded theoretically. The test and results are straightforward and easy to understand. It is generally less reliable than competing instruments, and no information about profile stability is offered. Such information would be tremendously helpful.

The standardization sample and research base for the PSCA are also a fraction of those for the Strong Interest Inventory (SVIB-SCII; 374) or Myers-Briggs Type Indicator (MBTI; T4:1702). Although there is far less research evidence behind the PSCA than for its competitors, the validity information given in the manual suggests that the PSCA might be a viable alternative to the SVIB-SCII or MBTI. Further evidence of validity is the fact that the scale scores do not correlate with grade-point average. This is an important point for users who believe that career exploration should be independent of ability. The PSCA is worth considering as a career counseling tool.

REVIEWER'S REFERENCES

Marston, W. M. (1928). *Emotions of normal people.* New York: Harcourt, Brace, & Company.

Marston, W. M., King, C. D., & Marston, E. H. (1931). *Integrative psychology.* New York: Harcourt, Brace, & Company.

Picha, R. E. (1981). C.H.I.P.S. Script™. Oak Brook, IL: PsychoGraphics.

Westbrook, B. W. (1985). [Review of the Strong-Campbell Interest Inventory.] In J. V. Mitchell, Jr. (Ed.), *The ninth mental measurements yearbook* (pp. 1481-1483). Lincoln, NE: The Buros Institute of Mental Measurements.

Picha, R. E. (1990). C.H.I.P.S. Script™. Oak Brook, IL: PsychoGraphics.

Review of the Picha-Seron Career Analysis by BERTRAM C. SIPPOLA, Associate Professor of Psychology, University of New Orleans, New Orleans, LA:

The Picha-Seron Career Analysis (PSCA) is a personality/interest inventory designed for "career assessment" for somewhat differing populations by providing the user with a choice of three parallel versions of analyses of the test taker's responses. The PSCA-CP (Career Profile) is designed for use with middle and high school students for self-exploration and early career planning. The PSCA-OP (Occupational Profile) is designed for college and adult populations who need information about themselves for making decisions about career or validating current career choices. The PSCA-PP (Personnel Profile) is designed for employer use in personnel selection and assessment to match individuals to job profiles.

Seron, a practicing counselor, has designed a test and manual for "career counselors" with little or no technical background. He notes that PSCA-like instruments have been used primarily in non-academic settings, such as "franchise operations." Especially in its introduction, his manual has a chatty and informal style. The PSCA is a "humanistically" oriented instrument originally developed for use by teachers and counselors working with inner city and rural youths. It is designed to focus on "who an individual is at the present time" (p. 2), and seems to discount the necessity of also assessing the student's knowledge, skills, or abilities as a part of the career counseling process. With goals of "increasing aspirations" and "raising expectations" of respondents, the PSCA uses only technical, managerial, and professional occupations.

The PSCA is one of a number of instruments developed over the years (e.g., Personal Profile System [10:280]) based on W. M. Marston's (1928) theory that behavior can be categorized according to four clusters of emotions: Dominance, Inducement of Others, Submission, and Compliance (Submission has been relabeled as Adaptance, although in the Technical Report #1 (TR) there is instead a category labeled Steadiness). With this theoretical base, Seron has modified more recent work by Picha (1981, 1990) to produce an instrument which uses these four "work-style traits" (DIAC) to rate the respondent's match to "successful people" in each of six general occupational areas into which his 178 occupations are organized (Picha, 1993). The makeup of these occupational scales, as described in the TR, is based on cluster analysis and discriminant function analysis. (These seem to approximate Holland's [1985] widely used six vocational interest types.) The PSCA also indicates the rating on each of three "learning styles": Internality/Externality, Cognitive Organization, and Time Orientation.

The PSCA manual does not discuss the general issues raised in the literature (e.g., Lowman, 1991) as to what (and how many) career-relevant personality dimensions there are. The manual specifically cites the PSCA as having been developed to be an alternative to the SVIB, SDS, and Myers-Briggs (MBTI). The first two are generally considered as dealing with what are typically called "interests," whereas the MBTI is usually described as a "personality" measure. While glossing over this distinction, the manual cites a recent study that concludes that both the PSCA and the MBTI measure several of the same personality characteristics, but that the PSCA is preferable on the basis of time needed and the quality of the feedback the respondent receives (which would ordinarily seem to be partly a function of the interpretive skills of the professional using the test). This may be a comparison of "print-outs" that are formula-determined standard descriptions.

The PSCA's sixth grade reading level allows it to be used with a wide variety of individuals, although most of the reported data on its use come from studies using college students. The PSCA consists of 24 sets of four statements, each presumably characteristic of one of the four workstyles; the respondent is required to choose one of the four as "least-like-you" and one as "most-like-you." According to the reported data, most subjects should be able to finish the PSCA in under 15 minutes. The manual states that the discriminations within each set become progressively finer. It could be that some respondents may find it somewhat difficult to choose appropriately "most" and "least" statements applying to themselves.

The manual describes in some detail the development and standardization of the multidimensional DIAC scales on a reference group of 1,628 community college students. Despite this, it is still not clear how many of the scaled scores are derived (e.g., the workstyle graphs for "ideal self" as opposed to "self under pressure").

The PSCA can be scored by the publisher directly, either individually or in batches of 26 or more, or the user can purchase software and a counter to generate [up to 32,000!] score reports locally. The report for the PSCA-OP provides graphs showing DIAC workstyle profiles for the respondent under "ideal," "pressure," and "usual" conditions, followed by standard descriptive phrases based on the scaled scores. There is then a graphic display showing how the respondent's DIAC scores compare with successful persons in each of the 178 occupations, followed by a list of the "fourteen occupations that you most resemble" (manual, Appendix D). These use a unidimensional index score summing across the DIAC differences between each respondent and the norm group scores for each occupation. The PSCA-CP differs from the PSCA-OP in providing only a "usual self" workstyle graph and descriptions. The PSCA-PP differs from the PSCA-OP in replacing the 178 occupational scales with an "in-depth" interpretation of the respondent's highest and lowest DIAC workstyle categories.

Reliability data are based on community college samples. Internal consistency of the DIAC scales was assessed using Cronbach's alpha; the range of alphas was .40 to.74, which is claimed to be "generally internally consistent" (manual, p. 16). Test-retest correlations of the DIAC scales over a 5- to 6-week interval range from .52 to.80 (lowest for Compliance, highest for Dominance), not impressive, but apparently acceptable.

The manual reports one study as demonstrating concurrent validity of the PSCA scales with theoretically similar scales on the Comrey Personality Scales, and also with the Leiter Scale (which measures situational locus of control in an educational setting) and the Hidden Figures Test, "an experimental test purporting to measure field dependence-independence and/or cognitive orientation" (p. 17). There need to be further concurrent validity studies with other, more widely used interest inventories and personality assessments, especially with samples from the younger populations for which the PSCA is, in part, designed. (No validity data are reported from this age range.)

The manual reports that there was no significant correlation between raw DIAC scores and community college grade-point averages. Although this may support Seron's contention that personality/interests measured by the PSCA are independent of a person's background, that background cannot be ignored in career counseling as this manual seems at times to suggest.

If you buy all the assumptions and want a quick, relatively inexpensive, canned career assessment instrument, you might find the PSCA useful. However, do not use it by itself! A relatively minor cavil concerns writing style. In addition to a number of typographical errors, the manual has a continual problem with subject/number disagreements.

REVIEWER'S REFERENCES

Marston, W. M. (1928). *Emotions of normal people*. New York: Harcourt, Brace.

Picha, R. (1981). C.H.I.P.S. Script™. Oak Brook, IL: Psychographics Corp.

Holland, J. L. (1985). *Making vocational choices: A theory of vocational choices and work environments* (2nd ed.). Englewood Cliffs, NJ: Prentice-Hall.

Picha, R. (1990). C.H.I.P.S. Script™. Oak Brook, IL: Psychographics Corp.

Lowman, R. L. (1991). *The clinical practice of career assessment: Interests, abilities, and personality*. Washington, DC: American Psychological Association.

Picha, R. (1993). *Assembly of C.H.I.P.S. Job Data Base*. Oak Brook, IL: Psychographics Corp.

[296]

PLAN.

Purpose: Measures knowledge and skills attained early in secondary education in four curriculum areas: English, mathematics, reading, and science reasoning, to provide students "with information they will need to plan and prepare for future academic and career success."
Population: Grade 10.
Publication Dates: 1989–92.
Administration: Group.
Price Data: Available from publisher.
Time: 115 minutes for 4 academic tests; (60–70) minutes for student information, Interest Inventory, Study Power Assessment, and High School Course information.
Comments: Formerly called P-ACT+.
Author: American College Testing.
Publisher: American College Testing .

a) PLAN ENGLISH TEST.
Purpose: Measures understanding of the conventions of standard written English.
Scores, 7: Usage/Mechanics (Punctuation, Basic Grammar, Sentence Structure), Rhetorical Skills (Strategy, Organization, Style), Total.
Time: 30 minutes.

b) PLAN MATHEMATICS TEST.
Purpose: Measures level of mathematics achievement.

Scores, 5: Algebra (Pre-Algebra, Elementary Algebra), Geometry (Coordinate Geometry, Plane Geometry), Total.
Time: 40 minutes.
c) PLAN READING TEST.
Purpose: Measures reading comprehension as a product of referring and reasoning skills.
Scores: Total score only.
Time: 20 minutes.
d) PLAN SCIENCE REASONING TEST.
Purpose: Measures scientific reasoning skills.
Scores: Total score only.
Time: 25 minutes.

Review of the PLAN by MARTHA BLACKWELL, Associate Professor of Psychology, Auburn University at Montgomery, Montgomery, AL:

The PLAN, formerly named P-ACT+, is actually the academic part of a battery of instruments produced by The American College Testing (ACT) Program. The PLAN is designed to measure knowledge and skills attained by beginning 10th graders. The battery consists of assessments of students' educational development; self-reported study skills, needs, and interests; and an educational/occupational plans sections. Information about the student from PLAN program participation could be used to help the student and his or her parents decide about future course work in high school and career goals, counselors in guiding the student in course selection and postsecondary planning, and school personnel in studying the relationship between curriculum and student performance on these tests.

The educational development test of the PLAN is somewhat like a pretest to the Enhanced ACT Assessment (139; an outgrowth of the original ACT Assessment) with similar content areas and test format, timed group administration, comparability of performances, and estimates of test performances between the PLAN given in the 10th grade and ACT given 2 years later in the 12th grade. The PLAN and ACT differ in the time expectations for educational attainment. The PLAN measures learning prior to or early in secondary education; ACT measures more complex reasoning and learning accrued throughout the entire secondary school experience.

The PLAN is designed to measure the educational development of beginning 10th graders. The PLAN is to be group administered on days designated by and monitored in a single session requiring 165 minutes total administration time and 115 minutes in actual test-taking time.

It is important to note that this review focuses on one single PLAN (formerly named P-ACT+, Form 08B) academic test. ACT's constant formative evaluation of its programs results in continuous creation of new items, item tryouts, item analyses, and new test booklets annually. Thus, comments appropriate to this particular PLAN academic test booklet may not hold across all test booklets.

Academic tests within the battery are English, Mathematics, Reading, and Science Reasoning. The total number of items is 145. Items for all the tests are multiple choice with four or five alternatives. Test content and vocabulary level are appropriate for 10th grade students. Descriptions for content area tests follow.

The English test (50 items, 30 minutes) measures conventions of standard written English in two content areas: Usage/Mechanics (30 items) and Rhetorical Skills (20 items). Categories comprising Usage/Mechanics are Punctuation, Basic Grammar, and Sentence Structure. Categories comprising Rhetorical Skills are Strategy, Organization, and Style. The Student Report provides three scores: English total and two subscores for Usage/Mechanics and Rhetorical Skills.

The Mathematics test (40 items, 40 minutes) measures quantitative reasoning, content, and skills usually acquired before the second year of high school. Content areas include Algebra (22 items) with categories Pre-Algebra and Elementary Algebra, and Geometry (18 items) with categories Coordinate Geometry and Plane Geometry. The Student Report provides three scores: Mathematics total score and two subscores for Algebra and Geometry.

The Reasoning test (25 items, 20 minutes) measures reading comprehension requiring referring and reasoning skills. Test content consists of prose passages from fiction, humanities, and social science. The Student Report provides one total test score for Reading. No subscores are reported.

The Science Reasoning test (30 items, 25 minutes) measures scientific reasoning skills applied to five sets of scientific information in the formats of data representation, research summaries, and conflicting viewpoints related to inconsistent hypotheses. The Student Report provides one total test score for Science Reasoning. No subscores are reported.

Potentially valuable information for curricular planning can be purchased by high schools that PLAN-test 25 or more students. More definitive delineation by category performances can be obtained as an Optional Research and Reporting Service (1992–93 PLAN P-ACT+ Program Guide, p. 17) entitled "Item-Response Summary Report." Thus, for English in the Usage/Mechanics area, performances are delineated by categories of Punctuation, Basic Grammar, and Sentence Structure; in the Rhetorical Skills area, by Strategy, Organization, and Style. Presumably, information for Mathematics might be available for Algebra categories of Pre-Algebra and Elementary Algebra, as well as for Geometry categories of Coordinate Geometry and Plane Geometry. For reading and for Science Reasoning it is doubtful that categorical analyses are available inasmuch as the type of content for stems is presented rather than the performance of an operation or skill.

One blatant error in test format was noted. The technical manual claims that each item is reviewed at least 12 times before selection; perhaps more attention should be given to test format. Content (stem) from which Item 11 and Item 12 were to be answered appeared on page 3; the questions (alternatives) appeared on page 4, the *back* of page 3 (P-ACT+, Form 08B, pp. 3, 4). Each of the four academic tests is timed separately. Thus, the placement of body content (stem) on one page and placement of questions (alternatives) on the back of that page may unduly penalize examinees and is unacceptable test format practice.

Tests are scored by ACT. Score results are produced only after item analyses. The raw scores (number of correct responses) for each of the four content area tests—English, Mathematics, Reading, Science Reasoning—are converted to scale scores. Because subscores and test scores were scaled separately, there is no arithmetic relationship between subscores and test scores.

The range of scores on all four tests and the Composite is 1 to 32. The Composite score is the average of the four scale scores rounded to the nearest whole number. Subscore scale range is 1 to 16. The standard error of measurement is approximately 2 points for each of the four test scores and four subscores (i.e., two subscores each for English and for Mathematics). The standard error of measurement for the Composite score is one. For 10th grade students, test means hover around 16 and subscores around 8 with standard errors of measurement from 1.73 to 2.39 for the four test scores and 1.4 to 1.81 for subscores. For 12th grade students planning to attend college, test means are 18 and subscore means are 9.

With approximately 68% confidence, an estimated range of scores within which a student's Composite score would be expected to fall when she or he takes the enhanced ACT Assessment 2 years later can be made. Two scale score points, used as the standard error of difference, are added and subtracted to the 10th grade P-ACT+ (PLAN) Composite score. Higher scores tended to have smaller standard errors. Caution is urged in interpretation of estimates because the intervals produced were on marginal distributions rather than on the conditional distribution.

Norms and score scales were derived from data provided by a sample of 15,878 students from 100,000 examinees, from one of the four samples intended to be nationally representative, and from 145 of 399 participating schools. Data were collected in the Academic Skills Study of high school students in October 1988. The target population consisted of students enrolled in private as well as public schools in the 10th, 11th, or 12th grade.

Two sets of norms for the PLAN (P-ACT+) test scores were derived from this special norming and scaling study. One set of norms is intended to represent the performance of all 10th grade students; the second set of norms is intended to represent the performance of "college-bound" 10th grade students. "College-bound" designates students who reported planning to attend a 2-year or 4-year college or university. It is important to note that the "college-bound" students are also included in the "national" norms.

A systematic sample selection from each stratum of school characteristics was drawn. Stratification variables were: region of the country, school size, public versus private status, and ACT Assessment user versus non-ACT Assessment user. A school defined as an ACT Assessment user was one located in the Mountain/Plains, Southwest, or Midwest regions or that had at least one student who took the ACT Assessment in the 1987–88 academic year. Attempts to match sample composition to U.S. Census demographics were close, but not completely representative. The greatest variations by geography were overrepresentation of the Southeast (.19 national, .25 average participation) and underrepresentation of the Northeast (.22 national, .18 participation); by race, underrepresentation of blacks (.16 national, .10 participation).

Variations in test administrations and in participation by schools and by students make suspect a truly national representation of students and schools. Schools were asked to test all students in each grade. Variations included: A few schools were allowed to administer the test batteries to randomly selected subsamples of their own students; makeup testing for absent students was strongly encouraged; and some schools with questionably prepared students did not participate.

Three test batteries were administered—the enhanced ACT Assessment, a lengthened form of the P-ACT+, and a lengthened form of the original ACT Assessment. To obtain random sampling of tests, booklets were stacked so that every third booklet was the same battery (spiraling) and tests were administered in that specified order; thus, all batteries at each school were taken presumably by randomly equivalent groups of examinees within each grade.

Examinee sample sizes for the 10th, 11th, and 12th grades for the national sample and for the college-bound sample follow. It is important to recall that the college-bound examinees are a subset of the national examinees and, therefore, are included in the national sample performances, also. Sample sizes by grade for the national sample and for the college-bound samples were, respectively: grade 10—5,630 and 4,838; grade 11—5,315 and 4,547; grade 12—4,933 and 4,253.

Weighting was applied for the sampling and norming processes. Individual examinee records were multiplied by weights to aid in achieving representation on the explicit stratification variables (i.e., the less likelihood of being chosen for the sample, the greater the assigned weight). Despite attempts to adjust statistically for nonresponse among schools and low participation by students at some schools, it is highly likely that bias in results may exist.

ACT's constant formative evaluation of its programs results in several test booklets annually. Standards for content specifications and statistical specifications are sought across test forms. Content specifications, determined through curricular analyses, help to ensure that the proportions of content areas are maintained across test forms. Statistical specifications, determined through item analyses, set acceptable levels of item difficulty and of discrimination indices. Distribution of item difficulties permits differentiation among students who vary widely in level of achievement. Tests are constructed to have a mean item difficulty of about .58 for the PLAN national population and a range of difficulties from about .20 to .85. To meet discrimination standards, items differing in level of difficulty require different biserial correlations on tests measuring comparable content. Thus, items in the difficulty range of .20–.29 should have a biserial correlation of .20 or higher with total scores on a test; items in the difficulty range of .30–.85 should have a biserial correlation of .30 or higher with scores on a test.

Item analyses on tryout units divide the sample into low, medium, and high groups by the individual's total tryout test score. The cutting scores for the three groups are the 27th and the 73rd percentile points. Biserial and point-biserial correlation coefficients as well as the differences between proportion of students answering the item correctly in each of the three groups are used as indices of the discriminating power of the tryout items. Each item is reviewed following item analysis.

Two kinds of reliability were not mentioned in the technical manual. These were test-retest reliability (stability) and parallel form/alternate form (equivalence) test reliability. Two facts necessitate such information: the cost to a school system in dollars, personnel, and time upon school-wide test adoption and the continuous production of new forms of ACT academic tests.

Internal consistency reliability was reported. Kuder-Richardson 20 reliability coefficients were computed for raw scores of 12th grade students used in the norms scale scores in Sample 1 of the 1988 Academic Skills Study. Reliability coefficients range from .70–.90. The KR20 coefficients for both national and college-bound students on the four tests were: English, .89; Mathematics, .84; Reading, .80; Science Reasoning, .71 national and .72 college-bound. KR20 coefficients for subscores for national, then college-bound students were: Usage/Mechanics, .83, .82; Rhetorical Skills, .78, .77; Pre-Algebra/Algebra, .78, .78. Insufficient reliability coefficients range from 0–.70. KR20 coefficients for subscores in Geometry for the national group and the college-bound group were both .64.

Validity discussions included content validity, intercorrelations between scale scores on pairs of tests and on the Composite for both national and college-bound groups, and comparisons of groups differing in educational background and goals. Content validity was declared established in test development procedures which include critical examination on each item at least 12 times, standard content specifications derived from high school curricular analyses, and review of test content by staff, teachers, measurement specialists, and experts in the content field. Comparisons of students differing in educational status, planned courses, and goals were made. Higher PLAN test scores were made by students who were in higher grades, planning to take more courses in English and Math, and planning to attend a 2- or 4-year college. Planned years of study in English and Mathematics investigations indicated that 10th grade and 12th grade students who had taken/planned to take 3.5 years of English and Math performed better than did students who had taken/planned to take 2.5 to 3 years who performed more like students who had taken/planned to take 2 or less years. College-bound students' observed correlations for scale scores ranged from .56 to .71 (adequate) indicating that examinees who score well on one test also tend to score well on another. College-bound students at the 10th, 11th, and 12th grade levels performed better on all four tests and the Composite than did the national group.

The PLAN, an academic test, is one part of an ambitious and comprehensive program intended to be all things to students, parents, counselors, teachers, and schools. The use of the PLAN by a school system is appropriate to the extent that a school's curriculum is similar to the test in educational objectives and content specifications and that their student population is similar to the normative sample. For schools that already administer the ACT, the PLAN would seem to be a logical addition to the testing program. The impact upon normative representation and test score interpretation resulting from the use of sophisticated statistical techniques to estimate normal curve performances and to make up for gaps in sample representation is unknown.

Review of the PLAN by MARY HENNING-STOUT, Associate Professor of Counseling Psychology, Lewis & Clark College, Portland, OR:

The PLAN uses the American College Testing (ACT) academic achievement tests as the centerpiece of its career-planning curriculum. Because of its basis in this college-preparatory testing instrument, the PLAN is aimed at students who intend to pursue post-secondary education. Although the literature accompanying the PLAN, and the array of job/career options listed for student, parent, and counselor use suggest relevance for the broad range of students, the PLAN program remains best suited for college-bound youth.

CONTENT. The PLAN program includes a battery of testing materials and a set of manuals and workbooks for facilitating the use of those materials. The PLAN assessment battery includes Tests of Educational Development (P-ACT+), a Study Power Assessment, a Needs Assessment, and an Interest Inventory. Of these tests, the P-ACT+, which also serves as a preparatory test for the ACT college entrance exam, is the most emphasized. Detailed and impressive information on the development of this test are provided in the Technical Manual. The psychometric thoroughness of the test developers as reported in this manual (summarized below) is impeccable. The centrality of the P-ACT+ with its tests in English, Mathematics, Reading, and Science Reasoning is clear in the authors' description of these tests and interpretation of each of the other tests in the context set by the results of achievement testing.

Noticeably less information is provided on the norming and item development of the other three tests of inventories. The information provided for the Study Power Assessment (referred to as the Study Skills Assessment in the Technical manual) indicates that it is a 60-item, 15-minute true/false test for measuring "students' knowledge of effective study skills related to managing time and study environment, reading textbooks, taking class notes, using information resources, and preparing for and taking test" (Technical Manual, p. 33). According to the Technical Manual, the items for this assessment were developed based upon literature review and consultation with experts in the area of study skills. The nature of the literature review and expert consultation are not specified.

The Needs Assessment is described as allowing students to identify their "perception of personal academic and planning needs" (PLAN Program Guide, p. 20) in 10 specified areas (e.g., expressing ideas in writing, developing public-speaking skills, developing test-taking skills, choosing a college or technical school to attend after high school). Accompanying the Needs Assessment is a student information section which surveys plans for attending college, general areas of career/job interest, ethnicity, and religious affiliation. This latter area seems an unusual addition, particularly because the list of 22 religious groups contains only one non-Christian listing (i.e., Jewish). The PLAN authors give no rationale for the inclusion of this question.

The Interest Inventory (UNIACT, in the Technical Manual) is the assessment tool most clearly focused upon career/job planning. This inventory contains 60 items, half in a Data/Ideas Scale, and half in a Things/People Scale. Both scales are described as having substantial empirical and theoretical bases as the two most general and inclusive continua along and around which vocations can be located. These continua serve as perpendicular and intersecting axes of the World of Work Map, a graphic upon which the results of students' responses to the Interest Inventory are located. The World of Work Map has four levels, the first containing six general job clusters which are located in a circle around the axes of the two scales (arts, science, technical, business operations, business contract, social service). The second level contains from two to six groups (families) of careers/jobs (e.g., applied arts, marketing and sales, vehicle operation and repair) that fit into each of the job clusters. The third level indicates three types of normal preparation for each job cluster (high school, high school plus 1 or 2 years, and high school plus 4 or more years). The fourth level lists specific occupations according to combinations of the first three levels, job clusters, families, and types of preparation. The Interest Inventory in combination with the other tests, and a High School Course Plan form, completes the battery of tests and inventories upon which students, parents, and counselors may draw for using PLAN as a career guidance program.

Additional printed resources accompany the PLAN tests and serve to set the sequence of events for implementing the program in its entirety. Initially, students and parents review the PLAN Student/Parent Planning Guide that introduces them to the career planning process. Next, students complete the PLAN test battery. Once scores are available, students are provided with a publication entitled *Using Your PLAN Results*. This document, when used with the guidance of a career counselor, could prove invaluable as a tool for both planning a student's high-school coursework and for empowering that student as an agent of her or his own vocational destiny. Finally, the PLAN curriculum includes resources for counselors (including the Technical Manual and PLAN Program Guide), which provide helpful information for using the program to support job/career and high-school course planning.

PSYCHOMETRIC CHARACTERISTICS. As mentioned above, the achievement tests of the P-ACT+ are the centerpiece of the PLAN program. The P-ACT+ is designed to compare students with each other and with the standardization group to describe their levels of academic achievement. These tests fit precisely with accepted and current psychometric theory and technique. Extensive evidence is provided in the Technical Manual for the rigor of item development, sampling, and norm construction. The internal consistency reliability of the four tests ranges from $r = .61$ (Science Reasoning) to $r = .88$ (English) for scale scores. The standard error of measurement ranges from 1.72 (English) to 2.39 (Reading) with all tests having a maximum scale score of 32.

The authors place substantial emphasis on the content validity of the P-ACT+, indicating that these tests are "designed to be curriculum-based" (Plan Program Guide, p. 19). The Technical Manual contains a description of the manner in which test developers canvass educators and review state-adopted textbooks as bases for item development. The authors see these attempts as sufficient for removing P-ACT+ from the company of aptitude tests, which they describe as "often purposefully chosen to be dissimilar to instructional materials" (Technical Manual, p. 2). Additional validity claims are based on evidence of correlations among the four tests of P-ACT+ (ranging from $r = .56$ to $r = .71$), which are interpreted to indicate that "examinees who score well on one test also tend to do well on another" (Technical Manual, p. 29). Discriminant validity is evident in the relationship between P-ACT+ scores and students' stated educational aspirations, students' current grade levels (e.g., 9th, 10th, 11th, or 12th), and the amount of coursework completed or planned in a given academic area.

Descriptions of the other tests or inventories included in the PLAN program provide scantier psychometric information. The norms of the Study Power Assessment (SPA) are based on the responses of 6,072 9th grade students in 32 schools who completed the test in spring, 1987. The spring assessment is justified as providing information most similar to the fall 10th grade students for whom the test is intended. The demographic characteristics of these 9th grade students and schools is not clarified. Internal consistency reliability for SPA is reported at $r = .89$. Validity is supported only through content standards related to the aforementioned literature review and expert consultation.

No psychometric data are presented for the Needs Assessment, nor is any rationale provided for specifying the 10 need areas. In contrast, norms for the Interest Inventory are based on probability samples of 8th, 10th, and 12th grade students drawn from 51,000 U.S. public and private schools. The authors explain that similarities in the norms of 8th and 10th grade students allowed the extrapolation of 9th and 11th grade norms (assuming the latter's consistency with 12th grade students, but providing no additional rationale for this assumption). A potential weakness of these norms is their age, having been established in 1983. Finally, the authors provide no explicit data on the Interest Inventory's reliability and validity referring the reader to an unreferenced ACT (1985) document describing the norming of the Career Planning Program.

SUMMARY. Administration of the entire battery should require "a half day during school-supervised sessions" (Technical Manual, p. 3). In addition to the instructional time required for testing, this program would also require time for the individual counseling of each student tested. The opportunity for career counseling provided with the PLAN program is its most powerful feature. The relevance of the PLAN to the lives of high school students is in the opportunity for students to gain guidance in clarifying their career/job interests and to establish a match between those interests and their high-school coursework.

The basis of the PLAN program is the P-ACT+, a standardized measure of academic achievement. The authors provide a thorough program for moving from that test to career/job and high school course planning. However, there is no discussion of the limitations of the achievement testing results as they apply to predicting interest or success in the range of career/job options. The extent to which the P-ACT+ can be described as curriculum-based is also questionable, because it is a nationally normed instrument and is, therefore, necessarily removed substantially from the everyday curricular experiences of high school students.

Although success in school does predict success in some careers, the PLAN program has its best application with college-bound students interested in careers as professionals. That focus is consistent with ACT's focus on measuring competitive suitability for college entrance. Students who have not been supported toward professional careers and students who have other vocational interests will be less well served with the PLAN program. The PLAN rests on the vocational status quo. This program does not provide a vehicle to disturbing employment patterns seen most clearly in career/job distributions across gender, race, and class. The PLAN supports existing trends in career choice, preparation, and definition; and its developers make no claims to do otherwise.

[297]

Portland Digit Recognition Test.

Purpose: "Designed for neuropsychological assessment of exaggeration and malingering."
Population: Adults.
Publication Dates: 1989–92.
Acronym: PDRT.
Scores, 3: Easy Items, Hard Items, Total.
Administration: Individual.
Price Data, 1994: $89 per complete kit including cards, 50 answer sheets, instructions, and manual ('92, 10 pages); $9 per 50 answer sheets; $60 per cards only; $29 per manual.
Time: (40–50) minutes.
Author: Laurence M. Binder.

Publisher: Laurence M. Binder (the author).
Cross References: See T4:2052 (1 reference).

TEST REFERENCES

1. Binder, L. M., Salinsky, M. C., & Smith, S. P. (1994). Psychological correlates of psychogenic seizures. *Journal of Clinical and Experimental Neuropsychology, 16*, 524-530.

Review of the Portland Digit Recognition Test by CHARLES J. LONG, Professor of Psychology, and STEPHANIE WESTERN, Research Assistant, Psychology Department, The University of Memphis, Memphis, TN:

The Portland Digit Recognition Test (PDRT) is designed to detect malingering in patients who have a monetary incentive to perform poorly on neuropsychological tests. More specifically it proposes to measure the tendency to exaggerate memory deficits on a forced-choice number recognition test modeled after Hiscock and Hiscock (1989). Although the PDRT does help identify malingerers, there is no evidence that it can differentiate malingerers from people with factitious disorders.

Forced-choice testing or symptom validity testing has been used to measure tendencies to exaggerate symptoms such as memory impairment. The assumption is that, in a two-choice task, correct responses of less than 50% suggest the possibility of malingering. The sensitivity of malingering detection procedures was apparently increased by Hiscock and Hiscock, whose task involves recognizing which of two five-digit numbers had been seen prior to a delay of variable length. The PDRT modified the Hiscock and Hiscock procedure by introducing an interpolated task of backward counting. However, no rationale is provided for this modification, nor is any comparison research reported.

The PDRT consists of 36 cards, each with two five-digit numbers printed on them, one above the other. Four sets of 18 trials are administered. In each trial, a five-digit number is read aloud by the administrator, the subject counts backward from a specified integer for a specified amount of time, and the subject is asked to identify which of the two five-digit numbers presented visually on a card is the one previously read by the administrator. The interpolated time increases across the first three trials but is identical in Trials 3 and 4. Forty minutes or more are required for the test. A short form is discussed, but it may be premature to consider its use.

The score sheets are adequate and the stimulus cards are readable, but because the administrator has numerous items to manipulate, it might be better to have the cards freestanding and bound so that they could be turned easily.

The manual is poor. It describes briefly the results of previous research findings that are better described in the original sources. There are several nontrivial errors, such as indicating that "each recognition probe card is used twice for items 1–36" (p. 2) when each is used only once. Several details are left unexplained, such as why there are 72 trials and how the five-digit numbers were chosen. The entire description of the procedure is much clearer in the Binder and Willis (1991) study. The "PDRT Instructions to the Patient" section of the manual is especially unsatisfactory. Lines to be read directly to the subject are not differentiated from explanatory text. The suggested use of praise is unclear. There are no instructions concerning the transition from Set 3 to Set 4. Obviously much remains to be done to improve the PDRT manual.

Three scores are obtained: number correct on "easy" trials (Sets 1 and 2), number correct on "hard" trials (Sets 3 and 4), and total number correct. The manual provides cutoff scores for easy, hard, and total scores. Scores significantly below chance (50%) are assumed to reflect deliberate production of errors. Caution is advised when interpreting scores not significantly below chance, but below the worst scores obtained by people with brain dysfunction and no financial incentives. The manual suggests that other measures designed to identify malingering also be employed when there is uncertainty.

The manual states that "the hard items are more likely to yield evidence of motivation to exaggerate than the easy items" (p. 6). However, in one validation study, groups not applying for compensation ("nonmalingerers") as well as groups applying for compensation ("malingerers") were incorrect on more "hard" than "easy" trials, though the differences were small. An investigation of the differences questions whether they were statistically significant and the original source does not discuss this (Binder & Willis, 1991).

Reliability measures were obtained by comparing performance on Set 3 with performance on Set 4. Other measures of reliability such as odd/even or test-retest are not discussed. For nonpatient controls, reliability is reported to be .92. For patients with brain dysfunction who were not seeking compensation, it is .82.

A major methodological problem relates to the fact that there are no external criteria for determination of "true" malingerers. Many studies on detection of malingering rely on one of two general strategies. In the first, evaluators attempt to differentiate subjects (often college students) instructed to malinger from subjects given standard instructions. In the second strategy, subjects (patients) with financial incentives are assumed to be malingerers, and subjects without incentives are assumed to be nonmalingerers. There remains a question as to the extent that members of the group labeled "malingerers" are in fact malingering. Validation studies on the PDRT have incorporated both strategies. People instructed to malinger received lower PDRT scores than all other groups considered. People with brain dysfunction and no identified incentives to perform poorly received high scores relative to the groups seeking compensation (Binder & Willis, 1991).

The Portland Digit Recognition Test might best be considered an early attempt to develop some method for determining tendencies to exaggerate cognitive dysfunction in patients with the potential for financial gain. Although it may be an improvement over simple symptom validity testing, no data are presented to support this claim. Considerable caution should be taken in relying on a single test in this regard. The authors state that performance that is significantly below chance indicates that a patient has deliberately provided wrong answers. However, this test measures several cognitive functions and patients impaired on one or more of these cognitive functions may be reduced to chance level of performance. Obviously, the test is not designed for such patients and should be used only where there are concerns regarding the possibility of malingering on the neuropsychological test battery. It should also be used in conjunction with more traditional strategies for interpreting neuropsychological test scores. More data are needed to justify the time required by the PDRT.

REVIEWER'S REFERENCES

Hiscock, M., & Hiscock, C. K. (1989). Refining the forced-choice method for the detection of malingering. *Journal of Clinical and Experimental Neuropsychology, 11*, 967-974.

Binder, L. M., & Willis, S. C. (1991). Assessment of motivation after financially compensable minor head trauma. *Psychological Assessment: A Journal of Consulting and Clinical Psychology, 3*, 175-181.

Review of the Portland Digit Recognition Test by OREST E. WASYLIW, Senior Clinical Psychologist, Isaac Ray Center, Chicago, IL:

A critical distinction between forensic assessments and standard clinical practice is the consideration of malingering or exaggeration of symptoms (Rogers, 1988). The presentation of being disordered can be of legal benefit, as in exculpation for a criminal offense through the defense of insanity, or through the acquisition of monetary benefits in claims of personal injury or malpractice. This has led to increased interest and research by forensic psychologists and neuropsychologists in the development of various guidelines and instruments for the evaluation of malingering (Binder, 1992; Schretlen, 1988; Golden & Strider, 1986; Wasyliw & Golden, 1985; Zielinski, 1994). One major reason for the need for quantitative, psychometric procedures is that clinical insight or intuition has not been shown to be useful in the assessment of exaggerated or invented symptoms (Schacter, 1986a, 1986b; Ziskin & Faust, 1988).

The Portland Digit Recognition Test (PDRT) is a very commendable attempt to develop an empirical, quantitative procedure designed to assess the intentional fabrication or gross exaggeration of cognitive deficits. Additionally, the basic principle underlying this procedure is robust, and was originally based on similar procedures developed by audiologists to assess malingered hearing impairments (Pankratz, 1988). This principle is simply that in any equal-probability, two-alternative, forced-choice task, the highest probability of error in the long run should not exceed 50%. Any performance significantly lower than 50% implies that the subject knew the correct answer and purposely chose the incorrect one. Significance levels can then be computed using the binomial theorem. Additionally, Hiscock and Hiscock (1989) demonstrated that lengthening the stimulus-response interval increased the sensitivity of this procedure.

The PDRT stimuli consist of up to 72 presentations of five-digit numbers, printed on white 3-inch x 5-inch cards. A number is read to the subject. Then a distractor task is given, followed by presentation of two numbers simultaneously, one of which is the originally presented number. The subject must then state which number is correct. There are 18 initial trials, which include 5 seconds of interpolated activity (counting backward, aloud). A second block of 18 trials includes 15 seconds of interpolated activity; and the last two 18-block trials involve a 30-second period of interpolated activities. This form of presentation allows the subject to believe that each subsequent series is more difficult, with the expectation that if performance is being malingered, the subject will do worse with greater lengths of interpolated activities. The stimuli are composed of 18 correct numbers and 36 target cards. The 18 items and their distractors are all administered four times. Half of the time, the correct item appears above the incorrect one on recognition tasks, and half of the time it appears below. Between each block, the subject is told that the following block of items will be more difficult because the interpolated delay will be longer. If subjects perform at better than a predetermined level, they are told they are doing well.

The authors report reliability and validity data for several populations. They report split-half reliabilities of .92 on nonpatient controls and .82 for patients with documented brain dysfunction (Binder & Willis, 1991). The same study reported comparisons of six groups: Three had no monetary incentive to malinger. These were nonpatient, honest controls, patients with documented brain damage, and patients with affective disorders (but no evidence of brain damage). The latter two groups were not in any litigation. The three remaining groups were considered to have motivation to exaggerate or malinger deficits. These were a group claiming compensation for minor head injury, patients with moderate to severe brain damage (confirmed by neuropsychological testing or EEG) who were also in litigation, and normal experimental subjects instructed to malinger (dissimulators). All groups were equated on age, education, and gender. Honest controls performed better on the PDRT than any other group. Noncompensation brain-damaged and affective patients did better than the remaining groups and were about equal with each other. Litigating patients did worse, and instructed dissimulators performed worst of all. Interestingly, the experimental simulators performed at an essentially random level (49.8% correct) on the hard items of the PDRT. Some of the most severely brain-damaged subjects also performed at near-chance levels. Recommended cutoffs for simple and hard components of the PDRT are suggested. Similar, verifying data have been published following publication of the PDRT manual (Binder, 1993a; Greiffenstein, Baker, & Gola, 1994). A short form of the PDRT is described in the manual, with data subsequently published (Binder, 1993b).

A few comments are in order. First, the authors introduce the PDRT by referring to the role of effort in neuropsychological test performance. Little effort, if any, may be necessary to perform at chance levels on the PDRT, but considerable effort would be necessary to achieve scores significantly below chance levels. To do so would require that the subject remember and consciously inhibit the correct response. Parenthetically, this implies at least some efficiency in prefrontal functioning. Second, the authors make no mention of any psychological scenarios (a possible example could be Ganzer's Syndrome) in which subjects might *unconsciously* select wrong answers. A discussion of this possibility would be welcome. Third, the PDRT assesses malingering of cognitive deficits. However, patients claiming organic damage could decide to malinger emotional rather than cognitive sequelae (Wasyliw & Cavanaugh, 1989). In the classic study by Heaton, Smith, Lehman, and Vogt (1978), for example, one of the few test scores significantly differentiating malingerers from genuine patients was the *F* scale of the MMPI. Therefore, a comprehensive evaluation of neuropsychological malingering should include assessment of exaggerated psychiatric complaints. Finally, the PDRT is a fairly obvious procedure and may not fool more sophisticated malingerers. Thus, the PDRT may best be considered as a "pathognomonic sign" approach (Lezak, 1983). That is, malingering is highly likely if performance is below cutoff levels, and virtually certain if performance is significantly lower than chance. However, good performance cannot conclusively rule out malingering, and other, possibly more subtle instruments, such as the Rey 15-Item Test (Rey, 1964; Lezak, 1983) could be added for this purpose.

The PDRT has gained popularity rapidly in forensic and neuropsychological practice, and has generated considerable research (Ailinski, 1994; Nies & Sweet, 1994). The utility of this instrument has received support in a variety of contexts. It has the advantage of being relatively simple, and allows for straightforward interpretation. The authors note that the PDRT should not be used exclusively in evaluating the veracity of cognitive complaints, and appropriately emphasize the pejorative consequences of rashly labeling anyone as a malingerer. Altogether, inclusion of the PDRT should be considered in any neuropsychological evaluation when malingering is suspected.

REVIEWER'S REFERENCES

Rey, A. (1964). *L'examen clinque en psychologie* [The clinical exam in psychology]. Paris: Presses Universitaires de France.

Heaton, S. K., Smith, H. H., Jr., Lehman, R. A. W., & Vogt, A. T. (1978). Prospects for faking believable deficits on neurological testing. *Journal of Consulting and Clinical Psychology, 46*(5), 892-900.

Lezak, M. (1983). *Neuropsychological assessment* (2nd ed.). New York: Oxford University Press.

Wasyliw, O. E., & Golden, C. J. (1985). Neuropsychological evaluation in the assessment of personal injury. *Behavioral Sciences & the Law, 3*, 149-164.

Golden, C. J., & Strider, M. A. (Eds.). (1986). *Forensic neuropsychology*. New York: Plenum Press.

Schacter, D. L. (1986a). Amnesia and crime: How much do we really know? *American Psychologist, 41*(3), 286-295.

Schacter, D. L. (1986b). On the relation between genuine and simulated amnesia. *Behavioral Sciences and the Law, 4*, 47-64.

Pankratz, L. (1988). Malingering on intellectual and neuropsychological measures. In R. Rogers (Ed.), *Clinical assessment of malingering and deception* (pp. 169-194). New York: Guilford.

Rogers, R. (Ed.). (1988). *Clinical assessment of malingering and deception*. New York: Guilford.

Schretlen, D. J. (1988). The use of psychological tests to identify malingered symptoms of mental disorder. *Clinical Psychology Review, 8*, 451-476.

Ziskin, J., & Faust, D. (1988). *Coping with psychiatric and psychological testimony*. (4th ed., vol. II: Special Topics). Los Angeles: Law and Psychology Press.

Hiscock, M., & Hiscock, C. K. (1989). Refining the forced-choice method for the detection of malingering. *Journal of Clinical and Experimental Neuropsychology, 11*, 967-974.

Wasyliw, O. E., & Cavanaugh, J. C. (1989). Simulation of brain damage: Assessment and decision rules. *Bulletin of the American Academy of Psychiatry and Law, 17*(4), 373-386.

Binder, L. M., & Willis, S. C. (1991). Assessment of motivation after financially compensable minor head trauma. *Psychological Assessment: A Journal of Consulting and Clinical Psychology, 3*, 175-181.

Binder, L. M. (1992). Deception and malingering. In A. E. Puente & R. J. McCaffrey (Eds.), *Handbook of neuropsychological assessment: A biopsychosocial perspective* (pp. 353-372). New York: Plenum.

Binder, L. M. (1993a). Assessment of malingering after mild head trauma with the Portland Digit Recognition Test. *Journal of Clinical and Experimental Neuropsychology, 15*, 170-182.

Binder, L. M. (1993b). An abbreviated form of the Portland Digit Recognition Test. *The Clinical Neuropsychologist, 7*, 104-107.

Ailinski, J. J. (1994). Malingering and defensiveness in the neuropsychological assessment of mild traumatic brain injury. *Clinical Psychology: Science and Practice, 1*(2), 169-194.

Greiffenstein, W., Baker, J., & Gola, T. (1994). Validation of malingered amnesia measures with a large sample. *Psychological Assessment, 6*(3), 218-224.

Niles, K. J., & Sweet, J. J. (1994). Neuropsychological assessment and malingering: A critical review of past and present strategies. *Archives of Clinical Neuropsychology, 9*(6), 501-552.

Zielinski, J. J. (1994). Malingering and defensiveness in the neuropsychological assessment of mild traumatic brain injury. *Clinical Psychology: Science and Practice, 1*(2), 169-184.

[298]

Portuguese Speaking Test.

Purpose: "To evaluate the level of oral proficiency in Portuguese attained by American and other English-speaking learners of Portuguese."

Population: College students and adults.

Publication Date: 1988.

Acronym: PST.

Scores: Total score only.

Administration: Individual.

Forms: 3 parallel forms (A, B, C).

Restricted Distribution: Restricted to qualified test supervisors.

Price Data, 1989: $60 per examinee, including use of test booklet, master tape(s), blank cassette for examinee responses, examinee handbook, test manual (28 pages), and score report by publisher (all materials must be returned to publisher after testing).
Foreign Language Edition: Master tape available in 2 versions: Brazilian Portuguese, Lusitanian Portuguese.
Time: (40–50) minutes.
Comments: Examinee's oral responses are recorded on tape and sent to publisher for scoring; test administered by tape recording in language laboratory setting or individually by using 2 tape recorders.
Authors: Charles W. Stansfield and Dorry Kenyon.
Publisher: Center for Applied Linguistics.

Review of the Portuguese Speaking Test by ANDREW D. COHEN, Professor of English as a Second Language and Applied Linguistics, University of Minnesota, Minneapolis, MN:

There has been a recent move to design semidirect tests to facilitate assessment of oral proficiency in cases where there are few trained interviewers to conduct oral interviews. Although the earliest semidirect oral proficiency test, that of English as a foreign language, appeared a decade ago (see Stansfield, Kenyon, Paiva, Doyle, Ulsh, & Cowles, 1990), the Center for Applied Linguistics has just recently begun developing a series of semidirect oral language tests, all using the ACTFL (American Council on the Teaching of Foreign Languages) guidelines and employing visual as well as aural stimuli.

The Portuguese Speaking Test (PST) consists of six sections:

1. *Personal Conversation*, in which the respondent hears 10 questions about family, education, hobbies, etc., in Portuguese, and is to respond to each in order.
2. *Giving Directions*, in which the respondent is shown a map in the test booklet and is instructed to give directions between two points. In this and in all subsequent sections, all instructions are provided in English.
3. *Detailed Description*, in which the respondent is shown a drawing representing a variety of objects and actions, and is instructed to describe the picture in detail.
4. *Picture Sequence*, in which the respondent is instructed to speak in a narrative fashion about two sets of four or five pictures in sequence, each time being called upon to use different tenses in the narration.
5. *Topical Discourse*, in which the respondent is instructed to talk about five topics, each involving specialized content. The topics are read aloud on the tape and are also written in English in the text booklet.
6. *Situations*, in which the respondent hears and reads, in English, five printed descriptions of situations in which a specified audience and communicative task are identified. The task tests the ability to handle interactive situations through simulated role-play—involving the use of appropriate speech acts such as requesting, complaining, apologizing, and giving a formal toast.

Recently, the authors of the test have also developed a complete set of rater training materials. These include a rater training tape that contains examples of at least three examinee responses representing different levels of proficiency, and a rater training manual that describes the typical rhetorical characteristics of performance at different proficiency levels, as well as procedures for deriving the global rating. The ratings the examinee receives are recorded on a scoring sheet, and are then analyzed using the rules in the rater training manual to determine the global rating. These materials may be used independently by ACTFL trained raters. Individuals without prior experience applying the ACTFL Proficiency Guidelines may attend a 2-day workshop to learn to score the test. Raters are also given the manual and the training tape, so that they may retrain themselves prior to actually scoring the test at a later date.

The authors of the test manual conducted a validation study of the PST, and report high interrater reliability (.93 and higher) and high parallel-form reliability (again .93 and higher). Furthermore, when results on the PST were correlated with ratings of performance on a live interview (the Oral Proficiency Interview), the resulting correlations apparently ranged between .90 and .96, depending on the test form and the rater.

In a survey of 30 respondents, a majority (86%) preferred a live interview over the semidirect test. The authors of the test attribute this rating to the respondents' unfamiliarity with a semidirect test—the perceived unnaturalness of speaking to a machine. However, the high correlations between performance on the live interview and the semidirect test encouraged the test's authors to promote the PST as an important second choice in situations where direct testing is impractical or impossible. One argument raised in favor of a semidirect test is that it eliminates the interviewer effect, for example, variations in the degree of nervousness on the part of the respondent or different interpersonal relations between the respondent and the interviewer (Stansfield et al., 1990).

The first section, Personal Conversation, is intended to help the respondents begin thinking in the target language while being asked questions about their personal life that might come up in a normal conversation. Some of the questions would not, however, come up in a conversation. Instead, they seem to be the traditional types of questions containing linguistic curiosities in their structure in order to test certain verb tenses (e.g., conditionals).

In the second section, Giving Directions, the map in one of the three forms does not have the usual array of streets at right angles to each other. Hence, problems in preparing directions may be based in part on conceptual difficulties in relating to the map rather than on language deficiency.

The third section, Detailed Description, is not communicative in the modern sense of the term. The task seems to test extensively for specialized vocabulary. As with the preceding section, the fourth section, Picture Sequence, also tests for specialized vocabulary with somewhat more emphasis on verb tense.

In the fifth section, Topical Discourse, each of the five topic areas seems to call for more preparation time than the 15 seconds allowed in order to make a truly cohesive and coherent response. Part of the difficulty is due to the fact that the prompt is in English whereas the response is to be in Portuguese. In a truly communicative context, a native would, in fact, give clues to vocabulary in the very asking of the question.

The sixth section, Situations, calls upon the respondent to be creative in the use of linguistically and socially appropriate responses. Bilingual instructions would have been invaluable as several of the situations evolve around some defective item for which a complaint is being lodged and the item reflects low-frequency vocabulary (e.g., "bedroom slippers").

In summary, the aim of the semidirect test is to shorten test time while obtaining a broader sampling of the speaker's interlanguage than an oral interview would generally do—in a reliable, valid, and efficient manner. The PST would appear to be doing this well. Nevertheless, paying closer attention to item design in future revisions of this test would be advisable—issues such as authenticity in conversational questions, adequacy of time to prepare a response, problems of cognitive ability in map reading, the language of instructions, and the human interest value of the situations.

Whereas performance on the Hebrew version of the semidirect test and the Oral Interview have correlated highly (Shohamy & Stansfield, 1990), the semidirect test was found to have more features of a literary genre and the Oral Interview more features of an oral text (Shohamy, 1991). For example, there was more paraphrasing and self-correction on the semidirect test than on the Oral Interview, and more switches to native language on the Oral Interview.

In addition, the holistic scoring of the semidirect test is problematic. Whereas this instrument provides an array of speaking samples, it uses a single rating instead of multiple ratings of content vocabulary, function, and contextualized use of structure. The same criticism leveled against the Oral Proficiency Interview—that the single scale is too limiting (Bachman, 1988; Lantolf & Frawley, 1988)—can be leveled against the scales used in the semidirect test. The single rating scale lumps together different behaviors in a presumed unidimensional scale of speaking that often does not reflect reality. Hence, the test constructors deserve praise for producing this test, but attention needs to be paid to potential limitations both in this test and in others like it as the semidirect testing effort progresses.

REVIEWER'S REFERENCES

Bachman, L. F. (1988). Problems in examining the validity of the ACTFL Oral Proficiency Interview. *Studies in Second Language Acquisition, 10*(2), 149-164.

Lantolf, J. P., & Frawley, W. (1988). Proficiency: Understanding the construct. *Studies in Second Language Acquisition, 10*(2), 181-195.

Shohamy, E., & Stansfield, C. W. (1990). The Hebrew speaking test: An example of international cooperation in test development and validation. *AILA Review, 7*, 79-90.

Stansfield, C. W., Kenyon, D. M., Paiva, R., Doyle, F., Ulsh, I., & Cowles, M. A. (1990). The development and validation of the Portuguese Speaking Test. *Hispania, 73*, 641-651.

Shohamy, E. (1991). *The validity of concurrent validity: Qualitative validation of the Oral Interview with the Semi-Direct Test.* Paper presented at the 13th Language Testing Research Colloquium, Educational Testing Service, Princeton, NJ.

[299]

Position Analysis Questionnaire.

Purpose: Constructed to analyze "jobs in terms of work activities and work-situation variables."
Population: Business and industrial jobs.
Publication Dates: 1969–89.
Acronym: PAQ.
Scores: 45 dimensions in 7 divisions: Information Input, Mental Processes, Work Output, Relationships with Other Persons, Job Context, Other Job Characteristics, Overall Dimensions.
Administration: Individual.
Price Data: Available from publisher.
Time: Administration time not reported.
Comments: Ratings by 2 or more analysts; also provides estimates of selected employment tests useful for personnel selection and job evaluation points.
Authors: Ernest J. McCormick, Robert C. Mecham, and P. R. Jeanneret.
Publisher: Consulting Psychologists Press, Inc.
Cross References: See T4:2054 (17 references) and T3:1855 (12 references); for a review by Alan R. Bass, see 8:983 (17 references).

TEST REFERENCES

1. Matsui, T., & Tsukamoto, S-I. (1990). Relation between career self-efficacy measures based on occupational titles and Holland codes and model environments: A methodological contribution. *Journal of Vocational Behavior, 38*, 78-91.

2. Macan, T. H. (1994). Time-management: Test of a process model. *Journal of Applied Psychology, 79*, 381-391.

Review of the Position Analysis Questionnaire by RONALD A. ASH, Professor of Business and Psychology, Director of Doctoral Program, School of Business, University of Kansas, Lawrence, KS:

The Position Analysis Questionnaire (PAQ) is *not* a test or measure of one or more human attributes (i.e., knowledge, skill, ability, interest, trait, temperament, etc.) as is typically covered in the *Mental Measurements Yearbook*. Rather, it is a structured *job* analysis questionnaire—it is used to analyze directly the content of jobs, work, bundles of tasks, etc., as opposed to measuring directly attributes of individual human beings. The PAQ contains 195 job elements (items). The first 187 job elements relate to job activities of the work situation, whereas the last eight report the type of compensation received by the incumbents on the job, and whether or not the job is considered "exempt" (from required overtime payment) under the U.S. Fair Labor Standards Act (FLSA).

PAQ job elements (items) are *worker-oriented* rather than *job-oriented*. That is, worker-oriented elements tend to characterize the generalized human behaviors involved in work activities, or what the worker *does to accomplish* the end result of his or her actions. In contrast, job-oriented elements are descriptions of job content that typically describe *what is accomplished* by the worker, and characterize the technological aspects of jobs (McCormick, 1959). PAQ elements tap the degree of importance or the extent of use of generalized human behaviors while avoiding detailed task and technology-specific job descriptors. The PAQ was designed so that virtually any type of position or job could be analyzed with it (McCormick, Jeanneret, & Mecham, 1972).

The PAQ job elements are organized into six divisions. The first three—Information Input, Mental Processes, and Work Output—represent a stimulus-organism-response frame of reference in thinking about the major aspects of virtually any job. Generally, a person obtains information from one or more sources in the work environment, uses that information along with information that has been learned previously, and performs some physical activity resulting in some type of work output. Thus, elements in the Information Input division provide data on where and how information needed to perform the job is gained; elements in the Mental Processes division provide data on what reasoning, decision-making, planning, and information processing activities are needed to perform the job; elements in the Work Output division provide data on what physical activities are required to perform the job, and what tools or devices are used. Elements in the fourth division, Relationships with Other Persons, provide for analysis of interpersonal aspects of jobs such as the nature of communications, the types of persons with whom the job incumbent communicates, and supervisory-subordinate relationships. Elements in the fifth division, Job Context, provide for describing the work situation or environment within which the job incumbent works. The sixth division, Other Job Characteristics, consists of a variety of job elements that do not lend themselves to being classified into the other divisions (e.g., type of apparel worn, yearly continuity of work, regularity of work hours, and the presence or absence of various job demands—specified work place, time pressure, vigilance for infrequent events, travel, etc.).

The recommended approach to analyzing a job with the PAQ involves a *trained job analyst* (*a*) obtaining initial information about the job from a *preinterview job description form* (two pages) completed by the job incumbent or the immediate supervisor of the job, (*b*) conducting a semistructured interview with the job incumbent and/or supervisor using the PAQ Interview Guide (eight pages), and then (*c*) rating the job on all 195 PAQ job elements using the Position Analysis Questionnaire and the tailored machine-scorable answer sheet. A number of different response scales are used for items throughout the PAQ. The two most widely used are *extent of use* (0 = Does not apply, 1 = Nominal/very infrequent . . . 5 = Very substantial) and *importance to this job* (0 = Does not apply, 1 = Very minor . . . 5 = Extreme). Although the scale anchors correspond with the whole numbers 0 through 5, ratings between these whole numbers (e.g., 0.5, 1.5, 4.5) are permitted. Other items are rated using a dichotomous *applicability* scale (0 = Does not apply, 1 = Does apply), and still other items have unique scales (e.g., *noise intensity*—1 = Very quiet, 2 = Quiet, 3 = Moderate, 4 = Loud, 5 = Very loud).

For professional, managerial, supervisory, office jobs, and the like (generally *white collar* jobs) the job analysis data can be collected directly from incumbents and supervisors who complete the PAQ. When this procedure is used, the PAQ authors recommend that considerable guidance be provided by someone who is very knowledgeable about job analysis and the PAQ (McCormick & Jeanneret, 1988). This expert would serve as a discussion leader to interpret the PAQ items in terms directly related to the jobs being analyzed for those incumbents and supervisors who actually complete PAQs. When using this procedure it is desirable to have three or four incumbents who hold the same job plus the supervisor of the job complete separate PAQs independently. This allows for a reliability check of the data, and computation of composite (average) answers for each PAQ item, which can serve as the final job analysis data. This method generally is *not* recommended for *blue collar* jobs/employees due to the relatively high verbal ability required to read and understand the PAQ (Ash & Edgell, 1975).

When job analysis data have been collected for all jobs to be analyzed, the data are sent to PAQ Services for processing. This can be accomplished by mailing the optically scannable PAQ answer sheets, or by sending data via modem using a PAQ data management microcomputer software package called Enter-Act. Standard data processing reports provided include a listing of PAQ item ratings for visual inspection and error detection, a consistency check pointing out related items which may have been answered inconsistently (e.g., the total time the worker spends in BODY POSITIONS/POSTURES exceeds 100%), a reliability analysis when multiple records are submitted for the same job, a job profile, and a job attribute profile for each job analyzed.

To produce the job profile, the PAQ job elements are used to compute 32 division job dimension scores (the job elements within each division were subjected to principal components factor analysis with varimax rotation to derive the division job dimensions), and 13 overall job dimensions scores (almost all of the PAQ job elements were subjected to a similar principal components factor analysis to derive the overall job dimensions). These two sets of job dimensions were derived through factor analysis of a sample of 2,200 jobs considered to be representative of the American labor force (technical manual). The job profile also lists the PAQ items with the highest percentile scores, job evaluation points (indicating the relative dollar value of the job), probability that the job is exempt under FLSA, a job prestige score, predictions of the range of test scores expected for persons employed in this job for nine aptitudes measured by the General Aptitude Test Battery (GATB) (e.g., verbal, numerical, spatial, clerical perception, motor coordination), and estimated Myers-Briggs Type Indicator (MBTI) information for persons holding this type of job.

The job attribute profile reports expert opinions about the human attributes required to perform the work behaviors necessary for the job. The job attribute scores are based on psychologists' ratings of the relevance of 76 human attributes to each of the PAQ job elements. Forty-nine of these are aptitudes (e.g., mechanical ability, perceptual speed, arithmetic reasoning); the other attributes are of an interest or temperament nature (e.g., dealing with things or objects, pressure of time, dealing with people). Other reports can be generated upon request by selecting options specified in the User's Manual for the PAQ.

How reliable is job analysis data based upon the PAQ? The Technical manual for the PAQ reports average interanalyst reliability of $r = .68$ for 325 jobs in the administrative offices of an insurance company, and an average "rate-rerate" reliability over a 90-day period of $r = .78$ for 427 "pairs" of jobs. However, the manual also notes that in cases of the analysis of jobs with many zero or "Does not apply" ratings for the PAQ job elements, inflated reliability coefficients can result.

How useful is PAQ job analysis information and how practical is the PAQ system to use relative to other methods of job analysis? Levine, Ash, Hall, and Sistrunk (1983) report on perhaps the most comprehensive comparative evaluation of seven job analysis methods conducted to date. Ninety-three job analysts working in both private and public sector organizations evaluated seven different job analysis methods in terms of 11 organizational purposes and 11 practical considerations. The PAQ was rated as highly useful for 7 of the 11 purposes, including job classification, job evaluation, (identification of) personnel requirements and specifications, worker mobility, efficiency/safety, manpower/work force planning, and (meeting) legal/quasi-legal requirements. Task Inventory and Functional Job Analysis methods were rated higher than the PAQ for purposes of job description, job design, performance appraisal, and worker training. The PAQ was rated high on virtually all aspects of practicality, including occupational versatility/suitability, standardization, respondent/user acceptability, sample size required, reliability, cost, quality of outcome, and time to completion, among others. However, the PAQ does require a relatively high amount of job analyst training for effective use.

The Position Analysis Questionnaire (PAQ) is a structured *job analysis* instrument using generic job elements that permit the analysis of virtually any job in the world of work in terms of work activities and work-situation variables. PAQ results provide descriptions of job content in terms of standardized scores on 32 division job dimensions or 13 overall job dimensions, and levels of various human attributes likely required for successful performance in the job or occupation in question. It is one of the highest rated job analysis methods in overall practicality, and for the purposes of job evaluation, job classification, and the identification of personnel requirements and specifications. On the other hand, task-based approaches to job analysis appear to be superior to the PAQ for purposes of job description, job design, and development of worker training programs. The PAQ system is sophisticated, and requires a knowledgeable job analyst for effective use.

REVIEWER'S REFERENCES

McCormick, E. J. (1959). The development of processes for indirect or synthetic validity: III. Applications of job analysis to indirect validity, A symposium. *Personnel Psychology, 12*, 402-413.

McCormick, E. J., Jeanneret, P. R., & Mecham, R. C. (1972). A study of job characteristics and job dimensions as based on the Position Analysis Questionnaire (PAQ). *Journal of Applied Psychology, 56*, 347-368.

Ash, R. A., & Edgell, S. L. (1975). A note on the readability of the Position Analysis Questionnaire (PAQ). *Journal of Applied Psychology, 60*, 765-766.

Levine, E. L., Ash, R. A., Hall, H., & Sistrunk, F. (1983). Evaluation of job analysis methods by experienced job analysts. *Academy of Management Journal, 26*, 339-348.

McCormick, E. J., & Jeanneret, P. R. (1988). Position Analysis Questionnaire (PAQ). In S. Gael (Ed.), *The job analysis handbook for business, industry, and government* (vol. 2; pp. 825-842). New York: John Wiley & Sons.

Review of the Position Analysis Questionnaire by GEORGE C. THORNTON III, Professor of Psychology, Colorado State University, Fort Collins, CO:

The purpose of the Position Analysis Questionnaire (PAQ) is to provide a quantitative analysis of job activities in virtually any job in business or industry. Ratings on 187 job elements are computer scored to yield evaluations of 45 job dimensions. Further derivations of this information are useful for specifying personnel selection requirements, conducting job evaluation and setting compensation rates, identifying job families, and developing performance appraisal systems. I have found that the PAQ is not particularly helpful for developing a training program or for identifying differences among jobs within a job family, especially at the managerial level.

The PAQ is designed to analyze worker-oriented job requirements (McCormick, 1979) in terms of worker behaviors and work-situation variables, rather than job-oriented requirements such as tasks completed. An advantage of a worker-oriented analysis is applicability across a wide range of jobs; a limitation is that it does not tell what work is accomplished.

The job elements consist of rating scales that ask the analyst to judge the importance or extent of use of behaviors falling into the following a priori categories: Information Input, Mental Processes, Work Output, Relations with Other Persons, Job Context, and Other Characteristics. The 1989 edition of the PAQ has been reformatted, but the job elements remain the same as earlier editions. For some rating scales, the points are anchored only with general adjectives; for other scales, the levels are anchored with behavioral examples or illustrative jobs. The reading level of many PAQ elements is quite high, but revisions in the format and slight revisions in wording have made the questionnaire easier to follow. Many sophisticated judgments are still required. These judgments are aided by an excellent job analysis manual that includes descriptions of each element and examples of jobs rated at each level of all rating scales.

Acceptable levels of interrater agreement (median correlations of two raters = .68) and rate-rerate reliability (median correlation = .78) have been found. It is generally recommended that the ratings of two analysts are averaged, but acceptable data result from one well-trained analyst.

A strength of the PAQ is that it provides information relevant to a variety of applications (Levine, Ash, Hall, & Sistrunk, 1983). I have found the PAQ particularly helpful for hypothesizing what aptitude tests will be valid for personnel selection and for conducting job evaluation. In one organization, the PAQ predicted that a general intelligence test, a mechanical reasoning test, and an eye-hand coordination test would probably be valid for selecting applicants for a manufacturing maintenance job. Justification for this use of the PAQ comes from extensive research in which the job elements were linked to human attributes. As an example of a job evaluation application, we used the PAQ to set pay rates for all jobs in a city government. Since that time, the PAQ has been useful for classifying new jobs and for conducting audits of jobs that allegedly changed over time. Justification for this use comes from evidence that PAQ dimension scores have been found to be systematically related to existing wage rates.

Numerous factor analyses using different job samples and scoring methods support the stability of the 13 overall dimensions (e.g., having decision, communicating, and general responsibility; operating machines/equipment) and 32 divisional dimensions (e.g., interpreting what is sensed; performing skilled/technical activities). Studies have shown that the type of rater influences the results (i.e., self and supervisor ratings yield higher dimension scores in comparison with ratings by a third-party independent analyst). I have experienced particular difficulty asking job incumbents to fill out the PAQ in job evaluation studies.

The supporting materials for the PAQ are exemplary. The new technical manual gives an updated and detailed description of the 30-year research program behind the PAQ, evidence of reliability and validity, and its many uses. An elaborate user's manual is provided to aid job analysts in completing the PAQ and interpreting the results.

PAQ Services is particularly helpful in identifying ways that the PAQ can be used in individual organizations, providing answers to questions, and providing data for research studies. For example, it provided average dimension ratings for selected jobs from the extensive PAQ data base, which we then related to the acceptability of drug testing (Murphy, Thornton, & Prue, 1991).

REVIEWER'S REFERENCES

McCormick, E. J. (1979). *Job analysis: Methods and applications.* New York: AMACOM.

Levine, E. L., Ash, R. A., Hall, H., & Sistrunk, F. (1983). Evaluation of job analysis methods by experienced job analysts. *Academy of Management Journal, 26*, 339-348.

Murphy, K. R., Thornton, G. C., III, & Prue, K. (1991). Influence of job characteristics on the acceptability of employee drug testing. *Journal of Applied Psychology, 76*, 447-453.

[300]

Positive and Negative Syndrome Scale.

Purpose: Designed to assist in the assessment of schizophrenia.
Population: Psychiatric patients.
Publication Dates: 1986–92.
Acronym: PANSS.
Scores: 9 clinical dimensions: Positive Syndrome, Negative Syndrome, Composite Index, General Psychopathology, Anergia, Thought Disturbance, Activation, Paranoid Belligerence, Depression.
Administration: Individual.
Price Data, 1993: $95 per complete kit including manual ('86, 59 pages), 25 QuikScore™ forms, and 25 Structured Clinical Interview forms; $30 per manual, $30 per 25 QuikScore™ forms; $50 per 25 SCI-PANSS Structured Clinical Interview forms.
Time: (30–40) minutes.
Authors: Stanley R. Kay, Lewis A. Opler, and Abraham Fiszbein.
Publisher: Multi-Health Systems, Inc.
Cross References: See T4:2055 (1 reference).

TEST REFERENCES

1. Sevy, S., Kay, S. R., Opler, L. A., & Van Praag, H. M. (1990). Significance of cocaine history in schizophrenia. *The Journal of Nervous and Mental Disease, 178*, 642-648.

2. Weiner, R. U., Opler, L. A., Kay, S. R., Merriam, A. E., & Papouchis, N. (1990). Visual information processing in positive, mixed, and negative schizophrenic syndromes. *The Journal of Nervous and Mental Disease, 178*, 616-626.

3. Fenton, W. S., & McGlashan, T. H. (1992). Testing systems for assessment of negative symptoms in schizophrenia. *Archives of General Psychiatry, 49*, 179-184.

4. McGlashan, T. H., & Fenton, W. S. (1992). The positive-negative distinction in schizophrenia: Review of natural history validators. *Archives of General Psychiatry, 49*, 63-72.

5. Dollfus, S., Petit, M., & Menard, J. F. (1993). Relationship between depressive and positive symptoms in schizophrenia. *Journal of Affective Disorders, 28*, 61-69.

6. Caton, C. L. M., Shrout, P. E., Eagle, P. F., Opler, L. A., & Felix, A. (1994). Correlates of codisorders in homeless and never homeless indigent schizophrenic men. *Psychological Medicine, 24*, 681-688.

7. Cournos, F., Guido, J. R., Coomaraswamy, S., Meyer-Bahlburg, H., Sugden, R., & Horwath, E. (1994). Sexual activity and risk of HIV infection among patients with schizophrenia. *American Journal of Psychiatry, 151*, 228-232.

8. Docherty, N. M., Sledge, W. H., & Wexler, B. E. (1994). Affective reactivity of language in stable schizophrenic outpatients and their parents. *The Journal of Nervous and Mental Disease, 182*, 313-318.

9. Fields, J. H., Grochowski, S., Lindenmayer, J. P., Kay, S. R., Grosz, D., Hyman, R. B., & Alexander, G. (1994). Assessing positive and negative symptoms in children and adolescents. *American Journal of Psychiatry, 151*, 249-253.

10. Javitt, D. C., Zylberman, I., Zukin, S. R., Heresco-Levy, U., & Lindenmayer, J. (1994). Amelioration of negative symptoms in schizophrenia by glycine. *American Journal of Psychiatry, 151*, 1234-1236.

11. Lysaker, P., Bell, M., Beam-Goulet, J., & Milstein, R. (1994). Relationship of positive and negative symptoms to cocaine abuse in schizophrenia. *The Journal of Nervous and Mental Disease, 182*, 109-112.

12. Marder, S. R., & Meibach, R. C. (1994). Risperidone in the treatment of schizophrenia. *American Journal of Psychiatry, 151*, 825-835.

13. Opler, L. A., Caton, c. L. M., Shrout, P., Dominguez, B., & Kass, F. I. (1994). Symptom profiles and homelessness in schizophrenia. *The Journal of Nervous and Mental Disease, 182*, 174-178.

14. Lysaker, P., & Bell, M. (1995). Work rehabilitation and improvements in insight in schizophrenia. *The Journal of Nervous and Mental Disease, 183*, 103-106.

15. McDermott, B. E. (1995). Development of an instrument for assessing self-efficacy in schizophrenic spectrum disorders. *Journal of Clinical Psychology, 51*, 320-331.

Review of the Positive and Negative Syndrome Scale by BARBARA J. KAPLAN, Psychologist, Western New York Institute for the Psychotherapies, Orchard Park, NY:

Use of the Positive and Negative Syndrome scale (PANSS) requires that the individuals to be assessed already be diagnosed as schizophrenic. This 30-item instrument looks at the symptomatology of schizophrenia primarily in terms of two clusters of "positive" and "negative" symptoms. Positive symptoms are those that represent an addition of certain specific characteristics in schizophrenia compared to normal mental status, such as hallucinations, delusions, grandiosity, and suspiciousness. Negative symptoms are those that represent absences in schizophrenia compared to normal mental status, such as blunted affect, emotional withdrawal, passivity, and difficulty in abstract thinking. Additional scales include a Composite (Positive minus Negative), General Psychopathology, and Aggression Risk. A series of studies covering the various scales, their standardization, reliability, and validity has been published.

The original normative sample consisted of 240 schizophrenic inpatients, with a high proportion of minorities and males. Several additional studies have since been conducted that enhance the validity of the instrument and indicate its usefulness in discriminating chronic from acute schizophrenics, helping to direct the choice of pharmacological treatment and evaluating posttreatment effects. Particularly interesting are the studies of the PANSS that address the PANSS' validity in predicting drug responsiveness and aggression.

Administration and scoring of the PANSS are fairly straightforward; however, this is not a diagnostic instrument. It is most usefully administered to schizophrenic patients when some additional information as to the profile of symptoms is desirable. It should not be administered or interpreted by someone without considerable knowledge of schizophrenic patients. The ratings of severity are made on a 7-point scale by the person administering the test. Although there are guidelines in rating the severity of symptoms, it is important that interrater reliability be established and periodically reassessed when the PANSS is used because the instrument itself depends to a great extent on clinical experience. The anchor points for the scales are likely to drift without reestablishing interrater reliability on a periodic basis.

The scoring manual for the test details the limitations and aptness of the instrument for various purposes. Although the PANSS is not a diagnostic instrument, the information it provides should function to illuminate some of the finer differentiations in schizophrenic patients.

The PANSS appears to be most appropriately used in trying to determine whether patients will be drug-responsive or drug-resistant to neuroleptics. The profile of symptoms focuses on what psychopharmacological agent might be effective. In addition, the PANSS offers some provocative data relevant to improving predictions of the risk of violent behavior. Additional use of the PANSS for these purposes would provide useful and welcome information.

Review of the Positive and Negative Syndrome Scale by CECIL R. REYNOLDS, Professor of Educational Psychology, Texas A&M University, College Station, TX:

The Positive and Negative Syndrome Scale (PANSS) was originally made available in 1986 and subsequently published in 1992. The PANSS was developed and standardized to differentiate dimensions of schizophrenia that are noted in the current diagnostic nomenclature as being primarily positive or negative symptom types. The PANSS includes 33 items scored for a Positive scale, Negative scale, Composite, a General Psychopathology scale, and a supplemental aggression index. Additional scores derived after the initial conceptualization of the scale include symptom clusters named Anergia, Thought Disturbance, Activation, Paranoid/Belligerence, and Depression. The PANSS was adapted from two prior psychiatric rating instruments, the Brief Psychiatric

Rating Scale and the Psychopathology Rating Schedule, published in the 1960s and 1970s. In developing the PANSS, the authors state that their objective was to provide a well-defined, standardized technique for positive-negative evaluation that attends to the methodological and psychometric considerations related to developing an understanding of schizophrenic syndromes.

The PANSS is, in fact, a structured interview completed over a period of 30 to 40 minutes by a mental health professional in direct contact with the patient. Based upon the responses to the structured interview recorded in the PANSS interview booklet, a rating scale is completed from which *T*-scores are derived. The entire process is estimated by the reviewer at just over one hour. Data gathered from the structured interview are rated on a 7-point rating scale ranging from *absent* to *minimal* to *mild* and on up to *severe* and *extreme*. No rationale for choosing a 7-point rating scale is provided. The manual also recommends that in order to achieve reliability with the PANSS, two or more trained individuals should independently complete the PANSS ratings, based on the completed structured interview schedule. Thus, the scale begins very quickly to involve a substantial amount of professional time and may not be an efficacious approach to diagnosis.

The PANSS is well conceptualized but has a host of psychometric problems in addition to being lengthy and consuming an inordinate amount of professional time relative to the information gleaned.

The PANSS was standardized on a sample of 240 schizophrenics with a DSM-III diagnosis that is indicated as "confirmed" but no indication as to how this occurred is noted. The norms are provided in a single table of *T*-scores for the entire age range of 18 years to 68 years, with no data to support this grouping and numerous developmental reasons for other groupings. Schizophrenia also differs in presentation to some extent by age of onset also arguing against the lack of age-graduated norms. The sample likely does not reflect the demographic distribution of schizophrenics as it was composed of 179 males, 61 females, 106 Blacks, 60 Whites, and 74 Hispanics. The *T*-scores derived from the PANSS are described in a somewhat confusing manner in the manual. The four-page chapter on interpretation of the PANSS indicates that PANSS *T*-scores are linear *T*-scores that do not transform the actual distribution of the variables. Subsequently, we are told that on the profile form in the column next to the *T*-scores, percentiles are given which are based on the normal curve and represent an algebraic transformation of the *T*-score. The *T*-scores for the various scales have common percentile rankings, thus it appears that the *T*-scores have been normalized, yet the narrative in the manual remains contradictory in this regard.

Just over three pages of the manual are devoted to issues of reliability and validity. The alpha reliability coefficients reported for the primary scales are consistently above .70 and appear to be quite good given the nature of the scale and the construct assessed. However, the reliability coefficients are based on an age range of 48 years and include a host of demographic characteristics that do not mimic population parameters. Because this may increase item variance artificially, the reliability estimates may be spuriously inflated. Test-retest reliability appears satisfactory as well yet significant sample problems are evident and we are not told whether raw scores or scaled scores were used in their derivation.

Several studies of criterion-related validity are reported in the manual and indicate that, in fact, the positive and negative items on the PANSS are negatively correlated as one would predict. Patients classified independently as having negative versus positive schizophrenia also showed a difference in the predicted direction on the various PANSS scales. Improvement in PANSS ratings following treatment with neuroleptic medication is also noted as providing validity data for the PANSS. In general, however, the validity studies reported provide scanty information; much more detail would be helpful to those who use the scale.

A factor analytic study of the PANSS is reported using the 30 items that make up the rating scales completed on the basis of responses to the interview from the normative sample of 240 schizophrenic inpatients. The method of principal components with equimax rotation was used and yielded seven orthogonal factors accounting for just under *65%* of the total variance. These results are interpreted in the manual as providing support for the PANSS. However, it appears that the factor structure is extremely complex and a full matrix of factor loadings is absent from the manual, which reports only factor loadings chosen by the authors. A full table of factor loadings would have been more useful in deciding upon the true patterns represented in the data. With only *65%* of the variance attributable to the intercorrelations of the items using a principal components approach, adequacy of domain sampling and the strength of the PANSS must be questioned.

The PANSS represents an interesting approach to differential diagnosis within the schizophrenic disorders. It is conceptualized well and provides systematic information. The quantitative application of the PANSS, however, is sorely lacking due to the psychometric problems represented and the length of the procedure. It is not clear that a traditional mental status exam and clinical interview with the patient would not yield equivalent diagnostic information and consume far less professional resources. Demonstration of the superiority of the PANSS to traditional diagnostic approaches that require less professional be necessary prior to investing in the use of this diagnostic technique. When applied to research studies of differential diagnosis within schizophrenic subtypes, the PANSS has much to offer and its use therein is encouraged. If revised, psychometric concerns and developmental phenomena deserve considerably more attention.

[301]

Practical Maths Assessments.

Purpose: Designed to assess knowledge and skills in practical mathematics.
Publication Date: 1990.
Administration: Group.
Price Data: Available from publisher.
Time: Administration time not reported.
Comments: Other test materials (e.g., dice, calculators) must be supplied by examiner.
Authors: Derek Foxman, Neil Hagues, and Graham Ruddock.
Publisher: NFER-Nelson Publishing Co., Ltd. [England].

a) TEST A.
Population: Age 9.
Scores, 4: Dice, Calculator, Length, Squares and Counters.
Comments: Orally administered.

b) TEST B.
Population: Ages 10–11.
Scores, 4: Same as *a* above.

c) TEST C.
Population: Ages 12–13.
Scores, 4: Making Lengths, Area, Calculator, Making Boxes.

Review of the Practical Maths Assessments by ANTHONY J. NITKO, Professor of Education, University of Pittsburgh, Pittsburgh, PA:

The Practical Maths Assessments is a series of performance tests in basic mathematics. The authors recommend that teachers use the tests in the context of the United Kingdom's National Curriculum. The assessments are organized into three nonoverlapping tests: A, B, and C. Test A is for primary school (Year 4), Test B for the last two years of primary school (Years 5 and 6), and Test C for the first two years of secondary school (Years 7 and 8).

Each test contains four subtests (called "topics"). Students perform these activities under standardized conditions, then answer the accompanying questions. Test A's topics are Dice, Calculator, Length, and Squares and Counters; Test B's are Squares and Counters, Length, Calculator, and Dice; and Test C's are Making Lengths, Area, Calculator, and Making Boxes. Although the subtests of the different levels have identical names, the activities and questions differ, being appropriate to the grade levels for which the test is targeted.

The authors want teachers to use these standardized materials and administration procedures to obtain performance information useful for diagnosing students' misconceptions and misunderstandings of mathematics concepts keyed to the National Curriculum Attainment Targets. Because the materials and directions for administration are standardized, teachers are able to (*a*) assess students in a group and (*b*) reference subtest scores to percentile norms.

The diagnosis itself, however, must be carried out under nonstandardized conditions. Teachers must: (*a*) carefully review each student's test booklet responses, (*b*) personally observe the way a student solves the problems and responds to the materials, and (*c*) personally interview a student to discover how and why the student responded as he or she did. Using a standard set of materials makes the process convenient for a teacher and permits comparisons across students.

Each task and question is accompanied by a marking key that provides a rubric for assigning marks (including partial credit in some cases). When the subtests are scored in this way, each subtest's scores range from a possible zero to 10 marks. These scores are referenced to percentile charts to obtain a norm-referenced profile for each student.

If teachers are to interpret percentile ranks properly, they must know how representative the sample is of the nation. The manual says that the norming sample is "proportionately stratified" (p. 122) to represent England. The strata are mentioned, but we are not told how many schools or children come from each school type, region, or type of county. Neither are we told how the sample was selected. We are told that Test A norms are based on 732 children from 28 schools, Test B norms on 1,235 children from 52 schools, and Test C on 1,619 children from 69 schools. There is a breakdown for each school year (4, 5, 6, 7, and 8) as well. Because the degrees of representativeness of the norming samples are unknown, it is entirely possible that a teacher who interprets a student's performance as indicating the student's relative standing in England will be incorrect.

The word reliability is used in the manual, but it is dismissed as inappropriate! For example, the authors say KR20 cannot be used because the items are not scored dichotomously. They never mention, however, that there are many appropriate procedures for assessing reliability from a single administration (e.g., coefficient alpha, intraclass correlation, and many generalizability coefficients). They acknowledge that it is possible to obtain test-retest reliability but dismiss failing to carry out such studies because they want teachers to focus on the diagnostic information in the students' answers. No mention is made of the reliability of the marking (scoring) by different teachers or the reliability of the diagnosis different teachers might make from the identical written responses of pupils. The authors have done England's mathematics teachers a disservice by failing to conceptualize for them the need for having consistent scores and diagnostic identifications. The authors' failure to conduct and report reliability studies illustrates the lack of a technical basis for score interpretation.

Just over 100 words are devoted to the topic of validity, none of which address the topic meaningfully. Messick (1989), among others, describes the dangers of using the tripartite content, criterion, and construct validity. Modern validity theorists describe how some persons select one of these three "types" and claim their test usage is valid. The Practical Maths Assessments' authors represent a good illustration of this type of inappropriate validation claim. Again, the authors' failure to present a solid technical case for the validity of the interpretations and uses they recommend is a disservice to England's teachers.

Are there redeeming features of this assessment? Perhaps. The tasks appear to offer teachers the opportunity to assess students' performance on meaningful mathematics skills. The assessment focuses on performance tasks and not multiple-choice items. However, the performances are "closed" in the sense that a single answer is required. It would be useful to supplement this set of tasks with "open" ones for which multiple solutions are possible and for which a teacher could observe a richer display of mathematical thinking skills.

The manual authors offer useful suggestions to teachers for interpreting student responses. The authors provide appropriate cautions concerning possible nonmathematics-related factors (such as language) that may affect the students' responses. The strategies students in the standardization used to complete the tasks are often described in detail sufficient for teachers to identify conceptual errors in their own students. The authors provide clear explanations of the main features of correct performance, major types of errors and misconceptions, and how to extend the assessment to similar tasks.

For many tasks, the authors describe the percent of students in the standardization sample who received various marks and committed types of errors. It would have been very useful if the authors had focused less on describing the distribution of task *marks* (scores), and more on the distribution in the standardization sample of the percent of students who demonstrated various types of mathematical thinking on each of the tasks. The "benchmarks" of the Toronto Board of Education provides an example of this latter approach (Clark, 1992).

SUMMARY. The Practical Maths Assessments cannot be defended as a scientifically sound measuring instrument based on the technical data provided by the authors. The basis for the percentile norms is unknown. It lacks appropriate data on reliability of marking and diagnosis. Its validity has not been fleshed out. The tasks appearing in the assessment are useful and appropriate, both inside and outside of Great Britain. The tasks, however, are generally "closed" and focus on obtaining a single correct answer. This is a drawback if your mathematics curriculum claims to foster broader and more open views of appropriate mathematical thinking. The manual contains useful descriptions of typical pupil responses to the tasks. The authors give suggestions for identifying and remediating students' errors during classroom instruction. The Practical Maths Assessments' main utility appears to be its use as an informal assessment of students' attainment of an important, but limited, set of mathematics learning targets.

REVIEWER'S REFERENCE

Messick, S. (1989). Validity. In R. L. Linn (Ed.), *Educational measurement* (3rd ed.) (pp. 13-104). Phoenix: The Oryx Press.

Clark, J. L. (1992). The Toronto Board of Education's Benchmarks in mathematics. *The Arithmetic Teacher: Mathematics Education Trhough the Middle Grades*, *39*(6), 51-55.

Review of the Practical Maths Assessments by MICHAEL S. TREVISAN, Assistant Professor of Educational Leadership and Counseling Psychology, Washington State University, Pullman, WA:

The Practical Maths Assessments are a collection of mathematics performance assessments designed to assess a portion of England's National Curriculum Attainment Targets. These assessments provide student achievement data on practical mathematics problems typically found in activities of daily living, such as measuring and calculating. More specifically, the results from the assessment are diagnostic, providing information for teachers concerning the strengths and weaknesses of students in relation to the achievement targets. There are three tests designed for ages 9 through 12. Test A, which is given to the younger students, is administered orally. This product is relatively new, having been normed in 1989. The specimen set contains sample tests, an easy-to-read teacher's manual, and is copyrighted 1990.

STANDARDIZATION. A proportionately stratified random sample of schools was chosen to establish the norming group. Region, type of school, and metropolitan or nonmetropolitan counties were variables chosen to obtain the most accurate representation of England. The number of students participating was 3,586 across 149 schools. The sample spanned grades 4 through 8 (referred to as National Curriculum Years). Test A is appropriate for National Curriculum Years 4, Test B for Years 5 and 6, and Test C for Years 7 and 8. Directions for administration were provided to participating teachers. These same directions are supplied in the Teacher's Manual obtained with the purchase of the test.

ADMINISTRATION. There are three options for administering this assessment. The first option follows the administration procedures used during standardization. This is the appropriate option for comparing assessment scores to the percentile norms. The second option allows some flexibility in administration, providing the opportunity for the teacher to interact with the students. The third option is less formal than the others, and provides for interaction among students as well as with the teacher. All procedures are well documented in the Teacher's Manual. The test can be administered with large or small groups. There is no time requirement for the test but should comparison to the norms be necessary, the publisher recommends administering the test in two sessions with a break in between. The publisher admonishes the user against making comparisons to the norm group unless the *formal* administration procedure used during standardization is followed. Some equipment is needed for this assessment, such as dice, paper clips, and a calculator. This equipment is not supplied with the purchase of the assessment.

SCORING. Scoring of the Practical Mathematics Assessments is based on a maximum of 10 points assigned per task based on the observation and judgment of the scorer. The higher the score the better the student has performed. This is true for all exercises across the three tests. A rubric indicating standards and associated points is supplied for each problem in the Teacher's Manual.

DIAGNOSTIC INFORMATION. Located in the Teacher's manual are suggestions for interpretation and use of the test results. This information is supplied for each task within each test. The information is predominantly narrative, suggesting why students make mistakes in general and why mistakes might be made specific to the topics tested. Additional information is provided concerning the task difficulty. The task difficulty is presented in two ways. First, the percentage of students in the standardization sample who obtained 0 to 2 points and 8 to 10 points for each task is given. Second, the percentage of students in the standardization sample who attained a certain degree of accuracy in relation to each task is also provided. For example, students in the standardization sample taking Test B were asked to draw a circle with a radius of 5 centimeters. The percentage of students drawing these circles within .1 and .2 centimeters of the required radius are reported. Percentile norms are also available relating the number of points obtained on a topic to a percentile range. For example, if a student obtained a score of 4 on the calculator topic for Test A, this student would be said to have performed as well or better than between 42% and 57% of the standardization sample. The task difficulty data, percentile norms, and narrative information provide a comprehensive approach for teachers to diagnose student strengths and weaknesses in relation to the targets assessed. The publisher does a fine job of integrating this information in the Teacher's Manual, maximizing diagnostic power.

NEW VALIDATION CRITERIA FOR PERFORMANCE ASSESSMENTS. Establishing validity evidence has plagued the development of many conventional standardized tests. Performance assessments are no exception. The nature of these tasks along with scoring based on observation and judgment pose additional problems for obtaining validity evidence not found when validating traditional tests. These unique validation problems have stimulated some to offer validation criteria appropriate for the demand of ensuring high quality performance assessments (Linn, Baker, & Dunbar, 1990). These criteria include the consequences of the assessment, fairness, transfer and generalizability (in part, reliability), cognitive complexity, content quality, content coverage, meaningfulness, cost, and efficiency. Evaluating the Practical Maths Assessments with these criteria may prove revealing and instructive. It should be stated that because the criteria were proffered in 1990, after the development of the assessment, the authors of the test had no way of using these criteria. Nevertheless, given the rapid development of performance assessments in this country and the far-reaching influence testing companies have in educational assessment, a validity check of this sort is needed to protect the consumer from poor products and inform publishers and users of the standards needed to ensure quality. A critique of this type will also move away from the noncritical rhetoric of the performance assessment movement and toward a balanced, cohesive view of educational measurement. To this end, because these criteria are new, each will be defined. A brief analysis concerning how well the Practical Maths Assessments meets each criterion will be provided.

CONSEQUENCES. There are consequences to test score interpretation for all assessments, intended or unintended. On a performance assessment such as the Practical Mathematics Assessments a consequence that must be considered is whether or not teachers will narrow their teaching and instruction to what is assessed. Narrowing teaching and instruction to what is assessed leaves important achievement targets untaught. Students given this kind of instruction would have less of an education than others taught with a broader range of achievement targets. The number of targets on the Practical Maths Assessments is small so a shift in instructional emphasis to these targets may not have a large impact on instruction because ample time would be available for instruction on other achievement targets. Nevertheless, consequences of a performance assessment on test score interpretation should be carefully considered.

FAIRNESS. Fairness refers to whether or not scores received on each test actually reflect the true achievement level of the student and not the bias of the scorer. Although fairness for a diagnostic test may not warrant the same level of concern as on a high-stakes achievement test, the quality of the information is directly related to the objectivity of the scorer. Without training scorers, the objectivity of scores obtained through observation and judgment is suspect. For the Practical Maths Assessments, no evidence of training was stated in the documentation nor is any requirement for training indicated for users. This limits the validity of scores until the publisher provides evidence of some type of training in order to apply fairly and appropriately the rubrics for the assessment of tasks. In addition, fairness might also consider performance differences between segments of the population as an indicator of the lack of fairness. No analysis of this type of fairness (or lack of) was supplied by the publisher. Fairness then, is suspect for the Practical Maths Assessments.

TRANSFER AND GENERALIZABILITY. Transfer and generalizability refers to the validity of generalizing from the scores on an assessment to a larger domain. For the Practical Maths Assessments, the question is how well the scores on this test generalize to the achievement domains tested. Part of this question is answered through reliability information. However, traditional measures of reliability are insufficient for performance assessments. This reviewer agrees with the publisher that a measure of internal consistency, for example, is not appropriate for the Practical Maths Assessments. However, this does not relieve the publisher from supplying other, more appropriate reliability estimates. Unfortunately, no reliability information was provided with the Practical Maths Assessments. This is inadequate, especially given the nature of the test. Specifically, when observation and judgment are required for scoring, evidence of inter-observer reliability is a must (Trevisan, 1991). Another part to the transfer and generalizability issue is task variability. Variability from task to task is a problem with performance assessments (Shavelson, Baxter, & Pine, 1992). This variability limits valid generalizations. The publishers of the Practical Maths Assessments did not provide data on this issue. Therefore, the Practical Maths Assessments have not met the criterion of transfer and generalizability.

COGNITIVE COMPLEXITY. Much of the argument for using performance assessments is the potential to assess targets not easily assessed with conventional methods (i.e., cognitively complex targets). Just because an assessment is labeled a performance assessment, however, does not mean that it automatically assesses a complex cognitive target. Evidence for this must be provided. To the publisher's credit, evidence for this is provided in the Teacher's Manual in narrative form. Certainly, some of the information about the percentage of students obtaining the correct answer (or close to it) provides other information regarding cognitive complexity. However, the narrative information provided in the Teacher's Manual is excellent, informative, and publishers contemplating building performance assessments are asked to refer to the rich information provided with the Practical Maths Assessments.

CONTENT QUALITY. Content quality is presumed in this test because it is tied to England's National Curriculum. Tremendous time and effort is demanded for curriculum development of this magnitude. Decisions regarding appropriate targets are not considered lightly. Therefore, content quality for the Practical Maths Assessments is a safe assumption.

CONTENT COVERAGE. Content coverage in performance assessments is often lacking because the amount of time needed for any one task works against the total number of tasks on a test, decreasing the content coverage. With only four targets assessed on each test, the Practical Maths Assessments suffers from this problem as well. Potential users should consider the tradeoff between the information gained from these few targets and the lack of information on targets not assessed.

MEANINGFULNESS. Part of the appeal for performance assessments is the potential to present more relevant or meaningful experiences to students than might otherwise be found in conventional tests. An analysis of the tasks on the Practical Maths Assessments provides solid evidence for meaningfulness. The obvious need to solve problems required in activities of daily living is strong justification.

COST AND EFFICIENCY. The issue of cost and efficiency concerns the cost of the test and how easy it is to administer. Performance assessments often require a great deal of time to administer and special equipment for the assessment. The Practical Maths Assessments require other equipment that will increase the cost of the assessment. If this equipment is not in sufficient supply, added cost will be incurred to obtain the needed equipment. Or, the teacher will need to devise a way of assessing a few students at a time while providing activities for the others. Although this is by no means insurmountable, it does pose planning problems for the teacher.

COMMENTS ON USE IN THE UNITED STATES. The link to England's curriculum is strong, stated in the Teacher's manual, and reflected in the tests. The publisher should be commended for linking curriculum and assessment. However, this strength for England may be its weakness in the United States. The achievement targets assessed may not be achievement targets espoused by districts and states in the United States. The match between a state or district's curriculum and this assessment should be carefully considered before this assessment is adopted by educators in the United States.

The test requires equipment not supplied with its purchase. For example, calculators are required, comprising 25% of each test. The publisher believes this equipment is commonly found in schools and should, therefore, not pose a problem for users of the test. Although this may be true in England it is not true in the United States. This reviewer has had the opportunity to observe and work in dozens of classrooms and school buildings throughout the country. Calculators were noticeably absent in most of these places. Potential users in the United States should consider the cost of purchasing needed equipment as well as the test before its adoption. Even in fiscally solvent times the additional cost of equipment may be too much for many U.S. schools and districts. Given the small number of achievement targets assessed, the cost becomes even more difficult to justify.

If students in the United States are to be given this assessment they must also know something about the metric system and England's currency. Some of the exercises require measuring lengths in centimeters (centimetres) and adding or subtracting money in terms of the British pound. This issue alone may mitigate against the use of this assessment in the United States.

SUMMARY AND RECOMMENDATIONS. In summary, the Practical Maths Assessments are a collection of performance assessments in the beginning stages of development, most appropriate for use in England. Further development would include technical information on the assessments and validation issues addressed. With a few exceptions, the publisher has done an excellent job with a difficult task; that is, constructing sound performance assessments. At this time, however, the assessment is not recommended for use in the United States (for reasons previously addressed) and users in England should carefully consider the aforementioned issues before adoption.

REVIEWER'S REFERENCES

Linn, R. L., Baker, E. L., & Dunbar, S. B. (1991). Complex, performance-based assessment: Expectations and validation criteria. *Educational Researcher*, *20*(8), 15-21.

Trevisan, M. S. (1991, April). Reliability of performance assessments: Let's make sure we account for the errors. In P. Wolmut (Chair), *Measurement issues in performance assessment*. Symposium conducted at the annual meeting of the American Educational Research Association, Chicago, IL.

Shavelson, R. J., Baxter, G. P., & Pine, J. (1992). Performance assessments: Political rhetoric and measurement reality. *Educational Researcher*, *21*(4), 22-27.

[302]

The Pragmatics Profile of Early Communication Skills.

Purpose: Developed to provide a descriptive and qualitative analysis of a child's typical communicative behaviours by means of a structured interview with a parent or other caregiver.

Population: Infancy to age 5.

Publication Date: 1988.

Scores: No scores; provides summary of skills in 4 areas: Communicative Intentions, Response to Communication, Interaction and Conversation, Contextual Variation.

Administration: Individual.

Price Data, 1992: £28.75 per complete profile/manual (46 pages).

Time: [30] minutes.

Authors: Hazel Dewart and Susie Summers.

Publisher: NFER-Nelson Publishing Co., Ltd. [England].

Review of The Pragmatics Profile of Early Communication Skills by DAVID MacPHEE, Associate Professor of Human Development and Family Studies, Colorado State University, Fort Collins, CO:

Effective intervention with children depends on accurate information about their behavior in everyday environments. As well, P.L. 99-457 mandates collaboration with caregivers in the assessment of young children and in the design and implementation of intervention. The Pragmatics Profile is consistent with both of these aims. It is a structured interview that capitalizes on caregivers' more extensive experience with children's communication in various settings. The information gained is to be used in designing home- or school-based interventions directed at communication skills, and to monitor progress.

This instrument is distinctive for its emphasis on pragmatics and its developmental orientation. Unlike many language assessments that emphasize deficits in vocabulary or speech, the Pragmatics Profile focuses on a number of skills related to effective communication. These include the form of communication used to express various intentions (e.g., gain and direct attention, requests, express emotions); how the child responds to various inputs such as requests, questions, and directives; and conversational give-and-take—how the child initiates and maintains interactions, conversational repairs, and clarifications. The fourth area assessed, Contextual Variation, relates to the range of people, places, and topics that may affect communication as well as awareness of social conventions. The developmental foundation is apparent in a series of tables displaying major milestones in preschool communication. Thus, the Pragmatics Profile is somewhat unique in its assessment of the *social* as opposed to cognitive functions of language.

These pragmatic skills are assessed with 33 open-ended questions that focus on how rather than how often or well the child communicates. To avoid having caregivers make judgments about specific language delays or which aspects of language are important to note, the questions focus on concrete events and everyday experiences. Examples of relevant behaviors are provided as prompts but respondents are urged to provide their own examples of the child's typical behavior. Rather than numerical scores, the product is qualitative information that is grist for the professional's interpretation. Only the broadest of guidelines are given for interpreting caregivers' responses, and these are usually either select examples or general possibilities such as enhanced caregiver awareness or expansion of the range of intentions used by the child. Thus, different therapists may reach disparate conclusions at the interview's completion, depending on their familiarity with developmental patterns and deviations, and their skill at eliciting relevant information from the caregivers.

The Pragmatics Profile does provide a systematic framework for making clinical judgments about early communication skills. Yet the paucity of explicit guidelines for interpreting responses and for linking responses to specific intervention strategies could be frustrating for less experienced therapists. If the emphasis on pragmatics is a new clinical perspective, as the authors suggest, then professionals will need much more guidance on how to use the information gained from this assessment. The lack of validity data also is a significant problem. One study did find that language-delayed children used less mature forms of communication and had fewer opportunities for conversations with peers. The Profile's utility would be enhanced if it was shown to be sensitive to intervention effects and to discriminate between groups with different language disorders.

In sum, the Pragmatics Profile is a structured clinical interview that focuses on preschool children's communication. Its strengths include richness of information about pragmatics in everyday contexts, which can be used as the basis for intervention, and development of collaborative relationships with caregivers in language assessment and intervention. Drawbacks include lack of guidelines for interpreting caregiver responses and translating them into intervention strategies, and absence of research evidence for its clinical utility—either to monitor progress in intervention or to differentiate among children with distinct language disorders. Thus, the Pragmatics Profile is most profitably used as an adjunct in providing services to preschoolers with communication problems, not as a primary screening or diagnostic tool.

Review of The Pragmatics Profile of Early Communication Skills by SHERWYN MORREALE, Director, Center for Excellence in Oral Communication, University of Colorado at Colorado Springs, Colorado Springs, CO, and RAY FENTON, Supervisor of Assessment and Evaluation, Anchorage School District, Anchorage, AK:

The Pragmatics Profile of Early Communication Skills assesses the language development of young children through the collection of information outside of a clinical setting from adults who have had the opportunity to observe the child in a number of situations. Informants might be parents, teachers, or anyone who has had extensive experience with the child.

The Pragmatics Profile was developed to extend the assessment of children beyond the clinical setting and to improve the quality of information that a speech therapist, educational or clinical psychologist, or teacher might have concerning a client. The authors suggest that the measure would have utility for any teacher with a special interest in speech and language development, teachers of children with special needs, or teachers of children for whom English is a second language. It is also suggested as a tool for those who might wish to do research on language development.

Information is solicited in four general areas: Communication Intentions, Response to Communication, Interaction and Conversation, and Contextual Variation. Informants answer standard questions related to each of the general areas. For example, Communication Intentions are considered based on questions related to Attention Directing, Requesting, Rejecting, and Greeting. The informant/observer is asked to note specific examples of how the child behaves in regard to each area. The observations are then considered relative to the developmental expectations for that area, as described in the Profile.

The authors do provide a brief account of the major stages in language development. The developmental cycle is considered in five periods: birth to 9 months, 9 to 18 months, 18 months to 3 years, 3 to 4 years, and 4 years and beyond. Typical communication behaviors are identified for each age span. After considering the observed behaviors reported by the informant, as related to the typical developmental cycle, the data collector completes a summary sheet with comments on the four areas of communication being assessed.

The authors stress that the information collected is qualitative and that data may be collected over time. This may include information collected by various individuals in various contexts. Examples are provided of the types of observations that might be recorded. The authors point out that the examples given are not all-inclusive and are not meant to be considered as a scale of development. They suggest that the examples might be used as prompts when interviewing a person.

The manual comprising the first 21 pages of The Pragmatics Profile of Early Communication Skills provides information on the background of the instrument, the pragmatic approach to communication, the approach developed in the profile, information on the construction of the profile, a description of the profile, a guide to use and administration, and a discussion of the implications for intervention. The manual is well written and provides ideas, examples, and detailed information on administration and use of the tool.

No statistical information on the validity or reliability of the profile is provided, nor is there direct evidence presented of the tool's efficacy for planning interventions or measuring the success of specific interventions. A key word search of the ERIC system found no published references to the use of the instrument as either a clinical or research tool. However, the instrument has good face validity and should be useful in helping the clinician or teacher develop a better understanding of the communication behaviors of a student or client. The general nature of the observations and the open response format limit the utility of the instrument as a screening tool and work against the use of the instrument as a measure of growth. These limitations also affect the value of the measure for researchers.

Two alternative measures might be considered which address some of the same skill areas included in The Pragmatics Profile of Early Communication Skills. The Joliet 3-Minute Speech and Language Screen (Revised) (Kinzler & Johnson, 1992; T4:1324) provides a quick, standardized screening. It is an individually administered measure of vocabulary, grammar, phonology, voice, and fluency designed to identify students who may need additional assessment and review for speech and language services. Another alternative, which is more achievement oriented and includes some communication skills, is the Test of Auditory perceptual Skills (Gardner, 1985; T4:2742), which is one of a group of several early childhood abilities tests from the same publisher. Both of these alternative measures offer scaled scores and information on norming populations and past clinical use.

To summarize, The Pragmatics Profile of Early Communication Skills is a good tool for developing a profile of a child's communication skills based on the observations of those who have had the opportunity to see the child in a variety of situations. The Profile is limited by some of the various features which make it attractive. The lack of specific data and quantification of behavior indexes reduce its utility. It would be highly useful in getting to know a child, but less useful as a diagnostic or evaluative tool.

REVIEWER'S REFERENCES

Gardner, M. F. (1985). Test of Auditory Perceptual Skills. Burlingame, CA: Psychological and Educational Publications, Inc.

Kinzler, M. C., & Johnson, C. C. (1992). Joliet 3-Minute Speech and Language Screen (Revised). Tucson, AZ: Communication Skill Builders.

[303]

Preschool Screening Test.

Purpose: "Designed to assess the [developmental] skills of preschool-aged, early elementary or mentally handicapped children."

Population: Age 2 through Grade 2 level children.

Publication Dates: 1983–89.

Scores: 7 developmental areas: Fine Motor, Personal/Social Visual, Visual Identification, Number Concepts, Discrimination/Matching, Readiness/Academic.

Administration: Individual.

Price Data, 1989: $150 per complete kit; $10 per 50 answer sheets; $15 per 50 fine motor drawing sheets.

Time: [20–30] minutes.

Author: Carol Lepera.

Publisher: Preschool Screening Test.

Review of the Preschool Screening Test by RUTH E. TOMES, Assistant Professor of Family Relations and Child Development, Oklahoma State University, Stillwater, OK:

The Preschool Screening Test, according to its author, was designed to measure academic functioning level as well as to provide a basis for setting "academic goals in a chronological developmental order" (p. 1) for children from age 2 years through grade 2. The name of this test is misleading. It is neither a screening test in the usual sense (i.e., as an indication that a child may have a problem that should be further investigated) nor is it suitable for preschoolers given the characteristics of the norming sample (described later). The test grew out of the author's work with mentally handicapped school-aged children. Its use was later extended to preschool-aged, developmentally disabled, and (apparently) nondisabled early elementary children as a "quick, yet accurate, screening instrument" (p. 1).

The Preschool Screening Test consists of 100 items arranged in seven developmental areas: Fine Motor, Personal/Social, Visual Identification, Language Concepts, Number Concepts, Visual Discrimination/Matching, and Readiness/Academic. Each area is further divided into seven age/grade levels: 24–30 months, 30–36 months, 36–48 months, 48–60 months, 60–72 months, grade 1, and grade 2. All materials for administration and scoring are included in the test kit. The attractive spiral-bound manual contains instructions for the examiner, stimuli for most test items, and technical information; additional materials are manipulatives that consist of counting blocks, colored discs, beads, crayons, and scissors. Included in the cost of the test is permission to copy the 4-page answer forms and 14-page fine motor drawing forms. This information, as well as some of the other information omitted from the manual (e.g., test administration time), is contained in a brochure/order form distributed by the publisher.

Administration of the Preschool Screening Test takes 20–30 minutes and is easily accomplished by following the clearly written instructions in the manual. Visual-motor tasks are given first followed by personal/social items to obtain a basal and ceiling level. The examiner starts the remainder of the test at the age/grade level where all items are passed (basal) and just before failures begin to occur (ceiling). Items are scored as pass, emerging, or fail according to criteria established in the manual. Only passes are considered in determining starting points and in interpreting the results in terms of "readiness age level" to be used for writing educational goals. The test total raw score may be converted to a standard score (M = 100, SD = 15) for children in kindergarten, first, and second grade. The manual does not describe how the raw score is calculated. This is a serious omission because the raw score is the basis for the standard score that the author claims can be used for comparison purposes at these age levels.

The Preschool Screening Test was standardized on 170 school-aged children randomly selected from kindergarten, first, and second grade classes in an Indianapolis township and on 34 preschool-aged children from the same area. The school-age sample was composed of 63 kindergarten, 58 first grade, and 49 second grade children. Distribution by sex of the children at each level is reported. No information is reported on race, SES, or whether the samples included children with disabilities. Sample sizes are small at every age level. The problem becomes serious at the preschool level. Presumably children ranging in age from 2 to 5 years were included in the sample of 34. An age breakdown is not reported, but it would appear that as few as eight or nine children may have been tested at each of the preschool age levels into which the test is divided for purposes of determining basal, ceiling, and interpretation as "readiness age." Further, all statistical analyses reported in the manual and summarized in the following paragraphs were based on these samples and thus must be considered suspect.

Of concern also is the procedure used in developing the Preschool Screening Test. No information is provided in the manual for selection of test items nor for their placement within particular age/grade levels. A rationale for "readiness age" decisions is also lacking. Item analyses were performed to determine difficulty of items and correlations of individual items and correlations of individual items with total scores. In general, the results of these analyses support the overall ordering of test items by difficulty. However, these results are suspect given that they were derived from data obtained from the inadequate norming sample. Again, no empirical evidence is provided for age-placement of items.

Reliability evidence includes coefficient alpha and split-half correlation with Spearman-Brown adjustments. Both techniques provided evidence that the Preschool Screening Test has sufficient internal consistency. The coefficient for the total sample was .98 and alphas ranged from .78 (coefficient alpha for grade 2) to .98 (both techniques for preschool). No data pertaining to test-retest reliability are presented.

Validity data for the Preschool Screening Test were obtained for kindergarten, first, and second grade by correlating test total scores and developmental area scores with teacher evaluation of school performance by assigned grades. These values were relatively low, ranging from .14 for second grade academic readiness to .73 for first grade total test score with teacher evaluation of academic readiness. Some evidence for construct validity may be inferred from the data for kindergarten, first, and second grade in that the mean test scores increased as the students progressed from grade to grade. It must be noted that no validity data pertain to the preschool age group.

In summary, the Preschool Screening Test is attractive to children and easy to administer. Beyond this, there is little to recommend its use, especially at the preschool level. If one's purpose is to screen, then either the Battelle Developmental Inventory Screening Test (T4:264) or the AGS Early Screening Profiles (24) would be better choices. If one wishes to measure academic readiness, then the Battelle Developmental Inventory (T4:263) or the Metropolitan Readiness Tests (233) would provide more adequate bases for instructional goals.

[304]

The Prevocational Assessment and Curriculum Guide.

Purpose: Designed to "assess and identify the prevocational training needs of handicapped persons."
Population: Mentally retarded individuals.
Publication Date: 1978.
Acronym: PACG.
Scores: 9 categories: Attendance/Endurance, Independence, Production, Learning, Behavior, Communication, Social Skills, Grooming/Eating, Toileting.
Administration: Individual.
Price Data, 1994: $12 per complete kit including inventory, summary profile sheet, manual (6 pages), and curriculum guide.
Time: [15–20] minutes.
Comments: Ratings by professional acquainted with individual; title on test is PACG Inventory.
Authors: Dennis E. Mithaug, Deanna K. Mar, and Jeffrey E. Stewart.
Publisher: Exceptional Education.

Review of The Prevocational Assessment and Curriculum Guide by RICHARD A. WANTZ, Associate Professor of Human Services and Director of the Office for Counseling and Life Planning Services (OCLPS), and SUSAN K. SPILLE, Graduate Clinical Coordinator for the OCLPS, College of Education and Human Services, Wright State University, Dayton, OH:

The Prevocational Assessment and Curriculum Guide (PACG) is designed for developing training programs for moderately, severely and profoundly handicapped persons who are preparing for sheltered employment. The PACG represents about 15 years of development by the authors and may be administered by a professional or paraprofessional familiar with the person's behavior patterns in work situations similar to those described in the inventory. Administration can be accomplished by either direct observation of the person in situations where responses would be similar to those assessed in this instrument or an interview with an observer who has had the opportunity to witness the person in work situations.

The authors target four functions for the PACG:

1. To assess and identify the prevocational training needs of handicapped persons.

2. To analyze behavior and skill deficits in terms of sheltered employment expectations.

3. To prescribe training goals designed to reduce identified deficits, and

4. To evaluate client performance by administering the instrument at the beginning of training in order to define appropriate goal areas and then periodically after training has commenced to determine progress toward training goals (manual, p. 1).

The PACG is a single 11-inch x 17-inch sheet folded to form four pages 8.5 inches x 11 inches and is divided into three assessment categories that assess and identify: (*a*) "worker behavior" in areas of Attendance/Endurance, Independence, Production, Learning, and disruptive/deviational "Behavior"; (*b*) the worker's Communication and Social "interaction skills"; and (*c*) the worker's Grooming/Eating and Toileting "self-help skills." After completion of the inventory, skill and behavior deficits that require further training can be determined by noting areas where the person's levels of performance are found to be unacceptable for entry into sheltered employment. In this manner the person's prevocational needs can be addressed. The assessment package also includes a separate PACG Summary Profile Sheet for graphing the nine factors assessed and allows for gains over time and a PACG Curriculum Guide which specifies intervention goals for each factor.

Validation and stability indicators were assessed in the late 1970s. In the manual the authors outline procedures used to establish content validity, item selection, cross validation, discriminant validity, and reliability. The PACG content item selection procedures were conducted in five northwestern states. Cross validation procedures were conducted in 15 activity centers and workshops in Kansas. Predictive validity was not established for three factors; the instrument failed to discriminate accurately for average skill level for the diagnostic categories of Attendance/Endurance, Grooming/Eating, and Toileting. Internal consistency reliability was determined by the odd-even numbered items split-half procedure. This procedure resulted in a strong significant internal consistency. No evidence is provided regarding the stability of the inventory.

The weaknesses of the inventory are (*a*) that the PACG is based on the perceptions and descriptions of the person administering the assessment, hence there may be differences from one professional to the next if they are not equally competent with evaluation methods and knowledgeable of the examinee; (*b*) cross validation norms are 15 years old and have not been tested for specific subpopulations; (*c*) the manual lacks comprehensiveness, is only four pages in length, and has not been updated to comply with the *Standards for Educational and Psychological Testing* (AERA, APA, NCME, 1985); and (*d*) case studies are not provided in the manual.

This inventory addresses important issues for employment of persons with disabilities and could be a useful evaluation tool for the vocational rehabilitation counselor as well as the employer. The PACG is recommended as a tool to provide insight regarding the development of training programs for handicapped clients who are preparing for sheltered employment. Examiners should use the PACG as a method to structure the focus of observations. However, examiners must keep in mind the lack of predictive power of the Attendance/Endurance, Grooming/Eating, and Toileting factors.

REVIEWER'S REFERENCE

American Educational Research Association, American Psychological Association, & National Council on Measurement in Education. (1985). *Standards for educational and psychological testing.* Washington, DC: American Psychological Association, Inc.

Review of The Prevocational Assessment and Curriculum Guide by JEAN M. WILLIAMS, Director, Effective Practices Specialty Option, PRC Inc., Indianapolis, IN:

The Prevocational Assessment and Curriculum Guide (PACG) is designed to identify prevocational training needs of handicapped persons, analyze behavior and skill deficits in terms of sheltered employment expectations, prescribe training goals to reduce identified deficits, and evaluate performance. The assessment contains 46 items in the following subcategories: Attendance/Endurance, Independence, Production, Learning, Behavior, Communication, Social Skills, Grooming/Eating, and Toileting. The PACG is completed by a professional or paraprofessional who knows the student's behavior patterns in each of the nine subcategories. It is recommended that such knowledge be based upon observations of the students in situations where they display responses assessed by the instrument.

The answer sheet contains descriptive statements about behavior in each of the nine subcategories. Two to six alternative answers are provided for each statement to indicate the level of response or existence of behavior. Ratings are given both numerical scores and an indication of whether the observed behavior falls within goal level.

Identifying training needs and selecting training goals is done by noting those areas in which the student falls short of goal level. For each area, the rater is referred to a curriculum guide containing a series of goal statements corresponding to the nine subcategories listed above. Goal statements are used to develop a comprehensive educational program. Numerical scores are used to compare the student's scores with those of persons entering sheltered employment. Scores are plotted on a Summary Profile Sheet, which is used to track progress over time as the student is observed and rated at regular intervals.

The four-page manual contains a description of the test population of 179 handicapped persons from 10 to 60 years of age who were diagnosed as profoundly, severely, or moderately handicapped. Many of the subjects had multiple handicaps, and all were enrolled in state institutions, community habilitation centers, or public schools.

RELIABILITY AND VALIDITY. Validity evidence is based on two surveys that identified skills and behaviors supervisors consider to be important for entrance into sheltered employment. In the first, 56 sheltered workshop supervisors in five states identified skills and behaviors they considered necessary for employment in their workshops. The survey was replicated in 15 activity centers in a different state. The Pearson r correlation between the two surveys was .83 (p = .001). Items included on the PACG are those identified by 85% or more of respondents of both surveys as important for entry into sheltered employment. Response levels and goal areas were also based upon survey data.

Twenty-six teachers rated the 179 subjects on the PACG. A split-half (odd and even items) reliability coefficient of .92 (p = .001) was calculated.

SUMMARY. The Prevocational Assessment and Curriculum Guide is easy to use and quick to administer. The profile sheet and other accompanying materials are written for paraprofessionals, so they are easily understood and user friendly. The key to using this scale seems to be identifying persons who are sufficiently knowledgeable about students to rate them on the 46 items, many of which require judgements about the frequency and quality of activities and interactions between the subject and peers or supervisors.

The Summary Profile Sheet on which results are recorded provides a visual representation of students' strengths and weaknesses in the nine subcategories. This is the most effective part of the PACG as it provides a mechanism for tracking student progress over time and also indicates whether students are ready for sheltered employment. The manual does not indicate how these results should be interpreted. Some test results may create thorny questions about a student's readiness for sheltered employment. For instance, it is possible that a student would score above "Workshop Level" on eight subcategories but be deficient in a single category. Does this deficiency indicate lack of readiness for employment or merely a need for extra supervision once employed?

Cross referencing assessment items to curriculum goals is quickly and easily accomplished. Once deficiencies are identified, teachers need only look at the answer sheet to determine objectives to be included on an individualized educational plan. These objectives, however, appear to be very broad with no suggestions as to how they may be accomplished. Although the process of completing and scoring the inventory and cross referencing deficiencies to behavioral goals may be accomplished by a paraprofessional, a professional educator would need to address identified deficiencies by designing an educational plan or set of strategies designed to move students toward attainment of these goals.

The predictive validity of this approach may be of questionable value. Although assessment developers were able to categorize successfully 179 persons classified as moderately, severely, and profoundly mentally retarded on all of the subscales except Attendance/Endurance, Grooming/Eating, and Toileting, they also included a disclaimer to users that, "The results you obtain may differ widely from these data." They suggest that users should concentrate on training students rather than making comparisons to the test population. These comments suggest that this instrument does not accurately predict how well students will perform in a workshop environment.

[305]

Prevocational Assessment Screen.

Purpose: "Designed to assess a student's motor and perceptual abilities in relation to performance requirements within a local vocational training program."
Population: Grades 9–12.
Publication Date: 1985.
Acronym: PAS.
Scores, 16: Time and Error scores for 8 modules: Alphabetizing, Etch A Sketch Maze, Calculating, Small Parts, Pipe Assembly, O Rings, Block Design, Color Sort.
Administration: Individual.
Price Data, 1989: $1,195 per complete kit including manual (50 pages) and computer software for use in scoring and reporting.
Time: (60–65) minutes.
Author: Michele Rosinek.
Publisher: Piney Mountain Press, Inc.

Review of the Prevocational Assessment Screen by STEPHEN L. KOFFLER, Managing Director, Center for Occupational and Professional Assessment, Educational Testing Service, Princeton, NJ:

The Prevocational Assessment Screen (PAS) was designed to assess motor and perceptual abilities of 14- to 18-year-old handicapped students (defined by the PAS manual to be mildly learning disabled, mildly retarded, or mildly emotionally disturbed) or disadvantaged students (defined by the PAS manual to be economically or educationally deprived and functioning at least one grade below grade level) in relation to performance requirements within a local vocational training program. The PAS was initially developed in a special needs evaluation laboratory in the Cobb County, Georgia School System to provide special needs educators with an alternative to the Vocational Rehab/Department of Labor model of assessment.

A stated purpose of the PAS is to give a school's "vocational team an indication of what a student needs to successfully complete the training program in which he or she enrolls" (manual, Appendix B, p. 2). The PAS includes eight hands-on activities, each measuring a different trait, and a computerized scoring and reporting system (for both Apple and IBM). The activities—Alphabetizing, Etch A Sketch Maze, Calculating, Small Parts, Pipe Assembly, O Rings, Block Design, and Color Sort—can be administered in any order and over any time setting required. All materials required, including activities, manual, and computer disks, are included in the PAS package.

OVERALL EVALUATION. Based on the information provided in the manual, the PAS in its current form has little to offer and clearly must be considered as still under development and in need of further research. The PAS manual provides insufficient detail about the PAS development, interpretation, and other essential information one would expect. The manual itself needs much work in terms of grammar, spelling, punctuation, and English usage.

SCORING. There are two facets for the scoring of each of the PAS activities—the time it takes an examinee to complete the activity and the number of errors made by the examinee. However, there is no error score for the Small Parts activity, and the methods for scoring errors for the Color Sort and O Rings activities are questionable. Percentiles are provided separately for both time and errors. However, the manual instructs the administrators of the PAS to "obtain a combined rarting (*sic*) by adding the time and error percentile for each sample then divide by two" (manual, p. 8). Such a procedure is clearly problematic because percentiles are not on an interval scale and hence cannot be added. In addition, only selected percentile ranks are provided in the manual's norms table which makes that table difficult to use.

NORMS. The PAS norms were determined by "psychometric techniques and by predetermined time studies (MTM-1)" (manual, Appendix B, p. 5). The norms were generated in eight urban, suburban, and rural secondary and postsecondary vocational training schools in Georgia. According to the manual, additional normative data have been collected from different systems throughout the country; however, it is not clear whether the latter data are included in the manual's norms table. Finally, there is no indication provided to suggest that the students in the norm group are representative of a larger population. Thus, the generalizability of the data beyond the selected schools in Georgia may be questionable.

The manual indicates the "validation research samples" are based on 293 students, of which 112 are average students, 121 are handicapped students (ages 14–16, not 14–18), and 61 are disadvantaged students. However, it is not clear (*a*) why the average students were included in the norming group or how "average" is defined, (*b*) whether norms are based on all three groups of students (especially because the one norms table included in the manual has a heading that reads "average high school students"), or (*c*) whether error percentiles are based on empirical data on the MTM-1 study.

VALIDITY. The manual indicates the PAS "can be used in a variety of ways to assess the aptitudes, work behaviors, learning styles and cognitive performances of students pursuing an occupational course of study" (manual, Appendix B, p. 1). However, there is little, if any, validity evidence provided to substantiate this claim. There is also little evidence provided to show the PAS is valid for the special needs and disadvantaged populations for which it is intended.

In general, validity evidence is sparse. The manual indicates that content validity is established via a Vocational Performance Matrix which sets up a direct relationship between the eight traits and the importance of each activity in each vocational training area. However, no evidence is provided to show how the content validity evidence is established nor how the activities are valid measures of the traits.

The norms table divides the percentile distribution into five categories (superior, above average, average, below average, and needs improvement). There is no explanation about how these categories were developed nor of the validity of their use. Finally, the manual reports the results of an MTM-1 predetermined time study that was conducted to provide criterion-related validity evidence. However, there is no indication of what the MTM-1 predetermined time study is nor how its results or the data furnished provide such evidence.

RELIABILITY. Test-retest reliability data are provided for all of the activities except for the Color Sort and Calculating activities. No information is presented to explain the lack of reliability data for those activities. It is also not clear as to what scores are being compared (number of errors, time, or both). Further, the reliability data are based on 50 average students in the norming sample, not the handicapped nor the disadvantaged students.

In summary, the PAS manual states that "from the inception of PAS in 1981, the developers never intended the module to be a highly scientific or predictive testing instrument" (manual, Appendix B, p. 1). Rather, the intent of the PAS is "to provide secondary special needs educators with an informal, uncomplicated method of gathering vocationally relevant information so that when a student is mainstreamed into a regular vocational training program the curriculum can be modified to accommodate the student's special needs" (manual, Appendix B, pp. 1–2). Nevertheless, even informal instruments must satisfy the principles of measurement called for in the *Standards for Educational and Psychological Testing* (AERA, APA, & NCME, 1985). The PAS, in its current form, does not satisfy those principles. Much more research is needed to clarify the validity, reliability, and usefulness of the PAS in vocational settings, especially for its intended special populations. There are too many questions about the PAS that need resolution before it can be recommended for use.

REVIEWER'S REFERENCE

American Educational Research Association, American Psychological Association, & National Council on Measurement in Education. (1985). *Standards for educational and psychological testing*. Washington, DC: American Psychological Association, Inc.

Review of the Prevocational Assessment Screen by JAMES B. ROUNDS, Associate Professor of Educational Psychology, University of Illinois at Urbana-Champaign, Champaign, IL:

The Prevocational Assessment Screen (PAS) is designed to assess motor and perceptual abilities for mildly handicapped and disadvantaged youth. The PAS was developed to assist special needs educators in student placement in a vocational training program and seems to be modeled after the Department of Labor's (1970) General Aptitude Test Battery. Eight abilities are assessed with a single module (test) per ability (in parenthesis): clerical/verbal (Alphabetizing), motor coordination (Etch A Sketch Maze), clerical/numerical (Calculating), finger dexterity (Small Parts), manual dexterity (Pipe Assembly), form perception (O Rings), spatial perception (Block Design), and color perception (Color Sort). Two scores are reported for each ability test: an error score (the number of incorrect items), and a timed score consisting of the amount of time in minutes to complete the test. The actual test materials and the software that includes a scoring program and a local norms development system were not included with the manual and therefore are not reviewed here.

Once subtest time scores are obtained they can be converted into percentile scores based on PAS high school norms or compared to predetermined time criterion values (the average time it would take an average worker to perform the subtest). Five-point scale ratings varying from 1 = *superior* to 5 = *needs improvement* are then assigned separately to the student's percentile scores and the student's time criterion scores for each subtest. These rating scores for the eight abilities can be compared to a vocational performance matrix of ability (performance) requirements by vocational training programs. The PAS provides a vocational performance matrix with instructor ratings, varying from 1 = *critically significant* to 5 = *no significance*, of the eight abilities for 19 vocational training programs (e.g., auto mechanics). By matching the student's abilities with the ability requirements of training programs, it is assumed that recommendations can be offered for areas of remediation.

Conceptually, the PAS system, modeled after the Department of Labor referral system, has the potential to link student abilities to vocational curricula. The actual contents of the PAS system, however, are poorly constructed and documented. For example, the PAS high school norms are inadequate. The norms for the eight ability subtests are based on an accidental sample from the state of Georgia of 81 to 136 "average" students, aged 14–18 years, ranging in education levels from 9th to 12th grade. The authors, however, acknowledge limitations of the normative sample and urge users to develop local norms. The manual does not discuss: (*a*) how the cutting scores were determined for the high school percentile norms or the predetermined time criterion values that result in the 5-point ability rating scores, and (*b*) how instructor's ratings were developed for the vocational performance matrix. But the author does caution the user on the applicability of the PAS vocational performance matrix, again urging users to develop local norms.

More problematically, the manual simply does not provide information to support the intended uses of the PAS scores. The author makes several inaccurate claims about the PAS validity. The author asserts that the "Content validity is established via the Vocational Performance Matrix" (manual, Appendix B, p. 8). By no stretch of the imagination is the Vocational Performance Matrix an indicator of the content validity of the PAS. One study, a predetermined time study of the PAS subtests, is cited to support the criterion-related validity. This time motion study, however, does not provide information about what the subtests measure.

The author refers the reader to Appendix B for "a factor analysis" (of what is not indicated). I could not find the "factor analysis" in Appendix B. I then called the Piney Mountain Press and asked for information on the factor analysis. The press sent the technical manual for the Skills Assessment Module (SAM; 1985; T4:2472). In the SAM manual, I found an outline of a "non-technical factor analysis" (p. 10) of 12 SAM subtests (7 of the 8 PAS subtests have the same name as the SAM subtests). The outline contains a table of subtests crossed with the headings of primary, secondary, and tertiary factor; inserted in cells of the table are the labels: perceptual, cognitive, and motor. No further information is given concerning the factor analysis. It is unclear if a factor analysis on PAS time or error scores was performed.

The author recommends one other major use of the PAS subtests. It is claimed the subtests can be used to determine if a student has the ability to learn with practice. It is suggested that users readminister the subtests until the student shows no further improvement in completion times. Because norms for repeated testing and validity information for such a use of PAS subtest scores are not given, users should refrain from using the PAS to assess learning potential.

Similar to the "factor analysis" example discussed above, the manual contains errors that could have been identified through a close reading. The manual, for example, refers the reader to Appendix F for a list of commercially prepared "interest inventories and surveys" (p. 4) and "work samples" (p. 5). There is no Appendix F. (The information is included at the end of Appendix E.) The reader will find statements such as "Consult directions for using the MATRIX on page 00000" (p. 6), "follow the guidelines discussed on pages [blank]" (Appendix B, p. 13), and "See page 6 in manual on READMINISTRATION TECHNIQUES" (p. 7). In this last case, the READMINISTRATION TECHNIQUES are found on page 5 rather than page 6. Numerous typos can be found in the text and on the materials used for scoring and reporting. The quality of the manual reminds me of Thorndike, Cunningham, Thorndike, and Hagen's (1991) observation that "the care that has gone into preparing the test manual is often a good indicator of the care that has been exercised in constructing the test" (p. 151). It is surprising that a manual available since 1985, with so many errors that are easy to correct, has not been revised.

I cannot recommend the PAS: It does not meet the basic standards for a psychological test. I have several suggestions. Teacher evaluations and ratings probably provide the best sources of information on student weaknesses and strengths for specific curriculum areas. If testing needs to be conducted, the Armed Services Vocational Aptitude Battery (ASVAB; U.S. Department of Defense, 1984; T4:196) is recommended. The ASVAB is designed for use in high school vocational guidance programs and provides information to aid in matching student abilities to vocational training programs.

REVIEWER'S REFERENCES

U.S. Department of Labor. (1970). *Manual for the USES General Aptitude Test Battery, Section III: Development*. Washington, DC: Manpower Administration.

U.S. Department of Defense. (1984). *Test manual for the Armed Services Vocational Aptitude Battery* (DOD 1304.12AA). North Chicago, IL: U.S. Military Entrance Processing Command.

Piney Mountain Press. (1985). *Technical manual: Skills Assessment Module*. Cleveland, GA: Piney Mountain Press.

Thorndike, R. M., Cunningham, G. K., Thorndike, R. L., & Hagen, E. P. (1991). *Measurement and evaluation in psychology and education* (5th ed.). New York: Macmillan Publishing Co.

[306]

The Primary Language Screen.

Purpose:: Designed to screen speech language skills of kindergarten and first grade students.
Population: Ages 5–7.
Publication Date: 1990.
Acronym: TPLS.
Scores, 3: Expressive, Receptive, Total.
Administration: Individual or group.
Price Data, 1994: $29.95 per set including manual (48 pages) and reproducible forms.
Time: Administration time not reported.
Author: Diane L. Eger.
Publisher: United/DOK Publishers.

Review of The Primary Language Screen by THERESA H. ELOFSON, Program Specialist, Chapter 1/Learning Assistance Program, Federal Way School District #210, Federal Way, WA:

The Primary Language Screen (TPLS) is described as a language screening instrument. The TPLS originally was developed in 1981 in public school settings as a comprehensive, group screening instrument for language disorders. The Receptive portion of the screening can be administered to a small group, an entire classroom, or an individual in kindergarten or first grade in about 30 minutes. The Expressive portion of the test takes approximately 5 minutes with each individual.

The test materials are in a notebook format with three-hole punched pages and tabbed dividers. The tests, scoring sheets, and class summary sheets are on reproducible forms. The answer key for the Receptive screening is at the end of the administration and scoring section. Scoring is done on the individual record form in another section of the manual. If the answer key were added to the individual record form, all information would be conveniently listed on one page, thus saving time and reducing the risk of transposing errors. The increased possibility of errors and time required to score the test also exists in the awkward arrangement of the Expressive worksheet portion of the test. The administrator must read from and record information on the Expressive Speech and Language worksheet and then transfer every piece of data, including observational data, to the TPLS individual record form. Test administrators might find the process less cumbersome if they used the worksheet to administer the test and then recorded the data directly on the TPLS individual record form. The directions for giving the test are simple and direct; the process for recording the information is cumbersome; and the actual scoring procedures of the test are easy. The "Informal Screening Data" section at the end of the test has no directions given, nor is it addressed in the manual. This section could be completed only by a trained language specialist.

Nowhere in the manual is it clearly stated how the items were initially chosen or constructed. Normative and statistical data were not clearly identified as to samples chosen, characteristics of the groups, and time of test administration. The norming data from the first version and the second version of The Primary Language Screen were compiled with no further explanation. The lack of specificity in data collection reduces confidence as a useful test.

A revision of the test was based on correlations of items presented in the manual. However, on page 23 of the manual the author states, "The TPLS has been further refined by eliminating several items, redrawing several stimuli, and developing a new format for the score sheet." No data analysis for this third revision is identified.

A table containing concurrent validity coefficients between the TPLS and the Metropolitan Readiness Test (r = .78), the Metropolitan Achievement Test (r = .36), and the Stanford Early Achievement Test (r = .59) gives support, with small samples, that there are concurrent relationships between the TPLS and these other measures. The test version used for this analysis is not stated.

The Kuder-Richardson formula 20 was applied to a sample of 341 kindergartners and 341 first graders to evaluate the internal consistency of the screening. Acceptable coefficients were obtained for two versions of the screening.

The Primary Language Screen is an inexpensive, individual and group language screening instrument for kindergarten and first grade. The manual is awkwardly written and difficult to follow. However, the administration and scoring procedures are simple processes. According to the manual author, the students who score in the lower 20% of classes tested should be considered for further testing, although the manual does not include data to support this cutoff. Although the TPLS may have some useful applications with groups of children as a screening instrument, the lack of specific information about key psychometric qualities is a critical shortcoming.

Review of The Primary Language Screen by JANET NORRIS, Associate Professor of Communication Sciences and Disorders, Louisiana State University, Baton Rouge, LA:

The Primary Language Screen for Kindergarten and First Grade (TPLS) is designed to screen both receptive and expressive language abilities of children in kindergarten or at the beginning of first grade. The Receptive portion is group administered and measures semantic, syntactic, and grammatic structures of language. This portion requires approximately 30 minutes. The Expressive portion is individually administered at approximately 5 minutes per child, and assesses the ability to respond to opposites and analogies, sentence repetition, and grammatic closure. The reported purpose of the TPLS is to screen all areas of language to large numbers of children efficiently and effectively, and to identify those who require further assessment. Children performing in the lower 20% of those screened are considered "at risk" and the lowest 10% are failed and should be referred for a diagnostic evaluation.

Administration is easy if the children are familiar with pencil-and-paper tasks and can follow oral directions. These requirements result in the recommendation that the test not be given until the second semester of the kindergarten year. The Receptive section requires test booklets to be copied and compiled from reproducible forms. Oral instructions direct the children to find a page marked with a given picture (i.e., response page 1 is marked by a heart, page 2 by a pencil, and so forth) and then to locate a row of pictures on that page by finding a specified shape in the left margin. From a choice of three pictures in that row the child is to use a crayon to place an X on the picture that correctly represents the concept specified. Scoring amounts to simply counting the number of correct responses out of 20 possible by comparing the child's choice to the answer key.

The Expressive section requires the child to listen to single sentences and either complete them (Opposites and Analogies, and Grammatical Closure items), repeat them (Sentence Repetition), or respond to them (Pragmatic items). Each task is made up of two to five items, for a total of 13 responses on the Expressive section, each scored as correct or incorrect. In addition, informal screening information is obtained by noting behaviors such as whether the child can ask and answer questions, maintain appropriate eye contact, use language that is appropriate to the context, articulate speech sounds correctly, and exhibit acceptable voice quality and fluency. Because of the qualitative judgments that must be made, the manual author states the Expressive section must be administered by a speech-language pathologist. I infer the test developers prefer the same person administer the entire test, but this is not required.

No mention of test reliability is made in the TPLS manual, except on page 2 where the term is incorrectly used. This is particularly problematic in that the Receptive portion is group administered and many factors could contribute to performance, including the size of the group, amount of background noise, confusion regarding the task, and rate at which questions are delivered. The manual author does not address these issues, except to recommend that an aide be present if the group size is more than 12 children.

Several studies were conducted to evaluate the test's validity. A correlational matrix and biserial correlations were computed to investigate construct validity. The intratest relationships showed moderate to high correlations for all but two tasks. Concurrent validity was established by comparing performance between the TPLS and standardized achievement tests, with moderate correlations obtained. The highest correlations were found between the TPLS and subtests measuring word meaning and readiness, suggesting the TPLS did measure many of the same language abilities as these instruments. Validity also was measured relative to the success of the TPLS in discriminating between high and low achievers. Results of one study showed that performance on specific tasks, as well as the Receptive subtotal, Expressive subtotal, and Total TPLS score did discriminate between children with identified language disorders and children with no known problems, as well as those with articulation problems only. However, the small numbers of subjects in these studies and the questions about the reliability of the instrument suggest the results should be interpreted tentatively.

Despite efforts to establish evidence for validity, some of the items on the TPLS do not appear to test what they claim. On the expressive portion of the test, one item requires the child to "Show me your right hand," and nonverbal responses are accepted. This item, as well as stating your birthday comprise the entire core of pragmatics items, and neither measures pragmatics or the use of language to accomplish a goal or function. Only discrete aspects of language are tested, whereas much of the current literature shows that language problems are often most apparent within connected discourse. The sentence repetition items are absurd (i.e., "On my next vacation, I will take an elephant to Pittsburgh"), and the semantics or unusual meaning of these sentences may distract children and cause a failure to repeat them in their exact form, as required by the task.

The TPLS does not have norms, and all studies used in test construction and validation were conducted on small, relatively homogeneous populations of children from one region in Pennsylvania. Very little information is provided about the characteristics of the children beyond grade level. The manual author suggests that each group tested form its own normative population, because the criteria of performing in the lower 20% of any group places a child in the at-risk category, and a performance in the bottom 10% results in a recommendation for further testing. Statements are made regarding the relationship between these percentages and populations of children including those with severe language disorders, those identified for special education, and those who speak English as a second language, but these claims are not substantiated except by reports of the use of the test over a 10-year period and the resulting clinical impressions.

The major disadvantage of the TPLS is that because of the task demands for the group-administered Receptive portion of the test, it is recommended that it not be used at the beginning of the kindergarten year to screen children. The manual author indicates this is not a serious detriment to the early identification of at-risk children when early referrals are encouraged from teachers, parents, and other agencies. This is viewed positively as leading to a reduction in the beginning of the year delay in entering children into an intervention program. However, if teacher and parent referral is effective in identifying and referring children for further evaluation, there would be no need for administering the TPLS during the second semester, and its use would be superfluous. Conversely, if the TPLS identifies children who are missed by the referral process but really do require special assistance, then the delay in identification is a serious problem.

Developing a valid, discriminating, and efficient language screening instrument for kindergarten children has long presented a challenge. Unfortunately, the TPLS is not successful in overcoming many of the problems inherent in this endeavor. Most problematic is the inappropriateness of this instrument for screening children at the beginning of the school year, when the need for identification is most critical. The limited testing and development of the test results in claims made relative to the effectiveness of this instrument that are based more on impression than data.

[307]

Primary Test of Cognitive Skills.

Purpose: Designed to "measure verbal, spatial, memory, and conceptual abilities."
Population: Grades K–1.
Publication Date: 1990.
Acronym: PTCS.
Scores, 5: Spatial, Memory, Concepts, Verbal, Total.
Administration: Group.
Price Data: Price information available from publisher for test materials including manual (70 pages), norms book (82 pages), and technical bulletin (23 pages); scoring service available from publisher.
Time: (30) minutes per subtest; (120) minutes total test.
Authors: Janellen Huttenlocher and Susan Cohen Levine.
Publisher: CTB Macmillan/McGraw-Hill.

Review of the Primary Test of Cognitive Skills by SHERRY K. BAIN, Visiting Assistant Professor of Psychology, University of Southern Mississippi, Hattiesburg, MS:

DESCRIPTION. The Primary Test of Cognitive Skills (PTCS) is a group-administered ability test designed for use with kindergartners and first graders. The authors recommend the PTCS be used in screening for problems such as learning disability or developmental delay, and to identify referrals for gifted programming. The authors also state the PTCS can be used for planning instructional programs both for individuals and for groups of children.

TEST MATERIALS, ADMINISTRATION, AND SCORING. Test items are presented in multiple-choice format, with students filling in the circle beneath the correct choice. Administration instructions are clearly written, and the graphic presentation of items is well designed for the age level.

Subtests of the PTCS are untimed. Recommendations are to allow 30 minutes for each of the four subtests and to spread the testing over at least 2 days. The minimum total testing time, not counting needed breaks, would therefore be 2 hours. The test may be administered by the teacher to small groups, with proctors in charge of 10 or fewer kindergartners and 15 or fewer first graders.

The PTCS can be hand scored by the examiner or machine scored by the publisher. Scale scores and standard errors of measurement by subscale are provided by a method based upon Item Response Theory or by a less accurate method based upon the number of correct responses. Percentile ranks based upon age and grade, and stanine scores are also available. Finally, a Cognitive Skills Index provides an age-based standard score ($X = 100$, $SD = 16$), giving an indication of the student's overall performance.

STANDARDIZATION, RELIABILITY, AND VALIDITY. PTCS standardization was carried out on a national sample of 7,562 kindergartners and 8,504 first graders in Fall 1988 and Spring 1989. The authors state that students were selected from public, private, and Catholic schools and represented diverse geographic areas, socioeconomic levels, and ethnic backgrounds. Demographic characteristics of the standardization sample are fairly representative of the U.S. population. A breakdown of means and standard deviations for correct responses by ethnic groups and gender is presented in the Norms Book.

Test-retest reliability is relatively low, but probably not unexpected for a group-administered test. Reliability coefficients range from .50 to .80 ($X = .66$) across the four subscales. Test-retest reliability for the PTCS Cognitive Skills Index is not presented in the Technical Bulletin but would be valuable information to include.

Internal consistency data were obtained, based upon the Kuder-Richardson Formula 20. Coefficients range from .60 to.78 for subscales, and .84 or above for the total test.

Support for predictive validity was obtained by comparing PTCS scores with scores from the California Achievement Test and the Comprehensive Test of Basic Skills. PTCS Total scores, compared to achievement subtests from both batteries, produced coefficients within an adequate range (.36 to .65).

Evidence of construct validity is presented only in intercorrelations among the four subscale areas, but not for the two subtests within each subscale. Factor analytic studies were not reported. For the kindergarten level, subscale intercorrelations ranged from .35 to .54. The Concepts subscale for the kindergartners correlated with both the Spatial and Verbal subscales at .50 or greater, raising the question of subscale specificity. For first graders, subscale intercorrelations ranged from .22 to .44, indicating better subscale specificity.

The PTCS Cognitive Skills Index correlated with PTCS subscale scores within a range of .60 to .80 for kindergartners and first graders. Memory produced the lowest coefficient (.60) when compared to PTCS Cognitive Skills Index for first graders.

Test bias was evaluated through statistical examination of tryout items, based upon recommended methods from Item Response Theory. The authors also stated they followed publisher's guidelines for developing nonbiased tests (guidelines were not presented in the Technical Bulletin), and had tryout items and final items reviewed by three people: the project director and two editorial staff members. A panel of independent experts was not apparently used, and no data were presented on predictive validity for various ethnic groups.

RECOMMENDATIONS. Of the authors' primary recommendations for using the PTCS, several seem questionable. When used as a screening test for learning disability and developmental delay, students' performances may be negatively influenced by PTCS format characteristics (e.g., multiple choice, group administration). Students' specific deficits such as poor fine motor skills or poor receptive language skills could interfere with task performance, giving misleading information. Developmentally based checklists, curriculum-based checklists, and normative-based group achievement tests would be more appropriate as screening instruments for developmentally delayed and learning disabled students. Other components of the CTB Early Childhood System, of which the PTCS is a member, might be appropriate screeners (e.g., The Early School Assessment).

The PTCS authors' recommendation that results of the test can be used for instructional planning for individuals and groups is a claim made by previous ability test authors, but not generally verified by research on Aptitude by Treatment Interaction (see Ysseldyke & Marston, 1990). Among the CTB Early Childhood System components, the Early School Assessment (127) and the Developing Skills Checklist (108) are based upon objectives that are matched to an activities package, the Instructional Activities for Kindergarten and First Grade. The PTCS test items, however, are not apparently matched to instructional objectives and are not actually tied to suggested interventions by publishers. In general, the information purportedly gained from PTCS administration for groups of students does not appear to outweigh the time required to administer the test, considering the lack of evidence that results can translate into instructional planning.

The PTCS may prove useful as a screening instrument for identifying gifted referrals, as the test authors suggested, if district guidelines allow group testing for this purpose. The Technical Bulletin does not present data correlating the PTCS scores with individually administered ability test scores, but local districts may wish to collect data on their own gifted referrals to determine the usefulness of the PTCS for screening this special group.

REVIEWER'S REFERENCE

Ysseldyke, J. E., & Marston, D. (1990). The use of assessment information to plan instructional interventions: A review of the research. In. T. B. Gutkin & C. R. Reynolds (Eds.), *The handbook of school psychology* (2nd ed.; pp. 661-682). New York: John Wiley & Sons.

Review of the Primary Test of Cognitive Skills by LAURA L. B. BARNES, Assistant Professor of Educational Research, and DAVID E. McINTOSH, Assistant Professor of School Psychology, Department of Applied Behavioral Studies, Oklahoma State University, Stillwater, OK:

The Primary Test of Cognitive Skills (PTCS) is a group-administered ability measure for the initial screening of giftedness and developmental delay and for instructional planning in kindergarten and first grade. In conjunction with the California Achievement Tests or the Comprehensive Tests of Basic Skills, the PTCS may be used in the initial screening of learning disabilities. The test is to be administered in paper-and-pencil format with visual and verbal stimuli from a test administrator. Practice exercises are included to familiarize young examinees with the mechanics of paper/pencil testing and with the item formats. The PTCS is one component of the Early Childhood System which includes the Early School Assessment (127), the Developing Skills Checklist (108), and an instructional activities book. Four tests with two subtests each make up the PTCS: Spatial (21 items)—Sequencing and Spatial Integration; Memory (21 items)—Spatial Memory and Associative Memory; Concepts (28 items)—Category and Spatial Concepts; and Verbal (24 items)—Object Naming and Syntax.

The PTCS may be given by teachers, psychologists, and others who have had some formal training in test administration. The practice exercises and test instructions to be read aloud to the children are printed in bold for ease of administration. Specific guidelines for preparing the examiner prior to testing with emphasis on the special concerns of assessing young children are provided in the manual. For all items, the child records his or her answer by darkening circles similar to those on computer-scoring sheets. Pilot studies indicated the children did not have difficulties with this task. Although the tests are generally easy to administer, the format in which the Spatial and Associative Memory subtests are administered may prove difficult in a group situation. For example, exposing the stimulus pictures in a standardized fashion so each child can view the pictures, maintaining each child's attention, and manipulating the stimulus books may be difficult. In addition, the phonetic pronunciation of the Associative Memory pictures would help increase consistency in administration.

Both machine and hand scoring are possible with the PTCS. Specific instructions for machine scoring required by the CTB/McGraw-Hill scoring service are in the manual. An answer key and instructions are provided for hand scoring. When hand scored, the number of correct responses (NCR) on each of the four tests is the basis for obtaining several derived scores from the Norms Book. Although subtests are mentioned in the manual and identified for administration purposes, subtest scores are not used and no norms are given for them. Types of derived scores available are scale scores, percentile ranks by grade and by age, stanines, and a Cognitive Skills Index (CSI). The CSI (total test IQ score) has a mean of 100 and standard deviation of 16. An Anticipated Achievement score may be obtained for comparison with obtained achievement scores.

Although the conversion of number correct scores to derived scores is relatively straightforward when only grade-based information is desired, the process is awkward and confusing if age-based norms are also used. Deriving all of the scores requires a great deal of flipping back and forth between sets of tables, making the process both time consuming and prone to recording errors. National stanines are obtainable from either of two sets of tables—one that provides grade-based norms and the other providing age-based norms. However, on the hand-scoring report form, the column is labeled only NS (national stanine) and none of the materials mention that there are actually two sets of stanine norms. Use of the two sets produce different results. The norms tables are organized and labeled in such a way that errors may easily go undetected.

Another potentially confusing aspect of scoring is that when the tests are machine scored, there is an option for either Item Response Theory (IRT)-based scoring or number correct scoring. Scale scores derived through the IRT-based scoring are a weighted function of examinee ability and item characteristics. Research indicates that in most cases, the IRT-based scoring leads to more accurate ability estimation than does number correct scoring, particularly at extreme ability ranges. The Norms Book contains a table presenting standard errors of measurement based upon both scoring methods where it may seem the IRT-based scores have their greatest relative advantage at the low ability ranges. However, the degree of precision gained through the IRT-based scoring must be weighed against the cost associated with machine scoring (because IRT-based scoring cannot reasonably be done by hand).

Little information is reported regarding the development of the test content other than mentioning that items were developed by national leaders in the study of cognitive development. Once developed, the initial item pool was subjected to rigorous screening, incorporating input from teachers and review panels, and statistical item analysis. Statistical methods guiding test development were based in the three-parameter IRT model. Considerable attention was given to preventing the inclusion of items that exhibited gender and/or ethnic bias in the final form. Both subjective reviews and IRT-based analyses were part of the bias studies. These procedures are fully described in the Technical Bulletin.

The norming sample consisted of 16,066 kindergarten and first grade children from locations throughout the United States with standardization occurring during Fall 1988 and Spring 1989. Sample selection was based upon region, school size, socioeconomic status, and type of community. Reported demographics include gender, ethnicity, and percent enrolled in special education programs. Age norms ranged from 61 to 90 months and have adequate sample sizes except for the 61-month age group which has fewer than 200. Less than 5% of the sample for each grade and norming period was composed of students with identified disabilities. The authors suggest these small numbers may be due to participating schools' exclusion of special program children from routine testing and/or the lack of formal diagnosis. In the latter case, the reported figures may underrepresent the actual percentage of these groups included in the norming sample.

Test score reliabilities were computed using traditional and IRT-based methods. Internal consistency (KR-20) reliabilities for the total scale are .88 (fall, kindergarten), .87 (spring, kindergarten), .86 (fall, first grade), and .84 (spring, first grade). Reliabilities for the four tests range from .60 to .78 (median reliability is .70). Median test-retest reliabilities with a 2-week interval for the individual tests are .64 (fall, kindergarten) and .69 (fall, first grade). In general, Memory had the lowest reported reliabilities. These reliabilities are perhaps better than expected considering this is a group-administered test for very young children; however, the total scale reliabilities should probably be considered too low to form a basis for individual decision making (e.g., achievement/ability discrepancies). Both IRT-based and traditional standard errors of measurement are reported in the Norms Book for each scale score. Regardless of the scoring method, measurement error is most pronounced at the extremes of the score range which may result in inaccurate assessment of low and high functioning children.

As with many group-based ability tests, validity evidence is rather weak. Neither content validity nor a specific content description of the types of abilities measured by each of the PTCS subtests are provided in the Technical Bulletin. This information would increase the interpretability of the scores. For example, the Sequences subtest appears to measure the perception of sequential patterns and nonverbal inductive reasoning, whereas the Spatial Integration subtest appears to measure spatial visualization/reasoning, part-whole relationships, and nonverbal reasoning. The Spatial Memory subtest appears to assess short-term visual recall, visual memory, and nonverbal reasoning. Short-term memory, visual memory, and recognition memory for pictures appeared to be measured by the Associative Memory subtest. The Category Concepts and Spatial Concepts subtests appear to measure nonverbal reasoning and visual attention to detail. Receptive language and short-term auditory memory appear to be measured by the Object Naming subtest, whereas the Syntax subtest appears to measure receptive language, understanding oral directions, short-term auditory memory, and using basic language concepts.

Predictive validity coefficients between the PTCS and the California Achievement Tests (CAT) and the Comprehensive Tests of Basic Skills (CTBS) are reported. The median correlation between individual PTCS tests and CAT Form E Level 11 is .39 (range .19 to .55); with CTBS/4, Level 10 the median correlation is .42 (range .23 to .61). The PTCS Spatial and Verbal tests generally had the highest correlations with the achievement tests; the PTCS Memory test had the lowest. The median PTCS Total score correlation with CAT scores is .54; for the CTBS the median correlation is .58. The magnitudes of these correlations together with low stability reliability seem to provide a rather weak basis for predicting achievement scores. No evidence was presented as to the test's relationship with individual measures of intelligence or with other individual screening measures (e.g., the Peabody Picture Vocabulary Test—Revised [T4:1945] and the Bracken Basic Concept Scale [T4:319]).

Evidence for construct validity is presented solely through tables of intercorrelations. The low to moderate correlations among the tests indicate they measure separate constructs (median r = .43 for kindergarten; median r = .35 for first grade). However, in the absence of other substantial validity evidence, the interpretation of those constructs is difficult. Correlations between the individual tests and the PTCS Total are lower than desired for an ability screening test; the highest correlation is r = .80 (Concepts with Total). One possible explanation is that the tests are assessing abilities that are not considered highly salient measures of intelligence. For example, the Associative Memory subtest appears to measure short-term visual memory skills. These have been shown to correlate only moderately with cognitive ability. Although each test is purported to measure two separate skills, no evidence is presented to indicate they do so. Evidence for the construct validity of the test would be enhanced through a detailed description of the rationale for the test content including a discussion of the theory from which the measured constructs were derived. The authors state that a unique feature of the PTCS is its clear distinction between verbal and nonverbal abilities. A more detailed explanation of this distinction and analyses to support this claim are crucial to interpreting the constructs. Correlations with other ability measures would also provide insight into what constructs are being measured.

The authors state the PTCS was created for the initial screening of learning disabilities and developmental delay. We recommend that such screening decisions be made cautiously because less than 1% of the norming sample included these populations and construct validity of the instrument is questionable.

The PTCS is a new ability test that is designed to be group administered during kindergarten and first grade to screen for giftedness, learning disabilities, and developmental delay. The technical aspects of its development, including item selection and bias reduction procedures, are excellent. Although designed to be as "child friendly" as possible, test performance is likely to be influenced by children's poor attention, misunderstanding of directions, and processing difficulties. The PTCS represents a novel approach to assessing ability and may be useful where an initial group screening is warranted. However, it should not be considered as an alternative to sound individually administered measures. The PTCS should be interpreted solely as a screening measure with predictions related to cognitive ability and future academic progress being made with caution.

[308]

Printing Performance School Readiness Test.

Purpose: Developed to identify preschool children who may be at risk for school failure.
Population: Ages 4-3 to 6-5.
Publication Dates: 1985–90.
Acronym: PPSRT.
Scores: Total score only.
Administration: Individual.
Price Data, 1990: $23 per complete kit including flash cards, 50 response sheets, 50 scoring sheets, and manual ('90, 62 pages); $8.50 per set of flash cards; $12.50 per 200 response sheets; $12.50 per 200 scoring sheets; $8.50 per manual.
Time: (10–15) minutes.
Author: Marvin L. Simner.
Publisher: Phylmar Associates.
Cross References: For a review by Carol Mardell-Czudnowski of an earlier edition, see 10:293.

Review of the Printing Performance School Readiness Test by JERRILYN V. ANDREWS, Assistant for Assessment and Data Collection, Office of School Administration, Montgomery County Public Schools, Rockville, MD:

The Printing Performance School Readiness Test (PPSRT) is designed to aid educators in identifying prekindergarten and kindergarten children who may be at risk of later school failure. Research has indicated that young children who exhibit a large number of "form errors" (i.e., addition, omission, or misalignment of parts of a letter or number) have a higher probability of later school failure than students who make smaller numbers of form errors. The test author should be commended for emphasizing that the PPSRT assesses just one early warning sign and that the test should not be used as the sole means of identifying students who may be at risk of later school failure.

The 1990 revised edition of the PPSRT appears to be identical to the earlier (1985) version; the test and supporting technical information match that reported in an earlier review (10:293). What is new is the abbreviated version of the PPSRT which is intended for preschool students ranging in age from 45 to 57 months. The manual says that the full test has been found to be too long for prekindergarten students. Because the current version of the full test has already been reviewed, this review will focus only on the abbreviated test.

The abbreviated test requires students to copy 18 letter and numbers directly below a sample. The 18 numbers and letters were selected, using item analysis procedures, from the 41 contained on the full test. The scoring procedures are straightforward and identical to those used on the full test. The individually administered test is untimed and the manual says testing takes approximately 3 minutes per child, considerably less than the 10–15 minutes per child needed for the full test. The two response sheets, each with nine letters and numbers, are pictured in the manual; the user is told to enlarge the 1.5 by 2 inch models to 8.5 by 11 inches. This will probably require that most users make their own response sheets rather than photocopy the models.

The manual provides little technical information about the abbreviated PPSRT; the reader is referred to a 1989 article by the test author for this information. That article (Simner, 1989) does provide adequate information except for the description of the sample; for that the reader is referred to yet another article (Simner, 1987). It would be better if the test manual itself contained all the information potential users need to evaluate the test.

According to Simner (1989) the study design closely parallels that used for the full PPSRT. For the abbreviated PPSRT, two samples containing a total of 171 prekindergarten students were tested in the fall of prekindergarten and then followed for the next 3 years. Interrater and test-retest reliabilities were both adequate and consistent with findings from the full PPSRT. Report card grades and standardized achievement test scores were used to assess predictive validity; again results were adequate and in line with the full PPSRT. The recommended cutoff score of

16 correctly identified 70–78% of the true positives and only produced 18–20% false positives. Thus, the results of the study of the abbreviated PPSRT closely follow those of the full PPSRT.

In summary, the PPSRT appears unchanged from the version reviewed earlier. The new, abbreviated PPSRT appears to have adequate technical properties as long as the reader follows the author's advice to use it as just one piece of screening information. Having every child ready for school has been called a national priority and will probably lead to more preschool programs. The abbreviated PPSRT may well provide a quick preliminary screening tool to help identify students who may need additional assistance.

REVIEWER'S REFERENCES

Simner, M. L. (1987). Predictive validity of the Teacher's School Readiness Inventory. *Canadian Journal of School Psychology*, *3*, 21-32.

Simner, M. L. (1989). Predictive validity of an abbreviated version of the Printing Performance School Readiness Test. *Journal of School Psychology*, *27*, 189-195.

Review of the Printing Performance School Readiness Test by AGNES E. SHINE, Assistant Professor of Educational Psychology, Mississippi State University, Mississippi State, MS:

The Printing Performance School Readiness Test (PPSRT) is an individually administered screening test developed to identify form errors in the printing of young children. Form errors occur in printing when the child adds, deletes, or misaligns parts of a letter or number, which results in a marked distortion. The author states that in young children form errors can be used as a warning sign for potential school failure. The ability to attend to a stimulus and coordinate fine muscle movements (e.g., copying, printing) is generally viewed as a measure or index of a child's maturity level. Designed for young children from age 4 to 6, the PPSRT can be administered in approximately 10–15 minutes. Extensive psychometric training is not necessary and with practice the PPSRT could be administered and interpreted by a variety of professionals such as a classroom teacher or public health nurse.

The test material includes a manual, 41 letter and number cards, response sheets, and an examiner protocol. The cards are exposed one at a time in sequential order. For prekindergarten children the test consists of copying 41 letters and numbers, whereas kindergarten children print the letter or number from memory after a 2- to 3-second exposure.

Norms and cutoff scores are provided for three time periods, late spring of prekindergarten (children 51–63 months), fall of kindergarten (children 57–69 months), and late spring of kindergarten (children 65–77 months). The scoring criteria are well written with visual examples of adequate performance and form errors. When scoring the PPSRT the examiner should note that only the child's first attempt is scored. Tracing over a letter or number is not considered a form error as long as the final reproduction closely resembles the presented stimulus. To help the examiner with scoring, the author provides the examiner with 10 practice scoring exercises.

According to the author the standardization sample consisted of 619 children from public schools in London, Ontario. However, the means and standard deviations for the PPSRT were based on the scores obtained from 859 protocols. Upon careful review of the six samples that comprise the subject pool, it was noted that some of the children were retested and their score included in the norming. This reviewer questions the wisdom of including the scores of subjects who had previous exposure to the test material because such exposure may have distorted the means. Because copying and printing tasks are often found in the curricula of young children, practice or remediation may have occurred between test administrations, possibly lowering the mean number of errors in the standardization sample. The mean number of errors for children tested in the fall of kindergarten was higher than the mean number of errors for children tested in late spring of prekindergarten. The rise in the number of form errors suggests that the tasks are not equivalent (e.g., copying to printing from memory).

The author uses cutoff scores with probabilities to describe the child's performance on the PPSRT. Specifically, children with odds of 10 to 1 would require immediate remediation and children with odds of 1 to 1 should be referred for additional assessment. The cutoff scores were calculated to identify approximately 75% of at-risk children. Standard scores or percentiles based on age may have been easier to use and more meaningful than cutoff scores.

The available reliability and validity data are difficult to understand and evaluate. Little information was provided in the manual concerning reliability studies. The author reports test-retest intervals from 1 month to 8 months. Test-retest reliability coefficients ranged from .73 to.87. It appears that as the number of months between test administrations increased, the reliability decreased. The amount or extent of training involved in achieving interscorer reliability was missing from the manual. Therefore, the meaning of the reported interscorer reliability studies (.97 and .98) was unclear given the lack of information.

Studies of criterion validity involved correlating the PPSRT with standardized achievement tests and school performance. When the PPSRT was correlated with achievement tests (e.g., Wide Range Achievement Test, KeyMath Diagnostic Arithmetic Test) the reported correlation coefficients ranged from .40 to .79. It is troubling to note the manual authors reported a correlation coefficient between the Wide Range Achievement Test (WRAT) and the PPSRT for prekindergarten children because the WRAT was normed on children 5 years of age and older. Correlating the PPSRT with school performance (grades) resulted in correlation coefficients that ranged from .27 to .63. The author indicated that these somewhat low correlations may be due to the removal of the children who failed, thus resulting in a restricted range.

Predictive validity was reported for the three different testing times. The sample was divided into high and low achievers. Thirty percent of the sample whose school achievement was described as "C" level were excluded from the analysis. Classification rates for the poor performance group (true positive) ranged from 71 to 85%, whereas the false positive hit rate ranged from 15 to 21%. Because the PPSRT is a screening device purportedly used to identify children at risk for school failure, it is also important to look at the false negative classification rates (e.g., student who had good test performance but poor school achievement). Using the present cutoff scores, 15 to 29% of the children were misclassified. Although the overall hit rate of the PPSRT may be adequate for a screening measure using the present cutoff scores it may result in overlooking children who may be at risk for school failure. The largest misclassification rates occurred in the prekindergarten sample with the lowest misclassifications rates in the sample tested in the late spring of kindergarten.

The author continually reminds the potential test user that the PPSRT is a screening test and should not be the sole instrument used to determine if a child is at risk for school failure. However, the author suggested the use of the PPSRT may avoid having to use longer, more specialized tests when screening young children. The author suggested that local norms be obtained and explained how this might be accomplished.

In summary, the PPSRT appears to be easy to administer. The test materials are well organized. At times the manual is difficult to read and understand. Sections dealing with reliability and validity data are somewhat confusing to this reviewer. Therefore, it is difficult to evaluate the PPSRT to determine if it is appropriate for the intended specific use. Because the test was normed on children in a specific geographic location, the generalizability of the test is questionable. Due to the limited sample of behaviors measured, clinicians should use the PPSRT with caution when screening young children.

[309]

Problem Experiences Checklist.

Purpose: Developed for use prior to the initial intake interview to identify potential problems for further discussion.
Population: Adolescents, adults.
Publication Date: 1991.
Scores: No scores.
Administration: Individual.
Editions, 2: Adolescent, Adult.
Manual: No manual.
Price Data, 1993: $14.50 per 25 checklists (specify Adult or Adolescent).
Time: [10–15] minutes.
Author: Leigh Silverton.
Publisher: Western Psychological Services.

Review of the Problem Experiences Checklist by MARK H. DANIEL, Senior Scientist, American Guidance Service, Circle Pines, MN:

The Problem Experiences Checklist (PEC) is designed to provide an easy and efficient way for a clinician or counselor to find out what kinds of problems are on a client's mind before the initial interview. The client reads a list of statements of problems, emotions, and potentially stressful circumstances and checks any that currently apply. There are no scores, and the PEC is not intended as a measuring instrument.

There are two versions, surveying similar domains but written differently to be appropriate for their intended age level. The Adult Version has 209 statements grouped into 11 categories, covering interpersonal and family relations; beliefs, emotions, and personal habits; job and financial situation; and stressful events. Each category also includes one or two open-ended "Other problems" items. The Adolescent Version is slightly longer, with 246 statements in 13 categories, but without the open-ended items. In addition to the topics covered by the Adult Version, it includes statements about school, recreation, and neighborhood circumstances.

The statements are concise, direct, and easy to read, and the layout of the forms is spacious and attractive. Clients should have no difficulty completing the checklist in the 10 to 15 minutes estimated by the publisher.

The absence of published documentation on these forms is acceptable considering their function and their lack of psychometric claims. One might, however, wonder how the problem domains were selected. The author has stated in personal communication (L. Silverton, October 21, 1991): "To construct the adult items, I reviewed DSM-III-R categories related to V-code diagnoses or problems not attributable to mental disorders . . . . I included all as categories." Silverton supplemented these categories with others commonly screened in intake interviews, such as self-care, beliefs and goals, and emotions. The Adolescent Version was constructed somewhat differently: "A review of the literature about psychosocial stressors in adolescence in general and more specific problems of adolescents seeking treatment suggested the general categories for the checklists" (L. Silverton, personal communication, October 21, 1991). Perusal of the forms suggests that the author's systematic approach resulted in broad and nonredundant coverage.

SUMMARY. The Problem Experiences Checklist appears to be a useful tool for surveying a client's concerns and learning about the psychosocial stressors in their life. It would complement, rather than substitute for, more clinical assessment devices.

Review of the Problem Experiences Checklist by MICHAEL J. SPORAKOWSKI, Professor of Family and Child Development, Virginia Polytechnic Institute and State University, Blacksburg, VA:

The Problem Experiences Checklist comes in two forms, the Adolescent Version and the Adult Version. Neither arrived on this reviewer's desk with any sort of manual or documentation beyond the checklists themselves. They appear to be a typical checklist approach towards a quick, face valid assessment of issues or problems that are concerning the respondent. It is most likely that this evaluation could be of use to the teacher, guidance counselor, clinical counselor, or therapist who might be working with the respondent as an initial self-appraisal of current functioning and/or difficulties. Because no data are presented with these checklists, they have no possibilities for comparison-to-norm scores for either clinical or research purposes.

Regarding the Adolescent Version, areas covered include: school, opposite-sex concerns, peers, family, goals, crises, emotions, recreation, habits, neighborhood circumstances, life transitions, beliefs and attitudes, and occupational and financial circumstances. The Adult Version covers: marital/relationship, children/parents, financial/legal, sexual/social, bereavement, personal habits, work adjustment, life transitions, beliefs and goals, painful memories, and emotions.

These checklists may be functional as part of an initial intake screening for counseling. They would be infinitely more valuable if descriptions of their construction, development, and use were included with them. If employed, users must develop their own normative bases for making comparisons and evaluating the instruments' psychometric qualities. As a counselor, these instruments might have value in stimulating discussion with some clients or offering quick, surface level insights into client's difficulties before they are actually seen. As a researcher or developer of assessments, the Problem Experiences Checklists offer me little.

[310]

Process Skills Rating Scales.

Purpose: "Designed for use in obtaining a rating of the student's facility in using process skills that develop his/her ability to think, reason, and search for knowledge independently, and to communicate and interact effectively with all members of society."

Population: Elementary and secondary school students.
Publication Date: 1990.
Acronym: PSRS.
Scores, 12: Verbal Communication Skills (Speech, Group Discussion, Interviewing, Debate), Scientific Research Skills, Independent Study Skills, Written Communication Skills, Receptive/Nonverbal Communication Skills, Critical Thinking and Reasoning Skills, Personal Growth and Human Relations Skills, Creative Thinking Skills, Library Research Skills.
Administration: Group.
Price Data, 1994: $29 per set including manual/forms (66 pages).
Time: Administration time not reported.
Authors: Frances A. Karnes and Suzanne Meriweather Bean.
Publisher: PRO-ED, Inc.

Review of the Process Skills Rating Scales by DEL EBERHARDT, Program Administrator, Greenwich Public Schools, Greenwich, CT:

The Process Skills Rating Scales (PSRS) by Karnes and Bean present the reviewer with a unique challenge. Many, if not most of the criteria by which we judge the adequacy of assessment devices are not present in the available resource material. Although some may argue it may not be critical for a rating scale that data on reliability, validity, norms, etc. are absent, it does place severe limitation on the review process.

The PSRS was "Designed for use in obtaining a rating of the student's facility in using process skills that develop his/her ability to think, reason, and search for knowledge independently, and to communicate and interact effectively with all members of society" (manual, p. 4). According to the authors the target population is elementary and secondary school students. The PSRS consists of 12 separate scales. They are presented as reproducible forms, suggesting that the user is free to make copies of the original set, hence avoiding the expense related to purchasing additional copies of the separate rating scales.

The 12 scales along with the number of items in each scale are as follows: Verbal Communication (Speech)—47 items; Verbal Communication (Group Discussion)—42 items; Verbal Communication (Interviewing)—17 items; Verbal Communication (Debate)—26 items; Written Communication—33 items; Receptive/Non Verbal Communication—15 items; Critical Thinking & Reasoning—71 items; Creative Thinking—43 items; Personal Growth & Human Relations—84 items; Library Research—83 items; Scientific Research—94 items; Independent Study—27 items.

The scales have a traditional four step response scale ranging from ALWAYS-FREQUENTLY-SELDOM to NEVER. The use of the absolutes "ALWAYS" and "NEVER" is very unusual in such scales and is probably not conducive to use. Suspect respondents would be inclined to choose the middle two categories, which would place severe restrictions on the utility of the response categories.

The PSRS has a user's manual that is simple in the extreme. On page 5 the authors indicate the scales should be "considered assessment tools" and should not be used for research. They further indicate that the scales have not been standardized and norms are not available.

The section of the manual devoted to the development of the PSRS is quite limited. We are told the PSRS was developed because the authors received many requests for instruments to assess process skills. I could find no explicit statement as to how the authors define process skills. Indirectly, they seem to be of the opinion that the 12 scales seem to define what they mean by process skills.

Section 3 of the manual contains only meager help on "use of results." In three pages the authors provide a very limited example of how one might use information from the Scientific Research skills scale. In addition, there are very brief descriptions as to how the scales might be used by district personnel, teachers, parents, students, and teacher educators.

Section 4 of the manual, "Suggestions for Activities" is only two pages in length. The authors offer an example as to how their INTRODUCE-REINFORCE-EXTEND view of the instructional process might be applied to teaching critical thinking and reasoning skills.

In summary, the PSRS, in my view, has a very limited realm for application at this stage of its development. It is difficult to determine whether the authors intended to create an instructional tool that looked like an assessment device or vice versa. The absence of sufficient information regarding construction, reliability, validity, and normative data severely limits its use. Special educators would be cautioned not to use the scales as part of the assessment process leading to the development of an Individualized Educational Plan (IEP). The results could easily be challenged by any party and it would be impossible to defend the PSRS on common psychometric characteristics.

The PSRS may be best used as a teaching tool in preservice education programs. Broader use awaits more and better quality control by the authors.

Review of the Process Skills Rating Scales by ANITA S. TESH, Assistant Professor, School of Nursing, University of North Carolina at Greensboro, Greensboro, NC:

The Process Skills Rating Scales (PSRS) consist of 12 scales addressing the areas listed above under "Scores." Scales are composed of 15 to 94 items. Items are statements of an ability (e.g., "Can effectively instruct a group of peers,") accompanied by a "Likert" response scale with points labeled *always*, *frequently*, *seldom*, and *never*. There are separate forms of each scale for use by students, teachers, and parents. These forms differ only in the instructions: Students are instructed to rate themselves; parents and teachers are instructed to rate the students.

The authors, Karnes and Bean, state the scales are intended for use with elementary and secondary students with "a wide range of abilities" (manual, p. 4). Many items contain words and constructs inappropriate for elementary students (e.g., "appropriate colloquial language"). Some items also address skills inappropriate for younger students or students who have not had certain educational experiences (e.g., use of Turabian Style).

TEST MANUAL. The test manual lacks information deemed primary in the *Standard for Educational and Psychological Testing* (1985, AERA, APA, & NCME; pp. 30, 36–37, 75, 79). For examples, qualifications for test administrators and conditions for test administration are not discussed. No information is provided regarding use of the test with the handicapped or with linguistic minorities. Although the test is designed to be scored by the user, no aids for interpreting test scores or scoring instructions are provided. Scoring must be inferred from the directions for use of test results.

SCORING. In most instruments with Likert response scales, responses are summed or averaged across items, as this enhances reliability. Although the PSRS items have Likert response scales, the authors do not describe summing across items. Items within a scale are said to be ordered from least to most difficulty, and each item is described as a subskill to be scored and interpreted individually (manual, p. 13). No validation of item order is provided, and the hazards of making inferences based on single items are not discussed (c.f., *Standards*, 1985, AERA, APA, & NCME; p. 14). Instructions are not provided for comparing, combining, and/or reconciling students' self-appraisals with those derived from teachers and parents. Instructions are also not given for age- or grade-appropriate interpretation of scores or adaptation of testing procedures.

NORMS. No norms are available.

RELIABILITY. No information on reliability of the PSRS is provided. The PSRS is intended for use in measuring students' knowledge and abilities, but has a format typically used in surveys and inventories. This format is almost certainly less reliable than more direct measurement would be. The response scale is subject to inconsistent interpretation. For example, does *always* mean "every time I've tried" or "under any imaginable circumstances"? If the first interpretation is used, responses will vary with circumstances of attempting the activity. If the second is used, responses will vary with the richness of the respondent's imagination.

There are numerous other threats to reliable measurement with the PSRS, including use of words and constructs which are difficult and may be unfamiliar to some cultural groups. Some items refer to activities not all students will have attempted. Some items refer to concrete activities, but others are abstract and difficult to relate to the response scale (e.g., "can develop a belief in own ability to succeed"). Many items contain subjective terms such as "easily" and "effectively" which may be interpreted inconsistently.

Responses provided by students and parents may also be influenced by their levels of confidence, and by personal or cultural characteristics such as modesty and self-effacement. Because their abilities are being assessed, some students (and parents) will feel that they should strive for a high score rather than answer honestly. Finally, inconsistent administration and scoring practices will impair reliability of the PSRS.

VALIDITY. No data on validity of the PSRS are provided. The processes of review of items by teachers, students, and parents to "ensure content validity" (manual, p. 7) are incompletely described. Threats to reliability cited above must also be considered to impair valid inference from test results.

Karnes and Bean (manual, p. 4) state the PSRS was designed to obtain ratings of a student's "facility in using process skills that *develop his/her ability to think, reason*, and search for knowledge independently, and to communicate and interact effectively with all members of society" (italics added). Although skills such as communication, study skills, and critical thinking may be fundamental to later learning and achievement, claims that they develop the ability to think and reason may be overstated.

CONCLUSIONS. Anastasi (1985, p. xxix) stated "the most effective tests are likely to be those developed for clearly defined purposes and for use within specific contexts." The PSRS lacks both clarity of purpose and specificity of context, thus it is difficult to deduce uses for which it would be effective. In the absence of evidence of the psychometric properties of the PSRS, test users bear sole responsibility for ensuring that their applications of the PSRS are reliable and valid. This is likely to be beyond the resources of many potential test users.

Among other uses, the authors suggest using the PSRS to assess students' functional levels and progress, and to guide instruction. Because reliability and validity of the PSRS is questionable, any use of the scales in summative evaluation of children's achievement, in grouping children, or in making similar discriminations among children is unwarranted and inappropriate. For the same reasons, the PSRS should not be used in evaluation of teachers' effectiveness.

Professional teachers regularly assess students' skills and needs by observing them perform tasks appropriate to their age and grade level, among other means. Parents have opportunities to make similar observations about their children, and to consult with teachers. Although the items on the PSRS may suggest interesting learning activities or discussion topics, the scales probably offer less trustworthy assessment information than would be obtained from careful observation of students' success in performing a variety of age- and grade-appropriate activities.

REVIEWER'S REFERENCES

American Educational Research Association, American Psychological Association, & National Council on Measurement in Education. (1985). *Standards for educational and psychological testing*. Washington, DC: American Psychological Association, Inc.

Anastasi, A. (1985). Mental measurement: Some emerging trends. In J. V. Mitchell (Ed.), *Ninth mental measurements yearbook* (pp. xxiii-xxix). Lincoln, NE: Buros Institute of Mental Measurements.

[311]

Professional and Managerial Position Questionnaire.

Purpose: Constructed for use in analyzing professional and managerial jobs.
Population: Professional and managerial jobs.
Publication Dates: 1980–92.
Acronym: PMPQ.
Scores: 3 categories: Job Functions, Personal Requirements, Other Information.
Administration: Group.
Price Data: Available from publisher.
Time: Administration time not reported.
Authors: J. L. Mitchell, E. J. McCormick, S. Morton McPhail (manual), P. Richard Jeanneret (manual), and Robert C. Mecham (manual).
Publisher: Consulting Psychologists Press, Inc.
Cross References: For reviews by Gregory H. Dobbins and George Thornton, see 9:993.

Review of the Professional and Managerial Position Questionnaire by MARY ANNE BUNDA, Professor of Educational Leadership, Western Michigan University, Kalamazoo, MI:

The technical manual developed for the original version of the Professional and Managerial Position Questionnaire (PMPQ) in 1979 has been supplemented by a single page reporting three uses of the instrument in the late 1970s. A new Job Analysis Manual was prepared by Consulting Psychologists Press in 1992. The new manual, as its title suggests, is designed to help organizations use the instrument to analyze positions. The procedures described in the manual suggest the instrument is used in an interview format with a "job analyst" performing the ratings while interviewing the incumbent of a position, or the supervisor of the incumbent, or for the original use of incumbent self-report. The manual contains no technical information on alternative data collection uses of the instrument. However, it might be noted that no published or fugitive uses of the instrument can be found in ERIC, PSYCHINFO, ABI inform, or the Business Periodical Index after the initial references to the development of the manual. The new job analysis manual has no technical information and a much shorter list of resources for the user.

As noted in previous reviews, the instrument was carefully constructed to fill a need of researchers for an instrument that could be used to measure administrative positions across a number of industries. A number of internally applied job classification and compensation systems in both the private and public sectors have been developed in the last two decades. Despite this, an instrument that crosses classification systems may still be worthwhile. However, the evidence set on this instrument does not take into consideration the growth in systems for classification of jobs. It does, however, offer the business community a number of ways to transfer files electronically.

The instrument yields three categories of scores. Within the Job Functions category, six different scores are possible. These scores range from Planning and Scheduling to Exercising Judgment and Communicating. There are two score types in the Personal Requirements section: Personal Development and Personal Qualities. The Other Information includes items relevant to certification, professional membership, and budget control. The item set that is aggregated for the scores requires essentially two dimensions of rating. The two dimensions are the extent to which the score area is a part of the position and the complexity of the score area as it is exhibited in the position. The rating scale in each dimension is a 10-point Likert type with the complexity scale anchored at every other point. The scope of the anchors for complexity show the range of positions that the test is designed to measure (e.g., the budgeting scale ranges from "estimating the costs of weekly office supplies" to "financial planning for a large state or a major corporation"). The reliability of the ratings has been addressed in the new manual in terms of rater consistency. However, no report is made of the study of raters. Nor has information been provided about the effects of incumbency on the ratings.

The validity evidence provided by the test developer is weak, primarily due to the use of salary as the major criterion variable. Correlational evidence from organizations with classification and compensation systems in place are likely to be spuriously high because of the overlap between the structure of most compensation systems and the PMPQ. No research has been reported on the efficacy of using the instrument across a number of different classification and compensation systems. Additionally, it should be noted that at least one user of the instrument noted that the accuracy of the ratings was not acceptable when the positions included a substantial component of professional or technical skill. That is, this instrument is primarily useful in the measurement of managerial responsibility rather than professional responsibilities. Furthermore, the instrument may overestimate positions at low level jobs and underestimate positions at high level jobs.

Researchers who have a need for information about managerial responsibility would be well advised to use this instrument only in conjunction with another measure.

Review of the Professional and Managerial Position Questionnaire by WILLIAM I. SAUSER, JR., Associate Vice President for Extension and Professor of Educational Foundations, Leadership, and Technology, Auburn University, Auburn, AL:

Job analysis has been defined as "the collection of data describing (a) observable (or otherwise verifiable) job behaviors performed by workers, including both *what is accomplished* as well as *what technologies are employed* to accomplish the end results and (b) verifiable characteristics of the job environment with which workers interact, including physical, mechanical, social, and informational elements" (Harvey, 1991, p. 74). Job analysis data can be used for a variety of purposes, including guiding vocational choice and work adjustment, establishing job requirements, designing jobs, and evaluating jobs in order to establish classification schemes and compensation systems (McCormick, 1979).

There are a variety of job analysis techniques, and each has particular strengths and weaknesses. The Professional and Managerial Position Questionnaire (PMPQ) is described in its technical manual as a "worker oriented" job analysis program. This type of job analysis instrument "describes even task-dissimilar jobs on a common set of descriptors that tend to be more behaviorally and technologically abstract than task statements" (Harvey, 1991, p. 94). Such instruments are, in the opinion of this reviewer, particularly well suited for classifying jobs and evaluating them for the purpose of establishing compensation systems. They are *not*, I believe, very useful for establishing a listing of tasks or duties associated with each job, or for designing training programs or performance review systems for jobs. Job analysts interested in these purposes should review Harvey (1991) and McCormick (1979) for more suitable techniques.

With respect to the construction or evaluation of tests to select employees, data provided by the PMPQ and other worker oriented job analysis procedures (such as the Position Analysis Questionnaire [299], which was developed by the same team who produced the PMPQ) may be useful when taking a construct validation approach to establishing job-relatedness, but they are not helpful when building content valid tests. Potential users of the PMPQ should consider carefully how they wish to use the resulting job analysis data. The PMPQ can be very helpful for some purposes, but of little utility for others.

The PMPQ is "a structured job analysis questionnaire for professional, managerial, and related positions such as those held by executives, supervisors, engineers, technicians, teachers, and other professionals" (test booklet, p. 1). The heart of the PMPQ is a set of 66 items designed to measure the job being analyzed in terms of (*a*) planning and scheduling, (*b*) processing information and ideas, (*c*) exercising judgment, (*d*) communicating, (*e*) interpersonal activities and relationships, and (*f*) technical activities. This is followed by a set of 17 items relating to such requirements for job success as education, training, experience, personal characteristics, and adaptability. The third set of questions—12 labeled as "other information"—gets at such matters as supervisory responsibilities, required licensing or certification, and basis of employment. Next there is a provision for 10 "extra" items to be provided at the option of the analyst using the PMPQ. The instrument concludes with a section describing how to calculate and provide confidential salary information about the job. This information presumably is used by the developers of the PMPQ to build the database against which the instrument is validated.

The PMPQ is a very complex instrument. It employs a variety of response scales, and is clearly designed to be used best by professional job analysts, *not* by job incumbents or supervisors. A well-prepared Job Analysis Manual guides the job analyst through every step of the procedure, which the manual authors state "can frequently be completed in about a day" (manual, p. 4). Raw data are recorded on an optical scan sheet, which is scored by PAQ Services, Inc. using proprietary formulae. Data entry via microcomputer at the analyst's site is an available option.

The current version of the PMPQ is much different in *appearance* from the original edition reviewed by Dobbins and Thornton (9:993). It is visually pleasing, with dark green ink on white paper (as opposed to the original brown on brown). Sexist language has been removed from the item descriptions, and the questionnaire and manual have been revised into a much more "user-friendly" format. The new Job Analysis Manual contains far more detailed information on how to conduct a successful job analysis interview. Descriptive information about each item is provided, eliminating much of the guesswork associated with the earlier edition.

However, *technically* this version appears identical to the original edition. Other than the editorial changes noted above, this is the same instrument as published in 1980; thus, Dobbins's and Thornton's evaluations are as relevant today as they were when originally published in 1985. The PMPQ remains an important and useful device, but it still suffers from the technical shortcomings noted in earlier reviews: (*a*) It is based on a review of older literature, (*b*) it has been validated against only one criterion (salary data), (*c*) the content is superficial in depth, and (*d*) it is lengthy and cumbersome to use. This reviewer also agrees with Harvey (1991), who found the PMPQ items much more "behaviorally abstract" (p. 150) than those of the other managerial instruments he reviewed—Lozada-Larsen's (1988) EXCEL and Page and Gomez's (1979) Position Description Questionnaire.

In summary, the PMPQ remains a valuable—though somewhat technically flawed—job analysis instrument for use with professional, managerial, and related positions held by executives, supervisors, engineers, technicians, teachers, and other professionals. The new edition is more visually appealing and "user-friendly" than the original version, and the new Job Analysis Manual contains much better guidance than the old manual. Technically, however, the new edition of the PMPQ is virtually identical to the original. If the job analyst's goal is to classify a variety of managerial and professional jobs and to construct a meaningful compensation system, the PMPQ may be a very useful tool. On the other hand, if the purpose is to identify in detail the tasks performed by the job incumbents in order to construct job sample tests or training programs, or to redesign the job ergonomically, the job analyst should consider some of the other job analysis methods described in McCormick (1979) and Harvey (1991).

REVIEWER'S REFERENCES

McCormick, E. J. (1979). *Job analysis: Methods and applications.* New York: AMACOM.

Page, K. C., & Gomez, L. R. (1979). *The development and application of job evaluation systems using the Position Description Questionnaire.* (Personnel Research Report No. 161-79). Minneapolis, MN: Control Data Corporation.

Lozada-Larsen, S. R. (1988). *Going beyond criticism: Management work theory and research.* Unpublished doctoral dissertation, Rice University, Houston.

Harvey, R. J. (1991). Job analysis. In M. D. Dunnette & L. M. Hough (Eds.), *Handbook of industrial and organizational psychology* (2nd ed. vol. 2; pp. 71-163). Palo Alto, CA: Consulting Psychologists Press, Inc.

[312]

Professional Employment Test.

Purpose: Designed to measure reading comprehension, reasoning, quantitative problem solving, and data interpretation for use in selecting personnel for professional, administrative, and managerial occupations.
Population: Potential professional state employees.
Publication Dates: 1986–87.
Acronym: PET.
Scores: Total score only.
Administration: Group.
Forms, 4: A, B, C, D.
Price Data: Available from publisher.
Time: 80(85) minutes for long form; 40(45) minutes for short form.
Authors: William W. Ruch, Richard H. McKillip, and Ricki Buckly.
Publisher: Psychological Services, Inc.

Review of the Professional Employment Test by GREGORY J. CIZEK, Assistant Professor of Educational Research and Measurement, University of Toledo, Toledo, OH:

The Professional Employment Test (PET) is a test of "abilities that are important for the successful performance of work behaviors in professional occupations" (manual, p. 1) in a written, multiple-choice format. The test is designed to assist in selection decisions for professional, administrative, and managerial positions in state and local governments.

The PET was developed to assess four cognitive abilities that have been demonstrated to be related to occupational success and productivity: Reading Comprehension, Quantitative Problem Solving, Data Interpretation, and Reasoning. The test consists of a sample item for each cognitive ability area with an explanation of the correct response, and 40 items on which examinees are scored. Succinct, complete directions for examinees are provided in each test booklet and a separate manual with detailed procedures for test administrators is available. The time limit for the test is 80 minutes.

Reading Comprehension items present the examinee with a paragraph; the examinee's task is to identify an accurate summarization or inference based on the paragraph. Quantitative Problem Solving tasks consist of two- or three-step arithmetic problems based on simple business scenarios. Reasoning items present syllogisms and require the examinee to evaluate the probable truth or falsehood of a conclusion from a set of premises. For the Data Interpretation items, examinees must deduce the values for missing entries in a table.

A transparent overlay is used to hand score examinees' responses. Scoring provides raw scores and percentile scores derived from a sample of 2,835 workers from one state. Nineteen occupations were represented in the sample.

RELIABILITY AND VALIDITY. Parallel forms reliability and an internal consistency estimate (KR-20) for the PET are reported to be .85 and .86, respectively. Parallel forms reliability was established by administering two forms of the test to a sample of 582 examinees. The technical manual does not include enough descriptive information about the sample used.

Validity for three occupations was examined (eligibility worker, probation and parole specialist, computer programmer/analyst). These occupations represented unique clusterings of abilities (facilitative; research and investigative; technical and administrative; respectively) resulting from a single state job analysis study. Validity studies were conducted using the same sample (n = 2,835) described above. In addition to PET scores, data consisted of supervisors' ratings and work samples; job knowledge test scores were gathered on the eligibility worker group only.

Validity of the PET (Form A) for predicting supervisory ratings was .31 for eligibility workers, .27 for probation and parole specialists, and .24 for programmer/analysts. Validity coefficients rose to .45, .40, and .35, respectively when corrected for both restriction of range and unreliability in the criterion. (An estimated reliability of .60 was used to adjust for unreliability in the criterion measure because reliability coefficients were unavailable for the supervisory ratings.)

Validity coefficients of the PET for predicting work samples for the three occupations were .42, .30, and .59, respectively. Corrected coefficients were .61, .44, and .84.

Job knowledge test scores were gathered only for eligibility workers; the validity of the PET for predicting this criterion was .56 (.75 when corrected). An "overall average" validity coefficient across the three occupations and criterion measures is reported to be .51.

Bias studies were also performed during item tryouts. The manual authors report "items that were disproportionately difficult for blacks were eliminated from the test" (manual, p. 7). No indication is provided regarding the disposition of items that may have been disproportionately difficult for whites nor is the criterion for "disproportionate difficulty." Also, no information is given regarding differential item functioning in other groups (e.g., Hispanics, males vs. females, etc.).

The manual includes references to the Equal Opportunity Employment Commission (EEOC) uniform guidelines on employee selection procedures. Also included are useful tables for estimating increases in employee performance and productivity that would be expected using various cutoffs. Information on "transportability," or the usefulness of the PET in contexts and occupations not addressed in its validity studies, is also in the manual.

RECOMMENDATIONS AND CAUTIONS. Overall, the test construction procedures, reliability and validity evidence, and documentation provided with the PET address many standards of sound testing practice. As with any instrument, the PET has relative strengths and weaknesses. The PET's strengths include: its foundation in job analyses; the availability of technical documentation, including validity studies and bias prevention procedures; sufficient guidelines for test administrators; and the fact that it can be administered quickly and scored easily.

As with all tests, potential users of the PET should be cautious in using the test and interpreting the results. First, although internal consistency and parallel forms reliability indices are reported, a test-retest coefficient is not. The stability of PET scores is critical to accurate decision making and would be worthy of future investigation.

Second, the validity information rests on a sample of three job classifications from a single state, raising some questions about generalizability. The validity coefficients—even corrected for unreliability and restriction of range—are modest. As indicated in the manual, users are cautioned to "transport" this validity evidence only to other situations in which employees perform "substantially the same major work behaviors" (manual, p. 25). Investigations were conducted to eliminate biased items; however, validity studies reported in the technical manual indicated that "the PET actually overpredicts job performance for blacks" (p. 19).

An additional weakness of the PET is more conceptual than technical. As described earlier, PET validity studies show differential validity for the three major work skills investigated (i.e., facilitative, research/investigative, and technical/administrative). Thus, the "overall average" validity coefficient of .51 for the PET is misleading for predicting performance in any individual work skill area; the individual validity coefficients are uniformly lower. For jobs that clearly fall in these major work areas, an instrument that assessed the dominant cognitive skill would be preferable.

Also, although norms are provided (see above), PET scores are most meaningful when compared to locally developed norms. However, most users of the PET may not have the ability to produce local norms. Unfortunately, information on local norm development is lacking, and insufficient cautions are given to guard against the inevitable improper use of the norms tables provided in the manual. Additional information and guidance should be presented regarding proper test use and interpretation of scores.

Finally, as other research has consistently revealed, the best predictors of job performance are the sets of knowledges, skills, and abilities that are specific to the job in question. Although tests of general ability like the PET may be good predictors, they are probably most useful in conjunction with other, reliable, job-specific information.

In summary, the PET is an easily administered test of important cognitive abilities that provides some useful information to agencies charged with screening applicants for professional, administrative, and managerial positions in state and local governments. The abilities tested show relationships to success in several occupations. The PET should be useful to governmental entities seeking additional information to supplement employment decisions, although it should not be used as a sole determinant, or when other, more job-relevant assessments are available.

Review of the Professional Employment Test by JAYNE E. STAKE, Professor of Psychology, University of Missouri-St. Louis, St. Louis, MO:

The Professional Employment Test (PET) was originally developed for personnel selection in state government. The PET was designed to assess aptitude for professional, administrative, and managerial occupations. Two parallel 40-item forms are available, each of which includes the following types of items: Data Interpretation, Reasoning (syllogisms), Quantitative Problem Solving, and Reading Comprehension. The content of most of the questions is relevant to business and state government settings.

Test items were selected from an initial item pool of 198 questions. All data interpretation and reading comprehension items in the original item pool were administered to 187 employees of a state government, and all syllogisms and quantitative problems in the pool were administered to a second group of 182 state employees. Criteria for item selection, as provided in the manual, were (*a*) moderate difficulty level, (*b*) success in discriminating high test scorers, (*c*) effective item distractors (foils), and (*d*) equal difficulty level for Black and White employees. The manual does not contain information concerning the actual item difficulty level, item discrimination, or distractor effectiveness of the questions that were selected for the PET. Furthermore, selected test items were not cross validated.

The reliability of both forms of the PET was .86, as measured by the KR-20 formula. The two forms were highly correlated (.85) and yielded equivalent means, standard deviations, and standard errors of measurement. Hence, the forms appear to be comparable. The validity of both forms was tested for three government occupations: eligibility worker, probation and parole specialist, and computer programmer.

Performance on the PET was correlated with three job performance criteria associated with these occupations: supervisory ratings, a work sample that simulated representative job tasks, and a job knowledge test (eligibility workers only). Correlations between PET scores and criterion measures ranged from .17 to .31 for supervisory ratings, .23 to .59 for work sample performance, and .55 to .56 for job knowledge test scores. The test authors reasoned that these correlations were attenuated by the restricted range of scores of the employees tested and the unreliability of criterion scores. The true correlations were estimated to be higher for supervisory ratings (.25 to .45), work sample performance (.34 to .84), and job knowledge (.74 to .75). Although these higher validity values are described in the test manual as the best estimates of validity, test users should note the higher values have not been empirically demonstrated. Validity studies have not been undertaken with a less restricted range of test scores or more reliable criterion measures. Furthermore, the validity of the PET has not been tested for other types of job performance, and test norms are available only for the three occupational groups in the validity study.

As acknowledged by the test authors, any measures developed for personnel selection should be carefully scrutinized for test fairness. The PET manual describes one study of test fairness. Relationships between PET scores and job criterion measures used in the validity study were determined separately for Black and White eligibility workers. The regression lines for the test score/criterion relationships were significantly different for Black and White examinees for two of the three criteria—work sample performance and job knowledge test performance. These findings suggest that the PET may underestimate the potential of White examinees, or overestimate the potential of Black examinees, to perform the job of eligibility worker. These results were unexpected and are difficult to interpret, but they provide evidence the PET does not disadvantage Black job applicants. No other studies of test bias have been undertaken, yet other types of test bias are possible. For example, the PET includes quantitative questions that may not be relevant to a particular job classification, such as probation and parole specialist. Because men tend to outperform women on tests of quantitative ability, the PET may underestimate the potential of women to perform as probation and parole specialists.

The authors calculate the value of the PET to an organization in terms of the improved quality of applicant selected. The test user is cautioned to regard these figures as speculative estimates. These calculations were based on two assumptions. First, the validity coefficient for the PET that was chosen for the calculations was .50. This value is an estimate of the true validity corrected for restriction of range and unreliability of criterion measures and may overestimate the true validity of the PET. Second, the calculation of the utility of the PET was based on the assumption that other predictive criteria would not be used in personnel selection. However, other information that is normally available when personnel decisions are made may have equal or greater power to predict job success. Employment history has been particularly useful for predicting later job performance.

In summary, the PET has proven to be a reliable instrument that has some ability to predict job performance variables in selected occupations. The PET may be useful as a rough estimate of cognitive ability, but caution should be used in interpreting test scores. The PET may not be test fair for all applicants and may not be as predictive of job performance as other factors, such as job history. Before using the PET as a selection tool, the relationship between PET scores and job performance should be determined for the specific job category and applicant pool in question.

[313]

Progressive Achievement Test of Mathematics [Revised].

Purpose: To assist classroom teachers in determining the mathematics skills of their students.
Population: Ages 8-0 to 14-11.
Publication Dates: 1974–94.
Acronym: PATM.
Scores: Total score only.
Administration: Group.
Levels: 7 overlapping levels called Parts 2 (Standard 2), 3(3), 4(4), 5(Form 1), 6(2), 7(3), 8(4) in three booklets (Primary, Parts 2–4; Intermediate, Parts 5 and 6; Secondary, Parts 7 and 8); 2 forms: A and B.
Price Data, 1995: NZ$5.85 per teacher's manual ('93, 46 pages); $1.53 per test booklet (Primary (S2-S4), Intermediate (F1 & F2), Secondary (F3 & F4); $.72 per marking key (Parts 2–8); $1.35 per answer sheet (Parts 2–8).
Time: (45–55) minutes.
Author: Neil A. Reid.
Publisher: New Zealand Council for Educational Research [New Zealand].
Cross References: See T3:1911 (1 reference) and 8:288 for a review of an earlier edition by Harold C. Trimble; see 11:309 for reviews by James C. Impara and A. Harry Passow of an earlier Australian edition.

TEST REFERENCES

1. Bornholt, L. J., Goodnow, J. J., & Cooney, G. H. (1994). Influences of gender stereotypes on adolescents' perception of their own achievement. *American Educational Research Journal, 31*, 675-692.

Review of the Progressive Achievement Test of Mathematics [Revised] by LINDA E. BRODY, Director, Study of Exceptional Talent, Center for Talented Youth, The Johns Hopkins University, Baltimore, MD:

The Progressive Achievement Test of Mathematics was designed to help teachers in New Zealand schools evaluate their students' knowledge of mathematics and develop an appropriate educational plan to meet their needs. Based on the assumption that students learn at different rates and that the pace and level of instruction should be adjusted to meet individual needs, the test authors suggest the test can be used by teachers to assist in: (*a*) grouping students with similar needs and competencies within a classroom for instructional purposes, (*b*) setting realistic goals and selecting materials appropriate for the differing achievement levels of their students, (*c*) identifying students requiring special diagnostic and remedial treatment, (*d*) selecting able students who require special mathematics programs, (*e*) providing a frame of reference within which to evaluate the mathematical competencies of their students and to help assess the extent to which the cognitive outcomes of the mathematics curriculum are being achieved, and (*f*) locating areas of weakness among students in a class. Teachers are cautioned, however, against using the test as an exclusive diagnostic measure and are told to supplement it with additional information.

The test battery includes seven 50-item multiple-choice tests, each designed for one grade level: Standard 2 through Form 4 (approximately grades 3 through 9). The tests are printed in three booklets: Primary for Standards 2, 3, and 4; Intermediate for Forms 1 and 2; and Secondary for Forms 3 and 4. Interestingly, the test is organized in an overlapping format so that students in adjacent grade levels repeat some of the same items. For example, students in Standard 2 answer questions 1–50 and students in Standard 3 answer questions 26–75 in the same booklet. Administered at the beginning of the school year, there are two forms of the test, A and B, used in alternate years.

Recall, computation, understanding, and application items are included to test students' knowledge of computation, fractions and decimals, measurement and money, elementary algebraic and geometric principles and procedures, and other pre-algebra topics. The items assess classic skills in mathematics as well as topics that are the results of recent efforts to reform mathematics education.

The test was developed on the basis of the mathematics syllabus used in New Zealand schools. The 1993 revised version was pilot tested in over 50 representative primary, intermediate, and secondary schools. As a result of the pilot testing, the most technically reliable items were retained for the final forms. Age and grade norms are provided and allow comparison of a child's performance to others of the same age or in the same grade in New Zealand schools.

The Teacher's Manual contains excellent instructions for administering, scoring, and interpreting the test. The technical information provided includes reliability coefficients for equivalent forms, split-half, and Kuder-Richardson; all are in the acceptable range. The items were reviewed for gender, ethnic, and other types of bias.

It appears this test serves a useful purpose for mathematics teachers in New Zealand because careful work has gone into relating the test to the curriculum in use in New Zealand schools. It is important, however, that teachers not use the test for diagnostic purposes. The test is too short for that. Although the author cautions against it in the manual, it may be tempting to use it that way. It is most useful as a gross measure for grouping students, or as an indicator of students in need of more in-depth diagnosis. In spite of the advantages of the national norms, it may actually be most useful for within-class comparisons of student performance.

For use outside of New Zealand, there are more limitations. Teachers or school systems considering using this test to assess mathematics achievement must consider the extent to which it reflects the curriculum in place in their school. There are also a few examples where spelling and usage reflect New Zealand practices, as well as the use of a space rather than a comma in numbers over 1,000, but students could be instructed in how to respond to these differences. The lack of normative information outside of New Zealand is another limitation for wider use; ideally, norms should be developed for other countries.

The manual author does not discuss out-of-level testing. It should be considered. The proximity of sequential, adjacent tests in the same booklets facilitate letting a student progress through several tests until difficulty with course content becomes apparent. Knowing that a student is capable of achieving well on an above-grade-level test would alert a teacher to the need to offer such a student more advanced coursework; at the same time, a teacher would have more information if below-grade-level testing is offered to a student who performs poorly on a grade-level assessment. The greater number of items available by asking students to take more than one test would also help offset the disadvantage of the small number of items on one test, although teachers are still encouraged to seek additional information before using this test for diagnostic and prescriptive purposes.

In summary, the Progressive Achievement Test of Mathematics is a technically sound instrument for use in New Zealand schools if it is used appropriately, bearing in mind the limitations expressed in the manual. It is less useful outside of New Zealand due to the absence of normative data from other countries or information about the relationship of test items to the mathematics curriculum in use outside of New Zealand. The strengths of the test, however, are the acknowledgment of individual differences in learning rate and achievement among students and its sequential evaluation of student performance. Thus, if teachers critique the content of the test items and deem it appropriate for their purposes, this test can serve as a valuable supplement to other indices of student achievement.

Review of the Progressive Achievement Test of Mathematics [Revised] by SUZANNE LANE, Associate Professor of Research Methodology, University of Pittsburgh, Pittsburgh, PA:

The Progressive Achievement Test (PAT) of Mathematics, Forms A and B is a group-administered test developed for use in schools in New Zealand and is "intended primarily to assist classroom teachers in determining the levels of development attained by their students in the basic skills and understandings of mathematics" (Teacher's Manual, p. 3). According to the author, it should be administered early in the school year and information obtained by the PAT of Mathematics can be used by teachers for several purposes such as grouping students for instruction within a classroom, identifying students requiring further diagnosis, selecting more able students for special mathematics programs, and providing a profile of weaknesses and strengths within a classroom.

The PAT: Mathematics Test provides seven different overlapping levels that collectively span seven grades (classes), which are Standard 2 to Form 4. The different levels are represented in three test booklets: Primary for Standards 2, 3, and 4; Intermediate for Forms 1 and 2; and Secondary for Forms 3 and 4.

The Primary test consists of 100 multiple-choice items with each Part represented by 50 items. The Intermediate and Secondary tests each consist of 75 multiple-choice items with each of their respective Parts represented by 50 items. Total administration time for each Part is 55 minutes with actual test time being 45 minutes.

Accompanying the test is the Teacher's Manual which contains technical information about the test and information on how to administer, score, and interpret/use the test results. The instructions for test administration and the directions for students taking the test are clear and easy to follow. Students record their choices on a separate answer sheet and teachers score the answer sheets to obtain each student's total score. Thus, teachers have access to the results for instructional purposes immediately following the administration of the test.

CONTENT AND TEST REVISION. The 1993 version of the PAT: Mathematics Test was revised "to achieve a balanced content coverage at each class level" (Teacher's Manual, p. 4). All items are classified in a content by process matrix. The content areas were determined by the syllabi of the New Zealand Ministry of Education and modifications were made based on the specifications of the draft *Mathematics in the National Curriculum*. Four processes were specified and are described in the manual: recall, computation, understanding, and application. In general, the proportion of items assessing understanding and application increases as the grade level increases.

Teachers, mathematics specialists, and Officers of the Ministry of Education in New Zealand were involved in the revision of the test. The original PAT: Mathematics Test was developed in the early 1970s and in the latter part of the 1980s mathematics advisors and teachers were consulted regarding the quality and relevancy of the test. A small panel of mathematics advisors and teachers made recommendations after a review of the original specifications and items. Also, a nationally representative sample of teachers and mathematics advisors were surveyed to obtain information on the "relevance and currency of the test content; the appropriateness of items, test length and timing; the format of test booklets, answer sheets and marking keys; and aspects of score information, presentation and interpretation" (Teacher's Manual, p. 31).

Based on the findings of the national survey and recommendations of the panel of mathematics teachers and advisors, the revision process began in 1991. The majority of the items developed by the selected teachers and staff were piloted at least three times on 120 or more students in 50 primary, intermediate, and secondary schools throughout the country. The author indicates the item characteristics on which the forms were matched included a number of variables such as process and content classifications and average difficulty and discrimination indices; however, discrimination indices and criteria used for selecting items are not reported in the manual. Although the author indicates the new items were piloted with items that were retained from the original test, there is no mention of the proportion of items on the 1993 version that were on the 1973–1974 version.

The items are written clearly and appear to be well constructed. Many items contain diagrams, graphs, maps, or tables, and there is use of "real world" representations such as surveys and recipes. As previously mentioned, many of the items assess students' understanding and application of mathematical concepts.

NORMS. The national standardization sample was tested at the end of March in 1992. The sample was selected in a multistage process in which the schools were systematically selected from the 12 education districts in New Zealand, according to level (primary, intermediate, and secondary) and to size of community (large urban, urban, town, rural). A total of 192 schools participated in the norming with each school weighted so that every child had an equal chance of participating. Within each school, 30 students at each grade level were randomly selected, with equal number of boys and girls selected at each grade level. There were approximately 1,000 students at each grade level. Ethnicity of students (e.g., Maori, Pacific Islanders, and immigrants from South-east Asian) was not directly controlled for in selecting the sample. Each student took both Form A and B of the appropriate grade level test with the order of administration varied systematically across schools.

Both age and grade norms are provided in terms of percentile ranks and stanines. Age percentile norms are provided for each half-year age group between 8 and 14 years. The norm conversion tables are clear and easy to use.

RELIABILITY. The Kuder-Richardson 20, equivalent form, and split-half reliability coefficients are provided for each form within each of the seven levels. The reliability coefficients are quite good; they are in the high .80s and the low .90s. The standard error of measurement is given for each form within each of the seven levels as are the reliability coefficients. The *SEM*s were calculated using the median reliability estimates. Also presented are the means and standard deviations for each form within each of the seven levels for boys and girls separately as well as combined.

VALIDITY. As previously mentioned, the test specifications and items were designed to reflect the national syllabi and were developed and reviewed by both teachers and mathematics advisors in New Zealand. The items appear to reflect the test specifications; however, prior to using the test, teachers would be advised to review the items to ensure the content and processes being assessed reflect their instruction.

Evidence for concurrent validity is provided by the correlation between scores on the PAT: Mathematics Test and other mathematics tests such as the Iowa Tests of Basic Skills. These correlations range from .67 to .81. Both logical and empirical studies were conducted to examine differential item functioning (DIF). Items that were identified as DIF by both of the implemented statistical procedures were retained after members of the culturally relevant group indicated that the source of differential responding did not appear to be a result of cultural differences. Reliability and validity evidence is both impressive and presented with unusual clarity.

MANUAL. As previously indicated, the Teacher's Manual is well written and informative. In particular, the sections on how to interpret the test scores are excellent. Clear descriptions are provided for teachers on how to convert raw scores to percentile ranks, how to interpret percentile ranks, and how not to interpret percentile ranks (e.g., they cannot be used to indicate score differences between students). Descriptions of how to interpret scores with respect to the standard error of measurement and confidence bands, and how to obtain percentile bands for given scores are informative and clearly written. A section on how to interpret test results to students and parents is also included.

In the section on uses of the test results, the author provides a table identifying common incorrect options and probable misconceptions underlying an incorrect option for each item. The author describes how teachers can use this information and the comparison of their classes' item difficulty indices with the provided national item difficulty indices to identify strengths and weaknesses of their classes. The author should be commended for cautioning teachers to use additional information in conjunction with the item-level information to identify their classes' strengths and weaknesses. The author further cautions classifying students as weak or strong in a particular content area such as fractions because of the small number of items measuring a content area.

SUMMARY. The PAT: Mathematics Test is a well-designed test that measures New Zealand students' basic skills and understanding in mathematics. The test results can be used by teachers to guide instruction and facilitate student learning. It appears the author's test development efforts adhere to the *Standards for Educational and Psychological Testing* (American Educational Research Association, American Psychological Association, & National Council on Measurement in Education, 1985). The revision and norming procedures were carefully crafted, reliability coefficients are relatively high, and efforts were made to ensure the test matched New Zealand's mathematics curricula. If the test were to be used outside of New Zealand, the content and wording of some of the items would require revision and appropriate norms would need to be developed.

REVIEWER'S REFERENCE

American Educational Research Association, American Psychological Association, & National Council on Measurement in Education. (1985). *Standards for educational and psychological testing*. Washington, DC: American Psychological Association, Inc.

[314]

Progressive Achievement Tests of Reading [Revised].

Purpose: Designed to assess the skills and abilities of the students in reading with a view to providing instruction adapted to their present stages of development.
Population: Standards 2–4, Forms 1–2, Forms 3–4 in New Zealand schools (Ages 8–14).
Publication Dates: 1969–91.
Scores, 2: Reading Comprehension, Reading Vocabulary.
Administration: Group.
Levels, 3: Primary, Intermediate, Secondary.
Forms, 2: A, B.
Price Data: Available from publisher.
Time: 55 minutes for Comprehension part, 40 minutes for Vocabulary part.
Comments: Raw scores convert to the Level scores (1–10), age percentile rank, and class percentile rank.
Authors: Neil A. Reid and Warwick B. Elley.
Publisher: New Zealand Council for Educational Research [New Zealand].
Cross References: See T4:2141 (7 references) and T3:1912 (2 references); for a review by Douglas A. Pidgeon, see 8:738 (1 reference); see also T2:1579 (1 reference); for excerpted reviews by Milton L. Clark and J. Elkins, see 7:699.

TEST REFERENCES

1. Fergusson, D. M., & Horwood, L. J. (1992). Attention deficit and reading achievement. *Journal of Child Psychology and Psychiatry and Allied Disciplines*, *33*, 375-385.
2. Fergusson, D. M., Lynskey, M. T., & Horwood, L. J. (1994). The effects of parental separation, the timing of separation and gender on children's performance on cognitive tests. *Journal of Child Psychology and Psychiatry and Allied Disciplines*, *35*, 1077-1092.
3. Fergusson, D. M., & Horwood, L. J. (1995). Early disruptive behavior, IQ, and later school achievement and delinquent behavior. *Journal of Abnormal Child Psychology*, *23*, 183-199.

Review of the Progressive Achievement Tests of Reading [Revised] by HERBERT C. RUDMAN, Professor of Measurement and Quantitative Methods, Department of Counseling, Educational Psychology and Special Education, Michigan State University, East Lansing, MI:

TEST CONTENT. The Progressive Achievement Tests of Reading (PATR), originally published in 1969, were designed to measure reading comprehension and reading vocabulary. This 1991 revision continues to measure just these two facets of the reading process. A test user looking for detailed information about enabling skills such as structural analysis (the ability to decode words by syllables, affixes, and root words), and phonetic analysis of consonants and vowels (the relationships between sounds and letters) will have to look elsewhere.

The original version of the PATR was designed to measure literal as well as inferential comprehension of prose material. According to the authors, a "sizable" sample of teachers in New Zealand determined the reading skills and materials to be included in the tests. These skills and materials were weighted by these teachers as well as by reading specialists from 10 regional committees. It would appear that those opinions have remained stable since 1969; the weightings and types of materials are still reflected in this newest version of the PATR.

The comprehension portion of the tests contains an approximately even distribution of factual and inferential items at each battery level. These items accompany passages 100 to 300 words in length. Although differing definitions of reading comprehension are available, most reading specialists would agree that content for such a test can also be identified by function, for example, paragraph reading, textual reading, functional reading (signs, newspapers, rules and regulations, directions), and recreational reading.

The Progressive Achievement Tests of Reading contain passages that the authors have classified under three rubrics: Narrative, Descriptive, and Expository. These passages are distributed rather evenly across grades and battery levels. Although it is possible that an American reviewer could misinterpret the terms, "narrative," "descriptive," and "expository" as used in New Zealand, a careful reading of the passages still indicates that of a total of 58 passages used across three battery levels, only one is drawn from a news magazine (Secondary Level, Form A, p. 12). When compared to reading materials used in comparable standardized achievement tests reviewed elsewhere in this *Mental Measurements Yearbook* series, The PATR's content more closely resembles textbook material than it does a variety of materials drawn from everyday life.

Any well-constructed test should be a reflection of an instructional theory that can be used to describe an instructional domain. Any critique of a test should be based, in part, on how well that domain has been sampled. The material sent for review does not adequately describe such a theory of reading comprehension. The domain appears to be, by definition, narrowly focused as exemplified by the authors' prefatory acknowledgments and their list of illustrative materials of suitable difficulty level (manual, pp. 2, 21).

The domain of words sampled by the various levels of vocabulary tests is defined as the 10,000 most commonly used words in the English language. The words were apparently drawn from one word list (Wright, 1965). This reviewer regrets that no other rationale for the choice of words to be tested was considered except the total number of common words defined. Because the vocabulary tests are school-related it would make some sense if they came from lists of words likely to be encountered in various school activities. Words do, sometimes, have special meanings in a context of academic disciplines. If the words were classified by content groupings, additional instructional use could be made of the data collected from vocabulary tests. Advances in the physical, biological, and social sciences have introduced into the common vocabulary a number of words which may have been considered specialized when Wright's common core vocabulary list was published in 1965. Surely, these words should have been incorporated into the 1991 revision of the PATR.

The Progressive Achievement Tests of Reading are organized into three battery levels: Primary, Intermediate, and Secondary. The Primary battery is used by students in grades 2, 3, and 4; the Intermediate level in grades 5 and 6; the Secondary battery for grades 7 and 8. Two forms, A and B, are available for measuring both reading comprehension and vocabulary. The New Zealand Educational Research Council (the developers and publishers of the PATR) recommend that Form A be administered in odd-numbered years and Form B in even-numbered years.

The authors use eight overlapping levels (or "parts") to measure Reading Comprehension and Reading Vocabulary content from Standard 2 (grade 2) to Form 4 (grade 8). The Primary battery contains 62 Reading Comprehension items divided into three different starting and ending points. Pupils in grade 2 complete "Part Two" (Items 1–41). Pupils in grade 3 begin with "Part Three" (Items 12–51), and those in grade 4 complete "Part Four" (Items 22–62). A similar scheme is used for Reading Vocabulary (45 items). The number of items across all three battery levels total 107 for Reading Comprehension and 125 for Reading Vocabulary. Each succeeding battery uses some of the same items and reading passages contained in the previous lower battery (Primary, Part 4 ranges from Item 22 to Item 62. Intermediate, Part 5 begins with Item 32 and ends with Item 72).

TECHNICAL ASPECTS. The PATR was constructed with considerable care. New items which were written and older items which were retained from the 1969 version were item analyzed in 44 primary, intermediate, and secondary schools throughout New Zealand. Extensive use was made of teachers and reading specialists throughout the item development phase. Reading vocabulary items were selected and calibrated for difficulty based upon previous renorming and item analyses conducted in 1981 and 1988. In some instances sentences used in 1969 were rewritten when "several" words had changed drastically. Neither the number of words nor the words themselves are identified. The basic source for these words remained the 1965 Wright word list used in the original edition of the PATR.

Conventional item analyses were conducted on the revised tests, and items that met the authors' specifications were incorporated into new item analysis versions for final standardization. Equivalent forms were prepared using the following variables for matching: numbers of items and reading passages, types of passages, readability indices, average difficulty and discrimination levels of the blocks of items related to the passages, and the balance of literal and inferential items. Vocabulary test forms were matched in blocks of five using difficulty and discrimination indices, as well as frequency of occurrence on the Wright list.

The PATR was standardized on a representative sample of 1,000 students at each class level from grade 2 (Standard 2) to grade 8 (Form 4). The total standardization sample consisted of 8,016 students and 180 schools drawn from the 12 education districts in New Zealand. The number of students tested represented 1 in 50 of the total population at each class level.

Care was taken to mitigate item bias, both cultural and statistical bias. Items in both the reading comprehension and vocabulary tests were examined for apparent gender, ethnic, or other types of cultural bias which could be offensive to a subgroup of the New Zealand population. Items that were so identified through a judgmental process were either rewritten or eliminated. Statistical control of bias was established through special studies in schools known to have large student populations consisting of Maori and Pacific Island students. Samples of European and non-European students were matched by grade level, gender, and total test score. Test results were then analyzed for differential item performance. A McNemar Chi-Square Test revealed statistical differences for only two items in both Forms A and B. Those items that showed differences between European and non-European students were reviewed by Maori members of the New Zealand Council for Educational Research and by "specialist Auckland advisers." The differences observed were judged to be "chance statistical fluctuations" and were retained in the test.

Reliability estimates for the reading comprehension test, grades 2–8 all yielded respectably high correlations: .85–.88 (equivalent forms); .88–.92 (split-half); and .87–.94 (KR20). Similar reliability estimates for the vocabulary test across the same grade levels were: .91–.94 (equivalent forms), .92–.95 (split-half), and .92–.96 (KR20).

Validity as discussed in the Teacher's Manual is puzzling. Although the importance of content validity of standardized achievement tests is very well stated the authors then seem to back away from the case they make for validity because it appears to be subjective. In their words they offer such sources of evidence of content validity as, "a detailed and thorough examination of the contents of the test–its structure and emphases, its correspondence with accepted syllabuses, commonly used graded reading series, and other resource materials . . . . This is largely a *subjective process*" [emphasis added] (p. 35). They then express concern that no statistical data can adequately establish content validity. Although one can argue that descriptive statistics dealing with frequencies and proportions can indeed help establish a base that relates the content of an instructional program with the content of the test, that really should be self-evident. However, no such specificity is offered in support of content validity except in the general terms just cited.

Examples are offered of concurrent validity in terms of correlations with other tests in the Progressive Achievement Test Series, as well as correlations with other standardized achievement tests in other English-speaking countries. This is impressive, but hardly necessary to establish a case for achievement test validity. I would have appreciated a more specific description of the sources that defined the domains measured in the reading test.

The greatest asset to the test user the PATR offers is the very practical suggestions for interpretation of the test scores. The caveats offered are sound, the case studies offered are realistic, and the discussions of the contributions and limitations of derived scores are as good as I have seen represented in other interpretive materials.

The Teacher's Manual has several tables of data that deal with item difficulty indices for both forms of the comprehension and vocabulary tests for all grades. Other norm tables consist of percentile rank norms by age and stanine (Forms A and B), and percentile rank norms by class and stanine. The tables are easy to interpret and allow individual as well as group interpretation.

SUMMARY. The reading passages are very interesting and should add pleasure to students who do not always view testing as a pleasurable experience. All told, the New Zealand Council for Educational Research has produced a good test for those programs more concerned with reading comprehension than with the measurement of enabling word study skills.

REVIEWER'S REFERENCE

Wright, C. W. (1965). *An English word count.* Pretoria: National Bureau of Educational and Social Research.

[315]

Prosody-Voice Screening Profile.

Purpose: Developed to assess speech characteristics of prosody and voice.

Population: Speech-delayed children.

Publication Date: 1990.

Acronym: PVSP.

Scores, 6: Prosody (Phrasing, Rate, Stress), Voice (Loudness, Pitch, Quality).

Administration: Individual.

Price Data: Not available.

Time: Administration time not reported.

Comments: Audiocassette recorder necessary for administration.

Authors: Lawrence D. Shriberg, Joan Kwiatkowski, and Carmen Rasmussen.

Publisher: Communication Skill Builders.
[The publisher advised in April 1994 that this test is now out of print—Ed.]

Review of the Prosody-Voice Screening Profile by LAURIE FORD, Assistant Professor of Psychology, University of South Carolina, Columbia, SC, and MICHAL NISSENBAUM, Graduate Student, Department of Educational Psychology, Texas A&M University, College Station, TX:

The Prosody-Voice Screening Profile (PVSP) is an instrument developed to screen prosody or intonation behaviors in six suprasegmental areas: Phrasing, Rate, Stress, Loudness, Pitch, and Quality. The tool was developed primarily for use with young children who have intelligibility problems. However, the authors report that the PVSP procedures may be used to screen clients of all ages and primary voice disorders. The PVSP requires the use of an audiocassette of a conversational speech sample of 12 to 25 or more utterances. Authors report that the coding procedure takes approximately 15 to 30 minutes. However, reviewers found that the actual coding time is likely to be somewhat longer for novices to the coding procedures.

Given the theoretical and methodological complexities that surface when one attempts to identify "prosody," the authors provide an excellent conceptual rationale for the development of their tool in the first chapter of the technical manual. In addition, methodological and procedural issues are clearly discussed. The tool was developed to address both "prosody," reflecting the perceptual consequences of inappropriate linguistic processing and "voice," reflecting the perceptual consequences of inappropriate vocal function. As a result "the hyphenated term *prosody-voice* was chosen purposefully to retain a distinction in levels of speech-language processing" (manual, p. 3).

Limited psychometric information on the tool is provided in the manual in the kit available from the publisher. Although the authors report that the validity of the PVSP "has been studied," this information is not readily available. The first test author provided us with two manuscripts (Shriberg, 1993; Shriberg & Kwiatkowski, in press) and a technical report of the tool (Shriberg, Kwiatkowski, Rasmussen, Lof, & Miller, 1992) all of which were helpful in gaining a better understanding of the psychometric properties of the instrument. However, the technical report made reference to "detailed" technical information in the training manual. It is our opinion that the psychometric data provided in the training manual is at best cursory and does not meet the recommendation of the *Standards for Educational and Psychological Testing* (1985). In the technical report provided by the author, adequate face, content, criterion, concurrent, and construct validity are reported. The information on the reliability of the tool is somewhat limited with the authors reporting that several studies were "in progress." The reliability information reported supports the technical adequacy of the tool with young children. However, given the relatively small sample sizes across the life span in many of the technical studies reported we advise some caution in interpreting the technical information reported. In the training manual the test authors caution that the validity of the instrument is highly dependent on the examiner's skill in coding responses. As a result we would stress that clinical decisions based on an evaluation of the subject's performance with this tool should only be made from administrations given by highly skilled examiners.

A strength of the information provided in the kit from the test publisher is the detailed administration and scoring procedures. Extensive examples are provided to assist the evaluator. However, prior experience in coding prosody and voice behavior is needed to ensure accuracy of results. The examples and audiotaped samples provided are also somewhat limited to difficulties likely exhibited by young children. If, as the authors report, the tool may be used with older children and adults more examples and audiotaped samples of these populations should be provided.

In summary, the Prosody-Voice Screening Profile has utility as a tool used by clinicians experienced in the evaluation of prosody and voice. However, considerable time is required to learn how to administer and score the tool with accuracy. In addition, the psychometric properties of the tool are in some areas adequate, with limited information on reliability reported. Given the limited number of standardized evaluation tools in this area, we recommend the PVSP be used only by highly qualified examiners. Given the limited psychometric properties reported, findings should be reported with caution and in conjunction with other evaluation information.

REVIEWER'S REFERENCES

American Educational Research Association, American Psychological Association, & National Council on Measurement in Education. (1985). *Standards for educational and psychological testing.* Washington, DC: American Psychological Association, Inc.

Shriberg, L. D., Kwiatkowski, J., Rasmussen, C., Lof, G. L., & Miller, J. F. (1992). *The Prosody-Voice Screening Profile (PVSP): Psychometric data and reference information for children* (Report No. 1). Tucson, AZ: Communication Skill Builders.

Shriberg, L. D. (1993). Four new speech and prosody-voice measures for genetics research and other studies in developmental phonological disorders. *Journal of Speech and Hearing Research, 36,* 105-140.

Shriberg, L. D., & Kwiatkowski, J. (in press). Developmental phonological disorders I: A clinical profile. *Journal of Speech and Hearing Research.*

Review of the Prosody-Voice Screening Profile by PENELOPE K. HALL, Associate Professor of Speech Pathology and Audiology, Wendell Johnson Speech and Hearing Center, The University of Iowa, Iowa City, IA:

The Prosody-Voice Screening Profile (PVSP) was developed to provide a standardized method for screening six suprasegmental areas which, if inappropriate, may contribute to problems with speech intelligibility. These areas are: Phrasing, Rate, Stress, Loudness, Pitch, and Quality. The PVSP authors state that the instrument was developed for use with young, unintelligible children, but can be used "with clients of all ages and primary disorders" (manual, p. vii).

Based on 12–25 audiotaped conversational utterances, the Profile coding procedures are reported to take 15–30 minutes to complete, after an examiner is proficient with the PVSP procedures and 32 codes. Included with the PVSP are a manual and training audiotapes.

The PVSP is based on sound rationales. The manual reviews a number of conceptual issues, including justification for such an instrument, use of spontaneous connected speech as stimuli, the necessary sample size, use of a bipolar appropriate/inappropriate judgment system, and the criteria levels to be used. Central is the importance of perceptual judgments made by listeners of the six suprasegmentals. The authors report that the PVSP is based on research they have conducted but which is reported elsewhere.

The procedures for using the PVSP are reported in meticulous detail, including the rules for glossing and segmenting the speech sample, the codes for excluding an utterance, and the codes for each of the six suprasegmentals. The training tapes are helpful as is the section of the manual dealing with this instruction. However, as with any subjective perceptually based judgment, there is likely to be disagreement with the PVSP authors as to the characteristics exhibited in the taped samples, despite their explanations of how their codes were applied. This may be particularly true in the area of nasality, due to dialectal and geographic differences in the degree to which this suprasegmental falls into the "acceptable" range. The Profile's authors also acknowledge that the instrument's coding decisions may reflect "behavior that is seldom salient to the community" (p. 52). They also acknowledge that "such differences may be accepted as stylistic variants and may not generate aversive consequences" (p. 52). Thus, some clients' PVSP results may describe inappropriate suprasegmental(s), but with no need for further clinical concern or involvement—a situation which some professionals would construe as false positives.

Information contained in the PVSP manual regarding the Profile's psychometric characteristics are sketchy. The authors report that the PVSP procedures were standardized on data of 70 subjects; 57 were preschool children with "speech delays of unknown origin" (p. 45) and 13 were children with "suspected apraxia of speech" (p. 45). Further information on the specifics of this population are not provided in the manual. The authors refer to descriptive and validity studies, and citations are listed in the references, but unfortunately are convention papers which are not readily available. The authors also state that a "comprehensive technical report" containing information on various aspects of validity and reliability "will be completed in 1991" (p. vii). However, efforts to obtain such a publication from the publisher were not successful—I was referred instead to the original 1990 manual.

In summary, the Prosody-Voice Screening Profile (PVSP) fills a need in the professional assessment library. The systematic and careful description of the procedures and codes used in the application of the Profile is to be commended. However, it is this same wealth of information that may be overwhelming to some professionals and may limit how extensively it is used. According to the PVSP authors, the Profile has undergone validity and reliability testing, although this information is presently not available with the Profile materials. The authors make references to a "revised text" (p. 46); it is hoped they will include psychometric information with a revised edition of the Profile. Nonetheless, the 1990 instrument would be helpful to speech-language pathologists to better describe the influence of suprasegmentals in the overall communication disorders of their clients, to practicing clinicians in an effort to "calibrate" their perceptual judgments, and to student clinicians learning the "art" of subjective perceptual judgments.

[316]

Psychoeducational Profile Revised.

Purpose: Designed "to assess skills and behaviors of autistic and communication-handicapped children who function between the ages of 6 months and 7 years."
Population: Autistic or communication-handicapped children whose chronological age is less than 12 years.
Publication Dates: 1979–90.
Acronym: PEP-R.
Scores, 12: Behavioral (Relating, Materials, Sensory, Language); Developmental (Imitation, Perception, Fine Motor, Gross Motor, Eye-Hand, Cognitive Performance, Cognitive Verbal, Total).
Administration: Individual.
Price Data, 1994: $59 per complete program; $49 per manual ('90, 182 pages); $14 per 10 Profile sheets.
Time: (45–90) minutes.
Authors: Eric Schopler, Robert Jay Reichler, Ann Bashford, Margaret D. Lansing, and Lee M. Marcus.
Publisher: PRO-ED, Inc.
Cross References: For reviews by Gerald S. Hanna and Martin J. Wiese, see 11:317.

TEST REFERENCES

1. Van Bourgondien, M. E., Marcus, L. M., & Schopler, E. (1992). Comparison of DSM-III-R and Childhood Autism Rating Scale diagnoses of autism. *Journal of Autism and Developmental Disorders, 22*(4), 493-506.
2. Myles, B. S., & Simpson, R. L. (1994). Facilitated communication with children diagnosed as autistic in public school settings. *Psychology in the Schools, 31*, 208-220.

Review of the Psychoeducational Profile Revised by PAT MIRENDA, Director of Research and Training, CBI Consultants, Ltd., Vancouver, British Columbia, Canada:

The Psychoeducational Profile Revised (PEP-R) is designed as an educational tool for planning individualized special education programs, especially for children with autism or related developmental disorders between the ages of 6 months and 7 years. The test can also be used with children from 7–12 years of age who perform at or below a first grade level in at least some areas. The complete PEP-R kit "consists of a set of toys and learning materials that are presented to a child within structured play activities" (manual, p. 3). The kit can either be purchased from the authors or constructed from items bought in stores and materials provided in the test manual. The examiner observes, evaluates, and records the child's responses during the test, assigning scores of "passing," "merging," or "failing" to each task. In the end, this results in production of a profile depicting the child's strengths and weaknesses in seven areas of development and four areas of behavior.

The test is uniquely designed to address some of the concerns typically voiced by examiners of children with autism or related disorders. Tasks in each of the seven developmental areas are designed at different levels of difficulty, to increase the likelihood that the child will experience success with at least some tasks. This allows the examiner to adjust task expectations and thus minimize the behavioral difficulties that may occur when task demands are too high. The items in the PEP-R can be presented in any order, allowing the examiner to be flexible to meet the individual child's needs. The tasks are presented in the context of structured play situations, thus avoiding the requirement of many tests that children be seated at a table facing the examiner (a requirement that is impossible for many children with autism to meet). The test is designed to minimize the amount and quality of language needed to communicate directions, and most of the required responses are nonverbal in nature. Both of these considerations are important for children with autism, who often have difficulty understanding or producing verbal language. Finally, the PEP-R includes a number of items for assessment of children functioning in the infant and toddler ranges.

The PEP-R was normed on a total sample of 420 "normal" children in several North Carolina communities. Of the 420 children, 276 were from the 1979 sample selected for the original test, and 144 were added in 1988 for the revision. The gender and racial (white, black, other) composition of the sample approximated that of the 1985 U.S. Census. Social class data are also provided in the manual, indicating that the majority of the white children in the sample were from the two highest socioeconomic groups, whereas the majority of black children were from the two lowest. This reflected the overall race-class distribution for North Carolina at the time of testing. The authors note the normative sample was not intended to be used for standardization; rather, it was used to establish "rough developmental hierarchies" within the seven developmental areas. Nonetheless, the small sample size and the restricted geographical region from which it was drawn is a limitation of the test.

The test is further hampered by its scant reliability data. The only reliability data provided are based on having five raters score one subject independently on the scale's seven developmental areas. Intraclass correlation (Guilford & Fruchter, 1978) was calculated for these scores, as an index of the similarity of observations among the different raters. The intraclass correlation was .92, indicating a high degree of similarity across the raters. In addition, a table is provided of test results (presumably, from an ANOVA) indicating that an F score of 5.30 was nonsignificant across raters. These two pieces of evidence suggest that, for the one subject involved in this test, the scores obtained were reasonably reliable. However, no information about this subject or about the five examiners and how they were trained is provided. Furthermore, the use of only one subject to establish reliability is not acceptable. Thus, the interrater reliability of the PEP-R cannot be assumed. No test-retest reliability measures are provided.

The manual contains a number of measures of validity, including correlations between the original PEP (not the PEP-R) with several well-known standardized tests. These include the Merrill-Palmer Scale (r = .85), the Vineland Social Maturity Scale (r = .84), the Bayley Scales of Development (r = .77), and the Peabody Picture Vocabulary Test (r = .71). Lower correlations were found with the Wechsler Intelligence Scale for Children—Revised (WISC-R) and Wechsler Preschool and Primary Scale of Intelligence (WPPSI) (r = .47) and the Leiter International Performance Scale (r = .24). Thus, it appears that scores from the PEP can be used with a similar degree of confidence as those from the first four tests listed. However, no validity data are provided for the PEP-R, which includes a number of new items for children below the preschool (i.e., 2.5-year) level. Thus, it is difficult to assess how the revised version of the test compares with other well-established developmental instruments.

Despite its psychometric limitations, the PEP-R is a widely used and potentially useful instrument for identifying strengths, weaknesses, and learning needs for children with autism and related disorders. The authors themselves note several cautions about the use of the PEP-R, which are important to reiterate here. It should *not* be used as an "IQ test," as that is not its intended purpose. It should *not* be used to develop individualized education plans (IEPs) directly from the test items, because most of the items are not particularly functional in and of themselves. Finally, it should *not* be used as the sole measure for providing a diagnosis of autism, although it can be used by a skilled examiner familiar with the syndrome to explore some of the behaviors and learning patterns common to these children. The PEP-R *can* be used as part of an effort to design effective teaching techniques and educational programs for young children with autism or related developmental disorders.

REVIEWER'S REFERENCE

Guilford, J. P., & Fruchter, B. (1978). *Fundamental statistics in psychology and education* (6th ed.). NY: McGraw-Hill.

Review of the Psychoeducational Profile Revised by GERALD TINDAL, Associate Professor of Special Education, University of Oregon, Eugene, OR:

The Psychoeducational Profile Revised (PEP-R) is designed for planning and evaluating teaching programs for children with autism, aged 6 months to 7 years. In the Introduction and Overview, Schopler, Reichler, Bashford, Lansing, and Marcus (the authors) emphasize an orientation toward assessing the learning needs: diagnostic, design of Individualized Educational Plans, and development of effective teaching techniques. The inventory provides estimates of performance in two major areas: (*a*) developmental functioning (with 131 items), comprising subscores (passing, emerging, and failing) in Imitation, Perception, Fine Motor, Gross Motor, Eye-Hand Integration, Cognitive Performance, and Cognitive Verbal Areas; and (*b*) behavioral abnormality (with 43 items), providing clinical judgments (appropriate, mild, and severe) in Relating and Affect, Play and Interest in Materials, Sensory Responses, and Language. "The total number of unusual or dysfunctional behaviors are quantified and qualified, indicating the severity of a child's behavioral difficulties" (manual, p. 3). A total Developmental Score and Developmental Quotient also can be obtained.

The technical manual (Volume I) contains a very extensive description of the scales and their development and content. Included are thorough descriptions of administration procedures and qualifications; such attention to detail is critical with this inventory because of many potential difficulties in assessing the target population of children with autism, and because many of the items require precise administration procedures to generate careful judgments of performance and behavior. For each of the 174 items, materials, administration and scoring guides are included in the manual for the developmental areas and observational questions, and scoring guides for behavioral areas. The authors should be commended for their description of these components of the inventory.

The technical sections of the manual, however, provide considerably less adequate information than is necessary. Interpretation of results references three outcomes that fail to be supported by their analyses of reliability and validity for the instrument:

1. A Developmental Profile provides an estimate of consistency of performance across the 131 items/tasks, giving the examiner "useful information on the nature of a child's learning skills and difficulties" (p. 67).
2. A Developmental Quotient (DQ) is thought to be "useful as an alternative or supplement to a standardized IQ" (p. 67).
3. A Behavioral Profile, based on the clinical judgments from 43 items, "provides a systematic means of describing a child's behavior" (p. 67).

The normative sample used to devise the DQ is woefully inadequate. Only 420 students were sampled for the standardization group; they fail to be appropriate in most uses of the inventory throughout the United States for three other reasons (*a*) the selected students are limited to a narrow geographic region (Carrboro and Chapel Hill, and surrounding communities in North Carolina); (*b*) the racial composition fails to reflect the proportions in most areas of the U.S. (86% white and only 11% black, with no other ethnicity represented); and (*c*) the socioeconomic status is heavily skewed to the high end of the scale (63% of the students are from the two highest SES groups). The authors acknowledge such problems, yet use the data to support the developmental functioning levels and hierarchies in two ways: (*a*) within each developmental area (and for the Total Developmental Score), the number of items passed are presented for a range of age levels and (*b*) percentages are presented of children within three major age groups of normal children (younger, at age, and older) who pass each item, including normative age levels. Both such reporting systems are inherently norm referenced and demand an adequate and representative standardization sample.

Within a 170-page test manual, only one page is devoted to reliability and validity. The data presented to support either component of technical adequacy are absent. The reliability analysis, which is crucial in any instrument so dependent upon judgments of developmental functioning (based on passing, emerging, or failing, as well as behavioral performance indicative of appropriate, mild, and severe functioning problems), is based on only *one* student who was assessed by five testers on seven developmental areas. No reliability data are presented for the Behavioral Areas. Validity data are equally lacking. Content validity is "established" by relating the sampling plan to another instrument devised by the same authors and a description of revisions made over the last 20 years. Concurrent validity information is presented by referencing correlations with several other instruments. These data do not reflect any description of subjects (e.g., sample size, classification, age, any demographics, etc.); neither is critical information presented about the study (when it was done and how it was conducted). Finally, although the authors query whether the "PEP-R [can] be used for effective educational and home programming" (p. 85), they simply reference its widespread adoption throughout North Carolina and other countries in the world as supportive of validity from its use. The authors abjectly fail to provide essential construct validity regarding the use for which it is purportedly designed: improvement in instructional decision making.

In summary, the PEP-R provides a wide sample of many behaviors in which most young children engage. The test is likely to be very difficult to administer and requires considerable familiarity before estimates of student performance can be made from the judgments, which form the core data upon which scores are based. The inventory is designed to guide instructional decisions but no information is provided whether such decisions are better or more effective as a function of using the results from the PEP-R. Although a normative sample is described and used to make judgments about performance, it is best avoided because of its narrow and biased composition. Furthermore, technical adequacy is lacking: Neither reliability nor validity data are sufficient to warrant using this instrument as it is described. In the end, the only use of this instrument is to interact with children and make a best first guess about some behaviors that may or may not be present. Ironically, though the instrument has been available for about 20 years and has received widespread adoption, the authors prefer to advocate use based on testimonials and not scientific evidence.

[317]

QUEST.

Purpose: A screening, diagnostic, and remediation kit designed to identify reading and number difficulties.
Population: Ages 7–8.
Publication Dates: 1983–91.
Administration: Group.
Price Data, 1992: £74.20 per teacher's set including manual ('91, 144 pages), spirit masters, test cards, posters, starter workbooks, reading skills workbooks, number skills workbooks, and diagnostic testing equipment; £12.65 per manual; £4.35 per 3 remediation starter workbooks; £4.60 per 3 reading skills workbooks; £4.60 per 3 number skills workbooks (specify Number Quest 1, Number Quest 2, or Money Quest); £5.50 per 3 number skills workbooks (specify Number Quest 3 or Number Quest 4).
Time: (30–40) minutes per test.
Comments: Teacher's manual includes information on remedial and individualized learning programs.
Authors: Alistair H. Robertson, Anne Henderson, Ann Robertson, Joanna Fisher, and Mike Gibson.
Publisher: NFER-Nelson Publishing Co., Ltd. [England].

a) READING SCREENING TEST.
Scores, 3: Word Identification, Reading Comprehension, Total.
Price Data: £13.80 per 12 spirit masters.

b) NUMBER SCREENING TEST.
Scores: Total score only.
Price Data: £7.80 per 3 posters.

c) DIAGNOSTIC READING TEST.
Scores, 11: Pre-reading (Auditory Discrimination, Visual Discrimination, Auditory Sequential Memory, Visual Sequential Memory, Visuo-motor Coordination), Word Attack Skills (Sight Vocabulary, Letter Recognition, Simple Blends, Beginnings and Endings, Diagraphs and the Silent e Rule, Reversals).
Price Data: £7.80 per 18 diagnostic test cards; £4.35 per diagnostic testing equipment.

d) DIAGNOSTIC NUMBER TEST.
Scores, 10: Pre-number (Visual Perception, Visuo-motor Coordination, Auditory Sequential Memory), Early Number Concepts (Sorting, Conservation, Ordering), Number Concepts (Addition, Subtraction); Number Skills (Ordering, Computation).
Price Data: Same as *c* above.

Review of the QUEST by G. GAGE KINGSBURY, Coordinator of Measurement Research, Portland Public Schools, Portland, OR:

QUEST is an assessment system designed to investigate the reading and number skills of students 7 to 8 years of age. The system includes group-administered screening tests, individually administered diagnostic tests, and remediation materials for use in the classroom. The tests are designed for administration by a classroom teacher or counselor. They have as their express purpose the identification of low-performing students, and the identification of particular skills in which these students need remedial instruction.

The screening tests are designed to be administered to groups of students, in order to identify a group of low performers who would go on in the assessment process to diagnostic testing and remediation. The screening tests each take 30 to 40 minutes to administer. The QUEST materials include complete scripts for administration of the screening tests. It is suggested that the students in the lowest 5% of the score distribution on the screening test be given the diagnostic tests.

The diagnostic tests are designed to be individually administered to students, to identify student skill areas that need further instruction. Each diagnostic test consists of a set of skill-area subtests (11 in reading and 10 in number skills). Administration takes approximately 30 minutes for either the reading or the number test. Again, a complete administration script is included in the QUEST materials. Scores from each of the subtests are consolidated to form the diagnostic profile for the student.

The diagnostic profile is used in conjunction with a flow diagram contained in the QUEST materials to identify the remediation materials students will need to improve their performance skills. These materials include work books for the students and suggestions for additional activities the student might find helpful in strengthening particular skill areas.

The major strength of the QUEST system is that it is a complete package. A teacher using QUEST can start with a group of unknown students, identify reading and number deficiencies in a relatively short period of time, and provide remediation materials for students for whom difficulties are identified. For a classroom teacher who wants to know that all students have the rudimentary reading and number skills they need to move on, QUEST might be a very useful tool.

Unfortunately, QUEST has four features that may make it less appealing for some educators. Three of these fall in the general categories of scoring, language, and measurement properties. In addition, there is a particular instructional approach that underlies QUEST. To the extent that an educator disagrees with the instructional approach, QUEST may be less appealing.

Test scoring and decision making in QUEST do not appear to have any strong theoretical basis. To identify the cutoff score on the screening test, the authors suggest scores that encompass the bottom 5% of students who took the screening test in the field test sample. No justification is given for this cutoff value other than to say that students below this score have "serious" difficulties. Although this may be true, it would be informative to know why they chose the 5% level, and the impact of choosing a different score level. In other words, can we be sure that only the bottom 5% will have serious learning problems? What about the bottom 8% or 10%?

Similarly, there is no explicit procedure described for identifying scores indicating that remediation is needed in the skill areas tapped by the diagnostic test. Different teachers might easily make different remediation decisions from the same set of test scores unless more rigorous guidelines are provided.

Language is another feature of QUEST that might limit its utility. QUEST uses many terms and phrasings that are specific to Great Britain. References to monetary units like pence and pounds, and words in common British usage like "lollies" and "tins" might make QUEST less useful in other English-speaking countries. Unless one is working in a country with similar monetary and measurement systems and similar speech patterns, QUEST should not be considered for use.

No information concerning the measurement properties of the QUEST tests is reported in the manual. Although a field test is described, no information is given concerning reliability, validity, or standard error of measurement. Because the decisions made with this test may have relatively high stakes for the student involved, it is important that the authors of QUEST provide information concerning the amount of error that we can expect in the test scores. The tests in the QUEST system are relatively short. The reliability of the scores will be, therefore, an important concern.

The instructional approach of the teachers implementing QUEST in a school district would also be important to the acceptance of the system. QUEST remediation materials are designed as drill and practice exercises in individual skill areas. Although this may be a fine way to learn the fundamental reading and number skills being considered here, it might require an adjustment in classrooms that are using integrated instructional approaches.

In conclusion, the QUEST system contains a coherent group of tools that may be used to identify and help students with difficulties in the fundamental skills underlying reading and mathematics. To implement QUEST in a new school district, however, I would suggest a small field test first, in order to validate cutoff scores and scoring procedures. In addition, I would suggest the authors provide additional information concerning the measurement characteristics of the tests, in order that users would have more data upon which to make decisions regarding the appropriateness of the tests for their settings.

Review of the QUEST by CHRISTINE NOVAK, Pediatric Psychologist, Division of Developmental Disabilities, University of Iowa, Iowa City, IA:

QUEST was developed in Great Britain as a result of a research project to help local authorities identify children who are failing in reading and/or number skills early in their school career and to design remedial programs to assist these children. The Screening tests were normed on over 2,000 children from 33 primary schools, in both urban and rural settings. "Failing" was arbitrarily defined by performance at or below the 5th percentile, due to the limited availability of resources for remediation activities; however, it was reported that an additional 10% of the sample could have benefited from remedial help. The Diagnostic tests and remedial activities were developed and field tested with the group of children who failed the Screening tests.

Test scores are compared to the group norm only at the level of screening. The distribution of scores is skewed to provide finer discrimination of failing performance; thus there is little separation of scores at the upper end of the distribution to discriminate accelerated performance. Normative comparisons are available for children under 6 years 9 months to children over 7 years 5 months, and at 3-month intervals in between these two ages. The exact upper and lower age limits are not specified, but the bulk of the standardization sample fell between the ages of 6-9 to 7-5. In addition to the ambiguity surrounding the ages for which the tests are appropriate, there is no discussion of the influence of educational placement, or more specifically, exposure to graded curriculum, on performance. One must use caution in assuming "failure" in a child who has not yet been exposed to the concepts and skills assessed, regardless of the child's age. This point is particularly salient for American children who may not be exposed to similar content as their English counterparts at various age levels.

Reliability of test scores is not discussed in the manual, nor are there any data to support the validity of the tests and the effectiveness of the remedial activities to improve academic performance. It is possible that published research exists, because the development of these materials was the result of a research project; however, no references are provided for the interested reader. Diagnostic and remedial activities include Auditory and Visual Discrimination, Auditory and Visual Sequential Memory, and Visual Motor Discrimination. Although these constructs may be helpful in understanding learning failure, direct instruction in these skills has not been shown to improve performance on academic tasks. Additionally, the reading materials focus primarily on word attack skills with minimal attention to comprehension. Comprehension can be an isolated area of weakness or a strength on which to capitalize in teaching compensatory strategies.

In summary, QUEST represents a collection of related tests and activities in beginning reading and number skills that appear to have good face validity. However, the utility of QUEST as a screening and diagnostic tool is limited by the questionable representativeness of the sample to American children (Screening tests) and the lack of empirical data to support the tests' reliability and validity. A better alternative for assessing the development of number skills is the Test of Early Mathematics Ability (T4:2750) which is based on a well-researched model and provides standard scores representing both low and high performance for children aged 4 years 0 months to 8 years 11 months. Specialized tests to assess reading skills which provide better norms and statistical properties are also available, such as the Durrell Analysis of Reading Difficulty (T4:822). The test taps skills similar to those evaluated by QUEST but all within the context of reading (e.g., visual memory of words).

[318]

Quick Phonics Survey.

Purpose: Designed to "assess a child's understanding of sound/symbol relationships, transfers, and associations."
Population: Grades 1–4.
Publication Date: 1976.
Acronym: QPS.
Scores: Total score only.
Administration: Individual.
Manual: No manual.
Price Data, 1991: $10 per plasticized reading card and 50 recording forms with directions.
Time: Administration time not reported.
Author: Bob Wright.
Publisher: Academic Therapy Publications (High Noon Division).

Review of the Quick Phonics Survey by BETH D. BADER, Assessment Specialist, Educational Issues Department, American Federation of Teachers, Washington, DC:

This assessment has a very limited purpose—that is to assess whether elementary students recognize English language symbols, both manuscript and cursive, and whether the students are able to understand the relationship between the symbol they see and its corresponding sound.

The laminated cards provided by the authors are very nice. However, the assessment fails to reach almost any standard deemed essential in conducting assessments. For example, the manual consists of one laminated sheet printed on both sides. There is no explanation of the purpose of the assessment, how to establish standards of reliability or validity, and no detailed explanation of how to administer the assessment. There are no instructions for assessment details such as guessing, time limits, procedures for marking the answer sheet, or elaboration of instructions for the student. The items in the assessment are taken out of context of good English and Language Arts instruction.

There is no standard for performance that would indicate to a teacher whether a student had performed acceptably. There are no rubrics or structures for scoring that would set norms for various grade levels. What is passing at grades 1, 2, or 3? Although the instructions set vague grade levels, in some cases the span in the levels is so wide it would be impossible to determine whether the student is demonstrating acceptable variation in learning or exhibiting instructional deficits. There are no suggestions about how to adjust for speech impairments. There are no suggestions for instructional resources, types of activities, or even directions to go to improve performance for particular deficiencies. There is no analysis of scores, individual tasks, or problems. In short, there is no guidance for teachers in how to administer the assessment, score the performance, interpret the results, or remedy the problems they might find. This test cannot be recommended.

Review of the Quick Phonics Survey by DAWN P. FLANAGAN, Assistant Professor of Psychology, St. John's University, Jamaica, NY:

The author of the Quick Phonics Survey (QPS) describes this instrument as "a rapid method of assessing a child's understanding of sound/symbol relationships, transfers, and associations" (Direction Sheet, p. 1). It is intended to be used by classroom teachers, aides, and educational diagnosticians to determine a child's level of phonetic skill proficiency. The QPS consists of a laminated Direction Sheet (i.e., administration guidelines), a laminated Sound/Symbol Card, and 25 response forms. There are 12 items on the QPS; each item assesses a different skill and is associated with a grade level (1, 2, 3, or 4), which has been interpreted by this reviewer as the grade at which that particular skill is expected to be mastered. The skills assessed by the QPS are as follows: (*a*) says/sings alphabet, (*b*) writes alphabet, (*c*) reads letter forms, (*d*) changes letters to sounds, (*e*) changes sounds to letters, (*f*) rhymes, (*g*) hears initial sounds in words, (*h*) hears terminal sounds in words, (*i*) pronounces blends in isolation, (*j*) writes blends in isolation, (*k*) discriminates between short /i/ and short /e/, and (*l*) recognizes syllables.

ADMINISTRATION, SCORING, AND INTERPRETATION. The administration guidelines of the QPS are not well written and, at times, are confusing or ambiguous. For example, the following instruction applies to 5 of the 12 items: "If there is any question regarding the child's ability to handle ten items only, that is, he/she is slow or uncertain, give all items in this section" (p. 2). This instruction appears counterintuitive. If a child is uncertain about what he or she is being asked to do, for example, then continuing to test is inappropriate because it will result in an inaccurate estimate of the child's skill or ability. The fact that the child cannot "handle" 10 items may also imply that he or she is frustrated or does not understand the task. Under these circumstances, it is recommended that the examiner discontinue testing or re-explain the task, respectively. Professional judgment must be exercised in these situations however, because standardized procedures are not available (e.g., the QPS has no basal and ceiling rules).

There are no procedures for scoring the QPS once the examiner records a child's responses on the Record Form. Although an examiner can calculate a total raw score for each skill, no norms or standard scores are provided by the test author. Thus, there is no way to compare a child's rate of acquisition of phonetic skills to other children of his or her own age.

There are no interpretation guidelines for the QPS. Although a grade level (1, 2, 3, or 4) appears at the end of the administration guidelines for each skill, it is not clear whether the child should have mastered the skill by that grade level or demonstrated a minimal level of competency. The only interpretive statements the test author makes appear in the directions to the examiner on Items 3 and 12. On Item 3, the author states that "by the end of the second grade, the child should be able to write it [the alphabet] in lower case, manuscript letters." On Item 12, the author states that "a score of 7 out of 10 indicates adequate auditory discrimination." These statements are virtually meaningless without normative data to substantiate or guide interpretation. Moreover, because the test author does not provide information regarding the appropriateness of the test content for its intended use, the criteria that were used to select specific items/skills, or a rationale for the inclusion of any of the items/skills on the QPS, interpretation of a child's performance in these skill areas is not recommended.

PSYCHOMETRIC PROPERTIES. The QPS is not standardized, reliability data are not available, and evidence of its content, construct, criterion-related, or diagnostic validity is not reported. There is no manual for the QPS and a review of the literature showed that no published reliability or validity studies were conducted prior to its publication and that it has not been used in any published research investigations since its publication.

CONCLUSIONS. There is certainly value in assessing a child's understanding of sound/symbol relationships and other phonetic skills and documenting those skills that have been mastered as well as the errors that are made by any given child. This descriptive information provides a foundation from which to select specific speech training objectives and develop remedial strategies. However, the QPS is not the best instrument to gather this type of qualitative data; it offers nothing more than a simple teacher-made test. A comprehensive assessment of a child's phonetic skills functioning as well as a complete analysis of the types of errors made by the child is perhaps best accomplished using a test such as the Woodcock Reading Mastery Tests—Revised (WRMT-R; Woodcock, 1987; T4:2976).

The QPS author has not explored any of the test's psychometric properties. Without reliability, validity, and normative data, the QPS cannot be used quantitatively and, therefore, cannot be used to make diagnostic *or screening* decisions. The QPS provides no means for teachers, educational diagnosticians, or other practitioners to elicit and evaluate systematically the appropriateness of a representative range of phonetic skills or document progress objectively in clinical or research settings. When the QPS is compared to competing phonetic evaluation procedures that have normative data, such as the WRMT-R, the Peabody Individual Achievement Test—Revised (PIAT-R; Markwardt, 1989; T4:1944), the Kaufman Test of Educational Achievement (K-TEA; Kaufman & Kaufman, 1985; T4:1348), or Ling's (1976) Phonetic Level Evaluation, it is clear that the QPS is narrow in scope, offers nothing unique to the assessment of phonetic skill acquisition in children, and is generally inferior to all other measures of phonetic skills. Given the many inadequacies of the QPS, it is not recommended.

REVIEWER'S REFERENCES

Ling, D. (1976). *Speech and the hearing impaired child: Theory and practice.* Washington, DC: Alexander Graham Bell Association for the Deaf.

Kaufman, A. S., & Kaufman, N. L. (1985). Kaufman Test of Educational Achievement. Circle Pines, MN: American Guidance Service.

Woodcock, R. W. (1987). Woodcock Reading Mastery Tests—Revised. Circle Pines, MN: American Guidance Service.
Markwardt, F. C., Jr. (1989). Peabody Individual Achievement Test—Revised. Circle Pines, MN: American Guidance Service.

[319]

Quick Screen of Phonology.

Purpose: Developed to estimate phonological development.
Population: Ages 3-0 to 7-11.
Publication Date: 1990.
Acronym: QSP.
Scores: Total score only.
Administration: Individual.
Price Data, 1991: $28.98 per picture stimulus book/manual (50 pages); $18.99 per 24 record forms.
Time: (5) minutes.
Comments: Abbreviated adaptation of the Bankson-Bernthal Test of Phonology (41).
Authors: Nicholas W. Bankson and John E. Bernthal.
Publisher: The Riverside Publishing Co.

Review of the Quick Screen of Phonology by SUSAN FELSENFELD, Assistant Professor of Communication, University of Pittsburgh, Pittsburgh, PA:

TEST STRUCTURE AND ADMINISTRATION. The Quick Screen of Phonology (QSP) is a shortened version of the longer and more thorough Bankson-Bernthal Test of Phonology (BBTOP; 41). Rather than providing a comprehensive assessment of a child's phonological system, the authors of the QSP intend this screening instrument to be used as a "quick estimate of a young child's phonological development" that "can then be used to determine the need for further phonological assessment" (manual, p. 1). This distinction is of critical important because, as a diagnostic tool, the QSP is clearly inadequate.

The QSP was designed to be administered to children between the ages of 3 and 7, with norms available for this age range. The test consists of 28 colored line-drawings of picturable nouns, housed in a spiral-bound book that also serves as the test manual. In general, the pictures are clear representations of the target stimuli, and most items should be in the productive repertoire of preschool children. Children are instructed to name each picture as it is presented, and, from these productions, judgements are made about the accuracy of each consonant within the word. Vowels are excluded from scoring. It should be noted that not all consonant phonemes are sampled in the QSP, and the test items reflect an extremely narrow range of syllable and word shapes. For example, 64% of the QSP items (18/28) are CVCs. Only five test words contain consonant clusters in any position, and only two targets are three-syllable words (telescope, potatoes). Because of this limited sampling, test users should be aware that the difficulty level of this test is very low, particularly for children in the upper age ranges who may possess more subtle speech production problems.

The QSP can be scored quickly by assigning one point for each item that had "all consonants correct" and zero points for items containing "any consonant error." Thus, for this test, higher scores indicate better performance. These raw scores may then be converted into two types of norm-referenced scores: standard scores (with a mean of 100 and a standard deviation of 15) and percentile ranks. Confidence intervals for these standard scores can also be calculated, using instructions and point ranges provided in the manual. Suggested cutoff scores for test failure by age are not provided.

PSYCHOMETRIC PROPERTIES. Most of the psychometric information about the QSP was obtained through a reinterpretation of results from the full BBTOP diagnostic test.

Norms: Norms for the QSP were developed using the 757 children from the larger BBTOP standardization sample who were between the ages of 3 and 7. In general, the standardization sample was representative of the United States population in terms of gender and geographical region of residence. In addition, there was some attempt to include ethnic minorities in the norming sample: 80% of the children were classified as "white," 10% were classified as "black," 5% were considered of "Spanish origin", and 5% were described as "other" race.

Reliability: Three reliability estimates are discussed in the QSP manual: internal consistency (split-half reliability), stability (test-retest reliability), and interrater agreement. The authors report generally high average internal consistency coefficients for ages 3–6 (.88), with a slightly lower value (.78) for age 7. Test-retest reliability was calculated by readministering the entire BBTOP to 34 4-year-old children approximately 8 weeks after the initial administration, and examining their responses on the items used in the QSP. The results of this small study yielded a test-retest correlation of .85, which indicates acceptable stability for this narrow sample. Interrater agreement was calculated by asking two trained examiners to score independently the protocols of these same 34 children. The agreement for raw score between these examiners was reported to be quite high (.99), indicating very acceptable interexaminer scoring agreement.

Validity. Validity estimates were obtained by comparing scores on the QSP with various aspects of the more comprehensive BBTOP test from which it was derived. In general, scores on the QSP were found to correlate well with those obtained on the BBTOP, an outcome which the authors used as evidence for high predictive and construct validity. Although high correlations between the QSP and the various components of the BBTOP do suggest that similar domains are being sampled by the screening and diagnostic versions of this test, it would have been desirable to compare the QSP results with those obtained on a completely independent measure of phonological ability.

SUMMARY. The QSP is a potentially useful tool for rapid identification of young children in need of a more comprehensive phonological assessment. Test users must, however, heed the authors' caution against relying upon the QSP to make diagnostic or treatment decisions. This test's strengths are in its ease of administration and interpretation, and its relatively comprehensive standardization sample. Its weaknesses are its very limited sampling of the phonological system, and, to a lesser extent, its traditional and unimaginative presentation format. For test users who need to sample the consonant production skills of large numbers of young children, the QSP is an acceptable addition to a screening armamentarium.

Review of the Quick Screen of Phonology by JOHN H. KRANZLER, Assistant Professor of School Psychology, University of Florida, Gainesville, FL:

The Quick Screen of Phonology (QSP) is an individually administered test of phonological development for children between the ages of 3-0 and 7-11 years. According the test's authors, the QSP "works well with other tests in a screening battery to identify delays in general language or cognitive-linguistic development" (manual, p. 1). Evidence supporting this assertion is not presented in the manual, however.

The QSP consists of 28 color pictures, which the examinee must name, and yields one estimate of phonological development (based on the number of words spoken without misarticulated consonants or consonant clusters). The QSP is easy to administer and score. The total testing time required is only about 5 minutes. Test administration requires no special examiner qualifications other than proficiency in judging the "articulatory/phonological accuracy of single-word productions" (p. 2). Administration and scoring instructions for the QSP are clearly explained in the manual, as are many relevant measurement concepts.

Two errors in the manual may confuse consumers with little testing experience, however. One concerns the use of the wrong standard score mean and standard deviation for the QSP in an example showing why one should not average percentile ranks; the other is a typographical error in the formula for the *SEM*.

STANDARDIZATION AND NORMS. The QSP was derived from the Bankson-Bernthal Test of Phonology (BBTOP; 41), a "longer and more thorough" (p. 11) test of phonology for children between the ages of 3 and 9 years. Items for the QSP were selected from the BBTOP on the basis of their ability to predict "performance on individual consonants, clusters, and phonological processes" (p. 11). The QSP items were also selected to represent a "systematically balanced sample of segments and phonological processes" (p. 2). The item selection procedures for the BBTOP are, unfortunately, not discussed.

Norms for the QSP are based on 757 of the 1,070 normal children from the standardization sample of the BBTOP, with an average of approximately 150 children at each age level. Subject selection procedures are not discussed. Tables are presented describing the QSP sample by geographic region, age, gender, race, educational setting, and Hispanic background. Conspicuously absent from this list of stratification variables is socioeconomic status. Nevertheless, for the variables reported the QSP sample compares reasonably well to the U.S. population, with the exception of an underrepresentation of African Americans. In the computation of the QSP norms the percentage of African Americans in the sample was weighted to increase its congruence with the national percentage. Analyses of possible gender, racial, or ethnic bias on the QSP are not reported. The test's authors, in fact, caution that the QSP may be biased for any group that differs markedly from the national norms in "dialect, ethnic backgroup, or socioeconomic/educational level" (p. 16). They therefore encourage the development of local norms when appropriate.

The QSP provides a normative table to convert the total raw score into a standard score. This is a normalized standard score ($M = 100$, $SD = 15$) within age groups. Information regarding the smoothing procedures is not presented. Percentile ranks are also provided. The normative table has four 3-month age levels within each year between the ages of 3-0 and 6-11 and two 6-month age levels between the ages of 7-0 and 7-11. No rationale is given for the change in the number of age levels for 7-year-olds. One *SEM* is provided for each year of age. Examination of the means and standard deviations across age levels suggests the possibility of a ceiling effect. For 7-year-olds, for example, the *mean* raw score correct is 27 out of 28 items. A *perfect* score at this age is equivalent to a standard score of only 106. Perhaps this explains why the 8 and 9-year-olds from the BBTOP standardization sample were not included in the QSP norms. These descriptive data also suggest that the distribution of raw scores is skewed (negatively), which raises the question of the appropriateness of the normalized standard scores.

RELIABILITY AND VALIDITY. The reliability and validity data reported in the manual are from analyses of the QSP items on the BBTOP, not from administration of the QSP itself. Because of the potential problems of item context effects, these data should be interpreted with caution. The split-half reliability of the QSP items, corrected by the Spearman Brown formula, is generally acceptable for a screening measure. For 7-year-olds, however, the reliability coefficient of .78 is marginal. The stability of the QSP items for 4-year-olds over an interval of 8 weeks is good. The stability of the QSP items at other ages is not reported. The interrater reliability of the QSP items is also acceptable.

The test's authors attempt to demonstrate predictive validity by correlating the total raw score correct for the QSP items on the BBTOP with the total correct for the remaining BBTOP items. Evidence that the QSP is related to other relevant criterion measures is not reported, yet badly needed. To establish construct validity, correlations among the total raw scores correct, consonant errors, and phonological process errors are provided. These variables are not statistically independent, however, so their intercorrelations may be spuriously inflated. Two principal components analyses of various intercorrelations among the QSP items were also conducted, but only for the children between the ages of 3 and 6 years. The 7-year-olds were omitted from these analyses without any explanation. This curious omission notwithstanding, results of the principal components analyses reveal that a number of components underlie individual differences on the QSP. The test's authors do not provide an interpretation of these components; nor do they discuss how the construct validity of the QSP is supported by these data. They merely state that these findings indicate that the QSP is a "multidimensional rather than unitary" (p. 23) measure of phonology. Given that principal components are orthogonal (uncorrelated) by definition, these data actually seem to question the appropriateness of using a single score to describe phonological development.

SUMMARY. The QSP is a screening measure of phonological development that can be quickly administered and easily scored. Scant information is presented regarding the item and subject selection procedures. A ceiling effect is also apparent, especially for older children. Although the QSP may have adequate reliability and stability, its validity remains an unanswered question. The QSP should thus be used with caution until further investigations have been conducted.

[320]

A Rating Inventory for Screening Kindergartners.

Purpose: Constructed "to assess the likelihood that kindergarten children will require future supplemental educational assistance."
Population: Kindergarten.
Publication Date: 1991.
Acronym: RISK.
Scores: 5 factor scores: School Competence, Task Orientation, Social, Behavior, Motor and ratings in 7 developmental areas: Hearing, Vision, Physical, Intellectual, Emotional, Language, Speech.
Administration: Individual.
Price Data, 1992: $190 per complete kit including 25 score sheets, diskette (select Apple II or IBM version), and manual (38 pages); $16 per 25 score sheets.
Time: Administration time not reported.
Comments: Ratings by teachers; Apple II or IBM microcomputer necessary for scoring.
Authors: J. Michael Coleman and G. Michael Dover.
Publisher: PRO-ED, Inc.

Review of A Rating Inventory for Screening Kindergartners by LeADELLE PHELPS, Associate Professor and Director, School Psychology Program, Department of Counseling and Educational Psychology, State University of New York at Buffalo, Buffalo, NY:

A Rating Inventory for Screening Kindergartners (RISK) is a screening instrument designed to identify kindergarten students who may require supplemental special education services. The scale consists of 34 Likert-type rating items (1 = *hardly ever*, 6 = *almost always*) that the classroom teacher completes during the spring of the kindergarten year. There are an additional eight items that require "yes or no" responses to questions dealing with health-related impairments (e.g., Does the child have any obvious hearing problems?), developmental delays (e.g., Does the child have any obvious speech problems?), and psychoeducational risk factors (e.g., Does the child have any obvious intellectual problems?). It would appear that the scale can be completed by teachers in approximately 5 minutes.

The scale is organized into five areas: (*a*) School Competence (12 questions), (*b*) Task Orientation (7 questions), (*c*) Sociability (6 questions), (*d*) Behavior (6 questions), and (*e*) Motor Skills (3 questions). These areas were derived using a principal components factor analysis followed by an orthogonal rotation.

School Competence consists of questions concerning the child's estimated level of intelligence, achievement motivation, academic performance, apparent learning problems, and special instructional needs. Not surprisingly, this area is statistically very robust with an eigenvalue of 14.41 and explained variance of 42.41% (explained variance for the total scale = 69.69%). Task Orientation is less robust but still adds 14.40% to the total explained variance. Task Orientation contains items assessing the likelihood of an attention deficit hyperactivity disorder.

The other three scores (Sociability, Behavior, and Motor) add very little to the explained variance or predictive power of the RISK. For example, the five RISK scores were correlated with the Otis-Lennon School Ability Test and the Stanford Achievement Test (SAT). The School Competence correlations with the SAT ranged from .50 (Reading) to .54 (Math). The correlation between School Competence and the Otis-Lennon was .51. Task Orientation correlations with the SAT ranged from .34–.40 and .44 with the Otis-Lennon. However, all the correlations among the other three RISK areas and the SAT/Otis-Lennon were in the .16–.25 range. Clearly, Sociability, Behavior, and Motor are not very accurate predictors of school achievement/aptitude. In addition, the five scores are generally highly correlated with one another with a mean correlation of .44. In summary, these statistics suggest that the RISK generally assesses one general factor with the five separate areas providing little distinct data of diagnostic or intervention relevance.

The reliability of the instrument is excellent with the authors reporting an alpha coefficient of .96 for the entire scale. The principal method used by the authors for establishing validity for the instrument was to ascertain if the RISK correctly identified students who later received special education placement. Using a series of discriminant function analyses, the authors determined that 78.7% of the children ultimately requiring resource room services were identified by the RISK. As many children are in need of special individualized assistance that can be offered via regular education placement, using special education placement (i.e., school failure) as the outcome variable is not viewed as efficacious in predicting specific achievement in core academic areas.

The greatest strength/weakness of the RISK (depending on your measurement orientation) resides in the use of teacher ratings. There are no national norms for this scale. Rather, each student's ratings are transformed to z-scores based on the ratings of *each teacher* within *each classroom*. The authors state that employing z-scores eliminates differences between how teachers anchored their ratings. Nevertheless, halo effects and leniency errors are very common pitfalls with rating scales. Having no impartial criteria and/or items that directly assess each youngster's competencies are questionable practices when the stated objective is to identify the "risk population."

In summary, the RISK is a quick and easily administered teacher rating scale. If a school district wishes to rely on such data for identifying children at risk, then this scale appears promising. However, scales that provide direct and objective assessments of children's academic aptitude may be a better alternative.

Review of A Rating Inventory for Screening Kindergartners by GENE SCHWARTING, Project Director of Early Childhood Special Education, Omaha Public Schools, Omaha, NE:

Interest has expanded significantly in recent years in the field of early childhood education, resulting in the development of new assessment techniques and instruments. In addition, concerns have surfaced regarding formal "tests" for this age group. A Rating Inventory for Screening Kindergartners (RISK) is an attempt to address both the interest and the concerns, through development of an informal teacher-based assessment tool to identify kindergartners in need of more formal diagnostic testing and at risk for future failure in school as well as placement into special education.

The RISK protocol consists of four pages containing 34 items on which the teacher assesses children near the end of the kindergarten year on a 6-point scale, along with eight indicators of specific concerns regarding the students. These 34 items are often highly subjective, such as to "estimate this child's intelligence," and reflect an informal review of the general skills found in kindergarten curricula at most schools. Resultant ratings are then converted to a z scale, with a score of less than -1.25 being considered significant. The authors indicate that further evaluation is needed if such scores are obtained in two or more domains, or if a score less than -2.0 is obtained for any one domain. Scores are entered into a computerized, menu-driven data bank; as a result of this process, ongoing local norms for "graduating" kindergartners are developed. The program allows for reporting information on an individual student profile, by class, or by school, with an additional feature allowing the previous year's data to be deleted.

The RISK was initially administered to the entire kindergarten population ($n = 2{,}306$) in two unidentified school districts selected as socioculturally homogeneous during the years 1980–1983. A follow-up in 1986 found 57% of these children still enrolled, of whom 86% were Caucasian—additional information regarding race, socioeconomic status, or other variables was not provided. At this time, information was also gathered as to placement into special education, Otis-Lennon group IQ scores, and national percentile rank on the Stanford Achievement Test (SAT).

Standardization data found coefficient alpha to be .96 with the correlation between the predictor variables based upon the suggested cutoff scores and later placement into special education to be .74. The School Competence scale accounted for 42% of the variance, followed by Task Orientation, Social, Behavior, and Motor in descending order (not surprisingly, this corresponds to the decreasing order of the number of items of each scale). Predictive validity for the norm group found the instrument to be 94% accurate for identifying children for special education, with a false positive rate of 3% and a false negative rate of 21%. It should be noted the special education placements predicted do not include speech therapy, and are for the most part (83.5%) in resource classrooms with type and severity of handicapping conditions not indicated. The SAT and Otis-Lennon scores are significantly below average for all groups except those predicted by the RISK to succeed in regular education. However, the correlations between these results and the RISK factor scores are .54 and lower.

In summary, it should be noted that the RISK is an attempt to make subjective information more objective and that the instrument is not so much an assessment tool as a reasonably priced data management system. Whether it is an improvement over informal teacher ratings would appear to be based upon the judgement of the teacher. Certainly, the applicability of the norm group to other schools, the high number of children placed into special education in the norm group schools (17.25%), and the 43% loss of the norm group population prior to the follow-up should also be considered by potential users of the instrument.

[321]

Rating Scale of Communication in Cognitive Decline.

Purpose: Designed to assess the communication abilities of patients with progressive dementia.
Population: Persons suffering from a prolonged illness.
Publication Date: 1991.
Acronym: RSCCD.
Scores, 3: Verbal, Nonverbal, Total.
Administration: Individual.
Price Data, 1994: $30 per manual including forms.
Time: Administration time not reported.
Authors: Rick Bollinger and Carole J. Hardiman.
Publisher: United/DOK Publishers.

Review of the Rating Scale of Communication in Cognitive Decline by MARK ALBANESE, Associate Professor of Preventive Medicine and Education, and Director, Office of Medical Education Research and Development, The University of Wisconsin-Madison Medical School, Madison, WI:

The Rating Scale of Communication in Cognitive Decline (RSCCD) is a short, 20-item form designed to classify the level of verbal and nonverbal communication behaviors of individuals previously diagnosed with dementia. Citing literature ranking communication difficulties in the top 6 of 20 behavioral problems most commonly reported by family caregiver(s) of Alzheimer's patients, the RSCCD is designed to be a resource for caregivers of demented individuals that will assist them in carefully defining and observing important communicative behaviors and to assist them in ongoing management by providing communication strategies that are compatible with overall ratings of communication. The utilitarian nature of the instrument is reflected in that it classifies individuals into 10 levels of communication abilities and then offers suggestions for how to manage communications for individuals in each level. The instrument is inappropriate for individuals who have had only a single cerebrovascular episode or persons who have specific language disorders, such as aphasia, following such an episode.

The form is simple and is administered by the caregiver during observation of abilities in situations where routine communications are expected to occur. It is recommended that multiple observations and ratings be done at different times of the day and in different situations over a week's time to get an idea of variability of performance. The instrument can also be administered by a health professional with assistance from a caregiver who knows the patient well. The form allows noting whether various behavior was directly observed or based upon caregiver report.

The RSCCD produces separate scores for Verbal and Nonverbal communication. The Verbal section emphasizes pragmatic categories of speech and language, concentrating on speaking and listening behaviors. The Nonverbal section assesses self-awareness and environmental awareness. Only half as much weight is given in scoring to the Nonverbal behaviors because they are considered functionally less effective than Verbal behaviors. The Total score is used to classify the person into 1 of 10 categories according to level of functioning (higher numbered categories reflect better functioning).

Two nicely detailed examples of how to use the RSCCD in patient care are given in the technical manual. Descriptions of classic communication behavior for each of the 10 levels plus strategies for communication management with individuals who are functioning at that level are also given.

Data on concurrent validity and inter- and intrarater reliability are presented in the technical report. Concurrent validity was assessed by correlating scores on the RSCCD with those on the Mini-Mental State Exam and the Global Deterioration Scale for 26 institutionalized patients diagnosed as demented. The RSCCD correlations ranged from .8 to .88 in absolute value with the two concurrent measures.

The reliability data were based upon ratings of residents in nursing homes in two Florida cities who were diagnosed as demented and who had no frank indication of focal lesion or specific indication of psychiatric disorder. The raters consisted of speech-language pathologists with 1 to 20 years of experience post graduate degree and caregivers who were registered nurses and licensed practical nurses employed in the facilities. Training given to the caregivers consisted of a 10–15-minute explanation of the rating scale and then the caregivers were shown an example of a rating completed on a patient known to them. The numbers of patients evaluated in several sets of data ranged from 4 to 27 and the time between retestings ranged from 3 to 12 weeks. The data report intrarater percentage agreement in category placement ranged from 75% to 89%, with the lower values reflecting longer intervals between ratings. The interrater percentages of agreement were 72% for the speech-language pathologists and 85% for the caregivers.

The greatest strength of the RSCCD is its "user-friendliness." The items are written in relatively nontechnical terms, for instance, "Expresses ideas, feelings, thoughts." The response scale is in terms of the percentage of time that the behavior occurs, with five levels available for checking (100%, 75%, 50%, 25%, 0%). The five levels also have verbal labels of *normal, mild, moderate, severe*, and *absent*, respectively, that correspond to the percentages of time. The instructions for how to compute total scores are very clear and excellent examples are given. The 10 categories into which examinees are placed are well described and recommendations are given for how to manage communication with individuals in each category. Finally, the authors give strong support for why communication is an important aspect of giving care to the demented and rationalizing the need for the instrument.

The weaknesses of the instrument are concentrated on what is a very limited assessment of the validity and reliability of the RSCCD. The validity data are somewhat troubling in that the correlations are so high (.8–.88) as to question whether unique characteristics are being assessed, particularly if the correlations were to be disattenuated for unreliability. Although the patient base used to conduct the reliability and validity study is described in terms of status with regard to dementia, issues related to sampling are largely lacking. This is made more problematic by the use of such small numbers of patients—at most 27 and in some analyses as few as 4. To further complicate matters, the analysis of the data is not adequately described and the reporting of percentage agreement, without a correction for chance agreement, may overreport the reliability of the data. It would also be useful to report generalizability coefficients, which would indicate the number of observations needed to obtain a classification that meets a specified level of reliability. The authors continue to conduct field tests, suggesting that more systematically collected and better analyzed data will be available in the future.

A final weakness is the technical manual alludes to use of the instrument by family members who are caregivers, but it does not elaborate on any special considerations that must be given for this population. Training becomes especially complex when dealing with the broader array of potential caregivers, especially those who are not health care providers, as prior education is likely to impact on use of the instrument. A more thorough treatment of the skills and training necessary to use the instrument would be of benefit.

In summary, the RSCCD is a simple, yet elegant instrument that has been developed to help caregivers improve their communication with demented individuals. The directions for use are very clear and well-chosen examples further enhance its use. More information on use of the instrument by nonhealth-care professionals and additional data on the reliability and validity of the instrument would be of benefit. In the meantime, use of the instrument should be governed by one's clinical judgment as to whether the RSCCD provides information more easily or whether the information is more useful than that provided by other competing instruments.

Review of the Rating Scale of Communication in Cognitive Decline by AYRES D'COSTA, Associate Professor of Education, The Ohio State University, Columbus, OH:

The Bollinger-Hardiman Rating Scale of Communication in Cognitive Decline (RSCCD) claims to be "designed to aid caregiver observation and rating of relevant communication abilities." "Relevant" is interpreted to mean those "that impact upon the patient's ability to meet self-care needs" (manual, p. 7).

The authors of the RSCCD claim it is a rating scale, rather than a test. It is intended to serve as an efficient means of quantifying a patient's communication ability levels for self-care after having been diagnosed with dementia. Developmental work for this scale was conducted at adult care centers in Florida.

The Verbal section of the RSCCD, which emphasizes speaking and listening, has 10 observation criteria, starting with "expressess ideas, feelings, thoughts," "expresses physical-emotional needs," "uses printed information," "initiates conversation or expression of need," to "completes what he/she is saying." The Nonverbal section, with emphasis on self and environmental awareness, also has 10 criteria, starting with "indicates physical needs in some way," "demonstrates appropriate emotional response," "evidences an awareness of routine," to "demonstrates awareness of and response to intense environmental stimuli."

Each of the 20 criteria is rated on a 5-point weighted scale: *normal, mild, moderate, severe, absent*. The weights in each section are added to provide a Verbal score (V) and a Nonverbal score (NV). These two scores are further weighted to provide a Total score, which is then linked by a table to one of 10 Communication Decline levels intended to help caregivers meet the specific needs of dementia patients in cognitive decline. Clinical interpretation is encouraged when a marked discrepancy occurs between the V and the NV scores. The RSCCD form also suggests developing a V/NV ratio without indicating how it might be utilized.

The manual provides some reliability figures, both intrarater and interrater, that seem reasonable but are based on very small patient samples (*N*s of 4, 8, 9, and 27). Comparisons were also made between different types of raters. It was disconcerting for this reviewer to note that these studies resulted in the authors concluding that "specialized training in communication observation is not a prerequisite for competent utilization of the RSCCD" (manual, p. 35). One wonders if the RSCCD observations and assessment would be worthy of professional consideration given this conclusion. Substantial concurrent validity correlations were reported with the Mini-Mental State Examination (MMSE), (Folstein, Folstein, & McHugh, 1975) and the Global Deterioration Scale (Reisberg, 1983). Although the MMSE is a commonly used instrument in dementia screening, it cannot validate the communications decline construct being assessed by the RSCCD. Moreover, MMSE scores were already known and utilized in the selection of the subjects for this study. Given these MMSE scores on the recording form of the RSCCD, one should worry about potential bias in the ratings.

If the RSCCD is to be evaluated as a psychometric instrument using AERA-APA-NCME *Standards* (1985), then it clearly falls short. Its manual is not a typical professional test manual. For instance, there is not enough justification provided for the 10 items selected for each section, nor was any study reported on the usefulness of each item for the proposed assessment. Considerable research has gone into item selection for comparable instruments, such as the MMSE, the Information-Memory-Concentration Test by Blessed, Tomlinson, and Roth (1968), etc. Several other instruments (e.g., Alzheimer's Disease Assessment Scale, Rosen, Mohs, & Davis, 1984), are currently available with cognitive (including communications) components that should have relevance to the development of a scale such as the RSCCD. As an assessment instrument, the RSCCD lacks a professional discussion of the domain that it proposes to sample.

The scoring technique proposed by the authors appears "cook-bookish" with little justification provided for the aggregation of ratings across the 10 criteria in each section. The development of the Total score seems to ignore the qualitative observations recorded in the Scale Form. The attribution of a Communication Decline Level (out of 10 levels proposed) based on the RSCCD Total score lacked both normative and clinical justification. Assigning communication decline levels to dementia patients requires more serious thought to DSM-IV diagnostic criteria (not mentioned in the manual), to the stages of cognitive degeneration reported by neurologists in Senile Dementia of Alzheimer Type (SDAT) and in other dementias, and to the recognition that all dementias do not result in similar cognitive or communication declines. Lest the scale become the victim of a lawsuit, care should be taken to emphasize that the proposed communication levels are designed purely for caregiving convenience, and not for diagnosis of severity of dementia.

This reviewer recognizes the need for better care for dementia patients, and the importance of communications in providing care. Recognition is given to the fact that the RSCCD is in its first edition, and that it is possibly just embarking on its research and development efforts. However, there seems to be little indication the authors have utilized the substantial resources of research knowledge and assessment instruments already available in the medical literature. To assert that "measures of self-care abilities are less affected by ethnic, cultural or educational background" (p. 6) stretches the findings of recent research. False positive as well as false negative and measurement biases have been reported for the MMSE based on age, gender, educational level, socioeconomic status, and cultural differences.

The RSCCD may be helpful to caregivers working with dementia patients. It should be used with caution and with full recognition of its limitations. It needs considerable developmental effort before it can merit professional status in neuropsychological assessment literature.

REVIEWER'S REFERENCES

Blessed, G., Tomlinson, B. E., & Roth, M. (1968). The association between quantitative measures of dementia and of senile change in the cerebral grey matter of elderly subjects. *British Journal of Psychiatry, 114*, 797-811.

Folstein, M. F., Folstein, S. E., & McHugh, P. R. (1975). "Mini-Mental State": A practical method for grading the cognitive state of patients for the clinician. *Journal of Psychiatric Research, 12*, 189-198.

Reisberg, B. (1983). Clinical presentation, diagnosis, and symptomatology of age-associated cognitive decline and Alzheimer's disease. In *Alzheimer's disease: The standard reference*. New York: Free Press.

Rosen, W. G., Mohs, R. C., & Davis, K. L. (1984). A new rating scale for Alzheimers' Disease. *American Journal of Psychiatry, 141*, 1356-1364.

American Educational Research Association, American Psychological Association, & National Council on Measurement in Education. (1985). *Standards for educational and psychological testing*. Washington, DC: American Psychological Association, Inc.

[322]

Reality Check Survey.

Purpose: Assesses "how managerial actions serve employee needs."
Population: Adults.
Publication Date: 1989.
Acronym: RCS.
Scores: Total score only.
Administration: Group.
Price Data, 1993: $6.95 per survey.
Time: Untimed.
Comments: Self-administered survey.
Author: Jay Hall.
Publisher: Teleometrics International.

Review of the Reality Check Survey by S. ALVIN LEUNG, Associate Professor in Educational Psychology, University of Houston, Houston, TX:

The Reality Check Survey (RCS) is a self-assessment inventory designed for employees in an organization to evaluate their preference for managerial style and behavior, and to assess whether these preferences have been met by the manager. The author does not provide specific information about the type of employees or organizations that would benefit from this survey.

The RCS has two sections. Each section has 20 items. A 7-point scale is used (*very true* to *very untrue*).

The first section consists of items related to the employee's preference for managerial styles and behavior. The second section consists of items related to whether the styles and behavior in the first section are judged to be present in the organization. The RCS is designed for self-scoring, and scoring instructions are provided for the test takers.

The RCS is not accompanied by a user manual or technical guide. A brief description of the theoretical basis of the instrument and the purpose of the inventory is presented in the test booklet. According to this description, the RCS is based on a theoretical model proposed by McGregor (1960) about managerial practices. Two managerial approaches are identified. The first approach is called "Theory X." This theory assumes that employees are not capable of fulfilling their work responsibilities unless there is a system of extrinsic reward and punishment. This approach usually results in a rigid, suspicious, and authoritarian work environment. The second approach is called "Theory Y." This theory suggests that employees are intrinsically motivated. They can take and fulfill responsibilities, and can identify creative solutions to problems. This approach usually results in a flexible, trusting, and collaborative work environment.

In the first section of the RCS, the items measure whether the employees prefer a Theory X (10 items) or a Theory Y (10 items) managerial approach. The second section measures whether the organizational environment is perceived by the employee as being a Theory X (10 items) or Theory Y (10 items) environment. The employees are instructed to compare their scores in the two sections and to consider what a manager can do differently to enhance work productivity.

The RCS is a simple device in which an employee can assess preferences for managerial styles. However, the RCS is far from being an acceptable psychological instrument. First, although the author described the theory on which the RCS is based, there is no information on how the test items were developed and how they are related to the theoretical foundation. Second, there is no normative information. The respondent cannot compare the obtained scores with those of a normative sample to determine where one stands. Third, there is no information about the reliability and validity of the RCS. The test developer and publication company have the ethical and professional responsibilities to accumulate and report technical information related to the psychometric properties, reliability, and validity of a test when it is published. A user manual documenting all these data should be compiled.

The objectives of the RCS are not clearly defined. For example, is the test designed to facilitate communication between an employee and a manager? Is the test designed to help an employee understand his or her expectations about management? What type of organizations and occupational groups can benefit from using the RCS?

The RCS test booklet does not describe how the scores are to be interpreted. A test score has little meaning if there is no normative information. Because the RCS is designed to assess managerial preference in terms of the Theory X scale and the Theory Y scale (in the first section), there has to be a method to determine how large a difference between the two sores denotes a meaningful and significant difference in preference. Similarly, to determine if the managerial practice is congruent with one's preference, there has to be a method to determine how big a difference between the correspondence scores in the two sections denotes a significant difference between preference and reality (e.g., comparing the Theory X score in the first section with the Theory X scores in the second section). The lack of interpretive guidelines has greatly reduced the utility of the RCS. A test user may misunderstand or misinterpret the significance of the test scores.

In conclusion, because of the above limitations, the RCS is not ready for general use. The scores of the RCS should not be used to make decisions about personnel management. There is no research evidence to support the RCS as a reliable and valid instrument. It is important for the author of the test to conduct research studies so that needed technical information can be made available to users.

REVIEWER'S REFERENCE

McGregor, D. (1960). *The human side of enterprise*. New York: McGraw-Hill.

Review of the Reality Check Survey by SHELDON ZEDECK, Chair and Professor of Psychology, University of California, Berkeley, CA:

The Reality Check Survey (RCS) is described as an instrument designed to allow respondents to provide their managers the opportunity to reflect on their (managers') beliefs regarding the capabilities, motives, and intentions of those they manage. Unfortunately, this is the most we can learn about the RCS based on the information that accompanies the instrument. Although the test booklet itself contains four pages on the underlying notion of the instrument (these pages are not to be reviewed by the respondent until after he or she has responded to the items), there is no manual containing reliability, validity, norms, or other psychometric data that one would want for purposes of evaluation and interpretation. A request of the test publisher for such information yielded the response: "No studies of reliability or validity have been reported" (personal communication, October 29, 1993).

The respondent first answers 20 questions (Part I) regarding the conditions they would prefer in order to do their best work and be most productive. Then, the respondent answers a parallel set of 20 questions (Part II), but this time from the perspective of whether the respondent views his or her manager as believing that the actions cited in the statements are necessary for the respondent to do his or her best work and be most productive. After completing Part II, the respondent tears along a perforated line and has available the scoring key that allows him or her to obtain both a "Theory X" and "Theory Y" score for each part. The respondent is told how to plot his or her scores, but is given absolutely no information as to what the scores mean, much less what "Theory X" or "Theory Y" mean. It is suggested, however, that the respondent *may* want to read the material on Managerial Philosophies that is found behind the Gold Seal. Breaking open the Gold Seal reveals about four pages that describe McGregor's classic "Theory X-Theory Y" philosophy (McGregor, 1960). The description of the philosophy is reasonably good, but no information is presented with respect to how to interpret the respondent's scores, either in an absolute or relative sense.

The very last paragraph of the four-page description suggests there is a form, the Managerial Philosophies Scale, the respondent's manager may have "hopefully" completed and discussed with the respondent for the purpose of the enhancement of their collective work experience.

Based on the available information, I have great difficulty in understanding the value of the instrument. Also, the reliance on a theory first espoused in 1960, and which to the best of my knowledge is no longer current, further contributes to my lack of enthusiasm. It would be interesting to know how the questions and underlying rationale relate to more current theories such as contingency theory, trait theory, sociotechnical theory, among others. Also, a comparison of the instrument to other management philosophy devices (see Clark & Clark, 1990, for alternative measures) would be most informative. In conclusion, there is very little to recommend the use of the RCS.

REVIEWER'S REFERENCES

McGregor, D. (1960). *The human side of enterprise.* New York: McGraw-Hill.

Clark, K. E., & Clark, M. B. (1990). *Measures of leadership.* West Orange, NJ: Leadership Library of America, Inc.

[323]

Receptive-Expressive Emergent Language Test, Second Edition.

Purpose: Designed to identify children who have specific language problems.
Population: Children from birth to 3 years of age.
Publication Dates: 1971–91.
Acronym: REEL-2.
Scores, 3: Expressive Language Age, Receptive Language Age, Combined Language Age.
Administration: Individual.
Price Data, 1994: $56 per complete kit; $29 per 25 profile/test forms; $29 per Examiner's Manual ('91, 50 pages).
Time: Administration time not reported.
Authors: Kenneth R. Bzoch and Richard League.
Publisher: PRO-ED, Inc.
Cross References: See T4:2238 (3 references) and T3:338 (5 references); for excerpted reviews by Alex Bannatyne, Dale L. Johnson and Barton B. Proger, see 8:956 (5 references); see also T2:2067 (2 references).

TEST REFERENCES

1. Kahn, J. V. (1992). Predicting adaptive behaviour of severely and profoundly mentally retarded children with early cognitive measures. *Journal of Intellectual Disability Research*, *36*, 101-114.

2. Owen, M. T., & Mulvihill, B. A. (1994). Benefits of a parent education and support program in the first three years. *Family Relations*, *43*, 206-212.

Review of the Receptive-Expressive Emergent Language Scale, Second Edition by LYLE F. BACHMAN, Professor of Applied Linguistics, University of California, Los Angeles, Los Angeles, CA:

The Receptive-Expressive Emergent Language Scale (REEL) was developed for the purpose of measuring "delays in emergent speech and language development in infants with congenital anomalies and medically related handicaps" (manual, p. 5) for use in diagnosis and remediation by appropriate individuals (e.g., speech clinicians and early childhood specialists). The authors state the Second Edition of this measure (REEL-2) continues to serve this purpose, as well as several others, such as screening "medically and environmentally at-risk populations," determining "the most facilitative behaviors for a particular age" for use in planning appropriate intervention, and determining "how well any planned interventions have served to change the disadvantaged status of individual children" (p. 5). The authors claim that the REEL-2 can be used in a variety of settings, including large pediatric indigent populations, clinical settings, educational settings, and settings with very high-risk infants with cleft palates and/or cerebral palsy. The authors assert the test measures the phonemic, morphenic, syntactic, and semantic development, in both receptive and expressive language skills, of children from birth to age 3. The REEL-2 yields scores in the form of age levels and quotients, norms the authors describe as "language-interactive behaviors that are optimal for infants and toddlers from birth to three years of age" (p. 4).

ADMINISTRATION. In administering the REEL-2, an interviewer uses the "items," or descriptive phrases, in the test form as a guide for asking questions of a caregiver about a child's "ongoing, typical behavior" (p. 13). Interviewers are specifically instructed to vary their questions in ways that they feel are appropriate to their informants. It is important for questions to be phrased appropriately, so as to obtain accurate responses from the informant. However, this variation in elicitation procedure across informants is potentially a major source of measurement error the authors fail to address in their discussion of reliability. A potentially more serious problem is the authors' assumption that equivalent measures can be obtained when the native language of the informant is not English, as long as the interviewer is familiar with both languages, or if an interpreter is used. This flies in the face of considerable research in the assessment of linguistic minorities that raises serious doubts about the validity of inferences and uses based on the administration of a given measure with individuals whose native language is not English (cf. Duran, 1989).

SCORING AND SCORE INTERPRETATION. The items in the test form are arranged into four groups, representing putative stages of development: Stage I: Phonemic level (0–3 months), Stage II: Morphemic level (3–9 months), Stage III: Syntactic level (9–18 months) and Stage IV: Semantic level (18–36 months). There are parallel sets of items for receptive and expressive language. The informant's responses are scored in three categories: "+" if the particular behavior specified in the item is "typical," "-" if it "has never been observed," and "+ -" if it is "only partly exhibited" (p. 14). The interviewer uses these scores to establish ceiling age levels that are reported as scores for Receptive Language Age (RLA), Expressive Language Age (ELA), and Combined Language Age (CLA), which is the average of the RLA and CLA scores. These three scores are converted to Receptive, Expressive, and Language Quotients, which are ratios of the age scores to chronological age. The interpretation of scores is made in terms of differences between the child's chronological age and the "expected levels," as defined in the REEL-2 scales, and specific intervention strategies are suggested for remediation of deficiencies indicated by REEL-2 scores.

TEST CONSTRUCTION. The items in the REEL-2 were selected from the research and existing scales in the developmental literature. The items are arranged sequentially into scales that consist of levels and categories that are derived from a stimulus-response model of language learning and a structuralist theory of linguistics, both of which have long since been abandoned by researchers in language acquisition. Since the mid-70s, work in first language acquisition has been largely informed by a cognitive information-processing view of learning (cf. Chomsky, 1959, 1982; McNeill, 1970; Brown, 1973; Slobin, 1973; Clark & Clark, 1977), whereas structuralist linguistic theory has been replaced by generative linguistic theory (cf. Chomsky, 1965, 1981). In short, both psychology of learning and linguistic theory have undergone major paradigm shifts since the time the REEL-2 scales were developed, and this raises serious questions about the theoretical viability of the constructs upon which the scales are based.

Items were field-tested and normed with a sample of "environmentally language-advantaged Caucasian infants" (p. 7), which raises questions about the appropriateness of the individual items for describing the language development of the "at-risk" children for whom the REEL-2 is intended. Items were selected for inclusion on the basis of statistical criteria: difficulty (Proportion correct between .15 and .85) and discrimination (item-total point biserial correlations of .3 or greater).

The use of this particular norm group is problematic on at least two counts. First, if the authors used this group because they felt it represented a "criterion group" in terms of language development, one must question the degree to which the developmental norms of advantaged white children are an appropriate criterion against which to compare the language development of infants for whom the test is intended, many of whom are likely to be either disadvantaged or linguistically and ethnically diverse. Second, selecting items for inclusion on the basis of item statistics derived from this norm group may mean that the test is less sensitive to individual differences in the intended population than it could have been, had a more appropriate norm group been used.

VALIDITY. The authors' discussion of validity is informed by an outdated view that considers content validity, criterion-related validity, and construct validity as essentially independent types of validity, rather than as a unitary concept (AERA, APA, & NCME, 1985). Furthermore, the evidence they cite pertains almost exclusively to the accuracy of the age score norms, with respect to score interpretability, and they provide virtually no evidence to support the validity of the intended uses recommended for the REEL-2.

Under content validity, the authors argue "the procedures used in building the REEL-2" (p. 10) provide evidence that the items in the REEL-2 represent the behavioral domain the test claims to measure. However, because items were selected on the basis of statistical criteria (discrimination and difficulty), with little mention of content criteria, this putative evidence of content coverage is questionable.

The studies cited as evidence of criterion-related validity are difficult to interpret and lack credibility. First, they are based on small samples (largest n = 50) and the subjects are not adequately described (e.g., no indication of the ages of the subjects in a longitudinal study, or of how many subjects at each age level in a cross-sectional study). Second, the criterion indicators are not always clearly defined (e.g., "normal expected levels of functioning" and "above their chronological ages," p. 10). Third, the statistics given are not adequate to support the claimed relationships (e.g., means, standard deviations, and standard errors for concurrent validity and no coefficients of determination or regression weights for a study of predictive validity).

Under construct validity the authors cite a single study, again inadequately described methodologically, and based on a small sample ($n = 45$). The authors claim this study demonstrates that differences in REEL-2 scores are not related to family income, sex, race, or language system. The problem is that this study does not demonstrate what construct differences in REEL-2 scores *are* related to, and hence provides no evidence for the construct validity of score interpretations. The authors also cite the high item discrimination indices as evidence for construct validity, but this is specious, because item-total correlations only tell us whether the items and the total score are correlated with each other, and say nothing about the construct that either may be measuring. The primary problem with any attempts to investigate the construct validity of REEL-2 score interpretations, however, is the lack of a credible construct, as mentioned above, in the section on Test Construction.

Another shortcoming in the authors' discussion of validity is the lack of any evidence supporting the many uses of the REEL-2 that they recommend. What users are given instead of evidence are allusions to "clinical use" and "long pragmatic experience" (p. 26). Because many of the claimed uses of the REEL-2 are related to programs of remediation or intervention, the consequences of misdiagnosis are potentially very serious, and test users should require more extensive research and documentation before using the REEL-2 for the purposes claimed by the authors.

RELIABILITY. The authors' discussion of reliability in inadequate on several counts: (*a*) their use of internal consistency and test-retest reliability estimates and associated standard error of measurement is of questionable relevance and appropriateness, (*b*) they fail to consider potential sources of measurement error associated with different interviewers, and (*c*) they fail to provide relevant information about measurement errors at the cut scores used to determine the criterion age levels.

The authors report coefficient alphas based on item statistics for each reported score by age level, but provide no descriptive statistics for the groups that were used in the study. Each item can be scored as "+," "-," or "+ -," and the authors do not indicate how these are coded numerically, it is difficult to know exactly how the coefficient alphas were calculated. In addition, the three age levels for which they report reliabilities (0–11, 12–23, and 24–36 months) do not correspond to the four developmental age periods in the scales themselves (0–3, 3–9, 9–18, and 18–36 months), so that it is not clear how potential users are to interpret the reported reliabilities with reference to particular age levels. The authors' estimation of test-retest reliability is equally problematic: It is based on very small samples (28 and 46), for which no descriptive statistics are provided, and the use of a 3-week interval between test administrations has to be questioned, given the rapid development from week to week that characterizes young children. Finally, classical standard errors of measurement, derived from the internal consistency estimates, are reported for REEL-2 standard scores, with no explanation of how the *SEM* was rescaled from raw scores to standard scores.

Because the REEL-2 is administered as an interview, there are potentially two sources of inconsistency associated with individual interviewers: inconsistencies in the way the questions are asked and inconsistencies in the way responses are scored. Neither of these are addressed in the discussion of reliability.

Finally, although the authors explicitly state the items and derived age levels are based on a criterion sample and hence criterion referenced, no agreement indices or standard errors of measurement for the different cut scores that are used for classification are provided. Furthermore, no domain-referenced dependability estimates are provided to permit test users to assess appropriately the degree to which the items in the REEL-2 adequately represent the domain from which they were sampled. Failure to provide such criterion-referenced information is a major omission because most of the putative uses of the test are related to classification decisions.

NORMS. The REEL-2 was normed with a sample "selected to represent the probable norm of environmentally language-advantaged Caucasian infants" (p. 7), so that serious questions must be raised about the use of the REEL-2 with children from linguistic minorities, many of whom may be misdiagnosed as "at-risk" because their native language is not English.

SUMMARY. The REEL-2 must be regarded as inadequate as a measure of early childhood language development. It is based on outdated models of both learning and language and its measurement qualities—validity and reliability—are undemonstrated. To its credit, the items included in its scales cover a wide range of behaviors, and the REEL-2 thus might be used, in conjunction with direct observation, to elicit information for developing a qualitative description of a child's early language development.

REVIEWER'S REFERENCES

Chomsky, N. (1959). A review of B. F. Skinner's Verbal Behavior. *Language*, *35*, 26-58.

Chomsky, N. (1965). *Aspects of the theory of syntax*. Cambridge, MA: M.I.T. Press.

McNeill, D. (1970). *The acquisition of language: The study of developmental psycholinguistics*. New York: Harper & Row.

Brown, R. W. (1973). *A first language: The early stages*. Cambridge, MA: Harvard University Press.

Slobin, D. (1973). Cognitive prerequisites for the development of grammar. In C. Ferguson & D. Slobin (Eds.). *Studies of child language development* (pp. 175-208). New York: Holt, Rinehart and Winston.

Clark, H. H., & Clark, E. V. (1977). *Psychology and language: An introduction to psycholinguistics*. New York: Harcourt, Brace, Jovanovich.

Chomsky, N. (1981). *Lectures on government and binding*. Dordrecht: Foris Publications.

Chomsky, N. (1982). *Some concepts and consequences of the theory of government and binding*. Cambridge, MA: M.I.T. Press.

American Educational Research Association, American Psychological Association, & National Council on Measurement in Education. (1985). *Standards for educational and psychological testing*. Washington, DC: American Psychological Association, Inc.

Duran, R. P. (1989). Testing of linguistic minorities. In R. L. Linn (Ed.), *Educational Measurement* (3rd ed., pp. 573-587). New York: American Council on Education/Macmillan.

Review of the Receptive-Expressive Emergent Language Test, Second Edition by LYNN S. BLISS, Professor of Communication Disorders and Sciences, Wayne State University, Detroit, MI:

The Receptive-Expressive Emergent Language Test, Second Edition (REEL-2) is an updated version of the original instrument. The changes involve revisions in the manual and an optional interview aimed at describing a child's language environment in order to plan intervention. The purpose of the instrument is to obtain information regarding the receptive and expressive language behaviors of infants and toddlers, from birth to 3 years. An interview procedure is used. The REEL-2 is based on a tridimensional model of language with semi-independent components of receptive, expressive, and inner language. All processes involve central nervous system function and reflect "stimulus-response modes of symbolic learned behavior" (manual, p. 3).

The contents of the REEL-2 have not been changed significantly from the original version. There are 132 items presented on a checklist that is divided into four stages of language development. Three items for receptive and for expressive behaviors are presented in 1-, 2-, and 3-month spans. The items are based on research findings obtained in the 1940s and 1970s.

The REEL-2 can be administered by anyone who is familiar with administration principles. Sample questions are located in the manual that assist the interviewer in obtaining appropriate information for each item. The interviewer begins with items in the receptive interval before the child's chronological age. After the interviewer asks the informant a question relating to specific behavior, the response is scored as + (behavior seems to be typical), - (behavior is not observed), or +- (behavior is emerging and variable). The last score is generally considered to be a plus. Ceiling scores are reached when the highest age interval contains at least two positive item scores in the receptive and in the expressive sections. A combined language age refers to the sum of the Receptive and Expressive Language Age divided by two. Receptive, Expressive, and Language quotients are also obtained by dividing the Receptive, Language, or Combined Ages by a child's chronological age and dividing the sum by 100. Data tables are presented in the manual to assist the clinician in deriving the age and quotient scores.

The infants used in the normative population represent children from language-advantaged Caucasian homes. The numbers of children used at each age level are not provided. Fifty protocols from each age level (one year or decoded cluster) were used as the basis for the final item analysis. No further information is given regarding standardization of the REEL in the original or updated version.

The description of the reliability and validity of the REEL-2 has been expanded from the original version. Data relating to internal consistency, test-retest, inter-examiner agreement, and standard error of measurement are presented and suggest that the REEL-2 is a reliable assessment measure. Internal consistency coefficients are reported to be above .92, reflecting a high degree of homogeneity among test items. All other data presented reflect high degrees of reliability. Validity of the REEL-2 was addressed by describing content, criterion-related, and construct validity. If the model on which the REEL is based is considered to be valid and the test selection process is assumed to be appropriate, construct and content validity might be accepted. The authors cite research that claims that the REEL-2 does not show differences in language development based on socioeconomic status, sex, race, or language system (i.e., receptive vs. expressive) contradicting the findings of many studies of language development. Criterion-related validity was addressed by describing the results of three studies that demonstrate the results of the REEL-2 relate to expectations of normal language development.

The advantages of the REEL-2 are in its easy administration and scoring. The manual contains clear instructions for the interviewer in asking questions, scoring responses, and obtaining equivalent age scores and quotients. The following disadvantages are evident. The model on which the instrument is based is outdated and restrictive. For example, pragmatic behaviors are not included. The standardization population is limited and data regarding standardization are not provided. Normative data are not presented. Guidelines for the optional clinical caregiver interview were not found in the manual.

In conclusion, although the REEL-2 is easy to administer and score, the limitations in standardization as well as an outdated model of linguistic functioning reduce the effectiveness of this instrument.

[324]

Reid Report.

Purpose: "The Report consists of a customized set of scales and questionnaires which focus on key, business-related employee behaviors. Measures attitudes toward conscientiousness and counterproductivity in the workplace and predicts overall work performance and counterproductive acts (turnover, absenteeism, tardiness, theft and inappropriate substance use)."

Population: Job applicants.

Publication Dates: 1969–92.

Scores: 1 of 4 possible evaluations (Recommended, Qualified, Not Recommended, No Opinion) in 4 parts (Integ-

rity Attitude, Antisocial History, Recent Drug Use, Work History) and overall evaluation.
Administration: Group.
Price Data: Price information available from publisher for test materials including examiner's manual ('89, 39 pages).
Time: (15–60) minutes.
Comments: Overall evaluation established by client organization, based upon specific organizational requirements.
Authors: Reid Psychological Systems, Paul Brooks (manual), and David Arnold (manual).
Publisher: Reid Psychological Systems.
Cross References: See T4:2243 (1 reference); for a review by Stanley L. Brodsky, see 8:658 (3 references); for integrated version of Reid Report/Reid Survey, see T2:1353 (1 reference) and 7:132 (1 reference).

TEST REFERENCES

1. Cunningham, M. R., Wong, D. T., & Barbee, A. D. (1994). Self-presentation dynamics on overt integrity tests: Experimental studies of the Reid Report. *Journal of Applied Psychology, 79*, 643-658.
2. Lilienfeld, S. O., Andrews, B. P., Stone-Romero, E. F., & Stone, D. (1994). The relations between a self-report honesty test and personality measures in prison and college samples. *Journal of Research in Personality, 28*, 154-169.

Review of the Reid Report by GEORGE DOMINO, Professor of Psychology, University of Arizona, Tucson, AZ:

The Reid Report (RR) is said to measure "attitudes toward honesty and integrity" and aims to "predict dishonest acts on the job" (manual, p. 1). The test booklet consists of four parts for a total of 320 items (oddly enough the first item is numbered 101), but it is only Part 1, made up of 80 yes-no items (only 70 are scored) and comprising the Integrity Attitude Inventory, that is scored and for which there is psychometric information available.

The Examiner's Manual is well written and presents considerable reliability and validity data, but does not seem to be written for the psychometrically sophisticated reader. The manual is perhaps more noteworthy for what is absent than what is presented.

There is in the manual no distinction made between the RR in its totality and Part 1, with Part 1 typically labelled as the RR. The manual indicates the RR contains 80 items, but the test booklet contains 83. For this reader there was considerable confusion over how scores are generated. The test information indicates that a four-fold evaluation is given (recommended, qualified, not recommended, no opinion), but most of the manual information indicates a two-fold evaluation (recommended vs. not recommended) with a cutoff score of 49–50. No indication is given how this particular score was selected. Although scores are reported as raw scores, as percentiles, and as probability (that the applicant will commit theft) scores, there is no table or other information that allows the reader to equate raw scores with percentiles. There is a table (Table 16) that equates "percent rank" with probability, but nowhere is there information on how the probability scores were computed, nor their degree of validity. The nature of the table strongly suggests that these probabilities are not empirically based, but were calculated "statistically."

The manual authors recommend the RR be administered only to applicants for positions "in which honesty and integrity are major job requirements" and where "dishonest behavior could cause significant economic, organizational or personal harm" (manual, p. 2). The RR has, however, been administered to over 5 million individuals, and what job descriptions are given suggest that many applicants were for relatively low-level positions such as parking lot attendants, laborers, assemblers, as well as salespersons, stock clerks, and warehouse workers.

The manual indicates that 18 internal consistency studies have been carried out, but Table 1 gives results for 14 samples, and it is not clear how the samples and the studies interface. Five of the coefficients are given as Cronbach's alphas, which is puzzling given the dichotomous nature of the item responses.

These aspects, like the misspelling of psychological on the inside frontispiece of the manual, are minor and only slightly irritating. There are, however, a number of more major and frustrating aspects to the RR. First, there is no discussion of the development of the test other than to indicate the authors. The conclusion is that the test was developed by "fiat" rather than by empirical procedures, and that internal consistency analyses or other item selection procedures were not followed. A few of the items are nearly identical with MMPI-CPI (Minnesota Multiphasic Personality Inventory—Californial Psychological Inventory) items, but no mention of this is made.

Secondly, given the aim of the test, its self-report format, and item transparency, faking is of central concern. The manual indicates that there is "extensive research on its resistance to faking" (p. 4), but what is presented does not support this claim. In one study, 51 college students were instructed to fake good, but the obtained mean was not significantly different from that obtained by a randomly selected group of employment applicants. Only when the two samples were "equated" for college education did a significant (but miniscule) difference appear. Incidentally, no means, standard deviations, or ANOVA results are presented in the manual, and of the 30 references cited only 9 are to publications in the public domain. In two other sets of studies the effects of different attitudes toward test-taking and different instruction conditions are explored. Attitudes are related to RR scores but instructions are not. Finally, one study is presented comparing incarcerated felons with randomly selected job applicants, with none of the felons earning a "recommended" score. The evidence presented on faking is neither convincing nor complete.

Two studies of the factorial structure of the RR are reported, suggesting four separate factors, but there is no evidence given for the separate validity (or lack) of these factors. Despite these results, the manual suggests that "integrity" (not one of the four factors) is what is being measured, and two studies are presented in which RR results are compared to multivariate personality inventories, showing that high scorers on the RR are better adjusted than low scorers. Somehow the leap between integrity and adjustment is made without specifying their equivalence.

Several predictive and concurrent validity studies are reported, most utilizing a self-report criterion. The results indicate substantial correlations between RR scores and self-reported criteria of honesty (those who say they are "honest" on the test say they are "honest" outside of the test), but low to marginal correlations when the criterion is not a self-report.

Cunningham, Trucott, and Wong (1990) studied employed college students in an experimental situation where the students were overpaid for their participation in the study, and could retain or return the overpayment. Those who returned the overpayment scored higher on the RR (r = .33). However, scores on the RR also correlated significantly with Mach IV scores (r = -.34), with the tendency to impress others (r = .55), and with the tendency to deny undesirable qualities (r = .38). Note that all these coefficients are greater in magnitude than the criterion one.

In summary, the RR has an impressive potential—it has been administered to over 5 million individuals, has apparently no adverse impact on minorities, and addresses an important issue in the workplace. The available evidence, however, provides more questions than answers, and leaves much to be desired from a psychometric point of view.

REVIWER'S REFERENCE

Cunningham, M. R., Trucott, M., & Wong, D. T. (1990). *An experimental investigation of integrity: Testing the predictive validity of the Reid Report.* Unpublished manuscript.

Review of the Reid Report by KEVIN R. MURPHY, Professor of Psychology, Colorado State University, Fort Collins, CO:

The Reid Report is designed to predict acts of dishonesty in the workplace (e.g., employee theft) on the basis of respondents' attitudes toward theft and dishonesty and their admissions of past misdeeds. Various versions of the inventory have been in use for over 40 years; according to Brodsky (1978), at least 19 revisions were undertaken in the first 30 years of its existence. The current Reid Report includes an 80-item Integrity Attitude Inventory, together with up to three optional supplements designed to assess work history, drug and alcohol abuse, and antisocial history. The Attitude Inventory includes 80 items measuring punitiveness toward self and others and projections of one's own honesty and others' dishonesty (Cunningham & Ash, 1988). The supplements include a variety of items, including many that request direct admissions of previous misdeeds, job dismissals, etc. For example, the antisocial history supplement inquires about committing and being convicted of a number of crimes and misdemeanors.

Each section of the test leads to one of four evaluations: (*a*) recommended, (*b*) qualified (i.e., recommended with qualifications), (*c*) not recommended, and (*d*) no opinion (e.g., if examinee does not complete the form). The overall evaluation resulting from the test is based on the least favorable recommendation from any part. Furthermore, evaluations of "qualified" on two or more parts lead to an overall evaluation of "not recommended." Test reports typically include the overall evaluation, evaluations on each part, and information about specific admissions made on each of the supplemental parts. Approximately 75% of those who complete the inventory receive evaluations of "recommended."

Percentile ranks are reported for the sections of the test on which an evaluation of "not recommended" is recorded. The examiner's manual reports normative data from a total sample of over 200,000 that links these percentile ranks to the probability of on-the-job theft. It is not clear how these probabilities were derived; given the evidence of differences in theft rates across occupations (Hollinger & Clark, 1983), it is not clear that these results could be generalized, even if we assume that they are approximately correct for at least some occupations.

Evidence of relatively high reliability (internal consistency and test-retest coefficients of appoximately .90 and .70, respectively) and of criterion-related validity, in terms of correlations with theft admissions, inventory shortfalls, and self-reports of time theft and substance abuse is reviewed in the manual. Given the fact the three supplements contain many questions that themselves call for these same admissions, these "validity" coefficients seem conceptually more similar to test-retest reliability coefficients than to independent demonstrations of the predictive power of the test. Nevertheless, they do provide some evidence to support the hypothesis that test scores are related to dishonest behavior.

Correlations between scores on the Reid Report and scores on several personality inventories (e.g., the Minnesota Multiphasic Personality Inventory [MMPI]) are presented as evidence of construct validity (Kochkin, 1987). Because no clear definition of the construct this test is designed to measure is ever presented, this type of evidence is hard to evaluate. It is useful to know that individuals who receive unfavorable recommendations on the Reid Report also show elevated scores on a number of personality and psychopathology scales, but until the construct is more clearly defined, it is difficult to sort supportive evidence from evidence *against* the construct validity of this measure.

In 1991, a task force of the American Psychological Association carried out an evaluation of integrity tests. Although the evaluation was on the whole more positive than negative, the use of categorical scoring systems in integrity testing (e.g., recommended vs. not recommended) was strongly criticized. The scoring system employed by the Reid Report presents a number of potentially serious problems, notably the use of the least favorable of the four possible evaluations as the determinant of the overall evaluation reported for each examinee. Although the test manual warns consumers not to use the Reid Report as the sole basis for hiring decisions, the fact that the test labels a person as "not recommended" if *any* of four scores falls below a cutting point that seems arbitrary does not seem likely to encourage the optimal use of information from the test.

On the whole, the Reid Report is representative of a growing class of tests that are used to make inferences about the trustworthiness of job applicants and incumbents. As the APA task force pointed out, this class of tests should be evaluated according to the same standards as other psychological tests, in which case the Reid Report appears to have demonstrated more than adequate reliability, as well as some evidence (independent of admissions similar to those on the test itself) of criterion-related validity. The scoring system and normative data for the test are both far from optimal, but if the limitations of tests of this type (particularly those that report categorical scores) are kept firmly in mind, this test can provide a potentially useful component of a personnel selection program.

REVIEWER'S REFERENCES

Brodsky, S. L. (1978). [Review of the Reid Report]. In O. K. Buros (Ed.), *Eighth mental measurements yearbook* (pp. 1025-1026). Highland Park, NJ: Gryphon Press.

Hollinger, R. C., & Clark, J. P. (1983). *Theft by employees*. Lexington, MA: Lexington Books.

Kochkin, S. (1987). Personality correlates of a measure of honesty. *Journal of Business and Psychology*, *1*, 236-247.

Cunningham, M. R., & Ash, P. (1988). The structure of honesty: Factor analysis of the Reid Report. *Journal of Business and Psychology*, *3*, 54-66.

APA Task Force. (1991). *Questionnaires used in the prediction of trustworthiness in pre-employment selection decisions: An A.P.A. Task Force report*. Washington, DC: American Psychological Association.

[325]

Responsibility and Independence Scale for Adolescents.

Purpose: Measures adaptive behaviors.
Population: Ages 12.0–19.11.
Publication Date: 1990.
Acronym: RISA.
Scores, 3: Responsibility, Independence, Adaptive Behavior Total.
Subscales, 9: Self-Management, Social Maturity, Social Communication, Domestic Skills, Money Management, Citizenship, Personal Organization, Transportation Skills, Career Skills.
Administration: Individual.
Price Data, 1991: $115 per complete set including test book, 25 response forms, and examiner's manual (175 pages); $24 per 25 response forms; $40 per examiner's manual.
Time: (30–45) minutes.
Comments: Administered in a standardized interview format to a respondent who is familiar with the adolescent.
Authors: John Salvia, John T. Neisworth, and Mary W. Schmidt.
Publisher: The Riverside Publishing Company

TEST REFERENCES

1. Brooke, S. L. (1993). Critical analysis of the Responsibility and Independence Scale for Adolescents. *Measurement and Evaluation in Counseling and Development*, *26*, 105-109.

2. Salvia, J. (1993). A different analysis of RISA. *Measurement and Evaluation in Counseling and Development*, *26*, 110-112.

Review of the Responsibility and Independence Scale for Adolescents by D. JOE OLMI, Assistant Professor of School Psychology, Department of Psychology, University of Southern Mississippi, Hattiesburg, MS:

The Responsibility and Independence Scale for Adolescents (RISA) is a 136-item norm-referenced instrument designed to assess adolescent adaptive behavior in individuals between the ages of 12-0 and 19-11 years. A parent, guardian, or individual who is very familiar with the adolescent should serve as respondent. Presented in an interview format, the RISA should take approximately 30–45 minutes to administer, with an additional 15 minutes needed for scoring and interpretation.

The justification for the instrument is couched in the model of adaptive behavior developed in 1984 by Schmidt and Salvia that posed three major emphases: "(1) a focus on adolescent adaptive behavior, (2) a need for appraisal that has utility for least restrictive environment/mainstream placement decisions, and (3) a solid foundation in learning theory" (examiner's manual, p. 56). The RISA can be used by a variety of professionals from diagnostic personnel, including school psychologists and educational assessment specialists, to counselors who have expertise in interviewing and assessment. Specialized training is not required. The test's primary purposes include serving as a component in diagnosis and identification in accordance with special education laws, and as an assessment device to aid in program planning.

As proposed by the authors, there are two domains to adolescent adaptive behavior: Responsibility and Independence. Within each domain are "functional" areas. Within each functional area are specific adolescent adaptive skills. The functional areas within the responsibility domain include Self-Management, Social Maturity, and Social Communication. Examples of adolescent adaptive skills within this domain include having constructive friendships, respecting others and their property, and using a telephone appropriately. The Independence domain includes Domestic Skills, Money Management, Citizenship, Personal Organization, Transportation Skills, and Career Skills. Examples of adaptive skills within this area are selecting and preparing foods, banking, conservation, driving legally and skillfully, and applying for employment.

The RISA consists of the examiner's manual, the testing book, and the record form. The examiner's manual is very well organized and contains information pertinent for administration, scoring, interpretation, technical support, and development. Chapter 5 of the examiner's manual contains a training model for the professional who might be self-teaching or the university trainer who is teaching the RISA in a formal assessment course. The practice exercise portion of the chapter is an asset and guides one through the scoring and interpretation procedures of two presented hypothetical cases.

Each item of the RISA is in question format as "Does ________ take care of his/her belongings?" (pp. 14–15). Black-and-white pictures correspond with each item to serve as additional prompts, and extra text directions are offered for the interviewer if the respondent does not reply within 5 seconds. Each item is scored 1 (Yes), 0 (No), DK (Don't Know) or NA (Not Applicable). Item sections for each "functional" area are appropriately labeled in the test booklet.

As the respondent is attending to the presented item card, the interviewer is also cued by a similar stimulus card containing the directions and scoring options for that particular item. A potential drawback to the design of the test booklet is that the respondent might be distracted by the interviewer's card, thus affecting a response. A free-standing easel format for the test booklet would have avoided the possibility of this occurring. No other shortcomings of the test booklet were noted.

The record form for the RISA is simple and well organized, containing sections for demographics, calculation of scores, and scoring of individual items. Item scores yield a Responsibility and an Independence standard score with a mean of 100 and standard deviation of 15. The Responsibility score is a measure of "a broad class of adaptive behaviors that meet social expectation and standards of reciprocity, accountability, and fairness and that enable personal development through self- and social management, age-appropriate behavior, and social communication" (p. 26). The Independence score is an indication of adaptive behaviors "that allow individuals to live separately and free from the control or determination of others and to conduct themselves effectively in matters concerning domestic and financial management, citizenship, personal organization, transportation, and career development" (p. 26).

These standard scores are totaled and converted to arrive at an Adaptive Behavior Total, also a standard score with a mean of 100 and standard deviation of 15. Confidence intervals are determined for the Responsibility percentile and standard score, the Independence percentile and standard score, and the Adaptive Behavior Total. The Standard Score Difference is calculated based on the authors' position that responsibility and independence are separate aspects of adaptive behavior. This score allows the interviewer to determine relative strengths and weaknesses of each aspect, potentially critical to program design. The Standard Difference Score is also converted to a percentile. For interpretation purposes, there are five classifications of percentiles denoting an adolescent's relative standing with same-age peers ranging from superior (95th or above) to deficient (5th or below).

It is important to note that the RISA standard scores and percentiles are not synonymous with normal distribution standard scores and percentiles. An additional table necessary for conversion of RISA percentiles to "normalized" standard scores is provided. This would be a necessary step before comparing RISA scores to standard scores from other frequently used measures such as the Wechsler Intelligence Scale for Children—Third Edition (412).

Items were selected from an initial item pool of 250. Standardization sites were then selected based on 1980 U.S. Census categories. Public and private secondary schools and community agencies serving adolescents within 70 communities were selected from 20 states across the country. Nineteen hundred predominantly European-American adolescents comprised the sample. Inadequate information is presented regarding the non-White composition of the standardization sample. Of the respondents, 84% were natural mothers and 13% were natural fathers, with the remainder consisting of primarily female guardians. Weighting within age groups was conducted to make the sample consistent with census data.

Psychometrically, the RISA is very sound. Corrected split-half correlations by age for the weighted sample ranged from .76 to .95, with the majority in the .90s. Test-retest reliabilities for intervals up to approximately 2 weeks exceeded .90. Content, criterion-related, and construct validity information is more than adequate. The authors cautiously note that the RISA is to be used only with individuals similar in demographic characteristics to the standardization sample.

In summary, the RISA is a sound assessment device that contributes to a much needed area: the assessment of adolescent behavior. Its strengths are its organization, design, and technical adequacy. Shortcomings are few, and one would do well to add the RISA to his or her diagnostic and program evaluation repertoire.

Review of the Responsibility and Independence Scale for Adolescents by JAMES P. VAN HANEGHAN, Assistant Professor of Educational Psychology, Counseling, and Special Education, Northern Illinois University, De-Kalb, IL:

The Responsibility and Independence Scale for Adolescents (RISA) is a normative measure of adaptive behavior designed to be used for adolescents (ages 12 years to 19 years 11 months). It is purported to have two distinguishing characteristics that separate it from other measures of adaptive behavior. First, it is targeted specifically at adolescents. The authors believe there are elements of adaptive behavior that are relatively unique to adolescence not dealt with adequately by other scales of adaptive behavior. Additionally, there are unique issues in dealing with adolescents in special education who are making the transition into the adult world. A valid index of how well these adolescents are prepared for the adult world could prove very useful. Second, as its title connotes, it purports to measure both reports of responsible and independent behavior in adolescents. Although the idea of independence is common to many scales of adaptive behavior, the *prominence* of the notion of responsibility is a distinguishing characteristic of the RISA.

The RISA contains items from nine subareas that fall under one of these two larger constructs of Responsibility and Independence. No attempt is made to develop scale scores for these nine subareas. Three subdomains fall under the domain of Responsibility: Self-Management, Social Maturity, and Social Communication. The other six subdomains, Domestic Skills, Money Management, Citizenship, Personal Organization, Transportation Skills, and Career Skills, all fall in the domain of Independence. The items tend to be focused toward the upper end of adolescence (high school and beyond). The inclusion of slightly more items toward the upper end of the scale was done for psychometric reasons. Practically, having more items biased toward the upper end of the scale reinforces the notion of using the RISA for questions about making the transition from school to adult life.

The authors see the instrument as useful for clinical, research, and training purposes. The authors suggest that most professionals involved in individualized testing should be able to administer the RISA with little training. As a clinical tool, the authors view the RISA as an instrument that can be used in conjunction with others for diagnostic, placement, or program planning purposes for adolescents in special education or counseling. They also suggest that particular score patterns can be used as an indicator of risk for delinquency. As a research tool, they see it as useful for understanding the psychosocial development of various groups of adolescents.

For the most part, the materials that accompany the RISA are adequate for helping users to master administration and scoring. The manual includes sufficient information about the norming sample, rules for administration, and scoring. It includes some sample protocols and other training materials for helping to teach individuals to use the test. Especially useful are materials that help train examiners to create an optimal testing environment.

The RISA, like most adaptive behavior inventories, is administered via an informant (e.g., parent). Each item appears on a page with a line drawing and the appropriate question to show the informant. On the opposite page, a more detailed version of the question appears with a rephrasing for the tester. The 136 items are straightforward to administer. Credit is given for possessing an independent living or responsibility skill based on whether the adolescent performs the behavior at least half the time. If the adolescent does not carry out the skill at least half the time, then he or she is scored zero for that item. If the item does not apply to the cultural group a child belongs to, the item is marked "not applicable." Note that "not applicable" does not concern age appropriateness. The item is scored zero if the item is not age appropriate (e.g., an adolescent below 16 cannot get a license and therefore drive a car). Finally, if the respondent does not know whether the adolescent does or does not demonstrate the skill, then the item is marked "don't know."

Scoring of the protocol is also simple. The number of Independence items scored as "one" form a raw score that is transformed into a standard score with a mean of 100 and a standard deviation of 15 via one of the tables in the appendix of the manual. The same is done with the Responsibility items. To obtain the standard score for the Adaptive Behavior Total, the standard scores for Responsibility and Independence Scales are added together, and the score is converted via one of the tables in the appendix of the examiner's manual.

One caution needs to be considered in scoring the protocol. Standard scores are considered invalid if seven or more items are considered "not applicable" or are marked "don't know." A plethora of "don't know" responses suggests that the informant is not knowledgeable of the adolescent's behavior. A plethora of "not applicable" responses suggests that the test is not applicable to individuals from particular cultural groups or subgroups. How one judges whether an item is applicable to a particular group is a concern. This is especially true for the Independence scales. The examples given in the manual of a Native American living on a reservation, or an Amish adolescent are very clear, but there are some less clear-cut examples. For instance, consider the inner-city minority adolescent living in poverty. This adolescent might not have the need for or access to an automobile. Thus, items surrounding driving an automobile might not be applicable. Adolescents in poverty might not have access to credit, and therefore items surrounding use of credit and interest on loans may be foreign to them. Although some examiners might not consider these cultural differences, but rather socioeconomic ones, others may interpret them as cultural differences. This ambiguity might present some problems in interpretation. The authors are very careful to point out that one has to be sensitive to cultural applicability and that it is incumbent upon the examiner to be sure that the items are valid for a particular group. However, a bit more guidance from the test developers concerning when items are not applicable would be helpful.

This issue of when items are culturally inapplicable is an important one because there is an overrepresentation of minority, culturally different, and low socioeconomic children in some special education populations. If we cannot generate standard scores for children from these groups, then the RISA may not be the tool of choice for practitioners who work with these students. To the authors' credit, they are sensitive to cultural differences and point out that individual items can be of some use, even if the overall score cannot. However, given that a significant portion of one target audience might be from the groups mentioned above, it would make some sense to address applicability in more detail. Perhaps local norms could be generated to help make the test more applicable to culturally different groups.

The chapter in the examiner's manual on the norming sample does not contain any discussion of the number of invalid protocols from individuals in that sample. Based on completed protocols, the authors do point out that differences in the three scores generated from the test along ethnic and racial lines are very small or nonexistent. They also report little difference in urban versus rural scores. Thus, they suggest that the data do not show any bias in the instrument.

Aside from the concern with item inapplicability, the norming information and the psychometrics of the test are generally good. They used a normative sample of approximately 1,900 individuals whose selection was stratified along six dimensions: geographic region, community size, education, income, employment status, and occupational type. They used the empirical literature, expert judges, classic item analysis techniques, and factor analysis to generate their scales. Both internal consistency and test-retest reliability are very high for the scales (.90 and above). However, there are no data presented on respondent accuracy (e.g., observation of actual behavior), interrater reliability, or correspondence with the reports of the adolescents themselves. They confirmed their theoretical constructs of responsibility and independence via factor analysis. The test scores show moderate to small correlations with other scales of adaptive behavior. Additionally, scores in special populations like individuals with mild, moderate, and severe mental retardation, juvenile delinquency, and learning disabilities all turn out to be deficient in comparison to normally developing adolescents. They also claim that the RISA can help predict whether an adolescent is at risk for delinquency. They report that adolescents from delinquent populations show discrepancy between Independence and Responsibility scores. Further research is needed to determine whether this indicator will prove to be useful in identifying adolescents at risk for delinquency as well as those who are already identified juvenile offenders. At present, there is very little long-term predictive validity evidence for the scale.

In summary, the RISA is a promising tool for measuring adaptive behavior of adolescents. It is straightforward to administer, its psychometrics are relatively good, and it has a unique focus. However, there are still questions that need to be addressed concerning the RISA. First, the issue of item inapplicability must be addressed in more detail by the test authors. This issue is an important one, especially when measures of adaptive behavior are used diagnostically. The authors are clearly aware that cultural differences may invalidate the scores from the scale. However, they need to provide more guidance than they do in helping consumers of the test make "not applicable" judgments wisely. Second, like any relatively new test, we know little about the long-term predictive validity of the RISA. That knowledge should come with research use of the RISA to study developmental patterns of change in adaptive behavior.

[326]

Revised BRIGANCE® Diagnostic Inventory of Early Development.

Purpose:: Constructed to "determine the developmental or performance level of the infant or child."
Population: Birth to age 7.
Publication Dates: 1978–91.
Scores: 11 areas: Preambulatory Motor Skills and Behaviors, Gross-Motor Skills and Behaviors, Fine-Motor Skills and Behaviors, Self-Help Skills, Speech and Language Skills, General Knowledge and Comprehension, Social and Emotional Development, Readiness, Basic Reading Skills, Manuscript Writing, Basic Math.
Administration: Individual.
Price Data, 1991: $95 per manual with tests ('91, 298 pages); $19.90 per 10 record books; $9.90 per group record book; $35.95 per classroom testing kit.
Time: [15–20] minutes per child.
Comments: "Criterion-referenced"; 1978 edition still available.
Author: Albert H. Brigance.
Publisher: Curriculum Associates, Inc.
Cross References: For reviews of an earlier edition by Stephen J. Bagnato and Elliot L. Gory, see 9:164.

Review of the Revised BRIGANCE® Diagnostic Inventory of Early Development by C. DALE CARPEN-

TER, Professor of Special Education, Western Carolina University, Cullowhee, NC:

The Revised BRIGANCE Diagnostic Inventory of Early Development (Birth to 7 Years) (IED-R) is a 1991 revision of a 1978 instrument of the same name. The original edition was generally well received (Bagnato, 1985; Gory, 1985; Robinson & Kovacevich, 1985). Noted strengths were that the IED was developmental with norm-referenced and criterion-referenced qualities. It was easy to use and appropriate for normal and delayed children, and it had planning goals. Some weaknesses were a lack of psychometric information such as reliability and validity and lack of a section on social-emotional development. In summary, the IED was considered to be a practical, informal tool to inventory a wide range of skills and needed to be adapted to fit the needs of children with unique needs. The IED lacked supporting technical data.

The Revised BRIGANCE Diagnostic Inventory of Early Development retains most of the original version. Some tests have been omitted such as Ball Bouncing, Rhythm, and Wheel Toys from Gross Motor Skills and Behaviors. Some tests have fewer items, particularly in the section titled Preambulatory Motor Skills and Behaviors, and some have more items such as in the section titled Self-Help Skills. The IED-R, like the original, also has 11 sections, but it includes a new section called Social and Emotional Development. The IED-R combines two sections from the earlier edition, Pre-Speech and Speech and Language Skills, into one section called Speech and Language Skills.

The format for the IED-R is unchanged. It uses the same system of recording for multiple administrations. Each page on the Record Book of the IED-R has administration directions and an objective. Some pages are reproducible for consumable use; some are laminated.

New features exist. A kit of materials needed to administer the IED-R is available from the publisher although they are easy to assemble on one's own. The Class Record Book is particularly helpful to monitor up to 15 children and their skills. A new appendix of developmental skills is available for copying.

CRITIQUE. The changes from the original appear to be improvements. Most items eliminated in the revision were not essential. New items appear helpful. Perhaps that is because systematic efforts were undertaken to elicit feedback from users (A. H. Brigance, personal communication, October, 1991). Tests omitted in the revision do not weaken the instrument.

The addition of the section titled Social and Emotional Development was a response to a perceived weakness in the first edition. There are 122 items in three subsections. This reviewer thinks that these items could be reduced to yield a more efficient but still effective instrument. Perhaps user feedback will effect that change in a future revision.

Technical data to demonstrate reliability and validity which were lacking in the original are still lacking with the IED-R. The instrument relies on popular developmental scales and curriculum materials currently in use (Benner, 1992). Cautions about the rigidity of a certain item at a certain age are present. The lack of supporting psychometric data is a serious flaw. The utility of the instrument may depend on the validity of the reference sources used to develop the items and to place them developmentally.

SUMMARY. Users of the IED who were satisfied will find a more efficient instrument in the IED-R. The IED-R is easy to use with all of the features of the IED and more. A new section on Social and Emotional Development has been added to fill a need. Technical data are not available to support reliability and validity, although updated references have been used to select and sequence items. Although there is now more competition in this area than when the original version was published, the IED-R is a viable tool because of its flexibility and planning utility.

REVIEWER'S REFERENCE

Bagnato, S. J. (1985). [Review of the BRIGANCE Diagnostic Inventory of Early Development]. In. J. V. Mitchell, Jr., (Ed.), *The ninth mental measurements yearbook* (Vol. 1, pp. 219-220). Lincoln, NE: Buros Institute of Mental Measurements.

Gory, E. L. (1985). [Review of the BRIGANCE Diagnostic Inventory of Early Development]. In. J. V. Mitchell, Jr., (Ed.), *The ninth mental measurements yearbook* (Vol. 1, pp. 220-221). Lincoln, NE: Buros Institute of Mental Measurements.

Robinson, J. H., & Kovacevich, D. A. (1985). [Review of the BRIGANCE Inventories]. In D. J. Keyser & R. C. Sweetland (Eds.), *Test critiques* (Vol. III, pp. 79-98). Kansas City: Test Corporation of America.

Benner, S. M. (1992). *Assessing young children with special needs: An ecological perspective*. White Plains, NY: Longman.

Review of the Revised BRIGANCE® Diagnostic Inventory of Early Development by DOUGLAS A. PENFIELD, Professor of Education, Graduate School of Education, Rutgers University, New Brunswick, NJ:

The Revised BRIGANCE Diagnostic Inventory of Early Development provides a process for assessing and tracking the developmental skills of children from birth to approximately 7 years of age. It is a norm- and criterion-referenced instrument designed to identify the strengths and weaknesses of the child through the use of skill assessment and a comprehensive record-keeping system. Identified strengths and weaknesses may subsequently be used for diagnostic purposes.

The Inventory is broken into 11 broad skill areas (see above Inventory description). Each broad skill area is further divided into a number of subareas which in turn are linked to basic skills and behaviors useful in assessing area and subarea mastery. For example, under the (G) Social and Emotional Development Skills area, the subareas are labelled (G-1) General Social and Emotional Development, (G-2) Play Skills and Behaviors, and (G-3) Work-Related Skills and Behaviors. The first seven broad skill areas represent skills that are developmental in nature, whereas the last four areas place a greater emphasis on cognitive behavior. Methods used to assess skills include (*a*) parent interviews, (*b*) observing the child, (*c*) asking the child to perform tasks, (*d*) engaging the child in conversation, and (*e*) teacher interviews. Examiners are encouraged to use their judgment in determining which skills to evaluate and how to best elicit a child's response. Extensive assessment guidelines are provided for each skill area.

There is an important link between the basic skills being evaluated and the approximate developmental age at which mastery is normally achieved. Skills are sequenced within a subarea according to developmental age. Special efforts have been taken to validate the skill sequencing. Given the chronological age of the child, examiners can use developmental age as an index for choosing an appropriate starting point within a skill subarea. Due to the extensiveness of the Inventory, it is not possible to administer the entire Inventory at one time. Examiners are advised to use their judgment in deciding which areas to evaluate in a single sitting.

The Inventory is contained in a seven-ring binder which is easily manipulated. When administering the Inventory, the examiner and child sit opposite each other with the Inventory placed between them. While the examiner reads the instructions, the child observes the visual material and responds to questions. Each broad skill area is broken down into overall goals and objectives, methods of assessment, assessment directions, required test materials, and the references used to validate the sequencing of skills. Questions are presented along with helpful hints for determining successful mastery. Illustrations and drawings are displayed in a clear, concise fashion.

Record keeping is enhanced by using the Developmental Record Book, an intact booklet which consists of an ordered listing of all basic skills and behaviors. Recommended coding for each skill is (*a*) not assessed, (*b*) assessed and set as an objective, (*c*) introduced but not achieved, and (*d*) skill has been achieved. Examiners are encouraged to modify the coding to meet their individual needs. Instructions for administering the questions are well documented and succinct. One of the strengths of the Inventory is that little specialized training is required of the examiner. A color-coding system has been developed to highlight the record-keeping and tracking process.

It appears that great care has been taken in selecting and arranging the skills to be evaluated. Even though the skills presented in this Inventory represent only a subset of the potential pool of behaviors that could be evaluated within the birth to age 7 range, they do constitute a broad cross section of the behaviors and skills associated with early childhood development. Each basic skill is regarded as a distinct entity, thus there is no cumulative score associated with a skill area or subarea. It is left to the discretion of the examiner to determine when a sufficient number of questions have been answered correctly to justify area or subarea mastery. No reliability or validity coefficients are presented, however, based on the scope of skills assessed by the Inventory, I am comfortable with the content coverage. Assuming that an examiner believes mastery of the skills in this instrument are indicative of positive growth, the Revised BRIGANCE Diagnostic Inventory of Early Development provides a comprehensive method for identifying the strengths and weaknesses of a child's development up to the age of 7.

[327]

Revised Denver Prescreening Developmental Questionnaire.

Purpose: "To facilitate earlier identification of children whose development may be delayed."
Population: Ages 0–9 months, 9–24 months, 2–4 years, 4–6 years.
Publication Dates: 1975–86.
Acronym: R-PDQ.
Scores: Item scores only.
Administration: Individual.
Levels, 4: Ages 0–9 months, 9–24 months, 2–4 years, 4–6 years.
Manual: No manual.
Price Data, 1990: $11 per 100 questionnaires (specify level).
Time: Administration time not reported.
Comments: Ratings by parents.
Author: William K. Frankenburg.
Publisher: Denver Developmental Materials, Inc.

TEST REFERENCES

1. Benson, B. A., Gross, A. M., Messer, S. C., Kellum, G., & Passmore, L. A. (1991). Social support networks among families of children with craniofacial anomalies. *Health Psychology, 10*, 252-258.

Review of the Revised Denver Prescreening Developmental Questionnaire by STEPHEN N. AXFORD, School Psychologist, Academy District Twenty, Colorado Springs, CO and Counseling Department Chair, University of Phoenix-Colorado Campus, Aurora, CO:

The Revised Denver Prescreening Developmental Questionnaire (R-PDQ) is specific in purpose and finite in scope. According to its authors, the R-PDQ is the "first step" in a "two-step screening process" (Frankenburg, Fandal, & Thornton, 1987). Citing the American Academy of Pediatrics' "Guideline for Child Health Maintenance," the authors note the initial phase of a developmental (i.e., pediatric) assessment includes parent report in documenting the child's developmental progress, and identification of candidates in need of more in-depth objective assessment. The "second step" thus involves use of the Denver Developmental Screening Test (DDST; 9:311), as conceptualized by the authors.

The R-PDQ is essentially a taxonomic parent survey of child development, similar to the Gesell Child Developmental Age Scale (161) with regard to content but less comprehensive, as would be expected of a screening instrument designed for determining areas of needed additional assessment. Typically, this type of screening is conducted informally. The R-PDQ affords a simple systematic procedure for gathering developmental screening information. The revision involved extending the age range to include ages birth to 6 years, changing the item-response format (from "yes/no/no opportunity" to "yes/no"), and changing the structure of the test to "make it easier . . . to compare a child's performance with DDST norms" (p. 653; Frankenburg et al., 1987). Regarding the change in answer format, the test developers provide the following rationale:

> The screen's purpose is to determine if a child can or cannot do a task, not to answer *why* a child is unable to do a task (e.g., no opportunity). (p. 655, Frankenburg et al., 1987)

Given the particular purpose of the R-PDQ (i.e., identifying candidates for further assessment), this rationale is legitimate, despite the psychometric advantages of a broader range of response choices.

The R-PDQ does not provide standard scores. Instead, data are reported in terms of "delays" and normalcy. A "delay" is defined as "any item passed by 90% of children at a younger age . . . than the child being screened" (Information Sheet). The authors recommend that if a child has one delay, he/she should be reevaluated with the R-PDQ following a 1-month waiting period, whereupon if the delay continues to manifest, follow-up testing with the DDST should be conducted. If two or more delays are identified, then a DDST screening should be initiated as soon as possible, according to the authors. This procedure, fairly conservative in approach (likely erring on the side of caution), seems satisfactory for the purposes of prediagnostic screening, assuming the standardization sample is reasonably representative of the general population (an area of needed additional research).

Regarding materials, it is apparent that the R-PDQ developers were careful in insuring readability, meaningful sequence, and ease of scoring. The materials are well organized and should be easy to use for parents and specialists alike. In addition, regarding content, the R-PDQ has considerable face validity. It is noteworthy that the authors contacted 12 pediatricians to garner critical feedback before revising the PDQ.

In terms of technical merit, research addressing the R-PDQ's validity and reliability is limited. The authors note their research on the R-PDQ has not focused on validity issues, responding instead to "clinician's concerns" pertaining to administration and interpretation. Regardless, it seems appropriate that follow-up research be conducted to ascertain the validity of the revised form. Nevertheless, in identifying concordance for delayed subjects, a hit rate of 96% was obtained between the R-PDQ and DDST results, involving 193 children, 73 of whom had one or more delays identified by the R-PDQ. This lends credibility to the R-PDQ as an effective prescreening instrument for developmental delays.

Regarding reliability, test-retest data collected on 51 children revealed 94% agreement over a 1-week interval. In a separate study involving 71 children, 83% agreement was obtained between teacher and parent ratings, again supporting the reliability of the R-PDQ.

The R-PDQ standardization sample consisted of 1,434 Denver area children recruited from six private pediatric offices (n = 1,012), eight urban day care centers (n = 227), the University Outpatient Clinic (n = 109), and one Head Start center (n = 86). Of course, in terms of demographic representation and because of selective as opposed to random sampling, it is questionable as to whether interpretive data (i.e., range of scores considered "normal") can be generalized to special populations (i.e., various geographic regions, SES groups, etc.). Regarding SES, however, the authors cite research indicating the standardization results are, indeed, generalizable across SES groups. Nevertheless, ultimately it would be best if normative data representative of national demographics were compiled. Also, if this should occur, it may be useful to develop norms for specific populations (e.g., sex, SES, cultural groups, handicapped populations, etc.).

As a "prescreening" instrument designed to assess developmental progress for the purpose of determining need for additional assessment, the R-PDQ is satisfactory. It is sufficient in scope, quite readable, very easy to score, economical, and provides reasonable guidelines for interpretation and use. In addition, although additional validation and standardization is recommended, the R-PDQ appears appropriate for its intended use.

REVIEWER'S REFERENCE

Frankenburg, W. K., Fandal, A. W., & Thornton, S. M. (1987). Revision of Denver Prescreening Developmental Questionnaire. *The Journal of Pediatrics*, *110*(4), 653-657.

Review of the Revised Denver Prescreening Developmental Questionnaire by WILLIAM B. MICHAEL, Professor of Education and Psychology, University of Southern California, Los Angeles, CA:

Four forms of the Revised Denver Prescreening Developmental Questionnaire (R-PDQ) are intended to provide a simplified monitoring and screening of children's development in four domains referred to as Personal Social (PS), Fine Motor-Adaptive (FMA), Language (L), and Gross Motor (GM). These four forms contain items that cover age spans from zero to 9 months (30 items), 9 to 24 months (33 items), 2 to 4 years (25 items), and 4 to 6 years (24 items). Each item portrays an activity of the child to which the observer (typically a parent, teacher, or health care professional) responds with a "yes" or "no" answer.

There is no manual for the four forms. A two-page set of instructions for administration of the scales and for the interpretation of the scores is available.

Apparently, the only source of information regarding the research and field testing underlying the preparation of the R-PDQ appears in an article by Frankenburg, Fandal, and Thornton (1987). Only minimal data are presented regarding validity and reliability issues. In addition, no work has been done to develop scoring norms for the separate functions represented on the test. Before such work would be appropriate, factor analyses studies would be needed.

All instruments that rely on the responses and observations of others are vulnerable to the unreliability of such reports. This test is not immune from this potential source of error. Minimally, there should be a certain amount of standardized training for persons who serve as observers, examiners, or evaluators.

Although the R-PDQ has considerable face validity and intuitive appeal, the lack of adequate instructions for its administration and interpretation, as well as the absence of reliability, validity, and comprehensive normative data, suggests the R-PDQ be used most cautiously, primarily as an experimental or exploratory scale in research. The authors should carry out the necessary psychometric analyses so that this promising-looking scale can be employed in an appropriate and valid manner.

REVIEWER'S REFERENCE

Frankenburg, W. K., Fandal, A. W., & Thornton, S. M. (1987). Revision of Denver Prescreening Developmental Questionnaire. *The Journal of Pediatrics*, *110*(4), 653-657.

[328]

Revised Edinburgh Functional Communication Profile.

Purpose: Developed to assess "the ability to engage in and sustain interaction" including "the modalities, verbal and nonverbal, used to achieve communication."
Population: Adults with disordered communications.
Publication Date: 1990.
Acronym: EFCP.
Scores: Item scores only.
Administration: Individual.
Price Data: Not available.
Time: Administration time not reported.
Comments: Ratings by professionals.
Authors: Sheila L. Wirz, Christine Skinner, and Elizabeth Dean.
Publisher: Communication Skill Builders.
[The publisher advised in April 1994 that this test is now out of print—Ed.]

Review of the Revised Edinburgh Functional Communication Profile by ESTHER E. DIAMOND, *Educational and Psychological Consultant, Evanston, IL:*

BACKGROUND AND DESCRIPTION. The revised Edinburgh Functional Communication Profile (EFCP), originally developed for use with elderly adults with aphasia, has been field tested and revised on the basis of findings and the feedback from clinicians involved in the field test. Field-test results have shown the EFCP to be effective for use with children and adults with a variety of communicative disorders. It can supplement traditional assessments with information about ability to use linguistic skills in particular contexts. The clinician can note under what circumstances and using what modalities the individual communicates.

The EFCP is based on speech act theory. A *speech act*, the basic unit of communication, consists of the *proposition*, or the words or symbols used in a message, and the *illocutionary force*, or the speaker's intention in communicating. The EFCP is not a standardized instrument; the authors note that standardized tests in this area have been more concerned with *what* the individual says than *how* he or she says or communicates it. Use of linguistic structures, they concluded on the basis of their research and that of others in the field, must be considered in the context of interpersonal setting. Other researchers cited in the manual have found that "standardized linguistic assessment alone may provide an unrealistic base line of communication ability" (manual, p. 1). From its early narrow consideration of linguistic functioning, the focus of speech-language pathology has progressed to a perspective that encompasses the multiple aspects of communicative competence.

The original Edinburgh Profile was designed to overcome some of the limitations of available assessment batteries, none of which directly addressed communicative function. Use of a pragmatic framework and maintenance of a distinction between measurement and observation provided a broad picture of communicative functioning. The current revision includes a wider range of client groups and provides three options for profiling communicative functioning. It is now easier to collect both qualitative and quantitative data, increasing the profile's potential sensitivity to the inferences that can be drawn.

A second profile, the Interaction Analysis, has been added to the original Communicative Performance Analysis. It counters the subjectivity of efforts to judge communicative effectiveness by measuring the effectiveness of the client's contributions in maintaining the interaction. This profile yields a quantitative score that enables the user to take repeated measures of a client's performance noting changes over time. In addition, an optional Supplementary Interview provides the user with structured prompts that facilitate eliciting a variety of communicative functions in prompted versus spontaneous situations. Finally, the Communicative Performance Analysis incorporates a number of minor changes suggested by users.

The revised EFCP assesses both the ability to engage in and sustain interaction, and the verbal and nonverbal modalities the client uses to communicate. Accurate observation of such abilities, the authors point out, is rarely included in standardized linguistic assessment.

ADMINISTRATION. The EFCP can be used by any professional "who has developed analytical observation skills, who has a basic familiarity with the study of interaction, and who understands the principles upon which the profile is based" (p. 4). The profiles can be completed from either direct observation or from a videotape. Rating may be done by a qualified observer or from a videotape; the latter would also provide a permanent record as a baseline or for later analysis. Scoring should be done from a videotape if the rater is involved in the conversation with the client. During live scoring, it is suggested, the examiner should score selected samples of communicative behavior rather than try to score every interaction. Whether to inform clients of the purpose of the videotaping is left to the clinician's professional judgment. The number of participants in a conversation is also left to the clinician's professional judgment, as is the choice of conversational topic. To complete the profiles, observations of free conversation may need to be supplemented by structured probes from the Supplementary Interview.

The Interaction Analysis requires the scoring of 10 conversational exchanges, selected from a larger sample within a single conversation. The examiner determines, on a scale from 0 to 5, how effectively the individual functions during each conversational exchange (e.g., greeting, acknowledging, responding) and, on a six-item scale, how effectively he or she conveys information (e.g., inappropriately, inadequately, in a stereotyped response, adequately, or by adding information to an adequate response). The examiner also checks the modalities the individual uses—spoken language, gestures or sign language, facial expression, vocalization or intonation, and writing or drawing—and their effectiveness. Finally, the examiner notes whether the client attempts to revise inadequate or misunderstood responses. A thorough and meticulous explanation of the scoring and the decision making involved is provided in the manual. Precise and helpful examples are given throughout the manual.

The optional Supplementary Interview contains prompts designed to indicate whether the client is capable of a wider range of communicative functions not observed in spontaneous conversation—greeting, acknowledging, responding to nonverbal requests, responding to closed and to open questions, requesting attention, requesting an object or an action or information, contributing to an existing topic, or initiating a new topic. Again, each function is clearly described and illustrated with helpful examples.

FIELD TEST RESULTS. Field-test trials of a preliminary revision of the EFCP were conducted with 17 speech-language clinicians in the U.S., 12 clinicians in the United Kingdom, and 50 student clinicians participating. The field testers worked from written instructions; their comments resulted in a number of clarifying revisions, such as expansion and clarification of the administration procedures.

To verify that a representative sample of communicative behavior could be obtained from 10 conversational exchanges, at least 16 minutes of conversation were videotaped for each of six patients. The three authors then rated only 10 conversational exchanges for each patient, using the Interaction Analysis. Each author then rated a different set of 10 exchanges. Means for the complete conversational samples and each set of 10 conversational exchanges correlated highly. (Note: No figure was given in the manual.)

SUMMARY. The Edinburgh Functional Communication Profile (EFCP), originally developed for use with elderly adults with aphasia, has been revised on the basis of field-test findings that showed it to be effective with children and adults with a variety of communication disorders. It can supplement traditional assessments with important information about ability to use language skills in particular contexts. Based on speech-act theory, the EFCP is not a standardized instrument, but the Interaction Analysis, a profile added to the revised form, yields a quantitative score that makes it possible to take repeated measures of a client's performance and to make changes over time. An optional Summary Sheet and an optional Supplementary Interview are other convenient additions.

The Revised EFCP promises to be very helpful in dealing with children and adults with communicative disorders. Its emphasis on context and on *how* the individual communicates rather than what he or she says should provide insight into the various aspects of communicative disorders. The combination of measurement and observation provides an effective joining of quantitative and qualitative methodology. The structured prompts in the optional Supplementary Interview and the descriptions of functions and the accompanying examples are clear and should greatly enhance the qualitative aspects of the scoring. The authors have done their homework well and are to be commended on this revision.

Review of the Revised Edinburgh Functional Communication Profile by AIMÉE LANGLOIS, Professor of Child Development, Humboldt State University, Arcata, CA:

The Revised Edinburgh Functional Communication Profile (REFCP) is designed to help professionals structure and analyze observations of their patients' communicative skills during conversation. The authors specify that the REFCP is not a test but "a tool for structuring clinician observations" (p. 4). The procedure departs from traditional assessments of communicative skills. Instead of delineating and scoring what patients do (say, write, sign, etc.) in response to test items designed to elicit specific behaviors, clinicians rate how effectively their patients communicate in situations that occur spontaneously. The goal of the REFCP is to describe how patients with language impairments such as aphasia, cerebral palsy, traumatic head injury, and developmental language disorders communicate in spite of obvious linguistic difficulties.

Based on Searle's speech act theory (1969), the profile focuses on both propositional and illocutionary aspects of communicative behavior and provides two types of analysis: Interaction and Communication Performance. The first rates on a 6-point scale an individual's participation in 10 conversational exchanges according to his or her effectiveness and the modalities he or she used (speech, gestures, facial expressions, vocalizations, writing); the second allows for the delineation of a patient's overall efficacy as a communicator for the functions of greeting, acknowledging, responding, requesting, and initiating. The Communication Performance Analysis specifies communicative efficacy on a continuum from inappropriate to inadequate, stereotyped, adequate, and elaborate for any and all modalities used by a patient.

CRITIQUE. The REFCP presents a useful approach to the evaluation of aphasic and other patients' abilities to communicate in daily situations. As opposed to the Communicative Abilities in Daily Living test (Holland, 1980; T4:600), which uses role playing as a method of eliciting behaviors, the REFCP relies on observations of spontaneous interactions. For this reason the authors strongly recommend completing the profile from a videotape lest the examiner affect the interaction. However, a Supplementary Interview script is suggested for patients who fail to communicate spontaneously or if a more systematic assessment is preferred.

Although the authors present a sound rationale for the design of the profile, several weaknesses must be addressed before the REFCP can be considered a useful and valid addition to a test library. The absence of test-retest reliability data is by far the most glaring omission. Although the authors emphasize the need for repeated measures to document patient change over time, the lack of test-retest reliability information makes this process questionable if not useless. In addition, the only validity data available are those presented to support the selection of 10 conversational exchanges as representative of a patient's overall communicative behavior. However, the choice of greeting, acknowledging, and other communicative functions for analysis is not supported with a rigorous item analysis to document their validity. This is especially important in light of the fact that research upon which the selection of these functions is based was conducted with preverbal and nonverbal children. The assumption that communicatively impaired adults would demonstrate the same functions needs documentation. Furthermore, given on one hand the relationship between culture and pragmatic aspects of communication, and on the other the high number of patients from various cultures on speech-language pathologists' case loads, at least two questions beg to be answered: (*a*) Are the communicative functions identified for analysis manifested universally? (*b*) Are differential scoring criteria needed for either or both the Interaction and the Communicative Performance Analyses? Finally, the lack of concurrent validity with established tests fails to establish fully the value of the REFCP as an assessment tool.

Although the manual authors provide evidence of interrater reliability, it is doubtful that professionals who learn to administer the test strictly from the manual would be reliable. Intertester reliability was obtained after each of 14 raters was given an explanation of the test, saw a trial video, and was allowed to discuss the profile before scoring videotape samples. However, professionals who purchase the test will not have had such training; this is problematic given that the distinction made by the authors between inadequate and inappropriate communication is not clear nor are examples provided to highlight this distinction. In addition, the definition of a conversational exchange is open to interpretation as are scoring criteria and sample scenarios provided to help rate the effectiveness of communication. Finally, the qualifications deemed necessary for users of the REFCP are subjectively stated (analytical observation skills, familiarity with the study of interaction, and understanding of principles underlying the profile); this further supports the need for data on interrater reliability with untrained testers.

SUMMARY. Overall, the REFCP is a procedure based on a sound rationale; the assessment of the effectiveness of an individual's communicative skills in natural contexts meets a definite need. Furthermore, its possible use with various disorders and age groups may provide useful research avenues. However, its clinical usefulness cannot be certain until test-retest reliability, concurrent validity, the validity of some of its items, and the reliability of untrained observers are demonstrated.

REVIEWER'S REFERENCES

Searle, J. R. (1969). *Speech acts: An essay in the philosophy of language.* Cambridge: Cambridge University Press.

Holland, A. L. (1980). Communicative Abilities in Daily Living. Baltimore, MD: University Park Press.

[329]

Revised Evaluating Acquired Skills in Communication.

Purpose: Constructed to assess communication skills in the areas of semantics, syntax, morphology, and pragmatics.

Population: Children 3 months to 8 years with severe language impairments.
Publication Dates: 1984–91.
Acronym: EASIC.
Scores: Ratings in 10 areas: Labels/Nouns and Pronouns, Verbs and Action Commands, Comprehension of Three-Word Phrases, Affirmation and Negation, Prepositional Location Commands, Comprehension of Singular and Plural, Adjectives and Attributes, Money Concepts, Categorization and Association, Interrogatives.
Administration: Individual.
Price Data, 1991: $75 per complete kit including manual ('91, 54 pages).
Time: Administration time not reported.
Author: Anita Marcott Riley.
Publisher: Communication Skill Builders.Cross Reference: For reviews by Barry W. Jones and Robert E. Owens, Jr. of an earlier edition, see 10:109.

Review of the Revised Evaluating Acquired Skills in Communication by WILLIAM O. HAYNES, Professor of Communication Disorders, Auburn University, Auburn, AL:

The Revised Evaluating Acquired Skills in Communication (EASIC) is an updated version of the original instrument published in 1984. The inventory is organized in five levels. The first level (Pre-Language Level) deals with prelanguage skills of response to sensory stimulation, object relations, means-end causality, motor imitation, matching, rejection, negation, affirmation, comprehension/use of communicative gestures, social interaction, and nonverbal communicative functions. The second level (Receptive Level I) includes comprehension of nouns, verbs, two-word phrases, prepositions, classification and categorization, adjectives and attributes, and interrogatives. The third level (Expressive Level I) includes many of the same areas as Receptive Level I. Receptive Level II includes nouns/pronouns, verbs, three-word phrases, affirmation, negation, prepositions, singular/plural adjectives, money concepts, categorization, and interrogatives. The Expressive Level II includes all of the Receptive Level II areas plus social interaction, sequencing, sentence structure, and pragmatic analysis. The EASIC provides Individualized Educational Plan (IEP) goals related to the assessment levels and suggested treatment procedures for accomplishing these objectives. In the assessment portion, each student's responses are evaluated qualitatively using six performance categories: spontaneous, cued (using a sign, verbalization, gesture, phonetic cue or open-ended sentence), imitated, manipulated, no response, and wrong. The scoring system depicts whether skills are accomplished, emerging, or not developed.

Reviews of the 1984 version of the EASIC (MMY10:109) criticized the instrument on several grounds. First, the EASIC did not provide thorough guidelines for the examiner to use in selecting the initial level of assessment. It appears the appropriate level could be chosen only after the clinician had significant familiarity with the student or after a rather thorough assessment of abilities had already been accomplished. The revised version of the EASIC has not provided any additional guidelines for placement of a student on assessment levels and, therefore, the criticism regarding placing students at a particular level remains a valid concern.

A second complaint was the total absence of psychometric data in support of the reliability and validity of the instrument. Attention to psychometric considerations, even in cases of non-norm-referenced tests, is a basic requirement for any test instrument. It is not optional. The issue of interjudge reliability alone is critical.

Another prior concern about the 1984 version of the EASIC was a lack of bibliographic support for the items on the test. The current version contains a list of 33 references; however, they are never specifically referred to in the manual. The only reference to the bibliography is on page 3 where the manual authors state "The age ranges were compiled from numerous sources containing normative and developmental data (see Bibliography)" (p. 3). This in no way justifies the inclusion or particular ordering of items on the instrument.

An additional criticism of the earlier version of the instrument was that little attention was paid to the areas of semantic relations and communicative functions. The revised EASIC does have a small section on communicative intents and does mention semantic relations in the two- and three-word utterance sections of the Receptive/Expressive Levels I and II. One prior review of the test lamented the EASIC had no provision for coding the student's response mode (e.g., verbal, gestural, signed, augmentative) especially because the instrument purports to be ideally used with significantly involved students (e.g., mentally retarded, autistic). These differing response modes are mentioned in the goals sections of each level (e.g., "The student will verbalize, sign, or use an alternative or augmentative communication system to express the size adjectives" [p. 29]) in the current version of the EASIC.

Finally, the picture stimuli are black and white and may be too abstract for some of the students likely to be tested. This has not changed since the earlier version.

The manual does not provide any case examples or illustrations of how scoring is accomplished and interpreted. Such information would be helpful to novice administrators of the test. The EASIC provides only one page of instructions on administering the tasks included in the instrument. There are no verbatim instructions to read to the student and not enough detail on exactly how to go through the tasks on each level.

In its present form, the EASIC fails to provide essential information regarding a rationale for inclusion of and ordering of items, psychometric adequacy, and detailed instructions for administration and scoring. Overall, the author has not responded to prior reviews of the instrument. Many of the same weaknesses remain in the revised version. The present reviewer would not recommend the EASIC for widespread use in assessment of severely involved students until such time as more research is done to support its reliability and validity.

Review of the Revised Evaluating Acquired Skills in Communication by JOHN H. KRANZLER, Assistant Professor of School Psychology, University of Florida, Gainesville, FL:

The Revised Evaluating Acquired Skills in Communication (R-EASIC) is an individually administered communication skills inventory for children between the ages of 3 months to 8 years with severe language impairments. The R-EASIC was originally developed through work with 200 autistic individuals between the ages of 2 and 26 years. No information regarding their sex, race, ethnicity, or developmental level is reported, however. The test author states that the R-EASIC "provides examiners with a systematic tool for assessing a student's communication skills, a simple format for recording the student's performance, and a correlating means for translating that [*sic*] assessment data into an Individual Education Plan" (manual, p. 1).

MATERIALS. Materials provided for the R-EASIC include stimulus booklets that specify the skill assessed, instructions, and stimulus materials needed for each item. Skill profile sheets are included to summarize performance. They can be used to record the results of as many as five administrations of the R-EASIC. Also provided are a stimulus picture book and supplemental picture cards, each of which consists of black-and-white line drawings of isolated objects or actions. The stimuli in the picture book are presented in a multiple-choice format, typically with three pictures per page, and responses can be either by pointing or by uttering single word responses. The supplemental picture cards can be arranged to measure such functions as matching, sorting, and sequencing. A set of index cards with behavioral objectives (correlating to each inventory item) is included for use in instructional planning. In addition to these materials, administration of the R-EASIC requires that the examiner supply at least 50 additional stimulus items. Fortunately, many of these objects are common to most school classrooms.

TEST DESCRIPTION. The Informal Communication Skills Inventories that compose the R-EASIC are divided into five levels: Pre-Language, Receptive Level I, Expressive Level I, Receptive Level II, and Expressive Level II. The Pre-Language Level measures skills that are prerequisite to meaningful speech. According to the author, this level is primarily used to assess children at Piaget's "Sensory Motor Substage V" (p. 2). The Receptive and Expressive Level I inventories assess emerging comprehension and expression skills. The Level II inventories measure more complex semantic, pragmatic, morphologic, and syntactic receptive and expressive language skills. The items presented in the Informal Communication Skills Inventories are arranged according to skill clusters. There are 9 to 12 of these clusters within each level. Each skill cluster is composed of 1 to 10 items that are arranged according to difficulty (from easy to hard). Information is not presented regarding the procedures used in either test development or item selection; nor is the theoretical rationale for placement of the items at Level I and Level II discussed.

Responses on the R-EASIC are evaluated "qualitatively," that is, in terms of six performance categories. These categories are: spontaneous, cued, imitated, manipulated, no response (or noncompliant), and wrong. Based on the number of responses in each category, the skill clusters are judged to be either "accomplished," "emerging," or "not yet developed." Unfortunately, justification for these scoring criteria is not presented. Behavioral goals and objectives can be selected for instruction of the skills that are judged to be emerging. The author states these behavioral goals and objectives "must be functional and integrated into the student's daily routine" (p. 3). Nevertheless, the majority of them appear to require the drill of isolated communication skills.

A "developmental age chart" is provided to show the age range at which each skill is normally acquired. The test author states that these "age ranges were compiled from numerous sources containing normative and developmental data" (p. 3). These sources are listed in a bibliography. The age ranges presented in this chart are rather general estimates of development, however, and should not be used for diagnostic purposes. It is also important to note that the R-EASIC has not been standardized or normed. No other summary scores, such as standard scores or percentile ranks, are available.

TEST CRITIQUE. Guidelines provided in the R-EASIC manual for administration and scoring are minimal. Even the starting and stopping rules are ultimately left to clinical judgment. It also appears the items on the R-EASIC may be administered in any order and over any number of test sessions. In spite of the fact that some additional instructions are presented for assessing autistic children, the scoring of many items may be highly subjective. In addition, the black-and-white line drawings may be too abstract for some children with severe developmental delays or autism or both. Finally, and most importantly, no information at all regarding the reliability and validity of the R-EASIC is reported.

SUMMARY. The R-EASIC is an individually administered communication skills inventory for young children with severe language impairments. No information regarding the procedures used in test construction or item selection is presented; nor is there any information pertaining to the test's reliability and validity. Although a chart showing the age ranges at which each skill is normally acquired is provided, these age ranges are rough estimates of development and should not be used for diagnosis. Finally, the behavioral goals and objectives that accompany the R-EASIC tend to focus on the drilling of isolated communication skills and not on the more functional aspects of communication.

[330]

Revised NEO Personality Inventory.

Purpose:: To measure five major dimensions or domains of normal adult personality.
Population: Ages 17 and older.
Publication Dates: 1978–92.
Administration: Group.
Price Data, 1994: $21 per manual ('92, 101 pages); $10 per 25 summary feedback sheets.
Foreign Language Editions: Spanish version available (Inventario de Personalidad NEO Revisado); information on translations into other languages available from publisher.
Authors: Paul T. Costa, Jr. and Robert R. McCrae.
Publisher: Psychological Assessment Resources, Inc.

a) REVISED NEO PERSONALITY INVENTORY.
Acronym: NEO-PI-R.
Forms, 2: Form S (self-reports), Form R (observer ratings).
Scores, 35: 30 facets in 5 domains: Neuroticism (Anxiety, Angry Hostility, Depression, Self-Consciousness, Impulsiveness, Vulnerability, Total), Extraversion (Warmth, Gregariousness, Assertiveness, Activity, Excitement-Seeking, Positive Emotions, Total), Openness (Fantasy, Aesthetics, Feelings, Actions, Ideas, Values, Total), Agreeableness (Trust, Straight-Forwardness, Altruism, Compliance, Modesty, Tender-Mindedness, Total), Conscientiousness (Competence, Order, Dutifulness, Achievement Striving, Self-Discipline, Deliberation, Total).
Price Data: $92 per complete kit including manual, 10 reusable Form S item booklets, 10 reusable Form R item booklets (5 men and 5 women), 25 hand-scorable answer sheets, 25 Form S and 25 Form R adult profiles forms, and 25 feedback sheets; $18 per 10 reusable Form S item booklets; $19 per 10 reusable Form R item booklets (5 each men and women versions); $15 per 25 hand-scorable answer sheets; $15 per 25 Form S adult profile forms; $15 per 25 Form R adult profile forms; $15 per 25 college student profile forms.
Time: (30–40) minutes.
Comments: Form R has two parallel versions: male and female.

b) NEO FIVE-FACTOR INVENTORY.
Acronym: NEO-FFI.
Scores, 5: Neuroticism, Extraversion, Openness, Agreeableness, Conscientiousness.
Price Data: $71 per NEO-FFI including manual, 25 Form S test booklets, and 25 feedback sheets; $44 per 25 NEO-FFI Form S test booklets.
Time: (10–15) minutes.
Comment: Shortened version of Form S.

Cross References: See T4:2263 (49 references); for reviews by Allen K. Hess and Thomas A. Widiger of an earlier edition see 11:258 (5 references); for a review by Robert Hogan of an earlier edition of *a*, see 10:214 (6 references).

TEST REFERENCES

1. Costa, P. T., Jr., & McCrae, R. R. (1986). Cross-sectional studies of personality in a national sample: I. Development and validation of survey measures. *Psychology and Aging, 1*, 140-143.

2. Costa, P. T., Jr., McCrae, R. R., Zonderman, A. B., Barbano, H. E., Lebowitz, B., & Larson, D. M. (1986). Cross-sectional studies of personality in a national sample: 2. Stability in neuroticism, extraversion, and openness. *Psychology and Aging, 1*, 144-149.

3. McCrae, R. R., & Costa, P. T., Jr. (1991). Adding *Liebe und Arbeit*: The full five-factor model and well-being. *Personality and Social Psychology Bulletin, 17*, 227-232.

4. Wise, T. N., Fagan, D. J., Schmidt, C. W., Ponticas, Y., & Costa, D. T. (1991). Personality and sexual functioning of transvestitic fetishists and other paraphilics. *The Journal of Nervous and Mental Disease, 179*, 694-698.

5. Holden, R. R. (1992). Association between the Holden Psychological Screening Inventory and the NEO five-factor inventory in a nonclinical sample. *Psychological Reports, 71*, 1039-1042.

6. Ramanaiah, N. V., & Detwiler, F. R. J. (1992). Psychological androgyny and the NEO Personality Inventory. *Psychological Reports, 71*, 1216-1218.

7. Shaver, P. R., & Brennan, K. A. (1992). Attachment styles and the "Big Five" personality traits: Their connections with each other and with romantic relationship outcomes. *Personality and Social Psychology Bulletin, 18*, 536-545.

8. Vaillant, G. E., Roston, D., & McHugo, G. J. (1992). An intriguing association between ancestral mortality and male affective disorder. *Archives of General Psychiatry, 49*, 709-715.

9. Brooner, R. K., Herbst, J. H., Schmidt, C. W., Bigelow, G. E., & Costa, P. T. (1993). Antisocial personality disorder among drug abusers: Relations to other personality diagnoses and the five-factor model of personality. *The Journal of Nervous and Mental Disease, 181*, 313-319.

10. Cappeliez, P. (1993). The relationship between Beck's concepts of sociotropy and autonomy and the NEO Personality Inventory. *British Journal of Clinical Psychology, 32*, 78-80.

11. Deniston, W. M., & Ramanaiah, N. V. (1993). California Psychological Inventory and the five-factor model of personality. *Psychological Reports, 73*, 491-496.

12. Ramanaiah, N. V., & Deniston, W. M. (1993). NEO Personality Inventory profiles of assertive and nonassertive persons. *Psychological Reports, 73*, 336-338.

13. Sanderson, B., & Kurdek, L. A. (1993). Race and gender as moderator variables in predicting relationship satisfaction and relationship commitment in a sample of dating heterosexual couples. *Family Relations, 42*, 263-267.

14. Suarez, E. C., Harlan, E., Peoples, M. C., & Williams, R. B. Jr. (1993). Cardiovascular and emotional responses in women: The role of hostility and harrassment. *Health Psychology, 12*, 459-468.

15. Zuckerman, M., & Hodgins, H. S. (1993). Developmental changes in the effects of the physical and vocal attractiveness stereotypes. *Journal of Research in Personality, 27*, 349-364.

16. Ackerman, P. L., & Goff, M. (1994). Typical intellectual engagement and personality: Reply to Rocklin (1994). *Journal of Educational Psychology, 86*, 150-153.

17. Brookings, J. B., & Wilson, J. F. (1994). Personality and family-environment predictors of self-reported eating attitudes and behaviors. *Journal of Personality Assessment, 63*, 313-326.

18. Caruso, J. C., & Spirrison, C. L. (1994). Early memories, normal personality variation, and coping. *Journal of Personality Assessment, 63*, 517-533.

19. Church, T. (1994). Relating the Tellegen and Five Factor models of personality structure. *Journal of Personality and Social Psychology, 67*, 898-909.

20. Coolidge, F. L., Becker, L. A., DiRito, D. C., Durham, R. L., Kinlaw, M. M., & Philbrick, P. B. (1994). On the relationship of the five-factor personality model to personality disorders: Four reservations. *Psychological Reports, 75*, 11-21.

21. Elliot, T. R., Herrick, S. M., MacNair, R. R., & Harkins, S. W. (1994). Personality correlates of self-appraised problem solving ability: Problem orientation and trait affectivity. *Journal of Personality Assessment, 63*, 489-505.

22. Hahn, R., & Comrey, A. L. (1994). Factor analysis of the NEO-PI and the Comrey Personality Scales. *Psychological Reports, 75*, 355-365.

23. Hamid, P. N. (1994). Assertiveness and personality dimensions in Chinese students. *Psychological Reports, 75*, 127-130.

24. Hyer, L., Braswell, L., Albrecht, B., Boyd, S., Boudewyns, P., & Talbert, S. (1994). Relationship of NEO-PI to personality styles and severity of trauma in chronic PTSD victims. *Journal of Clinical Psychology, 50*, 699-707.

25. Koestner, R., Bernieri, F., & Zuckerman, M. (1994). Self-peer agreement as a function of two kinds of trait relevance: Personal and social. *Social Behavior and Personality, 22*, 17-30.

26. Lecci, L., Okun, M. A., & Karoly, P. (1994). Life regrets and current goals as predictors of psychological adjustment. *Journal of Personality and Social Psychology, 66*, 731-741.

27. MacDonald, D. A., Anderson, P. E., Tsagarakis, C. I., & Holland, C. J. (1994). Examination of the relationship between the Myers-Briggs Type Indicator and the NEO Personality Inventory. *Psychological Reports, 74*, 339-334.

28. Mann, L. S., Wise, T. N., Trinidad, A., & Kohanski, R. (1994). Alexithymia, affect recognition, and the five-factor model of personality in normal subjects. *Psychological Reports, 74*, 563-567.

29. Marshall, G. N., Wortman, C. B., Vickers, R. R., Jr., Kusulas, J. W., & Hervig, L. K. (1994). The five-factor model of personality as a framework for personality-health research. *Journal of Personality and Social Psychology, 67*, 278-286.

30. Mount, M. K., Barrick, M. R., & Strauss, J. P. (1994). Validity of observer ratings of the big five personality factors. *Journal of Applied Psychology, 79*, 272-280.

31. Piedmont, R. L., & Weinstein, H. P. (1994). Predicting supervisor ratings of job performance using the NEO Personality Inventory. *The Journal of Psychology, 128*, 255-265.

32. Ramanaiah, N. V., Byravan, A., & Detwiler, F. R. J. (1994). Revised NEO Personality profiles of machiavellian and non-machiavellian people. *Psychological Reports, 75*, 937-938.

33. Ramanaiah, N. V., Detwiler, F. R. J., & Byravan, A. (1994). Revised NEO Personality Inventory profiles of narcissistic and nonnarcissistic people. *Psychological Reports, 75*, 512-514.

34. Rocklin, T. (1994). Relation between typical intellectual engagement and openness: Comment of Goff and Ackerman (1992). *Journal of Educational Psychology, 86*, 145-149.

35. Rosse, J. G., Miller, J. L., & Stecher, M. D. (1994). A field study of job applicants' reactions to personality and cognitive ability testing. *Journal of Applied Psychology, 79*, 987-992.

36. Siegler, I. C., Dawson, D. V., & Welsh, K. A. (1994). Caregiver ratings of personality change in Alzheimer's disease patients: A replication. *Psychology and Aging, 9*, 464-466.

37. Tokar, D. M., & Swanson, J. L. (1994). Evaluation of the correspondence between Holland's vocational personality typology and the five-factor model of personality. *Journal of Vocational Behavior, 46*, 89-108.

38. Trull, T. J., & Sher, K. J. (1994). Relationship between the five-factor model of personality and axis I disorders in a nonclinical sample. *Journal of Abnormal Psychology, 103*, 350-360.

39. Zuroff, D. C. (1994). Depressive personality styles and the five-factor model of personality. *Journal of Personality Assessment, 63*, 453-472.

40. Belsky, J., Crnic, K., & Gable, S. (1995). The determinants of coparenting in families with toddler boys: Spousal differences and daily hassles. *Child Development, 66*, 629-642.

41. Costa, P. T., & McCrae, R. R. (1995). Domains and facets: Hierarchial personality assessment using the Revised NEO Personality Inventory. *Journal of Personality Assessment, 64*, 21-50.

42. Halberstadt, A. G., Cassidy, J., Stifter, C. A., Parke, R. D., & Fox, N. A. (1995). Self-expressiveness within the family context: Psychometric support for a new measure. *Psychological Assessment, 7*, 93-103.

43. Holland, D. C., Dollinger, S. J., Holland, C. J., & MacDonald, D. A. (1995). The relationship between psychometric intelligence and the five-factor model of personality in a rehabilitation sample. *Journal of Clinical Psychology, 51*, 79-88.

44. Lipkus, I. M., & Siegler, I. C. (1995). Do comparative self-appraisals during young adulthood predict adult personality? *Psychology and Aging, 10*, 229-237.

45. Paulhus, D. L., Bruce, M. N., & Trapnell, P. D. (1995). Effects of self-presentation strategies on personality profiles and their structure. *Personality and Social Psychology Bulletin, 21*, 100-108.

46. Rhodewalt, F., & Morf, C. C. (1995). Self and interpersonal correlates of the Narcissistic Personality Inventory: A review and new findings. *Journal of Research in Personality, 29*, 1-23.

47. Santor, D. A., Zuroff, D. C., Ramsay, J. Q., Cervantes, P., & Palacios, J. (1995). Examining scale discriminability in the BDI and CES-D as a function of depressive severity. *Psychological Assessment, 7*, 131-139.

48. Tokar, D. M., & Swanson, J. L. (1995). Evaluation of the correspondence between Holland's vocational personality typology and the five-factor model of personality. *Journal of Vocational Behavior, 46*, 89-108.

49. Trull, T. J. (1995). Borderline personality disorder features in nonclinical young adults: I. Identification and validation. *Psychological Assessment, 7*, 33-41.

50. Zuckerman, M., Miyake, K., & Elkin, C. S. (1995). Effects of attractiveness and maturity of face and voice on interpersonal impressions. *Journal of Research in Personality, 29*, 253-272.

Review of the Revised NEO Personality Inventory by MICHAEL D. BOTWIN, Assistant Professor of Psychology, California State University, Fresno, Fresno, CA:

Over the last 50 years the five-factor model (FFM) of personality has been construed as an adequate taxonomy (Norman, 1963), a Rosetta stone for personality models, or a robust taxonomy of personality (see Digman, 1990; Goldberg, 1993; John, 1991 for theoretical and historic reviews of the five-factor model). The NEO-PI-R is the most recent version of Paul Costa and Robert McCrae's instrument to assess normal adult personality using the FFM (see 10:214 and 11:258 for reviews of the previous version of the test, the NEO-PI). The NEO-PI-R represents one of the few commercially available tests based on this model of personality.

The NEO-PI-R assesses five major domains of personality: Neuroticism (N), Extraversion (E), Openness to Experience (O), Agreeableness (A), and Conscientiousness (C), each represented by six lower level facet scale scores (see scale description above). It is available in three formats: self-report and observer-report versions and the NEO-FFI, a 60-item short form of the instrument.

Domain level reliabilities are excellent ranging from .86 to .95 for both the self and observer rating forms of this instrument. Facet level reliabilities are good ranging from .56 to .90 for both self- and observer-report forms of the NEO-PI-R. Short-term test-retest reliability has been found with the NEO-FFI and the NEO-PI-R. Long-term test-retest reliability has been shown for the N, E, and O domains of the previous version of this instrument.

Norms are based on a sample of 1,000 subjects (500 males, 500 females) selected from three large scale studies of the NEO-PI-R. The normative sample was stratified to match 1995 U.S. Census projections for age, gender, and race. This careful selection of the normative sample is an important improvement over the previous NEO-PI norms that were not as representative of the general population as is the current norm group. Separate norms are also provided for college-aged samples based on findings that adolescent and early adult samples systematically score higher on the dimensions of N, E, and O and lower on the dimensions of A and C.

The validity of the NEO-PI-R scales has been demonstrated in a variety of ways. There is strong consensual validity between self, peer, and spouse reports of the test. Construct, convergent, and divergent validity evidence of the scales has been collected through a series of studies conducted by Costa, McCrae, and their colleagues. NEO-PI-R scales correlated with analogous scales from other instruments. These instruments represent a variety of theoretical perspectives on scale construction including career interests (Self Directed Search), Jungian Types (Meyers-Briggs Type Indicator), needs and motives (Personality Research Form), psychopathology (Minnesota Multiphasic Personality Inventory), and multidimensional personality instruments (revised California Psychological Inventory, Guilford-Zimmerman Temperament Survey, Adjective Check List, and the Interpersonal Adjective Scale, Revised). The authors have also found links between the five factors, psychological well-being (high scores on well-being scales relate to high scores on E, A, C, but low scores on N), and coping style (positive coping styles related to high E and O scores; negative coping styles are related to high N scores). The nomothetic net cast by the NEO-PI-R provides a useful frame of reference for understanding the relationships of the five factors and other assessment instruments.

Several improvements have been made in the NEO-PI-R. The major revision is the addition of six facet scales for the domains of Agreeableness and Conscientiousness. This corrects the major shortcoming of the NEO-PI that used unidimensional 18-item scales to assess both of these domains. Minor changes were made to several items and a small number of items were replaced. These changes have resulted in a cleaner factor structure and improved psychometrics for the test.

A welcome addition to the NEO-PI-R scoring procedures are details for assessing a variety of response biases including random responding, acquiescence, and nay saying. There is also a three-item validity check included to detect honesty and accuracy in the completion of the questionnaire. The authors do not provide a means for controlling social desirability in the light of findings that suggest that controlling for social desirability may hinder, rather than enhance, scale validity (McCrae & Costa, 1983). The authors make the assumption that individuals will respond honestly to the items under most conditions. They urge caution in the interpretation of scores obtained under conditions where motivating factors may lead the test-taker to respond inaccurately to the items.

The NEO-PI-R is most suited for use as a basic research instrument. There are, however, several applied areas of suggested use for the NEO-PI-R. Evidence suggests that the conscientiousness scales may be useful in assessing employee reliability (Barrick & Mount, 1991). It has also been shown that the NEO-PI-R may be useful as part of a larger assessment battery for psychopathology (see Costa & Widiger, 1994), behavioral medicine, and vocational counseling.

Costa and McCrae deserve praise for the thoughtful and careful development of the NEO-PI-R manual. The manual contains information for both the full version (NEO-PI-R) and the short version (NEO-FFI) of the test. The specimen set also contains a bibliography of research using the various iterations of the NEO inventory. This manual not only explicates the features of the NEO-PI-R, but educates the reader on the history, theory, and application of the five-factor model of personality.

There are few shortcomings in the NEO-PI-R. This version of the instrument admirably addresses many criticisms of the previous version. Work still needs to be done to further demonstrate the validity of the new facet scales for the Agreeableness and Conscientiousness domains. The other major shortcoming of the NEO-PI-R is its foundation in the taxonomic nature of the FFM. There is a wealth of evidence demonstrating the robust nature of the FFM. The theoretical underpinnings of why these factors are important have not been addressed. Both issues will be resolved through additional research in these areas.

Costa and McCrae provide personality psychologists with a substantive arsenal of superb scales to assess personality, grounded in their voluminous work in the structure of personality. These scales should be considered a standard set of useful tools for personality assessment and may provide a useful bridge between basic research in personality psychology and applied psychology.

REVIEWER'S REFERENCES

Norman, W. T. (1963). Toward an adequate taxonomy of personality attributes: Replicated factor structure in peer nomination personality ratings. *Journal of Abnormal and Social Psychology, 66*, 574-583.

McCrae, R. R., & Costa, P. T., Jr. (1983). Social desirability scales: More substance than style. *Journal of Consulting and Clinical Psychology, 51*, 882-888.

Digman, J. M. (1990). Personality structure: Emergence of the five factor model. In M. R. Rosenzweig & L. W. Porter (Eds.), *Annual Review of Psychology* (Vol. 41, pp. 417-440). Palo Alto, CA: Annual Reviews.

John, O. P. (1990). The "Big Five" factor taxonomy: Dimensions of personality in the natural language and in questionnaires. In L. A. Pervin (Ed.), *Handbook of personality: Theory and research* (pp. 66-100). New York: Guilford Press.

Barrick, M. R., & Mount, M. K. (1991). The Big Five personality dimensions and job performance: A meta-analysis. *Personnel Psychology, 44*, 1-26.

Goldberg, L. R. (1993). The structure of phenotypic personality traits. *American Psychologist, 48*, 26-34.

Costa, P. T., & Widiger, T. A. (Eds.). (1994). *Personality disorders and the five factor model of personality*. Washington, DC: American Psychological Association.

Review of the Revised NEO Personality Inventory by SAMUEL JUNI, Professor, Department of Applied Psychology, New York University, New York, NY:

The Revised NEO Personality Inventory (NEO-PI-R) is presented in promotional materials as a comprehensive overview of an individual's emotional, interpersonal, experiential, attitudinal, and motivational styles. Personality dynamics, as traditionally defined, are noticeably absent in the descriptions. This test and its rationale have essentially been critiqued comprehensively in previous editions in respective reviews by Drs. Hogan (1989), Hess (1992), and Widiger (1992). It is clear that the qualitative advantage of the Five Factor approach, as compared to other personality taxonomies, is negligible. The enthusiastic response by some to the approach and the instrument is a social phenomenon, fueled by a prolific research team. It is not indicative of superlative theorizing or psychometric workmanship.

The increments in the various editions are substantial in terms of the sheer magnitude of psychometric data that augmented the original blueprint, but not in terms of opening new dimensions in conceptualization. This review describes briefly the changes in the instrument, and dwells on areas not stressed in the earlier reviews. In addition, some conceptual points raised in the earlier reviews (which the test authors have attempted to address in their published works) are discussed. A section is also included on item format because this was not critiqued previously. The manual covers quite thoroughly the published theoretical and measurement issues. I restricted myself to only a few representative citations because the large literature base is unwieldy and repetitive.

THE TEST AND ITS PSYCHOMETRICS. The very name of the test is enigmatic, as it ignores two of the five domains. A footnote on the first page of the manual states: "Although derived from the initials of the first three domains measured . . . . 'NEO' is a proper name, not an abbreviation, and should not be spelled out in publications" (p. 1). This linguistic foundation is not further explained.

A phenomenological and atheoretical stance is apparent throughout. If at all, conceptualization is based on a codification of an implicit personality theory deduced from the clustering of descriptors ordinary people use in describing others. Derived from analyses of natural language trait adjectives, the NEO-PI originally appeared in 1985 measuring the five domains (noted above) as well as facet scales for the first three domains. Some changes in format were introduced in 1989 which did not modify the inventory. The NEO-PI-R added facet scales for the last two domains, and also replaced a small number of the items in the first three. The authors are fairly confident that they have developed the psychometric operationalization of the Five Factor Theory to its ultimate, as evidenced by their prediction on the first page of the manual: "We expect that new developments with the NEO-PI-R will take the form of additional uses rather than changes in the questionnaire, norms, or profile sheets" (p. 1). Given the rather limited conceptual base of the entire structure, I concur with this judgment, based on the finite scope of possible elaboration as well as the extensive work done by researchers with the instrument.

Self-Report (S) and Observer Report (R) ratings are offered as options for obtaining data for the instrument. Other than perfunctory discussions of the relative merits of the two approaches, no systematic method is presented for synthesizing findings from the two sources.

Translations of the instrument are offered to the user in a variety of languages. No data are presented in the manual on translation techniques, nor on whether standards were followed. More troubling is the very rationale of such translation. Cultural relativism cannot be ignored here. The simplistic (a posteriori) basis of the Five Factor Model, as it is derived from colloquial usage of language, makes the model and its tools intrinsically bound to the culture and language that spawned it. Different cultures and different languages should give rise to other models that have little chance of being five in number nor of having any of the factors resemble those derived from the linguistic/social network of middle-class Americans.

The instrument comes with an abridged version (NEO-FFI) that offers only domain scores but no facets. The psychometric properties are developed adequately for this version as well. This version is not published with an observer rating form.

The original data base for the inventory was a longitudinal study on aging conducted in Baltimore in 1980. Subjects were recruited by word of mouth and these subjects helped recruit others (the snowball technique). Representative sampling is obviously jeopardized in such an approach. Compounding this inadequacy, a major drive was then conducted among wives of respondents to increase the female *n*. (It is noted that subjects solicited in this manner are notorious for being unmotivated and haphazard in their responses.) Persisting with the faulty sampling approach, respondents were then asked to nominate friends or neighbors to serve as peer raters—hardly an appropriate method to solicit a source of independent raters for the R Form who are supposed to serve as an alternate information source about the very nominator. As an additional anomaly, it is noted that although College-Age norms are published, the authors argue that such norms are appropriate for individuals aged 17 through 20, regardless whether they attend college or not—a questionable argument.

The test packet includes an NEO Summary intended for presentation to clients. Its validity is based on published accolades of the summary by respondents. Dolliver (1991) aptly reminds the authors of the Barnum Effect. The authors report moderate correlations between expected ratings by respondents versus NEO ratings. These demonstrate that NEO findings correlate to respondents' understanding of their own traits. I fail to see the point of result validation by consumers who are not personality theorists. Indeed, in discussing the validity of the instrument, the authors are concerned with the implications of the self-report mode, arguing that some individuals may not understand their own personality. An error is being made here confusing the understanding of items and the understanding of personality theory by respondents. It does not matter whether a respondent understood the theory behind an instrument. In fact, such understanding might lead to response distortion, not to accuracy. At any rate, the correct way to ascertain the accuracy of reports, insofar as respondents are concerned, is to distribute actual test reports to some and randomly created ones to others, and compare accuracy ratings. As might well be expected, the Barnum Effect reigns supreme in such designs, although some variations in ratings can be expected among individuals (Juni, 1982).

The manual does a fine job outlining validity and reliability work with the scales. A good simplifying feature of the inventory is the fact that items are keyed to one scale only to avoid artifactual correlations between scales. The a priori method in factor analyzing first to identify domains and then, within domains, to identify facets, is indeed a good means to let theory guide the analyses. This orientation is shortlived, however. The authors noted that when they created some measures, they had no idea where these may lead. They cite, for example, Openness to Experience, which is a predictor of divergent thinking ability as well as of moral reasoning. The interpretive report indeed features these types of (theoretically distant) aspects. Such overinclusiveness, in fact, defies the content validity of the domains, where statistics take over and usurp any theory that may have been an ingredient in the initial approach.

The manual presents a wealth of data on convergent correlations with many scales. One wonders whether there were also other attempts at correlating the instrument with measures that did not pan out. Such presentations would save future researchers much work and also give the test consumer some idea of divergence. Based on the solid data published, the authors can well afford to publish such "negative findings" without jeopardizing their product.

TEST SCOPE AND INTERPRETATION. A troubling slant to the presentation of this measure of normal personality traits is to be found in the portrayal of its utility in clinical settings. Beginning with a disclaimer that the instrument was not designed to diagnose psychopathology, we are then confronted by reported documentation linking the Five Factor model and the Axis-II disorders, the suggestion that high Self-Consciousness scores indicate a diagnosis of Social Phobia, and the consistency of low Dutifulness scores with a diagnosis of an Antisocial Personality Disorder. These are examples of well over 100 associations of scale scores with personality disorders presented in the manual.

A crucial issue dots the literature of this instrument: Are scales of normal personality appropriate as clinical tools for the pathological (or aberrant processes in the nonpathological)? The conceptual debate on the relative status of Personality versus Psychopathology theory is alive and well here. To those of us who adhere to Clinical Theory, suggestions such as those proffered by Costa and McCrae (1992b) to use the NEO-PI-R as an alternative to the current classificatory system of personality disorders are inappropriate and indicate nonappreciation (as well as lack of understanding) of pathology (Ben-Porath & Waller, 1992). Indeed, the NEO-PI-R authors are quite comfortable relegating theory to a less paramount position as evidenced by their argument (1992a) that personality description must precede, not follow, personality theory.

The Domain scores differ from clinical scales in that being low or average on a scale can be as informative as being high. This is commendable, because all adjective descriptors are subject to extreme distortions at both polarities. However, rather than staying with the intuitive (content-related) approach, the manual confronts the reader with numerous qualifications and redefinitions of common characteristics. Esoteric assertions and counterintuitive definitions abound. Other than distancing the instrument from mainstream clinical tools, the intent of these assertions is not clear. One gets the impression that the authors began with the mass appeal of common character terminologies, which were then redefined arbitrarily. Examples include:

> Openness may sound healthier or more mature to many psychologists, but the value of openness or closedness depends on the requirements of the situation, and both open and closed individuals perform useful functions in society. (manual, p. 15)

> It is tempting to see the agreeable side of this domain as both socially preferable and psychologically healthier . . . . Just as neither pole of this dimension is intrinsically better from society's point of view, so neither is necessarily better in terms of the individual's mental health. (manual, p. 15)

> Alternative formulations of the five-factor model often label this factor [openness] *Intellect*, and O scores are modestly associated with both education and measured intelligence. (manual, p. 15)

> Conscientiousness is an aspect of what was once called *character* . . . . Low scorers are not necessarily lacking in moral principles . . . . There is some evidence that they are more hedonistic and interested in sex. (manual, p. 16)

The manual features a section that argues for a linkage of scale scores to behavioral medicine and health psychology. The narrative dwells on correlational studies of the scales with Type A behavior patterns, somatic complaints, health habits and attitudes, and coronary-prone behavior. Correlational studies are interpreted as having clear implications for predictive formulations. Differential findings lead the authors to split hairs in counterintuitive and strained arguments, as illustrated in the linkage of heart disease only to antagonistic hostility but not to neurotic hostility. I found no particular rhyme or reason for why some of these behaviors were studies in relation to the instrument. It all appears like a shotgun approach designed to hit any reportable statistically significant findings, where conceptualization and theorization are mere afterthoughts.

Quite a jump from such studies to intervention is evident in the speculations in the manual, based on suggested relationships between low Agreeableness and a profile that has been correlated with coronary-prone behavior. The authors suggest either developing a therapy to increase Agreeableness or targeting low scorers on this scale for behavioral intervention.

The instrument is also recommended as a useful complement to vocational counseling, although the authors note that it should not be used as a substitute for well-validated vocational scales. It is true that some of the scale scores can be shown to contribute to a specific proportion of variance in some behavioral patterns. But, just because a correlation is found with one particular score (or contrast) from among a huge set of possible permutations, getting carried away with assumptions of relevance is not appropriate.

The manual presents alternate scoring algorithms dealing with polarities that contrast domain scores with each other, as well as some that contrast facet scores both within and between domains. Although recognizing the astronomical possibilities of such permutations, the authors nonetheless offer some polarities as interpretive indices based on research findings. It is suggested that given the huge set of polar possibilities across domain facets, such findings may be random artifacts. This is especially salient when some of the rationales presented supporting the relevance of selected polarities are less than convincing.

As we have come to expect from instruments that load on social desirability, quite a defensive stir appears in the NEO-PI-R literature as well. Scale proponents present arguments ranging from claims that such responding is not debilitating for most subjects, to claims that social desirability is indeed intrinsic to the measure of interest so that it would not make sense to exclude it, to presenting evidence that screening for social desirability on the NEO-PI-R would be counterproductive. None of these arguments will impress the skeptic.

The manual gives a string of strained reasons why the test should not be edited by users who are interested only in specific subsets. These are not convincing, and nothing more than the traditional turf protection effort is evident here.

THE TEST ITEMS. There are a variety of problems in the format of the items, which a good course in item writing could have precluded. Clearly, quality control was lacking at this basic—and essential—level.

The manual states that the test items require a sixth grade reading level. I spent some time with my daughter, a bright seventh grader, as she read the test. The assertion about grade level is incorrect. My daughter could not define some words; in addition, she was able to define technically individual words in some phrases, but the meaning of these words in the item contexts were not well understood. Following are a few of the troubling examples:

9. I'm not crafty or sly.

47. When I do things, I do them vigorously.

74. Some people think of me as cold and calculating.

188. Sometimes when I am reading poetry or looking at a work of art, I feel a chill or wave of excitement.

230. I'm something of a "workaholic."

238. I believe that the "new morality" of permissiveness is no morality at all.

Three validity check items are featured on the answer sheet, leaving it to the respondent to share with us whether she or he tried to answer items honestly and accurately, whether all items were responded to, and whether responses were entered in the correct areas. I would hardly refer to the latter two as validity items, and would have little faith in the validity of the first as such. I am also puzzled by the inclusion of the "tried" adverb in the first item (an adverb that is incongruously interjected in test items as well); why not ask simply if items were answered honestly?

There are various anomalies in the construction of specific sentences which range from nuances to inadequacies. Based on the years of development of the instrument, I cannot imagine why time was not taken to run the items by a reading expert to iron out these features. As a rule, the reader is left with the impression of haphazard item construction.

Form R shows many items beginning "He is . . . ." Often (but inconsistently), the contraction "He's" is used. Similar differentials are common in the female version. In the self-report version, parallel variations appears for "I am" versus "I'm." No explanation is given for these different styles. Overall, the authors favor contractions (e.g., don't, they're, there's), which, in my opinion, detract from the professionalism expected in such scales.

Negatively worded items are potential sore points when respondents choose the negative pole of the scale. Not all respondents can handle the paired reversals inherent in disagreeing with, for example, "Item 87. I am not a cheerful person."

Some items feature strict and unyielding statements (e.g., Item 27. I have never literally jumped for joy). Many items are not categorically stated, featuring instead frequency-based qualifiers such as *rarely, seldom, sometimes, pretty much, something of, somewhat, often, too much, usually, completely,* or *tend to*. Although it is feasible that these qualifiers were included to tone down items that were too extreme, it is not clear if this was indeed the case. More importantly, qualifiers potentially confound responses as badly as double negatives do, because the scale values may be attached by a respondent to the qualifier rather than to the primary item root. (Dramatic accentuators, such as *jumping for joy* or *bubbling with happiness* are similar potential detractors from primary item intent.)

Qualifiers often take the form of conditionals. Consider, for example, "Item 39: If necessary, I am willing to manipulate people to get what I want." There are other items which end with the "when I need to be" qualifier. The problems here parallel those of the frequency-based qualifiers.

Some items refer to actual traits or behaviors (e.g., Item 12. I am dominant, forceful, and assertive). A good number, however, focus on the respondent's judgment of others' evaluations (e.g., Item 14. Some people think I'm selfish and egotistical). Other items refer to the respondent's self-reported reputation (how she or he is "known" among others). Other items refer to how the respondent *seems to be* (e.g., Item 167), again implying others' perspectives (in contrast to personal views). These divergent item foci are conceptually disturbing. Furthermore, is it really surprising when the authors report (in their validation study of the S and R forms) a strong correspondence between self and peer ratings, if some of the very S items are intrinsically peer based and not self-report at all?

Some items deal with the respondent's opinions of, and prescriptions for, others. For example, Item 28 focuses on students' abilities to deal with controversy. I was unable to discern the logic for orienting some items in this manner.

There is some confusion in the wording of test items regarding limitations in the age range of respondents. Consider, for example, Item 28 just cited. Is there an implicit assumption here regarding the age of the respondent? Not at all clear to me are the assumptions behind "Item 208. I think that if people don't know what they believe in by the time they're 23, there's something wrong with them." I doubt the authors would find high test-retest reliability for this item as the respondent ages from 22 to 26.

Some items refer to affect regarding a trait rather than the possession of the trait. Consider, for example, "Item 219. I pride myself on my shrewdness in handling people." It is doubtful that the intent of this item is indeed self-evaluative. In fact, the respondent is asked to rate a trait (which is presumed present), and its appropriateness, simultaneously. Such items put an unreasonable binder on the respondent when the trait is not perceived to be present.

There are items which put an actuarial burden squarely on the respondent. Rather than ascertain behavioral frequencies, and then evaluate these normatively, the authors seem to expect respondents to do the entire job. Consider, for example, "Item 181. I have fewer fears than most people," as it contrasts (for example) to "Item 197. My life is fast-paced." Surely the estimation of the respondent's own *relative* behavior frequencies (as compared to those of others), by the respondent, should not be an issue here.

Occasional items feature contrasts of precepts rather than focusing on a specific behavior or attitude of interest (e.g., Item 239. I would rather be known as "merciful" than as "just"). Such item construction is fraught with conceptual and response-set pitfalls (Juni & Koenig, 1982). Conceptually, it is assumed arbitrarily that the respondent shares with the test authors an acceptance of the dimension which forms the basis for the presented comparison or contrast. (In the above-noted example, it is, however, possible that the respondent may interpret *merciful* in contrast to *punitive*, for instance.) Practically, the combination of two item-roots in one item leaves the respondent to react at will to one or the other, rather than to both, in choosing a response.

To a lesser extent, combining two facets into one item becomes problematical even if these are not contrasted. Consider, for example, "Item 26. I often feel helpless and want someone else to solve my problems." How is a respondent who agrees (for example) with the first of these facets, but disagrees with the second, supposed to answer?

I am puzzled by the logic of specific examples that appear occasionally, but not consistently, in scales. Such examples tend to limit generalizability. For instance, the Impulsiveness facet in Neuroticism features many examples relating to overeating. Why?

Some items relate to past behavior rather than to current functioning. Examples include references to *over the years* or to childhood games. Surely an instrument with a phenomenological orientation must exclude such perspectives.

CONCLUSION. The NEO-PI-R is a reliable and well-validated test of personality features, which derive from a theoretical base lacking in conceptualization. Its applicability to clinical phenomena is equivocal. Item format and content criteria are not well developed. Validation studies are well constructed, plentiful, and impressive, yielding an instrument that represents a comprehensive operational translation of the Five Factor Model of personality.

REVIEWER'S REFERENCES

Juni, S. (1982). Use of the defense orientation construct as a predictor of acceptance of feedback. *Psychological Reports, 50*, 1215-1218.

Juni, S., & Koenig, E. J. (1982). Contingency validity as a requirement in forced-choice item construction: A critique of the Jackson Vocational Interest Survey. *Measurement and Evaluation in Guidance, 14*, 202-207.

Hogan, R. (1989). [Review of The NEO Personality Inventory]. In J. C. Conoley & J. J. Kramer (Eds.), *The tenth mental measurements yearbook* (pp. 546-547). Lincoln, NE: Buros Institute of Mental Measurements.

Dolliver, R. H. (1991). "I am from Missouri: You have got to show me": A response to McCrae and Costa. *Journal of Counseling and Development, 69*, 373-374.

Ben-Porath, Y. S., & Waller, N. G. (1992). Five big issues in clinical personality assessment: A rejoinder to Costa and McCrae. *Psychological Assessment, 4*, 23-25.

Costa, P. T., & McCrae, R. R. (1992a). "Four ways five factors are not basic": Reply. *Personality and Individual Differences, 13*, 861-865.

Costa, P. T., & McCrae, R. R. (1992b). The five-factor model of personality and its relevance to personality disorders. *Journal of Personality Disorders, 6*, 343-359.

Hess, A. K. (1992). [Review of The NEO Personality Inventory]. In J. J. Kramer & J. C. Conoley (Eds.), *The eleventh mental measurements yearbook* (pp. 603-605). Lincoln, NE: Buros Institute of Mental Measurements.

Widiger, T. A. (1992). [Review of The NEO Personality Inventory]. In J. J. Kramer & J. C. Conoley (Eds.), *The eleventh mental measurements yearbook* (pp. 605-606). Lincoln, NE: Buros Institute of Mental Measurements.

[331]

Reynell Developmental Language Scales [U.S. Edition].

Purpose: Developed to measure verbal comprehension and expressive language skills.
Population: Ages 1-0 to 6-11.
Publication Dates: 1977–90.
Acronym: RDLS.
Scores, 2: Verbal Comprehension, Expressive Language.
Administration: Individual.
Price Data, 1993: $575 per complete kit including a set of test materials, 25 record forms, and manual ('90, 91 pages); $49.50 per 25 record forms; $60 per manual.
Time: (30) minutes.
Comments: Two Verbal Comprehension scales available to accommodate simple oral responses or pointing responses; British version still available.
Authors: Joan K. Reynell and Christian P. Gruber.
Publisher: Western Psychological Services.
Cross References: See T4:2272 (2 references); for reviews by Doris V. Allen and Diane Nelson Bryen of the British version, see 9:1049 (5 references); see also T3:2018 (16 references); for reviews by Katharine G. Butler and Joel Stark of the British version, see 8:974 (3 references); see also T2:2025 (3 references).

TEST REFERENCES

1. Kasari, C., Sigman, M., & Yirmiya, N. (1993). Focused and social attention of autistic children in interactions with familiar and unfamiliar adults: A comparison of autistic, mentally retarded, and normal children. *Development and Psychopathology, 5*, 403-414.

2. Bryson, S. E., Landry, R., & Smith, I. M. (1994). Brief report: A case study of literacy and socioemotional development in a mute autistic female. *Journal of Autism and Developmental Disorders, 24*, 225-231.

3. Campbell, S. B. (1995). Behavior Problems in preschool children: A review of recent research. *Journal of Child Psychology and Psychiatry and Allied Disciplines, 36*, 113-149.

Review of the Reynell Developmental Language Scales [U.S. Edition] by DAWN P. FLANAGAN, Assistant Professor of Psychology, St. John's University, Jamaica, NY:

ADMINISTRATION. The stimulus materials of the Reynell Developmental Language Scales (RDLS) are engaging for young children. Objects (e.g., ball, spoon, car) are arranged in a series of scenes or vignettes and test items correspond to the presentation of these vignettes. For this reason, test items do not progress in order of increasing difficulty and the RDLS does not have "basal" or "ceiling" rules. It appears that only those practitioners most experienced in language development and assessment would make appropriate decisions regarding when to discontinue testing. In order to avoid underestimating a child's ability by discontinuing testing too soon, the test authors recommend that examiners administer all sections of the RDLS to every child. This practice, however, is time consuming and inefficient.

SCORING AND INTERPRETATION. Comprehensive scoring and interpretation guidelines and case examples are presented for each of the scales. Additional guidelines are available for children who are deaf and hearing impaired. Raw scores can be converted to standard scores and percentile ranks. Confidence intervals are provided for each 6-month age group based on the average standard error of estimation for each scale and are centered around a child's estimated true score. However, confidence intervals are reported only at 68% and only at five levels of test performance (i.e., standard scores of 70, 85, 100, 115, 130). The rationale for choosing 68% rather than the more traditional 95% is unclear. The test authors recommend that examiners double the upper and lower bounds of the intervals reported at 68% when 95% confidence intervals are desired. Also, when a child's standard score falls midway between two of the five levels of performance reported, examiners must average the upper and lower bounds of the two reported scores to obtain a "new" confidence interval. This procedure is imprecise and may result in calculation errors. Confidence intervals are relatively simple to calculate and therefore, more complete and precise tables should have been constructed by the test authors.

Differences required for significance ($p<.05$) between the Verbal Comprehension and Expressive Language scales are provided for each 6-month age group. However, information regarding the percentage of the population that obtained Verbal Comprehension-Expressive Language discrepancies of a given magnitude is not available. Therefore, it cannot be determined whether a significant discrepancy is also *meaningful* or has clinical utility (i.e., occurred in a small percentage of the population).

In addition to a standard score interpretation, a developmental interpretation of a child's performance on the RDLS can be made. A developmental interpretation requires the use of the RDLS Ability/Difficulty Scale (ADS) which was constructed following Rasch modeling procedures. The Interpretation Form on the Test Booklet provides an ADS score for a child's "chronological level" and an ADS score for his or her "developmental level" (based on total number of correct responses). The difference between these two ADS scores provides a basis for interpreting delays or advances in a child's language development. One limitation to this approach is that it does not take into account the *mental age* of the child and, therefore, may lead to inappropriate classifications. That is, children who have language delays that are associated with cognitive deficits may be classified inappropriately as having a specific language disorder (Howlin & Kendall, 1991).

STANDARDIZATION. The RDLS was standardized on a sample of 619 children aged 1-0 through 6-11. The types of children included in the standardization sample were selected on a *nonrandom* basis to ensure that they approximated the 1987 U.S. Census data on the following demographic variables: geographic region, ethnicity, parental educational level, and sex. Sampling error was minimal with the exception of parental education, in which there was an overrepresentation (12.2%) of parents with 4-year degrees, and geographic region, in which there was an overrepresentation (8.9%) of subjects from the North-Central and an underrepresentation (5.5%) of subjects from the South. The number of subjects per each one-year age group ranged from 95 to 101 with the exception of 7-year-olds, of which only 27 were included. It is not clear why 7-year-olds were included in the standardization sample because normative data are not available for this age group. Overall, the normative characteristics of the RDLS are marginally acceptable because the size of the standardization sample is somewhat small and its representativeness is questionable because selection of subjects was not done randomly (Hammill, Brown, & Bryant, 1989).

RELIABILITY. Internal consistency reliability coefficients were reported for each RDLS scale for 12 six-month age groups encompassing the standardization sample. The Verbal Comprehension and Expressive Language scales for children aged 1-0–3-5 and 1-0–1-11, respectively, have reliability coefficients that cluster around .90 with some .80s. Therefore, examiners can be confident when making individual judgements regarding the test performance of very young children on the RDLS. The RDLS has reliability coefficients in the .80s for children aged 3-6 to 4-11 and may be used with these children for screening purposes. Reliability coefficients for children aged 5-0 through 6-11 generally fell below .80, indicating that the RDLS is unreliable at these ages and should not be used to make diagnostic or screening decisions for children at the upper age levels of this instrument. Test-retest reliability data were not reported, precluding an evaluation of the stability of the RDLS.

VALIDITY. Limited evidence is available for the construct validity of the RDLS. Internal consistency reliability coefficients were used to support the unitary nature of language development underlying the RDLS. Age trend data revealed gradual increases in performance with age and were used to support the developmental growth characteristic of the RDLS. Factor analytic studies should have been conducted to substantiate the existence of a Verbal Comprehension-Expressive Language dichotomy and to gain a more complete understanding of the factorial structure of the instrument.

The criterion-related validity evidence (concurrent and predictive) reported in the manual was weak. This evidence comes from a study that was conducted with New Zealand children over a decade ago, using the British revised edition of the RDLS. Although this edition of the RDLS had moderate correlations with seven tests, including tests of intelligence and psycholinguistic ability, the information has limited applicability for American children and demonstrates only preliminary support for the validity of the U.S. edition of the RDLS. Moreover, all the criterion measures used in this validation study have outdated norms (i.e., were published in the 1960s).

CONCLUSIONS. The RDLS is most useful for the assessment of very young children. It includes colorful and attractive test materials and is reliable at the youngest age levels. Caution is warranted in interpreting the test performance of any child on the RDLS, however, because of its technical inadequacies. Until additional studies are conducted to support or substantiate the reliability, validity, and clinical utility of this instrument, it cannot be used confidently to make diagnostic decisions and should be used to gather descriptive data only. It is recommended that only experienced speech pathologists use this instrument because their diagnostic-therapeutic knowledge will likely mitigate the possibility of misinterpretation as a result of insufficient psychometric data. Less experienced practitioners should use an instrument with better psychometric properties for assessing language development such as the Test of Language Development-2 Primary (Newcomer & Hammill, 1988; T4:2768).

REVIEWER'S REFERENCES

Newcomer, P. L., & Hammill, D. D. (1988). Test of Language Development-2 Primary. Austin, TX: PRO-ED, Inc.

Hammill, D. D., Brown, L., & Bryant, B. R. (1989). *A consumer's guide to tests in print*. Austin, TX: PRO-ED, Inc.

Howlin, P., & Kendall, L. (1991). Assessing children with language tests: Which tests to use? *British Journal of Disorders of Communication, 26*, 355-367.

Review of the Reynell Developmental Language Scales [U.S. Edition] by REBECCA J. McCAULEY, Associate Professor of Communication Sciences, University of Vermont, Burlington, VT:

TEST STRUCTURE. The U.S. Edition of the Reynell Developmental Language Scales (RDLS) consists of a 67-item Verbal Comprehension Scale and a 67-

item Expressive Language Scale. Based on a British version, it has undergone modest changes in vocabulary to make it appropriate for use with American children. The Verbal Comprehension Scale has two versions: one in which only pointing responses are required and a second in which simple oral responses are required. The instrument is designed for children covering a very wide range of ages—from 1 year to 6 years, 11 months. Test stimuli appear well suited to the intended population and consist of functional and toy-like objects, as well as a small number of picture stimuli.

TEST ADMINISTRATION AND INTERPRETATION. Instructions regarding test administration are generally clear. Also, they are consistent both with procedures required to achieve standardization conditions as well as with efforts to help younger children participate to the fullest extent possible. In particular, as a means of facilitating participation by younger, shy, or more involved children, a balance is struck between precision and a playful interactive style on the part of the tester and between the tester's direct collection of behavioral data and the use of carefully guided parental elicitation. Only one clear exception to the manual's overall clarity was found: the presence of conflicting instructions regarding selection of the appropriate version of the Verbal Comprehension Scale (i.e., in the manual's Introduction versus in the section dealing with that scale).

Test performance is to be interpreted using developmental and/or norm-referenced approaches. In the discussion of norm-referenced interpretations using standard scores, the authors emphasize the need to consider confidence intervals when scores on individual scales are evaluated or compared. Concerns often cited for developmental interpretations that make use of other types of developmental scores, such as age-equivalent scores, are somewhat reduced because the inclusion of standard errors of measurement based on a Rasch model allows developmental interpretations that address testing error. Conservative recommendations for the qualitative interpretation of performance on individual items are also included.

In a separate chapter, extensive recommendations are given for the interpretation of developmental scores obtained by hearing-impaired children when tested in various modes (e.g., lip-reading versus written language) and their performances compared to the norms for children with normal hearing. Although the authors argue persuasively for the value of this normative comparison, the absence of a normative sample with hearing impairment is a weakness. The authors plan to address this problem through additional norming studies.

NORMS. For the U.S. Edition, 619 children ages 1 year 0 months to 6 years 11 months were tested at nine sites. Sample sizes for each one-year age group were adequate (i.e., sample sizes approaching or exceeding 100), with the exception of the small sample (n = 27) included for the oldest age group (7 years). Within each age group, group composition by ethnicity, years of parental education, geographic region, and gender closely approximated those of the 1987 U.S. Census Bureau Report.

RELIABILITY. Data on reliability of the RDLS consist only of corrected split-half reliability coefficients for each scale and associated standard errors of measurement. The coefficients fall within acceptable levels for the younger groups of children, but then fall below the .80 level for most ages beyond 5 years. No information is reported regarding test-retest reliability or interexaminer reliability. The latter omission seems particularly unfortunate given the level of skill required of testers.

VALIDITY. A variety of evidence, much of it based on the British version of the RDLS, is presented to support the validity of the test for its use in the description of language skills in young children. Although evidence for the U.S. Edition would have provided the strongest possible evidence, the use of evidence obtained on the almost identical British Edition represents an acceptable alternative.

Evidence of content validity is supplied in the authors' descriptions of the process followed for the test's initial construction and the standardization of the British Edition through the later preparation of the United States Edition. Although much of this process falls in line with expectations of how a well-developed measure should evolve, the absence of a theoretical basis to the test is also evident and undermines all of the obtained validity data.

Criterion-related evidence of validity is supplied from a study (Silva, Bradshaw, & Spears, 1978) of 225 children assessed at age 4 and again at age 5 using the British Edition of the RDLS as well as several other cognitive and language measures. The two scales of the RDLS were shown to yield moderate, statistically significant correlations with other verbal measures and, as would be expected, lower correlations with nonverbal measures. In a follow-up to that study, the test's predictive criterion-related validity was demonstrated in comparisons of RDLS scores for 185 children from the original testing to their scores obtained 3 years later, at age 7, on the Wechsler Intelligence Scale for Children (Wechsler, 1949). Statistically significant, high correlations between verbal subtests and the two RDLS scales were obtained. The authors also cite an unpublished study conducted in Great Britain which produced similarly supportive results.

Evidence of construct validity in addition to that provided by evidence of criterion-related and content validity is reported in the form of studies showing that the RDLS differentiated children receiving speech therapy from a control group (Howell, Skinner, Gray, & Bloomfield, 1981) and that the RDLS scores correlated positively with experimental language measures among groups with and without language disorders (Udwin & Yule, 1982) as well as among children with autism (Cantwell, Howlin, & Rutter, 1977). In addition, the test developers report data suggesting that the test scores increase with chronological age, as is expected for a developmental measure.

SUMMARY AND CONCLUSIONS. Strengths of this U.S. Edition of a well-respected British test include its large and representative standardization samples and the strength of validity information provided for the almost identical British test. Weaknesses include the lack of test-retest and interexaminer reliability data as well as the absence of a theoretical basis behind the test's design. Nonetheless, this test appears to be a promising one for use with most U.S. children, particularly for those applications in which children from a broad range of ages are to be tested.

REVIEWER'S REFERENCES

Wechsler, D. (1949). Weschler Intelligence Scale for Children. New York: The Psychological Corporation.

Cantwell, D., Howlin, P., & Rutter, M. (1977). The analysis of language level and language function: A methodological study. *The British Journal of Disorders of Communication*, *12*, 119-135.

Silva, P. A., Bradshaw, J., & Spears, G. F. (1978). *A study of the concurrent and prediction validity of the Reynell Developmental Language Scales*. London: NFER-Nelson.

Howell, J., Skinner, C., Gray, M., & Bloomfield, S. (1981). A study of the comparative effectiveness of different language tests with two groups of children.

Udwin, O., & Yule, W. (1982). A comparison of performance on the Reynell Developmental Language Scales with the results of syntactical analysis of speech samples. *Child: Care, Health, and Development*, *8*, 337-343.

[332]

Riley Inventory of Basic Learning Skills.

Purpose: Evaluates a student's strengths and weaknesses in 13 process skills that are related to learning.
Population: Grades K–8.
Publication Date: 1992.
Acronym: RIBLS.
Scores, 18: Visual Processing (Sequencing, Memory, Abstraction, Total), Auditory Processing (Sequencing, Memory, Abstraction, Total), Verbal Processing (Vocabulary, Total), Kinesthetic Processing (Memory, Learning, Total), Abstract Processing (Integrative, Non Verbal Concept, Concentration, Total), Total.
Administration: Group.
Levels, 2: Primary, Upper.
Price Data, 1992: $17 per specimen set including manual (71 pages) and sample forms; $15 per Learning Process Skills manual (128 pages).
Time: 75 minutes.
Author: Stanley Riley.
Publisher: Academic Therapy Publications.

a) RILEY INVENTORY OF BASIC LEARNING SKILLS-PRIMARY LEVEL.
Population: Ages 6-0 to 7-11.
Price Data: $50 per RIBLS test kit-primary including manual, 10 test booklets, and 6 scoring templates.

b) RILEY INVENTORY OF BASIC LEARNING SKILLS-UPPER LEVEL.
Population: Ages 8-0 to 14+.
Price Data: $50 per RIBLS test kit-upper including manual, 10 test booklets, and 6 scoring templates.

Review of the Riley Inventory of Basic Learning Skills by ALICE J. CORKILL, Assistant Professor of Counseling and Educational Psychology, University of Nevada, Las Vegas, NV:

The Riley Inventory of Basic Learning Skills (RIBLS) was designed as a group test that would assess 12 learning process skills in five modalities. The 12 learning processes are: Visual Sequencing, Visual Memory, Visual Abstraction, Auditory Sequencing, Auditory Memory, Auditory Abstraction, Vocabulary, Kinesthetic Memory, Kinesthetic Learning, Integration, Nonverbal Concept Formation, and Concentration. The modalities are identified as: seeing selectively, hearing accurately, reading and understanding words, coordinating visual-motor activities, and thinking logically. Two levels of the test are included; the primary level is for ages 6 through 7 and the upper level is for ages 8 and above. The tests for each level are sometimes the same, sometimes similar (with the upper level test having additional items), and sometimes completely different.

The visual tests (modality: seeing selectively)—Visual Sequencing, Visual Memory, Visual Abstraction—purportedly assess perceiving logical visual sequences, retrieving visual patterns, and synthesizing visual patterns respectively. For both the primary and upper level tests several problems are apparent particularly with the tests of Visual Memory and Visual Abstraction. The test for Visual Sequencing requires the examinee to determine which shape logically extends a sequence. For example, the sequence "circle, plus, circle, plus, circle, plus" would be logically extended with a circle. The subtests for the primary and upper level differ in that the upper level subtest contains 17 additional problems.

For the test of Visual Memory, examinees are instructed to study a page of figures (for the primary test the figures are in the form of shapes and include things like: a circle, a triangle, a star, a circle and a square, a star and a circle, and a triangle; for the upper level test: a circle, a triangle, the letter "A," the letters "PN," the letters "SLJEC," the letters "VCMKZTL") and to then turn to a page further back in the test booklet and to find as many of the figures as they can from those previously studied. The examinee is given 5 minutes for this test. Because examinees are instructed to turn to the test page when they are ready, it is possible that an examinee might spend the entire 5 minutes studying the figures. These instructions should be altered so that all examinees, at some point, turn to the test page. Failing that, the examiner should be given instructions to either cue examinees to move on or to not, if that is something that provides information about the examinee's visual memory.

Beyond this seemingly insignificant difficulty, the tests for the primary and upper levels are qualitatively different and, as a result, cannot possibly be measuring the same construct. The primary level test requires memorization of shapes only. The upper level test requires the memorization of four solitary shapes (a circle, a square, a six-point star, and a triangle) and then moves on to memorization of one, two, even as many as seven letters. These two tests may be measuring very different memory skills or systems. If the subtest is to be considered as testing the same type of visual memory, then the tests for the primary and upper levels should more closely mirror one another. There is no reason to exclude letters and letter strings from the primary level test (as by age 6 or 7 most students recognize letters). Either the primary level test needs letters and letter strings or the upper level test should consist of only shapes and strings of shapes.

The test of visual abstraction requires that examinees find the missing portion of a picture. The pictures included on this subtest should have been more carefully selected. For example, Picture 6 is of a television with an antenna and a place on the left of the screen where there might have been a control panel. Most televisions today do not have control panels but are instead operated with a remote control unit. Are 6-year-old children expected to have such antiquated knowledge? Items 14 and 17 require specialized knowledge about smoke stacks on ships and engines on jet airplanes. Is it not possible that I, as a 6-year-old, have not seen large ships and airplanes? Further, Items 7 and 21 show reasonable representations of a wagon and a table with chairs respectively. What is missing is a portion of the wagon and chair that might not be visible in a regular photograph so why should we think they are missing in the drawings? In short, several of the items focus on minute details or specialized information that might inordinately penalize some examinees.

The auditory tests (modality: hearing accurately)—Auditory Sequencing, Auditory Memory, Auditory Abstraction—allegedly assess retrieving auditory information in a sequence, recalling auditory information, and understanding auditory information respectively. As with the visual subtests, for both the primary and upper level several problems are apparent particularly with the tests of auditory memory and auditory abstraction. The auditory sequencing subtest requires that examinees listen to and write strings of digits in the order in which they were read and in reverse order. This subtest is identical for both the primary and upper level.

The test of Auditory Memory requires that examinees remember a sequence of items and mark those items on their answer sheet. The primary level examinees are required to recall a string of digits whereas the upper level examinees are required to recall a string of words. For example, the first item for the primary examinees is to recall the numbers, 2, 5, and 8 (a series of numbers that follows a pattern or rule) and to mark those numbers on the answer sheet. The upper level examinees are required to recall the words "cat" and "ice" and to mark those words on the answer sheet. As with Visual Memory, the Auditory Memory subtest may be measuring different abilities. As a result, the two tests (primary and upper level) are not equivalent in terms of what, exactly they are measuring.

The test of Auditory Abstraction is also problematic. The test requires that the examinee listen to a string of words and he or she is to find the "answer" that best fits the meaning of the words. The primary examinees are given sometimes-difficult-to-decipher pictures but the upper level examinees are given words. Once again there is a discrepancy in how this "auditory abstraction" (whatever it may be) is being measured. The memory systems that serve for pictures and words are hypothesized to be substantially different (see, e.g., Paivio, 1986). Beyond the differences in what is being tested or measured, some of the pictures provided for the primary level examinees are obscure. For example, I understand why a police officer writing a ticket is different from one who is simply standing, but in their position as police officers do they not, perhaps, represent the same thing? Further, why should we assume that children have a representation of Easter (Item 10)? For Item 14 could not a school teacher picture fit the string of words, "chairs, envelopes, forms, computer, papers, card file" as well as the almost unidentifiable representation next to it?

The Vocabulary test (modality: reading and understanding words) ostensibly measures knowledge of words. Once again the primary and upper levels differ in the type of information provided to the examinee. Primary examinees are provided pictures (which would not result in a test of *reading* words) but upper level examinees are provided words. As with the Auditory Abstraction subtest, some of the pictures provided for the primary examinees are difficult to interpret. This is, however, not the most important consideration. The examinees should be given the same type of representation at both levels otherwise the examinations are not equivalent in terms of what they are allegedly measuring.

The two kinesthetic subtests—Kinesthetic Memory and Kinesthetic Learning—supposedly measure the modality of coordinating visual-motor activities. The Kinesthetic Memory subtests purports to measure visual-motor retention and does this by having examinees copy line drawings and then reproduce the line drawings without looking at the original figures. The

Kinesthetic Learning subtest purports to measure learning patterns of movement. This subtest requires that examinees at the primary level make faces out of geometrical figures (a square, a circle, a triangle, a diamond, and a hexagon) by learning what should go in each shape (which is given on the test paper) and then putting the eyes and mouth of the face in each shape. The circle, for example, gets two eyes and an upward-curved mouth. The diamond gets two eyes and a flat, horizontal line for a mouth. The upper level examinees, once again, are required to complete an entirely different activity. These examinees are to replace letters with a different lined representation. An "A," for example, is replaces by a "+"; a "B" by a "V"; and an "T" by a triangle. As with other subtests, these different tasks may be measuring different abilities and/or different memory systems. In addition, scoring numbers under the blanks on the answer sheet (or at the end of the rows of geometrical figures that become faces, in the primary test) indicate that the author of the test assumes that the examinee will fill in the blanks or faces in the order in which they appear. When I took this part of the test, I put plus signs under all the "A"s, then I did the replacement for the letter B, then I did the replacement for the letter C, and so on. When examinees approach the task as I did, scoring will be more difficult and the numbers provided to assist will be meaningless.

The modality "thinking logically" is examined by the final three subtests: Integration, Nonverbal Concept Formation, and Concentration. The test of Integration, which allegedly tests using combinations of processes, requires that examinees create words out of a provided list of letters. Identical credit is given for all words created. That is, longer, perhaps more sophisticated, words do not result in greater credit although they may be more difficult to invent. For this test, however, both primary and upper level examinees are given an identical test.

The test of Nonverbal Concept Formation measures concepts below the verbal level, although what this means is unclear. This is a test where subjects are asked to look at what appear to be puzzle pieces and imagine what they would be if they were put together. Primary and upper level subtests are identical in this instance also.

The final test is called Concentration. It allegedly measures an examinee's ability to pay attention to selected stimuli. This is basically a mental mathematics test where examinees are asked questions and are expected to calculate the answers mentally. The primary test and upper level test differ only in terms of the final items on the exam. The upper level test has three additional items.

The theoretical basis for the subtests has not been established by the author. That is, although the manual reports a number of studies suggesting that students who fail to master basic learning processes will be at a disadvantage during later learning, no where is there reported a theoretical foundation for any of the subtests. As a result, what this test actually measures has not been satisfactorily established.

Beyond the difficulties identified in the subtests themselves, problems with standardization were also noticed. The test was standardized on 2,115 students from schools in Northern, Central, and Southern California. The norm tables are reported in 6-month age increments beginning with 6 years, 0 months and ending with 13 years, 11 months. Although the test manual reports that "each age group included approximately fifty students on each test" (p. 41) a careful examination of the norm tables reveals that sample sizes in the age groups range from a low of 3 (8 years, 0 months to 8 years, 5 months for the subtest Auditory Memory) to a high of 108 (9 years, 6 months to 9 years, 11 months for the subtest Auditory Sequencing). This in itself might not be distressing except that further study of the norm tables reveals that 64.1% of the 192 age groupings reported have fewer than 50 examinees and 27.6% of these groups (of the 192 total) have less than 25 examinees. This casts serious doubts as to the generalizability of test results when current examinee scores are being compared to tables of norms where sample sizes may have been as small as 3, 5, or 8 examinees.

The test manual contains no information about reliability or validity.

The Riley Inventory of Basic Learning Skills has little to recommend it. The subtests themselves have apparently been designed without theoretical support. The two levels of the test—primary and upper—have, what are reported as, subtests that measure an ability or memory system using vastly different stimuli. The sample sizes in the standardization sample are frequently too low to offer stable means and standard deviations, thus the standard scores must be considered unstable. If all that has been cited is not enough, the lack of reliability and validity data render the test unusable.

REVIEWER'S REFERENCE

Paivio, A. (1986). *Mental representations: A dual coding approach.* New York: Oxford University Press.

Review of the Riley Inventory of Basic Learning Skills by TERRY M. WILDMAN, Professor of Curriculum and Instruction, Virginia Polytechnic Institute, Blacksburg, VA:

The Riley Inventory of Basic Learning Skills (RIBLS) is designed to assess 12 "learning process skills," which the author suggests are necessary for school achievement. The RIBLS can be group administered to individuals aged 6 years to adult. The 12 subtests are grouped in five categories: seeing selectively, hearing accurately, reading and understanding words, coordinating visual-motor activities, and thinking logically. For example, in the seeing selectively category, examinees are presented with three separate tasks (Visual Sequencing, Visual Memory, and Visual Abstraction) each requiring 5 minutes for administration. The Visual Sequencing task requires responding to a series of 15 simple forms (e.g., O+O+O+) and deciding which form (e.g., O) goes next in sequence. Visual Memory requires recognizing as many simple forms or form combinations (e.g., +O) as possible from a display of about 30 such items. The Visual Abstraction task involves examining simple pictures (e.g., watch, elephant, pistol) and placing an "X" over the location where a key part is missing. The remainder of the inventory can be characterized as focusing heavily on memory (for both auditorially and visually presented material) and vocabulary.

Clear directions are provided for the administration of each subtest. Any professional with classroom or other clinical testing experience should find the manual and test booklets to be user friendly. Very young children will likely need close supervision to follow the necessary procedures across the 12 tasks; otherwise group administration should present no special problems. In terms of time the manual recommends that one hour and 15 minutes be allocated for administration of the entire inventory, which is consistent with my own estimate. No provisions are suggested for dividing the inventory into two or more testing sessions for young children, but this should present no problem.

Test booklets are provided for primary levels (ages 6–7) and older individuals (age 8 and above). The booklets are 20 pages each, organized around the 12 separate tasks or subtests. Each subtest is scored on the basis of one point credit for each correct answer. Plastic scoring templates are available for several of the tests. Raw scores (number of correct answers) are recorded directly on each page and then transferred to the front page of the test booklet in preparation for conversion to scaled scores and subsequent plotting on a learning skills profile.

The RIBLS was standardized using a stratified sample of 2,115 students from 15 California schools. It is clear that considerable attention was given to the selection of a sample that would be representative of the general California population with respect to age, sex, race, socioeconomic status, and geographical region. Means and standard deviations are provided for each subtest across 16 age groups (6-month intervals are used). Approximately 800 students are represented in the sample with the number in each age-test category ranging from 3 to 108.

Unfortunately, there is no mention in the RIBLS manual of validity or reliability studies. What does the inventory actually measure? The items themselves will likely appear familiar in terms of their similarity to other school readiness or general intelligence tests, but the author has made no attempt in the technical manual to establish relationships between the RIBLS and other well-known inventories or tests. The only mention of a conceptual or theoretical basis for this inventory occurs within a brief (4-page) introduction in which vague references are made to the importance of acquiring basic learning processes during a "critical" early developmental period. The author defends his selection of "learning process skills" contained in this inventory as being "those which are evident and currently measurable" (p. 9).

Lack of data concerning the validity of this instrument is troubling at several levels. Within the various item categories (e.g., visual processing or thinking logically) the potential user will want evidence that the inventory assesses the skill or ability presumed in that category. No evidence is provided. Looking at the test as a whole, readers will wonder if the inventory really assesses five discrete skills or perhaps a single dimension of readiness or intelligence. Instead of citing factor analytic studies the author mentions simply that "The learning process skills presented here are interdependent and interacting" (p. 9). Finally, although the inventory is presumably being marketed to educators and others in the "helping professions" to facilitate diagnosis of learning process weaknesses, there is no discussion in the available materials to indicate how the items in this inventory relate to typical school learning in any domain.

In summary, the only conclusion that can be reached concerning this instrument is that the user will be flying blind in terms of how to interpret the learning skills profiles that can be so readily produced from the RIBLS. This will be especially troubling to those with little specialized training in assessment. At this point, despite the careful development of administrative procedures for this inventory, my recommendation to potential users is to seek a readiness inventory that reports essential data on validity and reliability. The present instrument should be reconsidered when these issues are fully explored in the technical manual.

[333]

Roeder Manipulative Aptitude Test.
Purpose: Measures manual and finger dexterity and hand-eye coordination.
Population: Elementary school to adult.
Publication Date: 1967.
Scores, 1 to 3: Left Hand Dexterity (optional), Right Hand Dexterity (optional), Total.
Administration: Group.
Price Data, 1991: $195 per test; $10.50 per 50 record blanks; $35 per test replacement parts.
Time: 5(10) minutes.
Author: Wesley S. Roeder.
Publisher: Lafayette Instruments Co.

Review of the Roeder Manipulative Aptitude Test by JEAN POWELL KIRNAN, Associate Professor of Psychology, Trenton State College, Trenton, NJ and SHAUNA FALTIN, System Reviewer, The Prudential Service Co., Roseland, NJ:

The Roeder Manipulative Aptitude Test (MAT) is designed as a measure of eye, hand, and finger coordination. It is suggested that the instrument be used in school settings as a vocational guidance tool and in employment settings where dexterity is the primary requirement. The test is recommended to be used as part of a comprehensive job selection process.

The instrument consists of a black styrene-plexiglass board with four horizontal rows of 10 threaded sockets, four receptacles to contain the washers, rods, caps, and nuts, as well as a socket where a T-bar is inserted. The instrument does not include storage space for the washers, rods, caps, and nuts that are used, making it easy to lose these small pieces. Furthermore, there is no mention of the number of pieces included in the test to determine whether or not pieces are missing. Missing pieces will affect the test's reliability because it becomes increasingly difficult to grasp a piece on the bottom of the receptacle. The socket that holds the T-bar is not threaded, hence, the T-bar in some cases will fall during testing unless it is tightly inserted. The materials used are sturdy and can withstand wear and tear.

The test involves four basic tasks that seem reasonable to a layperson. These tasks are: (*a*) Inserting rods into threaded sockets on the board and screwing a cap on top of each rod; (*b*) sliding a washer and nut alternately on each side of the T-bar using both hands; (*c*) sliding a washer and nut on the left side of the T-bar using the left hand; and (*d*) sliding a washer and nut on the right side of the T-bar using the right hand. The first task is timed for 3 minutes, and the second through fourth tasks are 40 seconds each. The test takes about 5 minutes, plus time for instructions, demonstration, and practice.

Three sets of administration instructions are provided: single administration, group administration, and administration to individuals with special needs. The test is easy to administer and requires no technical knowledge on the part of the administrator who must provide instruction, demonstration, careful examination, and, with individual administrations, scoring. The instructions in the manual allow the test taker to practice before being timed. There is no mention, however, of exactly how much time can be allotted for practice. Practice improves performance, so the administrator must give each person the same amount of practice time or the reliability will be affected. It is necessary that the test is taken in an appropriate setting with desks or tables and with chairs of heights comfortable for the test takers.

The recognition of accommodations in testing for special need individuals is quite helpful especially in light of the Americans with Disabilities Act of 1989. In this section, the administrator is told to instruct the examinee to ignore pieces that fall on the floor. This is an important test direction and should be provided to all, not just those with special needs. Examinees can waste a great deal of time picking up pieces that will inevitably drop on the floor or tables.

The administrator must be careful when reading the instructions in the manual as it contains numerous errors. The basic instructions include specific detail as to how the pieces should be placed, the hand(s) to use, a practice session, replacement of pieces, actual testing, scoring, and recording on the worksheet. Several spelling errors need correction, and a table on page 6 has no label and is assumed to be the format for users to submit their research data to the author. Most disturbing though, are the numerous errors found in the section on test administration and scoring. The errors include: omission of instructions to replace practice pieces before testing, instructions to place the score under the wrong heading on the scoring sheet, instructions to practice with the right hand followed by testing with the left hand, and instructions to test the same hand twice. Furthermore, utilization of the left hand is optional when testing individually; however, in the group administration and administration for special individuals, testing of the left hand is not optional. There seems to be no logical reason for this discrepancy other than a mistake by the publisher. These errors contribute to confusion when administering the test and can lead the administrators to "fix" these errors with individual and unique variations of instructions greatly reducing the reliability of the instrument.

The claim is made that the MAT can be used in group administration, whereas many other manual dexterity tests cannot be so administered. The modifications to the test, however, are limited to instructions to be "trustworthy" (p. 12) and directions as to how one should score the two sections. Certainly many other dexterity tests could be similarly adapted.

Scoring is easy, quick, and can be done by hand. Only simple addition is required and computation takes less than one minute. Individual and special individuals' scores are recorded by the proctor. In the case of group administration, each examinee must record his or her own score. This leaves open the possibility of cheating and relies too heavily on honest reports. Special notice should be taken when recording and instructing where to place the scores on the answer sheet due to the previously mentioned errors in the manual instructions. Scoring includes the summation of the scores from the first two tasks to obtain a "total manipulative aptitude score" (p. 26).

The scoring of the rods and caps does not require that a complete unit be correctly assembled to gain points. The number of rods and number of caps are added together. Should an individual screw in more rods than caps (and rods are easier to manipulate than the smaller caps), they would receive a higher score.

Answer forms are provided by means of a score sheet and a conversion sheet. The score sheet allows one to record the number of rods and caps that are correctly assembled, washers and nuts using both hands, washers and nuts using the left hand, and washers and nuts using the right hand. The conversion sheet is then used to convert the raw scores into percentiles. Only one table of normative data is provided for this conversion. The conversion formula is based on test results of 4,600 administrations in a sample of high school students in addition to various industrial groups. We assume the 4,600 administrations means 4,600 separate subjects. This wording choice is unusual and potentially confusing. The students consisted of males and females from various school districts and various industrial types in 27 states. The author should further define the sample as to the age level and whether the students were randomly selected from high school or if they came predominantly from vocational settings.

Because the conversion table is titled "High School Percentile Norms" one assumes that the normative data include only the high school subjects and not the industrial groups referred to earlier. No data on the industrial group norms are given. The normative data should be documented more fully and expanded to include separate norms for the various school groups and different occupational groups. The lack of separate occupational normative data leaves one in a dilemma as to how to use the raw scores. Applicants might be compared to one another and the high scorer selected. However, an argument could be made that job performance may not improve past a certain score on the MAT. Data from validity studies would be helpful in setting a minimum cutoff score for different occupations.

Reliability of the test by means of the test-retest method is .92. Much information, however, is omitted in the manual concerning additional facts such as the sample size, the individuals in the sample (age, occupation, sex), and the time interval between retests.

Two criterion-related predictive validity studies are reported. These studies provide evidence of the relationship between scores on the MAT and subsequent job performance. Both studies used supervisors' ratings as the criterion for job success and used subjects employed as assemblers of small electronic parts. The correlations obtained were .48 for the first study, using male subjects, and .49 for the second study, using a female sample. Tested before the job task, a minimum of 5 months on the job had elapsed prior to the supervisor ratings being taken. Supervisors' ratings are based on "various types of performance" (p. 6) but the manual does not state what types specifically were looked at.

The predictive validity study is an excellent research design and correlations in the high .40s are quite good. However, the sample size should be stated and additional information about the supervisors would be helpful. Also, although the use of supervisors' ratings is commonplace as a criterion, it is often subjective. It would seem likely that in an assembly-type job, a more objective measure of job performance such as the number assembled or reject rate would be available.

Because it is recommended in the manual that the test be used in many occupations and trades where dexterity is primarily employed, validity studies should be conducted in various industries other than the electronic industry. Some of the industries mentioned are auto mechanics, airplane mechanics, draftsman, machinists, and typists.

Measures of construct validity would provide additional support for the instrument and could easily be conducted. For example, other dexterity tests such as the Pennsylvania Bi-Manual Worksample (Packard, 1949) provide correlations between the test and similar dexterity tests such as the Minnesota Rate of Manipulation, the Revised Beta Examination, and the O'Connor Finger Dexterity Test. Furthermore, it would be helpful if the manual reported intercorrelations between the tasks to indicate whether it is necessary to administer all four tasks.

The test manual reports that additional research is underway to demonstrate the validity of the MAT in other occupational settings and asks for individuals using the test to share research findings with the author. This is an excellent idea as all assessment measures should have an ongoing program of research. What is disturbing in this case is that the manual has a copyright of 1967, and no additional research has been found on the MAT. Surely in 25 years additional research should have been conducted and provided for the test's users.

In conclusion, the MAT seems a reasonable measure of manual dexterity. It is face valid and reports acceptable reliability and validity. Users will have difficulty in interpreting and using scores due to lack of information about the normative group and the absence of separate normative data for a variety of occupations. The manual has not been updated in 25 years despite serious errors that will affect test scores and that are easily remedied. Thus, although the instrument may appear basically sound, the negative aspects (errors in instruction, lack of ongoing research, and unclear normative data) render it inferior to other readily available measures of the same construct.

REVIEWER'S REFERENCE

Packard, A. G. (1949). [Review of the Pennsylvania Bi-Manual Worksample.] In O. K. Buros (Ed.), *The third mental measurements yearbook* (p. 695). New Brunswick, NJ: Rutgers University Press.

Review of the Roeder Manipulative Aptitude Test by SUZANNE LANE, *Associate Professor of Research Methodology, University of Pittsburgh, Pittsburgh, PA:*

The Roeder Manipulative Aptitude Test (MAT) is designed to measure "eye, hand and finger coordination or [the] dexterity factor" (p. 4, Instruction Manual). The MAT is a speed test and can be group or individually administered. The author indicates that the MAT can be used for job selection and vocational guidance in conjunction with other aptitude tests and that it is appropriate for students in elementary and secondary school, college students, and adults. An Instruction Manual that accompanies the test is divided into five sections: purpose of the MAT, description of the MAT, reliability and validity of the MAT, directions for administering the MAT, and directions for scoring the MAT.

The MAT consists of a styrene-plexiglass board, a T-bar, washers, rods, caps, and nuts. The examinee is asked to perform two types of tasks: The first task asks the examinee to quickly and accurately screw rods into a socket and then to screw caps onto the rods, repeatedly, for a total of 3 minutes. For this task, the examinee is instructed to use only one hand, whichever is more comfortable. The second task asks the examinee to quickly and accurately slide washers and nuts onto the T-bar for a total of 40 seconds. The examinee is instructed to use both hands for this task. The washer and nuts task can be repeated with the examinee using the left hand only and/or the right hand only.

Three scores can be obtained: (*a*) the total score is the sum of the number of successes from the rods and caps task and the number of successes from the washers and nuts task (using both hands), (*b*) the left hand score is the number of successes from the washers and nuts task (using the left hand only), and (*c*) the right hand score is the number of successes from the washers and nuts task (using the right hand only).

Three sets of directions for administering the MAT are provided in the manual: individually administered test directions, group administered test directions, and individually administered test directions for "youngsters and individuals in remedial treatment, the handicapped, slow learners, etc." (p. 18, Instruction Manual). Within each section, the directions are separated for the rods and caps task, washers and nuts task (both hands), washers and nuts task (left hand only), and washers and nuts task (right hand only). The directions for the individual administration for the washers and nuts task (both hands) are in need of careful editing in that the directions indicate for the examiner to record the examinees' score in the box on the profile sheet labeled "washers and nuts—left hand" (p. 9). Moreover, within this same section the directions for the washers and nuts task (right hand) is provided twice prior to and after the directions for the left hand. Besides these two glaring editorial errors, the directions appear to be clear and easy to understand.

The norms provided in the manual are from "4,600 administrations given to high school students, in addition to various industrial groups" (p. 24, Instruction Manual). The author indicates that most of the data are reported by school districts (in 27 states) that are of different types and vary in size. The author provides no description of the industrial groups. Percentile norms are reported for the total score (rods and caps score plus the washers and nuts [both hands] score) as well as the washers and nuts (left hand) score and the washers and nuts (right hand) score. The author does not indicate whether these 4,600 administrations were individual or group administrations, or both. There is no discussion on whether special norms are needed for individuals with handicaps. Also, there is no rationale provided for combining the score from the rods and caps task with the score from the washers and nuts task (both hands) to obtain the total score.

The author indicates that the stability reliability coefficient for the MAT is .92. However, the time between the two testings and the sample size used are not reported in the manual. Although three scores can be obtained as indicated above, only one reliability coefficient is provided. It may be reasonable to assume that the reported coefficient of .92 is for the total score. No estimates of the standard error of measurement are provided.

A table providing the mean, standard deviation, and median for the total score, washers and nuts (right hand) score, and the washers and nuts (left hand) score for a sample of 454 examinees is included in the manual. Oddly, there is no reference to this table and therefore, no indication of the nature of the sample.

A validity coefficient of .48 was obtained by correlating supervisors' ratings of male assemblers of small electronic parts with the male assemblers' scores on the MAT. For female assemblers of small electronic parts the correlation between supervisors' ratings and their scores on the MAT was .49. The manual indicates that for both of these studies the examinees were tested before they were given their specific job assignments and supervisors' ratings were obtained after at least 5 months experience on their specific job assignments. The manual, however, provides no information regarding the sample size for either of the studies. Although the author states that additional predictive validity studies with examinees in different types of jobs are in progress, the manual has not been revised since 1967.

The *Standards for Educational and Psychological Testing* (AERA, APA, & NCME, 1985) indicate that test validation is the process of accumulating evidence to support the "appropriateness, meaningfulness, and usefulness of the specific inferences made from test scores" (p. 9). It is my opinion that the evidence for the validity and reliability of the MAT as well as the norms reported in this manual are inadequate and outdated. Thus, I cannot endorse the use of this test for selection purposes.

REVIEWER'S REFERENCE

American Educational Research Association, American Psychological Association, & National Council on Measurement in Education. (1985). *Standards for educational and psychological testing*. American Psychological Association, Inc.

[334]

Rokeach Value Survey.

Purpose: Constructed to identify values of importance to the respondent.

Population: Ages 11 and over.

Publication Dates: 1967–83.

Scores: No scores.

Administration: Group.

Price Data, 1992: $38 per 25 test booklets; $29.50 per manual ('73, 447 pages).

Time: (10–20) minutes.

Comments: Rankings of 18 terminal values ("end-states of existence") and 18 instrumental values ("modes of behavior"); manual title is The Nature of Human Values.

Author: Milton Rokeach.

Publisher: Consulting Psychologists Press, Inc.

Cross References: See T4:2290 (28 references); 9:1058 (17 references), and T3:2029 (49 references); for reviews by Jacob Cohen and Tom Kitwood, see 8:660 (155 references); see also T2:1355 (39 references).

TEST REFERENCES

1. Feather, N. T. (1988). Moral judgements and human values. *British Journal of Social Psychology, 27*, 239-246.
2. Feather, N. T. (1990). Reactions to equal reward allocations: Effects of situation, gender and values. *British Journal of Social Psychology, 29*, 315-329.
3. Schwartz, S. H. (1990). Individualism-collectivism: Critique and proposed refinements. *Journal of Cross-Cultural Psychology, 21*, 139-157.
4. Schwartz, S. H., Struch, N., & Bilsky, W. (1990). Values and intergroup social motives: A study of Israeli and German students. *Social Psychology Quarterly, 53*, 185-198.
5. Dickinson, J. (1991). Values and judgements of wage differentials. *British Journal of Social Psychology, 30*, 267-270.
6. Mayton, D. M., II, & Sangster, R. Y. (1992). Cross-cultural comparison of values and nuclear war attitudes. *Journal of Cross-Cultural Psychology, 23*, 340-352.
7. Shrum, L. J., & McCarty, J. A. (1992). Individual differences in differentiation in the rating of personal values: The role of private self-consciousness. *Personality and Social Psychology Bulletin, 18*, 223-230.
8. Diessner, R., Mayton, D. III, & Dolen, M. A. (1993). Values hierarchies and moral reasoning. *The Journal of Social Psychology, 133*, 869-871.
9. Gibbins, K., & Walker, I. (1993). Multiple interpretations of the Rokeach Value Survey. *The Journal of Social Psychology, 133*, 797-805.
10. Lester, D. (1993). Depression, suicidal preoccupation and scores on the Rokeach Value Survey: A correction. *Psychological Reports, 73*, 1202.
11. Madhere, S. (1993). The development and validation of the current Life Orientation Scale. *Psychological Reports, 72*, 467-472.
12. Allen, M. W. (1994). Reliability and accuracy of cultural-level judgements of personal values. *Perceptual and Motor Skills, 79*, 16-18.
13. Rudowicz, E., & Kitto, J. (1994). Empirical investigation into the value systems of Hong Kong Chinese students. *Psychological Reports, 75*, 211-216.
14. Suefeld, P., Bluck, S., Loewen, L., & Elkins, D. J. (1994). Sociopolitical values and integrative complexity of members of student political groups. *Canadian Journal of Behavioural Science, 26*, 121-141.

Review of the Rokeach Value Survey by SUSAN M. BROOKHART, Assistant Professor of Education, Duquesne University, Pittsburgh, PA:

The Rokeach Value Survey (RVS) is "to serve as an all-purpose instrument for research on human values" (p. 51) according to Rokeach's book, *The Nature of Human Values*. The instrument has in fact been widely used in research since 1967, most frequently in the 1970s and 1980s.

Values, in Rokeach's theoretical framework, are important because of their psychological significance to individuals and because of their effects on attitudes, social conduct, and judgment of others. Rokeach's definition of a value is "an enduring belief that a specific mode of conduct or end-state of existence is personally or socially preferable to an opposite or converse mode of conduct or end-state of existence" (p. 5). He calls the modes of conduct "instrumental values" and the end-states "terminal values." The task the RVS poses is for the respondent to rank, using stickers that can be moved until the respondent is satisfied with his or her choices, first 18 terminal values and then 18 instrumental values. The data the instrument yields are the rank orderings for each value.

Ranking as a method is consistent with Rokeach's theory about the comparative nature of values. He defines a value system as "an enduring organization of beliefs concerning preferable modes of conduct or end-states of existence along a continuum or relative importance" (p. 5), or a stable prioritizing of values in one's life.

The selection of the value terms was done carefully. For the 18 terminal values, a literature review, personal reflection, and empirical data were examined. The 18 instrumental values were based on Anderson's (1968) work on personality traits. Content and construct validity evidence were collected and reported. Nevertheless, there are two problems with operationalizing the theoretical construct "value system" as ranking two sets (terminal and instrumental, respectively) of 18 values each.

First, ranking 18 fixed-choice values is a somewhat arbitrary task, with list length determined in part by the upper limits on people's ability to rank order. The fixed choices stand in contrast to some of Rokeach's theoretical work on the personal nature of value systems. Rokeach's theory postulates that individuals base important judgments and actions on their sense of the relative importance of different values. It does not follow that the most important 18 values in one individual's value system would always match those in another individual's value system.

Second, ranking leads to ipsative measures. The ipsative scale causes difficulty in data analysis for many of the research applications for which the RVS was designed. Without transformation, the data are not appropriate for parametric tests. And ipsative measurement is measurement within individuals; it does not follow that two individuals who assign a value the same rank are governed by it, in their behavior or their judgments, to the same degree. It does follow that the RVS is a devilishly difficult task for a respondent with a strong value system. The manual author does note that most respondents reported the ranking task to be difficult; this reviewer thinks that is an understatement.

Test-retest reliabilities, measured with Spearman rho in studies with varying intervals between tests, are somewhat low. The best median reliabilities reported in the manual are for college students, using intervals of 3 to 7 weeks. Median *r* in three studies was from .78 to .80 for the 18 terminal values and .70 to .72 for the 18 instrumental values. These values are acceptable; however, reliabilities for 7th and 9th graders with a 3-week interval were .53 and .61 for instrumental values and .62 and .63 for terminal values. Other reliabilities, the results of other studies reported in the manual, were mostly in the .50s and .60s.

This reviewer thinks the reliabilities are acceptable under two conditions: *a*) the data are used for research with groups, not individuals; and (*b*) the data are used with college students or others who have ability with verbal abstractions. The RVS claims to be useful with ages 11 and above. The lower reliabilities for 7th graders give evidence there is less consistency of interpretation among young people than adults. It is true that some 11-year-olds have attained a formal operations stage of thought and can handle verbal abstractions. However, an 11-year-old's conception of, for example, "Wisdom—a mature understanding of life," or "An exciting life—a stimulating, active life," is necessarily still developing.

With these cautions, the simple ranking task and the global, philosophical items (inner harmony, equality, freedom, wisdom, etc.) do have some fascinating research possibilities. For example, the manual author reports the results of studies using the RVS to rank the results of content analyses of writers representing different political ideologies (Chapter 6). In other studies, the RVS allows group beliefs and reported behaviors to be examined within a theoretical framework.

The theoretical work and the norms presented in the manual (1973) are based on a national sample of 1,409 adult Americans obtained by the national Opinion Research Center. These RVS data were collected in April of 1968, along with demographic information, responses to questions about the assassination of Dr. Martin Luther King, responses to questions about civil rights, the poor, Vietnam, student protest, and the 1968 presidential candidates. As this list illustrates, the manual needs updating. These studies should be augmented with newer theoretical work and newer norm tables. For example, there is reason to suspect that gender differences in responses may have changed since 1968. Income categories have certainly changed since 1968, when $15,000+ was the top category; it would be good to see whether response distributions among relative income categories has changed. The norms also need updating because in the 1983 revision of the instrument, replacements were made in the lists of terminal values ("health" for "happiness") and instrumental values ("loyal" for "cheerful"). The norms reflect the original lists.

In sum, the RVS continues to be a useful research tool for theory development about the nature of human values. Its moderate reliability precludes its being used for any purposes that include making decisions with direct consequences for individuals. The RVS should be used with literate adults who are used to dealing with abstractions. The norms are based on data from 1968 and thus are of limited utility.

REVIEWER'S REFERENCE

Anderson, N. H. (1968). Likableness ratings of 555 personality-trait words. *Journal of Personality and Social Psychology*, 9, 272-279.

Review of the Rokeach Value Survey by ELEANOR E. SANFORD, Research Consultant, Division of Accountability Services/Research, North Carolina Department of Public Instruction, Raleigh, NC:

The Rokeach Value Survey by Milton Rokeach is designed to assess an individual's value system. In *The Nature of Human Values*, Rokeach defines a value as "an enduring belief that a specific mode of conduct or end-state of existence is personally or socially preferable to an opposite or converse mode of conduct or end-state of existence" and a value system as "an enduring organization of beliefs concerning preferable modes of conduct or end-states of existence along a continuum of relative importance" (p. 5). Terminal values—those that describe an individual's beliefs concerning desirable end-states of existence—include comfortable life, exciting life, sense of accomplishment, world at peace, world of beauty, equality, family security, freedom, happiness, inner harmony, mature love, national security, pleasure, salvation, self-respect, social recognition, true friendship, and wisdom. Instrumental values—those that describe an individual's beliefs concerning desirable modes of conduct—include being ambitious, broadminded, capable, cheerful, clean, courageous, forgiving, helpful, honest, imaginative, independent, intellectual, logical, loving, obedient, polite, responsible, and self-controlled.

The Rokeach Value Survey is simple to administer and takes approximately 10 to 20 minutes to complete. The individual is asked to rank each of the 18 terminal values by placing the gummed stickers next to the numbers from 1 to 18 (from most important to least important relative to all the other values). The procedure is then repeated with the 18 instrumental values.

All of the values are stated positively, and therefore social desirability is kept to a minimum. There is no actual scoring involved, each of the terminal and instrumental values is assigned the actual ranking.

The development of the instrument is based on Rokeach's theory of values and is briefly described in his book. Originally 12 terminal and 12 instrumental values were identified for use on Forms A and B of the instrument. The number of terminal and instrumental values was increased to 18 because of low reliabilities on the original forms of the survey. It was felt that individuals would not be able to rank order reliably more than 18 entities at one time. The 18 terminal values were identified by a consensus process from a review of the literature, the writer's own values, and interviews with individuals who described their value systems. The 18 instrumental values were derived from the work of H. N. Anderson and only values that were positive in nature and were deemed to be useful were included. The author does not describe any kind of review or field-testing process used to arrive at the specific set of 18 instrumental and 18 terminal values that appear on Forms C, D, and E. These three forms differ only in presentation format (without value descriptors, with value descriptors/gummed labels, and with value descriptors).

The Rokeach Value Survey exhibits adequate test-retest reliability estimates for this type of instrument: Spearman rho estimates for the terminal values ranged from .51 to .88 with a median of .65, and for the instrumental values ranged from .45 to .70 with a median of .61. The intercorrelations of the 36 values were small and it was assumed that each value was assessing a different dimension. The 36 values were also factor analyzed and seven factors were obtained that accounted for 41% of the variance in the value rankings. These factors are related to various aspects of the terminal and instrumental values, but according to Rokeach's theory two types of values (terminal and instrumental) were hypothesized.

The validity of the Rokeach Value Survey was determined by examining the rankings of values by contrasting groups (i.e., gender, income groupings, attained educational groupings, ethnicity, age, and various religious groupings). Significant ranking differences between groups were found for all of the groupings (gender: 12 terminal and 8 instrumental values; income: 9 terminal and 11 instrumental values; education: 14 terminal and 11 instrumental values). Several of these norm groups may not be appropriate for comparison with the values of individual in the 1990s. The top income grouping (>$15,000) is at or near the poverty level in today's world.

Respondents were also asked to respond to specific questions and/or statements concerning attitudes (i.e., civil rights for blacks and poor, student protest, international affairs, religion, and personality). Significant value ranking differences were obtained for all the values with at least one of the attitudinal measures except self-respect. A comfortable life, equality, salvation, and obedient exhibited significant ranking differences for at least 9 of the 11 attitudinal measures. Many of the attitudinal issues were very important during 1968 when the research was conducted, but they may not have as much importance in today's society. The age of the normative research is a weakness of the instrument.

The Rokeach Value Survey is useful for examining an individual's value system and for determining if change has occurred within the individual's value system. If the survey is to be used for comparing an individual's value system to the values of his or her society, then it should only be used after the norms are updated to reflect today's society.

[335]

Rotter Incomplete Sentences Blank, Second Edition.

Purpose: Primarily used "as a screening instrument of overall adjustment."
Population: College students, adults, high-school students.
Publication Dates: 1950–92.
Acronym: RISB.
Score: Index of Overall Adjustment.
Administration: Individual or group.
Forms, 3: College, Adult, High School.
Price Data, 1994: $20.50 per 25 response sheets (specify College, Adult, or High School); $50.50 per manual ('92, 256 pages).
Time: (20–40) minutes.
Authors: Julian B. Rotter, Michael I. Lah, and Janet E. Rafferty.
Publisher: The Psychological Corporation.
Cross References: See T4:2300 (11 references), T3:2037 (11 references), 8:663 (21 references), T2:1501 (48 references), P:472 (35 references), 6:239 (17 references), and 5:156 (18 references); for reviews by Charles N. Cofer and William Schofield of an earlier edition and an excerpted review by Adolf G. Woltmann, see 4:130 (6 references).

TEST REFERENCES

1. Engstrom, I. (1992). Mental health and psychological functioning in children and adolescents with inflammatory bowel disease: A comparison with children having other chronic illnesses and with healthy children. *Journal of Child Psychology and Psychiatry and Allied Disciplines*, *33*, 563-582.
2. Ames, P. C., & Riggio, R. E. (1995). Use of the Rotter Incomplete Sentences Blank with adolescent populations: Implications for determining maladjustment. *Journal of Personality Assessment*, *64*, 159-167.
3. Clark, A. J. (1995). Projective techniques in the counseling process. *Journal of Counseling and Development*, *73*, 311-316.

Review of the Rotter Incomplete Sentences Blank by GREGORY J. BOYLE, Associate Professor of Psychology, Bond University, Gold Coast, Queensland, Australia:

Like its predecessor, the Second Edition of the Rotter Incomplete Sentences Blank (RISB) is a projective measure of maladjustment with a semi-objective scoring system. Forms are available for high school students, college students, and the general adult population. The revised instrument remains essentially unchanged from the earlier version and provides direct information on personality conflicts. The original 40 sentence stems are retained with only two slight modifications. Only six stems are altered in the High School version, and only four stems in the Adult form. As scoring depends on intuitive clinical insights, cognizance of personality dynamics is essential for accurate interpretation. Although responses can also be scored qualitatively for projected motivational needs, as a general rule, interpretation of subjective scales is notoriously unreliable (cf. Fernandez, 1990).

Six practice-scoring examples (three each for males and females) based on the College form are included in the manual. For the sake of consistency in scoring protocols, detailed comparison of responses with the examples provided in the manual is essential. Responses are rated on a 7-point ordinal scale (higher scores suggesting greater maladjustment) on the basis of omissions and incomplete responses, conflict responses, positive responses, or neutral responses. Use of seven scale gradations is advantageous in enabling relatively fine discriminations between item responses. Overall scores generally range from 80 to 205 (on a scale from zero through 240). However, because of the diversity among individuals' idiosyncratic responses, the RISB cannot readily be computer scored. This inevitably raises questions as to the objectivity and scoring consistency of RISB responses.

Several studies reported in the RISB manual suggest uncertain reliability. Stability coefficients are reported as ranging from a low .38 (retest interval of 3 years) up to .82 (retest after only 1–2 weeks), so it cannot be assumed the instrument is always reliable. Some inconsistency in scoring is evident because although interscorer reliabilities range from .72 to .99, item-rater reliabilities range from .44 to .93. It is unlikely that scorers will always adhere closely to the examples provided, or interpret protocols judiciously. Because the scoring examples are based solely on college samples, there is the further question as to their applicability for high school and adult groups. This limitation has not been addressed in the revised instrument. Norms for noncollege groups have still not been developed. Like its predecessor, the revised manual also fails to provide scoring examples for noncollege groups.

Nevertheless, a positive feature of the RISB is its item homogeneity. The manual reports split-half estimates ranging from .74 to .86, and a Cronbach alpha coefficient of .69. This moderate level of item homogeneity suggests little item redundancy, and yet sufficient internal consistency to justify its use. As Boyle (1991) pointed out, moderate item homogeneities in psychometric scales facilitate *breadth* of measurement, minimizing redundant items.

The manual has been upgraded and incorporates several validation studies undertaken since 1950 for all three forms. However, no studies into the validity of using the College form with high school and general adult populations are reported. This is potentially problematic, because many studies over recent decades have inappropriately used the College form of the RISB with noncollege samples.

The RISB relies predominantly on face validity, so that item responses are readily amenable to distortion, depending on respondents' lack of self-insight, and their conscious and unconscious motives. Face validity is a major problem with personality tests, due to their susceptibility to motivational distortion, and is even more problematic with projective instruments (Boyle, 1988). As well, the instrument may act more effectively as a *trait* measure than as a *state* indicator of changes over time, and not be situationally sensitive, as for example, throughout the span of psychotherapeutic intervention. Despite these limitations, the RISB has received widespread use in both clinical and nonclinical settings (Cosden, 1985).

Factor analytic validity has been investigated for the College form, but not for the High School and Adult forms. However, little indication is given in the manual of the particular factor analytic methodology employed, nor any evaluation of the procedures adopted therein (e.g., along the lines suggested by Gorsuch, 1983). Consequently, the factor structure of the RISB remains somewhat uncertain.

In addition, there appears to be substantial overlap in scores obtained by normal and maladjusted individuals. According to the manual, a mean cutoff score of 145 correctly classifies from 40% to approximately 98% of individuals within both groups. In line with Cosden's (1985) suggestion, this cutoff score exceeds the 135 recommended originally. However, use of a cutoff score ignores the measurement error typically associated with psychometric scales, and fails to acknowledge that such cutoff scores can vary appreciably across different samples. Discussion in the manual of specific cutoff scores is problematic, because such scores are only meaningful with respect to specific groups. Furthermore, scores are likely to be distorted by response sets, confounding their direct interpretation.

Use of the RISB is often restricted to the earlier stages of clinical assessment, where it is useful as a quick screening device. Subsequently, more detailed assessment of psychological issues arising from an individual's specific responses can be undertaken. Allowing respondents the freedom to provide direct information about their concerns is a quick and efficient way of uncovering major conflicts. As the test authors point out, the revised manual includes updated scoring criteria and norms, and additional case studies reflecting many of the societal changes which have occurred since the instrument was first published. Overall, the revised RISB should serve a useful role within the clinical psychologist's armamentarium, although clearly, and unnecessarily to some extent, the accompanying manual still retains a number of the deficiencies of the earlier version.

REVIEWER'S REFERENCES

Gorsuch, R. L. (1983). *Factor analysis* (rev. 2nd ed.). Hillsdale, NJ: Erlbaum.

Cosden, M. (1985). [Review of Rotter Incomplete Sentences Blank.] In D. J. Keyser & R. C. Sweetland (Eds.), *Test critiques* (vol. 2; pp. 653-660). Kansas City, MO: Test Corporation of America.

Boyle, G. J. (1988). Elucidation of motivation structure by dynamic calculus. In J. R. Nesselroade & R. B. Cattell (Eds.), *Handbook of multivariate experimental psychology* (rev. 2nd ed.; pp. 737-787). New York: Plenum.

Fernandez, E. (1990). Artifact in pain ratings, its implications for test-retest reliability, and correction by a new scaling procedure. *Journal of Psychopathology and Behavioral Assessment, 12*, 1-15.

Boyle, G. J. (1991). Does item homogeneity indicate internal consistency or item redundancy in psychometric scales? *Personality and Individual Differences, 12*, 291-294.

Review of the Rotter Incomplete Sentences Blank, Second Edition by MARY J. McLELLAN, Assistant Professor of Educational Psychology, Northern Arizona University, Center for Excellence in Education, Flagstaff, AZ:

The Rotter Incomplete Sentences Blank, Second Edition (RISB) is a revised version of the 1950 edition. The revision of the test includes changing some items, an updated review of the literature, and updated normative information and scoring criteria. The authors recognized the need to provide scoring criteria that is more germane to today's society. This test is designed to provide an index of overall adjustment for high school, college, and adult populations. Although the test form may be administered by nonprofessional staff members, "only professionals with appropriate graduate-level training should score and interpret responses" (manual, p. 7).

The title accurately reflects the scope of the test, in that the examinee is required to write sentences for which a stem is provided. The stem is typically one or two words. There are 40 stems the examinee is required to complete. There are separate response sheets for the three groups of people in the standardization sample. The three response forms are similar and the differences are primarily reflective of current circumstances for the examinee. The test instructions require the examiner to hand the response form to the examinee and read the instructions in bold print if necessary. The examiner may encourage responding to every item, if necessary. Telling the examinee to skip an item and return to it later if the examinee "draws a blank" is acceptable. Reading the sentence stems to the examinee may be used with caution. Using the response form as it is designed is critical to the use of the scoring system because the size of the blank provided, to some extent, will control the length of the response. Long responses receive a score that affects the overall adjustment score. The objective scoring system and well-formulated examples are provided in the test manual.

The objective scoring system of the RISB is said to be unique by the authors. The test results yield a numerical score, which is reflective of overall adjustment. The scoring system consists of several principles. Incomplete responses or omissions are not scored, but do significantly affect the Overall Adjustment Score through a proration formula. Responses that reflect conflict receive scores of 4, 5, or 6 depending on the severity of the conflict expressed. The more severe conflict, the higher the score. Responses that reflect a healthy or hopeful frame of mind are scored as positive and receive scores of 1, 2, or 3 with the more positive responses receiving the lowest scores. Neutral responses receive a score of 3. When a long response is produced, the examiner adds 1 point to the score of that item. Examples of the scoring criteria are provided in the manual. The manual provides good examples and clear justifications why particular responses result in a specific score.

Suggested uses of the RISB include screening, tracking changes in scores over time, group comparisons, and research. Factor analytic studies have not successfully justified the use of specific item interpretation. The test authors make a sound defense of the objective scoring system for the uses suggested earlier and indicate that clinical interpretation and other methods of analysis are encouraged when the examiner needs additional information from the responses.

The reliability of the RISB is defined by the use of interscorer reliability, internal consistency, and test-retest reliability. Interscorer reliability is impressive, ranging from .72 to .99. The studies mentioned in the manual did not, however, specifically address the Second Edition scoring criteria (updated examples). Internal consistency is not the preferred measure of reliability to be used for this type of measure, but the authors do indicate that some information is available and the estimates are said to indicate a moderate degree of internal consistency. Test-retest reliability estimates range from .82 for short intervals to .38 through .70 for longer intervals (6 months to 3 years). The lower reliability coefficients for the longer intervals is defended as an indication that the RISB is a measure of stable traits versus momentary moods or reactive states. A comprehensive discussion of various validity studies is provided in the manual and adequate validity is confirmed. The authors conclude that the studies with both high school and adult populations provide adequate justification for use of the overall adjustment score. A discussion of the specific populations and issues addressed in the studies is included. Normative data were derived through the use of samples collected in 1977, 1988, and 1989. No new normative sample was reported for the second edition. The cutoff for adjustment versus maladjustment is discussed in the manual as being 145, but the authors qualify that score and suggest that the individual user determine the appropriate cutoff score based on the purpose of the test administration and the particular client population. Anyone using the test for the purposes of identification of particular types of individuals should read the manual carefully.

The RISB is a test that is extremely easy to administer. The objective scoring criteria are well developed by the test authors and excellent examples for assigning scores to specific responses are provided in the manual. The examiner needs to realize that the cutoff score is somewhat arbitrary depending on the purpose of testing. In addition, the scoring examples are specific to the College form and no examples for the Adult or High School form are provided. No specific normative data were reported in the manual for the Second Edition; however, the updated normative information included studies from 1977, 1988, and 1989. The authors do identify the importance of continued research into the changes in normative scores. The collection of local normative data is also recommended. In conclusion, the RISB has an objective scoring system that appears to have acceptable reliability and validity. When applied to the uses specified in the manual, the test administrator has a good tool to assess overall adjustment of high school and college students, and adults.

[336]

Safran Student's Interest Inventory, Third Edition.

Purpose: Developed to identify occupational interests.
Population: Grades 5–9, 9–12.
Publication Dates: 1960–85.
Scores, 7: Economic, Technical, Outdoor, Service, Humane, Artistic, Scientific.
Administration: Group.
Levels, 2: One, Two.
Price Data, 1992: \$39.50 per 35 test booklets (select level); \$24 per student's manual ('85, 8 pages); \$14.50 per counsellor's manual ('85, 39 pages); \$15 per examination kit.
Time: Administration time not reported.
Comments: Self-administered.
Authors: Carl Safran, Douglas W. Feltham, and Edgar N. Wright.
Publisher: Nelson Canada [Canada].
Cross References: For a review by Thomas T. Frantz of an earlier edition, see 7:1035; see also 6:1069 (1 reference).

Review of the Safran Student's Interest Inventory, Third Edition by ALBERT M. BUGAJ, Associate Professor of Psychology, University of Wisconsin—Marinette, Marinette, WI:

The Safran Student's Interest Inventory (SSII) was developed in Canada for use in determining the vocational interests of Canadian students. Previously for high school students, the third edition is also available in a version said to be suitable for grades 5 through 9. As a standard test the SSII is considerably lacking. Although it may provoke thought about career interests, its ability to do so in a valid and reliable manner must be questioned.

The SSII is based on an ipsative approach. Students' interests in an occupational area are compared with interest in each of six other areas, so their "highest raw score in an area indicates their greatest interest at a given time" (p. 6). A student completing the SSII can thus determine the strength of his or her own interest in any of seven areas, as compared to the other areas.

The manual indicates that a "powerful and unique feature" (p. 3) of the inventory is the method used to determine the consistency of the testees' responses. This involves arranging seven activities (one from each interest area examined) in pairs on each of the eight pages of the test. Each item is paired once with every other item. The manual authors assert, "if the student has been consistent, one item will have been chosen over all others (six choices), one over all but one (five choices), etc., to one that has been chosen over no others" (p. 39). If an item is chosen twice on a page, the student has been inconsistent. Given items numbered 1, 2, and 3, for example, an inconsistent testee might choose 1 over 2, 2 over 3, and 3 over 1, a logical impossibility. The manual stresses that approximately one-third of the inventories completed cannot be considered valid on the basis of the consistency check.

Before administrating the SSII, the manual authors suggest preparing the students with included background material. This curriculum is theoretically interesting and is one of the strongest points of the SSII.

Also commendable is the inclusion in the manual of lists of selected occupations found in each interest area examined by the test, and a second list examining pairs of interest areas. These occupational areas are further cross-referenced to other sources of information (the *Canadian Classification and Dictionary of Occupations*, and the Student Guidance Information System).

Despite these strengths of the manual, the test itself is questionable. A primary weakness is the small number of items used in deriving the scores for the seven interest areas examined, a stricture resulting from the consistency check. Although the complete test consists of 168 items, a mere 56 different statements are used, resulting in seven items per scale, each item being related to a different occupation.

Although the authors attempt to defend using such a small sampling of items by saying that activities, not occupations, are the focus of the test, one must question whether seven items per scale is sufficient. One hundred forty-two occupations, often involving a wide range of activities *in* an area are listed in the manual. The Economic area, for example, includes the occupations of lawyer, secretary, banker, and computer analyst, along with 17 others.

Although there may be a rationale for grouping the occupations into sets in occupational handbooks, no empirical basis for organizing them in such a way for standardized testing is apparent. This issue is related to the validity of the test itself, reported in the current manual using data collected with the first (1960) and second (1969) edition of the SSII. Apparently no data using the current edition have been collected, and the data from the earlier studies are sometimes presented in a slipshod manner.

Convergent validity was determined by administering the first edition of the SSII and the Kuder Preference Record to ninth graders. Correlations between scales on the tests ranged from a low of .20 in a first study to a high of .77 in a second. However, the first edition of the SSII contained 35 (not the current 56) items, so comparisons to the first edition cannot be made with certainty.

An attempt at assessing the criterion-related validity of the second edition of the SSII is also reported. Unfortunately, the authors chose to use as subjects "young adults" majoring in four areas at a polytechnic institute and a college, instead of sampling the population for which the second edition was designed. Of the 264 students tested, 31% provided inconsistent forms, which could not be used in the analysis.

The results of the analysis are poorly reported. No breakdown of how many subjects produced "usable" data in each major is reported. Although the authors report the results indicated the students' strongest interest areas corresponded with their chosen major, no statistical data are provided. In short, the validity of the second edition of the SSII is doubtful, and that of the present version is untested.

The reliability of the SSII is equally questionable. In this case, the data reported are based on the brief 1960 version. Based on a sample of high school students, the test-retest reliability of the version was high (.92), although the time between administrations is not reported. Kuder-Richardson reliability was also high. Like the validity data, however, the usefulness of such "old data" based on a previous version of the test is doubtful.

Thus far, all comments regarding technical data have been aimed toward Level II of the SSII, for use with grades 8 through 12. Nothing is reported regarding the reliability and validity of Level I, designed for grades 5 through 9. Ostensibly written at a lower reading level, no test of this assumption is reported, nor are data provided regarding its suitability for students in remedial and special education (a claim made in the publisher's advertisement).

The conception behind the SSII, most notably the consistency check, is interesting. However, too many questions remain about the test to recommend its use. The high number of inconsistently completed forms (about one-third of those administered) seems to result in an overly expensive test. The reliability and validity of the second edition were questionable, and this issue is even more true of the current edition. The low number of items used, and their method of selection, seem indefensible. Rather than select a small number of items to keep administration time brief (a strength, according to the manual), a larger number of items and more thorough testing of validity and reliability might result in a superior test. The SSII might promote discussion between a counselor and a student, but the Strong Vocational Interest Inventory (374), the Kuder Occupational Interest Survey (10:167), or the Jackson Vocational Interest Survey (10:158) should provide a more accurate assessment of interests in guiding students in making career decisions.

Review of the Safran Student's Interest Inventory, Third Edition by CAROLINE MANUELE-ADKINS, Professor of Educational Foundations and Counseling Programs, Hunter College, City University of New York, New York, NY:

The main objective of the Safran Student's Interest Inventory (SSII) is to initiate student's "vocational thinking." To do this students are asked to select their preferred career interests, provide self-ratings of ability in four areas (Academic, Mechanical, Social, and Clerical), and indicate which school subjects they like best and least. The SSII was developed in Canada and is primarily designed for Canadian students. This third edition is tied directly to the *Canadian Classification and Dictionary of Occupations* (CCDO) and the Student Guidance Information Service (SGIS). The third edition also provides two versions of the instrument: Level I (grades 5–9) and Level II (grades 9–12). This edition reflects a concern for including more current occupations and removing any bias against females.

Both levels of the SSII ask students to make forced-choice decisions about a set of preferred activities. This results in raw score totals for seven different interest areas: Economic, Technical, Outdoor, Service, Humane, Artistic, and Scientific. The items are simply stated (e.g., "Fix Airplanes or Design Jewelry" [Level I]; "Teaching Children at School or Growing and Harvesting Crops" [Level II]). They are repeated many times, in paired comparisons, for the purpose of providing a "consistency check." This technique is used to identify consistent and inconsistent interest patterns and is used to determine the validity of an individual's profile. Although this appears to be a measure of consistency, the constant repetition of items produces an inventory that respondents might find boring and uninteresting. The self-ratings of ability portion of the inventory asks respondents to compare themselves to other people and rate their ability in quartiles. This presents several problems in that there is no way of knowing to whom they are comparing themselves or what their definition of ability is. The school subjects interests section is fairly straightforward in that students are provided with a list of subjects and asked to indicate, on a continuum, which ones they like best and least.

Items and scales for the SSII were, according to the manual, selected by first defining them and then checking them against the Dictionary of Occupational Titles and the Minnesota Occupational Rating Scale. The criteria for defining the items and selecting them is unclear and no information is provided about item analyses, item scale correlations, or theoretical reasons for their inclusion. Scales for the inventory are also not defined so that the user is left to guess what Economic, Technical, Outdoor, Service, etc., really mean. Given the absence of these definitions the selection of occupations related to these areas or scales (used for students' further exploration) is questionable. It is difficult to ascertain how appropriate they are as examples of each occupational area.

Validity studies for the SSII include determining whether or not the inventory differentiated between students who were in Nursing, Electrical, Creative Arts, or Business Administration courses. According to the manual the results showed that "the test did differentiate among the programs" (p. 39) but there was also considerable overlap of interests in the various areas. The manual provided no technical data for these statements so it is difficult to determine the extent to which the results can be perceived as evidence for the validity of the measure. Two additional validity studies are provided that examine the relationship between the SSII and the Kuder Preference Record. The correlations (calculated on male only samples) range from .20 to .70 for one sample and .51 to .85 for another. The validity studies cited are all from 1960 and 1969. Apparently no further studies have been conducted. The absence of specific validity data, the scarcity of studies, and the lack of recent studies on the current version are important indicators that the user needs to question the validity of this measure.

Reliability data are also provided for earlier versions of the SSII but not for the current one. Internal reliability analyses ranged from .85 to .89. Test-retest reliability for 104 high school students is reported as a median of .92. These are robust reliability figures but we do not know what the relationship is between prior and current versions.

Normative data are also not provided for this version. The manual states that "norms were published for the 1969 edition as counsellors found them helpful in determining relative performance. After seven years of use in Canadian schools, it was found that the ipsative approach was a better method" (p. 39). The author here is suggesting that normative data are not particularly useful and advocates an approach whereby students' interests should be interpreted as "personal interests" and need not be compared to the interests of others. This information is rather confusing to interpret because the author tells us that counselors found the normative data useful. It is important to note that given the lack of normative data the SSII should not be used for research purposes and is recommended only for individual counseling sessions.

To assist counselors with interpreting individual scores on the SSII, examples of student profiles are provided with suggestions to the counselor about the meaning of scores and about what the students' next steps in their exploration should be. These examples are brief but helpful. An interesting aspect is the lesson plans for six sessions that demonstrate how one could conduct group activities to introduce students to the concepts of interests and abilities, administration, interpretation, the inventory, career exploration, and application. This context for preparation and knowledge is frequently ignored by test developers.

In summary, the SSII has some major test development areas that have been ignored. It appears to have no theoretical basis for its construction and no evidence is provided for how items were defined, selected, or grouped for the seven scales. Minimal data in support of validity and reliability are provided but these studies refer to earlier versions. Normative data are also absent. Although the Inventory is easy to read and understand, students, when confronted with so many repetitious items, may become disengaged and fail to respond seriously. There are many interest inventories that are superior to the SSII. These include the Self-Directed Search (for a simple assessment; 10:330), the Vocational Preference Inventory (10:382), versions of the Kuder (209, 10:167, T3:1271) and the Strong Vocational Interest Inventory (374). Although these inventories were not developed in Canada, they would provide results the user could use with more confidence.

[337]

Sales Personality Questionnaire.

Purpose: Developed to assess personality characteristics necessary for sales success.
Population: Sales applicants.
Publication Dates: 1987–90.
Acronym: SPQ.
Scores, 12: Interpersonal (Confidence, Empathy, Persuasive), Administration (Systematic, Conscientious, Forward Planning), Opportunities (Creative, Observant), Energies (Relaxed, Resilient, Results Oriented), Social Desirability.
Administration: Group.
Price Data, 1992: $27.50 per questionnaire booklet; $7.25 per answer sheet with prepaid mail-in Bureau scoring; $6.25 per answer sheet for on-site Optic Scan scoring

or handscoring; $31.50 per manual and user's guide ('90, 60 pages); $30 per sample set.
Time: (20–30) minutes.
Author: Saville & Holdsworth Ltd.
Publisher: Saville & Holdsworth Ltd USA, Inc.

Review of the Sales Personality Questionnaire by WAYNE J. CAMARA, Director of Scientific Affairs, American Psychological Association, Washington, DC:

The Sales Personality Questionnaire (SPQ) was developed in the United Kingdom in an attempt to identify the attributes required for success as agents for an insurance company. Five overall constructs, with a total of 12 dimensions, were identified from a job analysis and comprise the scales for the SPQ. The SPQ contains 108 items that can be completed in 20–30 minutes. Applicants or job incumbents are asked to read each item or statement and indicate the degree to which they agree or disagree with each, using a 5-point Likert scale. This instrument is part of the Selling Skills Series (SSS), which includes two aptitude tests, "Using Written Information" and "Reasoning with Data." Together, the publishers note, these instruments have been developed to measure "only skills that are specifically relevant to selling" (manual, p. 1).

The test is designed to measure personality characteristics associated with successful performance in a range of sales occupations. The five constructs and 12 scales are: Interpersonal (Confidence, Empathy, Persuasive), Administration (Systematic, Conscientious, Forward Planning), Opportunities (Creative, Observant), Energies (Relaxed, Resilient, Results Oriented), and Social Desirability (Social Desirability).

Test-retest reliability coefficients are reported for the 12 scales from a sample of 113 college students. Retesting of college students varied from 2 to 4 weeks, producing coefficients that ranged from .73 to .88. Internal consistency (Cronbach's coefficient alpha) ranged from .55 to .82 with the combined normative group of 245 sales staff and sales trainees. In a few cases, the internal consistency is too low to have confidence in the dimension measured. No descriptive data are available on the sample of college students, and what little information is reported on the combined normative sample is contradictory. Specifically, the combined normative sample ($n = 245$) is defined as "all persons in the United States who have taken the SPQ as of August, 1990" (manual, p. 51). Yet, breakouts by race and gender, which each include an unknown category, result in 234 cases and 300 cases, respectively. Interrelationships between the various scales are in some cases higher than would be desirable for independence of measures, yet they make intuitive sense. The combined normative group ($n = 245$) results from two samples, 187 sales manager trainees for a national shoe store chain and 58 sales representatives for manufacturing products. Separate norms are provided for these groups, yet the omission of descriptive information on jobs and samples would seem to prevent the user from selecting the most appropriate norm group.

The greatest weakness of the SPQ is the omission of any attempt to define or identify an underlying structure for the five constructs and 12 scales. The resulting scales were developed solely from a job analysis of sales jobs in one organization. Scales have not been confirmed with factor analytic techniques and there has been no attempt to examine relationships with other personality instruments that include similar scales. One available study ($n = 57$) does illustrate that a couple of scales from the SPQ have moderate correlations with three of the seven scales from the Sales Aptitude Test. However, intercorrelations with similar scales on well-established personality tests are required. The manual authors note that test respondents should be honest and that the questionnaire contains certain distortion or consistency checks. Yet, there is no mention of such items or any type of validity scale anywhere else in the materials or scoring profile.

In addition to content validity evidence from the initial job analysis, the publisher provides brief summaries of three criterion-related validity studies using the SPQ. These studies use supervisory ratings and rankings as criterion measures of job performance and provide mixed and often inconsistent results. For example, when ratings of selling skills are used as a criterion measure one study reports moderate, but significant, correlations with the Observant and Relaxed scales. Another study found manager's ratings of selling skills related to the Persuasive and Results-Oriented scales. In one study of sales assistants only 1 of the 12 scales was moderately correlated to actual individual sales ($r = .25$). Although the test does appear to identify important attributes for sales success and possesses a high degree of face validity, additional scientific evidence of validity with larger samples is required. Available studies are not described adequately and prevent potential users from determining if the positions and samples used would generalize to their situations.

The manual does not comply with the *Standards for Educational and Psychological Testing* (AERA, APA, & NCME, 1985) in providing adequate information on the samples used in developing norm tables and in the validation studies, criterion measures, evidence of differential prediction, the content domain of jobs included in job analyses, and appropriate uses of each test.

The test publisher provides little data that indicate if group differences exist across gender, race, or ethnic groups. Instead, they note that research is underway. The publisher does provide appropriate cautions that test users not rely on the test solely for employment decisions and the need to monitor test use.

The test materials are of sufficient quality. The 66-page test manual is adequate in describing administration and scoring procedures. Chapters on norms, validity, reliability, and profiling provide appropriate explanations of these technical measurement concepts. However, the manual is insufficient for determining how to actually use this instrument in employment settings. The manual also contains a number of typographical errors, which suggest that insufficient effort has been made to develop a quality product.

The SPQ can be administered in three ways: a booklet/answer sheet, booklet/pocket computer medium, or IBM compatible computer administration. Booklet/answer sheet administration requires bureau scoring by the publisher or machine scoring on location. Hand scoring is not available.

Until much more extensive psychometric research is conducted, extreme caution should be exercised when using this instrument in making decisions about individuals. At present, the SPQ does not have adequate evidence to support its use as an off-the-shelf test and should be used only when experts in psychometrics and employment testing are available to conduct appropriate job analyses, and normative and validation studies for an organization. Test users should consider specific scales contained within a number of broad-based personality tests, such as the Hogan Personality Inventory (10:140), the Hogan Personnel Selection Series (11:163), the California Psychological Inventory (11:54), and the Personality Research Form (11:282), which may be relevant to certain characteristics required for sales positions. Users should also consider the Sales Professional Assessment Inventory.

REVIEWER'S REFERENCE

American Educational Research Association, American Psychological Association, & National Council on Measurement in Education. (1985). *Standards for educational and psychological testing.* Washington, DC: American Psychological Association, Inc.

Review of the Sales Personality Questionnaire by MICHAEL J. ROSZKOWSKI, Director of Marketing Research and Associate Professor of Psychology, The American College, Bryn Mawr, PA:

Information about the Sales Personality Questionnaire (SPQ) is contained in a 66-page Manual & User's Guide, consisting of 10 chapters and two technical appendices. The manual presents detailed instructions about how to administer the questionnaire (including such details as to thank the person for participating). This spiral-bound booklet, which is under a corporate authorship (Saville & Holdsworth, Ltd.), discusses not only the SPQ but also provides a brief overview of fundamental psychometric issues.

Together with two aptitude tests, the SPQ constitutes a battery of tests known as the Selling Skills Series (SSS). The aptitude and the personality tests can be administered independently, but the authors recommend that the tests be used jointly in identifying a person's potential to succeed in a selling role. The 108 items constituting the SPQ are grouped into 12 domains: Confidence, Empathy, Persuasive, Systematic, Conscientious, Forward Planning, Creative, Observant, Relaxed, Resilient, Results Oriented, and Social Desirability. Although the first 11 domains are organized in the manual under more inclusive categories (i.e., Relations with People—Interpersonal; Thinking Style—Administration; Thinking Style—Opportunities; and Feelings and Emotions—Energies), the only scores derived from this questionnaire are on these 12 domains.

The manual authors describe the characteristics of a "low scorer" and a "high scorer" on each of the 12 domains and point to how each dimension may be important in a particular selling position. Although in general the selection process would favor the high scorer on each of the first 11 dimensions, in some sales positions, note the authors of the manual, the type of position will determine whether it is necessary to be high on a dimension like Resilient. Although high Resilient scorers are said to be good prospects for positions that involve cold calling and a large customer base, individuals with low Resilient scores may be successful in selling positions that require long-term relationships with a relatively few customers. The Social Desirability scale is meant to serve a "lie" detection function, but the manual makes reference to research suggesting that Social Desirability scores are positively related to performance in certain sales positions and, therefore, this scale too may serve a predictive role rather than simply determining whether the candidate is answering the questionnaire truthfully.

The items on the SPQ are answered on a 5-point Likert scale. There are no time limits, and it is reported that it typically takes 20–30 minutes to complete the questionnaire. If after 10 minutes the person has completed fewer than 40 items, the administrator is supposed to urge the test-taker to speed up the pace. Three means of taking the SPQ are possible: paper-and-pencil, Casio pocket calculator, or PC. A profile plotting the respondent's sten scores is the format for presenting the results.

Three norm tables are provided in the manual, each one presenting raw score to sten score conversions. The first table ($N = 245$), called the composite table, is based on the responses of all U.S. residents who had taken the SPQ as of August 1990. The other two tables are specific to the two groups that went into forming this composite, namely (*a*) 187 manager trainees at a national retail shoe store chain, and (*b*) 58 sales representatives of manufactured products. Summary descriptive statistics on these groups are reported for race, sex, and age. (The race of the latter group is unknown.) The manual's authors report that the test, originally developed in the United Kingdom, has only recently been introduced to the U.S. and that more extensive norm data are being collected. Users are urged to develop their own local norms and to share their data with the publishers of the test. Registered users are promised updated norms as they become available.

Two studies concerned with the SPQ's reliability are discussed. The first one, based on a sample of college students (N = 113), dealt with both the internal consistency and the test-retest reliability of the 12 domains making up this instrument. The average internal consistency reliability, measured using Cronbach's alpha, was .73 (ranging from .55 on Resilient to .84 on Creative). Test-retest reliability (2 to 4 weeks between administrations) was somewhat higher on all 12 scales, ranging from .73 to .88, with an average of .82; four domains had reliability coefficients above .85. The second study, using the 245 subjects who constitute the composite normative sample, explored the scale's internal consistency reliability, also using the Cronbach alpha technique. The average internal consistency was .68, with a low of .55 (Forward Planning) to a high of .82 (Creative).

The evidence generated to support the uniqueness of the 12 domains consists of intercorrelation coefficients between these domains. Although some of these correlations are in the .4 to .5 range, it is argued that none of the intercorrelations are "excessively high." On this basis the conclusion is drawn that each domain is measuring a unique dimension of behavior.

The validity of the SPQ was assessed in four criterion-related studies and one content validity study. Little detail is reported on the content validity study other than to indicate that it occurred in the United Kingdom and was based on a job analysis of the insurance agent role. In the first criterion-related validation effort, the concurrent validity of the SPQ was studied by (*a*) correlating SPQ scores to job performance ratings on six facets (i.e., dealing with customers, selling skills, administration/processing, organization of work, motivation, and an overall performance appraisal rating); and (*b*) correlating SPQ scores to rankings on two of these six criteria (selling skills, overall performance). The subjects were insurance agents (N = 151) who were rated by two of their managers. The correlations between the two raters were used to correct the criterion for unreliability. The uncorrected and corrected coefficients, which were significant at the .05 level, are reported in a table. Out of the 192 correlations (8 criteria x 12 SPQ domains x 2 raters), 38 (20%) were statistically significant. The uncorrected coefficients ranged from .14 to .32. When corrected for criterion unreliability, they went up slightly, ranging from .18 to .47; of these, 5% were in the teens, 53% were in the .20s, 34% were in the .30s, and 8% were in the .40s. Four of the domains did not correlate to any criterion (Systematic, Creative, Relaxed, Resilient). However, when the two managers' ratings were averaged, four significant correlations (in the upper teens) were found for the Creative and Relaxed domains.

In the second study, a sample of sales assistants (N = 121 to 158) in an electrical products retail outlet were rated by their managers on attendance record, enthusiasm, competitive spirit, and overall performance. Their SPQ scores were related to these ratings as well as to an individual sales figure. Of the 60 correlations, 9 (15%) were statistically significant, and ranged between .18 and .34 (average = .23). These correlations involved only half of the domains. The manual's authors explain the failure to find significant relationships between the other SPQ scores and job performance may be due to the nature of the sales assistant's role.

A sample of retail sales assistants (N = 105) served as subjects in the third study, which examined the relationship between SPQ scores and nine measures of job performance (confidence with customers, selling skills, general ability, communication skills, conscientiousness, product knowledge, motivation, team work, and overall job performance) derived from a job analysis. The average rating of two supervisors served as the criterion on each job aspect. Fourteen (13%) of the computed correlations were statistically significant, and involved 8 of the 12 SPQ domains. The statistically significant correlations ranged from .19 to .31 (average = .23). Interestingly, the highest correlation was negative in direction, between team work and Confidence, suggesting that sales assistants with low confidence were better team workers.

The last study discussed under validity deals with correlations between the SPQ and a test of selling principles (Sales Comprehension Test) and a series of tests (called The Sales Aptitude Test) that measure seven factors (i.e., sales judgment, selling interest, personality factors, identification of self with selling occupations, level of aspiration, insight into human nature, awareness of sales approach). The correlations involved SPQ sten scores, Sales Comprehension Test percentile scores, and 5-point risk indices from The Sales Aptitude Test. The subjects, on whom no descriptive data are available (according to the manual), consisted of "nation-wide sales representatives" (p. 65; N = 57). The 17 statistically significant correlations derived from this analysis, involving 8 SPQ domains, were in the .22 to .37 range, with an average of .27.

With respect to culture-fair testing, the manual authors suggest that an organization relying on the SPQ for selection purposes conduct a job analysis to determine if the SPQ matches the attributes necessary to perform a particular sales position. In other words, "local" validation is recommended whenever feasible. (The publisher of the SPQ is a consulting organization, which an be engaged for this purpose.) It is reported that three of the scales (Empathy, Resilient, and Social Desirability) show ethnic group differences, and that on five of the scales there are differences between the scores of males and females. However, as is acknowledged in the manual, the differences are relatively small, and the manual authors recommend that users not develop separate norms unless differential validity can be demonstrated.

After a careful consideration of the manual and the evidence contained therein supporting the psychometric integrity of the SPQ, several conclusions seem warranted. To begin with, aside from a few minor typos, the SPQ Manual & Users Guide is very well organized and written in clear, concise language. The presentation of psychometric concepts and not just the results of statistical calculations is an excellent idea, given the possibility that the intended consumers of this product may not be very sophisticated about these matters. The manual's authors do an excellent job of giving the test user an orientation to the fundamentals of psychological measurement.

On the other hand, data available in the manual in support of the uniqueness of each of the 12 domains are not very convincing. In order to demonstrate the nonoverlap of domains, it does not suffice to show that only low to moderate interdomain correlations exist. An item analysis indicating that the items on each domain are more highly correlated with the domain on which they are currently located than with the other domains would be more reassuring. Likewise, a factor analysis could be performed to demonstrate some correspondence between the domains and empirically derived factors. When the test-retest reliability on a scale is higher than its internal consistency, as is the case with the SPQ, it suggests that either the items within a given domain have low correlations with each other, or the number of items within a domain is too small.

Both the internal consistency and the temporal stability of the SPQ are low for an instrument meant for supporting decisions about individuals. Generally, a reliability of .85 or better is expected, but admittedly this level is hard to achieve for scales that measure noncognitive variables. If the item analysis discussed above has not been tried, perhaps relocating some items would help improve reliability.

The reported studies meant to demonstrate that the SPQ measures the intended characteristics resulted in modest validity coefficients, even when corrections for attenuation due to the unreliability in the criterion were made. Although the size of the validity coefficients is troublesome, it has been argued by some that even small correlations may have substantial impact on improving decision making. The number of correlations that were statistically significant is rather disappointing when one considers the large number of correlations that were actually computed. One could argue that a substantial portion of the relationships found to be significant were so by chance alone. It is puzzling that in one of the validity studies correlations were computed on percentile scores, especially in view of the cautions given in the manual about percentiles. The manual's authors note this instrument has been adapted only recently for use in the United States. If there are additional psychometric data on the SPQ based on British samples, I think such information should be included in the next manual so as to permit one to get a more comprehensive understanding of this selection tool.

The currently available norms on the SPQ are based on small samples of convenience and may be unique to a specific position in a particular industry. It is known that not all sales positions require the same skills, as the validation studies on the SPQ also seem to suggest. The expanded norms that are promised should make the instrument more useful from this perspective. I therefore recommend that users of the SPQ demonstrate its validity in their own setting, linking it to a job analysis. If group size permits, local norms should be developed.

[338]

SAQ-Adult Probation [Substance Abuse Questionnaire].

Purpose: "Designed specifically for adult probation department and corrections use as a risk and needs assessment instrument."
Population: Adult probationers.
Publication Dates: 1989–92.
Acronym: SAQ.
Scores: Behaviors/characteristics relevant to probation risk and needs assessment in 6 areas: Validity/Truthfulness Scale, Alcohol Scale, Drug Scale, Aggressivity Scale, Resistance Scale, Stress Coping Abilities.
Administration: Individual or group.
Price Data: $5–7 per test; other price data available from publisher.
Time: (25–30) minutes.
Comments: Self-administered, computer-scored test.
Author: Behavior Data Systems, Ltd.
Publisher: Behavior Data Systems, Ltd.

Review of the SAQ-Adult Probation [Substance Abuse Questionnaire] by TONY TONEATTO, Scientist, Addiction Research Foundation, Toronto, Ontario, Canada:

The Substance Abuse Questionnaire-Adult Probation (SAQ-AP) is a 153-item test, computer administered and scored, requiring approximately 30 minutes to complete. The SAQ-AP is designed to aid probation officers and parole staff in assessing the severity of substance abuse, violence proneness, and emotional disturbance of adult parolees. Risk levels for six scaled measures (Truthfulness, Alcohol, Drug, Aggressivity, Resistance, Stress Coping Abilities) are generated in percentile form with each scale accompanied by the appropriate, computer-generated, recommendations. The Truthfulness or Validity scale provides a measure of the validity of the client's response based on the degree of defensiveness demonstrated and is used to determine the validity of the individual's response profile.

The authors of the SAQ-AP suggest that it is suitable for use by staff who are neither clinicians nor diagnosticians but who must nevertheless identify potentially risky behavior on the part of their parolee clientele and develop appropriate courses of action. The SAQ-AP also identifies important attitudes towards, and motivation to change, risk behaviors, how the client perceives their problems, and degree of, and reasons for, involvement in the legal system. The authors also briefly describe a short form of the SAQ-AP to be used when time is at a premium or for clients who have difficulty reading. The short form consists of 64 items, requires 10 minutes to complete, but only provides scores on four scales (Truthfulness Scale, Alcohol Scale, Drug Scale, Risk Scale).

The SAQ-AP II, developed in 1993, includes two additional scales (Antisocial, Violence) and consists of 169 items. The SAQ-AP II also contains an additional 40 items measuring the degree to which various difficulties (e.g., insomnia), self-perceptions (e.g., self-control), and emotional states (e.g., tension) characterize the individual. However, at no point in the various literature describing the SAQ-AP is it explicitly stated if, and how, the responses to these items are utilized in the generation of the scaled measures. Because the SAQ-AP II is very recent and no evaluation of the psychometric properties of version II have yet been reported this review focuses on the SAQ-AP.

There is some concern about the nature of the computer-generated recommendations produced on the basis of the clients' response profiles. Such interpretive strategies are generally meaningful at an aggregate level but difficult to apply to any one individual. The recommendations provided by the SAQ-AP tend to be very brief, general, and highly restricted in the kinds of suggestions offered and typically direct the parole or probation official either to increase supervision of the parolee or to obtain treatment for the indicated problem (e.g., alcohol, violence). Although the ready availability of such recommendations may make them convenient and efficient it does raise the issue of how such advice improves upon the parole/probation official's own assessment and awareness of the parolee's history. For example, the SAQ-AP recommends that an individual who scores in the problem range on the Resistance scale be shown firm structure, clear behavioral expectations, and consequences for noncompliance. How should the parole official interpret this advice? What is firm structure? Expectations for what kind of behavior? What kinds of consequences and for which types of noncompliance? A major limitation of the SAQ-AP (and SAQ-AP II) is the difficulty in the interpretation and operationalization of what are essentially very general recommendations.

In addition, the SAQ-AP is unbalanced in its assessment because it focuses on risk assessment, deficiencies, and problems but fails to assess information that might be of greater utility in developing interventions such as the types of high-risk situations that elicit alcohol abuse or violence, client strengths and assets, or the nature of the coping skills the client does possess.

A great deal of data on the reliability of the SAQ-AP (but not for version II, which also includes the Antisocial scale and the Violence scale) is provided with a large number of subjects in various settings and geographic regions. Cronbach alphas tend to be high for all of the scales, generally greater than .80. Test-retest reliability coefficient of .71 (one-week time interval) is provided for parolee populations.

The validity of the SAQ-AP is much less established. Considerable data on the concurrent validity of the instrument are provided but only in its association with the Minnesota Multiphasic Personality Inventory (MMPI) (except for two studies with the polygraph test and the Driver Risk Inventory). Evidence of the association between the SAQ-AP and other measures of alcohol or drug dependence, aggressivity, antisocial behavior, or social desirability is not reported. Thus, the range of alternative and valid instruments that could be used to assess the concurrent validity of the SAQ-AP is severely limited; in any case the size of the correlations with the MMPI, albeit statistically significant, tend to be rather small and do not provide strong evidence of the SAQ-AP's concurrent validity. Predictive validity data for the SAQ-AP are conspicuously lacking. Such data, critical to evaluating whether the results generated by this instrument are actually associated with outcomes, are absent. For example, do individuals who score as high risk individuals have a higher rate of recidivism? Furthermore, there is no assessment of the construct validity of the SAQ-AP. For example, do individuals who score high on the alcohol or drug scales also meet diagnostic criteria for psychoactive substance use disorder? Do those who score high on measures of antisocial or aggressive behavior meet diagnostic criteria for antisocial personality disorder? Given the wide range of constructs that appear to be assessed by this instrument it is probably inaccurate to label this instrument as a measure of substance abuse as implied by the title. Thus, the overall evidence for the validity of the SAQ-AP is very poor.

The summary of research on the SAQ-AP does not report any norms for the population for which this test is designed. Although the authors state that the percentiles generated in their computer report incorporates such information, presentation of such data in the research summary would have been useful.

One positive feature of the SAQ-AP is that the authors appear committed to exploring gender differences and to that end report several studies showing that gender differences occur in only some geographic regions. The authors also claim that the SAQ-AP, when administered in these regions, is normed differently to reflect such gender differences.

In summary, although the reliability of the SAQ-AP is generally well established, the validity of the SAQ-AP is less well established. Concurrent validity is limited primarily to the MMPI; nothing can be said of its predictive or construct validity. It bears repeating that the SAQ-AP II has yet to be submitted to the psychometric evaluation conducted on the SAQ-AP. Conceptually, the question still remains as to whether the SAQ-AP conveys any useful information additional to simply asking the client if they have an alcohol-drug problem, if they are violent, and how they cope with stress. Integrating this in the context of their history is not addressed.

[339]

Scale for the Assessment of Negative Symptoms.

Purpose: To assess negative symptoms of schizophrenia.
Population: Psychiatric inpatients and outpatients of all ages.
Publication Dates: 1981–84.
Acronym: SANS.
Scores: 25 behavioral rating scores within 5 areas: Affective Flattening or Blunting, Alogia, Avolition-Apathy, Anhedonia-Asociality, Attention.
Administration: Individual.
Price Data: Available from publisher.
Foreign Language Editions: Available in Spanish, French, Italian, German, Portuguese, Japanese, Chinese, and Greek.
Time: [15–30] minutes.
Comments: May be used in conjunction with the Scale for the Assessment of Positive Symptoms (SAPS; 340).
Author: Nancy C. Andreasen.
Publisher: Nancy C. Andreasen.
Cross References: See T4:2325 (37 references); for information on an earlier edition, see 9:1069 (2 references).

TEST REFERENCES

1. Andreasen, N. C., Flaum, M., Swayze, V. W., II, Tyrrell, G., & Arndt, S. (1990). Positive and negative symptoms in schizophrenia. *Archives of General Psychiatry, 47*, 615-621.

2. Goldberg, T. E., Ragland, D., Torrey, F., Gold, J. M., Bigelow, L. B., & Weinberger, D. R. (1990). Neuropsychological assessment of monozygotic twins discordant for schizophrenia. *Archives of General Psychiatry, 47*, 1066-1072.

3. Hogg, B., Jackson, H. J., Rudd, R. P., & Edwards, J. (1990). Diagnosing personality disorders in recent-onset schizophrenia. *The Journal of Nervous and Mental Disease, 178*, 194-199.

4. Levinson, D. F., Simpson, G. M., Singh, H., Yadalam, K., Jain, A., Stephanos, M. J., & Silver, P. (1990). Fluphenazine dose, clinical response, and extrapyramidal symptoms during acute treatment. *Archives of General Psychiatry, 47*, 761-768.

5. Morrison, R. L., Bellack, A. S., Wixted, J. T., & Mueser, K. T. (1990). Positive and negative symptoms in schizophrenia: A cluster-analytic approach. *The Journal of Nervous and Mental Disease, 178*, 377-384.

6. Swayze, V. W., II, Andreasen, N. C., Alliger, R. J., Ehrhardt, J. C., & Yuh, W. T. C. (1990). Structural brain abnormalities in bipolar affective disorder. *Archives of General Psychiatry, 47*, 1054-1059.

7. Braff, D. L., Heaton, R., Kuck, J., Cullom, M., Moranville, J., Grant, I., & Zisook, S. (1991). A generalized pattern of neuropsychological deficits in outpatients with chronic schizophrenia with heterogeneous Wisconsin Card Sorting Test results. *Archives of General Psychiatry, 48*, 891-898.

8. Breier, A., Schreiber, J. L., Dyer, J., & Pickar, D. (1991). National Institute of Mental Health longitudinal study of chronic schizophrenia. *Archives of General Psychiatry, 48*, 239-246.

9. Fenton, W. S., & McGlashan, T. H. (1991). Natural history of schizophrenia subtypes. *Archives of General Psychiatry, 48*, 978-986.

10. McGorry, P. D., Chanen, A., McCarthy, E., Van Riel, R., McKenzie, D., & Singh, B. S. (1991). Posttraumatic stress disorder following recent-onset psychosis: An unrecognized postpsychotic syndrome. *The Journal of Nervous and Mental Disease, 179*, 253-258.

11. Andreasen, N. C., Flaum, M., & Arndt, S. (1992). The Comprehensive Assessment of Symptoms and History (CASH): An instrument for assessing diagnosis and psychopathology. *Archives of General Psychiatry, 49*, 615-623.

12. Andreasen, N. C., Rezai, K., Alliger, R., Swayze, V. W., II, Flaum, M., Kirchner, P., Cohen, G., & O'Leary, D. S. (1992). Hypofrontality in neuroleptic-naive patients and in patients with chronic schizophrenia. *Archives of General Psychiatry, 49*, 943-958.

13. Brown, K. W., & White, T. (1992). Sub-syndromes of tardive dyskinesia and some clinical correlates. *Psychological Medicine, 22*, 923-927.

14. Degreef, G., Ashtari, M., Bogerts, B., Bilder, R. M., Jody, D. N., Alvir, J. M. J., & Lieberman, J. A. (1992). Volumes of ventricular system subdivisions measured from magnetic resonance images in first-episode schizophrenic patients. *Archives of General Psychiatry, 49*, 531-537.

15. Tandon, R., Shipley, J. E., Taylor, S., Greden, J. F., Eiser, A., DeQuardo, J., & Goodson, J. (1992). Electroencephalographic sleep abnormalities in schizophrenia: Relationship to positive/negative symptoms and prior neuroleptic treatment. *Archives of General Psychiatry, 49*, 185-194.

16. Borod, J. C., Martin, C. C., Alpert, M., Brozgold, A., & Welkowitz, J. (1993). Perception of facial emotion in schizophrenic and right brain-damaged patients. *The Journal of Nervous and Mental Disease, 181*, 494-502.

17. Dollfus, S., Petit, M., & Menard, J. F. (1993). Relationship between depressive and positive symptoms in schizophrenia. *Journal of Affective Disorders, 28*, 61-69.

18. Goldberg, T. E., Torrey, E. F., Gold, J. M., Ragland, J. D., Bigelow, L. B., & Weinberger, D. R. (1993). Learning and memory in monozygotic twins discordant for schizophrenia. *Psychological Medicine, 23*, 71-85.

19. Hafner, H., Riecher-Rossler, A., an der Heiden, W., Maurer, K., Fatkenheuer, B., & Loffler, W. (1993). Generating and testing a causal explanation of the gender difference in age at first onset of schizophrenia. *Psychological Medicine, 23*, 925-940.

20. Jackson, H. J., & Pica, S. (1993). An investigation into the internal structure of DSM-III antisocial personality disorder. *Psychological Reports, 72*, 355-367.

21. Lieberman, J. A., Jody, D., Alvir, J., Ashtari, M., Levy, D. L., Bogerts, B., Degreef, G., Mayerhoff, D. I., & Cooper, T. (1993). Brain morphology, dopamine, and eye-tracking abnormalities in first-episode schizophrenia. *Archives of General Psychiatry, 50*, 357-368.

22. Lieberman, J., Jody, D., Geisler, S., Alvir, J., Loebel, A., Szymanski, S., Woerner, M., & Borenstein, M. (1993). Time course and biologic correlates of treatment response in first-episode schizophrenia. *Archives of General Psychiatry, 50*, 369-376.

23. McConaghy, N., Catts, S. V., Michie, P. T., Fox, A., Ward, P. B., & Shelley, A. (1993). P300 indexes thought disorder in schizophrenics, but allusive thinking in normal subjects. *The Journal of Nervous and Mental Disease, 181*, 176-182.

24. Ohaeri, J. U. (1993). Long-term outcome of treated schizophrenia in a Nigerian cohort. *The Journal of Nervous and Mental Disease, 181*, 514-516.

25. Parnas, J., Cannon, T. D., Jacobsen, B., Schulsinger, H., Schulsinger, F., & Mednick, S. A. (1993). Lifetime DSM-III-R diagnostic outcomes in the offspring of schizophrenic mothers: Results from the Copenhagen high-risk study. *Archives of General Psychiatry, 50*, 707-714.

26. Stirling, J., Tantam, D., Thomas, P., Newby, D., Montague, L., Ring, N., & Rowe, S. (1993). Expressed emotion and schizophrenia: The ontogeny of EE during an 18-month follow-up. *Psychological Medicine, 23*, 771-778.

27. Verbraak, M. J. P. M., Hoogduin, C. A. L., & Schaap, C. (1993). The heterogeneity of schizophrenic information processing and negative versus positive symptoms. *The Journal of Nervous and Mental Disease, 181*, 738-743.

28. Alpert, M., Clark, A., & Pouget, E. R. (1994). The syntactic role of pauses in the speech of schizophrenic patients with alogia. *Journal of Abnormal Psychology*, *103*, 750-757.

29. Amador, X. F., Flaum, M., Andreasen, N. C., Strauss, D. H., Yule, S. A., Clark, S. C., & Gorman, J. M. (1994). Awareness of illness in schizophrenia and schizoaffective and mood disorders. *Archives of General Psychiatry*, *51*, 826-836.

30. Aylward, E. H., Reiss, A., Barta, P. E., Tien, A., Han, W., Lee, J., & Pearlson, G. D. (1994). Magnetic resonance imaging measurement of posterior fossa structures in schizophrenia. *American Journal of Psychiatry*, *151*, 1448-1452.

31. Bell, R. C., Low, L. H., Jackson, H. J., Dudgeon, P. L., Copolov, D. L., & Singh, B. S. (1994). Latent trait modelling of symptoms of schizophrenia. *Psychological Medicine*, *24*, 335-345.

32. Berenbaum, S. A., Taylor, M. A., & Cloninger, C. R. (1994). Family study of schizophrenia and personality. *Journal of Abnormal Psychology*, *103*, 475-484.

33. Blanchard, J. J., Bellack, A. S., & Mueser, K. T. (1994). Affective and social-behavioral correlates of physical and social anhedonia in schizophrenia. *Journal of Abnormal Psychology*, *103*, 719-728.

34. Brier, A., Buchanan, R. W., Kirkpatrick, B., Orlando, R. D., Irish, D., Summerfelt, A., & Carpenter, W. T. (1994). Effects of clozapine on positive and negative symptoms in outpatients with schizophrenia. *American Journal of Psychiatry*, *151*, 20-26.

35. Buchanan, R. W., & Carpenter, W. T. (1994). Domains of psychopathology: An approach to the reduction of heterogeneity in schizophrenia. *The Journal of Nervous and Mental Disease*, *182*, 193-204.

36. Chakos, M. H., Lieberman, J. A., Bilder, R. M., Borenstein, M., Lerner, G., Bogerts, B., Wu, H., Kinon, B., & Ashtari, M. (1994). Increase in caudate nuclei volumes of first-episode schizophrenic patients taking antipsychotic drugs. *American Journal of Psychiatry*, *151*, 1430-1436.

37. Convit, A., Volavka, J., Czobor, P., DeAsis, J., & Evangelista, C. (1994). Effect of subtle neurological dysfunction on response to haloperidol treatment in schizophrenia. *American Journal of Psychiatry*, *151*, 49-56.

38. Docherty, N. M., Evans, I. M., Sledge, W. H., Seibyl, J. D., & Krystal, J. H. (1994). Affective reactivity of language in schizophrenia. *The Journal of Nervous and Mental Disease*, *182*, 98-102.

39. Fennig, S., Bromet, E. J., Jandorf, L., Schwartz, J. E., Lavelle, J., & Ram, R. (1994). Eliciting psychotic symptoms using a semi-structured diagnostic interview: The importance of collateral sources of information in a first-admission sample. *The Journal of Nervous and Mental Disease*, *182*, 20-26.

40. Fenton, W. S., & McGlashan, T. H. (1994). Antecedents, symptom progression, and long-term outcome of the deficit syndrome in schizophrenia. *American Journal of Psychiatry*, *151*, 351-356.

41. Goff, D. C., Amico, E., Dreyfuss, D., & Ciraulo, D. (1994). A placebo-controlled trial of trihexyphenidyl in unmedicated patients with schizophrenia. *American Journal of Psychiatry*, *151*, 429-431.

42. Gur, R. E., Mozley, P. D., Shtasel, D. L., Cannon, T. D., Gallacher, F., Turetsky, B., Grossman, R., & Gur, R. C. (1994). Clinical subtypes of schizophrenia: Differences in brain and CSF volume. *American Journal of Psychiatry*, *151*, 343-350.

43. Gureje, O., Bamidele, R., & Aderibigbe, Y. A. (1994). Heritability of schizophrenia: A controlled family history investigation in Nigeria. *British Journal of Psychiatry*, *164*, 481-486.

44. Hollister, J. M., Mednick, S. A., Brennan, P., & Cannon, T. D. (1994). Impaired autonomic nervous system habituation in those at genetic risk for schizophrenia. *Archives of General Psychiatry*, *51*, 552-558.

45. Katsanis, J., & Iacono, W. G. (1994). Electrodermal activity and clinical status in chronic schizophrenia. *Journal of Abnormal Psychology*, *103*, 777-783.

46. Kendler, K. S., McGuire, M., Gruenberg, A. M., & Walsh, D. (1994). An epidemiologic, clinical, and family study of simple schizophrenia in County Roscommon, Ireland. *American Journal of Psychiatry*, *151*, 27-34.

47. Koreen, A. R., Lieberman, J., Alvir, J., Chakos, M., Loebel, A., Cooper, T., & Kane, J. (1994). Relation of plasma fluphenazine levels to treatment response and extrapyramidal side effects in first-episode schizophrenic patients. *American Journal of Psychiatry*, *151*, 35-39.

48. Koreen, A. R., Lieberman, J., Alvir, J., Mayerhoff, D., Loebel, A., Chakos, M., Amin, F., & Cooper, T. (1994). Plasma homovanillic and levels in first-episode schizophrenia: Psychopathology and treatment response. *Archives of General Psychiatry*, *51*, 132-138.

49. Malla, A. K., & Norman, R. M. G. (1994). Prodromal symptoms in schizophrenia. *British Journal of Psychiatry*, *164*, 487-493.

50. Mayerhoff, D. I., Loebel, A. D., Alvir, J. M. J., Szymanski, S. R., Geisler, S. H., Borenstein, M., & Lieberman, J. A. (1994). The deficit state in first-episode schizophrenia. *American Journal of Psychiatry*, *151*, 1417-1422.

51. Mueser, K. T., Sayers, S. L., Schooler, N. R., Rosalind, M. M., & Haas, G. L. (1994). A multisite investigation of the reliability of the Scale for the Assessment of Negative Symptoms. *American Journal of Psychiatry*, *151*, 1453-1462.

52. Oke, S., Saatchi, R., Allen, E., Hudson, N. R., & Jervis, B. W. (1994). The contingent negative variation in positive and negative types of schizophrenia. *American Journal of Psychiatry*, *151*, 432-433.

53. Perry, W., & Braff, D. L. (1994). Information-processing deficits and thought disorder in schizophrenia. *American Journal of Psychiatry*, *151*, 363-367.

54. Poreh, A. M., Chapin, K., Rosen, M. D., & Youssef, I. (1994). Correlations between MMPI and the Scale for the Assessment of Positive Symptoms and the Scale for the Assessment of Negative Symptoms in schizophrenic patients. *Journal of Personality Assessment*, *63*, 275-283.

55. Schmand, B., Kuipers, T., van der Gaag, M., Bosveld, J., Bulthuis, F., & Jellema, M. (1994). Cognitive disorders and negative symptoms as correlates of motivational deficits in psychotic patients. *Psychological Medicine*, *24*, 869-884.

56. Seidenberg, M., Haltiner, A., Taylor, M. A., Hermann, B. B., & Wyler, A. (1994). Development and validation of a multiple ability self-report questionnaire. *Journal of Clinical and Experimental Neuropsychology*, *16*, 93-104.

57. Taylor, M. A., & Amir, N. (1994). The problem of missing clinical data for research in psychopathology: Some solution guidelines. *The Journal of Nervous and Mental Disease*, *182*, 222-229.

58. Taylor, M. A., Reed, R., & Berenbaum, S. (1994). Patterns of speech disorders in schizophrenia and mania. *The Journal of Nervous and Mental Disease*, *182*, 319-326.

59. van Kammen, D. P., Agren, H., Yao, J. K., O'Connor, D. T., Gurklis, J., & Peters, J. L. (1994). Noradrenergic activity and prediction of psychotic relapse following haloperidol withdrawal in schizophrenia. *American Journal of Psychiatry*, *151*, 379-384.

60. Wetzel, H., Hillert, H., Grunder, G., & Benkert, O. (1994). Roxindole, a dopamine autoreceptor agonist, in the treatment of positive and negative schizophrenic symptoms. *American Journal of Psychiatry*, *151*, 1499-1502.

61. Xiong, W., Phillips, M. R., Hu, X., Wang, R., Dai, Q., Kleinman, J., & Kleinman, A. (1994). Family-based intervention for schizophrenic patients in China: A randomised controlled trial. *British Journal of Psychiatry*, *165*, 239-247.

62. Arnold, S. E., Gur, R. E., Shapiro, R. M., Fisher, K. R., Moberg, P. J., Gibney, M. R., Gur, R. C., Blackwell, P., & Trojanowski, J. Q. (1995). Prospective clinicopathologic studies of schizophrenia: Accrual and assessment of patients. *American Journal of Psychiatry*, *152*, 731-737.

63. Catts, S. V., Shelley, A., Ward, P. B., Liebert, B., McConaghy, N., Andrews, S., & Michie, P. T. (1995). Brain potential evidence for an auditory sensory memory deficit in schizophrenia. *American Journal of Psychiatry*, *152*, 213-219.

64. Corey-Bloom, J., Jernigan, T., Archibald, S., Harris, M. J., & Jeste, D. V. (1995). Quantitative magnetic resonance imaging of the brain in late-life schizophrenia. *American Journal of Psychiatry*, *152*, 447-449.

65. Flaum, M., Swayze, V. W., O'Leary, D. S., Yuh, W. T. C., Erhardt, J. C., Arndt, S. V., & Andreasen, N. C. (1995). Effects of diagnosis, laterality, and gender on brain morphology in schizophrenia. *American Journal of Psychiatry*, *152*, 704-714.

66. Goldberg, T. E., Gold, J. M., Torrey, E. F., & Weinberger, D. R. (1995). Lack of sex differences in the neuropsychological performance of patients with schizophrenia. *American Journal of Psychiatry*, *152*, 883-888.

67. Jeste, D. V., Harris, M. J., Krull, A., Kuck, J., McAdams, L. A., & Heaton, R. (1995). Clinical and neuropsychological characteristics of patients with late-onset schizophrenia. *American Journal of Psychiatry*, *152*, 722-730.

68. Kendler, K. S., McGuire, M., Gruenberg, A. M., & Walsh, D. (1995). Examining the validity of DSM-III-R schizoaffective disorder and its putative subtypes in the Roscommon Family Study. *American Journal of Psychiatry*, *152*, 755-764.

69. Levinson, D. F., Simpson, G. M., Lo, E. S., Cooper, T. B., Singh, H., Yadalam, K., & Stephanos, M. J. (1995). Fluphenazine plasma levels, dosage, efficacy, and side effects. *American Journal of Psychiatry*, *152*, 765-771.

70. Paillere-Martinot, M., Lecrubier, Y., Martinot, J., & Aubin, F. (1995). Improvement of some schizophrenic deficit symptoms with low doses of amisulpride. *American Journal of Psychiatry*, *152*, 130-133.

71. Peralta, V., Cuesta, M. J., & DeLeon, J. (1995). Positive and negative symptoms/syndromes in schizophrenia: Reliability and validity of different diagnostic systems. *Psychological Medicine*, *25*, 43-50.

72. Slaghuis, W. L., & Bakker, V. J. (1995). Forward and backward visual masking of contour by light in positive- and negative-symptom schizophrenia. *Journal of Abnormal Psychology*, *104*, 41-54.

73. Szymanski, S., Lieberman, J. A., Alvir, J. M., Mayerhoff, D., Loebel, A., Geisler, S., Chakos, M., Koreen, A., Jody, D., Kane, J., Woerner, M., & Cooper. T. (1995). Gender differences in onset of illness, treatment

response, course, and biological indexes in first-episode schizophrenic patients. *American Journal of Psychiatry, 152,* 698-703.

74. Tyrka, A. R., Cannon, T. D., Haslam, N., Mednick, S. A., Schulsinger, F., Schulsinger, H., & Parnas, J. (1995). The latent structure of schizotypy: I. Premorbid indicators of a taxon of individuals at risk for schizophrenia-spectrum disorders. *Journal of Abnormal Psychology, 104,* 173-183.

75. Vita, A., Bressi, S., Perani, D., Invernizzi, G., Giobbio, G. M., Massimiliano, D., Garbarini, M., Del Sole, A., & Fazio, F. (1995). High resolution SPECT study of regional cerebral blood flow in drug-free and drug-naive schizophrenic patients. *American Journal of Psychiatry, 152,* 876-882.

Review of the Scale for the Assessment of Negative Symptoms by SUZANNE KING, Assistant Professor of Psychiatry, McGill University, Montreal, Quebec, Canada:

The Scale for the Assessment of Negative Symptoms (SANS) was the first scale developed specifically to measure the negative symptoms of schizophrenia. The SANS includes items reflecting the severity of 19 specific negative symptoms and signs regrouped into five symptom classes or subscales: Affective Flattening, Alogia, Avolition-Apathy, Anhedonia-Asociality, and Attention deficit. Each subscale also includes a global rating resulting in a total of 24 items. Symptoms are rated on a 6-point scale where 0 indicates *none*, and 5 is *severe*. One may average the ratings for symptoms within a subscale or use the global rating as a subscale score. Similarly, one may describe the severity of the negative symptom syndrome by either summing the five global ratings or by summing all 24 items.

Test materials for the 1984 edition include a 14-page manual and a scoring protocol for use with the SANS and the companion Scale for the Assessment of Positive Symptoms (SAPS; 340). The manual includes a single-paragraph description of each of the five subscales, descriptions of each of the 19 specific signs and symptoms measured, and brief descriptions of each possible rating.

The author recommends rating the severity of the symptoms over the previous month. Information required to make the ratings is derived from a clinical interview with the patient and, ideally, from additional information gathered from patient charts and from discussion with significant others.

For a description of the development of the SANS and its psychometric properties, one is referred to two journal articles (Andreasen, 1982; Andreasen & Olsen, 1982). The SANS was developed at a time when the distinction between positive and negative symptoms in schizophrenia was just beginning to emerge and reflects the author's conceptualization of negative symptoms at that time. Subsequent changes to the contents of the scale, consistent with research, were made between the publication of the 1982 articles and the current 1984 edition: Patient self-report items for each of the five subscales, and an item describing inappropriate affect (which had been included in the Affective Flattening subscale) were removed.

The author's report on reliability (Andreasen, 1982) is based on the study of 26 schizophrenic patients using the original, 30-item SANS. Interrater reliability was tested using two master's-level raters each of whom had more than 2 years experience conducting clinical psychiatric interviews. Interviewers administered the SANS jointly and gathered supplemental information from charts and from discussions with nurses. Intraclass correlations for the global ratings ranged from .70 for Affective Flattening to .88 for Alogia. For individual items, correlations ranged from .70 for lack of vocal inflections to .92 for grooming and hygiene and for inattentiveness.

Internal consistency (Cronbach's alpha) was lowest for the Anhedonia-Asociality subscale (.632) and highest for the Attentional Impairment subscale (.844). The alpha for the composite score was .885. Similar internal consistency scores have been reported in other studies of the SANS.

Andreason and Olsen (1982) describe efforts at establishing construct and predictive validity for the SANS using a sample of 52 schizophrenic patients. Using the SANS to measure negative symptoms, and two other scales to measure positive symptoms (the SAPS had not yet been developed), the authors classified subjects into three types: positive, negative, and mixed symptom types. Based on the literature, Andreason hypothesized that patients in the negative symptom group would have poorer premorbid adjustment, more cognitive deficits, larger ventricular brain ratios, and poorer work and educational attainment than those in the positive symptom group. She also predicted that patients in the negative symptom group would have lower Global Assessment Scale scores at both hospital admission and discharge than those in the positive symptom group. Results supported the construct and criterion validity of the SANS. Predictive validity was supported as patients in the negative symptom group were functioning less well at discharge than those in the positive symptom group. This study, using the SANS and, this time, the SAPS, was replicated with 110 schizophrenic patients (Andreason, Flaum, Swayze, Tyrrell, & Arndt, 1990). They obtained very similar results with the exception that patients with negative symptoms did not have significantly larger ventricular-brain ratios than those with mixed or positive symptom syndromes.

A final test of the validity of the SANS involved a factor analysis of all the items included in the assessment of both positive and negative symptoms. Four factors emerged in the results. The first factor explained nearly 43% of the variance and included all of the SANS global ratings, each with strong positive loadings. This first factor also included the hallmark positive symptoms (hallucinations and delusions) each with strong, negative loadings. These results suggest that positive and negative symptoms are at different ends of the same spectrum.

One strength of the SANS is that each of the five major negative symptoms is assessed by several items. The Brief Psychiatric Scale (BPRS; Overall & Gorham, 1961), for example, uses single items to assess each of the three symptoms in its negative symptom cluster. The larger number of items in the SANS used to assess the negative syndrome should make it a more reliable measure than shorter scales. The use of anchor points describing the behaviors that warrant each possible rating should enhance interrater reliability (although the equality of intervals between ratings may be threatened).

A major shortcoming of the SANS is its manual; it does not come close to meeting APA standards. It does not describe the development of the scale, nor make recommendations about the kinds of inferences that can be drawn from SANS scores. There is no support for the equal weighting of items within subscales nor for the equal weighting of subscales in the calculation of the total score. There are no guidelines for conducting the clinical interview and only one or two suggested questions for each item in only two of the five subscales. Standardization of assessment and, therefore, generalizability across patients and across studies is further compromised by the optional consideration of data obtained outside of the clinical interview. Although Andreason does offer training at the University of Iowa, and despite the existence of training tapes, training requirements and opportunities are not mentioned in the manual.

A danger inherent in all scales attempting to measure negative symptoms is the tendency for akinesia and depression to be confounded with negative symptoms such as flat affect. The manual ought to caution users about this danger.

In summary, there is some support for the reliability of the SANS as well as for its content, construct, and criterion-related validity. The scale does, however, require additional work to meet APA standards for reliability, validity, scaling and norming, and for test publication. The manual needs to be expanded to describe the development, validity, reliability, and standard errors of measurement, as well as norms for hospitalized and outpatient populations, all for the newer 24-item version. Although the scale requires improvement, this has not prevented the SANS from becoming a popular measure of negative symptoms, which is well-respected by the psychiatric community. Competing instruments, such as the Positive and Negative Symptom Scale (PANSS; Kay, Fiszbein, & Opler, 1987) and recent modifications of the BPRS (see Lukoff, Liberman, & Nuechterlein, 1986) are equally respectable.

REVIEWER'S REFERENCES

Overall, J., & Gorham, D. (1961). The Brief Psychiatric Rating Scale. *Psychological Reports, 10*, 799-812.

Andreasen, N. C. (1982). Negative symptoms in schizophrenia: Definition and reliability. *Archives of General Psychiatry, 39*, 784-788.

Andreasen, N. C., & Olsen, S. (1982). Negative v. positive schizophrenia: Definition and validation. *Archives of General Psychiatry, 39*, 789-794.

Lukoff, D., Liberman, R. P., & Nuechterlein, K. H. (1986). Symptom monitoring in the rehabilitation of schizophrenic patients. *Schizophrenia Bulletin, 12*, 578-602.

Kay, S. R., Fiszbein, A., & Opler, L. A. (1987). The Positive and Negative Syndrome Scale (PANSS) for schizophrenia. *Schizophrenia Bulletin, 13*, 261-275.

Andreason, N. C., Flaum, M., Swayze, V. W., II, Tyrrell, G., & Arndt, S. (1990). Positive and negative symptoms in schizophrenia. *Archives of General Psychiatry, 47*, 615-621.

Review of the Scale for the Assessment of Negative Symptoms by NIELS G. WALLER, Associate Professor of Psychology, University of California, Davis, Davis, CA:

Contemporary maps of the psychiatric terrain, such as the *DSM-IV* (American Psychiatric Association, 1994), acknowledge that most symptoms of mental illness are only stochastically related to diagnostic categories, and that few symptoms are singularly pathagnomonic. Nevertheless, a handful of diagnostic criteria have been particularly important in guiding psychiatric research on the major mental disorders. In schizophrenia research, for example, the so-called negative symptoms—such as affective blunting, alogia and avolition—have both endured and influenced over 100 years of nosological reorganization and refinement (see Sass, 1989, for a history of negative symptoms in psychiatric nosology). Currently, the negative symptoms represent one of five inclusion criteria for a *DSM-IV* schizophrenia diagnosis.

The Scale for the Assessment of Negative Symptoms (SANS), developed in the early 1980s by Nancy Andreasen, was the first rating scale designed specifically for the comprehensive assessment of negative symptoms in schizophrenia and related disorders. Although other negative symptoms scales are now available (see Kay, 1990, for an insightful review of six positive-negative symptoms scales), the SANS continues to merit close scrutiny because of its enduring popularity and historical importance (e.g., the SANS has been translated and studied in over a dozen languages and cultures, such as: Japanese, Chinese, Portuguese, Greek, Spanish, Italian, French, German, Dutch and Korean).

The SANS measures 19 specific negative symptoms (e.g., unchanging facial expression) and five global negative symptoms (e.g., affective flattening) that can be grouped into the following subscales: Affective Flattening or Blunting, Alogia, Avolition-Apathy, Anhedonia-Asociality, and Attentional Impairment. In some versions of the SANS the subscales contain illustrative behaviors, descriptive vignettes, and useful probes to elicit diagnostic information from the patient. For example, when rating grooming and hygiene behaviors, the clinician can ask: "How often do you bathe or shower?" "Do you change your clothes every day?" and "How often do you do laundry?"

Each item on the SANS is rated on a 6-point Likert scale that quantifies the presence, intensity, or severity of the specific negative symptom. On some versions of the instrument the rater is provided with symptom-threshold exemplars to anchor his or her clinical impressions. For instance, possible scores on the Affective Flattening or Blunting item range from 0 to 5. A score of 3 on this item signifies that the "Subject's expressions are dulled overall, but not absent," whereas a score of 5 indicates that the "Subject's face looks 'wooden' and changes little, if at all throughout the interview." Andreasen acknowledges that "good reliability cannot usually be achieved [on the subscales] without adequate training, even when observation items are stressed" (SANS, p. 51). Consequently, she has developed "a comprehensive set of training materials . . . involving videotapes and case vignettes" (p. 51). These teaching aids were not included in our package of materials, so I am unable to assess their usefulness or thoroughness (interested readers should contact Dr. Andreasen for further information). In several published studies of schizophrenic patients the intersubject agreement (assessed via the kappa coefficient) and internal consistency reliabilities (assessed by Cronbach's alpha) for the five subscales are in the moderate to high range (median kappa = .75, median alpha = .74). In one representative study, the overall reliability (alpha) of the SANS was .85. These values suggest that the SANS can be used to obtain reliable ratings of negative symptoms in clinical populations. This conclusion must be tempered, however, because it is not clear whether similar values would be obtained without additional training in SANS scoring.

The factor structure of the SANS, and the joint factor structure of the SANS and its companion instrument, the Scale for the Assessment of Positive Symptoms (Andreasen, 1984; 340), have been reported in several recent studies. These studies have generally relied on factor analysis (Keefe et al., 1992; Lenzenweger, Dworking, & Wethington, 1989) or principal components analysis (Andreasen & Olsen, 1982; Bilder, Mukherjee, Rieder, & Pandurangi, 1985; Liddle, 1987) to elucidate the latent structure of the SANS item pool. Unfortunately, drawing firm conclusions from this work is well-nigh impossible. Most of the relevant studies used extremely small samples (*n*s from 32 to 52!) and/or questionable statistical procedures. For example, some studies used rotated principal components analysis to determine the latent correlation between the positive and negative symptom dimensions. The principal components model provides *biased* correlations between latent constructs, and thus should not be used for testing theoretical models (Widaman, 1993). Other studies used confirmatory factor analysis approaches to test competing models of the SANS factor structure. However, the maximum likelihood estimation technique that was used in this work yields unbiased chi-square fit statistics *only* when the joint distribution of the observed variables is multivariate normal (or approximately so; see Waller, 1994). With clinical data this assumption is rarely satisfied, and none of the studies I reviewed reported whether this assumption was satisfied with the SANS item pool.

If the SANS has a formal manual, we did not receive it. Our materials included two copies of the scale and a half dozen empirical reports of the SANS in psychiatric research. A manual is urgently needed that brings together basic psychometric information on this instrument, including (*a*) item endorsement frequencies broken down by gender and diagnosis, (*b*) interitem correlation matrices in various diagnostic groups, (*c*) scale and item distribution statistics (e.g., mean, median, skewness, kurtosis, and percentile tables), (*d*) internal consistency and test retest reliability coefficients for subscales and the total scale, and (*e*) a comprehensive review of the latent structure of the SANS. It can be hoped these negative symptoms will be cured in the near future.

REVIEWER'S REFERENCES

Andreasen, N. C., & Olsen, S. (1982). Negative v. positive schizophrenia: Definition and validation. *Archives of General Psychiatry, 39*, 789-794.

Andreasen, N. C. (1984). Scale for the Assessment of Positive Symptoms. Iowa City: University of Iowa.

Bilder, R. M., Mukherjee, S., Rieder, R. O., & Pandurangi, A. K. (1985). Symptomatic and neuropsychological components of defect states. *Schizophrenia Bulletin, 11*, 409-419.

Liddle, P. F. (1987). The symptoms of chronic schizophrenia: A re-examination of the positive-negative dichotomy. *British Journal of Psychiatry, 151*, 145-151.

Lenzenweger, M. F., Dworkin, R. H., & Wethington, E. (1989). Examining the underlying structure of schizophrenic phenomonology: Evidence for a three-process model. *Schizophrenia Bulletin, 17*(3), 515-524.

Sass, H. (1989). The historical evolution of the concept of negative symptoms in schizophrenia. *British Journal of Psychiatry, 155* (Suppl. 7), 26-31.

Kay, S. R. (1990). Positive-negative symptom assessment in schizophrenia: Psychometric issues and scale comparison. *Psychiatric Quarterly, 61*, 163-178.

Keefe, R. S. E., Harvey, P. D., Lenzenweger, M. F., Davidson, M., Apter, S. H., Schmeidler, J., Mohs, R. C., & Davis, K. L. (1992). Empirical assessment of the factorial structure of clinical symptoms in schizophrenia: Negative symptoms. *Psychiatry Research, 44*, 153-165.

Widaman, K. F. (1993). Common factor analysis versus principal component analysis: Differential bias in representing model parameters? *Multivariate Behavioral Research, 28*, 263-311.

American Psychiatric Association. (1994). *Diagnostic and statistical manual of mental disorders* (4th ed.). Washington, DC: American Psychiatric Press.

Waller, N. G. (1994). Seven confirmatory factor analysis programs: EQS, EzPATH, LINCS, LISCOMP, LISREL 7, SIMPLIS, and CALIS. *Applied Psychological Measurement, 17*, 73-100.

[340]

Scale for the Assessment of Positive Symptoms.

Purpose: "Designed to assess positive symptoms, principally those that occur in schizophrenia."

Population: Psychiatric inpatients and outpatients of all ages.

Publication Date: 1984.

Acronym: SAPS.

Scores: 35 behavior ratings within 5 areas: Hallucinations, Delusions, Bizarre Behavior, Positive Formal Thought Disorder, Inappropriate Affect.

Administration: Individual.

Price Data: Available from publisher.

Time: [15–30] minutes.

Comments: Intended to serve as a complementary instrument to the Scale for the Assessment of Negative Symptoms (SANS; 339).

Author: Nancy C. Andreasen.

Publisher: Nancy C. Andreasen.

Cross References: See T4:2326 (24 references).

TEST REFERENCES

1. Andreasen, N. C., Flaum, M., Swayze, V. W., II, Tyrrell, G., & Arndt, S. (1990). Positive and negative symptoms in schizophrenia. *Archives of General Psychiatry, 47*, 615-621.

2. Hogg, B., Jackson, H. J., Rudd, R. P., & Edwards, J. (1990). Diagnosing personality disorders in recent-onset schizophrenia. *The Journal of Nervous and Mental Disease, 178*, 194-199.

3. Swayze, V. W., II, Andreasen, N. C., Alliger, R. J., Ehrhardt, J. C., & Yuh, W. T. C. (1990). Structural brain abnormalities in bipolar affective disorder. *Archives of General Psychiatry, 47*, 1054-1059.

4. Braff, D. L., Heaton, R., Kuck, J., Cullom, M., Moranville, J., Grant, I., & Zisook, S. (1991). A generalized pattern of neuropsychological deficits in outpatients with chronic schizophrenia with heterogeneous Wisconsin Card Sorting Test results. *Archives of General Psychiatry, 48*, 891-898.

5. Fenton, W. S., & McGlashan, T. H. (1991). Natural history of schizophrenia subtypes. *Archives of General Psychiatry, 48*, 978-986.

6. Andreasen, N. C., Flaum, M., & Arndt, S. (1992). The Comprehensive Assessment of Symptoms and History (CASH): An instrument for assessing diagnosis and psychopathology. *Archives of General Psychiatry, 49*, 615-623.

7. Andreasen, N. C., Rezai, K., Alliger, R., Swayze, V. W., II, Flaum, M., Kirchner, P., Cohen, G., & O'Leary, D. S. (1992). Hypofrontality in neuroleptic-naive patients and in patients with chronic schizophrenia. *Archives of General Psychiatry, 49*, 943-958.

8. Bellini, L., Gatti, F., Gasperini, M., & Smeraldi, E. (1992). A comparison between delusional and non-delusional depressives. *Journal of Affective Disorders, 25*, 129-138.

9. Dollfus, S., Petit, M., & Menard, J. F. (1993). Relationship between depressive and positive symptoms in schizophrenia. *Journal of Affective Disorders, 28*, 61-69.

10. Jackson, H. J., & Pica, S. (1993). An investigation into the internal structure of DSM-III antisocial personality disorder. *Psychological Reports, 72*, 355-367.

11. McConaghy, N., Catts, S. V., Michie, P. T., Fox, A., Ward, P. B., & Shelley, A. (1993). P300 indexes thought disorder in schizophrenics, but allusive thinking in normal subjects. *The Journal of Nervous and Mental Disease, 181*, 176-182.

12. Parnas, J., Cannon, T. D., Jacobsen, B., Schulsinger, H., Schulsinger, F., & Mednick, S. A. (1993). Lifetime DSM-III-R diagnostic outcomes in the offspring of schizophrenic mothers: Results from the Copenhagen high-risk study. *Archives of General Psychiatry, 50*, 707-714.

13. Verbraak, M. J. P. M., Hoogduin, C. A. L., & Schaap, C. (1993). The heterogeneity of schizophrenic information processing and negative versus positive symptoms. *The Journal of Nervous and Mental Disease, 181*, 738-743.

14. Woodruff, P. W. R., Pearlson, G. D., Geer, M. J., Barta, P. E., & Chilcoat, H. D. (1993). A computerized magnetic resonance imaging study of corpus callosum morphology in schizophrenia. *Psychological Medicine, 23*, 45-56.

15. Amador, X. F., Flaum, M., Andreasen, N. C., Strauss, D. H., Yule, S. A., Clark, S. C., & Gorman, J. M. (1994). Awareness of illness in schizophrenia and schizoaffective and mood disorders. *Archives of General Psychiatry, 51*, 826-836.

16. Aylward, E. H., Reiss, A., Barta, P. E., Tien, A., Han, W., Lee, J., & Pearlson, G. D. (1994). Magnetic resonance imaging measurement of posterior fossa structures in schizophrenia. *American Journal of Psychiatry, 151*, 1448-1452.

17. Bell, R. C., Low, L. H., Jackson, H. J., Dudgeon, P. L., Copolov, D. L., & Singh, B. S. (1994). Latent trait modelling of symptoms of schizophrenia. *Psychological Medicine, 24*, 335-345.

18. Berenbaum, S. A., Taylor, M. A., & Cloninger, C. R. (1994). Family study of schizophrenia and personality. *Journal of Abnormal Psychology, 103*, 475-484.

19. Buchanan, R. W., & Carpenter, W. T. (1994). Domains of psychopathology: An approach to the reduction of heterogeneity in schizophrenia. *The Journal of Nervous and Mental Disease, 182*, 193-204.

20. Docherty, N. M., Evans, I. M., Sledge, W. H., Seibyl, J. D., & Krystal, J. H. (1994). Affective reactivity of language in schizophrenia. *The Journal of Nervous and Mental Disease, 182*, 98-102.

21. Fenton, W. S., & McGlashan, T. H. (1994). Antecedents, symptom progression, and long-term outcome of the deficit syndrome in schizophrenia. *American Journal of Psychiatry, 151*, 351-356.

22. Gur, R. E., Mozley, P. D., Shtasel, D. L., Cannon, T. D., Gallacher, F., Turetsky, B., Grossman, R., & Gur, R. C. (1994). Clinical subtypes of schizophrenia: Differences in brain and CSF volume. *American Journal of Psychiatry, 151*, 343-350.

23. Hollister, J. M., Mednick, S. A., Brennan, P., & Cannon, T. D. (1994). Impaired autonomic nervous system habituation in those at genetic risk for schizophrenia. *Archives of General Psychiatry, 51*, 552-558.

24. Malla, A. K., & Norman, R. M. G. (1994). Prodromal symptoms in schizophrenia. *British Journal of Psychiatry, 164*, 487-493.

25. McCarley, R. W., Shenton, M. E., O'Donnell, B. F., & Nestor, P. G. (1994). Neural circuits in schizophrenia. *Archives of General Psychiatry, 51*, 515.

26. Oke, S., Saatchi, R., Allen, E., Hudson, N. R., & Jervis, B. W. (1994). The contingent negative variation in positive and negative types of schizophrenia. *American Journal of Psychiatry, 151*, 432-433.

27. Perry, W., & Braff, D. L. (1994). Information-processing deficits and thought disorder in schizophrenia. *American Journal of Psychiatry, 151*, 363-367.

28. Poreh, A. M., Chapin, K., Rosen, M. D., & Youssef, I. (1994). Correlations between MMPI and the Scale for the Assessment of Positive Symptoms and the Scale for the Assessment of Negative Symptoms in schizophrenic patients. *Journal of Personality Assessment, 63*, 275-283.

29. Seidenberg, M., Haltiner, A., Taylor, M. A., Hermann, B. B., & Wyler, A. (1994). Development and validation of a multiple ability self-report questionnaire. *Journal of Clinical and Experimental Neuropsychology, 16*, 93-104.

30. Taylor, M. A., & Amir, N. (1994). The problem of missing clinical data for research in psychopathology: Some solution guidelines. *The Journal of Nervous and Mental Disease, 182*, 222-229.

31. Taylor, M. A., Reed, R., & Berenbaum, S. (1994). Patterns of speech disorders in schizophrenia and mania. *The Journal of Nervous and Mental Disease, 182*, 319-326.

32. Wetzel, H., Hillert, H., Grunder, G., & Benkert, O. (1994). Roxindole, a dopamine autoreceptor agonist, in the treatment of positive and negative schizophrenic symptoms. *American Journal of Psychiatry, 151*, 1499-1502.

33. Xiong, W., Phillips, M. R., Hu, X., Wang, R., Dai, Q., Kleinman, J., & Kleinman, A. (1994). Family-based intervention for schizophrenic patients in China: A randomised controlled trial. *British Journal of Psychiatry, 165*, 239-247.

34. Arnold, S. E., Gur, R. E., Shapiro, R. M., Fisher, K. R., Moberg, P. J., Gibney, M. R., Gur, R. C., Blackwell, P., & Trojanowski, J. Q. (1995). Prospective clinicopathologic studies of schizophrenia: Accrual and assessment of patients. *American Journal of Psychiatry, 152*, 731-737.

35. Catts, S. V., Shelley, A., Ward, P. B., Liebert, B., McConaghy, N., Andrews, S., & Michie, P. T. (1995). Brain potential evidence for an auditory sensory memory deficit in schizophrenia. *American Journal of Psychiatry, 152*, 213-219.

36. Corey-Bloom, J., Jernigan, T., Archibald, S., Harris, M. J., & Jeste, D. V. (1995). Quantitative magnetic resonance imaging of the brain in late-life schizophrenia. *American Journal of Psychiatry, 152*, 447-449.

37. Flaum, M., Swayze, V. W., O'Leary, D. S., Yuh, W. T. C., Erhardt, J. C., Arndt, S. V., & Andreasen, N. C. (1995). Effects of diagnosis, laterality, and gender on brain morphology in schizophrenia. *American Journal of Psychiatry, 152*, 704-714.

38. Jeste, D. V., Harris, M. J., Krull, A., Kuck, J., McAdams, L. A., & Heaton, R. (1995). Clinical and neuropsychological characteristics of patients with late-onset schizophrenia. *American Journal of Psychiatry, 152*, 722-730.

39. Paillere-Martinot, M., Lecrubier, Y., Martinot, J., & Aubin, F. (1995). Improvement of some schizophrenic deficit symptoms with low doses of amisulpride. *American Journal of Psychiatry, 152*, 130-133.

40. Peralta, V., Cuesta, M. J., & DeLeon, J. (1995). Positive and negative symptoms/syndromes in schizophrenia: Reliability and validity of different diagnostic systems. *Psychological Medicine, 25*, 43-50.

41. Petty, R. G., Barta, P. E., Pearlson, G. D., McGilchrist, I. K., Lewis, R. W., Tien, A. Y., Pulver, A., Vaughn, D. D., Casanova, M. F., & Powers, R. E. (1995). Reversal of asymmetry of the planum temporale in schizophrenia. *American Journal of Psychiatry, 152*, 715-721.

42. Slaghuis, W. L., & Bakker, V. J. (1995). Forward and backward visual masking of contour by light in positive- and negative-symptom schizophrenia. *Journal of Abnormal Psychology, 104*, 41-54.

43. Tyrka, A. R., Cannon, T. D., Haslam, N., Mednick, S. A., Schulsinger, F., Schulsinger, H., & Parnas, J. (1995). The latent structure of schizotypy: I. Premorbid indicators of a taxon of individuals at risk for schizophrenia-spectrum disorders. *Journal of Abnormal Psychology, 104*, 173-183.

44. Vita, A., Bressi, S., Perani, D., Invernizzi, G., Giobbio, G. M., Massimiliano, D., Garbarini, M., Del Sole, A., & Fazio, F. (1995). High resolution SPECT study of regional cerebral blood flow in drug-free and drug-naive schizophrenic patients. *American Journal of Psychiatry, 152,* 876-882.

Review of the Scale for the Assessment of Positive Symptoms by JOHN D. KING, Professor of Special Education and Educational Administration, The University of Texas at Austin, Austin, TX:

DESCRIPTION. The Scale for the Assessment of Positive Symptoms (SAPS), available since 1984, is designed to aid in assessing "positive symptoms, principally those that occur in schizophrenia" (p. 2) by adding specific structure to standard diagnostic interviews. It is intended for use in conjunction with the Scale for Assessment of Negative Symptoms (SANS; 339), which serves a similar purpose for negative symptoms. It is suggested for use in clinical practice as well as in psychopharmacologic research in order to make weekly ratings and chart the subject's response to treatment.

The SAPS contains descriptions of major positive symptom groups, suggested interview probes, and 5-point Likert-type scales for assessing the severity of each symptom. There is also a summary sheet for combining and summarizing results from both the SAPS and the SANS. No information is provided on the development of the scale. Symptoms included and their descriptions are consistent with *DSM-III-R* (American Psychiatric Association, 1987, pp. 189–190) diagnostic criteria. In most cases, the symptom descriptions are more complete than those provided in the *DSM-III-R*.

RELIABILITY AND VALIDITY. Although the instrument has been available since 1984, no information is provided on reliability or validity of the SAPS, nor is the user directed to any relevant research. The lack of any information concerning interrater or repeated measures reliability significantly impairs interpretive confidence for research purposes.

STRENGTHS. Used in conjunction with the SANS, the SAPS can provide a useful adjunct to standard diagnostic interviews. It encourages greater specificity in describing symptom clusters, leading to a more exact and individualized account of each patient. The generally quite good symptom descriptions provided should prove helpful in differentiating similar but distinct symptom types, especially for those who lack formal training in psychiatric diagnosis. Most of the scales are well anchored and should facilitate decision making as to the relative severity of a given symptom.

LIMITATIONS. The Hallucination scales all refer to the relative frequency of "voices" regardless of the type of hallucination involved. This oversight needlessly complicates use of the scale. Anchor points for the Bizarre Behavior scales are vague and invite subjective interpretation of severity. This seems likely to reduce interrater reliability. In a similar vein, the Global Rating for each symptom group lacks a specified relationship to the individual symptoms from which it is derived. Again, this invites an overly subjective use of the scale which is likely to reduce reliability.

The lack of any reliability or validity information makes it difficult to interpret observed changes in scale scores over time. There is no empirically derived way to set reasonable confidence intervals for deciding if they reflect real changes in the patient's condition or merely normal variability associated with imperfect reliability. This shortcoming seriously undermines the usefulness of the SAPS for research purposes as suggested by the author.

SUMMARY. The Scale for the Assessment of Positive Symptoms (SAPS) is a guide for the assessment of positive symptoms, particularly those associated with schizophrenia. Along with its companion instrument, the Scale for the Assessment of Negative Symptoms (SANS), it is designed to augment a standard diagnostic interview to track progress in a clinical setting and as a research tool to monitor the effectiveness of psychopharmacological interventions. It promises to provide a more detailed and quantified picture of a given patient's constellation of symptoms than is ordinarily obtained through interview means alone. However, the lack of information about its psychometric properties reduces its appropriateness as a research instrument. Furthermore, some of the wording used as scale anchor points is at times inconsistent with the symptom being assessed. At other times, the wording is not sufficiently specific such that it invites subjective interpretation of the patient's symptoms.

REVIEWER'S REFERENCE

American Psychiatric Association. (1987). *Diagnostic and statistical manual of mental disorders* (3rd ed., rev.). Washington, DC: Author.

Review of the Scale for the Assessment of Positive Symptoms by SUZANNE KING, Assistant Professor of Psychiatry, McGill University, Montreal, Quebec, Canada:

The Scale for the Assessment of Positive Symptoms (SAPS) is a 34-item scale used to rate the severity of four positive symptoms of schizophrenia: Hallucinations, Delusions, Bizarre Behavior, and Formal Thought Disorder. Each symptom cluster, or subscale, is evaluated on the basis of a global rating plus between 4 and 12 ratings of specific symptoms.

Symptoms are rated on a 6-point scale ranging from zero, for "none," to 5 for "severe." Each possible rating has a brief definition in terms of severity, frequency, and so on. To summarize the ratings, one may either take the mean of the ratings for all items within a subscale, or use the global rating for each subscale. Similarly, a general rating of the severity of positive symptoms can be computed by taking the average of either all individual items, or of the global ratings for all subscales. A 35th item for inappropriate affect is included in the SAPS although research suggests that it does not fit into either a positive symptom or a negative symptom factor. Although inappropriate affect is a symptom of schizophrenia, the score for this item is not to be added into the total SAPS score.

The "test kit" includes a 20-page manual and a 7-page test protocol for use with the SAPS and with the companion instrument, Scale for Assessment of Negative Symptoms (SANS; 339), by the same author. The manual (dated June 25, 1992) includes a half-page introduction followed by one-paragraph descriptions of each of the four subscales, brief descriptions of each item within subscales, one or two suggested probes for items in three of the four symptom clusters, and objective anchors for each possible rating. There is no discussion in the manual of the development of the test, its psychometric properties, norms, scoring procedures, nor the training required to administer the SAPS appropriately. No references to other sources that may provide such information are included. The manual indicates that ratings are to be made on the basis of information gathered and observations made during the course of a "standard clinical interview," which is not described, and that additional information should be gathered from discussions with significant others familiar with the patient. Although no mention of this is made in the manual, training may be received at the University of Iowa. In addition, video tapes of interviews, along with written commentaries for training purposes and for monitoring interrater reliability, can be obtained from the author.

One must search the psychiatric literature for reports of psychometric properties of the SAPS. Walker, Harvey, and Perlman (1988) report that, from their study of 51 schizophrenic and 21 manic patients, the interrater reliability of symptoms in the SAPS and SANS ranged from .72 to.93 and that the average interrater reliability (Kappa) for SAPS scores was .84 (.82 for the SANS). These authors report internal consistency estimates (Cronbach's alpha) for the SAPS of .65 for schizophrenic patients and .41 for manic patients.

Walker et al. (1988) also lend support for the construct validity of the SAPS. Current theory suggests that positive and negative symptoms ought to be independent of each other in schizophrenia, although perhaps not in other psychotic disorders such as mania. These authors found a nonsignificant correlation of .19 between the total SAPS and SANS scores in their schizophrenic sample. Similar results, suggesting the independence of the SAPS and the SANS, have been found by other authors including Gur et al. (1991). Walker and her colleagues (1988) found a significant correlation of .47 ($p<.05$) between the total scores on the SAPS and SANS for manic patients. In addition, their results suggest that schizophrenic and manic patients differ significantly on two of the four positive symptoms from the SAPS as well as the total SAPS score, and on four of the five negative symptoms from the SANS, as well as on the total negative symptom score. These results support the ability of the SAPS and the SANS to discriminate between diagnostic groups. Gur et al. (1991) support the concurrent validity of the SAPS and SANS by showing significant correlations with the thought disorder and anergia factors (respectively) from the Brief Psychiatric Rating Scale (BPRS).

A strength of the SAPS is its use with the SANS to operationally define three groups of patients with schizophrenia: those with the positive symptom syndrome, those with the negative symptom syndrome, and those with mixed symptoms. Although further study is needed into the validity of the distinction among these three groups, recent research supports the notion that background and clinical characteristics of the groups may differ (Andreasen & Olsen, 1982; Andreasen, Flaum, Swayze, Tyrrell, & Arndt, 1990). These results, if replicated, will have important implications for our understanding of the etiology and course of schizophrenia.

The use of anchors for rating levels represents both a strength and a weakness of the SAPS. Although operational definitions of ratings ought to improve interrater reliability, the definitions used in the SAPS may threaten the assumption of equal intervals, calling into question the appropriateness of many statistical analyses with these data. In addition, although definitions for some items are not mutually exclusive, for other items they are not comprehensive.

The lack of a detailed guide to the clinical interview used to gather information needed to make ratings is an important shortcoming of the SAPS. Although there is seldom a guarantee that any two semistructured interviews will ever be identical, leaving the format and content of the interview completely up to the discretion, and mood, of the interviewer threatens the comparability of scores across subjects and the generalizability of results across studies.

Summary information about the SAPS may be misleading: Although the time needed to administer the SAPS is indicated as "15 to 30 minutes," the description of the positive formal thought disorder subscale states that the "anchor points for these ratings assume that the subject has been interviewed for a total of approximately forty-five minutes. If the interview is shorter, the ratings should be adjusted accordingly" (manual, p. 15).

In summary, the SAPS, along with its companion scale the SANS, is a very detailed measure of positive symptoms which, in the hands of a well-trained interviewer, could have adequate reliability and even validity for research purposes. Both scales appear to have gained acceptance in the psychiatric community. The documentation for the instrument, however, is sufficiently poor that caution is urged before this scale is selected. Competing instruments, such as the UCLA version of the BPRS (Lukoff, Liberman, & Nuechterlein, 1986), which is shorter than the SAPS and for which a new manual should be available by the end of 1993, and the Positive and Negative Symptom Scale (PANSS, Kay, Fiszbein, & Opler, 1987), which is gaining in popularity, may be considered as appropriate alternatives to the SAPS and the SANS.

REVIEWER'S REFERENCES

Andreasen, N. C., & Olsen, S. (1982). Negative v positive schizophrenia. *Archives of General Psychiatry, 39*, 789-794.

Lukoff, D., Liberman, R. P., & Nuechterlein, K. H. (1986). Symptom monitoring in the rehabilitations of schizophrenic patients. *Schizophrenia Bulletin, 12*, 578-602.

Kay, S. R., Fiszbein, A., & Opler, L. A. (1987). The Positive and Negative Syndrome Scale (PANSS) for schizophrenia. *Schizophrenia Bulletin, 13*, 261-276.

Walker, E. F., Harvey, P. D., & Perlman, D. (1988). The positive/negative symptom distinction in psychoses: A replication and extension of previous findings. *The Journal of Nervous and Mental Disease, 176*, 359-363.

Andreasen, N. C., Flaum, M., Swayze, V. W., Tyrrell, G., & Arndt, S. (1990). Positive and negative symptoms in schizophrenia. *Archives of General Psychiatry, 47*, 615-621.

Gur, R. E., Mozley, P. D., Resnick, S. M., Levick, S., Erwin, R., Saykin, A. J., & Gur, R. C. (1991). Relations among clinical scales in schizophrenia. *American Journal of Psychiatry, 148*, 472-478.

[341]

Scaled Curriculum Achievement Levels Test.

Purpose: Assesses individual and group achievement in mathematics computation, reading, and language usage.
Population: Grades 3–8.
Publication Date: 1992.
Acronym: SCALE.
Administration: Group.
Levels: 9 levels in each of 3 subtests: Mathematics Computation (M1–M9), Reading (R1–R9), Language Usage (L1–L9).
Price Data, 1995: $89.50 per complete kit including 6 administration booklets (2 each for Mathematics Computation, Reading, and Language Usage), 10 class placement/record sheets; 30 answer forms (10 each for Mathematics Computation, Reading, and language Usage), and manual (135 pages); $15 per 100 class placement/record sheets; $47.50 per manual.
Authors: Victor W. Doherty and Gale H. Roid.
Publisher: Western Psychological Services.

a) MATHEMATICS COMPUTATION.
Scores: Total score only.
Price Data: $24.50 per administration booklet; $12.50 per 10 answer forms.
Time: (20–25) minutes.

b) READING.
Scores: Same as *a* above.
Price Data: $34.50 per administration booklet; $12.50 per 10 answer forms.
Time: Same as *a* above.

c) LANGUAGE USAGE.
Scores: $31.50 per administration booklet; $12.50 per answer forms.
Price Data: Same as *a* above.
Time: (15–20) minutes.

Review of the Scaled Curriculum Achievement Levels Test by RUSSELL N. CARNEY, Associate Professor of Psychology, Southwest Missouri State University, Springfield, MO:

The Scaled Curriculum Achievement Levels Test (SCALE) is an achievement test battery covering grades 3 through 8. It consists of separate subtest booklets in Mathematics Computation, Reading, and Language Usage. The entire test may be completed in about one hour. According to the manual, uses of the SCALE include: measuring individual or group achievement, facilitating first-of-the-year grouping and placement decisions, special education screening "*that precedes diagnostic testing*" [italics added], "identifying general areas of educational dysfunction," testing children who miss regular achievement tests, and finally, "planning individual and group instruction using the direct link between test items and curriculum goals" (manual, p. 1).

The authors of the manual are to be commended for acknowledging limitations of the test. For example, they state that "short tests like those in the SCALE battery cannot provide highly reliable diagnostic information about each of several goals" (p. 20). Also, the tests "do not measure all major goals in each subject" (p. 20). Test users are further cautioned that "interpretation and instructional plans based on SCALE results should be limited to curricula covered by the SCALE tests at the level actually administered" (p. 20).

ADMINISTRATION. A unique feature of the SCALE is that, prior to testing, a teacher or other education professional assigns *each* student to the level of the test matching their ability level in Mathematics Computation, Reading, and Language Usage. The procedure for doing this is spelled out clearly in the manual, and is based on such information as prior test scores, grades, teacher reports, etc. The goal is to have students take only the level of the subtest most suited to their abilities. Those few students receiving extremely low or high scores should be retested by starting them at a more appropriate level of the test. This adjustment, of course, is limited by the lower and upper bounds of the nine overlapping test levels.

SCORING AND NORMS. Ease of scoring is facilitated by the use of "WPS AutoScore Answer Forms." Following testing, the first sheet of the answer form is torn away to reveal a second sheet upon which the students' responses and the correct answers are marked. Then, using the norms tables in Appendix B of the manual, raw scores may be converted to standard scores (M = 50, SD = 10), percentiles, and Normal Curve Equivalents (NCEs). Both fall and spring norms are available. Wisely, the SCALE does not report grade-equivalence (GE) scores—due to the inherent problems of such scores.

Additionally, "SCALE scores" are provided, which "represent an equal-interval progression from mastery of the easiest to the most difficult curriculum tasks in each subject area" (p. 16). These serve as an index of the relative difficulty of a curriculum task.

On the back of the answer sheet, all of the item reference numbers comprising that test are arranged in order of difficulty based on the SCALE scores, and are also grouped into strands representing various categories for that subtest (e.g., for math, strands represent multiplication, division, fractions, etc.). This arrangement is called the Curriculum Scales. The student's item-by-item performance can be marked here by the examiner, and lines drawn representing mastery, instructional, and frustration levels. Examination of the SCALE scores and Curriculum Scales in concert yields a clear snapshot of what the student can and cannot do, and should aid the user in making instructional decisions.

RELIABILITY. Despite the short administration time, the SCALE exhibits good reliability. A major factor contributing to its reliability is the procedure of assigning the student to the appropriate level of each subtest prior to administration. As the authors of the manual observe, "the very structure of the SCALE system of test levels is designed to increase test reliability and precision when levels are appropriately assigned" (p. 39).

Both conventional and IRT-based (Item Response Theory) estimates of reliability are provided in the manual. Internal consistency (Guilford, 1965, p. 463) was estimated for each of the 23-item levels for each subtest. These estimates ranged from .80 to .87 in Mathematics Computation, from .68 to .87 in Reading, and from .73 to .83 in Language Usage. As the authors point out, "these estimates will provide a lower-bound approximation of the reliability of the SCALE, since the tests were designed not only as individual short tests, but as a series of nine levels along an entire curriculum scale" (p. 39). One type of reliability data notably lacking from the technical information provided in the manual is that of test stability over time (e.g., test-retest reliability). Guidelines in the *Standards for Educational and Psychological Testing* (AERA, APA, & NCME, 1985) emphasize that measures of internal consistency are not substitutes for measures of stability over time (see Standard 2.6, p. 21).

Two IRT-based measures of reliability are mentioned: the standard error of measurement (*SEM*) at each level, and test information functions. Regarding *SEM*s, the authors observe that the "ranges of standard error are quite similar across levels and curriculum areas, with most levels having a standard error of approximately 4 SCALE points near the center of the raw score distribution (12 items correct [out of 23]), and remaining within 5 or 6 points throughout the most effective ranges of each level (7–20 items correct)" (p. 41). Higher values occur outside this range, and as already stated, students earning extreme scores should be retested. It would have been helpful had *SEM* values been presented in terms of standard score units.

Test information functions are defined as "an indicator of the precision of measurement of a test across a range of ability" (p. 41). Nine test information functions are graphed in the manual for each of the nine levels of the three content areas. The authors state that the overlapping nature of the curves illustrates that the most accurate measurement results when students are tested at their functional level.

VALIDITY. Guidelines in the *Standards* state that "ideal validation" should include evidence spanning the three traditional categories of validity: content, criterion-related, and construct (AERA, APA, & NCME, 1985, p. 9). Content validity represents the match between the content a test covers and what was taught. Thus, it is up to test users to compare their curriculum with the test content of the SCALE, and *all* test items have been included in the manual's appendix. In Reading and Language Usage, SCALE content areas compare closely with other achievement tests, such as the Metropolitan Achievement Tests, the Stanford Achievement Tests, and the California Achievement Test (CAT).

According to the *Standards*, concurrent validity is the preferred type of criterion-related validity for an achievement test (AERA, APA, & NCME, 1985, p. 11). Regarding the SCALE, concurrent validity was established by correlating the test with two other achievement tests in 1984. Compared with the Portland Achievement Levels Test (PALT) at selected grade levels, correlations ranged from .75 to .84 in Mathematics Computation, .78 to .87 in Reading, and .72 to .83 in Language Usage. Similarly, correlations with the CAT (Form C) ranged from .74 to .84 in Reading, and from .69 to .75 in Language Usage. Another line of evidence was that mathematics placements made using the PALT were "quite accurate" (manual, p. 45). The PALT was developed from the same extensive item bank as the SCALE—an item bank resulting from a large test development program in the Portland, Oregon Public Schools over a period of 15 years.

It is commendable that several lines of evidence regarding construct validity—specifically the constructs of Arithmetic Computation, Reading, and Language Usage achievement—are provided. These include: (*a*) information regarding the unidimensionality of SCALE tests; (*b*) correlations among the three achievement tests (Reading vs. Language Usage = .72; Reading vs. Mathematics Computation = .51); (*c*) information regarding "pre-to-post change studies" (manual, p. 47) (i.e., SCALE scores seem to reflect the effects of instruction designed to raise achievement); (*d*) an examination of students' means on the SCALE at the different grade levels shows increase with grade level; and (*e*) the PALT (highly correlated with the SCALE) correlates well with other standardized achievement batteries.

SUMMARY. The SCALE appears to be a well-designed achievement test battery, for which the principal strength is that it takes only about one hour to administer, and yet exhibits good reliability. Use of modern IRT procedures (based on the one-parameter logistic or Rasch model) have made possible the design of the test, and the test's ability to produce both norm-referenced (group norms) and criterion-referenced (curriculum scale) scores. In particular, a "distinct advantage of the Rasch-based score [i.e., the SCALE score] is that it can be reanchored to a new normative based without losing its equal-interval or curriculum-referenced characteristics" (manual, p. 36). As already indicated, the Curriculum Scales are quite helpful in pinpointing what the student has, and has not, mastered.

The format of test materials (e.g., test booklets and answer sheets) is simple and easy to follow. The WPS AutoScore Answer Forms yield a wealth of information when scored and completed as directed. Finally, the manual itself is clearly and expertly written, with ample use of figures and tables to support the text. Appendices include (*a*) a table to facilitate testing placement; (*b*) norms; (*c*) a listing of *all* test items; (*d*) an introduction to the Rasch model; (*e*) item difficulty, content, and use; and (*f*) item statistics. In particular, the section on the Rasch model (designed as a nonmathematical introduction) will be appreciated by the lay reader.

A potential drawback of the SCALE is the extra time required of the test user. First, each student's ability must be estimated, and the test booklet marked at that level, prior to administration. Although not an overwhelming task, this feature is relatively unique to the SCALE. Second, students scoring quite low or high need to be retested. Third, scoring is done by hand. Although the WPS AutoScore Answer Forms simplify this procedure, hand scoring—and especially looking up scores in the norms table—does take time. Despite the time consideration, the SCALE should be seriously considered by those desiring a brief, yet dependable, achievement test battery in the areas of mathematics computation, reading, and language usage.

REVIEWER'S REFERENCES

Guilford, J. P. (1965). *Fundamental statistics in psychology and education.* New York: McGraw-Hill.

American Educational Research Association, American Psychological Association, & National Council on Measurement in Education. (1985). *Standards for educational and psychological testing.* Washington, DC: American Psychological Association, Inc.

Review of the Scaled Curriculum Achievement Levels Test by ROBERT K. GABLE, Professor of Educational Psychology, and Associate Director, Bureau of Educational Research and Service, University of Connecticut, Storrs, CT:

The Scaled Curriculum Achievement Levels Test (SCALE) provides a fairly quick assessment of student mastery of curriculum tasks in global areas and selected content strands within these global areas. Although these tests parallel the respective content of most achievement batteries, they are not designed to provide highly reliable diagnostic information more properly obtained from follow-up testing with longer batteries. A feature of the tests is the use of Rasch item-response-theory procedures to create nine overlapping test levels covering the curriculum from grade 3 to grade 8. Students are tested on items within their range of ability (i.e., functional level testing); a clear description of locating proper test levels and individual and group administration procedures is provided. Normative data are provided for fall and spring testing times. The grade level (grade equivalent) norms were developed over a 5-year period using approximately 15,000–17,000 students per grade level in the Portland, Oregon school system. The students in this system perform close to the national average and represent high-, middle-, and low-income groups. The key to the utility of the norm data lies in the use of the item-response-theory item bank, which allows both norm-referenced and criterion-referenced interpretations.

Traditional normative scores in the form of standard scores derived using the Rasch procedures are based on the relative difficulty of curriculum tasks and, thus, "represent an equal-interval progression from mastery of the easiest to the most difficult curriculum tasks in each subject area" (p. 16). Levels of curriculum mastery can be estimated because each item is uniquely placed on a Curriculum Scale based on the level of difficulty. Procedures are described for using the Math, Reading, and Curriculum Scales to estimate probabilities of student success at three levels: Frustration (50%), Instructional (75%), and Mastery (90%). The information is then referenced to breakouts of the content area into curriculum strands identified for each item. For example, two of the Math Curriculum Scale content strands are: WA–addition of whole numbers, and WD–division of whole numbers. These materials are the key to the test user because they suggest ability-level-appropriate instruction for the student as well as areas in need of further diagnosis using other achievement batteries.

Content validity is highly supported through a curriculum and test development process involving teachers, curriculum specialists, and measurement experts. For several years items were written to match curriculum goals and piloted on thousands of students at each grade level. The SCALE manual provides very adequate test blueprints and descriptions of curriculum content. Also included is a comparison of SCALE item content with the Metropolitan Achievement Tests (MAT), the Stanford Achievement Tests (SAT), and the California Achievement Tests (CAT). (Note that the edition of the test compared was not indicated.) The SCALE limits the assessment of Mathematics to Computational Skills. For Reading and Language Usage the authors report approximately 90% match with the three well-known tests. The SCALE does not cover spelling and reference materials in Language Usage or phonics and word attack skills in Reading. In addition, the three batteries compared with the SCALE include more items in each area and often more diagnostic information. Criterion-related validity information is offered in the form of correlations with the Portland Achievement Levels Test, which was constructed from a longer set of items from the same Rasch-calibrated item bank, and Reading and Language Usage data for selected grade levels using the CAT. The most convincing evidence of construct validity is presented in the form of extensive analyses of test data and item-response-theory model fit. Across time and samples of students the stability of the Rasch difficulty and student ability estimates were examined during item selection and calibration. These studies supported the meaningfulness of the equal interval SCALE scores which provide the important link to curriculum planning based on the test scores.

Conventional internal consistency reliability estimates and three IRT-based reliability estimates are reported. The IRT estimates report the standard error of measurement at each level of the SCALE, test information functions listing precision of the tests in each curriculum area, and a set of summary estimates translated into conventional reliabilities. The reliability estimates are in the high 80s and low 90s when functional level testing is employed and most students are assigned to levels where they master approximately 50% of the items.

In summary, developers of the SCALE have successfully designed a series of tests that can be used at the functional level of each student for assessment and curriculum planning. We do note, however, that the materials appear quite expensive.

[342]

Scales of Early Communication Skills for Hearing-Impaired Children.

Purpose: "Designed to evaluate speech and language development of hearing-impaired children between the ages of two and eight years."
Population: Ages 2-0 to 8-11.
Publication Date: 1975.
Acronym: SECS.
Scores, 4: Receptive Language Skills, Expressive Language Skills, Nonverbal Receptive Skills, Nonverbal Expressive Skills.
Administration: Individual.
Price Data, 1992: $12 per manual (42 pages); $6 per 25 rating forms.
Time: [60] minutes (through observation).
Comments: Ratings by teachers.
Authors: Jean S. Moog and Ann E. Geers.
Publisher: Central Institute for the Deaf.

Review of the Scales of Early Communication Skills for Hearing-Impaired Children by VINCENT J. SAMAR, Associate Professor, and MARC MARSCHARK, Professor, National Technical Institute for the Deaf at the Rochester Institute of Technology, Rochester, NY:

DESCRIPTION OF THE INSTRUMENT. The Scales of Early Communication Skills for Hearing-Impaired Children is presented as an instrument designed to evaluate the communication, speech and language development of hearing-impaired children between the ages of 2 and 8 years. It is divided into four separately scored sections: Verbal Receptive (VR), Verbal Expressive (VE), Nonverbal Receptive (NVR), and Nonverbal Expressive (NVE). Each section is composed of a number of items (VR-5 items, VE-9 items, NVR-3 items, NVE-3 items), organized putatively in increasing order of steps in the acquisition of language or nonverbal skills (hierarchical ordering). Each of the 20 items requires a teacher to manipulate or observe situations in which a child may demonstrate a particular skill. The two verbal sections are further subdivided into an "A" scale and a "B" scale. The "A" scale putatively rates a child's behavior in relatively structured teaching/modeling situations. The "B" scale putatively rates a child's behavior in more natural, spontaneous situations. The scale items are intended to elicit the recognition and production of speech and nonverbal gesture and body language.

The manual presents an extended discussion of each scale item, including a rationale, the criteria for rating, and hypothetical examples of skill demonstration. No validation and incomplete reliability data are presented. The scales were standardized on a sample of 372 children between the ages of 2 years 0 months and 8 years 11 months from 14 oral programs for hearing-impaired children. Tables are provided for converting raw scores to equal-interval scale values for the Verbal "A" and "B" scales. Additional tables allow the user to determine the percentile ranks and standard scores by age for each verbal scale, and separately for Combination Receptive and Combination Expressive scales that merge their respective "A," "B," and nonverbal scores into a single measure. The nonverbal scores are not scaled or normed separately.

RATIONALE FOR THE INSTRUMENT. Noting that communication behaviors are easily influenced by the subtleties of a situation, the authors present this instrument as a better alternative to more typical one-time, highly structured, adult-child testing situations for assessing the language development of children with hearing losses. They imply that this scale will afford children the opportunity to exhibit their best performance. The instrument is specifically intended for use by trained professionals like teachers, rather than untrained providers like parents, on the assumption that a child's teacher both knows the child and knows how to evaluate language. The basic motivation for this instrument is the assumption stated in the manual that "the description of the child's communication skill is a necessary first step in establishing realistic teaching objectives" and determining "where he should go next" (manual, p. v). Scores on this instrument, then, are intended to be diagnostic of a child's stage of communication development, and to influence teachers' decisions about placement and language training for individual children.

GENERAL INSTRUMENT ADEQUACY. Any diagnostic language test for young children should possess some basic characteristics before it is adopted for use. First, the instrument should be justifiably appropriate for the population. Second, the scope of the measured construct should be clearly defined and should be specifically addressed by the test items. Third, the test should have clearly established validity and reliability statistics justifying its benefits and defining its limits. In other words, it should be convincingly clear to every potential professional user who the instrument is intended to evaluate and who it is not, what the scores are intended to mean, and whether the score interpretations are accurate. The Scales of Early Communication Skills for Hearing-Impaired Children fails to meet any of these conditions in its present form.

Target population: The target population for the instrument is ill defined. The instrument's title and the manual give the impression, through omission of stated restrictions, that it is intended for use with the general "hearing-impaired" child population, regardless of hearing loss or sociolinguistic background. Yet, the only normative data presented in the manual are for apparently severely to profoundly deaf and hard-of-hearing children from largely oral school programs. These children are no longer in the majority in the United States, and there is good reason to believe that they would approach this instrument with very different expectations, understandings, cooperativeness, and performance levels than children with less severe hearing losses, children in largely manual language programs, or children from primarily Deaf cultural backgrounds whose first language is ASL. Such children could easily subvert the response expectations of the teacher without necessarily failing to comprehend the communication situations.

Minimally, if the authors intend this instrument to be used as a norm-referenced test for a general population, then they must norm it on that population. Otherwise, the manual should clearly warn users *not* to apply the currently available norms to deaf and hard-of-hearing children from inapplicable subpopulations, of which there are several, and it should tell them why in persuasive terms. However, simply including members of a subpopulation in a normative sample does not guarantee that the test is applicable to that subpopulation. In fact, the construct scope of the present instrument suggests that it would be biased against most deaf and hard-of-hearing children as a measure of communication skill, simply because it does not comprehensively measure their relevant communication skills, especially manual language skills.

Construct Scope: The scope of the measured construct for this instrument is poorly defined, and presented in misleading terms by the manual. To begin with, the instrument is billed as assessing communication skills. Yet, an examination of the instrument items themselves reveals that it is intended to be a test of spoken communication, almost exclusively involving multimodal speech reception and production, with accessory score adjustments afforded by two vaguely defined nonverbal and gestural scales. The instrument's title belies this fact with its reference to the much broader construct of "communication skills."

Children whose first language is ASL, for example, may have excellent communication skills without having good speech skills, yet there is no recognition of this fact in the title of manual. This is not a small point. Educators concerned with deafness have often taken divided stands on the linguistic status and communicative value of sign languages. In this context it is crucial that a test of specific language skills should not appear insensitive to these issues. Minimally, the title should be changed in a revision to "Scales of Early Spoken Communication Skills for Hearing-Imapired Children."

Beyond the title issue, the manual liberally interchanges the terms speech development, communication skills development, language development, and language acquisition, as if this instrument were a kind of one-a-day solution to the general language assessment and placement issue throughout the deaf and hard-of-hearing children's early development. In fact, the scope of the communication skills assessed by this instrument is extremely limited; it is primarily restricted to relatively gross ratings of speech reception and expression, and specifically fails to assess sign language development.

VALIDITY AND RELIABILITY. The most serious objection that we have to the Scales of Early Communication Skills for Hearing-Impaired Children is that it is presented and marketed without a shred of validity data and with inadequate reliability data, even 20 years after the original copyright. This generally invites inappropriate, biased, and invalid assessment. Several validity issues must be resolved before this instrument may be regarded as appropriate for use with children.

POPULATION ASSESSMENT BIAS. Without a clear, frank, and unbiased discussion of the population restrictions and limitations of construct scope associated with the Scales of Early Communication Skills for Hearing-Impaired Children, this instrument possesses the potential for biased assessment of large segments of the population, especially those children whose preferred communication mode is through manual language. Children used to communicating through the use of manual language, for example, may not automatically regard spontaneous or structured vocalizations on the part of teachers as important communicative events, whether or not they are capable of understanding them as signals or even messages. Because there is no instruction in the manual about how to ensure that children understand the evaluation situation, especially the teacher-structured components, there is no guarantee that a child's failure to orient or react to a vocalizing teacher indicates an inability to do so. Furthermore, teachers may vary in their understanding of the communication and cultural issues involved in the valid use of communication tests with deaf and hard-of-hearing children. The manual for the Scales of Early Communication Skills for Hearing-Impaired Children, as it stands, is misleading and does nothing to protect children against overgeneralized assessment decisions based on that instrument.

ELICITATION AND ADMINISTRATION PROCEDURES. A serious validity concern is the vagueness of the language elicitation procedures considered necessary to rate children's progress. The manual is sometimes explicit about the need to control various aspects of the communication situation, such as the use of gesture and experience. However, it is left to the imagination and skill of the teacher to define adequately controlled elicitation procedures. In fact, there does not appear to be a requirement that the teacher actually directly examine children with item-specific protocols. Rather, the manual states that ratings may be based either on general observation of a child or on situations specifically designed to elicit communication behaviors. No validation studies are presented to confirm that these two approaches produce the same rating result. Without such studies, it remains possible that teacher biases may determine children's ratings more than children's situation-specific behaviors.

Inconsistencies in some item descriptions make clear the difficulty that a teacher might face in determining how to establish the correct environment for evaluation. For example, the third Expressive Scale B item, E IIIb, is supposed to determine whether a child "uses at least 4 different words or expressions to communicate" spontaneously (according to the stated purpose of the Expressive B scale on page 12 of the manual). However, the authors suggest for this item, but oddly for no others in the scale, that "it may still be necessary to elicit the child's use of the word through contrived situations (e.g., using pictures or objects to stimulate the response)." Are props permissible for the other items? What about providing partial sentence frames for a child to fill in words? Can you cue a child with the first letter sound of a word? All of these procedures still require a child to generate words or expressions. Are they all acceptable, and, more importantly, apart from direct modeling (imitation conditions) what is *not* an acceptable method of eliciting speech behavior, and why?

Another general descriptive confusion is the presentation of "required minimum vocabulary" values as criteria for rating at particular levels, followed by statements like "some children may need more" than the required minimum vocabulary to be rated at a given level (Expressive scale Item E IVb), or "It is the child's facility in imitating speech rather than the precise number of words he can imitate that qualifies him to be rated at this level" (Expressive scale Item E IIIa). There is little point in having a required minimum if it is not a precise value. The authors should simply refer to an estimated or approximate vocabulary size as a benchmark indicator. More importantly, it is not clear why the particular vocabulary levels chosen (1, 4, 20 words) for Items E II–E IV were singled out as developmental benchmarks. The same question arises with respect to the minimum word combinations, word classes, and sentences in other items.

Such vagaries and inconsistencies are not conducive to accurate, teacher-independent scaling. If these scales are intended to yield results that characterize a child's communication knowledge on some absolute dimension of spoken language development, independent of teacher biases, then it seems inappropriate to leave so much of the structure of the instrument up to individual teachers on the simplistic and questionable assumption that teachers necessarily know how to assess language (without bias). There are no clear protocols for even the supposedly structured components of this instrument, significantly weakening any claims to teacher-independent measurement. Teachers may be well acquainted with a child and may offer expert and educated opinions, but they are not necessarily objective observers, and scales are not automatically insensitive to bias.

SCALE STRUCTURE. Both the Receptive and the Expressive Verbal scales are composed of two parallel subscales, the A scales and the B scales. There is no information provided on the factor structure of these four scales, or on any other measures of their scale distinctiveness. Therefore, we do not know empirically whether they represent truly distinct subscales or merely a single underlying dimension of spoken language development which has been redundantly measured. It would be useful to know whether these scales truly span four dimensions of a child's spoken language knowledge, with ratings for individual children lying reliably at distinct points in the space defined by those dimensions. If so, then the instrument would presumably have the sort of diagnostic specificity that the authors imagine it to have. If not, then the instrument might unnecessarily obfuscate the individual differences in language knowledge among children and confound the language assessment and placement process. The distinctiveness of the nonverbal components is likewise unattested. In fact, the items that comprise the nonverbal components tend to confound verbal and nonverbal communication, so it is really not clear what they measure or how they modify the combination scale scores.

Regardless of their actual empirical distinctiveness, there are some conceptual difficulties with the definition of the four verbal scales. The distinction between the A and B scales for the Receptive scales is stated to be the distinction between teacher-structured and natural, spontaneous comprehension situations. However, it is sometimes difficult to see this distinction in actual test items. For example, the second item of the Receptive scale, R II, is intended to determine whether a child "DEMONSTRATES COMPREHENSION OF A FEW WORDS OR EXPRESSIONS." The "teacher-structured" A-scale situation is exemplified by asking a child to select a stated food from among several foods on a table. The "natural" B-scale situation is exemplified by asking a child to get a spoon from a drawer with which to eat ice cream. Both situations seem quite natural and highly situationally constrained. In fact, the A–B distinction used here and throughout the Receptive scales seems to be between relatively limited response sets (a fixed set of visible foods) and relatively open response sets (a kitchen full of utensils), *not* between artificial and natural situational structure. Curiously, some of the items intended to be natural require "minimal" situational cues and "no gestures" (e.g., Item R IIb). One of the five Receptive scale items (R V), in attempting to be natural, is exemplified by a coherent child-teacher conversation that ends up hopelessly corrupting the Receptive scale with expressive speech, as if the Receptive and Expressive scales of this instrument were not designed to separate the two skills in the first place.

The distinction between the A and B scales for the Expressive scales is the distinction between teacher-elicited imitation of speech sounds, words, and phrases on the one hand, and spontaneous production of speech on the other. Whereas with the Receptive scales the A and B versions are conceptually parallel, in that both require of a child relatively natural acts of comprehension, the relationship between the A and B scales of the Expressive scales seems artificial and strained. Verbatim or partial imitation is not a naturally motivated speech act throughout most of development. Furthermore, for some items the A scale does not even require verbatim imitation, with its useful requirement for reproduction of the grammatical structure of utterances. Rather, it only requires the child to produce an unstructured set of words from the utterance. Also, as utterances become longer, the imitation task becomes increasingly dependent on the child's verbal memory. So, it is not at all clear what is being measured by this scale. The B scale, on the other hand, attempts to assess the child's increasing grammatical sophistication directly. Although there are no data available on the response distributions for these two scales, it seems possible that a child could score high on the Expressive A scale and low on the Expressive B scale simply because the scales are not measuring the same general skill. Nevertheless, the manual defines the A–B item pairs at each level of the Expressive scales as a conceptually coherent developmental benchmark, as if the two scales really measured the same underlying thing.

BENCHMARK AND INDICATOR VALIDITY. The motivation for the specific benchmarks used in these scales is not justified by the authors on the grounds of any specific developmental milestones, and their indicators often seem superficial and arbitrary. For example, for the E VII benchmark "DEMONSTRATES THE ABILITY TO USE SENTENCES CONTAINING A MODIFYING WORD OR PHRASE," the A-scale indicator is "Imitates at Least 4 Words of a Sentence or Recalls at Least 4 Words of a Practice Sentence Pattern" (p. 24). It is difficult to see the relationship between the benchmark and the indicator.

Generally, the benchmarks are intended to track increases in the size and variety of vocabulary and grammatical word category groupings. Although such increases in language behavior would naturally be expected to correlate with English language development both in hearing and in deaf and hard-of-hearing children, these measures could yield only the crudest indication of developmental stage. They certainly do not probe the complexities of lexical knowledge, or the details of grammatical knowledge under development in the brains of deaf and hard-of-hearing children. Furthermore, there is nothing by way of validation for these scales that takes into account that deaf and hard-of-hearing children, who may be seriously restricted in their access to primary English language data, might show patterns of English language development (for fundamental linguistic reasons) that depart significantly from the patterns of hearing children, especially for the latter stages of the Expressive scale (Berent & Samar, 1990). There is no evidence presented that deaf and hard-of-hearing children normally follow all of these stages in the particular hierarchical order on their way to more adult forms of language behavior.

PREDICTIVE VALIDITY. Most importantly, this is a scale intended to aid teachers in making effective recommendations for instruction of individual children. Yet, there are no data available to show that use of this scale predicts a child's success to any extent in subsequent language training programs for any subpopulation of deaf and hard-of-hearing children.

RELIABILITY. The reliability information presented in the manual is inadequate. No data are presented on the presumably language-critical age range of 2–3 years, despite the claim that the Scales of Early Communication Skills for Hearing-Impaired Children is intended to rate children this young and help to place them (presumably reliably) in language training programs. Furthermore, the reliability sample is rather small (31), and the coefficients are not impressive (58–83% of variance accounted for depending on the scale), considering that the goal is individual child assessment rather than population research and that no data are presented on the homogeneity of error variance over the entire scale range. It is entirely possible that reliability in the midrange of skills is much worse than indicated by the overall reliability coefficients.

SUMMARY. The Scales of Early Communication Skills for Hearing-Impaired Children is an elaborately structured instrument, requiring considerable assessment time if it is to be applied by contriving actual evaluation situations for each child. We presume that the motivation for the elaborate administrative and quantitative structure of this instrument is to improve the general properties of the assessment for an individual child (e.g., reliability, validity, generalizability) over simple, unstructured observations and global descriptive characterization of the child's skills by the child's teachers. Yet, there is no empirical evidence that this instrument does so. Do scores on this instrument improve the delivery of educational services to deaf and hard-of-hearing children compared with more traditional assessment methods? Do children evaluated by this instrument make greater or earlier gains in their development of spoken communication skills? Does the instrument reduce the probability of misplacement? If not, why bother? Surely a teacher's reflective recommendation is a simpler result to obtain, and it does not risk the masquerade of false quantitative respectability that a numerical rating by an unvalidated instrument does. The burden of proof is clearly on the authors.

In summary, the Scales of Early Communication Skills for Hearing-Impaired Children is lacking in procedural precision, has no validity statistics, is limited in assessment scope, and is potentially biased against several subpopulations of deaf and hard-of-hearing children. We recommend that it not be used with deaf and hard-of-hearing children until such time as the instrument is adequately revised and validated.

REVIEWERS' REFERENCE

Berent, G. P., & Samar, V. J. (1990). The psychological reality of the subset principle: Evidence from the governing categories of prelingually deaf adults. *Language, 66*, 714-741.

Review of the Scales of Early Communication Skills for Hearing-Impaired Children by E. W. TESTUT, Associate Professor of Audiology, Department of Speech Pathology/Audiology, Ithaca College, Ithaca, NY:

The Scales of Early Communication Skills for Hearing-Impaired Children (SECS) provides a criterion-referenced means for assessing the receptive and expressive language behaviors and receptive and expressive nonverbal communication skills of hearing-impaired children between the ages of 2 to 8 years for the purpose of determining appropriate and targetable teaching objectives. The SECS assesses communication by providing checklists of verbal and nonverbal communication behaviors thought to reflect the developmental, expressive, and receptive language and communication stages of hearing-impaired children between the ages of 2 to 8 years. As such, items are hierarchically ordered so that a behavior not observed would preclude the existence of succeeding, higher level behaviors. The SECS, therefore, presumes (*a*) a universal, irreversible, linear model of English language acquisition; (*b*) that this linearity is reflected in the individual's expressive and receptive communication skills, including nonverbal communication; and (*c*) that the behaviors selected for inclusion in the SECS accurately reflect the presumed developmental model of language. Additionally, the SECS assumes a continuum of language development such that nonverbal communication precedes verbal communication and that possession of verbal communication may be seen as an indication that related level, nonverbal communication has been established.

Scoring is done by teachers or, presumably, speech-language pathologists familiar with the children being evaluated. According to the authors, the SECS is intended for use by the teacher because the teacher is most likely to understand language development and its assessment and to know the individual child. Additionally, because the intended purpose of the scale is to assist in the development of appropriate teaching behaviors, its application would be more meaningful for that individual most responsible for the development of these communication behaviors (i.e., the teacher and/or the speech-language pathologist). Specific verbal and nonverbal communication behaviors are identified by the manual in a level-ordered fashion, such that the test may be concluded when the individual is judged to lack specific behaviors appropriate to an identified level. Samples are specifically elicited under structured settings and, also, are observed in more natural, less structured, more spontaneous communication settings. Although two sets of samples are obtained this way, no rank order of importance of the two evaluative situations is intended by the authors. Additionally, rationales and sample behaviors are provided to assist the test user in determining the appropriateness of the child's communication sample relative to each level. All communication behavior is scored as observed (+) or not (-) or as only occasionally being seen (+/-), the latter suggesting an Incomplete, but developing acquisitional stage. The results are then tabulated, converted to a raw score, which by comparing to tables included in the SECS manual, can be converted to a percentile rank for both the structured and the spontaneously elicited receptive and expressive communication behaviors. It is also possible to obtain "Combined Expressive" and "Combined Receptive" percentile rank scores by combining verbal communication skill raw scores with nonverbal communication skill raw scores. All of the scale scores may be converted to a standard score where the individual's performance may be compared to the average for his or her age group. Additionally, an indication of the individual's relative distance from the average for his or her age group can be determined. No interpretation is given relative to the individual's performance compared to the normal language development of normally hearing, normal language functioning children.

The SECS has many strengths. It offers readily identifiable behaviors with simple instructions, rationales, and sample behaviors for each step of the evaluation. As such, it is easy to administer and, if the tester is truly familiar with the child as intended by the authors, requires a relatively short time to administer. Additionally, the interpretation of the SECS is easily accomplished and provides a means for comparing the development of hearing-impaired children with normative data. Finally, to the degree the behaviors reflect a universal, linear, irreversible model of language acquisition by hearing-impaired children, the results should permit the teacher to establish realistic, identifiable, communication skill teaching goals.

The SECS possesses some limitations. For example, how the specific stages of the SECS reflect normal communication development and/or relative validity are not explained. Additionally, no indication of intratester reliability and only a limited evaluation of intertester reliability are mentioned. Furthermore, little concrete information is given concerning the demographic makeup of subjects from whom normative data were obtained other than chronological age and average hearing levels at selected frequencies. It might have been helpful to have information concerning the composition of the normative group with respect to age, sex, race, ethnicity, and socioeconomic status, developmental level, geographic region, and primary language spoken in the home. Finally, if the language model on which the SECS is based is universal, linear, and irreversible, a normal language/communication skill acquisition, age level indication for normal hearing children might provide additional valuable information, especially where placement or performance in an integrated educational setting may be a consideration.

In summary, the SECS is a flexible, relatively straightforward means for assessing the communication development of young hearing-impaired children between the ages of 2 to 8 years. It is probably best used as a tool for targeting appropriate teaching goals rather than as an absolute measure of an individual's communication performance, but, as such, its application should prove valuable.

[343]

Schedule for Affective Disorders and Schizophrenia, Third Edition.

Purpose: "To record information regarding a subject's functioning and psychopathology."
Population: Adults.
Publication Dates: 1977–88.
Acronym: SADS.
Administration: Individual.
Price Data, 1993: $.50 per SADS/SADS-L suggested procedures; $2 per SADS/SADS-L instructions and clarifications ('85, 24 pages).
Time: Administration time not reported.
Authors: Robert L. Spitzer, Jean Endicott, Jo Ellen Loth (SADS-LB, SADS-LI), Patricia McDonald-Scott (SADS-LI), and Patricia Wasek (SADS-LI).
Publisher: Department of Research Assessment and Training, New York State Psychiatric Institute.

a) SCHEDULE FOR AFFECTIVE DISORDERS AND SCHIZOPHRENIA.

Scores, 24: Current Syndromes (Depressive Mood/Ideation, Endogenous Features, Depressive-Associated Features, Suicidal Ideation/Behavior, Anxiety, Manic Syndrome, Delusions-Hallucinations, Formal Thought Disorder, Impaired Functioning, Alcohol or Drug Abuse, Behavioral Disorganization, Miscellaneous Psychopathology, GAS [worst period], Extracted Hamilton); Past Week Functioning (Depressive Syndrome, Endogenous Features, Manic Syndrome, Anxiety, Delusions-Hall-Disorganization, GAS rating, Extracted Hamilton, Miscellaneous Psychopathology); Past Other than Diagnosis (Social Functioning, Suicidal Behavior).

Price Data: $3 per SADS booklet; $.50 per SADS score sheet; $1.50 per SADS summary scales scores; $.25 per editing and coding instructions; $2 per instructions/clarifications.

b) SCHEDULE FOR AFFECTIVE DISORDERS AND SCHIZOPHRENIA LIFETIME (VARIOUS VERSIONS).

1) *SADS-L.*

Purpose:: To record information regarding a subject's functioning and psychopathology; includes current disturbance.

Price Data: $2 per SADS-L booklet; $.50 per SADS-L score sheet.

2) *SADS-LB.*

Purpose:: To record information regarding a subject's functioning and psychopathology; includes current disturbance and additional items related to bipolar affective disorder.

Price Data: $2 per SADS-LB booklet; $.50 per SADS-LB score sheet.

3) *SADS-LI.*

Purpose:: To record information regarding a subject's functioning and psychopathology; specifies follow-up interval.

Price Data: $2 per SADS-LI booklet; $.50 per SADS-LI score sheet.

Cross References: See T4:2340 (152 references).

TEST REFERENCES

1. Lewinsohn, P. M., Fenn, D. S., Stanton, A. K., & Franklin, J. (1986). Relation of age at onset to duration of episode in unipolar depression. *Psychology and Aging, 1*, 63-68.

2. O'Hara, M. W., Hinrichs, J. V., Kohout, F. J., Wallace, R. B., & Lemke, J. H. (1986). Memory complaint and memory performance in the depressed elderly. *Psychology and Aging, 1*, 208-214.

3. Downey, J., Ehrhardt, A. A., Gruen, R., Bell, J. J., & Morishima, A. (1989). Psychopathology and social functioning in women with Turner syndrome. *The Journal of Nervous and Mental Disease, 177*, 191-201.

4. Green, B. L., Lindy, J. D., Grace, M. C., & Gleser, G. C. (1989). Multiple diagnosis in posttraumatic stress disorder: The role of war stressors. *The Journal of Nervous and Mental Disease, 177*, 329-335.

5. Guelfi, G. D., Faustman, W. O., & Csernansky, J. G. (1989). Independence of positive and negative symptoms in a population of schizophrenic patients. *The Journal of Nervous and Mental Disease, 177*, 285-290.

6. Joffe, R. T., & Regan, J. J. (1989). Personality and response to tricyclic antidepressants in depressed patients. *The Journal of Nervous and Mental Disease, 177*, 745-749.

7. Marmar, C. R., Gaston, L., Gallagher, D., & Thompson, L. W. (1989). Alliance and outcome in late-life depression. *The Journal of Nervous and Mental Disease, 177*, 464-472.

8. Mason, J. W., Kennedy, J. L., Kosten, T. R., & Giller, E. L. (1989). Serum thyroxine levels in schizophrenic and affective disorder diagnostic subgroups. *The Journal of Nervous and Mental Disease, 177*, 351-358.

9. Niederche, G., & Yoder, C. (1899). Metamemory perceptions in depressions of young and older adults. *The Journal of Nervous and Mental Disease, 177*, 4-14.

10. Reich, J. H. (1989). Familiality of DSM-II dramatic and anxious personality clusters. *The Journal of Nervous and Mental Disease, 177*, 96-100.

11. Riley, W. T., Treiber, F. A., & Woods, M. G. (1989). Anger and hostility in depression. *The Journal of Nervous and Mental Disease, 177*, 668-674.

12. Speed, N., Engdahl, B., Schwartz, J., & Eberly, R. (1989). Posttraumatic stress disorder as a consequence of the POW experience. *The Journal of Nervous and Mental Disease, 177*, 147-153.

13. Vaglum, S., & Vaglum, P. (1989). Comorbidity for borderline and schizotypal personality disorders: A study of alcoholic women. *The Journal of Nervous and Mental Disease, 177*, 279-284.

14. Asarnow, J. R., & Horton, A. A. (1990). Coping and stress in families of child psychiatric inpatients: Parents of children with depressive and schizophrenia spectrum disorders. *Child Psychiatry and Human Development, 21*, 145-157.

15. Bastani, B., Nash, F., & Meltzer, H. Y. (1990). Prolactin and cortisol responses to MK-212, a serotonin agonist, in obsessive-compulsive disorder. *Archives of General Psychiatry, 47*, 833-839.

16. Bulik, C. M., Carpenter, L. L., Kupfer, D. J., & Frank, E. (1990). Features associated with suicide attempts in recurrent major depression. *Journal of Affective Disorders, 18*, 29-37.

17. Cannon, T. D., Mednick, S. A., & Parnas, J. (1990). Antecedents of predominantly negative- and predominantly positive-symptom schizophrenia in a high-risk population. *Archives of General Psychiatry, 47*, 622-632.

18. Coryell, W. (1990). DST abnormality as a predictor of course in major depression. *Journal of Affective Disorders, 19*, 163-169.

19. Coryell, W., Keller, M., Lavori, P., & Endicott, J. (1990). Affective syndromes, psychotic features, and prognosis. *Archives of General Psychiatry, 47*, 651-657.

20. Dahl, R. E., Puig-Antich, J., Ryan, N. D., Nelson, B., Dachille, S., Cunningham, S. L., Trubnick, L., & Klepper, T. P. (1990). EEG sleep in adolescents with major depression: The role of suicidality and inpatient status. *Journal of Affective Disorders, 19*, 63-75.

21. DePaulo, J. R., Jr., Simpson, S. G., Gayle, J. O., & Folstein, S. E. (1990). Bipolar II disorder in six sisters. *Journal of Affective Disorders, 19*, 259-264.

22. Deutscher, S., & Cimbolic, P. (1990). Cognitive processes and their relationship to endogenous and reactive components of depression. *The Journal of Nervous and Mental Disease, 178*, 351-359.

23. Dew, M. A., Ragni, M. V., & Nimorwicz, P. (1990). Infection with human immunodeficiency virus and vulnerability to psychiatric distress. *Archives of General Psychiatry, 47*, 737-744.

24. Faravelli, C., Degl'Innocenti, G. B., Aiazzi, L., Incerpi, G., & Pallanti, S. (1990). Epidemiology of mood disorders: A community survey in Florence. *Journal of Affective Disorders, 20*, 135-141.

25. Fava, G. A., Grandi, S., Canestrari, R., & Molnar, G. (1990). Prodromal symptoms in primary major depressive disorder. *Journal of Affective Disorders, 19*, 149-152.

26. Finn, P. R., Kleinman, I., & Pihl, R. O. (1990). The lifetime prevalence of psychopathology in men with multigenerational family histories of alcoholism. *The Journal of Nervous and Mental Disease, 178*, 500-509.

27. Frank, E., Kupfer, D. J., Perel, J. M., Cornes, C., Jarrett, D. B., Mallinger, A. G., Thase, M. E., McEachran, A. B., & Grochocinski, V. J. (1990). Three-year outcomes for maintenance therapies in recurrent depression. *Archives of General Psychiatry, 47*, 1093-1099.

28. Garvey, M., DeRubeis, R. J., Hollon, S. D., Evans, M. D., & Tuason, V. B. (1990). Does 24-h urinary MHPG predict treatment response to antidepressants? II. Association between imipramine response and low MHPG. *Journal of Affective Disorders, 20*, 181-184.

29. Garvey, M., Noyes, R., Jr., Cook, B., Barrickman, L., Noel, M., & Ghosheh, R. (1990). Elevated levels of N-acetyl-B-glucosaminidase in affective disorders and chemical dependence. *Journal of Affective Disorders, 19*, 279-285.

30. Green, B. L., Grace, M. C., Lindy, J. D., & Gleser, G. C. (1990). War stressors and symptom persistence in posttraumatic stress disorder. *Journal of Anxiety Disorders, 4*, 31-39.

31. Harrow, M., Goldberg, J. F., Grossman, L. S., & Meltzer, H. Y. (1990). Outcome in manic disorders: A naturalistic follow-up study. *Archives of General Psychiatry, 47*, 665-671.

32. Harvey, P. D., & Serper, M. R. (1990). Linguistic and cognitive failures in schizophrenia: A multivariate analysis. *The Journal of Nervous and Mental Disease, 178*, 487-493.

33. Irwin, M., Caldwell, C., Smith, T. L., Brown, S., Schuckit, M. A., & Gillin, C. (1990). Major depression disorder, alcoholism, and reduced natural killer cell cytotoxicity. *Archives of General Psychiatry, 47*, 713-719.

34. Joffe, R. T., & Swinson, R. P. (1990). Tranylcypromine in primary obsessive-compulsive disorder. *Journal of Anxiety Disorders, 4*, 365-367.

35. Kasper, S., Rogers, S. L. B., Madden, P. A., Joseph-Vanderpool, J. R., & Rosenthal, N. E. (1990). The effects of phototherapy in the general population. *Journal of Affective Disorders, 18*, 211-219.

36. Klein, D. N., Taylor, E. B., Harding, K., & Dickstein, S. (1990). The unipolar-bipolar distinction in the characterological mood disorders. *The Journal of Nervous and Mental Disease, 178*, 318-323.

37. Kravitz, H. M., Edwards, J. H., Fawcett, J., & Fogg, L. (1990). Challenging the amphetamine challenge test: Report of an antidepressant treatment study. *Journal of Affective Disorders, 20*, 121-128.

38. Kupfer, D. J., Frank, E., McEachran, A. B., & Grochocinski, V. J. (1990). Delta sleep ratio. *Archives of General Psychiatry, 47*, 1100-1105.

39. Levinson, D. F., Simpson, G. M., Singh, H., Yadalam, K., Jain, A., Stephanos, M. J., & Silver, P. (1990). Fluphenazine dose, clinical response, and extrapyramidal symptoms during acute treatment. *Archives of General Psychiatry, 47*, 761-768.

40. Maj, M., & Perris, C. (1990). Patterns of course in patients with a cross-sectional diagnosis of schizoaffective disorder. *Journal of Affective Disorders, 20*, 71-77.

41. Mannuzza, S., Fyer, A. J., Liebowitz, M. R., & Klein, D. F. (1990). Delineating the boundaries of social phobia: Its relationship to panic disorder and agoraphobia. *Journal of Anxiety Disorders, 4*, 41-59.

42. Morphy, M. A., Fava, G. A., Pedersen, R. C., Zielezny, M., Sonino, N., & Brownie, A. C. (1990). Effects of metyrapone and dexamethasone upon pro-gamma-MSH plasma levels in depressed patients and healthy controls. *Journal of Affective Disorders, 19*, 183-189.

43. Morrison, R. L., Bellack, A. S., Wixted, J. T., & Mueser, K. T. (1990). Positive and negative symptoms in schizophrenia: A cluster-analytic approach. *The Journal of Nervous and Mental Disease, 178*, 377-384.

44. Noyes, R., Jr., Reich, J., Christiansen, J., Suelzer, M., Pfohl, B., & Coryell, W. A. (1990). Outcome of panic disorder: Relationship to diagnostic subtypes and comorbidity. *Archives of General Psychiatry, 47*, 809-818.

45. Pande, A. C., Grunhaus, L. J., Haskett, R. F., & Greden, J. F. (1990). Electroconvulsive therapy in delusional and non-delusional depressive disorder. *Journal of Affective Disorders, 19*, 215-219.

46. Pearlstein, T. B., Frank, A., Rivera-Tovar, A., Thoft, J. S., Jacobs, E., & Mieczkowski, T. A. (1990). Prevalence of Axis I and Axis II disorders in women with late luteal phase dysphoric disorder. *Journal of Affective Disorders, 20*, 129-134.

47. Reynolds, C. F., III, Buysse, D. J., Kupfer, D. J., Hoch, C. C., Houck, P. R., Matzzie, J., & George, C. J. (1990). Rapid eye movement sleep deprivation as a probe in elderly subjects. *Archives of General Psychiatry, 47*, 1128-1136.

48. Rihmer, Z., Barsi, J., Arató, M., & Demeter, E. (1990). Suicide in subtypes of primary major depression. *Journal of Affective Disorders, 18*, 221-225.

49. Sautter, F. J., McDermott, B. E., & Garver, D. L. (1990). A family study of lithium-responsive psychosis. *Journal of Affective Disorders, 20*, 63-69.

50. Schweizer, E., Rickels, K., Case, G., & Greenblatt, D. J. (1990). Long-term therapeutic use of benzodiazepines. *Archives of General Psychiatry, 47*, 908-915.

51. Siever, L. J., Silverman, J. M., Horvath, T. B., Klar, H., Coccaro, E., Keefe, R. S. E., Pinkham, L., Rinaldi, P., Mohs, R. C., & Davis, K. L. (1990). Increased morbid risk for schizophrenia-related disorders in relatives in schizotypal personality disordered patients. *Archives of General Psychiatry, 47*, 634-640.

52. Stark, K. D., Brookman, C. S., & Frazier, R. (1990). A comprehensive school-based treatment program for depressed children. *School Psychology Quarterly, 5*, 111-140.

53. Stein, M. B., Tancer, M. E., & Uhde, T. W. (1990). Major depression in patients with panic disorder: Factors associated with course and recurrence. *Journal of Affective Disorders, 19*, 287-296.

54. Stinson, D., & Thompson, C. (1990). Clinical experience with phototherapy. *Journal of Affective Disorders, 18*, 129-135.

55. Stunkard, A. J., Fernstrom, M. H., Price, R. A., Frank, E., & Kupfer, D. J. (1990). Direction of weight change in recurrent depression. *Archives of General Psychiatry, 47*, 857-860.

56. Targum, S. D., Clarkson, L. L., Magac-Harris, K., Marshall, L. E., & Skwerer, R. G. (1990). Measurement of cortisol and lymphocyte subpopulations in depressed and conduct-disordered adolescents. *Journal of Affective Disorders, 18*, 91-96.

57. Weddington, W. W., Brown, B. S., Haertzen, C. A., Cone, E. J., Dax, E. M., Herring, R. I., & Michaelson, B. S. (1990). Changes in mood, craving, and sleep during short-term abstinence reported by male cocaine addicts. *Archives of General Psychiatry, 47*, 861-868.

58. Weiner, R. U., Opler, L. A., Kay, S. R., Merriam, A. E., & Papouchis, N. (1990). Visual information processing in positive, mixed, and negative schizophrenic syndromes. *The Journal of Nervous and Mental Disease, 178*, 616-626.

59. Wolkowitz, O. M., Rubinow, D., Doran, A. R., Breier, A., Berrettini, W. H., Kling, M. A., & Pickar, D. (1990). Prednisone effects on neurochemistry and behavior. *Archives of General Psychiatry, 47*, 963-968.

60. Yehuda, R., Southwick, S. M., Nussbaum, G., Wahby, V., Giller, E. L., & Mason, J. W. (1990). Low urinary cortisol excretion in patients with posttraumatic stress disorder. *The Journal of Nervous and Mental Disease, 178*, 366-369.

61. Young, M. A., Fogg, L. F., Scheftner, W. A., & Fawcett, J. A. (1990). Concordance of symptoms in recurrent depressive episodes. *Journal of Affective Disorders, 20*, 79-85.

62. Young, M. A., Fogg, L. F., Scheftner, W. A., Keller, M. B., & Fawcett, J. A. (1990). Sex differences in the lifetime prevalence of depression: Does varying the diagnostic criteria reduce the female/male ratio? *Journal of Affective Disorders, 18*, 187-192.

63. Young, M. A., Scheftner, W. A., Fawcett, J., & Klerman, G. L. (1990). Gender differences in the clinical features of unipolar major depressive disorder. *The Journal of Nervous and Mental Disease, 178*, 200-203.

64. Alterman, A. I., & Cacciola, J. S. (1991). The antisocial personality disorder diagnosis in substance abusers: Problems and issues. *The Journal of Nervous and Mental Disease, 179*, 401-409.

65. Blackwood, D. H. R., St. Clair, D. M., Muir, W. J., & Duffy, J. C. (1991). Auditory P300 and eye tracking dysfunction in schizophrenic pedigrees. *Archives of General Psychiatry, 48*, 899-909.

66. Breier, A., Schreiber, J. L., Dyer, J., & Pickar, D. (1991). National Institute of Mental Health longitudinal study of chronic schizophrenia. *Archives of General Psychiatry, 48*, 239-246.

67. Carone, B. J., Harrow, M., & Westermeyer, J. F. (1991). Posthospital course and outcome in schizophrenia. *Archives of General Psychiatry, 48*, 247-253.

68. Cohn, J. F., Campbell, S. B., & Ross, S. (1991). Infant response in the still-face paradigm at 6 months predicts avoidant and secure attachment at 12 months. *Development and Psychopathology, 3*, 367-376.

69. Costello, E. J., Benjamin, R., Angold, A., & Silver, D. (1991). Mood variability in adolescents: A study of depressed, nondepressed and comorbid patients. *Journal of Affective Disorders, 23*, 199-212.

70. Davidson, M., Kahn, R. S., Knott, P., Kaminsky, R., Cooper, M., DuMont, K., Apter, S., & Davis, K. L. (1991). Effects of neuroleptic treatment on symptoms of schizophrenia and plasma homovanillic acid concentrations. *Archives of General Psychiatry, 48*, 910-913.

71. Davidson, M., Kahn, R. S., Powchik, P., Warne, P., Losonczy, M. F., Kaminsky, R., Apter, S., Jaff, S., & Davis, K. L. (1991). Changes in plasma homovanillic acid concentrations in schizophrenic patients following neuroleptic discontinuation. *Archives of General Psychiatry, 48*, 73-76.

72. DeMulder, E. K., & Radke-Yarrow, M. (1991). Attachment with affectively ill and well mothers: Concurrent behavioral correlates. *Development and Psychopathology, 3*, 227-242.

73. Denham, S. A., Zahn-Waxler, C., Cummings, E. M., & Iannotti, R. J. (1991). Social competence in young children's peer relations: Patterns of development and change. *Child Psychiatry and Human Development, 22*, 29-44.

74. Devanand, D. P., Sackeim, H. A., Lo, E., Cooper, T., Huttinot, G., Prudic, J., & Ross, F. (1991). Serial dexamethasone suppression tests and plasma dexamethasone levels. *Archives of General Psychiatry, 48*, 525-533.

75. Drennan, M. D., Klauber, M. R., Kripke, D. F., & Goyette, L. M. (1991). The effects of depression and age on the Horne-Ostberg morningness-eveningness score. *Journal of Affective Disorders, 23*, 93-98.

76. Duggan, C. F., Sham, P., Lee, A. S., & Murray, R. M. (1991). Can future suicidal behaviour in depressed patients be predicted? *Journal of Affective Disorders, 22*, 111-118.

77. Fava, G. A., Grandi, S., Canestrari, R., Grasso, P., & Persarin, F. (1991). Mechanisms of change of panic attacks with exposure treatment of agoraphobia. *Journal of Affective Disorders, 22*, 65-71.

78. Gasperini, M., Battaglia, M., Scherillo, P., Sciuto, G., Diaferia, G., & Bellodi, L. (1991). Morbidity risk for mood disorders in the families of borderline patients. *Journal of Affective Disorders, 21*, 265-272.

79. Gelernter, C. S., Uhde, T. W., Cimbolic, P., Arnkoff, D. B., ViHone, B. H., Tancer, M. E., & Bartko, J. J. (1991). Cognitive-behavioral and pharmacological treatments of social phobia. *Archives of General Psychiatry, 48*, 938-945.

80. Gillin, J. C., Sutton, L., Ruiz, C., Kelsoe, J., Dupont, R. M., Darko, D., Risch, S. C., Golshan, S., & Janowsky, D. (1991). The cholinergic rapid eye movement induction test with grecoline in depression. *Archives of General Psychiatry, 48*, 264-270.

81. Goetz, R. R., Puig-Antich, J., Dahl, R. E., Ryan, N. D., Asnis, G. M., Rabinovich, H., & Nelson, B. (1991). EEG sleep of young adults with major depression: A controlled study. *Journal of Affective Disorders, 22*, 91-100.

82. Herz, M. I., Glazer, W. M., Mostert, M. A., Sheard, M. A., Szymanski, H. V., Hafez, H., Mirza, M., & Vana, J. (1991). Intermittent vs. maintenance medication in schizophrenia. *Archives of General Psychiatry, 48*, 333-339.

83. Hsu, L. K. G., Clement, L., Santhouse, R., & Ju, E. S. Y. (1991). Treatment of bulimia nervosa with lithium carbonate: A controlled study. *The Journal of Nervous and Mental Disease, 179*, 351-355.

84. Jarrett, R. B., Giles, D. Z., Gullion, C. M., & Rush, A. J. (1991). Does learned resourcefulness predict response to cognitive therapy in depressed outpatients? *Journal of Affective Disorders, 23*, 223-229.

85. Joffe, R. T., & Levitt, A. J. (1991). Seasonal variation of peripheral thyroid hormone levels in major depression. *Journal of Affective Disorders, 23*, 49-51.

86. Kalus, O., Asnis, G. M., Rubinson, E., Kahn, R., Friedman, J. M. K., Iqbal, N., Grosz, D., van Praag, H., & Cahn, W. (1991). Desipramine treatment in panic disorder. *Journal of Affective Disorders, 21*, 239-244.

87. Keller, M. B., Lavori, P. W., Beardslee, W. R., Wunder, J., & Ryan, N. (1991). Depression in children and adolescents: New data on "undertreatment" and a literature review on the efficacy of available treatments. *Journal of Affective Disorders, 21*, 163-171.

88. Kosten, T. R., Rounsaville, B. J., Kosten, T. A., & Merikangas, K. (1991). Gender differences in the specificity of alcoholism transmission among the relatives of opioid addicts. *The Journal of Nervous and Mental Disease, 179*, 392-400.

89. Leonard, H. L., Lenane, M. C., Swedo, S. E., Rettew, D. C., & Rapoport, J. L. (1991). A double-blind comparison of clomipramine and desipramine treatment of severe onychophagia (nail biting). *Archives of General Psychiatry, 48*, 821-827.

90. Levitt, A. J., Joffe, R. T., & MacDonald, C. (1991). Life course of depressive illness and characteristics of current episode in patients with double depression. *The Journal of Nervous and Mental Disease, 179*, 678-682.

91. Limson, R., Goldman, D., Roy, A., Lamparski, D., Ravitz, B., Adinoff, B., & Linnoila, M. (1991). Personality and cerebrospinal fluid monoamine metabolites in alcoholics and controls. *Archives of General Psychiatry, 48*, 437-441.

92. Loranger, A. W., Lenzenweger, M. F., Gartner, A. F., Susman, V. L., Herzig, J., Zammit, G. K., Gartner, J. D., Abrams, R. C., & Young, R. C. (1991). Trait-state artifacts and the diagnosis of personality disorders. *Archives of General Psychiatry, 48*, 720-728.

93. Mitchell, P., Waters, B., Morrison, N., Shine, J., Donald, J., & Eisman, J. (1991). Close linkage of bipolar disorder to chromosome 11 markers is excluded in two large Australian pedigrees. *Journal of Affective Disorders, 21*, 23-32.

94. Moises, H. W., Gelernter, J., Giuffra, L. A., Zarcone, V., Wetterberg, L., Civelli, O., Kidd, K. K., & Cavalli-Sforza, L. L. (1991). No linkage between D_2 dopamine receptor gene region and schizophrenia. *Archives of General Psychiatry, 48*, 643-647.

95. O'Hara, M. W., Schlechte, J. A., Lewis, D. A., & Wright, E. J. (1991). Prospective study of postpartum blues. *Archives of General Psychiatry, 48*, 801-806.

96. Obarzanek, E., Lesem, M. D., Goldstein, D. S., & Jimerson, D. C. (1991). Reduced resting metabolic rate in patients with bulimia nervosa. *Archives of General Psychiatry, 48*, 456-462.

97. Peselow, E. D., Corwin, J., Fiere, R. R., Rotrosen, J., & Cooper, T. B. (1991). Disappearance of memory deficits in outpatient depressives responding to imipramine. *Journal of Affective Disorders, 21*, 173-183.

98. Pettegrew, J. W., Keshavan, M. S., Panchalingam, K., Strychors, S., Kaplan, D. B., Tretta, M. G., & Allen, M. (1991). Alterations in brain high-energy phosphate and membrane phospholipid metabolism in first-episode, drug-naive schizophrenics. *Archives of General Psychiatry, 48*, 563-568.

99. Rettew, D. C., Cheslow, D. L., Rapoport, J. L., Leonard, H. L., & Lenane, M. C. (1991). Neuropsychological test performance in trichotillomania: A further link with obsessive-compulsive disorder. *Journal of Anxiety Disorders, 5*, 225-235.

100. Rifkin, A., Doddi, S., Karajgi, B., Borenstein, M., & Wachspress, M. (1991). Dosage of haloperidol for schizophrenia. *Archives of General Psychiatry, 48*, 166-170.

101. Rounsaville, B. J., Anton, S. F., Carroll, K., Budde, D., Prusoff, B. A., & Gawin, F. (1991). Psychiatric diagnoses of treatment-seeking cocaine abusers. *Archives of General Psychiatry, 48*, 43-51.

102. Rounsaville, B. J., Kosten, T. R., Weissman, M. M., Prusoff, B., Pauls, D., Anton, S. F., & Merikangas, K. (1991). Psychiatric disorders in relatives of probands with opiate addiction. *Archives of General Psychiatry, 48*, 33-42.

103. Roy, A., DeJong, J., Lamparski, D., Adinoff, B., George, T., Moore, V., Garnett, D., Kerich, M., & Linnoila, M. (1991). Mental disorders among alcoholics. *Archives of General Psychiatry, 48*, 423-427.

104. Roy, A., DeJong, J., Lamparski, D., George, T., & Linnoila, M. (1991). Depression among alcoholics. *Archives of General Psychiatry, 48*, 428-432.

105. Rubin, K. H., Both, L., Zahn-Waxler, C., Cummings, E. M., & Wilkinson, M. (1991). Dyadic play behaviors of children of well and depressed mothers. *Development and Psychopathology, 3*, 243-251.

106. Saviotti, F. M., Grandi, S., Savron, G., Ermentini, R., Bartoulucci, G., Conti, S., & Fava, G. A. (1991). Characterological traits of recovered patients with panic disorder and agoraphobia. *Journal of Affective Disorders, 23*, 113-117.

107. Schneier, F. R., Fyer, A. J., Martin, L. Y., Ross, R. N. D., Mannuzza, S., Liebowitz, M. R., Gorman, J. M., & Klein, D. F. (1991). A comparison of phobic subtypes within panic disorder. *Journal of Anxiety Disorders, 5*, 65-75.

108. Servant, D., Bailly, D., Allard, C., & Parquet, P. J. (1991). Major depression in panic disorder: Role of recent life events. *Journal of Affective Disorders, 22*, 79-82.

109. Small, J. G., Klapper, M. H., Milstein, V., Kellams, J. J., Miller, M. J., Marhenke, J. D., & Small, I. F. (1991). Carbamazepine compared with lithium in the treatment of mania. *Archives of General Psychiatry, 48*, 915-921.

110. Stein, M. B., & Uhde, T. W. (1991). Endocrine, cardiovascular, and behavioral effects of intravenous protirelin in patients with panic disorder. *Archives of General Psychiatry, 48*, 148-156.

111. Van Cauter, E., Linkowski, P., Kerkhofs, M., Hobain, P., L'Hermite-Baleriaux, M., Leclercq, R., Brasseur, M., Copinschi, G., & Mendlewicz, J. (1991). Circadian and sleep-related endocrine rhythms in schizophrenia. *Archives of General Psychiatry, 48*, 348-356.

112. Warshaw, M. G., Klerman, G. L., & Lavori, P. W. (1991). The use of conditional probabilities to examine age-period-cohort data: Further evidence for a period effect in major depressive disorder. *Journal of Affective Disorders, 23*, 119-129.

113. Westermeyer, J. F., Harrow, M., & Marengo, J. T. (1991). Risk for suicide in schizophrenia and other psychotic and nonpsychotic disorders. *The Journal of Nervous and Mental Disease, 179*, 259-266.

114. Young, E. A., Haskett, R. F., Murphy-Weinberg, V., Watson, S. J., & Akil, H. (1991). Loss of glucocorticoid fast feedback in depression. *Archives of General Psychiatry, 48*, 693-699.

115. Andreasen, N. C., Flaum, M., & Arndt, S. (1992). The Comprehensive Assessment of Symptoms and History (CASH): An instrument for assessing diagnosis and psychopathology. *Archives of General Psychiatry, 49*, 615-623.

116. Austin, M. P., Dougall, N., Ross, M., Murray, C., O'Carroll, R. E., Moffoot, A., Ebmeier, K. P., & Goodwin, G. M. (1992). Single photon emission tomography with 99mTc-exametazime in major depression and the pattern of brain activity underlying the psychotic/neurotic continuum. *Journal of Affective Disorders, 26*, 31-44.

117. Austin, M.-P., Ross, M., Murray, C., O'Carroll, R. E., Ebmeier, K. P., & Goodwin, G. M. (1992). Cognitive function in major depression. *Journal of Affective Disorders, 25*, 21-30.

118. Bagby, R. M., Cox, B. J., Schuller, D. R., Levitt, A. J., Swinson, R. P., & Joffe, R. T. (1992). Diagnostic specificity of the dependent and self-critical personality dimensions in major depression. *Journal of Affective Disorders, 26*, 59-64.

119. Baxter, L. R., Jr., Mazziotta, J. C., Pahl, J. J., Grafton, S. T., St. George-Hyslop, P., Haines, J. L., Gusella, J. F., Szuba, M. P., Sclin, C. E., Guze, B. H., & Phelps, M. E. (1992). Psychiatric, genetic, and positron emission tomographic evaluation of persons at risk for Huntington's disease. *Archives of General Psychiatry, 49*, 148-154.

120. Baxter, L. R., Jr., Schwartz, J. M., Bergman, K. S., Szuba, M. P., Guze, B. H., Mazziotta, J. C., Alzraki, A., Selin, C. E., Ferng, H., Monford, P., & Phelps, M. E. (1992). Claudate glucose metabolic rate changes with both drug and behavior therapy for obsessive-compulsive disorder. *Archives of General Psychiatry, 49*, 681-689.

121. Belfer, P. L., & Glass, C. R. (1992). Agoraphobic anxiety and fear of fear: Test of a cognitive-attentional model. *Journal of Anxiety Disorders, 6*, 133-146.

122. Bench, C. J., Friston, K. J., Brown, R. G., Scott, L. C., Frackowiak, R. S. J., & Dolan, R. J. (1992). The anatomy of melancholia—focal abnormalities of cerebral blood flow in major depression. *Psychological Medicine, 22*, 607-615.

123. Black, D. W., Goldstein, R. B., Mason, E. E., Bell, S. E., & Blum, N. (1992). Depression and other mental disorders in the relatives of morbidly obese patients. *Journal of Affective Disorders, 25*, 91-96.

124. Black, D. W., Noyes, R., Jr., Goldstein, R. B., & Blom, N. (1992). A family study of obsessive-compulsive disorder. *Archives of General Psychiatry, 49*, 362-368.

125. Braff, D. L., Grillon, C., & Geyer, M. A. (1992). Gating habituation of the startle reflex in schizophrenic patients. *Archives of General Psychiatry, 49*, 206-215.

126. Brewerton, T. D., Mueller, E. A., Lesem, M. D., Brandt, H. A., Quearry, B., George, D. T., Murphy, D. L., & Jimerson, D. C. (1992). Neuroendocrine response to M-chlorophenylpiperazine and L-tryptophan in bulimia. *Archives of General Psychiatry, 49*, 852-861.

127. Breznitz, Z. (1992). Verbal indicators of depression. *The Journal of General Psychology, 119*, 351-363.

128. Campbell, S. B., Cohn, J. F., Flanagan, C., Popper, S., & Meyers, T. (1992). Course and correlates of postpartum depression during the transition to parenthood. *Development and Psychopathology, 4*, 29-47.

129. Caplan, R., Guthrie, D., Shields, W. D., & Mori, L. (1992). Formal thought disorder in pediatric complex partial seizure disorder. *Journal of Child Psychology and Psychiatry and Allied Disciplines, 33*, 1399-1412.

130. Carlson, G. A., Rapport, M. D., Pataki, C. S., & Kelly, K. L. (1992). Lithium in hospitalized children at 4 and 8 weeks: Mood, behavior and cognitive effects. *Journal of Child Psychology and Psychiatry and Allied Disciplines, 33*, 411-425.

131. Carroll, K. M., & Rounsaville, B. J. (1992). Contrast of treatment-seeking and untreated cocaine abusers. *Archives of General Psychiatry, 49*, 464-471.

132. Coryell, W., Endicott, J., & Keller, M. (1992). Major depression in a nonclinical sample: Demographic and clinical risk factors for first onset. *Archives of General Psychiatry, 49*, 117-125.

133. Coryell, W., Endicott, J., & Keller, M. (1992). Rapidly cycling affective disorder: Demographics, diagnosis, family history, and course. *Archives of General Psychiatry, 49*, 126-131.

134. Coryell, W., Winokur, G., Keller, M., Scheftner, W., & Endicott, J. (1992). Alcoholism and primary major depression: A family study approach to co-existing disorders. *Journal of Affective Disorders, 24*, 93-99.

135. da Roza Davis, J. M., Sharpley, A. L., Solomon, R. A., & Cowen, P. J. (1992). Sleep and 5-HT_2 receptor sensitivity in recovered depressed patients. *Journal of Affective Disorders, 24*, 177-182.

136. Degreef, G., Ashtari, m., Bogerts, B., Bilder, R. M., Jody, D. N., Alvir, J. M. J., & Lieberman, J. A. (1992). Volumes of ventricular system subdivisions measured from magnetic resonance images in first-episode schizophrenic patients. *Archives of General Psychiatry, 49*, 531-537.

137. Delvenne, V., Kerkhofs, M., Appleboom-Fondu, J., Lucas, F., & Mendlewicz, J. (1992). Sleep polygraphic variables in anorexia nervosa and depression: A comparative study in adolescents. *Journal of Affective Disorders, 25*, 167-172.

138. Diamond, R., White, R. F., Myers, R. H., Mastromauro, C., Koroshetz, W. J., Butters, N., Rothstein, D. M., Moss, M. B., & Vasterling, J. (1992). Evidence of presymptomatic cognitive decline in Huntington's disease. *Journal of Clinical and Experimental Neuropsychology, 14*, 961-975.

139. Downey, G., & Walker, E. (1992). Distinguishing family-level and child-level influences on the development of depression and aggression in children at risk. *Development and Psychopathology, 4*, 81-95.

140. Evans, D. L., Folds, J. D., Petitto, J. M., Golden, R. N., Pedersen, C. A., Corrigan, M., Gilmore, J. H., Silva, S. G., Quade, D., & Ozer, H. (1992). Circulating natural killer cell phenotypes in men and women with major depression: Relation to cytotoxic activity and severity of depression. *Archives of General Psychiatry, 49*, 388-395.

141. Fava, G. A., Grandi, S., Rafanelli, C., & Canestrari, R. (1992). Prodromal symptoms in panic disorder with agoraphobia: A replication study. *Journal of Affective Disorders, 26*, 85-88.

142. Frank, E., Kupfer, D. J., Hamer, T., Grochocinski, V. J., & McEachran, A. B. (1992). Maintenance treatment and psychobiologic correlates of endogenous subtypes. *Journal of Affective Disorders, 25*, 181-190.

143. Freund, L. S., Reiss, A. L., Hagerman, R., & Vinogradov, S. (1992). Chromosome fragility and psychopathology in obligate female carriers of the fragile X chromosome. *Archives of General Psychiatry, 49*, 54-60.

144. Hallmayer, J., Kennedy, J. L., Wetterberg, L., Sjogren, B., Kidd, K. K., & Cavalli-Sforza, L. L. (1992). Exclusion of linkage between the serotonin receptor and schizophrenia in a large Swedish kindred. *Archives of General Psychiatry, 49*, 216-219.

145. Hay, D. F., Zahn-Waxler, C., Cummings, E. M., & Iannotti, R. J. (1992). Young children's view about conflict with peers: A comparison of the daughters and sons of depressed and well women. *Journal of Child Psychology and Psychiatry and Allied Disciplines, 33*, 669-683.

146. Hickie, I., & Parker, G. (1992). The impact of an uncaring partner on improvement in non-melancholic depression. *Journal of Affective Disorders, 25*, 147-160.

147. Hollon, S. D., DeRubeis, R. J., Evans, M. D., Wiemer, M. J., Garvey, M. J., Grove, W. M., & Tuason, V. B. (1992). Cognitive therapy and pharmacotherapy for depression: Singly and in combination. *Archives of General Psychiatry, 49*, 774-781.

148. Hunt, N., Bruce-Jones, W., & Silverstone, T. (1992). Life events and relapse in bipolar affective disorder. *Journal of Affective Disorders, 25*, 13-20.

149. Irwin, M., Lacher, U., & Caldwell, C. (1992). Depression and reduced natural killer cytotoxicity: A longitudinal study of depressed patients and control subjects. *Psychological Medicine, 22*, 1045-1050.

150. Jimerson, D. C., Lesem, M. D., Kaye, W. H., & Bewerton, T. D. (1992). Low serotonin and dopamine metabolite concentrations in cerebrospinal fluid from bulimic patients with frequent binge episodes. *Archives of General Psychiatry, 49*, 131-138.

151. Khanna, R., Gupta, N., & Shanker, S. (1992). Course of bipolar disorder in eastern India. *Journal of Affective Disorders, 24*, 35-41.

152. Kruesi, M. J. P., Fine, S., Valladares, L., Phillips, R. A., Jr., & Rapoport, J. L. (1992). Paraphilics: A double-blind crossover comparison of clomipramine versus desipramine. *Archives of Sexual Behavior, 21*, 587-593.

153. Kruesi, M. J. P., Hibbs, E. D., Zahn, T. P., Keyser, C. S., Hamburger, S. D., Bartko, J. J., & Rapoport, J. L. (1992). A 2-year prospective follow-up study of children and adolescents with disruptive behavior disorders: Prediction by cerebrospinal fluid 5-hydroxyindoleacetic acid, homovanillic acid, and autonomic measures? *Archives of General Psychiatry, 49*, 429-435.

154. Lora, A., & Fava, E. (1992). Provoking agents, vulnerability factors and depression in an Italian setting: A replication of Brown and Harris's model. *Journal of Affective Disorders, 24*, 227-236.

155. Maier, W., Lichtermann, D., Minges, J., & Heun, R. (1992). The familial relation of personality disorders (DSM-III-R) to unipolar major depression. *Journal of Affective Disorders, 26*, 151-156.

156. Maier, W., Lichtermann, D., Minges, J., & Heun, R. (1992). Personality traits in subjects at risk for unipolar major depression: A family study perspective. *Journal of Affective Disorders, 24*, 153-164.

157. Mannuzza, S., Aronowitz, B., Chapman, T., Klein, D. F., & Fyer, A. J. (1992). Panic disorder and suicide attempt. *Journal of Anxiety Disorders, 6*, 261-274.

158. Marks, M. N., Wieck, A., Checkley, S. A., & Kumar, R. (1992). Contribution of psychological and social factors to psychotic and non-psychotic relapse after childbirth in women with previous histories of affective disorder. *Journal of Affective Disorders, 24*, 253-264.

159. Mitchell, P., Selbie, L., Waters, B., Donald, J., Vivero, C., Tully, M., & Shine, J. (1992). Exclusion of close linkage of bipolar disorder to dopamine D_1 and D_2 receptor gene markers. *Journal of Affective Disorders, 25*, 1-12.

160. Mufson, L., Weissman, M. M., & Warner, V. (1992). Depression and anxiety in parents and children: A direct interview study. *Journal of Anxiety Disorders, 6*, 1-13.

161. Muir, W. J., St. Clair, D. M., Blackwood, D. H. R., Roxburgh, H. M., & Marshall, I. (1992). Eye-tracking dysfunction in the affective psychoses and schizophrenia. *Psychological Medicine, 22*, 22, 573-580.

162. Murray, L. (1992). The impact of postnatal depression on infant development. *Journal of Child Psychology and Psychiatry and Allied Disciplines, 33*, 543-561.

163. Neylan, T. C., van Kammen, D. P., Kelley, M. E., & Peters, J. L. (1992). Sleep in schizophrenic patients on and off haloperidol therapy: Clinically stable vs. relapsed patients. *Archives of General Psychiatry, 49*, 643-649.

164. Pauls, D. L., Morton, L. A., & Egeland, J. A. (1992). Risks of affective illness among first degree relatives of bipolar I old-order Amish probands. *Archives of General Psychiatry, 49*, 703-708.

165. Rice, J. P., Rochberg, N., Endicott, J., Lavori, P. W., & Miller, C. (1992). Stability of psychiatric diagnoses: An application to the affective disorders. *Archives of General Psychiatry, 49*, 824-830.

166. Romans, S. E., & McPherson, H. M. (1992). The social networks of bipolar affective disorder patients. *Journal of Affective Disorders, 25*, 221-228.

167. Roth, W. T., Margraf, J., Ehlers, A., Taylor, B., Maddock, R. J., Davies, S., & Agras, S. (1992). Stress test reactivity in panic disorder. *Archives of General Psychiatry, 49*, 301-310.

168. Roy, A., Karoum, F., & Pollack, S. (1992). Marked reduction in indexes of dopamine metabolism among patients with depression who attempt suicide. *Archives of General Psychiatry, 49*, 447-450.

169. Rubin, R. T., Heist, E. K., McGeoy, S. S., Hanada, K., & Lesser, I. M. (1992). Neuroendocrine aspects of primary endogenous depression. *Archives of General Psychiatry, 49*, 558-567.

170. Ryan, N. D., Birmaher, B., Perel, J. M., Dahl, R. E., Meyer, V., Al-Shabbout, M., Iyengar, S., & Puig-Antich, J. (1992). Neuroendocrine response to L-5-Hydroxytryptophan challenge in prepubertal major depression: Depressed vs. normal children. *Archives of General Psychiatry, 49*, 843-851.

171. Schittecatte, M., Charles, G., Machowski, R., Garcia-Valentin, J., Mendlewicz, J., & Wilmotte, J. (1992). Reduced clonidine rapid eye movement steep suppression in patients with primary major affective illness. *Archives of General Psychiatry, 49*, 637-642.

172. Staner, L., De La Fuente, J. M., Kerkhofs, M., Linkowski, P., & Mendlewicz, J. (1992). Biological and clinical features of recurrent brief depression: A comparison with major depressed and healthy subjects. *Journal of Affective Disorders, 26*, 241-246.

173. Stuart, S., Simons, A. D., Thase, M. E., & Pilkonis, P. (1992). Are personality assessments valid in acute major depression? *Journal of Affective Disorders, 24*, 281-290.

174. Tandon, R., Shipley, J. E., Taylor, S., Greden, J. F., Eiser, A., DeQuardo, J., & Goodson, J. (1992). Electroencephalographic sleep abnormalities in schizophrenia: Relationship to positive/negative symptoms and prior neuroleptic treatment. *Archives of General Psychiatry, 49*, 185-194.

175. Volavka, J., Cooper, T., Czobor, P., Bitter, I., Meisner, M., Laska, E., Gastanaga, P., Krakowski, M., C-Ychou, J., Crowner, M., & Douyon, R. (1992). Haloperidol blood levels and clinical effects. *Archives of General Psychiatry, 49*, 354-361.

176. Zipursky, R. B., Lim, K. O., Sullivan, E. V., Brown, B. W., & Pfefferbaum, A. (1992). Widespread cerebral gray matter volume deficits in schizophrenia. *Archives of General Psychiatry, 49*, 195-205.

177. Apter, A., Pouls, D. L., Bleich, A., Zohar, A. H., Kron, S., Ratzoni, G., Dycian, A., Kotler, M., Weizman, A., Gadot, N., & Cohen, D. J. (1993). An epidemiologic study of Giles de la Tourette's syndrome in Israel. *Archives of General Psychiatry, 50*, 734-738.

178. Bench, C. J., Friston, K. J., Brown, R. G., Frackowiak, R. S. J., & Dolan, R. J. (1993). Regional cerebral blood flow in depression measured by positron emission tomography: The relationship with clinical dimensions. *Psychological Medicine, 23*, 579-590.

179. Benson, K. L., & Zarcone, V. P. (1993). Rapid eye movement sleep eye movements in schizophrenia and depression. *Archives of General Psychiatry, 50*, 474-482.

180. Biederman, J., Faraone, S. V., Doyle, A., Lehman, B. K., Kraus, I., Perrin, J., & Tsuang, M. T. (1993). Convergence of the Child Behavior Checklist with structured interview-based psychiatric diagnoses of ADHD children with and without comorbidity. *Journal of Child Psychology and Psychiatry and Allied Disciplines, 34*, 1241-1251.

181. Borod, J. C., Martin, C. C., Alpert, M., Brozgold, A., & Welkowitz, J. (1993). Perception of facial emotion in schizophrenic and right brain-damaged patients. *The Journal of Nervous and Mental Disease, 181*, 494-502.

182. Carlson, G. A., & Weintraub, S. (1993). Childhood behavior problems and bipolar disorder: Relationship or coincidence? *Journal of Affective Disorders, 28*, 143-153.

183. Carroll, K. M., Ball, S. A., & Rounsaville, B. J. (1993). A comparison of alternate systems for diagnosing antisocial personality disorder in cocaine abusers. *The Journal of Nervous and Mental Disease, 181*, 436-443.

184. Conrad, M., & Hammen, C. (1993). Protective and resource factors in high- and low-risk children: A comparison of children with unipolar, bipolar, medically ill, and normal mothers. *Development and Psychopathology, 5*, 593-607.

185. Denham, S. (1993). Maternal emotional responsiveness and toddlers' social-emotional competence. *Journal of Child Psychology and Psychiatry and Allied Disciplines, 34,* 715-728.
186. Docherty, N. M. (1993). Communication deviance, attention, and schizotypy in parents of schizophrenic patients. *The Journal of Nervous and Mental Disease, 181,* 750-756.
187. Faraone, S. V., Biederman, J., Lehman, B. K., Spencer, T., Norman, D., Seidman, L. J., Kraus, I., Perrin, J., Chen, W. J., & Tsuang, M. T. (1993). Intellectual performance and social failure in children with attention deficit hyperactivity disorder and in their siblings. *Journal of Abnormal Psychology, 102,* 616-623.
188. Fine, S., Haley, G., Gilbert, M., & Forth, A. (1993). Self-image as a predictor of outcome in adolescent major depressive disorder. *Journal of Child Psychology and Psychiatry and Allied Disciplines, 34,* 1399-1407.
189. Fyer, A. J., Mannuzza, S., Chapman, T. F., Liebowitz, M. R., & Klein, D. F. (1993). A direct interview family study of social phobia. *Archives of General Psychiatry, 50,* 286-293.
190. Garnet, K. E., Glick, M., & Edell, W. S. (1993). Anhedonia and premorbid competence in young, nonpsychotic, psychiatric inpatients. *Journal of Abnormal Psychology, 102,* 580-583.
191. Gill, M., McGuffin, P., Parfitt, E., Mant, R., Asherson, P., Collier, D., Vallada, H., Powell, J., Shaikh, S., Taylor, C., Sargeant, M., Clements, A., Nanko, S., Takazawa, N., Llewellyn, D., Williams, J., Whatley, S., Murray, R., & Owen, M. (1993). A linkage study of schizophrenia with DNA markers from the long arm of chromosome II. *Psychological Medicine, 23,* 27-44.
192. Goodman, S. H., Brogan, D., Lynch, M. E., & Fielding, B. (1993). Social and emotional competence in children of depressed mothers. *Child Development, 64,* 516-531.
193. Goodwin, G. M., Austin, M. P., Curran, S. M., Ross, M., Murray, C., Prentice, N., Ebmeier, K. P., Bennie, J., Carroll, S., Dick, H., & Fink, G. (1993). The elevation of plasma B-endorphin levels in major depression. *Journal of Affective Disorders, 29,* 281-289.
194. Goodwin, G. M., Austin, M.-P., Dougall, N., Ross, M., Murray, C., O'Carroll, R. E., Moffoot, A., Prentice, N., & Ebmeier, K. P. (1993). State changes in brain activity shown by the uptake of 99mTc-exametazine with single photon emission tomography in major depression before and after treatment. *Journal of Affective Disorders, 29,* 243-253.
195. Goodyer, I. M., Cooper, M. J., Vize, C. M., & Ashby, L. (1993). Depression in 11–16-year-old girls: The role of past parental psychopathology and exposure to recent life events. *Journal of Child Psychology and Psychiatry and Allied Disciplines, 34,* 1103-1115.
196. Gotlib, I. H., Lewinsohn, P. M., Seeley, J. R., Rohde, P., & Redner, J. E. (1993). Negative cognitions and attributional style in depressed adolescents: An examination of stability and specificity. *Journal of Abnormal Psychology, 102,* 607-615.
197. Hamilton, E. B., Jones, M., & Hammen, C. (1993). Maternal interaction style in affective disordered, physically ill, and normal women. *Family Process, 32,* 329-340.
198. Heun, R., & Maier, W. (1993). The role of obstetric complications in schizophrenia. *The Journal of Nervous and Mental Disease, 181,* 220-226.
199. Joffe, R. T., Singer, W., Levitt, A. J., & MacDonald, C. (1993). A placebo-controlled comparison of lithium and triiodothyronine augmentation of tricyclic antidepressants in unipolar refractory depression. *Archives of General Psychiatry, 50,* 387-393.
200. Kazdin, A. E., Mazurick, J. L., & Bass, D. (1993). Risk for attrition in treatment of antisocial children and families. *Journal of Clinical Child Psychology, 22,* 2-16.
201. Keller, M. B., Lavori, P. W., Coryell, W., Endicott, J., & Mueller, T. I. (1993). Bipolar I: A five-year prospective follow-up. *The Journal of Nervous and Mental Disease, 181,* 238-245.
202. Kitamura, T., Shima, S., Sugawara, M., & Toda, M. A. (1993). Psychological and social correlates of the onset of affective disorders among pregnant women. *Psychological Medicine, 23,* 967-975.
203. Kring, A. M., Kerr, S. L., Smith, D. A., & Neale, J. M. (1993). Flat affect in schizophrenia does not reflect diminished subjective experience of emotion. *Journal of Abnormal Psychology, 102,* 507-517.
204. Leonard, H. L., Swedo, S. E., Lenane, M. C., Rettew, D. C., Hamburger, S. D., Bartko, J. J., & Rapoport, J. L. (1993). A 2- to 7-year follow-up study of 54 obsessive-compulsive children and adolescents. *Archives of General Psychiatry, 50,* 429-439.
205. Lepine, J. P., Chignon, J. M., & Teherani, M. (1993). Suicide attempts in patients with panic disorder. *Archives of General Psychiatry, 50,* 144-149.
206. Levav, I., Kohn, R., Dohrenwend, B. P., Shrout, P. E., Skodol, A. E., Schwartz, S., Link, B. G., & Naveh, G. (1993). An epidemiological study of mental disorders in a 10-year cohort of young adults in Israel. *Psychological Medicine, 23,* 691-707.
207. Levitt, A. J., Joffe, R. T., Brecher, D., & MacDonald, C. (1993). Anxiety disorders and anxiety symptoms in a clinical sample of seasonal and non-seasonal depressives. *Journal of Affective Disorders, 28,* 51-56.
208. Lieberman, J. A., Jody, D., Alvir, J., Ashtari, M., Levy, D. L., Bogerts, B., Degreef, G., Mayerhoff, D. I., & Cooper, T. (1993). Brain morphology, dopamine, and eye-tracking abnormalities in first-episode schizophrenia. *Archives of General Psychiatry, 50,* 357-368.
209. Lieberman, J., Jody, D., Geisler, S., Alvir, J., Loebel, A., Szymanski, S., Woerner, M., & Borenstein, M. (1993). Time course and biologic correlates of treatment response in first-episode schizophrenia. *Archives of General Psychiatry, 50,* 369-376.
210. Luthar, S. S., Merikangas, K. R., & Rounsaville, B. J. (1993). Parental psychopathology and disorders in offspring: A study of relatives of drug abusers. *The Journal of Nervous and Mental Disease, 181,* 351-357.
211. Maier, W., Lichtermann, D., Minges, J., Hallmayer, J., Heun, R., Benkert, O., & Levinson, D. F. (1993). Continuity and discontinuity of affective disorders and schizophrenia. *Archives of General Psychiatry, 50,* 871-883.
212. Marcus, J., Hans, S. L., Auerbach, J. G., & Auerbach, A. G. (1993). Children at risk for schizophrenia: The Jerusalem infant development study. *Archives of General Psychiatry, 50,* 797-809.
213. McCarley, R. W., Shenton, M. E., O'Donnell, B. F., Faux, S. F., Kikinis, R., Nestor, P. G., & Jolesz, F. A. (1993). Auditory P300 abnormalities and left posterior superior temporal gyros volume reduction in schizophrenia. *Archives of General Psychiatry, 50,* 190-197.
214. McLeod, J. D. (1993). Spouse concordance for depressive disorders in a community sample. *Journal of Affective Disorders, 27,* 43-52.
215. Moldin, S. O., Scheftner, W. A., Rice, J. P., Nelson, E., Knesevich, M. A., & Akiskal, H. (1993). Association between major depressive disorder and physical illness. *Psychological Medicine, 23,* 755-761.
216. Morgenstern, H., & Glazer, W. M. (1993). Identifying risk factors for tardive dyskinesia among long-term outpatients maintained with neuroleptic medications. *Archives of General Psychiatry, 50,* 723-733.
217. Mukherjee, S., Schnur, D. B., Reddy, R., & Decina, P. (1993). Birth weight and CT scan findings in chronic schizophrenic patients. *The Journal of Nervous and Mental Disease, 181,* 672-675.
218. Nofzinger, E. A., Thase, M. E., Reynolds, C. F., III, Frank, E., Jennings, R., Garamoni, G. L., Fasiczka, A. L., & Kupfer, D. J. (1993). Sexual function in depressed men. *Archives of General Psychiatry, 50,* 24-30.
219. Oppenheimer, K., & Frey, J. (1993). Family transactions and developmental processes in panic-disordered patients. *Family Process, 32,* 341-352.
220. Orbach, I., Kedem, P., Gorchover, O., Apter, A., & Tyano, S. (1993). Fears of death in suicidal and nonsuicidal adolescents. *Journal of Abnormal Psychology, 102,* 553-558.
221. Pardoen, D., Bauwens, F., Tracy, A., Martin, F., & Mandlewicz, J. (1993). Self-esteem in recovered bipolar and unipolar out-patients. *British Journal of Psychiatry, 163,* 755-762.
222. Parnas, J., Cannon, T. D., Jacobsen, B., Schulsinger, H., Schulsinger, F., & Mednick, S. A. (1993). Lifetime DSM-III-R diagnostic outcomes in the offspring of schizophrenic mothers: Results from the Copenhagen high-risk study. *Archives of General Psychiatry, 50,* 707-714.
223. Radke-Yarrow, M., & Brown, E. (1993). Resilience and vulnerability in children of multiple-risk families. *Development and Psychopathology, 5,* 581-592.
224. Radke-Yarrow, M., Nottelmann, E., Belmont, B., & Welsh, J. D. (1993). Affective interactions of depressed and nondepressed mothers and their children. *Journal of Abnormal Child Psychology, 21,* 683-695.
225. Reich, J. H., & Vasile, R. G. (1993). Effect of personality disorders on the treatment outcome of Axis I conditions: An update. *The Journal of Nervous and Mental Disease, 181,* 475-484.
226. Rickels, K., Downing, R., Schweizer, E., & Hassmen, H. (1993). Antidepressants for the treatment of generalized anxiety disorder: A placebo-controlled comparison of imipramine, trazodone, and diazepam. *Archives of General Psychiatry, 50,* 884-895.
227. Roxborough, H., Muir, W. J., Blackwood, D. H. R., Walker, M. T., & Blackburn, I. M. (1993). Neuropsychological and P300 abnormalities in schizophrenics and their relatives. *Psychological Medicine, 23,* 305-314.
228. Schiavi, R. C., White, D., Mandeli, J., & Schreiner-Engel, P. (1993). Hormones and nocturnal penile tumescence in healthy aging men. *Archives of Sexual Behavior, 22,* 207-215.
229. Schittecatte, M., Ansseau, M., Charles, G., Machowski, R., Papart, P., Pichot, W., & Wilmotte, J. (1992). Growth hormone response to clonidine in male patients with panic disorder untreated by antidepressants. *Psychological Medicine, 22,* 1059-1062.
230. Schmidt, P. J., Grover, G. N., & Rubinow, D. R. (1993). Alprazolam in the treatment of premenstrual syndrome. *Archives of General Psychiatry, 50,* 467-473.
231. Simons, A. D., Angell, K. L., Monroe, J. M., & Thase, M. E. (1993). Cognition and life stress in depression: Cognitive factors and the definition, rating, and generation of negative life events. *Journal of Abnormal Psychology, 102,* 584-591.

232. Soloff, P. H., Cornelius, J., George, A., Nathan, S., Perel, J. M., & Ulrich, R. F. (1993). Efficacy of phenelzine and haloperidol in borderline personality disorder. *Archives of General Psychiatry*, *50*, 377-385.

233. Spangler, D. L., Simons, A. D., Monroe, S. M., & Thase, M. E. (1993). Evaluating the hopelessness model of depression: Diathesis-stress and symptoms components. *Journal of Abnormal Psychology*, *102*, 592-600.

234. Sturmey, P. (1993). The use of DSM and ICD diagnostic criteria in people with mental retardation: A review of empirical studies. *The Journal of Nervous and Mental Disease*, *181*, 38-41.

235. Swann, A. C., Secunda, S. K., Katz, M. M., Croughan, J., Bowden, C. L., Koslow, S. H., Berman, N., & Stokes, P. E. (1993). Specificity of mixed affective states: Clinical comparison of dysphoric mania and agitated depression. *Journal of Affective Disorders*, *28*, 81-89.

236. Ullrich, H. E. (1993). Cultural shaping of illness: A longitudinal perspective on apparent depression. *The Journal of Nervous and Mental Disease*, *181*, 647-649.

237. Weissman, M. M., Wickramaratne, P., Adams, P. B., Lish, J. D., Horwath, E., Charney, D., Woods, S. W., Leeman, E., & Frosch, E. (1993). The relationship between panic disorder and major depression: A new family study. *Archives of General Psychiatry*, *50*, 767-780.

238. Winokur, G., Coryell, W., Keller, M., Endicott, J., & Akiskal, H. (1993). A prospective follow-up of patients with bipolar and primary unipolar affective disorder. *Archives of General Psychiatry*, *50*, 457-465.

239. Young, E. A., Kotun, J., Haskett, R. F., Grunhaus, L., Greden, J. F., Watson, S. J., & Akil, H. (1993). Dissociation between pituitary and adrenal suppression to dexamethasone in depression. *Archives of General Psychiatry*, *50*, 395-403.

240. Young, L. T., Cooke, R. G., Robb, J. C., Levitt, A. J., & Joffe, R. T. (1993). Anxious and non-anxious bipolar disorder. *Journal of Affective Disorders*, *29*, 49-52.

241. Alpert, M., Clark, A., & Pouget, E. R. (1994). The syntactic role of pauses in the speech of schizophrenic patients with alogia. *Journal of Abnormal Psychology*, *103*, 750-757.

242. Asarnow, J. R. (1994). Annotation: Childhood-onset schizophrenia. *Journal of Child Psychology & Psychiatry & Allied Disciplines*, *35*, 1345-1371.

243. Asarnow, J. R., Tompson, M., Hamilton, E. B., Goldstein, M. J., & Guthrie, D. (1994). Family-expressed emotion, childhood-onset depression, and childhood-onset schizophrenia spectrum disorders: Is expressed emotions a nonspecific correlate of child psychopathology or a specific risk factor for depression? *Journal of Abnormal Child Psychology*, *22*, 129-146.

244. Asherson, P., Walsh, C., Williams, J., Sargeant, M., Taylor, C., Clements, A., Gill, M., Owen, M., & McGuffin, P. (1994). Imprinting and anticipation: Are they relevant to genetic studies or schizophrenia? *British Journal of Psychiatry*, *164*, 619-624.

245. Bagby, R. M., Schuller, D. R., Parker, J. D. A., Levitt, A., Joffe, R. T., & Shafir, S. (1994). Major depression and the self-criticism and dependency personality dimensions. *American Journal of Psychiatry*, *151*, 597-599.

246. Ball, S. A., Carroll, K. M., & Rounsaville, B. J. (1994). Sensation seeking, substance abuse, and psychopathology in treatment-seeking and community cocaine abusers. *Journal of Consulting and Clinical Psychology*, *62*, 1053-1057.

247. Berenbaum, S. A., Taylor, M. A., & Cloninger, C. R. (1994). Family study of schizophrenia and personality. *Journal of Abnormal Psychology*, *103*, 475-484.

248. Bernstein, V. J., & Hans, S. L. (1994). Predicting the developmental outcome of two-year-old children born exposed to methadone: Impact of social-environmental risk factors. *Journal of Clinical Child Psychology*, *23*, 349-359.

249. Bilder, R. M., Wu, H., Bogerts, B., Degreef, G., Ashtari, M., Alvir, J. M. J., Snyder, P. J., & Lieberman, J. A. (1994). Absence of regional hemispheric volume asymmetries in first-episode schizophrenia. *American Journal of Psychiatry*, *151*, 1437-1447.

250. Blanchard, J. L., & Neale, J. M. (1994). The neuropsychological signature of schizophrenia: Generalized or differential deficit? *American Journal of Psychiatry*, *151*, 40-48.

251. Brown, G. W., Hams, T. O., & Hepworth, C. (1994). Life events and endogenous depression. *Archives of General Psychiatry*, *51*, 525-534.

252. Brown, R. G., Scott, L. C., Bench, C. J., & Dolan, R. J. (1994). Cognitive function in depression: Its relationship to the presence and severity of intellectual decline. *Psychological Medicine*, *24*, 829-847.

253. Bruce-Jones, W. D. A., White, P. D., Thomas, J. M., & Clare, A. W. (1994). The effect of social adversity on the fatigue syndrome, psychiatric disorders and physical recovery, following glandular fever. *Psychological Medicine*, *24*, 651-659.

254. Bruder, G. E., Schnur, D. B., Fergeson, P., Mukherjee, S., Leite, P., & Sackeim, H. A. (1994). Dichotic-listening measures of brain laterality in mania. *Journal of Abnormal Psychology*, *103*, 758-766.

255. Buckley, P., Thompson, P., Way, L., & Meltzer, H. Y. (1994). Substance abuse among patients with treatment-resistant schizophrenia: Characteristics and implications for clozapine therapy. *American Journal of Psychiatry*, *151*, 385-389.

256. Busatto, G. F., Costa, D. C., Ell, P. J., Pilowsky, L. S., David, A. S., & Kerwin, R. W. (1994). Regional cerebral flow (rCBF) in schizophrenia during verbal memory activation: A 99mTC-HMPAO single photon emission tomography (SPET) study. *Psychological Medicine*, *24*, 463-472.

257. Cannon, T. D., Mednick, S. A., Parnas, J., Schulsinger, F., Praestholm, J., & Vestergaard, A. (1994). Developmental brain abnormalities in the offspring of schizophrenic mothers: II. Structural brain characteristics of schizophrenia and schizotypal personality disorder. *Archives of General Psychiatry*, *51*, 955-962.

258. Caplan, R., Guthrie, D., Shields, W. D., & Yudovin, S. (1994). Communication deficits in pediatric complex partial seizure disorder and schizophrenia. *Development and Psychopathology*, *6*, 499-517.

259. Cawthron, P., James, A., Dell, J., & Seagroat, V. (1994). Adolescent onset psychosis. A clinical and outcome study. *Journal of Child Psychology and Psychiatry and Allied Disciplines*, *35*, 1321-1332.

260. Chakos, M. H., Lieberman, J. A., Bilder, R. M., Borenstein, M., Lerner, G., Bogerts, B., Wu, H., Kinon, B., & Ashtari, M. (1994). Increase in caudate nuclei volumes of first-episode schizophrenic patients taking antipsychotic drugs. *American Journal of Psychiatry*, *151*, 1430-1436.

261. Chapman, L. J., Chapman, J. P., Kwapil, T. R., Eckblad, M., & Zinser, M. C. (1994). Putatively psychosis-prone subjects 10 years later. *Journal of Abnormal Psychology*, *103*, 171-183.

262. Chapman, T. F., Mannuzza, S., Klein, D. F., & Fyer, A. J. (1994). Effects of informant mental disorder on psychiatric family history data. *American Journal of Psychiatry*, *151*, 574-579.

263. Chen, W. J., Faraone, S. V., Biederman, J., & Tsuang, M. T. (1994). Diagnostic accuracy of the Child Behavior Checklist scales for attention-deficit hyperactivity disorder: A receiver-operating characteristic analysis. *Journal of Consulting and Clinical Psychology*, *62*, 1017-1025.

264. Chochinov, H. M., Wilson, K. G., Enns, M., & Lander, S. (1994). Prevalence of depression in the terminally ill: Effects of diagnostic criteria and symptom threshold judgements. *American Journal of Psychiatry*, *151*, 537-540.

265. Coccaro, E. F., Silverman, J. M., Klar, H. M., Horvath, T. B., & Siever, L. J. (1994). Familial correlates to reduced central serotonergic system function in patients with personality disorders. *Archives of General Psychiatry*, *51*, 318-324.

266. Convit, A., Volavka, J., Czobor, P., DeAsis, J., & Evangelista, C. (1994). Effect of subtle neurological dysfunction on response to haloperidol treatment in schizophrenia. *American Journal of Psychiatry*, *151*, 49-56.

267. Coryell, W., Akiskal, H. S., Lean, A. C., Winokur, G., Maser, J. D., Mueller, T. I., & Keller, M. B. (1994). The time course of nonchronic major depressive disorder: Uniformity across episodes and samples. *Archives of General Psychiatry*, *51*, 405-410.

268. Coryell, W., Winokur, G., Shea, T., Maser, J. D., Endicott, J., & Akiskal, H. S. (1994). The long-term stability of depressive subtypes. *American Journal of Psychiatry*, *151*, 199-204.

269. Craddock, N., Brockington, I., Mant, R., Parfitt, E., McGuffin, P., & Owen, M. (1994). Bipolar affective puerperal psychosis associated with consanguinity. *British Journal of Psychiatry*, *164*, 359-364.

270. Craddock, N., Owen, M., Burge, S., Kurian, B., Thomas, P., & McGuffin, P. (1994). Familial cosegregation of major affective disorder and Darier's disease (keratosis follicularis). *British Journal of Psychiatry*, *164*, 355-358.

271. Dew, M. A., Reynolds, C. F., III, Monk, T. H., Buysse, D. J., Hoch, C. C., Jennings, J. R., & Kupfer, D. J. (1994). Psychological correlates and sequelae of electroencephalographic sleep in healthy elders. *Journal of Gerontology: Psychological Sciences, 49*(Pt.1), P8-P18.

272. Dilsaver, S. C., Chen, Y., Swann, A. C., Shoaib, A. M., & Krajewski, K. J. (1994). Suicidality in patients with pure and depressive mania. *American Journal of Psychiatry*, *151*, 1312-1315.

273. Docherty, N. M., Evans, I. M., Sledge, W. H., Seibyl, J. D., & Krystal, J. H. (1994). Affective reactivity of language in schizophrenia. *The Journal of Nervous and Mental Disease*, *182*, 98-102.

274. Docherty, N. M., Sledge, W. H., & Wexler, B. E. (1994). Affective reactivity of language in stable schizophrenic outpatients and their parents. *The Journal of Nervous and Mental Disease*, *182*, 313-318.

275. Dworkin, R. H., Lewis, J. A., Cornblatt, B. A., & Erlenmeyer-Kimling, L. (1994). Social competence deficits in adolescents at risk for schizophrenia. *The Journal of Nervous and Mental Disease*, *182*, 103-108.

276. Fendrich, M., & Warner, V. (1994). Symptom and substance use reporting consistency over two years for offspring at high and low risk depression. *Journal of Abnormal Child Psychology*, *22*, 425-439.

277. Fields, J. H., Grochowski, S., Lindenmayer, J. P., Kay, S. R., Grosz, D., Hyman, R. B., & Alexander, G. (1994). Assessing positive and negative symptoms in children and adolescents. *American Journal of Psychiatry*, *151*, 249-253.

278. Frank, E., Andersen, B., Reynolds, C. F., III, Ritenour, A., & Kupfer, D. J. (1994). Life events and the research diagnostic criteria endogenous subtype. *Archives of General Psychiatry, 51*, 519-524.

279. Gallagher-Thompson, D., & Steffen, A. M. (1994). Comparative effects of cognitive-behavioral and brief psychodynamic psychotherapists for depressed family categories. *Journal of Consulting and Clinical Psychology, 62*, 543-549.

280. Garbutt, J. C., Mayo, J. P., Little, K. Y., Gillette, G. M., Mason, G. A., Dew, B., & Prange, A. J., Jr. (1994). Dose-response studies with protirelin. *Archives of General Psychiatry, 51*, 875-883.

281. Garnet, K. E., Levy, K. N., Mattanah, J. J. F., Edell, W. S., & McGlashan, T. H. (1994). Borderline personality disorder in adolescents: Ubiquitous or specific? *American Journal of Psychiatry, 151*, 1380-1382.

282. Garvey, M. J., & Schaffer, C. B. (1994). Are some symptoms of depression age dependent? *Journal of Affective Disorders, 32*, 247-251.

283. Garvey, M. J., Hollon, S. D., & DeRubeis, R. J. (1994). Do depressed patients with higher pretreatment stress levels respond better to cognitive therapy than imipramine? *Journal of Affective Disorders, 32*, 45-50.

284. Goisman, R. M., Warshaw, M. G., Peterson, L. G., Rogers, M. D., Cuneo, P., Hunt, M. F., Tomlin-Albanese, J. M., Kazim, A., Gollan, J. K., Epstein-Kaye, T., Reich, J. H., & Keller, M. B. (1994). Panic, agoraphobia, and panic disorder with agoraphobia: Data from a multicenter anxiety disorders study. *The Journal of Nervous and Mental Disease, 182*, 72-79.

285. Goldstein, R. B., Weissman, M. M., Adams, P. B., Horwath, E., Lish, J. D., Charney, D., Woods, S. W., Sabin, C., & Wickramaratne, P. J. (1994). Psychiatric disorders in relatives of probands with panic disorder and/or major depression. *Archives of General Psychiatry, 51*, 383-394.

286. Goreje, O., Omigbodun, O. O., Gater, R., Acha, R. A., Ikuesan, B. A., & Morris, J. (1994). Psychiatric disorders in a paediatric primary care clinic. *British Journal of Psychiatry, 165*, 527-530.

287. Gorman, J. M., Papp, L. A., Coplan, J. D., Martinez, J. M., Lennon, S., Goetz, R. R., Ross, D., & Klein, D. F. (1994). Anxiogenic effects of CO_2 and hyperventilation in patients with panic disorder. *American Journal of Psychiatry, 151*, 547-553.

288. Green, M. F., Nuechterlein, K. H., & Mintz, J. (1994). Backward masking in schizophrenia and mania: I. Specifying a mechanism. *Archives of General Psychiatry, 51*, 939-944.

289. Grimes, K., & Walker, E. F. (1994). Childhood emotional expressions, educational attainment, and age at onset of illness in schizophrenia. *Journal of Abnormal Psychology, 103*, 784-790.

290. Grof, P., Alda, M., Grof, E., Zvolsky, P., & Walsh, M. (1994). Lithuim response and genetics of affective disorders. *Journal of Affective Disorders, 32*, 85-95.

291. Grunhaus, L., Pande, A. C., Brown, M. B., & Greden, J. F. (1994). Clinical characteristics of patients with concurrent major depressive disorder and panic disorder. *American Journal of Psychiatry, 151*, 541-546.

292. Harrington, R., Bredenkamp, D., Groothues, C., Rutter, M., Fudge, H., & Pickles, A. (1994). Adult outcomes of childhood and adolescent depression. III. Links with suicidal behaviours. *Journal of Child Psychology and Psychiatry and Allied Disciplines, 35*, 1309-1319.

293. Hay, A. G., Bancroft, J., & Johnstone, E. C. (1994). Affective symptoms in women attending a menopause clinic. *British Journal of Psychiatry, 164*, 513-516.

294. Hays, J. C., Kasl, S. V., & Jacobs, S. C. (1994). The course of psychological distress following threatened and actual conjugal bereavement. *Psychological Medicine, 24*, 917-927.

295. Hollister, J. M., Mednick, S. A., Brennan, P., & Cannon, T. D. (1994). Impaired autonomic nervous system habituation in those at genetic risk for schizophrenia. *Archives of General Psychiatry, 51*, 552-558.

296. Humes, D. L., & Humphrey, L. L. (1994). A multimethod analysis of families with a polydrug-dependent or normal adolescent daughter. *Journal of Abnormal Psychology, 103*, 676-685.

297. Keller, M. B., Yonkers, K. A., Warshaw, M. G., Pratt, L. A., Gollan, J. K., Massion, A. O., White, K., Swartz, A. R., Reich, J., & Lavori, P. W. (1994). Remission and relapse in subjects with panic disorder and panic with agoraphobia: A prospective short-interval naturalistic follow-up. *The Journal of Nervous and Mental Disease, 182*, 290-296.

298. Kendler, K. S., Gruenberg, A. M., & Kinney, D. K. (1994). Independent diagnoses of adoptees and relatives as defined by DSM-III in the provincial and national samples of the Danish adoption study of schizophrenia. *Archives of General Psychiatry, 51*, 456-468.

299. Kety, S. S., Wender, P. H., Jacobsen, B., Ingraham, L. J., Jansson, L., Faber, B., & Kinney, D. K. (1994). Mental illness in the biological and adoptive relatives of schizophrenic adoptees: Replication of the Copenhagen study in the rest of Denmark. *Archives of General Psychiatry, 51*, 442-455.

300. Koreen, A. R., Lieberman, J., Alvir, J., Chakos, M., Loebel, A., Cooper, T., & Kane, J. (1994). Relation of plasma fluphenazine levels to treatment response and extrapyramidal side effects in first-episode schizophrenic patients. *American Journal of Psychiatry, 151*, 35-39.

301. Koreen, A. R., Lieberman, J., Alvir, J., Mayerhoff, D., Loebel, A., Chakos, M., Amin, F., & Cooper, T. (1994). Plasma homovanillic and levels in first-episode schizophrenia: Psychopathology and treatment response. *Archives of General Psychiatry, 51*, 132-138.

302. Kosten, T. A., Ball, S. A., & Rounsaville, B. J. (1994). A sibling study of sensation seeking and opiate addiction. *The Journal of Nervous and Mental Disease, 182*, 284-289.

303. Kramer, T. L., Lindly, J. D., Green, B. L., Grace, M. C., & Leonard, A. C. (1994). The comorbidity of post-traumatic stress disorder and suicidality in Vietnam veterans. *Suicide and Life-Threatening Behavior, 24*, 58-67.

304. Le, F., Mitchell, P., Vivero, C., Waters, B., Donald, J., Selbie, L. A., Shine, J., & Schofield, P. (1994). Exclusion of close linkage of bipolar disorder to the Gs-alpha subunit gene in nine Australian pedigrees. *Journal of Affective Disorders, 32*, 187-195.

305. Lesage, A. D., Boyer, R., Grunberg, F., Vanier, C., Morissette, R., Ménard-Buteau, C., & Loyer, M. (1994). Suicide and mental disorders: A case-control study of young men. *The American Journal of Psychiatry, 151*, 1063-1068.

306. Lewinsohn, P. M., Roberts, R. E., Seeley, J. R., Rohde, P., Gotlib, I. H., & Hops, H. (1994). Adolescent psychopathology: II. Psychosocial risk factors for depression. *Journal of Abnormal Psychology, 103*, 302-315.

307. Lipsitz, J. D., Martin, L. Y., Mannuzza, S., Chapman, T. F., Liebowitz, M. R., Klein, D. F., & Fyer, A. J. (1994). Childhood separation anxiety disorder in patients with adult anxiety disorders. *American Journal of Psychiatry, 151*, 927-929.

308. Loranger, A. W., Sartorius, N., Andreoli, A., Berger, P., Buchheim, P., Channabasavanna, S. M., Coid, B., Dahl, A., Diekstra, R. F. W., Ferguson, B., Jacobsberg, L. B., Momboor, W., Pull, C., Ono, Y., & Regier, D. A. (1994). The international personality disorder examination: The World Health Organization alcohol, drug abuse, and mental health administration international pilot study of personality disorders. *Archives of General Psychiatry, 51*, 215-224.

309. Macciardi, F., Petronis, A., Van Tol, H. H. M., Marino, C., Cavallini, C., Smeraldi, E., & Kennedy, J. L. (1994). Analysis of the D_4 dopamine receptor gene variant in an Italian schizophrenia kindred. *Archives of General Psychiatry, 51*, 288-293.

310. Maj, M., Magliano, L., Pirozzi, R., Marasco, C., & Guarneri, M. (1994). Validity of rapid cycling as a course specifier for bipolar disorder. *The American Journal of Psychiatry, 151*, 1015-1019.

311. Marciano, P. L., & Kazdin, A. E. (1994). Self-esteem, depression, hopelessness and suicidal intent among psychiatrically disturbed inpatient children. *Journal of Clinical Child Psychology, 23*, 151-160.

312. Martin, C. S., Earleywine, M., Blackson, T. C., Vanyukov, M. M., Moss, H. B., & Tarter, R. E. (1994). Aggressivity, inattention, hyperactivity, and impulsivity in boys at high and low risk for substance abuse. *Journal of Abnormal Child Psychology, 22*, 177-203.

313. Matochik, J. A., Liebenauer, L. L., King, A. C., Szymanski, H. V., Cohen, R. M., & Zametkin, A. J. (1994). Cerebral glucose metabolism in adults with attention deficit hyperactivity disorder after chronic stimulant treatment. *American Journal of Psychiatry, 151*, 658-664.

314. Mayerhoff, D. I., Loebel, A. D., Alvir, J. M. J., Szymanski, S. R., Geisler, S. H., Borenstein, M., & Lieberman, J. A. (1994). The deficit state in first-episode schizophrenia. *American Journal of Psychiatry, 151*, 1417-1422.

315. McDougle, C. J., Goodman, W. K., Leckman, J. F., Lee, N. C., Heninger, G. R., & Price, L. H. (1994). Haloperidol addition in fluvoxamine-refractory obsessive-compulsive disorder. *Archives of General Psychiatry, 51*, 302-308.

316. McMahon, F. J., Stine, O. C., Chase, G. A, Meyers, D. A., Simpson, S. G., & DePaulo, J. R., Jr. (1994). Influence of clinical subtype, sex, and lineality on age at onset of major affective disorder in a family sample. *American Journal of Psychiatry, 151*, 210-215.

317. Nobler, M. S., Sackeim, H. A., Prohovnik, I., Moeller, J. R., Mukherjee, S., Schnor, D. B., Prudic, J., & Devanand, D. P. (1994). Regional cerebral blood flow in mood disorders. III. *Archives of General Psychiatry, 51*, 884-897.

318. O'Carroll, R. E., Curran, S. M., Ross, M., Murray, C., Riddle, W., Moffoot, A. P. R., Ebmeier, K. P., & Goodwin, G. M. (1994). The differentiation of major depression from dementia of the Alzheimer type using within-subject neuropsychological discrepency analysis. *British Journal of Clinical Psychology, 33*, 23-32.

319. Perry, W., & Braff, D. L. (1994). Information-processing deficits and thought disorder in schizophrenia. *American Journal of Psychiatry, 151*, 363-367.

320. Piven, J., Wzorek, M., Landa, R., Lainhart, J., Bolton, P., Chase, G. A., & Folstein, S. (1994). Personality characteristics of the parents of autistic individuals. *Psychological Medicine, 24*, 783-795.

321. Radke-Yarrow, M., Zahn-Waxler, C., Richardson, D. T., Susman, A., & Martinez, P. (1994). Caring behavior in children of clinically depressed and well mothers. *Child Development, 65*, 1405-1414.

322. Reich, J., Goldenberg, I., Goisman, R., Vasile, R., & Keller, M. (1994). A prospective, follow-along study of the course of social phobia: II. Testing for basic predictors of course. *The Journal of Nervous and Mental Disease, 182*, 297-301.

323. Rifkin, A., Doddi, S., Karajgi, B., Borenstein, M., & Munne, R. (1994). Dosage of haloperidol for mania. *British Journal of Psychiatry, 165*, 113-116.

324. Rogers, J. C., Holm, M. B., Goldstein, G., McCue, M., & Nussbaum, P. D. (1994). Stability and change in functional assessment of patients with geropsychiatric disorders. *The American Journal of Occupational Therapy, 48*, 914-918.

325. Rorty, M., Yager, J., & Rossotto, E. (1994). Childhood sexual, physical, and psychological abuse in bulimia nervosa. *American Journal of Psychiatry, 151*, 1122-1126.

326. Rose, D. T., Abramson, L. Y., Hodulik, C. J., Halberstadt, L., & Leff, G. (1994). Heterogeneity of cognitive style among depressed inpatients. *Journal of Abnormal Psychology, 103*, 419-429.

327. Roy, A., Wolkowitz, O. M., Bissette, G., & Nemeroff, C. B. (1994). Differences in CSF concentrations of thyrotropin-releasing hormone in depressed patients and normal subjects: Negative findings. *American Journal of Psychiatry, 151*, 600-602.

328. Sabaté, O., Campion, D., d'Amato, T., Martres, M. P., Sokoloff, P., Giros, B., Leboyer, M., Jay, M., Guedj, F., Thibaut, F., Dollfus, S., Preterre, P., Petit, M., Babron, M. C., Waksman, G., Mallet, J., & Schwartz, J. C. (1994). Failure to find evidence for linkage or association between the dopamine d3 receptor gene and schizophrenia. *American Journal of Psychiatry, 151*, 107-111.

329. Sack, W. H., McSharry, S., Clarke, G. N., Kinney, R., Seeley, J., & Lewinsohn, D. (1994). The Khmer Adolescent Project: I. Epidemiologic finding in two generations of Cambodian refugees. *The Journal of Nervous and Mental Disease, 182*, 387-395.

330. Sands, J. R., & Harrow, M. (1994). Psychotic unipolar depression at follow-up: Factors related to psychosis in the affective disorders. *The American Journal of Psychiatry, 151*, 995-1000.

331. Schittecatte, M., Charles, G., Machowski, R., Dumont, F., Garcia-Valentin, J., Wilmotte, J., Papart, P., Pitchot, W., Wauthy, J., Ansseau, M., Hoffmann, G., & Pelc, I. (1994). Effects of gender and diagnosis on growth hormone response to clonidine for major depression: A large-scale multicenter study. *American Journal of Psychiatry, 151*, 216-220.

332. Schuckit, M. A. (1994). Low level of response to alcohol as a predictor of future alcoholism. *American Journal of Psychiatry, 151*, 184-189.

333. Seidenberg, M., Haltiner, A., Taylor, M. A., Hermann, B. B., & Wyler, A. (1994). Development and validation of a multiple ability self-report questionnaire. *Journal of Clinical and Experimental Neuropsychology, 16*, 93-104.

334. Siever, L. J., Friedman, L., Moskowitz, J., Mitropoulou, V., Keefe, R., Roitman, S. L., Merhige, D., Trestman, R., Silverman, J., & Mohs, R. (1994). Eye movement impairment and schizotypal psychopathology. *American Journal of Psychiatry, 151*, 1209-1215.

335. Siris, S. G., Bermanzohn, P. C., Mason, S. E., & Shuwall, M. A. (1994). Maintenance imipramine therapy for secondary depression in schizophrenia: A controlled trial. *Archives of General Psychiatry, 51*, 109-115.

336. Soloff, P. H., Liss, J. A., Kelly, T., Cornelius, J., & Ulrich, R. (1994). Risk factors for suicidal behavior in borderline personality disorder. *American Journal of Psychiatry, 151*, 1316-1323.

337. Steinberg, M., Cicchetti, D., Buchanan, J., Rakfeldt, J., & Rounsaville, B. (1994). Distinguishing between multiple personality disorder (dissociative identity disorder) and schizophrenia using the Structured Clinical Interview for DSM-IV Dissociative Disorders. *The Journal of Nervous and Mental Disease, 182*, 495-502.

338. Tarullo, L. B., DeMulder, E. K., Martinez, P. E., & Radke-Yarrow, M. (1994). Dialogues with preadolescents and adolescents: Mother-child interaction patterns in affectively ill and well dyads. *Journal of Abnormal Child Psychology, 22*, 33-51.

339. Taylor, M. A., & Amir, N. (1994). The problem of missing clinical data for research in psychopathology: Some solution guidelines. *The Journal of Nervous and Mental Disease, 182*, 222-229.

340. Taylor, M. A., Reed, R., & Berenbaum, S. (1994). Patterns of speech disorders in schizophrenia and mania. *The Journal of Nervous and Mental Disease, 182*, 319-326.

341. Thase, M. E., Reynolds, C. F., Frank, E., Jennings, J. R., Nofzinger, E., Fasiczka, A. L., Garamoni, G., & Kupfer, D. J. (1994). Polysomnographic studies of unmedicated depressed men before and after cognitive behavioral therapy. *American Journal of Psychiatry, 151*, 1615-1622.

342. Thase, M. E., Reynolds, C. F., Frank, E., Simmons, A. D., McGeary, J., Fasiczka, A. L., Garamoni, G. G., Jennings, R., & Kupfer, D. J. (1994). Do depressed men and women respond similarly to cognitive behavior therapy. *American Journal of Psychiatry, 151*, 500-505.

343. Virkkunen, M., Rawlings, R., Tokola, R., Poland, R., Guidotti, A., Nemeroff, C., Bissette, G., Kalogeras, K., Karonen, S., & Linnoila, M. (1994). CSF biochemistries, glucose metabolism, and diurnal activity rhythms in alcoholic, violent offenders, fire setters, and healthy volunteers. *Archives of General Psychiatry, 51*, 20-27.

344. Yang, Z. W., Chengappa, K. N. R., Shurin, G., Brar, J. S., Rabin, B. S., Gubbi, A. V., & Ganguli, R. (1994). An association between anti-hippocampal antibody concentration and lymphocyte production of IL-2 in patients with schizophrenia. *Psychological Medicine, 24*, 449-455.

345. Young, E. A., Haskett, R. F., Grunhaus, L., Pande, A., Weinberg, V. M., Watson, S. J., & Akil, H. (1994). Increased evening activation of the hypothalamic-pituitary-adrenal axis in depressed patients. *Archives of General Psychiatry, 51*, 701-707.

346. Young, L. T., Li, P. P., Kamble, A., Siu, K. P., & Warsh, J. J. (1994). Mononuclear leukocyte levels of G proteins in depressed patients with bipolar disorder or major depressive disorder. *American Journal of Psychiatry, 151*, 594-596.

347. Young, M. A., Fogg, L. F., Scheftner, W. A., & Fawcett, J. A. (1994). Intractions of risk factors in predicting suicide. *American Journal of Psychiatry, 151*, 434-435.

348. Anita, I. J., Smith, C. E., Wood, A. J., & Aronson, J. K. (1995). The upregulation of Na^+, K^+-ATPase pump numbers in lymphocytes from the first-degree unaffected relatives of patients with manic depressive psychosis in response to in vitro lithium and sodium ethacrynate. *Journal of Affective Disorders, 34*, 33-39.

349. Asnis, G. M., McGinn, L. K., & Sanderson, W. C. (1995). Atypical depression: Clinical aspects and noradrenergic function. *American Journal of Psychiatry, 152*, 31-36.

350. Ball, S. A., Carroll, K. M., Babor, T. F., & Rounsaville, B. J. (1995). Subtypes of cocaine abusers: Support for a Type A-Type B distinction. *Journal of Consulting and Clinical Psychology, 63*, 115-124.

351. Barber, J. P., Luborsky, L., Crits-Christoph, P., & Diguer, L. (1995). A comparison of core conflictual relationship themes before psychotherapy and during early sessions. *Journal of Consulting and Clinical Psychology, 63*, 145-148.

352. Bench, C. J., Frackowiak, R. S. J., & Dolan, R. J. (1995). Changes in regional cerebral blood flow in recovery from depression. *Psychological Medicine, 25*, 247-261.

353. Bergman, A. J., & Walker, E. (1995). The relationship between cognitive function and behavioral deviance in children at risk for psychopathology. *Journal of Child Psychology and Psychiatry and Allied Disciplines, 36*, 265-278.

354. Bernstein, A. S., Schnur, D. B., Bernstein, P., Yeager, A., Wrable, J., & Smith, S. (1995). Differing patterns of electrodermal and finger pulse responsivity in schizophrenia and depression. *Psychological Medicine, 25*, 51-62.

355. Biederman, J., Faraone, S. V., Mick, E., Spencer, T., Wilens, T., Kiely, K., Guite, J., Ablon, J. S., Reed, E., & Warburton, R. (1995). High risk for attention deficit hyperactivity disorder among children of parents with childhood onset of the disorder: A pilot study. *American Journal of Psychiatry, 152*, 431-435.

356. Brown, S. A., Inaba, R. K., Gillin, J. C., Schuckit, M. A., Stewart, M. A., & Irwin, M. R. (1995). Alcoholism and affective disorder: Clinical course of depressive symptoms. *American Journal of Psychiatry, 152*, 45-52.

357. Campbell, S. B., Cohn, J. F., & Meyers, T. (1995). Depression in first-time mothers: Mother-infant interaction and depression chronicity. *Developmental Psychology, 31*, 349-357.

358. Coryell, W., Endicott, J., Maser, J. A., Keller, M. B., Leon, A. C., & Akiskal, H. S. (1995). Long-term stability of polarity distinctions in the affective disorders. *American Journal of Psychiatry, 152*, 385-390.

359. Coryell, W., Endicott, J., Maser, J. D., Mueller, T., Lavori, P., & Keller, M. (1995). The likelihood of recurrence in bipolar affective disorder: The importance of episode recency. *Journal of Affective Disorders, 33*, 201-206.

360. Craighead, W. E., Curry, J. F., & Ilardi, S. S. (1995). Relationship of Children's Depression Inventory factors to major depression among adolescents. *Psychological Assessment, 7*, 171-176.

361. Davis, C. G., Lehman, D. R., Wortman, C. B., Silver, R. C., & Thompson, S. C. (1995). The undoing of traumatic life events. *Personality and Social Psychology Bulletin, 21*, 109-124.

362. Faraone, S. V., Biederman, J., Chen, W. J., Milberger, S., Warburton, R., & Tsuang, M. T. Genetic heterogeneity in attention-deficit hyperactivity disorder (ADHD): Gender, psychiatric comorbidity, and maternal ADHD. *Journal of Abnormal Psychology, 104*, 334-345.

363. Faraone, S. V., Seidman, L. J., Kremen, W. S., Pepple, J. R., Lyons, M. J., & Tsuang, M. T. (1995). Neuropsychological functioning among the nonpsychotic relatives of schizophrenic patients: A diagnostic efficiency analysis. *Journal of Abnormal Psychology, 104*, 286-304.

364. Freeman, E. W., Rickels, K., Schweizer, E., & Ting, T. (1995). Relationships between age and symptom severity among women seeking medical treatment for premenstrual symptoms. *Psychological Medicine, 25*, 309-315.

365. Friedman, L., Jesberger, J. A., Siever, L. J., Thompson, P., Mohs, R., & Meltzer, H. Y. (1995). Smooth pursuit performance in patients with affective disorders of schizophrenia and normal controls: Analysis with specific oculomotor measures, RMS error and qualitative ratings. *Psychological Medicine, 25*, 387-403.

366. George, D. T., Lindquist, T., Nutt, D. J., Ragan, P. W., Alim, T., McFarlane, V., Leviss, J., Eckhardt, M. J., & Linnoila, M. (1995). Effect of chloride or glucose on the incidence of lactate-induced pain attacks. *American Journal of Psychiatry, 152*, 692-697.

367. George, M. S., Ketter, T. A., Parekh, P. I., Horwitz, B., Herscovitch, P., & Post, R. M. (1995). Brain activity during transient sadness and happiness in healthy women. *American Journal of Psychiatry, 152*, 341-351.

368. Gorwood, P., Leboyer, M., Jay, M., Payan, C., & Feingold, J. (1995). Gender and age at onset in schizophrenia: Impact of family history. *American Journal of Psychiatry, 152*, 208-212.

369. Gotlib, I. H., Lewinsohn, P. M., & Seeley, J. R. (1995). Symptoms versus a diagnosis of depression: Differences in psychosocial functioning. *Journal of Consulting and Clinical Psychology, 63*, 90-100.

370. Grilo, C. M., Levy, K. N., Becker, D. F., Edell, W. S., & McGlashan, T. H. (1995). Eating disorders in female inpatients with versus without substance disorders. *Addictive Behaviors, 20*, 255-260.

371. Haaga, D. A. F., Ahrens, A. H., Schulman, P., Seligman, M. E. P., DuRubeis, R. J., & Minarik, M. L. (1995). Metatraits and cognitive assessment: Application to attributional style and depressive symptoms. *Cognitive Therapy and Research, 19*, 121-142.

372. Haywood, T. W., Kravitz, H. M., Grossman, L. S., Cavanaugh, J. L., Jr., Davis, J. M., & Lewis, D. A. (1995). Predicting the "revolving door" phenomenon among patients with schizophrenic, schizoaffective, and affective disorders. *American Journal of Psychiatry, 152*, 856-861.

373. Hill, J., Fudge, H., Harrington, R., Pickles, A., & Rutter, M. (1995). The Adult Personality Functioning Assessment (APFA): Factors influencing agreement between subject and informant. *Psychological Medicine, 25*, 263-275.

374. Hobfoll, S. E., Ritter, C., Lavin, J., Hulsizer, M. R., & Cameron, R. P. (1995). Depression prevalence and incidence among inner-city pregnant and postpartum women. *Journal of Consulting and Clinical Psychology, 63*, 445-453.

375. Hunt, N., & Silverstone, T. (1995). Does puerperal illness distinguish a subgroup of bipolar patients? *Journal of Affective Disorders, 34*, 101-107.

376. Kawada, Y., Hattori, M., Fukuda, R., Arai, H., Inoue, R., & Nanko, S. (1995). No evidence of linkage or association between tyrosine hydroxylase gene and affective disorder. *Journal of Affective Disorders, 34*, 89-94.

377. Kuczynski, L., & Kochanska, G. (1995). Function and content of maternal demands: Developmental significance of early demands for competent action. *Child Development, 66*, 616-628.

378. Lahey, B. B., Loeber, R., Hart, E. L., Frick, P. J., Applegate, B., Zhang, Q., Green, S. M., & Russo, M. F. (1995). Four-year longitudinal study of conduct disorder in boys: Patterns and predictors of persistence. *Journal of Abnormal Psychology, 104*, 83-93.

379. Levinson, D. F., Simpson, G. M., Lo, E. S., Cooper, T. B., Singh, H., Yadalam, K., & Stephanos, M. J. (1995). Fluphenazine plasma levels, dosage, efficacy, and side effects. *American Journal of Psychiatry, 152*, 765-771.

380. Lovejoy, M. C., & Steuerwald, B. L. (1995). Subsyndromal unipolar and bipolar disorders: Comparisons on positive and negative affect. *Journal of Abnormal Psychology, 104*, 381-384.

381. Lyons, M. J., Toomey, R., Faraone, S. V., Kremen, W. S., Yeung, A. S., & Tsuang, M. T. (1995). Correlates of psychosis proneness in relatives of schizophrenic patients. *Journal of Abnormal Psychology, 104*, 390-394.

382. Mattanah, J. J. F., Becker, D. F., Levy, K. N., Edell, W. S., & McGlashan, T. H. (1995). Diagnostic stability in adolescents followed up 2 years after hospitalization. *American Journal of Psychiatry, 152*, 889-894.

383. McDermott, B. E. (1995). Development of an instrument for assessing self-efficacy in schizophrenic spectrum disorders. *Journal of Clinical Psychology, 51*, 320-331.

384. Meltzer, H. Y., & Okayli, G. (1995). Reduction of suicidality during clozapine treatment of neuroleptic-resistant schizophrenia: Impact on risk-benefit assessment. *American Journal of Psychiatry, 152*, 183-190.

385. Nofzinger, E. A., Reynolds, C. F., Thase, M. E., Frank, E., Jennings, R., Fasiczka, A. L., Sullivan, L. R., & Kupfer, D. J. (1995). REM sleep enhancement by bupropion in depressed men. *American Journal of Psychiatry, 152*, 274-276.

386. Nolen-Hoeksema, S., Wolfson, A., Mumme, D., & Guskin, K. (1995). Helplessness in children of depressed and nondepressed mothers. *Developmental Psychology, 31*, 377-387.

387. Pauls, D. S., Alsobrook, J. P., Goodman, W., Rasmussen, S., & Leckman, J. F. (1995). A family study of obsessive-compulsive disorder. *American Journal of Psychiatry, 152*, 76-84.

388. Peselow, E. D., Sanfilipo, M. P., & Fieve, R. R. (1995). Relationship between hypomania and personality disorders before and after successful treatment. *American Journal of Psychiatry, 152*, 232-238.

389. Power, M. J., Duggan, C. F., Lee, A. S., & Murray, R. M. (1995). Dysfunctional attitudes in depressed and recovered depressed patients and their first-degree relatives. *Psychological Medicine, 25*, 87-93.

390. Prigerson, H. G., Frank, E., Kasl, S. V., Reynolds, C. F., Anderson, B., Zubenko, G. S., Houck, P. R., George, C. J., & Kupfer, D. J. (1995). Complicated grief and bereavement-related depression as distinct disorders: Preliminary empirical validation in elderly bereaved spouses. *American Journal of Psychiatry, 152*, 22-30.

391. Radke-Yarrow, M., McCann, K., DeMulder, E., Belmont, B., Martinez, P., & Richardson, D. T. (1995). Attachment in the context of high-risk conditions. *Development and Psychopathology, 7*, 247-265.

392. Reschke, A. H., Mannuzza, S., Chapman, T. F., Lipsitz, J. D., Liebowitz, M. R., Gorman, J. M., Klein, D. F., & Fyer, A. J. (1995). Sodium lactate response and familial risk for panic disorder. *American Journal of Psychiatry, 152*, 277-279.

393. Rubenstein, C. S., Altemus, M., Pigott, T. A., Hess, A., & Murray, D. L. (1995). Symptom overlap between OCD and bulimia nervosa. *Journal of Anxiety Disorders, 9*, 1-9.

394. Rush, A. J., Laux, G., Giles, D. E., Jarrett, R. B., Weissenburger, J., Feldman-Koffler, F., & Stone, L. (1995). Clinical characteristics of outpatients with chronic major depression. *Journal of Affective Disorders, 34*, 25-32.

395. Sakamoto, K., Nakadaira, S., Kamo, K., Kamo, T., & Takahashi, K. (1995). A longitudinal follow-up study of seasonal affective disorder. *American Journal of Psychiatry, 152*, 862-868.

396. Sands, J. R., & Harrow, M. (1995). Vulnerability to psychosis in unipolar major depression: Is premorbid functioning involved? *American Journal of Psychiatry, 152*, 1009-1015.

397. Schiavi, R. C., Stimmel, B. B., Mandeli, J., & White, D. (1995). Chronic alcoholism and male sexual function. *American Journal of Psychiatry, 152*, 1045-1051.

398. Schittecatte, M., Garcia-Valentin, J., Charles, G., Machowski, R., Pena-Othaitz, M-J., Mendlewicz, J., & Wilmotte, J. (1995). Efficacy of the "Clonidine REM Suppression Test (CREST)" to separate patients with major depression from controls: A comparison with three currently proposed biological markers of depression. *Journal of Affective Disorders, 33*, 151-157.

399. Segal, Z. V., Gemar, M., Truchon, C., Guirguis, M., & Horowitz, L. M. (1995). A priming methodology for studying self-representation in major depressive disorder. *Journal of Abnormal Psychology, 104*, 205-213.

400. Simons, A. D., Gordon, J. S., Monroe, S. M., & Thase, M. E. (1995). Toward an integration of psychologic, social, and biologic factors in depression: Effects on outcome and course of cognitive therapy. *Journal of Consulting and Clinical Psychology, 63*, 369-377.

401. Southwick, S. M., Yehuda, R., & Giller, E. L. (1995). Psychological dimensions of depression in borderline personality disorder. *American Journal of Psychiatry, 152*, 789-791.

402. Swanson, S. C., Templer, D. I., Thomas-Dobson, S., Cannon, W. G., Streiner, D. L., Reynolds, R. M., & Miller, H. R. (1995). Development of a three-scale MMPI: The MMPI-TRI. *Journal of Clinical Psychology, 51*, 361-374.

403. Szymanski, S., Lieberman, J. A., Alvir, J. M., Mayerhoff, D., Loebel, A., Geisler, S., Chakos, M., Koreen, A., Jody, D., Kane, J., Woerner, M., & Cooper. T. (1995). Gender differences in onset of illness, treatment response, course, and biological indexes in first-episode schizophrenic patients. *American Journal of Psychiatry, 152*, 698-703.

404. Tarullo, L. B., DeMulder, E. K., Ronsaville, D. S., Brown, E., & Radke-Yarrow, M. (1995). Maternal depression and maternal treatment of siblings as predictors of child psychopathology. *Developmental Psychology, 31*, 395-405.

405. Tarullo, L. B., Richardson, D. T., Radke-Yarrow, M., & Martinez, P. E. (1995). Multiple sources in child diagnosis: Parent-child concordance in affectively ill and well families. *Journal of Clinical Child Psychology, 24*, 173-183.

406. Taylor, M. A., & Amir, N. (1995). Sinister psychotics: Left-handedness in schizophrenia and affective disorder. *The Journal of Nervous and Mental Disease, 183*, 3-9.

407. Tyrka, A. R., Cannon, T. D., Haslam, N., Mednick, S. A., Schulsinger, F., Schulsinger, H., & Parnas, J. (1995). The latent structure of schizotypy: I. Premorbid indicators of a taxon of individuals at risk for schizophrenia-spectrum disorders. *Journal of Abnormal Psychology, 104*, 173-183.

408. Warshaw, M. G., Massion, A. O., Peterson, L. G., Pratt, L. A., & Keller, M. B. (1995). Suicidal behavior in patients with panic disorder: Retrospective and prospective data. *Journal of Affective Disorders, 34*, 235-247.

409. West, S. A., McElroy, S. L., Strakowski, S. M., Keck, P. E., & McConville, B. J. (1995). Attention deficit hyperactivity disorder in adolescent mania. *American Journal of Psychiatry, 152*, 271-273.

410. Winokur, G., Coryell, W., Akiskal, H. S., Maswer, J. D., Keller, M. B., Endicott, J., & Mueller, T. (1995). Alcoholism in manic-depressive (bipolar) illness: Familial illness, course illness, and the primary-secondary distinction. *American Journal of Psychiatry, 152*, 365-372.

411. Wisner, K. L., Peindl, K. S., & Hanusa, B. H. (1995). Psychiatric episodes in women with young children. *Journal of Affective Disorders, 34*, 1-11.

412. Wood, A., Kroll, L., Moore, A., & Harrington, R. (1995). Properties of the mood and feelings questionnaire in adolescent psychiatric outpatients: A research note. *Journal of Child Psychology and Psychiatry and Allied Disciplines, 36*, 327-334.

413. Yager, J., Rorty, M., & Rossotto, E. (1995). Coping styles differ between recovered and nonrecovered women with bulimia nervosa, but not between recovered women and non-eating disordered control subjects. *The Journal of Nervous and Mental Disease, 183*, 86-94.

414. Yehuda, R., Keefe, R. S. E., Harvey, P. D., Levengood, R. A., Gerber, D. K., Geni, J., & Siever, L. J. (1995). Learning and memory in combat veterans with posttraumatic stress disorder. *American Journal of Psychiatry, 152*, 137-139.

Review of the Schedule for Affective Disorders and Schizophrenia, Third Edition by PAUL A. ARBISI, Assessment Clinic Director, Psychology Service, Minneapolis VA Medical Center, Minneapolis, MN:

The Schedule for Affective Disorders and Schizophrenia (SADS) was developed in the mid-1970s primarily as a research instrument designed to obtain homogeneous groups of subjects defined by functional psychiatric illness. The introduction of a semistructured interview that supplied established criteria and allowed for the description of the clinical features of the episode provided a means by which researchers could lend coherence to the field and opened the way for a better understanding of both the social and biological basis of psychopathology. Prior to the advent of the SADS, there was tremendous disparity in the rate of diagnoses of particular disorders across research centers that differed geographically as well as philosophically (Cooper et al., 1972). To a great extent, this was a result of the nonsystematic gathering of information during an unstructured clinical interview. The interview was often driven by the biases of the interviewer, and hence, reached an unreliable diagnosis. Consequently, the development of clinically meaningful and reliable diagnostic categories was hindered by the use of unstructured interviews. The SADS was one of the first systematic attempts to address the two major sources of clinician unreliability, information variance and criterion variance, by use of an organized progression of questions based on established criteria. In so doing, the SADS revolutionized the way in which information regarding mental illness was obtained during the interview and deserves to be recognized as a major force in the evolution and refinement of psychiatric diagnosis.

The SADS is divided into two parts and takes approximately 1.5 to 2 hours to administer. Part I provides a detailed description of the clinical features of the current episode when it is most severe, and during the week prior to the interview. Part II focuses on historical information required to obtain a lifetime diagnosis. Further, the SADS provides estimates of severity by rating each symptom along a behaviorally anchored dimension of impairment or frequency of occurrence. The organization of the instrument was designed to mimic a clinical interview bent on differential diagnosis based on the Research Diagnostic Criteria (RDC) (Spitzer, Endicott, & Robins, 1975) by providing a suitable progression of questions along with appropriate rule-in and rule-out criteria. The SADS contains relevant information necessary to make diagnoses defined in the RDC, both currently and over the course of the subject's life time. Further, some, but not all, DSM-III-R diagnoses can be extracted. The failure to address questions relating to most personality disorders as well as Post Traumatic Stress Disorder (PTSD) is noteworthy and limits the applicability of the interview. There are several versions of the SADS differing primarily in terms of the time period that is the focus of assessment. Additionally, investigators have modified the instrument to add coverage of additional areas of function or for use in specialized populations. The SADS-L version is similar to Part II except that the time period covered is not limited to the past and includes any current disturbance. Consequently, information regarding the current episode is less well detailed when obtained with the SADS-L. Therefore, it is more suitable to studies where there is no need for detailed information regarding the current episode or the subject is currently asymptomatic. The SADS-LB is similar to the SADS-L, but contains additional items related to the diagnosis of bipolar illness. There are two versions designed to assess change in psychiatric status subsequent to an initial assessment, the SADS-C (change) and the SADS-I (interval) versions corresponding to Parts I and II, respectively. Score sheets are provided for each version that allow for coding and entry into a computer data base.

Test-retest and joint reliabilities for major RDC diagnoses obtained across separate research centers range from excellent to good. For example, the diagnosis of Mania was generally reliably obtained, yet the diagnosis of hypomania or cyclothymia was considerably less reliable and consensus diagnosis was more difficult to achieve. Rationally constructed summary dimensions of psychopathology demonstrate internal consistency ranging from excellent (.97) for manic syndrome, to poor (.47) for formal thought disorder. The validity of a diagnostic instrument not only hinges on the reliability of the instrument, but also on the validity of the adopted diagnostic criteria. The RDC served as the basis for many diagnostic categories in DSM-III-R (American Psychiatric Association, 1987), but does not always directly correspond to DSM-III-R, and now DSM-IV, criteria. A discussion of the validity of psychiatric diagnosis exceed the scope of this review; however, suffice it to say, as is the case with DSM-III-R, some RDC diagnoses do a better job of capturing a real nosological entity than do others. Finally, the SADS gives short shrift to the personality disorders and does not allow for certain prominent DSM diagnoses such as PTSD. On the other hand, if the investigator is interested in particular aspects of Affective Disorder, the SADS-L provides a detailed description of severity, intensity, and frequency of occurrence as well as lifetime history of the disorder. The SADS also shows utility in making reliable lifetime diagnoses in nonpatient populations.

The SADS semistructured format presupposes prior knowledge of psychiatric concepts and the manual designates raters such as psychiatrists, clinical psychologists, or psychiatric social workers as appropriate users. Extensive additional training is recommended in the use of the SADS to include viewing of videotapes of SADS interviews conducted by master interviewers and joint interviews with more experienced SADS interviewers. This level of mastery is in contrast to fully structured diagnostic interviews such as the SCID (Spitzer, Williams, Gibbon, & First, 1990) or the DIS (Robins, Helzer, Croughan, & Ratcliff, 1981) that do not require as much prior background or training in the administration of the respective interviews, and can be successfully administered by trained lay interviewers. The manual and supplementary instructions for the use of the SADS and SADS-L are straightforward, but the interview format itself can be somewhat confusing and requires study and practice before an accomplished, unstilted style of delivery can be achieved. Again, the purpose of the SADS is to obtain homogenous groups of subjects who meet specific, reliable diagnostic criteria. This level of precision can only be achieved through intensive training and practice with the SADS.

The SADS was designed as a research tool and not as an aid for clinicians in reaching diagnoses. Given that premise, the SADS, in general, performs well and does an excellent job at providing reliable RDC based current and lifetime diagnoses. In sum, good diagnostic reliability is achieved for all major diagnoses with the SADS, but in order to reach an acceptable level of interrater reliability, a highly educated rater is required to undergo extensive training in the administration of the SADS. On principle, this degree of scrupulous attention to rater reliability is certainly desirable, yet many investigators do not have the resources necessary to achieve this level of expertise and will want to rely on a more rigidly structured interview, such as the SCID (Spitzer et al., 1990) or the DIS (Robins et al., 1981). Finally, if reliable DSM-III-R diagnosis is the goal or there is a need to systematically address character pathology, then the more accessible SCID is the structured interview of choice.

REVIEWER'S REFERENCES

Cooper, J. E., Kendell, R. E., Gurland, B. J., Sharpe, L., Copeland, J. R. M., & Simon, R. (1972). *Psychiatric diagnosis in New York and London: A comparative study of mental hospital admissions.* London: Oxford University Press.

Spitzer, R. L., Endicott, J., & Robins, E. (1975). Research Diagnostic Criteria (RDC). New York: Biometrics Research, New York State Psychiatric Institute.

Robins, L. N., Helzer, J. E., Croughan, J., & Ratcliff, K. S. (1981). National Institute of Mental Health diagnostic interview schedule: Its history, characteristics, and validity. *Archives of General Psychiatry, 38,* 381-389.

American Psychiatric Association. (1987). *Diagnostic and statistical manual of mental disorders* (3rd ed., rev.). Washington, DC: American Psychiatric Association.

Spitzer, R. L., Williams, J. B. W., Gibbon, M., & First, M. B. (1990). *User's guide for the Structured Clinical Interview for DSM-III-R: SCID.* Washington, DC: American Psychiatric Press.

Review of the Schedule for Affective Disorders and Schizophrenia, Third Edition by JAMES C. CARMER, Clinical Psychologist, Lincoln, NE:

The Schedule for Affective Disorders and Schizophrenia (SADS) consists of a structured interview and rating form pertaining to symptoms of major psychiatric disorders. The SADS was developed out of the multicentered National Institute of Health Collaborative Study of the Psychobiology of Depression. This ambitious project prompted the development of widely standardized interview techniques, which could facilitate the kind of data collection necessary to conduct large scale epidemiological studies involving large numbers of subjects in divergent geographical locations and across generations. A companion diagnostic rating scale, the Research Diagnostic Criteria, relates to the SADS items, resulting in suggested diagnostic classifications for the subject of the interview. The Research Diagnostic Criteria was the forerunner of the DSM-III.

The SADS interview process consists of two parts. Part I involves rating the subject's symptoms *at their most severe* during the past week, or if the focus of the study is on the current episode of illness, the Part I ratings pertain to the week of the current episode of illness when the symptoms were at their most severe. Part II of the SADS focuses on historical information. It is expected that a rater familiar with the SADS could complete the interview in less than 2 hours. An advantage of the structure and focus of the SADS is that the interview process is not necessarily time limited and information can be gathered over the course of several days.

Four versions of the SADS are described in the accompanying materials. The SADS-L is similar to Part II of the SADS and is focused on rating the subject's symptoms over the individual's lifetime. The SADS-LI is based on the SADS-L and is designed to be administered following specified intervals or events to individuals previously administered the SADS-L. The SADS-C is a modification of the SADS which emphasizes current symptoms. With its emphasis on present symptoms, the SADS-C is potentially useful for treatment outcome studies and ongoing monitoring of targeted symptom relief.

Because the SADS relies on the clinical judgment of the interviewer to shape the detail of the questions asked, the SADS should be administered by clinicians familiar with diagnostic issues who have been specifically trained in the SADS. The authors offer support in training interviewers. The SADS interview structure permits the clinician to use all sources of information available, including records and the reports of family members, using clinical judgment in instances where sources conflict. Depending on the focus of the study, the SADS also can be used "blind," with only the interview data available.

The interview forms are well laid out, with general instructions and recommended queries for the interviewer to make. Reference help comes in the form of various updates and journal article reprints included with the testing materials. Scoring of the SADS results in 24 scales including various symptom groupings, an extracted Hamilton Depression Rating Scale score, and a Global Assessment Scale.

Reliability data for the SADS are reported through the inclusion of reprints of several different studies reporting reliability across time, interviewer, geographical location, and diagnostic category. The reliabilities reported are acceptable, although, because it is an interview technique, studies utilizing the SADS should assess and report at least interrater agreement. Additional studies have demonstrated acceptable reliability for joint interview and test-retest conditions, as well as internal consistency.

Studies included with the test material comparing diagnoses obtained with the SADS with diagnoses obtained with the Diagnostic Interview Schedule (DIS) indicate that agreement of diagnoses obtained by the two instruments is unexpectedly weak. This finding has not yet been explained. The value of the SADS does not rest in the diagnoses obtained with it; the SADS is a powerful research tool in the investigation of psychiatric symptomatology independent of diagnosis over time and across generations and cultures. Researchers should carefully evaluate which instrument is best suited for their study, as diagnoses obtained with the SADS are not necessarily equivalent to diagnoses obtained with the DIS.

The authors urge potential researchers to contact them for assistance in interviewer training, scale modifications, and referral and support for the instrument. It is emphasized that the SADS and its related scales are to be utilized only by trained interviewers and researchers. This instrument is not for general use by clinicians untrained specifically in its administration and scoring. Fortunately, the authors are available for consultation and assistance in maintaining the coherence of the body of research which utilizes the SADS. The authors offer assistance in the training of raters, and offer themselves as resources for both audio and video recordings of interviews to promote the reliability of SADS ratings.

The SADS has found almost universal acceptance in research which focuses on epidemiological perspectives, and, as such, has been frequently used in studies assessing the impact of political and physical events on affected groups worldwide. The SADS has been translated into several languages, and has been revised repeatedly to sharpen its applicability to each new target group investigated. Somewhat independently, numerous revisions of the SADS have been developed to target different ages and developmental levels. For example, the Kiddie-Schedule for Affective Disorders and Schizophrenia (K-SADS) is a modification of the SADS targeting school-age children (Ambrosini, Metz, Prabucki, & Lee, 1989).

A disadvantage of the SADS is that its terminology relates to diagnostic classification as conceptualized in the 1970s, during the time of the development of the DSM III. Diagnostic classification has changed with the advents of the DSM III, DSM III-R, and DSM IV. Terminology and diagnostic entities used in the DSM IV now differ significantly from that used in the SADS. However, because the SADS is focused on determining the presence of symptoms in individuals, rather than determining a psychiatric diagnosis, its usefulness throughout ongoing changes in diagnostic classification is assured. Using the SADS in research involving diagnostic entities will require some conversion of SADS results into the diagnostic classification utilized.

The SADS lacks a clear, coherent manual. The testing packet includes various reprints, mimeographed monographs, and revised instructions which are not integrated. Given the enormous utilization of the SADS, a comprehensive and cogent manual should be developed.

The SADS obviously meets an almost overwhelming need for a standardized instrument for documenting the presence of various indications of psychopathology. With the SADS it is possible for multiple researchers to investigate a wide range of real world situations affecting individuals, groups, and even societies. The SADS provides a stable human perspective from which it is possible to comprehend the subjective impact of biological, physical, and political events. The rapidly growing body of research utilizing the SADS is forming the foundation for long-term studies that previously have been impossible to conduct. The SADS is a potentially powerful treatment outcome assessment instrument for all modalities of psychological and psychiatric treatment.

REVIEWER'S REFERENCE

Ambrosini, P. J., Metz, C., Prabucki, K., & Lee, J. (1989). Videotape reliability of the third revised edition of the K-SADS. *Journal of the American Academy of Child and Adolescent Psychiatry, 28*(5), 723-728.

[344]

Scholastic Abilities Test for Adults.

Purpose: "Designed to be a general measure of scholastic accomplishment."

Population: Ages 16 and over.
Publication Date: 1991.
Acronym: SATA.
Scores: 9 subtest scores: Verbal Reasoning, Nonverbal Reasoning, Quantitative Reasoning, Reading Vocabulary, Reading Comprehension, Math Calculation, Math Application, Writing Mechanics, Writing Composition, and 9 composite scores: Scholastic Abilities, General Aptitude, Total Achievement, Verbal, Quantitative, Reading, Mathematics, Writing, Achievement Screener.
Administration: Group.
Price Data, 1994: $114 per complete kit including 10 test books, 25 response booklets, 25 profile/examiner record forms, and manual (102 pages); $41 per 10 test books; $29 per 25 response booklets; $19 per 25 profile/examiner record forms; $29 per manual; $79 per scoring and report system software (Apple or IBM).
Time: (60–120) minutes.
Authors: Brian R. Bryant, James R. Patton, and Caroline Dunn.
Publisher: PRO-ED, Inc.

Review of the Scholastic Abilities Test for Adults by NAMBURY S. RAJU, Professor of Psychology, Georgia Institute of Technology, Atlanta, GA:

The Scholastic Abilities Test for Adults (SATA) is designed for assessing the general aptitudes and achievements of individuals aged 16 and older. The SATA consists of nine separate subtests, yielding nine different aptitude and achievement scores and nine derived composite scores. Of the nine subtests, three subtests (Nonverbal Reasoning, Reading Vocabulary, and Reading Comprehension) have a multiple-choice response format, five subtests (Verbal Reasoning, Quantitative Reasoning, Math Calculation, Math Application, and Writing Mechanics) have an open response format, and one subtest (Writing Composition) requires the examinee to write four stories based on four picture prompts. All subtests are designed for both timed and untimed administrations and can be locally scored. Computer programs for scoring the SATA on an IBM PC or an Apple Computer are also available.

The majority of the subtests have 25 items each; the exceptions are Reading Comprehension with 60 items, Writing Mechanics with 15 items, and Writing Composition with four picture prompts. Associated with the raw scores from each subtest are the standard scores, percentile scores, and grade equivalent scores. Scores for the nine composites were derived from the subtest standard scores and were later converted to quotients, percentiles, and grade equivalents. Also available are discrepancy scores for use in determining whether one is functioning up to capacity and in identifying the underachievers. The SATA manual offers a variety of quantitative information concerning the psychometric properties of the SATA subscores and composites.

NORMS. The standardization of the SATA was based on 1,005 examinees, representing 19 states and ranging in age from 16 to 70. The maximum sample size for any age group was 159 examinees (manual, p. 32). The initial age distribution was collapsed into five (timed norms) and four to six (untimed norms) nonoverlapping age categories for the purpose of developing subtest percentiles and standard scores. Each subtest raw score scale was linearly transformed to a standard score scale with a mean of 10 and standard deviation of 3, resulting in a 1–20 range. The percentile scores were based on the assumption that the distribution of raw scores was normal for each age group (manual, p. 32); no justification was offered for this assumption in the manual. Although this assumption may appear tenable for the lower age groups, one wonders about its tenability for the upper age groups; empirically derived (without the assumption of normality) and smoothed percentiles would have been a more defensible choice. It seems that the small sample sizes may have necessitated the need for the assumption of normality in developing percentile scores. Separate percentiles are available for the timed and untimed administrations of the SATA. (Pages 43–50 are missing from this reviewer's copy of the examiner's manual; some of these missing pages contained the norms for the timed administration.)

The discrepancy analysis for determining strengths and weaknesses and for identifying under- and overachievers is an attractive and useful feature. It was not clear from the information in the manual whether the recommended criterion for significance took the standard errors of measurement into account, as it is typically done with differences based on achievement and ability scores at the individual level.

RELIABILITY. Internal consistency estimates of reliability were provided for all subtest scores and the composites. Reliability information was offered for more (10) age groups than the five age groups used in developing the percentile untimed norms. The reported reliabilities were quite high, with the vast majority of them being substantially greater than .80. With respect to test-retest reliability, only limited data were presented. As expected, the test-retest coefficients were generally lower than the internal consistency estimates of reliability and appeared to be significantly lower for Numerical Reasoning, Reading Comprehension, and Writing Composition subtests.

On page 33 of the examiner's manual, it was stated that the reliabilities were averaged using the z-transformation technique. Because the internal consistency estimates of reliability are not correlation coefficients, one wonders about the appropriateness of the z-transformation technique in this context.

SEMS. Standard errors of measurement (*SEM*s) were reported in the standard score metric. The *SEM*s were all equal to 1 (when rounded to an integer) for the nine subtests, which should encourage counselors to use them in practice. Strictly speaking, the *SEM* interpretation given on page 34 of the manual is incorrect; as clearly articulated in Gulliksen (1987, pp. 17–22), probability statements can only be used with groups of examinees, not with individual examinees.

ITEM DATA. Median item-test correlations and item difficulties (*p*-values) were presented for the nine subtests. Some of the reported median *p*-values for the Writing Mechanics subtest were greater than 1.00 (Table 4.2, p. 31, manual). It was not clear from the manual whether these values were some type of extrapolations or simply typographical errors.

VALIDITY. Information was presented for three types of validity: content, criterion-related, and construct. As part of criterion-related validity, correlations between the SATA subtests and other well-known adult intelligence and achievement tests were reported. Most of the reported correlations were quite high. These correlations were corrected for unreliability in the criterion and only those that were statistically significant were reported in the manual (p. 37). It was not clear to me whether the observed correlations were tested for statistical significance before or after correcting them for unreliability in the criterion. It should be noted that the commonly used tests of significance for correlations are not valid for corrected correlations. It would have been more informative if both the corrected and uncorrected correlations were reported in the manual.

As evidence of construct validity, correlations between the SATA subtests and other similarly designed tests were presented. In addition, data were presented on how abilities varied as a function of age. Also presented were the SATA mean scores for three groups of examinees: college students with learning disabilities, students in adult basic education, and high school students with learning disabilities. The reported performance trends across these three groups were in the expected direction, providing additional support for the construct validation of the SATA.

In summary, the SATA appears to be a reliable and valid instrument for assessing the general aptitude and achievement of adults. Although substantial psychometric and normative data were presented in support of the SATA, there is still a need for obtaining more reliable norms based on larger samples and for fine tuning the current psychometric data as well as providing information on the differential functioning of items. There is certainly a need for better quality control on the development and production of the examiner's manual.

REVIEWER'S REFERENCE

Gulliksen, H. (1987). *The theory of mental tests*. Hillsdale, NJ: Lawrence Erlbaum Associates.

Review of the Scholastic Abilities Test for Adults by DOUGLAS K. SMITH, Professor of School Psychology, University of Wisconsin-River Falls, River Falls, WI:

The Scholastic Abilities Test for Adults (SATA) is designed to provide "estimates of general aptitude and achievement abilities for individuals aged 16 and older" (manual, p. 2). Major purposes of the SATA include (*a*) determination of an individual's relative strengths and weaknesses in both abilities and achievement areas; (*b*) identification of individuals who may need special assistance; (*c*) documentation of an individual's progress over time in an intervention program; and (*d*) conducting research.

The SATA is composed of nine subtests including three aptitude measures (Verbal Reasoning, Nonverbal Reasoning, and Quantitative Reasoning) and six achievement measures (Reading Vocabulary, Reading Comprehension, Math Calculation, Math Application, Writing Mechanics, and Writing Composition). The test may be administered in a group setting in a timed format or individually in an untimed format (except for Reading Comprehension and Writing Composition, which have 15-minute time limits). Individual administration utilizes subtest ceilings to shorten administration time. Group testing requires about 2 hours and individual testing requires 1 to 1½ hours. A screening version of the SATA, consisting of Reading Vocabulary, Math Calculation, and Writing Mechanics can be administered in 30 minutes.

Test materials include a test book in which test items are presented and a separate response booklet for individuals to record their responses. Practice items (one or two depending on subtest) are provided for each subtest except Writing Composition. Two sets of directions (Untimed and Timed) are presented for each subtest (except for Reading Comprehension and Writing Mechanics, which have one set of directions).

The test administration instructions are relatively clear and easy to follow. The wording on one subtest, Reading Vocabulary, is somewhat cumbersome and lengthy. the use of a separate test book and response booklet could be confusing to some examinees. This is most apt to be a problem in the group testing format. Otherwise, test materials are well designed and easy to use.

Items are scored either correct or incorrect except for Writing Composition. For this subtest scoring is based on a combination of the vocabulary used and the "content maturity" (p. 15) of the composition. Although scoring guidelines and sample compositions are provided, scoring of this subtest is somewhat subjective.

Subtest raw scores are converted into standard scores (mean of 10 and standard deviation of 3) and percentile ranks. Standard scores for the subtests composing the various composites are added together and converted into a quotient (a standard score with mean of 100 and standard deviation of 15). Grade equivalents can also be derived. The examiner's manual describes each type of score and their major advantages and disadvantages. The interpretation of scores from the SATA is discussed at length in the examiner's manual and the reader is provided with both advantages and disadvantages of each approach. A special section, Cautions in Interpreting Scores, alerts the user to common errors in test interpretation.

A detailed description of the development of the SATA is provide in the examiner's manual including the rationale for the development of each subtest. Seven of the composite scores (Scholastic Abilities, General Aptitude, Total Achievement, Reading, Mathematics, Writing, and Achievement Screener) are content based and two (Verbal and Quantitative) are based on factor analysis of the standardization data.

Standardization of the SATA took place between August 1989 and April 1990. The standardization sample consisted of 1,005 individuals in 19 states, which roughly corresponded to 1985 census estimates on the variables of gender, geographical region, race, and ethnicity. The number of cases per age level ranged from 62 for the 70–79-year level to 190 for the 20–29-year level.

Internal consistency of the SATA was established by calculating coefficient alpha for each age interval (16, 17, 18, 19, 20–29, 30–39, 40–49, 50–59, 60–69, 70–79) and for the timed and untimed formats. Average values for the subtests ranged from .83 to .96 (timed format) and .87 to .96 (untimed format) and for the composites the range was .93 to .98 (timed format) and .94 to .98 (untimed format). Test-retest reliability estimates for 23 individuals between ages 21 and 43 tested and retested at a 1-week interval ranged from .61 to .88 (timed format) and .65 to .90 (untimed format) for subtests and from .85 to .93 (timed format) and .85 to .94 (untimed format) for the composites.

Criterion and construct validity of the SATA were established by comparing performance of groups of individuals (25 to 42 per group) on the SATA and other measures of ability (e.g., Wechsler Intelligence Scale for Adults—Revised; Woodcock-Johnson Psychoeducational Battery) and achievement (e.g., Wide Range Achievement Test—Revised). Acceptable validity coefficients were indicated. Factor analyses of the standardization sample indicated the presence of a general factor (Scholastic Abilities) and two additional factors (Verbal, Quantitative).

The authors of the SATA are to be commended for their thorough discussion of test interpretation, sources of errors in test scores, and appropriate use of test scores. Unfortunately, the Profile/Examiner Record Form does not provide an area for the examiner to record the standard error of measurement or to calculate the confidence interval for test scores. Such information is especially important for the composite scores.

The individual or group testing format of the SATA adds to its flexibility. Although the test is easy to administer and score, interpretation of test results requires specialized training. Because the test can be administered in a group setting, the qualifications of test users assumes special importance. On this issue, the test authors indicate that examiners should have "some formal training in assessment" (p. 7). Although several examples of such training are provided, the exact level of training needed by examiners is not specified. Because the SATA is compared to both achievement measures which require a minimum level of training and to individual measures of intelligence such as the Wechsler Scales which require in-depth training, a potential user of the SATA may be unsure of the exact level of training required for use of the instrument.

Overall, the SATA is a promising, new measure of abilities and achievement for individuals ages 16-0 through 79-11 years. Development of the instrument is thoroughly documented in the examiner's manual and initial reliability/validity data are at an acceptable level. As with any new test, additional data are needed to determine how the test relates to existing measures of ability and achievement.

[345]

School Assessment Survey.

Purpose: "Designed to measure schoolwide characteristics."

Population: Elementary through senior high school teachers and administrators.

Publication Date: 1985.

Acronym: SAS.

Scores, 9: Goal Consensus, Facilitative Leadership, Centralization of Influence: Classroom Instruction, Centralization of Influence: Curriculum and Resources, Vertical Communication, Horizontal Communication, Staff Conflict, Student Discipline, Teaching Behavior.

Administration: Group.

Price Data, 1991: $16.95 per kit including manual (69 pages).

Time: [30–40] minutes.

Authors: Bruce L. Wilson and William A. Firestone.

Publisher: Research for Better Schools.

Cross References: See T4:2355 (1 reference).

TEST REFERENCES

1. DiPaola, M. F., & Hoy, W. K. (1994). Teacher militancy: A professional check on bureaucracy. *Journal of Research and Development in Education, 27*, 83-88.

Review of the School Assessment Survey by LeANN M. GAMACHE, Director, Psychometric Services, Professional Assessment Services Division, American College Testing, Iowa City, IA:

The criteria for evaluation of any measurement instrument should be determined by the intended use of that instrument. The manual indicates that the School Assessment Survey (SAS) can be used (*a*) as a research tool, (*b*) to identify areas of organizational strengths and weaknesses, or (*c*) to help determine action needed to implement a specific change. As discussed in more detail below, the technical and other characteristics described in the manual support only the first suggested use (i.e., as a research tool).

Technical considerations and relevant criteria for measurement instruments are embodied in the *Standards for Educational and Psychological Testing*, published jointly in 1985 by AERA, APA, and NCME. Although it may seem problematic to use these standards in judging the SAS, also published in 1985, use of the SAS in today's educational environment requires that such considerations be made. This review is based on information from the SAS 1985 technical manual. Potential users are encouraged to obtain and carefully review this well-written document with respect to the requirements of their particular situation.

CONTENT. One of the strengths of the SAS is the research-based approach to its development. The manual specifically matches the dimensions to selected school effectiveness and improvement research. Much of the research cited, however, is that of the early 1980s and of the two authors themselves. The definition of the content dimensions would benefit from update with respect to broader and current research literature. Because at least a decade has passed since the conduct of the research cited, potential users must bear the burden of assessing the currency of this instrument.

The developers appropriately gave specific attention to the need to balance the often competing priorities of technical considerations and the realities of logistics, time constraints, and resources available at the school level. The final set of 48 items was determined on statistical performance alone. Unfortunately, this may have inadvertently narrowed the domain of each of these dimensions. There is no table of content specifications against which to assess the final content distribution of items; thus, it cannot be assumed that the five to seven items that are used to measure each of the nine dimensions is an adequate sample of the domain of each of those dimensions.

The particular items used are generally clear and concise, although future development efforts might focus on (*a*) reducing the appearance of duplicate indicators, (*b*) balancing positive and negative phrasing to reduce problems of response biases, (*c*) eliminating competing format cues for the responses, and (*d*) deleting items or parts of items when responses are not used in the calculation of the scores. Users of the present SAS, however, might be asked by respondents to clarify the inconsistency of directions and response format of the Centralization dimension items. The user faces a dilemma, however, because additional clarification on the part of the user will tend to invalidate the normative comparisons.

RELIABILITY AND VALIDITY. To be of value, a measurement process must produce results that are sufficiently replicable (i.e., reliable) and appropriate (i.e., valid) for the intended use. As is appropriate, the SAS documentation provides reliability information for each of the nine dimensions. The coefficient alpha values (reported for a sample of 61 schools) are fairly high, even though few items are used to assess each dimension. This is, however, not surprising given that the final set of items was selected on a purely statistical basis specifically to maximize coherence. More technically complete reliability information would include estimates of rater response consistency and reliability of replication of the ratings across various occasions. To the degree that such types of reliability estimates are high, the SAS can be thought to provide stable results. The stability of the results is a fairly critical issue in considering the value of this assessment, given the diagnostic intent suggested by the developers.

Most of the information with respect to the validity of the results rests on the research-based definitions of the dimensions discussed above and on the statistical performance of the items and dimensions. Generally, the dimensions appear distinct: For the initial sample of 61 schools, correlations are higher for items within a dimension and lower with items in other dimensions. This is not surprising, however, given the statistically based item selection approach that was used in finalizing the test form. Even so, the pattern of item correlations is generally not considered sufficient to establish the appropriateness (validity) of the results for diagnosing strengths and weaknesses. The contemporary standards indicate that additional evidence is needed to support the diagnostic uses suggested for the SAS. For example, the sensitivity of these dimension scores to various interventions needs to be examined, as does the relationship of these dimension profiles to indicators of school effectiveness. To the extent that future research establishes a causal relationship between performance on these dimensions and school effectiveness, the user may be more able to make diagnostic use of scores.

SAS scores are reported with respect to performance of the final normative group of schools. This group includes the 61 schools that were administered the longer, draft version of the SAS and the 159 schools that participated in the subsequent administration of the shorter, final instrument. Unfortunately, the appropriateness of this combination of samples (without regard to form) cannot be evaluated given the available information. Further, the characteristics of these 220 schools are not clearly documented. Thus, the norming sample should be characterized as a sample of convenience, although the group of 159 schools was added for the express purpose of increasing the sample to be a more nationally representative set of schools. Appropriately, research was conducted to examine the need for separate elementary and secondary norms; separate sets of normative information are used for elementary or secondary schools.

OPERATIONAL COMPONENTS. The SAS adeptly addresses several likely concerns of respondents and sources of measurement noise on the front cover of the survey: The directions ask that informants complete the questionnaire frankly, indicate that their responses will be kept in strictest confidence, and (to facilitate this) ask that they submit their responses in the enclosed envelope directly to the designated person. The 30–40 minutes suggested appears generally sufficient for responding to the survey. (The proportion of missing data varies considerably by dimension and is more likely related to content or response concerns rather than time constraints.) With the format exceptions noted above, the survey seems fairly simple to administer and to complete.

Results are provided at the school level in a concise, information-packed graphic format. The school's position for each dimension is marked on a plot, which also shows the performance of the norm group. In addition, the raw score for the school is provided for each dimension. Users need to exercise extreme caution against overinterpretation of these results, however, because (*a*) dimension scores have been standardized to a scale that, given the actual number of items used, inadvertently implies considerably more precision than exists; and (*b*) estimates of measurement error such as confidence bands are not included around the estimate of the school's position or around the norm group estimates.

CONCLUSION. The SAS represented a heroic effort in identifying organizational characteristics of schools that might impact school effectiveness. The current educational reform efforts highlight the continued need for tools to inform and guide school improvement efforts. In its present form, the SAS might serve a useful research function. Certainly, various aspects of its developmental process can serve as a model for future such efforts. Users of the present form need to verify the content currency of the SAS with respect to their particular needs and to rigorously guard against overinterpretation of any results. It is hoped that the limitations of the present SAS, with respect to today's expectations, can be met in future editions so that the potential and promise of the SAS concept can be fulfilled.

REVIEWER'S REFERENCE

American Educational Research Association, American Psychological Association, & National Council on Measurement in Education. (1985). *Standards for educational and psychological testing*. Washington, DC: American Psychological Association, Inc.

Review of the School Assessment Survey by DEAN NAFZIGER, Executive Director, and JOANNE L. JENSEN, Research Associate, Far West Laboratory for Educational Research and Development, San Francisco, CA:

The School Assessment Survey (SAS) is designed to measure the organizational forms of schools. The development of the SAS has been guided by two theories of how schools function—schools as bureaucratic organizations and schools as loosely coupled systems. As a measure of such schoolwide characteristics, the SAS is to be completed by all teachers at a given school site, thus providing an opportunity for the full complement of perceptions about a school to be represented.

The SAS is a 55-item teacher self-report measure involving a variety of response formats including ranking, forced-choice, and Likert-type scales. Its development is based more on conceptual rather than empirical grounds. The authors, drawing from the organizational sociology and school effectiveness literature, have translated ideas from these fields into items based on consultation with school practitioners and trainers in school improvement. The instrument yields a total of nine scales including: Goal Consensus, Facilitative Leadership, Centralization: Classroom Instruction, Centralization: Curriculum and Resources, Vertical Communication, Horizontal Communication, Staff Conflict, Student Discipline, and Teaching Behavior.

RELIABILITY. The reliability indices are based on data collected in the third and fourth phases of instrument development. The respondents include 2,311 teachers representing 61 elementary and secondary schools in Pennsylvania and New Jersey. The version of the instrument used in this phase of the study included a total of 85 items. The item set is reduced to the 55-item version of the instrument based on an item's ability to differentiate among schools, to cohere to other items within a dimension, and its failure to cohere to items from other dimensions.

The authors report coefficient alphas all falling well within an acceptable range (.76–.96). They conclude that the alpha results provide "strong evidence that reliable measures of organizational properties of schools are obtained through the SAS instrument" (p. 20). This conclusion appears to be too strong. Although no data are provided to describe the nature of this sample, the reliance on schools in the northeast appears to limit the generalizability of these results. Further, stronger evidence of the reliability of the instrument would have been provided by replicating these results with a sample other than the one on which the final item selection was based.

VALIDITY. Validity analyses were performed in two phases. In Phase III, the authors compared the mean interitem correlation within each dimension (items on the diagonal) to the mean correlations for the items in the other dimensions (off-diagonal items). For each dimension, the mean within-item correlation was found to be roughly twice that of the mean of the off-diagonal correlation. The authors report these results as "providing strong confirmation of the convergent and discriminant validity of the organizational dimensions in this instrument" (p. 20). Although the reported results are promising, they must be interpreted in light of the sample from which they are based.

It is not clear why the authors did not use a factor analytic approach to determine whether items within a scale were tapping the same dimension and not loading on other factors. A further advantage of a factor analytic approach to construct validity is that it allows for a test of the replicability of the factor structure through confirmatory factor analysis. The factor structure of the final item set obtained in Phase III could have been confirmed by the sample used in Phase IV.

In Phase IV, the sample from Phase III is augmented by 4,087 teachers from 159 schools through the country. Although the authors describe the sample as being more nationally representative of schools, they offer no descriptive data to support this claim. In this phase, the authors investigate whether the dimensions measure empirically distinct organizational phenomena and whether the dimensions are systematically related to other known characteristics of schools.

To determine if the dimensions are empirically distinct, the correlations of the nine dimension scores for the 220 schools are reported. They range from -.59 to .64 with one-half of the correlations ranging in absolute magnitude from .02–.19. Although the correlations are distributed throughout the range of values, the magnitude of the values suggests, at best, only a modest relationship among the dimensions. Given the dimensions are designed to assess different aspects of school organization some correlation is to be expected, but uniqueness, as suggested by these data, is desirable.

To test the relationship of the dimensions to characteristics of schools, two-way ANOVA are reported for grade level and SES. Seven of the nine dimensions result in significance with at least one of the two variables. The two communication dimensions (vertical and horizontal) do not achieve significance. Correlations of the dimensions to two measures of student behavior also are reported. Significant correlations are reported for both social and academic indicators at both the elementary and secondary level. The number of significant correlations observed must be evaluated in light of the overall error rate for the study; each correlation is tested separately at the .05 level.

USE. The instrument is designed to be used in elementary, junior high, and high schools to describe the organizational conditions in the school. The authors describe two primary uses—as a needs assessment or as a tool to assist in change planning. To assist in the interpretation of the results, the scores are converted to a *t*-scale. Norms are reported separately for elementary and secondary schools (middle, junior high, and high schools). Results are reported in an easy-to-read graphical format that includes the school's mean raw and standardized score for each dimension and a comparison to that of the norming sample. This presentation makes it easy to compare relative strengths within a school as well as the school to the norm. Comparisons to the norm are limited by the lack of descriptive data on the norming sample itself.

The instrument is to be completed by all teachers at a given school, and the authors report the average proportion of teachers completing the SAS to be 86%. Although the response rate is high, it is important to investigate whether the attitudes held by nonrespondents mirror those of the respondents—particularly when trying to capture the climate of the entire school. Given that respondents are ensured confidentiality, special procedures would be required, and participants should be informed in advance of followup procedures. The authors do not report any investigation of nonrespondents, but users are encouraged to do so.

As presented, the survey is to be completed only by teachers. It would be interesting to have administrators complete the same survey. Whether the SAS is to be used as a needs assessment or as a technique to facilitate change, the comparison of teacher and administrator perceptions could prove valuable.

SUMMARY. The SAS is based on extensive research in the areas of school effectiveness and improvement. The authors have translated this work into an easily administered survey of teacher attitudes as they relate to school organization. The instrument possesses clear face validity, and the reliability and validity data support its use. The reporting format makes comparisons both within the school and to the norm group straightforward. The interpretation of the reliability, validity, and norming sample data must be tempered, however, by the limited sample on which the reliability analyses are based and the lack of descriptive information for the validity study norming sample.

[346]

School Readiness Test.

Purpose: Designed to test the student's readiness for first grade academics.
Population: End of Kindergarten through first 3 weeks of Grade 1.
Publication Dates: 1974–90.
Acronym: SRT.
Scores, 9: Vocabulary, Identifying Letters, Visual Discrimination, Auditory Discrimination, Comprehension and Interpretation, Number Knowledge, Handwriting Ability, Developmental Spelling Ability, Total.
Administration: Group.
Price Data, 1993: $41.60 per 35 test booklets, scoring key, class record sheet, and manual ('90, 26 pages); $4.15 per scoring key; $9.95 per manual; $2.15 per class record sheet; $20 per specimen set.

Time: (90) minutes.
Comments: Subtest scores convert to "OK," "Probably Needs Help," "Definitely Needs Help"; total score converts to "Gifted Ready," "Superior Ready," "Average Ready," "Marginal," "Short Delay," "Long Delay."
Authors: O. F. Anderhalter and Jan Perney.
Publisher: Scholastic Testing Service, Inc.
Cross References: For a review by Thorsten R. Carlson, see 8:808.

Review of the School Readiness Test by ESTHER STAVROU TOUBANOS, School Psychologist, Lawrence Public Schools, Lawrence, NY:

The School Readiness Test (SRT) is a group-administered test designed to provide the classroom teacher with information about students' "readiness for learning" and particularly "factors that might interfere with the learning process." No operational definition of readiness is provided, although the authors describe three uses for the test results:

1. To divide pupils into groups that are *ready* for formal learning, and groups that could use varying amounts of further *readiness experience*.

2. To diagnose the strengths and weaknesses of the individual pupils as related to readiness for formal learning in the different skill areas. . . .

3. To improve and individualize the teaching procedures (manual of directions, p. 24).

A potentially useful feature of this test is the availability of a Spanish version.

In addition to a total readiness score, part scores are provided for eight separate areas: Vocabulary, Identifying Letters, Visual Discrimination, Auditory Discrimination, Comprehension and Interpretation, Number Knowledge, Handwriting Ability, and Developmental Spelling Ability. No rationale is provided for the inclusion of various subtests or why some areas traditionally considered relevant to school success (i.e., expressive language, general knowledge, etc.) are excluded.

Total raw scores can be converted to percentile ranks based on norms for either the end of kindergarten or beginning of first grade. The composition of the norm group, however, is not specified in the manual. Verbal ratings are also provided for the Total Score which indicates readiness level according to six institutional groupings (G/R = Gifted Ready, S/R = Superior Ready, A/R = Average Ready, M = Marginal, S/D = Short Delay, or L/D = Long Delay). It is suggested that subtest or "part" scores be examined for pupils whose total score falls in the Marginal, Short Delay or Long Delay classification. Part scores can also be converted into percentiles as well as stanines and ratings of "ok," "probably needs help," or "definitely needs help."

The School Readiness Test appears to be a refinement of an earlier test by the same name. The Word Recognition subtest is now called Vocabulary, Number Readiness is now Number Knowledge, and a new subtest, Developmental Spelling Ability, was added. Although not considered a revision, this version addresses some of the weaknesses described in an earlier *MMY* review by Carlson (1978). However, some problems still remain, including the failure to provide a conceptualization of the nature of school readiness or to describe the instructional relevance of the test scores.

The SRT is designed to be administered at the end of kindergarten or before the third week of first grade. The authors suggest breaking the testing into two 40-minute sessions, though in trials by this examiner it was difficult to maintain most of the students' attention for even 40 minutes. The directions for administration are specific and clear for the examiner to follow, making it easily administered by the classroom teacher or paraprofessionals with little additional training. However, the directions are very confusing for young children who must attend to too much information at once. In general, most of the subtests involve too much information on one page, making it difficult for the child to focus on each item. Sophisticated linguistic concepts like "top," "left," and "corner" are often used in the task directions. Therefore, students' performances may reflect their understanding of these concepts rather than the purpose for which they are formally being tested. The Vocabulary subtest is particularly problematic in this respect because the directions involve knowledge of vocabulary that may be as complex as that which is formally being tested. For example, on the sample, the child is first instructed to find the page with a picture of a bird in the top left corner, then to "Look at the pictures in the top row, with the picture of a flower in the corner . . . There are pictures of a plate, a cup and a spoon. Draw a ring like this around the picture of the cup" (manual of directions, p. 5). Therefore, although the child is being tested on identification of a cup, he/she must also be able to identify a bird and a flower. Some other words used to identify the rows to which the child must attend include airplane, telephone, and scissors. In a group-administered test, it may be difficult to monitor students' understanding of the directions. Although the teacher is instructed to walk around during administration of the sample to make sure everyone has understood, this precaution is no longer taken once the test begins. Language is an appropriate and important part of school readiness that must be assessed but not in a manner that may confound the results.

The Handwriting Ability subtest is also problematic in that some of the figures to be reproduced are difficult even for older children and, without item analyses reported, it is difficult to determine whether these or any of the items are useful in discriminating between children. In addition, the amount of space provided in which to reproduce the figures is inadequate for young children. This is a timed subtest and although children are instructed not to spend too much time on any one picture, such instruction needs to be emphasized. Furthermore, more information must be provided regarding the scoring of figures. Additional scoring examples would help make decisions less subjective and arbitrary. Guidelines for what happens if a child copies upper case letters in lower case would also be helpful.

A general problem across subtests is the lack of a rationale for the manner in which behaviors are sampled. For example, Identifying Letters tests the child's knowledge of lower case letters. Why was lower case chosen over the more traditional upper case? Auditory Discrimination does not involve discrimination but rather sound recognition. It is unclear what the Comprehension and Interpretation subtest is measuring. It seems to involve visual discrimination and attention to detail, auditory comprehension, and understanding of relational concepts. Visual discrimination is also a factor on Items 17 and 18 of Number Knowledge, where the child must distinguish a penny from a dime drawn in the same color.

It would be helpful to know the authors' definition of "readiness" because many subtests involve more advanced skills than this reviewer considers necessary for "readiness." Number Knowledge measures actual mastery of advanced numerical skills like recognition of order, fractional parts, measures of time and money, rather than just readiness to learn these skills. Handwriting Ability is described as measuring "readiness for formal instruction in handwriting." It seems that if a child can successfully complete this subtest, he or she already has some handwriting skills. The usefulness of the Developmental Spelling Ability subtest in "predicting later student performance in reading" is also questionable.

The lack of technical data in the manual is a serious limitation and prevents the user from making meaningful conclusions from the scores. Although percentiles are provided, their relevance is unknown because no information is provided regarding the normative sample. Reliability information is not provided in the manual making it impossible for the reader to determine the usefulness of test results. It remains to be seen whether the results of the test can predict later school difficulties, however, validity cannot even be addressed without adequate reliability data.

In summary, the SRT appears to have been developed with little rationale for selection of domains and items sampled. Without evidence of adequate standardization, reliability, and validity, the SRT should not be used to make diagnostic and/or placement decisions. The authors' claim the results can be used to improve and individualize the teaching procedures is unfounded. Furthermore, no recommendations are provided regarding possible interventions that can be generated from the results other than additional time in readiness activities. Aside from the ease of administration, there appear to be few reasons to use this test over the more superior, Metropolitan Readiness Tests (233).

REVIEWER'S REFERENCE

Carlson, T. R. (1978). [Review of the School Readiness Test.] In O. K. Buros (Ed.), *The eighth mental measurements yearbook* (pp. 1348-1350). Highland Park, NJ: Gryphon Press.

Review of the School Readiness Test by LARRY WEBER, Professor of Education, Virginia Tech, Blacksburg, VA:

The School Readiness Test (SRT) was designed to assist the teacher in gathering information regarding entering students' readiness for learning. It is intended that the test be administered by the classroom teacher at the end of kindergarten or before the third full week of the first grade. Eight separate tests comprise the exam and a score is provided for each, in addition to a total readiness score.

There is no information covering why certain topics were chosen as important elements in determining school readiness. Neither is there sufficient justification for the inclusion of the test items. A priori beliefs about which abilities are consequential for success in first grade seem to have guided the choice of test content.

There are several problems associated with various facets of the SRT, beginning with its directions for administration. It is recommended the exam be administered in two sittings (it is 1 hour and 20 minutes long) but the manual states that it can be given in one sitting—with a rest period. A test of such length is too long, for 5- and 6-year-old children, to be taken in a single time period. Another direction is similarly tentative (i.e., "If possible, students should be seated so that they cannot see each other's work during the testing"). Such statements make one believe that conditions under which the exam is administered may be varied to fit the needs of the situation.

Regarding the examination itself, the test on Vocabulary, which requires students to identify pictures of words said by the examiner, seems flawed. In examples given the student before the test, the examinee is asked to identify specific items like "cup" and "mouse." On the actual examination items several of the terms are obtuse, for example requiring the student to identify a hammer as a "tool," a truck as a "vehicle," a violin as an "instrument," etc. It is hard to imagine that the difficulty indices for many of the items on the vocabulary test would be above the chance level.

Other subtests also contain deficiencies. The Identifying Letters subtest contains only lower case letters. The directions for the Visual Discrimination test seem too brief and complex for young children. The Auditory Discrimination subtest, with the possible exception of the rhyming items, will probably be incomprehensible for many examinees. The time limit, 5 seconds, for marking responses to answers on the Comprehension and Interpretation subtest appears insufficient, as does the time limit for several items in the Number Knowledge subtest, which in addition to containing items about numbers has questions about size, shape, time, money and fractions. The Handwriting and Spelling subtests are straightforward.

The scoring key and directions for scoring are adequate. The raw score for the first seven subtests is simply the number of correct answers for those tests. Each item for the Spelling subtest is scored on a 0–5 scale. The Handwriting subtest scoring scale, although admittedly subjective, contains reasonable guidelines for assisting the examiner in scoring that section of the SRT; and the Spelling subtest directions for scoring are rather comprehensive. The total score on the eight subtests comprises the total readiness score which, when converted to a percentile rank, provides a basis for "verbal ratings" that indicate each examinee's apparent readiness level. There are six verbal ratings: Gifted Ready = 96–99 percentile; Superior Ready = 76–95 percentile; Average Ready = 40–75 percentile; Marginal = 24–39 percentile; Short Delay = 5–23 percentile; Long Delay = 1–4 percentile.

One of the major faults with the SRT is its deficiency in providing data to support statements made about its value and usefulness. The statements that are made seem to reflect the test coordinators' opinions, and are not based on evidence provided in the test materials. For example, they state that "experience has suggested" that the six classifications (listed above) are useful in designating degrees of readiness. However, the system they use is nothing more than an application of stanine score categories to the verbal classifications. That is Gifted Ready = Stanine 9; Superior Ready = Stanines 7–8; Average Ready = Stanines 5–6; Marginal = Stanine 4; Short Delay = Stanines 2–3; Long Delay = Stanine 1. The manual contains nothing supporting the validity for claims that students whose scores fall into a given category will exhibit the type of verbal rating readiness described for that category.

There are other dangers in using the SRT scores for classifying students. One is the problem of interpreting the verbal ratings literally and assuming examinees possess the attributes or deficiencies of the class in which they are categorized. So care must be taken that the values suggested by the "verbal ratings" are not overemphasized. Moreover, it appears the scores earned by students on the test may be a measure of prior experience. Many of the items seem dependent on more or less formal training with similar material. As is stated in the manual, children who have had little training or assistance at home may earn low readiness ratings, yet progress rapidly once they enter school.

School readiness norm tables, which give percentile ranks for children earning specific raw scores, are provided for kindergarten and grade 1 examinees. Also provided are tables that classify students as "definitely needs help," "probably needs help," or "OK," according to their performance on the eight subtests. No suggestions are made as to the type of help a student needs nor is evidence provided regarding the basis for classifying students. There was no description in the manual of the norming population, other than they were "pupils in the national standardization group" (p. 24).

Another major fault with the SRT is the absence of reliability and validity data. Information about individual items (i.e., item difficulty and item discrimination) was not presented. In general there is a noted deficiency of information regarding the technical measurement characteristics of the test.

Because of the weaknesses described above, it is difficult to recommend the SRT as an instrument to be used for assessing readiness for formal learning in schools. The reasons for inclusion of the various subtests are weak; the classification of students into readiness categories is suspect; and evidence about the technical aspects of the exam (norms, validity, and reliability) is lacking. For those reasons alone the adoption of and use of findings from the SRT could be challenged.

[347]

School Situation Survey.

Purpose: Designed to measure "school-related student stress."
Population: Grades 4–12.
Publication Date: 1989.
Acronym: SSS.
Scores, 7: Sources of Stress (Teacher Interactions, Academic Stress, Peer Interactions, Academic Self-Concept), Manifestations of Stress (Emotional, Behavioral, Physiological).
Administration: Group.
Price Data, 1992: $16 per 25 test booklets/answer sheets; $6 per scoring key; $24 per manual (37 pages); $25 per specimen set.
Time: (10–15) minutes.
Authors: Barbara J. Helms and Robert K. Gable.
Publisher: Consulting Psychologists Press, Inc.

Review of the School Situation Survey by THEODORE COLADARCI, Associate Professor of Education, University of Maine, Orono, ME:

The School Situation Survey (SSS) is a 34-item instrument designed to assess "school-related student stress" in grades 4 through 12. Comprising seven scales, the SSS provides separate scores for four "sources" of stress: Teacher Interactions ("students' perceptions of their teachers' attitudes toward them"), Academic Stress ("situations that relate to academic performance or achievement"), Peer Interactions ("students' social interactions or their perceptions of their classmates' feelings toward them"), and Academic Self-Concept ("students' feelings of self-worth, self-esteem, or self-concept relevant to perceived ability"). The remaining three scales yield scores regarding "manifestations" of stress: Emotional ("feelings such as fear, shyness, and loneliness"), Behavioral ("actions, reactions, or behavior toward others, such as striking out or being hurtful or disrespectful"), and Physiological ("physical reactions or functions such as nausea, tremors, or rapid heart beat").

Students rate each item (e.g., "I feel upset") on a 5-point scale ranging from *never* to *always*. Answer sheets can be hand scored easily with the accompanying acetate overlay, or returned to Consulting Psychologists Press for machine scoring. In either case, a student receives seven scores; a composite score across the seven scales is not provided (nor do the authors recommend that such a score be used).

DOCUMENTATION. The SSS manual is a physically attractive document containing helpful information for SSS users and appraisers alike. However, I found the manual wanting in several respects. First, little attention is devoted to the intended uses, and possible misuses, of the SSS. For example, it would seem that different concerns would surface for practitioners than for researchers, yet the authors say little for either audience.

Second, the overall organization of the manual is awkward at times. Suggested strategies for reducing stress are presented after a section on norms, and information regarding factor analyses is alluded to in the construct validity section—where it belongs—but the reader must refer back to an earlier section on item development to see the specifics.

Finally, the authors' treatment of fundamental aspects of instrumentation (e.g., validity) appears to be intended for readers with a technical background. Although the language of psychometrics and statistics is unavoidable in a users' manual, it serves an important educative purpose when presented well. I fear that some of the authors' language will have the unintended effect of distancing many readers from the information needed to make an informed appraisal of the SSS.

STANDARDIZATION SAMPLE. Norms are based on 7,036 students from grades 3 through 12 in 16 Connecticut and Rhode Island school districts. In two appendices, the authors report means, standard deviations, and ranges for interpreting scores for each of four grade-level clusters: grades 3–5, 6–8, 9, and 10–12. Within each grade level, descriptive statistics are broken down by sex.

The impressive number of students notwithstanding, these norms should be used cautiously. Schools were drawn from rural, suburban, and urban communities, but nothing is said about demographic considerations such as ethnicity and socioeconomic status, both of which would seem relevant to the problem of school-related stress. Consequently, the degree to which these norms are appropriate for any one school district remains an open question.

The authors, furthermore, do not report the number of students who were sampled in each grade. Can we assume the sixth-, seventh-, and eighth-grade students are evenly distributed within the 6–8-grade-level cluster? This ambiguity has implications for how confidently the SSS norms can be employed for a particular grade. (Curiously, the authors do not explain why they included third-grade students in the norming group for a survey designed for grades 4 through 12.)

Finally, we are told that SSS norms can be used "to provide feedback on an individual *or group* [italics added] basis" (p. 7). In fact, because the norms are based on individuals, they cannot be used to form judgments about *groups* of individuals (e.g., students in a particular grade or building). Consequently, the authors' three categories for interpreting scores (low, medium, high), derived from individual-level distributions of scores, are inappropriate for interpreting group data.

RELIABILITY. Internal-consistency coefficients for the seven scales are moderate, ranging from .68 to .80 when based on the entire sample of 7,036 students; similar coefficients are reported within each of the four grade-level clusters. Importantly, a standard error of measurement (*SEM*) is reported for each coefficient. The *SEM*s, expressed on the SSS 5-point scale, range from roughly one-third to over one-half of a point (.31 to .58), depending on the scale and grade-level cluster. Combined, these data raise questions about the suitability of the SSS for forming judgments and making decisions about students, particularly at the individual level.

Test-retest reliability was determined over a 3-week period for a sample of seventh- to ninth-grade students ($n = 621$), resulting in coefficients ranging from .61 to .71. The lower value of these coefficients is not surprising insofar as affective characteristics are less stable than cognitive aptitudes or academic achievement. Users nonetheless should realize the implication: Students' perceptions of school-related stress today, as measured by the SSS, might well differ from their perceptions in a few weeks.

We do not know how these 621 students were selected for the test-retest reliability analyses, or why a group of students was designated that cuts across two of the four grade-level clusters. More troubling, however, the authors do not explain why test-retest reliabilities are not reported for students in the remaining grade-level clusters. Can we assume, for example, that comparable coefficients would obtain for the youngest cluster? My sense is that the stress perceptions among students in grades 3 through 5 would be less stable than for older students. In any case, the stability of the SSS remains unestablished for a large segment of the target population.

VALIDITY. The authors invested considerable time and effort in the validation of the SSS.

Content validity. The content-validity question is raised by the authors this way: "To what extent do the items of [the SSS] adequately sample from the intended content domain?" (p. 14). The reader is then referred back to an earlier section on item development, which touches on the authors' procedure for constructing an initial set of 56 items by consulting the literature and talking with groups of students, parents, educators, and specialists. In my view, this discussion falls short of establishing the universe from which these 56 items were drawn. Consequently, it is difficult to determine how well (*a*) each scale samples the domain of items represented by that scale or (*b*) how well the seven SSS scales represent all sources and manifestations of stress.

Construct validity. According to Messick (1989), "construct validity is evaluated by investigating what qualities a test measures, that is, by determining the degree to which certain explanatory concepts or constructs account for performance on the test" (p. 16). The authors approached this task in three ways.

Factor analysis. The initial 56 items were factor analyzed on a sample of 907 students from grades 5, 7, and 9. After some revisions, the instrument was administered to a new sample of 1,111 students (also from grades 5, 7, and 9) and again factor analyzed. From this second set of analyses, 7 of the 14 obtained factors "replicated the original constructs" (pp. 11–12) that earlier had emerged from the literature and the authors' discussions with various groups. It is these seven factors, and their 34 items, that constitute the SSS.

These factors, with the corresponding items and loadings, are clearly presented in the manual. Importantly, factor loadings show a relatively clean separation of the seven factors. And the manner in which the items cluster within each factor makes conceptual sense, as well. For example, each of the three items in the Academic Stress factor pertains to achievement situations in school. Together, these data support the authors' claim that the SSS gets at relatively distinct aspects of students' stress perceptions.

Surprisingly, no factor analyses were conducted on the six remaining grades for which the SSS is intended. Although I have no a priori reason to question the validity of this instrument for these six grades, their absence precludes an adequate appraisal of the construct validity of the SSS. And why did the authors not base their factor analyses on the standardization sample of 7,036 students, rather than the restricted sample of 1,111? After all, the standardization sample provides the basis for the norms and internal-consistency reliability estimates. It would seem that the authors passed up an important opportunity for cross-validation, based on a larger sample, and with all grades represented.

Correlations with the State-Trait Anxiety Inventory for Children. Any instrument, of course, should correlate with existing measures of similar constructs. Consequently, the authors correlated each of the seven SSS scales with the A-Trait scale of the State-Trait Anxiety Inventory for Children (STAIC; Spielberger, Edwards, Lushene, Montuori, & Platzek, 1973), based on the restricted sample of 1,111 students from grades 5, 7, and 9. The obtained correlations range considerably: rs = .10 to .71, with a median r of .33. In general, these correlations provide weak to moderate support for the construct validity of the SSS.

It also would be informative to know whether the SSS scales *fail* to correlate with measures of constructs *dis*similar to school-related student stress. That is, does the SSS demonstrate "discriminant" validity? Correlations with the STAIC, which speak to the "convergent" validity of the SSS, unfortunately provide only half of the story.

Path analysis. To examine further the construct validity of the SSS, the authors tested a series of causal models using the statistical procedure, "path analysis." In three separate models, the four sources of stress (and several other variables) were used to predict each of the three manifestations of stress.

I had considerable difficulty with these analyses. First, the authors do not clearly demonstrate the relevance of path analysis to the question of construct validity. Consequently, the import of these results remains unclear. Second, the logic of the general model rests on tacit—and highly questionable—assumptions regarding causality. For example, academic stress is presented as a *cause* of academic self-concept and academic achievement. In my view, the opposite assertion is equally plausible.

Third, no guidance is offered for interpreting these partial regression coefficients. Nor are we told that R^2—a fundamental summary statistic in path analysis—ranges from .17 to .39 across the three analyses. These modest values, which I derived from available information, would seem to carry important implications for the tenability of the model and, more specifically, the authors' premise that sources of stress have a causal influence on manifestations of stress.

Finally, some of the authors' interpretations are questionable: (*a*) conclusions appear to be made about interactions among variables when, in fact, the statistical analysis did not allow for interactive effects; and (*b*) statements about relations among variables are based on exceedingly low effects.

CONCLUSIONS. The SSS is an easily administered and scored instrument for assessing students' perceptions of sources and manifestations of school-related stress. However, questions remain about the adequacy both of the norms and of the information pertaining to reliability and validity. Consequently, the SSS presently would appear to be more appropriate for researchers than for practitioners, insofar as the former group would be less inclined to use the SSS as a basis for forming judgments or making decisions about students.

REVIEWER'S REFERENCE

Spielberger, C. D., Edwards, C. D., Lushene, R. E., Montuori, J., & Platzek, D. (1973). *Preliminary manual for the State-Trait Anxiety Inventory for Children*. Palo Alto, CA: Consulting Psychologists Press.

Messick, S. (1989). Validity. In R. L. Linn (Ed.), *Educational measurement* (3rd ed.; pp. 13-103). New York: Macmillan Publishing Co.

Review of the School Situation Survey by LeADELLE PHELPS, Associate Professor and Director, School Psychology Program, Department of Counseling and Educational Psychology, State University of New York at Buffalo, Buffalo, NY:

The School Situation Survey (SSS) is an instrument designed "to assess students' perceptions of school-related sources and manifestations of stress" (manual, title page). Appropriate for grades 4–12, the survey consists of 34 Likert-type rating items (1 = *never*, 5 = *always*) that students can complete in approximately 10 to 15 minutes. As a screening instrument, the SSS may be useful in identifying youngsters who could benefit from supplemental counseling or mental health services.

The SSS is organized into seven areas: (*a*) Teacher Interactions consisting of six items assessing perceived teacher attitudes towards the student, (*b*) Academic Stress with three items addressing anxiety regarding academic performance, (*c*) Peer Interactions containing six items related to perceived peer attitudes toward the student, (*d*) Academic Self-Concept consisting of four items dealing with academic standing, (*e*) Emotional containing six items assessing stress-related feelings of emotional discomfort, (*f*) Behavioral with six items measuring stress-outcome behaviors, and (*g*) Physiological containing three items indicating physical symptomatology of stress. The first four scales are viewed by the authors as assessing Sources of Stress; the remaining three scales reflect Manifestations of Stress. The seven areas were derived using principal components factor analyses (items for Sources of Stress and Manifestations of Stress were analyzed separately) followed by oblique rotations.

Item selection and the decision to divide the scale into two parts (i.e., Sources of Stress and Manifestations of Stress) was based on a review of the literature and content validity evidence. A pilot form of the scale, containing 56 items was administered to 907 fifth-, seventh-, and ninth-graders. Separate principal components factor analyses followed by oblique rotations were completed for the two areas. Based on the proposed framework and the statistical findings, the authors revised and deleted/added items. The revised form (also 56 items) was administered to a new sample of 1,111 students. The data were again submitted to principal components factor analyses followed by oblique rotations and examined for factors that best replicated the original constructs. Items/factors that did not contribute to a meaningful interpretation were eliminated, resulting in the current 34-item seven-area instrument. The final factor structure of the SSS appears strong with intercorrelations among the seven areas ranging from .01 to .56 (M = .23), indicating that the scales are sufficiently independent.

The reliability of the instrument is moderate with the authors reporting alpha coefficients (derived from item-level factor analyses) for the seven areas ranging from .68 to .80. Test-retest data (3-week interval) are acceptable with correlations ranging from .61 to .71. Given that the SSS measures affect, which is quite variable or "personal state dependent" (manual, p. 12), these correlations would be considered supportive of the stability of the instrument.

In addition to the factor analytic procedures used in the development of the instrument, path analyses were completed to provide the user with interpretative information. In addition to the seven SSS scores, five other variables (i.e., gender, grade level, grade-level structure, cognitive ability, and perceived family stress) were included in the path model. The path analyses indicated that (*a*) "males experienced greater behavioral responses to stress, while females experienced more emotional and physiological responses to stress" (p. 17), and (*b*) "the strongest causes of emotional manifestation were academic stress and peer interactions, while the strongest cause of behavioral manifestations was teacher interactions" (p. 19).

Concurrent validity was assessed by correlating the seven SSS scores with the A-Trait scale of the State-Trait Anxiety Inventory for Children (Spielberger, Edwards, Lushene, Montuori, & Platzek, 1973). The correlations illustrate the only weakness with the SSS (as well as similar instruments assessing stress). Is the SSS measuring anxiety, depression, or stress? Discriminant validity is imperative in scales assessing affective issues. Although the SSS is a stress scale that converges in the expected direction, the scale could (and most likely would) also display substantial correlations with other related, yet supposedly distinct, affective constructs such as anxiety and depression. Thus, convergent and discriminant data are needed to support the construct validity of scales such as the SSS.

In summary, the SSS is a solidly constructed instrument that should be strengthened by continued research efforts. It would be particularly useful as a screening device in school systems.

REVIEWER'S REFERENCE

Spielberger, C. D., Edwards, C. D., Lushene, R. E., Montuori, J., & Platzek, D. (1973). *Preliminary manual for the State-Trait Anxiety Inventory for Children*. Palo Alto, CA: Consulting Psychologists Press.

[348]

School Social Skills Rating Scale.

Purpose:: Developed to assess social skills exhibited in a school setting.
Population: Elementary school and junior high school and high school.
Publication Date: 1984.
Acronym: S^3 Rating Scale.
Scores: Ratings in 4 categories: Adult Relations, Peer Relations, School Rules, Classroom Behaviors.
Administration: Individual.
Price Data, 1992: $40 per complete kit including manual (25 pages); $22 per 50 rating scales.
Time: (10) minutes.
Comments: Ratings by teachers.
Authors: Laura J. Brown, Donald D. Black, and John C. Downs.
Publisher: Slosson Educational Publications, Inc.
Cross References: See T4:2370 (1 reference).

Review of the School Social Skills Rating Scale by BETH D. BADER, Assessment Specialist, Educational Issues Department, American Federation of Teachers, Washington, DC:

This assessment takes on heightened significance in this time of increasing school violence and antisocial behavior. Antisocial classroom behavior is being seen correctly as a formidable deterrent to effective instruction. It is therefore important for teachers, paraprofessionals, and other support professionals to have vehicles for modeling and shaping new behaviors that allow students to receive maximum benefit from their teachers' efforts and prevent them from disrupting the education of others.

This assessment, the School Social Skills Rating Scale, or S^3, adopts a positive orientation, thereby attempting to spotlight and model positive behaviors rather than spotlighting or punishing negative behaviors. The positive models approach has a sounder educational and psychological basis than the negative examples. However, the authors of this 10-year-old assessment should consider some revisions and additions to their instrument.

In line with the *Standards for Educational and Psychological Testing* (AERA, APA, & NCME, 1985), the assessment manual contains a careful explanation of statistical reliability and attempts to support its claims of validity. Also following the *Standards*, the administration of the assessment and the behaviors it is assessing are explained. In addition, the manual authors describe the development of the test and its rationale, and assist the administrator in interpreting the behaviors that are described in each item.

There are a number of weaknesses in this assessment, however. There is no explanation of how or why the particular behaviors assessed were chosen. The authors do not explain what psychological or educational principles were used to select these particular behaviors. Also, by assuming a positive stance, the assessment does not account for certain problem behaviors that have no clear positive opposites, such as carrying weapons or fighting. The assessment would also be stronger if it aggregated individual behaviors into more general descriptive categories such as "peer interactions," "motivation," "self-discipline," "confidence," "good citizenship," etc., that could then become more diagnostic. In addition, the examination does not differentiate between behaviors that are problems for others—such as not requesting permission to use others' materials or disagreeing in an argumentative or combative way—and behaviors that are indicators of shyness or introversion—such as not greeting adults. The second type of behavior should not be considered negative, and may not be appropriate for spotlighting and intervention.

Finally, the entire assessment falls short in its attempt to diagnose. It does not set a standard for acceptable overall behavior. There are no norms. There is no aggregate scoring or indication of levels of "proficiency." At what level of behavior, for example, might the teacher want to cease addressing individual behaviors and plan more extensive interventions or consult a counselor? When should substandard behaviors of more than one child be seen as possibly an indication that classwide behavioral interventions are in order? What should be the next steps in working with individual children who have been assessed as needing significant behavior modifications? Is a particular aggregate score acceptable at grade 1 but indicative of serious deficits at grade 5? The authors also ought to mention suggested programs that are effective in addressing problem behaviors and modeling positive alternatives, even though they decline to offer specific remedies.

REVIEWER'S REFERENCE

American Educational Research Association, American Psychological Association, & National Council on Measurement in Education. (1985). *Standards for educational and psychological testing*. Washington, DC: American Psychological Association, Inc.

Review of the School Social Skills Rating Scale by WILLIAM K. WILKINSON, Assistant Professor of Counseling and Educational Psychology, New Mexico State University, Las Cruces, NM:

The School Social Skills (S^3) Rating Scale, which includes a brief manual and rating scale, allows classroom teachers to evaluate students on 40 prosocial behaviors (e.g., gives compliments, apologizes). Teachers rate each behavior according to a 6-point "frequency" continuum as follows: 1 = *No Opportunity to Observe*, 2 = *Never Uses Skill*, 3 = *Rarely Uses Skill*, 4 = *Occasionally Uses Skill and/or Uses it at Incorrect Times*, 5 = *Often Uses Skill Under Appropriate Conditions*, 6 = *Always Uses Skill Under Appropriate Conditions*. Although the 40 items are grouped in four scales—Adult Relations, Peer Relations, School

Rules, and Classroom Behaviors—separate scores for these scales are unavailable. No overall score is obtained either. Rather, the instrument is purportedly a criterion-referenced measure, and therefore, the S^3 authors do not provide norm-referenced scores.

The test developers have appropriately delimited the use of the S^3 to function as a guide for teachers to determine students' prosocial skills, and when deficient, to suggest what specific prosocial components (each item is task analyzed) can be remediated. In this context, the S^3 serves as a curriculum guide and educational tool for teachers regarding the prosocial construct. It is important to note (and the authors do) the manual does not include a section on what instructional processes can be implemented to target social skills deficits (e.g., role playing).

A key question is whether the S^3 is valid for determining in which of 40 prosocial skills a student (or group of students) is competent or deficient? The authors suggest that if a teacher rates a student competent or deficient then the results are valid. There is no statistical proof of validity anywhere to be found in the manual. Apparently, the authors believe that because their test construction approach is descriptive and criterion based, the need for evidence of criterion and construct validity is negated. Fortunately, just because a test is criterion referenced does not mean it escapes commonly accepted psychometric standards (Kaplan & Saccuzzo, 1993).

Certainly, validity evidence could be obtained. For example, concurrent validity data could be gathered for each item (or the four category areas), using the S^3 to predict prosocial behavior using frequency data gathered during structured behavior observation. Further, because the authors developed S^3 items from a pool of items on other rating scales (not specifically measuring prosocial behavior), one would expect some convergence between numerical ratings on different scales for each item. As an example, the test developers note that Item 1, "Following Instructions," was generated from items on other scales which were given as "uncooperative," "doesn't follow directions," "does not obey teacher directives," etc. Appropriate correlational hypotheses would seem simple to develop.

In fact, the only psychometric data presented for the S^3 were in the reliability section. Unfortunately, these data were either minimally described or inherently confusing. For example, test-retest estimates are given for four samples for each of the four categories and the total score (even though these units are not scored). The number provided is the percentage agreement, using the agreement/agreement + disagreement formula, by item and between ratings over a 10- to 21-day period. One must infer that different raters (apparently $n = 23$) rated different children for each item, then these individual item agreements were averaged to yield a mean agreement within categories (e.g., Adult Relations). If so, the meaning of these data is questionable because it is unclear whether this is really test-retest reliability or a combination of intrascorer (same rater and student across time) and interscorer reliability (across raters, children, and time). In fact, the interscorer element is completely uninterpretable because three elements are simultaneously varying.

Even with validity issues aside, I doubt the 6-point rating sale is necessary. Consider the actual end result of the S^3. On the test rating form, item values of 2, 3, and 4 are shaded, and the rater is requested to write the item numbers given these values in another box. Although never explicitly stated, the criterion for each item is then 2–4 to indicate a problem, and 5 and 6 to indicate no problem (recall a rating of 1 means the prosocial behavior was never observed). Let us say a rater completes the form and 10 items are listed as problematic. Because this is all the information the S^3 provides, I suggest the rater simply list which of the 40 prosocial behaviors are deficient, without specifically quantifying degree of skill. Indeed, until the actual numerical values given each item are statistically validated, it is not advisable to do anything but read the target behaviors and subjectively determine which prosocial skill is deficient.

Given the aforementioned comments, the S^3 should not be viewed as a measuring device per se, but rather, as a teacher's guide to prosocial behavior. It may have value to teachers in this context, and apparently does, because the authors provide information that in a sample of 73 middle and high school teaches, 70% of the participants were "completely satisfied" with the S^3 rating scale. Certainly, raters will be impressed by the detailed operational definitions given in the manual (an extremely positive feature for a rating scale). It is this behavior precision that will likely help teachers plan efficacious intervention strategies.

REVIEWER'S REFERENCE

Kaplan, R. M., & Saccuzzo, D. P. (1993). *Psychological testing: Principles, applications, and issues.* Pacific Grove, CA: Brooks Cole.

[349]

Screening Assessment for Gifted Elementary Students—Primary.

Purpose: Assesses a child's aptitude and achievement level in order to identify academically gifted students.
Population: Ages 5-0 to 8-11.
Publication Date: 1992.
Acronym: SAGES-P.
Scores, 3: General Information, Reasoning, Total.
Administration: Group.
Price Data, 1992: $74 per complete kit including examiner's manual (40 pages), 25 student response booklets, and 25 profile and summary sheets; $28 per examiner's manual; $39 per 25 student response booklets; $10 per 25 profile and summary sheets.
Time: (30–45) minutes.
Authors: Susan K. Johnsen and Anne L. Corn.

Publisher: PRO-ED, Inc.

Review of the Screening Assessment for Gifted Elementary Students—Primary by LEWIS R. AIKEN, Professor of Psychology, Pepperdine University, Malibu, CA:

This paper-and-pencil instrument, which was designed to identify mental giftedness in children aged 5–8 years, is a downward extension of the original Screening Assessment for Gifted Elementary Students constructed by S. K. Johnsen and A. L. Corn in 1987. The Screening Assessment for Gifted Elementary Students—Primary (SAGES-P) consists of two subtests: Subtest 1: General Information and Subtest 2: Reasoning (Analogies). These two subtests were designed as measures of the achievement and aptitude areas, but not the divergent production area, of mental giftedness. The two subtests, contained in a single Student Booklet, consist of 33 (Subtest 1) and 29 (Subtest 2) five-option items. Two example items are provided for Subtest 1 and four example items for Subtest 2. Each item is identified by number and by a special picture symbol located next to it. The pictorial, numerical, or alphabetic letter options for each item are placed in large boxes below the question.

As stated in the Examiner's Manual, SAGES-P may be administered either individually or to groups as large as 25 children. The tests is untimed, but requires 30–45 minutes to administer to small groups of primary-school children. Kindergarten children may require two separate testing sessions of 20 minutes each. The subtests should be administered in the order in which they were standardized—first Subtest 1 and then Subtest 2.

Detailed instructions for administration are given in the manual. The teacher or test administrator reads the instructions for each item aloud, making certain the examinees are on the correct item. When testing a group of children, all items in both subtests are administered. When testing one child at a time, testing time may be shortened by determining basal and ceiling ages. In that case, testing on Subtest 1 begins with Item 1 for 5-year-olds, Item 5 for 6-year-olds, Item 10 for 7-year-olds, and Item 14 for 8-year-olds. Testing on Subtest 2 begins at Item 14 for 5-year-olds, Item 3 for 6-year-olds, Item 7 for 7-year-olds, and Item 9 for 8-year-olds. On either subtest, a basal age is established as five items in a row correct, and a ceiling age as four out of five items incorrect.

Scores and other pertinent information about the child and the examiner are recorded on a Profile and Response Form. Separate norms tables for converting raw scores (number correct) to percentile ranks and standard scores are given for "Normal" and "Gifted" groups. These norms are in half-year intervals from age 5 years through 8 years, 11 months. The standard scores have a mean of 10 and a standard deviation of 3. The sum of the standard scores on the two subtests may be converted to percentile rank and quotient scores. Finally, two profiles of the results from testing a child may be constructed—one based on the norms for "Normal" children and another based on "Gifted" children.

Guidelines for interpreting the standard scores and quotients are given on pages 23–24 of the manual. On the basis of these converted scores, a child's performance may be assigned to one of seven categories, ranging from *Very Poor* to *Very Superior*. Other suggestions for diagnostic uses of the SAGES-P, such as interpreting differences between scores on the two subtests and "testing the limits" by probing for answers to items, are also provided.

Information on item development, standardization, reliability, and validity is contained in chapter 4 of the manual. Item construction and selection were clearly based on a sound knowledge of the theoretical and research literature on assessment of the gifted. The SAGES-P was standardized between September, 1990 and June, 1991 on 2,581 normal children and 1,034 gifted children in 19 states. The demographic characteristics of the two samples are specified on pages 30–31 of the manual.

As expected, the median difficulty indexes of the items increase with age level for both normal and gifted groups. Differences between the normal and gifted groups are greater on the Reasoning subtest than on the General Information subtest. For both normal and gifted groups, the median discriminating indexes of the items range from the lower .40s to the mid .60s.

Internal consistency reliability coefficients were computed on 60 randomly selected protocols in the normal group and 60 in the gifted group. These coefficients, for the Reasoning, General Information, and Total test scores in both the gifted and normal groups, are quite respectable. The Cronbach alphas are mostly in the low to middle .90s and none lower than .87.

In a validation study described in the manual, correlations of SAGES-P scores with Wechsler Intelligence Scale for Children—Revised (WISC-R) and Stanford-Binet IQs in samples of 2nd and 3rd grade students ranged from .65 to .74. Other concurrent validity data are found in the significant positive correlations between SAGES-P scores and scores on the Survey of Basic Skills, the Educational Ability Series, the Peabody Individual Achievement Test—Revised, and the Otis-Lennon School Ability Test. Some evidence for the construct validity of SAGES-P is found in the significant positive correlations of the scores with chronological age. It is noteworthy that these correlations are higher for the General Information subtest—a measure of achievement, than for the Reasoning subtest—a measure of aptitude. Perhaps more supportive of the validity of SAGES-P as a measure of mental giftedness is the table of mean raw scores for the four age levels of the normal and gifted groups on the two subtests. Unfortunately, because the standard deviations of the raw scores are not provided in the manual, tests of significance between the "gifted" and "normal" means cannot be conducted to determine which means are significantly different from each other.

The overall impression of this reviewer is that SAGES-P is potentially useful as a measure of general knowledge and mental ability. To determine whether it is more effective than other psychometric measures for identifying giftedness in primary school children remains to be seen. What is needed to establish its superiority in that respect is a study in which the success of the SAGES-P in differentiating between normal and gifted children is compared with that of other measures of mental ability. More sophisticated statistical methods, including factor analysis an discriminant analysis, might also be helpful in establishing such a claim.

Be that as it may, SAGES-P does boast a theoretical foundation, good standardization, respectable reliability coefficients, and some evidence for validity. The test should also be easy for nonpsychologists to administer, and, by following the suggestions in the Examiner's Manual, useful in diagnosis and placement.

Review of the Screening Assessment for Gifted Elementary Students—Primary by SUSANA URBINA, Associate Professor of Psychology, University of North Florida, Jacksonville, FL:

The Screening Assessment for Gifted Elementary Students—Primary (SAGES-P) is a downward extension of the Screening Assessment for Elementary Students (SAGES), published in 1987. Like its predecessor, SAGES-P aims at assisting in the identification of gifted children. Whereas SAGES was designed for use with children from 7 to 12 years old, SAGES-P is for children aged 5 to 8.

The authors of SAGES-P determined they would assess two areas which they equate, respectively, with achievement and aptitude. The areas they selected make up the two subtests of SAGES-P, namely, General Information and Reasoning.

The General Information subtest consists of 33 multiple-choice questions that are printed on the test booklet *and* read aloud by the examiner. Test takers must reply by selecting the picture, number, word, or letter that represents the best answer out of five choices. About a third of the items deal with numerical or quantitative content; the rest cover an assortment of areas (e.g., facts about animals, properties of objects).

The Reasoning subtest is made up of 28 analogies presented in a pictorial or figural multiple-choice format with five options. In this subtest, examinees are guided only through four sample items and the first test item and are then left to finish the remainder on their own. Considering the abstract nature of the Reasoning subtest and the age of test takers, this does not seem to be a wise course of action.

The directions for administering SAGES-P appear easy to follow when the test is given individually. When used with as many as 25 children, as the manual allows, administration could become problematic. No attempt has been made to establish comparability of individual and group administrations, though due to the use of basal and ceiling levels only in the former, the length of the test can differ significantly depending on administration mode.

Test items are printed in black on a white background. The booklets are plain and unlikely to hold the interest of typical or gifted children of the ages in question for very long.

SCORING. The SAGES-P is scored by a simple count of correct responses; in individual administration, items below the basal are also counted. Once raw subtest scores have been tallied, they can be transformed into percentile ranks and standard scores with a mean of 10 and a standard deviation of 3. An excellent feature of SAGES-P is that it provides normative tables for gifted and normal children at every half-year interval from 5-0 to 8-11. The normal sample consisted of 2,581 children enrolled in regular classrooms with demographic characteristics comparable to those of the school-age population of the United States. The gifted sample consisted of 1,034 children enrolled in gifted classes whose demographic characteristics also resembled those of the school-age population, except for the considerably higher level of education of parents. Both samples were tested from September of 1990 to June of 1991 and were drawn from the same 19 states.

Standard scores on the two subtests are added and the sum is converted to a composite standard score (M = 100, SD = 15), which in a throwback to obsolete terminology is labeled as a "quotient." The misnaming of the composite score is one of several instances in which the SAGES-P manual is technically inaccurate. For example, the authors state that "standard scores are derived from the properties of the normal probability curve" and refer readers to a table showing the percentages that would fall in various score ranges *if* scores were normally distributed. However, the conversion tables show clearly that for some groups (i.e., the younger normal and older gifted children) score distributions were considerably skewed; this not only renders normal curve percentages inapplicable but also suggests inadequate item difficulty levels for those groups. Test users are also urged in the manual to compare SAGES-P scores to those of other tests, such as the Otis-Lennon School Ability Test (OLSAT; 11:274), by transforming their scores linearly into the same mean and *SD* units used in SAGES-P. This suggestion ignores differences in the content and norms of the tests and falsely implies that comparability is a function of uniformity of score formats.

RELIABILITY. Internal consistency was assessed by the coefficient alpha which was computed on a sample of 120 protocols randomly drawn from the normal and gifted standardization groups. Average alpha coefficients for the subtests, across intellectual classifications and ages, range from .87 to .96. The standard error of measurement is described as an additional "type" of reliability available on the SAGES-P, although it is just another way of expressing data from the alpha coefficients. No evidence of the stability of scores over time is cited. This would be desirable especially in light of the SAGES-P target age.

VALIDITY. In order for a test to show content-related validity, its items must be representative of "some defined universe or domain of content" (AERA, APA, & NCME, 1985, p. 10). "Giftedness" is, by definition, independent of domain and can be demonstrated in a great variety of intellectual, academic, creative, artistic, psychomotor, and interpersonal endeavors. Thus, the notion of content validity is clearly inappropriate when considering a test meant to assist in identifying giftedness. Nevertheless, Johnsen and Corn claim content validity for SAGES-P because "the test's contents are found in the majority of different schools' identification procedures" (p. 32) and because it "conforms to currently used tests" (p. 32) for identifying the gifted.

Data on criterion-related validity consist of correlations between SAGES-P and the Wechsler Intelligence Scale for Children—Revised and Stanford-Binet (unspecified edition), which are both identified as "aptitude" tests. The correlations listed are in the low .70s for the General Information subtest and Total score and in the .60s for the Reasoning subtest. Correlations are also given for all SAGES-P scores and scores on the SRA Survey of Basic Skills, the Education Ability Series, the Peabody Individual Achievement Test—Revised, and the OLSAT. These coefficients range from not significant to .77 and are based on samples apparently gathered on the basis of convenience. All coefficients were corrected for attenuation and for restriction of range; contrary to recommended practice, uncorrected figures are not listed.

For evidence of construct validity, Johnsen and Corn reiterate the findings on concurrent validity, cite correlations between SAGES-P scores and age, and point out that scores of gifted children were substantially higher than those of nongifted children at all ages. Although all these data are compatible with the hypothesis that SAGES-P measures some aspects of intelligence, they do not demonstrate that SAGES-P can help to discriminate gifted from nongifted youngsters. In addition, the data are fairly weak (e.g., correlations between Reasoning subtest scores and age are .39 and .46 for the normal and gifted samples, respectively). Moreover, although the means for both subtests are indeed higher for gifted than for normal students, no indication of the significance of those differences or of the overlap in the scores is given. Finally, although emphasis is placed on the distinctions between the SAGES-P subtests, data on their intercorrelations are missing.

OVERVIEW. The SAGES-P cannot be recommended for its intended purpose. Not only is it narrower in focus than the intelligence scales traditionally used to decide who is gifted, but its difficulty range is also insufficient, especially for 8-year-olds. The Wechsler scales (9:1351, 11:466), the Stanford Binet Intelligence Scale, Fourth Edition (10:342), and even the Slosson Intelligence Test—Revised (358) all provide wider difficulty ranges and greater breadth of coverage than SAGES-P. In addition, the use of an instrument like SAGES-P as a *group test* to make decisions about young children seems indefensible. In fact, the potential for measurement error inherent in using it as a group test should be a deterrent to its being used that way even for research. As an individual test, however, SAGES-P could be of value in a battery for identifying giftedness or as a tool in investigating the nonverbal abilities of young children.

REVIEWER'S REFERENCE

American Educational Research Association, American Psychological Association, & National Council on Measurement in Education. (1985). *Standards for educational and psychological testing*. Washington, DC: American Psychological Association, Inc.

[350]

Screening Instrument for Targeting Educational Risk.

Purpose: Developed to provide a "method by which children with hearing problems (either known or suspected) can be educationally screened."

Population: Students with suspected or known hearing loss.

Publication Date: 1989.

Acronym: S.I.F.T.E.R.

Scores, 5: Academics, Attention, Communication, Class Participation, School Behavior.

Administration: Individual.

Price Data, 1994: $24 per complete kit including 100 screening forms and manual (7 pages); $17 per 100 screening forms; $9 per manual.

Time: Administration time not reported.

Comments: Ratings by teachers.

Author: Karen L. Anderson.

Publisher: PRO-ED, Inc.

Review of the Screening Instrument for Targeting Educational Risk by STEPHEN J. BONEY, Assistant Professor of Communication Disorders, Department of Special Education and Communication Disorders, University of Nebraska-Lincoln, Lincoln, NE:

The Screening Instrument for Targeting Educational Risk (S.I.F.T.E.R.) is a 15-item checklist-format instrument for screening the classroom performance of children who are hearing impaired and mainstreamed in regular education classrooms. The author also suggests the S.I.F.T.E.R. is appropriate for screening the educational performance of children identified through hearing screening programs. Based on national field testing, the S.I.F.T.E.R. is most appropriate for use with elementary-age children with hearing losses up through the moderate degree range. The instrument samples information from five broad areas: Academics, Attention, Communication, Class Participation, and School Behavior. Three questions are proffered in each area. The child's classroom teacher is to rate the student in each area using a 1 to 5 Likert scale. Adjective descriptors (e.g., upper, middle, lower, never, occasionally, frequently) are used as metrics for the middle and endpoint values (e.g., 1, 3, and 5). Teachers mark their ratings on an accompanying standard form. Responses are summed from each content area and entered on a shaded profile grid. Shading on the grid delineates three areas: pass, marginal, and fail. From the grid, a profile is constructed for each child and used to make decisions as to whether further assessment or programming are needed. Sample profiles with suggested follow-up are included in the manual.

Standardization of the S.I.F.T.E.R. was based on data from 530 students with varying degrees of hearing loss and 50 control students. Demographics are given for the students with hearing loss; however, similar information is not available regarding the control subjects. Students in the standardization sample were predominantly Caucasian (92%). Therefore, this instrument may not be appropriate for other racial or ethnic groups. Further, there is no indication of the socioeconomic levels of the students. Validation information presented in the manual is limited. The information presented is primarily descriptive and lacking statistical analysis. The author does, however, indicate that more detailed information regarding the validation process is available upon request.

Interrater reliability was assessed by having two teachers rate the performance of the same 10 students. Reliability coefficients were calculated for each content area and ranged from a low of .33 for class participation to a high of .62 for communication. These values are low and may reflect the use of only a small sample of teachers and students. This area warrants further attention. Reliability may be improved by providing the rater with general guidelines as to criteria that should be used for each of the Likert ratings. Additionally, there are no data concerning intrarater reliability. It would also be useful to determine interrater reliability for students by grade.

To date, the S.I.F.T.E.R. remains virtually the only standardized instrument to screen the classroom performance of mainstreamed hearing-impaired children. The brevity of the instrument along with the cadre of content areas makes it appealing for use in educational settings. Responses to questions are based on the teacher's knowledge and observations of the student. It is not necessary for teachers to supply specific performance information in the various content areas. Simply filing out the instrument may raise the teacher's awareness of potential educational problems the student may be experiencing. Scoring is simple. Professional school personnel other than the classroom teacher (e.g., speech-language, pathologist, audiologist, or teacher of the hearing impaired) are intended to score the instrument. This frees the teacher from an extra time commitment. Interpretation of results is fairly straightforward. The response grid allows the scorer to note quickly areas of difficulty. Examples of various students' S.I.F.T.E.R. profiles are presented in the manual to aid in interpretation.

In summary, the S.I.F.T.E.R. is a simple, quick, and easily scored screening instrument for determining potential classroom problems for mainstreamed hearing-impaired children or those children identified with hearing losses through hearing screening programs. It might also be used for children who experience frequent episodes of otitis media. It should be noted, however, that normative information for this specific population has not been determined. The S.I.F.T.E.R. is most appropriate for use with Caucasian students in grades kindergarten through 5. Results with minority students should be interpreted cautiously. Further, the S.I.F.T.E.R. should be used for those students with hearing losses through the moderate degree range who are primarily served by regular classroom teachers. There are some concerns regarding intertester reliability. In addition, limited validation information is presented in the user's manual. Even with these shortcomings, I would recommend the S.I.F.T.E.R. as part of a screening process to identify potential classroom problems for mainstreamed hearing-impaired children.

Review of the Screening Instrument for Targeting Educational Risk by STEVEN H. LONG, Assistant Professor of Speech Pathology & Audiology, Ithaca College, Ithaca, NY:

The Screening Instrument for Targeting Educational Risk (S.I.F.T.E.R.) is a questionnaire about the classroom performance of students with hearing loss. The questionnaire is completed by a student's classroom teacher. Responses are then scored and compared to cutoff values to determine whether further assessment by school personnel is warranted.

TEST MATERIALS. The S.I.F.T.E.R. questionnaire is printed on a single sheet and consists of 15 questions that call for responses on a 5-point rating scale. On the back of the questionnaire informants may write other comments. Information about test development, cutoff scores, and guidelines for interpretation of results are given in a very brief manual.

TEST ADMINISTRATION. Copies of the S.I.F.T.E.R. are distributed to the teachers of hearing-impaired students. The teachers circle the appropriate response to each question and return the form. A scoring grid allows the test user to sum responses in five categories: Academics, Attention, Communication, Class Participation, and School Behavior. By comparing a child's scores in each category to cutoff values, a rating of pass, marginal, or fail is assigned. The ratings profile is then evaluated to determine the most appropriate course of action for each child.

PSYCHOMETRIC ADEQUACY. Content validity for the 15 questions included in the S.I.F.T.E.R. questionnaire was established through logical and statistical analyses. A pilot version of the questionnaire contained 40 questions in seven categories. Based on data gathered from 82 students, the items on the S.I.F.T.E.R. were reduced to their present number. The items not included were ones found to be most discriminating of children with impairments.

The population on which the S.I.F.T.E.R. was standardized consisted of 530 children who had a known hearing loss or had failed a hearing screening. Though the instrument is intended for all children with hearing impairment, the author notes that the standardization group was biased toward Caucasian regular classroom students in kindergarten through grade 5 with faint to moderate losses.

The poorest psychometric feature of the S.I.F.T.E.R. is its interscorer reliability. It was only minimally assessed, with just two teachers each rating the same 10 students. The resulting correlations ranged from .33 to .62 for the five question categories. The author reports the direction of ratings—above or below average—was more highly correlated than the numerical ratings. This suggest that, perhaps, the S.I.F.T.E.R. would have been better designed using a 3-point rather than a 5-point rating scale. As the ratings are assigned by classroom teachers, it is possible that reliability could be improved through inservice training that offered examples of students at each of the rating points. This issue is not discussed by the author of the S.I.F.T.E.R.

SUMMARY. The S.I.F.T.E.R. is a teacher questionnaire designed to assist in the screening of children with known or suspected hearing loss. The content of individual items on the questionnaire was well evaluated. The standardization sample is fairly diverse and its few biases are clearly stated. The instrument's greatest shortcoming is its poor interscorer reliability, which completely undermines its norm-referenced use. Therefore, the only value to be gained from the S.I.F.T.E.R. would be as an adjunct to a more comprehensive evaluation of student performance.

[351]

Screening Test for Educational Prerequisite Skills.

Purpose: Developed to screen for skills needed for beginning kindergarten.
Population: Ages 4-0 to 5-11.
Publication Dates: 1976–90.
Acronym: STEPS.
Scores: 5 areas: Motor Skills, Intellectual Skills, Verbal Information Skills, Cognitive Strategies, Attitudes.
Administration: Individual.
Price Data, 1995: $135 per complete kit including test materials (pictures, bears, pencil), 25 AutoScore forms, 25 AutoScore home questionnaires, and manual ('90, 68 pages); $35 per set of test materials; $47.50 per 25 AutoScore forms; $24.50 per 25 AutoScore home questionnaires; $37.50 per manual; $89.50 per 50-use IBM microcomputer disk; $15 per 100 microcomputer answer sheets for use with disk.
Time: (8–10) minutes.
Author: Frances Smith.
Publisher: Western Psychological Services.

Review of the Screening Test for Educational Prerequisite Skills by JOHN CHRISTIAN BUSCH, Associate Professor of Education, University of North Carolina at Greensboro, Greensboro, NC:

The Screening Test for Educational Prerequisite Skills (STEPS) is a brief, individually administered screen for children about to enter kindergarten. It is used to identify children who should be monitored in kindergarten, and/or for whom curriculum modifications may be appropriate or who may be recommended for diagnostic testing. Originally developed in 1976, a national standardization study has been recently undertaken. The test consists of 14 tasks and three observations that measure five capabilities: symbol copying, ability to tell information, ability to take in and use information, smooth motor coordination, and attitude in learning situations. Errors in speech are also noted. The author associates the five STEPS capabilities with five constructs (Intellectual Skills, Verbal Information Skills, Cognitive Strategies, Motor Skills, and Attitudes, respectively) of Gagne's learning theory (1985).

Separate reports for parents and the school summarize the child's performance on individual items and for the capabilities listed above. A summary recommendation for the child is a central part of the report. Five possible recommendations include: The child is likely to adapt well to kindergarten, the child's progress should be monitored or the curriculum modified in one or both of two capability areas, or the child should be referred for diagnostic assessment. The summary recommendation is based only on performance in the Intellectual Skills and Verbal Information components of the assessment. Reports are produced from overlaying carbon sheets that are used to record and score the child's responses. The teacher and parent report forms are well organized and present information unambiguously; however, neither form provides space to record the child's age or possible handicapping condition, although the Home Questionnaire does provide space for both. The manual provides detailed directions for administration and scoring.

When a measure can be placed in a theoretical network, its meaning and significance are enhanced; therefore, the association of STEPS items with the constructs of Gagne's respected learning theory is desirable. However, certain linkages may be somewhat arguable. For example, Task 5 requires the child to copy geometric figures and is described as measuring intellectual skill. However, it would seem that such performance more likely reflects motor skill. In any case, confidence in the alignment of the test items with certain theoretical constructs would be enhanced by assigning a panel of independent, expert judges to link items to learning capabilities (constructs), rather than depending solely on the author's expertise.

Two of the items are intended to measure attitude. In Task 14, the child selects from each of six pairs of drawings, the drawing most like her. Although the author argues without empirical evidence that the items (drawings) reflect a single attitudinal continuum (participation versus avoidance), it appears that multiple dimensions (e.g., sociability, general happiness, attitude toward task completion, enjoyment of school) might comprise the scale. In Observation 3, also thought to reflect "participation-avoidance," the child is assigned a single point on a 9-point scale. This scale incorporates traits that are difficult to assess reliably, such as "responds willingly," "is somewhat anxious," "willing to work" without extensive observer training. In addition, the scale also appears to reflect multiple traits. Factor analysis indicates that these two items do not load on the same dimension.

Reasonable and carefully selected passing scores are essential to valid decisions; therefore, a description of the rationale and method for setting cut scores should always be provided. Various scoring rules for the individual tasks, the capabilities subscores, and the summary recommendations of the STEPS utilize cut scores. For example, a score of at least 3 on Task 13 and a score of 6 on Observation 3 are required to pass the item. A different summary recommendation is made when the language score is "4" than when it is "5." What is significant about that particular level of test performance for the expected kindergarten experience that leads to a particular summary recommendation? Several of the STEPS cut scores lack a stated rationale and many of those that include a rationale appear to be based primarily on the author's judgment and experience, rather than on an appeal to external evidence or to expert opinion. A minor observation is that the criterion for Task 5 as stated in the manual is not the same as that used on the scoring sheet. The lack of evidence to support particular cut scores is a major weakness.

The evidence presented in support of claims for valid and reliable measurement is based on the correlation between a dichotomous STEPS recommendation regarding risk and a dichotomous criterion measure or a dichotomous retest measure. Classifications based on the STEPS utilized both a broad and a narrow definition of risk. Because STEPS recommendations are made utilizing five categories, the use of a dichotomous STEPS classification for reliability and validity assessment is a potential weakness because it is unclear how relevant the evidence will be to actual decision making with the STEPS.

Decision consistency evidence was obtained from 80 students retested after 1 week. Reliability estimates based on items were low. The median phi value for items was .55 and, therefore, there is insufficient evidence to support the interpretation of individual items, although such scores are included in the parent and school reports. Consistency of the summary recommendations and of the capabilities are summarized in contingency tables and various summary statistics. The hit rates for the summary recommendations were 89% (broad definition of risk) and 90% (narrow definition) and the corresponding phi coefficients were .68 and .50. Although these hit rates represent acceptable levels of agreement, longer, more representative retest intervals should have been included in the design.

Evidence pertaining to content, concurrent (four studies), and predictive validity is presented in the manual. Because it is most relevant, this review will focus on the sole predictive validity study which employed the Metropolitan Readiness Test (MRT) as the basis for criterion classifications. In this study of 186 children, 25 different correlations were produced; those analyses based on the STEPS summary recommendation using a broad definition of risk have been selected for review. Each of those five correlations is statistically significant, however, the strength of the relationships is low. For example, the phi coefficient for the correlation between STEPS risk category and the MRT total score is .33. In this situation, the test correctly assigned 86% of the children to risk or no-risk categories. Although that hit rate is satisfactory, only 44% of those children actually at risk were correctly predicted (valid positives) whereas 56% were incorrectly predicted to be not at risk (false negatives). Interpretation of the percentage of valid positive decisions should recognize that the test provides a marked improvement over chance prediction because the outcome risk level was only 10%. This information offers modest support for the ability of the test to predict criterion outcomes.

In deciding to use a particular screening test, one must assess the costs of different false decisions. For this test, the cost of a false negative decision is that a child actually at risk might not receive necessary follow-up attention and testing, an undesirable consequence. A false positive decision might increase costs, with more children incorrectly being referred for follow-up. The user of a screening test might obtain higher valid positive rates through the adoption of a less stringent definition of risk on the test, but would have to tolerate a greater number of false positive decisions and an increase in testing cost.

The STEPS has a number of positive features. It responds to the need for a brief instrument of modest cost, which can be administered prior to more expensive diagnosis. There are detailed directions for administration and scoring and the standardization study reflects an attempt to satisfy various technical requirements. However, because of the weaknesses described above, the STEPS is not recommended at the current time.

REVIEWER'S REFERENCE

Gagne, R. M. (1985). *The conditions of learning* (4th ed.). New York: Holt, Rinehart & Winston.

Review of the Screening Test for Educational Prerequisite Skills by M. ELIZABETH GRAUE, Assistant Professor of Curriculum and Instruction, University of Wisconsin-Madison, Madison, WI:

The Screening Test for Educational Prerequisite Skills (STEPS) is designed to facilitate the process of identifying children with disabilities as well as to help teachers begin instructional planning. The author takes great pains to distinguish the STEPS from existing instruments, claiming that it is a test of "current potential" (manual, p. 33) or "educational prerequisite skills" (p. 49) rather than a test of readiness or achievement. Understanding the meanings and implications of these terms is critical to evaluating the instrument because it determines the criteria used to judge its validity.

Based on Gagne's theory of instruction, the test contains 14 tasks representing: Intellectual Skills, Verbal Information Skills, Cognitive Strategies Skills, Motor Skills, and Attitudes. This foundation purportedly makes for a close connection between test items and curriculum. Basing a kindergarten screening test on Gagne's theories assumes a notion of linear and hierarchical relations in learning in which certain skills are prerequisites to others: We should be able to identify the capabilities needed to succeed in kindergarten, find out whether children have them, and make instructional placements so that they are acquired. This view does not match current conceptions of learning and development held by cognitive scientists or by early childhood professionals (Bredekamp, 1986; Resnick, 1989). From its foundation, STEPS is on shaky ground and all subsequent discussion must keep that in mind.

The 8- to 10-minute individually administered test can be given by paraprofessionals and volunteers in either spring or fall. The test includes an optional Home Questionnaire for parents. Scoring is very simple, making it efficient for most large-scale screening programs. It is estimated that approximately $^3/_4$ of students will be identified as showing adequate potential for adapting to kindergarten, 19% require monitoring or close monitoring during the early part of the school year, and 4% will require further evaluation with potential referral for special services. These recommendations are based only on the items representing "intellectual" or "verbal information skills" and relegates the other areas (including the parent questionnaire) to supporting information. Basing a recommendation on such a restricted conception of child development is contrary to contemporary research on early education, valuing an extremely narrow perspective of the child and curriculum (Goal One Technical Planning Group, 1995).

An array of technical information is provided. All evidence is presented in terms of categorical recommendations rather than scores such as developmental age or percentile. The test was piloted in spring and fall with a sample of 1,527 students ranging in age from 4.0 to 5.11 years. The overall sample was chosen to approximately mirror U.S. Census data (unspecified date) for demographic characteristics that the author suggests influence educational risk. Racially, the sample was 77% White and 20% African-American. Socioeconomic status was distributed across categories with a greater proportion of children from lower SES groups represented. Gender breakdown shows 49% female and 51% male. The sample is heavily represented by children from the southern region of the U.S. The standardization sample included children in Head Start and Title One programs, but it did not include children with disabilities or Limited English Proficiency. Considering the suggestion that the screener could be used for identifying a broad range of students, these exclusions are worrisome. Performance differences were shown by SES, race, and gender and are explained by the author as representing the reality in schools, with lower income children, African-Americans, and boys being more likely to be at risk. No discussion of possible bias is presented.

Because the test reports on categorical recommendations, all reliability and validity analyses rely on categorical data. No standard error of measurement, interrater, or split-half reliability are reported. Test-retest reliability evidence was provided using a one-week lag between administrations through recommendations at time one and two. Specificity ranged from 80% to 92% and sensitivity from 88–91% depending on risk definition.

Validity analyses required the creation of a cut point for the criterion measures selected so that assessments of like recommendations could be made. One problem with this approach is that it assumes that the same recommendations would result from both instruments even if they were constructed from philosophically and technically different perspectives. Another problem is indicative of the muddiness of the STEPS conceptualization—the correlates chosen represent a bewildering array of ideas about children's development. The correlates include a test that is designed to show maturity through a simple drawing task, a teacher checklist used to communicate student behavior to mental health workers, a criterion-referenced instrument without published reliability and validity data, and a group-administered readiness test designed to help teachers plan instruction. Data are presented for concurrent and predictive validity by comparing percentages identified as at risk by the STEPS and each criterion, specificity and sensitivity (and their converses), hit rate, and simple correlation between the two measures (phi coefficient). Sensitivity and specificity for concurrent measure are as follows: Goodenough-Harris Drawing Test: 39% and 83%; School Behavior Checklist: 48% and 89%; Test of Basic Experience: 69% and 58%; Brigance K and 1 Screen: 38% and 92%. Predictive validity is evidenced through comparison to the Metropolitan Readiness Test, with sensitivity of 44% and specificity of 91%. In all cases it appears that the STEPS is a conservative screener, under-referring more frequently than it over-refers. Regardless, these values are low enough to suggest that any risk interpretation should be made with caution.

SUMMARY. The Screening Test for Educational Prerequisite Skills looks like it would be perfect for screening large numbers of children as they come to kindergarten: It is quick, easy to use and score, and is relatively inexpensive. Unfortunately, it is premised on a view of development that is rather dated, it bases recommendations on a very narrow band of child learning and experience, and its relation to existing measures is weak enough to prompt questions about its technical quality. Together, these issues bring up serious questions about STEPS validity as a screening instrument.

REVIEWER'S REFERENCES

Bredekamp, S. (Ed.). (1986). *Developmentally appropriate practice in programs serving children from birth through age 8*. Washington, DC: National Association for the Education of Young Children.

Resnick, L. B. (Ed.). (1989). *Knowing, learning, and instruction: Essays in honor of Robert Glaser*. Hillsdale, NJ: Lawrence Erlbaum.

Goal 1 Technical Planning Group. (1995). *Reconsidering children's early development and learning: Toward shared beliefs and vocabulary*. A report to the National Education Goals Panel.

Review of the Screening Test for Educational Prerequisite Skills by JEFFREY K. SMITH, Professor of Educational Psychology, Rutgers, the State University, New Brunswick, NJ:

The Screening Test for Educational Prerequisite Skills (STEPS) is an individually administered screening measure designed for use with children who are about to enter kindergarten. The purpose of the measure is to identify children who should be referred for extensive evaluation or monitored closely during early instruction due to weaknesses in the areas measured by the test. The test can be administered by nonprofessional aides or volunteers, and takes roughly 8 to 10 minutes to give and another 5 minutes to produce a report for a child. There is also an optional Home Questionnaire which parents complete.

The measure consists of 14 tasks and three observations made while administering the tasks; these are grouped into five general headings: (*a*) Smooth Motor Coordination, (*b*) Ability to Copy Symbols Used in Learning, (*c*) Ability to Tell Information, (*d*) Ability to Take In and Use Information, and (*e*) Attitudes in Learning Situations. The general headings were derived from Gagne's (1985) five capabilities necessary for learning (respectively): (*a*) Motor Skills, (*b*) Intellectual Skills, (*c*) Cognitive Strategy Skills, (*d*) Verbal Skills, and (*e*) Attitudes. Tasks include having a child balance on one foot, grasp a pencil, copy lower case letters and shapes, group objects according to color, respond to directions involving terms such as "over," "under," "behind," and "in front of," and repeat digit strings. All of the tasks seem reasonable for the intended use and pretty much in the mainstream of what one would expect in such a screening measure. The Home Questionnaire contains 23 items to which parents respond in a "yes/no" fashion. Typical items are "My child is looking forward to starting school," and "My child usually understands what I say."

The STEPS measure seems appropriate with respect to the selection of headings and the items to represent those headings. Directions for administration and scoring are straightforward and are likely to be well within the grasp of a paraprofessional. Problems with the measure arise when one examines the number of items used for each heading and the way in which the information is put together to make recommendations. Also, the reporting of information, especially to parents, is weak. Furthermore, the technical data provided for the measure are poorly presented and do not make a strong case for the use of the instrument—certainly not as strong as the author claims.

To examine these criticisms more closely, consider the problem of an insufficient number of items used to measure several of the headings. Motor Skills is measured by two items, ability to balance on one foot and the ability to hold a pencil. For balancing on one foot, the child is requested to stand on each foot for up to 15 seconds. The total number of seconds is summed for both feet. A total of 8 seconds is all that is necessary to receive a "plus" on this item. The item for fine motor skill consists of recording whether a child holds a pencil properly. No other measure is taken. Attitude toward learning is measured by a six-item set of pictures, which seems only vaguely related to learning, and by the examiner's assessment of the child's attitude toward the test setting.

Although the author emphasizes the relationship to Gagne's (1985) five areas of learning, only two of them are used for referral purposes. The other three are relegated to something called "Additional Support Capabilities." In examining the mechanism through which the basic recommendations from the instrument are made, it becomes clear that small variations in performance can lead to large differences in outcome. Three items comprise the "Ability to Copy Symbols" category (purportedly representing Gagne's Intellectual Skills category) and six items comprise the "Ability to Tell Information" category (Gagne's Verbal Information Skills). If a child is deemed deficient in both of these categories, he/she received the lowest recommendation: "Likely to benefit from referral for multidisciplinary diagnostic assessment." Deficient is operationalized as failing on all three copying tasks, or failing on three or more of six telling information tasks. There are then three intermediary levels where the reporting form recommends varying levels of monitoring of the progress of the child. The highest level of performance is characterized as: "Likely to adapt and cope with the demands of a typical kindergarten curriculum." This level can be obtained by passing one more tasks in each of the two areas. That is, a score of 0/3 in copying and 3/6 in telling information will result in a recommendation for extended assessment (the lowest recommendation). A score of 1/3 in copying and 4/6 in telling information will result in a recommendation of likely success (the highest recommendation). These score differences can consist of getting a triangle a bit neater and counting eight teddy bears as eight and not seven. The actual differences in performance seem far more subtle than the resulting recommendations.

Although in the technical section of the manual the author cautions against interpreting individual tasks, plus/minus results by task name are presented to parents with no cautionary note. The ability to grasp a pencil becomes "Smooth Motor Coordination: Fine Motor" with a plus or a minus on the reporting form. Furthermore, the ability to write one's name, copy letters, or copy shapes becomes "Ability to Copy Symbols Used in Learning" on the parent report.

The final area of concern relates to the technical information presented. A fairly substantial amount of technical information is presented, representing a sincere effort to research the efficacy of the instrument. However, the author makes some questionable assumptions about the nature of the measure which lead to the omission of useful information. For example, the author believes that because the measure is a screening measure and recommendations for children are not based on normative samples, that norms, scales and standard errors of measurement are not useful. The reliability and validity studies conducted are presented in terms of true and false positives and negatives. To some extent this is acceptable. However, it would be nice to look at some distributions of performance on scales and individual items. For example, in the introduction to the manual the author claims children enjoy taking the test. One of the observational items on the test is a 9-point scale concerning the children's attitude toward taking the test. The earlier claim could be verified simply by presenting the distribution of performance on this item, but no distributions on any items are presented. Furthermore, the claims that are made for the reliability and validity of the measure are simply not substantiated by the data presented.

The goal of the STEPS measure is admirable: to provide school districts with a short, easily administered measure that will provide information on which children need special consideration in one form or another as they enter kindergarten. The efforts of the author to develop such a measure are commendable. However, in my opinion the STEPS does not live up to the expectations presented in the manual nor to the needs of school districts in this increasingly crucial area of the educational process.

REVIEWER'S REFERENCE

Gagne, R. M. (1985). *The condition of learning* (4th ed.). New York: Holt, Rinehart & Winston.

[352]

Self-Assessment in Writing Skills.

Purpose: Developed as a self-assessment tool to assess writing skills.
Population: Clerical, managerial, and sales employees.
Publication Date: 1990.
Scores, 3: Content and Style, Organization and Format, Total.
Administration: Group or individual.
Price Data, 1990: $60 per complete kit including 20 inventories, 20 scoring sheets for part 1, and 20 scoring sheets for part 2.
Time: [90–120] minutes.
Comments: Self-administered, self-scored.
Authors: Training House, Inc.
Publisher: Training House, Inc.

Review of the Self-Assessment in Writing Skills by GABRIEL M. DELLA-PIANA, Director of Evaluation, El Paso Collaborative for Academic Excellence, University of Texas at El Paso, El Paso, TX:

The Self-Assessment in Writing Skills (SAWS) comes with no data on validity, reliability, or norms. The test materials consist of two four-page booklets and one three-page booklet. These guide the test taker through critique and rewriting of a two-page business letter presented with numbered lines (1 through 52). The letter to be critiqued and rewritten is a response to a request for assistance on a "security problem" (test form, p. 2) at a manufacturer's warehouse in which there has been an excessive amount of theft. The test taker is told the task will take 1–2 hours and there are 60 points for Part One (conducting a line-by-line critique of the content and style) and 40 points for Part Two (outlining recommended changes in organization and format, rewriting the letter, and listing your objectives—"why you are writing to Mr. Mansonhurst [citing] at least three or four things you want your letter . . . to accomplish"). Guidelines for scoring one's responses are included. None of the booklets are labeled to suggest an order of use though one can soon figure out the order. In the process, one may well have examined the scoring guides in advance of one's analysis or writing.

INSTRUCTIONS FOR PART ONE. (Recommending line-by-line changes in content or style of the letter.) The instructions direct the user to use a separate sheet of paper and "indicate by number each line of the letter on which you would make improvements in content or style." Actually, what may be inferred from the example given, is that one should improve the letter line-by-line by rewriting what needs improvement. Thus, the one example given is:

> Line 4–5. Change "theft has occurred in recent months" to "theft of recent months." (p. 1)

Thus, the instructions alone (taken as both procedural statement and example) lead one to rewrite at the sentence level any part of the text where content or style needs "improvement."

What happens after one has completed the line-by-line rewriting and turns to the scoring guide? The scoring guide (not so labeled) consists of 60 changes, each worth one point, against which one may compare their responses. Local, within sentence changes, are not problematic in general because that is what one expects from the instructions. But one finds that changes may be suggested rather than actually rewritten and that some changes are more extensive than the instructions would lead one to expect. Word-choice improvements are not surprising. The word "premature" is improved by substituting the intended "preliminary" and the phrase "providing guilt" is improved by substituting "proving guilt." Colloquialisms and unnecessarily wordy phrases are also not surprising as when, "It is the recommendation of our organization in such cases," is changed to "We recommend that." However, it comes as a shock to one who followed the "instructions" to find that one suggested improvement advises that it is better "to go from line 8 to line 14." Such a large chunk skipped is hardly suggested as appropriate by the instructions as given. The other surprise in Part One is that it is a tedious, time-consuming process, which could easily take some test takers all of the "about 1–2 hours" estimated time for the total test. No data are given on time taken by a specified sample of test takers during the test development process.

INSTRUCTIONS FOR PART TWO. (Rewriting the letter.) The test taker is directed to "outline . . . changes you would make in the organization and form of the letter . . . . Then . . . rewrite the letter . . . [and finally, if one persists to the next paragraph] *Before* [emphasis added] outlining and rewriting the letter . . . list your objectives . . . . why you are writing to Mr. Masonhurst . . . . [citing] at least three or four things you want your letter to Mr. Masonhurst to accomplish" (p. 1, instructions). Presumably one then goes on to the scoring guide.

Although the examinees were told to list at least 3 or 4 things they wanted accomplished, the scoring key lists six objectives with 1 point awarded for any *five* of the six objectives.

The outline is worth up to 7 points. Considerable reorganization is involved for this rather lengthy and complex letter. Thus, one item in the outline suggests combining the ideas in lines 7–8 with lines 30–34 making this the second paragraph. Another item in the outline suggests distinguishing "between internal security measures and external ones" by rewriting lines 9 to 39 in two paragraphs, one of which deals with internal security measures and the other with external measures. The suggested changes are reasonable. Whether they are what one might expect from the instructions is debatable. In any case, the process is complex and takes considerable time. One easily surpasses the 1–2 hours suggested.

The rewritten letter in the scoring guide reduces the original approximately 750-word letter to about 330 words and changes the format to include two sections with listings in "bullet" form for methods of catching a thief and security measures. The rewritten letter in the scoring guide is excellent. However, in my opinion, the instructions do not orient the test taker to such a major revision.

One could learn much about one kind of business letter writing from doing this task and comparing one's responses with that of the authors. However, there are many kinds of letter writing and this is a time-consuming approach for testing oneself on one type of letter. Furthermore, given the lack of validity and reliability data, and the lack of any data on experiences from test administration during development (norms, time for completion, difficulties to avoid), I recommend potential test users wishing to conduct "self assessment" of business letter writing competency turn elsewhere until this test undergoes further development. The objectively scored, Test of Standard Written English (9:244) is one possibility. Another, more informal approach making use of actual writing is Communicating by Letter (Gilbert, 1978), an old self-instructional guide including many "self tests."

REVIEWER'S REFERENCE

Gilbert, M. B. (1978). *Communicating by letter*. New York: John Wiley & Sons, Inc.

Review of the Self-Assessment in Writing Skills by STEPHEN JURS, Professor of Educational Psychology, Research, and Social Foundations, College of Education and Allied Professions, University of Toledo, Toledo, OH:

The Self-Assessment in Writing Skills was clearly developed as a self-assessment and is currently limited to that role. It can be given in a group setting as well as to an individual. It is self-administered and self-scored. The assessment consists of a two-page letter the examinee critiques and rewrites. Testing time is considered to be "about 1–2 hours."

Part One of the assessment is concerned with the content and style of the letter and requires the examinee to suggest changes. The lines of the letter are numbered and examinees are asked to recommend line-by-line changes "on another sheet of paper." There are 52 lines in the letter, which provide many opportunities for changes.

The scoring of Part One is done by comparing the examinee's recommended changes in content and style to a list of 60 possible, specific improvements to the letter. The examinee is told to "compare your own rewrite with ours, line by line, and score yourself." There is a maximum of 60 points for Part One.

The scoring process is somewhat subjective as the examinee is given great latitude in deciding whether his or her suggested changes adequately match those on the list. It is implied the self-scorer could award points for recommended changes not in the list but that the examinee believes are appropriate. Unfortunately, there is no check on whether the examinee's suggested changes are in fact improvements.

Part Two of the assessment requires the examinee to list objectives for the letter, outline any changes in the organization and format, and to rewrite the letter. There are 40 points maximum for Part Two.

The scoring for Part Two contains several guidelines. Three points are earned for realizing the overall objective and there is 1 point each for identifying five of six specific objectives. There are seven items, for 1 point each, that should be in the outline and there are 25 points that can be earned in the rewrite of the letter.

The scoring of the rewrite is done by comparing the examinee's letter to a model answer. Scores are based on sentence length, percentage of one-syllable words, sentences per paragraph, and some suggestions about structure. About half of the maximum points in Part Two are determined by general impressions of how the revised format matches the model answer. Again, it is the examinee's judgment that determines whether the changes are actually improvements. Part Two could easily be adapted for use on a word processor and that might allow for automated scoring regarding sentence length, number of syllables, etc.

It is doubtful the self-assessment is an accurate measure of small differences among examinees because the flexibility in scoring makes the part scores or even the total score imprecise. The scores do not provide diagnostic information. Users will have difficulty interpreting the meaning of the scores because it is not clear what is an acceptable score. It is not likely that many examinees will approach the maximum score of 100 and yet there is no guideline for interpreting lower scores. Thus, there is the potential that the results will be misinterpreted.

Although correcting and rewriting a business letter is not an intrinsically engaging task, the self-assessment could be used effectively in a workshop or seminar on improving written communication. The self-scoring might reduce participants' anxieties concerning an evaluation of their work.

The assessment has the potential for other uses such as an outcome measure in an evaluation of a training program or as a criterion measure in a research study. It would be necessary, however, to standardize thoroughly the scoring procedures if comparisons were to be made between individuals or groups.

The self-assessment presents an authentic, realistic task and thereby has, by definition, some degree of validity. Unfortunately, there is no evidence presented about the relationship between scores on the self-assessment and scores on other measures of writing or performance on writing tasks in the workplace. There are no norms for the assessment and there is no evidence, not even a discussion, about the reliability of the assessment. Some data related to reliability and validity are greatly needed.

The contradiction about the Self-Assessment in Writing Skills is that the persons who could benefit the most from the assessment, those with poor writing skills, are the least capable of judging the adequacy of their recommended changes, as the self-scoring demands. However useful the Self-Assessment in Writing Skills may be as an instructional device, at this point in its development it is not a test and should not be used for placement, diagnosis, or selection.

[353]

Sensory Integration and Praxis Tests.

Purpose: Designed to assess several practic abilities, various aspects of sensory processing status, and behavioral manifestations of deficits in integration of sensory inputs from these systems.
Population: Ages 4–8.11.
Publication Date: 1989.
Acronym: SIPT.
Scores: 17 tests: Space Visualization, Figure-Ground Perception, Standing and Walking Balance, Design Copying, Postural Praxis, Bilateral Motor Coordination, Praxis Verbal Command, Constructional Praxis, Postrotary Nys-

tagmus, Motor Accuracy, Sequencing Praxis, Oral Praxis, Manual Form Perception, Kinesthesia, Finger Identification, Graphesthesia, Localization of Tactile Stimuli.
Administration: Individual.
Price Data, 1993: $1,100 per set including all test materials, 25 copies of each consumable test form, 10 complete sets of all 17 computer-scored answer sheets with 10 transmittal sheets, manual (307 pages), and carrying case.
Time: (10) minutes or less per individual test.
Comments: Extension and revision of the Southern California Sensory Integration Tests (SCSIT) and the Southern California Postrotary Nystagmus Test (SCPNT); computer-scoring only; stopwatch capable of recording 1/10 seconds needed (available from publisher).
Author: A. Jean Ayres.
Publisher: Western Psychological Services.
Cross References: See T4:2433 (9 references). For a review by Byron P. Rourke of the SCPNT, see 9:1157 (20 references); for information on the SCSIT, see 9:1158 (5 references) and T3:2244 (21 references); for reviews by Homer B. C. Reed, Jr. and Alida S. Westman of the SCSIT, see 8:875 (5 references); see also T2:1887 (18 references).

TEST REFERENCES

1. Cermak, S. A., Morris, M. L., & Koomar, J. (1990). Praxis on verbal command and imitation. *The American Journal of Occupational Therapy, 44,* 641-645.
2. Fanchiang, S., Snyder, C., Zobel-Lachiusa, J., Loeffler, C. B., & Thompson, M. E. (1990). Sensory integrative processing in delinquent-prone and non-delinquent-prone adolescents. *The American Journal of Occupational Therapy, 44,* 630-639.
3. Kimball, J. G. (1990). Using the Sensory Integration and Praxis Tests to measure change: A pilot study. *The American Journal of Occupational Therapy, 44,* 603-608.
4. Mailloux, Z. (1990). An overview of the Sensory Integration and Praxis Tests. *The American Journal of Occupational Therapy, 44,* 589-594.
5. McAtee, S., & Mack, W. (1990). Relations between design copying and other tests of sensory integrative dysfunction: A pilot study. *The American Journal of Occupational Therapy, 44,* 596-601.
6. Murray, E. A., Cermak, S. A., & O'Brien, V. (1990). The relationship between form and space perception, constructional abilities, and clumsiness in children. *The American Journal of Occupational Therapy, 44,* 623-628.
7. Stallings-Sahler, S. (1990). Certification in administration and interpretation of the Sensory Integration and Praxis tests. *The American Journal of Occupational Therapy, 44,* 655-657.
8. Case-Smith, J. (1991). The effects of tactile defensiveness and tactile discrimination on in-hand manipulation. *The American Journal of Occupational Therapy, 45,* 811-818.
9. Cermak, S. A., & Murray, E. A. (1991). The validity of the constructional subtests of the Sensory Integration and Praxis tests. *The American Journal of Occupational Therapy, 45,* 539-543.
10. Liu, L., Gauthier, L., & Gauthier, S. (1991). Spatial disorientation in persons with early senile dementia of the Alzheimer type. *The American Journal of Occupational Therapy, 45,* 67-74.
11. Hall, L., Robertson, W., & Turner, M. A. (1992). Clinical reasoning process for service provision in the public school. *The American Journal of Occupational Therapy, 46,* 927-936.
12. Leonardelli-Haertlein, C. A. (1992). Ethics in evaluation in occupational therapy. *The American Journal of Occupational Therapy, 46,* 950-953.
13. Richardson, P. K., Atwater, S. W., Crowe, T. K., & Deitz, J. C. (1992). Performance of preschoolers on the Pediatric Clinical Test of Sensory Interaction for balance. *The American Journal of Occupational Therapy, 46,* 793-800.
14. Tse, S., & Bailey, D. M. (1992). T'ai Chi and postural control in the well elderly. *The American Journal of Occupational Therapy, 46,* 295-300.
15. Wilson, B., Pollock, N., Kaplan, B. J., Law, M., & Faris, P. (1992). Reliability and construct validity of the clinical observations of motor and postural skills. *The American Journal of Occupational Therapy, 46,* 775-783.
16. Dewey, D. (1993). Error analysis of limb and orofacial praxis in children with developmental motor deficits. *Brain and Cognition, 23,* 203-221.
17. Exner, C. E. (1993). Content validity of the In-hand Manipulation Test. *The American Journal of Occupational Therapy, 47,* 505-513.
18. DeMaio-Feldman, D. (1994). Somatosensory processing abilities of very low-birth weight infants at school age. *The American Journal of Occupational Therapy, 48,* 639-645.

Review of the Sensory Integration and Praxis Tests by JAMES E. YSSELDYKE, Professor of Educational Psychology and Director of National Center on Educational Outcomes, University of Minnesota, Minneapolis, MN:

The Sensory Integration and Praxis Tests (SIPT) are a derivative of the Southern California Sensory Integration Tests (SCSIT) and the Southern California Postrotary Nystagmus Test (SCPNT). The SIPT is made up of four new praxis tests and revised versions of 12 of the original 16 tests that made up the SCSIT. Four of the SCSIT tests were revised in a major way (Design Copying, Manual Form Perception, Bilateral Motor Coordination, Standing Balance) and the rest were changed to a minor extent in administration and scoring.

The SIPT is based on an underlying theory, often referred to as Ayres Sensory Integration Theory or Praxis Theory. There is a $1^1/_2$-page description of the theory in the manual, a theory which is said to be evolving. Ayres (the test author) states that "Lacking a universally accepted conceptual framework of how the brain works as a whole, the theory presented in this chapter has been constructed to provide a unifying concept for heuristic purposes" (p. 11). The test itself provides an examiner with information of heuristic interest, but of questionable practical significance. The author describes the test as designed to help the clinician understand the nervous system. She states that "The SIPT does not predict academic achievement, behavior problems, or any diagnostic category" (p. 233).

All scoring of the SIPT must be done using computerized scoring services available only through the publisher. One submits protocols and obtains the Western Psychological Services Test Report. There is no other way to score the test or compare child performance to norms.

In developing the SIPT, the author selected test content that would discriminate between dysfunctional and nondysfunctional children of normal intelligence. In addition, the content had to be relevant to an aspect of sensory processing and "related foundational skills [that] are particularly vulnerable to disorder and associated with learning and behavior problems" (p. 177), the measures needed to be related as evidenced by factor analysis, and it had to be possible to measure the "parameter" reliably.

Standardization of the test was completed using examiners who responded to advertisements in journals and newsletters. Examiners were trained for 5 days and any individual not meeting "defined accuracy criteria" was dropped. The criteria are not specified in the manual. The sampling plan was drawn up by constructing an ideal sample and then selecting communities (urban or rural), schools, and then students. Urban was defined as 2,500+ residents and rural was defined as less than 2,500 residents. Examiners were selected in either urban or rural settings. The author states that a random approach could not be used in rural settings, so examiners were allowed to pick the rural area closest to them. Urban examiners picked from urban areas in their region. Some examiners failed to get permission from any urban communities in their region, so they were allowed to replace their selected urban area with a "nearby community having highly similar demographic characteristics" (p. 181).

This is an incredibly elaborate test, with elaborate names and elaborate constructs and skills to assess. The directions for some of the subtests are difficult to follow, and this may account for some of the low reliabilities noted for specific subtests. The manual is an exercise in obfuscation.

To be useful, a test must provide reliable information and it must measure what its author claims it measures. Reliability is a necessary, but not sufficient, condition for validity. The author defines validity as "the ability to draw meaningful inferences from test scores to meet an intended purpose" (p. 197). She states that the primary purpose of the SIPT is assessment of the sensory integrative and practic status of children with known or selected problems.

Reliability data are restricted to those derived from administering the test to 41 dysfunctional children and 10 normal children. On the basis of data provided in tables, it looks like all 41 dysfunctional children were labeled LD. The children are of unspecified characteristics except for gender. For the entire sample of 51 children a total of 78 test-retest reliabilities are reported. Three of the 78 exceed .90. Ten of the reliabilities reported for this test are below .40; 43 are at or below .70. Interrater reliabilities are also reported. The SIPT does not have the necessary reliability to be used for diagnostic purposes.

The SIPT manual includes 38 pages of data on validity. Much of this is on the previous tests. Given that the skills, behaviors, or constructs assessed cannot be reliably assessed, the data on validity are of little use.

SUMMARY. The SIPT provides interesting data on a set of 17 tests with interesting names. The information is supposed to be of heuristic interest in understanding brain function; it is not intended to be predictive of academic performance or of response to therapy. As have its predecessors, this test probably will be well received by occupational therapists who espouse sensory integration therapy to provide interesting information about neurological functioning, information that is of little if any predictive usefulness.

[354]

Sixteen Personality Factor Questionnaire, Fifth Edition.

Purpose: Designed to measure personality traits.

Population: Ages 16 and over.

Publication Dates: 1949–94.

Acronym: 16PF.

Scores, 24: 16 primary factor scores: Warm vs. Reserved (A), Abstract-Reasoning vs. Concrete-Reasoning (B), Emotionally Stable vs. Reactive (C), Dominant vs. Deferential (E), Lively vs. Serious (F), Rule-Conscious vs. Expedient (G), Socially Bold vs. Shy (H), Sensitive vs. Utilitarian (I), Vigilant vs. Trusting (L), Abstracted vs. Grounded (M), Private vs. Forthright (N), Apprehensive vs. Self-Assured (0), Open to Change vs. Traditional (Q1), Self-Reliant vs. Group-Oriented (Q2), Perfectionistic vs. Tolerates Disorder (Q3), Tense vs. Relaxed (Q4); 5 global factor scores: Extraverted vs. Introverted (EX), High Anxiety vs. Low Anxiety (AX), Tough-Minded vs. Receptive (TM), Independent vs. Accommodating (IN), Self-Controlled vs. Unrestrained (SC); 3 response style indices: Impression Management (IM), Infrequency (INF), Acquiescence (ACQ).

Administration: Group.

Price Data, 1994: $82 per complete kit including 10 test booklets, 25 answer sheets, 25 individual record forms, scoring keys, manual ('94, 162 pages), and one prepaid processing certificate for a basic interpretive report (BIR); $12.50 per 10 test booklets; $25 per scoring keys and norms tables; $12.50 per 25 answer sheets; $7.50 per 25 individual record forms; $20 per manual; $29.50 per trial packet including test booklet, answer sheet, manual, and certificate for a Basic Interpretive Report (BIR); price data for Basic Interpretive Report including profiles, scores, and descriptive comments and Basic Score Report (includes scores only) available from publisher.

Time: (25–50) minutes.

Comments: Computer administration and scoring available.

Authors: Raymond B. Cattell, A. Karen S. Cattell, Heather E. P. Cattell (16PF), Mary Russell, Darcie Karol (manual).

Publisher: Institute for Personality and Ability Testing, Inc.

Cross References: See T4:2470 (140 references); for reviews of an earlier edition by James N. Butcher and Marvin Zuckerman, see 9:1136 (67 references); see also T3:2208 (182 references); for reviews by Bruce M. Bloxam, Brian F. Bolton, and James A. Walsh, see 8:679 (619 references); see also T2:1383 (244 references); for reviews by Thomas J. Bouchard, Jr. and Leonard G. Rorer, see 7:139 (295 references); see also P:245 (249 references); for a review by Maurice Lorr, see 6:174 (81 references); for a review by C. J. Adcock, see 5:112 (21 references); for reviews by Charles M. Harsh, Ardie Lubin, and J. Richard Wittenborn, see 4:87 (8 references).

TEST REFERENCES

1. Lebovits, A. H., & Strain, J. J. (1990). The asbestos worker who smokes: Adding insult to injury. *Health Psychology*, *9*, 405-417.

2. Dadds, M., Smith, M., Webber, Y., & Robinson, A. (1991). An exploration of family and individual profiles following father-daughter incest. *Child Abuse & Neglect*, *15*, 575-586.

3. Reinehr, R. C. (1991). Demonstrating personality scale validation procedures. *Teaching of Psychology*, *18*, 241-242.

4. Stohs, J. M. (1991). Young adult predictors and midlife outcomes of "starving artists'" careers: A longitudinal study of male fine artists. *Journal of Creative Behavior*, *25*, 92-105.

5. Bartram, D. (1992). The personality of UK managers: 16PF norms for short-listed applicants. *Journal of Occupational and Organizational Psychology, 65*, 159-172.

6. Craig, R. J., & Olson, R. E. (1992). Relationship between MCMI-II scales and normal personality traits. *Psychological Reports, 71*, 699-705.

7. Delamatre, J. E., & Schuerger, J. M. (1992). Personality disorder concept scales and 16 PF dimensions. *Psychological Reports, 70*, 839-849.

8. Francis, C. R., Hughes, H. M., & Hitz, L. (1992). Physically abusive parents and the 16-PF: A preliminary psychological topology. *Child Abuse & Neglect, 16*, 673-691.

9. Leo, D. D., Capodieci, S., & Villa, A. (1992). Personality facors in monozygotic and dizygotic twins: A comparative study. *Psychological Reports, 71*, 1115-1122.

10. Melamed, T., & Bozionelos, N. (1992). Gender differences in the personality features of British managers. *Psychological Reports, 71*, 979-986.

11. Melamed, T., & Bozionelos, N. (1992). Managerial promotion and height. *Psychological Reports, 71*, 587-593.

12. Nakano, K. (1992). Role of personality characteristics in coping behaviors. *Psychological Reports, 71*, 687-690.

13. Siegel, C., & Shaughnessy, M. F. (1992). Personality of college students in calculus courses. *Psychological Reports, 71*, 1309-1310.

14. Spirrison, C. L. (1992). Validity of the 16 PF-E experimental norms for adults with mental retardation. *Psychological Reports, 70*, 1200-1202.

15. Aplin, D. Y. (1993). Psychological evaluation of adults in a cochlear implant program. *American Annals of the Deaf, 138*, 415-419.

16. Haywood, T. W., Grossman, L. S., & Hardy, D. W. (1993). Denial and social desirability in clinical evaluations of alleged sex offenders. *The Journal of Nervous and Mental Disease, 181*, 183-188.

17. Hosokawa, T., & Ohyama, M. (1993). Reliability and validity of a Japanese version of the short-form Eysenck Personality Questionnaire—Revised. *Psychological Reports, 72*, 823-832.

18. Mowrer-Popiel, E., Pollard, C., & Pollard, R. (1993). An examination of factors affecting the creative production of female professors. *College Student Journal, 27*, 428-436.

19. Radford, M. H. B., Mann, L., Ohta, Y., & Nakane, Y. (1993). Differences between Australian and Japanese students in decisional self-esteem, decisional stress, and coping styles. *Journal of Cross-Cultural Psychology, 24*, 284-297.

20. Spitz, R. T., & MacKinnon, J. R. (1993). Predicting success in volunteer community service. *Psychological Reports, 73*, 815-818.

21. Volling, B. L., & Belsky, J. (1993). Parent, infant, and contextual characteristics related to maternal employment decisions in the first year of infancy. *Family Relations, 42*, 4-12.

22. Aldwin, C. M., Levenson, M. R., & Spiro, A. (1994). Vulnerability and resilience to combat exposure: Can stress have lifelong effects? *Psychology and Aging, 9*, 34-44.

23. Bonaguidi, F., Trivella, M. G., Michelassi, C., Carpeggiani, C., & L'Abbate, A. (1994). The second-order factor structure of Cattell's 16PF in patients with coronary heart disease. *Psychological Reports, 75*, 1271-1275.

24. Cattell, R. B. (1994). Constancy of global, second-ordered personality factors over a twenty-year-plus period. *Psychological Reports, 75*, 3-9.

25. Guastello, S. J., & Shissler, J. E. (1994). A two-factor taxonomy of creative behavior. *Journal of Creative Behavior, 28*, 211-221.

26. Herman, K., & Usita, P. (1994). Predictive validity of the 16 PF in screening volunteers for Big Brothers/Big Sisters. *Psychological Reports, 74*, 249-250.

27. Lee, R. E. (1994). Personality characteristics of very desirable and undesirable childcare workers in a residential setting. *Psychological Reports, 74*, 579-584.

28. Lutzky, S. M., & Knight, B. G. (1994). Explaining gender differences in caregiver distress: The roles of emotional attentiveness and coping styles. *Psychology and Aging, 9*, 513-519.

29. Persinger, M. A. (1994). Sense of a presence and suicidal ideation following traumatic brain injury: Indications of right-hemispheric intrusions from neuropsychological profiles. *Psychological Reports, 75*, 1059-1070.

30. Schuerger, J. M., Ekeberg, S. E., & Kustis, G. A. (1994). 16PF scores and machine operators' performances. *Perceptual and Motor Skills, 79*, 1426.

31. Shaughnessy, M. F., Stockard, J., Moore, J., & Siegel, C. (1994). Scores on the 16 Personality Factor Questionnaire and success in college calculus. *Psychological Reports, 75*, 348-350.

32. Singh, S. (1994). Gender differences in work values and personality characteristics among Indian executives. *The Journal of Social Psychology, 134*, 699-700.

33. Spiro, A., Schnurr, P. P., & Aldwin, C. M. (1994). Combat-related posttraumatic stress disorder symptoms in older men. *Psychology and Aging, 9*, 17-26.

34. Strohmer, D. C., & Shivy, V. A. (1994). Bias in counselor hypothesis testing: Testing the robustness of counselor confirmatory bias. *Journal of Counseling and Development, 73*, 191-197.

35. Terpylak, O., & Schuerger, J. M. (1994). Broad factor scales of the 16 PF Fifth Edition and Millon personality disorder scales. *Psychological Reports, 74*, 124-126.

36. Tziner, A., Meir, E. I., Dahan, M., & Birati, A. (1994). An investigation of the predictive validity and economic utility of the assessment center for the high-management level. *Canadian Journal of Behavioural Science, 26*, 228-245.

37. Fisher, S. G., Macrosson, W. D. K., & Walker, C. A. (1995). FIRO-B: The power of love and the love of power. *Psychological Reports, 76*, 195-206.

38. Grossman, L. S., & Craig, R. J. (1995). Comparison of MCMI-II and 16 PF validity scales. *Journal of Personality Assessment, 64*, 384-389.

Review of the Sixteen Personality Factor Questionnaire, Fifth Edition by MARY J. McLELLAN, Assistant Professor of Educational Psychology, Northern Arizona University, Center for Excellence in Education, Flagstaff, AZ:

The first edition of the Sixteen Personality Questionnaire (16PF) was published in 1949. Later editions were published in 1956, 1962, 1967–69, and this edition in 1993. The 16PF is designed to identify primary personality traits of normal adults. The appropriateness of the 16PF within a variety of settings, including clinical/counseling, industrial/organizational, research, and schools is indicated in the manual. The potential uses within such settings is extremely diverse.

The 16PF may be administered to individuals or groups and may be hand or computer scored. Adults (ages 16 through 92 years) may complete the test with a paper-and-pencil or computer version. The test consists of 185 items with a three-choice format. In most cases the middle response choice is a question mark (?). There are 15 reasoning ability items at the end of the test that have three distinct choices. Average time to complete the test is 35 to 50 minutes when pencil-and-paper scoring is used and 25 to 35 minutes when the test is taken on a computer. The same score sheet is used regardless of whether the protocol is to be computer scored or handscored. The test booklet is reusable. The administrator encourages the examinee to respond to all questions and to choose the first response that comes to mind rather than spending too much time on any one response. The protocol is not considered scorable if 13 or more items are not completed.

The administrator's manual provides a careful description of the handscoring process as well as information about the computer-scoring material available through IPAT. The advantages of the computer-scoring system are also discussed. The handscoring method is relatively simple when the administrator has the necessary materials at hand while reading the manual. The possibility of error while handscoring material is evident when working with material, but the usual caution and checking of protocols should add to scorer reliability. The 16-factor raw scores are counted directly on the scoring sheet from the handscoring keys. Sten scores are then found on the General Population Norms sheet or in Appendix B of the manual. The factor scores are then transferred to the individual record form where charting of the sten scores is completed along with the calculation of the five global factors. The test administrator can then interpret the profile of the examinee.

The profile interpretation ascribed to in the manual involves three steps. The response style indices are to be reviewed first and they include the Impression Management Scale and the Acquiescence Scale. The administrator should note the Acquiescence Scale must be calculated without the use of a template and is quite laborious. The next step is to interpret the Global factor scores and then the Primary factor scores. This approach is certainly the most accepted because the Response style indices address the validity of the examinee's responses. The Global Scores are more reliable and valid than the Primary factor scores and would therefore be interpreted first once the validity of the responses has been established. Chapter 3 includes a table that provides correlations between the Global Factors and other personality measures. The same information is provided for the Primary Factor scores.

The test-retest reliability coefficients of the 16PF for a 2-week period were very good for the global factors (ranging from .84 to .91). The primary factors did not fare as well with reliability coefficients ranging from .69 to .87. The 2-month interval reliability ratings dropped to a mean of .78 for the global factors and a mean of .7 for the primary factors. Internal consistency was calculated with Cronbach's coefficient alpha and values ranged from .64 to .85 with a mean of .74. The standard error of measurement is within an acceptable range given the purpose and scope of the test. Construct and criterion validity are discussed in chapter 5 and the rationale of the 16PF structure is well defined. The authors of the administrator's manual do an excellent job of describing how validity was established and provide caution to the administrator about making prognostic or predictive decisions from test results.

The norm sample consisted of 2,500 people whose demographic characteristics matched the 1990 U.S. Census figures. The sample of 2,500 were randomly selected from the 4,449 people who were administered the final experimental form of the 16PF. Some discrepancies are noted between the percent in sample and the percent in the 1990 Census in the age group description of Table 8. For example, in the 15- to 17-year age group, the percent in sample was 13.2% and the percent in census was 4.6%. This discrepancy appears to be accounted for with the underrepresentation of people ages 65 and over. There is also a notable discrepancy in the educational level of the sample with an underrepresentation of high school graduates and overrepresentation of college graduates.

The 16PF is a widely used measure of various personality characteristics. This psychometrically sophisticated measure is a valuable contribution to the testing repertoire of counselors and clinicians. The interpretation of the results is relatively complex and the two computer-generated reports, the Basic Interpretive Report and Basic Score Report are recommended for the less sophisticated user. The test booklet is easy to read (a fifth grade reading level) and the scoring procedure is relatively easy to follow. In conclusion, the 16PF does accomplish its intended purpose with a few weaknesses noted that do not significantly discourage use.

Review of the Sixteen Personality Factor Questionnaire, Fifth Edition by PAMELA CARRINGTON ROTTO, Assistant Professor of Educational Psychology, University of Nebraska-Lincoln, Lincoln, NE:

The Sixteen Personality Factor Questionnaire, Fifth Edition (16PF) originally was developed by Raymond Cattell in 1949. This instrument is designed to be used as a broad measure of personality and to predict a wide range of life behaviors for adults ages 16 and older. The 16PF is intended for use across clinical and counseling, industrial and organizational, research, and school settings. It is recommended for use in numerous capacities such as predicting performance criteria, attaining behavioral ratings, assessing personality across groups, describing personality changes, and predicting other criterion and construct measures.

Use of the 16PF Fifth Edition is somewhat limited in that this measure of normal adult personality should not be used as an indicator of psychopathology because the standard 16 factors are not sufficient to assess dimensions of abnormal personality. The 16PF Fifth Edition also has a limited range of predictive value and must be used cautiously in situations involving occupational selection and appraisal of specific qualities. In other words, as indicated by the authors, this measure is useful in predicting specific behavioral criteria such as social skills, but does not adequately assess other factors that may affect or predict future behavior such as motivation. The authors appropriately caution the user to employ the 16PF Fifth Edition as one component of a battery of relevant measures.

The 16PF is based on Cattell's original identification of primary traits of personality through factor analysis of a broad range of personality descriptors. Thus, this measure is not based on constructs related to a particular theory of personality. In addition, unlike many personality tests, the 16PF is not designed to distinguish one group from another.

According to the authors, the primary personality factor scales for the 16PF Fifth Edition were extracted from the fourth edition scales on the basis of dual criteria, which ensured that each item correlated highly with its own factor scale and did not correlate more highly with another factor scale. Selected items were revised to update language, remove ambiguity, and diminish unnecessary length. Items also were reviewed for gender and racial bias. The essentially unchanged primary personality factor scales continue to be represented by letters; however, the updated edition also includes descriptive terms for each factor (e.g., Warmth), which do not appear to differ substantially from the descriptive terms used for the fourth edition. The broad personality domains under which the primary factors cluster are called "Global Factors," a term that replaces the previously used "Second-Order Factors."

According to its authors, the 16PF Fifth Edition includes several general improvements over prior editions such as a revised item content, consistently organized response choices, updated normative data, new administrative indices to assess response bias, and improved psychometric properties. At least two manuals have been prepared to accompany this instrument, including a currently available administrator's manual by Russell and Karol and a forthcoming technical manual (Conn & Rieke, in press). Although the administrator's manual adequately provides the fundamental information essential for test administration and scoring, data critical for proper interpretation and psychometric evaluation of this measure are lacking. The user repeatedly is referred to the technical manual, which was not available for this review, for developmental and interpretive data relating to the Fifth Edition.

The 16PF Fifth Edition consists of a single form with 185 items that comprise 16 personality factor scales, as well as newly developed administrative indices designed to evaluate test-taking response styles (i.e., Impression Management, Infrequency, and Acquiescence scales). This format represents a practical improvement over the more cumbersome fourth edition, which included five psychometrically inconsistent forms (Forms A–E) and required administration of all of these forms (total of 712 items) to attain the most optimally reliable assessment. Each scale is composed of 10 to 15 forced-response items, with an overall readability at the fifth-grade level and a consistent format across all personality items.

The authors acknowledge the brevity of the scales and, in response, identify confidence intervals for obtained results and caution the user against overinterpretation of standard score differences. The question mark (?) used for each middle response may be slightly problematic in that this symbol implies an unsure or "I don't know" response, yet is intended for use in situations where neither of the two available answers accurately represent the best response for the individual.

Normative data were updated using a sample stratified on the basis of gender, race, age, and educational variables. It should be noted that relative to the 1990 U.S. Census data, individuals whose education did not exceed high school graduation appear to have been underrepresented in the normative sample and college graduates were overrepresented. Adults over age 54 also were underrepresented in this sample. In addition, adolescents between the ages of 15 and 17 years were significantly overrepresented relative to census data, an interesting phenomenon given the authors' recommendation that an adolescent version of the 16PF (the High School Personality Questionnaire; T4:1159) is a more appropriate measure for individuals of ages 12 through 18. Given the intended use of this measure, it is likely that underrepresentation of the less highly educated group in the normative sample is undesirable.

Several alternatives for quick and convenient scoring of the 16PF Fifth Edition are available, including handscoring or computer scoring that may be completed through the publisher or on-site using purchased software. Combined-gender norms also are available as a scoring option in accordance with federal civil rights legislation. Two new computer-generated interpretive reports (i.e., Basic Interpretive Report and Basic Score Report) are available, and other report formats consistent with those accompanying the fourth edition reportedly are forthcoming. The empirical validation efforts concerning these interpretive reports are neither mentioned nor described in the administrator's manual; thus, users must consider the possibility that these reports may be based on content interpretation and face validity rather than substantial empirical validation efforts.

Interpretation of the 16PF Fifth Edition currently is limited by the absence of published data. Although a useful synthesis of findings from various studies is summarized in the administrator's manual (i.e., general interpretive information, a strategy for profile interpretation, specific scale descriptions), this interpretive information is based on the preliminary body of evidence for the 16PF Fifth Edition which is not available to the user but apparently will be included in the unpublished technical manual. The aforementioned information is absolutely necessary, but is not sufficient for accurate profile interpretation. The authors indicate that scale definitions will be refined in the future as a database on this edition is developed. This post hoc approach to data interpretation is problematic, particularly in relation to the unknown utility of scales such as the Acquiescence Scale (a response style index unique to the 16PF Fifth Edition). The authors indicate the utility of this scale will be determined by professionals who use the 16PF Fifth Edition in various applications. Current guidelines for interpretation of this and other scales are disconcertingly vague.

Perhaps the greatest strength of the 16PF Fifth Edition is that this well-known research instrument has stood the test of time and is supported by a vast body of data. However, although an extensive program of research has yielded a significant body of data on the fourth edition of the 16PF, similar documentation does not yet exist for the current edition. This instrument is most valuable as a measure of normal adult personality in settings where diagnostic issues of psychpathology are not of concern. Overall, the identified improvements appear to have strengthened the utility of this instrument; however, the lack of sufficient information in the form of an available technical manual currently is a significant limitation of the 16PF Fifth Edition. Complete evaluation of this measure and its improved psychometric properties will be necessary following availability of this critical documentation.

REVIEWER'S REFERENCES

Conn, S. R., & Rieke, M. L. (Eds.). (in press). *The 16PF Fifth Edition technical manual*. Champaign, IL: Institute for Personality and Ability Testing, Inc.

[355]

SKILLSCOPE for Managers.

Purpose: Assesses managerial strengths and developmental needs from managers and coworkers perspectives.
Population: Managers.
Publication Dates: 1988–93.
Scores: 15 Skill Areas: Getting Information, Communication, Taking Action, Risk Taking, Administration, Conflict Management, Relationships, Selecting/Developing, Influencing, Flexibility, Knowledge of Job, Energy/Drive, Time Management, Coping With Pressure, Self-Management.
Administration: Group.
Price Data, 1993: $125 per complete set including 9 survey instruments, The Results computer scoring, The Summary, The Action Plan, and The Trainer's Guide ('93, 22 pages).
Time: Administration time not reported.
Comments: SKILLSCOPE questionnaires are returned to the Center for Creative Leadership for confidential scoring; managers are rated by self and by coworkers.
Authors: Robert E. Kaplan (survey), Maxine Dalton (Trainer's Guide), Bob Kaplan, Jean Leslie, Russ Moxley, Patricia Ohlott, and Ellen VanVelsor.
Publisher: Center for Creative Leadership.

Review of the SKILLSCOPE for Managers by LINDA F. WIGHTMAN, Vice President—Operations, Testing, and Research, Law School Admission Services, Newtown, PA:

The SKILLSCOPE for Managers is a 98-item management skills rating instrument providing information in 15 skill areas. The instrument is neither criterion referenced nor norm referenced in its ratings. That is, its purpose is not to evaluate a manager either in terms of absolute or relative management skills. Rather, it provides an opportunity for managers to compare their own perceptions of their strengths and weaknesses in various management skill areas to the perceptions of their bosses and co-workers. The evaluation process seems to be designed to result in a generally positive experience for managers. Raters are asked to identify each and every one of the 98 items that describe a strength of the manager, but to select only a very few that describe areas in which the manager needs improvement. This practice could reduce both the reliability and the effectiveness of the instrument for the manager who is having performance difficulties. Perceptions of the most serious of the deficiencies might vary among the raters when there are too many to choose among, giving the manager the incorrect impression that the problems are not serious because there appears to be little consensus in the "Development Needed" ratings. Alternatively, the test-retest reliability could be lowered significantly if some improvement is made following initial feedback so that the later rating(s) would reflect the next most important area(s) in need of improvement.

TEST DEVELOPMENT. The utility of the instrument for the purpose described above can be no greater than the degree to which an organization agrees with the descriptions of the manager's role and of the work environment upon which this instrument is based. That is, the description of a manager's job as "largely oral and interactive, current focussed" and one in which there is "always more than one problem in need of attention" found in the Trainer's Guide (p. 4) will be appropriate neither for all organizations nor for all types of management jobs within an organization. Prospective users should evaluate carefully the philosophy of management and the content of the skill categories found in the rating inventory before adopting this program for use in their organization. No rationale for the inclusion of the 15 skill areas found on this inventory is provided. Further, there is no information about the development, evaluation, and selection of the items that appear under the different skill areas.

RELIABILITY. The Trainer's Guide contains alpha coefficients (KR-20) for each of the 15 scales and they are in an acceptable range to support internal homogeneity. However, as the authors acknowledge, the between scale correlations are nearly as high as the within scale coefficients. The authors attribute the high intercorrelations to the "blending of skills and talents" (p. 15) that are represented by managerial activities. A reasonable alternative explanation is the presence of a simple halo effect. A halo effect likely would contribute also to the apparent strong internal reliability. The test-retest reliability also is in an acceptable range but again is likely to be at least partially attributable to a halo effect.

A problem somewhat related to halo effects is the response bias that is likely to occur when using this instrument. There are two sources of potential response bias. First, the manager apparently selects the co-workers and subordinates to whom the rating scale is given, and second, there is no requirement for employees to complete and return the questionnaire. The Summary and Action Plan are based on those questionnaires that are returned.

VALIDITY. The authors offer correlation between SKILLSCOPE data and performance evaluation data from one large manufacturing company as evidence of concurrent validity. There is not sufficient data about the study to evaluate the quality of the results. The authors report correlations ranging from .17 to .32 between overall evaluation and 5 of the skill areas. The correlations between SKILLSCOPE data and performance evaluation data for 7 of the other 10 skill areas are less than .1. These correlations are quite low for two instruments that purportedly are measuring the same job performance skills and are being reported by the same observer (i.e., the manager's boss). One explanation may lie in the differing requirements between the skill rating instrument and the performance evaluation form. In the former, the rater is allowed to make general unsupported observations and is required to make only a small number of negative observations, whereas in the latter, the rater typically is required to provide examples and documentation to support general evaluations of both strengths and weaknesses in employee performance. Lack of appropriate and objective examples may limit the number and types of skill strengths described in the performance review, lowering the correlation between the two instruments. The validity information should be expanded to include some content-related evidence.

ANCILLARY MATERIALS. The Action Plan and the Summary are part of a personnel feedback process and are developed from the responses to the rating instrument. Again, their utility is dependent upon a good match between the definition of the manager's job that is the foundation of the rating instrument and the goals and expectations for managers in companies considering adopting this program. The utility also is dependent on an understanding of the limitations of the process by both the manager and the personnel trainer. These limitations include the subjectivity of the raters, possible bias in respondents, possible halo effect, and failure to require examples to support generalizations about management performance.

CONCLUSIONS. The criticisms of the statistical data provided with this instrument partly reflect the tension between an instrument that is designed to capture perceptions among people in a work setting and an instrument that has the psychometric properties of an evaluation instrument. As a rating instrument for perceptions of management strengths to be used to target areas of self-examination by managers and/or communication between managers and their peers, this instrument may work well for companies for whom the manager's job fits the definition upon which this instrument was developed. It should not be confused, however, with an instrument designed to evaluate management effectiveness.

[356]

Slingerland College-Level Screening for the Identification of Language Learning Strengths and Weaknesses.

Purpose: Developed to screen for strengths and weaknesses in language learning.
Population: College or college graduates.
Publication Date: 1991.
Scores, 10: Visual to Kinesthetic-Motor I, Visual to Kinesthetic-Motor II, Visual Perception-Memory, Visual Discrimination, Visual Perception and Memory to Kinesthetic-Motor, Auditory to Visual-Kinesthetic I, Auditory to Visual-Kinesthetic II, Auditory to Visual, Comprehension, Auditory to Kinesthetic.
Administration: Group.
Price Data: Available from publisher.
Time: (45–50) minutes.
Comments: Upward extension of the Slingerland Screening Tests (T4:2478).
Author: Carol Murray.
Publisher: Educators Publishing Service, Inc.
Cross References: See T4:2478 (2 references).

Review of the Slingerland College-Level Screening for the Identification of Language Learning Strengths and Weaknesses by MARY ANNE BUNDA, Professor of Educational Leadership, Western Michigan University, Kalamazoo, MI:

This instrument has been developed to be an extension of other Slingerland Screening Tests (i.e., the primary, intermediate, and adult forms). Although some study has been made of the other instruments that use the Slingerland model, this instrument comes with no technical information. The manual suggests that field test information has not yet been collected. Not only are no data available on the reliability and validity of the test, but there are no norms presented. Rather the manual presents two case studies of individual responses to each of the 10 subtests with commentary by the test scorer.

The lack of any technical information on the test makes it impossible to recommend this instrument for any use other than research. The efficacy of other instruments developed within the model developed by Slingerland should not stand as evidence in the case of this instrument. The use of the model in the diagnosis of learning disabilities at other levels was clearly supplemented by additional information from instruments with known reliability and validity. In the case of this instrument, specifically designed for individuals who have attended at least 1 year of higher education, the manual itself acknowledges that the users will have limited objective supplemental data. In one of the cases, the individual provides the scorer with objective information which is used in the diagnosis. In the other, there is a recommendation to use self-report information from the examinee to form a diagnosis. The kinds of supplemental information recommended range from educational quality and opportunity to intelligence and health. However, no attempt has been made in the manual to explain how these factors must be taken into account. In each of the cases, the individual was diagnosed as specific language disabled and a tutor was recommended. Although these recommendations are made, the author points out the test is not called a test and the word disabled is not used in the title. The title of the test is not enough protection for potential examinees.

This test should not be used as a diagnostic device until further study is made of its role in the diagnosis of language disorder in postsecondary adults. Additionally, whether the model of language development and learning ascribed to by the developer warrants it or not, the test should clearly have norms developed. Evidence of the relationship between this test and other measures of both achievement and academic aptitude are definitely in order. At the very least, some evidence of the reliability of the scores which result from a single use of this instrument should be provided. Although the sample of behavior drawn by this instrument is very small, it may provide additional information to a sensitive special educator. A clinical interview may, however, provide the same quality of information.

Review of the Slingerland College-Level Screening for the Identification of Language Learning Strengths and Weaknesses by THOMAS W. GUYETTE, Assistant Professor of Speech Pathology, University of Illinois at Chicago, Chicago, IL:

The purpose of the Slingerland College-Level Screening for the Identification of Language Learning Strengths and Weaknesses (SCLS) is to identify persons with specific language disabilities. The SCLS is "intended for use with adults who have already graduate from college or for students attending college currently" (p. 4). The SCLS can be administered either to a group or to individuals.

The screening test comes with a teacher's manual, a test booklet, and stimulus materials. The teacher's manual primarily describes the administration and scoring of the test. Scoring and interpretation are also illustrated with two case reports. The test booklet is 10 pages long and can be purchased in packages of 12. The stimulus materials are appropriate in terms of size (for group administration) and professional appearance.

The SCLS is divided into 10 subtests. Subtest I is a "distance copying" test. The student is asked to copy a short paragraph which is posted in the room. Subtest II is a "near point" copying task and involves copying a short outline presented on the test booklet. Both Subtests I and II are timed and the student has 5 minutes to complete each subtest. In Subtest III the student is exposed to a stimulus card for 5 seconds, asked to wait for 5 seconds, and then matches the memory of the stimulus card to stimuli in the test booklet. Subtest IV is a test of visual discrimination which involves matching words. In Subtest V the student is exposed to a stimulus card for 5 seconds, waits for 5 seconds, and then writes or draws what they remember on the stimulus card. In Subtest VI the student listens to dictation, waits for 5 seconds, and then writes down the dictation. In Subtest VII a word is dictated and the student is asked to write down a particular grapheme (either word initial, word final, or vowel) occurring in that word. In Subtest VIII an auditory stimulus is dictated; after a 5-second delay the student is asked to match the auditory memory with a visual symbol. Subtest IX is a comprehension task where the students listen to a paragraph read by the examiner and then write what they remember. There is a 10-minute time limit for this task. In Subtest X the student is asked to write down a word after it is dictated.

The documentation accompanying the test provides the examiner with adequate information to administer and score the test. The description of the subtests is sufficient. Various categories of errors are illustrated including reversals, transpositions, insertions, omissions, inversions, substitutions, and poor formations. A discussion of self-corrections and other performance factors noted during scoring is present.

There are several significant problems with the SCLS. First, there is insufficient rationale proposed for the content of the test. The manual would be significantly improved by the addition of a section which describes the model of language processing used to derive the 10 subtests.

Second, there are questions concerning the interpretation of test scores. For example, the manual does not indicate when a score is to be considered normal or abnormal. Also, there are no data describing normal test performance and the author states that "no attempt has been made to establish standardized norms" (p. 4). Finally, although the manual states that the test score should be interpreted in relationship to other information such as family history, intelligence, grade-level achievement, and opportunities for learning, the manual does not clearly indicate how this additional information is to be used when interpreting the test results.

Third, the manual lacks information on test reliability. There is no information on the internal consistency of test items, on the reliability of scoring procedures, and on test-retest consistency. The lack of information on consistency of scoring across examiners is a significant omission given the judgement involved in scoring many of the subtests.

Fourth, the manual lacks information on test validity. There are no reports of concurrent, predictive, or construct validity.

In conclusion, the documentation accompanying the test provides the examiner with adequate information to administer and score the test. However, the test has significant weaknesses including: (*a*) insufficient rationale for the content of the test, (*b*) inadequate guidelines for interpretation of test scores, (*c*) no information on normal test performance, (*d*) no information on test reliability and, (*e*) no information on test validity. I would not recommend this test because of the omission of important psychometric information.

[357]

Slosson Articulation, Language Test with Phonology.

Purpose: Measures the communicative competence of a child by combining into a single score the assessment of articulation, phonology and language.
Population: Ages 3-0 to 5-11.
Publication Date: 1986.
Acronym: SALT-P.
Scores, 4: Consonants + Vowels/Diphthongs, Phonological Processes, Language Errors, Composite Score.
Administration: Individual.
Price Data, 1992: $50 per complete kit; $14 per examiner's manual (12 pages); $20 per 50 scoring forms; $18 per test book/picture plates; $70 per video tape.
Time: (7–10) minutes.
Comments: Instructional video tape with taped administration of test available.
Author: Wilma Jean Tade.
Publisher: Slosson Educational Publications, Inc.

Review of the Slosson Articulation, Language Test with Phonology by CLINTON W. BENNETT, Professor of Speech Pathology and Audiology, James Madison University, Harrisonburg, VA:

The Slosson Articulation, Language Test with Phonology (SALT-P) is a criterion-based screening test for children ages 3:0–5:11 who are "normal or at risk in developing adequate communication" (manual, p. 1). The first five picture plates (eight test items) are prescreening probes (and are not used in the final composite cutoff score) to identify potential language processing and formulation problems. The remaining picture plates evaluate articulation of 22 word-initial consonants, 18 final consonants, 10 consonant clusters, and 8 vowels/diphthongs; 82 potential phonological process errors; and 31 expressive/receptive language concepts. Each plate has punch-holes so with the response form underneath the response for each item is easily recorded although initially cumbersome. Testing time is 7–10 minutes.

The cutoff scores for both the prescreening probes and the screening test are subjective and are not explained. The normative population was only 289 children (76% Anglos, 24% minorities) from Fort Worth, Texas and the minority children performed significantly poorer ($p<.03$) than whites, although this is not discussed in the manual. Norms for individual test items are dated (e.g., articulation from Templin, 1957) and from other tests (Vocabulary Comprehension Scale and Preschool Language Scale) and the author's experience.

Validity is mentioned only in terms of cautions to the user relating to "examinee related factors which affect how valid" (p. 1) the test score truly is. Content, construct, and concurrent validity are not addressed.

Overall reliability was calculated using a linear combination of the three subscales, which indicated that composite scores increased with increasing age. Interjudge reliability was assessed only for two groups (speech pathologists and nonprofessionals) and the resultant correlation was .85. Test-retest reliability is not reported.

The pictures are black and white with poor visual contrasts; most are of two white children and one picture (fish) is upside down.

Phonological processes are broadly defined. Consonant Cluster Reduction is used for both reduction and cluster deletion (typically termed CCR and CCD); fronting errors are counted only in context of back vowels (with no explanation); and stopping (a non-stop > stop) is a much broader process than most clinicians use.

The SALT-P does not meet accepted psychometric standards and a number of pass/fail screening tests offer more reliable and valid measures of articulatory, phonologic, and linguistic functioning.

Review of the Slosson Articulation, Language Test with Phonology by ROBERT A. REINEKE, Visiting Associate Professor of Curriculum and Instruction, University of Nebraska-Lincoln, Lincoln, NE, and VICKI GRATOPP, Speech Pathologist, Lincoln Public Schools, Lincoln, NE:

The Slosson Articulation, Language Test with Phonology (SALT-P) consists of a test booklet, test manual, and instructional video tape (not reviewed). This norm-referenced screening test is intended to assess communication skills, specifically articulation, phonology, and language in children aged 3 years to 5 years 11 months. A composite score is derived that provides an index of communication proficiency. The author states that the test should not be used for differential screening or diagnosis.

Testing begins with eight prescreening items designed to identify children who might be at risk in terms of adequate language processing and formulation skills. According to the author, failure to reach a designated cutoff score on the prescreening portion should result in the child being referred for a more complete speech and language evaluation. In instances where the child is successful in passing the prescreening cut score, the remaining items are presented. In cases where the entire battery is used, separate composite score ranges are provided for children aged 3, 4, and 5 that indicate passing or "borderline" scores along with a cut score to refer children for further testing. Administration time is stated as being between 7 and 10 minutes.

The test offers a single format for screening articulation, language, and phonology, and is fairly simple to score. Some questions arose during administration of the test to a small sample of five children, including difficulty in moving through the protocol (aligning the scoring key to the test booklet), some pictures in the test booklet did not appear to stimulate interest on the part of examinees, and target responses were sometimes difficult to elicit from younger children, particularly 3-year-olds.

The normative sample consisted of 289 children ranging in age from 3 years to 5 years 11 months. Children aged 3, 4, and 5 were similarly represented and both male and female children were included in the norming sample. Seventy-six percent were "anglos" and 24% were minorities. Results based on the norm group clearly demonstrated that average composite scores were age related. Specific validation information beyond that tied to the author's language constructs was not described. Interrater reliability was demonstrated by comparing scores generated by professional speech pathologists with those given by nonprofessionals (undergraduate students in speech-related fields). The relatively high correlation of .85 suggests that nonprofessionals may be trained to administer the test. Information about the agreement among the professionals who administered the test was not available. Scale reliabilities for the three subscales, based on odd-even split half (Articulation -.95; Phonology -.97; Language .92) and coefficient alpha (Articulation -.95; Phonology .93; Language .90) were acceptable.

The SALT-P appears to have merit as a screening device for identifying children who might benefit from more extensive speech and language evaluation. Its simple scoring procedure and straightforward, although somewhat mechanically cumbersome, administration protocol may offer an efficient tool to screen large numbers of children for possible further language testing. To the extent that the test validity measures actual language and speech behaviors of interest to the investigator and results in accurate screening, the SALT-P represents a potentially useful and efficient tool.

[358]

Slosson Intelligence Test [1991 Edition].

Purpose: Designed for use as a "quick estimate of general verbal cognitive ability."
Population: Ages 4-0 and over.
Publication Dates: 1961–91.
Acronym: SIT-R.
Scores: Total score only.
Administration: Individual.
Price Data, 1992: $57 per complete kit including 50 test forms, manual ('91, 45 pages), and norms tables/technical manual ('91, 39 pages); $16 per 50 test forms; $21 per norms tables/technical manual; $23 per manual.
Time: (10–20) minutes.
Authors: Richard L. Slosson, Charles L. Nicholson (revision), and Terry H. Hibpshman (revision).
Publisher: Slosson Educational Publications, Inc.
Cross References: See T4:2482 (43 references); for reviews of an earlier edition by Thomas Oakland and William M. Reynolds, see 9:1142 (11 references); see also T3:2217 (82 references), 8:227 (62 references), and T2:524 (12 references); for reviews by Philip Himelstein and Jane V. Hunt, see 7:424 (31 references).

TEST REFERENCES

1. Johns, J. L. (1989). Diagnostic insights for at-risk readers with the Slosson Intelligence Test. *Journal of Reading, 33*, 187-192.

2. Kibby, M. W. (1989). Teaching sight vocabulary with and without context before silent reading: A field test of the "Focus of Attention" hypothesis. *Journal of Reading Behavior, 21*, 261-278.

3. Mudre, L. H., & McCormick, S. (1989). Effects of meaning-focused cues in underachieving readers' context use, self-corrections, and literal comprehension. *Reading Research Quarterly, 24*, 89-113.

4. Sowell, E. J., Zeigler, A. J., Bergwall, L., & Cartwright, R. M. (1990). Identification and description of mathematically gifted students: A review of empirical research. *Gifted Child Quarterly, 34*, 147-154.

5. Dave, C. A. (1992). Effects of linear vestibular stimulation on body-rocking behavior in adults with profound mental retardation. *The American Journal of Occupational Therapy, 46*, 910-915.

6. Graham, S., Macarthur, C., Schwartz, S., & Page-Voth, V. (1992). Improving the compositions of students with learning disabilities using a strategy involving product and process goal setting. *Exceptional Children, 58*, 322-334.

7. Callahan, C. M., Lundberg, A. C., & Hunsaker, S. L. (1993). The development of the Scale for the Evaluation of Gifted Identification Instruments (SEGII). *Gifted Child Quarterly, 37*, 133-140.

8. Fuchs-Beauchamp, K. D., Karnes, M. B., & Johnson, L. J. (1993). Creativity and intelligence in preschoolers. *Gifted Child Quarterly, 37*, 113-117.

9. Macmann, G. M., & Barnett, D. W. (1993). Reliability of psychiatric and psychological diagnoses of mental retardation severity: Judgements under naturally occurring conditions. *American Journal on Mental Retardation, 97*, 559-567.

10. May, D. C., & Kundert, D. K. (1993). Pre-first placements: How common and how informed? *Psychology in the Schools, 30*, 161-167.

11. McBurnett, K., Harris, S. M., Swanson, J. M., Pfiffner, L. J., Tamm, L., & Freeland, D. (1993). Neuropsychological and psychophysiological differentiation of inattention/overactivity and aggression/defiance symptom groups. *Journal of Clinical Child Psychology, 22*, 165-171.

12. Ott, D. A., & Lyman, R. D. (1993). Automatic and effortful memory in children exhibiting attention-deficit hyperactivity disorder. *Journal of Clinical Child Psychology, 22*, 420-427.

13. Uhry, J. K., & Shepherd, M. J. (1993). Segmentation/spelling instruction as part of a first-grade reading program: Effects on several measures of reading. *Reading Research Quarterly, 28*, 219-233.

14. Wherry, J. N., Paal, N., Jolly, J. B., Adam, B., Holloway, C., Everett, B., & Vaught, L. (1993). Concurrent and discriminant validity of the Gordon Diagnostic System: A preliminary study. *Psychology in the Schools, 30*, 29-36.

15. Eaves, R. C., Williams, P., Winchester, K., & Darch, C. (1994). Using teacher judgement and IQ to estimate reading and mathematics achievement in a remedial-reading program. *Psychology in the Schools, 31*, 261-272.

16. Lysaker, P., & Bell, M. (1995). Work rehabilitation and improvements in insight in schizophrenia. *The Journal of Nervous and Mental Disease, 183*, 103-106.

Review of the Slosson Intelligence Test [1991 Edition] by RANDY W. KAMPHAUS, Associate Professor of

Educational Psychology, University of Georgia, Athens, GA:

The expressed purpose of the Slosson Intelligence Test [1991 Edition] (SIT-R) is to serve as "a quick estimate of general verbal cognitive ability" or "index of verbal intelligence" (manual, p. 1). The manual presents appropriate cautions about interpretation of the SIT-R as a screening measure, suggesting at several points that follow-up assessment is necessary to corroborate SIT-R results. The SIT-R may also be used as a second measure of intelligence.

The goals of this test revision were to (*a*) include a more even distribution of items from various content domains, (*b*) update the language used in items, (*c*) provide an updated norm sample, (*d*) liberalize scoring guidelines to give credit for English or metric measures, and (*e*) discard the term "Intelligence Quotient (IQ)" in favor of "Total Standard Score (TSS)." The degree to which these changes are advantages or disadvantages and other characteristics of the SIT-R will be addressed next.

The SIT-R has numerous advantages over its progenitor but there remains ample room for improvement. Among the strengths of this version are a more comprehensive manual, updated item pool, better norming, ease of administration and scoring, adequate reliability and concurrent validity data with the Wechsler Intelligence Scale for Children—Revised (WISC-R), and lack of an "IQ" score. Weaknesses in this edition include a lack of detail in the manual, lack of evidence of match of the norming to U.S. Census statistics, dependence on a score classification scheme that may encourage misuse, and dependence on English language fluency.

The SIT-R is extremely easy to administer and score. The use of a small number of verbal item types with a dichotomous item scoring system makes the measure intuitive to use. The SIT-R remains loyal to the original work of Binet (Kamphaus, 1993) by utilizing a variety of item types, ranging from recall of digits to quantitative items, that are ordered by difficulty. This administration format differs from that of the Wechsler tradition of using subtests. The stated administration time of 10 to 30 minutes is likely realistic.

The use of the back of the record form for some drawing items seems ill advised as it invites the older examinee to turn the page over and view his or her own scores. Similarly, although there are some advised starting points for various age groups, these are not marked on the record form. The record form could also benefit from more space to record responses and other examiner notes. The record form, for the most part, is easy to use.

Although the SIT-R manuals, one for administration and scoring and one for norm tables and technical data, contain many important topics they are substandard. The first manual contains only about 10 pages of relevant copy and the second manual 22. The remaining pages of each manual are devoted to norm tables and lists of items. The second manual reports only one concurrent validity study with the WISC-R and one with the WAIS-R (Wechsler Adult Intelligence Scale—Revised). Given that there are currently many alternatives to the WISC-R, studies of the relationship of the SIT-R to the Stanford-Binet Intelligence Scale, Fourth Edition (T4:2553) and the Kaufman Assessment Battery for Children (T4:1343) would seem to be central to such a manual. Information on content validity and the use of item response theory to gauge the distribution of item difficulty is welcome.

The norming of the SIT-R and scaling procedures are poorly described. Because the norm-referenced scores for the SIT-R are offered separately by age group, the representation of the norm sample by age, gender, race/ethnicity, and parental education/occupation should be reported by age group. The sample does significantly underrepresent cultural minorities for the total sample and it would be informative to see if this problem is specific to one or several age groups. The manual does report that "goodness-of-fit" tests were used to test for differences in educational level by age group and that no differences were found. The results of these analyses, however, were not reported.

The scaling procedures are not described adequately enough to determine how the norms were articulated across age groups. There is no indication of the smoothing method used or whether or not one was used to produce reasonable distributions of scores from age to age. Another curiosity is the decision to not offer separate age group norms above age 18. The last entry in the norm table simply reads "18+." According to the reliability data presented on page 7 of the second manual there were 118 cases at ages 35 through 44.9 and 76 cases at age 13. Norms were developed separately for the 12-year-olds but not for the older age group. There may be a very good reason for not showing an appreciation of adult development in the norms but it is not made clear in the manual.

The "Slosson Classification Chart" for the Total Standard Score may encourage misuse of scores. This interpretive chart seems at odds with the cautions against overinterpretation given elsewhere in the manual. Most disconcerting about this table is that it equates low scores with various levels of mental retardation. This classification system suggests that the TSS can be used to diagnose mental retardation or to confirm mental retardation. This chart may lead diagnosticians, or in this case teachers, to make the diagnosis of mental retardation without the assessment of adaptive behavior. The history of mental retardation diagnosis is fraught with problems that have resulted from elevating intelligence tests to preeminence over adaptive behavior measures even though the latter are central to all major diagnostic systems (Kamphaus, 1993). Use of this chart by the diagnostically unsophisticated could lead to the diagnosis of syndromes such as mental retardation and giftedness based solely on intelligence test scores. This is clearly an antiquated practice.

Other dated material is included in the percentile chart where the term "IQ" is used. The use of this term seems incongruous with other parts of the manual where the TSS terminology is favored.

A final concern regarding the SIT-R is its applicability in an increasingly multicultural society. Unlike other new screeners such as the Kaufman Brief Intelligence Test (K-BIT; Kaufman & Kaufman, 1990; 205) the SIT-R may not be used to screen for intellectual problems using less verbal item types. The SIT-R verbal item types are also less practical for the assessment of the undereducated.

In summary, the SIT-R has numerous strengths to recommend its use including a more comprehensive manual than previously included, an updated item pool, improved norming, ease of administration and scoring, adequate reliability and concurrent validity data with the WISC-R, and lack of use of the "IQ" score. Some of the more disconcerting weaknesses include limited evidence of concurrent validity, lack of evidence of a match of the norming to U.S. Census statistics, dependence on a classification system for total scores that may encourage misuse, and excessive dependence on English language fluency. Although the SIT-R is not fatally flawed as a screener there are many good alternatives available with better psychometric properties. Short forms of comprehensive intelligence test batteries can boast larger and better described norming samples that are a better fit to U.S. Census Bureau statistics. The K-BIT possesses strong evidence of concurrent validity and a less verbal screener. The availability of these latter alternatives suggests that for many users of intelligence screeners the SIT-R will have to be supported by a continuing stream of supportive research investigations to become a viable candidate for widespread use. At the time of this review, better alternatives than the SIT-R are readily available.

REVIEWER'S REFERENCES

Kaufman, A. S., & Kaufman, N. L. (1990). Kaufman Brief Intelligence Test. Circle Pines, MN: American Guidance Service.

Kamphaus, R. W. (1993). *Clinical assessment of children's intelligence: A handbook for professional practice*. Boston: Allyn & Bacon.

Review of the Slosson Intelligence Test [1991 Edition] by T. STEUART WATSON, Assistant Professor of Educational Psychology, Mississippi State University, Starkville, MS:

PURPOSE AND RATIONALE. The Slosson Intelligence Test [1991 Edition] (SIT-R) is primarily intended to be a brief screening measure of verbal crystallized intelligence. It is used less frequently to proffer tentative diagnoses and to confirm the results of other tests. The authors caution the SIT-R is measuring only verbal crystallized intelligence and inferences regarding ability in other intellectual domains (e.g., abstract/visual reasoning) are not supported.

Previous editions of the Slosson Intelligence Test were designed using the Stanford-Binet as a theoretical model. The 1991 revision does not model any one test as it purports to combine the components of several intellectual theories into one overarching framework. The theories of intelligence espoused by Wechsler, Thorndike, Hagen, Sattler, Guilford, Cattell, Jensen, and Sternberg are briefly reviewed in the technical manual and serve as the basis for the SIT-R.

TEST CONTENT. The test contains 187 untimed items assessing the cognitive domains of vocabulary, general information, similarities and differences, comprehension, quantitative ability, and auditory memory. More than half of the items from the old Slosson (SIT) remain on this edition. Content validity is said to exist because similar items are found on other major tests of intelligence and the cognitive aptitudes measured have a long and proven history. Item arrangement on the SIT-R represents a significant deviation from the SIT in that items are now arranged in ascending order of difficulty as opposed to by age ranges.

Conceptually, all items except those purportedly measuring auditory memory fall into Cattell's crystallized intelligence domain. Crystallized intelligence is said to be a product of native ability, culture, and life experiences, and reflective of individuals' achievements in their culture.

STANDARDIZATION AND NORMS. The non-random standardization sample of the SIT-R represents a noticeable improvement over that of the SIT. The sample of 1,854 subjects approximates the percentages found in the United States in terms of geographic region, occupational category, educational level, gender, and race. Minorities are underrepresented in the standardization sample as are those living in areas with populations below 5,000 and above 500,000. Most of the data were drawn from subjects residing in areas with a population between 5,000 and 100,000. This section of the technical manual could be improved by presenting stratified data instead of percentages within nominal categories and by indicating the number of subjects tested at each age level.

Despite its vast improvement in the area of standardization, serious questions remain regarding the appropriateness of using this test with persons who score at the extremes of the distribution and with those who evidence various types of handicaps. In addition, the procedure used to select the sample (examiners selecting subjects based on age only and the authors selecting subjects from that pool to match certain demographic characteristics) represents an unorthodox (semi-incidental) means to obtain normative data.

The SIT-R has a mean total standard score (TSS) of 100 and a standard deviation of 16. Raw scores are easily converted to total standard scores by age. Total standard scores may then be converted to standard scores on the Wechsler Scale (presumably the verbal scale, although not specifically stated), College Entrance Examination Board (CEEB), and General Aptitude Test Battery (GATB). One can also derive *z* scores, *T* scores, NCEs, stanines, and percentiles from the total standard score. Separate scores are not computed for each of the domains (e.g., vocabulary, comprehension).

A less desirable option is to convert raw scores to Mean Age Equivalents (MAE). The authors state in the technical manual that although MAE scores have "serious theoretical problems and can produce misleading results" (p. 22), they are provided anyway because some educational systems require the use of such scores. A full paragraph in the administration manual is devoted to explaining MAE scores. Doing so, in my opinion, has no virtue and violates the authors' and test publisher's ethical responsibility to provide interpretive data that have a sound theoretical and empirical basis. It also reinforces the continued use and misinterpretation of meaningless test data.

ADMINISTRATION AND SCORING. The age range for the test is 4 years to 18+ years. Administration of the SIT-R is simple and straightforward and requires approximately 10 to 30 minutes. All of the items are presented in a question-and-answer format. Six items require a visual stimulus on the reverse side of the scoring protocol. Basals and ceilings are established by 10 successive correct and incorrect responses, respectively. Responses are scored dichotomously on a one-page protocol. The raw score is computed by adding the highest item in the basal to the number of correct responses after the basal.

RELIABILITY. Kuder-Richardson 20 reliability coefficients by age level range from .88 to .97, indicating a high degree of interitem consistency. Test-retest reliability is reported to be .96, based on a weak sample size of 41 and a one-week administration interval. Split-half reliability, calculated using the Spearman-Brown correction and the Rulon procedure, was .97 for the entire sample.

Overall, the reported reliabilities are sufficient. However, the manual does not explain the reliabilities clearly nor does it give substantial explanations of what they mean for the test consumer. Test-retest reliability could be enhanced by including studies with larger sample sizes and longer administration intervals.

VALIDITY. Concurrent criterion-related validity is based on correlations between the SIT-R total standard score and WAIS-R (Wechsler Adult Intelligence Scale—Revised) and WISC-R (Wechsler Intelligence Scale for Children—Revised) IQs. In a study of 10 subjects, significant correlations were found between TSS and three IQ scores on the WAIS-R. Comparisons with the WISC-R were made utilizing 234 subjects between the ages of 6 and 16. At each of four age levels (6–8, 9–11, 12–14, and 15–16) the TSS correlated significantly with each of the WISC-R IQs.

Clearly, it cannot be said unequivocally that the SIT-R is measuring only verbal crystallized intelligence. Indeed, from the limited validity studies reported, it seems it is measuring a general intelligence factor, or *g*. Many more validity studies should be performed with larger samples and broader populations before even tentative conclusions can be made regarding what this test is actually measuring.

Test bias is a complex and pivotal issue. The authors devote a third of a page to treatment of test bias which does not adequately address the most salient features of this subject. Indeed, it appears from the data tendered, the authors are concluding that the absence of mean raw score differences for ethnicity or gender is sufficient to warrant this judgment. One must also question the appropriateness of analyzing raw scores instead of mean standard scores. When analyzing individual test items using the Rasch model (the most common latent trait model), raw scores are deemed useless for further analysis.

The most portentous information regarding test bias is found in the section on Latent Trait Analysis where discussions on slope and intercept bias and error of estimate are presented. Pairwise comparisons and regression analyses on raw scores did not detect slope or intercept biases for any pair of four ethnic subpopulations or gender.

One disturbing point is the authors' explanation that use of latent trait analysis precludes gaining a representative sample of the population to produce meaningful norms. Despite the assumptions regarding Latent Trait Analysis, there is no substitute for gathering representative data during the normative process when designing a test for use with a variety of populations.

SUMMARY. Overall, the SIT-R is much improved over the original and updated versions. However, a number of problems continue to plague this instrument. The first issue is the selection procedure used to obtain normative data. Subjects were first tested and then chosen for inclusion into the sample based on their demographic characteristics. Noticeably lacking in the data on the normative sample are the numbers of individuals with disabilities tested during standardization. Omitting the percentage of students with various disabilities included in the sample precludes its use with that population, despite the manual's suggestions for testing such individuals.

The second difficulty with the SIT-R is the lack of adequate reliability and validity data. The data that are presented come from studies with meager sample sizes, restricted populations, and do not wholly support the theoretical basis upon which the test was designed.

A third issue concerns the discrepancies between what the authors acknowledge as good practice and what they discuss and recommend in the manuals. Besides use of the Mental Age Equivalent discussed earlier, the authors provide recommendations for testing individuals with handicaps. On the same page, however, they caution that administering the test to subjects not represented in the normative sample "may yield invalid scores and lead to erroneous interpretations" (p. 9).

Like its predecessor, the SIT-R may be used cautiously as a preliminary screening device to crudely estimate overall IQ. If one's goal is to predict IQ on the Wechsler scales, a more valid and reliable procedure is to use the dyads, triads, or quatrads from the Wechslers, for which psychometric properties are more robust.

[359]

Slosson Oral Reading Test [Revised].

Purpose: Designed as a "quick estimate to target word recognition levels for children and adults."
Population: Preschool–adult.
Publication Dates: 1963–90.
Acronym: SORT-R.
Scores: Total score only.
Administration: Individual.
Price Data, 1992: $32 per complete kit; $14 per manual ('90, 38 pages); $16 per 50 score sheets; $7 per bound word lists; $3 per large print word lists.
Special Editions: Large print edition available for individuals with visual handicaps.
Time: (3–5) minutes.
Comments: Grade equivalent (GE) and age equivalent (AE) scores are also available.
Authors: Richard L. Slosson and Charles L. Nicholson.
Publisher: Slosson Educational Publications, Inc.
Cross References: See T3:2218 (15 references), T2:1688 (5 references), and 6:844.

TEST REFERENCES

1. Ehr, L. C., & Sweet, J. (1991). Fingerpoint-reading of memorized text: What enables beginners to process the print? *Reading Research Quarterly, 26*, 442-462.

2. Reutzel, D. R., & Fawson, P. (1991). Literature webbing predictable books: A prediction strategy that helps below-average, first-grade readers. *Reading Research and Instruction, 30*(4), 20-29.

3. Ehri, L. C., & Robbins, C. (1992). Beginners need some decoding skill to read words by analogy. *Reading Research Quarterly, 27*, 13-26.

4. Murphy, P. W., Davis, T. C., Long, S. W., Jackson, R. H., & Decker, B. C. (1993). Rapid estimate of adult literacy in medicine (REALM): A quick reading test for patients. *Journal of Reading, 37*, 124-130.

Review of the Slosson Oral Reading Test [Revised] by STEVEN R. SHAW, Assistant Professor of Psychology, Illinois State University, Normal, IL, and MARK E. SWERDLIK, Professor of Psychology, Illinois State University, Normal, IL:

The Slosson Oral Reading Test [Revised] (SORT-R) represents a revision of the original Slosson Oral Reading Test published in 1963. The SORT-R is designed to assess a subject's "level of oral word recognition, word calling or reading level" (p. 9). This instrument is not a diagnostic measure nor does it measure all aspects of reading such as word knowledge and comprehension. It is a "quick screening test to determine a student's reading level." The author also suggests the SORT-R may be used to assess a student's progress, determine a student's grade level in reading, and to determine if a student is in need of further diagnostic assessment. However, the primary use of the SORT-R is as a screening instrument.

The test is composed of 200 words arranged in ascending order of difficulty. The words are organized into 10 groups of 20 words each. Each group represented approximate grade levels, ranging from preschool to 9–12 grades. The SORT-R is designed for use with subjects from age 4 and above.

ADMINISTRATION AND SCORING. A basal level is attained when a subject can pronounce all 20 words in a group. A ceiling is reached when none of the 20 words in a group can be pronounced correctly. Subjects are allowed 5 seconds to pronounce a word. The 5-second limit is waived if the subject has a speech defect (e.g., stuttering) or visual impairment. Criteria for determining errors are provided. The correct pronunciations and several examples of incorrect pronunciation are provided. Examiner discretion is advised if the subject has an articulation difficulty or regional accent. The manual indicates that pronunciations of word endings and tenses must be pronounced in order for a word to be scored as correct. However, in a different section of the manual, the author suggests not counting words as errors if the pronunciation only slightly changes the meaning of a word such as sudden for suddenly, or rivers for river.

The test materials are attractive and easy to read for both examiner and examinee. For convenience, basic administration and scoring procedures are printed on each test protocol. Raw scores, grade and age equivalents, percentile rank, standard scores (including *t*-scores and normal curve equivalents), and confidence levels can also be determined and recorded directly on the protocol. Despite the limitations of grade equivalents, the author stresses the value of this scoring convention. Moreover, the grade equivalents in the tables are approximations and interpolation is required for some ages.

NORMATIVE DATA. The SORT-R was co-normed with the Slosson Intelligence Test. The sample included 1,331 subjects, ranging from preschool to adults. The author suggests the sample represents the U.S. population. However, close inspection reveals that large differences exist between sample and census data on geographic location and occupational status. There were also large differences in the number of subjects at different age levels. The manual author indicates that subjects were included from "special classes ranging from the retarded to gifted, learning disabled and regular" (p. 7). Yet, no data on special populations were provided. There is a list of participating school districts, but no demographic information about them or how they were selected is given. Thus, it is difficult to determine to whom these norms would be applicable.

RELIABILITY. Internal consistency (Spearman-Brown Split Half, Rulon, and Kuder-Richardson) and test-retest stability all yield coefficients above .95. Interestingly, the highest reliabilities were found in the youngest age groups. All reliability data were collected on the standardization sample with no separate reliability studies reported in the manual. The number of subjects in the test-retest study was only 16 and no age data were provided. The high reliability can be attributed to the SORT-R containing a large number of items, a good sampling of test items, and test specificity as only oral reading is being measured. Based on the data reported in the manual, the SORT-R appears to have satisfactory reliability.

CONTENT VALIDITY. The words on the SORT-R are the same as on the SORT. Words were drawn from the Dolch reading list and "other reading lists" (manual, p. 1), tests of reading, and reading lists in textbooks at selected grade levels. All words were reviewed by reading experts, textbook authors, and compared to various curriculum guides. Words were selected to reflect a steady progress in reading difficulty from preschool to high school level. Based on the Slosson norms, each word represents one-half month progress. The author notes that the added length of word lists improves the content validity of the test. However, without knowing the specifics regarding the origin of the word lists one cannot assume this to be true.

CONSTRUCT/CRITERION. The SORT-R has been administered concurrently with several tests of reading recognition and reading comprehension. The Woodcock-Johnson Test of Achievement (WJTA)—Letter Word Identification and the Peabody Individual Achievement Test (PIAT)—Reading Comprehension both correlate over .90 with the SORT-R. Passage Comprehension from the WJTA and Reading Comprehension from the PIAT correlate with the SORT-R .68 and .83, respectively. The subjects used in these validity studies were not described. The criterion instruments used in these studies are outdated forms of tests that have revised versions. No evidence is presented to support the construct of the SORT-R other than correlations with reading tests that have also been criticized for lack of supporting construct validity. The SORT-R is also correlated highly (.87) with the Slosson Intelligence Test—Revised. This may indicate the two tests do not assess independent constructs. In addition, no validity data supporting the uses of the SORT-R proposed by the author are presented.

SUMMARY. The SORT-R should only be used for initial screening or research purposes. It is a quick test that is easy to administer and score. Although the SORT-R has adequate reliability, the test has limited relevance to school-based instruction. The content and construct validity of the SORT-R is questionable. Estimating reading progress during the school year with a test of word calling appears inappropriate. If detailed diagnostic information is required, informal reading inventories or normative instruments such as the Stanford Diagnostic Reading Battery (T4:2555), the Gray Oral Reading Test (166), and/or curriculum-based assessment are better choices than the SORT-R. Thus, the SORT-R fills a very small niche in reading assessment. This niche may be filled better with teacher's judgment of a student's reading ability.

Review of the Slosson Oral Reading Test [Revised] by CAROL E. WESTBY, Senior Research Associate, Training and Technical Assistance Unit, University of New Mexico Medical School, Albuquerque, NM:

The Slosson Oral Reading Test [Revised] (SORT-R) is a restandardization of the Slosson Oral Reading Test that was originally published in 1963. The purpose of the SORT-R is to provide a quick estimate of a person's oral word recognition or "word calling" level. It takes about 3 minutes to give and score. The SORT-R is not intended to be a diagnostic instrument or to measure reading comprehension. The SORT-R consist of 10 lists of 20 words each presented in a spiral-bound book. There are separate lists for preprimer through grade 8 levels and a list for 9th through 12th grade. Words were chosen from a variety of reading lists and textbooks at selected grade levels so that they represent a steady progression of difficulty from the preprimer to high school level. Words were not chosen according to their phonic characteristics, and hence, the SORT-R cannot be used to determine a person's knowledge of grapheme/phoneme relationships. The print size of the lists reflects the print size in school textbooks. The grades K–4 word lists are in 14-point print and the grades 5–12 lists are in 10-point print. A single-page score sheet has all the lists on the front.

Scoring is based on total number read correctly. Words are considered read incorrectly if the reader pronounces them incorrectly, takes longer than 5 seconds to read them, changes their form (hides/hide), or omits reading them. The starting or basal list is the list at which the person reads all words correctly; the ceiling list is the list at which the person does not read any of the words correctly. The back of the score sheet contains the test directions, space for recording demographic information (name, age, school, examiner), and test results.

The SORT-R has retained the same lists as the original SORT, but contains updated norms as well as new scoring methodologies such as: age and grade equivalencies and standard scores, *T*-scores, and stanines by age and grade. The standardization sample consisted of 1,331 individuals from preschool to adult from all sections of the United States. Percentages of the SORT-R sample reflect the gender and racial percentages of the total U.S. population. In addition, the educational level of parents of students in the sample matched the percentage of persons at various educational levels in the general U.S. population.

The SORT-R manual authors provide information on construct, content, and concurrent validity and on split-half and test-retest reliability. The large number of words on the SORT-R (200) contributes to both good content validity and reliability. The SORT-R shows high concurrent validity coefficients (correlations $r = .90$) with the letter identification subtest of the Woodcock-Johnson Tests of Achievement and the reading recognition subtest of the Peabody Individual Achievement Test. Split-half reliability and test-retest after 1 week resulted in correlations of .98. The SORT-R provides a valid and highly reliable means for quickly determining a person's word recognition level.

[360]

Slosson Test of Reading Readiness.

Purpose: "Designed to identify children who are at risk of failure in programs of formal reading instruction."
Population: Latter kindergarten–grade 1.
Publication Date: 1991.
Acronym: STRR.
Scores, 12: Visual Skills (Recognition of Capital Letters, Recognition of Lower Case Letters, Matching Capital and Lower Case Letters, Visual Discrimination-Matching Word Forms, Total), Auditory Skills (Auditory Discrimination-Rhyming Words, Auditory Discrimination and Memory—Recognition of Beginning Sounds, Total), Cognitive Skills (Sequencing, Opposites, Total), Total Inventory.
Administration: Individual.
Price Data, 1992: $48 per complete kit; $18 per manual (24 pages); $12 per test stimulus booklet; $16 per 50 scoring booklets; $6 per 50 letter to parent.
Time: (15) minutes.
Authors: Leslie Anne Perry and Gary J. Vitali.
Publisher: Slosson Educational Publications, Inc.

Review of the Slosson Test of Reading Readiness by GERALD S. HANNA, Professor of Educational Psychology and Measurement, Kansas State University, Manhattan, KS:

The Slosson Test of Reading Readiness (STRR) is an individually administered screening test to identify pupils who are at risk of having difficulty if placed in formal reading instruction. The content seems conventional and appropriate for a reading readiness test.

SCORING. Manual authors state that extensive training of examiners is not required to administer the test. This reviewer finds the administration and scoring instructions to be inadequately detailed, even for professionals and especially for paraprofessionals. For example, in the Sequencing subtest, which consists of a single set of three pictures to be arranged in order, the examiner is not instructed whether to award credit if the pictures are correctly sequenced in a right-to-left order or whether to ask, "which comes first?" Moreover, the directions to the child address the order in which the pictures are put down, rather than arranging them into the proper sequence. Therefore, should credit be denied if the child achieves a correct arrangement by first placing the middle picture in the middle and then correctly sequencing the other two?

In the Opposites subtest, the only keyed answer to "clean" is "dirty"; would "unclean" or "filthy" merit no credit? The only key to "empty" (with no indication whether it is an adjective or a verb) is "full"; isn't "fill" just as correct? If the child answered "fill," should one (*a*) give credit, (*b*) count the response wrong, or (*c*) ask for another response? The only key to "open" is "close." Is "closed" really wrong? The subjectivity introduced into the scoring by the inadequate directions and key would be expected to erode both reliability and validity.

Scoring is complicated by the fact that items in the various subtests are counted different amounts; the items in two subtests count one-half point each, the questions in most subtests count one point each, and the items in two subtests count three points each. These differences complicate scoring and may increase the frequency of scoring errors.

RELIABILITY. With no description whatever of the sample—in size, demographics, or score means and standard deviations—the manual authors report K-R 20 reliabilities of.96, .85, .74, and .96, respectively, for the Visual Subtest Quotient, the Auditory Subtest Quotient, the Cognitive Subtest Quotient, and of the Total Test. (The variables of which these scores are "quotients" is not at all clear.)

Insofar as a condition necessary for the use of K-R 20 is the equal weight of all test items (Cronbach, 1990, p. 203), the K-R 20 of the total score cannot be computed, given that some subtests' items count one-half point, some count one point, and some count three points. Moreover, the nonindependence among the tasks of sequencing the three pictures in the Sequencing Subtest constitutes another violation of the assumptions of K-R 20 (see Cronbach, 1990, p. 205).

Although the manual authors misdefine reliability as "the extent the items within the test measure a common factor" (manual, p. 4), they report test-retest reliability coefficients over a period of one week for an undescribed sample of 70 pupils. Readers are not informed whether the same examiner tested children on the two occasions; if so, the results do not reflect the reduction of reliability to be expected from differences among examiners. The findings of this study corresponding to those above are reported to be .75, .81, .49, and .87.

Because the characteristics of the reliability samples—particularly their variability—are not reported, none of the reliability findings are meaningful. The data supplied in the manual fail to meet widely recognized professional standards such as those of primary Standard 2.2 of *Standards for Educational and Psychological Testing* (American Education Research Association, American Psychological Association, & National Council on Measurement in Education, 1985).

VALIDITY. Criterion-related validity data are presented for five major reading tests. The manual authors correctly assert the basis for judging a test such as the STRR "is its ability to *predict* what will happen *in the future*" (manual, p. 5) [italics added]. Yet there is no indication concerning how much time elapsed between administration of the STRR and administration of the achievement test used for criterion-related validation "following reading instruction" (manual, p. 5). Other than sample sizes, which ranged from 18 to 107, the samples are not described in either verbal description of demographic characteristics or in the vital attribute of mean and standard deviation of test scores. The failure to meet the conventions of research reporting (e.g., see Primary Standards 1.11 and 1.18, AERA, APA, & NCME, 1985) in matters of sample and research design description renders the validity data uninterpretable.

STANDARDIZATION. The standardization sample is "described" in a single vague paragraph. The test was normed on 497 students in five states. The children ranged in age from late 5 to late 7. Few demographic data are presented with which the prospective user can compare the norming sample with the national population. Perhaps more worrisome is the absence of socioeconomic data and the absence of means, standard deviations, or frequency distribution for age of participants. Even the grade of participants is vague; readers are told only that "the majority of children were tested toward the end of kindergarten" (manual, p. 4). Here too, a disregard for prevailing scholarly standards such as Primary Standard 4.4 (AERA, APA, & NCME, 1985) is evident.

INTERPRETATION. Interpretation is focused on the total score. The authors wisely discourage use of the instrument for differential diagnosis of the nature of difficulties.

Three interpretative methods are offered. The first, risk analysis, is apparently intended to report the likelihood of a child receiving a given STRR score being at risk in formal reading instruction. Although the development of these data was conducted by means that are not clear to this reviewer, it appears that a conventional expectancy table would serve as a better medium to support this useful kind of interpretation.

The second interpretative basis is a simple pass-fail based on an arbitrary cut score that is one standard deviation below the mean of the standardization sample. Finally, standard scores are provided. Unfortunately, percentile ranks, the most suitable kind of derived score for purposes of descriptive interpretation, are not provided.

Commendably, the manual authors encourage use of multiple data sources. "We urge that, in addition to the information from this test, other indicators of a child's readiness for reading be considered when formulating recommendations" (manual, p. 1).

SUMMARY. Although the STRR consists of appropriate content, the instrument cannot be recommended for applied use. The scoring directions are flawed. The test's norm-referenced interpretations are based on an insufficiently described reference group that was selected by unspecified methods. The reliability data are both methodologically flawed and too inadequately described to be useful. Finally, the criterion-related validation studies were not disclosed in enough detail to be credible.

REVIEWER'S REFERENCES

American Educational Research Association, American Psychological Association, & National Council on Measurement in Education. (1985). *Standards for Educational and Psychological Testing*. Washington, DC: American Psychological Association, Inc.

Cronbach, L. J. (1990). *Essentials of psychological testing* (5th ed.). New York: Harper & Row.

Review of the Slosson Test of Reading Readiness by DIANE J. SAWYER, Murfree Professor of Dyslexic Studies, Middle Tennessee State University, Murfreesboro, TN:

The stated purpose of the Slosson Test of Reading Readiness (STRR) is to assess a child's readiness to begin formal reading instruction. The authors suggest that it be administered at the end of kindergarten and the results sent on to first grade teachers to support instructional planning. A letter to parents of children who may be at risk of failure is provided and offers suggestions for supportive activities in the home.

The STRR consists of eight subtests. These include: letter recognition (upper and lower case), matching upper case letters with lower case, visual discrimination of word forms, producing rhyming words for words provided, identifying words that do not begin with the same sound as others in a series, sequencing pictures, and stating opposites for words given. These subtests are grouped to form three clusters: Visual Skills (Subtests 1–4), Auditory Skills (Subtests 5 and 6), Cognitive Skills (Subtests 7 and

8). Administration time is about 15 minutes. Raw scores for subtest clusters and the total test may be interpreted within three frames of reference—pass/fail, conversion to a standard score scale, conversion to a "likelihood of nonreadiness quotient" (manual, p. 12).

The STRR has been in development since 1973. This 1991 version is the fourth and represents a significant paring down of subtests from 21 to 8. The standardization sample for this version consisted of 497 children ranging from "late five years of age to late seven years of age" with "the majority . . . tested toward the end of kindergarten" (manual, p. 4). This sample was drawn from Missouri, New Mexico, Texas, North Carolina, and Mississippi. The authors note that this sample reflected the socioeconomic and racial characteristics of the U.S. population with 70% white, 25% black, and 5% other. Reliability coefficients associated with performance among this sample range from .74 (Cognitive subtest cluster) to .96 (Visual subtest cluster) with overall test reliability of .96. Test-retest reliability, estimated from the performance of 70 students on two administrations one week apart, is reported to be .49 (Cognitive cluster), .81 (Auditory cluster), .75 (Visual cluster), and .87 for the total test. Although the stability index for the cognitive cluster is low, all other estimates of reliability are within the acceptable range. Authors caution against use of the cognitive cluster as an independent measure of cognitive abilities.

Because the purpose of the STRR is to predict which students are at risk of failure in formal reading programs, the authors compared performance on four widely used achievement tests (Iowa Tests of Basic Skills, California Achievement Test, Stanford Achievement Test, and the Comprehensive Test of Basic Skills) with total scores on the STRR. Though not stated, it appears that achievement measures were collected at the end of grade one. The sample sizes associated with these investigations were quite small (N = 18, 30, 41, 107, and 92 for the Stanford combined with the Otis-Lennon School Ability Indicator). One test (Iowa) did not report a total reading score. Among the other tests, correlations range from .578 (CTBS) to .81 (Stanford with Otis-Lennon indicator) for total reading. Though correlations indicate a degree of association between the two performance measures, they are not adequate estimates of the strength of one measure to predict performance level on another. Larger samples and more sophisticated analyses (e.g., step-wise regression analysis including independent measures of intelligence, language, and socioeconomic status) should be undertaken to establish the predictive validity of the STRR.

The STRR, overall, is a reasonably reliable measure of potential for success in traditional beginning reading programs—programs in which letter and word discrimination, beginning sounds, and rhyming features are the principal components of a decoding driven definition of beginning reading. However, such traditional programs have, in recent years, been significantly tempered by the concept of "emergent literacy" wherein preschool and kindergarten children acquire positive attitudes toward reading, model skilled readers' behaviors in the presence of books, and take on the pursuit of meaning through the flexible application of various cueing systems (pictures, prior knowledge, context, sentence structure, *and* letter/sound knowledge) to establish meaning. In language/meaning-based early reading programs, variables such as exposure to books, mastery of concepts specific to print, ability to segment spoken language, as well as letter recognition and knowledge of sound spelling will probably be more useful in guiding instruction. Teachers and administrators in such programs may find it useful to consider The Early Detection of Reading Difficulties battery developed by Marie Clay (1985) and published by Heinemann Books, Inc. as they attempt to support students at risk of failure in reading.

REVIEWER'S REFERENCE

Clay, M. (1985). *The early detection of reading difficulties* (3rd ed.). Portsmouth, NH: Heinemann Books, Inc.

[361]

Social Behavior Assessment Inventory.

Purpose: Assesses social skill levels in students.
Population: Grades K–9.
Publication Dates: 1978–92.
Acronym: SBAI.
Scores, 30: Environmental Behaviors (Care for the Environment, Dealing with Emergencies, Lunchroom Behavior, Movement Around Environment), Interpersonal Behaviors (Accepting Authority, Coping with Conflict, Gaining Attention, Greeting Others, Helping Others, Making Conversation, Organized Play, Positive Attitude Toward Others, Playing Informally, Property: Own and Others), Self-Related Behaviors (Accepting Consequences, Ethical Behavior, Expressing Feelings, Positive Attitude Toward Self, Responsible Behavior, Self-Care), Task-Related Behaviors (Asking and Answering Questions, Attending Behavior, Classroom Discussion, Completing Tasks, Following Directions, Group Activities, Independent Work, On-Task Behavior, Performing Before Others, Quality of Work).
Administration: Individual or group.
Price Data, 1994: $86 per complete kit including *Social Skills in the Classroom—2nd ed.*, manual ('92, 34 pages), and 25 rating booklets; $19 per manual; $30 per 25 rating booklets.
Time: (30–45) minutes.
Comments: Observations made by teacher or trained paraprofessional.
Authors: Thomas M. Stephens and Kevin D. Arnold.
Publisher: Psychological Assessment Resources, Inc.
Cross References: See T4:2493 (1 reference); for a review by Ronald S. Drabman of an earlier edition, see 9:1148; see also T3:2226 (1 reference).

Review of the Social Behavior Assessment Inventory by KATHRYN A. HESS, Research Associate, Montgomery, AL:

OVERVIEW. The Social Behavior Assessment Inventory (SBAI) is a 136-item measure developed as part of the Directive Teaching Instructional Management System. The SBAI is coordinated to be used with a set of prescriptive behavioral interventions. Designed for K–9th grade students deficient in social skills, the manual notes that it may be used with institutionalized youth or mentally retarded adults with similar social skill deficits. Suggested uses of the SBAI include: (*a*) screening, and (*b*) instructional design and intervention planning. The SBAI's items are reduced to 30 subscales, which, in turn are grouped into four areas: Environmental Behaviors has 4 subscales, Interpersonal Behaviors has 10 subscales, Self-Related Behaviors has 6 subscales, and Task-Related Behaviors has 10 subscales, which are all plotted as profiles. However, two major factors result in the profiles being meaningless. First, only raw scores are used (no *z* score or other conversion is calculated), and some subscales have as few as two items (which may not even be rated for sundry reasons). Consequently, elevations on the subscales are not comparable. The "profile" has no true baseline such as a 50 *T* score or a uniform number of items/behaviors per subscale or any other base from which profiles could yield meaningful interpretations.

RELIABILITY. Twenty undergraduate special education majors served as judges of 20 learning-disabled and 20 nondisabled students for a 14-minute period. The manual states: "three separate reliability checks for each rater from the time sample data" (p. 25) were calculated, yielding a 96.9% interrater agreement. It is obscure as to whether all raters rated all students, or all raters were compared to each other, or whether only a rater's judgments were contrasted over time. Furthermore, the table reporting the nine subscale reliability study uses two-letter abbreviations that do not correspond to the abbreviations used in the rest of the manual.

No content area or subscale internal consistency data are presented, but the total SBAI had an estimated Cronbach's alpha of .95 in one study, and from .90 to .94 in another study. No test-retest data are presented.

VALIDITY. Content validity was assessed by asking 65 teachers to rate the subscales as to their educational importance. No effort was made to define the content domain other than this teacher opinion study. "Convergent validity" studies consisted of correlating the SBAI subscales with each other and an empathy scale. No effort was made to see whether the SBAI subscales differentially correlated with behaviors that they purportedly tapped (convergent validity) and did not correlate with behaviors they were not supposed to measure (discriminant validity). Four multivariate studies show 69.5% to 83% correct classification discerning disturbed versus nondisturbed students, and between learning-disabled and nondisabled students. Remember a 50% correct rate is given by chance classification, and behavior disturbances are notable to teachers. Consequently, the real test for the SBAI would be whether it adds to classification above chance levels, and whether it adds descriptive specificity for the teachers' use in remediation and referral. Neither proposition is assessed.

CONCLUSION. For a test in development for two decades, the SBAI has essentially no reliability studies nor criterion validity studies to support its use. The SBAI, marketed in 1992, must measure up to psychometric standards to warrant the label "inventory." As a heuristic way of beginning to assess behavior with a set of corresponding prescriptive treatments, it has promise. But this promise needs fulfilling by way of reliability and validity studies for it to be an accepted assessment-intervention system.

Review of the Social Behavior Assessment Inventory by DAVID MACPHEE, Associate Professor of Human Development and Family Studies, Colorado State University, Fort Collins, CO:

The main purpose of the Social Behavior Assessment Inventory (SBAI) is to guide curricular intervention for students who have behavior problems typically associated with learning disabilities, conduct disorder, and attention deficit disorder. To this end, each item on the SBAI is keyed to a section of a companion book on how to enhance children's social skills. Before using the SBAI, teachers should have observed the target student for at least 2 weeks, possess a solid background in childhood behavior disorders, and have experience in social-learning and cognitive behavioral interventions. The authors' concern with clinical utility also is evident in their attention to content validity: The SBAI assesses skills that teacher deem important to success in school, most of which relate to conformity to institutional rules or orderliness.

The SBAI also is purported to be a screening tool for students suspected of having behavior or emotional disorders but there are several reasons to be wary of this application. First, there is no empirical basis for selecting students for further diagnostic testing. Norms are not provided in the manual nor is there a technical analysis and rationale for setting the cut scores that define "elevated" versus "within expectations" (cf. Standard 6.9; AERA, APA, & NCME, 1985). Although there are references to various ethnic and age groups being studied, neither sample characteristics nor group means are given (cf. Standard 4.4; AERA, APA, & NCME, 1985). Minimally, one should be able to determine whether boys are overrepresented among those with elevated scores, as is the case with other behavior disorders. Also, ninth graders presumably possess more sophisticated social skills than kindergartners but the same raw score determines "elevated" behavior problems regardless of age. Thus, referral rates may be determined more by age than by individual social skills.

Second, the SBAI consistently discriminates between clinical and comparison groups, thus establishing its criterion validity. It accurately identifies 69% to 86% of cases and controls, with nonclinical samples being classified more successfully (i.e., specificity). Yet accuracy in classifying diagnosed students cannot be generalized to screening undiagnosed populations. Misclassifications are higher with low-base rate phenomena—3% to 9% for childhood behavior disorders—requiring better agreement between screening and diagnostic tests. Data from undiagnosed samples have not been collected on the SBAI nor were the diagnostic attributes of the criterion variable defined (cf. Standard 1.13; AERA, APA, & NCME, 1985). Further in several studies discriminant analyses were used to classify students but the equations were not given (cf. Standard 1.21; AERA, APA, & NCME, 1985) nor was it clear whether a subset of the 30 subscales would provide a more efficient means of screening students. If a handful of scales is as effective as all 30, then the SBAI would have more appeal as a screening instrument.

It is difficult to evaluate other psychometric data because the manual lacks technical detail. For example, convergent validity was demonstrated through correlations between the SBAI and on-task behavior as observed in the classroom but *p* values were not reported. Evidently, the SBAI has not been assessed in relation to other widely used inventories of child behavior problems, including ADDH and conduct disorders, nor in relation to peer status. Recent research demonstrates the importance of social skills to peer status, especially bullying (Crick & Dodge, 1994), and provides a crucial theoretical context that is missing in the SBAI manual. Interrater reliabilities exceed 91% but it is unclear how agreement was calculated, and reliabilities have been determined for only 9 of the 30 subscales. Internal reliabilities across various samples are in excess of .90 but are reported for the *total* score only. Alpha reliabilities were not reported for the four content areas nor were factor analyses done to determine whether the four scales or 30 subscales are independent dimensions. Further, alpha reliabilities may be inflated because multiple grade levels were included in each sample: Age should be partialled to control for developmental increases in social skills.

Incremental validity is the degree to which a test increases prediction beyond information that is already known. In cost/benefit terms (Kaye, 1986), it is not clear that the SBAI has incremental validity as a screening tool. It is time-consuming to complete, and age, gender, prior academic performance, and shorter rating scales may be as predictive of social skills. Until more research is done on its psychometrics, the SBAI is not recommended as a screening instrument. The Child Behavior Checklist (T4:433) and Revised Behavior Problem Checklist (T4:2254) have more extensive data on reliability and validity and are preferred assessments of child behavior problems. The SBAI may be more useful as a guide to social skills training in the schools but evidence should be provided relative to its sensitivity to intervention effects. Clearly, social skills are important to success in school but whether *this* approach works remains to be seen.

REVIEWER'S REFERENCES

American Educational Research Association, American Psychological Association, & National Council on Measurement in Education. (1985). *Standards for educational and psychological testing*. Washington, DC: American Psychological Association, Inc.

Kaye, K. (1986). A four-dimensional model of risk assessment and intervention. In D. C. Farran & J. D. McKinney (Eds.), *Risk in intellectual and psychosocial development*. Orlando, FL: Academic Press.

Crick, N. R., & Dodge, K. A. (1994). A review and reformulation of social information-processing mechanisms in children's social adjustment. *Psychological Bulletin, 115*, 74-101.

[362]

Social Skills Rating System.

Purpose: Constructed to screen and classify children suspected of having social behavior problems and to assist in the development of appropriate interventions for identified children.

Publication Date: 1990.

Acronym: SSRS.

Administration: Individual.

Price Data, 1992: $86.40 per preschool/elementary levels starter set including 10 copies of each form and level questionnaires, 10 assessment-intervention records, and manual (207 pages); $81 per secondary level starter set; $16.50 per 30 questionnaires (select level and form); $25 per 30 assessment-intervention records; $27 per manual.

Time: (15–25) minutes.

Comments: Ratings by teachers and parents as well as student self-ratings; expanded version of the Teacher Ratings of Social Skills.

Authors: Frank M. Gresham and Stephen N. Elliott.

Publisher: American Guidance Service.

a) PRESCHOOL.

Population: Ages 3-0 to 4-11.

Scores, 2: Social Skills, Problem Behaviors.

Forms, 2: Parent, Teacher.

b) ELEMENTARY.

Population: Grades K–6.

Scores, 3: Social Skills, Problem Behaviors (Parent and Teacher forms only), Academic Competence (Teacher form only).

Forms, 3: Student, Parent, Teacher.

c) SECONDARY.

Population: Grades 7–12.

Scores, 3: Same as *b* above.

Forms, 3: Same as *b* above.

TEST REFERENCES

1. Elliott, S. N., Busse, R. T., & Gresham, F. M. (1993). Behavior rating scales: Issues of use and development. *School Psychology Review, 22*, 313-321.

2. Margalit, M. (1993). Social skills and classroom behavior among adolescents with mild mental retardation. *American Journal on Mental Retardation, 97*, 685-691.

3. Powless, D. L., & Elliott, S. N. (1993). Assessment of social skills of Native American preschoolers: Teachers' and parents' ratings. *Journal of School Psychology, 31*, 293-307.

4. Bramlett, R. K., Smith, B. L., & Edmonds, J. (1994). A comparison of nonreferred, learning-disabled, and mildly mentally retarded students utilizing the Social Skills Rating System. *Psychology in the Schools, 31*, 13-19.

5. Colegrove, R. W., Jr., & Huntzinger, R. M. (1994). Academic, behavioral, and social adaptation of boys with hemophilia/HIV disease. *Journal of Pediatric Psychology, 19*, 457-473.

6. Frankel, F., & Myatt, R. (1994). A dimensional approach to the assessment of social competence in boys. *Psychological Assessment, 6*, 249-254.

7. Lemanek, K. L., Horwitz, W., & Ohene-Frempong, K. (1994). A multiperspective investigation of social competence in children with sickle cell disease. *Journal of Pediatric Psychology, 19*, 443-456.

8. Merrell, K. W., & Popinga, M. R. (1994). The alliance of adaptive behavior and social competence: An examination of relationships between the Scales of Independent Behavior and the Social Skills Rating System. *Research in Development Disabilities, 15*, 39-47.

9. Sadowski, C., Moore, L. A., & Kelley, M. L. (1994). Psychometric properties of the Social Problem Solving Inventory (SPSI) with normal and emotionally disturbed adolescents. *Journal of Abnormal Child Psychology, 22*, 487-500.

10. Maag, J. W., Vasa, S. F., Reid, R., & Torrey, G. K. (1995). Social and behavioral predictors of popular, rejected, and average children. *Educational and Psychological Measurement, 55*, 196-205.

Review of the Social Skills Rating System by KATHRYN M. BENES, Director of Counseling Services, Catholic Social Services, Lincoln, NE:

The Social Skills Rating System (SSRS) is a standardized, norm-referenced instrument designed to provide professionals with a means to screen and classify student social behavior in educational and family settings. Moreover, the SSRS facilitates the development of intervention strategies for youth from preschool through grade 12 who may experience difficulty because of social skills or performance deficits.

Although the SSRS was developed to broadly assess social skills, it not only samples the social skills domain, but the domains of academic competence and problem behavior as well. The authors indicate that information from these additional domains is critical in determining factors that contribute to social skills problems. Moreover, the additional information is necessary in order to develop treatment strategies.

The SSRS manual provides a clear and detailed description of the overall goals and objectives of the SSRS. The authors have developed a user friendly guide for professionals wanting to assess and plan interventions for students with social skills or performance deficits. Much of what is presented here can be found in more thorough detail in the SSRS manual.

CONTENT. The SSRS offers three methods of evaluating student social behavior: (*a*) Parent Form, (*b*) Teacher Form, and (*c*) Student Form. In addition, the parent and teacher versions of the SSRS are divided into three developmental levels: preschool, kindergarten through sixth grade, and seventh through twelfth grades. Because of the reading level, the student version is available for youth who are capable of reading at a third grade level.

The SSRS Parent Form is completed by the student's mother and/or father, or guardian. The number of items on the Parent Form range from 49 (Preschool Level) to 55 (Elementary Level). Items ask the parent to rate the frequency of a specified behavior (e.g., "Attempts household tasks before asking for help") on a 3-point scale (0, Never; 1, Sometimes; 2, Very Often). In addition, the parent is asked to rate the importance of the behavior (0, Not Important; 1, Important; 2, Critical).

The Parent Form yields four Social Skills Subscale raw scores (i.e., Cooperation, Assertive, Responsibility, and Self-Control) as well as a Social Skills Scale total raw score. In addition, two Problem Behaviors Subscale raw scores (i.e., Externalizing and Internalizing) are derived from the responses on each of the three levels of the Parent Form and a third Problem Behavior Subscale raw score is included for the Elementary Level form. A total Problem Behaviors raw score is also included. The Social Skills Scale and Problem Behaviors Scale raw score totals are then converted into Standard Scores (mean = 100; standard deviation = 15).

The Teacher Form is completed by the student's teacher or other school personnel who has had exposure to the student's classroom behavior for at least 2 months. The number of items on the Teacher Form ranges from 40 (Preschool Level) to 57 (Elementary Level). Similar to the Parent Form, the teacher is requested to respond to items (e.g., "Finishes classroom assignments within time limits") using the same 3-point frequency and importance scales.

The Teacher Form responses are collapsed into three Social Skills Subscale raw scores (i.e., Cooperation, Assertion, and Self-Control). These three raw scores compose the Social Skills Scale total raw score. Similar to the Parent Form, the Teacher Form also has two Problem Behaviors Subscale raw scores (i.e., Externalizing and Internalizing) that are combined to yield a total Problem Behavior raw score. As with the Parent Form, the Social Skills Scale and Problem Behaviors Scale raw score totals are then converted into Standard Scores (mean = 100; standard deviation = 15). In addition to the Social Skills and Problem Behavior Scales, the Teacher Form also includes an Academic Competence Scale at the Elementary and Secondary Level. This section of the SSRS consists of nine items (e.g., "In *mathematics*, how does this child compare with other students?") that are rated on a 5-point scale (Lowest 10%; Next Lowest 20%; Middle 40%; Next Highest 20%; Highest 10%). These ratings are also converted into standard scores.

There are two Student Forms (Elementary, grades 3–6; Secondary, grades 7–12) that are self-ratings. The response format of the Secondary Level form is similar to that of the Parent and Teacher Forms; however, the Elementary Level form requests frequency of behavior only. The Student Forms also differ from the Parent Form in that instead of the Responsibility Subscale being measured, an Empathy Subscale is included. In addition, the Problem Behaviors Scale is absent from the Student Forms.

The final component of the SSRS is the Assessment-Intervention Record (AIR). The AIR is an eight-page form that serves to integrate the information obtained from the Parent, Teacher, and Student Forms. The AIR provides an effective means for analysis of student strengths and weaknesses and for prioritizing areas of concern in regard to student social skills. But more importantly, the AIR functions to facilitate the critical link between assessment and intervention.

STANDARDIZATION SAMPLE. The authors describe their sampling procedure in detail in the SSRS manual. They indicate that the SSRS was developed over the course of a 5-year period. The SSRS emerged from a prior research instrument, the Teacher Ratings of Social Skills (TROSS).

The SSRS standardization sample included 4,170 self-ratings of children and youth, 1,027 parents, and 259 teachers. Approximately the same number of male and female students, representing "sufficient" numbers from each grade level were sampled. The student sample included regular education students, as well as self-contained special education and mainstreamed special education students. The special education students represented in the standardization sample included youth identified as Mentally Handicapped, Learning Disabled, Behaviorally Disordered, and "Other."

Ethnic and racial representation in the SSRS standardization sample included a slight overrepresentation of Whites and Blacks, and a slight underrepresentation of Hispanics. Minority students made up approximately 27% of the normative sample, although the authors report that the U.S. population consists of about 31% ethnic and racial minorities.

The standardization sample was drawn from 18 states in the Northeast, North Central, South, and Western regions of the United States. The sample also represented individuals from urban, suburban, and rural communities.

RELIABILITY AND VALIDITY. The authors addressed the psychometric properties of the SSRS in great detail. They report coefficient alpha, the correlational index of internal consistency, for all forms ranged from .83 to .94 in regard to the Social Skills Scale, from .73 to .88 for the Problem Behavior Scale, and .95 for Academic Competence. These coefficients represent a high level of homogeneity among items.

Test-retest reliabilities were computed using the Elementary standardization sample for a 4-week period. Correlations for teacher ratings were .85 for the Social Skills scale, .84 for the Problem Behavior scale, and .93 for Academic Competence. Correlations for parent ratings were .87 for the Social Skills scale and .65 for the Problem Behavior scale. Finally, test-retest correlations for the self-ratings of students for the Social Skills scale was .68. Although the reliability coefficient for student self-reports was lower than the coefficients from parent or teacher forms, they nonetheless suggest adequate stability of the SSRS for all three forms.

The authors also addressed interrater reliability and standard error of measurement. As they point out, one would not expect high agreement on a measure such as the SSRS, therefore the utility of interrater reliability is somewhat limited. For a more detailed description of the standard error of measurement for the SSRS for the various scales and forms, the reader is referred to Appendix E of the SSRS manual.

In regard to validity, the authors addressed content, social, criterion-related, and construct validity. Gresham and Elliott (SSRS manual) demonstrated content validity by indicating the SSRS items were developed based on extensive empirical research. They also provided evidence for social validity by referring to prior research and the use of the Importance Rating Scale for each item.

The authors dedicated much of the validity section in the manual to criterion-related and construct validity. They cited a number of studies where the SSRS correlated highly with other somewhat similar measures (e.g., Social Behavior Assessment, Stephens, 1978; Harter Teacher Rating Scale, Harter, 1985; Piers-Harris Children's Self-Concept Scale, Piers, 1984; and the Child Behavior Checklist, Achenbach & Edelbrock, 1983, 1986, 1987). The results of the construct validity studies of the SSRS suggest "strong evidence in support of the construct validity of the Social Skills Rating System" (manual, p. 142).

CONCLUSION. Gresham and Elliott, the authors of the SSRS, have provided a psychometrically sound means of measuring the perceived social skills of youth from preschool to secondary school. The manual and forms are written and designed to make administration and scoring convenient. In addition, the items are written in behavioral terms so the rater does not have to use a high level of inference in order to respond. The use of the multirater system provides critical information regarding the student's self-evaluation of his/her behaviors as well as how significant others perceive the student's behavior at home and school. The most noteworthy factor of the SSRS, however, is the Assessment-Intervention Record (AIR). The AIR provides a format to integrate social skills assessment information and link the assessment to planned intervention strategies. By including this simple eight-page form, the authors assist professionals in making the important connection between assessment and intervention.

REVIEWER'S REFERENCES

Stephens, T. (1978). *Social skills in the classroom.* Columbus, OH: Cedars Press.

Achenbach, T., & Edelbrock, C. (1983). *Manual for the Child Behavior Checklist and revised Child Behavior Profile.* Burlington, VT: University of Vermont Department of Psychiatry.

Piers, E. V. (1984). *Piers-Harris Children's Self-Concept Scale* (revised manual). Los Angeles: Western Psychological Services.

Harter, S. (1985). *Manual for the Self-Perception Profile for Children.* Denver, CO: University of Denver.

Achenbach, T., & Edelbrock, C. (1986). *Manual for the Teacher's Report Form and teacher version of the Child Behavior Profile.* Burlington, VT: University of Vermont Department of Psychiatry.

Achenbach, T., & Edelbrock, C. (1987). *Manual for the Youth Self-Report form and profile.* Burlington, VT: University of Vermont Department of Psychiatry.

Review of the Social Skills Rating System by MICHAEL FURLONG, Associate Professor, and MITCHELL KARNO, Doctoral Student, Graduate School of Education, University of California, Santa Barbara, Santa Barbara, CA:

A distinguishing feature of the Social Skills Rating System (SSRS) is a multirater approach involving teachers, parents, and students as well as the integration of assessment results with intervention planning. Social skills items assessing the domains of Cooperation (all forms), Assertion (all forms), Self-Control (all forms), Responsibility (Parent Form only), and Empathy (Student Form only) are rated for frequency and importance to success in the child's specific classroom (Teacher Form) or the child's development (Parent Form). A Problem Behavior subscale is rated by teachers and parents that taps Externalizing, Internalizing, and Hyperactive behaviors. The Teacher Form also includes a very general Academic Competence subscale.

The SSRS actually is a set of eight related rating scales: two preschool versions (parent and teacher), three elementary school versions (parent, teacher, and student [grades 3–6]), and three secondary school versions (parent, teacher, and student). The eight versions contain 34–57 items derived from existing social skills training programs and other social skills rating scales. The eight versions have an average of just 37% of the items in common (range = 33% to 42% by pairs). The manual contains comparatively little discussion of the Preschool Form; it was not included in the national standardization and normative data are available only for the tryout sample. The Preschool Form should be considered experimental because it requires additional validity evaluation as well as appropriate norms.

The SSRS was originally designed to be a "brief selection/screening measure" (Clark, Gresham, & Elliott, 1985, p. 348) that provided an alternative to the Social Behavior Assessment Inventory, a comprehensive social skills check list. Yet, the various forms of the rating scale take about 15–20 minutes to complete, which is too time consuming for general screening purposes. The SSRS will more typically be used as a post-referral assessment, such as part of a child study team process, or in a comprehensive evaluation.

This instrument is designed to be used with normal and mildly handicapped students for whom social skills deficits might limit academic performance. It does not replace other social skills and adaptive behavior instruments used with students who have more severe disabilities or special social skills needs associated with sensory impairment.

A testament to the fine detail provided in the protocols and the associate summary sheet is that it is possible to complete accurately all scoring and documentation procedures without referring to the manual for directions. However, educational personnel who have limited assessment and psychometric knowledge will find the interpretation procedures a challenge to understand.

RELIABILITY. The Teacher version was the first to be developed and is clearly psychometrically the soundest of the eight SSRS scales. Ninety-two percent of the alpha coefficients from the three Teacher Forms are .80 or higher, with 45.8% .90 or higher. In contrast, only 44% of the alpha coefficients from the three Parent Forms are .80 or higher, and only 20% of the alpha coefficients from the two Student Forms are that high (manual, p. 109). Users should have a very satisfactory degree of confidence in the Teacher Forms and a moderate level of confidence in the Parent Forms. The two Student Forms should be used with some caution. Only the Total Score of the Student Form has adequate reliability—the social skills subscales are not reliable enough to warrant individual interpretation.

VALIDITY. The manual includes an impressive array of data that systematically examine the SSRS's content, social, criterion-related, and construct validity. Criterion-related validity studies are reported for the elementary versions but not for the secondary versions. The construct validity of the Teacher and Parent versions are supported by moderate to high loading on factor analyses using the normative sample. In contrast, the Elementary Student Form contains 10 subscale items with factor loadings below .30. All but one of these items are on the Cooperation and Assertion subscales, suggesting that they should be interpreted independently with caution.

With respect to predictive validity, the authors suggest in the manual and elsewhere (Gresham & Elliott, 1989a; 1989b) that the SSRS can be used to identify students who have social skills deficits that require special education services. How such a system is to be established is not well articulated. Educational agencies that might carry out such a public policy should first carefully evaluate the reliability and validity of the SSRS scores used to assist in making such eligibility decisions.

NORMING. At first glance, the size of the standardization sample is very impressive, but each user should closely examine the normative sample to decide if it is valid for their use. Ratings were obtained from 4,170 students in grades 3–12, 922 parents, and 259 teachers (88% female) who completed ratings for 1,335 students. The 4,170 students were roughly representative of the U.S. population but the sample underrepresented rural communities, the Northeast and West regions of the country, and Hispanic children. In the West region all the students were from the intermountain states with no students sampled from the West coast. This undoubtedly is partially responsible for the underrepresentation of Hispanic children. This sample characteristic is particularly critical in some regions of the country, such as California, where Hispanic students are the majority in many school districts. SSRS users in specific regions of the country may need to develop local norms and validate its use with specific minority populations.

Yoked ratings (parent, teacher, and student ratings of the same child) were obtained for only 837 children: 352 teacher-parent-student ratings of upper elementary children (grades 3–6); 157 teacher-parent-student ratings of secondary children (grades 7–12); and 328 teacher-parent ratings of early elementary children (grades K–2; no student ratings available). Thus, the Parent and Teacher norms for the early elementary, upper elementary, and secondary groups considered separately are based on less than 1,100 ratings, which are not representative of the U.S. population. More than three-fourths of the teacher ratings were obtained from the South and North Central regions of the country. The secondary school norms are based on ratings provided by just 51 teachers. In a laudable attempt to develop norms for children with disabilities, special education teachers were over sampled, but this resulted in just 57% of the teachers working in regular classrooms. Because the teacher rating scale is the most psychometrically sound, it is unfortunate that the sample on which the norms for this portion of the test are based is composed of so few and so unrepresentative a group of teachers. In addition, the parent sample contained proportionately too few parents with less than high school education; caution should be taken when the SSRS is used with parents from a low SES background.

SCALING. A peculiar aspect of the SSRS is that normative data for the various subscales in each version are not provided. Instead, subscale raw scores and global scores are classified in terms of Behavior Levels: "Fewer," "Average," or "More." "Fewer" refers to fewer social skills than was common in the norming sample and so on. The scale is reversed for the Problem Behavior subscale so here "More" refers to more social problems than in the norm sample. These classifications were created by placing all scores within one standard deviation of the mean (85–115 range) into the "Average" category, scores below 85 into the "Fewer" category, and scores above 115 into the "More" category. The authors correctly suggest that the "Behavior Levels" should be used for screening and program development purposes only. Standard scores and *SEm* values are provided for the global scores, but not for the subscales. This information is needed to use the SSRS properly. Note, however, that this information can be estimated by using the means and standard deviations for the various subscales on pages 121–123 of the manual.

The authors indicate that, "Since each item on the Social Skills and Problem Behaviors Scales represents a specific behavior, the words 'Fewer,' 'Average,' and 'More' can be directly interpreted as referring to amounts, or frequencies, of behavior" (p. 48). The reader is cautioned that when interpreting the Behavior Levels it is possible to obtain nearly identical raw scores that do not reflect a similar incidence of social skills. Because the items are each rated for frequency (0 = never; 1 = sometimes; 2 = very often), identical raw scores can be obtained with different combinations of specific items and the comparative frequency of the items. To avoid misinterpretation of the Behavior Levels it is necessary to consider simultaneously both the number of social skills exhibited by each child and the frequency with which they occur. Furthermore, the items included in the rating scales do not represent discrete social skills but are broad skills within each domain.

The authors suggest that if just one social skills subscale is below average ("Fewer") across parent, teacher, or student ratings, then an analysis of specific Social Skill Performance Deficits (skills rated as important for success and occurring infrequently) and Social Skills Acquisition Deficits (skills rated as important for success and not occurring at all) is completed. This ultimately means that each item is scrutinized to see if it reflects a social skills deficit or strength. Given the fact the SSRS is likely to be used most commonly in situations when a student is referred because of social skills related concerns, it is likely that across raters at least one subscale will fall in the problem areas defined by the "Behavior Levels." It would have been useful for the publisher to provide information concerning the frequency of the "Fewer" rating within and across the parent, teacher, and student forms. If the incidence of at least one "Fewer" rating is common in the norm sample, then it raises questions about the utility of providing the "Behavior Levels" at all. The value of the "Behavior Levels" classification procedure without supportive norming information is not clear to these reviewers. The authors acknowledge that the Behavior Levels "are very general descriptors that have limited utility" (manual, p. 50).

UNIQUE CHARACTERISTICS. The strength of the SSRS as an assessment system lies in the attempt to link assessment findings with program planning and implementation. Users of the SSRS will appreciate the careful work the authors have done to present a model of social skills program planning that modifies the approach for responding to Acquisition Deficits, Performance Deficits, and Social Skills Strengths in the presence or absence of interfering behavior problems. The model presented is behavioral so users must be comfortable with the use of operant, social learning, and cognitive-behavioral intervention strategies.

Useful materials also have been developed to support appropriate scoring, interpretation, and prevention/intervention planning. A user-friendly computer scoring program (American Guidance Service, 1992) is available. Those choosing to use the computer program will find that they do not need to use the Assessment-Intervention Record Form because the program produces all the information that it contains. The authors have also compiled a structured intervention program that teaches 43 social skills within the five domains measured by the SSRS (Elliott & Gresham, 1991). In addition, Cartledge and Kleefeld (1991) have developed a program for preschool children.

RESEARCH APPLICATION. Given the negatively skewed distribution of the global and subscale scores, outcome studies may be influenced by a ceiling effect. For example, raw scores of 0–19 on the Teacher Form for elementary girls fall below the 2nd percentile. At the other end of the distribution, the top two percentiles are associated with raw scores of 59 and 60. The SSRS produces a better estimate of social skill deficits than well-developed social skills. This general principle applies to the Problem Behavior Scale as well—standard scores below 85 are unavailable. Researchers interested in evaluating the impact of an intervention beyond a broadly defined "normal" range should use another instrument, such as the Child Behavior Check List (Achenbach, 1983; 11:64). In addition, researchers should cautiously use the two Student Forms subscales to evaluate intervention effectiveness because of low reliabilities.

SUMMARY. The authors of the SSRS have articulated an excellent, comprehensive model of social skills assessment/intervention. As discussed in the manual and elsewhere (Elliott, Sheridan, & Gresham, 1989), the assessment of social skills requires a "multimethod" approach that encompasses rating scales, behavioral observations, and interviews. When a rating scale is used as part of such an assessment, the SSRS is recommended for it is currently the most comprehensive one available. Users attending to the cautions cited above will find it to be a valuable program planning guide and secondarily an assessment tool. It should prove to be even more valuable as future revisions address some of the limitations discussed above.

REVIEWERS' REFERENCES

Achenbach, T., & Edelbrock, C. (1983). *Manual for the Child Behavior Checklist and revised Child Behavior Profile*. Burlington, VT: University of Vermont Department of Psychiatry.

Clark, L., Gresham, F. M., & Elliott, S. N. (1985). Development and validation of a social skills assessment measure: The TROSS-C. *Journal of Psychoeducational Assessment, 4*, 347-356.

Elliott, S. N., Sheridan, S. M., & Gresham, F. M. (1989a). Scientific practitioner—Assessing and treating social skills deficits: A case study for the scientist practitioner. *Journal of School Psychology, 27*, 197-222.

Gresham, F. M., & Elliott, S. N. (1989a). Social skills assessment technology for LD students. *Learning Disability Quarterly, 12*, 141-152.

Gresham, F. M., & Elliott, S. N. (1989b). Social skills deficits as a primary learning disability. *Journal of Learning Disabilities, 22*, 120-124.

American Guidance Service. (1991). *ASSIST for the SSRS* [computer software]. Circle Pines, MN: American Guidance Service.

Cartledge, G., & Kleefeld, J. (1991). *Taking part: Introducing social skills to children*. Circle Pines, MN: American Guidance Service.

Elliott, S. N., & Gresham, F. M. (1991). *Social Skills Intervention Guide*. Circle Pines, MN: American Guidance Service.

[363]

Softball Skills Test.

Purpose: "To improve teaching and evaluation of softball skills."

Population: Grades 5–12 and college.

Publication Date: 1991.

Scores, 4: Batting, Fielding Ground Balls, Overhand Throwing, Baserunning.

Administration: Individual.

Price Data, 1992: $12.50 per manual (56 pages).

Time: Administration time not reported.

Author: Roberta E. Rikli.

Publisher: American Alliance for Health, Physical Education, Recreation and Dance.

Review of the Softball Skills Test by DON SEBOLT, Associate Professor, Department of Human Nutrition, Foods and Exercise Science, Virginia Tech, Blacksburg, VA:

The Softball Skills Test Manual contains a softball skills test designed for males and females at all academic levels. The four test items included in the manual measure batting for power and accuracy, fielding ground balls, throwing for distance and accuracy, and baserunning speed.

The introduction includes information relating to the history of softball skills testing, guidelines and procedures used in the development of skills tests, and instructions for using the manual.

Test item reliability and validity estimates were presented for male and female students at each academic level. Intraclass reliability estimates ranged from .69 to .97 across the four test items. Concurrent validity estimates ranged from .54 to .94.

National norms are presented for each test item by gender and academic level. Both percentile norms and *T*-score norms are provided. Graphics are included to allow for the conversion of raw test scores to standard scores.

Each test item contains a statement of purpose, needed equipment, dimensions of test site, testing procedures, and scoring parameters. Also included for each test item is a clearly drawn figure that shows the test markings.

Both individual and group recording forms and a sample softball skills rating scale are presented in the Appendices. The individual recording form could be duplicated and used to record the scores of each student taking the test. A summary table is provided to include the raw score, percentile score, and *T*-score for each test item.

This test manual is extremely well done. Numerous pilot studies using both males and females at all levels—elementary, junior high, high school, and college—were conducted in the design of the specific test items. The four test items meet the guidelines established by the Measurement and Evaluation Council of AAHPERD. Well-established statistical procedures were employed to estimate the reliability and validity of each test item. Two thirds of the intraclass reliability estimates were at or above .85, and the majority of the concurrent validity values were above .70. The test norms were constructed from a solid sample (N = 10,000) and represented balanced clusters of gender and academic levels.

The Softball Skills Test Manual provides a test battery that meets acceptable standards for reliability and validity, contains clearly written test direction and accurate scoring procedures, requires neither expensive nor extensive equipment, and requires no more than two class period to administer.

In summary, the AAHPERD Softball Skills Test Manual is recommended for use within multi-academic-level physical education classes. The manual will help teachers improve the learning process in the areas of motivation, skill level diagnosis, and evaluation.

[364]

A Spanish Computerized Adaptive Placement Exam.

Purpose: Designed to assist appropriate placement into college-level Spanish courses.
Population: College students.
Publication Dates: 1986–88.
Acronym: S-CAPE.
Scores: Total score only.
Administration: Individual.
Price Data: Available from publisher.
Time: (20–25) minutes.
Comments: IBM-PC or compatible computer necessary for administration.
Authors: Jerry W. Larson and Kim L. Smith.
Publisher: Brigham Young University, Humanities Research Center.

Review of A Spanish Computerized Adaptive Placement Exam by G. GAGE KINGSBURY, Coordinator of Measurement Research, Portland Public Schools, Portland, OR:

The Spanish Computerized Adaptive Placement Exam (S-CAPE) is a short, computerized adaptive test designed to place students into lower level college Spanish courses based on their current understanding of written Spanish. It administers individualized tests directly to students using an IBM PC or equivalent computer.

Questions on the S-CAPE are multiple-choice items, calibrated using the one-parameter logistic (Rasch) IRT model. Items are drawn from an item pool consisting of 459 items at 51 difficulty levels. There are 9 items available at each difficulty level, and adjacent difficulty levels differ by .1 logit. (A logit is a step along the Rasch difficulty scale.)

The S-CAPE uses a simple mechanical branching strategy to chose items for students. For the first six items, item difficulty increases by .6 logits following each correct response, and decreases by .5 logits following each incorrect response. For all subsequent items, item difficulty increases by .1 logit following each correct response, and decreases by .1 logit following each incorrect response.

The test is terminated when the student misses four items with the same difficulty value or when the student answers five questions correctly in succession at the highest difficulty level. The student's final score is the level of the final item administered. This final score is compared to a placement chart to identify the appropriate course placement for the student.

RELIABILITY AND VALIDITY. The authors of the S-CAPE present a fair amount of initial research concerning the IRT scale development, reliability, validity, and acceptability of the S-CAPE. They describe a calibration study and several additional research studies conducted at Brigham Young University (BYU) concerning the instrument.

The calibration study used a sample of 199 students enrolled in appropriate undergraduate Spanish courses, and five long test forms. The five calibration field test forms were linked with a 30-item anchor block of items. This linked scale was used to design the final item pool for the test.

A small study with 43 college students indicated a short-term test-retest reliability of .86 for the S-CAPE. The same study resulted in a correlation of .91 with scores from the Multiple Assessment Programs and Services Spanish test.

In a separate study of 179 students, the S-CAPE was used for student placement. In this study, teachers interviewed in midterm indicated that approximately 80% of the students had been placed correctly into their courses.

STRENGTHS AND WEAKNESSES. The S-CAPE has three primary strengths as a Spanish placement test. First, the S-CAPE is short compared to conventional tests. In trial studies, the S-CAPE took approximately 20 minutes to administer, compared to 60 or more minutes for a comparable conventional test. Second, the S-CAPE is always available for immediate administration. This allows the testing of a single student who arrives late in the term to be accomplished easily. Third, the S-CAPE is an adaptive test. This should reduce student frustration and/or boredom with the placement test because fewer inappropriate items will be administered.

The S-CAPE has two major areas of weakness as a useful Spanish placement test. The first area of weakness concerns the procedures for adaptation that are used in the test. The second area of weakness involves the transportability of the test.

The adaptive testing procedure in S-CAPE is less than optimal in several ways. First, the selection of items in S-CAPE uses a mechanical branching approach that is almost never used in modern adaptive tests because it fails to maximize score information. The result is a test that is longer and less informative than it could be with a more modern selection procedure. Second, the final score on the S-CAPE is the difficulty level of the last item administered. Although this is a simple procedure, it uses very little of the information available from the student's responses to the items. More informative scoring procedures are currently used in almost all adaptive tests. Finally, the S-CAPE does not seem to have any mechanism for controlling the content of items administered. This may result in some tests that overemphasize one content area or another, and therefore reduce content validity.

Another area in which the S-CAPE has a weakness is that it is currently specific to BYU. All reliability and validity studies have been done using BYU students and BYU courses. Although it is very likely that the results of these studies will generalize to other settings, it would be helpful to see such results. In addition, the specificity of the S-CAPE to BYU means that there is a need to create a new placement chart in each new university that uses the S-CAPE. Although there is no easy way around this problem, some tools for facilitating the creation of a new placement chart (such as the type of item represented by each difficulty level) might prove useful.

EVALUATION. In summary, I would recommend the use of the S-CAPE only for universities that are willing to do a little work evaluating test performance and creating placement charts. The S-CAPE provides an immediately available adaptive test for student placement, which has some research base. Although the adaptation procedure is not the best available, it still seems to provide some advantage over the conventional tests available for the same purpose.

Review of A Spanish Computerized Adaptive Placement Exam by STEVEN L. WISE, Associate Professor of Educational Psychology, University of Nebraska-Lincoln, Lincoln, NE:

The Spanish Computerized Adaptive Placement Exam (S-CAPE) is a computerized adaptive test (CAT) that was developed to guide the placement of students into college-level Spanish courses. In undertaking the development of the S-CAPE, the authors correctly identified the potential usefulness of a CAT in making placement decisions; its advantages include (*a*) a large reduction in testing time compared with conventional tests, (*b*) the capability to provide immediate feedback to examinees regarding test performance and recommended course placement, and (*c*) the potential to readily administer a test on short notice throughout an academic year. Hence, the needs of a college-level placement testing program are well served by implementation of a CAT format.

The test materials consist of an S-CAPE demonstration disk (on a 5.25-inch or 3.5-inch DOS-formatted computer disk) and two documents. The first, entitled "Test Manual," focuses primarily on computer issues concerning use of the S-CAPE. It discusses installation of the software, configuration of the software to operate properly on the user's computer, and a description of the information requested from an examinee at the beginning of a testing session, the format of the test items, and an explanation of the data file generated by the program. The second document, which by more conventional standards should be considered the test manual, is a manuscript that discusses the rationale and need for the S-CAPE, the development of the item bank, the computer algorithm used in the S-CAPE, and evidence of the test's reliability and validity.

The S-CAPE items were calibrated using the Rasch model with data from paper-and-pencil administrations of the items. During development of the item pool, misfitting items were identified and deleted; however, the criteria for misfit were not specified, nor was the number of items deleted. The size of the item pool used in the S-CAPE is unclear; although the test documentation states that the final item pool contained roughly 1,100 items, the authors indicate that each of the 51 difficulty strata contain 9 items—which implies that 459 unique items are used. In addition, the authors indicate that, after calibration, the items were screened for "spelling errors, inaccuracies, or any other possible problems." It is not clear whether identified problematic items were revised (which would likely alter their difficulties) or deleted from the pool.

Administration of the S-CAPE follows a two-stage, fixed-step adaptive algorithm. During the first six items, correct responses result in a six-level increase in item difficulty, whereas incorrect responses decrease item difficulty by five levels. After the sixth item, item difficulty changes by only a single level at a time. Although the item pool contains three types of items, there is no indication that the algorithm maintains a balanced administration of item types. The characteristics suggest that the S-CAPE algorithm is somewhat primitive and inefficient by current standards of CAT software. Regardless, the S-CAPE is probably adequate for its intended task.

Evidence for reliability of the S-CAPE is sketchy. The authors provide reliability estimates based on a single administration of the fixed-length test forms used in collecting the data used in item calibration. In addition, a group of students was administered the S-CAPE twice over a 2-day period. Given (*a*) the short time period between testings, and (*b*) the likelihood that students received some of the same items on both administrations, the accuracy of the test-retest reliability coefficient is questionable. It would be more useful if the authors provided information regarding either (*a*) the standard errors of proficiency estimation or (*b*) the consistency with which students are placed into courses.

The limited validity evidence for the S-CAPE is encouraging. After the S-CAPE had been used to place students into four levels of Spanish courses, the course instructors reported that about 80% of the students had been appropriately placed. This evidence suggests that the S-CAPE can play a useful role in Spanish course placement decisions.

In general, although the S-CAPE appears to be a potentially useful instrument for placing students into college-level Spanish courses, it is a bit dated. Potential users should compare the S-CAPE with more recently developed (and probably more powerful) CAT software before making a testing software decision. More powerful is not necessarily more useful, however, and many users should find the S-CAPE to be well suited to their placement decision needs.

[365]

SPAR Spelling and Reading Tests, Second Edition.

Purpose: Provides group testing of literacy.
Population: Ages 7-0 to 12-11.
Publication Dates: 1976–91.
Scores: Total score only.
Administration: Group.
Price Data, 1994: £3.75 per 20 Form A or Form B; £5.50 per manual ('89, 25 pages); £3.25 per scoring template A or B; £5.99 per specimen set.
Time: 13 minutes.
Comments: Uses same scoring templates as Group Reading Test (T4:1102); spelling items provided as "banks" in the manual.
Author: Dennis Young.
Publisher: Hodder & Stoughton Educational [England].
Cross References: See T4:2520 (3 references); for reviews by J. Douglas Ayers of earlier editions of the Spelling Test and the Reading Test, see 8:76 and 8:742.

TEST REFERENCES

1. Hitch, G. J., & McAuley, E. (1991). Working memory in children with specific arithmetical learning difficulties. *British Journal of Psychology, 82*, 375-386.

2. Lewis, C., Hitch, G. J., & Walker, P. (1994). The prevalence of specific arithmetic difficulties and specific reading difficulties: In 9- to 10-year-old boys and girls. *Journal of Child Psychology and Psychiatry and Allied Disciplines, 35*, 283-292.

Review of the SPAR Spelling and Reading Tests, Second Edition by CLEBORNE D. MADDUX, Professor and Chairman, of Curriculum and Instruction, University of Nevada, Reno, Reno, NV:

The SPAR Spelling and Reading Tests are group-administered, norm-referenced spelling and reading achievement tests intended for use in the United Kingdom with first-year, junior children, and with other children whose reading ages are lower than 9 years. Test materials include a single, well-written manual covering both tests, and consumable, single-page reading forms for each of the two equivalent reading tests.

The spelling test consists of 40 increasingly difficult words that are written by the student after the examiner pronounces each word, uses it in a sentence, and pronounces it again. In the manual, the words are listed in 20 sections, with each section containing three different choices for the two consecutively numbered items it contains. (For example, the first section offers the following choices for Items 1 and 2: top/sit; pan/wag; or sat/rag.) No spelling answer sheet is provided, and the examiner is advised to duplicate forms containing 40 numbered, blank lines on which the child is to write. There are no standardized instructions to be read by the examiner, and the manual author notes the suggested sentences may be changed. The test is untimed, but about 20 seconds is the time suggested for completion of each item. No basal or ceiling levels are included, although the author mentions examiners might want to use 10 cumulative errors as a cutoff point, or 10 consecutive errors if a more conservative approach is desired. The raw scores is the number of items spelled correctly.

The reading test is presented in two equivalent forms, Form A and Form B. The consumable test sheet for each form is color coded, and consists of two parts. In the first part, the child examines a stimulus picture and circles a word to describe the picture from a list of four or five choices printed beside the picture. There are three trial items, and 15 test items in this section. In part two, a cloze format is employed in which students complete a short sentence by circling the appropriate word from six choices. Part two contains three sample items followed by 30 test items. Unlike the spelling test, the manual for the reading subtest contains a standardized script of instructions to be read to students. Both parts of the reading test are timed, with 4 minutes alloted to the pictures and 9 minutes to sentences. Basal and ceiling levels are not mentioned, and every child is allowed to attempt every item. Although there are two parts to the reading test, only a single raw score is produced by counting the total number of correct items excluding the sample items.

The raw scores for both reading and spelling can be converted to age equivalents or normalized standard scores with a mean of 100 and a standard deviation of 15.

NORMATIVE DATA. The spelling and reading tests were standardized on large samples (first-year junior, aged 7-8 to 8-10, N = 1,861; and secondary children chosen by teachers as poor in spelling and reading, ages 11-2 to 14-3, N = 1,045). However, these samples are somewhat dated because they were taken between 1984 and 1986. An additional sample of 246 children, ages 6-8 to 7-10 was drawn for use in extending the reading norms down to age 7-0. Although the standardization sample is sufficiently large, the manual does not contain an adequate description of how or why they were selected. The sample is described as drawn from schools representative of national standards.

RELIABILITY. Alternate-form reliability was investigated using 297 first-year juniors aged 8-3, and is reported as .95. It is unclear, however, whether this was obtained through use of reading or spelling scores, or by some combination of both scores. An investigation of the equivalence of randomly chosen spelling tests generated through the pairing procedure described above produced a coefficient of reliability of .94. This is adequate, although the description of the procedure used and the sample size is confusing and ambiguous.

VALIDITY. Several manual pages are devoted to a discussion of validity. The authors correctly assert the content validity of a test cannot be determined independent of the skills of the children with whom it will be used. The authors then assert that the content validity of the SPAR reading test is limited to use with children whose reading is limited to reading isolated words, and who are just beginning to deal with short prose selections.

Items on the spelling test were originally drawn from a study of the vocabulary of young children, and were refined through various means explained in the manual. These are acceptable, although more detail concerning samples and criteria for final selection of words would be desirable. For example, reference is made to the use of facility values for word selection, but no details are included.

Concurrent validity is addressed by presenting correlations between scores on the SPAR reading and the cloze tests. These are reported at three different ages and are acceptably high (.86, .81, and .79). For spelling, the SPAR spelling scores were correlated with several reading tests and an intelligence test. However, no data are given concerning sample demographics or sample size on which any of these correlations were calculated.

The manual contains an excellent discussion of predictive validity, and includes an explanation of various regression equations used to predict reading and spelling scores. Unfortunately, it is impossible to determine if any of these equations were empirically produced using SPAR scores, or if they are general, theoretical equations derived from other studies.

SUMMARY. The SPAR Spelling and Reading Tests are attractively and professionally printed and bound, and are quick and simple to administer and score. The spelling test uses a traditional dictation format, whereas the reading test requires the reading of isolated words and short sentences in a multiple-choice cloze format. Standardization samples appear to be quite adequate and are probably competently drawn. However, data on standardization are insufficient, and should be expanded. Reliability is adequate, and validity has been addressed by the test author. However, once again, the manual contains only an incomplete description of many critical aspects of validity studies that were carried out. This problem pervades the technical data that are presented. The reader is left with the impression that technical considerations may have been properly addressed, but information provided in the manual fails to establish this. Thus, the manual should be expanded considerably, with special attention given to describing demographics of samples and the rationale for the methods used to constitute them.

Until this is done, the test cannot be fairly judged, and the best that can be said is that it is promising, but that the technical adequacy has not yet been established.

Review of the SPAR Spelling and Reading Tests, Second Edition by WILLIAM R. MERZ, SR., Professor and Coordinator, School Psychology Training Program, California State University, Sacramento, CA:

The Spelling and Reading Tests, Second Edition (SPAR) is designed to assess the spelling and word reading skills of children from 7-0 to 12-11 years old. It consists of three sections: a word reading section, a sentence reading section, and a spelling section. In the word reading section the child circles from a list of three to five nouns the word that best represents a stimulus picture. In the sentence reading section the child circles from a list of five to six words a word that best completes a sentence stem. In the spelling section, the child writes words from dictation; the words are read, then put into a sentence, and then read again. Administration time for the first two sections is 13 minutes with the word reading section containing 15 items, and the sentence reading section containing 30 items. The spelling section takes about 14 minutes to administer if words are presented in roughly 20-second intervals.

The test is designed for what the British call first-year junior students, as well as for older junior students and secondary students who are poor readers. In

American terminology this equates roughly to third through fifth grades. The test was first published in 1976 and revised in 1987. It is quite similar to the Group Reading Test (T4:1102) and may be viewed as an upward extension of that test with the addition of a spelling test.

There are two equivalent forms of the SPAR reading sections. The author examined two groups of over 1,000 children to assess equivalence between forms and showed roughly equal percentages at specific points along the score continuum. The spelling section uses a technique labeled by the author as "banking," which enables the examiner to compose across segments many permutations of the three word pairs presented in each segment of the spelling bank. The test is hand scored and yields separate reading and spelling total raw scores, which are converted to quotients (standard scores, which at the third grade level seem to have a mean of 100 and a standard deviation of 15). The distributions are truncated for children 9 years and older.

The author provides a brief rationale for the test in the first part of the manual. There are short sections on administration, marking, and using the norms tables, as well. Another short section on the use of test scores in teaching presents the author's views on using tests to help select reading material and improve instruction. Comments to teachers on assisting children with difficulties in learning to read are also included in the manual.

Technical information is provided in a section titled "Construction and Investigations." That section includes a very brief paragraph on item construction and selection for the reading sections. Much more space is devoted to the spelling section, specifically to the item banking technique and what advantages it yields. The equivalence of the two forms is discussed at some length. Standardization, validity, and reliability are discussed. Norms were derived from the performance of more than 3,500 boys and girls from 7-8 to 12-11; younger and older children were tested, too, in order to extend the norms. A common norm was constructed with the scores of boys and girls being given equal weight. An extensive description of the norm group is not presented. Although content-related evidence of validity and criterion-related evidence of validity are discussed, construct-related evidence is not presented. Reliability is discussed in terms of correlation coefficients, standard errors of estimate, standard errors of measurement, and differences between obtained and predicted scores. This information is presented a little differently from the way that American test authors and publishers present their findings on the reliability of the scores generated from test performance; the information is less detailed than one would expect, certainly in light of what was presented for the Group Reading Test; however, the available information is clear and logical.

One may address whether or not a test is appropriate for general use by answering three questions. First, do the test content and scores relate to the questions being asked of the quantitative results? Second, has the test been constructed in such a way that results are generalizable; that is, does the author offer adequate information on reliability and validity? Third, are the test results interpretable; that is, are there norms or criteria by which performance on the test may be judged?

In the case of the SPAR, the answer to the first question depends on the definition of reading and spelling in the intermediate grades. If reading is defined as word identification, then the test assesses that skill and answers a question about a child's skill in identifying nouns for which pictures are presented and identifying words in the context of an incomplete sentence. If spelling words correctly from dictation is the definition used, then this test assesses spelling. The second question is answered with evidence that the content addresses the question and that scores obtained correlate with the results of other tests. Evidence the scores are reliable is presented for the reading section; it is lacking for the spelling section. The third question deals with interpretability; that question is not addressed well because the description of the standardization group is restricted to age and school placement and does not report any other demographics.

Utilizing a test out of its cultural context is always problematic. The SPAR is designed for British children in schools in the United Kingdom. Whether or not it assesses the same skills taught in the curriculum of American schools or school districts requires careful critical analysis. Certainly the norm group is quite different from one you would find in American intermediate and upper grades. The manual author presents information about the test in a straightforward manner; yet, there is a paucity of information about the norm group. It is clear that the quotients for children over 9 years old are quite skewed; one would expect that. How maximum scores in the high 80s and low 90s are derived for the older children when maximum scores for younger child exceed 120 is not explained. There are technical gaps in the information presented on reliability, too. The usual Pearson Product-Moment Correlation Coefficients are presented, and there is discussion of a multiple linear regression model for presenting reliability. This is valuable, useful information. Nevertheless, as useful as this test has been found in the United Kingdom, it is probably not appropriate for general use in American schools. If this test assesses targeted skills with appropriate content, American school personnel might use it as a criterion referenced assessment. If a school system has staff knowledgeable in test construction, local norming could be undertaken. Otherwise, the test is of questionable value for American schools.

[366]

SPECTRUM-I: A Test of Adult Work Motivation.

Purpose: Measures the importance people place on four major goals or values related to career development decisions.

Population: Ages 16–Adult.

Publication Dates: 1985–87.

Acronym: SPECTRUM-I.

Scores, 5: Bias, Accomplishment, Recognition, Power, Affiliation.

Administration: Group or individual.

Price Data, 1994: $8.75 per manual ('87, 25 pages).

Time: (10–15) minutes.

Comments: Self-administered survey; mail-in to publisher for narrative report processing.

Authors: Larry A. Braskamp and Martin L. Maehr.

Publisher: MetriTech, Inc.

a) SPECTRUM-I NARRATIVE REPORTS.

Price Data: $39 per narrative report kit including manual, processing of 5 reports, and 5 pre-paid test booklets; $6.75–$9.75 per narrative report including processing and answer sheets.

Comments: Oriented to the test taker and features extensive interpretive information and guidelines for applying the test results to the test taker's career and life planning; based on parent program SPECTRUM.

b) SPECTRUM-I MICROCOMPUTER VERSION.

Price Data: $595 per microcomputer version; $27 per 50 test booklets/answer sheets; $18 per 50 decision model worksheets.

Comments: Supports both on-line and off-line testing; IBM version only.

Review of the SPECTRUM-I: A Test of Adult Work Motivation by CYRIL J. SADOWSKI, Professor of Psychology, Auburn University at Montgomery, Montgomery, AL:

SPECTRUM-I assesses the importance an individual places on four goals and values. These are labeled Accomplishment, Recognition, Power, and Affiliation. There also is a Bias scale to measure a tendency to present oneself in a positive light. The instrument is designed for use with individuals age 16 and above, is self-administered, and should take 10–15 minutes to complete.

The four value scales consist of 65 items scored on 5-point Likert-type scales. Items were rationally generated to address the content domains and the scales were derived empirically through factor analysis. Each scale consists of a common factor, which can be further differentiated into two oblique factors. Only the four common factors are scored. The Accomplishment and Recognition scales each consist of 19 items, the Power (perhaps better termed Competitiveness) scale consists of 13 items, and the Affiliation (perhaps better termed Cooperativeness) scale consists of 14 items. The Bias scale consists of 12 statements to which respondents indicate their perceived validity with *generally true*, *generally false*, or *uncertain*. This scale was empirically derived and scored for the socially desirable response. None of the items on the Bias scale is included on the other scales. Normative data for the scales are based on a sample of more than 1,000 adults who ranged in age from 18 to 79, with an average age of 37.3.

The internal consistencies of the four main scales are quite acceptable. Alpha coefficients from a sample of 1,095 men and women were .81 for Accomplishment, .82 for Recognition, .82 for Power, and .84 for Affiliation. The Bias scale has poor internal consistency. Alpha coefficients for samples of 281 and 612 adults were .33 and .45, respectively. Thus, its use in interpreting other responses is questionable.

Test-retest coefficients for a sample of 108 undergraduates over a 1-month period were .50 for Accomplishment, .66 for Recognition, .53 for Power, and .53 for Affiliation. For a sample of 33 employees over a 9-month period the test-retest coefficients were .80 for Accomplishment, .59 for Recognition, .66 for Power, and .64 for Affiliation.

Construct validity evidence for the four main value scales comes from a sample of 150 undergraduates who also completed the Myers-Briggs Type Indicator (MBTI). The pattern of correlations between the MBTI dimensions and the values scales was consistent with the expected interpretation of the scales. Other data provide correlations between the value scales and a variety of criteria from a number of different groups. However, much of this is difficult to interpret as there is no presented rationale for any particular pattern of relationships. Moreover, in some cases, multiple regression coefficients are presented without any individual weights or explanation of the outcomes.

Perhaps most problematic is that one of the stated objectives of the instrument is for use in career counseling. The relatively low test-retest correlations make this use somewhat questionable at the onset. Moreover, the manual authors report that the only reliable relationship between the values and the dimensions of the Holland Vocational Preference Inventory (VPI) was a correlation between the Spectrum-I Affiliation scale and the VPI Social scale.

Narrative reports are available for interpreting high and low scale scores. These include summary statements about the meaning of high and low scores as well as descriptive characterizations. However, there is no explanation as to how these descriptions were derived. Although they do appear to have content validity, more information about this is necessary along with supporting empirical data.

The SPECTRUM-I scales do seem to have some potential merit for use in a selection system. However, it will be necessary to demonstrate that the scales have rationally differential validity for different employment groups and that the scales differentially predict rationally distinct performance criteria for the same groups. Further research along these lines would be most useful and beneficial.

Review of the SPECTRUM-I: A Test of Adult Work Motivation by TERRY A. STINNETT, Associate Professor of Psychology, Eastern Illinois University, Charleston, IL:

The SPECTRUM-I, a 77-item self-report inventory appropriate for use with individuals aged 16 years or older, is designed to measure personal values thought to be related to career choice and satisfaction. The test assesses the importance the examinee places on these goals and values. The instrument's authors consider it to be a test of work motivation and contend that it should be useful as a career counseling tool. The scale might be used by employers to help select potential employees or with current employees to design incentive programs tailored to their unique needs.

There are four content scales included in the instrument: Accomplishment (19 items), Recognition (19 items), Power (13 items), and Affiliation (14 items). The content scales are referred to as personal incentives. A separate Bias scale (12 items) is also included to detect examinees who use a "socially desirable responding" response style. The items on the four content scales are descriptive statements and are presented in a 5-point Likert format: (1) = *Strongly Disagree*, (2) = *Disagree*, (3) = *Uncertain*, (4) = *Agree*, and (5) = *Strongly Agree*. The items that comprise the Bias Scale are presented in a 3-point forced-choice format: (T) = *Generally True*, (U) = *Uncertain*, and (F) = *Generally False*. These choices are clearly displayed at the top of each page of the protocol and the task demands are easily understandable. The general survey instructions are brief and are presented in writing on the first page of the answer sheet. The test-taker should also be told to avoid the middle response option (uncertain) as much as possible in order to obtain the most meaningful work motivation profile. The SPECTRUM-I should take about 10–15 minutes to complete for an average reader and can be group administered.

The Accomplishment scale reflects the value an individual places on challenge, excitement, variety, and opportunity for creative problem solving. The Recognition scale indicates the degree to which the individual values external reward and encouragement as a measure of success, status, and as a reason to perform his or her work. The Power scale identifies the person's attitudes toward being a leader, the need for competition, need for control, and ambition in the workplace. Affiliation reflects the worth the individual places on relationships with friends and other people and the opportunity to be with others. The Bias scale can measure the extent to which the examinee is responding stylistically to present a socially desirable image.

Unfortunately, the scoring system is not provided in the manual for SPECTRUM-I users. Respondents complete an answer sheet, which must be mailed to the publisher for scoring. The publisher provides a narrative interpretive feedback report. These reports are processed daily and can be returned by mail, overnight courier, or FAX. Interpretation is norm-referenced. Raw scores are converted to *T*-scores ($M = 50, SD = 10$) for each of the personal incentive scales and for the Bias scale. For the personal incentive scales, *T*-scores that are within $^1/_2$ standard deviation of the mean are considered average (45–55). Low scores fall at least $^1/_2$ standard deviation below the mean, whereas high scores are at least $^1/_2$ standard deviation above the mean. Interpretation of the Bias scale is different from that of the content scales. A *T*-score of 60 on the Bias scale is considered high and suggests the person might be deliberately trying to present himself or herself in a positive light. However, it is also possible that a high level of endorsement of these items actually reflects the person's behavior accurately (e.g., selection for clergy).

NORMATIVE INFORMATION. The norms for the SPECTRUM-I are based on adults who had been included in various research projects conducted with the instrument since 1983 ($N = 1{,}000$). The authors report that the sampling was not systematically representative of the U.S. population, but subjects reportedly are included from many different geographic regions. Table 4.2 in the manual provides the age distribution and the percentage of subjects found at each of five age groups. The age ranges included span 18 to 79 years. Most of the normative sample fall into the 26–35-year range (35.6%). There are slightly more men (58.7%) than women in the sample. Gender differences have been noted only on the Power scale and separate norms are used for this score. Combined norms are used for all other scores. An occupational breakdown of the norm sample is also provided in Table 4.3. Most of the sample were middle-level corporation managers or pilots (29.2%) followed by professionals (e.g., medicine, law, clergy, professors) (25%). Because the normative information is not very detailed in the manual, potential test users might have difficulty evaluating whether the SPECTRUM-I would be appropriate for their specific uses. The sampling procedure and selection of subjects also severely limits the test's generalizability.

INTERPRETIVE INFORMATION. A sample report is included in the test manual. The eight-page report contains the individual's motivational profile and identifies what the person considers to be important. The first page of the report, after the cover, provides information about how to interpret the results and includes general information about the personal incentive scales. The Bias scale and each of the four content scales are presented on a separate page. Each page includes the *T*-score for that scale for the examinee, and a description of the characteristics of people who fall above or below the mean for that scale. The *T*-scores for each area are also graphically displayed as a darkened area that appears to be a confidence interval, but this is not clearly described in the manual or the report. A confidence interval is a band of scores that has a high probability of including the examinee's true score and is based on the Standard Error of Measurement (SE_m) of the scale or test (Cohen, Swerdlik, & Smith, 1992). There are no SE_m estimates provided in the manual. To determine whether the darkened areas in the sample graphs did reflect confidence intervals, this reviewer calculated the SE_m for each of the scales using the alpha reliabilities reported in the test manual and constructed obtained-score confidence intervals based on the 68% confidence level. The (SE_ms) are: Accomplishment = 4.36, Recognition = 4.24, Power = 4.24, Affiliation = 4.00, and Bias = 7.42. Examining the graphed *T*-scores provided in the sample report reveals that the darkened areas in the graphs are not confidence intervals based on these reliability estimates. It is unclear why the scores are presented that way. The final page of the report is a summary of the individual's scaled scores and the individual item responses. The interpretive report is to be used for making decisions related to hiring, promotions, career development, and personal growth.

CONTENT VALIDITY. Five hundred items for the content scales of the SPECTRUM-I were developed from a series of formal and informal interviews with hundreds of adults. The interviewees were asked to describe "times in which they had experienced failure or success, felt good about themselves, or were proud of or satisfied with something they had experienced in their lives" (p. 16). The 500 items were reduced to 226 by the test authors based on judgments of item clarity, theoretical relevance, and redundancy and were written to reflect the range of personal incentives identified in the interviews.

CONSTRUCT VALIDITY. Two forced-choice response formats were used (e.g., *strongly agree* to *strongly disagree* and *almost all the time* to *very little or none of the time*) and both were scaled on a 1–5-point basis. The 226-item version was administered to a sample of adult workers and college students ($N = 70$). The scale was further reduced to 180 items based on item-characteristic data generated from the responses of subjects in this sample. The specific procedures are not reported in the manual. The 180-item instrument was then administered to samples of American ($n = 750$) and Japanese ($n = 500$) adults. Half of the subjects were from the public sector, whereas the others were in the private sector. Fifty-four percent were male and 46% were female. Ten percent were college students, about 27% were employed in middle management positions, and approximately 11% were in technical and clerical support positions. No further description of this sample is provided in the manual. A correlation matrix was generated to examine the intercorrelations among each of the subtests. The *r*s ranged from .11 to .51 and were uniformly positive, which suggests the subtests to a degree are measuring distinct constructs. The data were further analyzed with principal axis factor analyses with oblique rotation specified and an eight-factor solution was derived. After inspection of the factor matrix the authors suggested that four higher-order factors could explain the patterns of item covariation reasonably well. Items with loading of .30 or more were initially retained in the content scales and subsequent analyses discarded those items that resulted in lower internal consistency. The final instrument is a four-factor device.

Table 4.1 in the manual displays the factor-loading coefficients and the factor structure of the SPECTRUM-I. However, the item numbers are not provided with the factor structure matrix so the manual user is given a table of factor-loading coefficients that are not identified by the specific items. This omission might be to facilitate the authors' proprietary rights to the scoring scheme, but it makes careful analysis of this aspect of the SPECTRUM's construct validity difficult. Also, close inspection of the factor-loading coefficients reveals that three items in the Accomplishment scale, and one item each in the Power and Affiliation scales had loadings of less than .30. Two of these items actually had higher loadings on a factor other than the one in which they were included. The authors might have included them with their respective factors for theoretical reasons, but that is not stated and cannot be determined from the table.

Age effects were examined for each of the personal incentive scales and were found to be theoretically consistent (Maehr & Braskamp, 1986). Accomplishment and Affiliation scores increase with age, whereas Recognition scores tend to decrease as people become older. Power scores tend to be higher in the 36–45-year age range. Younger and older people have been noted to have lower Power scores. Because there were age effects noted, norms by age might be needed. However, the description of the norms does not specify that age-group comparisons are made.

Coefficient alpha internal consistency estimates for the personal incentive scales are acceptable (Accomplishment = .81, Recognition = .82, Power = .82, and Affiliation = .84) and provide support for the scale's construct validity. The Bias scale was developed by empirically identifying socially desirable alternatives, without regard to the personality content of the items and thus, high internal consistency would not be expected (Bias = .33 and .45).

CRITERION-RELATED VALIDITY. A number of studies are reported in the manual to support the

SPECTRUM-I's criterion-related validity. MetriTech (1987) noted the SPECTRUM-I Recognition and Affiliation scales have predicted success among life insurance agents and accounted for about 18% of the variance in the success criterion (cited in Braskamp & Maehr, 1987).

Hensler and Krug (1987) determined Power was related to several indices of performance in real estate agents (cited in Braskamp & Maehr, 1987). Modest correlations were obtained between Power and number of listings, number of sale, and dollar volume of sales.

Ahadi, Krug, and Scott (1989) in a study of nurse retention, commitment, and satisfaction, reported that Accomplishment and Power were positively related to self-esteem and annual earning, whereas Recognition was negatively related to tenure, satisfaction, and self-reliance. Affiliation was correlated positively with satisfaction and job commitment but was inversely related to self-reliance (cited in Braskamp & Maehr, 1987).

SPECTRUM-I scales have also been found to be related to enrollment in college academic programs, involvement in different co-curricular activities, perceived intellectual and personal/social gains, and general educational development in samples of university undergraduate students. However, they were generally not related to vocational preferences in college students (Braskamp & Braskamp, 1989; Huang & Braskamp, 1988; cited in Braskamp & Maehr, 1987).

In another sample of college students Krug and Braskamp (1989) found that the SPECTRUM-I Recognition and Power scales were related to self-reported concerns (cited in Braskamp & Maehr, 1987). Recognition was related to concerns about boredom, finding a job, managing finances, nutrition, physical attractiveness, self-confidence, self-image, and social life. Power was related to students' concerns about boredom, clubs, parties and socials, dating opportunities, finding a job, finding relevant courses, living conditions, nutrition, relations with parents, roommates, separated/divorced parents, social life, and sports recreational activities. These researchers also reported that the Accomplishment and Affiliation scales were related to satisfaction and commitment to school (*r*s ranged from .17 to .25). Accomplishment, Power, and Recognition were also able to explain 33% of the variance in self-esteem.

The SPECTRUM-I also has been shown to predict instructional leadership behaviors in a sample of primary and secondary school principals (Krug, 1988; cited in Braskamp & Maehr, 1987). Affiliation and Accomplishment were the best predictors of the instructional leadership dimensions. Variance accounted for in the criterion variables ranged from 9% (manages curriculum) to 14% (defines mission).

RELIABILITY. As noted earlier, the SPECTRUM-I content scales have adequate internal consistency. Test-retest reliability was also assessed in two samples: college students enrolled in an Educational psychology course (N = 108) and hospital employees who were participating in an organizational development program (N = 33). The college students were retested after a 1-month interval. Reliability coefficients were as follows: Accomplishment (.50), Recognition (.66), Power (.53), and Affiliation (.53). The hospital employees were retested after a 9-month interval. Reliability coefficients were as follows: Accomplishment (.80), Recognition (.59), Power (.66), and Affiliation (.64). No test-retest estimate was reported for the Bias scale. These data indicate the SPECTRUM-I content scales have inadequate stability over time.

SUMMARY. The SPECTRUM-I is a test of adult work motivation that has potential to be used for decision making with current and potential employees. The scale is quickly administered and is easy for examinees to complete. The test has adequate evidence of construct validity and a good theoretical foundation. However, there are a number of problems with the scale that hampers its overall utility. The manual contains too little information for potential users to critically evaluate the scale to determine if it is appropriate for their intended uses. The normative sample is not described well and limits the SPECTRUM-I's generalizability. The SPECTRUM-I has poor test-retest reliability and, thus, the personal incentive scores are not likely to be stable over time. Finally, it might be inconvenient for users to be unable to score and interpret the examinees' protocols on site.

REVIEWER'S REFERENCES

Maehr, M. L., & Braskamp, L. A. (1986). *The motivation factor: A theory of personal investment.* Lexington, MA: Lexington Books.

Braskamp, L. A., & Maehr, M. L. (1987). *SPECTRUM-I: Manual to accompany the Narrative Report.* Champaign, IL: MetriTech, Inc.

Cohen, R. J., Swerdlik, M. E., & Smith, D. K. (1992). *Psychological testing and assessment: An introduction to tests and measurement* (2nd ed.). Mountain View, CA: Mayfield Publishing.

[367]

Speech and Language Evaluation Scale.

Purpose: "Designed for in-school screening and referral of students with speech and language problems."

Population: Ages 4.5–18.

Publication Dates: 1989–90.

Acronym: SLES.

Scores, 7: Speech (Articulation, Voice, Fluency), Language (Form, Content, Pragmatics), Total.

Administration: Individual.

Price Data, 1993: $112 per complete kit including 50 pre-referral checklist forms, 50 pre-referral intervention strategies documentation forms, technical manual ('89, 47 pages), 50 rating forms, and Speech and Language Classroom Intervention Manual ('90, 205 pages); $25 per 50 pre-referral checklist forms; $25 per 50 pre-referral intervention strategies documentation forms; $12 per technical manual; $28 per 50 rating forms; $22 per Speech and Language Intervention Manual; $12 per quick score (IBM or Apple); $149 per computerized Speech and Language Intervention Manual.

Time: (15–20) minutes.
Comments: Ratings by teachers.
Authors: Diane R. Fressola, Sandra Cipponeri-Hoerchler, Jacquelyn S. Hagan, Steven B. McDannold, Jacqueline Meyer (manual), and Stephen B. McCarney (technical manual).
Publisher: Hawthorne Educational Services, Inc.

Review of the Speech and Language Evaluation Scale by KATHARINE G. BUTLER, Research Professor, Communication Sciences and Disorders, Syracuse University, Syracuse, NY:

The Speech and Language Evaluation Scale (SLES) is a 68-item scale designed, according to its authors, to permit teachers, whom they describe as trained observers (manual, p. 23) to rate a student for communication disorders in an objective and accurate fashion. However, they cite no research to support this assertion, nor is there agreement in the field of communication disorders regarding the advisability of other than a fully qualified speech-language pathologist as the best professional to conduct a speech and language evaluation. Teachers, as part of their preparation, rarely take coursework in speech-language pathology, phonetics, or communication assessment. In addition, the items utilized require considerable interpretation (e.g., "Speech causes unfavorable listener reaction," "Secondary characteristics are present while speaking," "Pitch is too high or too low for age or sex," and so forth). The authors do point out that "The SLES is most appropriately completed by teachers who have had adequate opportunity to observe and work directly with the student. No particular length of time can be identified as being necessary to become familiar with a student's speech and language before a rating can take place" (p. 23). The authors suggest that elementary level teachers would be expected to rate the child on the entire 68 items, whereas at the secondary level teachers might rate only particular subscales, and perhaps provide partial responses.

Given the fact that most screening is done at the beginning of a school year, when case loads are being established and students' communication assessed, the requirement that the teacher be knowledgeable about the child's articulation, voice, fluency, language (form, content, and use/pragmatics) would appear to be problematic.

The SLES is offered in two versions, a Pre-Referral Checklist which is noted to be "a condensed version of the actual scale" (p. 26) and a "standard rating form which is .... useful in determining the individual items for which the student is in need of intervention in the classroom" (p. 27). In actuality, the same 68 items appear on both forms; only the size of type for the questions is modified, and the Pre-Referral form has room for comments from the teacher, and the SLES itself has half a page devoted to the construction of a profile, with the teacher-examiner simply identifying "observed behaviors" on the Pre-Referral form, and the teacher(s) or paraprofessionals on the SLES being asked to rate each item as *Always* (0), *Occasionally* (1), or *Never* (2) occurring. The authors point out that the SLES is "not a test which requires a performance demonstration for each item on the scale. The observer should rely on observations of the student's ability to perform the items on the scale as those behaviors occur naturally in the educational environment" (p. 33).

The theoretical construct upon which the SLES items were selected is unclear. Some of the items fall within the phonological awareness and/or the metalinguistic realm under the Articulation subtests, some are particularly problematic for the bilingual and Limited-English-Proficient child, some are so general as to leave the underlying difficulty opaque, and some reflect little recognition of likely responses by those children from diverse cultural backgrounds, under the Language, Form, Content, and Pragmatics subtests.

The authors note that the SLES was normed on a total of 4,501 students from 82 school districts, representing 27 states, with the normative sample including regular education students and diagnosed speech- and language-impaired students. Insufficient evidence is provided regarding the normative sample, interrater reliability data, item analysis, and content and construct validity.

Standard scores are similar to those of many intelligence tests, with a mean of 10 and a standard deviation of 3. The authors recommend that a standard score more than 1 standard deviation below the mean on any of the six subscales represents "a deficit significant enough to qualify the student, along with documentation from other instruments, for special education services" (p. 35).

Percentile scores are provided, to be used "when it is desirable to make comparisons of the student's speech and language disorder(s) to the speech and language of the normative population" (p. 36). Percentile scores are probably less helpful in this regard, because the five subsystems of language (including phonology, morphology, syntax, semantics, and pragmatics) are intricately embedded in the language system and do not yield readily to a surface percentage approach.

Interestingly, male and female scores are provided separately in three age groups (Males 4.5 to 7.0 years, 7.0 to 15.0 years, and 15.0 to 18.0 years; Females, are divided into 4.5 to 8.0 years, 8.0 to 16.0 years, and 16.0 to 18.0 years). Documentation is insufficient to identify the rationale for collapsing the subscale standard scores in this manner. In fact, research, such as that conducted by Nippold (1988) or Ehren (1994), among others, would provide evidence that lumping boys (ages 7 to 15) and girls (ages 8 to 16) together does not reflect the typical developmental increases in spoken language. In fact, Ehren notes that most screening procedures are inappropriate for older children, noting that students with language-based learning problems typically have "sufficient social use of language to handle the type of language screenings they encounter, although they may lack the necessary linguistic base on which to build complex academic skills" (p. 402).

In summary, although the SLES would appear to be an efficient instrument, because the speech-language pathologist is not involved in the assessment or perhaps even in the intervention, as described by the authors, insufficient information is provided to demonstrate its efficacy in the treatment of several important student populations, including those with limited English proficiency and bilingual and culturally diverse populations. The 68 items selected fail to reflect current information on later language acquisition. There is little or no evidence presented on false positives or false negatives, based upon the screening instrument itself or upon follow-up data. The difficulty of creating excellent norm-based screening tests in speech and language is considerable; *A Consumer's Guide to Tests in Print* (Hammill, Brown, & Bryant, 1989) gives no such test a "passing score."

REVIEWER'S REFERENCES

Nippold, M. A. (1988). (Ed.). *Later language development*. Boston: Little Brown.

Hammill, D. D., Brown, L., & Bryant, B. R. (1989). *A consumer's guide to tests in print*. Austin, TX: PRO-ED, Inc.

Ehren, B. J. (1994). New directions for meeting the academic needs of adolescents with Language Learning Disabilities. In G. P. Wallach & K. G. Butler (Eds.), *Language learning disabilities in school-age children and adolescents* (pp. 393-417). Needham Heights, MA: Allyn & Bacon.

Review of the Speech and Language Evaluation Scale by PENELOPE K. HALL, Associate Professor of Speech Pathology and Audiology, Wendell Johnson Speech and Hearing Center, The University of Iowa, Iowa City, IA:

The Speech and Language Evaluation Scale (SLES), a 68-item scale to be completed by classroom teachers, was designed to be an "educationally relevant measure of speech and language" (manual, p. 12). The scale was developed to facilitate the active inclusion of teachers into the process of identifying and describing the communication problems of students in their classes. The behaviors on which the ratings are to be made "occur naturally in the educational environment" (p. 23). The scale's authors state that the information gained from the scale can be used in the diagnostic process to categorize the problems of Articulation, Voice, Fluency, and Language Form, Content, and Pragmatics. These six areas constitute the "logical" SLES subscales. The test authors state that the SLES also can be "translated directly" (p. 38) into the development of IEP statements. The authors also purport that the SLES can provide a measure of the "entry level needs" and the "exit points" (p. 37) of the student's intervention program. The same 68 SLES items are used as both a prereferral checklist and as an evaluation rating form. The checklist reportedly can be completed by classroom teachers in approximately 15 minutes, with 5 minutes needed for scoring. The Speech and Language Classroom Intervention Manual is a resource for designing classroom intervention strategies dealing with the 68 listed communicative behaviors. A review of the psychometric characteristics of the SLES follows.

STANDARDIZATION SAMPLE. The SLES was standardized on a normative sample of 4,501 randomly selected elementary and secondary school-aged students. The ratings were completed by 1,273 "unselected" classroom teachers from 82 school districts in 27 states. There was a range of 98–601 students at each of 13 standardization age levels from 4.5 years to 18+ years. The test authors provide demographic information and state that the characteristics "approximate" those statistics resulting from the 1980 U.S. Census.

TEST CONSTRUCTION AND ITEM ANALYSIS. The "original scale items" (p. 12) were written by two practicing speech-language clinicians, and then "refined and edited" (p. 12) by two additional speech-language clinicians (see discussion of content validity below). Unfortunately, the item analysis dealt only with the 68 items contained in the scale, which were determined a priori, and did not result from statistical analysis of a larger pool of potential items. Upon examination, the items seem to be most appropriate for younger children, with failure to provide a developmental continuum for the full age range for which the scale is to be used. Thus, the scale's ability to discriminate older students with communication problems from those who are communicating normally is in question.

However, according to the test authors, the item analysis was completed as a part of the standardization process, and consisted of three parts. The first was an analysis of the response distribution for each of the 68 scale items. On 85% (58) of the items at least 10% of the subjects were reported to have problems, and on 32% (22) of the items more than 30% of the subjects had difficulty. The distribution was thought to "adequately differentiate" (p. 16) among the items. Recall, however, that this item analysis dealt only with the 68 test items, and thus, did not determine whether these items were the *best* items from a larger item pool.

The second way in which the SLES items were reported to be analyzed was through correlations of each item within a subscale with the total score for that subscale. All were greater than .51, a modest correlation. The test authors state that the standard error of measurement, a reliability measure, was the third method by which item analysis was conducted for the SLES.

MEASURES OF CENTRAL TENDENCY. Two normative scores were developed for the SLES: (*a*) Subscale

Standard Scores (mean = 10, *s.d.* = 3) for each of the six subscales, derived from conversions of the Raw Scores; and (*b*) overall Percentile Scores. Tables for these conversions are included in the SLES technical manual.

Gender differences were found in the standardization data for all but the voice subscale; "boys exhibited more dysfunction" (p. 14) in the other five subscales. The scores on all scales "generally" increased with age for both boys and girls. However, breaks in scoring were noted and used to develop six normative groups: girls ages 4.5 to 8.0, 8.0 to 16.0, and 16.0 to 18.0+; and boys ages 4.5 to 7.0, 7.0 to 15.0, and 15.0 to 18.0+. These groups seem quite broad and it is feared that information on students at the ends of these large age groupings may be obscured or distorted. Standardization by yearly increments might be more helpful and meaningful to the practicing professional.

VALIDITY. The test authors report content validity was assured by the way in which the pool of potential items were developed—literature review and clinical experience. These original items were then reviewed by a second pair of clinicians, after which items were added, deleted, rewritten, and combined to the 68 contained in the scale.

Construct validity was attempted by comparing the SLES results from 102 randomly selected 7- to 18-year-old students from the standardization population, to those of "a corresponding group of identified speech and language impaired students" (p. 21). The students with communication problems were found to have mean total quotient scores "much lower" than those achieved by the "regular education students." The raw score mean differences were reported to be statistically significant for "most subscales and the Percentile Score" (p. 22), although no further information is provided. Specifics on how closely the groups matched, and descriptions of the communication disorders of the "impaired" students also are not included, nor is information on the construct validity with students under 7 years of age. Further, no information is provided on how well the SLES discriminates the older from the younger subjects because of large age groupings used for these comparisons. The test authors also cite construct validity via correlations between the six subscales, with correlations ranging from .332 to .819.

RELIABILITY. Test-retest reliability in completion of the scales for a group of 209 students after 30 days yielded a correlation coefficient of .98 with a range of .87 to .99. Interrater reliability also was determined by two educators with "equal knowledge" of students. Results of ratings on 292 students yielded a correlation coefficient of.64 on the total score, and a range of .49 to .75, which are modest correlations.

The SLES manual gives sufficient detail for the administration, interpretation, and use of the instrument, although there are minor editing problems.

SUMMARY. The Speech and Language Evaluation Scale (SLES) attempts to present a timely assessment concept based on classroom teachers' ratings of student communication skills as observed in the educational setting. With increasing emphasis on consultation and collaborative clinical delivery systems, this *concept* may add information to the diagnostic process and provide a vehicle that enables classroom educators to be an active part of both the diagnostic and intervention processes for their students with communication disorders.

However, problems with the way in which the actual SLES items were developed and analyzed, failure to include items appropriate for the entire age range for which the test purports to be useful, and the large age groupings covered by the normative data limits the scale's psychometric strength, and thus restricts its usefulness. Hopefully, the SLES will provide stimulation for future, more extensively and systematically developed instruments.

[368]

Speech-Ease Screening Inventory (K–1).

Purpose: "Designed to screen the articulation and language development" of kindergartners and first-graders.
Population: Grades K–1.
Publication Date: 1985.
Scores: Item scores only in 5 areas (Articulation, Language Association, Auditory Recall, Vocabulary, Basic Concepts) and in 4 optional areas (Auditory, Similarities and Differences, Language Sample, Linguistic Relationships) plus 5 observational ratings (Voice Quality, Fluency, Syntax, Oral-Peripheral, Hearing).
Administration: Individual.
Price Data, 1994: $59 per complete kit; $19 per 100 screening forms; $13 per 50 summary sheets (specify kindergarten or first grade); $18 per manual (32 pages).
Time: (7–10) minutes.
Authors: Teryl Pigott, Jane Barry, Barbara Hughes, Debra Eastin, Patricia Titus, Harriett Stensel, Kathleen Metcalf, and Belinda Porter.
Publisher: PRO-ED, Inc.

Review of the Speech-Ease Screening Inventory (K–1) by KRIS L. BAACK, Assistant Clinical Professor of Speech Pathology and Audiology, Department of Special Education and Communication Disorders, University of Nebraska-Lincoln, Lincoln, NE:

The intent of the Speech-Ease Screening Inventory (K–1) is to determine the articulation and language development of kindergartners and first graders. The authors purport this inventory will identify students in need of further diagnostic evaluation in the area of speech-language pathology. This instrument was designed "to bring order to the chaos that a public school speech-language pathologist experiences at the beginning of a school year when faced with the need to screen hundreds of young children" (manual, p. 5), and to provide uniform screening procedures for all schools in a district.

The test consists of a manual, stimulus pictures, student response form, and summary forms for entire kindergarten and first grade classes. All items fit in a plastic portfolio for easy storage and transporting of the screening inventory. The Speech-Ease Screening Inventory (K–1) examines five main areas and four optional areas. The tasks in the main section assess Articulation, Language Association, Auditory Recall, Expressive Vocabulary, and Basic Concept development. Optional areas assess additional Auditory items, Similarities and Differences, Connected Language, and Linguistic relationships. There is also an area on the scoring form to note observations for Voice Quality, Fluency, Syntax, Oral Structures and Functions, and Hearing.

The manual for the Speech-Ease Screening Inventory (K–1) includes instructions that are easy to understand for the administration of this instrument. Also included are examples of individual scoring forms and summary forms. Although the information provided is clear and concise, important, accountable information is omitted. There is no mention of a rationale for phonemes or language items selected, references, or normative data.

Stimulus pictures are black-and-white line drawings. They are easy to identify, appropriate for designated use, and durable. The student response form includes demographic information, instructions, specific stimulus items, error cut-off levels, space for student responses, and boxes in each task section to record scores, with a larger box at the top for the speech-language pathologist's professional recommendation (pass, watch, rescreen, and diagnostic).

The Articulation screening description purpose is as stated "to help determine any phonemes omitted, substituted, or distorted" (p. 11). However, not all phonemes are included in the screening nor is a rationale provided for why those phonemes that are screened were selected. The Articulation component is screened in an open-ended sentence format that provides the professional the opportunity to note other speech and language abilities and/or challenges.

Language Association consists of oppositional concepts and analogies, whereas Auditory Recall assesses the student's ability to understand and remember critical elements of a story he or she has just heard. During the retelling of the story the speech-language pathologist has the opportunity to observe the student's vocal quality, syntax, sequencing, and fluency. The Vocabulary screening indicates "whether the student understands and can describe selected nouns, verbs, and modifiers" (p. 17). Determining the student's ability to understand spatial, temporal, quantitative, and other concepts required for following directions is the emphasis of the Basic Concepts section.

The four optional tasks are made available to provide additional information to assist the speech-language pathologist in determining whether a diagnostic evaluation is necessary. In the Auditory area a variety of abilities are examined: language processing and memory, following sequential directions, repeating related and unrelated lists, and repeating a syntactically correct sentence. In Similarities and Differences the student's ability to explain how two items are the same and how two items are different by stating function, category, size, shape, etc. is demonstrated. The third optional section, Language Sample, examines the student's ability to identify and relate a logical sequence. This structured language example uses picture cards to facilitate a short story. Finally, Linguistic Relationships focuses on the student's ability "to make a judgement about a linguistic concept in the sentence. Comparative, spatial, temporal, and passive linguistic relationships are included" (p. 25).

The categories selected for screening provide the professional with a good overview of the student's skills. However, the optional tasks are as important, if not more important to examine than the stated "five main tasks." The students' actual use of their connected language and their ability to make relationships are vital components in deciding whether further evaluation is warranted. Although individual screening items appear cognitively appropriate, the author does not provide validation of their selection. References supporting item selection and field testing of their validity should be included.

All tasks except two (one in the main task group and one in the optional task group) are dependent on the student being able to respond to auditory stimuli. A student who has difficulty using only the auditory modality for taking in information would surely receive scores indicative of further evaluation. Finally, all screening tasks, except Basic Concepts, rely on the students expressing their responses verbally.

The format of the inventory response form is compact, and although cluttered, it is easy to administer and score. The organization of the individual task scoring boxes allows the professional to examine quickly all scores and make a recommendation. The inclusion of the grade-level summary sheets was an excellent addition to this screening inventory. This form assists speech-language pathologists in the organization of their screenings and provides an accountable record for continued use.

This screening inventory is designed to assist the speech-language pathologist in determining the need for further evaluation of kindergartners and first graders, and does not purport to be an instrument used to identify a handicapping condition. However, although this instrument does not have to adhere to the rigorous construction or normative procedures of a diagnostic test, information on the validity and reliability of this inventory is warranted. In addition, to use this inventory as intended, consistency in determining recommendations regarding further evaluation is essential. Thus, speech-language pathologists must know interrater and intrarater reliabilities to have confidence in the decisions they are making using this inventory.

Review of the Speech-Ease Screening Inventory (K–1) by ELEANOR E. SANFORD, Research Consultant, Division of Accountability Services/Research, North Carolina Department of Public Instruction, Raleigh, NC:

The Speech-Ease Screening Inventory (K–1) is designed to screen the articulation and language development of students in kindergarten and first grade who may have receptive and/or auditory communication problems.

The inventory consists of five main tasks, an observation section, and four optional tasks. Each task is clearly defined and the scoring criteria are specified. The main tasks include Articulation, which is "designed to help determine any phonemes omitted, substituted, or distorted" (manual, p. 11); Language Association, which gives an indication of the child's ability to make "auditory associations and includes oppositional concepts and analogies" (p. 14); Auditory Recall, which is "designed to assess the child's ability to understand and remember critical elements of a story he or she has just heard" (p. 15); Vocabulary, which "indicates whether the child understands and can describe selected nouns, verbs, and modifiers" (p. 17); Basic Concepts, which screens the child's ability to "understand spatial, temporal, quantitative, and other concepts needed to follow directions" (p. 19). The open-ended format of the tasks also enables the administrator to evaluate selected components of various tasks at one time. With the Auditory Recall task, the retelling-the-story format also provides the opportunity to observe skills in auditory sequencing, syntax, vocal quality, and fluency. The observation section of the inventory includes Voice Quality, Fluency, Syntax, Oral-Peripheral, and Hearing. The optional tasks (Auditory, Similarities and Differences, Language Sample, and Linguistic Relationships) are used to determine the appropriate type of diagnostic tools needed.

As indicated in the manual, the screening should be individually conducted by a speech-language pathologist. It takes approximately 7 to 10 minutes to determine an overall recommendation concerning speech remediation—pass, watch, rescreen, diagnostic (needs specific diagnostic evaluation). Almost everything needed to conduct the screening and determine the overall recommendation (items, space for responses, and scoring criteria) is found on the inventory form.

The authors state that 4 years of development have gone into the inventory. Unfortunately, the authors have not stated how the tasks were chosen, how the items/prompts within the tasks were chosen, and how the scoring criteria/cutoffs were determined. If the 4 years were spent on refining the tasks, items/prompts, and criteria, then these processes should be described in the manual. No information concerning the reliability of the inventory is provided. Only one study concerning the predictive validity of the inventory was discussed in the manual. In this study 1,560 students were screened using the Speech-Ease Screening Inventory and 298 (19%) were identified as needing further diagnostic evaluation. Upon further evaluation, 72% of the 298 identified students were enrolled in remedial speech or language services. Based on these results, the authors state the inventory "effectively identifies those students needing further professional speech-language diagnostic evaluation" (manual, p. 5). No other instruments were administered to all students to verify this claim and students not initially identified with the inventory were not further tested (the extent of false-negative decisions is unknown).

Although this instrument appears to measure what it purports and it is simple to administer and score, it cannot be recommended to make individual decisions concerning the need for speech and/or language remediation because there is almost no psychometric information (i.e., reliability, validity, development of instrument). Further work should be undertaken to support the construct validity of the inventory. Concurrent validity studies would be useful because the Illinois Test of Psycholinguistic Abilities (ITPA; T4:1202) measures some of the same constructs (language association) as does Speech-Ease.

The actual development of the inventory must be described specifically addressing the following issues: development of the items/prompts, criteria for selection of items/prompts and tasks from the domain of possible indicators of needing speech and/or language remediation, interrelationships of the items/prompts and tasks, and development of the scoring criteria. Much important work waits to be done on this instrument before it can be recommended for use.

[369]

Spiritual Well-Being Scale.

Purpose: "Developed as a general indicator of the subjective state of religious and existential well-being."

Population: Adults.

Publication Dates: 1982–91.

Acronym: SWBS.

Scores, 3: Religious Well-Being, Existential Well-Being, Total Spiritual Well-Being.

Administration: Group.

Price Data, 1992: $12 per specimen set including scale, manual ('91, 6 pages), and scoring and research informa-

tion; $2.25 or less per scale; volume discounts and student discounts available.
Time: (10–15) minutes.
Comments: Even-numbered items produce Existential Well-Being Scale (EWB); odd-numbered items produce Religious Well-Being Scale (RWB).
Authors: Craig W. Ellison and Raymond F. Paloutzian.
Publisher: Life Advance, Inc.
Cross References: See T4:2529 (1 reference).

TEST REFERENCES

1. Nathanson, I. G. (1995). Divorce and women's spirituality. *Journal of Divorce & Remarriage, 22*(3/4), 179-188.

Review of the Spiritual Well-Being Scale by AYRES D'COSTA, Associate Professor of Education, The Ohio State University, Columbus, OH:

The Spiritual Well-Being Scale (SWBS) is a well-conceived and reasonably well-researched 20-item paper-and-pencil rating scale. The authors believe that personal well-being is more than existential, and requires a religious dimension which can be nonsectarian.

The items in the SWBS are self-belief statements, divided equally between the existential and religious domains, which are rated on a 6-point Likert scale reflecting *Strongly Agree* at one end and *Strongly Disagree* at the other. The items are phrased equally in the positive and the negative modes, thereby forcing some responder attentiveness and reducing possible response-set bias.

The authors have demonstrated reasonable professional attempts at good instrument development. Judging from the perspective of the 1985 AERA-APA-NCME *Standards for Educational and Psychological Testing*, this instrument has a good basis in theory and in construct definition. The literature in the field appears to have been well scouted in selecting and representing the two domains of interest to the instrument. The religious well-being domain is particularly well differentiated from other related constructs, such as "religious cognition" and "religious commitment." The authors of the SWBS claim to have used a multidimensional conceptualization of spiritual well-being, such as that developed by Moberg (1979) incorporating "transcendent concerns . . . which involve meaning, ideals, faith, commitment, purpose in life, and relationship to God" (Ellison, 1983). The authors, however, do not indicate how the 10 items assigned to each domain are supposed to represent each domain.

The two well-being constructs, Religious and Existential, seem well differentiated, judging from the reported factor analysis, although the Religious appears to be more homogeneous than the Existential. To the authors' credit, a large number of concurrent validity studies have been conducted to substantiate the validity of the instrument as a direct general measure of spiritual well-being. This reviewer wishes these studies could have been synthesized and strengthened with multitrait multimethod analyses. The authors are aware of most of their instrument's limitations. They concede its inability to discriminate at the upper end of its scores, calling it a ceiling effect. Perhaps because the SWBS is so simple, direct, and easily scored, it is also easily faked. The authors report a negatively skewed distribution in its scores. This means that SWBS is unable to provide the discrimination typically desired, except to identify those from opposing sectarian or clinically troubled groups. Thus, the SWBS would not be useful in the selection of a spiritual leader from a religious group. Rather, as Bufford, Paloutzian, and Ellison (1991) succinctly indicate, "the scale is currently useful for research and as a global index of *lack* of well-being" (p. 56, italics added).

The authors claim the SWBS is useful for those whose primary task is to assess and correct dysfunctionality. This is an important claim that needs considerable clarification and illustration in the manual. The manual is skimpy (6 pages) and tends to underplay the depth of conceptual thinking underlying the scale. Much of the thinking available to the scholar in the research literature needs to be made available in appropriate form to the practitioner.

The administration instructions in the manual reflect a lack of adequate concern for possible misuse of the instrument. There is need to create a proper atmosphere both for the person administering the scale and the person taking it. None of this is evident either in the instrument or in the manual. The manual appears to have been targeted to a sophisticated and responsible counselor/psychologist, and neglects the need to ensure that the scale will be administered and used correctly.

The SWBS has good reliability, reasonable validity, and a sound conceptual basis. This reviewer noted commendable professionalism and effort on the part of the authors in developing a sound instrument and in avoiding undue claims for it. The authors have acknowledged the need for better describing norm groups, and for items with greater sensitivity. The SWBS also needs a professional technical manual and a helpful user manual. These are costly items that require commercial marketing resources for the scale.

REVIEWER'S REFERENCES

Moberg, D. O. (1979). *Spiritual well-being: Sociological perspectives*. Washington, DC: University Press of America.
Ellison, C. W. (1983). Spiritual well-being: Conceptualization and measurement. *Journal of Psychology and Theology, 11*, 330-340.
American Educational Research Association, American Psychological Association, & National Council on Measurement in Education. (1985). *Standards for educational and psychological testing*. Washington, DC: American Psychological Association, Inc.
Bufford, R. K., Paloutzian, R. F., & Ellison, C. W. (1991). Norms for the Spiritual Well-Being Scale. *Journal of Psychology and Theology, 19*, 56-70.

Review of the Spiritual Well-Being Scale by PATRICIA SCHOENRADE, Associate Professor of Psychology, William Jewell College, Liberty, MO:

The Spiritual Well-Being Scale (SWBS) was developed by Ellison and Paloutzian in response to increasing attention to holistic emphases and quality-of-life factors in the psychological literature. The authors are to be commended for willingness to venture into an area that some regard as too subjective for quantitative assessment. The SWBS is designed to indicate the "perceived spiritual quality of life" (manual, p. 2). Its two subscales, Religious Well-Being (RWB) and Existential Well-Being (EWB), parallel the authors' understanding of the two dimensions of spiritual well-being, a conceptualization supported by factor analysis on the entire SWBS. Ten items comprise each of the subscales, and the two subscales combine to form a total score. The RWB items refer to the respondent's perception of God and perceived involvement of God in life. The EWB items deal largely with one's sense of meaning in life and satisfaction with life's present direction. The authors provide clear instructions for the relatively straightforward scoring; they readily acknowledge that the scale assesses *perceived* spiritual well-being.

Extensive normative data gathered from various religious groups, clinical samples, and student populations are summarized in the manual. The religious samples reported are predominantly Christian based (with the exception of the Unitarian sample). This homogeneity is somewhat unfortunate, given the authors regard the scale as nonsectarian and recommend its use with individuals with a variety of beliefs. Further research with more varied religious populations may reduce concern over the apparent ceiling effect observed for the RWB scale among (largely Christian) religious samples.

Reliability coefficients for both subscales and the total scales are quite high. Test-retest reliability coefficients range from .82 to .99, with the exception of one sample in which a coefficient of .73 was observed for the EWB scale. The test-retest intervals range from 1–10 weeks, an adequate interval given the nature of the construct. Coefficient alphas from seven studies indicate satisfactory internal consistency, ranging from .78 to .82 for the RWB and .82 to .94 for the EWB. The reverse scoring of nine items helps to guard against response bias.

The items render the scale highly face valid, an asset in most settings, a potential liability when used for outcome assessment and in religious congregations, two of the several uses the authors suggest. Concurrent validity is difficult to pinpoint, as few measures of spiritual well-being exist. Correlations with related measures such as Crumbaugh's (1969) Purpose in Life Test (for the EWB, $r = .68$) and Allport and Ross's (1967) measure of Intrinsic Religion (for the RWB, $r = .79$) are encouraging.

Consideration of construct validity must take account of the user's conceptions of religion and spirituality. The items appear to relate clearly to the constructs the authors described, but little information is provided about the initial selection of the items, which appear to have remained constant over 10 years of research. Particularly with the RWB, it may be difficult to distinguish between Religious Well-Being and religiosity, belief in a personal God, or level of religious involvement, a concern reinforced by the relatively strong correlation with Intrinsic Religion. The extensive references to the involvement of God in the respondent's life and problems may place some limitation on the nonsectarian nature of the measure, at least where the RWB is concerned; the scale may be less applicable for those whose religion places less emphasis on a personal, caring God. Nevertheless, the conceptualization presented in the RWB is one congruent with many Western Christian and related belief systems. The issue of predictive validity has begun to be addressed through scale correlations with several personality variables, but for the most part must await further research, which the authors explicitly invite.

The attention to a spiritual dimension and to perceived well-being in the spiritual domain merits greater emphasis in clinical and outcome assessment. The Spiritual Well-Being Scale, capturing at least two dimensions of spiritual functioning while offering ease of administration and scoring, will prove useful for such assessment.

REVIEWER'S REFERENCES

Allport, G. W., & Ross, J. M. (1967). Personal religious orientation and prejudice. *Journal of Personality and Social Psychology*, 5, 432-443.

Crumbaugh, J. C., & Maholick, L. T. (1969). The Purpose in Life Test. Munster, IN: Psychometric Affiliates.

[370]

The Standard Timing Model.

Purpose: "Designed to simulate the motions, functions and operations of automatic production machines" for use in selection, evaluation, and training of employees.
Population: Mechanics.
Publication Date: 1971.
Scores: 4 tasks: Cam "F" Retarded, Rod "C" Lengthened 1/16 inch, Rod "E" Shortened 1/16 inch Spring "E" Disconnected at Lever "E", Cam "D" Retarded.
Administration: Individual.
Price Data: Available from publisher.
Time: [60] minutes.
Author: Scientific Management Techniques, Inc.
Publisher: Scientific Management Techniques, Inc.

Review of The Standard Timing Model by SAMI GULGOZ, Assistant Professor of Psychology, Koc University, Istanbul, Turkey:

The Standard Timing Model is designed for the evaluation, training, or selection of mechanics. It reproduces the way most automatic production machines work and is not a replica of any specific machine. The Standard Timing Model is a mechanical device that can be set up by the test administrator to malfunction in a standard way. The device is composed of "shafts, cams, cam followers, levers, springs, connecting rods, gears, racks, stops, and guides" (manual, p. 3). The administrator prepares the device to malfunction in a standard manner before each task and the examinee has up to 15 minutes to complete each task. The total number of tasks is four and they should be administered in the specified sequence.

The device is highly durable with a strong construction and it can withstand a large number of testings. The connections between parts are clearly visible as a result of the well-planned construction of the device.

The instructions to the candidate may be linguistically difficult for the examinees for whom this test is designed. Otherwise, the instructions are complete and adequate for the task. The manual also includes a sample of possible questions by the examinee and the permissible responses. The test administrators must be qualified examiners trained by Scientific Management Techniques, Inc. The proper tuning and adjustment of the equipment prior to testing is crucial. Therefore, only administrators who have completed a training by Scientific Management Techniques, Inc. are qualified to administrate the test. Considering the specialization and the precision that is required, this training is absolutely necessary. The test manual includes instructions for the test administrators. These instructions are clear and orderly for a novice. They are probably crystal clear for those who had the appropriate training.

Test scoring is primarily objective scoring using the amount of time an examinee spends on the task with a maximum of 15 minutes. The task is not scored if the amount of time spent on the task exceeds 15 minutes. Because larger scores mean longer time was spent on the task, smaller scores denote better performance. The scoring system includes a qualitative analysis to determine an examinee's strengths and weaknesses, especially for purposes of training. This qualitative scoring system is very structured and leaves little space for interpretation on the part of the examiners. if an examinee completes all four tasks, there will be four scores for that examinee. Most validation studies use and recommend using the three best scores out of the four tasks. The scores can be interpreted according to scores obtained within a company or according to percentiles reported in one of the large number of studies.

The reliability coefficients reported in various studies range from .77 to .97 indicating the Standard Timing Model is a very reliable instrument. Various validation studies using concurrent and predictor validity procedures generate validity coefficients between .03 and .76. Most coefficients are around .30. Although many of these coefficients are significant, the large number of subjects used in the studies may explain the significance of the coefficients. Available validity data are adequate. Higher validity coefficients would be desirable. Females and minorities perform lower on the Standard Timing Model. The same differences exist in criterion measures as well. It cannot easily be concluded the Standard Timing Model is an unfair test, but further studies are certainly necessary to investigate equity concerns.

In conclusion, The Standard Timing Model is probably the best test of its kind with high reliability and average concurrent and predictive validity. I strongly recommend the use of this test as long as the companies are careful about the match of the test to their job requirements and the fairness of the test.

Review of The Standard Timing Model by GARY L. MARCO, Executive Director, College Board Statistical Analysis, Educational Testing Service, Princeton, NJ:

The Standard Timing Model, a measure of mechanical ability or aptitude, is based on a mechanical device developed some 30 years ago for General Foods Corporation. The 18-inch cubical device consists of a number of mechanical parts that, when activated by a hand crank, simulate the action of automatic high-speed production machines. The examinee is required to diagnose and correct four specific mechanical malfunctions. The primary use of the measurement is to select production equipment adjuster-mechanics. Results may also be used in training and evaluation.

ADMINISTRATION. A trained administrator gives four adjustment tasks in a prescribed order to one examinee in testing sessions approximately one and a half hours long (including one hour of testing time). Before a particular task is administered, the examiner sets up the Standard Timing Model in a prescribed way. In each case the examinee is required, within 15 minutes, to correct one or two malfunctions that cause the machine to jam. Some specifics regarding the administration are missing in the instruction manual. The manual should be revised to reflect current administrative procedures and administrator instructions.

SCORING. The primary scoring procedure is simply the sum of the elapsed time required to make the machine operational across the four tasks or, alternatively, the sum across the three tasks that took the least amount of time. The examiner also provides a qualitative analysis of task performance.

NORMS. The instructional manual encourages users of the Standard Timing Model to develop local norms on candidates and employees to provide relevant standards. Still, norms on similar jobs across organizations, if available, could provide additional interpretive information to users whose studies are limited to small samples of job candidates. Given the emphasis on local norms, the information on how to develop these norms and to compute percentile ranks should be included.

RELIABILITY. Scientific Management Techniques, Inc. (1974) conducted a test-retest reliability study by administering the tasks of the Standard Timing Model to 32 Canadian Post Office mechanics and trainee mechanics approximately 90 days apart. Scores from the two administrations correlated .77. In a more recent study Stokes (1988) reported an alternate form reliability of .77 for scores on the original set of four tasks and scores on a parallel set. The sets were taken from 6 to 18 months apart by 106 mechanics in the clothing industry. These results indicate that the Standard Timing Model is probably reliable enough to be used for making decisions at the individual level.

VALIDITY. Over the years a reasonable number of validity studies have been conducted in specific job settings. These jobs include production machine adjusters and technicians in the tobacco industry, mechanics in the sewing industry, machine repairers and adjusters in an envelope manufacturing company, and set-up mechanics and packaging mechanic artisans in the pharmaceutical industry. Most of the 10 validity studies available to the reviewer have been done on small samples that ranged from 14 to 312 subjects.

Most of these studies used a concurrent validity study design in which mechanics already employed were tested with the Standard Timing Model and also rated by their managers. Scores on the Standard Timing Model were correlated with ratings to provide a validity coefficient. The correlations in these studies fell in the moderate range (.30 to .50) for the most part, although the correlation in one study of fabrications technicians (Rosentreter, Owens, Lee, & Warren, 1979) reached .76.

One study (Gilhooly, 1972) used data collected over time, and evaluated predictive validity rather than concurrent validity. Gilhooly attempted to identify machine repairmen most likely to benefit from a year-long training program. He found correlations in the .30s for performance on the Standard Timing Model with success in a pretraining course ($N = 133$) and also with training success ($N = 66$).

Several researchers (Rosentreter, 1983; Shaffer, Block, Sloan, Donnelly, & Reddy, 1987; Stokes & Bracken, 1988; Stokes, Palmer, & Allison, 1990) used the Position Analysis Questionnaire (McCormick, Jeanneret, & Mecham, 1972) to conduct job analyses. This step is important to validation because use of the Standard Timing Model is inappropriate unless mechanical elements are significantly represented in a job.

These validity studies, although of varying quality, are adequate to justify the use of the Standard Timing Model for selecting mechanics who might ultimately succeed on the job. They did not, however, address test fairness because of small sample sizes.

CONCLUSIONS. The Standard Timing Model holds a unique place among tests of mechanical ability or aptitude in that it is a performance test that requires examinees to use their mechanical skill in working through the four tasks. Thus, the Standard Timing Model has considerable face validity as a performance measure. However, the instrument takes over an hour of administration time and must be administered to examinees one at a time, thus making the testing logistics somewhat complicated.

Considerable validity information has accumulated over the years for various types of production mechanics. These reports are, however, not published and are available only from the researchers or Scientific Management Techniques, Inc. The testing company is encouraged to develop a technical manual for The Standard Timing Model to provide a single source of technical information about the instrument.

Existing research suggests The Standard Timing Model can be used reliably and validly across a fairly broad range of production mechanics. More research is needed on this instrument, however, to demonstrate the reliability and validity of the task-level scores, to evaluate the extent to which the four tasks measured by the instrument are reasonable samples of the domain of measurement, and to provide information about the fairness of the instrument for minority and gender groups. Nevertheless, sufficient reliability and validity information exists to warrant the use of The Standard Timing Model as a measure of mechanical ability for selecting employees for production mechanic jobs.

Organizations interested in using The Standard Timing Model are well advised to conduct their own job analyses and validity studies. Even if such studies are conducted, however, scores on this instrument should probably not be used alone but rather in conjunction with other information to select individuals for production mechanic jobs.

REVIEWER'S REFERENCES

Gilhooly, F. M. (1972, July). *An evaluation of the selection process for machine repairmen.* (Available from Caress, Gilhooly & Kestin, Inc., New York, NY)

McCormick, E. J., Jeanneret, P. R., & Mecham, R. C. (1972). A study of job characteristics of job dimensions as based on the Position Analysis Questionnaire. *Journal of Applied Psychology, 30*, 347-368.

Scientific Management Techniques, Inc. (1974, July). *Canada Post Office, Ontario postal region, Toronto MAPP district, Toronto, Canada: Report on the implementation of mechanic selection and evaluation techniques retest results.* (Available from Scientific Management Techniques, Inc., Boston, MA)

Gilhooly, F. M. (1978, December). *The validation of S.T.M. timed tasks as predictors of mechanical repairer effectiveness.* (Available from Caress, Gilhooly & Kestin, Inc., New York, NY)

Rosentreter, G. E., Owens, W. A., Lee, J., & Warren, P. C. (1979, July). *Summary report on validity and implementation of senior fabrication technician selection process.* (Available from Scientific Management Techniques, Inc., Boston, MA)

Rosentreter, G. (1983, May). *Cross validation of The Standard Timing Model as a predictor of mechanical repairer effectiveness.* (Available from Liggett & Myers Tobacco Company, Inc., Durham, NC)

Gilhooly, F. M. (1985, October). *The validation of S. T. M. timed tasks as predictors of mechanical/adjuster effectiveness.* (Available from Caress, Gilhooly & Kestin, Inc., New York, NY)

Schaffer, G. S., Block, L. K., Sloan, C. E., Donnelly, T. M., & Reddy, S. (1987, August). *Use of The Standard Timing Model for the selection of customer service representatives: Job analysis and validation.* (Available from Scientific Management Techniques, Inc., Boston, MA)

Stokes, G. S. (1988, January). *Comparison of alternate forms of The Standard Timing Model*. (Available from Scientific Management Techniques, Inc., Boston, MA)

Stokes, G. S., & Bracken, D. T. (1988, January). *Use of The Standard Timing Model for selection of operators and mechanics: Job analysis and validation*. (Available from Scientific Management Techniques, Inc., Boston, MA)

Stokes, G. S., Palmer, H., & Allison, I. (1990, July). *Validation of Standard Timing Model for selection of packaging mechanic artisans*. (Available from Scientific Management Techniques, Inc., Boston, MA)

[371]

Stanford Achievement Test—Abbreviated Version—8th Edition.

Purpose: "Measures student achievement in reading, mathematics, language, spelling, study skills, science, social science, and listening."

Population: Primary (1.5–4.5), Intermediate (4.5–7.5), Advanced (7.5–8.5), TASK (9.0–12.9).

Publication Dates: 1989–92.

Administration: Group.

Price Data, 1994: $22.50 per examination kit (for preview only) including complete battery test booklet, directions for administering, practice test with directions (Primary 1 through Advanced 2 only), and hand-scorable answer documents (Primary 3 through TASK 3 only); $53–$55 per complete/partial battery hand-scorable test booklets; $8.50 per copy of directions for administration (specify level); $3.50 per copy of class records; $27 per fall or spring national norms booklet (1988), and $43.50 per SAT abbreviated national norms booklet (1991).

Comments: For fall testing, the publisher recommends the use of the previous grade level test.

Author: The Psychological Corporation.

Publisher: The Psychological Corporation.

a) PRIMARY 1.

Population: Grades 1.5–2.5.

Scores, 12: Word Study Skills, Word Reading, Reading Comprehension, Total Reading, Language/English, Spelling, Listening, Concepts of Number, Mathematics Computation, Mathematics Applications, Total Mathematics, Environment.

Price Data: $69 per 25 complete battery machine-scorable test booklets; $55 per 25 hand-scorable test booklets.

Time: 167 minutes for Partial battery; 187 minutes for Basic battery; 210 minutes for Complete battery.

b) PRIMARY 2.

Population: Grades 2.5–3.5.

Scores, 12: Word Study Skills, Reading Vocabulary, Reading Comprehension, Total Reading, Language/English, Spelling, Listening, Concepts of Numbers, Mathematics Computation, Mathematics Applications, Total Mathematics, Environment.

Price Data: Same as *a* above.

Time: 160 minutes for Partial battery; 180 minutes for Basic battery; 203 minutes for Complete battery.

c) PRIMARY 3.

Population: Grades 3.5–4.5.

Scores, 16: Word Study Skills, Reading Vocabulary, Reading Comprehension, Total Reading, Language Mechanics, Language Expression, Total Language, Study Skills, Spelling, Listening, Concepts of Number, Mathematics Computation, Mathematics Applications, Total Mathematics, Science, Social Science.

Price Data: $69 per 25 complete battery machine-scorable test booklets; $55 per 25 hand-scorable test booklets; $67 per 25 partial battery machine-scorable test booklets; $53 per 25 hand-scorable test booklets; $55 per 25 complete battery reusable test booklets; $53 per 25 partial battery reusable test booklets; $52 per 100 complete/partial battery Type 2 machine-scorable answer folders; $13 per 25 Form J complete/partial battery hand-scorable answer folders.

Time: 152 minutes for Partial battery; $197 minutes for Basic battery; 233 minutes for Complete battery.

d) INTERMEDIATE 1–3.

Population: Grades 4.5–7.5.

Scores, 15: Reading Vocabulary, Reading Comprehension, Total Reading, Language Mechanics, Language Expression, Total Language, Study Skills, Spelling, Listening, Concepts of Numbers, Mathematics Computation, Mathematics Applications, Total Mathematics, Science, Social Science.

Price Data: $55 per 25 complete battery test booklets; $53 per 25 partial battery test booklets; $52 per 100 complete/partial battery Type 2 machine-scorable answer folders; $13 per 25 Form J complete/partial battery hand-scorable answer folders.

Time: 142 minutes for Partial battery; 187 minutes for Basic battery; 223 minutes for Complete battery.

e) ADVANCED 1–2.

Population: Grades 7–8.

Scores, 15: Reading Vocabulary, Reading Comprehension, Total Reading, Language Mechanics, Language Expression, Total Language, Study Skills, Spelling, Listening, Concepts of Numbers, Mathematics Computations, Mathematics Applications, Total Mathematics, Science, Social Science.

Price Data: Same as *d* above.

Time: 142 minutes for Partial battery; $186 minutes for Basic battery; 222 minutes for Complete battery.

f) TASK 1–3.

Population: Grades 9–12.

Scores, 9: Reading Vocabulary, Reading Comprehension, Total Reading, Language/English, Study Skills, Spelling, Mathematics, Science, Social Science.

Price Data: $49.50 per 25 complete battery test booklets; $52 per 100 complete/partial battery Type 2 machine-scorable answer folders; $13 per 25 Form J complete/partial battery hand-scorable answer folders.

Time: 95 minutes for Partial battery; 119 minutes for Basic battery; 155 minutes for Complete battery.

Review of the Stanford Achievement Test—Abbreviated Version—8th Edition by STEPHEN N. ELLIOTT, Professor of Educational Psychology, and JAMES A. WOLLACK, Lecturer, School of Education Testing Services, University of Wisconsin-Madison, Madison, WI:

In an age where the quality of public education is coming under attack, there is an increased need for a tool capable of assessing the caliber of instruction in our schools. Since 1923, the Stanford Achievement Test (SAT) has been available for this purpose. As would be expected of a test now in its eighth edition, the Stanford Achievement Test is widely regarded as "one of the best achievement batteries of its type" (Brown, 1992).

The SAT is designed to assess overall student achievement, as well as individual achievement in reading, mathematics, and language for students in grades 1 through 10. High school achievement in the Stanford series is measured by the Stanford Test of Academic Skills (TASK). These tests were crafted according to a set of educational specifications designed to reflect recent findings in educational research and standard educational curricula for each grade level across the United States. As a result, the SAT and TASK are valuable tools for gaining descriptive information about individual students' academic achievement relative to other students throughout the country. Still, in this era where teachers' instructional productivity is so heavily scrutinized, it is difficult, if not self-defeating, for teachers to create the time to administer a lengthy, comprehensive achievement test battery. The Stanford Achievement Test Series, Abbreviated is a shorter, more efficient way to sample a student's knowledge. The Complete abbreviated test requires 155–233 minutes (depending on the grade level), an improvement of an average of 170 minutes over the SAT and 70 minutes over the TASK. Given the limited amount of time teachers have with students in the classroom, this marks a significant improvement upon the full-length battery, especially for elementary and junior high school classrooms.

The test's publisher provides an extensive array of materials designed to assist in the administration and interpretation of results, including clear, word-for-word directions for administering the test and comprehensive norms tables broken down by grade, test form, and semester (fall versus spring). Each test form, except for TASK, includes a brief practice test so that students may familiarize themselves with the basic structure of the test and begin to relax and settle into the testing environment, thus increasing the probability of valid test results. In addition to these standard test materials, the test publisher has available (for a fee) resources for teachers and administrators providing assistance in planning instruction, reporting results to parents, and designing follow-up procedures after test results. A Technical Data Report is also available, although the contents of this document are not described, except for one sentence explaining that the manual "contains statistical data and other information about the research involved in the development and norming of the Stanford series" (Directions for Administering-TASK 1/2/3, p. 15). The information contained in these adjunct sources would greatly help teachers and school administrators to be more informed, sophisticated test users. Unfortunately, without these additional resources, many test users may be uncertain how to interpret test results because this information is given only scant coverage in the materials that customarily accompany the test, and perhaps only the most conscientious reader will find the reference to these other materials. Because of the lack of advertising and the expense involved in ordering each of these ancillary materials, we are afraid that few consumers will request them. In fact, because of the publisher's package plan, we did not review these adjunct materials.

TEST DESIGN AND CONTENT. In contrast to the SAT and TASK, the Stanford-Abbreviated is designed to "provide data descriptive of overall *group* achievement trends" (Spring Norms Booklet, p. 15), rather than individual achievement, because the individual domains are not measured with as much depth. Nevertheless, the content of the Stanford-Abbreviated does reflect the content of the full-length battery. Each subtest that appears on the SAT and TASK is also represented in the Stanford-Abbreviated. To make the test shorter, the Stanford-Abbreviated subtests contain only 20 or 30 items. These items were all selected from the full-length battery based upon their content and their high item discriminations. During the test construction phase of the SAT and TASK, each of these items underwent intense review by content and curriculum specialists to ascertain that they were well constructed, adhered to the test blueprint, and were seemingly free from cultural, ethnic, gender, and racial biases with regard to the content, style, and vocabulary. The test items also were subjected to statistical item analysis and were examined to ensure that they functioned similarly by gender and ethnicity.

The items that appear on the Stanford-Abbreviated appear to be quite good, as would be expected by the method used to select them. They appear to cover a broad range of material within each subject area. A nice range of item styles also is presented. Many items incorporate visual aids, several require students to apply knowledge, and others ask them to draw parallels between two different sets of variables. The test booklets and accompanying materials all are very well designed and aesthetically pleasing. Directions are clear and simple. Items are presented legibly and handsomely illustrated. Norms tables are thoughtfully laid out and are easy to read.

SCORES AND NORMS. As with the full-scale battery, scores are available for each subtest, as well as composite scores for total reading, mathematics, and language, and overall scores for the Partial, Basic, or Complete test battery. Several types of scores are available with the Stanford-Abbreviated. In addition to typical raw scores, percentile ranks, and scaled scores, the Stanford-Abbreviated provides stanines, grade equivalents, and normal curve equivalents. Brief, simple descriptions of each type of score are provided. Ultimately, users are urged to use stanine scores to assist them in interpreting achievement profiles. We find this advice puzzling because stanines contain less information about one's achievement than the more frequently used percentiles or standard scores, and are also inferior to the less familiar normal curve equivalents. This recommendation could only derive from the ease with which one can lump students with scores of 1, 2, and 3 into a below-average group, categorize students with scores of 4, 5, and 6 into an average group, and designate students with scores of 7, 8, and 9 as belonging in an above-average group. We believe that such a recommendation reflects a lack of confidence in school administrators to correctly use and interpret more meaningful scores, and does not reflect best measurement interpretation practices.

One particularly beneficial feature of the norms tables is the inclusion of the standard error of measurement associated with each standard score. This information should assist in making more accurate interpretations about individual and group test scores.

Separate norms tables are provided for students taking the exam during the fall or spring semesters. The eighth edition of the SAT originally was normed in the spring of 1988 on approximately 175,000 students and again in the fall of 1988 on approximately 135,000 participants. New, updated norms were established in 1991 when the forms were restandardized. In the spring standardization, approximately 150,000 participants were sampled, and around 120,000 more participants were included in the fall standardization in 1991.

The 1991 National Norms Booklet that accompanies the test contains the demographic characteristics of those participating in the 1991 standardization. The standardization sample was selected to be similar to the population of students, according to the 1980 U.S. national Census, with respect to geographic region, socioeconomic status, urbanicity, and ethnicity. The deviations between the census data and the representation never exceeded 3%, so we may say that the sample accurately reflected the population with respect to these variables. The table also shows the percent of students with various handicapping conditions in the standardization. In the spring standardization, 6.2% of the students had handicapping conditions, whereas in the fall, only 4.8% of the students had handicapping conditions. In both semesters, the vast majority of the students with handicapping conditions were classified as learning disabled. Although the National Census figures corresponding to handicapping condition are not provided for direct comparison, both samples fall considerably shy of the approximately 12% of students with disabilities in the total population. Norms for separate subgroups (e.g., gender or ethnicity) are not provided.

Although the restandardization in 1991 renders the 1988 test norms obsolete, booklets containing those old norms are still part of the test package. One must exercise caution when using these books, to ensure that the correct norms are being consulted because slightly different results may be obtained. As would be expected from the equating procedure, any particular raw score coincides with the same standard score in both the 1988 and 1991 norms, but it is possible for the corresponding percentile rank and stanine to change. As an example, consider an 11th grade student receiving a score of 159 on the complete battery of the TASK 3 test during the fall. Both norms tables agree that this student received a scaled score of 710; however, the 1991 norms list this student at the 79th percentile and in stanine 7, whereas the 1988 norms list this student at the 76th percentile and in stanine 6. The test booklets themselves do not mention this source of confusion and fail to instruct the user to consult the 1991 norms unless they are retesting a student who was originally tested using the 1988 norms!

The ultimate goal of an achievement test is to inform the school of the quality of education and the achievement levels of their students in an assortment of academic areas. Although multiple types of scores are available for this purpose, the manual does not provide a clear picture of how one should use the test output to identify areas of weakness and improve instruction and learning. It would be very helpful, and again representative of best measurement practices, if the manual provided a sample report of prototypical output for both an individual student and a group of students, along with reasonable interpretations for how to best use this information.

RELIABILITY. Kuder-Richardson-20 (KR-20) measures of internal consistency are given as evidence of reliability. KR-20 coefficients for each subtest and composite test are provided separately for fall and spring administrations and test form. For the spring administration, KR-20s are available for two adjacent grade levels. The manuals also provide the reliability estimate of the full-length battery.

In general, the KR-20s are excellent. For all ages and tests, most subscale coefficients are in excess of .85 or .90, and the total scores and composite scores are almost all in excess of .95. Reliabilities for the Listening, Environment, and Language Mechanics subtests tended to be in the upper .7s. The conservative test user should be cautious about overanalyzing the scores on these subtests. All subtest KR-20s are highly comparable to those for the full-length battery, indicating that the abbreviated form is measuring the material with virtually no loss in accuracy. No test-retest reliabilities are provided in the basic manual.

One troubling aspect of the reliability data is that the internal consistencies noted apply to the 1988 norms and are contained in the 1988 fall and spring norms booklets. Because the 1988 norms are outdated, the inclusion of this reliability information appears to be the only utility of the 1988 norms books. The 1991 National Norms Booklet contains no mention of the concept of reliability! Although it is likely that this information is contained in the Technical Data Report, it would be helpful to users if this material was included in the 1991 National Norms Booklet. In addition to providing the users with accurate information about the test reliability, it would allow the publishers to send only the 1991 norms and avoid a very confusing situation.

VALIDITY. In his review of the SAT, Eighth Edition, Brown (1992) argued that "A major shortcoming of the series is the lack of convincing arguments and data in support of the validity of the battery." We echo Brown's sentiments once again. In the manual's brief discussion of validity, it is mentioned that the content validity may be evaluated by comparison of the test content against any given curriculum. It is further argued that because the Stanford-Abbreviated is simply a shorter version of the SAT but is designed to measure the same material, it is a valid instrument. Such an argument is a difficult one to accept, and no evidence is provided to indicate that the subtests, even on the full-length SAT, truly measure the state goals.

A major omission is the failure to present the correlation between the full-scale SAT and TASK with the Stanford-Abbreviated. The similarity between the reliability coefficients on the full-length batteries and the Stanford-Abbreviated leads us to believe that this correlation should be quite high. There also are no correlations presented between the Stanford-Abbreviated and other measures of achievement. It is mentioned that the students in the standardization during the fall of 1988 also completed the Otis-Lennon School Ability Test, but the actual relationship in terms of correlations between the two tests was not provided in the materials we had. The authors also are remiss for failing to present information about known groups' performance on the test. Documentation of differences between males and females, racial groups, geographic regions, and students with disabilities and those without disabilities would be useful to establish the convergent validity of the Stanford-Abbreviated. In addition, given the importance of these student variables in discussions of achievement, it is surprising they were not discussed in the manual.

CONCLUSIONS. An accurate and efficient test to assess students' academic performance is sorely needed. The Stanford-Abbreviated may well be that test. It follows in the 70-year-old tradition of excellent, thoughtful tests produced in the Stanford series. Although the manual encourages use of the Stanford-Abbreviated for identifying group achievement trends only, the striking similarity between its reliability coefficients with those on the full-length battery suggest that it may be appropriate to use it for *descriptive* purposes at the individual level, also. Our criticisms of the battery are, in general, aimed at aspects of the manuals that are not user-friendly. In particular, there is confusion over which set of norms tables should be consulted and the lack of reliability and validity data presented in the manual makes it very difficult and inconvenient to evaluate the test. Many of these data are likely provided in the Technical Data Report, so access to this report should be made easy for all users by including such information in the standard package received by users at no extra cost.

Overall, the Stanford-Abbreviated is a solid instrument that can provide schools with useful information about how well their students are satisfying the desired outcomes specified by curriculum and content experts relative to other students nationwide. The Stanford-Abbreviated accomplishes this dubious task in half the time of the full-length battery. When weighing the amount and quality of information about student and group performance to be learned from a test alongside the time required to administer such a battery during school hours, one would be wise to seriously consider the Stanford-Abbreviated.

REVIEWER'S REFERENCE

Brown, F. G. (1992). [Review of the Stanford Achievement Test, Eighth Edition.] In J. J. Kramer & J. C. Conoley (Eds.), *The eleventh mental measurements yearbook* (pp. 861-863). Lincoln, NE: Buros Institute of Mental Measurements.

Review of the Stanford Achievement Test—Abbreviated Version—8th Edition by KEVIN L. MORELAND, Associate Professor of Psychology, Fordham University, Bronx, NY:

According to the publisher, the Stanford Achievement Test—Abbreviated Version—8th Edition (SAT-A) "is particularly appropriate for providing information about group trends in achievement and meets Chapter 1 requirements for reporting reading, mathematics, and language" (Multilevel Fall Norms Booklet, p. 14).

Because the SAT-A is, as its name implies, a short form of the Stanford Achievement Test, Eighth Edition, much of the information in reviews of the full-length battery applies to the SAT-A as well (Brown, 1992; Stoker, 1992). Readers should consult those reviews as background for the present one.

DEVELOPMENT. Information about the development of the SAT-A is sketchy: Items were chosen from Form J of the full-length battery "based on a combination of the statistical properties of each item and the content assessed by the group of items in each subtest at each level" (Multilevel Fall Norms Booklet, p. 14). The result is a complete (abbreviated) battery that is a little over 25% shorter than the full-length SAT. Some of the subtests at some levels have been reduced by nearly 45% (e.g., Word Study Skills), but other have not been shortened at all (e.g., Mathematics Applications). The SAT-A, unlike the parent battery, does not include forms appropriate for children in kindergarten or the first grade.

The SAT-A was equated with the full-length battery using Rasch procedures.

CONTENT. It is asserted that the SAT-A's "content reflects the content of the full-length battery . . . The difference between the two tests is primarily a function of the depth to which clusters/objectives are tested" (Multilevel Fall Norms Booklet, p. 14). Perusal of the *Compendium of Test Objectives*, the *Indices of Instructional Objectives*, and the test materials themselves suggests that this characterization is accurate. This verification was a laborious task: The publisher should provide comparative tables that make it easy for potential users to satisfy themselves in this regard.

RELIABILITY. KR20 reliability coefficients indicate that the item selection efforts were quite successful. The SAT-A subtests and total scores are frequently as internally consistent as their full-length counterparts, reductions that do occur are typically a matter of less than .05.

VALIDITY. No real information is provided about the SAT-A's validity. The potential user is told that the SAT-A is valid to the extent that its content reflects the content of the full-length battery. This is disturbing on two counts. As noted above, it is not easy for potential users to assess the extent to which the SAT-A's content reflects that of the parent instrument. Moreover, as Brown (1992) noted, information about the validity of the full-length battery is limited. At a bare minimum, the (doubtlessly high) correlations between the full-length battery and the SAT-A should be published.

CONCLUSION. My conclusions about the SAT-A echo Brown's (1992) conclusions about the full-length battery. Anyone needing a norm-referenced, survey achievement test battery to assess group trends would be well-advised to give the Stanford Achievement Test—Abbreviated Version strong consideration. The development of the full-length battery reflects the care that has typified the construction of this academic achievement battery throughout its long history and the procedures used to develop the abbreviation appear to be sound. The test materials and interpretive materials are attractive and easy to use. My criticisms of the battery, for the most part, result from the absence of detailed information about the construction of the battery and its psychometric properties. There is one further question that needs to be raised even though it has nothing to do with the merits of the SAT-A per se: Is it really justifiable to sacrifice instructional time to administer a test that is not recommended for use in providing feedback to individual students or developing individualized instructional plans for them?

REVIEWER'S REFERENCES

Brown, F. G. (1992). [Review of the Stanford Achievement Test, Eighth Edition.] In J. J. Kramer & J. C. Conoley (Eds.), *The eleventh mental measurements yearbook* (pp. 861-863). Lincoln, NE: Buros Institute of Mental Measurements.

Stoker, H. (1992). [Review of the Stanford Achievement Test, Eighth Edition.] In J. J. Kramer & J. C. Conoley (Eds.), *The eleventh mental measurements yearbook* (pp. 863-865). Lincoln, NE: Buros Institute of Mental Measurements.

[372]

Stenographic Skill-Dictation Test.

Purpose: "Measures speed and accuracy in taking shorthand notes from dictated material."
Population: Applicants for stenographic positions.
Publication Dates: 1950–90.
Scores, 3: Difficulty Level, Dictation Speed, Read-Back Ability.
Administration: Group.
Price Data, 1991: $135 per reusable test kit including 5 cassette tapes and manual (no date, 20 pages).
Time: Administration time not reported.
Comments: Formerly called Test for Stenographic Skill; test may be administered orally or by cassette recording.
Author: E. F. Wonderlic Personnel Test, Inc.
Publisher: E. F. Wonderlic Personnel Test, Inc.
Cross References: For reviews by Virginia E. Corgan and Michael J. Stahl, see 10:344; for additional information and reviews by Reign H. Bittner and Clifford E. Jurgensen of an earlier version, see 4:459.

Review of the Stenographic Skill-Dictation Test by DAVID O. ANDERSON, Senior Measurement Statistician, Educational Testing Service, Princeton, NJ:

The Stenographic Skill-Dictation Test is designed to measure speed and accuracy in taking shorthand notes from dictated materials; that is, "to find the highest difficulty and speed level which best describes the applicant's ability to take dictation comfortably" (manual, p. 3). The applicant's ability to read back their shorthand notes is also measured. Four cassette tapes are used to dictate letters of varying difficulty at speeds ranging from 40 to 160 words per minute (with an additional tape for warm-up purposes). Each letter contains 100 words; letter difficulty within each tape is varied by changing the number of syllables and the average sentence length across the letters. The test can be administered, scored, and interpreted in about 30 minutes.

The manual accompanying the tapes includes scoring information, transcripts of the letters being dictated, directions for verbally dictating the letters (rather than using the tapes), and directions for using the warm-up letters to determine the dictation speed at which testing should start. There is no technical report containing information about test development, results from validity and reliability studies, and norm data.

VALIDITY AND RELIABILITY. The test materials appear to have face validity, and having the speed, complexity, and length of dictation controlled by audiotape presentation certainly increases the reliability of this type of measurement. However, there is no information presented as to how the test letters were selected, nor how the dictation speeds and syllable densities were decided upon. A test-retest reliability study would require a second form of the test. In addition, there is only one letter dictated at each combination of speed, syllable density, and average sentence length. Furthermore, the scoring instructions are sufficiently vague that interrater and intrarater reliabilities are likely to be low.

SCORING. After the applicant completes a letter (or a complete tape—it is unclear from the manual), he or she reads back the letter(s) while the administrator follows the transcript and notes the errors. The scoring guide recommends the following performance scale: *Excellent* = no errors, letter reads back easily; *Good* = one or two minor errors, letter reads back very easily, or hesitantly but accurately; *Fair* = three or more errors or changes, but letter is still satisfactory and makes sense; *Failure* = anything other than the above, the letter is disorganized and makes little or no sense. The administrator is instructed to go to the next highest speed tape if the applicant successfully completes the highest level difficulty letter on a tape. No empirical evidence or rationale is presented to justify this scale. Likewise, "successful completion" of a letter is never defined.

SUMMARY. The Stenographic Skill-Dictation Test could be an adequate device to measure the highest speed at which an applicant can comfortably take shorthand notes and read them back. However, the lack of any technical information regarding test development procedures and validity and reliability data limits this test's professional usefulness.

Review of the Stenographic Skill-Dictation Test by JOSEPH C. CIECHALSKI, Associate Professor of Counselor and Adult Education, East Carolina University, Greenville, NC:

The Stenographic Skill-Dictation Test is an individually administered test designed to assess the speed and accuracy of taking shorthand from dictated letters of 100 words each. All letters are included on five cassette tapes and are also printed in the manual. Two "warm-up" letters are included to determine the speed to begin the test. Letters are graded according to three levels of difficulty (easy, medium, and hard). Difficulty level is determined by the number of syllables per 100 words (syllable density) and average sentence length. For example, easier letters contain six or seven sentences with about 140 syllables each, whereas the more difficult letters contain four or six sentences with about 180 syllables. In addition, letters may be dictated at various speeds from 40 to 120 words per minute (wpm) orally or from 40 to 160 wpm using the cassettes.

ADMINISTRATION. The Stenographic Skill-Dictation Test may be administered orally or by cassette tape. Although administration time is not reported, the author claims the test can be administered, scored, and interpreted in less than 30 minutes. Separate directions for administering the dictation tests by cassette or orally are presented in the test manual. If the administrator is interested in the consistency of testing examinees, then he or she should use the cassettes. On each cassette, a male or female dictates each letter clearly in a voice that is pleasing and clear. However, if the administrator desires to vary the pace of each letter, he or she may use the Vari-Speed Guide. With some practice, this guide will help an administrator needing to read the letters at various speeds ranging from 40 to 120 wpm.

To determine the dictation speed of the first letter, the examiner administers a "warm-up" letter which is read at increasing rates of speed. The first warm-up letter contains between 40 to 100 wpm and the second one between 60 and 120 wpm. It is unclear from the directions, however, how a test administrator chooses between the two warm-up letters. When the warm-up letter is completed, the examinee reads back the letter to the administrator who determines the examinee's comfort speed and level of difficulty at taking dictation. For example, according to the author, "if an applicant successfully reads back their 'Warm-Up' letter notes at 90 wpm, but begins to falter at 100 wpm, he/she should be given the lowest difficulty level at 90 wpm" (p. 3). Unfortunately, "successfully" and "falters" are not clearly defined.

Therefore, using the example above, the first letter is dictated at the lowest level of difficulty (Level I) and at a speed of 90 wpm. An administrator then dictates subsequent letters at increasing levels of difficulty at the same speed (90 wpm) until the highest level (Level II or III) is achieved. If the examinee attains the highest difficulty level (Level III), the method described above continues at the next higher speed (100 wpm).

SCORING. Total scores are not reported. Instead, letters are scored separately. Each letter is scored according to level of difficulty, speed, and accuracy. As each letter is read back, the examiner reads the copy in the manual and counts the number of errors made. To record the results, three symbols are used: I, II, III to indicate level of difficulty and 60, 80, 90, etc., for dictation speed for each letter. Grades of "A" (Excellent), "B" (Good, "C" (Fair), and "D" (Failure) are awarded to each letter depending on the number of errors and how well the letter is read back. For example, a grade of "A" would be assigned to a letter containing no errors and the letter reads back easily. Or, a grade of "C" would be assigned to a letter containing three or more errors and the letter is satisfactory and makes sense.

An examiner may choose to substitute percentages in place of letter grades. For example, 90–100 for a grade of "A," 80 to 90 for a grade of "B," etc. In addition, an examiner who wants to judge the neatness of typing may request the examinee type the letter. The author reminds the administrator, however, "that this does not constitute a test of typing skill" (p. 5).

NORMS. Norms are not provided in the manual. This is surprising because the Stenographic Skill-Dictation Test is not a new test. In fact, the author claims that it has been perfected in actual employment conditions over a period of 20 years. To interpret the results, an examiner reports level of difficulty, dictation speed, and read-back performance for each individual. Norming tables would enable examiners to compare an individual's results with others who have been tested or are currently employed by the company.

VALIDITY AND RELIABILITY. No evidence of validity nor reliability is reported. With over 20 years of use, this reviewer would expect a plethora of validity and reliability data.

SUMMARY. The Stenographic Skill-Dictation Test is easy to administer and score. Uniformity of testing conditions is guaranteed if the test is administered using the cassette tapes. However, serious limitations of the test include the lack of reliability, validity, and norming data. Studies are needed to provide users of the test with evidence for test-retest reliability, interrater reliability, and predictive validity. Until then, the Stenographic Skill-Dictation Test should be used with extreme caution.

[373]

Stress Impact Scale.

Purpose: Designed "to assess the perception . . . and impact of potentially stressful events and conditions."
Population: Ages 8-3 to 19-6.
Publication Date: 1990.
Acronym: SIS.
Scores, 3: Stress Occurrence, Stress Impact, Stress Impact Differential.
Administration: Group.
Price Data, 1990: $49 per complete kit including 50 profile/student response forms and manual (53 pages); $24 per 50 profile/student response forms; $27 per manual.
Time: Administration time not reported.
Authors: Jerry B. Hutton and Timothy G. Roberts.
Publisher: PRO-ED, Inc.

Review of the Stress Impact Scale by ROBERT J. DRUMMOND, Professor of Counselor Education, University of North Florida, Jacksonville, FL:

The Stress Impact Scale (SIS) is a 70-item self-appraisal instrument designed to measure the occurrence and impact of potentially stressful events and conditions of children and youth between the ages of 8 and 20. Students are asked to mark "yes" or "no" to whether the event had happened and then if they checked "yes," circle whether the event still bothers them "none," "some," or "a lot." The SIS yields three stress quotients: the Stress Occurrence Quotient, Stress Impact Quotient, and the Stress Impact Differential Quotient. The instrument is based upon the assumption that 8- to 20-year-olds can make reliable and valid reports about their life circumstances, and that the subjective judgment of the impact of events yields useful information. The items represent events and conditions that could happen in the lives of this group in school, at home, or in the community and represent dimensions of academic performance and behavior, social isolation and objectives, mobility, disturbed relationships, and the like.

The authors report criterion-referenced, construct, and item validity. The authors present studies comparing the SIS with the Children's Manifest Anxiety Scale, Children's Life Events Inventory, and Piers-Harris Self-Concept Scale—Revised. The coefficients tend to be significant and in the predicted direction. The cluster analysis of the items tends to support the scale and item validity of the instrument.

The SIS appears to have excellent reliability. Alpha coefficients are reported by age, grade, ethnicity, race, gender, and the like. The coefficients range from .80 to .92. Test-retest coefficients on the Occurrence and Impact scales by grade were equally as high and ranged from .83 to .93 across different grade levels. The authors report the alpha coefficients and standard errors of measurement for the scales by age, grade, ethnicity, gender, and residency. One set of norms is presented for the total age group. The characteristics of the standardization group are well described. Some questions that might help counselors in using the test are not clarified in the manual (e.g., are there differences in scores due to gender, grade, age, or ethnic/cultural group?). Also, does the SIS provide a limited snapshot of a student with problems? How does response set and social desirability affect how a student responds on the instrument? Would one of the problem checklists be equally effective and provide additional information?

Illustrative case studies are presented with suggestions for interventions that might be used. The manual provides an excellent summary of research and interventions dealing with stress.

Overall the SIS appears to be a psychometrically sound instrument and a potentially useful tool for child psychologists and school counselors.

Review of the Stress Impact Scale by SCOTT T. MEIER, Associate Professor of Counseling and Educational Psychology, State University of New York at Buffalo, Buffalo, NY:

The Stress Impact Scale (SIS) is a 70-item self-report scale designed to assess stressful life events for children and adolescents. The SIS produces two major scores: (*a*) Stress Occurrence, the total number of stressful events endorsed by the respondent; and (*b*) Stress Impact, a sum of ratings of the degree to which the respondent is "bothered" by the endorsed stressful events.

The authors developed items for the scale by reviewing the stress literature, interviewing distressed students, and examining related scales. The process resulted in items with apparent validity and a reading level appropriate for the intended population. The item analyses, however, contain several unusual or questionable procedures. First, the test developers administered the scale to a group of subjects and retained items if they correlated (with an uncorrected Pearson *r*) with the total score above .20. Second, the developers examined scale stability by calculating alpha coefficients across levels of age, grade, ethnicity, race, gender, and urban/rural residency; confirmatory factor analyses would be a preferable procedure. Third, the developers conducted cluster analyses instead of factor analyses to determine the underlying structure of the SIS.

SIS norms appear to be adequate and representative across levels of gender, urban/rural residency, race, ethnicity, parent education level, parent occupation, and national geographic area. Reliability levels also appear adequate to good, with scale alphas consistently above .85 and test-retest reliability at .90 over a 2-week period.

Although convergent validity data are presented, no information is offered for discriminant or predictive validity. Consequently, the SIS's chief weakness, like most other measures of negative affect, is construct validity. The Stress Occurrence and Stress Impact scores are highly intercorrelated ($r = .86$), suggesting they are interchangeable. Individual items which correlate most highly with a scale total (e.g., "Caught doing something wrong," [p. 18], "Teacher yelling at me" [p. 17]) appear to be tapping a conduct disorder or behavioral problems factor, although the test developers' cluster analysis classified these items into a grouping the developers labeled "Conditions/Hassles."

Interestingly, the manual does contain evidence for discriminant validity that is, apparently, unrecognized by the test developers. Correlations between the SIS scales are highest with another measure of children's stressful life events (*r*s around .70), next highest with an anxiety measure (around .55), and lowest with a self-concept measure (about -.34). This rank order of correlations magnitude provides validity support in that the SIS correlates most highly with measures of similar constructs and less so with different constructs.

Perhaps because of these construct validity questions, self-report scales like the SIS typically are not accompanied by evidence that they can predict behavior or performance. Although the SIS developers present a reference to the contrary, little evidence exists in the stress literature that demonstrates a consistent relation between stress and performance (e.g., Meier, 1991).

The stress-performance link is poorly understood and may be nonlinear. The next steps for the SIS developers, then, are to (*a*) examine the discriminant validity of the SIS, that is, does the scale measure stress or a conduct disorder factor; and (*b*) determine whether the SIS can predict performance measures such as grades, school attendance, or teacher/parent ratings of behavioral problems.

Scales like the SIS can probably best be conceived as global measures of such negative affective states as stress, depression, and anxiety. As such, most of these self-report scales, if developed with some attention to psychometric properties, are probably interchangeable for most users' purposes. Users who wish to screen children and adolescents for stress and behavioral problems may wish to use the SIS for that purpose.

REVIEWER'S REFERENCE

Meier, S. T. (1991). Tests of the construct validity of occupational stress measures with college students: Failure to support discriminant validity. *Journal of Counseling Psychology*, *38*, 91-97.

[374]

Strong Interest Inventory [Fourth Edition].

Purpose: Designed to "inquire about a respondent's interest in a wide range of occupations."
Population: Ages 16 and over.
Publication Dates: 1927–85.
Acronym: SVIB-SCII.
Scores, 264: 6 General Occupational Themes: Realistic, Investigative, Artistic, Social, Enterprising, Conventional; 23 Basic Interest Scales: Adventure, Agriculture, Art, Athletics, Business Management, Domestic Arts, Law/Politics, Mathematics, Mechanical Activities, Medical Science, Medical Service, Merchandising, Military Activities, Music/Dramatics, Nature, Office Practices, Public Speaking, Religious Activities, Sales, Science, Social Service, Teaching, Writing; 207 General Occupational Themes: Accountant (female, male), Advertising Executive (f, m), Agribusiness Manager (m), Air Force Enlisted Personnel (f, m), Air Force Officer (f, m), Architect (f, m), Army Enlisted Personnel (f, m), Army Officer (f, m), Art Teacher (f, m), Commercial Artist (f, m), Fine Artist (f, m), Athletic Trainer (f, m), Banker (f, m), Beautician (f, m), Biologist (f, m), Broadcaster (f, m), Bus Driver (f, m), Business Education Teacher (f, m), Buyer (f, m), Carpenter (f, m), Chamber of Commerce Executive (f, m), Chef (f, m), Chemist (f, m), Chiropractor (f, m), College Professor (f, m), Computer Programmer (f, m), Credit Manager (f, m), Dental Assistant (f), Dental Hygienist (f), Dentist (f, m), Dietitian (f, m), Elected Public Official (f, m), Electrician (f, m), Elementary Teacher (f, m), Emergency Medical Technician (f, m), Engineer (f, m), English Teacher (f, m), Executive Housekeeper (f, m), Farmer (f, m), Flight Attendant (f, m), Florist (f, m), Food Service Manager (f, m), Foreign Language Teacher (f, m), Forester (f, m), Funeral Director (f, m), Geographer (f, m), Geologist (f, m), Guidance Counselor (f, m), Home Economics Teacher (f), Horticultural Worker (f, m), Interior Decorator (f, m), IRS Agent (f, m), Investments Manager (f, m), Lawyer (f, m), Librarian (f, m), Life Insurance Agent (f, m), Marine Corps Enlisted Personnel (f, m), Marketing Executive (f, m), Mathematician (f, m), Mathematics Teacher (f, m), Medi-

cal Illustrator (f, m), Medical Technician (f, m), Medical Technologist (f, m), Minister (f, m), Musician (f, m), Navy Enlisted Personnel (f, m), Navy Officer (f, m), Nurse LPN (f, m), Nurse RN (f, m), Nursing Home Administrator (f, m), Occupational Therapist (f, m), Optician (f, m), Optometrist (f, m), Personnel Director (f, m), Pharmacist (f, m), Photographer (f, m), Physical Education Teacher (f, m), Physical Therapist (f, m), Physician (f, m), Physicist (f, m), Police Officer (f, m), Psychologist (f, m), Public Administrator (f, m), Public Relations Director (f, m), Purchasing Agent (f, m), Radiologic Technologist (f, m), Realtor (f, m), Recreation Leader (f, m), Reporter (f, m), Research & Development Manager (f, m), Respiratory Therapist (f, m), Restaurant Manager (f, m), School Administrator (f, m), Science Teacher (f, m), Secretary (f), Social Science Teacher (f, m), Social Worker (f, m), Sociologist (f, m), Special Education Teacher (f, m), Speech Pathologist (f, m), Store Manager (f, m), Systems Analyst (f, m), Travel Agent (f, m), Veterinarian (f, m), Vocational Agriculture Teacher (f, m), YWCA Director (f), YMCA Director (m); 2 Special Scales: Academic Comfort, Introversion-Extroversion; 26 Administrative Indexes: Total Response, Infrequent Response, Response Percentages (Like, Indifferent, Dislike) for each of the 7 inventory sections (Occupations, School Subjects, Activities, Leisure Activities, Types of People, Preference Between Two Activities, Characteristics) plus Total for all parts.

Administration: Group.

Price Data, 1992: $13 per 25 test booklets; $18 per 25 Spanish test booklets; $18 per Strong user's guide ('84, 92 pages); $23 per manual ('85, 189 pages); $9 per specimen prepaid scoring packet; $54 per 10 prepaid expendable test booklets; $53 per 10 prepaid profile answer sheets; $85 per 10 prepaid interpretive expendable test booklets; $84 per prepaid interpretive answer sheets; $13 per 50 not prepaid answer sheets; $3.50 per 10 profile reports; $5.75 per 10 interpretive reports; $6 per 10 expanded interpretive reports; $5 per 10 topical reports.

Foreign Language Editions: Available in Spanish (Form T325S), French Canadian (Form T325FC), and Hebrew (T325H) translations, and the wording has been adapted for use in Great Britain (Form T325B).

Time: (20–30) minutes.

Comments: Separate machine scored answer sheets may be used; test cannot be scored locally.

Authors: Edward K. Strong, Jr. (original inventory), David P. Campbell (test and manual revision), and Jo-Ida C. Hansen (manual).

Publisher: Consulting Psychologists Press, Inc.

Cross References: For reviews by Wilbur L. Layton and Bert W. Westbook, see 9:1195 (17 references); see also T3:2318 (99 references); for reviews by John O. Crites, Robert H. Dolliver, Patricia W. Lunneborg, and excerpted reviews by Richard W. Johnson, David P. Campbell, and Jean C. Steinhauer, see 8:1023 (289 references, these references are for SVIB-M, SBIV-W, and SCII). For references on the Strong Vocational Interest Blank For Men, see T2:2212 (133 references); for reviews by Martin R. Katz and Charles J. Krauskopf and excerpted reviews by David P. Campbell and John W. M. Rothney, see 7:1036 (485 references); for reviews by Alexander W. Astin and Edward J. Furst, see 6:1070 (189 references); see also 5:868 (153 references); for reviews by Edward S. Bordin and Elmer D. Hinckley, see 4:747 (98 references): see also 3:647 (102 references); for reviews by Harold D. Carter, John G. Darley, and N. W. Morton, see 2:1680 (71 references); for a review by John G. Darley, see 1:1178. For references on the Strong Vocational Interest Blank For Women, see T2:2213 (30 references); for reviews by Dorothy M. Clendenen and Barbara A. Kirk, see 7:1037 (92 references); see also 6:1071 (12 references) and 5:869 (19 references); for a review by Gwendolen Schneidler Dickson, see 3:649 (38 references); for a review by Ruth Strang, see 2:1681 (10 references); for a review by John G. Darley, see 1:1179.

TEST REFERENCES

1. Grotevant, H. D., Cooper, C. R., & Kramer, K. (1986). Exploration as a predictor of congruence in adolescents' career choices. *Journal of Vocational Behavior, 29*, 201-215.

2. Robbins, S. B. (1987). Predicting change in career indecision from a self-psychology perspective. *Career Development Quarterly, 35*, 288-296.

3. Johnson, R. W., & Hoese, J. (1988). Career planning concerns of SCII clients. *Career Development Quarterly, 36*, 251-258.

4. Swanson, J. L., & Hansen, J-I. C. (1988). Stability of vocational interests over 4-year, 8-year, and 12-year appraisal. *Journal of Vocational Behavior, 33*, 185-202.

5. Fouad, N. A., Hansen, J-I. C., & Galicia, F. A. (1989). Cross-cultural similarity of vocational interests of professional engineers. *Journal of Vocational Behavior, 34*, 88-99.

6. Lent, R. W., Larkin, K. C., & Brown, S. D. (1989). Relation of self-efficacy to inventoried vocational interests. *Journal of Vocational Behavior, 34*, 279-288.

7. White, M. J., Kruczek, T. A., & Brown, M. T. (1989). Occupational sex stereotypes among college students. *Journal of Vocational Behavior, 34*, 289-298.

8. Carter, R. T., & Swanson, J. L. (1990). The validity of the Strong Interest Inventory with Black Americans: A review of the literature. *Journal of Vocational Behavior, 36*, 195-209.

9. Douce, L. A., & Hansen, J-I. C. (1990). Willingness to take risks and college women's career choice. *Journal of Vocational Behavior, 36*, 258-273.

10. Morrow, P. C., Mullen, E. J., & McElroy, J. C. (1990). Vocational Behavior 1989: The year in review. *Journal of Vocational Behavior, 37*, 121-195.

11. Randahl, G. J. (1990). A typological analysis of the relations between measured vocational interests and abilities. *Journal of Vocational Behavior, 38*, 333-350.

12. Rounds, J. B. (1990). The comparative and combined utility of work value and interest data in career counseling with adults. *Journal of Vocational Behavior, 37*, 32-45.

13. Spokane, A. R., & Hawks, B. K. (1990). Annual review: Practice and research in career counseling and development, 1989. *Career Development Quarterly, 39*, 98-128.

14. Hatcher, M. A. (1991). The corporate woman of the 1990s: Maverick or Innovator. *Psychology of Women Quarterly, 15*, 251-259.

15. Kidd, G., & Naylor, F. (1991). The predictive power of measured interests in tertiary course choice: The case of science. *Australian Journal of Education, 35*, 261-272.

16. Lewin, M., & Wild, C. L. (1991). The impact of the feminist critique on tests, assessment and methodology. *Psychology of Women Quarterly, 15*, 581-596.

17. Fouad, N. A., & Dancer, L. S. (1992). Cross-cultural structure of interests: Mexico and the United States. *Journal of Vocational Behavior, 40*, 129-143.

18. Gallagher, S. A., Stepien, W. J., & Rosenthal, H. (1992). The effects of problem-based learning on problem solving. *Gifted Child Quarterly, 36*, 195-200.

19. Hesketh, B., McLachlan, K., & Gardner, D. (1992). Work adjustment theory: An empirical test using a fuzzy rating scale. *Journal of Vocational Behavior, 40*, 318-337.

20. Miller, M. J. (1992). Synthesizing results from an interest and a personality inventory to improve career decision making. *Journal of Employment Counseling, 29*, 50-59.

21. Miller, M. J., & Foxworth, C. L. (1992). Effects of response set on the infrequent response index of the Strong Interest Inventory. *Journal of Employment Counseling, 29*, 162-165.

22. Pedoto, J. P., & Hartman, B. W. (1992). Artistic orientation as a clinical indictor of chronic career indecision in adult children and grandchildren of alcoholics. *Psychological Reports, 71*, 971-976.

23. Swanson, J. L. (1992). Generating hypotheses from Rachel's Strong profile. *Career Development Quarterly, 41*, 31-35.

24. Swanson, J. L. (1992). The structure of vocational interests for African American college students. *Journal of Vocational Behavior, 40*, 144-157.

25. Toman, S. (1992). The career dilemma of an artistic client: The case of Rachel. *Career Development Quarterly, 41*, 27-31.

26. Breeden, S. A. (1993). Job and occupational change as a function of occupational correspondence and job satisfaction. *Journal of Vocational Behavior, 43*, 30-45.

27. Carson, A. D., & Mowsesian, R. (1993). Self-monitoring and private self-consciousness: Relations to Holland's vocational personality types. *Journal of Vocational Behavior, 42*, 212-222.

28. Hansen, J-I. C., & Sackett, S. A. (1993). Agreement between college major and vocational interests for female athlete and non-athlete college students. *Journal of Vocational Behavior, 43*, 298-309.

29. Hansen, J-I. C., Collins, R. C., Swanson, J. L., & Fouad, N. A. (1993). Gender differences in the structure of interests. *Journal of Vocational Behavior, 42*, 200-211.

30. Lawson, L. (1993). Theory of work adjustment personality constructs. *Journal of Vocational Behavior, 43*, 46-57.

31. Rounds, J., & Tracey, T. J. (1993). Prediger's dimensional representation of Holland's RIASEC circumplex. *Journal of Applied Psychology, 78*, 875-890.

32. Velozo, C. A. (1993). Work evaluations: Critique of the state of the art of functional assessment of work. *The American Journal of Occupational Therapy, 47*, 203-209.

33. Amabile, T. M., Hill, K. G., Hennessey, B. A., & Tighe, E. M. (1994). The Work Performance Inventory: Assessing intrinsic and extrinsic motivational orientations. *Journal of Personality and Social Psychology, 66*, 950-967.

34. Betsworth, D. G., Bouchard, T. J., Jr., Cooper, C. R., Grotevant, H. D., Hansen, J-I. C., Scarr, S., & Weinberg, R. A. (1994). Genetic and environmental influences on vocational interests assessing using adoptive and biological families and twins reared apart and together. *Journal of Vocational Behavior, 44*, 263-278.

35. Blustein, D. L., Pauling, M. L., DeMania, M. E., & Faye, M. (1994). Relation between exploratory and choice factors and decisional progress. *Journal of Vocational Behavior, 44*, 75-90.

36. Brown, S. D., & Gore, P. A., Jr. (1994). An evaluation of interest congruence indices: Distribution characteristics of and measurement properties. *Journal of Vocational Behavior, 45*, 310-327.

37. Croteau, J. M., & Slaney, R. B. (1994). Two methods of exploring interests: A comparison of outcomes. *Career Development Quarterly, 42*, 252-261.

38. Hansen, J-I. C., Kozberg, J. G., & Goranson, D. (1994). Accuracy of student recall of Strong Interest Inventory results 1 year after interpretation. *Measurement and Evaluation in Counseling and Development, 26*, 235-242.

39. Lenox, R. A., & Subich, L. M. (1994). The relationship between self-efficacy beliefs and inventoried vocational interests. *Career Development Quarterly, 42*, 302-313.

40. Cronin, C. (1995). Construct validation of the Strong Interest Inventory Adventure Scale using the Sensation Seeking scale among female college students. *Measurement and Evaluation in Counseling and Development, 28*, 3-8.

41. Hesketh, B., Hesketh, T., Hansen, J-I., & Goranson, D. (1995). Use of fuzzy variables in developing new scales from the Strong Interest Inventory. *Journal of Counseling Psychology, 42*, 85-99.

42. Lubinski, D., Benbow, C. P., & Ryan, J. (1995). Stability of vocational interests among the intellectually gifted from adolescence to adulthood: A 15-year longitudinal study. *Journal of Applied Psychology, 80*, 196-200.

43. Sackett, S. A., & Hansen, J-I. C. (1995). Vocational outcomes of college freshmen with flat profiles on the Strong Interest Inventory. *Measurement and Evaluation in Counseling and Development, 28*, 9-24.

Review of the Strong Interest Inventory [Fourth Edition] by JOHN CHRISTIAN BUSCH, Associate Professor of Education, University of North Carolina at Greensboro, Greensboro, NC:

The Strong Interest Inventory (SVIB-SCII) "compares a person's interests with the interests of people happily employed in a wide variety of occupations. It is a measure of interests, not of aptitude or intelligence" (Specimen Brochure, p. 1). The Strong has been used by counselors for about 60 years and reviews have appeared in at least seven previous editions of the *Mental Measurements Yearbook*. The inventory has a long and venerable history of use, in part because its authors have responded to changes during that period.

One of the marks of a professionally maintained testing instrument is a willingness to continually evaluate and revise. The Strong is a wonderful example of this standard. Major changes have occurred during the past 25 years and the following revisions have been made for the 1985 version. Seventeen new vocational-technical occupational groups have been sampled (actually 34 paired male and female scales). Six newly emerging professional occupations (12 scales) have been added. Old occupational norms have been updated. Additional male and female parallel occupational scales have been developed so that currently only five scales are not paired by gender. Sixteen smaller criterion group samples were increased in size. New Men-in-General (MIG) and Women-in-General (WIG) reference samples were constructed to better reflect societal changes. These revisions increase confidence that test results will be relevant for the 1990s.

Since the last MMY review, a fourth edition of the Manual for the SVIB-SCII, a Specimen Brochure, and an updated profile have been published. The manual is a comprehensive description of the purpose and development of three types of Strong scales, the evidence marshaled in support of claims for valid and reliable measurement, and recommendations for interpretation and use. The manual is so extensive, I would choose it for examination in a measurement course.

The Strong is especially good in presenting information to clients in a clear and understandable form; the profile sheet efficiently integrates information from the three types of scales. Numeric, graphical, and verbal score summaries, the arrangement of scores, and statements of appropriate test use in the profile increase the likelihood of appropriate interpretation. The authors emphasize the need for the counselor and the client to integrate test results with other sources of information and to consider carefully discrepant test outcomes. The meaning of each of the scales is completely described and information regarding interpretation of the scales is summarized in the User's Guide for the SVIB-SCII (Hansen, 1984) and the manual. Administrative scales are used to guard against misinterpretation; and the possibility of client-manipulated test results is also discussed. Overall, the interpretive information is outstanding.

A large number of research studies have been conducted on the Strong during the past 30 years. In some instances the number of studies cited in the technical manual seems sparse even allowing that the manual cannot provide a comprehensive review. For example, the evidence regarding racial differences consists of two studies, both of which utilized the pre-1974 version of the Strong. The User's Guide does cite a few additional studies; however, the manual should be the primary source for summary of relevant information regarding the integrity of the scale. Given the extensive research base of the Strong, the authors might consider including a selected bibliographic listing of key studies organized by important issue in the manual. In general, the manual reports a balanced set of studies in support of the claims made for validity and reliability.

Sampling of occupations was an immense project that involved a total of 40,197 individuals in 162 occupations in 1981 and more than satisfies the *Standards for Educational and Psychological Testing* (AERA, APA, & NCME, 1985), which require detailed description of the validation sample. A list of reasonable selection criteria for occupational groups (satisfaction and success in the occupation, minimal experience, etc.) is provided in the manual. The list contains descriptions of the 207 occupational samples that include the sampling frames used, the size of the sample, the year data were collected, the mean age, years of education, and years of experience; no information summarizing variability of those characteristics or racial composition of the sample is provided.

The authors of the manual appear to be somewhat defensive with regard to the occupational samples. This is shown in statements such as, "Percent return, then, has practically nothing to do with the quality of the final sample. A low rate of return does not necessarily project a poor sample, nor does a 100-percent response rate guarantee a useful sample" (p. 52) and "In any case sampling issues often have been overemphasized; the crucial issue is not the sampling method, but the characteristics of the final sample" (p. 52). I believe most reviewers would be realistic in evaluating sampling procedures because the Strong does have knotty problems in identifying sampling frames and obtaining responses. Adequate sampling procedures do not guarantee adequate results; however, procedures which follow accepted traditions for inquiry do make adequate results more *likely*. In the absence of knowledge of population parameters, we must depend on an evaluation of the adequacy of sampling procedures. Response rates for each of the occupational samples should be published.

Some occupational groups consist of subspecialties that are potentially quite different from each other. For example, the Psychologist Occupational Group includes experimental, clinical, counseling, developmental, school, industrial, and other subspecialties. Interest inventories should address the fact that a particular client may show varying patterns of similarity to different subspecialties within an occupation or profession. Because the Strong provides information based on three types of scales, the client will have the opportunity to examine scores on the Basic Interest and Occupational Themes scales as possible approaches to differentiating between interest in, for example, experimental versus clinical psychology.

There is a separate chapter in the manual discussing gender issues. The authors conclude that substantial gender differences exist even when men and women in the same occupation have been compared. They conclude "separate scales and separate norms are necessary, but we must be certain they are used as a means of expanding options, not of limiting them" (p. 86). Occupational Scales are scored on both male and female scales. Although this practice complicates interpretation, the authors wish "to encourage both men and women to consider occupations heretofore dominated by the other sex" (p. 86).

A variety of evidence supports claims that the Strong measures consistently. Although standard deviations and reliability coefficients are provided, standard errors of measurement would be helpful. Some of the Basic Interest Scales are short (at least one consists of five items); exact lengths of those scales should be reported.

Concepts of vocational interest on the Strong were initially defined only in empirical terms, but since 1974 they have been linked to Holland's theory of occupational interests. This theoretical grounding helps in understanding and defining the construct and it provides a theoretical structure to guide and direct inquiry regarding the construct.

Evidence in support of validity claims is organized separately for the three types of Strong scales. Various sources of evidence are cited: analyses of item content, concurrent and predictive validity studies, confirmation of theoretically predicted patterns of intercorrelations between Strong subscales, and factor analytic studies. Concurrent validity evidence for the Occupational Scales is based on the degree of overlap of scores for a particular occupational sample and the General Reference sample; there appears to be a reasonable degree of group separation on the 207 scales. Percent overlap has been approximated by the Tilton Index which assumes a normal distribution. It is unclear why exact solutions are not reported given modern computational capabilities.

The predictive validity evidence for the Occupational Scales examines the relationship between scores and occupational status at some future time and is provided in the form of "hit" rates. Studies conducted on the current (post 1974) SVIB-SCII and reported in the manual include just a few studies in which the criterion was occupational choice or choice of college major. Enough time has passed that we would hope that additional summaries of long-term predictive validity studies would be cited.

The Strong more than satisfies the standards for tests and testing that have been set by the profession.

As a vocational counseling instrument, it is among the very best and this reviewer recommends it without reservation.

REVIEWER'S REFERENCE

American Educational Research Association, American Psychological Association, & National Council on Measurement in Education. (1985). *Standards for educational and psychological testing*. Washington, DC: American Psychological Association, Inc.

Review of the Strong Interest Inventory [Fourth Edition] by BLAINE R. WORTHEN, Professor and Chair, Research and Evaluation Methodology Program, Department of Psychology, and PERRY SAILOR, Research Associate, Department of Psychology, Utah State University, Logan, UT:

In the *Ninth Mental Measurements Yearbook* review of the 1981 revision of the Strong Vocational Interest Blank (SVIB), the Strong-Campbell Interest Inventory (SCII), Layton (1985) concluded that it was the foremost interest inventory and was "better than ever" (p. 1480), and Westbrook (1985) called it "probably the best interest inventory available" (p. 1483). Since then, the 1985 revision has been completed, which incorporates normative and profile changes that make this venerable instrument even better, though not yet without flaw.

Test content and use.

The SCII, which can be administered to individuals or groups, measures interests by asking each person to: (*a*) respond "like," "indifferent," or "dislike" to 131 occupations, 36 school subjects, 90 activities (39 of which are ways of spending leisure time), and 24 "types of people"; (*b*) state, for each of 30 paired activities or occupations, which one they prefer; and (*c*) rate how well each of 14 characteristics describes them. The machine-scorable responses are then compared to norms consisting of expressions of interests of persons in a wide variety of occupations who are contented in their jobs. The results, reported on profile sheets, present scores on 6 General Occupational Themes, 23 Basic Interest Scales, and 207 Occupational Scales. Interpretive advice is intended primarily to aid respondents in making occupational choices or curricular decisions, and two other scales—Academic Comfort and Introversion-Extroversion—are offered as counseling tools.

The current edition of the SCII includes the inventory booklet (Strong, Campbell, & Hansen, 1985), a user's guide (Hansen, 1984), a manual (Hansen & Campbell, 1985), and several types of answer sheets, scoring profiles, and descriptive and interpretive aids.

Practical considerations.

The SCII takes an average of 25–35 minutes to complete. Administration requires no special training and can be done by any qualified psychologist, counselor, or personnel worker. In the Specimen Brochure, the authors point out the profile is largely self-explanatory, but "its scores, and patterns of scores, should be interpreted for the respondent by the counselor—after thorough study of the User's Guide and the Manual, and perhaps after participation in one of the regional workshops on the Strong" (p. 3). The reviewers cannot comment on the workshops but agree that the manual and user's guide should be mastered to make maximum use of the information to be gained from the SCII.

Special commendation should be given to the manual and the user's guide. The manual is the primary technical, psychometric resource for the SCII and contains invaluable information on the rationales underlying scale construction; item statistics; scale norms, reliability, validity, and interpretation; and detailed information on criterion samples. The manual also provides extensive information concerning the processes and criteria used in constructing the Occupational Scales, the Basic Interest Scales, and the General Occupational Theme Scales.

The user's guide overlaps the manual to some degree but is more oriented to the needs of professional practitioners who use the test with clients. It includes very useful information on guidelines for the use of the SCII, pretest orientation, pre-interpretation preparation, using the codes in interpretation, using the SCII with adults, and career-counseling and SCII interpretation sequences. Also included in the user's guide is a discussion of interpretation of the Special Scales and Administrative Indexes (including rules of thumb for checking profile validity), testing special populations and people from other cultures, and interpretation of depressed, flat, and elevated profiles. It is difficult to imagine a better guide for the counselor or other user.

INTERPRETATION. Extensive attention has been given to helping counselors and clients interpret scale scores and patterns of scores; indeed, this is one of the strong points of the SCII. Several areas of difficulty in interpreting scale scores and patterns are noted in both the manual and user's guide. Apparent inconsistencies between the Basic Interest and Occupational Scales, where obviously related pairs of scales (e.g., Art and Fine Artist, Mathematics and Mathematician) yield highly contrasting scores, are discussed. Such inconsistencies are viewed by the SCII developers as assets that aid interpretation by forcing clients and counselors to understand the meaning of the scales and thus to interpret the scales properly. The ability to make correct interpretations of such inconsistencies is hindered somewhat, however, by the fact that the exact item makeup of these scales is not disclosed. The manual's authors state that item information for the Basic Interest Scales and General Occupational Themes may be found in earlier editions of the manual or in other sources cited, but that information was not available in the current materials. Composition of the Occupational Scales has never been released because the test publisher uses test-scoring income to support the research that has gone into improving and updating the inventory through its successive revisions. But the net effect is to leave the counselor who is faced with interpreting a profile that is high on "Marketing Executive" but low on "Sales" wishing to see the precise scale items on which both those scores are based.

The empirically derived "Special Scales," Academic Comfort and Introversion-Extroversion, are handled similarly to the Occupational Scales: The process of constructing them is described at length, there is extensive reliability and validity information provided, but scale construction—even the numbers of items—is not disclosed. Several career counselors have mentioned to the reviewers that interpreting the Academic Comfort Scale can be uncomfortable in the absence of such information about scale items.

Revisions in the 1985 Edition to remove gender inequity.

The SCII's roots go back to 1927, when E. K. Strong first published the SVIB. Beginning with the first SCII in 1974, and continuing through publication of subsequent revisions in 1981 and 1985, Strong's successors, David Campbell and Jo-Ida Hansen, have led successful efforts to: Merge Strong's Men's and Women's forms into a single form; incorporate a theoretical scheme (Holland's hexagonal model of career types) into the inventory's basically empirical framework; expand the number of Occupational Scales, especially in nonprofessional and vocational/technical occupations; and update the norming samples and match them by gender.

The extensive research that culminated in the 1985 revision was largely a result of the women's movement, which focused attention not only on inequities in the job market but also inequities in the SCII's use of separate Occupational Scales and norms for men and women. The developers responded to these concerns with an active program of research on men's and women's measured interests that has served as the foundation for a sex-equalization process that continued for 15 years, "with each revision representing a fairer, more balanced instrument" (manual, p. v). The results have been impressive, leading to development of new normative samples ("Women-in-General" and "Men-in-General") for use in constructing the Occupational Scales and in renorming the Basic Interest Scales and General Occupational Themes. The 1985 revision also increased the number of occupations on which female-normed and male-normed scales could be matched for the same occupations. Of the 106 occupations represented, 101 now have matching scales for females and males.

The manual authors argue persuasively that *equal* treatment is not the same as *identical* treatment, that women and men differ considerably in their responses to about one-third of the inventory items, that these differences remain even among people in the same occupations, and that "Empirical scales constructed on the basis of same-sex criterion and reference samples work better (are more valid) than scales based on opposite-sex samples" (p. 86). The developers also emphasize that sex differences "should in no way be used to discriminate against or repress any individual of either sex . . . . separate scales and separate norms are necessary, but we must be certain that they are used as a means of expanding options, not of limiting them" (p. 86).

Other major revisions in the 1985 SCII.

Although the instrument's 325 items have not changed since 1974 (except for wording on seven items related to religious activities, to make them more generic and less specifically Christian), the profiles and manual have been revised extensively in areas unrelated to sex equity. Other major changes for the 1985 edition include:

1. Expansion of the Occupational Criterion Samples. For the 1981 profile, according to the Specimen Brochure, the development team embarked on "the largest testing program of employed adults in history" (p. 3). For the current edition, they expanded it still further, testing 142,610 people to get 48,238 sample members.

2. Extension of the Occupational Scales to reduce the overemphasis on professional occupations. This effort produced 34 new scales (male and female scales for 17 vocational-technical and nonprofessional occupations).

3. Addition of scales for newly emerging professional occupations. Twelve of these scales (six occupations) have been added.

4. Increase in overall number and breadth of Occupational Scales. In all, there are now 207 Occupational Scales, representing 106 occupations, of which 32% have mean educational levels of less than 16 years or do not require a college degree.

5. Upgrading and renorming the older Occupational Scales. All 207 scales are now reasonably current, being based on Occupation Criterion Samples collected since 1974.

Technical considerations.

Norming of the SCII has been a huge undertaking extended across many years, and notwithstanding concerns discussed in a later section, the SCII is clearly one of the best-normed instruments in print.

RELIABILITY. Scores on the SCII are highly reliable. Median test-retest correlations for the 1985 Occupational Scales over 2 weeks, 30 days, and 3 years were .92, .89, and .87, respectively; means were also quite stable for all intervals. Median test-retest correlations for the Basic Interest Scales, for the same sample and time periods, were .91, .88, and .82, respectively. The median coefficient alpha was .92 for males and .91 for females. For the General Occupational

Themes, they were .91, .86, and .81, respectively. The median coefficient alpha was .90 for both males and females.

The numbers of items for the Occupational Scales range from 28 to 71. The stated goal is to have around 60 items, and most scales approach this. It appears the General Occupational Theme Scales contain 20 items each, but the manual is not completely clear in this regard. The Basic Interest Scales range in length from 5 to 24 items, with a median length of 11 items. This may be too short for optimum stability, although the test-retest correlations are quite high nonetheless. Layton (1985) expressed concern that changing responses on only two or three items on such short scales could alter standard scores and interpretations, a potential problem that remains.

VALIDITY. Several types of validity evidence are offered for the SCII, combining to make its use generally well validated for the purposes for which it is intended.

Concurrent validity of the Occupational Scales is the power to discriminate between people currently in different occupations. Two relevant types of validity information are (*a*) contrasts between Occupational Samples and the Men-in-General or Women-in-General reference samples, and (*b*) mean scores of occupations on each other's scales. The former is measured by mean differences between samples expressed in standard deviation units (or, conversely, in the degree of overlap between the score distribution of the groups). The median overlap for both the women's and men's scales is 36%, which corresponds to 1.83 standard deviations (*SD*s) difference in means. The range is from 13% overlap (3.03 *SD*s) to 53% overlap (1.26 *SD*s). The range in overlaps indicates the Occupational Scales vary considerably in their validities. The authors say that scales with the highest validities (lowest overlaps) are usually those for occupations that are "tightly defined and quite distinct from most other occupations" (manual, p. 72).

Mean scores of occupations on the remaining Occupational Scales are not reported because of the huge number of means that would result (207 samples on 207 scales equals 42,849 means). According to information in the manual, mean scores for the various occupations on a given Occupational Scale tend to be normally distributed around the General Reference Sample mean, with a range of three to four standard deviations.

Predictive validity of the Occupational Scales is the power to distinguish between persons who will later enter different occupations (while recognizing that "final vocational choice" is an imperfect criterion, because not everyone enters occupations for which they are well suited). Several studies conducted with the earlier SVIB are presented in the manual with a conclusion that "between one-half and two-thirds of all college students enter occupations that are predictable from their earlier scores" (p. 74). One predictive validity study conducted with the 1974 SCII is reported, using college students and a span of $3^1/_2$ years; results were in line with the earlier SVIB studies.

The manual authors assert that content validity of the Basic Interest Scales is supported by procedures used in constructing them, where the emphasis was on pulling together related items. For example, the Science scale contains the items "Astronomer," "Biologist," "Chemist," and "Working in a research laboratory."

Lists of occupational groups scoring either very high or very low on the various Basic Interest Scales are given as evidence for concurrent validity, with the conclusion that "The patterns of high- and low-scoring occupations demonstrate that scores on these scales are substantially related to the occupations that people pursue" (p. 40). The reviewers concur with this assessment.

The manual authors claim that predictive validity of the Basic Interest Scales is good because "there is considerable agreement between the scores earned by students and their eventual occupations" (p. 40), but give no data, because "the nature of the scales does not permit detailed predictions, (so) there is no way of tallying 'hits' and 'misses'" (p. 40).

Construct validity of the General Occupational Themes is supported by theme intercorrelations, which are generally in line with Holland's hexagonal model; that is, the strongest correlations tend to occur between adjacent themes, the weakest between opposites, when points on the hexagon are labeled, in succession, Investigative, Artistic, Social, Enterprising, Conventional, and Realistic. For example, the Investigative scale correlates .60 with the adjacent Realistic, but .13 with the directly opposite Enterprising. This overall pattern is not as consistent as might be desired, however. In fact, the Social scale correlates lower with the adjacent Artistic (.22) than with the directly opposite Realistic (.26) and nearly opposite Conventional (.39) scales.

Construct validity for the General Occupational Themes is also supported by the correlations between them and the same-named scales on the Vocational Preference Inventory (10:382) (median = .765).

Issues and concerns.

Despite the general excellence of the SCII and its ancillary materials, there are still two areas where there is room for improvement or cause for concern. Although neither of these should deter career counselors, school psychologists, or other qualified persons from using the SCII, the following items suggest caution for the user and/or need for further refinement by the developer.

1. Prior criticisms about failure to report response rates in data collected on the Occupational Scales are

dismissed in the manual on two grounds: "First, in some cases the figure is not available . . . . Second, the return rate is a meaningless number" (p. 52). Arguments that response rates may result largely from the quality of the sampling frame are cogent, but the argument that representativeness of the sample is peripheral to whether or not the sample is valid seems strained at best. For an occupational scale to have predictive validity, the sample selected to represent the particular occupation must have one additional characteristic beyond the criteria of "experience, success, and satisfaction" (manual, p. 52) in that occupation. The sample must also be *representative of* the broad spectrum of those in that occupation, not only of one small slice of it. The issue is that of possible bias due to volunteer responding, a bias that is uncontrolled if potentially important differences between those who respond and those who do not are ignored. Borg and Gall (1989) have identified many empirically demonstrated differences between volunteers and nonvolunteers, many of which may interact with interest patterns. If "1,000 forms are sent to entertainers featured in nightclub advertisements and only 100 are returned" (manual, p. 52), is it possible that these 100 may be more successful than nonrespondents and, therefore, their scores may be different, as Westbrook (1985) suggests? Or might the 100 be those who are compulsive about details, most inclined to respond to authority, or highest in Academic Comfort, but not necessarily most satisfied, successful, or experienced as entertainers? If so, then they may not represent entertainers well, and many persons who use the SCII for career advice could be led away from an entertainment career (in which they might have been happy and successful) by use of an SCII norm group from which volunteer bias had excluded important, relevant, nonvolunteer segments of the occupation's population. Admittedly, obtaining high response rates (to control volunteer bias) and conducting nonresponse bias checks (to assess whether respondents and nonrespondents in the sample are similar) are formidable tasks, but difficulty does not excuse the developers of responsibility, and these reviewers feel that such steps are important to assure the validity of the SCII Occupational Scales for their intended purposes. Omitting such efforts and asserting that response rates are meaningless numbers and that self-selection (and therefore sampling bias) may actually be advantageous is unfortunate in an instrument for which development, in so many ways, represents a psychometric standard for instrument development and validation.

2. One part of the "Pre-test Orientation" section of the user's guide is troubling. In it, users are told that "at a minimum, the respondents should be told that: . . . . In general, people respond 'Like' to about one-third of the items, 'Dislike' to about a third, and 'Indifferent' to about a third" (p. 6). This information is not emphasized strongly and is not printed anywhere on the test booklet itself. It seems likely that many test-takers—especially those who are administered the test by mail—never receive this information. Although it obviously is impossible to administer all tests under exactly identical testing conditions, the situation should be made as standard as possible, especially for something as basic as instructions for responding. This seems to introduce an unnecessary source of variation in testing conditions. It is even more disconcerting when one considers that the Occupational Samples—the norming groups—were tested by mail. It is not reported whether they were told anything about the typical distribution of responses. Although the desire to increase variability and avoid the interpretive challenges of flat profiles is understandable, risking loss of standardization is a high price to pay.

SUMMARY. The SCII is a quick, easily taken, easily administered instrument of proven usefulness and psychometric soundness. Its norms are quite up-to-date and avoid sex inequity and other major concerns. The manual and user's guide are outstanding. With the 1985 revision, the SCII is better than ever, and is recommended by the present reviewers as by far the best available interest inventory, notwithstanding the few needed improvements cited herein.

REVIEWERS' REFERENCES

Hansen, J. C. (1984). *User's guide for the SVIB-SCII.* Stanford, CA: Stanford University Press.

Hansen, J. C., & Campbell, D. P. (1985). *Manual for the SVIB-SCII.* Stanford, CA: Stanford University Press.

Layton, W. L. (1985). [Review of the Strong-Campbell Interest Inventory]. In J. V. Mitchell, Jr. (Ed.), *The ninth mental measurements yearbook* (Vol. 2, pp. 1480-1481). Lincoln, NE: The Buros Institute of Mental Measurements.

Strong, E. K., Campbell, D. P., & Hansen, J. C. (1985). *Strong-Campbell Interest Inventory of the Strong Vocational Interest Blank.* Stanford, CA: Stanford University Press.

Westbrook, B. W. (1985). [Review of the Strong-Campbell Interest Inventory]. In J. V. Mitchell, Jr. (Ed.), *The ninth mental measurements yearbook* (Vol. 2, pp. 1481-1483). Lincoln, NE: The Buros Institute of Mental Measurements.

Borg, W. R., & Gall, M. D. (1989). *Educational research: An introduction* (5th ed.). New York: Longman.

[375]

Structured Interview of Reported Symptoms.

Purpose: Designed to "detect malingering and other forms of feigning of psychological symptoms."
Population: Ages 18 and over.
Publication Dates: 1986–92.
Acronym: SIRS.
Scores, 13: Primary Scales (Rare Symptoms, Symptom Combinations, Improbable or Absurd Symptoms, Subtle Symptoms, Blatant Symptoms, Severity of Symptoms, Selectivity of Symptoms, Reported vs. Observed Symptoms), Supplementary Scales (Direct Appraisal of Honesty, Defensive Symptoms, Symptom Onset and Resolution, Overly Specified Symptoms, Inconsistency of Symptoms).
Administration: Individual.
Price Data, 1995: $78 per complete kit including manual ('92, 47 pages) and 10 interview booklets; $34 per manual; $51 per 10 interview booklets.

Time: (30–45) minutes.
Authors: Richard Rogers, R. Michael Bagby, and Susan E. Dickens.
Publisher: Psychological Assessment Resources, Inc.

Review of the Structured Interview of Reported Symptoms by DAVID N. DIXON, Professor and Chair of Counseling Psychology, Ball State University, Muncie, IN:

The Structured Interview of Reported Symptoms (SIRS) was developed for the assessment of malingering and related response styles. The focus of the SIRS is on the deliberate distortions in self-presentation. Terms used almost interchangeably to describe the construct include malingering, dissimulation, feigning, defensiveness, and unreliable responding. Using a structured interview method feigning, malingering, etc. is assessed on eight primary scales: Rare Symptoms (infrequent symptoms), Symptom Combinations (bona fide psychiatric symptoms which rarely occur simultaneously), Improbable or Absurd Symptoms (symptoms having a fantastic or preposterous quality), Blatant Symptoms (overendorsement of obvious signs of mental disorder), Subtle Symptoms (everyday problems), Severity of Symptoms (symptoms with extreme or unbearable severity), Selectivity of Symptoms (nonselective or indiscriminant endorsement of psychiatric problems), and Reported vs. Observed Symptoms (comparison of observed and reported symptoms). In addition, five supplementary scores are reported for assisting in interpreting response styles. Most of these scales were chosed based on a review of the literature (both psychometric and case studies) related to malingering.

The manual reports that three studies found mean alpha coefficients of .86 for the primary scales and .75 for the supplementary scales. From two studies the mean interrater reliability for the structured interviews of six raters were .96 and .98. Validity evidence was developed by comparing honest responders with both those instructed to feign mental illness and suspected malingerers. In a number of studies the SIRS was effective in discriminating between groups across a variety of populations. Convergent validity evidence was found by comparing the SIRS and the Minnesota Multiphasic Personality Inventory (MMPI) fake-bad indicators. Given the recency of publication (i.e., 1992), the authors are to be commended for the extensive and impressive reliability and validity information.

However, results of factor analytic studies are somewhat problematic. Specifically, scale scores rather than item responses were entered into the factor analyses. This provides information about the factor structure underlying the 13 scales, suggesting an underlying three-factor structure. Perhaps a factor analysis of the individual items would find a different, simpler set of scales than the 13 now included. A larger sample would be required to support a factor analysis of the items.

The manual does a thorough job providing instructions for administration, scoring, and interpretation of the SIRS. Guidelines for ethical use (e.g., training requirements, integration with other methods of assessment) are frequent and appropriate. Sufficient case examples are provided to illustrate the scoring and interpretation process. Interpretation is guided by validity studies, with caution guiding most classification decisions. Special attention is given to the use of the SIRS in distinguishing between malingering and fictitious disorders (DSM-III). The manual and test booklet are clearly designed and usable. A question that remained after reviewing the test and manual was how the test taker responds to the test. Several of the items have a humorous quality to them (e.g., #67. Do you have strong religious thoughts and periods of giggling? and #35. Do you have any unusual beliefs about automobiles? Do you believe they have their own religion?). These types of items make sense as Improbable Symptom Combinations and Absurd Symptoms, but does the test taker take them seriously and will the test administrator do the same?

The development of the SIRS is based on an impressive program of research by Rogers, Bagby, Gillis, and colleagues. The instrument is useful for making some difficult decisions regarding diagnosis and treatment, judicial proceedings, etc. Used in conjunction with other indices of malingering/feigning it appears to make an important contribution to clinical decision making.

Review of the Structured Interview of Reported Symptoms by RONALD J. GANELLEN, Director, Neuropsychology Service, Michael Reese Hospital and Medical Center, and Assistant Professor of Psychiatry and Neurology, University of Illinois at Chicago, Chicago, IL:

Although mental health professionals often assume that clients are honest and genuine when they describe themselves, there are instances when clients report symptoms in a biased, distorted manner. It is often difficult to identify with certainty whether an individual is fabricating symptoms they do not have or is exaggerating the severity of symptoms they do have. A clinician who suspects a patient is feigning a psychological disorder often relies upon objective evidence, such as the validity scales of standard personality tests, to make this determination, particularly when their evaluation influences important outcomes such as the verdict in a legal case, being eligible for treatment, or receiving disability benefits.

The Structured Interview of Reported Symptoms (SIRS) was developed to provide an objective measure for clinicians to use to detect malingering of *psychological* disturbance. The SIRS should not be used when questions of feigned *neuropsychological* impairment are considered. Based upon the authors' extensive clinical experience and their sophisticated reading of the literature concerning malingering, a number of different strategies used by persons who attempt to malinger psychopathology were identified. These strategies were operationalized in a structured interview format. Some of the strategies include the number of rare symptoms reported by the client (e.g., being bothered by strange smells); reporting bona fide symptoms, which rarely occur simultaneously (e.g., washing one's hand frequently because one possesses special powers); acknowledging improbable or absurd symptoms (e.g., believing that cars have their own religion); or endorsing a greater number of blatant, obvious symptoms than do diagnosed psychiatric patients. One scale for each strategy was developed.

Scores on each scale of the SIRS are classified as being honest, indeterminate, probably feigning, or definite feigning based upon research with psychiatric patients, normal controls, simulators, and malingerers. Cut scores for probable and definite feigning were set with the goal of having a few false positives. The authors recommend that conclusions concerning malingering are strongest if three or more scales are above the cut scores. It would be helpful for clinical decision making if the authors identified which of the SIRS primary scales are the strongest predictors of malingering. This information would be most useful in the event that only one or two SIRS scales are in the definite malingered range.

Several studies by Rogers and colleagues are described showing that subjects instructed to simulate a psychiatric disorder score higher than honest psychiatric patients or a normal control group on most SIRS scales and that suspected malingerers scored higher on most SIRS scales than psychiatric inpatients. Furthermore, although simulators who were coached on how to respond to feign specific psychiatric disorders score lower on the SIRS than uncoached simulators, the SIRS accurately discriminated both coached and uncoached simulators from honest psychiatric inpatients.

Overall, the SIRS has a sound theoretical foundation and the strategies are operationalized well. The instructions in the manual are clearly written and easily understood so that users can quickly become adept at administering the interview. The psychometric properties of the scales are acceptable.

The most important question concerns the accuracy with which the SIRS discriminates between honest and malingering subjects. The studies using the SIRS to date strongly support its usefulness. As with any new instrument, additional studies by independent investigators are needed to demonstrate the validity of the SIRS. Future studies should report more carefully the diagnoses of psychiatric patients who report symptoms honestly. For example, one psychiatric control group used in the study by Rogers, Gillis, Dickins, and Bagby (1991) was identified only as being outpatients at the Clarke Institute of Psychiatry, whereas a second control group of psychiatric inpatients was described only as having an Axis I disorder. No further details concerning the diagnoses involved, the method used to reach a diagnosis, or interrater reliability of the clinicians were reported. This may be important as patients with nonpsychotic Axis I disorders or a personality disorder may experience and report few of the rare, improbable, or absurd symptoms represented on the SIRS and, thereby, lower the scores on the primary scales. That is, the scores for subjects attempting to feign a psychotic disorder may be higher than samples of psychiatric patients with a nonpsychotic disorder but may not differ from samples of honest patients with a psychotic disorder. Furthermore, because many of the SIRS items appear to relate to psychotic conditions, it is possible that the SIRS may be more sensitive to attempts to malinger psychosis than to attempts to malinger other disorders, such as depression or Post-Traumatic Stress Disorder.

Most studies using the SIRS relied upon simulated deceptions; in this research paradigm, subjects, often college students, are instructed to attempt to present as having a psychiatric disorder and often a reward is offered if the subject can deceive the examiner. This paradigm is certainly valuable. However, the degree to which results from studies of simulated malingering generalize to real-life malingering has not been adequately established. This is an important issue given potential differences between malingerers and simulators due to life circumstances (e.g., college vs. prison life) and motivation to achieve potential outcomes (e.g., obtaining class credit vs. avoiding the death penalty). The acid test for detection of malingering occurs in actual clinical settings. One limitation in use of the SIRS is that relatively little research has been conducted thus far showing the validity of the SIRS with verified malingerers identified by methods other than the SIRS.

Several demographic variables should be studied more carefully to insure that the SIRS can be used reliably with populations often seen in the legal system, one arena where determinations of malingering are of critical importance. For example, the population of the criminal justice system is predominantly young, relatively uneducated, and from a minority background. Eighty-five percent of the SIRS sample of simulators and 72.9% of the malingerers are white and high school graduates, whereas most surveys show that over 80% of the urban jail population are African-American and have limited education. Thus, it is of critical importance to show that the SIRS operates as effectively with a minority, uneducated population as with a predominantly white, well-educated population. Furthermore, the group of honest psychiatric patients was significantly older than the other groups. The authors do report one unpublished study which shows that race had no effect on SIRS scores. Still, these demographic variables deserve further study.

The authors appear to vacillate between describing the SIRS as being useful to augment other widely used tests of symptom validity, such as the Minnesota Multiphasic Personality Inventory (MMPI), and as "a substantial improvement over such traditional methods of assessment of dissimulation" (manual, p. 5). Although the SIRS assesses dissimulation comprehensively, empirical research has not yet established that the SIRS is more accurate at detecting malingering when compared to traditional methods of assessment. Only one study was reported in which both the SIRS and the MMPI were given. The correlations between SIRS scales and MMPI indicators of a fake-bad response set were quite high, as predicted. Future research should address the question of *incremental validity*, that is whether the information provided by the SIRS adds to the information provided by other measures used as a standard part of a clinical assessment. This would help clinicians determine when to administer the SIRS (i.e., as a routine part of a clinical evaluation or only if malingering is suspected on the basis of other information).

In summary, the SIRS is a promising, thoughtfully constructed measure which can enhance the clinician's armamentarium when detection of feigned psychopathology is an issue. I would recommend its use as a supplement to existing measures of the veracity of self-reported symptoms, such as the MMPI-2 and look forward with enthusiasm to additional research relating to its validity.

REVIEWER'S REFERENCE

Rogers, R., Gillis, J. R., Dickens, S. E., & Bagby, R. M. (1991). Standardized assessment of malingering: Validation of the SIRS. *Psychological Assessment: A Journal of Clinical and Consulting Psychology, 3*, 89-96.

[376]

Structured Photographic Articulation Test Featuring Dudsberry.

Purpose: Designed to assess the child's articulation and phonological skills.
Population: Ages 3–9.
Publication Date: 1989.
Acronym: SPAT-D.
Scores: Total score only.
Administration: Individual.
Price Data, 1992: $69 per SPAT-D kit including 48 color photographs, 25 response forms, and manual (24 pages); $10 per 25 response forms.
Time: [10–15] minutes.
Comments: Forty-eight photographs are used to assess 59 consonant singletons and 21 consonant blends.
Authors: Janet D. Kresheck and Pat Tattersall.
Publisher: Janelle Publications, Inc.

Review of the Structured Photographic Articulation Test Featuring Dudsberry by CLINTON W. BENNETT, Professor of Speech Pathology and Audiology, James Madison University, Harrisonburg, VA:

The Structured Photographic Articulation Test Featuring Dudsberry (SPAT-D) uses 48 actual photographs to elicit an individual's production of 59 single consonant and 21 consonant clusters of /s/, /r/, and /l/ in the traditional word-level analysis. The photographs of the puppy, Dudsberry, are used because "verbalization is easily evoked from the child" (manual, p. 1) using this stimulus.

The traditional phonemic positions of initial, medial, final, and consonant clusters are used *but* relate to position within a syllable rather than a word (e.g., the /s/ in *pencil* is considered medial). Although phoneme position based upon syllabic structure is an accepted practice, the authors incorrectly label /dʒ/ in *orange* as final (it is a consonant cluster) and /bl/ in *table* as a blend (because the /l/ is syllabic, /b/ is medial, and /l/ is final).

The manual is clear and concise and the response form is user friendly with a color-coded response record. Stimulability testing is recommended (although instructions range from imitative models to varied amount of cues) and some common phonological processes can be identified. Several contradictions exist in the manual. "The end result of this test is to identify children in need of intervention" is a quote from the manual (p. 9). The authors acknowledge, however, that further testing for consistency of errors and intelligibility should be evaluated with either a deep test or conversational speech sample. The SPAT-D is a screening test, not a diagnostic test, and as such, further in-depth assessment would be necessary to identify children who require intervention. The manual also incorrectly classifies /f,v/ as stridents.

Normative data—means, standard deviations, and percentile ranks—are presented in 1-year increments for 710 children (from "various geographical regions") from ages 3-0–9-11; no delineation of ethnicity, gender, or socioeconomic status is provided. A summary of technical data is presented for reliability and validity. Interjudge reliability (median percentage of 96.1) is reported for presence/absence of each error but not for specific errors. Test-retest reliability was .97 and concurrent reliability with the Goldman-Fristoe Test of Articulation was .92.

Construct validity was investigated by using the SPAT-D to differentiate children with normal and impaired articulation. A significant difference on test performance was found between the two groups. Content validity is related to "articulation errors for single words" (p. 15) but single word productions are not indicative of conversational speech. Although five disordered children's performance on the SPAT-D and 10-minute spontaneous speech samples yielded 97% agreement on specific phoneme errors, the predictive validity from single-word productions to conversational speech is questionable.

The SPAT-D appears to be a valid and reliable measure of articulatory performance at the word level; however, expanded normative data would strengthen this test. The use of photographs may be of high interest to children and easily elicit spontaneous speech.

Review of the Structured Photographic Articulation Test Featuring Dudsberry by SUSAN FELSENFELD, Assistant Professor of Communication, University of Pittsburgh, Pittsburgh, PA:

TEST STRUCTURE AND ADMINISTRATION. The Structured Photographic Articulation Test Featuring Dudsberry (SPAT-D) is a 48-item test of articulation designed to be used with children between the ages of 3 and 9 years. According to the test authors, this test can be used to "identify children in need of intervention" and can also "provide a focus for a treatment plan in articulation therapy" (manual, p. 9). Although norms are available for the SPAT-D, the authors suggest the descriptive information derived from their test may be of greatest or best use to the clinician, particularly for treatment planning.

The SPAT-D samples 23 consonant singletons and 21 consonant blends in pre-, inter-, and post-vocalic word positions by asking children to name common pictures in response to carrier phrases. In addition, the response form includes 21 optional words that are considered to be phonetically "complex" (e.g., shirts, weird, table) for imitation. These words are not to be counted in the test scoring. Once recorded, the child's responses can be placed in a consonant singleton matrix that displays results by word position and manner of articulation. Although the authors also indicate that responses can be analyzed according to "phonological processes" (p. 9), there is no mechanism to record this on the response form, and little discussion about the interpretation of this analysis in the test manual.

The SPAT-D is scored by obtaining the number of correct items (i.e., those containing no target sounds in error). This raw score may then be compared to means and standard deviations reported at one-year age intervals, and may also be used to derive percentile ranks and corresponding standard scores. If these scores are used, it should be noted that there is extremely restricted variability beginning at age 7-0, with virtual error-free performance in the normative sample beyond this point (mean scores of 79.4–79.5 out of a possible 80 at the upper ages, with standard deviations of less than 2.0). The effect of this compression is to skew the derived percentile ranks substantially. For example, a child who is age 7-0 and makes one error on the SPAT-D will score in the 25th percentile. Although this outcome may be accurate from a statistical standpoint, the implied interpretation (of moderately poor performance) may not reflect the child's performance in the most meaningful way.

What is unique about the SPAT-D is the presentation format. Rather than using colored line drawings to elicit the target stimuli, this test uses actual colored photographs of a dog ("Dudsberry") interacting with various objects and performing common activities (e.g., sleeping, swimming). These engaging stimuli are well photographed and should appeal to most test takers within this age range.

PSYCHOMETRIC PROPERTIES. The documentation of the technical attributes of the SPAT-D is terse and inadequate. Although studies assessing both the reliability and the validity of this test were apparently performed in 1989, they remain unpublished and, thus, cannot be readily evaluated. This is the primary shortcoming of this instrument.

Norms: The SPAT-D was normed on 710 children between the ages of 3-0 and 9-11 who were tested by "speech-language clinicians from various geographical locations throughout the country" (p. 10). There was not an equal distribution of children at each test age (e.g., only about 10% of the children in the norming sample were 3-year-olds, whereas 17% were 9-year-olds). No other information about the norming sample or data collection procedures was provided.

Reliability: Two reliability estimates are discussed in the SPAT-D manual: test-retest reliability and interjudge agreement. To determine test-retest reliability, the SPAT-D was re-administered to 378 of the original test takers in the normative sample within 2 weeks of its initial administration. Results of this unpublished study yielded a reported Pearson coefficient of .97, which indicates very satisfactory stability. Correlation coefficients were not reported by age, so it cannot be determined if the test is equally stable across the age span tested. No further details of the procedures of this large reliability study were provided. Interjudge reliability was established by having "four qualified speech-language clinicians" (p. 14) evaluate the recorded responses of eight randomly selected subjects. A *median* percent agreement for presence or absence of error was reported to be 96.1 (ranges unspecified). Given the small sample size, the unusual method of reporting results, and the lack of procedural specificity, the results of this latter reliability study are difficult to interpret.

Validity: Two forms of validity, concurrent and construct, received primary attention by the test authors. In order to establish concurrent validity, scores on the SPAT-D and the Goldman-Fristoe Test of Articulation were compared for 36 children with normal speech (ages 3 to 8). A highly acceptable correlation coefficient (.92) was reported from this sample, with reasonably good consistency reported across ages (ranges of .81–.96). It is not known if the results would be as satisfactory if children with disordered articulation (the population of interest to clinicians) had been tested. To establish construct validity, 20 children with "normal" articulation and 20 "articulation disordered" (p. 16) children were administered the SPAT-D. Results of this nonreferenced study demonstrated that the articulation-disordered children scored significantly lower than the control children on this measure (p<.001), suggesting that the instrument was effective in discriminating the groups. No additional substantive information about validity was reported.

SUMMARY. The SPAT-D is an easy-to-administer and visually engaging test of articulation for young children. Like many tests of its kind it samples the consonant system in a traditional way, by eliciting the production of a limited number of single word responses. Its unique feature is the use of actual photographs rather than line drawings to elicit target sounds. The primary shortcomings of this instrument involve inadequate information about its psychometric integrity and the questionable usefulness of the normative data beyond age 6. Until further information about technical aspects of this test are available in the literature (or in an updated and much expanded manual), the use of the SPAT-D as a diagnostic norm-referenced test of articulation is not recommended. However, clinicians may want to consider using the SPAT-D test stimuli as an innovative tool to engage children in spontaneous speech and to elicit a range of consonant phonemes for purely descriptive purposes.

[377]

Student Adjustment Inventory.

Purpose: Designed as "an instrument for identifying common affective-social problems."
Population: Upper elementary, junior high, senior high, and beginning college students.
Publication Dates: 1975–89.
Acronym: SAI.
Scores, 7: Self-Esteem, Group Interaction, Self-Discipline, Communication, Energy/Effort, Learning/Studying, Attitude Towards Learning Environment.
Administration: Group or individual.
Forms, 2: Available in pencil and paper or microcomputer versions.
Price Data, 1994: $29.75 per report kit including manual ('89, 23 pages); $10 per 10 reusable test booklets; $8 per 50 answer sheets; $8 per manual; $4.85-$6.35 per mail-in report; $195 per SAI microcomputer version (unlimited usage, specify IBM 5.25 or 3.5).
Time: (30) minutes.
Author: James R. Barclay.
Publisher: MetriTech, Inc.

Review of the Student Adjustment Inventory by PHILIP ASH, Director, Ash, Blackstone and Cates, Blacksburg, VA:

The Student Adjustment Inventory (SAI) is a 78-item, seven-scale instrument designed to assess student reactions to affective-social problems frequently faced by older children and adolescents, grades 7 to 13 (first year college). It was developed as an extension to the Barclay Classroom Climate Inventory (BCCI; Barclay, 1973, 1978), which provides 42 scores and is designed for younger children, grades 3 to 6.

Responses to the 78 problem statements are *Often*, *Sometimes*, or *Never* a problem. The paper-and-pencil group form uses a General Purpose NCS Answer Sheet scored by the publisher, who provides a computer-printed report. The microcomputer version permits administration of the Inventory and then printing out a 3-to-5 page report which includes: (*a*) Problem Profile graph showing percentile norm scores for the seven scales; (*b*) a Personal Report; (*c*) an item-response summary; and (*d*) a score summary exhibiting both raw scale scores and percentile equivalents. The Report gives a brief description of each scale, followed by a statement relevant specifically to the examinee (e.g., "Among individuals who have taken this inventory Judith reports relatively few problems in this area").

This reviewer ran the disk version for four "cases," ranging from a perfect "no problem" response to one with all scale scores in the "major problem" area (95th–99th percentiles). The other two were "average" profiles, with three or five scores in the "marginal severity" area and the remainder rated "minor." The printouts for the scales were almost identical with respect to scale descriptions, which were generally verbatim copies of the scale descriptions in a Supplementary Interpretive Guide (Appendix A in the manual). Typically, only the last sentence was examinee-specific, a verbalization of the Problem Profile score. However, for the perfect "no problems" case, the Report was preceded by a warning that the extremely low scores might be due to "responding in a socially desirable way," and hence the interpretations might be of questionable validity. For the "major problems" case, interventions such as supportive counseling were suggested. At least at extreme score ranges, the information provided might be helpful to the student's teachers, counselors, and possibly parents.

The SAI manual's text is devoted almost exclusively to an explication of how to install, run, and use the outputs of the computer program. The program ran very smoothly. It should present little or no problem to a naive test-taker. In addition to the report printout, it provides a variety of other data management functions including the options to enter responses copied from an answer sheet, and review, select, and list individual reports. The program does not include any routine for statistical summary over a set of cases.

A References and Related Bibliography includes books on personality theory and related topics, and items on the BCCI, but none on the SAI itself. Although the SAI copyright date is 1989, the 19 references extend from 1934 to 1978 only, with most of them dated 1974–78. Only 4 are cited anywhere in the manual.

The manual also includes two appendices. Appendix A, Supplementary Interpretive Guide, was referred to above.

Appendix B, Summary of Reliability and Validity Data, reports various statistical measures for the SAI. Internal consistency estimates are provided for the seven scales for "normative" samples of males (N = 781) and females (N = 691). All coefficients were in the range .80–.86. No age or grade data are provided for the samples.

No norms tables are provided, although "percentile norms" are given in the Personal Report, and are referred to in other contexts in the manual.

Based upon a subsample apparently from studies using both the SAI and BCCI (male N = 671, female N = 691), intercorrelations by sex are presented for the seven scales. "Social desirability" (a BCCI scale?) was correlated negatively (r = -.31 to -.47) with each SAI scale for both sexes. The SAI scales were all highly intercorrelated (median r = .78). The authors interpret a factor analysis of the SAI scales as showing "that the largest amount of variance is explained by teacher expectations, followed by a combination of verbal skill deficits and self-control deficits" (manual, p. 18). A more parsimonious explanation is that the seven scales all measure a common factor of student school-related affect. This reviewer ran a principal components factor analysis on the intercorrelation matrix for males, with the internal consistency reliability estimates as the first approximation to the commonalties. The first factor had loadings on the seven scales of .85 or higher, and accounted for 92.6% of the total variance explained.

An unpublished doctoral dissertation (Beltran, 1975) provides limited evidence (for college freshmen, N = 70) of criterion-related validity. Four of the seven scale scores correlated significantly with scores on the Nelson-Denny Reading Test (r = .28–.29, p<.05), and three with grade-point average (r = .32–.46, p<.01). In the same study, correlations of the order of .2 to .4 were found between the SAI scales and scales of the Personality Orientation Inventory, a seven-scale personality test. No evidence is provided of the generalizality of these results to upper elementary and lower high school students. To demonstrate the predictability, and hence stability, of student problems over time, multiple correlations are given between six BCCI scales administered in fifth grade and each of the seven SAI scales administered in the eighth grade (N = 44 males, 44 females). All the multiple Rs were statistically significant, ranging from .28 to .69. Because the SAI was derived primarily from the BCCI, however, many of the scales are similar in concept. High correlations are to be expected.

The computerized version of the SAI is technologically interesting, but requires individual administration (except perhaps in a computer class). In many classroom situations in which the teacher or counselor is interested in identifying those individuals with problems who may be among class members, group administration and hand scoring would be quicker and cheaper than the mail-in requirements for SAI group administration. The lack of published norms and the extremely limited validity data should encourage consideration of other group-administered student attitude/personality scales available, for example, the Eyberg Child Behavior Inventory (ECBI; T4:948, reviewed 9:404); Student Opinion Inventory (T4:2598); Study Process Questionnaire (SPQ; T4:2608, reviewed 11:389); and the Sutter-Eyberg Student Behavior Inventory (SESBI; T4:2668, reviewed 11:410). Additional measures (e.g., Student Evaluation and Counseling) can be accessed by consulting Sweetland and Keyser (1983, 1986).

REVIEWER'S REFERENCES

Barclay, J. R. (1973). Multiple input assessment and preventive intervention. *School Psychologist Digest*, *2*(2), 13-18.

Beltran, A. (1975). *College students' educational-personal needs and academic achievement*. Unpublished doctoral dissertation, University of Kentucky, Lexington, KY.

Barclay, J. R. (1978). *Manual of the Barclay Classroom Climate Inventory*. Lexington, KY: Educational Skills Development, Inc.

Sweetland, R. C., & Keyser, D. J. (Eds.). (1983). *Tests: A comprehensive reference for assessments in psychology, education, and business*. Kansas City: Test Corporation of America.

Sweetland, R. C., & Keyser, D. J. (Eds.). (1986). *Tests: A comprehensive reference for assessments in psychology, education, and business* (2nd ed.). Kansas City: Test Corporation of America.

Review of the Student Adjustment Inventory by MARK J. BENSON, Associate Professor of Family and Child Development, Virginia Polytechnic Institute and State University, Blacksburg, VA:

The Student Adjustment Inventory (SAI) has a valuable purpose. The SAI is designed to assess the self-reported problems of students. The measure includes 78 common academic and social problems such as: "having problems with reading," "worrying about my grades," and "being afraid of other people." For each item, the respondent indicates whether it is *hardly ever a problem*, *sometimes a problem*, or *often a problem*. Although the scoring for the items is absent from the manual, extrapolation from sample scores indicates that the items are scored as 0 for *hardly ever*, 2 for *sometimes*, and 5 for *often a problem*. The 78 items comprise seven scales.

Information about the items is omitted from the manual. The publisher, however, provided the item-scale correspondence for the purposes of this review. According to this information, the scales overlap. Of the total 78 items, 33 appear on more than one scale, and one item scores on six different scales. Four scales have 20 items (Self-Competency, Group Interaction, Energy/Effort, and Attitude), two scales have 19 items

(Self-Discipline and Communication Skills), and the Learning/Studying scale has 18 items. The internal consistencies for the seven scales are good (.80 to .86).

Limited data are presented to support the validity of the test. The strongest validity support is from a study of 70 college students. With reading level controlled, three scales successfully contributed to the prediction of grade point average (Attitude, Learning/Studying, and Energy/Effort). Other reported attempts to support validity, however, are questionable. Data correlating the SAI scales with the seven scales of the Personal Orientation Inventory and regressing the SAI scales on each of the six scales of the Barclay Classroom Climate Inventory are presented. Both of these measures are, however, self-report tests without direct relevance to academic or social problems.

In addition to the lack of adequate validity data, the manual includes data that argue against the construct validity of the SAI. Specifically, the seven subscales are highly intercorrelated (.59 to .90). The magnitude of these correlations suggest a single factor, not seven factors, comprise the test. Judging from the correlation matrix, it is likely this single factor is a self-confidence or self-perception factor.

The content of the items raises further questions about the validity of the measure. About 50 of the 78 items are academically oriented. Although these academic items form a logical set, the remaining social emotional items only haphazardly sample the broad domain of social emotional development. Strategies for improving the measure would be either to revise and broaden the social-emotional items or to eliminate the social-emotional items and redesign the test as a measure of self-perceived academic problems.

Because the item-scale correspondence is not open to the public, potential examiners are unable to evaluate this very important aspect of the test. If this information was made available to the examiner, the arbitrary placement of the items on scales would be quite evident.

To evaluate clearly the validity of the measure, several direct approaches should be employed. First, the items should be factor analyzed. Scales could then be constructed based on empirical convergence. Next, the self-reported problems on the SAI scales should be compared against objective ratings by teachers or judges. Finally, divergence from measures of self-esteem or self-perception should be demonstrated.

The most serious technical problem with the SAI, however, is not the lack of independence of the scales or even the weakness of the validity data. The most serious problem is the norm data. A vaguely defined norm group of sixth through ninth graders, high school students, and college students is mentioned. There are no indications about when the data were collected, whether it is an amalgam of several separate samples, or how many students were assessed at each grade. In short, there is no way to evaluate the quality of the norm sample.

The inadequate norm sample is made more serious by total omission of norm data. The manual fails to include means and standard deviations by gender, age, or even the overall sample. To obtain normative comparisons, the examiner can either submit the items to be individually scored (about $5) or purchase a software package ($195). In either case, however, means and standard deviations still remain concealed. The combination of an easily accessible software package that also conceals the norms and scoring procedure may encourage misuse of the test.

Further potential for misuse is promoted by the profile and form report produced by the software package. The profile consists of percentile scores based on the norm sample, which is never described. The report is at best useless and at worst potentially harmful. The respondent's name is inserted at various spots in the report implying a uniquely tailored report. Instead, the reports are identical in describing each scale. For some scales, prescriptive advice is inserted into the report, but no justification appears in the manual for the basis for prescriptions.

Problems with validity, norms, and use of the SAI have been identified in previous reviews. The SAI was previously reviewed in the 8th and 9th editions of the *Mental Measurements Yearbook* when it was called the Barclay Learning Needs Assessment Inventory. In the *Eighth Mental Measurements Yearbook*, the reviewer concluded, "Unless major revisions and improvements are made, the Barclay inventory cannot provide information that is useful to anybody" (Hartnett, 1978, p. 705). In the *Ninth Mental Measurements Yearbook* the reviewer concluded, "The revision does not provide any basis for changing the original reviewer's negative evaluation" (Brassard, 1985, p. 131).

There appear to be only minor alterations and no reduction of the problems identified in previous reviews. The test name has been substituted for a more marketable title, Student Adjustment Inventory, but the problems remain. In contrast to these weaknesses of the SAI, a much more sound measure has been developed for college populations, the Student Adaptation to College Questionnaire (SACQ; Baker & Siryk, 1984, 1989; T4:2590, reviewed 11:383).

The SAI is seriously flawed. The problems include the concealment of the item-scale correspondence, the absence of norm data, the lack of validity data, the high intercorrelation across the scales, and weakness of the content validity for assessing social-emotional problems. For those who are familiar with testing, this measure is likely to be ignored; for those who are not, the measure is at risk for misuse.

REVIEWER'S REFERENCES

Hartnett, R. T. (1978). [Review of the Barclay Learning Needs Assessment Inventory]. In O. K. Buros (Ed.), *The eighth mental measurements yearbook* (pp. 704-705). Highland Park, NJ: Gryphon Press.

Brassard, M. R. (1985). [Review of the Barclay Learning Needs Assessment Inventory]. In J. V. Mitchell, Jr. (Ed.), *The ninth mental measurements yearbook* (p. 131). Lincoln, NE: Buros Institute of Mental Measurements.
Baker, R. W., & Siryk, B. (1984). Measuring adjustment to college. *Journal of Counseling Psychology, 31*, 179-189.
Baker, R. W., & Siryk, B. (1989). *Student Adaptation to College Questionnaire manual.* Los Angeles, CA: Western Psychological Services.

[378]

Student Talent and Risk Profile.

Purpose: To identify talented students as well as students "at-risk" for counseling, guidance, and special teaching strategies.
Population: Grades 5–12.
Publication Date: 1990.
Acronym: STAR Profile.
Scores, 7: Academic Performance, Creativity, Artistic Potential, Leadership, Emotional Maturity, Educational Orientation, At Risk.
Administration: Group.
Price Data, 1990: $40 per 35 test booklets; $.05 per NCS answer sheet; $8 per manual (21 pages); $10 per specimen set; scoring service offered by publisher ($160 minimum charge plus $1.60 or less per subject over 100).
Time: (60–65) minutes.
Comments: Revision of Biographical Inventory Form U.
Author: The Institute for Behavioral Research in Creativity.
Publisher: The Institute for Behavioral Research in Creativity.
Cross References: For reviews by Christopher Borman and Courtland C. Lee of Biographical Inventory Form U, see 9:150.

Review of the Student Talent and Risk Profile by BARBARA KERR, Professor of Psychology in Education, Arizona State University, Tempe, AZ:

The Student Talent and Risk Profile (STAR) was developed to assist teachers in the identification of students who may benefit from gifted education programs and students who may be at risk for educational problems. It is based on the Biographical Inventory Form U (9:150), a well-known measure of a variety of constructs related to creativity, leadership, and outstanding performance. Additional items were added recently to yield measures of emotional maturity and at-risk status. It is a 150-item multiple-choice instrument that includes questions about childhood activities and experiences, attitudes and interests, value preferences, and other self-descriptions. The test can be scored only by the Institute for Behavioral Research in Creativity. Each of the seven scales of the Student Talent and Risk Profile was developed on a different group, or combination of norm groups. Therefore, validity will be considered for each scale as well as for the test as a whole.

VALIDITY. The Academic Performance Scale was developed with college freshmen but was normed on 10,000 North Carolina high school students. Significant correlations have been obtained between Academic Performance and achievement and I.Q. measures.

The Creativity Scale was developed on a group of NASA scientists and engineers, yielding cross validities in the .40s, and was rewritten for use with students. It has approximately .30 correlation with artistic potential scores.

The Artistic Potential Scale was developed in a study of high school students attending the Interlochen Arts Academy and regular high school students; it differentiated arts from non-arts students and correlated from .40 to .50 with measures of artistic performance.

The Leadership scale was developed on a combination of the above groups. A validity study with North Carolina Governor's School students identified as high in leadership ability showed this scale successfully differentiated between identified leadership students and regular high school students, with cross validities of approximately .70.

The Emotional Maturity Scale was developed to identify at-risk students in junior high school in Utah. No studies were done of relationships with independent criteria. Items were selected through item-test correlations.

The Educational Orientation Scale was developed in a study of high school dropouts to differentiate these from other students. Items were added to show positive attitudes toward school and college aspirations. A recent study showed inconsistent correlations with teacher ratings and activities ratings in school.

The At-Risk Scale is a measure that combines Emotional Maturity and Educational Orientation; it is intended to indicate not only risk of dropping out but also for emotional or substance abuse problems. A recent study failed to show consistent correlations with teacher ratings and activities ratings in school.

Overall, the scales derived from original Form U of the Biographical Inventory remain promising as predictors of outstanding performance in academics, creative activities, artistic endeavors, and leadership. However, the newer scales intended to identify at-risk status clearly need work. There is not enough evidence to support their validity for prediction of emotional maturity, educational orientation, or at-risk status. Rather than relying on item to test correlations, the authors must perform the same kind of painstaking studies they undertook for the development of the other scales.

One concern is the items are quite transparent. Even a young student would be able to guess the import of a great many of them. Students may be able to answer the items in the way in which they wish to be perceived by their teachers or test administrators. A social desirability scale or correction should be included.

RELIABILITY. Unfortunately, reliability estimates for the scales of the STAR Profile were derived only from measures of coefficient alpha, a measure of internal consistency. The coefficient alpha reliability estimates for the scales were fairly impressive, with several in the high .80s. The reliability estimates increased with age, with alphas for grade 10–12 samples being 3 to 7 points higher than those for grade 4–6 samples.

There were apparently no studies done of alternate form or test-retest reliability; therefore, it is unknown what the effects of practice or repeated administrations of this test might be on scores. This is an unfortunate oversight.

USEFULNESS. As stated above, this instrument may be useful for identifying talented students, but is not ready to be used to identify at-risk students. An instrument is sorely needed that can identify talented, at-risk students, that is, those students who have great potential for excellent performance in school but are at risk for social, behavioral, or emotional problems. It is hoped that with further research this instrument could be refined to be able to perform this task.

Another utility concern is the scoring procedure. Because the test can be scored only by the publisher, the test user must consider whether the inconvenience and delay incurred by the use of the test is outweighed by the benefits to be derived by the results. In the case of the STAR Profile, the best use of the instrument is probably as a part of a battery of achievement, intelligence, and personality tests. The user may be unwilling to use the test if this additional inconvenience is not justified by the quantity and quality of the information to be gained. Ideally, this test should be hand scorable and even more reasonably priced; that would make the test immediately attractive to users who want some helpful and potentially intriguing information about a particular student.

Review of the Student Talent and Risk Profile by JOHN W. SHEPARD, Associate Professor of Counselor Education, The University of Toledo, Toledo, OH:

The stated purpose of the Student Talent and Risk Profile (STAR Profile [SP]) is to make for an easier identification of "talented" and "at-risk" students. The present measure is an expanded version of the 1976 Biographical Inventory Form U (9:150). The SP is divided into seven subtest-like categories assessing student performance in: Academic Performance, Creativity, Artistic Potential, Leadership, Emotional Maturity, Educational Orientation, and At Risk status. A Talent Identification Feedback Report is computer generated to assist educators in identifying and advising/counseling talented and/or at-risk students. The instrument is normed for 5th–12th graders.

Inventory results are derived from student responses to a 150-item multiple-choice questionnaire. SP items require students to make self-reported judgements regarding personal and scholastic traits as well as demographic/biographical data. Student performance on each of the seven categories is reported by a percentile comparison with their norm age group. Scores falling in the "top" 25th percentile of any category are starred for significance and easy identification. Although there is no set time limit for taking the SP it would probably require about 60 minutes to complete. Inventory pricing is affected by group size. The cost to simultaneously assess more than 500 students would approximate $2.50 per testee. The cost for 100 students would be approximately $2.80 per student.

It is difficult to validate the SP authors' claims regarding its statistical qualities and overall effectiveness. Very little substantive information is given in the inventory's manual as to reliability, norming, or validity. Much of the manual is dedicated to describing the SP's history. Norming data are scattered throughout the manual and provide a very sketchy description of how norms were gathered. Five of the scales are normed on a 1979 multiaged group and two are normed on a 1990 group of 6th graders. Three tables provide sufficient data as to sample sizes' internal reliability, interscale correlations, means, and standard deviations. Sample sizes appear large enough but are generally restricted to samples in one state. Five of the scale's norms are based on a 1979 sample. Internal scale reliability is satisfactory (.77 to .91) but no test-retest coefficients are reported.

Only one contemporary concurrent validity study, contrasting the inventory's "academic performance" scale with SAT (Scholastic Aptitude Test) scores and teacher ratings of study habits, was cited. Correlations of .59 and .64 were reported, respectively. No data regarding predictive validity were given despite claims to the contrary. Content validity was developed from numerous studies and refinements to past versions of the instrument. The instrument's 5th grade reading level may be too high for many elementary and junior high students. Some questions appeared ambiguous and others could prove embarrassing for students to answer truthfully. Very little assistance is given to the manual's reader regarding how to followup with a student who is identified as talented and/or gifted.

In summary, the SP could indeed provide useful data to educators who wish to identify and assist talented and/or gifted students. The measure is cost and time effective and quite easy to interpret. However, much work must be done in assessing and describing the instrument's reliability and validity. The dated and limited restricted norm group also makes one question whether results can be generalized to urban, rural, and/or suburban populations throughout the nation.

[379]

Styles of Leadership Survey.

Purpose: Assesses individual leadership skills under a variety of conditions.

Population: Adults.
Publication Dates: 1968–86.
Scores, 5: Philosophy, Planning and Goal Setting, Implementation, Performance and Evaluation, Total.
Administration: Group.
Price Data, 1993: $6.95 per survey.
Time: Untimed.
Comments: Self-administered survey.
Authors: Jay Hall, Jerry B. Harvey, and Martha S. Williams.
Publisher: Teleometrics International.
Cross References: See T3:2351 (1 reference); for a review by Abraham K. Korman of [Styles of Leadership and Management], see 8:1185 (8 references).

TEST REFERENCES

1. Nwafor, S., & Eddy, J. (1993). Leadership styles: A study of administrative leadership styles of senior administrators of public universities in Texas. *College Student Journal*, 27, 102-105.

Review of the Styles of Leadership Survey by KENNETH N. ANCHOR, Dean, School of Health and Human Services, and Professor, Senior University, Center for Disability Studies, Nashville, TN:

Leadership is a multifaceted and elusive characteristic that has proven to be an enduring challenge for psychometricians. Consensus continues to be absent on how best to measure it. Certainly it is a highly desirable and marketable quality sought in the work force by both public and private sectors. Outside consultants and human resource personnel seek ways of identifying leadership potential not only among the pool of those employed in organizations but also among prospects to be hired for supervisory or management positions. The writings of Warren Bennis, Peter Drucker, and Tom Peters provide a good introduction to this challenging domain.

The Styles of Leadership Survey (SLS) is a tool worthy of consideration for helping organizations to evaluate leadership orientation. The SLS is a self-assessment form comprising 12 items with three each assigned to one of four themes: (*a*) Philosophy of Leadership, (*b*) Planning and Goal Setting, (*c*) Implementation, and (*d*) Performance and Evaluation. After reading a brief but lucid definition of what area each three-item cluster will address the subject is asked to rate him/herself on 12 leadership premises using a 10-point equal interval scale ranging from "completely characteristic" to "completely uncharacteristic." Two data points for each item are created for a total of 24 from among the 60 options presented (i.e., 5 for each premise). Instructions and items appear on the first four pages of the well-presented and meticulously organized test booklet. The interpretive materials constitute 13 informative pages. The basis for scoring and interpretation is the well-established Managerial Grid Model of Blake and Mouton.

A central thrust of this measure is to provide a learning opportunity for the respondent to gain understanding and insight into his or her management style. A detailed and richly descriptive chart presents criteria for each of the five predominant leadership styles: directive, supportive, bureaucratic, strategic, and collaborative. According to each of the four main content areas or themes of the scale, profile summaries are reportedly based upon normalized, standardized results from nearly 3 thousand leaders representing "educational, civic, business, industry, government and service organizations. The average age . . . was 37.7 years and the range was from 17 to 69 years. The average number of followers supervised by these individuals was 34 with a range of 4 to 403" (p. 9). Data gathered from over 800 individuals representing eight types of occupational settings for comparison are displayed in the booklet (e.g., sales and marketing, government, law enforcement and manufacturing).

Designing a versatile leadership instrument is a formidable task. Adoption of the Managerial Grid is worthwhile as it continues to be widely taught and timely. Even those for whom it is new will find it a conceptually sensible and relevant framework for comprehending and assessing their own results. The authors claim reliability and validity data are above threshold (though data provided are sparse).

A key objective of the SLS is to help persons who have undertaken (or are about to assume) supervisory roles to become more knowledgeable of real organizational issues. Completing this instrument may serve to sensitize respondents to actual choices required of managers on a regular basis in many work settings. The content carefully selected for this elegant measure addresses themes that are predictive of successful and adaptive leadership and consistent decision making and problem solving. Of course, one size does not fit all and a caveat is in order for those who tackle the SLS that no single style of leadership is the best for all occasions, and effective leaders are perceived as flexible and able to recognize the demands of wide-ranging situations.

Certain potential limitations should be considered. There is no mechanism to detect the respondent with a high need for social approval who simply responds in what is perceived as the socially desirable or politically correct direction. The instrument should be given under professional direction to insure that any needed consultation or follow-up debriefing may be provided. Not everyone will know what to do appropriately with the information generated. Detailed test-retest guidelines (and research findings) should be included (or, at least, a more complete list of reference materials for the inquisitive individual).

Much to the credit of the three authors, scoring criteria are adequately explained without relying on technical jargon. Moreover, the results reveal one's "system of backup styles" (p. 13) in addition to one's general or primary leadership orientation. Several illuminating case examples are presented which exemplify an array of profile outcomes.

In summary, the SLS is a useful tool for examining leadership values regardless of work setting or respondent's experience in management roles. It is a modern instrument theoretically rooted in the Managerial Grid Model. Items are lucid and written in nonsexist, first-person language. The scoring and interpretation substantially involves the respondent. It can be administered individually or in a group setting. Those with a reading level below high school may encounter comprehension difficulties. Research results that have examined these styles distinguish among groups for age, number of persons supervised, and occupation. The SLS lends itself to serving as a facilitative learning tool which can easily be readministered periodically to monitor shifts in leadership priorities and functioning. Scoring is easily completed without consuming a great deal of time. Interpretive material is excellent and could be a valuable element of the supervisory process. The SLS does not measure interests or aptitudes and may not be well suited as a personnel selection device—but could be used helpfully as a part of a comprehensive battery or employee survey. Though the paper-and-pencil measure may be numbered in this era of rapidly accelerating high technology, this test yields an abundance of useful information predictive of organizational leadership perceptions.

Review of the Styles of Leadership Survey by NORMAN SUNDBERG, Professor Emeritus, Department of Psychology, University of Oregon, Eugene, OR:

The Styles of Leadership Survey (SLS) is designed to depict the characteristics of the respondent according to five styles derived from the two dimensions of the Blake/Mouton leadership grid. The horizontal axis of the grid is Concern for Purpose, and the vertical axis is Concern for People. Four of the five leadership styles are defined by the extremes in the four corners, and the fifth falls in the center of the square. Thus, Directive Leadership is in the highest position on Concern for Purpose and the lowest position on Concern for People. The others are Supportive Leadership (high on People, low on Purpose), Bureaucratic Leadership (low on both), Collaborative Leadership (high on both), and Strategic Leadership (in the middle on both axes).

Although the instructions tell the respondent that there are no right or wrong answers, it is clear from the manual what kind of leadership the authors value most. Naively one might think that the middle style, Strategic Leadership, described as a position of moderation and balance, would be the most desirable, but the authors chose Collaborative Leadership, which is at the highest on both Concern for People and Concern for Purpose; they described a person with that style as ideal—competent, responsible, believing work is healthy for people, and neither avoiding nor overreacting to conflict. They say the associate of such a leader is "indeed fortunate" because that style creates feelings of commitment as well as high self-worth.

The SLS is self-administering and self-scoring. However, the procedure and the phraseology is complicated, and it is likely that many respondents may need help. The authors report nothing about reading level, or how the items were developed. The questionnaire is on four pages, each covering a different topic and having three situations briefly described for which the subject rates five possible ways he or she reacts as a leader on a 10-point scale. Each of the four pages covers one general topic of leadership—Philosophy, Planning, Implementation, and Performance Evaluation. A paraphrased example under philosophy would be the question, "How do you feel a leader should relate to other members of the organization?" followed by five choices, such as "I feel that leaders should help workers feel good, trusting them to get the job done pretty much by themselves," and "I feel that a leader must be prepared for 'give and take' and avoid being too bossy or too friendly." In total respondents do 60 self-ratings each of which may range from 1 to 10. (It is not clear in the instructions whether the subject can use the same ratings for more than one of the five choices.) Questions can be raised about variability in complexity, social desirability, and plausibility among the choices.

The scoring first involves copying the ratings on a form and totaling them. (Though the ratings can range from 1 to 10, the grid shown for interpretation shows only 1 to 9, and the difference is not explained.) The raw self-ratings are converted into *T*-scores for the five leadership styles, which can then be ranked from most to least dominant. The manual indicates that leaders should have a dominant style and an orderly system of backup styles. For each of the four components (Philosophy, Planning, Implementation, and Evaluation) there are charts which show whether the respondent is weaker or stronger than desirable. There is also a companion form, the Leadership Appraisal Survey (LAS; T4:1406) with similar items for associates to rank the SLS respondent. With the two together, one could compare leader's perceptions with those of followers or other organizational members. The manual also mentions briefly a Styles of Management Inventory and implies that it is very similar to the SLS. This review concentrates on the SLS, which is the focus of the manual.

In a short section of the manual (pp. 15–16) entitled "Where do you go from here," the authors state that answering and scoring the SLS has been a semi-objective exploration, and "The fact is that you control your behavior and are responsible for it . . . you may behave however you choose . . . If you so elect, these data are meant to be the basis for planned, conscious change." They suggest studying the SLS items and listing behaviors the respondent would like to start and stop. An overview of each of the five leadership styles provides rather extensive descriptions of the type of behavior to be expected.

With all the value-laden admonishment in the manual, one might expect that the credibility of the instrument itself was based on strong research support. However, the manual, which was revised in 1986, lists only one reference to the author's works, dated 1975, and one additional related work by another author dated 1981 and also published by Telemetrics. The psychometrics are meager. The manual gives a median coefficient of stability (.70) with undescribed groups, and no other forms of reliability. The only research that relates to validity are brief mentions that SLS styles correlate with personality traits in ways consistent with grid theory and that a discriminant function analysis shows two dimensions defined primarily by the Directive, Supportive, and Bureaucratic styles. (Incidentally, the Bureaucratic Leadership style is described in a very biased way as lacking concern for both results and relationships, and likely to be adopted by people who have gone as high as they can go.) Normative data for the five styles are reported in the *T*-score conversion tables as being based on 2,800 leaders from a variety of organizations with an average age of 37.7 years and an average number of supervisees of 34. In another table, the authors report *T*-score means for eight groups with *N*s ranging from 23 to 253. Human service workers come out the highest on the ideal Collaborative style, and law enforcement officers are the highest on the Strategic style. However, not much can be made of these group means which are close together and no standard scores are given. There are no reports of gender differences, though the general literature suggests the hypothesis that women would score higher on Concern for People and men on Concern for Purpose. Though the manual (p. 17) states that the SLS and LAS are "widely used as learning instruments," there are no reports of evaluation of self-learning or results of training.

In conclusion, the Styles of Leadership Survey has probably improved over the version reviewed in 1978 *Eighth Mental Measurements Yearbook*, where the reviewer inveighed against "learning aids" that masquerade as tests and urged that such procedures should be taken off the market. The present manual does give some attention to norms, reliability, and validity. If a potential user is interested in the SLS as a test, there is much lacking. If the user wants a learning tool in management training, she or he should be aware of the highly evaluative descriptions of the leadership styles and the complex answering and scoring procedures which might put off some respondents.

[380]

Styles of Management Inventory.

Purpose: Assesses individual management style under a variety of conditions.
Population: Adults.
Publication Dates: 1964–86.
Scores, 5: Philosophy, Planning and Goal Setting, Implementation, Performance Evaluation, Total.
Administration: Group.
Price Data, 1993: $6.95 per inventory.
Time: Untimed.
Comments: Self-administered survey.
Authors: Jay Hall, Jerry B. Harvey, and Martha S. Williams.
Publisher: Teleometrics International.
Cross References: See T3:2351 (1 reference); for a review by Abraham K. Korman of [Styles of Leadership and Management], see 8:1185 (8 references).

Review of the Styles of Management Inventory by Richard W. FAUNCE, Licensed Psychologist, Maple Grove, MN:

The Styles of Management Inventory is described by the authors as a learning instrument for providing users with information about their dominant and backup styles of managing. Nevertheless, the Inventory booklet does refer to its use as a test and it seems reasonable to subject it to the critical procedures used for evaluating tests. The Inventory presents 12 management situations covering four categories. Three of these situations relate to Philosophy of Management, three to Planning and Goal Setting, three to Implementation, and three to Performance Evaluation. The Performance Evaluation situations, for example, relate to performance review procedures, dealing with employee mistakes, and dealing with personnel toward whom one has strong negative feelings.

For each situation, five alternative ways of responding are presented. The respondent is asked to rank order these five responses on a 10-point scale ranging from *completely characteristic* to *completely uncharacteristic* of what he or she would do or feel. Scale values for each response are summed and converted to *T* scores for each of the five Blake-Mouton managerial grid styles (Blake & Mouton, 1964). Thus, each of the five grid styles is based on the sum of 12 response scores across the four management components of Philosophy, Planning, Implementation, and Evaluation.

The order of the scores represents the respondent's dominant and backup managerial styles, with the highest score indicating the dominant style. A companion piece to the Inventory, the Management Appraisal Survey, is mentioned in the test booklet. This instrument uses the same items used in the Inventory to obtain perceptions of the subject's managerial style from associates. No information on the development of this instrument is presented.

The Inventory is untimed. My times were 35 minutes for reading instructions and responding, 25 minutes for scoring and recording, and 55 minutes for interpreting results, for a total of 1 hour and 55 minutes. Respondents without prior knowledge of basic statistics and the Blake-Mouton Grid could be expected to take somewhat more than 2 hours. A recent video produced by the publisher provides scoring and interpretation instructions (Telemetrics International, undated, p. 212).

Although the video may be helpful, it is expensive and it is devoted mainly to describing a new model of managerial style, the Style Parallax, which also uses the same items as those used in the Inventory. The Inventory does not have a manual although the 21-page test booklet contains a modicum of information relating to developmental procedures.

STANDARDIZATION AND NORMS. A conversion table for *T* Scores is based on 12,809 "managers from business, industry, government, and service organizations" (p. 9). No other information is presented for this normative group. Missing are such things as a definition of management, age, and date of data collection. In short, there is not much to make a user comfortable about using the table.

RELIABILITY AND VALIDITY. Statistical underpinnings for the 1986 edition of the Inventory are given in two sentences in the test booklet:

> The median coefficient of stability for the Styles of Management Inventory is .72 and the instrument discriminates between high, average and low achieving managers. Construct validity is good as revealed by a canonical correlation of the instrument with the MMPI: R= .68 significant at the .038 level of confidence. (p. 18)

These are the only two sentences in the test booklet under the heading of Reliability/Validity. No descriptive information is given on sample sizes, subgroup breakdowns, dates, or selection criteria. It appears that these data, except for the MMPI canonical correlation, are the same data reported in Korman's (1978) review in *The Eighth Mental Measurements Yearbook*. Then, as now, the reviewer could only guess at what had taken place. The authors' claim for construct validity through the use of the MMPI (Minnesota Multiphasic Personality Inventory) correlation is equally mysterious.

SUMMARY. Despite recent claims from the test publisher that "All of our materials undergo intensive scrutiny for validity and utility . . . there's no other training company that concentrates on this issue as much as we do" (Teleometrics International, undated, p. 2), it appears that relatively little has been done since the late 1970s to improve the information available on the scientific bases of the Styles of Management Inventory. The lack of information led Korman (1978) to conclude that these types of measures should be taken off the market. His hope seems to have been dashed in view of the apparent commercial success of the Inventory and its related products. Score one for face validity . . . and marketing. Can the Inventory be recommended? No. If the publisher wishes to live up to its claims it should begin by publishing a manual that provides users with information about the development, validity, and utility of its product.

REVIEWER'S REFERENCES

Blake, R. R., & Mouton, J. S. (1964). *The managerial grid: Strategic new insights into a proven system for increasing organization productivity and individual effectiveness, plus a revealing examination of how your managerial style can affect your mental and physical health.* Houston: Gulf Publishing Co.

Korman, A. K. (1978). [Review of the Styles of Leadership and Management]. In O. K. Buros (Ed.), *The eighth mental measurements yearbook* (p. 1763). Highland Park, NJ: The Gryphon Press.

Teleometrics International. (Undated). *Training design reference guide*. The Woodlands, TX: Author.

Review of the Styles of Management Inventory by LINDA F. WIGHTMAN, Vice President—Operations, Testing, and Research, Law School Admission Services, Newtown, PA:

The Styles of Management Inventory is designed to provide managers with information about their management style in a variety of situations. The inventory consists of 12 self-administered and self-scored items designed, according to the authors, to assess "general management orientation plus component assessments of managerial philosophy, planning, implementation, and evaluation." The instrument is based on Blake and Mouton's Managerial Grid model—a model that purports that all managers have two major concerns, production and people. Like the other assessment instruments offered by this publisher, the Styles of Management Inventory is presented in a single booklet that includes the inventory itself, scoring and score interpretation instructions, and elements of a technical manual.

The test taker is presented with 60 management alternatives presented five at a time under each of 12 different management situations. More specifically, for each of the 12 situations, the test taker is presented with five of the alternatives and is asked to place the alternative that is most characteristic of her/his behavior and the alternative that is least characteristic of her/his behavior on a 10-point scale that is anchored by *Completely Characteristic* at the top (a value of 10) and *Completely Uncharacteristic* at the bottom (a value of 1). Next, the test taker is told to place the remaining three alternatives on the same scale relative to how characteristic the alternative is of the test taker's management behavior.

When the inventory is completed, the test taker is provided with scoring instructions. Scoring is accomplished by recording the rating scale number for each alternative on a scoring form provided in the booklet and then summing the ratings in each of five columns. The test taker can then convert the raw sums to *T*-scores using a conversion table of normalized-standardized scores based on data of 12,809 managers from business, industry, government, and service organizations. The five columns represent five management styles that are subsequently defined in the score interpretation section of the booklet. These styles are labeled 1/1, 1/9, 9/9, 9/1, and 5/5, and are placed on a 9 by 9 grid, with 1/9 representing the management style that has high concern for people and low concern for production and 9/1 depicting the style that has high concern for production and low concern for people. The authors define the 9/9 manager as the ideal manager. Finally, the test takers are instructed to calculate difference scores by subtracting the second highest *T*-score from the highest, the third from the second, the fourth from the third, and the fifth from the fourth. The booklet provides test takers with explanations of each of the dominant management styles, as well as information about how to interpret the difference scores.

TEST DEVELOPMENT. The authors provide no rationale or theoretical framework for the 12 situations that are included in the inventory as well as no information about how the questions were developed, pretested, or selected. This same criticism has been raised by other *MMY* reviewers in their reviews of different inventories by this same publisher that use the same 12 management situations (Bernardin, 1989; Geisinger, 1992), and it has not yet been addressed.

NORMS. Raw scores are converted to *T*-scores based on data from more than 12,000 managers, but the sample is not adequately described. For example, the table of mean *T*-scores provided in the booklet suggests that the standardization sample is dominated by managers from Science and Technology and from manufacturing, but there is no breakdown of representation by type of organization. A possible need for separate norms by type of industry is not addressed. Likewise, there is no information about the level of managers represented nor about the gender and ethnicity of those managers.

Difference scores are used to identify both a general management orientation and a system of backup styles. The authors report that when the difference scores are all less than 10, there is no dominant management style. The authors equate these small difference scores with the worst possible management characteristics. However, they provide no research or psychometric data to support their interpretation and they provide no analyses or documentation to support the validity of 10 as the critical cutoff score.

RELIABILITY AND VALIDITY. The reliability and validity data provided in the booklet are inadequate. The only validity information is that the Styles of Management Inventory correlates about .68 with the MMPI (Minnesota Multiphasic Personality Inventory), but there is no information about the sample studied or the MMPI scale(s) used. The authors also report a median coefficient of stability of .72 and claim that "the instrument discriminates between high, average, and low achieving managers" (p. 18), but they fail to provide any description of procedures, data, or references to support these claims.

CONCLUSION. The Styles of Management Inventory is an attractively packaged, attractively priced assessment instrument with little psychometric evidence to support its utility. It clearly is intended to serve as an evaluation component of the GRID model of managerial behavior developed by the authors, but this instrument's relationship to the model and its ability to distinguish managers reliably according to model parameters are not supported. More serious validity work is required in order to defend the test development work used to construct this inventory. Evidence of expert judgement beyond that of the authors and a systematic job analysis study are among the types of evidence that should be provided. In its current form, the Styles of Management Inventory does not meet critical minimum test development standards as called for in the AERA/APA/NCME joint *Standards for Psychological and Educational Testing* (1985).

REVIEWER'S REFERENCES

American Educational Research Association, American Psychological Association, & National Council on Measurement in Education. (1985). *Standards for educational and psychological testing*. Washington, DC: American Psychological Association, Inc.

Bernardin, H. J. (1989). [Review of the Management Appraisal Survey]. In J. C. Conoley & J. J. Kramer (Eds.), *The tenth mental measurements yearbook* (pp. 458-459). Lincoln, NE: Buros Institute of Mental Measurements.

Geisinger, K. F. (1992). [Review of the Managerial Competence Index]. In J. J. Kramer & J. C. Conoley (Eds.), *The eleventh mental measurements yearbook* (pp. 502-503). Lincoln, NE: Buros Institute of Mental Measurements.

[381]

Substance Abuse Subtle Screening Inventory.

Purpose: To "identify chemical abusers and differentiate them from social drinkers and general psychiatric clients."
Population: Ages 12–18, adults.
Publication Dates: 1983–90.
Acronym: SASSI.
Administration: Group.
Levels, 2: Adult, Adolescent.
Price Data, 1989: $75 per starter kit; $25 per 25 tests and profiles; $10 per scoring key; $60 per videotape summary of manual; $55 per manual ('85, 242 pages).
Time: [10–15] minutes.
Author: Glenn A. Miller.
Publisher: The SASSI Institute.

a) ADULT FORM.

Scores, 8: Obvious Attributes, Subtle Attributes, Denial, Defensive Abuser vs. Defensive Non-Abuser, Alcohol vs. Drug, Codependency, Risk Prediction Score-Alcohol, Risk Prediction Score-Drug.

b) ADOLESCENT FORM.

Scores, 8: Obvious Attributes, Subtle Attributes, Defensiveness, Defensive Abuser vs. Defensive Non-Abuser, Correctional, Random Answering Pattern, Face Valid Alcohol, Face Valid Other Drug.

TEST REFERENCES

1. Svanum, S., & McGrew, J. (1995). Prospective screening of substance dependence: The advantages of directness. *Addictive Behaviors, 20*, 205-213.

Review of the Substance Abuse Subtle Screening Inventory by BARBARA KERR, Professor of Psychology in Education, Arizona State University, Tempe, AZ:

The Substance Abuse Subtle Screening Inventory (SASSI) is an interesting attempt to deal with the tendency of substance abusers to deny or obscure their substance abuse. It is based on the assumption that self-report responses that do not include substance use in their content may serve as indicators of substance abuse. Most substance abuse screening measures have obvious items concerning the use of alcohol and drug use; substance abusers who deny their condition or for a variety of reasons wish to hide their substance abuse will usually "fake good" on these scales. Therefore, substance abuse screening inventories that do not take this response set into account are not likely to be effective. Mental health centers, university student health centers, and court-ordered substance abuse centers have a great need for this kind of scale, and have greeted the development of the SASSI with enthusiasm (Creager, 1989).

DEVELOPMENT OF THE SASSI. The SASSI is a single-page, paper-and-pencil questionnaire. On one side are 52 True-False questions that seem to be unrelated to chemical abuse. On the other side are the Risk Prediction Scales which allow clients to self-report on the 12 alcohol-related and 14 drug-related items. The test in intended to be readable at the fifth grade level and can also be administered orally. It takes from 10 to 15 minutes for clients to complete both tests. The SASSI can be hand scored in about 1 minute.

The items on the SASSI are empirically derived. Most other current substance abuse screening instruments are rationally constructed, based on theoretical formulations of the symptoms of alcoholism. This scale is composed predominantly of items from other empirically derived scales and new items. Items were borrowed from the Minnesota Multiphasic Personality Inventory (MMPI; 9:715), the Psychological Screening Inventory (PSI; 9:1015; Lanyon, 1973), the Michigan Alcoholism Screening Test (Selzer, 1971), and many other sources that promised to yield items which differentiated between abusers and non-abusers. The subtle items related to a wide variety of behaviors related to health, social interaction, emotional states, preferences, needs, interests, and values. Non-subtle items are asked directly about substance abuse and its usual consequences.

Approximately 1,000 items were administered to close to 300 people in the course of the validation studies. Discriminant analyses were used to develop the major subscales. The subscales are as follows:

The Obvious Attributes Scale (OAT) is intended to measure the openness or the willingness of the client to admit to symptoms or problems related to substance abuse. A high score on this scale means that there are similarities between the client's personal style and the personal style of chemically dependent people.

The Subtle Attributes Scale (SAT) score is probably the most important scale, because it is very resistant to faking. It measures a personal predisposition to develop a dependency on drugs or alcohol. High scores means that the client is similar biologically or in personal style to chemically dependent people.

The Denial (DEN) scale was created to identify the client's defensiveness to test taking, but high scores can result from unconscious denial or deliberate attempts to conceal. Both high and low scores indicate problems: High scores are associated with excessive denial and low scores with feelings of worthlessness and deficiency.

The Defensive Abuser vs. Defensive Non-Abuser Scale (DEN) is used with the Denial Scale score in determining whether a person is in fact an abuser or whether their responses are those of a defensive non-abuser.

The Alcohol vs. Drug Scale (ALD) is intended to show whether the client prefers alcohol or other drugs. Although this is not a strong scale, usually a high score indicates alcohol preference and a low score indicates drug preference.

The Family vs. Controls Scale (FAM) is meant to be a preliminary measure of codependency. It is a weak scale at this point; it is meant to show how similar the test taker is to family members of alcohol and drug abusers.

The second part of the SASSI is made up of two previously developed scales, the Face Valid Alcohol scale (originally the Risk Prediction Scale for alcohol) and the Face Valid Drug Scale (originally the Risk Prediction Scale for drugs [SASSI manual, Appendix B, p. 18, Copper & Robinson, in press]).

Scoring and interpretation of the SASSI involves attention to the elevation and slope of the scales as well as using a variety of decision rules that lead to the classification of abuser or nonabuser. An example of such a rule is: If either of the following two conditions is met, classify as chemical abuser:

1. Obvious Attributes (OAT) or Subtle Attributes (SAT) *T*-score is above 70.

2. Obvious Attributes and Subtle Attributes *T* scores are both above 60.

VALIDITY. In the validation section of the manual, the author shows that the SASSI and the RPS measures each did better in identifying low defensive late stage abusers already involved in a residential detoxification program than the more defensive early stage abusers. It is important, therefore, to specify the population on which validity testing takes place. The combination of the SASSI and the RPS was most effective with all populations: The combination identified 90% of the residential detoxification sample, 80%

of defensive early stage abusers in a family oriented intensive outpatient program, and 90% of nonabusers who were also codependents. The independent contribution of the SASSI was most important with individuals who were defensive early stage abusers. The subscales were shown to each contribute independently to the decision rules. The Subtle Attributes (SAT) scale did a good job of identifying defensiveness and the Denial (DEN) scale in identifying distortions. The Family (FAM) scale was not successful in identifying codependency.

A later study found the SASSI to be useful in identifying subtle substance abusers among rehabilitation clients in Texas; 87% of the cases already classified as substance abusers by the rehabilitation agency were identified by the SASSI. Also, 32.7% of clients who had not been previously identified as substance abusers by the agency, and about whom counselors were not aware, were classified as such by the SASSI (DiNitto & Schwab, 1991). A dissertation by Kilkunas (1988), using only the SASSI without the Face Valid Scales, still found reasonably good prediction, with the SASSI identifying 94% of controls, 78% of Alcoholics, 71% of Drug Addicts, and 96% of codependents (Creager, 1989).

The SASSI has high concurrent validity with the MacAndrew (1965) subscale of the MMPI (.87), although the use of some of these items and some very similar ones certainly contributes to the high concurrent validity.

RELIABILITY. The internal consistency of most of the subscales of the SASSI is quite low. Because of the discriminant analysis method of construction, each subscale except the RPSA, RPSD, and PAL5 is made up of heterogeneous items rather than items related to a unitary construct. Internal consistency analyses were performed for Detox patients, Outpatients, and Probation groups. Coefficient alpha ranges are reported as follows: OAT, .61–.73; SAT, .25–.49; DEN, .57–.68; DAN, .56–.82; ALD, .44–.49; FAM, .16–.60; RPSA, .90–.92; RPSD, .93–.96; PAL5, .78–.80.

The only study of test-retest reliability which has been performed was one in which the SASSI was used without the Face Valid Scales. Kilkunas (1988) tested 24 subjects on a 4- to 6-week interval and found moderate to good test-retest reliability. The reliability coefficients were reported as follows: OAT, .87; SAT, .91; DEN, .86; DAN, .91; ALD, .78; FAM, .76.

It was puzzling that the author, who obviously put tremendous thought and care into the validation of the SASSI, gave so little attention to reliability. Because of the inconsistent nature of responding of many substance abusers to psychological instruments, and because of the importance of decisions made based on the SASSI, more emphasis on its reliability should be given in future research. All indications so far are the instrument is a reliable one.

CLINICAL USEFULNESS. The SASSI is almost as good as its promotion claims it to be. It seems to have been responsibly developed, and it is clearly created with the practitioner in mind. Its ease of administration and scoring, its clear decision rules and suggestions for interpretation, and the informative and carefully written manual all make it very attractive to mental health providers who have difficult and important decisions to make about treatment.

The SASSI fits its population as well; it does seem to accurately identify those who are denying or obscuring their substance abuse, particularly among less advanced stage abusers. One quibble is that although it is supposed to be at the fifth grade reading level, it looks as though it actually would require a higher reading level, probably seventh or eighth grade.

There may be ethical issues which will require exploration if the SASSI becomes widespread in its use. It must never become the psychological equivalent of the Breathalyzer test; legal decisions about the label substance abuser must be made on the basis of interview material, this and other instruments, and on evidence of actual behavior.

REVIEWER'S REFERENCES

MacAndrew, C. (1965). The differentiation of male alcoholic outpatients from nonalcoholic psychiatric outpatients by means of the MMPI. *Quarterly Journal of Studies on Alcohol*, *26*, 238-246.

Selzer, M. L. (1971). The Michigan Alcoholism Screening Test: The quest for a new diagnostic instrument. *American Journal of Psychiatry*, *127*, 1653-1658.

Lanyon, R. I. (1973). Psychological Screening Inventory: Manual. Goshen, NY: Research Psychologists Press.

Kilkunas, W. (1988). [Title unavailable]. Unpublished doctoral dissertation. Muncie, IN: Ball State University.

Creager, C. (1989, July/August). SASSI test breaks through denial. *Professional Counselor*, p. 81-84.

DiNitto, D. M., & Schwab, A. J. (1991). *Substance abuse factors which interfere with entry or reentry into employment*. Report for Texas Rehabilitation Commission. Austin, TX: University of Texas at Austin School of Social Work.

Copper, S., & Robinson, D. A. (in press). Cross-validation of the Substance Abuse Subtle Screening Inventory on a college population. *American Journal of College Health*.

Review of the Substance Abuse Subtle Screening Inventory by NICHOLAS A. VACC, Professor and Chairperson, Department of Counselor Education, University of North Carolina at Greensboro, Greensboro, NC:

The Substance Abuse Subtle Screening Inventory (SASSI) consists of two separate questionnaires included in one response form. On one side of the response form is the SASSI, which is a one-page paper-and-pencil questionnaire containing 52 true and false questions designed to assess chemical abuse in an unobtrusive way; items appear unrelated to chemical abuse and, therefore, make them less threatening to the respondent. On the opposite side of the response form is the Risk Prediction Scales (RPS), which was designed to predict the degree of risk of abusing alcohol and other drugs. The RPS, which comes in two forms, was developed by Linda A. Morton (1978) in conjunction with the Department of Mental Health, Division of Addiction Services, State of Indiana. It consists of 26 items designed to assess the level of substance-abuse risk (i.e., non-users minimally at risk, non-problematic users minimally at risk, non-users moderately at risk, non-problematic users moderately at risk, problematic users substantially at risk, and dysfunctional users totally at risk). Use of the RPS enhances the value of the SASSI.

The SASSI was developed to assess chemical dependency by being insulated to the respondent's level of honesty or faking. The author reports the instrument is independent of age, education, and socioeconomic status. The instrument provides information concerning five scales (i.e., Obvious Attributes [OAT], which is designed to differentiate substance abusers who have admitted problems from non-abusers; Subtle Attributes [SAT], which is intended to differentiate substance abusers from non-substance abusers regardless of the respondent's degree of honesty; Denial [DEN], which is designed to identify those substance abusers who are denying their behavior; Personal-Family [FAM], which distinguishes between substance abusers and non-abusers who live with dependency (co-dependency); and Alcohol/Drug Preference [ALD], which is designed to differentiate alcohol abusers from those with a poly-drug abuse pattern). The SASSI takes about 10–15 minutes to complete and can be scored in 5–10 minutes.

A single form of the SASSI is available for both men and women and is designed for respondents 18 years of age through adulthood. Also available is an adolescent form of the SASSI designed for use with children ages 12–18. The adolescent form, which is a more recent development by the test author, appears, like the adult form, to be nonthreatening and is designed for screening adolescents who may be chemically dependent. Other materials related to this instrument that are available through the SASSI Institute are an instructional videotape that provides information concerning the administration, scoring, development, philosophy, and validity data of the SASSI; training workshops (for a fee) that provide participants with the SASSI feedback system to include how the SASSI can be used to assist clients to establish goals and conduct therapeutic interventions; a computer-disk form of the SASSI designed for IBM-compatible computers; and a telephone consultation service provided by the staff at the SASSI Institute. A toll-free number is provided for this free consultation service concerning profile interpretation and program development using the SASSI.

In consulting practitioners, it appears that the computer-assisted scoring disk for IBM or compatible computers is the method of choice. The computer-scoring procedure is easy to learn and operate; clear instructions are available for using the SASSI computer version. The examinee answers the questions by typing the appropriate letter on the keyboard, and the next question appears automatically. After completing the assessment, examinees are asked whether they would like to review their answers. The computer-assisted scoring disk, which requires a password by the practitioner, enhances the scoring process and provides a visual display of the profile on the screen as well as a printed copy of the profile and results. Both the paper-and-pencil and computer versions of the SASSI are user friendly for respondents.

The SASSI's primary purpose as identified by the author is to serve as an objective screening tool to differentiate substance abusers from non-abusers. However, in addition to screening, the SASSI is frequently used by practitioners as a clinical instrument when counseling individuals and families. Yet, the SASSI's value within counseling programs has not been empirically documented. The manual provides a section on clinical interpretation of the SASSI for practitioners, but it also includes a disclaimer that such use has not been validated through empirical research. To be addressed are such questions as how valuable are the subscales in developing treatment plans?

The author reports through informal correspondence accompanying the reviewer's manual, that test/retest reliability was reported for 24 subjects as .87 (OAT), .91 (SAT), .86 (DEN), .78 (ALD), and .76 (FAM) for the adult form. Overall reliability averages appear to be acceptable (G. Miller, personal communication, August 1990). Considerable validity testing is provided in the manual. Unfortunately, adequate description concerning representativeness of the populations involved in the reported validity data is not provided. Notably absent is empirical information concerning the chronological age, social economic status, and ethnic background of the samples. Also, woefully inadequate are some of the cell-sizes of the subsamples reported for the validity and normative information provided. For example, the intensive outpatient program samples of family chemical abusers had *N*s as small as 3 for the male subgroup, 11 for the female subgroup, and 7 for the male family non-chemical abusers subgroup.

The SASSI manual is somewhat confusing and difficult to use. Practitioners have recommended that it is advisable to take the SASSI training workshop with a representative in order to properly understand how to score and interpret the instruments to achieve maximum benefit. This recommendation applies to both the paper-and-pencil and computer version printouts (C. Woods, personal communication, May 2, 1992).

In summary, considering the reasonable cost of approximately $2 a test, the computer version of the

SASSI is the instrument of choice as a quick screening instrument in the area of substance abuse. Because it is widely used by individuals involved with the substance-abuse field, including Alcohol Safety Action Programs, the SASSI psychometric properties should meet or exceed professional norms. The information reported in the manual is less than reassuring that this has been achieved. Although the manual appears comprehensive and thorough on quick inspection, it is poorly developed; it does not provide adequate information and the reader has to "dig" in an attempt to judge the value of the instrument. The author should consider developing a technical manual addressing the *Standards for Educational and Psychological Testing* (AERA, APA, & NCME, 1985) and a separate test user's manual written for the practitioner.

Such information as sample descriptions to include ethnic background, chronological age, socioeconomic status, and/or educational level, and a reported reading level index of the two forms would be helpful additions to the manual. Also, the small number of cases used in the development of some of the scales, and the absence of current samples (some samples are pre-1977) are of concern. A more current data base for normative analysis is needed. For an instrument that is often used, additional data need to be systematically collected for the purpose of addressing psychometric issues.

The cost, short testing time, and ease of use by test takers are compelling reasons for the instrument's use. I would use the computer-assisted version and the paper-and-pencil version of the SASSI, but the former version would be my first choice. Additionally, I would suggest prospective users attend a SASSI Institute workshop to better prepare themselves for using the instruments.

REVIEWER'S REFERENCE

American Educational Research Association, American Psychological Association, & National Council on Measurement in Education. (1985). *Standards for educational and psychological testing*. Washington, DC: American Psychological Association, Inc.

[382]

Survey of Employee Access.

Purpose: Measures effective managerial behavior.
Population: Adults.
Publication Date: 1989.
Acronym: SEA.
Scores, 5: Access to the Problem, Access to People, Access to Information and Resources, Access to Emotional/Procedural Supports, Access to Solution.
Administration: Group.
Price Data, 1993: $6.95 per survey.
Time: Untimed.
Comments: Self-administered survey.
Author: Jay Hall.
Publisher: Teleometrics International.

Review of the Survey of Employee Access by MARCIA J. BELCHER, Associate Dean, Office of Institutional Research, Miami-Dade Community College, Miami, FL:

The Survey of Employee Access (SEA) is a 25-item instrument designed to inform managers of the extent to which their employees believe they provide access to the technical and social resources needed to be involved in participatory decision making. There are five items for each of five areas of access: the problem itself, the people involved in the problem, the needed information and resources to address the problem, the emotional and procedural supports, and the solution. The survey is followed by a six-item Personal Reaction Index that asks employees to provide ratings on the degree to which they participate in decision making, satisfaction with their involvement in decision making, feeling of responsibility for making decisions work, personal ownership of decisions, frustration with decisions made, and quality of decisions.

To complete the Survey of Employee Access, respondents read a stem that describes a situation (e.g., "If the people I work with were having chronic production problems of some sort, . . . my manager would . . ." [p. 1]) and then distribute 5 points between two alternatives. The survey is untimed and no estimates are given for the approximate amount of time needed to complete it. However, the amount of reading required and the distribution of points are both indicators that at least 30 minutes—and possibly much more—should be allowed to complete the instrument.

The survey is self-scoring. Respondents sum their responses for the five items related to each of the five areas and then chart them. The bands on the chart indicate the 25th, 50th, 75th, and 99th percentiles, so respondents can see where they have rated their manager compared to others who have taken the survey.

The accompanying information on interpreting the survey provides background on the concept but little information on the psychometric properties of the test. The author states the norms are based on "other working people" but does not even indicate the number of respondents used in calculating the percentiles. It would be useful to know the types of job roles held by respondents. A high school education or at least strong language skills would probably be required to complete the survey. The vocabulary is sophisticated, and much reading is required with the length of individual items ranging from almost 70 to over 130 words.

Reliability and validity information is also scant. Internal consistency reliability of .902 is reported. The only validity information reported is a correlation between the SEA and the "scales" (actually one item) of the Personal Reaction Index given at the end of the survey. In any case, a single correlation does not appear interpretable because there are five scales on the SEA and six scales/items on the Personal Reaction Index.

It appears the best use of this survey would be as a tool to provide summary feedback to managers on the perceptions of workers. However, the norms and materials are geared toward individual responding. Thus, it is not entirely clear even who the audience is or how the survey might best be used. Perhaps the SEA would be useful in a seminar setting under the guidance of a professional who could help fold the survey results into a larger context. Without information on norms, reliability, or validity, however, users should be very tentative in their interpretations.

Review of the Survey of Employee Access by ROBERT FITZPATRICK, Consulting Industrial Psychologist, Cranberry Township, PA:

The Survey of Employee Access (SEA) consists of 25 items, 5 for each of the scores. For each item, the respondent employee rates his or her manager on what is effectively a 6-point scale. High scores indicate the manager believes in, and acts in accordance with, the management philosophy that rank-and-file employees should be actively encouraged to participate in making decisions about their work. The author suggests the effective manager should arrange things so that employees have *access* to the (*a*) problems, (*b*) people, (*c*) information and resources, (*d*) emotional/procedural supports (reassurance and removal of red tape), and (*e*) solution options that may be needed to make sound work-related decisions.

The SEA items are, for the most part, written at a high level of reading difficulty. Many of them involve long and convoluted sentences containing fairly complex ideas. The SEA appears unsuitable for employees with limited verbal facility.

The allocation of items to the scales seems inconsistent in a few cases. For example, the premise of Item 17 is that the work group needs certain materials or services to solve a problem; the question is how willing the manager would be to ask higher management for money to buy what is needed. This item is scored on the Access to People scale, apparently on the rationale that the access to higher management is more important than the access to the needed resources. But Item 18, which involves the manager's convincing higher management to release confidential information, is scored on the Access to Information and Resources scale.

Also included in the survey booklet is A Personal Reaction Index (PRI), of six items covering overall degree of participation, feelings of satisfaction, feelings of responsibility, feelings of commitment, feelings of frustration, and perceived decision quality. Each PRI item is to be rated on a 9-point scale. Apparently, the PRI is also available separately (for two reviews, see 9:946).

The SEA and PRI are self-scored. Scores are to be interpreted in relation to percentile norms which are provided. For the PRI, the norms are said to be based on a group of "12,728 individuals like yourself"; there is no other description of the norm group in the booklet. No information is given about the size or composition of the norm group for the SEA.

The survey booklet includes several pages of discussion aimed at helping the respondent interpret his or her scores. This material is pitched at an intermediate level and seems likely to be persuasive at that level. However, it is probably too sophisticated for employees without previous background in modern ideas of participatory management, and somewhat simplified for human resource professionals. It argues for a fairly extreme version of employee participation as almost a panacea for problems related to productive work. It further suggests, without convincing evidence or argument, that management provision of access is a key element in making participation effective. Included in the discussion is a confusing description of a study that is apparently thought to show that the PRI distinguishes between managers who follow the prescribed course and those who do not.

No separate technical manual is provided. A brief section of the survey booklet is titled "Developmental Information." It is said that internal consistency of the SEA is "excellent as evidenced by an Alpha of .902 " (p. 17) but no information is given about the derivation of this statistic. It is plausible that the items are highly intercorrelated. It seems likely that the five subscores are also highly similar to each other; no information is provided to indicate whether there is any point in distinguishing five types of access.

Construct validity is claimed on the basis that the SEA and PRI are correlated. Because it is not clear just what the PRI measures (beyond general job satisfaction), this finding is not very helpful. No other validity evidence is cited.

The survey booklet does not explain what function the SEA and PRI are intended to serve. It appears that respondents are assumed to be nonmanagers, describing their current managers. But to what end? The interpretive discussion argues for the benefits of participation and access, but says nothing about how a worker might influence his or her manager to encourage or even allow them.

The SEA, along with the accompanying PRI, is presented with no clear purpose, essentially no evidence for validity, and inadequate information about reliability and norms. It is not recommended.

[383]

Survey of Work Values, Revised, Form U.

Purpose: Constructed to identify attitudes toward work.
Population: Employees.
Publication Dates: 1975–76.
Scores, 6: Social Status, Activity Preference, Upward Striving, Attitude Toward Earnings, Pride in Work, Job Involvement.

Administration: Group.
Manual: No manual.
Price Data, 1992: $21 per 100 test booklets; $5 per 100 answer sheets; $5 per 100 hand-scoring sheets; general instructions, free.
Time: [15] minutes.
Authors: Bowling Green State University.
Publisher: Bowling Green State University.
Cross References: See T4:2665 (1 reference).

TEST REFERENCES

1. Singh, S. (1994). Gender differences in work values and personality characteristics among Indian executives. *The Journal of Social Psychology, 134*, 699-700.

Review of the Survey of Work Values, Revised, Form U by JULIE A. ALLISON, Assistant Professor of Psychology, Pittsburg State University, Pittsburg, KS:

The Survey of Work Values, Revised, Form U (SWV, Form U) is designed to assess several different aspects of the secularized Protestant Ethic. The scale is based on a conceptualization that includes both intrinsic aspects of work: Pride in Work, Job Involvement, and Activity Preference, and extrinsic aspects of work: Attitude toward Earnings, and Social Status of the job. Additionally, one dimension was included that measures aspects of both internality and externality: Upward Striving. These six components are each represented by nine items in the SWV, resulting in a 54-item scale. Respondents are asked to indicate their degree of agreement or disagreement with each statement on a 5-point Likert scale.

Inclusion of the items for each subscale was based on the method of reallocation. Individuals from both industrial and academic settings were asked to place items under the most relevant category of the category labels provided. Retention of any item was based on the perceived relevancy of the item to the category label: Items with a 70% allocation rate to a single category and no more than 20% allocation to any second category were retained.

Reliability measures for each of the subscales were computed from both a sample of industrial workers and a sample of government workers. The reliability figures reported ranged from .53 to .66. Although these figures are relatively low, they are justifiable in light of the small number of items per subscale and a wide range of item means within each subscale.

The authors provide partial support for construct validity: The reallocation procedure was successful, internal consistency is adequate, and the SWV scores successfully discriminated among various occupational groups and correlated with background characteristics of employed and disadvantaged persons. However, evidence for both convergent validity and discriminant validity is lacking and is needed to finalize an overall evaluation of the construct validity. For example, the relationship of the SWV with other tests, such as the Work Values Inventory (Super, 1970; T4:2998) which has excellent psychometric foundations (but focuses more generally on the concept of values) should be documented.

Although the 1979 normative data for the SWV needs to be updated, the SWV could be useful for both academicians and employers interested in the conceptualization and assessment of the Protestant Ethic. Past use of the scale has included evaluation of orientation programs and identification of differences between supervisors and employees. Assistance in the selection of workers is also a potential use of the SWV.

REVIEWER'S REFERENCE

Super, D. E. (1970). Work Values Inventory. Chicago: Riverside Publishing Co.

Review of the Survey of Work Values, Revised, Form U by H. JOHN BERNARDIN, University Research Professor, and DONNA K. COOKE, Assistant Professor, College of Business, Florida Atlantic University, Boca Raton, FL:

The Survey of Work Values (SWV) is designed to measure a person's general opinions about work and is based on Weber's concept of Protestant Ethic (Weber, 1958). The focus of the instrument and the underlying theory is on work values rather than attitudes toward a specific job, a respondent's career, or a particular organization. Consequently, work values are hypothesized to be less a function of the immediate work circumstances and more a function of relatively stable, personal factors. The utility of the SWV lies in the belief that these work values are more enduring than specific attitudes such as organizational commitment and job satisfaction (cf., Morrow, 1983).

For the current version of the SWV, the gender-neutral Form U, respondents are instructed to place a check mark on a 5-point Likert scale to indicate degree of agreement or disagreement with 54 statements. The survey is separate from the answer sheet, allowing for its reuse. One weakness is that the only norms currently available are from student samples. A manual would be very helpful to interested researchers because articles oftentimes do not reference the SWV in their titles or abstracts, thus, detailed study of the instrument's characteristics is difficult.

The scales operationalize six secular or nonreligious aspects of Protestant Ethic: Pride in Work, Activity Preference, Job Involvement, Social Status of Job, Attitude toward Earnings, and Upward Striving. The first three dimensions represent the intrinsic value of work or the opinion that work is valued for its own sake. Social Status of Job and Attitude toward Earnings are dimensions of the extrinsic value of work, that is, work is valued as a means to other ends. Upward Striving is not classified as either an intrinsic or extrinsic dimension.

The scale was developed through a painstaking process. Faculty and graduate students developed 91 items for the subscales. Fifty-eight glass-manufacturing workers were given these items and the definitions of seven categories and one "other" and told to assign the items to corresponding categories. The criteria for acceptance were at least 70% placement into a single category and no more than 20% placement into a second. The surviving items along with some additions were again successively judged by two samples of undergraduates using the same criteria. Industrial and nonindustrial groups were used to improve the likelihood that the final items would be generalizable. Small samples of the same industrial and undergraduate groups (46 and 45, respectively) assigned scale values to the items presented in their categories by associating them with five hypothetical workers. This step rests on the assumption that the raters had stereotypical impressions of the hypothetical workers. Because one would strongly expect high levels of stereotyping about fictitious people, the fact that different samples were used is of debatable utility. Both samples were equally unfamiliar with the hypothetical workers. Although the correlation of both sets of scale values was .94 (N = 67), it should be noted that the sample size reported for this correlation is lower than the already small combined sample of 91 who did the scaling. A larger sample size would have been preferable. Presenting the items by category may have enhanced these correlations.

Four hundred and ninety-five employees from the same glass manufacturing company completed the 67 items using a 6-point agreement scale. The items were in mixed order. An item was retained if it correlated highly within its subscale, contributed to the scale's alpha, increased the subscale value range, and had low scale value variability. Form U uses the more customary 5-point scale and it is expected that the change should result in increased scale reliability.

Principal components analysis resulted in six factors which accounted for 36% of total variance. The first factor comprised mainly items from the intrinsic dimensions (Pride in Work, Activity Preference, and Job Involvement). Social Status of Job, Attitude toward Earnings, and Upward Striving loaded separately. Despite not loading on a common factor, Social Status of Job and Attitude toward Earnings are said to be on the extrinsic dimension. Their subscale intercorrelation is a very modest .27. Two other factors, Conventional Ethic and Organization-Man Ethic were also identified in the original study (Wollack, Goodale, Wijting, & Smith, 1971) but are not included in Form U. Factor loadings seem to indicate two orthogonal axes, one of which could be labeled "extrinsic" and one of which could be labeled "intrinsic." The data do indicate that a bi-polar, intrinsic-extrinsic scale is inappropriate.

Despite claims by DeMeuse (1985) that the SWV is a frequently used instrument, our literature search revealed very few studies. One of the authors of the instrument reported that an unpublished Master's thesis conducted at Wayne State University revealed that the "attitudes toward earning" subscale was negatively correlated with bank teller errors and performance appraisals. No other subscale was significantly correlated with the criteria under study (P. C. Smith, personal communication, January 9, 1992).

One weakness of the SWV is its low subscale reliabilities. Although they are expected to improve with the use of the 5-point rather than the 6-point agreement scale, they are still low, with alphas reported in the .53 to .66 range across two large samples. The test-retest reliabilities over a 1-month period are more respectable, ranging from .65 to .76. For a scale for which the main selling point is that it assesses stable work attitudes, such low reliabilities are problematic, although they can be explained by the differences in difficulty levels for the items comprising each subscale. They cast doubt on the construct validity of the SWV. Compared to related, and relatively stable concepts such as the various forms of commitment whose alphas typically range in the .80s and .90s with fewer items, the SWV does not fare well. Increasing the number of items for each subscale would most certainly improve internal consistency.

The SWV has been related to a number of demographic variables including race, sex, and education. According to the letter addressed to prospective test users, the SWV-U is being validated for selection purposes. It will be interesting to see if its use is likely to result in any adverse impact, or is confounded by social desirability. Scoring transparency could certainly be a problem in real selection situations. It remains to be seen if the assessed work values change over time as circumstances such as income and career stage change. Judging from the items (e.g., "A good job is a well paying job"), it is very likely that one's opinion could be a function of the immediate work situation and not largely a function of an enduring orientation towards work. As for the utility for researchers, the SWV is lengthy compared to other measures of Protestant Ethic (54 items to Mirels & Garrett's [1971] 19 items). Some of the items themselves are long and time and space considerations may sway surveyors away from the SWV.

In summary, the SWV-U was a very carefully developed operationalization of an important set of employee attitudes which appears to have great potential for use. However, many psychometric questions persist. Since the original work in 1971, the field has become more crowded with shorter questionnaires that purport to measure not only Protestant Ethic but similar stable attitudes. The need for a test manual updating the documentation, low subscale reliabilities, possible confounding with social desirability, insufficient evidence of temporal stability 20 years after the publication of the original study, and the length of the survey make it difficult for us to recommend its use. Although the research certainly started out on the right foot, the authors of the instrument should present a stronger case to potential users.

REVIEWER'S REFERENCES

Weber, M. (1958). *The Protestant Ethic and the spirit of capitalism* (T. Parsons, Trans.). New York: Scribner.
Mirels, H. L., & Garrett, J. B. (1971). The Protestant Ethic as a personality variable. *Journal of Consulting and Clinical Psychology, 36*, 40-44.
Wollack, S., Goodale, J. G., Wijting, J. P., & Smith, P. C. (1971). Development of the Survey of Work Values. *Journal of Applied Psychology, 55*, 331-338.
Morrow, P. C. (1983). Concept redundancy in organizational research: The case of work commitment. *Academy of Management Review, 8*, 486-500.
DeMeuse, K. P. (1985). A compendium of frequently used measures in industrial/organizational psychology. *The Industrial Psychologist, 23*, 53-59.

[384]

Symbolic Play Test, Second Edition.

Purpose: Developed to assess early concept formation and symbolization based on a child's spontaneous nonverbal play.
Population: Ages 1–3.
Publication Dates: 1976–88.
Scores: Total score only.
Administration: Individual.
Price Data, 1992: £117.30 per complete set including toys, 25 record forms, and manual ('88, 39 pages); £10.10 per 25 record forms; £19.85 per manual.
Time: (10–15) minutes.
Authors: Marianne Lowe and Anthony J. Costello.
Publisher: NFER-Nelson Publishing Co., Ltd. [England].
Cross References: See T4:2673 (2 references) and T3:2383 (1 reference).

Review of the Symbolic Play Test, Second Edition by ANTHONY W. PAOLITTO, Assistant Professor of Education, School Psychology Program, Tufts University, Medford, MA:

The underlying rationale of the Symbolic Play Test, Second Edition (SPT), is that early concept formation and symbolization are precursors to a child's receptive and expressive verbal language which then proceed to develop concomitantly. The SPT has been designed to serve as a diagnostic tool that evaluates the language potential of 1- to 3-year-old children who have for any reason not yet displayed evidence of receptive or expressive language abilities. The format through which the authors attempt to accomplish this is through structured observations of a child's nonverbal play with various toys and the child's purported interpretation of their symbolic meaning.

The Second Edition of the SPT succeeds the Symbolic Play Test, Experimental Edition, first published in 1976. Both of the editions were developed and published in England. The current form of the SPT does not represent an actual revision of the previous edition, with the original standardization sample still being utilized along with the administration guidelines, scoring procedures, and most of the toys remaining intact. The Second Edition does provide a new expanded record form, in addition to a revised examiner's manual that now includes supplemental interpretation guidelines and a new chapter highlighting six clinical studies conducted with the SPT.

The Symbolic Play Test is administered individually and consists of four separate presentations of different toys or manipulatives. The intent of each presentation is to elicit spontaneous and undirected play from the child, with minimal verbal direction. Nonverbal intervention and encouragement is permitted sparingly. Test items within each of the four situations are evaluated based on the presence or absence of particular developmental activities and are relatively free of ambiguity in regards to scoring criteria. The appropriate response to a toy (e.g., placing a cup on a saucer) translates to a "+" or a point, that can be tabulated to derive an age-equivalent score. The record form is well structured with clear prompts for totaling scores and conversions to age equivalents.

The different toys used with the four situations appear to be appropriate symbols of play for children of the intended age range of the test. However, the sophistication and quality of individual items varies considerably. A tractor that is to be hitched to a trailer in Situation IV is likely to be found authentic enough and worthy of exploration by almost any child, yet the upright man who is to be seated in the tractor is clearly of different quality. The man is dressed with glued-on felt clothing, with wire legs, arms, and torso that are rigid and likely to cause a young child difficulty in attempting to place him in a seated position. A child is likely to get the impression the toy may break. A different doll used in Situation II (with webbed hands) that may be seated on a chair for a scorable point is even stiffer, such that any attempt to bend the doll may again lead children to believe they were about to break it if they persisted further. Such factors can have the added implication of lower scores for children who are experiencing some degree of fine motor delay. Such a delay is not uncommon for this age range.

The standardization sample of the SPT is insufficient. The initial sample consisted of 137 children ranging in age from 12 to 36 months who were administered 241 tests. Children were chosen randomly at each age level from five different nurseries or welfare centers in north or inner London. Those children known to have either physical or unspecified mental handicaps were excluded from the sample. With a breakdown of seven different age groupings, standardization data are based upon samples ranging in size at each level from 27 to 42 children. Some children were tested repeatedly so the same children are found across several age levels. No information is submitted on race or ethnicity. Efforts were made successfully to have children representative of various socioeconomic and occupational classifications, along with including a small sample of children whose parents were non-English-speaking. The sample characteristics limit the use of the instrument.

Internal consistency for the total scale was .81, with additional coefficients being reported for the seven different age groups at 3- or 6-month age intervals. These varied from .52 to .92, with considerable fluctuation between some of the adjoining age intervals: .52 at 18 months to .79 at 21 months; .92 at 30 months to .74 at 36 months. Stability coefficients were determined for 3-, 6-, 9-, and 12-month intervals, varying from .71 to .81. These are more acceptable considering the very young ages of the sampled children. The authors suggest that a ceiling effect may be influencing the extreme end of the age range but provide no further elaboration on this point.

The concurrent validity data presented involved comparing the SPT with the expressive language scale of the Reynell Developmental Language Scales (1969) and with a measure of sentence length (McCarthy, 1954). The authors purport the validity of their test is at least partially derived from the ostensible nature of its content; a strong case can be made only intuitively to concur with this assertion. Nonetheless, correlations reported for specific age levels varied significantly, from only -.14 to .53, with overall correlations of .28 (Reynell) and .31 (McCarthy). Although predictive validity studies yield higher correlations (.40 to .77), the authors recognize that further study is warranted with more comprehensive measures of language development.

In summary, the attractiveness and potential utility of the second edition of the Symbolic Play Test must be considered in conjunction with its restricted standardization sample and other psychometric limitations. The ambitious intent of the SPT as a means to evaluate very young children's language potential through examination of their symbolic play skills is conceptually intriguing as well as intuitively appealing. The authors have presented an inherently interesting procedure of assessment that can be administered easily and scored in under 20 minutes. Unfortunately, they have not further revised or improved upon the standardization sample of the experimental edition which they originally introduced as a pilot project undergoing further evaluation. At this juncture the norms are not only from a limited sample, but are nearly 20 years old. Their exclusion of the mentally handicapped children from the sample also appears questionable given the instrument's aim to evaluate children with underdeveloped language abilities. Given the extent of its current development the SPT should not be used for placement eligibility decisions until further refinement and standardization is undertaken. Speech-language therapists, psychologists, and other personnel engaged in developmental assessment of younger preschool populations may find the SPT useful in generating information about a child's symbolic relationships and nonverbal play.

REVIEWER'S REFERENCE

McCarthy, D. (1954). Language development in children. In L. Carmichael (Ed.), *Manual of child psychology* (2nd ed.) (pp. 492-630). New York: Wiley.

Review of the Symbolic Play Test, Second Edition by HARVEY N. SWITZKY, Professor of Educational Psychology, Counseling, and Special Education, Northern Illinois University, DeKalb, IL:

The Symbolic Play Test (SPT) is a clinical tool developed to evaluate the verbal language potential of very young children who have failed to develop receptive or expressive language by examining their nonverbal "semantic" aspects of representational play (i.e., their world of meanings, experiences, and fantasies) in order to differentiate children who have developed sufficient concepts and symbols in play but whose language dysfunctions may be due to deafness or environmental deprivations versus children whose language development and their ability to acquire meaningful experiences and functional symbol usage in play may be due to more central "organic" causes such as general developmental delay or a specific deficit in the development of their symbol system (e.g., developmental aphasia, infantile autism).

However, the authors stress a functional analysis of behavior of the children's strengths and weaknesses in nonverbal symbolic thought rather than a diagnostic function of their language delay per se. Such an approach stresses the psychoeducational function of the SPT in providing speech therapists, teachers, and parents material on which to base and provide experiences to develop language functions in these language-delayed children.

The test consists of four independent structured and standardized play situations designed to appeal to both very young boys and girls with play materials drawn from the experiences of children with multiple cultural backgrounds. Situation I consists of a large girl doll (sitting), a plastic saucer, a spoon, a cup, a large brush, and a comb. Situation II consists of a bed, a pillow, a blanket, and a small girl doll. Situation III consists of a chair, a table, a tablecloth, a fork, a small boy doll, a knife, and a plate. Situation IV consists of a well-made metal tractor with moveable wheels, a man doll, and a set of four logs in random positions. The toys are well made and should survive a lot of handling from the children without breaking. The set of toys, record forms, and manual are presented in a well-made red-plastic carrying case.

After a warm-up period (presenting different toys than those presented in the SPT), the toys making up Situation I–IV are presented in a standard fashion.

Administration guidelines are well presented in the manual. The test is untimed and testing is stopped when the child appears restless or bored; or when "play becomes repetitive and the child apparently has exhausted his store of ideas" (p. 12).

I find this stop rule to be too vague and problematic for the average examiner. Scoring of play behaviors is based on a very detailed Scoring Guide and the manual authors wisely recommend the examiner to take very detailed notes of the child's behavior before any scoring is attempted. The total score is the sum of all "passed," from which an age equivalent is derived. The age equivalent can be compared on other developmental tests, of other measures of nonverbal abilities, receptive language, and expressive language.

The section of the manual on standardization and psychometric information is based on an English population of 137 children derived from a random sample of Day Nursery and Infant Welfare children between 12–36 months sampled at 3-month intervals. The material in the manual is confusing. At times the standardization sample of 135 children is referred to while in other discussions the 241 tests (evaluations?) carried out on the sample are cited. Sometimes psychometric information is presented in terms of the test data and sometimes the psychometric information is presented in terms of child data.

The SPT behavioral categories were derived from a study of representational play in infants from 1 to 3 years (Lowe, 1975). I am concerned about the suitability of the play material for both very young boys and girls from multiple and diverse cultural backgrounds. There is a lack of attention to this problem in the assessment of intelligence and adaptive behavior in children (Switzky & Utley, 1991). The manual authors do not make a convincing case that there are no sex or cultural differences in the observed play behaviors and even claim that there is no "reason to suppose that findings will not apply to immigrant children, even if their native language is not English" (p. 3).

Considering the smallness of the sample and the small number of items sampled by Situation I (5), Situation II (5), Situation III (8), and Situation IV (6), the reliabilities of the scale are fairly robust. The categories of behavior for each situation form satisfactory Guttman Scales with adequate coefficients of scaleability and reproducibility. Split-half reliabilities and test-retest reliabilities are adequate for a clinical test.

The evidence regarding the validity of the test as a clinical tool to assess language potential is weak. "If the test of play is to be used to assess language potential it should be expected: (a) that it may show some correlation with concurrent language ability; (b) that it will predict language ability at a later date" (p. 6). Concurrent validity using the expressive language scale of the Reynell Developmental Language Scales (Reynell, 1969) and sentence length showed fairly low correlations with SPT scores. Predictive validity using correlations with SPT scores and sentence length was more convincing showing higher correlations between measures as time progresses. There is a tendency for SPT scores to increase with the age of the child, with the test being most sensitive from 15 to 24 months. This suggests some tentative construct support. The manual contains guidelines in terms of assessing children's play maturity as a measure of symbolic activity and a set of clinical studies with the SPT.

In summary, the strengths of the SPT are its sound test construction and its good reliability of measurement. The SPT may provide an experienced clinician additional information concerning cognitive functioning in language-delayed children. I doubt the SPT can be used without additional training by inexperienced evaluators. The SPT may have value as a research tool as well. The major weaknesses of the SPT are its lack of convincing validity as a measure of language potential, the very small sample sizes from which it was derived, and its cavalier attitude toward sex and cultural differences as they affect test scores.

REVIEWER'S REFERENCES

Reynell, J. (1969). Reynell Developmental Language Scales. Windsor, England: NFER-Nelson Publishing Co., Ltd.

Lowe, M. (1975). Trends in the development of representational play in infants from one to three years—an observational study. *Journal of Child Psychology and Psychiatry*, *16*, 33-47.

Switzky, H. N., & Utley, C. (1991). Sociocultural perspectives on the classification of persons with mental retardation. *AAMR Psychology Division Newsletter*, *1*(2), 1-4.

[385]

System to Plan Early Childhood Services.

Purpose: "A decision-making system designed for use by early childhood service teams."
Population: Ages 2–6.
Publication Date: 1990.
Acronym: SPECS.
Scores: 19 ratings in 6 areas: Communication (Receptive Language, Expressive Language), Sensorimotor (Hearing, Vision, Gross Motor, Fine Motor), Physical (Health, Growth, Normalcy), Self-Regulation (Temperament, Play, Attention, Self-Control), Cognition (Basic Concepts, Problem Solving); Self/Social (Self-Esteem, Motivation, Social Competence, Self-Care).
Administration: Individual.
Price Data, 1993: $89.95 per starter set including 50 Developmental Specs, 25 Team Specs, 25 Program Specs, and manual; $44.95 per 50 Developmental Specs; $18.25 per 25 Team Specs; $36.95 per 25 Program Specs.
Time: (15–20) minutes.
Comments: Individual ratings are used to develop team specs and program specs.
Authors: Stephen J. Bagnato and John T. Neisworth.
Publisher: American Guidance Service, Inc.

Review of the System to Plan Early Childhood Services by RIC BROWN, Acting Director, University Grants and Research Office, California State University, Fresno, CA:

The System to Plan Early Childhood Services (SPECS) is described as a decision-making device to be used by early childhood service teams including professionals in developmental, educational, medical, and mental health fields; parents; and paraprofessionals. The use of the SPECS is intended to reduce team meeting time without sacrificing quality and to improve planning and accountability by linking assessment, intervention, and evaluation for handicapped and at-risk children between the ages of 2 and 6.

Included in the system is a clinical judgment instrument (19 dimensions of child development), an individual rater profile (to graph professional and parent judgment), a team summary, a service matrix (to identify a child's needs), a team consensus profile, a background information form, a program options section (to specify a child's service needs in nine intervention areas), a transition services subsection, an intensity ratings profile (to graph the scope and degree of services), and a progress summary.

The SPECS was developed to meet the mandates of PL 99-457 and grew from a need to coalesce parental and professional judgment. A detailed table is provided identifying PL 99-457 mandates matched with SPECS features and components. The SPECS is reported to be useful for determining program eligibility, incorporating parental judgment, coordination of team decision making, assessing child status and progress, documenting efficacy of intervention, doing program reviews, screening for kindergarten transition, and conducting applied research.

The administration manual contains fairly extensive data regarding reliability and validity. A technical supplement is referenced as having more specific details with respect to the sample used and a description of specific methodology. Reliability in the form of intrarater stability is displayed for 163 early childhood educators and 163 paraprofessional aides on 19 dimensions. The ratings were approximately 2 weeks apart. Additionally, a percentage of agreement for each of the 19 dimensions is presented. Acceptable stability coefficients in the .7 to .8 range were found for both the intrarater and percentage of agreement analysis. Additionally, data are reported in terms of both content and concurrent validity. A detailed section concerning content development and numerous tables comparing SPECS dimensions with other tests of specific abilities are included (Otis Lennon School Ability Test, K-ABC). The information provided is well written, clear, and compelling with respect to the SPECS content.

A full chapter is devoted to discussion of the use of the SPECS system. The discussion includes the composition of the assessment team, the sequence of events that must be followed for team decision making, and an explanation regarding filling out the SPECS forms. An eight-step approach is described in great detail and a complete explanation for the 19 developmental scales is given. Additionally, a very descriptive use and interpretation section is provided. Three realistic case studies are presented that clearly demonstrate the SPECS system.

SUMMARY. In general, the SPECS includes all the components of a comprehensive program from assessment to follow-through. Although implementing the system may be time consuming, it would certainly be thorough. One potential weakness is the measurement of children on the developmental dimensions. Each dimension is one generic behavior rated on a 5-point Likert-type scale. Although each item appears to represent a relevant behavior (e.g., attention, rated from rarely pays attention to typically pays attention), one marker of a rather complex trait may be problematic. This apparent deficiency is somewhat ameliorated, however, by the use of multiple respondents. The ratings are not averaged across team members so that differences and similarities in ratings are available for study by the team. A second potential weakness of the SPECS is the failure to specifically address differential implications of the process with regard to gender, ethnic, or language differences among children.

Review of the System to Plan Early Childhood Services by MARK H. FUGATE, Assistant Professor of School Psychology, Alfred University, Alfred, NY:

The System to Plan Early Childhood Services (SPECS) is designed to provide early childhood service teams with a system for comprehensive decision making. The SPECS provides parents, early intervention professionals, and paraprofessionals with a process for the collaborative assessment of children with special needs. In addition to assessment, the SPECS is designed to provide direct links to program planning, intervention, and continued progress monitoring.

There are three systems within the SPECS process: Developmental Specs, Team Specs, and Program Specs. Developmental Specs is a clinical judgment instrument used to evaluate a child's behavior and development across 19 dimensions. Within each dimension the child's level of functioning is appraised on a 5-point continuum. Parents and team members provide ratings based on information gained from observations, assessment data, interviews, or personal experience with the child.

Team Specs provides a format for comparing all the members' Developmental Specs ratings. Contained within this form are a team summary, a team consensus profile, and a service matrix to assist in defining the child's intervention needs and methods for service delivery.

Program Specs includes a brief background information section, a series of program option questionnaires, and a subsection for outlining the transition needs of $4^1/_2$- to 6-year-old children. Also included in Program Specs are an intensity rating profile that provides for a graphic representation of the degree services needed across the intervention areas, and a progress summary section for recording pre and post intervention data.

The SPECS administration manual includes chapters providing an overview of the SPECS system, instructions for use, examples of SPECS use and interpretation, and a brief review of the technical characteristics of the SPECS system. For SPECS users who desire additional psychometric information the SPECS technical supplement is available free of charge from the publisher.

According to the information provided in the SPECS administration manual, test-retest reliability coefficients for the Developmental Specs range from .62 to .87 across the 19 dimensions when children were rated by a group of early childhood educators. When rated by paraprofessional aides test-retest reliability coefficients range from .60 to .88 across the 19 developmental dimensions. Across both groups of raters the reliability coefficients for all but 3 of the 38 dimensions exceed .70 with coefficients for 21 dimensions exceeding .80. Although the authors of the SPECS consider these reliability coefficients to be adequate, none of the reliability coefficients meet Salvia and Ysseldyke's (1991) test selection criterion of .90 for instruments used to make important educational decisions about individual students. However, many of the Developmental Specs reliability coefficients meet the less stringent guideline of .80 for tests used for screening purposes (Salvia & Ysseldyke, 1991, p. 142).

The SPECS administration manual authors refer much of the discussion of content validity to the SPECS technical manual. The basic discussions of concurrent criterion-related validity and construct validity are adequate. Moderate to high levels of agreement are reported between the Developmental Specs and a variety of concurrently administered developmental and cognitive measures. The primary limitation of the concurrent validity data is the subjects in the studies are most representative of the upper end ($4^1/_2$- to 6-year-olds) of the SPECS age range of 2- to 6-year-olds).

Construct validity is demonstrated in reports of the use of the Developmental Specs ratings to discriminate among children across a variety of diagnostic categories. Overall correct classification scores range from a low of 75% for developmental delay to a high of 96% for hearing impairment. When ratings of a variety of childhood service team members are compared overall classification accuracy ranges from a low of 66% for psychologists to a high of 90% for early childhood special education teachers.

Overall, the SPECS seems to be a well-organized and practical system for facilitating appropriate decision making among early childhood intervention teams. The process of moving through the sequence from Developmental Specs, to Team Specs, then Program Specs provides an excellent guide through the team decision-making process. It also appears the SPECS process, and service plans that would be developed, fit very nicely into the guidelines outlined in U.S. Law 99-457 for the development of Individual Family Service Plans.

Each of the three Specs forms are relatively uncomplicated and easy to use. Developmental Specs is comprehensive in its review of pertinent developmental and behavioral dimensions. Although Developmental Specs provides an exemplary vehicle for all members of the team to share their views on an individual child, this instrument may not have adequate reliability to be used as a primary assessment device. Perhaps reliability could be enhanced by providing general developmental guidelines for rating children of each age group across the 19 dimensions. For example, what are the typical receptive language skills of a 2-year-old as compared to a 4-year-old?

Team Specs promotes total team involvement in determining the strengths and weaknesses of individual children and provides a natural flow toward intervention planning. Program Specs presents a thorough guide for basic intervention planning across the 19 behavioral and developmental dimensions. However, the planning guide is generally non-specific, and may better serve as a launching point for specific intervention plan development than as a comprehensive plan in and of itself. Also, it would be helpful if the progress monitoring section provided a format for long-term progress monitoring. At this point the format only allows for "Time 1" and "Time 2" evaluation.

The SPECS administration manual is quite useful. Instructions are concise and easy to follow, and the interpretation chapter includes clear examples of the use and interpretation of the SPECS. Of particular value is the chapter that details the basics of good team functioning. The technical information provided in the administration manual is generally adequate. However, it might be useful to provide more discussion of the content issues here, rather than referring the reader to the technical manual. There is also a need to demonstrate further the reliability and validity process with the 2-to-4-year old population.

Essentially, the SPECS appears to be an excellent tool for early childhood service team decision making. Despite its few limitations, the SPECS is comprehensive in its format and provide a practical guide for early childhood assessment, intervention planning, and continued progress monitoring.

REVIEWER'S REFERENCES

Salvia, J., & Ysseldyke, J. E. (1991). *Assessment in special and remedial education* (5th ed.). Boston: Houghton Mifflin Co.

[386]

Teacher Evaluation Scale.

Purpose: "Evaluates characteristics of teacher behavior which lead to success in the educational environment."
Population: Teachers.
Publication Date: 1986.
Acronym: TES.
Scores, 4: Management of Student Behavior, Professionally Related, Instructional, Total.
Administration: Individual.
Price Data, 1992: $50 per complete kit including 50 Option 1, 2 or 3 rating forms, 50 classroom observation forms, technical manual (35 pages), and Professional Improvement Manual (53 pages); $20 per 50 Option 1, 2 or 3 rating forms; $10 per 50 classroom evaluation forms, $10 per technical manual; $10 per Professional Improvement Manual.
Time: Administration time not reported.
Comments: Manual title is The Professional Improvement Manual; ratings by administrator.
Authors: Stephen B. McCarney and Kathy K. Cummins (The Professional Improvement Manual).
Publisher: Hawthorne Educational Services, Inc.

TEST REFERENCES

1. Follman, J. (1992). Secondary school students' ratings of teacher effectiveness. *The High School Journal, 75,* 168-178.

Review of the Teacher Evaluation Scale by GREGORY J. MARCHANT, Associate Professor of Educational Psychology, Ball State University, Muncie, IN:

The Teacher Evaluation Scale (TES) is an evaluation instrument designed to identify teachers' performances relative to behaviors defined as effective and representative of standard professional behaviors. Teaching practices are rated on a 1 to 5 Likert-type scale indicating the frequency of the practice as demonstrated by the teacher. This rating is made by an informed observer, usually the teacher's principal. The TES includes a technical manual; a "Classroom Observation Form," which serves as an observational worksheet; a "Teacher Evaluation Scale," which allows for rating 35 items across the three areas of management of student behavior, professionally related, and instructional; along with a rating summary and a profile. A professional improvement manual is available. Teaching practices relevant to each of the scale's items are included in the manual.

The scale was developed as a means of evaluating "those characteristics of teacher behavior which lead to success in the educational environment" (manual, p. 4). An early version of the instrument was created by reviewing teacher evaluation instruments from school systems in 20 states. The total number of items on the instrument was reduced from 42 to 35 based on the comments of 30 administrators who reviewed the initial item list. An underlying basis for the scale was universal teaching principles drawn from effective teaching research with particular emphasis placed on characteristics identified by Kounin (1970).

Although the scale ratings are based on observations of teacher performance, the instrument is not a low-inference observational record. There are no specific guidelines concerning the nature of observations or for the number or duration of observations. The author does emphasize the need to gather evidence when an administrator has no knowledge of the teacher's performance on a particular item.

The author provides a good review of the psychometric properties of the instrument including the results of normative standardization data, principal components analysis, item and scale analyses, reliability coefficients, and validity estimates. The good-sized normative sample of 2,212 teachers from nine states appears to be fairly representative geographically and demographically of U.S. teachers. Four standardization tables are presented based on grade level (elementary teachers, and intermediate and secondary teachers grouped together), and for each of these categories divided into two groups based on more than or less than 3 years of experience. The author does not provide the rationale nor statistical test results suggesting the specific groupings.

Although the author identifies three distinct subscales for the TES, there is little statistical evidence to support the distinctions. Interpretation of a scree plot of eigen values suggests one strong factor. All of the items cross load on more than one factor (when considering loadings greater than .30). All but one of the items load (>.30) on the first factor with 21 of the 35 items having their highest loading on the first factor. Fourteen of the items are included in subscales on which they do not have the highest loading. All of the subscales are highly correlated (r >.85).

The instrument demonstrated good reliability with high internal consistency within the subscales (item/total r >.61), reliability of subscales to the total instrument (KR-20 coefficients ≥ .95), test-retest on the whole scale ($r = .96, p < .01$), and interrater reliability ($r = .92, p < .01$). The high reliability is not surprising considering the nature of the instrument and ways in which the reliability was assessed. As suggested by the factor analysis, the instrument seems to be consistently measuring one thing. That one thing is not based on discrete observations of data, but rather an accumulation of information. Therefore, the fact that a total of 14 administrators rated one or more teachers in a similar manner after a period of one month is not surprising. The credibility of the interrater reliability is also hindered by the relationship of the raters (principals and their assistant principals).

The validity of the subscales comes into question for reasons related to previously mentioned analyses; however, the instrument on the whole does appear to be a valid measure of effective teaching practices as defined by teacher evaluation documents and administrators. Principals have demonstrated relatively strong support for research-based effective teaching behaviors (Marchant, 1992); however, they do not have a history of accurate judgements of effective teaching (Medley & Coker, 1987). Medley and Coker (1987) concluded that principals may not be good observers or that they may hold inadequate models of effective teaching. It is unlikely that the TES would do much to improve either of these possibilities. The instrument does not provide direction that would facilitate accurate observations of teaching behaviors and it provides a model of effective teaching defined primarily by the consensus of administrators. At this writing the search for generic or general effective teaching behaviors has all but come to an end. Currently there is an emphasis on situation-specific and content-specific pedagogy that suggests the need to consider the context in the evaluation of effective teaching. A decontextualized generic evaluation instrument would seem to run counter to this approach to understanding and improving instruction.

In summary, the TES provides a means for administrators to document their perceptions of a teacher's performance relative to a general set of accepted teaching practices. The TES should not be considered an objective measure of differentiated effective teaching behaviors.

REVIEWER'S REFERENCES

Kounin, J. (1970). *Discipline and group management in classrooms.* New York: Holt, Rinehart, & Winston.

Medley, D. M., & Coker, H. (1987). The accuracy of principals' judgments of teacher performance. *Journal of Educational Research, 80*(4), 242-247.

Marchant, G. J. (1992). Attitudes toward research-based effective teaching behaviors. *Journal of Instructional Psychology, 19,* 119-126.

Review of the Teacher Evaluation Scale by TERRY M. WILDMAN, Professor of Curriculum and Instruction, Virginia Polytechnic Institute, Blacksburg, VA:

The Teacher Evaluation Scale (TES) was designed to assist school administrators in the identification and documentation of teacher behaviors that lead to success in elementary, intermediate, and secondary classrooms. The scale is composed of 35 items, organized around the general categories of managing student behavior, instruction, and professionalism. The items are written in the form of a performance statement (e.g., "reinforces/rewards appropriate social and academic behavior") the administrator must rate on a 5-point scale ranging from *does not demonstrate* to *demonstrates consistently*. Each item is written to include, parenthetically, two or three brief examples of actions which would satisfy the performance expectations measured by that item.

The TES includes an easy-to-read technical manual, a two-page classroom observation form, a four-page teacher rating booklet, and a 53-page Professional Improvement Manual. The Professional Improvement Manual provides a laundry list of brief suggestions to improve teaching or professional behavior for each of the 35 items, and is designed to be used by the administrator and teacher in developing a plan for professional improvement. The potential utility of the manual seems limited considering no conceptual basis for teaching suggestions is given or discussed.

The items themselves were culled from examination of the evaluation procedures used by approximately 20 school systems across the United States. The authors suggest the items selected are in general accord with the process-product research on effective teaching, and thus are likely to be positively correlated with teacher success. Regardless of research relevance, the performance statements included in this scale will likely be very familiar to administrators and teachers who have even modest experience in schools.

The administration directions suggest the rating form for a teacher can be completed in about 15 minutes. The rating form can be completed, however, only after administrators are confident they can rate the teachers' typical performance across all 35 items. This may involve many observations over a period of time. The authors also suggest the TES provides for an objective performance assessment because the items are behaviorally stated. My own reading is that the user of this scale will actually be making relatively high-inference judgments. The items are stated in very general terms (e.g., follows school system's policies and procedures) and the rater must decide what behaviors apply and the extent to which the behaviors are in teachers' day-to-day repertoires.

Once the rating is completed, which involves assigning a score of 1–5 to each of the 35 items, the rater uses a set of conversion tables to derive a standard score (M = 10; SD = 3) for the three subscales, and an overall "quotient" score (M = 100; SD = 15). These standard score derivations are based upon norms generated from a standardization sample of 2,212 teachers, representing elementary and intermediate/secondary assignments, and low and high experience levels.

Overall, the TES appears to have been carefully constructed and based upon a broad review of existing teacher performance assessment procedures. In terms of content validity, this instrument probably represents fairly the performance areas considered most important across diverse school systems during the 1970s and early 1980s. Reliabilities for the three subscales are provided and are above .90. Norms are provided for a national sample of teachers, but I do not see how they will be of much benefit given (*a*) the small sample of teachers in some grade level-experience categories, and (*b*) the primary intended use of the scale for professional development purposes at the local level.

One major problem I see with this scale in terms of current use is that it does not relate very well to the present knowledge base on teaching and teacher performance. Examples of performance areas that current users will miss in the TES include emphasis on collaboration, teaming, reflective practice, teaching approaches based on cognitive-constructivist theory, and integrated curriculum practices, to name just a few areas of current interest. Further, although the technical manual claims the items are closely tied to the 1970s process-product research, I do not find any useful mechanism in this performance assessment system to relate the individual items even to the older research base.

In summary, the author contends that the TES provides a standard evaluation system that will contribute to improved service delivery. This assertion seems to hinge on the proposition that success in teaching is a matter of displaying appropriate behaviors that have been identified as important through practice or research. I am frankly skeptical of this approach, and concerned that the fragmentation of teaching into 35 behavior categories, or even 50 or 100, risks diverting attention from the rich understandings that teachers are constructing for themselves regarding their work. The dominant focus on discrete behaviors seem overly technical, highly susceptible to bureaucratic manipulation, and insensitive to the rich metaphors that teachers use conceptually to define themselves and their work. If we can put these concerns aside, the TES does provide a well-organized way to direct evaluators' and teachers' attention to a general set of performance expectations.

[387]

Teacher's School Readiness Inventory.

Purpose: Constructed to screen for children who are at risk for school failure.
Population: Pre-kindergarten to kindergarten children.
Publication Dates: 1986–88.
Acronym: TSRI.
Scores: Total score only.
Administration: Individual.
Price Data, 1991: $12.50 per 200 rating forms; $7.50 per manual ('88, 44 pages); $11.50 per specimen set.
Time: (2–3) minutes.
Comments: Ratings by teachers.
Author: Marvin L. Simner.
Publisher: Phylmar Associates.

Review of the Teacher's School Readiness Inventory by THEODORE COLADARCI, Associate Professor of Education, University of Maine, Orono, ME:

The Teacher's School Readiness Inventory (TSRI), developed by Marvin L. Simner of the University of Western Ontario, is a five-item teacher rating scale designed to help prekindergarten and kindergarten teachers "make proper referral decisions" (scoring manual, p. 2) for children who are "at risk for school failure" (p. 12). Using a 5-point Likert-type scale, a teacher rates each child on distractibility, attention span, and memory span; verbal fluency; interest and participation; letter-identification skills; and printing skills. These five ratings are then summed to form a total score (the only score Simner recommends for decision making). Children receiving a TSRI total score at or below the established cutoff point are considered to be academically at-risk and, in turn, are referred either for additional testing or for immediate remediation, depending on the child's score.

DOCUMENTATION. The TSRI manual is quite impressive, especially in light of this instrument's brevity. Simner offers a clear and generally comprehensive treatment of the essential aspects of his instrument: (*a*) item development, (*b*) administration and use, (*c*) definitions and rating criteria, and (*d*) reliability and validity. In short, the author does a commendable job providing readers with the necessary information to evaluate the TSRI.

Importantly, Simner also repeatedly reminds the reader of the need to be cautious and circumspect when making judgments about any student's at-risk status. At one point, he proffers the following caveat:

> We do *not* recommend using the TSRI as the sole means of identifying children who are at risk for school failure. Instead, we believe that it would be far more appropriate to employ the TSRI as the first stage in a two-stage early identification program. (scoring manual, p. 12)

Curiously, this admonition seemingly applies only to children falling at or just below the cutoff point, who, Simner correctly recommends, should undergo additional testing with such instruments as the Metropolitan Readiness Assessment Program or the McCarthy Scales of Children's Abilities. In contrast, teachers immediately should "refer for assistance" (p. 14) any child with a TSRI total score below 12. Contrary to the caveat above, however, this latter recommendation effectively renders the TSRI "the sole means" of identifying at-risk children—at least for this subset of children. In my view, additional testing would be necessary for *any* student flagged by a five-item rating scale.

STANDARDIZATION SAMPLE. All reliability and validity analyses were based on March data (1983–1984) from 581 prekindergarten and kindergarten children—two samples of each—and their 38 teachers from 22 public elementary schools in lower- and middle-income areas of London, Ontario. The relevance of this norming group for districts involving other curricula, grading practices, demographic groups, or geographic regions remains to be established. For this reason, particularly cogent is Simner's recommendation that users establish local norms—a process requiring at least 3 years—before using the TSRI for making referral decisions.

RELIABILITY. Interrater reliability was established by having seven pairs of raters independently rate children in their respective classes, which resulted in a reliability coefficient of .86 for the TSRI total score. The reader is told that .86 is "within the range generally considered acceptable for tests that are to be used solely for screening purposes" (pp. 18–19), and Salvia and Ysseldyke (1985) are cited as support. In fact, Salvia and Ysseldyke argue for a minimum reliability of .90 where a test is to inform "important educational decisions, such as tracking and placement in a special class" (Salvia & Ysseldyke, 1991, p. 142). It seems to me that the TSRI *is* used for important educational decisions, insofar as children with TSRI scores below 12 are singled out, not for further (and more sensitive) assessment, but for immediate "assistance." In my view, this consideration calls into question the adequacy of the TSRI reliability, particularly for children having TSRI scores below 12. (The absence of a reported standard error of measurement merely compounds the problem.)

VALIDITY. As Salvia and Ysseldyke (1991) state, "Since decisions made on the basis of readiness tests are so important, *the validity of the tests is crucial*" (p. 471; italics added). For this reason, I cover the TSRI validity information in some detail.

Content validity. The five items that make up the TSRI represent important aspects of school readiness. However, Simner provides no rationale for restricting the TSRI to *these* five items, other than a passing reference to supporting research. Rather than refer readers to a publication in which this rationale appears, Simner should bring the thrust of that argument directly into the TSRI manual.

Concurrent validity. The TSRI total score shows a strong relationship with the child's June "class standing," a mark provided by the teacher using a 12-point scale from D- to A+. For prekindergarten and kindergarten children alike, correlations between TSRI and class standing range from the mid-.70s to mid-.80s. As the author acknowledges, however, these correlations are difficult to interpret insofar as the same teachers provided both ratings. These values doubtless would be smaller had Simner secured independent ratings (Hoge & Coladarci, 1989).

Concurrent validity coefficients also were obtained between the TSRI and two standardized tests. Among prekindergarten children, the TSRI correlates .71 with the Developmental Tasks for Kindergarten Readiness and .69 with the Wide Range Achievement Test (WRAT); for kindergarten children, the TSRI correlates about .79 with the WRAT. These values suggest an acceptable level of concurrent validity, given these two criteria.

Predictive validity. Laudably, Simner attempted to secure longitudinal data on these 581 children through the second grade in order to assess predictive validity, "the most important type of validity for a readiness test" (Salvia & Ysseldyke, 1991, p. 488). For example, teacher marks in reading, written composition, and mathematics were obtained for many of these children at the end of their first- and second-grade years. Not surprisingly, correlations between teacher marks and the TSRI total score are slightly higher (*a*) when based on the earlier, first-grade criteria; and (*b*) when based on kindergarten children, irrespective of when criterion information was obtained. In any case, the correlations are modest, ranging from .39 to .62. Further, interpretation is rendered somewhat problematic by student attrition: Roughly 25% of the 581 TSRI children had moved before completing the first grade. For the second grade, the number grew to almost one half.

Simner also correlated the TSRI with the Woodcock Reading Mastery Test and the KeyMath Diagnostic Arithmetic Test, which were administered in the first grade. Correlations range from .52 to .58 for prekindergarten children and .57 to .65 for kindergarten children. As with the correlations involving teacher marks, these coefficients should be interpreted cautiously because of student attrition in the first grade, and also because roughly 20% of those children who *were* present were not tested.

Classification analyses. Does the TSRI permit accurate classification of children? To be sure, this is the most important question for a screening test. Using the most recent information available, Simner placed children in the "poor performance" category if they had not been promoted to the next grade or if they were assigned "to a slower or junior section of the next grade" (p. 24). These children generally received teacher marks in the *D* range. In contrast, the "good performance" category was reserved for children who later received overall-performance ratings of *B-* or higher. Simner then established the TSRI cutoff score that correctly identified at least 85% of the children in the poor-performance category (13 and 15 for the prekindergarten and kindergarten level, respectively).

In his Tables 3 and 4, Simner clearly reports these data for each of the four samples. For example, we see that 86% to 88% of poor-performance children had earlier received TSRI total scores at or below the cutoff point ("true positives") and 88% to 96% of the good-performance children had fallen above the TSRI cutoff point ("true negatives"). In assessment argot, the TSRI thus demonstrates both "sensitivity" and "specificity."

It follows, of course, that high "hit rates" also are obtained: 88% to 94% of children later demonstrating either "poor" or "good" performance in school had earlier received a TSRI total score consistent with their performance category. From these data, Simner concludes that "the overall predictive validity of the

TSRI not only equals but often exceeds the predictive validity achieved by the majority of psychometric screening devices in use today" (p. 25).

This conclusion, however, must be tempered by at least four considerations. First, claims regarding TSRI validity would be strengthened considerably if these results were replicated, both with additional samples and from other sites. (One independent study, also from the Ontario region, was presented in an endnote and reported favorable, albeit less positive, findings.)

Second, because of student attrition, criterion information for some students was taken from first grade, kindergarten, or even prekindergarten. As Simner warns the reader, had second-grade data been obtained for all 581 children in the four TSRI samples, the validity results "might have been somewhat different" (p. 24). *How* different, of course, is not known.

Third, the high hit rates reported by Simner reflect, in part, his definition of "good performance" (*B*- or higher). But if the TSRI is designed to flag children who are "at risk for school failure" (p. 12), then one would expect that children falling above the cutoff score would *not fail*. That is, these children later should receive teacher marks of *C*- or higher. Calculations based on the comparison of *this* group and Simner's poor-performance group yields hit rates of 71% to 88% across the four samples, which are lower than the figures reported in the manual. Curiously, Simner uses the relaxed definition of success (*C*- or higher) for classification analyses he reports elsewhere (Simner, 1987)—contrary to the methodology appearing in the TSRI manual.

Fourth, and most troubling, *one half* of all children identified by the TSRI as academically at risk actually went on to earn teacher marks in the *C* range or higher. This large percentage of "false positives" is not surprising in view of the modest correlations between TSRI and teacher marks (.39 to .62). If these data are generalizable, then one out of every two children who are flagged by the TSRI will be flagged unnecessarily.

CONCLUSIONS. The TSRI is a brief, inexpensive, and easily administered instrument for making referral decisions about prekindergarten and kindergarten children who are academically at risk. In school districts that do not regularly screen this population with more in-depth testing, the TSRI might be regarded as an attractive device for quickly identifying children for further assessment (once local norms have been established). Contrary to the recommendation of the author, however, decisions regarding "assistance"—whatever this term may suggest to the prospective user—should not be based solely on a one-page, five-item rating scale.

REVIEWER'S REFERENCES

Simner, M. L. (1987). Predictive validity of the Teacher's School Readiness Inventory. *Canadian Journal of School Psychology*, *3*, 21-32.

Hoge, R. D., & Coladarci, T. (1989). Teacher-based judgments of academic achievement: A review of literature. *Review of Educational Research*, *59*, 297-313.

Salvia, J., & Ysseldyke, J. E. (1991). *Assessment* (5th ed.). Boston: Houghton Mifflin.

Review of the Teacher's School Readiness Inventory by BETH DOLL, Assistant Professor of School Psychology, University of Colorado at Denver, Denver, CO:

The Teacher's School Readiness Inventory (TSRI) is a rating form intended to assist preschool and kindergarten teachers in identifying students at risk for school failure in later grades. The purpose of the inventory is to provide more accurate estimates of school readiness than global teacher ratings, using a format that is briefer and so more practical than other kindergarten screening inventories.

The TSRI is a five-item measure, every item of which has shown a meaningfully strong relationship to later school performance in previous research. After working with a student for a minimum of 2 to 3 months, teachers complete the inventory by rating a student on a scale of 1 to 5 for each item. Every item is a composite of several discrete characteristics. For example, the first item incorporates teacher judgements about the degree to which a student fidgets, is inattentive, and has poor memory for details. Raters are instructed to consider both the number of item characteristics a child has difficulty with as well as the degree of difficulty a child experiences when assigning a rating on an item. The end points of each rating scale are loosely described with descriptors such as *highly distractible* or *very good attention span*. To assist in the rating, the manual provides teachers with a one-to-five-paragraph descriptor of each item. However, the ultimate decision about when a student evidences a *2* instead of a *4* for any item is up to the discretion of the individual teacher. Despite this apparent laxity in item values, the TSRI manual reports cross-rater reliabilities of a respectable .86 in an early reliability study (Simner, 1987). If these results can be duplicated in subsequent research, the scoring format of the TSRI may prove to be adequate.

Ratings are summed across the five items for a total range of scores from 5 to 25. Total scores are then interpreted using both cutoff points, below which a student is considered to be at risk for subsequent school failure, and probability scores, representing the likelihood that a student with that score will experience subsequent school failure. The manual provides cutoff points and probability scores based on an unrepresentative sample of 581 public school children in Ontario, as well as instructions for developing local cutoff scores for the inventory. The instructions for gathering local norms are clearly written and accompanied by illustrations explaining their analysis; the process requires comparing kindergarten and prekindergarten TSRI scores to students' end-of-the-year teacher ratings in first and second grades. As it is described, local norming is an ambitious one requiring a period of 2 to 3 years to complete. Most users are likely to use the provided cutoffs instead.

The TSRI manual suggests setting cutoff scores such that 85% of the children who subsequently experience school failure are identified; in the Ontario sample, this cutoff also identified false positives (children who were rated low on the TSRI but subsequently performed adequately in school) at a rate of 10%. Probability scores were then computed by determining the proportion of kindergarten students with each TSRI score who experienced school failure in first or second grade. The probability scores were computed using those students who clearly experienced failure in subsequent grades (with end-of-the-year grades of D or lower) and with those who were clearly successful (with end-of-the-year grades of B or higher); students whose school success was less clear were eliminated from the probabilities computations. As a result, the probabilities are somewhat distorted, overrepresenting the likelihood that a child with low ratings will experience difficulty and underrepresenting the likelihood that a child with a high rating will. It may not be possible to derive probability scores that are not misleading without identifying a more precise criterion variable than teacher grades from which to derive the scores.

The validity of the TSRI has been rigorously tested by the scale's author using the Ontario samples. Rating scores on the measure were compared 1, 2, and 3 years later to teacher grades, and to standardized measures of academic skills such as the Woodcock Reading Mastery Test, the KeyMath Diagnostic Arithmetic Test, the Developmental Tasks for Kindergarten Readiness, and the Wide Range Achievement Test. Despite the brevity of the scale, ratings showed respectable correlations ranging from .52 to .67 with standardized measures administered 1 year later, and ranging from .47 to .64 with teacher grades or promotion rankings made 1 year later. Moreover, within this sample, the scale was able to identify nearly 90% of the Ontario students who subsequently had learning difficulties; over 80% of the students declared to be at risk using the TSRI did experience learning difficulties in subsequent grades. This degree of validity is strikingly strong for a five-item scale.

The TSRI is a promising kindergarten screening inventory that may be both effective and practical. However, despite its strong reliability and validity in the Ontario samples, the fact that it has been evaluated only relative to a single community cannot be overlooked. The TSRI can be used only as the author recommends—with the development of local norms and decision points, and with demonstration of ample reliability and validity in the alternative populations where it is being used. These restrictions may limit the utility of the inventory for many users.

REVIEWER'S REFERENCE

Simner, M. L. (1987). Predictive validity of the Teacher's School Readiness Inventory. *Canadian Journal of School Psychology, 3,* 21-32.

[388]

Team Effectiveness Survey.

Purpose: Designed to assess process issues associated with team dynamics.
Population: Team members.
Publication Dates: 1968–86.
Acronym: TES.
Scores: 4 scores for each team member: Exposure, Feedback, Defensive, Supportive, plus Total Team Effectiveness score.
Administration: Group.
Price Data, 1991: $6.95 per test booklet/manual.
Time: Administration time not reported.
Author: Jay Hall.
Publisher: Telemetrics International.
Cross References: For a review by William G. Mollenkopf, see 8:1055.

Review of the Team Effectiveness Survey by GREGORY H. DOBBINS, Associate Professor of Management, The University of Tennessee at Knoxville, Knoxville, TN:

The Team Effectiveness Survey (TES) is designed to assess process issues that affect team effectiveness. It is based upon the assumption that team effectiveness will improve as team members understand more about their own interactional tendencies and discuss these tendencies with team members. Hence, it is an instrument designed primarily for organizational development purposes.

The TES provides individual and team scores for exposure (the tendency to engage in open expressions of one's own feelings and knowledge) and feedback (the tendency to solicit information from others about their feelings and knowledge). These dimensions are proposed to influence the effectiveness of communication and problem solving. Based upon Exposure and Feedback scores, four types of individuals and/or groups can be identified: Type A—low feedback and low exposure; Type B—high feedback and low exposure; Type C—low feedback and high exposure; and Type D—high feedback and high exposure. Hall (the test author) argues that Type D groups are creative and have high levels of interpersonal trust and support. The performance of the other groups (Types A, B, and C) is restricted because information flow and the open exchange of ideas are prevented.

The TES also assesses supportive and defensive climates. Hall argues that if an individual's Defensive climate score is higher than his or her Supportive climate score, then the individual may have a constraining effect on the team and foster feelings of insecurity, vulnerability, and lack of trust among members. If the individual's Supportive climate score is higher than his or her Defensive climate score, it indicates that the individual helps the team work effectively and encourages feelings of well-being and warmth.

Both individual and team scores are calculated with the TES. Thus, each team member will have a score on the four dimensions (Exposure, Feedback, Defensive climate, and Supportive climate) and a group average for each dimension. These scores are used to discuss interactional and process problems in the group.

ADMINISTRATION AND SCORING PROCEDURES. The TES could probably be completed in less than 30 minutes. However, it may take an additional hour to score. Group members are asked to rate each other on 20 behaviors. After making ratings, each group member distributes his or her ratings to all other group members. Each group member then transcribes how they were rated by all other group members on a tally sheet. Team members then add the 10 items that assess exposure and the 10 items that assess feedback. This is done separately for ratings made by each team member. Thus, in a group that contains nine team members, each team member will hand calculate nine sets of scores (i.e., how they were rated by Person A, Person B, and so forth plus self-ratings).

Scoring the climate measures suffers from similar problems. It requires each team member to add the five items that form the Defensiveness and Supportive scales. In addition, team members are asked to calculate average scores for each scale. Once again, these calculations will be time consuming and cumbersome for team members. In addition, without careful instructions and guidance, some individuals will probably miscalculate their scores.

The scoring procedure should be computerized in future revisions of the TES. In addition to reducing the time commitments of team members, better feedback could be provided by a computerized scoring system (e.g., medians and ranges could be calculated for each group, organizational means could be determined, and normative data could be accumulated by the publisher).

PSYCHOMETRIC PROPERTIES. The psychometric characteristics of the TES are unknown at this time. In fact, it fails to meet almost every technical standard put forth in the *Standards for Educational and Psychological Testing* (AERA, APA, & NCME, 1985). The reliabilities of the scales are not presented. There is no discussion of the manner in which the scales were constructed. At a minimum, the author should calculate coefficient alphas for the scales on the TES. Furthermore, criterion-related validity studies have not been conducted. Clearly, the correlation between TES scales and team effectiveness should be determined. Finally, normative data are not available for the TES.

I am also concerned with the construct validity of the instrument. For example, the instrument proposes that exposure and feedback are independent constructs. Although the two constructs may be theoretically independent, the instrument may be assessing nothing more than social potency. I would not be surprised to find that individuals who actively participate in groups receive higher scores on both Feedback and Exposure than individuals who do not actively participate in groups. These findings would reflect opportunity for exhibiting behaviors, instead of actual feedback and exposure tendencies. In addition, the scales could be contaminated by friendship bias and all the other problems with peer ratings.

SUMMARY. The TES may prove to be a psychometrically sound instrument and have a positive effect on organizational effectiveness. At the present time, however, it should be used cautiously. Not only is there no evidence to indicate that it assesses the constructs that it purports to measure, but its use could actually cause friction and conflict in some work teams, especially if discussions of TES findings are not skillfully guided by facilitators.

As more and more organizations move to teams, it will be important for the testing industry to design instruments that assess team functioning accurately. The TES may be very valuable in this effort. Hence, Teleometrics International should make an intense effort to validate the TES. Furthermore, personnel managers and organizational consultants should demand evidence of sound psychometric properties before adopting instruments such as the TES. Such actions would send a strong message to publishers of organizational development instruments and force these instruments to meet the same standards as other psychological tests and inventories.

REVIEWER'S REFERENCE

American Educational Research Association, American Psychological Association, & National Council on Measurement in Education. (1985). *Standards for educational and psychological testing.* Washington, DC: American Psychological Association, Inc.

Review of the Team Effectiveness Survey by HARRISON G. GOUGH, Professor of Psychology, Emeritus, University of California, Berkeley, Berkeley, CA:

The Team Effectiveness Survey (TES) is not so much a test as a training and self-study device for working with teams or small groups. The materials envisage up to 10 persons in the team, plus the self. Each member rates self, and all other members, on 20 bipolar items, using a 10-point scale graduated for how consistently the defined behavior occurs. The 20 items are grouped into two broad categories: *Exposure*, or the degree to which open and candid expression of own feelings, attitudes, and strategies for dealing with others are disclosed; and *Feedback*, or the degree to which the feelings, opinions, and goals of others are elicited and respected. An example of an "exposure" item is "Is openly affectionate toward other members that he or she likes. (As opposed to being inhibited, restrained, or acting embarrassed.)" An example of a "feedback" item is "Presses for additional information when other members are apparently not leveling. (As opposed to letting the matter drop or changing the subject.)"

Five of the items are also classified as indicating defensiveness, and five as indicating supportiveness. Averaging of the ratings received from others on these two clusters will show whether the individual functions more within a "defensive climate" or a "supportive climate." Team averages can also be computed from the Defensive and Supportive vectors.

The Exposure and Feedback averaged scores for self, and for self described by others on the team, are plotted along two axes from which a four-fold classification is derived: The Arena (reported by both self and others), the Blindspot (reported by others but not by self), the Facade (reported by self but not by others), and the Unknown (reported by neither self or others). The larger the area covered by the Arena, the more effective the individual member, and the more effective the team.

Although all of the above is plausible enough if offered as hypotheses to be confirmed, no evidence whatsoever is given as to the empirical validity of the scores and inferences as indicators of either team or individual effectiveness. Among the other things absent from the manual are (*a*) correlations among the 20 items and their factor structure; (*b*) single-trial or test-retest reliability data for the four major scores and two additional scores; (*c*) norms for the scales, and for frequencies in the four categories; (*d*) gender differences on scales and items; (*e*) relationships of the scales to other tests that assess interpersonal style in groups, and group climates, such as FIRO-B (Schutz, 1958) and the Moos Social Climate Scales (Moos, 1976); (*f*) information on the vulnerability of the TES to willful manipulation and faking; and (*g*) references to published research on the instrument.

Under the guidance of a proficient and well-trained psychologist, the TES could furnish raw material, as it were, of possible utility for self-study and group discussions. However, as an assessment tool capable of providing valid, meaningful, and reliable information it must as of now be deemed unacceptable.

REVIEWER'S REFERENCES

Schutz, W. C. (1958). *FIRO: A three-dimensional theory of interpersonal behavior*. New York: Rinehart.

Moos, R. H. (1976). *The human context: Environmental determinants of behavior*. New York: Wiley.

[389]

Temple University Short Syntax Inventory [Revised].

Purpose: Designed to obtain descriptive information about selected aspects of delayed language.
Population: Ages 3-0 to 4-11.
Publication Dates: 1984–88.
Acronym: TUSSI.
Administration: Individual.
Price Data, 1992: $44 per complete kit including manual ('84, 29 pages).
Authors: Adele Gerber, Henry Goehl, and Reinhart Heuer (Diagnostic and Screening Test Supplementary Manual).
Publisher: Slosson Educational Publications, Inc.

a) TEMPLE UNIVERSITY SHORT SYNTAX INVENTORY.
Scores, 3: Imitated Response Errors, Elicited Response Errors, Total Errors.
Price Data: $14.95 per 25 scoring sheets/test forms.
Time: (10–15) minutes.

b) TUSSI DIAGNOSTIC AND SCREENING TESTS.
Scores: Total Errors.
Price Data: $12 per supplementary manual ('88, 12 pages) and 25 supplementary test forms; $5 per 25 supplementary test forms.
Time: (2–3) minutes.

Review of the Temple University Short Syntax Inventory [Revised] by STEVEN H. LONG, Assistant Professor of Speech Pathology & Audiology, Ithaca College, Ithaca, NY:

The Temple University Short Syntax Inventory (TUSSI) is designed to examine a child's productive mastery of free and bound morphemes that express grammatical relations. Twelve items are scores: 10 morphemes that were tracked in Brown's (1973) research (-ing, in/on, plural, irregular past, possessive noun, article, regular past, third person singular, copula, auxiliary) and the nominative and possessive third person pronouns (he, she, his, her).

TEST MATERIALS. The TUSSI was first published in 1984. In 1988 a revised version was issued with several changes: (*a*) Additional normative data were provided; (*b*) test stimuli were slightly altered; (*c*) the full version of the instrument was labeled a "diagnostic test," and a "screening test" was formed from a subset of items; and (*d*) a new scoring form was devised. For reasons that are not clear the revised TUSSI did not replace the older version but merely added to it. Thus, the complete test kit consists of a 1984 manual, 1984 test forms, 1984 scoring sheets, stimulus line drawings, 1988 manual, and 1988 test forms. Both manuals must be read to understand the test but some of the information in the older manual is no longer applicable. The 1984 test forms do not correspond to the revised sentence stimuli and should not be used.

TEST ADMINISTRATION. Responses are obtained in pairs by asking children to (*a*) repeat a target sentence (imitative mode) and then (*b*) create a sentence that parallels the one just imitated (elicited mode). Line drawings are used to provide an informational context for all the sentences produced. For example, two of the drawings show a girl holding an apple that is missing a bite and a boy holding a peeled banana. The child is shown the first picture and asked to repeat "The girl eats the apple." Then, showing the other picture, the child is asked "Say yours." The expected response in this case is, "The boy eats the banana." The targeted grammatical morphemes in these sentences are the two definite articles and the third person singular present tense inflection. For comparison with the normative data, all targeted forms—103 in the Diagnostic Test, 55 in the Screening Test—are scored as correct or incorrect. A more elaborate qualitative analysis is also possible. For this, it is necessary to score all morphemes in every sentence as correct, omitted, substituted, or other error. The Diagnostic Test includes a lotto game procedure to reward and motivate the child after each pair of responses. This was eliminated in the Screening Test to save time. The authors report a high correlation between the two tests. The lotto game may be an unnecessary feature of the Diagnostic Test.

PSYCHOMETRIC ADEQUACY. The construct validity of the TUSSI is based on its measurement of grammatical morphemes, which are believed to develop systematically as children acquire English syntax. Adequate predictive validity is claimed for the Screening Test from the finding that its results correlated highly with the results from the Diagnostic Test. Given the item and normative group overlap between these two tests, a high correlation is virtually guaranteed, however. There are no data given to correlate TUSSI scores with any other standardized language measure. The authors do report significant correlations between the order of morpheme acquisition yielded by TUSSI scores and the order reported by Brown (1973).

Different data on interexaminer reliability are reported in the two test manuals. Agreement in excess of 96% is reported for the Screening Test, which requires only correct-incorrect judgments. Agreement for the Diagnostic Test is reported in the first manual as ranging from 86% to 93%. In the second manual, a range of 95% to 96% is reported. No explanation is offered for the difference in reliability scores. It appears, however, that the second set of judges were provided additional training in scoring, beyond what would be gained from a one-time reading of the scoring instructions in the manual. Therefore, users of this test may find interexaminer reliability to be somewhat lower than claimed. No information on the test-retest reliability of the TUSSI is given in either of the test manuals.

Normative data and guidelines for test interpretation appear in both manuals. Though not stated, it appears the information in the first manual is superseded by that in the second. The standardization group for the TUSSI consisted exclusively of white children who spoke Standard American English. Roughly two-thirds of the children were classified as belonging to an "upper" socioeconomic group and the remaining children to a "lower" group. The authors do not report whether they found performance differences related to socioeconomic status. The age range for the TUSSI is limited to 3–4 years. Only 217 children make up the normative group; 99 children took both the Screening Test and the Diagnostic Test, and 118 took the Diagnostic Test only. There were far fewer than the recommended 100 subjects in each of the 6-month age intervals.

The reported normative data reveal a severe ceiling effect for both versions of the TUSSI. Over half the subjects committed no errors and the authors found no significant differences between any of the age groups on either version of the test. As a result, the only meaningful interpretation of the TUSSI comes from a comparison of normal children's performance to that of a small group ($n = 14$) of "language-impaired" children. The authors present cutoff scores that were found to distinguish between the two groups of children. No information is given, however, about the characteristics of the "language-impaired" children. Hence we have no idea what kind of child the TUSSI is able to identify. The authors suggest that differences in a child's elicited and imitative responses on the Diagnostic Test can be used to determine his or her mastery of a particular morpheme. However, this analysis is based on a small number of children (50 High Normal, 12 Low Normal, 14 Language Impaired) and a very small number of total errors.

SUMMARY. The TUSSI is a screening or diagnostic test of early-developing morphemes that can be used with children 3 or 4 years of age. Two versions of the test have been issued. The revised version of the test largely replaces the earlier version but information about the test is contained in both manuals and two sets of scoring forms are supplied. This duplication can cause confusion for the user. The test has a small standardization sample, especially for the diagnostic version, and contains no information about concurrent validity or test-retest reliability. Its greatest failing, however, is that it shows no difference in scores between children of different ages. This precludes its use as an effective diagnostic instrument. As a screening instrument, it may have some value, although users should consider the limitations of the normative sample.

REVIEWER'S REFERENCE

Brown, R. (1973). *A first language: The early stages*. Cambridge, MA: Harvard University Press.

Review of the Temple University Short Syntax Inventory [Revised] by REBECCA J. McCAULEY, Associate Professor of Communication Sciences, University of Vermont, Burlington, VT:

TEST STRUCTURE. The Temple University Short Syntax Inventory [Revised] (TUSSI) consists of a 103-item Diagnostic Test and a 55-item Screening Test, which examine specific expressive language forms in imitated and elicited productions of preschool children (aged 3-0 to 4-11). Changes made in the revision include the development of the Screening Test, the addition of new quantitative data, modest changes in scoring, and expansion of test content. The revised Diagnostic Test is designed for use in the assessment of at-risk children, analysis of abnormal language patterns, and for the examination of a child's performance before and after treatment; whereas, the Screening Test is designed for rapid screening of children without identified handicapping conditions.

Although the original manual was relatively well organized and continues to be relevant, the new supplementary manual is confusing. In particular, new users are likely to have difficulty determining when to refer to the older manual and whether specific sections refer to the Screening or Diagnostic Tests.

TEST ADMINISTRATION AND INTERPRETATION. Administration of the Diagnostic Test is essentially unchanged from the earlier version in which a picture-lotto game format is used to maintain the interest of young test takers. Testing is tape-recorded so that on-line scoring by the tester does not interrupt the flow of the interaction. Each item uses a pair of pictures—one picture for an imitated response and the other for an elicited response similar in form to the imitation. Specific instructions regarding intonation and timing are provided to help increase the likelihood that targeted forms will be attempted for both elicited and imitated items. Whereas test administration is brief (10 to 15 minutes), scoring is somewhat more time-consuming (30 minutes) and complicated. Fortunately, several sample sets of responses, scorings, and rationales for specific scoring choices are provided in the original test manual.

The Screening Test abandons the lotto-game format and makes use of on-line scoring, thus resulting in 2 to 3 minutes testing time per child. As with the Diagnostic Test, pairs of imitated and elicited utterances are evoked using pairs of pictures.

NORMS. In the earlier version, TUSSI scores were interpreted with reference to criteria based on the research literature and on data from a small number of subjects evaluated during field testing. For the revised Diagnostic Test, means and standard deviations, as well as quartiles are provided at 6-month intervals for somewhat larger, but still relatively small samples ($n<50$). The authors appear to suggest the total score on this measure can be examined against the quartile of the appropriate age group for purposes of assessing progress in treatment. However, the primary value of the Diagnostic Test appears to be as a descriptive tool.

For the Screening Test, means, standard deviations, and quartiles are provided for larger samples. Criterion levels for "pass," "rescreen," and "evaluate" are specified and are uniform across children in the 3- to 4-year age range covered by the instrument.

The combined normative population for the two tests consisted of 217 Caucasian children who were considered normal in their development and spoke English as their first language. Approximately 62% of the children were from middle- to upper-middle-class homes, and 38% were from working-class to lower-middle-class homes. Given these normative samples, these tests appear to be most useful for assessing Caucasian children who speak Standard American English.

RELIABILITY. Data on interscorer reliability are the only type of reliability information reported. For the Screening Test, a reliability study by one of the test authors and two speech-language pathologists for 15 and for 29 subjects yielded agreements of 98% and 96%, respectively. For the Diagnostic Test, similar procedures using the same test author and two graduate students trained in the test yielded agreements of 96% and 95%, respectively. These levels of agreement, although high, may be somewhat inflated by chance agreement on correct items because it appears that normally developing children were used.

VALIDITY. Evidence of criterion-related validity for the Diagnostic Test consists of findings from a study in which statistically significant differences in scores were obtained when children with language impairment versus children without impairment were tested. In the earlier manual, pertinent evidence for construct validity is provided in the authors' description of the theoretical rationale behind targeted language forms and specific developmental expectations.

Evidence supporting the validity of the Screening Test consists of findings of high, statistically significant correlations between subjects' performances on the items forming the Screening Test with overall Diagnostic Test scores and statistically significant differences in performance on the Screening Test items for children with versus those without language impairment.

Despite positive evidence of validity for both tests, data provided under the heading "Normative Data" cast doubt on the developmental sensitivity of the revised TUSSI. Specifically, when the performances of different age groups were compared, no significant differences were obtained for either the Diagnostic or Screening Test. These findings are inconsistent with usual expectations for developmental language measures, but may be due to the relatively small (2-year) age range covered by the test.

SUMMARY AND CONCLUSIONS. The revised TUSSI Diagnostic and Screening Tests address expressive language forms in both elicited and imitated formats. Data are presented in the test manual suggesting that each measure can successfully distinguish children with language impairment from normally developing children and that interscorer agreement is likely to be high. In addition, the specific forms targeted are rarely examined expressively by other available tests, thereby making the TUSSI of potential importance as a descriptive tool. Although use of the revised TUSSI should be limited to Caucasian children with English as their first language, the use of a large proportion of children from lower socioeconomic status groups suggests that it may be appropriate for that group of children as well as those from higher SES groups. Weaknesses of the two measures include a paucity of data regarding most forms of reliability and a lack of clarity in the organization of the supplementary manual.

[390]

Tennis Skills Test Manual.

Purpose: Designed to assess essential skills needed to play tennis.
Population: High school and college.
Publication Date: 1989.
Scores, 3: Ground Stroke, Serve, Volley.
Administration: Individual.
Price Data, 1991: $12.50 per manual (56 pages).
Time: Administration time not reported.
Authors: Larry Hensley, Graham Hatcher, Gloria Hook, Paul Hook, Carolyn Lehr, and Jacqueline Shick.
Publisher: American Alliance for Health, Physical Education, Recreation, and Dance.
Cross References: See T4:2724 (1 reference).

Review of the Tennis Skills Test Manual by CLAUDE A. SANDY, Vice President, Research Dimensions, Inc., Richmond, VA:

The Tennis Skills Test Manual was developed in 1989 by the American Alliance for Health, Physical Education, Recreation, and Dance (AAHPERD) primarily for the purpose of providing high school and college level tennis instructors with an objective resource for evaluating their students' early tennis skill development. Additionally, with the inclusion of a chapter entitled "Tennis Drills for the Basic Skills," the manual provides instructional strategies for improving the tennis skills tested (i.e., forehand and backhand Ground Strokes, forehand and backhand Volleys, and Serve).

The test is aimed at measuring the essential skills of tennis (i.e., those "skills representing the basics of play without which an individual could not effectively participate," p. 10). Included are those skills having been identified as essential through a task analysis and consultation with recognized tennis teachers and coaches (i.e., Ground Strokes and the Serve). An intermediate level skill, the Volley, is included as a optional test. All three are objectively scored, individually administered performance tests conducted under specified conditions on specially marked tennis courts. Both Ground Strokes and the Serve are scored for both placement and power, whereas Volley is scored for placement only. The manual suggests that students in an average-size class could be tested in two class periods.

Content validity was assumed based on the task analysis. Concurrent validity was established by correlating students' test performance at the conclusion of a beginning instructional unit on tennis with subjective ratings by experts. The experts' ratings were based on separate 5-point scales for each skill. The rating scales are described in an appendix to the manual. A minimum of 50 students per sex per academic level were included in this study. Concurrent validity coefficients ranged from .65 to .91, but the coefficients for the two essential skills, Ground Strokes and the Serve, did not fall below .76. The study included a second administration of the test with 10 days of the first administration, resulting in test-retest reliability coefficients of .69 to .95. Again, higher coefficients (.79 to.95) were reported for the tests of Ground Strokes and Serves.

Raw scores for each of the tested skills can be converted to percentiles and *T*-scores using the normative information contained in the manual. Norms are provided for males and females for grade levels 9, 10, 11, and 12, and for college. Norming was accomplished by testing 600 students per sex per academic level in a national sample of convenience. Although not stated in the manual, it was determined by a call to the publisher that students included in the norm group had recently completed a beginning instructional unit on tennis and were sampled in intact class groups. The resulting norms cannot be considered representative of the population from which they were drawn and, therefore, must be used cautiously.

The scoring of the three tests is based on observations by the test administrator or an assistant. The appendix contains a sample form for recording a student's scores. Although the scoring is objective, it will require close observations and good judgment when balls land close to the scoring lines. For both Ground Strokes and the Serve, two observations must be made for each stroke (i.e., where the ball hits the court on its first and second bounces). This would require at least as much skill as calling lines in a tennis match; therefore, determination of interrater reliability would have been beneficial.

The Tennis Skills Test covers the most essential aspects of early tennis skill development. Its value is in increasing the objectivity of the assessment; however, it is not likely to add significantly to a subjective assessment by an experienced tennis instructor. Its greatest value, therefore, will be for instructors who have limited experience in tennis.

Review of the Tennis Skills Test Manual by WILLIAM A. STOCK, Professor of Exercise Science and Physical Education, and KATHERINE S. JONES, Tennis Instructor, Arizona State University, Tempe, AZ:

Consistent with other tests of sports skills sponsored by AAHPERD, the three scales in this battery are easy to use. A clearly written manual has sections on: (*a*) test development (global testing objectives of AAHPERD, research on tennis skills tests, and general instructions are covered); (*b*) test administration (a diagram and one page of detailed instructions is given for each test); (*c*) norms (percentile ranks and *T*-score for males and females for each high school grade and for college); and (*d*) tennis drills. To administer each test, regular game equipment and a court specially, but easily, marked for scoring are required. Besides a test administrator, it is desirable to have a second person observe and score a student's performance. A scoring form is provided. Although the manual says students may be trained as scorers, no evidence is provided that students score these tests reliably. Also missing is a description of a standard method for training students to score the performance of others. The absence of a training procedure will decrease the reliability of the tests whenever students are used as scorers.

A summary of research on antecedent tests provided the evidence by which members of the authoring committee assumed adequate content validity for this battery. Given the research reviewed, the domain of behavior tested, and the comparability between the present tests and their antecedents, this assumption of content validity appears justified.

On the basis of a pilot study, the applicability of these tests was restricted to persons at or above grade 9. Results from the pilot study also led to a combination of the separate scales for forehand and backhand strokes into a single measure. Regrettably, no specific information is provided about the sample used in the pilot study, nor about the nature of testing conducted during the pilot study, nor about the types of analyses employed. Also absent were specific estimates of reliability, validity, and errors of measurement.

Following the pilot study, revised tests were administered in school settings (a sample of at least 50 persons was collected at each grade and gender level). In all cases, the data were collected after a unit of instruction on tennis. The manual fails to furnish information about how instruction varied across settings or about the effects this instruction may have had on estimates of reliability and validity. No other descriptive information is furnished about these samples. Concerning reliability, coefficients of stability (retesting occurred within 10 days of first testing) varied between .69 (college females on the Volley test) and .95 (high school males on the Serve test). The reliability estimates reported for high school students may be too high because collapsing the different grade levels will confound variation due to maturation and age differences with variation due to ability.

Estimates of concurrent validity were provided in the form of correlation coefficients between a test score and a corresponding rating of the behavior by experts. The three individual 5-point rating scale items used as criteria are provided in the manual. Estimates of concurrent validity varied from .65 (college females on the Volley test) to .91 (high school males on the Serve test). However, this evidence has limited utility because the experts rated the same behaviors being tested. There is a clear need to relate these scales to other types of performance, such as overall skill in competitive and other natural game settings. The manual should describe more fully the experts used, the conditions under which they made their ratings, the types of training and instructions they received, and whether or not these raters also administered the tests.

Although the instructions for administering the tests are clear, improvement is possible. The directions for each test should include both a standard demonstration of the expected behavior and specific verbal instructions to be read or said to the test taker.

The sample used for the primary norming study was a sample of convenience solicited primarily by advertisement in AAHPERD publications. The ultimate sample consisted of more than 7,000 students from 42 states. No information is provided about the level of tennis experience of these students or about descriptive variables such as gender, age, race, and socioeconomic status. No information is provided about the communities of the sampled schools. These omissions limit the utility of the norms. The tables of percentile ranks and *T*-scores are adequately explained, but not accompanied by any other descriptive statistics. In the section on norms, the text suggests that persons scoring below the 25th percentile should be provided with a program of exercise and drills. No evidence is cited to support a prescription this specific.

In sum, the manual describes three tests that are easy to administer and appear directly related to tennis skills. Improvements in training procedures and instructions would increase the reliability of these tests. The evidence for the validity of these scales is severely limited.

[391]

Test of Adolescent/Adult Word Finding.

Purpose: Developed to assess word finding skills.
Population: Ages 12–80.
Publication Date: 1990.
Acronym: TAWF.
Scores: 5 sections (Picture Naming: Nouns, Sentence Completion Naming, Description Naming, Picture Naming: Verbs, Category Naming) yielding 4 scores: Accuracy, Comprehension, Item Response Time, Word Finding Profile.
Administration: Individual.
Forms, 2: Complete, Brief.
Price Data, 1991: $150 per complete kit including test book, 25 response booklets, examiner's manual (204

pages), and technical manual (121 pages); $25 per 25 response forms.
Time: (20–30) minutes for complete test; [10] minutes for brief test.
Comments: Upward extension of the Test of Word Finding (T4:2799); speed can be measured in actual or estimated Item Response Time; tape recorder and stopwatch required on Section 1 only when using Actual Item Response Time Option.
Author: Diane J. German.
Publisher: The Riverside Publishing Company.

Review of the Test of Adolescent/Adult Word Finding by RONALD B. GILLAM, Assistant Professor of Speech Communication, The University of Texas at Austin, Austin, TX:

Like its predecessor, the Test of Word Finding (T4:2799), the Test of Adolescent/Adult Word Finding (TAWF) is divided into six sections. In the first section, Picture Naming: Nouns, subjects name objects that are represented by colored pictures. Section two, Sentence Completion Naming, requires subjects to complete open-ended sentences spoken by the examiner. In section three, Description Naming, subjects provide words in response to examiner descriptions. Section four, Picture Naming: Verbs, requires that subjects label actions that are depicted in colored pictures. Section five, Category Naming, requires subjects to provide category labels for three basic-level words spoken by the examiner. In section six, Comprehension Assessment, subjects point to pictures representing vocabulary items that were named incorrectly on earlier sections.

The TAWF assesses naming accuracy, response delay, and types of errors on tasks requiring single-word naming of nouns, verbs, and category words. Naming accuracy is evaluated on the five verbal sections. Examples of errors and acceptable substitutions provided in the appendices are helpful for determining whether a response is correct or incorrect. Examiners also calculate a percentage of target-word comprehension that is designed to represent the subjects' knowledge of target words that were named incorrectly on the five verbal sections.

To evaluate naming speed, item response time measures are computed for the Picture Naming: Nouns section. Two different timing procedures are available. Subjects are classified as slow or fast namers by comparing total delayed responses or average response time to grade- or age-level norms that are provided in the manual. Naming speed data and accuracy data are combined to determine whether subjects are fast and inaccurate namers, slow and inaccurate namers, fast and accurate namers, or slow and accurate namers. Finally, examiners may perform informal analyses of word substitutions. Useful forms for substitution analyses are available in the appendix of the administration manual.

The entire TAWF can be administered in 20 to 30 minutes. A shortened version of the TAWF, called the Brief Test, is provided for use with subjects who may not be able to complete the entire TAWF. The Brief Test consists of a subset of items from each section of the full test, requires less than half the administration time, and yields standard scores and percentiles.

The TAWF was standardized at 21 sites representing the four geographic regions defined in the 1980 U.S. Census. The standardization sample consisted of 1,200 adolescents in grades 7 through 12 and 553 adults between the ages of 20 and 80 years. Approximately 100 females and 100 males were sampled at each of nine levels (grades 7 through 12; adults between the ages of 20 and 40; adults between the ages of 40 and 60; and adults between the ages of 60 and 80). Distributions across sex, education levels, race, and ethnicity reasonably approximate distributions reported in the 1980 U.S. Census. Children and adults with learning disabilities, speech and language problems, behavioral disorders, brain trauma, neurological disease, cardiovascular strokes, or fluency disorders were excluded from the standardization sample.

Test reliability was evaluated in two ways. First, using the Rasch Latent Trait model, overall-fit mean squares were calculated for item fit and person fit. The overall-fit mean square for TAWF item fit was an acceptable .99 for both the full test and the brief scale. The overall-fit mean square for person fit was .80 for the full test and .65 for the brief scale. The author attributes these low values to ceiling effects. Apparently, there was less than optimum variability in the standardization sample because many subjects scored in the high range.

Correlations for accuracy of naming were .93 for adolescents and .85 for adults; correlations for average item response time were .81 for adolescents and .72 for adults. These results suggest that accuracy of naming scores are more stable than item response time scores, and adolescents' performance on the TAWF is more stable than that of adults.

Although content and concurrent validity of the TAWF are acceptable, some factors pertaining to construct validity are problematic. The TAWF is not very sensitive to developmental differences. Scores earned by 9th, 10th, 11th, and 12th graders did not differ at statistically significant levels. Results for the brief form were even less acceptable; mean scores actually decreased between grades 7 and 9, then plateaued for grades 9 through 12. In contrast to the trend for the full TAWF, adults' scores on the TAWF Brief Test increased rather than decreased with age.

One of the purposes of the TAWF is to assist in identifying adolescents and adults with word-finding problems. The technical manual summarizes three studies that found significant differences in TAWF scores earned by adolescents with and without previously diagnosed word-finding problems. However, in one reported study, 31% of a sample of students with prediagnosed word-finding problems earned TAWF scores that placed them in accurate or very accurate namer categories. Further, 23% of these students presented with average or above average response times. In this study, the TAWF failed to identify the word-finding problems of a relatively high percentage of adolescents with previously diagnosed word-retrieval deficits.

In summary, the TAWF provides a means for systematic observation of adolescents' and adults' word-finding abilities in constrained naming contexts. The administration and technical manuals contain useful reviews of word-finding problems and helpful examples of TAWF responses and profiles. Use of the TAWF can aid examiners in forming hypotheses about word-finding abilities that can be probed further in informal follow-up procedures. However, four problems limit the usefulness of this test. First, the TAWF does not discriminate between the performance of subjects between the 9th and 12th grades. Second, average item response time scores did not reach optimum reliability levels. Third, examiners cannot predict with a high level of certainty that subjects with word-finding problems will earn TAWF scores that fall outside the normal range. Finally, the TAWF Brief Test offers examiners even less precision than the full test and is less reliable.

Review of the Test of Adolescent/Adult Word Finding by RICHARD E. HARDING, Senior Vice President, Gallup, Inc., Lincoln, NE:

The Test of Adolescent/Adult Word Finding (TAWF) was developed to help professionals in the field pinpoint deficiencies in five areas. These are Picture Naming: Nouns, Sentence Completion Naming, Description Naming, Picture Naming: Verbs, and Category Naming. Intervention, according to the author, could then fall into three categories called remediation, compensatory programming, and self-awareness. The test is complete with response booklets, a test book, a technical manual, and an administrator's scoring and interpretation manual.

The technical manual contains excellent descriptions of the purpose of the test and the theoretical base from which the test was derived. There are several sections to help the professional understand the practical problems the test was designed to uncover. In fact, the first chapter of the technical manual provides an excellent section on theory.

The research processes utilized to develop the test are described in great detail. For example, a Rasch latent trait model was employed to select the items, and the authors do an excellent job in describing their procedures. The items were administered to 330 students, of which 300 were found to be normal learners (50 were selected from each grade level 7–12) and 30 students in those same grades were found to have word-finding problems. They were randomly selected from a group of 500 students residing in Racine, Wisconsin. The word-finding problem students were selected from suburban schools in the Chicago metropolitan area. The sample was balanced according to gender. The criterion for item selection was excellent according to the Rasch analysis.

Once items were selected, a normative sample was drawn to develop the standardization scales. This included a final sample of 1,200 adolescents and 553 adults. These were people in grades 7–12 and adults aged 20 to 80 years residing in 21 states. Population data from the 1980 U.S. Census were utilized to ascertain the degree of representation with respect to stratification variables of gender, ethnicity, or race, geographic region, and the education level of the adult subjects or the parents of the adolescents tested. These all appear to be appropriate.

From this sample, normative scores were derived with regard to the accuracy of the response as well as the time of response. A time lag of 4 seconds was utilized as the appropriate time criterion.

RELIABILITY. Reliability was assessed with regard to item scale reliability and the goodness-of-fit criterion for the Rasch model. The overall-fit mean squares for Rasch model goodness of fit was .99. Many different analyses were done with appropriate statistics being reported for every phase of this research. The more traditional Kuder-Richardson Formula 20 was reported to be .85 for all ages. KR-20 was also found to be .85 for the 36 subjects demonstrating word-finding problems. Test-retest studies were conducted on both adolescents and adults. The test-retest period was 14 days and included both accuracy and time assessments. The test-retest reliability correlation was .93 for adolescents and .85 for adults for the accuracy part of the study. For the time response, test-retest reliabilities were .81 for adolescents and .72 for the adults.

VALIDITY. Validity was assessed with regard to content validity, criterion-related validity, and construct validity. A concurrent validity study was conducted on 30 seventh and eighth graders who were considered to be average achievers by their classroom teachers. Additionally, they had not been referred for or had received speech or special education or psychological services. These students were administered the TAWF as well as other common naming and vocabulary tests. The TAWF was then correlated to these. The correlations were moderate. The authors suggest the TAWF, therefore, "does not yield a language assessment identical to these [other] confrontation naming tests" (technical manual, p. 77). The tests utilized were the Boston Naming Test (Kaplan, Goodglass, & Weintraub, 1976) and the Upper Extension of the Expressive One-Word Picture Vocabulary Test (Gardner, 1983). Various studies were completed to determine the construct validity of the test and these appear to be appropriate.

The author includes an excellent set of references in the technical manual. These were apparently found to be of some utility as the test was being developed. Both the technical manual and the administration, scoring, and interpretation manual are very complete. The author did an excellent job in presenting the research conducted to develop the test as well as making the test relatively easy for people to administer and score. The test book is extremely well done with colored pictures and a very functional layout.

SUMMARY. In summary, the TAWF is an extremely well-researched test. Adequate data are presented as to the efficacy of the test, scoring procedures are clear and easy to use, as is the entire test process. The authors present appropriate and adequate evidence of reliability and validity and, in most cases, research conducted on large samples necessary for this type of test. The author, Diane J. German, has done an excellent job.

REVIEWER'S REFERENCES

Kaplan, E., Goodglass, H., & Weintraub, S. (1976). Boston Naming Test (experimental ed.). Boston: Veterans Administration Hospital.

Gardner, M. F. (1983). Upper Extension of the Expressive One-Word Picture Vocabulary Test. Novato, CA: Academic Therapy Publications.

[392]

Test of Cognitive Style in Mathematics.

Purpose: Identifies preferences in mathematical computation methods and problem solving methods.
Population: Ages 8–adult.
Publication Date: 1986.
Acronym: TCSM.
Scores, 5: Mental Computation, Arithmetic, Geometry/Visual, Algebra, Total.
Administration: Individual.
Price Data, 1992: $54 per complete kit including manual (65 pages); $8 per 50 profile record forms; $15 per 50 worksheets; $15 per 50 observation folders.
Time: (20) minutes.
Authors: John B. Bath, Stephen J. Chinn, and Dwight E. Knox.
Publisher: Slosson Educational Publications, Inc.

Review of the Test of Cognitive Style in Mathematics by RICHARD C. PUGH, Professor of Education, Indiana University, Bloomington, IN:

The Test of Cognitive Style in Mathematics (TCSM) is a test designed to identify each individual's preferred computation method and/or preferred problem-solving method. The test manual authors state the test provides information to regular classroom teachers about each student in terms of learning style. Use of the test assumes that identification of the individual's learning style can make instruction more appropriate and effective. The authors state that instruction in strategies of both the preferred style as well as the opposing style can increase flexibility and skill in problem solving. For the special education teacher, the position is taken that knowledge of learning style can assist in remedial instruction by helping in the selection of methods more appropriate to the student. Additionally, the test is claimed to provide a more complete understanding of an individual's learning preferences through alternative styles of valid problem solving.

The two cognitive styles that serve as the foundation for this test are focused on observable behaviors at the extreme ends of a continuum that are labeled Grasshopper (high scores) and Inchworm (low scores). The Grasshopper style is depicted as a person who resists using paper and pencil, makes initial estimates of an answer, restricts the range of possible answers, and attempts several methods almost simultaneously. There is an initial emphasis on holistic concepts. In contrast, the Inchworm style person takes small, sequential steps and is likely to use paper and pencil in solving problems. They tend to pursue a solution through the use of formulas. These two frameworks are thoroughly described in the test manual by providing examples of solutions to each of the 20 questions following both cognitive styles.

The process used for item development appears satisfactory. The test booklet consists of 20 problems presented one at a time with one problem on a page in an easel format. The test is designed for students 12 years of age and older. (The various test materials are inconsistent regarding age. In one place the test is described as being appropriate for 8-year-olds.) There are four subtests with five problems for each subtest. The subtests are labeled Mental Computation, Arithmetic, Geometry/Visual, and Algebra.

The Mental Computation subtest examines the four operations with whole numbers and an emphasis on mental mathematical strategies. Examinees are directed to respond verbally to a problem the examinee reads while the examiner reads the same problem aloud. The response is required to be made without writing.

For the other three subtests the examinee has access to a worksheet and pencil. The Arithmetic subtest includes topics of whole number addition, decimal multiplication, digit series, number pattern analysis, and arithmetic average. The Geometry/Visual subtest addresses topics of single pattern analysis, areas, geometric progression, multi-pattern analysis, and volume. The Algebra subtest deals with first order equations, simultaneous equations word problems, first order equation word problems, and consecutive numbers problems. Emphasis is placed on a relaxed atmosphere for test administration with the method of solution of a problem being the primary focus of the scoring, not the actual solution itself. Encouragement is given to the examinee to explain how the problems could be solved.

There is no time constraint but the average time for taking the test is reported to be about 20 minutes. The scoring strategy involves making a judgment according to the cognitive style the answer represents. The Inchworm style scores 1 for correct answers, Grasshopper styles score 3 for correct answers, and intermediate strategies score 2. An examinee is allowed to miss only one question from each section before that section becomes invalid. The student is given the average (mean) score in that section for the question that he or she could not answer. A grand total score is reported on the profile record. It is the sum of the scores on the four sections. No information is reported in the manual regarding missing information accumulated from across the four sections. Scoring is assisted by the use of an Observation Folder that provides a structured format for the recording of responses and suggested appropriate observations. In addition, a Profile Record is available. Inchworm scores are reported to be in the range of 5, 6, or 7 on a subtest and Grasshopper scores are in the range of 13, 14, or 15 on a subtest. Examples of each style answer are provided in the test manual and the Observation Folder. These examples likely increase the consistency of scoring. Based on two samples of 23 students and 24 students each, test-retest reliability coefficients with an interval of 5 weeks ranged between .80 and .95 for subtests.

The most compelling evidence for validity is content validity. The items were developed carefully through many trials to evaluate whether each item satisfied seven criteria all reported in the test manual. Among the criteria for item selection were whether the question generated more than one strategy of solution, whether the strategies were identifiable as Grasshopper and Inchworm, whether the item was difficult enough to force the subject into a natural style of problem solving yet short and easy to read and comprehend, and easy enough to encourage the examinee to attempt a solution. Additional technical information is reported in the test manual that relates to the relationship between an item and the cognitive style identified based on the total test score. This evidence is reported as discrimination indices for all 20 items that show all items have a significant relationship to the overall classification. However, this is hardly evidence about item validity as reported in the test manual. Rather, it is an estimate of internal consistency between the total test score and item scores.

The most persuasive characteristic of the TCSM is its careful development of a scoring strategy that relates conceptually to the description of the two cognitive styles. The relationship of cognitive style to the uses of the test described in the manual such as the formulation of instructional groups and design of remedial instruction is not addressed with any empirical evidence. This connection is left up to the user to assume. Therefore, in conclusion, the test appears to sort examinees into two different cognitive styles but caution should be exercised about the uses reported in the manual. Supportive evidence on this connection is not reported.

Review of the Test of Cognitive Style in Mathematics by DAN WRIGHT, School Psychologist, Wyandotte Comprehensive Special Education Cooperative, Kansas City, KS:

The Test of Cognitive Style in Mathematics (TCSM) is an attempt to distinguish students who may function, at least in mathematics, in either of two generally incompatible cognitive styles. Students displaying characteristics of these styles are referred to as "Inchworms" and "Grasshoppers." They are presumed to differ in three approaches to mathematics: analyzing and identifying the problem (in which they are detail-oriented vs. holistic, respectively), methods of solving the problem (which appear to be sequential and constrained vs. simultaneous and flexible), and verification (involving repetition vs. alternate procedures). Identifying styles thusly is of purported benefit to regular education teachers in grouping for instruction, to special education teachers in planning remediation, and to students themselves in understanding their own strengths. The test is recommended for students 12 years of age and older although there is some discrepancy in the test materials regarding the age range. It is composed of 20 problems, presented in easel format, in four content areas: Mental Computation, Arithmetic, Geometry/Visual, and Algebra (optional). Probes are offered with each item to determine the student's strategy or method of approach. A profile sheet may be used to summarize the number of items correct and to record observations.

The TCSM is not a normed test, which leaves no basis for comparison of results. Judgements about the cognitive styles demonstrated are entirely subjective. Limited information is provided on the development or evaluation of test items. Minimal information from a woefully small sample is provided on reliability and validity, but these deal with the TCSM as a test of mathematics only (i.e., correct problem solution) and *not* as a test of cognitive style. The TCSM is not psychometrically inadequate—it is psychometrically nonexistent. No reference is made to the voluminous literature or other assessment instruments dealing with general cognitive style. A cursory literature review is offered of work on cognitive styles in mathematics teaching, and a brief foray is made into brain hemispheric functioning. Neither of these adequately supports the suggestions that are made for remedial strategies, nor is the subjective interpretation of test results integrated.

In summary, the TCSM inadequately assess a construct of unproven utility. Although it is apparent that different cognitive styles can actually be employed in mathematics, this instrument offers no effective means of determining, interpreting, or employing such information.

[393]

Test of Early Language Development, Second Edition.

Purpose: Designed to measure the early development of oral language in the areas of receptive and expressive language, syntax, and semantics.
Population: Ages 2-0 to 7-11.
Publication Dates: 1981–91.
Acronym: TELD-2.
Scores: Total score only.
Administration: Individual.
Price Data, 1994: $109 per complete kit; $29 per 25 Form A Profile Record Forms; $29 per 25 Form B Profile Record Forms; $26 per picture book; $29 per Examiner's Manual ('91, 74 pages).
Time: (20) minutes.
Authors: Wayne P. Hresko, D. Kim Reid, and Donald D. Hammill.
Publisher: PRO-ED, Inc.
Cross References: For reviews by Janice Arnold Dole and Elizabeth M. Prather, see 9:1250 (1 reference).

TEST REFERENCES

1. Cole, K. N., Mills, P. E., Dale, P. S., & Jenkins, J. R. (1991). Effects of preschool integration for children with disabilities. *Exceptional Children, 58*, 36-45.

2. Roskos, K. (1991). An inventory of literate behavior in the pretend play episodes of eight preschoolers. *Reading Research and Instruction, 30*(3), 39-52.

3. Cole, K. N., Dale, P. S., & Mills, P. E. (1992). Stability of the intelligence quotient-language quotient relation: Is discrepancy modeling based on a myth? *American Journal on Mental Retardation, 97*, 131-143.

4. Cole, K. N., Dale, P. S., Mills, P. E., & Jenkins, J. R. (1993). Interaction between early intervention curricula and student characteristics. *Exceptional Children, 60*, 17-28.

Review of the Test of Early Language Development, Second Edition by JAVAID KAISER, Associate Professor of Education, Virginia Polytechnic Institute & State University, Blacksburg, VA:

The primary purpose of the Test of Early Language Development, Second Edition (TELD-2) is to screen children for language deficiency. The test is designed for normal children of ages 2-0 through 7-11 but can be administered to special populations after making proper adjustments in administering the test and establishing separate norms. The TELD-2 is administered individually without time limits and is available in two parallel forms: Form A and Form B. Each form contains 68 items. The test is well grounded in theory and measures form and content of language development. The syntax, morphology, and semantics are measured in receptive as well as expressive modes. Phonology that was measured in the first edition of the Test of Early Language Development (TELD) has been deleted from this second edition.

The TELD-2 is very easy to administer and score. It comes with explicit item-by-item instructions. A shortened version of these instructions is printed directly on the Record form for experienced examiners. The Picture Book accompanying the test is well organized and is easy to use. Additional objects needed to administer certain items are completely specified. The testing time is efficiently reduced by identifying different entry points on the tests for different age groups. Examples explaining basals and ceilings have minimized the probability of making scoring errors.

Items are scored correct (1) or incorrect (0). The sum of item scores is called the raw score. Knowing the chronological age of the child (without rounding days to the next month), the raw score can be converted into language quotient (LQ), normal curve equivalent (NCE), or age equivalent scores by using tables given in the manual. The authors have also provided a conversion table to convert the language quotient of the child into percentile rank, *z*-score, *T*-score, or stanine with little interpolation. The ranges of LQ and NCE scores have been labeled from "very poor" to "very superior" to make the interpretation of test scores easier. The authors are to be commended for emphasizing the proper role of test scores in the process of clinical diagnosis and for discouraging users from using age equivalent scores. Normal curve equivalent scores should also be avoided whenever possible, because authors have smoothed the curve on visual inspection.

Although the normative sample of 1,329 children was selected from multiple sites, the selection of sites was arbitrary and was determined where friends and colleagues of the authors or past users of the TELD resided. The description of sampling procedure (p. 44) further suggests that the selection of children at individual sites was not under the control of authors and may have included children who had or were suspected of language deficiency. In addition, normative groups for various age levels were small and ranged from 178 to 268 children. Although the authors have included adjacent age groups to produce more stable norms, the representativeness of normative groups is still questionable.

The content validity of the test has been established adequately. The criteria for the final selection of items included item validity as expressed by 22 professional experts, item difficulty, item-total correlation, and item bias. Only items that were free of gender and racial bias were included in the test.

The test has excellent internal consistency for all age levels. The coefficient alpha ranged from .91 to .97 with a median value of .97. Test-retest and equivalent-form reliability (.97 to .98) is available for children of ages 6-5 to 7-5 and is based on small sample size (N = 55). The same estimates for other age levels are not reported. The evidence produced in support of criterion-related validity is also questionable. The use of the TELD as a criterion measure of the TELD-2 is inappropriate because the TELD-2 is an extension of the TELD and included items from its first edition. Moreover, the sample size is very small (N = 55) and included children of only upper age levels (6-0 to 7-5). The correlation of TELD-2 scores with The Test of Language Development-2, Receptive Expressive Emergent Language, Preschool Language Scale, and Peabody Picture Vocabulary Test, though statistically significant, had only 16%–36% variance in common. Again, these correlations are based on very small sample sizes (N = 30 to 45) and did not cover all age levels for which the TELD-2 was developed.

The construct validity of the TELD-2 has been demonstrated through its correlation with intelligence and other cognitive measures. Here again, one encounters the same problem of small sample sizes (N = 15 to 55) and lack of representation for all age levels. Although authors claimed that TELD-2 was successful in differentiating various levels of language impairment in the state of Texas, the correct classification rate of the TELD-2 when administered to children with normal and mild language impairment is not known.

SUMMARY. The authors should be commended for developing a test in a difficult area like language development. The test is content valid and internally consistent but lacks evidence in support of its construct validity. Test administration, scoring, and interpretation of test scores is easy. The manual is well written except chapter 4 where authors have caused confusion by introducing the performance statistics of the TELD.

Review of the Test of Early Language Development, Second Edition by DAVID A. SHAPIRO, Associate Professor of Communication Disorders, Department of Human Services, College of Education and Psychology, Western Carolina University, Cullowhee, NC:

The Test of Early Language Development, Second Edition (TELD-2) is designed to measure early oral language abilities. Results from the TELD-2 can be compared with relative strengths and weaknesses in cognitive aptitude and early academic achievement. The authors appropriately cautioned that "the test results should be treated as hypotheses to be investigated further and either validated or invalidated through direct observation, additional testing, or future events" (p. 34). They further indicated that "the TELD-2 was designed to complement rather than replace systematic, naturalistic observation" (p. 2). Within this context, the test lists five purposes. In abbreviated form, they are to: identify students who are significantly below their peers in early language development and may be candidates for intervention, identify strengths and weaknesses of individual students, document students' progress in intervention, aid in directing instruction, and serve as a measurement device in research studies pertaining to academic achievement. These purposes represent a significant expansion of those reported in the original TELD (1981).

The Examiner's Manual is well organized and presents information that is critical to using the TELD-2 and to the assessment process in general. Other materials include a Picture Book and Profile/Record Forms (A and B). The rationale and overview of the TELD-2 are addressed concisely, as is the model upon which the test is based (Bloom & Lahey, 1978). Although the model includes form (phonology, syntax, and morphology; i.e., the structural components of language), content (semantics; i.e., knowledge of objects, relations among objects, and relations among events), and use (pragmatics; i.e., appropriateness of the language to specific contexts and communicative purposes), the TELD-2 addresses form (syntax and morphology only) and content only. The authors highlighted significant changes in the TELD-2 including expanding the test range for children aged 2-0 to 7-11 years, increasing the number of items on two alternate forms to 68 items each, shortening item directions and scoring instructions, and expanding the norm tables to include normal curve equivalent (NCE) scores.

Administration and scoring procedures are clear. The TELD-2 is administered to individuals in approximately 15 to 40 minutes. No time limits are imposed and the test may be administered in more than one session if necessary. All responses are recorded as either correct (1 point) or incorrect (0 points) on the Profile/Record Form, summed to form the TELD-2 total raw score, and then converted into a language quotient (LQ). Testing begins with the item corresponding to the child's chronological age. Preliminary items require direct observation or parental report. Later items require children to repeat words and sentences, answer questions, and respond to instructions with and without accompanying pictures and other materials presented by the examiner. The basal and ceiling are established by determining that point at which the child passes or misses, respectively, five consecutive items. Useful examples for establishing basals and ceilings are provided in the manual. All pictures used as stimuli are contained within a conveniently organized Picture Book. Turning the book one way enables presentation of the Form A pictures. Turning the opposite way presents Form B pictures. A few additional and easily accessible materials are required for administration and are specified in the manual. Administration instructions are followed immediately by scoring directions that include examples of correct responses. Every attempt has been made to simplify the scoring and reduce the amount of inferential judgments required of the examiner.

During an administration and scoring pilot implemented by this reviewer, several concerns arose. For example, the earliest items are scored on the bases of either observed language behavior or parent/caregiver report. Although the authors have established a precedent for parental reporting in assessment (p. 39), the reliability between the child's language behaviors observed by the examiner and those inferred by parental report for the TELD-2 should be verified. Further, the picture stimuli are typically presented neatly and without distraction. However, several items seem potentially confounded by the child's visual discrimination ability. For example, it is not clear in Picture 2 (Form A, Item 24) if the car is part of the "day" picture or an individual picture itself. Other items seem confounded by the structure of the verbal instructions and/or the visual stimuli. For example, Item 30 (Form A) directs "Show me the ball that is bigger" and "Show me the house that is smaller." The contrastives (bigger/smaller) imply a comparison between two units. Picture 8, however, provides three units each for balls and houses. Either a comparison of only two units or use of superlatives (biggest/smallest) would be more appropriate. Assessing knowledge of prepositions, Item 36 (Form A, Picture 10) directs "Show me the rope going around the tree." Because there is no ongoing action, deleting "going" in the instruction would be more linguistically correct and would provide a more direct comparison (around vs. not around/at the base of). Assessing knowledge of same and different, Item 49 (Form A, Picture 21) directs the examiner to point to a cluster of blocks and say "These toys are the same." A careful look at the blocks reveals that they are not the same (i.e., identical). Similar questions are raised regarding test items on Form B. Item 21 (Form B, Picture 3) assesses knowledge of big/little and directs the child to "Show me the big bear. Show me the little bear." This wording implies a comparison between two units, whereas Picture 3 has three bears. Changing the wording or picturing only two bears would be more appropriate. Both Items 42 and 46 seem culturally/linguistically biased in the response expectation. Item 42 requires familiarity with television and asks "What's your favorite TV show?" Many children in mountain communities do not get television reception; others cannot afford television. Yet the response must contain a program name or indicate "I don't have one," implying one among others does not surface as the favorite. Item 46 assesses knowledge of morning/afternoon and asks "Do you take a nap in the morning or in the afternoon?" Some children nap in the morning, some afternoon, some neither, some both. Although item selection and content validity will be addressed later, this reviewer experienced difficulty regarding the structure of the verbal instructions and visual stimuli when administering the test. In addition, although examples of correct responses are provided, a longer list of both acceptable and unacceptable responses would facilitate scoring. Responses that did not fit the examples of correct responses in the manual and the Profile/Record Form rendered some scoring subjectivity. Finally, the following concern is of considerable magnitude. The test objectives listed above imply the TELD-2 is a diagnostic measure, one that helps identify language-related strengths and weaknesses, design instruction, and document progress through intervention. However, the method of scoring (1–correct vs. 0–incorrect only) compromises valuable diagnostic information. Some form of verbatim recording would permit an analysis of the errors in order to determine the child's linguistic knowledge and level of cognitive abstraction. For example, several items call for the child to analyze on the basis of causality and/or functionality. Item 34 (Form A) asks "Why does X go to work?" Item 48 (Form A) asks "What do you do with a (pencil, knife, bus, clock)?" Neither the bipolar scoring scale (1 vs. 0) nor the Diagnostic Profile (which quantifies the number of items passed under System [i.e., Receptive and Expressive], and Feature [i.e., Syntax and Semantics]) permits an understanding of the nature of the child's response, rendering the TELD-2 a screening test only.

Explicit directions are provided for completing the Profile/Record Form and for determining and interpreting the raw score, standard scores (language quotient and normal curve equivalent), percentile rank, language age (i.e., age equivalents), and overall rating. However, the data provided on the sample Profile/Record Form, Form A (specifically for the language quotient, normal curve equivalent, and percentile rank, p. 30) do not agree with that provided in the appropriate tables in Appendix A (pp. 60–64). The individual scores are discussed in terms of their proper use and interpretation. The language quotient has a mean of 100 and a standard deviation of 15, thus enabling comparison with other standard scores across other instruments. The normal curve equivalent has a mean of 50 and a standard deviation of 21.06, providing an exact match between NCEs and percentile ranks of 1 and 99, thus having the same range and midpoints. The authors advised against using age equivalent scores (language age) whenever possible, reviewed significant cautions in interpreting test results, and reminded test users that the TELD-2 results "augmented by additional test findings, direct observation, and knowledge acquired from secondary sources, will eventually result in proper diagnosis and program"

(p. 32). Furthermore, the TELD-2 "should be used as the first level of assessment" (p. 37). If a child demonstrates reduced early language skills on the TELD-2, "his or her abilities in this area should be more thoroughly investigated either by using specific language ability measures, or through language sampling, diagnostic observation, or other clinical language methods" (p. 37).

The authors provided a thorough review of item development, item analysis, standardization procedures, normative information, reliability, and validity. The original TELD (1981) items formed the basis of the TELD-2. The procedures to design a set of additional items to broaden the range of language abilities sampled were described adequately. Items were analyzed on the basis of discriminating power (i.e., by using the point biserial correlation technique where each item is correlated with the total raw score) and item difficulty (i.e., by determining proportions of examinees who get each item correct and incorrect). Some items with difficulties below 15% and above 85% were retained in order to account for both the lower and upper age ranges and language potentials. Although the authors reported having paid particular attention to eliminating bias on the bases of ethnicity and sex, several individual items may be problematic as noted earlier.

The TELD-2 was standardized on a sample of 1,329 children at varied settings from 30 states. The characteristics of the subjects seem to represent a national sample on the bases of gender, urban/rural residence, race, geographic region, parental occupation, ethnicity, and age. The rationale for using the four kinds of normative scores is clearly presented.

Reliability estimates were obtained using the techniques of coefficient alpha, test-retest, and alternative forms. These estimates focus on two types of reliability (internal consistency and stability) and two sources of test error (content sampling and time sampling). All coefficient alphas exceeded the established criterion of .90. Standard errors of measurement associated with the coefficient alphas for Forms A and B were sufficiently small. These data indicate that both forms have sufficient internal consistency. A Rasch analysis, where both forms were analyzed at two levels with a one-parameter item response modal analysis, was conducted as another method for determining internal consistency. Results indicate that there appears to be good measurement of a single dimension of the material covered. Estimates of test error were determined by time sampling including immediate and delayed test-retest with alternate forms and delayed test-retest with the same form. The coefficients that resulted indicated sufficient temporal stability and consistency of response to the different forms.

Evidence is reported for content validity, criterion validity (concurrent only), and construct validity. Content validity was supported by detailed reporting of procedures for test construction, item development, and item analysis; data regarding discriminating power; and the relationship of the items to the theoretical construct. Concurrent validity was established by correlating the TELD-2, Form A and B, with the total score of the original TELD on 55 children (language ability not specified) ranging in age from 6-0 to 7-5 years. Although this procedure was unfortunately limited to the older age range and on a relatively small sample, the correlations are high (.96 and .97). Additional evidence of concurrent validity was reported by correlating the TELD-2 raw scores for both forms with those of two selected criterion tests on a sample of 45 language-normal children between the ages of 5 and 6 years, and two other criterion tests on 30 children (language ability not specified) between 4 and 5 years old. Again representing a relatively small sample within limited age ranges, correlation coefficients, reportedly significant beyond the .01 level, ranged from .47 to.66. These data, within the limitations noted, reflect adequate evidence of concurrent validity. Construct validity was supported by delineating a core of assumptions that underlie the test and hypotheses generated by these assumptions, and by presenting data to verify these hypotheses. Specific premises that were addressed included the relationship of the TELD-2 to chronological age and experience, intelligence, academic and school-related ability, and group differentiation. Although coverage could have been more complete and precise, these data provide some evidence of construct validity. This reviewer concurs with the authors that "Further data gathered from varied samples of children throughout the country would add significantly to assumptions pertaining to the test's usefulness" (p. 52).

In summary, the TELD-2 presents a useful measure of expressive and receptive language abilities in the areas of semantics and syntax of children aged 2-0 to 7-11 years. The Examiner's Manual, Picture Book, and Profile/Record Forms are well organized. Although the bipolar method of scoring is intended to simplify the scoring process, some subjectivity exists regarding interpreting correct versus incorrect responses. Furthermore, the method of scoring diminishes the diagnostic value of the language-related data collected, thus rendering the test a screening tool only. Taking seriously the authors' caution that results gained from the TELD-2 must be supplemented by other formal and informal measures of language including conversational language analysis, this test should prove helpful as a preliminary component of an assessment plan.

REVIEWER'S REFERENCE

Bloom, L., & Lahey, M. (1978). *Language development and language disorders*. New York: John Wiley and Sons.

[394]

Test of Early Reading Ability—Deaf or Hard of Hearing.

Purpose: Designed to measure "children's ability to attribute meaning to printed symbols, their knowledge of the alphabet and its functions, and their knowledge of the conventions of print."

Population: Deaf and hard of hearing children ages 3-0 to 13-11.

Publication Date: 1991.

Acronym: TERA-D/HH.

Scores: Total score only.

Administration: Individual.

Forms, 2: A, B.

Price Data, 1994: $124 per complete kit including picture book, 25 Form A and 25 Form B profile/examiner record forms, and manual (49 pages); $41 per picture book; $29 per 25 profile/examiner record forms (select Form A or B); $29 per manual.

Time: (20–30) minutes.

Comments: Adaptation of the Test of Early Reading Ability-2 (T4:2751).

Authors: D. Kim Reid, Wayne P. Hresko, Donald D. Hammill, and Susal Wiltshire.

Publisher: PRO-ED, Inc.

Review of the Test of Early Reading Ability—Deaf or Hard of Hearing (TERA-D/HH) by BARBARA A. ROTHLISBERG, Associate Professor of Psychology in Educational Psychology and School Psychology I Program Director, Ball State University, Muncie, IN:

Early reading behavior or emergent literacy has become an area of increasing interest given education's growing concern for early identification and intervention with children experiencing special educational needs. Acknowledging that interest, Reid, Hresko, Hammill, and Wiltshire have introduced the Test of Early Reading Ability—Deaf or Hard of Hearing (TERA-D/HH), a specialized version of the earlier Test of Early Reading Ability (2nd edition; TERA-2; T4:2751). The TERA-D/HH is designed for 3- to 13-year-old children with moderate to profound degrees of hearing loss. It can be adapted for administration using simultaneous communication or American Sign Language (ASL).

Recognizing that learning to read may be especially problematic for the auditorily challenged child, the TERA-D/HH seeks to pick out key components of early print experiences and assess children's relative competence in deriving meaning from such print symbols. Three aspects of early reading behavior are specifically addressed: constructing meaning from print, knowledge of the alphabet, and understanding print conventions. Construction of meaning encompasses a child's ability to "read" frequently encountered signs, logos, and words; relate words to one another; and understand the contextual nature of written discourse. Alphabet knowledge is defined as letter and word decoding (either orally or through sign). Finally, assessment of print conventions looks at the child's awareness of text orientation and organization (i.e., book handling, the spatial orientation of print on a page, and ability to uncover textual or print errors). The authors propose that deaf or hard-of-hearing children go through the same stages of early literacy behaviors as their hearing counterparts albeit at a different rate—hence the norms for 3- to 13-year-olds. Therefore, the intent of the TERA-D/HH includes the charting of progress in reading and the identification of children who may differ significantly from the norm in their early reading development.

The authors present a convincing rationale for their view of early reading behaviors. Linked to the literature on emergent literacy, the argument that hearing-impaired children experience print in a similar fashion to hearing children is logically made. The unknown element is in the way auditorily challenged children interpret the visual references associated with oral language. However, the TERA-D/HH evidently seeks to put children's print knowledge in a common context and identify the relative acquisition of understanding both within the auditorily challenged population and between this group and hearing children (through comparison with the TERA-2).

The administrative structure of the TERA-D/HH appears to be straightforward with specific instructions given for each item; however, examiners must have general training in assessment and interpretation as well as be proficient in the communication method employed by the student. This could include ASL, manual English, total communication, and/or finger spelling. The basic testing package includes the two forms—A and B—of the instrument printed in a back-to-back item booklet. Each form consists of 44 items scored as correct or incorrect. One point is awarded for each correct response with total raw score then converted into a percentile, *T* score, standard score (reading quotient), Normal Curve Equivalent, and/or stanine. Basal and ceiling levels are used to shorten testing time. Children 3 to 5-5 (years-months) begin with Item 1, those 5-6 to 7-5 start at Item 10, and still older students begin at Item 25. Questions are asked in ascending order until five consecutive errors are obtained (ceiling). If, in establishing a ceiling, the examinee has not obtained five consecutive *correct* responses, the examiner would then proceed to test backward from the starting point until five consecutive responses are correct or Item 1 is reached. Examples of scoring variations are provided in the manual.

Items representing the three early reading constructs (e.g., knowledge of alphabet, constructing meaning, understanding print conventions) are interspersed throughout the test although questions relating to knowledge of alphabet tend to occur earlier in the item sequence. To insure optimal performance, any item can be repeated or reworded if the concept being tested appears unclear. Attention is paid to the familiarity of particular print components. That is, several items require that the examiner select regionally appropriate logos or labels so that the questions take advantage of the child's actual experiences with print. Item instructions specify if portions of an item must be signed or presented in a prescribed way (i.e., finger spelled). Item stimuli are presented simply in a black-and-white format which may limit examinee interest in the testing situation.

The student record form is complete and easy to follow. In addition to the expected sections for scoring and listings of score conversions, this form includes a sheet which allows the examiner to picture the student's "Instructional Target Zone" by examining item performance in the three components of early reading to identify the types of concepts that might be profitably taught. This may be especially useful with early elementary-aged students because the breadth of items increases at this point.

The design of the TERA-D/HH Forms A and B appears to be adequate. Preliminary item content and categorization (as an early reading construct) were reviewed by a panel of experts to judge item quality and relevance. Items then were field tested to determine those with the best discriminating power and difficulty level. However, a limited set of items seem to be geared for the youngest age levels (under 6).

Once items had been selected, the TERA-D/HH was normed on 1,146 deaf and hard-of-hearing children dispersed across 29 states and the District of Columbia. Given the variations in this population (i.e., ethnicity, degree of hearing loss, method of teaching, etc.) the sampling seemed to be adequate. Number of cases per age level differed across the sample with the smallest number of cases occurring at the extremes (e.g., 76 children at 3 years, 71 cases at 13 years). No information was provided as to the distribution of cases (i.e., mean age of testing in years and months) within each year level or on the actual distribution of performance obtained at each age (i.e., degree of skewness).

Reliability estimates of the TERA-D/HH were established through the use of coefficient alpha and alternate form test-retest procedures. Coefficient alphas were computed for the entire standardization sample and averaged .95 for Form A and .94 for Form B suggesting a high degree of item homogeneity and the interrelation among components of early reading. Thus, although knowledge of meaning, the alphabet, and print conventions are portrayed as different constructs, they exhibited a high level of association. Alternate form test-retest reliability was conducted over a 2-week period on a limited sample of 25, 6- to 9-year-olds. The obtained correlation coefficient between Form A and B from this sample was .83. No reliability information on preschool-aged groups was included.

Evidence of test validity seemed to be the most problematic for the TERA-D/HH. Although the concept of content-related evidence of validity is aided by the use of experts to identify and structure the items used, the real test of this content is in the relation of the test to reading itself. The test items are supposed to indicate the acquisition of skills necessary and related to early reading. The number of items representing each component of early reading was not stated explicitly but can be gleaned from the pupil record form with its "Instructional Target Zone." For instance, of the 44 items on Form A, 16 were devoted to construction of meaning, 13 to knowledge of the alphabet, and 15 to knowledge of print conventions. Unfortunately, the evidence provided in support of criterion-related validity was extremely weak and basically unrelated to non-test behavior. Instead of correlating responses on the TERA-D/HH to other reading situations to determine the TERA-D/HH's relevance to instruction, only correlations relating the TERA-D/HH to the TERA-2 for a sample of eleven 7- to 9-year-olds are noted in the manual. Intuitively, this type of analysis seems better associated to preliminary evidence of construct validity (i.e., the relation of this new test to the preexisting measure purported to assess the same concepts) than it does to concurrent or criterion-related utility. Indeed, no confirmation that TERA-D/HH test scores relate to other reading measures or behaviors was provided.

Arguments for construct validity were uniformly based on small samples of older subjects. For instance, 15 students diagnosed with learning disabilities (LD) were distinguished from 13 diagnosed as mentally retarded (MR). The manual states that the average scores for the LD students were "markedly different" from the MR students; however, the small samples used may not have allowed for significant differences to be obtained.

Perhaps the bit of evidence most damaging to the TERA-D/HH utility as a measure of early reading skill is related to the tabled information (Table 4.6) in the manual on the standardization sample's mean raw score performance on the TERA-D/HH; standard deviations were not offered. According to this information the mean raw score of 3-year-olds was 1.3 (Form A) and 2.2 (Form B), of 4-year-olds was 3.5 (Form A) and 4.3 (Form B), and of 5-year-olds was 10.2 (Form A) and 10.7 (Form B). Recognizing the potential delay in acquisition of print concepts as a contributing factor, it is nevertheless sobering to see the potential lack of skill differentiation at the very ages where identification of early reading needs would seem most beneficial. For instance, what assistance can the TERA-D/HH provide to the instructional planning of a deaf 4-year, 2-month-old whose raw score on Form A was 2 but placed her at the 55th percentile? Certainly, basing the child's "reading" ability on such a limited sample of behavior may gravely misrepresent her capabilities. The TERA-D/HH did not appear to have the necessary number of simple items to establish a reasonable "floor" for analysis. Diagnosis or remedial planning based on such limited samples of items probably will not improve instructional practice for the very young.

At this point, the TERA-D/HH would be better treated as a research instrument than as an approved diagnostic tool—especially with preschoolers. The severe limitations on reliability and validity information raise serious questions regarding the measure's actual capacity to provide more than a gross and limited overview of deaf and hard-of-hearing children's recognition of print. Although the TERA-D/HH is an intriguing attempt to address a necessary assessment need, until supporting documentation can firm up the TERA-D/HH's claims of reliability and validity this instrument should not take the place of existing evaluation procedures related to early reading behavior.

Review of the Test of Early Reading Ability—Deaf or Hard of Hearing by ESTHER STAVROU TOUBANOS, School Psychologist, Lawrence Public Schools, Lawrence, NY:

The Test of Early Reading Ability—Deaf or Hard of Hearing (TERA-D/HH) is a special edition of the Test of Early Reading Ability (TERA-2; T4:2751) designed for students with sensory hearing loss. It is intended to assess early reading behaviors through three constructs: (*a*) the child's ability to attribute meaning to printed symbols, (*b*) knowledge of the alphabet and its functions, and (*c*) knowledge of the conventions employed in reading and writing English. The TERA-D/HH is not considered a readiness test but rather a measure of early literacy behaviors which "gradually evolve into standard reading and writing." The stated purposes for the TERA-D/HH are to identify students who are significantly different from peers in the early development of reading, to document a student's progress in learning to read, to serve as a measure in research projects, and to suggest instructional practices. The rationale used for the development of the test and its items is clearly stated in the manual and incorporates both theory and research.

The TERA-2 and TERA-D/HH assess the same constructs but differ in that items incompatible with sign were replaced and the wording of some directions was changed to facilitate sign interpretation. Because deaf and hard-of-hearing children generally take longer in learning to read, the upper age range was extended beyond age 9 to age 13-11. A broader age range is desirable because children with hearing loss tend to display a great deal of variability in rates and patterns of language development. The authors suggest comparing the results of TERA-D/HH with TERA-2 norms to estimate how well a deaf or hard-of-hearing student is progressing in comparison to hearing peers; however, it has not clearly been established the two tests are comparable.

The TERA-D/HH was designed to be used with simultaneous communication or American Sign Language (ASL). The authors suggest using the TERA-2 for students who rely heavily or exclusively on oral/aural communication. Examiners using the TERA-D/HH must be proficient in the administration and interpretation of assessment data as well as the use of various manual communication methods. The use of a certified interpreter is also acceptable, providing standardization is maintained. Comprehensive information is provided regarding administration conditions and procedures. Because parts of the TERA-D/HH assess students' awareness of logos and other forms of environmental print that may differ regionally, the TERA-D/HH was standardized using local variations by including examiner-made items. This unique feature could potentially cause difficulties in standardization if examiners are given too much leeway. However, specific instructions for selecting and field testing logos are provided to minimize differences among examiners.

Administration instructions and scoring criteria are conveniently contained on the record form and most responses are easily scored as either right or wrong. The basal and ceiling rules are somewhat problematic in that it is possible for a child to fail many items before attaining the basal of five consecutive correct answers, and still have them counted as correct. As a result, even though it is common for children with hearing loss to perform inconsistently, these inconsistencies within the test are ignored. This also causes practical problems in that children can reach a ceiling without having established a basal and the examiner must awkwardly move from difficult items to much easier items.

Raw scores for the total test can be converted into percentile ranks, normal curve equivalents, and reading quotients. It was surprising and refreshing to note the authors resist the temptation to include age/grade equivalents and provide a strong argument for this decision. Instructional target zones intended to pinpoint areas for direct instruction are provided. Although instructional target zones are a potential useful feature, the procedure for determining the instructional target zone is confusing and requires access to the child's mental age or conversion of an IQ using the ratio method. Considering many of the arguments against the use of the mental age, this procedure is not recommended.

The technical section of the manual is comprehensive. Technical data are also provided on the record form, although it is questionable whether this is necessary, particularly if it adds to the expense of the already costly record forms. Nevertheless, if this information is to be included on the record form, it should at least be consistent with what is stated in the manual. This is not the case.

Test items were selected based on the research literature in emergent reading behaviors, systematic observation of print available in preschooler's environments, and the literature on literacy acquisition of the deaf and hard of hearing. They were then examined by a panel of experts in both reading and hearing impairment to determine their appropriateness for inclusion. Items were validated statistically through examination of item difficulties, and item discrimination indices calculated using the point biserial correlation method. The criterion for inclusion of an item was a "conservative" .30 index of discrimination. This fairly low criterion was, according to the authors, followed "for the most part." Median item discrimination indices tended to be higher on Form A than Form B, particularly at ages 3 and 10 where the differences between the two forms are very large. This leads one to wonder if the two forms are really equivalent at these ages. Table 4.1 in the manual is difficult to interpret (at least for this reviewer) but appears to be displaying the median difficulty values for the total number of items by age. Based on this table, it appears that items of a wide variety of difficulties were included, with median values ranging from .06 to .93, depending on age and test form.

The standardization group included 1,146 children, stratified based on sex, race, ethnicity, geographic region, urban/rural residence, degree of hearing loss, and age of onset of hearing loss. All students used their customary aids during norming. Inspection of the demographic characteristics of the standardization group indicate the inclusion of children with moderate (41–70 db), severe (71–90 db), and profound (91 and above) hearing loss. The degrees of hearing loss are inconsistent with what is described in the introductory chapter, which categorizes the moderate group as having a loss of 41–62 db and severe, 63–90 db.

The percentages in the normative sample closely approximate the national percentages of deaf and hard of hearing for each variable except ethnicity, where Hispanics are underrepresented. No information is provide on how the normative group compares to the nation in their primary method of teaching. The majority of the sample used sign and speech. Because a large percentage of those with moderate hearing losses are often multiply handicapped, with associated conditions such as epilepsy, cerebral palsy, brain damage, learning disabilities, and visual impairment, it would be helpful to have information on the presence of other handicapping conditions in the normative sample.

According to the PRO-ED catalog, normative data are provided at every 6-month interval from 3-0 to 13-11. However, this is inconsistent from the norm tables which provide only 1-year intervals for age 3 and from ages 8 to 13-11. One-year intervals may be too long at age 3. The 1-year interval may not permit enough sensitivity to rapid developmental changes at this age.

Reliabilities are reported in terms of internal consistency and test-retest using alternate forms. Depending on age, coefficient alphas range from .93 to .97 (M = .95) for Form A and from .87 to .97 (M = .94) for Form B indicating strong internal consistency except for age 3. Test-retest reliabilities were calculated based on a limited sample of 25 students between the ages of 6 and 9 who were given the two alternate forms after a 2-week interval. They were inconsistently reported as .87 on the record form and .88 in the manual and are not useful for children outside the age range of 6 to 9. Given the small size of the sample, it would have been helpful to provide a description of the subjects. For the reading quotients, the mean standard errors of measurement associated with coefficient alpha were 3 (Form A) and 4 (Form B). Because the TERA-D/HH is meant to be used to measure student progress through the use of alternate forms, it would be important to report the standard errors for test-retest reliabilities. In addition, evidence of interrater reliability would be important because there may be variability among examiners in sign interpretation that could affect performance.

The authors provide arguments for content validity based on the method of item selection. Criterion-related validity was demonstrated in terms of fairly high correlations between both forms of the TERA-D/HH and their respective forms of the TERA-2. However, these correlations were based on a small group of 11 subjects, ages 7 to 9, with moderate to severe hearing loss. Support for construct validity is based on high correlations between raw score and chronological age. A low negative correlation between TERA-D/HH scores and degree of hearing loss was also reported. The TERA-D/HH correlated moderately with the Wechsler Intelligence Scale for Children—Revised (WISC-R) (.78 and .77 for Forms A and B respectively). The scores of a group of 15 learning disabled and 13 mentally retarded subjects were examined and both groups earned mean scores within the expected range.

In summary, there are few psychological and educational tests specifically normed for hearing-impaired children, and although PL 94-142 mandates appropriate assessment practices with handicapped children, practitioners are forced to conduct assessments using tests without adequate norms for the hearing impaired. Because the TERA-D/HH is the only individually administered test of its kind normed on the hearing impaired, its development is important. Its actual value is yet to be determined, however. Studies are needed to show that testing and successful intervention are linked.

The authors of the TERA-D/HH provide a comprehensive and informative manual, despite some inconsistencies. The test materials themselves, however, are dull and uninteresting for young children. The availability of two forms is helpful in documenting student progress but further evidence needs to be provided as to whether the two forms are truly equivalent. In addition, there appear to be serious floor and ceiling effects for children at the lower and upper age ranges of the test. For example, on Form A it is not possible for a 3-year-old to earn a score lower than 89 even if every item is failed. If the child gets just two items correct, he or she earns a score of 109, placing that child in the high average range. Similar ceiling effects are noted. Given the authors' goal of identifying children who are delayed or gifted, this is a serious limitation.

The authors appropriately recommend supplementing test results with observational information. In addition, because variable performance is the rule rather than the exception for children with hearing loss, one needs to use multiple instruments in assessments. Users of the TERA-D/HH may also want to supplement the results with those from criterion-referenced tests.

[395]

Test of Economic Literacy, Second Edition.

Purpose: Designed to "evaluate a student's performance and make decisions about economics instruction at the senior high school level."
Population: Grades 11–12.
Publication Dates: 1978–87.
Acronym: TEL.
Scores: Total score only.
Administration: Group.
Forms, 2: A, B.
Price Data: Price information available from publisher for test materials including examiner's manual ('87, 76 pages).
Time: (40–50) minutes.
Comments: Revision of the Test of Economic Understanding ('64).
Authors: John C. Soper and William B. Walstad.
Publisher: National Council on Economic Education.
Cross References: For a review by Anna S. Ochoa, see 9:1256; see also T2:1968 (19 references); for reviews by Edward J. Furst and Christine H. McGuire, and an excerpted review by Robert L. Ebel, see 7:901 (10 references).

Review of the Test of Economic Literacy, Second Edition by JENNIFER J. FAGER, Assistant Professor of Teacher Education, University of New Hampshire at Manchester, Manchester, NH:

Forms A and B of the Test of Economic Literacy each contain 46 items for testing 11th and 12th grade students. The Second Edition of the test replaces the outdated First Edition of the Test of Economic Literacy published in 1978–79. The Table of Specifications that formed the framework for item development was based on recommendations from the 1984 Joint Council on Economic Education. The Council, in its Master Curriculum Guide *Framework*, recommended changes be made from the First Edition to include a greater emphasis on international economics concepts as well as changes in the fundamental and macroeconomics concept listings.

The test questions were drawn from four content categories and utilized five cognitive levels of Bloom's taxonomy: knowledge, comprehension, application, analysis, and evaluation. The four content categories representing 22 subcategories include: (*a*) Fundamental Economic Concepts, (*b*) Microeconomic Concepts, (*c*) Macroeconomic Concepts, and (*d*) International Economic Concepts. The test makers gave careful consideration to the structure of the test, which combined content and cognitive operations in producing a variety of questions.

The test writers have attended closely to the issues of reliability and validity. In terms of reliability they report a coefficient of .87 on Form A and .88 on Form B (Cronbach alpha). In addition they report a standard error of measurement of about 3.0 for both forms. The authors also examined the stability of the test over time, and after an administration of Form A to a sample of the population, they found a Pearson correlation coefficient of .85 indicating a stable instrument.

The test developers exercised great care on the issue of validity. To help insure content validity a large number of test items were created by a test development committee consisting of university economists and high school economics teachers. The items were then reviewed by the National Advisory Committee for relevancy to modern economic concepts. In addition, attention was given to the readability level as well as basic psychometric constructs. A reading expert was employed to examine the tests for reading levels appropriate for high school juniors and seniors and a psychometric consultant examined the forms and assisted the test developers in creating parallel forms of the test. In short, the test developers took appropriate measures to make certain the instruments measured what the economists, economics educators, and secondary school teachers of economics believed to be appropriate, while attending to basic test construction concepts.

The test developers suggest the primary value of the Test of Economic Literacy is to help assess students' understanding of basic economic concepts. Specific guidelines are included in the Examiner's Manual for Interpretation of the test results as well as uses of the test. The test developers caution that teachers who disagree with the content or the objectives emphasized by the Test of Economic Literacy might not find this a valid test.

It is a challenge for test developers to create an instrument to measure concepts without first developing a set of objectives for the content to be measured. The test developers of the Test of Economic Literacy attended to both content and measurement issues to create a test that is valid and reliable for any basic economics course. The test is not timed; however, the 46-question format is designed to be used in a traditional 40–50-minute secondary school classroom. Given the limited number of questions I believe the authors have accomplished the task of creating a test representative of appropriate content in basic economics. By altering the categories from the First Edition of the Test of Economic Literacy to include items with a greater emphasis in international economics concepts the test developers have also identified current trends in economics and have adjusted the curriculum and thus the test accordingly.

The Examiner's Manual contains appropriate uses for the Test of Economic Literacy that include pretesting, posttesting, and testing during instruction. These uses are clearly stated and allow for little misinterpretation for the test user. In addition, norming data are provided for use in various courses. The test developers suggest the test can be used for a variety of courses that might include specific economics or units within a social studies course. The authors also provide item-by-item information for use in courses that only teach a portion of the content identified in the curriculum guide for which the test is based. I found this data especially helpful in interpreting scores.

The test seems to be free from bias. Norms are presented on culturally different populations based on the extensive norming process the test developers used in creating the final version of the exam. Many of the cells are small and the test developers suggest caution be used when interpreting data on specific characteristics.

Overall, the Test of Economic Literacy is a strong one for use in courses adhering to the content specified in the curriculum guide developed by the National Advisory Council. No questions can be raised regarding the reliability of the tests. The validity of the test is insured by the great care the developers used in creating a sample of items basic to introductory economics. A teacher who agrees with the content outlined in the curriculum guide would be well served by this test.

Review of the Test of Economic Literacy, Second Edition by DAN WRIGHT, School Psychologist, Wyandotte Comprehensive Special Education Cooperative, Kansas City, KS:

Construction of the Second Edition of the Test of Economic Literacy was necessitated by changes in the Master Curriculum Guide developed by the Joint Council on Economic Education, with which it is aligned. As was its predecessor, the Second Edition is composed of two alternate forms, each with 46 items. These now correspond to 22 discrete, basic economic concepts in the following categories: (*a*) Fundamental Economic Concepts, (*b*) Microeconomic Concepts, (*c*) Macroeconomic Concepts, and (*d*) International Economic Concepts. As with its predecessor, items are written to tap five levels of Bloom's Taxonomy: knowledge, comprehension, application, analysis, and evaluation. Synthesis is again omitted as impractical for a multiple-choice format, and as generally unnecessary in a test at the high school level.

The Second Edition has been developed with the same care and attention to detail that distinguished its predecessor (see Ochoa, 1985 for a review). More than 8,000 students from 212 high schools in 41 states participated in the norming, and an interesting breakdown of results by gender, ethnicity, geographic region, and more is provided. Cronbach's alpha for the two forms is reported at .87 and .88, and standard errors of measurement are 3.06 and 3.04, again establishing very satisfactory reliability. Content validity is evidenced by the meticulous process of item construction and review. Construct validity is supported by comparison of results within the normative group of students with and without previous economics instruction. Concurrent validity is supported by small studies comparing the Second Edition with the First, and with a published test of college economics. The aggregate evidence for validity is satisfactory.

In her review of the previous edition, Ochoa (1985) offered two suggestions and one concern which appear to have been at least partially addressed in the present edition. Although the altered structure of the test makes it difficult to determine, it appears that items have been added dealing with concepts for evaluating economic activities and policies (these no longer compose a distinct category); there definitely is significantly more attention devoted to the world economy. Ochoa's concern dealt with the possibility of cultural bias, and it was suggested that norms be examined for culturally different groups. The present edition presents such information, and it appears that there are, indeed, significant differences among the groups represented. Such differences are not conclusive of bias, but leave this topic as one deserving further, serious attention in future editions.

In summary, the Test of Economic Literacy is a solid instrument which appears to be an improvement of a worthy predecessor. Although the topic of bias remains of potential concern, it remains a well-developed, comprehensive test of economics knowledge at the high school level.

REVIEWER'S REFERENCE

Ochoa, A. S. (1985). [Review of the Test of Economic Literacy.] In J. V. Mitchell, Jr. (Ed.), *The ninth mental measurements yearbook* (pp. 1567-1568). Lincoln, NE: Buros Institute of Mental Measurements.

[396]

Test of Learning Ability.

Purpose: Constructed to assess spatial, verbal, and numerical ability.
Population: Industrial and business applicants.
Publication Dates: 1947–89.
Scores: Total score only.
Administration: Group.
Forms, 2: S89, T89.
Price Data: Available from publisher.
Time: 12 minutes.
Comments: Previously known as RBH Test of Learning Ability.
Authors: Richardson, Bellows, Henry & Co., Inc.
Publisher: Richardson, Bellows, Henry & Co., Inc.
Cross References: See T3:1984 (1 reference) and T2:44 (1 reference); for a review by Erwin K. Taylor, see 7:379 (2 references); see also 6:504 (2 references).

Review of the Test of Learning Ability by SUE M. LEGG, Associate Director, Office of Instructional Resources, University of Florida, Gainesville, FL:

The Test of Learning Ability, drawn from the Army General Classification Test item pool, was first published in 1947. It includes 54 items that are to be completed in 12 minutes. Three skills are represented: vocabulary, arithmetic reasoning, and spatial reasoning. These skills are spiraled in sets of three items of ascending difficulty. The current revision updates the content in arithmetic due to change in prices, etc., and scrambles the item order. No substantive changes in computational operations were made. No mention was made of any changes in the vocabulary items.

The reliability and validity information included in the manual is based on the previous Forms S and T. Research is underway on the new forms (S89 and T89), but because the changes are primarily cosmetic, the publishers state that the comparability of the item statistics supports their contention that the two forms will operate in a similar fashion.

Reliability was calculated on Forms S and T for black-white groups with Kuder-Richardson 20 formula coefficients ranging from .87 to .95. Mean scores for minority examinees were lower than for white examinees even when black examinees' years of schooling were equal to or greater than years of schooling for white examinees. Nine studies of male-female comparisons in which the sexes were matched on years of schooling indicated that males scored slightly higher than females. The fact that there was an overlap of 94% in the distribution of scores is offered as justification for the lack of separate norms.

A substantial number of validity studies were reported in which correlations with other achievement tests tended to be in the .68–.71 range, and correlations with more vocationally oriented paper-and-pencil tests generally ranged in the low .50s. Validity was based on correlations with performance appraisal, ranking, or training grades that were generally in the low .20 to mid .35 range with occasional studies reporting coefficients as high as .62.

Test battery validation studies were conducted to explore the improvement in validity when the RBH Test of Learning Ability was combined with other achievement tests. The validity coefficient for the Refinery and Chemical Plant Worker study was the lowest at .18 based on three tests weighted equally and the validity coefficient for the Refinery Controlman and Operator Employees was highest at .63.

The publishers may be commended for the amount of reliability and validity information included in the manual. In addition, a norms table based on over 63,000 examinees is provided. Missing is a description of how the test is used. Only a reference to the original purpose of the U.S. Army General Classification Test is made. If this test stands alone as a requirement for selection to the many technical and trade schools in the Army, then these decisions are based not on any special ability for a particular trade, but on skills related to block counting, arithmetic word problems, and vocabulary. The rationale for using the Learning Ability Test as a measure for predicting success in various occupations is not stated. The American Psychological Association *Standards* state that the following standard for criterion-related validity is essential:

> All criterion measures should be described accurately, and the rationale for choosing them as relevant criterion should be made explicit . . . . When appropriate attention should be drawn to significant aspects of performance that the criterion measure does not reflect. (AERA, APA, & NCME, 1985: Standard 1.12)

With regard to content validity, the *Standards* also declare essential the "clear definition of the universe represented" (AERA, APA, & NCME, 1985; Standard 1.6). Why these three skills have been included in the Test of Learning Ability, why the Test is so clearly speeded, and what job analyses indicate that these are the essential skills, are questions not explained. There may be an assumption upon which this test is based that has not been revealed.

The Test of Learning Ability is a novel test, in a way. It requires the examinee to constantly shift between one skill and the next. The increase in difficulty is apparent and challenging. It may well select examinees who have strong basic literacy skills. It is less clear that it is sufficient for a vocational aptitude test.

REVIEWER'S REFERENCE

American Educational Research Association, American Psychological Association, & National Council on Measurement in Education. (1985). *Standards for educational and psychological testing.* Washington, DC: American Psychological Association, Inc.

Review of the Test of Learning Ability by VICTOR L. WILLSON, Professor of Educational Psychology, Texas A&M University, College Station, TX:

The Test of Learning Ability (TLA) is a simple 54-item multiple-choice test intended for use in job selection for lower level industrial and business applicants. The test consists of items alternating among verbal definitions, simple arithmetic problems, and line drawings of stacks of blocks. For the latter the test taker is to count the number of blocks, inferring the number hidden by the perspective of the drawing. The test allows 12 minutes and can be completed in significantly less time. Two parallel forms are provided, Forms S89 and T89. The items appear parallel for the two forms, with increasing difficulty apparent. The reviewer took Form T and missed three items, all block drawings toward the end of the test. All three items could be interpreted in several ways due to the drawings, and seem to be the weakest aspect of the test. The items may contribute somewhat to error at upper score levels but are unlikely to affect significantly overall scores.

Reported internal consistency coefficients are at or above .87 for both forms. Several race studies are reported in the technical manual. Black test takers scored significantly below whites on both forms, whereas reliabilities for blacks were higher than for whites, significantly higher on Form S89 (calculated by the reviewer using the F test for independent reliabilities). Gender differences were reported for nine studies. Males scored higher than females in seven of the studies, and the meta-analytic effect size (calculated by the reviewer) is .16. Although not large, it is consistent, equivalent to about one item on the test. Given the reported consistent differences in spatial performance favoring men, it seems appropriate to attribute the net effect to the block items, although no data are reported on the subgroups of items.

Extensive validity research is presented on tens of thousands of applicants and workers in a variety of industrial and business settings. Correlations with other achievement tests show fairly consistent correlations in the .5 to .7 range. This is to be expected because verbal and mathematics achievement are tested on both the Test of Learning Ability and the criterion tests. The flatness of the correlation range can also be attributed in part to the presence of the spatial ability items, which probably attenuate correlations of the total score with school achievement. Correlations with mechanical reasoning tests are in the .4–.5 range typically, also supporting the point made above.

Concurrent validities using job performance appraisals and rankings are presented and are impressive for the extent and variety of research conducted. Correlations corrected for attenuation are presented for studies in which there was selection contamination. Although correlations range from .1 to .6 (uncorrected), with a few negative values, the great majority of correlations are above .2, with quite a few in the .3 to .5 range. This appears quite good, given the unreliability of the criterion measures.

Finally, a number of studies are reported in which the Test of Learning Abilities was included as part of a test battery for performance validation. Although not usually the highest correlation, given the length of the test the TLA performed creditably across the studies.

As a quick screening test the TLA performs well. A wealth of information has been compiled about it since its development from the World War II Army General Classification Test. The primary issue for such a test in 1993 (when this review was written) is whether it has outlived its form, given that we know about learning and intellectual functioning.

To a great extent the TLA looks like a short form of a group intelligence test that might be constructed from a much longer battery. Verbal ability is represented by the 18 definition items. Arithmetic usually loads on the verbal scale for most intelligence tests, and the 18 arithmetic items are highly verbally loaded because each problem is stated verbally. Finally, nonverbal intelligence is represented by the block counting items.

From a theoretical perspective the verbal items tend to pick up crystallized intellectual functioning, generally dependent on schooling. The spatial test taps ability not particularly trainable, so that the sum of the items produces a score weighted toward schooling but not entirely schooling related. No construct validity evidence is presented to show how these parts work, together or separately. For the same number of items one could gain a broader assessment of intellectual functioning through inclusion of areas such as verbal analogies, that assess fluid verbal intellectual functioning, and figural analogies, that will assess fluid nonverbal intellectual functioning. Both types of items have been prominent in modern theories and studies of intellectual functioning.

The authors are encouraged to systematically investigate inclusion of such items to broaden the base for assessment. It would appear that the same length and time limits could be retained, with potential improvement in the validities, through broadening the conceptual base for the test.

The Test of Learning Ability has a dated name. It assesses selected areas of school curriculum and spatial ability. The test has a durability clearly evident due to its simplicity and ease of use in screening for lower level industrial and business employment. It exhibits small systematic gender differences and a dated conglomerate of items. The authors should begin to revise and update this test to bring it more closely into the mainstream of modern intelligence tests.

[397]

Test of Oral Structures and Functions.

Purpose: "Assesses oral structures and motor integrity during verbal and nonverbal oral functioning."
Population: Ages 7–Adults.
Publication Date: 1986.
Acronym: TOSF.
Scores, 16: Speech Survey (Articulation, Rate/Prosody, Fluency, Voice, Total); Verbal Oral Functioning (Resonance, Balance, Sequenced Syllables, Mixed Syllable Sequence, Sequenced Vowels, Sequenced Syllable Rates, Total); Nonverbal Oral Functions (Isolated Functioning, Sequenced Functioning); Survey of Orofacial Structures; History-Behavioral Survey.
Administration: Individual.
Price Data, 1992: $60 per TOSF complete kit including manual (36 pages), 25 test booklets, finger cots, tongue blades, penlight, and balloons; $22.50 per examiner's manual; $25 per 25 test booklets; $6 per oroscope penlight.
Time: (20) minutes.
Author: Gary J. Vitali.
Publisher: Slosson Educational Publications, Inc.

Review of the Test of Oral Structures and Functions by RONALD B. GILLAM, Assistant Professor of Speech Communication, The University of Texas at Austin, Austin, TX:

According to the author, the Test of Oral Structures and Functions (TOSF) can be used for screening, diagnosis, evaluation of treatment efficacy, assistance with caseload management decisions, and prosthesis evaluation for examinees who are 7 years of age or older. However, it is difficult to imagine how any test could adequately serve such a wide variety of purposes for such a wide range of ages (see McCauley & Swisher, 1984; Salvia & Ysseldyke, 1988), and the author fails to explain how many of these potential applications can be accomplished.

The TOSF is divided into five sections: Speech Survey, Verbal Oral Functioning, Nonverbal Oral Functioning, Orofacial Structures, and an optional History/Behavioral Survey. Each section has separate norms and can be administered individually. In addition to the manual and a score form, administration requires tongue blades, finger cots, a pen light, balloons, a stop watch, a glass of water, a drinking straw, and crackers or a similar food. Examiners rate responses to most test items as normal (0), inconsistently in error (1), or consistently in error (2). Thus, higher raw scores represent increased problems.

To complete Part I, Speech Survey, the examiner converses with the examinee for at least 5 minutes, then rates the consistency of difficulties with various aspects of articulation, rate/prosody, fluency, and voice. As with most sections of this test, specific scoring criteria are very general, so scoring decisions require a great deal of clinical judgment. Errors that are judged to occur less than 75% of the time are marked as inconsistent; errors that are judged to occur 75% of the time or more are marked as consistent.

In Part II, Verbal Oral Functioning, the examiner evaluates resonance, vowel accuracy, rate, and prosody. Elicited productions of sentences such as "Bob likes chocolate cake" (p. 2, test form) are scored for presence of hypernasality, nasal assimilation, visible valving, nasal emissions, glottal stops, pharyngeal fricatives, and hyponasality. Imitated productions of sequenced syllables (papapa) and trisyllables (basawa basawa) are judged for syllable and vowel production accuracy, rate, and prosody. The examiner also evaluates the examinee's production of sequences of vowels. In the only timed task in the battery, the examiner records the number of seconds required to produce 20 consecutive targeted syllables (pa, ba, sa, za). Separate norms are available for this diadochokinetic task.

Part III, Nonverbal Oral Functioning, concerns the performance of isolated and sequenced oral functions. Tasks such as repeatedly puckering one's lips and elevating the tongue (isolated functions), and quickly moving the tongue from right to left and sucking from a straw (sequenced functions) are rated for level of difficulty (unremarkable, minimal difficulty, marked difficulty). For many of the tasks, guidelines for differentiating between difficulty levels are circular. For example, minimal difficulty is defined as performance that is "minimally or inconsistently abnormal"; marked difficulty is defined as performance that is "abnormal" (p. 6).

The examiner rates the degree of anomaly of orofacial structures in Part IV, Survey of Orofacial Structures. As with previous sections, insufficient information is provided to help the examiner determine whether an anomaly is mild or marked. A marked anomaly is defined as, "A marked degree of anomaly on any one listed observation or mild anomalies on two or more listed observations per structure targeted" (p. 9).

Part V, History/Behavioral Survey, is a list of questions that are checked for presence or absence on the basis of examinee responses or examiner observation. Questions concern such topics as speech difficulties; speech anxiety; knowledge of speech, hearing, or vision difficulties; and prior history of various kinds of disorders.

Total scores for each subtest are converted to scaled scores that represent the proportion of persons with known impairment who obtained a particular raw score. Given the subjective nature of many of the scoring decisions, generalizability across scorers could be a problem. However, the author reports median interrater correlation coefficients of .96 for the Speech Survey and Survey of Oral Structures subtests. Interrater correlations were not reported for the Verbal Oral Functioning and Nonverbal Oral Functioning subtests. Coefficient alpha values of .95 and .89 were reported for these subtests, indicating an appropriate degree of internal consistency.

The majority of the manual is devoted to test interpretation as it relates to differential diagnosis. Subtest performance patterns are presented to assist with differential diagnosis of dysarthria, apraxia, Broca's aphasia, velopharyngeal insufficiency, velopharyngeal incompetence, and functional articulation disorder. Unfortunately, it is difficult to judge the credibility of the performance profiles. The normative sample included 175 individuals who represented "client groups" (p. 32), but there is no information about the specific constitution of this sample. It would certainly be useful to know how the six diagnostic categories were represented in the sample of disordered individuals. Further, factor analysis and/or discriminant function analyses could have been performed to demonstrate the reliability and validity of the performance profiles.

In summary, the TOSF provides a system for scoring structural and functional aspects of the speech mechanism. The majority of the tasks are similar to those found on other speech mechanism instruments. This test is normed, but the manual does not provide enough information about the standardization sample for prospective users to judge adequately the strength of the norms. The test's major strength, the performance profiles, may also be its major weakness because the author does not provide evidence of their reliability or validity.

REVIEWER'S REFERENCES

McCauley, R. J., & Swisher, L. (1984). Use and misuse of norm-referenced tests in clinical assessment: A hypothetical case. *Journal of Speech and Hearing Disorders*, *49*, 338-348.

Salvia, J., & Ysseldyke, J. E. (1988). *Assessment in special and remedial education*. Boston: Houghton Mifflin.

Review of the Test of Oral Structures and Functions by ROGER L. TOWNE, Assistant Professor of Speech Pathology and Audiology, Illinois State University, Normal, IL:

PURPOSE. The Test of Oral Structures and Functions (TOSF), as purported by the author, can be used as a screening, diagnostic, and pre- and posttreatment assessment of oral structures and functions. The test is designed to be administered to anyone 7 years of age and older who has the ability to be a cooperative participant. Because "neurological and structural disorders of the oral-speech mechanism do not manifest themselves in a continuous fashion" (pp. 30–31) the TOSF generates scores that suggest oral structures and functions to be normal or abnormal.

ADMINISTRATION, SCORING, AND INTERPRETATION. Administration of the TOSF requires materials such as tongue blades, a stop watch, and a drinking straw, which are included in the complete TOSF test kit or must be purchased separately. There are five subtests in the TOSF. Subtest 1, Speech Survey, assesses articulation, rate/prosody, fluency, and voice during spontaneous or elicited discourse. Subtest 2, Verbal Oral Functioning, includes tasks that systematically assess resonance and articulation sequencing via sentence repetition, syllable and vowel sequencing, and sequenced syllable rates (diadochokinesis). Subtest 3, Nonverbal Oral Functioning, includes tasks that assess volitional and nonvolitional oral functioning both on isolated and sequencing tasks. Subtest 4, Orofacial Structures, surveys intraoral and orofacial structures at rest. Finally, Subtest 5, History/Behavioral Survey, is an optional questionnaire of possible co-occurring behaviors.

Scoring involves a cutoff approach in which scores are used to reach conclusions regarding the relative normality of oral structures and functions. Individual items in tasks for Subtests 1–4 are assigned scores in which points are given only for responses that indicate a problem: (*a*) 0 points for normal structure or function, (*b*) 1 point for inconsistent error rates, and (*c*) 2 points for consistent error rates. A total score is then calculated for each task and the task scores are then summed to attain a score for each subtest. Subtest raw scores are entered in the TOSF profile and converted to scaled scores. Using scaled scores the performance of each subtest is identified as being unremarkable, borderline, impaired, or markedly impaired.

Interpretation of the TOSF involves assessing the relative patterning of subtest performance rather than the magnitude of individual subtest scores. As the author notes, differential diagnosis based on TOSF performance requires the examiner to have a "fundamental understanding of oral structures and functions, and disorders which compromise their functioning" (p. 13). To assist in interpretation, expected TOSF Profiles of six classic disorders are provided. These disorders represent classes of structural, functional, or neuromotor problems and include dysarthria, acquired and developmental apraxia, Broca (expressive) aphasia, velopharyngeal insufficiency, velopharyngeal incompetence, and functional articulation disorder.

EVALUATION OF TEST ADEQUACY. Due to the author's premise that the characteristics measured by the TOSF are not normally distributed, non-parametric statistics were used to establish validity and reliability. Validity was established using the Wilcoxon Rank Sum statistic between test scores of 379 persons predicted to have high scores and those predicted to have low scores. Z-scores ranged from 3.03 to 13.89 and all were significant at $p<.01$. Reliability was established for interexaminer agreement using correlations and coefficient alpha. Interexaminer agreement ranged between .89 and .96 for Subtests 1–4. For the purposes to which this test was designed, it appears to have sufficient construct validity and reliability for examiners to have confidence in the results.

Organization of the TOSF follows the established format of examining both the structure and function of orofacial and intraoral structures. The test is relatively short and, therefore, should not require an undue amount of time to administer or score. The test booklet is well organized, easy to follow, and designed to facilitate testing and scoring. Space also is provided for recording observations other than those specified by the subtest items.

There are, however, some inherent weaknesses of the TOSF that can potentially limit its usefulness. Although its short lengths can be an asset, it also limits the author's contention the test can be used as a diagnostic tool. Notable exclusions include measures of lip, tongue, and mandibular muscle strength, volitional versus reflexive movements, and tests for tongue evaluation with mandibular fixation. These and other behaviors have important diagnostic implications.

The use of the 3-point scoring system is a valid attempt to quantify differences in behaviors that are usually described or simply noted as occurring. However, such quantification has limited diagnostic usefulness. As acknowledged by the author, "when using the TOSF for diagnostic purposes . . . no single type of dysfunction or degree of severity is of itself pathognomonic of a specific diagnostic label" (p. 13). This caveat should also extend to the scores obtained on the individual subtests; it is still the qualitative differences in the patterns of behavior that one must rely on for an accurate diagnosis. Quantification of these behaviors does not appear to facilitate this process.

SUMMARY. The TOSF is a relatively short and easy-to-administer test that probably should best be considered an advanced screening tool. Although a considerable amount of useful information regarding oral structure and function can be obtained, additional information should be gathered before making a diagnosis. A more extensive and time-consuming diagnostic test is the Dworkin-Culatta Oral Mechanism Examination (Dworkin & Culatta, 1980). However, for non-diagnostic purposes the shorter, less time-consuming TOSF would be a reasonable compromise between a structured and nonstructured oral-motor assessment.

REVIEWER'S REFERENCE

Dworkin, J. P., & Culatta, R. A. (1980). Dworkin-Culatta Oral Mechanism Examination. Nicholasville, KY: Edgewood Press.

[398]

Test of Pragmatic Language.

Purpose: Designed "to provide an in-depth screening of the effectiveness and appropriateness of a student's pragmatic, or social, language skills."
Population: Ages 5-0 to 13-11.
Publication Date: 1992.
Acronym: TOPL.
Scores, 3: Listening Skills, Speaking Skills, Total.
Administration: Individual.
Price Data, 1994: $84 per complete kit; $29 per examiner's manual (35 pages); $29 per TOPL picture book; $29 per 25 TOPL profile/examiner record forms.
Time: (45) minutes.
Authors: Diana Phelps-Terasaki and Trisha Phelps-Gunn.
Publisher: PRO-ED, Inc.

Review of the Test of Pragmatic Language by SALVADOR HECTOR OCHOA, Assistant Professor of Educational Psychology, Texas A&M University, College Station, TX:

The Test of Pragmatic Language (TOPL) is designed to assess a student's ability to use language in social contexts. The TOPL was constructed to fit a model of pragmatic language developed by the test authors.

The standardization sample of the TOPL has many strengths. First, the sample was obtained from 24 states and the Ontario province. The standardization sample is representative of the U.S. population with respect to gender, urban/rural, ethnicity, and geographical location. A sufficient number of students were included for ages 5 to 11. An insufficient number of students were obtained at age 12 ($n = 77$) and at age 13 ($n = 62$). The TOPL provides the following normative scores: quotient scores (mean = 100, SD = 15), percentile ranks, and age equivalents.

With respect to reliability, the manual contains information only about internal consistency and interrater reliability. The TOPL's overall internal consistency coefficient alpha of .82 is good. Acceptable coefficient alphas were obtained for all ages except for age 6, which has a coefficient of .74. The coefficient alphas reported for each age group, however, were not obtained using the entire standardization sample but rather with 50 subjects at each age level. The authors provided no rationale why they deleted over half of the standardization sample ($n = 566$) when calculating the overall and age level coefficient alphas. The interrater reliability coefficient of .99 reported in the manual is more than acceptable. The manual, however, did not include any information pertaining to test-retest reliability.

Three major types of validity are addressed. With respect to content validity, the TOPL has a good theoretical model that consists of two context (physical and audience) and four message (topic, purpose, visual, and abstraction) variables. The extent to which and how well these six variables are assessed by the TOPL is difficult to ascertain given the authors' failure to include a blueprint indicating how each of the 44 items relate to these six variables. The two item selection procedures conducted prior to the final version ensured that all items had acceptable discrimination and difficulty levels. Acceptable levels of discrimination and difficulty were reported at each age level for the final TOPL version. The test authors, however, used only 50 subjects per age level rather than the entire standardization sample. Criterion-related validity of the TOPL is not well established. A coefficient of .82 between teacher ratings of pragmatic language and TOPL scores is reported, but the number of subjects in this study was small ($n = 30$). Moreover, little information is given on how teachers rated students' pragmatic skills. Construct validity is supported via age differentiation. Additionally, the TOPL was correlated with the Screening Children for Related Early Educational Needs (SCREEN) language test, school achievement, and the Scholastic Aptitude Scale (SAS). Although these validity coefficients were in the acceptable range, the sample for each of the studies was small (30 or below).

The test manual is well written and organized. The drawings in the test booklet are appropriate except for Items 20 and 28. Item 20 shows an album being played and Item 28 shows children building snowmen. Albums are no longer produced and, thus, may not be appropriate for young children. Children in some geographical locations may not have seen snow or be able to relate to snowmen. The scoring information criteria provided in the test protocol is straightforward.

The TOPL has a theoretical basis, strong norming procedures, and acceptable reliability. Its straightforward scoring procedures are a strength given that other language instruments are either difficult or ambiguous in this area. Additional and/or more extensive validity studies, however, are warranted. The TOPL is comparable to other frequently used language instruments in the field. This instrument should be used with other related measures when assessing children's language skills.

Review of the Test of Pragmatic Language by WILLIAM K. WILKINSON, Assistant Professor of Counseling and Educational Psychology, New Mexico State University, Las Cruces, NM:

Although most would agree the construct social language and communicative competence is an important area of individual differences, its formal measurement remains underdeveloped. Essentially, this is the purpose for the Test of Pragmatic Language (TOPL), a 44-item, individually administered instrument designed to measure an individual's understanding of the social context of language.

The TOPL is nicely packaged, and includes a well-organized examiner's manual (with technical and administrative information), a picture book for item administration, and a profile/examiner record form. As indicated in the manual, the test was normed on school-aged children in grades K–9, with corresponding ages of 5–12 (although standard score conversions exist for age 13). Elsewhere in the manual, the authors suggest the TOPL can be used with adolescents and adults exhibiting language or behavior difficulties. Yet, it is unclear which conversion age one would use to get a derived score for, for example, a 24-year-old aphasic (13-year-old? clinical judgment?).

Administratively, the authors suggest the test can be given by teachers, speech and language pathologists, and those in the mental health fields. The TOPL does seem simple to administer and score, with verbatim instructions clearly printed on the record form, and scorable responses listed directly adjacent to the stimulus instructions. Several pieces of information I would have included, however, in the administrative section are (*a*) the need to administer all items, and (*b*) a better caution to the examiner about accidentally administering a picture number instead of the item number, because not all items have corresponding pictures (8 of the 44 items do not have pictures).

Regarding the technical development of the TOPL, the authors present a well-organized and simple discussion of item statistics, normative sample, and reliability and validity data. In fact, in some places, especially regarding item statistics, the information is overly simplified and needs to be discussed further (e.g., the number of items dropped at each field test, why the discriminating power of items dramatically rises for the sample of 13-year-olds, why items are more difficult for the 5-year-old sample, etc.).

The TOPL normative sample was selected according to national census statistics for school-aged children with respect to age, residence, race, geographic region, and ethnicity. The resultant sample of 1,016 participants, selected from 24 states, does appear nationally representative. A nice feature of the TOPL is the basic categories of derived scores are all tabled in the examiner's manual, and include (*a*) a standard score conversion in the form of a quotient with a mean of 100 and an D of 15, (*b*) an area conversion (percentile rank), and (*c*) a developmental conversion (age equivalent).

Reliability data, in the form of internal consistency and interscorer, meet adequate standards. With respect to internal consistency, the authors incorrectly applied Cronbach's alpha to dichotomous items (instead of the Kuder-Richardson formula). Alpha is intended primarily for multipoint items (cf. Ebel & Frisbie, 1991). Interscorer reliability is excellent, but it was reported only between the two test authors. It would be interesting to see the interscorer reliability between the field testers. Perhaps in future publications these data will be forthcoming.

Most of the validity section is devoted to construct validity; apparently, the TOPL shows differential population validity, for example, raw score means go up by age, and those identified with language difficulties score significantly below the normative sample. Convergent validity evidence is via correlations with other measures of language, verbal abilities, and mental abilities.

The one aspect of the TOPL that concerned me (despite the authors' disclaimer on p. 19) was the consistent mention of it as a diagnostic test. For example, throughout the manual, assertions are made the test provides information regarding the six core areas of pragmatic language—physical setting, audience, topic, purpose, visual-gestural, and abstraction. Subsequently, the remainder of the introduction (roughly nine pages) is devoted to elaborating these core areas. In fact, the TOPL supposedly yields six scores because the inside of the record form reveals that item sets are totaled to yield scores (called subtotal a through f). Finally, the first page introducing the conversion table is given as, "Normative Scores for Subtests and Composites" (p. 29).

Clearly, the TOPL is marketed as a diagnostic test. Yet, there is not one sliver of technical information nor one conversion table regarding these six separate areas. In fact, the separate subtest scores supposedly derived on the test record form are not even mentioned in the manual chapters on scoring, interpretation, or technical information. The only score noted is the overall TOPL score (simply given as the sum of correct responses), and this is the only score that can be converted using the conversion tables. Indeed, the front of the record form provides no space for profiling the "elusive" six core areas.

One final point along these lines relates to content validity. Clearly, the authors go to great lengths to provide a model by which the item content on the TOPL was apparently derived. Yet, it is not at all clear what items on the final version of the test correspond to what aspects of the model. For example, is the first item related to school setting, audience of one other peer with an excited mood(?), topic(?), the purpose of which is a request? The test developers present a thorough model, and the model is apparently relevant to item selection but they do not specify which items are relevant to which parts of the model. Such a detailed analysis makes sense if, as the authors suggest, the TOPL can be used as an initial screen (another contradiction to its diagnostic use) to determine exactly what type of pragmatic language area needs further assessment.

In sum, I am suggesting that the TOPL does one thing well—it gives an overall index of pragmatic language. The instrument is *not diagnostic*, but rather, provides an overall screen regarding social use of language.

REVIEWER'S REFERENCE

Ebel, R. L., & Frisbie, D. A. (1991). *Essentials of educational measurement.* Engelwood Cliffs, NJ: Prentice Hall.

[399]

Test of Word Finding in Discourse.

Purpose: Designed to assess children's word-finding skills in discourse.
Population: Ages 6-6 to 12-11.
Publication Date: 1991.
Acronym: TWFD.
Scores, 2: Productivity Index, Word-Finding Behaviors Index.
Administration: Individual.
Price Data, 1992: $78.90 per complete test including manual (173 pages) and 25 test record forms; $25 per 25 test record forms.
Time: (15–20) minutes.
Author: Diane J. German.
Publisher: The Riverside Publishing Co.
Cross References: See T4:2800 (1 reference).

Review of the Test of Word Finding in Discourse by JAMES DEAN BROWN, Associate Professor of Applied Linguistics, Department of English as a Second Language, University of Hawaii at Manoa, Honolulu, HI:

"By definition, children with word-finding problems have difficulty naming target words in the presence of good comprehension of those words" (manual, p. 7). The Test of Word Finding in Discourse (TWFD) is designed to measure this construct in conjunction with the Test of Word Finding (TWF; German, 1986; T4:2799). The TWFD assesses word-finding abilities in a discourse context, whereas the TWF does the same in constrained naming contexts. Both tests together can be used to diagnose word-finding problems.

The TWFD manual covers the following topics: overview, literature review, administration, segmentation, interpretation, development and standardization, reliability and validity, and practice exercises. The TWFD record forms provide raters with charts for tallying specific word-finding behaviors and directions for calculating various counts and indices.

The TWFD allows the user to count two "Productivity" indices (i.e., the total number of words, and total number of T-units) and calculate a Word-Finding Behaviors Index (i.e., the percentage of T-units that have one or more indicators of word-finding problems).

The Productivity indices have one major flaw. Test users are told that they should collect a minimum of 21 T-units worth of data, but also that "examiners can stop transcribing a student's language sample at 60 T-units" (p. 23). Then, the test user is told to count up the total number of words in each sample and the total number of T-units and compare these totals to the normative sample results in order to find each student's standard scores and percentile ranks. The comparison of test data totals with the normative data makes no sense because there is no way of assuring that each student in the test group and normative sample had the same time to produce words or T-units. If the counts were converted to words per 10 minutes and T-units per 10 minutes, comparability might be possible. However, as it stands, where a student scores in terms of the normative sample is largely determined by how much data the test user decides to transcribe.

The Word-Finding Behaviors Index may be more useful. However, calculating it is laborious:

1. A face-to-face interview is conducted and recorded for each child. The interview procedures are clearly described in the manual with additional directions on the stimulus pictures. The interviews involve gathering biodata information and then using specific pictures and very precise questions and probes.

2. Each student's language production is then transcribed (which is typically a very time-consuming process). The author suggests using a recorder with a pause button. A recorder with a foot pedal might prove much more efficient.

3. Each transcript is then segmented, which means that it is broken up into its various T-units. Originally, T-units were used for written language (Kellog-Hunt, 1965), and even that was difficult to count. The counting of T-units in spoken discourse is considerably more demanding because of the truncated and fragmented nature of spoken data. On the TWFD, the task is made even more complex by the fact that children with word-finding problems produce numerous substitutions, word reformulations, insertions, repetitions, empty words, time fillers, and delays—all of which are to be included within the T-units under some conditions and excluded under others. In short, although segmentation is clearly explained, the process is very complex (as indicated by the large number of pages needed to cover it).

4. Finally, the language samples must be scored. This process is also adequately explained with plenty of examples, but it too is complex (requiring many pages of explanation).

Throughout the manual, the generalizability of the test's results tends to be overstated. What the author calls a "nationally standardized" (p. 3) test involved only 856 children from 17 states. Granted, these students are well described in terms of how they were selected and their demographic make-up (including sex, grade, age, region, race/ethnicity, and parents' educational level), but the sample is relatively small.

In addition, descriptive statistics are provided for the Productivity and Word-Finding Behaviors indices for the normative sample, as well as for two subsamples of 43 students each (sampled to compare normal learning students with students who have word-finding problems).

Initially, it appears that the TWFD is reasonably reliable. Average interrater correlations of .96, .96, and .86 were obtained for the Total T-Units, Total Words, and Word-Finding Behaviors Index, respectively. Considerably lower test-retest reliabilities of .71, .80, and .84 were reported for the same measures. Internal consistency for the Word-Finding Behaviors Index was .73 for children with word-finding disorders, and .78 for normal language children. However, closer examination reveals that: (*a*) the interrater correlations were based on only seven judges rating 12 language samples; (*b*) the test-retest coefficients were based on only 30 normal language learning third graders; and (*c*) the internal consistency estimates were based on 33 and 40 students, respectively.

The predictive validity of the TWFD was defended by using a discriminant analysis of the scores of normal language children ($n = 43$) and children with word-finding problems ($n = 43$). A significant discriminant function resulted, and 42 out of the 43 normal language children were correctly classified, as were 39 out of the 43 children with word-finding problems.

Concurrent validity was studied by calculating correlation coefficients between the TWFD and TWF. The author argued that the very low (and apparently chance) correlations between these two tests indicated that they "rank children differently," and that "findings of this nature actually provide support for the criterion validity of the TWFD" (p. 91).

Two of the construct validity arguments are no more convincing. One shows very small mean changes in T-unit length across grade levels, and the other is based on very low correlations among the two productivity indices and the various word-finding problem indicators.

Two other construct validity arguments are more interesting. A factor analysis (with Varimax rotation, $n = 856$) revealed a clear three-factor solution, and several small matched-groups studies showed that, in most cases, significant differences existed between the scores of language normal children and children with word-finding problems for all of the TWFD indices.

On the one hand, the TWFD provides adequate descriptive and normative information, the test appears to be moderately reliable, and some of the validity arguments are convincing. On the other hand, the TWFD is complex to administer, analyze, score, and interpret. In the end, because it is the only available measure of this construct, the TWFD will probably prove useful for a few very dedicated language and speech researchers, pathologists, and teachers.

REVIEWER'S REFERENCES

Kellog-Hunt, W. (1965). *Grammatical structures written at three grade levels.* Champaign, IL: National Council of Teachers of English.

German, D. J. (1986). Test of Word Finding. Chicago: The Riverside Publishing Co.

Review of the Test of Word Finding in Discourse by REBECCA J. KOPRIVA, Associate Professor of Educational Measurement, California State University, Fresno, Fresno, CA:

The purpose of the Test of Word Finding in Discourse (TWFD) is to identify word-finding behaviors exhibited by children, grades 1–6, when shown three stimulus pictures and probed to tell a story and respond to related information regarding the pictures.

Both strengths and weaknesses have been identified which would impact the quality of this test for providing diagnostic and normative information regarding word-finding behaviors in students.

BACKGROUND INFORMATION, AND TEST AND PROTOCOL LAYOUT AND DESCRIPTION. This section is clearly the author's strength. An extensive (pp. 5–18) and frank review of existing research to date is supplied. Dr. German clearly identifies the place her test occupies within this literature. The manual contains clear and useful information about the purpose and parameters of the test for use in discourse situations, and the constructs she wants to evaluate. This includes information about other types of data that are needed to provide a complete evaluation of word-finding skills in situations other than discourse.

She provides a meaningful way to organize and interpret word-finding data, allowing test administrators to develop a holistic profile while also providing useful information on seven specific types of behavior known to be associated with word-finding problems. She has included well-written interpretive summaries of all the holistic profiles, including case study exemplars. Graphing opportunities have been provided to help explain the findings to other professionals, parents, and the students themselves.

Dr. German provides clear administration directions for professionals using her test. These directions include specific discussions of parameters to be followed when probing for more information from students. She also provides well-written directions for transcribing and scoring student responses appropriately, including a rich set of examples of responses and how they should be interpreted, and practice exercises to help calibrate the administrators.

TEST DEVELOPMENT. All stated developmental data were collected using "an experimental form," supposedly one of the three stimulus pictures. It was not specified whether the probing instructions were the same as in the final test. Responses from only 56 students were evaluated, grade levels unknown, selection process unknown, other academic referents unknown, and all Caucasian and middle class. Test-retest and interrater reliability studies were conducted. Discriminant analyses were conducted on a subgroup of the norming sample, and a matched sample of students identified with word-finding problems. Because the analyses were conducted on the final instrument, my evaluation of these findings is discussed in the validity section below.

I find the development process inadequate. The other stimulus pictures, and attendant probing questions from all three pictures, do not appear to have ever been field tested. No "item" analyses were conducted to ascertain the validity and viability of this approach, and, specifically, of these stimuli and their probes. Further, no analyses for validity or viability were conducted by the subgroups apparently judged to be important (as surmised in the selection of the norming sample), including grade level analyses. The reliability indices were adequate, but results are suspect because of the sampling problems, and because there was no mention of how the raters were trained.

NORMATIVE INFORMATION. Volunteers were elicited to identify students who might be willing to take part in the norming and technical studies. Students identified with learning disabilities, speech and language problems, and/or reading disorders were excluded from participating. A total of 2,500 students, grades 1–6, were identified, from 19 communities in 17 states. The students were stratified by sex, age, race/ethnicity, SES, geographical region, and community size, and subsequently, students were randomly selected to reflect appropriate weights in each strata as reported in the 1980 U.S. census. After permission slips from parents were returned, the final norm sample consisted of 856 children from the 19 communities in the 17 states. Data from these students resulted in scaled scores for the holistic indices and percentile ranks.

Generally, the scaling procedures appear to be appropriate. The main concern is with the sample itself, and the subsequent interpretation of the normative data. The final numbers of students generally reflected U.S. census figures in all cases other than educational level of parents (greater than half the parents attended 13+ years of school, and greater than one fourth attended school for 16+ years in the sample, whereas only 20% of the U.S. population attended 13–15 years of school, and 18% attended 16+ years. No breakdown of less than 12 years of school was provided in the sample). Specific breakdown by SES was not provided. Descriptions of the communities were not provided, other than naming the towns, which generally appear to be suburbs or smaller cities.

Further, there were only about 65 males/females per grade, approximately 30 students from each of four geographic regions per grade, and about 20 African Americans, 9 Hispanic, and 7 "others" (Asian, American Indian, Eskimos, and Pacific Islanders) per grade. Also "because only minimal grade-level differences and no systematic trends were observed in the normative sample for either of the [holistic indices], norms for specific grade levels were not generated for the TWFD. Instead, norms were based on the entire 856-subject sample for each TWFD index" (p. 77).

The implications of the incomplete representation of subgroups per grade, and the decision to collapse the data over grades are obvious. The numbers are inadequate to get representation of the full range of scores per subgroup, suggesting that other than average scores were not adequately represented per subgroup, per grade. This is especially true, of course, when identifying representation in cross tabs of membership in two or more subgroups (other than probably cells for gender by Caucasian). Further, even with approximately 125 students sampled per grade, it is questionable whether there are enough data collected to expect adequate representation of a full spread of scores per grade, for the complete sample. Therefore, differential systematic trends per grade likely could not be detected, even though there might be differences with a more sufficient sample size. All that appears to be available is a general idea about how Caucasian, middle class, non-identified (not learning disabled, or having speech and/or language problems, or a reading disorder) students, over grades, from communities like those evaluated, would respond. This is not sufficient for a norming sample.

RELIABILITY. Interrater, test-retest, and internal consistency reliability indices were collected. The test-retest sample (n = 30, 3rd graders, not randomly selected) and the internal consistency samples (33 nonrandomly selected students with word-finding problems, and 40 nonrandomly selected from the normative sample) were inadequate to provide generalizable results. An unnamed split-half procedure was used in analyzing internal consistency. Depending on the method, results would be tentative, at best.

Seven volunteer special educator professionals scored language samples of 12 students identified as not having word-finding problems. Although the interrater correlations were sufficient, it is problematic that no samples from students with word-finding problems were scored. Additionally, no information was given about the training these scorers received, so it is not known if they received the same materials as are offered in the current testing package. It appears that these correlational results could not be generalized to professionals using this test.

VALIDITY. Dr. German reported content, criterion, and construct validity. The content validity section did not address the testing materials, but rather professional opinions about the viability of the construct. Therefore, there does not appear to be any evidence for content validity reported in the testing materials.

To determine criterion-related validity, misclassification analyses were conducted with 43 students with word-finding problems (selection process for these students was not provided, nor was there any definition of the parameters associated with how they were identified) and 43 students without word-finding problems matched on subgroup variables. Most students were classified correctly with the TWFD; however, the sample size was inadequate to generalize by subgroups or grades (i.e., two students were sampled at grade 6). Information showing no to negative relationships between word-finding skills in discourse, as measured by this test, and word-finding skills when single-word naming is called for, were also used to substantiate criterion-related validity. It was unclear how these data supported criterion-related validity.

Developmental differences in length of responses, intercorrelations, a factor analysis, and discriminant analyses were provided to show evidence of construct validity. Developmental differences here appear to question Dr. German's conclusion that grade level differences are negligible. Interholistic and interbehavior correlations showed low to moderate relationships, providing evidence for the unique characteristics of each of the holistic indices and each of the behaviors. The factor analysis identified three factors, one which recorded frequency information (productivity), and two which split the behaviors indicated in the test. It is unclear about how this provides validity evidence. The discriminant analyses provided evidence for different levels of behavior skills and frequencies between 43 students from the normative sample, and 43 students identified with word-finding problems.

SUMMARY. For the reasons stated above, it appears there is inconclusive and spotty evidence suggesting that this test is valid and reliable for evaluating word-finding behaviors in discourse for students at specific grade levels, and for students of ethnic/racial heritage other than Caucasian. The normative information appears to be of limited use because of the concerns raised above. The presentation of the test and protocol were well done.

[400]

The Time of Your Life.

Purpose: Constructed as a self-assessment tool to provide "insight" into time management.
Population: Employees.
Publication Date: 1988.
Scores: Total score only.
Administration: Group or individual.
Price Data, 1990: $40 per complete kit including 20 inventories and 20 scoring and interpretation sheets.
Time: [30] minutes.
Comments: Self-administered, self-scored.
Author: Training House, Inc.
Publisher: Training House, Inc.

Review of The Time of Your Life by RALPH F. DARR, JR., Professor of Education, Department of Educational Foundations and Leadership, The University of Akron, Akron, OH:

The Time of Your Life: A Self-Assessment Exercise kit contains 20 test booklet/answer sheets and 20 sheets for self-scoring one's response. It may be administered individually or in a group setting. The purpose of the instrument is to enable the respondent to gain insight into his or her ability to manage time. The instrument is composed of 25 incomplete statements that describe how the respondent feels about "different aspects of time management." Three options are printed immediately below each statement. The three-option set is different for each of the 25 stems. The respondent circles the response that best expresses her or his feelings or experience.

SCORING. The instrument is scored with an answer sheet that is identical to the test booklet except that a weight is assigned to each of the options for the 25 items. The "best" answer receives a weight of "4," the next best a "2," and least appropriate response a weight of zero. The respondent checks his or her answers against the key by identifying the weight of each of her or his responses. The weights are then totaled. On the basis of total points received the respondent is assigned to one of four categories: SLAVE, 1–39 points; BALANCED, 40–59; MASTER, 60–79; and OBSESSION, 80–100.

INTERPRETING RESULTS. A brief paragraph on the answer sheet describes the characteristics of individuals falling into each of the four categories. The SLAVE is one who has little idea how to manage time. Such individuals are generally very disorganized. The BALANCED individual is "neither slave nor master of time" but gets the job done. To this individual there are other things more important than high productivity levels. The MASTER is one who has "learned how to manage time" (i.e., well organized, knows the values of prioritizing tasks, and can handle a variety of tasks without becoming frustrated). For the person in the OBSESSION category, time drives life. It manages the individual. Such people are always racing the clock. Only total scores are interpreted. There is no attempt to interpret certain patterns of responses or particular aspects of time management.

CRITIQUE. The kit provides no information about the theoretical basis of the instrument, the source of the items, the developmental history of the instrument, or its reliability and criterion-related validity. From perusing the instrument, it is difficult to assess either its construct or content validity. Because all 25 items do seem to be related to some aspect of time management, there does appear to be some degree of "face" validity here. The user has no real notion what this instrument really measures or how consistently it does measure whatever it is supposed to measure.

A second problem relates to interpretation of results. The primary purpose of this instrument seems to be to classify the respondent according to one of the four categories. After assigning the respondent to a particular category, the author(s) offer few suggestions about what the individual might do about his or her plight. Only for the SLAVE is any suggestion offered. "Convert spurts of speed into a steady pace that is more relaxed and more contemplative" (Self-Assessment Exercise, p. 1). No suggestions are offered as to how the BALANCED individual might move toward the MASTER category or how the OBSESSION individual might develop a more healthful approach toward the utilization of time.

This instrument seems to have little value for research, for employee assessment, or for employee training. It may have some value as a tool in counseling. After the respondent has taken and scored the instrument and been assigned to a category, he or she is quite likely to feel cheated when no concrete suggestions for improvement are provided.

Review of The Time of Your Life by RICHARD W. FAUNCE, Licensed Psychologist, Maple Grove, MN:

The Time of Your Life is a 25-item, multiple-choice, self-scoring paper that purports to help the individual "gain insight into your effectiveness in managing your time . . . and with it, your life" (Self-Assessment Exercise, p. 1).

The Time of Your Life consists of two parts: A Self-Assessment Exercise that presents the 25 items and three response categories for each item and a Scoring Sheet with Interpretations. The Scoring Sheet presents interpretations of each item as well as four interpretive categories based on total scores. Users are cautioned that individual item scores might not be important because "In some of the items that follow, a score of 4 is desirable while on others 4 indicates excess . . . a compulsion" (Scoring Sheet, p. 1). It is up to the user to determine which is which. Each item response on the Self-Assessment Exercise is scored 0, 2, or 4. Total scores may range from 0 to 100. Four interpretive categories are given, with low scores (0–39) indicating the user is a Slave to time and high scores (80–100) indicating an Obsession with time management. Intermediate scores indicate the user has a Balanced approach to time management (scores of 40–59) or is a Master of time management (scores of 60–79).

Presumably, scores in the Balanced and Master range (scores of 40–79) are desirable, because no behavioral changes are suggested by the interpretation. Slaves to time are told, "You need to convert spurts of speed into a steady pace that is more relaxed and more contemplative" (p. 1). Obsessed respondents are told, "you need to learn to say no . . . to take time to recharge your batteries and reflect on priorities" (p. 1).

Because it is likely that few people will score in the extreme Slave or Obsession categories (this reviewer completed the exercise under true, random response, and obsessed set conditions and all three total scores fell in the Balanced range) and because no information is given describing how the total scores have any relation to behavior, it is impossible to see what value The Time of Your Life has for gaining "insight into your effectiveness in managing your time. . . and with it, your life" (Self-Assessment Exercise, p. 1).

If The Time of Your Life is to be viewed as a "test" then little needs to be said about it. It does not begin to meet even the barest minimum standards of scientific test development (e.g., Manual: None; Test development information including standardization and norms: None; Information on psychometric properties including validity, reliability, and item statistics: None; Theoretical base: None).

It is perhaps stretching things to suggest this exercise may be of value for stimulating discussions among groups where more definitive information about time management and a qualified counselor are available. Perhaps this is how the instrument is used. After all, the authors are Training House, Inc., implying that their major function may be training, not test development. However, the exercise does not come with information on how it may be used in conjunction with training by Training House, or anyone else.

SUMMARY. This self-assessment exercise designed to help users gain insight into their time management and their lives offers no evidence that it can do either. The exercise fails to meet even the barest minimum standards of scientific test development. If it is to be used as a training device, then much more information will be needed before its prescriptions for behavioral change can be considered valid. The track record of this publisher does not indicate that such information can be expected. The Time of Your Life is a product of Training House, Inc., an organization that produced a series of measures and "exercises" in the 70s and 80s that offered little or no evidence of having desirable psychometric properties (Kramer & Conoley, 1992, reviews for tests 11:20 [Assessment of Competencies for Instructor Development], 11:78 [Communication Response Style: Assessment], 11:220 [Management Style Inventory], 11:223 [Managerial Assessment of Proficiency MAP], 11:287 [Personal Style Assessment], 11:353 [Self-Awareness Profile], 11:406 [Survey of Organizational Climate]). Generally, developmental details and psychometric properties were simply ignored or unreported. The Time of Your Life is no exception.

REVIEWER'S REFERENCE

Kramer, J. J., & Conoley, J. C. (Eds.). (1992). *The eleventh mental measurements yearbook*. Lincoln, NE: Buros Institute of Mental Measurements.

[401]

The Time-Sample Behavioral Checklist.

Purpose: Developed to measure the level and nature of functioning of adult residential patients and also used to document how and where residents and staff spend their time.
Population: Adults in residential treatment settings.
Publication Date: 1987.
Acronym: TSBC.
Scores: 7 categories: Location, Position, Awake-Asleep, Facial Expression, Social Orientation, Concurrent Activities, Crazy Behavior combined in a variety of ways to produce 9 higher-order scores: Appropriate Behavior (Interpersonal Interaction, Instrumental Activity, Self-Maintenance, Individual Entertainment, Total), Inappropriate Behavior (Bizarre Motor Behavior, Bizarre Facial & Verbal, Hostile-Belligerence, Total).
Administration: Individual.
Price Data, 1991: $18.95 per manual/checklist (286 pages).
Time: 10 2-second observations.
Comments: Should be used in conjunction with the Staff-Resident Interaction Chronograph.
Authors: Gordon L. Paul, Mark H. Licht, Marco J. Mariotto, Christopher T. Power, and Kathryn L. Engel.
Publisher: Research Press.
Cross References: See T4:2840 (1 reference).

Review of The Time-Sample Behavioral Checklist by CYNTHIA ANN DRUVA-ROUSH, Assistant Director, Evaluation and Examination Service, The University of Iowa, Iowa City, IA:

The Time-Sample Behavioral Checklist (TSBC) is a "standardized direct observational coding (DOC) instrument that employs technician-level observers to collect objective data" (manual, p. xv). The TSBC, originally designed for client assessment, "was extended to clinical staff to provide ongoing assessment of how and where staff spend their time as well as for monitoring some less stable personal-social characteristics" (p. 4).

Measurement is based on a series of observations. Observational rounds are made hourly over a week's period. During a single round, several individuals are measured, each for a 2-second period. In each single 2-second observation, the presence or absence of 69 behavioral codes are recorded on the TSBC response sheet. The time and activity are also recorded for each observation. "*Occasions sampling* follows the specified hourly time-sampling schedules to cover all days of the week and all times of the day when clientele are scheduled to be awake, with stratification over all behavior settings ('activities') proportionate to their occurrence in the treatment program" (p. 4). At least a full week of hourly time-sampling is needed to attach an appropriate interpretation.

Behavior descriptions listed in diagnostic manuals, abnormal psychology and psychiatry texts, and items in psychiatric rating scales were supplemented by "free-field" diary samples in several treatment units to arrive at the characteristics coded. Code scores are calculated by adding the observed frequency across multiple observations and dividing the total frequency for each code by the number of opportunities for occurrence. The 69 codes are then combined into various higher-order indexes. In addition, a Stereotypy/Variability set of scores is composed of a Location Index (relative amount of movement among geographic areas), a Position Index (range of physical positions), a Social Orientation Index (range of classes of people with whom clients spend their time), Concurrent Activities Index, Facial Expression Index, and Crazy Behavior Index.

The most recent normative study involved 1,205 clients obtained from 35 treatment units in 17 facilities covering both urban and rural locales. The normative sample ranged in age from 18 to 99 years. An examination of score distributions across a relatively wide range of values indicated that discriminations among both individuals and groups may be made. All indexes except Instrumental Activity and Self-Maintenance showed significant discriminations among treatment units.

An examination of repeated assessment across time indicates that the TSBC Indexes based on one-day summaries are not representative and could not substitute for full-week summaries within any of the subgroups of a multi-institutional sample (alcohol and acute units, chronic and mixed units, mentally retarded units, and community facilities).

A study was then made of stability of scores for various subgroups of patients in a longer week-to-week analysis. Highest correlation coefficients were reported for the chronic client subgroups. Clients within a structured environment reported higher stability coefficients (.28–.95) than those in an unstructured environment (.14–.85). (Hostile Belligerence scores indicated .00 stability in both environments.)

The average intraclass replicability over all client weekly TSBC Indexes and Codes exceeded $r = .97$. Interobserver replicabilities for client TSBC scores based on one-day observations had a median $r = .97$ for all higher order indices and a median $r = .94$ for individual code scores. Users are warned that some care should be taken in use of the TSBC with geriatrics and/or profoundly mentally retarded as decisions based on summary scores from the usual minimum of 10 observations as interobserver replicability coefficients fall below $r = .80$. More than 10 observations should then be employed as a basis for summaries that are intended for testing rather than for generating hypotheses.

The discriminant and convergent interrelationships among the higher-order TSBC rate scores provide evidence for the intended interpretation of both total indexes, all inappropriate component indexes, and two appropriate component indexes (Interpersonal Interaction and Individual Entertainment). Limitations on intended interpretations were suggested for both the Instrumental Activities and Self-Maintenance indexes. The interrelationships among the Stereotypy/Variability indexes provided empirical support for interpreting both the Concurrent Activities and Crazy Behavior indexes only.

The convergent/discriminant relationships between TSBC indexes and other direct observational coding systems, as well as interviews, ward rating scales, and questionnaires were examined across various subgroups of institutional units. All component indexes except for Instrumental Activity and Self-Maintenance were supported. Of the six Stereotypy/Variability indexes, only Concurrent Activities and Crazy Behavior demonstrated convergent/discriminant relationships.

Comparisons were made of means for various demographic characteristics. No evidence of sex bias was suggested for any score. "The failure of any TSBC score to demonstrate consistent age differences across all subgroups in the normative samples provides evidence against the existence of systematic age bias" (p. 175). The pattern of convergent and discriminant differences among racial groups and socioeconomic status groups is apparently consistent with the literature assessing behavior among mental patients. Blacks and lower class patients score lower on appropriate behavior and higher on inappropriate behavior. No attempt is made to study a possible interaction of the two factors. The test developers caution that TSBC indexes for racial minorities should not be used as predictors nor employed with norm-referenced interpretations without extensive additional investigation of cultural norms in local circumstances.

The Standards for Educational and Psychological Testing (AERA, APA, & NCME, 1985) state that with clinical testing, establishing a high level of criterion-related validity is of great importance. These standards further state that when validity is appraised by comparing the level of agreement between test results and clinical diagnosis, the diagnostic terms or categories employed should be carefully defined, and the method by which a diagnosis was made should be specified. In response to this requirement, TSBC researchers attempt to compare only broad diagnostic disability groups. Groups were formed by combining institutional diagnoses into broad graded categories on the basis of overall severity and pervasiveness of disability (alcohol and drug abuse, neurotic and lesser disorders, major affective psychoses, organic brain syndromes, schizophrenic psychoses, and mentally retarded). No examination is made of the source of these diagnoses. Comparisons are then made between these relatively broad groups by comparing means and overlap of confidence intervals on the higher-order indexes. Further analyses were made for degrees of retardation and paranoia. All but the Social Orientation Stereotypy/Variability Index score could be interpreted as more general indicants of behavior.

Evidence collected previous to the most recent edition of the user manual had demonstrated the ability of the TSBC indexes to predict which clients achieved successful discharges and the level of client functioning in the community up to 18 months later (*r*s in the .60s and .70s). Score means for the various indexes were compared between groups that were successful for 30 days in not returning to equally restrictive mental or correctional facilities. All major indexes, except Self-Maintenance and Instrumental Activity, and Concurrent Activities and Crazy Behavior Stereotypy/Variability Indexes displayed significant differences in score means between successful and unsuccessful release clientele. A study was then made as to what combination of the indexes would successfully discriminate between those who were successfully released and those who were not. This decision was based on maximizing the decision success similar to a loss function approach, although no method was clearly described. The best discrimination resulted from a combination of cutoffs that consider levels of the Total Appropriate Behavior, Interpersonal Interaction jointly with levels of the Concurrent Activities Stereotypy/Variability Index. The 95.9% success rate for independent discharges within 2 weeks of meeting TSBC readiness guidelines and 97.8% success rate for community placements within 4 weeks of meeting TSBC readiness guidelines displays further predictive validity.

In summary, the TSBC is an instrument requiring immense training of the observer called to record behaviors. The high level of replicability recorded over time and between observers is testimony, however, that observers can be suitably trained. The researchers are to be commended in their exhaustive examination of reliability and validity for each of their higher order indexes. Precautions for use of their instrument and its interpretation are clearly given. Strong evidence for all higher order indexes except for the Instrumental Activities and Self-Maintenance is clearly provided. The Stereotypy/Variability indices do not stand well under close examination. My one recommendation is that an editor be found for their user's manual. Reading through paragraph-long sentences was both frustrating and a deterrent from examining their very thorough research process.

REVIEWER'S REFERENCE

American Educational Research Association, American Psychological Association, & National Council on Measurement in Education. (1985). *Standards for educational and psychological testing*. Washington, DC: American Psychological Association, Inc.

Review of The Time-Sample Behavioral Checklist by SUSAN L. CROWLEY, Assistant Professor, and BLAINE R. WORTHEN, Professor and Chair, Research and Evaluation Methodolgy Program, Department of Psychology, Utah State University, Logan, UT:

The Time-Sample Behavioral Checklist (TSBC) is a standardized direct observational coding (DOC) instrument for multiple-occasion use in residential treatment facilities for mentally ill or mentally retarded adults. The authors state that the TSBC is intended to provide all the objective information and documentation needed on client functioning to (*a*) support a variety of "rational" decisions regarding client care (e.g., placement and disposition, problem identification, and description), and (*b*) answer specific research questions. Additionally, the TSBC assesses where clients and staff spend their time. It is intended to be used in concert with the Staff-Resident Interaction Chronograph (SRIC) as an entire assessment protocol. However, the authors state that the TSBC can be used alone for more "limited purposes."

The technical manual for the TSBC is Volume 2 of the five-volume *Assessment in Residential Treatment Settings* series. However, continuous references to other volumes reveal that much pertinent information about the TSBC is contained in those other volumes, which is frustrating for the reader. For instance, norm-referenced interpretation information is in Volume 4, the rationale for construction and data on cost-effectiveness is contained in Volume 1, and Volume 5 contains crucial information regarding the implementation of the system. Scattering such crucial information across four volumes is a major impediment to those attempting to understand the TSBC.

Data for the TSBC are collected by trained technician-level observers using discrete 2-second observations taken on a stratified time-sampling schedule during each hour that residents are scheduled to be awake. The authors suggest a minimum of 10 observations to gain an accurate picture of a client's functioning. However, they also caution against interpreting data from a limited number of observations, urging a full-week summary (50–100 observations) for most TSBC uses.

The TSBC has seven categories, including 69 behavioral codes and 3 control codes. TSBC computer program provides four types of summary scores: detailed code scores, category stereotypy/variability scores, and higher-order functioning scores at both intermediate and global levels. Calculation of summary scores is straightforward, often depending on simple averages.

The administration and coding manual for the TSBC (in Volume 2 of the series) is commendably thorough and detailed. Observational rules and procedures are outlined in meticulous and sometimes excessive detail (e.g., suggestions for clothing and makeup observers should wear). Code definitions are clearly organized and explicit, providing (*a*) a description of the behavior being coded, and (*b*) both typical and rare/difficult examples. Descriptions and codes are described in behavioral terms, minimizing the need for inference. The one glaring exception to this is the "crazy behavior" category. Although some of the codes in this category can be viewed as "crazy" (e.g., incoherent speech), others clearly cannot (e.g., crying, swearing). Further, "crazy" is both imprecise and value-laden, and a less emotionally laden term, perhaps "maladaptive" would be better.

The origin of the items comprising the TSBC is not well described. A multidisciplinary group of 10 professionals participated in the development. The authors state that after a "pilot test with trained observers, the coding system was standardized" (p. 2.3), but how (or whether) these test results were used in selecting and/or modifying the final pool of items is not specified.

The authors do an excellent job of describing the TSBC summary scores and identifying what each score can and cannot do, repeatedly identifying confidence intervals and the amount of change necessary for statistical significance. Limitations and cautions in data interpretation are emphasized, including cautions against overinterpretation and making dispositional attributions. The authors carefully critique the data throughout the volume, identifying which recommended interpretations are supported by sufficient data.

TECHNICAL INFORMATION. Reliability, validity, and normative data are based on nearly 19 years of research by the authors. The manual summarizes previously published information but is focused more on new information from a multi-institutional generalizability/feasibility study. The selection of data collection sites is clearly described and the authors have collected TSBC data on an impressively diverse sample varying in degree of chronicity, type of facility, and type of client (psychiatric, mentally retarded, and "normal" hospitalized). The only serious weakness of the sample is the omission of private residential facilities.

The authors claim the TSBC can also be used to identify where staff spend their time; however, the technical information presented is focused primarily on the scores collected on clients. The practical significance of collecting staff information is mentioned only briefly. Consequently, staff uses of the TSBC are distracting. Perhaps these data would become more relevant when the instrument is employed as part of the broader TSBC/SRIC system.

NORMATIVE INFORMATION. The normative sample includes 1,205 clients on whom TSBC data were collected. Characteristics of the entire normative sample of 1,205 clients are presented in tabular form, along with characteristics of subsamples representing the primary types of residential settings. The authors attempted to collect data on the broadest range of treatment settings and clients to demonstrate the feasibility of using the TSBC in these diverse facilities (except for private residential centers). The authors recommend using separate norms for the two major facility types (public and community). Although the authors present data suggesting their sample is generally representative of gender and racial characteristics of the population at large, they acknowledge specific limitations, such as the underrepresentation of some ethnic groups.

RELIABILITY. The reliability of TSBC codes and scores depends primarily on interobserver replicability. Training of observers is reviewed and issues of observer reactivity, drift, bias, and decay are addressed. In all cases, the replicability coefficients were high, usually $r>.90$. Standard errors of measurement and standard errors of differences between two scores are also presented within each major facility grouping.

The authors apply generalizability theory to TSBC data, although rather half-heartedly. Variance components for Clients, Observers, and the Residual are presented for the total sample and public and community facilities. Unfortunately, the authors go no further in evaluating the replicability of the data within the framework of generalizability theory or contrasting it with the results of applied classical test score theory.

VALIDITY. The authors address validity issues for the TSBC in a variety of ways, including: internal relationships among codes and indexes, differential stability and sensitivity to change, discrimination among groups differing on clinically relevant characteristics, concurrent information from other assessment tools, and predictive relationships with other performance and outcome measures. Generally, the validity evidence presented for the TSBC is impressive and supports the intended uses of the instrument. There are few areas of weakness. Where a score does not perform as well as would be desired, the authors call this to the reader's attention, identifying the limitation in a forthright manner.

In all cases, the authors do an excellent job of presenting the data, supporting interpretive suggestions, identifying limitations, and presenting plausible alternative hypotheses. Within each validity section, the TSBC score/code is presented and data reviewed in a systematic and thorough manner. The level of detail presented is probably excessive for most readers, however. Acknowledging this, the authors include summary sections with references to specific sections in the text. For ease in understanding, tables follow a similar format across chapters. Although clearly presented, the authors chose to omit nonsignificant correlations from the tables. It would have been better to leave these correlations in for comparative purposes, especially considering the limitations of statistical significance testing.

SUMMARY. The TSBC is a direct-observation coding system for use in adult residential treatment facilities. The authors have made a valuable contribution by providing a way to assess change, improvement, and specify strengths and weaknesses in a residential population. Additionally, TSBC data can be used for program evaluation, group comparisons, and numerous research questions. In reality, the TSBC is a research and assessment protocol rather than merely an assessment tool.

The authors present an abundance of evidence attesting to the sound psychometric properties of TSBC data. The most frustrating aspect of this instrument is that one must root through several volumes to obtain all the information necessary to use it intelligently.

Whether this instrument will ever be widely used is still a question. The authors make a convincing argument regarding the cost effectiveness of implementing the TSBC (and SRIC), but they acknowledge that there are significant tangible and intangible startup costs. Because many residential facilities are plagued by tight budgets and nearsighted administrators, the adoption of the TSBC may be limited.

[402]

TMJ Scale.

Purpose: "Designed to measure the [clinical significance of] symptom patterns of dental patients with temporomandibular joint disorders and orofacial pain."
Population: TM [temporomandibular] dental patients ages 13 and over.
Publication Dates: 1984–87.
Scores, 10: Physical Domain (Pain Report, Palpation Pain, Perceived Malocclusion, Joint Dysfunction, Range of Motion Limitation, Non-TM Disorder), Psychosocial Domain (Psychological Factors, Stress, Chronicity), Global Scale.
Administration: Individual.
Price Data, 1994: $20 per specimen set including question booklet, manual ('87, 86 pages), and sample report.
Time: (10–15) minutes.
Comments: Self-administered; self-report.
Authors: Stephen R. Levitt, Tom F. Lundeen, and Michael W. McKinney.
Publisher: Pain Resource Center, Inc.
Cross References: See T4:2842 (3 references).

Review of the TMJ Scale by WILLIAM W. DEARDORFF, Clinical Faculty, U.C.L.A. School of Medicine, Los Angeles, CA:

The TMJ Scale is a 97-item self-report symptom inventory designed to measure symptoms of temporomandibular joint (TMJ) dysfunction. The measure can be done in the home or office and takes approximately 10 to 15 minutes to complete. All items are scored on a 5-point scale (0–4) and are written at about an eighth grade reading level. The items on the TMJ Scale comprise three domains: Physical, Psychosocial, and Global. The Physical Domain is subdivided into dimensions of Pain Report, Palpation Pain, Perceived Malocclusion, Joint Dysfunction, Range of Motion Limitation, and Non-TM Disorder. The Psychosocial Domain is subdivided into dimensions of Psychological Factors, Stress, and Chronicity. The Global Scale is a composite score "whose function it is to communicate in a single score the probability that the patient has a TM disorder" (manual, p. 7). Scoring is done by computer either through a mail-in service or scoring software.

The authors chose not to develop formal validity scales for the TMJ Scale reasoning that this would significantly increase its length. They have developed gross criteria for assessing validity. These include the following: (*a*) If more than 20% of the total inventory items are missing the entire test is "invalid," (*b*) if more than 40% of items on an individual scale are missing then that scale is invalidated, and (*c*) if one or two "highly improbable" items are endorsed the results are marked unreliable or invalid, respectively. Empirical testing of these criteria has yet to be completed.

The internal consistencies of the scales, as measured by coefficient alpha, are very acceptable ranging from a low of.76 on Perceived Malocclusion to a high of .95 on the Global Scale. The test-retest reliabilities (mean time = 4.5 days; range = 1 to 23 days) are also good ranging from a low of.76 on Perceived Malocclusion to a high of .91 on Stress. The authors make the point that test-retest reliabilities are difficult to ascertain as the symptoms of TMJ disorders are transient by nature. The TMJ Scale manual presents a thorough discussion of test construction and empirical validation.

The TMJ Scale manual discusses that convergent validity is studied by measuring a test's similarity to other measures of the same symptom dimensions. The authors point out that there are no other validated self-report measures of TMJ symptoms. Therefore, convergent validity was measured by using clinician ratings of the various scale dimensions. Clinician judges were given descriptions of TM disorders as well as a symptom rating form. They were then asked to rate each patient on these dimensions without knowledge of the TMJ Scale results. Correlations between clinician ratings and scale scores ranged from a low of .20 on Perceived Malocclusion to a high of .56 on Palpation Pain (manual, p. 33). Interrater reliability was not assessed in this sample; however, in another study (Lundeen, Levitt, & McKinney, 1988) it was assessed using two independent clinician ratings on 22 patients having TM disorders. Interrater reliabilities in that study ranged from a low of .30 on Chronicity to a high of.88 on Malocclusion.

Discriminant validity, as presented in the TMJ Scale manual, was judged by the sensitivity and specificity of the Global scale when used with a "mixed" population (TMJ patient and Non-TM dental patients). Sensitivity was judged to be 84.2% and specificity was determined to be 80.3%.

Construct validity has yet to be established for the TMJ Scale and may be the area of greatest concern at this time. The foundation of the TMJ Scale is based upon its ability to identify and describe TM disorders as defined by the test's authors. The TMJ Scale manual states that the authors "chose to avoid the present diagnostic controversies and focus test development on attempting to create an assessment tool which could measure the complex multidimensional symptom parameters which describe and clinically define TM disorders" (manual, p. 2). Although the authors claimed to have operationalized their definitions of TM disorders, interrater reliabilities were done using only two judges on a small sample of patients and these were not high by psychometric standards. This brings into question what is actually being identified by the TMJ Scale as being a "TM disorder."

Related to this issue, the field of craniomandibular disorders is just now constructing a Research Diagnostic Criteria (RDC; Dworkin & LeResche, 1992) in an attempt to carefully define and operationalize TM disorder symptoms and diagnoses. As diagnostic validity is necessarily limited by reliability, claims that the TMJ Scale can identify TM-disordered and Non-TM-disordered patients must be viewed skeptically. The test manual appropriately states that the measure does not make diagnoses and should only be used as an aid to evaluation. Even so, clinicians may be at risk for minimizing this caveat as the majority of the manual and the published research is focused on the TMJ Scale's ability to "screen" and identify TM and Non-TM disorders.

An additional problem is that of using a composite score index for TM disorder assessment. The TMJ Scale purportedly identifies presence or absence of a TM Disorder, which might include one or more of 16 specific diagnoses (e.g., capsulitis, myofascial pain dysfunction, TMJ arthrosis, etc.) as operationalized by the test authors. No research has been done on the usefulness of the test for identifying subcategories of TM disorders.

Lastly, is the issue of utility. This involves determining how much cost-effective and useful information is gained using the TMJ Scale in addition to procedures already used as part of routine practice (for example, a simple symptom checklist questionnaire, clinical examination and, perhaps, a depression inventory). Although the predictive value of the TMJ Scale has been found to be good (a test's ability to "predict" a disorder over the base-rate), its usefulness has not been compared to other simple assessment methods.

In summary, the TMJ Scale shows strengths in terms of adequate internal consistency, test-retest reliability, and certain indices of convergent validity. Current weaknesses include problems with construct validity and the usefulness of the test compared to other cost-effective measures. It is of concern that independent corroboration of the criteria used to validate the TMJ Scale has not yet been conducted. At this juncture, independent evaluation of the TMJ Scale is certainly appropriate using a "gold standard" of adequate reliability and validity. For example, this might include using the RDC to validate the TM Section and the DSM-IV (American Psychiatric Association, 1994) to validate the Psychosocial Domain scales (Rugh, Woods, & Dahlstrom, in press). Until this type of independent corroboration is completed the TMJ Scale results should be used with caution.

REVIEWER'S REFERENCES

Lundeen, T. F., Levitt, S. R., & McKinney, M. W. (1988). Evaluation of temporomandibular joint disorders by clinician ratings. *The Journal of Prosthetic Dentistry*, *59*, 202-211.

Dworkin, S. F., & LeResche, L. (1992). Research diagnostic criteria for temporomandibular disorders: Review, criteria, examinations and specifications, critique. Parts I-IV. *Journal of Craniomandibular Disorders: Facial and Oral Pain*, *6*, 301-355.

American Psychiatric Association. (1994). *Diagnostic and statistical manual of mental disorders: DSM-IV* (4th ed.). Washington, DC: Author.

Rugh, J. D., Woods, B. J., & Dahlstrom, L. (in press). Temporomandibular disorders: Assessment of psychological factor. *Advances in Dental Research*.

[403]

Trainer's Assessment of Proficiency (TAP).

Purpose: Constructed as a "self-assessment exercise that measures relative strengths in twelve instructional skills."
Population: Trainers.
Publication Date: 1991.
Acronym: TAP.
Scores, 12: Assessing Needs and Entering Behavior, Setting Objectives and Terminal Behavior, Analyzing Participants and Situations, Eliciting Relevant Responses and Testing, Applying Classroom Facilitation Skills, Forming Questions and Probes Effectively, Maintaining Adult Relationships, Giving Feedback and Reinforcement, Building Toward Transfer of Training, Getting All Learners to Participate, Managing Classroom Time Effectively, Displaying Good Flow/Logic/Organization.
Administration: Group.
Forms, 2: Long, Short.
Price Data: Available from publisher.
Time: (60) minutes for Short form; (180) minutes for Long form.
Comments: Videocassette recorder necessary for administration of inventory.
Author: Scott B. Parry.
Publisher: Training House, Inc.

Review of the Trainer's Assessment of Proficiency (TAP) by MARK W. ROBERTS, Professor of Psychology, Idaho State University, Pocatello, ID:

The Trainer's Assessment of Proficiency (TAP) evaluates instructors of adults in time-limited, workshop or continuing education formats. For example, corporate trainers of employee groups might assess their current skills using the TAP.

Two forms of the TAP have been constructed. Each respondent needs a workbook and two videotapes to complete the Short Form. The Long Form requires a scoring guide and an Individual Development Plan. An administration booklet is available if the TAP is used to evaluate a group of trainers. The Long Form of the TAP is a self-assessment device that yields scores on 12 dimensions of training skill (listed above), presumably representing relevant domains of trainer abilities. The scoring guide assists the user in interpreting each dimension and the Individual Developmental Plan facilitates the use of TAP information to enhance abilities in areas of identified deficits. In contrast, the Short Form of the TAP yields a single score of overall trainer proficiency. The Short Form's suggested use is to critique other instructors, to help plan a presentation, or as a quick, post-presentation self-evaluation. Because the two forms are procedurally and conceptually different, the Short Form should not be construed as an abbreviated form, nor as a psychometrically acceptable substitute for the Long Form.

The TAP Long Form presents the respondent with a high quality videotape of a training session, divided into five segments: "Starting the Class"; "Sandy Leads a Discussion"; "Some Problems Arise"; "The Final Objective and Wrap-Up"; and "Sandy's Lesson Plan and Overall Performance." After each segment the respondent is prompted to stop the videotape and answer seven to eight multiple-choice items about the preceding videotaped segment and, occasionally, specified written material available in the workbook. Each item describes a teaching activity used by "Sandy" (the instructor) and requires the respondent to agree or disagree with each of four statements regarding that teaching activity. Therefore, the TAP is really a 148-item true-false test. There is a decided bias for responding "true" to each item. The workbook informs the respondent that 89 of the 148 statements are true; the administration booklet instructs the examiner to inform the class that 60% of the items are true (61.8% are actually keyed as true). Each scale score is generated by summing 12 item scores, some of which are negatively keyed (i.e., "minus one" for agreeing with a false statement). An arithmetic adjustment corresponding to the sum of the negatively keyed items is added to each scale, yielding an upper limit score of 12 and a lower limit score of zero on each scale.

The 12 TAP scales lack psychometric verification. There are no reliability data. There is no evidence of within-scale internal consistency, nor is there any evidence that the scales measure independent dimensions. There are no published normative data nor validity indices. The author submitted "normative" data ($n = 162$) to this reviewer from a variety of field trials, as well as data indicating an association between mean TAP scale scores and years of trainer experience. These data, however, are neither published nor convincing. Consequently, TAP scale scores cannot be interpreted by the usual method of considering the raw score, the standard error, and the normative distribution.

The Short Form of the TAP suffers from similar limitations. Twelve items are presented, each reflecting a relatively specific trainer skill. Trainer performance is rated on each item as either *excellent* (4 points), *good* (3 points), *average* (2 points), *inadequate* (1 point), or *poor/omitted* (0 points). The Short Form total score is the sum of the 12 item scores. Again, there are no reliability, validity, or normative data.

Currently, the TAP should be viewed as a clinical tool. It may be very helpful. There is little doubt that the author (S. Parry) possesses considerable expertise in instructing trainers. Further, the content validity of the TAP may be quite good. This reviewer is not aware of any similar instruments. Moreover, there is certainly a need to evaluate trainers of adults in the widely used workshop or continuing education formats. A device pinpointing trainer deficiencies leading to remediation would be very useful. Unfortunately, the current lack of empirical information precludes the routine use of the TAP by corporate trainers or by evaluators of trainers.

Review of the Trainer's Assessment of Proficiency (TAP) by DANIEL E. VOGLER, Associate Professor of Education, Virginia Tech, Blacksburg, VA:

DESCRIPTIVE BACKGROUND. The Trainer's Assessment of Proficiency (TAP) is a central part of the Instructional Skills Series developed by Dr. Parry. The TAP is presented through a workshop video, instructor feedback video, workbook, scoring guide, and an individual development plan. Long and Short Form instruments are included in the workbook with both linked to 12 training competencies.

The workshop video is a short video of an instructor presenting a training session to trainers on the topic: How To Manage Time In Class. The video is broken into parts that allow the respondent to observe five aspects of training. Instructors and prospective instructors can easily identify with the situation presented in the video.

The instructor feedback video provides an excellent assessment of the training session. It is balanced with regard to weaknesses and strengths of the instructor. Dr. Parry provides excellent descriptive observations and couples each with suggestions for improvement.

The workbook contains supporting documentation for the video. Additionally, it includes the Short and Long instrument forms needed for the assessment. The Long Form includes 37 items in a multiple-choice format. The respondent may select any or all of the alternatives. The responses are ultimately linked to the 12 training competencies. The Short Form requires the respondent to rate each of the 12 training competencies on a 5-point rating scale ranging from *excellent* to *poor/omitted*.

The scoring guide for the Long Form has each of the 37 items coded for relationship to the 12 training competencies. The Short Form is simply a subjective comparison to the manner in which Dr. Parry responded.

Closure for the TAP is an individual development plan. The document is organized into eight parts and when completed provides a blueprint for improvement. The plan is closely linked to the specific things that must be accomplished to use the assessment information for improvement.

INSTRUMENT QUALITIES. The TAP is a commonsense approach to assessing the cognitive competence of a trainer or prospective trainer by having the trainer observe a video and assess the training actions taken by another trainer. This approach is at least one step removed from actually assessing a trainer. Hence, the respondent is assessing another trainer and thereby not being personally assessed.

There were no validity, reliability, normative, or other psychometric data provided for the instruments. Thus, all inferences must be based totally on common sense. Nonetheless, I found the TAP easy to follow and felt that the 37 items and the 12 training competencies made sense.

USER CAUTIONS. The strength of the instrument resides in its simplicity and face validity qualities. If used with the video, it can serve as an excellent heuristic training tool. The ideas provided will surely evoke comment, thought, and curiosity from the respondent. The TAP might be a predictor of those with knowledge about training although there are no data to support this notion. It should *not* be viewed as an assessment of training skills.

The question of who could benefit from this instrument is open-ended. Because it is so closely linked to an instructional training series, the most obvious user will be a trainer of trainers. Accordingly, the instrument best serves an instructional need and not necessarily an assessment need. The notion of teacher trainers using the TAP is also prompted. However, the teacher training would likely be competency based in nature, yet the materials provided do not mention teachers as a possible audience. Clearly, the instrument needs to be tested with various groups. The data collected would surely cause the developer to modify various aspects of the instrument and supporting documentation.

SUMMARY. The TAP is an instrument that appears to have evolved from an instructional training series for trainers. It possesses considerable appeal as a diagnostic tool of cognition about training and may be a good tool for separating those who know about training from those who do not know. It, however, should *not* be considered as an assessment tool of actual training skills.

[404]

Transition Behavior Scale.

Purpose: "Measures student's readiness for transition to employment and independent living."
Population: Grades 11–12.
Publication Date: 1989.
Acronym: TBS.
Scores, 4: Work-Related, Interpersonal Relations, Social/Community Expectations, Total.
Administration: Individual.
Price Data, 1992: $60 per complete kit including technical manual (32 pages), 50 rating forms, and IEP and intervention manual (230 pages); $10 per technical manual; $30 per 50 rating forms; $20 per IEP and intervention manual.
Time: (15) minutes.
Author: Stephen B. McCarney.
Publisher: Hawthorne Educational Services, Inc.

Review of the Transition Behavior Scale by MARTHA BLACKWELL, Associate Professor of Psychology, Auburn University at Montgomery, Montgomery, AL:

The Transition Behavior Scale (TBS) was designed to assess junior and senior high school students' behaviors indicative of readiness for moving from the school environment to the broader arenas of work and society. TBS behaviors exemplify what are also known as character or personality traits, attitudes, or values and have been shown by research to be associated with success in work and life in general. These qualities include responsibility, compliance, dependability, flexibility, persistence, productivity, organization, honesty, cooperation, self-control, stability, loyalty, and adjustability. Past school evaluations on conduct, citizenship, and work habits reveal similar information sought by the TBS. Identification and remediation of failure-prone behaviors should occur at much earlier ages when behavior is more malleable than during the teenage years.

Teachers, guidance counselors, supervisors, and employers who daily and directly observe students' performance rate each student on 62 behaviors: Does not perform the behavior, performs the behavior inconsistently, performs the behavior consistently. Rating results are to be used for identifying students with or without the desirable behaviors and for providing remediation for students lacking readiness behaviors. The Transition Behavior Scale IEP and Intervention manual keys detailed interventions to each item. There is much overlap across the three subscales and the prescribed interventions.

The standardization sample is described demographically in relation to the 1980 U.S. Census. Test users are cautioned to limit generalizing results due to likeness/difference between characteristics of the standardization sample and target population. For example, 90% of the standardization subjects were white (U.S. Census 86%) and 43% were from the North Central geographic area (U.S. Census 27%).

Statistical analyses were thorough and extensive. Only one very dominant factor emerged (eigenvalue = 33); however, four factors (eigenvalues = 3, 2, 2, 1) were manipulated to form the bases for three subscales. All item/total score correlations except two were .60 and higher, well above the acceptable .30. Very high levels of correlations (.84 to .87) among the three subscales—Work Related, Interpersonal Relations, and Social/Community Expectations—raise the question of whether the three subscales are distinct. The test author pointed to these high correlations as substantiation for internal consistency. Test-retest reliabilities for the subtests and total score were substantial (.87 and better). Pearson product moment correlation coefficients for interrater reliability teacher/teacher and teacher/employer ranged from .87 to .92 and .77 to .79, respectively.

Content, criterion-related, and construct validity were addressed. Content validity evidence included the method of selection of descriptors, item/total correlations, and inter-subscale correlations.

Criterion-related validity was investigated by comparing performances on the Behavior Evaluation Scale (BES) constructed by McCarney, Leigh, and Cornbleet (1983) and the TBS. BES subscales correlated with TBS subscales as follows: inability to learn not due to physical and mental factors with Work Related, .48; inability to establish or maintain satisfactory interpersonal relationships with peers or teachers with Interpersonal Relations, .69; and inappropriate types of behavior or feelings in normal circumstances with Social/Community Expectation, .61. All obtained correlations exceeded Guilford's (1965) levels of acceptability (.30 to .35) at the .001 level of significance.

Diagnostic validity was supported by significant differences by gender on all three subscales and total scale and by the ratings of a 20% minority who perform either inconsistently or not at all on 57 of the 62 items. TBS responses are positively skewed with the majority of the high school students exhibiting positive behaviors and with females generally scoring higher than males. The wide ranges of the sum of subscale standard scores and of the percentile ranks by gender beg the discrimination power for females.

Construct validity evidence included comparison of ratings on the TBS of identified behavior/adjustment problem students with rated performances of randomly selected junior and senior students from the normative sample. Results showed that the problem-behavior students obtained lower mean total percentile scores and statistically significant ($p < .001$) raw score mean differences than did students from the normative sample.

Administration guidelines are clear and easy to follow. Raters could be anyone familiar with the student's behavior and skills over a period of time. Rating definitions could be improved by stipulating percentages of behavior comprising "inconsistently" and "consistently."

Scoring guidelines for subscale performances are clear by gender and total population because the relevant conversion tables report the sum of raw scores corresponding to the percentile rank. Conversion tables also report subscale standard scores.

Scoring guidelines for overall percentile rank are extremely confusing. Trouble begins when using subscale standard scores to determine overall percentile rank. No warning is given that the subscale standard scores may differ by gender (Table A1 and Table A in the manual) as well as by total population (Table A3). Nor is warning given that the sum of all three subscale standard scores by gender is used for same-gender overall percentile rank conversion tables. Furthermore, no direction is given that the sum of subscale standard scores shown for the total population (Table A3) should be used for determining overall percentile rank comparisons for total population (Table B3).

The TBS and relevant past school evaluations could help justify student assignment to special programs.

REVIEWER'S REFERENCES

Guilford, J. P. (1965). *Fundamental statistics in psychology and education* (4th ed.). New York: McGraw-Hill.

McCarney, S. B., Leigh, J. E., & Cornbleet, J. E. (1983). Behavior Evaluation Scale. Columbia, MO: Educational Services.

Review of the Transition Behavior Scale by DAVID O. HERMAN, Associate Education Officer, Office of Educational Research, New York City Board of Education, Brooklyn, NY:

The Transition Behavior Scale (TBS) is designed primarily for use by high school teachers to describe the readiness of their junior and senior students for transition to employment or independent living. Its 62 items describe behavior that is considered predictive of post-school adjustment. All items are positively worded—that is, they describe desirable behavior. The wording is clear.

In describing their students, raters respond to each item on a 3-point scale: 1 = *Does not perform the behavior*; 2 = *Performs the behavior inconsistently*; and 3 = *Performs the behavior consistently*. The manual emphasizes that no items are to be omitted, so it is important that raters know their students well through frequent contact. The manual recommends that at least three such qualified persons rate each student independently in order to minimize bias and random error in the results. This goal is laudable, but perhaps it may be approached only in small schools with high staff-to-student ratios.

The items that make up the TBS were carefully developed. A group of 47 teachers, guidance counselors, other educational staff members, and employers supplied lists of behaviors they considered predictive of success in employment and independent living. After the author eliminated duplicates from the initial lists, the same group was asked to review the surviving list for items that were inappropriate or poorly worded, and to add any new material not on the list.

The resulting 62 items were now assigned on the basis of their content to one of the three subscales noted in the descriptive entry that precedes this review. After field testing, the scale was standardized on a sample of 2,665 junior and senior students in 70 school systems in 23 states. The students rated were chosen at random from the classes of the participating teachers, who themselves are said to have been randomly selected. Thus, the sample was selected to represent students-in-general, not a special clinical or disturbed group. The manual provides evidence that the sample approximately represents the U.S. population in terms of sex, race, urban-rural residence, and parental occupation; however, rural students and those in the North Central states are somewhat overrepresented in this normative sample. These national norms are an impressive strength of the TBS.

Study of the standardization data revealed significant sex differences (females were rated higher on the average) on all three subscales, so norms were prepared for males and females separately as well as for the standardization sample as a whole.

The raw score on each subscale is the sum of ratings given to the items on that subscale. Using the norms table appropriate to the student's gender (the technical manual offers no guidance on when the same-sex norms will be more or less appropriate than the combined-sex norms), the raw score is transformed to the corresponding percentile rank as well as to a standard score. The total score on the TBS is not the sum of the three raw subscale scores; rather, the sum of standard scores on the subscales is transformed to its percentile rank. The effect of this manipulation is to equalize the contributions of the subscales to the total score. (The three subscales are not of the same size—there are 25 items on the Work Related subscale, 15 items on Interpersonal Relations, and 22 on Social/Community Expectations.) The manual does not justify using this procedure, even though simply summing the item scores would be easier and less prone to clerical error, and the resulting total score would probably have about the same measurement properties as the recommended total score.

After converting the four scores to their national percentile equivalents, the user lists items for which the student received the low ratings of 1 and 2. The lists will document primary and secondary concerns about the student's behavior, and can identify areas for possible intervention. The IEP and Intervention Manual provides educators with intervention strategies specifically keyed to the TBS items. Many of the suggested interventions are imaginative and reflect practical experience in handling problematic students. Less happily, the same or nearly the same interventions are proposed for so many different TBS items that the lists of interventions take on a rather general air; furthermore, some of them seem tangentially related to the behavior in question. A computer program is available for scoring the scale and printing lists of the low-rated items.

The technical manual reports a variety of psychometric support for the TBS. Several studies were carried out on the full standardization sample. A factor analysis at the item level is described, but it offers only limited support for dividing the items among the three subscales. Internal consistency, reported as alpha coefficients, was .93 or greater for the three subscales. The subscale intercorrelations were .85 or greater. Although lower than the subscale reliabilities, these high intercorrelations hardly support the manual's claims of the "distinctiveness" (p. 13) of the subscales. I suggest that the total score and lists of the low-rated items are more useful than the subscale scores—another reason for simplifying the derivation of total scores.

Additional reliability studies were conducted using groups of a few hundred cases drawn from the standardization sample. Coefficients of one-month stability and of interrater reliability ranged from the high .70s to the low .90s.

The technical manual presents three kinds of validity evidence. The content validity of the TBS is said to inhere in the development of the scale, that is, the careful identification of target behaviors and the refinement of item statements. Criterion-related validity rests on the relationship of TBS ratings to ratings on the Behavior Evaluation Scale (McCarney, Leigh, & Cornbleet, 1983), a rather similar-sounding rating scale. The correlations of the latter instrument and the TBS subscales were .48 with Work Related, .69 with Interpersonal Relations, and .61 with Social/Community Expectations.

Evidence of the construct ("diagnostic") validity comes from differences in TBS results for 263 students selected at random from the normative sample and 263 high school juniors and seniors "who were identified as having behavior/adjustment problems" (p. 16). The problem students were rated significantly lower than the "normal" group on all four TBS scores.

Unhappily, something must be said about the careless editing of both the technical manual and the IEP and Intervention manual. Here are examples. Both manuals are notably repetitive. The same student sample is sometimes described as consisting of high school seniors, and sometimes juniors and seniors. The tables of reliability and validity coefficients for subsets of the standardization sample fail to report the supporting means and standard deviations, which would have provided a partial check on the representativeness of the special samples. Two separate sections of the technical manual describe a particular table as summarizing data on the "discriminating power" of the TBS, when what is actually presented are data summarizing TBS raw scores. The directions for obtaining the total score are seriously incomplete. Some of the lists of suggested interventions present the same intervention twice. These may be minor matters, but they should be addressed whenever the materials are revised.

In summary, the Transition Behavior Scale appears to have been carefully constructed for its special purpose. The availability of national norms enhances its usefulness, as does the set of suggested interventions that are linked to the behaviors sampled by the scale. At the same time the author and publisher must be criticized for the air of carelessness that pervades the supporting manuals.

REVIEWER'S REFERENCE

McCarney, S. B., Leigh, J. E., & Cornbleet, J. E. (1983). Behavior Evaluation Scale. Columbia, MO: Educational Services.

[405]

Understanding and Managing Stress.

Purpose: Assesses stress level and health-related behaviors.
Population: Adults.
Publication Date: 1989.
Scores: Continuum of risk scores (low, medium, high) for each of 22 areas: Changes on the Job/Total, Changes on the Job/High-Impact, Changes in Personal Life/Total, Changes in Personal Life/High-Impact, Chronic Stressful Conditions on the Job, Chronic Stressful Conditions in Personal Life, Strain Response, Psychological Outlook, General Lifestyle/Importance to Health, General Lifestyle/Present Effectiveness, Social Support, Nutritional Habits and Awareness/Total, Physical Exercise Habits and Awareness, Drinking Habits, Behavioral Habits, Tobacco, Systolic Blood Pressure Reading, Diastolic Blood Pressure Reading, Total Cholesterol, High-Density Lipoprotein (HDL) Level, Ratio of Total Cholesterol to HDL, Triglyceride Level.
Administration: Group.
Price Data, 1991: $9.95 per handbook (64 pages).
Time: Administration time not reported.
Comments: Self-administered, self-scored.
Author: John D. Adams.
Publisher: Pfeiffer & Company International Publishers.

Review of Understanding and Managing Stress by WILLIAM J. WALDRON, Administrator, Employee Assessment, Tampa Electric Company, Tampa, FL:

INTRODUCTION. Understanding and Managing Stress is a self-administered, self-scored collection of instruments designed to provide individuals with insights about their current stress levels, job and lifestyle factors that are contributing to these stress levels, and suggested strategies for reducing stress.

Rather than being marketed as a "test," the instruments are intended to be used within organizations as part of a stress management workshop; a participant workbook, a book of readings, and a facilitator's guide are also available from the publisher for this purpose.

The set of instruments reviewed are provided as part of a workbook containing three main portions: (*a*) the instruments themselves (including instructions to the respondent), (*b*) instructions for self-scoring and determination of relative risk levels, and (*c*) an educational/planning section discussing the nature of stress and suggested life-style improvements that can be implemented to reduce stress levels. There is no technical manual as such for the instruments.

The quality of the educational components of the booklet is quite high; however, this review focuses upon the instrumentation rather than on the educational/training portions of the Understanding and Managing Stress package.

DESCRIPTION OF THE INSTRUMENTS. Within the package there are 13 self-report inventories. The first five instruments are concerned with assessing *episodic* stress (both on the job and within the respondent's personal life), *chronic* stress (again, separated into work and nonwork scales), and the *strain* response. The remaining eight scales measure *outlook/lifestyle* factors that contribute to stress and one's response to it: Psychological Outlook, General Lifestyle, Social Support, Nutritional Habits and Awareness, Exercise Habits and Awareness, Drinking Habits, Behavioral Habits, Additional Lifestyle Habits, and Medical Information.

The scales contain various numbers of items (from 7 to 40) and utilize different types of response scales: Some are simple checklists, whereas others use Likert-type scales. The instructions to the respondent are generally clear and concise. Five of the scales were developed elsewhere, with the original published sources cited in footnotes; the remainder appear to have been developed by the author. No information about the scale development process is provided, however.

CRITIQUE. It is impossible to pass judgment on the psychometric quality of the instruments. Although the author states that the scales have been in numerous research studies, information about these studies is not provided, nor is any of the traditional psychometric information (reliability, validity, etc.). Although this information may not, in general, be demanded by the target audience of training and development staff, its absence causes concern in regard to reliability, scoring, and response validity.

RELIABILITY. As noted, the scales in the package vary in both length and response format; it is likely that they vary significantly in reliability as well. Why is this important? In the later sections of the booklet, the author states that the results obtained "provide only a snapshot of your risks at a point in time. It is advisable to reassess your stress and lifestyle situation periodically to ensure that you are keeping the risks at a safe, low level" (p. 37). Without taking into account the precision (i.e., standard errors) or the expected stability of the scale scores (without significant lifestyle changes), such reassessment could definitely provide misleading information.

SCORING. After completing the inventories and calculating their scores according to the instructions provided in Part 1 of the booklet, the respondents are asked in Part 2 to plot each of their scores on a graphic continuum that represents a percentile scale "constructed from the scores of a large number of people who have completed the same inventory" (p. 29). On each of these scales, scores at or below about the 30th percentile are labeled as "low risk," those from about the 40th to 70th as "moderate risk," and any higher percentile ranks as "high risk."

Although this may be useful as a rough rule of thumb, more information is clearly appropriate here. Without further description about the individuals comprising the normative group(s), the results are difficult to interpret. First, given that the scales were developed by various researchers, it seems possible that quite different types of individuals make up the reference groups for the various scales. For example, being at the 50th percentile in a representative random sample of working adults would mean something entirely different from having the same rank with reference to a group made up only of people referred to an employee assistance plan. Second, the actual level of risk associated with the same percentile rank might be quite different from scale to scale, depending upon the shape of the distributions in the population and the evidence linking scores on the various scales to negative outcomes.

RESPONSE VALIDITY. Another consideration that might be important to potential users of the instruments is the degree to which the results may be consciously manipulated by respondents. Although no data are provided on this subject, it appears that an individual motivated to do so could easily distort his or her responses. In other words, the scales and their scoring are relatively *transparent*: If certain people wanted to present themselves as facing very little (or very great) stress, it appears that they would easily be able to do so. This may not be a major concern in a training workshop made up of self-selected employees who are motivated to learn about stress and ways to manage it; however, researchers attempting to use these scales in other contexts with other types of samples would need to be concerned with this possibility.

SUMMARY. The above concerns should not be taken as a condemnation of the instruments; although important data are lacking, the quality of the package taken as a whole is higher than that of many others that primarily target organizational training and development staff. Used carefully, with professional guidance in interpretation of the results, Understanding and Managing Stress could prove quite useful in helping individuals to assess and manage the stress that they face in their work and personal lives. This endorsement must be a qualified one; however, one would be able to recommend these instruments with more confidence if specific and detailed psychometric and normative data were provided.

Review of Understanding and Managing Stress by WILLIAM K. WILKINSON, Assistant Professor of Counseling and Educational Psychology, New Mexico State University, Las Cruces, NM, and CHRISTOPHER P. MIGOTSKY, Doctoral Student, Department of Educational Measurement, University of Illinois, Champaign-Urbana, Champaign-Urbana, IL:

Understanding and Managing Stress (UMS) is a compilation of previous self-report instruments designed to assess an individual's stress level and health-related behaviors. It is unclear who can take the UMS, but it appears that anyone constituting the "working public" may be applicable respondents (working in that the first few inventories ask current job-related questions). The required reading level is not given.

All UMS materials are contained in a single 58-page manual consisting of the following three parts. In Part 1, 13 inventories related to stress and lifestyle habits are provided. Overall, these 13 instruments contain 253 items, supposedly comprising 24 different scales. Response scales vary with the scale. For example, the first two scales are titled, "Changes on the Job," and "Changes in Personal Life," and respondents are directed to mark an adjustment score (provided) next to any event that happened in the past 12 months (e.g., decrease in status, new boss, death of spouse, serious illness, etc.). Scores are obtained by totaling the adjustment scores. With two exceptions, the remaining scales involve a 5- or 6-point, Likert-type response, and responses are summed to achieve scale scores.

Part 2 is a brief, self-interpretive guide for the user. Here, 22 of the 24 raw scale scores can be converted to a percentile continuum represented in decile increments. The raw score values corresponding to each decile are provided. Further, each decile continuum is divided into three risk levels—low, moderate, or high. For the vast majority of scale scores, each risk level includes a third of the deciles. Thus, in cases where high scores mean more risk, low risk corresponds to the 10–30 deciles, moderate risk the 40–60 deciles, and high risk the 70–90 deciles. In general, if any scores are in the moderate to high risk area, the test-taker is directed to "begin acting immediately to lower these risks."

Finally, Part 3 contains prescriptions and strategies for those wanting to alter their response to stress. For example, specific recommendations for altering nutrition and improving physical fitness are provided.

It is important to review the UMS materials from two perspectives: (*a*) the "naive respondent," who simply wants to learn more about his or her stress and lifestyle habits; and (*b*) the mental health professional who wants to know whether the UMS demonstrates adequate test properties for clinic/agency use. The first perspective is important, especially given the UMS package was constructed in the spirit of "self-awareness" instruments. Indeed, the entire package is meant to be self-administered, self-scored, and self-interpreted. As such, the critical question is, "will the UMS provide useful information to 'lay' respondents." Solely from a face validity vantage, items do appear to tap sources of stress, coping mechanisms for stress, and health-related behaviors. Knowing this information may be useful to respondents and may stimulate more self-analysis and, perhaps, encourage individuals to engage in more successful lifestyle habits.

On the other hand, human service professionals will be interested in determining the meaningfulness of test data, by judging the UMS in terms of psychometric adequacy. Unfortunately, the UMS is a compilation of existing instruments only in terms of the tests themselves. No normative, reliability, or validity data are provided for any of the instruments. Primary citations are listed for 6 of the 13 instruments, and the interested professional will need to consult these references to learn more about the technical properties of these instruments. Sources for the other instruments are not provided.

Clearly, without any information on the development of the individual instruments, human service professionals must take a gigantic "leap of faith" and simply assume that the tests are appropriate for their clients, measure the constructs they purportedly measure, and do so consistently. Obviously, inserting 13 separate test manuals in one package would be absurd. Yet, in the absence of basic information about each of the instruments, the test purchaser cannot know whether the tests are appropriate for a particular client, whether the tests provide consistent information, or whether the tests even measure what they claim to measure. One recommendation is the creation of a companion "test development" manual, in which enough psychometric information is included to enable the test purchaser to make reasonable decisions regarding the relevancy and usefulness of the individual measures.

In sum, the UMS represents an admirable attempt to synthesize stress and lifestyle instruments into a single package. Because the UMS may be aimed at the "naive" public, the goal increasing self-awareness, the author's attitude appears to be "what the lay public doesn't know about the individual tests won't hurt them." In other words, psychometrically unsophisticated test takers (an obviously vast audience) may learn something useful about their stress and lifestyle habits, even if the instruments themselves are technically unsound. We doubt this approach will appeal to critical consumers, and, because these consumers will decide whether the test has any appeal in practical settings, it is our belief that the UMS will not gain widespread appeal.

[406]

Veterinary College Admission Test.

Purpose: Designed to measure general academic ability and scientific knowledge.
Population: Veterinary college applicants.
Publication Dates: 1951–91.
Acronym: VCAT.
Scores, 5: Verbal Ability, Biology, Chemistry, Quantitative Ability, Reading Comprehension.
Administration: Group.
Restricted Distribution: Distribution restricted and test administered at licensed testing centers; details may be obtained from publisher.
Price Data: Available from publisher.
Time: 175(205) minutes.
Comments: Formerly called the Veterinary Aptitude Test.
Author: The Psychological Corporation.
Publisher: The Psychological Corporation.
Cross References: See T2:2358 (1 reference), 7:1101, 6:1139 (3 references), and 5:957 (3 references).

Review of the Veterinary College Admission Test by JAMES B. ERDMANN, Associate Dean and Professor of Medicine (Education), Jefferson Medical College, Thomas Jefferson University, Philadelphia, PA:

"Publishers should provide enough information for a qualified user or a reviewer of a test to evaluate the appropriateness and technical adequacy of the test." "Technical data that are required prior to the release of the test for operational use are usually summarized with appropriate references in a *technical manual.*" "Test developers have a responsibility to provide evidence regarding reliability and validity for stated testing purposes, as well as manuals and norms, when appropriate, to guide proper interpretation."

The preceding quotes are taken verbatim from *Standards for Educational and Psychological Testing*, (pages 35 and 25), prepared by a joint committee of the American Educational Research Association, the American Psychological Association, and the National Council on Measurement in Education (1985). Unfortunately, from all appearances, the publisher/test developer of the Veterinary College Admission Test (VCAT) has been inexcusably delinquent in meeting its responsibilities. This version of an admission test for entrance to schools of veterinary medicine was copyrighted in 1989 and still essential information necessary for the Psychological Corporation to discharge its most elementary responsibilities is unavailable from the publisher/developer. It should be noted that the *Standards* call for technical data to be made available *prior* to the release of the test for operational use. It is now 6 years since the test was copyrighted and still no technical justification for use of the test is available from the publisher/developer. It is this kind of behavior that makes it very difficult for responsible publishers and developers of tests to defend their testing programs against the critics and opponents of standardized testing.

The published documents available for this review consisted of the Candidate Information Booklet, the Manual of Directions for Examiners, and a specimen test. The latter is a secure document, and the Manual of Directions for Examiners has limited distribution intended only for those responsible for the administration of the test; hence, only the Candidate Information Booklet is widely available to provide any information about the nature of the test, the justification for its use in the admissions process, and the appropriate interpretation of scores derived from it. If at all, this booklet treats these topics in only the most superficial manner. No reliability nor any type of validity information is provided, except that the booklet states "Surveys of colleges of veterinary medicine were used to determine the content areas needed for the test" (p. 24). Perhaps it is a case of imprecise narrative, but even that statement does not confirm that the actual content of the test was *decided* by the colleges. Each of the five content areas are described in two lines or less. A total of 13 sample questions are provided, hardly enough to give a fair indication of the breadth and depth of coverage because no outlines of covered material are included.

The interpretation of reported scores is treated in less than half a page. And the information that is provided is somewhat perplexing. For example, the narrative indicates that the scores reported for each section and the total test (the composite score) range from 100 to 300. The text further indicates that 200 corresponds to the 50th percentile. Even if the original anchor group had an identical mean and median, it is hard to understand how successive administrations equated to the anchor group would have the same characteristics unless successive groups had identical distributions of scores. Such has not been the experience with most national standardized test programs, where the means move up or down from cohort to cohort depending on the characteristics of the group.

In personal communications with the publisher/developer to confirm the status of published technical information the mean, standard deviation, and standard error of the raw composite scores together with the Kuder-Richardson 21 were provided for the November 1993 administration. The latter had a value of .93 and although this would be judged satisfactory from an internal consistency point of view, alternate form or test-retest estimates are important as recommended by the *Standards* for the purpose for which test scores from the Veterinary College Admission Test are used.

These same personal communications led to the provision by the publisher/developer of the technical manual for the Pharmacy College Admission Test. It was supplied as an example of the kind of manual that will be prepared for the Veterinary College Admission Test and as an indication of the test development and scoring processes that are used for the Veterinary College Admission Test. Although the information presented would go a long way toward satisfying the need for information about the Veterinary College Admission Test, the actual data on the Veterinary College Admission Test are still missing and thus a major void remains.

Despite the status of published information about the test, there is a positive note. The potential populations of users are quite restricted, thus making it relatively easy for the developer/publisher of the test to communicate effectively about the limitations that should be understood in interpreting and using Veterinary College Admission Test scores. For example, in communications with program staff in an attempt to learn more about validity, it was implied that individual users (schools of veterinary medicine) were expected to conduct their own validity studies. The assumption seems to be that the user would not make decisions on the basis of the results of the Veterinary College Admission Test until local research had justified their use. It is conceivable that the contract between the schools of veterinary medicine with the Psychological Corporation stipulates such an expectation. However, there is no evidence to indicate that has been systematically pursued. From an inspection of the test questions, one should probably expect a generally positive relationship with general measures of academic achievement, but the magnitude really needs to be known. Further, there does not seem to be anything about the test that would suggest it was specifically responsive to the needs of veterinary school admissions officers.

When the Veterinary College Admission Test was originally released I would not have recommended using the test without first having had some developer-supplied concurrent validity data. Given the passage of time since its initial use, there can be no justification for not having a developer-provided technical manual containing the kind of treatment of reliability and validity issues called for in the *Standards* which is needed to support the continued use of the test.

REVIEWER'S REFERENCE

American Educational Research Association, American Psychological Association, & National Council on Measurement in Education. (1985). *Standards for educational and psychological testing*. Washington, DC: American Psychological Association, Inc.

Review of the Veterinary College Admission Test by TERRY A. STINNETT, Associate Professor of Psychology, Eastern Illinois University, Charleston, IL:

The Veterinary College Admission Test (VCAT), formerly known as the Veterinary Aptitude Test (VAT), was initially developed in the late 1940s. The VCAT is described by its publisher as a specialized test designed to measure general academic ability and scientific knowledge. It is intended to identify qualified applicants for admission into colleges of veterinary medicine. The test is group administered three times per year at scheduled testing centers. According to the 1991 candidate information booklet, there is a $50 fee that the applicant must pay by money order and attach to the application to be preregistered for the test. If the applicant does not preregister, there is a $25 standby registration fee in addition to the regular test fee. There is a $15 fee to reschedule the location of testing, the date of testing, or both. Three score reports are provided in the application cost; additional score reports are $10 each. An examinee can have his or her answer sheet hand scored for $10 if he or she wishes to confirm the electronically scored results.

HISTORY OF THE VCAT. Owens (1950a; 1950b) and Payne (1953) developed the original versions of the test and validated them shortly after World War II. In its prototypical form the test contained four special purpose tests: two 50-item achievement tests in chemistry and zoology and two 50-item tests purported to measure aptitude for "Paragraph Comprehension" and "Verbal Memory." After preliminary study, the first two subtests were shortened and combined into one form known as the Iowa State Veterinary Medical Achievement Test. The paragraph comprehension test was revised and called the Iowa State Veterinary Medical Aptitude Test I and the verbal memory test was revised and became Aptitude Test II. Collectively these scales became known as the Veterinary Medical Aptitude Test (VMAT). Validity studies conducted with the VMAT demonstrated the test had satisfactory split-half reliability ($r = .88$) and that it was related to grade-point average (r_ts ranged from .48 to .72). The VMAT also predicted academic success during the first two quarters of professional veterinary training better than preveterinary grades or performance on the ACE psychological examination and it predicted most efficiently, within the validational group, from a relatively low cutoff score. Layton (1952) used the VMAT, the veterinary scale of the Strong Vocational Interest Blank, the Professional Aptitude Test, and preveterinary grade-point average to predict academic achievement of students enrolled in a veterinary medicine program. The best combination of predictors of first year grades in veterinary school was the veterinary section of the Strong, preveterinary grade-point average, and the achievement score of the VMAT ($R = .60$). The aptitude tests of the VMAT were not found to be highly correlated with the criterion.

Almost a decade later, Brown (1960) used student grade-point average prior to admission in veterinary school and the VAT total score to predict grade-point average in the first 2 years of veterinary training (preclinical) and in the last 2 years of training (clinical). Multiple *R*s of .64 and .70 were obtained for the preclinical and clinical years, respectively. Use of preveterinary grade-point average and the VAT was effective in identifying students who were successful in veterinary school.

CURRENT DESCRIPTION. Current forms of the VCAT consist of approximately 230 multiple-choice items in five content areas thought to be critical for predicting success in a basic veterinary medicine curriculum: (*a*) Verbal Ability, (*b*) Biology, (*c*) Chemistry, (*d*) Quantitative Ability, and (*e*) Reading Comprehension. No detailed information about the development of the VCAT is available from the publisher. The candidate information booklet reports that surveys of colleges of veterinary medicine were used to determine the content areas needed for the test. Questions were then written by veterinary medicine professionals and educators. Those questions were edited and categorized by professional staff at The Psychological Corporation.

Each content area is a separate section on the VCAT and examinees are given 35 minutes to complete each section. The Verbal Ability section contains approximately 50 items designed to measure general vocabulary and verbal reasoning. The items are of two types: antonyms and analogies. The Biology and Chemistry sections also contain about 50 items each. The Biology items are designed to measure knowledge of concepts and principles likely to be encountered in elementary college biology courses and the Chemistry items are meant to measure knowledge of principles and concepts from elementary college courses in both organic and inorganic chemistry. The Quantitative Ability section measures quantitative reasoning and understanding of mathematical concepts with 40 items of various types. Some of the items test basic mathematical skills and include both calculation problems and word problems. Other quantitative items require the interpretation and synthesis of data that are presented graphically or in charts and some require the examinee to make quantitative comparisons. The Reading Comprehension section also contains about 40 items that measure the examinee's ability to read and understand college-level reading passages.

The VCAT is a multiple-choice test and the examinee completes the test by marking his or her answers on an optical-scan answer sheet. Each item has four choices. Scores are based on the number of correct answers and there is no penalty for guessing. Standard scores and percentiles are computed for each of the specific five content areas and for the test as a whole (i.e., a test composite). The standard scores range from 100 to 300 and allow for comparison across different forms of the test. A scaled score of 200 corresponds to the 50th percentile. It is not clearly stated in the candidate information booklet, but it is implied that the percentile scores are based on the performance of the current group of applicants who are taking the test. Thus, the percentile for a given score might vary over the years, depending on the applicant group to which the score is compared. The Psychological Corporation reports that no passing or failing score has been set. The extent to which the test results are used to determine whether an applicant will be admitted to veterinary medical school is at the discretion of each college.

RELIABILITY AND VALIDITY. There are no current reliability or validity data available for the VCAT. A representative of the Psychological Corporation informed this reviewer verbally that a technical report was in the process of being compiled. No preliminary data are available. There are no guidelines established by the publisher to assist the various colleges in the use of the VCAT test score.

SUMMARY. It would not be appropriate to recommend this instrument for use at this time. Although the prototype of the VCAT performed well in achieving its stated purpose and had adequate psychometric qualities, the current form of the test has no empirical data available to help potential users determine whether it is suitable for their purposes. Payne (1953) indicated the VMAT was not designed to replace other methods of selection (e.g., review of previous grades, performance on other standard examinations, and personal interviews). Admissions committees would be well advised to follow that advice and rely on multiple sources of information to maximize their hit rate on candidates who are likely to be successful in veterinary medicine programs.

REVIEWER'S REFERENCES

Owens, W. A. (1950a). An aptitude test for veterinary medicine. *Journal of Applied Psychology, 34*, 295-299.

Owens, W. A. (1950b). Development of a test of aptitude for veterinary medicine. In *Proceedings of the fifty-second session of the Iowa Academy of Science for 1950* (vol. 57; pp. 417-423). Iowa City, IA: State of Iowa.

Layton, W. L. (1952). Predicting success of students in veterinary medicine. *Journal of Applied Psychology, 36*, 323-315.

Payne, L. C. (1953). *Development and validation of a veterinary medical aptitude test*. Unpublished doctoral dissertation, Iowa State College, Ames.

Brown, F. G. (1960). Predicting success in the clinical and preclinical years of veterinary medical school. *Journal of the American Veterinary Medical Association, 137*, 428-429.

[407]

Visual Search and Attention Test.

Purpose: Constructed to assess "ability to scan accurately and [to] sustain attention on each of four different visual cancellation tasks."

Population: Ages 18 and over.

Publication Dates: 1987–90.

Acronym: VSAT.

Scores, 3: Left, Right, Total.

Administration: Individual.

Price Data, 1995: $54 per complete kit including 25 test booklets and manual ('90, 18 pages); $42 per 25 test booklets; $15 per manual.

Time: 4(6) minutes.

Authors: Max R. Trenerry, Bruce Crosson, James DeBoe, and William R. Leber.

Publisher: Psychological Assessment Resources, Inc.

TEST REFERENCES

1. O'Donnell, J. P., Macgregor, L. A., Dabrowski, J. J., Oestreicher, J. M., & Romero, J. J. (1994). Construct validity of neuropsychological tests of conceptual and attentional abilities. *Journal of Clinical Psychology, 50*, 596-600.

Review of the Visual Search and Attention Test by STEPHEN R. HOOPER, Associate Professor of Psychiatry, University of North Carolina School of Medicine, Chapel Hill, NC:

The Visual Search and Attention Test (VSAT) was designed to be used as a screening tool or as a component part of a larger neuropsychological assessment in order to gain a measure of sustained attention. Administration time is approximately 6 minutes. The test procedures are straightforward and require little background knowledge on the part of the examiner. The test authors do state, however, that examiners should be trained by a qualified psychologist, and that interpretation requires appropriate training in neuropsychology or an applied area of psychology. The only test material required for administration is the VSAT Test Booklet, and it is clear that careful thought went into its organization and development. The test booklet consists of eight pages containing a color vision screening, directions for the patient, two sample tasks, and a scoring grid. Further, three of the pages are blank so as to eliminate interfering stimuli from other pages, and each page has been organized via random placement of the letters and symbols that represent the target stimuli, equal placement of the stimuli on each side of the midline, and a landscaped presentation of the test items. These latter features are extremely important given the attentionally based nature of the task. In contrast, the letters/symbols are quite small and these target stimuli are close in their colors, especially for the nonverbal items. Although the normative data should begin to take these features into account, it does create a potential confound with respect to item complexity.

The manual is detailed with respect to administration and scoring, but it would have been helpful to have more current citations on attention in the reference section. In general, the manual is relatively brief, but nicely organized and well written. The authors describe a reasonable rationale for the VSAT, based on a cursory review of the literature, although a well-developed neuropsychologically based model of attention was not presented. In fact, given the duration of 1 minute for each subtest, one has to wonder whether the test is not tapping into visual selective attention more so than sustained attention. Nonetheless, the VSAT was developed in accordance with other measures of attention in the literature. Furthermore, the authors are careful to point out that sustained attention is only one component part of a larger construct called attention.

Scoring is simple and straightforward. An appendix contains the normative tables, which are easily accessed and consumed. These tables are arranged as four 10-year age bands, an 18–19-year age band, and a 60+ age-band. All raw scores are transferred into percentile ranks. Scoring criteria were based on a sample of 372 subjects, with about one-third of these subjects (n = 100) comprising specific neurologically impaired groups. In addition to a total score, left and right visual field scores can be obtained. Examiners should be careful interpreting the half-fields, however, as the findings could be an artifact of the administration of the VSAT (i.e., if someone is working left to right, then they should have a higher score on the left side in nearly all instances outside of when neuropathology is present). Further, the authors note the half-field scores seem to be of little value, outside of what might be observed from a qualitative perspective.

The statistical properties of the VSAT appear adequate. The authors provide information relative to the influence of selective demographic factors on this test, such as age, gender, and education. Temporal stability was deemed highly reliable (i.e., .95) over at least a 2-month period of time. Such test-retest practices should be planned with caution, however, as normal adults showed approximately an 11% improvement secondary to practice effects. Consequently, the use of serial administrations of the VSAT with respect to monitoring recovery of attentional functioning should be considered carefully. A standard error of measurement also was presented for each scale.

The VSAT clearly maintains good face validity, and the authors describe several other validation components as well. The VSAT was capable of distinguishing between a normal group and heterogeneous groups of brain-damaged individuals. An appraisal of sensitivity and specificity produced good results (i.e., overall hit rates in the mid .80s), although the rates of false positives and false negatives were somewhat high (i.e., greater than 12%). The total score from the VSAT also demonstrated good convergent and discriminant validity.

Normative data were ascertained on 272 adults, although a clear, detailed description of these individuals and the ascertainment procedures were not presented in the manual. The sample size for each age band was modest, and ranged from 24 subjects in the 50–59 age-band to 59 subjects in the 18–19 age-band. The reliability of the normative data was increased by the application of the continuous norming procedure. This procedure accounts for irregularities in the score distributions across age bands, and it makes adjustments when age-band samples are less than 200. This should facilitate greater confidence in the normative data.

In summary, the VSAT was designed to measure a selective component of the multidimensional construct of attention. Although purportedly measuring sustained attention, one could argue that the VSAT taps visual selective attention to a greater degree. The test is based loosely on a neuropsychological model of attention, although this is not well described. The test materials are simple and straightforward, and the test administration requires only about 6 minutes. The psychometric properties of the VSAT appear adequate, and some sophisticated adjustments were made in the normative sample to increase the confidence in these data; however, the normative sample and its ascertainment are not described in any detail. In general, this test should provide examiners with a quick and easy screening of the visual attention process, although exactly what aspects of the attentional process the test is tapping primarily remains to be determined.

Review of the Visual Search and Attention Test by WILFRED G. VAN GORP, Associate Professor in Residence and Director, Neuropsychology Assessment Laboratory, UCLA School of Medicine, Department of Psychiatry and Biobehavioral Sciences and Interim Chief, Psychology Service, Department of Veterans Affairs Medical Center, West Los Angeles, CA:

The Visual Search and Attention Test (VSAT) purports to assess sustained attention and visual scanning. The 6-minute test consists of four tasks: In the first two tasks, the respondent must find and cross out each letter (Task 1) or symbol (Task 2) that matches the target from an array of 40 letters or symbols per line, 10 lines per page. Tasks 3 and 4 use the same format as Tasks 1 and 2, but the stimuli also vary by color and the respondent must respond to the matches by color as well as form. Because findings from the initial validity studies on the VSAT indicated that only Tasks 3 and 4 significantly distinguished patients from normals, the total score is derived only from these latter two tasks. The test is administered to individuals aged 18 and older (no upper age limit is given), and percentiles based upon the respondent's age are computed. Scores for performance on the left and right sides can also be computed to detect hemispatial neglect.

The VSAT fills a significant gap in the compendium of neuropsychological tests because few (if any) tests of sustained attention of this type with adequate norms have been published formally. The test appears to have adequate test-retest reliability ($r = .95$) though this must be viewed as tentative in that it is based only on a subsample of 28 subjects. Discriminant analysis has revealed acceptable sensitivity and specificity when classifying normals versus "brain damaged subjects" using VSAT score (overall hit rate was .84, sensitivity = .78, specificity = .87). Interestingly, patients with unilateral left versus right hemisphere lesions did not differ in their Left versus Right scores on the VSAT, although it was not reported if any of these patients had been diagnosed formally with hemispatial neglect. Because of a limited number of subjects in the normative sample ($N = 272$), the authors used statistical procedures to find the best mathematical fit for the norms. This approach is better than merely reporting means and standard deviations from the normative sample, but not as good as having a sufficiently large N that such an estimation is not needed.

The most troubling aspect of this test is the repeated theme throughout the manual that this test will be useful as a screening measure to detect brain damage. The concept of brain damage as a unitary construct has been criticized repeatedly, though the manual contains numerous statements that seem to accept this notion. If the goal were to actually develop a general screening measure to detect individuals with diffuse brain damage, it would have been useful to include data on how the VSAT performs in this regard relative to other standard neuropsychological screening measures currently in use.

An additional concern must be raised regarding the size of the test stimuli. They are not large, and this may pose a problem for those with mild visual difficulties, especially the elderly. This is even more relevant because the elderly constitute one group for whom neuropsychological screening measures and tests of attention are often given, yet the relatively small stimuli and the unclear upper age limit of the normative data (percentiles are calculated in the highest age group for "60+") makes the test of questionable appropriateness for some elderly. Future editions of this test might include larger stimuli and more information on norms for the elderly.

The strength of this test—as used in contemporary clinical neuropsychology—is its assessment of sustained attention and visual scanning. Additional validation studies are awaited to determine how well the test performs in assessing these cognitive functions. As is, however, this relatively new test seems to hold promise if one can go beyond the notion of brain damage as a unitary construct as implied in the manual.

[408]

Vocational Interest Inventory and Exploration Survey.

Purpose:: Designed to "assess a student's interest in school based training programs" and provide "information about the training area."
Population: Vocational education students.
Publication Date: 1991.
Scores: 15 vocational training interest areas: Auto Mechanics/Transportation, Business and Office, Construction, Cosmetology, Drafting, Electro-Mechanics, Electronics, Food Service, Graphic Arts, Health Occupations, Horticulture/Agriculture, Marketing, Metals, Occupational Home Economics, Technology Education.
Administration: Individual or group.
Price Data, 1991: $495 per set.
Time: (15–20) minutes.
Authors: Nancy L. Scott and Charles Gilbreath.
Publisher: Piney Mountain Press, Inc.

Review of the Vocational Interest Inventory and Exploration Survey by LARRY COCHRAN, Professor of Counseling Psychology, Faculty of Education, The University of British Columbia, Vancouver, British Columbia, Canada:

The Vocational Interest Inventory and Exploration Survey (VOC-TIES) is not so much a test as a test-like intervention to help prospective students to decide upon a vocational training program. It is composed of an audio-visual presentation (slides and prerecorded narration) in which 15 vocational training programs are described. After each program is described, the student is asked whether he or she "would be interested in vocational training" in that area. To respond, the student marks on an answer sheet either yes, maybe, or no. As optional forms of administration, the test administrator can read the program descriptions or stop the audio-visual presentation after each description to discuss the area, answer questions, and encourage comments. The 15 training programs include automobile mechanics, office work, construction, cosmetology, drafting, mechanical equipment repair, electronics, food service, graphic arts, health, horticulture and agriculture, marketing and distribution, metals, occupational home economics, and technician. As a vocational intervention, the VOC-TIES is intended to provide information to assist students in making more informed decisions about training programs and careers. Program descriptions introduce the general nature of an area of work, indicate some criteria for selection, specify training requirements, and provide examples of jobs that training would qualify one to pursue. Generally, the program descriptions seem clear and informative, introducing a wide range of programs in a short amount of time. The VOC-TIES is unusual in the sense that most interest tests were designed to assess a pattern of interests and to relate those interests to possible occupations. The VOC-TIES stresses an institutional perspective, attempting to inform individuals of and gauge interest in training programs likely to be offered by vocational training institutes.

Ordinarily, however, when one has designed a program, it is then evaluated through research to sharpen statements of purpose, and investigate what it does and does not do. Currently, there is no evidence the VOC-TIES is an effective intervention. There is no evidence that prospective students learn enough to make an informed decision, that the information is adequate (for example, why were salary ranges not mentioned?), or that it stimulates exploration, and so on. There is no information regarding the soundness of program construction and its effectiveness.

As a test of training interest, the VOC-TIES does not meet any standard of test construction. There were no reported reliabilities, no evidence of validity, no norm groups, and no technical information of any kind in the manual. It was assumed that a *yes* response would indicate a high level of interest, a *maybe* response would indicate the need for exploration, and a *no* response would indicate lack of interest with no need for exploration.

The VOC-TIES might fill a potential need of community colleges and vocational training institutes. Although it seems like a worthwhile intervention to try out, it has not yet earned credibility. As a test, it lacks substance and ought not to be regarded as such without further evidence. In summary, the VOC-TIES is an untried intervention and test that will require much more grounding to be used with confidence.

Review of the Vocational Interest Inventory and Exploration Survey by KEVIN R. MURPHY, Professor of Psychology, Colorado State University, Fort Collins, CO:

The Vocational Interest Inventory and Exploration Survey is not an interest inventory in the usual sense of the term. It consists of a series of descriptions, presented via videotape or narrated slides, of 15 areas or clusters of training found at most U.S. vocational training schools. It provides students with information about the content of each cluster, about vocational criteria and training requirements, and with examples of the types of jobs that might be pursued after receiving training in each cluster. Following the presentation of information about these training clusters, subjects are simply asked if they are interested in each (response categories are "yes," "maybe," and "no"). These answers, it is hoped, with help direct vocational counselors in providing additional information about training and careers to examinees.

The manual that describes this inventory provides no data that can be used to evaluate this rather simple instrument. However, given the controversy over expressed versus inventoried interests, this inventory cannot be accepted as a simpler substitute for more elaborate measures. In my opinion, vocational interest measurement represents one of the success stories of applied psychology, and a number of exemplary measurement instruments exist (e.g., the Jackson Vocational Interest Survey [T4:1297] and the Strong Interest Inventory [374]). This inventory does not seem to fill a well-defined need, nor does it stand up to the same level of psychometric scrutiny as do several other alternatives.

To the authors' credit, the idea of presenting information about vocational training opportunities as part of the process of interest assessment is a very reasonable one. However, simply asking examinees whether or not they are interested in an area that has just been described to them is not likely to provide as much information about career and training interests as could be obtained from a psychometrically sophisticated inventory.

[409]

Vocational Interest, Experience and Skill Assessment (VIESA), Canadian Edition.

Purpose: Designed to stimulate career exploration.
Population: Grades 8–10, 11–adults.
Publication Date: 1985.
Acronym: VIESA, Canadian Edition.
Scores: Scores for Interests, Skills, and Experiences in 4 areas: People, Data, Things, Ideas.
Administration: Group or individual..
Levels, 2: 1, 2.
Price Data, 1994: $57.45 per 25 guide books and job family charts (specify level); $17.45 per examination kit level 1 & 2; $18.95 per user's handbook (61 pages).
Time: (40–45) minutes.
Comments: Self-scored inventory of career-related interests, experiences, skills and values, with supporting materials for counselors; adapted from VIESA, Second Edition, U.S. Edition (1984).
Author: ACT Career Planning Services.
Publisher: Nelson Canada.
Cross References: For information for VIESA, 2nd Edition, see 9:1338; for a review by Charles J. Krauskopf of an earlier edition, see 8:1025.

Review of the Vocational Interest, Experience, and Skill Assessment (VIESA), Canadian Edition by DAVID J. BATESON, Associate Professor of Mathematics and Science Education and the Educational Measurement Research Group, University of British Columbia, Vancouver, British Columbia, Canada:

Authors of the Users Handbook state the Vocational Interest, Experience, and Skill Assessment (VIESA) is designed to stimulate and facilitate self/career explorations. The primary goals are to help counselees: (*a*) expand self-awareness, (*b*) develop career awareness, (*c*) identify relevant career options, and (*d*) begin exploring and evaluating their career options. Counselors are encouraged to be thoroughly familiar with the handbook and the counselee materials. The need for thorough counselor familiarity with all the materials, and also with the Canadian Classification and Dictionary of Occupations (CCDO) and other job classification systems such as the Holland and Roe typologies, cannot be understated and it seems essential to the successful use of the VIESA. As a self-administered and self-scored tool, which it claims to be, the VIESA can be very confusing; counselees must be provided continuous guidance and supervision as they work through the document.

Based on data from the 1977 scoring accuracy study, only infrequent errors were reported when examinees transcribe and summarize at various places in the instrument. Small measurement errors for the instrument are also reported. None of these errors have a great effect individually, but when taken together, and when one considers the decision consequences on individuals of such instruments, the effect can be quite serious. Reliability statistics provided do not appear adequate given that results of the VIESA apply only to individuals and not to groups. If the instrument leads to individual decision making regarding career choices, issues of reliability are very serious and require serious attention.

A study undertaken by F. M. Gault and H. H. Meyers (1987) showed that subjects using the instrument believed they had learned more about career decision making and most found that they were able to identify previously uncontemplated career options. However, the study also found that peer counselors tended to prefer the Self-Directed Search (SDS; T4:2414) to the VIESA.

It would seem that the instrument is probably much better suited to be a teaching and learning tool, or a framework for a guidance program or course, than an assessment instrument. If it were to be used in conjunction with a computer-based career information system such as CHOICES, the Student Guidance Information System (SGIS), or the Career Factory (Bridges, 1987), its potential would be greatly enhanced. The opportunities for counselees to explore their interests, their skills, and their career possibilities are considerable with these materials; they can be extremely valuable. However, used with insufficient guidance, the results of the VIESA could be totally misleading for some individuals.

In summary, as an assessment instrument, the VIESA appears confusing and of insufficient reliability for the serious individual decisions that might be made. However, as a teaching tool, the VIESA has much to commend it.

REVIEWER'S REFERENCE

Bridges, M. (1987). Resources to find and evaluate counseling software. *Career Planning and Adult Development Journal*, 3(2), 34-42.

Gault, F. M., & Meyers. H. H. (1987). A comparison of two career planning inventories. *The Career Development Quarterly*, 35(4), 332-336.

Review of the Vocational Interest, Experience, and Skill Assessment (VIESA), Canadian Edition by BRENDA H. LOYD, Professor of Education, University of Virginia, Charlottesville, VA:

The Vocational Interest, Experience, and Skill Assessment (VIESA) is a career planning inventory that assesses perceptions of career-related interests, experiences, skills, and values. The instrument's main purposes are to expand self-awareness, to develop career awareness, and to begin to identify, evaluate, and explore career options. The assessment is designed to be used by eighth grade students through adults and may be used individually, in small groups, and in instructional settings. The instrument may be self-administered and self-scored or may be administered under the supervision of a counselor.

The instrument includes eight units. An introductory unit explains the purpose of the assessment and introduces the key concepts PEOPLE, DATA, THINGS, and IDEAS as ways of understanding different kinds of jobs. The second unit presents an interest inventory divided into four sections corresponding to the four key concepts. For each of the four sections, examinees indicate which activities they would like to do or not like to do and score their results. The third unit asks the examinee to focus on identifying his/her best skills by choosing among sets of three choices under each main concept. In the fourth unit, a trial job choice is selected. Building upon this foundation, the individual examines a World-of-Work map in Unit 5 and identifies job possibilities that appear to be most consistent with his/her interests, skills, and trial job choice. In Unit 6 the individual is given tips about selecting job possibilities from available resources based in part on the results of the assessment, but is encouraged also to seek out experiences and opportunities in clear contrast to those which the assessment might suggest, in order to broaden the experience upon which decisions will be made. Unit 7 focuses on job values, to help identify the relative importance of security, availability, pay, etc. to the individual and to relate these values to the identified job possibilities. The final section of the student booklet is an "experience" inventory, which purports to compare the individual with other students in terms of the amount of their experience with PEOPLE, DATA, THINGS, and IDEAS in the world of work.

VALIDITY AND RELIABILITY. Validity and reliability information have been collected since the original form of the instrument was constructed in 1976, and interest profiles for more than 40,000 persons in 352 educational and occupational groupings have been examined and reviewed. One caution in interpreting the reliability and validity evidence is that the data supporting the instrument were gathered from examinees in the United States. In evaluating the Canadian edition, it must be considered that although many, if not most, of the findings may generalize to the Canadian population, additional information supporting this generalization would be a helpful addition to the supporting documentation for the instrument.

Content and construct validity of the VIESA is supported by the clear structure underlying each section of the instrument. The two bipolar dimensions of Data/Ideas and Things/People form the basis for the interests, experiences, and skills sections, as well as the organization of the work map and the listings of jobs. The Dimensions were identified by analyzing all occupations listed in the *Dictionary of Occupational Titles* (DOT) from the U.S. Department of Labor and were supported by analyzing interest scores of over 110,000 people in the U.S. This basic information on occupations was organized into 23–25 job families, then into six job clusters that relate directly to the World-of-Work map. The information has been restructured from general to specific within the assessment instrument so that an examinee begins at the general level of the map and then proceeds through job clusters and families to specific occupational titles.

Conversion of U.S. Department of Labor occupational titles to appropriate Canadian titles was accomplished by comparing the similarity of the work performed and the vocational preparation required of the U.S. DOT occupations and the occupations listed in the *Canadian Classification and Dictionary of Occupations*.

Construct validity of the assessment is also supported by evaluating the two bipolar dimensions and the interest structure represented by Holland's theory, as well as the interest structure represented by Roe's interest types. Supporting evidence suggests that the Holland's hexagonal and Roe's octagonal interest structure can be summarized on the Data/Ideas and Things/People dimensions.

In addition to the question of the validity of underlying dimensions, special consideration was given to producing an interest inventory that did not limit men and women in their consideration of job possibilities due to possible early differences between male and female interests or societal expectations. An attempt was made to select items that measure the dimensions but minimize sex differences at the item level. Several reported validity studies suggest that the use of sex-balanced items has been successful in minimizing sex differences (i.e., in minimizing the situations in which one set of career options is suggested to males and another set to females).

Evidence of reliability includes reports of several studies of scoring accuracy. The self-scored instrument requires examinees to follow fairly straightforward instructions on how to sum responses, determine the difference between scores, and graph the intersection of scores on a grid (on the World-of-Work map). Among high school students, 8% to 14% of those sampled made errors in scoring or mapping the results onto the correct regions of the map. These results suggest some of the limitations of self-scoring, and also suggest the value of having a counselor or teacher available to assist in scoring or to check the work of examinees.

SUMMARY. The VIESA is a well-developed and clearly presented interest assessment that seems appropriate for use with high school students and adults. The intent of the assessment is to give a wide-band approach to developing career awareness; thus it encourages examinees to consider many types of careers. The intent is not to help examinees make fine choices among a few occupations, but to facilitate exploration and evaluation of possibilities. This suggests that the instrument would have its most appropriate use as part of a more comprehensive approach to career development, either as part of an instructional program or as one of many sources of information in a counseling situation.

[410]

Vocational Learning Styles.

Purpose: "Developed to assess learning styles and preferred working conditions."
Population: Grades 7–12 and adults.
Publication Date: 1989.
Acronym: LSV2.
Scores: 25 subtopics in 5 areas: Physical Domain (Kinesthetic, Visual, Tactile, Auditory), Social Domain (Group, Individual), Environmental Domain (Formal Design, Informal Design, Bright Lights, Dim Lights, Warm Temperature, Cool Temperature, With Sound, Without Sound), Mode of Expression Domain (Oral Expressive, Written Expressive), Work Characteristics Domain (Outdoors, Indoors, Sedentary, Non-Sedentary, Lifting, Non-Lifting, Data, People, Things).
Administration: Group.
Price Data, 1990: $495 per complete kit including guide, software, video, filmstrip, and 100 response sheets.
Time: Administration time not reported.
Comments: Manual title is Learning Styles Media Kit Vocational Edition.
Author: Helena Hendrix-Frye.
Publisher: Piney Mountain Press, Inc.

Review of the Vocational Learning Styles by LEO M. HARVILL, Professor and Assistant Dean for Medical Education, James H. Quillen College of Medicine, East Tennessee State University, Johnson City, TN:

The Vocational Learning Styles is a 75-item inventory designed to assess learning styles and preferred working conditions. Individuals respond to each statement as it best describes them using a rating scale ranging from *Most Like Me* (4) to *Least Like Me* (1). It is to be used with regular and special needs individuals in grades 7–12 and in postsecondary facilities devised to train individuals in marketable skills.

The numerous methods for administration of the inventory are a positive factor for assessment of this clientele. The administration of the paper-and-pencil and computer versions are straightforward. The videotape version has misleading directions at the beginning concerning the marking of the answer form. The examinee is told to mark "4" if the statement is *Most like me*, mark "1" if the statement is *Least like me*, and "3 OR 2" if the examinee is somewhere in between. What is shown on the video screen at that time is the "3 AND 2" both marked out on the answer form. This leaves the impression that multiple responses are appropriate. With that exception, the material provided for the administration of the inventory is excellent with explicit instructions for each of the various methods.

There is no explanation in the manual concerning which items belong to various subtopics or how to score the inventory by hand. All scores from the computer analysis for the 25 subtopics range from 6 to 24. This seems appropriate if six items are scored for each subtopic. However, there are only three items for each of the subtopics. Perhaps the three items each for oral and written modes of expression are all scored to arrive at each of the two subscores for oral and written mode of expression; this is not stated in the manual. However, using that method, it is difficult to determine how the three items each for People, Data, and Things are combined to arrive at six items for scoring each of those three subtopics.

No information is included in the materials concerning the construction of the inventory. There is no information concerning the validity of the inventory either. Reliabilities were not reported in the administration manual; they were reported in a separate document (technical manual) furnished by the publisher. Concerning the reliabilities reported, no information was provided concerning the type of reliability coefficients, the size of the group, the characteristics of the group, or the date the data were obtained. The reported reliabilities for the various subtopics are reasonably high ranging from .56 for Auditory to .91 for Sound/Noise. The median reliability value listed is.82 among the 25 values given. Only 2 are below .70.

Means and standard deviations are given for males ($N = 615$) and females ($N = 585$) from a standardization sample of 1,200 in the technical manual. There is a brief description of the sample but no date is given. Means and standard deviations are also provided for preferred time to study (morning and evening) but these subtopics are not included on the current form of the inventory. Something called "area scores" are also provided. They are labeled as groups of percentiles (e.g., 75th–99th). However, the values given are difficult to understand. For example, the values given for Visual-Females are 75th–99th (202), 50th–70th (165), 25th–49th (99), and 0th–20th (119). The percentile categories are unclear and have gaps in them. It is unclear what the single value represents. Further, the values are not consistent with the minimum and maximum values of 6 and 24 for the various subtopics. The "area scores" are mysterious.

A "percentile chart" for the work characteristics is given in the technical manual. It is stated that these percentiles "were derived by simple mathematical calculations." The work characteristics part of the inventory was not field tested, it was "added as an appendix to the Vocational LSTest Inventory," and "no mean scores or standard deviation scores were obtained." These statements cause concern about the construction of the inventory. The scores in the chart ranged from 30 (99th percentile) to zero (0th percentile); a score of 15 is listed at the 50th percentile for all subtopics. These score values are also not consistent with a minimum and maximum of 6 and 24. It is unclear how this table was derived. There seems to be no basis for the interpretive statements that accompany this chart. The six headings in the table do not mention People in the Things/Data category but do include Service/Non (there is nothing in the current inventory about service-type occupations).

In summary, the 23-page "technical manual" appeared to be for a different version or form of the inventory and was very poorly written. It is of very little value in understanding the construction, norms, reliability, and validity of the inventory. Much remains to be done to make this a good technical manual. The administration manual does not contain any of this information. No explanation is provided for hand scoring. The inventory is straightforward in its administration with several alternatives for administration. The language of the instrument seems appropriate for the intended audience.

Review of the Vocational Learning Styles by CRAIG N. MILLS, Executive Director, Testing and Services, Graduate Record Examinations Program, Educational Testing Service, Princeton, NJ:

The purpose of the Vocational Learning Styles (Learning Styles Media Kit Vocational Edition) is to provide an assessment of individuals' preferred learning styles and working conditions. It consists of 75 statements that respondents characterize as *most like me* to *least like me* on a 4-point scale. The 75 statements are categorized into five major domains and 25 individual elements.

TEST DEVELOPMENT AND SCORING. No information was provided describing the process by which statements were developed, evaluated, pretested, or assigned to categories. Furthermore, there is no documentation that the domains and elements have any basis in what is known about cognition and learning styles. Nor is there any justification for why this assessment is appropriate for vocational settings as distinct from others. Scores are the simple sum of the scale values assigned to the statement multiplied by 2. No rationale is provided to support this scoring, nor to the equal weighting of all elements within each domain. No analyses are reported to support the reporting of the different elements or domains or to support that they are, in fact, different from one another.

The score reports include narrative profiles suggesting how an instructor (or employer) might structure a learning (working) environment. However, no support is provided that proscriptions such as "An informal learning environment with pillows, a soft chair or couch help this individual learn best" (p. 25) are valid.

TECHNICAL INFORMATION. No technical information is provided. There is no information on test, domain, or subscale reliability. It is hard to imagine that reliabilities of scores based on only three items can be sufficient for the scores to be useful. Furthermore, there is a complete absence of any validity information or conceptual basis for the instrument.

SUMMARY. The Learning Styles Media Kit Vocational Edition is designed to assess individuals' preferred learning styles so that instructors can modify the learning environment to promote learning. However, there is no evidence of a research basis for the measure and no technical information is provided. The complete lack of a conceptual basis for the instrument coupled with the technical deficiencies in its documentation raise serious questions about its usefulness.

[411]

Voc-Tech Quick Screener.

Purpose: Designed to identify job interests.
Population: Non-college bound high school students and adults.
Publication Dates: 1984–90.
Acronym: VTQS.
Scores, 14: Administrative Support/Clerical, Agriculture/Animals and Forestry, Construction Trades, Design/Graphics and Communication, Food/Beverage Services, Health Services, Health Technicians, Industrial Production Trades, Marketing/Sales, Mechanical/Craftsmanship Trades, Personal Services, Protective Services, Science/Engineering Technicians, Transportation/Equipment Operators.
Administration: Group.
Price Data, 1990: $.50 per folder/questionnaire; $89.95 per microcomputer software package (Apple or IBM).
Time: (20–25) minutes.
Authors: Robert Kauk and Robert Robinett.
Publisher: CFKR Career Materials, Inc.

Review of the Voc-Tech Quick Screener by ALBERT M. BUGAJ, Associate Professor of Psychology, University of Wisconsin—Marinette, Marinette, WI:

The Voc-Tech Quick Screener (VTQS) is ostensibly designed to assess the job interests of non-college-bound high school students and adults. However, the screener is only "quick" in the sense that upon its completion it supposedly identifies the occupations in which the test taker is most interested. It then encourages them to seek further information about those occupations through such tasks as visiting career information centers, training sites, and people already "on-the-job." Given the nature of the test, the information seeker might be better served going to those sources first, and not bother taking the VTQS.

On the first page of the test, the testee is asked to rate (on a 3-point scale) how interested he or she is in finding a job that would match one of six personality traits (doer, thinker, creator, helper, persuader, organizer). Three activities (working with data, people, and things) are similarly rated. No concern is apparently taken by the authors of the VTQS that these ratings might be affected by social desirability.

The next three pages involve matching the previous characteristics with 14 "vocational-technical occupational clusters." This task is performed by matching the self-ratings to profiles for the 14 clusters constructed by the authors. For example, a person interested in construction trades, would, in part, have a high interest in occupations requiring people to be doers, a moderate interest in being a thinker, and a low interest in being a creator. When the testee's self-rating of a trait or activity matches that for the profile, a point is earned (5 points for key characteristics).

The explanation in the user's guide of how the point values were assigned to each of the characteristics in the profiles is cryptic. However, the reader is assured they are based on "a rational judgemental procedure," using "expert" data, "rather than strictly quantitative data" (p. 2). Hence, the point values seem qualitative in nature, and have not been empirically tested.

The 14 cluster groups of occupations are equally non-empirical in nature. According to the user's guide they "ally closely with the 12 clusters (work groups) used in the GUIDE TO OCCUPATIONAL EXPLORATION, U.S. Dept. of Labor" (p. 3), although the correspondence is not direct, and exceptions were made. Two clusters were added because the authors felt they were significant enough to warrant distinct groups, whereas another grouping was split in two.

Each cluster typically contains over a dozen disparate occupations. The transportation/equipment operators cluster, for example, ranges from air traffic controller to taxi driver. No attention is paid to the varying degrees of training or education which may be needed in the various occupations. Further, no empirical data justifying these groups are provided. Although the Department of Labor may group various occupations together, this does not mean they form a construct for use on an interest inventory.

Once the testee's interests are matched to these profiles, he or she is instructed to complete the final portion of the VTQS, given the name "the Occuputer." Here, the test taker lists the three fields receiving the highest number of points, and then rates (on 5-point scales) his or her interests in gaining the skills and completing the studies needed, chances of success, and interest in jobs related to the fields (information to aid in each task is provided). Points earned are again summed, and the high score indicates the field in which the testee has the greatest interest. Again, no concern for social desirability or other problems inherent in self-ratings is noted.

Finally, the test taker is asked to review lists of related jobs in the preferred cluster, and write the three he or she would like best. No quantitative ratings are made at this point. The testee is then directed to seek further information from the previously mentioned sources (e.g., career centers) about those occupations.

Little data are provided about reliability and validity of the VTQS. The user's guide reports an 88% correlation of preferred job clusters (not individual jobs selected) over a 2-week period. However, the number and age of the students is not reported.

It is also stated that a "large sampling of junior and senior high school students and adults" (p. 3) reported the reading level and directions are understandable, and found the test interesting and motivational. One assumes this means the students were motivated to seek other sources of information, after taking the VTQS (this point is unclear in the user's guide). However, it should be noted that no measure of whether the students were motivated to seek information *prior to* taking the survey is reported. Without such knowledge (or a matched group not taking the VTQS for comparison) its effect on motivation cannot be known with certainty.

The user's guide authors further indicate that over 90% of 1,000 students (ages not reported) indicated they were highly satisfied with the objectives and results of the test. Unfortunately, it is not said whether this judgement was made soon after taking the test, or once the subjects had entered an occupation on its basis and found it satisfying. Whether the test led them to consider new occupations, or simply confirmed previously made decisions is not stated. No measures of convergent validity are reported.

The use of the VTQS cannot be recommended, and it cannot begin to compare with a test like the Strong Vocational Interest Inventories (374). It is most likely susceptible to a high social desirability bias. The major constructs (the occupational clusters) have no empirical basis. Reliability and validity data, as provided in the manual, are insufficient. Because the students are instructed to seek other, major sources of information which should aid greatly in making a career decision, students might be better off seeking out these resources without the use of the VTQS.

Review of the Voc-Tech Quick Screener by DEL EBERHARDT, Program Administrator, Greenwich Public Schools, Greenwich, CT:

The Voc-Tech Quick Screener (VTQS) was, according to the authors, designed and field tested "to meet a specific career interest assessment: to provide means for valid and reliable personal assessment of job interests and to relate that assessment to specific jobs in 'vocational technical' clusters—often referred to as the 'high tech' area of work" (p. 1, user's guide). To meet this need the VTQS is available in a printed as well as a computerized format. It is suggested that the printed form will require about 20 minutes to complete and the computerized version will require only 5–10 minutes. This review is based on the printed version of the VTQS.

The printed version consists of two documents. The response document is a six-page fan-fold document that compresses an impressive amount of print and information into these few pages. In fact, there is so much material here that the reader is apt to become confused. Page 1 of the response document provides the student with a brief statement of the purpose of the VTQS, a description of the steps required to complete the project, and a scale for rating their occupational interests.

The student then rates him/her self on each of six qualities of a job. The terms doer, thinker, creator, helper, persuader, and organizer are used and very brief definitions of each are provided. The authors acknowledge these variables were worded and coded to "inter-correlate" with the Holland-RIASEC types.

Finally, the student does a self-rating in terms of the traditional DATA, PEOPLE, THINGS categories. Following the completion of the rating on nine variables, the student begins transferring these ratings onto four pages of the form. These categories resemble the basic interest scales and the occupational scales of the Strong Interest Inventory. However, in contrast to the Strong, the student does no personal ratings on these categories. The student is led to understand that despite the terms "quick" and "screener" in the title, they can draw conclusions about careers. Like so many assessment devices that are termed "screening" devices, there is a real danger that the client may draw conclusions that are not warranted based on the limited number of variables considered. The omission of mention of abilities, especially in an area referred to as "high tech", seems worth noting and should serve as a note of caution to the user of the VTQS.

The second document provided for the printed form of the VTQS is a user's guide. It is a very brief four-page document that is intended to be an instructional guide to the printed and computerized versions of the VTQS. This user's guide contains a one-paragraph "forward," a section on the rationale of the instrument, and a section on the design of the instrument. Other sections review the construction of the variables and the results of field testing. The user of the VTQS will be somewhat concerned about the limited material in the user's guide. The target audience for the instrument is not specified, but it seems reasonable to assume that high school juniors and seniors might constitute the primary audience. Although the reading difficulty level of the instrument is not reported in reference to any of the standard techniques for determining readability, the authors report the VTQS is sufficiently "easy to enable over 90% of upper level high school students and adults" (p. 4) to complete the instrument.

For the professional accustomed to test manuals that provide psychometric information consistent with the AERA/APA/NCME *Standards for Educational and Psychological Testing* (1985), the VTQS user's guide will be a major disappointment. For example, in reference to field testing (norming?) the authors mention using a "large" sample of junior and senior high school students and adults. However, there is no mention of the nature of this sample in terms of geography, SES, or any of the other aspects of a norming sample one has come to expect from test publishers. This reviewer found one mention of reliability in the user's guide. The authors report "test-retest" of the VTQS given in a 2-week duration that "there was an 88% correlation of preferred job clusters" (p. 2). The authors made no reference to validity studies of the VTQS. In summary, this reviewer would suggest that the professional looking for career assessment instruments consider other instruments before using the VTQS. Certainly the Strong Interest Inventory (374) and Holland's Self-Directed Search (10:330) would provide better techniques. The VTQS may best serve as an educational device. It might help high school students gain new information about the technical occupations under the careful guidance of a teacher or guidance counselor. It is not recommended for serious career guidance.

REVIEWER'S REFERENCE

American Educational Research Association, American Psychological Association, & National Council on Measurement in Education. (1985). *Standards for educational and psychological testing.* Washington, DC: American Psychological Association, Inc.

[412]

Wechsler Intelligence Scale for Children—Third Edition.

Purpose: A "measure of a child's intellectual ability."
Population: Ages 6-0 to 16-11.
Publication Dates: 1971–91.
Acronym: WISC-III.
Scores, 13 to 16: Verbal (Information, Similarities, Arithmetic, Vocabulary, Comprehension, Digit Span [optional], Total); Performance (Picture Completion, Coding, Picture Arrangement, Block Design, Object Assembly, Symbol Search [optional], Mazes [optional], Total), Total.
Administration: Individual.
Price Data, 1994: $520 per complete kit including manual ('91, 294 pages), stimulus booklet, 25 record forms, object assembly puzzles, object assembly layout shield, block design cubes, picture arrangement cards, two mazes response booklets, two symbol search response booklets, coding scoring template, and symbol search scoring template; $55.50 per manual; $68 per stimulus booklet; $28.50 per 25 mazes response booklets; $28.50 per 25 symbol search response booklets; $55 per 25 record forms; $152 per 6 object assembly puzzles.
Time: (50–75) minutes.
Author: David Wechsler.
Publisher: The Psychological Corporation.
Cross References: See T4:2939 (911 references); for reviews of an earlier edition by Morton Bortner, Douglas K. Detterman, and Joseph C. Witt and Frank Gresham, see 9:1351 (299 references); see also T3:2602 (645 references); for reviews by David Freides and Randolph H. Whitworth, and excerpted reviews by Carol Kehr Tittle and Joseph Petrosko, see 8:232 (548 references); see also T2:533 (230 references); for reviews by David Freides and R. T. Osborne of the original edition, see 7:431 (518 references); for a review by Alvin G. Burnstein, see 6:540 (155 references); for reviews by Elizabeth D. Fraser, Gerald R. Patterson, and Albert I. Rabin, see 5:416 (111 references); for reviews by James M. Anderson, Harold A. Delp, and Boyd R. McCandless, and an excerpted review by Laurance F. Shaffer, see 4:363 (22 references).

TEST REFERENCES

1. Asbury, C. A., Stokes, A., Adderly-Kelly, B., & Knuckle, E. P. (1989). Effectiveness of selected neuropsychological, academic, and sociocultural measures for predicting Bannatyne pattern categories in black adolescents. *Journal of Negro Education, 58*, 177-188.

2. Bihrle, A. M., Bellugi, U., Delis, D., & Marks, S. (1989). Seeing either the forest or the trees: Dissociation in visuospatial processing. *Brain and Cognition, 11*, 37-49.

3. Chapman, M., & Lindenberger, U. (1989). Concrete operations and attentional capacity. *Journal of Experimental Child Psychology, 47*, 236-258.

4. Dewei, L. (1989). The effect of role change on intellectual ability and on the ability self-concept in Chinese children. *American Journal of Community Psychology, 17*, 73-81.

5. Johnston, R. S., & Thompson, G. B. (1989). Is dependence on phonological information in children's reading a product of instructional approach? *Journal of Experimental Child Psychology, 48*, 131-145.

6. Kee, D. W., Matteson, R., & Hellige, J. (1989). Lateralized finger-tapping interference produced by block design activities. *Brain and Cognition, 11*, 127-132.

7. Kelly, M. S., Best, C. T., & Kirk, U. (1989). Cognitive processing deficits in reading disabilities: A prefrontal cortical hypothesis. *Brain and Cognition, 11*, 275-293.

8. Lord, C., Rutter, M., Goode, S., Heemsbergen, J., Jordan, H., Mawhood, L., & Schopler, E. (1989). Autism Diagnostic Observation Schedule: A standardized observation of communicative and social behavior. *Journal of Autism and Developmental Disorders, 19*(2), 185-212.

9. Nass, R., Peterson, H. D., & Koch, D. (1989). Differential effects of congenital left and right brain injury on intelligence. *Brain and Cognition, 9*, 258-266.

10. Scruggs, T. E., & Mastropieri, M. A. (1989). Reconstructive elaborations: A model for content area learning. *American Educational Research Journal, 26*, 311-327.

11. Swanson, H. L. (1989). The effects of central processing strategies on learning disabled, mildly retarded, average, and gifted children's elaborative encoding abilities. *Journal of Experimental Child Psychology, 47*, 370-397.

12. Van Deusen, J. (1989). Alcohol abuse and perceptual-motor dysfunction: The occupational therapist's role. *The American Journal of Occupational Therapy, 43*, 384-390.

13. Asarnow, J. R., & Horton, A. A. (1990). Coping and stress in families of child psychiatric inpatients: Parents of children with depressive and schizophrenia spectrum disorders. *Child Psychiatry and Human Development, 21*, 145-157.

14. Benbow, C. P., & Minor, L. L. (1990). Cognitive profiles of verbally and mathematically precocious students: Implications for identification of the gifted. *Gifted Child Quarterly, 34*, 21-26.

15. Bentin, S., Deutsch, A., & Liberman, I. Y. (1990). Syntactic competence and reading ability in children. *Journal of Experimental Child Psychology, 49*, 147-172.

16. Bruck, M., & Treiman, R. (1990). Phonological awareness and spelling in normal children and dyslexics: The case of initial consonant clusters. *Journal of Experimental Child Psychology, 50*, 156-178.

17. Chase, C. H., & Tallal, P. (1990). A developmental, interactive activation model of the Word Superiority Effect. *Journal of Experimental Child Psychology, 49*, 448-487.

18. Egeland, B., Kalkoske, M., Gottesman, N., & Erickson, M. F. (1990). Preschool behavior problems: Stability and factors accounting for change. *Journal of Child Psychology and Psychiatry and Allied Disciplines, 31*, 891-909.

19. Gillberg, C., Ehlers, S., Schaumann, H., Jakobsson, G., Dahlgren, S. O., Lindblom, R., Bagenholm, A., Tjuius, T., & Blioner, E. (1990). Autism under 3 years: A clinical study of 28 cases referred for autistic symptoms in infancy. *Journal of Child Psychology and Psychiatry and Allied Disciplines, 31*, 921-934.

20. Guttman, R., Epstein, E. E., Amir, M., & Guttman, L. (1990). A structural theory of spatial abilities. *Applied Psychological Measurement, 14*, 217-236.

21. Hasselhorn, M. (1990). The emergence of strategic knowledge activation in categorical clustering during retrieval. *Journal of Experimental Child Psychology*, *50*, 59-80.

22. Hurford, D. P., & Sanders, R. E. (1990). Assessment and remediation of a phonemic discrimination deficit in reading disabled second and fourth graders. *Journal of Experimental Child Psychology*, *50*, 396-415.

23. Kolko, D. J., Loar, L. L., & Sturnick, D. (1990). Inpatient social-cognitive skills training groups with conduct disordered and attention deficit disordered children. *Journal of Child Psychology and Psychiatry and Allied Disciplines*, *31*, 737-748.

24. Nass, R., Baker, S., Sadler, A. E., & Sidtis, J. J. (1990). The effects of precocious adrenarche on cognition and hemispheric specialization. *Brain and Cognition*, *14*, 59-69.

25. Neistadt, M. E. (1990). A critical analysis of occupational therapy approaches for perceptual deficits in adults with brain injury. *The American Journal of Occupational Therapy*, *44*, 299-304.

26. Oliver, C. E. (1990). A sensorimotor program for improving writing readiness skills in elementary-age children. *The American Journal of Occupational Therapy*, *44*, 111-116.

27. Quadrel, M. J., & Lau, R. L. (1990). A multivariate analysis of adolescents' orientations toward physician use. *Health Psychology*, *9*, 750-773.

28. Reams, R., Chamrad, D., & Robinson, N. M. (1990). The race is not necessarily to the swift: Validity of WISC-R bonus points for speed. *Gifted Child Quarterly*, *34*, 108-110.

29. Redding, R. E. (1990). Learning preferences and skill patterns among underachieving gifted adolescents. *Gifted Child Quarterly*, *34*, 72-75.

30. Schulte, A. C., Osborne, S. S., & McKinney, J. D. (1990). Academic outcomes for students with learning disabilities in consultation and resource programs. *Exceptional Children*, *57*, 162-172.

31. Silver, S. J., & Clampit, M. K. (1990). WISC-R profiles of high ability children: Interpretation of verbal-performance discrepancies. *Gifted Child Quarterly*, *34*, 76-79.

32. Skuy, M., Gaydon, V., Hoffenberg, S., & Fridjhon, P. (1990). Predictors of performance of disadvantaged adolescents in a gifted program. *Gifted Child Quarterly*, *34*, 97-101.

33. Solanto, M. V. (1990). The effects of reinforcement and response-cost on a delayed response task in children with attention deficit hyperactivity disorder: A research note. *Journal of Child Psychology and Psychiatry and Allied Disciplines*, *31*, 803-808.

34. Stevenson, J., & Fredman, G. (1990). The social environmental correlates of reading ability. *Journal of Child Psychology and Psychiatry and Allied Disciplines*, *31*, 681-698.

35. Tompkins, C. A., Holland, A. L., Ratcliff, G., Costello, A., Leahy, L. F., & Cowell, V. (1990). Predicting cognitive recovery from closed head-injury in children and adolescents. *Brain and Cognition*, *13*, 86-97.

36. Vallicorsa, A. L., & Garriss, E. (1990). Story composition skills of middle-grade students with learning disabilities. *Exceptional Children*, *57*, 48-54.

37. Wolters, G., Beishuizen, M., Broers, G., & Knoppert, W. (1990). Mental arithmetic: Effects of calculation procedure and problem difficulty on solution latency. *Journal of Experimental Child Psychology*, *49*, 20-30.

38. Zigmond, N., & Baker, J. (1990). Mainstream experiences for learning disabled students (Project MELD): Preliminary report. *Exceptional Children*, *57*, 176-185.

39. Andrews, J. F., & Mason, J. M. (1991). Strategy usage among deaf and hearing readers. *Exceptional Children*, *57*, 536-545.

40. Beidel, D. C. (1991). Determining the reliability of psychophysiological assessment in childhood anxiety. *Journal of Anxiety Disorders*, *5*, 139-150.

41. Bhatia, M. S., Nigam, V. R., Bohra, N., & Malik, S. C. (1991). Attention deficit disorder with hyperactivity among paediatric outpatients. *Journal of Child Psychology and Psychiatry and Allied Disciplines*, *32*, 297-306.

42. Bowers, P. G., & Swanson, L. B. (1991). Naming speed deficits in reading disability: Multiple measures of a singular process. *Journal of Experimental Child Psychology*, *51*, 195-219.

43. Calev, A., Nigal, D., Shapira, B., Tubi, N., Chazan, S., Ben-Yehuda, Y., Kugelmass, S., & Lerer, B. (1991). Early and long-term effects of electroconvulsive therapy and depression on memory and other cognitive functions. *The Journal of Nervous and Mental Disease*, *179*, 526-533.

44. Carlson, C. L., Pelham, W. E., Swanson, J. M., & Wagner, J. L. (1991). A divided attention analysis of the effects of methylphenidate on the arithmetic performance of children with attention-deficit hyperactivity disorder. *Journal of Child Psychology and Psychiatry and Allied Disciplines*, *32*, 463-471.

45. Casey, J. E., Rourke, B. P., & Picard, E. M. (1991). Syndrome of nonverbal learning disabilities: Age differences in neuropsychological, academic, and socioemotional functioning. *Development and Psychopathology*, *3*, 329-345.

46. Cermak, S. A., & Murray, E. A. (1991). The validity of the constructional subtests of the Sensory Integration and Praxis tests. *The American Journal of Occupational Therapy*, *45*, 539-543.

47. Clark, J., & Tollefson, N. (1991). Differences in beliefs and attitudes toward the improvability of writing skills of gifted students who exhibit mastery-oriented and helpless behaviors. *Journal for the Education of the Gifted*, *14*, 119-133.

48. Cornell, D. G., Callahan, C. M., & Loyd, B. H. (1991). Personality growth of female early college entrants: A controlled, prospective study. *Gifted Child Quarterly*, *35*, 135-143.

49. Cornell, D. G., Callahan, C. M., & Loyd, B. H. (1991). Research on early college entrance: A few more adjustments are needed. *Gifted Child Quarterly*, *35*, 71-72.

50. Cornell, D. G., Callahan, C. M., & Loyd, B. H. (1991). Socioemotional adjustment of adolescent girls enrolled in a residential acceleration program. *Gifted Child Quarterly*, *35*, 58-66.

51. de Sonneville, L. M. J., Njiokiktjien, C., & Hilhorst, R. C. (1991). Methylphenidate-induced changes in ADDH information processors. *Journal of Child Psychology and Psychiatry and Allied Disciplines*, *32*, 285-295.

52. Demb, J. M. (1991). Reported hyperphagia in foster children. *Child Abuse & Neglect*, *15*, 77-88.

53. Gallagher, J. J. (1991). Personal patterns of underachievement. *Journal for the Education of the Gifted*, *14*, 221-233.

54. Grigoroiu-Serbănescu, M., Christodorescu, D., Măgureanu, S., Jipescu, I., Totoescu, A., Marinescu, E., Ardelean, V., & Popa, S. (1991). Adolescent offspring of endogenous unipolar depressive parents and of normal parents. *Journal of Affective Disorders*, *21*, 185-198.

55. Kee, D. W., Gottfried, A., & Bathurst, K. (1991). Consistency of hand preference: Predictions to intelligence and school achievement. *Brain and Cognition*, *16*, 1-10.

56. Kim, W. J., Hahn, S. U., Kish, J., Rosenberg, L., & Harris, J. (1991). Separation reaction of psychiatrically hospitalized children: A pilot study. *Child Psychiatry and Human Development*, *22*, 53-67.

57. Landau, S., Milich, R., & Widiger, T. A. (1991). Conditional probabilities of child interview symptoms in the diagnosis of attention deficit disorder. *Journal of Child Psychology and Psychiatry and Allied Disciplines*, *32*, 501-513.

58. Mannuzza, S., Klein, R. G., Bonagura, N., Malloy, P., Giampino, T. L., & Addalli, K. A. (1991). Hyperactive boys almost grown up. *Archives of General Psychiatry*, *48*, 77-83.

59. Montague, M. (1991). Gifted, and learning-disabled gifted students' knowledge and use of mathematical problem-solving strategies. *Journal for the Education of the Gifted*, *14*, 393-411.

60. Morrow, L. M., Sisco, L. J., & Smith, J. K. (1991). The effect of mediated story-retelling on listening comprehension, story structure, and oral language development in children with learning disabilities. *Yearbook of National Reading Conference*, *40*, 435-443.

61. Oliver, J. M., Hodge Cole, N., & Hollingsworth, H. (1991). Learning disabilities as functions of familial learning problems and developmental problems. *Exceptional Children*, *57*, 427-440.

62. Parker, R. I., Tindal, G., & Hasbrouck, J. (1991). Progress monitoring with objective measures of writing performance for students with mild disabilities. *Exceptional Children*, *58*, 61-73.

63. Piven, J., Tsai, G., Nehme, E., Coyle, J. T., Chase, G. A., & Folstein, S. E. (1991). Platelet serotonin, a possible marker for familial autism. *Journal of Autism and Developmental Disorders*, *21*(1), 51-59.

64. Saunders, E. B., & Awad, G. A. (1991). Male adolescent sexual offenders: Exhibitionism and obscene phone calls. *Child Psychiatry and Human Development*, *21*, 169-178.

65. Shapiro, E. S., & Lentz, F. E., Jr. (1991). Vocational-technical programs: Follow-up of students with learning disabilities. *Exceptional Children*, *58*, 47-59.

66. Simonian, S. J., Tarnowski, K. J., & Gibbs, J. C. (1991). Social skills and antisocial conduct of delinquents. *Child Psychiatry and Human Development*, *22*, 17-27.

67. Stanley, J. C. (1991). Critique of "Socioemotional adjustment of adolescent girls enrolled in a residential acceleration program." *Gifted Child Quarterly*, *35*, 67-70.

68. Urban, J., Carlson, E., Egeland, B., & Sroufe, L. A. (1991). Patterns of individual adaptation across childhood. *Development and Psychopathology*, *3*, 445-460.

69. van der Meere, J., Wekking, E., & Sergeant, J. (1991). Sustained attention and pervasive hyperactivity. *Journal of Child Psychology and Psychiatry and Allied Disciplines*, *32*, 275-284.

70. Van-Tassel-Baska, J. (1991). Serving the disabled gifted through educational collaboration. *Journal for the Education of the Gifted*, *14*, 246-266.

71. Wolery, M., Cybriwsky, C. A., Gast, D. L., & Boyle-Gast, K. (1991). Use of constant time delay and attentional responses with adolescents. *Exceptional Children*, *57*, 462-474.

72. Anastopoulos, A. D., Goevremont, D. C., Shelton, T. L., & DuPaul, G. J. (1992). Parenting stress among families of children with attention deficit hyperactivity disorder. *Journal of Abnormal Child Psychology*, *20*, 503-520.

73. Caplan, R., Guthrie, D., Shields, W. D., & Mori, L. (1992). Formal thought disorder in pediatric complex partial seizure disorder. *Journal of Child Psychology and Psychiatry and Allied Disciplines*, *33*, 1399-1412.

74. Clement-Heist, K., Siegel, S., Gaylord-Ross, R. (1992). Simulated and in situ vocational social skills training for youths with learning disabilities. *Exceptional Children*, *58*, 336-345.

75. Coleman, M. R. (1992). A comparison of how gifted/LD and average/LD boys cope with school frustration. *Journal for the Education of the Gifted*, *15*, 239-265.

76. Crombie, G., Bouffard-Bouchard, T., & Schneider, B. H. (1992). Gifted programs: Gender differences in referral and enrollment. *Gifted Child Quarterly*, *36*, 213-214.

77. Curry, J. F., Miller, Y., Waugh, S., & Anderson, W. B. (1992). Coping responses in depressed, socially maladjusted, and suicidal adolescents. *Psychological Reports*, *71*, 80-82.

78. David, A. S. (1992). Stroop effects within and between the cerebral hemispheres: Studies in normal and acallosals. *Neuropsychologia*, *30*, 161-175.

79. Downey, G., & Walker, E. (1992). Distinguishing family-level and child-level influences on the development of depression and aggression in children at risk. *Development and Psychopathology*, *4*, 81-95.

80. Filoteo, J. V., Delis, D. C., Massman, P. J., Demadura, T., Butters, N., & Salmon, D. P. (1992). Directed and divided attention in Alzheimer's disease: Impairment in shifting of attention to global and local stimuli. *Journal of Clinical and Experimental Neuropsychology*, *14*, 871-883.

81. Flicek, M. (1992). Social status of boys with both academic problems and attention-deficit hyperactivity disorder. *Journal of Abnormal Child Psychology*, *20*, 353-366.

82. Forceville, E. J. M., Dekker, M. J. A., Aldencamp, A. P., Alpherts, W. C., & Schelvis, A. J. (1992). Subtest profiles of the WISC-R and WAIS in mentally retarded patients with epilepsy. *Journal of Intellectual Disability Research*, *36*, 45-59.

83. Fristad, M. A., Topolosky, S., Weller, E. B., & Weller, R. A. (1992). Depression and learning disabilities in children. *Journal of Affective Disorders*, *26*, 53-58.

84. Frydman, M., & Lynn, R. (1992). The general intelligence and spatial abilities of gifted young Belgian chess players. *British Journal of Psychology*, *83*, 233-235.

85. Gajria, M., & Salvia, J. (1992). The effects of summarization instruction on text comprehension of students with learning disabilities. *Exceptional Children*, *58*, 508-516.

86. Gillberg, I. C., Gillberg, C., & Kopp, S. (1992). Hypothyroidism and autism spectrum disorders. *Journal of Child Psychology and Psychiatry and Allied Disciplines*, *33*, 531-542.

87. Gillis, J. J., Gilger, J. W., Pennington, B. F., & DeFries, J. C. (1992). Attention deficit disorder in reading-disabled twins: Evidence for a genetic etiology. *Journal of Abnormal Child Psychology*, *20*, 303-315.

88. Goswami, U., & Mead, F. (1992). Onset and rime awareness and analogies in reading. *Reading Research Quarterly*, *27*, 153-162.

89. Graham, S., Macarthur, C., Schwartz, S., & Page-Voth, V. (1992). Improving the compositions of students with learning disabilities using a strategy involving product and process goal setting. *Exceptional Children*, *58*, 322-334.

90. Huebner, R. A. (1992). Autistic disorder: A neuropsychological enigma. *The American Journal of Occupational Therapy*, *46*, 487-501.

91. Hyde, M. B., & Power, D. J. (1992). The receptive communication abilities of deaf students under oral, manual, and combined methods. *American Annals of the Deaf*, *137*, 389-398.

92. Janelle, S. (1992). Locus of control in nondisabled versus congenitally physically disabled adolescents. *The American Journal of Occupational Therapy*, *46*, 334-342.

93. Jarvis, P. A., & Justice, E. M. (1992). Social sensitivity in adolescents and adults with learning disabilities. *Adolescence*, *27*, 977-988.

94. Kalliopuska, M. (1992). Grouping of children's helping behaviour. *Psychological Reports*, *71*, 747-753.

95. Kamphaus, R. W., & Platt, L. O. (1992). Subtest specificities for the WISC-III. *Psychological Reports*, *70*, 899-902.

96. Keel, M. C., & Gast, D. L. (1992). Small-group instruction for students with learning disabilities: Observational and incidental learning. *Exceptional Children*, *58*, 357-368.

97. Koller, H., Richardson, S. A., & Katz, M. (1992). Families of children with mental retardation: Comprehensive view from an epidemiologic perspective. *American Journal on Mental Retardation*, *97*, 315-332.

98. Kruesi, M. J. P., Hibbs, E. D., Zahn, T. P., Keyser, C. S., Hamburger, S. D., Bartko, J. J., & Rapoport, J. L. (1992). A 2-year prospective follow-up study of children and adolescents with disruptive behavior disorders: Prediction by cerebrospinal fluid 5-hydroxyindoleacetic acid, homovanillic acid, and autonomic measures? *Archives of General Psychiatry*, *49*, 429-435.

99. Lamm, O., & Epstein, R. (1992). Are specific reading and writing difficulties causally connected with developmental spatial inability? Evidence from two cases of developmental agnosia and apraxia. *Neuropsychologia*, *30*, 459-469.

100. Lehman, E. B., Bovasso, M., Grout, L. A., & Happ, L. K. (1992). Orienting task effects on memory for presentation modality in children, young adults, and older adults. *The Journal of General Psychology*, *119*, 15-27.

101. Lorsbach, T. C., Sodoro, J., & Brown, J. S. (1992). The dissociation of repetition priming and recognition memory in language/learning-disabled children. *Journal of Experimental Child Psychology*, *54*, 121-146.

102. Lynn, R. (1992). Does Spearman's g decline at high IQ levels? Some evidence from Scotland. *The Journal of Genetic Psychology*, *153*, 229-230.

103. Malone, L. D., & Mastropieri, M. A. (1992). Reading comprehension instruction: Summarization and self-monitoring training for students with learning disabilities. *Exceptional Children*, *58*, 270-279.

104. Matthew, J. L., Golin, A. K., Moore, M. W., & Baker, C. (1992). Use of SOMPA in identification of gifted African-American children. *Journal for the Education of the Gifted*, *15*, 344-356.

105. McDowell, J. A., Schumm, J. S., & Vaughn, S. (1992). Assessing exposure to print: Development of a measure for primary children. *Yearbook of National Reading Conference*, *42*, 101-107.

106. McLeskey, J., & Grizzle, K. L. (1992). Grade retention rates among students with learning disabilities. *Exceptional Children*, *58*, 548-554.

107. Merril, E. C. (1992). Attentional resource demands of stimulus encoding for persons with and without mental retardation. *American Journal on Mental Retardation*, *97*, 87-98.

108. Norman, G., & Breznitz, Z. (1992). Differences in the ability to concentrate in first-grade Israeli pupils of low and high socioeconomic status. *The Journal of Genetic Psychology*, *153*, 5-17.

109. Northam, E., Bowden, S., Anderson, V., & Court, J. (1992). Neuropsychological functioning in adolescents with diabetes. *Journal of Clinical and Experimental Neuropsychology*, *14*, 884-900.

110. Rimm, S. B., & Lovance, K. J. (1992). The use of subject and grade skipping for the prevention and reversal of underachievement. *Gifted Child Quarterly*, *36*, 101-105.

111. Rossman, B. B. R., & Rosenberg, M. S. (1992). Family stress and functioning in children: The moderating effects of children's beliefs about their control over parental conflict. *Journal of Child Psychology and Psychiatry and Allied Disciplines*, *33*, 699-715.

112. Scott, M. S., Perou, R., Urbano, R., Hogan, A., & Gold, S. (1992). The identification of giftedness: A comparison of White, Hispanic, and Black families. *Gifted Child Quarterly*, *36*, 131-139.

113. Scruggs, T. E., & Mastropieri, M. A. (1992). Classroom application of mnemonic instruction: Acquisition, maintenance, and generalization. *Exceptional Children*, *58*, 219-229.

114. Shear, P. K., Tallal, P., & Delis, D. C. (1992). Verbal learning and memory in language impaired children. *Neuropsychologia*, *30*, 451-458.

115. Skuy, M., Apter, A., Dembo, Y., Tyano, S., Kaniel, S., & Tzuriel, D. (1992). Cognitive modifiability of adolescents with schizophrenia: A research note. *Journal of Child Psychology and Psychiatry and Allied Disciplines*, *33*, 583-589.

116. Slate, J. R., Jones, C. H., & Covert, T. L. (1992). Rethinking the instructional design for teaching the WISC-R: The effects of practice administrations. *College Student Journal*, *26*, 285-289.

117. Sonuga-Barke, E. J. S., Taylor, E., & Heptinstall, E. (1992). Hyperactivity and delay aversion—II. The effect of self versus externally imposed stimulus presentation periods on memory. *Journal of Child Psychology and Psychiatry and Allied Disciplines*, *33*, 399-409.

118. Sonuga-Barke, E. J. S., Taylor, E., Sembi, S., & Smith, J. (1992). Hyperactivity and delay aversion—I. The effect of delay on choice. *Journal of Child Psychology and Psychiatry and Allied Disciplines*, *33*, 387-398.

119. Soussignan, R., Tremblay, R. E., Schaal, B., Laurent, D., Larivee, S., Gagnon, C., LeBlanc, M., & Charlebois, P. (1992). Behavioural and cognitive characteristics of conduct disorder-hyperactive boys from age 6 to 11: A multiple informant perspective. *Journal of Child Psychology and Psychiatry and Allied Disciplines*, *33*, 1333-1346.

120. Tannenbaum, A. (1992). Early signs of giftedness: Research and commentary. *Journal for the Education of the Gifted*, *15*, 104-133.

121. Thompson, R. W., & Nichols, G. T. (1992). Correlations between scores on a continuous performance test and parents' ratings of attention problems and impulsivity in children. *Psychological Reports*, *70*, 739-742.

122. Venter, A., Lord, C., & Schopler, E. (1992). A follow-up study of high-functioning autistic children. *Journal of Child Psychology and Psychiatry and Allied Disciplines*, *33*, 489-507.

123. Williams, J., Morgan, S. B., & Kalthoff, R. A. (1992). Concrete operational thought in children with learning disabilities and children with normal achievement. *The Journal of Genetic Psychology*, *153*, 87-102.

124. Abbott, R. D., & Berninger, V. W. (1993). Structural equation modelling of relationships among developmental skills and writing skills in primary- and intermediate-grade writers. *Journal of Educational Psychology*, *85*, 478-508.

125. Abel, T., & Karnes, F. A. (1993). Self-perceived strengths in leadership abilities between suburban and rural gifted students using the Leadership Strengths Indicator. *Psychological Reports, 73*, 687-690.

126. Amin, K., Douglas, V. I., Mendelson, M. J., & Dufresne, J. (1993). Separable/integral classification by hyperactive and normal children. *Development and Psychopathology, 5*, 415-431.

127. Aplin, D. Y. (1993). Psychological evaluation of adults in a cochlear implant program. *American Annals of the Deaf, 138*, 415-419.

128. Bailey, A., Bolton, P., Butler, L., LeCouteur, A., Murphy, M., Scott, S., Webb, T., & Rutter, M. (1993). Prevalence of the fragile X anomaly amongst autistic twins and singletons. *Journal of Child Psychology and Psychiatry and Allied Disciplines, 34*, 673-688.

129. Ballard, M. E., Cummings, E. M., & Larkin, K. (1993). Emotional and cardiovascular responses to adults' angry behavior and to challenging tasks in children of hypertensive and normotensive parents. *Child Development, 64*, 500-515.

130. Berk, L. E., & Landau, S. (1993). Private speech of learning disabled and normally achieving children in classroom academic and laboratory contexts. *Child Development, 64*, 556-571.

131. Berninger, V. W., & Whitaker, D. (1993). Theory-based branching diagnosis of writing disabilities. *School Psychology Review, 22*, 623-642.

132. Bowers, P. G. (1993). Text reading and rereading: Determinants of fluency beyond word recognition. *Journal of Reading Behavior, 25*, 133-153.

133. Carpentieri, S. C., Mulhern, R. K., Douglas, S., Hanna, S., & Fairclough, D. L. (1993). Behavioral resiliency among children surviving brain tumors: A longitudinal study. *Journal of Clinical Child Psychology, 22*, 236-246.

134. Carvajal, H. H., Hayes, J. E., Lackey, K. L., Rathke, M. L., Wiebe, D. A., & Weaver, K. A. (1993). Correlations between scores on the Wechsler Intelligence Scale for Children-III and the General Purpose Abbreviated Battery of the Stanford-Binet IV. *Psychological Reports, 72*, 1167-1170.

135. Chiarenza, G. A. (1993). Movement-related brain macropotentials of persons with Down syndrome during skilled performance. *American Journal on Mental Retardation, 97*, 449-467.

136. Chittooran, M. M., D'Amato, R. C., Lassiter, K. S., & Dean, R. S. (1993). Factor structure of psychoeducational and neuropsychological measures of learning-disabled children. *Psychology in the Schools, 30*, 109-118.

137. Cicchetti, D., Rogosch, F. A., Lynch, M., & Holt, K. D. (1993). Resilience in maltreated children: Processes leading to adaptive outcome. *Development and Psychopathology, 5*, 629-647.

138. Cotugno, A. J. (1993). The diagnosis of Attention Deficit Hyperactivity Disorder (ADHD) in community mental health centers: Where and when. *Psychology in the Schools, 30*, 338-344.

139. Danoff, B., Harris, K. R., & Graham, S. (1993). Incorporating strategy instruction within the writing process in the regular classroom: Effects on the writing of students with and without learning disabilities. *Journal of Reading Behavior, 25*, 295-322.

140. Dumont, R., & Faro, C. (1993). A WISC-III short form for learning-disabled students. *Psychology in the Schools, 30*, 212-219.

141. Dykman, R. A., & Ackerman, P. T. (1993). Behavioral subtypes of attention deficit disorder. *Exceptional Children, 60*, 132-141.

142. Ehlers, S., & Gillberg, C. (1993). The epidemiology of Asperger syndrome: A total population study. *Journal of Child Psychology and Psychiatry and Allied Disciplines, 34*, 1327-1350.

143. Elia, J., Welsh, P. A., Gullotta, C. S., & Rapoport, J. L. (1993). Classroom academic performance: Improvement with both methylphenidate and dextroamphetamine in ADHD boys. *Journal of Child Psychology and Psychiatry and Allied Disciplines, 34*, 785-804.

144. Faraone, S. V., Biederman, J., Lehman, B. K., Spencer, T., Norman, D., Seidman, L. J., Kraus, I., Perrin, J., Chen, W. J., & Tsuang, M. T. (1993). Intellectual performance and social failure in children with attention deficit hyperactivity disorder and in their siblings. *Journal of Abnormal Psychology, 102*, 616-623.

145. Fazio, B. B., Johnston, J. R., & Brandl, L. (1993). Relation between mental age and vocabulary development among children with mild mental retardation. *American Journal on Mental Retardation, 97*, 541-546.

146. Feitelson, D., Goldstein, Z., Iraqi, J., & Share, D. L. (1993). Effects of listening to story reading on aspects of literacy acquisition in a diglossic situation. *Reading Research Quarterly, 28*, 71-79.

147. Fergusson, D. M., Horwood, L. J., & Lynskey, M. T. (1993). The effects of conduct disorder and attention deficit in middle childhood on offending and scholastic ability at age 13. *Journal of Child Psychology and Psychiatry and Allied Disciplines, 34*, 899-916.

148. Finlayson, S. B., & Obrzut, J. E. (1993). Factorial structure of the Quick Neurological Screening Test—Revised for children with learning disabilities. *Psychology in the Schools, 30*, 5-10.

149. Flanagan, D. P., & Alfonso, V. C. (1993). Differences required for significance between Wechsler verbal and performance IQs and WIAT subtests and composites: The predicted achievement method. *Psychology in the Schools, 30*, 125-132.

150. Flanagan, D. P., & Alfonso, V. C. (1993). WIAT subtest and composite-predicted-achievement values based on WISC-III verbal and performance IQs. *Psychology in the Schools, 30*, 310-320.

151. Floyd, F. J., & Phillippe, K. A. (1993). Parental interactions with children with and without mental retardation: Behavior management, coerciveness, and positive exchange. *American Journal on Mental Retardation, 97*, 673-684.

152. Friedrich, W. N., Shurtleff, D. B., & Shaeffer, J. (1993). Cognitive abilities and lipomyelomeningocele. *Psychological Reports, 73*, 467-470.

153. Fuerst, D. R., & Rourke, B. P. (1993). Psychosocial functioning of children: Relations between personality subtypes and academic achievement. *Journal of Abnormal Child Psychology, 21*, 597-608.

154. Halgren, D. W., & Clarizio, H. F. (1993). Categorical and programming changes in special education services. *Exceptional Children, 59*, 547-555.

155. Halperin, J. M., Newcorn, J. H., Schwartz, S. T., McKay, K. E., Bedi, G., & Sharma, V. (1993). Plasma catecholamine metabolite levels in ADHD boys with and without reading disabilities. *Journal of Clinical Child Psychology, 22*, 219-225.

156. Holmes, C. S., Dunlap, W. P., Chen, R. S., Cornwell, J., Weissman, L., Obach, M., & Frentz, J. (1993). Postpubertal disease status in diabetes and factor structure anomaly on the WISC-R. *Journal of Clinical and Experimental Neuropsychology, 15*, 843-848.

157. Hooper, S. R., & Roof, K. D. (1993). Utility of the Hobby WISC-R split-half short form for children and adolescents with severe head injury. *Psychological Reports, 72*, 371-376.

158. Howe, G. W., Feinstein, C., Reiss, D., Molock, S., & Berger, K. (1993). Adolescent adjustment to chronic physical disorders-I. Comparing neurological and non-neurological conditions. *Journal of Child Psychology and Psychiatry and Allied Disciplines, 34*, 1153-1176.

159. Hurford, D. P., & Shedelbower, A. (1993). The relationship between discrimination and memory ability in children with reading disabilities. *Contemporary Educational Psychology, 18*, 101-113.

160. Jackson, N. E., Donaldson, G. W., & Mills, J. R. (1993). Components of reading skill in postkindergarten precocious readers and level-matched second graders. *Journal of Reading Behavior, 25*, 181-208.

161. Jambaque, I., Dellatolas, G., Dulac, O., Ponsot, G., & Signoret, J. (1993). Verbal and visual memory impairment in children with epilspsy. *Neuropsychologia, 31*, 1321-1337.

162. Kail, R. (1993). Processing time decreases globally at an exponential rate during childhood and adolescence. *Journal of Experimental Child Psychology, 56*, 254-265.

163. Kolko, D. J., & Kazdin, A. E. (1993). Emotional/behavioral problems in clinic and nonclinic children: Correspondence among children, parent and teacher reports. *Journal of Child Psychology and Psychiatry and Allied Disciplines, 34*, 991-1006.

164. Koverola, C., Pound, J., Heger, A., & Lytle, C. (1993). Relationship of child sexual abuse to depression. *Child Abuse & Neglect, 17*, 393-400.

165. Kushch, A., Gross-Glenn, K., Jallad, B., Lubs, H., Robin, M., Feldman, E., & Duara, R. (1993). Temporal lobe surface area measurements on MRI in normal and dyslexic readers. *Neuropsychologia, 31*, 811-821.

166. Kusché, C. A., Cook, E. T., & Greenberg, M. T. (1993). Neuropsychological and cognitive functioning in children withanxiety, externalizing, and comorbid psychopathology. *Journal of Clinical Child Psychology, 22*, 172-195.

167. Manis, F. R., Custodio, R., & Szeszulski, P. A. (1993). Development of phonological and orthographic skill: A 2-year longitudinal study of dyslexic children. *Journal of Experimental Child Psychology, 56*, 64-86.

168. Mannuzza, S., Klein, R. G., Bessler, A., Malloy, P., & LaPadula, M. (1993). Adult outcome of hyperactive boys: Educational achievement, occupational rank, and psychiatric status. *Archives of General Psychiatry, 50*, 565-576.

169. Margalit, M. (1993). Social skills and classroom behavior among adolescents with mild mental retardation. *American Journal on Mental Retardation, 97*, 685-691.

170. McBurnett, K., Harris, S. M., Swanson, J. M., Pfiffner, L. J., Tamm, L., & Freeland, D. (1993). Neuropsychological and psychophysiological differentiation of inattention/overactivity and aggression/defiance symptom groups. *Journal of Clinical Child Psychology, 22*, 165-171.

171. McCall, R. B., & Carriger, M. S. (1993). A meta-analysis of infant habituation and recognition memory performance as predictors of later IQ. *Child Development, 64*, 57-79.

172. McConaughy, S. H., & Skiba, R. J. (1993). Comorbidity of externalizing and internalizing problems. *School Psychology Review, 22*, 421-436.

173. McDonnell, J., Hardman, M. L., Hightower, J., Keifer-O'Donnel, R., & Drew, C. (1993). Impact of community-based instruction on the development of adaptive behavior of secondary-level students with mental retardation. *American Journal on Mental Retardation, 97*, 575-584.

174. McEachin, J. J., Smith, T., & Lovaas, O. I. (1993). Long-term outcome for children with autism who received early intensive behavioral treatment. *American Journal on Mental Retardation*, *97*, 359-372.

175. McGough, J. J., Speier, P. L., & Cantwell, D. P. (1993). Obsessive-compulsive disorder in childhood and adolescence. *School Psychology Review*, *22*, 243-251.

176. Moffitt, T. E., Caspi, A., Harkness, A. R., & Silva, P. A. (1993). The natural history of change in intellectual performance: Who changes? How much? Is it meaningful? *Journal of Child Psychology and Psychiatry and Allied Disciplines*, *34*, 455-506.

177. Nabuzoka, D., & Smith, P. K. (1993). Sociometric status and social behaviour of children with and without learning difficulties. *Journal of Child Psychology and Psychiatry and Allied Disciplines*, *34*, 1435-1448.

178. Pinto, A., & Francis, G. (1993). Cognitive correlates of depressive symptoms in hospitalized adolescents. *Adolescence*, *28*, 661-672.

179. Plante, T. G., Goldfarb, L. P., & Wadley, V. (1993). Are stress and coping associated with aptitude and achievement testing performance among children? A preliminary investigation. *Journal of School Psychology*, *31*, 259-266.

180. Post, K. R., & Mitchell, H. R. (1993). The WISC-III: A reality check. *Journal of School Psychology*, *31*, 541-545.

181. Radke-Yarrow, M., & Brown, E. (1993). Resilience and vulnerability in children of multiple-risk families. *Development and Psychopathology*, *5*, 581-592.

182. Rasku-Puttonen, H., Lyytinen, P., Porkkeus, A. M., Laakso, M. L., & Ahonen, T. (1993). Communication deviances and clarity among the mothers of normally achieving and learning-disabled boys. *Family Process*, *33*, 71-80.

183. Reid, R., & Harris, K. R. (1993). Self-monitoring of attention versus self-monitoring of performance: Effects on attention and academic performance. *Exceptional Children*, *60*, 29-40.

184. Salend, S. J., Whitaker, C. R., & Reeder, E. (1993). Group evaluation: A collaborative, peer-mediated behavior management system. *Exceptional Children*, *59*, 203-209.

185. Sameroff, A. J., Seifer, R., Baldwin, A., & Baldwin, C. (1993). Stability of intelligence from preschool to adolescence: The influence of social and family risk factors. *Child Development*, *64*, 80-97.

186. Scarr, S., Weinberg, R. A., & Waldman, I. D. (1993). IQ correlations in transracial adoptive families. *Intelligence*, *17*, 541-555.

187. Schaper, M. W., & Reitsma, P. (1993). The use of speech-based recording in reading by prelingually deaf children. *American Annals of the Deaf*, *138*, 46-54.

188. Schneider, W., Gruber, H., Gold, A., & Opwis, K. (1993). Chess expertise and memory for chess positions in children and adults. *Journal of Experimental Child Psychology*, *56*, 328-349.

189. Shah, A., & Frith, U. (1993). Why do autistic individuals show superior performance on the block design task? *Journal of Child Psychology and Psychiatry and Allied Disciplines*, *34*, 1351-1364.

190. Short, E. J., Schatschneider, C. W., & Friebert, S. E. (1993). Relationship between memory and metamemory performance: A comparison of specific and general strategy knowledge. *Journal of Educational Psychology*, *85*, 412-423.

191. Slaghuis, W. L., Lovegrove, W. J., & Davidson, J. A. (1993). Visual and language processing deficits are concurrent in dyslexia. *Cortex*, *29*, 601-615.

192. Smith, T., McEachin, J. J., & Lovaas, O. I. (1993). Comments on replication and evaluation of outcome. *American Journal on Mental Retardation*, *97*, 385-391.

193. Smith, T., Smith, B., Matthews, N., & Kennedy, S. (1993). Subtest scatter and Kaufman regroupings on the WISC-R in the non-learning-disabled and learning-disabled children. *Psychology in the Schools*, *30*, 24-28.

194. Stevenson, J., Pennington, B. F., Gilger, J. W., DeFries, J. C., & Gillis, J. J. (1993). Hyperactivity and spelling disability: Testing for shared genetic aetiology. *Journal of Child Psychology and Psychiatry and Allied Disciplines*, *34*, 1137-1152.

195. Swanson, H. L. (1993). An information processing analysis of learning disabled children's problem solving. *American Educational Research Journal*, *30*, 861-893.

196. Swanson, H. L. (1993). Working memory in learning disability subgroups. *Journal of Experimental Child Psychology*, *56*, 87-114.

197. Szatmari, P., Saigal, S., Rosenbaum, P., & Campbell, D. (1993). Psychopathology and adaptive functioning among extremely low birthweight children at eight years of age. *Development and Psychopathology*, *5*, 345-357.

198. Taylor, H. G., Barry, C. T., & Schatschneider, C. (1993). School-age consequences of *haemophilus influenzae* Type b meningitis. *Journal of Clinical Child Psychology*, *22*, 196-206.

199. Truscott, D. (1993). Adolescent offenders: Comparison for sexual, violent, and property offences. *Psychological Reports*, *73*, 657-658.

200. Utens, E. M. W. J., Verhulst, F. C., Meijboom, F. J., Duivenvoorden, H. J., Erdman, R. A. M., Bos, E., Roelandt, J. T. C., & Hess, J. (1993). Behavioural and emotional problems in children and adolescents with congenital heart disease. *Psychological Medicine*, *23*, 415-424.

201. Utley, C. A., Hoehn, T. P., Soraci, S. A., & Baumeister, A. A. (1993). Motivational orientation and span of apprehension in children with mental retardation. *The Journal of Genetic Psychology*, *154*, 289-295.

202. Utley, C. A., Hoehn, T. P., Soracijr, S. A., & Baumeister, A. A. (1993). Span of apprehension in mentally retarded children: An initial investigation. *Journal of Intellectual Disability Research*, *37*, 183-187.

203. van Ijzendoorn, W. J. E., & Bus, A. G. (1993). How valid are experts' prognoses on children with learning problems? *Journal of School Psychology*, *31*, 317-325.

204. Waterman, J., & Lusk, R. (1993). Psychological testing in evaluation of child sexual abuse. *Child Abuse & Neglect*, *17*, 145-159.

205. Wielkiewicz, R. M., & Daood, C. J. (1993). Correlations between WISC-R subtests and scales of the Personality Inventory for Children. *Psychological Reports*, *73*, 1343-1346.

206. Wilkinson, S. C. (1993). WISC-R profiles of children with superior intellectual ability. *Gifted Child Quarterly*, *37*, 84-91.

207. Williams, J. P. (1993). Comprehension of students with and without learning disabilities: Identification of narrative themes and idiosyncratic text representations. *Journal of Educational Psychology*, *85*, 631-641.

208. Wilson, B. A., Ivani-Chalian, R., Besag, F. M. C., & Bryant, T. (1993). Adapting the Rivermead Behavioral Memory Test for use with children aged 5 to 10 years. *Journal of Clinical and Experimental Neuropsychology*, *15*, 474-486.

209. Ackerman, P. T., Dykman, R. A., & Ogesby, D. M. (1994). Visual event-related potentials of dyslexic children to rhyming and nonrhyming stimuli. *Journal of Clinical and Experimental Neuropsychology*, *16*, 138-154.

210. Allon, M., Gutkin, T. B., & Bruning, R. (1994). The relationship between metacognition and intelligence in normal adolescents: Some tentative but surprising findings. *Psychology in the Schools*, *31*, 93-97.

211. Althaus, M., Minderaa, R. B., & Dienske, H. (1994). The assessment of individual differences between young children with a pervasive developmental disorder by means of behavior scales which are derived from direct observation. *Journal of Child Psychology and Psychiatry and Allied Disciplines*, *35*, 333-349.

212. Anastopoulos, A. D., Spisto, M. A., & Maher, M. C. (1994). The WISC-III freedom from distractibility factor: Its utility in identifying children with attention deficit hyperactivity disorder. *Psychological Assessment*, *6*, 368-371.

213. Anderson, C. A., Hinshaw, S. P., & Simmel, C. (1994). Mother-child interactions in ADHD and comparison boys: Relationships with overt and covert externalizing behavior. *Journal of Abnormal Child Psychology*, *22*, 247-265.

214. Asarnow, J. R., Tompson, M., Hamilton, E. B., Goldstein, M. J., & Guthrie, D. (1994). Family-expressed emotion, childhood-onset depression, and childhood-onset schizophrenia spectrum disorders: Is expressed emotions a nonspecific correlate of child psychopathology or a specific risk factor for depression? *Journal of Abnormal Child Psychology*, *22*, 129-146.

215. Baron-Cohen, S., Cross, P., Crowson, M., & Robertson, M. (1994). Can children with Gilles de la Tourette Syndrome edit their intentions? *Psychological Medicine*, *24*, 29-40.

216. Beardsworth, E. D., & Zaidel, D. W. (1994). Memory for faces in epileptic children before and after brain surgery. *Journal of Clinical and Experimental Neuropsychology*, *16*, 589-596.

217. Bjorklund, D. F., Schneider, W., Cassel, W. S., & Ashley, E. (1994). Training and extension of a memory strategy: Evidence for utilization deficiencies in the acquisition of an organizational strategy in high- and low-IQ children. *Child Development*, *65*, 951-965.

218. Blennerhassett, L., Strohmeier, S. J., & Hibbett, C. (1994). Criterion-related validity of Raven's Progressive Matrices with deaf residential school students. *American Annals of the Deaf*, *139*, 104-110.

219. Bolton, P., MacDonald, H., Pickles, A., Rios, P., Goode, S., Crowson, M., Bailey, A., & Rutter, M. (1994). A case-control family history study of autism. *Journal of Child Psychology and Psychiatry and Allied Disciplines*, *35*, 877-900.

220. Bowey, J. A. (1994). Phonological sensitivity in novice readers and nonreaders. *Journal of Experimental Child Psychology*, *58*, 134-159.

221. Brookshire, B. L., Butler, I. J., Ewing-Cobbs, L., & Fletcher, J. M. (1994). Neuropsychological characteristics of children with Tourette syndrome: Evidence for a nonverbal learning disability. *Journal of Clinical and Experimental Neuropsychology*, *16*, 289-302.

222. Brown, D. T. (1994). Review of the Kaufman Adolescent and Adult Intelligence Test (KAIT). *Journal of School Psychology*, *32*, 85-99.

223. Buitelaar, J. K., Swinkels, S. H. N., de Vries, H., van der Gaag, R. J., & van Hooff, J. (1994). An ethological study on behavioural differences between hyperactive, aggressive, combined hyperactive/aggressive and control children. *Journal of Child Psychology & Psychiatry & Allied Disciplines*, *35*, 1437-1446.

224. Caplan, R., Guthrie, D., Shields, W. D., & Yudovin, S. (1994). Communication deficits in pediatric complex partial seizure disorder and schizophrenia. *Development and Psychopathology*, *6*, 499-517.

225. Carr, J. (1994). Annotation: Long term outcome for people with Down's syndrome. *Journal of Child Psychology and Psychiatry and Allied Disciplines*, *35*, 425-439.

226. Cohen, R., Duncan, M., & Cohen, S. (1994). Classroom peer relations of children participating in a pull-out enrichment program. *Gifted Child Quarterly*, *38*, 33-37.

227. Colegrove, R. W., Jr., & Huntzinger, R. M. (1994). Academic, behavioral, and social adaptation of boys with hemophilia/HIV disease. *Journal of Pediatric Psychology*, *19*, 457-473.

228. Cook, E. T., Greenberg, M. T., & Kusche, C. A. (1994). The relations between emotional understanding, intellectual functioning, and disruptive behavior problems in elementary-school-aged children. *Journal of Abnormal Child Psychology*, *22*, 205-219.

229. Dai, X. Y., & Lynn, R. (1994). Gender differences in intelligence among Chinese children. *The Journal of Social Psychology*, *134*, 123-125.

230. Daniels, J. K., Owen, M. J., McGuffin, P., Thompson, L., Petterman, D. K., Chorney, M., Chorney, K., Smith, D., Skuder, P., Vignetti, S., McClearn, G. E., & Plomin, R. (1994). IQ and variation in the number of fragile X CGG repeats: No association in a normal sample. *Intelligence*, *19*, 45-50.

231. de Sonneville, L. M. J., Njiokiktjien, C., & Bos, H. (1994). Methylphenidate and information processing. Part I: Differentiation between responders and nonresponders; Part 2: Efficacy in responders. *Journal of Clinical and Experimental Neuropsychology*, *16*, 877-897.

232. Deb, S., & Prasad, K. B. G. (1994). The prevalence of autistic disorder among children with a learning disability. *British Journal of Psychiatry*, *165*, 395-399.

233. DiGiulio, D. V., Seidenberg, M., O'Leary, D. S., & Raz, N. (1994). Procedural and declarative memory: A developmental study. *Brain and Cognition*, *25*, 79-91.

234. Dobson, E., & Rust, J. O. (1994). Memory for objects and faces by the mentally retarded and nonretarded. *The Journal of Psychology*, *128*, 315-322.

235. Donders, J. (1994). Academic placement after traumatic brain injury. *Journal of School Psychology*, *32*, 53-65.

236. Douglas, V. I., & Parry, P. A. (1994). Effects of reward and nonreward on frustration and attention in attention deficit disorder. *Journal of Abnormal Child Psychology*, *22*, 281-302.

237. Dulaney, C. L., Marks, W., & Devine, C. (1994). Global/local processing in mentally retarded and nonretarded persons. *Intelligence*, *19*, 245-261.

238. DuPaul, G. J., & Eckert, T. L. (1994). The effects of social skills curricula: Now you see them, now you don't. *School Psychology Quarterly*, *9*, 113-132.

239. Eaves, L. C., Ho, H. H., & Eaves, D. M. (1994). Subtypes of autism by cluster analyses. *Journal of Autism and Developmental Disorders*, *24*, 3-22.

240. Erhardt, D., & Hinshaw, S. P. (1994). Initial sociometric impressions of attention-deficit hyperactivity disorder and comparison boys: Predictions from social behaviors and from nonbehavioral variables. *Journal of Consulting and Clinical Psychology*, *62*, 833-842.

241. Fee, V. E., Matson, J. L., & Benavidez, D. A. (1994). Attention deficit-hyperactivity disorder among mentally retarded children. *Research in Development Disabilities*, *15*, 67-79.

242. Fergusson, D. M., Lynskey, M. T., & Horwood, L. J. (1994). The effects of parental separation, the timing of separation and gender on children's performance on cognitive tests. *Journal of Child Psychology and Psychiatry and Allied Disciplines*, *35*, 1077-1092.

243. Flannery, K. A., & Liederman, J. (1994). A test of the immunoreactive theory for the origin of neurodevelopmental disorders in the offspring of women with immune disorder. *Cortex*, *30*, 635-646.

244. Fletcher, J. M., Shaywitz, S. E., Shankweiler, D. P., Katz, L., Liberman, I. Y., Stuebing, K. K., Francis, D. J., Fowler, A. E., & Shaywitz, B. A. (1994). Cognitive profiles of reading disability: Comparisons of discrepancy and low achievement definitions. *Journal of Educational Psychology*, *86*, 6-23.

245. Frick, P. J., O'Brien, B. S., Wootton, J. M., & McBurnett, K. (1994). Psychopathy and conduct problems in children. *Journal of Abnormal Psychology*, *103*, 700-707.

246. Frick, P. J., Silverthorn, P., & Evans, C. (1994). Assessment of childhood anxiety using structured interviews: Patterns of agreement among informants and association with maternal anxiety. *Psychological Assessment*, *6*, 372-379.

247. Gass, C. S., Ansley, J., & Boyette, S. (1994). Emotional correlates of fluency test and maze performance. *Journal of Clinical Psychology*, *50*, 586-590.

248. Giedd, J. N., Castellanos, F. X., Casey, B. J., Kozuch, P., King, A. C., Hamburger, S. D., & Rapoport, J. L. (1994). Quantitative morphology of the corpus callosum in attention deficit hyperactivity disorder. *American Journal of Psychiatry*, *151*, 665-669.

249. Glutting, J. J., Oakland, T., & Konold, T. R. (1994). Criterion-related bias with the guide to the assessment of test-session behavior for the WISC-III and WIAT: Possible race/ethnicity, gender, and SES effects. *Journal of School Psychology*, *32*, 355-369.

250. Goldstein, D. J., & Britt, T. W., Jr. (1994). Visual-motor coordination and intelligence as predictors of reading, mathematics, and written language ability. *Perceptual and Motor Skills*, *78*, 819-823.

251. Goldstein, G., Minshew, N. J., & Siegel, D. J. (1994). Age differences in academic achievement in high-functioning autistic individuals. *Journal of Clinical and Experimental Neuropsychology*, *16*, 671-680.

252. Gomez, R., & Sanson, A. V. (1994). Effects of experimenter and mother presence on the attentional performance and activity of hyperactive boys. *Journal of Abnormal Child Psychology*, *22*, 517-529.

253. Gomez, R., & Sanson, A. V. (1994). Mother-child interactions and noncompliance in hyperactive boys with and without conduct problems. *Journal of Child Psychology and Psychiatry and Allied Disciplines*, *35*, 477-490.

254. Goodman, R. (1994). A modified version of the Rutter Parent Questionnaire including extra items on children's strengths: A research note. *Journal of Child Psychology & Psychiatry & Allied Disciplines*, *35*, 1483-1494.

255. Graf, M. H., & Hinton, R. N. (1994). A 3-year comparison study of WISC-R and WISC-III IQ scores for a sample of special education students. *Educational and Psychological Measurement*, *54*, 128-133.

256. Green, A., Steiner, R., & White, N. (1994). A follow-up dual-task investigation of lateralized effects in right- and left-handed males. *Brain and Cognition*, *25*, 207-219.

257. Gustafson, S. B. (1994). Female underachievement and overachievement: Parental contributions and long-term consequences. *International Journal of Behavioral Development*, *17*, 469-484.

258. Haddad, F. A., Juliano, J. M., & Vaughan, D. (1994). Long-term stability of individual WISC-R IQs of learning disabled children. *Psychological Reports*, *74*, 15-18.

259. Halperin, J. M., Sharma, V., Siever, L. J., Schwartz, S. T., Matier, K., Wornell, G., & Newcorn, J. H. (1994). Serotonergic function in aggressive and nonaggressive boys with attention deficit hyperactivity disorder. *American Journal of Psychiatry*, *151*, 243-248.

260. Hansen, J., & Bowey, J. A. (1994). Phonological analysis skills, verbal working memory, and reading ability in second-grade children. *Child Development*, *65*, 938-950.

261. Happé, F. (1994). An advanced test of theory of mind: Understanding of story characters' thoughts and feelings by able, autistic, mentally handicapped, and normal children and adults. *Journal of Autism and Developmental Disorders*, *24*, 129-154.

262. Happe, F. G. E. (1994). Wechsler IQ profile and theory of mind in autism: A research note. *Journal of Child Psychology & Psychiatry & Allied Disciplines*, *35*, 1461-1471.

263. Hatcher, P. J., Hulme, C., & Ellis, A. W. (1994). Ameliorating early reading failure by integrating the teaching of reading and phonological skills: The phonological linkage hypothesis. *Child Development*, *65*, 41-57.

264. Henderson, S. E., Barnett, A., & Henderson, L. (1994). Visuospatial difficulties and clumsiness: On the interpretation of conjoined deficits. *Journal of Child Psychology and Psychiatry and Allied Disciplines*, *35*, 961-969.

265. Howard-Rose, D., & Rose, C. (1994). Students' adaptation to taks environments in resource room and regular class settings. *Journal of Special Education*, *28*, 3-26.

266. Hugdahl, K., & Carlsson, G. (1994). Dichotic listening and focused attention in children with hemiplegic cerebral palsy. *Journal of Clinical and Experimental Neuropsychology*, *16*, 84-92.

267. Jaedicke, S., Storoschuk, S., & Lord, C. (1994). Subjective experience and causes of affect in high-functioning children and adolescents with autism. *Development and Psychopathology*, *6*, 273-284.

268. Janniro, F., Sapp, G. L., & Kohler, M. P. (1994). Validating the Street Survival Skills Questionnaire. *Psychological Reports*, *74*, 191-194.

269. Järvelin, M. R., Läärä, E., Rantakallio, P., Moilanen, I., & Isohanni, M. (1994). Juvenile delinquency, education, and mental disability. *Exceptional Children*, *$161*, 230-241.

270. Jensen, A. R., & Johnson, F. W. (1994). Race and sex differences in head size and IQ. *Intelligence*, *18*, 309-333.

271. John, O. P., Caspi, A., Robins, R. W., Moffitt, T. E., & Stouthamer-Loeber, M. (1994). The "little five": Exploring the nomological network of the five-factor model of personality in adolescent boys. *Child Development*, *65*, 160-178.

272. Kamphaus, R. W., Benson, J., Hutchinson, S., & Platt, L. O. (1994). Identification of factor models for the WISC-III. *Educational and Psychological Measurement*, *54*, 174-186.

273. Karnes, F. A., & McGinnis, J. C. (1994). Correlations among scores on the Matrix Analogies Test—Short Form and the WISC-R with gifted youth. *Psychological Reports*, *74*, 948-950.

274. Karnes, F. A., & McGinns, J. C. (1994). Persons who most impress gifted youth: A replication. *Psychological Reports, 74,* 851-857.

275. Kaufman, A. S. (1994). A reply to Macmann and Barnett. Lessons from the blind men and the elephant. *School Psychology Quarterly, 9,* 199-207.

276. Kazdin, A. E., & Mazurick, J. L. (1994). Dropping out of child psychotherapy: Distinguishing early and late dropouts over the course of treatment. *Journal of Consulting and Clinical Psychology, 62,* 1069-1074.

277. Keith, T. Z. (1994). Intelligence is important. Intelligence is complex. *School Psychology Quarterly, 9,* 209-221.

278. Klonman, R., Brumaghim, J. T., Fitzpatrick, P. A., Borgstedt, A. D., & Strauss, J. (1994). Clinical and cognitive effects of methylphenidate on children with attention deficit disorder as a function of aggression/oppositionality and age. *Journal of Abnormal Psychology, 103,* 206-221.

279. Kovacs, M., Ryan, C., & Obrosky, D. S. (1994). Verbal intellectual and verbal memory performance of youths with childhood-onset insulin-dependent diabetes mellitus. *Journal of Pediatric Psychology, 19,* 475-483.

280. Lamborn, S. D., Fischer, K. W., & Pipp, S. (1994). Constructive criticism and social ties: A developmental sequence for understanding honesty and kindness in social interactions. *Developmental Psychology, 30,* 495-508.

281. Lavoie, M. E., & Charlebois, P. (1994). The discriminant validity of the Stroop Color and Word Test: Toward a cost-effective strategy to distinguish subgroups of disruptive preadolescents. *Psychology in the Schools, 31,* 98-107.

282. Leather, C. V., & Henry, L. A. (1994). Working memory span and phonological awareness tasks as predictors of early reading ability. *Journal of Experimental Child Psychology, 58,* 88-111.

283. Leung, P. W. L., & Connolly, K. J. (1994). Attentional difficulties in hyperactive and conduct-disordered children: A processing deficit. *Journal of Child Psychology and Psychiatry and Allied Disciplines, 35,* 1229-1245.

284. Levinson, E. M., & Folino, L. (1994). Correlations of scores on the Gifted Evaluation Scale with those on WISC-III and Kaufman Brief Intelligence Test for students referred for gifted evaluation. *Psychological Reports, 74,* 419-424.

285. Levy-Shiff, R., Einat, G., Har-Even, D., Mogilner, M., Mogilner, S., Lerman, M., & Krikler, R. (1994). Emotional and behavioral adjustment in children born prematurely. *Journal of Clinical Child Psychology, 23,* 323-333.

286. Lewis, C. D., & Lorentz, S. (1994). Comparison of the Leiter International Performance Scale and the Wechsler Intelligence Scales. *Psychological Reports, 74,* 521-522.

287. Lewis, J. D. (1994). Self-actualization in gifted students. *Psychological Reports, 74,* 767-770.

288. Liederman, J., & Flannery, K. A. (1994). Fall conception increases the risk of neurodevelopmental disorder in offspring. *Journal of Clinical and Experimental Neuropsychology, 16,* 754-768.

289. Loehlin, J. C., Horn, J. M., & Willerman, L. (1994). Differential inheritance of mental abilities in the Texas Adoption Project. *Intelligence, 19,* 325-336.

290. Luo, D., Petrill, S. A., & Thompson, L. A. (1994). An exploration of genetic *g*: Hierarchical factor analysis of cognitive data from the western reserve twin project. *Intelligence, 18,* 335-347.

291. Lyness, S. A., Eaton, E. M., & Schneider, L. S. (1994). Cognitive performance in older and middle-aged depressed outpatients and controls. *Journal of Gerontology: Psychological Sciences, 49*(Pt.1), P129-P136.

292. Lynn, R. (1994). Some reinterpretations of the Minnesota transracial adoption study. *Intelligence, 19,* 21-27.

293. Macmann, G. M., & Barnett, D. W. (1994). Some additional lessons from the Wechsler scales: A rejoinder to Kaufman and Keith. *School Psychology Quarterly, 9,* 223-236.

294. Macmann, G. M., & Barnett, D. W. (1994). Structural analysis of correlated factors: Lessons from the verbal-performance dichotomy of the Wechsler scales. *School Psychology Quarterly, 9,* 161-197.

295. Marciano, P. L., & Kazdin, A. E. (1994). Self-esteem, depression, hopelessness and suicidal intent among psychiatrically disturbed inpatient children. *Journal of Clinical Child Psychology, 23,* 151-160.

296. Martin, C. S., Earleywine, M., Blackson, T. C., Vanyukov, M. M., Moss, H. B., & Tarter, R. E. (1994). Aggressivity, inattention, hyperactivity, and impulsivity in boys at high and low risk for substance abuse. *Journal of Abnormal Child Psychology, 22,* 177-203.

297. McDougall, S., Hulme, C., Ellis, A., & Monk, A. (1994). Learning to read: The role of short-term memory and phonological skills. *Journal of Experimental Child Psychology, 58,* 112-133.

298. McGhee, R., & Lieberman, L. (1994). Gf-Gc Theory of human cognition: Differentiation of short-term auditory and visual memory factors. *Psychology in the Schools, 31,* 297-304.

299. McGuire, S., Neiderhiser, J. M., Reiss, D., Hetherington, E. M., & Plomin, R. (1994). Genetic and environmental influences on perceptions of self-worth and competence in adolescence: A study of twins, full siblings, and step siblings. *Child Development, 65,* 785-799.

300. McIntosh, R., Vaughn, S., Schumm, J. S., Haager, D., & Lee, O. (1994). Observations of students with learning disabilities in general education classrooms. *Exceptional Children, 60,* 249-261.

301. McKeough, A., Yates, T., & Marini, A. (1994). Intentional reasoning: A developmental study of behaviorally aggressive and normal boys. *Development and Psychopathology, 6,* 285-304.

302. Miles, J., & Stelmack, R. M. (1994). Learning disability subtypes and the effects of auditory and visual priming on visual event-related potential to words. *Journal of Clinical and Experimental Neuropsychology, 16,* 43-64.

303. Minshew, N. J., Goldstein, G., Taylor, H. G., & Siegel, D. J. (1994). Academic achievement in high functioning autistic individuals. *Journal of Clinical and Experimental Neuropsychology, 16,* 261-270.

304. Morra, S. (1994). Issues in working memory measurement: Testing for M capacity. *International Journal of Behavioral Development, 17,* 143-159.

305. Morton, L. L. (1994). Interhemispheric balance patterns detected by selective phonemic dichotic laterality measures in four clinical subtypes of reading-disabled children. *Journal of Clinical and Experimental Neuropsychology, 16,* 556-567.

306. Mott, P., & Krane, A. (1994). Interpersonal cognitive problem-solving and childhood social competence. *Cognitive Therapy and Research, 18,* 127-141.

307. Noam, G. G., Paget, K., Valiant, G., Borst, S., & Bartok, J. (1994). Conduct and affective disorders in developmental perspective: A systematic study of adolescent psychopathology. *Development and Psychopathology, 6,* 519-532.

308. Ornduff, S. R., Freedenfeld, R. N., Kelsey, R. M., & Critelli, J. W. (1994). Object relations of sexually abused female subjects: A TAT analysis. *Journal of Personality Assessment, 63,* 223-238.

309. Orsini, A. (1994). Corsi's block-tapping test: Standardization and concurrent validity with WISC-R for children aged 11 to 16. *Perceptual and Motor Skills, 79,* 1547-1554.

310. Osterling, J., & Dawson, G. (1994). Early recognition of children with autism: A study of first birthday home videotapes. *Journal of Autism and Developmental Disorders, 24,* 247-257.

311. Ozonoff, S., & McEvoy, R. E. (1994). A longitudinal study of executive function and theory of mind development in autism. *Development and Psychopathology, 6,* 415-431.

312. Ozonoff, S., Strayer, D. L., McMahon, W. M., & Filloux, F. (1994). Executive function abilities in autism and Tourette syndrome: An information processing approach. *Journal of Child Psychology and Psychiatry and Allied Disciplines, 35,* 1015-1032.

313. Parker, K. C. H., & Atkinson, L. (1994). Factor space of the Wechsler Intelligence Scale for Children—Third Edition: Critical thoughts and recommendations. *Psychological Assessment, 6,* 201-208.

314. Payette, K. A., & Clarizio, H. F. (1994). Discrepant team decisions: The effects of race, gender, achievement, and IQ on LD eligibility. *Psychology in the Schools, 31,* 40-48.

315. Pearson, D. A., & Aman, M. G. (1994). Rating hyperactivity and developmental indices: Should clinicians correct for developmental level. *Journal of Autism and Developmental Disorders, 24,* 395-411.

316. Pianta, R. C., & Egeland, B. (1994). Predictors of instability in children's mental test performance at 24, 48, and 96 months. *Intelligence, 18,* 145-163.

317. Pine, D. S., Weese-Mayer, D. E., Silvestri, J. M., Davies, M., Whitaker, A. H., & Klein, D. F. (1994). Anxiety and congenital central hypoventilation syndrome. *American Journal of Psychiatry, 151,* 864-870.

318. Pistole, D. R., & Ornduff, S. R. (1994). TAT assessment of sexually abused girls: An analysis of manifest content. *Journal of Personality Assessment, 63,* 211-222.

319. Piven, J., Wzorek, M., Landa, R., Lainhart, J., Bolton, P., Chase, G. A., & Folstein, S. (1994). Personality characteristics of the parents of autistic individuals. *Psychological Medicine, 24,* 783-795.

320. Plante, T. G., & Sykora, C. (1994). Are stress and coping associated with WISC-III performance among children? *Journal of Clinical Psychology, 50,* 759-762.

321. Pogge, D. L., Stokes, J. M., & Harvey, P. D. (1994). Empirical evaluation of the factorial structure of attention in adolescent psychiatric patients. *Journal of Clinical and Experimental Neuropsychology, 16,* 344-353.

322. Poole, J. L., & Schneck, C. M. (1994). Developmental differences in praxis in learning-disabled and normal children and adults. *Perceptual and Motor Skills, 78,* 1219-1228.

323. Quamma, J. P., & Greenberg, M. T. (1994). Children's experience of life stress: The role of family social support and social problem-solving skills as protective factors. *Journal of Clinical Child Psychology, 23,* 295-305.

324. Rauch-Elnekave, H. (1994). Teenage motherhood: Its relationship to undetected learning problems. *Adolescence, 29,* 91-103.

325. Resta, S. P., & Eliot, J. (1994). Written expression in boys with attention deficit disorder. *Perceptual and Motor Skills, 79,* 1131-1138.

326. Rodgers, J. L., Rowe, D. C., & May, K. (1994). DF analysis of NLSY IQ/achievement data: Nonshared environmental influences. *Intelligence, 19*, 157-177.

327. Rousseau, M. K., Krantz, P. J., Poulson, C. L., Kitson, M. E., & McClannahan, L. E. (1994). Sentence combining as a technique for increasing adjective use in writing by students with autism. *Research in Development Disabilities, 15*, 19-37.

328. Rovet, J., Szekely, C., & Hockenberry, M. (1994). Specific arithmetic calculation deficits in children with Turner syndrome. *Journal of Clinical and Experimental Neuropsychology, 16*, 820-839.

329. Ruth, W. J. (1994). Goal setting, responsibility training, and fixed ratio reinforcement: Ten-month application to students with emotional disturbance in a public school setting. *Psychology in the Schools, 31*, 146-155.

330. Sabatino, D. A., & Vance, H. B. (1994). Is the diagnosis of Attention Deficit/Hyperactivity Disorders meaningful? *Psychology in the Schools, 31*, 188-196.

331. Sears, L. L., Finn, P. R., & Steinmetz, J. E. (1994). Abnormal classical eye-blink conditioning in autism. *Journal of Autism and Developmental Disorders, 24*, 737-751.

332. Shapiro, E. S., & Eckert, T. L. (1994). Acceptability of curriculum-based assessment by school psychologists. *Journal of School Psychology, 32*, 167-183.

333. Slate, J. R. (1994). WISC-III correlations with the WIAT. *Psychology in the Schools, 31*, 278-285.

334. Snowling, M. J., Hulme, C., Smith, A., & Thomas, J. (1994). The effects of phonetic similarity and list length on children's sound categorization performance. *Journal of Experimental Child Psychology, 58*, 160-180.

335. Sommerville, W., & Whissell, C. (1994). Differences among slopes and intercepts for regression lines predicting children's connotative and denotative knowledge of familiar and unfamiliar words on the basis of age. *Perceptual and Motor Skills, 79*, 219-225.

336. Stahl, S. A., & Murray, B. A. (1994). Defining phonological awareness and its relationship to early reading. *Journal of Educational Psychology, 86*, 221-234.

337. Stanovich, K. E., & Siegel, L. S. (1994). Phenotypic performance profile of children with reading disabilities: A regression-based test of the phonological-core variable difference model. *Journal of Educational Psychology, 86*, 24-53.

338. Steinhausen, H. C., Willms, J., & Spohr, H. L. (1994). Correlates of psychopathology and intelligence in children with fetal alcohol syndrome. *Journal of Child Psychology and Psychiatry and Allied Disciplines, 35*, 323-331.

339. Stewart, S. M., Kennard, B. D., Waller, D. A., & Fixler, D. (1994). Cognitive function in children who receive organ transplantation. *Health Psychology, 13*, 3-13.

340. Strauss, E., Wada, J., & Hunter, M. (1994). Callosal morphology and performance on intelligence tests. *Journal of Clinical and Experimental Neuropsychology, 16*, 79-83.

341. Strom, R., Strom, S., Strom, P., & Collinsworth, P. (1994). Parent competence in families with gifted children. *Journal for the Education of the Gifted, 18*, 39-54.

342. Summers, J. A., & Craik, F. I. M. (1994). The effects of subject-performed tasks on the memory performance of verbal autistic children. *Journal of Autism and Developmental Disorders, 24*, 773-783.

343. Truscott, S. D., Narrett, C. M., & Smith, S. E. (1994). WISC-R subtest reliability over time: Implications for practice and research. *Psychological Reports, 74*, 147-156.

344. van Daal, V. H. P., Reistma, P., & van der Leij, A. (1994). Processing units in word reading by disabled readers. *Journal of Experimental Child Psychology, 57*, 180-210.

345. Van Reusen, A. K., & Bos, C. S. (1994). Facilitating student participation in individualized education programs through motivation strategy instruction. *Exceptional Children, 60*, 466-475.

346. Wang, P. P., & Bellugi, U. (1994). Evidence from two genetic syndromes for a dissociation between verbal and visual-spatial short-term memory. *Journal of Clinical and Experimental Neuropsychology, 16*, 317-322.

347. White, J. L., Moffitt, T. E., Caspi, A., Bartusch, D. J., Needles, D. J., & Stouthamer-Loeber, M. (1994). Measuring impulsivity and examining its relationship to delinquency. *Journal of Abnormal Psychology, 103*, 192-205.

348. Wold, D. C., Evans, C. R., Montague, J. C., Jr., & Dancer, J. E. (1994). A pilot study of SPINE test scores and measures of tongue deviancy in speakers with severe-to-profound hearing loss. *American Annals of the Deaf, 139*, 352-357.

349. Yeates, K. O., & Mortensen, M. E. (1994). Acute and chronic neuropsychological consequences of mercury vapor poisoning in two early adolescents. *Journal of Clinical and Experimental Neuropsychology, 16*, 209-222.

350. Yirmiya, N., Sigman, M., & Zacks, D. (1994). Perceptual perspective-taking and seriation abilities in high-functioning children with autism. *Development and Psychopathology, 6*, 263-272.

351. Zimet, S. G., Farley, G. K., Adler, S. S., & Zimmerman, T. (1994). Intellectual competence of children who are beginning inpatient and day psychiatric treatment. *Journal of Clinical Psychology, 50*, 866-877.

352. Zolten, A. J., Bush, L. K., Green, A., & Harrell, E. H. (1994). Comparison of error rates and performance on Wechsler's Coding and Digit Symbol subtests and the Symbol-Symbol test for children and adults. *Perceptual and Motor Skills, 79*, 1627-1631.

353. Acklin, M. W. (1995). Rorschach assessment of the borderline child. *Journal of Clinical Psychology, 51*, 294-302.

354. Bailey, A., LeCouteur, A., Gottesman, I., Bolton, P., Simonoff, E., Yuzda, E., & Rutter, M. (1995). Autism as a strongly genetic disorder: Evidence from a British twin study. *Psychological Medicine, 25*, 63-77.

355. Bergman, A. J., & Walker, E. (1995). The relationship between cognitive function and behavioral deviance in children at risk for psychopathology. *Journal of Child Psychology and Psychiatry and Allied Disciplines, 36*, 265-278.

356. Blackson, T. C. (1995). Temperament and IQ mediate the effects of family history of substance abuse and family dysfunction on academic achievement. *Journal of Clinical Psychology, 51*, 113-122.

357. Blumberg, T. A. (1995). A practitioner's view of WISC-III. *Journal of School Psychology, 33*, 95-97.

358. Bolen, L. M., Aichinger, K. S., Hall, C. W., & Webster, R. E. (1995). A comparison of the performance of cognitively disabled children on the WISC-R and WISC-III. *Journal of Clinical Psychology, 51*, 89-94.

359. Canivez, G. L. (1995). Validity of the Kaufman Brief Intelligence Test: Comparisons with the Wechsler Intelligence Scale for Children—Third Edition. *Assessment, 2*, 101-111.

360. de Jong, P. F., & Das-Smaal, E. A. (1995). Attention and intelligence: The validity of the Star Counting Test. *Journal of Educational Psychology, 87*, 80-92.

361. Dixon, W. E., Jr., & Anderson, T. (1995). Establishing covariance continuity between the WISC-R and the WISC-III. *Psychological Assessment, 7*, 115-117.

362. Elwan, F. Z. (1995). Gender differences on simultaneous and sequential cognitive tasks among Egyptian school children. *Perceptual and Motor Skills, 80*, 119-127.

363. Faraone, S. V., Biederman, J., Chen, W. J., Milberger, S., Warburton, R., & Tsuang, M. T. Genetic heterogeneity in attention-deficit hyperactivity disorder (ADHD): Gender, psychiatric comorbidity, and maternal ADHD. *Journal of Abnormal Psychology, 104*, 334-345.

364. Feldman, J., Kerr, B., & Streisgauth, A. D. (1995). Correlational analyses of procedural and declarative learning performance. *Intelligence, 20*, 87-114.

365. Fergusson, D. M., & Horwood, L. J. (1995). Early disruptive behavior, IQ, and later school achievement and delinquent behavior. *Journal of Abnormal Child Psychology, 23*, 183-199.

366. Flaks, D. K., Ficher, I., Masterpasqua, F., & Joseph, G. (1995). Lesbians choosing motherhood: A comparative study of lesbian and heterosexual parents and their children. *Developmental Psychology, 31*, 105-114.

367. Flanagan, R. (1995). The utility of the Kaufman Assessment Battery for Children (K-ABC) and the Wechsler Intelligence Scales for linguistically different children: Clinical considerations. *Psychology in the Schools, 32*, 5-11.

368. Freedenfeld, R. N., Ornduff, S. R., & Kelsey, R. M. (1995). Object relations and physical abuse: A TAT analysis. *Journal of Personality Assessment, 64*, 552-568.

369. Gnys, J. A., Willis, W. G., & Faust, D. (1995). School psychologists' diagnoses of learning disabilities: A study of illusory correlation. *Journal of School Psychology, 33*, 59-73.

370. Goodman, R., Simonoff, E., & Stevenson, J. (1995). The impact of child IQ, parent IQ and sibling IQ on child behavioural deviance scores. *Journal of Child Psychology and Psychiatry and Allied Disciplines, 36*, 409-425.

371. Graham, S., MacArthur, C., & Schwartz, S. (1995). Effects of goal setting and procedural facilitation on the revising behavior and writing performance of students with writing and learning problems. *Journal of Educational Psychology, 87*, 230-240.

372. Gresham, K. M., MacMillan, D. L., & Siperstein, G. N. (1995). Critical analysis of the 1992 AAMR definition: Implications for school psychology. *School Psychology Quarterly, 10*, 1-19.

373. Happe, F. G. E. (1995). The role of age and verbal ability in the theory of mind task performance of subjects with autism. *Child Development, 66*, 843-855.

374. Harden, P. W., & Pihl, R. O. (1995). Cognitive function, cardiovascular reactivity, and behavior in boys at high risk for alcoholism. *Journal of Abnormal Psychology, 104*, 94-103.

375. Hickey, J. E., Suess, P. E., Newlin, D. B., Spurgeon, L., & Porges, S. W. (1995). Vagal tone regulation during sustained attention in boys exposed to opiates in utero. *Addictive Behaviors, 20*, 43-59.

376. Hinshaw, S. P., Simmel, C., & Heller, T. L. (1995). Multimethod assessment of covert antisocial behavior in children: Laboratory observations, adult ratings, and child self-report. *Psychological Assessment, 7*, 209-219.

377. Hodapp, R. M. (1995). Definitions in mental retardation: Effects on research, practice, and perceptions. *School Psychology Quarterly, 10*, 24-28.

378. Iaboni, F., Douglas, V. I., & Baker, A. G. (1995). Effects of reward and response costs on inhibition in ADHD children. *Journal of Abnormal Psychology, 104*, 232-240.

379. Kosslyn, S. M., Hamilton, S. E., & Bernstein, J. H. (1995). The perception of curvature can be selectively disrupted by prosopagnosia. *Brain and Cognition, 27*, 36-58.

380. Kovacs, M., Ho, V., & Pollock, M. H. (1995). Criterion and predictive validity of the diagnosis of adjustment disorder: A prospective study of youths with new-onset insulin-dependent diabetes mellitus. *American Journal of Psychiatry, 152*, 523-528.

381. Lahey, B. B., Loeber, R., Hart, E. L., Frick, P. J., Applegate, B., Zhang, Q., Green, S. M., & Russo, M. F. (1995). Four-year longitudinal study of conduct disorder in boys: Patterns and predictors of persistence. *Journal of Abnormal Psychology, 104*, 83-93.

382. Lerer, B., Shapira, B., Calev, A., Tubi, N., Drexler, H., Kindler, S., Lidsky, D., & Schwartz, J. E. (1995). Antidepressant and cognitive effects of twice- versus three-times weekly ECT. *American Journal of Psychiatry, 152*, 564-570.

383. Li,. A. K. F., & Adamson, G. (1995). Motivational patterns related to gifted students' learning of mathematics, science and English: An examination of gender differences. *Journal for the Education of the Gifted, 18*, 284-297.

384. Liederman, J., & Flannery, K. A. (1995). The sex ratios of families with a neurodevelopmentally disordered child. *Journal of Child Psychology and Psychiatry and Allied Disciplines, 36*, 511-517.

385. Luthar, S. S., Woolston, J. L., Sparrow, S. S., Zimmerman, L. D., & Riddle, M. A. (1995). Adaptive behaviors among psychiatrically hospitalized children: The role of intelligence and related attributes. *Journal of Clinical Child Psychology, 24*, 98-108.

386. Matson, J. L. (1995). Comments on Gresham, MacMillan, and Siperstein's paper "Critical analysis of the 1992 AAMR definition: Implications for school psychology." *School Psychology Quarterly, 10*, 20-23.

387. McBride-Chang, C. (1995). What is phonological awareness? *Journal of Educational Psychology, 87*, 179-192.

388. Moon, S. M., & Dillon, D. R. (1995). Multiple exceptionalities: A case study. *Journal for the Education of the Gifted, 18*, 111-130.

389. Plomin, R. (1995). Genetics and children's experiences in the family. *Journal of Child Psychology and Psychiatry and Allied Disciplines, 36*, 33-68.

390. Prewett, P. N. (1995). A comparison of two screening tests (the Matrix Analogies Test—Short Form and the Kaufman Brief Intelligence Test) with the WISC-III. *Psychological Assessment, 7*, 69-72.

391. Sabatino, D. A., Spangler, R. S., & Vance, H. B. (1995). The relationship between the Wechsler Intelligence Scale for Children—Revised and the Wechsler Intelligence Scale for Children—III scales and subtests with gifted children. *Psychology in the Schools, 32*, 18-23.

392. Saccuzzo, D. P., & Johnson, N. E. (1995). Traditional psychometric tests and proportionate representation: An intervention and program evaluation study. *Psychological Assessment, 7*, 183-194.

393. Schatz, J., & Hamdam-Allen, G. (1995). Effects of age and IQ on adaptive behavior domains for children with autism. *Journal of Autism and Developmental Disorders, 25*, 51-60.

394. Schweitzer, J. B., & Sulzer-Azaroff, B. (1995). Self-control in boys with Attention Deficit Hyperactivity Disorder: Effects of added stimulation and time. *Journal of Child Psychology and Psychiatry and Allied Disciplines, 36*, 671-686.

395. Serra, M., Minderaa, R. B., van Geert, P. L. C., Jackson, A. E., Althaus, M., & Til, R. (1995). Emotional role-taking abilities of children with a pervasive developmental disorder not otherwise specified. *Journal of Child Psychology and Psychiatry and Allied Disciplines, 36*, 475-490.

396. Shalev, R. S., Manor, O., Amir, N., Wertman-Elad, R., & Gross-Tsur, V. (1995). Developmental dyscalculia and brain laterality. *Cortex, 31*, 357-365.

397. Shapiro, S. K., & Simpson, R. G. (1995). Koppitz scoring system as a measure of Bender-Gestalt performance in behaviorally and emotionally disturbed adolescents. *Journal of Clinical Psychology, 51*, 108-112.

398. Slate, J. R. (1995). Two investigations of the validity of the WISC-III. *Psychological Reports, 76*, 299-306.

399. Slater, A. (1995). Individual differences in infancy and later IQ. *Journal of Child Psychology and Psychiatry and Allied Disciplines, 36*, 69-112.

400. Slomkowski, C., Klein, R. G., & Mannuzza, S. (1995). Is self-esteem an important outcome in hyperactive children? *Journal of Abnormal Child Psychology, 23*, 303-315.

401. Stein, M. A., Szumowski, E., Blondis, T. A., & Roizen, N. J. (1995). Adaptive skills dysfunction in ADD and ADHD children. *Journal of Child Psychology and Psychiatry and Allied Disciplines, 36*, 663-670.

402. Stothard, S. E., & Holme, C. (1995). A comparison of phonological skills in children with reading comprehension difficulties and children with decoding difficulties. *Journal of Child Psychology and Psychiatry and Allied Disciplines, 36*, 399-408.

403. Tannock, R., Schachar, R., & Logan, G. (1995). Methylphenidate and cognitive flexibility: Dissociated dose effects in hyperactive children. *Journal of Abnormal Child Psychology, 23*, 235-266.

404. Temple, C. M., & Carney, R. A. (1995). Patterns of spatial functioning in Turner's syndrome. *Cortex, 31*, 109-118.

405. van der Meere, J., Shalev, R., Borger, N., & Gross-Tsur, V. (1995). Sustained attention, activation and MPH in ADHD: A research note. *Journal of Child Psychology and Psychiatry and Allied Disciplines, 36*, 697-703.

406. Vasey, M. W., Daleiden, E. L., Williams, L. L., & Brown, L. M. (1995). Biased attention in childhood anxiety disorders: A preliminary study. *Journal of Abnormal Child Psychology, 23*, 267-279.

407. Vellutino, F. R., Scanlon, D. M., & Spearing, D. (1995). Semantic and phonological coding in poor and normal readers. *Journal of Experimental Child Psychology, 59*, 76-123.

408. Yates, C. M., Berninger, V. W., & Abbott, R. D. (1995). Specific writing disabilities in intellectually gifted children. *Journal for the Education of the Gifted, 18*, 131-155.

409. Zelkowitz, P., Papageorgiou, A., Zelazo, P. R., & Weiss, M. J. S. (1995). Behavioral adjustment in very low and normal birth weight children. *Journal of Clinical Child Psychology, 24*, 21-30.

Review of the Wechsler Intelligence Scale for Children, Third Edition by JEFFERY P. BRADEN, Associate Professor of Educational Psychology, University of Wisconsin-Madison, Madison, WI:

The WISC-III is the third generation of the Wechsler Intelligence Scale for Children. Its predecessor, the WISC-R, is simply the most popular and widely researched test of children's intelligence history (see reviews listed in the test description). The WISC-III promises to improve the WISC-R through contemporary and representative norms, better floors and ceilings for subtests, new artwork and items sensitive to multicultural and gender concerns, and improved clarity of factor structure—all while maintaining "the basic structure and content of the WISC-R" (manual, p. 11). This review will address the degree to which the WISC-III fulfills its dual promises to improve the WISC-R without radically altering it; or, to put it into advertising language, the degree to which the WISC-III reflects a "new and improved original recipe" for intellectual assessment.

DESCRIPTION. The WISC-III is a collection of 13 distinct subtests (see description) divided into two scales—a Verbal Scale and a Performance Scale. The six Verbal Scale tests use language-based items, whereas the seven Performance Scale tests use visual-motor items that are less dependent on language. The overlap between the WISC-R and WISC-III is substantial in all common subtests (approximately 72% of WISC-R items appear unchanged in WISC-III subtests versions), and many subtests now include colorful, gender- and minority-sensitive artwork. New items were added to subtests that had insufficient floors (i.e., not enough easy items) or ceilings (i.e., not enough difficult items). A new subtest (Symbol Search) was added to the Performance Scale. Practitioners familiar with the WISC-R will appreciate the cogent description of key subtest changes on pages 14–18, and the summary of administration rules (manual, Table 3.3, pp. 44-45).

Five of the subtests in each scale produce scale-specific IQs (i.e., Verbal IQ and Performance IQ), and the 10 subtest scores produce a Full Scale IQ (FSIQ). The Verbal/Performance distinction is popular for many reasons, including: (*a*) its consistency with preschool and adult versions of the Wechsler tests (providing a "womb-to-tomb" test sequence with the WPPSI-R, WISC-III, WAIS-R/WAIS-III), (*b*) the ability to estimate intelligence independently on language-loaded versus language-reduced tasks, and (*c*) the varied subtest format holds the interest of the client over the test session.

Most of these features are unchanged from the WISC-R. However, the recommended order of subtest administration is different (i.e., the WISC-III begins with Picture Completion), and the WISC-III now provides for direct calculation of Index scores. The last change is significant; WISC-R users often reorganized subtests into factor scores for Verbal Comprehension (VO), Perceptual Organization (PO), and Freedom from Distractibility (FFD) (e.g., Kaufman, 1979; Sattler, 1992). The new Symbol Search subtest (along with Coding) creates a fourth factor, named Processing Speed (PS). Norms and procedures for organizing 12 WISC-III subtests into four index scores (VC, PO, FFD, and PS) are described in the WISC-III manual. The Mazes subtest contributes only to the calculation of IQs as an alternate test; none of the four factors include it.

NORMS AND RELIABILITY. The normative sample is large (N = 2,200) and remarkably representative of 1988 U.S. Census data. Subtest reliabilities (expressed as internal consistencies for all but the speeded subtests of Symbol Search and Coding) are moderate to excellent (.61 to .92). The consistency of IQs and Indexes is very good to excellent (.80 to .97). Subtest stability coefficients, based on 353 children subdivided into three age groups, are adequate but slightly lower than WISC-R subtest stabilities (.56 to .89). IQ and Index stability is mostly good to excellent (.74 to .95; only one coefficient is below .80). The manual provides a wealth of technical data that consistently attest to the adequacy of the instrument. Interrater reliabilities for selected Verbal Scale subtests are excellent (all greater than .92). The contemporary norms yield IQs that are 2–7 points lower than those obtained on the WISC-R. A "drop" in IQ is expected because of population drift (see Flynn, 1984, 1987). Subtest specificities and guidelines for subtest interpretation are also available from independent sources (Bracken, McCallum, & Crain, 1993; Kamphaus & Platt, 1992).

VALIDITY. Although the WISC-III has been available for only 4 years at the time of this review, it already boasts a substantial body of research addressing its validity. If I included the literature addressing the WISC-R (much of which applies to the WISC-III), I would be writing well into the next century. Therefore, I will (*a*) limit my review only to studies of the WISC-III, and (*b*) I will organize the validity literature into five categories. These categories are factorial validity, convergent/divergent validity, theory-expected group differences, differential validity/bias, and clinical validity.

Factorial validity. The WISC-III factor structure is largely congruent with a four-factor hierarchical model (i.e., Full Scale IQs estimate broad intelligence, with VC, PO, FFD, and PS subfactors). Although the addition of index scores (and confirmatory factor analyses to support them) is a major improvement in the WISC-III over the WISC-R, these improvements are unlikely to resolve the question of "How many factors are in the Wechsler?" Factor analyses using orthogonal rotation or confirmatory procedures from the normative sample (manual, pp. 187-196) and other samples (e.g., Hishinuma & Yamakawa, 1993; Roid, Prifitera, & Weiss, 1993) generally support the four-factor "Index" model. However, hierarchical factor analyses cast doubt on the composition, stability, and uniqueness of indexes (Carroll, 1993). Even the confirmatory factor analyses presented in the manual and elsewhere (e.g., Kamphaus, Benson, Hutchinson, & Platt, 1994) are not entirely consistent in yielding a four-factor solution. The available data suggest the "Index" model in the WISC-III better approximates reality than the traditional Verbal/Performance/Full Scale approach in the WISC-R, but the number, reliability, composition, and interpretation of subfactors are not, and may never be, fully resolved.

Convergent/divergent validity. The manual reports strong correlations between WISC-III metrics and comparable metrics from the WPPSI-R, WISC-R, WAIS-R, Otis-Lennon School Ability Test, and Differential Ability Scales (*r*s between WISC-III IQs and comparable composites range from .59 to .92). Item analyses (Sattler & Atkinson, 1993) show appropriate gradations of difficulty from the WPPSI-R to the WISC-III. Additionally, independent studies report correlations between WISC-III IQS/Indexes and comparable metrics from other batteries are well within acceptable limits (see Bracken, 1993; Carvajal, Hayes, Lackey et al., 1993). These results imply good convergent validity for the WISC-III. Likewise, studies reported in the manual and elsewhere describe lower correlations among noncomparable metrics (e.g., the WISC-III PS and the Peabody Picture Vocabulary Test—Revised; Carvajal, Hayes, Miller, Wiebe, & Weaver, 1993). Taken together, these data attest to the convergent and divergent validity of the WISC-III.

Predictive validity. Studies presented in the manual and subsequent publications support the ability of the WISC-III to predict relevant outcomes. The most important of these is academic achievement in children. The WISC-III manual reports appropriate correlations with achievement (pp. 204–209), and studies published since test publication also report appropriate IQ-achievement correlations in children representing normal (Weiss, Prifitera, & Roid, 1993), referred (Wessel & Potter, 1994), learning disabled (LD) (Slate, Jones, Graham, & Bower, 1994), severely emotionally disturbed (SED) (Teeter & Smith, 1993), language/speech impaired (L/S) (Doll & Boren, 1993), and hearing-impaired/deaf (Maller & Braden, 1993) clinical categories.

Theory-expected group differences. The manual also summarizes studies evaluating the degree to which gifted, mentally deficient, SED, LD, epileptic, attention-deficit-disordered (ADD), hearing-impaired/deaf, and L/S children show atypical WISC-III scores or patterns. Although the numbers of subjects in these groups are limited, the results are consistent with expected values. Published studies (some of which are elaborations of studies summarized in the manual) corroborate theory-expected patterns of performance in children in the following clinical categories: gifted (e.g., Levinson & Folino, 1994); referred for assessment (Prewett & Matavich, 1994; Wessel & Potter, 1994); SED (Teeter & Smith, 1993); at-risk (Hishinuma & Yamakawa, 1993); LD (Dumont & Faro, 1993; Prifitera & Dersh, 1993; Roid et al., 1993; Slate et al., 1994; Smith, Buckley, & Pingatore, 1992); dyslexic (Newby, Recht, Caldwell, & Schaefer, 1993); generic special education (Post, 1992); ADD (Anastopoulos, Spisto, & Maher, 1994; Prifitera & Dersh, 1993; Schwean, Saklofske, Yackulic, & Quinn, 1993); L/S children (Doll & Boren, 1993; Phelps, Leguori, Nisewaner, & Parker, 1993), and hearing-impaired/deaf (Maller & Braden, 1993). There are two exceptions to theory-expected differences. First, although L/S children have lower Verbal than Performance IQs, their Performance IQs (and PO Indexes) are significantly lower than average (Doll & Boren, 1993; Phelps et al., 1993). Second, the Processing Speed Index was not lower than other Index scores in LD children (Smith et al., 1992).

Differential validity/bias. A thorough WISC-III bias study was conducted in conjunction with the standardization of the Wechsler Individual Achievement Tests (WIAT; T4:2938). Unfortunately, the results of this study are not in the WISC-III manual. Instead, the results are presented in Weiss et al. (1993). Although there was little evidence that the WISC-R was biased for gender or minority groups, the WISC-III renorming took many steps to eliminate bias, including (*a*) review of items by experts, (*b*) item analyses to revise or eliminate items with differential functioning, and (*c*) predictive validity contrasts (using WISC-III scores to predict achievement scores and classroom grades). The procedures employed in these efforts are consistent with contemporary practices. The WISC-III exhibits little predictive bias when used with males, females, whites, blacks, and Hispanics (Weiss et al., 1993). Marginal findings of intercept bias suggest that the WISC-III may overpredict achievement in blacks, and underpredict English grades for females. Additional studies of Tohono O'Odham native-American children (Tanner-Halverson, Burden, & Sabers, 1993) also support the validity of the Verbal/Performance distinction for assessing minority children. The magnitude and direction of these findings suggest the WISC-III is equally valid for native English-speaking children regardless of gender or ethnicity.

Clinical validity. Although all of the preceding types of validity contribute to the WISC-III's clinical use and interpretation, to what degree can the WISC-III be used to identify exceptionality? It is tempting to infer good clinical validity from strong theory-expected group differences, but it is wrong to do so. To say that a group of children (e.g., ADD) show WISC-III mean scores concordant with theoretical expectations is different from saying the WISC-III is sensitive to diagnosing ADD. Concluding diagnostic sensitivity from theory-expected observations would be analogous to the following reasoning: Squirrels eat nuts (confirmed theoretical prediction); my mother eats nuts (clinical observation); therefore, my mother is a squirrel (clinical diagnosis). Instead, tests must provide evidence of differential diagnosis (i.e., theory-expected differences occur in clinical groups, but not in normal groups).

The WISC-III goes well beyond its predecessor in providing support for clinical diagnosis. First, it lists the reliability of differences between IQs and indexes at commonly accepted clinical levels. Second, it lists the frequency of occurrence for comparisons between scores. The availability of both approaches to detecting intra-individual differences is a major improvement over the WISC-R (which only provided reliability data).

However, the evidence to date suggests that the WISC-III is not terribly sensitive to abnormal clinical conditions. For example, few ADD children exhibit popular WISC-III subtest profiles, IQs, and Index rules (e.g., low scores on the Arithmetic, Coding, Information, and Digit Span, or ACID profile) (Anastopoulos, Spisto, & Maher, 1994; Prifitera & Dersh, 1993). Strict application of diagnostic rules yields few false positives (i.e., few "normals" are identified as "abnormal"), but they also yield many false negatives (i.e., most "abnormals" are identified as "normal"). This means that practitioners can be reasonably confident that children with "abnormal" profiles are likely to be abnormal, but many abnormal children will not show abnormal profiles. Relaxing WISC-III diagnostic rules decreases false negatives, but also increases false positives (Prifitera & Dersh, 1993). Naglieri (1993) provides tables that can help practitioners correct for multiple WISC-III comparisons within an individual (i.e., if practitioners treat each score contrast as an independent comparison, they will artificially inflate the number of abnormal contrasts), and Kramer (1993) provides errors of estimate for subtest score comparisons.

Much like its predecessor and its companion batteries, the WISC-III does not provide "response validity" data. I define "response validity" evidence showing that test-defined typologies respond differently to treatments or interventions. The practice of (*a*) inferring psychological deficits based on test scores, and (*b*) suggesting psychoeducational programs on the basis of these classifications is widespread. Malpractice is also aided and abetted by "guides" to the Wechsler Scales, some of which fail to provide data to support their occasionally sensational recommendations and claims (e.g., Jones & James, 1993). This is unfortunate, because scholarly approaches to WISC-III diagnosis (e.g., Kaufman, 1994a; Sattler, 1992) are often brushed with the same broad strokes applied to less-than-scholarly works. The only reliable connection between test scores and differential responses to treatment is the tendency for high-IQ children to learn more, and learn faster, than average- or low-IQ children. However, those who demand a link between intra-individual conditions and differential treatment outcomes will be dissatisfied with the WISC-III (e.g., Little, 1992; Shaw, Swerdlik, & Laurent, 1993).

EVALUATION OF THE WISC-III. The popularity of the WISC-R insures that the WISC-III will be among the most widely studied, criticized, and used tests. As of this writing, I found 11 reviews of the WISC-III in the professional literature (Carroll, 1993; Edwards & Edwards, 1993; Little, 1992; Kaufman, 1992, 1994a, 1994b; Post & Mitchell, 1993; Roid, 1990; Sattler, 1992; Shaw, Swerdlik, & Laurent, 1993; Sternberg, 1993). These reviews, and my own analysis, largely concur in identifying many strengths and weaknesses in the WISC-III. They also extend some key disagreements surrounding the use and interpretation of cognitive tests.

Strengths. There are many improvements in the WISC-III that will make it more attractive and easier to administer and score. Subtest materials are contemporary, generally well made, and free from overt bias and dated material. The examiner's record form is designed well and contains all the materials needed to derive IQs and three of four Indexes. The WISC-III manual cover allows examiners to stand it up when testing, and all criteria for scoring children's verbal responses are located in the administration section. Confidence intervals for IQs and Indexes are tabled, and adjust for regression to the mean (but see Sattler, 1992, pp. 1037–1041 for the desirability of this practice).

The WISC-III is also strong from a scientific perspective. WISC-III norms are excellent, and its psychometric adequacy continues to set a standard for other tests. The manual provides a thorough and lucid presentation of reliability and validity data, which strongly support the adequacy of the WISC-III (with few exceptions). Modifications improved the reliability and validity of the WISC-III over its predecessors (and many rivals), including the four-factor model, improved scoring criteria for verbal tests, reduced "floor" and "ceiling" effects, reliability- and frequency-of-differences tables, and direct examination of ethnic and gender bias. One rarely mentioned advantage is the availability of a conormed achievement battery (the WIAT). This allows practitioners to identify discrepancies between aptitude and achievement while correcting for regression effects using conormed tests (as recommended by Braden, 1987; Reynolds et al., 1984; Shepard, 1980). The WIAT manual provides the information needed to determine discrepancies between FSIQ and WIAT subtests and composites. Flanagan and Alfonso (1993a, 1993b) provide the information needed to determine discrepancies between VIQ, PIQ, and WIAT subtests and composites.

Weaknesses. Although the WISC-III is undoubtedly one of the best intelligence tests available today, it is not perfect. Administration and scoring concerns include the relative flimsiness of the Coding answer template, the need to buy additional forms to administer Symbol Search (needed to derive the PS factor), possible confusion regarding Object Assembly pieces (some look the same on both sides), and questions about the actual amount of time needed to administer the test (the manual claims 50–70 minutes, but 80–90 minutes is a more reasonable estimate). These concerns fall in the "minor complaints" category, but they suggest room for improvement.

Other concerns are more critical. Despite improvements in WISC-III subtests, subtest stability is no better (and may be worse) than WISC-R stability. Some subtests added bonus points for speed, which may depress scores in bright children who are reflective or otherwise slow to respond. Item content changes may render the test more acceptable to contemporary sensitivities, but removal of items relating to violence and vice may also inhibit its clinical value (Kaufman, 1994b). The meaning and interpretation of the FFD and PS factors are largely unknown. Although the WISC-R and WISC-III factor structures are extremely similar (Parker & Atkinson, 1994), the PS factor is new and awaits research to document its clinical value and meaning. Available research (e.g., theory-expected differences) is largely supportive of the PS Index, but some research (e.g., Anastopoulos et al., 1994; Smith et al., 1993) fails to provide evidence of diagnostic utility.

Unresolved disputes. Critics have voiced other concerns regarding the WISC-III. Among the most popular is the failure to radically restructure the WISC-III (e.g., Carroll, 1993; Little, 1992; Shaw, Swerdlik, & Laurent, 1993; Sternberg, 1993). However, critics vary widely regarding *how* to restructure the WISC-III. For example, Sternberg (1993) argues for a test reflecting multiple intelligences (e.g., Gardner, 1983), whereas Carroll (1993) wants the test to reflect a singular, hierarchical cognitive model. Little (1992) questions the value of latent constructs (e.g., intelligence); but even reviewers who embrace intelligence nonetheless characterize the WISC-III as "a new and improved dinosaur" (e.g., Shaw et al., 1993, p. 159).

The dynamic tension between researchers and clinicians spawns these criticisms. Researchers (who write most reviews) adopt strong views about what intelligence should be, and then criticize the WISC-III for failing to fulfill that vision. Clinicians are less likely to assume what intelligence "should be," and are more concerned about practical methods for estimating cognitive abilities. The WISC-III clearly reaches out to clinicians. Given the diversity of opinion regarding the value and nature of intelligence, the pragmatic approach has a strong, non-nonsense appeal. I agree with Kaufman's (1994b) conclusion that "the WISC-III is excellent" (p. 354).

SUMMARY. The WISC-III handily achieves the goals that drove revision of the test (i.e., updated norms, improved subtest characteristics and content, and enhanced factor structure—all within the historical WISC-R structure). The changes are nearly all for the better from the perspectives of the practitioner and the psychometrician. Although the manual does not provide data in a few areas (most notably related to diagnostic utility and outcome validity), it provides substantially more information than any other in the Wechsler series—and most other tests as well. The WISC-III is likely to remain the test of choice among practitioners and clinical researchers for assessing children's intelligence, although the Differential Ability Scales (T4:800), Stanford Binet: Fourth Edition (T4:2553), and the Woodcock-Johnson Psycho-Educational Battery—Revised (415) are worthy (and more economical) contenders to the preschool through young adult testing throne. The WISC-III offers evolutionary, not revolutionary, progress towards better assessment of cognitive abilities. Those who want a revolution will be disappointed with the WISC-III, but those who value moderate advances in clinical practice will value the WISC-III.

REVIEWER'S REFERENCES

Kaufman, A. S. (1979). *Intelligent testing with the WISC-R.* New York: John Wiley & Sons.

Shepard, L. (1980). An evaluation of the regression discrepancy method for identifying children with learning disabilities. *Journal of Special Education, 14*, 79-91.

Gardner, H. (1983). *Frames of mind: The theory of multiple intelligences.* New York: Basic Books.

Flynn, J. R. (1984). The mean IQ of Americans: Massive gains 1932 to 1978. *Psychological Bulletin, 95*, 29-51.

Reynolds, C. R. (1984). Critical measurement issues in learning disabilities. *Journal of Special Education, 18*, 451-476.

Flynn, J. R. (1987). Massive IQ gains in 14 nations: What IQ tests really measure. *Psychological Bulletin, 101*, 171-191.

Braden, J. P. (1987). A comparison of regression and stnadard score discrepancy methods for learning disabilities identification: Effects on racial representation. *Journal of School Psychology, 25*, 23-29.

Roid, G. H. (1990, August). *Historical continuity in intelligence assessment: Goals of the WISC-III standardization.* Paper presented at the annual meeting of the American Psychological Association, Boston.

Kamphaus, R. W., & Platt, L. O. (1992). Subtest specificities for the WISC-III. *Psychological Reports, 70*(3), 899-902.

Kaufman, A. S. (1992). Evaluation of the WISC-III and WPPSI-R for gifted children. *Roeper Review, 14*(3), 154-158.

Little, S. G. (1992). The WISC-III: Everything old is new again. *School Psychology Quarterly, 7*(2), 148-154.

Post, K. R. (1992). *A comparison of WISC-R and WISC-III scores on urban special education students.* Unpublished educational specialist thesis, James Madison University, Harrisonburg, VA.

Sattler, J. M. (1992). *Assessment of children* (updated & revised 3rd ed.). San Diego: Jerome M. Sattler.

Smith, D. K., Buckley, S., & Pingatore, M. (1992, August). *WISC-III/KBIT relationships in students with learning disabilities.* Paper presented at the annual meeting of the American Psychological Association, Washington, DC.

Bracken, B. A. (Ed.). (1993). *Monograph series advances in psychoeducational assessment: Wechsler Intelligence Scale for Children: Third Edition; Journal of Psychoeducational Assessment.* Brandon, VT: Clinical Psychology Publishing Co., Inc.

Bracken, B. A., McCallum, R. S., & Crain, R. M. (1993). WISC-III subtest composite reliabilities and specificities: Interpretive aids. In B. A. Bracken (Ed.), *Monograph series advances in psychoeducational assessment: Wechsler Intelligence Scale for Children: Third Edition; Journal of Psychoeducational Assessment* (pp. 22-34). Brandon, VT: Clinical Psychology Publishing Co., Inc.

Carroll, J. B. (1993). What abilities are measured by the WISC-III? In B. A. Bracken (Ed.), *Monograph series advances in psychoeducational assessment: Wechsler Intelligence Scale for Children: Third Edition; Journal of Psychoeducational Assessment* (pp. 134-143). Brandon, VT: Clinical Psychology Publishing Co., Inc.

Carvajal, H. H., Hayes, J. E., Lackey, K. L., Rathke, M. L., Wiebe, D. A., & Weaver, K. A. (1993). Correlations between scores on the Wechsler Intelligence Scale for Children-III and the General Purpose Abbreviated Battery of the Stanford-Binet IV. *Psychological Reports, 72*(3), 1167-1170.

Carvajal, H., Hayes, J. E., Miller, H. R., Wiebe, D. A., & Weaver, K. A. (1993). Comparisons of the vocabulary scores and IQs on the Wechsler Intelligence Scale for Children-III and the Peabody Picture Vocabulary Test—Revised. *Perceptual and Motor Skills, 76*(1), 28-30.

Doll, B., & Boren, R. (1993). Performance of severely language-impaired students on the WISC-III, language scales, and academic achievement measures. In B. A. Bracken (Ed.), *Monograph series advances in psychoeducational assessment: Wechsler Intelligence Scale for Children: Third Edition; Journal of Psychoeducational Assessment* (pp. 77-86). Brandon, VT: Clinical Psychology Publishing Co., Inc.

Dumont, R., & Faro, C. (1993). A WISC-III short form for learning-disabled students. *Psychology in the Schools, 30*(3), 212-219.

Edwards, R., & Edwards, J. L. (1993). The WISC-III: A practitioner perspective. In B. A. Bracken (Ed.), *Monograph series advances in psychoeducational assessment: Wechsler Intelligence Scale for Children: Third Edition; Journal of Psychoeducational Assessment* (pp. 144-150). Brandon, VT: Clinical Psychology Publishing Co., Inc.

Flanagan, D. P., & Alfonso, V. C. (1993a). Differences required for significance between Wechsler Verbal and Performance IQs and WIAT subtests and composites: The predicted-achievement method. *Psychology in the Schools, 30*, 125-132.

Flanagan, D. P., & Alfonso, V. C. (1993b). WIAT subtest and composite predicted-achievement values based on WISC-III Verbal and Performance IQ. *Psychology in the Schools, 30*(4), 310-320.

Hishinuma, E. S., & Yamakawa, R. (1993). Construct and criterion-related validity of the WISC-III for exceptional students and those who are "at risk." In B. A. Bracken (Ed.), *Monograph series advances in psychoeducational assessment: Wechsler Intelligence Scale for Children: Third Edition; Journal of Psychoeducational Assessment* (pp. 94-104). Brandon, VT: Clinical Psychology Publishing Co., Inc.

Jones, D. R., & James, S. (1993). Best uses of the WISC-III. In H. B. Vance (Ed.), *Best practices in assessment for school and clinical settings* (pp. 231-269). Brandon, VT: Clinical Psychology Publishing Co., Inc.

Kramer, J. H. (1993). Interpretation of individual subtest scores on the WISC-III. *Psychological Assessment, 5*(2), 193-196.

Maller, S. J., & Braden, J. P. (1993). The construct and criterion-related validity of the WISC-III with deaf adolescents. In B. A. Bracken

(Ed.), *Monograph series advances in psychoeducational assessment: Wechsler Intelligence Scale for Children: Third Edition; Journal of Psychoeducational Assessment* (pp. 105-113). Brandon, VT: Clinical Psychology Publishing Co., Inc.

Naglieri, J. (1993). Pairwise and ipsatve comparisons of WISC-III IQ and index scores. *Psychological Assessment, 5*(1), 113-116.

Newby, R. F., Recht, D. R., Caldwell, J., & Schaefer, J. (1993). Comparison of WISC-III and WISC-R IQ changes over a 2-year time span in a sample of children with dyslexia. In B. A. Bracken (Ed.), *Monograph series advances in psychoeducational assessment: Wechsler Intelligence Scale for Children: Third Edition; Journal of Psychoeducational Assessment* (pp. 87-93). Brandon, VT: Clinical Psychology Publishing Co., Inc.

Phelps, L., Leguori, S., Nisewaner, K., & Parker, M. (1993). Practical interpretations of the WISC-III with language-disordered children. In B. A. Bracken (Ed.), *Monograph series advances in psychoeducational assessment: Wechsler Intelligence Scale for Children: Third Edition; Journal of Psychological Assessment* (pp. 71-85). Brandon, VT: Clinical Psychology Publishing Co., Inc.

Post, K. R., & Mitchell, H. R. (1993). The WISC-III: A reality check. *Journal of School Psychology, 31*(4), 541-545.

Prifitera, A., & Dersh, J. (1993). Base rates of WISC-III diagnostic subtest patterns among normal, learning-disabled, and ADHD samples. In B. A. Bracken (Ed.), *Monograph series advances in psychoeducational assessment: Wechsler Intelligence Scale for Children: Third Edition; Journal of Psychoeducational Assessment* (pp. 43-55). Brandon, VT: Clinical Psychology Publishing Co., Inc.

Roid, G. H., Prifitera, A., & Weiss, L. G. (1993). Replication of the WISC-III factor structure in an independent sample. In B. A. Bracken (Ed.), *Monograph series advances in psychoeducational assessment: Wechsler Intelligence Scale for Children: Third Edition; Journal of Psychoeducational Assessment* (pp. 6-21). Brandon, VT: Clinical Psychology Publishing Co., Inc.

Sattler, J. M., & Atkinson, L. (1993). Item equivalence across scales: The WPPSI-R and WISC-III. *Psychological Assessment, 5*(2), 203-206.

Schwean, V. L., Saklofske, D. H., Yackulic, R. A., & Quinn, D. (1993). WISC-III performance of ADHD children. In B. A. Bracken (Ed.), *Monograph series advances in psychoeducational assessment: Wechsler Intelligence Scale for Children: Third Edition; Journal of Psychoeducational Assessment* (pp. 56-70). Brandon, VT: Clinical Psychology Publishing Co., Inc.

Shaw, S. R., Swerdlik, S. E., & Laurent, J. (1993). [Review of the WISC-III.] In B. A. Bracken (Ed.), *Monograph series advances in psychoeducational assessment: Wechsler Intelligence Scale for Children: Third Edition; Journal of Psychoeducational Assessment* (pp. 151-159). Brandon, VT: Clinical Psychology Publishing Co., Inc.

Sternberg, R. J. (1993). Rocky's back again: A review of the WISC-III. In B. A. Bracken (Ed.), *Monograph series advances in psychoeducational assessment: Wechsler Intelligence Scale for Children: Third Edition; Journal of Psychoeducational Assessment* (pp. 161-164). Brandon, VT: Clinical Psychology Publishing Co., Inc.

Tanner-Halverson, P., Burden, T., & Sabers, D. (1993). WISC-III normative data for Tohono O'Odham Native-American Children. In B. A. Bracken (Ed.), *Monograph series advances in psychoeducational assessment: Wechsler Intelligence Scale for Children: Third Edition; Journal of Psychoeducational Assessment* (pp. 125-133). Brandon, VT: Clinical Psychology Publishing Co., Inc.

Teeter, P. A., & Smith, P. L. (1993). WISC-III and WJ-R: Predictive and discriminant validity for students with severe emotional disturbance. In B. A. Bracken (Ed.), *Monograph series advances in psychoeducational assessment: Wechsler Intelligence Scale for Children: Third Edition; Journal of Psychoeducational Assessment* (pp. 114-124). Brandon, VT: Clinical Psychology Publishing Co., Inc.

Weiss, L. G., Prifitera, A., & Roid, G. (1993). The WISC-III and the fairness of predicting achievement across ethnic and gender groups. In B. A. Bracken (Ed.), *Monograph series advances in psychoeducational assessment: Wechsler Intelligence Scale for Children: Third Edition; Journal of Psychoeducational Assessment* (pp. 35-42). Brandon, VT: Clinical Psychology Publishing Co., Inc.

Witworth, J. R., & Sutton, D. L. (1993). *WISC-III compilation*. Novato, CA: Academic Therapy Publications.

Anastopoulos, A. D., Spisto, M. A., & Maher, M. C. (1994). The WISC-III Freedom from Distractibility factor: Its utility in identifying children with Attention Deficit Hyperactivity Disorder. *Psychological Assessment, 6*(4), 368-371.

Kamphaus, R. W., Benson, J., Hutchinson, S., & Platt, L. O. (1994). Identification of factor models for the WISC-III. *Educational and Psychological Measurement, 54*(1), 174-186.

Kaufman, A. S. (1994a). *Intelligent testing with the WISC-III*. New York: Wiley.

Kaufman, A. S. (1994b). King WISC the third assumes the throne. *Journal of School Psychology, 31*, 345-354.

Levinson, E. M., & Folino, L. (1994). Correlations of scores on the Gifted Evaluation Scale with those on the WISC-III and Kaufman Brief Intelligence Test for students referred for gifted evaluation. *Psychological Reports, 74*(2), 419-424.

Parker, K. C. H., & Atkinson, L. (1994). Factor space of the Wechsler Intelligence Scale for Children—Third Edition: Critical thoughts and recommendations. *Psychological Assessment, 6*(3), 201-208.

Prewett, P. N., & Matavich, M. A. (1994). A comparison of referred students' performance on the WISC-III and the Stanford-Binet Intelligence Scale: Fourth Edition. *Journal of Psychoeducational Assessment, 12*(11), 42-48.

Slate, J. R., Jones, C. H., Graham, L. S., & Bower, J. (1994). Correlations of WISC-III, WRAT-R, KM-R, and PPVT-R scores in students with specific learning disabilities. *Learning Disabilities Research and Practice, 9*(2), 104-107.

Wessel, J., & Potter, A. (1994). *Analysis of WISC-III data from an urban population of referred children*. Paper presented at the annual meeting of the National Association of School Psychologists Association, Seattle, WA. (Eric Document Reproduction No. ED371051)

Review of the Wechsler Intelligence Scale for Children, Third Edition by JONATHAN SANDOVAL, Professor of Education, University of California, Davis, Davis, CA:

How much do you tamper with a classic? This is the dilemma for a test publisher of one of the world's best known and most commonly administered tests when the time comes for revision. The Wechsler Intelligence Scale for Children (WISC) is undoubtedly the test of choice for tens of thousands of school and child clinical psychologists who need an appraisal of a child's intellectual functioning. Does a test publisher make changes to lead the field or does it cater to the ready-made market by making minimal changes? In the case of the Wechsler Intelligence Scale for Children, Third Edition (WISC-III), the Psychological Corporation has taken a careful, middle-of-the-road approach.

Since their inception, tests of intellectual functioning have been revised every 20 years or so. This practice seems justified in that the performance of the norm group improves approximately half a standard deviation with each revision. Norms require updating. In addition, advances in research, theory, psychometric method, and sensitivity require that tests be reexamined periodically.

The modernizing and renorming of the WISC has been most successful. The artwork and general appearance of the new WISC-III materials are first rate. They are in a contemporary but neutral style and attractive to children. In this edition, stimulus materials are generally printed in color. The people portrayed in items represent various ethnic and racial groups and attention has been paid to avoiding item content that might give offense. Some new items have been added, although $^3/_4$ of the items remain from the WISC-R, and the general administrative procedures have not changed appreciably. New items have been added to the top and bottom ends of subtests so they may be used with more confidence when testing individuals who are high or low functioning. Completely new is an optional subtest, Symbol Search.

A practitioner familiar with a previous version of the WISC will be able to transition to WISC-III easily. There are subtle differences in features such as discontinuation rules, starting points, number of sample trials, and scoring details so that some study will be necessary by even experienced examiners before using the test. Welcome changes include an easel-style administration manual, the inclusion of scoring standards along with the directions for Similarities, Vocabulary, and Comprehension, and the disappearance of the "red pencil." Most psychologists familiar with previous versions will be pleased with the changes. The manual is quite good, containing technical information, directions for administration and scoring, and norms in one volume. Tabs in the manual allow the user to find the appropriate information quickly.

The new norms for this revision are excellent. The standardization sample does an outstanding job mirroring the demographics of the 1988 U.S. Census; the stratification on the basis of parent education, race/ethnicity, geographic region, and community size is quite accurate, although children from large urban areas are somewhat absent from the norms. In the standardization process, children from minority groups were oversampled, so that large enough groups would be available for item performance studies. Large demographic changes in the U.S. childhood population underway currently, however, suggest that a revision may be needed before 2010. The procedures used in administering and scoring the standardization version of the test seem exemplary. The result of a thoughtful revision and careful standardization is a technically superior test.

As might be expected, the test has outstanding psychometric properties. The internal consistency and stability reliability coefficients are as high or higher than other tests of this type and are among the highest of any psychological measures. An exception is Mazes with an average stability coefficient of .57, suggesting that this optional subtest be used only in an emergency. For the first time, the results of an interscorer agreement study are reported in the manual. This study suggests quite high agreement between trained scorers on the subtests Similarities, Vocabulary, Comprehension, and Mazes. These findings reflect the clearer standards for scoring provided in the manual and the increased number of carefully chosen examples. Also provided are a number of useful tables based on the reliability data that help the test user interpret test scores. This list of useful tables grows with each edition. Missing, however, is a table of subtest specificities, information valued by sophisticated examiners.

The most dramatic departure on the WISC-III is the addition of the Symbol Search subtest. This subtest was included on the basis of research on controlled attention, and was intended to contribute to the measurement of a factor of interest to those assessing children for possible inclusion in special education. Here is one example of a notable effort by the publisher to move research and theory forward. Ironically, as a result of adding this subtest, the factor structure of the whole test changed. The WISC-III still yields the familiar Verbal, Quantitative, and Full Scale IQ scores but also produces four "Index" scores of Verbal Comprehension, Perceptual Organization, Freedom from Distractibility (FD), and Processing Speed. The names for the first three factors come from tradition, but it is unfortunate that the label "Freedom from Distractibility" was retained. First, this is not a very good description of what the subtests Arithmetic and Digit Span measure (could it be labeled "auditory-numerical attention and memory"?). In the past the subtest Coding was included in this factor; because it has been moved, this would have been a good time to change the factor label. The four index scores are indicated as optional, but they are prominently present on the test protocol. The manual does not supply much guidance as to when they might be used. Careful examiners must view these index scores as experimental until further research validates the utility and robustness of the last two factor scores. This reviewer would have preferred them to be in the manual but not on the face sheet of the protocol.

The validity of the WISC is well established. It is one of the most thoroughly studied psychological tests and the network of studies with respect to prediction and relationship with other psychological measures, behaviors, and status has produced unique support for the construct underlying the test. The manual reports satisfactory concurrent validity, factorial validity, and special group studies. There is no better measure of general intellectual functioning, particularly the capacity to gain from instruction in school, than Full Scale IQ. The factor analytic studies continue to support the verbal/performance dichotomy and offer evidence of the reasonableness of the four-factor solution of the index scores. On the other hand, the two subtests making up Processing Speed and the subtest Mazes have the smallest correlations with Full Scale IQ and perhaps will not prove an indicator of an important individual difference as research accumulates.

Missing from this revision is information on the item response scaling of the subtests. Competing measures, the Differential Ability Scales (T4:800) and the Woodcock-Johnson Psycho-Educational Battery—Revised (415) have relied on this modern approach to test construction, and are very good tests. Future latent trait analyses on the WISC will be welcome.

In conclusion, the WISC-III has been improved in this revision. It may rightly retain its place as the premier test of its kind, although there may be competitors for the title.

[413]

What Do You Say?

Purpose: Designed as a self-assessment tool to identify communication style and relate it to two basic types of human interactions: parent-child (McGregor's Theory X) and adult-adult (Theory Y).
Population: Employees.
Publication Dates: 1986–91.
Scores, 4: Empathic, Critical, Searching, Advising.
Administration: Group or individual.
Price Data, 1990: $80 per complete kit including 20 inventories, 20 answer sheets, and 20 interpretation booklets.
Time: [20] minutes administration; [10] minutes scoring; [30–60] minutes interpretation.
Comments: Self-administered, self-scored.
Authors: Training House, Inc.
Publisher: Training House, Inc.

Review of What Do You Say? by WILLIAM L. DEATON, Professor and Dean, School of Education, Auburn University at Montgomery, Montgomery, AL:

The stated purpose of this self-assessment is to give an individual insight into the ways in which he or she responds to people in interpersonal communications. Twelve statements are provided and the respondent is instructed to "invest" 3 points in four possible responses for each statement. Sets of responses are identified as A, B, C, and D and 0, 1, 2, or 3 points are to be assigned to each response. An example is provided to illustrate the various possible ways of responding to a statement.

Answers are recorded on a two-part answer sheet. Scoring instructions allow the respondent to determine scores for Empathic, Critical, Searching, and Advising; scores are obtained by summing the responses to keys provided for E, C, S, and A boxes on the second part of the answer sheet. The instructions note that the sum of the four scores should equal 36 and, if not, you "better locate the problem."

Minimum and maximum values for Empathic, Critical, Searching, and Advising scores are 0 and 36, respectively. No information is provided to indicate what these composite scores might represent; no discussion is presented about what information, if any, may be contained in differences between or among scores; and nothing is said about the possible relationships between the four scores and gender, age, socioeconomic status, employment history, type of employment, or any other characteristic of respondents.

The scoring instructions refer the user to a four-page folder titled Interpretation for finding the meaning of the four scores. The Interpretation Sheet is eight pages in length, not four. Four of "the most common response modes in interpersonal communications" (manual, p. 2) are described with brief paragraphs. Three and one-half pages then follow that summarize the four quadrants used in transactional analysis: Parent, Adult, Child, and Sick—corresponding to I'm OK, You're OK axes. Page 5 of the Interpretation Sheet finally ties some things together by stating that Parent responses are reflected in the sum of the Critical and Advising scores and Adult scores are obtained by summing the Empathic and Searching responses. No references are provided to the *I'm OK—You're OK* book by Harris (1969) on which most of the Interpretation Sheet material is based.

The remainder of the Interpretation Sheet is devoted to a summary of McGregor's Theory X and Theory Y (this is referenced). Only on the last page, Questions for Your Consideration, is the user informed that his or her Theory X style is C + A and that the Theory Y style is S + E. Never is it stated that Theory X and Theory Y styles are identical to Parent and Adult scores, respectively.

One question presented on page 8 of the Interpretation Sheet is "What is your reaction to the ratio of your Theory X style (C + A) to your Theory Y style (S + E)?" This reviewer wonders why there would be any reaction to such a ratio other than to paraphrase the title of the instrument: What do I say?

No information is presented about reliability or validity of scores. No reference is made to normative data nor is any mention made concerning the construction of this instrument. In fairness, it should be noted that two weak comments about scores are made: The searching response is "usually one of the two higher scores of most people," and "most people find that the critical response is their lowest score" (manual, p. 8). Although the self-assessment procedure may be interesting, the only reason to consider using this instrument is for the potential entertainment of users. However, $80 for 20 sets of material is a high price for a few minutes of entertainment.

REVIEWER'S REFERENCE

Harris, T. A. (1969). *I'm OK—You're OK: A practical guide to transactional analysis.* New York: Harper & Row.

Review of What Do You Say? by GERALD L. STONE, Professor of Counseling Psychology and Director, University Counseling Service, The University of Iowa, Iowa City, IA:

What Do You Say? is a paper-and-pencil, self-assessment tool. The instrument is designed to identify four communication responses (Empathic, Critical, Searching, and Advising) and relate them to McGregor's management theory (e.g., Theory X involves parent-child interactions and Theory Y, adult-adult interactions). Although not clearly articulated, the tool appears to be focused on business settings and employee communications.

The instrument is composed of 12 communication situations to which the testee is requested to select the response(s) that seems most appropriate. Responses are selected from four response alternatives that follow each situation. The testee has 3 points to "invest," resulting in three different ways of investing in each episode (e.g., if only one response is appropriate, then that response would receive 3 points, and the others would get zero points). A mark-sensitive answer sheet is available. The second page of the answer sheet provides instructions for scoring, and a four-page interpretive piece provides meaning to the scores (e.g., Critical plus Advising equals Parent score; Empathy plus Searching equal Adult score).

This instrument is similar to other self-assessment tools published by Training House including the Personal Style Assessment (T4:1990; see Stone, 1992). In addition to particular format similarities, these tools provide no manual, no data, and lack any evidence of behavioral validation for their approach, episodes, or communication responses. These tools remain in the "parlor game" domain until instrument validation studies are conducted.

REVIEWER'S REFERENCES

Stone, G. L. (1992). [Review of the Personal Style Assessment.] In J. J. Kramer & J. C. Conoley (Eds.), *The eleventh mental measurements yearbook* (pp. 666-667). Lincoln, NE: Buros Institute of Mental Measurements.

[414]

Wide Range Achievement Test 3.

Purpose: To measure the skills needed to learn reading, spelling, and arithmetic.
Population: Ages 5–75.
Publication Dates: 1940–93.
Acronym: WRAT3.
Scores: 3 subtests: Reading, Spelling, Arithmetic.
Administration: Individual in part.
Forms: 2 equivalent forms: Blue, Tan.
Price Data, 1993: $95 per starter set including 25 Blue test forms, 25 Tan test forms, 25 profile/analysis forms, set of 2 plastic cards for Reading/Spelling, and manual ('93, 188 pages) in attache case; $20 per 25 test forms (specify Blue or Tan); $10 per 25 profile/analysis forms; $10 per set of 2 plastic cards for Reading/Spelling; $30 per manual; $20 per attache case.
Time: (15–30) minutes.
Author: Gary S. Wilkinson.
Publisher: Jastak Associates/Wide Range Inc.
Cross References: See T4:2956 (121 references); for reviews by Elaine Clark and Patti L. Harrison, see 10:389 (161 references); for reviews by Paula Matuszek of an earlier edition and Philip A. Saigh of an earlier edition, see 9:1364 (103 references); see also T3:2621 (249 references), 8:37 (117 references), and T2:50 (35 references); for reviews by Jack C. Merwin and Robert L. Thorndike of an earlier edition, see 7:36 (49 references); see also 6:27 (15 references); for reviews by Paul Douglas Courtney, Verner M. Sims, and Louis P. Thorpe of the 1946 edition, see 3:21.

TEST REFERENCES

1. Elias, P. K., Elias, M. F., Robbins, M. A., & Gage, P. (1987). Acquisition of word-processing skills by younger, middle-age, and older adults. *Psychology and Aging*, *2*, 340-348.

2. Lowman, R. L., & Williams, R. E. (1987). Validity of self-ratings of abilities and competence. *Journal of Vocational Behavior*, *31*, 1-13.

3. Geary, D. C., & Burlingham-Dubree, M. (1989). External validation of the strategy choice model for addition. *Journal of Experimental Child Psychology*, *47*, 175-192.

4. Kibby, M. W. (1989). Teaching sight vocabulary with and without context before silent reading: A field test of the "Focus of Attention" hypothesis. *Journal of Reading Behavior*, *21*, 261-278.

5. Reed, M. A. (1989). Speech perception and the discrimination of brief auditory cues in reading disabled children. *Journal of Experimental Child Psychology*, *48*, 270-292.

6. Ross, J. M., & Smith, J. O. (1989). Adult basic educators' perceptions of learning disabilities. *Journal of Reading*, *33*, 340-347.

7. Stanovich, K. E., & West, R. F. (1989). Exposure to print and orthographic processing. *Reading Research Quarterly*, *24*, 402-433.

8. Bruck, M., & Treiman, R. (1990). Phonological awareness and spelling in normal children and dyslexics: The case of initial consonant clusters. *Journal of Experimental Child Psychology*, *50*, 156-178.

9. D'Annunzio, A. (1990). A nondirective combinatory model in an adult ESL program. *Journal of Reading*, *34*, 198-202.

10. Jordan, B. T., & Jordan, S. G. (1990). Jordan Left-Right Reversal Test: An analysis of visual reversals in children and significance for reading problems. *Child Psychiatry and Human Development*, *21*, 65-73.

11. Juel, C. (1990). Effects of reading group assignment on reading development in first and second grade. *Journal of Reading Behavior*, *22*, 233-254.

12. Quadrel, M. J., & Lau, R. L. (1990). A multivariate analysis of adolescents' orientations toward physician use. *Health Psychology*, *9*, 750-773.

13. Wade, S. E., Trathen, W., & Schraw, G. (1990). An analysis of spontaneous study strategies. *Reading Research Quarterly*, *24*, 147-166.

14. Wise, B. W., Olson, R. K., & Treiman, R. (1990). Subsyllabic units in computerized reading instruction: Onset-rime vs. postvowel segmentation. *Journal of Experimental Child Psychology*, *49*, 1-19.

15. Zigmond, N., & Baker, J. (1990). Mainstream experiences for learning disabled students (Project MELD): Preliminary report. *Exceptional Children*, *57*, 176-185.

16. Capaldi, D. M. (1991). Co-occurence of conduct problems and depressive symptoms in early adolescent boys: I. Familiar factors and general adjustment at grade 6. *Development and Psychopathology*, *3*, 277-300.

17. Casey, J. E., Rourke, B. P., & Picard, E. M. (1991). Syndrome of nonverbal learning disabilities: Age differences in neuropsychological, academic, and socioemotional functioning. *Development and Psychopathology*, *3*, 329-345.

18. Fitzgerald, J., Spiegel, D. L., & Cunningham, J. W. (1991). The relationship between parental literacy level and perceptions of emergent literacy. *Journal of Reading Behavior*, *23*, 191-213.

19. Kee, D. W., Gottfried, A., & Bathurst, K. (1991). Consistency of hand preference: Predictions to intelligence and school achievement. *Brain and Cognition*, *16*, 1-10.

20. McCloskey, M., Aliminosa, D., & Macaruso, P. (1991). Theory-based assessment of acquired dyscalculia. *Brain and Cognition*, *17*, 285-308.

21. Shapiro, E. S., & Lentz, F. E., Jr. (1991). Vocational-technical programs: Follow-up of students with learning disabilities. *Exceptional Children*, *58*, 47-59.

22. Bederman, J., Faraone, S. V., Keenan, K., Benjamin, J., Krifcher, B., Moore, C., Sprich-Buckminster, S., Ugaglia, K., Jellinek, M. S., Steingard, R., Spencer, T., Norman, D., Kolodny, R., Kraus, I., Perrin, J., Keller, M. B., & Tsuang, M. T. (1992). Further evidence for family-genetic risk factors in attention deficit hyperactivity disorder: Patterns of comorbidity in probands and relatives in psychiatrically and pediatrically referred samples. *Archives of General Psychiatry*, *49*, 728-738.

23. Clement-Heist, K., Siegel, S., & Gaylord-Ross, R. (1992). Simulated and in situ vocational social skills training for youths with learning disabilities. *Exceptional Children*, *58*, 336-345.

24. Dreyer, L. G., Shankweiler, D., & Luke, S. D. (1992). Children's retention of word spellings in relation to reading ability. *Yearbook of National Reading Conference*, *42*, 405-412.

25. Filippelli, L. A., & Jason, L. A. (1992). How life events affect the academic adjustment and self-concept of transfer children. *Journal of Instructional Psychology*, *19*, 61-65.

26. Geary, D. C., Bow-Thomas, C. C., & Yao, Y. (1992). Counting knowledge and skill in cognitive addition: A comparison of normal and mathematically disabled children. *Journal of Experimental Child Psychology*, *54*, 372-391.

27. Gilger, J. W., Pennington, B. F., Green, P., Smith, S. M., & Smith, S. D. (1992). Reading disability, immune disorders and non-right-handedness: Twin and family studies of their relations. *Neuropsychologia*, *30*, 209-227.

28. Kotering, L., Haring, N., & Klockars, A. (1992). The identification of high-school dropouts identified as learning disabled: Evaluating the utility of a discriminant analysis function. *Exceptional Children*, *58*, 422-435.

29. Lorsbach, T. C., Sodoro, J., & Brown, J. S. (1992). The dissociation of repetition priming and recognition memory in language/learning-disabled children. *Journal of Experimental Child Psychology, 54*, 121-146.

30. Marmurek, H. H. C. (1992). The development of letter and syllable effects in categorization, reading aloud, and picture naming. *Journal of Experimental Child Psychology, 53*, 277-299.

31. Matthew, J. L., Golin, A. K., Moore, M. W., & Baker, C. (1992). Use of SOMPA in identification of gifted African-American children. *Journal for the Education of the Gifted, 15*, 344-356.

32. McLeskey, J., & Grizzle, K. L. (1992). Grade retention rates among students with learning disabilities. *Exceptional Children, 58*, 548-554.

33. Misra, A. (1992). Generalization of social skills through self-monitoring by adults with mild mental retardation. *Exceptional Children, 58*, 495-507.

34. Tannenbaum, A. (1992). Early signs of giftedness: Research and commentary. *Journal for the Education of the Gifted, 15*, 104-133.

35. Williams, J., Morgan, S. B., & Kalthoff, R. A. (1992). Concrete operational thought in children with learning disabilities and children with normal achievement. *The Journal of Genetic Psychology, 153*, 87-102.

36. Wise, B. W. (1992). Whole words and decoding for short term learning: Comparisons on a "talking-computer" system. *Journal of Experimental Child Psychology, 54*, 147-167.

37. Abbott, R. D., & Berninger, V. W. (1993). Structural equation modelling of relationships among developmental skills and writing skills in primary- and intermediate-grade writers. *Journal of Educational Psychology, 85*, 478-508.

38. Attkisson, C. C., & Rosenblatt, A. (1993). Enhancing school performance of youth with severe emotional disorder: Initial results from system of care research in three California counties. *School Psychology Quarterly, 8*, 277-290.

39. Baldwin, A. L., Baldwin, C. P., Kasser, T., Zax, M., Sameroff, A., & Seifer, R. (1993). Contextual risk and resiliency during late adolescence. *Development and Psychopathology, 5*, 741-761.

40. Berninger, V. W., & Hooper, S. R. (1993). Preventing and remediating writing disabilities: Interdisciplinary frameworks for assessment, consultation, and intervention. *School Psychology Review, 22*, 590-594.

41. Berninger, V. W., & Whitaker, D. (1993). Theory-based branching diagnosis of writing disabilities. *School Psychology Review, 22*, 623-642.

42. Chittooran, M. M., D'Amato, R. C., Lassiter, K. S., & Dean, R. S. (1993). Factor structure of psychoeducational and neuropsychological measures of learning-disabled children. *Psychology in the Schools, 30*, 109-118.

43. Cotugno, A. J. (1993). The diagnosis of Attention Deficit Hyperactivity Disorder (ADHD) in community mental health centers: Where and when. *Psychology in the Schools, 30*, 338-344.

44. Dykman, R. A., & Ackerman, P. T. (1993). Behavioral subtypes of attention deficit disorder. *Exceptional Children, 60*, 132-141.

45. Faraone, S. V., Biederman, J., Lehman, B. K., Spencer, T., Norman, D., Seidman, L. J., Kraus, I., Perrin, J., Chen, W.J., & Tsuang, M. T. (1993). Intellectual performance and social failure in children with attention deficit hyperactivity disorder and in their siblings. *Journal of Abnormal Psychology, 102*, 616-623.

46. Friedrich, W. N., Shurtleff, D. B., & Shaeffer, J. (1993). Cognitive abilities and lipomyelomeningocele. *Psychological Reports, 73*, 467-470.

47. Fuerst, D. R., & Rourke, B. P. (1993). Psychosocial functioning of children: Relations between personality subtypes and academic achievement. *Journal of Abnormal Child Psychology, 21*, 597-608.

48. Geva, E., Wade-Woolley, L., & Shany, M. (1993). The concurrent development of spelling and decoding in two different orthographies. *Journal of Reading Behavior, 25*, 383-406.

49. Halperin, J. M., Newcorn, J. H., Schwartz, S. T., McKay, K. E., Bedi, G., & Sharma, V. (1993). Plasma catecholamine metabolite levels in ADHD boys with and without reading disabilities. *Journal of Clinical Child Psychology, 22*, 219-225.

50. Johnson, D. J. (1993). Relationships between oral and written language. *School Psychology Review, 22*, 595-609.

51. Jolly, J. B., Aruffo, J. F., Wherry, J. N., & Livingston, R. (1993). The utility of the Beck Anxiety Inventory with inpatient adolescents. *Journal of Anxiety Disorders, 7*, 95-106.

52. Kushch, A., Gross-Glenn, K., Jallad, B., Lubs, H., Robin, M.,Feldman, E., & Duara, R. (1993). Temporal lobe surface area measurements on MRI in normal and dyslexic readers. *Neuropsychologia, 31*, 811-821.

53. Kusché, C. A., Cook, E. T., & Greenberg, M. T. (1993). Neuropsychological and cognitive functioning in children with anxiety, externalizing, and comorbid psychopathology. *Journal of Clinical Child Psychology, 22*, 172-195.

54. Lemoine, H. E., Levy, B. A., & Hutchison, A. (1993). Increasing the naming speed of poor readers: Representations formed across repetitions. *Journal of Experimental Child Psychology, 55*, 297-328.

55. Levy, B. A., Nicholls, A., & Kohen, D. (1993). Repeated readings: Process benefits for good and poor readers. *Journal of Experimental Child Psychology, 56*, 303-327.

56. Lucas, B. A., & Newmark, C. S. (1993). MMPI scale 9 changes in incarcerated felons. *Psychological Reports, 72*, 28-30.

57. Mannuzza, S., Klein, R. G., Bessler, A., Malloy, P., & LaPadula, M. (1993). Adult outcome of hyperactive boys: Educational achievement, occupational rank, and psychiatric status. *Archives of General Psychiatry, 50*, 565-576.

58. Murphy, P. W., Davis, T. C., Long, S. W., Jackson, R. H., & Decker, B. C. (1993). Rapid estimate of adult literacy in medicine (REALM): A quick reading test for patients. *Journal of Reading, 37*, 124-130.

59. Nagle, R. J. (1993). The relationship between the WAIS-R and academic achievement among EMR adolescents. *Psychology in the Schools, 30*, 37-39.

60. Randolph, C., Gold, J. M., Carpenter, C. J., Goldberg, T. E., & Weinberger, D. R. (1993). Implicit memory in patients with schizophrenia and normal controls: Effects of task demands on susceptibility to priming. *Journal of Clinical and Experimental Neuropsychology, 15*, 853-866.

61. Roberts, C., & Zubrick, S. (1993). Factors influencing the social status of children with mild academic disabilities in regular classrooms. *Exceptional Children, 59*, 192-202.

62. Smith, T., Smith, B., Matthews, N., & Kennedy, S. (1993). Subtest scatter and Kaufman regroupings on the WISC-R in the non-learning-disabled and learning-disabled children. *Psychology in the Schools, 30*, 24-28.

63. Swanson, H. L. (1993). An information processing analysis of learning disabled children's problem solving. *American Educational Research Journal, 30*, 861-893.

64. Swanson, H. L. (1993). Working memory in learning disability subgroups. *Journal of Experimental Child Psychology, 56*, 87-114.

65. Swanson, H. L., Cooney, J. B., & Brock, S. (1993). The influence of working memory and classification ability on children's word problem solution. *Journal of Experimental Child Psychology, 55*, 374-395.

66. Tannock, R., Schachar, R. J., & Logan, G. D. (1993). Does methylphenidate induce overfocusing in hyperactive children? *Journal of Clinical Child Psychology, 22*, 28-41.

67. Taylor, H. G., Barry, C. T., & Schatschneider, C. (1993). School-age consequences of *haemophilus influenzae* Type b meningitis. *Journal of Clinical Child Psychology, 22*, 196-206.

68. Treiman, R., Berch, D., & Weatherston, S. (1993). Children's use of phoneme-grapheme correspondences in spelling: Rules of position and stress. *Journal of Educational Psychology, 85*, 466-477.

69. Treiman, R., Berch, D., Tincoff, R., & Weatherston, S. (1993). Phonology and spelling: The case of syllabic consonants. *Journal of Experimental Child Psychology, 56*, 267-290.

70. Trueblood, W., & Schmidt, M. (1993). Malingering and other validity considerations in the neuropsychological evaluation of mild head injury. *Journal of Clinical and Experimental Neuropsychology, 15*, 578-590.

71. Velozo, C. A. (1993). Work evaluations: Critique of the state of the art of functional assessment of work. *The American Journal of Occupational Therapy, 47*, 203-209.

72. Zametkin, A. J., Liebenauer, L. L., Fitzgerald, G. A., King, A. C., Minkonas, D. V., Herscovitch, P., Yamada, E. M., & Cohen, R. M. (1993). Brain metabolism in teenagers with attention-deficit hyperactivity disorder. *Archives of General Psychiatry, 50*, 333-340.

73. Zentall, S. S. (1993). Research on the educational implications of attention deficit hyperactivity disorder. *Exceptional Children, 60*, 143-153.

74. Ackerman, P. T., Dykman, R. A., & Ogesby, D. M. (1994). Visual event-related potentials of dyslexic children to rhyming and nonrhyming stimuli. *Journal of Clinical and Experimental Neuropsychology, 16*, 138-154.

75. Anderson, S. W., & Rizzo, M. (1994). Hallucinations following occipital lobe damage: A pathological activation of visual representations. *Journal of Clinical and Experimental Neuropsychology, 16*, 651-663.

76. Brookshire, B. L., Butler, I. J., Ewing-Cobbs, L., & Fletcher, J. M. (1994). Neuropsychological characteristics of children with Tourette syndrome: Evidence for a nonverbal learning disability. *Journal of Clinical and Experimental Neuropsychology, 16*, 289-302.

77. Castle, J. M., Riach, J., & Nicholson, T. (1994). Getting off to a better start in reading and spelling: The effects of phonemic awareness instruction within a whole language program. *Journal of Educational Psychology, 86*, 350-359.

78. Crossman, L. L., Casey, T. A., & Reilley, R. R. (1994). Influence of cognitive variables on MMPI-2 scale scores. *Measurement and Evaluation in Counseling and Development, 27*, 151-157.

79. DCCT Research Group. (1994). A screening algorithm to identify clinically significant changes in neuropsychological functions in the diabetes control and complications trial. *Journal of Clinical and Experimental Neuropsychology, 16*, 303-316.

80. DiGiulio, D. V., Seidenberg, M., O'Leary, D. S., & Raz, N. (1994). Procedural and declarative memory: A developmental study. *Brain and Cognition, 25*, 79-91.

81. Faulkner, H. J., & Levy, B. A. (1994). How text difficulty and reader skill interact to produce differential reliance on word and content overlap in reading transfer. *Journal of Experimental Child Psychology, 58*, 1-24.

82. Flannery, K. A., & Liederman, J. (1994). A test of the immunoreactive theory for the origin of neurodevelopmental disorders in the offspring of women with immune disorder. *Cortex, 30*, 635-646.

83. Gold, J. M., Hermann, B. P., Randolph, C., Wyler, A. R., Goldberg, T. E., & Weinberger, D. R. (1994). Schizophrenia and temporal lobe epilepsy: A neuropsychological analysis. *Archives of General Psychiatry, 51*, 265-272.

84. Gomez, R., & Sanson, A. V. (1994). Effects of experimenter and mother presence on the attentional performance and activity of hyperactive boys. *Journal of Abnormal Child Psychology, 22*, 517-529.

85. Gomez, R., & Sanson, A. V. (1994). Mother-child interactions and noncompliance in hyperactive boys with and without conduct problems. *Journal of Child Psychology and Psychiatry and Allied Disciplines, 35*, 477-490.

86. Greenbaum, P. E., Dedrick, R. F., Prange, M. E., & Friedman, R. M. (1994). Parent, teacher, and child ratings of problem behaviors of youngsters with serious emotional disturbances. *Psychological Assessment, 6*, 141-148.

87. Halperin, J. M., Sharma, V., Siever, L. J., Schwartz, S. T., Matier, K., Wornell, G., & Newcorn, J. H. (1994). Serotonergic function in aggressive and nonaggressive boys with attention deficit hyperactivity disorder. *American Journal of Psychiatry, 151*, 243-248.

88. Howard-Rose, D., & Rose, C. (1994). Students' adaptation to task environments in resource room and regular class settings. *Journal of Special Education, 28*, 3-26.

89. Hyde, T. M., Nawroz, S., Goldberg, T. E., Bigelow, L. B., Strong, D., Ostrem, J. L., Weinberger, D. R., & Kleinman, J. E. (1994). Is there cognitive decline in schizophrenia? A cross-sectional study. *British Journal of Psychiatry, 164*, 494-500.

90. Jolly, J. B., & Dykman, R. A. (1994). Using self-report data to differentiate anxious and depressive symptoms in adolescents: Cognitive content specificity and global distress? *Cognitive Therapy and Research, 18*, 25-37.

91. Liederman, J., & Flannery, K. A. (1994). Fall conception increases the risk of neurodevelopmental disorder in offspring. *Journal of Clinical and Experimental Neuropsychology, 16*, 754-768.

92. Miles, J., & Stelmack, R. M. (1994). Learning disability subtypes and the effects of auditory and visual priming on visual event-related potential to words. *Journal of Clinical and Experimental Neuropsychology, 16*, 43-64.

93. Morton, L. L. (1994). Interhemispheric balance patterns detected by selective phonemic dichotic laterality measures in four clinical subtypes of reading-disabled children. *Journal of Clinical and Experimental Neuropsychology, 16*, 556-567.

94. Perez, C. M., & Widom, C. S. (1994). Childhood victimization and long-term intellectual and academic outcomes. *Child Abuse & Neglect, 18*, 617-633.

95. Rovet, J., Szekely, C., & Hockenberry, M. (1994). Specific arithmetic calculation deficits in children with Turner syndrome. *Journal of Clinical and Experimental Neuropsychology, 16*, 820-839.

96. Sabatino, D. A., & Vance, H. B. (1994). Is the diagnosis of Attention Deficit/Hyperactivity Disorders meaningful? *Psychology in the Schools, 31*, 188-196.

97. Siegel, L. S. (1994). Working memory and reading: A life-span perspective. *International Journal of Behavioral Development, 17*, 109-124.

98. Stanovich, K. E., & Siegel, L. S. (1994). Phenotypic performance profile of children with reading disabilities: A regression-based test of the phonological-core variable difference model. *Journal of Educational Psychology, 86*, 24-53.

99. Stewart, S. M., Kennard, B. D., Waller, D. A., & Fixler, D. (1994). Cognitive function in children who receive organ transplantation. *Health Psychology, 13*, 3-13.

100. Treiman, R., Cassar, M., & Zukowski, A. (1994). What types of linguistic information do children use in spelling? The case of flaps. *Child Development, 65*, 1318-1337.

101. Trieman, R. (1994). Use of consonant letter names in beginning spelling. *Developmental Psychology, 30*, 567-580.

102. Trueblood, W. (1994). Qualitative and quantitative characteristics of malingered and other invalid WAIS-R and clinical memory data. *Journal of Clinical and Experimental Neuropsychology, 16*, 597-607.

103. Bisanz, J., Morrison, F. J., & Dunn, M. (1995). Effects of age and schooling on the acquisition of elementary quantitative skills. *Developmental Psychology, 31*, 221-236.

104. Conger, R. D., Patterson, G. R., & Ge, X. (1995). It takes two to replicate: A mediational model for the impact of parents' stress on adolescent adjustment. *Child Development, 66*, 80-97.

105. Faraone, S. V., Biederman, J., Chen, W. J., Milberger, S., Warburton, R., & Tsuang, M. T. Genetic heterogeneity in attention-deficit hyperactivity disorder (ADHD): Gender, psychiatric comorbidity, and maternal ADHD. *Journal of Abnormal Psychology, 104*, 334-345.

106. Faraone, S. V., Seidman, L. J., Kremen, W. S., Pepple, J. R., Lyons, M. J., & Tsuang, M. T. (1995). Neuropsychological functioning among the nonpsychotic relatives of schizophrenic patients: A diagnostic efficiency analysis. *Journal of Abnormal Psychology, 104*, 286-304.

107. Liederman, J., & Flannery, K. A. (1995). The sex ratios of families with a neurodevelopmentally disordered child. *Journal of Child Psychology and Psychiatry and Allied Disciplines, 36*, 511-517.

108. Reichard, C. C., Camp, C. J., & Strub, R. L. (1995). Effects of sudden insight on long-term sentence priming in Alzheimer's disease. *Journal of Clinical and Experimental Neuropsychology, 17*, 325-334.

109. Slate, J. R. (1995). Two investigations of the validity of the WISC-III. *Psychological Reports, 76*, 299-306.

110. Slater, A. (1995). Individual differences in infancy and later IQ. *Journal of Child Psychology and Psychiatry and Allied Disciplines, 36*, 69-112.

111. Yates, C. M., Berninger, V. W., & Abbott, R. D. (1995). Specific writing disabilities in intellectually gifted children. *Journal for the Education of the Gifted, 18*, 131-155.

Review of the Wide Range Achievement Test 3 by LINDA MABRY, Assistant Professor of Counseling and Educational Psychology, College of Education, Indiana University, Bloomington, IN:

The Wide Range Achievement Test 3 (WRAT3) includes three subtests in Reading, Spelling, and Arithmetic for individuals aged 5–74 years. There are two forms, said to be equivalent, to be administered separately, used for pre- and posttesting, or combined for "a more comprehensive evaluation" (administration manual, p. 9).

The Reading subtest requires testees to read aloud 42 words. No text is read; comprehension is unassessed; no skills other than pronunciation of isolated words are included. On no grounds can this be considered a test of reading. Pronunciation alone is insufficiently relevant to or representative of the domain of reading.

The Spelling subtest requires the test administrator to dictate 40 words and a sentence for each from the manual, and testees are to write the words on the test form. For children age 7 and younger, a name/letter writing section of 15 additional items is provided. Claims that this covers skills and knowledge related to "general cognitive ability" (p. 175) are not well supported.

The Arithmetic subtest includes 40 problems, doubtful as sufficient coverage of the domain of arithmetic. No more than one problem per type is included, raising doubts about the validity of inferences based on scores. (What if a person calculates square roots with 80% accuracy but misses the single such problem on the test?) Moreover, the two forms do not test the same skills: Only the blue form includes an algebra problem with two unknown quantities and a function problem; only the tan form includes a compound interest and a logarithm problem.

Inadequate content coverage, discrepancies between forms, and dubious relationship between scores and "general cognitive ability" are complicated by the speeded nature of the test and by the targeted population. It is sheer nonsense to claim, "Each form of the WRAT3 takes 15 to 30 minutes to complete" depending upon testees' skills and behaviors (p. 9) when testees must read 42 words, write 40 dictated words, and work 40 problems within that time frame. That being the case for "normal" testees, description of the test as "a valuable tool in the determination of learning ability or learning disability" (p. 10) is ludicrous.

A stated purpose of WRAT3 is to "determine precisely where the individual is having difficulty and . . . prescribe those remedial/educational programs which will target treatment for the specific defect" (p. 10). This statement suggests a *deficit* philosophy of special education in which "broken" students need "fixing," rather than the current *inclusion* philosophy in which children with disabilities need and deserve to be with typically developing peers. WRAT3 developers tested some special education students "randomly selected from public schools . . . as randomization would allow. Subjects were only excluded if they were unable to physically respond to the test items" (p. 27). Of these, some were to be excluded by examiners if "uncooperative and/or unwilling to take the tests" (p. 28). Individuals should not be forced to take tests but, among the many charts—the bulk of the manual—there is no final reckoning as to how many disabled persons were tested, the nature of their disabilities, or their proportions among either testees or the general population. This calls into question the test's diagnostic capacity, even with the developers' last-page admonition that the WRAT3 should be merely one element in determining the need for special services.

The test, although revised in 1993, is outdated. On the rationale that "[t]he basic concepts of the test have not changed for nearly 60 years" (p. 27), "[m]any of the items were first developed with previous editions of the WRAT dating back to 1936" (p. 176). But basic concepts in education and special education *have* changed (e.g., constructivism and inclusion), and sensitivity to a variety of sociocultural factors has increased. The rigor of item bias studies for this test is questionable, and timeliness is lacking. "At the time of the WRAT3 publication, the item bias studies had not been completed" (p. 170). Studies for an earlier version revealed "a slight, but consistent, bias" on the Arithmetic Level 2 test, which developers addressed in the WRAT3 by extending the 10-minute test time to 15 minutes (p. 170). Whether this response was appropriate, who was disadvantaged by the bias, and results of the most recent item bias study are all unclear.

Content validity was reported based on the Rasch statistic of item separation. For Reading and Spelling, the content domain was "all the words in the English language"; for Arithmetic, "computation problems taught in grades Kindergarten through high school" (p. 176). The manual alludes to a table of specifications for selecting items "representative of that domain" (p. 176). On the basis of maximum item separation scores (1.00) for each subtest, developers claim "strong evidence that there is content validity on each of the WRAT3 measures" (p. 176). Problem: Item separation is not a direct measure of the representativeness and relevance of items to the domain (Messick, 1989).

Construct validity is insufficiently addressed. Among several claims about construct validity are: (*a*) that increase in scores corresponding to increase in the age of testees (up to age group 45–54 years) shows WRAT3 tests developmental skills; (*b*) that moderate to high intercorrelations among subtest scores show WRAT3 tests related academic skills; (*c*) that correlations among WRAT3 subtest scores and WISC-III subtest scores show these academic skills are positively associated with general cognitive ability; (*d*) that performance on the WRAT3 is hypothesized as being consistent with that on (unnamed) other standardized achievement tests; and (*e*) that the WRAT3 "can distinguish among groups of Gifted, Learning Disabled, Educable Mentally Handicapped and Normal Students" (p. 176).

PROBLEMS. (*a*) Rising scores *may* suggest the developmental nature of the skills tested but do nothing to support the contention that the WRAT3 tests the skills it claims to test, the essence of construct validity. (*b*) Correlations among subtest scores and with WISC-III scores do not definitively determine that the skills tested by either are academic or cognitive. (*c*) A *hypothesis* that WRAT3 scores will be consistent with scores on other achievement tests offers no validity evidence whatever. (*d*) Discriminate analysis based on empirical studies of 40 gifted, 47 learning disabled, 24 educable mentally handicapped, and 111 "normal" students revealed scores consistent with prior classifications of the students' abilities. However, obvious rival hypotheses were not pursued. Further, although special students were matched to controls by age, gender, and race, they were not matched by socioeconomic status, a more important variable affecting achievement. Finally, the sample size is of questionable sufficiency.

Reliability was claimed from three measures of internal consistency (coefficient alpha, alternate form, and person separation indices) and a test-retest study. The manual defines reliability conventionally (p. 170) such that only the test-retest study would yield acceptable evidence. Appropriateness of the sample size and age of subjects is doubtful: The mean age of the 142 individuals tested and retested (averaging 37.4 days later) was 10.5 years.

The adequacy of any instrument intended to test the cognitive or academic abilities of persons within a 69-year age range and an ability range from educable mentally handicapped to gifted is immediately suspect, even one with a 58-year history of use. Suspicions of inadequacy here are confirmed by test content, item formats, obsolescence, underlying philosophy, potential for bias, and insufficient evidence of validity or reliability.

REVIEWER'S REFERENCE

Messick, S. J. (1989). Validity. In R. L. Linn (Ed.), *Educational Measurement* (pp. 13-103). New York: American Council on Education.

Review of the Wide Range Achievement Test 3 by ANNIE W. WARD, President, The Techné Group, Inc., Daytona Beach, FL:

The Wide Range Achievement Test (WRAT3) is a very old test, having been first published in 1936. The WRAT3 is the seventh edition of the test. The durability of this test in spite of the lack of evidence of adequate psychometric qualities suggests that the test fills a perceived need. The fact that it can be administered and scored quickly also helps.

The test was originally designed to be administered along with the Wechsler-Bellevue Scales in order to "add other dimensions to those covered by the Wechsler" (manual, p. 3). This is still the way the test is most commonly used. The test is aptly called "wide range" because it is designed to be used with individuals aged 5–75. The edition of the test just previous to this (WRAT-R) was split into two levels of difficulty, but had only one form. This edition (WRAT3) is a single-level test, with two equivalent forms, which makes a retest feasible. Although the WRAT has undergone several revisions it is basically the same test it was originally, and many of the items are the same. Perhaps it is time for a change.

An obvious attempt has been made to address some of the problems identified in the reviews of the previous edition, the WRAT-R. However, the major problem has not been addressed: the failure to identify the *construct* for the test and to provide evidence to support that construct. The problems with the test are summarized below, then recommendations are presented.

VALIDITY. The lack of a construct was understandable in the 1930s; today it is unacceptable. As Messick (1989) makes clear, investigation of validity involves a summary of the evidence for and the potential consequences of score interpretation and use. The greatest problem with all editions of the WRAT is that there is really NO validity evidence, although a small attempt has been made with the WRAT3 to address this problem. The author continues to try to use item statistics indicating that the items range in difficulty from very easy to very hard to support *content* validity, and he poses some hypotheses, as Shepard (1993) recommends, in an attempt at establishing *construct* validity. The problem is that, in the absence of an explicit construct, the hypotheses have little meaning. Nor is there any rationale for use of the kinds of items that continue to be used or any data to support that scores on the WRAT3 contribute anything to a better evaluation of an individual's status. The discriminant analysis data indicating that individuals previously classified in one of three categories score differently than a comparison sample is suggestive. (Although the table is correctly labeled, the heading and text on page 184 of the manual use the term "discriminate" analysis.) However, it is not sufficient to support a recommendation that the WRAT3 be used as a part of the classification process. The correlations between WRAT3 scores and age are only moderate.

RELIABILITY. In addition to Rasch statistics, data are now also reported for the traditional statistics, coefficient alpha and test-retest coefficients. However, the *N*s are quite small.

NORMS. The description of the norms sample is still quite sketchy, although the statement is made that it is stratified, and the tables report the percent of the sample by geographic area, ethnic groups, and age and gender groups. The "non-white" group has been broken down into "Black," "Hispanic," and "Other"; however, the *N*s for many of these groups are extremely small. The "Other" group has only 3.9% of the 4,433 of the total sample, a total of less than 175 cases distributed across the 23 age groups. For "Blacks" with 13.6% the number is only 603, an average of 27 per age group, and for Hispanics, the total is 474, or 21 per age group. Although the proportions may be representative according to census data, and are acceptable for establishing norms, the *N*s are not sufficient to determine whether the test is biased for nonwhite groups. The manual does not report any bias data, but states that a separate bias study is underway.

The manual recommends that the *standard score* be used in interpreting scores, particularly if they are being used in conjunction with Wechsler scores, because the standard scores use the same scale as the Wechsler tests. However, this is extremely misleading. Comparability of these scales assumes that they are derived from a common population; however, the data reported indicate that the difference between the WRAT means and the Weschler means is equal to or exceeds the standard error of measurement. This makes it very questionable to compare standard scores on the two tests. The manual also reports "Absolute Scores," a Rasch concept, but there is no indication as to how these scores might be useful, except to compare the three WRAT scores. In response to numerous criticisms of previous editions, the manual correctly suggests caution in the use of "grade score," although they are reported.

RECOMMENDATIONS. To correct these problems, the following changes are recommended:

1. The test should be rewritten, starting with a careful identification of the construct and its domain, and sampling from that domain.

The construct might be defined by considering what people are looking for when they use the

WRAT3; is a measure of achievement to be compared with measures of ability as secured from an instrument such as one of the Wechsler tests? To be useful, the construct *Achievement* must be operationally defined.

The first WRAT Reading was developed by sampling a dictionary of the time. If the current WRAT is to be useful, there probably need to be at least three levels of achievement specified: preschool through grade 2, grades 2 through 8, and adult. This suggests that the single-level test is not a useful concept. It also suggests that the items should come from different domains and be based on the type of tasks faced by people of a given age range.

Also, a large enough pool of items should be prepared so that nonfunctioning items may be discarded, and so that multiple forms of the test may be prepared.

2. Norms should be gathered, using a carefully stratified sample, and administering the appropriate level of the Wechsler test to the same individuals. In this way, the standard score scales would be comparable for the two instruments. Norms should be limited to standard scores, unless a very large national sample can be secured so that grade and age equivalents may be established reliably.

3. A factor analysis of the WRAT3 and the WISC-R should also be made to investigate whether the WRAT3 contributes any unique variance to the measurement provided by the WISC-R alone.

Until the redevelopment is accomplished, the following recommendations of temporary expedients are made:

1. Administer the WRAT3 to a large stratified sample along with the appropriate level of the Wechsler test, in order to establish equivalent standard score scales.

2. Administer the WRAT3 to an adequate sample of students involved in the standardization sample of a nationally normed achievement battery, so that equivalent scores could be established. The problem with this procedure is that the WRAT3 was deliberately constructed not to measure some of the skills that more traditional achievement tests cover.

3. The administration manual should be rewritten, eliminating some useless and all misleading information. Users should be cautioned that the test was not designed to diagnose an individual's difficulty; that it is only a part of a diagnostic package and must be interpreted along with many other kinds of data. The diagnostic profile should be modified or abandoned.

REVIEWER'S REFERENCES

Messick, S. J. (1989). Validity. In R. L. Linn (Ed.), *Educational measurement* (pp. 13-103). New York: American Council on Education.

Shepard, L. A. (1993). Evaluating test validity. *Review of Research in Education, 19*, 405-450.

[415]

Woodcock-Johnson Psycho-Educational Battery—Revised.

Purpose: Designed to measure "cognitive abilities, scholastic aptitudes, and achievement."

Population: Ages 2–90.

Publication Dates: 1977–91.

Acronym: WJ-R.

Administration: Individual.

Parts, 2: Cognitive, Achievement.

Price Data, 1992: $475 per complete WJ-R kit (Cognitive and Form A Achievement); $29.95 per technical manual ('91, 367 pages); $195 per computer scoring system (select Apple or IBM).

Comments: Aptitude/Achievement discrepancies can be calculated using actual norms when the Cognitive and Achievement Sections have been administered; 1977 edition still available; the Early Development Scale for Preschool Children is composed of fewer tests.

Authors: Richard W. Woodcock (examiner's manuals and test books), M. Bonner Johnson (test books), Nancy Mather (examiner's manuals), Kevin S. McGrew (technical manual), and Judy K. Werder (technical manual).

Publisher: The Riverside Publishing Company.

a) TESTS OF ACHIEVEMENT.

Scores: 9 Standard Battery test scores: Letter-Word Identification, Passage Comprehension, Calculation, Applied Problems, Dictation, Writing Samples, Science, Social Studies, Humanities plus 5 Standard Battery cluster scores derived from combinations of the above test scores: Broad Reading, Broad Mathematics, Broad Written Language, Broad Knowledge, Skills and the Ability to Calculate Intra-Achievement Discrepancies, and 9 Supplemental Battery test scores: Word Attack, Reading Vocabulary, Quantitative Concepts, Proofing, Writing Fluency, Punctuation & Capitalization, Spelling, Usage, Handwriting plus 6 Supplemental Battery Cluster scores derived from combinations of scores from the Standard Battery and Supplemental Battery: Basic Reading Skills, Reading Comprehension, Basic Mathematics Skills, Mathematics Reasoning, Basic Writing Skills, Written Expression.

Forms, 2: A, B.

Price Data: $195 per complete kit including Standard and Supplemental test books, 25 test records, 25 subject response books, examiner's manual ('89, 230 pages), and norms tables ('89, 275 pages) (select Form A or B); $32 per set of 25 test records and 25 subject response books (select Form A or B).

Time: (50–60) minutes for the Standard Battery; additional administration time for the Supplemental Battery not reported.

Comments: Tests may be administered separately.

b) TESTS OF COGNITIVE ABILITY.

Scores: 7 Standard Battery test scores plus 1 cluster score: Memory for Names, Memory for Sentences, Visual Matching, Incomplete Words, Visual Closure, Picture Vocabulary, Analysis-Synthesis, Broad Cognitive Ability (Standard or Early Development) and 14 Supplemental Battery test scores: Visual-Auditory Learning, Memory for Words, Cross Out, Sound Blending, Picture Recognition, Oral Vocabulary, Concept Formation, Delayed Recall (Memory for Names, Visual-Auditory Learning), Numbers Reversed, Sound Patterns, Spatial Relations, Listening Comprehension, Verbal Analogies plus 14 Supplemental Battery cluster scores derived from combinations of scores from the

Standard Battery and Supplemental Battery: Broad Cognitive Ability-Extended Scale, Cognitive Factor (Long-Term Retrieval, Short-Term Memory, Processing Speed, Auditory Processing, Visual Processing, Comprehension-Knowledge, Fluid Reasoning), Scholastic Aptitude (Reading, Mathematics, Written Language, Knowledge), Oral Language (Oral Language, Oral Language Aptitude), and Ability to Calculate Intracognitive Discrepancies.

Price Data: $330 per complete kit including Standard and Supplemental test books, 25 test records, audiocassettes, examiner's manual ('89, 204 pages), and norms tables ('89, 297 pages); $195 per complete Standard kit; $180 per Supplemental expansion including test book, 25 test records, audiocassette, examiner's manual, and norms tables (to be used only in conjunction with the Standard Battery); $32 per 25 Standard and Supplemental test records; $25 per 25 Standard test records.

Time: (30–40) minutes for the Standard Battery; an additional 40 minutes required to administer the Supplemental Battery.

Cross References: For reviews of the 1977 edition by Jack A. Cummings and Alan S. Kaufman, see 9:1387 (6 references); see also T3:2639 (3 references).

TEST REFERENCES

1. Burns, J. M., & Richgels, D. J. (1989). An investigation of task requirements associated with the invented spellings of 4-year-olds with above average intelligence. *Journal of Reading Behavior*, *21*, 1-14.

2. Ross, J. M., & Smith, J. O. (1989). Adult basic educators' perceptions of learning disabilities. *Journal of Reading*, *33*, 340-347.

3. Scruggs, T. E., & Mastropieri, M. A. (1989). Reconstructive elaborations: A model for content area learning. *American Educational Research Journal*, *26*, 311-327.

4. Torgesen, J. K., Wagner, R. K., Balthazar, M., Davis, C., Morgan, S., Simmons, K., Stage, S., & Zirps, F. (1989). Developmental and individual differences in performance on phonological synthesis tasks. *Journal of Experimental Child Psychology*, *47*, 491-505.

5. Burns, J. M., Mathews, F. N., & Mason, A. (1990). Essential steps in screening and identifying preschool gifted children. *Gifted Child Quarterly*, *34*, 102-107.

6. Carroll, J. B. (1990). Estimating item and ability parameters in homogeneous tests with the person characteristic function. *Applied Psychological Measurement*, *14*, 109-125.

7. Hurford, D. P., & Sanders, R. E. (1990). Assessment and remediation of a phonemic discrimination deficit in reading disabled second and fourth graders. *Journal of Experimental Child Psychology*, *50*, 396-415.

8. Schulte, A. C., Osborne, S. S., & McKinney, J. D. (1990). Academic outcomes for students with learning disabilities in consultation and resource programs. *Exceptional Children*, *57*, 162-172.

9. Burns, J. M., Collins, M. D., & Paulsell, J. C. (1991). A comparison of intellectually superior preschool accelerated readers and nonreaders: Four years later. *Gifted Child Quarterly*, *35*, 118-124.

10. Carlson, C. L., Pelham, W. E., Swanson, J. M., & Wagner, J. L. (1991). A divided attention analysis of the effects of methylphenidate on the arithmetic performance of children with attention-deficit hyperactivity disorder. *Journal of Child Psychology and Psychiatry and Allied Disciplines*, *32*, 463-471.

11. Kee, D. W., Gottfried, A., & Bathurst, K. (1991). Consistency of hand preference: Predictions to intelligence and school achievement. *Brain and Cognition*, *16*, 1-10.

12. Miller, S. D., & Yochum, N. (1991). Asking students about the nature of their reading difficulties. *Journal of Reading Behavior*, *23*, 465-485.

13. Oliver, J. M., Hodge Cole, N., & Hollingsworth, H. (1991). Learning disabilities as functions of familial learning problems and developmental problems. *Exceptional Children*, *57*, 427-440.

14. Parker, R. I., Tindal, G., & Hasbrouck, J. (1991). Progress monitoring with objective measures of writing performance for students with mild disabilities. *Exceptional Children*, *58*, 61-73.

15. Wilson, C. L., & Sindelar, P. T. (1991). Direct instruction in math word problems: Students with learning disabilities. *Exceptional Children*, *57*, 512-519.

16. Bruck, M., & Treiman, R. (1992). Learning to pronounce words: The limitations of analogies. *Reading Research Quarterly*, *27*, 375-388.

17. Carlisle, J. F. (1992). Understanding passages in science textbooks: A comparison of students with and without learning disabilities. *Yearbook of National Reading Conference*, *42*, 235-242.

18. Dreyer, L. G., Shankweiler, D., & Luke, S. D. (1992). Children's retention of word spellings in relation to reading ability. *Yearbook of National Reading Conference*, *42*, 405-412.

19. Geary, D. C., Bow-Thomas, C. C., & Yao, Y. (1992). Counting knowledge and skill in cognitive addition: A comparison of normal and mathematically disabled children. *Journal of Experimental Child Psychology*, *54*, 372-391.

20. Graham, S., Macarthur, C., Schwartz, S., & Page-Voth, V. (1992). Improving the compositions of students with learning disabilities using a strategy involving product and process goal setting. *Exceptional Children*, *58*, 322-334.

21. McLeskey, J., & Grizzle, K. L. (1992). Grade retention rates among students with learning disabilities. *Exceptional Children*, *58*, 548-554.

22. Sinnett, E. R., Roog, K. L., Benton, S. L., Downey, R. G., & Whitfall, J. M. (1993). The Woodcock-Johnson Revised—Its factor structure. *Educational and Psychological Measurement*, *53*, 763-769.

23. Attkisson, C. C., & Rosenblatt, A. (1993). Enhancing school performance of youth with severe emotional disorder: Initial results from system of care research in three California counties. *School Psychology Quarterly*, *8*, 277-290.

24. Berninger, V. W., & Hooper, S. R. (1993). Preventing and remediating writing disabilities: Interdisciplinary framewords for assessment, consultation, and intervention. *School Psychology Review*, *22*, 590-594.

25. Berninger, V. W., & Whitaker, D. (1993). Theory-based branching diagnosis of writing disabilities. *School Psychology Review*, *22*, 623-642.

26. Bottge, B. A., & Hasselbring, T. S. (1993). A comparison of two approaches for teaching complex, authentic mathematics problems to adolescents in remedial math classes. *Exceptional Children*, *59*, 556-566.

27. Finlayson, S. B., & Obrzut, J. E. (1993). Factorial structure of the Quick Neurological Screening Test—Revised for children with learning disabilities. *Psychology in the Schools*, *30*, 5-10.

28. Halgren, D. W., & Clarizio, H. F. (1993). Categorical and programming changes in special education services. *Exceptional Children*, *59*, 547-555.

29. Howe, G. W., Feinstein, C., Reiss, D., Molock, S., & Berger, K. (1993). Adolescent adjustment to chronic physical disorders-I. Comparing neurological and non-neurological conditions. *Journal of Child Psychology and Psychiatry and Allied Disciplines*, *34*, 1153-1176.

30. Jackson, N. E., Donaldson, G. W., & Mills, J. R. (1993). Components of reading skill in postkindergarten precocious readers and level-matched second graders. *Journal of Reading Behavior*, *25*, 181-208.

31. Kushch, A., Gross-Glenn, K., Jallad, B., Lubs, H., Robin, M., Feldman, E., & Duara, R. (1993). Temporal lobe surface area measurements on MRI in normal and dyslexic readers. *Neuropsychologia*, *31*, 811-821.

32. McGrew, K. S., & Knopik, S. N. (1993). The relationship between the WJ-R Gf-Gc cognitive clusters and writing achievment across the life-span. *School Psychology Review*, *22*, 687-695.

33. Plante, T. G., Goldfarb, L. P., & Wadley, V. (1993). Are stress and coping associated with aptitude and achievement testing performance among children? A preliminary investigation. *Journal of School Psychology*, *31*, 259-266.

34. Reid, R., & Harris, K. R. (1993). Self-monitoring of attention versus self-monitoring of performance: Effects on attention and academic performance. *Exceptional Children*, *60*, 29-40.

35. Sitlington, P. L., Frank, A. R., & Carson, R. (1993). Adult adjustment among high school graduates with mild disabilities. *Exceptional Children*, *59*, 221-233.

36. Swanson, H. L. (1993). An information processing analysis of learning disabled children's problem solving. *American Educational Research Journal*, *30*, 861-893.

37. Yochum, N., & Miller, S. D. (1993). Parents', teachers' and children's views of reading problems. *Reading Research and Instruction*, *33*, 59-71.

38. Brookshire, B. L., Butler, I. J., Ewing-Cobbs, L., & Fletcher, J. M. (1994). Neuropsychological characteristics of children with Tourette syndrome: Evidence for a nonverbal learning disability. *Journal of Clinical and Experimental Neuropsychology*, *16*, 289-302.

39. Erhardt, D., & Hinshaw, S. P. (1994). Initial sociometric impressions of attention-deficit hyperactivity disorder and comparison boys: Predictions from social behaviors and from nonbehavioral variables. *Journal of Consulting and Clinical Psychology*, *62*, 833-842.

40. Fletcher, J. M., Shaywitz, S. E., Shankweiler, D. P., Katz, L., Liberman, I. Y., Stuebing, K. K., Francis, D. J., Fowler, A. E., & Shaywitz, B. A. (1994). Cognitive profiles of reading disability: Comparisons of discrepancy and low achievement definitions. *Journal of Educational Psychology*, *86*, 6-23.

41. Frick, P. J., O'Brien, B. S., Wootton, J. M., & McBurnett, K. (1994). Psychopathy and conduct problems in children. *Journal of Abnormal Psychology*, *103*, 700-707.

42. Giedd, J. N., Castellanos, F. X., Casey, B. J., Kozuch, P., King, A. C., Hamburger, S. D., & Rapoport, J. L. (1994). Quantitative morphology of the corpus callosum in attention deficit hyperactivity disorder. *American Journal of Psychiatry, 151*, 665-669.
43. Goldstein, D. J., & Britt, T. W., Jr. (1994). Visual-motor coordination and intelligence as predictors of reading, mathematics, and written language ability. *Perceptual and Motor Skills, 78*, 819-823.
44. Gottfried, A. E., Fleming, J. S., & Gottfried, A. W. (1994). Role of parental motivational practices in children's academic intrinsic motivation and achievement. *Journal of Educational Psychology, 86*, 104-113.
45. McGhee, R., & Lieberman, L. (1994). Gf-Gc Theory of human cognition: Differentiation of short-term auditory and visual memory factors. *Psychology in the Schools, 31*, 297-304.
46. McIntosh, R., Vaughn, S., Schumm, J. S., Haager, D., & Lee, O. (1994). Observations of students with learning disabilities in general education classrooms. *Exceptional Children, 60*, 249-261.
47. Payette, K. A., & Clarizio, H. F. (1994). Discrepant team decisions: The effects of race, gender, achievement, and IQ on LD eligibility. *Psychology in the Schools, 31*, 40-48.
48. Spencer, W. D., & Raz, N. (1994). Memory for facts, source, and context: Can frontal lobe dysfunction explain age-related differences? *Psychology and Aging, 9*, 149-159.
49. Taub, C. F., Fine, E., & Cherry, R. S. (1994). Finding a link between selective auditory attention and reading problems in young children: A preliminary investigation. *Perceptual and Motor Skills, 78*, 1153-1154.
50. Van Reusen, A. K., & Bos, C. S. (1994). Facilitating student participation in individualized education programs through motivation strategy instruction. *Exceptional Children, 60*, 466-475.
51. Gnys, J. A., Willis, W. G., & Faust, D. (1995). School psychologists' diagnoses of learning disabilities: A study of illusory correlation. *Journal of School Psychology, 33*, 59-73.
52. Hinshaw, S. P., Simmel, C., & Heller, T. L. (1995). Multimethod assessment of covert antisocial behavior in children: Laboratory observations, adult ratings, and child self-report. *Psychological Assessment, 7*, 209-219.
53. Hurford, D. D., & Sanders, R. E. (1995). Phonological recoding ability in young children with reading disabilities. *Contemporary Educational Psychology, 20*, 121-126.
54. Simpson, R. G., & Halpin, G. (1995). Psychometric effects of altering the ceiling criterion on the Passage Comprehension Test of the Woodcock-Johnson Psycho-Educational Battery—Revised. *Educational and Psychological Measurement, 55*, 630-636.
55. Stipek, D., Feiler, R., Daniels, D., & Milburn, S. (1995). Effects of different instructional approaches on young children's achievement and motivation. *Child Development, 66*, 209-223.
56. Stormont-Spurgin, M., & Zentall, S. S. (1995). Contributing factors in the manifestation of aggression in preschoolers with hyperactivity. *Journal of Child Psychology and Psychiatry and Allied Disciplines, 36*, 491-509.

Review of the Woodcock-Johnson Psycho-Educational Battery—Revised by JACK A. CUMMINGS, Chair, Department of Counseling and Educational Psychology, Indiana University, Bloomington, IN:

The Woodcock-Johnson Psycho-Educational Battery—Revised (WJ-R) was designed to sample various cognitive and academic achievement abilities for individuals ranging in age from 2 through 95 years. The 1989/1990 revision of the original 1977 version of the Woodcock-Johnson Psycho-Educational Battery (Woodcock & Johnson, 1977) reflects the wisdom of a distinguished group of consultants and advisors (among whom were Jack B. Carroll, H. Carl Haywood, John L. Horn, and Kevin McGrew). Unlike revisions in the tradition of the Wechsler Scales, the authors of the WJ-R did not follow the market-preserving formula of retaining 80% of the original items with very minor adjustments to the structure of the scale. In contrast, Woodcock and Johnson made substantive changes, especially to the revised Tests of Cognitive Ability. The most significant criticism of the 1977 Tests of Cognitive Ability was the lack of a theoretical framework for the user to interpret an individual's cognitive functioning.

The WJ-R is not intended to be administered in its entirety, but rather in a selective fashion. For instance, on both the cognitive and achievement sections of the battery, there are a reduced set of subtests that comprise the "standard battery" and additional subtests for supplemental testing. Thus, the examiner has the option of using the standard battery, and then using referral information and additional subtests to test hypotheses generated in the initial phase of testing.

This review will provide an overview of the WJ-R and address issues associated with the quality of the normative sample, test administration, reliability, validity, and interpretation. Finally, comments will be offered on the relative merit of the battery when compared to other available measures.

The 1989/1990 revision of the Woodcock-Johnson used the Horn-Cattell model of intellectual processing (Horn, 1976, 1985, 1988; Horn & Cattell, 1966) as the foundation for selecting and organizing cognitive subtests. Ten new subtests were added to the Tests of Cognitive Ability. From the Horn-Cattell model, seven broad abilities are assessed by the WJ-R: Fluid Reasoning, Gf; Comprehension-Knowledge, Gc; Visual Processing, Gv; Auditory Processing, Ga; Processing Speed, Gs; Long-Term Retrieval, Glr; and Short-Term Memory, Gsm. This factorial model of the Tests of Cognitive Ability was derived following analyses of the 1977 normative sample for the 12 subtests of the Woodcock-Johnson Tests of Cognitive Ability and the first 25% of the normative sample for the 1989/1990 revision of the scale. Appropriately, no adjustments were made in the model following the collection of the remaining 75% of the sample.

The standard battery of the WJ-R Tests of Cognitive Ability is composed of seven subtests, each representing one of the Horn-Cattell abilities. The first level of the supplemental cognitive battery consists of seven subtests, again with each assessing one of the seven Horn-Cattell abilities. Further assessment of Long-Term Retrieval, Short-Term Memory, and Fluid Reasoning is possible with subtests 15–21.

The WJ-R Tests of Achievement include a Standard Battery and Supplemental Battery. Two parallel forms (A & B) are available for the nine subtests that comprise the Standard Battery. Five achievement clusters may be interpreted from the Standard Battery: Broad Reading, Broad Mathematics, Broad Written Language, Broad Knowledge, and Skills. Five supplemental subtests may be administered to provide a more in-depth understanding of a child's abilities in reading, mathematics, and written language.

NORMATIVE SAMPLE. The normative sample included 6,359 individuals from "over 100 geographically diverse U.S. communities" (WJ-R Tests of Academic Achievement examiner's manual, p. 93). Normative tables are available for the following groups: age 2.0 through 90+ years. The inclusion of college students is an important addition as a potential normative comparison group. With the advent of greater sensitivity to college students with learning disabilities, the WJ-R may be used to assess their cognitive and academic functioning. Comparison of the demographic characteristics of the sample to the U.S. population reveals a close match. This means that the WJ-R sample faithfully represents the U.S. population as described by the 1980 census distribution. Frequently, racial and ethnic minorities are undersampled for test norms. This is not the case, and to the contrary there is slight oversampling of racial/ethnic minorities. All normative data were collected from September 1986 to August 1988. A continuous-year procedure for normative testing was employed, rather than testing to create separate fall and spring norms.

ADMINISTRATION. Incorporated in the examiner's manual are suggested activities to acquaint the new examiner with appropriate administration and scoring practices. Checklists of learning activities, sample protocols, pronunciation tape, and scoring exercises will undoubtedly increase the likelihood of accurate administration and scoring. Accurate administration of the WJ-R is facilitated by the design of the examiner's pages in easel kit (e.g., spoken directions are highlighted in bold blue print, answer keys list appropriate probes for borderline responses, and warnings against common administration or scoring errors are included). Although the easel format simplifies administration for the examiner, there is an inherent liability. The repetitive page flipping does not sustain some young children's interest as well as when manipulable tasks are interspersed with verbal subtests. Thus, the examiner must be extra sensitive to the child's need to take breaks.

RELIABILITY. The internal consistency reliability coefficients for the WJ-R fall in the mid .90s for the major clusters on the Cognitive and Achievement scales. The split-half method corrected by the Spearman-Brown formula was used to estimate internal consistency, except on timed subtests where test-retest stabilities were appropriately substituted. Reliabilities for the subtests on the Standard and Supplemental Cognitive Batteries ranged from the mid .70s to low .90s, with most falling in the .80s. These estimates compare favorably to other available cognitive measures.

The internal consistency reliabilities for the subtests on the Achievement scale were slightly higher, most falling in the high .80s and low .90s. The exception among the Achievement subtests was the Writing Fluency subtests, which had a median coefficient of $r = .76$. Compared to other measures of achievement the pattern of reliabilities is similar. Likewise, a review of test-retest reliabilities presented in the technical manual indicates adequate stability of the major cluster and composite scores. Hence, the WJ-R should be judged favorably with respect to reliability as indicated by internal consistency and stability estimates.

Although included in the technical manual, information on the test-retest stability of the Woodcock-Johnson clusters and subtests was not presented in the examiner's manuals. These data would have been appropriate to include in the examiner's manuals because interpretation of the practice effect is necessary in situations where retesting takes place (e.g., second opinion cases). Because differential practice effects have been observed for the Wechsler scales, information on mean standard score gains would provide insight for these interpretations.

VALIDITY. Content, concurrent, and construct validation efforts for the battery are discussed in the technical manual and in briefer versions in the examiner's manuals. Although the coverage of various validation approaches is generally very comprehensive for the WJ-R, the content validation efforts are covered in a superficial manner. It is stated that expert opinion was used in the process of selecting items. Whether individuals who would bring alternative racial/ethnic perspectives to the scrutiny of items were included in the content validation process is not stated.

Concurrent validity was investigated across different age levels and with different anchor measures. For instance, at the age 9 level, comparisons were made with scores on the Kaufman Assessment Battery for Children, the Stanford-Binet Intelligence Test, Fourth Revision, and the Wechsler Intelligence Scale for Children—Revised. The respective validity coefficients for the Broad Cognitive Ability standard scores were .46, .53, and .52. The authors of the examiner's manuals note the reported correlations may slightly underestimate the true correlations for the general population due to the standard deviations of the samples being smaller than 15. Data are also provided on samples of children age 3 and age 17, with independent measures including the Boehm Test of Basic Concepts, Bracken Basic Concept Scale, Peabody Picture Vocabulary Test—Revised, and the Wechsler Adult Intelligence Scale—Revised. When the Broad Cognitive Ability standard score is compared to composite indices for the other scales the coefficients were observed to be in the high .50s to mid .60s. When all 14 subtests of the Extended Battery were included the coefficients were larger (i.e., mid .60s to low .70s), indicating a slightly large degree of shared variance between the Woodcock-Johnson Tests of Cognitive Ability and the anchor measures.

To assess the concurrent validity of the Tests of Achievement, the BASIS, the Kaufman Test of Educational Achievement, the Peabody Individual

Achievement Test, and the Wide Range Achievement Test—Revised were administered to samples of children ages 9 and 17. The pattern of intercorrelations among the scales provides further support for the domains as they are labeled.

A surprising omission from the technical manual is any information on standard scores obtained from the revised Woodcock-Johnson and compared to other measures. This omission is curious, especially given the controversy surrounding mean score differences on the 1977 version of the battery (Cummings & Moscato, 1984a, 1984b; Thompson & Brassard, 1984; Woodcock, 1984). Information on the comparison of mean scores for the WJ-R with the original 1977 version of the Woodcock-Johnson and with other anchor measures of cognitive ability and measures of achievement would have provided a context for interpretation of any differences noted when comparing old scores to WJ-R scores in the situation of a 3-year re-evaluation.

McGrew, Werder, and Woodcock provide an erudite discussion of the construct validity of the Tests of Cognitive Ability in the WJ-R Technical Manual. Confirmatory and exploratory factor analyses across age levels (grades K–3; grades 4–7; grades 8–12; young adult, < age 40; middle adult, 40–59; older adult, > age 60) are reported and provide evidence of the fidelity of the Horn-Cattell model in the Tests of Cognitive Ability. Only at the older adult age level did the Goodness-of-Fit Indices (GFI) and root-mean-square residuals (rmr) reveal a slightly weaker match of the Horn-Cattell (Gf-Gc) model to the test. Additionally, the authors of the technical manual tested the Woodcock-Johnson against alternative models: first-order "g," nonverbal-verbal dichotomy, and hierarchical "g." These analyses again revealed that the Horn-Cattell model was superior, especially when compared to the first-order "g" and verbal/nonverbal models.

INTERPRETATION. The Broad Cognitive Ability standard score provides a "broad-based measure of intellectual ability" (WJ-R Tests of Cognitive Ability examiner's manual, p. 25) and consists of the seven subtest scores from the standard scale. The extended scale Broad Cognitive Ability score may be obtained from the 14 subtests of the standard and extended scales. In addition to the Horn-Cattell abilities, the cognitive subtests may be grouped to form four scholastic aptitude clusters: Reading, Mathematics, Written Language, and Knowledge. These clusters are recommended for use in determining aptitude/achievement discrepancies. The aptitude clusters may be used to predict achievement. For instance, four cognitive subtests (Memory for Sentences, Visual Matching, Sound Blending, Oral Vocabulary) are weighted to obtain a Reading Aptitude score. It should be noted the aptitude clusters correlate with their representative achievement domains in the .70s. Two more clusters may also be generated from combinations of the cognitive subtests: Oral Language and Oral Language Aptitude. The subtests that compose the Oral Language cluster include tasks associated with receptive language (listening comprehension) and mixed receptive and expressive language tasks. The Oral Language Aptitude cluster includes nonlanguage tasks, and may be used as a measure of nonverbal ability.

Multiple figures are included in the examiner's manual to assist the examiner in conceptualizing the skills assessed by the various subtests. The tables have the skills arranged on continua, delineating less to more complex tasks. The figure that describes the Writing subtest will illustrate this point. At the bottom of the figure is the less complex motoric output component of producing legible handwriting; next is writing production of isolated units as in spelling single words; and at the highest level is connected discourse such as recognizing usage errors in text and at a higher level in producing writing samples. These figures may assist the examiner conceptualize and interpret an individual's results.

To say there are many options when selecting derived scores would be an understatement. The options include: age equivalents, grade equivalents, Relative Mastery Indices (which was labeled the Relative Performance Index, RPI, on the 1977 version of the Woodcock-Johnson), percentile ranks, extended percentile ranks, standard scores, and extended standard scores. Woodcock and Mather (the examiner's manuals authors) appropriately caution the user not to calculate all the possible scores. Rather they recommend the user recognize the strengths and weaknesses of the various scores and select the scores that have the greatest likelihood of effectively communicating the individual's test results. To this end there is a lucid discussion of the advantages and disadvantages of the various derived scores included in the section of the manuals on test interpretation.

Unlike other batteries, the authors of the Woodcock-Johnson have incorporated tables for evaluating an individual's aptitude/achievement discrepancy. Although authors of other cognitive measures (Stanford-Binet Intelligence Scale, Fourth Revision; 10:342; Wechsler Intelligence Scale for Children, Third Edition, 412) suggest their measure is appropriate for assessing children with learning disabilities, no specific guidelines are provided or referenced.

CONCLUSION. The WJ-R Battery represents a significant contribution to norm-referenced psychoeducational assessment. The test authors selected a factor analytic model on cognitive functioning with an impressive empirical foundation. The Horn-Cattell model served as the framework for constructing the WJ-R Tests of Cognitive Ability. The data from the standardization sample provided evidence for the fidelity of the WJ-R with the Horn-Cattell model. Likewise, the inclusion of supplemental tests is a positive feature of the battery.

The Woodcock-Johnson Tests of Achievement are unlike most available achievement measures for two reasons. First, the results of a single subtest are not used to estimate skills in a broad domain. For example, the Wide Range Achievement Test—Revised (10:389) has a single subtest, "Reading," that involves only letter and word recognition. In contrast, the Woodcock-Johnson Reading cluster is based on letter-word recognition and on a modified cloze approach to reading comprehension. Second, the Woodcock-Johnson differs from other survey measures of achievement in that supplemental subtests are available. For example, if an examiner administers the two standard reading subtests and wishes to learn more about the individual's reading skills, a word attack subtest and a reading vocabulary subtest may be used. There are a total of five supplemental subtests for the domains of reading, mathematics, and written language.

In conclusion, the WJ-R merits the attention of all who are engaged in norm-referenced psychoeducational assessment. The standardization sample is representative. The cognitive portion of the battery is based on a theoretically sound model of intellectual functioning. The achievement section of the battery is designed to assess multiple facets of important academic skills. And finally, ample research has been conducted on the 1977 and new revised version of the battery.

REVIEWER'S REFERENCES

Horn, J. L., & Cattell, R. B. (1966). Refinement and test of the theory of fluid and crystallized intelligence. *Journal of Educational Psychology*, *57*, 253-270.

Horn, J. L. (1976). Human abilities: A review of research and theory in the early 1970s. *Annual Review of Psychology*, *27*, 437-485.

Woodcock, R. W., & Johnson, M. B. (1977). Woodcock-Johnson Psycho-Educational Battery. Allen, TX: DLM Teaching Resources.

Cummings, J. A., & Moscato, E. M. (1984a). Research on the Woodcock-Johnson Psycho-Educational Battery: Implications for practice and future investigations. *School Psychology Review*, *13*, 33-40.

Cummings, J. A., & Moscato, E. M. (1984b). Reply to Thompson and Brassard. *School Psychology Review*, *13*, 45-48.

Thompson, P. L., & Brassard, M. R. (1984). Cummings and Moscato soft on Woodcock-Johnson. *School Psychology Review*, *13*, 41-44.

Woodcock, R. W. (1984). A response to some questions raised about the Woodcock-Johnson I. The mean score discrepancy issue. *School Psychology Review*, *13*, 342-354.

Horn, J. L. (1985). Remodeling old models of intelligence. In B. B. Wolman (Ed.), *Handbook of intelligence* (pp. 267-300). New York: John Wiley & Sons.

Horn, J. L. (1988). Cognitive diversity: A framework of learning. In P. L. Ackerman, R. J. Sternberg, & R. Glaser (Eds.), *Learning and individual differences* (pp. 61-116). New York: W. H. Freeman.

Review of the Woodcock-Johnson Psycho-Educational Battery—Revised by STEVEN W. LEE, Associate Professor of Educational Psychology and Research, University of Kansas, Lawrence, KS, and ELAINE FLORY STEFANY, Certified School Psychologist, Lyons, KS:

The Woodcock-Johnson Psycho-Educational Battery—Revised (WJ-R) is a comprehensive measure of abilities and achievement spanning broad age ranges. The revised edition was normed on 6,359 subjects and represents a significant revision and expansion of the 1977 edition. The norming procedures are excellent and include the following randomly stratified variables: census region, community size, sex, race, origin, funding of college/university, type of college/university, education of adults, occupational status of adults, and occupation of adults in the labor force. Studies are cited which support the appropriateness of the WJ-R for special groups including learning disabled, mentally retarded, and gifted.

The authors state the test development measurement procedures are designed to ensure high technical quality and the *Standards for Educational and Psychological Testing* (American Educational Research Association, American Psychological Association, & National Council on Measurement in Education, 1985) were taken into account in developing the instrument. A review of the manuals supports this assertion.

Extensive information is provided in the test manuals. A spiral-bound examiner's manual and an additional book of norms tables accompany each of the two main sections, that is a measure of abilities (WJ-R COG) and a measure of achievement (WJ-R ACH). The examiner's manuals describe the underlying theory, test development, administration and scoring, interpretation, and reliability and validity studies. A 350-page technical manual covers both test sections and includes an appendix with additional supporting data and bibliographies.

The technical manual includes a section on theories of intelligence, with emphasis upon the Horn-Cattell Gf-Gc (fluid and crystallized abilities) theory of intellectual processing on which the WJ-R COG is based. Factor analytic support is provided for seven broad intellectual abilities, including Long-Term Retrieval, Short-Term Memory, Processing Speed, Auditory Processing, Visual Processing, Comprehension-Knowledge, and Fluid Reasoning. Evidence is provided that two of the cognitive subtests measure each of the seven broad abilities.

Detailed instructions for administration, including practice exercises and cautions, are given in the manuals. Specific wording for each item is color-coded on the reverse side of each page of the flip easel as it is shown to the subject. Some COG subtests are administered on audiotape to insure uniformity of presentation.

The authors describe the instrument as a tool kit intended for use in selective diagnostic testing. Each of the two main sections includes a standard and a supplemental battery bound in separate easels. Two forms of the achievement test (A and B) allow for more frequent retesting. However, no data regarding

Form A and B equivalence are cited in the manual. Detailed statistics are given for finding significant discrepancies, both within the cognitive and achievement sections as well as ability/achievement discrepancies. The norming of the COG and ACH sections on the same sample reduces measurement error in finding discrepancies.

Subtest reliabilities are very good. Split-half procedures corrected for test length were used for all except the three timed subtests, on which test-retest correlations were used. Reliability coefficients are reported for all COG and ACH standard and supplementary subtests across age ranges. Forty-nine of the 55 median reliabilities reported are at the .80 level or higher. Standard errors of measurement are reported with reliabilities.

Many validity studies covering wide age ranges from preschool to adulthood are cited. These studies provide a broad variety of content, criterion-related, and construct validity evidence supporting the WJ-R. Besides the typical criterion-related validity information, extensive evidence is provided from confirmatory factor analytic studies.

A range of interpretative information is available for each subtest and cluster of subtests. The manual outlines the types of scores available with their levels of interpretation. After obtaining the raw score, grade and age level equivalents are available on the test blank without resorting to the norms tables. Also available on the test page is the W score, or Rasch Ability Score. Criterion-referenced statistics available in the norms tables include Rasch Difference Scores, Relative Mastery Indexes, Developmental Level Band (WJ-R COG), and Instructional Ranges (WJ-R ACH). Norm-referenced statistics available include standard scores with a mean of 100 and standard deviation of 15, *T*-scores, NCEs, standard score discrepancies, and percentile ranks with discrepancies.

Overall, the WJ-R represents an outstanding contribution to the field of cognitive and achievement testing. Psychometric properties are exceptional. Some of its most notable advantages include the solid grounding in theory, the broad age range, the norming of the cognitive and achievement sections on the same sample to provide for more reliable comparisons, the usefulness for selective diagnostic assessment, and the broad variety of statistical data that may be obtained.

Any disadvantages of the WJ-R are fundamentally practical rather than technical. In order to be used effectively, the test necessitates a reorientation in philosophy and practice for evaluators and consumers accustomed to global measures of cognitive ability. Careful study and practice are essential before using the instrument. Otherwise, examiners might develop a routine subtest battery and fail to utilize its rich diagnostic potential. Because of the large amount of test materials (four stand-up easel books plus manuals), itinerant evaluators may find it a challenge to have appropriate sections of the test available for diagnostic testing when needed. Computer scoring is recommended, as hand scoring may become tedious and prone to error because of the large number of norms tables. Also, without computer scoring there may be a tendency for evaluators to obtain only the age and grade equivalent scores on the test form instead of taking advantage of the various statistics available.

Nevertheless, the advantages of the WJ-R far outweigh any disadvantages. The instrument represents a significant advancement in the field of cognitive and achievement testing, and it is this reviewer's hope that it will receive the attention and use that it deserves.

REVIEWER'S REFERENCE

American Educational Research Association, American Psychological Association, & National Council on Measurement in Education. (1985). *Standards for educational and psychological testing*. Washington, DC: American Psychological Association, Inc.

[416]

Woodcock Language Proficiency Battery—Revised.

Purpose: Intended to measure abilities and achievement in oral language, reading, and written language as well as English language competence.
Population: Ages 2–90+.
Publication Dates: 1980–91.
Acronym: WLPB-R.
Scores, 25: Oral Language (Memory for Sentences, Picture Vocabulary, Oral Vocabulary, Listening Comprehension, Verbal Analogies), Reading (Letter-Word Identification, Passage Comprehension, Work Attack, Reading Vocabulary), Written Language (Dictation, Writing Samples, Proofing, Writing Fluency), Punctuation and Capitalization, Spelling, Usage, Handwriting, Oral Language, Broad Reading, Basic Reading Skills, Reading Comprehension, Broad Written Language, Basic Writing Skills, Written Expression, Broad English Ability.
Administration: Individual.
Price Data, 1992: $204 per complete test including test book, audio cassette, 25 response booklets, 25 test records, examiner's manual ('91, 219 pages), and norm tables (258 pages); $29 per 25 response booklets and 25 test records.
Foreign Language Edition: Spanish edition available.
Time: (20–60) minutes.
Comments: Battery is a subset of the tests included in the Woodcock-Johnson Psycho-Educational Battery—Revised (415).
Author: Richard W. Woodcock.
Publisher: The Riverside Publishing Co.
Cross References: See T4:2974 (1 reference); for reviews by Ruth Noyce and Michelle Quinn, see 9:1388.

TEST REFERENCES

1. Johnson, J., & Pascual-Leone, J. (1989). Developmental levels of processing in metaphor interpretation. *Journal of Experimental Child Psychology*, *48*, 1-31.

2. Slavin, R. E., Madden, N. A., Kurweit, N. L., Livermon, B. J., & Dolan, L. (1990). Success for all: First-year outcomes of a comprehensive plan for reforming urban education. *American Educational Research Journal*, *27*, 255-278.

3. Hayes, S. C., & Farnill, D. (1992). A study of the concurrent validity of the Screening Test of Adolescent Language with recent immigrants. *Psychological Reports*, 71, 175-178.

Review of the Woodcock Language Proficiency Battery—Revised by IRVIN J. LEHMANN, Professor of Measurement, Michigan State University, East Lansing, MI:

It should be noted at the outset that this reviewer is a psychometrician rather than a reading specialist. Accordingly, this evaluation of the Woodcock Language Proficiency Battery—Revised (WLPB-R) will focus more upon psychometric issues than on the measurement of language proficiency, per se. I will focus my evaluation on technical issues of validity, reliability, norms, etc., rather than commenting on such areas as the weakness of the language development section because of its lack of attention to eye-hand coordination.

The WLPB-R maintains, in some instances surpasses, the excellence of the original edition. Both editions are wide-range in that they are designed for children as young as 2 years to adults 90+ years of age. Both tests are individually administered and assess oral language, written language, and reading proficiency; the first edition with 8 subtests, the revised edition with 13 subtests. There are 5 new subtests: 2 each are in Written Language and Oral Language and 1 in Reading. The subtests designed to measure Oral Language skill are Picture Vocabulary, Listening Comprehension, Memory for Sentences, Oral Vocabulary, and Verbal Analogies. Reading skill is assessed by Word Attack, Reading Vocabulary, Passage Comprehension, and Letter-Word Identification. Written Language is measured by Dictation, Writing Samples, Proofing, and Writing Fluency. Supplementing these 13 subtests are 4 additional subtests: Punctuation and Capitalization, Spelling, Usage, and Handwriting. Added to the original clusters—Oral Language, Broad Reading, Basic Reading Skills, Reading Comprehension, Broad Written Language, Basic Writing Skills, and Written Expression—are two new ones—Broad English Ability: Early Development and Broad English Ability: Standard Scale. Finally, an intra-English discrepancy analysis procedure has been added to identify subjects with "specific deficits in English language competence" (p. 82).

Woodcock claims the WLPB-R can be used for diagnosis, determining intra-English discrepancies, program placement, planning individual programs, guidance, assessing growth, program evaluation, research, and psychometric training. I am somewhat leery about the validity of the WLPB-R for this cornucopia of uses, and especially for psychometric training. I would be remiss, however, if I did not compliment Woodcock who was very careful not to leave the impression the training manual was a substitute for additional psychometric training. Woodcock said only that the battery is "an ideal instrument for training . . . experience with the WLPB-R provides a solid foundation for learning to administer and interpret other tests" (p. 7).

The examiner's manual of 230+ pages is a model of thoroughness and resembles a textbook in its detailed discussion of the test's development, administration, and scoring; how to interpret the scores; the test's psychometric characteristics; and how to train the examiner.

The WLPB-R uses an easel test booklet format with the stimuli—be they words or pictures—facing the examinee and the directions facing the examiner. The subject's responses are recorded in the Test Record except for the Writing Samples, Dictation, and Writing Fluency tests. The latter are completed in the Subject Response Booklet.

The Early Development Scale consists of four tests—Memory for Sentences, Picture Vocabulary, Letter-Word Identification, and Dictation; takes about 20 minutes; and is used for preschool children. For other subjects, experienced examiners will take from 20 to 90 minutes to administer all 13 tests. Because the type of language assessment may vary from one subject to another, seldom is it necessary to administer the total battery.

To minimize testing time, basal and ceiling levels have been established for each subtest except for Writing Fluency. Instructions for the Writing Sample indicate the examiner establishes a "starting point," which is based on the examiner's estimate of the subject's ability level. Then basal and ceiling levels are established. These vary from passing or failing four to six consecutive items.

Woodcock notes there may be instances (e.g., subjects with hearing impairments, preschool children, physically handicapped) where the examiner must deviate from standard testing procedures. In those instances, he cautions the user to be aware that such modifications could affect the test results. I would have also liked to see a caution noted that the norms might be invalid.

All tests are administered orally with the exception of the Memory for Sentences and Listening Comprehension, which are presented with a standardized audio-cassette test tape—a novel feature. Examiners are cautioned to use high quality equipment so as not to allow audio distortion to affect examinee performance.

With the exception of the Memory for Sentences and Writing Samples subtests (where a 2, 1, 0 scoring system is used), each correct response receives a score of 1 whereas an incorrect or no response is given a 0. There are special scoring rules for the Punctuation and Capitalization, Spelling, Usage, and Handwriting scales. Scoring can be completed during test administration except for Writing Samples.

Woodcock is to be complimented for cautioning users to be cognizant of the many factors that should be considered in interpreting a subject's performance. He also states that only qualified individuals should make interpretations and decisions. I hope the test publisher has established criteria governing who is qualified to purchase the test.

NORMING. The standardization sample was quite thorough. Normative data were collected from a stratified random sample of 6,359 subjects in over 100 American cities. The preschool sample consisted of 705 subjects 2–5 years old and *not* enrolled in kindergarten; the K–12th grade sample consisted of 3,245 subjects; the college/university sample involved 916 subjects; and the adult-non-school sample was 1,493 subjects 14 to 90+ years old. The sample was balanced according to sex, race, occupation, geographic location, occupational status of adults, type of college (public vs. private), education of adults, race (Hispanic/non-Hispanic), and type of community. Data were gathered over approximately 2 years.

An interesting feature of the test's norms—grade and age equivalents, percentile ranks, and standard scores—is that they are continuous rather than interpolated on the basis of data gathered in the fall and spring. The latter procedure assumes that for the percentile ranks and standard scores there is no change for the reference group's average score from the beginning to end of the interval. Special college/university norms are also provided.

TYPES OF SCORES. Raw scores can be converted to age and grade equivalents, percentile ranks, standard scores, and relative mastery indexes. In addition, extended age, extended grade, and extended percentile rank scales are available. W scores "which are a special transformation of the Rasch ability scale" (p. 59) can be calculated and used to compute cluster scores.

Although the calculation of the various scores initially looms as a formidable nightmare, very detailed instructions and examples are provided. With a little training (and Woodcock stresses that examiners be thoroughly trained not only for administering the battery but especially for scoring and interpretation of the score) any immediate fear and concern should be quickly alleviated.

RELIABILITY. Except for the Writing Fluency and Handwriting tests and for the P (Punctuation and Capitalization), S (Spelling), and U (Usage) scales, corrected split-half, internal consistency reliability coefficients, and standard errors of measurement are reported. On the whole, they are in the high .80s and low .90s for the tests and in the mid .90s for the clusters. The median *SEM*s for the tests are in the 5s and 6s and in the 3s for the clusters. Test-retest correlations were computed for the Writing Fluency test, and ranged from .60–.87. Alternate form reliabilities using four small samples were computed for the Handwriting scale and ranged from .72–.78.

Interrater reliability estimates for the three writing tests—Writing Sample, Writing Fluency, and Handwriting– showed median correlations of .95–.98 for the Writing Fluency scale; and .71–.85 for the Handwriting scale. I agree with Woodcock that "wherever possible, the Handwriting measure be jointly scored by two raters" (p. 96). In fact, if/when only one rating is possible, extreme caution should be exercised for the Handwriting scale.

The table dealing with test-retest reliability is, to say the least, very confusing in that it attempts to digest material contained in another report as well as presenting data that appear to have little relevance to the potential test user. Without having some graduate work in measurement, interpretation is essentially meaningless. I strongly suggest that in a future revision of the manual this table should only contain data that are actually relevant.

VALIDITY. Content, construct, and concurrent validity were stressed and empirical data were presented to support the latter two. This is a marked improvement from the original battery where "no validity data are actually presented" (Quinn, 1985). However, the manual is lacking in information as to the procedure used to study content validity.

A variety of established tests were used as criterion measures to establish the concurrent validity of the WLPB-R. Regretfully, the samples used were very small (less than 100). I would be remiss if I did not compliment Woodcock for drawing the user's attention to the above average restricted range of the 3rd/4th and 10th/11th grade samples noting that generalizations to a more representative population should be made with caution. Not only that, but even with this caveat, the very low intercorrelations could not be increased to a respectable range. Other studies for the Writing and Written Language tests shared the same deficiencies of very small samples.

I question the construct validity evidence presented. If the older definition of this term is used, the WLPB-R would have to show that a group of judges verified that the test items did do what they are designed to do. And, if one accepts the more recent definition of the term, evidence would have to be presented where criterion data are gathered. Intercorrelations of the WLPB-R subtests and clusters suggests an attempt to demonstrate the test, whatever it may be, has subtests that are measuring different behaviors. In a sense, such an approach may be more related to internal consistency vis-a-vis homogeneity of items than to construct validity.

In conclusion, the WLPB-R accomplishes what it sets out to do, that is, measure a subject's language proficiency skills. It does so with an instrument that provides the user with much information about a subject's strengths and weaknesses. Item quality is good and reproduction (both pictorial and written) is exemplary. Although I would like to see additional validity and reliability information, I recommend this battery with few reservations.

REVIEWER'S REFERENCE

Quinn, M. (1985). [Review of the Woodcock Language Proficiency Battery]. In J. V. Mitchell, Jr. (Ed.), *The ninth mental measurements yearbook* (p. 1767). Lincoln, NE: Buros Institute of Mental Measurements.

Review of the Woodcock Language Proficiency Battery—Revised by G. MICHAEL POTEAT, Associate Professor of Psychology, East Carolina University, Greenville, NC:

The Woodcock Language Proficiency Battery—Revised (WLPB-R) is a subset of the Woodcock-Johnson Psycho-Educational Battery—Revised (Woodcock & Johnson, 1989; 415) and a revision of the Woodcock Language Proficiency Battery. The revised version of the WLPB includes five new tests (two each of Oral and Written Language, and one of Reading) and two new clusters (Broad English Ability-Early Development and Broad English Ability-Standard Scale). The norms have also been extended to cover ages from 24 months to 90 years. Separate norms are also available for university students. The WLPB-R is described by the authors as "a comprehensive set of individually administered tests for measuring abilities and achievement in oral language, reading, and written language" (p. 1). The battery provides a measure of overall English language competence and the assessment of strengths and weaknesses among an individual's oral, written, and reading language abilities.

The WLPB-R consists of 13 tests divided into three language areas and four supplemental tests. The Oral Language area consists of Memory for Sentences, Picture Vocabulary, Oral Vocabulary, Listening Comprehension, and Verbal Analogies. Reading comprises four tests: Letter-Word Identification, Passage Comprehension, Word Attack, and Reading Vocabulary. Written Language includes Dictation, Writing Samples, Proofing, and Writing Fluency. Supplemental tests are Punctuation & Capitalization, Spelling, Usage, and Handwriting. The Broad Ability-Early Developmental Scale is based on Memory for Sentences, Picture Vocabulary, Letter-Word Identification, and Dictation. The Broad-Ability-Standard Scale also uses Oral Vocabulary, Listening Comprehension, Verbal Analogies, Passage Comprehension, and Writing Samples. Cluster scores include Oral Language (based on all of the Oral Language tests), Broad Reading Cluster (Letter-Word Identification and Passage Comprehension), Basic Reading Cluster (Letter-Word Identification and Word Attack), Reading Comprehension (Passage Comprehension and Reading Vocabulary), Broad Written Language (Dictation and Writing Samples), Basic Writing Skills (Dictation and Proofing), and Written Expression (Writing Samples and Writing Fluency). All 13 tests are administered by starting at the subject's estimated ability level and obtaining a basal and a ceiling. The examiner may administer the entire battery or select any combination of subtests.

Raw scores are converted to W-scores (a Rasch-type ability score with a score centered on 500), grade equivalents, and age equivalents. Other interpretative data include Relative Mastery Indexes (RMIs) that indicate how well the subject would be expected to perform compared to others in an age or grade comparison group. An RMI of, for example, 70/90 means that the subject is predicted to show 70% success on tasks that others in the comparison group would be expected to complete successfully 90% of the time. Standard scores, with a mean of 100 and a standard deviation of 15, and percentile ranks are also provided. Use of a conversion table provides the option of obtaining *T* scores, stanines, and normal curve equivalents. A variety of interpretative profiles are provided.

The WLPB-R uses normative data obtained from 6,359 subjects in 100 U.S. communities. The preschool sample (2 to 5 years of age and not in kindergarten) included 705 subjects. The kindergarten to 12th grade sample included 3,245 subjects; the college sample has 916 subjects; and the adult nonschool sample was composed of 1,493 subjects. Examination of the normative sampling variables suggests the norms are representative of the U.S. population and can be used with reasonable confidence.

Measures of internal consistency (test reliability data) are provided for all 16 tests and the nine separate clusters. Interrater reliability is presented for the three subtests (Writing Samples, Writing Fluency, and Handwriting) that require more subjective scoring of the responses. Alternate-forms reliability is provided for the Handwriting scale, and test-retest data (based on 504 subjects) are provided for 10 tests and three clusters of the WLPB-R. The profusion of reliability data varies but generally the WLPB-R appears to have satisfactory to excellent reliability.

The content validity of the WLPB-R is reportedly based on both expert opinion and item validity studies. Unfortunately, information on content validity is not adequately summarized in the examiner's manual. Evidence for concurrent criterion-related validity is presented in the form of a series of studies comparing the WLPB-R with a number of different achievement and ability tests. It is difficult to summarize these very diverse data succinctly, but the WLPB-R is positively correlated to measures of language development and ability. A more systematic examination of the relationship between the WLPB-R and language performance in the classroom (using criterion-based assessment) would be a welcome addition. Evidence of construct validity is presented in the form of seven pages of test intercorrelations, five pages of cluster intercorrelations, and four pages of test-cluster intercorrelations. This mass of data is very difficult to interpret and should be supplemented by multivariate data reduction analysis (e.g., factor analysis). Other evidence for the construct validity of the WLPB-R consists of comparisons made between groups of age-matched gifted, normal, learning disabled, and mentally retarded subjects. This developmental analysis shows the expected gain in scores across the four groups.

The administration and scoring of the WLPB-R is covered in elaborate detail. Individuals who have administered other Woodcock-Johnson products will be able to quickly learn the WLPB-R, and any professional with a background in educational or psychological assessment should be able to develop competence in administering the WLPB-R by following the procedures outlined in the examiner's manual. The number of subtests and variety of scores that can be generated is so large, however, that the purchase of the companion computer scoring program is advised.

The use of the WLPB-R as a measure of language competency can be recommended without any major reservation. It is a well-normed, reliable, and comprehensive test with no major faults. More information on the content and criterion-related validity would be welcome, but the scope of the WLPB-R is impressive. Examination of the factor structure should also be done to determine if the subtests are really measuring distinct aspect of language ability, but the groupings are logical. In scope of coverage, the WLPB-R has no rival and should be considered by professionals who want a detailed measure of language achievement.

[417]

Work Environment Scale, Second Edition.

Purpose: Developed to "measure the social environments of different types of work settings."
Population: Employees and supervisors.
Publication Dates: 1974–86.
Acronym: WES.
Scores, 10: Involvement, Peer Cohesion, Supervisor Support, Autonomy, Task Orientation, Work Pressure, Clarity, Control, Innovation, Physical Comfort.
Administration: Group.
Forms, 3: Real (R), Ideal (I), Expectations (E).
Price Data, 1992: $13 per 25 test booklets (Form R); $14 per 25 test booklets (select Form I or E); $10 per 50 answer sheets; $15 per 25 self-scorable answer sheets; $6 per set of scoring stencils; $8 per 50 profiles; $65 per 10 prepaid narratives; $15 per 25 interpretive report forms; $12 per manual ('86, 48 pages); $19 per specimen set.
Time: [15–20] minutes.
Comments: A part of the Social Climate Scales (T4:2495).
Authors: Rudolf H. Moos and Paul N. Insel (tests).
Publisher: Consulting Psychologists Press, Inc.
Cross References: See T4:2989 (19 references); for a review by Rabindra N. Kanungo, see 9:1398 (1 reference); see also T3:2652 (2 references) and 8:713 (3 references). For a review of the Social Climate Scales, see 8:681.

TEST REFERENCES

1. Pierce, C. M. B., & Molloy, G. N. (1990). Relations between school type, occupational stress, role perceptions and social support. *Australian Journal of Education*, *34*, 330-338.
2. Long, B. C. (1993). Coping strategies of male managers: A prospective analysis of predictors of psychosomatic symptoms and job satisfaction. *Journal of Vocational Behavior*, *42*, 184-199.
3. Amabile, T. M., Hill, K. G., Hennessey, B. A., & Tighe, E. M. (1994). The Work Performance Inventory: Assessing intrinsic and extrinsic motivational orientations. *Journal of Personality and Social Psychology*, *66*, 950-967.
4. Grimm-Thomas, K., & Perry-Jenkins, M. (1994). All in a day's work: Job experiences, self-esteem, and fathering in working-class families. *Family Relations*, *43*, 174-181.
5. Hershberger, S. L., Lichtenstein, P., & Knox, S. S. (1994). Genetic and environmental influences on perceptions of organizational climate. *Journal of Applied Psychology*, *79*, 24-33.
6. Wooten, K. C., Barner, B. O., & Silver, N. C. (1994). The influence of cognitive style upon work environment preferences. *Perceptual and Motor Skills*, *79*, 307-314.

Review of the Work Environment Scale, Second Edition by RALPH O. MUELLER, Associate Professor of Educational Research, Department of Educational Leadership, The George Washington University, Washington, DC:

The Work Environment Scale, Second Edition (WES)—part of the Social Climate Scales (T4:2495; see Moos, 1974)—was designed as a norm-referenced forced-choice instrument to "describe or contrast the social environments of work settings, to compare employee and manager perceptions, to compare actual and preferred work environments, and to assess and facilitate change in work settings. Various subgroups of employees or staff members also may be compared with one another" (manual, p. 12). Each of three forms of the WES (Form R: Real; Form I: Ideal; Form E: Expectations) consists of 90 true-false items, grouped into 10 subscales, and designed to assess three underlying domains of the work environment (Relationship, Personal Growth, and System Maintenance and System Change). Items on Form R of the WES ask for employees' opinions about their current or *real* work setting. Form I contains reworded Form R items to assess employees' thoughts and feelings regarding the *ideal* work setting, and items on Form E solicit respondents' *expectations* of future employment.

The accompanying manual contains brief discussions of most topics that should be of importance to potential users although its organization is somewhat unconventional (e.g., initial evidence of the validity and reliability of the instrument [reviewed below] is dispersed throughout the manual rather than presented in a single chapter). Chapter 1 contains some general information on the development of Form R of the WES including a brief discussion on how the 90 true-false items were chosen to compose the 10 subscales and how the latter relate to the three underlying dimensions. In chapter 2, a description of the norming sample (reviewed below) and some evidence of the validity/reliability of Form R is presented. Forms E and I of the WES are introduced in chapter 3. The usual instructions for the administration and scoring of the instrument are given in chapter 4.

Finally, instructive examples of interpretations of WES profiles based on actual data and an overview of the existing literature on practical and research application are given in chapters 5 and 6.

NORMING. A table of norms for Form R of the WES (based on San Francisco, CA employees from a general work group [*n* = 1,442] and a health-care work group [*n* = 1,607]) is provided in an appendix of the manual. Based on information given in the test booklet, a technical evaluation of the norming data and procedures was difficult because no information was given on the year of data collection and the sex, race, age, and socioeconomic status of participants. In the opinion of this reviewer, *these omissions constitute a serious violation of Primary Standard 4.4 in Standards for Educational and Psychological Testing* (American Educational Research Association, American Psychological Association, & National Council on Measurement in Education, 1985, p. 33) *and might impede valid interpretations of WES results across one or more of the commonly cited socio-demographic factors.*

The test author acknowledged that norms available for Forms E and I of the WES (table of group means and standard deviations) are preliminary because they were based on relatively small "general and health-care work groups" (p. 9; *n* = 81 and *n* = 348, respectively). No further description of the samples was provided.

VALIDITY AND RELIABILITY. Specific evidence on the validity of the WES is not provided in the manual (one study was reviewed briefly in chapter 6 that seems to have investigated the criterion-related validity of the instrument, not the content and construct validity, as the title of the subsection suggests). The test author cited a factor analysis of Forms E and R of the WES (Booth, Norton, Webster, & Berry, 1976) that seemed to support only 5 of the 10 subscales. However, a table of Form R subscale intercorrelations (*n* = 1,045; range between a magnitude of.03 and .54) could be interpreted by the reader as initial evidence of the construct validity of that form of the WES (subscale intercorrelations for Forms E and I were reported to be similar to those for Form R but no specific data were provided in the manual). *The omission of specific data regarding the validity of the instrument is in serious violation of Standards 1.1, 1.2, and 1.5 among others* (AERA, APA, & NCME, 1995, pp. 13–14): Global and potentially far-reaching claims such as "Form I may be used by itself to assess the value orientations or the value changes in a work setting over time .... [Form E] can be useful in employment counseling to clarify prospective employees' or managers' expectations of a new work situation" (p. 9) should be interpreted with caution because no specific evidence of their validity is provided.

Evidence of the reliability of Form R of the WES consists of Cronbach's alpha coefficients ranging from .69 to .86 (*n* = 1,045), 1-month test-retest correlations between .69 and .83 (*n* = 75), and 12-month test-retest coefficients ranging from .51 to .63 (*n* = 245). The test author reported "generally similar" (p. 9) internal consistency results for Forms E and I; again, no numerical data were provided to support that claim.

SUMMARY. This reviewer agrees with the authors of the *Standards* that "Validity is the most important consideration in test evaluation" (AERA, APA, & NCME, 1985, p. 9). The unavailability of specific data on the validity and norming of the WES in this second edition of the test manual made a technical evaluation difficult, if not impossible. The development and past use of the WES seems to be documented in literature from the late 1970s to the mid 1980s. Whether or not that body of literature contains detailed information regarding the psychometric properties of the instrument is unknown to the reviewer. Before using any of the three forms of the WES, the reader might want to consult some of the relevant studies cited in the manual to gain more insight into the instrument's development and its validity and reliability than can be gained from the current version of the test booklet.

REVIEWER'S REFERENCES

Moos, R. (1974). *The Social Climate Scales: An overview.* Palo Alto, CA: Consulting Psychologists Press.

Booth, R. F., Norton, R. S., Webster, E. G., & Berry, N. H. (1976). Assessing the psychosocial characteristics of occupational training environments. *Journal of Occupational Psychology, 49,* 85-92.

American Educational Research Association, American Psychological Association, & National Council on Measurement in Education. (1985). *Standards for educational and psychological testing.* Washington, DC: American Psychological Association, Inc.

Review of the Work Environment Scale, Second Edition by EUGENE P. SHEEHAN, *Associate Professor of Psychology, University of Northern Colorado, Greeley, CO:*

Over the last two decades there has been much interest in the topics of organizational culture and climate. Some of this interest involved an attempt to improve productivity. This interest also arose from a desire to provide employees with a work environment that meets their needs. The Work Environment Scale (WES) is designed to provide a measure of individuals' perceptions of their work milieu.

There are three forms of the WES. Form R (Real) measures perceptions of existing work environments. Forms I (Ideal) and E (Expectations) are special forms developed from Form R. Form I measures workers' perceptions of ideal work situations, whereas Form E assesses perceptions about future work environments. Items and instructions from Form R were reworded so that respondents could answer in terms of ideal or expected work environments. The manual contains psychometric information on Form R. The information provided on the special forms is limited and inadequate. Administration and scoring procedures for the three forms are clear and easy to follow.

The 90 true-false items on the WES are divided equally among 10 subscales. Each subscale purportedly assesses a different dimension of the work environment. The 10 subscales are organized under three broad domains. The Relationship domain includes the Involvement, Peer Cohesion, and Supervisor Support subscales. Autonomy, Task Orientation, and Work Pressure subscales comprise the Personal Growth domain. Clarity, Control, Innovation, and Physical Comfort subscales measure the System Maintenance and System Change domain.

The instrument was developed using large heterogeneous samples. Item writing and item selection criteria were appropriate. The manual authors provide normative data in the form of means, standard deviations, and tables for the conversion of raw scores to standard scores for each scale. These normative data are based on two different samples: a health-care work group (N = 1,607) and employees from a general work setting (N = 1,442). Although the health-care work group is adequately described, it would be helpful if the manual described the occupational backgrounds of the general work group in more detail.

The manual contains some useful psychometric data on the subscales. Both the internal consistency reliabilities and the test-retest reliabilities are adequate. The reliabilities range from .69 (Peer Cohesion) to .86 (Innovation). One- and 12-month test-retest reliabilities range from .69 to .83 and .51 to .63 respectively. The 1-month reliability is based on a small sample (N = 75). Future measures of reliability should be based on a larger population. Stability coefficients for the total profile, measured over a 12-month period, are also adequate, averaging .61.

Despite such promising psychometric data, the organization of the subscales into the three domains has neither solid theoretical nor solid empirical support. For example, at a theoretical level, the Involvement subscale does not appear to fit in the Relationship domain. Similarly, the Work Pressure subscale seems more related to the System Maintenance and System Change domain than the Personal Growth domain. It could also be argued that the Clarity subscale could be placed in the Personal Growth domain. Another example of the theoretical confusion occurs at a more general level where the manual authors state the WES measures the social environments of work settings. As can be seen from the subscale titles, the WES measures physical components of work in addition to social aspects.

The manual contains a matrix of Form R subscale intercorrelations. (A factor analysis of the relationship between the subscales would be more appropriate and more helpful.) This matrix supports the already noted theoretical ambiguity. The correlation matrix does not provide strong empirical support for the organization of the subscales into the three domains. For example, although the three subscales of the Relationship domain have intercorrelations ranging from .47 to .53, some of these subscales are correlated at equal or higher levels with subscales from the other two domains. The highest correlation in the matrix (.54) is between the Involvement and Task Orientation subscales from the Relationship and Personal Growth domains respectively. A similar observation can be made concerning correlations between subscales on the Personal Growth and System Maintenance and System Change domains. For example, the Innovation subscale has higher correlations with five subscales from the Relationship and Personal Growth domains than it does with the subscales from the System Maintenance and System Change domain with which it is supposedly most highly related. Thus, the organization of the WES needs to be reviewed at both theoretical and empirical levels.

The manual contains samples of clinical and consulting uses to which the WES can be put. These include comparing and interpreting the profiles of different work groups and work settings, including the real, expected, and ideal. Other applications include the provision of feedback, monitoring change, and promoting improvement. Also included in the manual are summaries of the research studies in which the WES has been used. Although these studies were not intended to provide information on construct validity, they do provide some evidence that the WES measures aspects of the work environment.

In summary, the WES provides an interesting way to measure employees' perceptions of their work environment. The instrument can be put to several uses. It has adequate internal consistency and test-retest reliability. However, problems pertaining to the organization of the subscales into the three domains suggest that conclusions drawn from use of the instrument may be ambiguous.

[418]

Work Skills Series Production.

Purpose: Designed to measure the ability to understand instructions, work with numbers, and accurately check machine settings visually.
Population: Manufacturing and production employees and prospective employees.
Publication Date: 1990.
Acronym: WSS.
Scores: Total score only for each of 3 tests: Understanding Instructions (VWP1), Working with Numbers (NWP2), Visual Checking (CWP3).
Administration: Individual or group.
Price Data, 1991: \$75 per administration set; \$19 per reusable test booklet; \$20 per hand-scoring key (specify test); \$5 per answer sheet; \$6.50 per bureau-scored answer sheet; \$5 per 25 test logs; \$8.50 per 10 practice leaflets; \$6 per administration cards (specify test); \$30 per manual (68 pages); \$50 per optic-scan capability file per test; \$30 per specimen set; scoring service offered by publisher.

Time: 12 minutes for VWP1; 10 minutes for NWP2; 7 minutes for CWP3; 29(40) minutes for complete battery.
Author: Saville & Holdsworth Ltd.
Publisher: Saville & Holdsworth Ltd.

Review of the Work Skills Series Production by BRIAN BOLTON, University Professor, Arkansas Research and Training Center in Vocational Rehabilitation, University of Arkansas, Fayetteville, AR:

The Work Skills Series Production (WSS) was developed for use in the selection of personnel for jobs in manufacturing and industrial production. The strength of the WSS would appear to be the relevance of the test content to manufacturing and production jobs. Unfortunately, the manual does not include a description of the test development process, beyond stating that standard job analysis, item generation, and item analysis procedures were involved.

The WSS consists of three paper-and-pencil tests, Understanding Instructions, Working with Numbers, and Visual Checking. All test items use a multiple-choice response format, which makes for easy hand scoring, although machine scoring is also available. Total testing time required is about 40 minutes, including instructions and practice items (actual testing time is 29 minutes). All three tests are speeded.

Because an innovative feature of the WSS is the claimed job relevance of the test tasks, these are briefly described for the three tests. Understanding Instructions consists of 13 short paragraphs of written instructions or job information, each followed by three questions. Working with Numbers contains three sections, each with 12 questions about addition and subtraction, multiplication and division, and combinations of two arithmetic operations. The tasks deal with stock levels and rates of usage for various industrial parts. Visual Checking requires identification of switch settings using a set of color-coded rules. The 30 items include three-, four-, and five-component switches, all using three colors.

Total raw scores for each of the WSS tests may be converted to sten scores or percentile equivalents using seven norm tables. Several of the normative samples are small and no demographic information is provided for any of the norm groups. Although statistical comparisons are not given, it appears that the seven groups represent just two different levels of WSS performance. Finally, only three of the conversion tables contain norm data for Visual Checking, and these were based on a preliminary version of the test.

Internal consistency coefficients for the three WSS tests range from .91 to .93. These figures suggest the total scores are substantially reliable, but the content homogeneity of the tests (i.e., all items are of the same type) renders the interpretation ambiguous. In situations like this, there is no substitute for test-retest reliability studies. It would also be helpful to know the intercorrelations among the tests, so that their independent contributions to personnel selection could be appreciated.

Four carefully reported WSS validity studies using supervisor performance ratings as criteria are summarized in the manual. Concurrent and predictive investigations of employees in food processing, automobile assembly, and textile production provided very little evidence supportive of the WSS. Only a few (six at most) of the performance criteria (which numbered from 10 to 29 in the four studies) were significantly correlated with the WSS tests, and some of these significant correlations were obtained only for subsamples of low-scoring workers. It must be concluded that the data are at best suggestive of the selection potential of Understanding Instructions and Working with Numbers. Visual Checking was included in just one study.

SUMMARY. The Work Skills Series Production may have promise as a selection battery for manufacturing and industrial production jobs, but the technical data to support its utility are not presented. No information is provided on the development of the tests, the norms are inadequate, reliability data are absent, and validity has not been demonstrated for the intended purpose. The WSS does include some commendable features, such as job-relevant test content, practice exercises to establish facility with the test tasks, and administration cards to enhance test standardization. However, the publisher's claim that "the WSS has been found to be a reliable and valid predictor of performance in manufacturing and production jobs" (manual, p. 42) is simply not true. In my opinion the WSS is not ready for use in personnel selection until additional research documentation is provided.

Review of the Work Skills Series Production by WAYNE J. CAMARA, Director of Scientific Affairs, American Psychological Association, Washington, DC:

The Work Skills Series (WSS) for Production was developed in 1990 and is designed to measure skills required by individuals working in production and manufacturing positions. Its principal use would be in the employment screening of entry-level workers in production and manufacturing positions who have limited formal education. The instrument comprises three separate measures of the following skills:

> Understanding Instructions: The ability to read and understand simple, written messages and carry out simple, written instructions.
>
> Working with Numbers: The ability to make simple calculations quickly and accurately.
>
> Visual Checking: The ability to check a machine visually to make sure settings are accurate and changes are being made properly. (manual, p. 2)

Each of these tests is scored separately and there is no provision given in the testing materials for combining tests to derive a total score. Separate testing booklets and machine- or hand-scorable answer sheets are provided for each test. The tests are each speeded and use a multiple-choice format.

Understanding Instructions contains 39 items, which should be completed in 12 minutes. Thirteen separate passages describing organizational policies (e.g., fire alarm, reporting faulty equipment) or job procedures (e.g., use of a telephone for internal and outside calls) are presented in the format of a memo. Three multiple-choice items follow each passage. The content of the passages is sufficiently broad to have relevance across a wide variety of production and manufacturing positions. Although items and passages are presented on the same page, the speededness of this test would preclude applicants from routinely rereading passages and implies that more than simple comprehension of written instructions is required for exemplary performance. It is likely that reading comprehension, short-term memory, and general intelligence are highly related to performance.

Working With Numbers contains 36 items that must be completed in 10 minutes. All items use the same format, which requires simple calculations (+, -, X, /) involving use and inventory of equipment parts. "Candidates are presented with numerical information concerning stock levels and rates of usage of various hypothetical components" (manual, p. 9). Candidates then select the correct response from five available options. Although the basic mathematical computations may generalize across a wide variety of production and manufacturing positions, the item format is much more relevant to individuals who maintain inventories or are required to account for work materials on a daily basis. In addition to measuring arithmetic calculations, this test requires candidates to demonstrate reasoning ability.

Visual Checking contains 30 items that must be completed in 7 minutes. It requires candidates to attend to two factors (color of lights and the numeric value above the lights) and select the appropriate visual code that is said to represent the settings of equipment. A series of 3, 4, or 5 colored lights with a number above are presented in each item. Candidates must quickly inspect the color and number of each light, code and distinguish this information from that associated with other lights, find the corresponding symbol in an accompanying table, and carry this information long enough to recognize the same symbol in the item. Unfortunately, this paper-and-pencil task lacks the physical and psychological fidelity required to establish the desired relevance to equipment settings for machinery. This task goes beyond simple visual attention, requiring speed, attentional skills, short-term memory, and visual acuity.

Each test uses a single-item format. Administration procedures are straight-forward. Instructions are contained in the manual and separate administration cards for each test. The manual contains basic instructions that should be sufficient to allow somewhat inexperienced test administrators to use the WSS. As with many employment tests there are no explicit provisions for accommodating persons with disabilities or handicapping conditions. The fairly rigorous time limits specified could pose additional problems to employers in the wake of the Americans with Disabilities Act.

The raw score for each test is the number of items answered correctly. Scoring can be done by hand, using the acetate key, or by machine, on site with optical mark reader, or by the test publisher. The reliability of each test is reported based on Cronbach's internal consistency coefficient alpha and standard errors of measurement (*SEm*). The internal consistency coefficients range from .91–.93 across tests with the *SEm* ranging from 1.87–1.99. Virtually, no information is provided on the selected sample with the exception of the size of each sample. Although respectable, the levels of internal consistency reported cannot be used to infer the stability of test scores over time.

Evidence of validity is sparse for these tests and suggests very limited applications for test use. Four validation studies are briefly described in the appendix, with three of these using rather small samples (N = 35–66). In the two predictive validation studies the manual author notes that no or few significant correlations with job-relevant criteria were found when the entire sample of applicants was used. The test publisher then examined below average performers separately and reports significant correlations with a small number of criteria identified from a job analysis. Remaining empirical evidence suggests that Understanding Instructions and Working with Numbers have moderate to low levels of validity with a small number of specific job-related criteria. These studies were conducted on specific jobs and the inconsistency of results across studies is troublesome. For example, two studies suggest that Understanding Instructions is significantly related to numeric ability, despite its design as a measure of one's ability to understand written messages, whereas Working with Numbers was found to be unrelated to numerical ability in one of the same studies. In addition, Understanding Instructions is then found to be unrelated to ability to make fast and accurate calculations in a third study. Only one validity study was conducted on the Visual Checking test, reporting that it was moderately related to one of 29 criteria for food process operators—working with machinery. Yet, the former two tests demonstrated equivalent validity with the same criteria, despite their design as measures of vastly different constructs. In any case, there appears to be no evidence to support the validity or utility of the Visual Checking test for any application.

At best, the former two tests have very limited applications. The manual author states that "abilities measured by the WSS . . . were found to be tied to key job tasks and, hence, required for the satisfactory performance of these key tasks" (manual, p. 39). Yet, the four studies provide no theoretical rationale for each measure and results do not generalize across criteria that appear similar. Unfortunately, the manual and studies do not include any explanation of how the criteria are operationally defined. Intercorrelations among these tests are not provided. Seven separate sets of norms, by occupation, are offered in the manual. Although the manual author cautions "the choice of norm table is crucial" (manual, p. 26), available norms do not cover all occupations within production and manufacturing areas for which the WSS tests are supposedly valid. Add to this that the tests are designed for entry-level workers with little formal education and that they demonstrate validity (in two of four studies) only when below average performers are singled out. Potential test users should proceed with great caution before using these measures.

At a minimum, test users should conduct a comprehensive job analysis to determine if these tests measure any criteria required for the specific job(s) in question. Even in these instances, there is insufficient evidence to rely on these tests as a major determinant for hiring decisions. A major concern for employers is adverse impact of employment tests. The test publisher provides no data that indicate if group differences exist across gender, race, or ethnic groups. Instead, they note that research is underway. Without such evidence in hand, it seems unlikely any employer would use these tests for hiring decisions unless they are prepared to conduct in-house differential prediction studies.

The test materials are of sufficiently high quality. The 66-page test manual is adequate in describing administration and scoring procedures. Chapters on norms, validity, reliability, and test use provide appropriate explanations of these technical measurement concepts. However, in other ways the manual is insufficient for determining how to use these tests and describing what they actually measure. The manual does not comply with the *Standards for Educational and Psychological Testing* (AERA, APA, & NCME, 1985) in providing adequate information on the samples used in developing norm tables and in the validation studies, criterion measures, evidence of differential prediction, the content domain of jobs included in job analyses, and appropriate uses of each test.

The publisher's claim that "The WSS has been found to be a reliable and valid predictor of performance in manufacturing and production jobs" (manual, p. 42) is overstated. There is no explanation of the conceptual basis for each of the three measures and available research does not offer any consistent and rational explanation of what each test measures uniquely. The highly speeded nature of the tests suggests that they might be capturing "g" and have limited utility with only very low-ability job applicants.

REVIEWER'S REFERENCE

American Educational Research Association, American Psychological Association, & National Council on Measurement in Education. (1985). *Standards for educational and psychological testing*. Washington, DC: American Psychological Association, Inc.

CONTRIBUTING TEST REVIEWERS

PHILLIP L. ACKERMAN, Professor of Psychology, University of Minnesota, Minneapolis, MN

TERRY A. ACKERMAN, Associate Professor of Educational Psychology, University of Illinois, Champaign, IL

SUSAN F. ADAMS, Intensive Treatment Service Unit Manager, Beatrice State Developmental Center, Beatrice, NE

LEWIS R. AIKEN, Professor of Psychology, Pepperdine University, Malibu, CA

MARK ALBANESE, Associate Professor of Preventive Medicine and Education, and Director, Office of Medical Education Research and Development, The University of Wisconsin-Madison Medical School, Madison, WI

BRUCE K. ALCORN, Director of Certification, Teachers College, Ball State University, Muncie, IN

LAWRENCE M. ALEAMONI, Professor of Educational Psychology, University of Arizona, Tucson, AZ

CHARLENE M. ALEXANDER, Assistant Professor of Counseling Psychology, Fordham University, New York, NY

SARAH J. ALLEN, Assistant Professor of School Psychology, University of Cincinnati, Cincinnati, OH

JULIE A. ALLISON, Assistant Professor of Psychology, Pittsburg State University, Pittsburg, KS

KENNETH N. ANCHOR, Dean, School of Health and Human Services, and Professor, Senior University, Center for Disability Studies, Nashville, TN

DAVID O. ANDERSON, Senior Measurement Statistician, Educational Testing Service, Princeton, NJ

JOHN O. ANDERSON, Associate Professor, Faculty of Education, University of Victoria, Victoria, British Columbia, Canada

JERRILYN V. ANDREWS, Assistant for Assessment and Data Collection, Office of School Administration, Montgomery County Public Schools, Rockville, MD

PAUL A. ARBISI, Assessment Clinic Director, Psychology Service, Minneapolis VA Medical Center, Minneapolis, MN

FRANCIS X. ARCHAMBAULT, JR., Professor and Department Head, Department of Educational Psychology, University of Connecticut, Storrs, CT

JOYCE A. ARDITTI, Assistant Professor of Family and Child Development, Virginia Polytechnic Institute and State University, Blacksburg, VA

EDWARD ARONOW, Associate Professor of Psychology, Montclair State College, Upper Montclair, NJ

RAOUL A. ARREOLA, Director of Educational Technology, The University of Tennessee, Memphis, TN

F. MARION ASCHE, Professor of Education, Virginia Polytechnic Institute and State University, Blacksburg, VA

PHILIP ASH, Director, Ash, Blackstone and Cates, Blacksburg, VA

RONALD A. ASH, Professor of Business and Psychology, Director of Doctoral Program, School of Business, University of Kansas, Lawrence, KS

DEBORAH H. ATLAS, Coordinator, Rehabilitation Speech Pathology, Mt. Sinai Medical Center, New York, NY

JEFFREY A. ATLAS, Deputy Chief Psychologist and Assistant Clinical Professor, Bronx Children's Psychiatric Center, Albert Einstein College of Medicine, Bronx, NY

JAMES T. AUSTIN, Assistant Professor of Psychology, The Ohio State University, Columbus, OH

STEPHEN N. AXFORD, School Psychologist, Academy District Twenty, Colorado Springs, CO and Counseling Department Chair, University of Phoenix-Colorado Campus, Aurora, CO

GLEN P. AYLWARD, Professor of Pediatrics, Psychiatry and Behavioral and Social Sciences, Southern

Illinois University School of Medicine, Springfield, IL

KRIS L. BAACK, Assistant Clinical Professor of Speech Pathology and Audiology, Department of Special Education and Communication Disorders, University of Nebraska-Lincoln, Lincoln, NE

PATRICIA A. BACHELOR, Professor of Psychology, California State University, Long Beach, CA

LYLE F. BACHMAN, Professor of Applied Linguistics, University of California, Los Angeles, Los Angeles, CA

BETH D. BADER, Assessment Specialist, Educational Issues Department, American Federation of Teachers, Washington, DC

SHERRY K. BAIN, Visiting Assistant Professor of Psychology, University of Southern Mississippi, Hattiesburg, MS

JANET BALDWIN, Assistant Director, GED Testing Program, Washington, DC

DEBORAH L. BANDALOS, Assistant Professor of Educational Psychology, University of Nebraska-Lincoln, Lincoln, NE

LAURA L. B. BARNES, Assistant Professor of Educational Research, Department of Applied Behavioral Studies, Oklahoma State University, Stillwater, OK

DAVID W. BARNETT, Professor of School Psychology, University of Cincinnati, Cincinnati, OH

RITA M. BARNETT, Teacher, Oak Hills Local School District, Cincinnati, OH

WILLIAM M. BART, Professor of Educational Psychology, University of Minnesota, Minneapolis, MN

DAVID J. BATESON, Associate Professor of Mathematics and Science Education and the Educational Measurement Research Group, University of British Columbia, Vancouver, British Columbia, Canada

ERNEST A. BAUER, Research, Evaluation and Testing Consultant, Oakland Schools, Waterford, MI

MICHAEL D. BECK, President, BETA, Inc., Pleasantville, NY

MARCIA J. BELCHER, Associate Dean, Office of Institutional Research, Miami-Dade Community College, Miami, FL

KATHRYN M. BENES, Director of Counseling Services, Catholic Social Services, Lincoln, NE

CLINTON W. BENNETT, Professor of Speech Pathology and Audiology, James Madison University, Harrisonburg, VA

MARK J. BENSON, Associate Professor of Family and Child Development, Virginia Polytechnic Institute and State University, Blacksburg, VA

PHILIP BENSON, Associate Professor of Management, New Mexico State University, Las Cruces, NM

STEPHEN L. BENTON, Professor of Educational Psychology, Kansas State University, Manhattan, KS

RONALD A. BERK, Professor, School of Nursing, The Johns Hopkins University, Baltimore, MD

HINSDALE BERNARD, Assistant Professor, College of Education, Cleveland State University, Cleveland, OH

H. JOHN BERNARDIN, University Research Professor, College of Business, Florida Atlantic University, Boca Raton, FL

JEAN-JACQUES BERNIER, Full Professor, University Laval, Quebec, Canada

FRANK M. BERNT, Associate Professor, Department of Education and Health Services, St. Joseph's University, Philadelphia, PA

FREDERICK BESSAI, Professor of Education, University of Regina, Regina, Saskatchewan, Canada

LISA G. BISCHOFF, Assistant Professor of Education and School Psychology, Indiana State University, Terre Haute, IN

BRUCE H. BISKIN, Senior Psychometrician, American Institute of Certified Public Accountants, Jersey City, NJ

MARTHA BLACKWELL, Associate Professor of Psychology, Auburn University at Montgomery, Montgomery, AL

LYNN S. BLISS, Professor of Communication Disorders and Sciences, Wayne State University, Detroit, MI

SONYA BLIXT, Professor of Evaluation and Measurement, Kent State University, Kent, OH

MARTIN E. BLOCK, Assistant Professor of Education, University of Virginia, Charlottesville, VA

LISA A. BLOOM, Assistant Professor of Special Education, Western Carolina University, Cullowhee, NC

NANCY B. BOLOGNA, Assistant Professor of Psychiatry, Louisiana State University School of Medicine, New Orleans, LA

BRIAN BOLTON, University Professor, Arkansas Research and Training Center in Vocational Rehabilitation, University of Arkansas, Fayetteville, AR

DAVID L. BOLTON, Assistant Professor for Education, West Chester University, West Chester, PA

STEPHEN J. BONEY, Assistant Professor of Communication Disorders, Department of Special Education and Communication Disorders, University of Nebraska-Lincoln, Lincoln, NE

ROGER A. BOOTHROYD, Research Scientist, Bureau of Evaluation and Services Research, New York State Office of Mental Health, Albany, NY

ROBERT A. BORNSTEIN, Professor and Associate Chairman, Department of Psychiatry, The Ohio State University, Columbus, OH

MICHAEL D. BOTWIN, Assistant Professor of Psychology, California State University, Fresno, Fresno, CA

GREGORY J. BOYLE, Associate Professor of Psychology, Bond University, Gold Coast, Queensland, Australia

J. DAVID BOYLE, Professor and Chairman, Department of Music Education and Music Therapy, School of Music, University of Miami, Coral Gables, FL

BRUCE A. BRACKEN, Professor of Psychology, The University of Memphis, Memphis, TN

JEFFERY P. BRADEN, Associate Professor of Educational Psychology, University of Wisconsin-Madison, Madison, WI

LINDA E. BRODY, Director, Study of Exceptional Talent, Center for Talented Youth, The Johns Hopkins University, Baltimore, MD

SUSAN M. BROOKHART, Assistant Professor of Education, Duquesne University, Pittsburgh, PA

JAMES DEAN BROWN, Associate Professor of Applied Linguistics, Department of English as a Second Language, University of Hawaii at Manoa, Honolulu, HI

RIC BROWN, Acting Director, University Grants and Research Office, California State University, Fresno, Fresno, CA

SCOTT W. BROWN, Professor of Educational Psychology, University of Connecticut, Storrs, CT

RICHARD BROZOVICH, Director, Psychology and Learning Clinic, Oakland Schools, Waterford, MI

ALBERT M. BUGAJ, Associate Professor of Psychology, University of Wisconsin—Marinette, Marinette, WI

ALAN C. BUGBEE, JR., Director of Educational Systems/Associate Professor of Psychology, The American College, Bryn Mawr, PA

MICHAEL B. BUNCH, Vice President, Measurement Incorporated, Durham, NC

MARY ANNE BUNDA, Professor of Educational Leadership, Western Michigan University, Kalamazoo, MI

LINDA K. BUNKER, Professor and Associate Dean of Education, University of Virginia, Charlottesville, VA

CHRISTINE W. BURNS, Assistant Professor of Educational Psychology, University of Utah, Salt Lake City, UT

JOHN CHRISTIAN BUSCH, Associate Professor of Education, University of North Carolina at Greensboro, Greensboro, NC

KATHARINE G. BUTLER, Research Professor, Communication Sciences and Disorders, Syracuse University, Syracuse, NY

CAROLYN M. CALLAHAN, Professor, Curry School of Education, University of Virginia, Charlottesville, VA

WAYNE J. CAMARA, Director of Scientific Affairs, American Psychological Association, Washington, DC:

KAREN T. CAREY, Associate Professor of Psychology, California State University, Fresno, Fresno, CA

JAMES E. CARLSON, Director of Research, Educational Testing Service, Princeton, NJ

JANET F. CARLSON, Assistant Professor of Counseling and Psychological Services, State University of New York at Oswego, Oswego, NY

JOELLEN CARLSON, Director of Testing Standards, New York Stock Exchange, Inc., New York, NY

JAMES C. CARMER, Clinical Psychologist, Lincoln, NE

ARLENE E. CARNEY, Associate Professor of Communication Disorders, University of Minnesota, Minneapolis, MN

RUSSELL N. CARNEY, Associate Professor of Psychology, Southwest Missouri State University, Springfield, MO

C. DALE CARPENTER, Professor of Special Education, Western Carolina University, Cullowhee, NC

DARREL N. CAULLEY, Senior Lecturer, Graduate School of Education, La Trobe University, Bundoora, Australia

JOSEPH C. CIECHALSKI, Associate Professor of Counselor and Adult Education, East Carolina University, Greenville, NC

GREGORY J. CIZEK, Associate Professor of Educational Research and Measurement, University of Toledo, Toledo, OH

CHARLES D. CLAIBORN, Professor, Division of Psychology in Education, Arizona State University, Tempe, AZ

ELAINE CLARK, Associate Professor of Educational Psychology, University of Utah, Salt Lake City, UT

LARRY COCHRAN, Professor of Counseling Psychology, Faculty of Education, The University of British Columbia, Vancouver, British Columbia, Canada

ANDREW D. COHEN, Professor of English as a Second Language and Applied Linguistics, University of Minnesota, Minneapolis, MN

ANNABEL J. COHEN, Assistant Professor of Psychology, University of Prince Edward Island, Charlottetown, Prince Edward Island, Canada

THEODORE COLADARCI, Associate Professor of Education, University of Maine, Orono, ME

DEBRA E. COLE, Director of Partial Hospitalization, Virginia Treatment Center for Children, Medical College of Virginia, Richmond, VA

DEBORAH COLLINS, Deputy Director, Center for Survey Research, Virginia Polytechnic Institute and State University, Blacksburg, VA

JUDITH CONGER, Professor of Psychology and Director of Clinical Training, Purdue University, West Lafayette, IN

COLLIE WYATT CONOLEY, Associate Professor of Educational Psychology, University of Nebraska-Lincoln, Lincoln, NE

NORMAN A. CONSTANTINE, Senior Associate, Far West Laboratory for Educational Research and Development, San Francisco, CA

DONNA K. COOKE, Assistant Professor, College of Business, Florida Atlantic University, Boca Raton, FL

ALICE J. CORKILL, Assistant Professor of Counseling and Educational Psychology, University of Nevada, Las Vegas, NV

MERITH COSDEN, Associate Professor of Counseling/Clinical/School Psychology, Department of Education, University of California, Santa Barbara, CA

KEVIN D. CREHAN, Associate Professor of Educational Psychology, University of Nevada, Las Vegas, Las Vegas, NV

LAWRENCE H. CROSS, Associate Professor of Educational Research and Measurement, Virginia Polytechnic Institute and State University, Blacksburg, VA

SUSAN L. CROWLEY, Assistant Professor of Psychology, Utah State University, Logan, UT

JACK A. CUMMINGS, Chair, Department of Counseling and Educational Psychology, Indiana University, Bloomington, IN

WILLIAM L. CURLETTE, Professor of Counseling and Psychological Services, Professor of Educational Policy Studies, and Director of the Educational Research Bureau, Georgia State University, Atlanta, GA

RIK CARL D'AMATO, Professor and Director, Programs in School Psychology, Division of Professional Psychology, University of Northern Colorado, Greeley, CO

LARRY G. DANIEL, Associate Professor of Educational Leadership and Research, University of Southern Mississippi, Hattiesburg, MS

MARK H. DANIEL, Senior Scientist, American Guidance Service, Circle Pines, MN

RALPH F. DARR, JR., Professor of Education, Department of Educational Foundations and Leadership, The University of Akron, Akron, OH

STEPHEN F. DAVIS, Professor of Psychology, Emporia State University, Emporia, KS

AYRES D'COSTA, Associate Professor of Education, The Ohio State University, Columbus, OH

GARY J. DEAN, Associate Professor and Department Chairperson, Department of Counseling, Adult Education, and Student Affairs, Indiana University of Pennsylvania, Indiana, PA

WILLIAM W. DEARDORFF, Clinical Faculty, U.C.L.A. School of Medicine, Los Angeles, CA

WILLIAM L. DEATON, Professor and Dean, School of Education, Auburn University at Montgomery, Montgomery, AL

GABRIEL M. DELLA-PIANA, Director of Evaluation, El Paso Collaborative for Academic Excellence, University of Texas at El Paso, El Paso, TX

GERALD E. DEMAURO, Director, Bureau of Statewide Assessment, New Jersey State Department of Education, Trenton, NJ

JENNIFER DENICOLIS, Instructor, Temple University, Philadelphia, PA

DENISE M. DEZOLT, Coordinator of Field Experiences and Adjunct Assistant Professor, University of Rhode Island, Kingston, RI

ESTHER E. DIAMOND, Educational and Psychological Consultant, Evanston, IL

ALLAN O. DIEFENDORF, Associate Professor, Department of Otolaryngology, Indiana University School of Medicine, Indianapolis, IN

THOMAS E. DINERO, Associate Professor of Evaluation and Measurement, Kent State University, Kent, OH

JONATHAN G. DINGS, Graduate Student, Measurement and Statistics Program, University of Iowa, Iowa City, IA

DAVID N. DIXON, Professor and Chair of Counseling Psychology, Ball State University, Muncie, IN

GREGORY H. DOBBINS, Associate Professor of Management, The University of Tennessee at Knoxville, Knoxville, TN

BETH DOLL, Assistant Professor of School Psychology, University of Colorado at Denver, Denver, CO

GEORGE DOMINO, Professor of Psychology, University of Arizona, Tucson, AZ

THOMAS F. DONLON, Director, Office of Test Development and Research, Thomas Edison State College, Trenton, NJ

E. THOMAS DOWD, Professor and Director of Counseling Psychology, Kent State University, Kent, OH

PENELOPE W. DRALLE, Associate Professor of Psychiatry, Louisiana State University School of Medicine, New Orleans, LA

ROBERT J. DRUMMOND, Professor of Counselor Education, University of North Florida, Jacksonville, FL

CYNTHIA ANN DRUVA-ROUSH, Assistant Director, Evaluation and Examination Service, The University of Iowa, Iowa City, IA

DEL EBERHARDT, Program Administrator, Greenwich Public Schools, Greenwich, CT

TIM ECK, Graduate Student, University of Central Oklahoma, Edmond, OK

ALLEN JACK EDWARDS, Professor of Psychology, Southwest Missouri State University, Springfield, MO

BRADLEY ELISON, Partial Hospitalization Program Team Leader, Virginia Treatment Center for Children, Virginia Commonwealth University, Richmond, VA

STEPHEN N. ELLIOTT, Professor of Educational Psychology, University of Wisconsin-Madison, Madison, WI

THERESA H. ELOFSON, Program Specialist, Chapter 1/Learning Assistance Program, Federal Way School District #210, Federal Way, WA

GEORGE ENGELHARD, JR., Associate Professor of Educational Studies, Emory University, Atlanta, GA

JOHN M. ENGER, Professor of Education, Arkansas State University, Jonesboro, AR

JAMES B. ERDMANN, Associate Dean and Professor of Medicine (Education), Jefferson Medical College, Thomas Jefferson University, Philadelphia, PA

DEBORAH ERICKSON, Associate Professor of Education, Niagara University, Niagara University, NY

CLAIRE B. ERNHART, Professor of Psychiatry, Case Western Reserve University and MetroHealth Medical Center, Cleveland, OH

JULIAN FABRY, Counseling Psychologist, Omaha Psychiatric Institute, Omaha, NE

JENNIFER J. FAGER, Assistant Professor of Teacher Education, University of New Hampshire at Manchester, Manchester, NH

DOREEN WARD FAIRBANK, Adjunct Assistant Professor of Psychology, Meredith College, Raleigh, NC

SHAUNA FALTIN, System Reviewer, The Prudential Service Co., Roseland, NJ

RICHARD W. FAUNCE, Licensed Psychologist, Maple Grove, MN

SUSAN FELSENFELD, Assistant Professor of Communication, University of Pittsburgh, Pittsburgh, PA

RAY FENTON, Supervisor of Assessment and Evaluation, Anchorage School District, Anchorage, AK

TRENTON R. FERRO, Assistant Professor of Adult and Community Education, Indiana University of Pennsylvania, Indiana, PA

CARMEN J. FINLEY, Research Psychologist, Santa Rosa, CA

ROBERT FITZPATRICK, Consulting Industrial Psychologist, Cranberry Township, PA

DAWN P. FLANAGAN, Assistant Professor of Psychology, St. John's University, Jamaica, NY

JOHN W. FLEENOR, Research Scientist, Center for Creative Leadership, Greensboro, NC

DONNA FORD, Research Assistant, University of Central Oklahoma, Edmond, OK

LAURIE FORD, Assistant Professor of Psychology, University of South Carolina, Columbia, SC

JIM C. FORTUNE, Professor of Research and Evaluation, Virginia Tech University, Blacksburg, VA

ROBERT B. FRARY, Professor and Director, Office of Measurement and Research Services, Virginia Polytechnic Institute and State University, Blacksburg, VA

NORMAN FREDMAN, Professor and Coordinator, Counselor Education Programs, Queens College, City University of New York, Flushing, NY

MARK H. FUGATE, Assistant Professor of School Psychology, Alfred University, Alfred, NY

SOLOMON M. FULERO, Professor and Chair of Psychology, Sinclair College, Dayton, OH

MICHAEL FURLONG, Associate Professor, Graduate School of Education, University of California, Santa Barbara, Santa Barbara, CA

ELAINE FURNISS, UNICEF, Hanoi, Vietnam

ROBERT K. GABLE, Professor of Educational Psychology, and Associate Director, Bureau of Educational Research and Service, University of Connecticut, Storrs, CT

LENA R. GADDIS, Assistant Professor of Educational Psychology, Northern Arizona University, Flagstaff, AZ

LEANN M. GAMACHE, Director, Psychometric Services, Professional Assessment Services Division, American College Testing, Iowa City, IA

RONALD J. GANELLEN, Director, Neuropsychology Service, Michael Reese Hospital and Medical Center, and Assistant Professor of Psychiatry and Neurology, University of Illinois at Chicago, Chicago, IL

KURT F. GEISINGER, Professor of Psychology and Dean, College of Arts and Sciences, State University of New York at Oswego, Oswego, NY

RONALD B. GILLAM, Assistant Professor of Speech Communication, The University of Texas at Austin, Austin, TX

JERRY S. GILMER, Assistant Research Scientist, College of Medicine, The University of Iowa, Iowa City, IA

BERT A. GOLDMAN, Professor of Education, University of North Carolina at Greensboro, Greensboro, NC

DIANE GOLDSMITH, Director, Transition & Women's Programs, Manchester Community Technical College, Manchester, CT

HARRISON G. GOUGH, Professor of Psychology, Emeritus, University of California, Berkeley, Berkeley, CA

JOHN R. GRAHAM, Professor and Chair, Department of Psychology, Kent State University, Kent, OH

STEVE GRAHAM, Professor of Special Education, University of Maryland, College Park, MD

LARRY B. GRANTHAM, Associate Professor of Counselor Education, Western Carolina University, Cullowhee, NC

VICKI GRATOPP, Speech Pathologist, Lincoln Public Schools, Lincoln, NE

M. ELIZABETH GRAUE, Assistant Professor of Curriculum and Instruction, University of Wisconsin-Madison, Madison, WI

KATHY E. GREEN, Associate Professor of Education, University of Denver, Denver, CO

FRANK GRESHAM, Professor and Director, School Psychology Program, University of California, Riverside, Riverside, CA

J. JEFFREY GRILL, Special Education Coordinator, Ingram State Community College, Deatsville, AL

ROBERT M. GUION, Distinguished University Professor Emeritus, Bowling Green State University, Bowling Green, OH

SAMI GULGOZ, Assistant Professor of Psychology, Koc University, Istanbul, Turkey

ARLEN R. GULLICKSON, Professor and Chief of Staff for The Evaluation Center, Western Michigan University, Kalamazoo, MI

THOMAS W. GUYETTE, Assistant Professor of Speech Pathology, University of Illinois at Chicago, Chicago, IL

NATASHA GWARTNEY, Graduate Student, University of Central Oklahoma, Edmond, OK

THOMAS M. HALADYNA, Professor of Educational Psychology, Arizona State University West, Phoenix, AZ

PENELOPE K. HALL, Associate Professor of Speech Pathology and Audiology, Wendell Johnson Speech and Hearing Center, The University of Iowa, Iowa City, IA

RONALD K. HAMBLETON, Professor of Education and Psychology, University of Massachusetts at Amherst, Amherst, MA

GERALD S. HANNA, Professor of Educational Psychology and Measurement, Kansas State University, Manhattan, KS

RICHARD E. HARDING, Senior Vice President, Gallup, Inc., Lincoln, NE

DELWYN L. HARNISCH, Associate Professor of Educational Psychology, University of Illinois at Urbana-Champaign, Champaign, IL

STUART N. HART, Associate Professor of Counseling and Educational Psychology, Indiana University-Purdue University at Indianapolis, Indianapolis, IN

LEO M. HARVILL, Professor and Assistant Dean for Medical Education, James H. Quillen College of Medicine, East Tennessee State University, Johnson City, TN

MICHAEL R. HARWELL, Associate Professor of Psychology and Education, University of Pittsburgh, Pittsburgh, PA

JOHN HATTIE, Professor of Education, The University of North Carolina, Greensboro, NC

KEITH HATTRUP, Assistant Professor of Psychology, New York University, New York, NY

WILLIAM O. HAYNES, Professor of Communication Disorders, Auburn University, Auburn, AL

MARTINE HÉBERT, Assistant Professor, Department of Measurement and Evaluation, University Laval, Quebec, Canada

NATALIE L. HEDBERG, Professor of Communication Disorders and Speech Science, University of Colorado, Boulder, CO

MARY HENNING-STOUT, Associate Professor of Counseling Psychology, Lewis & Clark College, Portland, OR

DAVID O. HERMAN, Associate Education Officer, Office of Educational Research, New York City Board of Education, Brooklyn, NY

ALLEN K. HESS, Professor and Department Head, Department of Psychology, School of Sciences, Auburn University at Montgomery, Montgomery, AL

KATHRYN A. HESS, Research Associate, Montgomery, AL

ROBERT M. HESS, Assistant Professor of Education, Arizona State University West, Phoenix, AZ

ROBERT W. HILTONSMITH, Associate Professor of Psychology, Radford University, Radford, VA

STEPHEN R. HOOPER, Associate Professor of Psychiatry, University of North Carolina School of Medicine, Chapel Hill, NC

CHARLES HOUSTON, Director of Research and Planning, Virginia Western Community College, Roanoke, VA

SELMA HUGHES, Professor, Department of Psychology and Special Education, East Texas State University, Commerce, TX

STEPHEN H. IVENS, Vice President, Research & Development, Touchstone Applied Science Associates, Brewster, NY

ANNETTE M. IVERSON, Assistant Professor of Educational Psychology and Foundations, University of Northern Iowa, Cedar Falls, IA

JEFFREY JENKINS, Attorney, Narvaez & Jenkins, P.A., Albuquerque, NM

JOANNE L. JENSEN, Research Associate, Far West Laboratory for Educational Research and Development, San Francisco, CA

RICHARD W. JOHNSON, Adjunct Professor of Counseling Psychology and Associate Director of Counseling & Consultation Center, University of Wisconsin-Madison, Madison, WI

RUTH JOHNSON, Professor of Linguistics, Southern Illinois University at Carbondale, Carbondale, IL

ELIZABETH L. JONES, Assistant Professor of Psychology, Western Kentucky University, Bowling Green, KY

JAMES A. JONES, Doctoral Candidate and Graduate Assistant in Evaluation and Measurement, Kent State University, Kent, OH

KATHERINE S. JONES, Tennis Instructor, Arizona State University, Tempe, AZ

KEVIN M. JONES, Research Associate, Louisiana State University, Baton Rouge, LA

SAMUEL JUNI, Professor, Department of Applied Psychology, New York University, New York, NY

STEPHEN JURS, Professor of Educational Psychology, Research, and Social Foundations, College of Education and Allied Professions, University of Toledo, Toledo, OH

JAVAID KAISER, Associate Professor of Education, Virginia Polytechnic Institute & State University, Blacksburg, VA

RANDY W. KAMPHAUS, Associate Professor of Educational Psychology, University of Georgia, Athens, GA

BARBARA J. KAPLAN, Psychologist, Western New York Institute for the Psychotherapies, Orchard Park, NY

MITCHELL KARNO, Doctoral Student, Graduate School of Education, University of California, Santa Barbara, Santa Barbara, CA

MICHAEL G. KAVAN, Director of Behavioral Sciences and Associate Professor of Family Practice, Creighton University School of Medicine, Omaha, NE

PATRICIA B. KEITH, Assistant Professor of Psychology, Alfred University, Alfred, NY

TIMOTHY Z. KEITH, Professor of Psychology, Alfred University, Alfred, NY

MARY LOU KELLEY, Professor of Psychology, Louisiana State University, Louisiana State University Medical Center, Baton Rouge, LA

KATHRYN W. KENNEY, Director, Kenney Associates, Certified Speech-Language Pathologists, Gilbert, AZ

BARBARA KERR, Professor of Psychology in Education, Arizona State University, Tempe, AZ

KATHY KESSLER, Clinical Lecturer, Department of Otolaryngology, Indiana University School of Medicine, Indianapolis, IN

KENNETH A. KIEWRA, Associate Professor of Educational Psychology, University of Nebraska-Lincoln, Lincoln, NE

JOHN D. KING, Professor of Special Education and Educational Administration, The University of Texas at Austin, Austin, TX

SUZANNE KING, Assistant Professor of Psychiatry, McGill University, Montreal, Quebec, Canada

G. GAGE KINGSBURY, Coordinator of Measurement Research, Portland Public Schools, Portland, OR

JEAN POWELL KIRNAN, Associate Professor of Psychology, Trenton State College, Trenton, NJ

KARYLL KISER, Research Assistant, University of Central Oklahoma, Edmond, OK

CATHARINE C. KNIGHT, Visiting Assistant Professor, College of Education, Cleveland State University, Cleveland, OH

HOWARD M. KNOFF, Professor of School Psychology, Department of Psychological Foundations, University of South Florida, Tampa, FL

WILLIAM R. KOCH, Professor of Educational Psychology, The University of Texas, Austin, TX

STEPHEN L. KOFFLER, Managing Director, Center for Occupational and Professional Assessment, Educational Testing Service, Princeton, NJ

REBECCA J. KOPRIVA, Associate Professor of Educational Measurement, California State University, Fresno, Fresno, CA

JOHN H. KRANZLER, Assistant Professor of School Psychology, University of Florida, Gainesville, FL

CAROLE M. KRAUTHAMER, Assistant Professor of Psychology, Trenton State College, Trenton, NJ

S. DAVID KRISKA, Personnel Psychologist, City of Columbus, Columbus, OH

PHYLLIS KUEHN, Associate Professor of Educational Research, Measurement, and Statistics, California State University, Fresno, Fresno, CA

DEBORAH KING KUNDERT, Associate Professor of Educational Psychology and Statistics, University at Albany, State University of New York, Albany, NY

SUZANNE LANE, Associate Professor of Research Methodology, University of Pittsburgh, Pittsburgh, PA

WILLIAM STEVE LANG, Assistant Professor of Measurement and Research, University of South Florida at St. Petersburg, St. Petersburg, FL

AIMÉE LANGLOIS, Professor of Child Development, Humboldt State University, Arcata, CA

RICHARD I. LANYON, Professor of Psychology, Arizona State University, Tempe, AZ

JOSEPH G. LAW, JR., Associate Professor of Behavioral Studies, University of South Alabama, Mobile, AL

STEVEN B. LEDER, Associate Professor of Surgery, Yale University School of Medicine, New Haven, CT

STEVEN W. LEE, Associate Professor of Educational Psychology and Research, University of Kansas, Lawrence, KS

SUE M. LEGG, Associate Director, Office of Instructional Resources, University of Florida, Gainesville, FL

IRVIN J. LEHMANN, Professor of Measurement, Michigan State University, East Lansing, MI

FREDERICK T. L. LEONG, Assistant Professor of Psychology, The Ohio State University, Columbus, OH

S. ALVIN LEUNG, Associate Professor in Educational Psychology, University of Houston, Houston, TX

MARY A. LEWIS, Manager, Human Resources, PPG Architectural Finishes, Pittsburgh, PA

RICK LINDSKOG, Director of School Psychology Program and Associate Professor of Psychology and Counseling, Pittsburg State University, Pittsburg, KS

STEVEN G. LOBELLO, Associate Professor of Psychology, Auburn University at Montgomery, Montgomery, AL

CHARLES J. LONG, Professor of Psychology, The University of Memphis, Memphis, TN

STEVEN H. LONG, Assistant Professor of Speech Pathology & Audiology, Ithaca College, Ithaca, NY

BRENDA H. LOYD, Professor of Education, University of Virginia, Charlottesville, VA

LINDA MABRY, Assistant Professor of Counseling and Educational Psychology, College of Education, Indiana University, Bloomington, IN

DAVID MACPHEE, Associate Professor of Human Development and Family Studies, Colorado State University, Fort Collins, CO

CLEBORNE D. MADDUX, Professor and Chairman of Curriculum and Instruction, University of Nevada-Reno, Reno, NV

RODERICK K. MAHURIN, Assistant Professor of Psychiatry, University of Texas Health Science Center, San Antonio, TX

CAROLINE MANUELE-ADKINS, Professor of Educational Foundations and Counseling Programs, Hunter College, City University of New York, New York, NY

GREGORY J. MARCHANT, Associate Professor of Educational Psychology, Ball State University, Muncie, IN

GARY L. MARCO, Executive Director, College Board Statistical Analysis, Educational Testing Service, Princeton, NJ

SUZANNE MARKEL-FOX, Post Doctoral Fellow, Center for Mental Health Policies and Services Research, University of Pennsylvania, Philadelphia, PA

MARC MARSCHARK, Professor, National Technical Institute for the Deaf at the Rochester Institute of Technology, Rochester, NY

KEVIN J. MCCARTHY, Ph.D. Candidate, Associate in Psychology Department, E. Hunt Correctional Center, St. Gabriel, LA

REBECCA J. MCCAULEY, Associate Professor of Communication Sciences, University of Vermont, Burlington, VT

ERIN MCCLURE, Research Associate, Department of Psychiatry, University of Texas Health Science Center, San Antonio, TX

DAVID E. MCINTOSH, Assistant Professor of School Psychology, Department of Applied Behavioral Studies, Oklahoma State University, Stillwater, OK

MARY J. MCLELLAN, Assistant Professor of Educational Psychology, Northern Arizona University, Center for Excellence in Education, Flagstaff, AZ

ROBERT F. MCMORRIS, Professor of Educational Psychology and Statistics, State University of New York at Albany, Albany, NY

MICHAEL MCNAMARA, Graduate School of Education, La Trobe University, Bundoora, Australia

SHARON MCNEELY, Associate Professor of Educational Foundations, Northeastern Illinois University, Chicago, IL

MALCOLM R. MCNEIL, Professor and Co-chair, Department of Communication and Director of Communication Science & Disorders, University of Pittsburgh, Pittsburgh, PA

DOUGLAS J. MCRAE, Educational Measurement Specialist, Private Consultant, Monterey, CA

WILLIAM A. MEHRENS, Professor of Educational Measurement, Michigan State University, East Lansing, MI

SCOTT T. MEIER, Associate Professor, Counseling and Educational Psychology, State University of New York at Buffalo, Buffalo, NY

GARY B. MELTON, Director, Institute for Families in Society, University of South Carolina, Columbia, SC

KEVIN MENEFEE, Assistant Professor in Special Education and Communication Disorders, University of Nebraska-Lincoln, Lincoln, NE

PETER F. MERENDA, Professor Emeritus of Psychology and Statistics, University of Rhode Island, Kingston, RI

WILLIAM R. MERZ, SR., Professor and Coordinator, School Psychology Training Program, California State University, Sacramento, CA

WILLIAM B. MICHAEL, Professor of Education and Psychology, University of Southern California, Los Angeles, CA

CHRISTOPHER P. MIGOTSKY, Doctoral Student, Department of Educational Measurement, University of Illinois, Champaign-Urbana, Champaign-Urbana, IL

M. DAVID MILLER, Associate Professor of Foundations of Education, University of Florida, Gainesville, FL

ROBERT J. MILLER, Assistant Professor of Special Education, Mankato State University, Mankato, MN

CRAIG N. MILLS, Executive Director, Testing and Services, Graduate Record Examinations Program, Educational Testing Service, Princeton, NJ

PAT MIRENDA, Director of Research and Training, CBI Consultants, Ltd., Vancouver, British Columbia, Canada

JUDITH A. MONSAAS, Visiting Associate Professor of Educational Studies, Emory University, Atlanta, GA

MARY ROSS MORAN, Professor of Special Education, University of Kansas, Lawrence, KS

KEVIN L. MORELAND, Associate Professor of Psychology, Fordham University, Bronx, NY

CLAUDIA J. MORNER, Associate University Librarian for Access Services, Boston College, Chestnut Hill, MA

SHERWYN MORREALE, Director, Center for Excellence in Oral Communication, University of Colorado at Colorado Springs, Colorado Springs, CO

GALE M. MORRISON, Associate Professor of Education, Graduate School of Education, University of California, Santa Barbara, CA

PAUL M. MUCHINSKY, Joseph M. Bryan Distinguished Professor of Business, University of North Carolina, Greensboro, NC

RALPH O. MUELLER, Associate Professor of Educational Research, Department of Educational Leadership, Graduate School of Education and Human Development, The George Washington University, Washington, DC

KEVIN R. MURPHY, Professor of Psychology, Colorado State University, Fort Collins, CO

DEAN NAFZIGER, Executive Director, Far West Laboratory for Educational Research and Development, San Francisco, CA

PHILIP NAGY, Associate Professor of Measurement, Evaluation, and Computer Applications, The Ontario Institute for Studies in Education, Toronto, Ontario, Canada

DEBRA NEUBERT, Associate Professor of Special Education, University of Maryland at College Park, College Park, MD

DIANNA L. NEWMAN, Associate Professor of Educational Theory and Practice, University at Albany/State University of New York, Albany, NY

ISADORE NEWMAN, Professor and Associate Director for the Institute of Life-Span Development and Gerontology, The University of Akron, and Adjunct Professor of Psychiatry, N.E. Ohio Universities College of Medicine, Akron, OH

LOIS NICHOLS, Teacher of Gifted and Talented, Oak Hills Local School District, Cincinnati, OH

MICHAL NISSENBAUM, Graduate Student, Department of Educational Psychology, Texas A&M University, College Station, TX

ANTHONY J. NITKO, Professor of Education, University of Pittsburgh, Pittsburgh, PA

JANET NORRIS, Associate Professor of Communication Sciences and Disorders, Louisiana State University, Baton Rouge, LA

CHRISTINE NOVAK, Pediatric Psychologist, Division of Developmental Disabilities, University of Iowa, Iowa City, IA

SALVADOR HECTOR OCHOA, Assistant Professor of Educational Psychology, Texas A&M University, College Station, TX

JUDY OEHLER-STINNETT, Associate Professor of Applied Behavioral Studies, Oklahoma State University, Stillwater, OK

STEPHEN OLEJNIK, Professor of Educational Psychology, University of Georgia, Athens, GA

D. JOE OLMI, Assistant Professor of School Psychology, Department of Psychology, University of Southern Mississippi, Hattiesburg, MS

ALBERT C. OOSTERHOF, Professor of Educational Research, Florida State University, Tallahassee, FL

STEVEN V. OWEN, Professor of Educational Psychology, University of Connecticut, Storrs, CT

ABBOT PACKARD, Research Assistant, Virginia Tech University, Blacksburg, VA

IAN C. PALMER, Program Officer for English and Orientation, Latin American Scholarship Program of American Universities, Harvard University, Cambridge, MA

ANTHONY W. PAOLITTO, Assistant Professor of Education, School Psychology Program, Tufts University, Medford, MA

CHARLES K. PARSONS, Professor of Organizational Behavior, Georgia Institute of Technology, Atlanta, GA

A. HARRY PASSOW, Professor Emeritus of Education, Teachers College, Columbia University, New York, NY

DOUGLAS A. PENFIELD, Professor of Education, Graduate School of Education, Rutgers University, New Brunswick, NJ

CHARLES A. PETERSON, Director of Training in Psychology, VA Minneapolis Medical Center, and Associate Clinical Professor of Psychology at the University of Minnesota, Minneapolis, MN

STEVEN IRA PFEIFFER, Director, Devereux Institute of Clinical Training & Research, Devon, PA

LEADELLE PHELPS, Associate Professor and Director, School Psychology Program, Department of Counseling and Educational Psychology, State University of New York at Buffalo, Buffalo, NY

JAMES W. PINKNEY, Professor of Counseling and Adult Education, East Carolina University, Greenville, NC

MARK POPE, President, Career Decisions, San Francisco, CA

DONALD B. POPE-DAVIS, Associate Professor, Department of Counseling and Personnel Services, University of Maryland, College Park, MD

G. MICHAEL POTEAT, Associate Professor of Psychology, East Carolina University, Greenville, NC

RICHARD C. PUGH, Professor of Education, Indiana University, Bloomington, IN

RUDOLF E. RADOCY, Professor of Music Education and Music Therapy, University of Kansas, Lawrence, KS

JEFFREY S. RAIN, Assistant Professor and Chairman, Industrial/Organizational Psychology Program, Florida Tech, Melbourne, FL

NAMBURY S. RAJU, Professor of Psychology, Georgia Institute of Technology, Atlanta, GA

BIKKAR S. RANDHAWA, Professor of Educational Psychology, University of Saskatchewan, Saskatoon, Canada

GLEN E. RAY, Assistant Professor of Psychology, Auburn University at Montgomery, Montgomery, AL

JAMES C. REED, Director of Psychology, St. Luke's Hospital, New Bedford, MA

BARBARA A. REILLY, Assistant Professor of Management, Georgia State University, Atlanta, GA

ROBERT C. REINEHR, Professor of Psychology, Southwestern University, Georgetown, TX

ROBERT A. REINEKE, Visiting Associate Professor of Curriculum and Instruction, University of Nebraska-Lincoln, Lincoln, NE

PAUL RETZLAFF, Associate Professor of Psychology, University of Northern Colorado, Greeley, CO

CECIL R. REYNOLDS, Professor of Educational Psychology, Texas A&M University, College Station, TX

MARK W. ROBERTS, Professor of Psychology, Idaho State University, Pocatello, ID

ERIC ROBINSON, Certified School Psychologist, Omaha, NE

BRUCE G. ROGERS, Professor of Educational Psychology and Foundations, University of Northern Iowa, Cedar Falls, IA

MARGARET R. ROGERS, Assistant Professor of School Psychology, University of Maryland-College Park, College Park, MD

DEBORAH D. ROMAN, Director, Neuropsychology Laboratory, PM & R and Neurosurgery Departments, University of Minnesota, Minneapolis, MN

MICHAEL J. ROSZKOWSKI, Director of Marketing Research and Associate Professor of Psychology, The American College, Bryn Mawr, PA

BARBARA A. ROTHLISBERG, Associate Professor of Psychology in Educational Psychology and School Psychology I Program Director, Ball State University, Muncie, IN

PAMELA CARRINGTON ROTTO, Assistant Professor of Educational Psychology, University of Nebraska-Lincoln, Lincoln, NE

JAMES B. ROUNDS, Associate Professor of Educational Psychology, University of Illinois at Urbana-Champaign, Champaign, IL

HERBERT C. RUDMAN, Professor of Measurement and Quantitative Methods, Department of Counseling, Educational Psychology and Special Education, Michigan State University, East Lansing, MI

LAWRENCE M RUDNER, Director, ERIC Clearinghouse on Assessment and Evaluation, The Catholic University of America, Washington, DC

JOHN RUST, Senior Lecturer in Psychometrics, Goldsmith's College, University of London, London, England

DARRELL L. SABERS, Professor of Educational Psychology, University of Arizona, Tucson, AZ

CYRIL J. SADOWSKI, Professor of Psychology, Auburn University at Montgomery, Montgomery, AL

PERRY SAILOR, Research Associate, Department of Psychology, Utah State University, Logan, UT

KENNETH SAKAUYE, Associate Professor of Clinical Psychiatry, LSU Medical School in New Orleans, New Orleans, LA

VINCENT J. SAMAR, Associate Professor, National Technical Institute for the Deaf at the Rochester Institute of Technology, Rochester, NY

JONATHAN SANDOVAL, Professor of Education, University of California, Davis, Davis, CA

CLAUDE A. SANDY, Vice President, Research Dimensions, Inc., Richmond, VA

ELEANOR E. SANFORD, Research Consultant, Division of Accountability Services/Research, North Carolina Department of Public Instruction, Raleigh, NC

WILLIAM I. SAUSER, JR., Associate Vice President for Extension and Professor of Educational Foundations, Leadership, and Technology, Auburn University, Auburn, AL

DIANE J. SAWYER, Murfree Professor of Dyslexic Studies, Middle Tennessee State University, Murfreesboro, TN

DALE P. SCANNELL, Professor of Education, Indiana University and Purdue University at Indianapolis, Indianapolis, IN

WILLIAM D. SCHAFER, Associate Professor of Educational Measurement, Statistics, and Evaluation, University of Maryland, College Park, MD

STEVEN SCHINKE, Professor, Columbia University School of Social Work, New York, NY

NEAL SCHMITT, Professor of Psychology and Management, Michigan State University, East Lansing, MI

PATRICIA SCHOENRADE, Associate Professor of Psychology, William Jewel College, Liberty, MO

GREGORY SCHRAW, Assistant Professor of Educational Psychology, University of Nebraska-Lincoln, Lincoln, NE

GENE SCHWARTING, Project Director of Early Childhood Special Education, Omaha Public Schools, Omaha, NE

DON SEBOLT, Associate Professor, Department of Human Nutrition, Foods and Exercise Science, Virginia Tech, Blacksburg, VA

MARCIA B. SHAFFER, School Psychologist (Retired), Lancaster, NY

DAVID A. SHAPIRO, Associate Professor of Communication Disorders, Department of Human Services, College of Education and Psychology, Western Carolina University, Cullowhee, NC

STEVEN R. SHAW, Assistant Professor of Psychology, Illinois State University, Normal, IL

EUGENE P. SHEEHAN, Associate Professor of Psychology, University of Northern Colorado, Greeley, CO

JOHN W. SHEPARD, Associate Professor of Counselor Education, The University of Toledo, Toledo, OH

JAMES W. SHERBON, Professor of Music, Director of Graduate Studies in Music, School of Music, University of North Carolina at Greensboro, Greensboro, NC

AGNES E. SHINE, Assistant Professor of Educational Psychology, Mississippi State University, Mississippi State, MS

KUSUM SINGH, Assistant Professor of Educational Research and Evaluation, Virginia Polytechnic and State University, Blacksburg, VA

BERTRAM C. SIPPOLA, Associate Professor of Psychology, University of New Orleans, New Orleans, LA

ALFRED L. SMITH, JR., Personnel Psychologist, Federal Aviation Administration, Washington, DC

DOUGLAS K. SMITH, Professor of School Psychology, University of Wisconsin-River Falls, River Falls, WI

JEFFREY K. SMITH, Professor of Educational Psychology, Rutgers, the State University, New Brunswick, NJ

JEFFREY H. SNOW, Neuropsychologist, Capital Rehabilitation Hospital, Tallahassee, FL

BROOKE SNYDER, Research Assistant, Trenton State College, Trenton, NJ

GARGI ROYSIRCAR SODOWSKY, Associate Professor of Educational Psychology, University of Nebraska-Lincoln, Lincoln, NE

STEVEN D. SPANER, Associate Professor of Educational Psychology, Department of Behavioral Studies, School of Education, University of Missouri-Saint Louis, Saint Louis, MO

DONNA SPIKER, Clinical Assistant Professor of Psychiatry and Behavioral Science, Stanford University, Stanford, CA

SUSAN K. SPILLE, Graduate Clinical Coordinator for the Office for Counseling and Life Planning Services (OCLPS), College of Education and Human Services, Wright State University, Dayton, OH

MICHAEL J. SPORAKOWSKI, Professor of Family and Child Development, Virginia Polytechnic Institute and State University, Blacksburg, VA

SCOTT SPREAT, Administrator of Clinical Services, The Woods Schools, Langhorne, PA

JAYNE E. STAKE, Professor of Psychology, University of Missouri-St. Louis, St. Louis, MO

ELAINE FLORY STEFANY, Certified School Psychologist, Lyons, KS

STEPHANIE STEIN, Associate Professor of Psychology, Central Washington University, Ellensburg, WA

HARLAN J. STIENTJES, School Psychologist, Grant Wood Area Education Agency, Cedar Rapids, IA

TERRY A. STINNETT, Associate Professor of Psychology, Eastern Illinois University, Charleston, IL

WILLIAM A. STOCK, Professor of Exercise Science and Physical Education, Arizona State University, Tempe, AZ

GERALD L. STONE, Professor of Counseling Psychology and Director, University Counseling Service, The University of Iowa, Iowa City, IA

GARY STONER, Associate Professor of School Psychology, University of Oregon, Eugene, OR

RICHARD K. STRATTON, Associate Professor of Education, Division of Health and Physical Education, Virginia Polytechnic Institute & State University, Blacksburg, VA

CHRISTINE F. STRAUSS, Graduate Assistant in Evaluation and Measurement, Kent State University, Kent, OH

RICHARD B. STUART, Professor Emeritus, Department of Psychiatry and Behavioral Sciences, School of Medicine, University of Washington, Seattle, WA

GABRIELLE STUTMAN, Adjunct Assistant Professor of Psychology, Bronx Community College/CUNY, Bronx, NY

MICHAEL J. SUBKOVIAK, Professor of Educational Psychology, University of Wisconsin-Madison, Madison, WI

HOI K. SUEN, Professor of Educational Psychology, The Pennsylvania State University, University Park, PA

NORMAN D. SUNDBERG, Professor Emeritus, Department of Psychology, University of Oregon, Eugene, OR

DONNA L. SUNDRE, Associate Assessment Specialist/Associate Professor of Psychology, James Madison University, Harrisonburg, VA

ROSEMARY E. SUTTON, Associate Professor, College of Education, Cleveland State University, Cleveland, OH

MARK E. SWERDLIK, Professor of Psychology, Illinois State University, Normal, IL

HARVEY N. SWITZKY, Professor of Educational Psychology, Counseling, and Special Education, Northern Illinois University, DeKalb, IL

HAROLD TAKOOSHIAN, Associate Professor of Psychology, Fordham University, New York, NY

CATHY TELZROW, Psychologist and Director, Educational Assessment Project, Cuyahoga Special Education Service Center, Cleveland, OH

JAMES S. TERWILLIGER, Professor of Educational Psychology, University of Minnesota, Minneapolis, MN

ANITA S. TESH, Assistant Professor, School of Nursing, University of North Carolina at Greensboro, Greensboro, NC

E. W. TESTUT, Associate Professor of Audiology, Department of Speech Pathology/Audiology, Ithaca College, Ithaca, NY

DONALD THOMPSON, Professor of Counseling Psychology, School of Education, The University of Connecticut, Storrs, CT

NORA M. THOMPSON, Clinical Assistant Professor, Department of Psychiatry, University of Texas Health Science Center, San Antonio, TX

GEORGE C. THORNTON, III, Professor of Psychology, Colorado State University, Ft. Collins, CO

PAMELA S. TIDWELL, Assistant Professor of Psychology, Auburn University at Montgomery, Montgomery, AL

GERALD TINDAL, Associate Professor of Special Education, University of Oregon, Eugene, OR

CAROL KEHR TITTLE, Professor of Educational Psychology, Graduate School, City University of New York, New York, NY

RUTH E. TOMES, Assistant Professor of Family Relations and Child Development, Oklahoma State University, Stillwater, OK

TONY TONEATTO, Scientist, Addiction Research Foundation, Toronto, Ontario, Canada

ESTHER STAVROU TOUBANOS, School Psychologist, Lawrence Public Schools, Lawrence, NY

ROGER L. TOWNE, Assistant Professor of Speech Pathology and Audiology, Illinois State University, Normal, IL

ROSS E. TRAUB, Professor of Measurement, Evaluation, and Computer Application, The Ontario Institute for Studies in Education, Toronto, Ontario, Canada

MICHAEL S. TREVISAN, Assistant Professor of Educational Leadership and Counseling Psychology, Washington State University, Pullman, WA

KERRI TURK, Graduate Student, Department of Educational Psychology, Texas A&M University, College Station, TX

LAWRENCE J. TURTON, Professor of Speech-Language Pathology, Indiana University of Pennsylvania, Indiana, PA

SUSANA URBINA, Associate Professor of Psychology, University of North Florida, Jacksonville, FL

NICHOLAS A. VACC, Professor and Chairperson, Department of Counselor Education, University of North Carolina at Greensboro, Greensboro, NC

WILFRED G. VAN GORP, Associate Professor in Residence and Director, Neuropsychology Assessment Laboratory, UCLA School of Medicine, Department of Psychiatry and Biobehavioral Sciences and Interim Chief, Psychology Service, Department of Veterans Affairs Medical Center, West Los Angeles, CA

JAMES P. VAN HANEGHAN, Assistant Professor of Educational Psychology, Counseling, and Special Education, Northern Illinois University, DeKalb, IL

WENDY VAN WYHE, Research Assistant, Department of Psychology, The University of Memphis, Memphis, TN

DANIEL E. VOGLER, Associate Professor of Education, Virginia Tech, Blacksburg, VA

WILLIAM J. WALDRON, Administrator, Employee Assessment, Tampa Electric Company, Tampa, FL

NIELS G. WALLER, Associate Professor of Psychology, University of California, Davis, Davis, CA

RICHARD A. WANTZ, Associate Professor of Human Services and Director of the Office for Counseling and Life Planning Services (OCLPS), College of Education and Human Services, Wright State University, Dayton, OH

ANNIE W. WARD, President, The Techńe Group, Inc., Daytona Beach, FL

OREST E. WASYLIW, Isaac Ray Center, Chicago, IL

T. STEUART WATSON, Assistant Professor of Educational Psychology, Mississippi State University, Starkville, MS

LARRY WEBER, Professor of Education, Virginia Tech, Blacksburg, VA

ELLEN WEISSINGER, Associate Professor of Educational Psychology, University of Nebraska-Lincoln, Lincoln, NE

BERT W. WESTBROOK, Professor of Psychology, North Carolina State University, Raleigh, NC

CAROL E. WESTBY, Senior Research Associate, Training and Technical Assistance Unit, University of New Mexico Medical School, Albuquerque, NM

STEPHANIE WESTERN, Research Assistant, Psychology Department, The University of Memphis, Memphis, TN

ALIDA S. WESTMAN, Professor of Psychology, Eastern Michigan University, Ypsilanti, MI

PATRICIA H. WHEELER, President, EREAPA Associates, Livermore, CA

MARTIN J. WIESE, Licensed Psychologist, Educational Service Unit No. 6, Milford, NE

LINDA F. WIGHTMAN, Vice President—Operations, Testing, and Research, Law School Admission Services, Newtown, PA

TERRY M. WILDMAN, Professor of Curriculum and Instruction, Virginia Polytechnic Institute, Blacksburg, VA

WILLIAM K. WILKINBSON, Assistant Professor of Counseling and Educational Psychology, New Mexico State University, Las Cruces, NM

JANICE G. WILLIAMS, Associate Professor of Psychology, Clemson University, Clemson, SC

JEAN M. WILLIAMS, Director, Effective Practices Specialty Option, PRC Inc., Indianapolis, IN

ROBERT T. WILLIAMS, Professor and Director, Student Literacy Corps, Colorado State University, Fort Collins, CO

W. GRANT WILLIS, Associate Professor of Psychology, University of Rhode Island, Kingston, RI

VICTOR L. WILLSON, Professor of Educational Psychology, Texas A&M University, College Station, TX

HILDA WING, Personnel Psychologist, Federal Aviation Administration, Washington, DC

STEVEN L. WISE, Associate Professor of Educational Psychology, University of Nebraska-Lincoln, Lincoln, NE

JOSEPH C. WITT, Professor of Psychology, Louisiana State University, Baton Rouge, LA

L. ALAN WITT, Human Resources Manager, Barnett Banks, Inc., Jacksonville, FL

DONNA WITTMER, Assistant Professor of Education, University of Colorado at Denver, Denver, CO

RICHARD M. WOLF, Professor of Psychology and Education, Teachers College, Columbia University, New York, NY

JAMES A. WOLLACK, Lecturer, School of Education Testing Services, University of Wisconsin-Madison, Madison, WI

BLAINE R. WORTHEN, Professor and Chair, Research and Evaluation Methodology Program, Department of Psychology, Utah State University, Logan, UT

CLAUDIA R. WRIGHT, Associate Professor of Educational Psychology, California State University, Long Beach, CA

DAN WRIGHT, School Psychologist, Wyandotte Comprehensive Special Education Cooperative, Kansas City, KS

LOGAN WRIGHT, Associate Professor of Psychology, University of Central Oklahoma, Edmond, OK

MICHAEL K. WYNNE, Associate Professor, Department of Otolaryngology, Indiana University School of Medicine, Indianapolis, IN

TAMELA YELLAND, Psychologist, Veterans Administration, Anaheim Vet Center, Anaheim, CA

JOHN W. YOUNG, Assistant Professor of Educational Statistics and Measurement, Rutgers University, New Brunswick, NJ

JAMES E. YSSELDYKE, Professor of Educational Psychology and Director of National Center on Educational Outcomes, University of Minnesota, Minneapolis, MN

SHELDON ZEDECK, Chair and Professor of Psychology, University of California, Berkeley, CA

LELAND C. ZLOMKE, Director of Clinical Psychology, Beatrice State Developmental Center, Beatrice, NE

DONALD G. ZYTOWSKI, Professor Emeritus of Psychology, Iowa State University, Ames, IA

INDEX OF TITLES

This title index lists all the tests included in The Twelfth Mental Measurements Yearbook*. Citations are to test entry numbers, not to pages (e.g., 54 refers to test 54 and not page 54). (Test numbers along with test titles are indicated in the running heads at the top of each page, whereas page numbers, used only in the Table of Contents but not in the indexes, appear at the bottom of each page.) Superseded titles are listed with cross references to current titles, and alternative titles are also cross referenced.*

Tests in this volume were previously listed in Tests in Print IV *(1994). An (N) appearing immediately after a test number indicates that the test is a new, recently published test, and/or that it has not appeared before in any Buros Institute publication prior to* Tests in Print IV. *An (R) indicates that the test has been revised or supplemented since last included in a* Mental Measurements Yearbook.

INDEX OF ACRONYMS

This Index of Acronyms refers the reader to the appropriate test in The Twelfth Mental Measurements Yearbook*. In some cases tests are better known by their acronyms than by their full titles, and this index can be of substantial help to the person who knows the former but not the latter. Acronyms are only listed if the author or publisher has made substantial use of the acronym in referring to the test, or if the test is widely known by the acronym. A few acronyms are also registered trademarks (e.g., SAT); where this is known to us, only the test with the registered trademark is referenced. There is some danger in the overuse of acronyms, but this index, like all other indexes in this work, is provided to make the task of identifying a test as easy as possible. All numbers refer to test numbers, not page numbers.*

CLASSIFIED SUBJECT INDEX

The Classified Subject Index classifies all tests included in The Twelfth Mental Measurements Yearbook *into 18 major categories: Achievement, Behavior Assessment, Developmental, Education, English, Fine Arts, Foreign Language, Intelligence and Scholastic Aptitude, Mathematics, Miscellaneous, Multi-Aptitude Batteries, Neuropsychological, Personality, Reading, Sensory-Motor, Social Studies, Speech and Hearing, and Vocations. Each category appears in alphabetical order and tests are ordered alphabetically within each category. Each test entry includes test title, population for which the test is intended, and the test entry number in* The Twelfth Mental Measurements Yearbook. *All numbers refer to test entry numbers, not to page numbers. Brief suggestions for the use of this index are presented in the introduction.*

ACHIEVEMENT

BEHAVIOR ASSESSMENT

DEVELOPMENT

EDUCATION

ENGLISH

FINE ARTS

FOREIGN LANGUAGES

INTELLIGENCE AND SCHOLASTIC APTITUDE

MATHEMATICS

MISCELLANEOUS

MULTI-APTITUDE

NEUROPSYCHOLOGICAL

PERSONALITY

READING

SENSORY-MOTOR

SOCIAL STUDIES

SPEECH AND HEARING

VOCATIONS

PUBLISHERS DIRECTORY AND INDEX

This directory and index give the addresses and test entry numbers of all publishers represented in The Twelfth Mental Measurements Yearbook. *Please note that all numbers in this index refer to test entry numbers, not page numbers. Publishers are an important source of information about catalogs, specimen sets, price changes, test revisions, and many other matters.*

Life Insurance Marketing and Research Association, Inc., P.O. Box 208, Hartford, CT 06141: 32, 225

Management & Personnel Systems, Inc., 1475 North Broadway, Suite 280, Walnut Creek, CA 94596: 160

Manatech, Management Technologies, Inc., 1200 Post Oak Blvd., Suite 520, Houston, TX 77056: 291

MAT, Boston University, School of Music, 855 Commonwealth Ave., Boston, MA 02215: 250

McCarron-Dial Systems, P.O. Box 45628, Dallas, TX 75245: 284

MetriTech, Inc., 111 N. Market Street, Champaign, IL 61820: 15, 20, 190, 275, 366, 377

Mind Garden, 3803 East Bayshore Road, Palo Alto, CA 94303: 35

Modern Curriculum Press, Customer Service Department, 13900 Prospect Road, Cleveland, OH 44136: 111

Multi-Health Systems, Inc., 908 Niagara Falls Blvd., North Tonawanda, NY 14120-2060: 177, 300

National Association of Secondary School Principals, P.O. Box 3250, 1904 Association Drive, Reston, VA 22091-1598: 217

National Computer Systems, Content Mastery Examinations for Educators (CMME), P.O. Box 30, Iowa City, IA 52244: 25, 59, 92, 238

The National Council on Economic Education, 1140 Avenue of the Americas, New York, NY 10036: 395

National Occupational Competency Testing Institute, 409 Bishop Hall, Ferris State University, 1349 Cramer Circle, Big Rapids, MI 49307-2737: 255, 256, 257

NCS Assessments—Sales Dept., 5605 Green Circle Drive, Minnetonka, MN 55343: 60, 236

Nelson Canada, 1120 Birchmount Road, Scarborough, Ontario M1K 5G4, Canada: 61, 180, 274, 336, 409

C. H. Nevins Printing Co., 311 Bryn Mawr Island, Bayshore Gardens, Bradenton, FL 34207: 170

New Zealand Council for Educational Research, Education House West, 178-182 Willis St., Box 3237, Wellington, New Zealand: 4, 313, 314

NFER-Nelson Publishing Co., Ltd., Darville House, 2 Oxford Road East, Windsor, Berkshire SL4 1DF, England: 29, 40, 54, 55, 98, 129, 156, 159, 164, 173, 197, 221, 231, 239, 252, 267, 285, 301, 302, 317, 384

Optometry Admission Testing Program, 211 East Chicago Avenue, Suite 1840, Chicago, IL 60611: 269

Pain Resource Center, Inc., P.O. Box 2836, Durham, NC 27715: 402

Pendrake, Inc., 3370 Southampton Drive, Reno, NV 89509: 49

Pfeiffer & Company International Publishers, 8517 Production Avenue, San Diego, CA 92121-2280: 123, 136, 213, 245, 405

Phylmar Associates, Educational Publishers and Consultants, 191 Iroquois Avenue, London, Ontario N6C 2K9, Canada: 65, 308, 387

Piney Mountain Press, Inc., P.O. Box 333, Cleveland, GA 30528: 218, 305, 408, 410

PRO-ED, Inc., 8700 Shoal Creek Blvd., Austin, TX 78757-6897: 30, 36, 48, 73, 100, 105, 106, 107, 112, 114, 124, 154, 166, 196, 241, 263, 264, 294, 310, 316, 320, 323, 344, 349, 350, 368, 373, 393, 394, 398

Psychological Assessment Resources, Inc., P.O. Box 998, Odessa, FL 33556-0998: 17, 19, 21, 45, 68, 72, 76, 93, 130, 229, 290, 330, 361, 375, 407

The Psychological Corporation, 555 Academic Court, San Antonio, TX 78204-2498: 3, 26, 117, 118, 119, 140, 141, 158, 232, 233, 235, 262, 273, 335, 371, 406, 412

Psychological Services, Inc., 100 West Broadway, Suite 1100, Glendale, CA 91210: 312

Psychologists and Educators, Inc., Sales Division, P.O. Box 513, Chesterfield, MO 63006: 70, 82, 161

Psychology Press Inc., Box 328, Brandon, VT 05733-0328: 292

Reid Psychological Systems, 200 South Michigan Avenue, Suite 900, Chicago, IL 60604-2401: 324

Research for Better Schools, Inc., 444 North Third Street, Philadelphia, PA 19123-4107: 34, 345

Research Press, Dept G, Box 9177, Champaign, IL 61826: 401

Richardson, Bellows, Henry & Co., Inc., 1140 Connecticut Ave., N.W., Washington, DC 20036: 62, 396

The Riverside Publishing Co., 8420 Bryn Mawr Avenue, Chicago, IL 60631: 41, 52, 69, 86, 99, 115, 132, 191, 195, 251, 319, 315, 391, 399, 415, 416

Rocky Mountain Behavioral Science Institute, Inc., P.O. Box 1066, Fort Collins, CO 80522: 27

The SASSI Institute, P.O. Box 5069, Bloomington, IN 47407: 381

Saville & Holdsworth Ltd USA, Inc., 575 Boylston St., Boston, MA 02116: 337, 418

Scholastic Testing Service, Inc., 480 Meyer Road, Bensenville, IL 60106-1617: 175, 346

Scientific Management Techniques, Inc., 581 Boylston Street, Boston, MA 02116: 370

Sigma Assessment Systems, Inc., Research Psychologists Press Division, 1110 Military St., P.O. Box 610984, Port Huron, MI 48061-0984: 42

Slosson Educational Publications, Inc., P.O. Box 280, East Aurora, NY 14052-0280: 1, 89, 120, 207, 348, 357, 358, 359, 360, 389, 392, 397

Stanard & Associates, Inc., 309 West Washington Street, Suite 1000, Chicago, IL 60606: 253

Stoelting Co., Oakwood Center, 620 Wheat Lane, Wood Dale, IL 60191: 80, 148, 193, 240

Teachers College Press, Teachers College, Columbia University, New York, NY 10027: 188

Telemetrics International, 1755 Woodstead Court, The Woodlands, TX 77380: 2, 90, 91, 227, 228, 322, 379, 380, 382, 388

Therapy Skill Builders, 3830 E. Bellevue, P.O. Box 42050, Tucson, AZ 85733: 142, 143, 144, 155, 271

INDEX OF NAMES

This analytical index indicates whether a citation refers to authorship of a test, a test review, or a reference for a specific test. Numbers refer to test entries, not to pages. The abbreviations and numbers following the names may be interpreted as follows: "test, 73" *indicates authorship of test 73;* "rev, 86" *indicates authorship of a review of test 86;* "ref, 45(30)" *indicates authorship of reference number 30 in the "Test References" section for test 45;* "ref, 13r" *indicates a reference (unnumbered) in one of the "Reviewer's References" sections for test 13. Names mentioned in cross references are also indexed.*

SCORE INDEX

This Score Index lists all the scores, in alphabetical order, for all the tests included in The Twelfth Mental Measurements Yearbook. *Because test scores can be regarded as operational definitions of the variable measured, sometimes the scores provide better leads to what a test actually measures than the test title or other available information. The Score Index is very detailed, and the reader should keep in mind that a given variable (or concept) of interest may be defined in several different ways. Thus the reader should look up these several possible alternative definitions before drawing final conclusions about whether tests measuring a particular variable of interest can be located in the* 12th MMY. *If the kind of score sought is located in a particular test or tests, the reader should then read the test descriptive information carefully to determine whether the test(s) in which the score is found is (are) consistent with reader purpose. Used wisely, the Score Index can be another useful resource in locating the right score in the right test. As usual, all numbers in the index are test numbers, not page numbers.*